Guide to Congress

Guide to Congress

FIFTH EDITION • VOLUME II

CQ PRESS

A Division of Congressional Quarterly Inc.
Washington, D.C.

CQ Press
A Division of Congressional Quarterly Inc.
1414 22nd Street, N.W.
Washington, D.C. 20037
(202) 822-1475; (800) 638-1710

www.cqpress.com

Book design and production by Kachergis Book Design,
Pittsboro, North Carolina

Printed in the United States of America

03 02 01 00 99   5 4 3 2 1

The paper used in this publication meets the minimum requirements of the American National Standard for Information Science—Permanence of Paper for Printed Library Materials, ANSI Z 39.48-1984.

Illustration credits and acknowledgments appear on pages 1353–1354, Volume II, which constitutes a continuation of the copyright page.

LIBRARY OF CONGRESS CATALOGING-IN-PUBLICATION DATA
Congressional Quarterly's guide to Congress.—5th ed.
    p. cm.
    Includes bibliographical references and index.
    ISBN 1-56802-476-2 (v. 1) — ISBN 1-56802-436-3 (v. 2)
  — ISBN 1-56802-477-0 (set)
    1. United States. Congress. I. Title: Guide to Congress.
  II. Congressional Quarterly, Inc.
  JK1021.C565 1999
  328.73—dc21   99-053914

Summary Table of Contents

Table of Contents

PART V

Housing and Support

CHAPTER 24

Capitol and Office Buildings

To MOST AMERICANS, the United States Capitol is the symbol of a proud nation and a great democracy. Some sections are a few years younger than the Constitution.

The Capitol has witnessed nearly two hundred years of the nation's history, and often it has been at the center of that history. It has seen the United States grow from a weak strand of former British colonies on the Atlantic seaboard into a continent-sized nation whose influence circles the globe.

In practical terms the Capitol is essentially a building serving a public purpose. It is a meeting place and a forum for national lawmakers. Designed for the business of government, the Capitol has been remodeled and expanded several times. It has changed as the nation has changed, and it doubtless will continue to change as time exacts new demands.

In its dual roles as symbol and edifice, the Capitol is as typically American as the Eiffel Tower is typically French. Yet it also is a hub of workaday activity for thousands of congressional employees. Moreover, it formerly housed the Library of Congress and the Supreme Court.

Conceived as a home for the Senate and the House of Representatives, the Capitol was made to serve other functions almost from the beginning. The Library of Congress did not leave until 1897; the Supreme Court stayed until 1935. Presidential inaugurations have taken place inside Capitol chambers and outside the East and West fronts. The bodies of national leaders have lain in state in the Rotunda. A vast collection of art, some priceless and some worthless, adorns most of the building's interior walls as well as many of its ceilings and floors.

Controversy has dogged the Capitol from the start. Designers failed to produce acceptable plans; builders quarreled with architects. In the end, members of Congress grumbled about the results. The Capitol has been enlarged, and congressional office buildings have been erected to serve it. There even have been suggestions that Congress abandon the Capitol for a more modern home elsewhere—in Denver, for example.

The Capitol has undergone four major periods of construction. The first, which included the original design work and early construction, stretched from 1792 to about 1811. The second, from 1815 to 1829, saw the completion of the originally planned building, on which work had ceased during the War of 1812. Throughout this period, extensive repairs were made to sections of the Capitol destroyed by the British in 1814. The third period, from 1851 to 1892, included erection of the present wings used by the House and Senate and landscaping of the grounds. The fourth period began in 1949 with repairs to the roofs of the House and Senate wings and included extension of the East Front in 1962. The West Front restoration from 1983 to 1987 did not expand the building.

Early Construction, 1792–1811

After the Constitution was adopted and ratified, Congress met first in New York and then in Philadelphia. The act of July 16, 1790, which shifted the seat of government to "a district or territory . . . on the river Potomac," made it clear that a new city would have to be laid out, sites selected for the government buildings, and the buildings themselves designed and erected.

The task of selecting a site for the Capitol fell to Pierre Charles L'Enfant, who had been appointed by President George Washington in March 1791 to prepare a plan for the new city.

Washington had instructed L'Enfant to locate the city on the Maryland side of the Potomac. L'Enfant made several tours of the area, studied maps of European cities, and developed his plan. In a letter to Washington June 22, 1791, L'Enfant outlined a plan that called for a rectangular grid of streets that would be intersected by broad avenues radiating from the "principal places." The Capitol would be one of the "principal places," and L'Enfant recommended putting it "on the west end of Jenkins Heights, which stand as a pedestal waiting for a monument."

The president accepted L'Enfant's recommendations and on December 13, 1791, forwarded them to Congress. Although Washington had to dismiss L'Enfant in February 1792 because his work was behind schedule, L'Enfant's plans were used in preparing maps of the city. His recommendation of a site for the Capitol was retained on the maps. The area has been known ever since as Capitol Hill.

The area had been occupied earlier by a subtribe of the Algonquin Indians, known as the Powhatans, whose council house had been at the foot of the hill. The original Capitol grounds were a part of Cerne Abbey Manor, owned by Daniel Carroll of Duddington. The land was purchased by the government for twenty-five pounds an acre, the equivalent at the time of $66.66.

DESIGN COMPETITION

The three commissioners appointed by Washington to oversee development of the city and the public buildings had expected L'Enfant to provide designs for the buildings as well as the city. But by early 1792 it had become clear that the commissioners could not rely on L'Enfant for the building designs, and they decided to conduct a public design competition.

EARLY SEATS OF CONGRESS

Before the seat of government was moved to Washington, D.C., in 1800, the Capitol of the United States was located first in New York City and then in Philadelphia.

FEDERAL HALL, NEW YORK

The first session of the First Congress opened March 4, 1789, in Federal Hall at Broad and Wall Streets, New York City. The building, on the site of the old city hall, had been used previously by the Continental Congress. Private citizens raised $32,500 for Pierre Charles L'Enfant to redesign the structure.

The House chamber was on the first floor and the Senate chamber on the second floor. The actual cost of the renovations was almost $65,000, with half the total paid from tax revenues and half from lottery receipts.

The House and the Senate met in Federal Hall until the end of the second session of the First Congress on August 12, 1790.

CONGRESS HALL, PHILADELPHIA

Congress met for a decade in Congress Hall at Sixth and Chestnut Streets, Philadelphia. The building, next to the famous Independence Hall, originally was the county courthouse. The House chamber was on the first floor, the Senate chamber on the second floor.

Congress Hall was used by the House and the Senate from the opening of the third session of the First Congress on December 6, 1790, to the closing of the first session of the Sixth Congress on May 14, 1800.

Throughout March the commissioners advertised for designs. They set July 15, 1792, as a deadline and offered a prize of five hundred dollars and a city lot for the winning entry.

The specifications laid down by the commissioners called for a brick building to include a conference room and a room for the representatives, each accommodating three hundred persons; a room of twelve hundred square feet for the Senate; twelve rooms of six hundred square feet each for committees and clerks' offices; and appropriate lobbies and anterooms. They recommended that the central part of the building be designed so that, while it appeared to be complete, additions could be made later.

There were few trained architects in the United States, and the response to the competition was disappointing. Dr. William Thornton, a physician and inventor, gained the president's approval with a design submitted after the deadline. Washington praised Thornton's design for its "grandeur, simplicity and convenience." Secretary of State Thomas Jefferson said Thornton's design "captivated the eyes and judgment of all."[1]

The winning design called for a stately, three-story building, surmounted by a low dome. For the design, Thornton received the $500 award and a lot on North Capitol Street, about two blocks from the building site.

Thornton was an amateur architect and his design was merely a sketch. The commissioners hired Stephen M. Hallet, a professional French architect whose design entry lost out to Thornton's, to prepare working drawings. A clash was inevitable. As modifications of Thornton's design (some of them required for structural and practical reasons) crept into Hallet's drawings, Thornton raised a series of noisy objections. To settle the dispute, Washington called a meeting of Thornton, Hallet, James Hoban (winner of the design competition for the White House), and two builders. The group agreed to some of the modifications proposed by Hallet.

Jefferson wrote to Washington that Hallet had "preserved the most valuable ideas of the original and rendered them acceptable of execution, so that it is considered Dr. Thornton's plan rendered into practical form."[2] Historians still are uncertain as to which man had greater influence over the Capitol's ultimate design.

CONSTRUCTION OF THE CAPITOL

The Capitol was laid out on a north-south axis, so that descriptions mention north and south wings (ends) and east and west fronts (sides).

The first cornerstone was laid September 18, 1793, by Washington amid colorful Masonic rites. Although contemporary accounts put the cornerstone at the southeast corner of the north wing, it was not found during the 1958–1962 extension of the East Front.

Hallet was placed in charge of the construction, under the supervision of Hoban. As work progressed, Hallet persisted in altering the design without approval of either the president or the commissioners. Hallet was tolerated for a year but finally was discharged on November 15, 1794. Two months earlier, on September 12, Washington had named Thornton to a vacancy on the three-man board of commissioners, giving Thornton for the first time direct authority over the construction.

Nearly a year passed before a successor to Hallet was appointed. In the interval, Hoban superintended construction of both the White House and the Capitol. Then, on October 15, 1795, the commissioners appointed as the new construction superintendent George Hadfield, a prize-winning student at the Royal Academy in London.

Although Thornton's basic design for the Capitol was executed by three other men—Hallet, Hoban, and Hadfield—only Thornton was appointed by the president to the position that has come to be called "architect of the Capitol." The other three were hired by the board of commissioners. Congress abolished the board in 1802, when its responsibilities were taken over by a superintendent of public buildings.

Despite the controversies, construction continued. It took slave labor to build the home of a free government. The Capitol workforce was composed in large part of black slaves hired out by their masters in the District of Columbia and nearby Maryland and Virginia, as was then a common custom. By March 1796 the foundations had been laid, and the north wing was rising above ground level. The roof of the north wing had been boarded, shingled, and painted by the fall of 1798. When Congress arrived from Philadelphia in the autumn of 1800, the foundations of the south wing had been completed. The two wings were not connected by a permanent structure for more than twenty years.

The first public function held at the Capitol was a reception given by the citizens of Washington for President John Adams on June 5, 1800.

ARRIVAL OF CONGRESS

The act of July 16, 1790, designating a Potomac site as the permanent seat of government, had set the first Monday in December 1800 as the deadline for moving the new capital to Washington. When it became clear that the government buildings would be ready before December, Congress on April 24, 1800, authorized the president to make an earlier transfer. By an act of May 13, 1800, Congress fixed November 17, 1800, as the date of convening in its new quarters in Washington.

Congress was late for its debut. It formally convened November 17 but for lack of a quorum did not actually sit until November 21. The next day representatives and senators attending the second session of the Sixth Congress filled the Senate chamber to hear President Adams deliver a message of welcome. It was not until 1913 that another president, Woodrow Wilson, came to the Capitol to make a speech to Congress. The citizens of Washington had planned a parade and a formal reception for Congress, but the plans collapsed in a dispute over selection of a master of ceremonies and because of a surprise three-inch snowfall. Thus the welcome for Congress consisted of a congratulatory letter from local residents and a newly written, and long since forgotten, song.

Both the House and the Senate were quartered in the north wing because it was the only part of the Capitol that had been completed. The wing was three stories high and faced with sandstone on three sides. The fourth (south) side, to be connected later to the center section and south wing, was enclosed temporarily with brick.

The north wing, and the entire Capitol until the 1850s, was built primarily of sandstone from the Aquia Creek Quarry in Virginia. The quarry, on an island in the Potomac about forty miles south of Washington, supplied the stone for all public buildings in the new capital from 1791 to 1837. The soft, light gray "freestone" could be quarried easily and shipped economically to Washington. But it did not wear well and was not used extensively after other quarries came into production. Most of the original sandstone in the Capitol has been replaced or covered over by subsequent construction.

Inside the north wing, both the House and Senate chambers were two stories high. The House chamber was on the west side of the second floor. The Senate chamber was on the east side of the first floor, a floor below the space it later was to occupy and still later would turn over to the Supreme Court. On the walls of the Senate chamber hung portraits of Louis XVI and Marie An-

---

WASHINGTON'S TOMB

In the Capitol basement, two stories below the Rotunda, is an area that was intended to serve as a tomb for George and Martha Washington.

Within a few days after Washington's death on December 14, 1799, Congress adopted a joint resolution providing that the first president was to be honored by placing his body in a special tomb in a section of the Capitol yet to be built. Meanwhile, Washington was buried at Mount Vernon in accordance with the terms of his will. In a letter of December 31, 1799, Martha Washington gave permission to have his body moved to the Capitol.

Interior construction of the Rotunda was completed by 1824, but nearly five years more were needed to finish the entire central section. A circular opening about ten feet in diameter was left in the center of the Rotunda floor, to permit visitors to look down upon a statue of Washington which was to have been placed in the crypt on the first floor. The tomb itself was to be one floor below the statue.

In 1828 the opening in the Rotunda floor was closed because dampness from the lower levels was damaging the John Trumbull paintings hung in the Rotunda four years earlier. In 1830 a House committee recommended that both Washington and his wife be reinterred in the basement tomb.

As the 1832 centennial of Washington's birth approached, Congress asked John A. Washington, grandnephew of the first president, and George Washington Parke Custis, grandson of Mrs. Washington, for permission to move the bodies to the Capitol. Custis consented but John Washington refused. In 1832 the General Assembly of Virginia also adopted a resolution objecting to reinterment. The bodies have remained at Mount Vernon.

The area for the tomb is used to store the Lincoln catafalque, which serves as a bier when bodies of prominent citizens lie in state in the Rotunda.

---

toinette, the first works of art in the Capitol. The portraits had been presented by the king to the Continental Congress in 1784. Both paintings are thought to have been burned by the British in 1814.

Bursting out of its admittedly temporary quarters in the north wing, the House ordered construction of other temporary quarters on the foundations of its own south wing. The result was a one-story, elliptical brick building. Because of its shape and the stifling summer temperatures inside, the structure quickly was nicknamed "the oven." The House met there from the beginning of the Seventh Congress on December 7, 1801, until the end of the first session of the Eighth Congress on March 27, 1804, when it abandoned the site so that construction of the south wing could continue. The House met again in its north wing chamber from November 5, 1804, to March 3, 1807.

CONSTRUCTION UNDER LATROBE

In 1803 President Jefferson appointed Benjamin Henry Latrobe, an English architect, as surveyor of public buildings and placed him in charge of finishing the Capitol.

After demolition of "the oven," work was resumed on the south wing. The completed north wing determined the exterior design of the south wing, and the completed foundations of the south wing set the form of the interior. But like Hallet and Hadfield before him, Latrobe, as a professional architect, found flaws in Thornton's design. Thornton replied on January 1, 1805, with an open letter to members of the House defending his design. The bitter pamphlet war that ensued rocked Congress and threatened to delay further construction appropriations. Jefferson supported Latrobe, while cautioning him to "deviate as little as possible from the plan approved by General Washington." Latrobe survived the criticism and remained in charge of the work.

The roof of the south wing was completed during the winter of 1806–1807, and by March 1807 construction of the wing was virtually completed. The House moved from the north wing into what then was considered its permanent home (later Statuary Hall) for the opening of the Tenth Congress on October 26, 1807. Problems arose almost at once. Latrobe had succeeded in changing Thornton's design for an elliptical House chamber into two semicircles joined by parallel lines, and the acoustics were horrible. Hanging curtains between the stone columns helped somewhat, but faulty acoustics plagued the House throughout its occupancy of the chamber.

Upon completion of the south wing, Latrobe turned to repairing some of the mediocre construction in the north wing. He replaced with stone some of the wood, plaster, and brick interiors. He raised the floor of the two-story Senate chamber, dividing the area into two one-story chambers. He designed cornstalk motifs on columns in 1809 for the vestibule outside the first floor chamber. Latrobe hired Italian sculptors to execute his plans for the Capitol's interior.

During the remodeling, occupants of the north wing were shunted about. After adjournment of the first session of the Tenth Congress on April 25, 1808, the Senate moved into a first floor room on the west side of the north wing. The Supreme Court moved into the old House chamber on the west side of the second floor, sharing the space with the Library of Congress. The Supreme Court had moved to Washington for the opening of its February 1801 term and had been sitting in a small room adjoining the south side of the Senate chamber. The room was so cold and inconvenient that the Court often sat in a nearby tavern. After the Court adjourned in 1809, the Senate moved upstairs to share the old House quarters with the library.

By the winter of 1809–1810, new quarters were ready for both the Senate and the Supreme Court. On January 1, 1810, the Senate moved into its remodeled chamber on the second floor. The Court opened its 1810 term in the first floor chamber beneath the Senate. Both chambers were used later for other purposes,

---

CAPITOL BUILDING FACTS

Site. On the western end of a plateau known previously as Jenkins Heights, eighty-eight feet above the Potomac River. Located at the intersection of the Mall and North, East, and South Capitol Streets.

Grounds. Total of about 181 acres, including the Capitol, several congressional office buildings, the Library of Congress, the Supreme Court, and surrounding grounds, sidewalks, and roads.

Dimensions. Overall length 751 feet, 4 inches. Greatest width, including approaches, 350 feet. Height 287 feet, 5.5 inches from the East Front base to the top of the Statue of Freedom. The Capitol covers about four acres.

Capacity. Floor area of 16.5 acres on five levels. Contains approximately 540 rooms devoted to offices, committee rooms, restaurants, storage, and other purposes. There are 658 windows and 850 doorways.

Statue of Freedom. Female figure cast in bronze from plaster original by Thomas Crawford. Height 19.5 feet. Weight 14,985 pounds.

Dome. Width at base 135 feet, 5 inches. Made of cast iron. Weight 4,454.6 tons, or nearly 9 million pounds. Receives light through 108 windows.

Rotunda. Interior of the dome is 96 feet in diameter. Height 180 feet, 3 inches.

House Chamber. Length 139 feet. Width 93 feet. Greatest height 42.5 feet.

Senate Chamber. Length 113 feet, 3 inches. Width 80 feet, 3 inches. Greatest height 42.5 feet.

Source: Architect of the Capitol.

---

but for the 1976 Bicentennial they were restored to their appearance of the 1850s.

The threat of an approaching war with Britain began to cut into construction appropriations for the Capitol. Work slowed, then halted. The two sections, the north wing and the south wing, stood apart, separated by the unfinished center section. In 1811, before work was completely suspended, a temporary wooden covered walk was built to connect the two wings.

Estimates of the cost of erecting the two wings are at best tentative. Part of the cost was defrayed by the original contributions of $72,000 from Maryland and $120,000 from Virginia for construction of public buildings in Washington. The first congressional appropriation for the Capitol, in 1803, provided $50,000, although Congress had appropriated $9,000 in 1800 for furnishings. After studying Treasury records, Glenn Brown, author of a two-volume history of the Capitol published in 1900, put the cost of the north and south wings at $788,077.98.[3]

Reconstruction and Expansion, 1815–1829

Most of the fighting during the War of 1812 took place far from Washington. But in response to American raids into Canada, and hoping to demoralize the government, Vice Adm. Sir Alexander Cochrane authorized a series of Atlantic seaboard raids. Carrying out one of those operations, a British force under the command of Maj. Gen. Robert Ross and Rear Adm. Sir George Cockburn moved up the Patuxent River in Maryland in August 1814. The troops were put ashore near Benedict, Maryland, and marched overland through Upper Marlboro and Bladensburg toward Washington. American troops offered ineffective resistance.

The capital city was nearly deserted. Many residents had fled before the approaching troops. Most members of Congress, after a routine adjournment April 18, had long since left for their homes. President James Madison and most of the cabinet had gone to Bladensburg with the American troops.

The British entered Washington around dusk on August 24, 1814. That night a detachment of troops headed by Ross and Cockburn set the Capitol afire. The building was burned, according to several accounts, after Cockburn had mounted the Speaker's chair in the House chamber and asked, "Shall this harbor of Yankee democracy be burned?" The soldiers shouted "Aye."[4]

Leaving the Capitol in flames, the troops moved through the city and burned the White House and the Treasury building.

Later on the night of August 24 a violent rainstorm drowned the flames, preventing complete destruction of the buildings. The British again roamed through the city on August 25. Before withdrawing that night, they also burned buildings used by the State and War departments and a government arsenal.

As the president and other government officials returned to Washington August 27, the slow work of reconstruction began.

On August 8, 1814, President Madison had called a special session of Congress for September 19. The Capitol had been damaged too heavily to meet there, and on September 17 Madison announced that Congress would convene in Blodget's Hotel, which had been taken over previously by the Post Office and the Patent Office. The huge structure, on E Street between 7th and 8th Streets, Northwest, was the only government building not burned by the British. It had been built by Samuel Blodget Jr., one of the competitors for the original Capitol design, and it once was offered as a lottery prize but never served as a hotel. (The building was demolished later in the nineteenth century.)

The special session in Blodget's lasted from September 19, 1814, to March 3, 1815. On October 15 the House by a 74–83 vote defeated a bill to transfer the seat of government elsewhere. The vote was part of an intermittent effort from 1800 until after the Civil War to move the capital out of Washington.

This engraving shows the Capitol and its surroundings in 1850. The original dome of the Capitol, much lower than the present dome and made of wood sheathed in copper, was completed in 1828.

An act of February 15, 1815, authorized the president to accept a $500,000 loan from Washington banks to pay for rebuilding the Capitol. On March 14 Latrobe was recalled to oversee the work. According to his reports, damage to the north wing was more extensive than that to the south wing. The wooden-covered walk between them had been completely destroyed.

In repairing the interiors, Latrobe again redesigned the House chamber, making it semicircular but failing to improve its acoustics. He designed the central section west of the Rotunda and the famous tobacco capitals of the small rotunda on the second floor. For the East Front, Latrobe designed the main portico and exterior steps. The new steps were to lead from the ground level to the second floor, which had become, and remains, the principal floor of the Capitol. *(See "Capitol Floor Plan," in Reference Materials, p. 1148, Vol. II.)*

Work on reconstruction was well under way when Latrobe became entangled in a dispute with Samuel Lane, who had been named in 1816 to the newly created post of commissioner of public buildings and grounds. Latrobe resigned November 20, 1817.

Meanwhile, Congress had moved from Blodget's Hotel into new quarters. A group of Washington landowners, worried that Congress might move to another city, had raised $25,000 to build a temporary "capitol" at First and A Streets, Northeast. The cornerstone was laid July 4, 1815, and both the House and Senate met in the new building at the opening of the 14th Congress on December 4, 1815. The Senate chamber was on the ground floor and the House met on the floor above. Known as the Brick Capitol, the three-story brick building was rented to Congress for $1,650 a year.

James Monroe's first inaugural took place in front of the Brick Capitol on March 4, 1817. Congress met in the building for two terms. Later it was used as a rooming house, a military prison during the Civil War, and, finally, as the headquarters of the National Woman's Party. The site today is occupied by the Supreme Court building. *(See box, Inaugural Sites, this page.)*

To succeed Latrobe, President Monroe on January 8, 1818, appointed Charles Bulfinch of Boston, the first American-born architect to hold the position of architect of the Capitol. Bulfinch completed the reconstruction of the north and south wings, enabling Congress to resume meeting in the Capitol at the beginning of the 16th Congress on December 6, 1819. The Supreme Court already had returned for its February 1819 term.

The principal contribution of Bulfinch was to supervise work on the central section, for which the cornerstone was laid August 24, 1818. With some modifications, Bulfinch completed the designs of Thornton and Latrobe for the center and the East and West fronts. There was some discussion of substituting a grand staircase and salon in place of an open rotunda, but Bulfinch decided in favor of the original plan.

In October 1824 the unfinished rotunda was used for a public reception for the Marquis de Lafayette. Then in his late sixties, the last surviving major general of the American Revolution was

---

INAUGURAL SITES

A president may take the oath of office anywhere, and either in public or private. Beginning with Andrew Jackson in 1829, thirty-five inaugural ceremonies were held outdoors near the East Front portico of the Capitol, which looks out on the Supreme Court and the Library of Congress. Ten inaugurations have taken place inside the Capitol. Seven presidents took the oath privately when they assumed the office during an emergency. Three presidents—Rutherford B. Hayes, Woodrow Wilson, and Dwight D. Eisenhower—took the oath in private on the day required by the Constitution, then repeated the oath in public ceremonies a day or two later. Breaking with custom, Ronald Reagan was inaugurated in 1981 on the West Front of the Capitol overlooking the Mall. His second inauguration on the same site was forced indoors by cold weather in 1985.

Following is a list of public inaugural sites other than the East Front portico of the Capitol:

Year	President	Location
1789	George Washington	Federal Hall, New York City
1793	George Washington	Congress Hall, Philadelphia
1797	John Adams	Congress Hall, Philadelphia
1801	Thomas Jefferson	Senate Chamber, Capitol
1805	Thomas Jefferson	Senate Chamber, Capitol
1809	James Madison	House Chamber, Capitol
1813	James Madison	House Chamber, Capitol
1817	James Monroe	Brick Capitol
1821	James Monroe	House Chamber, Capitol
1825	John Quincy Adams	House Chamber, Capitol
1833	Andrew Jackson	House Chamber, Capitol
1850	Millard Fillmore	House Chamber, Capitol
1909	William Howard Taft	House Chamber, Capitol
1945	Franklin D. Roosevelt	South Portico, White House
1974	Gerald R. Ford	East Room, White House
1981	Ronald Reagan	West Front, Capitol
1985	Ronald Reagan	Rotunda, Capitol
1989	George Bush	West Front, Capitol
1993	Bill Clinton	West Front, Capitol
1997	Bill Clinton	West Front, Capitol

---

greeted as a hero. The same year John Trumbull's four paintings of scenes from the Revolution, commissioned in 1817, were hung in the Rotunda.

The original Capitol dome, much lower than the present dome and made of wood sheathed in copper, was completed in 1827. The pediment over the east portico, Luigi Persico's *Genius of America*, was completed in 1828. The following year, construction of the original Capitol was at last completed. The office Bulfinch had held since 1818 was abolished June 25, 1829.

The Capitol as completed in 1829 was 351 feet, 7.5 inches long at ground level and 282 feet, 10.5 inches wide. It took thirty-seven years of construction and repairs for the Capitol to achieve its original design, which it was to retain for only twenty-two years.

Treasury records indicate that the cost of repairing the damage wrought by the British was $687,126. Erection of the central section of the Capitol cost $957,647.36. The Capitol architect's office lists the total cost of the original building, including repairs, restoration, and grading of the Capitol grounds, as $2,432,851.34 up to the year 1827.

Expansion, 1851–1892

Neither the House nor the Senate chambers proved to be comfortable. In addition to the acoustical problems in the House, both chambers were difficult to heat adequately in winter and ventilate in summer.

As the mid-point of the nineteenth century approached, a new problem arose. The two chambers were becoming overcrowded by the increase in the number of members of Congress representing newly admitted states. It was clear that the Capitol would have to be expanded.

In response to a congressional request in 1843, the War Department prepared plans for an addition to the south wing to provide an enlarged chamber for the House. No further action was taken, however.

In May 1850 another set of requested drawings was rejected, although the Capitol by then was crowded with 62 senators and 232 representatives. The new drawings had been prepared by Robert Mills, the architect of public buildings and grounds, at the request of the Senate Committee on Public Buildings. Mills had proposed adding two wings and enlarging the dome. Mills is more widely remembered as the architect of the Washington Monument, the Treasury Building, and the Patent Office.

In September 1850 Congress adopted a resolution for a design competition under the supervision of the House and Senate committees on public buildings. Plans were to be submitted by December 1, 1850, and the winning design was to receive a $500 award. As advertised in newspapers, "the plans and estimates shall provide for the extension of the Capitol, either by additional wings, to be placed on the north and south of the present building, or by the erection of a separate and distinct building" to the east of the existing Capitol.

A variety of plans was submitted. Some merely extended the old building further to the north and the south. Others proposed adding wings to the east and the west. At least one plan called for a duplicate building to the east. Four plans were selected, and Mills was asked to prepare a composite, incorporating certain features of each.

In the meantime, a Senate amendment had been added to a routine appropriations bill authorizing President Millard Fillmore to select a suitable plan and to appoint an architect. The appropriations measure, approved September 30, 1850, provided an initial $100,000 for the expansion. The legislation thwarted Mills's effort to develop a composite plan.

On June 10, 1851, Fillmore approved the general outline of a plan submitted by Thomas Ustick Walter, a Philadelphia architect who had designed Girard College, considered to be an outstanding example of the Greek Revival style then popular in America. Walter was sworn in as architect of the Capitol extension on June 11. His accepted design provided for the erection at either end of the old building of two new wings, which have been used by the House (south wing) and Senate (north wing) ever since.

NEW HOUSE AND SENATE WINGS

The president laid the cornerstone for the extension on July 4, 1851, in the northeast corner of the House wing. The ceremonies included an oration by Daniel Webster. Work began immediately, but it soon was halted. Congress blocked further appropriations in the winter of 1851, when a controversy arose over charges of fraud and poor construction. The charges apparently were initiated by unsuccessful contractors and by the commissioner of public buildings and grounds. President Fillmore had made the Interior Department responsible for the extensions, leaving the commissioner in charge only of the central section. Investigating committees found the charges groundless, and appropriations were resumed in April 1852.

After renewed congressional sniping at Capitol Architect Walter in 1853, President Franklin Pierce on March 23 transferred responsibility for the construction from the Interior Department to the War Department. Secretary of War Jefferson Davis, who as a senator had led the drive for expansion, named Capt. M. C. Meigs of the Corps of Engineers to superintend the construction, and Meigs began a review of Walter's plans.

Meigs's review left Walter's basic design intact but altered the location of the Senate and House chambers within their respective wings. At Meigs's suggestion, Walter redesigned the location of the chambers to place them in the center of their respective wings, with the Senate facing north and the House south.

By the fall of 1854, the walls of the House and Senate wings were up to the ceiling level, but the chambers were not covered over until 1856. The present House chamber was occupied December 16, 1857. As had been the case in the past, representatives were provided with individual desks and chairs. The desks were replaced by semicircular benches in 1859, but the benches were removed and the desks reinstalled in 1860. Not until 1913 were the desks replaced by semicircular rows of seats.

Adequate acoustics remained a problem for the House even when it moved into its new chamber in 1857. Finally, in 1939, a system of microphones and loudspeakers was installed. After years of opposition, the Senate had a public address system installed in 1970.

A delay in receiving certain ironwork held up completion of the north wing in the 1850s, so the Senate was unable to meet in its new chamber until January 4, 1859. The Senate's old desks were moved to the new chamber; new desks were added as the number of senators increased.

The exterior marble for the two wings came from quarries in Massachusetts, and marble for the columns was quarried in

CAPITOL FIRES, BOMBINGS SINCE 1814

Several fires and explosions, some accidental, some deliberately caused, have damaged the Capitol over the course of its history. The first incident occurred August 24, 1814, when a detachment of British troops led by Maj. Gen. Robert Ross and Rear Adm. Sir George Cockburn set fire to the Capitol, heavily damaging the interior.

On December 24, 1851, an accidental fire burned the west front quarters of the Library of Congress, destroying 35,000 of the library's 55,000 books.

A November 6, 1898, gas explosion and fire caused extensive damage to the Supreme Court Chamber, the room previously used by the Senate.

The Senate Reception Room was damaged July 2, 1915, by the explosion of a homemade bomb placed there by Erich Muenter (first identified as Frank Holt), a former instructor of German at Harvard University. He had been upset by private sales of U.S. munitions to the allies in World War I.

An explosion in the Capitol on March 1, 1971, caused extensive damage but no injuries. Coming at a time of rising opposition to U.S. policies in Vietnam, it resulted in an improved security system for the Capitol and in congressional offices. The perpetrator or perpetrators have never been found.

The site of the explosion was an unmarked rest room on the ground floor of the original Senate wing, the oldest part of the Capitol. The blast demolished the rest room and caused extensive damage to six other rooms, including the Senate barbershop, a hearing room of the Senate Appropriations Committee, and hideaway offices used by several senators.

The damage from the blast consisted of cracked and battered walls, weakened floors and arches, blown-out doors and windows, and damaged trim, chandeliers, and artwork.

The Capitol was closed briefly to visitors on the morning following the bombing. Thereafter, the Capitol Police were instructed to check all briefcases and large packages brought into the Capitol and into the Senate and House office buildings by employees as well as tourists.

After the bombing, a number of improvements were made in the Capitol's security system.

• Packages and briefcases were inspected at all entrances to the Capitol and congressional office buildings. At ten entrances the guards are aided by X-ray machines, installed at a total cost of $300,000. Guards at other stations inspect packages by hand.

• An electronic surveillance system using closed circuit television and automatic alarms was installed at strategic points throughout the Capitol complex. The system has more than one hundred TV cameras, which are monitored by the Capitol Police. It was fully installed by May 1975 at a cost of $4 million.

• The tunnels from the Capitol Power Plant to all buildings in the Capitol complex were wired with an alarm system.

• The Capitol Police force was increased from 622 officers in 1971 to 1,265 by 1990.

• A hazardous device unit was established by the Capitol Police to respond to bomb threats, search Capitol areas, and examine suspicious packages. A team of dogs, owned by the Capitol Police, was trained especially to detect explosives. Before the president or a foreign dignitary addresses a joint session of Congress, the Capitol is cleared and the dogs are dispatched throughout the building to sniff out any bombs.

• Potential hiding places for explosives in the Capitol were patched up or sealed off in a series of minor construction projects. For example, false walls of the sort where the 1971 bomb was hidden can no longer be opened. The public is directed away from the remote sections where bombs might be left.

The bombing also gave new life to a study authorized in 1970 to modify the House and Senate galleries, including the installation of bulletproof glass. Such a measure was first suggested in 1954, following the shooting of five representatives by Puerto Rican nationalists. The study concluded in 1973 that the glass was not advisable. But in January 1976 electronic metal detectors were installed at seven entrances to the House gallery. The walk-through sensors are similar to those used at airports.

Far-reaching as they were, these security measures failed to prevent yet another Capitol bombing, on November 7, 1983. Shortly before 11 p.m. that night, a powerful device exploded in a second-floor alcove about thirty feet from the Senate chamber. The blast blew out a wall partition and shattered the windows of the Republican cloakroom. There were no injuries or structural damage, however, and repairs began the next morning. FBI investigators said the bomb had been set hours before it exploded and apparently consisted of several sticks of dynamite with a pocket watch as a timer.

In a telephone call to the *Washington Post*, a member of a group calling itself the Armed Resistance Unit claimed responsibility for the bombing. The caller said the explosion was meant as a protest against U.S. military "aggression" in Grenada and Vietnam.

As in the aftermath of earlier bombings, Capitol building security was tightened. Visitor access was limited to four or six doors (about ten had been used previously), and metal detectors were installed at all entrances. Only persons entering the House and Senate galleries had been screened before.

In addition, lobbyists and tourists no longer were permitted in the hallways immediately outside the House and Senate chambers. Auto traffic and parking on the East Front lot were restricted, and delivery trucks were searched. However, a proposal to enclose the Capitol grounds with a fence was discarded.

In May 1988, seven people were indicted by a U.S. District Court grand jury in Washington on charges of conspiring to carry out the 1983 bombing. Three of the accused pleaded guilty on September 7, 1990, clearing the way for federal prosecutors to drop charges against the remaining defendants, one of whom was then under treatment in a local hospital for Hodgkin's disease.

Under President Abraham Lincoln's orders, construction of the large Capitol dome continued during the Civil War "as a sign we intend the Union shall go on."

Maryland. One hundred columns, each cut from a single block of marble, were dressed by stonemasons on the Capitol grounds. Granite was used for the foundations. Before this phase of the construction, the Capitol had been built almost entirely of sandstone.

CONSTRUCTION OF A NEW DOME

Although Walter's plans for extending the Capitol had made no provision for replacing the 1827 Bulfinch dome, it soon became apparent that the greatly enlarged building dwarfed the old dome. Consequently, on April 4, 1855, Congress authorized a replacement, and Walter drew up the plans.

The tiered dome Walter designed became the most distinguishing feature of the Capitol. It is a considerable accomplishment of art and engineering. The entire dome, including the thirty-six columns in its lower section, is made of cast iron painted to match the Capitol's stonework. It consists of inner and outer shells girded and bolted together. It was assembled with the help of an internal crane that Meigs built from the floor of the Rotunda. The dome is more than 135 feet wide at its base, and the Rotunda inside is ninety-six feet in diameter.

Work on the dome began in 1856 and was completed in 1865. Construction continued during the Civil War because President Abraham Lincoln wanted the expanding Capitol to be "a sign we intend the Union shall go on."

On December 20, 1863, the last section of the Statue of Freedom atop the dome was bolted into place, crowning the Capitol. Originally designed by sculptor Thomas Crawford as *Armed Liberty*, wearing a soft cap of freed Roman slaves, the female statue was modified at the request of Secretary of War Davis.

After installation of the dome's statue, work continued elsewhere on the Capitol. The pediment over the east portico of the Senate wing, *The Progress of Civilization*, by Crawford, was erected in 1863. The north and west porticoes of the Senate wing were completed several years later. The porticoes of the House wing were finished by 1867, but the pediment over the east portico, Paul Wayland Bartlett's *The Apotheosis of Democracy*, was not installed until 1916.

Walter resigned as architect on May 26, 1865, as a result of a conflict over enlarging the quarters of the Library of Congress, then situated near the West Front of the Capitol. A fire in 1851 had destroyed much of the library.

SHOOTINGS AND OTHER VIOLENCE IN THE CAPITOL

The Capitol has not been immune from violence, particularly during the nineteenth century. Strong personal feelings in Congress occasionally have led to brawls among members in both chambers. In 1835 Vice President Martin Van Buren regularly wore a brace of pistols while presiding over the Senate. The House became known in frontier days as the "Bear Garden" because of its many quarrels. A picture in the files of the Library of Congress shows a wild melee on the House floor during a debate in 1858 on the Kansas statehood bill. Private citizens also have attacked members of Congress and staffers in the Capitol.

Following is a list of major incidents:

Attempt on President Jackson. On January 30, 1835, a man later identified as Richard Lawrence fired two pistols at Andrew Jackson as the president stood in the Rotunda. Both pistols misfired. Jackson had come to the Capitol to attend funeral services in the House chamber for Rep. Warren R. Davis, Nullifier-S.C. Lawrence, who was captured immediately, was found to be insane.

Foote-Benton Quarrel. On April 17, 1850, during a debate on the Compromise of 1850, Sen. Henry S. Foote, D-Miss., a supporter of the Compromise, drew a pistol on Sen. Thomas Hart Benton, D-Mo., who opposed the Compromise. The incident occurred when Benton rushed to threaten Foote after Foote had directed bitter personal abuse at him. Other senators intervened before Foote could fire.

Beating of Sumner. On May 22, 1856, Rep. Preston S. Brooks, D-S.C., used a heavy cane in an attack on Sen. Charles Sumner, R-Mass., in the Senate chamber. The attack came during discussion of the Kansas-Nebraska bill, and it followed a May 20 speech in which Sumner had personally denounced Brooks's uncle, Sen. A. P. Butler, States Rights Democrat–S.C. Sumner was beaten unconscious and was not able to resume his Senate duties for more than three years. Brooks, censured, resigned his seat but was reelected.

Shooting of Taulbee. On February 28, 1890, Charles E. Kincaid, a correspondent for the *Louisville Times,* shot former Rep. William P. Taulbee, D-Ky., on the stairs leading from the east corridor of the House to the basement. The shooting argument resulted from *Times* stories of a scandal involving Taulbee. Taulbee died of the wounds on March 11, 1890.

Gunman in the House. On December 13, 1932, a young man entered the House gallery, drew a loaded revolver and began waving it wildly, demanding time to address the House. As bedlam broke loose on the House floor, Rep. Melvin J. Maas, R-Minn., approached the gunman, a department store clerk named Marlin R. M. Kemmerer, and talked him into dropping the gun. Police arrested Kemmerer without a shot being fired.

Bricker Shooting. On July 12, 1947, Sen. John W. Bricker, R-Ohio, was shot at twice as he entered the Senate subway. Both shots missed. The gunman was William L. Kaiser, a former Capitol policeman who had lost money when an Ohio building and loan firm was liquidated fifteen years earlier.

Puerto Rican Attack. Five representatives were shot March 1, 1954, on the floor of the House. Their assailants, three pistol-wielding Puerto Rican extremists of the Nationalist Party, fired about thirty shots from a visitors' gallery into a crowd of about two hundred representatives. Wounded were Reps. Alvin M. Bentley, R-Mich., Ben F. Jensen, R-Iowa, Clifford Davis, D-Tenn., George H. Fallon, D-Md., and Kenneth A. Roberts, D-Ala. The three assailants, and a fourth member of the group captured later, received prison sentences.

Capitol Police Slayings. On July 24, 1998, a gunman barged through a security checkpoint at the Capitol and fatally shot two Capitol Police officers, Jacob J. Chestnut and John M. Gibson, and wounded a tourist. The assailant, Russell Eugene Weston Jr., also wounded in the attack, was later found to be mentally incompetent to stand trial on murder charges.

The flag-draped coffins of Chestnut and Gibson lay in state July 28 in the Capitol Rotunda, a tribute normally reserved for presidents, generals, and lawmakers of unusual distinction.

The shootings sparked efforts to upgrade security in the Capitol area. The fiscal 1999 appropriations bill for the legislative branch, passed that September, increased spending for the Capitol Police by 12 percent. A separate, supplemental appropriations bill that cleared Congress the following month authorized $100 million to build an underground Capitol visitor center where people could be screened before entering the "People's House."

Impeachment Trial Incident. A former television anchor from Mississippi was apprehended by Capitol Police on January 20, 1999, as he attempted to gain admittance to the Senate impeachment trial of President Bill Clinton. Walter Wilson Johnson was stopped when a police search of his bag turned up an 18-inch knife and two explosive devices. In April 1999 Johnson was confined to a local correctional treatment facility pending trial.

CAPITOL DURING THE CIVIL WAR

Congress, or what was left of it following secession, had adjourned March 3, 1861, the day before Lincoln's inauguration. When the president on April 15 issued a call for 75,000 volunteers after the Confederates attacked Ft. Sumter, the Capitol was still vacant. When the requested troops began arriving, they were quartered in the building. Some fourteen units (three thousand troops in all) bivouacked in the Capitol at one time or another.

When Lincoln called a special session of Congress for July 4, 1862, the troops were cleared out and the Capitol was given a thorough scouring. After Congress adjourned on July 17, the Capitol again was temporarily requisitioned as a hospital for the wounded from the Second Bull Run and Antietam battles. About fifteen hundred cots were set up in the corridors, the Rotunda, and the House and Senate chambers. The patients were transferred to other hospitals before Congress returned December 1, and the Capitol once again was cleaned and refurbished.

FINAL TRIBUTES IN ROTUNDA

There is no law or written rule regulating whose body may lie in state in the Rotunda of the Capitol. Use of the Rotunda is controlled generally by House and Senate approval through concurrent resolutions, but it has been used without full concurrence during recesses or between sessions of Congress.

Twenty-nine Americans have lain in state in the Rotunda. They have included nine presidents, six military men, and the city planner who chose the site for the Capitol. The simple bier of cloth-covered boards constructed for Abraham Lincoln's coffin has been used for all tributes since 1865. The Lincoln catafalque was used also for services in the Senate chamber for Chief Justice Salmon P. Chase in 1873 and in the House chamber for Rep. Samuel Hooper in 1875.

Following is a list of persons who have been honored in the Rotunda and the dates on which their bodies lay in state:

Henry Clay	July 1, 1852
Abraham Lincoln	April 19–21, 1865
Thaddeus Stevens	August 13–14, 1868
Charles Sumner	March 13, 1874
Henry Wilson	November 25–26, 1875
James A. Garfield	September 21, 23, 1881
John A. Logan	December 30–31, 1886
William McKinley	September 17, 1901
Pierre Charles L'Enfant (reinterment)	April 28, 1909
George Dewey	January 20, 1917
Unknown Soldier of World War I	November 9–11, 1921
Warren G. Harding	August 8, 1923
William Howard Taft	March 11, 1930
John Joseph Pershing	July 18–19, 1948
Robert A. Taft	August 2–3, 1953
Unknown Soldiers of World War II and the Korean War[1] (2)	May 28–30, 1958
John F. Kennedy	November 24–25, 1963
Douglas MacArthur	April 8–9, 1964
Herbert Hoover	October 23–25, 1964
Dwight D. Eisenhower	March 30–31, 1969
Everett McKinley Dirksen	September 9–10, 1969
J. Edgar Hoover	May 3–4, 1972
Lyndon Baines Johnson	January 24–25, 1973
Hubert H. Humphrey	January 14–15, 1978
Unknown Soldier of the Vietnam Era	May 1984
Claude Pepper	June 1, 1989
Jacob J. Chestnut and John M. Gibson (slain Capitol Police officers)	July 28, 1998

1. A duplicate catafalque was constructed, and each coffin rested for a time on the Lincoln catafalque.

SOURCE: Architect of the Capitol.

LANDSCAPING THE GROUNDS

As work on the Capitol expansion drew to a close in the late 1860s, the task of landscaping the Capitol grounds remained. The most prominent landscape architect of the time was Frederick Law Olmsted, the designer of New York City's Central Park. On June 23, 1874, Congress commissioned Olmsted to landscape the Capitol grounds. The results of his work still surround the building.

Initial work on the grounds was carried out from 1874 to 1882. In 1881 additional funds were sought for the stairway and terraces on the west side of the Capitol, which Olmsted also designed. Congress approved the request, and work began in 1884. Space beneath the terraces was designed for use as committee rooms. With the landscaping virtually completed, Olmsted resigned in 1885. The final work on the terraces, finished in 1892, was supervised by Architect of the Capitol Edward Clark.

Twentieth Century Alterations

For seventy-five years after the completion of the dome, little important architectural work was done on the Capitol. The roofs of the old north and south wings over the original Senate chamber and Statuary Hall were rebuilt and fireproofed in 1902.

In 1940 Congress authorized remodeling of the House and Senate chambers and replacement of their cast-iron and glass ceilings with new ceilings of stainless steel and plaster. Temporary supports were installed under the old, weakened ceilings. But work on the new ones was delayed by World War II. The actual remodeling was carried out from July 1949 to January 1951. The work incorporated designs used by Thornton and Latrobe in the Supreme Court and Statuary Hall sections of the Capitol and in other buildings of the period on which they worked.

On three occasions the House and the Senate vacated their chambers to allow the renovation to progress. The Senate held its sessions in the old Senate chamber, or Supreme Court room. The House met in the caucus room of the Longworth House Office Building.

When temporary ceiling supports were being installed, the two bodies met in their substitute quarters from November 22, 1940, to January 3, 1941. During the first stage of construction work, the two bodies met there from July 1, 1949, to January 3, 1950. When construction on the final stage was under way, the Senate met in its old chamber from August 11, 1950, to January 3, 1951, and the House met in the Longworth Building from September 1, 1950, to January 1, 1951.

EAST FRONT EXTENSION

The most controversial recent alteration of the Capitol was the 1958–1962 extension of the East Front. Although such an extension had been discussed for years, in 1956 it became a major dispute.

When Capitol Architect Thomas Walter designed the wings for the House and Senate and the new dome, he suggested ex-

The Speaker's Lobby reflects the opulence of the Capitol's interior.

tending the east central section to make it symmetrical with the west central section and avoid any appearance of inadequate support for the larger dome. Walter wrote in his 1863 report to Congress: "The eastern portion of the old building will certainly be taken down at no very distant day, and the front extended eastward."[5] But the day was more distant than Walter expected.

As early as 1903 the House had passed a bill to extend the East Front, but the legislation died in the Senate. One year later, Congress established a joint commission to study the question. The commission asked the firm of Carrere and Hastings, which had just designed the first House and Senate office buildings, to prepare plans for the proposed extension. The architects submitted two proposals, but once again no action was taken. In 1935 and in 1937 the Senate passed bills providing for an extension, but the measures died in the House.

Finally, in 1955, Congress authorized a 32.5-foot extension that had been proposed a half century earlier by Carrere and Hastings. At first, there was little discussion. Contributing to its acceptance were the deteriorating condition of the sandstone facing and Congress's need for additional space. Speaker Sam Rayburn, D-Texas, was one of the strongest advocates of the extension.

As public awareness of the impending project grew, however, strong opposition developed among architectural and historic preservation groups. Opponents of the extension said the East Front should be repaired and preserved. They forced a one-day hearing February 17, 1958, before the Senate Public Works Subcommittee on Public Buildings and Grounds. On February 21 the extension commission ordered the project to go ahead.

Work began in 1958 under the supervision of Capitol Architect J. George Stewart. On July 4, 1959, President Dwight D. Eisenhower laid the cornerstone for the new marble East Front. The old sandstone walls were retained as part of the interior wall construction. The original stonework and carvings were copied exactly. The old sandstone columns were removed and stored at the Capitol Power Plant; eventually they were transferred to the National Arboretum. Crumbling statuary from the East Front finally was transferred to the Smithsonian Institution in 1975. The work was completed in 1962, although it was far enough along for President John F. Kennedy to hold his inauguration at the East Front on January 20, 1961.

The East Front extension added 100,000 square feet of space to the Capitol's five floors. It provided 102 new rooms, including fifty-four offices for individuals and committees, reception rooms, dining rooms and kitchens, document rooms, entrance foyers, additional elevators, and a private corridor for members between the Senate and House wings.

The construction project involved more than an extension of the East Front. The Capitol's cast iron dome was sandblasted and repainted; a subway terminal was built under the Senate wing steps and the steps were rebuilt; the exterior marble of the Senate and House wings was cleaned for the first time since 1872; the entire building was "birdproofed"; all new rooms were furnished; and lighting throughout the Capitol was improved.

WEST FRONT CONTROVERSY

As work on the East Front drew to a close in 1962, the question of whether to restore or extend the West Front began developing into perhaps the most controversial construction issue in the Capitol's long history. At the heart of the controversy was a critical problem that had to be addressed: a structural weakness in the west wall of the Capitol's central section. The last exposed portion of the original Capitol, the wall was made of sandstone on the outside, brick and stone on the inside, and was filled with rubble. The wall bore much of the lateral load of the building and had been moving slightly, perhaps as much as one-fourth of an inch each year, according to the Capitol architect. In 1965 the weakest portions of the West Front were shored with heavy timbers.

A storm of congressional protest erupted when details of a proposed 285-room extension were made public in 1966. The objections were based on economic, historical, and architectural grounds. Architect of the Capitol J. George Stewart, a former representative from Delaware, was criticized for his strong advocacy of the plan.

Opposing extension, the American Institute of Architects (AIA) said in a 1967 report: "The west front of the Capitol can be restored and its structural weaknesses corrected." While restoration would be costly and "would entail some inconvenience," the AIA said, it was "unlikely that the cost of the restoration would approach the total cost of extension." The AIA, stressing the historical importance of the existing West Front, also called for a "permanent policy prohibiting any further major alteration to the Capitol."

Stewart died in office May 24, 1970. President Richard Nixon on January 27, 1971, appointed George M. White as the ninth architect of the Capitol. White was the Capitol's first professional architect since Walter. (See box, The Capitol Architect, this page.)

THE CAPITOL ARCHITECT

The post of architect of the Capitol has existed as a permanent position since 1876, when Congress transferred to the architect the functions performed previously by the commissioner for public buildings and grounds. However, beginning with William Thornton in 1793, nine presidential appointees have had the architect's responsibility for construction and maintenance of the Capitol.

The architect of the Capitol need not be a professional architect, for the position today is largely an administrative one. The architect is charged with the structural and mechanical care of the following buildings: the Capitol and two hundred acres of grounds, the Senate and House office buildings, the Library of Congress buildings and grounds, the U.S. Supreme Court buildings and grounds, the Senate garage, the Robert A. Taft Memorial, and the Capitol Power Plant, which heats and cools some buildings in addition to the Capitol complex. The architect also is charged with the operation of the U.S. Botanic Garden and the Senate restaurants.

The architect performs these tasks under the direction of the Speaker of the House, the Senate Committee on Rules and Administration, the House Office Building Commission, and the Joint Committee on the Library. Employees working for the architect of the Capitol include tree surgeons, stone inspectors, nurses, subway car and elevator operators, garage workers, and flag clerks. Services provided for congressional committees and members of Congress by the architect's office include work-space design, furniture acquisition and delivery, housekeeping, painting, and catering.

Following is a list of persons who have been appointed by the president to serve as architect of the Capitol, although under other titles in the early years:

1793–1794	William Thornton
1803–1811; 1815–1817	Benjamin Henry Latrobe
1818–1829	Charles Bulfinch
1851–1865	Thomas Ustick Walter
1865–1902	Edward Clark
1902–1923	Elliott Woods
1923–1954	David Lynn
1954–1970	J. George Stewart
1971–1997	George M. White
1997–	Alan M. Hantman

After a yearlong study of the various proposals, White concluded that an extension was needed. The controversy continued, but it was cooled somewhat in the late 1970s by other issues and Congress's desire not to disrupt the 1976 Bicentennial observances.

By 1983 the advocates of restoration had won out. Congress appropriated $49 million to stabilize the deteriorated masonry. More than thirty layers of paint were removed and more than a thousand stainless steel reinforcing rods were inserted into blocks that were considered safe enough to remain. About one-

RAISING THE FLAGS

Much of the Capitol's daily business is conducted in places inaccessible to the casual visitor—on the roof, for instance. It is there that employees of the architect of the Capitol's flag office raise and lower thousands of American flags each year, all destined for shipment to citizens or organizations that request one in writing from their member of Congress.

The flag program began in 1937. By 1999 more than one hundred thousand flags a year—about three hundred a day on average—were being run up a flagpole set aside for that purpose and lowered almost instantly. When mailed, a certificate of authenticity accompanies each flag. The recipient is charged a fee pegged to the type of fabric used, cotton or nylon. Each senator and House member may forward to the flag office as many constituent requests as he or she wishes.

The all-time record for Capitol flag raising was set on July 4, 1976, the day the nation's Bicentennial was celebrated. On that day 10,471 flags were flown over the Capitol on eighteen temporary flagpoles. Flag raising began at 12:01 a.m. and was concluded at 9 p.m.

The flag office also distributes the flags that have flown on the flagpoles located over the east and west central fronts of the Capitol. Those flags are flown continuously and are not replaced until they become worn.

third of the sandstone was replaced with Indiana limestone. The work was completed ahead of schedule in 1987, finally permitting removal of the shoring and scaffolding that for years had marred the view of the Capitol from the Mall.

OTHER REMODELING PROJECTS

Besides the controversial construction projects that have plagued the Capitol, more modest remodeling goes on continually. The building requires a great deal of maintenance, including restoration of art and replacement of furnishings. Four remodeling projects were designed to prepare the Capitol for the Bicentennial. These were supervised by the architect of the Capitol and the Senate Commission on Art and Antiquities.

Rotunda

Early in 1975 the Rotunda was refurbished for the first time in more than seventy years. The stone walls were cleaned and cracks were sealed. The exposed iron parts of the dome were tinted and gilded according to a color drawing prepared by Walter in the 1860s. Six oil paintings were restored, special lighting was installed, and sixteen upholstered benches designed for the House chamber in 1859 were placed around the Rotunda.

Statuary Hall

In 1975 and 1976 Statuary Hall was partially restored to resemble its appearance in 1822 when it served as the House chamber. Some statues were moved to other parts of the Capitol. The ceiling was repainted; new scarlet draperies were hung; and two fireplaces were opened and restored. An electric replica of the chamber's original Argand chandelier was installed in 1976.

Old Supreme Court Chamber

On May 22, 1975, the public got its first look at the restored Supreme Court chamber on the first floor of the original Senate wing. The chamber, which the Court used for seventy-five years, from Latrobe's remodeling until Walter's expansion, was fully restored to its appearance of 1859. For twenty years it had been a storeroom.

Old Senate Chamber

Restoration of the old Senate chamber, on the second floor north of the Rotunda, was completed in 1976. The original lights, draperies, and furniture used by the Senate in the 1850s were restored, and carpeting and other period furnishings were reproduced, including members' desks, arranged in four semicircular rows, and reproductions of the red-upholstered sofas that accommodated privileged visitors to the chamber's "lower circle." The Senate met there from 1810 to 1859, at which time the chamber was remodeled and used by the Supreme Court for the next seventy-five years.

Statue of Freedom

In May 1993 a helicopter lifted the Statue of Freedom from its perch atop the Capitol dome and placed it on a platform on

During the renovation of the Capitol dome in 1999, a large inflated donut was placed under the Rotunda to catch falling debris.

the Capitol's east front plaza. The nineteen-foot-tall bronze figure then underwent weeks of renovation and repair, including removal of corrosion, caulk, and interior paint. When the $780,000 project was completed, the statue received protective coatings of lacquer and wax. Freedom was returned to its pedestal on the dome (again by helicopter) in October 1993.

Capitol Dome

To combat leaks and cracks in the Capitol dome, the office of the Architect of the Capitol launched a two-phase rehabilitation program in early 1999. A priority concern during the initial phase, expected to last eighteen months, was safeguarding the interior canopy of the Rotunda, site of Constantino Brumidi's beloved fresco, *The Apotheosis of [George] Washington.* The project's second phase, due to begin in the summer of 2000, was to feature installation of a new bird-proofing system on the dome's roof.

U.S. Botanic Garden

The U.S. Botanic Garden Conservatory, situated at the foot of Capitol Hill, was closed in September 1997 for an estimated three years of renovation and reconstruction. As part of the project, three acres of lawn adjacent to the conservatory were to be converted into a National Garden.

House and Senate Office Buildings

The construction of separate office buildings for senators and representatives occurred relatively recently in the history of Congress. The first congressional office building, for House members, opened in 1908. Until then, a member's office consisted of his desk in the House or Senate chamber and his Washington residence. His files were carried in his head or jacket pockets. This was because congressional service was at most a part-time occupation for the first hundred years of the Republic. Sessions were short. Standing committees were few. And Washington was both inaccessible and inhospitable, which served to protect members from visits by constituents.

In Washington, if a member was not on the floor he had virtually no sanctuary, except for his dwelling. The lobbies just off the chambers provided some relaxation. These were open to the public, and favor-seekers took advantage of the chance to buttonhole legislators; hence the term *lobbying.*

PRESSURE FOR OFFICE SPACE

Pressure for additional office space came first from the congressional committees. As standing committees increased in number in the second half of the nineteenth century, they quickly overflowed the rooms allocated to them in the unfinished Capitol. At times several Senate committees would meet in separate areas of the Senate chamber. When Bulfinch was at work on the Capitol's center section, he erected a temporary building for committees on the site of the present House wing. The long wooden building stood for only a few years, until the original Capitol was completed. The expansion of the Capitol by Walter in the 1850s provided more committee rooms, and much of the space beneath the terraces built in the 1880s was designated for committees.

The proliferation of committees devoured new space almost as fast as it was provided. Not all of the proliferation was dictated by the press of legislative business. A committee office in the Capitol frequently doubled as a personal office for the committee chairman. The committee clerks doubled as a personal staff. This dual role of committees was widely acknowledged and occasionally criticized.

As the committees outgrew the space provided even in the expanded Capitol, additional space was rented in nearby privately owned buildings. By 1891 the Maltby Building, at B Street and New Jersey Avenue, Northwest, had become known as the Senate Annex, housing eighty-one offices. By the end of the century, use of the converted building had become too inconvenient, if not hazardous because of the danger of fire. The Maltby

CAPITOL SUBWAYS

Rep. Bud Shuster, R-Pa., right, and his chief of staff, Jack Schenendorf, ride the House subway to the Capitol.

The Senate and House office buildings are linked to the Capitol by underground tunnels. Subway cars have shuttled from the Senate wing to the Russell Building since 1909, to the Dirksen Building since 1960, and to the Hart Building since 1982.

The only subway service on the House side operates from the Rayburn Building. The tunnel between the Capitol and the Cannon and Longworth buildings is restricted to pedestrian traffic.

Two Studebaker battery-operated vehicles with solid rubber tires provided the first subway transportation to and from the Russell Building. Faster service came in 1912 with two monorail cars powered by overhead wires. Two redesigned monorail cars, produced at the Washington Navy Yard and put into service in 1920, remained in use until 1961.

A new subway system connecting the Senate office buildings with the Capitol began service in 1960. It consists of four eighteen-passenger electric cars on two-rail tracks. At twenty miles an hour, their running time is forty-five seconds from the Russell Building, sixty seconds from the Dirksen Building, and sixty-five seconds from the Hart Building.

A similar system was installed between the Rayburn Building and the Capitol in 1966. Running time is forty seconds.

All Capitol subways operate during working hours when Congress is in session, and the public may ride free if space is available. When the cars are not running, all tunnels remain open to pedestrian traffic.

Building had been condemned as unsafe even before the Senate finally left it.

CONSTRUCTION OF OFFICE BUILDINGS

As the nation grew, increased congressional membership produced a demand for additional rooms to accommodate members. The House authorized its first office building in 1903, the Senate in 1904. Today, each has three office buildings.

For years the House buildings were unnamed, known simply as the House Office Building, or, when a second one was built, as the Old House Office Building and the New House Office Building. When a third building was under construction in 1962, the House decided to name each for the House Speaker in office during a major part of its construction. The old building was named for Joseph G. Cannon, R-Ill., the new one for Nicholas Longworth, R-Ohio, and the third building for Sam Rayburn, D-Texas.

The buildings on the Senate side for many years were called simply the Old and New Senate Office Buildings. In 1972 they were named for two former leaders of the Senate, the old building for Richard B. Russell, D-Ga., and the new one for Everett McKinley Dirksen, R-Ill.

In 1972 the Senate authorized an addition to the Dirksen Building, designated the Hart Building in memory of Sen. Philip A. Hart, D-Mich. After many delays and revised cost estimates, the building opened in 1982. It cost $137.7 million, making it the most expensive of the six congressional office buildings.

Most committees of Congress have space in the office buildings, although a handful of House and Senate and joint House-Senate committees have retained rooms in the Capitol. Miscellaneous organizations of members, such as the Democratic Study Group, the House Republican Conference, and various congressional and special interest caucuses, all have space in the office buildings. The buildings also house a number of noncongressional organizations, including branch offices of the U.S. Employment Service, Office of Personnel Management, and liaison offices of all the armed forces. Assignment of space in the office buildings is based on seniority. Senior members anxious to escape visiting constituents and lobbyists in the office buildings often are assigned unmarked hideaways in the Capitol.

EARLY OFFICE BUILDINGS

The first of the congressional offices, the Cannon Building, was authorized by Congress in 1903. President Theodore Roosevelt participated in cornerstone ceremonies April 14, 1906. Designed by Carrere and Hastings, the building was occupied January 10, 1908.[6]

When designed, it was large enough to accommodate the existing House membership. But Congress in 1911 authorized an increase in the size of the House to 435 members (the present limit), and an additional story was added in 1913–1914. Overall, the building contains about five hundred rooms. As part of the Rayburn House Office Building project in the 1960s, the Cannon Building was remodeled.

The first office building for the Senate was authorized in 1904. Adapted by Carrere and Hastings from the firm's plans for the Cannon Building, the Russell Building was occupied March 5, 1909.

Authorized in 1929, the second building for the House—the Longworth Building—was ready for occupancy April 20, 1933. The eight floors occupied by representatives contain 251 two-room suites and sixteen committee rooms.

The first congressional office building, completed in 1908, was the Cannon Building, named after Speaker Joseph G. Cannon. Today, the House and Senate have three office buildings each for members and staff.

Congress authorized the Senate's second building—the Dirksen Building—in 1948, and the site, next to the Russell Building, was purchased and cleared. But the Korean War delayed groundbreaking until 1955. The building was ready for occupancy October 15, 1958. It has 419,000 square feet of floor space.

CONTROVERSIAL RAYBURN BUILDING

The next congressional office project, the Rayburn Building, was conceived in controversy and completed in conflict. Its legislative history began in 1955 when the Dirksen Building was under construction and Speaker Rayburn reminded the House of Representatives of its own space needs.

With the aid of trusted lieutenants, Rayburn, then seventy-three years old, maneuvered the initial funding through an "emergency" amendment to a supplemental appropriations bill. Under House rules, appropriations bills are supposed to be limited to providing money for projects authorized by previous legislation, but no new building had been authorized by Congress.

Nevertheless, by the time the supplemental appropriations bill emerged from a House-Senate conference, it provided an initial $5 million for the new House office building. Congress gave its final approval April 20, 1955, and the Rayburn Building project was under way.

The total cost of the Rayburn Building was obscured by design changes and faulty estimates and because other Capitol Hill construction and renovation was going on at the same time. Appropriations exceeding $135 million included the Rayburn Building and its site, remodeling of the Cannon and Longworth buildings, and construction of three underground garages and House subways. According to the office of the architect of the Capitol, final cost of the Rayburn Building itself was $87.7 million, including land acquisition and furnishings.

Completed and occupied in the spring of 1965, the Rayburn Building is larger than the Capitol itself. When approached from the west along Independence Avenue, it appears to dominate Capitol Hill. It is 720 feet long and 450 feet wide (covering about two blocks) and has fifty acres of floor space on nine stories. It is served by twenty-five passenger elevators, twenty-three escalators, and a subway line to the Capitol.

Primary accommodations include 169 three-room suites for representatives, nine hearing rooms for standing committees,

U.S. CAPITOL POLICE: A VERSATILE FORCE

The U.S. Capitol Police is the private security force of Congress. Members of the force are responsible for security inside the Capitol, in the Senate and House office buildings, and on the grounds surrounding the Capitol. Because Capitol Police are stationed at one of the most popular tourist attractions in the United States, they must be to some extent tour guides and public relations officers as well as law enforcement officers. As of May 1999 there were 1,315 officers.

From 1800 (when Congress first met in Washington) to 1857, watchmen were hired to guard the inside of the Capitol; patrol of the Capitol grounds was left to the District of Columbia police. Congress appropriated $200 on March 3, 1857, to pay the watchmen, and for the first time these security men were referred to as the Capitol Police. By 1876 the police had become a thirty-one-man force with one captain, three lieutenants, twenty-two privates, and six watchmen at a cost of $33,700 a year. The responsibility of selecting men for the force was split evenly between the sergeants at arms of the Senate and House.

PATRONAGE AND PROFESSIONALISM

Until 1967 all members of the Capitol Police were patronage appointees (except for the special officers on loan from the Metropolitan Police). Their continued service depended on remaining in the good graces of their sponsors and on the sponsor's tenure in office. When a senior member of Congress was defeated or retired, the member's patronage appointees generally left the Capitol also.

The first break with the patronage recruitment tradition came in 1967, when the House needed more policemen to handle security for the two-year-old Rayburn Building. Instead of expanding the 250-member force through patronage appointments, the House adopted a resolution adding seventy-eight men to it "without regard to political affiliation and solely on the basis of fitness to perform the duties." The result was an increasingly professional force, which delighted Capitol Police Chief James M. Powell, a longtime advocate of hiring more career police officers.

Patronage on the force dropped from nearly 100 percent in 1966 to 41 percent by 1970 and to 25 percent in 1971. By mid-1999, with patronage fully phased out, politically related appointments accounted for well under 10 percent of all Capitol Police.

When rising crime in the late 1960s pushed the District of Columbia up among the ten metropolitan centers with the highest crime rate, members of Congress began to expand the Capitol Police. Mass demonstrations in Washington opposing the Vietnam War also emphasized the need for a larger and more professional force. A bomb explosion in the Capitol on March 1, 1971, resulted in greater police protection throughout the Capitol Hill complex.

The increase in staff was accompanied by increases in police equipment, such as scout cars, cruisers, motor scooters, buses, package X-ray machines, a closed-circuit TV system, and a dozen police dogs trained to detect explosives.

CONTROL, SELECTION, AND TRAINING

The Capitol Police are under direction and control of the sergeant at arms of the Senate and the sergeant at arms of the House. The force technically is divided into two parts—one for the House, one for the Senate. When one side of Congress needs additional security forces, officers are added to the appropriate part of the force.

The sergeants at arms and the architect of the Capitol are the three members of the Capitol Police board, which reviews recommendations for suspension of an officer, considers requests for more men, and submits reports to congressional committees. The Capitol Police chief is responsible for recommending promotions.

Candidates for professional positions must pass a physical exam and undergo a background investigation. Applicants must be between twenty-one and forty. The recruit initiation program begins with two weeks of training conducted by the Capitol Police training division in Washington. The appointees then attend an ten-week course at the Federal Law Enforcement Training Center in Glynco, Ga., where they receive instruction in constitutional law, first aid, tactics, firearms use, pursuit driving, and other procedures.

A final ten-week training period is then conducted back in Washington, during which candidates receive instruction on matters such as survival techniques, traffic regulations, the D.C. Code, and court systems. But that is not the end of the apprenticeship ordeal. After graduating from recruit school, officer candidates take part in an eight-week field exercise in which they are paired with veteran officers.

Moreover, new members of the force receive training on explosives and hazardous devices, criminal investigation, hostage negotiations, terrorism, and physical security. Senior members are nominated periodically to attend a security training course at the FBI Academy.

In December 1981 the force was given statutory responsibility for protecting members of Congress, their families, and staff, anywhere in the United States.

A provision of the fiscal 1990 supplemental appropriations act extended the jurisdiction of the Capitol Police to parking spaces at Union Station rented by the Senate and to contiguous areas. Legislation approved by Congress in 1992 authorized Capitol Police officers to make arrests elsewhere in the District of Columbia while they were on official business or when they encountered crimes of violence.

and sixteen rooms for subcommittees. Eight of the hearing rooms are two stories high. A typical suite is about fifty-four feet long and thirty-two feet wide. An underground garage for sixteen hundred cars takes up 42 percent of the building's gross floor space. Health facilities include a fully equipped gymnasium, a twenty-by-sixty foot swimming pool, and compartments identified as "slumber rooms."

Aside from the cost and charges of extravagance, most of the criticism leveled at the Rayburn Building has dealt with its architectural style. Built of marble and granite, it is known architecturally as "simplified classic." But critics derided it as "Mussolini Modern" and "Texas Penitentiary."

CONTROVERSY OVER THE HART BUILDING

In 1972 the Senate concluded that the Dirksen Building needed to be expanded. An addition, designated the Hart Building in memory of Senator Hart, was authorized. After many delays and revised cost estimates, the building was opened in December 1982 at a cost of about $138 million—making it even more costly than the much-criticized Rayburn Building. Capitol architect White laid most of the blame for the high cost on price inflation during the ten years of planning and construction.

The final plans, approved in late 1975, provided that the building would have 546,000 square feet of office space for fifty senators, a gymnasium, and a two-story hearing room with built-in television lights and glass booths for broadcasters.

White testified in March 1981 that "major portions" would remain unfinished because of economies imposed in 1979, when senators were fretting about the steadily climbing estimates of the building's cost. Among the features left out of the final contracts were the gym, a rooftop restaurant, and the hearing room especially designed for television coverage.

HOUSE FIRETRAPS?

House Inspector General John W. Lainhart IV created a stir in December 1998 by asserting in a report that persons working in or visiting the three House office buildings, two House annexes, or the House side of the Capitol faced "undue risk of loss of life and property" because of inadequate fire protection. Lainhart stated that the Architect of the Capitol bore responsibility for the deficiencies he cited.

In a letter printed in the appendix of Lainhart's report, Architect of the Capitol Alan M. Hantman said he agreed "that

buildings in the House complex are not fully protected by modern, state of the art fire protection systems meeting current codes." But because "there is no legal requirement to continually retrofit buildings to meet current codes, . . . it is disingenuous to characterize all existing fire protection systems in the House complex as 'deficient' unless they are being compared to standards applicable to a recently completed building," he added. "In my judgment, that is not a reasonable standard to use."

Hantman received no comparable criticism from the Senate, which does not have an inspector general.

NOTES

1. Lonnelle Aikman, *We, the People: The Story of the United States Capitol,* 13th ed. (Washington, D.C.: United States Capitol Historical Society, 1985), 19.

2. Glenn Brown, *History of the United States Capitol* (Washington, D.C.: Government Printing Office, 1900), vol. 1, 12. This work is the principal source for the account of the Capitol through the nineteenth century.

3. Brown, *History of the United States Capitol,* vol. 1, 32, 101.

4. Aikman, *We, the People,* 31.

5. *The Capitol: A Pictorial History,* 6th ed. (Washington, D.C.: Joint Committee on Printing, Government Printing Office, 1973), 10.

6. For information about office buildings see *1991–1992 Congressional Directory, 102nd Congress* (Washington, D.C.: Government Printing Office, 1991), 646–648.

SELECTED BIBLIOGRAPHY

Aikman, Lonnelle. *We, the People: The Story of the United States Capitol.* 13th ed. Washington, D.C.: United States Capitol Historical Society, 1985.

Brown, Glenn. *History of the United States Capitol.* 2 vols. Washington, D.C.: Government Printing Office, 1903. Reprint. New York: Da Capo Press, 1970.

Bryan, Wilhelmus B. *A History of the National Capital.* 2 vols. New York: Macmillan, 1914–1916.

Frary, Ihna T. *They Built the Capitol.* Plainview, N.Y.: Books for Libraries, 1940.

Hazelton, George C., Jr. *The National Capitol.* New York: F. Taylor, 1902.

Leech, Margaret. *Reveille in Washington.* New York: Grosset & Dunlap, 1941.

U.S. Congress. *The Capitol: A Pictorial History.* 9th ed. Washington, D.C.: Government Printing Office, 1988.

U.S. Congress. House of Representatives, Office of Inspector General. *Fire Protection Systems Do Not Adequately Protect the House.* Audit Report 98-HOC-20, Dec. 18, 1998.

U.S. Congress. Senate. *The United States Congress and Capitol: A Walking Tour Handbook.* 2 vols. Washington, D.C.: Government Printing Office, 1999.

Wolanin, Barbara A. *Constantino Brumidi: Artist of the Capitol.* Washington, D.C.: Government Printing Office, 1998.

CHAPTER 25

Library of Congress

SENATORS AND REPRESENTATIVES are fortunate to have at their disposal one of the world's great repositories of information, the Library of Congress. In 1999 the library owned more than 115 million items, housed in three sprawling buildings on Capitol Hill. Each year over 2 million people troop through those buildings to use the library or simply to view its architecture or exhibits.

The Library of Congress may be the largest in the world. Whether it is the greatest is a matter of opinion. There is no standard measurement of library quality, and in measuring greatness it is difficult to compare the library's treasures, such as Thomas Jefferson's rough draft of the Declaration of Independence or James Madison's notes from the Constitutional Convention, with, for example, the British Museum's two signed copies of the Magna Charta.

By any measure the Library of Congress's collections are unparalleled and of astonishing variety. Although the library does not acquire every book published, its holdings increase at the rate of ten a minute. Works in more than 460 languages are owned by the library; about two-thirds of its books are not in English.

Besides the Jefferson and Madison items, the library's most valuable holdings include one of three known perfect copies of the Gutenberg Bible, a set of string instruments made by Antonio Stradivari, a nearly complete set of Mathew Brady's photographs of the Civil War, and the personal papers of twenty-three presidents, from Washington to Coolidge. (See box, Treasures in the Library of Congress, p. 748.)

The library has the dual role of assisting Congress and serving as the nation's library. The librarian of Congress oversees both functions, which are carried out by a staff of more than 4,000. The annual budget exceeds $391 million. The librarian is a presidential appointee, confirmed by the Senate, and reports to Congress and its ten-member Joint Committee on the Library. The thirteenth librarian of Congress, James H. Billington, was appointed in 1987 to succeed another historian, Daniel J. Boorstin.

DUAL ROLE

The library's dual role causes considerable strain throughout the organization. As a national library it maintains its huge collections and provides central services to authors, scholars, government agencies, and the public, as well as to other libraries throughout the United States to which it provides services in book preservation, interlibrary loans, sales of cataloging cards, and computer linkups.

But Congress established the library for its own use, and senators and representatives are its most privileged users. A 1975 library pamphlet stated the relationship clearly: "The primary role of the Library of Congress is to perform research work for members and committees of Congress."[1]

Congressional requests for books or background information are handled by a separate division, the Congressional Research Service, which receives and answers more than 560,000 inquiries from Congress each year. The library also maintains a Legislative Liaison Office, which handles matters relating to the library. (See "Congressional Research Service," p. 759.)

The Law Library provides reference and research services for all known legal systems, present and past. The library's attorneys consult with individual members of Congress and may testify as expert witnesses before congressional committees.

Located within the Madison Memorial Building is the Congressional Reading Room, which provides members with individual reference service. Another congressional reading room is located in the Jefferson Building.

Senators and representatives, their families, and specific members of their staffs are among the few who may borrow books from the Library of Congress. Books are delivered directly to congressional offices.

SCOPE OF HOLDINGS

In 1999 the Library of Congress's collection of more than 115 million items included 51 million manuscript pieces; more than 9 million books in large type, monographs and serials, music, bound newspapers, pamphlets, technical reports, and other printed materials; more than 4 million maps; 13 million movies, videos, prints, and other visual materials; and 12 million microforms. The library's holdings include the nation's largest collection of incunabula (books printed before 1500), many donated by Lessing J. Rosenwald and housed in Jenkintown, Pennsylvania.

The library has the world's most extensive collection of aeronautical literature. It has more than a thousand miniature books, none more than four inches high. In the graphic arts, two highly valued collections are the Joseph Pennell collection of Whistleriana and the Brady Civil War photographs.

The library's Russian collection is the largest outside the former Soviet Union, and its Chinese and Japanese collections are

TREASURES IN THE LIBRARY OF CONGRESS

The Library of Congress has a number of exceedingly rare and valuable possessions among its approximately 115 million books, manuscripts, recordings, photographs, and other items. Some have been displayed in the library, but most are in fragile condition and must be preserved and stored with great care. Some of the library's major treasures are described below:

Gutenberg Bible. One of three known perfect copies on vellum in the world. Other Bibles in the library include the manuscript Giant Bible of Mainz (1452) and the Necksei-Lipozc Bible in two illuminated volumes from fourteenth-century Hungary.

Bay Psalm Book. One of only eleven copies extant of John Eliot's translation of the Psalms. Published in Cambridge, Massachusetts, in 1640, the book is the first example of printing in North America that has survived.

Smallest Book. The smallest book in the Library of Congress, *Old King Cole,* measures one twenty-fifth of an inch by one twenty-fifth of an inch, or about the size of the period at the end of this sentence.

Stradivari Instruments. A set of five stringed instruments made by Antonio Stradivari (1644?–1737). The Julliard String Quartet plays them regularly in concert series at the library.

Declaration of Independence. Thomas Jefferson's rough draft of the Declaration in his handwriting, with changes written in by Benjamin Franklin and John Adams. The library also has two copies of the first published edition of the Declaration, printed on the night of July 4, 1776, by John Dunlop of Philadelphia.

Madison's Notes. James Madison's personal notes of debates during the 1787 Constitutional Convention in Philadelphia.

Bill of Rights. One of the original engrossed and certified copies. The library also has George Mason's 1776 draft of the Virginia bill of rights.

Gettysburg Address. Lincoln's first and second drafts of his Gettysburg Address, written on ruled paper. The Lincoln collection includes his manuscript for the second inaugural address.

Civil War Photographs. A nearly complete set of Mathew Brady's photographs of the Civil War. Others in the library's collection include pictures taken during the Depression by Walker Evans and others.

Folk Music. The library's Archive of Folk Culture has 26,000 cylinders, discs, and tapes of traditional American (including Indian) and foreign folk music, most of it preserved nowhere else. These are noncommercial archival recordings made in the field by folklorists.

Presidential Papers. The personal papers of twenty-three presidents, from Washington through Coolidge. The 2 million documents include Washington's 1775 commission as commander in chief, Monroe's journal of negotiations for the Louisiana Purchase, and Wilson's penciled draft announcing the 1918 armistice.

Music Manuscripts. Examples from virtually all twentieth-century composers and many earlier masters, including Bach, Beethoven, Haydn, Mozart, Schubert, and the largest collection anywhere of Johannes Brahms's manuscripts. The library also has a copy of the first printed book of music, *Odhecaton,* published by Petrucci in Venice in 1504.

the largest outside Asia. The library acquires books from some countries by standing orders with publishers and dealers for every important book published.

However, as the eighth librarian of Congress, Herbert Putnam, wrote in one of his forty annual reports: "The progress of the library which is more significant cannot be expressed in figures. It consists in the gradual perfection of its equipment and of its service, in a development of its collections appropriate to its purpose as a library of research, and in a wider appreciation and acceptance of its functions as a national library, with a duty to the entire country."

Library's History

Late in 1784, when the Continental Congress was preparing to move from Trenton to New York City, the New York Society offered to make its library of about 5,000 books available to the legislators. Congress began using the library in January 1785. The First Congress under the Constitution, which convened in New York in 1789, also used the society's library until the seat of the federal government was moved to Philadelphia in 1790. From 1790 to 1800 Congress had access to the collection of the Library Company of Philadelphia, the oldest library in America,

established in 1731 and superintended for a time by Benjamin Franklin. It had about 7,700 volumes in the 1790s.

When Congress decided in 1800 to transfer the new United States government to Washington, the legislators set aside $5,000 to buy books and set up a congressional library. London booksellers supplied 152 works in 740 volumes, and the Library of Congress was given a room in the original north wing of the Capitol, under the supervision of the secretary of the Senate and the clerk of the House. Supervision of the library by a single person was intended by an act of January 26, 1802, which authorized the president to appoint a librarian of Congress. But President Thomas Jefferson thought the post was not a full-time job and appointed John Beckley, clerk of the House, to serve also as librarian of Congress. Beckley did so until his death in April 1807.

1814: FIRE AND RECOVERY

In November 1807 Jefferson appointed Patrick Magruder to succeed Beckley both as clerk of the House and as librarian. Members of Congress were critical of Magruder in 1814 for what they deemed his lack of diligence in trying to save the library when British troops entered Washington. On the night of August 24 the invaders burned or pillaged most of the books that remained in the Capitol, including all of the library's original purchase. A newspaper published in Nottingham, England, not long afterward condemned the burning as "an act without example in modern wars." Magruder, insisting that he had done all that was reasonably within his power, resigned as House clerk and automatically gave up his position as librarian of Congress.

During the fall and winter of 1814–1815, while Congress was meeting temporarily in Blodget's Hotel several blocks northwest of the damaged Capitol, Jefferson, then in retirement at Monticello, offered to sell his 6,487-volume library to the government to make up for the loss sustained in the book burning. Jefferson wrote of his collection, "I have been 50 years making it, & have spared no pains, opportunity or expence to make it what it is." But anti-Jeffersonian members of Congress opposed the offer because Jefferson's library included books by Voltaire and other unorthodox thinkers. After considerable debate, the House authorized the purchase by an 81–71 vote. A total of $23,950 was appropriated, pricing each book on the basis of its format. President James Madison signed the bill on January 30, 1815, and the books were transported to Washington by horse cart.

Jefferson's library became the nucleus of the Library of Congress as it exists today, even though most of his books have been lost. Its 6,487 volumes contained 4,931 works in forty-four categories. Jefferson's classification system, which followed Sir Francis Bacon's table of science, was the basis for the library's entire catalog until 1897.

The acquisition of Jefferson's library, wrote author Lucy Salamanca, "proved to be the life-stream that restored energy and enterprise to the expiring . . . Library of Congress."[2] Whereas the library's previous collection had been narrowly utilitarian, Jefferson's library took all knowledge for its province. Recognizing the new importance in store for the library, Madison on January 21, 1815, appointed the first full-time librarian of Congress. The man he chose, George Watterston, was a lawyer, novelist, playwright, and newspaper editor. Watterston, through his wit and zeal, made the Library of Congress the cultural center of life in Washington. In December 1818 the library was moved from Blodget's Hotel to the Capitol, where it remained, though it was moved from time to time within the building, until 1897, when a separate building was constructed.

1851: ANOTHER FIRE

The library suffered from another major fire in 1851, when 35,000 of its 55,000 books were lost. After the Civil War, though, the library benefited from a new, stronger copyright law, passed in 1865. It required anyone applying for a copyright to deposit a copy of the publication in the library.

A major advocate of that law was Ainsworth R. Spofford, who in 1864 began thirty-two years of service as the librarian of Congress. Spofford, a bookseller and publisher, was one of three librarians to serve more than three decades. The others were John S. Meehan (1829–1861), a newspaper publisher, and Herbert Putnam (1899–1939), a professional librarian and member of a family of book publishers.

Others who have served as librarian are John Beckley (1802–1807), Patrick Magruder (1807–1814), George Watterston (1815–1829), John G. Stephenson (1861–1897), John R. Young (1897–1899), Archibald MacLeish (1939–1944), Luther H. Evans (1945–1953), L. Quincy Mumford (1954–1974), Daniel J. Boorstin (1975–1987), and John H. Billington (1987–).

Library Buildings

The Library of Congress was housed in the Capitol during most of the nineteenth century. William W. Bishop, librarian of the University of Michigan, writing of the library's expansion under Spofford in the first three decades after the Civil War, remarked: "Dr. Spofford waxed old, and the Frankenstein he had created overwhelmed the Capitol."[3]

Congress, by an act of April 15, 1886, authorized the construction of a separate building for the Library of Congress. In 1888 Gen. Thomas L. Casey, chief of engineers of the U.S. Army, was appointed to supervise the construction. The building was designed by John L. Smithmeyer and Paul J. Pelz, but architect Edward Pearce Casey was in charge of the building from 1892, including the interior design.

JEFFERSON BUILDING

The main Library of Congress building, now called the Jefferson Building, was completed in 1897 at a cost of $6,360,000. It is near the Capitol, filling the block bounded by East Capitol Street, Independence Avenue, and First and Second streets, Southeast. The library's old quarters in the Capitol were closed in July 1897, and the new building was opened November 1. One million books and pamphlets were transferred in the intervening period. A system of underground conveyor belts was used to move books and reference material between the library and the Capitol.

The inspiration for the gray granite building was the Paris Opera, built in the 1860s. It is in the ornate style of the Italian Renaissance, decorated more richly inside than out, with stairs, walls, and floors of multicolored marble from Tennessee, Italy, France, and Algeria. It is considered a landmark of public building decoration in the United States. The spectacular Great Hall features staircases of sculpture by Philip Martiny, and the corridors contain murals by John W. Alexander and paintings and a marble mosaic by Elihu Vedder. A clock over the entrance to the main reading room is decorated with sculptured figures representing Father Time and the four seasons.

The main reading room was closed from May 4, 1964, to August 16, 1965, to install new heating and air-conditioning systems and new lighting, to improve the book-carrying machinery, and to build temporary offices in the mezzanine of the great hall and the balconies of the main reading room. The partitions—which obscured much of the library's detailed art work—began to be removed in 1979 as library personnel moved into the new Madison Memorial Building. Another major renovation of the main reading room, completed in 1991, added thirty-eight more reading desks, for a new total of 250.

The Library of Congress's 1897 Jefferson Building was inspired by the Paris Opera. It is connected by pedestrian tunnels to the Adams and Madison buildings.

ADAMS BUILDING

The main building, after three decades of use, was filling its available space faster than had been anticipated. Congress in June 1930 authorized construction of an annex immediately east of the main building. Completed in April 1939 at a cost of $9 million, the library annex is of white marble, five stories high with three additional stories below ground and a tunnel to the main building. Bas-relief sculpture on its bronze doors represent twelve historic figures credited with giving the art of writing to their people.

In 1980 Congress changed the names of the two buildings. The main building was designated the Thomas Jefferson Building. The annex, previously known as the Thomas Jefferson Building, became the John Adams Building.

MADISON MEMORIAL BUILDING

About twenty years after the annex was occupied, the need for additional space again became evident. By the mid-1950s all bookshelves were filled, even though temporary additions brought the total shelf length to 336 miles.[4] L. Quincy Mumford noted that during his twenty years as librarian the collections increased by over 100 percent while library space increased by only 42 percent. By the end of fiscal 1974 the library occupied twelve buildings in Washington, Virginia, Maryland, and Ohio. There was hardly room anywhere for materials or library employees, who numbered nearly 4,000 by late 1975.

An article in *Parade* magazine in 1975 described some of the problems caused by lack of space: "Each year the Library is inundated with 16 million pieces of printed matter. The staff must sift through this paper avalanche, selecting the 3 or 4 million items judged worthy of admission to its shelves. Each book has to be cataloged, then stack attendants must try to squeeze them into the already overloaded shelves. There hasn't been enough room and the books get piled knee-deep on the floor. People seeking to use the Library may sit hour upon hour in the reading room, often vainly waiting. . . . Stack attendants freely admit that as many as 30 percent of book requests cannot be filled."[5]

Recognizing the need for additional space, Congress October 19, 1965, authorized $75 million for a building that would serve the double purpose of providing a second annex to the library and memorializing President James Madison. An act of March 16, 1970, raised the authorized expenditure to $90 million. Con-

The ornate Great Hall of the Jefferson Building is one of Washington's showplaces.

gress had been stung by architectural criticism of the Rayburn House Office Building, so the 1965 law said that plans for the Madison Memorial Building were to be drawn up "after consultation with the American Institute of Architects [AIA]." But Architect of the Capitol J. George Stewart commissioned the firm of Dewitt, Poor, and Shelton without the knowledge of the AIA consultants.

Congress for years put off appropriating the money to erect the Madison Memorial Building, largely because of budget constraints. There was no ground-breaking ceremony, and the building's cornerstone was not laid until March 8, 1974. After numerous delays the building was dedicated April 24, 1980. Construction funds totaled more than $130 million. In December 1979 the first staff contingent from the Congressional Research Service moved into the library's new quarters.

The massive 1.5 million square foot building has nine floors of 5.4 acres each, including two floors underground, and is topped by a terraced penthouse housing mechanical equipment, a restaurant, and executive suites. It has eight reading rooms. The building is connected by tunnels to the two other library buildings on Capitol Hill and to the Cannon House Office Building.

With the new structure in operation the three buildings of the Library of Congress covered 64.5 acres of floor space and contained 535 miles of bookshelves, mostly in the Jefferson and Adams buildings. The Madison Memorial Building is used mainly for nonbook storage and offices for the Congressional Research Service and other divisions.

Like the Rayburn Building and the Hart Senate Office Building, the Madison Memorial Building has been subjected to considerable criticism on aesthetic grounds. Writing in the March 15, 1980, *Washington Post*, the paper's architectural critic Wolf Von Eckhardt commented, "Its architecture seeks not to please and serve people but to impress them. It seeks simplistic solutions to complex problems. It seeks a massive monumentality symbolizing power. . . . Everything is very slick and in exquisitely bad taste, resembling the lobby of an insurance company headquarters building."

1990S MODERNIZATION

A restoration and renovation project encompassing the entire the Library of Congress complex (but mainly the Jefferson Building) officially got under way in May 1985 after years of planning. Reconstruction of the fountains and statuary in the Neptune Plaza at the west front of the Jefferson Building was the first high-profile undertaking.

Other highlights of the renovation included closure of the Jefferson Building's Main Reading Room and relocation of its card catalog and reference collections to the Adams Building, in December 1987; closure of the Jefferson Building's west front entrance and Great Hall, in June 1990; reopening of the Main Reading Room, newly equipped with a computer catalog center, in 1991; completion of interior repair work in the Jefferson and Adams buildings, in 1995; and beginning of repair work on the

Jefferson Building's copper roof and Elizabeth Sprague Coolidge Auditorium, in 1996.

The restoration job reached its climax in 1997, the centennial year of the Jefferson Building's opening. On October 30 the Coolidge Auditorium reopened to the public with a concert by the Juilliard String Quartet. The Torch of Learning atop the Jefferson Building dome was lighted for the first time and was to remain illuminated every night.

The decades-long project, under the general guidance of the Architect of the Capitol, did not go unrecognized. In early 1999 the American Institute of Architects and the American Library Association recognized the Jefferson Building's restoration with awards.

Wide-Ranging Services

Whether it is serving Congress specifically or the public in general, the library does its job by acquiring, organizing, stor-

---

TYPES OF HOLDINGS

The approximately 115 million items in the Library of Congress collections include a vast array of material, ranging from a Stradivarius to a film reel of *Star Wars*. The library's extensive comic book collection was acquired in its capacity as register of copyrights. The variety of the library's collections is indicated list below:

Artifacts, instruments, and mementos
Books in the ordinary sense
Books and magazines in Braille
Books and magazines recorded for the blind
Drawings, etchings, prints, and other graphic
    representations and designs
Incunabula (books published before 1500)
Manuscripts in scrolls, sheets, notebooks, and codex form
Maps
Microfilms and microfiches
Motion pictures, silent and sound
Music in written and printed notations
Music on phonograph records and cylinders
Music on tapes and wires
Music on compact disks
Newspapers, loose and in bound volumes
Pamphlets
Periodicals and magazines
Photocopies and photostats
Photographic negatives, prints, and slides
Posters and broadsides
Processed materials—usually typewritten material
    reproduced by near-print processes
Speeches, recitations, narratives, poetry, and dramatic
    performances on film, phonograph records, compact
    disc, tape
Technical reports

Renovations on the Library of Congress's circular main reading room were completed in 1990.

ing, and dispensing human knowledge. The information for which it is responsible is not confined to the written word but includes many other devices for recording, storing, preserving, and communicating ideas.

One of the library's major services is the cataloging of books. The library assigns to every book published in the United States, and many published abroad, a catalog number that indicates the book's subject matter. In fiscal 1998 the library cataloged 374,570 titles. Since 1981 the library's manual card catalog has been closed and all book control computerized.

In fiscal 1998, the library registered more than 558,000 claims to copyright. Many of the books and other works deposited for copyright protection are kept, adding to the permanent collection.

Any person over high school age may use the Library of Congress's two general reading rooms: the main reading room located in the Jefferson Building and another reading room on the fifth floor of the Adams Building. In addition, there are distributed among those buildings and the newer Madison Memorial Building the Law Library and specialized reading rooms for the blind and physically handicapped, and in subject areas including geography and maps, Hispanic material, local history and

genealogy, manuscripts, microfilms, music, newspaper and current periodicals, Orientalia, prints and photographs, rare books, science, and Slavic materials.

All are open to the public. Each of the rooms has a catalog, reference collection, and reference librarians to provide assistance. Readers may use computer terminals to search the library's databases for new titles, for sources of information on a variety of subjects, and for legislative histories.

The Library of Congress Information System, popularly known as SCORPIO, contains several files or databases available for use by the public. Four that are most useful for public policy research are: the legislative information file, the Bibliographic Citation file, the Library of Congress Computer Catalog, and the National Referral Center Master File.

Admission to the reading rooms is free, but materials may not be removed from the library. Books requested by readers are delivered to them in the reading rooms, and readers may use the reference books available on the open shelves without filling in a request slip. The main reading room reopened in 1991 with a collection of 45,000 reference books and desks for 250 readers.

During fiscal 1998, nearly 2 million users and visitors entered the library's Capitol Hill buildings. The three main library buildings display changing exhibits prepared by the Exhibits Office. The Gutenberg Bible is on permanent display in the Great Hall of the Jefferson Building.

The library presents films in the Mary Pickford Theater on an irregularly scheduled basis and, in the Coolidge Auditorium, concerts, readings, and dramatic performances. The Gertrude Clark Whittall Foundation supports concerts featuring the Stradivari instruments, played for many years by the Budapest String Quartet and currently by the Julliard String Quartet. Other concerts at the library have included the Boehm Quintette, the Contemporary Chamber Players of the University of Chicago, and the New York Chamber Soloists. Readings, lectures, and literary conferences have featured Herman Wouk, Sandra McPherson, Barbara W. Tuchman, and many others.

Hundreds of publications and recordings produced by the library are available to the public. Approximately 400 publications, based mainly on the library's collections, cover an enormous range of subjects. They include scholarly studies, guides to collections, bibliographies, lectures, checklists and directories, and papers presented at such meetings as the Library of Congress Symposium on the American Revolution.

The library also publishes facsimiles of historic documents, manuscripts, and posters, and a variety of greeting cards and gift items. In addition, the library sells compact discs and long-playing record albums produced from its vast collection of folk music and other recordings.

The Library of Congress provides special services to users who are blind, partially sighted, or otherwise physically unable to read conventional printed materials. The library and 140 cooperating regional libraries throughout the nation have books in raised characters (Braille) and books in large type, "talking books" on discs and tapes, and other recorded aids for the physically handicapped. Compact disc, tape, and record players are provided free. In fiscal 1998 the library circulated more than 22 million disc, cassette, and Braille items to 769,000 persons.

NOTES

1. *The Library of Congress* (Washington, D.C.: Government Printing Office, 1975).

2. Lucy Salamanca, *Fortress of Freedom: The Story of the Library of Congress* (Philadelphia: Lippincott, 1942), 107.

3. William W. Bishop and Andrew Keogh, eds., *Essays Offered to Herbert Putnam by His Colleagues and Friends on His Thirtieth Anniversary as Librarian of Congress, 5 April 1929* (New Haven, Conn.: Yale University Press, 1929).

4. Fred Kline, "Library of Congress: The Nation's Bookcase," *National Geographic*, November 1975, 674.

5. James Ridgeway and Alexander Cockburn, "The World's Largest Library and Its Large Problems," *Parade*, July 6, 1975, 14.

SELECTED BIBLIOGRAPHY

Adams, James T. *The Epic of America.* Boston: Atlantic Monthly Press, 1931.

Angle, Paul M. *The Library of Congress: An Account, Historical and Descriptive.* Kingsport, Tenn.: Kingsport Press, 1958.

Cole, John Y. *Jefferson's Legacy: A Brief History of the Library of Congress.* Washington, D.C.: U.S. Government Printing Office, 1993.

Goodrum, Charles A. *The Congressional Research Service of the United States Congress.* Washington, D.C.: Library of Congress, 1974.

Goodrum, Charles A., and Helen W. Dalrymple. *Guide to the Library of Congress.* Rev. ed. Washington, D.C.: Library of Congress, 1988.

———. *The Library of Congress.* Boulder, Colo.: Westview Press, 1982.

———. *Treasures of the Library of Congress.* Rev. ed. New York: Abrams, 1991.

Highsmith, Carol M., and Ted Landphair. *The Library of Congress: America's Memory.* Golden, Colo.: Fulcrum, 1994.

Library of Congress. *Annual Report of the Librarian of Congress.* Washington, D.C.: Library of Congress, 1999.

Nelson, Josephus, and Judith Farley. *Full Circle: Ninety Years of Service in the Main Reading Room.* Washington, D.C.: Library of Congress, 1991.

Simpson, Andrew L. *The Library of Congress.* New York: Chelsea House, 1989.

CHAPTER 26

Supporting Organizations

MEMBERS OF CONGRESS are backed by a number of supporting organizations that help keep Capitol Hill running. Among the largest of these are the General Accounting Office (GAO), the Congressional Budget Office (CBO), the Government Printing Office (GPO), and the Library of Congress's Congressional Research Service (CRS).

Each of the four agencies has its own specialized functions. CRS, for example, will research and analyze any issue or problem a member requests. The GPO prints, or contracts with commercial companies to print, thousands of congressional and other governmental publications each year.

GAO is Congress's examiner of executive branch spending. It conducts independent reviews, audits, and investigations of federal activities; develops standards for the government's accounting systems; provides legal opinions on government fiscal practices, and settles claims for and against the government.

CBO deals only with budgetary and economic matters. It helps Congress with the budget process and provides economic and policy analysis as lawmakers determine budget priorities and set spending and revenue levels. When the federal deficit soared in the 1980s, CBO's estimates of the budget gap became increasingly important as Congress worked to keep the deficit within the limits of the Gramm-Rudman antideficit law.

Although the GAO, CBO, and CRS have been given their own tasks, their jobs overlap to some extent. This has led in some cases to duplication and waste, and even to competition among the different groups. It has become increasingly common for congressional committees to ask two or all three agencies to do essentially the same study on an issue. This is done, it is argued, to provide a variety of perspectives.

General Accounting Office: Congressional Watchdog

The General Accounting Office is an arm of the legislative branch that was created to oversee the expenditures of the executive branch. Since it was established in 1921, GAO's duties have been expanded from routine audits of the accounts of executive departments to probing analyses of program management and planning, and often to controversial investigations of how federal agencies are spending the taxpayers' money.[1]

GAO, often referred to as the "watchdog of Congress," has been called a "one-eyed watchdog" by critics who feel it is too responsive to political pressures. The agency has sometimes found itself caught in a tug of war between Congress and the executive branch.

In countering its critics, the agency cites its own estimate that it saved taxpayers $79 billion over a five-year period in the late 1980s. GAO investigative audits have triggered hundreds of well-publicized news stories about everything from multimillion-dollar cost overruns for a weapons system to the remodeling of a cabinet member's office.

GAO's scope has expanded over the years, but its focus remains on helping Congress. When lawmakers need information about a program that will require additional funds, GAO is asked to conduct an investigation. The agency is required to perform investigations requested by committee chairmen and, as a matter of policy, assigns equal status to requests from ranking minority members. If possible, GAO responds to individual members' requests. When the House and Senate Appropriations committees are working on the annual appropriations bills, GAO staff members act as consultants.

Congressionally requested work has taken up a larger proportion of GAO's caseload in recent years. In fiscal 1998 congressional requests and mandates accounted for 96 percent of GAO's workload, up from an average of 61 percent in previous years and 38 percent in 1980. The agency issued 1,136 reports (popularly known as "blue-cover" reports) in fiscal 1998.

Moreover, GAO officials testified 256 times before 107 congressional committees and subcommittees in fiscal 1998. Each testimony was issued in printed form, as were transcripts of 181 briefings by agency officials. In contrast, GAO officials testified an average of 156 times a year between 1976 and 1980, and thirty times a year during 1966–1970.

EXPANDING ROLE

GAO's activities are wide-ranging. Late in 1972 the agency confirmed the existence of a secret "slush fund" at the Committee to Re-Elect the President (CREEP), a disclosure that spurred the Watergate investigations of the Nixon White House. In the 1980s, as defense spending rose, the agency conducted numerous investigations on how well the Pentagon was spending its new-found billions. As budget cuts hit domestic programs, GAO documented those effects as well. For example, GAO studies that were critical of the chemical Bigeye bomb and the Sgt. York antiaircraft gun led to the weapons' demise. And favorable reviews of the Head Start program helped keep it alive, despite pressure from the Reagan administration.

The Government Accounting Office is the legislative watchdog of executive branch spending.

Honduras. GAO said that the action should have required congressional authorization.

The development of GAO's wide-ranging role as a policy critic was made possible in 1950, when Congress freed the office from the task of performing regular audits of agencies. That chore was transferred to the agencies themselves.

In the 1960s doubts about the cost effectiveness of federal programs led GAO deeper into policy evaluation. Members of Congress were disturbed over cost overruns in development of the C-5A transport airplane and other military projects. At the request of Sen. William Proxmire, D-Wis., GAO launched a massive study of defense contractor profits.

GAO's aggressive tack against the defense industry raised hackles in Congress. During 1965 hearings on GAO's defense work, the agency was criticized for producing "inflammatory, colored, and sensational" studies. Comptroller General Joseph Campbell resigned.

Since then Congress has added provisions to numerous agency-authorization and grant-creation bills mandating GAO examination. In fiscal 1980 twenty-one laws were passed that expanded GAO's activities and powers. As GAO's workload grew, so did its budget—rising from $109.5 million in 1974 to $204.3 million in 1980 and $419.1 million in 1991. The 1990s brought a wave of downsizing to many federal agencies. GAO staff, which had expanded from 4,100 in the mid-1960s to about 5,100 in 1991, was scaled back to about 3,300 by 1999. The GAO's budget had also fallen to $363 million by 1999.

In 1985, with the passage of the Gramm-Rudman antideficit law, GAO was handed another responsibility. Under the law, the agency would have reviewed CBO and OMB estimates of military and domestic spending cuts required to meet Gramm-Rudman targets, adjusted them if necessary, and issued a report to the president that, in essence, would have mandated the cuts. The arrangement did not pass constitutional muster. In 1986 the Supreme Court ruled that GAO's role in the process was unconstitutional, and Congress in 1987 passed a new version of the law that excluded GAO from the process. *(See "Gramm-Rudman-Hollings," p. 175, Vol. I.)*

COMPTROLLER GENERAL

The comptroller general of the United States, a presidential appointee with a single fifteen-year term, heads GAO. The lengthy term, and the fact that the comptroller general can only be removed by a joint congressional resolution signed by the president, is designed so that an appointee can remain politically invulnerable.

In 1980 Congress gave itself a say in selecting the comptroller general. It created a ten-member commission to submit at least three suggested (nonbinding) nominees to the president. The commission was composed of the House Speaker, the Senate president pro tempore, the majority and minority leaders of both chambers, and the chairmen and ranking minority members of the House Government Operations Committee and the Senate Governmental Affairs Committee.

GAO investigates big and small problems. A 1988 report on the savings and loan industry provided much-needed data to members crafting a thrift institution bailout bill. The report said that 505 of the nation's 3,147 thrifts were insolvent at the end of 1987. At the other end of the spectrum, a 1991 report found that the Defense Department was doing an inadequate job in blocking consumer access to dangerous, easily tipped-over M151 Jeeps that were being disposed of by the army. The agency was a leader in focusing attention on safety and environmental problems at the nation's nuclear weapons plants, long before the Department of Energy or Congress paid attention to the problem.

In the early 1980s GAO conducted investigations at the behest of congressional critics of the Reagan administration's Central American policies. In 1982 the agency issued a report saying U.S. advisers in El Salvador were in danger and Congress should consider implementing the War Powers act to pull them out. In 1984 GAO said the Defense Department had illegally used "operation and maintenance" funds to build military facilities in

The first nominee to emerge from the process was Charles Bowsher, a partner with the Arthur Andersen accounting firm. He was among a list of eight recommended by the commission. President Ronald Reagan nominated Bowsher July 9, 1981; he was confirmed September 29. On November 9, 1998, David M. Walker became comptroller general. The salary of the position in 1999 was $136,700 a year.

Other 1980 legislation created an independent personnel system for GAO, to eliminate a potential conflict of interest. Until then, the law required the agency to monitor the activities of the executive branch, including two agencies—the Office of Personnel Management and the Merit Systems Protection Board—that had oversight over GAO's own personnel practices.

While the agency's basic mission is to review federal spending and management for Congress, GAO has several other functions. It offers legal opinions to government agencies, settles disputed claims by or against the United States, and prescribes accounting standards for government-wide use.

With the appointment of Bowsher in 1981, GAO became increasingly feisty, attracting criticism from its investigative targets and others who said the agency had gone in over its head by attempting to evaluate complex matters such as weapons technology. One Pentagon official asserted that some GAO investigators had "low levels of engineering competence and minimal knowledge" of the weapons they investigated.

Also, detractors contended, GAO should not be passing judgment on policy decisions that were more properly the province of Congress. They said the office should simply give Congress the facts and let the members make up their own minds.

Although scrupulous about maintaining its nonpartisan image, GAO nonetheless encountered accusations that its activities were politically motivated. The agency came under attack in

1991 when Republicans, frustrated by what they said was GAO's partisan slant, unsuccessfully tried to slash its budget by more than $100 million. "The General Accounting Office used to be prestigious and reliable," said House GOP Whip Newt Gingrich of Georgia. Now, he argued, it is the agency that "ought to be audited."

"It is uncoordinated. It is ideological. It is increasingly sloppy in its behavior," Gingrich said. "On some occasions its reports are technically incompetent. In other cases they are politically motivated."

GOP critics charged that the agency had endorsed Canada's national health care system, poorly handled an investigation into alleged talks between Ronald Reagan's 1980 presidential campaign and Iranian operatives concerning U.S. hostages, and kept secret from Republicans an agency report critical of the National Aeronautic and Space Agency's space station cost estimates.

But agency defender Rep. John D. Dingell, D-Mich., said GAO investigations had meant that "billions of dollars have been saved, and audits of things like the safety of the blood supply, misbehaviors at colleges and universities and by defense contractors . . . have been carried out by the General Accounting Office."

While GAO churns out in-depth audits of how the executive agencies perform, it rarely turns its sharp eye on its benefactor, Congress. One exception occurred in 1991, when Republicans broadened a GAO investigation of White House Chief of Staff John Sununu's travel habits to include an examination of Congress.

Although it sometimes has been criticized, GAO generally has been a highly regarded and frequently used resource. Dingell said in 1991: "It audits on its own, as it is chartered to do by the Congress, to find out whether there is waste, fraud, or abuse in the executive branch, or whether there is a failure to carry out the letter, spirit or intent of the law. . . . It has saved the taxpayers in the last year $15 billion."

Congressional Budget Office: Backstop on Fiscal Affairs

The Congressional Budget Office is a nonpartisan organization established under the 1974 budget act to provide Congress with budget-related information and analyses of alternative fiscal and program policies. The office does not make recommendations on matters of policy; its principal tasks are to present Congress with options for consideration and to study their possible budgetary impact. It works most closely with the House and Senate Budget committees.[2]

CBO's functions include: estimates of the five-year budgetary costs of proposed legislation; tracking congressional budgetary actions against spending levels preset in the budget resolution; periodic forecasts of economic trends and alternative fiscal policies; analyses of program issues that affect the federal budget; analyses of the inflationary impact of proposed legislation; and an annual report on major budgetary options. CBO was given additional responsibilities under deficit control legislation enacted in 1985 and 1990 and under legislation enacted in 1995 to control unfunded federal mandates. *(See box, Congressional Budgeting in Brief, p. 176, Vol. I.)*

In the 1980s, as the federal budget deficit ballooned, CBO's deficit estimates often were viewed as more accurate than OMB's. During the late 1980s, when so-called budget summits between administration officials and congressional leaders became a means of passing spending bills, CBO experts played an important role in supplying negotiators with speedy cost estimates of a wide variety of legislative initiatives.

STRUCTURE AND ACTIVITIES

Only two positions in the office are specified by statute—director and deputy director. The director is appointed for a four-year term by the Speaker of the House and the president pro tempore of the Senate on recommendation of both Budget committees.

Robert D. Reischauer, an economist from the Brookings Institution, was named in 1989 to be the third director of the CBO. He remained in the post until January 1995. Reischauer had been a deputy to CBO's first director, Alice M. Rivlin, who served from 1975 to 1983. Rudolph Penner filled the post from 1983 to 1987. Reischauer's appointment ended a two-and-a-half-year hiatus during which Senate and House leaders were unable to agree on a candidate.

The staff has grown only modestly, from 193 employees in 1975 to 226 in 1991, but dropping to 210 in 1999. The office is divided into eight major departments: budget analysis; macroeconomic analysis; tax analysis; natural resources and commerce; health and human resources; national security; administration and information; and special studies.

CBO's mandate differs from that of the president's Office of Management and Budget, which has the power to recommend spending increases or cuts in agency budgets. Under the 1974 budget act, Congress retained that power for its Budget committees and limited CBO's role to that of information analyst.[3]

With a budget of about $26 million in fiscal 1999, CBO prepared more than 2,000 "work products" in fiscal 1998. These included 678 federal cost estimates, plus numerous special reports, studies, papers, and memoranda. Cost estimates are studies of how much a bill would cost over a five-year period. CBO prepares such estimates for every bill reported by a congressional committee.

Providing bill cost estimates puts CBO analysts in close contact with committee staffs. Special reports prepared by the agency have included studies of the costs of verifying and complying with arms control treaties, the effects of taxing fossil fuels, and the costs of the federal government's liabilities under hazardous waste laws.

Since 1982 the agency also has prepared estimates of the costs to state and local governments of congressional directives. This added task resulted from pressure by state and local governments that were concerned about the increasing costs of congressional mandates. In 1990 the agency prepared 720 state and local cost estimates. However, CBO officials said congressional debates have generally ignored CBO's state and local cost estimates, because they do not directly affect the federal budget.

CAUGHT IN THE CROSSFIRE

A problem for CBO is that it often is caught between political factions that want budget figures to help make a point, not a decision.

Some economists questioned CBO's objectivity. They charged that the agency was tilted toward generous government spending—a possibility that worried the House Budget Committee when the office was established. House members wanted CBO to resemble the neutral, analytical General Accounting Office, but the Senate preferred a policy-oriented agency that would recommend alternatives to the budget of the administration in power.

CBO was criticized in 1988 over its conflicting estimates of the cost of raising the minimum wage. The agency issued two reports on the costs of a House Education and Labor Committee bill to raise the minimum wage from $3.35 to $5.05 over five years. The first report contained estimates of the bill's impact on the economy and estimated that the higher wages could lead to higher consumer prices and the loss of nearly 500,000 jobs.

But that report, dated March 25, barely saw the light of day before it was superseded March 29 by a second version, which omitted any reference to the bill's effect on the economy.

However, the majority staff of the committee, having seen the estimates, which were damaging to the bill's chances, "decided that they didn't want it," according to CBO staffer Michael Pogue, who prepared both reports. Thus, the second report, minus the impact assessment, was sent to the committee.

"It may be that the committee didn't like the answers we gave," said acting CBO director James L. Blum. "I think they were hoping it would have less of an impact."

And Reischauer was accused of partisanship in 1990 when, after the release of President George Bush's budget he said, "It's a 'Play it Again Sam' budget. We've seen this before."

"I heard from members about that," Reischauer later said. "It was perceived as partisan. I didn't mean it in a partisan sense, but I've learned how careful you have to be in this job."

June E. O'Neill, who inherited Reischauer's post, also was a target of partisan sniping during her four years as head of CBO. She stepped down in January 1999 to return to her teaching and administrative duties at New York City's Baruch College.

Throughout her tenure, O'Neill was criticized often by Republican congressional leaders. They complained that CBO's analyses and forecasts tended to be off-target, thus hobbling GOP budget and tax-policy initiatives. O'Neill's successor in 1999 was Dan L. Crippen, a former chief counsel to Senate Majority Leader Howard H. Baker Jr., R-Tenn., in 1984–1985.

CBO received a major new responsibility when Congress approved legislation in 1995 to curb "unfunded federal mandates"—requirements that Congress or federal agencies imposed on state and local governments, or private businesses, without providing money to pay for them. The law directed CBO to identify all such mandates costing state or local governments $50 million or more a year, as well as requirements costing private businesses $100 million or more a year.

To this end, CBO reviewed more than 500 reported congressional bills and other legislative proposals in calendar year 1998. The agency found that sixty-four of the measures contained intergovernmental mandates, and seventy-five contained private-sector mandates. CBO further determined that six of the intergovernmental mandates, and eighteen of the private-sector mandates, had costs exceeding the thresholds established in the 1995 law.

Congressional Research Service: Prized "Information Factory"

The Congressional Research Service, a department of the Library of Congress, has been described as Congress's "think tank, policy consultant, and information factory."[4] It provides much of the research and reference work on public policy issues prepared for members of Congress, committees, and staff.

Congress depends heavily on CRS support. The 700-member CRS staff annually responds to more than a half-million requests for information and analysis. CRS maintains several research and information centers throughout the Capitol complex to deal with these matters. One researcher offered this testimony to CRS research efficiency: "My all-time favorite . . . is the call we got from a frantic staffer whose boss was, at that moment, appearing on a TV talk show. The commercial had just come on and he needed to verify an obscure statistic. We came through before he had to go back on."[5]

Policy analysis and long-term research projects are the province of six research divisions: American law; domestic social policy; foreign affairs, defense, and trade; government and finance; information research; and resources, science and industry. In addition, CRS includes twenty-seven [in 1999] senior specialists—nationally recognized experts, many of whom have published widely and have had extensive careers outside CRS.

Members of Congress may request any kind of public policy research from CRS. Its reports are prized for their objectivity and nonpartisanship, and the service seldom meets criticism from its congressional overlords.

CRS tries to anticipate congressional needs for information, and some of its studies look far into the future, but it can respond with alacrity if circumstances require. When NATO air strikes against Yugoslavia began in 1999, an interdivisional team of CRS researchers moved quickly to assemble information lawmakers might need as the Kosovo crisis developed.

In addition to in-depth analyses prepared for congressional committees and individual members, CRS products and services include the following:

• Issue briefs, fifteen-page analyses of major policy issues. At the beginning of each session of Congress CRS identifies major issues most likely to result in hearings or legislation. The list provides a focus for CRS activity.

• *Major Legislation of the Congress.* Issued two to three times a year, *Major Legislation* provides a summary of bills in Congress and their legislative status.

CRS maintains four automated databases: legislation (Bill Digest) for the current and two preceding Congresses, major issues (issue briefs), bibliography (public policy literature), and an index to the daily *Congressional Record.* Computer users on Capitol Hill may access these files through the SCORPIO retrieval system.

OFFICE OF TECHNOLOGY ASSESSMENT

The Office of Technology Assessment (OTA) was a major supporting agency of Congress that ceased operations in 1995. OTA originated in 1972, when Congress established the nonpartisan analytical support agency to help Congress evaluate scientific and technical legislative proposals. Congress, which had few scientists, realized that it was poorly suited to evaluate the myriad of scientific questions before it.

The staff of OTA and a large corps of consultants conducted studies to assess both the beneficial and adverse consequences of new technologies and prepared analyses of alternate policies for congressional committees. Most of the agency's work centered on comprehensive, in-depth assessments that took a year or more to complete, although OTA also responded to congressional committee queries on technical matters.

With a full-time staff numbering above 100 during its heyday, OTA delivered several dozen reports and other studies to Congress annually. Although the agency's reports were generally respected, OTA released a number of controversial studies, the most contentious being a 1985 critique of President Ronald Reagan's Strategic Defense Initiative (SDI).

In 1995 Congress voted to eliminate OTA. The agency's critics said its reports took too long to produce and that other sources, government or private, could supply information on technology just as readily. OTA thus became the first federal agency to fall victim to the "Republican Revolution" of 1995, when the GOP took control of both houses of Congress.

HISTORY

Today's Congressional Research Service had its origins in the Legislative Reference Bureau—later known as the Legislative Reference Service (LRS)—which was created in the Library of Congress in 1914.

Beginning in 1935, Congress directed the service to prepare and publish a digest of public bills introduced in Congress. The 1946 Reorganization Act made this task a regular part of the LRS program. The 1946 law also made LRS a separate department within the Library of Congress. It enlarged the service and shifted the predominant staff from librarians to subject specialists. It added pro-and-con studies, comparative analyses, and subject-oriented reports to the service's continued information support.

The Legislative Reorganization Act of 1970 transformed LRS into the Congressional Research Service and gave it greater responsibilities. The law required CRS to maintain continuous liaison with all congressional committees. This has involved evaluating legislative proposals and alternatives, estimating results of proposed legislation, identifying all expiring programs at the beginning of each Congress, and citing policy areas that the committees might consider.

The 1970 law also directed CRS to prepare "purpose and effect" reports on all bills scheduled for hearings. It authorized the CRS director to prepare the budget for the service independently, for inclusion in the library's annual budget. The act directed the librarian of Congress to "encourage and assist the service in performing its work, and to grant it complete research independence and the maximum administrative independence."

Other electronic products and services supplied by CRS include:

• CRS Web site *(http://www.loc.gov/crs):* The site provides House and Senate offices and legislative branch agencies with round-the-clock access to such material as the full text of issues briefs, reports, and analyses of appropriations bills.

• *Legislative Alert:* A weekly compendium of CRS material relevant to expected floor action. The service is distributed by fax and e-mail subscription to all members of Congress as well as congressional committees and subcommittees.

CRS also has cosponsored three-day briefings for new members at the beginning of a Congress.

With about 700 employees in 1999, CRS had more than double the 306-person staff twenty years earlier. CRS employees are not patronage appointees. They are covered by a merit employment system and include lawyers, economists, engineers, information scientists, librarians, defense and foreign affairs analysts, political scientists, public administrators, and physical and behavioral scientists.

The service is housed in the Madison Memorial Building of the Library of Congress. It had a fiscal 1999 budget of $67 million.

Government Printing Office

Congress established the Government Printing Office (GPO) in 1861 to print for "the Senate and House of Representatives, the executive and judicial departments, and the Court of Claims." Buildings, equipment, and machinery were acquired from Cornelius Wendell, a private printer, for $135,000. The original plant stood on the site now occupied by the newest of the GPO buildings. It was staffed by a workforce of 350.

By its own reckoning, GPO has become one of the largest and best-equipped printing plants in the world, with more than 5,000 employees. Besides manufacturing and buying printing, it runs a sizable distribution and sales operation. Its Public Documents Division, established in 1895, maintains twenty-three bookstores throughout the nation. In addition, many GPO publications are distributed free to Congress, government agencies, private organizations, and the public.

In 1980 GPO established a Congressional Information Division that makes the services of printing specialists available to the offices and committees of Congress.

GPO is responsible for printing congressional bills, resolutions, and amendments; committee reports; House and Senate calendars; supplements to the *Code of Federal Regulations;*

The presses at the Government Printing Office turn out thousands of federal publications every year.

franked envelopes; the *Federal Register;* the *United States Government Manual;* the weekly compilation of *Presidential Documents;* the *Public Papers of the President;* and the *Congressional Record.* It also publishes numerous government reports and pamphlets. These publications may now be ordered through its Web site at *www.access.GPO.gov.*

NOTES

1. *United States Government Manual, 1996/97* (Washington, D.C.: Government Printing Office, 1996), 47–49.

2. Ibid., 62–63.

3. John Cranford, *Budgeting for America,* 2nd ed. (Washington, D.C.: Congressional Quarterly, 1989) 89–91.

4. Helen Dalrymple, "Congressional Research Service," *Library of Congress Information Bulletin,* September 24, 1990, 322.

5. Ibid., 320.

SELECTED BIBLIOGRAPHY

Brown, Richard E. *The GAO: Untapped Source of Congressional Power.* Knoxville: University of Tennessee Press, 1970.

Cranford, John. *Budgeting for America,* 2nd ed. Washington, D.C.: Congressional Quarterly, 1989.

Goodrum, Charles A. *Treasures of the Library of Congress.* Rev. ed. New York: Abrams, 1991.

Goodrum, Charles A., and Helen W. Dalrymple. *Guide to the Library of Congress.* Rev. ed. Washington, D.C.: Library of Congress, 1988.

Kolodny, Robin. *Pursuing Majorities: Congressional Campaign Committees in American Politics.* Norman: University of Oklahoma Press, 1998.

Mansfield, Harvey C. *The Comptroller General: A Study in the Law and Practice of Financial Administration.* New Haven, Conn.: Yale University Press, 1939.

Penner, Rudolph G., ed. *The Congressional Budget Process after Five Years.* Washington, D.C.: American Enterprise Institute, 1981.

Rivlin, Alice M., ed. *Economic Choices, 1984.* Washington, D.C.: Brookings Institution, 1984.

Rothstein, Samuel. "The Origins of Legislative Reference Services in the United States." *Legislative Studies Quarterly* 25, no. 3 (August 1990): 401–411.

Simpson, Andrew L. *The Library of Congress.* New York: Chelsea House, 1989.

Stanley, Eliot. *The General Accounting Office: One-Eyed Watchdog?* Citizens Advocate Center, 1970.

Trask, Roger R. *Defender of the Public Interest: The General Accounting Office, 1921–1966.* Washington, D.C.: Government Printing Office, 1996.

United States Government Manual, 1996–97. Washington, D.C.: Government Printing Office, 1996.

U.S. General Accounting Office. *The U.S. General Accounting Office: Responsibilities and Services to Congress.* Washington, D.C.: Government Printing Office, 1985.

PART VI

Pay and Perquisites

Members' Retiring Room in Capitol

CHAPTER 27

Pay and Honoraria

ISPUTES OVER PAY and benefits have been a constant feature of congressional politics throughout the nation's history. The American public is perennially unconvinced that senators and representatives are underpaid, and fights over pay increases inevitably provoke blunt displays of public scorn. Congress's first pay raise, in 1816, had to be repealed after many members were driven from office by public outcry.

Fear of criticism from the voters made members of Congress skittish about voting to increase their own pay, even when their salaries failed to keep up with inflation. Over the years they found ingenious ways to increase their income without having to cast a direct vote on a pay raise. These steps included using independent commissions to set pay levels, providing tax deductions for members' Washington living expenses, and participating in automatic salary increases established for federal workers.

Until the practice was banned in 1991, many lawmakers augmented their government salaries with honoraria—speaking fees and other payments from private interests. Members of Congress collected more than $9 million in honoraria in 1989.

The widespread practice of making speeches for honoraria was assailed as, at best, a source of distraction from the business of government and, at worst, a form of legalized bribery. Criticism of honoraria mounted through the 1980s, as outside interests became more and more brazen about using the payments to gain access to members of Congress. Stories of politicians picking up a $2,000 check for dropping by at a breakfast increasingly tainted the whole system.

A spate of congressional scandals in the late 1980s gave new impetus to proposals to curb outside income. In 1989 the House voted to ban honoraria as of 1991 and hiked representatives' pay to $125,100 to make up for the financial loss. The Senate refused to go along immediately, but in 1991 it also adopted the ban on honoraria and boosted its pay to the $125,100 House level. By 1999, members of Congress earned $136,700 annually.

Congressional Pay: Perennial Political Issue

Article I, Section 6, of the Constitution provides that "Senators and Representatives shall receive a Compensation for their Services, to be ascertained by Law, and paid out of the Treasury of the United States."

The constitutional language settled one sensitive contemporary issue—whether a member's salary should be drawn from state or national funds—but it left the resolution of a far more delicate question up to Congress itself—deciding what that salary should be. The inevitable result was to make congressional salaries a political issue that has plagued Congress throughout its history.

In trying to minimize the adverse political fallout from periodically raising its own salary, Congress fell into the practice of incorporating such pay increases in general pay legislation granting raises for most government workers, including at times the judiciary and the president. But even that tactic often failed to blunt critical reaction.

Public opposition to congressional pay increases has been particularly strong at various times in the nation's history, leading to wholesale election defeats of members who voted for increases their constituents considered unwarranted. On two occasions controversial salary increases were repealed by succeeding Congresses. Frequently, a few members refuse their pay raises, returning the increase to the Treasury or donating it to a public charity. Technically, all members must accept full pay. After receiving their salary, however, they may return any portion to the Treasury.

Despite the resistance both within and outside Congress, congressional pay has risen steadily, particularly in recent years. A member's pay in 1789 was $6 a day; by 1999 it had risen to $136,700 a year and was scheduled to rise to $141,300 in 2000. Although the salary of members remained unchanged for long periods, only rarely was it reduced. The last salary cut was during the Great Depression years of 1932 and 1933.

EARLY PAY LEGISLATION

During the Constitutional Convention of 1787 a principal question surrounding compensation of members was the source of the funds. Members of Congress under the Articles of Confederation had been paid by the states (members of the British Parliament at that time were not compensated). It was felt, however, that members of Congress under the Constitution should be paid, and paid by the national government.

Another question raised at the convention was whether senators and representatives should receive equal pay. Charles Pinckney of South Carolina twice moved "that no salary should be allowed" members of the Senate. "As this branch was meant to represent the wealth of the country," Pinckney asserted, "it ought to be composed of persons of wealth; and if no allowance was to be made, the wealthy alone would undertake the service." Pinckney's motion was seconded by Benjamin Franklin but twice was rejected, by votes of six states to five.[1]

Per Diem Compensation

One of the first, and most controversial, measures enacted by the new Congress in 1789 was a bill fixing the compensation of members. As originally approved by the House, representatives and senators alike were to be paid $6 a day. The proposal for equal pay developed into a dispute over whether senators, by reason of greater responsibilities and presumably higher qualifications, should receive a pay differential.

At the heart of the debate was an amendment by Rep. Theodore Sedgwick, a Massachusetts Federalist, to lower House pay to $5 a day, thus creating a $1-a-day differential in favor of senators. But the amendment was defeated by voice vote. On August 10, 1789, the House by a 30–16 roll call passed a bill providing for payment of $6 a day to members of both chambers.

In the Senate the bill was amended to provide that senators be paid at the $6 rate until March 4, 1795, when their pay would be increased to $8 a day; the pay of representatives would remain at $6. The amended bill passed the Senate on August 28, 1789.

After a House-Senate conference on the issue, the House on September 11 by a 29–25 vote agreed to fix the pay of senators at $7 a day after March 4, 1795, and by a 28–26 vote set March 4, 1796, as the expiration date of the legislation. The Senate agreed to the House amendments on September 12, and the bill was signed into law on September 22, 1789, seven days before the end of the first session of Congress.

As enacted, the measure provided the first congressional perquisite: a travel allowance for senators and representatives of $6 for each twenty miles. It also provided a $6-a-day differential for the House Speaker (making his pay $12 a day) and compensation for a number of lesser House and Senate officials.

When a new pay law was enacted in 1796, only a glancing reference was made to continuing the differential for the Senate. Both the House and the Senate passed a bill equalizing the pay at $6 a day.

Short-Lived Salary Law

In 1816 Congress voted itself a pay increase and a shift from per diem compensation to an annual salary. An act of March 19, 1816, raised congressional pay to $1,500 a year and made the raise retroactive to December 4, 1815, when the first session of the 14th Congress convened. The pay raise had been passed easily by both houses, but it was roundly condemned by the population at large. A number of members who had voted for the bill were defeated in the 1816 general election, and nine members resigned over the issue. One of the election victims was Rep. Daniel Webster, a New Hampshire Federalist. He was not elected to Congress again until 1822.

REMEDY FOR ABSENTEEISM: DOCKING MEMBERS' PAY

One suggestion as a way to curb absenteeism in Congress is to dock a member's pay for each day the person fails to appear on the floor of the House or Senate. The Constitution makes no provision for this, saying only that "each House shall be the Judge of the Elections, Returns and Qualifications of its own Members, and a Majority of each shall constitute a Quorum to do Business; but a smaller Number may adjourn from day to day, and may be authorized to compel the Attendance of absent Members, in such Manner, and under such Penalties as each House may provide." (Article I, Section 5)

Nevertheless, the first session of the First Congress in 1789 provided for an automatic docking of pay. Salaries were $6 a day for each day of attendance.

A law enacted in 1856 provided that "the Secretary of the Senate and the Sergeant at Arms of the House, respectively, shall deduct from the monthly payments of each member or delegate the amount of his salary for each day that he has been absent from the Senate or House, . . . unless such member or delegate assigns as the reason for such absence the sickness of himself or of some member of his family."

Since then a few isolated attempts to compel attendance have cited this law. During the 53rd Congress in 1894, after a ruling of the chair that the 1856 law was still in force, portions of some House members' salaries were withheld.

The 1894 incident was recalled in 1914 when the House adopted a resolution revoking all leaves of absence granted to members and directing the sergeant at arms to reduce members' pay for each day they were absent. The 1914 resolution was enforced stringently for a brief time.

But soon the practice of docking a member's pay for absenteeism was abandoned. The House parliamentarian's office argued there was no way of knowing when a member was away from his official duties.

In 1975 the Senate inserted a provision repealing the 1856 law in the fiscal 1976 legislative branch appropriations bill, but it was dropped from the final version of that bill.

In 1981 a U.S. district court judge rejected a California taxpayer's complaint that federal lawmakers should not be paid for days when they are absent from Congress without an excuse. In a brief opinion, Judge Spencer Williams of the Northern District of California dismissed the suit, ruling that merely being a taxpayer did not give the Californian sufficient standing to file the suit. Williams added that it would be "inappropriate for the courts to inquire into or supervise the attendance of members of a coordinate branch of government."

In a similar 1972 suit, a federal judge had dismissed a suit seeking to recover salaries and allowances paid several members of Congress who were away from Washington campaigning for the presidency.

The short session of the 14th Congress in 1817 repealed the $1,500 salary act, effective at the end of that Congress March 3, 1817. An act of January 22, 1818, restored per diem compensation and set the rate at $8, retroactive to March 3, 1817.

1850S TO 1930S

Almost four decades after Congress had returned to per diem compensation, a successful conversion to annual congressional salaries finally was achieved. An act of August 16, 1856, replaced the $8-a-day rate with a $3,000 annual salary, retroactive to the start of the 34th Congress December 3, 1855. Another retroactive pay increase—to $5,000—was approved July 28, 1866, and made effective as of December 4, 1865, when the 39th Congress convened for its first session.

In the closing days of the 42nd Congress in 1873, still another retroactive pay raise was enacted, increasing salaries to $7,500. The higher salary was made retroactive to the beginning of the 42nd Congress, in effect providing members with a $5,000 windfall ($2,500 per year for the two preceding years). Despite precedents for making the increase retroactive, the size of the increase and the windfall effect boomeranged. Criticism of Congress already was at a high level because of the Crédit Mobilier scandal, and the pay increase was immediately condemned as a "salary grab" and a "back-pay steal." Some members returned their pay to the Treasury; others donated it to colleges or charities.

When the 43rd Congress opened in December 1873, scores of bills were introduced to repeal the increase. By an act of January 20, 1874, congressional pay reverted to the previous $5,000 annual rate, where it stayed until a $7,500 salary was sanctioned in February 1907. A raise to $10,000 was approved in March 1925.

Government austerity was the byword as the Great Depression of the 1930s deepened. Salaries of federal employees were reduced, and members of Congress likewise had to take a pay cut. The Economy Act of June 30, 1932, provided for a 10 percent cutback in members' salaries, dropping them from $10,000 to $9,000. The cutback was increased another 6 percent, meaning a further drop to $8,500, by the Economy Act of March 20, 1933. Gradually the cutbacks were rescinded, and by the end of 1935 congressional salaries had been restored to the $10,000 level.

1940S TO 1960S

No further salary changes occurred until passage of the Legislative Reorganization Act of 1946, which increased congressional salaries from $10,000 to $12,500 and retained an existing $2,500 nontaxable expense allowance for all members. The increase took effect at the beginning of the 80th Congress in 1947. A $15,000 annual salary and elimination of the expense allowance had been recommended in committee, but the legislation was amended in the House, and the House provision was retained in the final version of the act. The measure provided $20,000 salaries for the vice president and Speaker of the House.[2]

Expense Allowance Controversy

Provision for the $2,500 expense allowance for representatives had been made in 1945 when the House Appropriations Committee included funding for it in a legislative branch appropriations bill. Although the bill did not so stipulate, the committee said the allowance probably would be tax-exempt. When the measure reached the House floor, opponents called the allowance an opening wedge for inflation and a pay increase by subterfuge. But a special rule drafted by the Rules Committee waived all points of order against the bill, thus thwarting efforts to eliminate the allowance on the floor. The legislation subsequently was adopted, 229–124. Other attempts to eliminate or change the proposal also failed, and the House approved the bill.

The Senate Appropriations Committee reported the bill after adding a $2,500 expense allowance for senators. But the committee amendment was defeated by the Senate, 9–43, and two compromise amendments also failed. An amendment to delete the House expense allowance was narrowly defeated, 22–28. The Senate thus passed the bill, which later was enacted, with the allowance for representatives but not for senators.

The question came up again during Senate action on a fiscal 1946 supplemental appropriations bill. The Senate committee offered an amendment to extend the expense allowance to senators, but the Senate again rejected the plan, 24–47. Senators ultimately received the $2,500 expense allowance in 1946 through the fiscal 1947 legislative branch appropriations bill.

In the Revenue Act of 1951 Congress eliminated the tax-free expense allowances, effective January 3, 1952. Also made subject to taxation were the expense allowances of the president, vice president, and Speaker of the House.

Congress in 1953 created a Commission on Judicial and Congressional Salaries to study the salary question and make recommendations to Congress. As approved by the Senate, the commission would have been empowered to raise salaries, but the House amended the measure to require congressional approval for any pay increase. The commission's report recommended a $10,000 salary boost, but Congress took no action.

In 1955, however, Congress enacted legislation raising both congressional and judicial salaries. The bill increased members' salaries to $22,500 (from $12,500 plus the $2,500 expense allowance). It also provided $35,000 for the Speaker and the vice president (up from $30,000) and retained the existing $10,000 taxable expense allowance for both positions. The increases became effective March 1, 1955.

The chief difference between the House and Senate bills was over the $2,500 expense allowance, which the House wanted to retain. But the Senate deleted it. Then the Senate rejected the final conference version because it retained an expense allowance provision. After that provision had been deleted, a second conference bill without the allowance was approved by Congress.

In 1964 Congress again approved raises in its own salaries, and those of other federal government employees. Members' salaries were raised by $7,500, to $30,000, effective in 1965. Salaries of the Speaker and the vice president were raised to $43,000. The bill was enacted after the House first killed a version of the bill raising congressional salaries by $10,000. The second measure was strongly backed by President Lyndon B. Johnson. Congress acted on the bill after most of the 1964 congressional primary elections had been held. It was passed in the House by a vote of 243–157 and in the Senate by 58–21.

Automatic Salary Increases

In 1967 Congress established a nine-member Commission on Executive, Legislative, and Judicial Salaries to review the salaries of members of Congress, federal judges, and top officers of the executive branch every four years and to recommend changes.

Creation of the commission plan was designed to relieve members of Congress of the politically risky task of periodically having to raise their own salaries. And it was hoped that the commission would set the salaries of top officials high enough to attract and keep the best qualified persons.

Three members of the commission were to be appointed by the president, two by the president of the Senate, two by the Speaker of the House, and two by the chief justice. Beginning in fiscal 1969, the commission was to submit its recommendations to the president, who was to propose in his annual budget message the exact rates of pay "he deems advisable" for federal executives, judges, and members of Congress. His recommendations could be either higher or lower than those of the commission, or he could propose that salaries not be altered. The recommendations were to take effect within thirty days unless Congress either disapproved all or part of the recommendations or enacted a separate pay measure.

The law did not work as well as its sponsors had hoped, although in its first test, in 1969, it worked as planned. Congressional salaries were increased from $30,000 to $42,500. But in 1973 President Richard Nixon delayed naming a pay commission, and pay proposals were not sent to Congress until 1974, an election year. The Senate, uneasy about a pay raise at that time, killed the proposed increases.

1975 PAY RAISE

Congressional salaries were not increased again for almost seven years, during which period the cost of living had risen 47.5 percent. But in 1975, Congress, with sleight of hand, approved a pay raise for itself and other top officials of the government. Congress opted to make itself and other top officials eligible for the annual government-wide pay increase, which was designed to maintain pay comparability between government workers and those in the private sector. The increase would be received automatically unless members of the House or Senate decided not to take it.

The plan was worked out secretly over several months by congressional leaders in consultation with the Ford administration. It was cleared by Congress only five days after most members had first heard of it. One representative called the debate "vicious, one of the ugliest, most disgusting things I've ever seen. . . . Members who rarely say a thing during floor debate were shouting and screaming at each other, saying, 'Don't be a hero, you want this raise as much as we do.' It was ugly."

The result was a 5 percent pay increase for members, bringing congressional salaries to $44,600 annually. The raise was much criticized by the voters, and in 1976 Congress decided it was prudent to pass up the automatic increase for that year. A provision denying the comparability pay raise to members of Congress scheduled for October was added to the fiscal 1977 legislative branch appropriations bill.

1977 PAY RAISE

Congress in 1977 made up for lost time by giving itself and other top government officials of the executive, legislative, and judicial branches a $12,900 pay raise, increasing lawmakers' salaries to $57,500 annually. This amounted to a pay hike of about 28.9 percent. It was the second increase in pay since 1969.

The raise had been recommended by the third quadrennial Commission on Executive, Legislative, and Judicial Salaries, chaired by businessman Peter G. Peterson. It conditioned its proposals for a salary increase upon adoption of a strong ethics code governing congressional conduct. And the panel called for public disclosure of members' financial worth, rigorous restrictions on outside earned income and on potential conflicts of interest, fully accountable expense allowances, and publicly reported auditing of the ethics codes' provisions.

Repeal of Automatic Procedure

Senators and representatives paid a price when they raised their salaries in 1977. Congress repealed the process that had allowed raises to take effect without a congressional vote under the commission procedure. And the new ethics codes adopted by both chambers as part of the 1977 pay increase negotiations included a ban on so-called slush funds—unofficial office accounts maintained with cash gifts from members' friends and supporters—and tight limits on outside income. (In 1979, however, the Senate suspended those outside income limits for four years.)

Congress also denied itself the scheduled 1977 comparability increase. Even so, criticism of the earlier raise that year was widespread.

In 1978 Congress also voted to forgo that year's comparability increase. Also affected were the top congressional aides, judges, and all other federal officials at or over the $47,500 pay level. Some sixteen thousand persons were affected. Other federal workers got the raise, which was 5.5 percent.

Tax Break for 1977

Congress cleared legislation in July 1977 exempting members of Congress from paying income taxes in those jurisdictions where they lived while attending sessions of Congress. A similar bill was passed by Congress in 1976 but was vetoed by President Gerald R. Ford on grounds that it unfairly created a special class of citizens with special privileges.

The 1977 tax exemption was challenged in the courts, but it was upheld by the Supreme Court in 1981.

As a practical matter, Maryland was the only state affected by the law because Virginia and the District of Columbia already had exempted members of Congress from their income tax laws. In 1977 there were about 125 members living in Maryland, and that number of members was estimated to be living there when the Supreme Court upheld the law in 1981.

1979 SENATE-HOUSE FEUD

The political sensitivity of congressional pay was apparent once again in 1979 when the issue set off a Senate-House feud. That dispute forced the government to begin fiscal 1980 without spending authority for many federal agencies.

As 1979 began, members were earning $57,500 a year. Moreover, they were due for a 7 percent pay hike that October under the comparability pay procedures then in effect. Under the 1975 salary law Congress was automatically entitled to the annual raise granted federal employees, unless it voted to block the increase.

Besides the proposed 7 percent increase, members hoped to recoup the 5.5 percent comparability adjustment from 1978 that Congress had voted not to take in that election year. The 1978 hike had not been repealed; it had just been suspended for a year. Thus if Congress took no action on it, members would receive both pay hikes, plus interest on the 5.5 percent raise, for a total increase of 12.9 percent, or more than $7,400.

With another election just a year away, however, a move was launched to limit or deny the congressional pay hikes altogether. Also caught up in the politics of the pay issue were federal judges and top-level executive branch bureaucrats making at least $47,500; past pay freezes had covered them as well.

The House Appropriations Committee recommended that the raise be limited to 7 percent, but in June the House knocked that limit down to 5.5 percent and then rejected the appropriations bill because it thought that increase too high.

Then, in late September, Congress became bogged down over an emergency stopgap funding bill that was being used as the vehicle for the pay hike. That measure was needed to fund agencies whose regular appropriations bills had not yet been approved. The House, in a nonrecorded vote, accepted a compromise 5.5 percent hike. The Senate knocked that out and said "no raise."

But just two days before the new fiscal year was to begin, the House insisted on the raise and adjourned for a week's recess, leaving the Senate with an unenviable choice: it could either approve the emergency funding resolution, thus keeping the government in business but also accepting the 5.5 percent pay increase, or kill the funding resolution, thus permitting the automatic 12.9 percent increase to go into effect but depriving most

of the government of authority to spend money as of October 1. An angry Senate voted to kill the resolution.

Finally, on October 12, almost two weeks after the new fiscal year had begun and just before thousands of federal workers were about to be denied a paycheck, Congress approved an emergency funding measure that rolled back the 12.9 percent increase to 5.5 percent. The new raise brought congressional salaries up to $60,662.50 beginning October 1, 1979.

While the increases for members of Congress and top executive branch officials were rolled back, federal judges were able to retain the entire 12.9 percent pay hike because under the Constitution Congress is prohibited from reducing the compensation of judges during their term of office.

1980-1981 PAY CONTROVERSIES

In 1980 Congress denied itself a 9.11 percent comparability increase that President Jimmy Carter had recommended for federal workers. The following year lawmakers included a provision prohibiting the pay adjustment in a fiscal 1981 continuing appropriations bill. The prohibition was extended through the end of fiscal 1981 in two subsequent laws.[3]

In 1981, citing the need to cut federal spending, Congress rejected another large pay raise—amounting to 16.9 percent—for lawmakers and high-level government employees. (President Carter in 1980 had recommended a pay raise to $70,896 based on the recommendation of the Commission on Executive, Legislative, and Judicial Salaries. President Ronald Reagan, who originally supported the increase, changed his mind, citing budgetary considerations.)

The proposed 1981 pay raise was debated amid disagreement between House and Senate members over the proper procedure for acting on proposed congressional salary hikes. The House and Senate each followed a different path in rejecting the pay raise. The Senate took a recorded vote on four separate resolutions of disapproval; the House merely took a voice vote on a resolution affirming "the sense of the House."

In 1977 Congress had amended the 1969 pay law by requiring each house to approve a presidential pay recommendation within sixty days in order for the proposed increase to take effect. The amendment stated that each chamber must take recorded votes on raising the pay of each branch of government. The approval of both chambers was required to raise the pay of employees in any of the three branches of government.

Future Automatic Raises

Congress had hoped to avoid controversy by voting in 1975 to make itself eligible for the automatic annual comparability pay raise granted federal employees. But because Congress had to appropriate the funds each year for its raise, the issue still came up annually. In an effort to further depoliticize congressional pay, lawmakers voted to fund congressional salaries through a permanent appropriation, effective October 1982. The new pay procedure was approved in October 1981 as a rider attached to an emergency funding bill. The move eliminated one avenue for rejecting the annual raise, but members opposed to congressional pay hikes continued to find ways to bring up the pay raise issue.

The final version of that legislation did not contain a 4.8 percent congressional pay raise for 1981 sought by House members.

1981 TAX DEDUCTIONS

In the same 1981 emergency appropriations bill containing the comparability adjustment procedure, Congress approved a change in congressional tax laws that enabled senators and representatives to deduct from their income taxes the expenses they incurred while residing in Washington. Under a 1952 law members had been allowed a maximum deduction of $3,000.

The Joint Taxation Committee estimated in 1981 that the change would cost the Treasury $3 million a year and provide a typical member in the 45 percent tax bracket with the equivalent of a $10,500 pay raise.

Though a similar proposal was pushed earlier in 1981 by House Appropriations Committee Chairman Jamie L. Whitten, D-Miss., it never came to a vote in the House. But Sen. Ted Stevens, R-Alaska, won approval of the plan in the Senate. Besides the tax deduction change, Stevens had shepherded through to enactment measures increasing legislators' official perquisites, loosening restrictions on outside earnings by lawmakers, and modifying provisions of the Senate's ethics code that placed strict limits on senators' honoraria.

Resolving Conflicting Statutes

After the tax change had been enacted, it was discovered that the new deductions conflicted with a provision of a 1976 statute limiting the amount of deductions a person living alone could take on second homes used in connection with a trade or business.

Under the combined effect of the 1976 and 1981 laws, a member of Congress who lived alone while working in Washington could, in the same tax year, depreciate the cost of a second home in the capital area as well as deduct from his taxes his Washington housing expenses. But a member whose family resided with him in Washington for more than fourteen days a year was not eligible for both tax breaks.

To remedy the situation Congress in December 1981 tacked a nongermane tax provision onto an unrelated bill and passed that measure without a roll-call vote. The bill enabled members living with their families in Washington to claim the same tax benefits as members living alone. Congress also instructed the Treasury secretary to prescribe the "appropriate" business deduction a member could take for each day Congress was in session without actually having to substantiate his business expenses.

Treasury Ruling for 1981

Under regulations approved by the Treasury in January 1982, the 1981 deduction would result in a saving of at least $19,200 for senators and $19,650 for House members. Since previous law allowed members a maximum deduction of $3,000 a year for their Washington expenses, the new legislation provided an additional deduction of at least $16,200 for senators and $16,650 for House members for that year. (The deduction would vary from year to year, depending on how many days each house was in session.)

A married member with two children and typical deductions who lived on his congressional salary alone during 1981 was able to keep about $7,000 that otherwise would have been paid in taxes, according to Congressional Quarterly calculations based on figures supplied by the Internal Revenue Service. Members with high Washington living expenses or with outside incomes in addition to their salaries could qualify for even bigger tax breaks.

1982 TAX DEDUCTION REPEAL

The tax breaks provoked a public outcry. Taxpayers flooded Capitol Hill and the Internal Revenue Service with angry letters and phone calls protesting the new deductions. Common Cause, the citizens' lobby group, criticized the tax deductions as unjustified and inequitable and launched a nationwide "Give Taxpayers A Break" campaign to repeal the 1981 tax deduction. It pledged to get all representatives and senators to publicly disclose the amount of the deductions for Washington living expenses they took in 1981. According to Common Cause President Fred Wertheimer, "Congress's failure to provide regular cost-of-living adjustments for itself cannot justify enacting extravagant and unjustified tax breaks that turn members of Congress into a privileged class of taxpayers. This is bound to undermine public confidence in the fairness of our tax system."

In response to the pressure, Congress in 1982 repealed the 1981 deductions. The measure was enacted into law July 18, but was made retroactive to January 1. It nevertheless allowed members to keep the lucrative deductions they took on their 1981 tax returns. The repeal restored the $3,000 annual limit on a member's deductions for Washington expenses—the limit that had been in force before 1981. The repeal, initiated by Sen. William Proxmire, D-Wis., was tacked onto a fiscal 1982 supplemental appropriations bill for federal agencies.

Earlier that year, the House threatened not to approve the repeal unless senators agreed to limit their outside earned income to the maximum allowed representatives. That dispute stalled final action on the spending bill/tax deduction repeal and exacerbated a bitter struggle between the House and Senate over the twin issues of members' tax breaks and honoraria. But the House backed down when it looked as if the honoraria provision might tie up the funding bill indefinitely.

1982 PAY DIFFERENTIAL

Breaking nearly two hundred years of tradition, Congress ended its 97th term with House members earning higher salaries than senators. But at the same time the Senate repealed a rule that would have limited outside earnings, thus allowing senators to earn as much as they wanted from business income, legal fees, and honoraria for appearances and speeches.

The changes in pay and honoraria were enacted in 1982 during a lame duck session, after members initially shunned a preelection salary increase. With help from members who did not have to worry about reelection, the House in December approved a 15 percent pay raise, increasing representatives' pay to $69,800 as of December 18.

The Senate rejected the pay raise but voted to kill a cap on outside earnings, passed in 1977 and scheduled to take effect January 1, 1983. Outside earnings for House members remained limited to 30 percent of a representative's salary—$20,940.

In 1981 some senators had earned as much as $48,000 in honoraria, leading some House members to remark that the Senate actually got a better arrangement.

Preelection Jitters

Before the November election the House turned back initial attempts by the Senate to raise congressional salaries. On August 17, House members rejected, 266–145, a conference report on a budget reconciliation bill because it contained a provision that would have required the Commission on Executive, Legislative, and Judicial Salaries to convene a special session and recommend a congressional pay increase by November 15. Congress would then have had thirty days to reject the raise or it would have taken effect.

The Senate went along with the House, and the offending provision was removed before the reconciliation bill was enacted.

On August 18 the House also killed, by voice vote, an identical provision that had been inserted in a fiscal 1982 supplemental appropriations bill.

The upcoming elections had members particularly gun-shy. Said Rep. Vic Fazio, D-Calif., "Obviously, we are in an election period, and it is not a good time to talk about these things."

But Rep. Ken Holland, D-S.C., who was leaving Congress because of the pay, said, "Somebody like me with four children, the first beginning college next week, just cannot remain in Washington under the pay that is provided."

As the elections drew closer, members also voted to forgo a 4 percent increase recommended by President Reagan for federal workers. Under a 1975 law, members of Congress were slated to get the same comparability raise as federal employees. But in September Congress included a provision in a stopgap budget measure that barred lawmakers and senior bureaucrats from getting the increase, which took effect October 1.

Final Action

Both the House pay increase and the Senate change in honoraria were included in the final fiscal 1983 continuing appropriations measure, cleared by Congress December 20. The legislation made the $9,138 House raise effective December 18.

The House voted 303–109 for the increase, but the key vote came when members rejected an amendment to keep pay at the

Rep. Ken Holland, D-S.C., left Congress after four terms because "somebody like me with four children . . . just cannot remain in Washington under the pay that is provided."

existing level. The amendment failed 208–208, with outgoing Rep. Robert K. Dornan, R-Calif., casting the tying no vote and seventy other lame ducks also voting no.

The House also added a section limiting all members of Congress to outside earnings of 30 percent. The Senate deleted the pay raise and the outside earnings cap. The compromise resulted in a salary increase for House members and no limit on outside earnings for senators.

1983 PAY-HONORARIA DISPUTE

In 1983, six months after the House had voted itself a 15 percent pay raise, senators followed suit, accepting a $9,138 increase effective July 1. That brought both House and Senate salaries to $69,800 a year.

Senators also agreed to limit their honoraria earnings to 30 percent of their salaries, the same amount House members could earn in total outside income. The limit on honoraria would take effect January 1, 1984. The change in Senate pay and honoraria was included in a fiscal 1983 supplemental appropriations bill that cleared Congress July 29.

The pay raise arose out of an attempt by House members to limit senators' honoraria earnings. When 1982 figures revealed that more than half of the Senate took in honoraria totaling more than 30 percent of their salaries and that some senators' honoraria earnings exceeded their salaries, outraged House members slapped a 30 percent limit on the amount senators could earn in speaking and writing fees. *(See "Honoraria: A Vanishing Perquisite," p. 778.)*

The amendment, added during the House Appropriations Committee's markup of the fiscal 1983 supplemental bill, was not contested during House floor debate.

The issue, however, impeded Senate action on the bill until Senate leaders worked out an agreement. During the pay raise debate, senators were forced to vote on a variety of options and at one point agreed 51–41 to cap honoraria without raising annual salaries. One week later senators approved, 49–47, an amendment limiting honoraria to 30 percent of their salaries and increasing Senate pay to $69,800.

1984 "BACKDOOR" INCREASE

In 1984 congressional salaries rose from $69,800 to $72,600, despite the Senate's attempt to prevent a pay hike.

Lawmakers automatically got a 3.5 percent pay increase as of January 1, 1984, under the 1975 comparability pay law that gave members of Congress the same cost-of-living raises as those received by federal workers. (President Reagan had recommended the increase in 1983 but had delayed its effective date from October 1, 1983, to January 1, 1984.)

In April Congress raised its pay another one-half percent in the 1983 Budget Reconciliation Act. The raise was retroactive to January.

The actual increase in take-home pay in 1984 amounted to less than $270, however, because lawmakers began paying Social Security taxes that year. Until 1984 members of Congress, like federal workers, were not covered by the Social Security system and instead received pension benefits from a separate retirement plan. But to keep the Social Security system solvent, Congress cleared legislation in 1983 that required members of Congress and all federal workers to join the system.

Senate Objections

Because Congress did not have to vote on the 3.5 percent pay increase, several Senate Republicans objected to what they called the "backdoor" pay hike.

In January the Senate took up a bill by Don Nickles, R-Okla., that would have rescinded the 3.5 percent increase for members of Congress but not other federal employees. During debate on the measure, Nickles said, "The country is going broke with deficits. It is hard for those of us who like to see cuts in every area, including defense, to accept a raise."

"If Congress wants a pay raise, they ought to be willing to have it up on the floor for everyone to see and vote up or down," said Jake Garn, R-Utah, a cosponsor of the bill. "We have had sneaky ones over the years, but this is the worst one."

Opponents of the bill argued that the salary rollback—which would have saved about $1.3 million in 1984—was a feeble gesture at budget austerity in the face of $200 billion budget deficits.

"If we really want to get down to the core, we will get into the areas where we are really spending money," said Barry Goldwater, R-Ariz. "Take a look at the welfare state."

Others warned that if salaries were not adequate to cover the high cost of maintaining homes both in their states and in Washington, members would be forced to rely more heavily on honoraria and other outside earnings.

Even Nickles, who said he would be "disappointed" if the House did not pass the measure, conceded that most senators would be relieved if the bill died in the House, which is what happened.

On January 26, senators voted 66–19 to revoke the $2,400 comparability increase. But the bill never made it to the House floor.

House leaders from both parties wanted to protect members from a politically risky vote during an election year. "I would think it is extraordinarily unwise for us to follow the action of the Senate and interrupt the cost-of-living adjustment," said Majority Whip Thomas S. Foley, D-Wash.

By referring the measure to the House Post Office and Civil Service Committee, whose chairman, William D. Ford, D-Mich., was known to favor regular pay increases, leaders ensured the bill's demise.

Second Raise

Congress got another slight salary increase when the Senate on April 5 cleared, 67–26, a budget reconciliation bill left over from 1983. Several senators were unhappy about the half percent increase in congressional pay included in the House-passed measure. But Senate Budget Committee Chairman Pete V. Domenici, R-N.M., said he did not want to change the House version and jeopardize the other savings that would be achieved under the legislation.

1985–1986 PAY FREEZE

Members of Congress again got a 3.5 percent comparability increase on January 1, 1985, along with their staffs and federal workers. The pay hike boosted congressional salaries to $75,100 a year.

The raise, which had been proposed by President Reagan in August 1984 for federal employees, applied to members of Congress under a 1975 law. (Like the previous comparability increase, this one had been scheduled to take effect October 1, 1984, but was delayed until January 1, 1985.)

The Commission on Executive, Legislative, and Judicial Salaries, which met every four years to recommend major adjustments in pay for top federal officials, did not recommend a congressional salary increase in 1985. Instead, it called for procedural changes in the way Congress rejected the president's recommendation for a pay raise and also proposed that another commission then convene in 1986 to recommend salary changes.

In August 1985 the president recommended a pay freeze rather than a comparability raise for federal employees for January 1986. Congress included a freeze on its own salaries in a budget reconciliation bill, which cleared March 20, 1986. Late in 1985, Congress increased the limit on honoraria earnings by senators to 40 percent from 30 percent of salary.

President Ronald Reagan meets with congressional leaders at the White House. Reagan was supportive of efforts to raise congressional pay rates in the 1980s.

1987 REAGAN PLAN

The next increases in congressional pay came in 1987, when members' salaries jumped from $75,100 to $77,400 on January 1, then to $89,500 on February 4. Lawmakers first got a 3 percent comparability raise on January 1 along with federal employees. The pay hike was included in a catchall fiscal 1987 appropriations bill passed in 1986.

In February members accepted a $12,100 increase that had been proposed by President Reagan based on the study of the specially convened Commission on Executive, Legislative, and Judicial Salaries.

The commission had proposed a 75 percent increase for lawmakers and argued that the purchasing power of a congressional salary, badly eroded by inflation, had dropped 40 percent since 1969. Instead, Reagan recommended a 16 percent hike.

On January 29 the Senate passed, 88–6, a measure to reject the commission's proposed raise, after members said it was wrong for Congress to pay itself more while the government was running record deficits. "Social Security recipients were given a 1.3 percent increase last year," said Strom Thurmond, R-S.C., who sponsored the resolution to block the increase. "Yet we consider giving ourselves a 16 percent increase. There is no rational justification for such action."

Senators then added an amendment blocking the pay raise to a House-passed bill to aid the homeless. The move infuriated House Democrats, who had made homeless aid a top priority.

The Senate action also underscored institutional rivalries. House members felt that senators, many of whom were wealthy to begin with, were also more in demand for appearances before special interest groups and thus able to raise more in honoraria than House lawmakers. They said senators were denying them a chance to earn enough to support their families and two homes, in Washington and in their districts. "Their position is you have to be a millionaire to be in Congress, or else they're for special interests having control," said Rep. Mike Lowry, D-Wash.

But maneuvering by House Democratic leaders enabled members to go on record against the proposed raise and still pocket the increase. House Speaker Jim Wright, D-Texas, made sure that the House vote on the pay raise came after the thirty-day deadline for disapproving pay proposals under the law. On February 4, 1987, the House cleared the homeless aid measure, including the provision rejecting the pay raise, but the action came one day after the deadline.

President Reagan declared the raise in effect. Opponents, who included six members of Congress led by Sen. Gordon J. Humphrey, R-N.H., went to court to repeal the increase, arguing that the raise was enacted unconstitutionally. On June 30 a U.S. district court judge dismissed the lawsuit.

In August Reagan recommended a 2 percent pay hike for federal workers and lawmakers, delayed from October 1, 1987, to January 1, 1988. But Congress denied itself the increase in a fiscal 1988 catchall spending bill that cleared on December 22, 1987.

1989–1990 PAY RAISES

After a storm of public criticism, Congress rejected a 51 percent pay raise in February 1989. Nine months later, in the Ethics Reform Act, members approved a hike of almost 40 percent over two years, in 1990 and 1991, for representatives and top federal officials and 9.9 percent for senators in 1990, while tightening ethics rules and limiting outside income.

As a result, House salaries rose to $96,600 in 1990 and $125,100 in 1991. Senators' salaries increased to $98,400 in 1990, but they were allowed to continue receiving honoraria. Representatives were no longer permitted to do so.

The measure, which cleared November 18, eliminated a loophole in a 1979 law that had allowed House members who had been in office at the beginning of 1980 to convert campaign funds to personal use once they retired. The legislation also limited expense-paid travel for nongovernmental trips and tightened rules on gifts.

By tying the pay raise to ethics reforms, congressional leaders sought to make the measure more palatable to critics. House Speaker Thomas Foley insisted on calling the measure an "ethics bill," correcting reporters who referred to it as a pay raise.

In the end it was the bipartisanship support of the leadership that pushed the bill through.

The legislation also changed the system for raising congressional pay. In place of the Commission on Executive, Legislative, and Judicial Salaries, the bill established an eleven-member Citizens' Commission on Public Service and Compensation, which was required to meet every four years and report to the president by December 15. The president's pay recommendations, made after receiving the commission's report, would take effect after the next congressional election and only if both the House and the Senate adopted a resolution of approval by recorded vote within sixty days.

The method for providing annual comparability increases also was revised to eliminate the president's role in recommending them. Instead, the congressional comparability raise was automatic and based on certain private sector wage increases as measured by one component of the Employment Cost Index.

Background

On December 13, 1988, the Commission on Executive, Legislative, and Judicial Salaries recommended that members of Congress get a 51 percent pay raise if they agreed to ban honoraria. That would have brought congressional salaries to $135,000, a $45,500 increase.

Members of the commission said that a 51 percent pay raise was necessary to make up for two decades of inflation and to provide incentive for members to wean themselves of honoraria.

The higher pay level would have been more than enough to make up for the loss of honoraria income, even for those who collected the maximum allowed under the law. But because the majority of Americans understood little about honoraria, a promise to give up these speaking fees in exchange for a pay raise failed to provide political cover.

"The honoraria ban never caught on with the public," said former Rep. William R. Ratchford, D-Conn., a member of the commission. "They can relate to a dollar figure on salary, but outside the Beltway, they're not sure what honorarium is."

President Reagan endorsed the 51 percent hike on January 9, which meant that unless Congress passed legislation blocking the increase within thirty days, the raise would take effect.

Advocates of the raise said that continued erosion of congressional salaries would turn lawmaking into a profession only the wealthy could afford. They emphasized that members faced unusually high living costs, including maintaining two residences, one back home and another in Washington.

California's Fazio, a leading pay-raise advocate, told his colleagues that even if they personally were comfortable living on the salary at that time, they should not block a raise for members from more expensive parts of the country. If their constituents did not think the raise was justified, Fazio said, members did not have to accept the extra money.

"If you can't justify it in South Dakota, don't tell someone who lives in the suburbs of San Francisco to live by the same standard," Fazio said.

But editorial writers slammed Congress not only for the size of the raise but also for attempting to avoid a vote on the issue. Congressional offices were flooded with mail from angry constituents.

Some of the harshest criticism came from consumer activist Ralph Nader and a network of radio talk-show hosts around the country who gave people a forum for venting their outrage against the raise. One radio station urged its listeners to send tea bags to congressmen with the slogan, "Read my lips: No pay raise," and thousands did.

Members of Congress started going public against the pay raise, even though, in many cases, they were privately hoping to get the money.

The Senate voted 95–5 on February 2, 1989, to disapprove of the proposed raise for members of Congress and senior officials in the executive, legislative, and judicial branches. The vote increased pressure on the House.

House Speaker Wright, who had promised to keep pay raise legislation off the House floor, was forced to reverse his position when a majority of members voted for consideration of the matter.

During debate on the raise, Ways and Means Chairman Dan Rostenkowski, D-Ill., gave an emotional defense of the raise. "I can't remember a more disheartening or embarrassing debate," he said. "I am proud of what I do and you, my colleagues, should feel the same way."

But after the outpouring of criticism, few were willing to test their worth at the voting booth.

On February 7, one day before the raise was to take effect, the

Speaker Tom Foley, D-Wash., was instrumental in pushing through the House pay raise of 1989.

House voted 380–48 to kill the pay raise for all three branches. The Senate quickly followed suit, 94–6.

Round Two

As soon as he became Speaker June 6, Foley urged a bipartisan task force that had been named by Wright to look at ethics laws to report quickly. It was understood that the centerpiece of that effort, eliminating honoraria payments, could only fly if members' lost income was offset by a salary increase.

The task force, headed by Fazio and Lynn Martin, R-Ill., came up with a plan intended to avoid the pitfalls of the previous pay hike effort. The plan called for a two-stage increase and delayed the larger hike until after the next election so voters could decide whether incumbents deserved the raise. And from the beginning, leaders said they would put the proposal to a roll-call vote. Proponents decided to leave it to the Senate to set its own salary and ethics rules.

The ethics–pay raise package came to the House floor on November 16. House Speaker Foley and Minority Leader Robert H. Michel, R-Ill., put the full weight and prestige of their offices behind the pay raise, in a show of bipartisanship missing in the earlier pay-raise drive.

"The Speaker and minority leader were behind this 100 percent—that was the key," said John P. Murtha, D-Pa., a veteran from the front lines of past fights for pay raises.

Few spoke in opposition to the bill. "We told people, if they couldn't be for it, at least don't be a leader of the opposition," said Steve Gunderson of Wisconsin, a deputy GOP whip.

The House approved the measure 252–174.

Senate Action

Senate leaders of both parties presented a united front in support of the two-step pay increase. But despite concerted arm-twisting in the closing hours of the session, they failed to muster the votes for the House package and had to quickly come up with a smaller raise to apply to senators.

When the initial pay-raise proposal appeared to be foundering, Assistant Senate Republican leader Alan K. Simpson of Wyoming called his House counterpart, Minority Whip Newt Gingrich of Georgia, for lobbying help from House members. House members descended onto the Senate floor to buttonhole their colleagues.

Unpersuaded were several Democratic senators with presidential ambitions—Sam Nunn of Georgia, Bill Bradley of New Jersey, and Al Gore of Tennessee—and some of the richest members, including Herb Kohl, D-Wis., and John D. Rockefeller IV, D-W.Va.

The House plan never came to a direct vote in the Senate. After off-the-floor discussions, Senate leaders conceded failure and offered a proposal that left the raise intact for House members and top government officials but raised Senate salaries by 9.9 percent and provided automatic annual adjustments in the future. The 9.9 percent raise was determined by restoring the previously denied 1988, 1989, and 1990 annual pay adjustments of 2 percent, 4.1 percent, and 3.6 percent, compounded, effective February 1, 1990. The vote on the plan was 56–43, with more than three-quarters of those facing reelection voting no. The House agreed to the Senate's changes, and, as a result, senators' pay increased to $98,400 from $89,500 on February 1.

Provisions for Representatives' Pay

The House-Senate compromise gave representatives two separate pay increases, one in 1990 and a second in 1991. Effective February 1, 1990, their pay increased by 7.9 percent, to $96,600 from $89,500. This raise reflected a restoration of the previously denied 1989 and 1990 annual adjustments of 4.1 percent and 3.6 percent, compounded. Effective January 1, 1991, representatives received a 25 percent increase. On that date, representatives also received a separate 3.6 percent annual adjustment, and with the 25 percent raise compounded by the subsequent 3.6 percent increase, representatives' pay went up 29.5 percent, to $125,100 from $96,600.

1991 PAY AND HONORARIA TRADE-OFF

Senators also received the 3.6 percent raise on January 1, 1991, taking their pay to $101,900 from $98,400. This adjustment was the first to which members were entitled pursuant to an automatic annual adjustment procedure established in the ethics package. Neither chamber challenged it on the floor to prohibit it from taking effect. As 1991 began, senators were paid less than representatives, but House members were barred from accepting honoraria. Senators, while still able to accept speaking fees, were limited to a smaller overall amount. However, between pay

TABLE 27-1 Congressional Pay

Year	Salary
1789–1795	$6 per diem
1795–1796	$6 per diem (House)
	$7 per diem (Senate)
1796–1815	$6 per diem
1815–1817	$1,500 per year
1817–1855	$8 per diem
1855–1865	$3,000 per year
1865–1871	$5,000 per year
1871–1873	$7,500 per year
1873–1907	$5,000 per year
1907–1925	$7,500 per year
1925–1932	$10,000 per year
1932–1933	$9,000 per year
1933–1935	$8,500 per year
1935–1947	$10,000 per year
1947–1955	$12,500 per year
1955–1965	$22,500 per year
1965–1969	$30,000 per year]
1969–1975	$42,500 per year
1975–1977	$44,600 per year
1977–1979	$57,500 per year
1979–1982	$60,662.50 per year[a]
December 1982–1983	$69,800 per year (House)
July 1983	$69,800 per year (Senate)
1984	$72,600 per year
1985–1986	$75,100 per year
January 1987	$77,400 per year
February 1987–1989	$89,500 per year
1990	$96,600 per year (House)
1990	$98,400 per year (Senate)
January 1991	$125,100 per year (House)
	$101,900 per year (Senate)
August 1991	$125,100 per year (Senate)
1992	$129,500 per year
1993–1997	$133,600 per year
1998–1999	$136,700 per year
2000[b]	$141,300

NOTE: The top six leaders of Congress—the Speaker of the House, the Senate president pro tempore, and the majority and minority leaders of both chambers—receive additional pay. Highest paid is the House Speaker, who earned $175,400 in 1999. The Speaker's pay was scheduled to rise to $181,400 in 2000 as the result of a 3.4 percent pay increase for all members of Congress under the annual adjustment procedures of law.

a. Percentage increases in congressional salaries generally are rounded to the nearest $100. The 1979 increase was not rounded because of specific language in the enacting legislation.   b. Scheduled as of October 1999.

SOURCE: Congressional Research Service; House Sergeant at Arms; Senate Disbursing Office.

and honoraria, senators could earn roughly as much as House members.

Annual Adjustment Formula

The size of the automatic annual adjustment was determined by a formula linking congressional salaries to private sector pay, instead of federal worker increases, as in the past.

The new method for figuring the increase was set in the 1989 law and replaced the procedure for automatic annual increases that had been in effect since 1975. By basing annual congressional pay increases on the Bureau of Labor Statistics' Employment Cost Index, a quarterly index of wages and salaries for private industry, lawmakers hoped to ensure annual pay raises for themselves without having to revisit the politically painful issue year after year.

1991: Senate Pay Raise

Before departing for the August congressional recess, the Senate voted to give itself a 22.8 percent raise to bring senators' annual salaries up to the House level of $125,100, to prohibit their acceptance of honoraria, and to limit outside earned income to 15 percent of their pay.

The Senate made its move when the legislative branch appropriations bill arrived on the floor July 17. Though it was widely known that a pay raise was in the works, the bill was brought up suddenly once Appropriations Committee Chairman Robert C. Byrd, D-W.Va., had the votes in hand. The Senate adopted his amendment, 53–45. The House agreed to go along, but only after forcing Senate negotiators to ease congressional limits on accepting gifts and to join the House and the rest of the federal government in banning honoraria. Both the raise and the honoraria ban took effect August 14, 1991.

1992 AND 1993 ANNUAL INCREASES

Without congressional disapproval of them, the annual adjustments for the next two years went into effect as scheduled. The appropriations bills as reported contained no language to ban them, nor were any floor amendments offered in either house to do so. As a result, representatives' and senators' pay increased by 3.5 percent in 1992, to $129,500 from $125,100, and by 3.2 percent in 1993, further raising their salary to $133,600.

1994–1997 ANNUAL ADJUSTMENTS BLOCKED

Although members received the first three scheduled annual salary adjustments under the 1989 ethics and pay law, Congress blocked them by amendments each year for the next four years (those scheduled for 1994, 1995, 1996, and 1997). The first year, Congress adopted an amendment to the Emergency Unemployment Compensation bill, and in 1995–1997 it adopted amendments to the Treasury–Postal Service appropriations bill.

Senate Majority Leader George J. Mitchell, D-Maine, and House Speaker Foley announced on February 24, 1993, that lawmakers would forgo an annual adjustment they were scheduled to receive in January 1994.

In 1994 opposition to the adjustment scheduled for January 1995 came not from the congressional leadership but from Rep. Jim Ross Lightfoot, R-Iowa, who blocked the increase in pay. Rep. Steny H. Hoyer, D-Md., chairman of the House Treasury, Postal Service and General Government Appropriations Subcommittee, wrote into the fiscal 1995 Treasury–Postal Service appropriations bill a provision giving federal workers an average raise of 1 percent higher than that recommended in the president's budget. Included in the provision was language blocking an increase in congressional salary to fend off criticism that his pay-raise proposal would trigger a higher annual adjustment for Congress. After President Bill Clinton agreed to Hoyer's higher pay increase, Hoyer's provision was no longer needed, and House and Senate conferees made plans to drop it, along with the language blocking the congressional pay raise.

But Lightfoot on September 19, 1994, vowed that he would force a vote on the congressional raise if it was retained in the bill. Hoyer said that he supported the $3,473 pay raise but that no more than fifty members would vote for it on the floor. The Senate relented and cut the annual adjustment, although Sen. Christopher S. Bond of Missouri accused Lightfoot, a fellow Republican, of playing politics.

In 1995 Sen. Fred Thompson, R-Tenn., introduced an amendment to the fiscal 1996 Treasury–Postal Service appropriations bill blocking the automatic annual adjustment of 2.3 percent. That increase was scheduled for January 1996.

The House in 1996 accepted a provision in the fiscal 1997 Treasury–Postal Service appropriations bill to block the automatic increase scheduled for January 1997. The amendment was offered by Jack Metcalf, R-Wash. Similar language was introduced in the Senate by Jesse Helms, R-N.C. Helms's amendment would have allowed federal judges to get the annual adjustment, but in the end the House language prevailed.

1998 ANNUAL INCREASE

In September 1997 lawmakers allowed the first pay raise for members of Congress in five years, boosting their yearly salary by 2.3 percent, from $133,600 to $136,700, effective in January 1998.

A number of younger lawmakers who had come to office on the promise that they would eliminate congressional pay and perks opposed the pay raise. But leaders from both parties worked to squelch opposition before it could gain momentum. The leadership was encouraged by public opinion polls showing a reversal in the negative attitude about Congress and by the majority of members who wanted a raise.

The Senate on July 17 had attached to the fiscal 1998 Treasury–Postal Service bill language offered by Sam Brownback, R-Kan., that eliminated the annual adjustment. The Senate passed its version of the bill July 22 by a vote of 99–0. Subsequently, the House Appropriations Committee reported its version of the bill without language eliminating the annual adjustment.

However, House leaders caught opponents of the pay increase off guard by scheduling a vote on the appropriations bill without warning. Opponents, led by Linda Smith, R-Wash., did not have time to organize an effort to block the annual adjustment with an amendment to the House bill. The bill passed 231–192 on September 17. The House and Senate conferees agreed on September 29 to a final version of the bill that dropped the Senate pay-freeze language, granting lawmakers an extra $3,073 per year, which was rounded up to $3,100.

House Speaker Newt Gingrich argued that the bill included a cost-of-living adjustment, not a pay raise. "I think it is vastly healthier to establish a pattern where [members] get a cost-of-

living adjustment that's routine," he said. "The only alternative to that is every 10 or 12 or 15 years you have to have a massive pay increase that is extraordinarily hard to pass and that causes enormous turmoil."[4]

1999 ANNUAL ADJUSTMENT BLOCKED

Congress blocked the 3.1 percent adjustment scheduled for 1999 by adding language to the fiscal 1999 Treasury–Postal Service bill, the conference version of which was incorporated in the fiscal 1999 Omnibus Consolidated and Emergency Supplemental Appropriations bill. The House agreed by a vote of 218–201 on July 16, 1998, to a rule that ensured that language in the reported Treasury–Postal Service bill prohibiting the 1999 pay increase would not be procedurally challenged during floor debate.

The effect of this rule was to protect the pay ban provision and not other language, including that providing federal health plan coverage for contraceptives. By not protecting the contraceptive language, Republicans hoped to strike the language when the bill came to the floor. Republicans put pressure on Democrats, a significant number of whom wanted to protect the contraceptive and other language, to vote for the rule by claiming that a vote against it was a vote in support of a congressional pay increase.

The following day, Democrats, still upset with the Republican effort to turn the debate on the rule into a vote on the pay raise, offered an amendment to strike the pay freeze language. The amendment was defeated by a vote of 79–342. The Senate Appropriations Committee also reported pay prohibition language in its version of the 1999 Treasury bill; no challenge to the language was made on the floor. As a result, the pay freeze went into effect, killing the pending January 1999 adjustment.

2000 ANNUAL INCREASE

Members were scheduled to receive a 3.4 percent pay increase in January 2000, raising their salary to $141,300. The increase was based on the formula established in the 1989 law, which took effect unless Congress blocked or reconsidered it, or unless the annual base adjustment for general schedule federal employees was lower than the increase. If lower, members of Congress were to receive the lower rate because by law members' annual adjustment cannot be greater than the adjustment in base pay for general schedule federal employees. Base pay is that rate before locality pay is added.

An unsuccessful attempt to allow a vote to block the pay raise was made in the House in July 1999, during consideration of the rule on HR 2490, the fiscal year 2000 Treasury–Postal Service appropriations bill. Several members sought parliamentary approval from the Rules Committee to allow a floor amendment that would prohibit the increase for Congress but permit it to go into effect for other top-level federal officials. Approval was sought because the rule allowed only germane amendments, and an amendment blocking the pay adjustment was not considered germane. Attempts to change the rule were defeated in a procedural vote, 276–147, and an amendment to prohibit the pay raise was not in order. No other efforts were made to block the increase on the House or Senate floors, and President Bill Clinton signed it into law on September 29, 1999. (In addition to the congressional pay hikes, the legislation also doubled the salary of presidents after Clinton to $400,000.)

Honoraria: A Vanishing Perquisite

Succumbing to pressure from voters, public interest lobbying groups, and a growing number of members, first the House and then the Senate agreed to give up one of their most cherished perquisites. Beginning in 1991, House members could no longer keep for themselves honoraria—the payment of money or anything of value an organization makes to a legislator in return for a speech, appearance, or article. The Senate approved the honoraria ban in mid-1991, as part of the annual legislative branch appropriations bill. The ban took effect upon enactment of the bill, but senators were permitted to keep speaking fees received prior to August 14, 1991 (up to the $23,068 limit that previously had been set for the year).

"I think it's the end of honoraria," Sen. Howard M. Metzenbaum, D-Ohio, said after the Senate voted in favor of the ban in July 1991. "We're never going to go back to that," added Assistant Republican Leader Alan K. Simpson, Wyo.[5]

Always reluctant to raise their own salaries for fear of the political repercussions that inevitably followed, members of Congress had long viewed the acceptance of honoraria as a supplement to their regular pay. As inflation eroded congressional salaries, honoraria became an even more important source of income for many legislators of modest means.

Honoraria were also a time-honored way for private organizations and associations to get an "insider's view" of Washington. Most of the honoraria members earned came from speeches to conventions held by trade associations, other business groups, and labor unions. Education groups, schools and colleges, foreign policy associations, religious, ethnic, and civic groups, and so-called single issue organizations (such as pro- and antiabortion groups) that often have an ideological bias also paid legislators in exchange for a briefing or speech.

Honoraria also were used by corporate boards of directors or small groups of business executives, lawyers, lobbyists, and others for intimate meetings with members of Congress, perhaps over breakfast or lunch. These groups said a meal and a chat with a prominent senator or representative was worth the $1,000 or $2,000 payment because of the opportunity it provided for an off-the-record exchange of views. For many smaller interest groups that could not afford campaign contributions on the same scale as bigger organizations, honoraria were particularly valuable in reaching lawmakers.

Organizations that gave honoraria—and members of Congress who accepted them—denied any impropriety. Many freely admitted, however, that inviting a member to address an organization's annual convention or meet with executives—and paying him or her for the appearance—could have important benefits. Top management at the organization gained a better understanding of the Washington scene and got an expert assessment of the chances for passage of legislation of interest to the organization. Such meetings also provided an occasion to get to know an important member, to apprise him of the organization's views, and to ensure easier access to the member in the future. These meetings also could be used to let the member know he had the support of influential groups in his state or congressional district.

In the opinion of many, however, paying legislators for speeches or appearances smacked of legalized bribery. Like campaign funds, the payment of honoraria could be construed as a means to ensure that a legislator would, at the least, give special consideration to the viewpoint of the organization making the payment. When a member accepts a $2,000 honorarium from an industry group, said Rep. Tom Harkin, D-Iowa, in 1981, "he's going to tell them what they want to hear."[6]

In the mid-1970s critics of the practice succeeded in placing limits on the amount of honoraria that a lawmaker could collect for any one speech or appearance or keep in any one year (any amount taken in over the total had to be donated to charity). Despite those restrictions, the total amount of honoraria paid to members of Congress increased steadily. In 1989 lawmakers collected more than $9 million overall in honoraria, compared with a total of $2.7 million just ten years earlier. The amount of honoraria declined in 1990, totaling $7.7 million.[7]

Movements to place tighter restrictions on honoraria or to ban them altogether faltered in the early and mid-1980s. Members acknowledged their growing political vulnerability to charges of impropriety. "I personally always got all the honoraria I could," said Rep. Charles Wilson, D-Texas, in 1987. "But in the future it could be a bad campaign issue."[8] At least 20 senators and 110 representatives reported that they received no honoraria in 1989, while at least 2 senators and 22 House members donated all of their honoraria earnings to charity. Many other members did not keep the full amount allowed under the rules.

Nonetheless, many lawmakers were unwilling to give up honoraria without a compensatory pay increase. But the public outcry that arose whenever the question of raising congressional pay came up made members reluctant to act on either front.

A breakthrough came in late 1989, when the House agreed to accept a substantial pay raise in return for a ban on honoraria. The decision might have been driven more by political expediency than ethical imperatives. During the 1988 election campaigns, challengers had needled several incumbents about their acceptance of honoraria. Criticisms that Sen. Lowell P. Weicker Jr. was making speeches for pay when he should have been voting in the Senate helped Democrat Joseph I. Lieberman unseat the veteran Republican from Connecticut. At the same time Speaker Jim Wright, D-Texas, was defending himself, unsuccessfully, against several charges of impropriety, including one that he had engaged in a scheme to avoid the House limits on honoraria. *(See "Wright," p. 925.)*

Even more reluctant than the House to abandon honoraria, the Senate in 1989 settled for a smaller pay increase and a system for phasing down the amount of honoraria each senator could legally accept. But pressure continued in the Senate, and in July 1991 the Senate finally voted to raise its salary to the same level as the House and to bar senators from pocketing any honoraria. Like House members, senators must donate any fees they receive for speeches, appearances, or articles to charity.

INITIAL LIMITATIONS ON HONORARIA

Until 1975 there were no restrictions on such earnings, and it was not unusual for prominent members of Congress to earn more from honoraria than from their salary.

The era of completely unregulated honoraria payments ended on January 1, 1975, when Congress's first campaign finance law took effect. That measure limited honoraria payments to members and other federal officials to $1,000 for a single speaking engagement or article and set a cap of $15,000 a year on total honoraria that a member could keep. The restrictions had an effect: eighty-one senators reported earning $637,893 in 1975, down more than $300,000 from the previous year. (House members were not required to report honoraria until 1978.)

The restrictions were loosened considerably by provisions of the Federal Election Campaign Act Amendments of 1976. That law raised the ceiling on payments for a single speech or article to $2,000 and raised the annual amount permitted to $25,000. The $25,000 was a net amount and did not include booking agents' fees, travel expenditures, subsistence, and expenses for an aide or a spouse accompanying the lawmaker. (See "1976 Amendments," p. 882.)

The 1976 law permitted members to deduct any funds donated to charity or used to pay out-of-pocket expenses from their total yearly honoraria earnings for the purpose of complying with the $25,000 limitation.

In addition, under the 1976 law House and Senate members could receive honoraria earned in previous years without applying those payments to their current year's limit. In 1977, the first year in which the campaign act amendments were in effect, eighty-one senators earned almost $1.1 million.

ETHICS CODES LIMITS

The House and Senate further limited the amount of honoraria lawmakers could accept when both chambers passed new ethics codes in 1977. As of January 1, 1979, no member of either the House or the Senate could accept more than 15 percent of his or her annual salary in outside earned income, including honoraria. The House further limited the honorarium a representative could accept for a single speech, appearance, or article to $750; the Senate limit was set at $1,000. (The House limit was raised to $1,000 in January 1979, the first month the limitations were in effect.)

The codes did not affect unearned income, such as dividends, interest payments, or rent from properties. The codes also exempted from the limitations income members earned from family farms and small businesses.

In both chambers the limits on outside earned incomes were the most controversial provisions of the ethics codes. House Speaker Thomas P. O'Neill Jr., D-Mass., and Senate Majority Leader Robert C. Byrd, D-W.Va., made passage of a strong ethics code a condition for approval of salary increases for Congress and top executive officials, which the two men believed were sorely needed. Both leaders said that a limit on outside income was essential to a strong code. O'Neill called the provision "the heart and soul of the entire package" of ethical standards.

Nonetheless, members in both chambers tried to strike the provisions from the two codes. Their principal argument was that the limitations would discriminate in favor of wealthy lawmakers. The restrictions, argued Rep. Otis G. Pike, D-N.Y., would "create a Congress of two kinds of people. Some will have large unearned incomes and the rest will need their political jobs in order to feed and clothe and educate their families. Whether this will be a more ethical Congress only time will tell, but I think not."

But backers of the limit on earned income argued that it was necessary to cut down the large amounts of money that special interest groups could contribute to members. "I believe that there is a real potential for conflict of interest when a senator takes large sums of money for speaking to groups who have a direct interest in legislation before this body," said Sen. Dick Clark, D-Iowa.[9]

The leaders prevailed in the end. The House rejected a move to delete the limitations on earned income, 79–344; the Senate defeated a similar amendment, 35–62.

SENATE DELAY

The Senate limitation was never implemented. In March 1979, the year the cap was to take effect, the Senate voted to delay implementation of those requirements until 1983. The delay had the effect of leaving a senator's maximum honorarium payment at $2,000 and annual honoraria earnings at $25,000—the ceilings set in the 1976 campaign finance law.

Senators were being paid $57,500 at the beginning of 1979, and the 15 percent limitation on total honoraria would have allowed them to earn another $8,625. Financial disclosure figures for 1978 showed that fifty-nine senators in office in 1979 had earned more than that in honoraria and would likely have suffered a reduction in their total income if the delay had not been approved. Instead, eighty-six senators received total honoraria payments of $1.2 million in 1979, an average of nearly $14,000 for each member who accepted honoraria.

Senate action on the delay came on short notice and passed by voice vote with only a handful of members on the floor. Although some senators complained about the way the delay was handled, the Senate three weeks later rejected an attempt to overturn the delay, 44–54.

ANNUAL LIMITS LIFTED

In October 1981 the Senate repealed the $25,000 limit on outside earned income imposed by the 1976 campaign finance act (although it left the $2,000 limit on the amount a senator could accept for a single speech or article). Sen. Ted Stevens, R-Alaska, argued that since senators had an unlimited income from other sources they should be entitled to unlimited payments from speeches. Although the change came late in 1981, twenty-five senators still earned more than $25,000 in honoraria that year. Several senators, however, continued to give all or part of their honoraria to charity.

After the Senate removed its annual honoraria limit, representatives complained that they deserved equal treatment. In a surprise move, the House leadership on December 15, 1981, brought to the floor a change in House rules that would double House members' allowable outside earnings, from 15 percent to 30 percent of their official salary. The change was approved unanimously in less than half a minute. Only a handful of members were present.

At an annual salary of $60,662.50, House members could earn up to $18,198.75 a year in honoraria, beginning in 1981. That compared to a ceiling of $9,099.37 under the lower limit. Since the ceiling was lifted so late in the year, members had only about two weeks to earn the additional income. Despite the deadline, more than seventy representatives reported outside income in excess of $9,100 for 1981.

The Senate's 1981 action eliminated the limits on accepting honoraria for 1981 and 1982. But the 15 percent cap on outside earnings contained in the Senate Ethics Code was still scheduled to take effect in 1983. In December 1982 the Senate repealed that cap; the only restriction on honoraria continued to be the $2,000 maximum for each appearance or speech. In return for lifting the cap, the Senate agreed to forgo a 15 percent pay increase that the House had voted itself.

ANNUAL LIMIT IMPOSED IN SENATE

The pay and honoraria differentials between the two chambers were short-lived. In May 1983 congressional financial disclosure statements were released showing that more than half of the senators earned honoraria totaling more than 30 percent of their salaries.

Pressured by the public and the House, the Senate in 1983 agreed to put a 30 percent limit on the total amount of honoraria a member could accept in a single year in exchange for a pay raise. The controversial measure was passed by a vote of 49–47. Senate action meant that both chambers were again paid the same amount, $69,800, and that legislators could accept no more than $20,940 in honoraria.

Two years later the Senate raised the cap on honoraria and other outside earned income to 40 percent of a senator's official salary. Early in 1986, by voice vote and with few members on the floor, the House also raised its cap to 40 percent. The following day, the House reversed that vote, leaving the cap at 30 percent.

HONORARIA BARRED IN HOUSE

Neither chamber dealt with the question of honoraria again until 1988, when the Commission on Executive, Legislative, and Judicial Salaries voted in December to recommend a 51 percent pay increase and a ban on honoraria. Members of the commission said that salaries had to be hiked that much to compensate for two decades of inflation—and to provide incentive for the Senate as well as the House to abandon the honoraria system.

From the moment it was announced, however, the pay boost drew criticism. Members quickly discovered that constituents knew little about honoraria, and that a ban gave them little political cover from the outrage the public was expressing about the proposed pay hike. "As far as I can tell, the only people you get money from are the rich," one House member reported a constituent as saying, "and if the rich are so bored, and have nothing better to do, let 'em pay it."[10] In an embarrassing defeat for House Speaker Jim Wright, the House finally voted down the pay raise. *(See "1989–1990 Pay Raises," p. 774.)*

Despite the defeat, pressure continued both for a pay increase and for stronger ethics rules, including a ban on honoraria. The resignations of Speaker Wright and Democratic Whip Tony Coelho, Calif., following allegations that they had violated House rules, made House members particularly eager to find ways to improve Congress's image with the voters. It was clear that a ban on honoraria was likely to be at the heart of any ethics reform.

The plan developed by a bipartisan House task force would raise congressional pay by a third over two years and at the same time overhaul ethics rules and ban honoraria payments. It called for a 7.9 percent increase for legislators and for top executive and judicial branch officials in 1990, to be followed by a 25 percent increase, plus a cost-of-living adjustment, in 1991.

The details of the plan were a closely held secret until the week it was to go to the floor. House Speaker Foley and Republican Leader Robert H. Michel of Illinois insisted on strong presidential support and did not go public with the task force recommendations until they had a letter of endorsement from President George Bush. In their final drive for rank-and-file backing, members of the Democratic leadership attended a GOP party caucus to drum up support for the package; Republican leaders, including Wright's nemesis, Newt Gingrich of Georgia, attended the caucus.

The resulting discipline was evident when the bill went to the floor on November 16. Few spoke in opposition to the bill, and rhetoric was muted.

The House approved a modification of the package, 252–174. Under the terms of the bill, House members, their staff, and other federal officials could not accept honoraria after January 1, 1991, but they could request that charitable contributions be made in their name. Such contributions could not exceed $2,000 and could not be made to any organization that benefited the legislator or his relatives. Federal employees quickly sought and won support for a repeal of the ban on honoraria

Sen. Robert C. Byrd, D-W.Va., almost single-handedly delivered the votes in 1991 for a pay increase/honoraria ban. Said Byrd: "There is nothing honorable about honoraria. It is simply a way for special interests to gain access to senators. . . ."

that applied to them. Effective also in 1991, the bill limited outside income earned by House members to 15 percent of the salary earned by employees at Executive Level II of the federal executive pay scale. In January 1991 Executive Level II employees earned $125,000, setting the outside earned income cap at $18,765. In 1999 the cap was raised to $20,505.

BAN ACCEPTED IN SENATE

As in the House, Senate leaders of both parties presented a united front on the pay raise–honoraria ban, and at first momentum seemed to be in favor of the House package. Senators met in an unusual two-party caucus to plan strategy, and in an early test the Senate voted overwhelmingly to invoke cloture on the bill. But a nose count showed that the leadership was four or five votes short of winning, even after several House members came over to lobby their Senate colleagues.

As a result the House plan never came to a direct vote in the Senate. After several hours of off-the-floor discussions, Senate

leaders conceded failure and offered an amendment that left the House-approved pay provisions for representatives intact, along with the executive and judicial branch salaries, but raised Senate salaries by only 9.9 percent, effective February 1, 1990, and provided future annual raises. Instead of banning them outright, the Senate bill reduced the ceiling on honoraria that senators could keep from 40 percent of salary in 1989 to 27 percent, or $26,568, effective January 1, 1990. The total permissible honoraria was $27,337: for one month during 1990, senators were allowed to earn 40 percent of that month's salary (or $2,983—that is, 40 percent of $7,458.33, one-twelfth of their annual salary of $89,500) and for the next eleven months they were allowed to earn 27 percent of their salary (or $24,354). (Senate leaders earned slightly higher salaries than rank-and-file members and therefore could retain slightly more in honoraria.) Any annual pay adjustment implemented after December 31, 1990, was to be accompanied by an equivalent reduction in the ceiling on honoraria until it reached zero. The Senate approved that amendment, 56–43, and the House cleared the bill by accepting the Senate changes.

In August 1990 the Senate for the first time voted to ban honoraria, but the amendment, offered by Christopher J. Dodd, D-Conn., was attached to a controversial campaign finance bill that died in conference. Dodd offered his amendment to another campaign finance bill in May 1991, and the Senate passed it by a wide margin. But again passage of the campaign finance bill was in doubt; President Bush had threatened to veto the bill. "In fact," said Republican Leader Bob Dole, Kan., "many of my colleagues are counting on the president's veto as a way to vote 'yes' on the honoraria ban today while taking honoraria tomorrow."[11]

The House ban left the Senate in the embarrassing position of being the only part of the federal government where acceptance of honoraria was not illegal. Senators took in nearly $2 million in honoraria in 1990, down about $700,000 from the total in the previous year. At least twenty-seven senators accepted no honoraria in 1990, and another five gave all their honoraria to charity. Senators were also piqued that their salaries were not only less than the amount that House members received but also less than what several House staffers earned.

When the fiscal 1992 legislative appropriations bill came to the Senate floor on July 17, Appropriations Committee Chairman Robert Byrd, backed by the Democratic and Republican leaders, offered an amendment to raise senators' pay 25 percent in exchange for a ban on honoraria. The pay hike would mean that, effective August 14, 1991, senators and representatives would once again earn the same salary, $125,100, and senators could no longer accept honoraria. The legislation also limited senators' outside income to 15 percent of their salary. The amendment was approved, 53–45.

Even though both houses had apparently closed the door on keeping honoraria, a loophole remained open. Besides the fee, members (and frequently their wives) often receive expense-paid trips to the sites where the speeches are given, as well as lodging and meals. In 1989 both chambers curbed the length of the trips that members could accept from private organizations but set no limits on the amounts of expenses that members could accept. *(See box, Types of Travel, p. 789.)*

The 1989 regulations were slightly revised with the congressional gift ban rules adopted in 1995. Members and their staffs may continue to accept free trips for meetings, speeches, and fact-finding tours related to their official duties. Domestic travel within the contiguous forty-eight states is capped at four days in the House and three days in the Senate; foreign travel is limited to a week, and lawmakers have thirty days from the end of the trip to report who paid for the trip, the destination, the purpose, and the cost.

NOTES

1. James Madison, *Notes of Debates in the Federal Convention of 1787* (Athens: Ohio University Press, 1966), 198.

2. Unless otherwise noted, the account of action on congressional pay is drawn from *Congress and the Nation* Vol. VIII and the *Congressional Quarterly Almanac* and *Weekly Report* for various years.

3. Paul E. Dwyer, "Salaries of Members of Congress: Congressional Votes, 1967–1989," Congressional Research Service, March 3, 1989.

4. Ronald D. Elving, "On Pay Adjustments, Timing Is All," *Congressional Quarterly Weekly Report,* October 4, 1997, 2438.

5. Janet Hook, "Senate's Ban on Honoraria Marks End of an Era," *Congressional Quarterly Weekly Report,* July 22, 1991, 1955.

6. *Congressional Quarterly Almanac 1981* (Washington, D.C.: Congressional Quarterly, 1982), 287.

7. "Members' 1989 Honoraria Receipts," *Congressional Quarterly Weekly Report,* June 2, 1990, 1749–1753; "Members' 1990 Honoraria Receipts," *Congressional Quarterly Weekly Report,* June 22, 1991, 1694–1698.

8. Janet Hook, "Proposal for 51 Percent Pay Hike Sets Up Fracas," *Congressional Quarterly Weekly Report,* December, 17, 1988, 3527.

9. *Congressional Quarterly Almanac 1977* (Washington, D.C.: Congressional Quarterly, 1978), 768, 773.

10. Beth Donovan, "Parties Find Ethics Tough Sell as Local Campaign Issue," *Congressional Quarterly Weekly Report,* July 15, 1989, 1813.

11. Phil Kuntz, "Honoraria Ban Still Just an Idea," *Congressional Quarterly Weekly Report,* May 25, 1991, 1353.

SELECTED BIBLIOGRAPHY

Congressional Quarterly. *Congressional Pay and Perquisites: History, Facts, and Controversy.* Washington, D.C.: Congressional Quarterly, 1992.

Davidson, Roger H., and Walter J. Oleszek. *Congress and Its Members.* 7th ed. Washington, D.C.: CQ Press, 2000.

Dwyer, Paul E. "Salaries of Members of Congress: Congressional Votes, 1967–1989." Congressional Research Service, March 3, 1989.

Elving, Ronald D. "On Pay Adjustments, Timing Is All." *Congressional Quarterly Weekly Report,* October 4, 1997.

Fiorina, Morris P. *Congress: Keystone of the Washington Establishment.* 2nd ed. New Haven, Conn.: Yale University Press, 1989.

Henry, H. Lon. *Congress, America's Privileged Class.* Rocklin, Calif.: Prima Publishing, 1993.

Parker, Glenn R. *Characteristics of Congress: Politics and Congressional Behavior.* Englewood Cliffs, N.J.: Prentice-Hall, 1989.

CHAPTER 28

Allowances and Other Benefits

FROM THE DAY newly elected members arrive in Washington to the day they leave Congress, lawmakers are presented with an array of allowances and benefits that help to ease the pressures of congressional life. Some of the perquisites of office, however, have been either trimmed in recent years or are now made available through a fee.

Members of Congress continue to enjoy free mailing privileges for official business and use of free office space in federal buildings in their home states or districts. Each member receives, in addition to salary, an official expense allowance for home office space rental, travel, telecommunications services, stationery, printing, computer services, postage mass mailings, office equipment, and other expenses.

Members are allowed free storage of files and records, the use of office decorations and furniture, use of recording and photographic studios, authority to make a limited number of appointments, and free publications. They also can receive various health protection plans and emergency care while at work, life insurance, and a generous retirement pension.

Senators and representatives have access to elaborate computerized mailing and legislative analysis systems and to gym facilities, including swimming pools, saunas, and masseurs. Legislative counsels, legal counsels, chaplains, and photographers stand by at the Capitol to assist members. Attractive dining rooms, barber and beauty shops, and convenient rail and airline ticket offices are available in the Capitol and congressional office buildings.

Trying to calculate the total amount of money Congress spends on itself can be very difficult. Most information is readily available in the semiannual reports of the secretary of the Senate and quarterly reports of the clerk of the House of Representatives. These publications list the salaries for all congressional employees and all expenditures made by members in their official duties. But it is hard to attach a dollar value to many fringe benefits.

The annual legislative branch appropriations, which includes funding for Congress itself and for several related agencies, such as the Library of Congress, came to $2.6 billion in fiscal 1999. This includes a fiscal year 1999 emergency supplemental appropriation of $100 million for design and construction of a Capitol visitors' center, $106.8 million for enhanced security for the Capitol complex and the Library of Congress, and $16.9 million for year 2000 conversion of "information technology systems." It also includes a supplemental of $5.6 million for renovation of the House page dormitory and for life-safety renovations to the O'Neill House Office Building. (*See boxes, The Cost of Congress, p. 797; Expanding Cost of Running Congress, p. 800.*)

The Franking Privilege: A Potent Perquisite

The franking privilege is one of the most valuable and controversial of members' perquisites of office. Every year millions of American households receive pieces of mail that bear a facsimile of the signature of a member of Congress, known as the frank, in place of a stamp. Mailing letters and packages under one's signature at taxpayers' expense is one of the nation's oldest privileges. The Continental Congress adopted the practice in 1775.

Through newsletters and other mailings, sent at government expense, legislators can communicate directly with their constituents, informing them about congressional decisions and passing on useful news about the federal government.

The franked envelope might contain a legislator's response to a constituent question or request, a copy of his newsletter, a survey, a press release, a packet of voting information, government publications or reports, or other printed matter that in some way relates to the legislator's "official duties."

Mailings related to political campaigns or political parties, personal business, or friendships may not be franked. A lawmaker, for example, cannot use the frank on a holiday greeting, a message of sympathy, an invitation to a party fund-raiser, or a request for political support. Nonetheless, opponents of the frank argue that it gives incumbents running for reelection a great boost over challengers who do not have the same cheap access to the voters.

Although no stamp is needed, a franked letter is not actually mailed free of charge. Each year, as part of the legislative appropriations bill, Congress appropriates a certain amount of money to cover the cost of members' franking.

The U.S. Postal Service keeps records on the franked mail it handles and periodically sends Congress what amounts to a bill. If Congress has not appropriated enough money to cover the costs of franked mail, it does so in a supplemental appropriations bill.

The Postal Service, however, is obligated to send all franked mail whether or not Congress appropriates enough money to cover the costs.

The concept of the frank goes back to 1775, when the first Continental Congress enacted a law giving its members mailing privileges—permitting members of Congress to communicate directly with their constituents at government expense. This 1869 wood engraving shows free bags of mail leaving the Washington, D.C. post office.

COSTS AND CONTROVERSIES

Until recently, cost was one of the most criticized aspects of the franking privilege. The cost of franked mail jumped dramatically in the 1970s and 1980s because of increases in both mailing rates and the amount of mail legislators sent under the frank. Mailing costs increased more than fourfold from 1972 to 1988; even adjusted for inflation, that represented an 86 percent increase. But new regulations since then have pushed the cost down considerably.

An even more controversial issue has been the advantage that the franking privilege gives incumbents over challengers. Despite restrictions on political content and self-promotion, members can and do take advantage of loopholes and lax regulation. For example, although members are cautioned against mass mailings of *Congressional Record* reprints containing statements of praise by another member, the mailings may be prefaced by a colleague's comments on the member's insightful analysis. Members' newsletters regularly report awards presented to the lawmaker as well as favorable ratings of his or her voting record by various interest groups. Although members are cautioned about the overuse of the word "I" and their name and photograph in franked material, there is little enforcement of the guidelines.

As the use of computerized mailings has grown more sophisticated, members increasingly have used the frank to target mass mailings, telling a selected group of people what they want to hear and, probably just as important, avoiding arousing groups thought to be unsympathetic. Lawmakers, for example, may tell farmers of their support for wheat exports, teachers of their support for education, small businesses of their opposition to an increase in the minimum wage.

Despite restrictions on use of the frank during the sixty days preceding primary and general elections, the amount spent on the frank has invariably gone up in election years. According to the Congressional Research Service, which works exclusively for Congress, the House spent $27 million in fiscal 1996, an election year, and $24.6 million in fiscal 1995, a nonelection year.[1]

Common Cause, a citizens' lobbying group, fights for different limitations on the use of the frank, such as an extended prohibition on the franking privilege before an election. For example, campaign finance legislation that passed the House in 1998 had a provision that would extend the two-month prohibition to six months. Other legislation proposed banning the frank during an entire election year. The legislation stalled in the 105th Congress.

By the late 1980s Congress was forced to deal with the way it used the frank, just as it had been forced to reexamine its use of other perquisites. The results of that examination were new rules in each chamber that allotted each member a specific mail budget and required each to disclose publicly the amount spent on franked mail. Individual disclosure was expected to slow increases in the cost of franked mail, perhaps even to reduce it. But critics continued to argue that even with the new limitations, the frank still gave members an unfair political advantage.

FRANKING REGULATIONS

Under the regulations in the U.S. Code dealing with the franking privilege, persons authorized to use the frank include the vice president, members and members-elect of Congress (senators, representatives, delegates, and resident commissioners), and officers of the House and Senate. A former Speaker of the House is entitled to use of the frank upon expiration of his term as a representative for the administration of matters relating to his service in the House and as Speaker. In addition, the surviving spouse of a member who dies is permitted to use the frank for nonpolitical correspondence related to the death of the member. The authorization expires 180 days after the member's death.

Members and others vested with the franking privilege are entitled, on a restricted basis, to use the frank during the ninety days immediately following the date on which they leave office. During this period use of the frank is limited to matters directly related to the closing of the member's congressional office. Former members may not send newsletters, questionnaires, or other mass-mailed material.

Standing, select, special, or joint committees of Congress, as well as subcommittees and commissions, may send mail under the frank of the chairman, the ranking minority member, or any other member of the committee. Exceptions are "informal" or "ad hoc" groups of lawmakers—such as the House Democratic Caucus or the House Republican Conference—whose business relates to political, party policy, or special interest matters.

The franking regulations prohibit a person entitled to use the frank from lending it to any nonmember, private committee, organization, or association. Use of the frank for the benefit of charitable organizations, political action committees, trade organizations, and other groups is expressly forbidden. Nor may the frank be used for mail delivered to a foreign country.

What May Be Franked

Despite these restrictions, a wide range of material may be sent out under the frank. The law states that the frank is designed to "assist and expedite the conduct of the official business, activities, and duties of the Congress of the United States." The terms "official business and activities" are broadly defined to cover "all matters which directly or indirectly pertain to the legislative process or to any congressional representative functions generally, or to the functioning, working, or operating of the Congress and the performance of official duties in connection therewith, and shall include, *but not be limited to,* the con-

veying of information to the public, and the requesting of the views of the public, or the views and information of other authority of government, as a guide or a means of assistance in the performance of those functions." (Emphasis added)

Among the major categories of mail eligible for the franking privilege are:

Newsletters and News Releases. The law authorizes use of the congressional frank for "the usual and customary congressional newsletter or press release, which may deal with such matters as the impact of laws and decisions on State and local government and individual citizens; reports on public and official actions taken by Members of Congress; and discussions of proposed or pending legislation of governmental actions and the position of the Members of Congress on, and arguments for or against, such matters."

Examples of frankable material in newsletters or news releases include tabulations of a member's voting record; reports on the lawmaker's position on various legislative proposals; notices that the member will visit his or her district on official business; statements that are critical of administration or congressional policies—provided they are not presented in a partisan manner; invitations to meet and participate with another lawmaker in a public discussion or report on Congress if the meeting is not held under political auspices; and a member's financial disclosure statement.

Questionnaires. Members may mail under the frank "the usual and customary congressional questionnaire seeking public opinion on any law, pending or proposed legislation, public issue, or subject." Members may not permit the frank to be used for the return of responses, but the results of the member's surveys may be included in a newsletter or other form of allowable franked correspondence. A member may not ask the recipient of a questionnaire to indicate whether he or she is a Republican or Democrat.

Mailgrams. Members may also send Mailgrams under the frank, provided the material conforms to the same guidelines used in sending mail under the franking law.

Other Material. Other materials that may be franked include mail to any individual or agency and to officials at any level of government regarding programs and proposed legislation; mail concerning congressional committee and floor action and other related matters of public concern or public service; mail between members, mail from a member's Capitol Hill office to his or her congressional district offices (or between district offices), or mail from a member to a state or local legislator; nonpartisan voter registration or election information or assistance; biographical or autobiographical material of a member or the member's family that is mailed as a part of a federal publication or in response to a specific request and is not intended for publicity purposes; and mail, including general mass mailings, that consists of federal laws or regulations, government publications or publications purchased with federal funds, and publications containing items of general information.

Government publications include, among others, the *Con-*

FRANKING PRIVILEGE UPHELD

On May 2, 1983, the Supreme Court rejected a challenge to the free mailing privileges of members of Congress. Putting an end to a decade-old lawsuit, the Court voted 6–3 not to consider the case. The vote left standing a lower court decision upholding the constitutionality of the congressional franking privilege.

The suit had been brought in 1973 by Common Cause, the self-styled public interest lobby, which charged that the frank was unconstitutional because it promoted the reelection of incumbents and therefore placed an unfair disadvantage on challengers. On September 7, 1982, a special three-judge panel of the U.S. District Court for the District of Columbia dismissed the Common Cause suit. The panel said the franking privilege "confers a substantial advantage to incumbent congressional candidates over their challengers" but found no constitutional violation.

Despite its ultimate rejection, the Common Cause suit *(Common Cause v. William F. Bolger)* had a substantial impact on the franking privilege. Between 1973, when the suit was first filed, and 1983, Congress had placed several restrictions on use of the frank meant to limit the most egregious abuses of its use.

The changes did not satisfy Common Cause, which continued to maintain that the frank conferred unfair campaign advantages on incumbents. In its effort to persuade the Supreme Court to hear the case, the lobby group said Congress either should not allow the frank to be used for mass mailings or should also allow nonincumbent challengers to use the frank. In its brief to the Court, Common Cause also suggested that franked mail should not be allowed for mailings to groups of people whose selection identified the mailing as political.

In 1998 Common Cause continued its fight for placing limitations on using the frank for different purposes. For example, the group supported a provision included in legislation that would have changed the financing of political campaigns. The provision would have extended the two-month prohibition of the frank before an election to six months. Provisions in other campaign finance legislation would have extended the prohibition an entire year. The legislation stalled in Congress.

---

gressional Record or a reprint of any part of the *Record*, and pamphlets and reports. The scope of the frank is not limited to these categories, however, and members are advised to seek the opinion of the House Commission on Congressional Mailing Standards or the Senate Ethics and Rules committees, which are authorized to enforce the franking rules and laws.

What May Not Be Franked

In contrast to the broad scope of material that can be franked, the specific prohibitions on use of the frank are defined narrowly. They include "purely personal mailings"; mailings "laudatory and complimentary" of a member "on a purely personal or political basis"; letters consisting solely of condolences to a person who has suffered a loss or congratulations to a per-

son who has achieved some personal distinction (expressions of congratulations to a person who has achieved a public distinction, such as election to public office, graduation from high school, or attainment of U.S. citizenship, may be franked); holiday greetings; reports on how a member spends time other than in connection with his legislative, representative, or "other official functions"; and mailings that "specifically solicit political support."

RESTRICTIONS ON USE

Before 1973 the only standards dealing with the franking privilege were those formulated by the U.S. Postal Service and its predecessor, the U.S. Post Office Department, and by the courts. However, neither postal service actively enforced the regulations, investigating alleged abuses only when private citizens filed official complaints. Conflicting court decisions and the reluctance of many judges to rule on questions of congressional propriety resulted in general confusion about proper use of the frank.

Several disputes about proper use of the frank arose during the 1972 election campaigns. A blatant case of abuse occurred in Georgia, where Rep. Fletcher Thompson, a Republican who was running for the Senate, used the frank to send mail to voters across the state, not just to those in his congressional district. The mailing, which cost taxpayers more than $200,000, became a campaign issue, and a key factor in Thompson's loss to Democrat Sam Nunn. Altogether, twelve cases of abuse reached the courts, helping to convince lawmakers that new regulations were necessary.

1973 Regulations

In 1973 Rep. Morris K. Udall, D-Ariz., introduced a bill establishing specific guidelines for using the franking privilege. The issue, Udall argued, was whether Congress would define the privilege or whether "the judges are going to write the law for us."

The bill, approved by Congress in December 1973, defined the types of mail members could send under the frank, set up mechanisms to rule on individual cases, and restricted the sending of mass mailings (defined as more than five hundred pieces of identical mail) during the four weeks preceding congressional primary and general elections. The law also established in the House a Commission on Congressional Mailing Standards, composed of three Republicans and three Democrats appointed by the Speaker, to resolve franking disputes arising under the law. The Senate Select Committee on Standards and Conduct—later renamed the Select Ethics Committee—was assigned a similar function.

The new regulations, however, did not anticipate every kind of abuse. In 1975 Congress voted to close a loophole in the 1973 law that had allowed former Rep. Frank M. Clark, D-Pa., to send out a franked newsletter to his former constituents two months after his term had expired. The 1975 change permitted former members to use the frank for ninety days after leaving Congress, but only for mailings related to closing down the legislators' offices.

1977 Ethics Code Restrictions

Early in 1977, when new ethics codes were passed, both chambers agreed to additional restrictions on the franking privilege. The House amended its standing rules to impose new limitations on use of the "postal patron" designation—mail that does not specify a recipient's name. The volume of postal patron mail that a member could send annually under the frank was limited to an amount equal to six times the number of addresses in a member's district. All franked postal-patron mailings had to be submitted to the House Commission on Congressional Mailing Standards, which was to advise the member whether the mailing met franking regulations.

In addition, both the House and Senate imposed new regulations on mass mailings—whether sent to a postal-patron address or to a specific person. Mass mailings under the frank were prohibited unless preparation and printing costs were paid entirely from public funds. This restriction was designed to end free political mailings and criticisms that mail printed for a member by special interest groups or political organizations was being sent at government expense. The codes also lengthened the cutoff for sending franked mail before a primary or general election to sixty days from twenty-eight.

The Senate included rules in its ethics code that required all franked mass mailings to be registered with the secretary of the Senate. The registration had to include a copy of the material, the number of pieces sent, and a description of the groups receiving the mailing. The information was to be made available for public inspection.

The Senate also provided that its central computer facilities could not be used to store any political or campaign lists and that other mail-related uses of the computer would be subject to guidelines issued by the Senate Ethics Committee.

Changes in the Early 1980s

Sporadically during the 1980s the House and Senate amended their rules and regulations on the frank, sometimes tightening the restrictions, sometimes loosening them. Amendments passed in 1981, for example, gave the Senate Select Ethics Committee and the House Commission on Congressional Mailing Standards statutory authority to enforce the franking rules and laws and to further regulate use of the frank.

The 1981 amendments also allowed senators to make postal-patron mailings, a privilege the House had held since 1973. But in 1982 the Senate Rules and Administration Committee decided to delay implementation of the law after the Senate sergeant at arms reported that if every senator made four such mailings a year, the Senate would have to hire an additional 166 employees and would exceed its mail budget by $57 million. After continued wrangling over the issue, the Rules Committee in November 1983 decided to allow senators to use postal-patron mailings only to announce town meetings.

On the House side, the franking commission in 1983 proposed a new set of rules to blunt criticisms that the frank gave members an unfair political advantage over election challengers. The rules placed limits on the use of photos in newsletters, on the size of the newsletters themselves, and on the size of a member's name in a headline. But after many legislators complained about the proposed restrictions, the commission backed down and issued them as guidelines, rather than rules. "The primary responsibility for ensuring proper and cost-efficient use of the franking privilege," the commission wrote, "lies with each individual member of the House who uses the privilege."

The Senate took a first step toward gaining control of the costs of franked mail in 1986, when it allocated a specific amount of its mail allowance to each senator and required senators to disclose publicly how they had spent their mail allotments. (In 1989 disclosure was shown to be an effective cost-cutter. During the first five months of the year, the Senate spent $6 million on official mail; when disclosure was lifted for the next seven months, spending shot up to $29 million, according to the Senate Rules Committee.)

Individual Budgets, Accountability

Nonetheless, costs continued to mount, as did the criticisms that the frank was an unfair political tool. One limit was imposed in 1989 when both chambers agreed to restrict the mass mailings to three a year, down from six. (Mass mailings notifying constituents of a town meeting or other appearance of the legislator did not count in this limitation, however.)

But the House refused to join the Senate in giving each member a mail budget and making him or her publicly accountable for it. In 1989 the two chambers agreed to set up two separate mail funds, one for the Senate and one for the House, giving each house more control over its budget for the frank.

In separate legislation the Senate made part of its permanent rules its procedure for allocating mail funds to members. A senator was authorized a specific dollar amount for franked mail based on the population of the senator's state. Senators also were permitted to transfer up to $100,000 of their allocation from their official mail accounts to their personnel and office expense accounts.

The rules still allowed senators to earmark part of their mail money for colleagues, leaving intact a system that let senators up for reelection use mail money from their colleagues who were not facing election. The rules did strike a blow at another cherished Senate perquisite. House members had complained that Senate rules allowed senators to use funds from their campaign accounts to supplement official spending on mass mailings, a practice the House barred. The new rules required any mass mailings to be paid for with appropriated funds.

The Senate also reinstated allocation and disclosure rules that it had suspended for part of the year.

Efforts to force House members to adopt similar disclosure rules were unsuccessful in 1989. But in 1990 the House, succumbing to pressure, agreed to give every member a mail budget and require each legislator to disclose the amount spent on franked mail.

The House plan was accepted with great reluctance on the part of many lawmakers. "There is a real concern that we should not retreat" on our use of the frank, said Chief Deputy Whip David E. Bonior, D-Mich., after hearing from colleagues at a meeting of Democratic whips. "Going into a critical campaign in 1992 after redistricting, this is a poor time to start undermining the advantages of incumbency," said another House Democrat. But eventually a majority realized that such restrictions on the frank were "not only necessary but politically inevitable," in the words of Pat Williams, D-Mont.[2]

The restrictions, adopted by voice vote, gave each member an individual mail budget equal to the amount needed to make three first-class mailings to every residential address in the district. Members could supplement their mail budgets by transferring up to $25,000 a year from accounts for other office expenses, but once the budget was depleted, the member had to stop using the frank. Members were required to make quarterly reports on the amount they spent. The House agreed to require that all mailings to more than five hundred recipients be submitted to the House franking commission for approval. By 1997 the average mail allowance for representatives was $113,299.[3]

In 1998 the House Administration Committee (formerly the House Oversight Committee) issued a regulation that removed the limit on the amount a representative could spend, allowing the member to spend as desired from the office account. That account was used as well to meet all other expenses of official business.

The Senate also tightened its restrictions a bit more in 1990. It barred the transfer of mail funds from one senator to another, and allowed a senator to carry over unused mail funds only to the next fiscal year. Previously, this carryover authority had been unlimited. The Senate also allowed members to transfer $100,000 from their mail accounts to their official personnel and office expense accounts, and in 1996 authorized them to use up to $50,000 of their office expense allowance for mass mailings.

Other reforms in the 1990s helped bring down the cost of the frank. For example, the House in 1992 changed its rules to prevent a member from sending newsletters to voters outside his or her district in years when postcensus reapportionment would change the district's boundaries and require the member to face new voters.

According to the U.S. Postal Service, Congress spent $18.8 million on the frank in fiscal 1997, with $15.4 million spent by the House and $3.4 million by the Senate. That spending total represented a reduction of approximately 40 percent from the total in fiscal 1996, when Congress spent $32 million on official mail. In 1996 franking expenditures had already declined significantly from the fiscal 1988 high of $113.4 million.

Foreign Travel: Business and Pleasure

"An overseas tour by a congressman or candidate," wrote William L. Safire, "is described by him as a fact-finding trip and as a junket by his opponents, who usually add 'at the taxpayer's expense.'"[4] Members who travel abroad at government expense defend the practice as a valuable way to learn about world problems, especially those that are debated in Congress. Detractors say such trips are usually a waste of taxpayers' money, although the critics have not kept members at home. But lawmakers are increasingly accepting privately funded trips to avoid the perception that they are traveling on the government tab. The mid-1990s gift ban permits lawmakers to go on fact-finding missions for up to seven days if the trips are connected with official duties and are disclosed within thirty days of their completion. But critics complain that when a corporation or organization pays for a member's trip abroad, that group gains an unfair advantage in promoting its agenda.

Members generally undertake foreign travel on committee business, in delegations appointed by the Speaker of the House or by the president pro tempore of the Senate, or by executive branch request or appointment. Travel reports detailing the costs of such trips must be made public quarterly. Travel reports do not have to be filed for foreign travel funded by the executive branch or by private organizations. However, members must include in their regular financial disclosure reports any privately funded foreign travel whose total value was $250 or more. (See box, Types of Travel, p. 789.)

PROS AND CONS OF FOREIGN TRAVEL

Ever since members of Congress began taking trips abroad at government expense, there have been opposing arguments on the value of such travel. Supporters defend foreign travel on three bases: fact-finding, overseeing government operations, and monitoring the administration of U.S. aid. Travel, these defenders argue, enables members to develop insights they would not otherwise obtain, and such firsthand information is needed for intelligent legislating. "It is absolutely preposterous for people to think [senators] can be well-informed without having visited the places they're making policy for. Senators are so insulated. . . . It makes sense to travel. It's stupid not to," said Sen. Joseph R. Biden Jr., D-Del., in 1981.[5]

Members argue similarly when corporations or nonprofit organizations pay for the overseas travel. They say that the travel educates lawmakers who must vote on complex issues, such as expansion of the NATO Alliance. "People would take a dim view of members of the Education Committee if they did not want to see any of the schools," said Rep. Stephen J. Solarz, D-N.Y., who served on the Foreign Affairs Committee during his eighteen years in the House and was a frequent traveler.[6]

Legislators also note that the travel is not always the luxurious vacation that critics depict. Often tedious, occasionally arduous, foreign travel is sometimes dangerous. In 1989 Rep. Mickey Leland, D-Texas, was killed during travel when his plane

TYPES OF TRAVEL

Listed below are the different types of travel that House members frequently engage in, both domestic and foreign.

1. Official congressional travel, domestic to member's district office. Travel to the district is authorized for a member and his or her staff in pursuit of the member's "official and representational duties." The member is not required to include this travel on the financial disclosure report; it is reported by the clerk of the House.

2. Official congressional travel, domestic committee business. This travel is permitted to members and committee staff members for official committee business, including hearings, studies, and the conduct of investigations. Such trips are reported to the clerk of the House.

3. Official congressional travel, foreign committee business. This travel is permitted to members for official business requested by the committee chairman. The traveler must submit an itemized report to the committee chairman, who submits consolidated reports to the clerk of the House, who publishes them in the *Congressional Record* and maintains them for public inspection.

4. Official congressional travel, foreign House business. The Speaker of the House authorizes travel for individual members and delegations on official business, primarily to represent the House at ceremonies and to conduct investigations. Travel reports must be submitted to the Speaker, who must submit such reports to the clerk of the House. The clerk then publishes the report in the *Congressional Record* and maintains it for public inspection.

5. Travel provided by a federal, state, or local government. Members are permitted to travel on official business at the request of a government. Travelers need not report travel sponsored by the federal government, but beginning in 1991 members must include travel sponsored by state or local governments in their financial disclosure statements.

6. Travel provided by a foreign government. As a general rule, a member may accept travel provided by a foreign government or a multinational organization only if the travel is wholly outside the United States. An exception is made for approved exchange programs. The member must report the travel within thirty days to the Committee on Standards of Official Conduct.

7. Campaign and political travel. Travel is permitted for a bona fide campaign or political purpose and must be reported on Federal Election Commission reports. This type of travel is not reimbursable from each member's representational allowance.

8. Privately sponsored fact-finding travel. A House member and a spouse or another family member may accept travel paid for by a private organization for "connection with" official duties. Unless prior approval is obtained from the House Ethics Committee, the sponsor may pick up the tab for a maximum of four days, including travel time, if the trip is within the United States, and seven days, excluding travel time, if it is abroad.

9. Substantial participation in a private event. A member, accompanied by a spouse or other family member, may accept travel expenses from a private sponsor for speaking or otherwise substantially participating in a private event. As for privately sponsored fact-finding travel, a sponsor may pay for only four days' expenses if the trip is domestic, seven days if the trip is abroad.

Members are required to report in their financial disclosure statements any reimbursements for travel expenses from a single source aggregating more than $250 in a year. Members may no longer accept honoraria for speeches or appearances, but members can request that contributions up to $2,000 per event be made in their name to a qualified charity in lieu of honoraria.

Senate rules on travel are similar except for the limitations on what private organizations can pay for. Under Senate rules private sources can pay travel expenses for no more than three days of domestic travel and seven days for foreign trips. Both limits exclude travel time.

---

crashed in Ethiopia where he had been on a hunger relief mission. In 1978 Rep. Leo J. Ryan, D-Calif., was shot and killed while investigating a religious cult in Guyana, South America.

Still, some foreign travel does have the appearance of being more pleasure than business, and some legislators will find their opponents trying to win votes by criticizing the trips. "If you travel a lot, your opponent will put a map of the world on the screen and have you, like a Ping-Pong ball, zigging and zagging all over the world," said Rep. Ileana Ros-Lehtinen, R-Fla., in 1997. She pointed out that no matter who foots the bill, special interests or taxpayers, travel can be a political liability.[7]

Critics contend that legislators traveling abroad spend only a minimal amount of time on official business, make unreasonable demands on U.S. embassy personnel in the countries they visit, sometimes damage American prestige through tactless acts or comments while abroad, and often confound foreign officials by giving the impression that their comments reflect official U.S. policy.

Most official trips are made under the auspices of congressional committees, although House and Senate leaders get additional travel allowances. In the past, leaders have been criticized for their use of these funds, but the criticism declined in the latter part of the 1990s. In April 1981, for instance, Speaker Thomas P. O'Neill Jr., D-Mass., and fourteen colleagues flew to New Zealand and Australia for two weeks to hold discussions with leaders in those countries on national security and economic issues. Many viewed the trip, which came in the midst of a congressional battle over President Ronald Reagan's program to cut the federal budget, as a blatant example of wasteful spending. Even some Democrats said O'Neill should have been in Washington lining up votes against the Reagan economic program.

Similar criticisms were voiced in 1988 when Speaker Jim Wright, D-Texas, invited thirteen members and seven staffers to accompany him to Australia for the centennial celebration of that country's parliament. In 1985 Rep. Bill Alexander, an Arkansas Democrat, used a military plane, at a cost of $50,000,

Members of Congress from time to time travel abroad in fact-finding missions. Here participants in a congressional observer group at the 1997 U.N. conference on global warming in Kyoto, Japan, talk with reporters. From left are Rep. Henry A. Waxman, D-Calif., Sen. Joseph Lieberman, D-Conn., Sen. John Kerry, D-Mass., and Rep. George Miller, D-Calif.

for a solo trip to Brazil; Democratic colleagues later reacted by ousting him as chief deputy whip.

One of the most celebrated junketeers in congressional history was Rep. Adam Clayton Powell Jr., D-N.Y. In one trip in 1962, Powell traveled through Europe for six weeks accompanied by two female assistants. According to one report, Powell requested State Department assistance in obtaining reservations at various European nightclubs and in arranging a six-day cruise on the Aegean Sea. Powell's extravagant travel contributed to his eventual ouster as chairman of the House Education and Labor Committee. (See "Powell," p. 921.)

Winter recess appears to be a popular time for lawmakers to go on fact-finding trips, generally in climates more temperate than Washington's. Senate Majority Leader Trent Lott, R-Miss., in January 1998 led a total of twenty-three staffers and senators on a government-paid trip through Central America and Mexico, staying one night in Antigua Guatemala at a luxury hotel built from a seventeenth-century monastery. Lott's office said the purpose of the trip was to study trade and efforts to curb smuggling of drugs and immigrants.[8]

WHEN CORPORATIONS PAY FOR TRIPS

New ethics laws and regulations in 1989 established the parameters for funding of fact-finding trips by corporations, foundations, and interest groups. They were slightly revised with the gift-ban rule in 1995. Members and their staffs are allowed to accept free trips for meetings, speeches, and fact-finding tours related to their official duties. Domestic travel is limited to four days including travel time and foreign travel to seven days excluding travel time. Lawmakers have thirty days to report to the clerk of the House the purpose of the trip, who paid for it, the destination, and the cost.

According to disclosure documents, House and Senate lawmakers took hundreds of trips from December 1996 to December 1997 that were paid for by corporations, nonprofit organizations, and educational groups. Israel, China, and Taiwan were popular destinations, although lawmakers attended seminars on U.S.-Russia relations in Dresden, Germany; discussed France's high-speed rail system in Paris; and took fact-finding tours of Congo and Libya.

Ralph Nader's Public Citizen, a private-sector watchdog group, monitors lawmakers' privately-sponsored overseas travel. Bob Schiff, a staff attorney with the group, said that privately funded travel provides special interest groups with access to lawmakers. He asserted that if members can justify the travel to their constituents, the trips should be paid for by taxpayers.[9]

"The lines of debate between what may be a unique means to buy influence and the notion of educating lawmakers from the world's only superpower can easily blur," according to a journalist who followed the story closely. For example, the Corporate Council on Africa paid for Reps. Bill Archer, R-Texas, E. Clay Shaw Jr., R-Fla., and their wives to go on a weeklong trade mission to Congo in January 1997 at a cost of $13,060 per couple. Ten months later, Shaw, the chair of the House Ways and Means Committee's Trade to Congo panel, was considering legislation strongly backed by the Corporate Council that would promote economic development and U.S. private-sector investments in sub-Saharan Africa.[10] The legislation stalled in 1998.

EFFORTS TO CONTROL TRAVEL

Congress first initiated some control over federally funded foreign travel when it passed the Mutual Security Act of 1954. In addition to appropriated funds, the act for the first time allowed congressional committees to use counterpart funds (foreign currencies credited to the United States in return for aid, which may be spent only in the country of origin). It also required legislators to make a full report to the House Administration Committee or the Senate Rules and Administration Committee (later changed to the Senate Appropriations Committee) on the amount of counterpart funds they spent. Beginning in 1959 these reports were required to be published annually in the *Congressional Record.*

In 1958 members and staff were required to prepare itemized reports of their use of foreign currencies to the chairs of committees, who in turn were required to submit consolidated travel reports within the first sixty days Congress was in session each year. Reports were then required to be published in the *Congressional Record.* It was not until 1961, however, that members were required to account publicly for appropriated funds they had spent on overseas trips. Not only committee reports but also individual itemized expenditures of both appropriated and counterpart funds now had to be reported in the *Record,* beginning that year.

In 1963 the House took further steps to curb foreign travel by allowing only five House committees to use appropriated and counterpart funds for travel abroad. Ten other committees could sponsor foreign trips only with permission from the House Rules Committee. And in 1967 and 1968 the House took steps to curb abuses of per diem expenses.

In October 1973 Congress reversed field and, as part of the State Department authorization bill, eliminated the requirement that foreign travel reports from committees and individual members be published in the *Congressional Record,* but stipulated that committees maintain travel reports in their offices for public inspection. Nor were the House and Senate oversight committees any longer required to make public a separate accounting of tax dollars spent on congressional travel.

The change was engineered by Rep. Wayne L. Hays, D-Ohio, chairman of the subcommittee in which the bill originated. Hays, who was also chairman of the House Administration Committee and a champion of generous perquisites for his colleagues, claimed his purpose was to trim the size of the *Record.* "We decided we weren't going to spend eight or nine thousand dollars to let you guys [reporters] do your stories on congressional travel," he said, adding that "there was no desire on anyone's part to cover up anything."[11]

Newspapers throughout the country editorialized against the change. As a result, in August 1974 Congress decided to make the reports public. But instead of requiring that they be published in the *Record,* which was readily available throughout the country, the reports were to be made available by the clerk of the House and the secretary of the Senate. In 1975 Hays gained control over the House reports when Congress specified that the reports be filed with the House Administration Committee, rather than the clerk's office.

Barely a year later, however, Hays was caught at the center of a sex-payroll scandal and was forced to resign as chairman of the House Administration Committee. In the aftermath of the

scandal, Congress passed several reforms, including one that required the annual foreign travel expense reports prepared by House and Senate committees to be printed once again in the *Record.* *(See "Hays," p. 947.)*

Basic disclosure laws for official foreign travel have remained the same since 1978. Members and staff are required to prepare individual travel reports and submit them to the committee or delegation chair within sixty days of completion of travel. Their reports include their names, the time spent in each country, and the amount spent on per diem, transportation, and other expenses; however, the purpose is rarely reported. Each quarter, committee and delegation chairs prepare a consolidated travel report for each trip and submit the reports to the clerk of the House or the secretary of the Senate. Within ten days of receipt, both officers must publish the consolidated reports in the *Record* and make them publicly available.

Official Allowances

The travel allowance provided in an act of September 22, 1789, fixing the compensation of members of Congress was the first of what has become a plethora of special allowances lawmakers have created for themselves through the years.

One of the biggest today is the official office expense allowance, which is separate from the clerk-hire allowance senators and representatives receive for staff assistance. The expense allowance covers domestic travel, stationery, computer services, postage, printing, telecommunications, office expenses in Washington, D.C., and in the member's congressional district or state, and other expenses. *(See "The Cost and Pay of Congressional Staff," p. 598, Vol. I.)*

In the 1970s both the House and Senate consolidated their allowances for basic office supplies and services, such as stationery, postage, computer services, telephone and telegraph, travel, office expenses in their state, and other official expenses, with no restrictions on the amount they could spend in any one category.

Until 1977 the House had nine separate special allowances, and representatives often had to adhere to certain limits on spending in each account. Special allowances generally were less generous and flexible for representatives than for senators. For example, most House allowances had to be spent a month at a time, whereas Senate allowances usually were cumulative over an entire calendar year. But the rules were changed in 1977, after Hays was forced to resign as chairman of the House Administration Committee, the panel that set expense guidelines.

In 1995 the rules were changed once more, and expense allowances were further consolidated. Today, the House Administration panel continues to oversee members' allowances. *(See Table 28-1, p. 792.)*

HOUSE EXPENSE ALLOWANCE

In 1977 separate House functions were consolidated into three main accounts: official expenses, clerk-hire allowances,

TABLE 28-1 Members' Allowances, 1999

Members of Congress have given themselves a variety of expense allowances. Today they are generally considered a necessary accessory to members' regular salary. They range from generous staff assistance and office space to free use of video recording facilities and sophisticated computer services. Congressional leaders receive additional remuneration.

Listed below are the major allowances and, where available, the dollar value of those benefits as of 1999. No value is given to some of the allowances because of the difficulty in determining the range of reimbursed costs; this would be the case for travel and telephone usage, for example. Most of the allowances were transferable from one account to another.

	House	*Senate*
Washington, D.C., office		
Official personnel, office allowances	$952,777 (average)[1]	$1,734,828–$3,023,971[2]
Clerk-hire	$632,355	$1,210,967–$2,157,222[3]
Committee legislative assistants	(some included in above)	$396,477
General office expenses	$200,000	$127,384–$470,272
Office space	Provided	Provided
Official mail allowances	Based on a formula using addresses in district	Based on a formula using state population
Paper and letterhead	Paper provided in office allowance	1.8–30.4 million sheets of paper
Envelope allowance	40,000 public document envelopes	50,000–100,000 public document envelopes
Furnishings and equipment	Provided[1]	Provided[1]
District/state offices		
Rental space allowed	2,500 square feet.[1]	4,800–8,000 square feet.[4]
Furnishings/equipment	Provided[4]	Provided[4]
Mobile office	none	one[4]
Travel, by formula	$6,200–$67,200	—

1. Funds for House members' offices are provided in the "Members' Representational Allowance." This figure includes funds for official (franked) mail; it does not include funds for personnel. Members may shift money among accounts.

2. Senators operate their offices from their "Official Personnel and Office Expense Allowances." With some limitations, senators may shift money between accounts. These figures include funds for senators' clerk-hire and general office expenses; they do not include funds for official (franked) mail, which are paid from a separate Senate account.

3. The allowance is based on a sliding scale linked to the senators' state populations.

4. These allowances are provided in addition to the official office expenses allowances.

SOURCE: Adapted from Roger H. Davidson and Walter J. Oleszek, *Congress and Its Members*, 7th ed. (Washington, D.C.: CQ Press, 2000), 154.

and official (franked) mail allowances. Official expenses covered the costs incurred in running congressional offices, both in Washington and in members' home districts. The clerk-hire account was used to pay the eighteen permanent and four nonpermanent employees representatives are allowed to hire.

The consolidated account system replaced the nine separate special allowances for travel, office equipment leasing, district office leasing, telecommunications, stationery, constituent communications, postage, computer services, and other official expenses.

In November 1995 members' three expense allowances were consolidated into one members' representational allowance (MRA). Although the MRA was calculated based on three parts—clerk-hire costs, office expenses, and mail costs—members could spend the allowance as they saw fit. The average MRA in 1999 was $952,777, including a base office expense allowance of $122,500. This allowance was in addition to the funds for each member that were calculated by assigning dollar values based both on the distance between the District of Columbia and the farthest point in a member's district and on the size of a member's district office space in a federal or private building. A California legislator, for example, received more than a New York legislator because the travel costs were higher. The amount of the official mail account was based on a formula using the

number of nonbusiness addresses in a member's district. The clerk-hire allowance was the same for each member.

Overall, the House allocated $385 million in fiscal 1999 for members' representational allowances. In 1999 the clerk-hire allowance was $632,355 for each member.

Starting in 1977, members were required to file quarterly reports detailing how they were using their expense allowances. Official expenses were defined as "ordinary and necessary business expenses incurred by the member . . . in support of the member's official and representational duties."

The House Administration Committee issued strict rules on what members can and cannot be reimbursed for. Under the panel's guidelines, House members could not be reimbursed from their expense accounts for the following types of expenditures:

• Employment service fees, moving allowances, and other expenses relating to hiring staff.

• Purchase or rental of items "having an extended useful life," such as the rental of a tuxedo. But members could charge office equipment relating to their duties to their official expense account.

• Greeting cards, flowers, trophies, donations, and dues for groups other than congressional organizations approved by the House Administration Committee. (Members who had claimed these expenses protested that constituents expected their representatives to send flowers to funerals, award sports trophies, and join lodges.)

• Radio or television time or advertisements, except for notices of meetings relating to congressional business.

• Tuition or fees for education and training unless a need for a special skill, relating to House activities, could be proved.

Flexibility of Allowance

With the consolidated system, it is easier for members to use up their entire expense account funds each year since representatives may freely transfer funds from one category to another without limitation. They may not spend more for official expenses than they are entitled to when the three allowances are combined. Otherwise, they must pay out of pocket. House rules require members to submit documentation of expenses incurred in order to be reimbursed. The documentation is reviewed by the clerk's office but is not available for public inspection until its quarterly report is published.

SENATE EXPENSE ALLOWANCE

Senators have three official allowances: administrative and clerical, official office, and legislative assistance. Although the legislative allowance ($396,477 for up to three persons) is set, the other funds, like those for a representative, vary. For a senator they are determined by the size of his or her state and the distance between the state and Washington, D.C. In 1999 the official office expense allowance ranged from $127,384 to $470,272. The administrative and clerical allowance varies from $1.2 million for a senator representing a state with a population of fewer than five million to $2.2 million for a senator from a state with 28 million or more people.[12] There are twenty-five population categories.

According to the "Senate Handbook," prepared by the Senate Rules and Administration Committee, the Senators' Official Personnel and Office Expense Account is a "multipurpose account" authorized each year. At the end of the year, any unused balance may not be carried over to the next year. In fiscal 1999 the Senate allocated over $239.2 million for these expense accounts.

Before 1979 a senator was able to request reimbursement for office expenses on his signature alone. The senator merely had to sign his name beneath a statement printed on an itemized voucher that said, "I certify that the above expenses were officially incurred." But the Senate has tightened its regulations on allowances by requiring senators to document each expense greater than $35. Expenses of $35 or less must either be itemized or documented. The rules also require each voucher for reimbursement to be "personally signed" by a senator.

The Senate expense allowance may be used to pay expenses of the following categories:

• Telecommunications equipment and service.

• Stationery and other office supplies purchased through the Senate Stationery Room or elsewhere for official business.

• Mass mailings.

• Preparation of required official reports, acquisition of mailing lists, and the mailing, delivery, and transmittal of material relating to official business.

• Publications, including subscriptions, clipping, and other information services.

• Additional office equipment for Washington, D.C., and home state offices.

• Official office expenses in senators' home states.

• Official travel within the United States.

• Expenses incurred by individuals selected by a senator to serve on panels or other bodies making recommendations on nominees to the service academies or federal judgeships.

• "Other official expenses as the senator determines are necessary."

There is no limit on the amount that can be spent in any one category, except for the latter category of "other official expenses." That discretionary allowance is unique to the Senate and permits a senator to spend up to 10 percent of his or her total available funds for any "official expenses."

Definition of Official Expenses

Though the Senate spends millions of dollars annually on "official expenses," until the last decade it had never defined what was an official expense. Finally, in 1980, the Senate agreed that official expenses were "ordinary and necessary business expenses incurred by a senator and his staff in the discharge of their official duties." All expenses are required to be published in the semiannual report of the secretary of the Senate.

The following expenses specifically are excluded: commuting and commuter parking fees; greeting cards; flowers; trophies; awards or certificates; donations or gifts of any type (except gifts of flags flown over the United States Capitol, and copies of an illustrated history book of Congress and calendar, both entitled *We, the People*); dues or assessments; purchase of broadcast time or print advertising time except classified advertising for personnel to be employed in a senator's office; expenses incurred by an individual who is not an employee (except those individuals selected by a senator to serve on panels or other bodies making recommendations on nominees to service academies or federal judgeships); travel expenses by employees in excess of those authorized by law; relocation expenses; pay for personal services performed in a normal employer-employee relationship; entertainment and meals; additional pay to employees; expenses for private vehicles; and furniture for home state offices.

A subsequent revision adopted by the Senate excluded supplemental allowances—which are separate from the expense allowances—given the vice president, president pro tempore, majority and minority leaders, and majority and minority whips.

DOMESTIC TRAVEL ALLOWANCE

The restrictions on congressional travel have eased a great deal. In the early 1960s senators and representatives were al-

Members of Congress are given official expense allowances for running their Washington and home offices. Staff salaries make up the largest budget item.

lowed three government-paid trips home each year. The number was raised repeatedly in the following two decades so that by the late 1970s senators could take more than forty trips home and representatives were allowed thirty-three. By 1980 there were no limits on the number of trips that could be taken.

House

Travel allowances are calculated based on the proximity of the member's district to Washington, D.C., and are added to his or her base official office expense account, which may be spent how the member sees fit. Before expense accounts were first consolidated in 1977, representatives received a separate travel allowance that permitted them twenty-six free round trips each year to and from their home district plus extra trips for their staff. Members could also choose to withdraw their travel allowance in cash, up to a maximum of $2,250 a year; any amount not used for travel could go toward members' personal expenses so long as they paid income taxes on it. Changes to the rules in 1976 ended the "cash-out" option.

The House calculates a domestic travel allowance for each member and uses that figure in determining the official expense allowances. In 1999 the figure was the equivalent of sixty-four multiplied by the rate per mile (23 cents per mile for three thousand miles or more, and 39 cents per mile for travel under five hundred miles), multiplied by the mileage between the District of Columbia and the farthest point in the member's district, plus 10 percent.

Members are reimbursed for the actual cost of travel, including rail and airfare, food, and lodging. When a member travels in a privately owned or leased vehicle, he or she is reimbursed at a maximum rate per mile of 31 cents for an automobile, 25 cents for a motorcycle, and 85 cents for an airplane. Members also may be reimbursed for travel on official business that is in addition to visits to their home district or state. The Defense Department also provides members of Congress with free transportation in the line of official business. But department officials do not release figures on the cost of such special shuttle service.

The federal government has contracted with participating air carriers for a fare-discount program for travel on official business only.

Senate

Travel is one of several items authorized as part of senators' official expense accounts. Reimbursable travel expenses include:

• Per diem and actual transportation expenses. The maximum per diem within the continental United States in 1998 was $162 (the rate differed in Alaska and Hawaii). Per diem expenses covered food, lodging, tips, laundry, and other incidental charges. There was no reimbursement for entertainment, nor could reimbursement for transportation (airfare and rail fare) exceed actual expenses. Under previous rules reimbursement claims had been limited under certain circumstances to less than actual expenses.

• Privately owned automobile mileage not to exceed 30 cents per mile.

• Motorcycle mileage not to exceed 24.5 cents per mile.

• Airplane mileage not to exceed 88.5 cents per mile.

• Actual costs of parking fees, ferry fares, and bridge, road, and tunnel tolls.

There is a statutory travel allowance for a senator-elect and up to two employees. The allowance covers one round trip between a senator-elect's home and Washington, D.C. The reimbursement is automatic; it is not paid from the official office expense account. The travel allowance for each senator used to be based on the cost of forty round trips a year for states with fewer than 10 million people and forty-four round trips for states with more than 10 million. A state's distance from Washington was figured in the computation. The travel allowance for senators no longer sets limits on the number of trips that can be taken each year. Senate regulations state that office staff must make round trips since the Senate will not pay the expenses of aides who relocate—for example, a staffer who moves to Washington after serving in a member's district office. (Although the House does not have any specific regulation governing round trips for staff, it also does not pay personnel relocation costs.)

Unlike the House, which permits travel outside the district only for educational seminars or authorized meetings, the Senate will reimburse for travel expenses that include official travel anywhere within the United States. (Before 1977 senators could be reimbursed only for travel within or to a senator's home state.) It also authorized per diem expenses for travel within a senator's home state. But neither the travel allowance nor the per diem allowance were permitted in the sixty-day period immediately prior to a contested primary or general election in which the senator was a candidate for office. In addition, the Senate required members to make public how they used the per diem and travel allowance funds. Senators also can accept free domestic transportation from the Defense Department on an availability basis or from company noncommercial carriers.

STATIONERY, NEWSLETTERS, AND POSTAGE

House

A representative's funds for stationery, postage, and newsletters come from his official expense account. There is no limit, within the account, on the amount he can spend on any one item.

By 1999 the base amount of a representative's official expense account came to $122,500. (The size of the allowance varies from representative to representative, depending on distance between Washington and the member's congressional district and rental rates charged by the General Services Administration for district office space.)

In addition to this expense account, each representative is allowed forty thousand brown "Public Document" envelopes a month without charge.

In 1989 and 1990 curbs were placed on mailing privileges for both House and Senate members. For the first time separate House and Senate "franking" accounts were established, with the belief that it would make each member more accountable for the spending. (See "Restrictions on Use," p. 786.)

The franking privilege has always been a frequent target for its abuse in reelection efforts—particularly from members of the minority party who are frustrated by their difficulty in ousting majority incumbents.

Attempts to keep down mail spending have worked. According to the Congressional Research Service report, "Official Congressional Mail Costs," reforms took place from 1989 to 1997, when postal rates increased dramatically. First-class mail rates increased by 28 percent, while third-class rates increased by 40 percent. As a result, the amount of official mail members could send to their constituents was reduced. Congress spent about $19 million on the frank in fiscal 1997, down from $32 million in fiscal 1996. The all-time high for the frank, $113 million, was reached just over a decade ago. For years many lame duck members have been criticized for taking their remaining expense account funds in the form of postage stamps. Critics have argued that lame duck representatives do not need regular postage because they are allowed to use the frank for ninety days after they leave office to clean up all remaining official correspondence.

Senate

Funds for Senate stationery and postage come from the member's personnel and office expense account. Each senator also receives allotments of white envelopes and letterheads, blank sheets, and brown "Public Document" envelopes, all based on the state's population.

Some services for printing and bulk mailing of newsletters, questionnaires, excerpts from the *Congressional Record,* and other items are provided without charge by the Senate's Service Department.

As in the House, changes to franking rules have held down spending. (Franked mail spending was just $17 million in fiscal 1990 after senators were forced to disclose individual spending. Mail costs in the Senate continued to drop throughout the decade: In fiscal 1997 the Senate spent $3 million on the frank, down from approximately $5 million in fiscal 1996 and fiscal 1995 and $10.6 million in fiscal 1994.

TELECOMMUNICATIONS ALLOWANCE

House

Before the House consolidated its allowances, the yearly telephone allowance was computed based on a formula. Members now use their representational allowances to pay for everything, including long-distance telephone service.

Senate

Since the Senate consolidated accounts in 1973, the Rules and Administration Committee has fixed senators' telephone and telegraph rates. The allowance was based on a fixed number of long-distance calls totaling no more than a fixed number of minutes for calls to and from Washington. The committee used a complicated formula to determine the telegraph allowance, based on state population and Western Union rates from Washington. Both formulas were used to determine a senator's total consolidated allowance, now called the official office expense account.

Senators have access to a long-distance WATS line provided by the telephone companies and paid for by the sergeant at arms. Senators from states with more than seven million residents are provided access to four long-distance WATS lines. Those from states with fewer than seven million residents have access to three lines.

OFFICE ALLOWANCES

House

The Washington office of a representative, typically a two- or three-room suite, is provided free of charge. Office furnishings and decorations, housekeeping, and maintenance also are free. Additional storage space and trunks are available free of charge. Representatives pay for electrical and mechanical office equipment, including computers, from their official expense account.

In recent years a handful of representatives have used their office expense accounts to pay for outside consultants to help them cope with the organizational demands of running a congressional office. Consultants have set up the Washington offices of freshmen representatives, trained new staffers, and improved mail flow, among other things. Neither the consulting firms nor the members are eager to advertise this use of the expense account since consultants are expensive.

Members pay for district expenses out of their consolidated office expense accounts. Until 1977 members were given separate allowances for their districts, which covered up to twenty-five hundred square feet of office space.

Senate

The Washington offices and furnishings for senators are provided free, as are housekeeping and maintenance services. Senators do not have allowances to buy or lease office equipment; it is provided by the sergeant at arms of the Senate.

A senator's home state office space is allocated according to the state's population. Within the allowed square footage there is no limit to the number of offices he may open. Offices are provided free in federal buildings or leased from private owners at the General Services Administration (GSA) regional rate. Senators receive an aggregate furniture and equipment allowance. The minimum allowance, the amount received by senators from the smallest states, is $30,000 for 4,800 square feet. The amount is increased for each authorized increase of square footage. All furnishings are provided through GSA. Each senator also is allowed to rent one mobile office for use throughout the state.

Rent and furnishings for senators' state offices are not chargeable to the official office account. These allowances also are provided through the GSA and are paid for by the Senate sergeant at arms.

PUBLICATIONS ALLOWANCE

In addition to their official expense allowance covering office operations, communications, and travel, members of Congress receive a number of free publications. In recent years, however, some of these publications have been made available on the Internet and are no longer automatically issued to members. Some used directly in members' work—for example, a complete set of the *U.S. Code* and District of Columbia codes and supplements—must be ordered. Other publications made available include the *Federal Register,* and office copies of the *Congressional Record* and *Congressional Directory.* All of these publications are printed by the United States Government Printing Office.

Members of Congress are allotted two subscriptions to the *Record;* they may receive up to five by request.

Each senator and representative receives a cloth-bound copy of the annual *Congressional Directory,* with his or her name engraved on it. It is also maintained electronically online through the Government Printing Office. Members receive ten copies of the directory. Until recent years they received an additional allotment: forty to each senator and twenty to each representative. Committees receive twenty copies to be equally distributed to the majority and minority staff. Also until recent years, members received allotments of special publications to send to constituents. One of the most popular was the *Yearbook* of the Department of Agriculture, which was discontinued in 1993. Each representative was allotted 400 copies, worth $4,800. Senators had an allotment of 550. The Government Printing Office used to permit members to turn in unused *Yearbooks* and certain other publications for exchange or credit toward other books or pamphlets, but no longer does so.

Pamphlets and Wall Calendars

Among the items members may choose to distribute are pamphlets on American history and the legislative process, historic documents, and calendars, including "We, the People" wall calendars.

"We, the People" calendars are full-color, glossy photo calendars that carry the name of the member. They are published by the U.S. Capitol Historical Society and are popular with constituents.

Senators and representatives also receive an unabridged dictionary and stand as part of their office furnishings.

Additional Benefits

In addition to their expense allowances, foreign travel compensation, and franking privileges, members of Congress benefit from numerous services and courtesies that go along with the job. Because of the difficulty of defining and isolating types of benefits, it is not possible to compile a complete list or compute their precise value. Although in recent years fees have been added to once-free services, members continue to have easy ac-

THE COST OF CONGRESS

The cost of running Congress grew dramatically from 1960 to the early 1990s, when it began to level off. In fiscal 1960 the legislative budget—including the operations of Congress and the related agencies—totaled $118.2 million. Legislative branch appropriations in fiscal 1999 totaled $2.3 billion, not including an emergency supplemental, close to the $2.2 billion the legislative branch received in fiscal 1991. Including emergency and other supplemental appropriations of $229.2 million, the total fiscal year 1999 budget was $2.6 billion. These emergency funds were made available for security at the Capitol building, a Capitol visitors' center, and support of year 2000 software and computer compliancy. A second fiscal year 1999 supplemental provided $3.8 million for renovation of the House page dormitory and $1.8 million for life safety renovations to the O'Neill House Office Building. The increase over nearly

four decades reflected the growth of the legislative bureaucracy. In 1960 House and Senate employees numbered about 6,500; some thirty years later that total exceeded 18,700. But growth has slowed in recent years because of cuts in committee and support agency staff, and termination of some congressional offices. By 1999 there were about 16,100 House and Senate employees.

The legislative branch must request funds for its programs and activities in an annual budget. The process generally is the same as that for the executive branch: proposed funding for Congress and related agencies is incorporated in a legislative appropriations bill, which must be approved by the House and Senate. Neither chamber, normally, delves into the requests of the other, and the executive branch does not review congressional funding decisions.

Fiscal 1960 Legislative Funds		*Fiscal 1999 Legislative Funds*[a]			
		Congressional Operations		*Related Agencies*	
Senate	$28,218,205	Senate	$474,891,000	Botanic Garden	$3,052,000
House of Representatives	46,732,200	House of Representatives	740,481,000	Library of Congress	
Architect of the Capitol	13,552,200	Joint Items	204,916,000	(except CRS)[b]	296,516,000
Botanic Garden	328,000	Office of Compliance	2,086,000	Architect of the Capitol	
Library of Congress	14,329,000	Congressional Budget Office	25,671,000	(library buildings)	12,672,000
Government Printing Office	15,020,000	Architect of the Capitol	289,746,000	Architect of the Capitol	
Total	$118,179,605	Congressional Research		(congressional cemetery)	1,000,000
		Service (CRS)	67,124,000	Government Printing Office	
		Government Printing Office		(noncongressional printing)	29,264,000
		(congressional printing)	$74,465,000	General Accounting Office	359,268,000
				Total	$2,581,152,000

a. Includes fiscal year 1999 emergency and other supplemental appropriations.
b. The library also was authorized to use $28 million in receipts.

cess to these programs. Selected additional benefits are described below.

Life Insurance

Regardless of age or state of health, every member receives term life insurance under the Federal Employees Group Life Insurance. The amount of coverage is determined by a formula based on the elected coverage. In 1999 the monthly premium was $.36 per $1,000 coverage and was an automatic payroll deduction. Additional $10,000 policies as well as coverage of from one to five times a member's annual pay are available, with the extra premiums determined by the age of the member. Family members also are eligible under these plans.

Health Insurance

Lawmakers are eligible for a variety of health insurance plans through the Federal Employees' Health Benefits Program, financed in part by the government. Participation is on a voluntary, contributory basis.

Capitol Hill Health Facilities

A staff of doctors, nurses, and other medical personnel stands by in the Capitol to give members medical care while at work. The Office of the Attending Physician is staffed and operated by the navy. Until 1991 the staff's services were free; now members are charged an annual fee. Services available to senators and representatives include physical examinations, laboratory work, electrocardiograms, periodic health preventive programs, physiotherapy, immunizations for foreign travel, and ambulance service. First aid stations in most House and Senate office buildings also offer help for minor ailments to members, their staffs, and visitors.

Library Services

The Library of Congress provides members with free analytical research services and facilities, and information that can be sent to constituents or used to answer constituents' questions. More than 740 employees in the Library's Congressional Re-

Senators and guests can enjoy meals in the opulent Senate restaurant at the Capitol.

search Service work exclusively for members. *(See "Congressional Research Service," p. 759.)*

Surplus Books

The Library of Congress gives away to members and their staffs surplus books that are not needed for the library's collections. Most of these volumes are duplicate copies of books already held by the library or discarded publications sent from various agencies or offices. Members may select and keep books for their own use or send volumes to libraries and schools in their districts or states. *(See "Publications Allowance," p. 796.)*

Legislative Counsel

The Office of Legislative Counsel, with offices on both sides of Capitol Hill, assists members in drafting bills, resolutions, and amendments. Its staff provides confidential help to committees and members on legislative matters only; it does not perform personal legal work for members. *(See box, Legislative Counsel, p. 759.)*

Legal Counsel

The Office of Senate Legal Counsel, created by the Ethics in Government Act of 1978, provides advice and handles legal matters relating to official work of Senate members, committees, and staffers. Functions of the office include defending the Senate against outside suits; filing civil actions to enforce subpoenas; and identifying pending legal proceedings that might affect congressional powers and responsibilities. The House counterpart to the Senate's legal counsel is the general counsel's office.

Chaplains

Both the House and Senate have their own chaplain, who is responsible for opening each daily session with a prayer and for serving generally as spiritual counselor to members, their families, and their staffs. The chaplains are officers of their respective chambers. In 1999 the House chaplain received a salary of $132,100; the Senate chaplain, $118,400.

Recreation

Members of Congress have their own health club, including a modern fitness center in the Rayburn House Office Building and an exercise room in the Russell Senate Office Building. Until recently, members could use the facilities for free; now there is an annual fee. For example, in 1998 senators paid $435 per year to use the gym. Facilities include swimming pools, exercise machines, and saunas as well as court facilities for volleyball, paddleball, and basketball.

Capitol Hill Restaurants

Food and eating facilities are available to members, staff, and visitors. The House side of the Capitol includes a member's dining room and a carry-out. Senators have two dining rooms: one private and one that permits guests. There are also cafeterias, snack bars, and coffee shops in House and Senate office buildings open to the public. In addition, members may reserve several private dining rooms or arrange catered banquets and parties in caucus rooms. By 1998 the House contracted out its catering jobs to private businesses that charged the going rate. Senate restaurants provide catering services through their own banquet manager.

Merchandise

Stationery stores located in the House and Senate office buildings used to sell many gift items as well as normal office supplies, all at cost or slightly above. In the 1990s, however, both the House and Senate buildings opened gift shops for the public, separate from the stationery stores. At the gift shops, members, their spouses, and their staffs can buy such things as wallets, briefcases, pocket calculators, and drinking glasses and ashtrays with the seal of either the House or the Senate. The stationery stores and gift shops no longer offer members a discount; in 1999 the stores maintained that their prices were comparable to those in the Washington area.

Free Parking

Each representative gets a free Capitol Hill garage space for personal use, plus five additional spaces and two outside parking permits for staff use. Each senator receives a limited number of parking spaces for personal use and for senior staff, plus a limited number of outside permits for staff, determined by the population of the senator's state. By 1998 parking rates around Capitol Hill were valued at up to $290 a month. Free parking for an unlimited time period is provided for members at Washington-area airports (Ronald Reagan Washington National, Dulles International, and Baltimore-Washington International).

Grooming

The House and Senate provide three barber and beauty shops in the Capitol and office buildings that give haircuts to members and staff. Although charges for haircuts formerly were at reduced rates, all of these facilities in 1999 maintained their prices were comparable to those in the Washington area.

Office Decorations

The U.S. Botanic Garden will loan to senators' offices six potted plants per year. Representatives received potted plants until the early 1990s, when the House voted to take away the privilege. Members used to be able to request cut flowers as well.

Depending on availability, members may decorate their offices upon request with free wall maps and charts, scenic photographs, and reproductions of paintings and prints, all of which may be framed and installed at no cost to members but remain government property. There are quotas on paintings and certain maps.

Ticket Offices

Two ticket offices run by the airlines in the Longworth (House) and Russell (Senate) Office Buildings and an Amtrak railroad ticket office in the Capitol make reservations and issue

One the many perquisites of members of Congress are designated parking areas at Washington, D.C., area airports.

tickets for members. Special rates for rail travel are available for members and staff traveling on official government business. Congress provides these offices with operating space, utilities, and janitorial services.

Photographs

Both the House and Senate provide official photographic services for members at public expense. Members may have photographs taken with constituents and at official functions or ceremonial events for news and publicity use. The Senate and House have separate staff darkrooms. There are no longer separate studios for the Democrats and Republicans.

Senators purchase photographic services through their expense accounts or excess campaign funds. The money is put into a photographic/recording studio revolving fund and is used to purchase photographic supplies. House funds are used to purchase cameras, film, and supplies.

Recording Studios

Both the House and Senate have extensive radio and television recording facilities that are available to all members. In theory the recording studios are designed to help members communicate with their constituents. Radio or television tapes recorded at the studios can be mailed to local stations for use in local news or public affairs programming.

The studios produce radio programs and videotape programs for television, usually within twenty-four hours. The studios also are equipped with speaker-phone service for two-way interviews with local radio or TV stations. In all cases, members must design their own programs and write their own scripts, but the studios provide such services as teleprompters and set makeup. Members must make appointments for filming and taping; appointments may be made on a standing basis. Tapes

EXPANDING COST OF RUNNING CONGRESS

The cost of running the U.S. Congress in the nearly forty years after 1960 expanded far faster than the general cost of living as measured by the consumer price index. The comparison below shows actual fiscal 1960 legislative appropriations and, in the middle column, the 1960 funds converted to 1999 dollars to account for inflation. The right column is the actual fiscal 1999 appropriations for the legislative branch. The nearly fourfold increase over a straight line increase that would have paralleled the cost of living is explained by the expanding activities and staff in Congress. Notable events during the thirty-nine years were the 1970 Legislative Reorganization Act, which among other things, laid the groundwork for more staff and increasing numbers of subcommittees, and passage of the 1974 Congressional Budget and Impoundment Control Act, which created the House and Senate Budget Committees and the Congressional Budget Office.

	Legislative Funds		
	Actual 1960	1960 in 1999 dollars	Actual 1999
Senate	$28,218,205	$159,299,394	$474,891,000
House of Representatives	46,732,200	263,815,899	740,481,000
Joint Items[a]	—	204,916,000	
Architect of the Capitol	13,552,200	76,505,832	303,418,000
Botanic Garden	328,000	1,851,649	3,052,000
Library of Congress	14,329,000	80,891,078	363,640,000
Government Printing Office	15,020,000	84,791,960	103,729,000
General Accounting Office	—	359,268,000	
Congressional Budget Office	—	25,671,000	
Office of Compliance	—	2,086,000	
Total	$118,179,605	$667,155,812	$2,581,152,000

a. There was no joint items account in 1960. Some legislative activities funded under joint items in 1999 were funded under Senate and Houses appropriations accounts in 1960.

and films are produced at cost, and representatives and senators may use their expense allowances to purchase audio and videotapes.

Other Benefits

Miscellaneous services and perquisites available to members include:

• Special congressional license tags provided by the city permit unrestricted parking by members on official business anywhere in Washington.

• American flags flown over the Capitol and certified by the Architect of the Capitol may be purchased with a member's al-

lowance and presented as gifts. (See box, Raising the Flag, p. 740.)

Discontinued: Tax Preparation

Until 1997, the Internal Revenue Service maintained temporary offices in both the House and Senate between January and April each year to help members and staff prepare their income tax returns. Public criticism of the special services these offices provided for members and staff resulted in demands that the IRS close these facilities.

Patronage: Waning Advantage of Office

Once one of the major advantages of holding public office, political patronage, especially that dispensed by members of Congress, has declined to virtually nothing. Unlike many of the other vanishing perks, the loss of patronage has not been particularly lamented; many legislators regarded it as a nuisance.

Senators and representatives once pulled the political strings on thousands of federal jobs. On Capitol Hill and back home, a powerful member could place scores of people in such jobs as local postmaster, health inspector, tax collector, welfare commissioner, and even custodian of public morals. The congressional patronage empire thus provided members with a long list of jobs with which to pay off political supporters.

Today on Capitol Hill the only jobs remaining under patronage are those that do not require specialized skills or technical knowledge, such as elevator operators and doorkeepers. All in all, a member now finds the available patronage jobs of little help in strengthening his political position or rewarding his campaign supporters back home.

GROWTH AND DECLINE

The practice of considering political loyalty when filling jobs began with President George Washington, but Andrew Jackson was the first president to openly back political patronage. Convinced that political loyalty was of paramount importance, he made a clean sweep of the government and filled vacancies with his men at all levels. But when Jackson spoke out in favor of patronage, the number of government jobs requiring technical skills was not large. The few persons given menial jobs through patronage appointments seemed to do little damage to the general efficiency of the government.

As the business of government expanded and grew more complex, the inadequacies of a system that put a premium on loyalty rather than ability became glaringly apparent. Criticism of patronage increased sharply after the assassination of President James A. Garfield by a disappointed job seeker in 1881. In response, Congress enacted the first major civil service reform in America. The 1883 Pendleton Act set up a three-member bipartisan board, the Civil Service Commission, and gave it authority to certify applicants for federal employment after they took competitive examinations.

The 1883 act covered only about 10 percent of federal employees in the executive branch, but its key provision gave the president power to expand the civil service classifications by executive order. A series of such orders, and additional legislation in the years that followed, removed from politics nearly all non-policy-making jobs in the federal government.

The last blow to the patronage system was dealt in 1969, when the Nixon administration decided to remove 63,000 postmaster and rural carrier appointments from politics. Instead, special boards were set up to select candidates for these positions. The Postal Reorganization Act of 1970, which established the U.S. Postal Service, put an end to patronage in the post office.

While the value of patronage to members declined, Congress retained an influential voice in presidential appointments to high-level government positions. Jobs filled by the administration in that category today include cabinet and subcabinet positions, positions on the federal judiciary, major diplomatic and military posts, and top positions on independent boards and regulatory agencies, as well as some lesser positions exempt from the civil service.

Most of those appointments require Senate confirmation, although the administration is not required to consult with Congress before submitting its selections. The degree of influence a member has over those nominations generally depends on his personal relationship with the president and his power on Capitol Hill.

The tradition of "senatorial courtesy" still plays a role in some nominations. *(See Chapter 7, Confirmation Power, Vol. I.)*

Until recently, most congressional employees could be hired and fired at the whim of the members who employed them.

They did not enjoy the elaborate job security provided by civil service regulations covering job qualifications, equitable application procedures, minimum starting salaries, and the specific pay raise and promotion policies of the executive branch and the private sector. But in 1995 Congress enacted the Congressional Accountability Act, which applied eleven federal labor and antidiscrimination laws to all congressional employees. *(See box, Congress and Workplace Compliance, p. 602, Vol. I.)*

ALLOCATING PATRONAGE JOBS

A patronage committee was first established by a caucus of Democratic representatives in 1911. When the Republicans gained control of the House in 1918, they set up their own patronage committee with rules that generally followed the Democrats' practices. The Republicans disbanded their committee in the early 1980s; the Democrats later abolished their patronage committee.

In the Senate, patronage allocation is handled through the office of the secretary of the majority party, which gives the sergeant at arms a list of those senators entitled to patronage slots. Seniority is the general criterion used for distributing patronage. The minority is entitled to fill one-third of the patronage positions; these are allocated through the office of the minority party secretary.

Patronage is more difficult to track in the House. The number of patronage positions was public knowledge until 1992, when there were roughly six hundred patronage jobs. Reductions in these positions came that year in the wake of scandals involving the House bank and post office. The House voted to bring its nonlegislative functions under the control of a professional, nonpartisan House administrator and to prohibit patronage controlled by the new position. The new director of nonlegislative and financial services was given responsibility for member and staff payrolls, the computer system, internal mail, office furnishings and supplies, restaurants, telecommunications, barber and beauty shops, the child care center, the photography office, tour guides, and the nonlegislative functions of the House printing services, recording studio, and records office. The House specified that its new administrator was to "hire and fire his or her staff on the basis of competency and qualifications, not patronage."

The first person to fill the position was retired army lieutenant general Leonard P. Wishart III. When he assumed the position in fall 1992, less than half of the patronage jobs had been transferred to his control. Wishart abruptly resigned in 1994 after he was blocked from taking control of certain operations that the House had voted to give him. When Republicans won control of the House in 1995, they eliminated the post and created a new position called chief administrative officer (CAO), whose goal was to professionalize the administrative functions of the House.[13] As of 1998 the CAO had not made public the number of patronage positions remaining in the House.

Still, the sergeant at arms is responsible for overseeing the largest number of patronage jobs in the House. The sergeant at arms supervises the officers of the press galleries, the doormen for the visitors' gallery and for the House chamber, the custodians, barbers, pages, and employees of the House document room, and employees of the folding room, which distributes newsletters, speeches, and other materials for representatives.

The sergeant at arms of the Senate supervises most of the patronage appointments in the Senate, including the Senate pages, doormen, elevator operators, custodians, officers of the Senate press galleries, and employees of the Senate post office.

Patronage in the Capitol Police force was sharply reduced in the early 1970s. In 1971 patronage appointments constituted 25 percent of the total force. As of the mid-1980s, members were no longer allowed to make patronage appointments to the Capitol Police force; all applicants had to meet certain professional standards in order to be hired. *(See box, U.S. Capitol Police, p. 744.)*

Although they are not technically patronage employees, there is a small group of Capitol Hill officials whose jobs depend on the influence of sponsors or on the party in control and the favor of the party leadership. The House and Senate sergeants at arms, the secretary of the Senate, and the clerk of the House work for all members of their respective houses, but they are elected by the members on strict party-line votes.

THE YOUNGEST PATRONAGE APPOINTEES: CAPITOL PAGES

Senate pages pose during the 1910s on the Capitol steps with Vice President Thomas R. Marshall, who entertained them at Christmas dinner. Records show that boys worked as pages as early as 1827. The first female page was appointed in 1970.

The youngest patronage employees on Capitol Hill are the House and Senate pages, who serve as messengers and perform other errands for members of Congress. Pages must be juniors in high school and at least sixteen years of age; they serve for one or two semester, or a summer session. They attend school early in the morning and then go to work in the Capitol, where until early evening, or later if there is a night session, they answer phones, run errands, deliver messages, or distribute information. A House description of the page program, noting the extensive walking required on the job, said, "We cannot stress enough that pages bring well broken-in, comfortable shoes."

Although demands on a page's time are high, hundreds of young men and women vie for the positions each year. Those nominated by more senior legislators have the best chance of being selected to fill the approximately seventy-two page positions in the House and thirty in the Senate. The opportunity to observe Congress is unsur-passed, and the pay is good for people so young. In 1999 House pages earn $14,138 a year, and Senate pages earn $12,988. House pages are housed on two floors of a congressional office building. In mid-1999 Congress approved $3.8 million for a new dormitory for House pages. Senate pages are housed in the Daniel Webster Page Residence near the Senate.

HISTORY OF PAGES

Working as a page has not always been so lucrative. The House and Senate have always used messengers, usually men, but began to use boys to fill these positions in 1827, when three youngsters were employed as "runners," or pages, in the House. Many of the runners were orphans or children of poor families, whose plight had come to the attention of a representative. There apparently was no law authorizing the use of young boys for these patronage jobs, yet hundreds

APPOINTMENTS TO MILITARY ACADEMIES

One remnant of the patronage system continues to flourish. Congressional appointees to the three major service academies account for about three-fourths of these academies' combined enrollment. Although occasional efforts have been made to remove all academy appointments from the patronage system, members of Congress have been reluctant to let the last sizable group in the congressional patronage system slip away from them.

Until 1902 the privilege of appointing candidates for admission to the academies was enjoyed only by representatives, the idea being to apportion academy enrollment on the basis of national population. Each congressional district was to supply one appointee every four years, thus giving each class maximum geographic variance and assuring equal distribution of appointments throughout the nation.

Eventually senators and representatives alike were authorized to have as many as five appointees enrolled at each academy at

were appointed over the years as a matter of practice. Members often paid the boys a bonus if they performed their duties well, but this practice was discontinued in 1843 after a special review of financial allocations in the House.

The Senate's first page was nine-year-old Grafton Hanson, who was appointed under the august sponsorship of Senators Daniel Webster and Henry Clay. Hanson served his sponsors for ten years and later became Senate postmaster. Although messengers were recognized as pages in the House in 1827, and in the Senate in 1829, the name "pages" appeared for the first time in the *Congressional Globe*, predecessor of the *Congressional Record*, in the 26th Congress (1839–1841). At about that time, a page was paid $1.50 a day.

A dress code was established for pages during the era when knickers were in vogue for boys. Until 1963, the Supreme Court, which had a small corps of pages until 1975, required its pages to wear knickers, long black stockings, and double-breasted jackets. Even more remarkable, until 1950, court pages could be no taller than five feet, four inches—the height of the backs of the justices' chairs.

Today, House pages wear dark blue jackets and dark gray slacks (girls wear dark gray skirts), navy blue ties, black shoes and socks, and long-sleeved white shirts. They must wear their jackets at all times. Senate pages wear navy blue suits and ties; the code is the same for both males and females. The Senate does not require its pages to wear jackets in the summer months.

Until 1971 all pages were boys. In December 1970 Sen. Jacob K. Javits, R-N.Y., appointed the first girl page, but she was not allowed to serve until May 1971, after the Senate passed a resolution permitting the appointment of female pages in the Senate. Earlier Javits broke another long-standing tradition, appointing in 1965 the first black page in congressional history.

PAGE DUTIES

Pages are under the direction of the House Clerk (who is supervised by the House Page Board, or the Senate sergeant at arms. Pages assigned to the House and Senate floors distribute pertinent documents to each legislator's seat in preparation for the day's business. When the House is called to order, the pages retire to a bench in the rear of the chamber to await a representative's call. A button next to a member's seat triggers a light on a board in the rear of the chamber signaling that a page is wanted. Senate pages sit on the rostrum at the front of the chamber and are called to run errands by the snapping of

a senator's fingers or the wave of a hand. Other pages in both chambers may answer phones in the minority or majority cloakroom, deliver messages, and distribute documents.

Pages are also required to attend school. Not until the Legislative Reorganization Act of 1946 became law were pages provided with any kind of uniform schooling. They had to rely on private tutors if they wanted to continue their education while working on Capitol Hill. With passage of the 1946 act, however, Congress set up the Capitol Page School in the Library of Congress, which was a public school operated by the District of Columbia with money appropriated for the purpose. Presently, House pages attend the House Page School in the Library; Senate pages attend the Senate Page School in their residence hall.

SCANDALS IN THE EARLY 1980S

Two related scandals in the early 1980s led to several changes in the page program. In news reports in 1982, two unidentified pages told of sexual misconduct on the part of House members involving pages. Later, after a House investigation, the two recanted their stories. Joseph A. Califano Jr., a former cabinet secretary who headed the investigation, said most of "the allegations and rumors of misconduct were the product of teenage exaggeration, gossip, or even out-and-out fabrication that was often repeated mercilessly in a political capital that thrives on rumor."

In 1983, however, the House censured two of its members after the House Committee on Standards of Official Conduct reported that they had sexual relations with pages. Daniel B. Crane, an Illinois Republican with a wife and six children, admitted that he had had an affair in 1980 with a seventeen-year-old female page. Gerry E. Studds, a Massachusetts Democrat, was found to have had a homosexual relationship in 1973 with a seventeen-year-old male page. *(See "Studds, Crane," p. 937.)*

As a result of these scandals, Congress agreed that only juniors in high school should serve as pages. Previously, pages had ranged in age from fourteen to eighteen, which, among other things, made it difficult to provide an appropriate school curriculum.

Congress also set up the Page Residence Hall in early 1983 and set curfews. Before then pages were required to find their own housing and provide their own meals.

Some members still argued that the page system should be abolished and the pages' duties taken over by adults.

---

one time. In 1998–1999 the total enrollment at the U.S. Military Academy at West Point, New York, was set by law at 4,000. Of that number, about 75 percent were congressional appointees. The number of cadets at the U.S. Naval Academy at Annapolis, Maryland, was 4,021 in 1998–1999, approximately 80 percent of whom were appointed by Congress. About 80 percent of the 4,066 cadets enrolled at the U.S. Air Force Academy at Colorado Springs, Colorado, in 1998–1999 were congressional appointees.

No candidate for appointment to the academies may be old-

er than twenty-one. He or she must be "of good moral character," a U.S. citizen, and unmarried with no dependents. Candidates must also pass a medical examination and physical and scholastic aptitude tests. Within those minimum standards, members of Congress have great leeway in making their appointments. Most senators and many representatives do not personally handle the screening of applicants, but leave the job to an assistant in the state or district office.

Legislators may also nominate as many as ten candidates for

appointment to the Merchant Marine Academy in Kings Point, New York. The candidates must take a nationally competitive examination to win appointment. No nominee on the member's list is guaranteed appointment; instead, the highest-scoring candidates are appointed to the freshman class, regardless of who nominated them. Members of Congress play no role in the selection of candidates to the U.S. Coast Guard Academy at New London, Connecticut.

NOTES

1. John Pontius, "Official Congressional Mail Costs," Congressional Research Service, March 19, 1997, 3.

2. *Congressional Quarterly Almanac 1990* (Washington, D.C.: Congressional Quarterly, 1991), 76.

3. Paul Dwyer, "Salaries and Allowances: The Congress," Congressional Research Service, June 27, 1997, 4.

4. William L. Safire, *The New Language of Politics: A Dictionary of Catchwords, Slogans, and Political Usage,* rev. ed. (New York: Collier, 1972), 196.

5. Richard Whittle, "Maligned and Controversial, Congressional Travel May Decline in Popularity," *Congressional Quarterly Weekly Report,* August 22, 1981, 1543.

6. Donna Cassata, "Corporations Pick Up the Tab for Globe-Hopping Members," *Congressional Quarterly Weekly Report,* December 6, 1997, 3032.

7. Roger H. Davidson and Walter J. Oleszek, *Congress and Its Members,* 7th ed. (Washington, D.C.: CQ Press, 2000), 340.

8. Juliana Gruenwald, "'Tis the Season for Mixing Business with Pleasure," *Congressional Quarterly Weekly Report,* January 10, 1998, 87.

9. Cassata, "Corporations Pick Up the Tab," 3032.

10. Ibid.

11. *Congress and the Nation,* Vol. IV (Washington, D.C.: Congressional Quarterly, 1977), 780.

12. Dwyer, "Salaries and Allowances," 6.

13. *Congressional Quarterly Almanac 1992* (Washington, D.C.: Congressional Quarterly, 1993).

SELECTED BIBLIOGRAPHY

Amer, Mildred L. *Selected Courtesies and Privileges Extended to Former Members of the House of Representatives.* Washington, D.C.: Congressional Research Service, 1990.

Congressional Quarterly. *Congressional Pay and Perquisites: History, Facts, and Controversy.* Washington, D.C.: Congressional Quarterly, 1992.

Davidson, Roger H., and Walter J. Oleszek. *Congress and Its Members.* 7th ed. Washington, D.C.: CQ Press, 2000.

Dodd, Lawrence C., and Bruce I. Oppenheimer. *Congress Reconsidered.* 6th ed. Washington, D.C.: CQ Press, 1997.

Fenno, Richard F., Jr., *Home Style: House Members in Their Districts.* Boston: Little, Brown, 1978.

Fiorina, Morris P. *Congress: Keystone of the Washington Establishment.* 2nd ed. New Haven, Conn.: Yale University Press, 1989.

Henry, H. Lon. *Congress: America's Privileged Class.* Rocklin, Calif.: Prima Publishing, 1994.

Jones, Charles O. *The United States Congress: People, Place, and Policy.* Chicago: Dorsey, 1982.

Ornstein, Norman J., Thomas E. Mann, and Michael J. Malbin. *Vital Statistics on Congress 1997–1998.* Washington, D.C.: Congressional Quarterly, 1998.

Parker, Glenn R. *Characteristics of Congress: Politics and Congressional Behavior.* Englewood Cliffs, N.J.: Prentice-Hall, 1989.

Congress and the Electorate

CHAPTER 29

Who Elects Congress

F EW ELEMENTS of the American political system have changed so markedly over the years as has the electorate. Since the early days of the nation, when the voting privilege was limited to the upper economic classes, one voting barrier after another has fallen to pressures for wider suffrage. First, men who did not own property, then women, then African Americans, and finally young people obtained the franchise. By the early 1970s virtually every adult citizen eighteen and older had won the right to vote.

But by the end of the 1990s only about half of those eligible to vote were exercising that right in high-profile presidential elections and barely one-third of those eligible were bothering to vote in midterm congressional elections. The comparatively low turnout led some observers to speculate that people stayed away from the polls because they were disillusioned with the political process. Others said concern about low turnout was overblown.

Broadening the Franchise

During the nation's first decades, all thirteen of the original states restricted voting to adult male property holders and taxpayers. The framers of the Constitution apparently were content to continue this time-honored practice. The Constitutional Convention adopted without dissent the recommendation of its Committee of Detail that qualifications for the electors of the House of Representatives "shall be the same . . . as those of the electors in the several states of the most numerous branch of their own legislatures."[1]

Under this provision fewer than half of the adult white men in the United States were eligible to vote in federal elections. With women and indentured servants disqualified, fewer than one of every four white adults could cast a ballot. Slaves also were ineligible to vote, although freed slaves could vote in some states if they met whatever other qualifications the state placed on its voters.

Those practices actually represented a liberalization of restrictions on voting that had prevailed at one time in the colonial period. Roman Catholics had been disenfranchised in almost every colony; Jews in most colonies; Quakers and Baptists in some. Not until 1842 did Rhode Island permit Jews to vote.

For half a century before the Civil War, the electorate was steadily broadened. The new western settlements supplied a stimulus for allowing all men to vote, and Jacksonian democracy encouraged its acceptance. Gradually, seven states that had limited voting strictly to men who owned property substituted a taxpaying qualification, and by the middle of the century most states had removed even that requirement.

The Fourteenth Amendment, ratified in 1868, made everyone born or naturalized in the United States a citizen and directed Congress to reduce the number of representatives from any state that disenfranchised adult male citizens for any reason other than commission of a crime. Although no such reduction was ever made, that amendment—together with the Fifteenth Amendment, which said that the right to vote could not be denied on the basis of "race, color, or previous condition of servitude"—legally opened the polling booths to black men.

Former slaves did vote in the years immediately following the Civil War, but by the turn of the century, most southern states had in place laws and election practices that effectively barred blacks from voting. Not until passage of the Voting Rights Act of 1965 would the promise held out by the Fifteenth Amendment begin to be fulfilled.

Women fought for nearly ninety years to win their right to vote; success came with ratification of the Nineteenth Amendment in 1920. Residents of the District of Columbia were given the right to vote in presidential elections with ratification of the Twenty-third Amendment in 1961. And in 1970 Congress authorized residents of the nation's capital to elect a nonvoting delegate to the House of Representatives.

In 1971 the Twenty-sixth Amendment lowered the voting age to eighteen for federal, state, and local elections. A Supreme Court ruling in 1972 effectively required states to reduce the time citizens had to live there to be eligible to vote; no state now requires more than a thirty-day residency. By the beginning of the 1990s, only insanity, a felony conviction, or failure to meet a residency requirement barred voting-age citizens from going to the polls.

TURNOUT TRENDS

Most significant liberalizations of election law have resulted in a sharp increase in voting. From 1824 to 1856, a period of gradual relaxation in the states' property and taxpaying qualifications for voting, voter participation in presidential elections increased from 3.8 percent to 16.7 percent of the population. In 1920, when the Nineteenth Amendment gave women the franchise, it rose to 25.1 percent.

Between 1932 and 1976 both the voting-age population and the number of voters in presidential elections roughly doubled. Except for the 1948 presidential election, when barely half the

Figure 29-1   Voter Turnout, 1789–1998

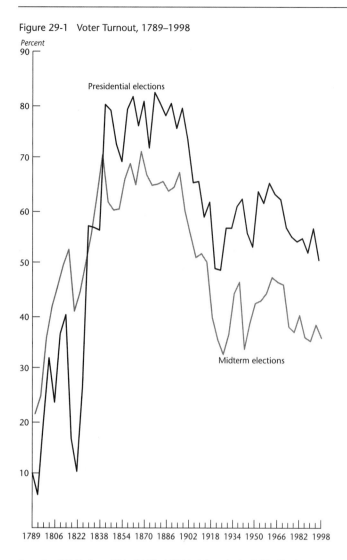

Source: Harold W. Stanley and Richard G. Niemi, *Vital Statistics on American Politics,* 7th ed. (Washington, D.C.: Congressional Quarterly, 1999).

people of voting age went to the polls, the turnout in the postwar years through 1968 was approximately 60 percent, according to Census Bureau surveys. This relatively high figure was attributed to a high sense of civic duty that permeated American society in the immediate postwar years, a population more rooted than it was to be later in the century, and to new civil rights laws encouraging blacks to vote.

Despite larger numbers of people voting, the rate of voter participation slumped after 1968. In that year's presidential election, 61 percent of the voting-age population went to the polls. Through successive stages, that mark fell below 50 percent in the 1996 election, the lowest level of voter turnout since 1924. Voting in the midterm elections, always lower than in presidential years, also declined.

The famous postwar baby boom, together with a lower voting age, had produced by the early 1970s a disproportionate number of young voters—voters who are the least likely to vote. In the 1972 presidential election, the first in which eighteen-year-olds could vote nationwide, some 11 million young voters

entered the electorate. But the actual number of voting participants was only 4.4 million greater than in 1968, resulting in a five-point drop in the ratio of eligible to actual voters. (*See Chapter 30, Political Parties and Elections.*)

Voting participation continued to decrease throughout the rest of the century even as the baby boomers grew older. There were a few upticks in turnout in both the 1980s and 1990s, most notably in the election of 1992—when the excitement of the nation's first baby-boom ticket (Democrats Bill Clinton and Al Gore), a well-financed independent candidate (H. Ross Perot), and the widespread perception of recession pushed the turnout above 100 million for the first and only time in the nation's history. By the late 1990s, however, turnout was again on the wane, with the presidential election of 1996 and the midterm congressional contests of 1998 posting the lowest turnout rates for elections of their type since the end of World War II.

Many reasons for the declining turnouts have been offered. Mark Mellman, a Democratic campaign consultant, has been among those who said they have detected public cynicism about the political process. "There's a sense that the political system is out of their control on one hand and not responsive on the other," Mellman has said. Campaigns that once thrived at the grassroots level—with storefront political headquarters manned by volunteers and stocked with buttons and stickers—were being waged through the more impersonal medium of television.

But another school of thought has contended that low turnout might be overrated as an indicator of voter apathy and cynicism. As expressed by Richard Scammon, former director of the U.S. Bureau of the Census: "Peace and prosperity can generally operate to keep the vote down. . . . In a sense, a low voter turnout is consent. A pool of disinterest may be valuable for a democracy."[2]

One question frequently asked is whether the results would be different if everyone voted. In a paper that they wrote in 1998, two University of California political scientists, Benjamin Highton and Raymond E. Wolfinger, answered: probably not. "The two most common demographic features of nonvoters are their residential mobility and youth, two characteristics that do not suggest political distinctiveness," they wrote. "To be sure, the poor, less educated, and minorities are overrepresented among nonvoters. But the young and the transient are even more numerous. . . . What our findings have demonstrated is that the 'party of nonvoters' is truly heterogeneous. Taken as a whole, nonvoters appear well represented by those who vote."[3]

Nonetheless, studies by the Census Bureau have shown marked differences in participation among various classes of voters. Older voters tend to vote at a higher rate than younger voters. Well-educated voters tend to vote at a higher rate than those less educated. Whites tend to vote at a higher rate than blacks and Hispanics. (*See Table 29-1, page 809.*)

GROWTH OF INDEPENDENTS

Although more people identify themselves as Democrats than Republicans, there has been a steady rise over the last half

TABLE 29-1 The Nation's Voters, 1980–1996
(Percentages of voting-age Americans who said they had voted)

	Presidential election years					Congressional election years			
	1980	1984	1988	1992	1996	1982	1986	1990	1994
Race/ethnicity									
White	61	61	59	64	56	50	47	47	47
Black	51	56	52	54	51	43	43	39	37
Hispanic	30	33	29	29	27	25	24	21	20
Gender									
Male	59	59	56	60	53	49	46	45	45
Female	59	61	58	58	56	48	46	45	45
Region									
Northeast	59	60	57	61	55	50	44	45	46
Midwest	66	66	63	67	59	55	50	49	49
South	56	57	55	59	52	42	43	42	41
West	57	59	56	59	52	51	48	45	47
Age									
18–20	36	37	33	39	31	20	19	18	17
21–24	43	44	38	46	33	28	24	22	22
25–44	59	58	54	58	49	45	41	41	39
45–64	69	70	68	70	64	62	59	56	57
65 and older	65	68	69	70	67	60	61	60	61
Employment									
Employed	62	62	58	64	55	50	46	45	46
Unemployed	41	44	39	46	37	34	31	28	29
Not in labor force	57	59	57	59	54	49	48	47	46
Education									
8 years or less	43	43	37	35	30	36	33	28	24
1–3 years high school	46	44	41	41	34	38	34	31	27
4 years high school	59	59	55	58	49	47	44	42	41
1–3 years college	67	68	65	69	61	53	50	50	50
4 or more years college	80	79	78	81	73	67	63	63	64
Total	59	60	57	61	54	49	46	45	45

SOURCE: U.S. Bureau of the Census, Current Population Reports on voting and registration in general elections, 1980–1996.

century in voters who do not identify with either party. A Gallup poll released in April 1999 found that 34 percent of the American voters considered themselves Democrats, 28 percent Republicans, and 38 percent independents, with polls showing the independent strain strongest among white, young, northern, and rural voters.

Yet when it comes to the act of voter registration, most voters still sign up with one of the two major parties; at least that is the case in the twenty-seven states (and the District of Columbia) where there is such a choice to be made. According to a compilation by the political newsletter *Ballot Access News* in late 1998, Democrats had the registration advantage in thirteen states plus the District of Columbia (a total that included the four most populous states where voters can register by party—California, Florida, New York, and Pennsylvania). Republicans led in eight states (with the exception of New Hampshire, all in the Plains or Rocky Mountain region), and independents had the edge in six states, four of them in the Northeast (Connecticut, Maine, Massachusetts, and New Jersey).

The number of registered voters nationwide at any given time is impossible to calculate. States have different registration deadlines; people who move may be registered in more than one state at the same time, or temporarily may not be recorded in any state; and some states do not require preregistration before voting, while others do not require towns and municipalities to keep registration records.

The Black Vote: A Long, Painful Struggle

In no period of American history were all black people excluded from the polls. At the time of the Constitutional Convention, free blacks had the right of suffrage in all the original states except Georgia, South Carolina, and Virginia. Their right to vote stemmed from the fact that the first black people were brought to America not as slaves but as indentured servants, who could expect freedom after a fixed number of years' service to a master. By 1800, however, the majority of black people were held in slavery. As it grew, so did disenfranchisement. At the outbreak of the Civil War, black Americans were disfranchised,

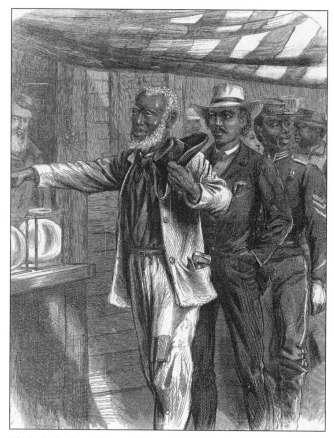

Blacks, including a Union soldier, are depicted casting their first ballots in an image published November 16, 1867. In fact, it would take another hundred years to secure voting rights for African Americans.

solely on the basis of their race, in all except six of the thirty-three states.

President Abraham Lincoln's Emancipation Proclamation of 1863 freed the slaves but did not accord them voting rights. To ease the impact of change on the South, Lincoln preferred to move cautiously in expanding the black electorate. After the Civil War several southern states promptly enacted "Black Codes" barring the newly liberated slaves from voting or holding office. Radical Republicans in Congress responded by passing the Reconstruction Act of 1867, which established provisional military governments in the Southern states. The return of civilian control was conditioned on their ratification of the Fourteenth Amendment, which buttressed individual liberty with "due process" and "equal protection" under the law. The amendment's second section threatened to reduce any state's representation in Congress for denying the vote to any male citizen twenty-one years of age or older.

The Reconstruction Act further stated that a secessionist state could not be readmitted to the Union unless it extended the franchise to all adult males, white and black. Congress followed in February 1869 by submitting the Fifteenth Amendment, prohibiting racial discrimination in voting, to the states. It was ratified twelve months later.

The Radical Republican majority in Congress feared that unless blacks were allowed to vote, Democrats and ex-rebels would quickly regain control of the national government. In the presidential election of 1868, in fact, Gen. Ulysses S. Grant defeated his Democratic opponent, Horatio Seymour, by fewer than 305,000 votes; the new black vote probably decided the election.

Former slaves obtained important positions in the governments formed under the Reconstruction Act of 1867. P. B. S. Pinchback served briefly as acting governor of Louisiana; Mississippi, South Carolina, and Louisiana had black lieutenant governors. Between 1870 and 1900, southern states sent twenty-two black men to Congress—two of them, Hiram R. Revels and Blanche Kelso Bruce, represented Mississippi as senators. Bruce served a full six-year term (1875–1881) and was a presiding officer of the Republican National Convention of 1880.

The white South did not yield gracefully to this turn of events. Gunnar Myrdal noted in his landmark study of black people in America, *An American Dilemma,* that: "The Fourteenth and Fifteenth Amendments were . . . looked upon as the supreme foolishness of the North and, worse still, as an expression of ill-will of the Yankees toward the defeated South. The Negro franchise became the symbol of the humiliation of the South."[4]

AFTER RECONSTRUCTION

Congress in 1870 passed an enforcement act to protect black voting rights in the South, but the Supreme Court in 1876 ruled that Congress had exceeded its authority. In the case of *United States v. Reese,* the Court held that the Fifteenth Amendment did not give anyone the right to vote; it simply guaranteed the right to be free from racial discrimination in exercising that right. The extension of the right to vote itself, the Court said, was up to the states, not the federal government. Therefore, the Court said, Congress had overreached its power to enforce the Fifteenth Amendment when it enacted the 1870 law that penalized state officials who denied blacks the right to vote, or refused to count their votes, or obstructed them from voting.

At the same time, the North clearly was growing weary of the crusade for betterment of the condition of blacks. When the first federal troops were withdrawn in April 1877, the remaining Radical Reconstruction governments in the South quickly disintegrated. Some of the newly enfranchised citizens continued to vote, but by 1900, according to historian Paul Lewinson in his book *Race, Class and Party,* "all factions united in a white man's party once more, to put the Negro finally beyond the pale of political activity."[5]

Mississippi led the way in prohibiting black political activity. A new state constitution drawn up in 1890 required prospective voters to pay a poll tax of two dollars and to demonstrate their ability to read any section of the state constitution or to interpret it when read to them.

Literacy Tests for Voters

In Mississippi and other southern states that adopted voter literacy tests, care was taken not to disfranchise illiterate whites. Five states exempted white voters from literacy and some other requirements by "grandfather clauses"—regulations allowing prospective voters, if not otherwise qualified, to register if they were descended from persons who had voted, or served in the state's military forces, before 1867. Other provisions allowed illiterates to register if they owned a certain amount of property or could show themselves to be of good moral character—requirements easily twisted to exclude only blacks.

At one time or another, twenty-one states imposed literacy requirements as a condition for voting. The first to do so, Connecticut in 1855 and Massachusetts in 1857, sought to disqualify a flood of European immigrants. Between 1890 and 1910, Mississippi, South Carolina, Louisiana, North Carolina, Alabama, Virginia, Georgia, and Oklahoma adopted literacy tests—primarily to restrict the black vote.

Nineteen of the twenty-one states demanded that voters be able to read English, and all but four of them (New York, Washington, Alaska, and Hawaii) required the reading of some legal document or passage from the state or federal Constitution. Either in lieu of or in addition to the reading requirements, fourteen states required an ability to write.

As applied in the South, literacy tests and other voting restrictions virtually disenfranchised black citizens. Outside the South the New York test was by far the most stringent, although there were seldom any complaints that it was applied in a discriminatory way. Despite pressures by civil libertarians, Congress declined for years to void literacy tests on grounds that to do so would violate a state's right to impose its own voting requirements.

Reports of extreme voter discrimination in the South gradually moved Congress to search for remedial legislation. In 1965 it passed a sweeping Voting Rights Act that suspended literacy tests in seven southern states and parts of another. Five years later Congress expanded the law to bar all voter-literacy tests.

Poll-Tax Barrier to Voting

The first poll taxes in America were substitutes for property ownership and were intended to enlarge the voting franchise. But only a few states retained them at the time of the Civil War. They were afterward revived for a far different purpose—to restrict the franchise—in all eleven states of the old Confederacy: Florida (1889), Mississippi and Tennessee (1890), Arkansas (1892), South Carolina (1895), Louisiana (1898), North Carolina (1900), Alabama (1901), Virginia and Texas (1902), and Georgia (1908).

The ostensible purpose was to "cleanse" elections of mass abuses, but the records of constitutional conventions held in five southern states during the period revealed statements praising the poll tax as a measure to bar blacks and poor whites from the polls. Some historians have asserted that the main intent of these measures was to limit the popular base of a so-called agrarian revolt inspired by the Populist Party against the existing political structure.[6]

After the Populist era many states voluntarily dropped use of the poll tax, including six southern states—North Carolina (1920), Louisiana (1934), Florida (1937), Georgia (1945), South Carolina (1951), and Tennessee (1953). Proposals to abolish the poll tax were introduced in every Congress from 1939 to 1962. By 1960 only four states still required its payment by voters. In August 1962, the House approved a constitutional amendment—already accepted by the Senate—that outlawed poll taxes in federal elections, and that amendment, the Twenty-fourth, was ratified in January 1964. In 1966 the Supreme Court held that the poll tax was an unconstitutional requirement for voting in state and local elections as well. "Voter qualifications have no relation to wealth nor to paying or not paying this or any other tax. Wealth, like race, creed, or color, is not germane to one's ability to participate intelligently in the electoral process," Justice William O. Douglas wrote for the majority in *Harper v. Virginia Board of Elections*.

White Primaries

Even more than literacy tests or poll taxes, perhaps the most effective disfranchisement of southern blacks was their exclusion from the Democratic Party's primary elections. In the solidly Democratic South of the post-Reconstruction era, winning the party's nomination virtually assured election. Being excluded from voting in the primary was equivalent to being excluded from voting altogether.

Not until 1941 did the Supreme Court make clear that Congress had the power to regulate primary, as well as general, elections. Indeed, in a 1921 decision involving campaign spending, *Newberry v. United States*, the Court seemed to say that Congress lacked power to regulate primary elections. This doubt about the reach of federal power encouraged the eleven states that had composed the Confederacy to begin systematic exclusion of black voters from the primary. The Democratic Party was often organized on a statewide or county basis as a private club or association that could freely exclude blacks.

The effort of Texas to use the white primary to shut blacks out of the political process came before the Supreme Court in five cases, brought over a span of twenty-five years. In 1923 the Texas Legislature passed a law forbidding blacks to vote in the state Democratic primary. Dr. L. A. Nixon, a black resident of El Paso, challenged the law, arguing that it clearly violated the Fourteenth and Fifteenth Amendments. In the case of *Nixon v. Herndon*, decided in 1927, the Supreme Court agreed with Nixon's Fourteenth Amendment claim.

After the 1927 *Herndon* decision, the Texas Legislature authorized the executive committees of state political parties to establish their own qualifications for voting in the primary. Dr. Nixon again sued, challenging the law as racially discriminatory. Attorneys for the state argued that the Fourteenth Amendment's equal protection clause did not apply because the party, not state officials, set up the allegedly discriminatory standards.

With Justice Benjamin N. Cardozo writing for a five-man majority, the Court held in 1932 that the executive committee of the Democratic Party acted as a delegate of the state in setting voter qualifications and that its action was equivalent to state action and was thus within the scope of the equal protection guarantee, which it violated *(Nixon v. Condon)*.

The Texas Democratic Party responded by acting without state authorization to put itself off-limits to black voters. Confronted with this situation, the Court in 1935 retreated to its *Newberry* reasoning and ruled, in *Grovey v. Townsend*, that in this instance the party had acted not as a creature of the state but as a voluntary association of individuals. As such, its actions—even in controlling access to the vote—were not restricted by the Constitution.

In 1941 the Court switched signals again, discarding the *Newberry* doctrine in the case of *United States v. Classic. Classic* was not a racial discrimination case but instead concerned a man convicted of falsifying election returns. His conviction was based on a federal law that made it a crime "to injure, oppress, threaten, or intimidate any citizen in the free exercise or enjoyment of any right or privilege secured to him by the Constitution." He challenged his conviction, arguing that the right to vote in a primary election was not a right secured by the Constitution.

But the Court upheld the conviction, ruling that the primary was an integral part of the election process. The authority of Congress under Article I, Section 4, to regulate elections included the authority to regulate primary elections, wrote Justice Stone, "when, as in this case, they are a step in the exercise by the people of their choice of representatives in Congress."

Three years later, in 1944, the Court overturned *Grovey* and held the all-white primary unconstitutional. This case, *Smith v. Allwright*, arose out of the refusal of S. S. Allwright, a county election official, to permit Lonnie E. Smith, a black man, to vote in the 1940 Texas Democratic primary. Smith sued, saying Allwright had deprived him of his civil rights. Smith was represented by two attorneys for the National Association for the Advancement of Colored People (NAACP), William H. Hastie and Thurgood Marshall. Both were later made judges, with Marshall becoming the first black member of the Supreme Court.

The relentless effort of Texas Democrats to maintain the white primary at last came to an end in 1953 with another Supreme Court decision. In one Texas county an all-white Democratic organization conducted all-white primary elections under the name of Jaybird Club, a self-declared private club. In *Terry v. Adams* the Court declared this a ploy in violation of the Fifteenth Amendment.

Physical and Psychic Coercion

Throughout this period legal devices to curtail black political activity were buttressed by physical and economic intimidation. As Myrdal wrote: "Physical coercion is not so often practiced against the Negro, but the mere fact that it can be used with impunity . . . creates a psychic coercion that exists nearly everywhere in the South. . . . [I]t is no wonder that the great majority of Negroes in the South make no attempt to vote and—if they make attempts which are rebuffed—seldom demand their full rights under the federal Constitution."[7]

Any who summoned up the courage to try to register encountered various delays and harassment. The scornful question "What do you want here, nigger?" often sufficed to send a black person away. If the applicants persisted, the registrar was likely to ignore them, tell them that there were no more registration forms, or direct them to another place of registration, which, if it existed, was usually closed. Southern registrars also displayed a tendency to lose registration forms filled out by black applicants.

More subtle practices limited black political participation in the North as well. With the exception of Chicago, white-controlled city machines excluded black people from any significant role in politics for the first half of the twentieth century. During that time, Congress did virtually nothing to encourage black voting.

CIVIL RIGHTS LEGISLATION

Not until the 1950s, when the civil rights movement began to gather force, did Congress, at the urging of the executive branch, begin to reassert federal power to ensure the right of black citizens to vote. Its first action was passage of the Civil Rights Act of 1957, which was intended to enforce the voting guarantee set out in the Fifteenth Amendment.

The 1957 act authorized the attorney general to bring lawsuits to halt public and private interference with the right of black people to vote, and expanded federal jurisdiction over such suits. The law also created the Civil Rights Commission to investigate and publicly disclose problems of racial discrimination, including voting problems. The investigatory procedures of the commission and the authorization of the federal lawsuits were upheld by the Supreme Court in 1960, in *United States v. Raines*.

Responding to reports that progress in securing voting rights for blacks still was slow even under the provisions of the 1957 act, Congress in 1960 passed a measure that permitted the U.S. attorney general to sue a state for deprivation of voting rights even if the individuals named initially as defendants—usually voting registrars—had left office. This provision remedied a situation that had arisen in a suit brought by the United States against Alabama voting officials. In addition, Title VI of the 1960 law authorized the appointment of special federal "voting referees" to oversee voter registration in counties where a federal court detected a pattern of voter discrimination.

The Civil Rights Act of 1964 mandated state adoption of standard procedures and requirements for all persons seeking to register to vote. The law also required local officials to justify rejecting an applicant who had completed the sixth grade or had

Voting rights were one of many reforms sought by the civil rights supporters, including Martin Luther King Jr. (front row, second from left), who marched in Washington in August 1963. Prodded by the civil rights movement, Congress began to reassert federal power to ensure the right of black citizens to vote.

equivalent evidence of intellectual competence. Other provisions of the 1964 law expedited the movement of voting rights cases to the Supreme Court.

In two cases brought under the 1964 act, *United States v. Louisiana* and *United States v. Mississippi*, the Supreme Court in 1965 sanctioned the government's efforts to break the pattern of case-by-case litigation of voting rights violations. The Court upheld federal power to challenge a state's entire constitutional legal framework for voter registration and conduct of elections.

The Voting Rights Act

But progress still was slow. In Dallas County, Alabama, three new federal laws and four years of litigation had produced the registration of only 383 black voters out of a potential pool of fifteen thousand. On March 8, 1965, the Rev. Martin Luther King Jr. led a "Walk for Freedom" to dramatize the need for additional efforts in behalf of registering black voters in Selma, the county seat, and elsewhere in the South. The violence of the reaction of local white law enforcement officers and white bystanders to the peaceful demonstration drew nationwide attention to the dimensions of the problem.

A week later, President Lyndon B. Johnson addressed a joint session of Congress to ask for passage of a new voting rights measure to close legal loopholes that enabled local officials to stall black voter registration. Johnson explained that "no law that we now have on the books . . . can ensure the right to vote when local officials are determined to deny it." Later that month, NAACP official Roy Wilkins appeared before a Senate committee on behalf of the Leadership Conference on Civil Rights to urge Congress to "transform this retail litigation method of registration into a wholesale administration procedure registering all who seek to exercise their democratic birthright." Within five months Congress had approved the sweeping Voting Rights Act of 1965.

The law suspended literacy tests and provided for the appointment of federal supervisors of voter registration in all states and counties where literacy tests or similar qualifying devices were in effect on November 1, 1964, and where fewer than 50 percent of the voting-age residents had registered to vote or voted in the 1964 presidential election.

The law established criminal penalties for persons found guilty of interfering with the voting rights of others. State or county governments in areas of low voter registration were required to obtain federal approval of any new voting laws, standards, practices, or procedures before implementing them. A state or county covered by the act could escape from the law's provisions if it could persuade a three-judge federal court in the District of Columbia that no racial discrimination in registration or voting had occurred in the previous five years.

The act placed federal registration machinery in six southern states (Alabama, Georgia, Mississippi, South Carolina, Louisiana, and Virginia), Alaska, twenty-eight counties in North Carolina, three counties in Arizona, and one in Idaho.

Passage of the voting rights act heralded a significant increase in the number of blacks registered to vote. Within four years, almost a million blacks had registered to vote under its provisions. The Civil Rights Commission reported in 1968 that registration of blacks had climbed to more than 50 percent of the black voting-age population in every southern state. Before the act, black registration had exceeded 50 percent in only three: Florida, Tennessee, and Texas. The most dramatic increase occurred in Mississippi, where black registration rose from 6.7 percent to 59.8 percent of the voting-age population.[8]

Voting Law Extended

In renewing the act in 1970 for an additional five years, its supporters turned back the efforts of southern senators to dilute key provisions. State and local governments were forbidden to use literacy tests or other voter-qualifying devices, and the triggering formula was altered to apply to any state or county that used a literacy test for voting and where less than 50 percent of the voting-age residents were registered on November 1, 1968, or had voted in the 1968 general election.

Under the 1970 law, the preclearance requirement applied to those areas affected by the 1965 law and ten more: three Alaska districts; Apache County, Arizona; Imperial County, California; Elmore County, Idaho; the Bronx, Kings (Brooklyn), and New York (Manhattan) counties, New York; and Wheeler County, Oregon.

By the time the act was due for its second extension in 1975, an estimated 2 million black people had been added to the voting rolls in the South, more than doubling the previous total. The number of blacks holding elective office also increased. The Joint Center for Political Studies reported that the number of black elected officials in the seven southern states covered by the Voting Rights act had gone up from fewer than one hundred in 1964 to 963 in just ten years. The total included one member of the House of Representatives, thirty-six state legislators, and 927 county and municipal officials.

The Voting Rights Act was renewed for seven years and substantially expanded in 1975. The triggering formula was amended to bring under coverage of the law any state or county that was using a literacy test in 1972 and where less than 50 percent of the residents eligible to vote had registered as of November 1, 1972. Two additional provisions gave greater protection to certain language minorities, defined as persons of Spanish heritage, Native Americans, Asian Americans, and Alaskan natives.

The federal preclearance provisions were expanded to apply to any jurisdiction where:

• The Census Bureau determined that more than 5 percent of the voting-age citizens were of a single language minority.

• Election materials had been printed only in English for the 1972 presidential election.

• Fewer than 50 percent of the voting-age citizens had registered for or voted in the 1972 presidential election.

These amendments significantly expanded coverage of the act, bringing in all of Alaska, Texas, and Arizona, and selected counties in several other states, including California and Florida. In addition, provisions were added requiring certain parts of the country to provide bilingual voting materials.

Congress approved a third extension of the act on June 23, 1982, two months before the law was due to expire. The 1982 legislation represented a major victory for a coalition of civil rights groups that included black, Hispanic, labor, religious, and civic organizations. Many of them had criticized President Ronald Reagan's administration for its hesitation and reservations about earlier versions and certain features of the measure.

However, the bill received widespread bipartisan support and strong backing from members of both chambers, including southerners. More than twice as many southern Democrats in both the Senate and House voted for passage in 1982 than in 1965 when the law was first approved. The steady upward trend in southern support for the act reflected changing social and political mores, and a great increase in black voting in the South.

The 1982 law had four main elements. First, it extended for twenty-five years provisions that required nine states and portions of thirteen others to obtain Justice Department approval for any changes in their election laws and procedures. Second, starting in 1984, a jurisdiction could be released from the restrictions by showing a clean voting rights record for the previous ten years. Third, it overturned a 1980 Supreme Court ruling that "intent to discriminate" must be shown to prove a violation. Fourth, it extended the bilingual election provisions through 1992.

The requirement for Justice Department approval of election-law changes figured prominently in redistricting being carried out in the affected states on the basis of the 1990 census. While that proved to be a matter of considerable controversy, there is little doubt that the Voting Rights Act has had a positive effect on the numbers of blacks winning elective office. Nationwide in January 1997, according to a compilation by the Joint Center for Political Studies, the number of black elected officials included forty members of Congress; 579 state legislators; 387 mayors and more than 3,700 other municipal officials; more than 800 judges or magistrates; and nearly fifty police chiefs, sheriffs, and local marshals. (These totals were from the fifty states, the District of Columbia, and the Virgin Islands.)

CONSTITUTIONAL PROVISIONS FOR HOUSE AND SENATE ELECTIONS

ARTICLE I, SECTION 2

The House of Representatives shall be composed of Members chosen every second Year by the People of the several States, and the Electors in each State shall have the Qualifications requisite for Electors of the most numerous Branch of the State Legislature.

No Person shall be a Representative who shall not have attained to the age of twenty five Years, and been seven Years a Citizen of the United States, and who shall not, when elected, be an Inhabitant of that State in which he shall be chosen.

Representatives and direct Taxes shall be apportioned among the several States which may be included within this Union, according to their respective Numbers, which shall be determined By adding to the whole Number of free Persons, including those bound to Service for a Term of Years, and excluding Indians not taxed, three fifths of all other Persons. The actual Enumeration shall be made within three Years after the first Meeting of the Congress of the United States, and within every subsequent Term of ten Years, in such Manner as they shall by Law direct. The Number of Representatives shall not exceed one for every thirty Thousand, but each State shall have at Least one Representative; and until such enumeration shall be made, the State of New Hampshire shall be entitled to chuse three, Massachusetts eight, Rhode-Island and Providence Plantations one, Connecticut five, New York six, New Jersey four, Pennsylvania eight, Delaware one, Maryland six, Virginia ten, North Carolina five, South Carolina five, and Georgia three.

When vacancies happen in the Representation from any State, the Executive Authority thereof shall issue Writs of Election to fill such Vacancies.

ARTICLE I, SECTION 3

The Senate of the United States shall be composed of two Senators from each State, chosen by the Legislature thereof, for six years; and each Senator shall have one Vote.

Immediately after they shall be assembled in Consequence of the first Election, they shall be divided as equally as may be into three Classes. The Seats of the Senators of the first Class shall be vacated at the Expiration of the second Year, of the second class at the Expiration of the fourth Year, and of the third class at the Expiration of the sixth Year, so that one third may be chosen every second Year; and if Vacancies happen by Resignation, or otherwise, during the Recess of the Legislature of any State, the Executive thereof may make temporary Appointments until the next Meeting of the Legislature, which shall then fill such Vacancies.

No Person shall be a Senator who shall not have attained to the Age of thirty Years, and been nine Years a Citizen of the United States, and who shall not, when elected, be an Inhabitant of that State for which he shall be chosen.

ARTICLE I, SECTION 4

The Times, Places and Manner of holding Elections for Senators and Representatives, shall be prescribed in each State by the Legislature thereof; but the Congress may at any time by Law make or alter such Regulations, except as to the Places of chusing Senators.

The Congress shall assemble at least once in every Year, and such Meeting shall be on the first Monday in December, unless they shall by Law appoint a different day.

ARTICLE I, SECTION 5

Each House shall be the Judge of the Elections, Returns and Qualifications of its own Members, and a Majority of each shall constitute a Quorum to do Business; but a smaller Number may adjourn from day to day, and may be authorized to compel the Attendance of absent Members in such Manner, and under such Penalties as each House may provide.

AMENDMENT XIV
(RATIFIED JULY 28, 1868)

Section 2. Representatives shall be apportioned among the several States according to their respective numbers, counting the whole number of persons in each State, excluding Indians not taxed. But when the right to vote at any election for the choice of electors for President and Vice President of the United States, Representatives in Congress, the Executive and Judicial officers of a State, or the members of the Legislature thereof, is denied to any of the male inhabitants of such State, being twenty-one years of age, and citizens of the United States, or in any way abridged, except for participation in rebellion, or other crime, the basis of representation therein shall be reduced in the proportion which the number of such male citizens shall bear to the whole number of male citizens twenty-one years of age in such State.

AMENDMENT XVII
(RATIFIED MAY 31, 1913)

The Senate of the United States shall be composed of two Senators from each State, elected by the people thereof, for six years; and each Senator shall have one vote. The electors in each State shall have the qualifications requisite for electors of the most numerous branch of the State legislatures.

When vacancies happen in the representation of any State in the Senate, the executive authority of such State shall issue writs of election to fill such vacancies: *Provided,* That the legislature of any State may empower the executive thereof to make temporary appointments until the people fill the vacancies by election as the legislature may direct.

This amendment shall not be so construed as to affect the election or term of any Senator chosen before it becomes valid as part of the Constitution.

AMENDMENT XX
(RATIFIED JANUARY 23, 1933)

Section 1. The terms of the President and Vice President shall end at noon on the 20th day of January, and the terms of Senators and Representatives at noon on the 3d day of January, of the years in which such terms would have ended if this article had not been ratified; and the terms of their successors shall then begin.

Section 2. The Congress shall assemble at least once in every year, and such meeting shall begin at noon on the 3rd day of January, unless they shall by law appoint a different day.

JUDICIAL SUPPORT

Not surprisingly, the unprecedented assertion of federal power over electoral and voting matters embodied in the Voting Rights Act was immediately challenged as exceeding the constitutional authority of Congress and encroaching on states' rights. But in 1966, in direct contrast to its post–Civil War rulings, the Supreme Court firmly backed the power of Congress to pass such a law. In that case, *South Carolina v. Katzenbach*, the state argued that Congress had exceeded its authority in suspending South Carolina voting standards, permitting the use of federal election examiners, and adopting a "triggering" formula that affected some states but not others. At the Court's invitation, Alabama, Georgia, Louisiana, Mississippi, and Virginia filed briefs in support of South Carolina's challenge. Twenty other states filed briefs in support of the law.

Strong Court Backing

The Supreme Court rejected all constitutional challenges to the act. "Congress," wrote Chief Justice Earl Warren for the decision's 8–1 majority, "has full remedial powers [under the Fifteenth Amendment] to effectuate the constitutional prohibition against racial discrimination in voting." The federal approval requirement for new voting rules in the states covered by the act, Warren observed, "may have been an uncommon exercise of congressional power, as South Carolina contends, but the Court has recognized that exceptional conditions can justify legislative measures not otherwise appropriate."

Also in 1966, in *Katzenbach v. Morgan*, the Court upheld the portion of the Voting Rights Act that permitted persons educated in accredited "American-flag" schools to vote even if they were unable to read and write English. The provision was aimed at enfranchising Puerto Ricans educated in such schools, living in the United States, but unable to demonstrate literacy in English.

Although the basic constitutionality of the Voting Rights Act was now settled, a steady stream of voting rights cases came to the Court in the late 1960s and the 1970s, testing the scope and application of the law. But the Court continued to back and broadly interpret the act. In the 1969 case of *Gaston County v. United States*, for example, the Court refused to let a North Carolina county reinstate a literacy test.

Some Exceptions Allowed

In 1975, however, the Court held in *Richmond v. United States* that a federally approved annexation plan did not violate the Voting Rights Act—even if it reduced the percentage of black voters in the city's population—so long as there were legitimate reasons for the annexation. Despite its willingness to affirm the sweeping provisions of the 1965 law, the Court refused to interpret it as forbidding all use of racial criteria in legislative redistricting or as requiring that blacks be given proportional representation on elected bodies.

In a 1976 decision, *Beer v. United States*, the Court upheld a city's reapportionment of the districts from which city council members were chosen. The change resulted in an increase in the number of black council members, but not in a proportional representation of black voters among the council members. The Court held that the Voting Rights Act was satisfied so long as such changes did not reduce the voting strength of racial minorities.

The next year, in *United Jewish Organizations of Williamsburgh v. Cary*, the Court upheld New York's 1974 redistricting law, which purposely redrew certain districts to give them nonwhite majorities. The county (Kings) affected in the case was one of three in New York that had been brought under the coverage of the Voting Rights Act by the 1970 amendments to that law. The Hasidic Jewish community of the Williamsburgh section of Brooklyn objected that the new boundaries divided their voting strength between two districts. The objectors argued that such use of racial criteria in the redistricting deprived them of equal protection guaranteed by the Fourteenth Amendment and diluted their voting strength in violation of the Fifteenth Amendment.

The Constitution did not prevent all use of racial criteria in districting and apportionment, wrote Justice Byron R. White for the seven-member Supreme Court majority in that case. Nor, he continued, did it "prevent a State subject to the Voting Rights Act from deliberately creating or preserving black majorities in particular districts in order to ensure that its reapportionment plan complies with [the act]. . . ."

"There is no doubt," White continued, that the state, in drawing new district lines, "deliberately used race in a purposeful manner. But its plan represented no racial slur or stigma with respect to whites or any other race, and we discern no discrimination violative of the Fourteenth Amendment nor any abridgment of the right to vote on account of race within the meaning of the Fifteenth Amendment."

In the 1980 case of *Mobile v. Bolden*, the Court for the first time narrowed the reach of the Voting Rights Act. Justice Potter Stewart wrote on behalf of a 6–3 majority that the fact that no black person had ever been elected city commissioner in Mobile, Alabama, under the city's challenged system of at-large elections was not enough to prove the system was in violation of the Voting Rights Act and the Constitution. "The Fifteenth Amendment does not entail the right to have Negro candidates elected," Stewart wrote, but only guaranteed that blacks would be able to "register and vote without hindrance."

Mobile Decision Overturned

The decision set off a reaction in Congress that resulted in specific language being written into the 1982 extension of the Voting Rights Act declaring that a voting practice or law that had the effect of discriminating was in violation of the federal law, whatever the local intent might have been. In 1986 the Court applied the new test to *Thornburg v. Gingles*, ruling that six of North Carolina's multimember legislative districts impermissibly diluted the strength of black votes in the state. The fact that very few black candidates had been elected from those districts was enough to prove that the system was in violation of the law, the Court held.

In 1991 the Supreme Court relied on the 1982 revisions of the Voting Rights Act to rule that the act applied to the election of judges.

Court Decisions in the 1990s

Entering the 1990s, blacks and Hispanics were still underrepresented in Congress. To remedy this situation, the Justice Department sought to use the "preclearance" provision of the Voting Rights Act to encourage states with histories of minority voting rights violations to create so-called majority-minority districts—districts where black or Hispanic populations were in the majority. *(See "Minority Representation," p. 909.)*

With newly drawn majority-minority districts, the 1992 election produced a large increase in the total of black and Hispanic House members. The number of blacks jumped from twenty-six to thirty-nine, the number of Hispanics from eleven to seventeen. But some of the districts were sharply criticized as a form of racial gerrymandering because of their irregular shapes, and the Supreme Court in 1993 demonstrated that these districts would come under tough legal scrutiny.

At issue in 1993 was a district that wound its way in a snake-like fashion through central North Carolina, picking up black neighborhoods in four metropolitan areas. The district, drawn at the urging of the Justice Department, was challenged by a group of white voters who alleged that North Carolina had set up "a racially discriminatory voting process" and deprived them of the right to vote in "a color-blind" election. Their suit was dismissed by a federal district court but reinstated by the Supreme Court in a 5–4 decision, *Shaw v. Reno* (1993).

In her opinion for the Court, Justice Sandra Day O'Connor acknowledged that racial considerations could not be excluded from the redistricting process. But she said that in "some exceptional cases" a plan could be "so highly irregular that, on its face, it rationally cannot be understood as anything other than an effort to segregate voters on the basis of race." To justify such a plan, O'Connor said, the government must show that it is narrowly tailored to serve a compelling government interest.[9]

The *Shaw v. Reno* decision returned the case to a lower court for further hearings. Meanwhile, challenges to racially drawn redistricting plans were proceeding in other states, which the Court used to refine its position on racial redistricting. In 1995 the Court struck down a Georgia plan that had created three black-majority districts, including one that stretched from the Atlanta suburbs across half the state to the coastal city of Savannah. The 5–4 vote in *Miller v. Johnson* was the same as in the North Carolina case, but the Court made clear that challenges were not limited to plans with irregularly shaped districts.

Writing for the majority, Justice Anthony M. Kennedy argued that government should not treat citizens as members of a racial class, and he said that the Georgia map could not be justified on the grounds that it was necessary to comply with the Voting Rights Act because the Justice Department had incorrectly interpreted the law to require the maximum number of majority-black districts be created. Redistricting plans were subject to challenge, Kennedy said, if race was "the predominant factor motivating the legislature's decision to place a significant number of voters within or without a particular district."

The decision was widely criticized. President Bill Clinton called the ruling "a setback in the struggle to ensure that all Americans participate fully in the electoral process." But the criticism did not sway the Court's majority. In 1996 the same five-justice majority in *Shaw v. Hunt* rejected the serpentine North Carolina district that it had scrutinized in 1993, arguing that the state had neglected traditional districting criteria, such as compactness, while overemphasizing the importance of race. The Court in *Bush v. Vera* also found that Texas had improperly used racial considerations in the drawing of three congressional districts. District maps in parts of Florida, Louisiana, New York, and Virginia were also successfully challenged on the basis of race. The Court, however, let stand Illinois' Hispanic majority-minority district after the state argued successfully that it had a "compelling state interest" in it.

Civil rights groups complained that the effect of the rulings would make it more difficult for minorities to be elected to Congress. But their warnings were tempered by the election results. In 1999 there were thirty-seven blacks in the House (down two from 1993) and eighteen Hispanics (up one from 1993).

Women's Vote: A Victory in Stages

The drive for women's suffrage, which began in the late 1830s, was closely related in the beginning to the movement for abolition of slavery. Women, because of their extensive legal disadvantages under the common law, often compared their lot to that of slaves and thus directed the bulk of their political activity against proposals for extending slavery. Women were disfranchised at every level of government. Only in New Jersey did they have a theoretical right to vote. That right had been included inadvertently in the state constitutions of 1776 and 1797, but the state legislature repealed the provision at the outset of the nineteenth century when some women actually attempted to vote.

Early victories for the women's suffrage movement came mostly in connection with school elections. Kentucky in 1838 gave the right to vote in such elections to widows and unmarried women with property that was subject to taxation for school purposes. Kansas in 1861 gave women the vote on all school questions, and by 1880 Michigan, Utah, Minnesota, Colorado, New Hampshire, and Massachusetts had followed suit.

The Woman's Rights Convention at Seneca Falls, New York, in July 1848 is generally cited as the beginning of the women's suffrage movement in the United States. But the Declaration of Principles, which Elizabeth Cady Stanton read at that meeting and which thereafter became a sacred text for the movement, was a much broader and more revolutionary document than a simple claim for the franchise.

STEPS TOWARD THE VOTE

Direct-action tactics first were applied by suffragists shortly after the Civil War, when Susan B. Anthony urged women to go to the polls and claim the right to vote under terms of the newly adopted Fourteenth Amendment. In the national elections of 1872, Anthony voted in her home city of Rochester, New York; she subsequently was tried and convicted of the crime of "voting without having a lawful right to vote." For almost a quarter of a century, Anthony and her followers pressed Congress for a constitutional amendment granting women's suffrage. On January 25, 1887, the Senate finally considered the proposal but rejected it by a 16–34 vote.

The suffrage forces had more success in some western states. As a territory, Wyoming extended full suffrage to women in 1869 and retained it upon becoming a state in 1890. Colorado, Utah, and Idaho granted women voting rights before the turn of the century. But after that the advocates of suffrage for women encountered stronger opposition, and it was not until the height of the Progressive movement that other states, mostly in the West, gave women full voting rights. Washington granted equal suffrage in 1910, California in 1911, Arizona, Kansas, and Oregon in 1912, Montana and Nevada in 1914, and New York in 1917.

Opponents argued that women were the "weaker sex," that their temperament was unsuited to make the kinds of decisions necessary in casting a ballot, and that suffrage might alter the relationship between the sexes. In the two decades preceding women's enfranchisement, extravagant claims were made by extremists on both sides. Radical feminists often insisted that women voters would be able to cleanse American politics of its corruption and usher in some ill-defined, utopian golden age. Antifranchise forces were as far-reaching in their claims. During World War I, Henry A. Wise Wood, president of the Aero Club

of America, told the House Committee on Woman Suffrage that giving women the vote would mean "the dilution with the qualities of the cow of the qualities of the bull upon which all the herd's safety must depend." And the January 1917 issue of *Remonstrance,* an antisuffrage journal, cautioned that women's suffrage would lead to the nationalization of women, free love, and communism.[10]

CONSTITUTIONAL AMENDMENT

On the eve of World War I, the advocates of militant tactics took the lead in a national campaign for women's rights. In the congressional elections of 1914, they set out to defeat all Democratic candidates in the nine states (which had increased to eleven by election day) where women had the right to vote. They held the majority Democrats in Congress responsible for not submitting a constitutional amendment to the states for their approval of women's voting rights. Only twenty of the forty-three challenged candidates were elected. However, this showing of electoral strength did not move President Woodrow Wilson to take up their cause.

President Wilson's opposition to a constitutional amendment prompted a series of stormy demonstrations by the suffragettes around the White House and other sites in Washington after the United States had entered World War I. The demonstrators insisted that it was unconscionable for this country to be denying its own female citizens a right to participate in government while at the same time it was fighting a war on the premise of "making the world safe for democracy."

At the direction of the administration, thousands of the women demonstrators were arrested and brought to trial. Some were beaten by hostile crowds—often made up of soldiers and sailors who viewed the demonstrations as unpatriotic. At their

Supporters of the Nineteenth Amendment—giving women the right to vote—picket the White House in 1916. The Nineteenth Amendment was ratified in 1920.

trials, many of the women stood mute or made speeches advocating suffrage and attacking President Wilson for his refusal to endorse the constitutional amendment.

The jailing of many of these women caused a severe housing problem for District of Columbia penal authorities and created a wave of sympathy for the suffragettes. Public support for their position was heightened by the prisoners' claims that they had been treated inhumanely and had been subjected to unsanitary conditions in prison. To protest these conditions, some of the prisoners went on a hunger strike, and the authorities resorted to forced feeding, an action that aroused even greater public sympathy.

President Wilson capitulated, announcing on January 9, 1918, his support for the proposed suffrage amendment. The House approved it the next day by a 274–136 vote, one vote more than the necessary two-thirds majority. But the Senate fell short of the two-thirds majority in October 1918 and again in February 1919. However, when the Congress elected in November 1918 met for the first time on May 19, 1919, it took little more than two weeks to gain the required majorities in both chambers.

On August 18, 1920, Tennessee became the thirty-sixth state to approve the amendment, enough for ratification. On August 26, Secretary of State Bainbridge Colby signed a proclamation formally adding the Nineteenth Amendment to the Constitution. It stated simply that "The right of citizens of the United States to vote shall not be denied or abridged by the United States or any state on account of sex." *(See "Women's Suffrage," p. 368, Vol. 1.)*

In the 1920 presidential election, the first in which women could vote, it was estimated that only about 30 percent of those who were eligible actually voted. Analyses of the 1924 election indicated that scarcely one-third of all eligible women voted while more than two-thirds of the eligible men had done so. The women's electoral performance came as a bitter blow to the suffragists. In more recent national elections, however, surveys by the Census Bureau have found that voting participation by women is about the same as that of men.

By the end of the twentieth century, women's representation in Congress, though, was well below half. The 106th Congress began in 1999 with sixty-five women members—nine in the Senate and fifty-six in the House—representing 12 percent of the seats in Congress. The United States ranked thirty-ninth among 160 legislatures in female representation, according to the Inter-Parliamentary Union. Sweden ranked first.

The Eighteen-Year-Old Vote

Twenty-one was the minimum voting age in every state until 1943, when Georgia lowered it to eighteen—the age at which young men were being drafted to fight in World War II. The slogan "Old enough to fight, old enough to vote" had a certain logic and public appeal. But no other state followed Georgia's lead until after the war. In 1946 South Carolina Democrats authorized eighteen-year-olds to vote in party primaries, but later

withdrew that privilege. In 1955 Kentucky voters lowered the voting age to eighteen. Alaska and Hawaii, upon entering the Union in 1959, adopted minimum voting ages of nineteen and twenty, respectively.

Meanwhile, in 1954, President Dwight D. Eisenhower had proposed a constitutional amendment granting eighteen-year-olds the right to vote nationwide, but the proposal was rejected by the Senate. Eventually Congress was persuaded—perhaps by the demographics of America's fast-expanding youth population, which during the 1960s had begun to capture the nation's attention; perhaps by the separate hopes of Republicans and Democrats to win new voters; perhaps by the Vietnam War in which the young were called on to fight again. In the Voting Rights Act of 1970, Congress added a provision to lower the voting age to eighteen in all federal, state, and local elections, effective January 1, 1971.

On signing the bill into law, President Richard Nixon restated his belief that the provision was unconstitutional because Congress had no power to extend suffrage by statute, and directed Attorney General John N. Mitchell to ask for a swift court test of the law's validity. The Supreme Court, ruling in *Oregon v. Mitchell* only weeks before the law was due to take effect, sustained its application to federal elections but held it unconstitutional in regard to state and local elections.

After the Court ruled, Congress wasted little time in approving and sending to the states a proposed Twenty-sixth Amendment to the Constitution, stating: "The right of citizens of the United States, who are eighteen years of age or older, to vote shall not be denied or abridged by the United States or any State on account of age. The Congress shall have power to enforce this article by appropriate legislation." The proposal received final congressional approval March 23, 1971, and was ratified by the necessary three-fourths of the states by July 1, record time for a constitutional amendment. *(See "The Vote for Eighteen-Year-Olds," p. 373, Vol. 1.)*

More than 25 million Americans became eligible to vote for the first time in the 1972 presidential election. It was the biggest influx of potential voters since women won the right to vote in 1920. But the younger age group has never fulfilled its potential power at the polls; in election after election, younger voters have had the lowest turnout rate of any age category.

Removing Obstacles to Voting

In the late twentieth century the federal government and the states took steps to increase participation in the electoral process. The Voting Rights Act of 1970 helped pave the way in removing residency restrictions on new voters. Another major federal initiative, the "motor-voter" law of 1993, was designed to increase the ease of voter registration. Other measures to increase voter turnout came at the state level, with a number of states experimenting with new voting methods, such as mail-in ballots.

Figure 29-2   Partisan Identification, 1952–1998

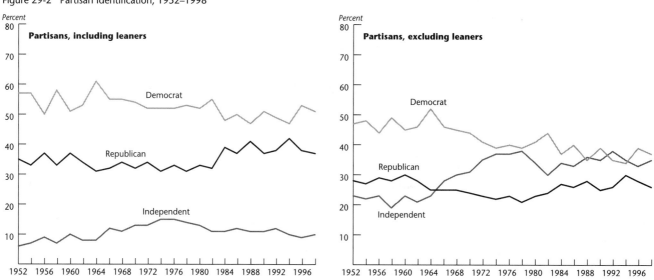

Note: "Leaners" are independents who consider themselves closer to one party.

   Source: Harold W. Stanley and Richard G. Niemi, *Vital Statistics on American Politics,* 7th ed. (Washington, D.C.: Congressional Quarterly, 1999). Calculated by the authors from National Election Studies codebooks and data sets.

REDUCING RESIDENCY REQUIREMENTS

Every state at some time has imposed a minimum period of residence in the state (and some of them a shorter period of residence in a county or voting district) as a qualification for voting. The rationale for this practice has been that individuals cannot vote intelligently, at least on state and local affairs, until they have lived in an area for a given period of time. Until the 1970s most of the states required one year's residence for voting. At one time or another, Alabama, Louisiana, Mississippi, Rhode Island, and South Carolina required residency of as much as two years.

In 1970 thirty-three states imposed residency requirements of one year, fifteen required six months, and two (New York and Pennsylvania) three months. As another condition for voting in 1970, every state except New Hampshire required voters to have lived in the same county or voting district for a stipulated period of time. The most stringent of these requirements were in Maryland and Texas, where six months was required in the county and voting district.

Federal voting rights legislation in 1970 permitted voting in presidential elections after thirty days of residence. This provision, upheld by the Supreme Court, extended the franchise to about 5 million people who might otherwise have been disqualified from voting in the 1972 presidential election. Soon thereafter the Court decided (*Dunn v. Blumstein*) that a state cannot constitutionally restrict the franchise to persons who lived in the state at least one year and in the county at least three months. The 6–1 opinion, rendered March 21, 1972, caused all the states to change their residency requirements. By 1980, nineteen states and the District of Columbia had no minimum residency requirement, and no other state imposed more than a

thirty-day residence requirement except Arizona, which required fifty days. Ten years later, Arizona lowered its requirement to twenty-nine days.[11]

VOTERS LIVING ABROAD

In 1976 President Gerald R. Ford signed legislation establishing uniform voting procedures for American citizens who lived overseas. The law gave Americans abroad the right to vote by absentee ballot in federal elections in the state in which they had their last voting address. The Senate Rules Committee had reported in May 1975 that studies showed that "nearly all of these private citizens outside of the United States in one way or another are strongly discouraged, or are even barred by the rules of the states of their last domicile, from participation in presidential and congressional elections."[12]

In 1978 Congress approved legislation that prevented states from using evidence that an American living overseas voted in a state or federal election as proof of residency for tax purposes. Sponsors said many Americans living abroad did not vote because they feared they might have to pay additional taxes.

MOTOR-VOTER: EASING REGISTRATION FURTHER

In most Western nations government agencies sign up voters, but the United States places the burden for qualifying for electoral participation on the citizen. Although the procedure is still somewhat cumbersome, a variety of state and federal legislation, capped by the National Voter Registration Act or so-called motor-voter act, has made voter registration more convenient.

Signed into law by President Bill Clinton on May 20, 1993,

motor-voter required states to provide all eligible citizens the opportunity to register when they applied for or renewed a driver's license. It also required states to allow mail-in registration and to provide voter registration forms at agencies that supplied public assistance, such as welfare checks or help for people with disabilities. Compliance with the federally mandated program was required by 1995. Costs were to be borne by the states.

Partly as a result of the legislation, a record number of new voters, some 10 million, signed up in the first three years following implementation of the act. The Federal Election Commission reported to Congress in 1996 that the United States had 143 million registered voters, or 72.8 percent of the voting-age population. The percentage was the highest since 1960, when national registration figures first became available.

Congressional Republicans had opposed the legislation on political grounds, namely that it would allow citizens of traditional Democratic constituencies—the urban poor and minorities, among others—easier access to the voting booth. Opponents also argued that easier registration could lead to election fraud.

But motor-voter had neither the negative results that critics feared nor the positive impact that supporters hoped. One year after the law was enacted, Republicans won control of both houses of Congress, which they retained in 1996 and 1998. Meanwhile, in spite of the increased number of registered voters, election turnout continued to decline in the late 1990s.

OTHER STATE MEASURES

By the end of the twentieth century states were also experimenting with various other measures designed to increase voter turnout, including election-day voter registration, easier absentee balloting, and elections by mail.

In the late 1970s President Jimmy Carter proposed federal legislation to allow voters to register at the polls on election day, but it was not enacted. Several states, though, have adopted election-day registration on their own, including Minnesota. In 1998, when Reform Party candidate Jesse Ventura closed fast to win the Minnesota governorship, more than 330,000 citizens registered to vote on election day (which represented 16 percent of the ballots cast).

Still, in today's busy world, when many potential voters may not have the time or capability to travel to the polls on a given day, the idea of absentee voting for all has been gaining wider acceptance. About half the states have an "early voting" option, including "no-fault" absentee voting open to all voters with no need to plead sickness, disability, or any other reason for wanting to vote before election day. A few states, such as Colorado, Texas, and Tennessee, have tried opening voting-style booths before election day in stores or other public places.

A couple of states have tested another alternative: dispensing with voting booths altogether and conducting elections by mail to encourage higher participation. Proponents argue that the benefits of voting by mail—including convenience, speed, and lower costs—outweigh the disadvantages, including the possible abuse of the system, and the lost sociability that comes with gathering at the polls.

In Nevada the 1996 Republican presidential primary was held by mail-in vote. But the largest test took place in Oregon, which used mail-in votes to fill a vacant Senate seat. The winner was Democrat Ron Wyden, the first senator elected by mail.

The new procedure received good reviews. More than three-quarters of those Oregonians polled said they preferred voting by mail over going to the polling places. Women and older voters were strongest in favor of mail voting.

Oregon subsequently became the first state to decide to hold all elections by mail, approving a ballot measure in 1998 requiring vote by mail in biennial primary and general elections. The measure eliminated polling places, but it did not affect existing law allowing absentee ballots or voting at local election offices.

NOTES

1. Max Farrand, ed., *The Records of the Federal Convention of 1787* (New Haven, Conn.: Yale University Press, 1966), vol. 2, 178.
2. Mellman and Scammon are quoted in *President Bush, The Challenge Ahead* (Washington, D.C.: Congressional Quarterly, 1989), 3.
3. Benjamin Highton and Raymond E. Wolfinger, "The Political Implications of Higher Turnout" (paper presented at the 1998 annual meeting of the American Political Science Association), Boston, September 1998, 10.
4. Gunnar Myrdal, *An American Dilemma: The Negro Problem and Modern Democracy* (New York: Harper and Row, 1944), 445.
5. Paul Lewinson, *Race, Class and Party: A History of Negro Suffrage and White Politics in the South* (New York: Oxford University Press, 1932), 194.
6. Frederic D. Ogden, *The Poll Tax in the South* (University: University of Alabama Press, 1958), 2–4.
7. Myrdal, *An American Dilemma,* 485.
8. U.S. Commission on Civil Rights, *Voter Participation* (May 1968), 223. See also U.S. Commission on Civil Rights, *The Voting Rights Act: Ten Years Later* (January 1975), 60.
9. Joan Biskupic and Elder Witt, *Guide to the U.S. Supreme Court* (Washington, D.C.: Congressional Quarterly, 1997), 529.
10. Mary Costello, "Women Voters," *Editorial Research Reports* (Washington, D.C.: Congressional Quarterly, 1972), 776.
11. Information from annual editions of *The Book of the States* (Washington, D.C.: The Council of State Governments), and from the Arizona Secretary of State's Office.
12. Senate Committee on Rules and Administration, "Overseas Citizens Voting Rights Act of 1975," 94th Cong., 1st sess., 1975, S Rept 94-121, 2.

SELECTED BIBLIOGRAPHY

Abramson, Paul R., John H. Aldrich, and David W. Rohde. *Change and Continuity in the 1996 and 1998 Elections.* Washington, D.C.: CQ Press, 1999.
Berelson, Bernard, Paul F. Lazarsfeld, and William A. McPhee. *Voting: A Study of Opinion Formation in a Presidential Campaign.* Chicago: University of Chicago Press, 1954
Campbell, Angus. *The Voter Decides.* New York: Harper and Row, 1954.
Campbell, Angus, Philip E. Converse, Warren E. Miller, and Donald E. Stokes. *The American Voter.* New York: Wiley, 1960.
Campbell, James E. *The Presidential Pulse of Congressional Elections.* 2nd ed. Lexington: University Press of Kentucky, 1997.
Claude, Richard. *The Supreme Court and the Electoral Process.* Baltimore: Johns Hopkins University Press, 1970.

Conway, M. Margaret. *Political Participation in the United States.* 2nd ed. Washington, D.C.: CQ Press, 1991.

Cummings, Milton C. *Congressmen and the Electorate: Elections for the U.S. House and the President, 1920–1964.* New York: Free Press, 1966.

Farrand, Max, ed. *The Records of the Federal Convention of 1787.* 4 vols. New Haven, Conn.: Yale University Press, 1966.

Fiorina, Morris P. *Retrospective Voting in American National Elections.* New Haven, Conn.: Yale University Press, 1981.

Flanigan, William H., and Nancy H. Zingale. *Political Behavior of the American Electorate.* 9th ed. Washington, D.C.: CQ Press, 1998.

Guide to U.S. Elections. 3rd ed. Washington, D.C.: Congressional Quarterly, 1994.

Hamilton, Alexander, James Madison, and John Jay. *The Federalist Papers.* Introduction by Clinton Rossiter. New York: New American Library, 1961.

Haynes, George H. *The Election of Senators.* New York: Henry Holt, 1906.

Heard, Alexander, and Donald S. Strong. *Southern Primaries and Elections, 1920–1949.* University: University of Alabama Press, 1950. Reprint. Plainview, N.Y.: Books for Libraries Press, 1970.

Herrnson, Paul S. *Congressional Elections: Campaigning at Home and in Washington.* 2nd ed. Washington, D.C.: CQ Press, 1998.

Jacobson, Gary C. *The Politics of Congressional Elections.* 4th ed. New York: Longman, 1997.

Key, V. O. *The Responsible Electorate.* New York: Vintage Books, 1966.

Lewinson, Paul. *Race, Class and Party: A History of Negro Suffrage and White Politics in the South.* New York: Oxford University Press, 1932.

Mann, Thomas E. *Unsafe at Any Margin: Interpreting Congressional Elections.* Washington, D.C.: American Enterprise Institute, 1978.

Mayhew, David R. *Congress: The Electoral Connection.* New Haven, Conn.: Yale University Press, 1974.

McGovney, Dudley O. *The American Suffrage Medley.* Chicago: University of Chicago Press, 1949.

Myrdal, Gunnar. *An American Dilemma: The Negro Problem and Modern Democracy.* New York: Harper & Row, 1944.

Nie, Norman H., Sidney Verba, and John R. Petrocik. *The Changing American Voter.* Cambridge: Harvard University Press, 1976.

Ogden, Frederic D. *The Poll Tax in the South.* University: University of Alabama Press, 1958.

Pomper, Gerald M., et al. *The Election of 1996: Reports and Interpretations.* Chatham, N.J.: Chatham House, 1997.

Rosenstone, Steven J., and John Mark Hansen. *Mobilization, Participation, and Democracy in America.* New York: Macmillan, 1993.

Teixeira, Ruy A. *The Disappearing American Voter.* Washington, D.C.: Brookings Institution, 1992.

Wolfinger, Raymond E., and Steven J. Rosenstone. *Who Votes?* New Haven, Conn.: Yale University Press, 1980.

CHAPTER 30

Political Parties and Elections

POLITICAL PARTIES are vital elements in the life and work of Congress and its members. Although they are not specifically mentioned in the Constitution, political parties have been important in Congress almost since its creation. The chief functions of the parties in Congress are to help select and then elect candidates for Congress, through the electoral process, and to organize and distribute power within the institution. The party that holds a majority of seats in each chamber controls all key positions of authority.

In the broadest sense, a political party is a coalition of people who join together to try to win governmental power by winning elections. Members of a party supposedly share a loosely defined set of common beliefs, although members of the same party often hold extremely different opinions and outlooks. Citizens rely on political parties to define issues, to support or oppose candidates on the basis of those issues, and then to carry out the agreed-upon policies when the party is in power.

Functions of Parties

Political parties in America serve many functions. Most important, parties help elect the president, by nominating candidates for the office and then working to get them elected. Political parties also put forward candidates for most state and local offices and help elected leaders mobilize support for their programs.

Before the Civil War a number of different parties played significant roles in Congress. Since the mid-nineteenth century, almost all members of Congress have belonged either to the Democratic or the Republican Party. Occasionally, however, some members of other parties—the Progressive Party in the early 1900s, for example—have been elected. Sometimes, a member is elected as an independent, with no affiliation to any political party.

The Democrats and Republicans each have been dominant in Congress at different times. For much of the period between the Civil War and the Great Depression of the 1930s, Republicans held majorities in both the House and the Senate. Democrats dominated through much of the rest of the century, controlling both chambers for fifty-two of the sixty-two years from the election of 1932 until the election of 1994. From 1995 to the end of the twentieth century, the Republicans held the upper hand in both the House and the Senate.

CHOOSING CONGRESSIONAL CANDIDATES

One essential function of the parties is to provide a mechanism for choosing and supporting congressional candidates. In pre-Jacksonian times, the legislative caucus was the usual method of nominating candidates for both state and federal office. From 1800 to 1824 congressional Democratic-Republicans even used the caucus to select the party's nominee for the presidency. In 1824 Andrew Jackson's followers, realizing their candidate had no chance of winning endorsement in the party caucus, set out to discredit "King Caucus" and substitute party conventions as a more democratic means of selecting the party's candidate. By 1828 most states had abandoned the caucus for the convention, and in 1832 Jacksonian Democrats sent delegates to Baltimore, where they nominated Jackson for president and Martin Van Buren for vice president.

In the early 1900s the Progressives worked to abolish the convention and replace it with the direct primary. Proponents of the primary contended that powerful organizations had seized control of the nominating conventions and frequently had ignored the preferences of the party rank and file. Under the leadership of its governor, Robert M. La Follette Sr., a leading Progressive who later served in Congress, Wisconsin in 1903 enacted the first mandatory primary law. By 1917 the direct primary had been adopted in almost every state; the convention persisted only for the selection of presidential candidates and candidates for a few state offices, and for Republican Party nominations in the Democratic South.

During this same period, the Progressives also succeeded in pushing through Congress a constitutional amendment calling for direct election of senators; they had been chosen by their state legislatures. Beginning in 1914 senators were not only elected by popular vote, but also nominated in most states through party primaries.

The direct primary considerably broadened the range of positions that a political party might take. Political scientist V. O. Key Jr., noted in his book *Politics, Parties, and Pressure Groups* that "rival factions and leaders could now fight out their differences in a campaign directed to the electorate—or a substantial segment of it—rather than be bound by the decision of an assembly of delegates."[1]

ORGANIZING CONGRESS

Parties also play an essential role in the internal organization of Congress. All formal authority in Congress is arranged ac-

Figure 30–1   American Political Parties 1789–1996

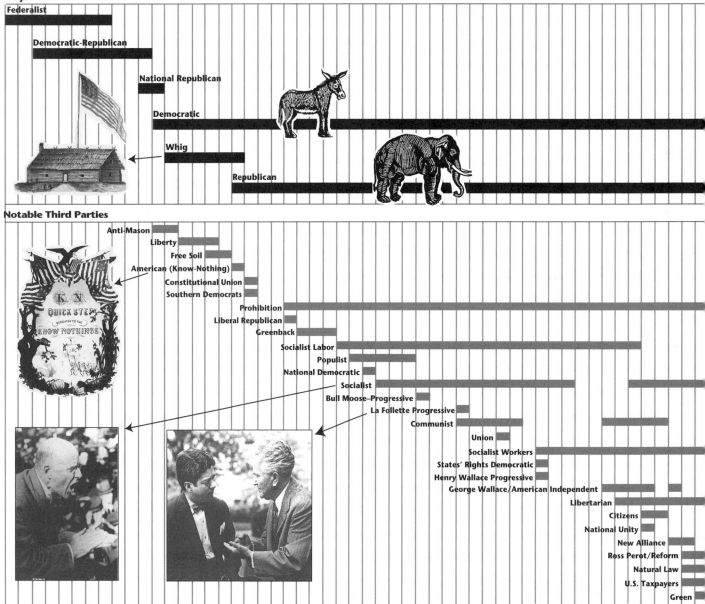

Note: Throughout U.S. history there have been more than 1,500 political parties. For this chart Congressional Quarterly editors have selected those parties that achieved national significance during presidential election years. The spaces between the rules on this chart indicate the election year only. For example, the Constitutional Union Party and the Southern Democrats were in existence for the 1860 election only and were gone by 1864. Similarly, the Green Party first fielded a presidential candidate in 1996.

cording to party. The party that holds the majority in each chamber has the votes to select leaders such as Speaker of the House and the majority leader in the Senate. All committee and subcommittee chairmen are members of the majority party and majority party leaders control the legislative agenda. Within each party a whip system enables party leaders to pressure party members to support the party position on key issues. (See Chapter 14, Party Leadership in Congress.)

Without structures for bringing together like-minded members for common action, Congress might find itself in constant

chaos as each member fought to advance his or her individual agenda. Instead, the parties help to create a system in which leaders and followers can work together in pursuit of a common program. Members, however, are under no obligation to support party positions or obey party leaders. And in recent decades, individual legislators have built their constituencies with little reference to party labels. But with the Republican takeover of Congress in 1995, partisanship—reflected in the amount of party-line voting—reached some of its highest levels in the last half of the twentieth century on both sides of Capitol Hill.

Party System: Unforeseen Development

The Founders never envisioned the importance that political parties would develop in Congress and the nation. The authors of the Constitution had little understanding of the functions of political parties; they were ambivalent, if not hostile, to the new party system as it developed in the early years of the Republic. "If I could not go to heaven but with a party, I would not go there at all," Thomas Jefferson said in 1789.[2]

The Constitution did not mention parties, either to authorize them or prohibit them. It made possible a permanent role for parties, however, by giving citizens civil liberties and the right to organize. At the same time it erected safeguards against partisan excesses by creating a system of checks and balances within the government. The "great object" of the new government, wrote James Madison in *Federalist* No. 10, was "to secure the public good and private rights against the danger of such a faction [party], and at the same time to preserve the spirit and the form of popular government."[3]

EMERGENCE OF PARTIES

Parties emerged soon after the adoption of the Constitution. Those who favored the strong central government embodied in the Constitution came to be called Federalists. Led by Treasury Secretary Alexander Hamilton, they were drawn mostly from merchants and bankers in the Northeast, who favored strong government action to protect the currency from losing its value through inflation. They were opposed by a group that later became known as the Democratic-Republicans. Led by Jefferson and Madison, the Democratic-Republicans were largely southern and western farmers, who opposed a strong central government and sought government policies to make it easier to borrow money.

Party lines were fluid in the first Congresses, with members drifting between one loose coalition and the other. By the mid-1790s, however, the factions had hardened enough for one senator to observe that "the existence of two parties in Congress is apparent." Federalists generally held the upper hand in these early years, controlling the Senate and contending equally for power with the Democratic-Republicans in the House.

Although George Washington identified himself with no political party, John Adams, his successor, was unabashedly Federalist. But by 1800 Jefferson's supporters had gained a majority, and from 1801, when Jefferson replaced Adams, Democratic-Republicans occupied the White House and controlled Congress until 1829. The 1816 elections signaled the effective end of the Federalist Party, whose representation in Congress dropped off to a small minority; even the semblance of a two-party system disappeared.

Along with the dominance of the Democratic-Republicans, the first twenty years of the nineteenth century saw growth in the power of the party caucus over Congress's operations. Important decisions were made in private meetings of the Demo-cratic-Republicans, and party members in Congress were pressed to follow the party's position.

The size and power of the Democratic-Republican Party soon led to the development of internal factions, as different regional groups struggled for influence within the only national political organization. By the mid-1820s two groups emerged: the National Republicans, a coalition of eastern manufacturers, large southern plantation owners, and westerners who favored internal economic development projects and a protective tariff against foreign goods; and the Democrats, who represented agrarian interests from the South and West and held that the common people, not the rich, should have the dominant voice in government.

The Democrats captured control of Congress in 1826 and the White House in 1828 and were to remain the dominant party in Congress for the next three decades. Showing their disgust with what they considered to be the "mob rule" of the Jacksonians, the National Republicans in 1834 changed their name to Whigs, an English political term signifying antagonism to excessive use of executive power. The Whigs twice won the presidency, in 1840 and 1848, and always held a substantial number of seats in Congress. But the Whigs were able to capture a majority of either body on only a few occasions—the 1840 and 1846 elections in the House and the 1840 and 1842 elections in the Senate.

REPUBLICAN PARTY FOUNDED

The Whigs faded rapidly during the 1850s and went out of existence in 1856. In their place rose the Republican Party of today. Initially, the party was composed of "Free Soil" Democrats and Whigs who opposed the extension of slavery into new territories. The party won control of the House in 1854 but lost it in 1856, even as its first presidential candidate, John Charles Fremont, was winning a third of the popular vote. During the next four years the party broadened its appeal to small farmers and owners of small businesses by promising a homestead law for western settlement and a protective tariff. In 1858 the party recaptured control of the House and in 1860 it won the Senate and, with the election of Abraham Lincoln, the presidency.

The Republican Party controlled Congress and the presidency for most of the next seventy years. Democrats sometimes were able to win a majority of House seats and, on occasion, a Senate majority. But the Republicans, who soon gained the nickname of "Grand Old Party" (GOP), dominated the era. Backed by eastern business interests, they favored high tariffs and tight controls on the amount of money in the economy. The Democrats were the party of the South and of disaffected agricultural interests from the West. They generally sought low tariffs and liberal credit.

TWO-PARTY DOMINANCE

It was during this period of Republican rule that the role of the parties themselves became much more important in Congress. Although the Congress of the pre–Civil War period tend-

The Republican convention of 1860 in Chicago nominated Abraham Lincoln for the presidency. Republicans controlled Congress and the presidency for most of the next seventy years. They became known as the "Grand Old Party" (GOP).

ed to be dominated by brilliant individuals, the postwar Senate and House were the arenas of powerful party leaders. This trend was particularly apparent in the Senate, where many of the members were "party bosses" who had gained power through political organizations in their own states. These men placed a high value on party loyalty and on the need for party discipline. They were often ready to compromise their ideals to maintain harmony within the party.

The first attempt at developing a strong party structure came in the 1870s, when New York Republican Roscoe Conkling organized a faction that controlled the Senate on procedural matters. Conkling's group had little effect on legislation, however, and the Senate returned to individualistic ways after Conkling left the Senate.

The birth of modern party discipline came in the 1890s. Republican Senators William B. Allison of Iowa and Nelson W. Aldrich of Rhode Island organized an informal group of senators, who first met only for poker and relaxation. After Allison was elected chairman of the Senate Republican Caucus, the organization of party members, in 1897, the group assumed control of the Senate. Allison used his office to solidify his control of his party and his party's control of the Senate.

Allison controlled the Steering Committee, which directed floor proceedings, and the Committee on Committees, which made committee assignments. Although chairmanship of committees was determined primarily by seniority, Allison had great leeway to appoint members to committees who would follow his wishes. Access to positions of influence soon depended on the favor and support of the party leaders.

Republicans used the caucus to work out party positions in private and then to speak in a unified voice on the Senate floor. Although they were not bound to obey the party position, members who ignored it risked losing most of their power in the Senate. The Democrats soon followed the Republicans by organizing their own internal power structure.

On the House side, Republican Speakers Thomas Bracket Reed of Maine in the 1890s and Joseph G. Cannon of Illinois in the first decade of the 1900s elicited a similar degree of party control over their rank and file. Reed's rule firmly established the authority of the majority to prevail over the minority, ending a period in which the minority used obstructionist tactics that frequently brought legislative activity in the House to a standstill.

ATTACKS ON THE SYSTEM

The system of strict party control was not popular among many people outside of Congress, who saw it as violating the principles of representative democracy. There were also critics of the system within Congress, including the Liberal Republicans of the 1870s and the "mugwump" antileadership Republicans of the 1880s. In addition, representatives of third parties attacked the system.

The most important of these were the Populists, who represented an agrarian reform movement based in the Midwest and West. The Populists won three Senate seats and eleven House seats in 1892. They reached their peak in the crucial election of 1896 when they and their allies won seven Senate seats and thirty House seats. Much of their program, which stressed loosening of controls on the amount of money circulated in the economy, was adopted by the Democrats, and the Populists soon faded from the scene.

The cause of reform was soon taken up by the progressives. This movement sought both economic changes, such as antitrust legislation and introduction of the income tax, and political measures aimed at opening up the system, such as direct election of senators and laws against corrupt election practices. The progressives were composed of reformist Republicans and members of the separate Progressive Party. The Bull Moose–Progressives, as they were called in honor of their leader, former president Theodore Roosevelt, elected seventeen House members in 1912. The progressives played key roles in the congressional reform movement of the early 1900s, working to reduce the autocratic power of House Speaker Cannon, and pushing for curbs on the filibuster.

Despite these attacks, the system of party control of Congress developed into a formal institution. During the 1910s, Senate Democrats and then Senate Republicans elected a single member to serve both as chairman of the party caucus and as floor leader. Soon the majority and minority leaders were the acknowledged spokespeople for their parties in the Senate. In the House the revolt against the power of the Speaker led to a great increase in the power of the party caucuses. The Democrats, who controlled the House from 1911 to 1919, worked out most legislative decisions within party meetings, and party rules obliged members to vote for the party position if it was endorsed by a two-thirds majority.

Republicans regained control of both houses of Congress in 1918, and they maintained their power until the early years of the Great Depression. However, the party was torn by deep divisions between regular forces and the progressives, who often cooperated with the Democrats in pushing legislation favorable to the economic interests of western farmers. Progressive Republicans who tried to challenge their party leadership were quickly punished by the loss of seats on important committees.

DEMOCRATS AS MAJORITY PARTY

The Republicans lost their exclusive control of Congress in 1930, when Democrats gained a narrow majority in the House. That election proved to be a warning sign of what was to come two years later. The 1932 elections were a watershed in the history of partisan divisions in Congress. Led by presidential candidate Franklin D. Roosevelt, who promised relief from the economic disaster that had befallen the nation, the Democrats swept to commanding majorities in both the House and Senate. By the 1936 elections, the Republicans had been reduced to a small minority. The Democrats held 331 House seats as a result of that election; the Republicans 89. The Democratic majority in the Senate was an overwhelming 76–16.

With few exceptions, the Democrats remained in complete control of Congress from then until the mid-1990s. Between 1930 and 1994, they lost their House majority only twice, in the 1946 and 1952 elections. Those elections also gave Republicans brief control of the Senate; Democrats regained control again in 1948 and 1954. The GOP also controlled the Senate during the first six years of Ronald Reagan's presidency, 1981–1987. However, Democrats regained a substantial majority in the 1986 elections, which they maintained into the early 1990s.

In 1992 Democrats won the White House for only the second time in a quarter century. But their control of both ends of Pennsylvania Avenue was short-lived. Redistricting at the beginning of the 1990s had created plenty of opportunities for the GOP, especially in the South, where the formation of a number of new majority-minority districts lowered the minority share in myriad other districts, thus enhancing Republican chances in the latter.

Democrats, as well, had suffered nationally from the perception of an arrogance of power, epitomized by a House banking scandal that was a major factor in the defeat of nineteen House incumbents (mainly Democrats) in the 1992 primary season; the number was a postwar record. Nor were the Democrats helped in 1993 and 1994 by the struggling start of the new Clinton administration, which in 1994 lobbied Congress for a complex overhaul of the nation's health care system that died in spite of the Democratic majorities in both the House and Senate.

The confluence of these factors produced a tidal wave in the 1994 elections that propelled the Republicans into power in both houses of Congress for the first time in forty years.

Divided Government

The Republican congressional takeover in 1995 returned Washington to the divided government that it has known in most of the second half of the twentieth century. Yet the combination of a Democratic president and a Republican Congress was the reverse of the combination that had existed before. (See Table 30-1, p. 828.)

In 1952 and 1956, Gen. Dwight D. Eisenhower, a war hero, carried the Republicans to the White House, as the GOP in 1954 slumped into its long-running minority status on Capitol Hill. Recurrent economic recessions under President Eisenhower and the vigorous campaign of presidential candidate John F. Kennedy enabled the Democrats to recapture the White House in 1960 and retain it with Lyndon B. Johnson's election in 1964.

But Republicans regained the presidency in 1968 from a

TABLE 30-1 Divided Government, 1860–1998

During the last half of the twentieth century, it was not unusual for one party to occupy the White House and for the other party to dominate Congress. But for almost a century before that, beginning with the election of the first Republican president (Abraham Lincoln) in 1860, one party or the other tended to control both ends of Pennsylvania Avenue. The chart below indicates the party that won control of the House and Senate in each national election since 1860, and notes the president that was either elected then or serving at the time (in the case of midterm elections). Changes in the presidency between elections are indicated by a slash.

Election	President	Party winning control House	Senate	Control of presidency and Congress[a]	Election	President	Party winning control House	Senate	Control of presidency and Congress[a]
1860	Lincoln (R)	R	R	All Republican	1930	Hoover (R)	D	R	Congress Split
1862	Lincoln (R)	R	R	All Republican	1932	F. Roosevelt (D)	D	D	All Democrat
1864	Lincoln/A. Johnson (R)	R	R	All Republican[b]	1934	F. Roosevelt (D)	D	D	All Democrat
1866	A. Johnson (R)	R	R	All Republican	1936	F. Roosevelt (D)	D	D	All Democrat
1868	Grant (R)	R	R	All Republican	1938	F. Roosevelt (D)	D	D	All Democrat
1870	Grant (R)	R	R	All Republican	1940	F. Roosevelt (D)	D	D	All Democrat
1872	Grant (R)	R	R	All Republican	1942	F. Roosevelt (D)	D	D	All Democrat
1874	Grant (R)	D	R	Congress Split	1944	F. Roosevelt/Truman (D)	D	D	All Democrat
1876	Hayes (R)	D	R	Congress Split	1946	Truman (D)	R	R	Divided
1878	Hayes (R)	D	D	Divided	1948	Truman (D)	D	D	All Democrat
1880	Garfield/Arthur (R)	R	R	All Republican	1950	Truman (D)	D	D	All Democrat
1882	Arthur (R)	D	R	Congress Split	1952	Eisenhower (R)	R	R	All Republican
1884	Cleveland (D)	D	R	Congress Split	1954	Eisenhower (R)	D	D	Divided
1886	Cleveland (D)	D	R	Congress Split	1956	Eisenhower (R)	D	D	Divided
1888	B. Harrison (R)	R	R	All Republican	1958	Eisenhower (R)	D	D	Divided
1890	B. Harrison (R)	D	R	Congress Split	1960	Kennedy (D)	D	D	All Democrat
1892	Cleveland (D)	D	D	All Democrat	1962	Kennedy/L. Johnson (D)	D	D	All Democrat
1894	Cleveland (D)	R	R	Divided	1964	L. Johnson (D)	D	D	All Democrat
1896	McKinley (R)	R	R	All Republican	1966	L. Johnson (D)	D	D	All Democrat
1898	McKinley (R)	R	R	All Republican	1968	Nixon (R)	D	D	Divided
1900	McKinley/T. Roosevelt (R)	R	R	All Republican	1970	Nixon (R)	D	D	Divided
1902	T. Roosevelt (R)	R	R	All Republican	1972	Nixon/Ford (R)	D	D	Divided
1904	T. Roosevelt (R)	R	R	All Republican	1974	Ford (R)	D	D	Divided
1906	T. Roosevelt (R)	R	R	All Republican	1976	Carter (D)	D	D	All Democrat
1908	Taft (R)	R	R	All Republican	1978	Carter (D)	D	D	All Democrat
1910	Taft (R)	D	R	Congress Split	1980	Reagan (R)	D	R	Congress Split
1912	Wilson (D)	D	D	All Democrat	1982	Reagan (R)	D	R	Congress Split
1914	Wilson (D)	D	D	All Democrat	1984	Reagan (R)	D	R	Congress Split
1916	Wilson (D)	D	D	All Democrat	1986	Reagan (R)	D	D	Divided
1918	Wilson (D)	R	R	Divided	1988	Bush (R)	D	D	Divided
1920	Harding (R)	R	R	All Republican	1990	Bush (R)	D	D	Divided
1922	Harding/Coolidge (R)	R	R	All Republican	1992	Clinton (D)	D	D	All Democrat
1924	Coolidge (R)	R	R	All Republican	1994	Clinton (D)	R	R	Divided
1926	Coolidge (R)	R	R	All Republican	1996	Clinton (D)	R	R	Divided
1928	Hoover (R)	R	R	All Republican	1998	Clinton (D)	R	R	Divided

NOTES: Key to abbreviations: D—Democrat; R—Republican. a. "All" indicates that one party controlled the White House and both houses of Congress. "Divided" indicates that one party held the presidency while the other party controlled both houses of Congress. "Congress Split" indicates that control of Congress was split, with one party holding the House and the other the Senate. b. The pro-Republican majority in Congress elected in 1864 was designated Unionist.

Democratic Party badly split over the Vietnam War and under attack from third party candidate George C. Wallace. Richard Nixon, reelected by a huge majority in 1972, tried to create a new party alignment by courting the once solidly Democratic South with conservative domestic programs. But the results were mixed, and the party was badly damaged when the Watergate scandal forced Nixon to resign in 1974. The scandal paved the way for Democrat Jimmy Carter to triumph in 1976.

But in 1980 a conservative tide, economic problems, and the Iranian hostage crisis swept Republican Ronald Reagan into the presidency. Eight years later his vice president, George Bush, succeeded Reagan, and in his first two years in office scored some of the highest popularity ratings of any modern president, Democrat or Republican.

As the 1990s began, there was considerable conjecture as to why the Democratic Party was able to thrive in congressional and state elections while repeatedly losing the presidency. It had become the "oddest riddle of American politics of recent years," political analyst Alan Ehrenhalt wrote in his book *The United States of Ambition.* Ehrenhalt, executive editor of *Governing* magazine and former political editor of the *Congressional Quarterly Weekly Report,* recalled that some observers believed voters elected Democrats to Congress to impose a deliberate check on the Republicans they sent to the White House.

Another theory—"more plausible" to the author—was that Republicans won the presidency by offering an ideology the electorate liked to hear but did not want to practice. According to this reasoning, Democrats won the lesser offices because they

TABLE 30-2 The House in the 1990s: From Democrat to Republican

The House of Representatives went from Democratic to Republican in the 1990s, fueled by the GOP upsurge in the South. But since winning control of the House in 1994, Republicans lost ground in every region except the South.

	South			West			Midwest			East				Total House			
	R	D		R	D		R	D		R	D	I		R	D	I	
1990	44	85	D	37	48	D	45	68	D	41	66	1	D	167	267	1	D
1992	52	85	D	38	55	D	44	61	D	42	57	1	D	176	258	1	D
1994	73	64	R	53	40	R	59	46	R	45	54	1	D	230	204	1	R
1996	82	55	R	51	42	R	55	50	R	39	60	1	D	227	207	1	R
1998	82	55	R	49	44	R	54	51	R	38	61	1	D	223	211	1	R
Net GOP Change [a]	+38			+12			+9			−3				+56			

NOTES: Key to abbreviations: D—Democrat; I—Independent; R—Republican. Traditionally, Congressional Quarterly has defined the four regions as follows: East—Connecticut, Delaware, Maine, Maryland, Massachusetts, New Hampshire, New Jersey, New York, Pennsylvania, Rhode Island, Vermont, West Virginia; Midwest—Illinois, Indiana, Iowa, Kansas, Michigan, Minnesota, Missouri, Nebraska, North Dakota, Ohio, South Dakota, Wisconsin; South—Alabama, Arkansas, Florida, Georgia, Kentucky, Louisiana, Mississippi, North Carolina, Oklahoma, South Carolina, Tennessee, Texas, Virginia; West—Alaska, Arizona, California, Colorado, Hawaii, Idaho, Montana, Nevada, New Mexico, Oregon, Utah, Washington, Wyoming.   a. Change in GOP seats, 1990–1998.

delivered the services and generated the government programs that the voters did not want to give up.

But the best answer, according to Ehrenhalt, was that the Democratic Party—"the party of government"—tended to attract career politicians and to benefit from their growing presence. Ehrenhalt contended that during the previous two decades in most constituencies, "Democrats have generated the best supply of talent, energy, and sheer ambition," which over time "enabled them to win an extra 10 percent of the seats in a state legislature, or an extra two or three seats in a congressional delegation. It adds up. . . ."[4]

The era that Ehrenhalt described was interrupted dramatically by the election of 1994, when Republicans not only won both houses of Congress, but also captured a majority of the nation's governorships and made inroads in the state legislatures. But whether the era of Democratic congressional dominance was over for good was open to conjecture. In the elections of 1996 and 1998, the Democrats inched back toward parity in the House and continued to hold more seats than the Republicans in the state legislatures, still a prime source of congressional candidates. *(See Table 30-2, this page.)*

PARTY AFFILIATION

It is probably no coincidence that the rise in divided government in the latter half of the twentieth century has coincided with the proliferation of independent voters—voters who profess no party choice. They accounted for only 16 percent of the electorate in 1937, but 32 percent—nearly a third—in 1990, and 38 percent in early 1999, according to Gallup surveys. In early 1999, 34 percent of the American voters considered themselves Democrats, 28 percent Republicans.

Yet the two major parties were still held in relatively high regard by the end of the century. When independents were asked in the 1999 Gallup survey whether they leaned to the Republican or Democratic Parties, the number that defined themselves as

staunchly independent dropped to about 10 percent. Still, there was no denying that the last half of the twentieth century saw a rise in ticket-splitting, a willingness by voters of all stripes to go back and forth across the ballot rather than vote a straight-party ticket. *(See Table 30-3, p. 830.)*

Even party regulars sometimes vote for candidates in the opposing party, according to findings reported by political scientists William H. Flanigan and Nancy H. Zingale. "The proportion of strong partisans who report having voted for different parties has increased substantially since 1952," they wrote.[5]

In a comparison of voting habits in the 1952 and 1988 elections, Flanigan and Zingale noted that southern whites "have become dramatically less Democratic, while blacks throughout the country have become slightly more Democratic and the most consistently loyal Democratic group." The authors found that Jews "have shifted away from their extremely one-sided Democratic identification" but toward independent, rather than Republican, status. Independents also made inroads among Catholics and white Protestants in the North, at the expense of both parties. Despite change, Flanigan and Zingale wrote, "there is partisan stability among both Republicans and Democrats, and the shifting of political fortunes is accomplished without intensity or extreme political appeals."[6]

Overall, according to Gallup Polls, Democrats have experienced a gradual decline in favor since 1964, when 53 percent of the voters—a record number—identified themselves with that party. However, over the course of the 1990s, voter identification with the Democrats has stayed roughly the same, while identification with the Republicans has declined and the number of self-described independents has increased.

The Gallup survey of early 1999 found a continuation of the gender gap, which had been a visible feature of American politics for the previous quarter century. While men were almost evenly divided between the Democrats and Republicans as their party of choice, women preferred the Democrats by a margin of

TABLE 30-3 Ticket-Splitting Between Presidential
and House Candidates, 1900–1996

Year	Districts[a]	Districts with split results[b]	
		Number	Percentage
1900	295	10	3.4
1904	310	5	1.6
1908	314	21	6.7
1912	333	84	25.2
1916	333	35	10.5
1920	344	11	3.2
1924	356	42	11.8
1928	359	68	18.9
1932	355	50	14.1
1936	361	51	14.1
1940	362	53	14.6
1944	367	41	11.2
1948	422	90	21.3
1952	435	84	19.3
1956	435	130	29.9
1960	437	114	26.1
1964	435	145	33.3
1968	435	139	32.0
1972	435	192	44.1
1976	435	124	28.5
1980	435	143	32.8
1984	435	196	45.0
1988	435	148	34.0
1992	435	100	23.0
1996	435	111	25.5

NOTES: a. Before 1952 complete data are not available on every congressional district.   b. Congressional districts carried by a presidential candidate of one party and a House candidate of another party.

SOURCE: Norman J. Ornstein, Thomas E. Mann, and Michael J. Malbin, eds., *Vital Statistics on Congress, 1997–1998* (Washington, D.C.: Congressional Quarterly, 1998), 71.

10 percentage points. The survey also indicated that the Democrats were supported by a "May-September" coalition of the young and elderly. Democrats were preferred by a margin of 11 percentage points over the Republicans among voters age eighteen to twenty-nine and by 10 percentage points among those age sixty-five and older. The Democrats were preferred over the Republicans by a less pronounced margin among voters in age groups in between.[7]

PARTY DECLINE IN CONGRESS

During the years after World War II in which Democrats dominated Capitol Hill, the parties suffered a noticeable decline in their influence on Congress. Parties and party leaders had much less power than they did at the beginning of the century. Members of Congress increasingly functioned as individuals rather than loyal party members, both in their electoral campaigns and in the way they voted in committee and on the floor.

In many respects, the increasing individualism was a natural outgrowth of divided government. While many districts were voting Republican for president, they were electing a Democrat to Congress. It created a situation where many members of

Congress felt they had to buck their party often in order to stay in favor with their constituents.

At the same time, the growth of party primaries as a means for selecting congressional candidates added to the decline of the importance of parties. Originally introduced to reduce the power of corrupt party bosses, by giving the choice of the party nominee to party members as a whole, primaries have had the unintended effect of undermining the parties as institutions. Congressional candidates today often bypass the established party leadership in their area and appeal directly to the voters.

Other factors have contributed to the decline of the parties within Congress. In the 1950s and 1960s the conservative coalition of Republicans and southern Democrats effectively controlled both the House and Senate, and for many years it was able to frustrate efforts by the Democratic leadership to push through civil rights and other legislation. In the 1970s the congressional reform movement stripped away much of the power of the old-line party leaders. That has made it possible for members to ignore the position of the party leadership and to vote according to their own interests, without fear of much punishment. And as the century waned, interest groups took an increasingly active role in congressional campaigns, often independent of both the parties and the candidates.

Republicans and Democrats in Congress have made strong efforts in recent years to restore some of their influence in electoral politics. Each party has a House and Senate campaign committee, and all four committees play key roles in recruiting, training, organizing, and funding campaigns. The Republicans in particular have developed their campaign committees into wealthy, high-technology centers able to wage a coordinated national campaign for GOP candidates.

But nothing has rejuvenated the parties in Congress as much as the Republican takeover in 1995. Democrats were stunned. Republicans were ebullient and quickly began to push their conservative reform agenda called the Contract with America. By the end of 1995 the proportion of votes in which a majority of one party had voted against the majority of another had reached a forty-year high in both the House and Senate. The proportion of party-unity votes declined in both 1996 and 1997, but spiked upward again in 1998, a year capped in the House by the highly partisan votes to impeach President Bill Clinton.

Election of Members: Evolving Process

The creation of the U.S. Senate was a result of the "Great Compromise" at the Constitutional Convention in 1787. The small states wanted equal representation in Congress, fearing domination by the large states under a population formula. The larger states, however, naturally wished for a legislature based on population, where their strength would prevail. In resolving this dispute, delegates simply split the basis of representation between the two chambers—population for the House of Representatives, equal representation by state for the Senate. Each state was entitled to two senators.

SENATE ELECTIONS

The Founders let state legislatures, instead of the people themselves, elect U.S. senators. The argument was that legislatures were more able than the electorate to give sober and reflective thought to the selection, and by doing so would take a greater supportive interest in the fledgling national government. The legislatures, after all, had chosen the members of the Continental Congress and the delegates to the Constitutional Convention.

Some legislatures looked upon the senators as their "ambassadors" to the federal government and went so far as to instruct them on how to vote. This raised severe problems of conscience among senators on occasion and resulted in several resignations.

At first, the legislatures made their own arrangements for electing senators. Many states required the two houses of the legislature, sitting separately, to agree on the same candidate. Others required a ballot of the two houses in a joint session. In 1866 Congress decided to exercise its authority. Procedures requiring concurrent majorities in both houses resulted in numerous delays and vacancies. So Congress established procedures for the legislatures to follow in the election of senators, as was authorized by the Constitution.

Article I, Section 4 states in part: "The times, places and manner of holding elections for Senators and Representatives shall be prescribed in each state by the legislature thereof; but the Congress may at any time by law make or alter such regulations, except as to the places of chusing Senators."

The new federal law required the first ballot for senator to be taken by the two houses separately. If no candidate received a majority of the vote in both houses—that is, if a deadlock resulted—then the two houses were to meet and vote jointly until a majority choice emerged. However, the new system did not have the desired effect. The requirement for a majority vote continued to result in voting deadlocks.

A notable instance occurred in Delaware at the turn of the last century. With the legislators divided between two factions of the Republican Party, and the Democrats in the minority, they could not reach agreement by the time Congress went into session on March 4, 1899. So bitter was the Republican factional dispute that neither side would support a candidate acceptable to the other. Nor would the Democrats play kingmaker by siding with one group or the other. The dispute continued throughout the 56th Congress (1899–1901), leaving the seat unfilled.

Furthermore, the term of Delaware's other Senate seat ended in 1901, necessitating another election. The same pattern prevailed, with the legislature failing to fill either Senate seat, leaving the state unrepresented in the Senate from March 4, 1901, until March 1, 1903, when at last the deadlock was broken by the choice of one faction's Senate candidate to one seat, and the other faction's candidate to the other seat.

The system had other faults besides election deadlocks. The party caucuses in the state legislatures and individual members were subject to intense and unethical lobbying by supporters of various senatorial candidates. Because of the frequency of allegations of illegal methods used in securing election, the Senate found itself involved in election disputes. The Constitution makes Congress the judge of its own members. Article I, Section 5 states that "Each House shall be the Judge of the Elections, Returns, and Qualifications of its own Members. . . ."

Critics of the legislative election of senators had still another grievance. They contended that elections to the state legislatures often were overshadowed by senatorial contests. Thus when voters went to the polls to choose their state legislators, they would sometimes be urged to disregard state and local issues and vote for a legislator who promised to support a certain candidate for the U.S. Senate. This, the critics said, led to a neglect of state government. Moreover, drawn-out Senate contests tended to hold up the consideration of state business.

The main criticism of legislative elections was that they distorted, or even blocked, the will of the people. Throughout the nineteenth century, a movement for popular elections had in several states taken away from legislatures the right to choose governors and presidential electors. Now attention focused on the Senate.

Toward the turn of the century, the House on five occasions approved proposed constitutional amendments for popular Senate elections. But each time the Senate refused to act. Frustrated in Congress, the reformers began implementing various formulas for selecting Senate candidates. In some cases, party conventions endorsed nominees for senator, enabling the voters to know which candidates the legislature was likely to support.

Oregon took the lead in instituting nonbinding popular elections. Under a 1901 law, voters expressed their choice for senator in popular ballots. While the results of the vote had no legal force, the law required that the election returns be formally announced to the state legislature. When first tried, in 1902, the Oregon legislators ignored the ballot winner. But the reformers increased their pressure, including demands that candidates for the legislature sign a pledge to vote for the winner of the popular vote. By 1908 the plan was working as its authors had hoped, with a Republican legislature electing Democrat George Chamberlain, the winner of the popular contest. Within a few years Colorado, Kansas, Minnesota, Montana, Nevada, and Oklahoma adopted the Oregon method.

It was not until 1911 that the Senate, infused with a number of progressives, both Democrats and Republicans, approved a constitutional amendment for the popular election of senators. It did so that June 12, by a vote of 64–24. The House concurred in the Senate version on May 13, 1912, by a vote of 238–39. The Seventeenth Amendment was then put before the states for their approval. It was ratified April 8, 1913.

The amendment did not bring a wholesale changeover in the Senate's membership. In fact, all but two of the twenty-five incumbents who sought election in November 1914 were successful. Seven other senators had retired or died.

In 1938 Gen. Walter Faulkner of Tennessee lost his bid for a seat in the House. Here he pursues the farm vote.

HOUSE ELECTIONS

The House of Representatives was designed by the Founders to be the branch of government closest to the people. Its members, unlike the Senate or the president, were to be chosen directly by the voters. They were given two-year terms, so the people would have a chance to monitor and pass judgment on their activities at brief intervals. In addition, members of the House, the larger of the two legislative bodies, would have relatively small constituencies.

The lower houses of the colonial and state legislatures served as a model for the U.S. House. In each state, at least one house was elected by popular vote.

The Constitution left the qualification of voters to the states, with one exception: the qualifications could be no more restrictive than for the most numerous branch of a state's own legislature. At first, property qualifications for voting were general. But a democratic trend early in the nineteenth century swept away most property qualifications, producing practically universal white male suffrage by the 1830s.

Many delegates to the Constitutional Convention preferred annual elections for the House, believing that the body should reflect as closely as possible the wishes of the people. James Madison, however, argued for a three-year term, to let the representatives gain knowledge and experience in national and local affairs. The result was a compromise on a two-year term.

The two-year term has not been universally popular. From time to time, proposals have been made to extend it. President Lyndon B. Johnson advocated a four-year term in his 1966 State of the Union address. That proposal received more applause than any other part of his speech, but it came to nothing.

The size of the original House of Representatives was written into Article I, Section 2 of the Constitution, along with directions to apportion the House according to population, as recorded in the first census in 1790. Until then, the original thirteen states were assigned the following members: New Hampshire three, Massachusetts eight, Rhode Island one, Connecticut five, New York six, New Jersey four, Pennsylvania eight, Delaware one, Maryland six, Virginia ten, North Carolina five, South Carolina five, and Georgia three. This apportionment of seats—sixty-five in all—remained in effect during the First and Second Congresses (1789–1793).

Congress in 1792 determined that the House should have one

representative for every 33,000 inhabitants, 105 members in all, and fixed the number for each state. This method of dividing the population of the various states by 33,000 was devised by Thomas Jefferson and known as "rejected fractions," for all remainders were disregarded. Congress enacted a new apportionment measure, including the mathematical formula to be used, every ten years (except 1920) until a permanent law became effective in 1929. *(See Chapter 33, Reapportionment and Redistricting.)*

Changing Election Practices

Five New England states at one time or another required a majority vote (50.01 percent) to win election to the House. If no candidate gained a majority, new elections were held until one contender managed to do so. But all of the states had phased out the requirement by the end of the nineteenth century. Multiple races were necessary sometimes because none of the candidates could win a majority. In the Fourth District of Massachusetts in 1848–1849, for example, twelve successive elections were held to try to choose a representative. None was successful, and the district remained unrepresented in the House during the 31st Congress (1849–1851).

Prior to ratification of the Twentieth Amendment in 1933, regular sessions of Congress began in December of odd-numbered years. There was, therefore, a long period between elections in November of even-numbered years until the beginning of the regular congressional session. As a consequence, several states moved congressional elections to odd-numbered years—a practice that continued until late in the nineteenth century.

Practices in the South

Many of the anomalies in election of U.S. representatives occurred in the South. That region's experience with slavery, Civil War, Reconstruction, and racial antagonisms created special problems for the regular electoral process.

Article I, Section 2 of the Constitution contained a formula for counting slaves for apportionment purposes: every five slaves would be counted as three persons. Thus, the total population of a state to be used in determining its congressional representation would be the free population plus three-fifths of the slave population.

After the Civil War and the emancipation of the slaves, blacks were fully counted for the purposes of apportionment. The Fourteenth Amendment, ratified in 1868, required that apportionment be based on "the whole number of persons in each State. . . ." On this basis, several southern states tried to claim immediate additional representation on their readmission to the Union. Tennessee, for example, chose an extra U.S. representative, electing him at large in 1868. Virginia took similar action in 1869 and 1870, and South Carolina in 1868 and 1870. But the House declined to seat the additional representatives, ruling that the states would have to await reapportionment after the 1870 census for any changes in their representation.

Another provision of the Fourteenth Amendment provided for reducing the House representation of any state that denied the voting franchise to any male citizen over twenty-one. This effort to prevent the southern states from denying the vote to newly freed slaves was never applied. Congress instead frequently considered election challenges filed against members-elect from the South. Between 1881 and 1897, eighteen Democrats from the former Confederate states were unseated by the House, often on charges that black voting rights were abused in their districts.

CONTESTED ELECTIONS

Decentralization of control over elections in the United States may have strengthened participatory democracy, but it has led frequently to controversy over election results. Losing candidates and their supporters believe in many cases that more voters were on their side than the official count showed. Floyd M. Riddick wrote in *The United States Congress: Organization and Procedure:* "Seldom if ever has a Congress organized without some losing candidate for a seat in either the Senate or House contesting the right of the member-elect to be senator or representative, as the case might be, as a result of the election in which the losing candidate participated."[8]

To avert partisanship, a 1798 law established procedures to settle contested House elections. The law expired in 1804. A new law was passed in 1851 and amended in 1873 and 1875. These laws sought to give a judicial rather than partisan character to contested election proceedings, but party loyalty usually governed the outcomes.

The Federal Contested Election Act of 1969 superseded the earlier legislation. The new law, which also applied only to House contests, prescribed procedures for instituting a challenge and presenting testimony but did not establish criteria to govern decisions. It was more restrictive than earlier laws because it allowed only candidates on the ballot or bona fide write-in candidates to contest election results. Previously, anyone having an interest in a congressional election could initiate proceedings.

Senators were chosen by state legislatures until the adoption in 1913 of the Seventeenth Amendment, providing for direct popular elections. Before then, contested senatorial elections often involved accusations of corruption in the legislatures. Congress never passed a law on contested Senate elections comparable to that for the House.

The number of contested congressional elections since 1789 probably is in the hundreds, most experts agree. But an exact number has never been determined because students of the subject disagree on what constitutes a contested election.

Senate Cases

Lorimer. Four contested Senate elections in the twentieth century illustrate the complexity of such proceedings. William Lorimer, R-Ill., was elected a senator by the Illinois Legislature and took his seat on June 18, 1909. In May 1910 he requested that the Committee on Privileges and Elections examine press reports of bribery and corruption in the election. The Senate on March 1, 1911, rejected a resolution declaring that Lorimer had not been "duly and legally elected." The vote was 40–46.[9]

The case was reopened in the next Congress and the decision reversed after a specially appointed committee heard more testimony. While the committee majority favored dropping the charges, the minority pressed to overturn Lorimer's election. On June 13, 1912, the Senate adopted a resolution, 55–28, declaring the election invalid. Throughout the proceedings on Lorimer, his Republican Party held almost a 2-to-1 majority in the Senate.

Vare. Corruption also was the central issue in the case of Republican William S. Vare of Pennsylvania. During the primaries in 1926, newspapers reported illegal activities by Vare supporters to aid their candidate. Vare won the primary and the November election.

The Senate meanwhile, on May 19, 1926, had appointed a committee to investigate Pennsylvania's senatorial primaries and the fall election. Vare's Democratic rival, former secretary of labor William B. Wilson, charged that Vare's victory was won illegally. When Congress met, Vare was asked to stand aside while other senators-elect were sworn in.

Proceedings dragged on for two years. The Senate received a series of reports on the case, including one from a special committee, February 22, 1929, that said Vare, because of excessive use of money to get nominated and elected, was not entitled to a seat. On December 5, the Senate Committee on Privileges and Elections reported that Vare had received a plurality of the legal votes cast in the election. But the Senate the following day voted 58–22 to deny Vare a seat and 66–15 that Wilson had not been elected. The Pennsylvania governor later appointed Republican Joseph R. Grundy to the vacant Senate seat. Republicans controlled the Senate throughout the proceedings on Vare.

Wyman-Durkin Contest. The closest Senate election since popular voting for the Senate was instituted in 1913 occurred November 5, 1974, in New Hampshire, where Republican Louis C. Wyman led Democrat John A. Durkin by only two votes after the ballots were counted and recounted.

The election spawned a long, bitter, and embarrassing dispute in the Senate covering seven months and forty-one roll-call votes. It ended when the Senate for the first time declared a vacancy because of its inability to decide an election contest.[10]

The dispute began when final unofficial returns gave Wyman a 355-vote margin over Durkin. A recount then found Durkin the winner by ten votes. The state ballot commission examined the recount and found Wyman the winner by two votes.

(Wyman actually served for a short period. His predecessor, Sen. Norris Cotton, R, who was retiring, resigned late in December 1974 to take advantage of a special early-retirement pension bonus. The New Hampshire governor appointed Wyman to fill the remaining sixty hours of Cotton's term, until noon January

In 1975 the Senate for the first time declared a vacancy because of its inability to decide an election contest. In a new election, New Hampshire voters chose Democrat John A. Durkin, above, over Republican Louis C. Wyman.

3, 1975. Had Wyman been seated, the few extra hours would have helped establish seniority rights over other newly elected senators.)

Durkin filed a petition of contest with the Senate December 27, 1974, challenging Wyman's right to the seat and defending the validity of his own recount victory. On January 5, 1975, Wyman filed a petition in the Senate urging that Durkin's petition be dismissed. He also asked that the seat be declared vacant, to open the way for a new election in New Hampshire. Wyman and his supporters feared Durkin would win if the Senate, with its 61–38 Democratic majority, reviewed the ballot commission findings as the Democratic candidate requested.

The first skirmish occurred soon after the Senate convened. On January 28, the Senate turned aside Republican attempts to seat Wyman temporarily and to declare the seat vacant and voted, 58–34, to send the dispute to the Senate Rules and Administration Committee. The Senate thus accepted the arguments of Senate Majority Leader Mike Mansfield, D-Mont., and Rules Chairman Howard W. Cannon, D-Nev., who cited the constitutional provision that each house of Congress should be the judge of its own elections and said the Rules Committee should at least try to determine who won before calling for a new election.

Democrats also said that the conflicting rulings of the New Hampshire authorities precluded seating either of the contestants, even though Wyman had the most recent certification. Republicans claimed that precedent dictated the temporary seating of Wyman, without prejudice to Durkin's challenge. But the motion to temporarily seat Wyman failed on a 34–58 vote, while a motion to declare the seat vacant lost, 39–53.

The Rules Committee agreed to examine and recount the ballots in dispute. By April 25 nearly one thousand ballots had been examined. But the committee failed to agree on twenty-seven of the ballots, splitting on 4–4 tie votes. Tie votes also occurred on eight legal and procedural issues. The eight issues and twenty-seven ballots were sent to the Senate floor to be resolved.

Floor consideration of the disputed election began June 12 with a second attempt by the Republicans to declare the seat vacant. The motion was defeated, 43–55, and a filibuster by Republicans and several southern Democrats supporting the Republican position began. An unprecedented six attempts were made to invoke cloture (shut off debate), but they all failed to obtain the required sixty votes. An attempt to settle one of the eight disputed issues in Wyman's favor July 15 was defeated on a 44–49 vote. After this loss, the Republicans charged that a Democratic "steamroller" was in operation and refused to allow a vote on any other issue.

The Senate began to spend less and less time each day on the New Hampshire dispute and returned to debate on substantive legislation. But neither side appeared ready to compromise. In the absence of any definitive Senate action, public pressure mounted for a vacancy to be declared and a new election held.

Finally, Durkin relented and asked for a new election. Durkin's change of mind was a surprise to the Senate Democratic leadership, but there was a feeling of relief that the impasse had been broken. The Senate June 30 voted 71–21 to declare the seat vacant as of August 8.

Durkin won the special September 16 election with a plurality of 27,771 votes (taking 53.6 percent of the vote) and was sworn in September 18, 1975.

Landrieu-Jenkins Contest. The last contested Senate election of the twentieth century was a throwback to those at the beginning of the century, when corruption was cited as the main issue.

At issue was a 1996 open-seat election in Louisiana that Democrat Mary L. Landrieu narrowly won over Republican state representative Louis "Woody" Jenkins by 5,788 votes out of 1.7 million cast. Republican Gov. Mike Foster certified Landrieu as the winner barely two weeks after the election. But Jenkins, who had the strong backing of conservatives and the Republican right, alleged that skullduggery endemic to Louisiana's Democratic Party cost him the election and propelled Landrieu to victory.

Sen. Mary Landrieu of Louisiana talks to the press after the release of the 1997 bipartisan Senate committee report that recommended the dismissal of the seat challenge against her 1996 election.

He leveled no specific charges at Landrieu but alleged that systematic illegality marred the contest. Jenkins's charges included vote buying, multiple voting, fraudulent voter registration, campaign finance violations, voting machine malfunctions, election commissioner wrongdoing, and the illegal transporting of voters to the polls.

Jenkins initially pursued a challenge of the election results in the Louisiana courts, but he abandoned that effort for lack of time. Knowing that the Senate is the final arbiter of its membership, he petitioned that body to unseat Landrieu and order a new election.

The Senate Rules and Administration Committee hired two outside counsels to investigate the charges and then, under pressure from conservatives who turned the case into a cause célèbre, rejected its independent lawyers' recommendations for a limited probe. On a party-line vote April 17, the panel chose to pursue an aggressive inquiry.

Over a six-month period, the investigation was marked by partisan fits and starts. Democrats delayed the investigation until ground rules were firmly established on the use of federal investigators and on the authority to issue subpoenas. John W.

Warner, R-Va., chairman of the committee, directed that election-law attorneys from one of his home state's top law firms spearhead the investigation.

In June, a few weeks after the second phase of the probe had begun, Democrats withdrew from the inquiry, saying investigators had found that a political operative for Jenkins had paid witnesses to invent stories of voter fraud. The committee's minority referred incidents of alleged election tampering to the Justice Department's criminal division.

In July, over the strong objections of the panel's Democrats, Republicans decided to widen their open-ended investigation and granted Warner unprecedented subpoena power. The next month, the chairman was a one-man show in New Orleans, questioning Democratic officials and representatives from the gambling industry, which had placed a gambling initiative on the ballot and had spent liberally during the 1996 campaign.

On October 1, the committee concluded there were isolated incidences of fraud, election irregularities, and lax record-keeping, but nothing on the scale of Jenkins's allegations of widespread, organized wrongdoing. The committee voted 16–0 to end its investigation, saying "the evidence collected to date does not meet the applicable burden to justify further consideration" of Jenkins's petition.

In a final action, the committee decided against reimbursing either Landrieu or Jenkins for their legal fees, as lawmakers were leery of encouraging a losing candidate to challenge an election knowing that the taxpayers would eventually fit the bill.

House Cases

William F. Willoughby stated in *Principles of Legislative Organization and Administration* in 1934: "The whole history of the handling of election contests by the House has constituted one of the major scandals of our political system."[11]

Willoughby noted that after enactment of the 1851 law on procedures for adjudicating elections "for many years the House made little or no pretense of settling election contests on any basis of equity, political considerations in practically all cases determining the decision reached." In 1955 John T. Dempsey, a doctoral candidate at the University of Michigan, made a case-by-case examination of the 546 contested election cases he had counted in the House. He found that only on forty-seven occasions, less than 10 percent of the total, did the controlling party award a contested seat to a member of the minority party.

Mississippi Dispute. Perhaps the most dramatic election dispute settled by the House in recent years was that of the Mississippi Five in 1965. The governor of Mississippi certified the election to the House in 1964 of four Democrats and one Republican. The Democrats were Thomas G. Abernethy, William M. Colmer, Jamie L. Whitten, and John Bell Williams; the Republican was Prentiss Walker.

Their right to be seated was contested by a biracial group, the Mississippi Freedom Democratic Party, formed originally to challenge the seating of an all-white delegation from the state to the 1964 Democratic National Convention. This group, when unsuccessful in getting its candidates on the 1964 congressional election ballot, conducted a rump election in which Annie Devine, Virginia Gray, and Fannie L. Hamer were the winners.[12]

The three women, when they sought entrance to the House floor, were barred. However, Speaker John W. McCormack, D-Mass., asked the regular Mississippi representatives-elect to stand aside while the other members of the House were sworn in. William F. Ryan, D-N.Y., sponsor of the challenge, contended that the regular congressional election in Mississippi was invalid because blacks had been systematically prevented from voting. A resolution to seat the regular Mississippi delegation was adopted on January 4, 1965, by a voice vote.

Later that year Congress enacted the Voting Rights Act of 1965, which contained strict sanctions against states that practiced discrimination against minority voters.

McCloskey-McIntyre Contest. Three 1984 House races were so close that the losers contested the results. One race, in Indiana, led to four months of acrimony between Democrats and Republicans over what appeared to be the closest House contest in the twentieth century. Debate on the race took up far more time than almost any other issue the House considered in 1985.

After the November 6 election, incumbent Democrat Frank McCloskey appeared to have won reelection to his Indiana Eighth District seat by seventy-two votes. But correction of an arithmetical error (ballots in two precincts were counted twice) gave Republican challenger Richard D. McIntyre an apparent thirty-four-vote victory. On that basis, the Indiana secretary of state December 14 certified McIntyre the winner.

But when Congress convened January 3, 1985, the Democratic-controlled House refused to seat McIntyre, voting instead to declare the seat vacant pending an investigation of alleged irregularities in the election. Three times after that—in February, March, and April—Republicans pushed the seating of McIntyre to a vote, losing each time while picking up no more than a handful of votes from the Democrats.

A recount completed January 22 showed McIntyre's lead had increased to 418 votes, after more than 4,800 ballots were thrown out for technical reasons. But a House Administration Committee task force, with auditors from the General Accounting Office, conducted its own recount and, on a 2–1 partisan split, found McCloskey the winner by four votes. Republicans then tried to get a new election by declaring the seat vacant. Their attempt lost, 200–229. Nineteen Democrats joined 181 Republicans in voting for a new election.

The next day, before the House Administration Committee's recommendation to seat McCloskey came to a vote, Republicans moved to send the issue back to the panel with orders to count thirty-two controversial absentee ballots that the task force had decided, on a 2–1 vote, not to count. That motion was rejected, 183–246.

The House then approved the resolution 236–190, with ten

Democrats joining the Republicans in voting against it. GOP members walked out of the House chamber in protest, accusing Democrats of stealing the election.

The Supreme Court May 28 refused to get involved in the dispute. Without a dissenting vote, it denied Indiana permission to sue the House in the Supreme Court.

A U.S. district court judge in Washington, D.C., dismissing a suit brought by McIntyre against House Democrats and House officers, ruled March 1 that the House had the constitutional right to judge its own membership.

On February 7, a federal district court in Indiana had dismissed a separate suit filed by McIntyre challenging recount procedures in two of the district's counties and ruled that the House alone was responsible for determining the validity of contested ballots.

Ultimately, McIntyre challenged McCloskey to a rematch in 1986, but he lost by more than 13,000 votes.

Other 1984 Contested Elections. Results in two other close House races also were contested, but those challenges, in Guam and Idaho, were unsuccessful. On July 24, the House agreed by voice vote to a resolution dismissing a challenge by Democrat Antonio Borja Won Pat, the former nonvoting delegate from Guam, against Republican Ben Blaz. Won Pat, who had represented Guam in Congress since 1973, had lost the November 1984 election by about 350 votes. Won Pat had protested, among other things, that Blaz had not won an absolute majority of the votes cast, as required by law. On October 2, the House threw out a challenge by former representative George Hansen, R-Idaho, against Democrat Richard H. Stallings. Hansen, who was convicted in 1984 of filing false financial disclosure forms, charged, among other things, vote fraud in his 170-vote loss to Stallings. The House dismissed the challenge by a 247–4 vote, with 169 members, mostly Republicans, voting "present." *(See "Hansen," p. 938.)*

Sanchez-Dornan Contest. Thirteen months of acrimonious debate with ethnic overtones ended in February 1998 when the Republican-led House refused to overturn the election of California Democrat Loretta Sanchez. Republican Robert K. Dornan. claimed that Sanchez had unseated him by 984 votes in 1996 because of a rash of illegal voting by noncitizens in his demographically changing Orange County district. Sanchez, who was Hispanic, contended Dornan's charges were racially motivated.

A three-member task force within the House Oversight Committee conducted the investigation. It focused particularly on Hermandad Mexicana Nacional, a group that helped register Hispanic voters in California in 1996. The task force found evidence of 748 illegal votes cast by noncitizens, a total that fell short of Sanchez's margin of victory. But Republicans said the results showed that Dornan's challenge was not frivolous and that the GOP was not unfairly targeting Hispanics.

As the House probe proceeded through the fall of 1997, Dornan began using his privileges as a former member to visit the House floor. After his verbal altercation with Robert Menendez, D-N.J., about the probe, Dornan's floor access was denied. More than one hundred Republicans joined a nearly unanimous bloc of Democrats to adopt a resolution that barred Dornan from the House floor or surrounding areas until the contested election was resolved.

Meanwhile, Democrats were raising a ruckus on the House floor, introducing a slew of privileged resolutions to halt the probe, charging that it targeted Hispanic voters. While none of the resolutions succeeded, Democrats did bring action on the floor to a halt several times. Minority Leader Richard A. Gephardt, D-Mo., in October offered a privileged resolution calling for an end to the probe. The House rejected the proposal, 204–222.

Through the following months Republicans and Democrats conducted behind-the-scenes talks to find a face-saving way to end the probe. Finally in February 1998 the House ended the investigation by agreeing there had been vote fraud in Sanchez's election but not enough to justify continuation of Dornan's challenge. The House first defeated, 194–215, a Democratic motion to return the resolution to the House Oversight Committee and strip most of its findings of election fraud. Then, the House voted 378–33 for a resolution to drop the inquiry into Dornan's challenge. All thirty-three votes against the resolution were cast by Republicans.

Dornan subsequently sought to regain his seat in the 1998 general election, but he lost to Sanchez by nearly 15,000 votes.

NOTES

1. V. O. Key Jr., *Politics, Parties, and Pressure Groups*, 5th ed. (New York: Crowell, 1964), 378.

2. Letter to Francis Hopkinson, March 3, 1789. Quoted in Elizabeth Frost, ed., *The Bully Pulpit: Quotations from America's Presidents* (New York: Facts on File, 1988), 149.

3. *The Federalist Papers*, with an introduction by Clinton Rossiter (New York: New American Library, 1961), 80.

4. Alan Ehrenhalt, *The United States of Ambition: Politicians, Power, and the Pursuit of Office* (New York: Times Books, 1991), 23.

5. William H. Flanigan and Nancy H. Zingale, *Political Behavior of the American Electorate* (Washington, D.C.: CQ Press, 1991), 43–44.

6. Ibid., 68, 83.

7. Lydia Saad, "Independents Rank as Largest U.S. Political Group" (Gallup News Service, April 9, 1999), 1–3.

8. Floyd M. Riddick, *The United States Congress: Organization and Procedure* (Washington, D.C.: National Capitol Publishers, 1949), 12.

9. George H. Haynes, *The Senate of the United States* (Boston: Houghton-Mifflin, 1938), 131.

10. For more background, see *Congressional Quarterly Almanac 1975*, 699.

11. William F. Willoughby, *Principles of Legislative Organization and Administration* (Washington, D.C.: Brookings Institution, 1934), 277.

12. For more background, see *Congressional Quarterly Almanac 1965*, 609.

SELECTED BIBLIOGRAPHY

Abramson, Paul R., John H. Aldrich, and David W. Rohde. *Change and Continuity in the 1996 and 1998 Elections.* Washington, D.C.: CQ Press, 1999.

American Political Science Association. Committee on Political Parties. *Toward a More Responsible Two-Party System: A Report.* New York: Rinehart, 1950.

Bibby, John F., and L. Sandy Maisel. *Two Parties, or More? The American Party System.* Boulder, Co.: Westview Press, 1998.

Bone, Hugh A. *American Politics and the Party System.* New York: McGraw-Hill, 1955.

Brady, David W., and Craig Volden. *Revolving Gridlock: Politics and Policy from Carter to Clinton.* Boulder, Colo.: Westview Press, 1998.

Cox, Gary W., and Samuel Kernell, ed. *The Politics of Divided Government.* Boulder, Colo.: Westview Press, 1991.

Ehrenhalt, Alan. *The United States of Ambition: Politicians, Power, and the Pursuit of Office.* New York: Times Books, 1991.

Flanigan, William H., and Nancy H. Zingale. *Political Behavior of the American Electorate.* 9th ed. Washington, D.C.: CQ Press, 1998.

Green, John C., and Daniel M. Shea. *The State of the Parties: The Changing Role of Contemporary American Parties.* 3rd ed. Lanham, Md.: Rowan and Littlefield, 1999.

Ladd, Everett Carll, and Charles D. Hadley. *Transformation of the American Party System.* 2nd ed. New York: Norton, 1978.

Maisel, L. Sandy, ed. *The Parties Respond: Changes in American Parties and Campaigns.* 2nd ed. Boulder: Westview Press, 1994

Nelson, Michael. *The Elections of 1996.* Washington, D.C.: CQ Press, 1997.

Nichols, Roy F. *The Invention of the American Political Parties.* New York: Macmillan, 1967.

Reichley, James. *The Life of the Parties: A History of American Political Parties.* New York: Free Press, 1992.

Schattschneider, E. E. *Party Government.* New York: Holt, Rinehart and Winston, 1942.

———. *The Semisovereign People: A Realist's View of Democracy in America.* New York: Holt, Rinehart and Winston, 1960.

Schlesinger, Arthur M., Jr., ed. *History of U.S. Political Parties.* 4 vols. New York: Bowker, 1981.

Schlesinger, Joseph A. *Political Parties and the Winning of Office.* Ann Arbor: University of Michigan Press, 1991.

Shea, Daniel M., and John C. Green. *The State of the Parties: The Changing Role of Contemporary American Parties.* Lanham, Md: Rowan and Littlefield, 1994.

Sundquist, James L. *Dynamics of the Party System: Alignment and Realignment of Political Parties in the United States.* Rev. ed. Washington, D.C.: Brookings Institution, 1983.

Tarrance, V. Lance, Jr., Walter De Vries, and Donna L. Mosher. *Checked and Balanced: How Ticket-Splitters Are Shaping the New Balance of Power in American Politics.* Grand Rapids, Mich.: Eerdmans, 1998.

Wattenberg, Martin P. *The Decline of American Political Parties: 1952–1994.* Cambridge: Harvard University Press, 1996.

CHAPTER 31

Who Gets Elected

Americans elect a new Congress on the first Tuesday after the first Monday in November of even-numbered years. Early the following January the elected representatives and senators begin their first session of that Congress. Those elected November 3, 1998, for instance, were sworn in January 6, 1999, on the opening day of the 106th Congress. They included many new faces—eight new senators and forty freshmen representatives—as is inevitable in each Congress.

As an institution, Congress has suffered public criticism almost since the nation's beginnings. Alexis de Tocqueville, the astute French visitor of the late 1820s, observed the "vulgar demeanor" of the House of Representatives, where often he could not detect even one "distinguished man." In contrast, as he further wrote in his classic *Democracy in America*, the Senate was "composed of eloquent advocates, distinguished generals, wise magistrates, and statesmen of note, whose arguments would do honor to the most remarkable parliamentary debates of Europe."[1]

Subsequent views of the entire Congress at times seemed no more charitable than de Tocqueville's opinion of the House. Gallup polls assessing the amount of trust and confidence that Americans have in various institutions indicate that Congress consistently ranks third among the three branches of government. In December 1998 Gallup found that 63 percent of the Americans questions had "a great deal" or "fair amount" of confidence in the executive branch, and 78 percent said they had confidence in the judicial branch. Yet 61 percent of those Americans polled expressed trust and confidence in the legislative branch, up seven percentage points from May 1997.[2] But paradoxically, election results often indicate that while Congress as an institution may not be held in high regard, voters are more generous in returning the incumbents who represent them.

In the modern era the power of incumbency has remained strong with the turnover rate averaging at about 10 percent or less—historically a very low level. This turnover rate included deaths and resignations of incumbents, as well as defeat at the polls. Political scientists suggest that the incumbent's appeal rests on more than his or her record in Congress. In an era of high campaign costs, especially for television advertising, the incumbent has usually achieved greater voter recognition than any challenger and is better positioned to raise campaign funds.

Incumbents looked less secure, however, in the congressional elections of 1992 and 1994—in which more than eighty incumbents lost their reelection bids. In the early 1990s voters were increasingly wary of "career politicians," and many challengers ran antigovernment campaigns presenting themselves positively as having never served in an elected office. Many new members vowed to serve only a limited number of terms, so as to avoid becoming too cozy in Congress.

The landmark 1994 elections swept Republicans to power in both chambers. Democrats had controlled either the House or Senate, and usually both, since 1955. Since 1933, when the Great Depression realigned political power, Republicans had managed to control both houses only twice—in the 80th Congress (1947–1949) and the 83rd Congress (1953–1955). Republicans also held a Senate majority from 1981 to 1987.

In 1996 the GOP maintained its majority, losing nine seats in the House, but gaining two in the Senate. It was the first time that the GOP had won a back-to-back majority in the House since the 1920s. In 1998 the Republican Party again held onto both chambers, but its majority was further trimmed by five seats in the House. There were signs that the power of incumbency had returned. All but seven of the 401 House members (98 percent) seeking reelection were successful. Just three of thirty-four senators up in 1998 were defeated.

Characteristics of Members

Whether the turnover is large or small, a certain uniformity pervades Congress. Congress has been dominated since its inception by middle-aged white men with backgrounds in law or business. Their levels of income and education have consistently been above the national average. But for many of the lawmakers today, business occupations are past activities. In recent years, ethics rules have limited the income that can be earned outside of Congress. Moreover, serving in Congress has become a full-time job. And since the 1970s it has attracted career politicians, whose primary earnings have come from government service.

Ever so slowly, other changes also have crept into the makeup of Congress. The numbers of women, African American, and Hispanic American members have increased in recent decades, although still not in proportion to their share of the total population. Of the 535 members of Congress at the beginning of 1999, sixty-five were women, thirty-seven were black, eighteen were Hispanic, five were of Asian or Pacific Islands descent, and one senator, Ben Nighthorse Campbell of Colorado, was of Native American heritage. In addition, of the five nonvoting delegates sent to the House, two were black women, one was Hispanic, and two were of Pacific Island descent.

TABLE 31–1 Age Structure of Congress

Average ages of members at the beginning of each Congress.

Year	House	Senate	Congress
1949	51.0	58.5	53.8
1951	52.0	56.6	53.0
1953	52.0	56.6	53.0
1955	51.4	57.2	52.2
1957	52.9	57.9	53.8
1959	51.7	57.1	52.7
1961	52.2	57.0	53.2
1963	51.7	56.8	52.7
1965	50.5	57.7	51.9
1967	50.8	57.7	52.1
1969	52.2	56.6	53.0
1971	51.9	56.4	52.7
1973	51.1	55.3	52.0
1975	49.8	55.5	50.9
1977	49.3	54.7	50.3
1979	48.8	52.7	49.5
1981	48.4	52.5	49.2
1983	45.5	53.4	47.0
1985	49.7	54.2	50.5
1987	50.7	54.4	52.5
1989	52.1	55.6	52.8
1991	52.8	57.2	53.6
1993	51.7	58.0	52.9
1995	50.9	58.4	52.2
1997	51.6	57.5	52.7
1999	52.6	58.3	53.7

SOURCE: Congressional Quarterly.

AVERAGE AGE

The average age of members of Congress went up substantially between the post–Civil War period and the 1950s but remained fairly constant until the mid-1970s. In the 41st Congress (1869–1871), the average was 44.6 years; by the 85th Congress (1957–1959), it was 53.8. Over the next eighteen years, the average fluctuated only slightly. But when the 94th Congress met in January 1975, the average age dropped to 50.9 years. *(See Table 31-1, this page.)*

The difference was made in the House, where ninety-two freshmen members reduced the average age of representatives to 49.8 years, the first time since World War II that the average in either chamber had fallen below 50. The 96th Congress (1979–1981) was the youngest since 1949; the overall average age for both chambers had slipped to 49.5 years. It dropped again in January 1981, when the House had eight members under 30, the most since World War II. The younger trend bottomed out in 1983 when the average hit 47 years.

After that came a gradual increase, continuing through the beginning of the 106th Congress in 1999, when the average age climbed to 53.7. That aging trend was partly attributable to the aging trend of the nation's population. But low turnover in Congress was also a big factor. The youngest Congress of the 1990s was the 104th, when the Republicans took control. The average age in January 1995 was 52.2, with House members averaging 50.9 years.

OCCUPATIONS

The legal profession has been the dominant occupational background of members of Congress since its beginning. In the First Congress, more than one-third of the House members had legal training. The proportion of lawyers in Congress crested at 70 percent in 1840 but remained high. From 1950 to the mid-1970s it was in the 55–60 percent range.

The first significant decline in members with a law background began with the 96th Congress. Although sixty-five of the one hundred senators were lawyers in 1979, for the first time in at least thirty years lawyers made up less than a majority of the House. That situation continued through the 1990s. When the 106th Congress convened in January 1999, 169 of the 435 representatives and fifty-seven of the one hundred senators were lawyers. *(See Table 31-2, p. 841.)*

After lawyers, members with a business or banking background make up the second largest group in Congress. In the 106th Congress, 159 House members claimed such a background, down from 181 in the 105th Congress. The November 1998 election also sent eighty-four members with a background in education, twenty-two who listed agriculture as their occupation, twenty who had real estate experience, and eighteen from the medical or health care profession.

Members of the clergy continue to be underrepresented in Congress. Only a handful of Protestant ministers have served in Congress, and no Catholic priest had done so until 1971, when Rep. Robert F. Drinan, D-Mass., a Jesuit, took a House seat. (Father Gabriel Richard was the nonvoting delegate of the Territory of Michigan from 1823 to 1825.) Drinan served five terms but declined to run again in 1980, the year that Pope John Paul II ordered priests not to hold public office. The pope's directive also prompted Robert J. Cornell, a Catholic priest and former U.S. House member, to halt his political comeback bid in Wisconsin. Cornell, a Democrat elected in 1974, had served two terms before he was defeated in 1978. Only two members of the 106th Congress listed their occupation as clergy.

A new breed of legislator emerged in the 1970s: the career politician whose primary earnings had always come from political office at the local, state, or federal level. This trend became possible because states and localities had begun to think of political positions as full-time jobs and had raised salaries accordingly. In addition, the demands of modern political campaigns left less time for the pursuit of other careers.

Members of the 106th Congress continued this trend. Thirty-three of forty House freshmen had held another elected office, and the chamber as a whole had 311 members who claimed a successful election to local or state office in their background. The picture is much the same in the Senate, where seven of eight newcomers had prior political experience. Eighty-six of the one hundred senators in the 106th Congress held a previous elected office.

New members of Congress also tend to lack military experience, continuing a trend that had been prevalent in the 1990s. At

TABLE 31-2 Members' Occupations, 106th Congress

| | House | | | Senate | | | Congress |
Occupation	Dem.	Rep.	Total	Dem.	Rep.	Total	Total
Actor/entertainer	0	1	1	0	1	1	2
Aeronautics	0	1	1	0	0	0	1
Agriculture	8	14	22	1	5	6	28
Arts/creative	1	1	2	0	0	0	2
Business/banking	53	106	159	6	18	24	183
Clergy	0	1	1	0	1	1	2
Education	49	34	84[a]	5	8	13	97
Engineering	1	8	9	0	0	0	9
Health care	2	1	3	0	0	0	3
Journalism	2	6	9[a]	2	6	8	17
Labor organizing	1	0	1	0	0	0	1
Law	87	76	163	27	28	55	218
Law enforcement	8	2	10	0	0	0	10
Medicine	5	10	15	0	2	2	17
Military	0	1	1	0	1	1	2
Professional sports	0	2	2	0	1	1	3
Public service/politics	57	49	106	10	8	18	124
Real estate	3	17	20	2	2	4	24
Technical/trade	1	2	3	0	0	0	3
Miscellaneous	1	5	6	0	0	0	6

NOTES: Because some members have more than one occupation, totals are larger than the number of members.

   a. Includes Independent Bernard Sanders of Vermont.

   SOURCE: Congressional Quarterly.

the start of the 101st Congress in 1989, seventy senators and 216 House members cited military service. In 1999 at the start of the 106th Congress, only 179 of the 535 members claimed military service (forty-three in the Senate and 136 in the House).

RELIGIOUS AFFILIATIONS

Among religious groups, Protestants have comprised nearly three-fourths of the membership of both houses in recent years. However, Roman Catholics form the biggest single religious group—a distinction they have held since taking the lead from Methodists in 1965.

In the 106th Congress Roman Catholics made up the largest religious congregation in both chambers with a total of 151. Among Protestant denominations, Baptists were the most numerous (70), followed by Methodists (62), Presbyterians (48), Episcopalians (43), and Lutherans (22). In all, the members listed affiliations with some nineteen religious groups, including Jewish (34), Mormon (17), Eastern Christian (6), Christian Scientist (5), Unitarian (3), and Pentecostal (3). Eight did not specify a religious preference, and forty-two simply listed "Protestant." No one was designated Moslem, Hindu, or Buddhist.[3]

Women in Congress

By January 1999 a total of 197 women had sat in Congress, starting with Rep. Jeannette Rankin, R-Mont., elected in 1917. Her state gave women the right to vote before the Nineteenth Amendment to the Constitution enfranchising women was ratified in 1920. Of the 197 women, 169 served in the House only, twenty in the Senate only, and five—Margaret Chase Smith, R-Maine; Barbara A. Mikulski, D-Md.; Barbara Boxer, D-Calif.; Olympia J. Snowe, R-Maine; and Blanche Lincoln, D-Ark.—in both chambers. *(See Table 31-3, p. 842.)*

In her 1996 book about women who had served in Congress, Rep. Marcy Kaptur, D-Ohio, wrote

From the first woman to serve in Congress—Jeannette Rankin of Montana, elected to the House in 1917—to the fifty-eight who serve today, their personal stories have varied tremendously. More than one-third of these women were widows who succeeded their husbands in office and went on to surpass them. Some were self-actualized women who either rose through the ranks of political parties and institutions or took them on and got elected to Congress on their own. Most encountered and rose above incredible adversity and tragedy; a few were blessed with vast wealth. All exhibited insight into the human condition, a persevering determination to overcome obstacles, and a conscience formed in the knowledge that women have always been, and may always be, charged with nurturing, teaching and enlightening the human race.[4]

Several women served out unexpired terms of less than one year. Rebecca L. Felton, the first woman to serve in the Senate, did so for only one day. Felton, a Georgia Democrat, was appointed October 1, 1922, to fill the Senate vacancy created by the death of Thomas E. Watson. She was not sworn in until November 21, and the next day yielded her seat to Walter F. George, who had meanwhile been elected to fill the vacancy.

Gladys Pyle, a South Dakota Republican, was elected Novem-

TABLE 31-3 Women in Congress, 1947–1999

Congress	Senate	House
80th (1947–1949)	1	7
81st (1949–1951)	1	9
82nd (1951–1953)	1	10
83rd (1953–1955)	1	12
84th (1955–1957)	1	17
85th (1957–1959)	1	15
86th (1959–1961)	1	17
87th (1961–1963)	2	18
88th (1963–1965)	2	12
89th (1965–1967)	2	11
90th (1967–1969)	1	10
91st (1969–1971)	1	10
92nd (1971–1973)	1	13
93rd (1973–1975)	1	16
94th (1975–1977)	0	17
95th (1977–1979)	2	18
96th (1979–1981)	1	16
97th (1981–1983)	2	19
98th (1983–1985)	2	22
99th (1985–1987)	2	22
100th (1987–1989)	2	23
101st (1989–1991)	2	28
102nd (1991–1993)	3	29
103rd (1993–1995)	7	48
104th (1995–1997)	8	48
105th (1997–1999)	9	51
106th (1999–2001)	9	56

NOTE: House totals exclude nonvoting delegates. See Reference Materials for roster of women who have served in Congress.

ber 9, 1938, to fill the unexpired term of Rep. Peter Norbeck, who died in office. But his term ended the following January 3 before Congress convened and thus Pyle never took the oath of office.

In 1996 Kansas Lt. Gov. Sheila Frahm was appointed by Gov. Bill Graves to fill the Senate seat of Majority Leader Bob Dole, who had resigned from the Senate to run full time for president. Frahm held the seat less than five months. A special primary was held in August to fill Dole's seat, and Frahm lost it to a more conservative Republican, Sam Brownback, who went on to win the November general election.

THE WIDOW'S MANDATE

In many jurisdictions it became customary for the office-holder's party to run his widow for the seat in the hope of tapping a sympathy vote. Sometimes she filled the office by brief appointment until the governor or party leaders could agree on a candidate.

The "widow's mandate," as such, marked the beginning of political careers for some women. Edith Nourse Rogers, a Massachusetts Republican, entered the House after her husband died in 1925 and remained there until her death in 1960. Margaret Chase Smith filled her late husband's House seat in 1940 and went on to serve four terms in the Senate (1949–1973). Hattie W. Caraway, an Arkansas Democrat, who was appointed to the Senate seat of her late husband in 1931, was returned to Congress by Arkansas voters in 1932 and 1938.

Rep. Charlotte T. Reid, R-Ill., and Rep. Marilyn Lloyd, D-Tenn., became their parties' nominees when their husbands died between the primary and general elections (in 1962 and 1974, respectively). As women became more active in politics at all levels, the congressional tradition of the widow's mandate has weakened.

In the 106th Congress, three women held the House seats of their late husbands. Jo Ann Emerson, R-Mo., won a special election in 1996 to fill out the term of her husband, Bill Emerson. She later won the general election to win a full term in the 105th Congress. Two years later, Republican Mary Bono won the California seat, which had been represented by her husband, former pop singer Sonny Bono. She won reelection easily in November 1998. Lois Capps, D-Calif., won the Santa Barbara district of her husband, Walter Capps, who died in 1997.

Marriages have also linked members of Congress. Rep. Emily Taft Douglas, D-Ill., was elected to Congress in 1944, four years before her husband, Sen. Paul H. Douglas, D-Ill., was. Another woman, Rep. Martha Keys, D-Kan., married Rep. Andrew Jacobs, D-Ind., in 1976. This marriage between colleagues was the first of its kind in congressional history. Rep. Olympia J. Snowe, R-Maine, in 1989 married the governor of Maine, John R. McKernan Jr., a former U.S. representative. In 1994 Rep. Susan Molinari wed her New York state colleague, Rep. Bill Paxon, joining together two House Republican leaders. In the 105th Congress, Molinari served as Republican conference vice chairman and Paxon served as chairman of the National Republican Congressional Committee. In 1996 Molinari gave birth to the couple's daughter.

Molinari earned another distinction as one of the few women in Congress who were daughters of representatives. She won the Staten Island seat of her father, Rep. Guy Molinari, who left the House to become Staten Island borough president. California Democrat Lucille Roybal-Allard also shared that distinction by winning the House seat of her father, Edward R. Roybal, whose congressional career lasted thirty years. California Democrat Nancy Pelosi, who entered the House since 1987, was the daughter of Thomas J. D'Alesandro Jr., a House member from 1939 to 1947 and then mayor of Baltimore.

SLOW GAIN IN NUMBERS

It has been a long, slow climb in women's membership since Rankin's election to Congress in 1916. Her seating was not followed by a surge of women members, even after women received the vote in 1920. The first notable increase came in 1928, when nine women were elected to the House. The number had scarcely more than doubled by 1961, when nineteen women (two senators, seventeen representatives) served in Congress.

After that women's membership declined slightly and did not regain the 1961 level until 1975. Another slippage followed until 1981, when the membership reached twenty for the first time.

The thirty women sworn in as members of the 102nd Congress in January 1991 represented a record number to be elected in a single election. Thirty women also served in the 101st Congress, but only twenty-seven of them were elected in the 1988 general elections. Three others—Ileana Ros-Lehtinen, R-Fla.; Jill L. Long, D-Ind.; and Susan Molinari—came to the House through special elections in 1989 and 1990.

The elections of 1992 found record numbers of women running for and being elected to Congress. The 103rd Congress, which opened in 1993, included forty-seven women in the House, an increase of nineteen, and six in the Senate, an increase of four.

Several factors contributed to the success of women candidates in 1992. Many capitalized on an unusually large number of retirements to run in open seats. They also benefited from reapportionment, which created dozens of opportunities for newcomers in the South and West. Another factor was public dissatisfaction with Congress, which allowed women to portray themselves positively as outsiders. The Senate's questioning of law professor Anita F. Hill's accusations of sexual harassment in the 1991 confirmation hearings of Supreme Court Justice Clarence Thomas also had an impact. The televised image of an all-male Senate Judiciary panel sharply questioning Hill brought home dramatically to many women their lack of representation in Congress.

By the last Congress of the decade, the 106th, there was an all-time high of sixty-seven women—fifty-six in the House and nine in the Senate—on Capitol Hill. (The House total does not include two nonvoting delegates.)

The number of women elected to full Senate terms increased dramatically in the 1990s. By 1999 the nine women serving in the Senate were all elected to full Senate terms, and two states—California and Maine—were represented in the Senate solely by women. Democrats Barbara Boxer and Dianne Feinstein were both elected to the Senate from California in 1992; and Republicans Olympia J. Snowe and Susan Collins were elected from Maine in 1994 and 1996, respectively.

In 1992 the first African American woman was elected to the Senate, Democrat Carol Moseley-Braun of Illinois. The daughter of a police officer and a medical technician, Moseley-Braun grew up in Chicago. She served in the state legislature from 1979 to 1988, where she rose to become the first woman assistant majority leader. She also served as the Cook County recorder of deeds (1988–1992). The outrage over the Senate's handling of the Thomas confirmation hearings propelled Moseley-Braun into the 1992 Illinois Senate race. She won that election with 53 percent of the vote, but lost in 1998 in her bid for reelection.

Before 1987, only six women ever won election to full Senate

On the steps of the Capitol, Democrats Loretta Sanchez of California, left, and Carolyn McCarthy of New York talk to reporters about their 1996 election to the House. In 1999 Sanchez and McCarthy were among the sixty-five women serving in Congress.

terms. They were Maurine B. Neuberger, D-Ore. (1960), Nancy Landon Kassebaum, R-Kan. (1978, 1984, 1990), Paula Hawkins, R-Fla. (1980), and Barbara A. Mikulski, D-Md. (1986). Kassebaum was the first woman ever elected to the Senate without being preceded in Congress by her husband.

LEADERSHIP POSITIONS

Although women have been entering Congress in record numbers, at the end of the twentieth century they still were finding it difficult to move to the top of the committee and party leadership ladders. In 1995 Kassebaum became the first woman to chair a major Senate committee, Labor and Human Resources. She was joined in the House by fellow Kansas Republican, Jan Meyers, who chaired the Small Business Committee. Before Meyers, no woman had chaired a full House committee since 1977, when Merchant Marine Committee Chairwoman Leonor K. Sullivan, D-Mo., left Congress. Mae Ella Nolan, a California Republican who served from 1923 to 1925, was the first woman to chair a congressional committee; she headed the House Committee on Expenditures in the Post Office Department.

In 1989 Barbara Mikulski became the first woman to chair a Senate Appropriations subcommittee, the VA, HUD and Related Agencies panel. She became its ranking minority member when the GOP took control of the Senate in 1995. On the House Appropriations Committee, Barbara Vucanovich, R-Nev., chaired the Military Construction Subcommittee in the 104th Congress. In the 106th Congress, Ohio's Marcy Kaptur served as the ranking member of the Agriculture subcommittee and California's Nancy Pelosi was the ranking member of the Foreign Operations panel.

In the wake of the 1998 elections, two women—Jennifer Dunn, R-Wash., and Rosa DeLauro, D-Conn.—challenged their party's leaders for a larger role in running the House, and each one was rebuffed. When the Republicans held leadership races for the 106th Congress, Dunn challenged Majority Leader Dick Armey of Texas for his job. Early in the 105th Congress, she had been elevated to an official leadership position, winning election as conference secretary. In July 1997 she moved further up in the leadership by winning the position of conference vice chairman. But her effort to move Armey out of the second highest party slot failed. If she had won, she would have been the first woman majority leader.

During the Democrats' November 1998 organizational meetings, DeLauro challenged Martin Frost of Texas for the position of chairman of the House Democratic Caucus. Ten Democrats made nominating speeches on behalf of DeLauro, the caucus' outspoken chief deputy whip, but she still did not prevail.

Congress has been an important starting point for women seeking national office, however. Shirley Chisholm, a Democratic representative from New York, ran for president in 1972, and Geraldine Ferraro, another New York Democrat who served in the House, was her party's vice presidential nominee in 1984.

Blacks in Congress

In 129 years, from 1870 to 1999, one hundred black Americans served in Congress—four in the Senate and ninety-six in the House. John W. Menard holds the distinction of being the first black person elected to Congress. But his 1868 election in Louisiana was disputed and the House denied him a seat in the 40th Congress. Hiram R. Revels of Mississippi, who filled an unexpired Senate term from February 1870 to March 1871, thus became the first black person actually to serve in Congress. The first black person to serve in the House was Joseph H. Rainey of South Carolina, from December 1870 to March 1879. (See Table 31-4, p. 845.)

Menard, Revels, and Rainey were elected during the post–Civil War Reconstruction era (1865–1877), when many white voters were disenfranchised and Confederate veterans were barred from holding office. During that period sixteen black men were sent to Congress from Alabama, Georgia, Florida, Louisiana, Mississippi, North Carolina, and South Carolina. But from the end of Reconstruction until the end of the century, only seven black men were elected to Congress, all from the Carolinas and Virginia. They, like their predecessors, were Republicans.

As federal controls were lifted in the South, literacy tests, poll taxes, and sometimes threats of violence eroded black voting rights. From the time Blanche K. Bruce of Mississippi left the Senate in 1881, no other black person served in that body until Edward W. Brooke, R-Mass., did from 1967 to 1979. In 1992 Illinois Democrat Carol Moseley-Braun was elected to the Senate, becoming the first black woman to gain a Senate seat. She served one term.

The last black person elected to the House in the nineteenth century was Republican George Henry White of North Carolina; he was elected in 1896 and 1898 but did not seek renomination in 1900. For nearly three decades there were no black members of Congress—not until Oscar De Priest, R-Ill., entered the House in 1929 and served three terms. During the next quarter-century only three other blacks were elected to Congress: Arthur W. Mitchell in 1934, William L. Dawson in 1942, and Adam Clayton Powell Jr. in 1944. All three represented big-city black constituencies, in Chicago (Mitchell and Dawson) and New York (Powell).

Moreover, all three were Democrats, reflecting a switch in black voting habits. President Franklin D. Roosevelt had pulled a majority of black voters away from the party of Abraham Lincoln into a coalition of Depression-era urban laborers, farmers, and intellectuals. Mitchell, the first black Democrat elected to the House, was brought in by the Democratic sweep in the 1934 election.

That election also removed the Republican, De Priest, and marked the beginning of a fifty-six-year absence of black representation among House Republicans. That drought was broken in November 1990 when Connecticut elected Gary Franks, a

TABLE 31-4 Blacks in Congress, 1947–1999

Congress	Senate	House
80th (1947–1949)	0	2
81st (1949–1951)	0	2
82nd (1951–1953)	0	2
83rd (1953–1955)	0	2
84th (1955–1957)	0	3
85th (1957–1959)	0	4
86th (1959–1961)	0	4
87th (1961–1963)	0	4
88th (1963–1965)	0	5
89th (1965–1967)	0	6
90th (1967–1969)	1	5
91st (1969–1971)	1	9
92nd (1971–1973)	1	12
93rd (1973–1975)	1	15
94th (1975–1977)	1	16
95th (1977–1979)	1	16
96th (1979–1981)	0	16
97th (1981–1983)	0	17
98th (1983–1985)	0	20
99th (1985–1987)	0	20
100th (1987–1989)	0	22
101st (1989–1991)	0	24
102nd (1991–1993)	0	26
103rd (1993–1995)	1	39
104th (1995–1997)	1	38
105th (1997–1999)	1	37
106th (1999–2001)	0	37

NOTE: House totals exclude nonvoting delegates. See Reference Materials for roster of blacks who have served in Congress.

black Republican real-estate investor from Waterbury who had once captained Yale's basketball team. Franks was defeated for reelection in 1996.

House Democrats, in contrast, steadily gained black members. Only two were added in the 1950s—Charles C. Diggs Jr., D-Mich., and Robert N.C. Nix, D-Pa.—but after that the pace quickened. Five more were elected in the 1960s, and fourteen each in the 1970s and 1980s. The number of black Americans elected to Congress more than doubled during the 1990s—thirty-six were elected to the House and one to the Senate.

The Supreme Court's "one-person, one-vote" rulings in the early 1960s, ratification of the Twenty-fourth Amendment in 1964, and congressional passage of the 1965 Voting Rights Act are credited with opening up the polls to black voters as never before.

The Voting Rights Act provided for federal oversight in jurisdictions where black registration and voting was exceptionally low; the Twenty-fourth Amendment outlawed poll taxes and similar restrictions on voting; and the courts eventually ended a southern practice of diluting black voting power by gerrymandering voting districts. As black voter turnouts increased, so did black representation in Congress.

In 1968 Rep. Shirley Chisholm, D-N.Y., became the first black woman to be elected to Congress. She was joined in the House by Yvonne Brathwaite Burke, D-Calif., and Barbara C. Jordan, D-Texas, who both served from 1973 until 1979. In a 1973 special

election, Cardiss Collins won the House seat previously held by her late husband, George W. Collins. Next came Katie Hall, D-Ind., the winner of a special election in November 1982, followed by two victors in the November 1990 general election, Maxine Waters, D-Calif., and Barbara-Rose Collins, D-Mich.

Jordan and Andrew Young, D-Ga., both elected in 1972, were the first blacks in the twentieth century to go to Congress from states of the Old Confederacy. Both Georgia and Texas later sent other black representatives, who were joined by black House members from Tennessee (Harold E. Ford), Mississippi (Mike Espy), and Louisiana (William J. Jefferson).

The 103rd Congress (1993–1995) had included several firsts for black Americans. In addition to Moseley-Braun becoming the first black woman ever elected to the Senate, for the first time since the Reconstruction era, the House delegations from Alabama, Florida, North Carolina, South Carolina, and Virginia included black members. Georgia elected its first black woman representative, Cynthia McKinney. The dramatic gains for African Americans in the 1992 elections was in large measure a result of redistricting aimed at increasing minority strength in Congress—a legacy of the civil rights era. This effort to draw so-called majority-minority districts, however, came under heated attack as the decade of the 1990s wore on. By 1999 the Supreme Court in a number of decisions had set new standards that greatly limited this method of increasing black representation in Congress. (See "Redistricting Battles," p. 846, and Chapter 33, Reapportionment and Redistricting.)

In 1998 all of the thirty-seven black members elected to Congress were Democrats except one, Republican J.C. Watts of Oklahoma, a former professional football player and youth minister. In addition, Democrats Eleanor Holmes Norton of the District of Columbia and Donna M. C. Christensen of the Virgin Islands were elected as nonvoting delegates.

Despite the steady gains of blacks being elected to Congress and the growing power of senior black members, African Americans remained numerically underrepresented in Congress. In 1999 they made up about 12 percent of the population, but only 9 percent of the House and had no representation in the Senate.

As the number of black Americans continued to increase in the House, those elected earlier gained seniority and, in some instances, committee chairmanships. Dawson served as chairman of the Committee on Expenditures in the Executive Departments (later renamed the Government Operations Committee) from 1949 until his death in 1970 (except for 1953–1955, when the Republicans controlled the House). Other notable black chairmen included Powell (Education and Labor Committee, 1961–1967); William H. Gray III, D-Pa. (Budget Committee, 1985–1989); Augustus F. Hawkins, D-Calif. (Education and Labor, 1984–1991); and Louis Stokes, D-Ohio (Permanent Select Committee on Intelligence, 1987–1989, and Standards of Official Conduct, 1981–1985, 1991–1993).

In 1989 Democrats elected Gray to majority whip, the third-highest ranking job in the House. Gray held the post until 1991 when he resigned from Congress to become president of the

Jesse Jackson Jr., pictured here standing with his father, Jesse Jackson, said the recent gains of blacks in Congress should be viewed in the historical context: although he was the ninety-first African American elected to Congress in 1995, more than 11,000 other people had served by then.

United Negro College Fund. In 1991 Rep. John Lewis, D-Ga., a veteran of the civil rights movement, moved up into the House Democratic leadership as a chief deputy whip.

By the end of the century, a few black members of Congress had served in the House for more than twenty-five years. California Democrat Ronald V. Dellums, who retired from the House in the 105th Congress after fourteen terms, served as chairman of the Armed Services Committee in the 103rd Congress. In the 106th Congress, William L. Clay of Missouri, a former chairman of the Post Office and Civil service Committee, served as the ranking member on the Education and Workforce Committee; John Conyers Jr. of Michigan, a former chairman of the Government Operations Committee, was the ranking member on the Judiciary Committee; and Charles Rangel of New York, ranking member of the Ways and Means Committee.

The new generation of African Americans elected to Congress in the 1990s reflected the changes begun during the civil rights era. Many came to Congress with considerable experience in state legislatures and other local government positions. Bobby L. Rush of Illinois, a leader of the militant Black Panther movement during the 1960s, had served for a decade on the Chicago city council. Earl F. Hilliard, Alabama's first black representative since Reconstruction, was an eighteen-year veteran of his state's legislature. Cynthia McKinney had been a member of the Georgia state legislature, and Corrine Brown had served in the Florida legislature.

In a 1995 special election, Jesse L. Jackson Jr., whose father, the Rev. Jesse Jackson, was a civil rights crusader and two-time Democratic presidential contender, was elected from Illinois. He

was thirty-one years old when he was sent to Congress. In 1996 Julia Carson of Indiana won the seat of her former boss, Democrat Andrew Jacobs Jr., and became the first black to represent Indianapolis in the House. She had served in both the Indiana House and Senate. Another African American woman, Carolyn Cheeks Kilpatrick, won her House seat after serving seventeen years in the Michigan House. In 1998 the Cleveland district seat of retiring black Rep. Louis Stokes was won by African American Democrat Stephanie Tubbs Jones, a judge and prosecutor in Cuyahoga County.

REDISTRICTING BATTLES

Following the 1990 census, many states redrew congressional district lines under the provisions of the 1965 Voting Rights Act, which required that interests of minority voters be protected. Districts in which minorities made up a majority of the voting age population were known as majority-minority districts. As state mapmakers pulled districts this way and that to pick up minority voters, many old boundaries were tugged out of shape. In some states, oddly shaped majority-minority districts emerged.

Congressional remapping that went to extreme lengths to elect minorities quickly came under scrutiny by the Supreme Court. In 1993 in *Shaw v. Reno,* the Court ruled against North Carolina's bizarrely shaped majority-minority districts, inviting a new round of lawsuits challenging the constitutionality of districts drawn to ensure the election of minorities. Two years later in *Miller v. Johnson,* the Court struck down a Georgia redistricting plan that created three black-majority districts. The Court cast heavy doubt on any district lines for which race was the "predominant factor." In 1995 a panel of three federal judges imposed a new plan that reduced the black population share to about one-third in two of the districts.

Even though the black-majority 11th District in Georgia was invalidated by the Supreme Court decision, Cynthia A. McKinney, the district's black representative, scored a comfortable victory in 1996 in the newly drawn white-majority 4th District. Only one-third of the new district's voting age population was black, compared with 64 percent in her old district. In fact, all three of Georgia's black Democrats in the House were reelected to redrawn districts in 1996.

The thrust of the Court's opinions threatened those who defended majority-minority districts as a way to empower minority voters. But the justices did not make sweeping determinations affecting all such districts, they seemed inclined to carve out new limits in a sequence of slightly different cases. The following states faced redistricting challenges between 1993–1998: Alabama, Georgia, Florida, Illinois, Louisiana, North Carolina, New York, Ohio, South Carolina, Texas and Virginia. *(See Chapter 33, Reapportionment and Redistricting.)*

Hispanics in Congress

The fast-expanding population of Hispanic Americans has sparked predictions that they would emerge as a powerful voting bloc. However, Hispanic voter turnouts traditionally have fallen well below the national average.

By 1999 at the start of the 106th Congress, only eighteen members and one nonvoting delegate from Puerto Rico identified themselves as Hispanics—people of Spanish ancestry. *(See Table 31-5, this page.)*

Still, the number of Hispanic members currently in Congress should be two times greater (thirty-eight) if it were in proportion to the Hispanic population, which the 1990 census measured as 9 percent of the nation's total, up from 6 percent in 1980. Hispanic activists attribute low voting participation to poverty, lack of education, language barriers, alienation resulting from discrimination, large numbers of young people, immigration status, and often a continuing attachment to their homelands.

As of January 1999, a total of thirty-eight Hispanics had served in Congress—two in the Senate and thirty-six in the House. Several other Hispanics represented territories as nonvoting delegates or resident commissioners. The 106th Congress included Carlos A. Romero-Barceló, the resident commissioner of Puerto Rico.

The growth of Hispanic representation in the House was in large part the result of judicial interpretations of the Voting Rights Act requiring that minorities be given maximum opportunity to elect members of their own group to Congress. After the 1990 census, congressional district maps in states with significant Hispanic populations were redrawn with the aim of sending more Hispanics to Congress, a goal accomplished by

TABLE 31-5 Hispanics in Congress, 1947–1999

Congress	Senate	House
80th (1947–1949)	1	1
81st (1949–1951)	1	1
82nd (1951–1953)	1	1
83rd (1953–1955)	1	1
84th (1955–1957)	1	1
85th (1957–1959)	2	0
86th (1959–1961)	2	0
87th (1961–1963)	2	1
88th (1963–1965)	1	3
89th (1965–1967)	0	4
90th (1967–1969)	0	4
91st (1969–1971)	0	5
92nd (1971–1973)	0	6
93rd (1973–1975)	0	6
94th (1975–1977)	0	6
95th (1977–1979)	0	5
96th (1979–1981)	0	6
97th (1981–1983)	0	7
98th (1983–1985)	0	10
99th (1985–1987)	0	11
100th (1987–1989)	0	11
101st (1989–1991)	0	11
102nd (1991–1993)	0	11
103rd (1993–1995)	0	17
104th (1995–1997)	0	17
105th (1997–1999)	0	18
106th (1999–2001)	0	18

NOTE: House totals exclude nonvoting delegates. See Reference Materials for roster of Hispanics who have served in Congress.

the 1992 elections. Before the 1992 elections, there were only thirteen Hispanic members of Congress.

No Hispanic candidate has been elected to the Senate since 1970 when Joseph Montoya won his second and last term. Dennis Chavez, his fellow Democrat from New Mexico, was the first Hispanic to serve in the Senate (1935–1962).

Rep. Romualdo Pacheco, R-Calif., was the only Hispanic to serve in Congress during the nineteenth century. Mexican-born, with an English stepfather and an English education, Pacheco helped to bridge the cultural gap between the Spanish-speaking settlers of California and the newly arrived Americans. After California was taken from Mexico and given statehood, Pacheco moved upward in a succession of political offices to the governorship in 1875, filling out the term of his predecessor who resigned to become a U.S. senator.

The next year Pacheco ran for Congress and was certified the victor in a disputed election and took his seat early in 1877. But the House subsequently decided that his opponent was the rightful winner. Pacheco returned home and ran again—successfully—twice more. Upon leaving Congress he became ambassador to Honduras and then Guatemala. No other Hispanic American was elected to Congress until 1912. After that, only in 1927–1931 and 1941–1943 was Congress without any Hispanic American members. By 1999 Hispanic members had been elected from Texas (10 members), California (9), New Mexico (8),

New York (4), Louisiana (2), Florida (2), Arizona (1), Illinois (1), and New Jersey (1).

Fifteen of the Hispanics elected in 1998 were Democrats, and three were Republicans. Among the group were two Democratic freshmen—Grace F. Napolitano from California and Charlie Gonzalez of Texas, who succeeded his father Henry B. Gonzalez, a thirty-seven-year veteran of the House and the former chairman and ranking member of the Banking Committee.

Other notable Hispanics who had long congressional careers were Rep. E. "Kika" de la Garza, D-Texas, a former chairman and ranking member of the House Agriculture Committee, who served thirty-two years in the House; Rep. Manuel Lujan Jr., R-N.M., who served ten House terms before becoming President George Bush's secretary of the interior in 1989; and Bill Richardson, D-N.M., who left the House in 1993 after ten years to became U.S. Representative to the United Nations and then energy secretary in the Clinton administration.

Turnover in Membership

Congress experienced high turnover rates in the nineteenth and early twentieth centuries, principally in the House. The Senate experienced more stability because its members were selected for six-year terms and because state legislatures tended to send the same men to the Senate time after time. The Senate's turnover rate began to increase only after the popular election of senators was instituted by the Seventeenth Amendment in 1913. In the middle decades of the twentieth century, congressional turnover held steady at a relatively low rate. For a quarter-century after World War II each Congress had an average of about seventy-eight new members. An increase began in the 1970s; more than one hundred new members entered Congress in 1975. Turnover remained fairly high through the early 1980s, and then came a spell of strong incumbency and relatively low turnover that lasted through the 1990 election.

LIMITING TERMS

Although a push for term limits for elected officials became popular in the early 1990s, both the House and Senate in the 104th Congress failed to pass a constitutional amendment limiting the terms of members of Congress. When another try in the House failed in the 105th Congress, the momentum for term limits seemed to stall and future for term limits at the end of the twentieth century looked uncertain.

The term limits movement was kicked off in 1990 when Colorado became the first state to seek to limit the number of terms that members of Congress could serve. A referendum approved by more than two-thirds of Colorado voters limited House members to six two-year terms and senators to two six-year terms. The measure also set term limits on state legislators and statewide elected offices.

By 1995 backers of term limits had won ballot initiatives or laws in at least twenty-three states. In 1995 the Supreme Court ruled in *U.S. Term Limits v. Thornton* and *Bryant v. Hill* that states could not impose limits on congressional terms. These rulings left term limits supporters only one solution: a constitutional amendment. But constitutional amendments are difficult to pass: they must receive a two-thirds majority vote from both chambers of Congress and then be ratified by three-fourths (thirty-eight) of the states.

Term limits supporters argued that mandatory retirement after twelve years was necessary to bring new people and viewpoints into Congress, to reduce the constant pressure to get reelected, and to control federal spending, which they said resulted from career politicians getting too close to special interest groups seeking federal funds. Opponents countered that term limits would strip Congress of experienced legislators, diminish the political power of less-populated states that were helped by their members gaining seniority, and would merely speed up, not solve, the problem of legislators getting too friendly with special interest groups. Depriving voters the right to vote for an incumbent would be undemocratic, opponents added.

In the House the term limits constitutional amendment ran into trouble from the start. The House Judiciary Committee agreed on February 28, 1995, to send its version of the measure to the floor without recommendation. Committee Chairman Henry J. Hyde, R-Ill., staunchly opposed term limits, calling the concept "a terrible mistake, a kick in the stomach of democracy." He even filed a brief outlining his opposition when the Supreme Court took up the issue in its 1994–1995 term.

On March 29, the House rejected a term limits constitutional amendment that proposed a twelve-year lifetime limit on members of each chamber. The 227–204 vote fell 61 votes short of a two-thirds majority. Forty Republicans voted against the measure, and thirty of the forty who opposed it chaired a committee or subcommittee.

In the Senate, a term limits constitutional amendment limiting senators to two six-year terms and representatives to six two-year terms stalled on the Senate floor in April 1996. A vote to shut off debate on the measure failed, 58–42, two short of the 60 votes needed. All fifty-three Senate Republicans voted for cloture, even though some opposed limiting congressional terms, leaving the Democrats to take the heat for blocking the Senate from moving to an up-or-down vote.

Term limits supporters again tried to pass a constitutional amendment through the House in 1997. In February members voted on eleven versions of the term limits amendment based on different initiatives begun in nine states. The underlying broad measure—restricting House members to six years and senators to twelve—received a simple majority of 217–211. The tally was 69 votes short of the necessary two-thirds majority needed for passage. The House then considered ten proposals beyond the underlying measure. Some would have made the limits retroactive, given the states the authority to adopt stricter limits, or restricted House members to six or eight years. All were soundly defeated.

The 1988 election brought only thirty-three new faces to the House and ten to the Senate, the smallest turnover in history, both numerically and as a share (8 percent) of total membership. Another small turnover followed in 1990; the combined turnover for both chambers, including retirement, amounted to just 10 percent. The 1990 Senate incumbent reelection rate of 96.9 percent was the highest since direct elections began in 1914.

Several factors contributed to the turnover rates in the 1970s and early 1980s. The elections of 1972 and 1974 were affected by redistricting that followed the 1970 census; many House veterans retired rather than face strong new opposition. Those two elections also were the first in which eighteen-year-olds could vote. Probably the chief reason for change in 1974 was the Watergate scandal, which put an end to the Nixon administration and badly damaged the Republican Party. Democrats gained forty-three seats in the House that year, and the following January seventy-five of the ninety-two freshman representatives in the 94th Congress were Democrats.

Most of those Democrats managed to hold onto their seats in the 1976 elections. The upheavals in that year's voting were in Senate races. Eighteen new senators took their oath of office in January 1977, marking the Senate's largest turnover since 1959.

An even larger Senate turnover came in the 1978 elections. It resulted in a 1979 freshman class of twenty senators, the biggest since the twenty-three member class of 1947. In 1978 ten incumbent senators retired, more than in any year since World War II. Three other incumbents were beaten in primaries, the most in a decade. And seven more were defeated for reelection, the second-highest number in twenty years. In the House a record number of fifty-eight seats had been cast open by retirement,

death, primary defeat, and other causes. Moreover, nineteen incumbents fell in the general election, giving the House seventy-seven freshmen when the 96th Congress opened in January 1979.

In 1980, when Ronald Reagan won the White House, Republicans took control of the Senate for the first time since 1957, ending the longest one-party dominance in that body in its history. They also netted thirty-three House seats, the biggest Republican gain since 1966. But the Democrats made a comeback in 1982 midterm elections: of the eighty-one new representatives, fifty-seven were Democrats. Republicans lost twenty-six seats in the House, half of them held by freshmen.

As in the early 1970s, redistricting was an important factor in the 1982 election. The 1980 census shifted seventeen seats from the Northeast and Midwest to the Sun Belt states of the South and West. Democrats took ten of these seats despite the Sun Belt's propensity to vote for Republican presidential candidates.

In 1984, a presidential election year, Republicans gained fourteen House seats and Democrats two Senate seats in an election that resulted in little turnover. Forty-three new representatives and seven new senators entered the 99th Congress. On only four previous occasions since 1914 had there been fewer than ten Senate newcomers. In 1986 Democrats regained control of the Senate, electing eleven of the thirteen freshmen senators.

The 1986 House elections were extraordinarily good for incumbents of both parties. Only six House members lost in the general election; two others had been defeated in the primaries. But enough seats were open from retirement and death to yield a freshman House class of fifty members—twenty-three Republicans and twenty-seven Democrats.

TABLE 31-6 Longest Service in Congress

Member	Years of Service	Total Years[a]
Carl T. Hayden, D-Ariz.	1912–1927(H), 1927–1969(S)	57
Jamie L. Whitten, D-Miss.	1941–1995(H)	53
Carl Vinson, D-Ga.	1914–1965(H)	50
Emanuel Celler, D-N.Y.	1923–1973(H)	50
Sam Rayburn, D-Texas	1913–1961(H)	49
Wright Patman, D-Texas	1929–1976(H)	47
Joseph G. Cannon, R-Ill.	1873–1891(H), 1893–1913(H), 1915–1923(H)	46
Adolph J. Sabath, D-Ill.	1907–1952(H)	46
Strom Thurmond, R-S.C.	1955–1956(S), 1957– (S)	45[b]
John D. Dingell, D-Mich.	1955– (H)	45[b]
Lister Hill, D-Ala.	1923–1938(H), 1938–1969(S)	45
George H. Mahon, D-Texas	1935–1979(H)	44
Warren G. Magnuson, D-Wash.	1937–1944(H), 1944–1981(S)	44
Justin S. Morrill, R-Vt.	1855–1867(H), 1867–1898(S)	44
Melvin Price, D-Ill.	1945–1988(H)	44
William B. Allison, R-Iowa	1863–1871(H), 1873–1908(S)	43
Henry M. Jackson, D-Wash.	1941–1953(H), 1953–1983(S)	43

NOTES: H = House, S = Senate.

a. As of October 1999. Totals, based on exact dates of service, are rounded to nearest year. Minor differences in days or months of service determine rankings of members with the same total of years.

b. Service record as of October 1999. Thurmond was reelected in 1996; Dingell was reelected in 1998.

SOURCES: Congressional Research Service, Congressional Quarterly.

In 1988 George Bush became the first Republican in sixty years to hold the White House for his party for a third consecutive term. But he also became the first candidate since John F. Kennedy in 1960 to win the presidential election while his party lost seats (three) in the House. Again in 1990, for the third straight election, Democrats gained House seats (nine). That feat had not been accomplished since the string of Democratic victories in 1954, 1956, and 1958.

In the presidential election year of 1992, voters opted to give the Democrats a chance to run both Congress and the White House by electing Democrat Bill Clinton, the former governor of Arkansas, as president. Clinton was elected with only 43 percent of the popular vote over Bush and independent candidate Ross Perot. Not since Democrat Jimmy Carter had relinquished the White House to Republican Ronald Reagan in 1981 had Congress been controlled by the president's party.

Heading into the 1992 campaign, there was grumbling that the American political system had lost its capacity for renewal—low turnover in the 1980s fostered a perception of Congress as an incumbency club, fueled by special interest cash that nearly always defeated any challengers. But 1992 redistricting as a result of the 1990 census dramatically reshaped many districts, prodding some members into retirement and forcing others to run in unfamiliar constituencies. Reports of lax management and overdrawn checks at the House Bank also contributed to a high congressional turnover.

All this tumult resulted in 110 new members entering the House in January 1993, an influx of freshmen exceeding anything Washington had seen in more than forty years. In the postwar era, only one House freshman class was larger—the 118 newcomers to the 81st Congress in 1949. And no other freshman class had so many women (twenty-five) and minorities, including sixteen African Americans, eight Hispanics, and one Korean American.

The Senate freshman class of the 103rd Congress was the largest since 1981, with nine men and five woman, including the chamber's first black woman (Moseley-Braun of Illinois) and its first Native American (Democrat Ben Nighthorse Campbell of Colorado) since Charles Curtis, a Republican from Kansas who stepped down in 1929 to become vice president under Herbert Hoover.

The midterm elections of 1994 brought even more upheaval as the Republicans gained control of both the House and Senate for the first time since 1955. The Democratic loss was truly national in scope. Republicans won 37 million votes in 1994—nearly 9 million more than the party had won in the 1990 midterm elections. It was the first time since 1946 that Republican House candidates received a majority (52.3 percent) of the total House vote. Democrats in 1994 drew almost one million fewer votes than in 1990, continuing a general downward slide in their congressional voting strength that had begun in the mid-1980s.

The GOP tide of 1994 was caused by large surges in voter support for the Republicans and voter apathy for the Democrats. The election marked the middle of Democratic president Bill Clinton's first term, and the president's party had difficulty motivating its core constituency. Although Clinton had some successes during his first two years in office, most notably deficit reduction and the North American Free Trade Agreement, his failure in getting Congress to agree to comprehensive health care reform seemed to stall his administration's programs. In addition, Republican candidates reaped the gains they had anticipated from redistricting after the 1990 census. The remapping was largely favorable to the GOP.

Money also made the difference for some Republican challengers. According to the Federal Election Commission, Republican candidates had an easier time raising money from political action committees and other sources than in previous years. Conservative groups—from the National Rifle Association to term limit advocates—played active roles in several congressional races. Several GOP freshmen were elected with the prominent support of conservative Christian activists.

In 1994 Republicans gained fifty-two House seats, increasing their number from 178 to 230. The Democrats dropped from 256 to 204 seats. For the Republicans, seventy-three freshmen were elected, 157 incumbents were reelected, and thirty-four incumbents were defeated.

At the start of the 104th Congress, Georgia Rep. Newt Gingrich became the first Republican Speaker of the House from the South. His ascendancy accompanied the long-anticipated realignment of the South. For the first time since the end of Reconstruction in the 1870s, Republicans won a majority of southern congressional districts.

Republicans also swept the Senate in 1994, after eight years in the minority. The Republicans captured all nine open seats and ousted two Democratic incumbents, gaining control with 52–48 seats. Adding insult to injury, the day after the general election, Democratic Sen. Richard C. Shelby of Alabama announced that he was switching parties. The incoming Senate freshman class had eleven Republicans and no Democrats. Since 1914, when the popular election of senators began, there had never been an all-GOP Senate freshman class.

The 1996 elections also ended up in the record books. Never before had voters reelected a Democratic president and at the same time entrusted both the House and the Senate to the Republican Party. Clinton, who was almost written off after the disastrous 1994 midterm elections, scored a political comeback by winning handily in November 1996. And the Republicans won their first back-to-back majority in the House since the 1920s. The Democrats managed, however, to cut into the GOP's numbers. Democrats gained a net of nine seats, leaving a party breakdown in the House of 227 Republicans and 207 Democrats, and Bernard Sanders of Vermont as the lone independent.

In 1996 a total of twenty incumbents were defeated; all but three were Republicans. The heaviest toll in 1996 was among the mainly conservative and contentious GOP freshman class—eleven freshmen Republicans were defeated. The GOP held on to its majority in the House by its performance in the open

DELEGATES IN CONGRESS

In addition to the 435 members of the House of Representatives, there are also five nonvoting members, who represent the District of Columbia and the four U.S. territories—American Samoa, Guam, Puerto Rico, and the U.S. Virgin Islands. All elect delegates who serve two-year terms, except for Puerto Rico, which sends a "resident commissioner" to the House for a four-year term. The four delegates and the resident commissioner may vote in committee, give floor speeches, and even hold chairmanships, but they are not allowed to vote on the House floor. Because the House Resources Committee has jurisdiction over U.S. territorial affairs, the four overseas delegates serve on that committee.

DISTRICT OF COLUMBIA

In 1871 Congress established a territorial form of government over the entire District of Columbia. The new city administration included an elected nonvoting delegate to the House of Representatives—Republican Norton P. Chipman—as well as an appointed governor; a territorial assembly, with one elected and one appointed chamber; and a new board of public works. Gross financial mismanagement by Alexander Shepherd, board member and later District governor, led Congress to replace the District territorial government with three commissioners appointed by the president. The territorial assembly and the position of House delegate were abolished. Chipman's term expired in 1875.

Although it was clear that permanent suppression of representative government for the District was not intended, the changes made were incorporated in the 1878 act that established the capital city's government. For the next century Congress acted as the city's governing council while the president chose its administrators.

In 1970 Congress finally cleared legislation providing for the first nonvoting delegate from the District of Columbia since 1875. Democrat Walter E. Fauntroy, a black Baptist minister, was elected to the U.S. House on March 23, 1971. The D.C. delegate was given all House privileges except that of voting on the floor—the delegate could vote in committee. It also amended city election laws to provide for primary and general elections for the post.

The measure had been briefly detained in the Senate, as Edward M. Kennedy, D-Mass., requested that action be held up until senators considered his proposal to give the District voting representation in both the House and Senate. In a subsequent meeting with city officials, Kennedy agreed to release the bill, saying that the delay had highlighted his view that the nonvoting delegate is important but only as an interim measure.

The D.C. delegate still has limited voting rights, causing some city residents to complain of taxation without full representation. D.C. residents pay federal income taxes. At the start of the 106th Congress in 1999, Democrat Eleanor Holmes Norton, elected in 1990, was the D.C. delegate.

TERRITORIES

A U.S. possession since 1898, Puerto Rico became a commonwealth in 1952. The first resident commissioner from Puerto Rico, Federico Degetau, was sent to the House in 1900. With a popula-

tion of over three million in the 1990s, Puerto Rico is the largest U.S. territory. Democrat Carlos Romero-Barceló, elected in 1992, was the resident commissioner in 1999.

The United States acquired Guam from Spain in the treaty of Paris after the Spanish-American War of 1898. The United States bought the Virgin Islands from Denmark in 1917. Under acts passed by Congress, both territories are governed by locally elected legislatures. Proposals for representation of the two territories was considered by every Congress since the mid-1950s. In 1972 Congress authorized one nonvoting House delegate each from Guam and the Virgin Islands. In the 106th Congress, Democrat Robert A. Underwood, elected in 1992, represented Guam and Donna M. C. Christensen, elected in 1996, was the delegate from the Virgin Islands.

The United States gained the islands of American Samoa from the United Kingdom and Germany under the 1899 Treaty of Berlin. These South Pacific islands are administered by the Department of Interior. American Samoa sent its first delegate to the House in 1979. In 1999 Democrat Eni F. H. Faleomavaega, first elected in 1988, was the delegate.

VOTING RIGHTS

In December 1992, while organizing for the 103rd Congress, Democrats approved a proposal to give the nonvoting delegates the right to vote on the floor when the House considered legislation in the Committee of the Whole—a parliamentary framework under which House members meet to debate and amend legislation. The full House accepted the proposal as part of a package of rule changes in January 1993.

D.C. Delegate Eleanor Holmes Norton persuaded her fellow Democrats that no legal distinction existed between voting in committee, which the delegates had the right to do, and voting on the floor in the Committee of the Whole. Some Democrats had reservations about giving the delegates the right to floor votes and the caucus eventually approved a compromise measure. The compromise required that whenever a question was decided on the strength of delegate votes, regardless of whether it was approved or rejected, the committee would dissolve and the House would immediately vote on the issue again without the delegates. Of the 404 times that the five delegates were eligible to vote during the 103rd Congress, only three times did their votes prove decisive, thus triggering an automatic revote.

Republicans were not happy with the rules change—at the time all five delegates were Democrats. On January 7, 1993, House Minority Leader Robert H. Michel, R-Ill., a dozen GOP members and three citizens filed suit in U.S. District Court challenging the delegates new voting rights. District Judge Harold H. Greene ruled that the delegate voting procedure was constitutional because "the votes . . . are meaningless." Greene went on to say that, without the provision for a second vote in close calls, the rule plainly would have been unconstitutional. Not surprisingly, the delegates' limited floor-voting privileges were stripped away at the beginning of the 104th Congress, when the Republicans gained the House majority.

seats. Of fifty-three open seats, Republicans won twenty-nine, ten of them given up by Democratic incumbents. Democrats won twenty-four, only four of which had been held by Republicans.

In the Senate, the Republicans built on their gains in the 1994 election. For the 105th Congress, the GOP had a solid 55–45 majority over the Democrats. That was the Republicans highest total in the Senate following any election since 1928.

By 1998 the turnover in the House and Senate seemed to have settled down. All but seven of the 401 House members seeking reelection were returned to office. The Democrats also regrouped in 1998—Clinton's second midterm election—and managed to close the partisan gap even further in the House. The Democrats picked up five House seats, giving 106th Congress 223 Republicans, 211 Democrats, and one independent. This twelve-seat majority was the slimmest majority in the House since 1955.

The Senate's partisan breakdown remained the same in 1999 with fifty-five Republicans and forty-five Democrats. Just three of the thirty-four senators up for reelection in 1998 were defeated. Eight Senate freshmen joined the 106th Congress—four Democrats and four Republicans.

Shifts Between Chambers

From the early days of Congress, members have sometimes shifted from one chamber to the other. Far fewer former senators have gone to the House than vice versa. In the 1790s, nineteen former representatives became senators and three former senators moved to the House. The same pattern continued through the nineteenth century and into the twentieth. By the end of the twentieth century, it was common to find House members running for the Senate, but senators rarely, if ever, returned to the House. Former senators were more likely to return home to pursue a race for governor, run as their party's vice presidential candidate, or seek the office of president.

Although both chambers are equal under the law, the Senate's six-year terms offer the officeholder greater stability. That body also has larger staffs and more generous perquisites. A senator's opportunity to make his mark are undoubtedly better in a chamber of one hundred members than in the 435-member House. The Senate's role in foreign affairs may add to its luster, and senators enjoy the prestige of a statewide constituencies.

Perhaps the most notable shift from the Senate to the House was Henry Clay's journey in 1811. Giving up a Senate seat from Kentucky, he entered the House and was promptly elected Speaker, a position he used to prod the country to go to war with Britain in 1812. After five terms in the House, Clay returned to the Senate in 1823. Another prominent transfer was that of John Quincy Adams of Massachusetts; he served in the Senate (1803–1808), as secretary of state (1817–1825), as president (1825–1829), and finally in the House (1831–1848).

Only one other former president, Andrew Johnson, returned to Congress in later years. Like Adams, he had served in both houses of Congress (from Tennessee) before he entered the White House. As vice president in 1865, Johnson was elevated to the presidency upon Abraham Lincoln's assassination. He left office in 1869 a bitter man, having survived impeachment charges instigated by his own Republican Party. The Tennessee legislature sent him back to the U.S. Senate in 1875, where he served the last five months of his life. *(See "Members of Congress Who Became President," p. 1110, in Reference Materials.)*

NOTES

1. Alexis de Tocqueville, *Democracy in America*, vol. 1 (New York: Vintage Books, 1971), 231.

2. The Gallup Poll: Public Trust in Federal Government Remains High, Jan. 8, 1999. (From Gallup Organization Web site.)

3. Charles Pope, "New Congress Is Older, More Politically Seasoned," *CQ Weekly Report*, January 9, 1999, 60–63.

4. Marcy Kaptur, *Women of Congress: A Twentieth-Century Odyssey* (Washington, D.C.: Congressional Quarterly, 1996), 1–2.

SELECTED BIBLIOGRAPHY

Berg, John C. *Unequal Struggle: Class, Gender, Race, and Power in the U.S. Congress.* Boulder, Colo.: Westview Press, 1995.

Canon, David T. *Actors, Athletes, and Astronauts: Political Amateurs in the United State Congress.* Chicago: University of Chicago Press, 1990.

Davidson, Roger H., and Walter J. Oleszek. *Congress and Its Members.* 7th ed. Washington, D.C.: CQ Press, 2000.

Duncan, Phil, ed. *Politics in America 2000: The 106th Congress.* Washington, D.C.: Congressional Quarterly, 1999.

Ehrenhalt, Alan. *United States of Ambition: Politicians, Power, and the Pursuit of Office.* New York: Times Books, 1991.

Fenno, Richard F. *Home Style: House Members and Their Districts.* Boston: Little, Brown, 1978.

———. *Senators on the Campaign Trail: The Politics of Representation.* Norman: University of Oklahoma Press, 1996.

Fowler, Linda, and Robert D. McClure. *Political Ambition: Who Decides to Run for Congress.* New Haven, Conn.: Yale University Press, 1989.

Gertzog, Irwin N. *Congressional Women: Their Recruitment, Integration, and Behavior.* 2nd ed. Westport, Conn.: Praeger, 1995.

Hibbing, John R. *Congressional Careers: Contours of Life in the U.S. House of Representatives.* Chapel Hill: University of North Carolina Press, 1991.

Jacobson, Gary C. *The Politics of Congressional Elections.* Boston: Little, Brown, 1983.

Kaptur, Marcy. *Women of Congress: A Twentieth-Century Odyssey.* Washington, D.C.: Congressional Quarterly, 1996.

Merriner, James L., and Thomas P. Senter. *Against Long Odds: Citizens Who Challenge Congressional Incumbents.* Westport, Conn.: Praeger, 1999.

Ragsdale, Bruce A., and Joel D. Treese. *Black Americans in Congress, 1870–1989.* Office of the Historian, U.S. House of Representatives. Washington, D.C.: Government Printing Office, 1990.

Reedy, George, *The U.S. Senate.* New York: Crown, 1983.

U.S. Congress. House. Commission on the Bicentenary. *Women in Congress, 1917–1990.* Washington, D.C.: Government Printing Office, 1991

White, William S. *Citadel: The Story of the U.S. Senate.* New York: Harpers & Brothers, 1956.

CHAPTER 32

Campaign Financing

IN THE EARLY YEARS of the twentieth century Congress attempted to devise a system to limit the influence of money in politics. In the closing years of the century Congress was still at it.

Although campaign finance had changed dramatically over the century—from its early freewheeling days to a heavily regulated system—the public demands for reform at the beginning and end of the century were much the same: to curb the ability of special interests and wealthy individuals to dominate the flow of campaign money and to try to establish level playing fields for challengers as well as incumbents, for politicians of modest means as well as wealthier campaigners.

The costs of elections had spiraled upward in modern times. The price tag for the 1998 congressional elections was $740 million.[1] Members of Congress were finding themselves under relentless pressure to raise funds for their campaigns—a time-consuming task that critics said was taking its toll not only on the members personally but on Congress as an institution. When members announced their retirement from Congress, more often than not the demands of campaign fund-raising were among the reasons for their decision.

But, judging from the electoral success of congressional incumbents, the system was paying off for members willing to keep playing the game. For those choosing to run again, the re-election rate in 1998 for House members was 98 percent and nearly 90 percent for senators.

Controversy Surrounds Financing System

Critics of the campaign financing system became increasingly vocal in the 1980s and 1990s. But there was no consensus on what was wrong with the system, let alone what would make it right.

For those who expressed dismay at skyrocketing campaign costs, there were others who said the costs were small when compared with a major corporation's advertising budget or the price tag of a nuclear submarine.

For those who called for limits on campaign spending, there were others who charged that limits would only further entrench incumbents and put challengers at a disadvantage.

For those who deplored the role special interests, particularly political action committees (PACs), played in American politics, there were those who defended this role as a manifestation of democracy's pluralism.

For those who saw public money as the way to eliminate outside influences in politics, there were others who scoffed at the use of taxpayer money, even in times of budget surpluses.

For those who deplored the influx of unlimited and basically unregulated "soft" money to the political parties, there were those who welcomed the resulting resurgence of parties as major players in electoral politics.

For those who wanted to regulate advertising they said crossed the line between advocating issues to advocating particular candidates, there were those who defended the ads as important tools in educating voters.

For those who criticized independent expenditures for or against candidates, there were those who saw such spending as part of their First Amendment rights.

Beyond specific policy disagreements was the less tangible love-hate relationship legislators had with the system. Members were faced with the dilemma of having to change a system that returned the vast majority of them to the halls of Congress election after election. Reform advocate Sen. Robert C. Byrd, D-W.Va., explained: "We are afraid to let go of the slick ads and the high-priced consultants, afraid to let go of the PAC money and the polls, unsure that we want to change the rules of the game that we all understand and know so well."[2]

UNCERTAINTIES IN CHANGE

Reformers faced the enormous task of proposing legislation that would bridge the differences between Democrats and Republicans, representatives and senators, incumbents and challengers. Members were afraid of the unknowns that surrounded change—how each party would adapt to it and whether it might give the opposing party an advantage.

Their caution was well-founded. It was, indeed, difficult to calculate all the ramifications of the many reform proposals on the table at any one time. As political scientist Frank J. Sorauf described it: "Available money seeks an outlet, and if some outlets are narrowed or closed off, money flows with increased pressure to the outlets still open. It is the law that systems of campaign finance share with hydraulic systems."[3] Members feared that those outlets might benefit their opponents more than themselves.

There had been ample examples of changes with unanticipated results. Congressional attempts to curtail the influence of the wealthy "fat cat" donors in the wake of the 1970s Watergate scandal resulted in more stringent limits on individual contributions than on political committees. This made contributions through PACs much more attractive to some givers and in turn became a significant factor in the rise of PACs.

The dramatic growth of soft money was another example of a development many did not anticipate. Soft money refers to the unlimited, largely unregulated money contributed primarily to political parties for activities and expenses not directly related to specific federal elections. It is called "soft" to distinguish it from the "hard money" that is used for federal election campaigns and regulated by the Federal Election Campaign Act (FECA)— money that is "hard" to raise because of the FECA's limits and restrictions. Corporations and labor unions have been prohibited from participating directly in federal elections for a good part of the twentieth century, and in the 1970s an aggregate contribution limit was placed on individual donors. But there was no limit on the amount of soft money they could contribute to the parties or spend on nonfederal activities.

In the 1970s the Federal Election Commission (FEC), the independent agency charged with overseeing compliance with the federal election laws, relaxed some of the rules covering the separation of federal campaign funds from state and local parties' nonfederal money. The FEC allowed the state and local parties for the first time to use nonfederal soft money to pay for a portion of their administrative expenses, as well as voter drives and generic party activities, even if they had an indirect effect on federal campaigns. Congress then passed legislation to encourage greater participation of these parties in presidential election campaigns, allowing them to spend unlimited amounts of hard money on things like voter drives and campaign materials.

The combination of these actions by the FEC and Congress triggered the surge in soft money. Once the national parties determined that they, too, could use soft money for certain expenses, they began raising millions of dollars for their nonfederal accounts. Soon the money was being spent not only for get-out-the-vote drives but for major advertising campaigns said to promote party issues, not candidates.

Being able to use soft money for certain party expenses had the added advantage of freeing up more hard dollars for direct aid to federal candidates, further fueling the upward spiral of campaign spending. And extra hard dollars came in handy when the Supreme Court allowed political parties to make independent expenditures on their candidates' behalf.

The parties' enthusiasm for soft money in the 1996 election campaign helped produce the most significant campaign finance scandal since Watergate.

1996 SCANDAL

Public attention was riveted on the flaws of the campaign finance system by actions taken during the 1996 presidential election campaign. At the root of the scandal were allegations that foreign money—particularly Chinese—had made it into the campaign in violation of federal law and that the parties' pursuit and use of soft money may have crossed the line into illegal activity.

Much of the focus was on the Democrats. As the scandal unfolded, it was revealed that the Democratic National Committee (DNC) had accepted nearly $3 million in illegal or suspect contributions, money the DNC said it would return. The fund-raising tactics of President Bill Clinton and Vice President Al Gore were also central to the scandal. The news media provided accounts of the Clintons entertaining large donors at private White House coffees and inviting some contributors for overnight stays in the Lincoln bedroom or to go along on government foreign trade missions, and of Gore making fund-raising calls from his office and accepting donations from Buddhist nuns at a temple in California.

The GOP-led Congress launched investigations in both chambers, which seemed to do little more than embarrass the Democrats for their fund-raising excesses. Senate Governmental Affairs Committee investigators in 1997 came up with no proof of allegations that the Chinese government had conspired to influence U.S. elections through large campaign contributions or that the White House had knowingly accepted illegal foreign contributions or that the Clinton administration ever changed policy in exchange for campaign contributions. And along the way, Democrats managed to reveal that a Republican National Committee (RNC) think tank, the National Policy Forum, had also accepted foreign money that may have been passed onto the RNC. A parallel campaign finance investigation by the House Government Reform and Oversight Committee was still under way as of mid-1999.

Various requests were made for the appointment of an independent counsel to look into alleged Democratic fund-raising abuses, but Attorney General Janet Reno concluded that the allegations did not meet the standard for such an appointment. Reno declined to get into the area of soft money because it did not fall under the provisions of the FECA. The attorney general looked at fund-raising calls made by Clinton from the White House and Gore from his office but determined that they were to solicit soft money and therefore did not violate the ban on soliciting hard money contributions on federal property. Moreover, according to Reno, Clinton's calls were from the White House residence, which was not covered by the solicitation ban.

The attorney general also examined the question of whether the Clinton-Gore campaign committees had been illegally involved in the political issue ad campaign financed by the DNC. A preliminary investigation by FEC auditors had concluded that both the DNC and the RNC had coordinated millions of dollars worth of issue ads with their respective presidential candidates' campaign committees, making the ads an in-kind contribution in violation of federal spending limits for presidential candidates who accept public funding. But Reno found no criminal intent to violate the law by Clinton or Gore, based on the fact that they had been advised by counsel that the advertising campaign complied with the law. (The FEC subsequently rejected the auditors' findings.)

While rejecting calls for independent counsels, Reno empha-

CAMPAIGN FINANCE GLOSSARY

Following is a glossary of some commonly used terms in the campaign finance field. It was drawn from documents produced by the Federal Election Commission, Center for Responsive Politics, Congressional Research Service of the Library of Congress, and Congressional Quarterly. The definitions reflect the laws and regulations in force as of October 1999.

Bundling. The practice of aggregating separate contributions from various individuals for delivery to a candidate, thereby generating clout for the individual or organization that collects and delivers the contributions. The bundler could focus on employees of a particular business, members of a particular profession, or activists committed to a particular policy. Because the bundler merely forwarded batches of checks made out by individuals to a candidate, the contributions did not count against the bundler's own contribution limits.

Hard Money. Money raised and spent for federal election campaigns under the limitations and prohibitions of the Federal Election Campaign Act (FECA).

Independent Expenditures. Money spent for communications (such as broadcast advertisements or direct mail) that expressly advocated the election or defeat of a candidate. Such spending was deemed "independent" so long as the individual or group making the expenditure did not coordinate, cooperate, or consult in any way with the candidate's campaign.

These expenditures were regulated by federal election laws. Thus, while individuals or groups could spend unlimited amounts of money on independent campaign efforts, they had to report these expenditures to the Federal Election Commission (FEC) once they reached a certain level. In addition, the entity sponsoring the independent advertising campaign had to identify itself in its ads and note that the ad was not authorized by the candidate's committee.

Issue Advocacy Advertising. Advertisements advocating a particular position on an issue. Such advertising often implicitly supported the candidates of one political party by advocating the same position they held on an issue. But because the focus was on an issue—such as congressional term limits or family values—none of the campaign laws applied. As long as individuals or groups avoided expressly urging people to vote for or against a specific candidate, they could raise and spend unlimited amounts of money. There were no disclosure or reporting requirements in campaign finance law for issue ads, unless the group was a federal PAC or party committee.

Political Action Committee (PAC). Organizations created to raise and spend money for candidates for federal office. They were typically begun by corporations, industries, trade associations, labor unions, ideology groups, or others with shared policy interests.

A "leadership PAC" was such a committee run by one or more congressional leaders, or other members who aspired to leadership positions. When members outside the leadership structure started creating PACs, the term "personal PAC" also came into use. Contributions to this type of PAC were considered separate from contributions to the campaign committee of the individual member who sponsored the PAC. A contributor who had given the maximum amount allowed to the House Speaker's campaign committee, for example, still could give to the Speaker's leadership PAC. These PACs were subject to the same constraints as other PACs.

Soft Money. Money raised and spent outside the limitations and prohibitions of the Federal Election Campaign Act and, therefore, not to be used for activities directly related to federal election campaigns. This money was raised primarily by the national, state, and local Republican and Democratic parties for grassroots and party-building activities. The parties could use the funds for get-out-the-vote efforts, administrative costs, generic party advertising, and to help state and local candidates. (Activities that benefited both federal and state and local candidates had to be funded in part by hard money.) There was no limit on the amount of money that a donor (an individual, corporation, labor union, or PAC) could give to a party's soft money account, but the party had to disclose the source of contributions in excess of $200.

---

sized that the Justice Department's Campaign Financing Task Force was conducting an ongoing investigation into allegations of wrongdoing in the 1996 election cycle. The task force had brought charges involving campaign finance violations against eighteen Democratic contributors or fund-raisers, as of mid-1999. Various charges included making illegal foreign or corporate contributions and channeling donations through conduit or "straw" contributors who were later reimbursed, a violation of federal law.

DISSATISFACTION WITH SYSTEM

Whether what went on in the 1996 campaign was legal or not, the scandal did little to shore up public confidence in the system.

A 1997 public opinion survey found that a majority (57 per-cent) of Americans were dissatisfied with the state of the political system, and the role of money was one of the main sources of that discontent. About two-thirds of those polled cited as major problems the excessive influence of political contributions on elections and government policy, as well as the conflict of interest created when elected officials solicited or took contributions while making policy decisions. Majorities also said that elected officials spent too much time fund-raising and that the high cost of campaigns discouraged good people from running for office.[4]

Many members of Congress also were dissatisfied with the system but ran into roadblocks when they tried to fix it. A bill to ban soft money and restrict issue advocacy ads won bipartisan approval in the House in 1998, but a companion bill in the Senate fell victim to a GOP-led filibuster. In 1999, the House again passed a bill, but Senate action on a scaled-back bill was blocked by a filibuster in October.

ONGOING SEARCH FOR SOLUTIONS

Attempts to reform the campaign finance system were nothing new. Campaign finance reformers over the years have sought to curb campaign spending by limiting and regulating campaign expenditures and donations made to candidates as well as by informing voters of the amounts and sources of the donations, and the amounts, purposes, and recipients of the expenditures. Disclosure was intended to reveal which candidates, if any, were unduly indebted to interest groups, in time to forewarn the voters.

Congress had argued the issues of campaign finance since the first law regulating campaigns was enacted during the administration of Theodore Roosevelt in 1907. Major new laws, however, came only after the scandals of Teapot Dome in the 1920s and Watergate in the 1970s.

In 1925 the Teapot Dome scandal yielded the Federal Corrupt Practices Act, an extensive statute governing the conduct of federal campaigns. That act codified earlier laws limiting campaign expenditures, but the limits were so unrealistically low and the law so riddled with loopholes that it was ineffectual.

Watergate, though, changed all that. The June 1972 break-in at Democratic national headquarters in Washington's Watergate office building touched off a scandal that became the 1970s' code word for governmental corruption. Although the scandal had many aspects, money in politics was at its roots. Included in Watergate's catalog of misdeeds were specific violations of campaign spending laws, violations of other criminal laws facilitated by the availability of virtually unlimited campaign contributions, and still other instances where campaign funds were used in a manner that strongly suggested influence peddling.

Congress had begun to move on campaign finance even before Watergate. Less than six months before the break-in, Congress had adopted two pieces of legislation containing some of the ground rules under which elections were still being conducted in the 1990s. First, Congress approved legislation allowing a one-dollar tax checkoff to finance presidential campaigns. (The amount was increased to three dollars by 1993 legislation.) Congress also passed the Federal Election Campaign Act (FECA), requiring comprehensive disclosure of campaign contributions and expenditures by candidates for federal office and placing a limit on the amount of money candidates could spend on media advertising. (The media spending limits were repealed in 1974.) The 1971 FECA ultimately had a limited impact on controlling campaign spending.

But Watergate focused public attention on campaign spending at all levels of government and produced a mood in Congress that even the most reluctant legislators found difficult to resist. In the aftermath came the most significant overhaul in campaign finance legislation in the nation's history. Major legislation passed in 1974 (the House had passed its version on the day Richard Nixon announced he would resign the presidency) and 1976, coming on the heels of the 1971 legislation, radically altered the system of financing federal elections.

The FECA Amendments of 1974 set limits on contributions and expenditures for congressional and presidential elections, established the FEC, and created the framework for providing presidential candidates with public financing.

Before the sweeping 1974 act received its first real test, it was extensively pruned by the Supreme Court. The Court in its 1976 decision in *Buckley v. Valeo* upheld the FECA's disclosure requirements, contribution limitations, and public financing of presidential elections. But it struck down spending limits for congressional and presidential races, including restraints on the use of a candidate's personal assets, except for presidential candidates who accepted public financing. It also struck down limits on independent expenditures, expenditures made in support of or opposition to a candidate but without the knowledge or cooperation of the candidate.

The justices weighed First Amendment rights against the 1974 act's underlying purpose: prevention of the abuses that surfaced during Watergate. In the case of contributions, the Court concluded that First Amendment considerations were outweighed because "the quantity of communication by the contributor does not increase perceptibly with the size of his contribution." But it found limiting expenditures to be a "substantial" restraint on free speech that could preclude "significant use of the most effective modes of communication."

Many subsequent congressional efforts to change the campaign finance system were driven by the desire to find a way to limit congressional campaign spending without violating the mandates of the Court decision. With the ceilings on expenditures removed, campaign costs grew apace and candidates became increasingly dependent on raising money in the easiest and most cost-effective way—from PACs.

In striking down restraints on independent expenditures, the Supreme Court opened the door for individuals and PACs to spend millions of dollars independently; such spenders were generally derided by candidates and party leaders as unwelcome "loose cannons" in the political process. The decision spurred the rise of independent expenditures by nonconnected, or ideological, PACs. Sharply negative ads underwritten by such groups gained the enmity of both parties.

In 1979 Congress amended the FECA, in part to encourage more grassroots and political party activity in federal campaigns. Included in the package of amendments was the section allowing state and local parties to underwrite voter drives in behalf of presidential tickets without regard to financial limits.

Throughout the late 1970s reformers sought to extend public financing to congressional races, but their efforts failed. A bill to limit the role of PACs was passed by the House in 1979 but blocked by the threat of a filibuster in the Senate.

After the 1970s Congress proved less amenable to further major changes in campaign financing. Proposals were debated but it would be a decade before either chamber passed a major cam-

In the late 1990s Republican John McCain, left, of Arizona and Democrat Russell D. Feingold of Wisconsin led the drive for campaign finance reform in the Senate.

paign finance bill. And once again it would be scandals that provided the impetus.

In 1989 allegations of ethical violations and questionable financial dealings involving Speaker Jim Wright, D-Texas, intensified pressures on House Democrats to act on campaign finance legislation. Wright, facing charges that would lead to his resignation from Congress, embraced campaign finance reform and created a bipartisan task force to develop a reform plan. *(See "Wright," p. 925.)*

Further pressure for change came the following year in the form of the Keating Five scandal, so named for five senators suspected of doing favors for a wealthy campaign contributor, Charles H. Keating Jr. The controversy, an offshoot of the savings and loan scandal, added fuel to a fire that Common Cause, a public interest lobby, had lit under Congress to revise the campaign system.

At the heart of the Keating Five scandal was $1.5 million in contributions made or solicited by Keating, the powerful owner of a thrift and real estate empire, for the campaigns or other political causes of the five senators. More than half of the money—$850,000—was paid out of corporate funds to nonprofit voter registration organizations with which one of the senators, Alan Cranston, D-Calif., was affiliated. Keating also employed a technique called "bundling," through which he raised many individual contributions from family members, associates, and employees of his companies and handed the contributions over in a lump sum designed to impress the recipient politicians. Televised hearings and news stories revealing Keating's use of his fund-raising skills to assemble clout in Washington proved far more effective at raising questions about the relationship between elected officials and major contributors than the flood of statistics about PACs that were issued by good government groups. *(See box, The Keating Five Scandal, p. 962.)*

Both chambers passed bills in 1990, over GOP objections, but action came late in the session and the bills died when Congress adjourned and went home for the elections.

Both chambers again passed bills in 1991. There were vast differences between the two versions and compromise seemed unlikely. But this time scandals at the House bank and post office sent Democratic leaders on a reform mission and reignited the campaign finance issue. Conferees reconciled differences in 1992 by letting each chamber live by its own rules. But President George Bush objected to that approach, along with the bill's spending limits and public funding provisions, and vetoed the bill.

Reformers' hopes were high, when Clinton came into the White House vowing to overhaul the system. Both chambers approved radically different bills in 1993 but the Democrats did not work out a compromise until late the next year. At that point Senate Democrats were unable to shut off a GOP-led filibuster. Some questioned the Democrats' sincerity in pursuing campaign reform and wondered if they had purposely waited until it was too late in the session to overcome Republican opposition.

Many expected that the scandal surrounding the 1996 election would renew fervor for reform. And it did, but not enough to lead to enactment of a new law. The House passed its bill in 1998 but the Senate bill was again blocked by a GOP filibuster.

The effort was renewed in 1999, but the outcome was the same when the Senate debated a bill in October.

The battle had been a familiar one. As then–Common Cause president Fred Wertheimer once put it: "There are no fights like campaign finance fights because they are battles about the essence of politics and power."[5]

Congressional Candidates' Contributions and Expenditures

The modern congressional election is a complex financial affair. Fund-raisers, accountants, lawyers, and a variety of consultants play crucial roles in today's campaigns. Decisions on how to raise money and how to marshal a campaign's resources can be key to electoral success.

Money pours in from a vast array of sources—not all of them controlled by the candidate—including individuals, PACs, party committees, candidates themselves and their families, and independent organizations running their own campaigns to influence the outcome. Money flows out for rent, computers, salaries, polls, consulting fees, printing, postage, and radio, television, and newspaper advertising.

Much of the money that at one time moved in the shadows of campaigns is now a matter of public record, thanks to the stringent disclosure provisions of the FECA. All candidates for federal office, once they cross a certain threshold, periodically must submit to the FEC itemized accounts of contributions and expenditures in excess of $200 and debts and obligations owed to or by the candidate or committee. These detailed reports, which are made public by the FEC, provide a window on the modern political campaign.

POLITICAL CONTRIBUTIONS

FEC figures indicated that congressional candidates raised a total of more than $781 million during the 1997–1998 election cycle. House and Senate incumbents together raised $430 million; challengers raised $210.5 million. An additional $141 million was raised by candidates for open seats.

When broken down by chamber, the figures showed that Senate candidates raised a total of nearly $288 million, with incumbents attracting $135.5 million, challengers $114 million, and open-seat candidates almost $38 million.

House candidates took in a total of just under $494 million. The incumbents' share was more than $294 million, while challengers raised about $96 million and open-seat candidates about $103 million.

Much of this money came from two principal sources: individual contributions and PACs. Candidates' loans to their campaigns also were a significant source of funding in Senate races, but much less so in House campaigns. Lesser amounts came from the political parties.

Individual Contributions

Political campaigns have traditionally been financed by the contributions of individual donors. The biggest difference today is that many more contributors are now involved in the process. The pre-Watergate contributors of unlimited amounts of money to federal candidates—the so-called "fat cats"—have been largely replaced by smaller donors, who either give directly to a candidate or contribute through a political party committee or PAC. The big donors, of course, have not disappeared. After coming up against statutory limits on direct contributions to federal campaigns, they found other outlets, such as soft money contributions to the parties.

Under the FECA, individuals are limited to $1,000 per candidate per election (a primary election, general election, and special election are considered separate elections with separate limits), $20,000 a year to a national party committee, and $5,000 a year to a PAC, with an overall limit of $25,000 per calendar year. (See Table 32-1, p. 859.)

Individual donors' reasons for giving are varied, as political scientist Paul Herrnson pointed out in a study of House races. They may give simply because they want to see a change in Congress. They may want access to influential incumbent members or they may like hobnobbing with political elites. They may want to support those with whom they share a common ethnic, racial, or religious bond.[6]

Whatever the motive, individual contributions to major party congressional candidates in 1997–1998 amounted to nearly $420 million, or 54 percent of their total receipts of $776 million. When broken down by chamber, individual contributions accounted for about 58 percent ($166.5 million) of Senate candidates' receipts and nearly 52 percent ($253 million) of House candidates'. Only a decade before there was a much wider gap in the two chambers' dependence on individual contributions. In the 1987–1988 election cycle, 64 percent of Senate candidates' money came from individual donors but not quite 47 percent in House campaigns.

FEC figures for all House and Senate candidates in 1997–1998 indicate that the gifts came in all sizes. About 31 percent were for less than $200 and 40 percent were for $750 or more.

Although scarcely used by individuals in congressional elections, an "independent expenditure" is another avenue for affecting elections. This is an expenditure for communications advocating the election or defeat of a candidate that is made without the knowledge or cooperation of the candidate or the candidate's campaign organization. Congress had placed a limit on such expenditures in the 1974 FECA amendments but this, along with most other limits, was thrown out by the Supreme Court in 1976 as a violation of First Amendment rights. PACs and, more recently, political parties have used independent expenditures on a far larger scale than individual donors have, but a $1.1 million expenditure in 1984 by businessman Michael Goland urging the defeat of Sen. Charles Percy, R-Ill., reportedly because of his Middle East stance, highlighted the potential of such spending when Percy lost. Independent expenditures must be reported to the FEC when they exceed $250 per year.

TABLE 32-1 Contribution Limits

Donors	Candidate committee	PAC[a]	Local party committee[b]	State party committee[b]	National party committee[c]	Special limits
			Recipients			
Individual	$1,000 per election[d]	$5,000 per year	$5,000 per year combined limit		$20,000 per year	$25,000 per year overall limit[e]
Local party committee[b]	$5,000 per election[d] combined limit	$5,000 per year combined limit	unlimited transfers to other party committees			
State party committee[b] (multicandidate)[f]			unlimited transfers to other party committees			
National party committee[c] (multicandidate)[f]	$5,000 per election[d]	$5,000 per year	unlimited transfers to other party committees			$17,500 to Senate candidate per campaign[g]
PAC[a] (multicandidate)[f]	$5,000 per election[d]	$5,000 per year	$5,000 per year combined limit		$15,000 per year	
PAC[a] (not multicandidate)[f]	$1,000 per election[d]	$5,000 per year	$5,000 per year combined limit		$20,000 per year	

NOTES: a. These limits apply to separate segregated funds and nonconnected PACs. Affiliated PACs share the same set of limits on contributions received and made.
b. A state party committee shares its limits with local party committees in that state unless a local committee's independence can be demonstrated.
c. A party's national committee, Senate campaign committee, and House campaign committee are each considered national party committees and each have separate limits except for contributions to Senate candidates. See Special limits column.   d. Each of the following is considered a separate election with a separate limit: primary election, caucus or convention with authority to nominate, general election, and special election.   e. A contribution to a party committee or a PAC counts against the annual limit for the year in which the contribution is made. A contribution to a candidate counts against the limit for the year of the election for which the contribution is made.   f. A multicandidate committee is a political committee that has been registered for at least six months, has received contributions from more than fifty contributors and, with the exception of a state party committee, has made contributions to at least five federal candidates.   g. This limit is shared by the national committee and the Senate campaign committee.
SOURCE: Federal Election Commission.

Political Action Committees

Labor unions, corporations, and incorporated trade and membership organizations are prohibited by law from using their general treasury funds to make contributions or expenditures in federal elections. They, therefore, participate indirectly in the electoral process through what are called "separate segregated funds." These funds, along with the political committees of other organizations (such as ideological and issue groups) that raise money for candidates, are known as political action committees. Most PACs are permitted to contribute $5,000 per candidate per election, with no overall limit. They also may give $15,000 per year to a national party committee.

PACs have been around for some time. The Congress of Industrial Organizations (CIO) founded the first modern PAC in 1943 when labor unions were barred from contributing directly. But their significance increased dramatically in the 1970s and 1980s. The number of registered PACs was 608 at the end of 1974, when the FEC first began its PAC count. It reached a high of 4,268 at the end of 1988 but had dropped to 3,798 a decade later. Registration, however, does not necessarily imply that the PAC actually made contributions during an election cycle. Nearly half of the decline between 1988 and 1998 was the result of the FEC's removal of inactive groups from its PAC list.

The more telling statistics on PAC growth are those on PAC giving. In the 1977–1978 election cycle, PACs contributed $34 million to congressional candidates; in the 1987–1988 election cycle, they reported contributions of $151 million. And by 1997–1998 the total had reached nearly $207 million. PAC contributions in the 1998 cycle constituted 32 percent of House candidates' receipts and not quite 17 percent of contributions to Senate candidates.

Why the explosive growth in PAC numbers and dollars? The answer can be found in part in the reform legislation of the 1970s. In 1971 Congress sanctioned the use of regular corporate and union funds to pay the overhead costs of PACs. Legislation in 1974 placed more stringent limits on individual contributions than on those of PACs. Most PACs, in fact, could give five times more than an individual contributor to a candidate—$5,000 versus $1,000. That same year Congress also lifted restrictions on the formation of PACs by government contractors.

PACs also tended to fill a void left by weakened political parties in the 1970s. "As citizen loyalties to political parties waned, as the party organizations weakened, and as the parties lost control of campaigns to the media and candidates, interest groups became the political organization of choice for many Americans concerned about specific (and even narrow) interests and issues," explained Sorauf.[7]

Further impetus for growth came in 1975 when the FEC

ruled that the Sun Oil Co. could establish a PAC and solicit contributions to SunPAC from stockholders and employees; the ruling eliminated the last barrier that had prevented corporations from forming PACs. FEC figures show that the number of corporate PACs jumped from 139 at the time of the SunPAC ruling in November 1975 to 433 by the end of 1976. PACs also reaped benefits from the Supreme Court's 1976 decision striking down restrictions on independent spending. *(See "1976 Amendments," p. 882.)*

Reaction to the rapid growth of PAC numbers and influence varied dramatically. Some saw it as a manifestation of democracy at work in a pluralist society, while others perceived it as a threat by special interests to the integrity of the electoral system and governmental process. *(See "PAC Phenomenon," p. 867.)*

But certain facts about PACs have been beyond dispute. One is that PACs have been overwhelmingly oriented toward incumbents. FEC figures showed that of the nearly $207 million that candidates reported receiving from PACs during the 1998 campaign, about $158 million went to incumbents, while only about $21.5 million went to challengers and about $27 million to open-seat candidates.

While some critics contend that PACs are out to buy votes with their contributions, many observers believe that their aim is to buy access to members in positions to help—or hinder—their cause. An example of this could be seen in the jump in contributions business PACs made to Democratic incumbents in the House during the 1980s. This increase was attributed to the persuasive powers of California Rep. Tony Coelho, chairman of the Democratic Congressional Campaign Committee in the early 1980s, who was said to have convinced traditionally conservative PACs of the logic of having access to a sitting member of the House instead of wasting money on a challenger who was likely to lose.

Thus, pragmatism won out over ideology, as corporate PAC contributions to Democrats edged up to more than 50 percent. But with the Republican takeover of Congress in the mid-1990s, corporate PACs were able to return to old loyalties. "Their ideological brethren had taken control of Congress. At the same time, the newly powerful House Republicans launched an aggressive campaign to cajole the PACs into making up for their past indiscretions by cutting off the Democrats and giving as much money as possible to Republicans," wrote Larry Makinson of the Center for Responsive Politics, a nonpartisan research organization.[8]

The overall PAC contribution figures for the 1998 campaign were fairly evenly divided between the two parties, although there was a definite tilt toward the GOP. And when the figures were broken down by type of PAC, the fact that the corporate PACs were well on their way home became obvious: they gave twice as much to the Republicans as to the Democrats in both chambers.

Labor PACs in the 1990s, however, showed none of the corporate PACs' pragmatism. They were in the Democratic camp when the Democrats controlled Congress; they were in the Democratic camp when the GOP was in control. Of the $6 million labor PACs gave to Senate candidates in the 1998 election cycle, $5.4 million went to Democrats. Of the $37 million they gave to House candidates, $34 million went to Democrats.

Independent Expenditures. In addition to direct contributions to candidates, PACs also can make independent expenditures. PACs reported independent expenditures of $7.5 million for congressional candidates in the 1998 races and nearly $1.5 million against candidates.

The numbers were small compared to overall PAC spending but the potential for larger expenditures did exist because there were no statutory limits on them. One often-cited example occurred in 1980 when the National Conservative Political Action Committee (NCPAC) spent more than $1 million against six liberal Senate incumbents, four of whom were defeated. But independent spending did not become a major PAC tactic because, as Sorauf pointed out, independent expenditures can earn more enmity than gratitude from candidates and do not produce the close political relationship with candidates that PACs are seeking.[9]

Leadership PACs. Although PACs are usually associated with interest groups outside Congress, a small but influential group of PACs called "leadership PACs"—also known as "personal PACs," "member PACs," or "politicians' PACs"—exists within Congress. These are separate PACs formed by members of Congress or other political leaders independent of their own campaign committees. They often are the PACs of presidential hopefuls, congressional leaders, or would-be leaders. "In almost all cases—and this is central to their role as brokers—sponsoring individuals are raising and giving money at least in part to support their own political careers, positions, or goals," Sorauf wrote.[10]

Leadership PACs offer several other advantages, according to former FEC Commissioner Trevor Potter. If they qualify as multicandidate committees, the PACs can accept $5,000 from individual donors instead of the $1,000 a candidate's campaign committee can accept. Since these PACs are considered to be separate from a candidate's campaign committee, the candidate can accept contributions from the same source twice—once for the campaign committee and once for the leadership PAC. These PACs also are increasingly being used as a source of funding for a member's travel or other political expenses.[11]

By the late 1990s, several dozen leadership PACs had set up soft money nonfederal accounts to assist state candidates and to cover certain operating expenses.

Political Parties

Political parties traditionally have provided direct assistance to candidates in two ways: through contributions, and through payments to vendors in a candidate's behalf. The latter, known as "coordinated expenditures," fund any number of campaign services such as polling, research, direct mailings, advertising, or buying TV time.

Party committees also persuade others to contribute. Convincing PACs, individuals, and incumbents to support a party's most competitive challengers and open-seat candidates has been one of the major tasks of the congressional campaign committees.[12] These congressional, or Hill, committees are the Democratic Senatorial Campaign Committee, National Republican Senatorial Committee, Democratic Congressional Campaign Committee, and the National Republican Congressional Committee.

Parties have found other ways to aid candidates, creating a great deal of controversy along the way. This type of assistance includes everything from get-out-the vote drives to advertising that stops just short of asking for a vote (so-called issue ads) to independent expenditures in support of a party's candidates.

Direct Contributions. National committees, which include the party's national committee as well as the House and Senate campaign committees, are each permitted to make contributions of $5,000 per candidate per election. That amounts to a total of $20,000 in party money for candidates' primary and general election races for the House, but for Senate candidates there is a $17,500 limit. State and local party committees may give a combined total of $5,000 per election.

Coordinated expenditures are made only in general elections, and the amount the parties may spend on behalf of a candidate is set by formula. For House candidates in states with more than one member, the national party expenditure limit is set at $10,000, adjusted for inflation, which translated into a $32,550 limit in 1998. For House candidates in states with only one member, the national parties could spend up to the limit for Senate candidates in those states, which in 1998 was $65,100. For Senate candidates, the party could spend the greater of either $20,000, adjusted for inflation—$65,100 in 1998—or two cents for every person of voting age, again adjusted for inflation. According to this formula, coordinated expenditures for Senate candidates in 1998 ranged from the base figure of $65,100 in the less populous states to a high of $1.5 million in California. *(See "Independent Expenditures," this page.)*

State party committees are also allowed to make coordinated expenditures in the same amounts as the national party. State parties, however, often do not have that kind of money, so the national party is permitted to use its money to make the expenditures on behalf of the state, in effect doubling its expenditure limit for a particular state or district.

The Republican Party has proven itself over the years to be the more successful fund-raiser of the two parties. GOP fund-raising prowess certainly could be expected when it was the majority party in Congress but Herrnson wrote that some of their advantage was more permanent, including a superior direct-mail fund-raising list and a wealthier constituency.[13]

In the 1997–1998 election cycle, national, state, and local Republican Party committees reported federal (hard dollar) receipts of $285 million and expenditures of nearly $276 million. Of this, they contributed $2.6 million directly to congressional candidates and made coordinated expenditures of $15.7 million. Democrats raised a total of $160 million and spent about $155

million. They contributed $1.2 million to congressional candidates and spent $18.6 million in their behalf. The bulk of the federal money (hard dollars) the party raises goes for party-building, electoral, and fund-raising activities.

Direct contributions and expenditures by the parties constitute a comparatively small percentage of the overall receipts of candidates. Parties, however, help candidates in other ways.

Soft Money. Parties can raise unlimited amounts of so-called soft money—essentially unregulated money—from unions, corporations, trade associations, and individuals for state and local party activities. Although this money cannot by law be used for federal candidates, when it is channeled into such grassroots activities as voter registration, education, and turnout, party candidates at all levels benefit. The money may be used to pay a portion of the overhead expenses of party committees, thus freeing up additional funds for direct contributions to candidates. Moreover, soft money has become an increasingly significant source for funding issue advocacy advertising—which are ads that promote the party's positions but do not "expressly advocate" the election or defeat of candidates.

Reports on soft money at one time were based largely on voluntary disclosures; however, at the beginning of 1991, regulations went into effect requiring that the money be reported to the FEC and the reports be made available to the public. During the 1997–1998 election cycle, Republican soft money accounts raised $131.6 million, a 151 percent increase over 1993–1994, the last midterm election cycle. Democrats collected $92.8 million, an 89 percent increase. *(See Figure 32-1, this page.)*

Independent Expenditures. A new avenue for parties' use of hard dollars was opened in 1996 when the Supreme Court threw

Figure 32–1 National Party Soft Money Receipts

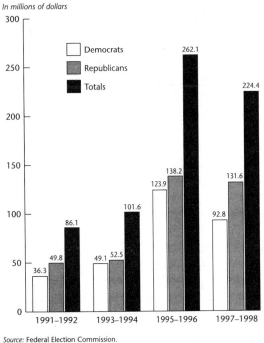

In millions of dollars

Source: Federal Election Commission.

out restrictions on independent expenditures by political parties (*Colorado Republican Federal Campaign Committee v. Federal Election Commission*). The ruling meant that the parties could spend unlimited amounts on such things as advertising that called for the election—or defeat—of specific candidates, as long as they did not coordinate those expenditures with the campaigns of their candidates.

The Court, however, left open the question of whether limits on coordinated expenditures were even constitutional. The issue was remanded to the lower courts.

The Republican Party jumped right in, making $10 million in independent expenditures in the 1996 election campaign. Democrats spent $1.5 million. GOP independent expenditures dropped off significantly in the 1998 midterm election campaign—less than $264,000 was reported. Democrats again spent $1.5 million.

Other Assistance. Political parties like to act as conduits, passing contributions through their committees to candidates. Thanks to sophisticated computers and mass mailings, a party can target those who might be interested in a race and encourage them to contribute. Through a practice called "earmarking," a contributor can direct money to a candidate or committee through an intermediary, such as the party. The money counts against the donor's contribution limits.

Computers and such techniques as electronic bank drafts have also facilitated the practice of "bundling," in which checks from a number of contributors are grouped together and presented as a package to a candidate. For bundling to be legal, however, the original donors must retain control over designation of the eventual recipient.

Candidate's Own Money

Another source of money for campaigns is the candidate's own bank account. Candidates can reach as deeply into their own pockets as they want because there are no limits on how much candidates may contribute or loan to their own campaigns. Deep personal pockets are not only welcomed by the parties but are sometimes even expected. Political scientists David Magleby and Candice Nelson wrote in 1990 that the political parties may expect challengers and open-seat candidates to give or loan their campaigns $25,000 or more in House races and even more for Senate campaigns.[14]

Candidates usually opt to loan the money to their campaigns in the hope that, if they win, they may be able to get some of it back from fund-raising after the election.

In 1974 Congress attempted to set limits on how much House and Senate candidates could contribute to their own campaigns, but before the limits could take effect they were ruled unconstitutional by the Supreme Court in the 1976 *Buckley* decision. The Court ruled that "the candidate, no less than any other person, has a First Amendment right to engage in the discussion of public issues and vigorously and tirelessly to advocate his own election."

In keeping with the law's intent to clean up campaign finance

activities, the justices also wrote that "the use of personal funds reduces the candidate's dependence on outside contributions and thereby counteracts the coercive pressure and attendant risks of abuse to which the act's contribution limitations are directed."

Most political observers agreed that the Court had given wealthy contenders a tremendous advantage. Simply having access to money and a willingness to pour a lot of it into a campaign does not guarantee victory in November—or even in a primary. But wealthy candidates are able to afford expensive, professional consultants and plan their strategy with greater assurance than candidates without a personal fortune.

And money enables the wealthy, but unknown, candidate to make the first splash in a crowded field of relatively obscure contenders for an open seat in Congress. While dozens of potential candidates may jockey for position, the one who can begin a campaign with an early television blitz is likely to start several lengths ahead.

Television stations require campaigns to pay their bills before any material is aired. For this reason, candidates who have the ability to loan or contribute a sizable sum can purchase expensive television advertising whenever they want. Those who are less well-off financially are forced to wait until the money comes in before beginning their media buy.

As the campaign progresses, especially after the primary, the advantage of personal wealth diminishes. Candidates without a personal fortune then have greater access to other sources of money, particularly from party coffers; the field is smaller, making it easier for voters to draw clear distinctions between the candidates; and more free publicity is available as the general election draws nearer. There are many cases where a rich candidate was able to clear out the primary field but then lost in the general election.

While being able to bankroll a large portion of one's own campaign has many advantages, it also has several clear disadvantages. The most obvious and frequently encountered is that it opens self-financed candidates to charges that they are trying to "buy" the election. Sometimes the opposition levels the charge; often the media raise it.

Another disadvantage is that outside money is harder to raise. Potential contributors often assume the rich candidates do not need their money. In some cases that may be true. But from a political standpoint a healthy list of contributors can give a campaign more credibility by indicating that the candidate, besides having a fat war chest, has a broad base of support.

FEC figures for the 1997–1998 election cycle showed that congressional candidates loaned themselves $100.4 million—about $52 million in the Senate and $48 million in the House. Candidates contributed more than $6.7 million to their campaigns—nearly $1.4 million in the Senate and $5.4 million in the House.

The largest user of personal money in the 1998 elections was Peter G. Fitzgerald of Illinois, who loaned his winning Senate campaign about $14 million. But Fitzgerald's loan was just half of what first-term Republican Rep. Michael Huffington put into his 1994 campaign to unseat Democratic Sen. Dianne Feinstein of California. Huffington spent $28.3 million of his own money—$16 million in contributions and $12 million in loans—but lost the race by a margin of only 2 percent.

CAMPAIGN EXPENDITURES

Congressional candidates spent approximately $740 million in the 1997–1998 election cycle, about $25 million less than the previous election cycle. Of the nearly $736 million spent by major party candidates, House and Senate incumbents together spent a total of $394 million, while challengers spent $203.6 million and open-seat candidates, $138 million. Incumbents ended the campaign with a $115 million cash surplus—proof that they had plenty of firepower to summon had they felt the need.

Figures for Senate major party candidates showed total expenditures of $287.5 million. Incumbents spent $137 million; challengers, $112 million; and open-seat candidates, $38 million. House Democrats and Republicans spent $448 million, with incumbents spending just under $257 million; challengers, $91.4 million; and open-seat candidates, $100 million.

How money is spent varies from one campaign to another. The needs of a House candidate are different from those of a Senate candidate. The needs of a challenger are different from those of an incumbent. A Senate candidate in a large state runs a different campaign than a candidate in a small state. Representatives of urban, suburban, and rural congressional districts run vastly different campaigns. Costs skyrocket in hotly contested races and are negligible in races with little or no opposition.

But some generalizations may be made. Campaigns have to pay for staff and rent. They hire consultants, media experts, and polling firms. They send out computerized mailings. They buy postage, buttons, bumper stickers, billboards, newspaper ads, radio spots, and television time—lots of television time.

Television Costs

Television advertising plays a significant role in campaigns. Being on or off the air wins elections. "The hard fact of life for a candidate is that if you are not on TV, you are not truly in the race," Sen. Ernest F. Hollings, D-S.C., told a congressional committee in 1990.[15]

And it is costly. "You simply transfer money from contributors to television stations," as Sen. Bill Bradley, D-N.J., put it in 1991.[16]

The Congressional Research Service (CRS), in a 1997 report on proposals to give candidates free or reduced-rate television time, found electronic media advertising to be the single largest category of aggregate Senate and House campaign expenditures. (This category included radio and TV airtime, production costs, and consultant fees.) Studies of the 1990, 1992, and 1994 elections cited by CRS found these costs consumed about 27 percent of campaign budgets in House races and about 40–45 percent in Senate races. The percentages went up for more competitive races and in Senate races in larger states, as well as for challengers and open seat contenders.[17]

Although television has been an important tool in House campaigns, it has not been consistently so. For example, Sara Fritz and Dwight Morris in a *Los Angeles Times* study found that in the 1990 campaign more than a quarter of House incumbents reported spending no money on broadcast advertising.[18] In urban centers such as Los Angeles, New York, and Chicago, it has not been cost effective, as an assistant to Rep. Howard L. Berman, D-Calif., who represented the San Fernando Valley suburbs of Los Angeles, explained:

You spend thousands for one thirty-second spot on one TV station, in a city where cable is rampant and there are a zillion channels. There are sixteen to seventeen congressional districts in L.A., so the vast majority of those who see it are not your constituents and can't vote for you anyway.[19]

Other Costs

Congressional candidates face a variety of other costs in their pursuit of a seat in the House or Senate. As with media costs, there are many variables. Incumbents, challengers, and open-seat candidates will allocate funds differently, depending on the competitiveness of the race, the size of their constituency, and, of course, their resources.

In their study of the 1992 races Dwight Morris and Murielle E. Gamache found that House incumbents on average spent about 25 percent of their money on overhead, which included everything from rent and office furniture to telephones and computers to salaries and taxes to travel and food. About 15 percent was spent on fund-raising (events, direct mail, and telemarketing); 4 percent on polling; 27 percent on electronic and other advertising; 20 percent on other campaign activity (voter contact mail, actual campaigning, and food, gifts, etc., for staff and volunteers); 5 percent on donations (to other candidates, political parties, and civic organizations); and 4 percent on miscellaneous gifts and expenses. Senate incumbents reported about 25 percent on overhead, 21 percent on fund-raising, 3 percent on polling, 41 percent on advertising, 8 percent on other campaign activity, 1 percent on donations, and 2 percent on miscellaneous items.[20]

Campaign Finance Issues and Proposals

The debates on campaign finance proposals after the 1970s highlighted the vastly different views members held on the system and what, if anything, needed fixing. Democrats and Republicans took opposing views on issue after issue, with many votes routinely dividing along partisan lines. The chamber they belonged to was also a factor in their views.

Despite the lack of consensus, there were some issues that repeatedly surfaced.

CONTROVERSIES

For many, there were certain basic problems in the campaign finance system. One was the high cost of running for office. That in turn led to another problem: the incessant search for contributions to pay the bills, a problem that had both personal and institutional ramifications.

The relentless search for money would then spawn other controversies. For a time, PACs were seen by many reformers as the villains. Others saw the fund-raising advantage of incumbents as a nearly insurmountable obstacle for challengers.

But by the 1990s new campaign finance controversies had erupted and the targets for reform changed. Soft money contributions and issue advocacy ads were seen by many as major loopholes in the system. Also troubling to many reformers were independent expenditures, especially by the political parties, and the practice of an intermediary pulling together, or "bundling," political contributions to a member from a number of donors.

Campaigns' High Costs

"Politics has got so expensive that it takes lots of money to even get beat with," humorist Will Rogers remarked in 1931.[21] If it was true then, it is much more so today.

The $740 million congressional candidates spent during the 1997–1998 election cycle was less than the $765 million spent in the previous election. But it was a great deal more than the $459 million spent just a decade earlier in 1987–1988. *(See Figure 32-2, this page.)*

For some that cost is too high. These people see "[t]he high cost of elections and the perception that they are 'bought and sold' . . . as contributing to public cynicism about the political process," observed CRS analyst Joseph E. Cantor. Others have raised concerns that the cost of running for office has given wealthy candidates the advantage over others of more modest means and that it may have fueled reliance on more sophisticated—often negative—media advertising. But on the other side of the issue, Cantor pointed out, are those who say that the expenditures are not too high—maybe not even high enough—when compared to overall government spending or commercial advertising. For example, "the nation's two leading commercial advertisers, Proctor and Gamble and General Motors, spent more in promoting their products in 1996 ($5 billion) than was spent on all U.S. elections that year."[22]

Senate Costs. A study by Cantor found that average Senate campaign costs went from $595,000 to $3.3 million between 1976 and 1996. This represented a 459 percent increase. When adjusted for inflation, the average rose by 102 percent and actually declined in five out of ten times.

The CRS study also gave statistics on just the winning candidates. For Senate winners, average spending rose from $609,000 to $3.8 million during the twenty-year period.[23]

The most expensive Senate race on record through the 1998 election was the 1994 California race between Feinstein and Huffington. Together they spent about $44.4 million. Huffington spent nearly $30 million, including the more than $28 million of his own money.[24]

House Costs. Cantor's study for CRS found average spending by House candidates rose from $73,000 in 1976 to $493,000 in

Figure 32–2   Campaign Spending by Election Year

In millions of dollars

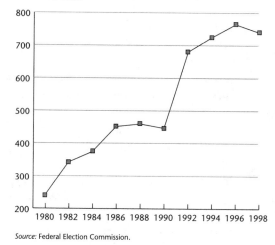

Source: Federal Election Commission.

1996, a 575 percent increase. When adjusted for inflation the average rose by 143 percent and declined three out of ten times. The average House winner spent $680,000 in 1996, a 682 percent rise from the $87,000 in 1976.[25]

The most expensive House race on record through 1998 was the race in Georgia's sixth district that year. Newt Gingrich, the Republican Speaker of the House, and his Democratic challenger, Gary Pelphrey, spent a combined $7.6 million. Of that total, Pelphrey spent $11,232 and Gingrich spent the rest![26] But apparently much of Gingrich's money was not spent to defeat Pelphrey. A study by the Center for Responsive Politics of the first fifteen months of the election cycle found that Gingrich had spent $3.7 million by that point, even though he did not yet have a registered opponent and that the "bulk of Gingrich's expenditures supported a direct-mail fund-raising operation, a costly technique used primarily to develop a wider base, especially useful for candidates contemplating a presidential run."[27] Moreover, Gingrich used a sizable portion of his campaign funds to assist other candidates and committees. For example, his reports to the FEC indicated a "transfer of excess funds" in the amount of $500,000 to the National Republican Campaign Committee in October 1998 and of $100,000 to his personal PAC in November 1998.

Why So Costly? Several factors account for the spiraling costs of congressional campaigns. The most obvious cause, as the above figures have indicated, has been inflation. As the costs of other goods and services in the economy inflated, so too did those of campaigns.

But even when inflation is accounted for, the cost of campaigns has increased dramatically in recent decades. A key reason has been the rise in the cost of fund-raising and of educating the electorate.

Since the 1960s congressional campaigns have undergone tremendous change. Most have been transformed from the volunteers-stuffing-envelopes-and-canvassing voters type of campaign to highly technical, mechanized campaigns that are likely to use computerized mass mailings to solicit contributions and thirty-second TV ads to get their message across to voters. Candidates hire political consultants to direct their campaigns and polling companies to tell them how they are doing. All of the high-tech trappings of modern campaigns cost money—big money.

Population growth affects campaigns—as the electorate expands so too does the cost of reaching voters. Individual campaigns' costs are also affected by the demographics of districts. Candidates in urban, suburban, or rural districts run very different campaigns with very different price tags. TV ads may not be cost-effective in an urban district, but they may be the only way a rural candidate can reach far-flung constituents.

The proliferation of media outlets has increased the cost as well. People are listening to or watching many more stations than they used to, so to reach them, campaigns have to spread their ads around.

The level of competition in a campaign also drives up the price of a campaign. Costs stay down if an incumbent has little or no opposition, but they rise sharply if an electoral threat appears. This is also true of contests for an open seat, which frequently are the most competitive races. In open-seat races, according to political scientist Gary Jacobson, "neither candidate enjoys the benefits of incumbency, both parties normally field strong candidates, and the election is usually close." Senate races also tend to attract money, according to Jacobson, because incumbent senators are often perceived as vulnerable, most of their challengers are well-known public figures, and elections to the 100-member Senate have a greater political impact than do those to the 435-member House.[28]

Some observers believe that so much money is raised in campaigns because so much money is available. But incumbents have reasons to raise as much money as they can. One of these is "deterrence." They want to use their campaign "war chests" to scare off potential opponents. And if deterrence does not work, they want to be ready for any surprises their opponents may come up with.

Incumbents also feel more secure with sizable reserves in the bank. They want to be ready in case a millionaire opponent decides to run against them. They want to be able to counter negative issue ads or independent expenditures. House members may anticipate a tough challenge because of an upcoming redistricting. Others stockpile money in case they decide to run for higher office, such as a House member running for the Senate or a senator running for the presidency.

Quest for Money

By many accounts, one of the most onerous tasks a legislator faces is fund-raising. It "takes a toll of the time, energy, and attention of legislators," according to Sorauf. "It is a task that tires even the most enthusiastic fund-raisers, and it depresses those incumbents who find it distasteful."[29]

Facing reelection contests every two years, members of the House are essentially campaigning and fund-raising all the time. One election campaign runs into the next. And even in the Senate, where the six-year term was once considered a luxury, members are beginning their campaigns earlier and earlier. The multimillion dollar price tags on some races require increasing attention to fund-raising.

For some that price is too high. When Democratic Sen. Frank R. Lautenberg of New Jersey announced that he would not seek a fourth term in the Senate in 2000, he said that a powerful factor in his decision was "the searing reality" that he would have had to spend half of every day between his mid-February 1999 announcement and the November 2000 election fund-raising. He explained:

To run an effective campaign, I would have to ask literally thousands of people for money. I would have had to raise $125,000 a week, or $25,000 every working day. That's about $3,000 an hour—more than lots of people earn in a month—distracted from the job I was hired to do.[30]

And more than a few find the task demeaning as well. At one Democratic Party training session, candidates were offered the following advice: "Learn how to beg, and do it in a way that leaves you some dignity."[31] That may be easier said than done, as Sen. Tom Daschle, D-S.D., found during his successful 1986 campaign to unseat an incumbent senator: "You're with people you have nothing in common with. You have a cosmetic conversation. You paint the best face you can on their issues and feel uncomfortable through the whole thing. You sheepishly accept their check and leave feeling not very good."[32]

At least he left with the check, which is more than can be said for many challengers. Attempting to unseat a sitting member of Congress is an enormously difficult task for a number of reasons, not the least of which is the obstacle of having to bankroll a campaign. Rep. David E. Price, D-N.C., a political scientist who ran successfully against an incumbent in 1986, said that he had undertaken few ventures as difficult and discouraging as raising money for his primary campaign. He held small fund-raisers, sent mail appeals to party activists, and approached potential large contributors, with mixed success. He and his wife contacted people on their old Christmas card lists, as well as professional colleagues and family members. They took out a second mortgage on their home. Price won the primary but still found fund-raising for the general election a continuing struggle. He later reflected on his campaign:

I will . . . never forget how difficult it was to raise the first dollars. I understand quite well why many potentially strong challengers and potentially able representatives simply cannot or will not do what it takes to establish financial "viability" and why so many who do reach that point can do so only on the basis of personal wealth. The modus operandi of most large contributors, PACs, and even party committees often makes their calculations of an incumbent's "safety" a self-fulfilling prophecy.[33]

The difficulties that surround fund-raising have institutional, as well as personal, consequences. For one thing, the time members spend raising money is time away from the business of legislating. Sen. Robert Byrd, D-W.Va., said that one of his

"WHEW—IT'S OVER! TOMORROW WE START RAISING MONEY FOR THE NEXT ELECTION"

Of the 402 House incumbents who sought reelection in 1998, 395 won—a 98.3 percent reelection rate. The last time the reelection rate in the House had dipped below 90 percent was in 1992 and the time before that was in 1974. On the Senate side the reelection rates have been much more erratic. But in the 1998 election twenty-six of twenty-nine incumbents seeking reelection won, which put the reelection rate at 89.7 percent. (*See Figure 32-3, p. 867.*)

This very decided advantage of incumbents at the polls has produced much study and speculation. According to Roger H. Davidson and Walter J. Oleszek, political scientists have launched "a veritable cottage industry" to answer the question of why incumbents are so formidable.[36]

Several reasons can be cited. Incumbents have name recognition. They have a public record to run on, which can be especially helpful if they can demonstrate they have voted to protect the interests of their constituents and have brought home federal grants and projects. Incumbents are highly visible because of easy and regular access to the media.

A real plus for incumbents is that they continue to receive their salary throughout the campaign. Many challengers are not so lucky. The prospect of doing without a salary while campaigning full-time for a year or more probably has deterred many a potential candidate from running.

Moreover, incumbents enjoy a number of perquisites, the most important being large staffs on Capitol Hill and in state or district offices ready to respond to the needs and inquiries of constituents. Thanks to the franking privilege, most letters and newsletters to constituents can be mailed free of charge, although there are restrictions aimed at curtailing blatant use of the privilege for political purposes. Members also benefit from allowances for phone calls and for travel back to their home district or state.

Incumbents also enjoy a distinct advantage in raising money for their reelection campaigns. FEC figures showed that House incumbents had a fund-raising advantage over challengers of more than three to one in 1997–1998. Incumbents raised $294 million, compared with $96 million raised by challengers. And incumbents clearly had more to spend—altogether, they had a surplus of almost $94 million.

The advantage of incumbents in the Senate was not as great. Senate incumbents in the 1997–1998 election cycle raised $135.5 million, while challengers raised about $114 million. Incumbents finished the campaign with a combined reserve of $21 million.

Both individual donors and PACs favored incumbents. Fifty-seven percent of all individual contributions went to incumbents. The percentage was much higher for PAC contributions—nearly 77 percent went to incumbents.

Over the years the implications of the tilt toward incumbents have preoccupied members, reformers, and observers of Congress alike. Some warned of a trend toward a "permanent Congress" with little turnover, and they deplored PACs "buying" access to members of Congress. But others dismissed the notion

biggest problems when he served as Senate majority leader was accommodating the senators' need for time away from the floor to raise money for their campaigns. "They have to go raise the money and they don't want any roll-call votes," Byrd lamented. "Now how can a majority leader run the Senate under such circumstances?" To Byrd the culprit was clear: "Mad, seemingly limitless escalation of campaign costs."[34] Byrd ended up revamping the Senate's work schedule in 1988 to give members time off to campaign and attend fund-raisers.

As Rep. Price indicated, there is another institutional consequence: the high cost of elections discourages people from running for Congress. "Potential challengers or candidates for open seats realize that unless they can raise a lot of money, they have little chance of winning," wrote Magleby and Nelson. As a result, party committees have found "it is increasingly hard to convince people to run, given the low probability of success and the high investment of time and money necessary to even hope to be competitive."[35]

Incumbent Advantage

Voters in 1998 returned congressional incumbents to Washington en masse, as they pretty much had been doing for years.

Figure 32–3 Incumbent Advantage in Reelection, 1946–1998

Winning percentages of those seeking reelection

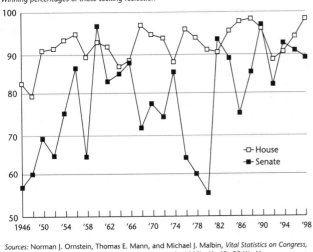

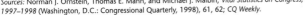

Sources: Norman J. Ornstein, Thomas E. Mann, and Michael J. Malbin, *Vital Statistics on Congress, 1997–1998* (Washington, D.C.: Congressional Quarterly, 1998), 61, 62; *CQ Weekly.*

and framed these contributions in a more positive light—contributors wanted to go with a winner, and most incumbents were seen as sure bets.

Fears of incumbents' advantage were allayed somewhat after the 1994 midterm election when the Republicans took control of both houses of Congress for the first time in forty years.

PAC Phenomenon

The rapid growth in the 1970s and 1980s of PAC money and influence in the electoral process generated much controversy. Defenders of PACs insisted they were an outgrowth of a democratic society. "PACs are both natural and inevitable in a free, pluralist democracy," political scientist Larry J. Sabato wrote. "In fact, the vibrancy and health of a democracy depend in good part on the flourishing of interest groups and associations among its citizenry."[37]

But critics branded PACs as a source of tainted money because their giving often was tied to specific legislation, to a leadership position, to membership on a certain committee, or to the mere fact of incumbency. Wertheimer voiced Common Cause's view before the Senate Rules Committee in 1989: "It is increasingly clear that PAC participation represents a threat to the public trust in the integrity of our electoral and congressional decision-making processes."[38]

One member of Congress who renounced PAC contributions said he thought PACs symbolized why voters had become alienated from politics. "People feel like it's big money, big business, big labor, the lobbyists who are represented, that little by little the playing field has been tilted," Romano L. Mazzoli, D-Ky., stated in 1990.[39]

However, a fellow Democrat in the House held the opposite view. In an opinion piece in the *Washington Post* in 1994, John Lewis, D-Ga., argued that PACs "give working people and people with little means the ability to participate in the political process." He went on: "Many of these people who contribute

through a 'checkoff,' or small deduction from their paycheck each week, would effectively be denied participation in the process if it weren't for their union or company PAC."[40]

PACs became a dominant issue in campaign finance debates. But the question of what to do, if anything, about them was a particularly divisive one between the parties and the chambers. Democrats were more dependent on PAC contributions than were Republicans, and House members relied on them more than senators. Those who wanted to curb PAC influence put forward proposals ranging from banning them completely to limiting how much PACs could give or candidates could receive from PACs.

But the urgency to do something about PACs diminished, as their numbers leveled off and other issues began to overshadow them. "The PAC issue has been greatly supplanted by more fundamental issues of electoral regulation, with observers finding new appreciation for the limited and disclosed nature of PAC money," explained Cantor.[41]

Soft Money

Campaign finance law bars corporations and unions from contributing to federal campaigns, and sets an annual ceiling of $25,000 on an individual's aggregate contributions to federal candidates and the national party committees. They can, however, give "soft" money, which refers to the unlimited and largely unregulated contributions to political party committees for activities ostensibly unrelated to federal candidates. It is called "soft" to distinguish it from the tightly regulated "hard" dollars (money that is "hard" to raise within the limitations) that can go straight to parties, PACs, and candidates for direct use in federal campaigns.

Soft money donations skyrocketed in the 1990s, as did the controversy surrounding them. For some, soft money represented a return to the Watergate era when fat cat contributors won special access with six-figure donations. But party officials lauded the contributions, saying they kept party organizations relevant and strong.

Soft money was an outgrowth of the tough post-Watergate reforms that sought to clamp down on flagrant campaign finance abuses. The 1974 Federal Election Campaign Act (FECA) set limits on contributions and introduced some public financing of presidential elections. But the new law was so strict that candidates, party committees, and even academics joined in protest following the 1976 election cycle, arguing that the new rules were stifling volunteer and grassroots party activity. For example, bumper stickers, lawn signs, and the like were considered in-kind contributions to the candidates. Also, public financing of presidential campaigns had brought with it restrictions on spending and tight limits on additional fund-raising by parties and campaign committees. The campaigns opted to spend their resources on advertising rather than local party activities. Party leaders complained that the new law had almost completely eliminated state and local party organizations from presidential campaigns.

Responding to those complaints, the FEC issued a controversial ruling in 1978 allowing a state party to use money that was not permitted under federal campaign finance law—in this case, corporate and labor contributions—to pay for a portion of grassroots and generic party activities, even if they indirectly aided federal candidates. Previously, the FEC had allowed the use of nonfederal money to pay a portion of a party's overhead and administrative costs but had barred the use of such money to pay for any portion of get-out-the-vote or voter registration activities because of their indirect effect on federal races.

FEC Commissioner Thomas E. Harris issued a sharp dissent to the agency's 1978 ruling, arguing that it would allow the use of corporate and union money to pay most of the costs of voter drives because there usually were more state and local elections than federal races in a state. "His point was not lost on party leaders, who quickly began to adapt their financial strategies to take advantage of the new opportunities inherent in the FEC's decision," political scientist Anthony Corrado observed. Because the national parties also were involved in state and local election activities, it was assumed that they too could use money not permitted under the FECA for certain expenses as long as they kept this nonfederal money in a separate account.[42]

And then in 1979 Congress approved amendments to the FECA allowing state and local parties to spend as much as they wanted on campaign materials for volunteer activities to promote any federal candidate. Such items included buttons, bumper stickers, handbills, brochures, posters, and yard signs. Also, those party organizations were allowed to conduct, without financial limit, certain kinds of voter registration and get-out-the-vote drives on behalf of presidential tickets.

The 1978 FEC ruling and the 1979 amendments gave rise to the soft money phenomenon. The FEC had sanctioned the use of both federal and nonfederal money for election activities as long as it was kept in separate accounts and the 1979 law allowed state parties to spend unlimited amounts of hard dollars for activities that would aid their entire slate of candidates, including federal candidates. With traditional funding sources restricted by the FECA contribution limits, there was a strong incentive for parties to find other sources of money so they could take advantage of the new avenues opened to them.

Republicans were faster to seize on soft money's possibilities in the 1980 presidential campaign, but Democrats quickly caught up and resisted early calls to abolish the practice. The rapid growth of soft money led Common Cause to sue the FEC to force it to tighten its regulations. In a partial victory, a federal judge ordered the agency to amend its rules; one of the effects of the new rules, which went into effect in 1991, was to make most soft money reportable.

In the 1992 election cycle, the first in which soft money had to be reported, the national party committees reported soft money receipts of $86 million—$49.8 million went to the Republicans and $36 million to the Democrats. By the 1996 cycle, the parties were aggressively seeking soft money and managed to raise $262 million—$138 million went to the GOP and $123.9

million to the Democrats. Moreover, they had found an important new use for it: television issue advocacy advertising. "To a certain extent, there was only so much money you could spend on get-out-the-vote," explained Corrado. "But once you started moving to advertising, the demand for soft money rose dramatically."[43]

The parties' pursuit of soft money played a key role in the scandal that erupted in the 1996 presidential election. It was the most significant campaign finance scandal since Watergate. (See "1996 Scandal," p. 854.)

Despite the scandal and resulting embarrassment, the parties' appetite for soft money continued unabated. In fact, soft money, which previously had been largely a phenomenon of presidential politics, became a major factor in congressional politics as well. One study found the growth in party soft money activity, including party issue advocacy, to be "the most important money and politics development in the 1998 congressional elections."[44]

Democratic Party committees raised $92.8 million in the 1997–1998 election cycle compared with $49 million in the last midterm election in 1994, while Republicans raised $131.6 million compared with $52.5 million. A breakdown of those figures showed the four congressional campaign committees posting record gains in soft money receipts in 1998 compared with 1994. The Democratic Senate and House campaign committees raised $42.7 million in 1998 and $5.5 million in 1994; the Republican congressional committees raised $64.8 million in 1998 and $13 million in 1994.

The booming soft money business on Capitol Hill had some wondering why, if soft money was to be used for generic party-building activities and for state and local elections, were the congressional campaign committee raising so much of it? Most of the committees claimed to be taking on broader party functions and therefore were giving to state and local candidates. Soft money also became an attractive option for congressional fund-raisers who believed that the two national committees were so focused on presidential contests that they had neglected voter turnout in competitive House and Senate races. But a big reason for their aggressive pursuit of soft money was the purchase of issue ads.[45]

Issue Advocacy Ads

Issue advocacy advertising is a type of communication that is supposed to promote certain ideas or issues, as opposed to express advocacy ads that call for the election or defeat of particular candidates. The line between the two types of advertising, however, can be rather thin at times. As a study by the University of Pennsylvania's Annenberg Public Policy Center put it: "To the naked eye, these issue advocacy ads are often indistinguishable from ads run by candidates."[46]

Issue ads may be broadcast on TV or radio, conveyed by telephone, or printed in fliers or mailers. They usually point out a particular candidate's position on a given issue, painting either a dark or glowing picture of the candidate based on that one position, be it abortion or term limits or environmental protection or whatever. But, most importantly, the ads stop just short of specifically asking for a vote for or against a candidate.

The Supreme Court in its 1976 *Buckley* decision ruled that limits on campaign contributions applied only to "communications that in express terms advocate the election or defeat of a clearly identified candidate for federal office." A footnote in the ruling defined express terms to include such phrases as "vote for," "elect," or "support." As a result, many took the position that if issue ads did not include such terms, they were not subject to any reporting requirements or spending limits.

The use of issue ads by the parties and outside groups grew dramatically in the 1990s. Studies by the Annenberg Public Policy Center estimated that seventy-seven groups and committees spent between $275 million and $340 million on issue ads during the 1997–1998 election cycle, compared with the $135 million to $150 million spent in 1995–1996. About 40 percent of the ads in both election cycles fell in what was said to be the "pure attack" category, which meant that the ads made a case only against the opposing position. The 1996 study said this contributed to the negative tone of political campaigns.

Republicans learned in the 1998 campaign that negative issue ads can sometimes backfire. In the final week of the campaign, the National Republican Congressional Committee (NRCC) began running three ads addressing President Bill Clinton's affair with White House intern Monica Lewinsky. Many analysts thought the ads, which had the approval of Speaker Gingrich, were a mistake and that the GOP should have kept their focus on basic issues that affect voters' everyday lives, such as education and jobs. The ad campaign contributed to the ill will in the House that ultimately caused Gingrich to step down as Speaker.

The upward spiral of issue advocacy had been vividly illustrated in the 1996 election cycle, when the AFL-CIO spent $35 million on an issue ad campaign—$25 million on paid media and the rest on direct mail and related organizing activities. The ads, which focused on such issues as Medicare, minimum wage, education, and pensions, ran heavily in vulnerable Republican districts. A coalition of business groups, formed to counter labor's effort, spent $5 million on issue ads. The Annenberg study also indicated that the Democratic National Committee spent $44 million on issue advocacy ads, while the Republican National Committee and the NRCC spent $34 million in the 1996 election cycle.

Opponents of issue ads say they are nothing more than thinly veiled pitches for or against individual candidates and represent a giant loophole in campaign spending laws. But supporters insist that issue ads educate the public and help create a better-informed electorate. And they argue that any limits on issue advocacy would impede their constitutional right to free speech.

Soft money was used for the first time in a big way to pay for such ads in the 1996 election. Federal regulations barred the national parties from using soft money for more than 40 percent

Campaign finance reformers in the House in the 1990s were led by Republican Christopher Shays of Connecticut, left, and Democrat Martin T. Meehan of Massachusetts, right.

of the costs of such ads, while limits on state parties varied depending on the ratio of federal to nonfederal candidates. Interest groups and individuals, however, had no restrictions on how much unregulated money they could spend on the ads.

Independent Expenditures

The Supreme Court in the *Buckley* decision ruled that the 1974 FECA's $1,000 ceiling on independent expenditures was a clear violation of the First Amendment right of free expression. Independent expenditures are defined as communications that expressly advocate the election or defeat of a candidate but are made without consultation or coordination with the candidate.

Although there no longer is a limit on the amount that can be spent, independent expenditures are subject to FECA disclosure requirements and must be paid for with funds legally permitted in a federal election campaign. In other words, an independent expenditure could not be financed by labor or most corporate money (certain small, ideologically based nonprofit corporations are exempt), nor by a contribution from a foreign national.

Independent expenditures have been controversial for several reasons. Some question whether such expenditures are truly independent. Others criticize the clout it gives a wealthy individual or an organization to influence the outcome of an election. Still others point out that candidates themselves sometimes resent this outside interference even when the communication favors their campaigns. *(See "Individual Contributions," p. 858; "Political Action Committees," p. 859.)*

The debate over independent expenditures intensified when

the Supreme Court issued its 1996 ruling that political parties could make independent expenditures. In the *Colorado Republican Federal Campaign Committee v. Federal Election Commission* decision, the Court held that state and national parties were free to make unlimited expenditures in a congressional campaign as long as the party and the candidate were not working together. The Court thus rejected the prevailing assumption that a party was uniquely connected to its candidates—especially given the coordinated expenditures it made on behalf of its candidates—and could not act independently of them.

Bundling of Contributions

Bundling refers to an intermediary pulling together contributions to a certain candidate from a number of individual donors and passing those checks on in a "bundle" to the candidate. (The checks could also be sent separately but it still would be obvious who had instigated the flow.) The intermediary earns the gratitude of the candidate without having the money count against its own contribution limits. Bundling can be done by an individual, PAC, or political party committee.

Critics argue that, because there are no limits on the overall amount a conduit group may collect and pass on to a candidate, bundling essentially allows the group to circumvent election law. But bundlers say they are simply matching donors with like-minded candidates.

The Council for a Livable World, a nuclear arms control lobbying group, first bundled checks in 1962, sending contributions to an obscure Democratic Senate candidate from South Dakota named George McGovern. But it was EMILY's List, which backed Democratic women candidates who favored abortion rights, that perfected the practice. In addition to its regular PAC contributions, EMILY's List required its members to contribute a minimum of $100 to at least two candidates endorsed by the group.

EMILY's List was something of an exception. In most cases, according to Sorauf, bundlers and the interests they represented were not publicly known. In a discussion of PAC bundling, Sorauf wrote: "Virtually all the important information that PACs must and do disclose to the FEC is lost if organized giving is simply bundled instead."[47]

ONGOING DEBATE

Congress revisited the campaign finance debate regularly beginning in the mid-1980s but made little progress on the fundamental issues that divided the parties. Each party wanted to capitalize on its strong points and curb those of the other party.

The Democrats contended that the system operated like an arms race—that candidates engaged in a never-ending quest for a financial edge. Hence, most Democrats insisted that any new law had to limit campaign spending. They advocated partial public funding of candidates who promised to abide by spending limits, which they said would allow challengers to spend on a level equal to incumbents.

But most Republicans strenuously opposed taxpayer financing of congressional campaigns, which they likened to welfare for politicians. Many Republicans also argued that spending limits locked in incumbent advantages. They said challengers needed the option to outspend incumbents to make themselves equally visible to voters. For Republicans, the problem was one of tainted sources of money. Instead of capping spending, they proposed curbing specific sources, such as PACs and large out-of-state contributions. And they wanted to encourage political parties to spend even more money in behalf of their candidates.

Further complicating matters was the fact that incumbent factions in each party savored the easy flow of money from Washington fund-raisers. House Democrats in particular found it difficult to think of parting with PAC dollars. Some accused the Senate of posturing in their attempts to ban PACs, knowing full well that House members, who received a much higher portion of their contributions from PACs than did senators, would vote to preserve PACs or that the Supreme Court ultimately would declare the ban unconstitutional.

Proposals to limit but not ban PACs generated another type of controversy. Although PACs could give $10,000 to a candidate in an election cycle ($5,000 for the primary and $5,000 for the general), most gave far less. However, labor PACs often gave Democrats in close races the full $10,000 permitted—money they did not want to lose.

Democrats also objected to Republican proposals to let political parties give more to, or spend more in behalf of, their candidates than existing law allowed, primarily because the GOP was better at raising money.

The debate went on in Congress after Congress. Rep. Bob Franks, R-N.J., described it as "an intricate game of ping-pong. . . . One chamber would pass a law, knowing the other would not. It was playing politics."[48] Legislation was passed, rejected, filibustered, never made it to conference, or vetoed.

In the mid-1990s the explosive growth of soft money and issue advocacy advertising added a new urgency to the campaign finance debate. Congress's preoccupation with PACs, spending limits, and public funding gave way to efforts to curtail the new types of campaign spending. But partisan divisions existed on these issues as well. Republicans, for example, complained that clamping down on soft money without inhibiting labor's independent spending on behalf of Democrats would amount to unilateral disarmament by the GOP.

And so the heated debate over the financing of elections continued, as it had throughout the history of American politics.

Financing Campaigns: Historical Development

In early American politics the source of money to finance a political campaign was never a question. Politics was a gentleman's pursuit and the gentleman was to pay. But, as political scientist Robert Mutch points out, the expenses were small and campaigns in the modern sense were few. "Candidates were supposed to attract support by virtue of their reputations, not by actually mingling with voters," Mutch wrote.[49] Candidates' expenses might have included the costs of printing and distributing campaign literature or perhaps providing food and drink for the voters on election day.

George Washington, for example, during his campaign for the House of Burgesses in Virginia in 1757, dispensed twenty-eight gallons of rum, fifty gallons of rum punch, thirty-four gallons of wine, forty-six gallons of beer, and two gallons of cider royal! "Even in those days this was considered a large campaign expenditure," writer George Thayer observed, "because there were only 391 voters in his district, for an average outlay of more than a quart and a half per person."[50]

By the early nineteenth century politics no longer was the exclusive domain of the wealthy merchant or the gentleman farmer. The professional politician had emerged. Lacking personal wealth, the new breed was dependent on others for campaign support and on salaries for their livelihood. Modern political parties also began to emerge, and with them came the spoils system. When a new president came in, government jobs were transferred to his supporters. It was not long before the new appointees were having to pay for the privilege of a government job, with the political parties exacting percentages from the salaries of federal employees.

The first known cases of assessments on government workers were levied by the Democratic Party on U.S. customs employees in New York City during the 1830s. But attempts to legislate against the practice went nowhere because, as Mutch noted, "few politicians were willing to eliminate such a valuable source of party funds, and the system of assessments continued to grow."[51]

The first provision of federal law relating to campaign finance was incorporated into an act of March 2, 1867, making naval appropriations for fiscal 1868. The final section of the act read:

And be it further enacted, That no officer or employee of the government shall require or request any workingman in any navy yard to contribute or pay any money for political purposes, nor shall any workingman be removed or discharged for political opinion; and any officer or employee of the government who shall offend against the provisions of this section shall be dismissed from the service of the United States.

Reports circulated the following year that at least 75 percent of the money raised by the Republican Congressional Committee came from federal officeholders. Continuing agitation on this and other aspects of the spoils system in federal employment—tragically highlighted by the assassination in 1881 of President James A. Garfield by a disappointed office seeker—led to adoption of the 1883 Civil Service Reform Act. The act, also known as the Pendleton Act, authorized the establishment of personnel rules, one of which stated, "That no person in the public service is for that reason under any obligation to contribute to any political fund . . . and that he will not be removed or otherwise prejudiced for refusing to do so." The law made it a crime for any federal employee to solicit campaign funds from another federal employee.

Links between money and politics were a target for editorial cartoonists even before Thomas Nast drew this in 1871.

But shrewd campaign managers found money elsewhere. Business money had become increasingly important in the post–Civil War period and was dominant by the close of the century. In the legendary 1896 campaign between Republican William McKinley and Democrat-Populist William Jennings Bryan, McKinley's successful effort was managed by Marcus A. (Mark) Hanna, a wealthy Ohio financier and industrialist who turned the art of political fund-raising into a system for assessing campaign contributions from banks and corporations.

As these political contributions grew, so too did public concern over the role of corporate money in politics. "The concern among the electorates of the industrialized nineteenth century was that their elected representatives might not be the real policymakers, that government might still be controlled by those who provided campaign funds," Mutch wrote.[52] In the late 1800s several states enacted campaign finance laws, some requiring disclosure of information on the sources and uses of campaign contributions and others actually prohibiting corporate contributions. The push was on for action on the national level.

EARLY LEGISLATION

Reacting to the increasingly lavish corporate involvement in political campaigns, the hearty band of reformers known as the "muckrakers" pressed for the nation's first extensive campaign finance legislation. During the first decade of the twentieth century, they worked to expose big business's influence on government through unrestrained spending on behalf of favored candidates.

Corporate Contribution Ban

Revelations during congressional hearings that several corporations had secretly financed Theodore Roosevelt's 1904 presidential campaign provided impetus for change. The establishment of the National Publicity Law Organization, headed by former Rep. Perry Belmont, D-N.Y., focused further attention on the issue. President Roosevelt, in his annual message to Congress, proposed on December 5, 1905, that "all contributions by corporations to any political committee or for any political purpose should be forbidden by law." Roosevelt repeated the proposal the following December, suggesting that it be the first item of congressional business.

Congress in 1907 passed the first federal campaign finance law, the Tillman Act, which made it unlawful for a corporation or a national bank to make "a money contribution in connection with any election" of candidates for federal office. Although Roosevelt is generally regarded as having initiated the series of actions leading to the 1907 law, Mutch points out that the bill passed by Congress had actually been written and introduced five years earlier.[53]

In his December 1907 annual message, Roosevelt joined those calling for the "very radical measure" of public funding of party organizations. But no action was taken.

Disclosure Mandated

Three years later the first Federal Corrupt Practices Act (also known as the Publicity Act of 1910) was passed, establishing disclosure requirements for U.S. House candidates. Specifically, the law required every political committee "which shall in two or more states influence the result or attempt to influence the result of an election at which Representatives in Congress are to be elected" to file with the clerk of the House of Representatives, within thirty days after the election, the name and address of each contributor of $100 or more, the name and address of each recipient of $10 or more from the committee, and the total amounts that the committee received and disbursed. Individuals who engaged in similar activities outside the framework of committees also were required to submit such reports.

The following year legislation was passed extending the filing requirements to committees influencing Senate elections and requiring candidates for House and Senate seats to file financial reports. (Popular election of senators, in place of election by state legislatures, was mandated by the Seventeenth Amendment, approved by Congress in 1912 and ratified in 1913.) Both pre- and postelection reports were required. The most important innovation of the 1911 act was the limit that was placed on the amount a candidate could spend campaigning for his nomination and election: a candidate for the Senate, no more than $10,000 or the maximum amount permitted in his state, whichever was less; for the House, no more than $5,000 or the maximum amount permitted in his state, whichever was less.

1925 Corrupt Practices Act

No further changes in federal campaign law were made for more than a decade. But then the system was overhauled with passage of the Federal Corrupt Practices Act of 1925, which served as the basic campaign finance law until the early 1970s.

The Teapot Dome scandal gave Congress the push it needed to pass reform legislation. During a congressional investigation of alleged improprieties in the Harding administration's leasing of naval oil reserves to private operators, it had been discovered that an official of the company that had leased the Teapot Dome reserve in Wyoming had not only bribed the official in charge of the leasing but had also contributed generously to the Republican Party to help retire its 1920 campaign debt. The contribution had been made in a nonelection year and therefore did not have to be reported under existing law—a loophole that was closed by the 1925 act's requirement that contributions of $100 or more be reported, whether made in an election year or not. (See "Teapot Dome," p. 267, Vol. I.)

The 1925 act regulated campaign spending and disclosure of receipts and expenditures by House and Senate candidates, as well as disclosure by national political committees and their subsidiaries and by other committees seeking to influence elections in more than one state. The 1925 act limited its restrictions to general election campaigns because the Supreme Court in 1921 had ruled that Congress did not have jurisdiction over primaries. (See "Restrictions on Primaries," p. 873.)

The act revised the amounts that candidates could legally spend. Unless a state law prescribed a smaller amount, the act set the ceilings at $10,000 for a Senate candidate and $2,500 for a House candidate; or an amount equal to three cents for each vote cast in the last preceding election for the office sought, but not more than $25,000 for the Senate and $5,000 for the House.

The 1925 act incorporated the existing prohibition against campaign contributions by corporations and national banks, the ban on solicitation of political contributions from federal employees by candidates or other federal employees, and the requirement that reports on campaign finances be filed. It prohibited giving or offering money to anyone in exchange for his or her vote. In amending the provisions of the 1907 act on contributions, the new law substituted for the word "money" the phrase "a gift, subscription, loan, advance, or deposit of money, or anything of value."

The Corrupt Practices Act, however, was riddled with loopholes and contained no provisions for enforcement. It did not mandate publication of the reports or review of the reports for errors and omissions. It did not require reports of contributions and expenditures in either presidential or congressional primary campaigns, nor in connection with a party's presidential nomination. It did not require reports by political committees so long as they confined their activities to a single state and were not actual subsidiaries of a national political committee. Frequently, congressional candidates reported they had received and spent nothing on their campaigns, maintaining that the campaign committees established to elect them to office had been working without their "knowledge and consent."

Candidates were able to evade the spending limitations by channeling most of their campaign expenditures through separate committees that were not required to report federally, thus making the federal ceilings, from a practical standpoint, meaningless.

No candidate for the House or the Senate ever was prosecuted under the 1925 act, although it was widely known that most candidates spent more than the act allowed and did not report all they spent. Only two persons elected to Congress—Republicans William S. Vare of Pennsylvania and Frank L. Smith of Illinois, both elected to the Senate in 1926—ever were excluded from office for spending in excess of the act's limits.

The 1925 act's requirement that political committees seeking to influence the election of presidential electors in two or more states file contribution and spending reports was challenged in the courts as an unconstitutional infringement on states' rights. The Supreme Court in 1934, in *Burroughs and Cannon v. United States*, upheld the act's applicability to the election of presidential electors and implicitly sanctioned federal regulation of campaign financing in congressional elections.

On the topic of disclosure, the Court stated: "Congress reached the conclusion that public disclosure of political contributions, together with the names of contributors and other details, would tend to prevent the corrupt use of money to affect elections. The verity of this conclusion reasonably cannot be denied."

Hatch Act and Labor Restrictions

During the period between the early efforts to regulate spending and the broad reforms of the 1970s, some laws related to campaign financing were enacted, although they had less direct effects than the corrupt practices laws.

A 1939 law, commonly called the Hatch Act but also known as the Clean Politics Act, barred federal employees from active participation in national politics and prohibited collection of political contributions from persons receiving relief funds provided by the federal government.

A 1940 amendment to the Hatch Act made several significant additions to campaign finance law. It placed a ceiling of $3 million in a calendar year on expenditures by a political committee operating in two or more states. (In practice, however, the parties easily evaded this stipulation.) The 1940 amendment forbade federal contractors, whether individuals or companies, to contribute to any political committee or candidate. It also asserted Congress's right to regulate primary elections for the nomination of candidates for federal office and made it unlawful for anyone to contribute more than $5,000 to a federal candidate or political committee in a single year. But Congress opened a big loophole when it specifically exempted from this limitation "contributions made to or by a state or local committee."

Three years later Congress passed the War Labor Disputes Act (Smith-Connally Act), temporarily extending the 1907 prohibition on political contributions by national banks and corporations to include labor unions. This prohibition was made permanent by the Labor-Management Relations Act of 1947 (Taft-Hartley Act).

Restrictions on Primaries

Legislative and judicial decisions in the first half of the twentieth century repeatedly redefined the relationship of campaign finance laws to primary elections. The 1911 act limiting campaign expenditures in congressional elections covered primaries as well as general elections. In 1921, however, the Supreme Court in the case of *Newberry v. United States* struck down the law's application to primaries on the ground that the power the Constitution gave Congress to regulate the "manner of holding election" did not extend to party primaries and conventions. The Corrupt Practices Act of 1925 exempted primaries from its coverage.

The Hatch Act amendments of 1940 made primaries again subject to federal restrictions on campaign contributions despite the *Newberry* decision. This legislation was upheld in 1941, when the Supreme Court in *United States v. Classic* reversed its *Newberry* decision by ruling that Congress has the power to regulate primary elections when the primary is an integral part of the process of selecting candidates for federal office. The *Classic* decision was reaffirmed by the Court in 1944 in *Smith v. Allwright*. When the Taft-Hartley Act was adopted in 1947, its prohibition of political contributions by corporations, national banks, and labor organizations was phrased to cover primaries as well as general elections.

LOOPHOLES ABOUND

Even with the revisions of the 1930s and 1940s, the campaign system was filled with loopholes. In a 1967 message to Congress proposing election reforms, President Lyndon B. Johnson said of the Corrupt Practices and Hatch acts: "Inadequate in their scope when enacted, they are now obsolete. More loophole than law, they invite evasion and circumvention."

Contributors' Loopholes

The Corrupt Practices Act required the treasurer of a political committee active in two or more states to report at specified times the name and address of every donor of $100 or more to a campaign. To evade such recording, a donor could give less than $100 to each of numerous committees supporting the candidate of his choice. A Senate subcommittee in 1956 checked the contributions of sums between $50 and $99.99 to one committee. It found that of ninety-seven contributions in that range, eighty-eight were over $99, including fifty-seven that were exactly $99.99.

Technically, an individual could not contribute more than $5,000 to any national committee or federal candidate. However, he or she could contribute unlimited funds to state, county, and local groups that passed along the money in the organization's name.

Members of the same family could legally contribute up to $5,000 each. A wealthy donor wanting to give more than $5,000 to a candidate or a political committee could privately subsidize gifts by relatives. Each such subsidized gift could amount to

$5,000. In this way, the donor could arrange for a spouse, child, aunt, uncle, brother, or sister to make a $5,000 gift as well.

According to data from the Survey Research Center at the University of Michigan, only about 8 percent of the population contributed in 1968. Both parties relied on big contributors. In every presidential election in the 1950s and 1960s, with one exception, the Democratic National Committee relied on contributors of more than $500 for more than 60 percent of its funds. For the same period, again with the exception of one election year, the Republican National Committee received more than 50 percent of its contributions from donations of more than $500.

Each party could count on support from certain wealthy contributors. Among the Republicans were the Mellons, Rockefellers, and Whitneys. Among the Democrats were the Laskers, Kennedys, and Harrimans. Large contributions also came from foreigners.

Corporations. Corporations could skirt the prohibition of contributions to a political campaign by giving bonuses or salary increases to executives in the expectation that as individuals they would make corresponding political contributions to candidates favored by the corporation.

Political campaign managers learned to watch for contribution checks drawn directly on corporate funds and to return them to avoid direct violation of the law. Often this money made its way back to the political managers in some other form.

Corporations were allowed to place advertisements in political journals, even though there was no apparent benefit to the corporations from the ads, and they could lend billboards, office furniture, equipment, mailing lists, and airplanes to candidates or political committees. If a loan of this kind was deemed a violation of the letter of the law, the corporation could rent these items to a candidate or committee, instead of lending them, and then write off the rental fee as uncollectible.

Unions. Labor unions could contribute to a candidate or political committee funds collected from members apart from dues. Money could be taken directly from union treasuries and used for technically "nonpartisan" purposes, such as promoting voter registration, encouraging members to vote, or publishing the voting records of members of Congress or state legislators.

Organized labor's registration and get-out-the-vote drives overwhelmingly supported Democratic candidates, being keyed to areas where regular Democratic efforts were considered deficient or where an overwhelming Democratic vote was traditionally necessary to overcome a Republican plurality in some other section of the district, state, or country.

Public service activities, such as union newspapers or radio programs, could be financed directly from regular union treasuries. As with corporate newspapers and radio programs, a sharply partisan viewpoint could be, and often was, expressed.

Candidates' Loopholes

Federal or state limitations on the amount of money a candidate might knowingly receive or spend were easily evaded. A loophole in the law enabled numerous candidates to report that

they received and spent not one cent on their campaigns because any financial activity was conducted without their "knowledge or consent." In 1964 four senators reported that their campaign books showed zero receipts and zero expenditures—Vance Hartke, D-Ind.; Roman L. Hruska, R-Neb.; Edmund S. Muskie, D-Maine; and John C. Stennis, D-Miss.

Four years later, when Sen. George McGovern, D-S.D., reported no receipts or expenditures, one of his staff explained that they were careful to make sure that McGovern never saw the campaign receipts. Two senators elected in 1968—William B. Saxbe, R-Ohio, and Richard S. Schweiker, R-Pa.—reported general election expenditures of $769,614 and $664,614, respectively, to their state authorities, but expenditures of only $20,962 and $5,736, respectively, to the secretary of the Senate.

Another measure of the recorded figures' incompleteness was the contrast between the reported total political spending in 1960—$28,326,322—and the $175 million spending estimate by political experts. In 1962, $18,404,115, was reported spent in congressional races, but Congressional Quarterly estimated the actual total at almost $100 million.

The credibility gap fostered by the "knowledge or consent" loophole was widened further because the Federal Corrupt Practices Act applied only to political committees operating in two or more states. If a committee operated in one state only and was not a subdivision of a national committee, the law did not apply. If a committee operated in the District of Columbia only, receiving funds there and mailing checks to candidates in a single state, the law did not cover it.

Limits on the expenditures that a political committee might make were evaded by establishing more than one committee and apportioning receipts and expenditures among them, so that no one committee exceeded the limit. Because the law limited annual spending by a political committee operating in two or more states to $3 million annually, the major parties formed committees under various names, each of which was free to spend up to $3 million.

Although the Corrupt Practices Act provided criminal penalties for false reporting or failure to report, successive administrations ignored them, even though news reporters repeatedly uncovered violations. Eisenhower administration Attorney General Herbert Brownell stated in 1954 the Justice Department's position that the initiative in such cases rested with the secretary of the Senate and the clerk of the House, and that policy was continued.

Secretaries of the Senate and clerks of the House for many years winked at violations of the filing requirements. The situation changed in 1967 when former Rep. W. Pat Jennings, D-Va., became House clerk. He began sending lists of violations to the Justice Department for prosecution, but then the department refused to act.

Attempts at Reform

Attempts to rewrite the 1925 act were made regularly during the late 1950s and the 1960s but with little success.

In April 1962 the President's Commission on Campaign Costs issued a report recommending proposals to encourage greater citizen participation in financing presidential campaigns. The commission had been named in October 1961 by President John F. Kennedy. Alexander Heard, then-dean of the University of North Carolina Graduate School, was the chairman and Herbert Alexander, then-director of the Citizens' Research Foundation, was the executive director. Among the commission's recommendations were that:

• Tax credits or deductions be given for certain levels of individuals' political contributions.

• The existing limits on expenditures of interstate political committees and individual contributions to those committees be repealed, leaving no limit.

• All candidates for president and vice president and committees spending at least $2,500 a year be required to report expenditures made in both primary and general election campaigns.

• A Registry of Election Finance be established to help enforce political financing regulations.

• The government pay the transition costs of a president-elect during the period between election and inauguration.

In May 1962 President Kennedy submitted to Congress five draft bills encompassing proposals identical or similar to the commission's. But the only bill reported was one to finance transition costs, and it died on the House floor.

Tax Checkoff Attempt. Congress did not act again in the area of campaign finance until the mid-1960s, when it passed a tax checkoff plan to provide government subsidies to presidential election campaigns. An act approved in 1966 authorized any individual paying federal income tax to direct that one dollar of the tax due in any year be paid into a Presidential Election Campaign Fund. The fund, to be set up in the U.S. Treasury, was to disburse its receipts proportionately among political parties whose presidential candidates had received 5 million or more votes in the preceding presidential election. Congress, however, failed to adopt the required guidelines for distribution of the funds, so the 1966 act was in effect voided in 1967.

Skyrocketing Costs. But the mood in Washington was beginning to change. In addition to growing irritation with the toothlessness of the disclosure laws, uneasiness was increasing over campaign costs.

Rising campaign costs were evident soon after World War II. Heard wrote in 1960:

Radio and television broadcasting eat up millions. Thousands go to pay for rent, electricity, telephone, telegraph, auto hire, airplanes, airplane tickets, registration drives, hillbilly bands, public relations counsel, the Social Security tax on payrolls. Money pays for writers and for printing what they write, for advertising in many blatant forms, and for the boodle in many subtle guises. All these expenditures are interlarded with outlays for the hire of donkeys and elephants, for comic books, poll taxes and sample ballots, for gifts to the United Negro College Fund and the Police Relief Association, for a $5.25 traffic ticket in Maryland and $66.30 worth of "convention liquor" in St. Louis.[54]

Radio and television ads came to occupy a greater and greater portion of campaign budgets, as broadcasting emerged as the dominant political medium in the 1960s. "Overall, political broadcasting increased from 17.3 percent of the estimated total of all political spending ($200 million) in 1964 to 19.6 percent (of $300 million) in 1968, ensuring its position as the largest single cost in political campaigns," according to Herbert Alexander.[55]

Congressional incumbents feared that limits on media costs were needed to prevent them from draining campaign treasuries, and making candidates increasingly dependent on wealthy contributors and powerful lobbying groups. Many Democrats saw a limit on TV outlays as a way to overcome what they viewed as the Republicans' lopsided advantage in raising money.

In addition, incumbents of both parties feared that rich challengers could use TV "blitzes" to overpower them, a fear that had been fanned in 1970 by the high-cost campaigns of two relative unknowns—Rep. Richard L. Ottinger of New York and Ohio parking-lot magnate Howard M. Metzenbaum—who succeeded in winning Democratic primary races for the U.S. Senate, although they lost in the general election.

Against this backdrop of skyrocketing campaign costs, the administration of Richard Nixon tightened enforcement of the Federal Corrupt Practices Act, successfully pressing charges in 1969 against corporations (mostly in California) that had contributed money in 1968.

Major Reform Laws Enacted in the 1970s

By the 1970s all sides acknowledged the need for new campaign finance legislation. Within a five-year period—between 1971 and 1976—Congress passed four major laws that changed the way political campaigns for national office were financed and conducted. Stunned by the campaign abuses that came to light during the Watergate scandal, state governments and the courts also moved to alter the methods of campaign financing.

1971 REFORM LAWS

In 1971 Congress passed two separate pieces of legislation: the Federal Election Campaign Act (FECA) of 1971, which for the first time set a ceiling on the amount federal candidates could spend on media advertising and required full disclosure of campaign contributions and expenditures; and the Revenue Act of 1971, which included a tax checkoff section to allow taxpayers to contribute to a general public campaign fund for eligible presidential candidates.

FECA: Limits and Disclosure

The 1971 act was the first major piece of campaign finance legislation passed since 1925. It combined two sharply different approaches to reform. One section clamped limits on how much a federal candidate could spend on all forms of communications media. The second part provided, for the first time, for relatively complete and timely public reports by candidates on who was financing their campaigns and how much they were spending. Meaningful disclosure would reduce the likelihood of corruption and unfair advantage, it was theorized.

Media Limits. The bill went into effect April 7, 1972, sixty days after President Richard Nixon signed it. The heart of the new law was the section placing ceilings on media costs, which was applicable separately to the primary campaign and to the general election. For a House candidate, the limit was set at $50,000 or ten cents for each voting-age person in the congressional district, whichever was greater. For a Senate candidate, the limit was $50,000 or ten cents for each voting-age person in the state.

The ceiling, which was to rise automatically with the cost of living, applied to spending for television, radio, newspaper, magazine, billboard, and automated telephone advertising. The centerpiece of this section was the restriction that no more than 60 percent of the overall media total could go for radio and television advertising. In practice, this meant in the 1972 elections that a candidate for the House could spend no more than $52,150 for *all* media outlays in the primary campaign and no more than $52,150 in the general election campaign. (The cost-of-living factor had raised these figures from the initial $50,000.) In each case, only $31,290 of the overall media total could go for radio and television.

Because of population differences between states, the figures for Senate races ranged from an overall media limit of $52,150 in thinly populated states such as Alaska and Montana (of which only $31,290 could be for radio and TV) to as much as $1.4 million in California (of which about $840,000 could be for radio and TV).

Presidential limits also were computed on the basis of ten cents per voting-age person. For each presidential candidate, the overall media limit was $14.3 million, of which less than $8.6 million could be used for radio and TV.

Disclosure Requirements. The 1971 FECA required that any candidate or political committee in a federal campaign file quarterly spending and receipts reports that itemized receipts or expenditures of $100 or more by listing the name, address, occupation, and place of business of the contributor or recipient. During election years, added reports were required to be filed fifteen and five days before an election, and any contribution of $5,000 or more had to be reported within forty-eight hours if received after the last preelection report.

Closing numerous loopholes in previous law, the statute applied the reporting requirements to primaries, conventions, and runoffs as well as to the general election. Any political committee had to report, even if it operated in only one state, provided it spent or received in excess of $1,000 a year. This meant, in effect, that the loophole of avoiding reports by having separate campaign fund groups in each state was eliminated for presidential candidates and that members of Congress with campaign fund groups operating only in their home states would henceforth have to report their receipts and expenditures.

The reports were to be filed with the House clerk for House candidates, secretary of the Senate for Senate candidates, and General Accounting Office (GAO) for presidential candidates. These would be made available for public inspection within forty-eight hours of being received and periodically published; reports also were required to be filed with the secretary of state of each state and made available for public inspection by the end of the day on which received.

On the theory that disclosure alone would eliminate corruption, all the ineffective spending and contribution limits were repealed, except provisions barring contributions directly from corporate funds and directly from union funds raised from dues money. (However, *voluntary* funds raised from union members and administered by a union unit were permitted.)

Proponents of reform, cognizant of the partisan considerations that could have threatened any revision of campaign laws, worked to avoid writing a law that would favor any political party or candidate. Republicans, aware of the relatively healthy financial condition of their party in 1971, were eager to protect their coffers; Democrats did not want to jeopardize their large contributions from organized labor.

The reform movement also included various groups outside Congress, such as the National Committee for an Effective Congress, the chief pressure group; Common Cause; labor unions; and some media organizations.

Income Tax Checkoff

The Revenue Act of 1971 containing the income tax checkoff cleared Congress on December 9, 1971, after a bitter partisan debate dominated by the approaching 1972 presidential election. President Nixon reluctantly signed the bill but forced a change in the effective date of the fund from the 1972 election to 1976 as the price of his acquiescence.

The plan gave each taxpayer the option beginning in 1973 of designating one dollar of his or her annual federal income tax payment for a general campaign fund to be divided among eligible presidential candidates. Those filing joint returns could designate two dollars.

Democrats, whose party was $9 million in debt following the 1968 presidential election, said the voluntary tax checkoff was needed to free presidential candidates from obligations to their wealthy campaign contributors. Republicans, whose party treasury was well stocked, charged that the plan was a device to rescue the Democratic Party from financial difficulty.

THE WATERGATE ELECTION

Both 1971 laws were campaign finance milestones, but they left intact the existing system of private financing for the 1972 presidential campaign. While the FECA drew high marks for improving campaign disclosure and received some credit for reducing media costs, its successes were overshadowed by the massive misuse of campaign funds that characterized Watergate, one of the nation's worst political scandals.

The predominant theory at the time of passage was that

President Richard Nixon announces his resignation in August 1974. Revelations about campaign finance abuses tied to the Watergate scandal, which had brought about Nixon's downfall, spurred the most significant overhaul of campaign finance laws in the nation's history.

merely by writing a good, tight campaign finance law emphasizing disclosure, Congress could reduce excessive contributions from any one source to any one candidate. Candidates, according to this theory, would want to avoid the appearance of being dominated by a few large donors. Good disclosure would allow the public to identify the political activities of special interest groups and take necessary corrective action at the polls.

But it did not work that way. Huge individual and corporate donations were near the center of the Watergate scandal as largely unreported private contributions financed the activities of the 1972 Nixon reelection campaign. Of the $63 million collected by the Nixon camp, nearly $20 million was in contributions from 153 donors giving $50,000 or more. More than $11 million was raised during the month before the FECA disclosure rules took effect on April 7, 1972, including $2.3 million on April 5 and $3 million on April 6.[56]

The Finance Committee for the Reelection of the President kept its pre–April 7 lists confidential until a Common Cause lawsuit sought disclosure under provisions of the old Federal Corrupt Practices Act and forced them into the open in 1973. Such reticence was partly explained by the existence of questionable contributions to the Nixon campaign: $200,000 in financier Robert Vesco's attaché case; a $100,000 secret donation from millionaire industrialist Howard Hughes, which Nixon confidant Bebe Rebozo purportedly kept locked in a safe deposit box; and $2 million pledged to Nixon by the dairy industry.

Illegal corporate gifts also motivated secrecy. In a report issued in July 1974, the Senate Select Committee on Presidential Campaign Activities (known as the Senate Watergate Committee) charged that "during the 1972 presidential campaign, it appears that at least thirteen corporations made contributions totaling over $780,000 in corporate funds. . . . Of these, twelve gave approximately $749,000 to the president's reelection campaign, which constituted the bulk of the illegal corporate contributions."

The primary sources of such corporate money, according to the Senate committee, were "foreign subsidiaries." Other sources included corporate reserves and expense accounts. The committee added that "although the bulk of the contributions preceded April 7, 1972, there was no disclosure of any of the contributions until July 6, 1973—or fifteen months after almost all of them were made."

Presidential lawyer Herbert Kalmbach, who headed the corporate gifts campaign, in June 1974 was sentenced to six to eighteen months in jail and fined $10,000 after pleading guilty to illegal campaign operations. Kalmbach collected more than $10 million from U.S. corporations, the bulk of it prior to April 7, 1972.

According to staff reports of the Senate Watergate Committee, Kalmbach and other fund-raisers sought donations on an industry-by-industry basis, using an influential corporate executive to raise money among other executives in his industry.

The leading individual giver in the 1972 campaign was Chicago insurance executive W. Clement Stone, chairman of the Combined Insurance Co. of America. In the April 7–December 31, 1972, reporting period monitored by the GAO, Stone was listed as giving $73,054 to reelect Nixon. But even before the revelations forced by Common Cause, Stone had admitted to pre-April giving of $2 million. The second highest giver was Richard Scaife, heir to the Mellon banking and oil fortune, who contributed $1 million to Nixon's reelection before April 7.

John Gardner, then the head of Common Cause, said in April 1973:

Watergate is not primarily a story of political espionage, nor even of White House intrigue. It is a particularly malodorous chapter in the annals of campaign financing. The money paid to the Watergate conspirators before the break-in—and the money passed to them later—was money from campaign gifts.[57]

Gardner's charge was dramatically confirmed by President Nixon's August 5, 1974, release of a June 23, 1972, tape recording of conversations between himself and his chief of staff, H. R. Haldeman. The tape revealed that Nixon was told at that time of the use of campaign funds in the June 17, 1972, Watergate break-in and agreed to help cover up that fact. Nixon's resignation August 9, 1974, followed the August 5 disclosure.

Disclosure Provisions

The campaign disclosure provisions of the 1971 FECA proved extremely useful, enabling scholars and the relevant committees of Congress to get a clear picture for the first time of patterns of contributions and spending. Emerging from the reports were data on enormous contributions by the milk industry, on corporate contributions, on formerly concealed large contributions by individuals, and on "laundered money"—information that played a key role in uncovering misconduct in the Watergate scandal.

Although thousands of reports were late or faulty, overall compliance with the disclosure law probably was fairly good. Nevertheless, a great many problems remained. The reports, especially those made in the last few days before the election, were extremely difficult for a reporter or a rival political camp to collate and decipher. Multiple contributions by a wealthy individual made to one candidate through a system of dummy organizations with cryptic names were difficult to track rapidly. Investigating an industrywide campaign of financial support to a candidate or a group of candidates proved to be an extremely tedious task.

State finance committees and other committees—with titles such as Democrats for Nixon or Writers for McGovern—were created to prevent big contributors from being inhibited by high gift taxes. An individual could give up to $3,000, tax-free, to an independent campaign committee. Records showed that the Nixon campaign benefited from 220 of these finance committees. McGovern had 785 such committees, according to his national campaign treasurer, Marian Pearlman, "created for Stewart Mott." General Motors heir Mott, who donated about $400,000 to McGovern, even declared himself a campaign committee.

The Internal Revenue Service interpreted campaign committees as being independent if one out of three officers was different from officers for other committees, if the candidates supported by the committees were different, or if the committees' purposes were different. As a result, campaign finance committees proliferated in 1972, and contributors were hardly deterred from giving large sums to one candidate.

More important, the crucial element in effectiveness of the law was enforcement. The Justice Department was given sole power to prosecute violations, despite its forty-six-year record of somnolence in enforcing previous regulations. It was traditionally understood that Justice Department bureaucrats feared to undertake vigorous enforcement lest they endanger the party in power and be fired.

The question became: Would the department make a powerful, massive effort not only to round up serious violators but to require that reports be on time and complete? Without such action from the department the practice of filing sloppy, incomplete, or even misleading reports, and filing them late, would clearly vitiate much of the effect of the law and render it null in practice.

Although thousands of violations—some serious but most technical (late or incomplete)—were referred to the Justice Department in 1972 and 1973 by the House, Senate, and GAO, only a handful of prosecutions resulted. During the 1972 campaign the department had only one full-time attorney supervising enforcement of the act, according to reports.

Another provision in the law requiring periodic reporting of contributions and expenditures further impeded enforcement. According to many members of Congress, the frequent filing of these reports during primary and general election campaigns by all political committees of candidates created monumental bookkeeping chores for the candidates. Correspondingly, the mammoth number of reports filed with the House clerk, the Senate secretary, and the comptroller general made closer scrutiny practically impossible.

To remedy the latter problem, Common Cause, at a cost of more than $250,000 and thousands of hours from volunteer workers, organized teams of people in 1972 to collect and collate information on reports, which it then distributed to the press in time for use before election day.

Fred Wertheimer, who was then the legislative director of Common Cause, said the aim was to make the law work and to give it a good start. But it was clear that depending on private organizations alone probably would be inadequate. Unless some permanent way were found, perhaps at government expense, to speed up collation and distribution of the materials—particularly late in the campaign—the objectives of disclosure would be undermined.

Media Expenditures

The 1972 election was more expensive than any that preceded it. About $425 million was spent in all races, with the Senate Watergate Committee estimating that the presidential race cost about $100 million, more than double the $44.2 million spent in the 1968 presidential election. During the 1972 campaign, presidential and Senate outlays for radio and television campaign advertising dropped sharply compared with 1968 and 1970, but whether this decline resulted from the FECA's media advertising limits was unclear.

In the presidential race, part of the drop was due to the

strength of the incumbent, who had loads of free airtime available to him when he chose to address the nation in "nonpolitical" speeches as president, instead of seeking paid time as merely a candidate.

The drop in Senate spending was less easily explained, but many senators said one factor was the realization that electronic media, while enormously effective, did not provide the quantum leap in campaigning techniques that had been expected. The notion that television could "do it all," which was virtually an article of faith in the late 1960s and in 1970, had begun to fade, and more resources were put into other forms of advertising and into traditional organizational and legwork efforts. Broadcast spending totals also were reduced by the requirement in the 1971 law that TV stations charge politicians the lowest unit rate for any time slot.

Also, many senators learned in 1972 that TV station coverage was not well designed for campaign purposes in many areas. In some large states, such as Kentucky, it was impossible to cover the whole state with stations broadcasting only within that state. To cover border areas, it was necessary to buy time on stations located in other states, only a portion of whose viewers were in Kentucky. To send a message to one corner of the state a candidate had to pay for coverage outside the state as well, a wasteful and costly practice.

The same was true in some large central metropolitan areas located between two or three states. For northern New Jersey, a candidate had to pay rates for New York too, since many of the stations in that area broadcast simultaneously to New York City, Connecticut, and northern New Jersey.

Some senators found it cheaper under these conditions to use other ways of reaching the voters. Federal Communications Commission reports showed that while a handful of senators went slightly over their campaign limits, the TV limits as a whole were observed. Because of the TV "targeting" problems, many in Congress began to argue that a flat spending limit for TV was too inflexible. They said an overall spending limit for all campaign costs—similar to that repealed in 1971, but with real scope and enforcement teeth—would be better. Such a proposal, they argued, would still limit any massive use of TV because a candidate would not be able to exceed his total campaign spending limit. But it would allow greater flexibility as to which portion of overall costs went to TV and which to other items.

The media limits were repealed in 1974.

1974 REFORM LAW

Almost two and a half years after it passed the FECA of 1971, Congress, reacting to presidential campaign abuses and public opinion favoring reform, enacted another landmark campaign reform bill that substantially overhauled the existing system of financing election campaigns. Technically, the 1974 law was a set of amendments to the 1971 legislation, but in fact it was the most comprehensive campaign finance bill Congress had ever passed.

The new measure, which President Gerald R. Ford signed into law October 15, repealed some provisions of the 1971 law,

expanded others, and broke new ground in such areas as public financing and contribution and expenditure limitations.

The Federal Election Campaign Act Amendments of 1974:

• Established a Federal Election Commission consisting of six voting members—two appointed by the president and four designated by congressional leaders—as well as two nonvoting members, the clerk of the House and secretary of the Senate. All six voting members had to be confirmed by both the House and Senate.

• Instituted numerous contribution limitations, including: for individuals, a limit of $1,000 per candidate per primary, runoff, or general election, not to exceed $25,000 to all federal candidates annually; for political committees, a limit of $5,000 per candidate per election, with no aggregate limit; for presidential and vice presidential candidates and their families, a limit of $50,000 to their own campaigns. A limit of $1,000 was established for independent expenditures on behalf of a candidate. Cash contributions of more than $100 were prohibited, as were foreign contributions in any amount.

• Set limits on spending by federal candidates and the national parties, including: a total of $10 million per candidate for all presidential primaries, $20 million per candidate in the presidential general election, and $2 million for each major political party's nominating convention and lesser amounts for minor parties' conventions; $100,000 or eight cents per voting-age person in their state, whichever was greater, for Senate primary candidates and $150,000 or twelve cents per voting-age person, whichever was greater, for Senate general election candidates; $70,000 for House primary candidates and $70,000 for House general election candidates. National party spending was limited to $10,000 per candidate in House general elections; $20,000 or two cents per the voting-age population in the state, whichever was greater, for each candidate in Senate general elections; and two cents for every voting-age person in presidential general elections. (The party expenditures were above the candidates' individual spending limits.) Senate spending limits were applied to House candidates who represented a whole state. The act exempted certain expenditures from the limits and provided that the limits would increase with inflation. The act repealed the media spending limits adopted in 1971.

• Extended public funding for presidential campaigns to include not only general election campaigns but also prenomination campaigns and national nominating conventions. Eligible candidates seeking presidential nomination would receive public funds matching their privately raised money within prescribed limits. Eligible candidates in a general election would each receive $20 million U.S. Treasury grants (to be adjusted for inflation) to finance their campaigns. Eligible political parties would receive grants of $2 million (to be adjusted for inflation) to conduct their nominating conventions. The amendments stipulated that if the level of money in the tax checkoff fund established by the 1971 Revenue Act was insufficient to finance all three stages of the electoral process, the funds would be dis-

With congressional leaders looking on, President Gerald R. Ford signs the Federal Election Campaign Act amendments of 1974.

bursed for the general election, the conventions, and the primaries, in that order.

• Created a number of disclosure and reporting procedures, including: establishment by each candidate of one central campaign committee through which all contributions and expenditures on behalf of that candidate would be reported; reporting names and addresses, as well as occupation and place of business, of those contributing more than $100; filing of full reports of contributions and expenditures with the FEC ten days before and thirty days after each election, and within ten days of the close of each quarter. Presidential candidates were not required, however, to file more than twelve reports in any one year.

The final bill did not contain Senate-passed provisions for partial public financing of congressional campaigns. Senate conferees dropped the fight for some form of public financing for House and Senate races in return for higher spending limits for congressional campaigns and a stronger independent election commission to enforce the law.

BUCKLEY V. VALEO

As soon as the 1974 law took effect, it was challenged in court by a diverse array of plaintiffs, including Sen. James L. Buckley, C-N.Y.; former Sen. Eugene J. McCarthy, D-Minn.; the New York Civil Liberties Union; and *Human Events,* a conservative publication. They filed suit on January 2, 1975.

Their basic arguments were that the law's new limits on campaign contributions and expenditures curbed the freedom of contributors and candidates to express themselves in the political marketplace and that the public financing provisions discriminated against minor parties and lesser-known candidates in favor of the major parties and better-known candidates.

The U.S. Court of Appeals for the District of Columbia on August 14, 1975, upheld all of the law's major provisions, thus setting the stage for Supreme Court action. The Supreme Court handed down its ruling, *Buckley v. Valeo,* on January 30, 1976, in an unsigned 137-page opinion. In five separate, signed opinions, several justices concurred with and dissented from separate issues in the case.

In its decision, the Court upheld the provisions that:

• Set limits on how much individuals and political committees could contribute to candidates.

• Provided for the public financing of presidential primary and general election campaigns.

• Required the disclosure of campaign contributions of more than $100 and campaign expenditures of more than $100.

But the Court overturned other features of the law, ruling that the campaign spending limits were unconstitutional violations of the First Amendment guarantee of free expression. For presidential candidates who accepted federal matching funds, however, the ceiling on the expenditures remained intact. The Court also struck down the method for selecting members of the FEC.

Spending Limits Overturned

The Court stated: "A restriction on the amount of money a person or group can spend on political communication during a campaign necessarily reduces the quantity of expression by restricting the number of issues discussed, the depth of their exploration and the size of the audience reached. This is because virtually every means of communicating ideas in today's mass society requires the expenditure of money."

Only Justice Byron R. White dissented on this point; he would have upheld the limitations. Rejecting the argument that money is speech, White wrote that there are "many expensive campaign activities that are not themselves communicative or remotely related to speech."

Although the Court acknowledged that contribution and spending limits had First Amendment implications, it distinguished between the two by saying that the act's "expenditure ceilings impose significantly more severe restrictions on protected freedom of political expression and association than do its limitations on financial contributions."

The Court removed all the limits imposed on political spending and, by so doing, weakened the effect of the contribution ceilings. The law had placed spending limits on House, Senate, and presidential campaigns and on party nominating conventions. To plug a loophole in the contribution limits, the bill also had placed a $1,000 annual limit on how much an individual could spend independently on behalf of a candidate.

The independent expenditure ceiling, the opinion said, was a clear violation of the First Amendment. The Court wrote:

While the . . . ceiling thus fails to serve any substantial governmental interest in stemming the reality or appearance of corruption in the electoral process, it heavily burdens core First Amendment expression. . . . Advocacy of the election or defeat of candidates for federal office is no less entitled to protection under the First Amendment than the discussion of political policy generally or advocacy of the passage or defeat of legislation.

The Court also struck down the limits on how much of their own money candidates could spend on their campaigns. The law had set a $25,000 limit on House candidates, $35,000 on

Sen. James L. Buckley, C-N.Y., was the lead plaintiff in the lawsuit that prompted the Supreme Court to overturn several provisions of the 1974 campaign finance law.

Senate candidates, and $50,000 on presidential candidates. "The candidate, no less than any other person, has a First Amendment right to engage in the discussion of public issues and vigorously and tirelessly to advocate his own election and the election of other candidates," the opinion said.

The ruling made it possible for a wealthy candidate to finance his own campaign and thus to avoid the limits on how much others could give him. The Court wrote that "the use of personal funds reduces the candidate's dependence on outside contributions and thereby counteracts the coercive pressures and attendant risks of abuse to which the act's contribution limitations are directed."

Justice Thurgood Marshall rejected the Court's reasoning in striking down the limit on how much candidates may spend on their campaigns. "It would appear to follow," he said, "that the candidate with a substantial personal fortune at his disposal is off to a significant 'head start.'" Moreover, he added, keeping the limitations on contributions but not on spending "put[s] a premium on a candidate's personal wealth."

FEC Makeup Faulted

The Court held unanimously that the FEC was unconstitutional. The Court said the method for appointing commissioners violated the Constitution's separation-of-powers and

FEDERAL ELECTION COMMISSION

Given all the controversy that has surrounded the campaign finance system, it is no surprise that the agency established to monitor that system has been steeped in controversy as well. Critics charge that the Federal Election Commission (FEC) has been weak and ineffective in its enforcement of federal campaign finance law. And many also say that is exactly what Congress had in mind when it created the agency.

FEC MANDATE

The Federal Election Commission (FEC) was created by Congress in 1974 to administer and enforce the Federal Election Campaign Act (FECA) of 1971 and its amendments. The FEC's duties include receiving and making public the campaign finance reports mandated by the FECA. These reports are available for examination at the FEC, as well as at the FEC Web site: *http://www.fec.gov.*

FEC staff members review the reports for omissions and may request additional information. If the FEC finds an apparent law violation, it has the authority to seek a conciliation agreement, sometimes with a fine. If a conciliation agreement cannot be reached, the FEC may sue for enforcement in U.S. District Court. The commission may refer possible criminal violations to the Justice Department for prosecution.

The FEC also administers the Presidential Election Campaign Fund, which makes possible the public funding of presidential primaries, national party conventions, and presidential general elections.

FEC MEMBERS

The 1974 amendments established the FEC as a six-member commission, with the clerk of the House and secretary of the Senate serving as nonvoting ex officio members. No more than three of the six commissioners were to be from the same political party.

The 1974 law stipulated that four of the six members would be selected by Congress, a provision the Supreme Court soon found, among others, to be unconstitutional. In its 1976 *Buckley v. Valeo* decision, the Court declared the method violated the separation of powers clauses of the Constitution because the four commissioners were appointed by congressional officials but exercised executive powers.

Amendments passed in 1976 reconstituted the FEC as a six-member commission appointed by the president and confirmed by the Senate. However, Congress in effect continued to control four of the appointments by providing the White House with a list of acceptable nominees for these slots.

The makeup of the FEC was again called into question when the D.C. Circuit Court of Appeals in 1993 ruled that the commission had violated the constitutional separation of powers by including the two nonvoting congressional staff members in its deliberations. The FEC reconstituted itself without the clerk of the House and the secretary of the Senate but asked the Supreme Court to review the decision. The Court in 1994 rejected the appeal on technical grounds, ruling that the agency lacked authority to appeal the matter to the Supreme Court (*Federal Election Commission v. NRA Political Victory Fund*). The Court held that the FECA gave only the solicitor general the authority to make such appeals.

In other action affecting the makeup of the commission, Congress in 1997 limited, beginning in 1998, future nominees for FEC commissioner slots to one six-year term. An attempt to place term limits on the FEC's general counsel and staff director failed in 1998.

AGENCY CRITICS

The FEC has not lacked its critics. Some have objected to actions taken by the agency, but for many others the problem has been its inaction.

In a front-page article entitled "The Little Agency That Can't," the *Washington Post* in 1997 detailed the complaints against the FEC. "Once hailed as the two-fisted enforcer that would protect the body politic from future Watergate scandals and the corrupting scourge of unregulated campaign cash, the commission has proved to be weak, slow-footed and largely ineffectual."[1]

Many critics have placed much of the blame for FEC shortcom-

appointments clauses because some members were named by congressional officials but exercised executive powers. The justices refused to accept the argument that the commission, because it oversaw congressional as well as presidential elections, could have congressionally appointed members. The Court wrote:

We see no reason to believe that the authority of Congress over federal election practices is of such a wholly different nature from the other grants of authority to Congress that it may be employed in such a manner as to offend well established constitutional restrictions stemming from the separation of powers.

According to the decision, the commission could exercise only those powers Congress was allowed to delegate to congressional committees—investigating and information gathering. The Court ruled that only if the commission's members were appointed by the president, as required under the Constitution's appointments clause, could the commission carry out the administrative and enforcement responsibilities the law originally gave it.

The last action put Congress on the spot, because the justices stayed their ruling for thirty days, until February 29, 1976, to give the House and Senate time to "reconstitute the commission by law or adopt other valid enforcement mechanisms." As it developed, Congress was to take much longer than thirty days to act, and instead of merely reconstituting the commission, it was to pass a whole new campaign finance law.

1976 AMENDMENTS

The Court decision forced Congress to return to campaign finance legislation once again. The 1976 election campaign was

ings on Congress. In 1997 Thomas E. Mann, then-director of Governmental Studies at the Brookings Institution, wrote that ". . . Congress had no interest in an independent, powerful FEC. It designed the agency carefully to ensure that it would operate on a tight leash held firmly by its master."

For starters, Mann pointed out, Congress gave itself the authority to appoint four of the six commissioners and supply two of its officers as ex officio members. The requirement that no more than three commissioners could be from the same party resulted in a three Democrat–three Republican commission, making it nearly impossible to take serious action against either party. Congress subsequently required an affirmative vote of four members for the commission to issue regulations and advisory opinions and initiate civil actions and investigations. In addition, the FEC was given no authority to impose sanctions and had to depend instead on the federal court and the Justice Department to pursue violators. Congress even had veto power over FEC rules and regulations until the Supreme Court declared all legislative vetoes unconstitutional in 1983.

Moreover, according to Mann, Congress took other steps "to ensure that delay and timidity would become the watchwords of the agency." These included denying the FEC the multiyear budgeting authority enjoyed by other independent agencies, skeptically reviewing FEC requests for budget increases despite the agency's expanding workload, banning random audits of candidates, insisting on time-consuming procedures, and keeping up "a barrage of criticism that weakened the FEC's legitimacy and reinforced the contempt with which political operatives came to view the Commission."[2]

The *Post* article also placed blame on Congress for creating an agency that "no individual could control—or lead" and that "guaranteed partisan gridlock and timidity in challenging the political status quo." The article criticized the federal courts as well for having "repeatedly gutted the agency's enforcement efforts" and a succession of presidents for having "appointed pliant commissioners who rarely displayed get-tough independence."

1996 SCANDAL

Critics of the FEC were particularly vocal in the wake of the 1996 campaign finance scandal because of the agency's inaction in the face of numerous allegations of campaign funding irregularities. The FEC indirectly exposed some of the 1996 irregularities through its required disclosure reports but did little more as the Senate and House launched investigations and the Justice Department pursued possible criminal violations.

At the center of the controversy was the frenzied raising of millions of dollars in unregulated soft money by the political parties. The parties insisted the money went for party-building activities, but others argued that much of it was used to support the candidacies of President Bill Clinton and Republican challenger Bob Dole, even though each received $61.8 million in public funding and was limited by law to spending only that amount. An FEC staff audit charged that both presidential campaigns had illegally coordinated with the Democratic and Republican national committees to spend millions of dollars on issue ads that benefited their candidacies, which amounted to spending in excess of the federal grants. FEC commissioners, however, unanimously rejected the staff recommendations that the campaigns be required to return that excess money to the federal Treasury. (*See "1996 Scandal," p. 854.*)

Supporters of campaign finance overhaul attacked the commissioners' decision. "This is an agency that is supposed to protect the public interest, and instead it's protecting the two parties who have joined hands to run roughshod over the law," said Donald Simon, executive vice president of Common Cause, a government watchdog group.

1. Benjamin Weiser and Bill McAllister, "The Little Agency That Can't: Election-Law Enforcer Is Weak by Design, Paralyzed by Division," *Washington Post*, February 12, 1997, A1, 16–17.

2. Thomas E. Mann, "The Federal Election Commission: Implementing and Enforcing Federal Campaign Finance Law," in *Campaign Finance Reform: A Sourcebook*, ed. Anthony Corrado et al. (Washington, D.C.: Brookings Institution, 1997), 277–278.

already under way, but the Court said that the FEC could not continue to disburse public funds to presidential candidates so long as some commission members were congressional appointees.

President Ford had wanted only a simple reconstitution of the commission, but Congress insisted on going much further. The new law, arrived at after much maneuvering and arguing between Democrats and Republicans, closed old loopholes and opened new ones, depending on the point of view of the observer.

In its basic provision, the law signed by the president May 11, 1976, reconstituted the FEC as a six-member panel appointed by the president and confirmed by the Senate. Commission members were not allowed to engage in outside business activities. The commission was given exclusive authority to prosecute civil violations of the campaign finance law and was vested with jurisdiction over violations formerly covered only in the criminal code, thus strengthening its enforcement power. But the bill also required an affirmative vote of four members for the commission to issue regulations and advisory opinions and initiate civil actions and investigations. The commission was limited to issuing advisory opinions only for specific fact situations. And Congress was given the power to disapprove proposed regulations.

A major controversy that delayed enactment stemmed from organized labor's insistence that corporate fund-raising activity through PACs be curtailed. Labor was angered by the FEC's SunPAC decision in November 1975 that encouraged the growth of corporate PACs.

In the wake of Watergate many corporations had been skittish about what they were permitted to do. Not until the FEC released its landmark ruling in the case involving the Sun Oil Co.'s political action committee, SunPAC, did many businesses feel comfortable in establishing PACs. The FEC decision was in response to Sun Oil's request to use general funds to create, administer, and solicit voluntary contributions to its political action committee. Besides approving the request, the decision allowed business PACs to solicit all employees and stockholders for contributions. Labor PACs had been restricted to soliciting only their members.

Eventually a compromise was reached between the Democrats, who did not hesitate to use their overwhelming numerical strength to make changes that would have severely restricted the ability of business to raise political money, and the Republicans, who lacked the strength to fend off the antibusiness amendments but had the votes to sustain a filibuster and a veto.

Labor won some but not all of its goal. The final law permitted company committees to seek contributions only from stockholders and executive and administrative personnel and their families. It continued to restrict union PACs to soliciting contributions from union members and their families. Twice a year, however, union and corporate PACs were permitted to seek campaign contributions, by mail only, from all employees. Contributions would have to remain anonymous and would be received by an independent third party that would keep records but pass the money on to the PACs.

The final bill contained another provision prompted by the Supreme Court decision. Besides finding the FEC's makeup unconstitutional, the Court had thrown out the 1974 law's limitations on independent political expenditures as a clear violation of the First Amendment. To plug the potential loophole, Congress required political committees and individuals making independent political expenditures of more than $100 to swear that the expenditures were not made in collusion with the candidate.

The 1976 legislation also set some new contribution limits: An individual could give no more than $5,000 a year to a PAC and $20,000 to the national committee of a political party (the 1974 law set a $1,000 per election limit on individual contributions to a candidate and an aggregate contribution limit for individuals of $25,000 a year; no specific limits, except the aggregate limit, applied to contributions to political committees). A PAC could give no more than $15,000 a year to the national committee of a political party (the 1974 law set only a limit of $5,000 per election per candidate). The Democratic and Republican senatorial campaign committees could give up to $17,500 a year to a candidate (the 1974 law had set a $5,000 per election limit).

HILL PUBLIC FUNDING DEFEATED

Following the 1976 election, the spotlight in campaign finance quickly focused on extending public financing to House and Senate races. Prospects for passage seemed far better than they had been in 1974, the last time the proposal had been considered. At that time, leading officials, from the White House on down, had been either opposed or seemingly indifferent to its passage.

But in 1977 Jimmy Carter, a strong advocate of public funding, was in the White House. Key congressional leaders favored the proposal. And the Democrats had an overwhelming advantage in the House, far larger than during the 93rd Congress (1973–1975), when the House rejected congressional public financing after it had been approved by the Senate.

Despite the high hopes of public financing supporters, legislation to extend the concept to congressional races was blocked in 1977 by a filibuster in the Senate and opposition in the House Administration Committee. Renewed attempts to push the legislation in 1978 and 1979 also went nowhere.

1979 FECA AMENDMENTS

In a rare demonstration of harmony on a campaign finance measure, Congress in late 1979 passed legislation to eliminate much of the red tape created by the FECA and to encourage political party activity. Agreement was not difficult because the drafters concentrated on solving FECA's noncontroversial problems.

The amendments, signed into law January 8, 1980, reduced FECA's paperwork requirements in several ways. First, the act decreased the maximum number of reports a federal candidate would have to file with the FEC during a two-year election cycle from twenty-four to nine. For Senate candidates, the number of reports mandated over the six-year election cycle was reduced from twenty-eight to seventeen. Second, candidates who raised or spent less than $5,000 in their campaigns would not have to file reports at all. In 1978 about seventy House candidates, including five winners, fell below the $5,000 threshold. Previously, all candidates were required to report their finances regardless of the amount. Also, candidates would have to report in less detail. The legislation raised the threshold for itemizing both contributions and expenditures to $200 from $100. The threshold for reporting independent expenditures was also increased, from $100 to $250.

In 1976 political party leaders had complained that the FECA almost completely precluded state and local party organizations from helping with the presidential campaign. Because they had only limited federal funds to spend, both the Democratic and Republican presidential campaigns focused on media advertising. At the same time, they cut back expenditures on items such as buttons and bumper stickers that traditionally were used in promoting grassroots activity.

The 1979 bill permitted state and local party groups to purchase, without limit, campaign materials for volunteer activities to promote any federal candidate. Those items included buttons, bumper stickers, handbills, brochures, posters, and yard signs. Also, those party organizations were allowed to conduct, without financial limit, certain kinds of voter registration and get-out-the-vote drives on behalf of presidential tickets.

The incidental mention of a presidential candidate on the campaign literature of local candidates was no longer counted as a campaign contribution. Previously, such references had been counted, which created paperwork problems in reporting those costs to the FEC. Local party groups would be required to report their finances only if annual spending for volunteer activities exceeded $5,000 or if costs for nonvolunteer projects were more than $1,000. Before, such groups had to file campaign reports if total spending exceeded $1,000 a year.

Volunteer political activity by individuals was encouraged by raising to $1,000, from $500, the amount of money a person could spend in providing his home, food, or personal travel on behalf of a candidate without reporting it to the FEC as a contribution. If the volunteer activity was on behalf of a political party, the person could spend up to $2,000 before the amount was treated as a contribution.

The 1979 act also prohibited members from converting leftover campaign funds to personal use. However, those in Congress at the time of the law's enactment were exempted. Because Senate rules flatly prohibited personal use of such funds by former members as well as incumbents, the bill's exemption was of benefit only to sitting House members. The loophole became a target for reformers and caused resentment among senators and younger House members who could not take advantage of it. In 1989 Congress moved to close it by including a provision in an ethics-and-pay law that forced the grandfathered House members to either leave Congress before the beginning of the 103rd Congress in 1993 or lose their right to take the money. The funds that could be converted were frozen at no more than what they had on hand when the 1989 ethics law was enacted.

Congressional Stalemates on Campaign Reform Proposals

Congress repeatedly visited the issue of campaign finance reform in the next two decades but no major legislation had been enacted as of October 1999. Reform fell victim to differences between the parties and the chambers over what was wrong with the system and how it should be remedied.

PAC ISSUE DEBATE

PACs came to the forefront of the campaign finance debate in the 1980s. The rise in the number of PACs and their influence in political campaigns put lawmakers on the defensive against a public perception that special interest groups had undue influence on politicians.

The House in 1979 passed a bill to reduce PAC contributions, but the bill died in the Senate the following year under threat of a filibuster. Although the bill applied only to House races, opponents in the Senate feared that its passage could renew interest in public financing or could lead to PAC spending ceilings in Senate races.

Several years passed before the issue was debated again. This time, in 1986, the Senate went on record twice in favor of strict new controls on PACs. The Senate first adopted an amendment offered by the Democrats that would have set caps on what a candidate could take from PACs overall and singly and also would have closed loopholes on PAC giving that generally favored Republicans. The Senate then adopted a Republican counterproposal to prohibit PAC contributions to national party organizations, which Democrats relied on more heavily than the GOP. But the legislation got caught in partisan maneuvering over who should get the credit—or blame—for reforming campaign finance guidelines, and which party would suffer the most under the proposed restrictions. A final vote was never taken.

COMPREHENSIVE REFORM ATTEMPT

In the next Congress, the Senate debated the most comprehensive campaign finance bill to come before Congress since 1974. But the legislation ultimately was shelved after a record-setting eight cloture votes in 1987–1988 failed to cut off a Republican filibuster.

The cornerstone of the Senate Democrats' bill was a proposal for campaign spending limits, which backers saw as the key to curbing skyrocketing election costs. But such limits were bitterly opposed by Republicans, who thought a spending cap would institutionalize the Democrats' majority in Congress. Another key element that many Republicans abhorred was a provision for public financing for Senate candidates who agreed to abide by the spending limits. Most Republicans said it represented a government intrusion into what generally had been a private realm. Republicans also criticized the bill's aggregate limit on what Senate candidates could accept from PACs on the ground that the provision would favor the well-organized, well-funded PACs that could donate early in an election cycle, freezing out other PACs that wanted to donate later.

The protracted debate over the bill was marked by extraordinary partisanship and elaborate parliamentary maneuvering. Majority Leader Robert Byrd attempted to break the GOP filibuster by keeping the Senate in session around the clock. During one of two all-night sessions Republicans responded in kind, by repeatedly moving for quorum calls and then boycotting the floor. That forced Democrats to keep enough members present to maintain the quorum needed for the Senate to remain in session. Byrd then decided to resort to a little-known power of the Senate, last used in 1942, to have absent members arrested and brought to the floor. This led to the spectacle of Oregon Republican Bob Packwood being arrested and physically carried onto the Senate floor in the wee hours of February 24, 1988.

A truce was eventually reached, the final unsuccessful cloture vote taken, and the bill was pulled from the floor. A later attempt to adopt a constitutional amendment to overcome the *Buckley v. Valeo* decision forbidding mandatory campaign spending limits suffered a similar fate, as it would in later Congresses.

Protesters from the National Campaign Finance Reform Coalition wave signs and shout slogans intent on convincing President George Bush not to veto campaign finance reform legislation in 1992. Bush vetoed the bill and an override attempt in the Senate failed.

REPEATED IMPASSES IN 1990S

The movement in the next Congress (1989–1991) to rewrite campaign finance laws ended where it began, mired in disagreement. The House and Senate passed separate bills—both generally backed by Democrats and strongly opposed by Republicans—containing voluntary spending limits and reducing the influence of PACs. But the two chambers' proposals differed substantially. The Senate would have dismantled PACs, while the House would have set limits on their contributions. The bills also were wide apart on the issue of soft money. The Senate would have taken a big step toward imposing federal rules on state election activities; the House limited itself primarily to abuses that cropped up in the 1988 presidential campaigns. Facing these broad differences late in the session, as well as a threat from President George Bush to veto any bill with campaign spending limits, conferees on the two bills never met.

Bush in 1989 had proposed what he called a "sweeping system of reform" that sought to eliminate most PACs, enhance the role of political parties, and grind down the electoral advantages enjoyed by incumbents (including one of the major weapons in an incumbent's arsenal, the frank, by banning "unsolicited mass mailings" from congressional offices). Democrats had assailed

the Bush plan as baldly partisan. Even within the GOP, there was no consensus on major items such as curbing the frank and eliminating certain PACs. (See "Franking Privilege," p. 783.)

With campaign finance overhaul presumed dead for the year, lawmakers attempted to peel off the one part of the effort that every politician could agree on: getting broadcasters to lower advertising rates for candidates. But neither chamber acted on the proposal because the effort encountered opposition not only from broadcasters but also from Common Cause, which said the legislation would provide a major benefit to incumbents without dealing with the fundamental problems in the campaign finance system.

Scandals in the next Congress (1991–1993) heightened pressure on both chambers to enact some type of reform measure. The Senate was rocked by the Keating Five savings and loan investigation of 1990–1991, which Common Cause characterized as "the smoking gun" that proved the corruption of the election finance system. On the House side, scandals at the House bank and post office reignited the campaign finance issue in 1992, as House Democratic leaders grasped for reform measures large and small. (See boxes, The Keating Five Scandal, p. 962, and House Bank, Post Office Scandals, p. 974.)

Both chambers passed bills in 1991 to limit spending and subsidize campaigns with public dollars. The bills, however, were vastly different and finding common ground seemed unlikely. But with the impetus of the ethics scandals, conferees came up with a compromise bill, in part by letting each chamber live by its own rules on public financing. The Senate backed off from its ban on PACs and the House went along with the Senate's more restrictive language on soft money. But in the end what they produced was a Democratic bill and, without bipartisan support, it was doomed. President Bush—objecting to its spending limits, public funding, and creation of separate systems for House and Senate campaigns—vetoed the bill. The Senate fell nine votes short of overriding Bush's veto. In the wake of the legislation's failure in 1992, both Democrats and Republicans aggressively argued that the other side stymied their efforts at reform.

Given the strong backing from Democrats in the previous Congress and incoming President Bill Clinton's vow to overhaul the system, the 103rd Congress (1993–1995) opened with high expectations for enactment of a new campaign finance law. Both chambers did pass bills in 1993, but again they were radically different. The Senate bill banned PACs, while the House bill set an aggregate cap on PAC contributions to a campaign. Both measures contained spending limits but offered vastly different incentives to encourage candidates to comply. House and Senate Democrats worked out a compromise but the bill died late in the 1994 session when a GOP-led filibuster blocked the Senate from sending its bill to conference.

Failure to enact the bill in 1994 was a major defeat for Clinton and Democratic congressional leaders. Democrats, however, had set the stage for defeat by waiting until the eleventh hour to come up with a compromise version. Indeed, the long history of the legislation was rich with evidence that many Democrats in both chambers shared GOP objections to establishing a system that would provide congressional candidates with federal subsidies. Other Democrats, particularly in the House, were deeply, if privately, opposed to an overhaul of the system that had protected their seats and majority status for years. In the end, it was the inability of Democrats to iron out their internal differences that delayed the bill so long that it became vulnerable to procedural snags. Some supporters of the legislation blamed Clinton, who had campaigned on the issue but brought little to bear on it in 1994.

The Republican takeover in the next Congress (1995–1997) made little difference in campaign finance legislation. Despite promises to overhaul the system, Republicans had no more success than their Democratic predecessors. The most memorable development on campaign finance in 1995 turned out to be the least important: a much-publicized handshake by President Clinton and House Speaker Newt Gingrich on agreement to create a commission to explore changes in the system. Nothing came of it.

With their new majority status in Congress helping to fill GOP election coffers, many Republicans found themselves loath to change the system. Although rank-and-file members managed to force the leadership to allow floor debates on the issue, they failed to pass legislation in either chamber. A bipartisan effort to revise campaign finance laws was stopped once again by a filibuster in the Senate. The bill called for voluntary spending limits in return for certain incentives and would have banned PAC and soft money contributions. In the House, a GOP bill that would have set new contribution limits for individuals and PACs was defeated, in part because of an unrelated provision that would have required labor unions to get signed agreements from workers before using their dues for political contributions. A House Democratic alternative was defeated as well.

SOFT MONEY, ISSUE ADS DEBATE

Advocates of a campaign finance overhaul failed again in the 105th Congress (1997–1999). They had hoped revelations of campaign abuses in the 1996 election would outrage the public sufficiently to put pressure on Congress to move legislation, but Republican leaders focused instead on investigations into Democratic fund-raising activities. The House passed a sweeping measure after its backers surmounted attempts by the GOP leadership to block its consideration on the House floor. The leaders relented in the face of a growing number of signatures on a discharge petition to bring the bill to the floor without committee action, a procedural move that would have cost the leadership control of the floor and allowed backers to debate a variety of campaign finance bills on their own terms. A Senate bill succumbed once again to a filibuster.

But what was interesting this time around was how much the focus of the campaign finance debate had changed. PAC contributions, spending limits, and public funding were no longer the dominant themes. In fact, the House-passed bill included no provisions in those areas. And on the Senate side, sponsors of campaign finance legislation dropped those provisions in an attempt to broaden GOP support for their bill. The House and Senate bills focused instead on soft money and issue advocacy advertising, reflecting the dramatic growth of both in the 1990s and the enormous controversy surrounding them. The bills would have banned national parties from receiving or spending soft money and would have prohibited state and local parties from using soft money for federal election activity. They also would have redefined express advocacy so that more of what was then classified as issue advocacy advertising would be regulated.

Backers of the legislation renewed their efforts early in the 106th Congress (1999–2001). House Democrats again gathered signatures on a discharge petition in hopes of preempting the leadership's plan to put off consideration of the bill until the fall of 1999. But the issue did not come to the floor until September. The House at that time passed an amended campaign finance overhaul bill that was substantively the same as the legislation it had approved in 1998.

And so the fate of the legislation once again was in the Senate's hands. Senate sponsors quickly unveiled a new strategy aimed at avoiding yet another death by filibuster. They put aside—at least for the time being—their proposal to more closely regulate issue ads and opted instead for a narrow bill that focused on banning soft money. They hoped this move would neutralize GOP opponents' argument that the bill was a violation of free speech rights. But the new strategy failed to attract enough votes to cut off a filibuster when the Senate took up the bill in October. The bill was shelved, but sponsors vowed to continue to press for a vote.

NOTES

1. Unless otherwise noted, the figures in this chapter on campaign receipts and expenditures in the 1998 elections were from the Federal Election Commission and include money that moved during the 1997–1998 election cycle in all congressional races, including those of primary losers. (Figures for just general election candidates or for just major party candidates are noted as such in the text of this chapter.) The main source was "FEC Reports on Congressional Fundraising for 1997–98," a Federal Election Commission press release of April 28, 1999. Other FEC press releases used included "FEC Announces 1998 Party Spending Limits," March 6, 1998; "Major Parties Report Record Amounts in 'Soft Money' Contributions," March 19, 1998; "FEC Issues Semi-Annual Federal PAC Count," February 12, 1999; and "FEC Reports on Political Party Activity for 1997–98," April 9, 1999; "FEC Releases Information on PAC Activity for 1997–98," June 8, 1999.

2. Quoted in Chuck Alston, "Image Problems Propel Congress Back to Campaign Finance Bills," *Congressional Quarterly Weekly Report*, February 2, 1991, 281.

3. Frank J. Sorauf, *Money in American Elections* (Glenview, Ill.: Scott, Foresman, 1988), 73–74.

4. Center for Responsive Politics and Princeton Survey Research Associates, "Money and Politics: A National Survey of the Public's Views on How Money Impacts Our Political System" (Washington, D.C.: Center for Responsive Politics, April–May 1997).

5. Quoted in Larry J. Sabato, *PAC Power: Inside the World of Political Action Committees* (New York: Norton, 1984), 171.

6. Paul S. Herrnson, "Money and Motives: Spending in House Elections," in *Congress Reconsidered*, 6th ed., ed. Lawrence C. Dodd and Bruce I. Oppenheimer (Washington, D.C.: CQ Press, 1997), 114.

7. Frank J. Sorauf, "Political Action Committees," in *Campaign Finance Reform: A Sourcebook,* ed. Anthony Corrado et al. (Washington, D.C.: Brookings Institution, 1997), 123.

8. Larry Makinson, "The Big Picture: Money Follows Power Shift on Capitol Hill" (Washington, D.C.: Center for Responsive Politics, 1997), 10.

9. Sorauf, "Political Action Committees," 126.

10. Sorauf, *Money in American Elections,* 174.

11. Trevor Potter, "Where Are We Now? The Current State of Campaign Finance Law," in *Campaign Finance Reform: A Sourcebook,* 7.

12. Herrnson, "Money and Motives," in *Congress Reconsidered,* 107–108.

13. Ibid., 105.

14. David B. Magleby and Candice J. Nelson, *The Money Chase: Congressional Campaign Finance Reform* (Washington, D.C.: Brookings Institution, 1990), 58.

15. Senate Committee on the Judiciary, Subcommittee on the Constitution, "Hearing on Campaign Finance Reform," 100th Cong., 2nd sess., February 28, 1990, 7.

16. Quoted in Chuck Alston, "Forcing Down Cost of TV Ads Appeals to Both Parties," *Congressional Quarterly Weekly Report,* March 16, 1991, 647.

17. Joseph E. Cantor, Denis Steven Rutkus, and Kevin B. Greely, "Free and Reduced-Rate Television Time for Political Candidates," Library of Congress, Congressional Research Service, Rept 97-680 GOV, July 7, 1997, iii, 3–4.

18. Sara Fritz and Dwight Morris, *Gold-Plated Politics: Running for Congress in the 1990s* (Washington, D.C.: CQ Press, 1992), 128.

19. Quoted in Alston, "Forcing Down Cost of TV Ads Appeals to Both Parties," 648.

20. Dwight Morris and Murielle E. Gamache, *Handbook of Campaign Spending: Money in the 1992 Congressional Races* (Washington D.C.: Congressional Quarterly, 1994), 8–12.

21. Quoted in Larry J. Sabato, *Paying for Elections: The Campaign Finance Thicket* (New York: Twentieth Century Fund/Priority Press, 1989), 11.

22. Joseph E. Cantor, "Campaign Financing," Library of Congress, Congressional Research Service, Rept. IB87020, August 6, 1998, 2.

23. Joseph E. Cantor, "Congressional Campaign Spending: 1976–1996," Library of Congress, Congressional Research Service, Rept. 97-793 GOV, August 19, 1997, 3–4.

24. Common Cause News, April 8, 1999.

25. Cantor, "Congressional Campaign Spending: 1976–1996," 3–4.

26. Common Cause News, April 8, 1999.

27. Sheila Krumholz, "Tracking the Cash: Candidate Fund-Raising in the 1998 Elections" (Washington, D.C.: Center for Responsive Politics, 1988).

28. Gary C. Jacobson, "Money in the 1980 and 1982 Congressional Elections," in *Money and Politics in the United States: Financing Elections in the 1980s,* ed. Michael J. Malbin (Washington, D.C.: American Enterprise Institute, 1984), 58.

29. Sorauf, *Money in American Elections,* 333.

30. Helen Dewar, "Lautenberg to Retire from Senate in 2000," *Washington Post,* February 18, 1999, A3.

31. Diane Granat, "Parties' Schools for Politicians Grooming Troops for Elections," *Congressional Quarterly Weekly Report,* May 5, 1984, 1036.

32. Quoted in Andy Plattner, "The High Cost of Holding—and Keeping—Public Office," *U.S. News & World Report,* June 22, 1987, 30.

33. David E. Price, "The House of Representatives: A Report from the Field," in *Congress Reconsidered,* 4th ed., ed. Lawrence C. Dodd and Bruce I. Oppenheimer (Washington, D.C.: CQ Press, 1989), 417–418.

34. Senate Committee on Rules and Administration, *Hearings on Senate Campaign Finance Proposals,* 100th Cong., 1st sess., March 5 and 18, April 22 and 23, 1987, 7–8.

35. Magleby and Nelson, *The Money Chase,* 44.

36. Roger H. Davidson and Walter J. Oleszek, *Congress and Its Members,* 7th ed. (Washington, D.C.: CQ Press, 2000), 68.

37. Sabato, *Paying for Elections,* 4.

38. Senate Committee on Rules and Administration, Hearings on Campaign Finance Reform, 101st Cong., 1st sess., Fred Wertheimer testimony, April 20, 1989, committee handout, 30.

39. Quoted in Chuck Alston, "A Political Money Tree Waits for Incumbents in Need," *Congressional Quarterly Weekly Report,* June 30, 1990, 2026.

40. John Lewis, "In Defense of PACs," *Washington Post,* July 1, 1994, A25.

41. Cantor, "Campaign Financing," 2.

42. Anthony Corrado, "Party Soft Money," in *Campaign Finance Reform: A Sourcebook,* 172.

43. Quoted in Alan Greenblatt, "Soft Money: The Root of All Evil or a Party-Building Necessity?" *Congressional Quarterly Weekly Report,* September 6, 1997, 2065.

44. David B. Magleby and Marianne Holt, ed., "Outside Money: Soft Money & Issue Ads in Competitive 1998 Congressional Elections" (Provo, Utah: Brigham Young University, 1999), 12.

45. Jackie Koszczuk, "'Soft Money' Speaks Loudly on Capitol Hill This Season," *CQ Weekly,* June 27, 1998, 1738.

46. Deborah Beck et al.,"Issue Advocacy Advertising During the 1996 Campaign: A Catalog" (Philadelphia: University of Pennsylvania, Annenberg Public Policy Center, 1997), 3.

47. Sorauf, "Political Action Committees," *Campaign Finance Reform: A Sourcebook,* 128.

48. Quoted in Rebecca Carr, "Campaign Finance: Lingering Doubts," *Congressional Quarterly Weekly Report,* February 8, 1997, 353.

49. Robert E. Mutch, *Campaigns, Congress, and Courts: The Making of Federal Campaign Finance Law* (New York: Praeger, 1988), xv.

50. George Thayer, *Who Shakes the Money Tree? American Campaign Financing Practices from 1789 to the Present* (New York: Simon and Schuster, 1973), 25.

51. Mutch, *Campaigns, Congress, and Courts*, xvi.

52. Ibid., xvii.

53. Ibid., 4.

54. Alexander Heard, *The Costs of Democracy* (Chapel Hill: University of North Carolina Press, 1960), 388.

55. Herbert E. Alexander, *Financing the 1968 Election* (Lexington, Mass.: D.C. Heath, 1971), 93.

56. Herbert E. Alexander, *Financing the 1972 Election* (Lexington, Mass.: D.C. Heath, 1976), 7.

57. *Facts on File*, April 29–May 5, 1973, 357.

SELECTED BIBLIOGRAPHY

Adamany, David, and George E. Agree. *Political Money: A Strategy for Campaign Financing in America*. Baltimore: Johns Hopkins University Press, 1975.

Alexander, Herbert E. *Financing Politics: Money, Elections, and Political Reform*. 4th ed. Washington, D.C.: CQ Press, 1992.

Alexander, Herbert E., and Anthony Corrado. *Financing the 1992 Election*. Armonk, N.Y.: M. E. Sharpe, 1995. (Ninth in quadrennial series by Alexander and the Citizens' Research Foundation that began with the 1960 elections.)

Beck, Deborah, Paul Taylor, Jeffrey Stanger, and Douglas Rivlin. "Issue Advocacy Advertising During the 1996 Campaign: A Catalog." Philadelphia: University of Pennsylvania, Annenberg Public Policy Center, 1997.

Biersack, Robert, Paul S. Herrnson, and Clyde Wilcox. *After the Revolution: PACs, Lobbies, and the Republican Congress*. Boston: Allyn and Bacon, 1999.

Cantor, Joseph E. "Campaign Financing." Rept. No. IB87020. Library of Congress, Congressional Research Service, August 6, 1998.

———. "Congressional Campaign Spending: 1976–1996." Library of Congress, Congressional Research Service, Rept. 97-793 GOV, August 19, 1997.

———. "Political Action Committees: Their Role in Financing Congressional Elections." Rept. No. 98-255 GOV. Library of Congress, Congressional Research Service, March 11, 1998.

Cantor, Joseph E., Denis S. Rutkus, and Kevin B. Greely. "Free and Reduced-Rate Television Time for Political Candidates." Library of Congress, Congressional Research Service, Rept 97-680 GOV, July 7, 1997.

Center for Responsive Politics. "Who's Paying? Stats At-a-Glance on the Funding of U.S. Elections." Washington, D.C.: Center for Responsive Politics, 1997.

Center for Responsive Politics and Princeton Survey Research Associates. "Money and Politics: A National Survey of the Public's Views on How Money Impacts Our Political System." Washington, D.C.: Center for Responsive Politics, April–May 1997.

Corrado, Anthony, Thomas E. Mann, Daniel R. Ortiz, Trevor Potter, and Frank J. Sorauf, eds. *Campaign Finance Reform: A Sourcebook*. Washington, D.C.: Brookings Institution, 1997.

Dodd, Lawrence C., and Bruce I. Oppenheimer. *Congress Reconsidered*. 6th ed. Washington, D.C.: CQ Press, 1997.

Drew, Elizabeth. *The Corruption of American Politics: What Went Wrong and Why*. New York: Birch Lane Press, 1999.

Eismeier, Theodore J., and Philip H. Pollock III. *Business, Money and the Rise of Corporate PACs in American Elections*. New York: Quroum Books, 1988.

Federal Election Commission. "Annual Report." Washington, D.C., 1974–.

———. "FEC Disclosure Series." Washington, D.C., 1975–76.

———. "FEC Reports on Financial Activities." Washington, D.C., 1977–.

———. "Twenty Year Report." Washington, D.C., 1995.

Fritz, Sara, and Dwight Morris. *Gold-Plated Politics: Running for Congress in the 1990s*. Washington, D.C.: CQ Press, 1992.

Goidel, Robert K., Donald A. Gross, and Todd G. Shields. *Money Matters: Consequences of Campaign Finance Reform in U.S. House Elections*. Lanham, Md.: Rowan and Littlefield, 1999.

Green, John, Paul Herrnson, Lynda Powell, and Clyde Wilcox. "Individual Congressional Campaign Contributors: Wealthy, Conservative and Reform-Minded." Washington, D.C.: Center for Responsive Politics, 1998.

Heard, Alexander. *The Costs of Democracy*. Chapel Hill: University of North Carolina Press, 1960.

Herrnson, Paul S. *Congressional Elections: Campaigning at Home and in Washington*. 2nd ed. Washington, D.C.: CQ Press, 1998.

Jackson, Brooks. *Broken Promise: Why the Federal Election Commission Failed. A Twentieth Century Fund Report*. New York: Priority Press, 1990.

———. *Honest Graft: Big Money and the American Political Process*. Rev. ed. Washington, D.C.: Farragut, 1990.

Jacobson, Gary C. *Money in Congressional Elections*. New Haven, Conn.: Yale University Press, 1980.

———. *The Politics of Congressional Elections*. 4th ed. New York: Longman, 1997.

Krasno, Jonathan S. *Challengers, Competition, and Reelection: Comparing Senate and House Elections*. New Haven, Conn.: Yale University Press, 1994.

Kubiak, Greg D. *The Gilded Dome: The U.S. Senate and Campaign Finance Reform*. Norman: University of Oklahoma Press, 1994.

Magleby, David B., and Marianne Holt, eds. "Outside Money: Soft Money & Issue Ads in Competitive 1998 Congressional Elections." Provo, Utah: Brigham Young University, 1999.

Magleby, David B., and Candice J. Nelson. *The Money Chase: Congressional Campaign Finance Reform*. Washington, D.C.: Brookings Institution, 1990.

Makinson, Larry. "The Big Picture: Money Follows Power Shift on Capitol Hill." Washington, D.C.: Center for Responsive Politics, 1997.

Makinson, Larry, and Joshua F. Goldstein. *The Cash Constituents of Congress*. 2nd ed. Washington, D.C.: Congressional Quarterly, 1994.

———. *Open Secrets: The Encyclopedia of Congressional Money and Politics*. 4th ed. Washington, D.C.: Congressional Quarterly, 1996.

Malbin, Michael J., ed. *Money and Politics in the United States: Financing Elections in the 1980s*. Chatham, N.J.: Chatham House/American Enterprise Institute, 1984.

Morris, Dwight, and Murielle E. Gamache. *Handbook of Campaign Spending: Money in the 1992 Congressional Races*. Washington, D.C.: Congressional Quarterly, 1994.

Mutch, Robert E. *Campaigns, Congress, and Courts: The Making of Federal Campaign Finance Law*. New York: Praeger, 1988.

Nugent, Margaret L., and John R. Johannes. *Money, Elections, and Democracy: Reforming Congressional Campaign Finance*. Boulder, Colo.: Westview, 1990.

Ornstein, Norman J. *Campaign Finance: An Illustrated Guide*. Washington, D.C.: American Enterprise Institute, 1997.

Ornstein, Norman J., Thomas E. Mann, and Michael J. Malbin. *Vital Statistics on Congress, 1997–1998*. Washington, D.C.: Congressional Quarterly, 1998.

Overacker, Louise. *Money in Elections*. New York: Macmillan, 1932.

Pollock, James K. *Party Campaign Funds*. New York: Knopf, 1926.

Sabato, Larry J. *PAC Power: Inside the World of Political Action Committees*. New York: Norton, 1984.

———. *Paying for Elections: The Campaign Finance Thicket*. New York: Priority Press/Twentieth Century Fund, 1989.

Sorauf, Frank J. *Inside Campaign Finance: Myths and Realities*. New Haven, Conn.: Yale University Press, 1994.

———. *Money in American Elections*. Glenview, Ill.: Scott, Foresman/Little, Brown, 1988.

Thayer, George. *Who Shakes the Money Tree? American Campaign Financing from 1789 to the Present*. New York: Simon and Schuster, 1973.

CHAPTER 33

Reapportionment and Redistricting

REAPPORTIONMENT, the redistribution of the 435 House seats among the states to reflect shifts in population, and redistricting, the redrawing of congressional district boundaries within the states, are among the most important and contentious processes in the U.S. political system. They help to determine whether Democrats or Republicans, or liberals or conservatives, will dominate the House, and whether districts will be drawn to favor the election of candidates from particular racial or ethnic groups.

Reapportionment and redistricting occur every ten years on the basis of the decennial population census. States where populations grew quickly during the previous ten years typically gain congressional seats, while those that lost population or grew much more slowly than the national average stand to lose seats. The number of House members for the rest of the states remains the same.

The states that gain or lose seats usually must make extensive changes in their congressional maps. Even those states with stable delegations must make modifications to take into account population shifts within their boundaries, in accordance with Supreme Court "one-person, one-vote" rulings.

In most states, the state legislatures are responsible for drafting and enacting the new congressional district map. Thus, the majority party in each state legislature is often in a position to draw a district map that enhances the fortunes of its incumbents and candidates at the expense of the opposing party. "Some members may find their old district no longer recognizable, or their home located in someone else's district. Others will find the music has stopped and they are, quite literally, without a seat. Or they will find themselves thrown together in a single district with another incumbent—often from the same party," wrote one reporter. "The scramble to prevent or minimize such political problems involves some of the most brutal combat in American politics, for the power to draw district lines is the power not only to end one politician's career but often to enfranchise or disenfranchise a neighborhood, a city, a party, a social or economic group or even a race by concentrating or diluting their votes within a given district."[1]

Among the many unique features to emerge in the remarkable nation-creating endeavor of 1787 was a national legislative body whose membership was to be elected by the people and apportioned on the basis of population. In keeping with the nature of the Constitution, however, only fundamental rules and regulations were provided. The interpretation and implementation of the instructions contained in the document were left to future generations.

Within this flexible framework many questions soon arose. How large was the House of Representatives to be? What mathematical formula was to be used in calculating the distribution of seats among the various states? Were the representatives to be elected at large or by districts? If by districts, what standards should be used in fixing their boundaries? Congress and the courts have been wrestling with these questions for more than two hundred years.

Until the mid-twentieth century such questions generally remained in the hands of the legislators. But with the population increasingly concentrated in urban areas, variations in populations among rural and urban districts in a single state grew more and more pronounced. Efforts to persuade Congress and state legislatures to address the issue of heavily populated but underrepresented areas proved unsuccessful. Legislators from rural areas were so intent on preventing power from slipping from their hands that they managed to block reapportionment of the House after the 1920 census.

Not long afterward, litigants began trying to persuade the Supreme Court to order the states to revise congressional district boundaries to reflect population shifts. For years they found the Court unreceptive, but then there was incremental progress, and a breakthrough finally occurred in 1964 in the case of *Wesberry v. Sanders*. In that case, the Court declared that the Constitution required that "as nearly as practicable, one man's vote in a congressional election is to be worth as much as another's."

In the years that followed, the Court repeatedly reaffirmed its one-person, one-vote requirement. Following the 1980 census, several states adopted new maps with districts of nearly equal population that were designed to benefit one party at the expense of the other. These partisan gerrymanders disregarded other traditional tenets of map-drawing, such as making districts compact and respecting the integrity of county and city lines. But as long as the districts in such maps were drawn to be equal in population, these gerrymanders seemed unassailable in the courts. In 1986, a slim majority of the Supreme Court held that partisan gerrymanders were subject to constitutional review by federal courts. But the Court offered no opinion on what might constitute an impermissible partisan gerrymander, and maps drawn with a clear partisan slant continued to appear in the 1990s round of redistricting.

Starting in the mid-1980s and continuing through the 1990s, the focus of much redistricting controversy and litigation shifted to the practice of racial gerrymandering—designing constituencies to favor the election of candidates from racial or ethnic groups whose numbers in Congress are lower than their proportion in the general population.

In a landmark 1986 ruling (*Thornburg v. Gingles*), the Supreme Court not only said that gerrymandering that deliberately diluted minority voting strength was illegal, but went even further, imposing a requirement that mapmakers do all they can to maximize minority voting strength. The expansion of minority rights sparked by *Gingles* changed redistricting dramatically. After the 1990 census, redistricting in many states was done with an eye toward creating constituencies designed to elect minority candidates. Those new maps resulted in record numbers of blacks and Hispanics winning House seats in 1992.

As if taken aback by the pace of change wrought by *Gingles*, the Supreme Court issued a series of rulings in the 1990s that seemed aimed at discouraging states from going to extremes to draw districts for minorities. So with the approach of the 2000 census and the first round of redistricting in the new century, mapmakers faced the challenge of striking a balance between going far enough, but not too far, in giving minorities a chance to win House districts.

Early History of Reapportionment

Modern legislative bodies are descended from the councils of feudal lords and gentry that medieval kings summoned for the purpose of raising revenues and armies. The councils represented only certain groups of people, such as the nobility, the clergy, the landed gentry, and town merchants; the notion of equal representation for equal numbers of people or even for all groups of people had not yet begun to develop.

Beginning as little more than administrative and advisory arms of the throne, royal councils in time developed into lawmaking bodies and acquired powers that eventually eclipsed those of the monarchs they served. In England the king's council became Parliament, with the higher nobility and clergy making up the House of Lords and representatives of the gentry and merchants making up the House of Commons. The power struggle between king and council climaxed in the mid-1600s, when the king was executed and a "benevolent" dictatorship was set up under Oliver Cromwell. Although the monarchy was soon restored, by 1800 Parliament was clearly the more powerful branch of government.

The growth of the powers of Parliament, as well as the development of English ideas of representation during the seventeenth and eighteenth centuries, had a profound effect on the colonists in America. Representative assemblies were unifying forces behind the breakaway of the colonies from England and the establishment of the newly independent nation.

Colonists in America generally modeled their legislatures after England's, using both population and land units as bases for apportionment. Patterns of early representation varied. "Nowhere did representation bear any uniform relation to the number of electors. Here and there the factor of size had been crudely recognized," Robert Luce noted in his book *Legislative Principles*.[2]

The Continental Congress, with representation from every colony, proclaimed in the Declaration of Independence in 1776 that governments derive "their just powers from the consent of the governed" and that "the right of representation in the legislature" is an "inestimable right" of the people. The Constitutional Convention of 1787 included representatives from all the states. However, in neither of these bodies were the state delegations or voting powers proportional to population.

In New England the town was usually the basis for representation. In the Middle Atlantic region the county frequently was used. Virginia used the county with additional representation for specified cities. In many areas, towns and counties were fairly equal in population, and territorial representation afforded roughly equal representation for equal numbers of people. Delaware's three counties, for example, were of almost equal population and had the same representation in the legislature. But in Virginia the disparity was enormous (from 951 people in one county to 22,015 in another). Thomas Jefferson criticized the state's constitution on the ground that "among those who share the representation, the shares are unequal."[3]

THE FRAMERS' INTENTIONS

What, then, did the Framers of the Constitution have in mind about who would be represented in the House of Representatives and how?

The Constitution declares only that each state is to be allotted a certain number of representatives. It does not state specifically that congressional districts must be equal or nearly equal in population. Nor does it explicitly require that a state create districts at all. However, it seems clear that the first clause of Article I, Section 2, providing that House members should be chosen "by the people of the several states," indicates that the House of Representatives, in contrast to the Senate, was to represent people rather than states. (*See box, Constitutional Provisions, p. 893.*)

The third clause of Article I, Section 2, provided that congressional apportionment among the states must be according to population. "There is little point in giving the states congressmen 'according to their respective numbers' if the states do not redistribute the members of their delegations on the same principle," Andrew Hacker argued in his book *Congressional Districting*. "For representatives are not the property of the states, as are the senators, but rather belong to the people who happen to reside within the boundaries of those states. Thus, each citizen has a claim to be regarded as a political unit equal in value to his neighbors."[4]

Hacker also examined the Constitutional Convention, *The Federalist Papers* (essays written by Alexander Hamilton, John Jay, and James Madison in defense of the Constitution), and the

CONSTITUTIONAL PROVISIONS

ARTICLE I, SECTION 2

The House of Representatives shall be composed of Members chosen every second Year by the People of the several States, and the Electors in each State shall have the Qualifications requisite for Electors of the most numerous Branch of the State Legislature. . . .

Representatives and direct Taxes shall be apportioned among the several States which may be included within this Union, according to their respective Numbers, which shall be determined by adding to the whole Number of free Persons, including those bound to Service for a Term of Years, and excluding Indians not taxed, three fifths of all other Persons. The actual Enumeration shall be made within three Years after the first Meeting of the Congress of the United States, and within every subsequent Term of ten Years, in such Manner as they shall by Law direct. The Number of Representatives shall not exceed one for every thirty thousand, but each State shall have at least one Representative. . . .

ARTICLE I, SECTION 4

The Times, Places and Manner of holding Elections for Senators and Representatives, shall be prescribed in each State by the Legislature thereof; but the Congress may at any time by Law make or alter such Regulations, except as to the Place of Chusing Senators. . . .

AMENDMENT XIV
(RATIFIED JULY 28, 1868)

Section 2. Representatives shall be apportioned among the several States according to their respective numbers, counting the whole number of persons in each State, excluding Indians not taxed. But when the right to vote at any election for the choice of electors for President and Vice President of the United States, Representatives in Congress, the Executive and Judicial officers of a State, or the members of the Legislature thereof, is denied to any of the male inhabitants of such State, being twenty-one years of age, and citizens of the United States, or in any way abridged, except for participation in rebellion, or other crime, the basis of representation therein shall be reduced in the proportion which the number of such male citizens shall bear to the whole number of male citizens twenty-one years of age in such State.

---

state conventions ratifying the Constitution for evidence of the Framers' intentions with regard to representation. He found that the issue of unequal representation arose only once during debate in the Constitutional Convention. The occasion was Madison's defense of Article I, Section 4, of the proposed Constitution, giving Congress the power to override state regulations on "the times . . . and manner" of holding elections for members of Congress. Madison's argument related to the fact that many state legislatures of the time were badly malapportioned: "The inequality of the representation in the legislatures of particular states would produce a like inequality in their representation in the national legislature, as it was presumable that the counties having the power in the former case would secure it to themselves in the latter."[5]

The implication was that states would create congressional districts and that unequal districting was undesirable and should be prevented.

Madison made this interpretation even more clear in his contributions to *The Federalist Papers*. Arguing in favor of the relatively small size of the projected House of Representatives, he wrote in No. 56: "Divide the largest state into ten or twelve districts and it will be found that there will be no peculiar local interests . . . which will not be within the knowledge of the Representative of the district."

In the same paper Madison said, "The Representatives of each state will not only bring with them a considerable knowledge of its laws, and a local knowledge of their respective districts, but will probably in all cases have been members, and may even at the very time be members, of the state legislature, where all the local information and interests of the state are assembled, and from whence they may easily be conveyed by a very few hands into the legislature of the United States." And, finally, in the *Federalist* No. 57 Madison stated that "each Representative of the United States will be elected by five or six thousand citizens." In making these arguments, Madison seems to have assumed that all or most representatives would be elected by districts rather than at large.[6]

In the states' ratifying conventions, the grant to Congress by Article I, Section 4, of ultimate jurisdiction over the "times, places and manner of holding elections" (except the places of choosing senators) held the attention of many delegates. There were differences over the merits of this section, but no justification of unequal districts was prominently used to attack the grant of power. Further evidence that individual districts were the intention of the Founding Fathers was given in the New York ratifying convention, when Alexander Hamilton said, "The natural and proper mode of holding elections will be to divide the state into districts in proportion to the number to be elected. This state will consequently be divided at first into six."[7]

From his study of the sources relating to the question of congressional districting, Hacker concluded,

There is, then, a good deal of evidence that those who framed and ratified the Constitution intended that the House of Representatives have as its constituency a public in which the votes of all citizens were of equal weight. . . . The House of Representatives was designed to be a popular chamber, giving the same electoral power to all who had the vote. And the concern of Madison . . . that districts be equal in size was an institutional step in the direction of securing this democratic principle.[8]

Reapportionment: The Number of Seats

The Constitution made the first apportionment, which was to remain in effect until the first census was taken. No reliable figures on the population were available at the time. The Constitution's apportionment yielded a sixty-five member House. The seats were allotted among the thirteen states as follows: New Hampshire, three; Massachusetts, eight; Rhode Island and Providence Plantations, one; Connecticut, five; New York, six; New Jersey, four; Pennsylvania, eight; Delaware, one; Maryland, six; Virginia, ten; North Carolina, five; South Carolina, five; and Georgia, three. This apportionment remained in effect during the First and Second Congresses (1789–1793).

Apparently realizing that apportionment of the House was likely to become a major bone of contention, the First Congress submitted to the states a proposed constitutional amendment containing a formula to be used in future reapportionments. The amendment provided that following the taking of a decennial census one representative would be allotted for every 30,000 people until the House membership reached 100. Once that level was reached, there would be one representative for every 40,000 people until the House membership reached 200, when there would be one representative for every 50,000 people.

FIRST APPORTIONMENT BY CONGRESS

The states, however, refused to ratify the reapportionment-formula amendment, which forced Congress to enact apportionment legislation after the first census was taken in 1790. The first apportionment bill was sent to the president in March 1792. President George Washington sent the bill back to Congress without his signature—the first presidential veto.

The bill had incorporated the constitutional minimum of 30,000 as the size of each district. But the population of each state was not a simple multiple of 30,000; significant fractions were left over. For example, Vermont was found to be entitled to 2.85 representatives, New Jersey to 5.98, and Virginia to 21.02. A formula had to be found that would deal in the fairest possible manner with unavoidable variations from exact equality.

Accordingly, Congress proposed in the first apportionment bill to distribute the members on a fixed ratio of one representative for each 30,000 inhabitants, and to give an additional member to each state with a fraction exceeding one-half. Washington's veto was based on the belief that eight states would receive more than one representative for each 30,000 people under this formula.

A motion to override the veto was unsuccessful. A new bill meeting the president's objections, approved in April 1792, provided for a ratio of one member for every 33,000 inhabitants and fixed the exact number of representatives to which each state was entitled. The total membership of the House was to be 105. In dividing the population of the various states by 33,000, all remainders were to be disregarded. Thomas Jefferson devised the solution, known as the method of rejected fractions.

A method of reapportionment devised by Thomas Jefferson resulted in great inequalities among states. This method was in use until 1840.

JEFFERSON'S METHOD

Jefferson's method of reapportionment resulted in great inequalities among districts. A Vermont district would contain 42,766 inhabitants, a New Jersey district 35,911, and a Virginia district only 33,187. Jefferson's method emphasized what was considered to be the ideal size of a congressional district rather than what the size of the House ought to be.

The reapportionment act based on the census of 1800 continued the ratio of 33,000, which provided a House of 141 members. The third apportionment bill, enacted in 1811, fixed the ratio at 35,000, yielding a House of 181 members. Following the 1820 census Congress set the ratio at 40,000 inhabitants per district, which produced a House of 213 members. The act of May 22, 1832, fixed the ratio at 47,700, resulting in a House of 240 members.

Dissatisfaction with inequalities produced by the method of rejected fractions grew. Launching a vigorous attack against it, Daniel Webster urged adoption of a method that would assign an additional representative to each state with a large fraction. Webster outlined his reasoning in a report he submitted to Congress in 1832:

The Constitution, therefore, must be understood not as enjoining an absolute relative equality—because that would be demanding an impossibility—but as requiring of Congress to make the apportionment of Representatives among the several states according to their respective numbers, *as near as may be.* That which cannot be done perfectly must be done in a manner as near perfection as can be. . . . In such a case approximation becomes a rule.[9]

Following the 1840 census Congress adopted a reapportionment method similar to that advocated by Webster. The method fixed a ratio of one representative for every 70,680 people. This figure was reached by deciding on a fixed size of the House in advance (223), dividing that figure into the total national "representative population," and using the result (70,680) as the fixed ratio. The population of each state was then divided by this ratio to find the number of its representatives and the states were assigned an additional representative for each fraction more than one-half. Under this method the actual size of the House dropped. *(See Table 33-1, p. 896.)*

The modified reapportionment formula adopted by Congress in 1842 was more satisfactory than the previous method, but another change was made following the census of 1850. Proposed by Rep. Samuel F. Vinton of Ohio, the new system became known as the Vinton method.

VINTON APPORTIONMENT FORMULA

Under the Vinton formula Congress first fixed the size of the House and then distributed the seats. The total qualifying population of the country was divided by the desired number of representatives, and the resulting number became the ratio of population to each representative. The population of each state was divided by this ratio, and each state received the number of representatives equal to the whole number in the quotient for that state. Then, to reach the required size of the House, additional representatives were assigned based on the remaining fractions, beginning with the state having the largest fraction. This procedure differed from the 1842 method only in the last step, which assigned one representative to every state having a fraction larger than one-half.

Proponents of the Vinton method pointed out that it had the distinct advantage of fixing the size of the House in advance and taking into account at least the largest fractions. The concern of the House turned from the ideal size of a congressional district to the ideal size of the House itself.

Under the 1842 reapportionment formula, the exact size of the House could not be fixed in advance. If every state with a fraction more than one-half were given an additional representative, the House might wind up with a few more or a few less than the desired number. However, under the Vinton method, only states with the largest fractions were given additional House members and only up to the desired total size of the House.

Vinton Apportionments

Six reapportionments were carried out under the Vinton method. The 1850 census act contained three provisions not included in any previous law. First, it required reapportionment not only after the census of 1850 but also after all the subsequent censuses; second, it purported to fix the size of the House permanently at 233 members; and third, it provided in advance for an automatic apportionment by the secretary of the interior under the method prescribed in the act.

Following the census of 1860 an automatic reapportionment was to be carried out by the Interior Department. However, because the size of the House was to remain at the 1850 level, some states faced loss of representation and others were to gain fewer seats than they expected. To avert that possibility, an act was approved in 1862 increasing the size of the House to 241 and giving an extra representative to eight states—Illinois, Iowa, Kentucky, Minnesota, Ohio, Pennsylvania, Rhode Island, and Vermont.

Apportionment legislation following the 1870 census contained several new provisions. The act fixed the size of the House at 283, with the proviso that the number should be increased if new states were admitted. A supplemental act assigned one additional representative each to Alabama, Florida, Indiana, Louisiana, New Hampshire, New York, Pennsylvania, Tennessee, and Vermont.

With the Reconstruction era at its height in the South, the reapportionment legislation of 1872 reflected the desire of Congress to enforce Section 2 of the new Fourteenth Amendment. That section attempted to protect the right of blacks to vote by providing for reduction of representation in the House of a state that interfered with the exercise of that right. The number of representatives of such a state was to be reduced in proportion to the number of inhabitants of voting age whose right to go to the polls was denied or abridged. The reapportionment bill repeated the language of Section 2, but the provision never was put into effect because of the difficulty of determining the exact number of people whose right to vote was being abridged.

The reapportionment act of 1882 provided for a House of 325 members, with additional members for any new states admitted to the Union. No new apportionment provisions were added. The acts of 1891 and 1901 were routine as far as apportionment was concerned. The 1891 measure provided for a House of 356 members, and the 1901 statute increased the number to 386.

Problems with Vinton Method

Despite the apparent advantages of the Vinton method, certain difficulties revealed themselves as the formula was applied. Zechariah Chafee Jr. of the Harvard Law School summarized these problems in an article in the *Harvard Law Review* in 1929. The method, he pointed out, suffered from what he called the "Alabama paradox." Under that aberration, an increase in the total size of the House might be accompanied by an actual loss of a seat by some states, even though there had been no corresponding change in population. This phenomenon first appeared in tables prepared for Congress in 1881, which gave Alabama eight members in a House of 299 but only seven members in a House of 300. It could even happen that the state that

TABLE 33-1 Congressional Apportionment, 1789–1990

	Constitution[b]															Year of Census[a]					
	(1789)	1790	1800	1810	1820	1830	1840	1850	1860	1870	1880	1890	1900	1910	1930[c]	1940	1950	1960	1970	1980	1990
Ala.				1[d]	3	5	7	7	6	8	8	9	9	10	9	9	9	8	7	7	7
Alaska																	1[d]	1	1	1	1
Ariz.														1[d]	1	2	2	3	4	5	6
Ark.						1[d]	1	2	3	4	5	6	7	7	7	7	6	4	4	4	4
Calif.							2[d]	2	3	4	6	7	8	11	20	23	30	38	43	45	52
Colo.										1[d]	1	2	3	4	4	4	4	4	5	6	6
Conn.	5	7	7	7	6	6	4	4	4	4	4	4	5	5	6	6	6	6	6	6	6
Del.	1	1	1	2	1	1	1	1	1	1	1	1	1	1	1	1	1	1	1	1	1
Fla.							1[d]	1	1	2	2	2	3	4	5	6	8	12	15	19	23
Ga.	3	2	4	6	7	9	8	8	7	9	10	11	11	12	10	10	10	10	10	10	11
Hawaii																	1[d]	2	2	2	2
Idaho												1[d]	1	1	2	2	2	2	2	2	2
Ill.				1[d]	1	3	7	9	14	19	20	22	25	27	27	26	25	24	24	22	20
Ind.				1[d]	3	7	10	11	11	13	13	13	13	13	12	11	11	11	11	10	10
Iowa							2[d]	2	6	9	11	11	11	11	9	8	8	7	6	6	5
Kan.									1	3	7	8	8	8	7	6	6	5	5	5	4
Ky.		2	6	10	12	13	10	10	9	10	11	11	11	11	9	9	8	7	7	7	6
La.				1[d]	3	3	4	4	5	6	6	6	7	8	8	8	8	8	8	8	7
Maine				7[d]	7	8	7	6	5	5	4	4	4	4	3	3	3	2	2	2	2
Md.	6	8	9	9	9	8	6	6	5	6	6	6	6	6	6	6	7	8	8	8	8
Mass.	8	14	17	13[e]	13	12	10	11	10	11	12	13	14	16	15	14	14	12	12	11	10
Mich.						1[d]	3	4	6	9	11	12	12	13	17	17	18	19	19	18	16
Minn.								2[d]	2	3	5	7	9	10	9	9	9	8	8	8	8
Miss.				1[d]	1	2	4	5	5	6	7	7	8	8	7	7	6	5	5	5	5
Mo.					1	2	5	7	9	13	14	15	16	16	13	13	11	10	10	9	9
Mont.											1[d]	1	1	2	2	2	2	2	2	2	1
Neb.									1[d]	1	3	6	6	6	5	4	4	3	3	3	3
Nev.									1[d]	1	1	1	1	1	1	1	1	1	1	2	2
N.H.	3	4	5	6	6	5	4	3	3	3	2	2	2	2	2	2	2	2	2	2	2
N.J.	4	5	6	6	6	6	5	5	5	7	7	8	10	12	14	14	14	15	15	14	13
N.M.														1[d]	1	2	2	2	2	3	3
N.Y.	6	10	17	27	34	40	34	33	31	33	34	34	37	43	45	45	43	41	39	34	31
N.C.	5	10	12	13	13	13	9	8	7	8	9	9	10	10	11	12	12	11	11	11	12
N.D.											1[d]	1	2	3	2	2	2	2	1	1	1
Ohio			1[d]	6	14	19	21	21	19	20	21	21	21	22	24	23	23	24	23	21	19
Okla.														5[d]	8	9	8	6	6	6	6
Ore.							1[d]	1	1	1	2	2	3	3	4	4	4	4	4	5	5
Pa.	8	13	18	23	26	28	24	25	24	27	28	30	32	36	34	33	30	27	25	23	21
R.I.	1	2	2	2	2	2	2	2	2	2	2	2	2	3	2	2	2	2	2	2	2
S.C.	5	6	8	9	9	9	7	6	4	5	7	7	7	7	6	6	6	6	6	6	6
S.D.											2[d]	2	2	3	2	2	2	2	2	1	1
Tenn.		1	3	6	9	13	11	10	8	10	10	10	10	10	9	10	9	9	8	9	9
Texas							2[d]	2	4	6	11	13	16	18	21	21	22	23	24	27	30
Utah												1[d]	1	2	2	2	2	2	2	3	3
Vt.		2	4	6	5	5	4	3	3	3	2	2	2	2	1	1	1	1	1	1	1
Va.	10	19	22	23	22	21	15	13	11	9	10	10	10	10	9	9	10	10	10	10	11
Wash.											1[d]	2	3	5	6	6	7	7	7	8	9
W.Va.										3	4	4	5	6	6	6	6	5	4	4	3
Wis.							2[d]	3	6	8	9	10	11	11	10	10	10	10	9	9	9
Wyo.											1[d]	1	1	1	1	1	1	1	1	1	1
TOTAL	65	106	142	186	213	242	232	237	243	293	332	357	391	435	435	435	437[f]	435	435	435	435

NOTES: a. Apportionment effective with congressional election two years after census.   b. Original apportionment made in Constitution, pending first census.   c. No apportionment was made in 1920.   d. These figures are not based on any census, but indicate the provisional representation accorded newly admitted states by Congress, pending the next census.   e. Twenty members were assigned to Massachusetts, but seven of these were credited to Maine when that area became a state.   f. Normally 435, but temporarily increased two seats by Congress when Alaska and Hawaii became states.

SOURCES: *Biographical Directory of the American Congress* and Bureau of the Census.

lost a seat was the one state that had expanded in population, while all the others had fewer people.

Chafee concluded from his study of the Vinton method:

Thus, it is unsatisfactory to fix the ratio of population per Representative before seats are distributed. Either the size of the House comes out haphazard, or, if this be determined in advance, the absurdities of the "Alabama paradox" vitiate the apportionment. Under present conditions, it is essential to determine the size of the House in advance; the problem thereafter is to distribute the required number of seats among the several states as nearly as possible in proportion to their respective populations so that no state is treated unfairly in comparison with any other state.[10]

MAXIMUM MEMBERSHIP OF HOUSE

In 1911 the membership of the House was fixed at 433. Provision was made for the addition of one representative each from Arizona and New Mexico, which were expected to become states in the near future. Thus, the size of the House reached 435, where it has remained with the exception of a brief period, 1959–1963, when the admission of Alaska and Hawaii raised the total temporarily to 437.

Limiting the size of the House amounted to recognition that the body soon would expand to unmanageable proportions if Congress continued the practice of adding new seats every ten years to match population gains without depriving any state of its existing representation. Agreement on a fixed number made the task of reapportionment even more difficult when the population not only increased but also became much more mobile. Population shifts brought Congress up hard against the politically painful necessity of taking seats away from slow-growing states to give the fast-growing states adequate representation.

A new mathematical calculation was adopted for the reapportionment following the 1910 census. Devised by W. F. Willcox of Cornell University, the new system established a priority list that assigned seats progressively, beginning with the first seat above the constitutional minimum of at least one seat for each state. When there were forty-eight states, this method was used to assign the forty-ninth member, the fiftieth member, and so on, until the agreed upon size of the House was reached. The method was called major fractions and was used after the censuses of 1910, 1930, and 1940. There was no reapportionment after the 1920 census.

1920S STRUGGLE

The results of the fourteenth decennial census were announced in December 1920, just after the short session of the 66th Congress convened. The 1920 census showed that for the first time in history most Americans were urban residents. This came as a profound shock to people accustomed to emphasizing the nation's rural traditions and the virtues of life on farms and in small towns as Thomas Jefferson had. Jefferson once wrote:

Those who labor in the earth are the chosen people of God, if ever He had a chosen people, whose breasts He had made His peculiar deposit for substantial and genuine virtue. . . . The mobs of great cities add just as much to the support of pure government as sores do to the strength of the human body. . . . I think our governments will remain virtuous for many centuries as long as they are chiefly agricultural: and this shall be as long as there shall be vacant lands in any part of America. When they get piled up upon one another in large cities as in Europe, they will become corrupt as in Europe.[11]

As their power waned throughout the latter part of the nineteenth century and the early part of the twentieth, farmers clung to the Jeffersonian belief that somehow they were more pure and virtuous than the growing number of urban residents. When faced with the fact that they were in the minority, these country residents put up a strong rearguard action to prevent the inevitable shift of congressional districts to the cities. They succeeded in postponing reapportionment legislation for almost a decade.

Rural representatives insisted that, because the 1920 census was taken as of January 1, the farm population had been undercounted. In support of this contention, they argued that many farm laborers were seasonally employed in the cities at that time of year. Furthermore, midwinter road conditions probably had prevented enumerators from visiting many farms, they said, and other farmers were said to have been uncounted because they were absent on winter vacation trips. The change of the census date to January 1 in 1920 had been made to conform to recommendations of the U.S. Department of Agriculture, which had asserted that the census should be taken early in the year if an accurate statistical picture of farming conditions was to be obtained.

Another point raised by rural legislators was that large numbers of unnaturalized aliens were congregated in northern cities, with the result that these cities gained at the expense of constituencies made up mostly of citizens of the United States. Rep. Homer Hoch, R-Kan., submitted a table showing that in a House of 435 representatives, exclusion from the census count of people not naturalized would have altered the allocation of seats in sixteen states. Southern and western farming states would have retained the number of seats allocated to them in 1911 or would have gained, while northern industrial states and California would have lost or at least would have gained fewer seats.

A constitutional amendment to exclude all aliens from the enumeration for purposes of reapportionment was proposed during the 70th Congress (1927–1929) by Hoch, Sen. Arthur Capper, R-Kan., and others. But nothing further came of the proposals.

Reapportionment Bills Opposed

The first bill to reapportion the House according to the 1920 census was drafted by the House Census Committee early in 1921. Proceeding on the principle that no state should have its representation reduced, the committee proposed to increase the total number of representatives from 435 to 483. But the House voted 267–76 to keep its membership at 435. The bill then was blocked by a Senate committee, where it died when the 66th Congress expired March 4, 1921.

TABLE 33-2 State Population Totals, House Seat Changes in the 1990s

	1980 Population[a]	1990 Population[a]	% change	1982 to 1990 seats	1992 to 2000 seats	Seat change in 1990s
Ala.	3,983,888	4,040,587	3.8	7	7	0
Alaska	401,851	550,043	36.9	1	1	0
Ariz.	2,718,215	3,665,228	34.8	5	6	+1
Ark.	2,286,435	2,350,725	2.8	4	4	0
Calif.	23,667,902	29,760,021	25.7	45	52	+7
Colo.	2,889,964	3,294,394	14.0	6	6	0
Conn.	3,107,576	3,287,116	5.8	6	6	0
Del.	594,338	666,168	12.1	1	1	0
D.C.[b]	638,333	606,900	–4.9	—	—	—
Fla.	9,746,324	12,937,926	32.7	19	23	+4
Ga.	5,463,105	6,478,216	18.6	10	11	+1
Hawaii	964,691	1,108,229	14.9	2	2	0
Idaho	943,935	1,006,749	6.7	2	2	0
Ill.	11,426,518	11,430,602	—	22	20	–2
Ind.	5,490,224	5,544,159	1.0	10	10	0
Iowa	2,913,808	2,776,755	–4.7	6	5	–1
Kan.	2,363,679	2,477,574	4.8	5	4	–1
Ky.	3,660,777	3,685,296	0.8	7	6	–1
La.	4,205,900	4,219,973	0.3	8	7	–1
Maine	1,124,660	1,227,928	9.2	2	2	0
Md.	4,216,975	4,781,468	13.4	8	8	0
Mass.	5,737,037	6,016,425	4.9	11	10	–1
Mich.	9,262,078	9,295,297	0.4	18	16	–2
Minn.	4,075,970	4,375,099	7.3	8	8	0
Miss.	2,520,638	2,573,216	2.1	5	5	0
Mo.	4,916,686	5,117,073	4.1	9	9	0
Mont.	786,690	799,065	1.6	2	1	–1
Neb.	1,569,825	1,578,385	0.5	3	3	0
Nev.	800,493	1,201,833	50.1	2	2	0
N.H.	920,610	1,109,252	20.5	2	2	0
N.J.	7,364,823	7,730,188	5.0	14	13	–1
N.M.	1,302,894	1,515,069	16.3	3	3	0
N.Y.	17,558,072	17,990,455	2.5	34	31	–3
N.C.	5,881,766	6,628,637	12.7	11	12	+1
N.D.	652,717	638,800	–2.1	1	1	0
Ohio	10,797,630	10,847,115	0.5	21	19	–2
Okla.	3,025,290	3,145,585	4.0	6	6	0
Ore.	2,633,105	2,842,321	7.9	5	5	0
Pa.	11,863,895	11,881,632	0.1	23	21	–2
R.I.	947,154	1,003,464	5.9	2	2	0
S.C.	3,121,820	3,486,703	11.7	6	6	0
S.D.	690,768	696,004	0.8	1	1	0
Tenn.	4,591,120	4,877,185	6.2	9	9	0
Texas	14,229,191	16,986,510	19.4	27	30	+3
Utah	1,461,037	1,722,850	17.9	3	3	0
Vt.	511,456	562,758	10.0	1	1	0
Va.	5,346,818	6,187,358	15.7	10	11	+1
Wash.	4,132,156	4,866,692	17.8	8	9	+1
W.Va.	1,949,644	1,793,477	–8.0	4	3	–1
Wis.	4,705,767	4,891,769	4.0	9	9	0
Wyo.	469,557	453,588	–3.4	1	1	0
U.S.[c]	226,545,805	248,709,873	9.8	435	435	19

NOTES: a. For comparative purposes, the 1980 and 1990 figures do not include citizens living overseas.   b. The District of Columbia, which has one nonvoting delegate to the House, is not included in determination of apportionment.   c. Total population for 1980 and 1990 includes the District of Columbia.

Early in the 67th Congress, the House Census Committee again reported a bill, this time fixing the total membership at 460, an increase of 25. Two states—Maine and Massachusetts—would have lost one representative each, and sixteen states would have gained seats. On the House floor an unsuccessful attempt was made to fix the number at the existing 435, and the House sent the bill back to committee.

During the 68th Congress (1923–1925), the House Census Committee failed to report any reapportionment bill. In April 1926, midway through the 69th Congress (1925–1927), it became apparent that the committee would not produce a reapportionment measure. A motion to discharge a reapportionment bill from the committee failed, however, and the matter once again was put aside.

Coolidge Intervention

President Calvin Coolidge, who previously had made no reference to reapportionment in his communications to Congress, announced in January 1927 that he favored passage of a new apportionment bill during the short session of the 69th Congress, which would end in less than two months. The House Census Committee refused to act. Its chairman, Rep. E. Hart Fenn, R-Conn., therefore moved in the House to suspend the rules and pass a bill he had introduced authorizing the secretary of commerce to reapportion the House immediately after the 1930 census. The motion was voted down 183–197.

The Fenn bill was rewritten early in the 70th Congress (1927–1929) to give Congress itself a chance to act before the proposed reapportionment by the secretary of commerce should go into effect. The House passed an amended version of the Fenn bill in January 1929, and it was quickly reported by the Senate Commerce Committee. Repeated efforts to bring it up for floor action ahead of other bills failed. Its supporters gave up the fight when it became evident that senators from states slated to lose representation were ready to carry on a filibuster that would have blocked not only reapportionment but all other measures.

Hoover Intervention

President Herbert Hoover listed provision for the 1930 census and reapportionment as "matters of emergency legislation" that should be acted upon in the special session of the 71st Congress, which was convened on April 15, 1929. In response to this urgent request, the Senate on June 13 passed, 48–37, a combined census-reapportionment bill that had been approved by voice vote of the House two days earlier.

The 1929 law established a permanent system of reapportioning the 435 House seats following each census. It provided that immediately after the convening of the 71st Congress for its short session in December 1930, the president was to transmit to Congress a statement showing the population of each state together with an apportionment of representatives to each state based on the existing size of the House. Failing enactment of new apportionment legislation, that apportionment would go into effect without further action and would remain in effect for ensuing elections to the House of Representatives until another census had been taken and another reapportionment made.

Because two decades had passed between reapportionments, a greater shift than usual took place following the 1930 census. California's House delegation was almost doubled, rising from eleven to twenty. Michigan gained four seats, Texas three, and New Jersey, New York, and Ohio two each. Twenty-one states lost a total of twenty-seven seats; Missouri lost three, and Georgia, Iowa, Kentucky, and Pennsylvania each lost two.

To test the fairness of two allocation methods—the familiar major fractions and the new equal proportions system—the 1929 act required the president to report the distribution of seats by both methods. But, pending legislation to the contrary, the method of major fractions was to be used.

The two methods gave an identical distribution of seats based on 1930 census figures. However, in 1940 the two methods gave different results: under major fractions, Michigan would gain a seat lost by Arkansas; under equal proportions, no change would occur in either state. The automatic reapportionment provisions of the 1929 act went into effect in January 1941. But

the House Census Committee moved to reverse the result, favoring the method of equal proportions and the certain Democratic seat in Arkansas over a possible Republican gain if the seat were shifted to Michigan. The Democratic-controlled Congress went along, adopting equal proportions as the method to be used in reapportionment calculations after the 1950 and subsequent censuses, and making this action retroactive to January 1941 to save Arkansas its seat.

While politics doubtless played a part in the timing of the action taken in 1941, the method of equal proportions had come to be accepted as the best available: It had been worked out by Edward V. Huntington of Harvard in 1921. At the request of the Speaker of the House, all known methods of apportionment were considered in 1929 by the National Academy of Sciences Committee on Apportionment. The committee expressed its preference for equal proportions.

METHOD OF EQUAL PROPORTIONS

The method of equal proportions involves complicated mathematical calculations. In brief, each of the fifty states is ini-

Figure 33–1   1990 Reapportionment: Gainers and Losers

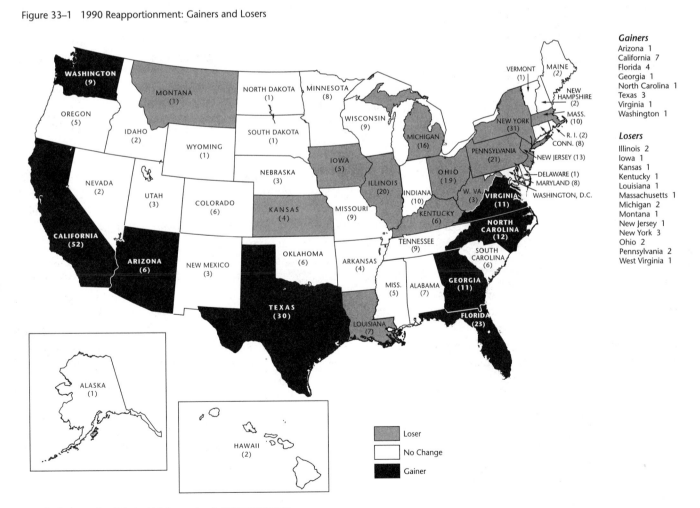

Note: Number in parentheses indicates state's House seats under 1990 reapportionment.

tially assigned the one seat to which it is entitled by the Constitution. Then "priority numbers" for states to receive second seats, third seats, and so on are calculated by dividing the state's population by the square root of n(n-1), where "n" is the number of seats for that state. The priority numbers are then lined up in order and the seats given to the states with priority numbers until 435 are awarded.

The method is designed to make the proportional difference in the average district size in any two states as small as possible. After the 1981 reapportionment, for example, South Dakota's single district was the most populous, with 690,768 residents, while Montana's two districts, each with slightly fewer than 400,000 people, were the least populous. Under the 1990 apportionment, Montana lost a seat; its remaining district was the most populous, with 803,655 residents. With 455,975 people, Wyoming's single district was the least populous. The mean population per district nationwide was about 572,500.

QUESTIONING THE COUNT IN THE 1980S AND 1990S

While the method of equal proportions came to accepted as the best way to apportion House seats among the states, the 1980s and 1990s brought heated debate over a more fundamental issue: the accuracy of the census itself.

Members of Congress as well as state and local officials have a keen interest in an accurate population count. In addition to being the basis for reapportionment and redistricting, the census also is used to determine the allocation of funding for many federal aid programs.

Concern about the census "undercount" grew after 1980, when the Census Bureau estimated that it counted about 99 percent of the white population but only about 94 percent of the blacks. Democrats, especially those representing inner-city districts where the undercount was comparatively high, argued unsuccessfully for a statistical adjustment to compensate for undercounting.

The controversy over the 1990 count began even before the census was taken, when the Commerce Department, the parent agency to the Census Bureau, announced in 1987 that it would not statistically adjust the 1990 data. New York City, along with other cities, states, and civil rights organizations, pressed a case in court to force the Census Bureau to make a statistical adjustment to account for people who were missed, including sizable numbers of blacks, Hispanics, and Native Americans. In 1996 the Supreme Court rejected adjusting the census.

But by then, the White House had passed from Republican to Democratic hands, and Commerce Department officials were laying plans to have the Census Bureau use statistical sampling techniques that they said would enhance the accuracy of the 2000 census. The Republican majority in Congress gave statistical sampling a cold eye, worrying that it might lead to politically motivated manipulating of the census. (*See box, How Should the Census Count the Population? p. 904.*)

Redistricting: Drawing the Lines

Although the Constitution contained provisions for the apportionment of U.S. House seats among the states, it was silent about how the members should be elected. From the beginning most states divided their territory into geographic districts, permitting only one member of Congress to be elected from each district.

But some states allowed would-be House members to run at large, with voters able to cast as many votes as there were seats to be filled. Still other states created what were known as multimember districts, in which a single geographic unit would elect two or more members of the House. At various times, some states used combinations of these methods. For example, a state might elect ten representatives from ten individual districts and two at large.

In the first few elections to the House, New Hampshire, Pennsylvania, New Jersey, and Georgia elected their representatives at large, as did Rhode Island and Delaware, the two states with only a single representative. Districts were used in Massachusetts, New York, Maryland, Virginia, and South Carolina. In Connecticut a preliminary election was held to nominate three times as many people as the number of representatives to be chosen at large in the subsequent election. In 1840 twenty-two of the thirty-one states elected their representatives by districts. New Hampshire, New Jersey, Georgia, Alabama, Mississippi, and Missouri, with a combined representation of thirty-three House seats, elected their representatives at large. Three states, Arkansas, Delaware, and Florida, had only one representative each.

Those states that used congressional districts quickly developed what came to be known as the gerrymander. The term refers to the practice of drawing district lines so as to maximize the advantage of a political party or interest group. The name originated from a salamander-shaped congressional district created by the Massachusetts Legislature in 1812 when Elbridge Gerry was governor. (*See box, Origins of Gerrymander, p. 901.*)

Constant efforts were made during the early 1800s to lay down national rules, by means of a constitutional amendment, for congressional districting. The first resolution proposing a mandatory division of each state into districts was introduced in Congress in 1800. In 1802 the legislatures of Vermont and North Carolina adopted resolutions in support of such action. From 1816 to 1826 twenty-two states adopted resolutions proposing the election of representatives by districts.

In Congress Sen. Mahlon Dickerson, R-N.J., proposed such an amendment regularly almost every year from 1817 to 1826. It was adopted by the Senate three times, in 1819, 1820, and 1822, but each time it failed to reach a vote in the House. Although the constitutional amendment was unsuccessful, a law passed in 1842 required contiguous single-member congressional districts. That law required representatives to be "elected by districts composed of contiguous territory equal in number to the representatives to which said state may be entitled, no one district electing more than one Representative."

The districting provisions of the 1842 act were not repeated in the legislation that followed the 1850 census. But in 1862 an act separate from the reapportionment act revived the provisions of the act of 1842 requiring districts to be composed of contiguous territory.

The 1872 reapportionment act again repeated the districting provisions and went even further by adding that districts should contain "as nearly as practicable an equal number of inhabitants." Similar provisions were included in the acts of 1881 and 1891. In the act of 1901, the words "compact territory" were added, and the clause then read "contiguous and compact territory and containing as nearly as practicable an equal number of inhabitants." This requirement appeared also in the legislation of 1911. The "contiguous and compact" provisions of the act subsequently lapsed, and Congress has never replaced them.

Several unsuccessful attempts were made to enforce redistricting provisions. Despite the districting requirements enacted in 1842, New Hampshire, Georgia, Mississippi, and Missouri elected their representatives at large that autumn. When the new House convened for its first session, on December 4, 1843, objection was made to seating the representatives of the four states.

The House debated the matter in February 1844. With the Democratic Party holding a majority of more than sixty, and with eighteen of the twenty-one challenged members being Democrats, the House decided to seat the members. However, by 1848 all four states had come around to electing their representatives by districts.

The next challenge a representative encountered over federal districting laws occurred in 1901. A charge was leveled that the existing Kentucky redistricting law did not comply with the reapportionment law of 1901; the charge aimed at preventing the seating of Rep. George G. Gilbert, D, of Kentucky's Eighth District. The committee assigned to investigate the matter turned aside the challenge, asserting that the federal act was not binding on the states. The reasons given were practical and political:

Your committee are therefore of opinion that a proper construction of the Constitution does not warrant the conclusion that by that instrument Congress is clothed with power to determine the boundaries of Congressional districts, or to revise the acts of a State Legislature in fixing such boundaries; and your committee is further of opinion that even if such power is to be implied from the language of the Constitution, it would be in the last degree unwise and intolerable that it should exercise it. To do so would be to put into the hands of Congress the ability to disfranchise, in effect, a large body of the electors. It would give Congress the power to apply to all the States, in favor of one party, a general system of gerrymandering. It is true that the same method is to a large degree resorted to by the several states, but the division of political power is so general and diverse that notwithstanding the inherent vice of the system of gerrymandering, some kind of equality of distribution results.[12]

ORIGINS OF THE GERRYMANDER

The practice of "gerrymandering"—the excessive manipulation of the shape of a legislative district to benefit certain persons or groups—is probably as old as the Republic, but the name originated in 1812.

In that year the Massachusetts Legislature carved out of Essex County a district which historian John Fiske said had a "dragonlike contour." When the painter Gilbert Stuart saw the misshapen district, he penciled in a head, wings, and claws and exclaimed: "That will do for a salamander!"—to which editor Benjamin Russell replied: "Better say a Gerrymander"—after Elbridge Gerry, then governor of Massachusetts.

By the 1990s the term had broadened to include the modern-day practice of drawing maps to benefit racial and ethnic groups. In the past the term was applied largely to districts drawn to benefit incumbents or political parties.

In 1908 the Virginia Legislature transferred Floyd County from the Fifth District to the Sixth District. As a result, the population of the Fifth was reduced from 175,579 to 160,191 and that of the Sixth was increased from 181,571 to 196,959. The average for the state was 185,418. The newly elected representative from the Fifth District, Edward W. Saunders, D, was challenged by his opponent in the election on the ground that the Virginia law of 1908 was null and void because it did not conform with the federal reapportionment law of 1901, or with the constitution of Virginia. Had the district included the counties that were a part of it before enactment of the 1908 state legislation, Saunders's opponent would have had a majority of the votes.

The majority of the congressional investigating committee upheld the challenge and recommended that Saunders's opponent be seated. For the first time, it appeared that the districting legislation would be enforced, but the House did not take action on the committee's report and Saunders was seated.

COURT ACTION ON REDISTRICTING

After the long and desultory battle over reapportionment in the 1920s, those who were unhappy over the inaction of Congress and the state legislatures began taking their cases to court. At first, the protesters had no luck. But as the population disparities grew in both federal and state legislative districts and the Supreme Court began to show a tendency to intervene, the objectors were more successful.

Finally, in a series of decisions beginning in 1962 with *Baker v. Carr* the Court exerted great influence over the redistricting process, ordering that congressional districts as well as state and local legislative districts be drawn so that their populations would be as nearly equal as possible.[13]

Supreme Court's 1932 Decision

Baker v. Carr essentially reversed the direction the Court had taken in 1932. *Wood v. Broom* was a case challenging the constitutionality of a Mississippi redistricting law because it violated the standards of the 1911 federal redistricting act. The question was whether the federal act was still in effect. That law, which required that districts be separate, compact, contiguous, and equally populated, had been neither specifically repealed nor reaffirmed in the 1929 reapportionment act.

Speaking for the Court, Chief Justice Charles Evans Hughes ruled that the 1911 act, in effect, had expired with the approval of the 1929 apportionment act and that the standards of the 1911 act therefore were no longer applicable. The Court reversed the decision of a lower federal court, which had permanently enjoined elections under the new Mississippi redistricting act.

That the Supreme Court upheld a state law that failed to provide for districts of equal population was almost less important than the minority opinion that the Court should not have heard the case. Justices Louis D. Brandeis, Harlan F. Stone, Owen J. Roberts, and Benjamin N. Cardozo, while concurring in the majority opinion, said they would have dismissed the *Wood* case for "want of equity." The "want-of-equity" phrase in this context suggested a policy of judicial self-limitation with respect to the entire question of judicial involvement in essentially "political" questions.

"Political Thicket"

Not until 1946, in *Colegrove v. Green*, did the Court again rule in a significant case dealing with congressional redistricting. The case was brought by Kenneth Colegrove, a political science professor at Northwestern University, who alleged that congressional districts in Illinois, which varied between 112,116 and 914,053 in population, were so unequal that they violated the Fourteenth Amendment's guarantee of equal protection of the laws. A seven-member Supreme Court divided 4–3 in dismissing the suit.

Justice Felix Frankfurter gave the opinion of the Court, speaking for himself and Justices Stanley F. Reed and Harold H. Burton. Frankfurter's opinion cited *Wood v. Broom* to indicate that Congress had deliberately removed the standard set by the 1911 act. He also said that he, Reed, and Burton agreed with the minority that the Court should have dismissed the case. The issue, Frankfurter said, was of

a peculiarly political nature and therefore not meant for judicial interpretation. . . . The short of it is that the Constitution has conferred upon Congress exclusive authority to secure fair representation by the states in the popular House and has left to that House determination whether states have fulfilled their responsibility. If Congress failed in exercising its powers, whereby standards of fairness are offended, the remedy lies ultimately with the people. . . . To sustain this action would cut very deep into the very being of Congress. Courts ought not to enter this political thicket. The remedy for unfairness in districting is to secure state legislatures that will apportion properly, or to invoke the ample powers of Congress.

Frankfurter also said that the Court could not affirmatively remap congressional districts and that elections at large would be politically undesirable.

In a dissenting opinion Justice Hugo L. Black, joined by Justices William O. Douglas and Frank Murphy, maintained that the district court did have jurisdiction over congressional redistricting. The three justices cited as evidence a section of the U.S. Code that allowed district courts to redress deprivations of constitutional rights occurring through action of the states. Black's opinion also rested on an earlier case in which the Court had indicated that federal constitutional questions, unless "frivolous," fall under the jurisdiction of the federal courts. Black asserted that the appellants had standing to sue and that the population disparities violated the equal protection clause of the Fourteenth Amendment.

With the Court split 3–3 on whether the judiciary had or should exercise jurisdiction, Justice Wiley B. Rutledge cast the deciding vote in *Colegrove v. Green*. On the question of justiciability, Rutledge agreed with Black, Douglas, and Murphy that the issue could be considered by the federal courts. Thus a majority of the Court participating in the *Colegrove* case felt that congressional redistricting cases were justiciable.

Yet on the question of granting relief in this specific instance, Rutledge agreed with Frankfurter, Reed, and Burton that the case should be dismissed. He pointed out that four of the nine justices in *Wood v. Broom* had felt that dismissal should be for want of equity. Rutledge saw a "want-of-equity" situation in *Colegrove v. Green* as well. "I think the gravity of the constitutional questions raised [are] so great, together with the possibility of collision [with the political departments of the government], that the admonition [against avoidable constitutional decision] is appropriate to be followed here," Rutledge said. Jurisdiction, he thought, should be exercised "only in the most compelling circumstances." He thought that "the shortness of time remaining [before the forthcoming election] makes it doubtful whether action could or would be taken in time to secure for petitioners the effective relief they seek." Rutledge

GERRYMANDERING: THE SHAPE OF THE HOUSE

There are basically three types of gerrymanders. One is the partisan gerrymander, where a single party draws the lines to its advantage. Another is the proincumbent (sometimes called the "bipartisan" or "sweetheart") gerrymander, where the lines are drawn to protect incumbents, with any gains or losses in the number of seats shared between the two parties. In states where control of the state government is divided, proincumbent gerrymanders are common.

A third form of gerrymandering is race-based, where lines are drawn to favor the election of candidates from particular racial or ethnic groups. Initially, racial redistricting referred to the practice of drawing lines to scatter minority voters across several districts, so they would not have a dominant influence in any. But the impact of the 1965 Voting Rights Act and numerous court rulings has resulted in a new version of racial gerrymandering: designing constituencies to concentrate minority voters. These majority-minority districts are more likely to elect a minority candidate.

Sweetheart gerrymandering rarely attracts much attention. But this method of mapping has a powerful effect on the House. "Districts get more Democratic for Democrats and more Republican for Republicans. Competition is minimized," said Bernard Grofman, a political scientist at the University of California at Irvine. Incumbent reelection rates have been high since World War II, in part because a proincumbent spin in much of the line drawing diminishes the prospects for dramatic change in the House's membership.

Still, redistricting at least increases the possibility of turnover, because most states must redraw their districts to accommodate population shifts within the state as well as the gain or loss of any

seats. Typically, some House members choose to retire rather than stand for election in redesigned districts.

Partisan gerrymanders do not always achieve their goals. Indiana Republicans redrew their map in 1981 with the hope that it would turn the Democrats' congressional majority into a 7–3 Republican edge. Instead, by the end of the decade Democrats held a 7–3 advantage.

But without question, gerrymandering during redistricting is an important determinant of which party controls the House. Many political analysts predicted that the 1980 reapportionment would alter the political makeup of the House, because most of the states that lost seats tended to favor liberal Democrats, while the states that gained seats were more likely to favor Republicans or conservative Democrats. But in part because of the Democrats' gerrymandering successes in the state redistricting battles, their party remained in control of the House throughout the 1980s.

In the 1990 reapportionment, the shift of House seats to more conservative areas in the South and West continued, but successful gerrymandering by Democrats helped the party hold its House majority in 1992. Finally in 1994 a broad surge of support for Republican candidates helped the GOP take control of the House. However, the Republican majority shrank in 1996 and 1998. Looking ahead to redistricting after the 2000 census, both parties in the late 1990s began girding for new battles over gerrymandering.

SOURCE: Robert Benenson, Peter Bragdon, Rhodes Cook, Phil Duncan, and Kenneth E. Jaques, *Jigsaw Politics: Shaping the House after the 1990 Census* (Washington, D.C.: Congressional Quarterly, 1990), 38.

---

warned that congressional elections at large would deprive citizens of representation by districts, "which the prevailing policy of Congress demands." In the case of at-large elections, Rutledge said, "the cure sought may be worse than the disease." For all these reasons he concluded that the case was "one in which the Court may properly, and should, decline to exercise its jurisdiction."

Changing Views

In the ensuing years, law professors, political scientists, and other commentators increasingly criticized the *Colegrove* doctrine and grew impatient with the Supreme Court's reluctance to intervene in redistricting disputes. At the same time, the membership of the Court was changing, and the new members were more inclined toward judicial action on redistricting.

In the 1950s the Court decided two cases that laid some groundwork for its subsequent reapportionment decisions. The first was *Brown v. Board of Education*, the historic school desegregation case, in which the Court decided that an individual citizen could assert a right to equal protection of the laws under the Fourteenth Amendment, contrary to the "separate but equal" doctrine of public facilities for white and black citizens.

Six years later, in *Gomillion v. Lightfoot*, the Court held that

the Alabama Legislature could not draw the city limits of Tuskegee so as to exclude nearly every black vote. In his opinion Justice Frankfurter drew a clear line between redistricting challenges based on the Fourteenth Amendment, such as *Colegrove*, and challenges to discriminatory redistricting based on the Fifteenth Amendment's voting rights protections, as in *Gomillion*. But Justice Charles E. Whittaker said that the equal protection clause was the proper constitutional basis for the decision. One commentator later remarked that *Gomillion* amounted to a "dragon" in the "political thicket" of *Colegrove*.

By 1962 only three members of the *Colegrove* Court remained: Justices Black and Douglas, dissenters in that case, and Justice Frankfurter, aging spokesperson for restraint in the exercise of judicial power.

By then it was clear that malapportionment within the states no longer could be ignored. By 1960 not a single state legislative body existed in which there was not at least a 2-to-1 population disparity between the most and the least heavily populated districts. For example, the disparity was 242–1 in the Connecticut House, 223–1 in the Nevada Senate, 141–1 in the Rhode Island Senate, and 9–1 in the Georgia Senate. Studies of the effective vote of large and small counties in state legislatures between 1910 and 1960 showed that the effective vote of the most populous counties had slipped while their percentage of the national population had more than doubled. The most lightly populated counties, on the other hand, advanced from a position of slight overrepresentation to one of extreme overrepresentation, holding almost twice as many seats as they would be entitled to by population size alone. Predictably, the rural-dominated state legislatures resisted every move toward reapportioning state legislative districts to reflect new population patterns.

Population imbalance among congressional districts was substantially lopsided but by no means so gross. In Texas the 1960 census showed the most heavily populated district had four times as many inhabitants as the most lightly populated. Arizona, Maryland, and Ohio each had at least one district with three times as many inhabitants as the least populated. In most cases rural areas benefited from the population imbalance in congressional districts. As a result of the postwar population movement out of central cities to the surrounding areas, the suburbs were the most underrepresented.

Baker v. Carr

Against this background a group of Tennessee city dwellers successfully broke the long-standing precedent against federal court involvement in legislative apportionment problems. For more than half a century, since 1901, the Tennessee Legislature had refused to reapportion itself, even though a decennial reapportionment based on population was specifically required by the state's constitution. In the meantime, Tennessee's population had grown and shifted dramatically to urban areas. By 1960 the House legislative districts ranged from 3,454 to 36,031 in population, while the Senate districts ranged from 39,727 to 108,094. Appeals by urban residents to the rural-controlled Tennessee Legislature proved fruitless. A suit brought in the state courts to force reapportionment was rejected on grounds that the courts should stay out of legislative matters.

City dwellers then appealed to the federal courts, stating that they had no redress: the legislature had refused to act for more than half a century, the state courts had refused to intervene,

HOW SHOULD THE CENSUS COUNT THE POPULATION?

Counting the number of people in the United States has never been as easy as one, two, three, and that is not just because of logistical problems. When it comes to the decennial census, the political stakes are huge, and so is the interest in how the count is conducted. The constitutionally mandated census not only provides crucial information for reapportioning U.S. House seats among the states, but it also supplies the data for drawing district boundaries for state and local public officials and for determining how billions in federal spending is distributed through dozens of grant programs, including Medicaid, educational assistance to poor children, community development block grants, and job training.

Questions about the accuracy of the census are as old as the Republic. A 1998 report issued by the General Accounting Office (GAO) said, "The census has never counted 100 percent of those it should, in part, because American sensibilities would probably not tolerate more foolproof census-taking methods." For instance, the census could be made more precise if people were required to register with the government. But even proposing such a mandate would stir a huge public fuss.

Disputes over the accuracy of the census have intensified since 1911, when Congress fixed the number of representatives at 435. Since then, a gain of representation in any one state can come only at the loss of representation in another. After the 1920 census showed for the first time that the majority of Americans lived in cities, rural interests objected that the farm population had been undercounted. They pressed their case with such tenacity that legislation reapportioning House seats for the 1920s never passed. In 1941 concerns about the accuracy of the census arose when the number of men turning out for the wartime draft was considerably higher than expectations based on the 1940 census.

In the latter years of the twentieth century, there was intense controversy about the census's undercounting of certain groups, espe-

cially minorities. It became more difficult for government census takers to make an accurate population count in crowded inner-city neighborhoods and in some sparsely settled rural areas. The undercount issue became a particular concern for major cities and for the Democrats who tended to represent them. They were in the forefront of an effort to persuade the Census Bureau to use a statistical method to adjust the census for the undercount.

The Census Bureau estimated that it did not count 1.4 percent of the total population in 1980, including roughly 5.9 percent of the nation's blacks. In 1991 Commerce Secretary Robert A. Mosbacher, serving in the administration of Republican president George Bush, said that he would not adjust the 1990 census, even though a post-census survey found that blacks were undercounted by 4.8 percent, Native Americans by 5 percent, and Hispanics by 5.2 percent. Mosbacher said he was "deeply troubled" by the disproportionate undercount of minorities but decided that sticking with the head count would be "fairest for all Americans."

Several states and cities pursued the matter in court, pressing a suit requesting a statistical adjustment of the census to compensate for the undercount. A 1996 Supreme Court ruling went against them.

By then, though, Democrat Bill Clinton was in the White House, and the Census Bureau was laying the groundwork for a 2000 census that bureau officials said would produce a more accurate count by combining traditional head-tallying methods with large-scale use of statistical sampling techniques. Their plan was to count at least 90 percent of the people in each census tract by tabulating surveys returned in the mail and sending census-takers to interview those who did not respond by mail. Then the remaining population would be estimated by statistically extrapolating the demographics of 750,000 randomly selected homes nationwide.

However, this proposal met with fierce resistance in the Republi-

and Tennessee had no referendum or initiative laws. They charged that there was "a debasement of their votes by virtue of the incorrect, obsolete and unconstitutional apportionment" to such an extent that they were being deprived of their right to equal protection of the laws under the Fourteenth Amendment.

The Supreme Court on March 26, 1962, handed down its historic decision in *Baker v. Carr*, ruling 6–2 in favor of the Tennessee city dwellers. In the majority opinion, Justice William J. Brennan Jr. emphasized that the federal judiciary had the power to review the apportionment of state legislatures under the Fourteenth Amendment's equal protection clause. "The mere fact that a suit seeks protection as a political right," Brennan wrote, "does not mean that it presents a political question" that the courts should avoid.

In a vigorous dissent, Justice Frankfurter said the majority decision constituted "a massive repudiation of the experience of our whole past" and was an assertion of "destructively novel judicial power." He contended that the lack of any clear basis for relief "catapults the lower courts" into a "mathematical quagmire." Frankfurter insisted that "there is not under our Constitution a judicial remedy for every political mischief." Appeal for relief, Frankfurter maintained, should not be made in the courts, but "to an informed civically militant electorate."

The Court had abandoned the view that malapportionment questions were outside its competence. But it stopped there and in *Baker v. Carr* did not address the merits of the challenge to the legislative districts, stating only that federal courts had the power to resolve constitutional challenges to maldistribution of voters among districts.

Gray v. Sanders

The one-person, one-vote rule was set out by the Court almost exactly one year after its decision in *Baker v. Carr*. But the case in which the announcement came did not involve congressional districts.

In *Gray v. Sanders* the Court found that Georgia's county-

can-controlled Congress. The GOP majority complained that sampling was unconstitutional and open to political manipulation. "Our Constitution calls for an 'actual enumeration' of citizens, not just an educated guess by Washington bureaucrats," Rep. John A. Boehner, R-Ohio, said. Democrats in Congress retorted that conservatives opposed statistical sampling because they feared it would cost the GOP seats in the House. "They believe not counting certain minorities and the poor is to their political advantage," said Rep. Carolyn B. Maloney, D-N.Y.

With the Republican House and the Democratic White House at a standoff on allowing statistical sampling in the 2000 census, the dispute headed to the courts. When the Supreme Court heard arguments on the case in late 1998, justices expressed reluctance to get involved in what looked essentially like a partisan fight.

In January 1999 in *Department of Commerce v. House of Representatives*, the court issued an equivocal 5–4 ruling that seemed likely to spur further litigation. Pleasing Republicans, the court majority said that amendments to the Census Act added in 1976 forbade "the use of sampling in calculating the population for purposes of apportionment." House Speaker Dennis Hastert, R-Ill., declared, "The administration should abandon its illegal and risky polling scheme and start preparing for a true head count."

But Democrats took some solace in the Court majority's position that the Census Act "required" that sampling be used for other purposes (such as establishing the population formulas used to distribute some federal grant monies) if the Census Bureau and the secretary of Commerce deem it "feasible."

The ruling led the Clinton administration to plot a course to produce two sets of numbers in the 2000 census—a count based on traditional methods to be used for reapportionment, and an adjusted count to be used for distributing federal money and other purposes, possibly including redistricting within the states. That decision drew a harsh response from Republicans in Congress. Rep. Dan Miller, R-Fla., chairman of the House Census Committee, said, "It will absolutely be a disaster if we have a two-number census. . . . If we try to divide the census, we'll have two failed censuses."

ILLEGAL ALIENS

Members of Congress and other public officials also have taken a strong interest in the traditional inclusion of illegal aliens in the census. Some complain that the Census Bureau's effort to count all people living in the United States has unfair political ramifications.

The Fourteenth Amendment states that "representatives shall be apportioned among the several states according to their respective numbers, counting the whole number of persons in each state, excluding Indians not taxed." The Census Bureau has never attempted to exclude illegal aliens from the census—a policy troubling to states that fear losing House seats and clout to states with large numbers of illegal aliens.

The Census Bureau does not have a method for excluding illegal aliens, although it has studied some alternatives. Some supporters of the current policy say that any questions used to separate out illegal aliens could discourage others from responding, thus undermining the accuracy of the census.

OVERSEAS PERSONNEL

For the 1990 census the Commerce Department reversed a long-standing policy and counted military personnel and dependents stationed overseas. "Historically we have not included them because the census is based on the concept of usual residence," said Charles Jones, associate director of the Census Bureau. "People overseas have a 'usual residence' overseas." An exception was made once in 1970 during the Vietnam War. For the purposes of reapportionment, overseas personnel, who in 1990 numbered 923,000, were assigned to the state each individual considered home.

unit primary system for electing state officials—a system that weighted votes to give advantage to rural districts in statewide primary elections—denied voters equal protection of the laws. All votes in a statewide election must have equal weight, the Court held:

> How then can one person be given twice or 10 times the voting power of another person in a statewide election merely because he lives in a rural area or because he lives in the smallest rural county? Once the geographical unit for which a representative is to be chosen is designated, all who participate in the election are to have an equal vote—whatever their race, whatever their sex, whatever their occupation, whatever their income, and wherever their home may be in that geographical unit. This is required by the Equal Protection Clause of the Fourteenth Amendment. The concept of "we the people" under the Constitution visualizes no preferred class of voters but equality among those who meet the basic qualification. The idea that every voter is equal to every other voter in his State, when he casts his ballot in favor of one of several competing candidates, underlies many of our decisions. . . . The conception of political equality from the Declaration of Independence to Lincoln's Gettysburg Address, to the Fifteenth, Seventeenth, and Nineteenth Amendments can mean only one thing—one person, one vote.

The Rule Applied

The Supreme Court's rulings in *Baker and Gray* concerned the equal weighting and counting of votes cast in state elections. In 1964, deciding the case of *Wesberry v. Sanders*, the Court applied the one-person, one-vote principle to congressional districts and set equality as the standard for congressional redistricting.

Shortly after the *Baker* decision was handed down, James P. Wesberry Jr., an Atlanta resident and a member of the Georgia Senate, filed suit in federal court in Atlanta claiming that gross disparity in the population of Georgia's congressional districts violated Fourteenth Amendment rights of equal protection of the laws. At the time, Georgia districts ranged in population from 272,154 in the rural Ninth District in the northeastern part of the state to 823,860 in the Fifth District in Atlanta and its suburbs. District lines had not been changed since 1931. The state's number of House seats remained the same in the interim, but Atlanta's district population—already high in 1931 compared with the others—had more than doubled in thirty years, making a Fifth District vote worth about one-third that of a vote in the Ninth.

In June 1962 the three-judge federal court divided 2–1 in dismissing Wesberry's suit. The majority reasoned that the precedent of *Colegrove* still controlled in congressional district cases. The judges cautioned against federal judicial interference with Congress and against "depriving others of the right to vote" if the suit should result in at-large elections. They suggested that the Georgia Legislature (under court order to reapportion itself) or the U.S. Congress might better provide relief. Wesberry then appealed to the Supreme Court.

On February 17, 1964, the Supreme Court ruled in *Wesberry v. Sanders* that congressional districts must be substantially equal in population. The Court, which upheld Wesberry's challenge by a 6–3 decision, based its ruling on the history and wording of Article I, Section 2, of the Constitution, which states that representatives shall be apportioned among the states according to their respective numbers and be chosen by the people of the several states. This language, the Court stated, meant that "as nearly as is practicable, one man's vote in a congressional election is to be worth as much as another's."

The majority opinion, written by Justice Black and supported by Chief Justice Earl Warren and Justices Brennan, Douglas, Arthur J. Goldberg, and Byron R. White, said: "While it may not be possible to draw congressional districts with mathematical precision, that is no excuse for ignoring our Constitution's plain objective of making equal representation for equal numbers of people the fundamental goal for the House of Representatives."

In a strongly worded dissent, Justice John M. Harlan asserted that the Constitution did not establish population as the only criterion of congressional districting but left the matter to the discretion of the states, subject only to the supervisory power of Congress. "The constitutional right which the Court creates is manufactured out of whole cloth," Harlan concluded.

The *Wesberry* opinion established no precise standards for districting beyond declaring that districts must be as nearly equal in population "as is practicable." In his dissent Harlan suggested that a disparity of more than 100,000 between a state's largest and smallest districts would "presumably" violate the equality standard enunciated by the majority. On that basis, Harlan estimated, the districts of thirty-seven states with 398 representatives would be unconstitutional, "leaving a constitutional House of 37 members now sitting."

Neither did the Court's decision make any reference to gerrymandering, since it discussed only the population, not the shape of districts. In a separate opinion handed down the same day as *Wesberry,* the Court dismissed a challenge to congressional districts in New York City, which had been brought by voters who charged that Manhattan's "silk-stocking" Seventeenth District had been gerrymandered to exclude blacks and Puerto Ricans.

Strict Equality

Five years elapsed between *Wesberry* and the Court's next application of constitutional standards to congressional districting. In 1967 the Court hinted at the strict stance it would adopt two years later. With two unsigned opinions, the Court sent back to Indiana and Missouri for revision those two states' congressional redistricting plans because they allowed variations of as much as 20 percent from the average district population.

Two years later Missouri's revised plan returned to the Court for full review. By a 6–3 vote, the Court rejected the plan. It was unacceptable, the Court held in *Kirkpatrick v. Preisler* (1969), because it allowed a variation of as much as 3.1 percent from perfectly equal population districts. Thus the Court made clear its stringent application of the one-person, one-vote rule to congressional districts.

There was no "fixed numerical or percentage population variance small enough to be considered *de minimis* and to satisfy without question the 'as nearly as practicable' standard," Justice Brennan wrote for the Court. "Equal representation for equal numbers of people is a principle designed to prevent debasement of voting power and diminution of access to elected Representatives. Toleration of even small deviations detracts from these purposes."

The only permissible variances in population, the Court ruled, were those that were unavoidable despite the effort to achieve absolute equality or those that could be legally justified. The variances in Missouri could have been avoided, the Court said.

None of Missouri's arguments for the plan qualified as "legally acceptable" justifications. The Court rejected the argument that population variance was necessary to allow representation of distinct interest groups. It said that acceptance of such variances to produce districts with specific interests was "antithetical" to the basic purpose of equal representation.

Justice White dissented from the majority opinion, which he characterized as "an unduly rigid and unwarranted application of the Equal Protection Clause which will unnecessarily involve the courts in the abrasive task of drawing district lines." White added that some "acceptably small" population variance could be established. He indicated that considerations of existing political boundaries and geographical compactness could justify to him some variation from "absolute equality" of population.

Justice Harlan, joined by Justice Potter Stewart, dissented, saying that "whatever room remained under this Court's prior decisions for the free play of the political process in matters of reapportionment is now all but eliminated by today's Draconian judgments."

PRACTICAL RESULTS

As a result of the Court's decisions of the 1960s, nearly every state was forced to redraw its congressional district lines—sometimes more than once. By the end of the decade, thirty-nine of the forty-five states with more than one representative had made the necessary adjustments.

However, the effect of the one-person, one-vote standard on congressional districts did not bring about immediate population equality in districts. Most of the new districts were far from equal in population, because the only official population figures came from the 1960 census. Massive population shifts during the decade rendered most post-*Wesberry* efforts to achieve equality useless.

But redistricting based on the 1970 census resulted in districts that differed only slightly in population from the state average. Among House members elected in 1972, 385 of 435 represented districts that varied by less than 1 percent from the state average district population.

By contrast, only nine of the districts in the 88th Congress (elected in 1962) deviated less than 1 percent from the state aver-

The national census is conducted every ten years to determine, among other things, how many representatives each state will have in Congress. Here a census taker prepares to collect information in person.

age; eighty-one were between 1 and 5 percent; eighty-seven from 5 to 10 percent; and in 236 districts the deviation was 10 percent or greater. Twenty-two House members were elected at large.

The Supreme Court made only one major ruling concerning congressional districts during the 1970s. In 1973 the Court declared the Texas congressional districts, as redrawn in 1971, unconstitutional because of excessive population variance among districts. The variance between the largest and smallest districts was 4.99 percent. The Court returned the case to a three-judge federal panel, which adopted a new congressional district plan.

Precise Equality

Following the 1980 census, several federal courts accepted or imposed redistricting maps that achieved population equality but were drawn for blatant partisan purposes. In Missouri a federal court accepted the Democrats' remap proposal over the Republican plan because its districts were more nearly equal in population. The Democratic map obtained population equality by dismantling a district in a part of the state where population was growing and preserving a district in inner-city St. Louis that had been losing population. The plan cost one Republican incumbent his seat.

Michigan's map for the 1980s offered an extreme example of fealty to precise population equality. In 1982 a court-imposed redistricting plan created sixteen congressional districts with exactly equal populations—514,560. The state's two other districts each had a population of just one person fewer—514,559. To achieve that equality, however, the line for many districts cut through many small cities and towns, dividing their residents between two or three different districts.

Although maps such as these raised the question whether partisan gerrymandering was also a violation of an individual's voting rights, the Supreme Court in 1983 appeared to make it even more difficult to challenge a redistricting map on grounds other than population deviation. In a 5–4 decision, the Court ruled in *Karcher v. Daggett* that states must adhere as closely as possible to the one-person, one-vote standard and bear the burden of proving that deviations from precise population equality were made in pursuit of a legitimate goal. The decision overturned New Jersey's congressional map because the variation between the most populated and the least populated districts was 0.69 percent.

Brennan, who wrote the Court's opinion in *Baker* and *Kirkpatrick,* also wrote the opinion in *Karcher,* contending that population differences between districts "could have been avoided or significantly reduced with a good-faith effort to achieve population equality."

"Adopting any standard other than population equality, using the best census data available, would subtly erode the Constitution's ideal of equal representation," Brennan wrote. "In this case, appellants argue that a maximum deviation of approximately 0.7 percent should be considered *de minimis.* If we accept that argument, how are we to regard deviations of 0.8 percent, 0.95 percent, 1.0 percent or 1.1 percent? . . . To accept the legitimacy of unjustified, though small population deviations in this case would mean to reject the basic premise of *Kirkpatrick* and *Wesberry.*"

Brennan said that "any number of consistently applied legislative policies might justify" some population variation. These included "making districts compact, respecting municipal boundaries, preserving the cores of prior districts, and avoiding contests between incumbent Representatives." However, he cautioned, the state must show "with some specificity that a particular objective required the specific deviations in its plan, rather than simply relying on general assertions."

In his dissent Justice White criticized the majority for its "unreasonable insistence on an unattainable perfection in the equalizing of congressional districts." He warned that the decision would invite "further litigation of virtually every congressional redistricting plan in the nation."

Partisan Gerrymandering

In *Karcher* the Court did not address the underlying political issue in the New Jersey case, which was that its map had been drawn to serve Democratic interests. As a partisan gerrymander, the map had few peers, boasting some of the most oddly shaped districts in the country. One constituency, known as the "fishhook" by its detractors, twisted through central New Jersey's industrial landscape, picking up Democratic voters along the way. Another stretched from the suburbs of New York to the fringes of Trenton.

In separate dissents Justices Lewis F. Powell Jr., and John Paul Stevens broadly hinted that they were willing to hear constitutional challenges to instances of partisan gerrymandering. "A legislator cannot represent his constituents properly—nor can voters from a fragmented district exercise the ballot intelligently—when a voting district is nothing more than an artificial unit divorced from, and indeed often in conflict with, the various communities established in the State," wrote Powell.

The Court's opportunity to address that issue came in *Davis v. Bandemer.* On June 30, 1986, the Court ruled that political gerrymanders are subject to constitutional review by federal courts, even if the disputed districts meet the one-person, one-vote test. The case arose from a challenge by Indiana Democrats who argued that the Republican-drawn map so heavily favored the Republican Party that Democrats were denied appropriate representation. But the Court rejected the Democrats' challenge to the alleged gerrymander, saying that one election was insufficient to prove unconstitutional discrimination. Left unclear were what standards the Court would use to find a partisan gerrymander legally unacceptable.

National Republicans expressed delight with the *Bandemer* decision. The GOP had long held that Democratic control over most state legislatures had allowed them to draw congressional and legislative districts to their partisan advantage. In particular, Republicans expressed confidence that the *Bandemer* decision lay the groundwork for overturning California's congressional district map, created by Democratic Rep. Phillip Burton in the early 1980s.

Widely recognized as a classic example of a partisan gerrymander, the map featured a number of oddly shaped districts, drawn neither compactly nor with respect to community boundaries, but all with nearly equal populations. As one commentator described it, "Burton carefully stretched districts from one Democratic enclave to another—sometimes joining them with nothing but a bridge, a stretch of harbor, or a spit of land . . .—avoiding Republicans block for block and household for household."[14] Before the 1982 elections, Democrats held twenty-two congressional districts, Republicans twenty-one. With the

Burton map in place for the 1982 elections, Democrats held twenty-eight seats, Republicans only seventeen.

Republican Rep. Robert E. Badham filed a lawsuit against the Burton plan in federal district court in 1983. In the wake of the *Bandemer* decision, that court held a hearing on *Badham v. Eu* but dismissed the Republican complaint by a 2–1 vote. The court in essence ruled that a party seeking to overturn a gerrymandered map must show a general pattern of exclusion from the political process, which the California Republican Party, in control of the governorship, a Senate seat, and 40 percent of the House seats, could not do. The Republicans appealed to the Supreme Court, but the Court refused to become involved, voting 6–3 in 1989 to reaffirm the lower court's decision without comment.

MINORITY REPRESENTATION

One form of gerrymandering is expressly forbidden by law: redistricting for the purpose of racial discrimination. The Voting Rights Act of 1965, extended in 1970, 1975, and 1982, banned redistricting that diluted the voting strength of black communities. Other minorities, including Hispanics, Asian Americans, American Indians, and native Alaskans, subsequently were brought under the protection of the law.

In 1980 the Supreme Court for the first time narrowed the reach of the Voting Rights Act in the case of *Mobile v. Bolden*, a challenge to the at-large system of electing city commissioners used in Mobile, Alabama.[15] By a vote of 6–3, the Court ruled that proof of discriminatory intent by the commissioners was necessary before a violation could be found; the fact that no black had ever been elected under the challenged system was not proof enough.

The *Mobile* decision set off an immediate reaction on Capitol Hill. In extending the Voting Rights Act in 1982, Congress amended it to outlaw any practice that has the effect of discriminating against blacks or other minorities—regardless of the intent of lawmakers.

The Justice Department later adopted a similar "results test" for another part of the act (Section 5), which requires certain states and localities with a history of discrimination to have their electoral plans "precleared" by the department. In 1986 the Supreme Court applied this test in *Thornburg v. Gingles*, ruling that six of North Carolina's multimember legislative districts impermissibly diluted black voting strength. Sharply departing from *Mobile*, the Court held that since very few blacks had been elected from these districts, the system must be in violation of the law.

The Court also used the *Thornburg* decision to develop three criteria that, if met, should lead to the creation of a minority legislative district: the minority group must be large and geographically compact enough to constitute a majority in a single-member electoral district; the group must be politically cohesive; and the white majority must vote as a bloc to the degree that it usually can defeat candidates preferred by the minority.

Thus, within a period of ten years the burden of proof was shifted from minorities, who had been required to show that lines were being drawn to dilute their voting strength, to lawmakers, who had to show that they had done all they could to maximize minority voting strength.

But maps drawn for the 1990s that went to extraordinary lengths to elect minorities came quickly under scrutiny by the Supreme Court. In a 1993 ruling on districts in North Carolina *Shaw v. Reno*, Justice Sandra Day O'Connor wrote for the Court

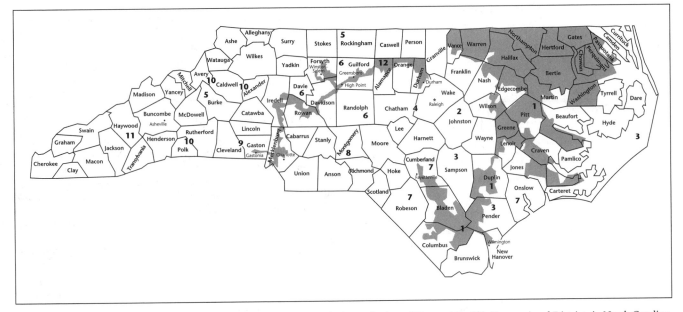

The Supreme Court in 1993 ruled in *Shaw v. Reno* that a lawsuit against the bizarrely shaped First and Twelfth Congressional Districts in North Carolina (shaded on map) could go forward. In the 1990s several districts like these were eventually struck down because they were too heavily reliant on race.

majority that any map that groups people "who may have little in common with one another but the color of their skin bears an uncomfortable resemblance to political apartheid." The ruling reinstated a suit by five white North Carolinians who contended that the state's congressional district map, which created two oddly shaped majority-minority districts, violated their right to "equal protection under law" by diluting their votes.

And in a 1995 case involving districts in Georgia *Miller v. Johnson*, the Court ruled that using race as "the predominant factor" in drawing districts is presumed to be unconstitutional, unless it serves a compelling government interest. The decision struck down a redistricting plan that created three black-majority districts.

Those two rulings represented a speedy swing of the judicial pendulum away from the 1986 Gingles doctrine of maximizing minority voting strength in redistricting. As the 1990s unfolded, the constitutionality of majority-minority districts was widely challenged, and eventually, federal courts ordered a number of states—including North Carolina, Georgia, Florida, Louisiana, New York, Texas, and Virginia—to redraw districts that were adjudged to be unconstitutional racial gerrymanders.

But the Supreme Court did not make sweeping determinations affecting all majority-minority districts. In Illinois, a majority-minority district was allowed to stand after the state argued successfully that it had a "compelling state interest" in giving Chicago's large Hispanic population the opportunity to elect one representative of its own. And in a 1999 North Carolina case *Hunt v. Cromartie*, the Court unanimously ruled that mapmakers could create a district with a "supermajority" of black Democrats as long as the primary reason for doing so was political rather than racial.

Even though numerous majority-minority districts were redrawn in the mid- and late 1990s to reduce minority populations, nearly all those districts retained members of minority groups as their representatives by the end of the twentieth century.

CONGRESS AND REDISTRICTING

Congress considered several proposals in the post–World War II period to enact new legislation on redistricting. Only one of these efforts was successful—enactment of a measure barring at-large elections in states with more than one House seat.

In January 1951 President Harry S. Truman asked for a ban on gerrymandering, an end to at-large seats in states having more than one representative, and a sharp reduction in the huge differences in size among congressional districts within most states. On behalf of the administration, Emanuel Celler, D-N.Y., chairman of the House Judiciary Committee, introduced a bill reflecting these requests, but the committee took no action.

Celler regularly introduced his bill throughout the 1950s and early 1960s, but it made no headway until the Supreme Court handed down the *Wesberry* decision in 1964. The House passed a version of the Celler bill in 1965, largely to discourage the

Supreme Court from imposing even more rigid criteria. The Senate, however, took no action and the measure died.

In 1967, after defeating a conference report that would have prevented the courts from ordering a state to redistrict or to hold at-large elections until after the 1970 census, Congress approved a measure to ban at-large elections in all states entitled to more than one representative. Exceptions were made for New Mexico and Hawaii, which had a tradition of electing their representatives at large. Both states, however, soon passed districting laws, New Mexico for the 1968 elections and Hawaii for 1970.

Bills to increase the size of the House to prevent states from losing seats as a result of population shifts have been introduced after most recent censuses, but Congress has given little consideration to any of them.

NOTES

1. Ronald D. Elving, "Redistricting: Drawing Power with a Map," *Editorial Research Reports,* February 15, 1991, 99.

2. Robert Luce, *Legislative Principles* (New York: Houghton Mifflin, 1930; New York: DaCapo Press, 1971), 342.

3. Thomas Jefferson, *The Portable Thomas Jefferson,* ed. Merrill D. Peterson, part 3, *Notes on the State of Virginia* (New York: Viking, 1965), 163.

4. Andrew Hacker, *Congressional Districting: The Issue of Equal Representation,* rev. ed. (Washington, D.C.: Brookings Institution, 1964), 6–7.

5. Max Farrand, ed., *The Records of the Federal Convention of 1787* (New Haven, Conn.: Yale University Press, 1911, 1966), vol. 2, 241.

6. *The Federalist Papers,* with an introduction by Clinton Rossiter (New York: New American Library, 1961), 347–48, 354.

7. Quoted in Laurence F. Schmeckebier, *Congressional Apportionment* (Washington, D.C.: Brookings Institution, 1941), 131.

8. Hacker, *Congressional Districting,* 14.

9. Quoted in Schmeckebier, *Congressional Apportionment,* 113.

10. Zechariah Chafee, "Congressional Reapportionment," *Harvard Law Review* (1929): 1015–1047.

11. Jefferson, *Notes on the State of Virginia,* 217.

12. Schmeckebier, *Congressional Reapportionment,* 137.

13. The following summary is based on *Congressional Quarterly's Guide to the U.S. Supreme Court,* 2nd ed. (Washington, D.C.: Congressional Quarterly, 1990), 483–493.

14. Elving, "Redistricting," 107.

15. The discussion of minority representation is based on Rhodes Cook, "Map-Drawers Must Toe the Line in Upcoming Redistricting," *Congressional Quarterly Weekly Report,* September 1, 1990, 2786–2793.

SELECTED BIBLIOGRAPHY

Baker, Gordon E. *The Reapportionment Revolution: Representation, Political Power, and the Supreme Court.* New York: Random House, 1966.

Benenson, Robert, et al. *Jigsaw Politics: Shaping the House after the 1990 Census.* Washington, D.C.: Congressional Quarterly, 1990.

Butler, David, and Bruce Cain. *Congressional Redistricting: Comparative and Theoretical Perspectives.* New York: Macmillan, 1992.

Cortner, Richard C. *The Apportionment Cases.* Knoxville: University of Tennessee Press, 1970.

Davidson, Chandler, ed. *Minority Vote Dilution.* Washington, D.C.: Howard University Press, 1984.

DeGrazia, Alfred. *Essay on Apportionment and Representative Government.* Washington, D.C.: American Enterprise Institute, 1963. Reprint. Westport, Conn.: Greenwood Press, 1983.

Ehrenhalt, Alan. "Reapportionment and Redistricting." In *The American Elections of 1982,* edited by Thomas E. Mann and Norman J. Ornstein. Washington, D.C.: American Enterprise Institute, 1983.

Farrand, Max, ed. *The Records of the Federal Convention of 1787.* 4 vols. New Haven, Conn.: Yale University Press, 1973.

Grofman, Bernard, ed. *Race and Redistricting in the 1990s.* New York: Agathon Press, 1998.

Hacker, Andrew. *Congressional Districting: The Issue of Equal Representation.* Rev. ed. Washington, D.C.: Brookings Institution, 1964.

Hamilton, Alexander, James Madison, and John Jay. *The Federalist Papers.* Introduction by Clinton Rossiter. New York: New American Library, 1961.

Hamilton, Howard D. *Legislative Apportionment: Key to Power.* New York: Harper and Row, 1964.

Hanson, Royce. *The Political Thicket: Reapportionment and Constitutional Democracy.* Englewood Cliffs, N.J.: Prentice-Hall, 1966.

Herrnson, Paul S. *Congressional Elections: Campaigning at Home and in Washington.* 2nd ed. Washington, D.C.: CQ Press, 1998.

Hinckley, Barbara. *Congressional Elections.* Washington, D.C.: CQ Press, 1981.

Krousser, J. Morgan. *Colorblind Justice: Minority Voting Rights and the Undoing of the Second Reconstruction.* Chapel Hill: University of North Carolina Press, 1999.

Luce, Robert. *Legislative Principles.* Boston: Houghton Mifflin, 1930. Reprint. New York: Da Capo Press, 1971.

Parker, Frank R. *Black Votes Count: Political Empowerment in Mississippi after 1965.* Chapel Hill: University of North Carolina Press, 1990.

Rush, Mark. *Does Redistricting Make a Difference? Partisan Representation and Electoral Behavior.* Baltimore: Johns Hopkins University Press, 1993.

Scher, Richard K., Jon L. Mills, and John J. Hotaling. *Voting Rights and Democracy: The Law and Politics of Districting.* Chicago: Nelson-Hall, 1997.

Schmeckebier, Laurence F. *Congressional Apportionment.* Washington, D.C.: Brookings Institution, 1941. Reprint. Westport, Conn.: Greenwood Press, 1976.

Schubert, Glendon, ed. *Reapportionment.* New York: Scribner, 1965.

Schwab, Larry M. *The Impact of Congressional Reapportionment and Redistricting.* Lanham, Md.: University Press of America, 1988.

Thernstrom, Abigail M. *Whose Votes Count? Affirmative Action and Minority Voting Rights.* Cambridge: Harvard University Press, 1987.

PART VIII

Qualifications and Conduct

Closed-door meeting of the House ethics committee.

CHAPTER 34

Seating and Disciplining Members

A NUMBER OF ethical controversies involving members of Congress closed out the twentieth century, culminating in the first-ever reprimand of a sitting Speaker of the House of Representatives. A mixture of heightened public awareness, tighter rules regarding the conduct of members of Congress, and increased scrutiny by the press resulted in the 1990s in the punishment of members who had played too close to the edge. Some members who came under scrutiny for behavior that in the not-so-distant past was overlooked or was considered acceptable remained defiant in the face of the situation in which they found themselves.

In an investigation that became known as the Keating Five, five prominent senators were accused of improperly intervening with federal regulators in behalf of a savings and loan, whose president had made generous contributions to their reelection campaigns. At issue was whether a connection existed between government favoritism and campaign contributions.

In the end, only one of the five—Alan Cranston, D-Calif.— faced disciplinary action. The Senate Ethics Committee in 1991 reprimanded him for conduct that veered too close to a quid pro quo. While Cranston expressed some regret over his actions, he refused to admit any wrongdoing. Cranston said, "I now realize that what I did looked improper. But I differ, and I differ very, very deeply, with the committee's statement . . . that my conduct violated established norms of behavior in the Senate." He compared the Ethics Committee with a "tyrant king" for deciding ex post facto that any such norms existed. And he said he could produce "example after example of comparable" conduct among his colleagues.

Members looking for a lesson from the Keating Five case likely were left unsatisfied. The Senate's ethics watchdogs said that they could not define improper conduct. The committee could only advise members to be careful when helping constituents and raising money.

The Senate in 1991 felt the anger and frustration of women across America in response to its handling of allegations of sexual harassment lodged against Supreme Court nominee Clarence Thomas. As a result, when numerous female staff members and campaign workers accused Sen. Bob Packwood, R-Ore., of sexual misconduct, the charges were taken seriously by the chamber. The Senate Ethics Committee began an inquiry soon after the *Washington Post* published the allegations in 1992. It was the first time the panel was publicly known to have undertaken a sexual harassment investigation.

Packwood announced his intention to resign from the Senate one day after the Ethics Committee unanimously adopted a resolution calling for his expulsion. However, he had fought the charges for years and left the Senate maintaining that he was guilty of no more than "overeager kissing," despite evidence to the contrary. Many members, particularly women senators, saw the committee's actions as reflecting a heightened sensitivity in the society as a whole about sexual conduct in the workplace.

The highest-profile congressional ethics case in the 1990s involved House Speaker Newt Gingrich, R-Ga. In a state of turmoil, the House in 1997 voted to reprimand and fine Gingrich. After years of saying no truth existed to the charges and implying that he was the victim of Democratic political machinations, Gingrich admitted that he improperly managed the financing of his political activities through charitable foundations. Gingrich also acknowledged giving the House Committee on Standards of Official Conduct (ethics committee) misleading information regarding its investigation into his activities. However, he publicly blamed his lawyer for the error. Seventeen days after he made his confession and two weeks before he was reprimanded, Gingrich was reelected Speaker by House Republicans.

As the millennium approached, the debate continued over what constituted fitness to serve as senators and representatives.

Constitutional Power to Punish Members

In dealing with disciplinary cases, the Senate exercises its sole authority to seat, unseat, and punish its own members. Likewise, under the Constitution, only the House had the right to penalize errant representatives. While members of both chambers were subject to prosecution in courts for criminal offenses, they were immune to any kind of prosecution for anything they did or did not do in performance of their legislative actions.

The Constitutional Convention of 1787 bestowed that authority and immunity in keeping with one of its favorite concepts: checks and balances. It put bounds on the seating power by listing certain mandatory qualifications for membership in Congress. And under the balance of power concept, the judicial branch has been called on at various times to interpret the extent of Congress's authority to admit members or expel them for misconduct.

The power of Congress to pass on the fitness of its members

sometimes comes into conflict with the right of voters in each state to decide who shall represent them. Occasionally it is a question of citizenship or competence, but more often such disputes arise over whether the person was duly elected. Although Congress has had to determine the winner in many contested elections, the clear choice of the voters has been rejected, for lack of the requisite qualifications, in fewer than twenty cases since 1789. *(See "Contested Elections," p. 833.)*

Congress also has sparingly used its disciplinary powers. As of mid-1999 the Senate had expelled only fifteen members (including one later rescinded), the House only four. Only nine senators, twenty-one representatives, and one territorial delegate have been formally censured, although lesser punishments have been meted out in some cases.

Congress's authority to judge and punish members rests on two clauses in Article I of the Constitution. The first is clause 1 of Article I, Section 5, which reads in part: "Each House shall be the Judge of the Elections, Returns and Qualifications of its own members." This clause would appear to give each house carte blanche in the validation of elections and the seating of members-elect. However, the election of members of Congress is regulated elsewhere in Article I and in the Seventeenth Amendment, which provides for direct election of senators. In addition, the Constitution specifically lists the qualifications required for membership in Congress.

The second clause on seating, unseating, and punishment of members is clause 2 of Article I, Section 5, reading: "Each House may determine the Rules of its Proceedings, punish its Members for disorderly Behavior, and, with the Concurrence of two thirds, expel a Member." The original draft of this clause did not include the words "with the concurrence of two thirds." When the clause was considered in the Constitutional Convention, August 10, 1787, James Madison of Virginia said that the right of expulsion was "too important to be exercised by a bare majority of a quorum, and in emergencies might be dangerously abused."[1] He proposed requiring a two-thirds vote for expulsion.

Gouverneur Morris of Pennsylvania opposed Madison's proposal. "This power may be safely trusted to a majority," he said. "To require more may produce abuses on the side of the minority. A few men from fractious motives may keep in a member who ought to be expelled." But Edmund Randolph and George Mason of Virginia and Daniel Carroll of Maryland spoke in support, and Madison's two-thirds proposal was adopted by a vote of ten states in favor, one (Pennsylvania) divided, and none opposed.

Pertinent litigation that reached the Supreme Court in the late nineteenth century focused mainly on legalistic questions such as the power of Congress to subpoena witnesses when considering members' qualifications. These suits gave the Court an opportunity to indicate bases for judging qualifications and suggesting the scope of allowed punishments. In the twentieth century, the Court has ruled more directly on what Congress can and cannot do in such cases.

The legality of excluding a member-elect has raised more questions than the right to punish a member already seated. The Supreme Court in 1969 said a state may send to Congress anyone it chooses if that person meets the qualifications in the Constitution and is legally elected. It reversed the House's exclusion of Adam Clayton Powell Jr., because Powell met the basic constitutional requirements. Earlier, in 1926, the Court ruled that William S. Vare of Pennsylvania had not been legally elected to a Senate seat because of corruption in the election campaign. The Court ruling said that exclusion in such a case did not violate a state's rights. *(See "Vare," p. 834; "Powell," p. 921.)*

The Supreme Court in its 1880–1881 term upheld the right of Congress to punish its members. Although the case, *Kilbourn v. Thompson,* directly involved only private persons under investigation by the House, it occurred at a time when the Crédit Mobilier scandal had aroused suspicions of financial misdeeds by several members of the House, including Speaker James G. Blaine, R-Maine.

The scandal moved the Court to go beyond its ruling on private citizen Kilbourn and discuss the power to punish members of Congress. Speaking in the context of calls for punishing members accused of unethical financial involvement in the business under investigation, it said:

• "The Constitution expressly empowers each House to punish its own members for disorderly behavior. We see no reason to doubt that this punishment may in a proper case be imprisonment."

• "Each House is by the Constitution made the judge of the election and qualifications of its members. In deciding on these it has an undoubted right to examine witnesses and inspect papers, subject to the usual rights of witnesses in such cases; and it may be that a witness would be subject to like punishment at

---

CONSTITUTIONAL STANDARDS FOR MEMBERS OF CONGRESS

• Article I, Section 3, clause 3: A senator must be at least thirty years old and have been a citizen of the United States not less than nine years.

• Article I, Section 2, clause 2: A representative must be at least twenty-five years old and have been a citizen not less than seven years.

• Article I, Section 2, clause 2, and Section 3, clause 3: Every member of Congress must be, when elected, an inhabitant of the state that he or she is to represent.

• Article I, Section 6, clause 2: No one may be a member of Congress who holds any other "Office under the United States."

• Fourteenth Amendment, Section 3: No person may be a senator or a representative who, having previously taken an oath as a member of Congress to support the Constitution, has engaged in rebellion against the United States or given aid or comfort to its enemies, unless Congress has removed such disability by a two-thirds vote of both houses.

the hands of the body engaged in trying a contested election, for refusing to testify, that he would if the case were pending before a court of judicature."

In a later case, *In re Chapman,* decided in 1897, the Court reaffirmed the right of Congress to compel testimony on matters within its jurisdiction. It also defined the circumstances under which either chamber might expel one of its members: "The right to expel extends to all cases where the offense is such as in the judgment of the Senate is inconsistent with the trust and duty of a member."

AUTOMATIC EXPULSION

The reference to expulsion in the Court's opinion of 1897 was supplemented in an opinion handed down in 1906 interpreting an act of Congress approved June 11, 1864. The act provided that any senator or representative found guilty of illegally receiving compensation for services provided in connection with a claim, contract, or other proceeding before a government agency "shall . . . be rendered forever thereafter incapable of holding any office . . . under the government of the United States." Sen. Joseph R. Burton, R-Kan., had been convicted under this law. In fighting to keep his seat, Burton's lawyers contended that the 1864 law violated the constitutional right of the Senate to decide on expulsion of its members.

In the Court's decision May 21, 1906, Justice John M. Harlan said that "the final judgment of conviction did not operate, ipso facto, to vacate the seat of the convicted senator nor compel the Senate to expel him or to regard him as expelled by force alone of the judgment" *(Burton v. United States).* On the following day, the Senate asked its Committee on Privileges and Elections to recommend what action, if any, should be taken. Burton resigned on June 4, 1906, before the committee reported.

PRIMARY ELECTION MISCONDUCT

Misconduct by a member-elect provided the next major case for the Supreme Court to rule on congressional power to judge members' qualifications. This case came from the Federal Corrupt Practices Act of June 25, 1910, as amended August 19, 1911. The two laws limited the amount of money that a candidate for Congress could spend on a campaign.

Truman H. Newberry, R-Mich., and sixteen others were found guilty of conspiring to violate the corrupt practices legislation in the Democratic senatorial primary election of August 27, 1918, in Michigan. Newberry's opponent was carmaker Henry Ford. Acting on Newberry's appeal *(Newberry v. United States),* the Supreme Court ruled May 2, 1921, that Congress did not have power to control in any way a state's party primaries or conventions for designating Senate or House candidates.

Twenty years after *Newberry,* the Supreme Court reversed itself on the right of Congress to legislate on primary elections. In a decision issued on May 26, 1941, *United States v. Classic,* the Court said that the power to regulate national elections, assigned by the Constitution to Congress, "includes the authority to regulate primary elections when, as in this case, they are a

step in the exercise by the people of their choice of representatives in Congress."

DENIAL OF REPRESENTATION

The Court did not have to rule until 1929 on whether exclusion of a member-elect by Congress deprives a state, even temporarily, of its right to representation. The issue was before the justices only peripherally, but they decided the matter anyway. The case concerned the November 2, 1926, Senate election of Pennsylvania Republican William Vare, which the Senate had voided because of corruption. The Court, in *Barry et al. v. United States ex rel. Cunningham,* said the Senate had authority "to exclude persons asserting membership who either had not been elected or, what amounts to the same thing, had been elected by resort to fraud, bribery, corruption, or other sinister methods having the effect of vitiating the election."

The Court then went on to the key issue of representation. The justices said that the Article V language guaranteeing equal representation prohibited a state from being deprived of its equal suffrage in the Senate. But, the Court said, this language was "a limitation upon the power of amendment" and did not apply in the Vare situation. "The temporary deprivation of equal representation" from not seating a person while an election controversy is resolved, the Court said, "is the necessary consequence of the exercise of a constitutional power, and no more deprives the state of its 'equal suffrage' in the constitutional sense than would a vote of the Senate vacating the seat of a sitting member or a vote of expulsion."

The Vare case was significant for one other question the Supreme Court answered: whether Congress, in judging election cases, violated the principle of separation of powers by exercising a judicial function. The Court said that, by authorizing Congress to be the judge of its members' qualifications, the Constitution conferred on each house "certain powers which are not legislative but judicial in character," including the power "to render a judgment which is beyond the authority of any other tribunal to review."

BASIC MEMBERSHIP STANDARDS

The Supreme Court in 1969 acknowledged that a chamber could expel a member for misconduct, but it limited the grounds for refusing to seat a member-elect to those specified in the Constitution. The issue arose when the House in 1967 refused to seat New York Democrat Adam Clayton Powell Jr. on the grounds that he had misappropriated public funds. Powell and thirteen voters in his district brought suit against the officers of the House.

The central legal issues in the Powell suit were:

• Could the House add to the Constitution's three qualifications for House membership? Those three standards required the member be at least twenty-five years old, have been a U.S. citizen for at least seven years, and, when elected, be an inhabitant of the state from which he was elected.

• Did the courts have the power to examine the actions of the

House? U.S. District Judge George L. Hart Jr. ruled April 7, 1967, that he had no jurisdiction in the case and dismissed the suit.

The U.S. Court of Appeals for the District of Columbia on February 28, 1968, affirmed Hart's action. The Court of Appeals stated that the case involved a political question, which, if decided, would constitute a violation of the separation of powers and produce an embarrassing confrontation between Congress and the courts.

While the case was before the Supreme Court, the next Congress seated Powell, who had been reelected again in 1968. But the Court decided that even though he had been seated, the issues, including Powell's claim for back pay, required settlement. By a 7–1 vote on June 16, 1969, the Supreme Court reversed the lower court. Chief Justice Earl Warren, delivering the opinion, said the House had improperly excluded Powell because he met the constitutional requirements of age, residence, and citizenship.

On the question of the lower court's jurisdiction, Warren acknowledged that five members of Congress who were defendants (the Speaker of the House, the majority and minority leaders, and the ranking members of the committee that investigated Powell) were immune under the speech or debate clause of the Constitution. However, three other defendants, functionaries of the House who had withheld Powell's pay and denied him such perquisites as an office and staff, were liable for action, the Court said. A claim for back pay was sent back to a lower court, but Powell never pursued the matter. *(See "Powell," p. 921.)*

The Right to a Seat: Subject to Challenge

The Constitution provides in Article VI that senators and representatives "shall be bound by Oath or Affirmation, to support this Constitution."

Congress has enacted laws, adopted rules, and made ad hoc decisions under this provision. It has prescribed the form of the oath and procedures for administering it, and it has grappled with such questions as whether a challenged member-elect should take an oath before the dispute is settled. The ad hoc decisions have gone both ways.

The congressional oath of office was prescribed by an act of June 1, 1789: "I, A B, do solemnly swear (or affirm) that I will support the Constitution of the United States." In the light of Civil War experience, this language was expanded in 1868 to read:

I, A B, do solemnly swear (or affirm) that I will support and defend the Constitution of the United States against all enemies, foreign and domestic; that I will bear true faith and allegiance to the same; that I take this obligation freely, without any mental reservation or purpose of evasion; and that I will well and faithfully discharge the duties of the office on which I am about to enter. So help me God.

Before the first meeting of each Congress, Senate and House officials compile lists of members-elect on the basis of certifica-

tions signed by the state governors and secretaries of state. At the first meeting of each chamber in a new Congress, the presiding officer (the Speaker in the House and the vice president in the Senate) administers the oath orally in the form of a question beginning, "Do you solemnly swear (or affirm). . .?" and the answer by each new member is, "I do." New members chosen between regular elections are sworn in the same way.

A member's right to take the oath and be seated may be challenged by an already seated member or by a private individual or group. A member-elect whose right to a seat is questioned presents himself or herself in the usual way to take the oath. The presiding officer, either on the officer's own authority or, more often, on the basis of a motion, may ask the individual to stand aside while the oath is administered to other members-elect. Sometimes, a member-elect takes the oath without prejudice, and a resolution to investigate the person's right to the seat is introduced later.

A member-elect who has stood aside still may go onto the chamber floor. The House in particular has allowed a challenged member to argue his or her claim to the seat. House Rule XXXII, which lists those who may be "admitted to the Hall of the House," includes "contestants in election cases during the pendency of their cases in the House." The Senate rule on floor access does not mention persons involved in election contests. Traditionally, however, contestants have been present during consideration of their cases.

The House in 1997 took the unusual step of barring a former member from gaining access to the House floor. Robert K. Dornan, R-Calif., a nine-term member, had contested his defeat in the 1996 elections. After Dornan got into a nasty confrontation with Rep. Robert Menendez, D-N.J., about a House Oversight Committee task force probe into the matter, the House voted 289–65 to bar Dornan from the floor until the investigation was completed. While the special investigating committee found evidence of voting problems, it declined to overturn the election, allowing Loretta Sanchez, D-Calif., to retain the seat.

A disputed-seat controversy usually is sent to a committee. Sometimes, a select committee is established for this purpose; at other times, the question is referred to the Senate Rules or House Administration or another standing committee. The committee often holds hearings and usually presents a report and a draft resolution incorporating its recommendations.

Until the Powell case, Congress had acted from time to time as if it were entitled to add qualifications as well as to wink at failure to meet them.

Alexander Hamilton in No. 60 of *The Federalist* wrote: "The qualifications of the persons who may . . . be chosen are defined and fixed in the Constitution, and are unalterable by the legislature."

Later authorities, including a House committee in 1900 considering the seating of a Mormon convicted of polygamy, argued that the Constitutional Convention intended to empower Congress to add qualifications. The committee concluded that if the Convention meant to restrict qualifications to the three in the Constitution, it would have phrased them affirmatively. For example, the Framers would have written: "Every member of the House of Representatives shall be of the age of twenty-five years at least," rather than deliberately using the supposedly more flexible negative phrasing of Article I, Section 2: "No Person shall be a Representative who shall not have attained to the Age of twenty five Years."

The qualifications issue was a dilemma. If Congress followed only the three requirements, it had to seat individuals regarded as obnoxious. If it excluded such individuals, it could be charged with exceeding its powers. The Civil War turmoil focused the issue.

Both houses added a qualification for membership in 1862 known as the "Ironclad Oath Law" or the "Test Oath Law." It required members to swear, before taking the oath of office, that they had never voluntarily borne arms against the United States or aided, recognized, or supported a jurisdiction hostile to the United States. This law remained in effect until the Fourteenth Amendment was ratified in 1868.

SENATE EXCLUSIONS

Only three senators-elect have been denied seats for lack of the requisite qualifications:

• Albert Gallatin, born in Geneva, became a U.S. citizen in 1785. When elected to the Senate by the Pennsylvania Legislature in 1793, he had not been a citizen nine years as required by the Constitution. He contended that every man who had taken part in the Revolution was a citizen according to the law of reason and nature. The Senate on February 28, 1794, by a vote of 14–12, disagreed and said his election was void.

• James Shields, a native of Ireland, was elected a senator from Illinois in 1848. Shields had been naturalized October 21, 1840, but would not be a citizen until October 20, 1849. He ap-

peared March 5, 1849, to take his seat. Although Shields was seated on March 6, the Senate on March 15 adopted a resolution declaring his election void on the ground of insufficient years of citizenship. Shields then was elected to fill the vacancy thus created and was allowed to serve beginning October 27, 1849.

• Phillip F. Thomas of Maryland had given $100 to his son when the son entered Confederate military service. When the Maryland Legislature elected Thomas a U.S. senator in 1866, he was charged with being disloyal for giving aid and comfort to the enemy. The Senate voted 27–20 to exclude Thomas on grounds of noncitizenship.

Exclusion proceedings based on the age qualification for senators were avoided, in two cases, by different means. When Henry Clay of Kentucky arrived in Washington to take his seat, he lacked five months of the required thirty years. The Senate tacitly ignored this fact, and he was sworn in, November 19, 1806. Rush D. Holt, D-W.Va., also had not reached the age of thirty when the time came for him to enter the Senate in 1935. He delayed the presentation of his credentials until his thirtieth birthday and was then admitted. The Senate later rejected, 62–17, a proposal to declare Holt's election invalid on the grounds of age.

Exclusion Cases Rejected

Exclusion proceedings have not always blocked a member from taking a seat. Severe illness prevented Democrat John M. Niles from taking the Senate seat to which the Connecticut Legislature had elected him in 1843. Because Niles showed signs of mental strain when he arrived in Washington in April 1844, the Senate appointed a committee to consider his case. The committee reported that Niles was "laboring under mental and physical debility, but is not of unsound mind." It said there was "no sufficient reason why he be not qualified and permitted to take his seat," which he did within a month.

TABLE 34-1 Senate Cases Involving Qualifications for Membership

Congress	Session	Year	Member-elect	Grounds	Disposition
3rd	1st	1793	Albert Gallatin, D-Pa.	Citizenship	*Excluded*
11th	1st	1809	Stanley Griswold, D-Ohio	Residence	Admitted
28th	1st	1844	John M. Niles, D-Conn.	Sanity	Admitted
31st	Special	1849	James Shields, D-Ill.	Citizenship	*Excluded*
37th	2nd	1861	Benjamin Stark, D-Ore.	Loyalty	Admitted
40th	1st	1867	Phillip F. Thomas, D-Md.	Loyalty	*Excluded*
41st	2nd	1870	Hiram R. Revels, R-Miss.	Citizenship	Admitted
41st	2nd	1870	Adelbert Ames, R-Miss.	Residence	Admitted
59th	2nd	1907	Reed Smoot, R-Utah	Mormonism	Admitted[a]
69th	2nd	1926	Arthur R. Gould, R-Maine	Character	Admitted
74th	1st	1935	Rush D. Holt, D-W.Va.	Age	Admitted
75th	1st	1937	George L. Berry, D-Tenn.	Character	Admitted
77th	2nd	1942	William Langer, R-N.D.	Character	Admitted[a]
80th	1st	1947	Theodore G. Bilbo, D-Miss.	Character	Died before Senate acted
83rd	2nd	1964	Pierre Salinger, D-Calif.	Residence	Admitted

NOTE: a. The Senate decided that a two-thirds majority, as in expulsion cases, would be required for exclusion. The resolution proposing exclusion did not receive a two-thirds majority.

SOURCE: Senate Committee on Rules and Administration, Subcommittee on Privileges and Elections, *Senate Election, Expulsion, and Censure Cases from 1793 to 1972*, compiled by Richard D. Hupman, 92nd Cong. 1st sess., 1972, S Doc 92-7.

Hiram R. Revels, R-Miss., a former slave elected to the Senate in 1870, was challenged because he had not become a citizen until 1868, when the Fourteenth Amendment was ratified. The Senate ruled that the amendment made Revels retroactively a citizen and seated him.

Reed Smoot, R-Utah, a senator-elect in 1903, was challenged by Utah citizens who said that as a Mormon he favored polygamy and opposed the separation of church and state. Smoot was given the oath on a tentative basis while the Committee on Privileges and Elections studied his eligibility. The committee concluded that Smoot was not entitled to his seat.

When the issue came to a vote in 1907, Philander C. Knox, R-Pa., argued that a two-thirds vote was required because the action involved expulsion, not exclusion. "There is no question as to Senator Smoot's possessing the qualifications prescribed by the Constitution, and therefore we cannot deprive him of his seat by a majority vote," Knox said. The two-thirds requirement was approved, but it never mattered. In voting, the Senate rejected motions to expel and exclude Smoot by 27–43 and 28–42 votes.

When Arthur R. Gould, R-Maine, was elected to the Senate in 1926, a controversy arose over an accusation that some fourteen years earlier he had been involved in bribery. In the Privileges and Elections Committee's hearings, Gould contended that denying him a seat denied the right of Maine's citizens to select their own senator. The committee reported that Gould's alleged part in the bribery case had not been proved.

In 1941 the claim of William Langer, R-N.D., to a Senate seat was challenged over alleged misconduct during his service as governor and in other North Dakota state government posts. When an investigating committee recommended that Langer be excluded, the Senate added a two-thirds requirement, as it had done in the case of Reed Smoot, and then on March 27, 1942, voted down the proposed resolution.

In January 1947 senator-elect Theodore G. Bilbo, D-Miss., a two-term Senate veteran who had been accused of fraud, violence in preventing blacks from voting, and other offenses, was asked to stand aside when other senators-elect took the oath. He died in August 1947 before the Senate settled the question of his right to the seat.

HOUSE EXCLUSIONS

Ten members-elect have been excluded from the House of Representatives as not qualified to serve. John Bailey of Massachusetts was the first excluded. He was challenged on the ground that he was not a resident of the district he purported to represent. The House, by a resolution of March 18, 1824, declared that Bailey was not entitled to his seat. He returned home, was elected to fill the vacancy created by his exclusion, and was seated December 13, 1824.

In 1867 southern states elected to Congress four men whom the House found to be tainted with acts of disloyalty during the Civil War. They were Democrats John Y. Brown and John D. Young of Kentucky and independents W. D. Simpson of South Carolina and John A. Wimpy of Georgia.

South Carolina had another representative-elect excluded three years later. Benjamin F. Whittemore, a Republican, was censured by the House in 1870 for selling appointments to the U.S. Military Academy and resigned on February 24 of that year. When Whittemore was reelected to the same Congress, John A. Logan, R-Ill., discussed his case on the House floor: "It is said that the constituency has the right to elect such member as they deem proper. I say no. We cannot say that he shall be of a certain politics, or of a certain religion, or anything of that kind; but, Sir, we have the right to say that he shall not be a man of infamous character." The House on June 21, 1870, excluded Whittemore by a vote of 130–76.

The House based two exclusions on polygamy. George Q. Cannon was elected in 1872 as a delegate from the Utah Territory. In the first and second sessions of the 43rd Congress, the question of his eligibility was raised and settled in his favor. Cannon served in the House until 1881 without being challenged, but in 1882 the issue arose again. The House, taking account both of Cannon's practice of polygamy and of doubts about the validity of his election, declared the seat vacant, in effect excluding Cannon.

In 1900 members of the House questioned the right of Brigham H. Roberts, elected as a representative from Utah, to take his seat. Roberts had been found guilty some years earlier of violating an 1882 law that prohibited polygamy. This was the case in which an investigating committee argued that the Founders had not foreclosed the right of Congress to establish qualifications for membership other than those mentioned in the Constitution. The House refused to seat Roberts, 268–50.

Exclusion cases in which the House ultimately admitted the representative-elect evoked various memorable exchanges on the floor. An example is the case of John C. Conner, D-Texas, who was accused of having whipped black soldiers under his command in 1868 and of having boasted in 1869 that he would escape conviction in a military court by bribing witnesses. James A. Garfield, R-Ohio, speaking in the House on March 31, 1870, raised a constitutional question on this case: "Allow me to ask . . . if anything in the Constitution of the United States . . . forbids that a 'moral monster' shall be elected to the Congress?" Ebon C. Ingersoll, R-Ill., replied: "I believe the people may elect a moral monster to Congress if they see fit, but I believe that Congress has a right to exclude that moral monster from a seat if they see fit." Nonetheless, a resolution allowing Conner to take his seat was adopted the same day.

Berger

In the twentieth century, only Victor L. Berger, Wisconsin Socialist, and Adam Clayton Powell Jr. have been excluded from the House. Berger had been convicted in 1919 of violating the Espionage Act of 1917 by publishing antiwar statements. While an appeal was pending, he was elected to the 66th Congress. By

TABLE 34-2 House Cases Involving Qualifications for Membership

Congress	Session	Year	Member-elect	Grounds	Disposition
1st	1st	1789	William L. Smith, Fed-S.C.	Citizenship	Admitted
10th	1st	1807	Philip B. Key, Fed-Md.	Residence	Admitted
10th	1st	1807	William McCreery,—Md.	Residence	Admitted
18th	1st	1823	Gabriel Richard, Ind-Mich. Terr.	Citizenship	Admitted
18th	1st	1823	John Bailey, Ind-Mass.	Residence	*Excluded*
18th	1st	1823	John Forsyth, D-Ga.	Residence	Admitted
27th	1st	1841	David Levy, R-Fla. Terr.	Citizenship	Admitted
36th	1st	1859	John Y. Brown, D-Ky.	Age	Admitted
40th	1st	1867	William H. Hooper, D-Utah Terr.	Mormonism	Admitted
40th	1st	1867	Lawrence S. Trimble, D-Ky.	Loyalty	Admitted
40th	1st	1867	John Y. Brown, D-Ky.	Loyalty	*Excluded*
40th	1st	1867	John D. Young, D-Ky.	Loyalty	*Excluded*
40th	1st	1867	Roderick R. Butler, R-Tenn.	Loyalty	Admitted
40th	1st	1867	John A. Wimpy, Ind-Ga.	Loyalty	*Excluded*
40th	1st	1867	W.D. Simpson, Ind-S.C.	Loyalty	*Excluded*
41st	1st	1869	John M. Rice, D-Ky.	Loyalty	Admitted
41st	2nd	1870	Lewis McKenzie, Unionist-Va.	Loyalty	Admitted
41st	2nd	1870	George W. Booker, Conservative-Va.	Loyalty	Admitted
41st	2nd	1870	Benjamin F. Whittemore, R-S.C.	Malfeasance	*Excluded*
41st	2nd	1870	John C. Conner, D-Texas	Misconduct	Admitted
43rd	1st	1873	George Q. Cannon, R-Utah Terr.	Mormonism	Admitted
43rd	2nd	1874	George Q. Cannon, R-Utah Terr.	Polygamy	Admitted
47th	1st	1881	John S. Barbour, D-Va.	Residence	Admitted
47th	1st	1882	George Q. Cannon, R-Utah Terr.	Polygamy	Seat vacated[a]
50th	1st	1887	James B. White, R-Ind.	Citizenship	Admitted
56th	1st	1899	Robert W. Wilcox, Ind-Hawaii Terr.	Bigamy, treason	Admitted
56th	1st	1900	Brigham H. Roberts, D-Utah	Polygamy	*Excluded*
59th	1st	1905	Anthony Michalek, R-Ill.	Citizenship	Admitted
66th	1st	1919	Victor L. Berger, Socialist-Wis.	Sedition	*Excluded*
66th	2nd	1920	Victor L. Berger, Socialist-Wis.	Sedition	*Excluded*
69th	1st	1926	John W. Langley, R-Ky.	Criminal misconduct	Resigned
70th	1st	1927	James M. Beck, R-Pa.	Residence	Admitted
71st	1st	1929	Ruth B. Owen, D-Fla.	Citizenship	Admitted
90th	1st	1967	Adam C. Powell Jr., D-N.Y.	Misconduct	*Excluded*[b]
96th	1st	1979	Richard A. Tonry, D-La.	Vote fraud	Resigned

NOTES: a. Discussions of polygamy and an election contest led to a declaration that the seat was vacant. b. The Supreme Court June 16, 1969, ruled that the House had improperly excluded Powell.

SOURCES: Hinds and Cannon, *Precedents of the House of Representatives of the United States,* 11 vols. (1935–1941); Joint Committee on Congressional Operations, *Exclusion, Censure, and Expulsion Cases from 1789 to 1973,* 93rd Cong., 1st sess., 1973, committee print.

resolution adopted November 10, 1919, the House said Berger was "not entitled to take the oath of office as a representative." He was reelected during the same Congress and excluded again on January 10, 1920. But after the Supreme Court had reversed Berger's conviction, he was elected to the House three more times—1922, 1924, and 1926—and was seated without question.

Powell

One of the stormiest episodes in congressional history was the precedent-shattering case of Rep. Adam Clayton Powell Jr., D-N.Y. It was Powell's exclusion from the House that led to the Supreme Court decision prohibiting Congress from adding to the constitutional qualifications for membership in the House or Senate.

In 1937 Powell succeeded his father as pastor of the Abyssinian Baptist Church in Harlem, one of the largest congregations in the country. Seven years later Powell was elected to the 79th Congress with the nomination of both the Democratic and Re-

publican parties. He took his seat with the Democrats, was reelected regularly by large majorities, served as chairman of the House Committee on Education and Labor from 1961 to 1967, and was considered by many observers the most powerful black in the United States. Throughout his legislative career, he retained his pastorate.

Powell's troubles stemmed in part from his flamboyant personality and his apparent disregard for the law. On the eve of Powell's 1952 reelection bid, the Internal Revenue Service said that he had underestimated his 1945 income tax by $2,749. A 1960 trial for criminal tax evasion resulted in a hung jury, and Powell eventually paid $27,833 in back taxes and penalties. Meanwhile he lost two suits brought by a widow in his district, Esther James, whom he had described in a television interview as a "bag woman" or graft collector for New York City police. During these legal difficulties, Powell was held in contempt of court on four occasions.

In the 1950s and the early 1960s Powell repeatedly went on

The Supreme Court ruled that the House acted unconstitutionally in excluding Rep. Adam Clayton Powell Jr. in 1967. Powell, who was reelected in 1968, took his seat in 1969 after the Court decision.

costly pleasure trips at government expense. In addition, he incurred criticism for taking a staff member, Corinne A. Huff, on many trips to Bimini Island in the Bahamas. Out of government funds, he paid his wife $20,578 a year as a clerk while she lived in Puerto Rico. She was ordered dropped from the payroll in 1967.

In 1966 Powell's committee colleagues effectively stripped him of his powers as chairman of the House Education and Labor Committee. He had angered committee Democrats by long absences that delayed House action on President Lyndon B. Johnson's antipoverty bill. By a vote of 27–1, the committee September 22, 1966, adopted new rules, one of which provided that if the chairman failed to bring a bill to the floor, one of the six subcommittee chairmen could do so.

The House Democratic Caucus on January 9, 1967, removed Powell from his chairmanship for the duration of the 90th Congress. This was the first time since 1925 that a committee chairman had been deposed in either house of Congress. Powell, who attended the caucus, called the action "a lynching, northern style." A day later, Powell was embroiled in a challenge to his seat in the House.

When members of the House convened January 10, 1967, a resolution submitted by Morris K. Udall, D-Ariz., proposed that Powell be sworn in, pending the result of a sixty-day investiga-

tion of his conduct by a select committee. Udall contended that stripping Powell of his chairmanship was punishment enough because his malfeasance was based on his misuse of that position. But the resolution was rejected on a 126–305 vote.

The House then adopted a resolution offered by Minority Leader Gerald R. Ford, R-Mich., that denied Powell his seat pending an investigation. The vote was 363–65.

House Judiciary Committee Chairman Emanuel Celler, D-N.Y., was chairman of the select committee appointed to investigate Powell's qualifications for his seat. The committee conducted hearings beginning February 8, 1967, and submitted its report February 23. The committee proposed that Powell be sworn in; that his seniority be based on the date of his swearing in; that he be censured for "gross misconduct" through misuse of funds of the Committee on Education and Labor, refusal to pay the judgment against him, and noncooperation with House investigating committees; and that he be fined $40,000, to be paid to the clerk of the House in the form of a monthly deduction of $1,000 from Powell's salary, to "offset any civil liability of Mr. Powell to the United States."[2] The recommendation for a fine was unprecedented in congressional history.

The House on March 1, 1967, rejected the committee's proposals and adopted instead a resolution excluding Powell from the 90th Congress—the first exclusion since Victor L. Berger was barred in 1919 and 1920. On the select committee's proposals, the vote was 202 in favor, 222 against; on the exclusion resolution, 307 in favor, 116 against.

As in his ouster from his committee chairmanship, Powell ascribed his exclusion to racism. That racial feeling played a part in the vote to exclude Powell seemed probable. Celler said on television and on the House floor that he saw "an element of racism in the vote." Arlen J. Large, a Washington correspondent, wrote in the Wall Street Journal March 22, 1967: "Disclaimers of race as a factor in Mr. Powell's exclusion don't jibe with the nearly solid anti-Powell votes of southern congressmen, reflecting the bitterly worded letters from white voters back home."

In his appearances before the select committee, Powell responded only to questions relating to the constitutional requirements for House membership—his age, citizenship, and residency. These were the only questions that the House could properly inquire into, Powell and his lawyers claimed. Upon his exclusion, Powell filed suit. The case eventually reached the Supreme Court, which on June 16, 1969, ruled that the House had improperly excluded Powell, a duly elected representative who met the constitutional requirements for membership.

His district reelected Powell in a special election April 11, 1967, but he did not apply to the House to be seated while appealing his exclusion to the courts. Reelected in 1968, Powell was sworn in and seated but subjected to loss of seniority and fined $25,000. The resolution imposing these penalties was adopted, 254–158.

Although he had won the right to be seated, Powell rarely attended Congress, preferring instead his retreat in Bimini. In 1970 Charles B. Rangel successfully challenged Powell in the

Democratic primary and went on to win the general election. Powell died in Miami, April 4, 1972.

Degrees of Discipline: Mild to Harsh

For offenses of sufficient gravity, each house of Congress may punish its members by expulsion or censure (the words "condemn" and "denounce" have been used as synonyms for censure). Of the two degrees of punishment, censure is milder and requires a simple majority vote while expulsion requires a two-thirds majority. Censure also has the advantage of not depriving constituents of their elected senators or representatives. Grounds for disciplining members usually consist of a member's action during service in Congress. Both houses have sparingly used their power to penalize a member for prior offenses and have been shy about punishing misdeeds committed during a previous Congress.

For minor transgressions of the rules, the presiding officer of either chamber may call a member to order, without a formal move to censure. For example, Russell B. Long, D-La., presiding over the Senate on January 14, 1955, called Joseph R. McCarthy, R-Wis., to order after McCarthy questioned the motives of some senators who had voted on a resolution continuing an investigation of communists in government. Long said: "The statement of the junior senator from Wisconsin was that other senators were insincere. In making that statement, the senator from Wisconsin spoke contrary to the rules of the Senate. . . . He must take his seat."[3] Later on the same day, Long again called McCarthy to order.

In recent years Congress has turned to other methods when it has wanted to discipline members while avoiding the strong measures of expulsion or censure. These methods have included denouncement, reprimand, denial of the member's right to vote, stripping of chairmanships, and fines.

EXPULSION

Fifteen senators have been expelled, one in 1797 and fourteen during the Civil War. One of the latter actions was reversed after the expelled senator had died. Formal expulsion proceedings in the Senate have been instituted nine times since the Civil War, always without success. (*See Table 34-3, p. 924.*)

In the House, only four members have been expelled, three in 1861 and one in 1980. Ten representatives have been censured as a lesser form of punishment during expulsion proceedings against them. (*See Table 34-4, p. 926.*)

In both houses, embattled members have resigned rather than risk expulsion or other punishment.

Grounds for Expulsion

The Abscam investigation of 1980, in which FBI agents posing as Arab sheiks or businessmen offered bribes to members of Congress, resulted in the first ouster of a member for corruption. Until then, the only grounds on which a member had been expelled was conspiracy against a foreign country (the 1797 case

in the Senate) and support of a rebellion (the Civil War cases of fourteen senators and three representatives).

Other cases dealing with corruption had been unsuccessful, as had cases concerned with the killing of a representative in a duel, the assaulting of a senator or a representative, treasonable or offensive utterances, sedition, and Mormonism.

Prior Offenses. The most important question raised about the power to expel has been whether a member of either house may be ousted for offenses committed before the person was elected.

John Quincy Adams, while serving in the Senate before he became president, submitted a committee report supporting the Senate's power to expel a member for preelection conduct that came to light after he had taken his seat. The case concerned John Smith, D-Ohio, who allegedly had been connected with Aaron Burr's conspiracy to separate several of the western states from the Union. Adams's committee, in its report of December 31, 1807, said:

When a man whom his fellow citizens have honored with their confidence on the pledge of a spotless reputation has degraded himself by the commission of infamous crimes, which become suddenly and unexpectedly revealed to the world, defective, indeed, would be that institution which should be impotent to discard from its bosom the contagion of such a member.

Smith retained his seat by a single vote on April 9, 1808, when 19 yeas, not enough to make up the required two-thirds, were cast for expulsion, against 10 nays. (Smith's counsel was Francis Scott Key, who later wrote the poem that became the national anthem.)

Incompatible Office. The Constitution, in Article I, Section 6, provides: "No Person holding any Office under the United States, shall be a Member of either House during his Continuance in Office." When a senator or representative has accepted appointment to another "Office under the United States," the member has jeopardized but not always lost the privilege of remaining in Congress, depending on the type of office the member accepted and the attitude of the chamber in which he or she was serving. If a position in Congress is forfeited by acceptance of another office, the member is not considered to have been expelled; the seat is treated as having been vacated.

Cases arising in the Civil War and subsequent wars in which members of Congress served in the armed forces generally did not result in vacating of their seats. In the war with Spain, a House committee recommended adoption of a resolution declaring vacant the seats of four representatives who had accepted commissions in the U.S. Army to serve in the war with Spain. "No mere patriotic sentiment," it said, "should be permitted to override the plain language of the fundamental written law." On March 2, 1899, the House, by a vote of 77 yeas and 163 nays, declined to consider the proposed resolution.

Members of both chambers have been appointed to serve as commissioners to negotiate peace and arbitrate disputes, as members of "blue ribbon" boards of inquiry, and so forth, without losing their seats in Congress. The House in 1919 authorized members who had been absent on military service to be paid

TABLE 34-3 Cases of Expulsion in the Senate

Year	Member	Grounds	Disposition
1797	William Blount, Ind-Tenn.	Anti-Spanish conspiracy	Expelled
1808	John Smith, D-Ohio	Disloyalty	Not expelled
1858	Henry M. Rice, D-Minn.	Corruption	Not expelled
1861	James M. Mason, D-Va.	Support of rebellion	Expelled
1861	Robert M. T. Hunter, D-Va.	Support of rebellion	Expelled
1861	Thomas L. Clingman, D-N.C.	Support of rebellion	Expelled
1861	Thomas Bragg, D-N.C.	Support of rebellion	Expelled
1861	James Chestnut Jr., States Rights-S.C.	Support of rebellion	Expelled
1861	Alfred O. P. Nicholson, D-Tenn.	Support of rebellion	Expelled
1861	William K. Sebastian, D-Ark.	Support of rebellion	Expelled[a]
1861	Charles B. Mitchel, D-Ark.	Support of rebellion	Expelled
1861	John Hemphill, State Rights D-Texas	Support of rebellion	Expelled
1861	Louis T. Wigfall, D-Texas	Support of rebellion	Not expelled[b]
1861	Louis T. Wigfall, D-Texas	Support of rebellion	Expelled
1861	John C. Breckinridge, D-Ky.	Support of rebellion	Expelled
1861	Lazarus W. Powell, D-Ky.	Support of rebellion	Not expelled
1862	Trusten Polk, D-Mo.	Support of rebellion	Expelled
1862	Jesse D. Bright, D-Ind.	Support of rebellion	Expelled
1862	Waldo P. Johnson, D-Mo.	Support of rebellion	Expelled
1862	James F. Simmons, Whig-R.I.	Corruption	Not expelled
1873	James W. Patterson, R-N.H.	Corruption	Not expelled
1893	William N. Roach, D-N.D.	Embezzlement	Not expelled
1905	John H. Mitchell, R-Ore.	Corruption	Not expelled
1907	Reed Smoot, R-Utah	Mormonism	Not expelled
1919	Robert M. La Follette, R-Wis.	Disloyalty	Not expelled
1934	John H. Overton, D-La.	Corruption	Not expelled
1934	Huey P. Long, D-La.	Corruption	Not expelled
1942	William Langer, R-N.D.	Corruption	Not expelled
1982	Harrison A. Williams Jr., D-N.J.	Corruption	Not expelled[c]
1995	Bob Packwood, R-Ore.	Sexual harassment	Not expelled[d]

NOTES: a. The Senate reversed its decision on Sebastian's expulsion March 3, 1877. Sebastian had died in 1865, but his children were paid an amount equal to his Senate salary between the time of his expulsion and the date of his death. b. The Senate took no action on an initial resolution expelling Wigfall because he represented a state that had seceded from the Union; three months later he was expelled for supporting the Confederacy.   c. Facing probable expulsion, Williams resigned March 11, 1982.   d. Facing probable expulsion, Packwood resigned Sept. 7, 1995.

SOURCES: Senate Committee on Rules and Administration, Subcommittee on Privileges and Elections, *Senate Election, Expulsion, and Censure Cases from 1793 to 1972,* comp. Richard D. Hupman, 92nd Cong., 1st sess., 1972, S Doc 92–7; *Congress and the Nation 1981–1984,* vol. 6. (Washington, D.C.: Congressional Quarterly, 1985); *Congress and the Nation 1993–1996,* vol. 9 (Washington, D.C.: Congressional Quarterly, 1988).

their salaries minus the amount they were paid for military service.

During the Vietnam War, Judge Gerhard A. Gesell of the U.S. District Court for the District of Columbia ruled on April 2, 1971, that the 117 members who held commissions in military reserve units were violating the incompatible-office clause of the Constitution. The decision reached the Supreme Court, which ruled June 25, 1974, that the plaintiffs—current and former reservists opposed to the war—did not have legal standing to make the challenge (*Schlesinger v. Reservists Committee to Stop the War*).

Civil War Cases

After the Senate's expulsion of William Blount of Tennessee in 1797 for conspiracy to incite members of two Indian tribes to attack Spanish Florida and Louisiana, the only successful expulsion cases were those resulting from the Civil War. (*See "Congressional Impeachment," p. 347, Vol. I.*)

On January 21, 1861, Jefferson Davis, D-Miss., like a number of other southern senators before and after that date, announced his support of secession and withdrew from the Senate. He became president of the Confederacy. On March 14, 1861, ten days after Abraham Lincoln's inauguration, the Senate adopted a resolution ordering that, because the seats of these southerners had "become vacant, . . . the Secretary be directed to omit their names respectively from the roll." Although Davis and the five other southern senators had left voluntarily, they had not formally resigned. Hence the Senate's action resembled expulsion.

Senate. On a single day, July 11, 1861, the Senate expelled ten members—two each from Arkansas, North Carolina, Texas, and Virginia, and one each from South Carolina and Tennessee—for failure to appear in their seats and for participation in secession. The vote was 32 in favor of expulsion, 10 against. John C. Breckinridge, D-Ky., who had been vice president of the United States from 1857 to 1861, was expelled December 4, 1861, by the following resolution: "Whereas John C. Breckinridge, a member of this body from the State of Kentucky, has joined the enemies of his country, and is now in arms against the Government he had sworn to support: Therefore, Resolved, That said John C. Breckinridge, the traitor, be, and he hereby is, expelled from the Senate." On this resolution the vote was 37–0.

Of the ten expulsions voted by the Senate on July 11, 1861, one was later annulled posthumously. In 1877 the Committee on Privileges and Elections reviewed the expulsion of William K. Sebastian, D-Ark., decided that the Senate had a right to reverse its earlier action, and recommended such reversal. The Senate on March 3, 1877, adopted the committee's recommendation, which was based on its findings that the charges made against Sebastian in 1861 had been "occasioned by want of information, and by the overruling excitement of a period of great public danger." Sebastian, who remained loyal to the Union throughout the war, had been dead twelve years when his expulsion was reversed.

In 1862 the Senate expelled three senators, all for disloyalty to the government: Missouri Democrats Trusten Polk and Waldo P. Johnson and Indiana Democrat Jesse D. Bright. Polk was accused of stating in a widely published letter his hopes that Missouri would secede from the Union. Johnson reportedly held similar feelings and did not appear to take his Senate seat. Bright was charged with treason for giving an arms salesman a letter of introduction to former senator Jefferson Davis, who by then had become president of the Confederacy.

House. On July 13, 1861, the House expelled John B. Clark, D-Mo., who had served in the House since 1857. After a brief debate on Clark's entrance into the Confederate forces, and without referring the case to a committee, the House adopted the expulsion order by slightly more than a two-thirds vote, 94–45.

Two other representatives were expelled in December 1861: John W. Reid, D-Mo., for taking up arms against the country, and Henry C. Burnett, D-Ky., for open rebellion against the federal government.

Efforts to Expel Other Senators

No senators have been expelled since the Civil War, but World War I brought the first of several attempts in modern times to dismiss members for disloyalty or, more commonly, for corruption. All were unsuccessful, but one resulted in resignation.

Sen. Robert M. La Follette, R-Wis., spoke at St. Paul, Minnesota, September 20, 1917, decrying American participation in the war in Europe. On the basis of that speech, Minnesota's Public Safety Commission petitioned the Senate to expel La Follette for sedition. The Senate by a 50–21 vote dismissed the petition on January 16, 1919.

In 1932–1934 the two senators from Louisiana, Democrats Huey P. Long and John H. Overton, were accused of fraud and corruption in connection with their nomination and election. The Committee on Privileges and Elections investigated but eventually asked to be taken off the cases. The Senate did so on

June 16, 1934, in effect burying expulsion resolutions that had been introduced.

Charges of corruption against William Langer, then a senator-elect from North Dakota, prompted an effort to block his admission or to expel him should he be seated. On March 27, 1941, the Senate first rejected a resolution stating that the case did not fall within the constitutional provisions for expulsion. It then rejected a resolution declaring that Langer was not entitled to his seat.

Harrison A. Williams Jr., D-N.J., the only senator caught in the Abscam net, was convicted of accepting stock in a titanium mining company in return for his promise to get government contracts for the mine's output. On August 24, 1981, the Senate Ethics Committee unanimously recommended that the Senate expel Williams. After numerous delays, the Senate began debate on the committee's resolution March 3, 1982. On March 11, when it was clear that more than two-thirds of the senators would vote for expulsion, Williams resigned his Senate seat.

House Expulsion of Myers

More than one hundred years after the Civil War cases, the House expelled another member, only the fourth such event. Michael J. "Ozzie" Myers, D-Pa., one of seven members of Congress caught in the FBI's Abscam trap, was expelled on October 2, 1980. The vote was 376–30. Videotapes made by the FBI had shown Myers accepting a bribe of $50,000 in cash and boasting of his familiarity with Philadelphia officials and the Mafia. (*See "The Court Cases," p. 955.*)

Notable Resignations

As in the case of Williams in the Senate, two House members convicted in the Abscam scandal resigned from the House to avoid expulsion proceedings: John W. Jenrette Jr., D-S.C., and Raymond F. Lederer, D-Pa. Others implicated did not seek reelection or were defeated. (*See "Abscam Investigation," p. 953.*)

The 1980s also saw two House leaders resign rather than risk expulsion or other humiliation because of investigations into their financial affairs.

Wright. The House ethics committee opened a formal investigation of Speaker Jim Wright, D-Texas, on June 9, 1988. Wright had publicly invited such an inquiry after the government-watchdog group Common Cause joined longtime critic Newt Gingrich, R-Ga., in urging an investigation.

Republicans, especially Gingrich, had been criticizing Wright since he became Speaker in 1987. Democrats generally closed ranks around the Speaker, saying that questions about his finances were a Republican tactic to deflect attention from allegations of misconduct in the Reagan administration. But the call by Common Cause for an investigation made it difficult for Democrats, many of whom had strong ties to the nonpartisan organization, to dismiss the attacks on Wright as purely partisan.

Republican leaders in September filed another complaint seeking a second, unrelated inquiry into allegations that Wright

TABLE 34-4 Cases of Expulsion in the House

Year	Member	Grounds	Disposition
1798	Matthew Lyon, Anti-Fed.-Vt.	Assault on representative	Not expelled
1798	Roger Griswold, Fed.-Conn.	Assault on representative	Not expelled
1799	Matthew Lyon, Anti-Fed.-Vt.	Sedition	Not expelled
1838	William J. Graves, Whig-Ky.	Killing of representative in duel	Not expelled
1839	Alexander Duncan, Whig-Ohio	Offensive publication	Not expelled
1856	Preston S. Brooks, State Rights Dem.-S.C.	Assault on senator	Not expelled
1857	Orsamus B. Matteson, Whig-N.Y.	Corruption	Not expelled
1857	William A. Gilbert, Whig-N.Y.	Corruption	Not expelled
1857	William W. Welch, American-Conn.	Corruption	Not expelled
1857	Francis S. Edwards, American-N.Y.	Corruption	Not expelled
1858	Orsamus B. Matteson, Whig-N.Y.	Corruption	Not expelled
1861	John B. Clark, D-Mo.	Support of rebellion	Expelled
1861	Henry C. Burnett, D-Ky.	Support of rebellion	Expelled
1861	John W. Reid, D-Mo.	Support of rebellion	Expelled
1864	Alexander Long, D-Ohio	Treasonable utterance	Not expelled[a]
1864	Benjamin G. Harris, D-Md.	Treasonable utterance	Not expelled[a]
1866	Lovell H. Rousseau, R-Ky.	Assault on representative	Not expelled[a]
1870	Benjamin F. Whittemore, R-S.C.	Corruption	Not expelled[a]
1870	Roderick R. Butler, R-Tenn.	Corruption	Not expelled[a]
1873	Oakes Ames, R-Mass.	Corruption	Not expelled[a]
1873	James Brooks, D-N.Y.	Corruption	Not expelled[a]
1875	John Y. Brown, D-Ky.	Insult to representative	Not expelled[a]
1875	William S. King, R-Minn.	Corruption	Not expelled
1875	John G. Schumaker, D-N.Y.	Corruption	Not expelled
1884	William P. Kellogg, R-La.	Corruption	Not expelled
1921	Thomas L. Blanton, D-Texas	Abuse of leave to print	Not expelled[a]
1979	Charles C. Diggs Jr., D-Mich.	Misuse of clerk-hire funds	Not expelled[a]
1980	Michael J. "Ozzie" Myers, D-Pa.	Corruption	Expelled
1988	Mario Biaggi, D-N.Y	Corruption	Not expelled[b]
1990	Barney Frank, D-Mass.	Discrediting House	Not expelled[c]

NOTES: a. Censured after expulsion move failed or was withdrawn.   b. Facing probable expulsion, Biaggi resigned from Congress on August 8, 1988.   c. Reprimanded after expulsion and censure moves failed.

SOURCES: Hinds and Cannon, *Precedents of the House of Representatives of the United States*, 11 vols. (1935–1941); Joint Committee on Congressional Operations, *House of Representatives Exclusion, Censure, and Expulsion Cases from 1789 to 1973*, 93rd Cong., 1st sess., 1973, committee print; *Congressional Quarterly Almanac* 1980; *Congressional Quarterly Weekly Report*, selected issues.

improperly disclosed security secrets in comments he made relating to activities of the CIA in Nicaragua. The ethics panel did not rule on the complaint in the 100th Congress.

The panel opened its preliminary investigation into the allegations of financial misconduct in June by unanimous vote after a marathon eight-and-a-half-hour session that extended into the night. It announced that it would investigate six allegations against Wright, including the publication and sale of a 117-page book by Wright called *Reflections of a Public Man*.

The "preliminary inquiry" voted by the committee was a grand jury-like investigation, in which the panel gathered evidence and took testimony from witnesses. The preliminary inquiry was to lead to a staff report to the committee, with recommendations about whether to issue the equivalent of an indictment, known as a "statement of alleged violations," that would be followed by a trial-like phase of the investigation known as a disciplinary hearing. In a move to enhance the credibility of the inquiry, the ethics committee in July hired an outside attorney, Chicago trial lawyer Richard J. Phelan, to head it.

The inquiry offered Wright a chance to testify before the panel—an opportunity he had been seeking in the days before the committee action. The Speaker testified for more than five hours September 14. But the panel did not finish its investigation by the end of the 100th Congress (1987–1989), much to the disappointment of Wright's supporters. The issue began to overshadow the legislative accomplishments of Wright's first term as Speaker and lingered over Democrats' plans for the 101st Congress.

After a ten-month investigation, the ethics committee April 17, 1989, formally charged Wright with accepting improper gifts from Texas developer George Mallick, who had paid Wright's wife, Betty, an $18,000-a-year salary and given her use of a company car and condominium—benefits the committee valued at a total of $145,000 over ten years. The committee also alleged that bulk sales of Wright's book were intended as an "overall scheme to evade the House outside earned income limits." Wright had earned about $55,000 from the book, with a royalty of about 55 percent.

Those allegations were spelled out in a statement of alleged violations, citing sixty-nine instances in five broad categories

One day after the Senate Ethics Committee unanimously adopted a resolution calling for his expulsion, Sen. Bob Packwood in a floor speech emotionally tells his colleagues that he will resign in the face of sexual harassment charges.

where the committee found "reason to believe" Wright violated House rules over the previous ten years. The committee also announced it was continuing to investigate a previously undisclosed allegation concerning an oil well deal that resulted in huge profits for Wright. But the committee decided not to pursue half of the 116 possible rule violations Phelan had identified. Among those dropped were questions about Wright's investment in a lucrative oil well and allegations that he had been too heavy-handed in his dealings with federal thrift-industry regulators.

Procedural and legal delays pushed the next phase, the disciplinary hearing, into June. In the meantime, the press pummeled Wright with new allegations about his conduct, and negotiations to have key charges against him dismissed were unsuccessful. On May 31 Wright announced that he would resign as Speaker and would leave the House, which he did on June 30.

Coelho. A *Newsweek* story in 1987 alleged that Democratic Majority Whip Tony Coelho of California might have violated House rules and federal law in his dealings with a Texas savings and loan. At issue was Coelho's use of the company's yacht for eight fund-raisers in 1986, when he headed the Democratic Congressional Campaign Committee.

No investigation was launched into those allegations, despite calls from conservatives for a probe. But in 1989 Coelho resigned from Congress rather than face a protracted ethics investigation of his personal finances in the wake of a controversy surrounding a "junk bond" deal. Coelho announced his intention to resign just days before Wright announced his. Coelho resigned effective June 15, 1989.

Packwood. Oregon Republican Sen. Bob Packwood resigned in 1995 rather than face near-certain expulsion.

On September 7, 1995, the day after the Senate Ethics Committee voted unanimously to recommend his expulsion on sex-

ual and official misconduct charges, Packwood announced his intention to resign. Packwood was elected to the Senate in 1968 and was serving his fifth term. Upon his announcement, he agreed to relinquish his chairmanship of the Senate Finance Committee immediately. His resignation spared the Senate a wrenching televised trial—a potential spectacle that had many lawmakers aghast, especially considering the explicit sexual nature of the charges.

The end to the saga came after a lengthy and frequently bitter investigation. The probe was prompted by allegations that were published in the *Washington Post* in November 1992. Packwood apologized for any misconduct and said he was dealing with a potential alcohol problem. The Senate Ethics Committee began its investigation into the allegations on December 1. Packwood subsequently signaled that he would present an aggressive defense, a decided shift from the apologetic stance he initially took. Over the course of its investigation, the ethics panel held more than fifty closed-door meetings and engaged in a legal fight over subpoenas that went all the way to the Supreme Court. The panel assembled a startling 10,145-page dossier, some from Packwood's own diaries, showing that the senator had made unwanted sexual advances to at least seventeen women, tampered with evidence, and abused his office by pressuring lobbyists to find his estranged wife a job.

Ethics Committee Chairman Mitch McConnell, R-Ky., and Vice Chairman Richard H. Bryan, D-Nev., at a news conference dismissed Packwood's claim that he had only snatched kisses and that he was the victim of changed mores. "There was a habitual pattern of aggressive, blatantly sexual advances, mostly directed at members of his own staff or others whose livelihoods were connected in some way to his power and authority as a senator," McConnell said. McConnell and Bryan also blasted Packwood for soliciting jobs for his ex-wife from lobbyists, and they accused him of deliberately altering his diaries to deceive the panel in its quest for evidence.

Packwood's diaries were one of the most damning pieces of evidence the committee compiled. Packwood at first tried to use part of the 8,200 pages to support his version of events but fought the ethics committee's request for, then subpoena of, the diaries. The Senate voted to enforce the subpoena in court. On March 2, 1994, Supreme Court Chief Justice William H. Rehnquist rejected Packwood's appeal of a district court decision requiring him to turn over the diaries. On March 14, Packwood dropped his appeals and turned over the diaries.

Packwood resigned from the Senate on October 1, 1995.

CENSURE

In the first two centuries of Congress, through mid-1999, only nine senators and twenty-two representatives had been censured as punishment. In the Senate, censure proceedings are carried out with a degree of moderation typical of that chamber's proceedings. The alleged offender, for example, is allowed to speak in his own defense. The House treats an offender more harshly, often denying him the privilege of defending himself. In most cases, a censured member is treated like a felon; the Speaker calls the person to the bar of the House and makes a solemn pronouncement of censure.

On October 27, 1921, for example, Speaker Frederick H. Gillett, R-Mass., directed the sergeant at arms to bring to the bar of the House Rep. Thomas L. Blanton, D-Texas, who was being disciplined for inserting indecent matter in the *Congressional Record*. The Speaker then made the following statement:

Mr. Blanton, by a unanimous vote of the House—yeas, 293; nays, none—I have been directed to censure you because, when you had been allowed the courtesy of the House to print a speech which you did not deliver, you inserted in it foul and obscene matter, which you knew you could not have spoken on the floor; and that disgusting matter, which could not have been circulated through the mails in any other publication without violating the law, was transmitted as part of the proceedings of this House to thousands of homes and libraries throughout the country, to be read by men and women, and worst of all by children, whose prurient curiosity it would excite and corrupt. In accordance with the instructions of the House and as its representative, I pronounce upon you its censure.

Censure by the Senate

Timothy Pickering, F-Mass., was the first member to be censured by the Senate. In December 1810 he had read aloud in the chamber secret documents relating to the 1803 convention with France for the cession of Louisiana. The Senate on January 2, 1811, adopted the following resolution of censure:

Resolved, That Timothy Pickering, a Senator from the State of Massachusetts, having, . . . whilst the Senate was in session with open doors, read from his place certain documents confidentially communicated by the President of the United States to the Senate, the injunction of secrecy not having been removed, has, in so doing, committed a violation of the rules of this body.

Twenty senators voted for the resolution; seven, against it.

A tongue-in-cheek dramatization of the moment during a heated debate when Sen. Henry S. Foote of Mississippi drew a pistol on Sen. Thomas Hart Benton of Missouri. A committee recommendation to censure both Foote and Benton was not pursued by the full Senate.

Benjamin Tappan, D-Ohio, was similarly censured on May 10, 1844, when the Senate adopted a two-part resolution concerning his release to the press of confidential material relating to a treaty for the annexation of Texas. The first part, adopted 35–7, censured Tappan for releasing the documents in "flagrant violation" of Senate rules. The second, adopted 39–3, accepted Tappan's apology and said that no further censure would "be inflicted on him."

Threatened violence was involved in the next censure case in the Senate. On the Senate floor April 7, 1850, Thomas Hart Benton, D-Mo., made menacing gestures and advanced toward Henry S. Foote, U-Miss., while Foote was making a speech. Foote drew a pistol from his pocket and cocked it. Before any damage was done, other senators intervened and restored order. A committee appointed to consider the incident said in its report, July 30, that what the two men had done was deplorable. The committee recommended that both Benton and Foote be censured, but the Senate took no action. This was the only Senate case in which an investigating committee's recommendation of censure was not adopted.

More than half a century later, on February 22, 1902, while the Senate was debating Philippine affairs, Benjamin R. Tillman, D-S.C., questioned the integrity of John L. McLaurin, D-S.C. When McLaurin branded the statement as "a willful, malicious, and deliberate lie," Tillman advanced toward McLaurin and they engaged in a brief fistfight. After they had been separated, the Senate by a vote of 61–0 declared them to be "in contempt of the Senate" and referred the matter to the Committee on Privileges and Elections. The committee on February 27 recommended censure for both men, and the Senate adopted the resolution by a vote of 54–12.

Hiram Bingham, R-Conn., was censured in 1929 after he hired Charles L. Eyanson, a secretary to the president of the Connecticut Manufacturers' Association, as a staff member to assist him in dealing with tariff legislation. Sen. George W. Norris, R-Neb., introduced a resolution declaring that Bingham's action was "contrary to good morals and senatorial ethics." During consideration of the resolution on November 4, 1929, the Senate added language stating that Bingham's actions were "not the result of corrupt motives," but that they nonetheless brought the Senate into disrepute. The resolution was then adopted by a vote of 54–22, with eighteen senators (including Bingham) not voting.

McCarthy. The sixth member of the Senate to be censured— "condemned" was the actual language used by the Senate—was Joseph R. McCarthy, R-Wis. Proceedings on this case began in the 82nd Congress in 1951 and were concluded in the 83rd in 1954. William Benton, D-Conn., in August 1951 offered a resolution calling on the Committee on Rules and Administration to investigate, among other things, McCarthy's participation in the defamation of Democrat Millard E. Tydings during the Maryland senatorial campaign, to determine whether expulsion proceedings should be instituted against McCarthy. On April 10, 1952, McCarthy submitted a resolution calling on the same com-

---

SENATE CONDEMNATION OF MCCARTHY

Resolution relating to the conduct of the Senator from Wisconsin, Mr. McCarthy. [S Res 301, 83rd Cong., 2nd sess., adopted December 2, 1954.]

Section 1. Resolved, that the Senator from Wisconsin, Mr. McCarthy, failed to cooperate with the Subcommittee on Privileges and Elections of the Senate Committee on Rules and Administration in clearing up matters referred to that Subcommittee which concerned his conduct as a Senator and affected the honor of the Senate and, instead, repeatedly abused the Subcommittee and its Members who were trying to carry out assigned duties, thereby obstructing the constitutional processes of the Senate, and that this conduct of the Senator from Wisconsin, Mr. McCarthy, is contrary to Senatorial traditions and is hereby condemned.

Section 2. The Senator from Wisconsin (Mr. McCarthy), in writing to the chairman of the Select Committee to Study Censure Charges (Mr. Watkins) after the Select Committee had issued its report and before the report was presented to the Senate charging three members of the Select Committee with "deliberate deception" and "fraud" for failure to disqualify themselves;

In stating to the press on November 4, 1954, that the special Senate session that was to begin November 8, 1954, was a "lynch party";

In repeatedly describing this special Senate Session as a "lynch bee" in a nationwide television and radio show on November 7, 1954;

In stating to the public press on November 13, 1954, that the chairman of the Select Committee (Mr. Watkins) was guilty of "the most unusual, most cowardly thing I've ever heard of" and stating further: "I expected he would be afraid to answer the questions, but didn't think he'd be stupid enough to make a public statement"; and in characterizing the said Committee as the "unwilling handmaiden," "involuntary agent," and "attorneys-in-fact" of the Communist party and in charging that the said Committee in writing its report "imitated Communist methods—that it distorted, misrepresented, and omitted in its efforts to manufacture a plausible rationalization" in support of its recommendations to the Senate, which characterizations and charges were contained in a statement released to the press and inserted into the *Congressional Record* of November 10, 1954, acted contrary to Senatorial ethics and tended to bring the Senate into dishonor and disrepute, to obstruct the constitutional processes of the Senate, and to impair its dignity.

And such conduct is hereby condemned.

---

mittee to investigate Benton's activities as assistant secretary of state, campaign contributions Benton had received, and other matters. After conducting an investigation, a Rules subcommittee submitted an inconclusive report on January 2, 1953.

In the spring of 1954, the Senate Permanent Investigations Subcommittee conducted hearings on mutual accusations of misconduct by McCarthy and U.S. Army officials. *(See "Censure of McCarthy," p. 273, Vol. I.)*

Sen. Ralph E. Flanders, R-Vt., on July 30 introduced a resolu-

TABLE 34-5 Censure Proceedings in the Senate

Year	Member	Grounds	Disposition
1811	Timothy Pickering, Fed-Mass.	Breach of confidence	Censured
1844	Benjamin Tappan, D-Ohio	Breach of confidence	Censured
1850	Thomas H. Benton, D-Mo.	Disorderly conduct	Not censured
1850	Henry S. Foote, Unionist-Miss.	Disorderly conduct	Not censured
1902	John L. McLaurin, D-S.C.	Assault	Censured
1902	Benjamin R. Tillman, D-S.C.	Assault	Censured
1929	Hiram Bingham, R-Conn.	Bringing Senate into disrepute	Condemned [a]
1954	Joseph R. McCarthy, R-Wis.	Obstruction of legislative process, insult to senators, etc.	Condemned [a]
1967	Thomas J. Dodd, D-Conn.	Financial misconduct	Censured
1979	Herman E. Talmadge, D-Ga.	Financial misconduct	Denounced [b]
1990	Dave Durenberger, R-Minn.	Financial misconduct	Denounced [b]
1991	Alan Cranston, D-Calif.	Improper conduct	Reprimanded [c]

NOTES: a. The word *condemned* as used in the Bingham and McCarthy cases is regarded as the same as *censured*. b. As in the Bingham and McCarthy cases, the word *denounced* as applied to Talmadge and Durenberger is considered virtually synonymous with *censured*.   c. The Ethics Committee reprimanded Cranston on behalf of the full Senate, after determining that it lacked the authority to issue a censure in the same manner. The reprimand was delivered on the Senate floor by committee leaders, but there was no vote or formal action by the full Senate. It was the first use of *reprimand* in the Senate.

SOURCES: Senate Committee on Rules and Administration, Subcommittee on Privileges and Elections, *Senate Election, Expulsion, and Censure Cases from 1793 to 1972*, comp. Richard D. Hupman, 92nd Cong., 1st sess., 1972, S Doc 92-7; *Congress and the Nation 1977–1980*, vol. 5 (Washington, D.C.: Congressional Quarterly, 1981); *Congressional Quarterly Almanac 1990*.

tion to censure McCarthy for his refusal to testify before the Rules subcommittee in 1952, his refusal to repudiate the "frivolous and irresponsible" conduct of Investigations Subcommittee Counsel Roy M. Cohn and consultant G. David Schine on their 1953 European trip investigating subversion, and his "habitual contempt for people."[4] The Senate on August 2 adopted, by a vote of 75–12, a proposal to refer Flanders's censure resolution to a select committee. Three days later, Vice President Richard Nixon appointed the select committee.

The Select Committee to Study Censure Charges held hearings from August 31 to September 13, 1954. In defending himself before the committee, McCarthy contended that the Senate could not punish a member for what he did in a previous Congress. The committee rejected that contention and on September 27 submitted a forty-thousand-word report unanimously recommending censure. After a recess during the congressional election campaign, the Senate reconvened November 8 to consider the censure proposal. Proceedings in the next few weeks led to modifications of that proposal and substitution of the word "condemned" for "censured." (Historians nonetheless count the Senate's rebuke of McCarthy as a censure; its denouncement of Sen. Herman E. Talmadge, D-Ga., in 1979 is, however, considered an action short of censure.) *(See box, Senate Condemnation of McCarthy, p. 929.)*

The Senate adopted the resolution of condemnation on December 2 by a vote of 67–22. Republicans split evenly, twenty-two favoring and twenty-two opposing the resolution. All forty-four Democrats, together with Wayne Morse, I-Ore., voted for the resolution. In January 1955, when control of Congress passed to the Democrats, McCarthy lost his committee and subcom-

mittee chairmanships. His activities thereafter attracted less public attention, and he died May 2, 1957.

Dodd. House Speaker Sam Rayburn, D-Texas, often said that the ethics of a member of Congress should be judged not by his peers but by the voters at reelection time. By the mid-1960s, it had become clear that neither Congress nor the public felt judgment at the polls was sufficient.

In 1964 the Senate was jolted by publicity over charges that Robert G. "Bobby" Baker had used his office as secretary to the Senate majority to promote his business interests. To allay public misgivings, the Senate on July 24 of that year established a Select Committee on Standards and Conduct with responsibility for investigating "allegations of improper conduct" by senators and Senate employees. In September, however, the Senate assigned jurisdiction over the Baker case to the Rules and Administration Committee. *(See box, Two Aides' Misuse of Power, p. 949.)*

The new select committee's first inquiry, begun in 1966, concerned the Dodd case. On January 24, 1966, and later dates, columnists Drew Pearson and Jack Anderson accused Sen. Thomas J. Dodd, D-Conn., of having used campaign funds for personal expenses, double-billed the government for travel expenses, and improperly exchanged favors with Julius Klein, a public relations representative of West German interests. On the last charge, the columnists said that Dodd had gone to Germany to intercede with Chancellor Konrad Adenauer in behalf of Klein's accounts, although the trip was supposedly made on Senate business.

Dodd on February 23, 1966, requested the Select Committee on Standards and Conduct to investigate his relationship with

Klein. The committee conducted hearings on all three of the Pearson-Anderson charges in June–July 1966 and March 1967. Dodd testified in his own defense.

On the first charge, Dodd said he "truly believed" the proceeds from the testimonial dinners "to be donations to me from my friends." The second charge, he said, stemmed from "sloppy bookkeeping" by Michael V. O'Hare, who had been an employee of Dodd. O'Hare and other former Dodd employees reportedly had taken documents from Dodd's files and made copies of them available to the committee. In the course of the hearings, Dodd called O'Hare a liar.[5] On charge three, Dodd denied that he had been a mere errand boy for Klein on the trip to Europe.

The committee on April 27, 1967, submitted its report on the Dodd case. It recommended that Dodd be censured for spending campaign contributions for personal purposes and for billing seven trips to both the Senate and private organizations. The committee dropped the third charge, saying that while Dodd's relations with Klein were indiscreet, there was not sufficient evidence of wrongdoing.

Voting on the committee's recommendations, June 23, 1967, the Senate censured Dodd on the first charge, by a vote of 92–5, but refused by a vote of 45 yeas to 51 nays to censure him on the second charge. The resolution as adopted recorded the judgment of the Senate that Dodd

for having engaged in a course of conduct . . . from 1961 to 1965 of exercising the influence and favor of his office as a United States Senator . . . to obtain, and use for his personal benefit, funds from the public through political testimonials and a political campaign, deserves the censure of the Senate; and he is so censured for his conduct, which is contrary to accepted morals, derogates from the public trust expected of a Senator, and tends to bring the Senate into dishonor and disrepute.

Dodd declined to seek the Democratic nomination for senator from Connecticut in 1970 but ran in the general election as an independent. He placed third, with 24 percent of the votes, while the Democratic nominee lost to Republican Lowell P. Weicker Jr., 34 percent to 42 percent. Dodd died May 24, 1971. His son, Christopher J. Dodd, D-Conn., was elected to the House in 1974 and served there until his election to the Senate in 1980.

Talmadge. Twelve years after the censure of Thomas Dodd, the Senate voted to discipline Georgia Democrat Herman E. Talmadge for financial misconduct. Talmadge was formally "denounced"—a punishment regarded at the time as virtually synonymous with censure.

In 1978 both a federal grand jury and the Senate Ethics Committee (by then a permanent, standing committee) began investigating reports that Talmadge used campaign funds and office accounts for personal purposes. The reports, which first arose during his divorce proceedings and were reported extensively by the *Washington Star,* stemmed principally from Talmadge's ex-wife Betty and his former administrative assistant Daniel Minchew, a member of the Interstate Commerce Commission.

Financial information made public during his bitterly contested divorce settlement revealed that Talmadge had written only one check to "cash" during the entire period from 1970 to 1976. Talmadge said he was able to live without cashing checks because he accepted small amounts of cash from his constituents, friends, and supporters throughout his public career. He also admitted to accepting meals, lodging, and most of his clothes. "Wherever I go [in Georgia], people entertain me, lodge me, give me small amounts of money," Talmadge told the *Star* in May 1978. Talmadge also acknowledged that he had not reported the money, goods, or services as "income" or as campaign contributions because they were "gifts." A spokesperson said the senator was unable to remember a single individual who had given him such gifts of cash and goods.

During a one-day appearance before the Ethics Committee in 1979, Betty Talmadge told the committee that her husband had for years kept a roll of cash, most of it in hundred dollar bills, in his overcoat pocket in a closet of their Washington residence. Talmadge denied that.

At the committee hearings, which began April 30, 1979, Talmadge delivered an unsworn statement that called the bulk of the charges against him "trivial" and "petty" and said the remaining, serious charges were untrue or the result of negligence. For example, the failure in his initial 1974 campaign report (a year when he was reelected) to list campaign receipts and expenditures was caused by "confusion" by his staff, he said.

Although he was reimbursed "around $12,000" by his campaign committee in January 1975 for his 1974 expenses—a total not reported to the Federal Election Commission (FEC) until 1978—Talmadge told the Ethics panel that "there is not the slightest basis for concluding that those errors were due to anything but inadvertence and confusion."

Talmadge said the fact that he repaid the Senate more than $37,000 in 1978 for expenses that were claimed in prior years, but were not reimbursable under Senate rules, should put that charge to rest. He laid the improper claims to his staff. Talmadge reserved his harshest words for former aide Minchew, whom he called "a proven liar, cheat, and embezzler."

In June Minchew testified for eight days before the committee. He said his role in laundering campaign contributions and Senate expense funds through a secret Washington bank account was to provide the senator with "insulation" and "deniability" in case the scheme ever was uncovered. By the end of his testimony, several committee members and the special counsel expressed doubts of Minchew's credibility, which was shaken by questioning from Talmadge's attorney.

On October 3 the Ethics Committee recommended that the Senate denounce Talmadge for financial misconduct. The committee rejected a censure proposal. Instead, the committee resolution said Talmadge's conduct "is reprehensible and tends to bring the Senate into dishonor and disrepute and is hereby denounced."

The committee skirted the question of Talmadge's direct involvement in the financial misconduct. Instead, it said "Talmadge either knew, or should have known, of these improper

In 1979 the Senate voted to discipline Sen. Herman E. Talmadge, D-Ga., for financial misconduct. Talmadge was formally "denounced"—a punishment regarded at the time as slightly less severe than censure. Many senators gave testimony to Talmadge's long service in the Senate.

acts and omissions, and, therefore, by the gross neglect of his duty to faithfully and carefully administer the affairs of his office, he is responsible for these acts and omissions." Talmadge called the committee's action "a personal victory" and said the findings "support my basic contention . . . that I was negligent in the oversight of my office, but that I have committed no intentional wrongdoing."

The committee said that Talmadge:

• Improperly collected $43,435.83 in reimbursements after submitting false, unsigned expense vouchers from 1973 to 1978;

• Filed inaccurate reports and failed to file other reports in a timely fashion in accounting for the use of funds during his 1974 Senate race;

• Filed "inaccurate" Senate financial disclosure reports for 1972 through 1977;

• Failed to report more than $10,000 in campaign contributions deposited in the secret Washington bank account.

The committee said that allegations of improper conduct by Talmadge in real estate transactions were "without foundation." It also said that charges of nonpayment of gift taxes were "not substantiated."

On October 11, 1979, the Senate voted 81–15 to denounce Talmadge as recommended by the committee. Despite the overwhelming vote, many senators gave testimonials to Talmadge's

service in the Senate, where he was fifth in seniority, chairman of the Agriculture and Forestry Committee, and ranking Democrat on the Finance Committee.

In May 1980 the Justice Department announced it had completed its investigation of Talmadge's financial affairs and decided not to seek an indictment. The senator lost his 1980 try for reelection.

Durenberger. In 1990 another senator was denounced. On July 25 the Senate voted 96–0 to denounce Dave Durenberger, R-Minn., for conduct it called "clearly and unequivocally unethical." The charges against Durenberger focused mainly on a 1985–1986 book deal the senator had with a Minnesota publishing company and on Senate reimbursement Durenberger received for rent he paid on a Minneapolis condominium from August 1983 to November 1989.

More than a year after it opened its investigation, and five months after it first met with Durenberger about the case, the Ethics Committee on July 18 unanimously called for Durenberger to be formally denounced for his financial dealings. The panel went beyond the recommendation of special counsel Robert S. Bennett—who also handled the committee's investigation of Sen. Harrison Williams in 1982 and the Keating Five in 1990–1991—by calling for Durenberger to pay more than $124,000 in restitution.

The Ethics Committee's June 12–13 formal public hearings on the Durenberger case marked the first time in its twenty-six-year history that it had conducted business before television cameras.

Bennett's investigation produced twenty-three volumes of evidence, the result of 198 subpoenas for internal documents, 240 interviews with witnesses, numerous depositions, and at least 75 affidavits. Bennett focused on the book deal with Piranha Press and on the Minneapolis condominium. Piranha Press was owned by Gary L. Diamond, a friend of Durenberger's who also published trade journals for the restaurant and hospitality industries. He published two books by Durenberger: *Neither Madmen nor Messiahs,* a collection of white papers on defense policy, in 1984; and *Prescription for Change,* a collection of speeches about health care, in 1986. The only other book Diamond had published, Bennett said, was about wrestling holds.

Piranha Press paid Durenberger $100,000 in quarterly installments of $12,500 that began in 1985 and ended in early 1987 in return for his making 113 appearances to promote the book. Bennett contended that the arrangement "was little more than a pretext to sanitize what were honestly honoraria payments." Bennett traced the deal to Durenberger's need to replace lost honoraria income. The senator reported $92,750 in honoraria in 1983, the last year the Senate permitted members to collect unlimited speech fees. New Senate rules capped Durenberger's honoraria income at $22,530 in 1985 and $30,040 in 1986, the years of the book deal.

In those two years, Durenberger made traditional honoraria speeches until he reached the limit. At that point, speeches would be designated as "Piranha Press events," Bennett said.

The senator's attorney, Michael C. Mahoney of Minneapolis, asked the Federal Election Commission to rule on the nature of the publishing agreement. The FEC ruled that Durenberger's stipend from Piranha was acceptable—a ruling Durenberger would repeatedly use as a shield. The request for the opinion, however, never mentioned what Bennett said were three crucial facts: Durenberger's contract called for the groups he addressed to pay the publisher a fee; the appearances stemmed from requests for speeches, not book promotions; and the promotional events were identical to traditional honorarium events.

Groups wanting to hear Durenberger were referred by his staff to Mahoney, the agent for Piranha Press. With a call or a letter, Mahoney would tell the organizations that Durenberger's appearance was a book promotion. "What were honoraria events one day magically became book promotion events the next," Bennett said. Never in the 113 times Durenberger appeared for Piranha did an organization ask Durenberger to promote his book, Bennett said. Some organizations and constituencies important to the senator objected to the arrangement.

"This very hungry fish, Piranha Press, was allowed to engage in a feeding frenzy on responsible organizations who thought they were sponsoring traditional honorarium events," Bennett said. "And unfortunately, the evidence shows that Senator Durenberger . . . allowed himself and the stature of his office to be used as the bait, and he got $100,000 for his trouble."

Bennett depicted Durenberger's handling of his Minneapolis condominium as a "search for loopholes." It began in 1983, when Durenberger decided he could not afford two residences—a house in McLean, Virginia, and the one-bedroom condominium. Owning the Minneapolis condo where he stayed also prevented the Senate from reimbursing him for living expenses on his frequent trips to Minnesota.

Durenberger took two steps in 1983 to change this situation. First, he changed his legal residence to his parents' address in Avon, Minnesota. Second, he sought to change the ownership of the condo to a partnership with Roger Scherer, a friend and political backer who owned another condo in the same building.

From August 1983 until mid-November 1989, Durenberger collected $40,055 from the U.S. Treasury for per diem expenses while staying at the condo. After the Senate Rules Committee ruled in January 1990 that Durenberger's resident city for the purposes of reimbursement was Minneapolis, not Avon, during these periods, the senator paid back $11,005 to the Treasury.

Before seeking reimbursement for staying in the condo, Durenberger said, his staff consulted the Senate's Rules and Ethics committees, which raised no objections at the time.

The denouncement said that Durenberger's conduct "has been reprehensible and has brought the Senate into dishonor and disrepute." He was ordered to repay more than $124,000 in restitution, including $29,050 plus interest for reimbursements he received for the cost of staying in his Minneapolis condominium. That sum was owed on top of the $11,005 Durenberger already had repaid. The Senate also required Durenberger to

give charities an amount equal to the honoraria he allegedly obtained improperly, approximately $95,000.

Though Durenberger had called denouncement too harsh a penalty, he did not challenge the sanction or the version of events Ethics Committee Chairman Howell Heflin, D-Ala., presented to the Senate.

Avoiding a trial on felony charges, former senator Durenberger pleaded guilty on August 22, 1995, to five misdemeanor charges of hiding his ownership of a Minnesota condominium to collect reimbursement for lodging when he traveled home. His guilty plea covered ten specific days, for which he had claimed $425 in reimbursement. On November 29, 1995, Durenberger was fined $1,000 and placed on a year's probation.

Cranston. One of the most divisive ethics cases in the history of the Senate came to a novel close November 20, 1991, after two years of investigation. The Senate Ethics Committee invented a new punishment to reprove Alan Cranston, D-Calif., for his

Sen. Alan Cranston, D-Calif., is sworn in before testifying at the Keating Five hearings in 1991. Cranston was later reprimanded for improper conduct—the first time the Senate used reprimand as a form of punishment.

conduct in the Keating Five case. Almost nine months earlier, the committee had issued much milder rebukes to the other four senators involved in the scandal—Democrats John Glenn, Ohio, Donald W. Riegle Jr., Mich., and Dennis DeConcini, Ariz., and Republican John McCain, Ariz. *(See box, The Keating Five Scandal, p. 962.)*

The committee had begun hearings on the complicated case in November 1990; the senators and their attorneys presented their rebuttal in January 1991. The committee issued its preliminary recommendations on February 27, 1991, when it chastised McCain, Glenn, Riegle, and DeConcini for their poor judgment in dealings with thrift owner Charles H. Keating Jr. and instituted formal proceedings against Cranston.

The key issue in this case was whether any link existed between Keating's prodigious fund-raising ($1.5 million for senators' campaign or political causes) and the help he received from the senators in fending off regulations he perceived to be problematic for his thrift, Lincoln Savings and Loan Association. The thrift went bankrupt in 1989, costing taxpayers an estimated $2 billion. All five senators had met with bank regulators to try to persuade them not to issue regulations that would have restricted Lincoln's investment options. But the committee found that only Cranston's actions deserved greater scrutiny.

After months of acrimonious and often partisan debate, the Ethics Committee concluded that Cranston had gone too far in his advocacy for Keating with federal banking regulators. In looking at Cranston's dealings with Keating, the panel decided that the implicit quid pro quo of doing favors for a top contributor veered too close to the explicit. No one episode sealed Cranston's fate, said Committee Chairman Howell Heflin, D-Ala., rather it was "the totality of the circumstances."

Cranston had accepted about $1 million, most of it for non-profit voter-drive groups at a time when Keating was marshaling political clout in a bitter fight with federal regulators over Lincoln. Large donations were given or solicited close in time to specific official actions by Cranston on Keating's behalf, mostly calls to regulators. The committee called this "linkage" and said it breached "established norms of behavior in the Senate and was improper conduct which reflects upon the Senate," in violation of a long-standing general Senate rule.

To break an internal stalemate, the panel created a new form of punishment halfway between a committee rebuke and a full-Senate censure. While the panel took the matter to the floor, there was no vote or formal action by the full body. Instead, ethics leaders told the assembled Senate that the panel itself was reprimanding Cranston for "an impermissible pattern of conduct in which fundraising and official actions were substantially linked."

The ninety-five senators who had somberly gathered to hear the verdict found themselves the subject of attack by Cranston, the defendant. While he apologized for making the Senate look bad, he rejected many of the committee's findings and then implied that some of his colleagues had done worse. He maintained that he had not done anything wrong. "My behavior did

not violate any established norms," he said. "Here, but for the grace of God, stand you."

His unrepentant speech infuriated Ethics Committee members. "After accepting this committee's recommendation, what I heard is a statement I can only describe as arrogant, unrepentant and a smear on this institution. Everybody does not do it," raged Warren B. Rudman, R-N.H., the top Republican on the Ethics Committee. Cranston did not take back his remarks.

Members looking for retribution were left unsatisfied because the Ethics Committee had entered into an unprecedented deal with Cranston: in return for not facing the prospect of sanction by the full Senate, the seventy-seven-year-old Cranston, who was suffering from prostate cancer and had announced he would not run for reelection, agreed to accept the reprimand. "The resolution we bring before the Senate today," said Rudman, "is not a perfect solution. It is, however, for this institution an acceptable result, and it certainly is better than no resolution at all."

Censure by the House

A House rule, first adopted in 1789, reads: "If any member, in speaking or otherwise, transgress the rules of the House, the Speaker shall, or any member may, call him to order; . . . and if the case require it, he shall be liable to censure or such punishment as the House may deem proper." The censure clause of this rule has been invoked thirty-six times, and censure has been voted twenty-two times, two-thirds of them in the 1860s and 1870s. Grounds for censure have included assault on a fellow member of the House, insult to the Speaker, treasonable utterance, corruption, and other offenses. In the twentieth century, five representatives have been censured. *(See Table 34-6, p. 935.)*

The first censure motion in the House was introduced after Matthew Lyon, Anti-Fed-Vt., physically attacked Roger Griswold, F-Conn., on the House floor in January 1798. Griswold had taunted Lyon on his allegedly poor military record. The censure motion failed. The following month, Lyon and Griswold engaged in an affray with tongs and cane, again on the House floor. Again a motion was introduced to censure both members, and again the motion failed.

In 1832 William Stanbery, JD-Ohio, became the first House member to be formally censured. He had insulted the Speaker by saying, in objection to a ruling by the chair, "The eyes of the Speaker [Andrew Stevenson, D-Va.] are too frequently turned from the chair you occupy toward the White House." There were 93 votes for censuring Stanbery; 44 were opposed. Censure for unacceptable language or offensive publication was imposed in seven other cases. For example, John W. Hunter of New York was censured on January 26, 1867, for saying, about a statement made by a colleague, "So far as I am concerned, it is a base lie."

In 1842 censure was considered and rejected in the case of one of the most distinguished representatives in American history, John Quincy Adams, a former president of the United States. Adams had presented to the House, for forty-six of his constituents, a petition asking Congress to dissolve the Union

TABLE 34-6 Censure Proceedings in the House

Year	Member	Grounds	Disposition
1798	Matthew Lyon, Anti-Fed.-Vt.	Assault on representative	Not censured
1798	Roger Griswold, Fed.-Conn.	Assault on representative	Not censured
1832	William Stanbery, JD-Ohio	Insult to Speaker	Censured
1836	Sherrod Williams, Whig-Ky.	Insult to Speaker	Not censured
1838	Henry A. Wise, Tyler Dem.-Va.	Service as second in duel	Not censured
1839	Alexander Duncan, Whig-Ohio	Offensive publication	Not censured
1842	John Q. Adams, Whig-Mass.	Treasonable petition	Not censured
1842	Joshua R. Giddings, Whig-Ohio	Offensive paper	Censured
1856	Henry A. Edmundson, D-Va.	Complicity in assault on senator	Not censured
1856	Laurence M. Keitt, D-S.C.	Complicity in assault on senator	Censured
1860	George S. Houston, D-Ala.	Insult to representative	Not censured
1864	Alexander Long, D-Ohio	Treasonable utterance	Censured
1864	Benjamin G. Harris, D-Md.	Treasonable utterance	Censured
1866	John W. Chanler, D-N.Y.	Insult to House	Censured
1866	Lovell H. Rousseau, R-Ky.	Assault on representative	Censured
1867	John W. Hunter, Ind-N.Y.	Insult to representative	Censured
1868	Fernando Wood, D-N.Y.	Offensive utterance	Censured
1868	E. D. Holbrook, D-Idaho[a]	Offensive utterance	Censured
1870	Benjamin F. Whittemore, R-S.C.	Corruption	Censured
1870	Roderick R. Butler, R-Tenn.	Corruption	Censured
1870	John T. Deweese, D-N.C.	Corruption	Censured
1873	Oakes Ames, R-Mass.	Corruption	Censured
1873	James Brooks, D-N.Y.	Corruption	Censured
1875	John Y. Brown, D-Ky.	Insult to representative	Censured[b]
1876	James G. Blaine, R-Maine	Corruption	Not censured
1882	William D. Kelley, R-Pa.	Offensive utterance	Not censured
1882	John D. White, R-Ky.	Offensive utterance	Not censured
1883	John Van Voorhis, R-N.Y.	Offensive utterance	Not censured
1890	William D. Bynum, D-Ind.	Offensive utterance	Censured
1921	Thomas L. Blanton, D-Texas	Abuse of leave to print	Censured
1978	Edward R. Roybal, D-Calif.	Lying to House committee	Not censured[c]
1979	Charles C. Diggs Jr., D-Mich.	Misuse of clerk–hire funds	Censured
1980	Charles H. Wilson, D-Calif.	Financial misconduct	Censured
1983	Gerry E. Studds, D-Mass.	Sexual misconduct	Censured
1983	Daniel B. Crane, R-Ill.	Sexual misconduct	Censured
1990	Barney Frank, D-Mass.	Discrediting House	Not censured[c]

NOTES: a. Holbrook was a territorial delegate, not a representative.   b. The House later rescinded part of the censure resolution against Brown.   c. Reprimanded after censure resolution failed or was withdrawn.

SOURCES: Hinds and Cannon, *Precedents of the House of Representatives of the United States*, 11 vols. (1935–1941); Joint Committee on Congressional Operations, *House of Representatives Exclusion, Censure, and Expulsion Cases from 1789 to 1973*, 93rd Cong., 1st sess., 1973, committee print; *Congress and the Nation 1977–1980, 1981–1984, 1985–1988, 1992–1996*, vols. 5, 6, 7, 9 (Washington, D.C.: Congressional Quarterly); *Congressional Quarterly Almanac 1990*.

and allow the states to go their separate ways. A resolution proposing to censure him for this act was worded so strongly that Adams asserted his right, under the Sixth Amendment to the Constitution, to a trial by jury. He succeeded in putting his opponents on the defensive, and the resolution was not put to a vote.

Lovell H. Rousseau, R-Ky., during the evening of June 14, 1866, assaulted Josiah B. Grinnell, R-Iowa, with a cane in the portico on the East Front of the Capitol. On the House floor, earlier in the month, Grinnell had imputed cowardice to Rousseau. A committee appointed to report on the case recommended that Rousseau be expelled. That recommendation was rejected, but the House voted on July 17, 1866, that he "be summoned to the bar of this House, and be there publicly reprimanded by the Speaker for his violation of its rights and privileges." The order was carried out July 21, despite Rousseau's

announcement that he had sent his resignation to the governor of Kentucky.

Corruption was the basis for censure or proposed censure in a number of cases. The House on February 27, 1873, by a vote of 182–36, censured Oakes Ames, R-Mass., and James Brooks, D-N.Y., for their part in a financial scandal involving Crédit Mobilier stock given to members of Congress. Three years later, Speaker James G. Blaine, R-Maine, was accused of involvement in that scandal as well as of receiving excessive payments from the Union Pacific Railroad Co. for bonds sold to the company. Two months before the convention at which Blaine hoped to be chosen the Republican candidate for president, he spoke in the House on the charges against him. By selective reading of a series of allegedly incriminating letters, Blaine managed to confuse the evidence sufficiently to rout the proponents of censure. (*See "Crédit Mobilier," p. 266, Vol. I.*)

ASSAULT ON SUMNER

Charles Sumner of Massachusetts, in a Senate speech May 20, 1856, denounced in scathing language supporters of the Kansas-Nebraska Act of 1854, which repealed the Missouri Compromise of 1820 and permitted the two new territories to decide whether slavery would be allowed there.

Two days later, while Sumner was seated at his desk on the Senate floor after the day's session had ended, he heard his name called. Looking up, he saw a tall stranger, who berated him for his speech and then struck him on the head repeatedly with a heavy walking stick, which was broken by the blows. Sumner fell bleeding and unconscious to the floor. He was absent from the Senate, because of the injuries suffered in the assault, for three and a half years, until December 5, 1859.

The attacker was Rep. Preston S. Brooks, SRD-S.C., nephew of one of those whom Sumner had excoriated—Sen. A. P. Butler, SRD-S.C. Expulsion proceedings against Brooks failed, on a strictly party vote. He resigned his House seat July 15, 1856, but was elected to fill the vacancy caused by his resignation.

Rep. Laurence M. Keitt, D-S.C., was censured by the House on July 15, 1856, for having known of Brooks's intention to assault Sumner, for having taken no action to discourage or prevent the assault, and for having been "present on one or more occasions to witness the same." Keitt resigned July 16, 1856, and was elected to fill the vacancy caused by his resignation. A resolution similar to the one censuring Keitt but directed against Rep. Henry A. Edmundson, D-Va., failed of adoption July 15, 1856.

In one instance, the House rescinded part of a censure resolution. During debate on a bill in 1875, John Y. Brown, D-Ky., referred to Benjamin Butler, R-Mass., as "outlawed in his own home from respectable society; whose name is synonymous with falsehood; and who is the champion, and has been on all occasions, of fraud; who is the apologist of thieves; who is such a prodigy of vice and meanness that to describe him would sicken imagination and exhaust invective." Brown was censured February 4, 1875, for that insult and for lying to the Speaker in order to continue his insulting speech. But a year later, on May 2, 1876, the House agreed to rescind that portion of the censure resolution condemning Brown for lying to the Speaker. The charge of insulting another member remained, however.

Diggs. The first member censured since 1921 was Charles C. Diggs Jr., D-Mich., who was publicly chastised by the House July 31, 1979, for misuse of his clerk-hire funds. An attempt to expel him from the House was rejected.

Diggs had been convicted October 7, 1978, on twenty-nine felony counts centering on charges that he illegally diverted more than $60,000 of his congressional employees' salaries to his personal and official use. He was reelected to the House in November 1978 despite the conviction.

When Congress convened January 9, 1979, House Republicans announced they would seek to expel Diggs from the House

as a convicted felon. The ethics committee began an investigation of his case but moved too slowly to satisfy Newt Gingrich, a freshman Republican from Georgia. If Diggs chose to vote despite his conviction, Gingrich informed Diggs in a February 22 letter, Gingrich would move to expel Diggs from the House. Existing House rules recommended—but did not require—that convicted House members refrain from voting unless they were reelected after their conviction.

On the House floor February 28, Diggs voted "yea" on a bill to increase the public debt limit. The next day, Gingrich offered a resolution to expel Diggs from the House. Majority Leader Jim Wright immediately moved to refer the resolution to the ethics committee, and this carried, 322–77.

The committee filed formal charges against Diggs for violating House rules and negotiated with him for an admission of guilt. On June 27 Diggs wrote to the committee admitting to some of the charges. He agreed to be censured by his colleagues in return for ending the committee's investigation into his financial affairs.

In the letter, Diggs admitted he had padded his office payroll and accepted kickbacks from five current and former employees. He said his personal gain from the kickbacks totaled $40,031.66, and he offered to repay the sum with interest. Diggs said he thought the agreement with the committee would help his pending appeal of his conviction. (It did not. The appeal was turned down by the Supreme Court in June 1980, and Diggs resigned from Congress the next day and began serving his three-year jail sentence.)

In recommending censure instead of expulsion, the committee explained in its July 19 report that it had "considered his admission of guilt of serious offenses against the House rules, his apology to the House therefor, his agreement to make restitution of substantial amounts by which he was unjustly enriched, and the nature of the offenses charged." On July 30, 1979, a move by a Republican group of representatives trying to force a vote on an expulsion resolution was tabled—and thus killed—by a 205–197 vote. The next day censure of Diggs was approved by a vote of 414–0, with four members voting present.

Wilson. Rep. Charles H. Wilson, D-Calif., was censured by the House June 10, 1980, for financial misconduct. The action came just a week after Wilson lost his bid for renomination in the June 3 California primary. The House approved the censure resolution on a voice vote after rejecting 97–308 a move to reduce Wilson's punishment from a censure to a reprimand. In voting to censure Wilson, the House found him guilty of improperly converting almost $25,000 in campaign funds to his personal use and accepting $10,500 in gifts from an individual with a direct interest in legislation before Congress.

Following the vote, Wilson was called to the front of the chamber, where House Speaker Thomas P. O'Neill Jr., D-Mass., read the censure resolution to him. Wilson then turned and quickly left the chamber. It was the second time in two years that the House had disciplined Wilson. The California Democrat was reprimanded in October 1978 after he first denied—and then acknowledged—receiving wedding gifts, including $600 in cash, from South Korean businessman Tongsun Park. (See "Mc-Fall, Roybal, Wilson," p. 938.)

The individual the committee said was placed on Wilson's payroll and who allegedly had kicked back to the California Democrat was Lee Rogers, president of a Los Angeles mail order firm called the American Holiday Association. At ethics committee hearings a committee lawyer produced a letter from Wilson to Rogers boasting that the representative's "strong opposition" to a bill opposed by Rogers had killed the legislation in subcommittee. "You may be certain that I will work with you to see it stays buried in the subcommittee," the letter concluded.

After the censure vote a new Democratic rule forced Wilson to give up his chairmanship of the House Post Office Subcommittee on Postal Operations. House Democrats had voted in May to automatically deprive censured members of their chairmanships.

Studds, Crane. The 1980s brought the first censures arising from House members' sexual conduct. Daniel B. Crane, R-Ill., and Gerry E. Studds, D-Mass., became the twenty-first and twenty-second censured representatives. Others involved in sex-related scandals received lesser punishments.

The House's action capped a year-long investigation by the ethics panel into allegations of sexual misconduct and drug use by members and congressional pages. The investigation was led by special counsel Joseph A. Califano Jr., who served as secretary of health, education, and welfare in the Carter administration.

On July 14, 1983, the committee issued its report on the investigation, along with separate reports on Studds and Crane. The committee asserted that both Studds and Crane had had sexual relationships with teenage pages and thus had committed a "serious breach of duty owed by the House and its individual members to the young people who serve the House as its pages."

The panel reported that in 1973 Studds had a sexual relationship with a seventeen-year-old male page, who might have been sixteen at the time the relationship began. In addition, the committee said Studds made sexual advances to two other male pages in 1973. Studds told his House colleagues July 14 that he was homosexual.

Crane, the panel said, had a sexual relationship with a seventeen-year-old female page in 1980. Because the legal age of consent in the District of Columbia was sixteen, the panel accused neither Studds nor Crane of a crime. Nevertheless, the panel felt that even a consensual sexual relationship between a member and a page constituted improper conduct.

In choosing an appropriate penalty for Studds and Crane, Califano cited as precedents the two most recent cases of severe discipline, the censure of Charles Wilson and the expulsion of Michael Myers. Califano concluded, "Measured against the precedents, neither expulsion nor censure is warranted." He recommended a reprimand, and the committee agreed by an 11–1 vote.

In the House debate on the ethics committee's recommendation, Gingrich argued that a reprimand was too mild. "With no

CENSURE FOR DUELING WITHHELD

The killing of one representative by another in a duel in 1838 went uncensured by the House. Rep. Jonathan Cilley, JD-Maine, had made statements on the floor reflecting on the character of James W. Webb, prominent editor of a New York City newspaper that was a Whig organ. When Webb sent Cilley a note by the hand of Rep. William J. Graves, Whig-Ky., demanding an explanation of the statements, Cilley refused to receive the note. Further correspondence led to a challenge by Graves and agreement by Cilley to a duel with rifles.

The duel took place on February 24, 1838, on the Marlboro Pike in Maryland, close to the District of Columbia. Graves and Cilley each fired twice, with no result. In the third volley, Cilley was shot fatally in the abdomen.

Four days later, the House appointed a committee to investigate the affair. A majority recommended on April 21 that Graves be expelled from the House and that the seconds in the duel, Rep. Henry A. Wise, W-Va., and George W. Jones (a member of the Tennessee House of Representatives who served in the national House of Representatives, 1843–1859), be censured. One of the minority group on the committee, Rep. Franklin H. Elmore, SRD-S.C., observed that dueling by members had been frequent and generally had gone unnoticed by the House. A motion to table the committee's report and print the testimony was agreed to May 10, and an attempt on July 4 to take up the report was unsuccessful. Graves was not expelled, and Wise and Jones were not censured.

malice toward any individual," he said, "I cannot see how a reprimand is in any way adequate." Gingrich wanted the two expelled.

House Minority Leader Robert H. Michel, R-Ill., moved to change the recommendation from reprimand to censure. Michel said he sensed that members wanted a more severe punishment.

Michel's motion in Crane's case was agreed to 289–136. The censure resolution then was adopted 421–3. In Studds's case, Michel's motion was agreed to 338–87, and the House voted to censure Studds by a 420–3 vote. Crane voted for his own censure. Studds voted "present" when the House voted on his censure.

Crane faced his silent colleagues as Speaker O'Neill read the resolution of censure to him. Studds faced the Speaker, hands clasped behind him, as his censure was read. Studds was reelected in 1984 and again in 1986, 1988, and 1990; Crane lost his next reelection bid.

In light of the incidents, Congress revised the page system to tighten control over the pages' housing and schooling. (See box, The Youngest Patronage Appointees: Capitol Pages, p. 802, Vol I.)

OTHER FORMS OF DISCIPLINE

As lesser forms of punishment than expulsion or censure, the House has from time to time reprimanded members or forced them to give up chairmanships. Members who remained in the House after criminal indictments have been urged to refrain from voting on the floor or in committee. Since 1975, convicted members have been denied that right. *(See "Suspension," p. 941.)*

Reprimand

House ethics committee chairman John J. Flynt Jr., D-Ga., said in 1976 that he saw no real difference between reprimand and censure. In the case of a reprimand, however, no further action is taken against a member. When censured, a member must stand in the well of the House and be publicly admonished by the Speaker.

Sikes. Flynt's statement came after his committee recommended a reprimand for Robert L. F. Sikes, D-Fla., for failing to disclose financial holdings in defense business and a conflict of interest. Sikes was the first member of the House investigated by the newly created ethics committee.

The complaint against Sikes was filed by the public affairs lobby Common Cause and forwarded to the committee by forty-four representatives. After collecting information and testimony from Sikes and his counsel, the committee recommended a formal reprimand.

On July 29, 1976, the House approved the reprimand by a vote of 381–3. Sikes won reelection that November, but in January 1977 the House Democratic Caucus voted 189–93 to unseat Sikes as chairman of the Appropriations Subcommittee on Military Construction.

McFall, Roybal, Wilson. The House ethics committee conducted highly publicized hearings in 1977–1978 into reports of congressional lobbying by agents of the South Korean government and of lavish gifts to representatives by Korean businessman Tongsun Park. The investigations ended with slaps on the wrist to three California Democrats—John J. McFall, Edward R. Roybal, and Charles Wilson. The committee charged McFall and Roybal with failing to report campaign contributions from Park. Wilson was accused of failing to report, on a committee questionnaire, wedding gifts from Park that included $600 in cash. The recommended punishment was a reprimand for McFall and Wilson and censure for Roybal because the committee concluded he had lied to it.

The House October 13, 1978, rejected the resolution to censure Roybal on a 170–219 vote, and he was reprimanded instead, as were McFall and Wilson. Several Roybal supporters suggested that as a Hispanic he was a victim of bias. *(See "Korean Influence Buying," p. 952.)*

Two years later the House censured Wilson for financial misconduct in another matter. *(See "Wilson," p. 936.)*

Hansen. The House July 31, 1984, reprimanded George V. Hansen, R-Idaho, for failing to reveal various financial dealings that he was required to disclose under the 1978 Ethics in Government Act. Hansen's conviction and reprimand stemmed from his failure to report nearly $334,000 in loans and profits between 1978 and 1981. A seven-term House member, Hansen was sentenced June 15 to between five and fifteen months in prison and a $40,000 fine following his April 2 federal felony conviction on the disclosure charges. He was narrowly defeated in his subsequent election bid.

The vote for a reprimand was 354–52 with six members voting present. Leaders of the House ethics committee, which had recommended the reprimand by an 11–1 vote, used a parliamentary tactic to block a House vote to change the penalty to a censure or to include other House members. During the debate, a defiant Hansen maintained his innocence, insisting that Reagan administration officials and other members of Congress had been caught in questionable financial reporting snags similar to his.

Hansen's 1984 conviction was not his first legal problem. In 1975 he pleaded guilty to two misdemeanor charges of filing late and false campaign finance reports from his 1974 House primary. He received a two-month prison sentence that was suspended and instead paid a $2,000 fine.

Murphy. Accepting the recommendation of its ethics committee, the House December 18, 1987, voted 324–68 to reprimand Austin J. Murphy, D-Pa., for diverting government resources to his former law firm, for allowing another member to vote for him on the House floor, and for keeping a "no-show" employee on his payroll.

Murphy claimed he been made a scapegoat to appease conservative Republicans who all year had lambasted the House ethics committee for being slow to act on charges of misconduct by some Democratic members, silent or secretive about others, and hesitant to recommend sanctions when it did find violations of law or ethics codes.

"We are not scapegoating anybody," ethics panel member Vic Fazio, D-Calif., said on the floor. "We've taken heat before; we'll take heat again."

Frank. The House of Representatives on July 26, 1990, formally reprimanded Barney Frank, D-Mass., for improperly using his office to help a male prostitute. The House voted 408–18 to reprimand Frank after a roiling, unusually partisan debate about how harshly to punish him.

Despite politicians' election-year jitters about ethics issues—heightened in a case involving homosexuality—the House turned back efforts to overturn the recommendation of its ethics committee and punish Frank more severely. That came in the wake of a passionate appeal by House ethics committee Chairman Julian C. Dixon, D-Calif., for his colleagues to stand by the panel as their bulwark against political attacks. "We will throw no one to the wolves," Dixon said.

The House rejected a resolution to expel Frank, the ultimate sanction, 38–390. The intermediate penalty of censure was turned down largely along party lines, 141–287.

Frank did not contest the ethics committee's finding that he "reflected discredit upon the House" by using his status as a member of Congress to fix thirty-three parking tickets and by writing a misleading memorandum in behalf of Steve Gobie, a male prostitute with whom Frank associated in 1985–1987.

Frank, who had publicly acknowledged his homosexuality in

TABLE 34-7 Reprimand Proceedings in the House

Congress	Session	Year	Member	Grounds	Disposition
94th	2nd	1976	Robert L. F. Sikes, D-Fla.	Financial misconduct	Reprimanded
95th	2nd	1978	John J. McFall, D-Calif.	Financial misconduct	Reprimanded
95th	2nd	1978	Edward R. Roybal, D-Calif.	Financial misconduct	Reprimanded
95th	2nd	1978	Charles H. Wilson, D-Calif.	Financial misconduct	Reprimanded
98th	2nd	1984	George V. Hansen, R-Idaho	Financial misconduct	Reprimanded
100th	1st	1987	Austin J. Murphy, D-Pa.	Misuse of office	Reprimanded
101st	2nd	1990	Barney Frank, D-Mass.	Discrediting House	Reprimanded
105th	1st	1997	Newt Gingrich, R-Ga.	Discrediting House	Reprimanded

NOTE: The only significant difference between *censure* and *reprimand* in the House is that censured members must stand before the House as the Speaker reads the censure resolution. This is not required in reprimand cases.

SOURCES: *Congress and the Nation 1973– 1976, 1977–1980, 1981–1984, 1985–1988, 1989–1992*, vols. 4–8 (Washington, D.C.: Congressional Quarterly, various years); *Congressional Quarterly Almanac 1997* (Washington, D.C.: Congressional Quarterly, 1998).

1987, went to the well of the House near the end of debate to apologize to his colleagues. Attributing his misconduct to the strain of concealing his homosexuality at the time, Frank said, "I should have known better. I do now."

In the eyes of other participants in the debate, more was at stake than just one member's conduct. "We are here to repair the integrity of the United States House of Representatives," said House GOP Whip Gingrich, who proposed upping the sanction to censure.

Dixon, indignant at challenges to his committee's unanimous verdict, cast the debate as a referendum on the ethics panel itself. "This case boils down to, really, who do you trust?" said Dixon.

The political crosscurrents in the Frank investigation were strong from the day the committee opened its investigation in September 1989. The *Washington Times* a few weeks earlier had disclosed Frank's relationship with Gobie, a felon on probation. After buying sex from Gobie in 1985, Frank befriended him and paid him to help with household chores.

In its report on the inquiry filed July 20, the panel said it found no conclusive evidence that Frank knew Gobie was running a prostitution service out of his apartment until his landlady told him that she had seen suspicious activity in his absence. But the panel criticized Frank for a misleading memo written in support of ending Gobie's probation. The memo included assertions that Gobie had met Frank through "mutual friends"— when in fact Frank had responded to Gobie's escort-service ad in a gay newspaper—and that Gobie was adhering to his probation requirements, when Frank knew Gobie was engaged in prostitution. Frank said candor on those two points would have revealed his own homosexuality.

Although the panel concluded that Frank had not improperly pressured probation officials, it said that the memo "could be perceived as an attempt to use political influence." The panel also ordered Frank to pay the parking tickets because it was not clear whether they were incurred on official business. Having agreed on those two areas of impropriety, many Democrats on the ethics committee had sought a light sanction that would have avoided action by the House—a letter of reproval.

But members on and off the committee were concerned that Frank might receive too light a punishment. George "Buddy" Darden, D-Ga., said a letter of rebuke would have been too mild. The publicity surrounding Frank's case, he said, had "held the House up to a certain amount of public embarrassment. There's no other way to look at it." On July 19 the House ethics committee unanimously agreed to recommend a reprimand for Frank after it became clear that the committee would be overturned by the House if it did not send something stronger to the floor.

From the beginning, it was all but certain that the effort to expel Frank would be rejected. Expulsion had been reserved for more serious transgressions such as treason. Its proponent in the Frank case, California Republican William E. Dannemeyer, was not considered an influential advocate because even some of his own Republican colleagues regarded him as an antigay zealot.

Anticipating the effort to censure Frank, a task force of Democrats sympathetic to him had worked for months to drum up support for Frank among his colleagues. Under House rules, censure was considered harsher than a reprimand because the chastised member must stand in the well of the House when the charges were read and could not hold a chairmanship for the rest of that Congress. Frank was chairman of a Judiciary subcommittee.

Frank's effort to avoid censure was also aided by Gingrich's advocacy of it. Many Democrats still resented Gingrich's part in the 1989 resignation of Speaker Jim Wright. Democrats were also annoyed that Gingrich was criticizing the same committee that he once praised for clearing his own name. The ethics committee in March had dismissed formal complaints against Gingrich over his own financial dealings. Republicans had tried but failed to persuade someone other than Gingrich to offer the censure motion. GOP leader Michel voted for censure but did not speak on the floor. In the end, only twelve Democrats, most of them southerners, joined 129 Republicans in supporting censure.

Despite the reprimand from his colleagues, Frank had little trouble winning reelection.

Newt Gingrich, R-Ga., became the first Speaker in the history of the House to be reprimanded by his colleagues. Gingrich, who acknowledged he had provided the House ethics committee with misleading information, also had to pay a $300,000 penalty.

Gingrich. On January 21, 1997, Newt Gingrich, R-Ga., became the first Speaker in the history of the House to be formally punished by his colleagues. The House voted 395–28 to reprimand Gingrich and require that he pay the government $300,000 for behavior that lengthened the investigation. Five members voted present.

Gingrich had also been the target of earlier ethics complaints. *(See "Gingrich," p. 964.)*

Gingrich taught a college course, which he created, called "Renewing American Civilization" between 1993 and 1995. The course was financed through donations solicited by tax-exempt groups, an arrangement that allowed supporters to make undisclosed contributions and claim tax write-offs as well—two benefits not available to them under election laws that required full disclosure and provided no such tax write-offs. While Gingrich maintained that the course was nonpartisan and thus eligible for tax-exempt support, an ethics investigatory subcommittee found that it was probably tied to party politics and to Gingrich's quest to lead a Republican takeover of Congress. Gingrich did not admit to improperly using tax-exempt groups for partisan purposes but instead acknowledged a lesser crime of failing to seek legal advise in his use of foundations to finance the course as well as town meetings.

After nearly two years of investigation and repeated denials of wrongdoing, Gingrich surprised many when he agreed to a plea bargain with the ethics committee on December 21, 1996. In return for the committee not pursuing the case any further, Gingrich pleaded guilty to not seeking proper tax advice and also to providing the committee with misleading information during the course of its investigation.

After an intense campaign by his top party leaders, Gingrich was narrowly reelected Speaker on January 7, 1997, by a vote of 216–205, with six Republicans voting present and four voting for other GOP candidates.

To arrive at what his punishment should be, the ethics committee held a televised hearing on January 17, 1997. While the special counsel James M. Cole and panel Democrats wanted a harsher penalty, the committee decided to reprimand him—a form of punishment less severe than censure. The reprimand weakened Gingrich as Speaker, and he had to put down an abortive coup against him in July 1997. After his party lost seats in the 1998 elections, Gingrich resigned from the House.

Loss of Chairmanship

Depriving members of chairmanships has been a common form of punishment since the 1960s:

• Removal from his chairmanship was one of several disciplinary actions taken against Representative Powell in 1966–1967. *(See "Powell," p. 921.)*

• Wayne L. Hays, D-Ohio, in mid-1976 gave up the chairmanship of both the Democratic Congressional Campaign Committee and the House Administration Committee after it was alleged that he had kept a mistress on the latter committee's payroll. Hays was pressured to resign the posts by the House Democratic leadership, and it was evident that the Democratic Caucus would have forced him to do so if he had not stepped aside voluntarily. Hays resigned from Congress September 1, 1976. (See "Hays," p. 947.)

• Representative Sikes lost his appropriations subcommittee chairmanship in 1977. (See "Sikes," p. 938.)

• In January 1979 House Democratic leaders persuaded Representative Diggs to resign as chairman of the House Foreign Affairs Subcommittee on Africa after his conviction for taking kickbacks. Diggs voluntarily gave up his chairmanship of the Committee on the District of Columbia. He was later censured by the House. (See "Diggs," p. 936.)

The House Democratic Caucus May 29, 1980, changed its rules to take away automatically a committee or subcommittee chairmanship from any party member who was censured by the House or indicted or convicted of a felony carrying a sentence of at least two years. Democrats backed the revision in caucus rules because of their concern about the precedent in the then-pending censure resolution against Rep. Charles Wilson, which would also have stripped him of a subcommittee chairmanship. Democrats feared that letting the entire House vote on a chairmanship would rob the party caucuses of an important prerogative. House Republicans adopted a similar rule on August 4, 1993. The new policy did not apply to pending cases, thus exempting Joseph M. McDade of Pennsylvania, the ranking Republican on the House Appropriations Committee. McDade had been indicted in 1992 on charges of taking favors, bribes, and illegal gratuities.

By the beginning of the 106th Congress (1999–2000), nine members had been stripped of their chairmanships since 1980: Wilson, John M. Murphy, D-N.Y., Frank Thompson Jr., D-N.J., Studds, Mario Biaggi, D-N.Y., Harold E. Ford, D-Tenn., Robert Garcia, D-N.Y., Nicholas Mavroules, D-Mass., and Dan Rostenkowski, D-Ill.

Wilson was denied the chairmanship of the House Post Office Subcommittee on Postal Operations after he was censured. Following their indictments in the Abscam investigation, Murphy lost the chairmanship of the House Merchant Marine and Fisheries Committee and its Merchant Marine Subcommittee; Thompson, the House Administration Committee, the Education and Labor Subcommittee on Labor-Management Relations, and the Joint Committee on Printing. Studds lost his chairmanship of the Merchant Marine and Fisheries Subcommittee on Coast Guard and Navigation as the result of his censure for sexual misconduct. Upon being indicted for accepting an illegal gratuity and of interstate travel and obstruction of justice in connection with that charge, Biaggi stepped down as chairman of the Merchant Marine Subcommittee of House Merchant Marine and Fisheries and of the House Select Aging Subcommittee on Human Services. Ford relinquished the chairmanship of the House Ways and Means Subcommittee on Public Assistance and Unemployment Compensation when indicted on charges of bank, mail, and tax fraud; when acquitted years later, he assumed the top spot on the Ways and Means Subcommittee on Human Resources. Facing federal influence-peddling charges, Garcia gave up the chairmanship of the House Banking, Finance, and Urban Affairs Subcommittee on International Finance, Trade, and Monetary Policy and later its Subcommittee on Policy Research and Insurance. Mavroules lost the chairmanship of the House Armed Services Subcommittee on Investigations after being indicted on charges of extortion, racketeering, tax evasion, and abuse of office. Rostenkowski stepped down from his powerful perch as chairman of the House Ways and Means Committee, as well as vice chairman of the Joint Taxation Committee, after being indicted on charges connected to the House Post Office scandal. (See "Wilson," p. 936; "Abscam Investigation," p. 953; "Studds, Crane" p. 938; "Biaggi," p. 961; "Ford," p. 969; "Garcia," p. 962; "Mavroules," p. 968; "Rostenkowski," p. 975; box, House Bank, Post Office Scandal, p. 974.)

Suspension

In 1972 the House began to formalize an unwritten rule that a member indicted for or convicted of a crime should refrain from voting on the House floor or in committee. Before that, no member had voluntarily refrained from voting since 1929 when, under indictment in the District of Columbia, Frederick N. Zihlman, R-Md., did not vote on the floor and temporarily turned over his chairmanship of the House Committee on the District of Columbia to the committee's ranking member.

The move to formalize that unwritten rule was prompted by the case of John Dowdy, D-Texas, who was convicted December 31, 1971, of bribery, conspiracy, and perjury charges. While Dowdy appealed his conviction, the ethics committee reported a resolution May 3, 1972, stating that any House member convicted of a crime for which he could receive a sentence of two or more years in prison should not participate in committee business or House votes. The maximum sentence for the crimes Dowdy was convicted of was forty years in prison and a $40,000 fine.

Because the Rules Committee failed to act, the resolution was not enacted. But Dowdy, in a June 21, 1972, letter to Speaker Carl Albert, D-Okla., promised he would refrain from voting.[6] He retired from the House at the beginning of 1973. Later that year a federal court cleared him of the conspiracy and bribery charges but left standing his conviction for perjury.

Not until April 16, 1975, did the House enact a resolution similar to the one proposed in 1972. Under the 1975 rule, the voluntary prohibition against voting would apply during an appeal of the conviction but would end on reversal or when the member was reelected subsequent to conviction, even if the verdict was upheld on appeal. The House adopted the new rule April 16, 1975, by a vote of 360–37. Later, it was incorporated in the House Code of Official Conduct. (See box, Government's Code of Ethics, p. 945.)

Diggs took advantage of the rule's leniency in 1979 until he was censured on July 31 of that year. Convicted of taking kickbacks in October 1978, Diggs was reelected by his Detroit constituents in November and continued to vote in the House until the censure resolution passed.

In the Senate, the question of voting arose with the conviction of Senator Williams in the Abscam scandal. Unlike the House, the Senate had no requirement for mandatory or voluntary restraint from voting in such cases. Until he resigned, Williams continued to vote on the floor and in committee, although some colleagues urged him to refrain from doing so.

In the early 1900s it had been the custom for indicted senators to stay off the floor and avoid voting. But the custom was reversed in 1924 by Sen. Burton K. Wheeler, D-Mont., who insisted on the right to protest his innocence to the Senate after being indicted for bribery. Wheeler continued to vote and ultimately was cleared of wrongdoing. *(See box, Senators Convicted or Indicted While in Office, p. 957.)*

NOTES

1. Unless otherwise noted, information sources for this chapter were Asher C. Hinds and Clarence Cannon, *Hinds' and Cannon's Precedents of the House of Representatives of the United States* (Washington, D.C.: Government Printing Office, 1935–1941), vols. 1 and 2; Senate Committee on Rules and Administration, *Senate Election, Expulsion, and Censure Cases,* compiled by Richard D. Hupman, 92nd Cong., 1st sess., 1972, S Doc 92-7; Joint Committee on Congressional Operations, *House of Representatives Exclusion, Censure, and Expulsion Cases,* 93rd Cong., 1st sess., 1973, committee print; William F. Willoughby, *Principles of Legislative Organization and Administration* (Washington, D.C.: Brookings Institution, 1934).

2. Kent M. Weeks, *Adam Clayton Powell and the Supreme Court* (New York: Dunellen Publishing, 1971), 79, 134.

3. *Congressional Record,* 84th Cong., 1st sess., January 14, 1955, 373.

4. *Congressional Record,* 83rd Cong., 2nd sess., July 30, 1954, 12730.

5. Senate Committee on Standards and Conduct, *Investigation of Senator Thomas J. Dodd, Hearings before the Select Committee on Standards and Conduct,* 89th Cong., 2nd sess., 1966, 846–847.

6. Dowdy voted three times by proxy in the House District of Columbia Committee June 22, 1972, after he had said he would not vote in committee or on the floor. Dowdy explained the votes by saying that he had given his proxy to the committee for use at a June 21 meeting that was postponed until June 22 without his knowledge. Dowdy's pledge to refrain from voting was made the evening of June 21.

SELECTED BIBLIOGRAPHY

Alexander, De Alva S. *History and Procedure of the House of Representatives.* New York: Lenox Hill, 1916.

Amer, Mildred. *House Committee on Standards of Official Conduct: A Brief History of Its Evolution and Jurisdiction.* Washington, D.C.: Congressional Research Service, Library of Congress, 1997.

Baker, Richard A. *The Senate of the United States: A Bicentennial History.* Malabar, Fla.: Krieger, 1988.

Butler, Anne M., and Wendy Wolff. *United States Senate Election, Expulsion, and Censure Cases, 1793–1990.* Washington, D.C.: Government Printing Office, 1995.

Currie, James T. *The United States House of Representatives.* Malabar, Fla.: Krieger, 1988.

Getz, Robert S. *Congressional Ethics: The Conflict of Interest Issue.* New York: Van Nostrand, 1966.

Hupman, Richard D. *House of Representatives Exclusion, Censure, and Expulsion Cases from 1789 to 1973.* 93rd Cong., 1st sess., 1973, committee print. Washington, D.C.: Government Printing Office, 1973.

Maskell, Jack. *Expulsion and Censure Actions Taken by the Full Senate against Members.* Washington, D.C.: Congressional Research Service, Library of Congress, 1990, 1993.

———. *Removal of Members of Congress from Office and the Issue of Recall of Legislators.* Congressional Research Service, Library of Congress, 1999.

———. *Reports concerning Investigations and/or Disciplinary Recommendations from the House Committee on Standards of Official Conduct since Its Inception in 1968.* Congressional Research Service, Library of Congress, 1989.

Riddick, Floyd M., and Alan S. Frumin. *Riddick's Senate Procedure, Precedents, and Practices.* Rev. ed. 101st Cong., 2nd sess., 1992. Senate Doc. 101-28.

Thompson, Dennis F. *Ethics in Congress: From Individual to Institutional Corruption.* Washington, D.C.: Brookings Institution, 1995.

Tiefer, Charles. *Congressional Practice and Procedure: A Reference, Research, and Legislative Guide.* New York: Greenwood Press, 1989.

Tienken, Robert L. *House of Representatives Exclusion, Censure, and Expulsion Cases from 1789 to 1973.* Washington, D.C.: Government Printing Office, 1973.

U.S. Congress. House. Committee on Standards of Official Conduct. *Historical Summary of Conduct Cases in the House of Representatives,* Washington, D.C.: Government Printing Office, 1992.

Weeks, Kent M. *Adam Clayton Powell and the Supreme Court.* New York: Dunellen, 1971.

CHAPTER 35

Ethics and Criminal Prosecutions

THE UNITED STATES CONGRESS polices itself. It is empowered by the Constitution to keep its members in line, and by and large it succeeds in doing so.

While Mark Twain could joke that "there is no distinctly native American criminal class except Congress," the vast majority of senators and representatives have not been lawbreakers or even home wreckers.

But some of them have broken laws or marriages, and their illegal acts and embarrassing antics have posed some of the most difficult decisions their peers have ever had to face. In a handful of extreme cases Congress has resorted to its ultimate punishment: kicking out the offender—an action formally known as expulsion.

More commonly the discipline administered has been a good old-fashioned tongue lashing, euphemized as a "censure" or "reprimand." Little or no difference exists between the terms, except that in the House censure entails a public chastisement; a reprimand does not. In the Senate, the censured or reprimanded member is spared the indignity of being chastised publicly. (See Chapter 34, Seating and Disciplining.)

The Senate shies away from both expulsion and censure. As of mid-1999, no senator had been expelled since 1862 or censured since 1967. (Two senators, Harrison Williams, D-N.J., in 1982 and Bob Packwood, R-Ore., in 1995, however, resigned in the face of certain expulsion.) Only three senators were disciplined between 1968 and 1999: two were "denounced" and one was "repimanded," although, here again, there is no clear distinction between the meanings of the two words and "censure."

Nor, apparently, does calling a censure by another name make it any more palatable to the senators handing out the punishment. William L. Armstrong of Colorado, who participated in the unanimous denouncement of his Republican colleague, Minnesota's Dave Durenberger, in 1990, put it this way: "When this is all over and after we have voted to denounce him, we will still want him to be our friend. We will still want to go down to the dining room and have lunch with him." (See "Durenberger," p. 932.)

Senators and representatives have even less enthusiasm for another aspect of the disciplinary process: serving on the ethics committees. Most members avoid those committees, which must deal with all the behavior problems of their colleagues, not just those that reach the Senate or House floor, and thus require every member to take a stand. The two relatively unpopular panels are the Senate Ethics Committee and the House Committee on Standards of Official Conduct

Julian C. Dixon, D-Calif., who stepped down as chairman in 1991 after leading the House ethics committee through a mine field of cases in the 1980s, reflected at one point: "Members always think you're not being fair to them, and the public thinks you're bending over backwards for the member. It's a no-win situation."

The proliferation of ethics cases in both chambers has not made the job any easier. The larger House, particularly, handled a massive docket of difficult cases in the 1980s and 1990s, including for the first time three that resulted in censure or reprimand of members for sexual misbehavior. (See box, Modern Congresses Still Prey to Old Enemies of Sex, Alcohol, p. 970.)

The increase of cases paralleled a rise in morals problems throughout American society, but that alone could not explain the rash of arrests, indictments, complaints, and exposés that brought the cases before the ethics committees for investigation. Some thought that just having such committees, which are fairly new in their current form, was enough to generate business for them. When there was no mechanism for handling complaints, there was less incentive to file them.

Heightened awareness of the moral climate, akin to the "green" concern for the physical environment, may also have contributed to the reduced tolerance of questionable or unethical behavior. Misdeeds winked at in years past were no longer acceptable. Comprehensive ethics laws enacted in 1977 and in 1989 gave members of Congress clearer guidelines of behavior, and these in turn removed some of the guesswork in deciding whether a member deserved punishment.

As recently as 1976, House members had shouted down a move to throw out a colleague, California Republican Andrew J. Hinshaw, who had been convicted of bribery. Four years later the climate had changed enough that representatives could overcome their distaste for the job and expel a member of the Democratic majority, Michael J. "Ozzie" Myers of Pennsylvania, who had been snared in the FBI's bribery sting operation, Abscam. By 1989 House members exerted sufficient pressure in a far less clear-cut case to bring about the first resignation of a Speaker, Democrat Jim Wright of Texas. (See "The Court Cases," p. 955; "Wright," p. 925.)

Over in the Senate, an even more complex case—one involving five senators accused of interfering with federal regulation of a troubled savings and loan institution—posed new dilemmas and set new precedents as Congress began its third century of existence. Senators were also called on to decide how to punish one of their own accused of sexual harassment, Bob Packwood, R-Ore. *(See box, The Keating Five Scandal, p. 962; "Pack-wood," p. 927.)*

Ethics Codes 1958–1978: The Cleanup Begins

The source of power for each house of Congress to punish its members for misconduct is contained in Article I, Section 5, of the Constitution, which states: "Each House may determine the Rules of its Proceedings, punish its Members for disorderly Behavior, and with the concurrence of two thirds, expel a Member."

Congress has been particularly reluctant to use expulsion, the most severe punishment it can impose. Only fifteen senators and four representatives have ever been expelled (although others have resigned to avoid expulsion), and almost all such cases arose during the Civil War. Lesser disciplinary actions—censure and reprimands—have been almost as rare.

Besides the natural human inclination to avoid confrontation or hurting someone's feelings, there are philosophical and legal reasons for Congress's reluctance to punish. Some members and scholars believe that, except in cases where a member's actions are illegal and punishable by the courts, the electorate, not the member's colleagues, must be the ultimate judge of his or her behavior. Loyalty among members, especially of the same party, and toward Congress as an institution is another factor. The difficulty of agreeing on what constitutes a conflict of interest and misuse of power has also clouded the question.

Members' traditional distaste for passing judgment on colleagues was apparent in the 1960s, when a series of scandals led to formation of the ethics committees as they exist today.

The 1960s scandals involved senators Thomas J. Dodd, D-Conn., and Daniel B. Brewster, D-Md.; secretary to the Senate Majority Bobby Baker; and several representatives, including the flamboyant Adam Clayton Powell Jr., D-N.Y., who was almost expelled from the House. The Powell case and several criminal prosecutions produced notable court rulings on the exclusion of members and the extent of their immunity from prosecution. *(See "Powell," p. 921.)*

The Framers of the Constitution saw Congress's powers to judge the elections and qualifications of its members and to punish them for disorderly behavior as essential to the legislature's ability to function as a coequal branch of the government, free from harassment and domination by the other branches.

Those powers are reinforced by the speech or debate clause of the Constitution (Article I, Section 6), which the courts have broadly interpreted as granting members of Congress immunity from prosecution for nearly all actions related to their legislative functions. *(See, "Congressional Immunity: Shielding Legislators," p. 984.)*

POST-WATERGATE REFORMS

The 1972–1974 Watergate affair, in which the central crime was abuse of power in the White House, also focused attention on influence-buying in the federal government. Among the key findings of other congressional investigations were a milk lobby's deal with President Richard Nixon and illegal campaign contributions to the president from powerful corporations. *(See "Watergate," p. 273, Vol I.)*

Several years after Watergate, congressional investigating committees found a foreign government, the Republic of South Korea, guilty of spending hundreds of thousands of dollars, often as campaign contributions, to influence Congress.

In the post-Watergate period, Congress strengthened the public disclosure law on election campaign contributions and then turned to its own ethical standards. Meanwhile the Justice Department began to give more attention to "white-collar crime," including alleged misdeeds by individual members of Congress.

The result in the 1970s was a more thoroughgoing congressional reform movement than any previous one in history. Like most waves of reform this one was followed by countermovements and some backsliding, but its major achievements remained historic: For the first time the law required members of Congress to disclose the source and amount of major campaign contributions. And they and top officers of the executive and judicial branches were also required to disclose their financial holdings. *(See "Major Reform Laws Enacted in the 1970s," p. 875.)*

Nevertheless, Congress showed somewhat less determination to punish ethical indiscretions by its own members. The "Koreagate" investigations (1977–1978) resulted in little more than wrist-slapping of several members involved. But the Abscam trials (1980–1981), in which seven members of Congress were prosecuted by the Justice Department and found guilty by juries, produced Myers's expulsion, the first since the Civil War. The other six members either resigned from Congress or were turned out of office by their constituents before their probable expulsion could occur. The Abscam cases were the first involving a bloc of members of Congress since the Crédit Mobilier scandal of 1872. *(See Crédit Mobilier, p. 266, Vol. I.)*

CODES OF CONDUCT

Because of its reluctance to deal harshly with members, Congress generally was content to turn away from a member's ethics problems until outside pressures forced it to act. Occasionally the instigation came from the executive branch, through its Justice Department, which from time to time sued a member of Congress, usually for income tax evasion. But mainly the news media spotlighted congressional scandals, generating public pressure for reform that Congress could not ignore.

Newspaper stories on congressional nepotism and withholding of payroll information prompted the Senate in 1959 to open its employees' payroll to public scrutiny. Similar information had been available in the House since 1932. Beginning in 1960, critical stories on congressional junkets led to a series of curbs on travel expense by members. *(See "Questionable Hiring Practices," p. 605, Vol. I; "Foreign Travel," p. 788.)*

Congress took no effective action, however, to establish

GOVERNMENT'S CODE OF ETHICS

Congress in 1958 approved the following Code of Ethics (H Con Res 175, 85th Congress, 2nd session) for all government employees, including members of Congress.[1]

Any person in Government service should:

1. Put loyalty to the highest moral principles and to country above loyalty to persons, party, or Government department.

2. Uphold the Constitution, laws, and legal regulations of the United States and of all governments therein and never be a party to their evasion.

3. Give a full day's labor for a full day's pay; giving to the performance of his duties his earnest effort and best thought.

4. Seek to find and employ more efficient and economical ways of getting tasks accomplished.

5. Never discriminate unfairly by the dispensing of special favors or privileges to anyone, whether for remuneration or not; and never accept, for himself or his family, favors or benefits under circumstances which might be construed by reasonable persons as influencing the performance of his governmental duties.

6. Make no private promises of any kind binding upon the duties of office, since a Government employee has no private word which can be binding on public duty.

7. Engage in no business with the Government, either directly or indirectly, which is inconsistent with the conscientious performance of his governmental duties.

8. Never use any information coming to him confidentially in the performance of government duties as a means for making private profit.

9. Expose corruption wherever discovered.

10. Uphold these principles, ever conscious that public office is a public trust.

1. The report of the House Committee on Standards of Official Conduct, *In the Matter of a Complaint Against Rep. Robert L. F. Sikes* (H Rept 94-1364, July 23, 1976), stated that "although the Code of Ethics for Government Service was adopted as a concurrent resolution, and as such, may have expired with the adjournment of the 85th Congress, the standards of ethical conduct expressed therein represent continuing traditional standards of ethical conduct to be observed by Members of the House at all times, which were supplemented in 1968 by a specific Code of Official Conduct."

guidelines on sweeping conflict-of-interest problems, such as outside employment and income, dealings with regulatory agencies, voting on matters in which the member had a personal stake, and relations with lobbyists and campaign contributors. No formal code of ethics for members existed until 1958, when Congress enacted a code applying throughout the government. The code was part of the reaction to the 1957–1958 investigation of Sherman Adams, chief of staff to President Dwight D. Eisenhower. Adams accepted gifts from a businessman, Bernard Goldfine, who was seeking favorable treatment from federal agencies. In the aftermath Adams resigned.

The code of ethics was hortatory. It had no legal force. Ten years later the House and Senate separately adopted new rules intended to help prevent conflicts of interest in Congress. The

new rules were largely a response to the internal investigations of Representative Powell, Senator Dodd, and Bobby Baker. *(See "Powell," p. 921; "Dodd," p. 930; box, Two Aides' Misuse of Power, p. 949.)*

Special committees on ethics also were established. After seeing the partisan bickering during the Senate Rules and Administration Committee's investigation of Bobby Baker, senators in 1964 voted to set up a strictly bipartisan committee to investigate allegations of improper conduct by senators and Senate employees. The Select Committee on Standards and Conduct had as its first chairman a respected elder, John C. Stennis, D-Miss. Its first case was the investigation and censure of Thomas Dodd.

The new rules declared that a senator should use the power and perquisites the people entrusted to him "only for their benefit and never for the benefit of himself or of a few." The Senate code also:

• Spelled out conditions under which senators could accept money from fund-raising events and the uses to which contributions could be put. In addition to campaign expenses, contributions could be used for travel and for printing or broadcasting reports to constituents. These accounts were popularly known as "slush funds."

• Prohibited all except designated Senate employees from soliciting or distributing campaign funds.

• Required senators and employees above a certain income to file confidential financial disclosure statements annually with the U.S. comptroller general. Contributions received at fundraisers and honoraria of $300 or more were to be disclosed to the public.

The House in 1967, after the Powell case, established a twelve-member bipartisan Committee on Standards of Official Conduct to recommend a code of conduct for representatives and the powers it might need to enforce it. The first chairman was Rep. Melvin Price, D-Ill. The committee recommended a code of conduct in 1968, along with a requirement for financial disclosure. In adopting these the House also made the committee permanent and gave it investigative and enforcement powers.

The Code of Official Conduct, among other things, declared that a member may "accept no gift of substantial value, directly or indirectly, from any person, organization or corporation having a direct interest in legislation before the Congress" or accept an honorarium for a speech or article "in excess of the usual and customary value for such services."

The House rule on financial disclosure, unlike the Senate rule, required that the information be available to the general public. The Senate had rejected a similar requirement by a vote of 40–44. Representatives were told to list their financial interests of more than $5,000 or income of more than $1,000 from companies doing substantial business with the government or regulated by the government and their sources of income for services exceeding $5,000 annually.

In 1970 the House broadened the public disclosure requirements to include two new items—the source of each honorarium of $300 or more earned in one year, and the names of creditors to whom $10,000 or more was owed for ninety days or longer without the pledge of specific security.

1970S SCANDALS

Until 1976 the House ethics committee proved reluctant to make any public investigation of misconduct. For example, *Life* magazine on August 9, 1968, raised charges of wrongdoing against Rep. Cornelius E. Gallagher, D-N.J., calling him a "tool and collaborator" of a reputed Mafia figure in New Jersey. The committee, after looking into the *Life* allegations, chose not to release any information on its inquiry and took no action against Gallagher. Chairman Price said "there was no proof of any violation" of the House's code of ethics.

In 1972 Gallagher was indicted for income tax evasion, perjury, and conspiracy to hide kickbacks. He pleaded guilty to the tax charge, was sentenced to two years in prison, and did not seek reelection. In 1978, during the so-called Koreagate hearings, businessman Tongsun Park testified that among his payments to members of Congress in the early 1970s was $211,000 to Gallagher.

Eight years after its establishment as a permanent committee, the House Committee on Standards of Official Conduct undertook its first investigation of a member, Robert L. F. Sikes, D-Fla., in May 1976, which resulted in the House's reprimanding Sikes. A few weeks after it opened the Sikes probe, the committee began investigating another member, Wayne L. Hays, D-Ohio.

Hays's sex scandal came on the heels of the escapades of Argentine striptease dancer Fanne Foxe and Rep. Wilbur Mills, D-Ark., the influential chairman of the Ways and Means Committee. Publicity about the Mills-Foxe affair began October 9, 1974, when Foxe jumped out of Mills's car and into the Potomac River tidal basin and was rescued by a policeman. Mills later appeared on a Boston burlesque stage with Foxe to praise her dance performance. The adverse publicity culminated in December when Mills resigned his chairmanship, acknowledged his alcoholism, and decided not to seek reelection in 1976.

Besides the Sikes and Hays cases, five criminal proceedings against members of Congress in 1976 helped to create the climate for the ethics codes of 1977:

• Representative Andrew J. Hinshaw, R-Calif., was convicted January 26, 1976, of two bribery charges stemming from his previous service as assessor of Orange County, California.

• Rep. James R. Jones, D-Okla., pleaded guilty January 29, 1976, of failing to report a cash campaign contribution from Gulf Oil Corp. in 1972, a misdemeanor, not a felony.

• Rep. Henry J. Helstoski, D-N.J., was indicted June 2, 1976, on charges he accepted money in return for introducing private bills in Congress to permit certain aliens to remain in the United States. Three years later his congressional immunity led to dismissal of the charges. *(See "1979 Rulings," p. 987.)*

• Rep. Allan T. Howe, D-Utah, was convicted July 23, 1976, in

---

BAN ON NEPOTISM

In a surprise move in 1967, Congress curbed what had been a widespread practice on Capitol Hill: putting family members on the payroll.

The proposal to prohibit nepotism by federal officials, including senators and representatives, was offered by Rep. Neal Smith, D-Iowa, as a floor amendment to a postal rate and federal pay bill. The House adopted it by a 49–33 standing vote and the Senate later accepted the Smith proviso, with language extending it to less immediate relatives (sons-in-law, for example). Thus the ban was written into permanent law.

Smith said his amendment was aimed in particular at postmasters in small post offices who were inclined to hire their wives as post office clerks. But nepotism by members of Congress—the hiring of wives, children, siblings, and other close relatives for work on a member's own staff—was a frequent source of critical press comment. Columnists over the years had charged certain members with padding their official staffs or district offices with relatives who did no work for their government paycheck. Though the ban prohibited members from paying relatives to work on their staffs, several members employed their spouses in their congressional offices with no pay.

The nepotism ban prohibited officers or employees of the federal or District of Columbia governments from appointing, or recommending for appointment or promotion, a relative to serve in the same agency or department as the official.

Salt Lake City for soliciting two policewomen posing as prostitutes.

• Rep. James F. Hastings, R-N.Y., was convicted in December 1976 for taking payroll kickbacks from his congressional employees.

The Sikes and Hays cases resulted in disciplinary action against the two members. A later criminal case, against Rep. Daniel J. Flood, D-Pa., resulted in his resignation.

Sikes

The House reprimanded Sikes on July 29, 1976, accepting 381–3 the ethics committee's findings that he was guilty of financial misconduct. Sikes, the longtime chairman of the House Appropriations Subcommittee on Military Construction, was found in three instances to "have violated standards of conduct applicable to all members of Congress."

He was charged with failing to disclose his investments in a defense contractor, Fairchild Industries, in a bank he helped to establish on a naval base in his district, and in Florida land parcels that he tried to upgrade in value through legislation.

Forty-four House members lodged a complaint against Sikes with the ethics committee, an unprecedented action at the time. The complaint was based on information developed by Florida newspaper reports and groups outside Congress. After an initial inquiry the committee voted May 12 to hold a formal investigation of Sikes's actions. By elevating the probe from the status of an inquiry to an investigation, the panel gave itself the authority to subpoena financial records and question witnesses under oath.

Hays

Less than a month after undertaking the Sikes investigation, the ethics committee began a probe of a sex-and-public-payroll scandal involving Ohio's Wayne Hays, the powerful chairman of the House Administration Committee and House Democrats' fund-raising committee, the Democratic National Congressional Committee. In a story that broke in the *Washington Post* May 23, 1976, Elizabeth Ray accused Hays of giving her a $14,000-a-year job on the House Administration Committee in exchange for sexual favors. Ray described herself as having no qualifications for an office job. She said, "I can't type. I can't file. I can't even answer the phone."

Hays at first denied the Ray charge but then admitted to the House May 25 that he had had a "personal relationship" with Ray. He denied, however, that he had hired her to be his mistress.

On May 25 Hays asked the ethics committee to investigate the matter. The same day twenty-eight House members, in a letter to ethics Chairman John J. Flynt Jr., D-Ga., asked the committee to take up the Hays case. The Justice Department and FBI had entered the case soon after Ray made her charges, and by May 26 a federal grand jury in Washington, D.C., began hearing testimony relating to her allegations. On June 2 the committee voted 11–0 to begin an immediate investigation into the charges.

Pressure built up quickly in the House to oust Hays from his leadership positions. On June 3 he relinquished his chairmanship of the Democratic Congressional Campaign Committee. Hays won renomination to his House seat in a close Democratic primary in Ohio's Eighteenth District June 8. Then, bowing to pressure from the House Democratic leadership, Hays resigned the chairmanship of the House Administration Committee June 18 and on August 13 announced he would not run for reelection to Congress in November. On September 1 Hays resigned. The ethics panel then voted, 12–0, to end its investigation of him.

Flood

Rep. Daniel J. Flood, D-Pa., chairman of the Appropriations subcommittee that controlled federal health, education, and welfare spending, was indicted on thirteen criminal charges in 1978. Nevertheless, he was reelected in the November elections that year.

Flood, a mustachioed former actor and one of the House's most colorful characters, was charged with lying to a grand jury about payoffs allegedly made to him and a former aide, Stephen Elko. He was also, along with Elko, indicted for bribery.

The indictment alleged that Flood received payments—ranging from $5,000 to $27,000—from several individuals in ex-

Rep. Daniel J. Flood, one of the House's most colorful characters, was indicted in 1978 on thirteen criminal charges, including bribery and perjury. He resigned his seat in 1980.

change for his help in getting them grants or other forms of federal aid or approval. One of the bribery counts also alleged that Flood was promised $100,000 for another favor for a Pennsylvania home builder.

Elko and a business associate had been found guilty in 1977 of accepting bribes in exchange for helping several private vocational schools get federal aid. Testimony alleged that persistent pressure from Flood's congressional office caused the U.S. Office of Education to grant temporary accreditation to the business schools. Flood was charged with perjury in his grand jury testimony in the Elko case.

A mistrial was declared February 3, 1979, shortly after Flood's trial began. In very poor health and facing a second trial plus a House ethics investigation, Flood resigned in January 1980. On February 26 he pleaded guilty to a single misdemeanor charge and was placed on probation.

Flood was also linked with charges brought in 1978 against Rep. Joshua Eilberg, D-Pa., for illegally helping Hahnemann Medical College and Hospital in Philadelphia to obtain a $14.5 million federal construction grant. Eilberg was defeated for reelection after being indicted, and he pleaded guilty in February 1979.

Elko testified that he recommended Eilberg's law firm to the hospital and that Flood was to receive $50,000 from the firm for arranging an appropriation for the grant.

CODE, PAY RELATIONSHIP

In 1977 the House and Senate adopted separate, but largely similar, codes of ethics for their members and employees. The following year Congress passed a law, the Ethics in Government Act, to enforce the codes and to apply the congressional financial disclosure requirements to the other two branches of government. *(See "1978 Ethics in Government Act," p. 949.)*

Impetus for the 1977 codes of conduct came from the congressional scandals of 1976, from heightened post-Watergate concern about integrity in government, and from the recommendations of two public commissions. One was the quadrennial Commission on Executive, Legislative, and Judicial Salaries, chaired in 1976–1977 by businessman Peter G. Peterson, a former secretary of commerce. The other was the special Commission on Operations of the Senate, headed by former senator Harold E. Hughes, D-Iowa.

Both commissions recommended pay increases for Congress on the condition that the two chambers adopt effective codes of ethics. The Hughes commission, saying the Senate had "insufficient safeguards against conflicts of interest," urged adoption of a ban on honoraria and full financial disclosure by senators and the chamber's top employees.

The Peterson commission also called for financial disclosure plus additional steps: a limit on the outside income members could earn in addition to their congressional salaries, accountable expense allowances, and public audits of compliance with the conflict-of-interest restrictions. The commission was regarded as having significant influence because it was the originating body for salary increases at the highest levels of government, including Supreme Court justices and cabinet members.

Limits and Disclosure

President Gerald R. Ford, with the concurrence of president-elect Jimmy Carter, approved the Peterson commission recommendations for pay increases and a congressional code of ethics and forwarded them to Congress on January 17, 1977. Under the proposal congressional salaries would rise 28.9 percent, from $44,600 to $57,500. Other officials, including the top grades of the civil service, would get comparable increases.

Congressional leaders moved swiftly to put the twin proposals for Congress on track. Believing the pay raise was needed but keenly aware of public opinion against it, House Speaker Thomas P. O'Neill Jr., D-Mass., and Senate Majority Leader Robert C. Byrd, D-W.Va., made passage of strong ethics codes a condition for approval of the salary increase. Both leaders said that a limit on outside income was essential to a strong code; O'Neill called the provision "the heart and soul of the entire package" of ethical standards. The outside income limit, which became the most bitterly fought section of the code in each

house, did not apply to "unearned" income such as dividends and capital gains.

O'Neill assigned responsibility for drawing up an ethics code to a bipartisan Commission on Administrative Review headed by Rep. David R. Obey, D-Wis., which began work in late 1976. The commission released a proposed code on February 7, 1977, and the House passed it 402–22 on March 2, after heated debate on the outside income issue.

The Senate used the Obey Commission's work as the basis for a code that paralleled the House code in most respects. The Senate approved its code April 1 after two weeks of debate and action on sixty-four amendments. The 86–9 vote in favor of passage by no means reflected the depth of feeling in the Senate against elements of the new code. Gaylord Nelson, D-Wis., floor manager for the bill, said afterward that many senators who voted for it feared the political consequences of a negative vote. Nevertheless, Nelson said, Senate acceptance of full financial disclosure was a "milestone" because past efforts to force senators to make public their financial operations had been hotly contested.

In both chambers the earned income limit produced the bitterest opposition, but in each case it was approved by lopsided margins. The House vote was 344–79 and the Senate's was 62–35. The limit continued to be attacked, however, both before and after its January 1, 1979, effective date. In March 1979 the Senate voted 54–44 to defer imposing the limit on senators for four years, to 1983.

Provisions of 1977 Codes

The limit on outside earned income—set at 15 percent of the congressional salary, or $8,625 at the salary level existing in 1977—was directed at conflict-of-interest problems raised by large honoraria given by interest groups and at the continuing but declining practice of members carrying on as private lawyers or insurance agents while supposedly working full time as members of Congress. The source and amount of this income had to be reported.

The codes also abolished office accounts, which put an end to the last remaining device by which members could accept unreported contributions from organizations or individuals and use the funds for virtually any purpose. Members also were faced with new restrictions on their use of the franking privilege to send mail.

And finally, the idea that personal financial activities were nobody's business but the member's own was put to rest. As passed, the codes required members to make public data on their income, gifts received, financial holdings, debts, securities, commodity transactions, and real estate dealings. Spouses had to report much the same information.

Members were not required to report the exact value of their holdings of different kinds but only a range of value—the scale ran from not more than $5,000 to greater than $5 million (later reduced to $250,000 and over). In the 1978 Ethics in Govern-

TWO AIDES' MISUSE OF POWER

Misuses of power and conflicts of interest have not been limited to members of Congress. Occasionally congressional aides have used their positions and their employers' prestige for personal gain. Following are two of the most famous cases.

BAKER: SENATE PAGE TO MILLIONAIRE

Robert G. "Bobby" Baker began his Capitol Hill career as a teenage page in the Senate. Ambitious and aggressive, Baker rose to the position of secretary to the Senate majority, making himself right-hand man to his mentor, Majority Leader Lyndon B. Johnson, D-Texas, in the late 1950s. When he quit his post under fire a few years later, Baker on paper was worth $2 million, most of it gained, the subsequent court records showed, from combining law practice with influence peddling. The notoriety caused by the Baker case is credited with moving the Senate to create an ethics committee.

Baker resigned in 1963 after a civil suit was brought against him, charging that he used his influence to obtain contracts for a vending machine concern in which he had a financial interest. Senate investigations conducted over the next two years concluded that Baker was guilty of "gross improprieties." The investigating committee recommended that the Senate require full financial disclosures by senators and top employees of the Senate.

Baker meanwhile was brought to trial on charges of income tax evasion, theft, and conspiracy to defraud the government. He was found guilty in January 1967; after appeals had been exhausted, he began his prison term four years later. The major charge on which he was found guilty was that he had collected more than $99,000 from a group of California savings and loan executives, ostensibly as campaign contributions, but in reality had kept about $80,000 for himself.

At the trial two of the California executives testified that in 1962 they gave Baker about $66,000 for campaign contributions to seven senators and one House member, Ways and Means Committee Chairman Wilbur D. Mills, D-Ark. Mills and one of the senators, Foreign Relations Committee Chairman J. W. Fulbright, D-Ark., testified that they had received none of the funds. Defense counsel stipulated that none of the other six senators had received any of the funds. One of the savings and loan executives testified that Baker told him the California savings and loan associations could improve their standing in Congress with a "very impressive" contribution to certain senators and House members and could "win friends" in Congress at a time when a bill was pending to increase taxes on the associations.

Baker testified that he turned the money over to Sen. Robert S. Kerr, D-Okla., a power on the Senate Finance Committee, for his re-election campaign. Kerr was dead by the time Baker told his story.

SWEIG: ILLEGAL USE OF SPEAKER'S OFFICE

A congressional scandal that attracted nationwide attention when it was revealed in 1969 involved influence peddling in the office of Speaker John W. McCormack, D-Mass. In the end, one of his top aides, Dr. Martin Sweig, was convicted on July 9, 1970, of perjury, and on January 28, 1972, of misusing the Speaker's office to influence government decisions.

Sweig, who had worked for McCormack twenty-four years and was drawing an annual salary of $36,000 in 1969, was implicated with Nathan M. Voloshen, a New York City lawyer-lobbyist and longtime McCormack friend. On June 17, 1970, Voloshen pleaded guilty to charges of conspiring to use the Speaker's office to influence matters before federal government agencies and to three counts of lying to a federal grand jury about the charges.

---

ment Act, Congress applied roughly the same disclosure rules to high officials of the executive and judicial branches.

Both codes prohibited members and employees from accepting gifts of $100 or more from lobbyists and foreign nationals and forbade the conversion of testimonial or campaign funds to personal use. They also set a maximum amount a member could accept as an honorarium.

The Senate code contained three significant sections not in the House code. One was a provision prohibiting senators or employees from engaging in a professional practice, such as law, for compensation. Strom Thurmond of South Carolina, the Republican floor manager of the code, had proposed the flat ban in committee, arguing that senators had "no business" practicing other professions. It was modified on the floor to permit senators and employees to practice a profession so long as they were not affiliated with any firm and their work was not carried out during Senate office hours. *(See box, Members of Congress and the Practice of Law, p. 950.)*

The Senate code also prohibited former senators from lobbying in the Senate for one year after leaving office and prohibited former staff members for a senator or committee from lobbying their former employer or committee member and staff for one year. Unlike the House code, the Senate code declared that no member, officer, or employee could refuse to hire an individual, discharge an individual, or discriminate with respect to promotion, pay, or terms of employment on the basis of race, color, religion, sex, national origin, age, or state of physical handicap.

1978 ETHICS IN GOVERNMENT ACT

In October 1978 Congress enacted the Ethics in Government Act, which gave legal force to the financial disclosure requirements of the 1977 House and Senate ethics codes and required the same disclosures by high-ranking members of the executive and judicial branches. The law set civil penalties for violations.

The act contained other strong conflict-of-interest provisions covering executive employees who leave the government

Until World War II, to be a member of Congress was to hold a part-time job. Consequently, certain occupations that demand almost full-time attention—running a business or teaching school, for example—sent few representatives to Congress while others, notably the law, sent many. For years more than half of all members of Congress were lawyers, but the percentage has been dropping. In the 106th Congress (1999–2001) it was 40.7 percent. Men and women from business and banking accounted for the second-highest category, 34.2 percent. *(See "Characteristics of Members," p. 839.)*

LEGAL PRACTICE AND PAST SCANDALS

The combination of two professions—law and congressional office—has led to numerous scandals. Sen. Daniel Webster's retainer from the Bank of the United States is familiar to many. What is not so well known is that Webster's professional relationship with the bank was no secret; he represented the bank in forty-one cases before the Supreme Court.

It was not an unusual arrangement for the time; neither was it universally condoned. John Quincy Adams, for example, as a member of Congress declined to practice before federal courts.

It was not until the 1850s that members were forbidden to represent claimants against the U.S. government. This restriction grew out of a scandal surrounding senator, and later secretary of the Treasury, Thomas Corwin of Ohio. Corwin successfully recovered half a million dollars (an enormous sum for those days) in a mining case; scandal erupted when it was disclosed that both the claimant and silver mine were frauds.

Legal practice played a supporting role in the great railroad robbery known as the Crédit Mobilier scandal of the Grant administration. In that case, as brought out in a congressional hearing, promoters of the Union Pacific Railroad used stock in Crédit Mobilier, a joint stock company they controlled, to bribe members of Congress to keep up federal subsidies to the railroad. *(See "Crédit Mobilier," p. 266, Vol. I.)*

The early 1900s again brought congressional ethics to a low spot in public opinion. Heavily promoted by publisher William Randolph Hearst, a series of articles by David Graham Phillips called *Treason of the Senate* alleged corrupt behavior by twenty-one senators. The series played a major role in promoting direct election of senators. Only one of the twenty-one senators replied publicly to Phillips's charges. He was Sen. Joseph W. Bailey, D-Texas, who had received more than $225,000 in legal fees for several months' services to a Texas oilman. Bailey vehemently defended his practice of law while serving in the Senate:

I despise those public men who think they must remain poor in order to be considered honest. I am not one of them. If my constituents want a man who is willing to go to the poorhouse in his old age in order to stay in the Senate during his middle age, they will have to find another senator. I intend to make every dollar that I can honestly make without neglecting or interfering with my public duty.

BAR ASSOCIATION ACTIONS

The legal profession moved to discourage congressional law practice in the late 1960s. The move came after a series of scandals that involved, sometimes indirectly, congressional law practices. Among those cases were those of Rep. Thomas F. Johnson, D-Md., Senate Majority Secretary Bobby Baker, Sen. Thomas J. Dodd, D-Conn., and Rep. Cornelius Gallagher, D-N.J.

The American Bar Association revised its canons in 1969. Its new Code of Professional Responsibility provided that the name of a public official should not be used in the name of a law firm or in the firm's professional notices "during any significant period in which he is not actively and regularly practicing law as a member of the firm." Most state bar associations adopted the code, as did a number of state supreme courts, thus clearing the way for formal grievance proceedings if violated.

Following an extensive study of congressional ethics, conducted in 1967–1969, a special committee of the Association of the Bar of the City of New York made several recommendations on members of Congress who were engaged in the legal profession. The committee recommended that members voluntarily refrain from any form of law practice, except for first-termers who foresaw little prospect for reelection. The committee also recommended that Congress enact legislation to forbid "double-door" law partnerships (under which the law partner of a member of Congress engages in federal agency practice prohibited by law to the member) and to prohibit members from appearing for compensation in the courts. The longtime chairman of the House Judiciary Committee, Emanuel Celler, D-N.Y., was a practitioner of a double-door partnership.

The New York City Bar Association in 1970 published the committee's report by James C. Kirby under the title *Congress and the Public Trust: Report of the Association of the Bar of the City of New York Special Committee on Congressional Ethics.*

In 1978 Rep. Joshua Eilberg, D-Pa., was indicted on charges he illegally received legal fees for helping a Philadelphia hospital get a federal construction grant. The House Committee on Standards of Official Conduct said he received more than $100,000 from his law firm under circumstances suggesting he was influenced in "the performance of his government duties." Eilberg was defeated for reelection that fall and pleaded guilty to reduced charges in 1979.

INCOME FROM LAW PRACTICES

In the 1990s lawyers continued to make up a significant segment of Congress, but the practice of law all but disappeared as a source of outside income for members. Fifteen years earlier, in financial disclosure reports for the year 1975, fifty-three representatives reported at least $1,000 in income from a law practice. Eight House members noted that they had withdrawn from practice. Disclosure reports on 1980 income gave approximately the same figures on present and withdrawn legal practice, but the ethics codes' limit on outside earned income appeared to have reduced the twenty practicing lawyers' income considerably.

A Senate rule effective January 1, 1983, barred the practice of law and other professions for compensation, and the Ethics Reform Act of 1989 extended the same prohibition to House members effective in 1991.

(known as "revolving-door" restrictions) but did not apply those constraints to members and employees of the legislative branch.

President Jimmy Carter had given impetus to these new precautions even before he assumed the presidency. He required his appointees to meet guidelines for financial disclosure, divestiture of holdings that could create conflicts between private and government interests, and postgovernment employment restrictions. He asked Congress to enact these requirements into law.

As a direct outgrowth of the Watergate investigations, the Ethics in Government Act established procedures for court appointment of a special prosecutor to substitute for Justice Department prosecutors whenever a high-ranking federal official was accused of criminal action. The Watergate special prosecutor had been appointed under the attorney general's general authority to name special counsel. The new law set forth a step-by-step process for initiating and carrying out such an investigation.

The act set up an office of legal counsel in the Senate to represent that body and its members in court. The House decided not to be covered by this new office.

The act also established the Office of Government Ethics in the Office of Personnel Management, which Carter created in 1978 by splitting the Civil Service Commission in two. The new ethics office would develop rules and regulations on government conflicts of interest and other ethical problems, and it would monitor and investigate compliance with federal ethics laws.

HONORARIA

Congress first limited how much its members could earn from honoraria in the 1974 campaign finance law. For 1975 senators and representatives could receive no more than $15,000 annually for giving speeches and writing articles and were limited to $1,000 for each item.

Under pressure from the Senate, that ceiling was raised in the 1976 amendments to the campaign law to allow members of Congress to receive $2,000 for each individual event and an aggregate amount of $25,000 a year. However, the $25,000 limit was a net figure because members were allowed to deduct certain expenses such as booking agents' fees and travel expenditures.

The 1977 House and Senate ethics codes, with their 15 percent limit on earned income, cut the ceiling on total honoraria to less than $10,000 and the limit on a single honorarium to $1,000. But the Senate subsequently put off its income limit and repealed the $25,000 honorarium ceiling, keeping only the campaign law's $2,000-a-speech maximum. Critics said senators were placing themselves in bond to interest groups willing to pay generous honoraria. Supporters replied that without the opportunity to earn honoraria the Senate would become even more a rich man's club.

The principal purpose of the limits on earned income and honoraria was to reduce potential conflicts of interest. It was recognized that organizations often gave honoraria to members of Congress serving on committees that handled legislation sought by the donor organization. Getting legislators to speak to a conference and mingle with organization representatives could be an effective lobbying technique.

Under the 1977 House and Senate ethics rules a member had to report gifts of transportation, food, lodging, or entertainment aggregating $250 or more from any one source during the preceding calendar year. The rule applied to individuals and groups that did not have a direct interest in legislation.

But the codes specifically barred members and employees from accepting gifts aggregating more than $100 during a calendar year from persons having direct interests in legislation, or from foreign nationals. Both chambers defined persons with direct interests in legislation as lobbyists (even if they were not registered lobbyists), businesses, labor unions, and organizations that maintained political action committees.

Subsequent advisory opinions, however, made it clear that a member could accept more than $100 in food, lodging, transportation, and other "necessary expenses" so long as the member "renders personal services sufficient to constitute 'equal consideration' for the expenses provided by the sponsoring organization." As long as the service performed "is more than perfunctory in nature," the payment was considered an honorarium.

Any travel provided to the member in connection with speechmaking is counted as a reimbursement, not a gift, the codes stated. In other words, according to a House ethics committee aide, if a member goes to "a company's moose hunting lodge for the weekend, that's a gift." If the member "goes to the lodge to make a speech," however, then the member should disclose his food, lodging, and transportation as a reimbursement.

The Senate's action early in 1979, deferring the limit on senators' outside income for four years, to 1983, created bitter resentment among House members. It enabled senators to collect honoraria up to $2,000 for each speech and $25,000 each year, while representatives were limited to earning no more than $9,099 beyond their salaries and $1,000 for each honorarium. (Because the cap on representatives' outside income was pegged at 15 percent of their salaries, subsequent cost-of-living salary raises also pushed up the earnings ceiling.)

Two years later the Senate poured more salt into representatives' wounds. It voted 45–43 on September 24, 1981, to remove entirely the $25,000 ceiling on honoraria. That galvanized the House Rules Committee to approve a resolution raising the earnings limit to 40 percent of representatives' salaries. When brought to a roll-call vote on the House floor, however, the resolution was defeated 147–271 on October 28.

Six weeks later House leaders arranged a quiet flip-flop without a recorded vote. The turnabout occurred December 15 with surprising swiftness and little warning. During a lull in House business, John P. Murtha, D-Pa., rose and asked for unanimous consent to approve a resolution increasing the ceiling on House members' outside earnings from 15 percent of their official salary to 30 percent. When no one objected, Murtha returned to his seat. The entire process took about ten seconds.

Supporters said privately that surprise was necessary because members needed higher pay—either directly or indirectly—but were unwilling to go on record for it for fear of a public outcry. They compounded their public relations problems the next day, however, when both houses increased the congressional tax deduction for Washington, D.C., living expenses. The doubling of representatives' earned income limit raised it to $18,198, while senators remained free of any limit. Both chambers continued to accept honoraria until 1991 when, again to help justify pay raises for themselves, the House and then the Senate banned the practice altogether. *(See "Honoraria: A Vanishing Perquisite," p. 778.)*

Criminal Probes: Spur to Ethics Actions

The creation of House and Senate ethics committees in the 1960s institutionalized Congress's responsibility to police itself. Left open was the question of how much initiative the committees should take in rooting out unethical behavior.

At first the committees tended to wait until criminal proceedings had started before investigating a member. Critics of this approach argued that the congressional ethics codes spelled out higher standards of behavior than just avoidance of criminal activity. They suggested that members must be answerable to their colleagues for questionable legislative actions that could not be prosecuted in court because of the Constitution's immunity clause.

The committees' procedures, in which they acted as investigator, prosecutor, and jury, came under criticism. And because of members' reluctance to serve on the committees, turnover was rapid and the caliber of the panels was not widely respected in Congress.

In both of the committees' major investigations between 1977 and 1982, the executive branch had acted first. One investigation centered on the South Korean government's long effort to buy influence in Congress, which the Justice Department had secretly been examining, and the other was a follow-up to the FBI's Abscam net for corrupt legislators.

KOREAN INFLUENCE BUYING

On October 24, 1976, the *Washington Post* broke the story that the Justice Department was probing "the most sweeping allegations of congressional corruption ever investigated by the federal government." The *Post* said that South Korean agents dispensed between $500,000 and $1 million a year in cash and gifts to members of Congress to help maintain "a favorable legislative climate" for South Korea. Tongsun Park, a South Korean businessman operating in Washington, was named as the principal dispenser of favors.

Follow-up reports said an influence-buying plan had been hatched in the Blue House, the South Korean equivalent of the White House, in late 1970 or early 1971 by President Park Chung

In the Korean influence buying scandal, former representative Richard Hanna, D-Calif., admitted that he had used his congressional office illegally.

Hee, Tongsun Park, high Korean Central Intelligence Agency (KCIA) officials, and Pak Bo Hi, later a chief aide to Korean evangelist Sun Myung Moon.

President Park reportedly was concerned about a Nixon administration plan to withdraw about a third of the U.S. troops in Korea. Growing opposition in the United States to the war in Vietnam also raised fears in Korea that a pullout would lessen American ability to protect it against another invasion from North Korea. The Park regime thus put a high priority on continued U.S. congressional support.

In January 1977 the House ethics committee began a slow-moving investigation of the involvement of representatives in the South Korean scheme. The Senate Ethics Committee conducted a separate investigation of senators' reported roles.

Soon after the initial *Post* story, Tongsun Park fled the country. Indicted by the U.S. government September 6, 1977, Park stayed in Korea while lengthy negotiations were carried out by his government and the U.S. Justice Department. Finally he agreed to testify before the House ethics committee if granted immunity from prosecution.

The indictment charged Park with thirty-six counts of conspiracy to defraud the United States, bribery, mail fraud, failure to register as a foreign agent, and making illegal political contributions. Former representative Richard Hanna, D-Calif., was named as an unindicted coconspirator, as were former KCIA directors Kim Hyung Wook and Lee Hu Rak.

The indictment charged that Park and Hanna, around 1967, concocted a scheme to collect large commissions from sales of U.S. rice to South Korea and to use some of that money to buy friends for Korea in Congress. The KCIA directors were alleged to have cooperated in the scheme. Park, a lavish party-giver in Washington, reportedly received more than $9 million in commissions on rice sales from 1969 to 1976.

Hanna had retired from Congress in 1974 after serving six terms. As a sponsor of the Asian Development Bank, he had made numerous trips to Asia and to Korea. He was later indicted and in March 1978 pleaded guilty to one count of conspiracy to defraud the government. He admitted that he had agreed to use his office to help Tongsun Park and had received $200,000 for his efforts between 1969 and 1975. He began serving a thirty-month prison term in May 1978.

Before holding hearings, both ethics committees asked House and Senate members to report any contacts they had with South Korean government representatives and any gifts or political contributions received from Tongsun Park or others.

Park's testimony before the House ethics committee began February 28, 1978, and ran for more than a week. While he named members to whom he had given contributions, he denied being a representative of the South Korean government or conspiring to buy influence in Congress. He did, however, describe the help he had received from Rep. Otto E. Passman, D-La., in retaining his lucrative commissions on sales of rice to South Korea. As chairman of the House Appropriations subcommittee that dealt with rice and other Food for Peace commodity sales abroad, Passman had been in a good position to help his rice-growing constituents as well as Park. (Passman was defeated for reelection in the 1976 congressional primary, indicted in 1978 for bribery and conspiracy to defraud the U.S. government, but acquitted of all charges the next year.)

During his testimony, Park said that most of his payments went to three men who had since left the House—Passman, who Park testified received cash and gifts of between $367,000 and $407,000; Hanna, who allegedly received $262,000; and Cornelius Gallagher, D-N.J., who Park said got $211,000. (Hanna admitted receiving $200,000.)

Four sitting representatives became the objects of disciplinary hearings by the House ethics committee. They were California Democrats John J. McFall, Edward R. Roybal, and Charles H. Wilson, and New Jersey Democrat Edward J. Patten. The committee's report said McFall had converted a $3,000 campaign contribution from Park to his personal use, Roybal had done the same with a $1,000 contribution and then lied under oath about it, Wilson had denied receiving money from Park despite the latter's testimony that he gave Wilson $600 in cash as a wedding gift, and Patten had forwarded a contribution he received from Park as a personal contribution to a New Jersey political organization.

The committee cleared Patten and recommended reprimands for McFall and Wilson and censure of Roybal for deliberately lying under oath. The probe ended in October 1978 when the House voted to reprimand all three Californians, its mildest form of punishment. (*See "McFall, Roybal, Wilson," p. 938.*)

The Senate Ethics Committee concluded its Korean investigation in October 1978 with a report that recommended no disciplinary action against any incumbent or former senator.

ABSCAM INVESTIGATION

An FBI undercover operation known as Abscam, a combination of the words Arab and scam, in 1980 implicated seven members of Congress in criminal wrongdoing. By May 1981 juries had convicted the seven—six House members and one senator—for their role in the affair, and by March 11, 1982, none of the seven was still in Congress.

The House members were John W. Jenrette Jr., D-S.C., Richard Kelly, R-Fla., Raymond F. Lederer, D-Pa., John M. Murphy, D-N.Y., Michael J. "Ozzie" Myers, D-Pa., and Frank Thompson Jr., D-N.J. Another House member, John P. Murtha, D-Pa., was named an unindicted coconspirator and testified for the government in the trial of Murphy and Thompson. The senator was Harrison A. Williams Jr., D-N.J.

In summary, Abscam led to the following congressional actions with respect to the convicted seven:

Myers was expelled from the House of Representatives on October 2, 1980, only the fourth representative ever expelled and the first since the Civil War. (*See "House Expulsion of Myers," p. 925.*)

Three others—Jenrette, Lederer, and Williams—resigned from Congress to avoid almost certain expulsion.

Kelly, Murphy, and Thompson were defeated for reelection before being convicted in court.

The unindicted conspirator, Murtha, was cleared by the House ethics committee over the objections of the committee counsel.

Two elements made Abscam far more than a routine corruption case. One was the FBI's use of videotapes to record the meetings of phony sheiks, members of Congress, and others—a development that allowed the public to see one representative stuffing money into bulging pockets. The other unusual element was the prominence of three of those convicted—senior committee chairmen, two of whom (Thompson and Williams) were generally considered leaders within their party.

The Scam

According to published accounts and subsequent court evidence, undercover FBI agents approached an undisclosed number of members of Congress offering to introduce them to representatives of wealthy Arabs interested in making investments in their districts. Some of the members were asked if they could use their Capitol Hill positions to help the Arabs obtain U.S. residency. Others were asked to use their influence in government to obtain federal grants and gambling licenses or to arrange real estate deals.

Five of the accused—Williams, Kelly, Lederer, Myers, and Thompson—were videotaped accepting cash or stock. Jenrette

RULES GOVERNING MEMBERS' CONDUCT: CONSTITUTION, HILL RULES, AND CRIMINAL LAWS

Concern for the ethical conduct of members of Congress is reflected in the Constitution, federal statutes, and Senate and House rules. Some key provisions affecting members' conduct follow:

CONSTITUTIONAL PROVISION

Article I, Section 5, clause 2: "Each House may determine the Rules of its Proceedings, punish its Members for disorderly Behavior, and, with the Concurrence of two thirds, expel a Member."

Article I, Section 6, clause 1: "They shall in all Cases, except Treason, Felony and Breach of the Peace, be privileged from Arrest during their Attendance at the Session of their respective Houses, and in going to and returning from the same; and for any Speech or Debate in either House, they shall not be questioned in any other Place."

Article I, Section 6, clause 2: "No Senator or Representative shall, during the Time for which he was elected, be appointed to any civil Office under the Authority of the United States, which shall have been created, or the Emoluments whereof shall have been encreased during such time; and no Person holding any Office under the United States, shall be a Member of either House during his Continuance in Office."

Article I, Section 9, clause 8: "No Title of Nobility shall be granted by the United States; And no Person holding any Office of Profit or Trust under them, shall, without the Consent of the Congress, accept of any present, Emolument, Office, or Title, of any kind whatever, from any King, Prince, or foreign State."

Article VI, clause 3: "The Senators and Representatives before mentioned . . . shall be bound by Oath or Affirmation, to support this Constitution."

CRIMINAL STATUTES

A series of laws in Title 18 of the U.S. Code make it a federal crime for members of Congress to engage in certain actions. Prohibited acts, excluding those relating to campaign spending, include:

• Soliciting or receiving a bribe for the performance of any official act, for the violation of an official duty, or for participating in or permitting any fraud against the United States. The penalty is a $20,000 fine or three times the monetary equivalent of the thing of value, whichever is greater, or imprisonment for not more than fifteen years, or both, plus possible disqualification from holding office.

• Soliciting or receiving anything of value for himself or because of any official act performed or to be performed by him. The penalty is a $10,000 fine or imprisonment for not more than two years, or both.

• Soliciting or receiving any compensation for services in relation to any proceeding, contract, claim, or controversy in which the United States is a party or has a direct and substantial interest, before any department, agency, court martial, officer, or civil or military commission. The penalty is a $10,000 fine and imprisonment for not more than two years, or both, plus disqualification from holding office.

• Practicing in the Court of Claims. The penalty is a $10,000 fine and imprisonment for not more than two years, or both, plus disqualification from holding office.

• Receiving, as a political contribution or otherwise, anything of value for promising use of or using influence to obtain for any person an appointive office or place under the United States. The penalty is a $1,000 fine, or imprisonment for not more than one year, or both.

• The campaign laws prohibit buying a vote, promising employment, soliciting political contributions from federal employees, and threatening the job of a federal employee who fails to give a campaign contribution. *(See Chapter 32, Campaign Financing.)*

CHAMBER RULES

Prior to the adoption of formal codes of conduct beginning in 1958, the chief ethical curbs on members' activities related to voting. *(See box, Government's Code of Ethics, p. 945.)*

In 1801, when he was vice president and presiding over the Senate, Thomas Jefferson wrote in *Jefferson's Manual*:

Where the private interests of a Member are concerned in a bill or question he is to withdraw. And where such an interest has appeared, his voice has been disallowed. . . . In a case so contrary, not only to the laws of decency, but to the fundamental principle of the social compact, which denies to any man to be a judge in his own cause, it is for the honor of the House that this rule of immemorial observance should be strictly adhered to.

Jefferson's rule gave rise to Rule VIII of the House, which requires each member present to vote "unless he has a direct personal or pecuniary interest in the event of such question." In most cases this decision has been left to the member. Under an 1874 ruling a representative may vote for his or her private interests if the measure is not for the member's exclusive benefit, but for that of a group.

Under Rule XII senators may be excused from voting, provided they give their reasons for abstaining, and senators have been excused in the past because of such a direct interest in the outcome.

---

was tape-recorded saying he had been given the cash by an associate. Murphy allegedly told an associate to accept the cash. The defendants' claim that the government had entrapped them won support in some legal and congressional circles, and leaks to the press were generally condemned.

Although Attorney General Benjamin Civiletti asked congressional committees to hold up investigations until the crimi-

nal trials were completed, both the Senate Select Ethics Committee and the House Committee on Standards of Official Conduct began their own investigations.

In the end, the House committee waited until Myers, Jenrette, and Lederer had been convicted in court before taking final action. Using court evidence as the basis for its probe, the panel recommended that Myers be expelled, and the full House

Rep. Michael J. "Ozzie" Myers was expelled from the House in 1980 as a result of his role in the Abscam affair. He was the fourth representative in history to be expelled.

agreed. Jenrette resigned from the House just as the Standards Committee was ready to hand down a recommendation for his expulsion. Lederer resigned in 1981 after the committee recommended his expulsion. Because Kelly, Murphy, and Thompson were defeated for reelection, no congressional disciplinary action against them was taken.

The Senate committee unanimously recommended in August 1981 that Williams be expelled. After numerous delays the Senate debated the recommendation for five days in March 1982 before Williams submitted his resignation.

The Court Cases

Myers and three codefendants were convicted August 30, 1980, of bribery, conspiracy, and interstate travel to aid racketeering. The codefendants were Camden, New Jersey, mayor Angelo J. Errichetti, Philadelphia attorney Howard L. Criden, and Philadelphia city councilman Louis C. Johanson, a partner in Criden's law firm.

Jurors saw videotapes of Myers accepting an envelope with $50,000 in cash from an agent. The government charged that Myers took the money in return for promises to introduce a private immigration bill to help the agent's supposed Arab employer gain permanent U.S. residence. Myers then boasted of his familiarity with Philadelphia government officials and members of the Mafia and agreed to accept an additional $85,000. On the stand, Myers acknowledged that he had accepted money from the undercover agents. He maintained that he was not bribed, however, because he had never intended to do anything in return for the money.

Following a five-week trial, Jenrette was convicted October 7, 1980, on two counts of bribery and a single count of conspiracy. Convicted with him was a business associate, John R. Stowe. During the trial, government prosecutors charged that Jenrette and Stowe had accepted $50,000 in cash from an undercover FBI agent. Prosecutors described the payment as the first installment of a $100,000 bribe to be paid the two men in return for Jenrette's promise to introduce a private immigration bill on behalf of the agent's supposed Arab employer. "I've got larceny in my blood," jurors saw Jenrette say during a videotaped meeting with the agent.

Jenrette was defeated in the November 1980 election. In December the ethics committee recommended that the House discipline him and on December 10 he resigned just before the committee was to vote on his expulsion. Jenrette began serving a two-year prison term in 1985.

Murphy and Thompson on December 3, 1980, became the third and fourth members of Congress to be convicted for their involvement in Abscam. After their indictments both men were required by House rules to yield their committee chairmanships until the criminal charges were resolved. Murphy was chairman of the House Merchant Marine and Fisheries Committee and its Merchant Marine Subcommittee. Thompson chaired the House Administration Committee, the Education and Labor Committee Subcommittee on Labor-Management Relations, and the Joint Committee on Printing.

According to the indictment, Philadelphia attorney Criden introduced Thompson to the undercover agents at an October 1979 meeting in Washington. At that meeting, Thompson agreed to use his official position to help a group of Arab businessmen—the agents' supposed employers—on "an immigration matter," the indictment alleged. At a second meeting, Thompson and Criden were given $50,000, the indictment said, which they shared with "others."

The indictment said Thompson then agreed to introduce the agents to other members of Congress willing to take bribes. He subsequently met with Murphy, the indictment said, after which Murphy and Criden met with two FBI agents in a hotel near New York's Kennedy International Airport, where they were given $50,000 in return for Murphy's promise of help on the immigration matter. Murphy, Thompson, Criden, and "others" shared the cash, the indictment said.

Thompson then introduced Criden to Murtha, the indictment said. In a subsequent meeting with the FBI agents, Criden received an additional $50,000 payment, which he shared with Thompson and Murphy, according to the indictment. The indictment said Murtha agreed to use his official position to help the Arab businessmen gain U.S. residency, but he did not share in the cash payments.

The indictment further alleged that Murphy agreed to find investment opportunities in shipping companies for the agents' supposed employers and to use his position as chairman of the Merchant Marine Committee to advance those companies' interests. The indictment said that Murphy and an unnamed associate intended to benefit both directly and indirectly from the investments.

Thompson also sought investments from the Arab businessmen, the indictment said. It added that benefits from the investments were to accrue to Thompson as well as to unnamed former law partners.

During the trial, Thompson took the stand to deny he had ever received any bribe money. Murtha, who was not indicted in the case, testified, however, that Thompson had approached him on the House floor during 1979 to tell him he could share with Thompson and Murphy $50,000 in "walking around" money in return for meeting with the undercover agents. Murtha subsequently met with the agents but accepted no cash from them. Murphy did not testify in his own defense.

A Brooklyn jury convicted both Thompson and Murphy of conspiracy and accepting unlawful gratuities. Thompson also was convicted of bribery, but Murphy was exonerated of that charge. The convictions came a month after the two lost their reelection bids.

Kelly, the only Republican caught by Abscam, was convicted January 26, 1981, of bribery and conspiracy. He had been defeated for reelection in the September 9, 1980, Florida primary. The July 15 indictment alleged that Kelly accepted $25,000 in cash from an FBI undercover agent in return for agreeing to use his influence to help people emigrate to the United States. The indictment alleged further that Kelly was later to have received $75,000 as part of the conspiracy.

When Kelly's name surfaced in February news accounts of the Abscam probe, he admitted to reporters that he took $25,000 in FBI money. But Kelly said it was part of his own investigation of "shady characters."

During the trial, Kelly was seen on videotape at a Washington home rented by the FBI stuffing money into his pockets and asking before he left whether the money made visible bulges in his clothing. A federal district court overturned Kelly's conviction in 1982 on his claim that he had been denied civil rights, but a higher court reinstated the conviction in 1983. On November 4, 1985, Kelly began serving six to eighteen months at the minimum security prison at Eglin Air Force Base, Florida.

Lederer was convicted January 9, 1981, in a Brooklyn federal district court, of bribery, conspiracy, accepting an illegal gratuity, and interstate travel to aid racketeering. An indictment, handed down May 28, 1980, charged that Lederer in September 1979 accepted a $50,000 bribe in a hotel room near Kennedy Airport in New York from an undercover FBI agent who said he represented Arab businessmen. Lederer promised to introduce private bills to give the Arabs permanent U.S. residency, the indictment said. Lederer shared the $50,000 payment with Errichetti, Criden, and Johanson, the indictment charged.

As the only Abscam figure reelected to the House in 1980, Lederer faced disciplinary action by the new Congress. Supported by the Philadelphia Democratic organization, he had easily won his primary election over six opponents April 22 and was reelected in November with 55 percent of the vote. On April 28, 1981, the Standards Committee recommended that Lederer be expelled from the House. The following day he announced that he would resign from the House May 5. Lederer began serving a prison term in 1985.

Senator Williams

Williams was convicted May 1, 1981, of all nine counts brought against him. They included bribery, conspiracy, accepting outside compensation for the performance of official duties, and aid to a racketeering enterprise. He was only the fourth senator convicted of criminal wrongdoing while in office. *(See box, Senators Convicted or Indicted While in Office, p. 957.)*

Harrison A. Williams Jr. resigned from the Senate in 1982 as his colleagues debated expelling him. Williams had been convicted on criminal charges in the Abscam scandal.

SENATORS CONVICTED OR INDICTED WHILE IN OFFICE

Four sitting senators have been convicted of criminal wrongdoing while in office:

- Harrison A. Williams Jr., D-N.J., was convicted of criminal wrongdoing in the Abscam scandal in 1981.
- Truman H. Newberry, R-Mich., who was found guilty in March 1920 of election irregularities. The Supreme Court reversed Newberry's conviction in May 1921, but he resigned in November 1922 after realizing that, despite the Court's finding, "his position could never be other than uncomfortable," according to *Senate Election, Expulsion, and Censure Cases* (S Doc 92-7).
- John H. Mitchell, R-Ore., convicted in July 1905 on charges of accepting compensation for services rendered before a U.S. department. He died in late 1905 while his conviction was on appeal.
- Joseph R. Burton, R-Kan., convicted in November 1905 for allegedly using the mails for fraudulent purposes and accepting compensation for services rendered before a U.S. department. Burton resigned in June 1906 after the Supreme Court upheld his conviction, and he served five months in prison.

PLEADED GUILTY TO MISDEMEANOR CHARGES

Former Minnesota Republican senator David Durenberger (1978–95) on August 23, 1995, pleaded guilty to five misdemeanor charges related to his reimbursement for stays at a condominium he owned in Minneapolis. On November 29, Durenberger was fined $1,000 and put on a year's probation. According to the Justice Department's Public Integrity Section, Durenberger received $3,825 for stays at his condominium from April to August 1987. The Justice Department said that Durenberger knew he was not eligible to get paid back for the time spent in his own condominium. The misdemeanor charges were filed instead of the more serious felony charges for conspiracy and making false claims that Justice filed against him in 1994. Each of those charges carried maximum sentences of ten years in prison. In 1990 the Senate denounced Durenberger after the Ethics Committee found that he had "brought the Senate into dishonor and disrepute." He did not seek reelection in 1994. *(See "Durenberger," p. 932.)*

INDICTED BUT NOT CONVICTED

Five other senators were charged with criminal offenses while in office but not convicted. They were:

- John Smith, D-Ohio, indicted in 1806 along with Vice President Aaron Burr for treason. He was acquitted.
- Charles H. Dietrich, R-Neb., indicted in December 1903 on bribery and conspiracy charges in connection with the appointment of a postmaster and the leasing of a post office. The charges were dropped on a technicality in January 1904.
- Burton K. Wheeler, D-Mont., indicted in April 1924 on a bribery charge. Wheeler was acquitted.
- Edward J. Gurney, R-Fla., indicted in April 1974 for alleged election law violations. The indictment was dismissed in May 1974. Gurney was again indicted in July 1974, this time on charges of perjury and soliciting bribes. He was acquitted on the bribery solicitation charge in August 1975 and on the perjury charge in October 1976.
- Kay Bailey Hutchison, R-Texas, indicted September 27, 1993, (charges dropped because a grand juror was found to have been ineligible), reindicted December 8, 1993. Cleared of all five charges that she had misused Texas state workers and equipment for personal and political gain while she was state treasurer. *(See "Hutchison," p. 972.)*

Standing seventh in seniority among Senate Democrats, Williams was chairman of the Senate Labor and Human Resources Committee until Republicans gained control of the Senate in 1981. He also was ranking member of the Banking Committee, former chairman of its Securities Subcommittee, and a member of the Rules and Administration Committee.

Like the other Abscam defendants, he was convicted of promising to introduce a private immigration bill for what turned out to be a phony sheik (actually an FBI agent in disguise). Unlike the others he was charged not with accepting a large cash payment but with accepting shares in a titanium mine in return for a promise to help the enterprise get government contracts. Prosecutors said the stock certificates omitted Williams's name to conceal his interest in the mine. The stock was in the name of a close associate who was an unindicted co-conspirator in the case. The scam concerned a scheme to secure a $100 million loan for the mine and processing facility in Piney River, Virginia, from the supposed sheik.

Denying the charges, Williams said he only intended to help friends who owned the mine to obtain a loan from a wealthy Arab. Williams also acknowledged that he had boasted of his influence with high government officials "to an uncomfortable degree" in the presence of the bogus Arab and that he had accepted stock in the mine. But he said he believed the stock certificates to be worthless.

After his conviction Williams continued to vote on the Senate floor while pursuing an appeal to higher courts. He followed a precedent set in 1924 by Sen. Burton K. Wheeler, D-Mont., after his indictment for bribery. The Montana senator, however, was never convicted.

Wheeler at the time of the indictment headed a special committee investigating the failure of the Warren G. Harding administration to prosecute federal officials suspected of influence-peddling in the Teapot Dome scandal. Wheeler maintained he had been framed by the very officials he was investigating. Instead of keeping off the floor, Wheeler demanded the right to speak to declare his innocence and to ask the Senate to investigate the charge. During the ensuing probe, he continued to vote. Wheeler subsequently was cleared of any wrongdoing both by the Senate and by a federal jury. Since then, indicted senators have remained active in Senate affairs until they either were cleared or left the Senate.

House rules urged—but did not require—a convicted member to refrain from voting in committee and on the floor until the member either was cleared or reelected. *(See "Suspension," p. 941.)*

The Senate Ethics Committee, after reviewing the evidence in the court case and hearing Williams present his defense again, voted unanimously August 24, 1981, to recommend that the Senate expel him. That would have been the sixteenth expulsion from the Senate and the first since the Civil War. *(See Table 34-3, p. 924.)*

After numerous delays the Senate began debating the recommendation March 3, 1982. Noting Williams's claim that the government tried "to manufacture crime out of nothing," Ethics Vice Chairman Howell Heflin, D-Ala., a former judge, argued that the evidence upheld the case against Williams regardless of the government's conduct. "At any point in this drawn out, sordid affair," Heflin said, "Senator Williams could have said, 'Wait a minute. What you're proposing is wrong. That is not what I had in mind. I can't be involved in this.' But he didn't. He stayed; he discussed; he agreed; he promised; he pledged—to abuse his office, his public trust, for which now he must be expelled."

The Democratic whip, Alan Cranston of California, worked on Williams's behalf to reduce the punishment to a censure motion. But when closer friends of Williams reluctantly endorsed expulsion, it became clear that Cranston's motion would fail and that well over the required two-thirds of the Senate was ready to vote to expel Williams. On March 11, 1982, he resigned from the Senate.

1980s and 1990s: Bumper Crop of Cases

The 1980s and 1990s produced an unprecedented number of congressional ethics cases. While some speculation arose that Congress was attracting a lower quality of candidates than in the past, other factors seemed a more likely explanation for the increase, such as: the availability of a place to file complaints—the ethics committees; the new activism of the committees themselves; the clearer guidelines offered by the House and Senate codes and the 1978 and 1989 ethics acts; sharper vigilance by the media and law enforcement agencies; and less tolerance generally for immoral or amoral behavior that was once considered a politician's own business.

The following list of members investigated during this period deals primarily with nonsexual alleged offenses. Those of a sexual nature, sometimes drug or alcohol related, are treated in a separate box on page 000. Those caught up in Abscam were discussed earlier. Also not included here are those members who in the 1980s and 1990s faced disciplinary action in their respective chambers. *(See "Abscam Investigation," p. 953; Chapter 34, Seating and Disciplining.)*

ETHICS CASES IN THE 1980S

Morgan

The Senate Ethics Committee voted unanimously June 26, 1980, to clear Sen. Robert Morgan, D-N.C., of a charge that he acted improperly by taking advice from John Stirk, a former Morgan military affairs aide employed as a lawyer by General Dynamics Corp., a large defense contractor.

During the Senate Armed Services Committee's markup of the fiscal 1981 weapons procurement bill, Morgan persuaded the committee to add $91 million to convert 155 F-111D and FB-111A aircraft for use as a manned nuclear bomber. The F-111 was made by General Dynamics, but Morgan said he favored altering the aircraft before he met Stirk in 1977. The Senate subsequently took the program out of the bill.

The Ethics Committee also rejected a North Carolina Republican Party charge that Morgan improperly accepted campaign contributions from defense contractor political action committees.

Bayh

The Senate Ethics Committee ruled in March 1980 that Birch Bayh, D-Ind., violated Senate franking regulations when he used public funds to send out a mass mailing that had been printed with campaign funds. Bayh termed the rules violation "an honest mistake" and reimbursed the Senate for the postage.

The franked mailing—setting out the senator's views on federal aid to the Chrysler Corp.—was sent to fifteen thousand employees of the ailing automobile firm in December 1979. Bayh used campaign funds to pay a private firm to print and address the mailing. Address labels were furnished by the United Auto Workers union.

The committee said the mailing violated a provision of the 1977 Senate ethics code requiring that only official funds be used to print material mailed under a senator's frank. Furthermore, senators were prohibited by federal law from "loaning" their franking privileges to any organization outside the Senate such as a campaign committee or private printing firm.

Richmond

Rep. Fred W. Richmond, D-N.Y., pleaded guilty August 25, 1982, to charges of tax evasion, possession of marijuana, and making an illegal payment to a government employee. At the same time, he announced his resignation from the House and, as part of an unusual plea bargain with federal prosecutors, agreed not to run for office again.

In return for his guilty plea and resignation, the government agreed not to prosecute him for other actions it had been investigating, including cocaine possession and his arranging for a prison escapee, using an alias, to be put on the House payroll. The House Committee on Standards of Official Conduct, which had been investigating the allegations against Richmond, dropped its probe when he resigned.

The part of the plea bargain involving Richmond's resignation and promise not to run for reelection was voided November 10, 1982, by U.S. District Judge Jack B. Weinstein as an "unconstitutional interference by the executive with the legislative branch of government" that "conflicted with the fundamental right of the people to elect their representatives."

Judge Weinstein sentenced Richmond to a year and a day in federal prison and fined him $20,000. He began his prison sentence at the federal prison camp at Allenwood, Pennsylvania, on December 6.

The only felony charge to which he pleaded guilty—tax evasion—involved Richmond's 1980 income, which he admitted in court was understated on his tax return. He did not report funds paid by his company, Walco National Corp., for his New York apartment. This reduced Richmond's tax liability by approximately $50,000.

Richmond had had an earlier brush with the law in 1978, when he was arrested on a morals charge. The charges were dropped after he completed a psychiatric treatment program. (See "Richmond," p. 970.)

Ferraro

The Democratic Party's 1984 vice presidential candidate, Rep. Geraldine A. Ferraro of New York, was found by the House ethics committee to have technically violated the 1978 Ethics in Government Act. The committee ruled December 3, 1984, that Ferraro committed the technical violations about ten times in failing to report or reporting incorrectly a number of items on her financial disclosure forms from 1978 through 1983. The committee's vote, reportedly 8–2, was taken in secret.

The forty-six-page report also concluded that Ferraro failed to meet the standards necessary for claiming to exempt her husband's financial interests from her financial disclosure forms. But the panel did not investigate that question. Ferraro told reporters she felt "completely vindicated" by the ethics committee's report.

No action was taken against Ferraro before her term expired January 3, 1985. As Walter F. Mondale's running mate she had not sought reelection. The panel decided the House would not have time to act on the complaint against her while she was still a member.

Hatfield

The Senate Ethics Committee investigated Sen. Mark O. Hatfield, R-Ore., in 1984 because of questions arising from his wife's business dealings with a Greek businessman, Basil A. Tsakos. Antoinette Hatfield had received $55,000 from Tsakos in connection with a trans-African pipeline project. Hatfield, chairman of the Senate Appropriations Committee, insisted that the payment had been for legitimate work his wife had done on the project. He later said it had been "a mistake" for his wife to take the money while he was supporting the pipeline in Congress. The committee voted September 25, 1984, that there was insufficient evidence of wrongdoing against Hatfield to justify a full-scale inquiry. A final report was issued January 10, 1985.

Concluding a fifteen-month investigation, the Ethics Committee rebuked Hatfield on August 12, 1992, for accepting and failing to report gifts worth nearly $43,000 between 1983 and 1988 as well as three travel reimbursements of unspecified value. The committee found that Hatfield had violated the 1978 Ethics in Government Act and Senate rules and deemed his actions "improper conduct reflecting upon the Senate." The ethics panel found no evidence of criminal violations or willful wrongdoing, and no connection was made between Hatfield's official actions and acceptance of the gifts. The committee did not recommend discipline by the full Senate, thus closing the case.

Daniel

In a 343-page report released February 10, 1986, the House ethics committee reported that Rep. Dan Daniel, D-Va., a member of the Armed Services Committee, had accepted at least sixty-eight and perhaps more than two hundred free trips on a defense contractor's corporate jet. The panel concluded that Daniel had broken rules prohibiting gifts totaling $100 or more from sources with an interest in legislation, barring use of private funds to augment office allowances, and requiring that members report gifts totaling $250 or more a year. All three rules were based on the 1978 Ethics in Government Act.

Daniel told the committee that he was aware of the ethics law and House rules but had not realized that the thresholds were aggregate amounts, not individual amounts, for gifts received in a year.

The panel also had discovered that, after nineteen of the flights on which he was a passenger, Daniel had submitted vouchers seeking reimbursement for auto mileage. Daniel testified that long drives aggravated injuries he had suffered in a 1982 auto accident and that he mistakenly thought he was entitled to repayment when his wife or aides drove his car between Washington, D.C., and his Virginia district, even if he was not in the car.

The committee concluded that Daniel had misunderstood federal laws and House rules and decided no sanctions were necessary because he had subsequently complied by repaying the defense contractor—Beech Aircraft Corp.—and the government and by updating his annual financial disclosure statements, which were required of all federal officeholders.

The panel said it was satisfied by Daniel's testimony that he had not violated federal criminal statutes against submitting false claims and embezzling from the government. The committee also found no improper relationship between the nine-term lawmaker and the defense contractor. It did express "concern regarding at least an appearance of impropriety."

Daniel easily won reelection in 1986, but he died January 23, 1988, before completing the term.

Weaver

In a unanimous decision, the House ethics committee found that Rep. James Weaver, D-Ore., in borrowing $81,667 from campaign funds in 1981–1984 for commodity market trades, had violated a House rule against using campaign funds for any-thing other than "bona fide campaign purposes." His reports on commodity trading, listed only in broad summaries, violated a second rule requiring details of each transaction to be reported on annual financial statements that members were required by law to file.

Weaver variously described the $81,667 in borrowings either as repayment to him for earlier loans he had made to the cam-paign or as loans he meant to repay—with interest and, if lucky, profits from his investments. Because Weaver had reported his borrowings and made partial disclosure of his investments on his campaign and financial-worth reports, the committee ruled out sanctions. "There was no evidence of an intent to avoid public notice" of the loans, the panel's report said. As for the commodities trading, it added, "disclosure was attempted—al-beit inadequately."

The committee's 258-page report, released October 7, 1986, ended an eight-month probe. During that period, Weaver won Oregon's Democratic nomination for the Senate and then abruptly dropped out in August, citing the cloud of the unre-solved ethics case. He retired from the House in January 1987 af-ter six terms.

Banking Committee Chairman Fernand J. St Germain lost his House seat in a November 1988 upset after an ethics committee investigation of his behavior.

Fiedler

The Los Angeles district attorney dropped political corrup-tion charges against Rep. Bobbi Fiedler, R-Calif., on February 19, 1986, saying that the evidence was "not sufficient" to pursue the case. Fiedler, who unsuccessfully sought the GOP nomination for the U.S. Senate seat held by Democrat Alan Cranston, had been indicted January 23, along with an aide, on charges of vio-lating an obscure California law by offering a rival candidate money to withdraw from the GOP primary. The statute, passed in 1893, apparently had never been used in criminal proceed-ings.

Boner

An investigation into allegations against Bill Boner, D-Tenn., was ended when he left the House on October 5, 1987, to become mayor of Nashville. An inconclusive ethics committee report, released December 15, left many questions unresolved, because the inquiry was incomplete when Boner left Congress and the committee thus lost the power to continue investigating him. Ethics committee chairman Julian Dixon denied suggestions that the committee deliberately delayed the release of the report until after Boner was elected mayor.

The committee began its inquiry into Boner in February 1986. For a year beginning in April 1986, the investigation was suspended at the request of Justice Department officials. It was resumed after Justice announced it would not seek indictments.

The staff report did conclude that Boner violated House rules when he used campaign funds to pay for a side trip he and his wife took from Taiwan to Hong Kong and when he accepted use of a speedboat from a Nashville company for two years

without reporting it as a gift. The staff did not complete its in-vestigation of charges by a defense contractor, who was a former friend of Boner, that he paid the representative nearly $50,000 in bribes by paying Boner's wife legal fees for work she never did. But the staff report suggested that Boner's dealings with the contractor "could be construed by reasonable persons as influ-encing the performance of his governmental duties."

St Germain

After a fourteen-month investigation, the ethics panel April 15, 1987, absolved Fernand J. St Germain, D-R.I., of allegations that he grew rich through abuse of his office. The committee did find that the chairman of the Banking, Finance, and Urban Affairs Committee repeatedly violated provisions of the 1977 House ethics code and the 1978 Ethics in Government Act, which required members to disclose their finances annually. But it recommended no punishment. St Germain hailed the report as a total vindication.

The ethics committee report did not dispute the accuracy of 1985 articles in the *Wall Street Journal* that led to the inquiry. The report's fifty pages of text and 1,355 pages of supporting ma-terial further documented the newspaper's contention that St Germain, who boasted of his working-class background, had built a multimillion-dollar fortune with what the *Journal* called "lots of investment help from people and institutions that have benefited from his official actions."

Summarizing the various violations, the panel concluded that "the identified improprieties do not rise to such a level war-ranting further action by this committee." As for the potentially more damaging allegations of abuse of office for personal gain, the panel said those "were not substantiated by clear and convincing evidence."

Earlier in 1987 more than one-fourth of St Germain's Democratic colleagues had voted against his reelection as Banking chairman. He won, 182–70, but lost his House seat in a November 1988 upset. As Banking Committee chairman, St Germain had played a major role in the regulatory changes that helped to bring about the savings and loan industry collapse and the investigation of five senators' involvement in the rescue of one of the S&Ls. (See box, The Keating Five Scandal, p. 962.)

Oakar

Questions about Rep. Mary Rose Oakar's payroll led to allegations of conflict of interest and fraud. After an informal review, the ethics committee June 17, 1987, found that the Ohio Democrat broke House rules and federal laws when she paid a former staff member more than $45,000 in salary for nearly two years after the aide had moved to New York.

Personnel rules formulated by the House Administration Committee on which Oakar sat required House employees to work in Washington or in a member's district. Members certified monthly that their payroll was in compliance. Federal law prohibited false claims against the government, under penalty of up to five years in prison and a $10,000 fine.

Oakar was directed to repay the funds, which she said she had already done. Beyond that, the committee concluded, "no disciplinary action is warranted in this matter." In addition, the committee absolved Oakar of any improprieties related to her purchase of a town house with a second aide, who had been given a $10,000-a-year raise the same month they purchased the property.

Oakar lost her bid for reelection in 1992 amid allegations that she had misused her account at the defunct House bank. She was indicted February 22, 1995, on seven felony counts. She was charged with lying to the FBI about asking the House bank to stop payment on three checks, writing a $16,000 check even though she knew not enough money was in the account to cover it, trying to evade campaign finance law, and failing to report a $50,000 loan on her 1991 financial disclosure form. Two of the seven counts were dismissed March 21, 1996: lying to Congress by filing false financial statements and writing an overdraft check at the House bank. Oakar pleaded guilty on September 30, 1997, to a misdemeanor conspiracy charge and a misdemeanor campaign finance violation. When her 1992 campaign accounts came under scrutiny as a part of the Justice Department investigation of the House bank, investigators found that she had shifted $16,000 in campaign contributions from her House bank account to her campaign using false names to evade the individual contributions limits. She admitted giving false information to the Federal Election Commission. On January 21, 1998, she was sentenced to two years of probation and fined $32,000. Oakar was further required to perform two hundred hours of community service.

Stallings

In a report issued October 19, 1987, the ethics panel concluded that Rep. Richard Stallings, D-Idaho, had violated House rules by improperly borrowing campaign funds to buy a car and lend money to an aide. The committee issued a letter rebuking him but called for no other disciplinary action.

While the panel concluded Stallings's loans did not meet the rules criterion of being for use solely by the campaign, it said that the violation arose from a misunderstanding—Stallings's incorrect assumption that the loans were governed by a less restrictive federal law allowing campaign funds to be used for "any legal purpose."

Stallings's problems occurred because he reported the $5,800 he had borrowed on his July 1987 Federal Election Commission report. The same report showed that Stallings had repaid part of the loan with interest. The ethics committee accepted Stallings's assertion that he did not intend to avoid public disclosure of the loans.

The issue was politically sensitive for the Idaho Democrat because of his narrow 1984 victory over former Republican member George Hansen, who was convicted that year for failing to report $334,000 in loans and profits from 1978 to 1981. (See "Hansen," p. 938.)

Biaggi

Facing near-certain expulsion from the House, Mario Biaggi, D-N.Y., resigned from Congress four days after his August 4, 1988, conviction on felony charges in connection with bribes allegedly paid by a defense contractor to get no-bid government contracts. It was his second conviction in less than a year.

Biaggi had been convicted in September 1987 on charges related to accepting Florida vacations after using his influence to help a Brooklyn ship-repair company. Having been found guilty of accepting an illegal gratuity, obstructing justice, and other criminal charges, Biaggi was fined $500,000 and sentenced to thirty months in prison but was freed pending appeal.

A preliminary report by the House ethics committee staff in November 1987 concluded that Biaggi's offenses violated House rules as well as the laws governing financial disclosure, travel, and acceptance of gifts and brought "discredit upon the House of Representatives." The ethics panel recommended Biaggi's expulsion from the House, but floor action on the resolution of expulsion, which had been filed February 18, 1988, was put off while Biaggi stood trial in the second, unrelated case.

The New York representative was convicted in 1988 of racketeering, conspiracy, extortion, and accepting bribes in connection with a scandal involving the Wedtech Corp., a South Bronx concern that began as a machine shop and grew into a multimillion-dollar defense contractor that earned the acclamation of President Ronald Reagan. Wedtech's primary source of business was a federal program that set aside contracts, without bids, for minority-owned companies. It briefly came to symbolize the possibilities of free enterprise in the impoverished South

THE KEATING FIVE SCANDAL

When does the relationship between members' two most time-consuming tasks—helping constituents and raising money—become improper and unethical? That was the fundamental question posed, but not entirely answered, by the Senate ethics case known as the Keating Five.

The Senate Ethics Committee in 1989–1991 investigated five senators—Alan Cranston, D-Calif.; Dennis DeConcini, D-Ariz.; John Glenn, D-Ohio; John McCain, R-Ariz.; and Donald W. Riegle Jr., D-Mich.—who were suspected of doing favors between 1987 and 1989 for a wealthy campaign contributor, Charles H. Keating Jr. Keating was the head of a California-based thrift, Lincoln Savings and Loan Association, that failed in 1989, costing taxpayers $2 billion. Lincoln became a symbol of one of the largest financial debacles in U.S. history, the near collapse of the savings and loan industry. Keating gave a total of $1.5 million to the campaigns and political causes of the senators. In the end, on November 20, 1991, the committee reprimanded Cranston, in a new ethics punishment. The other four had been let off nearly ten months earlier with letters of reprimand.

The committee held televised hearings from November 15, 1990, through January 16, 1991, to investigate whether any of the five senators had violated Senate rules against exerting improper influence in return for compensation. The hearings were technically only a preliminary inquiry into whether the Ethics Committee should proceed to a formal investigation of the charges. The committee named Washington lawyer Robert S. Bennett as special counsel to handle the investigation.

All five senators denied wrongdoing, arguing that their efforts on behalf of Keating were proper representation of a constituent having troubles with a federal agency. They denied that they had helped Keating in return for his prodigious fund-raising and maintained that their actions did not influence the decisions of government regulators with regard to Lincoln. In the mid-1980s, Lincoln began a bitter feud with federal regulators. Bank regulators charged that the thrift's rapid, high-risk growth had violated federal regulations. Keating fought back, charging that he was the victim of a "vendetta." Keating successfully lined up well-placed politicians to help him in his fight as things heated up in late 1986 and early 1987. Among them were Cranston, DeConcini, Glenn, McCain, and Riegle.

The key events found by Bennett concerned two meetings held in April 1987. In the first, on April 2, four of the senators (all but Riegle) met privately in DeConcini's office with Edwin J. Gray, chairman of the Federal Home Loan Bank Board, which was responsible for regulating the thrift industry. Gray contended that the senators pressured him to withdraw the direct investment rule, which would rein in Lincoln's ability to pursue its high-flying investment strategy. Bennett emphasized that Gray had told to bring no aides to the meeting. "Under all of the circumstances, including the articulated purpose of the meeting, it is at best strange that there was a purposeful effort made to exclude staff," said Bennett during the televised hearings.

Details of the second meeting, on April 9, 1987, taken by one of the regulators seemed to be very accurate, said Bennett, and they indicated that DeConcini seemed to be negotiating for Lincoln.

Bennett made clear that he viewed Cranston's efforts in Keating's behalf to be the most questionable. He received the most money from Keating, he allowed his fund-raisers to serve as an important link with Keating, he remained active in helping Keating after others had stopped, and he seemed the most ideologically incompatible with Keating.

In summing up the facts and standards that he believed should apply to the case, Bennett distinguished carefully among the five senators. He urged the committee to find that Cranston, DeConcini, and Riegle had acted improperly. He said that Glenn and McCain's acceptance of contributions was far removed in time from their actions, eliminating any taint from their fund-raising.

Bennett argued that DeConcini had gone beyond the bounds of proper behavior to negotiate for Keating with regulators in 1987, and he noted that DeConcini weighed in with them again in 1989 on the pending sale of Lincoln, despite knowledge that the regulators had referred evidence of possible criminal conduct at Lincoln to the Justice Department.

Bennett argued that Cranston's case provided the closest connection between money and action. He cited four separate occasions in which Cranston took action for Keating after soliciting or receiving large amounts of cash for his own campaign or for voter registration groups with which he was affiliated.

Of Riegle, Bennett also drew a connection between fund-raising and action, all of which occurred in a three-month period in 1987. And he made a damning accusation that Riegle had misled the committee, perhaps intentionally, about his role in the Keating affair.

As for the senator's contention that their meetings with and repeated phone calls to regulators were merely "status inquiries" to find out whether the Lincoln case was being handled properly, Bennett was derisive. "If I'm sitting on a park bench, and an eight-hundred-pound gorilla comes along and says, 'Excuse me, I'm just

Bronx. But Wedtech was at the center of a wide-ranging scandal by the time it went out of business.

Biaggi was sentenced to eight years in prison, to run concurrently with the previous thirty-month sentence.

Garcia

On November 21, 1988, Rep. Robert Garcia faced federal influence-peddling charges stemming from the investigation into the Wedtech Corp. The charges against Garcia were conspiracy, two counts of receipt of bribes, two counts of extortion, and two counts of receipt of gratuities. The seven-count indictment came less than two weeks after voters endorsed Garcia for a sixth full term, giving him 92 percent of the vote.

Under House Democratic Caucus rules, Garcia had to step down from the chairmanship of the House Banking Subcommittee on International Development, Finance, Trade, and Monetary Policy for the remainder of the 100th Congress. Given that Congress had adjourned, there was little impact on the

making a status inquiry if there are any seats available,' you say, 'You're damn right, there's a seat available.' And there's a lot of eight-hundred-pound gorillas around this place."

Bennett reiterated his position that the senators' actions had been wrong and that they should have known how wrong they would appear to the public. *(See box, Violating the 'Appearance Standard,' p. 965.)*

Establishing the facts of the case, while time-consuming, proved to be easier for the Ethics Committee then deciding the central question of at what point a senator's conduct crossed the bounds of ethics. After more than thirty-three hours of closed-door deliberations spread over six weeks, the Ethics Committee announced on February 27, 1991, that the only senator they would proceed against was Cranston. The panel found evidence that some of Cranston's official actions were "substantially linked" with his fund-raising. The other four senators were criticized in written statements for poor judgment, with DeConcini and Riegle also rebuked for the appearance of acting improper. But the panel decided that existing rules did not warrant further action against the four senators.

The committee on November 19, 1991, voted 5–0, with Jesse Helms, R-N.C., abstaining, for a new, unique punishment for Cranston. In a seventy-nine-page report, the Ethics Committee found that while there was no evidence of a corrupt bargain—an illegal exchange of contributions for official action—Cranston's conduct did veer too close to a quid pro quo. The panel said that evidence seemed to show that Cranston solicited and accepted much more money than the other four senators—$100,000 and more at a clip—and repeatedly did so at times when Keating was successfully seeking his assistance.

No one episode sealed Cranston's fate; instead Ethics Committee Chairman Howell Heflin, D-Ala., said it was "the totality of the circumstances." The panel walked a fine line in attempting to articulate what was improper about Cranston's conduct. His behavior was found to fall somewhere between actually being dishonest and merely looking dishonest. Fund-raising and official actions were linked, Heflin said, but not "causally connected."

But the committee's report offered little in the way of guidance to senators seeking to avoid "linkage." The "cardinal principle," the report said, was to make decisions "without regard to whether the individual had contributed or promised to contribute." It cautioned members to consider the following: the merits of the constituent's request; how much money the constituent had contributed; whether the type of official action to be taken in behalf of the constituent deviated from the senator's usual conduct; and the "proximity of money and action." The report, however, did not say how to evaluate these considerations.

The Ethics Committee report was challenged by Helms, who issued a twenty-seven-page report showing why he believed the committee had not gone far enough in its actions against Cranston, and by Cranston, who responded with a sixty-six-page report he said showed the committee had gone too far in its conclusions.

Key to the panel's final compromise was the desire by all concerned to avoid a full-scale floor fight. For that, the committee needed Cranston to accept its decision. Cranston's bottom line: "If the committee had called for any action by the full Senate against me, I would have fought it tooth and nail." Perhaps for this reason, the question of whether there would be a floor vote was a tightly held secret. It became clear by the morning of November 20, 1991, that the committee would not ask members to vote. When speculation arose that someone might try to force a vote, President Pro Tempore Robert C. Byrd, D-W.Va., quashed the notion when he took the presiding officer's chair and said, "The order does not provide for the taking of any votes by the Senate."

The punishment for Cranston was halfway between a committee rebuke and a full-scale Senate censure. The Ethics Committee leaders told the assembled Senate that the committee had reprimanded Cranston for "an impermissible pattern of conduct in which fund raising and official activities were substantially linked." It was the Senate's first use of the word "reprimand" in place of its more traditional "censure," and it was the first time that the action was taken by the committee, not the full Senate.

The Senate tied up one loose end from the Keating investigation on July 2, 1992, when it adopted a resolution that was designed to spell out when a senator could properly intervene with federal agencies on behalf of constituents. Senate Majority Leader George J. Mitchell, D-Maine, had appointed a task force in April 1991 to review Senate rules governing "constituent service." The measure was criticized by the government watchdog group Common Cause as flawed, partly because it did not attempt to define what was improper use of influence. The resolution said only that the "decision to provide assistance to petitioners may not be made on the basis of contributions or services, or promises of contributions or services, to the member's political campaigns or to other organizations in which a member had a political, personal or financial interest."

committee, and the House ethics committee could not consider action against Garcia.

Garcia and his wife, Jane Lee Garcia, were found guilty October 20, 1989, of two counts of extortion and one count of conspiracy. They were accused of taking more than $170,000 in payments and interest-free loans, plus a diamond necklace, from the defunct Wedtech. Both Garcias were acquitted of four counts of bribery and receipt of illegal gratuities.

Garcia, who had become chairman of another Banking sub-committee, Policy Research and Insurance, in the 101st Congress, stepped down in 1989 to devote full time to an appeal of his conviction. He resigned from Congress January 7, 1990, twelve days before he was sentenced to three years in prison for extortion.

A federal appeals court overturned the Garcias' convictions on June 29, 1990. The appellate court said the Garcias' actions fell short of extortion. "Garcia never even hinted that he was prepared to use his power to harm Wedtech," a three-judge panel of the U.S. Court of Appeals for the Second Circuit wrote. "In making the payments, the company was motivated by desire, not fear." U.S. District Judge Leonard Sand refused, however, on December 3 to block a new trial.

The Garcias argued that a new trial would violate the double jeopardy clause of the Constitution because they would be tried twice for the same offense. Sand ruled, though, that the Constitution did not bar the retrial of a defendant who obtained a reversal of a conviction on appeal.

Both Garcias were convicted again in 1991, a verdict that was overturned in April 1993. And on September 15, 1993, prosecutors announced they would not attempt to retry either of the Garcias. Later that year, Garcia set up shop as a lobbyist in Washington.

Sunia

Fofo I. F. Sunia, the Democratic delegate from American Samoa, pleaded guilty on August 3, 1988, to charges of conspiring to defraud the government by keeping on his House payroll "ghost employees" who did no congressional work. The House ethics committee had opened a preliminary investigation of Sunia's payroll practices in October 1987, but his resignation on September 6, 1988, ended its jurisdiction over him.

Swindall

Rep. Pat Swindall, R-Ga., was indicted October 17, 1988, on charges that he lied about a transaction in which he almost borrowed money that allegedly came from illegal drug profits. Swindall was defeated for reelection the next month.

The former representative was sentenced in 1989 to a year in prison.

Rose

The ethics panel concluded in 1988 that Rep. Charlie Rose, D-N.C., violated House rules by putting campaign funds to personal use and by failing to report certain aspects of his financial affairs. But the panel recommended no punishment. The committee announced its conclusion March 23, when it sent Rose a formal "letter of reproval" for breaking House rules. But it said it believed formal sanctions were not warranted because of mitigating circumstances.

In its report, released March 31, the panel concluded that Rose had wrongly borrowed $63,995 from his campaign in eight transactions from 1978 to 1985 and had improperly put up a $75,000 certificate of deposit held by his campaign as collateral for a personal loan. In both cases, the panel said, Rose violated a House rule that barred members from converting campaign funds to personal use and required that funds be used solely for "bona fide campaign purposes."

The committee also concluded that Rose violated House rules by failing to disclose in his House financial reports the loans from his campaign and others from several banks. Although it never spelled out which mitigating circumstances led it to conclude formal punishment of Rose was not warranted,

the committee noted that he had voluntarily amended his financial disclosure forms and had repaid the money.

On October 27, 1994, Rose settled a five-year lawsuit by the Justice Department stemming from this ethics investigation when he agreed to pay a civil fine of $12,500. The Justice Department had sued him for "knowingly and willfully" filing inaccurate financial disclosure statements and had sought fines totaling $30,000.

Rose had gone to court to block the government's suit, filed in May 1989, on constitutional grounds, but a panel of the U.S. Court of Appeals for the District of Columbia Circuit on July 12, 1994, unanimously rejected arguments by Rose and House lawyers that the civil suit violated the Constitution's separation of powers doctrine because the Justice Department relied on Rose's statements to the House ethics committee and because that panel already had investigated and rebuked him for the same false statements.

Durenberger

Before being denounced and subsequently convicted on charges related to making false reimbursement claims, Sen. Dave Durenberger, R-Minn., was criticized in 1988 by the Senate Ethics Committee for appearing to disclose "sensitive national security information" about U.S. espionage. The panel, however, recommended no punishment for the senator. (See "Durenberger," p. 932.)

At issue were remarks Durenberger made in 1987 about Jonathan Jay Pollard, who was sentenced to life in prison for spying on the United States for Israel. Speaking to a Jewish group, Durenberger said that the United States had recruited an Israeli spy in the 1980s, before Israel employed Pollard. The investigation focused on whether his comments violated Senate rules prohibiting the disclosure of classified intelligence information provided to the Intelligence Committee, of which Durenberger served as chairman in 1985–1986.

Dickinson

The House ethics committee in October 1989 asked Bill Dickinson, R-Ala., to explain a transaction involving $300,000 he obtained from Bill Collier, an Alabama friend and defense contractor. According to press accounts, Dickinson turned over the money to an investor for one-third of the profits even though he put up no money of his own. Dickinson said the business deal, which ultimately failed, was unrelated to—and came along after—his efforts to help Collier's company, the district's largest private employer.

No formal complaint was ever lodged against Dickinson, and the committee did not formally investigate him.

Gingrich

Before he became in 1997 the first sitting Speaker of the House to be reprimanded, Newt Gingrich of Georgia, while House GOP whip, was the target of another ethics committee investigation. (See "Gingrich," p. 940.)

VIOLATING THE 'APPEARANCE STANDARD'

Can a legislator's conduct be improper merely because it looks bad? In the Keating Five case, Special Counsel Robert S. Bennett urged the Senate Ethics Committee to conclude that, even absent a finding of actual improper conduct, members could be disciplined just for looking as though they behaved improperly—for violating what he called the "appearance standard." *(See box, The Keating Five Scandal, p. 962.)*

"Legislators who appear to reasonable persons to do wrong actually do wrong by eroding the trust between citizens and their representatives," Bennett told the panel. He argued that long-standing traditions, Senate and House precedents, previous Ethics Committee pronouncements, and common sense supported his position. However, although Bennett cited several past ethics cases in which appearances came into play, he offered no example of a lawmaker having been punished merely because his or her behavior looked improper.

Bennett formulated the suggested standard this way: "A senator should not engage in conduct which would appear to be improper to a reasonable, nonpartisan, fully informed person." Senators were required to follow not just written rules and laws, Bennett said; they also had to adhere to certain unwritten standards of conduct. He cited numerous precedents going back to the late 1700s to show that senators could be punished, even expelled, for violating unwritten standards.

In 1964 the Ethics Committee's report on its investigation of Bobby Baker, a top Senate employee who was found to have used his office to promote outside business interests, said that "officials have an obligation . . . to refrain not only from actual wrongdoing but from conduct leaving the appearance of wrongdoing."

When the Select Committee on Standards and Conduct first proposed a code of conduct in 1968, it stated in a report that "the Senate must not only be free of improper influence but must also be . . . free from the appearance of impropriety."

In its 1978 report on the Korean influence scandal, the Ethics Committee said "a key element" of previous conduct-related Senate resolutions "is that a senator must avoid the appearance of impropriety, as well as impropriety itself." *(See box, Two Aides' Misuse of Power," p. 949; "Korean Influence Buying," p. 952)*

Bennett said that the standard had been invoked in the 1989–1990 case against Dave Durenberger, R-Minn. Before the Senate unanimously voted to denounce Durenberger for unethical financial dealings, Warren B. Rudman, R-N.H., vice chairman of the Ethics Committee, said his colleague "failed his obligation of protecting both the appearance and reality of propriety." Bennett cited three House cases as well, those of Robert L. F. Sikes, D-Fla., in 1976; Raymond F. Lederer, D-Pa., in 1981; and Mario Biaggi, D-N.Y., in 1988. All four of Bennett's precedents involved more than just appearances, however. The committee found that Durenberger violated rules on speech fees, financial disclosure, gifts, and campaign contributions. Lederer and Biaggi were charged with violating criminal bribery statutes, while Sikes was found to have violated House disclosure requirements.

Opponents argued that the existing Senate rule prohibiting members from engaging in "improper conduct which may reflect upon the Senate" was, in effect, a two-step test. First, the conduct in question must be found to be improper; then it must be shown to reflect badly on the Senate. That is, the appearance standard could not be imposed independently. Furthermore, they argued, voters should be left to decide if any appearance problem exists and punish members at the polls accordingly.

Dismissing two formal complaints filed by Rep. Bill Alexander, D-Ark., the panel on March 7, 1990, said in its report, "The committee is of the firm view that no adequate basis exists for initiating a preliminary inquiry. . . . The facts alleged in the complaints, even if true, have been generally deemed not to state violations" of House rules or law, said the Committee on Standards of Official Conduct. The panel did, however, scold Gingrich for relatively minor violations: an omission from his financial disclosure form and an aide's misuse of congressional stationery.

But the committee found no impropriety in the central focus of the complaint—a partnership, financed largely by his political backers, set up to promote a 1984 book cowritten by Gingrich.

Interest in the case was high because Gingrich instigated the 1988–1989 investigation that led to the resignation of Democratic Speaker Jim Wright of Texas. At a news conference March 8, Gingrich dismissed the accusations as a "political smear. . . . I am glad the committee was thorough, and I am happy the

charges have been exposed as politically inspired nonsense." He narrowly won reelection in 1990.

The controversy surrounding Gingrich's book deal began when the *Washington Post* on March 20, 1989, published an article detailing the formation of a partnership to promote Gingrich's book, *A Window of Opportunity*. The partnership, managed by Gingrich's wife, Marianne, raised $105,000 to supplement the publisher's meager promotional budget. The enterprise had twenty-two partners, including fourteen who had also made political contributions to Gingrich.

Alexander filed a complaint with the committee April 11, raising questions about whether the arrangement was a means to circumvent House rules on outside income, acceptance of gifts, and conversion of campaign funds or government resources to personal use. Alexander amended his complaint in July and again in October, when he added a long list of allegations unrelated to the book deal.

Among them, the complaint cited Gingrich's failure to mention on his annual financial disclosure report a mortgage he cosigned with his daughter when she bought a house. The complaint also alleged that Gingrich improperly used official stationery to help recruit cruise participants for a Florida travel agency. An aide sent a letter providing information about a senior citizens' cruise the agency was sponsoring.

Alexander's initial complaint was reviewed by the ethics committee staff, which concluded that many of the allegations were conjectural and that others were not supported by facts, were based on unusual legal arguments, or were accompanied by no facts that amounted to rule violations. The staff concluded in a June 1989 memo that the reams of paper Alexander provided did not meet the threshold required for opening a preliminary investigation: that the allegations "merit further inquiry."

The same conclusion was reached by the committee's outside counsel in the case, the Chicago law firm of Phelan, Pope & John, which also handled the Wright investigation. In October the firm presented the committee with its conclusion that there was no basis for opening a formal investigation. After further questioning Gingrich, the committee concurred and voted 11–0 on March 7 to dismiss all of Alexander's allegations. "Representative Alexander's complaint asserts that the partnership was, in fact, a scheme whereby influential friends of the Gingriches sought to funnel to them either gifts, campaign contributions or both," the committee report said. "In the committee's view, there is no support for this proposition."

The committee did conclude, however, that Gingrich should have reported his participation in his daughter's home purchase, and it directed him to amend his financial disclosure forms to include the transaction. The panel also concluded that a Gingrich aide violated House rules in sending out the cruise promotion on official stationery under the congressional frank.

Gingrich said he had not known of the mailing and that neither he nor the aide profited from it. But the committee told Gingrich he was "remiss in your oversight and administration of your congressional office" and directed him to guard against future abuse of mail and office resources.

ETHICS CASES IN THE 1990S

Stangeland

The Minnesota Democratic Farmer-Labor Party the week of April 2, 1990, filed a complaint with the House ethics committee against Minnesota Republican Rep. Arlan Stangeland over a series of telephone calls Stangeland charged to his House credit card. The committee took no action against Stangeland, who lost his 1990 reelection bid.

In a January story, the *St. Cloud Times* reported that Stangeland made 341 long-distance calls, at a cost of $762, to or from phones of a Virginia woman who Stangeland said was a friend and lobbyist. Although he initially said that some of the calls may have been personal, Stangeland later said that all were made for business reasons. A former staff aide, he said, stole phone records from his office to try to smear him.

Dyson

The House ethics committee on February 2, 1990, dropped an investigation into election and sex discrimination accusations against Roy Dyson, D-Md. A Republican official had filed the complaint just before election day 1988, alleging that Dyson misused official funds for campaign purposes and discriminated against women in hiring.

Dyson's office practices had been thrust into the public eye in mid-1988 when his administrative aide, Tom Pappas, committed suicide after a *Washington Post* article reported on his unorthodox personnel practices.

Despite the dismissal of the charges, ethics remained a major issue in Dyson's unsuccessful bid for reelection in November 1990.

Fauntroy

The Justice Department, after deciding not to prosecute Delegate Walter E. Fauntroy, D-D.C., on allegations of padding his payroll, referred the case to the House ethics committee in May 1990. The committee took no action against Fauntroy, who gave up his seat that year to run unsuccessfully for mayor of Washington.

Fauntroy, the District of Columbia's nonvoting delegate, had been the subject of a fifteen-month federal investigation concerning allegations that he improperly kept Thomas John Savage, son of Illinois Democratic Rep. Gus Savage, on his payroll at the same time the younger Savage was living in Chicago and running for the Illinois legislature. House rules required staff members to work in Washington, D.C., or in the representative's district.

Former delegate Fauntroy pleaded guilty March 24, 1995, to a felony charge stemming from the House Bank scandal. Fauntroy admitted falsely reporting a $23,887 donation to a church on his financial disclosure form for 1988. The charge was reduced to a misdemeanor, after the Supreme Court May 15 ruled that the law Fauntroy had been prosecuted under did not include lying to Congress. He instead was charged with a misdemeanor under D.C. law.

According to the Justice Department, Fauntroy wrote a check to New Bethel Baptist Church with instructions to hold it until he had funds to cover the check. The check was not cashed until June 1989, a month after he had reported the gift on his 1988 financial disclosure form. On August 9, 1995, Fauntroy was sentenced to two years' probation, fined $1,000, and required to serve three hundred hours of community service.

Sikorski

An investigation of allegations against Gerry Sikorski, D-Minn., was dropped by the House ethics committee February 2, 1990. The case had been filed after newspapers reported staffers' complaints that Sikorski required them to do personal chores and campaign work.

Rep. Julian Dixon, center, stepped down as chairman of the House ethics committee in 1991 after leading the panel through a mine field of cases in the 1980s. Most members of Congress avoid serving on the ethics committees.

Flake

The government dropped embezzlement and tax evasion charges against New York Democratic Rep. Floyd H. Flake on April 3, 1991, after a federal judge barred what prosecutors called the "heart" of the government's case concerning financial dealings for a housing project sponsored by a church Flake had headed for fifteen years. The indictment alleged that Flake siphoned off $75,000 in transportation funds from the Allen Senior Citizens Apartments and used $66,000 in other church funds for personal purposes.

After the three-week trial ended, jurors told reporters that they found the government's case weak. Much of it was based on confusing financial records and testimony from church members sympathetic to the Flakes. Prosecutors denied allegations by Flake, who is black, that racism and politics may have been behind the charges against him.

As pastor of the Allen African Methodist Episcopal church, Flake had organized efforts to obtain projects to assist local low-income residents. One of his successes was a $10 million federal grant to the church to build the three-hundred-unit seniors' housing project.

Alexander

The House ethics committee in 1991 dropped its inquiry into the business ties between Rep. Bill Alexander, D-Ark., and the two managers of a foundation that got federal funds with his help, when Alexander severed his connection with the managers.

Alexander had asked the panel June 17 whether his Appropriations Committee work in behalf of the Marine Resources Development Foundation was a conflict of interest with his business investments with Neil Monney and Ian Koblick, its directors. The *Wall Street Journal* June 14 reported that Alexander had helped direct up to $400,000 a year since fiscal 1988 to the foundation. In 1986 Alexander invested $20,000 in a venture by Monney and Koblick to build a small underwater "hotel" and related facilities in the same lagoon as the foundation's educational programs.

The committee June 27 declined to declare that Alexander had not broken House rules, saying it needed more information about his financial dealings.

D'Amato

The Senate Ethics Committee rebuked Sen. Alphonse M. D'Amato, R-N.Y., on August 2, 1991, for running his office in an "improper and an inappropriate manner." At the same time it closed its nineteen-month investigation into sixteen allegations that D'Amato had been influenced by campaign contributors and favor-seeking family members. The committee said it found no or insufficient evidence to support the charges, which initially had been filed by Mark Green, D'Amato's 1986 Democratic opponent.

The most publicized allegations suggested that D'Amato had improperly pressured Housing and Urban Development Department (HUD) officials to finance housing projects that benefited his relatives and political contributors. The *New York Times* reported that D'Amato in March 1984 wrote to HUD in support of a Buffalo housing renovation project whose partners included two of his political backers, Angelo Sedita and Peter Elia. *Newsday* reported that D'Amato, in a July 1986 letter, urged HUD to finance a project at Sackets Harbor in upstate New York represented by his brother Armand's law firm and developed by a construction firm whose executives were political contributors. D'Amato said that he supported projects that benefited his constituents based "solely on merit and need." He said that HUD documents indicating he had requested funding for certain projects in Puerto Rico were mistaken. His support for the Sackets Harbor project predated the involvement of his political contributors, he said.

D'Amato also was accused of helping Wedtech, the Bronx company at the center of the convictions of two New York House members, Democrats Mario Biaggi and Robert Garcia, in return for $30,000 in illegal campaign contributions and of being the beneficiary of a system under which Unisys, a defense contractor with offices in New York, told executives to donate thousands of dollars to D'Amato's campaign and then to seek reimbursement. D'Amato said he did not know about either contribution scheme.

The *Wall Street Journal* reported that D'Amato, as chairman of the Senate subcommittee overseeing the securities industry in 1985, dropped his backing for legislation restricting high-risk "junk bonds" after receiving $70,000 in donations from the pioneers of junk-bond financing, Drexel Burnham Lambert. D'Amato said no connection existed between the contributions and his position on the legislation.

The Ethics Committee rebuked D'Amato for allowing his brother to misuse his office in behalf of the Unisys Corp. Concerning the allegations of help for contributors in Puerto Rico, the committee said its investigations were hampered because essential witnesses invoked the Fifth Amendment to avoid testifying.

In a separate action, the Senate Ethics Committee on September 18, 1996, cleared D'Amato of wrongdoing for any special treatment he might have received from the New York brokerage firm Stratton Oakmont that earned him a $37,125 one-day stock profit. The Congressional Accountability Project, a group affiliated with consumer advocate Ralph Nader, filed the ethics complaint June 11.

A Securities and Exchange Commission (SEC) report, released June 5, found that Stratton Oakmont in a 1993 transaction gave D'Amato "atypical" treatment that yielded the lucrative profit. The firm allowed the senator to open an account, purchase shares in an initial public offering of a computer company, and buy more shares of the company than other investors with similarly valued accounts, even though he did not meet the company's financial criteria.

At the time of the profit, the SEC was investigating Stratton Oakmont and D'Amato was the ranking Republican on the Senate Banking Committee. Stratton executives contributed $12,000 to D'Amato's 1992 reelection campaign, though he returned most of the money after the SEC filed charges against the firm. D'Amato disclosed the profit on his 1994 financial disclosure form. The SEC report did not say that D'Amato violated any laws.

Bustamante

Former representative Albert G. Bustamante, D-Texas, was convicted on July 21, 1993, of racketeering and accepting an illegal gift. He was first elected to the House in 1984 and was defeated by Republican Henry Bonilla in 1992.

The jury found Bustamante had accepted a $35,000 bribe in 1986 from a food service company in exchange for influencing the Air Force to renew a contract with the company. He was also found guilty of accepting a no-risk loan during a failed bid to buy a San Antonio television station. Bustamante was found not guilty on eight other charges, including allegations that he had accepted money from a real estate company and his wife's law firm.

Bustamante on October 1, 1993, was sentenced to three and half years in prison and fined $55,100.

Mavroules

Former representative Nicholas Mavroules, D-Mass., pleaded guilty on April 15, 1993, to fifteen offenses, including accepting illegal gratuities and failing to report all his income. In return, prosecutors dropped two racketeering charges. On June 29, he was sentenced to fifteen months in prison, three years of probation, and a fine of $15,000.

Prosecutors indicted Mavroules on August 27, 1992, accusing him of soliciting and accepting free cars and cash for a variety of favors during twenty years in public office. He was indicted on counts of racketeering, extortion, tax evasion, and abuse of office. The charges included one that Mavroules extorted $25,000 from the owners of a liquor store for his assistance in securing a liquor license, when he was mayor of Peabody. He also was accused of extorting $12,000 in 1985 in return for arranging a prison transfer for a convicted drug trafficker and soliciting and receiving a discount for the use of a beach house in Gloucester, Mass. The developer who owned the house allegedly received federal grants and other assistance from Mavroules and his staff.

Upon being indicted, Mavroules was required to relinquish the chairmanship of the House Armed Services Subcommittee on Investigations. Mavroules was first elected to Congress in 1978 and served seven terms before being defeated by Republican Peter G. Torkildsen in 1992.

Smith

Former representative Lawrence J. Smith, D-Fla., pleaded guilty on May 25, 1993, to charges that he had evaded taxes and lied to the Federal Election Commission. On August 2, Smith was sentenced to three months in jail and two years' probation. Smith had been elected to the House in 1982 and retired in 1992.

The charges Smith admitted to included a scheme in which Smith funneled $10,000 from his campaign fund to his personal use. He was given a $10,000 check from a former law partner, allegedly as a campaign reimbursement, and Smith converted it into two $5,000 cashier's checks.

Ford

Ending three days of deliberations following a five-week trial in federal court in Memphis, a jury of eleven whites and one black on April 19, 1993, found Democrat Harold E. Ford, Tennessee's first African American congressman, not guilty of one count of conspiracy, three counts of bank fraud, and fourteen counts of mail fraud. The jury also acquitted two codefendents. U.S. District Court Judge Jerome Turner had thrown out one mail fraud count against Ford and eleven counts against the other two.

The trial was the second on the same charges for Ford. The first trial ended April 27, 1990, in a hung jury with eight blacks voting to acquit and four whites voting to convict.

At the heart of the case was Ford's relationship with Jacob and C. H. Butcher Jr., who controlled a system of Tennessee banks that failed. The two brothers ultimately pleaded guilty to crimes connected with the failures and served time in jail.

Prosecutors charged Ford and two other friends of the Butcher brothers with conspiring with the brothers to defraud several of the banks in their system by using them to make loans to Ford to support his "extravagant and lavish lifestyle." In return, prosecutors alleged that Ford promised to "use his political influence as a United States congressman to further the political and business goals" of the Butchers. The loans totaled some $1 million. Once the banks failed, Ford settled a $350,000 loan for $25,000.

Ford said that the loans were legitimate business transactions involving the family funeral home. He said that he had used some of the money to pay off personal debts, but only because the funeral business owed him the money. And he denied being anything but a friend to the Butcher brothers.

Upon his initial indictment, Ford was required to give up his chairmanship of the House Ways and Means Subcommittee on Public Assistance and Unemployment Compensation. When acquitted, Ford assumed the top spot on the Ways and Means Subcommittee on Human Resources.

Robb

A federal grand jury on January 12, 1993, voted not to indict Sen. Charles S. Robb, D-Va., on conspiracy and obstruction of justice charges. Robb maintained his innocence throughout the investigation.

The case centered on the release of an illegally recorded cellular phone call involving Gov. L. Douglas Wilder, D-Va., a longtime Robb rival. In the tape, recorded in October 1988, Wilder speculated that rumors about Robb's attendance at Virginia Beach parties where cocaine was used would ruin his career. The tape was leaked to the media more than two years later, when rumors about Robb's private life were refueled by a beauty queen's claim that she had had an affair with the senator. Robb's aides apparently believed that the rumors would be discounted if they could be traced to a rival, particularly when they seemed so inconsistent with the image of Robb—a square-jawed former Marine, a son-in-law to President Lyndon B. Johnson, and a prospective presidential candidate.

Robb appeared twice before the grand jury, and three aides implicated him in plea agreements they made to criminal charges. Virginia Beach businessman Bruce Thompson was indicted on three charges, including witness tampering, related to the case. The indictment included allegations that Robb declined to listen to the tapes, although he knew their contents, so he could maintain "plausible deniability." Similar allegations were contained in the plea agreements.

Hubbard

Former representative Carroll Hubbard, D-Ky., pleaded guilty on April 5, 1994, to charges that he misused congressional employees, violated federal election laws and obstructed justice. His wife, Carol Brown Hubbard, pleaded guilty to a misdemeanor charge in the case. Hubbard served in the House from 1975 to 1993.

Hubbard also was caught by the Justice Department probe of the House bank, but his case was only tangentially related to the scandal. Hubbard admitted he had falsified his campaign reports to hide disbursements to himself and others. Some of the funds were secretly funneled to his wife's unsuccessful campaign for a House seat. Hubbard also admitting stealing federal property by having his staff perform personal tasks and work on both his and his wife's campaigns.

On November 9, Hubbard was sentenced to three years in prison for three felony convictions and ordered to pay $153,000 in restitution.

Perkins

Former representative Carl Perkins, D-Ky., pleaded guilty December 20, 1994, to writing bad checks, filing false financial disclosure statements, and lying on his campaign finance reports. Perkins, who served from 1985 to 1993, admitted to bank fraud for his part in a check-kiting scheme from April 1990 through July 1990 that involved several institutions, including the House bank.

On March 13, 1995, Perkins was sentenced to twenty-one months in prison, three years' probation, and 250 hours of community service. He also was ordered to complete an alcohol treatment program.

Tucker

Rep. Walter R. Tucker III, D-Calif., resigned from the House on December 15, 1995, after being convicted of seven federal counts of extortion and two counts of tax evasion. He was sen-

The temptations of the flesh can be fatal attractions for members of Congress. Despite the obvious dangers, numerous members have become ensnared in sex scandals that ruined or damaged their careers.

Among the most publicized downfalls were those of Reps. Wilbur D. Mills, D-Ark., in 1974 and Wayne L. Hays, D-Ohio, in 1976. Mills cavorted with a stripper, Fanne Foxe, and blamed his actions on alcoholism, and Hays allegedly put his mistress, Elizabeth Ray, on the House payroll. Ray had told a reporter that Hays hired her even though she could not type, take dictation, or "even answer the phone." *(See "1970s Scandals," p. 946.)*

Besides Hays, three other House members were involved in 1976 sex scandals: John Young, D-Texas, Joe D. Waggonner Jr., D-La., and Allan T. Howe, D-Utah. House aide Colleen Gardner charged that Young kept her on the payroll primarily to have sex with him. Waggonner was arrested in Washington on charges of soliciting a police decoy for purposes of prostitution. Howe was convicted July 23, 1976, in Salt Lake City for soliciting two policewomen posing as prostitutes. The House took no action against Young, Waggonner, or Howe.

CASES IN THE 1980S

Even the 1980 Abscam bribery investigation had a sex angle. Rita Jenrette, the wife of one of those convicted, Rep. John W. Jenrette Jr., D-S.C., told the press that she and her husband had once made love on the Capitol steps. She later posed for *Playboy,* and John Jenrette entered an alcoholism program. *(See "Abscam Investigation," p. 953.)*

The House in the 1980s began to show less tolerance of sexual misbehavior. In 1983 Gerry E. Studds, D-Mass., and Daniel B. Crane, R-Ill., were censured for having sexual relationships with teenage congressional pages, Studds with a male and Crane with a female. Barney Frank, D-Mass., was reprimanded in 1990 for his relationship with a male prostitute. *(See "Studds, Crane," p. 937; "Frank," p. 938.)*

Bauman. Rep. Robert E. Bauman, R-Md., pleaded not guilty October 3, 1980, to a misdemeanor charge of sexual solicitation and agreed to undergo court-supervised treatment for alcoholism in return for dropping the charge. Bauman was accused of committing oral sodomy on a teenage boy in Washington, D.C.

Bauman was defeated for reelection by Democrat Roy Dyson, whose own House office was later touched by an incident with overtones of homosexuality. A male staff member committed suicide in New York following newspaper disclosure of bizarre demands that the aide had made of his male subordinates. Both Dyson and the aide, before his death, denied homosexuality. *(See "Dyson," p. 966.)*

Hinson. Jon C. Hinson, R-Miss., resigned from the House April 13, 1981, after being arrested in a Capitol Hill men's room February 4 on a misdemeanor charge of attempted sodomy. He received a suspended thirty-day jail sentence and a year's probation after pleading no contest and agreeing to continue medical treatment.

Hinson had disclosed in 1980, while seeking election to a second House term, that he had been arrested in 1976 for committing an indecent act in a homosexual trysting place in Arlington, Virginia. He also disclosed that he had been among the survivors of a 1977 fire at a Washington theater frequented by homosexuals, but he denied being a homosexual.

Richmond. Fred W. Richmond, D-N.Y., resigned from the House in 1982 after pleading guilty to marijuana possession and other charges. In an earlier brush with the law, Richmond pleaded not guilty in 1978 to a charge that he solicited homosexual sex for pay. Because he had acknowledged the truth of the morals charge, the plea was a technicality to make him eligible for the District of Columbia's first-offender program. The charges were dropped May 3, 1978, after he completed the program. *(See "Richmond," p. 958.)*

Lukens. Donald E. "Buz" Lukens, confronted with new allegations of sexual misconduct, resigned from Congress in 1990 rather than face ethics sanctions in his final days in the House. The Ohio Republican, who lost his bid for reelection in a May primary, announced his resignation two days after the House ethics committee on October 22 adopted a resolution revealing new charges that he made "unwanted and unsolicited sexual advances to a congressional employee."

The panel had planned to look into the new allegations, which centered on reports that Lukens had fondled and propositioned an elevator operator in the Capitol. The ethics committee first began investigating Lukens in August 1989, after his conviction in May of that year of contributing to the delinquency of a minor for having sex with a sixteen-year-old girl in Columbus, Ohio. He was sentenced to thirty days in jail and given a $500 fine.

Savage. In a report released February 2, 1990, the House ethics committee concluded that Gus Savage, D-Ill., made improper sexual advances to a young woman while on an official trip to Africa and that his actions were contrary to the House rule requiring members' behavior to "reflect creditably" on the House. The committee did not propose disciplinary action because Savage had apologized to the woman in writing.

The committee concluded the inquiry without a formal disciplinary hearing. The panel based its conclusion on interviews with Savage and others on the tour as well as on a sworn deposition from the woman, a Peace Corps worker who was not further identified. Savage denied any impropriety—including the woman's allegations that he kissed her and asked her to spend the night with him. But Savage wrote to the woman November 20, 1989, saying: "I never intended to offend and was not aware that you felt offended at the time."

Accusations of impropriety by Savage surfaced in the *Washington Post* on July 19, 1989. Savage's problems, though, did not end with the committee's conclusion of its inquiry. His criticism of three colleagues who called for the investigation of him prompted the House on February 7 to consider revising its rules that allowed members to change their floor remarks before they were published in the *Congressional Record.* The proposal to review the rules was approved 373–30 after Savage's remarks were omitted from the *Record's* account of his February 1 speech, in which he contended that he was a victim of racism in politics and the media.

Most members of Congress routinely edited their remarks before submitting them for the record, but they typically made minor changes, such as corrections of grammar, rather than wholesale omissions.

Bates. On October 18, 1989, the House ethics committee sent Jim Bates, D-Calif., a "letter of reproval" for sexually harassing women on his congressional staff. Former aides had complained that Bates patted their buttocks, asked for hugs, and made suggestive remarks and gestures.

"Your improper conduct and concurrent violations of relevant standards deserve reproval," the committee said in its letter to Bates. It directed him to apologize formally to the complainants. Bates was defeated for reelection in 1990.

CASES IN THE 1990S

Sex- and alcohol-related trouble continued to dog members of Congress in the 1990s.

Packwood. Sen. Bob Packwood, R-Ore., came under fire when the *Washington Post* reported in late 1992 the allegations of sexual misconduct lodged against him by numerous women. The more-than-two-year investigation by the Senate Ethics Committee included rare court action to force Packwood to turn over his personal diaries. Packwood resigned in 1995 in the face of near-certain expulsion. *(See "Packwood," p. 927.)*

Adams. The Senate Ethics Committee May 22, 1992, dismissed a complaint against Brock Adams, D-Wash., because the allegations of sexual misconduct were based on anonymous sources and because the alleged incidents occurred before he was a senator. Adams denied the charges.

Inouye. The Senate Ethics Committee announced April 7, 1993, that it had decided against pursuing sexual misconduct allegations against Daniel K. Inouye, D-Hawaii, because no alleged victims would cooperate in the investigation. The charges against Inouye surfaced during his 1992 reelection campaign.

Robb. A federal grand jury in 1993 declined to bring conspiracy and obstruction of justice charges against Sen. Charles S. Robb, D-Va. The charges involved allegations that Robb had had a sexual relationship with a former beauty queen and had seen cocaine used at a party. *(See "Robb," p. 969.)*

Kennedy. On October 13, 1994, the Senate Ethics Committee announced that it had decided not to open a formal investigation into allegations that Sen. Edward M. Kennedy, D-Mass., had harassed a female staffer and used illegal drugs. The committee announcement came after a conservative media watchdog group, Accuracy in Media, quoted former Kennedy aide Richard E. Burke, author of *The Senator: My Ten Years with Ten Kennedy,* as saying the panel had received sworn statements alleging harassment from women who had worked for Kennedy. The committee said it never received such statements and not only denounced the charges but also criticized Burke, saying it found "no basis for his allegations nor anyone who could substantiate those allegations."

Kennedy's name had come up in connection with a rape charge brought against his nephew, William Kennedy Smith, in 1991. The woman said she was raped on the Kennedy family's Palm Beach compound, where Kennedy and his son Patrick were staying at the time. Smith was acquitted.

Kleczka. Rep. Gerald D. Kleczka, D-Wis., was arrested May 13, 1995, on drunken driving charges in Alexandria, Virginia. He subsequently entered an alcohol abuse treatment center. Kleczka had pleaded guilty to driving while intoxicated in Fairfax County, Virginia, in 1987 and was sentenced to thirty days in jail. That punishment was lifted after he completed an alcohol awareness course. He also was charged with public drunkenness in Fairfax County in 1990.

Reynolds. Rep. Mel Reynolds, D-Ill., was sentenced on September 29, 1995, to five years in prison for having sex with teenage campaign worker Beverly Heard, soliciting child pornography from her, and then trying to impede the state's investigation of the matter. Heard charged that Reynolds and she began their relationship when she was sixteen. She testified against Reynolds only after serving thirteen days in jail in contempt of court for initially refusing to take the stand. Reynolds admitted to having a weakness for phone sex but denied ever having sexual contact with Heard. Reynolds was convicted in Illinois on August 22.

tenced on April 17, 1996, to twenty-seven months in federal prison.

Tucker, who was elected in 1992, was indicted on August 11, 1994, for taking $30,000 from a company that wanted to build a trash incinerator plant in Compton, Calif., while he was mayor there. He was also accused of trying to get another $250,000 from the company. Tucker was charged with failure to report the $30,000 on his income tax forms.

On June 1, 1995, a federal grand jury handed up additional indictments, charging Tucker with taking a $5,000 bribe from a firm that collected garbage in Compton and with taking $2,500 to help extend the company's municipal contract.

Tucker maintained that he was innocent and that he had been set up by federal prosecutors.

Hutchison

Sen. Kay Bailey Hutchison, R-Texas, was exonerated February 11, 1994, of criminal ethics charges—five counts of misusing Texas state workers and equipment for personal and political gains when she was state treasurer and tampering with state records relating to the case. Judge John Onion Jr. told the jury to find Hutchison not guilty after prosecutors indicated that they were not prepared to go forward. Onion had refused to indicate whether he would allow the prosecutors to submit as evidence phone and computer records that were gathered in a raid of Hutchison's office five days after she won a 1993 special election to the U.S. Senate.

Hutchison was first indicted September 27, 1993, on five felony charges of misconduct. The indictments were thrown out October 26 because one person was not qualified to sit on the grand jury.

Hutchison was re-indicted December 8 on four felony counts and one misdemeanor similar to the original counts. Four of the new indictments were dismissed December 29 for being too vague. Prosecutors were given time to redraw the indictments. The charges were reinstated, and Hutchison pleaded not guilty on January 7, 1994.

The case did not go to the Senate Ethics Committee because it involved actions taken before Hutchison became a senator.

Frost

The House ethics committee announced November 29, 1994, that it had dismissed a complaint brought by Dallas County GOP Chairman Robert Driegert over congressional redistricting work for the 1992 elections done by the staff of Rep. Martin Frost, D-Texas. The committee wrote to Frost: "The committee accepts your statement that you were unaware of the prohibition on utilizing official funds for activities relating to redistricting and is of the opinion that you could have reasonably relied on House approvals for related activities in forming your belief that the expenditures were properly made."

Frost said he would reimburse the Treasury for any money spent on redistricting.

Hatch, Gorton

The Senate Ethics Committee in 1995 dismissed separate complaints alleging that Sens. Orrin G. Hatch, R-Utah, and Slade Gorton, R-Wash., allowed lobbyists to have improper influence in the bill drafting process.

The complaints were based on news accounts that Gorton had sought drafting help from the Endangered Species Reform Coalition and that Hatch's Judiciary Committee staff had permitted utility lobbyists to brief committee aides on provisions in a pending regulatory reform bill. The Ethics Committee concluded that Senate rules did not prohibit lobbyists from providing information to members or staff.

In other action, the Senate Ethics Committee announced November 20, 1993, that it found unanimously that Hatch had acted neither illegally nor unethically in his dealings with the scandal-ridden Bank of Credit and Commerce International (BCCI). Contacts between Hatch, one of his aides, and key insiders of BCCI had been the subject of numerous news reports since 1991. Hatch called for an ethics investigation in August 1992 after denying wrongdoing.

Daschle

The Senate Ethics Committee on November 30, 1995, dismissed allegations that Senate Minority Leader Tom Daschle, D-S.D., improperly intervened with federal regulators to help a friend's air charter company.

The complaint sought an investigation into Daschle's dealings with federal airline regulators in behalf of B&L Aviation of Rapid City, S.D. A second request for an investigation came from the widows of three Indian Health Service doctors killed when one of B&L's planes crashed.

Daschle came under scrutiny because in 1992 he began efforts to get federal regulators to consolidate aviation inspections under the Federal Aviation Administration (FAA). Other federal agencies had been involved in safety inspections because the charters ferried government officials into less-than-hospitable areas, such as back-country wilderness.

While B&L's planes passed FAA inspections, the U.S. Forest Service found a number of violations during its safety reviews, and the charter company consequently was banned in 1994 from flying Forest Service employees. The plane that crashed had passed both FAA and Forest Service inspections. The National Transportation Safety Board blamed the crash on pilot error and bad weather.

"Contracts and actions by Sen. Daschle and his staff were routine and proper constituent service," the committee said.

Gramm

The Senate Ethics Committee in 1995 decided not to investigate when Phil Gramm, R-Texas, attempted to violate federal campaign laws in helping Sen. Bob Packwood, R-Ore., in his 1992 reelection effort.

At issue was whether Gramm, then chairman of the National

Republican Senatorial Committee, intended to spend $100,000 for Packwood in excess of federal spending limits. The issue arose from Packwood's March 6, 1992, diary entry, which detailed a promise by an unnamed senator, later identified as Gramm, to raise the money for party building activities that instead would go for Packwood's reelection. The diaries served as evidence in a separate ethics investigation into Packwood's activities. *(See "Packwood," p. 927.)*

"What was said in that room would be enough to convict us all of something," Packwood wrote. "He [Sen. X] says, now, of course you know there can't be any legal connection between this money and Sen. Packwood, but we know that it will be used for his benefit." Gramm said the discussion was about so-called soft money, which was used for party building and get-out-the-vote drives and was not subject to the same limits as contributions to federal candidates.

Faircloth

North Carolina Republican Sen. Lauch Faircloth's multimillion-dollar investment in hog farming did not conflict with his responsibilities on Capitol Hill, the Senate Ethics Committee said February 22, 1995.

Senate Rule XXXVII said senators could not push for legislation that would benefit themselves or their families, or "the financial interests of a limited class to which such individuals belong." The Ethics Committee said the hog industry affected too many people that Faircloth's actions did not violate the rule.

Armey

The House ethics committee on June 13, 1995, cited Majority Leader Dick Armey, R-Texas, for improperly writing a letter on a facsimile of House stationery that was mailed by an outside group, but the committee said it would take no action.

Armey's letter was mailed April 12, 1995, to business leaders by the Capital Research Center, a conservative advocacy group that had criticized corporate executives for contributing to liberal advocacy groups.

Greene Waldholtz

Utah Rep. Enid Greene Waldholtz saw her congressional career collapse as a federal grand jury in 1995 began investigating possible bank fraud schemes by her estranged husband, Joseph P. Waldholtz, to fund her 1994 campaign. Investigators in 1996 concluded that no proof was found that she was part of her husband's crimes and did not charge her in the case. In 1996 the freshman representative was divorced, dropped her husband's name, and declined to run for reelection.

Greene spent a record $1.8 million to unseat incumbent Democrat Karen Shepherd in 1994. In 1995 Greene admitted that the money came principally not from her and her husband's funds—as she had said at the time—but from her father. But she said her husband, a GOP political operative who she said handled virtually all financial transactions, had tricked her

father and herself. Federal law limited donations from individuals other than the candidate to $1,000 per election.

Greene acknowledged filing a false financial disclosure statement but she did so unknowingly because of her husband's deceptions. Her lawyers also acknowledged that she had made mistakes in her campaign disclosure forms filed with the Federal Election Commission in 1992, when she ran unsuccessfully for Congress.

Gephardt

The House ethics committee September 28, 1996, dismissed an ethics complaint failed against Minority Leader Richard A. Gephardt, D-Mo., but the panel upbraided him for failing to properly disclose income from a vacation property.

At issue was property in Duck, N.C., that Gephardt traded in 1991 for a piece of beachfront land in nearby Corolla. By trading instead of selling the Duck home, Gephardt was able to avoid capital gains taxes. Such tax-free exchanges were permitted for investment properties only. However, Gephardt listed the Duck property as a "vacation home" and did not disclose any rental income from the property on his 1991 financial disclosure form.

The ethics committee in 1992 questioned Gephardt about not disclosing the exchange on his 1991 report. Gephardt said he did not think the exchange of the home needed "to be disclosed if it was not used for rental purposes."

In 1992 the Gephardts received permanent financing for the Corolla property, on which they and another couple with equal interests in the property built a large home. The complaint alleged that Gephardt told a mortgage company in applying for a loan that he planned to use the new home as personal vacation property. But Gephardt subsequently listed rental income from the property in his financial disclosure statements.

On the day before the committee dropped the complaint, Gephardt filed an amended financial disclosure form listing rental income of $25,000 to $50,000 on the property for 1992. In a terse letter to Gephardt, the panel said that it expected him to be "more diligent in the future and adhere strictly to the requirements to file timely and accurate financial disclosure statements."

Bonior

The House ethics committee refused to pursue a series of complaints lodged against House Democratic Whip David E. Bonior of Michigan by the conservative Landmark Legal Foundation.

In 1995 and 1996, the foundation sought to have the ethics committee investigate whether Bonior broke House rules in writing his 1984 book *The Vietnam Veteran: A History of Neglect*; whether his employment of his wife violated nepotism rules; and whether he misused his public office to wage a political war against House Speaker Newt Gingrich, R-Ga.

On May 8, 1996, the committee said it found no substance to the nepotism charge. On May 9, the panel rejected the com-

HOUSE BANK, POST OFFICE SCANDALS

At the time—in the early 1990s—that the public's opinion of Congress was sinking astoundingly low, two scandals broke that involved the inner-workings of the House.

HOUSE BANK

The General Accounting Office (GAO) on September 18, 1991, reported that hundreds of sitting and former House members for years routinely overdrew their House bank accounts without penalty. Infuriated voters, who viewed the practice as further proof that members of Congress refused to play by the rules that governed everybody else, drove scores of representatives from office in the 1992 elections. Of the 269 sitting members with overdrafts, seventy-seven, or one in four, retired, were defeated for reelection, or lost election to another office.

According to the GAO, House members had bounced 8,331 checks between July 1989 and June 1990. The bank covered the overdrafts, which included 581 checks of $1,000 or more written by 134 members.

Responding to the criticism, the House voted 390–8 on October 3, 1991, to shut down the sergeant at arms's bank and check-cashing service and send its audit records to the House Standards of Official Conduct Committee (ethics committee) for review.

On March 11, 1992, the ethics committee issued its official report, which said nineteen sitting House members and five former members abused their banking privileges. The panel had devised a standard that drew a line between abuses that were "routine, repeated and significant" and lesser offenses that would not be disclosed. However, shortly after the report's release, many Democrats said publicly that they wanted all names released.

The House voted 391–36 on March 12 to name those members cited by the ethics committee. Then, in the early hours of March 13, the House voted to reveal the names of all other sitting and former members who floated checks during the period surveyed by the committee—from July 1, 1988, to October 3, 1991. Each member's total number of bad checks also would be disclosed. The ethics committee on April 16 released the names of the additional 252 sitting and 51 former lawmakers who overdrew their accounts.

Attorney General William P. Barr on March 20 had appointed retired federal appeals judge Malcolm P. Wilkey to conduct a preliminary inquiry into whether the House bank affair involved any federal crimes. A controversy arose over Wilkey's subpoena demanding all the House bank's microfilm records. In the end, however, the House voted 347–64 to turn over the data.

Wilkey issued his report on December 16, 1992. In it, he said,

"Actual criminal conduct by some members appears to have taken place, but it is quite limited. Where criminal violations were indicated, a full-scale investigation will be undertaken."

Former House sergeant at arms Jack Russ, whose job it was to oversee the bank, became the first person to be prosecuted for passing bad checks. Members who faced charges stemming from the bank scandal included former representative Carl Perkins, D-Ky., and former delegate Walter E. Fauntroy, D-D.C. *(See "Perkins," p. 969; "Fauntroy," p. 966.)*

The GAO issued its final audit of the House bank on April 28, 1993.

HOUSE POST OFFICE

The House Post Office ran its postal operations under a contract with the U.S. Postal Service, and it was headed by a postmaster that was elected by the House. In 1991 the attorney general for the District of Columbia began an investigation into allegations that stamp clerks had been stealing funds from the House Post Office and dealing drugs there. Several Post Office employees eventually pleaded guilty to various charges.

Investigations depicted a sloppily run operation where cash and stamps were treated casually and where workers were beholden to political sponsors, not to professional managers. Its status as a House office was ended and its operations turned over to the Postal Service in 1992.

The first word of the possible involvement of House members came in May 1992, when the House learned that the grand jury probing the House Post Office had subpoenaed records of Reps. Dan Rostenkowski, D-Ill., Joe Kolter, D-Pa., and Austin J. Murphy, D-Pa. On July 19, 1993, Robert V. Rota, the former House postmaster, pleaded guilty to three misdemeanors—one count of conspiracy to embezzle and two of aiding and abetting members who he called Congressman A and Congressman B "in willfully and knowingly embezzling" U.S. funds. Documents related to Rota's plea bargain detailed certain stamp purchases as fake. The alleged scheme made by Congressman A matched stamp purchases attributed in public House records to Rostenkowski; Congressman B, Kolter.

Rostenkowski pleaded guilty in 1996 to two counts of felony mail fraud stemming from his misuse of public funds to purchase gifts and to pay employees who did little or no official work. Kolter pleaded guilty in 1996 to one count of conspiring to steal money by converting stamps to cash. *(See "Rostenkowski," p. 975; "Kolter," p. 976.)*

---

plaint about the book because House rules prohibited the investigation of an incident that took place more than three Congresses (six years) before the complaint was filed, unless it could be shown that it was directly related to a more recent incident under investigation. The committee also said the foundation lacked standing to file the complaint about Bonior's battle with Gingrich, and no members were willing to file it on the organization's behalf.

McIntosh

The House ethics committee the week of March 23, 1996, dismissed two complaints against David M. McIntosh, R-Ind., clearing him of violating House rules when he distributed documents created by his staff using an advocacy group's letterhead. But the committee admonished McDermott privately against doing it again.

The complaints grew from hearings held in 1995 by the Government Reform and Oversight Subcommittee on National Economic Growth, Natural Resources, and Regulatory Affairs, which McIntosh chaired, on the lobbying activities of organizations that received federal grants. During the hearing, McIntosh displayed a poster and distributed press releases produced by his staff on Alliance for Justice—a coalition of civil rights and advocacy groups—letterhead, which claimed to show the value of federal grants that the alliance's member organizations had received. The documents included no disclaimer, and the groups complained that they were incorrect. McIntosh, who also displayed the poster on the House floor, said his staff had mistakenly failed to include a disclaimer.

Solomon

The House ethics committee on May 9, 1996, dismissed a complaint against Rules Committee Chairman Gerald B. H. Solomon, R-N.Y., but warned him to be more careful in the language he used on official letterhead.

Democratic New York State Assemblyman Richard L. Brodsky alleged that Solomon had threatened to take political reprisals against him if he did not cease a state investigation of a controversial environmental cleanup deal. Brodsky was disturbed that the state Department of Environmental Conservation proposed setting a major environmental violation by General Electric (GE) by asking the company to spend $200,000 to erect a boat launch. State environmental officials said that GE, a major employer in Solomon's congressional district and a contributor to Solomon's campaigns, had illegally dumped hazardous materials into the soil and allowed a hazardous wastes fire at its site in Albany for nearly a year.

Solomon took exception to Brodsky's queries into the matter. "New York state has had enough of media-hungry liberals looking for political gain at the expense of business and jobs for New Yorkers," Solomon wrote to Brodsky on February 1, 1996, on official congressional letterhead. "As chairman of the Rules Committee," he wrote, "I could easily retaliate by involving myself in the activities of your Assembly district."

In dismissing Brodsky's complaint, the ethics committee issued Solomon a written warning to "avoid even the appearance of impropriety and be judicious in the language used on official letterhead." The committee said "a reader of your letter to Mr. Brodsky could form the impression that you did intend to retaliate against him in some way."

McDade

Eight years after the FBI began investigating him, Rep. Joseph M. McDade, R-Pa., on August 1, 1996, was found not guilty of charges of influence peddling. The government had accused McDade of accepting $100,000 in illegal gifts, favors, and bribes from defense contractors in return for helping them get federal contracts.

The facts of the case were not in dispute. McDade admitting to taking many of the gifts and had listed most on his financial disclosure statements. What was in question was McDade's in-

tent. The prosecution called his intent criminal. They charged him with violating the 1970 Racketeer Influenced and Corrupt Organizations (RICO) act, saying he ran his office like a criminal enterprise. Prosecutors attempted to prove that McDade extorted items ranging from a golf jacket to a $7,500 Georgetown University Law School scholarship for his son from five defense firms and a lobbyist in the years between 1983 and 1988. They alleged that McDade, in return, helped the companies get $68 million in federal contracts. The defense argued that McDade was not doing anything different from anyone else on the Hill.

McDade's May 5, 1992, indictment had been upheld June 15, 1994, by the Third U.S. Circuit Court of Appeals. The Supreme Court decided March 6, 1995, not to hear a constitutional challenge to the McDade indictment. The issues brought to the Court focused not on the merits of the case but on whether the Justice Department, under the Constitution, could indict McDade at all. McDade's lawyers contended that the Constitution prohibited officials of the other branches of government from interfering with Congress's legislative duties. The Justice Department argued that that constitutional provisions could be cited by McDade as part of his defense at trial but did not prevent indictment. Upholding a lower court ruling, an appeals court in 1996 rejected McDade's argument that the charges should be thrown out because prosecutors were applying criminal penalties to House rules, thus clearing the way for trial.

Rostenkowski

Former representative Dan Rostenkowski, D-Ill. (1959–1995) pleaded guilty April 9, 1996, to two counts of felony mail fraud stemming from his misuse of public funds to purchase gifts and to pay employees who did little or no official work. Federal prosecutors dropped eleven other corruption charges in a plea agreement worked out with Rostenkowski. Four other counts, charging him with lying to Congress, were thrown out in March 1996 in response to a 1995 Supreme Court decision in *Hubbard v. United States* that said a law that had been widely used to prosecute individuals for lying to Congress applied only to untruthful statements made to executive branch officials.

As a result of the original seventeen-count indictment handed down May 31, 1994, Rostenkowski was required to step down as chairman of the powerful House Ways and Means Committee and as vice chairman of the Joint Taxation Committee. He was defeated for reelection in 1994.

According to figures cited in the indictment, Rostenkowski misused $668,000 in public funds and $52,267 in campaign funds. The government said he padded his payroll with fourteen so-called ghost employees for personal, business, or campaign services provided to Rostenkowski and his family. Public funds totaling $529,200 were paid to these employees between July 1971 and July 1992. Rostenkowski was accused of spending about $42,200 in taxpayers funds for items at the House stationery store that he and his family gave away as gifts or kept for personal use. The indictment alleged that Rostenkowski pocketed at least $49,300 in cash from the House Post Office through sham

Rep. Dan Rostenkowski, the former powerful House Ways and Means chairman, pleaded guilty in 1996 to two counts of felony mail fraud. Rostenkowski was sentenced to seventeen months in prison and fined $100,000.

transactions made to look like stamp purchases. He allegedly got the cash in three ways: (1) He traded stamps he previously procured with House expense vouchers for cash; (2) he traded stamps or stamp vouchers for cash; and (3) he cashed in checks from his campaign and political action committee and reported them as postage purchases on Federal Election Commission reports. Furthermore, Rostenkowski allegedly obtained personal ownership and clear title to seven vehicles for himself and his family by paying the dealership $73,500 in House funds and $28,267 in campaign funds.

On June 30, 1994, Rep. Christopher Shays, R-Conn., filed an ethics complaint against Rostenkowski based on the indictment. The House ethics committee subsequently voted to defer an investigation.

On August 5, 1994, Rostenkowski's lawyers went to court asking to have the indictment dismissed on separation-of-powers grounds. They argued that the charges violated constitutional provisions giving Congress the power to make and enforce its own rules and shielding members from prosecutions based on legislative acts. They also said House rules on office budgets and campaign funds were so vague and gave members so much discretion that the case was "ill-suited for judicial resolution." U.S. District Judge Norma Holloway Johnson October 14 rejected Rostenkowski's arguments. A unanimous three-judge federal appeals court panel July 18, 1995, refused to dismiss any charges

against Rostenkowski. Johnson on November 14, 1995, turned down a request by Rostenkowski's lawyers to shift the case to Chicago, Rostenkowski's hometown.

Rostenkowski was sentenced to seventeen months in prison and fined $100,000.

Kolter

Former representative Joe Kolter, D-Pa., was sentenced July 31, 1996, to six months in prison, fined $20,000, and ordered to pay $9,300 in restitution for his role in the House Post Office scandal. Kolter had pleaded guilty May 7 to one count of conspiring to steal thousands of dollars in taxpayers' money by converting government-purchased stamps at the House Post Office into cash.

Kolter, who served from 1983 to 1993, admitted to conspiring with postmaster Robert V. Rota to steal $9,300 in cash after converting stamps and stamp vouchers into cash. Documents also showed that Kolter and Rota took steps to conceal the scheme. For example, they used blank House office vouchers, instead of those from Kolter's office, when preparing the fake vouchers, to hide the transactions from Kolter's staff.

U.S. District Judge Norma Holloway Johnson in April 1996 dropped two of the five original embezzlement counts against Kolter, citing a Supreme Court decision that covered lying to Congress, and narrowed a third count to conspiracy, to which Kolter pleaded guilty. As part of the plea agreement, prosecutors dropped the remaining charges against Kolter, who was also accused of bilking taxpayers of $33,000 worth of china, timepieces, pins, and gold necklaces from the House stationery store.

Kim

Rep. Jay C. Kim, R-Calif., and his wife, June, pleaded guilty August 11, 1997, to a total of ten counts stemming from the receipt of more than $230,000 in illegal campaign contributions. Kim subsequently was sentenced to two months of home detention, one year of probation, two hundred hours of community service, and a $5,000 fine.

On behalf of his campaign committee, Kim pleaded guilty to five felony counts. However, he was not personally liable for any fines imposed. He was culpable for three misdemeanor charges to which he pleaded guilty: that he knowingly accepted a $50,000 campaign contribution from a Taiwanese national and laundered it through his personal bank account; that he accepted an illegal $12,000 corporate contribution from Nikko Enterprises Inc.; and that he directed his firm, JayKim Engineers Inc., to give more than $83,000 in illegal corporate contributions to his campaign.

June Kim pleaded guilty to two charges related to her acceptance of more than $19,000 in illegal corporate contributions.

On October 9, 1998, the House ethics committee announced that Kim had violated federal campaign laws and House rules in at least six instances. However, the panel said it would take no

Rep. Jay C. Kim, R-Calif., convicted in 1997 of violating federal campaign laws, served two months of home detention while in Congress and lost a reelection bid in 1998.

action because Kim had been defeated in a June 1998 GOP primary.

Collins

The House ethics committee January 2, 1997, said Rep. Barbara-Rose Collins, D-Mich., violated laws and House rules. The committee found that Collins allowed improper campaign activities by her congressional staff, that she used official funds for campaign and personal purposes, that she misused funds intended for a scholarship program, and that she gave huge, temporary raises to some members of her staff to give them enough money to accompany her on a trip to Africa.

Collins was defeated for reelection in an August 1996 primary.

Cooley

Rep. Wes Cooley, R-Ore., was found guilty March 18, 1997, of lying about his military record in official state voters' pamphlets. He was sentenced to two years' probation and ordered to perform community service and pay fines and expenses.

Cooley, who had served one term, 1995–1997, withdrew his bid for reelection under pressure from fellow Republicans after questions were raised about whether Cooley had served in the Army Special Forces in Korea during that war as he had claimed. During his trial, prosecutors told the court that they

could prove that Cooley had been in the United States during the Korean War. Cooley had been indicted December 10, 1996.

McDermott

U.S. District Judge Thomas F. Hogan on July 28, 1998, dismissed a lawsuit by Rep. John A. Boehner, R-Ohio, against Rep. Jim McDermott, D-Wash., for disclosing a taped cell phone conversation concerning the ethics investigation of Speaker Newt Gingrich, R-Ga.

Hogan ruled that McDermott's First Amendment rights were paramount in the case. He said McDermott had obtained the tape legally and had a constitutional right to disclose its contents. But the judge chastised McDermott because he was serving on the House ethics committee at the time.

On December 21, 1996, Boehner, head of the House GOP Conference, was driving in Florida, talking to other Republican leaders on a cell phone about the predicament facing Gingrich. The call was intercepted by a Florida couple listening to their police scanner. They said they taped the call because they thought it had historical value. The contents of the tape eventually showed up in the *New York Times* and the *Atlanta Journal-Constitution*. Democrats immediately charged that the tape showed that Gingrich had violated an agreement not to rally opposition to an ethics committee decision to reprimand him.

The House ethics committee on July 24, 1996, had dismissed an ethics complaint against McDermott filed by Peter T. King, R-N.Y., that called for the appointment of an outside counsel to probe McDermott's conduct in the Gingrich ethics investigation.

DeLay

The House ethics committee on May 11, 1999, took Majority Whip Tom DeLay, R-Texas, to task for threatening to punish a trade group because it hired a Democrat as its president. The panel cited House rules that prohibited lawmakers from using their offices to take punitive action for partisan reasons.

The admonition was in response to DeLay's role in the fall of 1998 in attempting to dissuade the Electronic Industries Alliance from hiring as its president former representative Dave McCurdy, D-Okla. (1981–1995). House leaders, including DeLay, postponed for one day a vote on an international treaty, which was opposed by some members of the alliance, to show displeasure with the selection of McCurdy for a job they felt should go to a Republican. Of the leaders involved, DeLay may have been singled out because of his reputation for using bare-knuckled tactics to persuade Washington business interests not only to support Republicans but also to withhold money and support from Democrats.

Shuster

As of mid-1999, the House ethics committee was continuing an investigation into whether House Transportation and Infrastructure Committee Chairman Bud Shuster, R-Pa., violated illegal gratuities law as a result of his relationship with an ex-staffer.

The complaint was initially filed September 5, 1996, by the Congressional Accountability Project, a Ralph Nader group. Because no members of Congress was willing to file the complaint, the group was allowed to do so under House rules. However, the complaint died at the end of the 104th Congress because the ethics committee had not reached a conclusion.

The committee November 14, 1997, launched a probe into Shuster, again upon request of the Congressional Accountability Project. Citing a slew of newspaper accounts, the watchdog group asked the committee to investigate Shuster's relationship with Ann Eppard, who was his chief of staff from 1973 to 1994 and became a lobbyist specializing in transportation for businesses with an interest in legislation before Shuster's committee. Eppard also continued to serve as Shuster's campaign fund-raiser, soliciting contributions from many of those same transportation clients, according to the news stories. Shuster also often stayed with Eppard at her $823,000 waterfront home, perhaps violating House gift rules by accepting free lodging. The investigation also focused on whether Shuster did favors for developer Maurice A. Lawruk, who was a financial backer of a car dealership owned by Shuster's two sons.

The panel announced June 10, 1998, that it was curtailing its investigation to steer clear of an ongoing Justice Department criminal probe. Shuster reportedly was being investigated for helping two businessmen get better deals for property acquired for Boston's $11 billion "Big Dig" highway project in exchange for their campaign contributions.

The committee subsequently expanded its investigation to include possible ethical violations during several of Shuster's re-election campaigns. New questions surfaced in January 1999 when documents were filed in connection with a federal grand jury investigation of Eppard and another lobbyist, Vernon A. Clark. A filing in the case included a list of "gratuities provided" to Eppard and paid for by Richard Goldberg, a businessman with an interest in Big Dig. The filing showed that Eppard and Shuster stayed together for a total of seven nights at two vacation homes on Cape Cod rented by Goldberg; it placed the accommodations' value at $980 apiece.

Brown

The House ethics committee on June 9, 1999, voted to open a formal inquiry into allegations that Rep. Connie Brown, D-Fla., received a luxury car from a West African businessman after Brown lobbied to keep him out of prison.

In 1998 the *St. Petersburg Times* reported that businessman Foutanga Dit Babani Sissoko told aides to buy a Lexus automobile for Shantrel Brown, Brown's adult daughter, in 1997. Sissoko had been sentenced to prison on a bribery charge. Brown had lobbied to have him deported instead of sent to jail.

The committee also would investigate lodging provided to Brown in 1997 "at premises owned or controlled" by Sissoko.

Changes in Ethics Rules

Congressional pay raises and codes of ethics continued to be intertwined in the 1990s. Whenever Congress voted itself a big pay increase, it usually tried to dampen public opposition by coupling the action with some offsetting reduction in other benefits or tightening the rules of conduct for members.

The most conspicuous "perk" eliminated in this manner was the acceptance of honoraria payments for speeches or articles. Fees for speeches to groups with an interest in legislation had been particularly controversial. In 1989 Congress banned honoraria for House members as part of the new Ethics Reform Act, the most sweeping rewrite of the congressional conduct code in twelve years.

1989 ETHICS LAW REVISION

The 1989 act gave Congress a two-tiered pay system, with higher salaries for representatives than for senators. After chafing under the lower pay for more than a year, the Senate in July 1991 also voted to give up honoraria in exchange for a $23,200 raise that put senators' salaries on a par with House members' $125,100 a year. *(See "Honoraria: A Vanishing Perquisite," p. 778.)*

As part of the deal under which the House agreed to the Senate pay raise, Congress in 1991 eased some of the gift rules that it had passed less than two years earlier. The new rules allowed senators, representatives, and their employees to accept more expensive gifts (worth up to $250) than permitted under the 1989 rules and an unlimited number of lesser gifts (worth $100 or less). The rules eliminated almost all requirements to disclose the receipt of gifts.

The 1989 Ethics Reform Act, which President George Bush signed into law, incorporated new restrictions on lobbying by government officials, including members of Congress, after they left office. *(See box, 'Revolving Door' Slowed, p. 979.)*

The changes received little debate on the floor, but they addressed several areas that had brought bad publicity to members for years. The measure eliminated a loophole in a 1979 law that had allowed House members who had been in office at the beginning of 1980 to convert campaign funds to personal use once they retired. Members serving in the 103rd Congress (1993–1995) would lose their ability to take advantage of the loophole. Senate rules had previously prohibited the practice.

The measure limited expense-paid travel for nongovernmental trips to no more than seven days for trips abroad. The Senate limited domestic trips to three days; the House, four days. Both chambers tightened rules on gifts—limiting senators to $300 worth of gifts a year from any source other than relatives; the cap on gifts to House members was set at $200 a year. House members were barred from accepting fees for professional services, including the practice of law and serving on boards of directors.

But the measure also loosened restrictions in some areas. For instance, it exempted from the annual limit on gifts all meals in

'REVOLVING DOOR' SLOWED

Congress rewrote restrictions on lobbying by former executive branch officials—and, for the first time, applied such limits to its own members and staff—as part of the 1989 pay-and-ethics package.

The provisions were an attempt to clamp down on the "revolving-door" problem—officials trading top government positions for high-paying jobs lobbying former colleagues on issues they previously oversaw.

For the first time, members of Congress were prohibited from lobbying in the legislative branch for a year after leaving office. In addition, former government officials were barred from using confidential information concerning trade and treaty negotiations to advise clients for a year.

Cabinet secretaries and other top White House officials were banned from lobbying any other senior executive branch officials for a year after leaving office, a broader restriction than one that had prohibited contacts with their own former office. Similar legislation cleared Congress in 1988 but was vetoed by President Ronald Reagan.

The revolving-door provisions resurfaced only in the closing weeks of the session, when congressional leaders saw an opportunity to gain a pay raise in exchange for accepting new restrictions on a host of ethics issues, including postemployment lobbying.

But while tightening some limits, Congress rolled back others already in law that the administration said were leading key procurement officials to quit their jobs.

At the last minute, administration officials demanded that the president remain exempt from the lobbying restrictions. They argued that the bill might bar ex-presidents from offering advice to other administrations. Sponsors maintained that the bill would not prevent a former president from expressing his personal views but agreed to go along.

Another price on the bill imposed at the last minute was an administration demand that Congress roll back controversial lobbying restrictions already in law. A 1988 law (PL 100-679) barred former federal employees from working on a procurement contract for two years if they played a role in awarding that contract.

Early in 1989 top-level employees in the National Aeronautics and Space Administration (NASA), the Defense Department, and other agencies began resigning in droves to avoid being covered.

Guidelines to implement the law were issued May 11, but Congress, at the administration's request, passed new legislation that delayed imposition of the new rules.

House sponsors were willing to go along with a repeal of the 1988 law and several others that restricted lobbying by former Defense and Energy Department employees. However, Senate negotiators would not accept a full repeal, and lawmakers agreed to suspend the laws for a year to allow further review.

Washington. The law also exempted as "nominal" gifts worth less than $75—up from the previous threshold of $35.

Honoraria were not eliminated altogether, but House members could not keep the payments. They had to be returned or channeled to charities.

Following are major provisions of the law, as signed by President Bush on November 30, 1989:

Pay

House, Other Federal Officials. Provided, in February 1990, a 7.9 percent pay increase to House members, federal judges, and top executive branch officials who did not receive cost-of-living increases for 1989 and 1990.

• Provided a 25 percent increase for House members and other top executive- and judicial-branch officials on January 1, 1991.

Senate. Provided, in February, a 9.9 percent pay increase for senators.

Future Increases. Provided for automatic, annual cost-of-living adjustments (COLAs) for members of Congress and top federal officials of 0.5 percentage point less than the previous year's Economic Cost Index, which measures inflation of private industry salaries. A ceiling on annual COLAs was set at 5 percent.

• Required the House and Senate to take recorded votes on all future congressional pay increases other than annual COLAs.

• Replaced the "quadrennial commission" that met every four years to recommend salary hikes for top federal officials with an eleven-member Citizens' Commission on Public Service and Compensation, to include five people chosen by lot from voter-registration lists, two by the president, two by congressional leaders, and one by the chief justice of the United States.

• Required the commission to meet every four years and report to the president by December 15.

• Specified that the president's pay recommendations, made after receiving the commission's report, would take effect after the next congressional election and only if both the House and the Senate adopted a resolution of approval by recorded vote within sixty days of its submission.

Honoraria

House. Froze at 1989 levels the honoraria and other outside income House members could keep in 1990—$26,850 for most.

• Barred House members, staff, and other federal officials from keeping any honoraria beginning January 1, 1991.

• Allowed House members and others subject to the honoraria ban to request that charitable contributions be made in their name in lieu of honoraria for speeches and appearances.

• Limited such charitable contributions to $2,000 per speech or appearance and prohibited them from being made to any organization that benefited the speaker or his or her relatives.

• Barred those who had such charitable contributions made on their behalf from getting tax advantages—such as deductions or increases in the amount they could shelter in tax-free Keogh accounts—as a result of those donations.

Senate. Reduced the ceiling on honoraria that senators could keep from 40 percent of salary in 1989 to 27 percent in 1990—$26,568 for most.

• Provided that any cost-of-living pay increase after December 31, 1990, be accompanied by an equivalent reduction in the ceiling on honoraria until it reached zero.

Other Outside Income

House. Barred House members and senior staff from keeping more than 15 percent of the Executive Level II salary ($96,600) in outside earned income beginning January 1, 1991.

• Prohibited House members and senior staff from being paid for working or affiliating with a law or other professional firm. They would be allowed to teach for pay if the ethics committee approved.

• Prohibited House members and senior staff from being paid for serving on boards of directors.

• Applied the above limits on outside income also to federal, noncareer employees at the GS-16 salary level or higher.

• Repealed the House ban on honoraria and other limits on outside income if the 25 percent pay raise in 1991 was repealed.

• Clarified House rules exempting copyright royalties from the cap on outside income to specify that exempt royalties must be paid by an established trade publisher, in line with customary contract terms.

Campaign Funds

• Eliminated, by the time the 103rd Congress began in 1993, an exemption in election law that allowed House members elected before 1980 to convert campaign funds to personal use when they retired from Congress.

• Froze what such funds members could convert, if they retired before the end of the 102nd Congress, at no more than what they had on hand when the 1989 ethics law was enacted.

Gifts and Travel

• Authorized the Office of Government Ethics to issue rules for receipt of gifts by all federal employees.

House. Amended rules governing House members and employees to bar receiving gifts from any one person, except relatives, valued at more than the ceiling set by the Foreign Gifts Act—a cap that was set at $200 beginning January 1, 1990, and would be automatically adjusted for inflation every three years.

• Exempted from the annual gift limit the value of meals and drinks, unless they were part of overnight lodging.

• Raised from $35 to $75 the threshold below which gifts would not count toward the annual ceiling.

• Limited the exemption on gifts of "personal hospitality" to bar receiving more than thirty days of lodging a year from someone other than a relative and to require members to ensure that any hospitality extended for more than four days was personal—not corporate-financed or being claimed as a business expense.

• Allowed private sources to pay travel expenses for no more than four days of domestic travel and seven days (excluding travel time) for international trips.

• Allowed travel expenses for one accompanying relative.

• Allowed the Committee on Standards of Official Conduct to waive gift and travel restrictions in exceptional circumstances.

Senate. Amended rules governing senators and Senate employees to prohibit their receiving more than $300 a year in gifts from any one source other than relatives and kept the $100 limit on gifts from people with a direct interest in legislation.

• Dropped an exemption allowing unlimited gifts of entertainment.

• Allowed private sources to pay travel expenses for no more than three days of domestic travel and seven days for international trips. Both limits excluded travel time.

• Allowed travel expenses to be paid for one accompanying Senate aide or a spouse.

Ethics Committee

House. Expanded the Committee on Standards of Official Conduct, beginning in the 102nd Congress, from twelve to fourteen members and limited each member to no more than three terms during any five successive Congresses.

• Required the committee to divide its investigative and adjudicative functions by naming a four- or six-member subcommittee to review allegations whenever a preliminary inquiry was opened. The other members would hold disciplinary hearings when the investigative subcommittee found reason to believe that rules were violated and issued a statement of alleged violation.

• Prohibited the committee from making public a statement of alleged violation until the accused could draft a response, and required that the two documents be released simultaneously.

• Required the committee to issue a report on any investigation, regardless of the case's disposition.

• Allowed the committee to investigate only violations alleged to have occurred in the three most recent Congresses, unless older violations related to more recent ones or unless specifically instructed by the House.

• Allowed members facing ethics sanctions to bring an attorney onto the House floor during consideration of the committee's recommendations.

• Directed the committee to establish an Office on Advice and Education to guide members and employees.

Financial Disclosure

• Brought all three branches of government under the same financial disclosure law, although each would continue to be responsible for administering requirements for its own employees.

• Raised from $100 to $200 the threshold below which income from any source need not be disclosed and raised from $35 to $75 the threshold below which gifts need not be reported.

• Required members of Congress and other federal officials

who had charitable contributions made on their behalf in lieu of honoraria to disclose the source and amount of such contributions beginning in 1991. The charities receiving such contributions would not have to be publicly reported, but their identities would have to be disclosed in confidential reports to the House Committee on Standards of Official Conduct or other ethics offices.

• Required disclosure of the source and amount of any honoraria spouses of reporting officials earned.

• Required more detailed disclosure of travel reimbursements, including an itinerary and dates of travel.

• Specified that underlying assets of regulated investment companies did not have to be reported if the firm was widely diversified and the reporting official had no control over it.

• Required all federal officials, including members of Congress, to file a final financial disclosure form, known as a "termination report," after they left office.

• Extended the time within which financial disclosure reports must be made available to the public from fifteen days to thirty days after they were filed.

• Doubled from $5,000 to $10,000 the maximum civil penalty for violation of financial disclosure law and established a $200 penalty fee for late filing.

Postemployment Lobbying

• Barred members and officers of Congress from lobbying the legislative branch for a year after they left office.

• Barred former congressional staff members for a year after leaving employment from lobbying the member, office, or committee for which they had worked. Leadership staff members were barred from lobbying the members and employees of the leadership for the chamber in which they served.

• Kept a lifetime ban on all former executive branch employees from lobbying on matters in which they were "personally and substantially involved" while in office and kept a two-year ban on matters that were "under their official responsibility within the year preceding termination of government service." No such prohibitions would be applied to the legislative branch, however.

• Barred former Executive Level I officials throughout the government and Level II officials in the White House for a year after leaving office from lobbying any officials at Levels I through V.

• Imposed a one-year ban on lobbying by former executive employees and military officers at the GS-17 pay level or above at the agency they had served. Although the civil service pay scale did not apply to congressional staff, any legislative branch employees paid at the GS-17 level or higher would be barred for a year from lobbying the members who employed them or the committees for which they had worked. Former employees would also be barred from "representing, aiding or advising" foreign governments or foreign political parties for a year.

• Barred executive branch employees who were "personally and substantially" involved in trade or treaty negotiations with-

With public disapproval rising in the 1980s and 1990s in the wake of scandals and internal investigations, Congress heeded the calls for reform by adopting stricter ethics standards.

in a year before leaving office from representing or advising people concerned with such negotiations. The ban would last a year.

Miscellaneous Provisions

Conflict of Interest. Barred House employees from participating in contacts with the judiciary or government agencies with respect to nonlegislative matters in which they had a significant financial interest.

• Added civil and misdemeanor penalties to the criminal ones already available that may be imposed on federal employees for violating conflict-of-interest law.

Procurement Law. Postponed for one year implementing procurement-reform laws that barred former federal employees from working on a procurement contract for two years if they played a role in awarding the contract.

Car Rentals. Relaxed rules barring government officials from using officially leased cars for incidental personal use.

Senior Executive Service. Required members of the executive branch's Senior Executive Service to be recertified in that status every three years beginning in 1991, unless they had been employed as a senior executive for at least thirteen years.

1995 CHANGES IN GIFT RULES

The Senate and House in 1995 adopted new rules that placed restrictions on gifts that lawmakers could accept. The changes were made in the form of separate Senate and House resolutions that applied only to the chamber that passed it and did not have the force of law.

Senate Resolution

The major provisions of the resolution passed by the Senate July 28 are as follows:

Gifts. A $50 limit was placed on the value of gifts, including meals and entertainment, that senators and their staff could accept. The resolution placed a $100 annual limit on gifts from any one source, with no gift permitted to exceed $50 in value. The resolution did not, however, cap the cumulative total of gifts that any single senator or Senate staff member could accept in a year.

Senators and their staff could accept unlimited gifts from family members and close personal friends, although they had to get Ethics Committee approval for gifts valued at more than $250.

Gifts to the sponsors and dependents of senators or their staff were subject to the same restrictions if the senator or staff member had reason to believe the gifts were given in connection with his or her official position.

Charity Outings and Events. Senators were barred from accepting free travel to events that were substantially recreational. The provision applied to the so-called charity trips where senators and lobbyists golfed and skied together to raise money for charities.

Trips. Senators and their staff could continue to accept free travel for meetings, speaking engagements, and fact-finding tours that were in connection with their official duties. The trips were capped at seven days for international travel, exclusive of travel time, and three days for domestic trips. Spouses were permitted on such trips if they were "appropriate to assist in the representation of the Senate."

Legal Defense Funds. Lobbyists could not contribute to a senator's or staff member's legal defense fund. Previous rules had permitted such contributions, up to $10,000 per person, if they were disclosed.

Charitable Contributions. Lobbyists were barred from contributing to charities maintained or controlled by a senator or a Senate staffer. However, lobbyists could continue to make contributions of up to $2,000 to any charity designated by a member in lieu of paying a speaking fee to a senator or Senate staffer.

Exceptions and Clarifications. Senators and their staff could continue to accept: campaign contributions from lobbyists; contributions to a legal defense fund from those who were not registered lobbyists; gifts from other senators and staffers; anything of value resulting from an outside business not connected with official business; pensions and benefits; informational materials, such as books and videotapes; honorary degrees, including travel to ceremonies; items of little intrinsic value, such as plaques and trophies; inheritances; or any gift for which the Senate Ethics Committee provided a waiver.

House Resolution

The major provisions of the resolution passed by the House November 16, which went into effect January 1, 1996, are as follows:

Gifts. House members no longer could accept any gifts, except those from close personal friends or family. Members could still accept unlimited gifts from family and friends, but such gifts valued at more than $250 required a waiver from the House Committee on Standards of Official Conduct.

Widely Attended Events. Members could attend conventions, charity events, and similar occasions with their expenses picked up by the sponsor, as long as the event was connected with a member's official duties. Members could take their spouse or another individual to widely attended events when the sponsoring organization, and not a lobbyist, was paying their way. Members could not solicit such trips.

Charity Outings. The resolution eliminated the practice of members taking lobbyist-paid trips to participate in golf, skiing, and tennis tournaments to raise money for charity. The sponsor of such an event could waive the entrance fee for members, but not provide any travel expenses, such as transportation, food, and lodging.

Trips. Members could continue accepting all-expense paid trips for fact-finding purposes or associated with a member's official duties, such as flying to a private group's convention to speak about Congress. Lobbyists and foreign agents, though, were specifically prohibited from paying a member's travel expenses for such trips. International trips were limited to seven days, excluding travel time, and domestic trips were capped at four days. Members could bring along a spouse or family member.

1996 Clarifications

The House and Senate ethics committees in 1996 clarified the new rules for accepting gifts from lobbyists.

Clubs and Charity Events. House members and their staffs were prohibited from accepting honorary memberships in organizations that waived initiation and periodic fees. Members were allowed to accept free memberships in Rotary and other private clubs under some circumstances.

House members and staff could accept free attendance to golf tournaments and other charity events only if the primary purpose of the event was to raise funds for an organization eligible to receive tax-deductible contributions. Such invitations had to come from an event sponsor and not be solicited.

House members and staff were allowed to accept offers of local transportation by a sponsor but prohibited from accepting reimbursement for housing and other transportation costs to a charity event. Members could accept items of nominal value given to all participants in a group setting at a charity event. Members could accept all items given to other participants if they paid the entrance fee. Members could also accept a "skill" prize, such as for the lowest score in a golf tournament, and any door prize worth more than $250, provided they listed such prizes on their annual financial disclosure statements.

Party Conventions. House members were permitted to attend most of the receptions, parties, and meals that were customary at national political conventions. The organizer of the event had to issue the invitation. Events sponsored by local and state governments and the political parties also were permitted.

House members and staff were allowed to accept meals, lodging, transportation, and tickets to sporting, theatrical, and other entertainment events, as long as they came from one of the two major political parties, a campaign fund-raising committee, or a local or state party organization. Members could accept the gifts and handouts that convention delegates got as long as they were items given to everybody, not just lawmakers. But members could not accept gifts from lobbyists.

Senators attending conventions could accept free food, lodging, entertainment, gifts, and transportation if they were provided by local, state, or federal governments or the host city's official committee.

Senators could accept invitations to privately financed functions that were "widely attended events," defined as gatherings of at least twenty-five people from outside of Congress. Senators were allowed to attend receptions and to accept t-shirts and items of "little intrinsic value."

ILLEGAL GRATUITIES

In a unanimous decision April 27, 1999, the Supreme Court rejected an expansive reading of a 1962 law against the giving or taking of gratuities that has been used to prosecute public officials, including executive branch officials and members of Congress.

Simply presenting a gift to a public official is not a crime. To break the law, the Court held in *U.S. v. Sun-Diamond Growers of California,* a gift-giver's generosity must be tied to some specific action taken by the official who received the present. The ruling will make it more difficult for government officials to be prosecuted for taking gifts.

The 1962 law was designed to create a new crime for accepting things of value that did not rise to the level of an outright bribe. While bribe-taking by a federal official is punishable by fifteen years in prison, the maximum sentence for accepting an illegal gratuity is only two years. The quid pro quo between the payment and the action by a public official, the defining feature of bribery, is somewhat nebulous in the illegal gratuities law, which barred the giving of gifts to an official "for or because any official act performed or to be performed by such public official."

1997 HOUSE ETHICS OVERHAUL

The House in 1997 revamped its self-policing process in the aftermath of the highly partisan atmosphere surrounding the ethics investigation of House Speaker Newt Gingrich. *(See "Gingrich," p. 940.)*

Leaders of both parties put together a task force to study the chamber's ethics process and recommend changes to the full House. While the task force deliberated, the ethics committee was not constituted and there was a moratorium on filing ethics complaints against members.

The task force issued its report on June 18. The House September 18 adopted 258–154 new rules based largely on the group's recommendations, aimed at making the ethics process more timely and bipartisan. That action came after the House made two major changes to the package put forth by the task force and defeated a third. Many Democrats voted against the final resolution because they opposed the changes.

In what was the most controversial change adopted by the House, the new rules barred nonmembers from filing complaints with the ethics committee. The task force had recommended that outside groups be allowed to file complaints if they had "personal knowledge" of a transgression. Advocates for the ban argued that members needed to be protected from frivolous ethics complaints, especially from their political foes during reelection campaigns. Under the approved change, outsiders were required to find a lawmaker to sponsor the complaint, which meant they had to go a long extra mile to find a member willing to risk political oblivion by bringing a formal complaint against a House leader or an influential committee chairman.

A second modification approved by the House required a majority vote of the full committee to expand the scope of a subcommittee investigation when additional information was uncovered. The task force had recommended that the investigative subcommittee that handled the initial steps of a case have the power to expand the scope. The intent was to safeguard the subcommittee's autonomy.

The House rejected an amendment to require that complaints against members be dismissed if the committee deadlocked for six months over the issue of whether to open an investigation. Supporters argued that lawmakers needed protection from election-year challengers who filed baseless ethics complaints with the intent of having them linger long enough to do political damage. Critics said the proposed change would encourage stalemate by giving committee members favoring dismissal an incentive to dig in and wait for the clock to run out.

The rules changes adopted by the House also included:

• A time limit of forty-five days during which the committee was required to either dismiss a complaint, resolve it with a letter to the lawmaker, or establish a subcommittee to open an investigation. If the committee failed to act within forty-five calendar days—or five legislative days, whichever was longer—a complaint would automatically go to the investigation stage. But the panel also could extend the review period for an additional forty-five calendar days.

• Enhanced powers for the chairman and ranking member, who could refer a complaint to an investigative subcommittee on their own. Under previous rules, only a vote of the full committee could kick off an investigation. The ranking member also was given greater power to place items on the committee's agenda.

• Creation of a nonpartisan professional staff and a twenty-member pool of lawmakers who could be called on to serve on the subcommittee.

Overall, the House opted to maintain the existing bifurcated system, in which an investigatory subcommittee reviewed a complaint and then made recommendations to an adjudicatory subcommittee that took over the trial-like phase of the process.

Congressional Immunity: Shielding Legislators

The concept of congressional immunity from certain legal actions was a well-established principle in England when it was added to the American Constitution. Article I, Section 6 provides that senators and representatives "shall in all Cases, except Treason, Felony and Breach of the Peace, be privileged from Arrest during their Attendance at the Session of their respective Houses, and in going to and returning from the same; and for any Speech or Debate in either House, they shall not be questioned in any other Place."

The privilege-from-arrest clause has become practically obsolete, as various court decisions have excluded more and more acts and proceedings from the protection of the clause. As currently interpreted, the clause applies only to arrests in civil suits, such as nonpayment of debts or breach of contract; and most state constitutions or statutes prohibit arrest generally in such actions. Civil arrests were more common when the Constitution was adopted.

Long v. Ansell in 1934 and *United States v. Cooper* in 1800 declared that the clause does not apply to service of process in civil or criminal cases; nor does it apply to arrest in any criminal case. Furthermore, *Williamson v. United States* in 1908 interpreted the phrase "treason, felony and breach of the peace" as excluding all criminal offenses from coverage by the privilege.

The speech or debate clause has been cited more frequently by members seeking immunity from actions against them. Various court decisions have broadly interpreted the phrase "speech or debate" to include virtually everything a member does in carrying out legislative responsibilities.

'SPEECH OR DEBATE' CLAUSE

The first Supreme Court interpretation of the speech or debate clause occurred in 1881 in *Kilbourn v. Thompson.* The case is also widely cited for its ruling on the limits of congressional investigations. *(See "Judicial Review," p. 252, Vol. I.)*

It involved a contempt of Congress citation against Hallet Kilbourn, manager of a real estate pool, for refusing to answer questions before the House Select Committee on the Real Estate Pool and Jay Cooke Indebtedness. The House ordered Kilbourn jailed for contempt. He won release on a writ of habeus corpus and sued the Speaker, members of the investigating committee,

---

IMMUNITY IN WASHINGTON

Members of Congress apparently were no longer to be immune from arrest in Washington, D.C., for crimes such as drunk driving and soliciting prostitutes, according to a 1976 Justice Department ruling.

Reports occasionally had appeared in the press of such incidents involving a member of Congress. Invariably, once police confirmed that the suspect was a member, action against the person would be dropped.

The July 23 Justice Department ruling, which had been requested by the District of Columbia chief of police, stemmed from a case involving Rep. Joe D. Waggonner Jr., D-La. Waggonner had been arrested after he allegedly solicited a District policewoman posing as a prostitute. He was released when police identified him as a member of Congress.

On the basis of the ruling, D.C. police said, members "and all other elected and appointed federal, state, and local officials are subject to arrest for the commission of criminal offenses to the same extent and in the same manner as all other citizens." An exception would be continued for most parking violations by private automobiles bearing congressional license plates.

The nonarrest policy, which had been in effect for more than one hundred years, had been based on "a misinterpretation of the meaning" of the Privilege from Arrest Clause in Article I, Section 6, of the Constitution, a police spokesperson said.

At least since *Williamson v. United States* in 1908, this language was believed to have been inserted in the Constitution to prevent political harassment through civil arrest. The more sweeping policy against arrest was thought to have been aimed at not offending the legislators, who controlled the D.C. Police Department budget.

Since the decision, several members of Congress were arrested in Washington, D.C., and surrounding suburbs for driving under the influence of alcohol and were subjected to punishments such as fines. None served jail time for such offenses.

---

and Sergeant at Arms John G. Thompson for false arrest. The Supreme Court upheld Kilbourn's claim, on the grounds that it had not been a legitimate investigation.

The Court decided the case on the basis of Congress's investigatory powers. But the defendants raised the speech or debate clause as a defense, and the Court commented on this issue in its opinion. The Court said the protection of the clause was not only limited to words spoken in debate, but also was applicable to written reports, to resolutions offered, to the act of voting, and to all things generally done in a session of the House by one of its members in relation to the business before it.

LEGISLATIVE ACTS PROTECTED

The Supreme Court on February 24, 1966, held in a 7–0 decision that in prosecuting a former member of Congress the executive branch may not constitutionally inquire into the member's motives for making a speech on the floor, even though the speech was made for a bribe and was part of an unlawful conspiracy.

The holdings in *United States v. Johnson* left members immune from prosecution for their words and legislative deeds on the floor of Congress, with one exception reserved by the Court—prosecution under a "narrowly drawn" law enacted by Congress itself "to regulate the conduct of its Members." Members of Congress already were immune from libel suits for speeches made on the floor.

Johnson was the first case of its kind. The Court was unable to find among the English or American cases any direct precedent. The Court did discuss cases holding that legislators were protected from private suits for their legislative words and deeds; and it cited approvingly a Supreme Court decision, the force of which appeared to extend the *Johnson* doctrine to state legislators.

The *Johnson* case arose out of the conviction of former representative Thomas F. Johnson, D-Md., on June 13, 1963, by a federal jury in Baltimore. The government charged that Johnson, former representative Frank W. Boykin, D-Ala., and two officers of a Maryland savings and loan company then under indictment, J. Kenneth Edlin and William L. Robinson, entered into a conspiracy whereby Johnson and Boykin would approach the Justice Department to urge a "review" of the indictment and Johnson would make a speech on the floor of the House defending savings and loan institutions. Johnson made the speech June 30, 1960, and it was reprinted by the indicted company and distributed to the public. Johnson and Boykin allegedly received money in the form of "campaign contributions." Johnson's share was more than $20,000.

Johnson was convicted on seven counts of violating the federal conflict-of-interest law and on one count of conspiring to defraud the United States; the others were convicted of the same charges. President Lyndon B. Johnson December 17, 1965, granted Boykin a full pardon.

The Fourth Circuit Court of Appeals September 16, 1964, set aside Thomas Johnson's conspiracy conviction on grounds that it was unconstitutional under the speech or debate clause. The court ordered a new trial on the other counts on grounds that evidence taken about Johnson's speech on the conspiracy count "infected" the entire case.

The Supreme Court affirmed the lower court's ruling, thus foreclosing further prosecution on the conspiracy count but permitting retrial on the other counts. In the majority opinion, Justice John Marshall Harlan said the purpose of the speech or debate clause was "prophylactic," that it had been adopted by the Constitutional Convention (without discussion or opposition) because of the English experience with efforts of the Crown to intimidate and punish Parliament. The clause was intended to protect the independence and integrity of Congress, the Court said, and to reinforce the separation of powers by preventing an "unfriendly" executive and a "hostile" judiciary appointed by the executive from reaching into congressional activity for evidence of criminality.

The government's theory, rejected by the Court, was that Johnson's criminal act—acceptance of a bribe and entering into a conspiracy—predated his floor speech. Justice Harlan said the indictment particularized the speech as part of the conspiracy charged, and evidence about the speech was taken at trial.

On January 26, 1968, Johnson was convicted for a second time on the conflict-of-interest charges by the U.S. District Court in Baltimore. He was sentenced to six months in prison.

IMMUNITY PROTECTION NARROWED

On June 29, 1972, the Supreme Court in effect narrowed the category of protected actions under the immunity clause. The Court's ruling was issued in a case involving former senator Daniel B. Brewster, D-Md.

A federal grand jury on December 1, 1969, had indicted Brewster, Spiegel Inc., a Chicago mail-order firm, and Cyrus T. Anderson, a lobbyist for the firm, on charges of violating federal bribery laws. The indictment charged that Brewster received $24,500 from Spiegel Inc. and Anderson to influence his "action, vote and decision" on postal rate legislation.

The grand jury said the payments were made in five installments between January 10, 1966, and January 31, 1968. Brewster was a member of the Senate Post Office and Civil Service Committee during a 1967 debate on postal rate increases for regular third-class mail. Spiegel was a major user of such rates. Brewster had been defeated for reelection in 1968.

Ten months after Brewster's indictment, a U.S. district court judge dismissed it on the grounds that the senator was immune from prosecution because of the speech or debate clause.

The government took an appeal directly to the Supreme Court, which issued a decision June 29, 1972, narrowing the category of protected actions under the immunity clause. A six-justice Court majority ruled that "taking a bribe is, obviously, no part of the legislative process or function" (*United States v. Brewster*).

Chief Justice Warren E. Burger, writing the opinion, continued: "The illegal conduct is taking or agreeing to take money for a promise to act in a certain way. There is no need for the government to show that [Brewster] fulfilled the alleged illegal bargain . . . for it is taking the bribe, not performance of the illicit compact, that is a criminal act." Importantly, the Court upheld the validity of the indictment, making it unnecessary for the government to inquire into legislative acts or their motivations to prove a violation of the bribery statute. Brewster was ordered to stand trial and was convicted November 17, 1972.

The jury found Brewster guilty of a lesser bribery charge, that of accepting an unlawful gratuity. Following the verdict, Spiegel Inc. pleaded guilty. Brewster was sentenced to two to six years in prison and fined $30,000. In August 1974 a federal appeals court reversed the conviction on grounds the jury had not been given proper instructions. A new trial was scheduled for August 1975. But on June 25, 1975, Brewster pleaded no contest to a felony charge of accepting an illegal gratuity while he was a senator.

PROTECTED ACTS SPECIFIED

On June 29, 1972, the Supreme Court took the unusual step of specifying in some detail certain acts of a legislator that were protected by the immunity clause. The case involved Sen. Mike Gravel, D-Alaska, and his actions in releasing portions of the then-classified Pentagon Papers history of United States' involvement in the Vietnam War.

During the controversy over publication of the Pentagon Papers in 1971 by the *New York Times,* the *Washington Post,* and several other newspapers, Gravel on June 29, 1971, convened a special meeting of the Public Works Subcommittee on Public Buildings, of which he was chairman. With the press and the public in attendance, Gravel read classified documents from the Pentagon Papers into the subcommittee record. Subsequently, the senator arranged for the verbatim publication of the subcommittee record by Beacon Press, the nonprofit publishing arm of the Unitarian-Universalist Association.

In August 1971 a federal grand jury in Boston, investigating the release of the Pentagon Papers, ordered an aide to Gravel, Leonard S. Rodberg, to appear before it. Rodberg had been hired the night Gravel called the session of his subcommittee to read excerpts from the secret documents. Rodberg subsequently helped Gravel edit the papers and make arrangements for their publication. The grand jury also subpoenaed several persons associated with Beacon Press who were involved in publication of the papers.

Rodberg moved to quash the subpoena on the grounds he was protected from the questioning by congressional immunity, contending such immunity extended to staff members. Gravel filed a motion to intervene on Rodberg's behalf, claiming Rodberg was acting under the senator's orders, which were immune from judicial inquiry.

The Justice Department, in a brief filed in the case September 8, 1971, said no immunity existed for either Rodberg or Gravel. While not saying so directly, the department's action left open the possibility it might subpoena Gravel himself to testify.

A lower court ruled in October 1971 that the grand jury could not question any witness about Gravel's conduct at the special meeting or about his preparation for the meeting. The grand jury also was prohibited from questioning Rodberg about his own actions taken at Gravel's direction relating to the meeting.

In January 1972 the court of appeals held that Gravel could be questioned about the subsequent publication of the subcommittee record by Beacon Press but not about the subcommittee meeting itself. The same immunities extended to Gravel were also to be applied to Rodberg, the court ruled. But third parties, the court ruled, could be questioned about any of their own ac-

Following Sen. Mike Gravel's disclosure of the classified Pentagon Papers in 1972, the Supreme Court enumerated the acts of a legislator that were protected by the immunity clause.

tions regarding the publication and the ad hoc committee session.

In a 5–4 decision on June 29, 1972, the Supreme Court specifically enumerated the activities of Gravel and Rodberg that were protected by the immunity clause *(Gravel v. United States).*

The Court said no witness could be questioned concerning: (1) the conduct of Gravel or his aides at the meeting of the Subcommittee on Public Buildings and Grounds of the Senate Public Works Committee on June 29, 1971; (2) the motives and purposes behind the conduct of Gravel or his aides at the June 29 meeting; (3) communications between Gravel and his aides during the terms of their employment and related to the June 29 meeting or any other legislative act of the senator; or (4) any act, in itself not criminal, performed by the senator or by his aides in the course of their employment in preparation for the subcommittee meeting, except as it proved relevant to investigating possible third-party crime.

The ruling held that Gravel's constitutional immunity did not shield him or his aides from grand jury questioning regarding their activities not directly related to their legislative responsibilities. "While the Speech or Debate Clause recognizes speech, voting and other legislative acts as exempt from liability that might attach," the Court stated, "it does not privilege either senator or aide to violate an otherwise valid criminal law in preparing for or implementing legislative acts."

The Court concluded that the immunity of Gravel's aide was identical to that of his employer and defined the latter's as immunity from "prosecutions that directly impinge upon or threaten the legislative process."

The Court majority concurred with the lower court ruling that the negotiations leading to unofficial publication of the committee record were outside the protection of the speech or debate clause. However, it also held that both Gravel and Rodberg were vulnerable to grand jury questioning and possible liability regarding their roles in the Pentagon Papers publication.

LEGISLATIVE PROTECTION RESTATED

The Supreme Court on October 9, 1973, upheld an appellate court ruling that had reversed five of eight conspiracy, bribery, and perjury convictions against former representative John Dowdy, D-Texas, on grounds that they violated the immunity clause.

A federal grand jury in Baltimore indicted Dowdy on March 31, 1970. The indictment alleged he had accepted a $25,000 bribe at the Atlanta airport on September 22, 1965, to intervene in a federal and District of Columbia investigation of the Monarch Construction Co. of Silver Spring, Maryland.

Dowdy was convicted on December 30, 1971, in U.S. District Court in Baltimore of crossing a state line to receive a bribe, conspiracy to obstruct justice, conspiracy to violate conflict of interest statutes, and five counts of perjury. He was sentenced to eighteen months in prison and fined $25,000.

On March 13, 1973, the Fourth Circuit Court of Appeals reversed five of the eight convictions and reduced Dowdy's sentence to six months in prison and a $3,000 fine. Convictions on three counts of perjury were sustained (Dowdy v. United States).

The court held that evidence used in the trial that violated Dowdy's immunity "was an examination of the defendant's actions as a congressman, who was chairman of a subcommittee investigating a complaint, in gathering information in preparation for a possible subcommittee investigatory hearing."

Although the alleged criminal act—bribery—was the same in both the Brewster and Dowdy cases, the major difference, which resulted in one prosecution's being upheld and the other's being reversed, was the source of the evidence. In Brewster's case there was sufficient evidence available outside of Brewster's legislative activities to permit the case to go forward. In Dowdy's case so much of the evidence was based on Dowdy's legislative activities that the court reversed five of the eight convictions.

On October 9, 1973, the Supreme Court upheld the ruling of the lower court (Dowdy v. United States). After losing a bid to stay out of prison for health reasons, Dowdy began serving his sentence January 28, 1974.

1979 RULINGS

In June 1979 the Supreme Court released two decisions concerning congressional immunity.

In United States v. Helstoski, the Court forbade federal prosecutors to use any evidence of past legislative actions in prosecuting former representative Henry Helstoski, D-N.J. He had been indicted in 1976 on charges he accepted money in return for introducing private bills allowing certain aliens to remain in the United States. As a result of the decision the prosecutors dropped seven bribery-related counts against Helstoski and sought reindictment of him on remaining obstruction of justice counts. The district judge, however, dismissed these counts also, ruling they were "tainted" by Helstoski's legislative actions.

In Hutchinson v. Proxmire, the Court held that congressional immunity did not protect Sen. William Proxmire, D-Wis., from being sued for libel by a scientist who charged that he had been injured by Proxmire's remarks ridiculing his research. The allegedly libelous remarks were made on the Senate floor in 1975 and then published in a press release and newsletter. The Court ruled that only the remarks on the floor were protected by the speech or debate clause.

Proxmire had been sued by Dr. Ronald Hutchinson, a researcher at the Kalamazoo State Hospital, after the Wisconsin Democrat gave the National Aeronautics and Space Administration and the Office of Naval Research his satiric "Golden Fleece Award." Those agencies had awarded Hutchinson $500,000 in grants for research into how monkeys exhibit aggression. Proxmire garnered considerable publicity by periodically giving Golden Fleece Awards to spotlight what he considered outstanding cases of government waste.

In a 1975 Senate speech, Proxmire said Hutchinson had "made a monkey out of the American taxpayer." He also referred to the Golden Fleece Award in a newsletter, in a press release, and on a television interview program. His legislative assistant, Morton Schwartz, telephoned the agencies funding Hutchinson's research, and they subsequently cut off the grants. Repetition of Proxmire's Senate remarks outside the Capitol were ruled to be beyond the reach of his immunity.

Proxmire made an out-of-court settlement with Hutchinson, announcing the settlement in a March 24, 1980, speech on the Senate floor. Although he did not say so in the speech, the senator agreed to pay the scientist $10,000 in return for ending further litigation. Proxmire used the floor speech to "clarify" his 1975 Golden Fleece statements, which had led to the suit in the first place.

Although Hutchinson paid his own legal fees in the lengthy suit, the Senate picked up the $124,351 tab for Proxmire's defense.

SELECTED BIBLIOGRAPHY

Beard, Edmund, and Stephen Horn. *Congressional Ethics: The View from the House.* Washington, D.C.: Brookings Institution, 1975.

Drew, Elizabeth. *Politics and Money: The New Road to Corruption.* New York: Macmillan, 1983.

Getz, Robert S. *Congressional Ethics: The Conflict of Interest Issue.* New York: Van Nostrand, 1966.

Jennings, Bruce, and Daniel Callahan, eds. *Representation and Responsibility: Exploring Legislative Ethics.* New York: Plenum Press, 1985.

Rudman, Warren B. *Combat: Twelve Years in the U.S. Senate.* New York: Random House, 1996.

Simon, Paul. *The Glass House: Politics and Morality in the Nation's Capital.* New York: Continuum, 1984.

Stern, Philip M. *The Best Congress Money Can Buy.* New York: Pantheon Books, 1988.

Thompson, Dennis F. *Ethics in Congress: From Individual to Institutional Corruption.* Washington, D.C.: Brookings Institution, 1995.

U.S. Congress. House. Committee on Standards of Official Conduct. *Ethics Manual for Members, Officers, and Employees of the U.S. House of Representatives.* 100th Cong., 1st sess., 1987.

U.S. Congress. Senate. Select Committee on Ethics. *In re: The Matter of Senator Alan Cranston, Senator Dennis DeConcini, Senator John Glenn, Senator John McCain, Senator Donald Riegle. Prepared Text of the Opening Statement of Special Counsel Robert S. Bennett.* 101st Cong., 2nd sess., 1990, committee print.

————. *Interpretive Rulings of the Select Committee on Ethics.* Washington, D.C.: Government Printing Office, 1993.

————. *Senate Ethics Manual.* Washington, D.C.: Government Printing Office, 1996.

APPENDIX A

Reference Materials

Constitution of the United States

The United States Constitution was written at a convention that Congress called on February 21, 1787, for the purpose of recommending amendments to the Articles of Confederation. Every state but Rhode Island sent delegates to Philadelphia, where the convention met that summer. The delegates decided to write an entirely new constitution, completing their labors on September 17. Nine states (the number the Constitution itself stipulated as sufficient) ratified by June 21, 1788.

We the People of the United States, in Order to form a more perfect Union, establish Justice, insure domestic Tranquility, provide for the common defence, promote the general Welfare, and secure the Blessings of Liberty to ourselves and our Posterity, do ordain and establish this Constitution for the United States of America.

ARTICLE I

Section 1. All legislative Powers herein granted shall be vested in a Congress of the United States, which shall consist of a Senate and House of Representatives.

Section 2. The House of Representatives shall be composed of Members chosen every second Year by the People of the several States, and the Electors in each State shall have the Qualifications requisite for Electors of the most numerous Branch of the State Legislature.

No Person shall be a Representative who shall not have attained to the age of twenty five Years, and been seven Years a Citizen of the United States, and who shall not, when elected, be an Inhabitant of that State in which he shall be chosen.

[Representatives and direct Taxes shall be apportioned among the several States which may be included within this Union, according to their respective Numbers, which shall be determined by adding to the whole Number of free Persons, including those bound to Service for a Term of Years, and excluding Indians not taxed, three fifths of all other Persons.][1] The actual Enumeration shall be made within three Years after the first Meeting of the Congress of the United States, and within every subsequent Term of ten Years, in such Manner as they shall by Law direct. The Number of Representatives shall not exceed one for every thirty Thousand, but each State shall have at Least one Representative; and until such enumeration shall be made, the State of New Hampshire shall be entitled to chuse three, Massachusetts eight, Rhode-Island and Providence Plantations one, Connecticut five, New-York six, New Jersey four, Pennsylvania eight, Delaware one, Maryland six, Virginia ten, North Carolina five, South Carolina five, and Georgia three.

When vacancies happen in the Representation from any State, the Executive Authority thereof shall issue Writs of Election to fill such Vacancies.

The House of Representatives shall chuse their Speaker and other Officers; and shall have the sole Power of Impeachment.

Section 3. The Senate of the United States shall be composed of two Senators from each State, [chosen by the Legislature thereof,][2] for six Years; and each Senator shall have one Vote.

Immediately after they shall be assembled in Consequence of the first Election, they shall be divided as equally as may be into three Classes. The Seats of the Senators of the first Class shall be vacated at the Expiration of the second Year, of the second Class at the Expiration of the fourth Year, and of the third Class at the Expiration of the sixth Year, so that one third may be chosen every second Year; [and if Vacancies happen by Resignation, or otherwise, during the Recess of the Legislature of any State, the Executive thereof may make temporary Appointments until the next Meeting of the Legislature, which shall then fill such Vacancies.][3]

No Person shall be a Senator who shall not have attained to the Age of thirty Years, and been nine Years a Citizen of the United States, and who shall not, when elected, be an Inhabitant of that State for which he shall be chosen.

The Vice President of the United States shall be President of the Senate, but shall have no Vote, unless they be equally divided.

The Senate shall chuse their other Officers, and also a President pro tempore, in the Absence of the Vice President, or when he shall exercise the Office of President of the United States.

The Senate shall have the sole Power to try all Impeachments. When sitting for that Purpose, they shall be on Oath or Affirmation. When the President of the United States is tried, the Chief Justice shall preside: And no Person shall be convicted without the Concurrence of two thirds of the Members present.

Judgment in Cases of Impeachment shall not extend further than to removal from Office, and disqualification to hold and enjoy any Office of honor, Trust or Profit under the United States: but the Party convicted shall nevertheless be liable and subject to Indictment, Trial, Judgment and Punishment, according to Law.

Section 4. The Times, Places and Manner of holding Elections for Senators and Representatives, shall be prescribed in each State by the Legislature thereof; but the Congress may at any time by Law make or alter such Regulations, except as to the Places of chusing Senators.

The Congress shall assemble at least once in every Year, and such Meeting shall [be on the first Monday in December],[4] unless they shall by Law appoint a different Day.

Section 5. Each House shall be the Judge of the Elections, Returns and Qualifications of its own Members, and a Majority of each shall constitute a Quorum to do Business; but a smaller Number may adjourn from day to day, and may be authorized to compel the Attendance of absent Members, in such Manner, and under such Penalties as each House may provide.

Each House may determine the Rules of its Proceedings, punish its Members for disorderly Behaviour, and, with the Concurrence of two thirds, expel a Member.

Each House shall keep a Journal of its Proceedings, and from time to time publish the same, excepting such Parts as may in their Judgment require Secrecy; and the Yeas and Nays of the Members of either House on any question shall, at the Desire of one fifth of those Present, be entered on the Journal.

Neither House, during the Session of Congress, shall, without the Consent of the other, adjourn for more than three days, nor to any other Place than that in which the two Houses shall be sitting.

Section 6. The Senators and Representatives shall receive a Compensation for their Services, to be ascertained by Law, and paid out of the Treasury of the United States. They shall in all Cases, except Treason, Felony and Breach of the Peace, be privileged from Arrest during their Attendance at the Session of their respective Houses, and in going to and returning from the same; and for any Speech or Debate in either House, they shall not be questioned in any other Place.

No Senator or Representative shall, during the Time for which he was elected, be appointed to any civil Office under the Authority of the United States, which shall have been created, or the Emoluments whereof shall have been encreased during such time; and no Person holding any Office under the United States, shall be a Member of either House during his Continuance in Office.

Section 7. All Bills for raising Revenue shall originate in the House of Representatives; but the Senate may propose or concur with Amendments as on other Bills.

Every Bill which shall have passed the House of Representatives and the Senate, shall, before it become a Law, be presented to the President of the United States; If he approve he shall sign it, but if not he shall return it, with his Objections to that House in which it shall have originated, who shall enter the Objections at large on their Journal, and proceed to reconsider it. If after such Reconsideration two thirds of that House shall agree to pass the Bill, it shall be sent, together with the Objections, to the other House, by which it shall likewise be reconsidered, and if approved by two thirds of that House, it shall become a Law. But in all such Cases the Votes of both Houses shall be determined by yeas and Nays, and the Names of the Persons voting for and against the Bill shall be entered on the Journal of each House respectively. If any Bill shall not be returned by the President within ten Days (Sundays excepted) after it shall have been presented to him, the Same shall be a Law, in like Manner as if he had signed it, unless the Congress by their Adjournment prevent its Return, in which Case it shall not be a Law.

Every Order, Resolution, or Vote to which the Concurrence of the Senate and House of Representatives may be necessary (except on a question of Adjournment) shall be presented to the President of the United States; and before the Same shall take Effect, shall be approved by him, or being disapproved by him, shall be repassed by two thirds of the Senate and House of Representatives, according to the Rules and Limitations prescribed in the Case of a Bill.

Section 8. The Congress shall have Power To lay and collect Taxes, Duties, Imposts and Excises, to pay the Debts and provide for the common Defence and general Welfare of the United States; but all Duties, Imposts and Excises shall be uniform throughout the United States;

To borrow Money on the credit of the United States;

To regulate Commerce with foreign Nations, and among the several States, and with the Indian Tribes;

To establish an uniform Rule of Naturalization, and uniform Laws on the subject of Bankruptcies throughout the United States;

To coin Money, regulate the Value thereof, and of foreign Coin, and fix the Standard of Weights and Measures;

To provide for the Punishment of counterfeiting the Securities and current Coin of the United States;

To establish Post Offices and post Roads;

To promote the Progress of Science and useful Arts, by securing for limited Times to Authors and Inventors the exclusive Right to their respective Writings and Discoveries;

To constitute Tribunals inferior to the supreme Court;

To define and punish Piracies and Felonies committed on the high Seas, and Offences against the Law of Nations;

To declare War, grant Letters of Marque and Reprisal, and make Rules concerning Captures on Land and Water;

To raise and support Armies, but no Appropriation of Money to that Use shall be for a longer Term than two Years;

To provide and maintain a Navy;

To make Rules for the Government and Regulation of the land and naval Forces;

To provide for calling forth the Militia to execute the Laws of the Union, suppress Insurrections and repel Invasions;

To provide for organizing, arming, and disciplining, the Militia, and for governing such Part of them as may be employed in the Service of the United States, reserving to the States respectively, the Ap-

pointment of the Officers, and the Authority of training the Militia according to the discipline prescribed by Congress;

To exercise exclusive Legislation in all Cases whatsoever, over such District (not exceeding ten Miles square) as may, by Cession of particular States, and the Acceptance of Congress, become the Seat of the Government of the United States, and to exercise like Authority over all Places purchased by the Consent of the Legislature of the State in which the Same shall be, for the Erection of Forts, Magazines, Arsenals, dock-Yards, and other needful Buildings;—And

To make all Laws which shall be necessary and proper for carrying into Execution the foregoing Powers, and all other Powers vested by this Constitution in the Government of the United States, or in any Department or Officer thereof.

Section 9. The Migration or Importation of such Persons as any of the States now existing shall think proper to admit, shall not be prohibited by the Congress prior to the Year one thousand eight hundred and eight, but a Tax or duty may be imposed on such Importation, not exceeding ten dollars for each Person.

The Privilege of the Writ of Habeas Corpus shall not be suspended, unless when in Cases of Rebellion or Invasion the public Safety may require it.

No Bill of Attainder or ex post facto Law shall be passed.

No Capitation, or other direct, Tax shall be laid, unless in Proportion to the Census or Enumeration herein before directed to be taken.[5]

No Tax or Duty shall be laid on Articles exported from any State.

No Preference shall be given by any Regulation of Commerce or Revenue to the Ports of one State over those of another; nor shall Vessels bound to, or from, one State, be obliged to enter, clear, or pay Duties in another.

No Money shall be drawn from the Treasury, but in Consequence of Appropriations made by Law; and a regular Statement and Account of the Receipts and Expenditures of all public Money shall be published from time to time.

No Title of Nobility shall be granted by the United States: And no Person holding any Office of Profit or Trust under them, shall, without the Consent of the Congress, accept of any present, Emolument, Office, or Title, of any kind whatever, from any King, Prince, or foreign State.

Section 10. No State shall enter into any Treaty, Alliance, or Confederation; grant Letters of Marque and Reprisal; coin Money; emit Bills of Credit; make any Thing but gold and silver Coin a Tender in Payment of Debts; pass any Bill of Attainder, ex post facto Law, or Law impairing the Obligation of Contracts, or grant any Title of Nobility.

No State shall, without the Consent of the Congress, lay any Imposts or Duties on Imports or Exports, except what may be absolutely necessary for executing it's inspection Laws: and the net Produce of all Duties and Imposts, laid by any State on Imports or Exports, shall be for the Use of the Treasury of the United States; and all such Laws shall be subject to the Revision and Controul of the Congress.

No State shall, without the Consent of Congress, lay any Duty of Tonnage, keep Troops, or Ships of War in time of Peace, enter into any Agreement or Compact with another State, or with a foreign Power, or engage in War, unless actually invaded, or in such imminent Danger as will not admit of delay.

ARTICLE II

Section 1. The executive Power shall be vested in a President of the United States of America. He shall hold his Office during the Term of four Years, and, together with the Vice President, chosen for the same Term, be elected, as follows

Each State shall appoint, in such Manner as the Legislature thereof may direct, a Number of Electors, equal to the whole Number of Senators and Representatives to which the State may be entitled in the Congress: but no Senator or Representative, or Person holding an Office of Trust or Profit under the United States, shall be appointed an Elector.

[The Electors shall meet in their respective States, and vote by Ballot for two Persons, of whom one at least shall not be an Inhabitant of the same State with themselves. And they shall make a List of all the Persons voted for, and of the Number of Votes for each; which List they shall sign and certify, and transmit sealed to the Seat of the Government of the United States, directed to the President of the Senate. The President of the Senate shall, in the Presence of the Senate and House of Representatives, open all the Certificates, and the Votes shall then be counted. The Person having the greatest Number of Votes shall be the President, if such Number be a Majority of the whole Number of Electors appointed; and if there be more than one who have such Majority, and have an equal Number of Votes, then the House of Representatives shall immediately chuse by Ballot one of them for President; and if no Person have a Majority, then from the five highest on the list the said House shall in like Manner chuse the President. But in chusing the President, the Votes shall be taken by States, the Representation from each State having one Vote; A quorum for this Purpose shall consist of a Member or Members from two thirds of the States, and a Majority of all the States shall be necessary to a Choice. In every Case, after the Choice of the President, the Person having the greatest Number of Votes of the Electors shall be the Vice President. But if there should remain two or more who have equal Votes, the Senate shall chuse from them by Ballot the Vice President.][6]

The Congress may determine the Time of chusing the Electors, and the Day on which they shall give their Votes; which Day shall be the same throughout the United States.

No Person except a natural born Citizen, or a Citizen of the United States, at the time of the Adoption of this Constitution, shall be eligible to the Office of President; neither shall any Person be eligible to that Office who shall not have attained to the Age of thirty five Years, and been fourteen Years a Resident within the United States.

In Case of the Removal of the President from Office, or of his Death, Resignation, or Inability to discharge the Powers and Duties of the said Office,[7] the Same shall devolve on the Vice President, and the Congress may by Law provide for the Case of Removal, Death, Resignation or Inability, both of the President and Vice President, declaring what Officer shall then act as President, and such Officer shall act accordingly, until the Disability be removed, or a President shall be elected.

The President shall, at stated Times, receive for his Services, a Compensation, which shall neither be encreased nor diminished during the Period for which he shall have been elected, and he shall not receive within that Period any other Emolument from the United States, or any of them.

Before he enter on the Execution of his Office, he shall take the following Oath or Affirmation:—"I do solemnly swear (or affirm) that I will faithfully execute the Office of President of the United States, and will to the best of my Ability, preserve, protect and defend the Constitution of the United States."

Section 2. The President shall be Commander in Chief of the Army and Navy of the United States, and of the Militia of the several States, when called into the actual Service of the United States; he may require the Opinion, in writing, of the principal Officer in each of the executive Departments, upon any Subject relating to the Duties of their respective Offices, and he shall have Power to grant Reprieves and Pardons for Offences against the United States, except in Cases of Impeachment.

He shall have Power, by and with the Advice and Consent of the Senate, to make Treaties, provided two thirds of the Senators present concur; and he shall nominate, and by and with the Advice and Consent of the Senate, shall appoint Ambassadors, other public Ministers and Consuls, Judges of the supreme Court, and all other Officers of the United States, whose Appointments are not herein otherwise provided for, and which shall be established by Law: but the Congress may by Law vest the Appointment of such inferior Officers, as they think proper, in the President alone, in the Courts of Law, or in the Heads of Departments.

The President shall have Power to fill up all Vacancies that may happen during the Recess of the Senate, by granting Commissions which shall expire at the End of their next Session.

Section 3. He shall from time to time give to the Congress Information of the State of the Union, and recommend to their Consideration such Measures as he shall judge necessary and expedient; he may, on extraordinary Occasions, convene both Houses, or either of them, and in Case of Disagreement between them, with Respect to the Time of Adjournment, he may adjourn them to such Time as he shall think proper; he shall receive Ambassadors and other public Ministers; he shall take Care that the Laws be faithfully executed, and shall Commission all the Officers of the United States.

Section 4. The President, Vice President and all civil Officers of the United States, shall be removed from Office on Impeachment for, and Conviction of, Treason, Bribery, or other high Crimes and Misdemeanors.

ARTICLE III

Section 1. The judicial Power of the United States, shall be vested in one supreme Court, and in such inferior Courts as the Congress may from time to time ordain and establish. The Judges, both of the supreme and inferior Courts, shall hold their Offices during good Behaviour, and shall, at stated Times, receive for their Services, a Compensation, which shall not be diminished during their Continuance in Office.

Section 2. The judicial Power shall extend to all Cases, in Law and Equity, arising under this Constitution, the Laws of the United States, and Treaties made, or which shall be made, under their Authority; —to all Cases affecting Ambassadors, other public Ministers and Consuls; —to all Cases of admiralty and maritime Jurisdiction; —to Controversies to which the United States shall be a Party; —to Controversies between two or more States; —between a State and Citizens of another State;[8] —between Citizens of different States; —between Citizens of the same State claiming Lands under Grants of different States, and between a State, or the Citizens thereof, and foreign States, Citizens or Subjects.[8]

In all Cases affecting Ambassadors, other public Ministers and Consuls, and those in which a State shall be Party, the supreme Court shall have original Jurisdiction. In all the other Cases before mentioned, the supreme Court shall have appellate Jurisdiction, both as to Law and Fact, with such Exceptions, and under such Regulations as the Congress shall make.

The Trial of all Crimes, except in Cases of Impeachment, shall be by Jury; and such Trial shall be held in the State where the said Crimes shall have been committed; but when not committed within any State, the Trial shall be at such Place or Places as the Congress may by Law have directed.

Section 3. Treason against the United States, shall consist only in levying War against them, or in adhering to their Enemies, giving them Aid and Comfort. No Person shall be convicted of Treason unless on the Testimony of two Witnesses to the same overt Act, or on Confession in open Court.

The Congress shall have Power to declare the Punishment of Treason, but no Attainder of Treason shall work Corruption of Blood, or Forfeiture except during the Life of the Person attainted.

ARTICLE IV

Section 1. Full Faith and Credit shall be given in each State to the public Acts, Records, and judicial Proceedings of every other State. And the Congress may by general Laws prescribe the Manner in which such Acts, Records and Proceedings shall be proved, and the Effect thereof.

Section 2. The Citizens of each State shall be entitled to all Privileges and Immunities of Citizens in the several States.

A Person charged in any State with Treason, Felony, or other Crime, who shall flee from Justice, and be found in another State, shall on Demand of the executive Authority of the State from which he fled, be delivered up, to be removed to the State having Jurisdiction of the Crime.

[No Person held to Service or Labour in one State, under the Laws thereof, escaping into another, shall, in Consequence of any Law or Regulation therein, be discharged from such Service or Labour, but shall be delivered up on Claim of the Party to whom such Service or Labour may be due.]⁹

Section 3. New States may be admitted by the Congress into this Union; but no new State shall be formed or erected within the Jurisdiction of any other State; nor any State be formed by the Junction of two or more States, or Parts of States, without the Consent of the Legislatures of the States concerned as well as of the Congress.

The Congress shall have Power to dispose of and make all needful Rules and Regulations respecting the Territory or other Property belonging to the United States; and nothing in this Constitution shall be so construed as to Prejudice any Claims of the United States, or of any particular State.

Section 4. The United States shall guarantee to every State in this Union a Republican Form of Government, and shall protect each of them against Invasion; and on Application of the Legislature, or of the Executive (when the Legislature cannot be convened) against domestic Violence.

ARTICLE V

The Congress, whenever two thirds of both Houses shall deem it necessary, shall propose Amendments to this Constitution, or, on the Application of the Legislatures of two thirds of the several States, shall call a Convention for proposing Amendments, which, in either Case, shall be valid to all Intents and Purposes, as Part of this Constitution, when ratified by the Legislatures of three fourths of the several States, or by Conventions in three fourths thereof, as the one or the other Mode of Ratification may be proposed by the Congress; Provided [that no Amendment which may be made prior to the Year One thousand eight hundred and eight shall in any Manner affect the first and fourth Clauses in the Ninth Section of the first Article; and]¹⁰ that no State, without its Consent, shall be deprived of its equal Suffrage in the Senate.

ARTICLE VI

All Debts contracted and Engagements entered into, before the Adoption of this Constitution, shall be as valid against the United States under this Constitution, as under the Confederation.

This Constitution, and the Laws of the United States which shall be made in Pursuance thereof; and all Treaties made, or which shall be made, under the Authority of the United States, shall be the supreme Law of the Land; and the Judges in every State shall be bound thereby, any Thing in the Constitution or Laws of any State to the Contrary notwithstanding.

The Senators and Representatives before mentioned, and the Members of the several State Legislatures, and all executive and judicial Officers, both of the United States and of the several States, shall be bound by Oath or Affirmation, to support this Constitution; but no religious Test shall ever be required as a Qualification to any Office or public Trust under the United States.

ARTICLE VII

The Ratification of the Conventions of nine States, shall be sufficient for the Establishment of this Constitution between the States so ratifying the Same.

Done in Convention by the Unanimous Consent of the States present the Seventeenth Day of September in the Year of our Lord one thousand seven hundred and Eighty seven and of the Independence of the United States of America the Twelfth. IN WITNESS whereof We have hereunto subscribed our Names,

George Washington,
President and deputy from Virginia.

New Hampshire:
John Langdon,
Nicholas Gilman.

Massachusetts:
Nathaniel Gorham,
Rufus King.

Connecticut:
William Samuel Johnson,
Roger Sherman.

New York:
Alexander Hamilton.

New Jersey:
William Livingston,
David Brearley,
William Paterson,
Jonathan Dayton.

Pennsylvania:
Benjamin Franklin,
Thomas Mifflin,
Robert Morris,
George Clymer,
Thomas FitzSimons,
Jared Ingersoll,
James Wilson,
Gouverneur Morris.

Delaware:
George Read,
Gunning Bedford Jr.,
John Dickinson,
Richard Bassett,
Jacob Broom.

Maryland:
James McHenry,
Daniel of St. Thomas Jenifer,
Daniel Carroll.

Virginia:
John Blair,
James Madison Jr.

North Carolina:.
William Blount,
Richard Dobbs Spaight,
Hugh Williamson.

South Carolina:
John Rutledge,
Charles Cotesworth Pinckney,
Charles Pinckney,
Pierce Butler.

Georgia:
William Few,
Abraham Baldwin.

[The language of the original Constitution, not including the Amendments, was adopted by a convention of the states on September 17, 1787, and was subsequently ratified by the states on the following dates: Delaware, December 7, 1787; Pennsylvania, December 12, 1787; New Jersey, December 18, 1787; Georgia, January 2, 1788; Connecticut, January 9, 1788; Massachusetts, February 6, 1788; Maryland, April 28, 1788; South Carolina, May 23, 1788; New Hampshire, June 21, 1788.

Ratification was completed on June 21, 1788.

The Constitution subsequently was ratified by Virginia, June 25, 1788; New York, July 26, 1788; North Carolina, November 21, 1789; Rhode Island, May 29, 1790; and Vermont, January 10, 1791.]

AMENDMENTS

AMENDMENT I

(First ten amendments ratified December 15, 1791.)

Congress shall make no law respecting an establishment of religion, or prohibiting the free exercise thereof; or abridging the freedom of speech, or of the press; or the right of the people peaceably to assemble, and to petition the Government for a redress of grievances.

AMENDMENT II

A well regulated Militia, being necessary to the security of a free State, the right of the people to keep and bear Arms, shall not be infringed.

AMENDMENT III

No Soldier shall, in time of peace be quartered in any house, without the consent of the Owner, nor in time of war, but in a manner to be prescribed by law.

AMENDMENT IV

The right of the people to be secure in their persons, houses, papers, and effects, against unreasonable searches and seizures, shall not be violated, and no Warrants shall issue, but upon probable cause, supported by Oath or affirmation, and particularly describing the place to be searched, and the persons or things to be seized.

AMENDMENT V

No person shall be held to answer for a capital, or otherwise infamous crime, unless on a presentment or indictment of a Grand Jury, except in cases arising in the land or naval forces, or in the Militia, when in actual service in time of War or public danger; nor shall any person be subject for the same offence to be twice put in jeopardy of life or limb; nor shall be compelled in any criminal case to be a witness against himself, nor be deprived of life, liberty, or property, without due process of law; nor shall private property be taken for public use, without just compensation.

AMENDMENT VI

In all criminal prosecutions, the accused shall enjoy the right to a speedy and public trial, by an impartial jury of the State and district wherein the crime shall have been committed, which district shall have been previously ascertained by law, and to be informed of the nature and cause of the accusation; to be confronted with the witnesses against him; to have compulsory process for obtaining witnesses in his favor, and to have the Assistance of Counsel for his defence.

AMENDMENT VII

In Suits at common law, where the value in controversy shall exceed twenty dollars, the right of trial by jury shall be preserved, and no fact tried by a jury, shall be otherwise re-examined in any Court of the United States, than according to the rules of the common law.

AMENDMENT VIII

Excessive bail shall not be required, nor excessive fines imposed, nor cruel and unusual punishments inflicted.

AMENDMENT IX

The enumeration in the Constitution, of certain rights, shall not be construed to deny or disparage others retained by the people.

AMENDMENT X

The powers not delegated to the United States by the Constitution, nor prohibited by it to the States, are reserved to the States respectively, or to the people.

AMENDMENT XI *(Ratified February 7, 1795)*

The Judicial power of the United States shall not be construed to extend to any suit in law or equity, commenced or prosecuted against one of the United States by Citizens of another State, or by Citizens or Subjects of any Foreign State.

AMENDMENT XII *(Ratified June 15, 1804)*

The Electors shall meet in their respective states and vote by ballot for President and Vice-President, one of whom, at least, shall not be an inhabitant of the same state with themselves; they shall name in their ballots the person voted for as President, and in distinct ballots the person voted for as Vice-President, and they shall make distinct lists of all persons voted for as President, and of all persons voted for as Vice-President, and of the number of votes for each, which lists they shall sign and certify, and transmit sealed to the seat of the government of the United States, directed to the President of the Senate; — The President of the Senate shall, in the presence of the Senate and House of Representatives, open all the certificates and the votes shall then be counted; — The person having the greatest number of votes for President, shall be the President, if such number be a majority of the whole number of Electors appointed; and if no person have such majority, then from the persons having the highest numbers not exceeding three on the list of those voted for as President, the House of Representatives shall choose immediately, by ballot, the President. But in choosing the President, the votes shall be taken by states, the representation from each state having one vote; a quorum for this purpose shall consist of a member or members from two-thirds of the states, and a majority of all the states shall be necessary to a choice. [And if the House of Representatives shall not choose a President whenever the right of choice shall devolve upon them, before the fourth day of March next following, then the Vice-President shall act as President, as in the case of the death or other constitutional disability of the President. —][11] The person having the greatest number of votes as Vice-President, shall be the Vice-President, if such number be a majority of the whole number of Electors appointed, and if no person have a majority, then from the two highest numbers on the list, the Senate shall choose the Vice-President; a quorum for the purpose shall consist of two-thirds of the whole number of Senators, and a majority of the whole number shall be necessary to a choice. But no person constitutionally ineligible to the office of President shall be eligible to that of Vice-President of the United States.

AMENDMENT XIII *(Ratified December 6, 1865)*

Section 1. Neither slavery nor involuntary servitude, except as a punishment for crime whereof the party shall have been duly convicted, shall exist within the United States, or any place subject to their jurisdiction.

Section 2. Congress shall have power to enforce this article by appropriate legislation.

AMENDMENT XIV *(Ratified July 9, 1868)*

Section 1. All persons born or naturalized in the United States, and subject to the jurisdiction thereof, are citizens of the United States and of the State wherein they reside. No State shall make or enforce any law which shall abridge the privileges or immunities of citizens of the United States; nor shall any State deprive any person of life, liberty, or property, without due process of law; nor deny to any person within its jurisdiction the equal protection of the laws.

Section 2. Representatives shall be apportioned among the several States according to their respective numbers, counting the whole number of persons in each State, excluding Indians not taxed. But when the right to vote at any election for the choice of electors for President and Vice President of the United States, Representatives in Congress, the Executive and Judicial officers of a State, or the members of the Legislature thereof, is denied to any of the male inhabitants of such State, being twenty-one years of age,[12] and citizens of the United States, or in any way abridged, except for participation in rebellion, or other crime, the basis of representation therein shall be reduced in the proportion which the number of such male citizens shall bear to the whole number of male citizens twenty-one years of age in such State.

Section 3. No person shall be a Senator or Representative in Congress, or elector of President and Vice President, or hold any office, civil or military, under the United States, or under any State, who, having previously taken an oath, as a member of Congress, or as an officer of the United States, or as a member of any State legislature, or as an executive or judicial officer of any State, to support the Constitution of the United States, shall have engaged in insurrection or rebellion against the same, or given aid or comfort to the enemies thereof. But Congress may by a vote of two-thirds of each House, remove such disability.

Section 4. The validity of the public debt of the United States, authorized by law, including debts incurred for payment of pensions and bounties for services in suppressing insurrection or rebellion, shall not be questioned. But neither the United States nor any State shall assume or pay any debt or obligation incurred in aid of insurrection or rebellion against the United States, or any claim for the loss or emancipation of any slave; but all such debts, obligations and claims shall be held illegal and void.

Section 5. The Congress shall have power to enforce, by appropriate legislation, the provisions of this article.

AMENDMENT XV *(Ratified February 3, 1870)*

Section 1. The right of citizens of the United States to vote shall not be denied or abridged by the United States or by any State on account of race, color, or previous condition of servitude.

Section 2. The Congress shall have power to enforce this article by appropriate legislation.

AMENDMENT XVI *(Ratified February 3, 1913)*

The Congress shall have power to lay and collect taxes on incomes, from whatever source derived, without apportionment among the several States, and without regard to any census or enumeration.

AMENDMENT XVII *(Ratified April 8, 1913)*

The Senate of the United States shall be composed of two Senators from each State, elected by the people thereof, for six years; and each Senator shall have one vote. The electors in each State shall have the qualifications requisite for electors of the most numerous branch of the State legislatures.

When vacancies happen in the representation of any State in the Senate, the executive authority of such State shall issue writs of election to fill such vacancies: *Provided,* That the legislature of any State may empower the executive thereof to make temporary appointments until the people fill the vacancies by election as the legislature may direct.

This amendment shall not be so construed as to affect the election or term of any Senator chosen before it becomes valid as part of the Constitution.

AMENDMENT XVIII *(Ratified January 16, 1919)*

Section 1. After one year from the ratification of this article the manufacture, sale, or transportation of intoxicating liquors within, the importation thereof into, or the exportation thereof from the United States and all territory subject to the jurisdiction thereof for beverage purposes is hereby prohibited.

Section 2. The Congress and the several States shall have concurrent power to enforce this article by appropriate legislation.

Section 3. This article shall be inoperative unless it shall have been ratified as an amendment to the Constitution by the legislatures of

the several States, as provided in the Constitution, within seven years from the date of the submission hereof to the States by the Congress.][13]

AMENDMENT XIX *(Ratified August 18, 1920)*

The right of citizens of the United States to vote shall not be denied or abridged by the United States or by any State on account of sex.

Congress shall have power to enforce this article by appropriate legislation.

AMENDMENT XX *(Ratified January 23, 1933)*

Section 1. The terms of the President and Vice President shall end at noon on the 20th day of January, and the terms of Senators and Representatives at noon on the 3d day of January, of the years in which such terms would have ended if this article had not been ratified; and the terms of their successors shall then begin.

Section 2. The Congress shall assemble at least once in every year, and such meeting shall begin at noon on the 3d day of January, unless they shall by law appoint a different day.

Section 3.[14] If, at the time fixed for the beginning of the term of the President, the President elect shall have died, the Vice President elect shall become President. If a President shall not have been chosen before the time fixed for the beginning of his term, or if the President elect shall have failed to qualify, then the Vice President elect shall act as President until a President shall have qualified; and the Congress may by law provide for the case wherein neither a President elect nor a Vice President elect shall have qualified, declaring who shall then act as President, or the manner in which one who is to act shall be selected, and such person shall act accordingly until a President or Vice President shall have qualified.

Section 4. The Congress may by law provide for the case of the death of any of the persons from whom the House of Representatives may choose a President whenever the right of choice shall have devolved upon them, and for the case of the death of any of the persons from whom the Senate may choose a Vice President whenever the right of choice shall have devolved upon them.

Section 5. Sections 1 and 2 shall take effect on the 15th day of October following the ratification of this article.

Section 6. This article shall be inoperative unless it shall have been ratified as an amendment to the Constitution by the legislatures of three-fourths of the several States within seven years from the date of its submission.

AMENDMENT XXI *(Ratified December 5, 1933)*

Section 1. The eighteenth article of amendment to the Constitution of the United States is hereby repealed.

Section 2. The transportation or importation into any State, Territory, or possession of the United States for delivery or use therein of intoxicating liquors, in violation of the laws thereof, is hereby prohibited.

Section 3. This article shall be inoperative unless it shall have been ratified as an amendment to the Constitution by conventions in the several States, as provided in the Constitution, within seven years from the date of the submission hereof to the States by the Congress.

AMENDMENT XXII *(Ratified February 27, 1951)*

Section 1. No person shall be elected to the office of the President more than twice, and no person who has held the office of President, or acted as President, for more than two years of a term to which some other person was elected President shall be elected to the office of the President more than once. But this Article shall not apply to any person holding the office of President when this Article was proposed by the Congress, and shall not prevent any person who may be holding the office of President, or acting as President, during the term within which this Article becomes operative from holding the office of President or acting as President during the remainder of such term.

Section 2. This article shall be inoperative unless it shall have been ratified as an amendment to the Constitution by the legislatures of three-fourths of the several States within seven years from the date of its submission to the States by the Congress.

AMENDMENT XXIII *(Ratified March 29, 1961)*

Section 1. The District constituting the seat of Government of the United States shall appoint in such manner as the Congress may direct:

A number of electors of President and Vice President equal to the whole number of Senators and Representatives in Congress to which the District would be entitled if it were a State, but in no event more than the least populous State; they shall be in addition to those appointed by the States, but they shall be considered, for the purposes of the election of President and Vice President, to be electors appointed by a State; and they shall meet in the District and perform such duties as provided by the twelfth article of amendment.

Section 2. The Congress shall have power to enforce this article by appropriate legislation.

AMENDMENT XXIV *(Ratified January 23, 1964)*

Section 1. The right of citizens of the United States to vote in any primary or other election for President or Vice President, for electors for President or Vice President, or for Senator or Representative in Congress, shall not be denied or abridged by the United States or any State by reason of failure to pay any poll tax or other tax.

Section 2. The Congress shall have power to enforce this article by appropriate legislation.

AMENDMENT XXV *(Ratified February 10, 1967)*

Section 1. In case of the removal of the President from office or of his death or resignation, the Vice President shall become President.

Section 2. Whenever there is a vacancy in the office of the Vice President, the President shall nominate a Vice President who shall take office upon confirmation by a majority vote of both Houses of Congress.

Section 3. Whenever the President transmits to the President pro tempore of the Senate and the Speaker of the House of Representatives his written declaration that he is unable to discharge the powers and duties of his office, and until he transmits to them a written declaration to the contrary, such powers and duties shall be discharged by the Vice President as Acting President.

Section 4. Whenever the Vice President and a majority of either the principal officers of the executive departments or of such other body as Congress may by law provide, transmit to the President pro tempore of the Senate and the Speaker of the House of Representatives their written declaration that the President is unable to discharge the powers and duties of his office, the Vice President shall

immediately assume the powers and duties of the office as Acting President.

Thereafter, when the President transmits to the President pro tempore of the Senate and the Speaker of the House of Representatives his written declaration that no inability exists, he shall resume the powers and duties of his office unless the Vice President and a majority of either the principal officers of the executive departments or of such other body as Congress may by law provide, transmit within four days to the President pro tempore of the Senate and the Speaker of the House of Representatives their written declaration that the President is unable to discharge the powers and duties of his office. Thereupon Congress shall decide the issue, assembling within forty-eight hours for that purpose if not in session. If the Congress, within twenty-one days after receipt of the latter written declaration, or, if Congress is not in session, within twenty-one days after Congress is required to assemble, determines by two-thirds vote of both Houses that the President is unable to discharge the powers and duties of his office, the Vice President shall continue to discharge the same as Acting President; otherwise, the President shall resume the powers and duties of his office.

AMENDMENT XXVI *(Ratified July 1, 1971)*

Section 1. The right of citizens of the United States, who are eighteen years of age or older, to vote shall not be denied or abridged by the United States or by any State on account of age.

Section 2. The Congress shall have power to enforce this article by appropriate legislation.

AMENDMENT XXVII *(Ratified May 7, 1992)*

No law varying the compensation for the services of the Senators and Representatives shall take effect, until an election of Representatives shall have intervened.

SOURCE: U.S. Congress, House, Committee on the Judiciary, *The Constitution of the United States of America, as Amended,* 100th Cong., 1st sess., 1987, H Doc 100–94.

NOTES: 1. The part in brackets was changed by section 2 of the Fourteenth Amendment.

2. The part in brackets was changed by the first paragraph of the Seventeenth Amendment.

3. The part in brackets was changed by the second paragraph of the Seventeenth Amendment.

4. The part in brackets was changed by section 2 of the Twentieth Amendment.

5. The Sixteenth Amendment gave Congress the power to tax incomes.

6. The material in brackets was superseded by the Twelfth Amendment.

7. This provision was affected by the Twenty-fifth Amendment.

8. These clauses were affected by the Eleventh Amendment.

9. This paragraph was superseded by the Thirteenth Amendment.

10. Obsolete.

11. The part in brackets was superseded by section 3 of the Twentieth Amendment.

12. See the Nineteenth and Twenty-sixth Amendments.

13. This amendment was repealed by section 1 of the Twenty-first Amendment.

14. See the Twenty-fifth Amendment.

Acts of Congress Held Unconstitutional

1. ACT OF SEPTEMBER 24, 1789 (1 STAT. 81, § 13, IN PART).

Provision that ". . . [the Supreme Court] shall have power to issue . . . writs of mandamus, in cases warranted by the principles and usages of law, to any . . . persons holding office, under authority of the United States" as applied to the issue of mandamus to the Secretary of State requiring him to deliver to plaintiff a commission (duly signed by the President) as justice of the peace in the District of Columbia *held* an attempt to enlarge the original jurisdiction of the Supreme Court, fixed by Article III, § 2.

Marbury v. Madison, 1 Cr. (5 U.S.) 137 (1803).

2. ACT OF FEBRUARY 20, 1812 (2 STAT. 677).

Provisions establishing board of revision to annul titles conferred many years previously by governors of the Northwest Territory were *held* violative of the due process clause of the Fifth Amendment.

Reichart v. Felps, 6 Wall. (73 U.S.) 160 (1868).

3. ACT OF MARCH 6, 1820 (3 STAT. 548, § 8, PROVISO).

The Missouri Compromise, prohibiting slavery within the Louisiana Territory north of 36° 30', except Missouri, *held* not warranted as a regulation of Territory belonging to the United States under Article IV, § 3, clause 2 (and *see* Fifth Amendment).

Scott v. Sandford, 19 How. (60 U.S.) 393 (1857).

4. ACT OF FEBRUARY 25, 1862 (12 STAT. 345, § 1); JULY 11, 1862 (12 STAT. 532, § 1); MARCH 3, 1863 (12 STAT. 711, § 3), EACH IN PART ONLY.

"Legal tender clauses," making noninterest-bearing United States notes legal tender in payment of "all debts, public and private," so far as applied to debts contracted before passage of the act, *held* not within express or implied powers of Congress under Article I, § 8, and inconsistent with Article I, § 10, and Fifth Amendment.

Hepburn v. Griswold, 8 Wall. (75 U.S.) 603 (1870); overruled in *Knox v. Lee (Legal Tender Cases),* 12 Wall. (79 U.S.) 457 (1871).

5. ACT OF MAY 20, 1862 (§ 35, 12 STAT.); ACT OF MAY 21, 1862 (12 STAT. 407); ACT OF JUNE 25, 1864 (13 STAT. 187); ACT OF JULY 23, 1866 (14 STAT. 216); REVISED STATUTES RELATING TO THE DISTRICT OF COLUMBIA, ACT OF JUNE 22, 1874 (§§ 281, 282, 294, 304, 18 STAT. PT. 2).

Provisions of law requiring, or construed to require, racial separation in the schools of the District of Columbia, *held* to violate the equal protection component of the due process clause of the Fifth Amendment.

Bolling v. Sharpe, 347 U.S. 497 (1954).

6. ACT OF MARCH 3, 1863 (12 STAT. 756, § 5).

"So much of the fifth section . . . as provides for the removal of a judgment in a State court, and in which the cause was tried by a jury to the circuit court of the United States for a retrial on the facts and law, is not in pursuance of the Constitution, and is void" under the Seventh Amendment.

The Justices v. Murray, 9 Wall. (76 U.S.) 274 (1870).

7. ACT OF MARCH 3, 1863 (12 STAT. 766, § 5).

Provision for an appeal from the Court of Claims to the Supreme Court—there being, at the time, a further provision (§ 14) requiring an estimate by the Secretary of the Treasury before payment of final judgment, *held* to contravene the judicial finality intended by the Constitution, Article III.

Gordon v. United States, 2 Wall. (69 U.S.) 561 (1865). (Case was dismissed without opinion; the grounds upon which this decision was made were stated in a posthumous opinion by Chief Justice Taney printed in the appendix to volume 117 U.S. 697.)

8. ACT OF JUNE 30, 1864 (13 STAT. 311, § 13).

Provision that "any prize cause now pending in any circuit court shall, on the application of all parties in interest . . . be transferred by that court to the Supreme Court. . . ," as applied in a case where no action had been taken in the Circuit Court on the appeal from the district court, *held* to propose an appeal procedure not within Article III, § 2.

The Alicia, 7 Wall. (74 U.S.) 571 (1869).

9. ACT OF JANUARY 24, 1865 (13 STAT. 424).

Requirement of a test oath (disavowing actions in hostility to the United States) before admission to appear as attorney in a federal court by virtue of any previous admission, *held* invalid as applied to an attorney who had been pardoned by the President for all offenses during the Rebellion—as *ex post facto* (Article I, § 9, clause 3) and an interference with the pardoning power (Article II, § 2, clause 1).

Ex parte Garland, 4 Wall. (71 U.S.) 333 (1867).

10. ACT OF MARCH 2, 1867 (14 STAT. 484, § 29).

General prohibition on sale of naphtha, etc., for illuminating purposes, if inflammable at less temperature than 110 F., *held* invalid "except so far as the section named operates within the United States, but without the limits of any State," as being a mere police regulation.

United States v. Dewitt, 9 Wall. (76 U.S.) 41 (1870).

11. REVISED STATUTES 5132, SUBDIVISION 9 (ACT OF MARCH 2, 1867, 14 STAT. 539).

Provision penalizing "any person respecting whom bankruptcy proceedings are commenced . . . who, within 3 months before the commencement of proceedings in bankruptcy, under the false color and pretense of carrying on business and dealing in the ordinary course of trade, obtains on credit from any person any goods or chattels with intent to defraud. . . ," *held* a police regulation not within the bankruptcy power (Article I, § 4, clause 4).

United States v. Fox, 95 U.S. 670 (1878).

12. ACT OF MAY 31, 1870 (16 STAT. 140, §§ 3, 4).

Provisions penalizing (1) refusal of local election official to permit voting by persons offering to qualify under State laws, applicable to any citizens; and (2) hindering of any person from qualifying or voting, *held* invalid under Fifteenth Amendment.

United States v. Reese, 92 U.S. 214 (1876).

13. REVISED STATUTES 5507 (ACT OF MAY 31, 1870, 16 STAT. 141, § 4).

Provision penalizing "every person who prevents, hinders, controls, or intimidates another from exercising . . . the right of suffrage, to whom that right is guaranteed by the Fifteenth Amendment to the Constitution of the United States, by means of bribery. . . ," *held* not authorized by the Fifteenth Amendment.

James v. Bowman, 190 U.S. 127 (1903).

14. REVISED STATUTES 1977 (ACT OF MAY 31, 1870, 16 STAT. 144).

Provision that "all persons within the jurisdiction of the United States shall have the same right in every State and Territory to make and enforce contracts . . . as is enjoyed by white citizens. . . ," *held* invalid under the Thirteenth Amendment.

Hodges v. United States, 203 U.S. 1 (1906), overruled in *Jones v. Alfred H. Mayer Co.,* 392 U.S. 409, 441-443 (1968).

15. REVISED STATUTES OF THE DISTRICT OF COLUMBIA, § 1064 (ACT OF JUNE 17, 1870, 16 STAT. 154 § 3).

Provision that "prosecutions in the police court [of the District of Columbia] shall be by information under oath, without indictment by grand jury or trial by petit jury," as applied to punishment for conspiracy *held* to contravene Article III, § 2, requiring jury trial of all crimes.

Callan v. Wilson, 127 U.S. 540 (1888).

16. REVISED STATUTES 4937–4947 (ACT OF JULY 8, 1870, 16 STAT. 210), AND ACT OF AUGUST 14, 1876 (19 STAT. 141).

Original trademark law, applying to marks "for exclusive use within the United States," and a penal act designed solely for the protection of rights defined in the earlier measure, *held* not supportable by Article I, § 8, clause 8 (copyright clause), nor Article I, § 8, clause 3, by reason of its application to intrastate as well as interstate commerce.

Trade-Mark Cases, 100 U.S. 82 (1879).

17. ACT OF JULY 12, 1870 (16 STAT. 235).

Provision making Presidential pardons inadmissible in evidence in Court of Claims, prohibiting their use by that court in deciding claims or appeals, and requiring dismissal of appeals by the Supreme Court in cases where proof of loyalty had been made otherwise than as prescribed by law, *held* an interference with judicial power under Article III, § 1, and with the pardoning power under Article II, § 2, clause 1.

United States v. Klein, 13 Wall. (80 U.S.) 128 (1872).

18. REVISED STATUTES 5519 (ACT OF APRIL 20, 1871, 17 STAT. 13, § 2).

Section providing punishment in case "two or more persons in any State . . . conspire . . . for the purpose of depriving . . . any person . . . of the equal protection of the laws . . . or for the purpose of preventing or hindering the constituted authorities of any State . . . from giving or securing to all persons within such State . . . the equal protection of the laws. . . ," *held* invalid as not being directed at state action proscribed by the Fourteenth Amendment.

United States v. Harris, 106 U.S. 629 (1883).

In *Baldwin v. Franks,* 120 U.S. 678 (1887), an attempt was made to distinguish the *Harris* case and to apply the statute to a conspiracy directed at aliens within a State, but the provision was *held* not enforceable in such limited manner.

19. ACT OF MARCH 3, 1873 (CH. 258 § 2, 17 STAT. 599, RECODIFIED IN 39 U.S.C. § 3001(e)(2)).

Comstock Act provision barring from the mails any unsolicited advertisement for contraceptives, as applied to circulars and flyers promoting prophylactics or containing information discussing the desirability and availability of prophylactics, violates the free speech clause of the First Amendment.

Bolger v. Youngs Drug Products Corp., 463 U.S. 60 (1983).

20. ACT OF JUNE 22, 1874 (18 STAT. 1878, § 4).

Provision authorizing federal courts, in suits for forfeitures under revenue and custom laws, to require production of documents, with allegations expected to be proved therein to be taken as proved on failure to produce such documents, was *held* violative of the search and seizure provision of the Fourth Amendment and the self-incrimination clause of the Fifth Amendment.

Boyd v. United States, 116 U.S. 616 (1886).

21. ACT OF MARCH 1, 1875 (18 STAT. 336, §§ 1, 2).

Provision "That all persons within the jurisdiction of the United States shall be entitled to the full and equal enjoyment of the accommodations . . . of inns, public conveyances on land or water, theaters, and other places of public amusement; subject only to the conditions and limitations established by law, and applicable alike to citizens of every race and color, regardless of any previous condition of servitude"—subject to penalty, *held* not to be supported by the Thirteenth or Fourteenth Amendments.

Civil Rights Cases, 109 U.S. 3 (1883), as to operation within States.

22. ACT OF MARCH 3, 1875 (18 STAT. 479, § 2).

Provision that "if the party [i.e., a person stealing property from the United States] has been convicted, then the judgment against him shall be conclusive evidence in the prosecution against [the] receiver that the property of the United States therein described has been embezzled, stolen, or purloined," *held* to contravene the Sixth Amendment.

Kirby v. United States, 174 U.S. 47 (1899).

23. ACT OF JULY 12, 1876 (19 STAT. 80, § 6, IN PART).

Provision that "postmasters of the first, second, and third classes . . . may be removed by the President by and with the advice and consent of the Senate," *held* to infringe the executive power under Article II, § 1, clause 1.

Myers v. United States, 272 U.S. 52 (1926).

24. ACT OF AUGUST 11, 1888 (25 STAT. 411).

Clause, in a provision for the purchase or condemnation of a certain lock and dam in the Monongahela River, that ". . . in estimating the sum to be paid by the United States, the franchise of said corporation to collect tolls shall not be considered or estimated. . . ," *held* to contravene the Fifth Amendment.

Monongahela Navigation Co. v. United States, 148 U.S. 312 (1893).

25. ACT OF MAY 5, 1892 (27 STAT. 25, § 4).

Provision of a Chinese exclusion act, that Chinese persons "convicted and adjudged to be not lawfully entitled to be or remain in the United States shall be imprisoned at hard labor for a period not exceeding 1 year and thereafter removed from the United States . . . (such conviction and judgment being had before a justice, judge, or commissioner upon a summary hearing)," *held* to contravene the Fifth and Sixth Amendments.

Wong Wing v. United States, 163 U.S. 228 (1896).

26. JOINT RESOLUTION OF AUGUST 4, 1894 (28 STAT. 1018, NO. 41).

Provision authorizing the Secretary of the Interior to approve a second lease of certain land by an Indian chief in Minnesota (granted to lessor's ancestor by art. 9 of a treaty with the Chippewa Indians), *held* an interference with judicial interpretation of treaties under Article III, § 2, clause 1 (and repugnant to the Fifth Amendment).

Jones v. Meehan, 175 U.S. 1 (1899).

27. ACT OF AUGUST 27, 1894 (28 STAT. 553–560, §§ 27–37).

Income tax provisions of the tariff act of 1894. "The tax imposed by §§ 27 and 37, inclusive . . . so far as it falls on the income of real estate and of personal property, being a direct tax within the meaning of the Constitution, and, therefore, unconstitutional and void because not apportioned according to representation [Article I, § 2, clause 3], all those sections, constituting one entire scheme of taxation, are necessarily invalid" (158 U.S. 601, 637).

Pollock v. Farmers' Loan & Trust Co., 157 U.S. 429 (1895), and rehearing, 158 U.S. 601 (1895).

28. ACT OF JANUARY 30, 1897 (29 STAT. 506).

Prohibition on sale of liquor ". . . to any Indian to whom allotment of land has been made while the title to the same shall be held in trust by the Government. . . ," *held* a police regulation infringing state powers, and not warranted by the commerce clause, Article I, § 8, clause 3.

Matter of Heff, 197 U.S. 488 (1905), overruled in *United States v. Nice,* 241 U.S. 591 (1916).

29. ACT OF JUNE 1, 1898 (30 STAT. 428).

Section 10, penalizing "any employer subject to the provisions of this act" who should "threaten any employee with loss of employment . . . because of his membership in . . . a labor corporation, association, or organization" (the act being applicable "to any common carrier . . . engaged in the transportation of passengers or property . . . from one State . . . to another State. . . ," etc.), *held* an infringement of the Fifth Amendment and not supported by the commerce clause.

Adair v. United States, 208 U.S. 161 (1908).

30. ACT OF JUNE 13, 1898 (30 STAT. 448, 459).

Stamp tax on foreign bills of lading, *held* a tax on exports in violation of Article I, § 9.

Fairbank v. United States, 181 U.S. 283 (1901).

31. SAME (30 STAT. 448, 460).

Tax on charter parties, as applied to shipments exclusively from ports in United States to foreign ports, *held* a tax on exports in violation of Article I, § 9.

United States v. Hvoslef, 237 U.S. 1 (1915).

32. SAME (30 STAT. 448, 461).

Stamp tax on policies of marine insurance on exports, *held* a tax on exports in violation of Article I, § 9.

Thames & Mersey Marine Ins. Co. v. United States, 237 U.S. 19 (1915).

33. ACT OF JUNE 6, 1900 (31 STAT. 359, § 171).

Section of the Alaska Code providing for a six-person jury in trials for misdemeanors, *held* repugnant to the Sixth Amendment, requiring "jury" trial of crimes.

Rassmussen v. United States, 197 U.S. 516 (1905).

34. ACT OF MARCH 3, 1901 (31 STAT. 1341, § 935).

Section of the District of Columbia Code granting the same right of appeal, in criminal cases, to the United States or the District of Columbia as to the defendant, but providing that a verdict was not to be set aside for error found in rulings during trial, *held* an attempt to take an advisory opinion, contrary to Article III, § 2.

United States v. Evans, 213 U.S. 297 (1909).

35. ACT OF JUNE 11, 1906 (34 STAT. 232).

Act providing that "every common carrier engaged in trade or commerce in the District of Columbia . . . or between the several States . . . shall be liable to any of its employees . . . for all damages which may result from the negligence of any of its officers . . . or by reason of any defect . . . due to its negligence in its cars, engines . . . roadbed," etc., *held* not supportable under Article I, § 8, clause 3 because it extended to intrastate as well as interstate commercial activities.

The Employers' Liability Cases, 207 U.S. 463 (1908). (The act was upheld as to the District of Columbia in *Hyde v. Southern R. Co.,* 31 App. D.C. 466 (1908); and as to the Territories, in *El Paso & N.E. Ry. v. Gutierrez,* 215 U.S. 87 (1909).)

36. ACT OF JUNE 16, 1906 (34 STAT. 269, § 2).

Provision of Oklahoma Enabling Act restricting relocation of the State capital prior to 1913, *held* not supportable by Article IV, § 3, authorizing admission of new States.

Coyle v. Smith, 221 U.S. 559 (1911).

37. ACT OF FEBRUARY 20, 1907 (34 STAT. 889, § 3).

Provision in the Immigration Act of 1907 penalizing "whoever . . . shall keep, maintain, control, support, or harbor in any house or other place, for the purpose of prostitution . . . any alien woman or girl, within 3 years after she shall have entered the United States," *held* an exercise of police power not within the control of Congress over immigration (whether drawn from the commerce clause or based on inherent sovereignty).

Keller v. United States, 213 U.S. 138 (1909).

38. ACT OF MARCH 1, 1907 (34 STAT. 1028).

Provisions authorizing certain Indians "to institute their suits in the Court of Claims to determine the validity of any acts of Congress passed since . . . 1902, insofar as said acts . . . attempt to increase or extend the restrictions upon alienation . . . of allotments of lands of Cherokee citizens. . . ," and giving a right of appeal to the Supreme

Court, *held* an attempt to enlarge the judicial power restricted by Article III, § 2, to cases and controversies.

Muskrat v. United States, 219 U.S. 346 (1911).

39. ACT OF MAY 27, 1908 (35 STAT. 313, § 4).

Provision making locally taxable "all land [of Indians of the Five Civilized Tribes] from which restrictions have been or shall be removed," *held* a violation of the Fifth Amendment, in view of the Atoka Agreement, embodied in the Curtis Act of June 28, 1898, providing tax-exemption for allotted lands while title in original allottee, not exceeding 21 years.

Choate v. Trapp, 224 U.S. 665 (1912).

40. ACT OF FEBRUARY 9, 1909 (§ 2, 35 STAT. 614, AS AMENDED).

Provision of Narcotic Drugs Import and Export Act creating a presumption that possessor of cocaine knew of its illegal importation into the United States, *held,* in light of the fact that more cocaine is produced domestically than is brought into the country and in absence of any showing that defendant could have known his cocaine was imported, if it was, inapplicable to support conviction from mere possession of cocaine.

Turner v. United States, 396 U.S. 398 (1970).

41. ACT OF AUGUST 19, 1911 (37 STAT. 28).

A proviso in § 8 of the Federal Corrupt Practices Act fixing a maximum authorized expenditure by a candidate for Senator "in any campaign for his nomination and election," as applied to a primary election, *held* not supported by Article I, § 4, giving Congress power to regulate the manner of holding elections for Senators and Representatives.

Newberry v. United States, 256 U.S. 232 (1921), overruled in *United States v. Classic,* 313 U.S. 299 (1941).

42. ACT OF JUNE 18, 1912 (37 STAT. 136, § 8).

Part of § 8 giving the Juvenile Court of the District of Columbia (proceeding upon information) concurrent jurisdiction of desertion cases (which were, by law, punishable by fine or imprisonment in the workhouse at hard labor for 1 year), *held* invalid under the Fifth Amendment which gives right to presentment by a grand jury in case of infamous crimes.

United States v. Moreland, 258 U.S. 433 (1922).

43. ACT OF MARCH 4, 1913 (37 STAT. 988, PART OF PAR. 64).

Provision of the District of Columbia Public Utility Commission Act authorizing appeal to the United States Supreme Court from decrees of the District of Columbia Court of Appeals modifying valuation decisions of the Utilities Commission, *held* an attempt to extend the appellate jurisdiction of the Supreme Court to cases not strictly judicial within the meaning of Article III, § 2.

Keller v. Potomac Elec. Co., 261 U.S. 428 (1923).

44. ACT OF SEPTEMBER 1, 1916 (39 STAT. 675).

The original Child Labor Law, providing "that no producer . . . shall ship . . . in interstate commerce . . . any article or commodity the product of any mill . . . in which within 30 days prior to the removal of such product therefrom children under the age of 14 years have been employed or permitted to work more than 8 hours in any day or more than 6 days in any week. . . ," *held* not within the commerce power of Congress.

Hammer v. Dagenhart, 247 U.S. 251 (1918).

45. ACT OF SEPTEMBER 8, 1916 (39 STAT. 757, § 2(a), IN PART).

Provision of the income tax law of 1916, that a "stock dividend shall be considered income, to the amount of its cash value," *held* invalid (in spite of the Sixteenth Amendment) as an attempt to tax something not actually income, without regard to apportionment under Article I, § 2, clause 3.

Eisner v. Macomber, 252 U.S. 189 (1920).

46. ACT OF OCTOBER 6, 1917 (40 STAT. 395).

The amendment of §§ 24 and 256 of the Judicial Code (which prescribe the jurisdiction of district courts) "saving . . . to claimants the rights and remedies under the workmen's compensation law of any State," *held* an attempt to transfer federal legislative powers to the States—the Constitution, by Article III, § 2, and Article I, § 8, having adopted rules of general maritime law.

Knickerbocker Ice Co. v. Stewart, 253 U.S. 149 (1920).

47. ACT OF SEPTEMBER 19, 1918 (40 STAT. 960).

Specifically, that part of the Minimum Wage Law of the District of Columbia which authorized the Wage Board "to ascertain and declare . . . (a) Standards of minimum wages for women in any occupation within the District of Columbia, and what wages are inadequate to supply the necessary cost of living to any such women workers to maintain them in good health and to protect their morals. . . ," *held* to interfere with freedom of contract under the Fifth Amendment.

Adkins v. Children's Hospital, 261 U.S. 525 (1923), overruled in *West Coast Hotel Co. v. Parrish,* 300 U.S. 379 (1937).

48. ACT OF FEBRUARY 24, 1919 (40 STAT. 1065, § 213, IN PART).

That part of § 213 of the Revenue Act of 1919 which provided that ". . . for the purposes of the title . . . the term 'gross income' . . . includes gains, profits, and income derived from salaries, wages, or compensation for personal service (including in the case of . . . judges of the Supreme and inferior courts of the United States . . . the compensation received as such) . . ." as applied to a judge in office when the act was passed, *held* a violation of the guaranty of judges' salaries, in Article III, § 1.

Evans v. Gore, 253 U.S. 245 (1920). *Miles v. Graham,* 268 U.S. 501 (1925), held it invalid as applied to a judge taking office subsequent to the date of the act. Both cases were overruled by *O'Malley v. Woodrough,* 307 U.S. 227 (1939).

49. ACT OF FEBRUARY 24, 1919 (40 STAT. 1097, § 402(c)).

That part of the estate tax law providing that "gross estate" of a decedent should include value of all property "to the extent of any interest therein of which the decedent has at any time made a transfer or with respect to which he had at any time created a trust, in contemplation of or intended to take effect in possession or enjoyment at or after his death (whether such transfer or trust is made or created before or after the passage of this act), except in case of a *bona fide* sale . . ." as applied to a transfer of property made prior to the act and intended to take effect "in possession or enjoyment" at death of grantor, but not in fact testamentary or designed to evade taxation, *held* confiscatory, contrary to Fifth Amendment.

Nicholds v. Coolidge, 274 U.S. 531 (1927).

50. ACT OF FEBRUARY 24, 1919, TITLE XII (40 STAT. 1138, ENTIRE TITLE).

The Child Labor Tax Act, providing that "every person . . . operating . . . any . . . factory . . . in which children under the age of 14 years have been employed or permitted to work . . . shall pay . . . in addition to all other taxes imposed by law, an excise tax equivalent to 10 percent of the entire net profits received . . . for such year from the sale . . . of the product of such . . . factory. . . ," *held* beyond the taxing power under Article I, § 8, clause 1, and an infringement of state authority.

Bailey v. Drexel Furniture Co. (Child Labor Tax Case), 259 U.S. 20 (1922).

51. ACT OF OCTOBER 22, 1919 (41 STAT. 298, § 2), AMENDING ACT OF AUGUST 10, 1917 (40 STAT. 277, § 4).

(a) Section 4 of the Lever Act, providing in part "that it is hereby made unlawful for any persons willfully . . . to make any unjust or unreasonable rate or charge in handling or dealing in or with any necessaries . . ." and fixing a penalty, *held* invalid to support an indictment for charging an unreasonable price on sale—as not setting up an ascertainable standard of guilt within the requirement of the Sixth Amendment.

United States v. L. Cohen Grocery Co., 255 U.S. 81 (1921).

(b) That provision of § 4 making it unlawful "to conspire, combine, agree, or arrange with any other person to . . . exact excessive prices for any necessaries" and fixing a penalty, *held* invalid to support an indictment, on the reasoning of the *Cohen Grocery* case.

Weeds, Inc. v. United States, 255 U.S. 109 (1921).

52. ACT OF AUGUST 24, 1921 (42 STAT. 187, FUTURES TRADING ACT).

(a) Section 4 (and interwoven regulations) providing a "tax of 20 cents a bushel on every bushel involved therein, upon each contract of sale of grain for future delivery, except . . . where such contracts are made by or through a member of a board of trade which has been designated by the Secretary of Agriculture as a 'contract market'. . . ," *held* not within the taxing power under Article I, § 8.

Hill v. Wallace, 259 U.S. 44 (1922).

(b) Section 3, providing "That in addition to the taxes now imposed by law there is hereby levied a tax amounting to 20 cents per bushel on each bushel involved therein, whether the actual commodity is intended to be delivered or only nominally referred to, upon each . . . option for a contract either of purchase or sale of grain. . . ," *held* invalid on the same reasoning.

Trusler v. Crooks, 269 U.S. 475 (1926).

53. ACT OF NOVEMBER 23, 1921 (42 STAT. 261, § 245, IN PART).

Provision of Revenue Act of 1921 abating the deduction (4 percent of mean reserves) allowed from taxable income of life insurance companies in general by the amount of interest on their tax-exempts, and so according no relative advantage to the owners of the tax-exempt securities, *held* to destroy a guaranteed exemption.

National Life Ins. v. United States, 277 U.S. 508 (1928).

54. ACT OF JUNE 10, 1922 (42 STAT. 634).

A second attempt to amend §§ 24 and 256 of the Judicial Code, relating to jurisdiction of district courts, by saving "to claimants for compensation for injuries to or death of persons other than the master or members of the crew of a vessel, their rights and remedies under the workmen's compensation law of any State . . ." *held* invalid on authority of *Knickerbocker Ice Co. v. Stewart.*

Washington v. Dawson & Co., 264 U.S. 219 (1924).

55. ACT OF JUNE 2, 1924 (43 STAT. 313).

The gift tax provisions of the Revenue Act of 1924, applicable to gifts made during the calendar year, were *held* invalid under the Fifth Amendment insofar as they applied to gifts made before passage of the act.

Untermeyer v. Anderson, 276 U.S. 440 (1928).

56. ACT OF FEBRUARY 26, 1926 (44 STAT. 70, § 302, IN PART).

Stipulation creating a conclusive presumption that gifts made within two years prior to the death of the donor were made in contemplation of death of donor and requiring the value thereof to be included in computing the death transfer tax on decedent's estate was *held* to effect an invalid deprivation of property without due process.

Heiner v. Donnan, 285 U.S. 312 (1932).

57. ACT OF FEBRUARY 26, 1926 (44 STAT. 95, § 701).

Provision imposing a special excise tax of $1,000 on liquor dealers operating in States where such business is illegal, was *held* a penalty, without constitutional support following repeal of the Eighteenth Amendment.

United States v. Constantine, 296 U.S. 287 (1935).

58. ACT OF MARCH 20, 1933 (48 STAT. 11, § 17, IN PART).

Clause in the Economy Act of 1933 providing ". . . all laws granting or pertaining to yearly renewable term war risk insurance are hereby repealed," *held* invalid to abrogate an outstanding contract of insurance, which is a vested right protected by the Fifth Amendment.

Lynch v. United States, 292 U.S. 571 (1934).

59. ACT OF MAY 12, 1933 (48 STAT. 31).

Agricultural Adjustment Act providing for processing taxes on agricultural commodities and benefit payments therefor to farmers, *held* not within the taxing power under Article I, § 8, clause 1.

United States v. Butler, 297 U.S. 1 (1936).

60. ACT OF JOINT RESOLUTION OF JUNE 5, 1933 (48 STAT. 113, § 1).

Abrogation of gold clause in Government obligations, *held* a repudiation of the pledge implicit in the power to borrow money (Article I, § 8, clause 2), and within the prohibition of the Fourteenth Amendment, against questioning the validity of the public debt. (The majority of the Court, however, held plaintiff not entitled to recover under the circumstances.)

Perry v. United States, 294 U.S. 330 (1935).

61. ACT OF JUNE 16, 1933 (48 STAT. 195, THE NATIONAL INDUSTRIAL RECOVERY ACT).

(a) Title I, except § 9.

Provisions relating to codes of fair competition, authorized to be approved by the President in his discretion "to effectuate the policy" of the act, *held* invalid as a delegation of legislative power (Article I, § 1) and not within the commerce power (Article I, § 8, clause 3).

Schechter Poultry Corp. v. United States, 295 U.S. 495 (1935).

(b) § 9(c).

Clause of the oil regulation section authorizing the President "to prohibit the transportation in interstate . . . commerce of petroleum . . . produced or withdrawn from storage in excess of the amount permitted . . . by any State law . . ." and prescribing a penalty for violation of orders issued thereunder, *held* invalid as a delegation of legislative power.

Panama Refining Co. v. Ryan, 293 U.S. 388 (1935).

62. ACT OF JUNE 16, 1933 (48 STAT. 307, § 13).

Temporary reduction of 15 percent in retired pay of judges, retired from service but subject to performance of judicial duties under the Act of March 1, 1929 (45 Stat. 1422), was *held* a violation of the guaranty of judges' salaries in Article III, § 1.

Booth v. United States, 291 U.S. 339 (1934).

63. ACT OF APRIL 27, 1934 (48 STAT. 646, § 6) AMENDING § 5(I) OF HOME OWNERS LOAN ACT OF 1933.

Provision for conversion of state building and loan associations into federal associations, upon vote of 51 percent of the votes cast at a meeting of stockholders called to consider such action, *held* an encroachment on reserved powers of State.

Hopkins Savings Assn. v. Cleary, 296 U.S. 315 (1935).

64. ACT OF MAY 24, 1934 (48 STAT. 798).

Provision for readjustment of municipal indebtedness, though "adequately related" to the bankruptcy power, was *held* invalid as an interference with state sovereignty.

Ashton v. Cameron County Dist., 298 U.S. 513 (1936).

65. ACT OF JUNE 19, 1934 (CH. 652, 48 STAT. 1088, § 316, 18 U.S.C. § 1304).

Section 316 of the Communications Act of 1934 (which prohibits radio and television broadcasters from carrying advertisements for privately operated casino gambling regardless of the station's or casino's location, violates the First Amendment's protections for commercial speech as applied to prohibit advertising of private casino gambling broadcast by stations located within a state where such gambling is illegal.

Greater New Orleans Broadcasting Ass'n v. United States, 119 S. Ct. 1923 (1999).

66. ACT OF JUNE 27, 1934 (48 STAT. 1283).

The Railroad Retirement Act, establishing a detailed compulsory retirement system for employees of carriers subject to the Interstate Commerce Act, *held* not a regulation of commerce within the meaning of Article I, § 8, clause 3, and violative of the due process clause (Fifth Amendment).

Railroad Retirement Board v. Alton R. Co., 295 U.S. 330 (1935).

67. ACT OF JUNE 28, 1934 (48 STAT. 1289, CH. 869).

The Frazier-Lemke Act, adding subsection (5) to § 75 of the Bankruptcy Act, designed to preserve to mortgagors the ownership and enjoyment of their farm property and providing specifically, in paragraph 7, that a bankrupt left in possession has the option at any time within 5 years of buying at the appraised value—subject meanwhile to no monetary obligation other than payment of reasonable rental, *held* a violation of property rights, under the Fifth Amendment.

Louisville Bank v. Radford, 295 U.S. 555 (1935).

68. ACT OF AUGUST 24, 1935 (49 STAT. 750).

Amendments of Agricultural Adjustment Act *held* not within the taxing power.

Rickert Rice Mills v. Fontenot, 297 U.S. 110 (1936).

69. ACT OF AUGUST 29, 1935 (CH. 814 § 5(e), 49 STAT. 982, 27 U.S.C. § 205(e)).

The prohibition in section 5(e)(2) of the Federal Alcohol Administration Act of 1935 on the display of alcohol content on beer labels is inconsistent with the protections afforded to commercial speech by the First Amendment. The government's interest in curbing strength wars among brewers is substantial, but, given the "overall irrationality" of the regulatory scheme, the labeling prohibition does not directly and materially advance that interest.

Rubin v. Coors Brewing Co., 514 U.S. 476 (1995).

70. ACT OF AUGUST 30, 1935 (49 STAT. 991).

Bituminous Coal Conservation Act of 1935, *held* to impose, not a tax within Article I, § 8, but a penalty not sustained by the commerce clause (Article I, § 8, clause 3).

Carter v. Carter Coal Co., 298 U.S. 238 (1936).

71. ACT OF FEBRUARY 15, 1938 (CH. 29, 52 STAT. 30).

District of Columbia Code § 22-1115, prohibiting the display of any sign within 500 feet of a foreign embassy if the sign tends to bring the foreign government into "public odium" or "public disrepute," violates the First Amendment.

Boos v. Barry, 485 U.S. 312 (1988).

72. ACT OF JUNE 25, 1938 (52 STAT. 1040).

Federal Food, Drug, and Cosmetic Act of 1938, § 301(f), prohibiting the refusal to permit entry or inspection of premises by federal officers *held* void for vagueness and as violative of the due process clause of the Fifth Amendment.

United States v. Cardiff, 344 U.S. 174 (1952).

73. ACT OF JUNE 30, 1938 (52 STAT. 1251).

Federal Firearms Act, § 2(f), establishing a presumption of guilt based on a prior conviction and present possession of a firearm, *held* to violate the test of due process under the Fifth Amendment.

Tot v. United States, 319 U.S. 463 (1943).

74. ACT OF AUGUST 10, 1939 (§ 201(d), 53 STAT. 1362, AS AMENDED, 42 U.S.C. § 402(g)).

Provision of Social Security Act that grants survivors' benefits based on the earnings of a deceased husband and father covered by the Act to his widow and to the couple's children in her care but that grants benefits based on the earnings of a covered deceased wife and mother only to the minor children and not to the widower *held* violative of the right to equal protection secured by the Fifth Amendment's due process clause, since it unjustifiably discriminates against female wage earners required to pay social security taxes by affording them less protection for their survivors than is provided for male wage earners.

Weinberger v. Wiesenfeld, 420 U.S. 636 (1975).

75. ACT OF OCTOBER 14, 1940 (54 STAT. 1169, § 401(g)); AS AMENDED BY ACT OF JANUARY 20, 1944 (58 STAT. 4, § 1).

Provision of Aliens and Nationality Code (8 U.S.C. § 1481(a)(8)), derived from the Nationality Act of 1940, as amended, that citizenship shall be lost upon conviction by court martial and dishonorable discharge for deserting the armed services in time of war, *held* invalid as imposing a cruel and unusual punishment barred by the Eighth Amendment and not authorized by the war powers conferred by Article I, § 8, clauses 11 to 14.

Trop v. Dulles, 356 U.S. 86 (1958).

76. ACT OF NOVEMBER 15, 1943 (57 STAT. 450).

Urgent Deficiency Appropriation Act of 1943, § 304, providing that no salary should be paid to certain named federal employees out of moneys appropriated, *held* to violate Article I, § 9, clause 3, forbidding enactment of bill of attainder or *ex post facto* law.

United States v. Lovett, 328 U.S. 303 (1946).

77. ACT OF SEPTEMBER 27, 1944 (58 STAT. 746, § 401(J)); AND ACT OF JUNE 27, 1952 (66 STAT. 163, 267–268, § 349(a)(10)).

Section 401(J) of Immigration and Nationality Act of 1940, added in 1944, and § 49(a)(10) of the Immigration and Nationality Act of 1952 depriving one of citizenship, without the procedural safeguards guaranteed by the Fifth and Sixth Amendments, for the offense of leaving or remaining outside the country, in time of war or national emergency, to evade military service *held* invalid.

Kennedy v. Mendoza-Martinez, 372 U.S. 144 (1963).

78. ACT OF JULY 31, 1946 (CH. 707, § 7, 60 STAT. 719).

District court decision *holding* invalid under First and Fifth Amendments statute prohibiting parades or assemblages on United States Capitol grounds is summarily affirmed.

Chief of Capitol Police v. Jeannette Rankin Brigade, 409 U.S. 972 (1972).

79. ACT OF JUNE 25, 1948 (62 STAT. 760).

Provision of Lindbergh Kidnapping Act which provided for the imposition of the death penalty only if recommended by the jury *held* unconstitutional inasmuch as it penalized the assertion of a defendant's Sixth Amendment right to jury trial.

United States v. Jackson, 390 U.S. 570 (1968).

80. ACT OF AUGUST 18, 1949 (63 STAT. 617, 40 U.S.C. § 13k)

Provision, insofar as it applies to the public sidewalks surrounding the Supreme Court building, which bars the display of any flag, banner, or device designed to bring into public notice any party, organization, or movement *held* violative of the free speech clause of the First Amendment.

United States v. Grace, 461 U.S. 171 (1983).

81. ACT OF MAY 5, 1950 (64 STAT. 107).

Article 3(a) of the Uniform Code of Military Justice subjecting civilian ex-servicemen to court martial for crime committed while in military service *held* to violate Article III, § 2, and the Fifth and Sixth Amendments.

Toth v. Quarles, 350 U.S. 11 (1955).

82. ACT OF MAY 5, 1950 (64 STAT. 107).

Insofar as Article 2(11) of the Uniform Code of Military Justice subjects civilian dependents accompanying members of the armed forces overseas in time of peace to trial, in capital cases, by court martial, it is violative of Article III, § 2, and the Fifth and Sixth Amendments.

Reid v. Covert, 354 U.S. 1 (1957).

Insofar as the aforementioned provision is invoked in time of peace for the trial of noncapital offenses committed on land bases overseas by employees of the armed forces who have not been inducted or who have not voluntarily enlisted therein, it is violative of the Sixth Amendment.

McElroy v. United States, 361 U.S. 281 (1960).

Insofar as the aforementioned provision is invoked in time of peace for the trial of noncapital offenses committed by civilian dependents accompanying members of the armed forces overseas, it is violative of Article III, § 2, and the Fifth and Sixth Amendments.

Kinsella v. United States, 361 U.S. 234 (1960).

Insofar as the aforementioned provision is invoked in time of peace for the trial of a capital offense committed by a civilian employee of the armed forces overseas, it is violative of Article III, § 2, and the Fifth and Sixth Amendments.

Grisham v. Hagan, 361 U.S. 278 (1960).

83. ACT OF AUGUST 16, 1950 (64 STAT. 451, AS AMENDED).

Statutory scheme authorizing the Postmaster General to close the mails to distributors of obscene materials *held* unconstitutional in the absence of procedural provisions which would assure prompt judicial determination that protected materials were not being restrained.

Blount v. Rizzi, 400 U.S. 410 (1971).

84. ACT OF AUGUST 28, 1950 (§ 202(c)(1)(D), 64 STAT. 483, 42 U.S.C. § 402(c)(1)(C)).

District court decision *holding* invalid as a violation of the equal protection component of the Fifth Amendment's due process clause a Social Security provision entitling a husband to insurance benefits through his wife's benefits, provided he received at least one-half of his support from her at the time she became entitled, but requiring no such showing of support for the wife to qualify for benefits through her husband, is summarily affirmed.

Califano v. Silbowitz, 430 U.S. 934 (1977).

85. ACT OF AUGUST 28, 1950 (§ 202(f)(1)(E), 64 STAT. 485, 42 U.S.C. § 402(f)(1)(D)).

Social Security Act provision awarding survivors' benefits based on earnings of a deceased wife to widower only if he was receiving at least half of his support from her at the time of her death, whereas widow receives benefits regardless of dependency, *held* violative of equal protection element of Fifth Amendment's due process clause because of its impermissible gender classification.

Califano v. Goldfarb, 430 U.S. 199 (1977).

86. ACT OF SEPTEMBER 23, 1950 (TITLE 1, § 5, 64 STAT. 992).

Provision of Subversive Activities Control Act making it unlawful for member of Communist front organization to work in a defense plant *held* to be an overbroad infringement of the right of association protected by the First Amendment.

United States v. Robel, 389 U.S. 258 (1967).

87. ACT OF SEPTEMBER 23, 1950 (64 STAT. 993, § 6).

Subversive Activities Control Act of 1950, § 6, providing that any member of a Communist organization, which has registered or has been ordered to register, commits a crime if he attempts to obtain or use a passport, *held* violative of due process under the Fifth Amendment.

Aptheker v. Secretary of State, 378 U.S. 500 (1964).

88. ACT OF SEPTEMBER 28, 1950 (TITLE I, §§ 7, 8, 64 STAT. 993).

Provisions of Subversive Activities Control Act of 1950 requiring in lieu of registration by the Communist Party registration by Party members may not be applied to compel registration or to prosecute for refusal to register of alleged members who have asserted their privilege against self-incrimination inasmuch as registration would expose such persons to criminal prosecution under other laws.

Albertson v. Subversive Activities Control Board, 382 U.S. 70 (1965).

89. ACT OF OCTOBER 30, 1951 (§ 5(f)(ii), 65 STAT. 683, 45 U.S.C. § 231a(c)(3)(ii)).

Provision of Railroad Retirement Act similar to section voided in *Goldfarb. (See No. 85 on p. 1004.)*

Railroad Retirement Bd. v. Kalina, 431 U.S. 909 (1977).

90. ACT OF JUNE 27, 1952 (CH. 477, § 244(e)(2), 66 STAT. 214, 8 U.S.C. § 1254 (c)(2)).

Provision of the immigration law that permits either House of Congress to veto the decision of the Attorney General to suspend the deportation of certain aliens violates the bicameralism and presentation requirements of lawmaking imposed upon Congress by Article I, §§ 1 and 7.

INS v. Chadha, 462 U.S. 919 (1983).

91. ACT OF JUNE 27, 1952 (TITLE III, § 349, 66 STAT. 267).

Provision of Immigration and Nationality Act of 1952 providing for revocation of United States citizenship of one who votes in a foreign election *held* unconstitutional under § 1 of the Fourteenth Amendment.

Afroyim v. Rusk, 387 U.S. 253 (1967).

92. ACT OF JUNE 27, 1952 (66 STAT. 163, 269, § 352(a)(1)).

§ 352(a)(1) of the Immigration and Nationality Act of 1952 depriving a naturalized person of citizenship for "having a continuous residence for three years" in state of his birth or prior nationality *held* violative of the due process clause of the Fifth Amendment.

Schneider v. Rusk, 377 U.S. 163 (1964).

93. ACT OF AUGUST 16, 1954 (CH. 736, 68A STAT. 521, 26 U.S.C. § 4371(1)).

A federal tax on insurance premiums paid to foreign insurers not subject to the federal income tax violates the Export Clause, Art. I, § 9, cl. 5, as applied to casualty insurance for losses incurred during the shipment of goods from locations within the United States to purchasers abroad.

United States v. IBM Corp., 517 U.S. 843 (1996).

94. ACT OF AUGUST 16, 1954 (68A STAT. 525, INT. REV. CODE OF 1954, §§ 4401–4423).

Provisions of tax laws requiring gamblers to pay occupational and excise taxes may not be used over an assertion of one's privilege against self-incrimination either to compel extensive reporting of activities, leaving the registrant subject to prosecution under the laws of all the States with the possible exception of Nevada, or to prosecute for failure to register and report, because the scheme abridged the Fifth Amendment privilege.

Marchetti v. United States, 390 U.S. 39 (1968), and *Grosso v. United States,* 390 U.S. 62 (1968).

95. ACT OF AUGUST 16, 1954 (68A STAT. 560, MARIJUANA TAX ACT, §§ 4741, 4744, 4751, 4753).

Provisions of tax laws requiring possessors of marijuana to register and to pay a transfer tax may not be used over an assertion of the privilege against self-incrimination to compel registration or to prosecute for failure to register.

Leary v. United States, 395 U.S. 6 (1969).

96. ACT OF AUGUST 16, 1954 (68A STAT. 728, INT. REV. CODE OF 1954, §§ 5841, 5851).

Provisions of tax laws requiring the possessor of certain firearms, which it is made illegal to receive or to possess, to register with the Treasury Department may not be used over an assertion of the privilege against self-incrimination to prosecute one for failure to register or for possession of an unregistered firearm since the statutory scheme abridges the Fifth Amendment privilege.

Haynes v. United States, 390 U.S. 85 (1968).

97. ACT OF AUGUST 16, 1954 (68A STAT. 867, INT. REV. CODE OF 1954, § 7302).

Provision of tax laws providing for forfeiture of property used in violating internal revenue laws may not be constitutionally used in face of invocation of privilege against self-incrimination to condemn money in possession of gambler who had failed to comply with the registration and reporting scheme held void in *Marchetti v. United States,* 390 U.S. 39 (1968).

United States v. United States Coin & Currency, 401 U.S. 715 (1971).

98. ACT OF JULY 18, 1956 (§ 106, STAT. 570).

Provision of Narcotic Drugs Import and Export Act creating a presumption that possessor of marijuana knew of its illegal importation into the United States *held,* in absence of showing that all marijuana in United States was of foreign origin and that domestic users could know that their marijuana was more likely than not of foreign origin, unconstitutional under the due process clause of the Fifth Amendment.

Leary v. United States, 395 U.S. 6 (1969).

99. ACT OF AUGUST 10, 1956 (70A STAT. 35, § 772(F)).

Proviso of statute permitting the wearing of United States military apparel in theatrical productions only if the portrayal does not tend to discredit the armed force imposes an unconstitutional restraint upon First Amendment freedoms and precludes a prosecution under 18 U.S.C. § 702 for unauthorized wearing of uniform in a street skit disrespectful of the military.

Schacht v. United States, 398 U.S. 58 (1970).

100. ACT OF AUGUST 10, 1956 (70A STAT. 65, UNIFORM CODE OF MILITARY JUSTICE, ARTICLES 80, 130, 134).

Servicemen may not be charged under the Act and tried in military courts because of the commission of non-service connected crimes committed off-post and off-duty which are subject to civilian court jurisdiction where the guarantees of the Bill of Rights are applicable.

O'Callahan v. Parker, 395 U.S. 258 (1969).

101. ACT OF SEPTEMBER 2, 1958 (§ 5601(b)(1), 72 STAT. 1399).

Provision of Internal Revenue Code creating a presumption that one's presence at the site of an unregistered still shall be sufficient for conviction under a statute punishing possession, custody, or control of an unregistered still unless defendant otherwise explained his presence at the site to the jury *held* unconstitutional because the presumption is not a legitimate, rational, or reasonable inference that defendant was engaged in one of the specialized functions proscribed by the statute.

United States v. Romano, 382 U.S. 136 (1965).

102. ACT OF SEPTEMBER 2, 1958 (§ 1(25)(B), 72 STAT. 1446), AND ACT OF SEPTEMBER 7, 1962 (§ 401, 76 STAT. 469).

Federal statutes providing that spouses of female members of the Armed Forces must be dependent in fact in order to qualify for certain dependent's benefits, whereas spouses of male members are statutorily deemed dependent and automatically qualified for allowances, whatever their actual status, *held* an invalid sex classification under the equal protection principles of the Fifth Amendment's due process clause.

Frontiero v. Richardson, 411 U.S. 677 (1973).

103. ACT OF SEPTEMBER 2, 1958 (PUB. L. 85-921, § 1, 72 STAT. 1771, 18 U.S.C. § 504(1)).

Exemptions from ban on photographic reproduction of currency "for philatelic, numismatic, educational, historical, or newsworthy purposes" violates the First Amendment because it discriminates on the basis of the content of a publication.

Regan v. Time, Inc., 468 U.S. 641 (1984).

104. ACT OF SEPTEMBER 14, 1959 (§ 504, 73 STAT. 536).

Provision of Labor-Management Reporting and Disclosure Act of 1959 making it a crime for a member of the Communist Party to serve as an officer or, with the exception of clerical or custodial positions, as an employee of a labor union *held* to be a bill of attainder and unconstitutional.

United States v. Brown, 381 U.S. 437 (1965).

105. ACT OF OCTOBER 11, 1962 (§ 305, 76 STAT. 840).

Provision of Postal Services and Federal Employees Salary Act of 1962 authorizing Post Office Department to detain material determined to be "communist political propaganda" and to forward it to the addressee only if he requested it after notification by the Department, the material to be destroyed otherwise, *held* to impose on the addressee an affirmative obligation which amounted to an abridgment of First Amendment rights.

Lamont v. Postmaster General, 381 U.S. 301 (1965).

106. ACT OF OCTOBER 15, 1962 (76 STAT. 914).

Provision of District of Columbia laws requiring that a person to be eligible to receive welfare assistance must have resided in the District for at least one year impermissibly classified persons on the basis of an assertion of the right to travel interstate and therefore *held* to violate the due process clause of the Fifth Amendment.

Shapiro v. Thompson, 394 U.S. 618 (1969).

107. ACT OF DECEMBER 16, 1963 (77 STAT. 378, 20 U.S.C. § 754).

Provision of Higher Education Facilities Act of 1963 which in effect removed restriction against religious use of facilities constructed with federal funds after 20 years *held* to violate the establishment clause of the First Amendment inasmuch as the property will still be of considerable value at the end of the period and removal of the restriction would constitute a substantial governmental contribution to religion.

Tilton v. Richardson, 403 U.S. 672 (1971).

108. ACT OF JULY 30, 1965 (§ 339, 79 STAT. 409).

Section of Social Security Act qualifying certain illegitimate children for disability insurance benefits by presuming dependence but disqualifying other illegitimate children, regardless of dependency, if the disabled wage earner parent did not contribute to the child's support before the onset of the disability or if the child did not live with the parent before the onset of disability *held* to deny latter class of children equal protection as guaranteed by the due process clause of the Fifth Amendment.

Jimenez v. Weinberger, 417 U.S. 628 (1974).

109. ACT OF SEPTEMBER 3, 1966 (§ 102(b), 80 STAT. 831), AND ACT OF APRIL 8, 1974 (§§ 6(a)(1)AMENDING § 3(d) OF ACT, 6(a)(2) AMENDING § 3(e)(2)(c), 6(a)(5) AMENDING § 3(s)(5), AND 6(a)(6) AMENDING § 3(x)).

Those sections of the Fair Labor Standards Act extending wage and hour coverage to the employees of state and local governments *held* invalid because Congress lacks the authority under the commerce clause to regulate employee activities in areas of traditional governmental functions of the States.

National League of Cities v. Usery, 426 U.S. 833 (1976).

110. ACT OF NOVEMBER 7, 1967 (PUB. L. 90-129, § 201(8), 81 STAT. 368), AS AMENDED BY ACT OF AUGUST 13, 1981 (PUB. L. 97-35, § 1229, 95 STAT. 730, 47 U.S.C. § 399).

Communications Act provision banning noncommercial educational stations receiving grants from the Corporation for Public Broadcasting from engaging in editorializing violates the First Amendment.

FCC v. League of Women Voters, 468 U.S. 364 (1984).

111. ACT OF JANUARY 2, 1968 (§ 163(a)(2), 81 STAT. 872).

District court decisions *holding* unconstitutional under Fifth Amendment's due process clause section of Social Security Act that reduced, perhaps to zero, benefits coming to illegitimate children upon death of parent in order to satisfy the maximum payment due the wife and legitimate children are summarily affirmed.

Richardson v. Davis, 409 U.S. 1069 (1972).

112. ACT OF JANUARY 2, 1968 (§ 203, 81 STAT. 882).

Provision of Social Security Act extending benefits to families whose dependent children have been deprived of parental support because of the unemployment of the father but not giving benefits when the mother becomes unemployed *held* to impermissibly classify on the basis of sex and violate the Fifth Amendment's due process clause.

Califano v. Westcott, 443 U.S. 76 (1979).

113. ACT OF JUNE 22, 1970 (CH. III, 84 STAT. 318).

Provision of Voting Rights Act Amendments of 1970 which set a minimum voting age qualification of 18 in state and local elections *held* to be unconstitutional because beyond the powers of Congress to legislate.

Oregon v. Mitchell, 400 U.S. 112 (1970).

114. ACT OF DECEMBER 29, 1970 (§ 8(a), 84 STAT. 1598, 29 U.S.C. § 637 (a)).

Provision of Occupational Safety and Health Act authorizing inspections of covered work places in industry without warrants *held* to violate Fourth Amendment.

Marshall v. Barlow's, Inc., 436 U.S. 307 (1978).

115. ACT OF JANUARY 11, 1971 (§ 2, 84 STAT. 2048).

Provision of Food Stamp Act disqualifying from participation in program any household containing an individual unrelated by birth, marriage, or adoption to any other member of the household violates the due process clause of the Fifth Amendment.

Department of Agriculture v. Moreno, 413 U.S. 528 (1973).

116. ACT OF JANUARY 11, 1971 (§ 4, 84 STAT. 2049).

Provision of Food Stamp Act disqualifying from participation in program any household containing a person 18 years or older who had been claimed as a dependent child for income tax purposes in the present or preceding tax year by a taxpayer not a member of the household violates the due process clause of the Fifth Amendment.

Dept. of Agriculture v. Murry, 413 U.S. 508 (1973).

117. ACT OF DECEMBER 10, 1971 (PUB. L. 92-178, § 801, 85 STAT. 570, 26 U.S.C. § 9012(f)).

Provision of Presidential Election Campaign Fund Act limiting to $1,000 the amount that independent committees may expend to further the election of a presidential candidate financing his campaign with public funds is an impermissible limitation of freedom of speech and association protected by the First Amendment.

FEC v. National Conservative Political Action Comm., 470 U.S. 480 (1985).

118. FEDERAL ELECTION CAMPAIGN ACT OF FEBRUARY 7, 1972 (86 STAT. 3), AS AMENDED BY THE FEDERAL CAMPAIGN ACT AMENDMENTS OF 1974 (88 STAT. 1263), ADDING OR AMENDING 18 U.S.C. §§ 608(a), 608(e), AND 2 U.S.C. § 437(c).

Provisions of election law that forbid a candidate or the members of his immediate family from expending personal funds in excess of specified amounts, that limit to $1,000 the independent expenditures of any person relative to an identified candidate, and that forbid expenditures by candidates for federal office in excess of specified amounts violate the First Amendment speech guarantees; provisions of the law creating a commission to oversee enforcement of the Act are an invalid infringement of constitutional separation of powers in that they devolve responsibilities upon a commission four of whose six members are appointed by Congress and all six of whom are confirmed by the House of Representatives as well as by the Senate, not in compliance with the appointments clause.

Buckley v. Valeo, 424 U.S. 1 (1976).

119. ACT OF APRIL 8, 1974 (PUB. L. 93-259, §§ 6(a)(6), 6(d)(1), 29 U.S.C. §§ 203(x), 216(b)).

Fair Labor Standards Amendments of 1974 subjecting non-consenting states to suits for damages brought by employees in state courts violates the principle of sovereign immunity implicit in the constitutional scheme. Congress lacks power under Article I to subject non-consenting states to suits for damages in state courts.

Alden v. Maine, 119 S. Ct. 2240 (1999).

120. ACT OF MAY 11, 1976 (PUB. L. 92-225, § 316, 90 STAT. 490, 2 U.S.C. § 441)(b)).

Provision of Federal Election Campaign Act requiring that independent corporate campaign expenditures be financed by voluntary contributions to a separate segregated fund violates the First Amendment as applied to a corporation organized to promote political ideas, having no stockholders, and not serving as a front for a business corporation or union.

FEC v. Massachusetts Citizens for Life, Inc., 479 U.S. 238 (1986).

121. ACT OF MAY 11, 1976 (PUB. L. 94-283, § 112(2), 90 STAT. 489, 2 U.S.C. § 441a(d)(3)).

The Party Expenditure Provision of the Federal Election Campaign Act, which limits expenditures by a political party "in connection with the general election campaign of a [congressional] candidate," violates the First Amendment when applied to expenditures that a political party makes independently, without coordination with the candidate.

Colo. Repub. Federal Campaign Comm. v. FEC, 518 U.S. 604 (1996).

122. ACT OF OCTOBER 1, 1976 (TITLE II, 90 STAT. 1446); ACT OF OCTOBER 12, 1979 (101(c), 93 STAT. 657).

Provisions of appropriations laws rolling back automatic pay increases for federal officers and employees is unconstitutional as to Article III judges because, the increases having gone into effect, they violate the security of compensation clause of Article III, § 1.

United States v. Will, 449 U.S. 200 (1980).

123. ACT OF OCTOBER 19, 1976 (PUB. L. 94-553, § 101(c)), 17 U.S.C § 504(c).

Section 504(c) of the Copyright Act, which authorizes a copyright owner to recover statutory damages, in lieu of actual damages, "in a sum of not less than $500 or more than $20,000 as the court considers just," does not grant the right to a jury trial on the amount of statutory damages. The Seventh Amendment, however, requires a jury determination of the amount of statutory damages.

Feltner v. Columbia Pictures Television, 118 S. Ct. 1279 (1998).

124. ACT OF NOVEMBER 6, 1978 (§ 241(a), 92 STAT. 2668, 28 U.S.C. § 1471)

Assignment to judges who do not have tenure and guarantee of compensation protections afforded Article III judges of jurisdiction over all proceedings arising under or in the bankruptcy act and over all cases relating to proceedings under the bankruptcy act is invalid, inasmuch as judges without Article III protection may not receive at least some of this jurisdiction.

Northern Pipeline Const. Co. v. Marathon Pipe Line Co., 458 U.S. 50 (1982).

125. ACT OF NOVEMBER 9, 1978 (PUB. L. 95-621, § 202(c)(1), 92 STAT. 3372, 15 U.S.C. § 3342(c)(1)).

Decision of Court of Appeals holding unconstitutional provision giving either House of Congress power to veto rules of Federal Energy Regulatory Commission on certain natural gas pricing matters is summarily affirmed on the authority of *Chadha. (See No. 90 on p. 1005.)*

Process Gas Consumers Group v. Consumer Energy Council, 463 U.S. 1216 (1983).

126. ACT OF MAY 30, 1980 (94 STAT. 399, 45 U.S.C. § 1001 ET. SEQ.) AS AMENDED BY THE ACT OF OCTOBER 14, 1980 (94 STAT. 1959).

Acts of Congress applying to bankruptcy reorganization of one railroad and guaranteeing employee benefits is repugnant to the requirement of Article I, § 8, cl. 4, that bankruptcy legislation be "uniform."

Railway Labor Executives' Assn. v. Gibbons, 455 U.S. 457 (1982).

127. ACT OF MAY 28, 1980 (PUB. L. 96-252, § 21(A), 94 STAT. 393, 15 U.S.C. § 57a-1(a)).

Decision of Court of Appeals holding unconstitutional provision of FTC Improvements Act giving Congress power by concurrent resolution to veto final rules of the FTC is summarily affirmed on the basis of *Chadha. (See No. 90 on p. 1005)*

United States Senate v. FTC, 463 U.S. 1216 (1983).

128. ACT OF JANUARY 12, 1983 (PUB. L. 97-459, § 207, 96 STAT. 2519, 25 U.S.C. § 2206).

Section of Indian Land Consolidation Act providing for escheat to tribe of fractionated interests in land representing less than 2% of a tract's total acreage violates the Fifth Amendment's takings clause by completely abrogating rights of intestacy and devise.

Hodel v. Irving, 481 U.S. 704 (1987).

129. ACT OF OCTOBER 30, 1984 (PUB. L. 98-608, § 1(4)), 98 STAT. 3173, 25 U.S.C. § 2206.

Section 207 of the Indian Land Consolidation Act, as amended in 1984, effects an unconstitutional taking of property without compensation by restricting a property owner's right to pass on property to his heirs. The amended section, like an earlier version held unconstitutional in *Hodel v. Irving (No. 128),* provides that certain small interests in Indian land will escheat to the tribe upon death of the owner. None of the changes made in 1984 cures the constitutional defect.

Babbitt v. Youpee, 519 U.S. 234 (1997).

130. ACT OF JANUARY 15, 1985 (PUB. L. 99-240, § 5(D)(2)(C), 99 STAT. 1842, 42 U.S.C. § 2021E(D)(2)(C)).

"Take-title" incentives contained in the Low-Level Radioactive Waste Policy Amendments Act of 1985, designed to encourage states to cooperate in the federal regulatory scheme, offend principles of federalism embodied in the Tenth Amendment. These incentives, which require that non-participating states take title to waste or become liable for generators' damages, cross the line distinguishing encouragement from coercion. Congress may not simply commandeer the legislative and regulatory processes of the states, nor may it force a transfer from generators to state governments. A required choice between two unconstitutionally coercive regulatory techniques is also impermissible.

New York v. United States, 505 U.S. 144 (1992).

131. ACT OF DECEMBER 12, 1985 (PUB. L. 99-177, § 251, 99 STAT. 1063, 2 U.S.C. § 901).

That portion of the Balanced Budget and Emergency Deficit Control Act which authorizes the Comptroller General to determine the amount of spending reductions which must be accomplished each year to reach congressional targets and which authorizes him to report a figure to the President which the President must implement violates the constitutional separation of powers inasmuch as the Comptroller General is subject to congressional control (removal) and cannot be given a role in the execution of the laws.

Bowsher v. Synar, 478 U.S. 714 (1986).

132. ACT OF OCTOBER 30, 1986 (PUB. L. 99-591, TITLE VI, § 6007(F), 100 STAT. 3341, 49 U.S.C. APP. § 2456(f)).

The Metropolitan Washington Airports Act of 1986, which transferred operating control of two Washington, D.C., area airports from the Federal Government to a regional airports authority, violates separation of powers principles by conditioning that transfer on the establishment of a Board of Review, composed of Members of Congress and having veto authority over actions of the airports authority's board of directors.

Metropolitan Washington Airports Auth. v. Citizens for the Abatement of Aircraft Noise, 501 U.S. 252 (1991).

133. ACT OF NOVEMBER 17, 1986 (PUB. L. 99-662, TITLE IV, § 1402(A), 26 U.S.C. §§ 4461, 4462).

The Harbor Maintenance Tax (HMT) violates the Export Clause of the Constitution, Art. I, § 9, cl. 5, to the extent that the tax applies to goods loaded for export at United States ports. The HMT, which requires shippers to pay a uniform charge of 0.125 percent of cargo value on commercial cargo shipped through the Nation's ports, is an impermissible tax rather than a permissible user fee. The value of export cargo does not correspond reliably with federal harbor services used by exporters, and the tax does not, therefore, represent compensation for services rendered.

United States v. United States Shoe Corp., 523 U.S. 360 (1998).

134. ACT OF APRIL 28, 1988 (PUB. L. 100-297, § 6101, 102 STAT. 424, 47 U.S.C. § 223(B)).

Provision insofar as it bans indecent as well as obscene commercial interstate telephone messages violates the speech clause of the First Amendment.

Sable Communications v. FCC, 492 U.S. 115 (1989).

135. ACT OF OCTOBER 17, 1988 (PUB. L. 100-497, § 11(D)(7), 102 STAT. 2472, 25 U.S.C. § 2710(d)(7)).

A provision of the Indian Gaming Regulatory Act authorizing an Indian tribe to sue a State in federal court to compel performance of a duty to negotiate in good faith toward the formation of a compact violates the Eleventh Amendment. In exercise of its powers under Article I, Congress may not abrogate States' Eleventh Amendment immunity from suit in federal court. *Pennsylvania v. Union Gas Co.*, 491 U.S. 1 (1989), is overruled.

Seminole Tribe of Florida v. Florida, 517 U.S. 44 (1996).

136. ACT OF OCTOBER 28, 1989 (PUB. L. 101-131, 103 STAT. 777, 18 U.S.C. § 700).

The Flag Protection Act of 1989, criminalizing burning and certain other forms of destruction of the United States flag, violates the First Amendment. Most of the prohibited acts involve disrespectful treatment of the flag, and evidence a purpose to suppress expression out of concern for its likely communicative impact.

United States v. Eichman, 496 U.S. 310 (1990).

137. ACT OF NOVEMBER 30, 1989 (PUB. L. 101-194, § 601, 103 STAT. 1760, 5 U.S.C. APP. § 501).

Section 501(b) of the Ethics in Government Act, as amended in 1989 to prohibit Members of Congress and federal employees from accepting honoraria, violates the First Amendment as applied to Executive Branch employees below grade GS-16. The ban is limited to expressive activity and does not include other outside income, and the "speculative benefits" of the ban do not justify its "crudely crafted burden" on expression.

United States v. National Treasury Employees Union, 513 U.S. 454 (1995).

138. ACT OF NOVEMBER 29, 1990 (PUB. L. 101-647, § 1702, 104 STAT. 4844, 18 U.S.C. § 922Q).

The Gun Free School Zones Act of 1990, which makes it a criminal offense to knowingly possess a firearm within a school zone, exceeds congressional power under the Commerce Clause. It is "a criminal statute that by its terms has nothing to do with 'commerce' or any sort of economic enterprise." Possession of a gun at or near a school "is in no sense an economic activity that might, through repetition elsewhere, substantially affect any sort of interstate commerce."

United States v. Lopez, 514 U.S. 549 (1995).

139. ACT OF DECEMBER 19, 1991 (PUB. L. 102-242, § 476, 105 STAT. 2387, 15 U.S.C. § 78AA-1).

Section 27A(b) of the Securities Exchange Act of 1934, as added in 1991, requiring reinstatement of any section 10(b) actions that were dismissed as time barred subsequent to a 1991 Supreme Court decision, violates the Constitution's separation of powers to the extent that it requires federal courts to reopen final judgments in private civil actions. The provision violates a fundamental principle of Article III that the federal judicial power comprehends the power to render dispositive judgments.

Plaut v. Spendthrift Farm, Inc., 514 U.S. 211 (1995).

140. ACT OF OCTOBER 5, 1992 (PUB. L. 102-385, §§ 10(b) AND 10(c), 106 STAT. 1487, 1503; 47 U.S.C. § 532(j) AND § 531 NOTE, RESPECTIVELY).

Section 10(b) of the Cable Television Consumer Protection and Competition Act of 1992, which requires cable operators to segregate and block indecent programming on leased access channels if they do not prohibit it, violates the First Amendment. Section 10(c) of the Act, which permits a cable operator to prevent transmission of "sexually explicit" programming on public access channels, also violates the First Amendment.

Denver Area Educ. Tel. Consortium v. FCC, 518 U.S. 727 (1996).

141. ACT OF OCTOBER 24, 1992, TITLE XIX, 106 STAT. 3037 (PUB. L. 102-486), 26 U.S.C. §§ 9701-9722.

The Coal Industry Retiree Health Benefit Act of 1992 is unconstitutional as applied to the petitioner Eastern Enterprises. Pursuant to the Act, the Social Security Commissioner imposed liability on Eastern for funding health care benefits of retirees from the coal industry who had worked for Eastern prior to 1966. Eastern had transferred its coal-related business to a subsidiary in 1965. Four Justices viewed the imposition of liability on Eastern as a violation of the Takings Clause, and one Justice viewed it as a violation of substantive due process.

Eastern Enterprises v. Apfel, 524 U.S. 498 (1998).

142. ACT OF OCTOBER 27, 1992 (PUB. L. 102-542, 15 U.S.C. § 1122).

The Trademark Remedy Clarification Act, which provided that states shall not be immune from suit under the Trademark Act of 1946 (Lanham Act) "under the Eleventh Amendment . . . or under any other doctrine of sovereign immunity," did not validly abrogate state sovereign immunity. Congress lacks power to do so in exercise of Article I powers, and the TRCA cannot be justified as an exercise of power under section 5 of the Fourteenth Amendment. The right to be free from a business competitor's false advertising is not a "property right" protected by the Due Process Clause.

College Savings Bank v. Florida Prepaid Postsecondary Educ. Expense Bd., 119 S. Ct. 2219 (1999).

143. ACT OF OCTOBER 28, 1992 (106 STAT. 4230, PUB. L. 102-560, 29 U.S.C. § 296).

The Patent and Plant Variety Remedy Clarification Act, which amended the patent laws to expressly abrogate states' sovereign immunity from patent infringement suits, is invalid. Congress lacks power to abrogate state immunity in exercise of Article I powers, and the Patent Remedy Clarification Act cannot be justified as an exercise of power under section 5 of the Fourteenth Amendment. Section 5 power is remedial, yet the legislative record reveals no identified pattern of patent infringement by states and the Act's provisions are "out of proportion to a supposed remedial or preventive object."

Florida Prepaid Postsecondary Edu. Expense Bd. v. College Savings Bank, 119 S. Ct. 2199 (1999).

144. ACT OF NOVEMBER 16, 1993 (PUB. L. 103-141, 107 STAT. 1488, 42 U.S.C. §§ 2000BB TO 2000BB-4).

The Religious Freedom Restoration Act, which directed use of the compelling interest test to determine the validity of laws of general applicability that substantially burden the free exercise of religion, exceeds congressional power under section 5 of the Fourteenth Amendment. Congress's power under Section 5 to "enforce" the Fourteenth Amendment by "appropriate legislation" does not extend to defining the substance of the Amendment's restrictions. This RFRA appears to do. RFRA "is so far out of proportion to a supposed remedial or preventive object that it cannot be understood as responsive to, or designed to prevent, unconstitutional behavior."

City of Boerne v. Flores, 117 S. Ct. 2157 (1997).

145. ACT OF NOVEMBER 30, 1993 (PUB. L. 103-159, 107 STAT. 1536).

Interim provisions of the Brady Handgun Violence Prevention Act that require state and local law enforcement officers to conduct background checks on prospective handgun purchasers are inconsistent with the Constitution's allocation of power between Federal and State governments. In *New York v. United States,* 505 U.S. 144 (1992), the Court held that Congress may not compel states to enact or enforce a federal regulatory program, and "Congress cannot circumvent that prohibition by conscripting the State's officers directly."

Printz v. United States, 521 U.S. 98 (1997).

146. ACT OF FEBRUARY 8, 1996 (110 STAT. 56, 133-34, PUB. L. 104-104, TITLE V, § 502, 47 U.S.C. §§ 223(a), 223(d)).

Two provisions of the Communications Decency Act of 1996—one that prohibits knowing transmission on the Internet of obscene or indecent messages to any recipient under 18 years of age, and the other that prohibits the knowing sending or displaying of patently offensive messages in a manner that is available to anyone under 18 years of age—violate the First Amendment.

Reno v. ACLU, 117 S. Ct. 2329 (1997).

147. ACT OF APRIL 9, 1996 (110 STAT. 1200, PUB. L. 104-130, 2 U.S.C. §§ 691 ET SEQ).

The Line Item Veto Act, which gives the President the authority to "cancel in whole" three types of provisions that have been signed into law, violates the Presentment Clause of Article I, section 7. In effect, the law grants to the President "the unilateral power to change the text of duly enacted statutes." This Line Item Veto Act authority differs in important respects from the President's constitutional authority to "return" (veto) legislation: the statutory cancellation occurs after rather than before a bill becomes law, and can apply to a part of a bill as well as the entire bill.

Clinton v. City of New York, 524 U.S. 417 (1998).

SOURCES: Compiled from Library of Congress, *The Constitution of the United States of America; Analysis and Interpretation,* S. Doc., 103-6, 1992; 1996 supplement, S. Doc., 104-14, 1996; 1998 supplement, S. Doc., 106-8; Library of Congress, Congressional Research Service.

Rules of the House of Representatives, 106th Congress

RULE I

THE SPEAKER

APPROVAL OF THE JOURNAL

1. The Speaker shall take the Chair on every legislative day precisely at the hour to which the House last adjourned and immediately call the House to order. Having examined and approved the Journal of the last day's proceedings, the Speaker shall announce to the House his approval thereof. The Speaker's approval of the Journal shall be deemed agreed to unless a Member, Delegate, or Resident Commissioner demands a vote thereon. If such a vote is decided in the affirmative, it shall not be subject to a motion to reconsider. If such a vote is decided in the negative, then one motion that the Journal be read shall be privileged, shall be decided without debate, and shall not be subject to a motion to reconsider.

PRESERVATION OF ORDER

2. The Speaker shall preserve order and decorum and, in case of disturbance or disorderly conduct in the galleries or in the lobby, may cause the same to be cleared.

CONTROL OF CAPITOL FACILITIES

3. Except as otherwise provided by rule or law, the Speaker shall have general control of the Hall of the House, the corridors and passages in the part of the Capitol assigned to the use of the House, and the disposal of unappropriated rooms in that part of the Capitol.

SIGNATURE OF DOCUMENTS

4. The Speaker shall sign all acts and joint resolutions passed by the two Houses and all writs, warrants, and subpoenas of, or issued by order of, the House. The Speaker may sign enrolled bills and joint resolutions whether or not the House is in session.

QUESTIONS OF ORDER

5. The Speaker shall decide all questions of order, subject to appeal by a Member, Delegate, or Resident Commissioner. On such an appeal a Member, Delegate, or Resident Commissioner may not speak more than once without permission of the House.

FORM OF A QUESTION

6. The Speaker shall rise to put a question but may state it sitting. The Speaker shall put a question in this form: "Those in favor (of the question), say 'Aye.'"; and after the affirmative voice is expressed, "Those opposed, say 'No.'". After a vote by voice under this clause, the Speaker may use such voting procedures as may be invoked under rule XX.

DISCRETION TO VOTE

7. The Speaker is not required to vote in ordinary legislative proceedings, except when his vote would be decisive or when the House is engaged in voting by ballot.

SPEAKER PRO TEMPORE

8. (a) The Speaker may appoint a Member to perform the duties of the Chair. Except as specified in paragraph (b), such an appointment may not extend beyond three legislative days.

(b)(1) In the case of his illness, the Speaker may appoint a Member to perform the duties of the Chair for a period not exceeding 10 days, subject to the approval of the House. If the Speaker is absent and has omitted to make such an appointment, then the House shall elect a Speaker pro tempore to act during the absence of the Speaker.

(2) With the approval of the House, the Speaker may appoint a Member to act as Speaker pro tempore only to sign enrolled bills and joint resolutions for a specified period of time.

TERM LIMIT

9. A person may not serve as Speaker for more than four consecutive Congresses (disregarding for this purpose any service for less than a full session in any Congress).

DESIGNATION OF TRAVEL

10. The Speaker may designate a Member, Delegate, Resident Commissioner, officer, or employee of the House to travel on the business of the House within or without the United States, whether the House is meeting, has recessed, or has adjourned. Expenses for such travel may be paid from applicable accounts of the House described in clause 1(i)(1) of rule X on vouchers approved and signed solely by the Speaker.

COMMITTEE APPOINTMENT

11. The Speaker shall appoint all select, joint, and conference committees ordered by the House. At any time after an original appointment, the Speaker may remove Members, Delegates, or the Resident Commissioner from, or appoint additional Members, Delegates, or the Resident Commissioner to, a select or conference committee. In appointing Members, Delegates, or the Resident Commissioner to conference committees, the Speaker shall appoint no less than a majority who generally supported the House position as determined by the Speaker, shall name those who are primarily responsible for the legislation, and shall, to the fullest extent feasible, include the principal proponents of the major provisions of the bill or resolution passed or adopted by the House.

DECLARATION OF RECESS

12. To suspend the business of the House for a short time when no question is pending before the House, the Speaker may declare a recess subject to the call of the Chair.

OTHER RESPONSIBILITIES

13. The Speaker, in consultation with the Minority Leader, shall develop through an appropriate entity of the House a system for drug testing in the House. The system may provide for the testing of a Member, Delegate, Resident Commissioner, officer, or employee of the House, and otherwise shall be comparable in scope to the system for drug testing in the executive branch pursuant to Executive Order 12564 (Sept. 15, 1986). The expenses of the system may be paid from applicable accounts of the House for official expenses.

RULE II

OTHER OFFICERS AND OFFICIALS

ELECTIONS

1. There shall be elected at the commencement of each Congress, to continue in office until their successors are chosen and qualified, a Clerk, a Sergeant-at-Arms, a Chief Administrative Officer, and a Chaplain. Each of these officers shall take an oath to support the Constitution of the United States, and for the true and faithful exercise of the duties of his office to the best of his knowledge and ability, and to keep the secrets of the House. Each of these officers shall appoint all of the employees of his department provided for by law. The Clerk, Sergeant-at-Arms, and Chief Administrative Officer may be removed by the House or by the Speaker.

CLERK

2. (a) At the commencement of the first session of each Congress, the Clerk shall call the Members, Delegates, and Resident Commissioner to order and proceed to record their presence by States in alphabetical order, either by call of the roll or by use of the electronic voting system. Pending the election of a Speaker or Speaker pro tempore, the Clerk shall preserve order and decorum and decide all questions of order, subject to appeal by a Member, Delegate, or Resident Commissioner.

(b) At the commencement of every regular session of Congress, the Clerk shall make and cause to be printed and delivered to each Member, Delegate, and the Resident Commissioner a list of the reports that any officer or Department is required to make to Congress, citing the law or resolution in which the requirement may be contained and placing under the name of each officer the list of reports he is required to make.

(c) The Clerk shall—

(1) note all questions of order, with the decisions thereon, the record of which shall be appended to the Journal of each session;

(2) enter on the Journal the hour at which the House adjourns;

(3) complete the printing and distribution of the Journal to Members, Delegates, and the Resident Commissioner, together with an accurate and complete index, as soon as possible after the close of a session; and

(4) send a printed copy of the Journal to the executive of and to each branch of the legislature of every State as may be requested by such State officials.

(d) The Clerk shall attest and affix the seal of the House to all writs, warrants, and subpoenas issued by order of the House and certify the passage of all bills and joint resolutions.

(e) The Clerk shall cause the calendars of the House to be printed and distributed each legislative day.

(f) The Clerk shall—

(1) retain in the library at the Office of the Clerk for the use of the Members, Delegates, Resident Commissioner, and officers of the House, and not to be withdrawn therefrom, two copies of all the books and printed documents deposited there; and

(2) deliver or mail to any Member, Delegate, or the Resident Commissioner an extra copy, in binding of good quality, of each document requested by that Member, Delegate, or Resident Commissioner that has been printed by order of either House of Congress in any Congress in which the Member, Delegate, or Resident Commissioner served.

(g) The Clerk shall provide for his temporary absence or disability by designating an official in the Office of the Clerk to sign all papers that may require the official signature of the Clerk and to do all other official acts that the Clerk may be required to do under the rules and practices of the House, except such official acts as are provided for by statute. Official acts done by the designated official shall be under the name of the Clerk. The designation shall be in writing and shall be laid before the House and entered on the Journal.

(h) The Clerk may receive messages from the President and from the Senate at any time when the House is not in session.

(i)(1) The Clerk shall supervise the staff and manage the office of a Member, Delegate, or Resident Commissioner who has died, resigned, or been expelled until a successor is elected. The Clerk shall perform similar duties in the event that a vacancy is declared by the House in any congressional district because of the incapacity of the person representing such district or other reason. Whenever the Clerk is acting as a supervisory authority over such staff, he shall have authority to terminate employees and, with the approval of the Committee on House Administration, may appoint such staff as is required to operate the office until a successor is elected.

(2) For 60 days following the death of a former Speaker, the Clerk shall maintain on the House payroll, and shall supervise in the same manner, staff appointed under House Resolution 1238, Ninety-first Congress (as enacted into permanent law by chapter VIII of the Supplemental Appropriations Act, 1971) (2 U.S.C. 31b-5).

(j) In addition to any other reports required by the Speaker or the Committee on House Administration, the Clerk shall report to the Committee on House Administration not later than 45 days following the close of each semiannual period ending on June 30 or on December 31 on the financial and operational status of each function under the jurisdiction of the Clerk. Each report shall include financial statements and a description or explanation of current operations, the implementation of new policies and procedures, and future plans for each function.

(k) The Clerk shall fully cooperate with the appropriate offices and persons in the performance of reviews and audits of financial records and administrative operations.

SERGEANT-AT-ARMS

3. (a) The Sergeant-at-Arms shall attend the House during its sittings and maintain order under the direction of the Speaker or other presiding officer. The Sergeant-at-Arms shall execute the commands of the House, and all processes issued by authority thereof, directed to him by the Speaker.

(b) The symbol of the office of the Sergeant-at-Arms shall be the mace, which shall be borne by him while enforcing order on the floor.

(c) The Sergeant-at-Arms shall enforce strictly the rules relating to the privileges of the Hall of the House and be responsible to the House for the official conduct of his employees.

(d) The Sergeant-at-Arms may not allow a person to enter the room over the Hall of the House during its sittings; and from 15 minutes before the hour of the meeting of the House each day until 10 minutes after adjournment, he shall see that the floor is cleared of all persons except those privileged to remain.

(e) In addition to any other reports required by the Speaker or the Committee on House Administration, the Sergeant-at-Arms shall report to the Committee on House Administration not later than 45 days following the close of each semiannual period ending on June 30 or on December 31 on the financial and operational status of each function under the jurisdiction of the Sergeant-at-Arms. Each report shall include financial statements and a description or explanation of current operations, the implementation of new policies and procedures, and future plans for each function.

(f) The Sergeant-at-Arms shall fully cooperate with the appropriate offices and persons in the performance of reviews and audits of financial records and administrative operations.

CHIEF ADMINISTRATIVE OFFICER

4. (a) The Chief Administrative Officer shall have operational and financial responsibility for functions as assigned by the Committee on House Administration and shall be subject to the policy direction and oversight of the Committee on House Administration.

(b) In addition to any other reports required by the Committee on House Administration, the Chief Administrative Officer shall report to the Committee on House Administration not later than 45 days following the close of each semiannual period ending on June 30 or December 31 on the financial and operational status of each function under the jurisdiction of the Chief Administrative Officer. Each report shall include financial statements and a description or explanation of current operations, the implementation of new policies and procedures, and future plans for each function.

(c) The Chief Administrative Officer shall fully cooperate with the appropriate offices and persons in the performance of reviews and audits of financial records and administrative operations.

CHAPLAIN

5. The Chaplain shall offer a prayer at the commencement of each day's sitting of the House.

OFFICE OF INSPECTOR GENERAL

6. (a) There is established an Office of Inspector General.

(b) The Inspector General shall be appointed for a Congress by the Speaker, the Majority Leader, and the Minority Leader, acting jointly.

(c) Subject to the policy direction and oversight of the Committee on House Administration, the Inspector General shall only—

(1) conduct periodic audits of the financial and administrative functions of the House and of joint entities;

(2) inform the officers or other officials who are the subject of an audit of the results of that audit and suggesting appropriate curative actions;

(3) simultaneously notify the Speaker, the Majority Leader, the Minority Leader, and the chairman and ranking minority member of the Committee on House Administration in the case of any financial irregularity discovered in the course of carrying out responsibilities under this clause;

(4) simultaneously submit to the Speaker, the Majority Leader, the Minority Leader, and the chairman and ranking minority member of the Committee on House Administration a report of each audit conducted under this clause; and

(5) report to the Committee on Standards of Official Conduct information involving possible violations by a Member, Delegate, Resident Commissioner, officer, or employee of the House of any rule of the House or of any law applicable to the performance of official duties or the discharge of official responsibilities that may require referral to the appropriate Federal or State authorities under clause 3(a)(3) of rule XI.

OFFICE OF THE HISTORIAN

7. There is established an Office of the Historian of the House of Representatives. The Speaker shall appoint and set the annual rate of pay for employees of the Office of the Historian.

OFFICE OF GENERAL COUNSEL

8. There is established an Office of General Counsel for the purpose of providing legal assistance and representation to the House. Legal assistance and representation shall be provided without regard to political affiliation. The Office of General Counsel shall function pursuant to the direction of the Speaker, who shall consult with a Bipartisan Legal Advisory Group, which shall include the majority and minority leaderships. The Speaker shall appoint and set the annual rate of pay for employees of the Office of General Counsel.

RULE III

THE MEMBERS, DELEGATES, AND RESIDENT COMMISSIONER OF PUERTO RICO

VOTING

1. Every Member shall be present within the Hall of the House during its sittings, unless excused or necessarily prevented, and shall vote on each question put, unless he has a direct personal or pecuniary interest in the event of such question.

2. (a) A Member may not authorize any other person to cast his vote or record his presence in the House or the Committee of the Whole House on the state of the Union.

(b) No other person may cast a Member's vote or record a Member's presence in the House or the Committee of the Whole House on the state of the Union.

DELEGATES AND THE RESIDENT COMMISSIONER

3. (a) Each Delegate and the Resident Commissioner shall be elected to serve on standing committees in the same manner as Members of the House and shall possess in such committees the same powers and privileges as the other members of the committee.

(b) The Delegates and the Resident Commissioner may be appointed to any select committee and to any conference committee.

RULE IV

THE HALL OF THE HOUSE

USE AND ADMITTANCE

1. The Hall of the House shall be used only for the legislative business of the House and for caucus and conference meetings of its Members, except when the House agrees to take part in any ceremonies to be observed therein. The Speaker may not entertain a motion for the suspension of this clause.

2. (a) Only the following persons shall be admitted to the Hall of the House or rooms leading thereto:

(1) Members of Congress, Members-elect, and contestants in election cases during the pendency of their cases on the floor.

(2) The Delegates and the Resident Commissioner.

(3) The President and Vice President of the United States and their private secretaries.

(4) Justices of the Supreme Court.

(5) Elected officers and minority employees nominated as elected officers of the House.

(6) The Parliamentarian.

(7) Staff of committees when business from their committee is under consideration.

(8) Not more than one person from the staff of a Member, Delegate, or Resident Commissioner when that Member, Delegate, or Resident Commissioner has an amendment under consideration (subject to clause 5).

(9) The Architect of the Capitol.

(10) The Librarian of Congress and the assistant in charge of the Law Library.

(11) The Secretary and Sergeant-at-Arms of the Senate.

(12) Heads of departments.

(13) Foreign ministers.

(14) Governors of States.

(15) Former Members, Delegates, and Resident Commissioners; former Parliamentarians of the House; and former elected officers and minority employees nominated as elected officers of the House (subject to clause 4).

(16) One attorney to accompany a Member, Delegate, or Resident Commissioner who is the respondent in an investigation undertaken by the Committee on Standards of Official Conduct when a recommendation of that committee is under consideration in the House.

(17) Such persons as have, by name, received the thanks of Congress.

(b) The Speaker may not entertain a unanimous consent request or a motion to suspend this clause.

3. (a) Except as provided in paragraph (b), all persons not entitled to the privilege of the floor during the session shall be excluded at all times from the Hall of the House and the cloakrooms.

(b) Until 15 minutes of the hour of the meeting of the House, persons employed in its service, accredited members of the press entitled to admission to the press gallery, and other persons on request of a Member, Delegate, or Resident Commissioner by card or in writing, may be admitted to the Hall of the House.

4. (a) Former Members, Delegates, and Resident Commissioners; former Parliamentarians of the House; and former elected officers and minority employees nominated as elected officers of the House shall be entitled to the privilege of admission to the Hall of the House and rooms leading thereto only if—

(1) they do not have any direct personal or pecuniary interest in any legislative measure pending before the House or reported by a committee; and

(2) they are not in the employ of, or do not represent, any party or organization for the purpose of influencing, directly or indirectly, the passage, defeat, or amendment of any legislative measure pending before the House, reported by a committee, or under consideration in any of its committees or subcommittees.

(b) The Speaker shall promulgate such regulations as may be necessary to implement this rule and to ensure its enforcement.

5. A person from the staff of a Member, Delegate, or Resident Commissioner may be admitted to the Hall of the House or rooms leading thereto under clause 2 only upon prior notice to the Speaker. Such persons, and persons from the staff of committees admitted under clause 2, may not engage in efforts in the Hall of the House or rooms leading thereto to influence Members with regard to the legislation being amended. Such persons shall remain at the desk and are admitted only to advise the Member, Delegate, Resident Commissioner, or committee responsible for their admission. A person who violates this clause may be excluded during the session from the Hall of the House and rooms leading thereto by the Speaker.

GALLERY

6. (a) The Speaker shall set aside a portion of the west gallery for the use of the President, the members of the Cabinet, justices of the Supreme Court, foreign ministers and suites, and the members of their respective families. The Speaker shall set aside another portion of the same gallery for the accommodation of persons to be admitted on the cards of Members, Delegates, or the Resident Commissioner.

(b) The Speaker shall set aside the southerly half of the east gallery for the use of the families of Members of Congress. The Speaker shall control one bench. On the request of a Member, Delegate, Resident Commissioner, or Senator, the Speaker shall issue a card of admission to his family, which may include their visitors. No other person shall be admitted to this section.

PROHIBITION ON CAMPAIGN CONTRIBUTIONS

7. A Member, Delegate, Resident Commissioner, officer, or employee of the House, or any other person entitled to admission to the Hall of the House or rooms leading thereto by this rule, may not knowingly distribute a political campaign contribution in the Hall of the House or rooms leading thereto.

RULE V

BROADCASTING THE HOUSE

1. The Speaker shall administer a system subject to his direction and control for closed-circuit viewing of floor proceedings of the House in the offices of all Members, Delegates, the Resident Commissioner, and committees and in such other places in the Capitol and the House Office Buildings as he considers appropriate. Such system may include other telecommunications functions as the Speaker considers appropriate. Any such telecommunications shall be subject to rules and regulations issued by the Speaker.

2. (a) The Speaker shall administer a system subject to his direction and control for complete and unedited audio and visual broadcasting and recording of the proceedings of the House. The Speaker shall provide for the distribution of such broadcasts and recordings to news media, for the storage of audio and video recordings of the proceedings, and for the closed-captioning of the proceedings for hearing-impaired persons.

(b) All television and radio broadcasting stations, networks, services, and systems (including cable systems) that are accredited to the House Radio and Television Correspondents' Galleries, and all radio and television correspondents who are so accredited, shall be provided access to the live coverage of the House.

(c) Coverage made available under this clause, including any recording thereof—

(1) may not be used for any political purpose;

(2) may not be used in any commercial advertisement; and

(3) may not be broadcast with commercial sponsorship except as part of a bona fide news program or public affairs documentary program.

3. The Speaker may delegate any of his responsibilities under this rule to such legislative entity as he considers appropriate.

RULE VI

OFFICIAL REPORTERS AND NEWS MEDIA GALLERIES

OFFICIAL REPORTERS

1. Subject to the direction and control of the Speaker, the Clerk shall appoint, and may remove for cause, the official reporters of the House, including stenographers of committees, and shall supervise the execution of their duties.

NEWS MEDIA GALLERIES

2. A portion of the gallery over the Speaker's chair as may be necessary to accommodate representatives of the press wishing to report debates and proceedings shall be set aside for their use. Reputable reporters and correspondents shall be admitted thereto under such regulations as the Speaker may prescribe from time to time. The Standing Committee of Correspondents for the Press Gallery, and the Executive Committee of Correspondents for the Periodical Press Gallery, shall supervise such galleries, including the designation of its employees, subject to the direction and control of the Speaker. The Speaker may assign one seat on the floor to Associated Press reporters and one to United Press International reporters, and may regulate their occupation. The Speaker may admit to the floor, under such regulations as he may prescribe, one additional representative of each press association.

3. A portion of the gallery as may be necessary to accommodate reporters of news to be disseminated by radio, television, and similar means of transmission, wishing to report debates and proceedings, shall be set aside for their use. Reputable reporters and correspondents shall be admitted thereto under such regulations as the Speaker may prescribe. The Executive Committee of the Radio and Television Correspondents' Galleries shall supervise such gallery, including the designation of its employees, subject to the direction and control of the Speaker. The Speaker may admit to the floor, under such regulations as he may prescribe, one representative of the National Broadcasting Company, one of the Columbia Broadcasting System, and one of the American Broadcasting Company.

RULE VII

RECORDS OF THE HOUSE

ARCHIVING

1. (a) At the end of each Congress, the chairman of each committee shall transfer to the Clerk any noncurrent records of such committee, including the subcommittees thereof.

(b) At the end of each Congress, each officer of the House elected under rule II shall transfer to the Clerk any noncurrent records made or acquired in the course of the duties of such officer.

2. The Clerk shall deliver the records transferred under clause 1, together with any other noncurrent records of the House, to the Archivist of the United States for preservation at the National Archives and Records Administration. Records so delivered are the permanent property of the House and remain subject to this rule and any order of the House.

PUBLIC AVAILABILITY

3. (a) The Clerk shall authorize the Archivist to make records delivered under clause 2 available for public use, subject to paragraph (b), clause 4, and any order of the House.

(b)(1) A record shall immediately be made available if it was previously made available for public use by the House or a committee or a subcommittee.

(2) An investigative record that contains personal data relating to a specific living person (the disclosure of which would be an unwarranted invasion of personal privacy), an administrative record relating to personnel, or a record relating to a hearing that was closed under clause 2(g)(2) of rule XI shall be made available if it has been in existence for 50 years.

(3) A record for which a time, schedule, or condition for availability is specified by order of the House shall be made available in accordance with that order. Except as otherwise provided by order of the House, a record of a committee for which a time, schedule, or condition for availability is specified by order of the committee (entered during the Congress in which the record is made or acquired by the committee) shall be made available in accordance with the order of the committee.

(4) A record (other than a record referred to in subparagraph (1), (2), or (3)) shall be made available if it has been in existence for 30 years.

4. (a) A record may not be made available for public use under clause 3 if the Clerk determines that such availability would be detrimental to the public interest or inconsistent with the rights and privileges of the House. The Clerk shall notify in writing the chairman and ranking minority member of the Committee on House Administration of any such determination.

(b) A determination of the Clerk under paragraph (a) is subject to later orders of the House and, in the case of a record of a committee, later orders of the committee.

5. (a) This rule does not supersede rule VIII or clause 9 of rule X and does not authorize the public disclosure of any record if such disclosure is prohibited by law or executive order of the President.

(b) The Committee on House Administration may prescribe guidelines and regulations governing the applicability and implementation of this rule.

(c) A committee may withdraw from the National Archives and Records Administration any record of the committee delivered to the Archivist under this rule. Such a withdrawal shall be on a temporary basis and for official use of the committee.

DEFINITION OF RECORD

6. In this rule the term "record" means any official, permanent record of the House (other than a record of an individual Member, Delegate, or Resident Commissioner), including—

(a) with respect to a committee, an official, permanent record of the committee (including any record of a legislative, oversight, or other activity of such committee or a subcommittee thereof); and

(b) with respect to an officer of the House elected under rule II, an official, permanent record made or acquired in the course of the duties of such officer.

WITHDRAWAL OF PAPERS

7. A memorial or other paper presented to the House may not be withdrawn from its files without its leave. If withdrawn certified copies thereof shall be left in the office of the Clerk. When an act passes for the settlement of a claim, the Clerk may transmit to the officer charged with the settlement thereof the papers on file in his office relating to such claim. The Clerk may lend temporarily to an officer or bureau of the executive departments any papers on file in his office relating to any matter pending before such officer or bureau, taking proper receipt therefor.

RULE VIII

RESPONSE TO SUBPOENAS

1. When a Member, Delegate, Resident Commissioner, officer, or employee of the House is properly served with a subpoena or other judicial order directing appearance as a witness relating to the official functions of the House or for the production or disclosure of any document relating to the official functions of the House, such Member, Delegate, Resident Commissioner, officer, or employee shall comply, consistently with the privileges and rights of the House, with the subpoena or other judicial order as hereinafter provided, unless otherwise determined under this rule.

2. Upon receipt of a properly served subpoena or other judicial order described in clause 1, a Member, Delegate, Resident Commissioner, officer, or employee of the House shall promptly notify the Speaker of its receipt in writing. Such notification shall promptly be laid before the House by the Speaker. During a period of recess or adjournment of longer than three days, notification to the House is not required until the reconvening of the House, when the notification shall promptly be laid before the House by the Speaker.

3. Once notification has been laid before the House, the Member, Delegate, Resident Commissioner, officer, or employee of the House shall determine whether the issuance of the subpoena or other judicial order described in clause 1 is a proper exercise of jurisdiction by the court, is material and relevant, and is consistent with the privileges and rights of the House. Such Member, Delegate, Resident Commissioner, officer, or employee shall notify the Speaker before seeking judicial determination of these matters.

4. Upon determination whether a subpoena or other judicial order described in clause 1 is a proper exercise of jurisdiction by the court, is material and relevant, and is consistent with the privileges and rights of the House, the Member, Delegate, Resident Commissioner, officer, or employee of the House shall immediately notify the Speaker of the determination in writing.

5. The Speaker shall inform the House of a determination whether a subpoena or other judicial order described in clause 1 is a proper exercise of jurisdiction by the court, is material and relevant, and is

consistent with the privileges and rights of the House. In so informing the House, the Speaker shall generally describe the records or information sought. During a period of recess or adjournment of longer than three days, such notification is not required until the reconvening of the House, when the notification shall promptly be laid before the House by the Speaker.

6. (a) Except as specified in paragraph (b) or otherwise ordered by the House, upon notification to the House that a subpoena or other judicial order described in clause 1 is a proper exercise of jurisdiction by the court, is material and relevant, and is consistent with the privileges and rights of the House, the Member, Delegate, Resident Commissioner, officer, or employee of the House shall comply with the subpoena or other judicial order by supplying certified copies.

(b) Under no circumstances may minutes or transcripts of executive sessions, or evidence of witnesses in respect thereto, be disclosed or copied. During a period of recess or adjournment of longer than three days, the Speaker may authorize compliance or take such other action as he considers appropriate under the circumstances. Upon the reconvening of the House, all matters that transpired under this clause shall promptly be laid before the House by the Speaker.

7. A copy of this rule shall be transmitted by the Clerk to the court when a subpoena or other judicial order described in clause 1 is issued and served on a Member, Delegate, Resident Commissioner, officer, or employee of the House.

8. Nothing in this rule shall be construed to deprive, condition, or waive the constitutional or legal privileges or rights applicable or available at any time to a Member, Delegate, Resident Commissioner, officer, or employee of the House, or of the House itself, or the right of such Member, Delegate, Resident Commissioner, officer, or employee, or of the House itself, to assert such privileges or rights before a court in the United States.

RULE IX

QUESTIONS OF PRIVILEGE

1. Questions of privilege shall be, first, those affecting the rights of the House collectively, its safety, dignity, and the integrity of its proceedings; and second, those affecting the rights, reputation, and conduct of Members, Delegates, or the Resident Commissioner, individually, in their representative capacity only.

2. (a)(1) A resolution reported as a question of the privileges of the House, or offered from the floor by the Majority Leader or the Minority Leader as a question of the privileges of the House, or offered as privileged under clause 1, section 7, article I of the Constitution, shall have precedence of all other questions except motions to adjourn. A resolution offered from the floor by a Member, Delegate, or Resident Commissioner other than the Majority Leader or the Minority Leader as a question of the privileges of the House shall have precedence of all other questions except motions to adjourn only at a time or place, designated by the Speaker, in the legislative schedule within two legislative days after the day on which the proponent announces to the House his intention to offer the resolution and the form of the resolution. Oral announcement of the form of the resolution may be dispensed with by unanimous consent.

(2) The time allotted for debate on a resolution offered from the floor as a question of the privileges of the House shall be equally divided between (A) the proponent of the resolution, and (B) the Majority Leader, the Minority Leader, or a designee, as determined by the Speaker.

(b) A question of personal privilege shall have precedence of all other questions except motions to adjourn.

RULE X

ORGANIZATION OF COMMITTEES

COMMITTEES AND THEIR LEGISLATIVE JURISDICTIONS

1. There shall be in the House the following standing committees, each of which shall have the jurisdiction and related functions assigned by this clause and clauses 2, 3, and 4. All bills, resolutions, and other matters relating to subjects within the jurisdiction of the standing committees listed in this clause shall be referred to those committees, in accordance with clause 2 of rule XII, as follows:

(A) COMMITTEE ON AGRICULTURE.

(1) Adulteration of seeds, insect pests, and protection of birds and animals in forest reserves.

(2) Agriculture generally.

(3) Agricultural and industrial chemistry.

(4) Agricultural colleges and experiment stations.

(5) Agricultural economics and research.

(6) Agricultural education extension services.

(7) Agricultural production and marketing and stabilization of prices of agricultural products, and commodities (not including distribution outside of the United States).

(8) Animal industry and diseases of animals.

(9) Commodity exchanges.

(10) Crop insurance and soil conservation.

(11) Dairy industry.

(12) Entomology and plant quarantine.

(13) Extension of farm credit and farm security.

(14) Inspection of livestock, poultry, meat products, and seafood and seafood products.

(15) Forestry in general and forest reserves other than those created from the public domain.

(16) Human nutrition and home economics.

(17) Plant industry, soils, and agricultural engineering.

(18) Rural electrification.

(19) Rural development.

(20) Water conservation related to activities of the Department of Agriculture.

(B) COMMITTEE ON APPROPRIATIONS.

(1) Appropriation of the revenue for the support of the Government.

(2) Rescissions of appropriations contained in appropriation Acts.

(3) Transfers of unexpended balances.

(4) Bills and joint resolutions reported by other committees that provide new entitlement authority as defined in section 3(9) of the Congressional Budget Act of 1974 and referred to the committee under clause 4(a)(2).

(C) COMMITTEE ON ARMED SERVICES.

(1) Ammunition depots; forts; arsenals; and Army, Navy, and Air Force reservations and establishments.

(2) Common defense generally.

(3) Conservation, development, and use of naval petroleum and oil shale reserves.

(4) The Department of Defense generally, including the Departments of the Army, Navy, and Air Force, generally.

(5) Interoceanic canals generally, including measures relating to the maintenance, operation, and administration of interoceanic canals.

(6) Merchant Marine Academy and State Maritime Academies.

(7) Military applications of nuclear energy.

(8) Tactical intelligence and intelligence-related activities of the Department of Defense.

(9) National security aspects of merchant marine, including financial assistance for the construction and operation of vessels, maintenance of the U.S. shipbuilding and ship repair industrial base, cabotage, cargo preference, and merchant marine officers and seamen as these matters relate to the national security.

(10) Pay, promotion, retirement, and other benefits and privileges of members of the armed forces.

(11) Scientific research and development in support of the armed services.

(12) Selective service.

(13) Size and composition of the Army, Navy, Marine Corps, and Air Force.

(14) Soldiers' and sailors' homes.

(15) Strategic and critical materials necessary for the common defense.

(D) COMMITTEE ON BANKING AND FINANCIAL SERVICES.

(1) Banks and banking, including deposit insurance and Federal monetary policy.

(2) Bank capital markets activities generally.

(3) Depository institutions securities activities generally, including activities of any affiliates (except for functional regulation under applicable securities laws not involving safety and soundness).

(4) Economic stabilization, defense production, renegotiation, and control of the price of commodities, rents, and services.

(5) Financial aid to commerce and industry (other than transportation).

(6) International finance.

(7) International financial and monetary organizations.

(8) Money and credit, including currency and this issuance of notes and redemption thereof; gold and silver, including the coinage thereof; valuation and revaluation of the dollar.

(9) Public and private housing.

(10) Urban development.

(E) COMMITTEE ON THE BUDGET.

(1) Concurrent resolutions on the budget (as defined in section 3(4) of the Congressional Budget Act of 1974), other matters required to be referred to the committee under titles III and IV of that Act, and other measures setting forth appropriate levels of budget totals for the United States Government.

(2) Budget process generally.

(3) Establishment, extension, and enforcement of special controls over the Federal budget, including the budgetary treatment of off-budget Federal agencies and measures providing exemption from reduction under any order issued under part C of the Balanced Budget and Emergency Deficit Control Act of 1985.

(F) COMMITTEE ON COMMERCE.

(1) Biomedical research and development.

(2) Consumer affairs and consumer protection.

(3) Health and health facilities (except health care supported by payroll deductions).

(4) Interstate energy compacts.

(5) Interstate and foreign commerce generally.

(6) Exploration, production, storage, supply, marketing, pricing, and regulation of energy resources, including all fossil fuels, solar energy, and other unconventional or renewable energy resources.

(7) Conservation of energy resources.

(8) Energy information generally.

(9) The generation and marketing of power (except by federally chartered or Federal regional power marketing authorities); reliability and interstate transmission of, and ratemaking for, all power; and siting of generation facilities (except the installation of interconnections between Government waterpower projects).

(10) General management of the Department of Energy and management and all functions of the Federal Energy Regulatory Commission.

(11) National energy policy generally.

(12) Public health and quarantine.

(13) Regulation of the domestic nuclear energy industry, including regulation of research and development reactors and nuclear regulatory research.

(14) Regulation of interstate and foreign communications.

(15) Securities and exchanges.

(16) Travel and tourism.

The committee shall have the same jurisdiction with respect to regulation of nuclear facilities and of use of nuclear energy as it has with respect to regulation of nonnuclear facilities and of use of nonnuclear energy.

(G) COMMITTEE ON EDUCATION AND THE WORKFORCE.

(1) Child labor.

(2) Gallaudet University and Howard University and Hospital.

(3) Convict labor and the entry of goods made by convicts into interstate commerce.

(4) Food programs for children in schools.

(5) Labor standards and statistics.

(6) Education or labor generally.

(7) Mediation and arbitration of labor disputes.

(8) Regulation or prevention of importation of foreign laborers under contract.

(9) Workers' compensation.

(10) Vocational rehabilitation.

(11) Wages and hours of labor.

(12) Welfare of miners.

(13) Work incentive programs.

(H) COMMITTEE ON GOVERNMENT REFORM.

(1) Federal civil service, including intergovernmental personnel; and the status of officers and employees of the United States, including their compensation, classification, and retirement.

(2) Municipal affairs of the District of Columbia in general (other than appropriations).

(3) Federal paperwork reduction.

(4) Government management and accounting measures generally.

(5) Holidays and celebrations.

(6) Overall economy, efficiency, and management of government operations and activities, including Federal procurement.

(7) National archives.

(8) Population and demography generally, including the Census.

(9) Postal service generally, including transportation of the mails.

(10) Public information and records.

(11) Relationship of the Federal Government to the States and municipalities generally.

(12) Reorganizations in the executive branch of the Government.

(I) COMMITTEE ON HOUSE ADMINISTRATION.

(1) Appropriations from accounts for committee salaries and expenses (except for the Committee on Appropriations); House Information Resources; and allowance and expenses of Members, Delegates, the Resident Commissioner, officers, and administrative offices of the House.

(2) Auditing and settling of all accounts described in subparagraph (1).

(3) Employment of persons by the House, including staff for Members, Delegates, the Resident Commissioner, and committees; and reporters of debates, subject to rule VI.

(4) Except as provided in paragraph (q)(11), the Library of Congress, including management thereof; the House Library; statuary and pictures; acceptance or purchase of works of art for the Capitol; the Botanic Garden; and purchase of books and manuscripts.

(5) The Smithsonian Institution and the incorporation of similar institutions (except as provided in paragraph (q)(11)).

(6) Expenditure of accounts described in subparagraph (1).

(7) Franking Commission.

(8) Printing and correction of the Congressional Record.

(9) Accounts of the House generally.

(10) Assignment of office space for Members, Delegates, the Resident Commissioner, and committees.

(11) Disposition of useless executive papers.

(12) Election of the President, Vice President, Members, Senators, Delegates, or the Resident Commissioner; corrupt practices; contested elections; credentials and qualifications; and Federal elections generally.

(13) Services to the House, including the House Restaurant, parking facilities, and administration of the House Office Buildings and of the House wing of the Capitol.

(14) Travel of Members, Delegates, and the Resident Commissioner.

(15) Raising, reporting, and use of campaign contributions for candidates for office of Representative, of Delegate, and of Resident Commissioner.

(16) Compensation, retirement, and other benefits of the Members, Delegates, the Resident Commissioner, officers, and employees of Congress.

(J) COMMITTEE ON INTERNATIONAL RELATIONS.

(1) Relations of the United States with foreign nations generally.

(2) Acquisition of land and buildings for embassies and legations in foreign countries.

(3) Establishment of boundary lines between the United States and foreign nations.

(4) Export controls, including nonproliferation of nuclear technology and nuclear hardware.

(5) Foreign loans.

(6) International commodity agreements (other than those involving sugar), including all agreements for cooperation in the export of nuclear technology and nuclear hardware.

(7) International conferences and congresses.

(8) International education.

(9) Intervention abroad and declarations of war.

(10) Diplomatic service.

(11) Measures to foster commercial intercourse with foreign nations and to safeguard American business interests abroad.

(12) International economic policy.

(13) Neutrality.

(14) Protection of American citizens abroad and expatriation.

(15) The American National Red Cross.

(16) Trading with the enemy.

(17) United Nations organizations.

(K) COMMITTEE ON THE JUDICIARY.

(1) The judiciary and judicial proceedings, civil and criminal.

(2) Administrative practice and procedure.

(3) Apportionment of Representatives.

(4) Bankruptcy, mutiny, espionage, and counterfeiting.

(5) Civil liberties.

(6) Constitutional amendments.

(7) Federal courts and judges, and local courts in the Territories and possessions.

(8) Immigration and naturalization.

(9) Interstate compacts generally.

(10) Claims against the United States.

(11) Meetings of Congress; attendance of Members, Delegates, and the Resident Commissioner; and their acceptance of incompatible offices.

(12) National penitentiaries.

(13) Patents, the Patent and Trademark Office, copyrights, and trademarks.

(14) Presidential succession.

(15) Protection of trade and commerce against unlawful restraints and monopolies.

(16) Revision and codification of the Statutes of the United States.

(17) State and territorial boundary lines.

(18) Subversive activities affecting the internal security of the United States.

(L) COMMITTEE ON RESOURCES.

(1) Fisheries and wildlife, including research, restoration, refuges, and conservation.

(2) Forest reserves and national parks created from the public domain.

(3) Forfeiture of land grants and alien ownership, including alien ownership of mineral lands.

(4) Geological Survey.

(5) International fishing agreements.

(6) Interstate compacts relating to apportionment of waters for irrigation purposes.

(7) Irrigation and reclamation, including water supply for reclamation projects and easements of public lands for irrigation projects; and acquisition of private lands when necessary to complete irrigation projects.

(8) Native Americans generally, including the care and allotment of Native American lands and general and special measures relating to claims that are paid out of Native American funds.

(9) Insular possessions of the United States generally (except those affecting the revenue and appropriations).

(10) Military parks and battlefields, national cemeteries administered by the Secretary of the Interior, parks within the District of Columbia, and the erection of monuments to the memory of individuals.

(11) Mineral land laws and claims and entries thereunder.

(12) Mineral resources of public lands.

(13) Mining interests generally.

(14) Mining schools and experimental stations.

(15) Marine affairs, including coastal zone management (except for measures relating to oil and other pollution of navigable waters).

(16) Oceanography.

(17) Petroleum conservation on public lands and conservation of the radium supply in the United States.

(18) Preservation of prehistoric ruins and objects of interest on the public domain.

(19) Public lands generally, including entry, easements, and grazing thereon.

(20) Relations of the United States with Native Americans and Native American tribes.

(21) Trans-Alaska Oil Pipeline (except ratemaking).

(M) COMMITTEE ON RULES.

(1) Rules and joint rules (other than those relating to the Code of Official Conduct) and the order of business of the House.

(2) Recesses and final adjournments of Congress.

(N) COMMITTEE ON SCIENCE.

(1) All energy research, development, and demonstration, and projects therefor, and all federally owned or operated nonmilitary energy laboratories.

(2) Astronautical research and development, including resources, personnel, equipment, and facilities.

(3) Civil aviation research and development.

(4) Environmental research and development.

(5) Marine research.

(6) Commercial application of energy technology.

(7) National Institute of Standards and Technology, standardization of weights and measures, and the metric system.

(8) National Aeronautics and Space Administration.

(9) National Space Council.

(10) National Science Foundation.

(11) National Weather Service.

(12) Outer space, including exploration and control thereof.

(13) Science scholarships.

(14) Scientific research, development, and demonstration, and projects therefor.

(O) COMMITTEE ON SMALL BUSINESS.

(1) Assistance to and protection of small business, including financial aid, regulatory flexibility, and paperwork reduction.

(2) Participation of small-business enterprises in Federal procurement and Government contracts.

(P) COMMITTEE ON STANDARDS OF OFFICIAL CONDUCT.

The Code of Official Conduct.

(Q) COMMITTEE ON TRANSPORTATION AND IN- FRASTRUCTURE.

(1) Coast Guard, including lifesaving service, lighthouses, lightships, ocean derelicts, and the Coast Guard Academy.

(2) Federal management of emergencies and natural disasters.

(3) Flood control and improvement of rivers and harbors.

(4) Inland waterways.

(5) Inspection of merchant marine vessels, lights and signals, lifesaving equipment, and fire protection on such vessels.

(6) Navigation and laws relating thereto, including pilotage.

(7) Registering and licensing of vessels and small boats.

(8) Rules and international arrangements to prevent collisions at sea.

(9) The Capitol Building and the Senate and House Office Buildings.

(10) Construction or maintenance of roads and post roads (other than appropriations therefor).

(11) Construction or reconstruction, maintenance, and care of buildings and grounds of the Botanic Garden, the Library of Congress, and the Smithsonian Institution.

(12) Merchant marine (except for national security aspects thereof).

(13) Purchase of sites and construction of post offices, customhouses, Federal courthouses, and Government buildings within the District of Columbia.

(14) Oil and other pollution of navigable waters, including inland, coastal, and ocean waters.

(15) Marine affairs, including coastal zone management, as they relate to oil and other pollution of navigable waters.

(16) Public buildings and occupied or improved grounds of the United States generally.

(17) Public works for the benefit of navigation, including bridges and dams (other than international bridges and dams).

(18) Related transportation regulatory agencies.

(19) Roads and the safety thereof.

(20) Transportation, including civil aviation, railroads, water transportation, transportation safety (except automobile safety), transportation infrastructure, transportation labor, and railroad retirement and unemployment (except revenue measures related thereto).

(21) Water power.

(R) COMMITTEE ON VETERANS' AFFAIRS.

(1) Veterans' measures generally.

(2) Cemeteries of the United States in which veterans of any war or conflict are or may be buried, whether in the United States or abroad (except cemeteries administered by the Secretary of the Interior).

(3) Compensation, vocational rehabilitation, and education of veterans.

(4) Life insurance issued by the Government on account of service in the Armed Forces.

(5) Pensions of all the wars of the United States, general and special.

(6) Readjustment of servicemen to civil life.

(7) Soldiers' and sailors' civil relief.

(8) Veterans' hospitals, medical care, and treatment of veterans.

(S) COMMITTEE ON WAYS AND MEANS.

(1) Customs, collection districts, and ports of entry and delivery.

(2) Reciprocal trade agreements.

(3) Revenue measures generally.

(4) Revenue measures relating to insular possessions.

(5) Bonded debt of the United States, subject to the last sentence of clause 4(f).

(6) Deposit of public monies.

(7) Transportation of dutiable goods.

(8) Tax exempt foundations and charitable trusts.

(9) National social security (except health care and facilities programs that are supported from general revenues as opposed to payroll deductions and except work incentive programs).

GENERAL OVERSIGHT RESPONSIBILITIES

2. (a) The various standing committees shall have general oversight responsibilities as provided in paragraph (b) in order to assist the House in—

(1) its analysis, appraisal, and evaluation of—

(A) the application, administration, execution, and effectiveness of Federal laws; and

(B) conditions and circumstances that may indicate the necessity or desirability of enacting new or additional legislation; and

(2) its formulation, consideration, and enactment of changes in Federal laws, and of such additional legislation as may be necessary or appropriate.

(b)(1) In order to determine whether laws and programs addressing subjects within the jurisdiction of a committee are being implemented and carried out in accordance with the intent of Congress and whether they should be continued, curtailed, or eliminated, each standing committee (other than the Committee on Appropriations) shall review and study on a continuing basis—

(A) the application, administration, execution, and effectiveness of laws and programs addressing subjects within its jurisdiction;

(B) the organization and operation of Federal agencies and entities having responsibilities for the administration and execution of laws and programs addressing subjects within its jurisdiction;

(C) any conditions or circumstances that may indicate the necessity or desirability of enacting new or additional legislation addressing subjects within its jurisdiction (whether or not a bill or resolution has been introduced with respect thereto); and

(D) future research and forecasting on subjects within its jurisdiction.

(2) Each committee to which subparagraph (1) applies having more than 20 members shall establish an oversight subcommittee, or require its subcommittees to conduct oversight in their respective jurisdictions, to assist in carrying out its responsibilities under this clause. The establishment of an oversight subcommittee does not limit the responsibility of a subcommittee with legislative jurisdiction in carrying out its oversight responsibilities.

(c) Each standing committee shall review and study on a continuing basis the impact or probable impact of tax policies affecting subjects within its jurisdiction as described in clauses 1 and 3.

(d)(1) Not later than February 15 of the first session of a Congress, each standing committee shall, in a meeting that is open to the public and with a quorum present, adopt its oversight plan for that Congress. Such plan shall be submitted simultaneously to the Committee on Government Reform and to the Committee on House Administration. In developing its plan each committee shall, to the maximum extent feasible—

(A) consult with other committees that have jurisdiction over the same or related laws, programs, or agencies within its jurisdiction with the objective of ensuring maximum coordination and cooperation among committees when conducting reviews of such laws, programs, or agencies and include in its plan an explanation of steps that have been or will be taken to ensure such coordination and cooperation;

(B) give priority consideration to including in its plan the review of those laws, programs, or agencies operating under permanent budget authority or permanent statutory authority; and

(C) have a view toward ensuring that all significant laws, programs, or agencies within its jurisdiction are subject to review every 10 years.

(2) Not later than March 31 in the first session of a Congress, after consultation with the Speaker, the Majority Leader, and the Minority Leader, the Committee on Government Reform shall report to the House the oversight plans submitted by committees together with any recommendations that it, or the House leadership group described above, may make to ensure the most effective coordination of oversight plans and otherwise to achieve the objectives of this clause.

(e) The Speaker, with the approval of the House, may appoint special ad hoc oversight committees for the purpose of reviewing specific matters within the jurisdiction of two or more standing committees.

SPECIAL OVERSIGHT FUNCTIONS

3. (a) The Committee on Appropriations shall conduct such studies and examinations of the organization and operation of executive departments and other executive agencies (including an agency the majority of the stock of which is owned by the United States) as it considers necessary to assist it in the determination of matters within its jurisdiction.

(b) The Committee on the Budget shall study on a continuing basis the effect on budget outlays of relevant existing and proposed legislation and report the results of such studies to the House on a recurring basis.

(c) The Committee on Commerce shall review and study on a continuing basis laws, programs, and Government activities relating to nuclear and other energy and nonmilitary nuclear energy research and development including the disposal of nuclear waste.

(d) The Committee on Education and the Workforce shall review, study, and coordinate on a continuing basis laws, programs, and Government activities relating to domestic educational programs and institutions and programs of student assistance within the jurisdiction of other committees.

(e) The Committee on Government Reform shall review and study on a continuing basis the operation of Government activities at all levels with a view to determining their economy and efficiency.

(f) The Committee on International Relations shall review and study on a continuing basis laws, programs, and Government activities relating to customs administration, intelligence activities relating to foreign policy, international financial and monetary organizations, and international fishing agreements.

(g) The Committee on Armed Services shall review and study on a continuing basis laws, programs, and Government activities relating to international arms control and disarmament and the education of military dependents in schools.

(h) The Committee on Resources shall review and study on a continuing basis laws, programs, and Government activities relating to Native Americans.

(i) The Committee on Rules shall review and study on a continuing basis the congressional budget process, and the committee shall report its findings and recommendations to the House from time to time.

(j) The Committee on Science shall review and study on a continuing basis laws, programs, and Government activities relating to nonmilitary research and development.

(k) The Committee on Small Business shall study and investigate on a continuing basis the problems of all types of small business.

ADDITIONAL FUNCTIONS OF COMMITTEES

4. (a)(1)(A) The Committee on Appropriations shall, within 30 days after the transmittal of the Budget to Congress each year, hold hearings on the Budget as a whole with particular reference to—

(i) the basic recommendations and budgetary policies of the President in the presentation of the Budget; and

(ii) the fiscal, financial, and economic assumptions used as bases in arriving at total estimated expenditures and receipts.

(B) In holding hearings under subdivision (A), the committee shall receive testimony from the Secretary of the Treasury, the Director of the Office of Management and Budget, the Chairman of the Council of Economic Advisers, and such other persons as the committee may desire.

(C) A hearing under subdivision (A), or any part thereof, shall be held in open session, except when the committee, in open session and with a quorum present, determines by record vote that the testimony to be taken at that hearing on that day may be related to a matter of national security. The committee may by the same procedure close one subsequent day of hearing. A transcript of all such hearings shall be printed and a copy thereof furnished to each Member, Delegate, and the Resident Commissioner.

(D) A hearing under subdivision (A), or any part thereof, may be held before a joint meeting of the committee and the Committee on Appropriations of the Senate in accordance with such procedures as the two committees jointly may determine.

(2) Pursuant to section 401(b)(2) of the Congressional Budget Act of 1974, when a committee reports a bill or joint resolution that provides new entitlement authority as defined in section 3(9) of that Act, and enactment of the bill or joint resolution, as reported, would cause a breach of the committee's pertinent allocation of new budget authority under section 302(a) of that Act, the bill or joint resolution may be referred to the Committee on Appropriations with instructions to report it with recommendations (which may include an amendment limiting the total amount of new entitlement authority provided in the bill or joint resolution). If the Committee on Appropriations fails to report a bill or joint resolution so referred within 15 calendar days (not counting any day on which the House is not in session), the committee automatically shall be discharged from consideration of the bill or joint resolution, and the bill or joint resolution shall be placed on the appropriate calendar.

(3) In addition, the Committee on Appropriations shall study on a continuing basis those provisions of law that (on the first day of the first fiscal year for which the congressional budget process is effective) provide spending authority or permanent budget authority and shall report to the House from time to time its recommendations for terminating or modifying such provisions.

(4) In the manner provided by section 302 of the Congressional Budget Act of 1974, the Committee on Appropriations (after consulting with the Committee on Appropriations of the Senate) shall subdivide any allocations made to it in the joint explanatory statement accompanying the conference report on such concurrent resolution, and promptly report the subdivisions to the House as soon as practicable after a concurrent resolution on the budget for a fiscal year is agreed to.

(b) The Committee on the Budget shall—

(1) review on a continuing basis the conduct by the Congressional Budget Office of its functions and duties;

(2) hold hearings and receive testimony from Members, Senators, Delegates, the Resident Commissioner, and such appropriate representatives of Federal departments and agencies, the general public, and national organizations as it considers desirable in developing concurrent resolutions on the budget for each fiscal year;

(3) make all reports required of it by the Congressional Budget Act of 1974;

(4) study on a continuing basis those provisions of law that exempt Federal agencies or any of their activities or outlays from inclusion in the Budget of the United States Government, and report to the House from time to time its recommendations for terminating or modifying such provisions;

(5) study on a continuing basis proposals designed to improve and facilitate the congressional budget process, and report to the House from time to time the results of such studies, together with its recommendations; and

(6) request and evaluate continuing studies of tax expenditures, devise methods of coordinating tax expenditures, policies, and programs with direct budget outlays, and report the results of such studies to the House on a recurring basis.

(c)(1) The Committee on Government Reform shall—

(A) receive and examine reports of the Comptroller General of the United States and submit to the House such recommendations as it considers necessary or desirable in connection with the subject matter of the reports;

(B) evaluate the effects of laws enacted to reorganize the legislative and executive branches of the Government; and

(C) study intergovernmental relationships between the United States and the States and municipalities and between the United States and international organizations of which the United States is a member.

(2) In addition to its duties under subparagraph (1), the Committee on Government Reform may at any time conduct investigations of any matter without regard to clause 1, 2, 3, or this clause conferring jurisdiction over the matter to another standing committee. The findings and recommendations of the committee in such an investigation shall be made available to any other standing committee having jurisdiction over the matter involved and shall be included in the report of any such other committee when required by clause 3(c)(4) of rule XIII.

(d)(1) The Committee on House Administration shall—

(A) examine all bills, amendments, and joint resolutions after passage by the House and, in cooperation with the Senate, examine all bills and joint resolutions that have passed both Houses to see that they are correctly enrolled and forthwith present those bills and joint resolutions that originated in the House to the President in person after their signature by the Speaker and the President of the Senate, and report to the House the fact and date of their presentment;

(B) provide policy direction for, and oversight of, the Clerk, Sergeant-at-Arms, Chief Administrative Officer, and Inspector General;

(C) have the function of accepting on behalf of the House a gift, except as otherwise provided by law, if the gift does not involve a duty, burden, or condition, or is not made dependent on some future performance by the House; and

(D) promulgate regulations to carry out subdivision (C).

(2) An employing office of the House may enter into a settlement of a complaint under the Congressional Accountability Act of 1995 that provides for the payment of funds only after receiving the joint approval of the chairman and ranking minority member of the Committee on House Administration concerning the amount of such payment.

(e)(1) Each standing committee shall, in its consideration of all public bills and public joint resolutions within its jurisdiction, ensure that appropriations for continuing programs and activities of the Federal Government and the government of the District of Columbia will be made annually to the maximum extent feasible and consistent with the nature, requirement, and objective of the programs and activities involved. In this subparagraph programs and activities of the Federal Government and the government of the District of Columbia includes programs and activities of any department, agency, establishment, wholly owned Government corporation, or instrumentality of the Federal Government or of the government of the District of Columbia.

(2) Each standing committee shall review from time to time each continuing program within its jurisdiction for which appropriations are not made annually to ascertain whether the program should be modified to provide for annual appropriations.

BUDGET ACT RESPONSIBILITIES

(f)(1) Each standing committee shall submit to the Committee on the Budget not later than six weeks after the President submits his budget, or at such time as the Committee on the Budget may request—

(A) its views and estimates with respect to all matters to be set forth in the concurrent resolution on the budget for the ensuing fiscal year that are within its jurisdiction or functions; and

(B) an estimate of the total amounts of new budget authority, and budget outlays resulting therefrom, to be provided or authorized in all bills and resolutions within its jurisdiction that it intends to be effective during that fiscal year.

(2) The views and estimates submitted by the Committee on Ways and Means under subparagraph (1) shall include a specific recommendation, made after holding public hearings, as to the appropriate level of the public debt that should be set forth in the concurrent resolution on the budget and serve as the basis for an increase or decrease in the statutory limit on such debt under the procedures provided by rule XXIII.

ELECTION AND MEMBERSHIP OF STANDING COMMITTEES

5. (a)(1) The standing committees specified in clause 1 shall be elected by the House within seven calendar days after the commencement of each Congress, from nominations submitted by the respective party caucus or conference. A resolution proposing to change the composition of a standing committee shall be privileged if offered by direction of the party caucus or conference concerned.

(2)(A) The Committee on the Budget shall be composed of members as follows:

(i) Members, Delegates, or the Resident Commissioner who are members of other standing committees, including five who are members of the Committee on Appropriations and five who are members of the Committee on Ways and Means;
(ii) one Member from the elected leadership of the majority party; and
(iii) one Member from the elected leadership of the minority party.

(B) Except as permitted by subdivision (C), a member of the Committee on the Budget other than one from the elected leadership of a party may not serve on the committee during more than four Congresses in a period of six successive Congresses (disregarding for this purpose any service for less than a full session in a Congress).

(C) A member of the Committee on the Budget who served as either the chairman or the ranking minority member of the committee in the immediately previous Congress and who did not serve in that respective capacity in an earlier Congress may serve as either the chairman or the ranking minority member of the committee during one additional Congress.

(3)(A) The Committee on Standards of Official Conduct shall be composed of 10 members, five from the majority party and five from the minority party.

(B) Except as permitted by subdivision (C), a member of the Committee on Standards of Official Conduct may not serve on the committee during more than three Congresses in a period of five successive Congresses (disregarding for this purpose any service for less than a full session in a Congress).

(C) A member of the Committee on Standards of Official Conduct may serve on the committee during a fourth Congress in a period of five successive Congresses only as either the chairman or the ranking minority member of the committee.

(4)(A) At the beginning of a Congress, the Speaker or his designee and the Minority Leader or his designee each shall name 10 Members, Delegates, or the Resident Commissioner from his respective party who are not members of the Committee on Standards of Official Conduct to be available to serve on investigative subcommittees of that committee during that Congress. The lists of Members, Delegates, or the Resident Commissioner so named shall be announced to the House.

(B) Whenever the chairman and the ranking minority member of the Committee on Standards of Official Conduct jointly determine that Members, Delegates, or the Resident Commissioner named under subdivision (A) should be assigned to serve on an investigative

subcommittee of that committee, each of them shall select an equal number of such Members, Delegates, or Resident Commissioner from his respective party to serve on that subcommittee.

(b)(1) Membership on a standing committee during the course of a Congress shall be contingent on continuing membership in the party caucus or conference that nominated the Member, Delegate, or Resident Commissioner concerned for election to such committee. Should a Member, Delegate, or Resident Commissioner cease to be a member of a particular party caucus or conference, that Member, Delegate, or Resident Commissioner shall automatically cease to be a member of each standing committee to which he was elected on the basis of nomination by that caucus or conference. The chairman of the relevant party caucus or conference shall notify the Speaker whenever a Member, Delegate, or Resident Commissioner ceases to be a member of that caucus or conference. The Speaker shall notify the chairman of each affected committee that the election of such Member, Delegate, or Resident Commissioner to the committee is automatically vacated under this subparagraph.

(2)(A) Except as specified in subdivision (B), a Member, Delegate, or Resident Commissioner may not serve simultaneously as a member of more than two standing committees or more than four subcommittees of the standing committees.

(B)(i) Ex officio service by a chairman or ranking minority member of a committee on each of its subcommittees under a committee rule does not count against the limitation on subcommittee service.

(ii) Service on an investigative subcommittee of the Committee on Standards of Official Conduct under paragraph (a)(4) does not count against the limitation on subcommittee service.

(iii) Any other exception to the limitations in subdivision (A) must be approved by the House on the recommendation of the relevant party caucus or conference.

(C) In this subparagraph the term "subcommittee" includes a panel (other than a special oversight panel of the Committee on Armed Services), task force, special subcommittee, or other subunit of a standing committee that is established for a cumulative period longer than six months in a Congress.

(c)(1) One of the members of each standing committee shall be elected by the House, on the nomination of the majority party caucus or conference, as chairman thereof. In the temporary absence of the chairman, the member next in rank (and so on, as often as the case shall happen) shall act as chairman. Rank shall be determined by the order members are named in resolutions electing them to the committee. In the case of a permanent vacancy in the elected chairmanship of a committee, the House shall elect another chairman.

(2) A member of a standing committee may not serve as chairman of the same standing committee, or of the same subcommittee of a standing committee, during more than three consecutive Congresses (disregarding for this purpose any service for less than a full session in a Congress).

(d)(1) Except as permitted by subparagraph (2), a committee may have not more than five subcommittees.

(2) A committee that maintains a subcommittee on oversight may have not more than six subcommittees. The Committee on Appropriations may have not more than 13 subcommittees. The Committee on Government Reform may have not more than seven subcommittees.

(e) The House shall fill a vacancy on a standing committee by election on the nomination of the respective party caucus or conference.

EXPENSE RESOLUTIONS

6. (a) Whenever a committee, commission, or other entity (other than the Committee on Appropriations) is granted authorization for the payment of its expenses (including staff salaries) for a Congress, such authorization initially shall be procured by one primary expense

resolution reported by the Committee on House Administration. A primary expense resolution may include a reserve fund for unanticipated expenses of committees. An amount from such a reserve fund may be allocated to a committee only by the approval of the Committee on House Administration. A primary expense resolution reported to the House may not be considered in the House unless a printed report thereon was available on the previous calendar day. For the information of the House, such report shall—

(1) state the total amount of the funds to be provided to the committee, commission, or other entity under the primary expense resolution for all anticipated activities and programs of the committee, commission, or other entity; and

(2) to the extent practicable, contain such general statements regarding the estimated foreseeable expenditures for the respective anticipated activities and programs of the committee, commission, or other entity as may be appropriate to provide the House with basic estimates of the expenditures contemplated by the primary expense resolution.

(b) After the date of adoption by the House of a primary expense resolution for a committee, commission, or other entity for a Congress, authorization for the payment of additional expenses (including staff salaries) in that Congress may be procured by one or more supplemental expense resolutions reported by the Committee on House Administration, as necessary. A supplemental expense resolution reported to the House may not be considered in the House unless a printed report thereon was available on the previous calendar day. For the information of the House, such report shall—

(1) state the total amount of additional funds to be provided to the committee, commission, or other entity under the supplemental expense resolution and the purposes for which those additional funds are available; and

(2) state the reasons for the failure to procure the additional funds for the committee, commission, or other entity by means of the primary expense resolution.

(c) The preceding provisions of this clause do not apply to—

(1) a resolution providing for the payment from committee salary and expense accounts of the House of sums necessary to pay compensation for staff services performed for, or to pay other expenses of, a committee, commission, or other entity at any time after the beginning of an odd-numbered year and before the date of adoption by the House of the primary expense resolution described in paragraph (a) for that year; or

(2) a resolution providing each of the standing committees in a Congress additional office equipment, airmail and special-delivery postage stamps, supplies, staff personnel, or any other specific item for the operation of the standing committees, and containing an authorization for the payment from committee salary and expense accounts of the House of the expenses of any of the foregoing items provided by that resolution, subject to and until enactment of the provisions of the resolution as permanent law.

(d) From the funds made available for the appointment of committee staff by a primary or additional expense resolution, the chairman of each committee shall ensure that sufficient staff is made available to each subcommittee to carry out its responsibilities under the rules of the committee and that the minority party is treated fairly in the appointment of such staff.

(e) Funds authorized for a committee under this clause and clauses 7 and 8 are for expenses incurred in the activities of the committee.

INTERIM FUNDING

7. (a) For the period beginning at noon on January 3 and ending at midnight on March 31 in each odd-numbered year, such sums as may be necessary shall be paid out of the committee salary and expense accounts of the House for continuance of necessary investigations and studies by—

(1) each standing and select committee established by these rules; and

(2) except as specified in paragraph (b), each select committee established by resolution.

(b) In the case of the first session of a Congress, amounts shall be made available under this paragraph for a select committee established by resolution in the preceding Congress only if—

(1) a resolution proposing to reestablish such select committee is introduced in the present Congress; and

(2) the House has not adopted a resolution of the preceding Congress providing for termination of funding for investigations and studies by such select committee.

(c) Each committee described in paragraph (a) shall be entitled for each month during the period specified in paragraph (a) to 9 percent (or such lesser percentage as may be determined by the Committee on House Administration) of the total annualized amount made available under expense resolutions for such committee in the preceding session of Congress.

(d) Payments under this paragraph shall be made on vouchers authorized by the committee involved, signed by the chairman of the committee, except as provided in paragraph (e), and approved by the Committee on House Administration.

(e) Notwithstanding any provision of law, rule of the House, or other authority, from noon on January 3 of the first session of a Congress until the election by the House of the committee concerned in that Congress, payments under this paragraph shall be made on vouchers signed by—

(1) the member of the committee who served as chairman of the committee at the expiration of the preceding Congress; or

(2) if the chairman is not a Member, Delegate, or Resident Commissioner in the present Congress, then the ranking member of the committee as it was constituted at the expiration of the preceding Congress who is a member of the majority party in the present Congress.

(f)(1) The authority of a committee to incur expenses under this paragraph shall expire upon adoption by the House of a primary expense resolution for the committee.

(2) Amounts made available under this paragraph shall be expended in accordance with regulations prescribed by the Committee on House Administration.

(3) This clause shall be effective only insofar as it is not inconsistent with a resolution reported by the Committee on House Administration and adopted by the House after the adoption of these rules.

TRAVEL

8. (a) Local currencies owned by the United States shall be made available to the committee and its employees engaged in carrying out their official duties outside the United States or its territories or possessions. Appropriated funds, including those authorized under this clause and clauses 6 and 8, may not be expended for the purpose of defraying expenses of members of a committee or its employees in a country where local currencies are available for this purpose.

(b) The following conditions shall apply with respect to travel outside the United States or its territories or possessions:

(1) A member or employee of a committee may not receive or expend local currencies for subsistence in a country for a day at a rate in excess of the maximum per diem set forth in applicable Federal law.

(2) A member or employee shall be reimbursed for his expenses for a day at the lesser of—

(A) the per diem set forth in applicable Federal law; or

(B) the actual, unreimbursed expenses (other than for transportation) he incurred during that day.

(3) Each member or employee of a committee shall make to the chairman of the committee an itemized report showing the dates each country was visited, the amount of per diem furnished, the cost of transportation furnished, and funds expended for any other official purpose and shall summarize in these categories the total foreign

currencies or appropriated funds expended. Each report shall be filed with the chairman of the committee not later than 60 days following the completion of travel for use in complying with reporting requirements in applicable Federal law and shall be open for public inspection.

(c)(1) In carrying out the activities of a committee outside the United States in a country where local currencies are unavailable, a member or employee of a committee may not receive reimbursement for expenses (other than for transportation) in excess of the maximum per diem set forth in applicable Federal law.

(2) A member or employee shall be reimbursed for his expenses for a day, at the lesser of—

(A) the per diem set forth in applicable Federal law; or
(B) the actual unreimbursed expenses (other than for transportation) he incurred during that day.

(3) A member or employee of a committee may not receive reimbursement for the cost of any transportation in connection with travel outside the United States unless the member or employee actually paid for the transportation.

(d) The restrictions respecting travel outside the United States set forth in paragraph (c) also shall apply to travel outside the United States by a Member, Delegate, Resident Commissioner, officer, or employee of the House authorized under any standing rule.

COMMITTEE STAFFS

9. (a)(1) Subject to subparagraph (2) and paragraph (f), each standing committee may appoint, by majority vote, not more than 30 professional staff members to be compensated from the funds provided for the appointment of committee staff by primary and additional expense resolutions. Each professional staff member appointed under this subparagraph shall be assigned to the chairman and the ranking minority member of the committee, as the committee considers advisable.

(2) Subject to paragraph (f) whenever a majority of the minority party members of a standing committee (other than the Committee on Standards of Official Conduct or the Permanent Select Committee on Intelligence) so request, not more than 10 persons (or one-third of the total professional committee staff appointed under this clause, whichever is fewer) may be selected, by majority vote of the minority party members, for appointment by the committee as professional staff members under subparagraph (1). The committee shall appoint persons so selected whose character and qualifications are acceptable to a majority of the committee. If the committee determines that the character and qualifications of a person so selected are unacceptable, a majority of the minority party members may select another person for appointment by the committee to the professional staff until such appointment is made. Each professional staff member appointed under this subparagraph shall be assigned to such committee business as the minority party members of the committee consider advisable.

(b)(1) The professional staff members of each standing committee—

(A) may not engage in any work other than committee business during congressional working hours; and
(B) may not be assigned a duty other than one pertaining to committee business.

(2) Subparagraph (1) does not apply to staff designated by a committee as "associate" or "shared" staff who are not paid exclusively by the committee, provided that the chairman certifies that the compensation paid by the committee for any such staff is commensurate with the work performed for the committee in accordance with clause 8 of rule XXIV.

(3) The use of any "associate" or "shared" staff by a committee

shall be subject to the review of, and to any terms, conditions, or limitations established by, the Committee on House Administration in connection with the reporting of any primary or additional expense resolution.

(4) This paragraph does not apply to the Committee on Appropriations.

(c) Each employee on the professional or investigative staff of a standing committee shall be entitled to pay at a single gross per annum rate, to be fixed by the chairman and that does not exceed the maximum rate of pay as in effect from time to time under applicable provisions of law.

(d) Subject to appropriations hereby authorized, the Committee on Appropriations may appoint by majority vote such staff as it determines to be necessary (in addition to the clerk of the committee and assistants for the minority). The staff appointed under this paragraph, other than minority assistants, shall possess such qualifications as the committee may prescribe.

(e) A committee may not appoint to its staff an expert or other personnel detailed or assigned from a department or agency of the Government except with the written permission of the Committee on House Administration.

(f) If a request for the appointment of a minority professional staff member under paragraph (a) is made when no vacancy exists for such an appointment, the committee nevertheless may appoint under paragraph (a) a person selected by the minority and acceptable to the committee. A person so appointed shall serve as an additional member of the professional staff of the committee until such a vacancy occurs (other than a vacancy in the position of head of the professional staff, by whatever title designated), at which time that person is considered as appointed to that vacancy. Such a person shall be paid from the applicable accounts of the House described in clause 1(i)(1) of rule X. If such a vacancy occurs on the professional staff when seven or more persons have been so appointed who are eligible to fill that vacancy, a majority of the minority party members shall designate which of those persons shall fill the vacancy.

(g) Each staff member appointed pursuant to a request by minority party members under paragraph (a), and each staff member appointed to assist minority members of a committee pursuant to an expense resolution described in paragraph (a) of clause 6, shall be accorded equitable treatment with respect to the fixing of the rate of pay, the assignment of work facilities, and the accessibility of committee records.

(h) Paragraph (a) may not be construed to authorize the appointment of additional professional staff members of a committee pursuant to a request under paragraph (a) by the minority party members of that committee if 10 or more professional staff members provided for in paragraph (a)(1) who are satisfactory to a majority of the minority party members are otherwise assigned to assist the minority party members.

(i) Notwithstanding paragraph (a)(2), a committee may employ nonpartisan staff, in lieu of or in addition to committee staff designated exclusively for the majority or minority party, by an affirmative vote of a majority of the members of the majority party and of a majority of the members of the minority party.

SELECT AND JOINT COMMITTEES

10. (a) Membership on a select or joint committee appointed by the Speaker under clause 11 of rule I during the course of a Congress shall be contingent on continuing membership in the party caucus or conference of which the Member, Delegate, or Resident Commissioner concerned was a member at the time of appointment. Should a Member, Delegate, or Resident Commissioner cease to be a member

of that caucus or conference, that Member, Delegate, or Resident Commissioner shall automatically cease to be a member of any select or joint committee to which he is assigned. The chairman of the relevant party caucus or conference shall notify the Speaker whenever a Member, Delegate, or Resident Commissioner ceases to be a member of a party caucus or conference. The Speaker shall notify the chairman of each affected select or joint committee that the appointment of such Member, Delegate, or Resident Commissioner to the select or joint committee is automatically vacated under this paragraph.

(b) Each select or joint committee, other than a conference committee, shall comply with clause 2(a) of rule XI unless specifically exempted by law.

PERMANENT SELECT COMMITTEE ON INTELLIGENCE

11. (a)(1) There is established a Permanent Select Committee on Intelligence (hereafter in this clause referred to as the "select committee"). The select committee shall be composed of not more than 16 Members, Delegates, or the Resident Commissioner, of whom not more than nine may be from the same party. The select committee shall include at least one Member, Delegate, or the Resident Commissioner from each of the following committees:

(A) the Committee on Appropriations;
(B) the Committee on Armed Services;
(C) the Committee on International Relations; and
(D) the Committee on the Judiciary.

(2) The Speaker and the Minority Leader shall be ex officio members of the select committee but shall have no vote in the select committee and may not be counted for purposes of determining a quorum thereof.

(3) The Speaker and Minority Leader each may designate a member of his leadership staff to assist him in his capacity as ex officio member, with the same access to committee meetings, hearings, briefings, and materials as employees of the select committee and subject to the same security clearance and confidentiality requirements as employees of the select committee under this clause.

(4)(A) Except as permitted by subdivision (B), a Member, Delegate, or Resident Commissioner, other than the Speaker or the Minority Leader, may not serve as a member of the select committee during more than four Congresses in a period of six successive Congresses (disregarding for this purpose any service for less than a full session in a Congress).

(B) A member of the select committee who served as either the chairman or the ranking minority member of the select committee in the immediately previous Congress and who did not serve in that respective capacity in an earlier Congress may serve as either the chairman or the ranking minority member of the select committee during one additional Congress.

(b)(1) There shall be referred to the select committee proposed legislation, messages, petitions, memorials, and other matters relating to the following:

(A) The Central Intelligence Agency, the Director of Central Intelligence, and the National Foreign Intelligence Program as defined in section 3(6) of the National Security Act of 1947.

(B) Intelligence and intelligence-related activities of all other departments and agencies of the Government, including the tactical intelligence and intelligence-related activities of the Department of Defense.

(C) The organization or reorganization of a department or agency of the Government to the extent that the organization or reorganization relates to a function or activity involving intelligence or intelligence-related activities.

(D) Authorizations for appropriations, both direct and indirect, for the following:

(i) The Central Intelligence Agency, the Director of Central Intelligence, and the National Foreign Intelligence Program as defined in section 3(6) of the National Security Act of 1947.

(ii) Intelligence and intelligence-related activities of all other departments and agencies of the Government, including the tactical intelligence and intelligence-related activities of the Department of Defense.

(iii) A department, agency, subdivision, or program that is a successor to an agency or program named or referred to in (i) or (ii).

(2) Proposed legislation initially reported by the select committee (other than provisions solely involving matters specified in subparagraph (1)(A) or subparagraph (1)(D)(i)) containing any matter otherwise within the jurisdiction of a standing committee shall be referred by the Speaker to that standing committee. Proposed legislation initially reported by another committee that contains matter within the jurisdiction of the select committee shall be referred by the Speaker to the select committee if requested by the chairman of the select committee.

(3) Nothing in this clause shall be construed as prohibiting or otherwise restricting the authority of any other committee to study and review an intelligence or intelligence-related activity to the extent that such activity directly affects a matter otherwise within the jurisdiction of that committee.

(4) Nothing in this clause shall be construed as amending, limiting, or otherwise changing the authority of a standing committee to obtain full and prompt access to the product of the intelligence and intelligence-related activities of a department or agency of the Government relevant to a matter otherwise within the jurisdiction of that committee.

(c)(1) For purposes of accountability to the House, the select committee shall make regular and periodic reports to the House on the nature and extent of the intelligence and intelligence-related activities of the various departments and agencies of the United States. The select committee shall promptly call to the attention of the House, or to any other appropriate committee, a matter requiring the attention of the House or another committee. In making such report, the select committee shall proceed in a manner consistent with paragraph (g) to protect national security.

(2) The select committee shall obtain annual reports from the Director of the Central Intelligence Agency, the Secretary of Defense, the Secretary of State, and the Director of the Federal Bureau of Investigation. Such reports shall review the intelligence and intelligence-related activities of the agency or department concerned and the intelligence and intelligence-related activities of foreign countries directed at the United States or its interests. An unclassified version of each report may be made available to the public at the discretion of the select committee. Nothing herein shall be construed as requiring the public disclosure in such reports of the names of persons engaged in intelligence or intelligence-related activities for the United States or the divulging of intelligence methods employed or the sources of information on which the reports are based or the amount of funds authorized to be appropriated for intelligence and intelligence-related activities.

(3) Within six weeks after the President submits a budget under section 1105(a) of title 31, United States Code, or at such time as the Committee on the Budget may request, the select committee shall submit to the Committee on the Budget the views and estimates described in section 301(d) of the Congressional Budget Act of 1974 regarding matters within the jurisdiction of the select committee.

(d)(1) Except as specified in subparagraph (2), clauses 6(a), (b), and (c) and 8(a), (b), and (c) of this rule, and clauses 1, 2, and 4 of rule XI shall apply to the select committee to the extent not inconsistent with this clause.

(2) Notwithstanding the requirements of the first sentence of clause 2(g)(2) of rule XI, in the presence of the number of members required under the rules of the select committee for the purpose of taking testimony or receiving evidence, the select committee may vote to close a hearing whenever a majority of those present determines that the testimony or evidence would endanger the national security.

(e) An employee of the select committee, or a person engaged by contract or otherwise to perform services for or at the request of the select committee, may not be given access to any classified information by the select committee unless such employee or person has—

(1) agreed in writing and under oath to be bound by the Rules of the House, including the jurisdiction of the Committee on Standards of Official Conduct and of the select committee concerning the security of classified information during and after the period of his employment or contractual agreement with the select committee; and

(2) received an appropriate security clearance, as determined by the select committee in consultation with the Director of Central Intelligence, that is commensurate with the sensitivity of the classified information to which such employee or person will be given access by the select committee.

(f) The select committee shall formulate and carry out such rules and procedures as it considers necessary to prevent the disclosure, without the consent of each person concerned, of information in the possession of the select committee that unduly infringes on the privacy or that violates the constitutional rights of such person. Nothing herein shall be construed to prevent the select committee from publicly disclosing classified information in a case in which it determines that national interest in the disclosure of classified information clearly outweighs any infringement on the privacy of a person.

(g)(1) The select committee may disclose publicly any information in its possession after a determination by the select committee that the public interest would be served by such disclosure. With respect to the disclosure of information for which this paragraph requires action by the select committee—

(A) the select committee shall meet to vote on the matter within five days after a member of the select committee requests a vote; and

(B) a member of the select committee may not make such a disclosure before a vote by the select committee on the matter, or after a vote by the select committee on the matter except in accordance with this paragraph.

(2)(A) In a case in which the select committee votes to disclose publicly any information that has been classified under established security procedures, that has been submitted to it by the executive branch, and that the executive branch requests be kept secret, the select committee shall notify the President of such vote.

(B) The select committee may disclose publicly such information after the expiration of a five-day period following the day on which notice of the vote to disclose is transmitted to the President unless, before the expiration of the five-day period, the President, personally in writing, notifies the select committee that he objects to the disclosure of such information, provides his reasons therefor, and certifies that the threat to the national interest of the United States posed by the disclosure is of such gravity that it outweighs any public interest in the disclosure.

(C) If the President, personally in writing, notifies the select committee of his objections to the disclosure of information as provided in subdivision (B), the select committee may, by majority vote, refer the question of the disclosure of such information, with a recommendation thereon, to the House. The select committee may not publicly disclose such information without leave of the House.

(D) Whenever the select committee votes to refer the question of disclosure of any information to the House under subdivision (C), the chairman shall, not later than the first day on which the House is in session following the day on which the vote occurs, report the matter to the House for its consideration.

(E) If the chairman of the select committee does not offer in the House a motion to consider in closed session a matter reported under subdivision (D) within four calendar days on which the House is in session after the recommendation described in subdivision (C) is reported, then such a motion shall be privileged when offered by a Member, Delegate, or Resident Commissioner. In either case such a motion shall be decided without debate or intervening motion except one that the House adjourn.

(F) Upon adoption by the House of a motion to resolve into closed session as described in subdivision (E), the Speaker may declare a recess subject to the call of the Chair. At the expiration of the recess, the pending question, in closed session, shall be, "Shall the House approve the recommendation of the select committee?".

(G) Debate on the question described in subdivision (F) shall be limited to two hours equally divided and controlled by the chairman and ranking minority member of the select committee. After such debate the previous question shall be considered as ordered on the question of approving the recommendation without intervening motion except one motion that the House adjourn. The House shall vote on the question in open session but without divulging the information with respect to which the vote is taken. If the recommendation of the select committee is not approved, then the question is considered as recommitted to the select committee for further recommendation.

(3)(A) Information in the possession of the select committee relating to the lawful intelligence or intelligence-related activities of a department or agency of the United States that has been classified under established security procedures, and that the select committee has determined should not be disclosed under subparagraph (1) or (2), may not be made available to any person by a Member, Delegate, Resident Commissioner, officer, or employee of the House except as provided in subdivision (B).

(B) The select committee shall, under such regulations as it may prescribe, make information described in subdivision (A) available to a committee or a Member, Delegate, or Resident Commissioner, and permit a Member, Delegate, or Resident Commissioner to attend a hearing of the select committee that is closed to the public. Whenever the select committee makes such information available, it shall keep a written record showing, in the case of particular information, which committee or which Member, Delegate, or Resident Commissioner received the information. A Member, Delegate, or Resident Commissioner who, and a committee that, receives information under this subdivision may not disclose the information except in a closed session of the House.

(4) The Committee on Standards of Official Conduct shall investigate any unauthorized disclosure of intelligence or intelligence-related information by a Member, Delegate, Resident Commissioner, officer, or employee of the House in violation of subparagraph (3) and report to the House concerning any allegation that it finds to be substantiated.

(5) Upon the request of a person who is subject to an investigation described in subparagraph (4), the Committee on Standards of Official Conduct shall release to such person at the conclusion of its investigation a summary of its investigation, together with its findings. If, at the conclusion of its investigation, the Committee on Standards of Official Conduct determines that there has been a significant breach of confidentiality or unauthorized disclosure by a Member, Delegate, Resident Commissioner, officer, or employee of the House, it shall report its findings to the House and recommend appropriate

action. Recommendations may include censure, removal from committee membership, or expulsion from the House, in the case of a Member, or removal from office or employment or punishment for contempt, in the case of an officer or employee.

(h) The select committee may permit a personal representative of the President, designated by the President to serve as a liaison to the select committee, to attend any closed meeting of the select committee.

(i) Subject to the Rules of the House, funds may not be appropriated for a fiscal year, with the exception of a bill or joint resolution continuing appropriations, or an amendment thereto, or a conference report thereon, to, or for use of, a department or agency of the United States to carry out any of the following activities, unless the funds shall previously have been authorized by a bill or joint resolution passed by the House during the same or preceding fiscal year to carry out such activity for such fiscal year:

(1) The activities of the Central Intelligence Agency and the Director of Central Intelligence.

(2) The activities of the Defense Intelligence Agency.

(3) The activities of the National Security Agency.

(4) The intelligence and intelligence-related activities of other agencies and subdivisions of the Department of Defense.

(5) The intelligence and intelligence-related activities of the Department of State.

(6) The intelligence and intelligence-related activities of the Federal Bureau of Investigation, including all activities of the Intelligence Division.

(j)(1) In this clause the term "intelligence and intelligence-related activities" includes—

(A) the collection, analysis, production, dissemination, or use of information that relates to a foreign country, or a government, political group, party, military force, movement, or other association in a foreign country, and that relates to the defense, foreign policy, national security, or related policies of the United States and other activity in support of the collection, analysis, production, dissemination, or use of such information;

(B) activities taken to counter similar activities directed against the United States;

(C) covert or clandestine activities affecting the relations of the United States with a foreign government, political group, party, military force, movement, or other association;

(D) the collection, analysis, production, dissemination, or use of information about activities of persons within the United States, its territories and possessions, or nationals of the United States abroad whose political and related activities pose, or may be considered by a department, agency, bureau, office, division, instrumentality, or employee of the United States to pose, a threat to the internal security of the United States; and

(E) covert or clandestine activities directed against persons described in subdivision (D).

(2) In this clause the term "department or agency" includes any organization, committee, council, establishment, or office within the Federal Government.

(3) For purposes of this clause, reference to a department, agency, bureau, or subdivision shall include a reference to any successor department, agency, bureau, or subdivision to the extent that a successor engages in intelligence or intelligence-related activities now conducted by the department, agency, bureau, or subdivision referred to in this clause.

(k) Clause 12(a) of rule XXII does not apply to meetings of a conference committee respecting legislation (or any part thereof) reported by the Permanent Select Committee on Intelligence.

RULE XI

PROCEDURES OF COMMITTEES AND UNFINISHED BUSINESS

IN GENERAL

1. (a)(1)(A) Except as provided in subdivision (B), the Rules of the House are the rules of its committees and subcommittees so far as applicable.

(B) A motion to recess from day to day, and a motion to dispense with the first reading (in full) of a bill or resolution, if printed copies are available, each shall be privileged in committees and subcommittees and shall be decided without debate.

(2) Each subcommittee is a part of its committee and is subject to the authority and direction of that committee and to its rules, so far as applicable.

(b)(1) Each committee may conduct at any time such investigations and studies as it considers necessary or appropriate in the exercise of its responsibilities under rule X. Subject to the adoption of expense resolutions as required by clause 6 of rule X, each committee may incur expenses, including travel expenses, in connection with such investigations and studies.

(2) A proposed investigative or oversight report shall be considered as read in committee if it has been available to the members for at least 24 hours (excluding Saturdays, Sundays, or legal holidays except when the House is in session on such a day).

(3) A report of an investigation or study conducted jointly by more than one committee may be filed jointly, provided that each of the committees complies independently with all requirements for approval and filing of the report.

(4) After an adjournment sine die of the last regular session of a Congress, an investigative or oversight report may be filed with the Clerk at any time, provided that a member who gives timely notice of intention to file supplemental, minority, or additional views shall be entitled to not less than seven calendar days in which to submit such views for inclusion in the report.

(c) Each committee may have printed and bound such testimony and other data as may be presented at hearings held by the committee or its subcommittees. All costs of stenographic services and transcripts in connection with a meeting or hearing of a committee shall be paid from the applicable accounts of the House described in clause 1(i)(1) of rule X.

(d)(1) Each committee shall submit to the House not later than January 2 of each odd-numbered year a report on the activities of that committee under this rule and rule X during the Congress ending at noon on January 3 of such year.

(2) Such report shall include separate sections summarizing the legislative and oversight activities of that committee during that Congress.

(3) The oversight section of such report shall include a summary of the oversight plans submitted by the committee under clause 2(d) of rule X, a summary of the actions taken and recommendations made with respect to each such plan, a summary of any additional oversight activities undertaken by that committee, and any recommendations made or actions taken thereon.

(4) After an adjournment sine die of the last regular session of a Congress, the chairman of a committee may file an activities report under subparagraph (1) with the Clerk at any time and without approval of the committee, provided that—

(A) a copy of the report has been available to each member of the committee for at least seven calendar days; and

(B) the report includes any supplemental, minority, or additional views submitted by a member of the committee.

ADOPTION OF WRITTEN RULES

2. (a)(1) Each standing committee shall adopt written rules governing its procedure. Such rules—

(A) shall be adopted in a meeting that is open to the public unless the committee, in open session and with a quorum present, determines by record vote that all or part of the meeting on that day shall be closed to the public;

(B) may not be inconsistent with the Rules of the House or with those provisions of law having the force and effect of Rules of the House; and

(C) shall in any event incorporate all of the succeeding provisions of this clause to the extent applicable.

(2) Each committee shall submit its rules for publication in the Congressional Record not later than 30 days after the committee is elected in each odd-numbered year.

REGULAR MEETING DAYS

(b) Each standing committee shall establish regular meeting days for the conduct of its business, which shall be not less frequent than monthly. Each such committee shall meet for the consideration of a bill or resolution pending before the committee or the transaction of other committee business on all regular meeting days fixed by the committee unless otherwise provided by written rule adopted by the committee.

ADDITIONAL AND SPECIAL MEETINGS

(c)(1) The chairman of each standing committee may call and convene, as he considers necessary, additional and special meetings of the committee for the consideration of a bill or resolution pending before the committee or for the conduct of other committee business, subject to such rules as the committee may adopt. The committee shall meet for such purpose under that call of the chairman.

(2) Three or more members of a standing committee may file in the offices of the committee a written request that the chairman call a special meeting of the committee. Such request shall specify the measure or matter to be considered. Immediately upon the filing of the request, the clerk of the committee shall notify the chairman of the filing of the request. If the chairman does not call the requested special meeting within three calendar days after the filing of the request (to be held within seven calendar days after the filing of the request) a majority of the members of the committee may file in the offices of the committee their written notice that a special meeting of the committee will be held. The written notice shall specify the date and hour of the special meeting and the measure or matter to be considered. The committee shall meet on that date and hour. Immediately upon the filing of the notice, the clerk of the committee shall notify all members of the committee that such special meeting will be held and inform them of its date and hour and the measure or matter to be considered. Only the measure or matter specified in that notice may be considered at that special meeting.

TEMPORARY ABSENCE OF CHAIRMAN

(d) A member of the majority party on each standing committee or subcommittee thereof shall be designated by the chairman of the full committee as the vice chairman of the committee or subcommittee, as the case may be, and shall preside during the absence of the chairman from any meeting. If the chairman and vice chairman of a committee or subcommittee are not present at any meeting of the committee or subcommittee, the ranking majority member who is present shall preside at that meeting.

COMMITTEE RECORDS

(e)(1)(A) Each committee shall keep a complete record of all committee action which shall include—

(i) in the case of a meeting or hearing transcript, a substantially verbatim account of remarks actually made during the proceedings, subject only to technical, grammatical, and typographical corrections authorized by the person making the remarks involved; and

(ii) a record of the votes on any question on which a record vote is demanded.

(B)(i) Except as provided in subdivision (B)(ii) and subject to paragraph (k)(7), the result of each such record vote shall be made available by the committee for inspection by the public at reasonable times in its offices. Information so available for public inspection shall include a description of the amendment, motion, order, or other proposition, the name of each member voting for and each member voting against such amendment, motion, order, or proposition, and the names of those members of the committee present but not voting.

(ii) The result of any record vote taken in executive session in the Committee on Standards of Official Conduct may not be made available for inspection by the public without an affirmative vote of a majority of the members of the committee.

(2)(A) Except as provided in subdivision (B), all committee hearings, records, data, charts, and files shall be kept separate and distinct from the congressional office records of the member serving as its chairman. Such records shall be the property of the House, and each Member, Delegate, and the Resident Commissioner shall have access thereto.

(B) A Member, Delegate, or Resident Commissioner, other than members of the Committee on Standards of Official Conduct, may not have access to the records of that committee respecting the conduct of a Member, Delegate, Resident Commissioner, officer, or employee of the House without the specific prior permission of that committee.

(3) Each committee shall include in its rules standards for availability of records of the committee delivered to the Archivist of the United States under rule VII. Such standards shall specify procedures for orders of the committee under clause 3(b)(3) and clause 4(b) of rule VII, including a requirement that nonavailability of a record for a period longer than the period otherwise applicable under that rule shall be approved by vote of the committee.

(4) Each committee shall make its publications available in electronic form to the maximum extent feasible.

PROHIBITION AGAINST PROXY VOTING

(f) A vote by a member of a committee or subcommittee with respect to any measure or matter may not be cast by proxy.

OPEN MEETINGS AND HEARINGS

(g)(1) Each meeting for the transaction of business, including the markup of legislation, by a standing committee or subcommittee thereof (other than the Committee on Standards of Official Conduct or its subcommittee) shall be open to the public, including to radio, television, and still photography coverage, except when the committee or subcommittee, in open session and with a majority present, determines by record vote that all or part of the remainder of the meeting on that day shall be in executive session because disclosure of matters to be considered would endanger national security, would compromise sensitive law enforcement information, would tend to defame, degrade, or incriminate any person, or otherwise would violate a law or rule of the House. Persons, other than members of the committee and such noncommittee Members, Delegates, Resident Commissioner, congressional staff, or departmental representatives as the committee may authorize, may not be present at a business or markup session that is held in executive session. This subparagraph does not apply to open committee hearings, which are governed by clause 4(a)(1) of rule X or by subparagraph (2).

(2)(A) Each hearing conducted by a committee or subcommittee (other than the Committee on Standards of Official Conduct or its subcommittees) shall be open to the public, including to radio, television, and still photography coverage, except when the committee or subcommittee, in open session and with a majority present, determines by record vote that all or part of the remainder of that hearing on that day shall be closed to the public because disclosure of testimony, evidence, or other matters to be considered would endanger national security, would compromise sensitive law enforcement information, or would violate a law or rule of the House.

(B) Notwithstanding the requirements of subdivision (A), in the presence of the number of members required under the rules of the committee for the purpose of taking testimony, a majority of those present may—

(i) agree to close the hearing for the sole purpose of discussing whether testimony or evidence to be received would endanger national security, would compromise sensitive law enforcement information, or would violate clause 2(k)(5); or

(ii) agree to close the hearing as provided in clause 2(k)(5).

(C) A Member, Delegate, or Resident Commissioner may not be excluded from nonparticipatory attendance at a hearing of a committee or subcommittee (other than the Committee on Standards of Official Conduct or its subcommittees) unless the House by majority vote authorizes a particular committee or subcommittee, for purposes of a particular series of hearings on a particular article of legislation or on a particular subject of investigation, to close its hearings to Members, Delegates, and the Resident Commissioner by the same procedures specified in this subparagraph for closing hearings to the public.

(D) The committee or subcommittee may vote by the same procedure described in this subparagraph to close one subsequent day of hearing, except that the Committee on Appropriations, the Committee on Armed Services, and the Permanent Select Committee on Intelligence, and the subcommittees thereof, may vote by the same procedure to close up to five additional, consecutive days of hearings.

(3) The chairman of each committee (other than the Committee on Rules) shall make public announcement of the date, place, and subject matter of a committee hearing at least one week before the commencement of the hearing. If the chairman of the committee, with the concurrence of the ranking minority member, determines that there is good cause to begin a hearing sooner, or if the committee so determines by majority vote in the presence of the number of members required under the rules of the committee for the transaction of business, the chairman shall make the announcement at the earliest possible date. An announcement made under this subparagraph shall be published promptly in the Daily Digest and made available in electronic form.

(4) Each committee shall, to the greatest extent practicable, require witnesses who appear before it to submit in advance written statements of proposed testimony and to limit their initial presentations to the committee to brief summaries thereof. In the case of a witness appearing in a nongovernmental capacity, a written statement of proposed testimony shall include a curriculum vitae and a disclosure of the amount and source (by agency and program) of each Federal grant (or subgrant thereof) or contract (or subcontract thereof) received during the current fiscal year or either of the two previous fiscal years by the witness or by an entity represented by the witness.

(5)(A) Except as provided in subdivision (B), a point of order does not lie with respect to a measure reported by a committee on the ground that hearings on such measure were not conducted in accordance with this clause.

(B) A point of order on the ground described in subdivision (A) may be made by a member of the committee that reported the measure if such point of order was timely made and improperly disposed of in the committee.

(6) This paragraph does not apply to hearings of the Committee on Appropriations under clause 4(a)(1) of rule X.

QUORUM REQUIREMENTS

(h)(1) A measure or recommendation may not be reported by a committee unless a majority of the committee is actually present.

(2) Each committee may fix the number of its members to constitute a quorum for taking testimony and receiving evidence, which may not be less than two.

(3) Each committee (other than the Committee on Appropriations, the Committee on the Budget, and the Committee on Ways and Means) may fix the number of its members to constitute a quorum for taking any action other than the reporting of a measure or recommendation, which may not be less than one-third of the members.

LIMITATION ON COMMITTEE SITTINGS

(i) A committee may not sit during a joint session of the House and Senate or during a recess when a joint meeting of the House and Senate is in progress.

CALLING AND QUESTIONING OF WITNESSES

(j)(1) Whenever a hearing is conducted by a committee on a measure or matter, the minority members of the committee shall be entitled, upon request to the chairman by a majority of them before the completion of the hearing, to call witnesses selected by the minority to testify with respect to that measure or matter during at least one day of hearing thereon.

(2)(A) Subject to subdivisions (B) and (C), each committee shall apply the five-minute rule during the questioning of witnesses in a hearing until such time as each member of the committee who so desires has had an opportunity to question each witness.

(B) A committee may adopt a rule or motion permitting a specified number of its members to question a witness for longer than five minutes. The time for extended questioning of a witness under this subdivision shall be equal for the majority party and the minority party and may not exceed one hour in the aggregate.

(C) A committee may adopt a rule or motion permitting committee staff for its majority and minority party members to question a witness for equal specified periods. The time for extended questioning of a witness under this subdivision shall be equal for the majority party and the minority party and may not exceed one hour in the aggregate.

INVESTIGATIVE HEARING PROCEDURES

(k)(1) The chairman at an investigative hearing shall announce in an opening statement the subject of the investigation.

(2) A copy of the committee rules and of this clause shall be made available to each witness.

(3) Witnesses at investigative hearings may be accompanied by their own counsel for the purpose of advising them concerning their constitutional rights.

(4) The chairman may punish breaches of order and decorum, and of professional ethics on the part of counsel, by censure and exclusion from the hearings; and the committee may cite the offender to the House for contempt.

(5) Whenever it is asserted that the evidence or testimony at an investigative hearing may tend to defame, degrade, or incriminate any person—

(A) notwithstanding paragraph (g)(2), such testimony or evidence shall be presented in executive session if, in the presence of the number of members required under the rules of the committee for the purpose of taking testimony, the committee determines by vote of a majority of those present that such evidence or testimony may tend to defame, degrade, or incriminate any person; and

(B) the committee shall proceed to receive such testimony in open session only if the committee, a majority being present, determines that such evidence or testimony will not tend to defame, degrade, or incriminate any person.

In either case the committee shall afford such person an opportunity voluntarily to appear as a witness, and receive and dispose of requests from such person to subpoena additional witnesses.

(6) Except as provided in subparagraph (5), the chairman shall receive and the committee shall dispose of requests to subpoena additional witnesses.

(7) Evidence or testimony taken in executive session, and proceedings conducted in executive session, may be released or used in public sessions only when authorized by the committee, a majority being present.

(8) In the discretion of the committee, witnesses may submit brief and pertinent sworn statements in writing for inclusion in the record. The committee is the sole judge of the pertinence of testimony and evidence adduced at its hearing.

(9) A witness may obtain a transcript copy of his testimony given at a public session or, if given at an executive session, when authorized by the committee.

SUPPLEMENTAL, MINORITY, OR ADDITIONAL VIEWS

(l) If at the time of approval of a measure or matter by a committee (other than the Committee on Rules) a member of the committee gives notice of intention to file supplemental, minority, or additional views for inclusion in the report to the House thereon, that member shall be entitled to not less than two additional calendar days after the day of such notice (excluding Saturdays, Sundays, and legal holidays except when the House is in session on such a day) to file such views, in writing and signed by that member, with the clerk of the committee.

POWER TO SIT AND ACT; SUBPOENA POWER

(m)(1) For the purpose of carrying out any of its functions and duties under this rule and rule X (including any matters referred to it under clause 2 of rule XII), a committee or subcommittee is authorized (subject to subparagraph (2)(A))—

(A) to sit and act at such times and places within the United States, whether the House is in session, has recessed, or has adjourned, and to hold such hearings as it considers necessary; and

(B) to require, by subpoena or otherwise, the attendance and testimony of such witnesses and the production of such books, records, correspondence, memoranda, papers, and documents as it considers necessary.

(2) The chairman of the committee, or a member designated by the chairman, may administer oaths to witnesses.

(3)(A)(i) Except as provided in subdivision (A)(ii), a subpoena may be authorized and issued by a committee or subcommittee under subparagraph (1)(B) in the conduct of an investigation or series of investigations or activities only when authorized by the committee or subcommittee, a majority being present. The power to authorize and issue subpoenas under subparagraph (1)(B) may be delegated to the chairman of the committee under such rules and under such limitations as the committee may prescribe. Authorized subpoenas shall be signed by the chairman of the committee or by a member designated by the committee.

(ii) In the case of a subcommittee of the Committee on Standards of Official Conduct, a subpoena may be authorized and issued only by an affirmative vote of a majority of its members.

(B) A subpoena duces tecum may specify terms of return other than at a meeting or hearing of the committee or subcommittee authorizing the subpoena.

(C) Compliance with a subpoena issued by a committee or subcommittee under subparagraph (1)(B) may be enforced only as authorized or directed by the House.

COMMITTEE ON STANDARDS OF OFFICIAL CONDUCT

3. (a) The Committee on Standards of Official Conduct has the following functions:

(1) The committee may recommend to the House from time to time such administrative actions as it may consider appropriate to establish or enforce standards of official conduct for Members, Delegates, the Resident Commissioner, officers, and employees of the House. A letter of reproval or other administrative action of the committee pursuant to an investigation under subparagraph (2) shall only be issued or implemented as a part of a report required by such subparagraph.

(2) The committee may investigate, subject to paragraph (b), an alleged violation by a Member, Delegate, Resident Commissioner, officer, or employee of the House of the Code of Official Conduct or of a law, rule, regulation, or other standard of conduct applicable to the conduct of such Member, Delegate, Resident Commissioner, officer, or employee in the performance of his duties or the discharge of his responsibilities. After notice and hearing (unless the right to a hearing is waived by the Member, Delegate, Resident Commissioner, officer or employee), the committee shall report to the House its findings of fact and recommendations, if any, for the final disposition of any such investigation and such action as the committee may consider appropriate in the circumstances.

(3) The committee may report to the appropriate Federal or State authorities, either with the approval of the House or by an affirmative vote of two-thirds of the members of the committee, any substantial evidence of a violation by a Member, Delegate, Resident Commissioner, officer, or employee of the House, of a law applicable to the performance of his duties or the discharge of his responsibilities that may have been disclosed in a committee investigation.

(4) The committee may consider the request of a Member, Delegate, Resident Commissioner, officer, or employee of the House for an advisory opinion with respect to the general propriety of any current or proposed conduct of such Member, Delegate, Resident Commissioner, officer, or employee. With appropriate deletions to ensure the privacy of the person concerned, the committee may publish such opinion for the guidance of other Members, Delegates, the Resident Commissioner, officers, and employees of the House.

(5) The committee may consider the request of a Member, Delegate, Resident Commissioner, officer, or employee of the House for a written waiver in exceptional circumstances with respect to clause 4 of rule XXIV.

(b)(1)(A) Unless approved by an affirmative vote of a majority of its members, the Committee on Standards of Official Conduct may not report a resolution, report, recommendation, or advisory opinion relating to the official conduct of a Member, Delegate, Resident Commissioner, officer or employee of the House, or, except as provided in subparagraph (2), undertake an investigation of such conduct.

(B)(i) Upon the receipt of information offered as a complaint that is in compliance with this rule and the rules of the committee, the chairman and ranking minority member jointly may appoint members to serve as an investigative subcommittee.

(ii) The chairman and ranking minority member of the committee jointly may gather additional information concerning alleged conduct that is the basis of a complaint or of information offered as a complaint until they have established an investigative subcommittee or either of them has placed on the agenda of the committee the issue of whether to establish an investigative subcommittee.

(2) Except in the case of an investigation undertaken by the com-

mittee on its own initiative, the committee may undertake an investigation relating to the official conduct of an individual Member, Delegate, Resident Commissioner, officer, or employee of the House only—

(A) upon receipt of information offered as a complaint, in writing and under oath, from a Member, Delegate, or Resident Commissioner and transmitted to the committee by such Member, Delegate, or Resident Commissioner; or

(B) upon receipt of information offered as a complaint, in writing and under oath, from a person not a Member, Delegate, or Resident Commissioner provided that a Member, Delegate, or Resident Commissioner certifies in writing to the committee that he believes the information is submitted in good faith and warrants the review and consideration of the committee.

If a complaint is not disposed of within the applicable periods set forth in the rules of the Committee on Standards of Official Conduct, the chairman and ranking minority member shall establish jointly an investigative subcommittee and forward the complaint, or any portion thereof, to that subcommittee for its consideration. However, if at any time during those periods either the chairman or ranking minority member places on the agenda the issue of whether to establish an investigative subcommittee, then an investigative subcommittee may be established only by an affirmative vote of a majority of the members of the committee.

(3) The committee may not undertake an investigation of an alleged violation of a law, rule, regulation, or standard of conduct that was not in effect at the time of the alleged violation. The committee may not undertake an investigation of such an alleged violation that occurred before the third previous Congress unless the committee determines that the alleged violation is directly related to an alleged violation that occurred in a more recent Congress.

(4) A member of the committee shall be ineligible to participate as a member of the committee in a committee proceeding relating to the member's official conduct. Whenever a member of the committee is ineligible to act as a member of the committee under the preceding sentence, the Speaker shall designate a Member, Delegate, or Resident Commissioner from the same political party as the ineligible member to act in any proceeding of the committee relating to that conduct.

(5) A member of the committee may disqualify himself from participating in an investigation of the conduct of a Member, Delegate, Resident Commissioner, officer, or employee of the House upon the submission in writing and under oath of an affidavit of disqualification stating that the member cannot render an impartial and unbiased decision in the case in which the member seeks to be disqualified. If the committee approves and accepts such affidavit of disqualification, the chairman shall so notify the Speaker and request the Speaker to designate a Member, Delegate, or Resident Commissioner from the same political party as the disqualifying member to act in any proceeding of the committee relating to that case.

(6) Information or testimony received, or the contents of a complaint or the fact of its filing, may not be publicly disclosed by any committee or staff member unless specifically authorized in each instance by a vote of the full committee.

(7) The committee shall have the functions designated in titles I and V of the Ethics in Government Act of 1978, in sections 7342, 7351, and 7353 of title 5, United States Code, and in clause 11(g)(4) of rule X.

(c)(1) Notwithstanding clause 2(g)(1) of rule XI, each meeting of the Committee on Standards of Official Conduct or a subcommittee thereof shall occur in executive session unless the committee or subcommittee, by an affirmative vote of a majority of its members, opens the meeting to the public.

(2) Notwithstanding clause 2(g)(2) of rule XI, each hearing of an adjudicatory subcommittee or sanction hearing of the Committee on Standards of Official Conduct shall be held in open session unless the committee or subcommittee, in open session by an affirmative vote of a majority of its members, closes all or part of the remainder of the hearing on that day to the public.

(d) Before a member, officer, or employee of the Committee on Standards of Official Conduct, including members of a subcommittee of the committee selected under clause 5(a)(4) of rule X and shared staff, may have access to information that is confidential under the rules of the committee, the following oath (or affirmation) shall be executed:

"I do solemnly swear (or affirm) that I will not disclose, to any person or entity outside the Committee on Standards of Official Conduct, any information received in the course of my service with the committee, except as authorized by the committee or in accordance with its rules."

Copies of the executed oath shall be retained by the Clerk as part of the records of the House. This paragraph establishes a standard of conduct within the meaning of paragraph (a)(2). Breaches of confidentiality shall be investigated by the Committee on Standards of Official Conduct and appropriate action shall be taken.

(e)(1) If a complaint or information offered as a complaint is deemed frivolous by an affirmative vote of a majority of the members of the Committee on Standards of Official Conduct, the committee may take such action as it, by an affirmative vote of a majority of its members, considers appropriate in the circumstances.

(2) Complaints filed before the One Hundred Fifth Congress may not be deemed frivolous by the Committee on Standards of Official Conduct.

AUDIO AND VISUAL COVERAGE OF
COMMITTEE PROCEEDINGS

4. (a) The purpose of this clause is to provide a means, in conformity with acceptable standards of dignity, propriety, and decorum, by which committee hearings or committee meetings that are open to the public may be covered by audio and visual means—

(1) for the education, enlightenment, and information of the general public, on the basis of accurate and impartial news coverage, regarding the operations, procedures, and practices of the House as a legislative and representative body, and regarding the measures, public issues, and other matters before the House and its committees, the consideration thereof, and the action taken thereon; and

(2) for the development of the perspective and understanding of the general public with respect to the role and function of the House under the Constitution as an institution of the Federal Government.

(b) In addition, it is the intent of this clause that radio and television tapes and television film of any coverage under this clause may not be used, or made available for use, as partisan political campaign material to promote or oppose the candidacy of any person for elective public office.

(c) It is, further, the intent of this clause that the general conduct of each meeting (whether of a hearing or otherwise) covered under authority of this clause by audio or visual means, and the personal behavior of the committee members and staff, other Government officials and personnel, witnesses, television, radio, and press media personnel, and the general public at the hearing or other meeting, shall be in strict conformity with and observance of the acceptable standards of dignity, propriety, courtesy, and decorum traditionally observed by the House in its operations, and may not be such as to—

(1) distort the objects and purposes of the hearing or other meeting or the activities of committee members in connection with that hearing or meeting or in connection with the general work of the committee or of the House; or

(2) cast discredit or dishonor on the House, the committee, or a Mem-

ber, Delegate, or Resident Commissioner or bring the House, the committee, or a Member, Delegate, or Resident Commissioner into disrepute.

(d) The coverage of committee hearings and meetings by audio and visual means shall be permitted and conducted only in strict conformity with the purposes, provisions, and requirements of this clause.

(e) Whenever a hearing or meeting conducted by a committee or subcommittee is open to the public, those proceedings shall be open to coverage by audio and visual means. A committee or subcommittee chairman may not limit the number of television or still cameras to fewer than two representatives from each medium (except for legitimate space or safety considerations, in which case pool coverage shall be authorized).

(f) Each committee shall adopt written rules to govern its implementation of this clause. Such rules shall contain provisions to the following effect:

(1) If audio or visual coverage of the hearing or meeting is to be presented to the public as live coverage, that coverage shall be conducted and presented without commercial sponsorship.

(2) The allocation among the television media of the positions or the number of television cameras permitted by a committee or subcommittee chairman in a hearing or meeting room shall be in accordance with fair and equitable procedures devised by the Executive Committee of the Radio and Television Correspondents' Galleries.

(3) Television cameras shall be placed so as not to obstruct in any way the space between a witness giving evidence or testimony and any member of the committee or the visibility of that witness and that member to each other.

(4) Television cameras shall operate from fixed positions but may not be placed in positions that obstruct unnecessarily the coverage of the hearing or meeting by the other media.

(5) Equipment necessary for coverage by the television and radio media may not be installed in, or removed from, the hearing or meeting room while the committee is in session.

(6)(A) Except as provided in subdivision (B), floodlights, spotlights, strobelights, and flashguns may not be used in providing any method of coverage of the hearing or meeting.

(B) The television media may install additional lighting in a hearing or meeting room, without cost to the Government, in order to raise the ambient lighting level in a hearing or meeting room to the lowest level necessary to provide adequate television coverage of a hearing or meeting at the current state of the art of television coverage.

(7) In the allocation of the number of still photographers permitted by a committee or subcommittee chairman in a hearing or meeting room, preference shall be given to photographers from Associated Press Photos and United Press International Newspictures. If requests are made by more of the media than will be permitted by a committee or subcommittee chairman for coverage of a hearing or meeting by still photography, that coverage shall be permitted on the basis of a fair and equitable pool arrangement devised by the Standing Committee of Press Photographers.

(8) Photographers may not position themselves between the witness table and the members of the committee at any time during the course of a hearing or meeting.

(9) Photographers may not place themselves in positions that obstruct unnecessarily the coverage of the hearing by the other media.

(10) Personnel providing coverage by the television and radio media shall be currently accredited to the Radio and Television Correspondents' Galleries.

(11) Personnel providing coverage by still photography shall be currently accredited to the Press Photographers' Gallery.

(12) Personnel providing coverage by the television and radio media and by still photography shall conduct themselves and their coverage activities in an orderly and unobtrusive manner.

PAY OF WITNESSES

5. Witnesses appearing before the House or any of its committees shall be paid the same per diem rate as established, authorized, and regulated by the Committee on House Administration for Members,

Delegates, the Resident Commissioner, and employees of the House, plus actual expenses of travel to or from the place of examination. Such per diem may not be paid when a witness has been summoned at the place of examination.

UNFINISHED BUSINESS OF THE SESSION

6. All business of the House at the end of one session shall be resumed at the commencement of the next session of the same Congress in the same manner as if no adjournment had taken place.

RULE XII

RECEIPT AND REFERRAL OF MEASURES AND MATTERS

MESSAGES

1. Messages received from the Senate, or from the President, shall be entered on the Journal and published in the Congressional Record of the proceedings of that day.

REFERRAL

2. (a) The Speaker shall refer each bill, resolution, or other matter that relates to a subject listed under a standing committee named in clause 1 of rule X in accordance with the provisions of this clause.

(b) The Speaker shall refer matters under paragraph (a) in such manner as to ensure to the maximum extent feasible that each committee that has jurisdiction under clause 1 of rule X over the subject matter of a provision thereof may consider such provision and report to the House thereon. Precedents, rulings, or procedures in effect before the Ninety-Fourth Congress shall be applied to referrals under this clause only to the extent that they will contribute to the achievement of the objectives of this clause.

(c) In carrying out paragraphs (a) and (b) with respect to the referral of a matter, the Speaker—

(1) shall designate a committee of primary jurisdiction;

(2) may refer the matter to one or more additional committees for consideration in sequence, either initially or after the matter has been reported by the committee of primary jurisdiction;

(3) may refer portions of the matter reflecting different subjects and jurisdictions to one or more additional committees;

(4) may refer the matter to a special, ad hoc committee appointed by the Speaker with the approval of the House, and including members of the committees of jurisdiction, for the specific purpose of considering that matter and reporting to the House thereon;

(5) may subject a referral to appropriate time limitations; and

(6) may make such other provision as may be considered appropriate.

(d) A bill for the payment or adjudication of a private claim against the Government may not be referred to a committee other than the Committee on International Relations or the Committee on the Judiciary, except by unanimous consent.

PETITIONS, MEMORIALS, AND PRIVATE BILLS

3. If a Member, Delegate, or Resident Commissioner has a petition, memorial, or private bill to present, he shall endorse his name, deliver it to the Clerk, and may specify the reference or disposition to be made thereof. Such petition, memorial, or private bill (except when judged by the Speaker to be obscene or insulting) shall be entered on the Journal with the name of the Member, Delegate, or Resident Commissioner presenting it and shall be printed in the Congressional Record.

4. A private bill or private resolution (including an omnibus claim or pension bill), or amendment thereto, may not be received or considered in the House if it authorizes or directs—

(a) the payment of money for property damages, for personal injuries or death for which suit may be instituted under the Tort Claims Procedure provided in title 28, United States Code, or for a pension (other than to carry out a provision of law or treaty stipulation);

(b) the construction of a bridge across a navigable stream; or

(c) the correction of a military or naval record.

PROHIBITION ON COMMEMORATIONS

5. (a) A bill or resolution, or an amendment thereto, may not be introduced or considered in the House if it establishes or expresses a commemoration.

(b) In this clause the term "commemoration" means a remembrance, celebration, or recognition for any purpose through the designation of a specified period of time.

EXCLUDED MATTERS

6. A petition, memorial, bill, or resolution excluded under this rule shall be returned to the Member, Delegate, or Resident Commissioner from whom it was received. A petition or private bill that has been inappropriately referred may, by direction of the committee having possession of it, be properly referred in the manner originally presented. An erroneous reference of a petition or private bill under this clause does not confer jurisdiction on a committee to consider or report it.

SPONSORSHIP

7. (a) All other bills, memorials, petitions, and resolutions, endorsed with the names of Members, Delegates, or the Resident Commissioner introducing them, may be delivered to the Speaker to be referred. The titles and references of all bills, memorials, petitions, resolutions, and other documents referred under this rule shall be entered on the Journal and printed in the Congressional Record. An erroneous reference may be corrected by the House in accordance with rule X on any day immediately after the Pledge of Allegiance to the Flag by unanimous consent or motion. Such a motion shall be privileged if offered by direction of a committee to which the bill has been erroneously referred or by direction of a committee claiming jurisdiction and shall be decided without debate.

(b)(1) The primary sponsor of a public bill or public resolution may name cosponsors. The name of a cosponsor added after the initial printing of a bill or resolution shall appear in the next printing of the bill or resolution on the written request of the primary sponsor. Such a request may be submitted to the Speaker at any time until the last committee authorized to consider and report the bill or resolution reports it to the House or is discharged from its consideration.

(2) The name of a cosponsor of a bill or resolution may be deleted by unanimous consent. The Speaker may entertain such a request only by the Member, Delegate, or Resident Commissioner whose name is to be deleted or by the primary sponsor of the bill or resolution, and only until the last committee authorized to consider and report the bill or resolution reports it to the House or is discharged from its consideration. The Speaker may not entertain a request to delete the name of the primary sponsor of a bill or resolution. A deletion shall be indicated by date in the next printing of the bill or resolution.

(3) The addition or deletion of the name of a cosponsor of a bill or resolution shall be entered on the Journal and printed in the Congressional Record of that day.

(4) A bill or resolution shall be reprinted on the written request of the primary sponsor. Such a request may be submitted to the Speaker only when 20 or more cosponsors have been added since the last printing of the bill or resolution.

(5) When a bill or resolution is introduced "by request," those words shall be entered on the Journal and printed in the Congressional Record.

EXECUTIVE COMMUNICATIONS

8. Estimates of appropriations and all other communications from the executive departments intended for the consideration of any committees of the House shall be addressed to the Speaker for referral as provided in clause 2 of rule XIV.

RULE XIII

CALENDARS AND COMMITTEE REPORTS

CALENDARS

1. (a) All business reported by committees shall be referred to one of the following three calendars:

(1) A Calendar of the Committee of the Whole House on the state of the Union, to which shall be referred public bills and public resolutions raising revenue, involving a tax or charge on the people, directly or indirectly making appropriations of money or property or requiring such appropriations to be made, authorizing payments out of appropriations already made, releasing any liability to the United States for money or property, or referring a claim to the Court of Claims.

(2) A House Calendar, to which shall be referred all public bills and public resolutions not requiring referral to the Calendar of the Committee of the Whole House on the state of the Union.

(3) A Private Calendar as provided in clause 5 of rule XV, to which shall be referred all private bills and private resolutions.

(b) There is established a Corrections Calendar as provided in clause 6 of rule XV.

(c) There is established a Calendar of Motions to Discharge Committees as provided in clause 2 of rule XV.

FILING AND PRINTING OF REPORTS

2. (a)(1) Except as provided in subparagraph (2), all reports of committees (other than those filed from the floor as privileged) shall be delivered to the Clerk for printing and reference to the proper calendar under the direction of the Speaker in accordance with clause 1. The title or subject of each report shall be entered on the Journal and printed in the Congressional Record.

(2) A bill or resolution reported adversely shall be laid on the table unless a committee to which the bill or resolution was referred requests at the time of the report its referral to an appropriate calendar under clause 1 or unless, within three days thereafter, a Member, Delegate, or Resident Commissioner makes such a request.

(b)(1) It shall be the duty of the chairman of each committee to report or cause to be reported promptly to the House a measure or matter approved by the committee and to take or cause to be taken steps necessary to bring the measure or matter to a vote.

(2) In any event, the report of a committee on a measure that has been approved by the committee shall be filed within seven calendar days (exclusive of days on which the House is not in session) after the day on which a written request for the filing of the report, signed by a majority of the members of the committee, has been filed with the clerk of the committee. The clerk of the committee shall immediately notify the chairman of the filing of such a request. This subparagraph does not apply to a report of the Committee on Rules with respect to a rule, joint rule, or order of business of the House, or to the reporting of a resolution of inquiry addressed to the head of an executive department.

(c) All supplemental, minority, or additional views filed under clause 2(l) of rule XI by one or more members of a committee shall be included in, and shall be a part of, the report filed by the committee with respect to a measure or matter. When time guaranteed by clause 2(l) of rule XI has expired (or, if sooner, when all separate views have been received), the committee may arrange to file its report with the Clerk not later than one hour after the expiration of such time. This clause and provisions of clause 2(l) of rule XI do not preclude the immediate filing or printing of a committee report in the absence of a timely request for the opportunity to file supplemental, minority, or additional views as provided in clause 2(l) of rule XI.

CONTENT OF REPORTS

3. (a)(1) Except as provided in subparagraph (2), the report of a committee on a measure or matter shall be printed in a single volume that—

(A) shall include all supplemental, minority, or additional views that have been submitted by the time of the filing of the report; and

(B) shall bear on its cover a recital that any such supplemental, minority, or additional views (and any material submitted under paragraph (c)(3) or (4)) are included as part of the report.

(2) A committee may file a supplemental report for the correction of a technical error in its previous report on a measure or matter.

(b) With respect to each record vote on a motion to report a measure or matter of a public nature, and on any amendment offered to the measure or matter, the total number of votes cast for and against, and the names of members voting for and against, shall be included in the committee report. The preceding sentence does not apply to votes taken in executive session by the Committee on Standards of Official Conduct.

(c) The report of a committee on a measure that has been approved by the committee shall include, separately set out and clearly identified, the following:

(1) Oversight findings and recommendations under clause 2(b)(1) of rule X.

(2) The statement required by section 308(a) of the Congressional Budget Act of 1974, except that an estimate of new budget authority shall include, when practicable, a comparison of the total estimated funding level for the relevant programs to the appropriate levels under current law.

(3) An estimate and comparison prepared by the Director of the Congressional Budget Office under section 402 of the Congressional Budget Act of 1974 if timely submitted to the committee before the filing of the report.

(4) A summary of oversight findings and recommendations by the Committee on Government Reform under clause 4(c)(2) of rule X if such findings and recommendations have been submitted to the reporting committee in time to allow it to consider such findings and recommendations during its deliberations on the measure.

(d) Each report of a committee on a public bill or public joint resolution shall contain the following:

(1) A statement citing the specific powers granted to Congress in the Constitution to enact the law proposed by the bill or joint resolution.

(2)(A) An estimate by the committee of the costs that would be incurred in carrying out the bill or joint resolution in the fiscal year in which it is reported and in each of the five fiscal years following that fiscal year (or for the authorized duration of any program authorized by the bill or joint resolution if less than five years);

(B) A comparison of the estimate of costs described in subdivision (A) made by the committee with any estimate of such costs made by a Government agency and submitted to such committee; and

(C) When practicable, a comparison of the total estimated funding level for the relevant programs with the appropriate levels under current law.

(3)(A) In subparagraph (2) the term "Government agency" includes any department, agency, establishment, wholly owned Government corporation, or instrumentality of the Federal Government or the government of the District of Columbia.

(B) Subparagraph (2) does not apply to the Committee on Appropriations, the Committee on House Administration, the Committee on Rules, or the Committee on Standards of Official Conduct, and does not apply when a cost estimate and comparison prepared by the Director of the Congressional Budget Office under section 402 of the Congressional Budget Act of 1974 has been included in the report under paragraph (c)(3).

(e)(1) Whenever a committee reports a bill or joint resolution proposing to repeal or amend a statute or part thereof, it shall include in its report or in an accompanying document—

(A) the text of a statute or part thereof that is proposed to be repealed; and

(B) a comparative print of any part of the bill or joint resolution proposing to amend the statute and of the statute or part thereof proposed to be amended, showing by appropriate typographical devices the omissions and insertions proposed.

(2) If a committee reports a bill or joint resolution proposing to repeal or amend a statute or part thereof with a recommendation that the bill or joint resolution be amended, the comparative print required by subparagraph (1) shall reflect the changes in existing law proposed to be made by the bill or joint resolution as proposed to be amended.

(f)(1) A report of the Committee on Appropriations on a general appropriation bill shall include—

(A) a concise statement describing the effect of any provision of the accompanying bill that directly or indirectly changes the application of existing law; and

(B) a list of all appropriations contained in the bill for expenditures not previously authorized by law (except classified intelligence or national security programs, projects, or activities).

(2) Whenever the Committee on Appropriations reports a bill or joint resolution including matter specified in clause 1(b)(2) or (3) of rule X, it shall include—

(A) in the bill or joint resolution, separate headings for "Rescissions" and "Transfers of Unexpended Balances"; and

(B) in the report of the committee, a separate section listing such rescissions and transfers.

(g) Whenever the Committee on Rules reports a resolution proposing to repeal or amend a standing rule of the House, it shall include in its report or in an accompanying document—

(1) the text of any rule or part thereof that is proposed to be repealed; and

(2) a comparative print of any part of the resolution proposing to amend the rule and of the rule or part thereof proposed to be amended, showing by appropriate typographical devices the omissions and insertions proposed.

(h)(1) It shall not be in order to consider a bill or joint resolution reported by the Committee on Ways and Means that proposes to amend the Internal Revenue Code of 1986 unless—

(A) the report includes a tax complexity analysis prepared by the Joint Committee on Internal Revenue Taxation in accordance with section 4022(b) of the Internal Revenue Service Restructuring and Reform Act of 1998; or

(B) the chairman of the Committee on Ways and Means causes such a tax complexity analysis to be printed in the Congressional Record before consideration of the bill or joint resolution.

(2) A report from the Committee on Ways and Means on a bill or joint resolution designated by the Majority Leader, after consultation with the Minority Leader, as major tax legislation may include a dynamic estimate of the changes in Federal revenues expected to result from enactment of the legislation. The Joint Committee on Internal Revenue Taxation shall render a dynamic estimate of such legislation only in response to a timely request from the chairman of the Committee on Ways and Means, after consultation with the ranking minority member. A dynamic estimate under this paragraph may be used only for informational purposes.

(3) In this paragraph the term "dynamic estimate" means a projection based in any part on assumptions concerning probable effects of macroeconomic feedback. A dynamic estimate shall include a statement identifying all such assumptions.

AVAILABILITY OF REPORTS

4. (a)(1) Except as specified in subparagraph (2), it shall not be in order to consider in the House a measure or matter reported by a committee until the third calendar day (excluding Saturdays, Sundays, or legal holidays except when the House is in session on such a day) on which each report of a committee on that measure or matter has been available to Members, Delegates, and the Resident Commissioner.

(2) Subparagraph (1) does not apply to—

(A) a resolution providing a rule, joint rule, or order of business reported by the Committee on Rules considered under clause 6;

(B) a resolution providing amounts from the applicable accounts described in clause 1(i)(1) of rule X reported by the Committee on House Administration considered under clause 6 of rule X;

(C) a resolution presenting a question of the privileges of the House reported by any committee;

(D) a measure for the declaration of war, or the declaration of a national emergency, by Congress; and

(E) a measure providing for the disapproval of a decision, determination, or action by a Government agency that would become, or continue to be, effective unless disapproved or otherwise invalidated by one or both Houses of Congress. In this subdivision the term "Government agency" includes any department, agency, establishment, wholly owned Government corporation, or instrumentality of the Federal Government or of the government of the District of Columbia.

(b) A committee that reports a measure or matter shall make every reasonable effort to have its hearings thereon (if any) printed and available for distribution to Members, Delegates, and the Resident Commissioner before the consideration of the measure or matter in the House.

(c) A general appropriation bill reported by the Committee on Appropriations may not be considered in the House until the third calendar day (excluding Saturdays, Sundays, and legal holidays except when the House is in session on such a day) on which printed hearings of the Committee on Appropriations thereon have been available to Members, Delegates, and the Resident Commissioner.

PRIVILEGED REPORTS, GENERALLY

5. (a) The following committees shall have leave to report at any time on the following matters, respectively:

(1) The Committee on Appropriations, on general appropriation bills and on joint resolutions continuing appropriations for a fiscal year after September 15 in the preceding fiscal year.

(2) The Committee on the Budget, on the matters required to be reported by such committee under titles III and IV of the Congressional Budget Act of 1974.

(3) The Committee on House Administration, on enrolled bills, on contested elections, on matters referred to it concerning printing for the use of the House or the two Houses, on expenditure of the applicable accounts of the House described in clause 1(i)(1) of rule X, and on matters relating to preservation and availability of noncurrent records of the House under rule VII.

(4) The Committee on Rules, on rules, joint rules, and the order of business.

(5) The Committee on Standards of Official Conduct, on resolutions recommending action by the House with respect to a Member, Delegate, Resident Commissioner, officer, or employee of the House as a result of an investigation by the committee relating to the official conduct of such Member, Delegate, Resident Commissioner, officer, or employee.

(b) A report filed from the floor as privileged under paragraph (a) may be called up as a privileged question by direction of the reporting committee, subject to any requirement concerning its availability to Members, Delegates, and the Resident Commissioner under clause 4 or concerning the timing of its consideration under clause 6.

PRIVILEGED REPORTS BY THE COMMITTEE ON RULES

6. (a) A report by the Committee on Rules on a rule, joint rule, or the order of business may not be called up for consideration on the same day it is presented to the House except—

(1) when so determined by a vote of two-thirds of the Members voting, a quorum being present;

(2) in the case of a resolution proposing only to waive a requirement of clause 4 or of clause 8 of rule XXII concerning the availability of reports; or

(3) during the last three days of a session of Congress.

(b) Pending the consideration of a report by the Committee on Rules on a rule, joint rule, or the order of business, the Speaker may entertain one motion that the House adjourn. After the result of such a motion is announced, the Speaker may not entertain any other dilatory motion until the report shall have been disposed of.

(c) The Committee on Rules may not report—

(1) a rule or order proposing that business under clause 7 of rule XV be set aside by a vote of less than two-thirds of the Members voting, a quorum being present;

(2) a rule or order that would prevent the motion to recommit a bill or joint resolution from being made as provided in clause 2(b) of rule XIX, including a motion to recommit with instructions to report back an amendment otherwise in order, if offered by the Minority Leader or a designee, except with respect to a Senate bill or resolution for which the text of a House-passed measure has been substituted.

(d) The Committee on Rules shall present to the House reports concerning rules, joint rules, and the order of business, within three legislative days of the time when they are ordered. If such a report is not considered immediately, it shall be referred to the calendar. If such a report on the calendar is not called up by the member of the committee who filed the report within seven legislative days, any member of the committee may call it up as a privileged question on the day after the calendar day on which the member announces to the House his intention to do so. The Speaker shall recognize a member of the committee who rises for that purpose.

(e) An adverse report by the Committee on Rules on a resolution proposing a special order of business for the consideration of a public bill or public joint resolution may be called up as a privileged question by a Member, Delegate, or Resident Commissioner on a day when it is in order to consider a motion to discharge committees under clause 2 of rule XV.

(f) If the House has adopted a resolution making in order a motion to consider a bill or resolution, and such a motion has not been offered within seven calendar days thereafter, such a motion shall be privileged if offered by direction of all reporting committees having initial jurisdiction of the bill or resolution.

(g) Whenever the Committee on Rules reports a resolution providing for the consideration of a measure, it shall (to the maximum extent possible) specify in the resolution the object of any waiver of a point of order against the measure or against its consideration.

RESOLUTIONS OF INQUIRY

7. A report on a resolution of inquiry addressed to the head of an executive department may be filed from the floor as privileged. If such a resolution is not reported to the House within 14 legislative days after its introduction, a motion to discharge a committee from its consideration shall be privileged.

RULE XIV

ORDER AND PRIORITY OF BUSINESS

1. The daily order of business (unless varied by the application of other rules and except for the disposition of matters of higher precedence) shall be as follows:

First. Prayer by the Chaplain.

Second. Reading and approval of the Journal, unless postponed under clause 9(a) of rule XX.

Third. The Pledge of Allegiance to the Flag.

Fourth. Correction of reference of public bills.

Fifth. Disposal of business on the Speaker's table as provided in clause 2.

Sixth. Unfinished business as provided in clause 3.

Seventh. The morning hour for the consideration of bills called up by committees as provided in clause 4.

Eighth. Motions that the House resolve into the Committee of the Whole House on the state of the Union subject to clause 5.

Ninth. Orders of the day.

2. Business on the Speaker's table shall be disposed of as follows:

(a) Messages from the President shall be referred to the appropriate committees without debate.

(b) Communications addressed to the House, including reports and communications from heads of departments and bills, resolutions, and messages from the Senate, may be referred to the appropriate committees in the same manner and with the same right of correction as public bills and public resolutions presented by Members, Delegates, or the Resident Commissioner.

(c) Motions to dispose of Senate amendments on the Speaker's table may be entertained as provided in clauses 1, 2, and 4 of rule XXII.

(d) Senate bills and resolutions substantially the same as House measures already favorably reported and not required to be considered in the Committee of the Whole House on the state of the Union may be disposed of by motion. Such a motion shall be privileged if offered by direction of all reporting committees having initial jurisdiction of the House measure.

3. Consideration of unfinished business in which the House may have been engaged at an adjournment, except business in the morning hour and proceedings postponed under clause 9 of rule XX, shall be resumed as soon as the business on the Speaker's table is finished, and at the same time each day thereafter until disposed of. The consideration of all other unfinished business shall be resumed whenever the class of business to which it belongs shall be in order under the rules.

4. After the unfinished business has been disposed of, the Speaker shall call each standing committee in regular order and then select committees. Each committee when named may call up for consideration a bill or resolution reported by it on a previous day and on the House Calendar. If the Speaker does not complete the call of the committees before the House passes to other business, the next call shall resume at the point it left off, giving preference to the last bill or resolution under consideration. A committee that has occupied the call for two days may not call up another bill or resolution until the other committees have been called in their turn.

5. After consideration of bills or resolutions under clause 4 for one hour, it shall be in order, pending consideration thereof, to entertain a motion that the House resolve into the Committee of the Whole House on the state of the Union or, when authorized by a committee, that the House resolve into the Committee of the Whole House on the state of the Union to consider a particular bill. Such a motion shall be subject to only one amendment designating another bill. If such a motion is decided in the negative, another such motion may not be considered until the matter that was pending when such motion was offered is disposed of.

6. All questions relating to the priority of business shall be decided by a majority without debate.

RULE XV

BUSINESS IN ORDER ON SPECIAL DAYS

SUSPENSIONS, MONDAYS AND TUESDAYS

1. (a) A rule may not be suspended except by a vote of two-thirds of the Members voting, a quorum being present. The Speaker may not entertain a motion that the House suspend the rules except on Mondays and Tuesdays and during the last six days of a session of Congress.

(b) Pending a motion that the House suspend the rules, the Speaker may entertain one motion that the House adjourn. After the result of such a motion is announced, the Speaker may not entertain any other motion until the vote is taken on the suspension.

(c) A motion that the House suspend the rules is debatable for 40 minutes, one-half in favor of the motion and one-half in opposition thereto.

DISCHARGE MOTIONS, SECOND AND FOURTH MONDAYS

2. (a) Motions to discharge committees shall be in order on the second and fourth Mondays of a month.

(b)(1) A Member may present to the Clerk a motion in writing to discharge—

(A) a committee from consideration of a public bill or public resolution that has been referred to it for 30 legislative days; or

(B) the Committee on Rules from consideration of a resolution that has been referred to it for seven legislative days and that proposes a special order of business for the consideration of a public bill or public resolution that has been reported by a standing committee or has been referred to a standing committee for 30 legislative days.

(2) Only one motion may be presented for a bill or resolution. A Member may not file a motion to discharge the Committee on Rules from consideration of a resolution providing for the consideration of more than one public bill or public resolution or admitting or effecting a nongermane amendment to a public bill or public resolution.

(c) A motion presented under paragraph (b) shall be placed in the custody of the Clerk, who shall arrange a convenient place for the signatures of Members. A signature may be withdrawn by a Member in writing at any time before a motion is entered on the Journal. The Clerk shall make signatures a matter of public record, causing the names of the Members who have signed a discharge motion during a week to be published in a portion of the Congressional Record designated for that purpose on the last legislative day of the week and making cumulative lists of such names available each day for public inspection in an appropriate office of the House. The Clerk shall devise a means for making such lists available to offices of the House and to the public in electronic form. When a majority of the total membership of the House shall have signed the motion, it shall be entered on the Journal, printed with the signatures thereto in the Record, and referred to the Calendar of Motions to Discharge Committees.

(d)(1) On the second and fourth Mondays of a month (except during the last six days of a session of Congress), immediately after the Pledge of Allegiance to the Flag, a motion to discharge that has been on the calendar for at least seven legislative days shall be privileged if called up by a Member whose signature appears thereon. When such a motion is called up, the House shall proceed to its consideration under this paragraph without intervening motion except one motion to adjourn. Privileged motions to discharge shall have precedence in the order of their entry on the Journal.

(2) When a motion to discharge is called up, the bill or resolution to which it relates shall be read by title only. The motion is debatable for 20 minutes, one-half in favor of the motion and one-half in opposition thereto.

(e)(1) If a motion prevails to discharge the Committee on Rules from consideration of a resolution, the House shall immediately consider the resolution, pending which the Speaker may entertain one motion that the House adjourn. After the result of such a motion to adjourn is announced, the Speaker may not entertain any other dilatory motion until the resolution has been disposed of. If the resolution is adopted, the House shall immediately proceed to its execution.

(2) If a motion prevails to discharge a standing committee from consideration of a public bill or public resolution, a motion that the House proceed to the immediate consideration of such bill or resolution shall be privileged if offered by a Member whose signature appeared on the motion to discharge. The motion to proceed is not debatable. If the motion to proceed is adopted, the bill or resolution shall be considered immediately under the general rules of the House. If unfinished before adjournment of the day on which it is called up, the bill or resolution shall remain the unfinished business until it is disposed of. If the motion to proceed is rejected, the bill or resolution shall be referred to the appropriate calendar, where it shall have the same status as if the committee from which it was discharged had duly reported it to the House.

(f)(1) When a motion to discharge originated under this clause has once been acted on by the House, it shall not be in order to entertain during the same session of Congress—

(A) a motion to discharge a committee from consideration of that bill or resolution or of any other bill or resolution that, by relating in substance to or dealing with the same subject matter, is substantially the same; or

(B) a motion to discharge the Committee on Rules from consideration of a resolution providing a special order of business for the consideration of that bill or resolution or of any other bill or resolution that, by relating in substance to or dealing with the same subject matter, is substantially the same.

(2) A motion to discharge on the Calendar of Motions to Discharge Committees that is rendered out of order under subparagraph (1) shall be stricken from that calendar.

ADVERSE REPORT BY THE COMMITTEE ON RULES, SECOND AND FOURTH MONDAYS

3. An adverse report by the Committee on Rules on a resolution proposing a special order of business for the consideration of a public bill or public joint resolution may be called up under clause 6(e) of rule XIII as a privileged question by a Member, Delegate, or Resident Commissioner on a day when it is in order to consider a motion to discharge committees under clause 2.

DISTRICT OF COLUMBIA BUSINESS, SECOND AND FOURTH MONDAYS

4. The second and fourth Mondays of a month shall be set apart for the consideration of such District of Columbia business as may be called up by the Committee on Government Reform after the disposition of motions to discharge committees and after the disposal of such business on the Speaker's table as requires reference only.

PRIVATE CALENDAR, FIRST AND THIRD TUESDAYS

5. (a) On the first Tuesday of a month, the Speaker shall direct the Clerk to call the bills and resolutions on the Private Calendar after disposal of such business on the Speaker's table as requires reference only. If two or more Members, Delegates, or the Resident Commissioner object to the consideration of a bill or resolution so called, it shall be recommitted to the committee that reported it. No other business shall be in order before completion of the call of the Private Calendar on this day unless two-thirds of the Members voting, a quorum being present, agree to a motion that the House dispense with the call.

(b)(1) On the third Tuesday of a month, after the disposal of such business on the Speaker's table as requires reference only, the Speaker may direct the Clerk to call the bills and resolutions on the Private Calendar. Preference shall be given to omnibus bills containing the texts of bills or resolutions that have previously been objected to on a call of the Private Calendar. If two or more Members, Delegates, or the Resident Commissioner object to the consideration of a bill or resolution so called (other than an omnibus bill), it shall be recommitted to the committee that reported it. Two-thirds of the Members voting, a quorum being present, may adopt a motion that the House dispense with the call on this day.

(2) Omnibus bills shall be read for amendment by paragraph. No amendment shall be in order except to strike or to reduce amounts of money or to provide limitations. An item or matter stricken from an omnibus bill may not thereafter during the same session of Congress be included in an omnibus bill. Upon passage such an omnibus bill shall be resolved into the several bills and resolutions of which it is composed. The several bills and resolutions, with any amendments adopted by the House, shall be engrossed, when necessary, and otherwise considered as passed severally by the House as distinct bills and resolutions.

(c) The Speaker may not entertain a reservation of the right to object to the consideration of a bill or resolution under this clause. A bill or resolution considered under this clause shall be considered in the House as in the Committee of the Whole. A motion to dispense with the call of the Private Calendar under this clause shall be privileged. Debate on such a motion shall be limited to five minutes in support and five minutes in opposition.

CORRECTIONS CALENDAR, SECOND AND FOURTH TUESDAYS

6. (a) After a bill has been favorably reported and placed on either the Union or House Calendar, the Speaker, after consultation with the Minority Leader, may direct the Clerk also to place the bill on the "Corrections Calendar." At any time on the second and fourth Tuesdays of a month, the Speaker may direct the Clerk to call a bill that has been on the Corrections Calendar for three legislative days.

(b) A bill called from the Corrections Calendar shall be considered in the House, is debatable for one hour equally divided and controlled by the chairman and ranking minority member of the primary committee of jurisdiction, and shall not be subject to amendment except those recommended by the primary committee of jurisdiction or offered by the chairman of the primary committee or a designee. The previous question shall be considered as ordered on the bill and any amendments thereto to final passage without intervening motion except one motion to recommit with or without instructions.

(c) The approval of three-fifths of the Members voting, a quorum being present, shall be required to pass a bill called from the Corrections Calendar. The rejection of a bill so called, or the sustaining of a point of order against it or against its consideration, does not cause its removal from the Calendar to which it was originally referred.

CALENDAR CALL OF COMMITTEES, WEDNESDAYS

7. (a) On Wednesday of each week, business shall not be in order before completion of the call of the committees (except as provided by clause 4 of rule XIV) unless two-thirds of the Members voting, a quorum being present, agree to a motion that the House dispense with the call. Such a motion shall be privileged. Debate on such a motion shall be limited to five minutes in support and five minutes in opposition.

(b) A bill or resolution on either the House or the Union Calendar, except bills or resolutions that are privileged under the Rules of the House, may be called under this clause. A bill or resolution called up from the Union Calendar shall be considered in the Committee of the Whole House on the state of the Union without motion, subject to clause 3 of rule XVI. General debate on a measure considered under this clause shall be confined to the measure and may not exceed two hours equally divided between a proponent and an opponent.

(c) When a committee has occupied the call under this clause on one Wednesday, it shall not be in order on a succeeding Wednesday to consider unfinished business previously called up by that committee until the other committees have been called in their turn unless—

(1) the previous question has been ordered on such unfinished business; or

(2) the House adopts a motion to dispense with the call under paragraph (a).

(d) If any committee has not been called under this clause during a session of a Congress, then at the next session of that Congress the call shall resume where it left off at the end of the preceding session.

(e) This rule does not apply during the last two weeks of a session of Congress.

(f) The Speaker may not entertain a motion for a recess on a Wednesday except during the last two weeks of a session of Congress.

RULE XVI

MOTIONS AND AMENDMENTS

MOTIONS

1. Every motion entertained by the Speaker shall be reduced to writing on the demand of a Member, Delegate, or Resident Commissioner and, unless it is withdrawn the same day, shall be entered on the Journal with the name of the Member, Delegate, or Resident Commissioner offering it. A dilatory motion may not be entertained by the Speaker.

WITHDRAWAL

2. When a motion is entertained, the Speaker shall state it or cause it to be read aloud by the Clerk before it is debated. The motion then shall be in the possession of the House but may be withdrawn at any time before a decision or amendment thereon.

QUESTION OF CONSIDERATION

3. When a motion or proposition is entertained, the question, "Will the House now consider it?" may not be put unless demanded by a Member, Delegate, or Resident Commissioner.

PRECEDENCE OF MOTIONS

4. (a) When a question is under debate, only the following motions may be entertained (which shall have precedence in the following order):

(1) To adjourn.
(2) To lay on the table.
(3) For the previous question.
(4) To postpone to a day certain.
(5) To refer.
(6) To amend.
(7) To postpone indefinitely.

(b) A motion to adjourn, to lay on the table, or for the previous question shall be decided without debate. A motion to postpone to a day certain, to refer, or to postpone indefinitely, being decided, may not be allowed again on the same day at the same stage of the question.

(c)(1) It shall be in order at any time for the Speaker, in his discretion, to entertain a motion—

(A) that the Speaker be authorized to declare a recess; or
(B) that when the House adjourns it stand adjourned to a day and time certain.

(2) Either motion shall be of equal privilege with the motion to adjourn and shall be decided without debate.

DIVISIBILITY

5. (a) Except as provided in paragraph (b), a question shall be divided on the demand of a Member, Delegate, or Resident Commissioner before the question is put if it includes propositions so distinct in substance that, one being taken away, a substantive proposition remains.

(b)(1) A motion or resolution to elect members to a standing committee of the House, or to a joint standing committee, is not divisible.

(2) A resolution or order reported by the Committee on Rules providing a special order of business is not divisible.

(c) A motion to strike and insert is not divisible, but rejection of a motion to strike does not preclude another motion to amend.

AMENDMENTS

6. When an amendable proposition is under consideration, a motion to amend and a motion to amend that amendment shall be in order, and it also shall be in order to offer a further amendment by way of substitute for the original motion to amend, to which one amendment may be offered but which may not be voted on until the original amendment is perfected. An amendment may be withdrawn in the House at any time before a decision or amendment thereon. An amendment to the title of a bill or resolution shall not be in order until after its passage or adoption and shall be decided without debate.

GERMANENESS

7. No motion or proposition on a subject different from that under consideration shall be admitted under color of amendment.

READINGS

8. Bills and joint resolutions are subject to readings as follows:

(a) A first reading is in full when the bill or joint resolution is first considered.

(b) A second reading occurs only when the bill or joint resolution is read for amendment in a Committee of the Whole House on the state of the Union under clause 5 of rule XVIII.

(c) A third reading precedes passage when the Speaker states the question: "Shall the bill [or joint resolution] be engrossed [when applicable] and read a third time?" If that question is decided in the affirmative, then the bill or joint resolution shall be read the final time by title and then the question shall be put on its passage.

RULE XVII

DECORUM AND DEBATE

DECORUM

1. (a) A Member, Delegate, or Resident Commissioner who desires to speak or deliver a matter to the House shall rise and respectfully address himself to "Mr. Speaker" and, on being recognized, may address the House from any place on the floor. When invited by the Chair, a Member, Delegate, or Resident Commissioner may speak from the Clerk's desk.

(b)(1) Remarks in debate shall be confined to the question under debate, avoiding personality.

(2)(A) Except as provided in subdivision (B), debate may not include characterizations of Senate action or inaction, references to individual Members of the Senate, or quotations from Senate proceedings.

(B) Debate may include references to actions taken by the Senate or by committees thereof that are a matter of public record; references to the pendency or sponsorship in the Senate of bills, resolutions, and amendments; factual descriptions relating to Senate action or inaction concerning a measure then under debate in the House; and quotations from Senate proceedings on a measure then under debate in the House that are relevant to the making of legislative history establishing the meaning of that measure.

RECOGNITION

2. When two or more Members, Delegates, or the Resident Commissioner rise at once, the Speaker shall name the Member, Delegate, or Resident Commissioner who is first to speak. A Member, Delegate, or Resident Commissioner may not occupy more than one hour in debate on a question in the House or in the Committee of the Whole House on the state of the Union except as otherwise provided in this rule.

MANAGING DEBATE

3. (a) The Member, Delegate, or Resident Commissioner who calls up a measure may open and close debate thereon. When general debate extends beyond one day, that Member, Delegate, or Resident Commissioner shall be entitled to one hour to close without regard to the time used in opening.

(b) Except as provided in paragraph (a), a Member, Delegate, or Resident Commissioner may not speak more than once to the same question without leave of the House.

(c) A manager of a measure who opposes an amendment thereto is entitled to close controlled debate thereon.

CALL TO ORDER

4. (a) If a Member, Delegate, or Resident Commissioner, in speaking or otherwise, transgresses the Rules of the House, the Speaker shall, or a Member, Delegate, or Resident Commissioner may, call to order the offending Member, Delegate, or Resident Commissioner, who shall immediately sit down unless permitted on motion of another Member, Delegate, or the Resident Commissioner to explain. If a Member, Delegate, or Resident Commissioner is called to order, the Member, Delegate, or Resident Commissioner making the call to order shall indicate the words excepted to, which shall be taken down in writing at the Clerk's desk and read aloud to the House.

(b) The Speaker shall decide the validity of a call to order. The House, if appealed to, shall decide the question without debate. If the decision is in favor of the Member, Delegate, or Resident Commissioner called to order, the Member, Delegate, or Resident Commissioner shall be at liberty to proceed, but not otherwise. If the case requires it, an offending Member, Delegate, or Resident Commissioner shall be liable to censure or such other punishment as the House may consider proper. A Member, Delegate, or Resident Commissioner may not be held to answer a call to order, and may not be subject to the censure of the House therefor, if further debate or other business has intervened.

COMPORTMENT

5. When the Speaker is putting a question or addressing the House, a Member, Delegate, or Resident Commissioner may not walk out of or across the Hall. When a Member, Delegate, or Resident Commissioner is speaking, a Member, Delegate, or Resident Commissioner may not pass between the person speaking and the Chair. During the session of the House, a Member, Delegate, or Resident Commissioner may not wear a hat or remain by the Clerk's desk dur-

ing the call of the roll or the counting of ballots. A person may not smoke or use any personal, electronic office equipment, including cellular phones and computers, on the floor of the House. The Sergeant-at-Arms is charged with the strict enforcement of this clause.

EXHIBITS

6. When the use of an exhibit in debate is objected to by a Member, Delegate, or Resident Commissioner, its use shall be decided without debate by a vote of the House.

GALLERIES

7. During a session of the House, it shall not be in order for a Member, Delegate, or Resident Commissioner to introduce to or to bring to the attention of the House an occupant in the galleries of the House. The Speaker may not entertain a request for the suspension of this rule by unanimous consent or otherwise.

CONGRESSIONAL RECORD

8. (a) The Congressional Record shall be a substantially verbatim account of remarks made during the proceedings of the House, subject only to technical, grammatical, and typographical corrections authorized by the Member, Delegate, or Resident Commissioner making the remarks.

(b) Unparliamentary remarks may be deleted only by permission or order of the House.

(c) This clause establishes a standard of conduct within the meaning of clause 3(a)(2) of rule XI.

SECRET SESSIONS

9. When confidential communications are received from the President, or when the Speaker or a Member, Delegate, or Resident Commissioner informs the House that he has communications that he believes ought to be kept secret for the present, the House shall be cleared of all persons except the Members, Delegates, Resident Commissioner, and officers of the House for the reading of such communications, and debates and proceedings thereon, unless otherwise ordered by the House.

RULE XVIII

THE COMMITTEE OF THE WHOLE HOUSE ON THE STATE OF THE UNION

RESOLVING INTO THE COMMITTEE OF THE WHOLE

1. Whenever the House resolves into the Committee of the Whole House on the state of the Union, the Speaker shall leave the chair after appointing a Chairman to preside. In case of disturbance or disorderly conduct in the galleries or lobby, the Chairman may cause the same to be cleared.

2. (a) Except as provided in paragraph (b) and in clause 7 of rule XV, the House resolves into the Committee of the Whole House on the state of the Union by motion. When such a motion is entertained, the Speaker shall put the question without debate: "Shall the House resolve itself into the Committee of the Whole House on the state of the Union for consideration of this matter?", naming it.

(b) After the House has adopted a resolution reported by the Committee on Rules providing a special order of business for the consideration of a measure in the Committee of the Whole House on the state of the Union, the Speaker may at any time, when no question is pending before the House, declare the House resolved into the Committee of the Whole for the consideration of that measure without intervening motion, unless the special order of business provides otherwise.

MEASURES REQUIRING INITIAL CONSIDERATION IN THE COMMITTEE OF THE WHOLE

3. All bills, resolutions, or Senate amendments (as provided in clause 3 of rule XXII) involving a tax or charge on the people, raising revenue, directly or indirectly making appropriations of money or property or requiring such appropriations to be made, authorizing payments out of appropriations already made, releasing any liability to the United States for money or property, or referring a claim to the Court of Claims, shall be first considered in the Committee of the Whole House on the state of the Union. A bill, resolution, or Senate amendment that fails to comply with this clause is subject to a point of order against its consideration.

ORDER OF BUSINESS

4. (a) Subject to subparagraph (b) business on the calendar of the Committee of the Whole House on the state of the Union may be taken up in regular order, or in such order as the Committee may determine, unless the measure to be considered was determined by the House at the time of resolving into the Committee of the Whole.

(b) Motions to resolve into the Committee of the Whole for consideration of bills and joint resolutions making general appropriations have precedence under this clause.

READING FOR AMENDMENT

5. (a) Before general debate commences on a measure in the Committee of the Whole House on the state of the Union, it shall be read in full. When general debate is concluded or closed by order of the House, the measure under consideration shall be read for amendment. A Member, Delegate, or Resident Commissioner who offers an amendment shall be allowed five minutes to explain it, after which the Member, Delegate, or Resident Commissioner who shall first obtain the floor shall be allowed five minutes to speak in opposition to it. There shall be no further debate thereon, but the same privilege of debate shall be allowed in favor of and against any amendment that may be offered to an amendment. An amendment, or an amendment to an amendment, may be withdrawn by its proponent only by the unanimous consent of the Committee of the Whole.

(b) When a Member, Delegate, or Resident Commissioner offers an amendment in the Committee of the Whole House on the state of the Union, the Clerk shall promptly transmit five copies of the amendment to the majority committee table and five copies to the minority committee table. The Clerk also shall deliver at least one copy of the amendment to the majority cloakroom and at least one copy to the minority cloakroom.

QUORUM AND VOTING

6. (a) A quorum of a Committee of the Whole House on the state of the Union is 100 Members. The first time that a Committee of the Whole finds itself without a quorum during a day, the Chairman shall invoke the procedure for a quorum call set forth in clause 2 of rule XX, unless he elects to invoke an alternate procedure set forth in clause 3 or clause 4(a) of rule XX. If a quorum appears, the Committee of the Whole shall continue its business. If a quorum does not appear, the Committee of the Whole shall rise, and the Chairman shall report the names of absentees to the House.

(b)(1) The Chairman may refuse to entertain a point of order that a quorum is not present during general debate.

(2) After a quorum has once been established on a day, the Chairman may entertain a point of order that a quorum is not present only when the Committee of the Whole House on the state of the Union is operating under the five-minute rule and the Chairman has put the pending proposition to a vote.

(3) Upon sustaining a point of order that a quorum is not present, the Chairman may announce that, following a regular quorum call

under paragraph (a), the minimum time for electronic voting on the pending question shall be five minutes.

(c) When ordering a quorum call in the Committee of the Whole House on the state of the Union, the Chairman may announce an intention to declare that a quorum is constituted at any time during the quorum call when he determines that a quorum has appeared. If the Chairman interrupts the quorum call by declaring that a quorum is constituted, proceedings under the quorum call shall be considered as vacated, and the Committee of the Whole shall continue its sitting and resume its business.

(d) A quorum is not required in the Committee of the Whole House on the state of the Union for adoption of a motion that the Committee rise.

(e) In the Committee of the Whole House on the state of the Union, the Chairman shall order a recorded vote on a request supported by at least 25 Members.

(f) In the Committee of the Whole House on the state of the Union, the Chairman may reduce to five minutes the minimum time for electronic voting without any intervening business or debate on any or all pending amendments after a record vote has been taken on the first pending amendment.

DISPENSING WITH THE READING OF AN AMENDMENT

7. It shall be in order in the Committee of the Whole House on the state of the Union to move that the Committee of the Whole dispense with the reading of an amendment that has been printed in the bill or resolution as reported by a committee, or an amendment that a Member, Delegate, or Resident Commissioner has caused to be printed in the Congressional Record. Such a motion shall be decided without debate.

CLOSING DEBATE

8. (a) Subject to paragraph (b) at any time after the Committee of the Whole House on the state of the Union has begun five-minute debate on amendments to any portion of a bill or resolution, it shall be in order to move that the Committee of the Whole close all debate on that portion of the bill or resolution or on the pending amendments only. Such a motion shall be decided without debate. The adoption of such a motion does not preclude further amendment, to be decided without debate.

(b) If the Committee of the Whole House on the state of the Union closes debate on any portion of a bill or resolution before there has been debate on an amendment that a Member, Delegate, or Resident Commissioner has caused to be printed in the Congressional Record at least one day before its consideration, the Member, Delegate, or Resident Commissioner who caused the amendment to be printed in the Record shall be allowed five minutes to explain it, after which the Member, Delegate, or Resident Commissioner who shall first obtain the floor shall be allowed five minutes to speak in opposition to it. There shall be no further debate thereon.

(c) Material submitted for printing in the Congressional Record under this rule shall indicate the full text of the proposed amendment, the name of the Member, Delegate, or Resident Commissioner proposing it, the number of the bill or resolution to which it will be offered, and the point in the bill or resolution or amendment thereto where the amendment is intended to be offered. The amendment shall appear in a portion of the Record designated for that purpose. Amendments to a specified measure submitted for printing in that portion of the Record shall be numbered in the order printed.

STRIKING THE ENACTING CLAUSE

9. A motion that the Committee of the Whole House on the state of the Union rise and report a bill or resolution to the House with the recommendation that the enacting or resolving clause be stricken

shall have precedence of a motion to amend, and, if carried in the House, shall constitute a rejection of the bill or resolution. Whenever a bill or resolution is reported from the Committee of the Whole with such adverse recommendation and the recommendation is rejected by the House, the bill or resolution shall stand recommitted to the Committee of the Whole without further action by the House. Before the question of concurrence is submitted, it shall be in order to move that the House refer the bill or resolution to a committee, with or without instructions. If a bill or resolution is so referred, then when it is again reported to the House it shall be referred to the Committee of the Whole without debate.

CONCURRENT RESOLUTION ON THE BUDGET

10. (a) At the conclusion of general debate in the Committee of the Whole House on the state of the Union on a concurrent resolution on the budget under section 305(a) of the Congressional Budget Act of 1974, the concurrent resolution shall be considered as read for amendment.

(b) It shall not be in order in the House or in the Committee of the Whole House on the state of the Union to consider an amendment to a concurrent resolution on the budget, or an amendment thereto, unless the concurrent resolution, as amended by such amendment or amendments—

(1) would be mathematically consistent except as limited by paragraph (c); and

(2) would contain all the matter set forth in paragraphs (1) through (5) of section 301(a) of the Congressional Budget Act of 1974.

(c)(1) Except as specified in subparagraph (2), it shall not be in order in the House or in the Committee of the Whole House on the state of the Union to consider an amendment to a concurrent resolution on the budget, or an amendment thereto, that proposes to change the amount of the appropriate level of the public debt set forth in the concurrent resolution, as reported.

(2) Amendments to achieve mathematical consistency under section 305(a)(5) of the Congressional Budget Act of 1974, if offered by direction of the Committee on the Budget, may propose to adjust the amount of the appropriate level of the public debt set forth in the concurrent resolution, as reported, to reflect changes made in other figures contained in the concurrent resolution.

UNFUNDED MANDATES

11. (a) In the Committee of the Whole House on the state of the Union, an amendment proposing only to strike an unfunded mandate from the portion of the bill then open to amendment, if otherwise in order, may be precluded from consideration only by specific terms of a special order of the House.

(b) In this clause the term "unfunded mandate" means a Federal intergovernmental mandate the direct costs of which exceed the threshold otherwise specified for a reported bill or joint resolution in section 424(a)(1) of the Congressional Budget Act of 1974.

APPLICABILITY OF RULES OF THE HOUSE

12. The Rules of the House are the rules of the Committee of the Whole House on the state of the Union so far as applicable.

RULE XIX

MOTIONS FOLLOWING THE AMENDMENT STAGE

PREVIOUS QUESTION

1. (a) There shall be a motion for the previous question, which, being ordered, shall have the effect of cutting off all debate and bringing the House to a direct vote on the immediate question or questions on which it has been ordered. Whenever the previous question has been ordered on an otherwise debatable question on which there has been no debate, it shall be in order to debate that question for 40 minutes, equally divided and controlled by a proponent of the question and an opponent. The previous question may be moved and ordered on a single question, on a series of questions allowable under the rules, or on an amendment or amendments, or may embrace all authorized motions or amendments and include the bill or resolution to its passage, adoption, or rejection.

(b) Incidental questions of order arising during the pendency of a motion for the previous question shall be decided, whether on appeal or otherwise, without debate.

RECOMMIT

2. (a) After the previous question has been ordered on passage or adoption of a measure, or pending a motion to that end, it shall be in order to move that the House recommit (or commit, as the case may be) the measure, with or without instructions, to a standing or select committee. For such a motion to recommit, the Speaker shall give preference in recognition to a Member, Delegate, or Resident Commissioner who is opposed to the measure.

(b) Except as provided in paragraph (c), if a motion that the House recommit a bill or joint resolution on which the previous question has been ordered to passage includes instructions, it shall be debatable for 10 minutes equally divided between the proponent and an opponent.

(c) On demand of the floor manager for the majority, it shall be in order to debate the motion for one hour equally divided and controlled by the proponent and an opponent.

RECONSIDERATION

3. When a motion has been carried or lost, it shall be in order on the same or succeeding day for a Member on the prevailing side of the question to enter a motion for the reconsideration thereof. The entry of such a motion shall take precedence over all other questions except the consideration of a conference report or a motion to adjourn, and may not be withdrawn after such succeeding day without the consent of the House. Once entered, a motion may be called up for consideration by any Member. During the last six days of a session of Congress, such a motion shall be disposed of when entered.

4. A bill, petition, memorial, or resolution referred to a committee, or reported therefrom for printing and recommitment, may not be brought back to the House on a motion to reconsider.

RULE XX

VOTING AND QUORUM CALLS

1. (a) The House shall divide after the Speaker has put a question to a vote by voice as provided in clause 6 of rule I if the Speaker is in doubt or division is demanded. Those in favor of the question shall first rise from their seats to be counted, and then those opposed.

(b) If a Member, Delegate, or Resident Commissioner requests a recorded vote, and that request is supported by at least one-fifth of a quorum, the vote shall be taken by electronic device unless the Speaker invokes another procedure for recording votes provided in this rule. A recorded vote taken in the House under this paragraph shall be considered a vote by the yeas and nays.

(c) In case of a tie vote, a question shall be lost.

2. (a) Unless the Speaker directs otherwise, the Clerk shall conduct a record vote or quorum call by electronic device. In such a case the

Clerk shall enter on the Journal and publish in the Congressional Record, in alphabetical order in each category, the names of Members recorded as voting in the affirmative, the names of Members recorded as voting in the negative, and the names of Members answering present as if they had been called in the manner provided in clause 3. Except as otherwise permitted under clause 9 or 10 of this rule or under clause 6 of rule XVIII, the minimum time for a record vote or quorum call by electronic device shall be 15 minutes.

(b) When the electronic voting system is inoperable or is not used, the Speaker or Chairman may direct the Clerk to conduct a record vote or quorum call as provided in clause 3 or 4.

3. The Speaker may direct the Clerk to conduct a record vote or quorum call by call of the roll. In such a case the Clerk shall call the names of Members, alphabetically by surname. When two or more have the same surname, the name of the State (and, if necessary to distinguish among Members from the same State, the given names of the Members) shall be added. After the roll has been called once, the Clerk shall call the names of those not recorded, alphabetically by surname. Members appearing after the second call, but before the result is announced, may vote or announce a pair.

4. (a) The Speaker may direct a record vote or quorum call to be conducted by tellers. In such a case the tellers named by the Speaker shall record the names of the Members voting on each side of the question or record their presence, as the case may be, which the Clerk shall enter on the Journal and publish in the Congressional Record. Absentees shall be noted, but the doors may not be closed except when ordered by the Speaker. The minimum time for a record vote or quorum call by tellers shall be 15 minutes.

(b) On the demand of a Member, or at the suggestion of the Speaker, the names of Members sufficient to make a quorum in the Hall of the House who do not vote shall be noted by the Clerk, entered on the Journal, reported to the Speaker with the names of the Members voting, and counted and announced in determining the presence of a quorum to do business.

5. (a) In the absence of a quorum, a majority comprising at least 15 Members, which may include the Speaker, may compel the attendance of absent Members.

(b) Subject to clause 7(b) a majority of those present may order the Sergeant-at-Arms to send officers appointed by him to arrest those Members for whom no sufficient excuse is made and shall secure and retain their attendance. The House shall determine on what condition they shall be discharged. Unless the House otherwise directs, the Members who voluntarily appear shall be admitted immediately to the Hall of the House and shall report their names to the Clerk to be entered on the Journal as present.

6. (a) When a quorum fails to vote on a question, a quorum is not present, and objection is made for that cause (unless the House shall adjourn)—

(1) there shall be a call of the House;

(2) the Sergeant-at-Arms shall proceed forthwith to bring in absent Members; and

(3) the yeas and nays on the pending question shall at the same time be considered as ordered.

(b) The Clerk shall record Members by the yeas and nays on the pending question, using such procedure as the Speaker may invoke under clause 2, 3, or 4. Each Member arrested under this clause shall be brought by the Sergeant-at-Arms before the House, whereupon he shall be noted as present, discharged from arrest, and given an opportunity to vote; and his vote shall be recorded. If those voting on the question and those who are present and decline to vote together make a majority of the House, the Speaker shall declare that a quorum is constituted, and the pending question shall be decided as the requisite majority of those voting shall have determined. Thereupon further proceedings under the call shall be considered as dispensed with.

(c) At any time after Members have had the requisite opportunity to respond by the yeas and nays, but before a result has been announced, the Speaker may entertain a motion that the House adjourn if seconded by a majority of those present, to be ascertained by actual count by the Speaker. If the House adjourns on such a motion, all proceedings under this clause shall be considered as vacated.

7. (a) The Speaker may not entertain a point of order that a quorum is not present unless a question has been put to a vote.

(b) Subject to paragraph (c) the Speaker may recognize a Member, Delegate, or Resident Commissioner to move a call of the House at any time. When a quorum is established pursuant to a call of the House, further proceedings under the call shall be considered as dispensed with unless the Speaker recognizes for a motion to compel attendance of Members under clause 5(b).

(c) A call of the House shall not be in order after the previous question is ordered unless the Speaker determines by actual count that a quorum is not present.

POSTPONEMENT OF PROCEEDINGS

8. (a)(1) When a recorded vote is ordered, or the yeas and nays are ordered, or a vote is objected to under clause 6 on any of the questions specified in subparagraph (2), the Speaker may postpone further proceedings on that question to a designated place in the legislative schedule on that legislative day (in the case of the question of agreeing to the Speaker's approval of the Journal) or within two legislative days (in the case of any other question).

(2) The questions described in the subparagraph (1) are as follows:

(A) The question of passing a bill or joint resolution.

(B) The question of adopting a resolution or concurrent resolution.

(C) The question of agreeing to a motion to instruct managers on the part of the House (except that proceedings may not resume on such a motion under clause 7(c) of rule XXII if the managers have filed a report in the House).

(D) The question of agreeing to a conference report.

(E) The question of agreeing to a motion to recommit a bill considered under clause 6 of rule XV.

(F) The question of ordering the previous question on a question described in subdivision (A), (B), (C), (D), or (E).

(G) The question of agreeing to an amendment to a bill considered under clause 6 of rule XV.

(H) The question of agreeing to a motion to suspend the rules.

(b) At the time designated by the Speaker for further proceedings on questions postponed under paragraph (a), the Speaker shall resume proceedings on each postponed question in the order in which it was considered.

(c) The Speaker may reduce to five minutes the minimum time for electronic voting on a question postponed under this clause, or on a question incidental thereto, that follows another electronic vote without intervening business, so long as the minimum time for electronic voting on the first in any series of questions is 15 minutes.

(d) If the House adjourns on a legislative day designated for further proceedings on questions postponed under this clause without disposing of such questions, then on the next legislative day the unfinished business is the disposition of such questions in the order in which they were considered.

FIVE-MINUTE VOTES

9. The Speaker may reduce to five minutes the minimum time for electronic voting—

(a) after a record vote on a motion for the previous question, on any underlying question that follows without intervening business, or on a question incidental thereto;

(b) after a record vote on an amendment reported from the Committee of the Whole House on the state of the Union, on any subsequent amendment to that bill or resolution reported from the Committee of the Whole, or on a question incidental thereto;

(c) after a record vote on a motion to recommit a bill, resolution, or conference report, on the question of passage or adoption, as the case may be, of such bill, resolution, or conference report, or on a question incidental thereto, if the question of passage or adoption follows without intervening business the vote on the motion to recommit; or

(d) as provided in clause 6(b)(3) of rule XVIII, clause 6(f) of rule XVIII, or clause 8 of this rule.

AUTOMATIC YEAS AND NAYS

10. The yeas and nays shall be considered as ordered when the Speaker puts the question on passage of a bill or joint resolution, or on adoption of a conference report, making general appropriations, or increasing Federal income tax rates (within the meaning of clause 5 of rule XXI), or on final adoption of a concurrent resolution on the budget or conference report thereon.

BALLOT VOTES

11. In a case of ballot for election, a majority of the votes shall be necessary to an election. When there is not such a majority on the first ballot, the process shall be repeated until a majority is obtained. In all balloting blanks shall be rejected, may not be counted in the enumeration of votes, and may not be reported by the tellers.

RULE XXI

RESTRICTIONS ON CERTAIN BILLS

RESERVATION OF CERTAIN POINTS OF ORDER

1. At the time a general appropriation bill is reported, all points of order against provisions therein shall be considered as reserved.

GENERAL APPROPRIATION BILLS AND AMENDMENTS

2. (a)(1) An appropriation may not be reported in a general appropriation bill, and may not be in order as an amendment thereto, for an expenditure not previously authorized by law, except to continue appropriations for public works and objects that are already in progress.

(2) A reappropriation of unexpended balances of appropriations may not be reported in a general appropriation bill, and may not be in order as an amendment thereto, except to continue appropriations for public works and objects that are already in progress. This subparagraph does not apply to transfers of unexpended balances within the department or agency for which they were originally appropriated that are reported by the Committee on Appropriations.

(b) A provision changing existing law may not be reported in a general appropriation bill, including a provision making the availability of funds contingent on the receipt or possession of information not required by existing law for the period of the appropriation, except germane provisions that retrench expenditures by the reduction of amounts of money covered by the bill (which may include those recommended to the Committee on Appropriations by direction of a legislative committee having jurisdiction over the subject matter) and except rescissions of appropriations contained in appropriation Acts.

(c) An amendment to a general appropriation bill shall not be in order if changing existing law, including an amendment making the availability of funds contingent on the receipt or possession of information not required by existing law for the period of the appropria-

tion. Except as provided in paragraph (d), an amendment proposing a limitation not specifically contained or authorized in existing law for the period of the limitation shall not be in order during consideration of a general appropriation bill.

(d) After a general appropriation bill has been read for amendment, a motion that the Committee of the Whole House on the state of the Union rise and report the bill to the House with such amendments as may have been adopted shall, if offered by the Majority Leader or a designee, have precedence over motions to amend the bill. If such a motion to rise and report is rejected or not offered, amendments proposing limitations not specifically contained or authorized in existing law for the period of the limitation or proposing germane amendments that retrench expenditures by reductions of amounts of money covered by the bill may be considered.

(e) A provision other than an appropriation designated an emergency under section 251(b)(2) or section 252(e) of the Balanced Budget and Emergency Deficit Control Act, a rescission of budget authority, or a reduction in direct spending or an amount for a designated emergency may not be reported in an appropriation bill or joint resolution containing an emergency designation under section 251(b)(2) or section 252(e) of such Act and may not be in order as an amendment thereto.

(f) During the reading of an appropriation bill for amendment in the Committee of the Whole House on the state of the Union, it shall be in order to consider en bloc amendments proposing only to transfer appropriations among objects in the bill without increasing the levels of budget authority or outlays in the bill. When considered en bloc under this paragraph, such amendments may amend portions of the bill not yet read for amendment (following disposition of any points of order against such portions) and is not subject to a demand for division of the question in the House or in the Committee of the Whole.

TRANSPORTATION OBLIGATION LIMITATIONS

3. It shall not be in order to consider a bill, joint resolution, amendment, or conference report that would cause obligation limitations to be below the level for any fiscal year set forth in section 8103 of the Transportation Equity Act for the 21st Century, as adjusted, for the highway category or the mass transit category, as applicable.

APPROPRIATIONS ON LEGISLATIVE BILLS

4. A bill or joint resolution carrying an appropriation may not be reported by a committee not having jurisdiction to report appropriations, and an amendment proposing an appropriation shall not be in order during the consideration of a bill or joint resolution reported by a committee not having that jurisdiction. A point of order against an appropriation in such a bill, joint resolution, or amendment thereto may be raised at any time during pendency of that measure for amendment.

TAX AND TARIFF MEASURES AND AMENDMENTS

5. (a) A bill or joint resolution carrying a tax or tariff measure may not be reported by a committee not having jurisdiction to report tax or tariff measures, and an amendment in the House or proposed by the Senate carrying a tax or tariff measure shall not be in order during the consideration of a bill or joint resolution reported by a committee not having that jurisdiction. A point of order against a tax or tariff measure in such a bill, joint resolution, or amendment thereto may be raised at any time during pendency of that measure for amendment.

PASSAGE OF TAX RATE INCREASES

(b) A bill or joint resolution, amendment, or conference report carrying a Federal income tax rate increase may not be considered as passed or agreed to unless so determined by a vote of not less than three-fifths of the Members voting, a quorum being present. In this paragraph the term "Federal income tax rate increase" means any amendment to subsection (a), (b), (c), (d), or (e) of section 1, or to section 11(b) or 55(b), of the Internal Revenue Code of 1986, that imposes a new percentage as a rate of tax and thereby increases the amount of tax imposed by any such section.

CONSIDERATION OF RETROACTIVE TAX RATE INCREASES

(c) It shall not be in order to consider a bill, joint resolution, amendment, or conference report carrying a retroactive Federal income tax rate increase. In this paragraph—

(1) the term "Federal income tax rate increase" means any amendment to subsection (a), (b), (c), (d), or (e) of section 1, or to section 11(b) or 55(b), of the Internal Revenue Code of 1986, that imposes a new percentage as a rate of tax and thereby increases the amount of tax imposed by any such section; and

(2) a Federal income tax rate increase is retroactive if it applies to a period beginning before the enactment of the provision.

RULE XXII

HOUSE AND SENATE RELATIONS

SENATE AMENDMENTS

1. A motion to disagree to Senate amendments to a House bill or resolution and to request or agree to a conference with the Senate, or a motion to insist on House amendments to a Senate bill or resolution and to request or agree to a conference with the Senate, shall be privileged in the discretion of the Speaker if offered by direction of the primary committee and of all reporting committees that had initial referral of the bill or resolution.

2. A motion to dispose of House bills with Senate amendments not requiring consideration in the Committee of the Whole House on the state of the Union shall be privileged.

3. Except as permitted by clause 1, before the stage of disagreement, a Senate amendment to a House bill or resolution shall be subject to the point of order that it must first be considered in the Committee of the Whole House on the state of the Union if, originating in the House, it would be subject to such a point under clause 3 of rule XVIII.

4. When the stage of disagreement has been reached on a bill or resolution with House or Senate amendments, a motion to dispose of any amendment shall be privileged.

5. (a) Managers on the part of the House may not agree to a Senate amendment described in paragraph (b) unless specific authority to agree to the amendment first is given by the House by a separate vote with respect thereto. If specific authority is not granted, the Senate amendment shall be reported in disagreement by the conference committee back to the two Houses for disposition by separate motion.

(b) The managers on the part of the House may not agree to a Senate amendment described in paragraph (a) that—

(1) would violate clause 2(a)(1) or (c) of rule XXI if originating in the House; or

(2) proposes an appropriation on a bill other than a general appropriation bill.

6. A Senate amendment carrying a tax or tariff measure in violation of clause 5(a) of rule XXI may not be agreed to.

CONFERENCE REPORTS; AMENDMENTS REPORTED IN DISAGREEMENT

7. (a) The presentation of a conference report shall be in order at any time except during a reading of the Journal or the conduct of a record vote, a vote by division, or a quorum call.

(b)(1) Subject to subparagraph (2) the time allotted for debate on a motion to instruct managers on the part of the House shall be equally divided between the majority and minority parties.

(2) If the proponent of a motion to instruct managers on the part of the House and the Member, Delegate, or Resident Commissioner of the other party identified under subparagraph (1) both support the motion, one-third of the time for debate thereon shall be allotted to a Member, Delegate, or Resident Commissioner who opposes the motion on demand of that Member, Delegate, or Resident Commissioner.

(c)(1) A motion to instruct managers on the part of the House, or a motion to discharge all managers on the part of the House and to appoint new conferees, shall be privileged—

(A) after a conference committee has been appointed for 20 calendar days without making a report; and

(B) on the first legislative day after the calendar day on which the Member, Delegate, or Resident Commissioner offering the motion announces to the House his intention to do so and the form of the motion.

(2) The Speaker may designate a time in the legislative schedule on that legislative day for consideration of a motion described in subparagraph (1).

(3) During the last six days of a session of Congress, the period of time specified in subparagraph (1)(A) shall be 36 hours.

(d) Each conference report to the House shall be printed as a report of the House. Each such report shall be accompanied by a joint explanatory statement prepared jointly by the managers on the part of the House and the managers on the part of the Senate. The joint explanatory statement shall be sufficiently detailed and explicit to inform the House of the effects of the report on the matters committed to conference.

8. (a)(1) Except as specified in subparagraph (2), it shall not be in order to consider a conference report until—

(A) the third calendar day (excluding Saturdays, Sundays, or legal holidays except when the House is in session on such a day) on which the conference report and the accompanying joint explanatory statement have been available to Members, Delegates, and the Resident Commissioner in the Congressional Record; and

(B) copies of the conference report and the accompanying joint explanatory statement have been available to Members, Delegates, and the Resident Commissioner for at least two hours.

(2) Subparagraph (1)(A) does not apply during the last six days of a session of Congress.

(b)(1) Except as specified in subparagraph (2), it shall not be in order to consider a motion to dispose of a Senate amendment reported in disagreement by a conference committee until—

(A) the third calendar day (excluding Saturdays, Sundays, or legal holidays except when the House is in session on such a day) on which the report in disagreement and any accompanying statement have been available to Members, Delegates, and the Resident Commissioner in the Congressional Record; and

(B) copies of the report in disagreement and any accompanying statement, together with the text of the Senate amendment, have been available to Members, Delegates, and the Resident Commissioner for at least two hours.

(2) Subparagraph (1)(A) does not apply during the last six days of a session of Congress.

(3) During consideration of a Senate amendment reported in dis-

agreement by a conference committee on a general appropriation bill, a motion to insist on disagreement to the Senate amendment shall be preferential to any other motion to dispose of that amendment if the original motion offered by the floor manager proposes to change existing law and the motion to insist is offered before debate on the original motion by the chairman of the committee having jurisdiction of the subject matter of the amendment or a designee. Such a preferential motion shall be separately debatable for one hour equally divided between its proponent and the proponent of the original motion. The previous question shall be considered as ordered on the preferential motion to its adoption without intervening motion.

(c) A conference report or a Senate amendment reported in disagreement by a conference committee that has been available as provided in paragraph (a) or (b) shall be considered as read when called up.

(d)(1) Subject to subparagraph (2), the time allotted for debate on a conference report or on a motion to dispose of a Senate amendment reported in disagreement by a conference committee shall be equally divided between the majority and minority parties.

(2) If the floor manager for the majority and the floor manager for the minority both support the conference report or motion, one-third of the time for debate thereon shall be allotted to a Member, Delegate, or Resident Commissioner who opposes the conference report or motion on demand of that Member, Delegate, or Resident Commissioner.

(e) Under clause 6(a)(2) of rule XIII, a resolution proposing only to waive a requirement of this clause concerning the availability of reports to Members, Delegates, and the Resident Commissioner may be considered by the House on the same day it is reported by the Committee on Rules.

9. Whenever a disagreement to an amendment has been committed to a conference committee, the managers on the part of the House may propose a substitute that is a germane modification of the matter in disagreement. The introduction of any language presenting specific additional matter not committed to the conference committee by either House does not constitute a germane modification of the matter in disagreement. Moreover, a conference report may not include matter not committed to the conference committee by either House and may not include a modification of specific matter committed to the conference committee by either or both Houses if that modification is beyond the scope of that specific matter as committed to the conference committee.

10. (a)(1) A Member, Delegate, or Resident Commissioner may raise a point of order against nongermane matter, as specified in subparagraph (2), before the commencement of debate on—

(A) a conference report;

(B) a motion that the House recede from its disagreement to a Senate amendment reported in disagreement by a conference committee and concur therein, with or without amendment; or

(C) a motion that the House recede from its disagreement to a Senate amendment on which the stage of disagreement has been reached and concur therein, with or without amendment.

(2) A point of order against nongermane matter is one asserting that a proposition described in subparagraph (1) contains specified matter that would violate clause 7 of rule XVI if it were offered in the House as an amendment to the underlying measure in the form it was passed by the House.

(b) If a point of order under paragraph (a) is sustained, a motion that the House reject the nongermane matter identified by the point of order shall be privileged. Such a motion is debatable for 40 minutes, one-half in favor of the motion and one-half in opposition thereto.

(c) After disposition of a point of order under paragraph (a) or a motion to reject under paragraph (b), any further points of order under paragraph (a) not covered by a previous point of order, and any consequent motions to reject under paragraph (b), shall be likewise disposed of.

(d)(1) If a motion to reject under paragraph (b) is adopted, then after disposition of all points of order under paragraph (a) and any consequent motions to reject under paragraph (b), the conference report or motion, as the case may be, shall be considered as rejected and the matter remaining in disagreement shall be disposed of under subparagraph (2) or (3), as the case may be.

(2) After the House has adopted one or more motions to reject nongermane matter contained in a conference report under the preceding provisions of this clause—

(A) if the conference report accompanied a House measure amended by the Senate, the pending question shall be whether the House shall recede and concur in the Senate amendment with an amendment consisting of so much of the conference report as was not rejected; and

(B) if the conference report accompanied a Senate measure amended by the House, the pending question shall be whether the House shall insist further on the House amendment.

(3) After the House has adopted one or more motions to reject nongermane matter contained in a motion that the House recede and concur in a Senate amendment, with or without amendment, the following motions shall be privileged and shall have precedence in the order stated:

(A) A motion that the House recede and concur in the Senate amendment with an amendment in writing then available on the floor.

(B) A motion that the House insist on its disagreement to the Senate amendment and request a further conference with the Senate.

(C) A motion that the House insist on its disagreement to the Senate amendment.

(e) If, on a division of the question on a motion described in paragraph (a)(1)(B) or (C), the House agrees to recede, then a Member, Delegate, or Resident Commissioner may raise a point of order against nongermane matter, as specified in paragraph (a)(2), before the commencement of debate on concurring in the Senate amendment, with or without amendment. A point of order under this paragraph shall be disposed of according to the preceding provisions of this clause in the same manner as a point of order under paragraph (a).

11. It shall not be in order to consider a conference report to accompany a bill or joint resolution that proposes to amend the Internal Revenue Code of 1986 unless—

(a) the joint explanatory statement of the managers includes a tax complexity analysis prepared by the Joint Committee on Internal Revenue Taxation in accordance with section 4022(b) of the Internal Revenue Service Restructuring and Reform Act of 1998; or

(b) the chairman of the Committee on Ways and Means causes such a tax complexity analysis to be printed in the Congressional Record before consideration of the conference report.

12. (a)(1) Subject to subparagraph (2), a meeting of each conference committee shall be open to the public.

(2) In open session of the House, a motion that managers on the part of the House be permitted to close to the public a meeting or meetings of their conference committee shall be privileged, shall be decided without debate, and shall be decided by a record vote.

(b) A point of order that a conference committee failed to comply with paragraph (a) may be raised immediately after the conference report is read or considered as read. If such a point of order is sustained, the conference report shall be considered as rejected, the House shall be considered to have insisted on its amendments or on disagreement to the Senate amendments, as the case may be, and to have requested a further conference with the Senate, and the Speaker may appoint new conferees without intervening motion.

RULE XXIII

STATUTORY LIMIT ON PUBLIC DEBT

1. Upon adoption by Congress of a concurrent resolution on the budget under section 301 or 304 of the Congressional Budget Act of 1974 that sets forth, as the appropriate level of the public debt for the period to which the concurrent resolution relates, an amount that is different from the amount of the statutory limit on the public debt that otherwise would be in effect for that period, the Clerk shall prepare an engrossment of a joint resolution increasing or decreasing, as the case may be, the statutory limit on the public debt in the form prescribed in clause 2. Upon engrossment of the joint resolution, the vote by which the concurrent resolution on the budget was finally agreed to in the House shall also be considered as a vote on passage of the joint resolution in the House, and the joint resolution shall be considered as passed by the House and duly certified and examined. The engrossed copy shall be signed by the Clerk and transmitted to the Senate for further legislative action.

2. The matter after the resolving clause in a joint resolution described in clause 1 shall be as follows: "That subsection (b) of section 3101 of title 31, United States Code, is amended by striking out the dollar limitation contained in such subsection and inserting in lieu thereof '$————'.", with the blank being filled with a dollar limitation equal to the appropriate level of the public debt set forth pursuant to section 301(a)(5) of the Congressional Budget Act of 1974 in the relevant concurrent resolution described in clause 1. If an adopted concurrent resolution under clause 1 sets forth different appropriate levels of the public debt for separate periods, only one engrossed joint resolution shall be prepared under clause 1; and the blank referred to in the preceding sentence shall be filled with the limitation that is to apply for each period.

3. (a) The report of the Committee on the Budget on a concurrent resolution described in clause 1 and the joint explanatory statement of the managers on a conference report to accompany such a concurrent resolution each shall contain a clear statement of the effect the eventual enactment of a joint resolution engrossed under this rule would have on the statutory limit on the public debt.

(b) It shall not be in order for the House to consider a concurrent resolution described in clause 1, or a conference report thereon, unless the report of the Committee on the Budget or the joint explanatory statement of the managers complies with paragraph (a).

4. Nothing in this rule shall be construed as limiting or otherwise affecting—

(a) the power of the House or the Senate to consider and pass bills or joint resolutions, without regard to the procedures under clause 1, that would change the statutory limit on the public debt; or

(b) the rights of Members, Delegates, the Resident Commissioner, or committees with respect to the introduction, consideration, and reporting of such bills or joint resolutions.

5. In this rule the term "statutory limit on the public debt" means the maximum face amount of obligations issued under authority of chapter 31 of title 31, United States Code, and obligations guaranteed as to principal and interest by the United States (except such guaranteed obligations as may be held by the Secretary of the Treasury), as determined under section 3101(b) of such title after the application of section 3101(a) of such title, that may be outstanding at any one time.

RULE XXIV

CODE OF OFFICIAL CONDUCT

There is hereby established by and for the House the following code of conduct, to be known as the "Code of Official Conduct":

1. A Member, Delegate, Resident Commissioner, officer, or employee of the House shall conduct himself at all times in a manner that shall reflect creditably on the House.

2. A Member, Delegate, Resident Commissioner, officer, or employee of the House shall adhere to the spirit and the letter of the Rules of the House and to the rules of duly constituted committees thereof.

3. A Member, Delegate, Resident Commissioner, officer, or employee of the House may not receive compensation and may not permit compensation to accrue to his beneficial interest from any source, the receipt of which would occur by virtue of influence improperly exerted from his position in Congress.

4. A Member, Delegate, Resident Commissioner, officer, or employee of the House may not accept gifts except as provided by clause 5 of rule XXVI.

5. A Member, Delegate, Resident Commissioner, officer, or employee of the House may not accept an honorarium for a speech, a writing for publication, or other similar activity, except as otherwise provided under rule XXVI.

6. A Member, Delegate, or Resident Commissioner—

(a) shall keep his campaign funds separate from his personal funds;

(b) may not convert campaign funds to personal use in excess of an amount representing reimbursement for legitimate and verifiable campaign expenditures; and

(c) may not expend funds from his campaign account that are not attributable to bona fide campaign or political purposes.

7. A Member, Delegate, or Resident Commissioner shall treat as campaign contributions all proceeds from testimonial dinners or other fund-raising events.

8. (a) A Member, Delegate, Resident Commissioner, or officer of the House may not retain an employee who does not perform duties for the offices of the employing authority commensurate with the compensation he receives.

(b) In the case of a committee employee who works under the direct supervision of a member of the committee other than a chairman, the chairman may require that such member affirm in writing that the employee has complied with clause 8(a) (subject to clause 7 of rule X) as evidence of compliance by the chairman with this clause and with clause 7 of rule X.

9. A Member, Delegate, Resident Commissioner, officer, or employee of the House may not discharge and may not refuse to hire an individual, or otherwise discriminate against an individual with respect to compensation, terms, conditions, or privileges of employment, because of the race, color, religion, sex (including marital or parental status), disability, age, or national origin of such individual, but may take into consideration the domicile or political affiliation of such individual.

10. A Member, Delegate, or Resident Commissioner who has been convicted by a court of record for the commission of a crime for which a sentence of two or more years' imprisonment may be imposed should refrain from participation in the business of each committee of which he is a member, and a Member should refrain from voting on any question at a meeting of the House or of the Committee of the Whole House on the state of the Union, unless or until judicial or executive proceedings result in reinstatement of the presumption of his innocence or until he is reelected to the House after the date of such conviction.

11. A Member, Delegate, or Resident Commissioner may not authorize or otherwise allow an individual, group, or organization not under the direction and control of the House to use the words "Congress of the United States," "House of Representatives," or "Official Business," or any combination of words thereof, on any letterhead or envelope.

12. (a) Except as provided in paragraph (b), an employee of the House who is required to file a report under rule XXVII may not participate personally and substantially as an employee of the House in a contact with an agency of the executive or judicial branches of Government with respect to nonlegislative matters affecting any nongovernmental person in which the employee has a significant financial interest.

(b) Paragraph (a) does not apply if an employee first advises his employing authority of a significant financial interest described in paragraph (a) and obtains from his employing authority a written waiver stating that the participation of the employee in the activity described in paragraph (a) is necessary. A copy of each such waiver shall be filed with the Committee on Standards of Official Conduct.

13. Before a Member, Delegate, Resident Commissioner, officer, or employee of the House may have access to classified information, the following oath (or affirmation) shall be executed:

"I do solemnly swear (or affirm) that I will not disclose any classified information received in the course of my service with the House of Representatives, except as authorized by the House of Representatives or in accordance with its Rules."

Copies of the executed oath (or affirmation) shall be retained by the Clerk as part of the records of the House.

14. (a) In this Code of Official Conduct, the term "officer or employee of the House" means an individual whose compensation is disbursed by the Chief Administrative Officer.

(b) An individual whose services are compensated by the House pursuant to a consultant contract shall be considered an employee of the House for purposes of clauses 1, 2, 3, 4, 8, 9, and 13 of this rule.

RULE XXV

LIMITATIONS ON USE OF OFFICIAL FUNDS

LIMITATIONS ON USE OF OFFICIAL AND UNOFFICIAL ACCOUNTS

1. A Member, Delegate, or Resident Commissioner may not maintain, or have maintained for his use, an unofficial office account. Funds may not be paid into an unofficial office account.

2. Notwithstanding any other provision of this rule, if an amount from the Official Expenses Allowance of a Member, Delegate, or Resident Commissioner is paid into the House Recording Studio revolving fund for telecommunications satellite services, the Member, Delegate, or Resident Commissioner may accept reimbursement from nonpolitical entities in that amount for transmission to the Clerk for credit to the Official Expenses Allowance.

3. In this rule the term "unofficial office account" means an account or repository in which funds are received for the purpose of defraying otherwise unreimbursed expenses allowable under section 162(a) of the Internal Revenue Code of 1986 as ordinary and necessary in the operation of a congressional office, and includes a newsletter fund referred to in section 527(g) of the Internal Revenue Code of 1986.

LIMITATIONS ON USE OF THE FRANK

4. A Member, Delegate, or Resident Commissioner shall mail franked mail under section 3210(d) of title 39, United States Code at the most economical rate of postage practicable.

5. Before making a mass mailing, a Member, Delegate, or Resident Commissioner shall submit a sample or description of the mail matter involved to the House Commission on Congressional Mailing Standards for an advisory opinion as to whether the proposed mailing is in compliance with applicable provisions of law, rule, or regulation.

6. A mass mailing that is otherwise frankable by a Member, Delegate, or Resident Commissioner under the provisions of section 3210(e) of title 39, United States Code, is not frankable unless the cost of preparing and printing it is defrayed exclusively from funds made available in an appropriation Act.

7. A Member, Delegate, or Resident Commissioner may not send a mass mailing outside the congressional district from which he was elected.

8. In the case of a Member, Delegate, or Resident Commissioner, a mass mailing is not frankable under section 3210 of title 39, United States Code, when it is postmarked less than 60 days before the date of a primary or general election (whether regular, special, or runoff) in which he is a candidate for public office. If the mail matter is of a type that is not customarily postmarked, the date on which it would have been postmarked, if it were of a type customarily postmarked, applies.

9. In this rule the term "mass mailing" means, with respect to a session of Congress, a mailing of newsletters or other pieces of mail with substantially identical content (whether such pieces of mail are deposited singly or in bulk, or at the same time or different times), totaling more than 500 pieces of mail in that session, except that such term does not include a mailing—

(a) of matter in direct response to a communication from a person to whom the matter is mailed;

(b) from a Member, Delegate, or Resident Commissioner to other Members, Delegates, the Resident Commissioner, or Senators, or to Federal, State, or local government officials; or

(c) of a news release to the communications media.

PROHIBITION ON USE OF FUNDS BY MEMBERS NOT ELECTED TO SUCCEEDING CONGRESS

10. Funds from the applicable accounts described in clause 1(i)(1) of rule X, including funds from committee expense resolutions, and funds in any local currencies owned by the United States may not be made available for travel by a Member, Delegate, Resident Commissioner, or Senator after the date of a general election in which he was not elected to the succeeding Congress or, in the case of a Member, Delegate, or Resident Commissioner who is not a candidate in a general election, after the earlier of the date of such general election or the adjournment sine die of the last regular session of the Congress.

RULE XXVI

LIMITATIONS ON OUTSIDE EARNED INCOME AND ACCEPTANCE OF GIFTS

OUTSIDE EARNED INCOME; HONORARIA

1. (a) Except as provided by paragraph (b), a Member, Delegate, Resident Commissioner, officer, or employee of the House may not—

(1) have outside earned income attributable to a calendar year that exceeds 15 percent of the annual rate of basic pay for level II of the Executive Schedule under section 5313 of title 5, United States Code, as of January 1 of that calendar year; or

(2) receive any honorarium, except that an officer or employee of the House who is paid at a rate less than 120 percent of the minimum rate of basic pay for GS-15 of the General Schedule may receive an honorarium unless the subject matter is directly related to the official duties of the individual, the payment is made because of the status of the individual with the House, or the person offering the honorarium has interests that may be substantially affected by the performance or nonperformance of the official duties of the individual.

(b) In the case of an individual who becomes a Member, Delegate, Resident Commissioner, officer, or employee of the House, such individual may not have outside earned income attributable to the portion of a calendar year that occurs after such individual becomes a Member, Delegate, Resident Commissioner, officer, or employee that exceeds 15 percent of the annual rate of basic pay for level II of the Executive Schedule under section 5313 of title 5, United States Code, as of January 1 of that calendar year multiplied by a fraction, the numerator of which is the number of days the individual is a Member, Delegate, Resident Commissioner, officer, or employee during that calendar year and the denominator of which is 365.

(c) A payment in lieu of an honorarium that is made to a charitable organization on behalf of a Member, Delegate, Resident Commissioner, officer, or employee of the House may not be received by that Member, Delegate, Resident Commissioner, officer, or employee. Such a payment may not exceed $2,000 or be made to a charitable organization from which the Member, Delegate, Resident Commissioner, officer, or employee or a parent, sibling, spouse, child, or dependent relative of the Member, Delegate, Resident Commissioner, officer, or employee, derives a financial benefit.

2. A Member, Delegate, Resident Commissioner, officer, or employee of the House may not—

(a) receive compensation for affiliating with or being employed by a firm, partnership, association, corporation, or other entity that provides professional services involving a fiduciary relationship;

(b) permit his name to be used by such a firm, partnership, association, corporation, or other entity;

(c) receive compensation for practicing a profession that involves a fiduciary relationship;

(d) serve for compensation as an officer or member of the board of an association, corporation, or other entity; or

(e) receive compensation for teaching, without the prior notification and approval of the Committee on Standards of Official Conduct.

COPYRIGHT ROYALTIES

3. (a) A Member, Delegate, Resident Commissioner, officer, or employee of the House may not receive an advance payment on copyright royalties. This paragraph does not prohibit a literary agent, researcher, or other individual (other than an individual employed by the House or a relative of a Member, Delegate, Resident Commissioner, officer, or employee) working on behalf of a Member, Delegate, Resident Commissioner, officer, or employee with respect to a publication from receiving an advance payment of a copyright royalty directly from a publisher and solely for the benefit of that literary agent, researcher, or other individual.

(b) A Member, Delegate, Resident Commissioner, officer, or employee of the House may not receive copyright royalties under a contract entered into on or after January 1, 1996, unless that contract is first approved by the Committee on Standards of Official Conduct as complying with the requirement of clause 4(d)(1)(E) (that royalties are received from an established publisher under usual and customary contractual terms).

DEFINITIONS

4. (a)(1) In this rule, except as provided in subparagraph (2), the term "officer or employee of the House" means an individual (other

than a Member, Delegate, or Resident Commissioner) whose pay is disbursed by the Chief Administrative Officer, who is paid at a rate equal to or greater than 120 percent of the minimum rate of basic pay for GS-15 of the General Schedule, and who is so employed for more than 90 days in a calendar year; and

(2) when used with respect to an honorarium, the term "officer or employee of the House" means an individual (other than a Member, Delegate, or Resident Commissioner) whose salary is disbursed by the Chief Administrative Officer.

(b) In this rule the term "honorarium" means a payment of money or a thing of value for an appearance, speech, or article (including a series of appearances, speeches, or articles) by a Member, Delegate, Resident Commissioner, officer, or employee of the House, excluding any actual and necessary travel expenses incurred by that Member, Delegate, Resident Commissioner, officer, or employee (and one relative) to the extent that such expenses are paid or reimbursed by any other person. The amount otherwise determined shall be reduced by the amount of any such expenses to the extent that such expenses are not so paid or reimbursed.

(c) In this rule the term "travel expenses" means, with respect to a Member, Delegate, Resident Commissioner, officer or, employee of the House, or a relative of such Member, Delegate, Resident Commissioner, officer, or employee, the cost of transportation, and the cost of lodging and meals while away from his residence or principal place of employment.

(d)(1) In this rule the term "outside earned income" means, with respect to a Member, Delegate, Resident Commissioner, officer, or employee of the House, wages, salaries, fees, and other amounts received or to be received as compensation for personal services actually rendered, but does not include—

(A) the salary of a Member, Delegate, Resident Commissioner, officer, or employee;

(B) any compensation derived by a Member, Delegate, Resident Commissioner, officer, or employee of the House for personal services actually rendered before the adoption of this rule or before he became a Member, Delegate, Resident Commissioner, officer, or employee;

(C) any amount paid by, or on behalf of, a Member, Delegate, Resident Commissioner, officer, or employee of the House to a tax-qualified pension, profit-sharing, or stock bonus plan and received by him from such a plan;

(D) in the case of a Member, Delegate, Resident Commissioner, officer, or employee of the House engaged in a trade or business in which he or his family holds a controlling interest and in which both personal services and capital are income-producing factors, any amount received by the Member, Delegate, Resident Commissioner, officer, or employee, so long as the personal services actually rendered by him in the trade or business do not generate a significant amount of income; or

(E) copyright royalties received from established publishers under usual and customary contractual terms; and

(2) outside earned income shall be determined without regard to community property law.

(e) In this rule the term "charitable organization" means an organization described in section 170(c) of the Internal Revenue Code of 1986.

GIFTS

5. (a)(1)(A) A Member, Delegate, Resident Commissioner, officer, or employee of the House may not knowingly accept a gift except as provided in this clause.

(B) A Member, Delegate, Resident Commissioner, officer, or employee of the House may accept a gift (other than cash or cash equivalent) that the Member, Delegate, Resident Commissioner, officer, or employee reasonably and in good faith believes to have a value of less than $50 and a cumulative value from one source during a calendar year of less than $100. A gift having a value of less than $10 does not count toward the $100 annual limit. Formal recordkeeping is not required by this subdivision, but a Member, Delegate, Resident Commissioner, officer, or employee of the House shall make a good faith effort to comply with this subdivision.

(2)(A) In this clause the term "gift" means a gratuity, favor, discount, entertainment, hospitality, loan, forbearance, or other item having monetary value. The term includes gifts of services, training, transportation, lodging, and meals, whether provided in kind, by purchase of a ticket, payment in advance, or reimbursement after the expense has been incurred.

(B)(i) A gift to a family member of a Member, Delegate, Resident Commissioner, officer, or employee of the House, or a gift to any other individual based on that individual's relationship with the Member, Delegate, Resident Commissioner, officer, or employee, shall be considered a gift to the Member, Delegate, Resident Commissioner, officer, or employee if it is given with the knowledge and acquiescence of the Member, Delegate, Resident Commissioner, officer, or employee and the Member, Delegate, Resident Commissioner, officer, or employee has reason to believe the gift was given because of his official position.

(ii) If food or refreshment is provided at the same time and place to both a Member, Delegate, Resident Commissioner, officer, or employee of the House and the spouse or dependent thereof, only the food or refreshment provided to the Member, Delegate, Resident Commissioner, officer, or employee shall be treated as a gift for purposes of this clause.

(3) The restrictions in subparagraph (1) do not apply to the following:

(A) Anything for which the Member, Delegate, Resident Commissioner, officer, or employee of the House pays the market value, or does not use and promptly returns to the donor.

(B) A contribution, as defined in section 301(8) of the Federal Election Campaign Act of 1971 (2 U.S.C. 431 et seq.) that is lawfully made under that Act, a lawful contribution for election to a State or local government office, or attendance at a fundraising event sponsored by a political organization described in section 527(e) of the Internal Revenue Code of 1986.

(C) A gift from a relative as described in section 109(16) of title I of the Ethics in Government Act of 1978 (2 U.S.C. App. 109(16)).

(D)(i) Anything provided by an individual on the basis of a personal friendship unless the Member, Delegate, Resident Commissioner, officer, or employee of the House has reason to believe that, under the circumstances, the gift was provided because of his official position and not because of the personal friendship.

(ii) In determining whether a gift is provided on the basis of personal friendship, the Member, Delegate, Resident Commissioner, officer, or employee of the House shall consider the circumstances under which the gift was offered, such as:

(I) The history of his relationship with the individual giving the gift, including any previous exchange of gifts between them.

(II) Whether to his actual knowledge the individual who gave the gift personally paid for the gift or sought a tax deduction or business reimbursement for the gift.

(III) Whether to his actual knowledge the individual who gave the gift also gave the same or similar gifts to other Members, Delegates, the Resident Commissioners, officers, or employees of the House.

(E) Except as provided in paragraph (c)(3), a contribution or other payment to a legal expense fund established for the benefit of a Member, Delegate, Resident Commissioner, officer, or employee of the House that is otherwise lawfully made in accordance with the restrictions and disclosure requirements of the Committee on Standards of Official Conduct.

(F) A gift from another Member, Delegate, Resident Commissioner, officer, or employee of the House or Senate.

(G) Food, refreshments, lodging, transportation, and other benefits—

(i) resulting from the outside business or employment activities of the Member, Delegate, Resident Commissioner, officer, or employee of the House (or other outside activities that are not connected to his duties as an officeholder), or of his spouse, if such benefits have not been offered or enhanced because of his official position and are customarily provided to others in similar circumstances;

(ii) customarily provided by a prospective employer in connection with bona fide employment discussions; or

(iii) provided by a political organization described in section 527(e) of the Internal Revenue Code of 1986 in connection with a fundraising or campaign event sponsored by such organization.

(H) Pension and other benefits resulting from continued participation in an employee welfare and benefits plan maintained by a former employer.

(I) Informational materials that are sent to the office of the Member, Delegate, Resident Commissioner, officer, or employee of the House in the form of books, articles, periodicals, other written materials, audiotapes, videotapes, or other forms of communication.

(J) Awards or prizes that are given to competitors in contests or events open to the public, including random drawings.

(K) Honorary degrees (and associated travel, food, refreshments, and entertainment) and other bona fide, nonmonetary awards presented in recognition of public service (and associated food, refreshments, and entertainment provided in the presentation of such degrees and awards).

(L) Training (including food and refreshments furnished to all attendees as an integral part of the training) if such training is in the interest of the House.

(M) Bequests, inheritances, and other transfers at death.

(N) An item, the receipt of which is authorized by the Foreign Gifts and Decorations Act, the Mutual Educational and Cultural Exchange Act, or any other statute.

(O) Anything that is paid for by the Federal Government, by a State or local government, or secured by the Government under a Government contract.

(P) A gift of personal hospitality (as defined in section 109(14) of the Ethics in Government Act) of an individual other than a registered lobbyist or agent of a foreign principal.

(Q) Free attendance at a widely attended event permitted under subparagraph (4).

(R) Opportunities and benefits that are—

(i) available to the public or to a class consisting of all Federal employees, whether or not restricted on the basis of geographic consideration;

(ii) offered to members of a group or class in which membership is unrelated to congressional employment;

(iii) offered to members of an organization, such as an employees' association or congressional credit union, in which membership is related to congressional employment and similar opportunities are available to large segments of the public through organizations of similar size;

(iv) offered to a group or class that is not defined in a manner that specifically discriminates among Government employees on the basis of branch of Government or type of responsibility, or on a basis that favors those of higher rank or rate of pay;

(v) in the form of loans from banks and other financial institutions on terms generally available to the public; or

(vi) in the form of reduced membership or other fees for participation in organization activities offered to all Government employees by professional organizations if the only restrictions on membership relate to professional qualifications.

(S) A plaque, trophy, or other item that is substantially commemorative in nature and that is intended for presentation.

(T) Anything for which, in an unusual case, a waiver is granted by the Committee on Standards of Official Conduct.

(U) Food or refreshments of a nominal value offered other than as a part of a meal.

(V) Donations of products from the district or State that the Member, Delegate, or Resident Commissioner represents that are intended primarily for promotional purposes, such as display or free distribution, and are of minimal value to any single recipient.

(W) An item of nominal value such as a greeting card, baseball cap, or a T-shirt.

(4)(A) A Member, Delegate, Resident Commissioner, officer, or employee of the House may accept an offer of free attendance at a widely attended convention, conference, symposium, forum, panel discussion, dinner, viewing, reception, or similar event, provided by the sponsor of the event, if—

(i) the Member, Delegate, Resident Commissioner, officer, or employee of the House participates in the event as a speaker or a panel participant, by presenting information related to Congress or matters before Congress, or by performing a ceremonial function appropriate to his official position; or

(ii) attendance at the event is appropriate to the performance of the official duties or representative function of the Member, Delegate, Resident Commissioner, officer, or employee of the House.

(B) A Member, Delegate, Resident Commissioner, officer, or employee of the House who attends an event described in subdivision (A) may accept a sponsor's unsolicited offer of free attendance at the event for an accompanying individual.

(C) A Member, Delegate, Resident Commissioner, officer, or employee of the House, or the spouse or dependent thereof, may accept a sponsor's unsolicited offer of free attendance at a charity event, except that reimbursement for transportation and lodging may not be accepted in connection with the event.

(D) In this paragraph the term "free attendance" may include waiver of all or part of a conference or other fee, the provision of local transportation, or the provision of food, refreshments, entertainment, and instructional materials furnished to all attendees as an integral part of the event. The term does not include entertainment collateral to the event, nor does it include food or refreshments taken other than in a group setting with all or substantially all other attendees.

(5) A Member, Delegate, Resident Commissioner, officer, or employee of the House may not accept a gift the value of which exceeds $250 on the basis of the personal friendship exception in subparagraph (3)(D) unless the Committee on Standards of Official Conduct issues a written determination that such exception applies. A determination under this subparagraph is not required for gifts given on the basis of the family relationship exception in subparagraph (3)(C).

(6) When it is not practicable to return a tangible item because it is perishable, the item may, at the discretion of the recipient, be given to an appropriate charity or destroyed.

(b)(1)(A) A reimbursement (including payment in kind) to a Member, Delegate, Resident Commissioner, officer, or employee of the House from a private source other than a registered lobbyist or agent of a foreign principal for necessary transportation, lodging, and related expenses for travel to a meeting, speaking engagement, fact-finding trip, or similar event in connection with his duties as an officeholder shall be considered as a reimbursement to the House and not a gift prohibited by this clause, if the Member, Delegate, Resident Commissioner, officer, or employee—

(i) in the case of an employee, receives advance authorization, from the Member, Delegate, Resident Commissioner, or officer under whose direct supervision the employee works, to accept reimbursement; and

(ii) discloses the expenses reimbursed or to be reimbursed and the authorization to the Clerk within 30 days after the travel is completed.

(B) For purposes of subdivision (A), events, the activities of which are substantially recreational in nature, are not considered to be in connection with the duties of a Member, Delegate, Resident Commissioner, officer, or employee of the House as an officeholder.

(2) Each advance authorization to accept reimbursement shall be signed by the Member, Delegate, Resident Commissioner, or officer of the House under whose direct supervision the employee works and shall include—

(A) the name of the employee;

(B) the name of the person who will make the reimbursement;

(C) the time, place, and purpose of the travel; and

(D) a determination that the travel is in connection with the duties of the employee as an officeholder and would not create the appearance that the employee is using public office for private gain.

(3) Each disclosure made under subparagraph (1)(A) of expenses reimbursed or to be reimbursed shall be signed by the Member, Delegate, Resident Commissioner, or officer (in the case of travel by that Member, Delegate, Resident Commissioner, or officer) or by the Member, Delegate, Resident Commissioner, or officer under whose direct supervision the employee works (in the case of travel by an employee) and shall include—

(A) a good faith estimate of total transportation expenses reimbursed or to be reimbursed;

(B) a good faith estimate of total lodging expenses reimbursed or to be reimbursed;

(C) a good faith estimate of total meal expenses reimbursed or to be reimbursed;

(D) a good faith estimate of the total of other expenses reimbursed or to be reimbursed;

(E) a determination that all such expenses are necessary transportation, lodging, and related expenses as defined in subparagraph (4); and

(F) in the case of a reimbursement to a Member, Delegate, Resident Commissioner, or officer, a determination that the travel was in connection with his duties as an officeholder and would not create the appearance that the Member, Delegate, Resident Commissioner, or officer is using public office for private gain.

(4) In this paragraph the term "necessary transportation, lodging, and related expenses"—

(A) includes reasonable expenses that are necessary for travel for a period not exceeding four days within the United States or seven days exclusive of travel time outside of the United States unless approved in advance by the Committee on Standards of Official Conduct;

(B) is limited to reasonable expenditures for transportation, lodging, conference fees and materials, and food and refreshments, including reimbursement for necessary transportation, whether or not such transportation occurs within the periods described in subdivision (A);

(C) does not include expenditures for recreational activities, nor does it include entertainment other than that provided to all attendees as an integral part of the event, except for activities or entertainment otherwise permissible under this clause; and

(D) may include travel expenses incurred on behalf of either the spouse or a child of the Member, Delegate, Resident Commissioner, officer, or employee.

(5) The Clerk shall make available to the public all advance authorizations and disclosures of reimbursement filed under subparagraph (1) as soon as possible after they are received.

(c) A gift prohibited by paragraph (a)(1) includes the following:

(1) Anything provided by a registered lobbyist or an agent of a foreign principal to an entity that is maintained or controlled by a Member, Delegate, Resident Commissioner, officer, or employee of the House.

(2) A charitable contribution (as defined in section 170(c) of the Internal Revenue Code of 1986) made by a registered lobbyist or an agent of a foreign principal on the basis of a designation, recommendation, or other specification of a Member, Delegate, Resident Commissioner, officer, or employee of the House (not including a mass mailing or other solicitation di-

rected to a broad category of persons or entities), other than a charitable contribution permitted by paragraph (d).

(3) A contribution or other payment by a registered lobbyist or an agent of a foreign principal to a legal expense fund established for the benefit of a Member, Delegate, Resident Commissioner, officer, or employee of the House.

(4) A financial contribution or expenditure made by a registered lobbyist or an agent of a foreign principal relating to a conference, retreat, or similar event, sponsored by or affiliated with an official congressional organization, for or on behalf of Members, Delegates, the Resident Commissioner, officers, or employees of the House.

(d)(1) A charitable contribution (as defined in section 170(c) of the Internal Revenue Code of 1986) made by a registered lobbyist or an agent of a foreign principal in lieu of an honorarium to a Member, Delegate, Resident Commissioner, officer, or employee of the House is not considered a gift under this clause if it is reported as provided in subparagraph (2).

(2) A Member, Delegate, Resident Commissioner, officer, or employee who designates or recommends a contribution to a charitable organization in lieu of an honorarium described in subparagraph (1) shall report within 30 days after such designation or recommendation to the Clerk—

(A) the name and address of the registered lobbyist who is making the contribution in lieu of an honorarium;

(B) the date and amount of the contribution; and

(C) the name and address of the charitable organization designated or recommended by the Member, Delegate, or Resident Commissioner.

The Clerk shall make public information received under this subparagraph as soon as possible after it is received.

(e) In this clause—

(1) the term "registered lobbyist" means a lobbyist registered under the Federal Regulation of Lobbying Act or any successor statute; and

(2) the term "agent of a foreign principal" means an agent of a foreign principal registered under the Foreign Agents Registration Act.

(f) All the provisions of this clause shall be interpreted and enforced solely by the Committee on Standards of Official Conduct. The Committee on Standards of Official Conduct is authorized to issue guidance on any matter contained in this clause.

CLAIMS AGAINST THE GOVERNMENT

6. A person may not be an officer or employee of the House, or continue in its employment, if he acts as an agent for the prosecution of a claim against the Government or if he is interested in such claim, except as an original claimant or in the proper discharge of official duties.

RULE XXVII

FINANCIAL DISCLOSURE

1. The Clerk shall send a copy of each report filed with the Clerk under title I of the Ethics in Government Act of 1978 within the seven-day period beginning on the date on which the report is filed to the Committee on Standards of Official Conduct. By August 1 of each year, the Clerk shall compile all such reports sent to him by Members within the period beginning on January 1 and ending on June 15 of each year and have them printed as a House document, which shall be made available to the public.

2. For the purposes of this rule, the provisions of title I of the Ethics in Government Act of 1978 shall be considered Rules of the House as they pertain to Members, Delegates, the Resident Commissioner, officers, and employees of the House.

RULE XXVIII

GENERAL PROVISIONS

1. The provisions of law that constituted the Rules of the House at the end of the previous Congress shall govern the House in all cases to which they are applicable, and the rules of parliamentary practice comprised by Jefferson's Manual shall govern the House in all cases to which they are applicable and in which they are not inconsistent with the Rules and orders of the House.

2. In these rules words importing the masculine gender include the feminine as well.

RULE I

APPOINTMENT OF A SENATOR TO THE CHAIR

1. In the absence of the Vice President, the Senate shall choose a President pro tempore, who shall hold the office and execute the duties thereof during the pleasure of the Senate and until another is elected or his term of office as a Senator expires.

2. In the absence of the Vice President, and pending the election of a President pro tempore, the Acting President pro tempore or the Secretary of the Senate, or in his absence the Assistant Secretary, shall perform the duties of the Chair.

3. The President pro tempore shall have the right to name in open Senate or, if absent, in writing, a Senator to perform the duties of the Chair, including the signing of duly enrolled bills and joint resolutions but such substitution shall not extend beyond an adjournment, except by unanimous consent; and the Senator so named shall have the right to name in open session, or, if absent, in writing, a Senator to perform the duties of the Chair, but not to extend beyond an adjournment, except by unanimous consent.

RULE II

PRESENTATION OF CREDENTIALS AND QUESTIONS OF PRIVILEGE

1. The presentation of the credentials of Senators elect or of Senators designate and other questions of privilege shall always be in order, except during the reading and correction of the Journal, while a question of order or a motion to adjourn is pending, or while the Senate is voting or ascertaining the presence of a quorum; and all questions and motions arising or made upon the presentation of such credentials shall be proceeded with until disposed of.

2. The Secretary shall keep a record of the certificates of election and certificates of appointment of Senators by entering in a well-bound book kept for that purpose the date of the election or appointment, the name of the person elected or appointed, the date of the certificate, the name of the governor and the secretary of state signing and countersigning the same, and the State from which such Senator is elected or appointed.

3. The Secretary of the Senate shall send copies of the following recommended forms to the governor and secretary of state of each State wherein an election is about to take place or an appointment is to be made so that they may use such forms if they see fit.

THE RECOMMENDED FORMS FOR CERTIFICATE OF ELECTION AND CERTIFICATE OF APPOINTMENT ARE AS FOLLOWS:

"CERTIFICATE OF ELECTION FOR SIX-YEAR TERM

"To the President of the Senate of the United States:

This is to certify that on the — day of ——, 19—, A—— B—— was duly chosen by the qualified electors of the State of —— a Senator from said State to represent said State in the Senate of the United States for the term of six years, beginning on the 3d day of January, 19—.

"Witness: His excellency our governor ——, and our seal hereto affixed at —— this — day of ——, in the year of our Lord 19—.

"By the governor:

"C—— D——,
"Governor.

"E—— F——,
"Secretary of State."

"CERTIFICATE OF ELECTION FOR UNEXPIRED TERM

"To the President of the Senate of the United States:

"This is to certify that on the — day of ——, 19—, A—— B—— was duly chosen by the qualified electors of the State of —— a Senator for the unexpired term ending at noon on the 3d day of January, 19—, to fill the vacancy in the representation from said State in the Senate of the United States caused by the —— of C—— D——.

"Witness: His excellency our governor ——, and our seal hereto affixed at —— this — day of ——, in the year of our Lord 19—.

"By the governor:

"E—— F——,
"Governor.

"G—— H——,
"Secretary of State."

"CERTIFICATE OF APPOINTMENT

"To the President of the Senate of the United States:

"This is to certify that, pursuant to the power vested in me by the Constitution of the United States and the laws of the State of ——, I, A—— B——, the governor of said State, do hereby appoint C—— D—— a Senator from said State to represent said State in the Senate of the United States until the vacancy therein caused by the —— of E—— F——, is filled by election as provided by law.

"Witness: His excellency our governor ——, and our seal hereto affixed at —— this — day of ——, in the year of our Lord 19—.

"By the governor:

"G—— H——,
"Governor.

"I—— J——,
"Secretary of State."

RULE III

OATHS

The oaths or affirmations required by the Constitution and prescribed by law shall be taken and subscribed by each Senator, in open Senate, before entering upon his duties.

OATH REQUIRED BY THE CONSTITUTION AND BY LAW TO BE TAKEN BY SENATORS

"I, A—— B——, do solemnly swear (or affirm) that I will support and defend the Constitution of the United States against all enemies, foreign and domestic; that I will bear true faith and allegiance to the same; that I take this obligation freely, without any mental reservation or purpose of evasion; and that I will well and faithfully discharge the duties of the office on which I am about to enter: So help me God. " (5 U.S.C. 3331.)

RULE IV

COMMENCEMENT OF DAILY SESSIONS

1. (a) The Presiding Officer having taken the chair, following the prayer by the Chaplain, and a quorum being present, the Journal of the preceding day shall be read unless by nondebatable motion the reading shall be waived, the question being, "Shall the Journal stand approved to date?", and any mistake made in the entries corrected. Except as provided in subparagraph (b) the reading of the Journal shall not be suspended unless by unanimous consent; and when any motion shall be made to amend or correct the same, it shall be deemed a privileged question, and proceeded with until disposed of.

(b) Whenever the Senate is proceeding under paragraph 2 of rule XXII, the reading of the Journal shall be dispensed with and shall be considered approved to date.

(c) The proceedings of the Senate shall be briefly and accurately stated on the Journal. Messages of the President in full; titles of bills and resolutions, and such parts as shall be affected by proposed amendments; every vote, and a brief statement of the contents of each petition, memorial, or paper presented to the Senate, shall be entered.

(d) The legislative, the executive, the confidential legislative proceedings, and the proceedings when sitting as a Court of Impeachment, shall each be recorded in a separate book.

2. During a session of the Senate when that body is in continuous session, the Presiding Officer shall temporarily suspend the business of the Senate at noon each day for the purpose of having the customary daily prayer by the Chaplain.

RULE V

SUSPENSION AND AMENDMENT OF THE RULES

1. No motion to suspend, modify, or amend any rule, or any part thereof, shall be in order, except on one day's notice in writing, specifying precisely the rule or part proposed to be suspended, modified, or amended, and the purpose thereof. Any rule may be suspended without notice by the unanimous consent of the Senate, except as otherwise provided by the rules.

2. The rules of the Senate shall continue from one Congress to the next Congress unless they are changed as provided in these rules.

RULE VI

QUORUM—ABSENT SENATORS MAY BE SENT FOR

1. A quorum shall consist of a majority of the Senators duly chosen and sworn.

2. No Senator shall absent himself from the service of the Senate without leave.

3. If, at any time during the daily sessions of the Senate, a question shall be raised by any Senator as to the presence of a quorum, the Presiding Officer shall forthwith direct the Secretary to call the roll and shall announce the result, and these proceedings shall be without debate.

4. Whenever upon such roll call it shall be ascertained that a quorum is not present, a majority of the Senators present may direct the Sergeant at Arms to request, and, when necessary, to compel the at-tendance of the absent Senators, which order shall be determined without debate; and pending its execution, and until a quorum shall be present, no debate nor motion, except to adjourn, or to recess pursuant to a previous order entered by unanimous consent, shall be in order.

RULE VII

MORNING BUSINESS

1. On each legislative day after the Journal is read, the Presiding Officer on demand of any Senator shall lay before the Senate messages from the President, reports and communications from the heads of Departments, and other communications addressed to the Senate, and such bills, joint resolutions, and other messages from the House of Representatives as may remain upon his table from any previous day's session undisposed of. The Presiding Officer on demand of any Senator shall then call for, in the following order:

The presentation of petitions and memorials.
Reports of committees.
The introduction of bills and joint resolutions.
The submission of other resolutions.

All of which shall be received and disposed of in such order, unless unanimous consent shall be otherwise given, with newly offered resolutions being called for before resolutions coming over from a previous legislative day are laid before the Senate.

2. Until the morning business shall have been concluded, and so announced from the Chair, or until one hour after the Senate convenes at the beginning of a new legislative day, no motion to proceed to the consideration of any bill, resolution, report of a committee, or other subject upon the Calendar shall be entertained by the Presiding Officer, unless by unanimous consent: *Provided, however,* That on Mondays which are the beginning of a legislative day the Calendar shall be called under rule VIII, and until two hours after the Senate convenes no motion shall be entertained to proceed to the consideration of any bill, resolution, or other subject upon the Calendar except the motion to continue the consideration of a bill, resolution, or other subject against objection as provided in rule VIII, or until the call of the Calendar has been completed.

3. The Presiding Officer may at any time lay, and it shall be in order at any time for a Senator to move to lay, before the Senate, any bill or other matter sent to the Senate by the President or the House of Representatives for appropriate action allowed under the rules and any question pending at that time shall be suspended for this purpose. Any motion so made shall be determined without debate.

4. Petitions or memorials shall be referred, without debate, to the appropriate committee according to subject matter on the same basis as bills and resolutions, if signed by the petitioner or memorialist. A question of receiving or reference may be raised and determined without debate. But no petition or memorial or other paper signed by citizens or subjects of a foreign power shall be received, unless the same be transmitted to the Senate by the President.

5. Only a brief statement of the contents of petitions and memorials shall be printed in the Congressional Record; and no other portion of any petition or memorial shall be printed in the Record unless specifically so ordered by vote of the Senate, as provided for in paragraph 4 of rule XI, in which case the order shall be deemed to apply to the body of the petition or memorial only; and names attached to the petition or memorial shall not be printed unless specially ordered, except that petitions and memorials from the legislatures or conven-

tions, lawfully called, of the respective States, Territories, and insular possessions shall be printed in full in the Record whenever presented.

6. Senators having petitions, memorials, bills, or resolutions to present after the morning hour may deliver them in the absence of objection to the Presiding Officer's desk, endorsing upon them their names, and with the approval of the Presiding Officer, they shall be entered on the Journal with the names of the Senators presenting them and in the absence of objection shall be considered as having been read twice and referred to the appropriate committees, and a transcript of such entries shall be furnished to the official reporter of debates for publication in the Congressional Record, under the direction of the Secretary of the Senate.

RULE VIII

ORDER OF BUSINESS

1. At the conclusion of the morning business at the beginning of a new legislative day, unless upon motion the Senate shall at any time otherwise order, the Senate shall proceed to the consideration of the Calendar of Bills and Resolutions, and shall continue such consideration until 2 hours after the Senate convenes on such day (the end of the morning hour); and bills and resolutions that are not objected to shall be taken up in their order, and each Senator shall be entitled to speak once and for five minutes only upon any question; and an objection may be interposed at any stage of the proceedings, but upon motion the Senate may continue such consideration; and this order shall commence immediately after the call for "other resolutions", or after disposition of resolutions coming "over under the rule", and shall take precedence of the unfinished business and other special orders. But if the Senate shall proceed on motion with the consideration of any matter notwithstanding an objection, the foregoing provisions touching debate shall not apply.

2. All motions made during the first two hours of a new legislative day to proceed to the consideration of any matter shall be determined without debate, except motions to proceed to the consideration of any motion, resolution, or proposal to change any of the Standing Rules of the Senate shall be debatable. Motions made after the first two hours of a new legislative day to proceed to the consideration of bills and resolutions are debatable.

RULE IX

MESSAGES

1. Messages from the President of the United States or from the House of Representatives may be received at any stage of proceedings, except while the Senate is voting or ascertaining the presence of a quorum, or while the Journal is being read, or while a question of order or a motion to adjourn is pending.

2. Messages shall be sent to the House of Representatives by the Secretary, who shall previously certify the determination of the Senate upon all bills, joint resolutions, and other resolutions which may be communicated to the House, or in which its concurrence may be requested; and the Secretary shall also certify and deliver to the President of the United States all resolutions and other communications which may be directed to him by the Senate.

RULE X

SPECIAL ORDERS

1. Any subject may, by a vote of two-thirds of the Senators present, be made a special order of business for consideration and when the time so fixed for its consideration arrives the Presiding Officer shall lay it before the Senate, unless there be unfinished business in which case it takes its place on the Calendar of Special Orders in the order of time at which it was made special, to be considered in that order when there is no unfinished business.

2. All motions to change such order, or to proceed to the consideration of other business, shall be decided without debate.

RULE XI

PAPERS—WITHDRAWAL, PRINTING, READING OF, AND REFERENCE

1. No memorial or other paper presented to the Senate, except original treaties finally acted upon, shall be withdrawn from its files except by order of the Senate.

2. The Secretary of the Senate shall obtain at the close of each Congress all the noncurrent records of the Senate and of each Senate committee and transfer them to the National Archives and Records Administration for preservation, subject to the orders of the Senate.

3. When the reading of a paper is called for, and objected to, it shall be determined by a vote of the Senate, without debate.

4. Every motion or resolution to print documents, reports, and other matter transmitted by the executive departments, or to print memorials, petitions, accompanying documents, or any other paper, except bills of the Senate or House of Representatives, resolutions submitted by a Senator, communications from the legislatures or conventions, lawfully called, of the respective States, shall, unless the Senate otherwise order, be referred to the Committee on Rules and Administration. When a motion is made to commit with instructions, it shall be in order to add thereto a motion to print.

5. Motions or resolutions to print additional numbers shall also be referred to the Committee on Rules and Administration; and when the committee shall report favorably, the report shall be accompanied by an estimate of the probable cost thereof; and when the cost of printing such additional numbers shall exceed the sum established by law, the concurrence of the House of Representatives shall be necessary for an order to print the same.

6. Every bill and joint resolution introduced or reported from a committee, and all bills and joint resolutions received from the House of Representatives, and all reports of committees, shall be printed, unless, for the dispatch of the business of the Senate, such printing may be dispensed with.

RULE XII

VOTING PROCEDURE

1. When the yeas and nays are ordered, the names of Senators shall be called alphabetically; and each Senator shall, without debate, declare his assent or dissent to the question, unless excused by the Senate; and no Senator shall be permitted to vote after the decision shall have been announced by the Presiding Officer, but may for sufficient reasons, with unanimous consent, change or withdraw his vote. No

motion to suspend this rule shall be in order, nor shall the Presiding Officer entertain any request to suspend it by unanimous consent.

2. When a Senator declines to vote on call of his name, he shall be required to assign his reasons therefor, and having assigned them, the Presiding Officer shall submit the question to the Senate: "Shall the Senator for the reasons assigned by him, be excused from voting?" which shall be decided without debate; and these proceedings shall be had after the rollcall and before the result is announced; and any further proceedings in reference thereto shall be after such announcement.

3. A Member, notwithstanding any other provisions of this rule, may decline to vote, in committee or on the floor, on any matter when he believes that his voting on such a matter would be a conflict of interest.

4. No request by a Senator for unanimous consent for the taking of a final vote on a specified date upon the passage of a bill or joint resolution shall be submitted to the Senate for agreement thereto until after a quorum call ordered for the purpose by the Presiding Officer, it shall be disclosed that a quorum of the Senate is present; and when a unanimous consent is thus given the same shall operate as the order of the Senate, but any unanimous consent may be revoked by another unanimous consent granted in the manner prescribed above upon one day's notice.

RULE XIII

RECONSIDERATION

1. When a question has been decided by the Senate, any Senator voting with the prevailing side or who has not voted may, on the same day or on either of the next two days of actual session thereafter, move a reconsideration; and if the Senate shall refuse to reconsider such a motion entered, or if such a motion is withdrawn by leave of the Senate, or if upon reconsideration the Senate shall affirm its first decision, no further motion to reconsider shall be in order unless by unanimous consent. Every motion to reconsider shall be decided by a majority vote, and may be laid on the table without affecting the question in reference to which the same is made, which shall be a final disposition of the motion.

2. When a bill, resolution, report, amendment, order, or message, upon which a vote has been taken, shall have gone out of the possession of the Senate and been communicated to the House of Representatives, the motion to reconsider shall be accompanied by a motion to request the House to return the same; which last motion shall be acted upon immediately, and without debate, and if determined in the negative shall be a final disposition of the motion to reconsider.

RULE XIV

BILLS, JOINT RESOLUTIONS, RESOLUTIONS, AND PREAMBLES THERETO

1. Whenever a bill or joint resolution shall be offered, its introduction shall, if objected to, be postponed for one day.

2. Every bill and joint resolution shall receive three readings previous to its passage which readings on demand of any Senator shall be on three different legislative days, and the Presiding Officer shall give notice at each reading whether it be the first, second, or third: *Provided*, That each reading may be by title only, unless the Senate in any case shall otherwise order.

3. No bill or joint resolution shall be committed or amended until it shall have been twice read, after which it may be referred to a committee; bills and joint resolutions introduced on leave, and bills and joint resolutions from the House of Representatives, shall be read once, and may be read twice, if not objected to, on the same day for reference, but shall not be considered on that day nor debated, except for reference, unless by unanimous consent.

4. Every bill and joint resolution reported from a committee, not having previously been read, shall be read once, and twice, if not objected to, on the same day, and placed on the Calendar in the order in which the same may be reported; and every bill and joint resolution introduced on leave, and every bill and joint resolution of the House of Representatives which shall have received a first and second reading without being referred to a committee, shall, if objection be made to further proceeding thereon, be placed on the Calendar.

5. All bills, amendments, and joint resolutions shall be examined under the supervision of the Secretary of the Senate before they go out of the possession of the Senate, and all bills and joint resolutions which shall have passed both Houses shall be examined under the supervision of the Secretary of the Senate, to see that the same are correctly enrolled, and, when signed by the Speaker of the House and the President of the Senate, the Secretary of the Senate shall forthwith present the same, when they shall have originated in the Senate, to the President of the United States and report the fact and date of such presentation to the Senate.

6. All other resolutions shall lie over one day for consideration, if not referred, unless by unanimous consent the Senate shall otherwise direct. When objection is heard to the immediate consideration of a resolution or motion when it is submitted, it shall be placed on the Calendar under the heading of "Resolutions and Motions over, under the Rule," to be laid before the Senate on the next legislative day when there is no further morning business but before the close of morning business and before the termination of the morning hour.

7. When a bill or joint resolution shall have been ordered to be read a third time, it shall not be in order to propose amendments, unless by unanimous consent, but it shall be in order at any time before the passage of any bill or resolution to move its commitment; and when the bill or resolution shall again be reported from the committee it shall be placed on the Calendar.

8. When a bill or resolution is accompanied by a preamble, the question shall first be put on the bill or resolution and then on the preamble, which may be withdrawn by a mover before an amendment of the same, or ordering of the yeas and nays; or it may be laid on the table without prejudice to the bill or resolution, and shall be a final disposition of such preamble.

9. Whenever a private bill, except a bill for a pension, is under consideration, it shall be in order to move the adoption of a resolution to refer the bill to the Chief Commissioner of the Court of Claims for a report in conformity with section 2509 of title 28, United States Code.

10. No private bill or resolution (including so-called omnibus claims or pension bills), and no amendment to any bill or resolution, authorizing or directing (1) the payment of money for property damages, personal injuries, or death, for which a claim may be filed under chapter 171 of title 28, United States Code, or for a pension (other than to carry out a provision of law or treaty stipulation); (2) the construction of a bridge across a navigable stream; or (3) the correction of a military or naval record, shall be received or considered.

RULE XV

AMENDMENTS AND MOTIONS

1. All motions and amendments shall be reduced to writing, if desired by the Presiding Officer or by any Senator, and shall be read before the same shall be debated.

2. Any motion, amendment, or resolution may be withdrawn or modified by the mover at any time before a decision, amendment, or ordering of the yeas and nays, except a motion to reconsider, which shall not be withdrawn without leave.

3. If the question in debate contains several propositions, any Senator may have the same divided, except a motion to strike out and insert, which shall not be divided; but the rejection of a motion to strike out and insert one proposition shall not prevent a motion to strike out and insert a different proposition; nor shall it prevent a motion simply to strike out; nor shall the rejection of a motion to strike out prevent a motion to strike out and insert. But pending a motion to strike out and insert, the part to be stricken out and the part to be inserted shall each be regarded for the purpose of amendment as a question, and motions to amend the part to be stricken out shall have precedence.

4. When an amendment proposed to any pending measure is laid on the table, it shall not carry with it, or prejudice, such measure.

5. It shall not be in order to consider any proposed committee amendment (other than a technical, clerical, or conforming amendment) which contains any significant matter not within the jurisdiction of the committee proposing such amendment.

RULE XVI

APPROPRIATIONS AND AMENDMENTS TO GENERAL APPROPRIATION BILLS

1. On a point of order made by any Senator, no amendments shall be received to any general appropriation bill the effect of which will be to increase an appropriation already contained in the bill, or to add a new item of appropriation, unless it be made to carry out the provisions of some existing law, or treaty stipulation, or act or resolution previously passed by the Senate during that session; or unless the same be moved by direction of the Committee on Appropriations or of a committee of the Senate having legislative jurisdiction of the subject matter, or proposed in pursuance of an estimate submitted in accordance with law.

2. The Committee on Appropriations shall not report an appropriation bill containing amendments to such bill proposing new or general legislation or any restriction on the expenditure of the funds appropriated which proposes a limitation not authorized by law if such restriction is to take effect or cease to be effective upon the happening of a contingency, and if an appropriation bill is reported to the Senate containing amendments to such bill proposing new or general legislation or any such restriction, a point of order may be made against the bill, and if the point is sustained, the bill shall be recommitted to the Committee on Appropriations.

3. All amendments to general appropriation bills moved by direction of a committee having legislative jurisdiction of the subject matter proposing to increase an appropriation already contained in the bill, or to add new items of appropriation, shall, at least one day before they are considered, be referred to the Committee on Appropriations, and when actually proposed to the bill no amendment propos-

ing to increase the amount stated in such amendment shall be received on a point of order made by any Senator.

4. On a point of order made by any Senator, no amendment offered by any other Senator which proposes general legislation shall be received to any general appropriation bill, nor shall any amendment not germane or relevant to the subject matter contained in the bill be received; nor shall any amendment to any item or clause of such bill be received which does not directly relate thereto; nor shall any restriction on the expenditure of the funds appropriated which proposes a limitation not authorized by law be received if such restriction is to take effect or cease to be effective upon the happening of a contingency; and all questions of relevancy of amendments under this rule, when raised, shall be submitted to the Senate and be decided without debate; and any such amendment or restriction to a general appropriation bill may be laid on the table without prejudice to the bill.

5. On a point of order made by any Senator, no amendment, the object of which is to provide for a private claim, shall be received to any general appropriation bill, unless it be to carry out the provisions of an existing law or a treaty stipulation, which shall be cited on the face of the amendment.

6. When a point of order is made against any restriction on the expenditure of funds appropriated in a general appropriation bill on the ground that the restriction violates this rule, the rule shall be construed strictly and, in case of doubt, in favor of the point of order.

7. Every report on general appropriation bills filed by the Committee on Appropriations shall identify with particularity each recommended amendment which proposes an item of appropriation which is not made to carry out the provisions of an existing law, a treaty stipulation, or an act or resolution previously passed by the Senate during that session.

8. On a point of order made by any Senator, no general appropriation bill or amendment thereto shall be received or considered if it contains a provision reappropriating unexpended balances of appropriations; except that this provision shall not apply to appropriations in continuation of appropriations for public works on which work has commenced.

RULE XVII

REFERENCE TO COMMITTEES; MOTIONS TO DISCHARGE; REPORTS OF COMMITTEES; AND HEARINGS AVAILABLE

1. Except as provided in paragraph 3, in any case in which a controversy arises as to the jurisdiction of any committee with respect to any proposed legislation, the question of jurisdiction shall be decided by the presiding officer, without debate, in favor of the committee which has jurisdiction over the subject matter which predominates in such proposed legislation; but such decision shall be subject to an appeal.

2. A motion simply to refer shall not be open to amendment, except to add instructions.

3. (a) Upon motion by both the majority leader or his designee and the minority leader or his designee, proposed legislation may be referred to two or more committees jointly or sequentially. Notice of such motion and the proposed legislation to which it relates shall be printed in the Congressional Record. The motion shall be privileged, but it shall not be in order until the Congressional Record in which the notice is printed has been available to Senators for at least twenty-four hours. No amendment to any such motion shall be in order ex-

cept amendments to any instructions contained therein. Debate on any such motion, and all amendments thereto and debatable motions and appeals in connection therewith, shall be limited to not more than two hours, the time to be equally divided between, and controlled by, the majority leader and the minority leader or their designees.

(b) Proposed legislation which is referred to two or more committees jointly may be reported only by such committees jointly and only one report may accompany any proposed legislation so jointly reported.

(c) A motion to refer any proposed legislation to two or more committees sequentially shall specify the order of referral.

(d) Any motion under this paragraph may specify the portion or portions of proposed legislation to be considered by the committees, or any of them, to which such proposed legislation is referred, and such committees or committee shall be limited, in the consideration of such proposed legislation, to the portion or portions so specified.

(e) Any motion under this subparagraph may contain instructions with respect to the time allowed for consideration by the committees, or any of them, to which proposed legislation is referred and the discharge of such committees, or any of them, from further consideration of such proposed legislation.

4. (a) All reports of committees and motions to discharge a committee from the consideration of a subject, and all subjects from which a committee shall be discharged, shall lie over one day for consideration, unless by unanimous consent the Senate shall otherwise direct.

(b) Whenever any committee (except the Committee on Appropriations) has reported any measure, by action taken in conformity with the requirements of paragraph 7 of rule XXVI, no point of order shall lie with respect to that measure on the ground that hearings upon that measure by the committee were not conducted in accordance with the provisions of paragraph 4 of rule XXVI.

5. Any measure or matter reported by any standing committee shall not be considered in the Senate unless the report of that committee upon that measure or matter has been available to Members for at least two calendar days (excluding Sundays and legal holidays) prior to the consideration of that measure or matter. If hearings have been held on any such measure or matter so reported, the committee reporting the measure or matter shall make every reasonable effort to have such hearings printed and available for distribution to the Members of the Senate prior to the consideration of such measure or matter in the Senate. This paragraph—

(1) may be waived by joint agreement of the Majority Leader and the Minority Leader of the Senate; and

(2) shall not apply to—

(A) any measure for the declaration of war, or the declaration of a national emergency, by the Congress, and

(B) any executive decision, determination, or action which would become, or continue to be, effective unless disapproved or otherwise invalidated by one or both Houses of Congress.

RULE XVIII

BUSINESS CONTINUED FROM SESSION TO SESSION

At the second or any subsequent session of a Congress the legislative business of the Senate which remained undetermined at the close of the next preceding session of that Congress shall be resumed and proceeded with in the same manner as if no adjournment of the Senate had taken place.

RULE XIX

DEBATE

1. (a) When a Senator desires to speak, he shall rise and address the Presiding Officer, and shall not proceed until he is recognized, and the Presiding Officer shall recognize the Senator who shall first address him. No Senator shall interrupt another Senator in debate without his consent, and to obtain such consent he shall first address the Presiding Officer, and no Senator shall speak more than twice upon any one question in debate on the same legislative day without leave of the Senate, which shall be determined without debate.

(b) At the conclusion of the morning hour at the beginning of a new legislative day or after the unfinished business or any pending business has first been laid before the Senate on any calendar day, and until after the duration of three hours of actual session after such business is laid down except as determined to the contrary by unanimous consent or on motion without debate, all debate shall be germane and confined to the specific question then pending before the Senate.

2. No Senator in debate shall, directly or indirectly, by any form of words impute to another Senator or to other Senators any conduct or motive unworthy or unbecoming a Senator.

3. No Senator in debate shall refer offensively to any State of the Union.

4. If any Senator, in speaking or otherwise, in the opinion of the Presiding Officer transgress the rules of the Senate the Presiding Officer shall, either on his own motion or at the request of any other Senator, call him to order; and when a Senator shall be called to order he shall take his seat, and may not proceed without leave of the Senate, which, if granted, shall be upon motion that he be allowed to proceed in order, which motion shall be determined without debate. Any Senator directed by the Presiding Officer to take his seat, and any Senator requesting the Presiding Officer to require a Senator to take his seat, may appeal from the ruling of the Chair, which appeal shall be open to debate.

5. If a Senator be called to order for words spoken in debate, upon the demand of the Senator or of any other Senator, the exceptionable words shall be taken down in writing, and read at the table for the information of the Senate.

6. Whenever confusion arises in the Chamber or the galleries, or demonstrations of approval or disapproval are indulged in by the occupants of the galleries, it shall be the duty of the Chair to enforce order on his own initiative and without any point of order being made by a Senator.

7. No Senator shall introduce to or bring to the attention of the Senate during its sessions any occupant in the galleries of the Senate. No motion to suspend this rule shall be in order, nor may the Presiding Officer entertain any request to suspend it by unanimous consent.

8. Former Presidents of the United States shall be entitled to address the Senate upon appropriate notice to the Presiding Officer who shall thereupon make the necessary arrangements.

RULE XX

QUESTIONS OF ORDER

1. A question of order may be raised at any stage of the proceedings, except when the Senate is voting or ascertaining the presence of a quorum, and, unless submitted to the Senate, shall be decided by the Presiding Officer without debate, subject to an appeal to the Senate. When an appeal is taken, any subsequent question of order which may arise before the decision of such appeal shall be decided by the Presiding Officer without debate; and every appeal therefrom shall be decided at once, and without debate; and any appeal may be laid on the table without prejudice to the pending proposition, and thereupon shall be held as affirming the decision of the Presiding Officer.

2. The Presiding Officer may submit any question of order for the decision of the Senate.

RULE XXI

SESSION WITH CLOSED DOORS

1. On a motion made and seconded to close the doors of the Senate, on the discussion of any business which may, in the opinion of a Senator, require secrecy, the Presiding Officer shall direct the galleries to be cleared; and during the discussion of such motion the doors shall remain closed.

2. When the Senate meets in closed session, any applicable provisions of rules XXIX and XXXI, including the confidentiality of information shall apply to any information and to the conduct of any debate transacted.

RULE XXII

PRECEDENCE OF MOTIONS

1. When a question is pending, no motion shall be received but—
   To adjourn.
   To adjourn to a day certain, or that when the Senate adjourn it shall be to a day certain.
   To take a recess.
   To proceed to the consideration of executive business.
   To lay on the table.
   To postpone indefinitely.
   To postpone to a day certain.
   To commit.
   To amend.

Which several motions shall have precedence as they stand arranged; and the motions relating to adjournment, to take a recess, to proceed to the consideration of executive business, to lay on the table, shall be decided without debate.

2. Notwithstanding the provisions of rule II or rule IV or any other rule of the Senate, at any time a motion signed by sixteen Senators, to bring to a close the debate upon any measure, motion, other matter pending before the Senate, or the unfinished business, is presented to the Senate, the Presiding Officer, or clerk at the direction of the Presiding Officer, shall at once state the motion to the Senate, and one hour after the Senate meets on the following calendar day but one, he shall lay the motion before the Senate and direct that the clerk call the roll, and upon the ascertainment that a quorum is present, the Presiding Officer shall, without debate, submit to the Senate by a yea-and-nay vote the question:

"Is it the sense of the Senate that the debate shall be brought to a close?" And if that question shall be decided in the affirmative by three-fifths of the Senators duly chosen and sworn—except on a measure or motion to amend the Senate rules, in which case the necessary affirmative vote shall be two-thirds of the Senators present and voting—then said measure, motion, or other matter pending before the Senate, or the unfinished business, shall be the unfinished business to the exclusion of all other business until disposed of.

Thereafter no Senator shall be entitled to speak in all more than one hour on the measure, motion, or other matter pending before the Senate, or the unfinished business, the amendments thereto, and motions affecting the same, and it shall be the duty of the Presiding Officer to keep the time of each Senator who speaks. Except by unanimous consent, no amendment shall be proposed after the vote to bring the debate to a close, unless it had been submitted in writing to the Journal Clerk by 1 o'clock p. m. on the day following the filing of the cloture motion if an amendment in the first degree, and unless it had been so submitted at least one hour prior to the beginning of the cloture vote if an amendment in the second degree. No dilatory motion, or dilatory amendment, or amendment not germane shall be in order. Points of order, including questions of relevancy, and appeals from the decision of the Presiding Officer, shall be decided without debate.

After no more than thirty hours of consideration of the measure, motion, or other matter on which cloture has been invoked, the Senate shall proceed, without any further debate on any question, to vote on the final disposition thereof to the exclusion of all amendments not then actually pending before the Senate at that time and to the exclusion of all motions, except a motion to table, or to reconsider and one quorum call on demand to establish the presence of a quorum (and motions required to establish a quorum) immediately before the final vote begins. The thirty hours may be increased by the adoption of a motion, decided without debate, by a three-fifths affirmative vote of the Senators duly chosen and sworn, and any such time thus agreed upon shall be equally divided between and controlled by the Majority and Minority Leaders or their designees. However, only one motion to extend time, specified above, may be made in any one calendar day.

If, for any reason, a measure or matter is reprinted after cloture has been invoked, amendments which were in order prior to the reprinting of the measure or matter will continue to be in order and may be conformed and reprinted at the request of the amendment's sponsor. The conforming changes must be limited to lineation and pagination.

No Senator shall call up more than two amendments until every other Senator shall have had the opportunity to do likewise.

Notwithstanding other provisions of this rule, a Senator may yield all or part of his one hour to the majority or minority floor managers of the measure, motion, or matter or to the Majority or Minority Leader, but each Senator specified shall not have more than two hours so yielded to him and may in turn yield such time to other Senators.

Notwithstanding any other provision of this rule, any Senator who has not used or yielded at least ten minutes, is, if he seeks recognition, guaranteed up to ten minutes, inclusive, to speak only.

After cloture is invoked, the reading of any amendment, including House amendments, shall be dispensed with when the proposed amendment has been identified and has been available in printed form at the desk of the Members for not less than twenty-four hours.

RULE XXIII

PRIVILEGE OF THE FLOOR

Other than the Vice President and Senators, no person shall be admitted to the floor of the Senate while in session, except as follows:

The President of the United States and his private secretary.

The President elect and Vice President elect of the United States.

Ex-Presidents and ex-Vice Presidents of the United States.

Judges of the Supreme Court.

Ex-Senators and Senators elect.

The officers and employees of the Senate in the discharge of their official duties.

Ex-Secretaries and ex-Sergeants at Arms of the Senate.

Members of the House of Representatives and Members elect.

Ex-Speakers of the House of Representatives.

The Sergeant at Arms of the House and his chief deputy and the Clerk of the House and his deputy.

Heads of the Executive Departments.

Ambassadors and Ministers of the United States.

Governors of States and Territories.

Members of the Joint Chiefs of Staff.

The General Commanding the Army.

The Senior Admiral of the Navy on the active list.

Members of National Legislatures of foreign countries and Members of the European Parliament.

Judges of the Court of Claims.

The Mayor of the District of Columbia.

The Librarian of Congress and the Assistant Librarian in charge of the Law Library.

The Architect of the Capitol.

The Chaplain of the House of Representatives.

The Secretary of the Smithsonian Institution.

The Parliamentarian Emeritus of the Senate.

Members of the staffs of committees of the Senate and joint committees of the Congress when in the discharge of their official duties and employees in the office of a Senator when in the discharge of their official duties (but in each case subject to such rules or regulations as may be prescribed by the Committee on Rules and Administration). Senate committee staff members and employees in the office of a Senator must be on the payroll of the Senate and members of joint committee staffs must be on the payroll of the Senate or the House of Representatives.

RULE XXIV

APPOINTMENT OF COMMITTEES

1. In the appointment of the standing committees, or to fill vacancies thereon, the Senate, unless otherwise ordered, shall by resolution appoint the chairman of each such committee and the other members thereof. On demand of any Senator, a separate vote shall be had on the appointment of the chairman of any such committee and on the appointment of the other members thereof. Each such resolution shall be subject to amendment and to division of the question.

2. On demand of one-fifth of the Senators present, a quorum being present, any vote taken pursuant to paragraph 1 shall be by ballot.

3. Except as otherwise provided or unless otherwise ordered, all other committees, and the chairmen thereof, shall be appointed in the same manner as standing committees.

4. When a chairman of a committee shall resign or cease to serve on a committee, action by the Senate to fill the vacancy in such committee, unless specially otherwise ordered, shall be only to fill up the number of members of the committee, and the election of a new chairman.

RULE XXV

STANDING COMMITTEES

1. The following standing committees shall be appointed at the commencement of each Congress, and shall continue and have the power to act until their successors are appointed, with leave to report by bill or otherwise on matters within their respective jurisdictions:

(a) (1) Committee on Agriculture, Nutrition, and Forestry, to which committee shall be referred all proposed legislation, messages, petitions, memorials, and other matters relating primarily to the following subjects:

1. Agricultural economics and research.

2. Agricultural extension services and experiment stations.

3. Agricultural production, marketing, and stabilization of prices.

4. Agriculture and agricultural commodities.

5. Animal industry and diseases.

6. Crop insurance and soil conservation.

7. Farm credit and farm security.

8. Food from fresh waters.

9. Food stamp programs.

10. Forestry, and forest reserves and wilderness areas other than those created from the public domain.

11. Home economics.

12. Human nutrition.

13. Inspection of livestock, meat, and agricultural products.

14. Pests and pesticides.

15. Plant industry, soils, and agricultural engineering.

16. Rural development, rural electrification, and watersheds.

17. School nutrition programs.

(2) Such committee shall also study and review, on a comprehensive basis, matters relating to food, nutrition, and hunger, both in the United States and in foreign countries, and rural affairs, and report thereon from time to time.

(b) Committee on Appropriations, to which committee shall be referred all proposed legislation, messages, petitions, memorials, and other matters relating to the following subjects:

1. Appropriation of the revenue for the support of the Government, except as provided in subparagraph (e).

2. Rescission of appropriations contained in appropriation Acts (referred to in section 105 of title 1, United States Code).

3. The amount of new spending authority described in section 401(c)(2) (A) and (B) of the Congressional Budget Act of 1974 which is to be effective for a fiscal year.

4. New spending authority described in section 401(c)(2)(C) of the Congressional Budget Act of 1974 provided in bills and resolutions referred to the committee under section 401(b)(2) of that Act (but subject to the provisions of section 401(b)(3) of that Act).

(c) (1) Committee on Armed Services, to which committee shall be referred all proposed legislation, messages, petitions, memorials, and other matters relating to the following subjects:

1. Aeronautical and space activities peculiar to or primarily associated with the development of weapons systems or military operations.

2. Common defense.

3. Department of Defense, the Department of the Army, the Department of the Navy, and the Department of the Air Force, generally.

4. Maintenance and operation of the Panama Canal, including administration, sanitation, and government of the Canal Zone.

5. Military research and development.

6. National security aspects of nuclear energy.

7. Naval petroleum reserves, except those in Alaska.

8. Pay, promotion, retirement, and other benefits and privileges of members of the Armed Forces, including overseas education of civilian and military dependents.

9. Selective service system.

10. Strategic and critical materials necessary for the common defense.

(2) Such committee shall also study and review, on a comprehensive basis, matters relating to the common defense policy of the United States, and report thereon from time to time.

(d) (1) **Committee on Banking, Housing, and Urban Affairs,** to which committee shall be referred all proposed legislation, messages, petitions, memorials, and other matters relating to the following subjects:

1. Banks, banking, and financial institutions.

2. Control of prices of commodities, rents, and services.

3. Deposit insurance.

4. Economic stabilization and defense production.

5. Export and foreign trade promotion.

6. Export controls.

7. Federal monetary policy, including Federal Reserve System.

8. Financial aid to commerce and industry.

9. Issuance and redemption of notes.

10. Money and credit, including currency and coinage.

11. Nursing home construction.

12. Public and private housing (including veterans' housing).

13. Renegotiation of Government contracts.

14. Urban development and urban mass transit.

(2) Such committee shall also study and review, on a comprehensive basis, matters relating to international economic policy as it affects United States monetary affairs, credit, and financial institutions; economic growth, urban affairs, and credit, and report thereon from time to time.

(e) (1) **Committee on the Budget,** to which committee shall be referred all concurrent resolutions on the budget (as defined in section 3(a)(4) of the Congressional Budget Act of 1974) and all other matters required to be referred to that committee under titles III and IV of that Act, and messages, petitions, memorials, and other matters relating thereto.

(2) Such committee shall have the duty—

(A) to report the matters required to be reported by it under titles III and IV of the Congressional Budget Act of 1974;

(B) to make continuing studies of the effect on budget outlays of relevant existing and proposed legislation and to report the results of such studies to the Senate on a recurring basis;

(C) to request and evaluate continuing studies of tax expenditures, to devise methods of coordinating tax expenditures, policies, and programs with direct budget outlays, and to report the results of such studies to the Senate on a recurring basis; and

(D) to review, on a continuing basis, the conduct by the Congressional Budget Office of its functions and duties.

(f) (1) **Committee on Commerce, Science, and Transportation,** to which committee shall be referred all proposed legislation, messages, petitions, memorials, and other matters relating to the following subjects:

1. Coast Guard.

2. Coastal zone management.

3. Communications.

4. Highway safety.

5. Inland waterways, except construction.

6. Interstate commerce.

7. Marine and ocean navigation, safety, and transportation, including navigational aspects of deepwater ports.

8. Marine fisheries.

9. Merchant marine and navigation.

10. Nonmilitary aeronautical and space sciences.

11. Oceans, weather, and atmospheric activities.

12. Panama Canal and interoceanic canals generally, except as provided in subparagraph (c).

13. Regulation of consumer products and services, including testing related to toxic substances, other than pesticides, and except for credit, financial services, and housing.

14. Regulation of interstate common carriers, including railroads, buses, trucks, vessels, pipelines, and civil aviation.

15. Science, engineering, and technology research and development and policy.

16. Sports.

17. Standards and measurement.

18. Transportation.

19. Transportation and commerce aspects of Outer Continental Shelf lands.

(2) Such committee shall also study and review, on a comprehensive basis, all matters relating to science and technology, oceans policy, transportation, communications, and consumer affairs, and report thereon from time to time.

(g) (1) **Committee on Energy and Natural Resources,** to which committee shall be referred all proposed legislation, messages, petitions, memorials, and other matters relating to the following subjects:

1. Coal production, distribution, and utilization.

2. Energy policy.

3. Energy regulation and conservation.

4. Energy related aspects of deepwater ports.

5. Energy research and development.

6. Extraction of minerals from oceans and Outer Continental Shelf lands.

7. Hydroelectric power, irrigation, and reclamation.

8. Mining education and research.

9. Mining, mineral lands, mining claims, and mineral conservation.

10. National parks, recreation areas, wilderness areas, wild and scenic rivers, historical sites, military parks and battlefields, and on the public domain, preservation of prehistoric ruins and objects of interest.

11. Naval petroleum reserves in Alaska.

12. Nonmilitary development of nuclear energy.

13. Oil and gas production and distribution.

14. Public lands and forests, including farming and grazing thereon, and mineral extraction therefrom.

15. Solar energy systems.

16. Territorial possessions of the United States, including trusteeships.

(2) Such committee shall also study and review, on a comprehensive basis, matters relating to energy and resources development, and report thereon from time to time.

(h) (1) **Committee on Environment and Public Works,** to which committee shall be referred all proposed legislation, messages, petitions, memorials, and other matters relating to the following subjects:

1. Air pollution.

2. Construction and maintenance of highways.

3. Environmental aspects of Outer Continental Shelf lands.

4. Environmental effects of toxic substances, other than pesticides.

5. Environmental policy.

6. Environmental research and development.

7. Fisheries and wildlife.

8. Flood control and improvements of rivers and harbors, including environmental aspects of deepwater ports.

9. Noise pollution.

10. Nonmilitary environmental regulation and control of nuclear energy.

11. Ocean dumping.

12. Public buildings and improved grounds of the United States generally, including Federal buildings in the District of Columbia.

13. Public works, bridges, and dams.

14. Regional economic development.

15. Solid waste disposal and recycling.

16. Water pollution.

17. Water resources.

(2) Such committee shall also study and review, on a comprehensive basis, matters relating to environmental protection and resource utilization and conservation, and report thereon from time to time.

(i) **Committee on Finance,** to which committee shall be referred all proposed legislation, messages, petitions, memorials, and other matters relating to the following subjects:

1. Bonded debt of the United States, except as provided in the Congressional Budget Act of 1974.

2. Customs, collection districts, and ports of entry and delivery.

3. Deposit of public moneys.

4. General revenue sharing.

5. Health programs under the Social Security Act and health programs financed by a specific tax or trust fund.

6. National social security.

7. Reciprocal trade agreements.

8. Revenue measures generally, except as provided in the Congressional Budget Act of 1974.

9. Revenue measures relating to the insular possessions.

10. Tariffs and import quotas, and matters related thereto.

11. Transportation of dutiable goods.

(j) (1) **Committee on Foreign Relations,** to which committee shall be referred all proposed legislation, messages, petitions, memorials, and other matters relating to the following subjects:

1. Acquisition of land and buildings for embassies and legations in foreign countries.

2. Boundaries of the United States.

3. Diplomatic service.

4. Foreign economic, military, technical, and humanitarian assistance.

5. Foreign loans.

6. International activities of the American National Red Cross and the International Committee of the Red Cross.

7. International aspects of nuclear energy, including nuclear transfer policy.

8. International conferences and congresses.

9. International law as it relates to foreign policy.

10. International Monetary Fund and other international organizations established primarily for international monetary purposes (except that, at the request of the Committee on Banking, Housing, and Urban Affairs, any proposed legislation relating to such subjects reported by the Committee on Foreign Relations shall be referred to the Committee on Banking, Housing, and Urban Affairs).

11. Intervention abroad and declarations of war.

12. Measures to foster commercial intercourse with foreign nations and to safeguard American business interests abroad.

13. National security and international aspects of trusteeships of the United States.

14. Oceans and international environmental and scientific affairs as they relate to foreign policy.

15. Protection of United States citizens abroad and expatriation.

16. Relations of the United States with foreign nations generally.

17. Treaties and executive agreements, except reciprocal trade agreements.

18. United Nations and its affiliated organizations.

19. World Bank group, the regional development banks, and other international organizations established primarily for development assistance purposes.

(2) Such committee shall also study and review, on a comprehensive basis, matters relating to the national security policy, foreign policy, and international economic policy as it relates to foreign policy of the United States, and matters relating to food, hunger, and nutrition in foreign countries, and report thereon from time to time.

(k) (1) **Committee on Governmental Affairs**, to which committee shall be referred all proposed legislation, messages, petitions, memorials, and other matters relating to the following subjects:

1. Archives of the United States.

2. Budget and accounting measures, other than appropriations, except as provided in the Congressional Budget Act of 1974.

3. Census and collection of statistics, including economic and social statistics.

4. Congressional organization, except for any part of the matter that amends the rules or orders of the Senate.

5. Federal Civil Service.

6. Government information.

7. Intergovernmental relations.

8. Municipal affairs of the District of Columbia, except appropriations therefor.

9. Organization and management of United States nuclear export policy.

10. Organization and reorganization of the executive branch of the Government.

11. Postal Service.

12. Status of officers and employees of the United States, including their classification, compensation, and benefits.

(2) Such committee shall have the duty of—

(A) receiving and examining reports of the Comptroller General of the United States and of submitting such recommendations to the Senate as it deems necessary or desirable in connection with the subject matter of such reports;

(B) studying the efficiency, economy, and effectiveness of all agencies and departments of the Government;

(C) evaluating the effects of laws enacted to reorganize the legislative and executive branches of the Government; and

(D) studying the intergovernmental relationships between the United States and the States and municipalities, and between the United States and international organizations of which the United States is a member.

(l) **Committee on the Judiciary,** to which committee shall be referred all proposed legislation, messages, petitions, memorials, and other matters relating to the following subjects:

1. Apportionment of Representatives.

2. Bankruptcy, mutiny, espionage, and counterfeiting.

3. Civil liberties.

4. Constitutional amendments.

5. Federal courts and judges.

6. Government information.

7. Holidays and celebrations.

8. Immigration and naturalization.

9. Interstate compacts generally.

10. Judicial proceedings, civil and criminal, generally.

11. Local courts in the territories and possessions.

12. Measures relating to claims against the United States.

13. National penitentiaries.

14. Patent Office.

15. Patents, copyrights, and trademarks.

16. Protection of trade and commerce against unlawful restraints and monopolies.

17. Revision and codification of the statutes of the United States.

18. State and territorial boundary lines.

(m) (1) **Committee on Labor and Human Resources,** to which committee shall be referred all proposed legislation, messages, petitions, memorials, and other matters relating to the following subjects:

1. Measures relating to education, labor, health, and public welfare.

2. Aging.

3. Agricultural colleges.

4. Arts and humanities.

5. Biomedical research and development.

6. Child labor.

7. Convict labor and the entry of goods made by convicts into interstate commerce.

8. Domestic activities of the American National Red Cross.

9. Equal employment opportunity.

10. Gallaudet College, Howard University, and Saint Elizabeths Hospital.

11. Handicapped individuals.

12. Labor standards and labor statistics.

13. Mediation and arbitration of labor disputes.

14. Occupational safety and health, including the welfare of miners.

15. Private pension plans.

16. Public health.

17. Railway labor and retirement.

18. Regulation of foreign laborers.

19. Student loans.

20. Wages and hours of labor.

(2) Such committee shall also study and review, on a comprehensive basis, matters relating to health, education and training, and public welfare, and report thereon from time to time.

(n) (1) **Committee on Rules and Administration,** to which committee shall be referred all proposed legislation, messages, petitions, memorials, and other matters relating to the following subjects:

1. Administration of the Senate Office Buildings and the Senate wing of the Capitol, including the assignment of office space.

2. Congressional organization relative to rules and procedures, and Senate rules and regulations, including floor and gallery rules.

3. Corrupt practices.

4. Credentials and qualifications of Members of the Senate, contested elections, and acceptance of incompatible offices.

5. Federal elections generally, including the election of the President, Vice President, and Members of the Congress.

6. Government Printing Office, and the printing and correction of the Congressional Record, as well as those matters provided for under rule XI.

7. Meetings of the Congress and attendance of Members.

8. Payment of money out of the contingent fund of the Senate or creating a charge upon the same (except that any resolution relating to substantive matter within the jurisdiction of any other standing committee of the Senate shall be first referred to such committee).

9. Presidential succession.

10. Purchase of books and manuscripts and erection of monuments to the memory of individuals.

11. Senate Library and statuary, art, and pictures in the Capitol and Senate Office Buildings.

12. Services to the Senate, including the Senate restaurant.

13. United States Capitol and congressional office buildings, the Library of Congress, the Smithsonian Institution (and the incorporation of similar institutions), and the Botanic Gardens.

(2) Such committee shall also—

(A) make a continuing study of the organization and operation of the Congress of the United States and shall recommend improvements in such organization and operation with a view toward strengthening the Congress, simplifying its operations improving its relationships with other branches of the United States Government, and enabling it better to meet its responsibilities under the Constitution of the United States;

(B) identify any court proceeding or action which, in the opinion of the Committee, is of vital interest to the Congress as a constitutionally established institution of the Federal Government and call such proceeding or action to the attention of the Senate and

(C) develop, implement, and update as necessary a strategy planning process and a strategic plan for the functional and technical infrastructure support of the Senate and provide oversight over plans developed by Senate officers and others in accordance with the strategic planning process.

(o) (1) **Committee on Small Business,** to which committee shall be referred all proposed legislation, messages, petitions, memorials, and other matters relating to the Small Business Administration.

(2) Any proposed legislation reported by such committee which relates to matters other than the functions of the Small Business Administration shall, at the request of the chairman of any standing committee having jurisdiction over the subject matter extraneous to the functions of the Small Business Administration, be considered and reported by such standing committee prior to its consideration by the Senate; and likewise measures reported by other committees directly relating to the Small Business Administration shall, at the request of the chairman of the Committee on Small Business, be referred to the Committee on Small Business for its consideration of any portions of the measure dealing with the Small Business Administration, and be reported by this committee prior to its consideration by the Senate.

(3) Such committee shall also study and survey by means of research and investigation all problems of American small business enterprises, and report thereon from time to time.

(p) **Committee on Veterans' Affairs,** to which committee shall be referred all proposed legislation, messages, petitions, memorials, and other matters relating to the following subjects:

1. Compensation of veterans.

2. Life insurance issued by the Government on account of service in the Armed Forces.

3. National cemeteries.

4. Pensions of all wars of the United States, general and special.

5. Readjustment of servicemen to civil life.

6. Soldiers' and sailors' civil relief.

7. Veterans' hospitals, medical care and treatment of veterans.

8. Veterans' measures generally.

9. Vocational rehabilitation and education of veterans.

2. Except as otherwise provided by paragraph 4 of this rule, each of the following standing committees shall consist of the number of Senators set forth in the following table on the line on which the name of that committee appears:

Committee	Members
Agriculture, Nutrition, and Forestry	18
Appropriations	28
Armed Services	18
Banking, Housing, and Urban Affairs	18
Commerce, Science, and Transportation	20
Energy and Natural Resources	20
Environment and Public Works	18
Finance	20
Foreign Relations	18
Governmental Affairs	16
Judiciary	18
Labor and Human Resources	18

3. (a) Except as otherwise provided by paragraph 4 of this rule, each of the following standing committees shall consist of the number of Senators set forth in the following table on the line on which the name of that committee appears:

Committee	Members
Budget	22
Rules and Administration	16
Veterans' Affairs	2
Small Business	18

(b) Each of the following committees and joint committees shall consist of the number of Senators (or Senate members, in the case of a joint committee) set forth in the following table on the line on which the name of that committee appears:

Committee	Members
Aging	18
Intelligence	19
Joint Economic Committee	10

(c) Each of the following committees and joint committees shall consist of the number of Senators (or Senate members, in the case of a joint committee) set forth in the following table on the line on which the name of that committee appears:

Committee	Members
Ethics	6
Indian Affairs	14
Joint Committee on Taxation	5

4. (a) Except as otherwise provided by this paragraph—

(1) each Senator shall serve on two and no more committees listed in paragraph 2; and

(2) each Senator may serve on only one committee listed in paragraph 3 (a) or (b).

(b)(1) Each Senator may serve on not more than three subcommittees of each committee (other than the Committee on Appropriations) listed in paragraph 2 of which he is a member.

(2) Each Senator may serve on not more than two subcommittees of a committee listed in paragraph 3 (a) or (b) of which he is a member.

(3) Notwithstanding subparagraphs (1) and (2), a Senator serving as chairman or ranking minority member of a standing, select, or special committee of the Senate or joint committee of the Congress may serve ex officio, without vote, as a member of any subcommittee of such committee or joint committee.

(4) No committee of the Senate may establish any subunit of that committee other than a subcommittee, unless the Senate by resolution has given permission therefor. For purposes of this subparagraph, any subunit of a joint committee shall be treated as a subcommittee.

(c) By agreement entered into by the majority leader and the minority leader, the membership of one or more standing committees may be increased temporarily from time to time by such number or numbers as may be required to accord to the majority party a majority of the membership of all standing committees. When any such temporary increase is necessary to accord to the majority party a majority of the membership of all standing committees, members of the majority party in such number as may be required for that purpose may serve as members of three standing committees listed in paragraph 2. No such temporary increase in the membership of any standing committee under this subparagraph shall be continued in effect after the need therefor has ended. No standing committee may be increased in membership under this subparagraph by more than two members in excess of the number prescribed for that committee by paragraph 2 or 3(a).

(d) A Senator may serve as a member of any joint committee of the Congress the Senate members of which are required by law to be appointed from a standing committee of the Senate of which he is a member, and service as a member of any such joint committee shall not be taken into account for purposes of subparagraph (a)(2).

(e)(1) No Senator shall serve at any time as chairman of more than one standing, select, or special committee of the Senate or joint committee of the Congress, except that a Senator may serve as chairman of any joint committee of the Congress having jurisdiction with respect to a subject matter which is directly related to the jurisdiction of a standing committee of which he is chairman.

(2) No Senator shall serve at any time as chairman of more than one subcommittee of each standing, select, or special committee of the Senate or joint committee of the Congress of which he is a member.

(3) A Senator who is serving as the chairman of a committee listed in paragraph 2 may serve at any time as the chairman of only one subcommittee of all committees listed in paragraph 2 of which he is a member and may serve at any time as the chairman of only one subcommittee of each committee listed in paragraph 3 (a) or (b) of which he is a member. A Senator who is serving as the chairman of a committee listed in paragraph 3 (a) or (b) may not serve as the chairman of any subcommittee of that committee, and may serve at any time as the chairman of only one subcommittee of each committee listed in paragraph 2 of which he is a member. Any other Senator may serve as the chairman of only one subcommittee of each committee listed in paragraph 2, 3(a), or 3(b) of which he is a member.

(f) A Senator serving on the Committee on Rules and Administration may not serve on any joint committee of the Congress unless the Senate members thereof are required by law to be appointed from the Committee on Rules and Administration, or unless such Senator served on the Committee on Rules and Administration and the Joint Committee on Taxation on the last day of the Ninety-eighth Congress.

(g) A Senator who on the day preceding the effective date of title I of the Committee System Reorganization Amendments of 1977 was serving as the chairman or ranking minority member of the Committee on the District of Columbia or the Committee on Post Office and Civil Service may serve on the Committee on Governmental Affairs in addition to serving on two other standing committees listed in paragraph 2. At the request of any such Senator, he shall be appointed to serve on such committee but, while serving on such committee and two other standing committees listed in paragraph 2, he may not serve on any committee listed in paragraph 3 (a) or (b) other than the Committee on Rules and Administration. The preceding provisions of this subparagraph shall apply with respect to any Senator only so long as his service as a member of the Committee on Governmental Affairs is continuous after the date on which the appointment of the majority and minority members of the Committee on Governmental Affairs is initially completed.

RULE XXVI

COMMITTEE PROCEDURE

1. Each standing committee, including any subcommittee of any such committee, is authorized to hold such hearings, to sit and act at such times and places during the sessions, recesses, and adjourned periods of the Senate, to require by subpoena or otherwise the attendance of such witnesses and the production of such correspondence, books, papers, and documents, to take such testimony and to make such expenditures out of the contingent fund of the Senate as may be authorized by resolutions of the Senate. Each such committee may make investigations into any matter within its jurisdiction, may report such hearings as may be had by it, and may employ stenographic assistance at a cost not exceeding the amount prescribed by the Committee on Rules and Administration. The expenses of the committee shall be paid from the contingent fund of the Senate upon vouchers approved by the chairman.

2. Each committee shall adopt rules (not inconsistent with the Rules of the Senate) governing the procedure of such committee. The rules of each committee shall be published in the Congressional Record not later than March 1 of the first year of each Congress, except that if any such committee is established on or after February 1 of a year, the rules of that committee during the year of establishment shall be published in the Congressional Record not later than sixty days after such establishment. Any amendment to the rules of a committee shall not take effect until the amendment is published in the Congressional Record.

3. Each standing committee (except the Committee on Appropriations) shall fix regular weekly, biweekly, or monthly meeting days for the transaction of business before the committee and additional meetings may be called by the chairman as he may deem necessary. If at least three members of any such committee desire that a special meeting of the committee be called by the chairman, those members may file in the offices of the committee their written request to the chairman for that special meeting. Immediately upon the filing of the request, the clerk of the committee shall notify the chairman of the filing of the request. If, within three calendar days after the filing of the request, the chairman does not call the requested special meeting, to be held within seven calendar days after the filing of the request, a majority of the members of the committee may file in the offices of the committee their written notice that a special meeting of the committee will be held, specifying the date and hour of that special meeting. The committee shall meet on that date and hour. Immediately upon the filing of the notice, the clerk of the committee shall notify all members of the committee that such special meeting will be held and inform them of its date and hour. If the chairman of any such committee is not present at any regular, additional, or special meeting of the committee, the ranking member of the majority party on the committee who is present shall preside at that meeting.

4. (a) Each committee (except the Committee on Appropriations and the Committee on the Budget) shall make public announcement of the date, place, and subject matter of any hearing to be conducted by the committee on any measure or matter at least one week before the commencement of that hearing unless the committee determines that there is good cause to begin such hearing at an earlier date.

(b) Each committee (except the Committee on Appropriations) shall require each witness who is to appear before the committee in any hearing to file with the clerk of the committee, at least one day before the date of the appearance of that witness, a written statement of his proposed testimony unless the committee chairman and the ranking minority member determine that there is good cause for noncompliance. If so requested by any committee, the staff of the committee shall prepare for the use of the members of the committee before each day of hearing before the committee a digest of the statements which have been so filed by witnesses who are to appear before the committee on that day.

(c) After the conclusion of each day of hearing, if so requested by any committee, the staff shall prepare for the use of the members of the committee a summary of the testimony given before the committee on that day. After approval by the chairman and the ranking minority member of the committee, each such summary may be printed as a part of the committee hearings if such hearings are ordered by the committee to be printed.

(d) Whenever any hearing is conducted by a committee (except the Committee on Appropriations) upon any measure or matter, the minority on the committee shall be entitled, upon request made by a majority of the minority members to the chairman before the completion of such hearing, to call witnesses selected by the minority to testify with respect to the measure or matter during at least one day of hearing thereon.

5. (a) Notwithstanding any other provision of the rules, when the Senate is in session, no committee of the Senate or any subcommittee thereof may meet, without special leave, after the conclusion of the first two hours after the meeting of the Senate commenced and in no case after two o'clock postmeridian unless consent therefor has been obtained from the majority leader and the minority leader (or in the event of the absence of either of such leaders, from his designee). The prohibition contained in the preceding sentence shall not apply to the Committee on Appropriations or the Committee on the Budget. The majority leader or his designee shall announce to the Senate whenever consent has been given under this subparagraph and shall state the time and place of such meeting. The right to make such announcement of consent shall have the same priority as the filing of a cloture motion.

(b) Each meeting of a committee, or any subcommittee thereof, including meetings to conduct hearings, shall be open to the public, except that a meeting or series of meetings by a committee or a subcommittee thereof on the same subject for a period of no more than fourteen calendar days may be closed to the public on a motion made and seconded to go into closed session to discuss only whether the matters enumerated in clauses (1) through (6) would require the meeting to be closed, followed immediately by a record vote in open session by a majority of the members of the committee or subcommittee when it is determined that the matters to be discussed or the testimony to be taken at such meeting or meetings—

(1) will disclose matters necessary to be kept secret in the interests of national defense or the confidential conduct of the foreign relations of the United States;

(2) will relate solely to matters of committee staff personnel or internal staff management or procedure;

(3) will tend to charge an individual with crime or misconduct, to disgrace or injure the professional standing of an individual, or otherwise to expose an individual to public contempt or

obloquy, or will represent a clearly unwarranted invasion of the privacy of an individual;

(4) will disclose the identity of any informer or law enforcement agent or will disclose any information relating to the investigation or prosecution of a criminal offense that is required to be kept secret in the interests of effective law enforcement;

(5) will disclose information relating to the trade secrets of financial or commercial information pertaining specifically to a given person if—

(A) an Act of Congress requires the information to be kept confidential by Government officers and employees; or

(B) the information has been obtained by the Government on a confidential basis, other than through an application by such person for a specific Government financial or other benefit, and is required to be kept secret in order to prevent undue injury to the competitive position of such person; or

(6) may divulge matters required to be kept confidential under other provisions of law or Government regulations.

(c) Whenever any hearing conducted by any such committee or subcommittee is open to the public, that hearing may be broadcast by radio or television, or both, under such rules as the committee or subcommittee may adopt.

(d) Whenever disorder arises during a committee meeting that is open to the public, or any demonstration of approval or disapproval is indulged in by any person in attendance at any such meeting, it shall be the duty of the Chair to enforce order on his own initiative and without any point of order being made by a Senator. When the Chair finds it necessary to maintain order, he shall have the power to clear the room, and the committee may act in closed session for so long as there is doubt of the assurance of order.

(e) Each committee shall prepare and keep a complete transcript or electronic recording adequate to fully record the proceeding of each meeting or conference whether or not such meeting or any part thereof is closed under this paragraph, unless a majority of its members vote to forgo such a record.

6. Morning meetings of committees and subcommittees thereof shall be scheduled for one or both of the periods prescribed in this paragraph. The first period shall end at eleven o'clock antemeridian. The second period shall begin at eleven o'clock antemeridian and end at two o'clock postmeridian.

7. (a)(1) Except as provided in this paragraph, each committee, and each subcommittee thereof is authorized to fix the number of its members (but not less than one-third of its entire membership) who shall constitute a quorum thereof for the transaction of such business as may be considered by said committee, except that no measure or matter or recommendation shall be reported from any committee unless a majority of the committee were physically present.

(2) Each such committee, or subcommittee, is authorized to fix a lesser number than one-third of its entire membership who shall constitute a quorum thereof for the purpose of taking sworn testimony.

(3) The vote of any committee to report a measure or matter shall require the concurrence of a majority of the members of the committee who are present. No vote of any member of any committee to report a measure or matter may be cast by proxy if rules adopted by such committee forbid the casting of votes for that purpose by proxy; however, proxies may not be voted when the absent committee member has not been informed of the matter on which he is being recorded and has not affirmatively requested that he be so recorded. Action by any committee in reporting any measure or matter in accordance with the requirements of this subparagraph shall constitute the ratifi-

cation by the committee of all action theretofore taken by the committee with respect to that measure or matter, including votes taken upon the measure or matter or any amendment thereto, and no point of order shall lie with respect to that measure or matter on the ground that such previous action with respect thereto by such committee was not taken in compliance with such requirements.

(b) Each committee (except the Committee on Appropriations) shall keep a complete record of all committee action. Such record shall include a record of the votes on any question on which a record vote is demanded. The results of rollcall votes taken in any meeting of any committee upon any measure, or any amendment thereto, shall be announced in the committee report on that measure unless previously announced by the committee, and such announcement shall include a tabulation of the votes cast in favor of and the votes cast in opposition to each such measure and amendment by each member of the committee who was present at that meeting.

(c) Whenever any committee by rollcall vote reports any measure or matter, the report of the committee upon such measure or matter shall include a tabulation of the votes cast by each member of the committee in favor of and in opposition to such measure or matter. Nothing contained in this subparagraph shall abrogate the power of any committee to adopt rules—

(2) providing in accordance with subparagraph (a) for a lesser number as a quorum for any action other than the reporting of a measure or matter.

8. (a) In order to assist the Senate in—

(1) its analysis, appraisal, and evaluation of the application, administration, and execution of the laws enacted by the Congress, and

(2) its formulation, consideration, and enactment of such modifications of or changes in those laws, and of such additional legislation, as may be necessary or appropriate, each standing committee (except the Committees on Appropriations and the Budget), shall review and study, on a continuing basis the application, administration, and execution of those laws, or parts of laws, the subject matter of which is within the legislative jurisdiction of that committee. Such committees may carry out the required analysis, appraisal, and evaluation themselves, or by contract, or may require a Government agency to do so and furnish a report thereon to the Senate. Such committees may rely on such techniques as pilot testing, analysis of costs in comparison with benefits, or provision for evaluation after a defined period of time.

(b) In each odd-numbered year, each such committee shall submit, not later than March 31, to the Senate, a report on the activities of that committee under this paragraph during the Congress ending at noon on January 3 of such year.

9. (a) Except as provided in subparagraph (b), each committee shall report one authorization resolution each year authorizing the committee to make expenditures out of the contingent fund of the Senate to defray its expenses, including the compensation of members of its staff and agency contributions related to such compensation, during the period beginning on March 1 of such year and ending on the last day of February of the following year. Such annual authorization resolution shall be reported not later than January 31 of each year, except that, whenever the designation of members of standing committees of the Senate occurs during the first session of a Congress at a date later than January 20, such resolution may be reported at any time within thirty days after the date on which the designation of such members is completed. After the annual authorization resolution of a committee for a year has been agreed to, such committee may procure authorization to make additional expenditures out of the contingent fund of the Senate during that year only

by reporting a supplemental authorization resolution. Each supplemental authorization resolution reported by a committee shall amend the annual authorization resolution of such committee for that year and shall be accompanied by a report specifying with particularity the purpose for which such authorization is sought and the reason why such authorization could not have been sought at the time of the submission by such committee of its annual authorization resolution for that year.

(b) In lieu of the procedure provided in subparagraph (a), the Committee on Rules and Administration may—

(1) direct each committee to report an authorization resolution for a two-year budget period beginning on March 1 of the first session of a Congress; and

(2) report one authorization resolution containing more than one committee authorization resolution for a one-year or two-year budget period.

10. (a) All committee hearings, records, data, charts, and files shall be kept separate and distinct from the congressional office records of the Member serving as chairman of the committee; and such records shall be the property of the Senate and all members of the committee and the Senate shall have access to such records. Each committee is authorized to have printed and bound such testimony and other data presented at hearings held by the committee.

(b) It shall be the duty of the chairman of each committee to report or cause to be reported promptly to the Senate any measure approved by his committee and to take or cause to be taken necessary steps to bring the matter to a vote. In any event, the report of any committee upon a measure which has been approved by the committee shall be filed within seven calendar days (exclusive of days on which the Senate is not in session) after the day on which there has been filed with the clerk of the committee a written and signed request of a majority of the committee for the reporting of that measure. Upon the filing of any such request, the clerk of the committee shall transmit immediately to the chairman of the committee notice of the filing of that request. This subparagraph does not apply to the Committee on Appropriations.

(c) If at the time of approval of a measure or matter by any committee (except for the Committee on Appropriations), any member of the committee gives notice of intention to file supplemental, minority, or additional views, that member shall be entitled to not less than three calendar days in which to file such views, in writing, with the clerk of the committee. All such views so filed by one or more members of the committee shall be included within, and shall be a part of, the report filed by the committee with respect to that measure or matter. The report of the committee upon that measure or matter shall be printed in a single volume which—

(1) shall include all supplemental, minority, or additional views which have been submitted by the time of the filing of the report, and

(2) shall bear upon its cover a recital that supplemental, minority, or additional views are included as part of the report.

This subparagraph does not preclude—

(A) the immediate filing and printing of a committee report unless timely request for the opportunity to file supplemental, minority, or additional views has been made as provided by this subparagraph; or

(B) the filing by any such committee of any supplemental report upon any measure or matter which may be required for the correction of any technical error in a previous report made by that committee upon that measure or matter.

11. (a) The report accompanying each bill or joint resolution of a public character reported by any committee (except the Committee on Appropriations and the Committee on the Budget) shall contain—

(1) an estimate, made by such committee, of the costs which would be incurred in carrying out such bill or joint resolution in the fiscal year in which it is reported and in each of the five fiscal years following such fiscal year (or for the authorized duration of any program authorized by such bill or joint resolution, if less than five years), except that, in the case of measures affecting the revenues, such reports shall require only an estimate of the gain or loss in revenues for a one year period; and

(2) a comparison of the estimate of costs described in subparagraph (1) made by such committee with any estimate of costs made by any Federal agency; or

(3) in lieu of such estimate or comparison, or both, a statement of the reasons why compliance by the committee with the requirements of subparagraph (1) or (2), or both, is impracticable.

(b) Each such report (except those by the Committee on Appropriations) shall also contain—

(1) an evaluation, made by such committee, of the regulatory impact which would be incurred in carrying out the bill or joint resolution. The evaluation shall include (A) an estimate of the numbers of individuals and businesses who would be regulated and a determination of the groups and classes of such individuals and businesses, (B) a determination of the economic impact of such regulation on the individuals, consumers, and businesses affected, (C) a determination of the impact on the personal privacy of the individuals affected, and (D) a determination of the amount of additional paperwork that will result from the regulations to be promulgated pursuant to the bill or joint resolution, which determination may include, but need not be limited to, estimates of the amount of time and financial costs required of affected parties, showing whether the effects of the bill or joint resolution could be substantial, as well as reasonable estimates of the recordkeeping requirements that may be associated with the bill or joint resolution; or

(2) in lieu of such evaluation, a statement of the reasons why compliance by the committee with the requirements of clause (1) is impracticable.

(c) It shall not be in order for the Senate to consider any such bill or joint resolution if the report of the committee on such bill or joint resolution does not comply with the provisions of subparagraphs (a) and (b) on the objection of any Senator.

12. Whenever a committee reports a bill or a joint resolution repealing or amending any statute or part thereof it shall make a report thereon and shall include in such report or in an accompanying document (to be prepared by the staff of such committee) (a) the text of the statute or part thereof which is proposed to be repealed; and (b) a comparative print of that part of the bill or joint resolution making the amendment and of the statute or part thereof proposed to be amended, showing by stricken-through type and italics, parallel columns, or other appropriate typographical devices the omissions and insertions which would be made by the bill or joint resolution if enacted in the form recommended by the committee. This paragraph shall not apply to any such report in which it is stated that, in the opinion of the committee, it is necessary to dispense with the requirements of this subsection to expedite the business of the Senate.

13. (a) Each committee (except the Committee on Appropriations) which has legislative jurisdiction shall, in its consideration of all bills and joint resolutions of a public character within its jurisdiction, endeavor to insure that—

(1) all continuing programs of the Federal Government and of the government of the District of Columbia, within the jurisdiction of such committee or joint committee, are designed; and

(2) all continuing activities of Federal agencies, within the jurisdiction of such committee or joint committee, are carried on; so that, to the extent consistent with the nature, requirements, and objectives of those programs and activities, appropriations therefor will be made annually.

(b) Each committee (except the Committee on Appropriations) shall with respect to any continuing program within its jurisdiction for which appropriations are not made annually, review such program, from time to time, in order to ascertain whether such program could be modified so that appropriations therefor would be made annually.

RULE XXVII

COMMITTEE STAFF

1. Staff members appointed to assist minority members of committees pursuant to authority of a resolution described in paragraph 9 of rule XXVI or other Senate resolution shall be accorded equitable treatment with respect to the fixing of salary rates, the assignment of facilities, and the accessibility of committee records.

2. The minority shall receive fair consideration in the appointment of staff personnel pursuant to authority of a resolution described in paragraph 9 of rule XXVI.

3. The staffs of committees (including personnel appointed pursuant to authority of a resolution described in paragraph 9 of rule XXVI or other Senate resolution) should reflect the relative number of majority and minority members of committees. A majority of the minority members of any committee may, by resolution, request that at least one-third of all funds of the committee for personnel (other than those funds determined by the chairman and ranking minority member to be allocated for the administrative and clerical functions of the committee as a whole) be allocated to the minority members of such committee for compensation of minority staff as the minority members may decide. The committee shall thereafter adjust its budget to comply with such resolution. Such adjustment shall be equitably made over a four-year period, commencing July 1, 1977, with not less than one-half being made in two years. Upon request by a majority of the minority members of any committee by resolution, proportionate space, equipment, and facilities shall be provided for such minority staff.

4. No committee shall appoint to its staff any experts or other personnel detailed or assigned from any department or agency of the Government, except with the written permission of the Committee on Rules and Administration.

RULE XXVIII

CONFERENCE COMMITTEES; REPORTS; OPEN MEETINGS

1. The presentation of reports of committees of conference shall always be in order when available on each Senator's desk, except when the Journal is being read or a question of order or a motion to adjourn is pending, or while the Senate is voting or ascertaining the presence of a quorum; and when received the question of proceeding to the consideration of the report, if raised, shall be immediately put, and shall be determined without debate.

2. Conferees shall not insert in their report matter not committed to them by either House, nor shall they strike from the bill matter agreed to by both Houses. If new matter is inserted in the report, or if matter which was agreed to by both Houses is stricken from the bill, a point of order may be made against the report, and if the point of order is sustained, the report is rejected or shall be recommitted to the committee of conference if the House of Representatives has not already acted thereon.

3. (a) In any case in which a disagreement to an amendment in the nature of a substitute has been referred to conferees, it shall be in order for the conferees to report a substitute on the same subject matter; but they may not include in the report matter not committed to them by either House. They may, however, include in their report in any such case matter which is a germane modification of subjects in disagreement.

(b) In any case in which the conferees violate subparagraph (a), the conference report shall be subject to a point of order.

4. Each report made by a committee of conference to the Senate shall be printed as a report of the Senate. As so printed, such report shall be accompanied by an explanatory statement prepared jointly by the conferees on the part of the House and the conferees on the part of the Senate. Such statement shall be sufficiently detailed and explicit to inform the Senate as to the effect which the amendments or propositions contained in such report will have upon the measure to which those amendments or propositions relate.

5. If time for debate in the consideration of any report of a committee of conference upon the floor of the Senate is limited, the time allotted for debate shall be equally divided between the majority party and the minority party.

6. Each conference committee between the Senate and the House of Representatives shall be open to the public except when managers of either the Senate or the House of Representatives in open session determine by a rollcall vote of a majority of those managers present, that all or part of the remainder of the meeting on the day of the vote shall be closed to the public.

RULE XXIX

EXECUTIVE SESSIONS

1. When the President of the United States shall meet the Senate in the Senate Chamber for the consideration of Executive business, he shall have a seat on the right of the Presiding Officer. When the Senate shall be convened by the President of the United States to any other place, the Presiding Officer of the Senate and the Senators shall attend at the place appointed, with the necessary officers of the Senate.

2. When acting upon confidential or Executive business, unless the same shall be considered in open Executive session, the Senate Chamber shall be cleared of all persons except the Secretary, the Assistant Secretary, the Principal Legislative Clerk, the Parliamentarian, the Executive Clerk, the Minute and Journal Clerk, the Sergeant at Arms, the Secretaries to the Majority and the Minority, and such other officers as the Presiding Officer shall think necessary; and all such officers shall be sworn to secrecy.

3. All confidential communications made by the President of the United States to the Senate shall be by the Senators and the officers of the Senate kept secret; and all treaties which may be laid before the Senate, and all remarks, votes, and proceedings thereon shall also be

kept secret, until the Senate shall, by their resolution, take off the injunction of secrecy.

4. Whenever the injunction of secrecy shall be removed from any part of the proceedings of the Senate in closed Executive or legislative session, the order of the Senate removing the same shall be entered in the Legislative Journal as well as in the Executive Journal, and shall be published in the Congressional Record under the direction of the Secretary of the Senate.

5. Any Senator, officer, or employee of the Senate who shall disclose the secret or confidential business or proceedings of the Senate, including the business and proceedings of the committees, subcommittees, and offices of the Senate, shall be liable, if a Senator, to suffer expulsion from the body; and if an officer or employee, to dismissal from the service of the Senate, and to punishment for contempt.

6. Whenever, by the request of the Senate or any committee thereof, any documents or papers shall be communicated to the Senate by the President or the head of any department relating to any matter pending in the Senate, the proceedings in regard to which are secret or confidential under the rules, said documents and papers shall be considered as confidential, and shall not be disclosed without leave of the Senate.

RULE XXX

EXECUTIVE SESSION—PROCEEDINGS ON TREATIES

1. (a) When a treaty shall be laid before the Senate for ratification, it shall be read a first time; and no motion in respect to it shall be in order, except to refer it to a committee, to print it in confidence for the use of the Senate, or to remove the injunction of secrecy.

(b) When a treaty is reported from a committee with or without amendment, it shall, unless the Senate unanimously otherwise directs, lie over one day for consideration; after which it may be read a second time, after which amendments may be proposed. At any stage of such proceedings the Senate may remove the injunction of secrecy from the treaty.

(c) The decisions thus made shall be reduced to the form of a resolution of ratification, with or without amendments, as the case may be, which shall be proposed on a subsequent day, unless, by unanimous consent, the Senate determine otherwise, at which stage no amendment to the treaty shall be received unless by unanimous consent; but the resolution of ratification when pending shall be open to amendment in the form of reservations, declarations, statements, or understandings.

(d) On the final question to advise and consent to the ratification in the form agreed to, the concurrence of two-thirds of the Senators present shall be necessary to determine it in the affirmative; but all other motions and questions upon a treaty shall be decided by a majority vote, except a motion to postpone indefinitely, which shall be decided by a vote of two-thirds.

2. Treaties transmitted by the President to the Senate for ratification shall be resumed at the second or any subsequent session of the same Congress at the stage in which they were left at the final adjournment of the session at which they were transmitted; but all proceedings on treaties shall terminate with the Congress, and they shall be resumed at the commencement of the next Congress as if no proceedings had previously been had thereon.

RULE XXXI

EXECUTIVE SESSION—PROCEEDINGS ON NOMINATIONS

1. When nominations shall be made by the President of the United States to the Senate, they shall, unless otherwise ordered, be referred to appropriate committees; and the final question on every nomination shall be, "Will the Senate advise and consent to this nomination?" which question shall not be put on the same day on which the nomination is received, nor on the day on which it may be reported by a committee, unless by unanimous consent.

2. All business in the Senate shall be transacted in open session, unless the Senate as provided in rule XXI by a majority vote shall determine that a particular nomination, treaty, or other matter shall be considered in closed executive session, in which case all subsequent proceedings with respect to said nomination, treaty, or other matter shall be kept secret: *Provided,* That the injunction of secrecy as to the whole or any part of proceedings in closed executive session may be removed on motion adopted by a majority vote of the Senate in closed executive session: *Provided further,* That any Senator may make public his vote in closed executive session.

3. When a nomination is confirmed or rejected, any Senator voting in the majority may move for a reconsideration on the same day on which the vote was taken, or on either of the next two days of actual executive session of the Senate; but if a notification of the confirmation or rejection of a nomination shall have been sent to the President before the expiration of the time within which a motion to reconsider may be made, the motion to reconsider shall be accompanied by a motion to request the President to return such notification to the Senate. Any motion to reconsider the vote on a nomination may be laid on the table without prejudice to the nomination, and shall be a final disposition of such motion.

4. Nominations confirmed or rejected by the Senate shall not be returned by the Secretary to the President until the expiration of the time limited for making a motion to reconsider the same, or while a motion to reconsider is pending unless otherwise ordered by the Senate.

5. When the Senate shall adjourn or take a recess for more than thirty days, all motions to reconsider a vote upon a nomination which has been confirmed or rejected by the Senate, which shall be pending at the time of taking such adjournment or recess, shall fall; and the Secretary shall return all such nominations to the President as confirmed or rejected by the Senate, as the case may be.

6. Nominations neither confirmed nor rejected during the session at which they are made shall not be acted upon at any succeeding session without being again made to the Senate by the President; and if the Senate shall adjourn or take a recess for more than thirty days, all nominations pending and not finally acted upon at the time of taking such adjournment or recess shall be returned by the Secretary to the President, and shall not again be considered unless they shall again be made to the Senate by the President.

7. (a) The Official Reporters shall be furnished with a list of nominations to office after the proceedings of the day on which they are received, and a like list of all confirmations and rejections.

(b) All nominations to office shall be prepared for the printer by the Official Reporter, and printed in the Congressional Record, after the proceedings of the day in which they are received, also nominations recalled, and confirmed.

(c) The Secretary shall furnish to the press, and to the public upon request, the names of nominees confirmed or rejected on the day on which a final vote shall be had, except when otherwise ordered by the Senate.

RULE XXXII

THE PRESIDENT FURNISHED WITH COPIES OF RECORDS OF EXECUTIVE SESSIONS

The President of the United States shall, from time to time, be furnished with an authenticated transcript of the public executive records of the Senate, but no further extract from the Executive Journal shall be furnished by the Secretary, except by special order of the Senate; and no paper, except original treaties transmitted to the Senate by the President of the United States, and finally acted upon by the Senate, shall be delivered from the office of the Secretary without an order of the Senate for that purpose.

RULE XXXIII

SENATE CHAMBER—SENATE WING OF THE CAPITOL

1. The Senate Chamber shall not be granted for any other purpose than for the use of the Senate; no smoking shall be permitted at any time on the floor of the Senate, or lighted cigars, cigarettes, or pipes be brought into the Chamber.

2. It shall be the duty of the Committee on Rules and Administration to make all rules and regulations respecting such parts of the Capitol, its passages and galleries, including the restaurant and the Senate Office Buildings, as are or may be set apart for the use of the Senate and its officers, to be enforced under the direction of the Presiding Officer. The Committee shall make such regulations respecting the reporters' galleries of the Senate, together with the adjoining rooms and facilities, as will confine their occupancy and use to bona fide reporters of newspapers and periodicals, and of news or press associations for daily news dissemination through radio, television, wires, and cables, and similar media of transmission. These regulations shall so provide for the use of such space and facilities as fairly to distribute their use to all such media of news dissemination.

RULE XXXIV

PUBLIC FINANCIAL DISCLOSURE

1. For purposes of this rule, the provisions of title I of the Ethics in Government Act of 1978 (Pub. L. 95521) shall be deemed to be a rule of the Senate as it pertains to Members, officers, and employees of the Senate.

2. (a) The Select Committee on Ethics shall transmit a copy of each report filed with it under title I of the Ethics in Government Act of 1978 (other than a report filed by a Member of Congress) to the head of the employing office of the individual filing the report.

(b) For purposes of this rule, the head of the employing office shall be—

(1) in the case of an employee of a Member, the Member by whom that person is employed;

(2) in the case of an employee of a Committee, the chairman and ranking minority member of such Committee;

(3) in the case of an employee on the leadership staff, the Member of the leadership on whose staff such person serves; and

(4) in the case of any other employee of the legislative branch, the head of the office in which such individual serves.

3. In addition to the requirements of paragraph 1, Members, officers, and employees of the Senate shall include in each report filed under paragraph 1 the following additional information:

(a) For purposes of section 102(a)(1)(B) of the Ethics in Government Act of 1978 additional categories of income as follows:

(1) greater than $1,000,000 but not more than $5,000,000, or

(2) greater than $5,000,000.

(b) for purposes of section 102(d)(1) of the Ethics in Government Act of 1978 additional categories of value as follows:

(1) greater than $1,000,000 but not more than $5,000,000;

(2) greater than $5,000,000 but not more than $25,000,000;

(3) greater than $25,000,000 but not more than $50,000,000; and

(4) greater than $50,000,000.

(c) For purposes of this paragraph and section 102 of the Ethics in Government Act of 1978, additional categories with amounts or values greater than $1,000,000 set forth in section 102(a)(1)(B) and 102(d)(1) shall apply to the income, assets, or liabilities of spouses and dependent children only if the income, assets, or liabilities are held jointly with the reporting individual. All other income, assets, or liabilities of the spouse or dependent children required to be reported under section 102 and this paragraph in an amount or value greater than $1,000,000 shall be categorized only as an amount or value greater than $1,000,000.

4. In addition to the requirements of paragraph 1, Members, officers, and employees of the Senate shall include in each report filed under paragraph 1 an additional statement under section 102(a) of the Ethics in Government Act of 1978 listing the category of the total cash value of any interest of the reporting individual in a qualified blind trust as provided in section 102(d)(1) of the Ethics in Government Act of 1978, unless the trust instrument was executed prior to July 24, 1995 and precludes the beneficiary from receiving information on the total cash value of any interest in the qualified blind trust.

RULE XXXV

GIFTS

1. (a)(1) No Member, officer, or employee of the Senate shall knowingly accept a gift except as provided in this rule.

(2) A Member, officer, or employee may accept a gift (other than cash or cash equivalent) which the Member, officer, or employee reasonably and in good faith believes to have a value of less than $50, and a cumulative value from one source during a calendar year of less than $100. No gift with a value below $10 shall count toward the $100 annual limit. No formal recordkeeping is required by this paragraph, but a Member, officer, or employee shall make a good faith effort to comply with this paragraph.

(b)(1) For the purpose of this rule, the term "gift" means any gratuity, favor, discount, entertainment, hospitality, loan, forbearance, or other item having monetary value. The term includes gifts of services, training, transportation, lodging, and meals, whether provided in kind, by purchase of a ticket, payment in advance, or reimbursement after the expense has been incurred.

(2)(A) A gift to a family member of a Member, officer, or employee, or a gift to any other individual based on that individual's relationship with the Member, officer, or employee, shall be considered a gift to the Member, officer, or employee if it is given with the knowledge and acquiescence of the Member, officer, or employee and the Member, officer, or employee has reason to believe the gift was given because of the official position of the Member, officer, or employee.

(B) If food or refreshment is provided at the same time and place to both a Member, officer, or employee and the spouse or dependent thereof, only the food or refreshment provided to the Member, officer, or employee shall be treated as a gift for purposes of this rule.

(c) The restrictions in subparagraph (a) shall not apply to the following:

(1) Anything for which the Member, officer, or employee pays the market value, or does not use and promptly returns to the donor.

(2) A contribution, as defined in the Federal Election Campaign Act of 1971 (2 U.S.C. 431 et seq.) that is lawfully made under that Act, or attendance at a fundraising event sponsored by a political organization described in section 527(e) of the Internal Revenue Code of 1986.

(3) A gift from a relative as described in section 109(16) of title I of the Ethics Reform of 1989 (5 U.S.C. App. 6).

(4)(A) Anything, including personal hospitality, provided by an individual on the basis of a personal friendship unless the Member, officer, or employee has reason to believe that, under the circumstances, the gift was provided because of the official position of the Member, officer, or employee and not because of the personal friendship.

(B) In determining whether a gift is provided on the basis of personal friendship, the Member, officer, or employee shall consider the circumstances under which the gift was offered, such as:

(i) The history of the relationship between the individual giving the gift and the recipient of the gift, including any previous exchange of gifts between such individuals.

(ii) Whether to the actual knowledge of the Member, officer, or employee the individual who gave the gift personally paid for the gift or sought a tax deduction or business reimbursement for the gift.

(iii) Whether to the actual knowledge of the Member, officer or employee the individual who gave the gift also at the same time gave the same or similar gifts to other Members, officers, or employees.

(5) A contribution or other payment to a legal expense fund established for the benefit of a Member, officer, or employee, that is otherwise lawfully made, subject to the disclosure requirements of the Select Committee on Ethics, except as provided in paragraph 3(c).

(6) Any gift from another Member, officer, or employee of the Senate or the House of Representatives.

(7) Food, refreshments, lodging, and other benefits—

(A) resulting from the outside business or employment activities (or other outside activities that are not connected to the duties of the Member, officer, or employee as an office holder) of the Member, officer, or employee, or the spouse of the Member, officer, or employee, if such benefits have not been offered or enhanced because of the official position of the Member, officer, or employee and are customarily provided to others in similar circumstances;

(B) customarily provided by a prospective employer in connection with bona fide employment discussions; or

(C) provided by a political organization described in section 527(e) of the Internal Revenue Code of 1986 in connection with a fundraising or campaign event sponsored by such an organization.

(8) Pension and other benefits resulting from continued participation in an employee welfare and benefits plan maintained by a former employer.

(9) Informational materials that are sent to the office of the Member, officer, or employee in the form of books, articles, periodicals, other written materials, audiotapes, videotapes, or other forms of communication.

(10) Awards or prizes which are given to competitors in contests or events open to the public, including random drawings.

(11) Honorary degrees (and associated travel, food, refreshments, and entertainment) and other bona fide, nonmonetary awards presented in recognition of public service (and associated food, refreshments, and entertainment provided in the presentation of such degrees and awards).

(12) Donations of products from the State that the Member represents that are intended primarily for promotional purposes, such as display or free distribution, and are of minimal value to any individual recipient.

(13) Training (including food and refreshments furnished to all attendees as an integral part of the training) provided to a Member, officer, or employee, if such training is in the interest of the Senate.

(14) Bequests, inheritances, and other transfers at death.

(15) Any item, the receipt of which is authorized by the Foreign Gifts and Decorations Act, the Mutual Educational and Cultural Exchange Act, or any other statute.

(16) Anything which is paid for by the Federal Government, by a State or local government, or secured by the Government under a Government contract.

(17) A gift of personal hospitality (as defined in section 109(14) of the Ethics in Government Act) of an individual other than a registered lobbyist or agent of a foreign principal.

(18) Free attendance at a widely attended event permitted pursuant to subparagraph (d).

(19) Opportunities and benefits which are—

(A) available to the public or to a class consisting of all Federal employees, whether or not restricted on the basis of geographic consideration;

(B) offered to members of a group or class in which membership is unrelated to congressional employment;

(C) offered to members of an organization, such as an employees' association or congressional credit union, in which membership is related to congressional employment and similar opportunities are available to large segments of the public through organizations of similar size;

(D) offered to any group or class that is not defined in a manner that specifically discriminates among Government employees on the basis of branch of Government or type of responsibility, or on a basis that favors those of higher rank or rate of pay;

(E) in the form of loans from banks and other financial institutions on terms generally available to the public; or

(F) in the form of reduced membership or other fees for participation in organization activities offered to all Government employees by professional organizations if the only restrictions on membership relate to professional qualifications.

(20) A plaque, trophy, or other item that is substantially commemorative in nature and which is intended solely for presentation.

(21) Anything for which, in an unusual case, a waiver is granted by the Select Committee on Ethics.

(22) Food or refreshments of a nominal value offered other than as a part of a meal.

(23) An item of little intrinsic value such as a greeting card, baseball cap, or a T-shirt.

(d)(1) A Member, officer, or employee may accept an offer of free attendance at a widely attended convention, conference, symposium, forum, panel discussion, dinner, viewing, reception, or similar event, provided by the sponsor of the event, if

(A) the Member, officer, or employee participates in the event as a speaker or a panel participant, by presenting information related to Congress or matters before Congress, or by performing a ceremonial function appropriate to the Member's, officer's, or employee's official position; or

(B) attendance at the event is appropriate to the performance of the official duties or representative function of the Member, officer, or employee.

(2) A Member, officer, or employee who attends an event described in clause (1) may accept a sponsor's unsolicited offer of free attendance at the event for an accompanying individual if others in attendance will generally be similarly accompanied or if such attendance is appropriate to assist in the representation of the Senate.

(3) A Member, officer, or employee, or the spouse or dependent thereof, may accept a sponsor's unsolicited offer of free attendance at a charity event, except that reimbursement for transportation and lodging may not be accepted in connection with an event that does not meet the standards provided in paragraph 2.

(4) For purposes of this paragraph, the term "free attendance" may include waiver of all or part of a conference or other fee, the provision of local transportation, or the provision of food, refreshments, entertainment, and instructional materials furnished to all attendees as an integral part of the event. The term does not include entertainment collateral to the event, nor does it include food or refreshments taken other than in a group setting with all or substantially all other attendees.

(e) No Member, officer, or employee may accept a gift the value of which exceeds $250 on the basis of the personal friendship exception in subparagraph (c)(4) unless the Select Committee on Ethics issues a written determination that such exception applies. No determination under this subparagraph is required for gifts given on the basis of the family relationship exception.

(f) When it is not practicable to return a tangible item because it is perishable, the item may, at the discretion of the recipient, be given to an appropriate charity or destroyed.

2. (a)(1) A reimbursement (including payment in kind) to a Member, officer, or employee from an individual other than a registered lobbyist or agent of a foreign principal for necessary transportation, lodging and related expenses for travel to a meeting, speaking engagement, fact-finding trip or similar event in connection with the duties of the Member, officer, or employee as an officeholder shall be deemed to be a reimbursement to the Senate and not a gift prohibited by this rule, if the Member, officer, or employee

(A) in the case of an employee, receives advance authorization, from the Member or officer under whose direct supervision the employee works, to accept reimbursement, and

(B) discloses the expenses reimbursed or to be reimbursed and the authorization to the Secretary of the Senate within 30 days after the travel is completed.

(2) For purposes of clause (1), events, the activities of which are substantially recreational in nature, shall not be considered to be in connection with the duties of a Member, officer, or employee as an officeholder.

(b) Each advance authorization to accept reimbursement shall be signed by the Member or officer under whose direct supervision the employee works and shall include—

(1) the name of the employee;

(2) the name of the person who will make the reimbursement;

(3) the time, place, and purpose of the travel; and

(4) a determination that the travel is in connection with the duties of the employee as an officeholder and would not create the appearance that the employee is using public office for private gain.

(c) Each disclosure made under subparagraph (a)(1) of expenses reimbursed or to be reimbursed shall be signed by the Member or officer (in the case of travel by that Member or officer) or by the Member or officer under whose direct supervision the employee works (in the case of travel by an employee) and shall include—

(1) a good faith estimate of total transportation expenses reimbursed or to be reimbursed;

(2) a good faith estimate of total lodging expenses reimbursed or to be reimbursed;

(3) a good faith estimate of total meal expenses reimbursed or to be reimbursed;

(4) a good faith estimate of the total of other expenses reimbursed or to be reimbursed;

(5) a determination that all such expenses are necessary transportation, lodging, and related expenses as defined in this paragraph; and

(6) in the case of a reimbursement to a Member or officer, a determination that the travel was in connection with the duties of the Member or officer as an officeholder and would not create the appearance that the Member or officer is using public office for private gain.

(d) For the purposes of this paragraph, the term "necessary transportation, lodging, and related expenses"—

(1) includes reasonable expenses that are necessary for travel for a period not exceeding 3 days exclusive of travel time within the United States or 7 days exclusive of travel time outside of the United States unless approved in advance by the Select Committee on Ethics;

(2) is limited to reasonable expenditures for transportation, lodging, conference fees and materials, and food and refreshments, including reimbursement for necessary transportation, whether or not such transportation occurs within the periods described in clause (1);

(3) does not include expenditures for recreational activities, nor does it include entertainment other than that provided to all attendees as an integral part of the event, except for activities or entertainment otherwise permissible under this rule; and

(4) may include travel expenses incurred on behalf of either the spouse or a child of the Member, officer, or employee, subject to a determination signed by the Member or officer (or in the case of an employee, the Member or officer under whose direct supervision the employee works) that the attendance of the spouse or child is appropriate to assist in the representation of the Senate.

(e) The Secretary of the Senate shall make available to the public all advance authorizations and disclosures of reimbursement filed pursuant to subparagraph (a) as soon as possible after they are received.

3. A gift prohibited by paragraph 1(a) includes the following:

(a) Anything provided by a registered lobbyist or an agent of a foreign principal to an entity that is maintained or controlled by a Member, officer, or employee.

(b) A charitable contribution (as defined in section 170(c) of the Internal Revenue Code of 1986) made by a registered lobbyist or an agent of a foreign principal on the basis of a designation, recommendation, or other specification of a Member, officer, or employee (not including a mass mailing or other solicitation directed to a broad category of persons or entities), other than a charitable contribution permitted by paragraph 4.

(c) A contribution or other payment by a registered lobbyist or an agent of a foreign principal to a legal expense fund established for the benefit of a Member, officer, or employee.

(d) A financial contribution or expenditure made by a registered lobbyist or an agent of a foreign principal relating to a conference, retreat, or similar event, sponsored by or affiliated with an official congressional organization, for or on behalf of Members, officers, or employees.

4. (a) A charitable contribution (as defined in section 170(c) of the Internal Revenue Code of 1986) made by a registered lobbyist or an agent of a foreign principal in lieu of an honorarium to a Member, officer, or employee shall not be considered a gift under this rule if it is reported as provided in subparagraph (b).

(b) A Member, officer, or employee who designates or recommends a contribution to a charitable organization in lieu of honoraria described in subparagraph (a) shall report within 30 days after such designation or recommendation to the Secretary of the Senate—

(1) the name and address of the registered lobbyist who is making the contribution in lieu of honoraria;

(2) the date and amount of the contribution; and

(3) the name and address of the charitable organization designated or recommended by the Member.

The Secretary of the Senate shall make public information received pursuant to this subparagraph as soon as possible after it is received.

5. For purposes of this rule—

(a) the term "registered lobbyist" means a lobbyist registered under the Federal Regulation of Lobbying Act or any successor statute; and

(b) the term "agent of a foreign principal" means an agent of a foreign principal registered under the Foreign Agents Registration Act.

6. All the provisions of this rule shall be interpreted and enforced solely by the Select Committee on Ethics.

The Select Committee on Ethics is authorized to issue guidance on any matter contained in this rule.

RULE XXXVI

OUTSIDE EARNED INCOME

For purposes of this rule, the provisions of section 501 of the Ethics in Government Act of 1978 (5 U.S.C. App. 7 501) shall be deemed to be a rule of the Senate as it pertains to Members, officers, and employees of the Senate.

RULE XXXVII

CONFLICT OF INTEREST

1. A Member, officer, or employee of the Senate shall not receive any compensation, nor shall he permit any compensation to accrue to his beneficial interest from any source, the receipt or accrual of which would occur by virtue of influence improperly exerted from his position as a Member, officer, or employee.

2. No Member, officer, or employee shall engage in any outside business or professional activity or employment for compensation which is inconsistent or in conflict with the conscientious performance of official duties.

3. No officer or employee shall engage in any outside business or professional activity or employment for compensation unless he has reported in writing when such activity or employment commences and on May 15 of each year thereafter so long as such activity or employment continues, the nature of such activity or employment to his supervisor. The supervisor shall then, in the discharge of his duties, take such action as he considers necessary for the avoidance of conflict of interest or interference with duties to the Senate.

4. No Member, officer, or employee shall knowingly use his official position to introduce or aid the progress or passage of legislation, a principal purpose of which is to further only his pecuniary interest, only the pecuniary interest of his immediate family, or only the pecuniary interest of a limited class of persons or enterprises, when he, or his immediate family, or enterprises controlled by them, are members of the affected class.

5. (a) No Member, officer, or employee of the Senate compensated at a rate in excess of $25,000 per annum and employed for more than ninety days in a calendar year shall (1) affiliate with a firm, partnership, association, or corporation for the purpose of providing professional services for compensation; (2) permit that individual's name to be used by such a firm, partnership, association or corporation; or (3) practice a profession for compensation to any extent during regular office hours of the Senate office in which employed. For the purposes of this paragraph, "professional services" shall include but not be limited to those which involve a fiduciary relationship.

(b) A Member or an officer or employee whose rate of basic pay is equal to or greater than 120 percent of the annual rate of basic pay in effect for grade GS-15 of the General Schedule shall not—

(1) receive compensation for affiliating with or being employed by a firm, partnership, association, corporation, or other entity which provides professional services involving a fiduciary relationship;

(2) permit that Member's, officer's, or employee's name to be used by any such firm, partnership, association, corporation, or other entity;

(3) receive compensation for practicing a profession which involves a fiduciary relationship; or

(4) receive compensation for teaching, without the prior notification and approval of the Committee on Ethics.

6. (a) No Member, officer, or employee of the Senate compensated at a rate in excess of $25,000 per annum and employed for more than ninety days in a calendar year shall serve as an officer or member of the board of any publicly held or publicly regulated corporation, financial institution, or business entity. The preceding sentence shall not apply to service of a Member, officer, or employee as—

(1) an officer or member of the board of an organization which is exempt from taxation under section 501(c) of the Internal Revenue Code of 1954, if such service is performed without compensation;

(2) an officer or member of the board of an institution or organization which is principally available to Members, officers, or employees of the Senate, or their families, if such service is performed without compensation; or

(3) a member of the board of a corporation, institution, or other business entity, if (A) the Member, officer, or employee had served continuously as a member of the board thereof for at least two years prior to his election or appointment as a Member, officer, or employee of the Senate, (B) the amount of time required to perform such service is minimal, and (C) the Member, officer, or employee is not a member of, or a member of the staff of any Senate committee which has legislative jurisdiction over any agency of the Government charged with regulating the activities of the corporation, institution, or other business entity.

(b) A Member or an officer or employee whose rate of basic pay is equal to or greater than 120 percent of the annual rate of basic pay in effect for grade GS-15 of the General Schedule shall not serve for compensation as an officer or member of the board of any association, corporation, or other entity.

7. An employee on the staff of a committee who is compensated at a rate in excess of $25,000 per annum and employed for more than ninety days in a calendar year shall divest himself of any substantial holdings which may be directly affected by the actions of the committee for which he works, unless the Select Committee, after consultation with the employee's supervisor, grants permission in writing to retain such holdings or the employee makes other arrangements acceptable to the Select Committee and the employee's supervisor to avoid participation in committee actions where there is a conflict of interest, or the appearance thereof.

8. If a Member, upon leaving office, becomes a registered lobbyist under the Federal Regulation of Lobbying Act of 1946 or any successor statute, or is employed or retained by such a registered lobbyist for the purpose of influencing legislation, he shall not lobby Members, officers, or employees of the Senate for a period of one year after leaving office.

9. If an employee on the staff of a Member, upon leaving that position, becomes a registered lobbyist under the Federal Regulation of Lobbying Act of 1946 or any successor statute, or is employed or retained by such a registered lobbyist for the purpose of influencing legislation, such employee may not lobby the Member for whom he worked or that Member's staff for a period of one year after leaving that position. If an employee on the staff of a committee, upon leaving his position, becomes such a registered lobbyist or is employed or retained by such a registered lobbyist for the purpose of influencing legislation, such employee may not lobby the members of the committee for which he worked, or the staff of that committee, for a period of one year after leaving his position.

10. (a) Except as provided by subparagraph (b), any employee of the Senate who is required to file a report pursuant to rule XXXIV shall refrain from participating personally and substantially as an employee of the Senate in any contact with any agency of the executive or judicial branch of Government with respect to nonlegislative matters affecting any nongovernmental person in which the employee has a significant financial interest.

(b) Subparagraph (a) shall not apply if an employee first advises his supervising authority of his significant financial interest and obtains from his employing authority a written waiver stating that the participation of the employee is necessary. A copy of each such waiver shall be filed with the Select Committee.

11. For purposes of this rule—

(a) "employee of the Senate" includes an employee or individual described in paragraphs 2, 3, and 4(c) of rule XLI;

(b) an individual who is an employee on the staff of a subcommittee of a committee shall be treated as an employee on the staff of such committee; and

(c) the term "lobbying" means any oral or written communication to influence the content or disposition of any issue before Congress, including any pending or future bill, resolution, treaty, nomination, hearing, report, or investigation; but does not include—

(1) a communication (i) made in the form of testimony given before a committee or office of the Congress, or (ii) submitted for inclusion in the public record, public docket, or public file of a hearing; or

(2) a communication by an individual, acting solely on his own behalf, for redress of personal grievances, or to express his personal opinion.

12. For purposes of this rule—

(a) a Senator or the Vice President is the supervisor of his administrative, clerical, or other assistants;

(b) a Senator who is the chairman of a committee is the supervisor of the professional, clerical, or other assistants to the committee except that minority staff members shall be under the supervision of the ranking minority Senator on the committee;

(c) a Senator who is a chairman of a subcommittee which has its own staff and financial authorization is the supervisor of the professional, clerical, or other assistants to the subcommittee except that minority staff members shall be under the supervision of the ranking minority Senator on the subcommittee;

(d) the President pro tempore is the supervisor of the Secretary of the Senate, Sergeant at Arms and Doorkeeper, the Chaplain, the Legislative Counsel, and the employees of the Office of the Legislative Counsel;

(e) the Secretary of the Senate is the supervisor of the employees of his office;

(f) the Sergeant at Arms and Doorkeeper is the supervisor of the employees of his office;

(g) the Majority and Minority Leaders and the Majority and Minority Whips are the supervisors of the research, clerical, or other assistants assigned to their respective offices;

(h) the Majority Leader is the supervisor of the Secretary for the Majority and the Secretary for the Majority is the supervisor of the employees of his office; and

(i) the Minority Leader is the supervisor of the Secretary for the Minority and the Secretary for the Minority is the supervisor of the employees of his office.

RULE XXXVIII

PROHIBITION OF UNOFFICIAL OFFICE ACCOUNTS

1. (a) No Member may maintain or have maintained for his use an unofficial office account. The term "unofficial office account" means an account or repository into which funds are received for the purpose, at least in part, of defraying otherwise unreimbursed expenses allowable in connection with the operation of a Member's office. An unofficial office account does not include, and expenses incurred by a Member in connection with his official duties shall be defrayed only from—

(1) personal funds of the Member;

(2) official funds specifically appropriated for that purpose;

(3) funds derived from a political committee (as defined in section 301(d) of the Federal Election Campaign Act of 1971 (2 U.S.C. 431)); and

(4) funds received as reasonable reimbursements for expenses incurred by a Member in connection with personal services provided by the Member to the organization making the reimbursement.

(b) Notwithstanding subparagraph (a), official expenses may be defrayed only as provided by subsections (d) and (i) of section 311 of the Legislative Appropriations Act, 1991 (Pub. L. 101-520).

2. No contribution (as defined in section 301(e) of the Federal Election Campaign Act of 1971 (2 U.S.C. 431)) shall be converted to the personal use of any Member or any former Member. For the purposes of this rule "personal use" does not include reimbursement of expenses incurred by a Member in connection with his official duties.

RULE XXXIX

FOREIGN TRAVEL

1. (a) Unless authorized by the Senate (or by the President of the United States after an adjournment sine die), no funds from the United States Government (including foreign currencies made available under section 502(b) of the Mutual Security Act of 1954 (22 U.S.C. 1754(b)) shall be received for the purpose of travel outside the United States by any Member of the Senate whose term will expire at the end of a Congress after

(1) the date of the general election in which his successor is elected; or

(2) in the case of a Member who is not a candidate in such general election, the earlier of the date of such general election or the adjournment sine die of the second regular session of that Congress.

(b) The travel restrictions provided by subparagraph (a) with respect to a Member of the Senate whose term will expire at the end of a Congress shall apply to travel by—

(1) any employee of the Member;

(2) any elected officer of the Senate whose employment will terminate at the end of a Congress; and

(3) any employee of a committee whose employment will terminate at the end of a Congress.

2. No Member, officer, or employee engaged in foreign travel may claim payment or accept funds from the United States Government (including foreign currencies made available under section 502(b) of the Mutual Security Act of 1954 (22 U.S.C. 1754(b)) for any expense for which the individual has received reimbursement from any other source; nor may such Member, officer, or employee receive reimbursement for the same expense more than once from the United States Government. No Member, officer, or employee shall use any funds furnished to him to defray ordinary and necessary expenses of foreign travel for any purpose other than the purpose or purposes for which such funds were furnished.

3. A per diem allowance provided a Member, officer, or employee in connection with foreign travel shall be used solely for lodging, food, and related expenses and it is the responsibility of the Member, officer, or employee receiving such an allowance to return to the United States Government that portion of the allowance received which is not actually used for necessary lodging, food, and related expenses.

RULE XL

FRANKING PRIVILEGE AND RADIO AND TELEVISION STUDIOS

1. A Senator or an individual who is a candidate for nomination for election, or election, to the Senate may not use the frank for any mass mailing (as defined in section 3210(a)(6)(E)2 of title 39, United States Code) if such mass mailing is mailed at or delivered to any postal facility less than sixty days immediately before the date of any primary or general election (whether regular, special, or runoff) in which the Senator is a candidate for public office or the individual is a candidate for Senator, unless the candidacy of the Senator in such election is uncontested.

2. A Senator shall use only official funds of the Senate, including his official Senate allowances, to purchase paper, to print, or to prepare any mass mailing material which is to be sent out under the frank.

3. (a) When a Senator disseminates information under the frank by a mass mailing (as defined in section 3210(a)(6)(E) of title 39, United States Code), the Senator shall register quarterly with the Secretary of the Senate such mass mailings. Such registration shall be made by filing with the Secretary a copy of the matter mailed and providing, on a form supplied by the Secretary, a description of the group or groups of persons to whom the mass mailing was mailed.

(b) The Secretary of the Senate shall promptly make available for public inspection and copying a copy of the mail matter registered, and a description of the group or groups of persons to whom the mass mailing was mailed.

4. Nothing in this rule shall apply to any mailing under the frank which is (a) in direct response to inquiries or requests from persons to whom the matter is mailed; (b) addressed to colleagues in Congress or to government officials (whether Federal, State, or local); or (c) consists entirely of news releases to the communications media.

5. The Senate computer facilities shall not be used (a) to store, maintain, or otherwise process any lists or categories of lists of names and addresses identifying the individuals included in such lists as campaign workers or contributors, as members of a political party, or by any other partisan political designation, (b) to produce computer printouts except as authorized by user guides approved by the Committee on Rules and Administration, or (c) to produce mailing labels for mass mailings, or computer tapes and discs, for use other than in service facilities maintained and operated by the Senate or under contract to the Senate. The Committee on Rules and Administration shall prescribe such regulations not inconsistent with the purposes of this paragraph as it determines necessary to carry out such purposes.

6. (a) The radio and television studios provided by the Senate or by the House of Representatives may not be used by a Senator or an individual who is a candidate for nomination for election, or election, to the Senate less than sixty days immediately before the date of any primary or general election (whether regular, special, or runoff) in which that Senator is a candidate for public office or that individual is a candidate for Senator, unless the candidacy of the Senator in such election is uncontested.

(b) This paragraph shall not apply if the facilities are to be used at the request of, and at the expense of, a licensed broadcast organization or an organization exempt from taxation under section 501(c)(3) of the Internal Revenue Code of 1954.

RULE XLI

POLITICAL FUND ACTIVITY; DEFINITIONS

1. No officer or employee of the Senate may receive, solicit, be a custodian of, or distribute any funds in connection with any campaign for the nomination for election, or the election, of any individual to be a Member of the Senate or to any other Federal office. This prohibition does not apply to three assistants to a Senator, at least one of whom is in Washington, District of Columbia, who have been designated by that Senator to perform any of the functions described in the first sentence of this paragraph and who are compensated at an annual rate in excess of $10,000 if such designation has been made in writing and filed with the Secretary of the Senate and if each such assistant files a financial statement in the form provided under rule XXXIV for each year during which he is designated under this rule. The Majority Leader and the Minority Leader may each designate an employee of their respective leadership office staff as one of the 3 designees referred to in the second sentence. The Secretary of the Senate shall make the designation available for public inspection.

2. For purposes of the Senate Code of Official Conduct—

(a) an employee of the Senate includes any employee whose salary is disbursed by the Secretary of the Senate; and

(b) the compensation of an officer or employee of the Senate who is a reemployed annuitant shall include amounts received by such officer or employee as an annuity, and such amounts shall be treated as disbursed by the Secretary of the Senate.

3. Before approving the utilization by any committee of the Senate of the services of an officer or employee of the Government in accordance with paragraph 4 of rule XXVII or with an authorization provided by Senate resolution, the Committee on Rules and Administration shall require such officer or employee to agree in writing to comply with the Senate Code of Official Conduct in the same manner and to the same extent as an employee of the Senate. Any such officer or employee shall, for purposes of such Code, be treated as an employee of the Senate receiving compensation disbursed by the Secretary of the Senate in an amount equal to the amount of compensation he is receiving as an officer or employee of the Government.

4. No Member, officer, or employee of the Senate shall utilize the full-time services of an individual for more than ninety days in a calendar year in the conduct of official duties of any committee or office of the Senate (including a Member's office) unless such individual—

(a) is an officer or employee of the Senate,

(b) is an officer or employee of the Government (other than the Senate), or

(c) agrees in writing to comply with the Senate Code of Official Conduct in the same manner and to the same extent as an employee of the Senate.

Any individual to whom subparagraph (c) applies shall, for purposes of such Code, be treated as an employee of the Senate receiving compensation disbursed by the Secretary of the Senate in an amount equal to the amount of compensation which such individual is receiving from any source for performing such services.

5. In exceptional circumstances for good cause shown, the Select Committee on Ethics may waive the applicability of any provision of the Senate Code of Official Conduct to an employee hired on a per diem basis.

6. (a) The supervisor of an individual who performs services for any Member, committee, or office of the Senate for a period in excess of four weeks and who receives compensation therefor from any source other than the United States Government shall report to the Select Committee on Ethics with respect to the utilization of the services of such individual.

(b) A report under subparagraph (a) shall be made with respect to an individual—

(1) when such individual begins performing services described in such subparagraph;

(2) at the close of each calendar quarter while such individual is performing such services; and

(3) when such individual ceases to perform such services.

Each such report shall include the identity of the source of the compensation received by such individual and the amount or rate of compensation paid by such source.

(c) No report shall be required under subparagraph (a) with respect to an individual who normally performs services for a Member, committee, or office for less than eight hours a week.

(d) For purposes of this paragraph, the supervisor of an individual shall be determined under paragraph 11 of rule XXXVII.

RULE XLII

EMPLOYMENT PRACTICES

1. No Member, officer, or employee of the Senate shall, with respect to employment by the Senate or any office thereof—

(a) fail or refuse to hire an individual;

(b) discharge an individual; or

(c) otherwise discriminate against an individual with respect to promotion, compensation, or terms, conditions, or privileges of employment on the basis of such individual's race, color, religion, sex, national origin, age, or state of physical handicap.

2. For purposes of this rule, the provisions of section 509(a) of the Americans With Disabilities Act of 1990 shall be deemed to be a rule of the Senate as it pertains to Members, officers, and employees of the Senate.

RULE XLIII

REPRESENTATION BY MEMBERS

1. In responding to petitions for assistance, a Member of the Senate, acting directly or through employees, has the right to assist petitioners before executive and independent government officials and agencies.

2. At the request of a petitioner, a Member of the Senate, or a Senate employee, may communicate with an executive or independent government official or agency on any matter to—

(a) request information or a status report;

(b) urge prompt consideration;

(c) arrange for interviews or appointments;

(d) express judgments;

(e) call for reconsideration of an administrative response which the Member believes is not reasonable supported by statutes, regulations or considerations of equity or public policy; or

(f) perform any other service of a similar nature consistent with the provisions of this rule.

3. The decision to provide assistance to petitioners may not be made on the basis of contributions or services, or promises of contributions or services, to the Member's political campaigns or to other organizations in which the Member has a political, personal, or financial interest.

4. A Member shall make a reasonable effort to assure that representations made in the Member's name by any Senate employee are accurate and conform to the Member's instructions and to this rule.

5. Nothing in this rule shall be construed to limit the authority of Members, and Senate employees, to perform legislative, including committee, responsibilities.

Glossary of Congressional Terms

AA—*(See Administrative Assistant.)*

Absence of a Quorum—Absence of the required number of members to conduct business in a house or a committee. When a quorum call or roll-call vote in a house establishes that a quorum is not present, no debate or other business is permitted except a motion to adjourn or motions to request or compel the attendance of absent members, if necessary by arresting them.

Absolute Majority—A vote requiring approval by a majority of all members of a house rather than a majority of members present and voting. Also referred to as constitutional majority.

Account—Organizational units used in the federal budget primarily for recording spending and revenue transactions.

Act—(1) A bill passed in identical form by both houses of Congress and signed into law by the president or enacted over his veto. A bill also becomes an act without the president's signature if he does not return it to Congress within ten days (Sundays excepted) and if Congress has not adjourned within that period. (2) Also, the technical term for a bill passed by at least one house and engrossed.

Adjourn—A formal motion to end a day's session or meeting of a house or a committee. A motion to adjourn usually has no conditions attached to it, but it may specify the day or time for reconvening or make reconvening subject to the call of the chamber's presiding officer or the committee's chairman.

Adjourn for More Than Three Days—Under Article I, Section 5 of the Constitution, neither house may adjourn for more than three days without the approval of the other. The necessary approval is given in a concurrent resolution and agreed to by both houses, which may permit one or both to take such an adjournment.

Adjournment Sine Die—Final adjournment of an annual or two-year session of Congress; literally, adjournment without a day. The two houses must agree to a privileged concurrent resolution for such an adjournment. A sine die adjournment precludes Congress from meeting again until the next constitutionally fixed date of a session (January 3 of the following year) unless Congress determines otherwise by law or the president calls it into special session. Article II, Section 3 of the Constitution authorizes the president to adjourn both houses until such time as he thinks proper when the two houses cannot agree to a time of adjournment, but no president has ever exercised this authority.

Adjournment to a Day (and Time) Certain—An adjournment that fixes the next date and time of meeting for one or both houses. It does not end an annual session of Congress.

Administration Bill—A bill drafted in the executive office of the president or in an executive department or agency to implement part of the president's program. An administration bill is introduced in Congress by a member who supports it or as a courtesy to the administration.

Administrative Assistant (AA)—The title usually given to a member's chief aide, political advisor, and head of office staff. The administrative assistant often represents the member at meetings with visitors or officials when the member is unable (or unwilling) to attend.

Adoption—The usual parliamentary term for approval of a conference report. It is also commonly applied to amendments.

Advice and Consent—The Senate's constitutional role in consenting to or rejecting the president's nominations to executive branch and judicial offices and the treaties he submits. Confirmation of nominees requires a simple majority vote of senators present and voting. Treaties must be approved by a two-thirds majority of those present and voting.

Aisle—The center aisle of each chamber. When facing the presiding officer, Republicans usually sit to the right of the aisle, Democrats to the left. When a member speaks of "my side of the aisle" or "this side," he means his party.

Amendment—A formal proposal to alter the text of a bill, resolution, amendment, motion, treaty, or some other text. Technically, it is a motion. An amendment may strike out (eliminate) part of a text, insert new text, or strike out and insert—that is, replace all or part of the text with new text. The texts of amendments considered on the floor are printed in full in the *Congressional Record*.

Amendment in the Nature of a Substitute—Usually, an amendment to replace the entire text of a measure. It strikes out everything after the enacting clause and inserts a version that may be somewhat, substantially, or entirely different. When a committee adopts extensive amendments to a measure, it often incorporates them into such an amendment. Occasionally, the term is applied to an amendment that replaces a major portion of a measure's text.

Annual Authorization—Legislation that authorizes appropriations for a single fiscal year and usually for a specific amount. Under the rules of the authorization-appropriation process, an annually authorized agency or program must be reauthorized each year if it is to receive appropriations for that year. Sometimes Congress fails to enact the reauthorization but nevertheless provides appropriations to continue the program, circumventing the rules by one means or another.

Appeal—A member's formal challenge of a ruling or decision by the presiding officer. On appeal, a house or a committee may overturn the ruling by majority vote. The right of appeal ensures the body against arbitrary control by the chair. Appeals are rarely made in the House and are even more rarely successful. Rulings are more frequently appealed in the Senate and occasionally overturned, in part because its presiding officer is not the majority party's leader, as in the House.

Apportionment—The action, after each decennial census, of allocating the number of members in the House of Representatives to each state. By law, the total number of House members (not counting delegates and a resident commissioner) is fixed at 435. The number allotted to each state is based approximately on its proportion of the nation's total population. Since the Constitution guarantees each state one representative no matter how small its population, exact proportional distribution is virtually impossible. The mathematical formula currently used to determine the apportionment is called the Method of Equal Proportions. *(See Method of Equal Proportions.)*

Appropriated Entitlement—An entitlement program, such as veterans' pensions, that is funded through annual appropriations rather than by a permanent appropriation. Because such an entitlement law requires the government to provide eligible recipients the benefits to which they are entitled, whatever the cost, Congress must appropriate the necessary funds.

Appropriation—(1) Legislative language that permits a federal agency to incur obligations and make payments from the Treasury for specified purposes, usually during a specified period of time. (2) The specific amount of money made available by such language. The Constitution prohibits payments from the Treasury except "in Consequence of Appropriations made by Law." With some exceptions, the rules of both houses forbid consideration of appropriations for purposes that are unauthorized in law or of appropriation amounts larger than those authorized in law. The House of Representatives claims the exclusive right to originate appropriation bills—a claim the Senate denies in theory but accepts in practice.

At-Large—Elected by and representing an entire state instead of a district within a state. The term usually refers to a representative rather than to a senator. *(See Apportionment, Congressional District, Redistricting.)*

August Adjournment—A congressional adjournment during the month of August in odd-numbered years, required by the Legislative Reorganization Act of 1970. The law instructs the two houses to adjourn for a period of at least 30 days before the second day after Labor Day, unless Congress provides otherwise or if, on July 31, a state of war exists by congressional declaration.

Authorization—(1) A statutory provision that establishes or continues a federal agency, activity or program for a fixed or indefinite period of time. It may also establish policies and restrictions and deal with organizational and administrative matters. (2) A statutory provision that authorizes appropriations for an agency, activity, or program. The appropriations may be authorized for one year, several years, or an indefinite period of time, and the authorization may be for a specific amount of money or an indefinite amount ("such sums as may be necessary"). Authorizations of specific amounts are construed as ceilings on the amounts that subsequently may be appropriated in an appropriation bill, but not as minimums; either house may appropriate lesser amounts or nothing at all.

Authorization-Appropriation Process—The two-stage procedural system that the rules of each house require for establishing and funding federal agencies and programs: first, enactment of authorizing legislation that creates or continues an agency or program; second, enactment of appropriations legislation that provides funds for the authorized agency or program.

Automatic Roll Call—Under a House rule, the automatic ordering of the yeas and nays when a quorum is not present on a voice or division vote and a member objects to the vote on that ground. It is not permitted in the Committee of the Whole.

Backdoor Spending Authority—Authority to incur obligations that evades the normal congressional appropriations process because it is provided in legislation other than appropriation acts. The most common forms are borrowing authority, contract authority, and entitlement authority.

Baseline—A projection of the levels of federal spending, revenues, and the resulting budgetary surpluses or deficits for the upcoming and subsequent fiscal years, taking into account laws enacted to date and assuming no new policy decisions. It provides a benchmark for measuring the budgetary effects of proposed changes in federal revenues or spending, assuming certain economic conditions.

Bicameral—Consisting of two houses or chambers. Congress is a bicameral legislature whose two houses have an equal role in enacting legislation. In most other national bicameral legislatures, one house is significantly more powerful than the other.

Bill—The term for the chief vehicle Congress uses for enacting laws. Bills that originate in the House of Representatives are designated as H.R., those in the Senate as S., followed by a number assigned in the order in which they are introduced during a two-year Congress. A bill becomes a law if passed in identical language by both houses and signed by the president, or passed over his veto, or if the president fails to sign it within ten days after he has received it while Congress is in session.

Bills and Resolutions Introduced—Members formally present measures to their respective houses by delivering them to a clerk in the chamber when their house is in session. Both houses permit any number of members to join in introducing a bill or resolution. The first member listed on the measure is the sponsor; the other members listed are its cosponsors.

Bills and Resolutions Referred—After a bill or resolution is introduced, it is normally sent to one or more committees that have jurisdiction over its subject, as defined by House and Senate rules and precedents. A Senate measure is usually referred to the committee with jurisdiction over the predominant subject of its text, but it may be sent to two or more committees by unanimous consent or on a motion offered jointly by the majority and minority leaders. In the House, a rule requires the Speaker to refer a measure to the committee that has primary jurisdiction. The Speaker is also authorized to refer measures sequentially to additional committees and to impose time limits on such referrals.

Bipartisan Committee—A committee with an equal number of members from each political party. The House Committee on Standards of Official Conduct and the Senate Select Committee on Ethics are the only bipartisan, permanent full committees.

Borrowing Authority—Statutory authority permitting a federal agency, such as the Export-Import Bank, to borrow money from the public or the Treasury to finance its operations. It is a form of backdoor spending. To bring such spending under the control of the congressional appropriation process, the Congressional Budget Act requires that new borrowing authority shall be effective only to the extent and in such amounts as are provided in appropriations acts.

Budget—A detailed statement of actual or anticipated revenues and expenditures during an accounting period. For the national government, the period is the federal fiscal year (October 1–September 30). The budget usually refers to the president's budget submission to Congress early each calendar year. The president's budget estimates federal government income and spending for the upcoming fiscal year and contains detailed recommendations for appropriation, revenue, and other legislation. Congress is not required to accept or even vote directly on the president's proposals, and it often revises the president's budget extensively. *(See Fiscal Year.)*

Budget Act—Common name for the Congressional Budget and Impoundment Control Act of 1974, which established the basic procedures of the current congressional budget process; created the House and Senate Budget committees; and enacted procedures for reconciliation, deferrals, and rescissions. *(See Budget Process, Deferral, Impoundment, Reconciliation, Rescission. See Also Gramm-Rudman-Hollings Act of 1985.)*

Budget and Accounting Act of 1921—The law that, for the first time, authorized the president to submit to Congress an annual budget for the entire federal government. Prior to the act, most federal agencies sent their budget requests to the appropriate congressional committees without review by the president.

Budget Authority—Generally, the amount of money that may be spent or obligated by a government agency or for a government program or activity. Technically, it is statutory authority to enter into obligations that normally result in outlays. The main forms of budget authority are appropriations, borrowing authority, and contract authority. It also includes authority to obligate and expend the proceeds of offsetting receipts and collections. Congress may make budget authority available for only one year, several years, or an indefinite period, and it may specify definite or indefinite amounts.

Budget Process—(1) In Congress, the procedural system it uses (a) to approve an annual concurrent resolution on the budget that sets goals for aggregate and functional categories of federal expenditures, revenues, and the surplus or deficit for an upcoming fiscal year; and (b) to implement those goals in spending, revenue, and, if necessary, reconciliation and debt-limit legislation. (2) In the executive branch, the process of formulating the president's annual budget, submitting it to Congress, defending it before congressional committees, implementing subsequent budget-related legislation, impounding or sequestering expenditures as permitted by law, auditing and evaluating programs, and compiling final budget data. The Budget and Accounting Act of 1921 and the Congressional Budget and Impoundment Control Act of 1974 established the basic elements of the current budget process. Major revisions were enacted in the Gramm-Rudman-Hollings Act of 1985 and the Budget Enforcement Act of 1990.

Budget Resolution—A concurrent resolution in which Congress establishes or revises its version of the federal budget's broad financial features for the upcoming fiscal year and several additional fiscal years. Like other concurrent resolutions, it does not have the force of law, but it provides the framework within which Congress subsequently considers revenue, spending, and other budget-implementing legislation. The framework consists of two basic elements: (1) aggregate budget amounts (total revenues, new budget authority, outlays, loan obligations and loan guarantee commitments, deficit or surplus, and debt limit); and (2) subdivisions of the relevant aggregate amounts among the functional categories of the budget. Although it does not allocate funds to specific programs or accounts, the budget committees' reports accompanying the resolution often discuss the major program assumptions underlying its functional amounts. Unlike those amounts, however, the assumptions are not binding on Congress.

By Request—A designation indicating that a member has introduced a measure on behalf of the president, an executive agency, or a private individual or organization. Members often introduce such measures as a courtesy because neither the president nor any person other than a member of Congress can do so. The term, which appears next to the sponsor's name, implies that the member who introduced the measure does not necessarily endorse it. A House rule dealing with by-request introductions dates from 1888, but the practice goes back to the earliest history of Congress.

Calendar—A list of measures or other matters (most of them favorably reported by committees) that are eligible for floor consideration. The House has five calendars; the Senate has two. A place on a calendar does not guarantee consideration. Each house decides which measures and matters it will take up, when, and in what order, in accordance with its rules and practices.

Calendar Wednesday—A House procedure that on Wednesdays permits its committees to bring up for floor consideration nonprivileged measures they have reported. The procedure is so cumbersome and susceptible to dilatory tactics, however, that it is rarely used.

Call Up—To bring a measure or report to the floor for immediate consideration.

Casework—Assistance to constituents who seek assistance in dealing with federal and local government agencies. Constituent service is a high priority in most members' offices.

Caucus—(1) A common term for the official organization of each party in each house. (2) The official title of the organization of House Democrats. House and Senate Republicans and Senate Democrats call their organizations "conferences." (3) A term for an informal group of members who share legislative interests, such as the Black Caucus, Hispanic Caucus, and Children's Caucus.

Censure—The strongest formal condemnation of a member for misconduct short of expulsion. A house usually adopts a resolution of censure to express its condemnation, after which the presiding officer reads its rebuke aloud to the member in the presence of his colleagues.

Chairman—The presiding officer of a committee, a subcommittee, or a task force. At meetings, the chairman preserves order, enforces the rules, recognizes members to speak or offer motions, and puts questions to a vote. The chairman of a committee or subcommittee usually appoints its staff and sets its agenda, subject to the panel's veto.

Chamber—The Capitol room in which a house of Congress normally holds its sessions. The chamber of the House of Representatives, officially called the Hall of the House, is considerably larger than that of the Senate because it must accommodate 435 representatives, four delegates, and one resident commissioner. Unlike the Senate chamber, members have no desks or assigned seats. In both chambers, the floor slopes downward to the well in front of the presiding officer's raised desk. A chamber is often referred to as "the floor," as when members are said to be on or going to the floor. Those expressions usually imply that the member's house is in session.

Christmas Tree Bill—Jargon for a bill adorned with amendments, many of them unrelated to the bill's subject, that provide benefits for interest groups, specific states, congressional districts, companies, and individuals.

Classes of Senators—A class consists of the 33 or 34 senators elected to a six-year term in the same general election. Since the terms of approximately one-third of the senators expire every two years, there are three classes.

Clean Bill—After a House committee extensively amends a bill, it often assembles its amendments and what is left of the bill into a new measure that one or more of its members introduces as a "clean bill." The revised measure is assigned a new number.

Clerk of the House—An officer of the House of Representatives responsible principally for administrative support of the legislative process in the House. The clerk is invariably the candidate of the majority party.

Clerk-Hire—The personal staff to which a member is entitled. The House sets a maximum number of staff and a monetary allowance for each member. The Senate does not have a maximum staff level, but does set a monetary allowance for each member.

Cloakrooms—Two rooms with access to the rear of each chamber's floor, one for each party's members, where members may confer privately, sit quietly, or have a snack. The presiding officer sometimes urges members who are conversing too loudly on the floor to retire to their cloakrooms.

Closed Rule—A special rule reported from the House Rules Committee that prohibits amendments to a measure or that only permits amendments offered by the reporting committee.

Cloture—A Senate procedure that limits further consideration of a pending proposal to 30 hours in order to end a filibuster. Sixteen senators must first sign and submit a cloture motion to the presiding officer. One hour after the Senate meets on the second calendar day thereafter, the chair puts the motion to a yea-and-nay vote following a live quorum call. If three-fifths of all senators (60 if there are no vacancies) vote for the motion, the Senate must take final action on the cloture proposal by the end of the 30 hours of consideration and may consider no other business until it takes that action. Cloture on a proposal to amend the Senate's standing rules requires approval by two-thirds of the senators present and voting.

Code of Official Conduct—A House rule that bans certain actions by House members, officers, and employees; requires them to conduct themselves in ways that "reflect creditably" on the House; and orders them to adhere to the spirit and the letter of House rules and those of its committees. The code's provisions govern the receipt of outside compensation, gifts, and honoraria, and the use of campaign funds; prohibit members from using their clerk-hire allowance to pay anyone who does not perform duties commensurate with that pay; forbids discrimination in members' hiring or treatment of employees on the grounds of race, color, religion, sex, handicap, age, or national origin; orders members convicted of a crime who might be punished by imprisonment of two or more years not to participate in committee business or vote on the floor until exonerated or reelected; and restricts employees' contact with federal agencies on matters in which they have a significant financial interest. The Senate's rules contain some similar prohibitions.

College of Cardinals—A popular term for the subcommittee chairmen of the appropriations committees, reflecting their influence over appropriation measures. The chairmen of the full appropriations committees are sometimes referred to as popes.

Comity—The practice of maintaining mutual courtesy and civility between the two houses in their dealings with each other and in members' speeches on the floor. Although the practice is largely governed by long-established customs, a House rule explicitly cautions its members not to characterize any Senate action or inaction, refer to individual senators except under certain circumstances, or quote from Senate proceedings except to make legislative history on a measure. The Senate has no rule on the subject, but references to the House have been held out of order on several occasions. Generally, the houses do not interfere with each other's appropriations, although minor conflicts sometimes occur. A refusal to receive a message from the other house has also been held to violate the practice of comity.

Committee—A panel of members elected or appointed to perform some service or function for its parent body. Congress has four types of committees: standing, special or select, joint, and, in the House, a Committee of the Whole.

Committees conduct investigations, make studies, issue reports and recommendations, and, in the case of standing committees, review and prepare measures on their assigned subjects for action by their respective houses. Most committees divide their work among several subcommittees. With rare exceptions, the majority party in a house holds a majority of the seats on its committees, and their chairmen are also from that party.

Committee Jurisdiction—The legislative subjects and other functions assigned to a committee by rule, precedent, resolution, or statute. A committee's title usually indicates the general scope of its jurisdiction but often fails to mention other significant subjects assigned to it.

Committee of the Whole—Common name of the Committee of the Whole House on the State of the Union, a committee consisting of all members of the House of Representatives. Measures from the union calendar must be considered in the Committee of the Whole before the House officially completes action on them; the committee often considers other major bills as well. A quorum of the committee is 100, and it meets in the House chamber under a chairman appointed by the Speaker. Procedures in the Committee of the Whole expedite consideration of legislation because of its smaller quorum requirement, its ban on certain motions, and its five-minute rule for debate on amendments. Those procedures usually permit more members to offer amendments and participate in the debate on a measure than is normally possible. The Senate no longer uses a Committee of the Whole.

Committee Ratios—The ratios of majority to minority party members on committees. By custom, the ratios of most committees reflect party strength in their respective houses as closely as possible.

Committee Report on a Measure—A document submitted by a committee to report a measure to its parent chamber. Customarily, the report explains the measure's purpose, describes provisions and any amendments recommended by the committee, and presents arguments for its approval.

Committee Veto—A procedure that requires an executive department or agency to submit certain proposed policies, programs, or action to designated committees for review before implementing them. Before 1983, when the Supreme Court declared that a legislative veto is unconstitutional, these provisions permitted committees to veto the proposals. They no longer do so, and the term is now something of a misnomer. Nevertheless, agencies usually take the pragmatic approach of trying to reach a consensus with the committees before carrying out their proposals, especially when an appropriations committee is involved.

Concurrent Resolution—A resolution that requires approval by both houses but is not sent to the president for his signature and therefore cannot have the force of law. Concurrent resolutions deal with the prerogatives or internal affairs of Congress as a whole. Designated H. Con. Res. in the House and S. Con. Res. in the Senate, they are numbered consecutively in each house in their order of introduction during a two-year Congress.

Conferees—A common title for managers, the members from each house appointed to a conference committee. The Senate usually authorizes its presiding officer to appoint its conferees. The Speaker appoints House conferees, and under a rule adopted in 1993, can remove conferees "at any time after an original appointment" and also appoint additional conferees at any time. Conferees are expected to support the positions of their houses despite their personal views, but in practice this is not always the case. The party ratios of conferees generally reflect the ratios in their houses.

Each house may appoint as many conferees as it pleases. House conferees often outnumber their Senate colleagues; however, each house has only one vote in a conference, so the size of its delegation is immaterial.

Conference—(1) A formal meeting or series of meetings between members representing each house to reconcile House and Senate differences on a measure (occasionally several measures). Since one house cannot require the other to agree to its proposals, the conference usually reaches agreement by compromise. When a conference completes action on a measure, or as much action as appears possible, it sends its recommendations to both houses in the form of a conference report, accompanied by an explanatory statement. (2) The official title of the organization of all Democrats or Republicans in the Senate and of all Republicans in the House of Representatives. *(See Party Caucus.)*

Conference Committee—A temporary joint committee formed for the purpose of resolving differences between the houses on a measure or, occasionally, several measures. Voting in a conference committee is not by individuals, but by house as determined by a majority vote of each house's conferees respectively. Both houses require that conference committees open their meetings to the public although closed meetings can be held under certain circumstances. Otherwise, there are no congressional rules governing the organization of, or procedure in, a conference committee.

Conference Report—A document submitted to both houses that contains a conference committee's agreements for resolving their differences on a measure. It must be signed by a majority of the conferees from each house separately and must be accompanied by an explanatory statement. Both houses prohibit amendments to a conference report and require it to be accepted or rejected in its entirety.

Congress—(1) The national legislature of the United States, consisting of the House of Representatives and the Senate. (2) The national legislature in office during a two-year period. Congresses are numbered sequentially; thus, the 1st Congress of 1789–1791 and the

102nd Congress of 1991–1993. Before 1935, the two-year period began on the first Monday in December of odd-numbered years. Since then it has extended from January of an odd-numbered year through noon on January 3 of the next odd-numbered year. A Congress usually holds two annual sessions, but some have had three sessions and the 67th Congress had four. When a Congress expires, measures die if they have not yet been enacted.

Congressional Accountability Act of 1995 (CAA)—An act applying 11 labor, workplace, and civil rights laws to the legislative branch and establishing procedures and remedies for legislative branch employees with grievances in violation of these laws. The following laws are covered by the CAA: the Fair Labor Standards Act of 1938; Title VII of the Civil Rights Act of 1964; Americans with Disabilities Act of 1990; Age Discrimination in Employment Act of 1967; Family and Medical Leave Act of 1993; Occupational Safety and Health Act of 1970; Chapter 71 of Title 5, *U.S. Code* (relating to federal service labor-management relations); Employee Polygraph Protection Act of 1988; Worker Adjustment and Retraining Notification Act; Rehabilitation Act of 1973; and Chapter 43 of Title 38, *U.S. Code* (relating to veterans' employment and reemployment).

Congressional Budget Office (CBO)—A congressional support agency created by the Congressional Budget and Impoundment Control Act of 1974 to provide nonpartisan budgetary information and analysis to Congress and its committees. CBO acts as a scorekeeper when Congress is voting on the federal budget, tracking bills to make sure they comply with overall budget goals. The agency also estimates what proposed legislation would cost over a five-year period. CBO works most closely with the House and Senate Budget committees.

Congressional Directory—The official who's who of Congress, usually published during the first session of a two-year Congress.

Congressional District—The geographical area represented by a single member of the House of Representatives. For states with only one representative, the entire state is a congressional district. As of 1999, seven states had only one representative each: Alaska, Delaware, Montana, North Dakota, South Dakota, Vermont and Wyoming.

Congressional Record—The daily, printed, and substantially verbatim account of proceedings in both the House and Senate chambers. Extraneous materials submitted by members appear in a section titled "Extensions of Remarks." A "Daily Digest" appendix contains highlights of the day's floor and committee action plus a list of committee meetings and floor agendas for the next day's session.

Although the official reporters of each house take down every word spoken during the proceedings, members are permitted to edit and "revise and extend" their remarks before they are printed. In the Senate section, all speeches, articles, and other material submitted by senators but not actually spoken or read on the floor are set off by large black dots, called bullets. However, bullets do not appear when a senator reads part of a speech and inserts the rest. In the House section, undelivered speeches and materials are printed in a distinctive typeface. The term "permanent *Record*" refers to the bound volumes of the daily *Records* of an entire session of Congress.

Congressional Research Service (CRS)—Established in 1917, a department of the Library of Congress whose staff provide nonpartisan, objective analysis, and information on virtually any subject to committees, members, and staff of Congress. Originally the Legislative Reference Service, it is the oldest congressional support agency.

Congressional Terms of Office—A term normally begins on January 3 of the year following a general election and runs two years for representatives and six years for senators. A representative chosen in a special election to fill a vacancy is sworn in for the remainder of his predecessor's term. An individual appointed to fill a Senate vacancy usually serves until the next general election or until the end of the predecessor's term, whichever comes first. Some states, however, require their governors to call a special election to fill a Senate vacancy shortly after an appointment has been made.

Contempt of Congress—Willful obstruction of the proper functions of Congress. Most frequently, it is a refusal to obey a subpoena to appear and testify before a committee or to produce documents demanded by it. Such obstruction is a misdemeanor and persons cited for contempt are subject to prosecution in federal courts. A house cites an individual for contempt by agreeing to a privileged resolution to that effect reported by a committee. The presiding officer then refers the matter to a U.S. attorney for prosecution.

Continuing Body—A characterization of the Senate on the theory that it continues from Congress to Congress and has existed continuously since it first convened in 1789. The rationale for the theory is that under the system of staggered six-year terms for senators, the terms of only about one-third of them expire after each Congress and, therefore, a quorum of the Senate is always in office. Consequently, under this theory, the Senate, unlike the House, does not have to adopt its rules at the beginning of each Congress because those rules continue from one Congress to the next. This makes it extremely difficult for the Senate to change its rules against the opposition of a determined minority because those rules require a two-thirds vote of the senators present and voting to invoke cloture on a proposed rules change.

Continuing Resolution (CR)—A joint resolution that provides funds to continue the operation of federal agencies and programs at the beginning of a new fiscal year if their annual appropriation bills have not yet been enacted; also called continuing appropriations.

Contract Authority—Statutory authority permitting an agency to enter into contracts or incur other obligations even though it has not received an appropriation to pay for them. Congress must eventually fund them because the government is legally liable for such payments. The Congressional Budget Act of 1974 requires that new contract authority may not be used unless provided for in advance by an appropriation act, but it permits a few exceptions.

Controllable Expenditures—Federal spending that is permitted but not mandated by existing authorization law and therefore may be adjusted by congressional action in appropriation bills. (*See Appropriation.*)

Correcting Recorded Votes—The rules of both houses prohibit members from changing their votes after a vote result has been announced. Nevertheless, the Senate permits its members to withdraw or change their votes, by unanimous consent, immediately after the announcement. In rare instances, senators have been granted unanimous consent to change their votes several days or weeks after the announcement.

Votes tallied by the electronic voting system in the House may not be changed. But when a vote actually given is not recorded during an oral call of the roll, a member may demand a correction as a matter of right. On all other alleged errors in a recorded vote, the Speaker determines whether the circumstances justify a change. Occasionally, members merely announce that they were incorrectly recorded; announcements can occur hours, days, or even months after the vote and appear in the *Congressional Record*.

Cosponsor—A member who has joined one or more other members to sponsor a measure.

Credit Authority—Authority granted to an agency to incur direct loan obligations or to make loan guarantee commitments. The Congressional Budget Act of 1974 bans congressional consideration of credit authority legislation unless the extent of that authority is made subject to provisions in appropriation acts.

C-SPAN—Cable-Satellite Public Affairs Network, which provides live, gavel-to-gavel coverage of Senate floor proceedings on one cable television channel and coverage of House floor proceedings on another channel. C-SPAN also televises important committee hearings in both houses. Each house also transmits its televised proceedings directly to congressional offices.

Current Services Estimates—Executive branch estimates of the anticipated costs of federal programs and operations for the next and future fiscal years at existing levels of service and assuming no new initiatives or changes in existing law. The president submits these estimates to Congress with his annual budget and includes an explanation of the underlying economic and policy assumptions on which they are based, such as anticipated rates of inflation, real economic growth, and unemployment, plus program caseloads and pay increases.

Custody of the Papers—Possession of an engrossed measure and certain related basic documents that the two houses produce as they try to resolve their differences over the measure.

Dance of the Swans and the Ducks—A whimsical description of the gestures some members use in connection with a request for a recorded vote, especially in the House. When a member wants his colleagues to stand in support of the request, he moves his hands and arms in a gentle upward motion resembling the beginning flight of a graceful swan. When he wants his colleagues to remain seated in order to avoid such a vote, he moves his hands and arms in a vigorous downward motion resembling a diving duck.

Dean—Within a state's delegation in the House of Representatives, the member with the longest continuous service.

Debate—In congressional parlance, speeches delivered during consideration of a measure, motion, or other matter, as distinguished from speeches in other parliamentary situations, such as one-minute and special order speeches when no business is pending. Virtually all debate in the House of Representatives is under some kind of time limitation. Most debate in the Senate is unlimited; that is, a senator, once recognized, may speak for as long as he chooses, unless the Senate invokes cloture.

Debt Limit—The maximum amount of outstanding federal public debt permitted by law. The limit (or ceiling) covers virtually all debt incurred by the government except agency debt. Each congressional budget resolution sets forth the new debt limit that may be required under its provisions.

Deferral—An impoundment of funds for a specific period of time that may not extend beyond the fiscal year in which it is proposed. Under the Impoundment Control Act of 1974, the president must notify Congress that he is deferring the spending or obligation of funds provided by law for a project or activity. Congress can disapprove the deferral by legislation.

Deficit—The amount by which the government's outlays exceed its budget receipts for a given fiscal year. Both the president's budget and the annual congressional budget resolution provide estimates of the deficit or surplus for the upcoming and several future fiscal years.

Degrees of Amendment—Designations that indicate the relationships of amendments to the text of a measure and to each other. In general, an amendment offered directly to the text of a measure is an amendment in the first degree, and an amendment to that amendment is an amendment in the second degree. Both houses normally prohibit amendments in the third degree—that is, an amendment to an amendment to an amendment.

Delegate—A nonvoting member of the House of Representatives elected to a two-year term from the District of Columbia, the territory of Guam, the territory of the Virgin Islands, or the territory of American Samoa. By law, delegates may not vote in the full House, but they may participate in debate, offer motions (except to reconsider), and serve and vote on standing and select committees. On their committees, delegates possess the same powers and privileges as other members, and the Speaker may appoint them to appropriate conference committees and select committees.

Denounce—A formal action that condemns a member for misbehavior; considered by some experts to be equivalent to censure. *(See Censure.)*

Dilatory Tactics—Procedural actions intended to delay or prevent action by a house or a committee. They include, among others, offering numerous motions, demanding quorum calls and recorded votes at every opportunity, making numerous points of order and parliamentary inquiries, and speaking as long as the applicable rules permit. The Senate rules permit a battery of dilatory tactics, especially lengthy speeches, except under cloture. In the House, possible dilatory tactics are more limited. Speeches are always subject to time limits and debate-ending motions. Moreover, a House rule instructs the Speaker not to entertain dilatory motions and lets the Speaker decide whether a motion is dilatory. However, the Speaker may not override the constitutional right of a member to demand the yeas and nays, and in practice usually waits for a point of order before exercising that authority. *(See Cloture.)*

Discharge a Committee—Remove a measure from a committee to which it has been referred in order to make it available for floor consideration. Noncontroversial measures are often discharged by unanimous consent. However, because congressional committees have no obligation to report measures referred to them, each house has procedures to extract controversial measures from recalcitrant committees. Six discharge procedures are available in the House of Representatives. The Senate uses a motion to discharge, which is usually converted into a discharge resolution.

Division Vote—A vote in which the chair first counts those in favor of a proposition and then those opposed to it, with no record made of how each member votes. In the Senate, the chair may count raised hands or ask senators to stand, whereas the House requires members to stand; hence, often called a standing vote. Committees in both houses ordinarily use a show of hands. A division usually occurs after a voice vote and may be demanded by any member or ordered by the chair if there is any doubt about the outcome of the voice vote. The demand for a division can also come before a voice vote. In the Senate, the demand must come before the result of a voice vote is announced. It may be made after a voice vote announcement in the House, but only if no intervening business has transpired and only if the member was standing and seeking recognition at the time of the announcement. A demand for the yeas and nays or, in the House, for a recorded vote, takes precedence over a division vote.

Doorkeeper of the House—A former officer of the House of Representatives who was responsible for enforcing the rules prohibiting unauthorized persons from entering the chamber when the House is in session. The doorkeeper was usually the candidate of the majority party. In 1995, the office was abolished and its functions transferred to the sergeant at arms.

Effective Dates—Provisions of an act that specify when the entire act or individual provisions in it become effective as law. Most acts become effective on the date of enactment, but it is sometimes necessary or prudent to delay the effective dates of some provisions.

Electronic Voting—Since 1973 the House has used an electronic voting system to record the yeas and nays and to conduct recorded votes. Members vote by inserting their voting cards in one of the boxes at several locations in the chamber. They are given at least 15 minutes to vote. When several votes occur immediately after each other, the Speaker may reduce the voting time to five minutes on the second and subsequent votes. The Speaker may allow additional time on each vote, but he may also close a vote at any time after the minimum time has expired. Members can change their votes at any time before the Speaker announces the result. The House also uses the electronic system for quorum calls. While a vote is in progress, a large panel above the Speaker's desk displays how each member has voted. Smaller panels on either side of the chamber display running totals of the votes and the time remaining. The Senate does not have electronic voting.

Enacting Clause—The opening language of each bill, beginning "Be it enacted by the Senate and House of Representatives of the United States of America in Congress assembled..." This language gives legal force to measures approved by Congress and signed by the president or enacted over his veto. A successful motion to strike it from a bill kills the entire measure.

Engrossed Bill—The official copy of a bill or joint resolution as passed by one chamber, including the text as amended by floor action, and certified by the clerk of the House or the secretary of the Senate (as appropriate). Amendments by one house to a measure or amendments of the other also are engrossed. House engrossed documents are printed on blue paper; the Senate's are printed on white paper.

Enrolled Bill—The final official copy of a bill or joint resolution passed in identical form by both houses. An enrolled bill is printed on parchment. After it is certified by the chief officer of the house in which it originated and signed by the House Speaker and the Senate president pro tempore, the measure is sent to the president for his signature.

Entitlement Program—A federal program under which individuals, businesses, or units of government that meet the requirements or qualifications established by law are entitled to receive certain payments if they seek such payments. Major examples include Social Security, Medicare, Medicaid, unemployment insurance, and military and federal civilian pensions. Congress cannot control their expenditures by refusing to appropriate the sums necessary to fund them because the government is legally obligated to pay eligible recipients the amounts to which the law entitles them.

Ethics Rules—Several rules or standing orders in each house that mandate certain standards of conduct for members and congressional employees in finance, employment, franking, and other areas. The Senate Permanent Select Committee on Ethics and the House Committee on Standards of Official Conduct investigate alleged violations of conduct and recommend appropriate actions to their respective houses.

Exclusive Committee—(1) Under the rules of the Republican Conference and House Democratic Caucus, a standing committee whose members usually cannot serve on any other standing committee. As of 1999 the Appropriations, Commerce (beginning in the 105th Congress), Ways and Means, and Rules committees were designated as exclusive committees. (2) Under the rules of the two party conferences in the Senate, a standing committee whose members may not simultaneously serve on any other exclusive committee.

Executive Calendar—The Senate's calendar for committee reports on its executive business, namely treaties and nominations. The calendar numbers indicate the order in which items were referred to the calendar but have no bearing on when or if the Senate will consider them. The Senate, by motion or unanimous consent, resolves itself into executive session to consider them

Executive Document—A document, usually a treaty, sent by the president to the Senate for approval. It is referred to a committee in the same manner as other measures. Resolutions to ratify treaties have their own "treaty document" numbers. For example, the first treaty submitted in the 106th Congress would be "Treaty Doc 106-1."

Executive Order—A unilateral proclamation by the president that has a policy-making or legislative impact. Members of Congress have challenged some executive orders on the grounds that they usurped the authority of the legislative branch. Although the Supreme Court has ruled that a particular order exceeded the president's authority, it has upheld others as falling within the president's general constitutional powers.

Executive Privilege—The assertion that presidents have the right to withhold certain information from Congress. Presidents have based their claim on: (1) the constitutional separation of powers; (2) the need for secrecy in military and diplomatic affairs; (3) the need to protect individuals from unfavorable publicity; (4) the need to safeguard the confidential exchange of ideas in the executive branch; and (5) the need to protect individuals who provide confidential advice to the president.

Expulsion—A member's removal from office by a two-thirds vote of his house; the super majority is required by the Constitution. It is the most severe and most rarely used sanction a house can invoke against a member. Although the Constitution provides no explicit grounds for expulsion, the courts have ruled that it may be applied only for misconduct during a member's term of office, not for conduct before the member's election. Generally, neither house will consider expulsion of a member convicted of a crime until the judicial processes have been exhausted. At that stage, members sometimes resign rather than face expulsion. In 1977 the House adopted a rule urging members convicted of certain crimes to voluntarily abstain from voting or participating in other legislative business.

Federal Debt—The total amount of monies borrowed and not yet repaid by the federal government. Federal debt consists of public debt and agency debt. Public debt is the portion of the federal debt borrowed by the Treasury or the Federal Financing Bank directly from the public or from another federal fund or account. For example, the Treasury regularly borrows money from the Social Security trust fund. Public debt accounts for about 99 percent of the federal debt. Agency debt refers to the debt incurred by federal agencies like the Export-Import Bank, but excluding the Treasury and the Federal Financing Bank, which are authorized by law to borrow funds from the public or from another government fund or account.

Filibuster—The use of obstructive and time-consuming parliamentary tactics by one member or a minority of members to delay, modify, or defeat proposed legislation or rules changes. Filibusters are also sometimes used to delay urgently needed measures in order to force the body to accept other legislation. The Senate's rules permitting unlimited debate and the extraordinary majority it requires to impose cloture make filibustering particularly effective in that chamber. Under the stricter rules of the House, filibusters in that body are short-lived and therefore ineffective and rarely attempted

Fiscal Year—The federal government's annual accounting period. It begins October 1 and ends on the following September 30. A fiscal year is designated by the calendar year in which it ends and is often referred to as FY. Thus, fiscal year 1999 began October 1, 1998, ended September 30, 1999, and is called FY99. In theory, Congress is supposed to complete action on all budgetary measures applying to a fiscal year before that year begins. It rarely does so.

Five-Minute Rule—In its most common usage, a House rule that limits debate on an amendment offered in Committee of the Whole to five minutes for its sponsor and five minutes for an opponent. In practice, the committee routinely permits longer debate by two devices: the offering of pro forma amendments, each debatable for five minutes, and unanimous consent for a member to speak longer than five minutes. Also a House rule that limits a committee member to five minutes when questioning a witness at a hearing until each member has had an opportunity to question that witness.

Floor—The ground level of the House or Senate chamber where members sit and the houses conduct their business. When members are attending a meeting of their house, they are said to be on the floor. Floor action refers to the procedural actions taken during floor consideration, such as deciding on motions, taking up measures, amending them, and voting.

Floor Manager—A majority party member responsible for guiding a measure through its floor consideration in a house and for devising the political and procedural strategies that might be required to get it passed. The presiding officer gives the floor manager priority recognition to debate, offer amendments, oppose amendments, and make crucial procedural motions.

Frank—Informally, a member's legal right to send official mail postage free under his or her signature; often called the franking privilege. Technically, it is the autographic or facsimile signature used on envelopes instead of stamps that permits members and certain congressional officers to send their official mail free of charge. The franking privilege has been authorized by law since the first Congress, except for a few months in 1873. Congress reimburses the U.S. Postal Service for the franked mail it handles.

Function or Functional Category—A broad category of national need and spending of budgetary significance. A category provides an accounting method for allocating and keeping track of budgetary resources and expenditures for that function because it includes all budget accounts related to the function's subject or purpose such as agriculture, administration of justice, commerce and housing and energy. Functions do not necessarily correspond with appropriations acts or with the budgets of individual agencies.

Gag Rule—A pejorative term for any type of special rule reported by the House Rules Committee that proposes to prohibit amendments to a measure or only permits amendments offered by the reporting committee.

Galleries—The balconies overlooking each chamber from which the public, news media, staff, and others may observe floor proceedings.

General Accounting Office (GAO)—A congressional support agency, often referred to as the investigative arm of Congress. It evaluates and audits federal agencies and programs in the United States and abroad on its own initiative or at the request of congressional committees or members.

General Appropriation Bill—A term applied to each of the 13 annual bills that provide funds for most federal agencies and programs and also to the supplemental appropriation bills that contain appropriations for more than one agency or program.

Germane—Basically, on the same subject as the matter under consideration. A House rule requires that all amendments be germane. In the Senate, only amendments proposed to general appropriation bills and budget resolutions or under cloture must be germane. Germaneness rules can be evaded by suspension of the rules in both houses, by unanimous consent agreements in the Senate, and by special rules from the Rules Committee in the House.

Gerrymandering—The manipulation of legislative district boundaries to benefit a particular party, politician, or minority group. The term originated in 1812 when the Massachusetts legislature redrew the lines of state legislative districts to favor the party of Gov. Elbridge Gerry, and some critics said one district looked like a salamander. *(See also Congressional District, Redistricting.)*

Gramm-Rudman-Hollings Act of 1985—Common name for the Balanced Budget and Emergency Deficit Control Act of 1985, which established new budget procedures intended to balance the federal budget by fiscal year 1991. (The timetable subsequently was extended and then deleted.) The act's chief sponsors were senators Phil Gramm (R-Texas), Warren Rudman (R-N.H.), and Ernest Hollings (D-S.C.).

Grandfather Clause—A provision in a measure, law, or rule that exempts an individual, entity, or a defined category of individuals or entities from complying with a new policy or restriction. For example, a bill that would raise taxes on persons who reach the age of 65 after a certain date inherently grandfathers out those who are 65 before that date. Similarly, a Senate rule limiting senators to two major committee assignments also grandfathers some senators who were sitting on a third major committee prior to a specified date.

Grants-in-Aid—Payments by the federal government to state and local governments to help provide for assistance programs or public services.

Hearing—Committee or subcommittee meetings to receive testimony on proposed legislation during investigations or for oversight purposes. Relatively few bills are important enough to justify formal hearings. Witnesses often include experts, government officials, spokespersons for interested groups, officials of the General Accounting Office, and members of Congress.

Hold—A senator's request that his or her party leaders delay floor consideration of certain legislation or presidential nominations. The majority leader usually honors a hold for a reasonable period of time, especially if its purpose is to assure the senator that the matter will not be called up during his or her absence or to give the senator time to gather necessary information.

Hold (or Have) the Floor—A member's right to speak without interruption, unless he or she violates a rule, after recognition by the presiding officer. At the member's discretion, he or she may yield to another member for a question in the Senate or for a question or statement in the House, but may reclaim the floor at any time.

Hold-Harmless Clause—In legislation providing a new formula for allocating federal funds, a clause to ensure that recipients of those funds do not receive less in a future year than they did in the current year if the new formula would result in a reduction for them. Similar to a grandfather clause, it has been used most frequently to soften the impact of sudden reductions in federal grants. *(See Grandfather Clause.)*

Hopper—A box on the clerk's desk in the House chamber into which members deposit bills and resolutions to introduce them. In House jargon, to drop a bill in the hopper is to introduce it.

Hour Rule—A House rule that permits members, when recognized, to hold the floor in debate for no more than one hour each. The majority party member customarily yields one-half the time to a minority member. Although the hour rule applies to general debate in Committee of the Whole as well as in the House, special rules routinely vary the length of time for such debate and its control to fit the circumstances of particular measures.

House as in Committee of the Whole—A hybrid combination of procedures from the general rules of the House and from the rules of the Committee of the Whole, sometimes used to expedite consideration of a measure on the floor.

House Calendar—The calendar reserved for all public bills and resolutions that do not raise revenue or directly or indirectly appropriate money or property when they are favorably reported by House committees.

House Manual—A commonly used title for the handbook of the rules of the House of Representatives, published in each Congress. Its official title is *Constitution, Jefferson's Manual, and Rules of the House of Representatives.*

House of Representatives—The house of Congress in which states are represented roughly in proportion to their populations, but every state is guaranteed at least one representative. By law, the number of voting representatives is fixed at 435. Four delegates and one resident commissioner also serve in the House; they may vote in their committees but not on the House floor. Although the House and

Senate have equal legislative power, the Constitution gives the House sole authority to originate revenue measures. The House also claims the right to originate appropriation measures, a claim the Senate disputes in theory but concedes in practice. The House has the sole power to impeach, and it elects the president when no candidate has received a majority of the electoral votes. It is sometimes referred to as the lower body.

Immunity—(1) Members' constitutional protection from lawsuits and arrest in connection with their legislative duties. They may not be tried for libel or slander for anything they say on the floor of a house or in committee. Nor may they be arrested while attending sessions of their houses or when traveling to or from sessions of Congress, except when charged with treason, a felony, or a breach of the peace. (2) In the case of a witness before a committee, a grant of protection from prosecution based on that person's testimony to the committee. It is used to compel witnesses to testify who would otherwise refuse to do so on the constitutional ground of possible self-incrimination. Under such a grant, none of a witness's testimony may be used against him or her in a court proceeding except in a prosecution for perjury or for giving a false statement to Congress. *(See also Contempt of Congress.)*

Impeachment—The first step to remove the president, vice president, or other federal civil officers from office and to disqualify them from any future federal office "of honor, Trust or Profit." An impeachment is a formal charge of treason, bribery, or "other high Crimes and Misdemeanors." The House has the sole power of impeachment and the Senate the sole power of trying the charges and convicting. The House impeaches by a simple majority vote; conviction requires a two-thirds vote of all senators present.

Impoundment—An executive branch action or inaction that delays or withholds the expenditure or obligation of budget authority provided by law. The Impoundment Control Act of 1974 classifies impoundments as either deferrals or rescissions, requires the president to notify Congress about all such actions, and gives Congress authority to approve or reject them. The Constitution is unclear on whether a president may refuse to spend appropriated money, but Congress usually expects the president to spend at least enough to achieve the purposes for which the money was provided whether or not he agrees with those purposes.

Instruct Conferees—A formal action by a house urging its conferees to uphold a particular position on a measure in conference. The instruction may be to insist on certain provisions in the measure as passed by that house or to accept a provision in the version passed by the other house. Conferees are not bound by instructions and a conference report is not subject to a point of order on the ground that instructions were violated.

Investigative Power—The authority of Congress and its committees to pursue investigations, upheld by the Supreme Court but limited to matters related to, and in furtherance of, a legitimate task of the Congress. Standing committees in both houses are permanently authorized to investigate matters within their jurisdictions. Major investigations are sometimes conducted by temporary select, special, or joint committees established by resolutions for that purpose.

Some rules of the House provide certain safeguards for witnesses and others during investigative hearings. These permit counsel to accompany witnesses, require that each witness receive a copy of the committee's rules, and order the committee to go into closed session if it believes the testimony to be heard might defame, degrade, or incriminate any person. The committee may subsequently decide to hear such testimony in open session. The Senate has no rules of this kind.

Item Veto—A procedure (sometimes called a line-item veto), available between January 1997 and June 1998, that permitted the president to cancel amounts of new discretionary appropriations (budget authority), as well as new items of direct spending (entitlements) and certain limited tax benefits, unless Congress disapproved by law within a limited period of time. The item veto thus allowed the president to reject the funding level approved by Congress for specific programs without being forced to veto the entire legislation. But the Supreme Court in 1998 declared the 1996 Line-Item Veto Act unconstitutional. The Court found that the veto was "the functional equivalent of partial repeal of acts of Congress," even though "there is no provision in the Constitution that authorizes the president to enact, to ammend, or to repeal statutes."

Joint Committee—A committee composed of members selected from each house. The functions of most joint committees involve investigation, research, or oversight of agencies closely related to Congress. Permanent joint committees, created by statute, are sometimes called standing joint committees. Once quite numerous, only four joint committees remained as of 1999: Joint Economic, Joint Taxation, Joint Library, and Joint Printing. None has authority to report legislation.

Joint Resolution—A legislative measure that Congress uses for purposes other than general legislation. Like a bill, it has the force of law when passed by both houses and either approved by the president or passed over the president's veto. Unlike a bill, a joint resolution enacted into law is not called an act; it retains its original title.

Most often, joint resolutions deal with such relatively limited matters as the correction of errors in existing law, continuing appropriations, a single appropriation, or the establishment of permanent joint committees. Unlike bills, however, joint resolutions also are used to propose constitutional amendments; these do not require the president's signature and become effective only when ratified by three-fourths of the states. The House designates joint resolutions as H.J. Res., the Senate as S.J. Res. Each house numbers its joint resolutions consecutively in the order of introduction during a two-year Congress.

Joint Session—Informally, any combined meeting of the Senate and the House. Technically, a joint session is a combined meeting to count the electoral votes for president and vice president or to hear a presidential address, such as the State of the Union message; any other formal combined gathering of both houses is called a joint meeting.

Joint Sponsorship—Two or more members sponsoring the same measure.

Journal—The official record of House or Senate actions, including every motion offered, every vote cast, amendments agreed to, quorum calls, and so forth. Unlike the *Congressional Record,* it does not provide reports of speeches, debates, statements, and the like. The Constitution requires each house to maintain a *Journal* and to publish it periodically.

Junket—A member's trip at government expense, especially abroad, ostensibly on official business but, it is often alleged, for pleasure.

King of the Mountain (or Hill Rule)—*(See Queen of the Hill Rule.)*

LA—*(See Legislative Assistant.)*

Lame Duck—Jargon for a member who has not been reelected, or did not seek reelection, and is serving the balance of his or her term. Lame Duck Session: A session of a Congress held after the election for the succeeding Congress, so-called after the lame duck members still serving.

Law—An act of Congress that has been signed by the president, passed over the president's veto, or allowed to become law without the president's signature.

Legislation—(1) A synonym for legislative measures: bills and joint resolutions. (2) Provisions in such measures or in substantive amendments offered to them. (3) In some contexts, provisions that change existing substantive or authorizing law, rather than provisions that make appropriations.

Legislation on an Appropriation Bill—A common reference to provisions changing existing law that appear in, or are offered as amendments to, a general appropriation bill. A House rule prohibits the inclusion of such provisions in general appropriation bills unless they retrench expenditures. An analogous Senate rule permits points of order against amendments to a general appropriation bill that propose general legislation.

Legislative Assistant (LA)—A member's staff person responsible for monitoring and preparing legislation on particular subjects and for advising the member on them; commonly referred to as an LA.

Legislative Day—The day that begins when a house meets after an adjournment and ends when it next adjourns. Because the House of Representatives normally adjourns at the end of a daily session, its legislative and calendar days usually coincide. The Senate, however, frequently recesses at the end of a daily session, and its legislative day may extend over several calendar days, weeks, or months. Among other uses, this technicality permits the Senate to save time by circumventing its morning hour, a procedure required at the beginning of every legislative day

Legislative History—(1) A chronological list of actions taken on a measure during its progress through the legislative process. (2) The official documents relating to a measure, the entries in the *Journals* of the two houses on that measure, and the *Congressional Record* text of its consideration in both houses. The documents include all committee reports and the conference report and joint explanatory statement, if any. Courts and affected federal agencies study a measure's legislative history for congressional intent about its purpose and interpretation.

Legislative Process—(1) Narrowly, the stages in the enactment of a law from introduction to final disposition. An introduced measure that becomes law typically travels through reference to committee; committee and subcommittee consideration; report to the chamber; floor consideration; amendment; passage; engrossment; messaging to the other house; similar steps in that house, including floor amendment of the measure; return of the measure to the first house; consideration of amendments between the houses or a conference to resolve their differences; approval of the conference report by both houses; enrollment; approval by the president or override of the president's veto; and deposit with the Archivist of the United States. (2) Broadly, the political, lobbying, and other factors that affect or influence the process of enacting laws.

Legislative Veto—A procedure, declared unconstitutional in 1983, that allowed Congress or one of its houses to nullify certain actions of the president, executive branch agencies, or independent agencies. Sometimes called congressional vetoes or congressional disapprovals. Following the Supreme Courts 1983 decision, Congress amended several legislative veto statutes to require enactment of joint resolutions, which are subject to presidential veto, for nullifying executive branch actions.

Line Item—Generally, an amount in an appropriation measure. It can refer to a single appropriation account or to separate amounts within the account. In the congressional budget process, the term usually refers to assumptions about the funding of particular programs or accounts that underlie the broad functional amounts in a budget resolution. These assumptions are discussed in the reports accompanying each resolution and are not binding.

Line-Item Veto—*(See Item Veto.)*

Loan Guarantee—A statutory commitment by the federal government to pay part or all of a loan's principal and interest to a lender or the holder of a security in case the borrower defaults.

Lobby—To try to persuade members of Congress to propose, pass, modify, or defeat proposed legislation or to change or repeal existing laws. A lobbyist attempts to promote his or her own preferences or those of a group, organization, or industry. Originally the term referred to persons frequenting the lobbies or corridors of legislative chambers in order to speak to lawmakers. In a general sense, lobbying includes not only direct contact with members but also indirect attempts to influence them, such as writing to them or persuading others to write or visit them, attempting to mold public opinion toward a desired legislative goal by various means, and contributing or arranging for contributions to members election campaigns. The right to lobby stems from the First Amendment to the Constitution, which bans laws that abridge the right of the people to petition the government for a redress of grievances.

Logrolling—Jargon for a legislative tactic or bargaining strategy in which members try to build support for their legislation by promising to support legislation desired by other members or by accepting amendments they hope will induce their colleagues to vote for their bill.

Mace—The symbol of the office of the House sergeant at arms. Under the direction of the Speaker, the sergeant at arms is responsible for preserving order on the House floor by holding up the mace in front of an unruly member, or by carrying the mace up and down the aisles to quell boisterous behavior. When the House is in session, the mace sits on a pedestal at the Speaker's right; when the House is in Committee of the Whole, it is moved to a lower pedestal. The mace is 46 inches high and consists of 13 ebony rods bound in silver and topped by a silver globe with a silver eagle, wings outstretched, perched on it.

Majority Leader—The majority party's chief floor spokesman, elected by that party's caucus—sometimes called floor leader. In the Senate, the majority leader also develops the party's political and procedural strategy, usually in collaboration with other party officials and committee chairmen. He negotiates the Senate's agenda and committee ratios with the minority leader and usually calls up measures for floor action. The chamber traditionally concedes to the majority leader the right to determine the days on which it will meet and the hours at which it will convene and adjourn. In the House, the majority leader is the Speaker's deputy and heir apparent. He helps plan the floor agenda and the party's legislative strategy and often speaks for the party leadership in debate.

Managers—(1) The official title of members appointed to a conference committee, commonly called conferees. The ranking majority and minority managers for each house also manage floor consideration of the committee's conference report. (2) The members who manage the initial floor consideration of a measure. (3) The official title of House members appointed to present impeachment articles to the Senate and to act as prosecutors on behalf of the House during the Senate trial of the impeached person.

Mandatory Appropriations—Amounts that Congress must appropriate annually because it has no discretion over them unless it first amends existing substantive law. Certain entitlement programs, for example, require annual appropriations.

Markup—A meeting or series of meetings by a committee or subcommittee during which members mark up a measure by offering, debating, and voting on amendments to it.

Members' Allowances—Official expenses that are paid for or for which members are reimbursed by their houses. Among these are the costs of office space in congressional buildings and in their home states or districts; office equipment and supplies; postage-free mailings (the franking privilege); a set number of trips to and from home states or districts, as well as travel elsewhere on official business; telephone and other telecommunications services; and staff salaries.

Method of Equal Proportions—The mathematical formula used since 1950 to determine how the 435 seats in the House of Representatives should be distributed among the 50 states in the apportionment following each decennial census. It minimizes as much as possible the proportional difference between the average district population in any two states. Because the Constitution guarantees each state at least one representative, 50 seats are automatically apportioned. The formula calculates priority numbers for each state, assigns the first of the 385 remaining seats to the state with the highest priority number, the second to the state with the next highest number, and so on until all seats are distributed. *(See Apportionment.)*

Midterm Election—The general election for members of Congress that occurs in November of the second year in a presidential term.

Minority Leader—The minority party's leader and chief floor spokesman, elected by the party caucus; sometimes called minority floor leader. With the assistance of other party officials and the ranking minority members of committees, the minority leader devises the party's political and procedural strategy.

Minority Staff—Employees who assist the minority party members of a committee. Most committees hire separate majority and minority party staffs, but they also may hire nonpartisan staff.

Morning Business—In the Senate, routine business transacted at the beginning of the morning hour and by unanimous consent at the demand of any senator during the day.

Morning Hour—A two-hour period at the beginning of a new legislative day during which the Senate is supposed to conduct routine business, call the calendar on Mondays, and deal with other matters described in a Senate rule. In practice, it often does not occur because the Senate frequently recesses, rather than adjourns, at the end of a daily session and therefore the rule does not apply when it next meets.

Motion—A formal proposal for a procedural action, such as to consider, to amend, to lay on the table, to reconsider, to recess, or to adjourn. It has been estimated that at least 85 motions are possible under various circumstances in the House of Representatives, somewhat fewer in the Senate. Not all motions are created equal; some are privileged or preferential and enjoy priority over others. And some motions are debatable, amendable or divisible, while others are not.

Multiyear Appropriation—An appropriation that remains available for spending or obligation for more than one fiscal year; the exact period of time is specified in the act making the appropriation.

Multiyear Authorization—(1) Legislation that authorizes the existence or continuation of an agency, program, or activity for more than one fiscal year. (2) Legislation that authorizes appropriations for an agency, program, or activity for more than one fiscal year.

Nomination—A proposed presidential appointment to a federal office submitted to the Senate for confirmation. Approval is by majority vote. The Constitution explicitly requires confirmation for ambassadors, consuls, public Ministers (department heads), and Supreme Court justices. By law, other federal judges, all military promotions of officers, and many high-level civilian officials must be confirmed.

Oath of Office—Upon taking office, members of Congress must swear or affirm that they will "support and defend the Constitution . . . against all enemies, foreign and domestic," that they will "bear true faith and allegiance" to the Constitution, that they take the obligation "freely, without any mental reservation or purpose of evasion," and that they will "well and faithfully discharge the duties" of their office. The oath is required by the Constitution; the wording is prescribed by a statute. All House members must take the oath at the beginning of each new Congress.

Omnibus Bill—A measure that combines the provisions of several disparate subjects into a single and often lengthy bill.

Open Rule—A special rule from the House Rules Committee that permits members to offer as many floor amendments as they wish as long as the amendments are germane and do not violate other House rules.

Order of Business (House)—The sequence of events during the meeting of the House on a new legislative day prescribed by a House rule; also called the general order of business. The sequence consists of (1) the chaplain's prayer; (2) approval of the *Journal;* (3) pledge of allegiance (4) correction of the reference of public bills; (5) disposal of business on the Speaker's table; (6) unfinished business; (7) the morning hour call of committees and consideration of their bills (largely obsolete); (8) motions to go into Committee of the Whole; and (9) orders of the day (also obsolete). In practice, on days specified in the rules, the items of business that follow approval of the *Journal* are supplanted in part by the special order of business (for example, the corrections, discharge, or private calendars or motions to suspend the rules) and on any day by other privileged business (for example, general appropriation bills and special rules) or measures made in order by special rules. By this combination of an order of business with privileged interruptions, the House gives precedence to certain categories of important legislation, brings to the floor other major legislation from its calendars in any order it chooses, and provides expeditious processing for minor and noncontroversial measures.

Order of Business (Senate)—The sequence of events at the beginning of a new legislative day prescribed by Senate rules. The sequence consists of (1) the chaplain's prayer; (2) pledge of allegiance, (3)*Journal* reading and correction; (4) morning business in the morning hour; (5) call of the calendar during the morning hour; and (6) unfinished business.

Original Jurisdiction—The authority of certain committees to originate a measure and report it to the chamber. For example, general appropriation bills reported by the House Appropriations Committee are original bills, and special rules reported by the House Rules Committee are original resolutions.

Other Body—A commonly used reference to a house by a member of the other house. Congressional comity discourages members from directly naming the other house during debate.

Outlays—Amounts of government spending. They consist of payments, usually by check or in cash, to liquidate obligations incurred in prior fiscal years as well as in the current year, including the net lending of funds under budget authority. In federal budget accounting, net outlays are calculated by subtracting the amounts of refunds and various kinds of reimbursements to the government from actual spending.

Override a Veto—Congressional enactment of a measure over the president's veto. A veto override requires a recorded two-thirds vote of those voting in each house, a quorum being present. Because the president must return the vetoed measure to its house of origin, that house votes first, but neither house is required to attempt an override, whether immediately or at all. If an override attempt fails in the house of origin, the veto stands and the measure dies.

Oversight—Congressional review of the way in which federal agencies implement laws to ensure that they are carrying out the intent of Congress and to inquire into the efficiency of the implementation and the effectiveness of the law. The Legislative Reorganization Act of 1946 defined oversight as the function of exercising continuous watchfulness over the execution of the laws by the executive branch.

Parliamentarian—The official advisor to the presiding officer in each house on questions of procedure. The parliamentarian and his assistants also answer procedural questions from members and congressional staff, refer measures to committees on behalf of the presiding officer, and maintain compilations of the precedents. The House parliamentarian revises the House Manual at the beginning of every Congress and usually reviews special rules before the Rules Committee reports them to the House. Either a parliamentarian or an assistant is always present and near the podium during sessions of each house.

Party Caucus—Generic term for each party's official organization in each house. Only House Democrats officially call their organization a caucus. House and Senate Republicans and Senate Democrats call their organizations conferences. The party caucuses elect their leaders, approve committee assignments and chairmanships (or ranking minority members, if the party is in the minority), establish party committees and study groups, and discuss party and legislative policies. On rare occasions, they have stripped members of committee seniority or expelled them from the caucus for party disloyalty.

Permanent Appropriation—An appropriation that remains continuously available, without current action or renewal by Congress, under the terms of a previously enacted authorization or appropriation law. One such appropriation provides for payment of interest on the public debt and another the salaries of members of Congress.

Permanent Authorization—An authorization without a time limit. It usually does not specify any limit on the funds that may be appropriated for the agency, program, or activity that it authorizes, leaving such amounts to the discretion of the appropriations committees and the two houses.

Pocket Veto—The indirect veto of a bill as a result of the president withholding approval of it until after Congress has adjourned sine die. A bill the president does not sign, but does not formally veto while Congress is in session, automatically becomes a law ten days (excluding Sundays) after it is received. But if Congress adjourns its annual session during that ten-day period, the measure dies even if the president does not formally veto it.

Point of Order—A parliamentary term used in committee and on the floor to object to an alleged violation of a rule and to demand that the chair enforce the rule. The point of order immediately halts the proceedings until the chair decides whether the contention is valid.

Pork or Pork Barrel Legislation—Pejorative terms for federal appropriations, bills, or policies that provide funds to benefit a legislators district or state, with the implication that the legislator presses for enactment of such benefits to ingratiate himself or herself with constituents rather than on the basis of an impartial, objective assessment of need or merit.

The terms are often applied to such benefits as new parks, post offices, dams, canals, bridges, roads, water projects, sewage treatment plants, and public works of any kind, as well as demonstration projects, research grants, and relocation of government facilities. Funds released by the president for various kinds of benefits or government contracts approved by him allegedly for political purposes are also sometimes referred to as pork.

Postcloture Filibuster—A filibuster conducted after the Senate invokes cloture. It employs an array of procedural tactics rather than lengthy speeches to delay final action. The Senate curtailed the postcloture filibusters effectiveness by closing a variety of loopholes in the cloture rule in 1979 and 1986.

Power of the Purse—A reference to the constitutional power Congress has over legislation to raise revenue and appropriate monies from the Treasury. Article I, Section 8 states that Congress "shall have Power To lay and collect Taxes, Duties, Imposts and Excises, [and] to pay the Debts." Section 9 declares: "No Money shall be drawn from the Treasury, but in Consequence of Appropriations made by Law."

Preamble—Introductory language describing the reasons for and intent of a measure, sometimes called a whereas clause. It occasionally appears in joint, concurrent, and simple resolutions but rarely in bills.

Precedent—A previous ruling on a parliamentary matter or a long-standing practice or custom of a house. Precedents serve to control arbitrary rulings and serve as the common law of a house.

President of the Senate—The vice president of the United States in his constitutional role as presiding officer of the Senate. The Constitution permits the vice president to cast a vote in the Senate only to break a tie, but he is not required to do so.

President Pro Tempore—Under the Constitution, an officer elected by the Senate to preside over it during the absence of the vice president of the United States. Often referred to as the "pro tem," he is usually the majority party senator with the longest continuous service in the chamber and also, by virtue of his seniority, a committee chairman. When attending to committee and other duties, the president pro tempore appoints other senators to preside.

Presiding Officer—In a formal meeting, the individual authorized to maintain order and decorum, recognize members to speak or offer motions, and apply and interpret the chamber's rules, precedents, and practices. The Speaker of the House and the president of the Senate are the chief presiding officers in their respective houses.

Previous Question—A nondebatable motion which, when agreed to by majority vote, usually cuts off further debate, prevents the offering of additional amendments, and brings the pending matter to an immediate vote. It is a major debate-limiting device in the House; it is not permitted in Committee of the Whole or in the Senate.

Private Bill—A bill that applies to one or more specified persons, corporations, institutions, or other entities, usually to grant relief when no other legal remedy is available to them. Many private bills deal with claims against the federal government, immigration and naturalization cases, and land titles.

Private Calendar—Commonly used title for a calendar in the House reserved for private bills and resolutions favorably reported by committees. The private calendar is officially called the Calendar of the Committee of the Whole House.

Private Law—A private bill enacted into law. Private laws are numbered in the same fashion as public laws.

Privilege—An attribute of a motion, measure, report, question, or proposition that gives it priority status for consideration. Privileged motions and motions to bring up privileged questions are not debatable.

Privilege of the Floor—In addition to the members of a house, certain individuals are admitted to its floor while it is in session. The rules of the two houses differ somewhat, but both extend the privilege to the president and vice president, Supreme Court justices, cabinet members, state governors, former members of that house, members of the other house, certain officers and officials of Congress, certain staff of that house in the discharge of official duties, and the chamber's former parliamentarians. They also allow access to a limited number of committee and members' staff when their presence is necessary.

Pro Forma Amendment—In the House, an amendment that ostensibly proposes to change a measure or another amendment by moving "to strike the last word" or "to strike the requisite number of words." A member offers it not to make any actual change in the measure or amendment but only to obtain time for debate.

Pro Tem—A common reference to the president pro tempore of the Senate or, occasionally, to a Speaker pro tempore. *(See President Pro Tempore, Speaker Pro Tempore.)*

Proxy Voting—The practice of permitting a member to cast the vote of an absent colleague in addition to his own vote. Proxy voting is prohibited on the floors of the House and Senate, but the Senate permits its committees to authorize proxy voting, and most do. In 1995, House rules were changed to prohibit proxy voting in committee.

Public Bill—A bill dealing with general legislative matters having national applicability or applying to the federal government or to a class of persons, groups, or organizations.

Public Debt—Federal government debt incurred by the Treasury or the Federal Financing Bank by the sale of securities to the public or borrowings from a federal fund or account.

Public Law—A public bill or joint resolution enacted into law. It is cited by the letters P.L. followed by a hyphenated number. The digits before the hyphen indicate the number of the Congress in which it was enacted; the digits after the hyphen indicate its position in the numerical sequence of public measures that became law during that Congress. For example, the Budget Enforcement Act of 1990 became P.L. 101-508 because it was the 508th measure in that sequence for the 101st Congress. *(See also Private Law.)*

Queen of the Hill Rule—A special rule from the House Rules Committee that permits votes on a series of amendments, especially complete substitutes for a measure, in a specified order, but directs that the amendment receiving the greatest number of votes shall be the winning one. This kind of rule permits the House to vote directly on a variety of alternatives to a measure. In doing so, it sets aside the precedent that once an amendment has been adopted, no further amendments may be offered to the text it has amended. Under an earlier practice, the Rules Committee reported "king of the hill" rules under which there also could be votes on a series of amendments, again in a specified order. If more than one of the amendments was adopted under this kind of rule, it was the last amendment to receive a majority vote that was considered as having been finally adopted, whether or not it had received the greatest number of votes.

Quorum—The minimum number of members required to be present for the transaction of business. Under the Constitution, a quorum in each house is a majority of its members: 218 in the House and 51 in the Senate when there are no vacancies. By House rule, a quorum in Committee of the Whole is 100. In practice, both houses usually assume a quorum is present even if it is not, unless a member makes a point of no quorum in the House or suggests the absence of a quorum in the Senate. Consequently, each house transacts much of its business, and even passes bills, when only a few members are present.

For House and Senate committees, chamber rules allow a minimum quorum of one-third of a committee's members to conduct most types of business.

Quorum Call—A procedure for determining whether a quorum is present in a chamber. In the Senate, a clerk calls the roll (roster) of senators. The House usually employs its electronic voting system.

Ramseyer Rule—A House rule that requires a committee's report on a bill or joint resolution to show the changes the measure, and any committee amendments to it, would make in existing law.

Rank or Ranking—A member's position on the list of his party's members on a committee or subcommittee. When first assigned to a committee, a member is usually placed at the bottom of the list, then moves up as those above leave the committee. On subcommittees, however, a member's rank may not have anything to do with the length of his service on it.

Ranking Member—(1) Most often a reference to the minority member with the highest ranking on a committee or subcommittee. (2) A reference to the majority member next in rank to the chairman or to the highest ranking majority member present at a committee or subcommittee meeting.

Ratification—(1) The president's formal act of promulgating a treaty after the Senate has approved it. The resolution of ratification agreed to by the Senate is the procedural vehicle by which the Senate gives its consent to ratification. (2) A state legislature's act in approving a proposed constitutional amendment. Such an amendment becomes effective when ratified by three-fourths of the states.

Reapportionment—*(See Apportionment.)*

Recess—(1) A temporary interruption or suspension of a meeting of a chamber or committee. Unlike an adjournment, a recess does not end a legislative day. Because the Senate often recesses from one calendar day to another, its legislative day may extend over several calendar days, weeks, or even months. (2) A period of adjournment for more than three days to a day certain, especially over a holiday or in August during odd-numbered years.

Recess Appointment—A presidential appointment to a vacant federal position made after the Senate has adjourned sine die or has adjourned or recessed for more than 30 days. If the president submits the recess appointee's nomination during the next session of the Senate, that individual can continue to serve until the end of the session even though the Senate might have rejected the nomination. When appointed to a vacancy that existed 30 days before the end of the last Senate session, a recess appointee is not paid until confirmed.

Recommit—To send a measure back to the committee that reported it; sometimes called a straight motion to recommit to distinguish it from a motion to recommit with instructions. A successful motion to recommit kills the measure unless it is accompanied by instructions.

Recommit a Conference Report—To return a conference report to the conference committee for renegotiation of some or all of its agreements. A motion to recommit may be offered with or without instructions.

Recommit with Instructions—To send a measure back to a committee with instructions to take some action on it. Invariably in the House and often in the Senate, when the motion recommits to a standing committee, the instructions require the committee to report the measure "forthwith" with specified amendments.

Reconciliation—A procedure for changing existing revenue and spending laws to bring total federal revenues and spending within the limits established in a budget resolution. Congress has applied reconciliation chiefly to revenues and mandatory spending programs, especially entitlements. Discretionary spending is controlled through annual appropriation bills.

Recorded Vote—(1) Generally, any vote in which members are recorded by name for or against a measure; also called a record vote or roll-call vote. The only recorded vote in the Senate is a vote by the yeas and nays and is commonly called a roll-call vote. (2) Technically, a recorded vote is one demanded in the House of Representatives and supported by at least one-fifth of a quorum (44 members) in the House sitting as the House or at least 25 members in Committee of the Whole.

Recorded Vote by Clerks—A voting procedure in the House where members pass through the appropriate "aye" or "no" aisle in the chamber and cast their votes by depositing a signed green (yea) or red (no) card in a ballot box. These votes are tabulated by clerks and reported to the chair. The electronic voting system is much more convenient and has largely supplanted this procedure. *(See Committee of the Whole, Recorded Vote, Teller Vote.)*

Redistricting—The redrawing of congressional district boundaries within a state after a decennial census. Redistricting may be required to equalize district populations or to accommodate an increase or decrease in the number of a state's House seats that might have resulted from the decennial apportionment. The state governments determine the district lines. *(See Apportionment, Congressional District, Gerrymandering.)*

Referral—The assignment of a measure to committee for consideration. Under a House rule, the Speaker can refuse to refer a measure he believes is "of an obscene or insulting character."

Report—(1) As a verb, a committee is said to report when it submits a measure or other document to its parent chamber. (2) A clerk is said to report when he or she reads a measure's title, text, or the text of an amendment to the body at the direction of the chair. (3) As a noun, a committee document that accompanies a reported measure. It describes the measure, the committee's views on it, its costs, and the changes it proposes to make in existing law; it also includes certain impact statements. (4) A committee document submitted to its parent chamber that describes the results of an investigation or other study or provides information it is required to provide by rule or law.

Representative—An elected and duly sworn member of the House of Representatives who is entitled to vote in the chamber. The Constitution requires that a representative be at least 25 years old, a citizen of the United States for at least seven years, and an inhabitant of the state from which he or she is elected. Customarily, the member resides in the district he or she represents. Representatives are elected in even-numbered years to two-year terms that begin the following January.

Reprimand—A formal condemnation of a member for misbehavior, considered a milder reproof than censure. The House of Representatives first used it in 1976. The Senate first used in 1991. *(See also Censure, Code of Official Conduct, Denounce, Ethics Rules, Expulsion, Seniority Loss.)*

Rescission—A provision of law that repeals previously enacted budget authority in whole or in part. Under the Impoundment Control Act of 1974, the president can impound such funds by sending a message to Congress requesting one or more rescissions and the reasons for doing so. If Congress does not pass a rescission bill for the programs requested by the president within 45 days of continuous session after receiving the message, the president must make the funds available for obligation and expenditure. If the president does not, the comptroller general of the United States is authorized to bring suit to compel the release of those funds. A rescission bill may rescind all, part, or none of an amount proposed by the president, and may rescind funds the president has not impounded.

Reserving the Right to Object—A member's declaration that at some indefinite future time he or she may object to a unanimous consent request. It is an attempt to circumvent the requirement that a member may prevent such an action only by objecting immediately after it is proposed.

Resident Commissioner from Puerto Rico—A nonvoting member of the House of Representatives, elected to a four-year term. The resident commissioner has the same status and privileges as delegates. Like the delegates, the resident commissioner may not vote in the House or Committee of the Whole.

Resolution—(1) A simple resolution; that is, a nonlegislative measure effective only in the house in which it is proposed and not requiring concurrence by the other chamber or approval by the president. Simple resolutions are designated H. Res. in the House and S. Res. in the Senate. Simple resolutions express nonbinding opinions on policies or issues or deal with the internal affairs or prerogatives of a house. (2) Any type of resolution: simple, concurrent, or joint. *(See Concurrent Resolution, Joint Resolution.)*

Resolution of Inquiry—A resolution usually simple rather than concurrent calling on the president or the head of an executive agency to provide specific information or papers to one or both houses.

Resolution of Ratification—The Senate vehicle for agreeing to a treaty. The constitutionally mandated vote of two-thirds of the senators present and voting applies to the adoption of this resolution. However, it may also contain amendments, reservations, declarations, or understandings that the Senate had previously added to it by majority vote.

Revenue Legislation—Measures that levy new taxes or tariffs or change existing ones. Under Article I, Section 7, Clause 1 of the Constitution, the House of Representatives originates federal revenue measures, but the Senate can propose amendments to them. The House Ways and Means Committee and the Senate Finance Committee have jurisdiction over such measures, with a few minor exceptions.

Revise and Extend One's Remarks—A unanimous consent request to publish in the *Congressional Record* a statement a member did not deliver on the floor, a longer statement than the one made on the floor, or miscellaneous extraneous material.

Revolving Fund—A trust fund or account whose income remains available to finance its continuing operations without any fiscal year limitation.

Rider—Congressional slang for an amendment unrelated or extraneous to the subject matter of the measure to which it is attached. Riders often contain proposals that are less likely to become law on their own merits as separate bills, either because of opposition in the committee of jurisdiction, resistance in the other house, or the probability of a presidential veto. Riders are more common in the Senate.

Roll Call—A call of the roll to determine whether a quorum is present, to establish a quorum, or to vote on a question. Usually, the House uses its electronic voting system for a roll call. The Senate does not have an electronic voting system; its roll is always called by a clerk.

Rule—(1) A permanent regulation that a house adopts to govern its conduct of business, its procedures, its internal organization, behavior of its members, regulation of its facilities, duties of an officer, or some other subject it chooses to govern in that form. (2) In the House, a privileged simple resolution reported by the Rules Committee that provides methods and conditions for floor consideration of a measure or, rarely, several measures.

Second-Degree Amendment—An amendment to an amendment in the first degree. It is usually a perfecting amendment.

Secretary of the Senate—The chief administrative and budgetary officer of the Senate. The secretary manages a wide range of functions that support the operation of the Senate as an organization as well as those functions necessary to its legislative process, including recordkeeping, document management, certifications, housekeeping services, administration of oaths, and lobbyist registrations.

Section—A subdivision of a bill or statute. By law, a section must be numbered and, as nearly as possible, contain "a single proposition of enactment."

Select or Special Committee—A committee established by a resolution in either house for a special purpose and, usually, for a limited time. Most select and special committees are assigned specific investigations or studies, but are not authorized to report measures to their chambers.

Senate—The house of Congress in which each state is represented by two senators; each senator has one vote. Article V of the Constitution declares that "No State, without its Consent, shall be deprived of its equal Suffrage in the Senate." The Constitution also gives the Senate equal legislative power with the House of Representatives. Although the Senate is prohibited from originating revenue measures, and as a matter of practice it does not originate appropriation measures, it can amend both. Only the Senate can give or withhold consent to treaties and nominations from the president. It also acts as a court to try impeachments by the House and elects the vice president when no candidate receives a majority of the electoral votes. It is often referred to as "the upper body," but not by members of the House.

Senate Manual—The handbook of the Senate's standing rules and orders and the laws and other regulations that apply to the Senate, usually published once each Congress.

Senator—A duly sworn elected or appointed member of the Senate. The Constitution requires that a senator be at least 30 years old, a citizen of the United States for at least nine years, and an inhabitant of the state from which he or she is elected. Senators are usually elected in even-numbered years to six-year terms that begin the following January. When a vacancy occurs before the end of a term, the state governor can appoint a replacement to fill the position until a successor is chosen at the state's next general election or, if specified under state law, the next feasible date for such an election, to serve the remainder of the term. Until the Seventeenth Amendment was ratified in 1913, senators were chosen by their state legislatures.

Senatorial Courtesy—The Senate's practice of declining to confirm a presidential nominee for an office in the state of a senator of the president's party unless that senator approves.

Seniority—The priority, precedence, or status accorded members according to the length of their continuous service in a house or on a committee.

Seniority Loss—A type of punishment that reduces a member's seniority on his or her committees, including the loss of chairmanships. Party caucuses in both houses have occasionally imposed such punishment on their members, for example, for publicly supporting candidates of the other party.

Seniority Rule—The customary practice, rather than a rule, of assigning the chairmanship of a committee to the majority party member who has served on the committee for the longest continuous period of time.

Seniority System—A collection of long-standing customary practices under which members with longer continuous service than their colleagues in their house or on their committees receive various kinds of preferential treatment. Although some of the practices are no longer as rigidly observed as in the past, they still pervade the organization and procedures of Congress.

Sequestration—A procedure for canceling budgetary resources that is, money available for obligation or spending—to enforce budget limitations established in law. Sequestered funds are no longer available for obligation or expenditure.

Sergeant at Arms—The officer in each house responsible for maintaining order, security, and decorum in its wing of the Capitol, including the chamber and its galleries. Although elected by their respective houses, both sergeants at arms are invariably the candidates of the majority party.

Session—(1) The annual series of meetings of a Congress. Under the Constitution, Congress must assemble at least once a year at noon on January 3 unless it appoints a different day by law. (2) The meetings of Congress or of one house convened by the president under his constitutional authority, called a special session. (3) A house is said to be in session during the period of a day when it is meeting.

Severability (or Separability) Clause—Language stating that if any particular provisions of a measure are declared invalid by the courts, the remaining provisions shall remain in effect.

Slip Law—The first official publication of a measure that has become law. It is published separately in unbound, single-sheet form or pamphlet form. A slip law usually is available two or three days after the date of the law's enactment.

Speaker—The presiding officer of the House of Representatives and the leader of its majority party. The Speaker is selected by the majority party and formally elected by the House at the beginning of each Congress. Although the Constitution does not require the Speaker to be a member of the House, in fact, all Speakers have been members.

Speaker Pro Tempore—A member of the House who is designated as the temporary presiding officer by the Speaker or elected by the House to that position during the Speaker's absence.

Speaker's Vote—The Speaker is not required to vote, and his name is not called on a roll-call vote unless he so requests. Usually, the Speaker votes either to create a tie vote, and thereby defeat a proposal, or to break a tie in favor of a proposal. Occasionally, the Speaker also votes to emphasize the importance of a matter or his special interest in it.

Special Session—A session of Congress convened by the president, under his constitutional authority, after Congress has adjourned sine die at the end of a regular session. (See Adjournment Sine Die, Session.)

Spending Authority—The technical term for backdoor spending. The Congressional Budget Act of 1974 defines it as borrowing authority, contract authority, and entitlement authority for which appropriation acts do not provide budget authority in advance. Under the Budget Act, legislation that provides new spending authority may not be considered unless it provides that the authority shall be effective only to the extent or in such amounts as provided in an appropriation act.

Sponsor—The principal proponent and introducer of a measure or an amendment.

Staff Director—The most frequently used title for the head of staff of a committee or subcommittee. On some committees, that person is called chief of staff, clerk, chief clerk, chief counsel, general counsel, or executive director. The head of a committee's minority staff is usually called minority staff director.

Standing Committee—A permanent committee established by a House or Senate standing rule or standing order. The rule also describes the subject areas on which the committee may report bills and resolutions and conduct oversight. Most introduced measures must be referred to one or more standing committees according to their jurisdictions.

Standing Order—A continuing regulation or directive that has the force and effect of a rule, but is not incorporated into the standing rules. The Senate's numerous standing orders, like its standing rules, continue from Congress to Congress unless changed or the order states otherwise. The House uses relatively few standing orders, and those it adopts expire at the end of a session of Congress.

Standing Rules—The rules of the Senate that continue from one Congress to the next and the rules of the House of Representatives that it adopts at the beginning of each new Congress.

Standing Vote—An alternative and informal term for a division vote, during which members in favor of a proposal and then members opposed stand and are counted by the chair.

Star Print—A reprint of a bill, resolution, amendment, or committee report correcting technical or substantive errors in a previous printing; so called because of the small black star that appears on the front page or cover.

State of the Union Message—A presidential message to Congress under the constitutional directive that he shall "from time to time give to the Congress Information of the State of the Union, and recommend to their Consideration such Measures as he shall judge necessary and expedient." Customarily, the president sends an annual State of the Union Message to Congress, usually late in January.

Statutes at Large—A chronological arrangement of the laws enacted in each session of Congress. Though indexed, the laws are not arranged by subject matter nor is there an indication of how they affect or change previously enacted laws. The volumes are numbered by Congress, and the laws are cited by their volume and page number. The Gramm-Rudman-Hollings Act, for example, appears as 99 Stat. 1037.

Straw Vote Prohibition—Under a House precedent, a member who has the floor during debate may not conduct a straw vote or otherwise ask for a show of support for a proposition. Only the chair may put a question to a vote.

Strike from the *Record*—Expunge objectionable remarks from the *Congressional Record*, after a member's words have been taken down on a point of order.

Subcommittee—A panel of committee members assigned a portion of the committee's jurisdiction or other functions. On legislative committees, subcommittee's hold hearings, mark up legislation, and report measures to their full committee for further action; they cannot report directly to the chamber. A subcommittees party composition usually reflects the ratio on its parent committee.

Subpoena Power—The authority granted to committees by the rules of their respective houses to issue legal orders requiring individuals to appear and testify, or to produce documents pertinent to the committee's functions, or both. Persons who do not comply with subpoenas can be cited for contempt of Congress and prosecuted.

Subsidy—Generally, a payment or benefit made by the federal government for which no current repayment is required. Subsidy payments may be designed to support the conduct of an economic enterprise or activity, such as ship operations, or to support certain market prices, as in the case of farm subsidies.

Sunset Legislation—A term sometimes applied to laws authorizing the existence of agencies or programs that expire annually or at the end of some other specified period of time. One of the purposes of setting specific expiration dates for agencies and programs is to encourage the committees with jurisdiction over them to determine whether they should be continued or terminated.

Sunshine Rules—Rules requiring open committee hearings and business meetings, including markup sessions, in both houses, and also open conference committee meetings. However, all may be closed under certain circumstances and using certain procedures required by the rules.

Super Majority—A term sometimes used for a vote on a matter that requires approval by more than a simple majority of those members present and voting; also referred to as extraordinary majority.

Supplemental Appropriation Bill—A measure providing appropriations for use in the current fiscal year, in addition to those already provided in annual general appropriation bills. Supplemental appropriations are often for unforeseen emergencies.

Suspension of the Rules (House)—An expeditious procedure for passing relatively noncontroversial or emergency measures by a two-thirds vote of those members voting, a quorum being present.

Suspension of the Rules (Senate)—A procedure to set aside one or more of the Senate's rules; it is used infrequently, and then most often to suspend the rule banning legislative amendments to appropriation bills.

Task Force—A title sometimes given to a panel of members assigned to a special project, study, or investigation. Ordinarily, these groups do not have authority to report measures to their respective houses.

Tax Expenditure—Loosely, a tax exemption or advantage, sometimes called an incentive or loophole; technically, a loss of governmental tax revenue attributable to some provision of federal tax laws that allows a special exclusion, exemption, or deduction from gross income or that provides a special credit, preferential tax rate, or deferral of tax liability.

Televised Proceedings—Television and radio coverage of the floor proceedings of the House of Representatives have been available since 1979 and of the Senate since 1986. They are broadcast over a coaxial cable system to all congressional offices and to some congressional agencies on channels reserved for that purpose. Coverage is also available free of charge to commercial and public television and radio broadcasters. The Cable-Satellite Public Affairs Network (C-SPAN) carries gavel-to-gavel coverage of both houses.

Teller Vote—A voting procedure, formerly used in the House, in which members cast their votes by passing through the center aisle to be counted, but not recorded by name, by a member from each party appointed by the chair. The House deleted the procedure from its rules in 1993, but during floor discussion of the deletion a leading member stated that a teller vote would still be available in the event of a breakdown of the electronic voting system.

Third-Degree Amendment—An amendment to a second-degree amendment. Both houses prohibit such amendments.

Third Reading—A required reading to a chamber of a bill or joint resolution by title only before the vote on passage. In modern practice, it has merely become a pro forma step.

Tie Vote—When the votes for and against a proposition are equal, it loses. The president of the Senate may cast a vote only to break a tie. Because the Speaker is invariably a member of the House, he is entitled to vote but usually does not. He may choose to do so to break, or create, a tie vote.

Title—(1) A major subdivision of a bill or act, designated by a roman numeral and usually containing legislative provisions on the same general subject. Titles are sometimes divided into subtitles as well as sections. (2) The official name of a bill or act, also called a caption or long title. (3) Some bills also have short titles that appear in the sentence immediately following the enacting clause. (4) Popular titles are the unofficial names given to some bills or acts by common usage. For example, the Balanced Budget and Emergency Deficit Control Act of 1985 (short title) is almost invariably referred to as Gramm-Rudman (popular title). In other cases, significant legislation is popularly referred to by its title number (see definition (1) above). For example, the federal legislation that requires equality of funding for women's and men's sports in educational institutions that receive federal funds is popularly called Title IX.

Track System—An occasional Senate practice that expedites legislation by dividing a day's session into two or more specific time periods, commonly called tracks, each reserved for consideration of a different measure.

Transfer Payment—A federal government payment to which individuals or organizations are entitled under law and for which no goods or services are required in return. Payments include welfare and Social Security benefits, unemployment insurance, government pensions, and veterans benefits.

Treaty—A formal document containing an agreement between two or more sovereign nations. The Constitution authorizes the president to make treaties, but he must submit them to the Senate for its approval by a two-thirds vote of the senators present. Under the Senate's rules, that vote actually occurs on a resolution of ratification. Although the Constitution does not give the House a direct role in approving treaties, that body has sometimes insisted that a revenue treaty is an invasion of its prerogatives. In any case, the House may significantly affect the application of a treaty by its equal role in enacting legislation to implement the treaty.

Trust Funds—Special accounts in the Treasury that receive earmarked taxes or other kinds of revenue collections, such as user fees, and from which payments are made for special purposes or to recipients who meet the requirements of the trust funds as established by law. Of the more than 150 federal government trust funds, several finance major entitlement programs, such as Social Security, Medicare, and retired federal employees' pensions. Others fund infrastructure construction and improvements, such as highways and airports.

Unanimous Consent—Without an objection by any member. A unanimous consent request asks permission, explicitly or implicitly, to set aside one or more rules. Both houses and their committees frequently use such requests to expedite their proceedings.

Uncontrollable Expenditures—A frequently used term for federal expenditures that are mandatory under existing law and therefore cannot be controlled by the president or Congress without a change in the existing law. Uncontrollable expenditures include spending required under entitlement programs and also fixed costs, such as interest on the public debt and outlays to pay for prior-year obligations. In recent years, uncontrollables have accounted for approximately three-quarters of federal spending in each fiscal year.

Unfunded Mandate—Generally, any provision in federal law or regulation that imposes a duty or obligation on a state or local government or private sector entity without providing the necessary funds to comply. The Unfunded Mandates Reform Act of 1995 amended the Congressional Budget Act of 1974 to provide a mechanism for the control of new unfunded mandates.

Union Calendar—A calendar of the House of Representatives for bills and resolutions favorably reported by committees that raise revenue or directly or indirectly appropriate money or property. In addition to appropriation bills, measures that authorize expenditures are also placed on this calendar. The calendar's full title is the Calendar of the Committee of the Whole House on the State of the Union.

Upper Body—A common reference to the Senate, but not used by members of the House.

U.S. Code—Popular title for the *United States Code: Containing the General and Permanent Laws of the United States in Force on. . . .* It is a consolidation and partial codification of the general and permanent laws of the United States arranged by subject under 50 titles. The first six titles deal with general or political subjects, the other 44 with subjects ranging from agriculture to war, alphabetically arranged. A supplement is published after each session of Congress, and the entire Code is revised every six years.

User Fee—A fee charged to users of goods or services provided by the federal government. When Congress levies or authorizes such fees, it determines whether the revenues should go into the general collections of the Treasury or be available for expenditure by the agency that provides the goods or services.

Veto—The president's disapproval of a legislative measure passed by Congress. He returns the measure to the house in which it originated without his signature but with a veto message stating his objections to it. When Congress is in session, the president must veto a bill within ten days, excluding Sundays, after he has received it; otherwise it becomes law without his signature. The ten-day clock begins to run at midnight following his receipt of the bill. *(See also Committee Veto, Item Veto, Override a Veto, Pocket Veto.)*

Voice Vote—A method of voting in which members who favor a question answer aye in chorus, after which those opposed answer no in chorus, and the chair decides which position prevails.

Voting—Members vote in three ways on the floor: (1) by shouting "aye" or "no" on voice votes; (2) by standing for or against on division votes; and (3) on recorded votes (including the yeas and nays), by answering "aye" or "no" when their names are called or, in the House, by recording their votes through the electronic voting system.

War Powers Resolution of 1973—An act that requires the president "in every possible instance" to consult Congress before he commits U.S. forces to ongoing or imminent hostilities. If he commits them to a combat situation without congressional consultation, he must notify Congress within 48 hours. Unless Congress declares war or otherwise authorizes the operation to continue, the forces must be withdrawn within 60 or 90 days, depending on certain conditions. No president has ever acknowledged the constitutionality of the resolution.

Well—The sunken, level, open space between members' seats and the podium at the front of each chamber. House members usually address their chamber from their party's lectern in the well on its side of the aisle. Senators usually speak at their assigned desks.

Whip—The majority or minority party member in each house who acts as assistant leader, helps plan and marshal support for party strategies, encourages party discipline, and advises his leader on how his colleagues intend to vote on the floor. In the Senate, the Republican whip's official title is assistant leader.

Yeas and Nays—A vote in which members usually respond "aye" or "no" (despite the official title of the vote) on a question when their names are called in alphabetical order. The Constitution requires the yeas and nays when a demand for it is supported by one-fifth of the members present, and it also requires an automatic yea-and-nay vote on overriding a veto. Senate precedents require the support of at least one-fifth of a quorum, a minimum of 11 members with the present membership of 100.

How a Bill Becomes a Law

This graphic shows the most typical way in which proposed legislation is enacted into law. There are more complicated, as well as simpler, routes, and most bills never become law. The process is illustrated with two hypothetical bills, House bill No. 1 (HR 1) and

Senate bill No. 2 (S 2). Bills must be passed by both houses in identical form before they can be sent to the president. The path of HR 1 is traced by a gray line, that of S 2 by a black line. In practice, most bills begin as similar proposals in both houses.

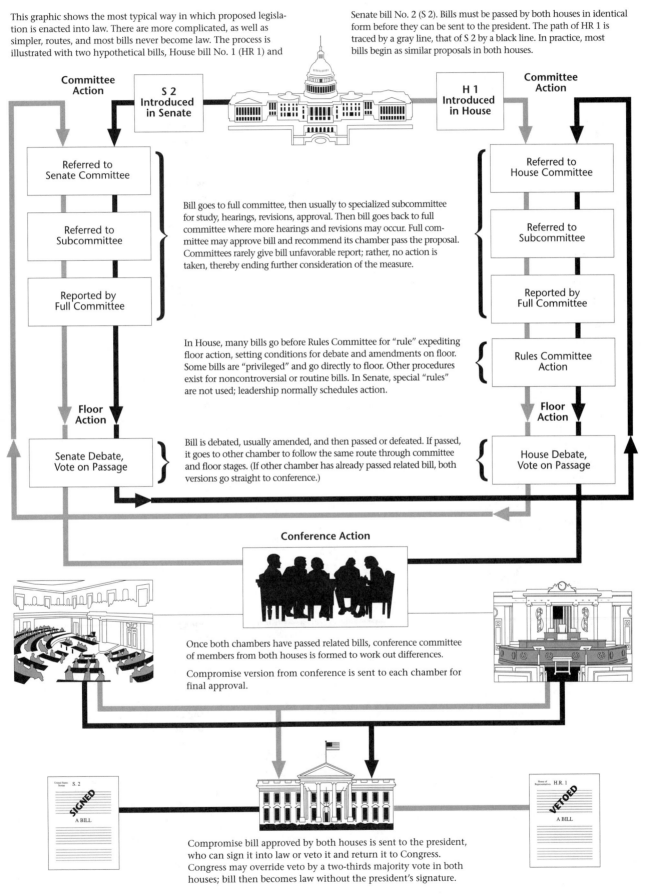

Committee Action

S 2 Introduced in Senate

H 1 Introduced in House

Committee Action

Referred to Senate Committee

Referred to Subcommittee

Reported by Full Committee

Bill goes to full committee, then usually to specialized subcommittee for study, hearings, revisions, approval. Then bill goes back to full committee where more hearings and revisions may occur. Full committee may approve bill and recommend its chamber pass the proposal. Committees rarely give bill unfavorable report; rather, no action is taken, thereby ending further consideration of the measure.

Referred to House Committee

Referred to Subcommittee

Reported by Full Committee

In House, many bills go before Rules Committee for "rule" expediting floor action, setting conditions for debate and amendments on floor. Some bills are "privileged" and go directly to floor. Other procedures exist for noncontroversial or routine bills. In Senate, special "rules" are not used; leadership normally schedules action.

Rules Committee Action

Floor Action

Senate Debate, Vote on Passage

Bill is debated, usually amended, and then passed or defeated. If passed, it goes to other chamber to follow the same route through committee and floor stages. (If other chamber has already passed related bill, both versions go straight to conference.)

Floor Action

House Debate, Vote on Passage

Conference Action

Once both chambers have passed related bills, conference committee of members from both houses is formed to work out differences.

Compromise version from conference is sent to each chamber for final approval.

S 2 — SIGNED — A BILL

H.R. 1 — VETOED — A BILL

Compromise bill approved by both houses is sent to the president, who can sign it into law or veto it and return it to Congress. Congress may override veto by a two-thirds majority vote in both houses; bill then becomes law without the president's signature.

Political Party Affiliations in Congress and the Presidency, 1789–1999

Year	Congress	House		Senate		President
		Majority party	*Principal minority party*	*Majority party*	*Principal minority party*	
1789–1791	1st	AD-38	Op-26	AD-17	Op-9	F (Washington)
1791–1793	2nd	F-37	DR-33	F-16	DR-13	F (Washington)
1793–1795	3rd	DR-57	F-48	F-17	DR-13	F (Washington)
1795–1797	4th	F-54	DR-52	F-19	DR-13	F (Washington)
1797–1799	5th	F-58	DR-48	F-20	DR-12	F (John Adams)
1799–1801	6th	F-64	DR-42	F-19	DR-13	F (John Adams)
1801–1803	7th	DR-69	F-36	DR-18	F-13	DR (Jefferson)
1803–1805	8th	DR-102	F-39	DR-25	F-9	DR (Jefferson)
1805–1807	9th	DR-116	F-25	DR-27	F-7	DR (Jefferson)
1807–1809	10th	DR-118	F-24	DR-28	F-6	DR (Jefferson)
1809–1811	11th	DR-94	F-48	DR-28	F-6	DR (Madison)
1811–1813	12th	DR-108	F-36	DR-30	F-6	DR (Madison)
1813–1815	13th	DR-112	F-68	DR-27	F-9	DR (Madison)
1815–1817	14th	DR-117	F-65	DR-25	F-11	DR (Madison)
1817–1819	15th	DR-141	F-42	DR-34	F-10	DR (Monroe)
1819–1821	16th	DR-156	F-27	DR-35	F-7	DR (Monroe)
1821–1823	17th	DR-158	F-25	DR-44	F-4	DR (Monroe)
1823–1825	18th	DR-187	F-26	DR-44	F-4	DR (Monroe)
1825–1827	19th	AD-105	J-97	AD-26	J-20	DR (John Q. Adams)
1827–1829	20th	J-119	AD-94	J-28	AD-20	DR (John Q. Adams)
1829–1831	21st	D-139	NR-74	D-26	NR-22	DR (Jackson)
1831–1833	22nd	D-141	NR-58	D-25	NR-21	D (Jackson)
1833–1835	23rd	D-147	AM-53	D-20	NR-20	D (Jackson)
1835–1837	24th	D-145	W-98	D-27	W-25	D (Jackson)
1837–1839	25th	D-108	W-107	D-30	W-18	D (Van Buren)
1839–1841	26th	D-124	W-118	D-28	W-22	D (Van Buren)
1841–1843	27th	W-133	D-102	W-28	D-22	W (W. Harrison)
						W (Tyler)
1843–1845	28th	D-142	W-79	W-28	D-25	W (Tyler)
1845–1847	29th	D-143	W-77	D-31	W-25	D (Polk)
1847–1849	30th	W-115	D-108	D-36	W-21	D (Polk)
1849–1851	31st	D-112	W-109	D-35	W-25	W (Taylor)
						W (Fillmore)
1851–1853	32nd	D-140	W-88	D-35	W-24	W (Fillmore)
1853–1855	33rd	D-159	W-71	D-38	W-22	D (Pierce)
1855–1857	34th	R-108	D-83	D-40	R-15	D (Pierce)
1857–1859	35th	D-118	R-92	D-36	R-20	D (Buchanan)
1859–1861	36th	R-114	D-92	D-36	R-26	D (Buchanan)
1861–1863	37th	R-105	D-43	R-31	D-10	R (Lincoln)
1863–1865	38th	R-102	D-75	R-36	D-9	R (Lincoln)
1865–1867	39th	U-149	D-42	U-42	D-10	R (Lincoln)
						R (A. Johnson)
1867–1869	40th	R-143	D-49	R-42	D-11	R (A. Johnson)
1869–1871	41st	R-149	D-63	R-56	D-11	R (Grant)
1871–1873	42nd	R-134	D-104	R-52	D-17	R (Grant)
1873–1875	43rd	R-194	D-92	R-49	D-19	R (Grant)
1875–1877	44th	D-169	R-109	R-45	D-29	R (Grant)
1877–1879	45th	D-153	R-140	R-39	D-36	R (Hayes)
1879–1881	46th	D-149	R-130	D-42	R-33	R (Hayes)
1881–1883	47th	R-147	D-135	R-37	D-37	R (Garfield)
						R (Arthur)
1883–1885	48th	D-197	R-118	R-38	D-36	R (Arthur)
1885–1887	49th	D-183	R-140	R-43	D-34	D (Cleveland)

Year	Congress	House		Senate		President
		Majority party	Principal minority party	Majority party	Principal minority party	
1887–1889	50th	D-169	R-152	R-39	D-37	D (Cleveland)
1889–1891	51st	R-166	D-159	R-39	D-37	R (B. Harrison)
1891–1893	52nd	D-235	R-88	R-47	D-39	R (B. Harrison)
1893–1895	53rd	D-218	R-127	D-44	R-38	D (Cleveland)
1895–1897	54th	R-244	D-105	R-43	D-39	D (Cleveland)
1897–1899	55th	R-204	D-113	R-47	D-34	R (McKinley)
1899–1901	56th	R-185	D-163	R-53	D-26	R (McKinley)
1901–1903	57th	R-197	D-151	R-55	D-31	R (McKinley)
						R (T. Roosevelt)
1903–1905	58th	R-208	D-178	R-57	D-33	R (T. Roosevelt)
1905–1907	59th	R-250	D-136	R-57	D-33	R (T. Roosevelt)
1907–1909	60th	R-222	D-164	R-61	D-31	R (T. Roosevelt)
1909–1911	61st	R-219	D-172	R-61	D-32	R (Taft)
1911–1913	62nd	D-228	R-161	R-51	D-41	R (Taft)
1913–1915	63rd	D-291	R-127	D-51	R-44	D (Wilson)
1915–1917	64th	D-230	R-196	D-56	R-40	D (Wilson)
1917–1919	65th	D-216	R-210	D-53	R-42	D (Wilson)
1919–1921	66th	R-240	D-190	R-49	D-47	D (Wilson)
1921–1923	67th	R-301	D-131	R-59	D-37	R (Harding)
1923–1925	68th	R-225	D-205	R-51	D-43	R (Coolidge)
1925–1927	69th	R-247	D-183	R-56	D-39	R (Coolidge)
1927–1929	70th	R-237	D-195	R-49	D-46	R (Coolidge)
1929–1931	71st	R-267	D-167	R-56	D-39	R (Hoover)
1931–1933	72nd	D-220	R-214	R-48	D-47	R (Hoover)
1933–1935	73rd	D-310	R-117	D-60	R-35	D (F. Roosevelt)
1935–1937	74th	D-319	R-103	D-69	R-25	D (F. Roosevelt)
1937–1939	75th	D-331	R-89	D-76	R-16	D (F. Roosevelt)
1939–1941	76th	D-261	R-164	D-69	R-23	D (F. Roosevelt)
1941–1943	77th	D-268	R-162	D-66	R-28	D (F. Roosevelt)
1943–1945	78th	D-218	R-208	D-58	R-37	D (F. Roosevelt)
1945–1947	79th	D-242	R-190	D-56	R-38	D (F. Roosevelt)
						D (Truman)
1947–1949	80th	R-245	D-188	R-51	D-45	D (Truman)
1949–1951	81st	D-263	R-171	D-54	R-42	D (Truman)
1951–1953	82nd	D-234	R-199	D-49	R-47	D (Truman)
1953–1955	83rd	R-221	D-211	R-48	D-47	R (Eisenhower)
1955–1957	84th	D-232	R-203	D-48	R-47	R (Eisenhower)
1957–1959	85th	D-233	R-200	D-49	R-47	R (Eisenhower)
1959–1961	86th	D-283	R-153	D-64	R-34	R (Eisenhower)
1961–1963	87th	D-263	R-174	D-65	R-35	D (Kennedy)
1963–1965	88th	D-258	R-177	D-67	R-33	D (Kennedy)
						D (L. Johnson)
1965–1967	89th	D-295	R-140	D-68	R-32	D (L. Johnson)
1967–1969	90th	D-247	R-187	D-64	R-36	D (L. Johnson)
1969–1971	91st	D-243	R-192	D-57	R-43	R (Nixon)
1971–1973	92nd	D-254	R-180	D-54	R-44	R (Nixon)
1973–1975	93rd	D-239	R-192	D-56	R-42	R (Nixon)
						R (Ford)
1975–1977	94th	D-291	R-144	D-60	R-37	R (Ford)
1977–1979	95th	D-292	R-143	D-61	R-38	D (Carter)
1979–1981	96th	D-276	R-157	D-58	R-41	D (Carter)
1981–1983	97th	D-243	R-192	R-53	D-46	R (Reagan)
1983–1985	98th	D-269	R-165	R-54	D-46	R (Reagan)
1985–1987	99th	D-252	R-182	R-53	D-47	R (Reagan)
1987–1989	100th	D-258	R-177	D-55	R-45	R (Reagan)
1989–1991	101st	D-259	R-174	D-55	R-45	R (Bush)
1991–1993	102nd	D-267	R-167	D-56	R-44	R (Bush)

Year	Congress	House		Senate		President
		Majority party	Principal minority party	Majority party	Principal minority party	
1993–1995	103rd	D-258	R-176	D-57	R-43	D (Clinton)
1995–1997	104th	R-230	D-204	R-53	D-47	D (Clinton)
1997–1999	105th	R-227	D-207	R-55	D-45	D (Clinton)
1999–2001	106th	R-222	D-211	R-55	D-45	D (Clinton)

NOTE: Figures are for the beginning of the first session of each Congress. Key to abbreviations: AD—Administration; AM—Anti-Masonic; D—Democratic; DR—Democratic-Republican; F—Federalist; J—Jacksonian; NR—National Republican; Op—Opposition; R—Republican; U—Unionist; W—Whig.

SOURCES: U.S. Bureau of the Census, *Historical Statistics of the United States, Colonial Times to 1970* (Washington, D.C.: Government Printing Office, 1975); and U.S. Congress, Joint Committee on Printing, *Official Congressional Directory* (Washington, D.C.: Government Printing Office, 1967–); *CQ Weekly,* selected issues.

Election Results, Congress and Presidency, 1860–1998

Election year	Congress	House Members elected Dem.	Rep.	Misc.	House Gains/losses Dem.	Rep.	Senate Members elected Dem.	Rep.	Misc.	Senate Gains/losses Dem.	Rep.	Presidency Popular vote Elected	Plurality
1860	37th	42	106	28	−59	−7	11	31	7	−27	+5	Lincoln (R)	485,706
1862	38th	80	103		+38	−3	12	39		+1	+8		
1864	39th	46	145		−34	+42	10	42		−2	+3	Lincoln (R)	405,581
1866	40th	49	143		+3	−2	11	42		+1	0	Johnson (R)	
1868	41st	73	170		+24	+27	11	61		0	+19	Grant (R)	304,906
1870	42nd	104	139		+31	−31	17	57		+6	−4		
1872	43rd	88	203		−16	+64	19	54		+2	−3	Grant (R)	763,474
1874	44th	181	107	3	+93	−96	29	46		+10	−8		
1876	45th	156	137		−25	+30	36	39	1	+7	−7	Hayes (R)	−254,235
1878	46th	150	128	14	−6	−9	43	33		+7	−6		
1880	47th	130	152	11	−20	+24	37	37	2	−6	+4	Garfield (R)	1,898
1882	48th	200	119	6	+70	−33	36	40		−1	+3	Arthur (R)	
1884	49th	182	140	2	−18	+21	34	41		−2	+2	Cleveland (D)	25,685
1886	50th	170	151	4	−12	+11	37	39		+3	−2		
1888	51st	156	173	1	−14	+22	37	47		0	+8	Harrison (R)	−90,596
1890	52nd	231	88	14	+75	−85	39	47	2	+2	0		
1892	53rd	220	126	8	−11	+38	44	38	3	+5	−9	Cleveland (D)	372,639
1894	54th	104	246	7	−116	+120	30	44	5	−5	+6		
1896	55th	134	206	16	+30	−40	34	46	10	−5	+2	McKinley (R)	596,985
1898	56th	163	185	9	+29	−21	26	53	11	−8	+7		
1900	57th	153	198	5	−10	+13	29	56	3	+3	+3	McKinley (R)	859,694
1902	58th	178	207		+25	+9	32	58		+3	+2	Roosevelt (R)	
1904	59th	136	250		−42	+43	32	58		0	0	Roosevelt (R)	2,543,695
1906	60th	164	222		+28	−28	29	61		−3	−3		
1908	61st	172	219		+8	−3	32	59		+3	−2	Taft (R)	1,269,457
1910	62nd	228	162	1	+56	−57	42	49		+10	−10		
1912	63rd	290	127	18	+62	−35	51	44	1	+9	−5	Wilson (D)	2,173,945
1914	64th	231	193	8	−59	+66	56	39	1	+5	−5		
1916	65th	210	216	9	−21	+23	53	42	1	−3	+3	Wilson (D)	579,511
1918	66th	191	237	7	−19	+21	47	48	1	−6	+6		
1920	67th	132	300	1	−59	+63	37	59		−10	+11	Harding (R)	7,020,023
1922	68th	207	225	3	+75	−75	43	51	2	+6	−8	Coolidge (R)	
1924	69th	183	247	5	−24	+22	40	54	1	−3	+3	Coolidge (R)	7,333,217

Election Year	Congress	House Members elected Dem.	Rep.	Misc.	House Gains/losses Dem.	Rep.	Senate Members elected Dem.	Rep.	Misc.	Senate Gains/losses Dem.	Rep.	Presidency Popular vote Elected	Plurality
1926	70th	195	237	3	+12	−10	47	48	1	+7	−6		
1928	71st	167	267	1	−28	+30	39	56	1	−8	+8	Hoover (R)	6,429,579
1930	72nd	220	214	1	+53	−53	47	48	1	+8	−8		
1932	73rd	313	117	5	+97	−101	59	36	1	+12	−12	Roosevelt (D)	7,068,817
1934	74th	322	103	10	+9	−14	69	25	2	+10	−11		
1936	75th	333	89	13	+11	−14	75	17	4	+6	−8	Roosevelt (D)	11,073,102
1938	76th	262	169	4	−71	+80	69	23	4	−6	+6		
1940	77th	267	162	6	+5	−7	66	28	2	−3	+5	Roosevelt (D)	4,964,561
1942	78th	222	209	4	−45	+47	57	38	1	−9	+10		
1944	79th	243	190	2	+21	−19	57	38	1	0	0	Roosevelt (D)	3,594,993
1946	80th	188	246	1	−55	+56	45	51		−12	+13	Truman (D)	
1948	81st	263	171	1	+75	−75	54	42		+9	−9	Truman (D)	2,188,054
1950	82nd	234	199	2	−29	+28	48	47	1	−6	+5		
1952	83rd	213	221	1	−21	+22	47	48	1	−1	+1	Eisenhower (R)	6,621,242
1954	84th	232	203		+19	−18	48	47	1	+1	−1		
1956	85th	234	201		+2	−2	49	47		+1	0	Eisenhower (R)	9,567,720
1958	86th	283	154		+49	−47	64	34		+17	−13		
1960	87th	263	174		−20	+20	64	36		−2	+2	Kennedy (D)	118,574[a]
1962	88th	258	176	1[b]	−4	+2	67	33		+4	−4		
1964	89th	295	140		+38	−38	68	32		+2	−2	Johnson (D)	15,951,378
1966	90th	248	187		−47	+47	64	36		−3	+3		
1968	91st	243	192		−4	+4	58	42		−5	+5	Nixon (R)	510,314
1970	92nd	255	180		+12	−12	55	45		−4	+2		
1972	93rd	243	192		−12	+12	57	43		+2	−2	Nixon (R)	17,999,528
1974	94th	291	144		+43	−43	61	38		+3	−3		
1976	95th	292	143		+1	−1	62	38		0	0	Carter (D)	1,682,970
1978	96th	277	158		−11	+11	59	41		−3	+3		
1980	97th	243	192		−33	+33	47	53		−12	+12	Reagan (R)	8,420,270
1982	98th	269	166		+26	−26	46	54		0	0		
1984	99th	253	182		−14	+14	47	53		+2	−2	Reagan (R)	16,877,890
1986	100th	258	177		+5	−5	55	45		+8	−8		
1988	101st	259	174		+2	−2	55	45		+1	−1	Bush (R)	7,077,023
1990	102nd	267	167	1	+9	−8	56	44		+1	−1		
1992	103rd	258	176	1	−9	+9	57	43		+1	−1	Clinton (D)	5,805,444
1994	104th	204	230	1	−52	+52	47	53		−8	+8[c]		
1996	105th	207	227	1	+3	−3	45	55		−2	+2	Clinton (D)	8,203,602
1998	106th	211	223	1	+5	−5	45	55		0	0		

NOTES: The seats totals reflect the makeup of the House and Senate at the start of each Congress. Special elections that shifted party ratios inbetween elections are not noted.

a. Includes divided Alabama elector slate votes.

b. Vacancy—Rep. Clem Miller, D–Calif. (1959–62) died Oct. 6, 1962, but his name remained on the ballot and he received a plurality.

c. Sen. Richard Shelby (Ala.) switched from the Democratic to the Republican Party the day after the election, bringing the total Republican gain to nine.

Speakers of the House of Representatives, 1789–1999

Congress		Speaker	Congress		Speaker
1st	(1789–1791)	Frederick A. C. Muhlenberg, Pa.	49th	(1885–1887)	Carlisle
2nd	(1791–1793)	Jonathan Trumbull, F-Conn.	50th	(1887–1889)	Carlisle
3rd	(1793–1795)	Muhlenberg	51st	(1889–1891)	Thomas Brackett Reed, R-Maine
4th	(1795–1797)	Jonathan Dayton, F-N.J.	52nd	(1891–1893)	Charles F. Crisp, D-Ga.
5th	(1797–1799)	Dayton	53rd	(1893–1895)	Crisp
6th	(1799–1801)	Theodore Sedgwick, F-Mass.	54th	(1895–1897)	Reed
7th	(1801–1803)	Nathaniel Macon, D-N.C.	55th	(1897–1899)	Reed
8th	(1803–1805)	Macon	56th	(1899–1901)	David B. Henderson, R-Iowa
9th	(1805–1807)	Macon	57th	(1901–1903)	Henderson
10th	(1807–1809)	Joseph B. Varnum, Mass.	58th	(1903–1905)	Joseph G. Cannon, R-Ill.
11th	(1809–1811)	Varnum	59th	(1905–1907)	Cannon
12th	(1811–1813)	Henry Clay, R-Ky.	60th	(1907–1909)	Cannon
13th	(1813–1814)	Clay	61st	(1909–1911)	Cannon
	(1814–1815)	Langdon Cheves, D-S.C.	62nd	(1911–1913)	James B. "Champ" Clark, D-Mo.
14th	(1815–1817)	Clay	63rd	(1913–1915)	Clark
15th	(1817–1819)	Clay	64th	(1915–1917)	Clark
16th	(1819–1820)	Clay	65th	(1917–1919)	Clark
	(1820–1821)	John W. Taylor, D-N.Y.	66th	(1919–1921)	Frederick H. Gillett, R-Mass.
17th	(1821–1823)	Philip P. Barbour, D-Va.	67th	(1921–1923)	Gillett
18th	(1823–1825)	Clay	68th	(1923–1925)	Gillett
19th	(1825–1827)	Taylor	69th	(1925–1927)	Nicholas Longworth, R-Ohio
20th	(1827–1829)	Andrew Stevenson, D-Va.	70th	(1927–1929)	Longworth
21st	(1829–1831)	Stevenson	71st	(1929–1931)	Longworth
22nd	(1831–1833)	Stevenson	72nd	(1931–1933)	John Nance Garner, D-Texas
23rd	(1833–1834)	Stevenson	73rd	(1933–1934)	Henry T. Rainey, D-Ill.[a]
	(1834–1835)	John Bell, W-Tenn.	74th	(1935–1936)	Joseph W. Byrns, D-Tenn.
24th	(1835–1837)	James K. Polk, D-Tenn.		(1936–1937)	William B. Bankhead, D-Ala.
25th	(1837–1839)	Polk	75th	(1937–1939)	Bankhead
26th	(1839–1841)	Robert M. T. Hunter, D-Va.	76th	(1939–1940)	Bankhead
27th	(1841–1843)	John White, W-Ky.		(1940–1941)	Sam Rayburn, D-Texas
28th	(1843–1845)	John W. Jones, D-Va.	77th	(1941–1943)	Rayburn
29th	(1845–1847)	John W. Davis, D-Ind.	78th	(1943–1945)	Rayburn
30th	(1847–1849)	Robert C. Winthrop, W-Mass.	79th	(1945–1947)	Rayburn
31st	(1849–1851)	Howell Cobb, D-Ga.	80th	(1947–1949)	Joseph W. Martin Jr., R-Mass.
32nd	(1851–1853)	Linn Boyd, D-Ky.	81st	(1949–1951)	Rayburn
33rd	(1853–1855)	Boyd	82nd	(1951–1953)	Rayburn
34th	(1855–1857)	Nathaniel P. Banks, R-Mass.	83rd	(1953–1955)	Martin
35th	(1857–1859)	James L. Orr, D-S.C.	84th	(1955–1957)	Rayburn
36th	(1859–1861)	William Pennington, R-N.J.	85th	(1957–1959)	Rayburn
37th	(1861–1863)	Galusha A. Grow, R-Pa.	86th	(1959–1961)	Rayburn
38th	(1863–1865)	Schuyler Colfax, R-Ind.	87th	(1961)	Rayburn
39th	(1865–1867)	Colfax		(1962–1963)	John W. McCormack, D-Mass.
40th	(1867–1869)	Colfax	88th	(1963–1965)	McCormack
	(1869)	Theodore M. Pomeroy, R-N.Y.	89th	(1965–1967)	McCormack
41st	(1869–1871)	James G. Blaine, R-Maine	90th	(1967–1969)	McCormack
42nd	(1871–1873)	Blaine	91st	(1969–1971)	McCormack
43rd	(1873–1875)	Blaine	92nd	(1971–1973)	Carl Albert, D-Okla.
44th	(1875–1876)	Michael C. Kerr, D-Ind.	93rd	(1973–1975)	Albert
	(1876–1877)	Samuel J. Randall, D-Pa.	94th	(1975–1977)	Albert
45th	(1877–1879)	Randall	95th	(1977–1979)	Thomas P. O'Neill Jr., D-Mass.
46th	(1879–1881)	Randall	96th	(1979–1981)	O'Neill
47th	(1881–1883)	Joseph Warren Keifer, R-Ohio	97th	(1981–1983)	O'Neill
48th	(1883–1885)	John G. Carlisle, D-Ky.	98th	(1983–1985)	O'Neill

Congress		Speaker	Congress		Speaker
99th	(1985–1987)	O'Neill	103rd	(1993–1995)	Foley
100th	(1987–1989)	Jim Wright, D-Texas	104th	(1995–1997)	Newt Gingrich, R-Ga.
101st	(1989)	Wright[b]	105th	(1997–1999)	Gingrich
	(1989–1991)	Thomas S. Foley, D-Wash.	106th	(1999–)	J. Dennis Hastert, R-Ill.
102nd	(1991–1993)	Foley			

NOTES: Key to abbreviations: D—Democrat; F—Federalist; R— Republican; W—Whig.

a. Rainey died in 1934, but was not replaced until the next Congress.

b. Wright resigned and was succeeded by Foley on June 6, 1989.

SOURCES: *1999–2000 Congressional Directory, 106th Congress* (Washington, D.C.: Government Printing Office, 1999); *CQ Weekly,* selected issues.

House Floor Leaders, 1899–1999

Congress		Majority	Minority
56th	(1899–1901)	Sereno E. Payne, R-N.Y.	James D. Richardson, D-Tenn.
57th	(1901–1903)	Payne	Richardson
58th	(1903–1905)	Payne	John Sharp Williams, D-Miss.
59th	(1905–1907)	Payne	Williams
60th	(1907–1909)	Payne	Williams/Champ Clark, D-Mo.[a]
61st	(1909–1911)	Payne	Clark
62nd	(1911–1913)	Oscar W. Underwood, D-Ala.	James R. Mann, R-Ill.
63rd	(1913–1915)	Underwood	Mann
64th	(1915–1917)	Claude Kitchin, D-N.C.	Mann
65th	(1917–1919)	Kitchin	Mann
66th	(1919–1921)	Franklin W. Mondell, R-Wyo.	Clark
67th	(1921–1923)	Mondell	Claude Kitchin, D-N.C.
68th	(1923–1925)	Nicholas Longworth, R-Ohio	Finis J. Garrett, D-Tenn.
69th	(1925–1927)	John Q. Tilson, R-Conn.	Garrett
70th	(1927–1929)	Tilson	Garrett
71st	(1929–1931)	Tilson	John N. Garner, D-Texas
72nd	(1931–1933)	Henry T. Rainey, D-Ill.	Bertrand H. Snell, R-N.Y.
73rd	(1933–1935)	Joseph W. Byrns, D-Tenn.	Snell
74th	(1935–1937)	William B. Bankhead, D-Ala.[b]	Snell
75th	(1937–1939)	Sam Rayburn, D-Texas	Snell
76th	(1939–1941)	Rayburn/John W. McCormack, D-Mass.[c]	Joseph W. Martin Jr., R-Mass.
77th	(1941–1943)	McCormack	Martin
78th	(1943–1945)	McCormack	Martin
79th	(1945–1947)	McCormack	Martin
80th	(1947–1949)	Charles A. Halleck, R-Ind.	Sam Rayburn, D-Texas
81st	(1949–1951)	McCormack	Martin
82nd	(1951–1953)	McCormack	Martin
83rd	(1953–1955)	Halleck	Rayburn
84th	(1955–1957)	McCormack	Martin
85th	(1957–1959)	McCormack	Martin
86th	(1959–1961)	McCormack	Charles A. Halleck, R-Ind.
87th	(1961–1963)	McCormack/Carl Albert, D-Okla.[d]	Halleck
88th	(1963–1965)	Albert	Halleck
89th	(1965–1967)	Albert	Gerald R. Ford, R-Mich.
90th	(1967–1969)	Albert	Ford
91st	(1969–1971)	Albert	Ford
92nd	(1971–1973)	Hale Boggs, D-La.	Ford
93rd	(1973–1975)	Thomas P. O'Neill Jr., D-Mass.	Ford/John J. Rhodes, R-Ariz.[e]
94th	(1975–1977)	O'Neill	Rhodes
95th	(1977–1979)	Jim Wright, D-Texas	Rhodes
96th	(1979–1981)	Wright	Rhodes
97th	(1981–1983)	Wright	Robert H. Michel, R Ill.
98th	(1983–1985)	Wright	Michel
99th	(1985–1987)	Wright	Michel

Congress		Majority	Minority
100th	(1987–1989)	Thomas S. Foley, D-Wash.	Michel
101st	(1989–1991)	Foley/Richard A. Gephardt, D-Mo.[f]	Michel
102nd	(1991–1993)	Gephardt	Michel
103rd	(1993–1995)	Gephardt	Michel
104th	(1995–1997)	Dick Armey, R-Texas	Richard A. Gephardt, D-Mo.
105th	(1997–1999)	Armey	Gephardt
106th	(1999–)	Armey	Gephardt

NOTES:

a. Clark became minority leader in 1908.

b. Bankhead became Speaker of the House on June 4, 1936. The post of majority leader remained vacant until the next Congress.

c. McCormack became majority leader on Sept. 26, 1940, filling the vacancy caused by the elevation of Rayburn to the post of Speaker of the House on Sept. 16, 1940.

d. Albert became majority leader on Jan. 10, 1962, filling the vacancy caused by the elevation of McCormack to the post of Speaker of the House on Jan. 10, 1962.

e. Rhodes became minority leader on Dec. 7, 1973, filling the vacancy caused by the resignation of Ford on Dec. 6, 1973, to become vice president.

f. Gephardt became majority leader on June 14, 1989, filling the vacancy created when Foley succeeded Wright as Speaker of the House on June 6, 1989.

SOURCES: Randall B. Ripley, *Party Leaders in the House of Representatives* (Washington, D.C.: Brookings Institution, 1967); *Biographical Directory of the American Congress, 1774–1996* (Alexandria, Va.: CQ Staff Directories, 1997); *CQ Weekly,* selected issues.

Senate Floor Leaders, 1911–1999

Congress		Majority	Minority
62nd	(1911–1913)	Shelby M. Cullom, R-Ill.	Thomas S. Martin, D-Va.
63rd	(1913–1915)	John W. Kern, D-Ind.	Jacob H. Gallinger, R-N.H.
64th	(1915–1917)	Kern	Gallinger
65th	(1917–1919)	Thomas S. Martin, D-Va.	Gallinger/Henry Cabot Lodge, R-Mass.[a]
66th	(1919–1921)	Henry Cabot Lodge, R-Mass.	Martin/Oscar W. Underwood, D-Ala.[b]
67th	(1921–1923)	Lodge	Underwood
68th	(1923–1925)	Lodge/Charles Curtis, R-Kan.[c]	Joseph T. Robinson, D-Ark.
69th	(1925–1927)	Curtis	Robinson
70th	(1927–1929)	Curtis	Robinson
71st	(1929–1931)	James E. Watson, R-Ind.	Robinson
72nd	(1931–1933)	Watson	Robinson
73rd	(1933–1935)	Joseph T. Robinson, D-Ark.	Charles L. McNary, R-Ore.
74th	(1935–1937)	Robinson	McNary
75th	(1937–1939)	Robinson/Alben W. Barkley, D-Ky.[d]	McNary
76th	(1939–1941)	Barkley	McNary
77th	(1941–1943)	Barkley	McNary
78th	(1943–1945)	Barkley	McNary
79th	(1945–1947)	Barkley	Wallace H. White Jr., R-Maine
80th	(1947–1949)	Wallace H. White Jr., R-Maine	Alben W. Barkley, D-Ky.
81st	(1949–1951)	Scott W. Lucas, D-Ill.	Kenneth S. Wherry, R-Neb.
82nd	(1951–1953)	Ernest W. McFarland, D-Ariz.	Wherry/Styles Bridges, R-N.H.[e]
83rd	(1953–1955)	Robert A. Taft, R-Ohio/ William F. Knowland, R-Calif.[f]	Lyndon B. Johnson, D-Texas
84th	(1955–1957)	Lyndon B. Johnson, D-Texas	William F. Knowland, R-Calif.
85th	(1957–1959)	Johnson	Knowland
86th	(1959–1961)	Johnson	Everett McKinley Dirksen, R-Ill.
87th	(1961–1963)	Mike Mansfield, D-Mont.	Dirksen
88th	(1963–1965)	Mansfield	Dirksen
89th	(1965–1967)	Mansfield	Dirksen
90th	(1967–1969)	Mansfield	Dirksen
91st	(1969–1971)	Mansfield	Dirksen/Hugh Scott, R-Pa.[g]
92nd	(1971–1973)	Mansfield	Scott
93rd	(1973–1975)	Mansfield	Scott
94th	(1975–1977)	Mansfield	Scott
95th	(1977–1979)	Robert C. Byrd, D-W.Va.	Howard H. Baker Jr., R-Tenn.
96th	(1979–1981)	Byrd	Baker
97th	(1981–1983)	Howard H. Baker Jr., R-Tenn.	Robert C. Byrd, D-W.Va.
98th	(1983–1985)	Baker	Byrd
99th	(1985–1987)	Bob Dole, R-Kan.	Byrd
100th	(1987–1989)	Byrd	Bob Dole, R-Kan.
101st	(1989–1991)	George J. Mitchell, D-Maine	Dole
102nd	(1991–1993)	Mitchell	Dole
103rd	(1993–1995)	Mitchell	Dole
104th	(1995–1997)	Bob Dole, R-Kan./Trent Lott, R-Miss.[h]	Tom Daschle, D-S.D.
105th	(1997–1999)	Lott	Daschle
106th	(1999–)	Lott	Daschle

NOTES:

a. Lodge became minority leader on Aug. 24, 1918, filling the vacancy caused by the death of Gallinger on Aug. 17, 1918.

b. Underwood became minority leader on April 27, 1920, filling the vacancy caused by the death of Martin on Nov. 12, 1919. Gilbert M. Hitchcock, D-Neb., served as acting minority leader in the interim.

c. Curtis became majority leader on Nov. 28, 1924, filling the vacancy caused by the death of Lodge on Nov. 9, 1924.

d. Barkley became majority leader on July 22, 1937, filling the vacancy caused by the death of Robinson on July 14, 1937.

e. Bridges became minority leader on Jan. 8, 1952, filling the vacancy caused by the death of Wherry on Nov. 29, 1951.

f. Knowland became majority leader on Aug. 4, 1953, filling the vacancy caused by the death of Taft on July 31, 1953. Taft's vacant seat was filled by Democrat Thomas Burke on Nov. 10, 1953. The division of the Senate changed to 48 Democrats, 47 Republicans, and 1 Independent, thus giving control of the Senate to the Democrats. However, Knowland remained as majority leader until the end of the 83rd Congress.

g. Scott became minority leader on Sept. 24, 1969, filling the vacancy caused by the death of Dirksen on Sept. 7, 1969.

h. Lott became majority leader on June 12, 1996, following the resignation of Dole on June 11.

SOURCES: *Biographical Directory of the American Congress, 1774–1996* (Alexandria, Va.: CQ Staff Directories, 1997); *Majority and Minority Leaders of the Senate,* comp. Floyd M. Riddick, 94th Cong., 1st sess., 1975, S Doc 66; *CQ Weekly,* selected issues.

Congressional Committee Chairs since 1947

Following is a list of House and Senate standing committee chairs from January 1947 through September 1999. The years listed reflect the tenure of the committee chairs. As committee names have changed through the years, the committees are listed by their names as of September 1999; former committee names are listed as well. This list also includes chairs of committees that were disbanded during the period.

HOUSE

Agriculture
Clifford R. Hope (R-Kan. 1947–1949)
Harold D. Cooley (D-N.C. 1949–1953)
Clifford R. Hope (R-Kan. 1953–1955)
Harold D. Cooley (D-N.C. 1955–1967)
W. R. Poage (D-Texas 1967–1975)
Thomas S. Foley (D-Wash. 1975–1981)
E. "Kika" de la Garza (D-Texas 1981–1995)
Pat Roberts (R-Kan. 1995–1997)
Bob Smith (R-Ore. 1997–1999)
Larry Combest (R-Texas 1999–)

Appropriations
John Taber (R-N.Y. 1947–1949)
Clarence Cannon (D-Mo. 1949–1953)
John Taber (R-N.Y. 1953–1955)
Clarence Cannon (D-Mo. 1955–1964)
George H. Mahon (D-Texas 1964–1979)
Jamie L. Whitten (D-Miss. 1979–1993)
William H. Natcher (D-Ky. 1993–1994)
David Obey (D-Wis. 1994–1995)
Robert L. Livingston (R-La. 1995–1999)
C. W. "Bill" Young (R-Fla. 1999–)

Armed Services
(formerly Armed Services, 1947–1995; National Security, 1995–1998)
Walter G. Andrews (R-N.Y. 1947–1949)
Carl Vinson (D-Ga. 1949–1953)
Dewey Short (R-Mo. 1953–1955)
Carl Vinson (D-Ga. 1955–1965)
L. Mendel Rivers (D-S.C. 1965–1971)
F. Edward Hébert (D-La. 1971–1975)
Melvin Price (D-Ill. 1975–1985)
Les Aspin (D-Wis. 1985–1993)
Ronald V. Dellums (D-Calif. 1993–1995)
Floyd D. Spence (R-S.C. 1995–)

Banking and Financial Services
(formerly Banking and Currency, 1947–1975; Banking, Currency and Housing, 1975–1977; Banking, Finance and Urban Affairs, 1977–1995)
Jesse P. Wolcott (R-Mich. 1947–1949)
Brent Spence (D-Ky. 1949–1953)
Jesse P. Wolcott (R-Mich. 1953–1955)
Brent Spence (D-Ky. 1955–1963)
Wright Patman (D-Texas 1963–1975)
Henry S. Reuss (D-Wis. 1975–1981)
Fernand J. St Germain (D-R.I. 1981–1989)
Henry B. Gonzalez (D-Texas 1989–1995)
Jim Leach (R-Iowa 1995–)

Budget
Brock Adams (D-Wash. 1975–1977)
Robert N. Giaimo (D-Conn. 1977–1981)
James R. Jones (D-Okla. 1981–1985)
William H. Gray III (D-Pa. 1985–1989)
Leon E. Panetta (D-Calif. 1989–1993)
Martin Olav Sabo (D-Minn. 1993–1995)
John R. Kasich (R-Ohio 1995–)

Commerce
(formerly Interstate and Foreign Commerce, 1947–1981; Energy and Commerce, 1981–1995)
Charles A. Wolverton (R-N.J. 1947–1949)
Robert Crosser (D-Ohio 1949–1953)
Charles A. Wolverton (R-N.J. 1953–1955)
J. Percy Priest (D-Tenn. 1955–1957)
Oren Harris (D-Ark. 1957–1966)
Harley O. Staggers (D-W.Va. 1966–1981)
John D. Dingell (D-Mich. 1981–1995)
Thomas J. Bliley Jr. (R-Va. 1995–)

District of Columbia
Everett McKinley Dirksen (R-Ill. 1947–1949)
John L. McMillan (D-S.C. 1949–1953)
Sidney Elmer Simpson (R-Ill. 1953–1955)
John L. McMillan (D-S.C. 1955–1973)
Charles C. Diggs Jr. (D-Mich. 1973–1979)
Ronald V. Dellums (D-Calif. 1979–1993)
Pete Stark (D-Calif. 1993–1995)
(Reorganized as a subcommittee of the Government Reform and Oversight in 1995)

Education and the Workforce
(formerly Education and Labor, 1947–1995; Economic and Educational Opportunities, 1995–1997)
Fred A. Hartley Jr. (R-N.J. 1947–1949)
John Lesinski (D-Mich. 1949–1950)
Graham A. Barden (D-N.C. 1950–1953)
Samuel K. McConnell Jr. (R-Pa. 1953–1955)
Graham A. Barden (D-N.C. 1955–1961)
Adam Clayton Powell Jr. (D-N.Y. 1961–1967)
Carl D. Perkins (D-Ky. 1967–1984)
Augustus F. Hawkins (D-Calif. 1984–1991)
William D. Ford (D-Mich. 1991–1995)
Bill Goodling (R-Pa. 1995–)

Government Reform
(formerly Expenditures in the Executive Departments, 1947–1952; Government Operations, 1952–1995; Government Reform and Oversight, 1995–1998)
Clare E. Hoffman (R-Mich. 1947–1949)
William L. Dawson (D-Ill. 1949–1953)
Clare E. Hoffman (R-Mich. 1953–1955)
William L. Dawson (D-Ill. 1955–1971)
Chet Holifield (D-Calif. 1971–1975)
Jack Brooks (D-Texas 1975–1989)
John Conyers (D-Mich. 1989–1995)
William F. Clinger (R-Pa. 1995–1997)
Dan Burton (R-Ind. 1997–)

House Administration
(formerly House Administration, 1947–1995; House Oversight, 1995–1998)
Karl M. LeCompte (R-Iowa 1947–1949)
Mary T. Norton (D-N.J. 1949–1951)
Thomas B. Stanley (D-Va. 1951–1953)
Karl M. LeCompte (R-Iowa 1953–1955)
Omar Burleson (D-Texas 1955–1968)
Samuel N. Friedel (D-Md. 1968–1971)
Wayne L. Hays (D-Ohio 1971–1976)
Frank Thompson Jr. (D-N.J. 1976–1980)
Augustus F. Hawkins (D-Calif. 1981–1984)
Frank Annunzio (D-Ill. 1985–1991)
Charlie Rose (D-N.C. 1991–1995)
Bill Thomas (R-Calif. 1995–)

Intelligence, Permanent Select Committee on
(formerly Select Committee on Intelligence, 1975–1976)
Lucien N. Nedzi (D-Mich. 1975)
Otis G. Pike (D-N.Y. 1975–1976)
Edward P. Boland (D-Mass. 1977–1985)
Lee H. Hamilton (D-Ind. 1985–1987)
Louis Stokes (D-Ohio 1987–1989)
Anthony C. Beilenson (D-Calif. 1989–1991)
Dave McCurdy (D-Okla. 1991–1993)
Dan Glickman (D-Kan. 1993–1995)
Larry Combest (R-Texas 1995–1997)
Porter J. Goss (R-Fla. 1997–)

Internal Security
(formerly Un-American Activities, 1947–1969)
J. Parnell Thomas (R-N.J. 1947–1949)
John S. Wood (D-Ga. 1949–1953)
Harold H. Velde (R-Ill. 1953–1955)
Francis E. Walter (D-Pa. 1955–1963)
Edwin E. Willis (D-La. 1963–1969)
Richard H. Ichord (D-Mo. 1969–1975)
(The panel was abolished in 1975)

International Relations
(formerly Foreign Affairs, 1947–1975; International Relations, 1975–1979; Foreign Affairs, 1979–1995)
Charles A. Eaton (R-N.J. 1947–1949)
John Kee (D-W.Va. 1949–1951)
James P. Richards (D-S.C. 1951–1953)
Robert B. Chiperfield (R-Ill. 1953–1955)
James P. Richards (D-S.C. 1955–1957)
Thomas S. Gordon (D-Ill. 1957–1959)
Thomas E. Morgan (D-Pa. 1959–1977)
Clement J. Zablocki (D-Wis. 1977–1983)
Dante B. Fascell (D-Fla. 1984–1993)
Lee H. Hamilton (D-Ind. 1993–1995)
Benjamin A. Gilman (R-N.Y. 1995–)

Judiciary

Earl C. Michener (R-Mich. 1947–1949)
Emanuel Celler (D-N.Y. 1949–1953)
Chauncey W. Reed (R-Ill. 1953–1955)
Emanuel Celler (D-N.Y. 1955–1973)
Peter W. Rodino Jr. (D-N.J. 1973–1989)
Jack Brooks (D-Texas 1989–1995)
Henry J. Hyde (R-Ill. 1995–)

Merchant Marine and Fisheries

Fred Bradley (R-Mich. 1947)
Alvin F. Weichel (R-Ohio 1947–1949)
Schuyler Otis Bland (D-Va. 1949–1950)
Edward J. Hart (D-N.J. 1950–1953)
Alvin F. Weichel (R-Ohio 1953–1955)
Herbert C. Bonner (D-N.C. 1955–1965)
Edward A. Garmatz (D-Md. 1966–1973)
Leonor K. Sullivan (D-Mo. 1973–1977)
John M. Murphy (D-N.Y. 1977–1981)
Walter B. Jones (D-N.C. 1981–1992)
Gerry E. Studds (D-Mass. 1992–1993)
George Miller (D-Calif. 1993–1995)
(Reorganized as a subcommittee of Transportation and Infrastructure in 1995.)

Post Office and Civil Service

Edward H. Rees (R-Kan. 1947–1949)
Tom Murray (D-Tenn. 1949–1953)
Edward H. Rees (R-Kan. 1953–1955)
Tom Murray (D-Tenn. 1955–1967)
Thaddeus J. Dulski (D-N.Y. 1967–1975)
David N. Henderson (D-N.C. 1975–1977)
Robert N. C. Nix Sr. (D-Pa. 1977–1979)
James M. Hanley (D-N.Y. 1979–1981)
William D. Ford (D-Mich. 1981–1991)
William L. Clay (D-Mo. 1991–1995)
(Reorganized as a subcommittee of Government Reform and Oversight in 1995.)

Resources

(formerly Public Lands, 1947–1951; Interior and Insular Affairs, 1951–1992; Natural Resources, 1993–1995)
Richard J. Welch (R-Calif. 1947–1949)
Andrew L. Somers (D-N.Y. 1949)
J. Hardin Peterson (D-Fla. 1949–1951)
John R. Murdock (D-Ariz. 1951–1953)
A. L. Miller (R-Neb. 1953–1955)
Claire Engle (D-Calif. 1955–1959)
Wayne N. Aspinall (D-Colo. 1959–1973)
James A. Haley (D-Fla. 1973–1977)
Morris K. Udall (D-Ariz. 1977–1991)
George Miller (D-Calif. 1991–1995)
Don Young (R-Alaska, 1995–)

Rules

Leo E. Allen (R-Ill. 1947–1949)
Adolph J. Sabath (D-Ill. 1949–1953)
Leo E. Allen (R-Ill. 1953–1955)
Howard W. Smith (D-Va. 1955–1967)
William M. Colmer (D-Miss. 1967–1973)
Ray J. Madden (D-Ind. 1973–1977)
James J. Delaney (D-N.Y. 1977–1978)

Richard Bolling (D-Mo. 1979–1983)
Claude Pepper (D-Fla. 1983–1989)
Joe Moakley (D-Mass. 1989–1995)
Gerald B. H. Solomon (R-N.Y. 1995–1999)
David Dreier (R-Calif. 1999–)

Science

(formerly Science and Astronautics, 1959–1975; Science and Technology, 1975–1987; Science, Space and Technology, 1987–1995)
Overton Brooks (D-La. 1959–1961)
George P. Miller (D-Calif. 1961–1973)
Olin E. Teague (D-Texas 1973–1979)
Don Fuqua (D-Fla. 1979–1987)
Robert A. Roe (D-N.J. 1987–1991)
George E. Brown Jr. (D-Calif. 1991–1995)
Robert S. Walker (R-Pa. 1995–1997)
F. James Sensenbrenner Jr. (R-Wis. 1997–)

Small Business

(formerly Select Committee on Small Business, 1947–1975)
Walter C. Ploeser (R-Mo. 1947–1949)
Wright Patman (D-Texas 1949–1953)
William S. Hill (R-Colo. 1953–1955)
Wright Patman (D-Texas 1955–1963)
Joe L. Ervins (D-Tenn. 1963–1977)
Neal Smith (D-Iowa 1977–1981)
Parren J. Mitchell (D-Md. 1981–1987)
John J. LaFalce (D-N.Y. 1987–1995)
Jan Meyers (R-Kan. 1995–1997)
James M. Talent (R-Mo. 1997–)

Standards of Official Conduct

Melvin Price (D-Ill. 1969–1975)
John J. Flynt Jr. (D-Ga. 1975–1977)
Charles E. Bennett (D-Fla. 1977–1981)
Louis Stokes (D-Ohio 1981–1985)
Julian C. Dixon (D-Calif. 1985–1991)
Louis Stokes (D-Ohio 1991–1993)
Jim McDermott (D-Wash. 1993–1995)
Nancy L. Johnson (R-Conn. 1995–1997)
James V. Hansen (R-Utah 1997–1999)
Lamar Smith (R-Texas 1999–)

Transportation and Infrastructure

(formerly Public Works, 1947–1975; Public Works and Transportation, 1975–1995)
George A. Dondero (R-Mich. 1947–1949)
William M. Whittington (D-Miss. 1949–1951)
Charles A. Buckley (D-N.Y. 1951–1953)
George A. Dondero (R-Mich. 1953–1955)
Charles A. Buckley (D-N.Y. 1955–1965)
George H. Fallon (D-Md. 1965–1971)
John A. Blatnik (D-Minn. 1971–1975)
Robert E. Jones Jr. (D-Ala. 1975–1977)
Harold T. Johnson (D-Calif. 1977–1981)
James J. Howard (D-N.J. 1981–1988)
Glenn M. Anderson (D-Calif. 1988–1991)
Robert A. Roe (D-N.J. 1991–1993)
Norman Y. Mineta (D-Calif. 1993–1995)
Bud Shuster (R-Pa. 1995–)

Veterans' Affairs

Edith Nourse Rogers (R-Mass. 1947–1949)
John E. Rankin (D-Miss. 1949–1953)
Edith Nourse Rogers (R-Mass. 1953–1955)
Olin E. Teague (D-Texas 1955–1973)
William Jennings Bryan Dorn (D-S.C. 1973–1975)
Ray Roberts (D-Texas 1975–1981)
G. V. "Sonny" Montgomery (D-Miss. 1981–1995)
Bob Stump (R-Ariz. 1995–)

Ways and Means

Harold Knutson (R-Minn. 1947–1949)
Robert L. Doughton (D-N.C. 1949–1953)
Daniel A. Reed (R-N.Y. 1953–1955)
Jere Cooper (D-Tenn. 1955–1957)
Wilbur D. Mills (D-Ark. 1958–1975)
Al Ullman (D-Ore. 1975–1981)
Dan Rostenkowski (D-Ill. 1981–1994)
Sam M. Gibbons (D-Fla. 1994–1995)
Bill Archer (R-Texas 1995–)

SENATE

Aeronautical and Space Sciences

Lyndon B. Johnson (D-Texas 1958–1961)
Robert S. Kerr (D-Okla. 1961–1963)
Clinton P. Anderson (D-N.M. 1963–1973)
Frank E. Moss (D-Utah 1973–1977)
(Abolished in 1977, when its jurisdiction was consolidated under Commerce.)

Agriculture, Nutrition, and Forestry

(formerly Agriculture and Forestry, 1947–1977)
Arthur Capper (R-Kan. 1947–1949)
Elmer Thomas (D-Okla. 1949–1951)
Allen J. Ellender (D-La. 1951–1953)
George D. Aiken (R-Vt. 1953–1955)
Allen J. Ellender (D-La. 1955–1971)
Herman E. Talmadge (D-Ga. 1971–1981)
Jesse Helms (R-N.C. 1981–1987)
Patrick J. Leahy (D-Vt. 1987–1995)
Richard G. Lugar (R-Ind. 1995–)

Appropriations

Styles Bridges (R-N.H. 1947–1949)
Kenneth McKellar (D-Tenn. 1949–1953)
Styles Bridges (R-N.H. 1953–1955)
Carl Hayden (D-Ariz. 1955–1969)
Richard B. Russell (D-Ga. 1969–1971)
Allen J. Ellender (D-La. 1971–1972)
John L. McClellan (D-Ark. 1972–1977)
Warren G. Magnuson (D-Wash. 1978–1981)
Mark O. Hatfield (R-Ore. 1981–1987)
John C. Stennis (D-Miss. 1987–1989)
Robert C. Byrd (D-W.Va. 1989–1995)
Mark O. Hatfield (R-Ore. 1995–1997)
Ted Stevens (R-Alaska 1997–)

Armed Services

Chan Gurney (R-S.D. 1947–1949)
Millard E. Tydings (D-Md. 1949–1951)

Richard B. Russell (D-Ga. 1951–1953)
Leverett Saltonstall (R-Mass. 1953–1955)
Richard B. Russell (D-Ga. 1955–1969)
John C. Stennis (D-Miss. 1969–1981)
John Tower (R-Texas 1981–1985)
Barry Goldwater (R-Ariz. 1985–1987)
Sam Nunn (D-Ga. 1987–1995)
Strom Thurmond (R-S.C. 1995–1999)
John W. Warner (R-Va. 1999–)

Banking, Housing, and Urban Affairs
(formerly Banking and Currency, 1947–1971)
Charles W. Tobey (R-N.H. 1947–1949)
Burnet R. Maybank (D-S.C. 1949–1953)
Homer E. Capehart (R-Ind. 1953–1955)
J. W. Fulbright (D-Ark. 1955–1959)
A. Willis Robertson (D-Va. 1959–1967)
John J. Sparkman (D-Ala. 1967–1975)
William Proxmire (D-Wis. 1975–1981)
Jake Garn (R-Utah 1981–1987)
William Proxmire (D-Wis. 1987–1989)
Donald W. Riegle Jr. (D-Mich. 1989–1995)
Alfonse M. D'Amato (R-N.Y. 1995–1999)
Phil Gramm (R-Texas 1999–)

Budget
Edmund S. Muskie (D-Maine 1975–1979)
Ernest F. Hollings (D-S.C. 1979–1981)
Pete V. Domenici (R-N.M. 1981–1987)
Lawton Chiles Jr. (D-Fla. 1987–1989)
Jim Sasser (D-Tenn. 1989–1995)
Pete V. Domenici (R-N.M. 1995–)

Commerce, Science, and Transportation
(formerly Interstate and Foreign Commerce, 1947–1961; Commerce, 1961–1977)
Wallace H. White (R-Maine 1947–1949)
Edwin C. Johnson (D-Colo. 1949–1953)
Charles W. Tobey (R-N.H. 1953)
John W. Bricker (R-Ohio 1953–1955)
Warren G. Magnuson (D-Wash. 1955–1978)
Howard W. Cannon (D-Nev. 1978–1981)
Bob Packwood (R-Ore. 1981–1985)
John C. Danforth (R-Mo. 1985–1987)
Ernest F. Hollings (D-S.C. 1987–1995)
Larry Pressler (R-S.D. 1995–1997)
John McCain (R-Ariz. 1997–)

District of Columbia
C. Douglass Buck (R-Del. 1947–1949)
J. Howard McGrath (D-R.I. 1949–1951)
Matthew M. Neely (D-W.Va. 1951–1953)
Francis Case (R-S.D. 1953–1955)
Matthew M. Neely (D-W.Va. 1955–1959)
Alan Bible (D-Nev. 1959–1969)
Joseph D. Tydings (D-Md. 1969–1971)
Thomas Eagleton (D-Mo. 1971–1977)
(Abolished in 1977 and its responsibilities transferred to Governmental Affairs.)

Energy and Natural Resources
Henry M. Jackson (D-Wash. 1977–1981)
James A. McClure (R-Idaho 1981–1987)

J. Bennett Johnston (D-La. 1987–1995)
Frank H. Murkowski (R-Alaska 1995–)

Environment and Public Works
(formerly Public Works, 1947–1977)
Chapman Revercomb (R-W.Va. 1947–1949)
Dennis Chavez (D-N.M. 1949–1953)
Edward Martin (R-Pa. 1953–1955)
Dennis Chavez (D-N.M. 1955–1962)
Pat McNamara (D-Mich. 1963–1966)
Jennings Randolph (D-W.Va. 1966–1981)
Robert T. Stafford (R-Vt. 1981–1987)
Quentin N. Burdick (D-N.D. 1987–1992)
Daniel Patrick Moynihan (D-N.Y. 1992)
Max Baucus (D-Mont. 1993–1995)
John H. Chafee (R-R.I. 1995–1999)

Ethics, Select Committee on
(formerly the Select Committee on Standards and Conduct, 1966–1977)
John C. Stennis (D-Miss. 1966–1975)
Howard W. Cannon (D-Nev. 1975–1977)
Adlai Ewing Stevenson III (D-Ill. 1977–1981)
Malcolm Wallop (R-Wyo. 1981–1983)
Ted Stevens (R-Alaska 1983–1985)
Warren B. Rudman (R-N.H. 1985–1987)
Howell Heflin (D-Ala. 1987–1991)
Terry Sanford (D-N.C. 1991–1993)
Richard H. Bryan (D-Nev. 1993–1995)
Mitch McConnell (R-Ky. 1995–1997)
Robert C. Smith (R-N.H. 1997–)

Finance
Eugene D. Millikin (R-Colo. 1947–1949)
Walter F. George (D-Ga. 1949–1953)
Eugene D. Millikin (R-Colo. 1953–1955)
Harry Flood Byrd (D-Va. 1955–1965)
Russell B. Long (D-La. 1965–1981)
Robert Dole (R-Kan. 1981–1985)
Bob Packwood (R-Ore. 1985–1987)
Lloyd Bentsen (D-Texas 1987–1993)
Daniel Patrick Moynihan (D-N.Y. 1993–1995)
Bob Packwood (R-Ore. 1995)
William V. Roth Jr. (R-Del. 1995–)

Foreign Relations
Arthur H. Vandenberg (R-Mich. 1947–1949)
Tom Connally (D-Texas 1949–1953)
Alexander Wiley (R-Wis. 1953–1955)
Walter F. George (D-Ga. 1955–1957)
Theodore Francis Green (D-R.I. 1957–1959)
J. W. Fulbright (D-Ark. 1959–1975)
John J. Sparkman (D-Ala. 1975–1979)
Frank Church (D-Idaho 1979–1981)
Charles Percy (R-Ill. 1981–1985)
Richard G. Lugar (R-Ind. 1985–1987)
Claiborne Pell (D-R.I. 1987–1995)
Jesse Helms (R-N.C. 1995–)

Governmental Affairs
(formerly Expenditures in Executive Departments, 1947–1952; Government Operations, 1952–1977)
George D. Aiken (R-Vt. 1947–1949)
John L. McClellan (D-Ark. 1949–1953)
Joseph R. McCarthy (R-Wis. 1953–1955)
John L. McClellan (D-Ark. 1955–1972)
Sam J. Ervin Jr. (D-N.C. 1972–1974)
Abraham A. Ribicoff (D-Conn. 1975–1981)
William V. Roth Jr. (R-Del. 1981–1987)
John Glenn (D-Ohio 1987–1995)
William V. Roth Jr. (R-Del. 1995–1996)
Ted Stevens (R-Alaska 1996–1997)
Fred Thompson (R-Tenn. 1997–)

Health, Education, Labor and Pensions
(formerly Labor and Public Welfare, 1947–1977; Human Resources, 1977–1979; Labor and Human Resources, 1979–1999)
Robert A. Taft (R-Ohio 1947–1949)
Elbert D. Thomas (D-Utah 1949–1951)
James E. Murray (D-Mont. 1951–1953)
H. Alexander Smith (R-N.J. 1953–1955)
Lister Hill (D-Ala. 1955–1969)
Ralph W. Yarborough (D-Texas 1969–1971)
Harrison A. Williams Jr. (D-N.J. 1971–1981)
Orrin G. Hatch (R-Utah 1981–1987)
Edward M. Kennedy (D-Mass. 1987–1995)
Nancy Landon Kassebaum (R-Kan. 1995–1997)
James M. Jeffords (R-Vt. 1997–)

Indian Affairs
(formerly a temporary select committee; redesignated as a permanent committee in 1993.)
Daniel Inouye (D-Hawaii 1993–1995)
John McCain (R-Ariz. 1995)
Ben Nighthorse Campbell (R-Colo. 1995–)

Intelligence Activities, Select Committee on
Daniel K. Inouye (D-Hawaii 1976–1978)
Birch Bayh (D-Ind. 1978–1981)
Barry Goldwater (R-Ariz. 1981–1985)
Dave Durenberger (R-Minn. 1985–1987)
David L. Boren (D-Okla. 1987–1993)
Dennis DeConcini (D-Ariz. 1993–1995)
Arlen Specter (R-Pa. 1995–1997)
Richard C. Shelby (R-Ala. 1997–)

Interior and Insular Affairs
(formerly Public Lands, 1947–1948)
Hugh Butler (R-Neb. 1947–1949)
Joseph C. O'Mahoney (D-Wyo. 1949–1953)
Hugh Butler (R-Neb. 1953–1954)
Guy Gordon (R-Ore. 1954–1955)
James E. Murray (D-Mont. 1955–1961)
Clinton P. Anderson (D-N.M. 1961–1963)
Henry M. Jackson (D-Wash. 1963–1977)
(Most of its jurisdiction transferred to Energy and Natural Resources in 1977.)

Judiciary

Alexander Wiley (R-Wis. 1947–1949)
Pat McCarran (D-Nev. 1949–1953)
William Langer (R-N.D. 1953–1955)
Harley M. Kilgore (D-W.Va. 1955–1956)
James O. Eastland (D-Miss. 1956–1978)
Edward M. Kennedy (D-Mass. 1979–1981)
Strom Thurmond (R-S.C. 1981–1987)
Joseph R. Biden Jr. (D-Del. 1987–1995)
Orrin G. Hatch (R-Utah 1995–)

Post Office and Civil Service

William Langer (R-N.D. 1947–1949)
Olin D. Johnston (D-S.C. 1949–1953)
Frank Carlson (R-Kan. 1953–1955)
Olin D. Johnston (D-S.C. 1955–1965)
A. S. Mike Monroney (D-Okla. 1965–1969)
Gale W. McGee (D-Wyo. 1969–1977)
(Abolished in 1977 and its jurisdiction transferred to Governmental Affairs.)

Rules and Administration

C. Wayland Brooks (R-Ill. 1947–1949)
Carl Hayden (D-Ariz. 1949–1953)
William E. Jenner (R-Ind. 1953–1955)
Theodore Francis Green (D-R.I. 1955–1957)
Thomas C. Hennings Jr. (D-Mo. 1957–1960)
Mike Mansfield (D-Mont. 1961–1963)
B. Everett Jordan (D-N.C. 1963–1972)
Howard W. Cannon (D-Nev. 1973–1977)
Claiborne Pell (D-R.I. 1978–1981)
Charles McC. Mathias Jr. (R-Md. 1981–1987)
Wendell H. Ford (D-Ky. 1987–1995)
Ted Stevens (R-Alaska 1995–1996)
John Warner (R-Va. 1996–1999)
Mitch McConnell (R-Ky. 1999–)

Small Business

(formerly the Select Committee on Small Business, 1950–1981)

John J. Sparkman (D-Ala. 1950–1953)
Edward J. Thye (R-Minn. 1953–1955)
John J. Sparkman (D-Ala. 1955–1967)
George A. Smathers (D-Fla. 1967–1969)
Alan Bible (D-Nev. 1969–1975)
Gaylord Nelson (D-Wis. 1975–1981)
Lowell P. Weicker Jr. (R-Conn. 1981–1987)
Dale Bumpers (D-Ark. 1987–1995)
Christopher S. Bond (R-Mo. 1995–)

Veterans' Affairs

Vance Hartke (D-Ind. 1971–1977)
Alan Cranston (D-Calif. 1977–1981)
Alan K. Simpson (R-Wyo. 1981–1985)
Frank H. Murkowski (R-Alaska 1985–1987)
Alan Cranston (D-Calif. 1987–1993)
John D. Rockefeller IV (D-W.Va. 1993–1995)
Alan K. Simpson (R-Wyo. 1995–1997)
Arlen Specter (R-Pa. 1997–)

Members of Congress Who Became President

When George Bush became president in 1989, he brought to twenty-four the number of presidents who had previous service in the House of Representatives or the Senate or both.

Following is a list of these presidents and the chambers in which they served previous to their White House service.

Three other presidents—George Washington, John Adams, and Thomas Jefferson—had served in the Continental Congress, as had two of those included below, James Madison and James Monroe. James A. Garfield was elected to the Senate in January 1880 for a term beginning March 4, 1881, but declined to accept in December 1880 because he had been elected president. John Quincy Adams served in the House for seventeen years after he had been president, and Andrew Johnson returned to the Senate five months before he died.

HOUSE ONLY	SENATE ONLY	BOTH CHAMBERS
James Madison	James Monroe	Andrew Jackson
James K. Polk	John Quincy Adams	William Henry Harrison
Millard Fillmore	Martin Van Buren	John Tyler
Abraham Lincoln	Benjamin Harrison	Franklin Pierce
Rutherford B. Hayes	Warren G. Harding	James Buchanan
James A. Garfield	Harry S. Truman	Andrew Johnson
William McKinley		John F. Kennedy
Gerald R. Ford		Lyndon B. Johnson
George Bush		Richard Nixon

SOURCE: *Biographical Directory of the American Congress, 1774–1996* (Alexandria, Va.: CQ Staff Directories, 1997).

Women Members of Congress, 1917–1999

As of September 1999, a total of 197 women had been elected or appointed to Congress. Of the 194 women who actually served in Congress (two others were never sworn in and another resigned her seat the day after she was sworn in), 169 served in the House only, twenty in the Senate only, and five—Maine Republicans Margaret Chase Smith and Olympia Snowe, Maryland Democrat Barbara Mikulski, California Democrat Barbara Boxer, and Arkansas Democrat Blanche Lambert Lincoln—in both chambers. Following is a list of the women members, their political affiliations and states, and the years in which they served. In addition, Mary E. Farrington, R-Hawaii (1954–1957), Eleanor Holmes Norton, D-D.C. (1991–), and Donna Christensen, D-V.I. (1997–), served as delegates.

SENATE

Rebecca L. Felton, Ind. D-Ga.[a]	1922
Hattie W. Caraway, D-Ark.	1931–1945
Rose McConnell Long, D-La.	1936–1937
Dixie Bibb Graves, D-Ala.	1937–1938
Gladys Pyle, R-S.D.[b]	1938–1939
Vera C. Bushfield, R-S.D.	1948
Margaret Chase Smith, R-Maine	1949–1973
Hazel H. Abel, R-Neb.	1954
Eva K. Bowring, R-Neb.	1954
Maurine B. Neuberger, D-Ore.	1960–1967
Elaine S. Edwards, D-La.	1972
Maryon Pittman Allen, D-Ala.	1978
Muriel Buck Humphrey, D-Minn.	1978
Nancy Landon Kassebaum, R-Kan.	1978–1997
Paula Hawkins, R-Fla.	1981–1987
Barbara Mikulski, D-Md.	1987–
Jocelyn B. Burdick, D-N.D.	1992
Dianne Feinstein, D-Calif.	1992–
Barbara Boxer, D-Calif.	1993–
Kay Bailey Hutchison, R-Texas	1993–
Carol Moseley-Braun, D-Ill.	1993–1999
Patty L. Murray, D-Wash.	1993–
Olympia J. Snowe, R-Maine	1995–
Sheila Frahm, R-Kan.	1996
Susan Collins, R-Maine	1997–
Mary L. Landrieu, D-La.	1997–
Blanche Lambert Lincoln, D-Ark.	1999–

HOUSE

Jeannette Rankin, R-Mont.	1917–1919; 1941–1943
Alice M. Robertson, R-Okla.	1921–1923
Winnifred S. M. Huck, R-Ill.	1922–1923
Mae E. Nolan, R-Calif.	1923–1925
Florence P. Kahn, R-Calif.	1925–1937
Mary T. Norton, D-N.J.	1925–1951
Edith N. Rogers, R-Mass.	1925–1960
Katherine G. Langley, R-Ky.	1927–1931
Ruth H. McCormick, R-Ill.	1929–1931
Pearl P. Oldfield, D-Ark.	1929–1931
Ruth B. Owen, D-Fla.	1929–1933
Ruth S. B. Pratt, R-N.Y.	1929–1933
Effiegene Locke Wingo, D-Ark.	1930–1933
Willa M. B. Eslick, D-Tenn.	1932–1933
Marian W. Clarke, R-N.Y.	1933–1935
Virginia E. Jenckes, D-Ind.	1933–1939
Kathryn O'Loughlin McCarthy, D-Kan.	1933–1935
Isabella S. Greenway, D-Ariz.	1933–1937
Caroline L. G. O'Day, D-N.Y.	1935–1943
Nan W. Honeyman, D-Ore.	1937–1939

Elizabeth H. Gasque, D-S.C.[b]	1938–1939
Clara G. McMillan, D-S.C.	1939–1941
Jessie Sumner, R-Ill.	1939–1947
Frances P. Bolton, R-Ohio	1940–1969
Florence R. Gibbs, D-Ga.	1940–1941
Margaret Chase Smith, R-Maine	1940–1949
Katherine E. Byron, D-Md.	1941–1943
Veronica G. Boland, D-Pa.	1942–1943
Clare Boothe Luce, R-Conn.	1943–1947
Winifred C. Stanley, R-N.Y.	1943–1945
Willa L. Fulmer, D-S.C.	1944–1945
Emily Taft Douglas, D-Ill.	1945–1947
Helen G. Douglas, D-Calif.	1945–1951
Chase G. Woodhouse, D-Conn.	1945–1947; 1949–1951
Helen D. Mankin, D-Ga.	1946–1947
Eliza J. Pratt, D-N.C.	1946–1947
Georgia L. Lusk, D-N.M.	1947–1949
Katharine P. C. St. George, R-N.Y.	1947–1965
Reva Z. B. Bosone, D-Utah	1949–1953
Cecil M. Harden, R-Ind.	1949–1959
Edna F. Kelly, D-N.Y.	1949–1969
Vera D. Buchanan, D-Pa.	1951–1955
Marguerite S. Church, R-Ill.	1951–1963
Maude E. Kee, D-W.Va.	1951–1965
Ruth Thompson, R-Mich.	1951–1957
Gracie B. Pfost, D-Idaho	1953–1963
Leonor K. Sullivan, D-Mo.	1953–1977
Iris F. Blitch, D-Ga.	1955–1963
Edith Starrett Green, D-Ore.	1955–1975
Martha W. Griffiths, D-Mich.	1955–1974
Coya G. Knutson, DFL-Minn.	1955–1959
Kathryn E. Granahan, D-Pa.	1956–1963
Florence P. Dwyer, R-N.J.	1957–1973
Catherine D. May, R-Wash.	1959–1971
Edna O. Simpson, R-Ill.	1959–1961
Jessica McCullough Weis, R-N.Y.	1959–1963
Julia B. Hansen, D-Wash.	1960–1974
Catherine D. Norrell, D-Ark.	1961–1963
Louise G. Reece, R-Tenn.	1961–1963
Corinne B. Riley, D-S.C.	1962–1963
Charlotte T. Reid, R-Ill.	1963–1971
Irene B. Baker, R-Tenn.	1964–1965
Patsy T. Mink, D-Hawaii	1965–1977; 1990–
Lera M. Thomas, D-Texas	1966–1967
Margaret M. Heckler, R-Mass.	1967–1983
Shirley A. Chisholm, D-N.Y.	1969–1983
Bella S. Abzug, D-N.Y.	1971–1977
Ella T. Grasso, D-Conn.	1971–1975
Louise Day Hicks, D-Mass.	1971–1973
Elizabeth B. Andrews, D-Ala.	1972–1973
Yvonne B. Burke, D-Calif.	1973–1979

Marjorie Sewell Holt, R-Md.	1973–1987		Jennifer B. Dunn, R-Wash.	1993–
Elizabeth Holtzman, D-N.Y.	1973–1981		Karan English, D-Ariz.	1993–1995
Barbara C. Jordan, D-Texas	1973–1979		Anna G. Eshoo, D-Calif.	1993–
Patricia Schroeder, D-Colo.	1973–1997		Tillie Fowler, R-Fla.	1993–
Corinne "Lindy" Boggs, D-La.	1973–1991		Elizabeth Furse, D-Ore.	1993–1999
Cardiss R. Collins, D-Ill.	1973–1997		Jane F. Harman, D-Calif.	1993–1999
Marilyn Lloyd, D-Tenn.	1975–1995		Eddie Bernice Johnson, D-Texas	1993–
Millicent Fenwick, R-N.J.	1975–1983		Blanche Lambert Lincoln, D-Ark.	1993–1997
Martha E. Keys, D-Kan.	1975–1979		Carolyn B. Maloney, D-N.Y.	1993–
Helen S. Meyner, D-N.J.	1975–1979		Cynthia Ann McKinney, D-Ga.	1993–
Virginia Smith, R-Neb.	1975–1991		Carrie P. Meek, D-Fla.	1993–
Gladys Noon Spellman, D-Md.	1975–1981		Marjorie Margolies-Mezvinsky, D-Pa.	1993–1995
Shirley N. Pettis, R-Calif.	1975–1979		Deborah D. Pryce, R-Ohio	1993–
Barbara A. Mikulski, D-Md.	1977–1987		Lucille Roybal-Allard, D-Calif.	1993–
Mary Rose Oakar, D-Ohio	1977–1993		Lynn Schenk, D-Calif.	1993–1995
Beverly Byron, D-Md.	1979–1993		Karen Shepherd, D-Utah	1993–1995
Geraldine Ferraro, D-N.Y.	1979–1985		Karen L. Thurman, D-Fla.	1993–
Olympia J. Snowe, R-Maine	1979–1995		Nydia M. Velazquez, D-N.Y.	1993–
Bobbi Fiedler, R-Calif.	1981–1987		Lynn Woolsey, D-Calif.	1993–
Lynn M. Martin, R-Ill.	1981–1991		Helen Chenoweth, R-Idaho	1995–
Marge Roukema, R-N.J.	1981–		Barbara Cubin, R-Wyo.	1995–
Claudine Schneider, R-R.I.	1981–1991		Sheila Jackson-Lee, D-Texas	1995–
Jean Spencer Ashbrook, R-Ohio	1982–1983		Sue W. Kelly, R-N.Y.	1995–
Barbara B. Kennelly, D-Conn.	1982–1999		Zoe Lofgren, D-Calif.	1995–
Katie Beatrice Hall, D-Ind.	1982–1985		Karen McCarthy, D-Mo.	1995–
Sala Burton, D-Calif.	1983–1987		Sue Myrick, R-N.C.	1995–
Barbara Boxer, D-Calif.	1983–1993		Lynn N. Rivers, D-Mich.	1995–
Nancy L. Johnson, R-Conn.	1983–		Andrea Seastrand, R-Calif.	1995–1997
Marcy Kaptur, D-Ohio	1983–		Linda Smith, R-Wash.	1995–1999
Barbara Farrell Vucanovich, R-Nev.	1983–1997		Enid Greene Waldholtz, R-Utah	1995–1997
Helen Delich Bentley, R-Md.	1985–1995		Juanita Millender-McDonald, D-Calif.	1996–
Jan Meyers, R-Kan.	1985–1997		Jo Ann Emerson, R-Mo.	1996–
Cathy Long, D-La.	1985–1987		Julia Carson, D-Ind.	1997–
Constance A. Morella, R-Md.	1987–		Diana DeGette, D-Colo.	1997–
Elizabeth J. Patterson, D-S.C.	1987–1993		Kay Granger, R-Texas	1997–
Patricia Saiki, R-Hawaii	1987–1991		Darlene Hooley, D-Ore.	1997–
Louise M. Slaughter, D-N.Y.	1987–		Carolyn Cheeks Kilpatrick, D-Mich.	1997–
Nancy Pelosi, D-Calif.	1987–		Carolyn McCarthy, D-N.Y.	1997–
Nita M . Lowey, D-N.Y.	1989–		Anne M. Northup, R-Ky.	1997–
Jolene Unsoeld, D-Wash.	1989–1995		Loretta Sanchez, D-Calif.	1997–
Jill L. Long, D-Ind.	1989–1995		Deborah Ann Stabenow, D-Mich.	1997–
Ileana Ros-Lehtinen, R-Fla.	1989–		Ellen O. Tauscher, D-Calif.	1997–
Susan Molinari, R-N.Y.	1990–1997		Mary Bono, R-Calif.	1998–
Barbara-Rose Collins, D-Mich.	1991–1997		Lois Capps, D-Calif.	1998–
Rosa DeLauro, D-Conn.	1991–		Barbara Lee, D-Calif.	1998–
Joan Kelly Horn, D-Mo.	1991–1993		Heather Wilson, R-N.M.	1998–
Maxine Waters, D-Calif.	1991–		Tammy Baldwin, D-Wis.	1999–
Eva M. Clayton, D-N.C.	1992–		Shelley Berkley, D-Nev.	1999–
Corrine Brown, D-Fla.	1993–		Judy Biggert, R-Ill.	1999–
Leslie L. Byrne, D-Va.	1993–1995		Stephanie Tubbs Jones, D-Ohio	1999–
Maria E. Cantwell, D-Wash.	1993–1995		Grace F. Napolitano, D-Calif.	1999–
Pat Danner, D-Mo.	1993–		Jan Schakowsky, D-Ill.	1999–

NOTES:

a. Felton was sworn in Nov. 21, 1922, to fill the vacancy created by the death of Thomas E. Watson, D. The next day she gave up her seat to Walter F. George, D, the elected candidate for the vacancy.

b. Never sworn in because Congress was not in session between election and expiration of term.

SOURCES: Commission on the Bicentenary of the U.S. House of Representatives, *Women in Congress, 1917–1990* (Washington, D.C.: Government Printing Office, 1991); *Biographical Directory of the American Congress, 1774–1996* (Alexandria, Va.: CQ Staff Directories, 1997); *CQ Weekly,* selected issues.

Black Members of Congress, 1870–1999

As of September 1999, one hundred black Americans had served in Congress; four in the Senate and ninety-six in the House. Following is a list of the black members, their political affiliations and states, and the years in which they served. In addition, John W. Menard, R-La., won a disputed election in 1868 but was not permitted to take his seat in Congress. In addition to those listed below, Walter E. Fauntroy, D-D.C. (1971–1991), Eleanor Holmes Norton, D-D.C. (1991–), and Donna Christensen, D-V.I. (1997–), served as delegates.

SENATE

Hiram R. Revels, R-Miss.	1870–1871
Blanche K. Bruce, R-Miss.	1875–1881
Edward W. Brooke III, R-Mass.	1967–1979
Carol Moseley-Braun, D-Ill.	1993–1999

HOUSE

Joseph H. Rainey, R-S.C.	1870–1879
Jefferson F. Long, R-Ga.	1870–1871
Robert C. De Large, R-S.C.	1871–1873
Robert B. Elliott, R-S.C.	1871–1874
Benjamin S. Turner, R-Ala.	1871–1873
Josiah T. Walls, R-Fla.	1871–1876
Richard H. Cain, R-S.C.	1873–1875; 1877–1879
John R. Lynch, R-Miss.	1873–1877; 1882–1883
Alonzo J. Ransier, R-S.C.	1873–1875
James T. Rapier, R-Ala.	1873–1875
Jeremiah Haralson, R-Ala.	1875–1877
John A. Hyman, R-N.C.	1875–1877
Charles E. Nash, R-La.	1875–1877
Robert Smalls, R-S.C.	1875–1879; 1882–1883; 1884–1887
James E. O'Hara, R-N.C.	1883–1887
Henry P. Cheatham, R-N.C.	1889–1893
John M. Langston, R-Va.	1890–1891
Thomas E. Miller, R-S.C.	1890–1891
George W. Murray, R-S.C.	1893–1895; 1896–1897
George H. White, R-N.C.	1897–1901
Oscar S. De Priest, R-Ill.	1929–1935
Arthur W. Mitchell, D-Ill.	1935–1943
William L. Dawson, D-Ill.	1943–1970
Adam Clayton Powell Jr., D-N.Y.	1945–1967; 1969–1971
Charles C. Diggs Jr., D-Mich.	1955–1980
Robert N. C. Nix, D-Pa.	1958–1979
Augustus F. Hawkins, D-Calif.	1963–1991
John Conyers Jr., D-Mich.	1965–
Shirley A. Chisholm, D-N.Y.	1969–1983
William L. Clay, D-Mo.	1969–
Louis Stokes, D-Ohio	1969–1999
George W. Collins, D-Ill.	1970–1972
Ronald V. Dellums, D-Calif.	1971–1998
Ralph H. Metcalfe, D-Ill.	1971–1978
Parren J. Mitchell, D-Md.	1971–1987
Charles B. Rangel, D-N.Y.	1971–
Yvonne B. Burke, D-Calif.	1973–1979
Cardiss Collins, D-Ill.	1973–1997
Barbara C. Jordan, D-Texas	1973–1979
Andrew J. Young Jr., D-Ga.	1973–1977
Harold E. Ford, D-Tenn.	1975–1997
Julian C. Dixon, D-Calif.	1979–
William H. Gray III, D-Pa.	1979–1991
George T. Leland, D-Texas	1979–1989
Bennett McVey Stewart, D-Ill.	1979–1981
George W. Crockett Jr., D-Mich.	1980–1991
Mervyn M. Dymally, D-Calif.	1981–1993
Gus Savage, D-Ill.	1981–1993
Harold Washington, D-Ill.	1981–1993
Katie B. Hall, D-Ind.	1982–1985
Charles A. Hayes, D-Ill.	1983–1993
Major R. Owens, D-N.Y.	1983–
Edolphus Towns, D-N.Y.	1983–
Alan D. Wheat, D-Mo.	1983–1995
Alton R. Waldon Jr., D-N.Y.	1986–1987
Mike Espy, D-Miss.	1987–1993
Floyd H. Flake, D-N.Y.	1987–1997
John Lewis, D-Ga.	1987–
Kweisi Mfume, D-Md.	1987–1996
Donald M. Payne, D-N.J.	1989–
Craig A. Washington, D-Texas	1990–1995
Barbara-Rose Collins, D-Mich.	1991–1997
Gary A. Franks, R.-Conn.	1991–1997
William J. Jefferson, D-La.	1991–
Maxine Waters, D-Calif.	1991–
Lucien E. Blackwell, D-Pa	1991–1995
Eva Clayton, D-N.C.	1992–
Sanford D. Bishop Jr., D-Ga.	1993–
Corrine Brown, D-Fla.	1993–
James E. Clyburn, D-S.C.	1993–
Cleo Fields, D-La.	1993–1997
Alcee L. Hastings, D-Fla.	1993–
Earl F. Hilliard, D-Ala.	1993–
Eddie Bernice Johnson, D-Texas	1993–
Cynthia McKinney, D-Ga.	1993–
Carrie P. Meek, D-Fla.	1993–
Melvin J. Reynolds, D-Ill.	1993–1995
Bobby L. Rush, D-Ill.	1993–
Robert C. Scott, D-Va.	1993–
Bennie Thompson, D-Miss.	1993–
Walter R. Tucker III, D-Calif.	1993–1995
Melvin Watt, D-N.C.	1993–
Albert R. Wynn, D-Md.	1993–
Chaka Fattah, D-Pa.	1995–
Jesse Jackson Jr., D-Ill.	1995–
Sheila Jackson-Lee, D-Texas	1995–
J. C. Watts Jr., R-Okla.	1995–
Elijah E. Cummings, D-Md.	1996–
Juanita Millender-McDonald, D-Calif.	1996–
Julia Carson, D-Ind.	1997–
Danny K. Davis, D-Ill.	1997–
Harold E. Ford Jr., D-Tenn.	1997–
Carolyn Cheeks Kilpatrick, D-Mich.	1997–
Barbara Lee, D-Calif.	1998–
Gregory W. Meeks, D-N.Y.	1998–
Stephanie Tubbs Jones, D-Ohio	1999–

SOURCES: Maurine Christopher, *America's Black Congressmen* (Crowell, 1971); *Biographical Directory of the American Congress, 1774–1996* (Alexandria, Va.: CQ Staff Directories, 1997); *CQ Weekly*, selected issues.

Hispanic Members of Congress, 1877–1999

As of September 1999, thirty-seven Hispanics had served in Congress, two in both the Senate and the House and thirty-five in the House only. Following is a list of the Hispanic members, their political affiliations and states, and the years in which they served. Not included are Hispanics who served as territorial delegates, resident commissioners of Puerto Rico, or delegates of Guam or the Virgin Islands.

SENATE

Dennis Chavez, D-N.M.	1935–1962
Joseph M. Montoya, D-N.M.	1957–1964

HOUSE

Romualdo Pacheco, R-Calif.	1877–1878; 1879–1883
Ladislas Lazaro, D-La.	1913–1927
Benigno Cardenas Hernandez, R-N.M.	1915–1917; 1919–1921
Nestor Montoya, R-N.M.	1921–1923
Dennis Chavez, D-N.M.	1931–1935
Joachim Octave Fernandez, D-La.	1931–1941
Antonio Manuel Fernandez, D-N.M.	1943–1956
Henry B. Gonzalez, D-Texas	1961–1999
Edward R. Roybal, D-Calif.	1963–1993
Joseph Manuel Montoya, D-N.M.	1964–1977
E. "Kika" de la Garza II, D-Texas	1965–1997
Manuel Lujan Jr., R-N.M.	1969–1989
Herman Badillo, D-N.Y.	1971–1977
Robert Garcia, D-N.Y.	1978–1990
Anthony Lee Coelho, D-Calif.	1979–1989
Matthew G. Martinez, D-Calif.	1982–
Solomon P. Ortiz, D-Texas	1983–
William B. Richardson, D-N.M.	1983–1997
Esteban E. Torres, D-Calif.	1983–1999
Albert G. Bustamante, D-Texas	1985–1993
Ileana Ros-Lehtinen, R-Fla.	1989–
José E. Serrano, D-N.Y.	1990–
Ed Pastor, D-Ariz.	1991–
Xavier Becerra, D-Calif.	1993–
Henry Bonilla, R-Texas	1993–
Lincoln Diaz-Balart, R-Fla.	1993–
Luis V. Gutierrez, D-Ill.	1993–
Robert Menendez, D-N.J.	1993–
Lucille Roybal-Allard, D-Calif.	1993–
Frank Tejeda, D-Texas	1993–1997
Nydia M. Velázquez, D-N.Y.	1993–
Rubén Hinojosa, D-Texas	1997–
Silvestre Reyes, D-Texas	1997–
Ciro D. Rodriguez, D-Texas	1997–
Loretta Sanchez, D-Calif.	1997–
Charlie Gonzalez, D-Texas	1999–
Grace Napolitano, D-Calif.	1999–

SOURCES: *Biographical Directory of the American Congress, 1774–1996* (Alexandria, Va.: CQ Staff Directories, 1997); Congressional Hispanic Caucus; *CQ Weekly,* selected issues.

Recorded Votes in the House and Senate, 1947–1998

Year	House	Senate	Year	House	Senate
1947	84	138	1973	541	594
1948	75	110	1974	537	544
1949	121	226	1975	612	611
1950	154	229	1976	661	700
1951	109	202	1977	706	636
1952	72	129	1978	834	520
1953	71	89	1979	672	509
1954	76	181	1980	604	546
1955	73	88	1981	353	497
1956	74	136	1982	459	469
1957	100	111	1983	498	381
1958	93	202	1984	408	292
1959	87	215	1985	439	381
1960	93	207	1986	451	359
1961	116	207	1987	488	420
1962	124	227	1988	451	379
1963	119	229	1989	368	312
1964	113	312	1990	511	326
1965	201	259	1991	428	280
1966	193	238	1992	473	270
1967	245	315	1993	597	395
1968	233	280[a]	1994	497	329
1969	177	245	1995	867	613
1970	266	422	1996	454	306
1971	320	423	1997	633	298
1972	329	532	1998	533	314

NOTES: Totals do not include quorum calls.　　a. This figure does not include one yea-and-nay vote that was ruled invalid for lack of a quorum.

SOURCES: *CQ Almanac,* selected volumes (Washington, D.C.: Congressional Quarterly, selected years); *Congressional Record's* Résumés of Congressional Activity; Norman J. Ornstein, Thomas E. Mann, and Michael J. Malbin, *Vital Statistics on Congress, 1997–1998* (Washington, D.C.: Congressional Quarterly, 1998), 166.

Attempted and Successful Cloture Votes, 1919–1999

Congress		First Session		Second Session		Total	
		Attempted	Successful	Attempted	Successful	Attempted	Successful
66th	(1919–1921)	1	1	0	0	1	1
67th	(1921–1923)	1	0	1	0	2	0
68th	(1923–1925)	0	0	0	0	0	0
69th	(1925–1927)	0	0	2	1	2	1
70th	(1927–1929)	5	2	0	0	5	2
71st	(1929–1931)	0	0	0	0	0	0
72nd	(1931–1933)	0	0	0	0	0	0
73rd	(1933–1935)	1	0	0	0	1	0
74th	(1935–1937)	0	0	0	0	0	0
75th	(1937–1939)	0	0	2	0	2	0
76th	(1939–1941)	0	0	0	0	0	0
77th	(1941–1943)	0	0	1	0	1	0
78th	(1943–1945)	0	0	1	0	1	0
79th	(1945–1947)	0	0	4	0	4	0
80th	(1947–1949)	0	0	0	0	0	0
81st	(1949–1951)	0	0	2	0	2	0
82nd	(1951–1953)	0	0	0	0	0	0
83rd	(1953–1955)	0	0	1	0	1	0
84th	(1955–1957)	0	0	0	0	0	0
85th	(1957–1959)	0	0	0	0	0	0
86th	(1959–1961)	0	0	1	0	1	0
87th	(1961–1963)	1	0	3	1	4	1
88th	(1963–1965)	1	0	2	1	3	1
89th	(1965–1967)	2	1	5	0	7	1
90th	(1967–1969)	1	0	5	1	6	1
91st	(1969–1971)	2	0	4	0	6	0
92nd	(1971–1973)	10	2	10	2	20	4
93rd	(1973–1975)	10	2	21	7	31	9
94th	(1975–1977)	23	13	4	4	27	17
95th	(1977–1979)	5	1	8	2	13	3
96th	(1979–1981)	4	1	17	9	21	10
97th	(1981–1983)	7	2	20	7	27	9
98th	(1983–1985)	7	2	12	9	19	11
99th	(1985–1987)	9	1	14	9	23	10
100th	(1987–1989)	24	6	20	6	44	12
101st	(1989–1991)	9	6	15	5	24	11
102nd	(1991–1993)	20	9	28	14	48	23
103rd	(1993–1995)	20	4	22	10	42	14
104th	(1995–1997)	21	4	29	5	50	9
105th	(1997–1999)	24	7	29	11	53	18

NOTE: The number of votes required to invoke cloture was changed March 7, 1975, from two-thirds of those present and voting, to three-fifths of the total Senate membership, as Rule XXII of the standing rules of the Senate was amended.

SOURCES: *Congress and the Nation,* selected volumes (Washington, D.C.: Congressional Quarterly, selected years); *CQ Almanac,* selected volumes (Washington, D.C.: Congressional Quarterly, selected years; Richard S. Beth, Congressional Research Service, Library of Congress.)

House Discharge Petitions since 1931

The discharge petition is a little-used but dramatic House device that enables a majority of representatives to bring to the floor legislation blocked in committee. The following table shows the frequency with which the discharge petition has been used since the present discharge procedure was adopted in 1931 through the first session of the 106th Congress.

While the procedure obviously is rarely used and even more rarely successful, it may on occasion indirectly succeed by impelling a legislative committee, the Rules Committee, or the leadership to act on a measure and thereby avoid the discharge. (*See box, p. 488, Vol. I*)

| Congress | | Discharge petitions filed | Discharge motion | | Committee Discharged | Underlying measure[c] | |
			Entered[a]	Called up[b]		Passed House	Received final approval[d]
72nd	(1931–33)	12	5	5	1	1	–
73rd	(1933–35)	31	6	1	1	1	–
74th	(1935–37)	33	3	2	2	–	–
75th	(1937–39)	43	4	4	3[e]	2	1
76th	(1939–41)	37[e]	2	2	2	2	–
77th	(1941–43)	15	1	1	1	1	–
78th	(1943–45)	21	3	3	3	3	1[f]
79th	(1945–47)	35	3	1	1	1	–
80th	(1947–49)	20	1	1	1	1	–
81st	(1949–51)	34	3[g]	1	1	1	–
82nd	(1951–53)	14	–	–	–	–	–
83rd	(1953–55)	10	1	1	1	1	–
84th	(1955–57)	6	–	–	–	–	–
85th	(1957–59)	7	1	1	1	1	–
86th	(1959–61)	7	1	1	1	1	1
87th	(1961–63)	6	–	–	–	–	–
88th	(1963–65)	5	–	–	–	–	–
89th	(1965–67)	6	1	1	1	1	–
90th	(1967–69)	4	–	–	–	–	–
91st	(1969–71)	12	1	1	1	1	–
92nd	(1971–73)	15	1	1	1	–	–
93rd	(1973–75)	10	–	–	–	–	–
94th	(1975–77)	15	–	–	–	–	–
95th	(1977–79)	11	–	–	–	–	–
96th	(1979–81)	14	2	1	1	–	–
97th	(1981–83)	24	1	–	–	–	–
98th	(1983–85)	13	1	–	–	–	–
99th	(1985–87)	10	1	–	–	–	–
100th	(1987–89)	5[h]	–	–	–	–	–
101st	(1989–91)	8	1	–	–	–	–
102nd	(1991–93)	8	1[i]	1[i]	1[i]	–	–
103rd	(1993–95)	26	2[i]	2[i]	2[i]	1	1[f]
104th	(1995–97)	15	–	–	–	–	–
105th	(1997–99)	8	–	–	–	–	–
	TOTALS	540	46	31	26	19	4

NOTE: As of September 1999.

a. A discharge motion is "entered" when the petition receives sufficient signatures for it to be entered on the Calendar of Motions to Discharge Committees. This number was 145 in the 72nd and 73rd Congresses, 219 in the 86th and 87th Congresses, and 218 for all other Congresses in the table.

b. A discharge motion may be offered on the floor on any second or fourth Monday falling at least seven legislative days after the discharge petition is entered. Each day on which the House convenes is usually a legislative day.

c. A discharge petition may be filed to bring to the floor either a substantive measure in committee or a "special rule" from the Committee on Rules providing for House consideration of such a measure that is either in committee or previously reported. The last two columns of this table reflect action on the underlying, substantive measure, not on the special rule, if any, on which discharge was directly sought.

d. Includes bills and joint resolutions becoming law; constitutional amendments submitted to the states for ratification; resolutions agreed to by the House; and concurrent resolutions finally agreed to by both chambers.

e. During this Congress, the Rules Committee was discharged from a special rule for consideration of one measure, and the measure was taken up but then recommitted. Subsequently, the Rules Committee was discharged from a second special rule for consideration of the measure. This measure accordingly appears twice under "Committee discharged" and earlier columns, but only once under "Passed House" and subsequently.

f. Resolution attempting to change House Rules.

g. Includes one petition entered with respect to a special rule on a measure and another on the same measure directly.

h. Includes one petition filed on a special rule for considering two measures.

i. Includes one measure in the 102nd Congress and two in the 103rd from which the committee was discharged, and which were brought to the floor, by unanimous consent after the discharge petition was entered.

SOURCE: Richard S. Beth, "The Discharge Rule in the House: Recent Use in Historical Context," Congressional Research Service, Library of Congress, September 15, 1997; update provided by CRS, September 1999.

Sessions of the U.S. Congress, 1789–1999

Congress	Session	Date of beginning[1]	Date of adjournment[2]	Length in days	President pro tempore of the Senate[3]	Speaker of the House of Representatives
1st	1	Mar. 4, 1789	Sept. 29, 1789	210	John Langdon of New Hampshire	Frederick A. C. Muhlenberg of Pennsylvania
	2	Jan. 4, 1790	Aug. 12, 1790	221		
	3	Dec. 6, 1790	Mar. 3, 1791	88		
2nd	1	Oct. 24, 1791	May 8, 1792	197	Richard Henry Lee of Virginia	Jonathan Trumbull of Connecticut
	2	Nov. 5, 1792	Mar. 2, 1793	119	John Langdon of New Hampshire	
3rd	1	Dec. 2, 1793	June 9, 1794	190	Langdon	Frederick A. C. Muhlenberg of Pennsylvania
					Ralph Izard of South Carolina	
	2	Nov. 3, 1794	Mar. 3, 1795	121	Henry Tazewell of Virginia	
4th	1	Dec. 7, 1795	June 1, 1796	177	Tazewell	Jonathan Dayton of New Jersey
					Samuel Livermore of New Hampshire	
	2	Dec. 5, 1796	Mar. 3, 1797	89	William Bingham of Pennsylvania	
5th	1	May 15, 1797	July 10, 1797	57	William Bradford of Rhode Island	Dayton
	2	Nov. 13, 1797	July 16, 1798	246	Jacob Read of South Carolina	George Dent of Maryland[5]
					Theodore Sedgwick of Massachusetts	
	3	Dec. 3, 1798	Mar. 3, 1799	91	John Laurence of New York	
					James Ross of Pennsylvania	
6th	1	Dec. 2, 1799	May 14, 1800	164	Samuel Livermore of New Hampshire	Theodore Sedgwick of Massachusetts
					Uriah Tracy of Connecticut	
	2	Nov. 17, 1800	Mar. 3, 1801	107	John E. Howard of Maryland	
					James Hillhouse of Connecticut	
7th	1	Dec. 7, 1801	May 3, 1802	148	Abraham Baldwin of Georgia	Nathaniel Macon of North Carolina
	2	Dec. 6, 1802	Mar. 3, 1803	88	Stephen R. Bradley of Vermont	
8th	1	Oct. 17, 1803	Mar. 27, 1804	163	John Brown of Kentucky	Macon
					Jesse Franklin of North Carolina	
	2	Nov. 5, 1804	Mar. 3, 1805	119	Joseph Anderson of Tennessee	
9th	1	Dec. 2, 1805	Apr. 21, 1806	141	Samuel Smith of Maryland	Macon
	2	Dec. 1, 1806	Mar. 3, 1807	93	Smith	
10th	1	Oct. 26, 1807	Apr. 25, 1808	182	Smith	Joseph B. Varnum of Massachusetts
	2	Nov. 7, 1808	Mar. 3, 1809	117	Stephen R. Bradley of Vermont	
					John Milledge of Georgia	

(Continued)

Congress	Session	Date of beginning[1]	Date of adjournment[2]	Length in days	President pro tempore of the Senate[3]	Speaker of the House of Representatives
11th	1	May 22, 1809	June 28, 1809	38	Andrew Gregg of Pennsylvania	Varnum
	2	Nov. 27, 1809	May 1, 1810	156	John Gaillard of South Carolina	
	3	Dec. 3, 1810	Mar. 3, 1811	91	John Pope of Kentucky	
12th	1	Nov. 4, 1811	July 6, 1812	245	William H. Crawford of Georgia	Henry Clay of Kentucky
	2	Nov. 2, 1812	Mar. 3, 1813	122	Crawford	
13th	1	May 24, 1813	Aug. 2, 1813	71	Crawford	Clay
	2	Dec. 6, 1813	Apr. 18, 1814	134	Joseph B. Varnum of Massachusetts	
	3	Sept. 19, 1814	Mar. 3, 1815	166	John Gaillard of South Carolina	Langdon Cheves of South Carolina[6]
14th	1	Dec. 4, 1815	Apr. 30, 1816	148	Gaillard	Henry Clay of Kentucky
	2	Dec. 2, 1816	Mar. 3, 1817	92	Gaillard	
15th	1	Dec. 1, 1817	Apr. 20, 1818	141	Gaillard	Clay
	2	Nov. 16, 1818	Mar. 3, 1819	108	James Barbour of Virginia	
16th	1	Dec. 6, 1819	May 15, 1820	162	John Gaillard of South Carolina	Clay
	2	Nov. 13, 1820	Mar. 3, 1821	111	Gaillard	John W. Taylor of New York[7]
17th	1	Dec. 3, 1821	May 8, 1822	157	Gaillard	Philip P. Barbour of Virginia
	2	Dec. 2, 1822	Mar. 3, 1823	92	Gaillard	
18th	1	Dec. 1, 1823	May 27, 1824	178	Gaillard	Henry Clay of Kentucky
	2	Dec. 6, 1824	Mar. 3, 1825	88	Gaillard	
19th	1	Dec. 5, 1825	May 22, 1826	169	Nathaniel Macon of North Carolina	John W. Taylor of New York
	2	Dec. 4, 1826	Mar. 3, 1827	90	Macon	
20th	1	Dec. 3, 1827	May 26, 1828	175	Samuel Smith of Maryland	Andrew Stevenson of Virginia
	2	Dec. 1, 1828	Mar. 3, 1829	93	Smith	
21st	1	Dec. 7, 1829	May 31, 1830	176	Smith	Stevenson
	2	Dec. 6, 1830	Mar. 3, 1831	88	Littleton Waller Tazewell of Virginia	
22nd	1	Dec. 5, 1831	July 16, 1832	225	Tazewell	Stevenson
	2	Dec. 3, 1832	Mar. 2, 1833	91	Hugh Lawson White of Tennessee	
23rd	1	Dec. 2, 1833	June 30, 1834	211	George Poindexter of Mississippi	Stevenson
	2	Dec. 1, 1834	Mar. 3, 1835	93	John Tyler of Virginia	John Bell of Tennessee[8]
24th	1	Dec. 7, 1835	July 4, 1836	211	William R. King of Alabama	James K. Polk of Tennessee
	2	Dec. 5, 1836	Mar. 3, 1837	89	King	
25th	1	Sept. 4, 1837	Oct. 16, 1837	43	King	Polk
	2	Dec. 4, 1837	July 9, 1838	218	King	
	3	Dec. 3, 1838	Mar. 3, 1839	91	King	
26th	1	Dec. 2, 1839	July 21, 1840	233	King	Robert M. T. Hunter of Virginia
	2	Dec. 7, 1840	Mar. 3, 1841	87	King	
27th	1	May 31, 1841	Sept. 13, 1841	106	Samuel L. Southard of New Jersey	John White of Kentucky
	2	Dec. 6, 1841	Aug. 31, 1842	269	Willie P. Mangum of North Carolina	
	3	Dec. 5, 1842	Mar. 3, 1843	89	Mangum	

(Continued)

Congress	Session	Date of beginning[1]	Date of adjournment[2]	Length in days	President pro tempore of the Senate[3]	Speaker of the House of Representatives
28th	1	Dec. 4, 1843	June 17, 1844	196	Mangum	John W. Jones of Virginia
	2	Dec. 2, 1844	Mar. 3, 1845	92	Mangum	
29th	1	Dec. 1, 1845	Aug. 10, 1846	253	David R. Atchison of Missouri	John W. Davis of Indiana
	2	Dec. 7, 1846	Mar. 3, 1847	87	Atchison	
30th	1	Dec. 6, 1847	Aug. 14, 1848	254	Atchison	Robert C. Winthrop of Massachusetts
	2	Dec. 4, 1848	Mar. 3, 1849	90	Atchison	
31st	1	Dec. 3, 1849	Sept. 30, 1850	302	William R. King of Alabama	Howell Cobb of Georgia
	2	Dec. 2, 1850	Mar. 3, 1851	92	King	
32nd	1	Dec. 1, 1851	Aug. 31, 1852	275	King	Linn Boyd of Kentucky
	2	Dec. 6, 1852	Mar. 3, 1853	88	David R. Atchison of Missouri	
33rd	1	Dec. 5, 1853	Aug. 7, 1854	246	Atchison	Boyd
	2	Dec. 4, 1854	Mar. 3, 1855	90	Jesse D. Bright of Indiana Lewis Cass of Michigan	
34th	1	Dec. 3, 1855	Aug. 18, 1856	260	Jesse D. Bright of Indiana	Nathaniel P. Banks of Massachusetts
	2	Aug. 21, 1856	Aug. 30, 1856	10	Bright	
	3	Dec. 1, 1856	Mar. 3, 1857	93	James M. Mason of Virginia Thomas J. Rusk of Texas	
35th	1	Dec. 7, 1857	June 14, 1858	189	Benjamin Fitzpatrick of Alabama	James L. Orr of South Carolina
	2	Dec. 6, 1858	Mar. 3, 1859	88	Fitzpatrick	
36th	1	Dec. 5, 1859	June 25, 1860	202	Fitzpatrick Jesse D. Bright of Indiana	William Pennington of New Jersey
	2	Dec. 3, 1860	Mar. 3, 1861	93	Solomon Foot of Vermont	
37th	1	July 4, 1861	Aug. 6, 1861	34	Foot	Galusha A. Grow of Pennsylvania
	2	Dec. 2, 1861	July 17, 1862	228	Foot	
	3	Dec. 1, 1862	Mar. 3, 1863	93	Foot	
38th	1	Dec. 7, 1863	July 4, 1864	209	Foot Daniel Clark of New Hampshire	Schuyler Colfax of Indiana
	2	Dec. 5, 1864	Mar. 3, 1865	89	Clark	
39th	1	Dec. 4, 1865	July 28, 1866	237	Lafayette S. Foster of Connecticut	Colfax
	2	Dec. 3, 1866	Mar. 3, 1867	91	Benjamin F. Wade of Ohio	
40th	1	Mar. 4, 1867[9]	Dec. 2, 1867	274	Wade	Colfax
	2	Dec. 2, 1867[10]	Nov. 10, 1868	345	Wade	
	3	Dec. 7, 1868	Mar. 3, 1869	87	Wade	Theodore M. Pomeroy of New York [11]
41st	1	Mar. 4, 1869	Apr. 10, 1869	38	Henry B. Anthony of Rhode Island	James G. Blaine of Maine
	2	Dec. 6, 1869	July 15, 1870	222	Anthony	
	3	Dec. 5, 1870	Mar. 3, 1871	89	Anthony	
42nd	1	Mar. 4, 1871	Apr. 20, 1871	48	Anthony	Blaine
	2	Dec. 4, 1871	June 10, 1872	190	Anthony	
	3	Dec. 2, 1872	Mar. 3, 1873	92	Anthony	
43rd	1	Dec. 1, 1873	June 23, 1874	204	Matthew H. Carpenter of Wisconsin	Blaine
	2	Dec. 7, 1874	Mar. 3, 1875	87	Carpenter Henry B. Anthony of Rhode Island	

(Continued)

Congress	Session	Date of beginning[1]	Date of adjournment[2]	Length in days	President pro tempore of the Senate[3]	Speaker of the House of Representatives
44th	1	Dec. 6, 1875	Aug. 15, 1876	254	Thomas W. Ferry of Michigan	Michael C. Kerr of Indiana[12] Samuel S. Cox of New York, pro tempore[13] Milton Sayler of Ohio, pro tempore[14]
	2	Dec. 4, 1876	Mar. 3, 1877	90	Ferry	Samuel J. Randall of Pennsylvania
45th	1	Oct. 15, 1877	Dec. 3, 1877	50	Ferry	Randall
	2	Dec. 3, 1877	June 20, 1878	200	Ferry	
	3	Dec. 2, 1878	Mar. 3, 1879	92	Ferry	
46th	1	Mar. 18, 1879	July 1, 1879	106	Allen G. Thurman of Ohio	Randall
	2	Dec. 1, 1879	June 16, 1880	199	Thurman	
	3	Dec. 6, 1880	Mar. 3, 1881	88	Thurman	
47th	1	Dec. 5, 1881	Aug. 8, 1882	247	Thomas F. Bayard of Delaware David Davis of Illinois	J. Warren Keifer of Ohio
	2	Dec. 4, 1882	Mar. 3, 1883	90	George F. Edmunds of Vermont	
48th	1	Dec. 3, 1883	July 7, 1884	218	Edmunds	John G. Carlisle of Kentucky
	2	Dec. 1, 1884	Mar. 3, 1885	93	Edmunds	
49th	1	Dec. 7, 1885	Aug. 5, 1886	242	John Sherman of Ohio	Carlisle
	2	Dec. 6, 1886	Mar. 3, 1887	88	John J. Ingalls of Kansas	
50th	1	Dec. 5, 1887	Oct. 20, 1888	321	Ingalls	Carlisle
	2	Dec. 3, 1888	Mar. 3, 1889	91	Ingalls	
51st	1	Dec. 2, 1889	Oct. 1, 1890	304	Ingalls	Thomas B. Reed of Maine
	2	Dec. 1, 1890	Mar. 3, 1891	93	Charles F. Manderson of Nebraska	
52nd	1	Dec. 7, 1891	Aug. 5, 1892	251	Manderson	Charles F. Crisp of Georgia
	2	Dec. 5, 1892	Mar. 3, 1893	89	Isham G. Harris of Tennessee	
53rd	1	Aug. 7, 1893	Nov. 3, 1893	89	Harris	Crisp
	2	Dec. 4, 1893	Aug. 28, 1894	268	Harris	
	3	Dec. 3, 1894	Mar. 3, 1895	97	Matt W. Ransom of North Carolina Isham G. Harris of Tennessee	
54th	1	Dec. 2, 1895	June 11, 1896	193	William P. Frye of Maine	Thomas B. Reed of Maine
	2	Dec. 7, 1896	Mar. 3, 1897	87	Frye	
55th	1	Mar. 15, 1897	July 24, 1897	131	Frye	Reed
	2	Dec. 6, 1897	July 8, 1898	215	Frye	
	3	Dec. 5, 1898	Mar. 3, 1899	89	Frye	
56th	1	Dec. 4, 1899	June 7, 1900	186	Frye	David B. Henderson of Iowa
	2	Dec. 3, 1900	Mar. 3, 1901	91	Frye	
57th	1	Dec. 2, 1901	July 1, 1902	212	Frye	Henderson
	2	Dec. 1, 1902	Mar. 3, 1903	93	Frye	
58th	1	Nov. 9, 1903	Dec. 7, 1903	29	Frye	Joseph G. Cannon of Illinois
	2	Dec. 7, 1903	Apr. 28, 1904	144	Frye	
	3	Dec. 5, 1904	Mar. 3, 1905	89	Frye	
59th	1	Dec. 4, 1905	June 30, 1906	209	Frye	Cannon
	2	Dec. 3, 1906	Mar. 3, 1907	91	Frye	
60th	1	Dec. 2, 1907	May 30, 1908	181	Frye	Cannon
	2	Dec. 7, 1908	Mar. 3, 1909	87	Frye	

(Continued)

Congress	Session	Date of beginning[1]	Date of adjournment[2]	Length in days	President pro tempore of the Senate[3]	Speaker of the House of Representatives
61st	1	Mar. 15, 1909	Aug. 5, 1909	144	Frye	Cannon
	2	Dec. 6, 1909	June 25, 1910	202	Frye	
	3	Dec. 5, 1910	Mar. 3, 1911	89	Frye	
62nd	1	Apr. 4, 1911	Aug. 22, 1911	141	Frye[15]	Champ Clark of Missouri
	2	Dec. 4, 1911	Aug. 26, 1912	267	Augustus O. Bacon of Georgia[16]	
					Frank B. Brandegee of Connecticut[17]	
					Charles Curtis of Kansas[18]	
					Jacob H. Gallinger of New Hampshire[19]	
					Henry Cabot Lodge of Massachusetts[20]	
	3	Dec. 2, 1912	Mar. 3, 1913	92	Bacon;[21] Gallinger[22]	
63rd	1	Apr. 7, 1913	Dec. 1, 1913	239	James P. Clarke of Arkansas	Clark
	2	Dec. 1, 1913	Oct. 24, 1914	328	Clarke	
	3	Dec. 7, 1914	Mar. 3, 1915	87	Clarke	
64th	1	Dec. 6, 1915	Sept. 8, 1916	278	Clarke[23]	Clark
	2	Dec. 4, 1916	Mar. 3, 1917	90	Willard Saulsbury of Delaware	
65th	1	Apr. 2, 1917	Oct. 6, 1917	188	Saulsbury	Clark
	2	Dec. 3, 1917	Nov. 21, 1918	354	Saulsbury	
	3	Dec. 2, 1918	Mar. 3, 1919	92	Saulsbury	
66th	1	May 19, 1919	Nov. 19, 1919	185	Albert B. Cummins of Iowa	Frederick H. Gillett of Massachusetts
	2	Dec. 1, 1919	June 5, 1920	188	Cummins	
	3	Dec. 6, 1920	Mar. 3, 1921	88	Cummins	
67th	1	Apr. 11, 1921	Nov. 23, 1921	227	Cummins	Gillett
	2	Dec. 5, 1921	Sept. 22, 1922	292	Cummins	
	3	Nov. 20, 1922	Dec. 4, 1922	15	Cummins	
	4	Dec. 4, 1922	Mar. 3, 1923	90	Cummins	
68th	1	Dec. 3, 1923	June 7, 1924	188	Cummins	Gillett
	2	Dec. 1, 1924	Mar. 3, 1925	93	Cummins	
69th	1	Dec. 7, 1925	July 3, 1926	209	George H. Moses of New Hampshire	Nicholas Longworth of Ohio
	2	Dec. 6, 1926	Mar. 3, 1927	88	Moses	
70th	1	Dec. 5, 1927	May 29, 1928	177	Moses	Longworth
	2	Dec. 3, 1928	Mar. 3, 1929	91	Moses	
71st	1	Apr. 15, 1929	Nov. 22, 1929	222	Moses	Longworth
	2	Dec. 2, 1929	July 3, 1930	214	Moses	
	3	Dec. 1, 1930	Mar. 3, 1931	93	Moses	
72nd	1	Dec. 7, 1931	July 16, 1932	223	Moses	John N. Garner of Texas
	2	Dec. 5, 1932	Mar. 3, 1933	89	Moses	
73rd	1	Mar. 9, 1933	June 15, 1933	99	Key Pittman of Nevada	Henry T. Rainey of Illinois[24]
	2	Jan. 3, 1934	June 18, 1934	167	Pittman	
74th	1	Jan. 3, 1935	Aug. 26, 1935	236	Pittman	Joseph W. Byrns of Tennessee[25]
	2	Jan. 3, 1936	June 20, 1936	170	Pittman	William B. Bankhead of Alabama[26]
75th	1	Jan. 5, 1937	Aug. 21, 1937	229	Pittman	Bankhead
	2	Nov. 15, 1937	Dec. 21, 1937	37	Pittman	
	3	Jan. 3, 1938	June 16, 1938	165	Pittman	

(Continued)

Congress	Session	Date of beginning[1]	Date of adjournment[2]	Length in days	President pro tempore of the Senate[3]	Speaker of the House of Representatives
76th	1	Jan. 3, 1939	Aug. 5, 1939	215	Pittman	Bankhead [27]
	2	Sept. 21, 1939	Nov. 3, 1939	44	Pittman	
	3	Jan. 3, 1940	Jan. 3, 1941	367	Pittman [28] William H. King of Utah [30]	Sam Rayburn of Texas [29]
77th	1	Jan. 3, 1941	Jan. 2, 1942	365	Pat Harrison of Mississippi[31] Carter Glass of Virginia [32]	Rayburn
	2	Jan. 5, 1942	Dec. 16, 1942	346		
78th	1	Jan. 6, 1943 [33]	Dec. 21, 1943	350	Glass	Rayburn
	2	Jan. 10, 1944 [34]	Dec. 19, 1944	345	Glass	
79th	1	Jan. 3, 1945 [35]	Dec. 21, 1945	353	Kenneth McKellar of Tennessee	Rayburn
	2	Jan. 14, 1946 [36]	Aug. 2, 1946	201	McKellar	
80th	1	Jan. 3, 1947 [37]	Dec. 19, 1947	351	Arthur H. Vandenberg of Michigan	Joseph W. Martin Jr. of Massachusetts
	2	Jan. 6, 1948 [38]	Dec. 31, 1948	361	Vandenberg	
81st	1	Jan. 3, 1949	Oct. 19, 1949	290	Kenneth McKellar of Tennessee	Sam Rayburn of Texas
	2	Jan. 3, 1950 [39]	Jan. 2, 1951	365	McKellar	
82nd	1	Jan. 3, 1951 [40]	Oct. 20, 1951	291	McKellar	Rayburn
	2	Jan. 8, 1952 [41]	July 7, 1952	182	McKellar	
83rd	1	Jan. 3, 1953 [42]	Aug. 3, 1953	213	Styles Bridges of New Hampshire	Joseph W. Martin Jr. of Massachusetts
	2	Jan. 6, 1954 [43]	Dec. 2, 1954	331	Bridges	
84th	1	Jan. 5, 1955 [44]	Aug. 2, 1955	210	Walter F. George of Georgia	Sam Rayburn of Texas
	2	Jan. 3, 1956 [45]	July 27, 1956	207	George	
85th	1	Jan. 3, 1957 [46]	Aug. 30, 1957	239	Carl Hayden of Arizona	Rayburn
	2	Jan. 7, 1958 [47]	Aug. 24, 1958	230	Hayden	
86th	1	Jan. 7, 1959 [48]	Sept. 15, 1959	252	Hayden	Rayburn
	2	Jan. 6, 1960 [49]	Sept. 1, 1960	240	Hayden	
87th	1	Jan. 3, 1961 [50]	Sept. 27, 1961	268	Hayden	Rayburn [51]
	2	Jan. 10, 1962 [52]	Oct. 13, 1962	277	Hayden	John W. McCormack of Massachusetts [53]
88th	1	Jan. 9, 1963 [54]	Dec. 30, 1963	356	Hayden	McCormack
	2	Jan. 7, 1964 [55]	Oct. 3, 1964	270	Hayden	
89th	1	Jan. 4, 1965	Oct. 23, 1965	293	Hayden	McCormack
	2	Jan. 10, 1966 [56]	Oct. 22, 1966	286	Hayden	
90th	1	Jan. 10, 1967 [57]	Dec. 15, 1967	340	Hayden	McCormack
	2	Jan. 15, 1968 [58]	Oct. 14, 1968	274	Hayden	
91st	1	Jan. 3, 1969 [59]	Dec. 23, 1969	355	Richard B. Russell of Georgia	McCormack
	2	Jan. 19, 1970 [60]	Jan. 2, 1971	349	Russell	
92nd	1	Jan. 21, 1971 [61]	Dec. 17, 1971	331	Russell[62] Allen J. Ellender of Louisiana[63]	Carl Albert of Oklahoma
	2	Jan. 18, 1972 [64]	Oct. 18, 1972	275	Ellender [65] James O. Eastland of Mississippi [66]	
93rd	1	Jan. 3, 1973 [67]	Dec. 22, 1973	354	Eastland	Albert
	2	Jan. 21, 1974 [68]	Dec. 20, 1974	334	Eastland	
94th	1	Jan. 14, 1975 [69]	Dec. 19, 1975	340	Eastland	Albert
	2	Jan. 19, 1976 [70]	Oct. 1, 1976	257	Eastland	

(Continued)

Congress	Session	Date of beginning[1]	Date of adjournment[2]	Length in days	President pro tempore of the Senate[3]	Speaker of the House of Representatives
95th	1	Jan. 4, 1977 [71]	Dec. 15, 1977	346	Eastland	Thomas P. O'Neill Jr. of Massachusetts
	2	Jan. 19, 1978 [72]	Oct. 15, 1978	270	Eastland	
96th	1	Jan. 15, 1979 [73]	Jan. 3, 1980	354	Warren G. Magnuson of Washington	O'Neill
	2	Jan. 3, 1980 [74]	Dec. 16, 1980	349	Magnuson	
97th	1	Jan. 5, 1981 [75]	Dec. 16, 1981	347	Strom Thurmond of South Carolina	O'Neill
	2	Jan. 25, 1982 [76]	Dec. 23, 1982	333	Thurmond	
98th	1	Jan. 3, 1983 [77]	Nov. 18, 1983	320	Thurmond	O'Neill
	2	Jan. 23, 1984 [78]	Oct. 12, 1984	264	Thurmond	
99th	1	Jan. 3, 1985 [79]	Dec. 20, 1985	352	Thurmond	O'Neill
	2	Jan. 21, 1986 [80]	Oct. 18, 1986	278	Thurmond	
100th	1	Jan. 6, 1987 [81]	Dec. 22, 1987	351	John C. Stennis of Mississippi	Jim Wright of Texas
	2	Jan. 25, 1988 [82]	Oct. 22, 1988	272	Stennis	
101st	1	Jan. 3, 1989 [83]	Nov. 22, 1989	324	Robert C. Byrd of West Virginia	Wright; Thomas S. Foley of Washington [84]
	2	Jan. 23, 1990 [85]	Oct. 28, 1990	260	Byrd	Foley
102nd	1	Jan. 3, 1991 [86]	Jan. 3, 1992	366	Byrd	Foley
	2	Jan. 3, 1992 [87]	Oct. 9, 1992	281	Byrd	
103rd	1	Jan. 5, 1993[88]	Nov. 26, 1993	326	Byrd	Foley
	2	Jan. 25, 1994[89]	Dec. 1, 1994	311	Byrd	
104th	1	Jan. 4, 1995[90]	Jan. 3, 1996	365	Strom Thurmond of South Carolina	Newt Gingrich of Georgia
	2	Jan. 3, 1996[91]	Oct. 4, 1996	276	Thurmond	
105th	1	Jan. 7, 1997[92]	Nov. 13, 1997	311	Thurmond	Gingrich
	2	Jan. 27, 1998[93]	Dec. 19, 1998	327	Thurmond	
106th[94]	1	Jan. 6, 1999[95]	—	—	Thurmond	J. Dennis Hastert of Illinois

NOTES: 1. The Constitution (art. I, sec. 4) provided that "The Congress shall assemble at least once in every year . . . on the first Monday in December, unless they shall by law appoint a different day." Pursuant to a resolution of the Continental Congress, the first session of the First Congress convened March 4, 1789. Up to and including May 20, 1820, 18 acts were passed providing for the meeting of Congress on other days in the year. After 1820 Congress met regularly on the first Monday in December until 1934, when the Twentieth Amendment to the Constitution became effective changing the meeting date to Jan. 3. (Until then, brief special sessions of the Senate only were held at the beginning of each presidential term to confirm Cabinet and other nominations—and occasionally at other times for other purposes. The Senate last met in special session from March 4 to March 6, 1933.) The first and second sessions of the First Congress were held in New York City. Subsequently, including the first session of the Sixth Congress, Philadelphia was the meeting place; since then, Congress has convened in Washington.

2. Until adoption of the Twentieth Amendment, the deadline for adjournment of Congress in odd-numbered years was March 3. However, the expiring Congress often extended the "legislative day" of March 3 up to noon of March 4, when the new Congress came officially into being. After ratification of the Twentieth Amendment, the deadline for adjournment of Congress in odd-numbered years was noon on Jan. 3.

3. At one time, the appointment or election of a president pro tempore was considered by the Senate to be for the occasion only, so that more than one appear in several sessions, and in others none was chosen. Since March 12, 1890, they have served until "the Senate otherwise ordered."

4. Elected to count the vote for president and vice president, which was done April 6, 1789, because there was a quorum of the Senate for the first time. John Adams, vice president, appeared April 21, 1789, and took his seat as president of the Senate.

5. Elected Speaker pro tempore for April 20, 1798, and again for May 28, 1798.

6. Elected Speaker Jan. 19, 1814, to succeed Henry Clay, who resigned Jan. 19, 1814.

7. Elected Speaker Nov. 15, 1820, to succeed Henry Clay, who resigned Oct. 28, 1820.

8. Elected Speaker June 2, 1834, to succeed Andrew Stevenson of Virginia, who resigned.

9. There were recesses in this session from Saturday, Mar. 30, to Wednesday, July 1, and from Saturday, July 20, to Thursday, Nov. 21.

10. There were recesses in this session from Monday, July 27, to Monday, Sept. 21, to Friday, Oct. 16, and to Tuesday, Nov. 10. No business was transacted subsequent to July 27.

11. Elected Speaker Mar. 3, 1869, and served one day.

12. Died Aug. 19, 1876.

13. Appointed Speaker pro tempore Feb. 17, May 12, June 19.

14. Appointed Speaker pro tempore June 4.

15. Resigned as president pro tempore Apr. 27, 1911.

16. Elected to serve Jan. 11–17, Mar. 11–12, Apr. 8, May 10, May 30 to June 1 and 3, June 13 to July 5, Aug. 1–10, and Aug. 27 to Dec. 15, 1912.

17. Elected to serve May 25, 1912.

18. Elected to serve Dec. 4–12, 1911.

19. Elected to serve Feb. 12–14, Apr. 26–27, May 7, July 6–31, Aug. 12–26, 1912.

20. Elected to serve Mar. 25–26, 1912.

21. Elected to serve Aug. 27 to Dec. 15, 1912, Jan. 5–18, and Feb. 2–15, 1913.

22. Elected to serve Dec. 16, 1912, to Jan. 4, 1913, Jan. 19 to Feb. 1, and Feb. 16 to Mar. 3, 1913.

23. Died Oct. 1, 1916.

24. Died Aug. 19, 1934.

25. Died June 4, 1936.

26. Elected June 4, 1936.

27. Died Sept. 15, 1940.

28. Died Nov. 10, 1940.

29. Elected Sept. 16, 1940.

30. Elected Nov. 19, 1940.

31. Elected Jan. 6, 1941; died June 22, 1941.

32. Elected July 10, 1941.

33. There was a recess in this session from Thursday, July 8, to Tuesday, Sept. 14.

34. There were recesses in this session from Saturday, Apr. 1, to Wednesday, Apr. 12; from Friday, June 23, to Tuesday, Aug. 1; and from Thursday, Sept. 21, to Tuesday, Nov. 14.

35. The House was in recess in this session from Saturday, July 21, 1945, to Wednesday, Sept. 5, 1945, and the Senate from Wednesday, Aug. 1, 1945, to Wednesday, Sept. 5, 1945.

36. The House was in recess in this session from Thursday, Apr. 18, 1946, to Tuesday, Apr. 30, 1946.

37. There was a recess in this session from Sunday, July 27, 1947, to Monday, Nov. 17, 1947.

38. There were recesses in this session from Sunday, June 20, 1948, to Monday, July 26, 1948, and from Saturday, Aug. 7, 1948, to Friday, Dec. 31, 1948.

39. The House was in recess in this session from Thursday, Apr. 6, 1950, to Tuesday, Apr. 18, 1950, and both the Senate and the House were in recess from Saturday, Sept. 23, 1950, to Monday, Nov. 27, 1950.

40. The House was in recess in this session from Thursday, Mar. 22, 1951, to Monday, Apr. 2, 1951, and from Thursday, Aug. 23, 1951, to Wednesday, Sept. 12, 1951.

41. The House was in recess in this session from Thursday, Apr. 10, 1952, to Tuesday, Apr. 22, 1952.

42. The House was in recess in this session from Thursday, Apr. 2, 1953, to Monday, Apr. 13, 1953.

43. The House was in recess in this session from Thursday, Apr. 15, 1954, to Monday, Apr. 26, 1954, and adjourned sine die Aug. 20, 1954. The Senate was in recess in this session from Friday, Aug. 20, 1954, to Monday, Nov. 8, 1954; from Thursday, Nov. 18, 1954, to Monday, Nov. 29, 1954, and adjourned sine die Dec. 2, 1954.

44. There was a recess in this session from Monday, Apr. 4, 1955, to Wednesday, Apr. 13, 1955.

45. There was a recess in this session from Thursday, Mar. 29, 1956, to Monday, Apr. 9, 1956.

46. There was a recess in this session from Thursday, Apr. 18, 1957, to Monday, Apr. 29, 1957.

47. There was a recess in this session from Thursday, Apr. 3, 1958, to Monday, Apr. 14, 1958.

48. There was a recess in this session from Thursday, Mar. 26, 1959, to Tuesday, Apr. 7, 1959.

49. The Senate was in recess in this session from Thursday, Apr. 14, 1960, to Monday, Apr. 18, 1960; from Friday, May 27, 1960, to Tuesday, May 31, 1960, and from Sunday, July 3, 1960, to Monday, Aug. 8, 1960. The House was in recess in this session from Thursday, Apr. 14, 1960, to Monday, Apr. 18, 1960; from Friday, May 27, 1960, to Tuesday, May 31, 1960, and from Sunday, July 3, 1960, to Monday, Aug. 15, 1960.

50. The House was in recess in this session from Thursday, Mar. 30, 1961, to Monday, Apr. 10, 1961.

51. Died Nov. 16, 1961.

52. The House was in recess in this session from Thursday, Apr. 19, 1962, to Monday, Apr. 30, 1962.

53. Elected Jan. 10, 1962.

54. The House was in recess in this session from Thursday, Apr. 11, 1963, to Monday, Apr. 22, 1963.

55. The House was in recess in this session from Thursday, Mar. 26, 1964, to Monday, Apr. 6, 1964; from Thursday, July 2, 1964, to Monday, July 20, 1964; from Friday, Aug. 21, 1964, to Monday, Aug. 31, 1964. The Senate was in recess in this session from Friday, July 10, 1964, to Monday, July 20, 1964; from Friday, Aug. 21, 1964, to Monday, Aug. 31, 1964.

56. The House was in recess in this session from Thursday, Apr. 7, 1966, to Monday, Apr. 18, 1966; from Thursday, June 30, 1966, to Monday, July 11, 1966. The Senate was in recess in this session from Thursday, Apr. 7, 1966, to Wednesday, Apr. 13, 1966; from Thursday, June 30, 1966, to Monday, July 11, 1966.

57. There was a recess in this session from Thursday, Mar. 23, 1967, to Monday, Apr. 3, 1967; from Thursday, June 29, 1967, to Monday, July 10, 1967; from Thursday, Aug. 31, 1967, to Monday, Sept. 11, 1967; and from Wednesday, Nov. 22, 1967, to Monday, Nov. 27, 1967.

58. The House was in recess this session from Thursday, Apr. 11, 1968, to Monday, Apr. 22, 1968; from Wednesday, May 29, 1968, to Monday, June 3, 1968; from Wednesday, July 3, 1968, to Monday, July 8, 1968; from Friday, Aug. 2, 1968, to Wednesday, Sept. 4, 1968. The Senate was in recess this session from Thursday, Apr. 11, 1968, to Wednesday, Apr. 17, 1968; from Wednesday, May 29, 1968, to Monday, June 3, 1968; from Wednesday, July 3, 1968, to Monday, July 8, 1968; from Friday, Aug. 2, 1968, to Wednesday, Sept. 4, 1968.

59. The House was in recess this session from Friday, Feb. 7, 1969, to Monday, Feb. 17, 1969; from Thursday, Apr. 3, 1969, to Monday, Apr. 14, 1969; from Wednesday, May 28, 1969, to Monday, June 2, 1969; from Wednesday, July 2, 1969, to Monday, July 7, 1969; from Wednesday, Aug. 13, 1969, to Wednesday, Sept. 3, 1969; from Thursday, Nov. 6, 1969, to Wednesday, Nov. 12, 1969; from Wednesday, Nov. 26, 1969, to Monday, Dec. 1, 1969. The Senate was in recess this session from Friday, Feb. 7, 1969, to Monday, Feb. 17, 1969; from Thursday, Apr. 3, 1969, to Monday, Apr. 14, 1969; from Wednesday, July 2, 1969, to Monday, July 7, 1969; from Wednesday, Aug. 13, 1969, to Wednesday, Sept. 3, 1969; from Wednesday, Nov. 26, 1969, to Monday, Dec. 1, 1969.

60. The House was in recess this session from Tuesday, Feb. 10, 1970, to Monday, Feb. 16, 1970; from Thursday, Mar. 26, 1970, to Tuesday, Mar. 31, 1970; from Wednesday, May 27, 1970, to Monday, June 1, 1970; from Wednesday, July 1, 1970, to Monday, July 6, 1970; from Friday, Aug. 14, 1970, to Wednesday, Sept. 9, 1970; from Wednesday, Oct. 14, 1970, to Monday, Nov. 16, 1970; from Wednesday, Nov. 25, 1970, to Monday, Nov. 30, 1970; from Tuesday, Dec. 22, 1970, to Tuesday, Dec. 29, 1970. The Senate was in recess this session from Tuesday, Feb. 10, 1970, to Monday, Feb. 16, 1970; from Thursday, Mar. 26, 1970, to Tuesday, Mar. 31, 1970; from Wednesday, Sept. 2, 1970, to Tuesday, Sept. 8, 1970; from Wednesday, Oct. 14, 1970, to Monday, Nov. 16, 1970; from Wednesday, Nov. 25, 1970, to Monday, Nov. 30, 1970; from Tuesday, Dec. 22, 1970, to Monday, Dec. 28, 1970.

61. The House was in recess this session from Wednesday, Feb. 10, 1971, to Wednesday, Feb. 17, 1971; from Wednesday, Apr. 7, 1971, to Monday, Apr. 19, 1971; from Thursday, May 27, 1971, to Tuesday, June 1, 1971; from Thursday, July 1, 1971, to Tuesday, July 6, 1971; from Friday, Aug. 6, 1971, to Wednesday, Sept. 8, 1971; from Thursday, Oct. 7, 1971, to Tuesday, Oct. 12, 1971; from Thursday, Oct. 21, 1971, to Tuesday, Oct. 26, 1971; from Friday, Nov. 19, 1971, to Monday, Nov. 29, 1971. The Senate was in recess this session from Thursday, Feb. 11, 1971, to Wednesday, Feb. 17, 1971; from Wednesday, Apr. 7, 1971, to Wednesday, Apr. 14, 1971; from Wednesday, May 26, 1971, to Tuesday, June 1, 1971; from Wednesday, June 30, 1971, to Tuesday, July 6, 1971; from Friday, Aug. 6, 1971, to Wednesday, Sept. 8, 1971; from Thursday, Oct. 21, 1971, to Tuesday, Oct. 26, 1971; from Wednesday, Nov. 24, 1971, to Monday, Nov. 29, 1971.

62. Died Jan. 21, 1971.

63. Elected Jan. 22, 1971.

64. The House was in recess this session from Wednesday, Feb. 9, 1972, to Wednesday, Feb. 16, 1972; from Wednesday, Mar. 29, 1972, to Monday, Apr. 10, 1972; from Wednesday, May 24, 1972, to Tuesday, May 30, 1972; from Friday, June 30, 1972, to Monday, July 17, 1972; from Friday, Aug. 18, 1972, to Tuesday, Sept. 5, 1972. The Senate was in recess this session from Wednesday, Feb. 9, 1972, to Monday, Feb. 14, 1972; from Thursday, Mar. 30, 1972, to Tuesday, Apr. 4, 1972; from Thursday, May 25, 1972, to Tuesday, May 30, 1972; from Friday, June 30, 1972, to Monday, July 17, 1972; from Friday, Aug. 18, 1972, to Tuesday, Sept. 5, 1972.

65. Died July 27, 1972.

66. Elected July 28, 1972.

67. The House was in recess this session from Thursday, Feb. 8, 1973, to Monday, Feb. 19, 1973; from Thursday, Apr. 19, 1973, to Monday, Apr. 30, 1973; from Thursday, May 24, 1973, to Tuesday, May 29, 1973; from Saturday, June 30, 1973, to Tuesday, July 10, 1973; from Friday, Aug. 3, 1973, to Wednesday, Sept. 5, 1973; from Thursday, Oct. 4, 1973, to Tuesday, Oct. 9, 1973; from Thursday, Oct. 18, 1973, to Tuesday, Oct. 23, 1973; from Thursday, Nov. 15, 1973 to Monday, Nov. 26, 1973. The Senate was in recess this session from Thursday, Feb. 8, 1973, to Thursday, Feb. 15, 1973; from Wednesday, Apr. 18, 1973, to Monday, Apr. 30, 1973; from Wednesday, May 23, 1973, to Tuesday, May 29, 1973; from Saturday, June 30, 1973, to Monday, July 9, 1973; from Friday, Aug. 3, 1973, to Wednesday, Sept. 5, 1973; from Thursday, Oct. 18, 1973, to Tuesday, Oct. 23, 1973; from Wednesday, Nov. 21, 1973, to Monday, Nov. 26, 1973.

68. The House was in recess this session from Thursday, Feb. 7, 1974, to Wednesday, Feb. 13, 1974; from Thursday, Apr. 11, 1974, to Monday, Apr. 22, 1974; from Thursday, May 23, 1974, to Tuesday, May 28, 1974; from Thursday, Aug. 22, 1974, to Wednesday, Sept. 11, 1974; from Thursday, Oct. 17, 1974, to Monday, Nov. 18, 1974; from Tuesday, Nov. 26, 1974, to Tuesday, Dec. 3, 1974. The Senate was in recess this session from Friday, Feb. 8, 1974, to Monday, Feb. 18, 1974; from Wednesday, Mar. 13, 1974, to Tuesday, Mar. 19, 1974; from Thursday, Apr. 11, 1974, to Monday, Apr. 22, 1974; from Wednesday, May 23, 1974, to Tuesday, May 28, 1974; from Thursday, Aug. 22, 1974, to Wednesday, Sept. 4, 1974; from Thursday, Oct. 17, 1974, to Monday, Nov. 18, 1974; from Tuesday, Nov. 26, 1974, to Monday, Dec. 2, 1974.

69. The House was in recess this session from Wednesday, Mar. 26, 1975, to Monday, Apr. 7, 1975; from Thursday, May 22, 1975, to Monday, June 2, 1975; from Thursday, June 26, 1975, to Tuesday, July 8, 1975; from Friday, Aug. 1, 1975, to Wednesday, Sept. 3, 1975; from Thursday, Oct. 9, 1975, to Monday, Oct. 20, 1975; from Thursday, Oct. 23, 1975, to Tuesday, Oct. 28, 1975; from Thursday, Nov. 20, 1975, to Monday, Dec. 1, 1975. The Senate was in recess this session from Wednesday, Mar. 26, 1975, to Monday, Apr. 7, 1975; from Thursday, May 22, 1975, to Monday, June 2, 1975; from Friday, June 27, 1975, to Monday, July 7, 1975; from Friday, Aug. 1, 1975, to Wednesday, Sept. 3, 1975; from Thursday, Oct. 9, 1975, to Monday, Oct. 20, 1975; from Thursday, Oct. 23, 1975, to Tuesday, Oct. 28, 1975; from Thursday, Nov. 20, 1975, to Monday, Dec. 1, 1975.

70. The House was in recess in this session from Wednesday, Feb. 11, 1976, to Monday, Feb. 16, 1976; from Wednesday, Apr. 14, 1976, to Monday, Apr. 26, 1976; from Thursday, May 27, 1976, to Tuesday, June 1, 1976; from Friday, July 2, 1976, to Monday, July 19, 1976; from Tuesday, Aug. 10, 1976, to Monday, Aug. 23, 1976; from Thursday, Sept. 2, 1976, to Wednesday, Sept. 8, 1976.

The Senate was in recess this session from Friday, Feb. 6, 1976, to Monday, Feb. 16, 1976; from Wednesday, Apr. 14, 1976, to Monday, Apr. 26, 1976; from Friday, May 28, 1976, to Wednesday, June 2, 1976; from Friday, July 2, 1976, to Monday, July 19, 1976; from Tuesday, Aug. 10, 1976, to Monday, Aug. 23, 1976; from Wednesday, Sept. 1, 1976, to Tuesday, Sept. 7, 1976.

71. The House was in recess this session from Wednesday, Feb. 9, 1977, to Wednesday, Feb. 16, 1977; from Wednesday, Apr. 6, 1977, to Monday, Apr. 18, 1977; from Thursday, May 26, 1977, to Wednesday, June 1, 1977; from Thursday, June 30, 1977, to Monday, July 11, 1977; from Friday, Aug. 5, 1977, to Wednesday, Sept. 7, 1977; from Thursday, Oct. 6, 1977, to Tuesday, Oct. 11, 1977. The Senate was in recess this session from Friday, Feb. 11, 1977, to Monday, Feb. 21, 1977; from Thursday, Apr. 7, 1977, to Monday, Apr. 18, 1977; from Friday, May 27, 1977, to Monday, June 6, 1977; from Friday, July 1, 1977, to Monday, July 11, 1977; from Saturday, Aug. 6, 1977, to Wednesday, Sept. 7, 1977.

72. The House was in recess this session from Thursday, Feb. 9, 1978, to Tuesday, Feb. 14, 1978; from Wednesday, Mar. 22, 1978, to Monday, Apr. 3, 1978; from Thursday, May 25, 1978, to Wednesday, May 31, 1978; from Thursday, June 29, 1978, to Monday, July 10, 1978; from Thursday, Aug. 17, 1978, to Wednesday, Sept. 6, 1978. The Senate was in recess this session from Friday, Feb. 10, 1978, to Monday, Feb. 20, 1978; from Thursday, Mar. 23, 1978, to Monday, Apr. 3, 1978; from Friday, May 26, 1978, to Monday, June 5, 1978; from Thursday, June 29, 1978, to Monday, July 10, 1978; from Friday, Aug. 25, 1978, to Wednesday, Sept. 6, 1978.

73. The House was in recess this session from Thursday, Feb. 8, 1979, to Tuesday, Feb. 13, 1979; from Tuesday, Apr. 10, 1979, to Monday, Apr. 23, 1979; from Thursday, May 24, 1979, to Wednesday, May 30, 1979; from Friday, June 29, 1979, to Monday, July 9, 1979; from Thursday, Aug. 2, 1979, to Wednesday, Sept. 5, 1979; from Tuesday, Nov. 20, 1979, to Monday, Nov. 26, 1979. The Senate was in recess this session from Friday, Feb. 9, 1979, to Monday, Feb. 19, 1979; from Tuesday, Apr. 10, 1979, to Monday, Apr. 23, 1979; from Friday, May 25, 1979, to Monday, June 4, 1979; from Friday, Aug. 3, 1979, to Wednesday, Sept. 5, 1979; from Tuesday, Nov. 20, 1979, to Monday, Nov. 26, 1979.

74. The House was in recess this session from Wednesday, Feb. 13, 1980, to Tuesday, Feb. 19, 1980; from Wednesday, Apr. 2, 1980, to Tuesday, Apr. 15, 1980; from Thursday, May 22, 1980, to Wednesday, May 28, 1980; from Wednesday, July 2, 1980, to Monday, July 21, 1980; from Friday, Aug. 1, 1980, to Monday, Aug. 18, 1980; from Thursday, Aug. 28, 1980, to Wednesday, Sept. 13, 1980. The Senate was in recess this session from Monday, Feb. 11, 1980, to Thursday, Feb. 14, 1980; from Thursday, Apr. 3, 1980, to Tuesday, Apr. 15, 1980; from Thursday, May 22, 1980, to Wednesday, May 28, 1980; from Wednesday, July 2, 1980, to Monday, July 21, 1980; from Wednesday, Aug. 6, 1980, to Monday, Aug. 18, 1980; from Wednesday, Aug. 27, 1980, to Wednesday, Sept. 3, 1980; from Wednesday, Oct. 1, 1980, to Wednesday, Nov. 12, 1980; from Monday, Nov. 24, 1980, to Monday, Dec. 1, 1980.

75. The House was in recess this session from Friday, Feb. 6, 1981, to Tuesday, Feb. 17, 1981; from Friday, Apr. 10, 1981, to Monday, Apr. 27, 1981; from Friday, June 26, 1981, to Wednesday, July 8, 1981; from Tuesday, Aug. 4, 1981, to Wednesday, Sept. 9, 1981; from Wednesday, Oct. 7, 1981, to Tuesday, Oct. 13, 1981; from Monday, Nov. 23, 1981, to Monday, Nov. 30, 1981. The Senate was in recess this session from Friday, Feb. 6, 1981, to Monday, Feb. 16, 1981; from Friday, Apr. 10, 1981, to Monday, Apr. 27, 1981; from Thursday, June 25, 1981, to Wednesday, July 8, 1981; from Monday, Aug. 3, 1981, to Wednesday, Sept. 9, 1981; from Wednesday, Oct. 7, 1981, to Wednesday, Oct. 14, 1981; from Tuesday, Nov. 24, 1981, to Monday, Nov. 30, 1981.

76. The House was in recess this session from Wednesday, Feb. 10, 1982, to Monday, Feb. 22, 1982; from Tuesday, Apr. 6, 1982, to Tuesday, Apr. 20, 1982; from Thursday, May 27, 1982, to Wednesday, June 2, 1982; from Thursday, July 1, 1982, to Monday, July 12, 1982; from Friday, Aug. 20, 1982, to Wednesday, Sept. 8, 1982; from Friday, Oct. 1, 1982, to Monday, Nov. 29, 1982. The Senate was in recess this session from Thursday, Feb. 11, 1982, to Monday, Feb. 22, 1982; from Thursday, Apr. 1, 1982, to Tuesday, Apr. 13, 1982; from Thursday, May 27, 1982, to Tuesday, June 8, 1982; from Thursday, July 1, 1982, to Monday, July 12, 1982; from Friday, Aug. 20, 1982, to Wednesday, Sept. 8, 1982; from Friday, Oct. 1, 1982, to Monday, Nov. 29, 1982.

77. The House adjourned for recess this session Friday, Jan. 7, 1983, to Tuesday, Jan. 25, 1983; Thursday, Feb. 17, 1983, to Tuesday, Feb. 22, 1983; Thursday, March 24, 1983, to Tuesday, Apr. 5, 1983; Thursday, May 26, 1983, to Wednesday, June 1, 1983; Thursday, June 30, 1983, to Monday, July 11, 1983; Friday, Aug. 5, 1983, to Monday, Sept. 12, 1983; Friday, Oct. 7, 1983, to Monday, Oct. 17, 1983. The Senate adjourned for recess this session Monday, Jan. 3, 1983, to Tuesday, Jan. 25, 1983; Friday, Feb. 4, 1983, to Monday, Feb. 14, 1983; Friday, March 25, 1983, to Tuesday, Apr. 5, 1983; Friday, May 27, 1983, to Monday, June 6, 1983; Friday, July 1, 1983, to Monday, July 11, 1983; Friday, Aug. 5, 1983, to Monday, Sept. 12, 1983; Monday Oct. 10, 1983, to Monday, Oct. 17, 1983.

78. The House adjourned for recess this session Thursday, Feb. 9, 1984, to Tuesday, Feb. 21, 1984; Friday, Apr. 13, 1984, to Tuesday, Apr. 24, 1984; Friday, May 25, 1984, to Wednesday, May 30, 1984; Friday, June 29, 1984, to Monday, July 23, 1984; Friday, Aug. 10, 1984, to Wednesday, Sept. 5, 1984. The Senate adjourned for recess this session Friday, Feb. 10, 1984, to Monday, Feb. 20, 1984; Friday, Apr. 13, 1984, to Tuesday, Apr. 24, 1984; from Friday, May 25, 1984, to Thursday, May 31, 1984; from Friday, June 29, 1984, to Monday, July 23, 1984; Friday, Aug. 10, 1984, to Wednesday, Sept. 5, 1984.

79. The House adjourned for recess this session Monday, Jan. 7, 1985, to Monday, Jan. 21, 1985; Thursday, Feb. 7, 1985, to Tuesday, Feb. 19, 1985; Thursday, March 7, 1985, to Tuesday, March 19, 1985; Thursday, Apr. 4, 1985, to Monday, Apr. 15, 1985; Thursday, May 23, 1985, to Monday, June 3, 1985; Thursday, June 27, 1985, to Monday, July 8, 1985; Thursday, Aug. 1, 1985, to Wednesday, Sept. 4, 1985; Thursday, Nov. 21, 1985, to Monday, Dec. 2, 1985. The Senate adjourned for recess this session Monday, Jan. 7, 1985, to Monday, Jan. 21, 1985; Thursday, Feb. 7, 1985, to Monday, Feb. 18, 1985; Tuesday, March 12, 1985, to Thursday, March 14, 1985; Thursday, Apr. 4, 1985, to Monday, Apr. 15, 1985; Friday, May 24, 1985, to Monday, June 3, 1985; Thursday, June 27, 1985, to Monday, July 8, 1985; Thursday, Aug. 1, 1985, to Monday, Sept. 9, 1985; Saturday, Nov. 23, 1985, to Monday, Dec. 2, 1985.

80. The House adjourned for recess this session Tuesday, Jan. 7, 1986, to Tuesday, Jan. 21, 1986; Friday, Feb. 7, 1986, to Tuesday, Feb. 18, 1986; Tuesday, March 25, 1986, to Tuesday, Apr. 8, 1986; Thursday, May 22, 1986, to Tuesday, June 3, 1986; Thursday, June 26, 1986, to Monday, July 14, 1986; Friday, Aug. 15, 1986, to Monday, Sept. 8, 1986. The Senate adjourned for recess this session Tuesday, Jan. 7, 1986, to Tuesday, Jan. 21, 1986; Friday, Feb. 7, 1986, to Monday, Feb. 17, 1986; Thursday, March 27, 1986, to Tuesday, Apr. 8, 1986; Wednesday, May 21, 1986, to Monday, June 2, 1986; Thursday, June 26, 1986, to Monday, July 14, 1986; Friday, Aug. 15, 1986, to Monday, Sept. 8, 1986.

81. The House adjourned for recess this session Thursday, Jan. 8, 1987, to Tuesday, Jan. 20, 1987; Wednesday, Feb. 11, 1987, to Wednesday, Feb. 18, 1987; Thursday, Apr. 9, 1987, to Tuesday, Apr. 21, 1987; Thursday, May 21, 1987, to Wednesday, May 27, 1987; Wednesday, July 1, 1987, to Tuesday, July 7, 1987; Wednesday, July 15, 1987, to Monday, July 20, 1987; Friday, Aug. 7, 1987, to Wednesday, Sept. 9, 1987; Tuesday, Nov. 10, 1987, to Monday, Nov. 16, 1987; Friday, Nov. 20, 1987, to Monday, Nov. 30, 1987. The Senate adjourned for recess this session Tuesday, Jan. 6, 1987, to Monday, Jan. 12, 1987; Thursday, Feb. 5, 1987, to Monday, Feb. 16, 1987; Friday, Apr. 10, 1987, to Tuesday, Apr. 21, 1987; Thursday, May 21, 1987, to Wednesday, May 27, 1987; Wednesday, July 1, 1987, to Tuesday, July 7, 1987; Friday, Aug. 7, 1987, to Wednesday, Sept. 9, 1987; Friday, Nov. 20, 1987, to Monday, Nov. 30, 1987.

82. The House adjourned for recess this session Tuesday, Feb. 9, 1988, to Tuesday, Feb. 16, 1988; Thursday, March 31, 1988, to Monday, Apr. 11, 1988; Thursday, May 26, 1988, to Wednesday, June 1, 1988; Thursday, June 30, 1988, to Thursday, July 7, 1988; Thursday, July 14, 1988, to Tuesday, July 26, 1988; Thursday, Aug. 11, 1988, to Wednesday, Sept. 7, 1988. The Senate adjourned for recess this session Thursday, Feb. 4, 1988, to Monday, Feb. 15, 1988; Friday, March 4, 1988, to Monday, March 14, 1988; Thursday, March 31, 1988, to Monday, Apr. 11, 1988; Friday, Apr. 29, 1988, to Monday, May 9, 1988; Friday, May 27, 1988, to Monday, June 6, 1988; Wednesday, June 29, 1988, to Wednesday, July 6, 1988; Thursday, July 14, 1988, to Monday, July 25, 1988, Thursday, Aug. 11, 1988, to Wednesday, Sept. 7, 1988.

83. The House adjourned for recess this session Wednesday, Jan. 4, 1989, to Thursday, Jan. 19, 1989; Thursday, Feb. 9, 1989, to Tuesday, Feb. 21, 1989; Thursday, March 23, 1989, to Monday, Apr. 3, 1989; Tuesday, Apr. 18, 1989, to Tuesday, Apr. 25, 1989; Thursday, May 25, 1989, to Wednesday, May 31, 1989; Thursday, June 29, 1989, to Monday, July 10, 1989; Saturday, Aug. 5, 1989, to Wednesday, Sept. 6, 1989. The Senate adjourned for recess this session Wednesday, Jan. 4, 1989, to Friday, Jan. 20, 1989; Friday, Jan. 20, 1989, to Wednesday, Jan. 25, 1989; Thursday, Feb. 9, 1989, to Tuesday, Feb. 21, 1989; Friday, March 17, 1989, to Tuesday, Apr. 4, 1989; Wednesday, Apr. 19, 1989, to Monday, May 1, 1989; Thursday, May 18, 1989, to Wednesday, May 31, 1989; Friday, June 23, 1989, to Tuesday, July 11, 1989; Friday, Aug. 4, 1989, to Wednesday, Sept. 6, 1989.

84. Elected Speaker June 6, 1989, to succeed Jim Wright, who resigned the Speakership that day.

85. The House adjourned for recess this session Wednesday, Feb. 7, 1990, to Tuesday, Feb. 20, 1990; Wednesday, Apr. 4, 1990, to Wednesday, Apr. 18, 1990; Friday, May 25, 1990, to Tuesday, June 5, 1990; Thursday, June 28, 1990, to Tuesday, July 10, 1990; Saturday, Aug. 4, 1990, to Wednesday, Sept. 5, 1990. The Senate adjourned for recess this session Thursday, Feb. 8, 1990, to Tuesday, Feb. 20, 1990; Friday, March 9, 1990, to Tuesday, March 20, 1990; Thursday, Apr. 5, 1990, to Wednesday, Apr. 18, 1990; Thursday, May 24, 1990, to Tuesday, June 5, 1990; Thursday, June 28, 1990, to Tuesday, July 10, 1990; Saturday, Aug. 4, 1990, to Monday, Sept. 10, 1990.

86. The House adjourned for recess this session Wednesday, Feb. 6, 1991, to Tuesday, Feb. 19, 1991; Friday, March 22, 1991, to Tuesday, Apr. 9, 1991; Thursday, June 27, 1991, to Tuesday, July 9, 1991; Friday, Aug. 2, 1991, to Wednesday, Sept. 11, 1991. The Senate adjourned for recess this session Wednesday, Feb. 6, 1991, to Tuesday, Feb. 19, 1991; Friday, March 22, 1991, to Tuesday, Apr. 9, 1991; Thursday, Apr. 25, 1991, to Monday, May 6, 1991; Friday, May 24, 1991, to Monday, June 3, 1991; Friday, June 28, 1991, to Monday, July 8, 1991; Friday, Aug. 2, 1991, to Tuesday, Sept. 10, 1991.

87. The House adjourned for recess this session Friday, Jan. 3, 1992, to Wednesday, Jan. 22, 1992; Friday, Apr. 10, 1992, to Tuesday, April 28, 1992; Thursday, July 2, 1992, to Tuesday, July 7, 1992; Friday, July 9, 1992, to Tuesday, July 21, 1992; Wednesday, Aug. 12, 1992, to Wednesday, Sept. 9, 1992. The Senate adjourned for recess this session Monday, Jan. 6, 1992, to Monday, Jan. 20, 1992; Monday, Feb. 10, 1992, to Monday, Feb. 17, 1992; Monday, Apr. 13, 1992, to Friday, Apr. 24, 1992; Monday, May 25, 1992, to Friday, May 29, 1992; Monday, July 6, 1992, to Friday, July 17, 1992; Thursday, Aug. 13, 1992, to Monday, Sept. 7, 1992.

88. The House adjourned for recess this session Thursday, Jan. 7, 1993, to Tuesday, Jan. 19, 1993; Friday, Feb. 5, 1993, to Monday, Feb. 15, 1993; Thursday, Apr. 8, 1993, to Sunday, Apr. 18, 1993; Friday, May 28, 1993, to Monday, June 7, 1993; Friday, July 2, 1993, to Monday, July 12, 1993; Saturday, Aug. 7, 1993, to Tuesday, Sept. 7, 1993. The Senate adjourned for recess this session Friday, Jan. 8, 1993, to Tuesday, Jan. 19, 1993; Friday, Feb. 5, 1993, to Monday, Feb. 15, 1993; Monday, Apr. 5, 1993, to Friday, Apr. 16, 1993; Monday, May 31, 1993, to Friday, June 4, 1993; Friday, July 2, 1993, to Friday, July 9, 1993; Monday, Aug. 9, 1993, to Monday, Sept. 6, 1993; Friday, Oct. 8, 1993, to Tuesday, Oct. 12, 1993; Friday, Nov. 12, 1993, to Monday Nov. 15, 1993.

89. The House adjourned for recess this session Thursday, Jan. 27, 1994, to Monday, Jan. 31, 1994; Saturday, Feb. 12, 1994, to Monday, Feb. 21, 1994; Friday, March 25, 1994, to Monday, Apr. 11, 1994; Friday, May 27, 1994, to Tuesday, June 7, 1994; Friday, July 1, 1994, to Monday, July 11, 1994; Saturday, Aug. 27, 1994, to Sunday, Sept. 11, 1994. The Senate adjourned for recess this session Monday, Feb. 14, 1994, to Monday, Feb. 21, 1994; Monday, March 28, 1994, to Friday, Apr. 8, 1994; Monday, May 30, 1994, to Monday, June 6, 1994; Monday, July 4, 1994, to Friday, July 8, 1994; Friday, Aug. 26, 1994, to Friday, Sept. 9, 1994.

90. The House adjourned for recess this session Saturday, Apr. 8, 1995, to Sunday, Apr. 30, 1995; Friday, May 26, 1995, to Monday, June 5, 1995; Saturday, July 1, 1995, to Sunday, July 9, 1995; Saturday, Aug. 5, 1995, to Tuesday, Sept. 5, 1995; Saturday, Sept. 30, 1995, to Thursday, Oct. 5, 1995. The Senate adjourned for recess this session Friday, Feb. 17, 1995, to Tuesday, Feb. 21, 1995; Saturday, Apr. 8, 1995, to Sunday, Apr. 23, 1995; Saturday, May 27, 1995, to Sunday, June 4, 1995; Saturday, July 1, 1995, to Sunday, July 9, 1995; Saturday, Aug. 12, 1995, to Monday, Sept. 4, 1995; Sunday, Oct. 1, 1995, to Monday, Oct. 9, 1995; Saturday, Nov. 21, 1995, to Sunday, Nov. 26, 1995.

91. The House adjourned for recess this session Wednesday, Jan. 10, 1996, to Sunday, Jan. 21, 1996; Saturday, March 30, 1996, to Sunday, Apr. 14, 1996; Saturday, June 29, 1996, to Sunday, July 7, 1996; Saturday, Aug. 3, 1996, to Tuesday, Sept. 3, 1996. The Senate adjourned for recess this session Thursday, Jan. 11, 1996, to Sunday, Jan. 21, 1996; Saturday, March 30, 1996, to Saturday, Apr. 14, 1996; Saturday, May 25, 1996, to Sunday, June 2, 1996; Saturday, June 29, 1996, to Sunday, July 7, 1996; Saturday, Aug. 3, 1996, to Monday, Sept. 2, 1996.

92. The House adjourned for recess this session Friday, Jan. 10, 1997, to Sunday, Jan. 19, 1997; Wednesday, Jan. 22, 1997, to Monday, Feb. 3, 1997; Friday, Feb. 14, 1997, to Monday, Feb. 24, 1997; Saturday, March 22, 1997, to Monday, Apr. 7, 1997; Friday, June 27, 1997, to Monday, July 7, 1997; Saturday, Aug. 2, 1997, to Tuesday, Sept. 2, 1997; Friday, Oct. 10, 1997, to Monday, Oct. 20, 1997. The Senate adjourned for recess this session Friday, Jan. 10, 1997, to Monday, Jan. 20, 1997; Friday, Feb. 14, 1997, to Sunday, Feb. 23, 1997; Saturday, March 22, 1997, to Sunday, Apr. 6, 1997; Saturday, May 24, 1997, to Sunday, June 1, 1997; Saturday, June 28, 1997, to Sunday, July 6, 1997; Saturday, Aug. 2, 1997, to Monday, Sept. 1, 1997; Friday, Oct. 10, 1997, to Sunday, Oct. 19, 1997.

93. The House adjourned for recess this session Friday, Feb. 13, 1998, to Monday, Feb. 23, 1998; Thursday, Apr. 2, 1998, to Monday, Apr. 20, 1998; Saturday, May 23, 1998, to Tuesday, June 2, 1998; Friday, June 26, 1998, to Monday, July 13, 1998; Saturday, Aug. 8, 1998, to Tuesday, Sept. 8, 1998. The House adjourned Oct. 21, 1998, and was called back by the Speaker for a resumption of the second session Thursday, Dec. 17, 1998, to Saturday, Dec. 19, 1998. The Senate adjourned for recess this session Thursday, Jan. 1, 1998, to Monday, Jan. 26, 1998; Saturday, Feb. 14, 1998, to Sunday, Feb. 22, 1998; Saturday, Apr. 4, 1998, to Sunday, Apr. 19, 1998; Saturday, May 23, 1998, to Sunday, May 31, 1998; Saturday, June 27, 1998, to Sunday, July 5, 1998; Saturday, Aug. 1, 1998, to Sunday, Aug. 30, 1998; Saturday, Sept. 5, 1998, to Monday, Sept. 7, 1998.

94. As of October 11, 1999.

95. The House adjourned for recess this session Wednesday, Jan. 6, 1999, to Tuesday, Jan. 19, 1999; Tuesday, Jan. 19, 1999, to Tuesday, Feb. 2, 1999; Friday, Feb. 12, 1999, to Tuesday, Feb. 23, 1999; Thursday, March 25, 1999, to Monday, April 12, 1999; Thursday, May 27, 1999, to Monday, June 7, 1999; Saturday, July 3, 1999, to Sunday, July 11, 1999; Saturday, Aug. 7, 1999, to Tuesday, Sept. 7, 1999. The Senate adjourned for recess this session Friday, Feb. 12, 1999, to Monday, Feb. 22, 1999; Thursday, March 25, 1999, to Monday, Apr. 12, 1999; Thursday, May 27, 1999, to Monday, June 7, 1999; Saturday, July 3, 1999, to Sunday, July 11, 1999; Saturday, Aug. 7, 1999, to Tuesday, Sept. 7, 1999; Saturday, Oct. 9, 1999, to Monday, Oct. 11, 1999.

SOURCES: For 1789–1990: *Official Congressional Directory*. For 1991–1999: Calendars of the U.S. House of Representatives and the U.S. Senate.

Lame Duck Sessions since 1945

Congress has held nine postelection sessions since 1945.

1948. The 1948 postelection session of the 80th Congress lasted only two hours. Both chambers swore in new members, approved several minor resolutions, and received last-minute reports from committees.

In addition to final floor action, several committees resumed work. The most active was the House Un-American Activities Committee, which continued its investigation of alleged communist espionage in the federal government.

1950. After the 1950 elections, President Harry S. Truman sent a "must" agenda to the lame-duck session of the 81st Congress. The president's list included supplemental defense appropriations, an excess profits tax, aid to Yugoslavia, a three-month extension of federal rent controls, and statehood for Hawaii and Alaska. During a marathon session that lasted until only a few hours before its successor took over, the 81st Congress acted on all of the president's legislative items except the statehood bills, which were blocked by a Senate filibuster.

1954. Only one chamber of the 83rd Congress convened after the 1954 elections. The Senate returned Nov. 8 to hold what has been called a "censure session," a continuing investigation into the conduct of Sen. Joseph R. McCarthy, R-Wis. (1947–57). By a 67–22 roll call, the Senate Dec. 2 voted to "condemn" McCarthy for his behavior.

In other postelection floor action, the Senate passed a series of miscellaneous and administrative resolutions and swore in new members.

1970. President Richard Nixon criticized the lame-duck Congress as one that had "seemingly lost the capacity to decide and the will to act." Filibusters and intense controversy contributed to inaction on the president's request for trade legislation and welfare reform.

Congress nevertheless claimed some substantive results during the session, which ended Jan. 2, 1971. Several major appropriations bills were cleared for presidential signature. Congress also approved foreign aid to Cambodia, provided interim funding for the supersonic transport (SST) plane, and repealed the Tonkin Gulf Resolution that had been used as a basis for American military involvement in Vietnam.

1974. In a session that ran from Nov. 18 to Dec. 20, 1974, the 93rd Congress cleared several important bills for presidential signature, including a mass transit bill, a Labor-Health, Education and Welfare appropriations bill, and a foreign assistance package. A House-Senate conference committee reached agreement on a major strip-mining bill, but President Gerald R. Ford vetoed it.

Congress approved the nomination of Nelson A. Rockefeller as vice president. It also overrode presidential vetoes of two bills—one broadening the Freedom of Information Act, a second authorizing educational benefits for Korean War and Vietnam-era veterans.

1980. The lame-duck session of the 96th Congress was productive, at least until Dec. 5, the original adjournment date set by congressional leaders. By that date a budget had been approved, along with a budget reconciliation measure. Ten regular appropriations bills had cleared, though one subsequently was vetoed. Congress had approved two major environmental measures—an Alaskan lands bill and toxic waste "superfund" legislation—as well as a three-year extension of general revenue sharing.

Year	Congress	Chamber	Dates
1948	80th	Senate House	Dec. 31, 1948 (2-hour session)
1950	81st	Senate House	Nov. 27, 1950–Jan. 2, 1951
1954	83rd	Senate	Nov. 8, 1954–Dec. 2, 1954
1970	91st	Senate House	Nov. 16, 1970–Jan. 2, 1971
1974	93rd	Senate House	Nov. 18, 1974–Dec. 20, 1974
1980	96th	Senate House	Nov. 12, 1980–Dec. 16, 1980
1982	97th	Senate House	Nov. 29, 1982–Dec. 23, 1982 Nov. 29, 1982–Dec. 21, 1982
1994	103rd	Senate House	Nov. 30, 1994–Dec. 1, 1994 Nov. 29, 1994
1998	105th	House	Dec. 18, 1998–Dec. 19, 1998

After Dec. 5, however, the legislative pace slowed noticeably. Action on a continuing appropriations resolution for those departments and agencies whose regular funding had not been cleared was delayed, first by a filibuster on a fair housing bill and later by more than one hundred "Christmas tree" amendments, including a $10,000-a-year pay raise for members. After the conference report failed in the Senate and twice was rewritten, the bill was shorn of virtually all its "ornaments" and finally cleared by both chambers on Dec. 16.

1982. Despite the reluctance of congressional leaders, President Ronald Reagan urged the convening of a postelection session at the end of the 97th Congress, principally to pass remaining appropriations bills.

Rising unemployment—and Democratic election gains in the House—made job creation efforts the focus of the lame-duck Congress, however. Overriding the objections of Republican conservatives, Congress passed Reagan-backed legislation raising the federal gasoline tax from four cents to nine cents a gallon to pay for highway repairs and mass transit. Supporters said the legislation would help alleviate unemployment by creating three hundred thousand jobs.

Congress eventually cleared four additional appropriations bills, packaging the remaining six in a continuing appropriations resolution that also included a pay raise for House members. Conferees dropped funding for emergency jobs programs to avert a threatened veto of the resolution.

The lame-duck session also was highlighted by Congress's refusal to fund production and procurement of the first five MX intercontinental missiles. This was the first time in recent history that either house of Congress had denied a president's request to fund production of a strategic weapon.

1994. Congress reconvened to reconsider, and ultimately approve, the Uruguay Round pact strengthening the General Agreement on Tariffs and Trade (GATT). The bill had been submitted Sept. 27, 1994, by President Bill Clinton under fast-track rules for trade legislation, which allowed each chamber only an up-or-down vote on the bill without amendments. But the rules also allowed every chairman with jurisdiction to take up to forty-five days to review the bill. Sen. Ernest F. Hollings, D-S.C., demanded his forty-five days, forcing the Senate leadership to schedule a two-day lame-duck session.

Clinton asked the House to approve the bill before the October adjournment, but the Democratic leadership delayed consideration. The House reconvened for a one-day session Nov. 29 and passed the GATT bill by a wide margin.

Following a twenty-hour debate Nov. 30 and Dec. 1, the Senate gave overwhelming approval to the bill.

1998. In a two-day postelection session, the House of the 105th Congress reconvened Dec. 18 to vote on four articles of impeachment against President Bill Clinton. Voting along party lines, the chamber on Dec. 19 impeached the president for only the second time in history, approving Articles I and III by votes of 228–206 and 221–212, respectively. The articles accused Clinton of perjury and obstruction of justice in the investigation of his affair with former White House intern Monica Lewinsky.

Before the historic action, Republicans on a procedural vote (230–204) prevented Democrats from offering a resolution of censure. Republicans also defeated a motion to adjourn the session, brought by Democrats to protest a decision by the Republican leadership to vote on impeachment even as the U.S. military conducted airstrikes against Iraq.

The day of the vote, Speaker-designate Robert L. Livingston, R-La., having admitted to extramarital affairs two days earlier, announced that he would not seek the speakership. Instead, he said, he would resign his seat in six months. Livingston had been expected to succeed Speaker Newt Gingrich, R-Ga., who resigned after Republicans lost a net five seats in the 1998 midterm elections.

The House concluded the session by appointing thirteen Republican Judiciary Committee members to prosecute the case in the Senate. The Senate of the 106th Congress voted on Feb. 12, 1999, to acquit Clinton of both charges.

Longest Sessions of Congress

Rank	Congress	Session	Dates	Length in days[a]	Recesses Senate	House
1	76th	3rd	Jan. 3, 1940–Jan. 3, 1941	367	July 11–July 22, 1940	July 11–July 22, 1940
2	102nd	1st	Jan. 3, 1991–Jan. 3, 1992	366	Feb. 6–Feb. 19, 1991 Mar. 22–Apr. 9, 1991 Apr. 25–May 6, 1991 May 24–June 3, 1991 June 28–July 8, 1991 Aug. 2–Sept. 10, 1991	Feb. 6–Feb. 19, 1991 Mar. 22–Apr. 9, 1991 May 23–May 29, 1991 June 27–July 9, 1991 Aug. 2–Sept. 11, 1991 Nov. 27, 1991–Jan. 3, 1992
3	77th	1st	Jan. 3, 1941–Jan. 2, 1942	365		
	81st	2nd	Jan. 3, 1950–Jan. 2, 1951	365	Sept. 23–Nov. 27, 1950	Apr. 6–Apr. 18, 1950 Sept. 23–Nov. 27, 1950
	104th	1st	Jan. 4, 1995–Jan. 3, 1996	365	Feb. 17–Feb. 21, 1995 Apr. 8–Apr. 23, 1995 May 27–June 4, 1995 July 1–July 9, 1995 Aug. 12–Sept. 4, 1995 Oct. 1–Oct. 9, 1995 Nov. 21–Nov. 26, 1995	Apr. 8–Apr. 30, 1995 May 26–June 5, 1995 July 1–July 9, 1995 Aug. 5–Sept. 5, 1995 Sept. 30–Oct. 5, 1995
6	80th	2nd	Jan. 6, 1948–Dec. 31, 1948	361	June 20–July 26, 1948 Aug. 7–Dec. 31, 1948	June 20–July 26, 1948 Aug. 7–Dec. 31, 1948
7	88th	1st	Jan. 9, 1963–Dec. 30, 1963	356		Apr. 11–Apr. 22, 1963
8	91st	1st	Jan. 3, 1969–Dec. 23, 1969	355	Feb. 7–Feb. 17, 1969 Apr. 3–Apr. 14, 1969 July 2–July 7, 1969 Aug. 13–Sept. 3, 1969 Nov. 26–Dec. 1, 1969	Feb. 7–Feb. 17, 1969 Apr. 3–Apr. 14, 1969 May 28–June 2, 1969 July 2–July 7, 1969 Aug. 13–Sept. 3, 1969 Nov. 6–Nov. 12, 1969 Nov. 26–Dec. 1, 1969
9	65th	2nd	Dec. 3, 1917–Nov. 21, 1918	354	Dec. 18, 1917–Jan. 3, 1918	Dec. 18, 1917–Jan. 3, 1918
	93rd	1st	Jan. 3, 1973–Dec. 22, 1973	354	Feb. 8–Feb. 15, 1973 Apr. 18–Apr. 30, 1973 May 23–May 29, 1973 June 30–July 9, 1973 Aug. 3–Sept. 5, 1973 Oct. 18–Oct. 23, 1973 Nov. 21–Nov. 26, 1973	Feb. 8–Feb. 19, 1973 Apr. 19–Apr. 30, 1973 May 24–May 29, 1973 June 30–July 10, 1973 Aug. 3–Sept. 5, 1973 Oct. 4–Oct. 9, 1973 Oct. 18–Oct. 23, 1973 Nov. 15–Nov. 26, 1973
	96th	1st	Jan. 15, 1979–Jan. 3, 1980	354	Feb. 9–Feb. 19, 1979 Apr. 10–Apr. 23, 1979 May 25–June 4, 1979 June 27–July 9, 1979 Aug. 3–Sept. 5, 1979 Nov. 20–Nov. 26, 1979 Adjourned *sine die* Dec. 20, 1979	Feb. 8–Feb. 13, 1979 Apr. 10–Apr. 23, 1979 May 24–May 30, 1979 June 29–July 9, 1979 Aug. 2–Sept. 5, 1979 Nov. 20–Nov. 26, 1979 Adjourned *sine die* Jan. 3, 1980
12	79th	1st	Jan. 3, 1945–Dec. 21, 1945	353	Aug. 1–Sept. 5, 1945	July 21–Sept. 5, 1945

Rank	Congress	Session	Dates	Length in days[a]	Recesses Senate	House
13	99th	1st	Jan. 3, 1985–Dec. 20, 1985	352	Jan. 7–Jan. 21, 1985 Feb. 7–Feb. 18, 1985 Mar. 12–Mar. 14, 1985 Apr. 4–Apr. 15, 1985 May 24–June 3, 1985 June 27–July 8, 1985 Aug. 1–Sept. 9, 1985 Nov. 23–Dec. 2, 1985	Jan. 7–Jan. 21, 1985 Feb. 7–Feb. 19, 1985 Mar. 7–Mar. 19, 1985 Apr. 4–Apr. 15, 1985 May 23–June 3, 1985 June 27–July 8, 1985 Aug. 1–Sept. 4, 1985 Nov. 21–Dec. 2, 1985
14	80th	1st	Jan. 3, 1947–Dec. 19, 1947	351	July 27–Nov. 17, 1947	July 27–Nov. 17, 1947
	100th	1st	Jan. 6, 1987–Dec. 22, 1987	351	Jan. 6–Jan. 12, 1987 Feb. 5–Feb. 16, 1987 Apr. 10–Apr. 21, 1987 May 21–May 27, 1987 July 1–July 7, 1987 Aug. 7–Sept. 9, 1987 Nov. 20–Nov. 30, 1987	Jan. 8–Jan. 20, 1987 Feb. 11–Feb. 18, 1987 Apr. 9–Apr. 21, 1987 May 21–May 27, 1987 July 1–July 7, 1987 July 15–July 20, 1987 Aug. 7–Sept. 9, 1987 Nov. 10–Nov. 16, 1987 Nov. 20–Nov. 30, 1987
16	78th	1st	Jan. 6, 1943–Dec. 21, 1943	350	July 8–Sept. 14, 1943	July 8–Sept. 14, 1943
17	91st	2nd	Jan. 19, 1970–Jan. 2, 1971	349	Feb. 10–Feb. 16, 1970 Mar. 26–Mar. 31, 1970 Sept. 2–Sept. 8, 1970 Oct. 14–Nov. 16, 1970 Nov. 25–Nov. 30, 1970 Dec. 22–Dec. 28, 1970	Feb. 10–Feb. 16, 1970 Mar. 26–Mar. 31, 1970 May 27–June 1, 1970 July 1–July 6, 1970 Aug. 14–Sept. 9, 1970 Oct. 14–Nov. 16, 1970 Nov. 25–Nov. 30, 1970 Dec. 22–Dec. 29, 1970
	96th	2nd	Jan. 3, 1980–Dec. 16, 1980	349	Feb. 11–Feb. 14, 1980 Apr. 3–Apr. 15, 1980 May 22–May 28, 1980 July 2–July 21, 1980 Aug. 6–Aug. 18, 1980 Aug. 27–Sept. 3, 1980 Oct. 1–Nov. 12, 1980 Nov. 24–Dec. 1, 1980	Feb. 13–Feb. 19, 1980 Apr. 2–Apr. 15, 1980 May 22–May 28, 1980 July 2–July 21, 1980 Aug. 1–Aug. 18, 1980 Aug. 28–Sept. 3, 1980 Oct. 2–Nov. 12, 1980 Nov. 21–Dec. 1, 1980

a. Includes days in recess.

SOURCE: *1999–2000 Congressional Directory, 106th Congress* (Washington, D.C.: Government Printing Office, 1999).

Joint Sessions, Joint Meetings, and Inaugurations, 1789–1999

Date	Type	Occasion, topic, or location	Name and position of dignitary *(where applicable)*
		NEW YORK CITY	
1st CONGRESS			
April 6, 1789	Joint session	Counting electoral votes	N.A.
April 30, 1789	Joint session	Inauguration and church service	President George Washington and the Senate-appointed chaplain
January 8, 1790	Joint session	Annual message	President Washington
		PHILADELPHIA	
December 8, 1790	Joint session	Annual message	President Washington
2nd CONGRESS			
October 25, 1791	Joint session	Annual message	President Washington
November 6, 1792	Joint session	Annual message	President Washington
February 13, 1793	Joint session	Counting electoral votes	N.A.
3rd CONGRESS			
March 4, 1793	Inauguration	Senate Chamber	President Washington
December 3, 1793	Joint session	Annual message	President Washington
November 19, 1794	Joint session	Annual message	President Washington
4th CONGRESS			
December 8, 1795	Joint session	Annual message	President Washington
December 7, 1796	Joint session	Annual message	President Washington
February 8, 1797	Joint session	Counting electoral votes	N.A.
5th CONGRESS			
March 4, 1797	Inauguration	Hall of the House	President John Adams
May 16, 1797	Joint session	Relations with France	President Adams
November 23, 1797	Joint session	Annual message	President Adams
December 8, 1798	Joint session	Annual message	President Adams
6th CONGRESS			
December 3, 1799	Joint session	Annual message	President Adams
December 26, 1799	Joint session	Funeral procession and oration in memory of George Washington	Rep. Henry Lee, F-Va.
		WASHINGTON, D.C.	
November 22, 1800	Joint session	Annual message	President Adams
February 11, 1801	Joint session	Counting electoral votes	N.A.
7th CONGRESS			
March 4, 1801	Inauguration	Senate Chamber	President Thomas Jefferson
8th CONGRESS			
February 13, 1805	Joint session	Counting electoral votes	N.A.
9th CONGRESS			
March 5, 1805	Inauguration	Senate Chamber	President Jefferson
10th CONGRESS			
February 8, 1809	Joint session	Counting electoral votes	N.A.
11th CONGRESS			
March 4, 1809	Inauguration	Hall of the House	President James Madison
12th CONGRESS			
February 10, 1813	Joint session	Counting electoral votes	N.A.
13th CONGRESS			
March 4, 1813	Inauguration	Hall of the House	President Madison

Date	Type	Occasion, topic, or location	Name and position of dignitary (where applicable)
14th CONGRESS			
February 12, 1817	Joint session	Counting electoral votes	N.A.
15th CONGRESS			
March 4, 1817	Inauguration	In front of Brick Capitol	President James Monroe
16th CONGRESS			
February 14, 1821	Joint session	Counting electoral votes	N.A.
17th CONGRESS			
March 5, 1821	Inauguration	Hall of the House	President Monroe
18th CONGRESS			
December 10, 1824	Joint meeting	Address	Speaker Henry Clay, Ky.; Gen. Gilbert du Motier, Marquis de Lafayette
February 9, 1825	Joint session	Counting electoral votes	N.A.
19th CONGRESS			
March 4, 1825	Inauguration	Hall of the House	President John Quincy Adams
20th CONGRESS			
February 11, 1829	Joint session	Counting electoral votes	N.A.
21st CONGRESS			
March 4, 1829	Inauguration	East Portico	President Andrew Jackson
22nd CONGRESS			
February 13, 1833	Joint session	Counting electoral votes	N.A.
23rd CONGRESS			
March 4, 1833	Inauguration	Hall of the House	President Jackson
December 31, 1834	Joint session	Lafayette eulogy	Representative and former president John Quincy Adams; ceremony attended by President Jackson
24th CONGRESS			
February 8, 1837	Joint session	Counting electoral votes	N.A.
25th CONGRESS			
March 4, 1837	Inauguration	East Portico	President Martin Van Buren
26th CONGRESS			
February 10, 1841	Joint session	Counting electoral votes	N.A.
27th CONGRESS			
March 4, 1841	Inauguration	East Portico	President William Henry Harrison
28th CONGRESS			
February 12, 1845	Joint session	Counting electoral votes	N.A.
29th CONGRESS			
March 4, 1845	Inauguration	East Portico	President James Knox Polk
30th CONGRESS			
February 14, 1849	Joint session	Counting electoral votes	N.A.
31st CONGRESS			
March 5, 1849	Inauguration	East Portico	President Zachary Taylor
July 10, 1850	Joint session	Oath of office to President Millard Fillmore	N.A.
32nd CONGRESS			
February 9, 1853	Joint session	Counting electoral votes	N.A.
33rd CONGRESS			
March 4, 1853	Inauguration	East Portico	President Franklin Pierce

Date	Type	Occasion, topic, or location	Name and position of dignitary (where applicable)
34th CONGRESS			
February 11, 1857	Joint session	Counting electoral votes	N.A.
35th CONGRESS			
March 4, 1857	Inauguration	East Portico	President James Buchanan
36th CONGRESS			
February 13, 1861	Joint session	Counting electoral votes	N.A.
37th CONGRESS			
March 4, 1861	Inauguration	East Portico	President Abraham Lincoln
February 22, 1862	Joint session	Reading of Washington's farewell address	John W. Forney, secretary of the Senate
38th CONGRESS			
February 8, 1865	Joint session	Counting electoral votes	N.A.
39th CONGRESS			
March 4, 1865	Inauguration	East Portico	President Lincoln
February 12, 1866	Joint session	Memorial to Abraham Lincoln	George Bancroft, historian; ceremony attended by President Andrew Johnson
40th CONGRESS			
February 10, 1869	Joint session	Counting electoral votes	N.A.
41st CONGRESS			
March 4, 1869	Inauguration	East Portico	President Ulysses S. Grant
42nd CONGRESS			
February 12, 1873	Joint session	Counting electoral votes	N.A.
43rd CONGRESS			
March 4, 1873	Inauguration	East Portico	President Grant
December 18, 1874	Joint meeting	Reception of King Kalakaua of Hawaii	Speaker James G. Blaine, R-Maine; David Kalakaua, King of the Hawaiian Islands
44th CONGRESS			
February 1, 1877	Joint session	Counting electoral votes	N.A.
February 10, 1877			
February 12, 1877			
February 19, 1877			
February 20, 1877			
February 21, 1877			
February 24, 1877			
February 26, 1877			
February 28, 1877			
March 1, 1877			
March 2, 1877			
45th CONGRESS			
March 5, 1877	Inauguration	East Portico	President Rutherford B. Hayes
46th CONGRESS			
February 9, 1881	Joint session	Counting electoral votes	N.A.
47th CONGRESS			
March 4, 1881	Inauguration	East Portico	President James A. Garfield
February 27, 1882	Joint session	Memorial to James A. Garfield	James G. Blaine, former Speaker, senator, and secretary of state; ceremony attended by President Chester A. Arthur

Date	Type	Occasion, topic, or location	Name and position of dignitary (where applicable)
48th CONGRESS			
February 11, 1885	Joint session	Counting electoral votes	N.A.
February 21, 1885	Joint session	Completion of Washington Monument	Rep. John D. Long, R-Mass.; Rep.-elect John W. Daniel, D-Va.; ceremony attended by President Arthur
49th CONGRESS			
March 4, 1885	Inauguration	East Portico	President Grover Cleveland
50th CONGRESS			
February 13, 1889	Joint session	Counting electoral votes	N.A.
51st CONGRESS			
March 4, 1889	Inauguration	East Portico	President Benjamin Harrison
December 11, 1889	Joint session	Centennial of George Washington's first inauguration	Melville W. Fuller, chief justice of the United States; ceremony attended by President Harrison
52nd CONGRESS			
February 8, 1893	Joint session	Counting electoral votes	N.A.
53rd CONGRESS			
March 4, 1893	Inauguration	East Portico	President Grover Cleveland
54th CONGRESS			
February 10, 1897	Joint session	Counting electoral votes	N.A.
55th CONGRESS			
March 4, 1897	Inauguration	In front of original Senate Wing of Capitol	President William McKinley
56th CONGRESS			
December 12, 1900	Joint meeting	Centennial of the Capital City	Reps. James D. Richardson, D-Tenn., and Sereno E. Payne, R-N.Y., and Sen. George F. Hoar, R-Mass.; ceremony attended by President McKinley
February 13, 1901	Joint session	Counting electoral votes	N.A.
57th CONGRESS			
March 4, 1901	Inauguration	East Portico	President McKinley
February 27, 1902	Joint session	Memorial to William McKinley	John Hay, secretary of state; ceremony attended by President Theodore Roosevelt and Prince Henry of Prussia
58th CONGRESS			
February 8, 1905	Joint session	Counting electoral votes	N.A.
59th CONGRESS			
March 4, 1905	Inauguration	East Portico	President Roosevelt
60th CONGRESS			
February 10, 1909	Joint session	Counting electoral votes	N.A.
61st CONGRESS			
March 4, 1909	Inauguration	Senate Chamber	President William Howard Taft
62nd CONGRESS			
February 12, 1913	Joint session	Counting electoral votes	N.A.
February 15, 1913	Joint session	Memorial for Vice President James S. Sherman	A group of twelve senators; House Speaker Champ Clark, D-Mo.; President Taft
63rd CONGRESS			
March 4, 1913	Inauguration	East Portico	President Woodrow Wilson
April 8, 1913	Joint session	Tariff message	President Wilson
June 23, 1913	Joint session	Currency and bank reform message	President Wilson
August 27, 1913	Joint session	Mexican affairs message	President Wilson
December 2, 1913	Joint session	Annual message	President Wilson

Date	Type	Occasion, topic, or location	Name and position of dignitary (where applicable)
January 20, 1914	Joint session	Trusts message	President Wilson
March 5, 1914	Joint session	Panama Canal tolls	President Wilson
April 20, 1914	Joint session	Mexico message	President Wilson
September 4, 1914	Joint session	War tax message	President Wilson
December 8, 1914	Joint session	Annual message	President Wilson
64th CONGRESS			
December 7, 1915	Joint session	Annual message	President Wilson
August 29, 1916	Joint session	Railroad message (labor-management dispute)	President Wilson
December 5, 1916	Joint session	Annual message	President Wilson
February 3, 1917	Joint session	Severing diplomatic relations with Germany	President Wilson
February 14, 1917	Joint session	Counting electoral votes	N.A.
February 26, 1917	Joint session	Arming of merchant ships	President Wilson
65th CONGRESS			
March 5, 1917	Inauguration	East Portico	President Wilson
April 2, 1917	Joint session	War with Germany	President Wilson
December 4, 1917	Joint session	Annual message/war with Austria-Hungary	President Wilson
February 11, 1918	Joint session	Peace message	President Wilson
May 27, 1918	Joint session	War finance message	President Wilson
November 11, 1918	Joint session	Terms of armistice signed by Germany	President Wilson
December 2, 1918	Joint session	Annual message	President Wilson
February 9, 1919	Joint session	Memorial to Theodore Roosevelt	Sen. Henry Cabot Lodge, R-Mass.; ceremony attended by former president Taft
66th CONGRESS			
August 8, 1919	Joint session	Cost of living message	President Wilson
September 18, 1919	Joint session	Address	President pro tempore Albert B. Cummins, R-Iowa; Speaker Frederick H. Gillett, R-Mass.; Representative and former Speaker Champ Clark; Gen. John J. Pershing
February 9, 1921	Joint session	Counting electoral votes	N.A.
67th CONGRESS			
March 4, 1921	Inauguration	East Portico	President Warren G. Harding
April 12, 1921	Joint session	Federal problem message	President Harding
December 6, 1921	Joint session	Annual message	President Harding
February 28, 1922	Joint session	Maintenance of the merchant marine	President Harding
August 18, 1922	Joint session	Coal and railroad message	President Harding
November 21, 1922	Joint session	Promotion of the American merchant marine	President Harding
December 8, 1922	Joint session	Annual message	President Harding
February 7, 1923	Joint session	British debt due to the United States	President Harding
68th CONGRESS			
December 6, 1923	Joint session	Annual message	President Calvin Coolidge
February 27, 1924	Joint session	Memorial to Warren G. Harding	Charles Evans Hughes, secretary of state; ceremony attended by President Coolidge
December 15, 1924	Joint session	Memorial to Woodrow Wilson	Dr. Edwin Anderson Alderman, president of the University of Virginia; ceremony attended by President Coolidge
February 11, 1925	Joint session	Counting electoral votes	N.A.
69th CONGRESS			
March 4, 1925	Inauguration	East Portico	President Coolidge
February 22, 1927	Joint session	George Washington birthday message	President Coolidge
70th CONGRESS			
February 13, 1929	Joint session	Counting electoral votes	N.A.

Date	Type	Occasion, topic, or location	Name and position of dignitary (where applicable)
71st CONGRESS			
March 4, 1929	Inauguration	East Portico	President Herbert Hoover
72nd CONGRESS			
February 22, 1932	Joint session	Bicentennial of George Washington's birth	President Hoover
February 6, 1933	Joint meeting	Memorial to Calvin Coolidge	Arthur Prentice Rugg, chief justice of the Supreme Judicial Court of Massachusetts; ceremony attended by President Hoover
February 8, 1933	Joint session	Counting electoral votes	N.A.
73rd CONGRESS			
March 4, 1933	Inauguration	East Portico	President Franklin Delano Roosevelt
January 3, 1934	Joint session	Annual message	President Roosevelt
May 20, 1934	Joint session	100th anniversary, death of Lafayette	André de Laboulaye, ambassador of France; President Roosevelt; ceremony attended by Count de Chambrun, great-grandson of Lafayette
74th CONGRESS			
January 4, 1935	Joint session	Annual message	President Roosevelt
May 22, 1935	Joint session	Veto message	President Roosevelt
January 3, 1936	Joint session	Annual message	President Roosevelt
75th CONGRESS			
January 6, 1937	Joint session	Counting electoral votes	N.A.
January 6, 1937	Joint session	Annual message	President Roosevelt
January 20, 1937	Inauguration	East Portico	President Roosevelt; Vice President John Nance Garner
January 3, 1938	Joint session	Annual message	President Roosevelt
76th CONGRESS			
January 4, 1939	Joint session	Annual message	President Roosevelt
March 4, 1939	Joint session	Sesquicentennial of the 1st Congress	President Roosevelt
June 9, 1939	Joint meeting	Reception	George VI and Elizabeth, King and Queen of the United Kingdom
September 21, 1939	Joint session	Neutrality address	President Roosevelt
January 3, 1940	Joint session	Annual message	President Roosevelt
May 16, 1940	Joint session	National defense message	President Roosevelt
77th CONGRESS			
January 6, 1941	Joint session	Counting electoral votes	N.A.
January 6, 1941	Joint session	Annual message	President Roosevelt
January 20, 1941	Joint session	Inauguration, East Portico	President Roosevelt; Vice President Henry A. Wallace
December 8, 1941	Joint session	War with Japan	President Roosevelt
December 26, 1941	Joint meeting	Address	Winston Churchill, prime minister of the United Kingdom
January 6, 1942	Joint session	Annual message	President Roosevelt
August 6, 1942	Joint meeting[a]	Address	Wilhelmina, Queen of the Netherlands
78th CONGRESS			
January 7, 1943	Joint session	Annual message	President Roosevelt
May 19, 1943	Joint meeting	Address	Winston Churchill, prime minister of the United Kingdom
November 18, 1943	Joint meeting	Moscow Conference	Cordell Hull, secretary of state
79th CONGRESS			
January 6, 1945	Joint session	Counting electoral votes	N.A.
January 6, 1945	Joint session	Annual message	President Roosevelt was not present. His message was read before the joint session of Congress
January 20, 1945	Inauguration	South Portico, White House	President Roosevelt; Vice President Harry S. Truman
March 1, 1945	Joint session	Yalta Conference	President Roosevelt

Date	Type	Occasion, topic, or location	Name and position of dignitary (where applicable)
April 16, 1945	Joint session	Prosecution of the War	President Harry S. Truman
May 21, 1945	Joint session	Bestowal of Congressional Medal of Honor on Tech. Sgt. Jake William Lindsey	Gen. George C. Marshall, chief of staff, U.S. Army; President Truman
June 18, 1945	Joint meeting	Address	Gen. Dwight D. Eisenhower, supreme commander, Allied Expeditionary Force
October 5, 1945	Joint meeting	Address	Adm. Chester W. Nimitz, commander-in-chief, Pacific Fleet
October 23, 1945	Joint session	Universal military training message	President Truman
November 13, 1945	Joint meeting	Address	Clement R. Attlee, prime minister of the United Kingdom
May 25, 1946	Joint session	Railroad strike message	President Truman
July 1, 1946	Joint session	Memorial to Franklin Delano Roosevelt	John Winant, U.S. representative on the Economic and Social Council of the United Nations; ceremony attended by President Truman and Mrs. Franklin Delano Roosevelt
80th CONGRESS			
January 6, 1947	Joint session	State of the Union Address	President Truman
March 12, 1947	Joint session	Greek-Turkish aid policy	President Truman
May 1, 1947	Joint meeting	Address	Miguel Aleman, president of Mexico
November 17, 1947	Joint session	Aid to Europe message	President Truman
January 7, 1948	Joint session	State of the Union Address	President Truman
March 17, 1948	Joint session	National security and conditions in Europe	President Truman
April 19, 1948	Joint session	50th anniversary, liberation of Cuba	President Truman; Guillermo Belt, ambassador of Cuba
July 27, 1948	Joint session	Inflation, housing, and civil rights	President Truman
81st CONGRESS			
January 5, 1949	Joint session	State of the Union Address	President Truman
January 6, 1949	Joint session	Counting electoral votes	N.A.
January 20, 1949	Joint session	Inauguration, East Portico	President Truman; Vice President Alben W. Barkley
May 19, 1949	Joint meeting	Address	Eurico Gaspar Dutra, President of Brazil
January 4, 1950	Joint session	State of the Union Address	President Truman
May 31, 1950	Joint meeting	Address	Dean Acheson, secretary of state
82nd CONGRESS			
January 8, 1951	Joint session	State of the Union Address	President Truman
February 1, 1951	Joint meeting[b]	North Atlantic Treaty Organization	Gen. Dwight D. Eisenhower
April 2, 1951	Joint meeting	Address	Vincent Auriol, president of France
April 19, 1951	Joint meeting	Return from Pacific Command	Gen. Douglas MacArthur
June 21, 1951	Joint meeting	Address	Galo Plaza, president of Ecuador
September 24, 1951	Joint meeting	Address	Alcide de Gasperi, prime minister of Italy
January 9, 1952	Joint session	State of the Union Address	President Truman
January 17, 1952	Joint meeting	Address	Winston Churchill, prime minister of the United Kingdom
April 3, 1952	Joint meeting	Address	Juliana, Queen of the Netherlands
May 22, 1952	Joint meeting	Korea	Gen. Matthew B. Ridgway
June 10, 1952	Joint session	Steel industry dispute	President Truman
83rd CONGRESS			
January 6, 1953	Joint session	Counting electoral votes	N.A.
January 20, 1953	Joint session	Inauguration, East Portico	President Dwight D. Eisenhower; Vice President Richard Nixon
February 2, 1953	Joint session	State of the Union Address	President Eisenhower
January 7, 1954	Joint session	State of the Union Address	President Eisenhower
January 29, 1954	Joint meeting	Address	Celal Bayar, president of Turkey
May 4, 1954	Joint meeting	Address	Vincent Massey, governor general of Canada
May 28, 1954	Joint meeting	Address	Haile Selassie I, Emperor of Ethiopia
July 28, 1954	Joint meeting	Address	Syngman Rhee, president of South Korea

Date	Type	Occasion, topic, or location	Name and position of dignitary (where applicable)
84th CONGRESS			
January 6, 1955	Joint session	State of the Union Address	President Eisenhower
January 27, 1955	Joint meeting	Address	Paul E. Magliore, president of Haiti
February 29, 1956	Joint meeting	Address	Giovanni Gronchi, president of Italy
May 17, 1956	Joint meeting	Address	Dr. Sukarno, president of Indonesia
85th CONGRESS			
January 5, 1957	Joint session	Middle East message	President Eisenhower
January 7, 1957	Joint session	Counting electoral votes	N.A.
January 10, 1957	Joint session	State of the Union Address	President Eisenhower
January 21, 1957	Joint session	Inauguration, East Portico	President Eisenhower; Vice President Nixon
May 9, 1957	Joint meeting	Address	Ngo Dinh Diem, president of Vietnam
January 9, 1958	Joint session	State of the Union Address	President Eisenhower
June 5, 1958	Joint meeting	Address	Theodor Heuss, president of West Germany
June 18, 1958	Joint meeting	Address	Carlos F. Garcia, president of the Philippines
86th CONGRESS			
January 9, 1959	Joint session	State of the Union Address	President Eisenhower
January 21, 1959	Joint meeting	Address	Arturo Frondizi, president of Argentina
February 12, 1959	Joint session	Sesquicentennial of Abraham Lincoln's birth	Fredric March, actor; Carl Sandburg, poet
March 11, 1959	Joint meeting	Address	Jose Maria Lemus, president of El Salvador
March 18, 1959	Joint meeting	Address	Sean T. O'Kelly, president of Ireland
May 12, 1959	Joint meeting	Address	Baudouin, King of the Belgians
January 7, 1960	Joint session	State of the Union Address	President Eisenhower
April 6, 1960	Joint meeting	Address	Alberto Lleras-Camargo, president of Colombia
April 25, 1960	Joint meeting	Address	Charles de Gaulle, president of France
April 28, 1960	Joint meeting	Address	Mahendra, King of Nepal
June 29, 1960	Joint meeting	Address	Bhumibol Adulyadej, King of Thailand
87th CONGRESS			
January 6, 1961	Joint session	Counting electoral votes	N.A.
January 20, 1961	Joint session	Inauguration, East Portico	President John F. Kennedy; Vice President Lyndon B. Johnson
January 30, 1961	Joint session	State of the Union Address	President Kennedy
May 4, 1961	Joint meeting	Address	Habib Bourguiba, president of Tunisia
July 12, 1961	Joint meeting	Address	Mohammad Ayub Khan, president of Pakistan
September 21, 1961	Joint meeting	Address	Manuel Prado, president of Peru
January 11, 1962	Joint session	State of the Union Address	President Kennedy
February 26, 1962	Joint meeting	Friendship 7: first United States orbital space flight	Lt. Col. John H. Glenn Jr., USMC, Friendship 7 astronaut
April 4, 1962	Joint meeting	Address	Joao Goulart, president of Brazil
April 12, 1962	Joint meeting	Address	Mohammad Reza Shah Pahlavi, Shahanshah of Iran
88th CONGRESS			
January 14, 1963	Joint session	State of the Union Address	President Kennedy
May 21, 1963	Joint meeting	Flight of Faith 7 spacecraft	Maj. Gordon L. Cooper Jr., USAF, Faith 7 astronaut
November 27, 1963	Joint session	Assumption of office	President Lyndon B. Johnson
January 8, 1964	Joint session	State of the Union Address	President Johnson
January 15, 1964	Joint meeting	Address	Antonio Segni, president of Italy
May 28, 1964	Joint meeting	Address	Eamon de Valera, president of Ireland
89th CONGRESS			
January 4, 1965	Joint session	State of the Union Address	President Johnson
January 6, 1965	Joint session	Counting electoral votes	N.A.
January 20, 1965	Inauguration	East Portico	President Johnson; Vice President Hubert H. Humphrey
March 15, 1965	Joint session	Voting rights	President Lyndon B. Johnson
September 14, 1965	Joint meeting	Flight of Gemini 5 spacecraft	Gemini 5 astronauts
January 12, 1966	Joint session	State of the Union Address	President Johnson
September 15, 1966	Joint meeting	Address	Ferdinand E. Marcos, president of the Philippines

Date	Type	Occasion, topic, or location	Name and position of dignitary (where applicable)
90th CONGRESS			
January 10, 1967	Joint session	State of the Union Address	President Johnson
April 28, 1967	Joint meeting	Vietnam policy	Gen. William C. Westmoreland
October 27, 1967	Joint meeting	Address	Gustavo Diaz Ordaz, president of Mexico
January 17, 1968	Joint session	State of the Union Address	President Johnson
91st CONGRESS			
January 6, 1969	Joint session	Counting electoral votes	N.A.
January 9, 1969	Joint meeting	Apollo 8: First flight around the moon	Apollo 8 astronauts
January 14, 1969	Joint session	State of the Union Address	President Johnson
January 20, 1969	Inauguration	East Portico	President Richard Nixon; Vice President Spiro T. Agnew
September 16, 1969	Joint meeting	Apollo 11: First lunar landing	Apollo 11 astronauts
January 22, 1970	Joint session	State of the Union Address	President Nixon
February 25, 1970	Joint meeting	Address	Georges Pompidou, president of France
June 3, 1970	Joint meeting	Address	Dr. Rafael Caldera, president of Venezuela
September 22, 1970	Joint meeting	Report on prisoners of war	Col. Frank Borman, representative to the president on prisoners of war
92nd CONGRESS			
January 22, 1971	Joint session	State of the Union Address	President Nixon
September 9, 1971	Joint session	Economic policy	President Nixon
September 9, 1971	Joint meeting	Apollo 15: lunar mission	Apollo 15 astronauts
January 20, 1972	Joint session	State of the Union Address	President Nixon
June 1, 1972	Joint session	European trip report	President Nixon
June 15, 1972	Joint meeting	Address	Luis Echeverria Alvarez, president of Mexico
93rd CONGRESS			
January 6, 1973	Joint session	Counting electoral votes	N.A.
January 20, 1973	Inauguration	East Portico	President Nixon; Vice President Agnew
December 6, 1973	Joint meeting	Oath of office to Vice President Gerald R. Ford	Vice President Gerald R. Ford; ceremony attended by President Nixon
January 30, 1974	Joint session	State of the Union Address	President Nixon
August 12, 1974	Joint session	Assumption of office	President Gerald R. Ford
October 8, 1974	Joint session	Economy	President Ford
94th CONGRESS			
January 15, 1975	Joint session	State of the Union Address	President Ford
April 10, 1975	Joint session	State of the World message	President Ford
June 17, 1975	Joint meeting	Address	Walter Scheel, president of West Germany
November 5, 1975	Joint meeting	Address	Anwar El Sadat, president of Egypt
January 19, 1976	Joint session	State of the Union Address	President Ford
January 28, 1976	Joint meeting	Address	Yitzhak Rabin, prime minister of Israel
March 17, 1976	Joint meeting	Address	Liam Cosgrave, prime minister of Ireland
May 18, 1976	Joint meeting	Address	Valery Giscard d'Estaing, president of France
June 2, 1976	Joint meeting	Address	Juan Carlos I, King of Spain
September 23, 1976	Joint meeting	Address	Dr. William R. Tolbert Jr., president of Liberia
95th CONGRESS			
January 6, 1977	Joint session	Counting electoral votes	N.A.
January 12, 1977	Joint session	State of the Union Address	President Ford
January 20, 1977	Inauguration	East Portico	President Jimmy Carter; Vice President Walter F. Mondale
February 22, 1977	Joint meeting	Address	Pierre Elliot Trudeau, prime minister of Canada
April 20, 1977	Joint session	Energy	President Carter
January 19, 1978	Joint session	State of the Union Address	President Carter
September 18, 1978	Joint session	Middle East Peace agreements	President Carter
96th CONGRESS			
January 23, 1979	Joint session	State of the Union Address	President Carter
June 18, 1979	Joint session	SALT II agreements	President Carter
January 23, 1980	Joint session	State of the Union Address	President Carter

Date	Type	Occasion, topic, or location	Name and position of dignitary (where applicable)
97th CONGRESS			
January 6, 1981	Joint session	Counting electoral votes	N.A.
January 20, 1981	Inauguration	West Front	President Ronald Reagan; Vice President George Bush
February 18, 1981	Joint session	Economic recovery	President Reagan
April 28, 1981	Joint session	Economic recovery—inflation	President Reagan
January 26, 1982	Joint session	State of the Union Address	President Reagan
January 28, 1982	Joint meeting	Centennial of birth of Franklin Delano Roosevelt	Several members of Congress; former Representative James Roosevelt, D-Calif., son of President Roosevelt; and other dignitaries
April 21, 1982	Joint meeting	Address	Beatrix, Queen of the Netherlands
98th CONGRESS			
January 25, 1983	Joint session	State of the Union Address	President Reagan
April 27, 1983	Joint session	Central America	President Reagan
October 5, 1983	Joint meeting	Address	Karl Carstens, president of West Germany
January 25, 1984	Joint session	State of the Union Address	President Reagan
March 15, 1984	Joint meeting	Address	Dr. Garett FitzGerald, prime minister of Ireland
March 22, 1984	Joint meeting	Address	François Mitterand, president of France
May 8, 1984	Joint meeting	Centennial of birth of Harry S. Truman	Several current or former members of Congress; and Margaret Truman Daniel, daughter of President Truman
May 16, 1984	Joint meeting	Address	Miguel de la Madrid, president of Mexico
99th CONGRESS			
January 7, 1985	Joint session	Counting electoral votes	N.A.
January 21, 1985	Inauguration	Rotunda	President Reagan; Vice President Bush
February 6, 1985	Joint session	State of the Union Address	President Reagan
February 20, 1985	Joint meeting	Address	Margaret Thatcher, prime minister of the United Kingdom
March 6, 1985	Joint meeting	Address	Bettino Craxi, prime minister of Italy
March 20, 1985	Joint meeting	Address	Raul Alfonsin, president of Argentina
June 13, 1985	Joint meeting	Address	Rajiv Gandhi, prime minister of India
October 9, 1985	Joint meeting	Address	Lee Kuan Yew, prime minister of Singapore
November 21, 1985	Joint session	Geneva Summit	President Reagan
February 4, 1986	Joint session	State of the Union Address	President Reagan
September 11, 1986	Joint meeting	Address	Jose Sarney, president of Brazil
September 18, 1986	Joint meeting	Address	Corazon C. Aquino, president of the Philippines
100th CONGRESS			
January 27, 1987	Joint session	State of the Union Address	President Reagan
November 10, 1987	Joint meeting	Address	Chaim Herzog, president of Israel
January 25, 1988	Joint session	State of the Union Address	President Reagan
April 27, 1988	Joint meeting	Address	Brian Mulroney, prime minister of Canada
June 23, 1988	Joint meeting	Address	Robert Hawke, prime minister of Australia
101st CONGRESS			
January 4, 1989	Joint session	Counting electoral votes	N.A.
January 20, 1989	Inauguration	West Front	President George Bush; Vice President Dan Quayle
February 9, 1989	Joint session	Building a Better America	President Bush
March 2, 1989	Joint meeting	Bicentennial of the 1st Congress	Several members of Congress and the executive branch; and other dignitaries
June 7, 1989	Joint meeting	Address	Benazir Bhutto, prime minister of Pakistan
October 4, 1989	Joint meeting	Address	Carlos Salinas de Gortari, president of Mexico
October 18, 1989	Joint meeting	Address	Roh Tae Woo, president of the Republic of Korea
November 15, 1989	Joint meeting	Address	Lech Walesa, chairman of Solidarność labor union, Poland

Date	Type	Occasion, topic, or location	Name and position of dignitary *(where applicable)*
January 31, 1990	Joint session	State of the Union Address	President Bush
February 21, 1990	Joint meeting	Address	Vaclav Hável, president of Czechoslovakia
March 7, 1990	Joint meeting	Address	Giulio Andreotti, prime minister of Italy
March 27, 1990	Joint meeting	Centennial of birth of Dwight D. Eisenhower	Several members of Congress; John S. D. Eisenhower, former ambassador to Belgium and son of President Eisenhower; and other dignitaries
June 26, 1990	Joint meeting	Address	Nelson Mandela, deputy president of the African National Congress, South Africa
September 11, 1990	Joint session	Invasion of Kuwait by Iraq	President Bush
102nd CONGRESS			
January 29, 1991	Joint session	State of the Union Address	President Bush
March 6, 1991	Joint session	Conclusion of Persian Gulf War	President Bush
April 16, 1991	Joint meeting	Address	Violeta B. de Chamorro, president of Nicaragua
May 8, 1991	c	Address	Gen. H. Norman Schwarzkopf, allied commander, Persian Gulf War
May 16, 1991	Joint meeting	Address	Elizabeth II, Queen of United Kingdom
November 14, 1991	Joint meeting	Address	Carlos Saul Menem, president of Argentina
January 28, 1992	Joint session	State of the Union Address	President Bush
April 30, 1992	Joint meeting	Address	Richard von Weizsacker, president of Germany
June 17, 1992	Joint meeting	Address	Boris Yeltsin, president of Russia
103rd CONGRESS			
January 6, 1993	Joint session	Counting electoral votes	N.A.
January 20, 1993	Inauguration	West Front	President William J. Clinton; Vice President Albert Gore
February 17, 1993	Joint session	Economic address	President Clinton
September 22, 1993	Joint session	Health care reform	President Clinton
January 25, 1994	Joint session	State of the Union Address	President Clinton
May 18, 1994	Joint meeting	Address	Narasimha Rao, prime minister of India
July 26, 1994	Joint meeting	Addresses	Hussein I, King of Jordan; Yitzhak Rabin, prime minister of Israel
October 6, 1994	Joint meeting	Address	Nelson Mandela, president of South Africa
104th CONGRESS			
January 24, 1995	Joint session	State of the Union Address	President Clinton
July 26, 1995	Joint meeting	Address	Kim Yong-sam, president of South Korea
October 11, 1995	Joint meeting	Close of the commemoration of the 50th anniversary of World War II	Speaker Newt Gingrich, R-Ga.; Vice President Gore; President pro tempore Strom Thurmond, R-S.C.; Reps. Henry J. Hyde, R-Ill., and G. V. "Sonny" Montgomery, D-Miss.; Sens. Daniel K. Inouye, D-Hawaii, and Robert Dole, R-Kan.; former representative Robert H. Michel, R-Ill.; Gen. Louis H. Wilson (ret.), former commandant of the Marine Corps
December 12, 1995	Joint meeting	Address	Shimon Peres, prime minister of Israel
January 30, 1996	Joint session	State of the Union Address	President Clinton
February 1, 1996	Joint meeting	Address	Jacques Chirac, president of France
July 10, 1996	Joint meeting	Address	Benjamin Netanyahu, prime minister of Israel
September 11, 1996	Joint meeting	Address	John Bruton, prime minister of Ireland
105th CONGRESS			
January 9, 1997	Joint session	Counting electoral votes	N.A.
January 20, 1997	Inauguration	West Front	President Clinton, Vice President Gore
February 4, 1997	Joint session	State of the Union Address[d]	President Clinton
February 27, 1997	Joint meeting	Address	Eduardo Frei, president of Chile
January 27, 1998	Joint session	State of the Union Address	President Clinton
June 10, 1998	Joint meeting	Address	Kim Dae-jung, president of South Korea
July 15, 1998	Joint meeting	Address	Emil Constantinescu, president of Romania

Date	Type	Occasion, topic, or location	Name and position of dignitary (where applicable)
106th CONGRESS[e]			
January 19, 1999	Joint session	State of the Union Address	President Clinton

NOTES: The parliamentary difference between a joint session and joint meeting has evolved over time. In recent years the distinctions have become clearer. A joint session is more formal, and it occurs upon the adoption of a concurrent resolution; a joint meeting occurs when each body adopts a unanimous consent agreement to recess to meet with the other legislative body. Inaugurations that were not joint sessions are listed in the second column; those that were joint sessions are so identified and described in the third column.

   a. An address to the Senate in the Senate chamber, to which members of the House informally were invited.
   b. An informal meeting in the Library of Congress.
   c. Not an official joint meeting. Schwarzkopf addressed the House in the House chamber and members of the Senate were invited.
   d. First State of the Union Address carried live on the Internet.
   e. Through June 15, 1999.

SOURCES: *1999–2000 Congressional Directory, 106th Congress* (Washington, D.C.: Government Printing Office, 1999); Senate Historical Office.

Special Sessions of the Senate, 1789–1933

From 1789 to 1933 presidential and congressional terms began on March 4, although Congress generally did not meet until the first Monday in December. When a new president was to take office, his predecessor would call the Senate into special session to confirm the nominations for the cabinet and other significant posts. Special sessions also were convened to consider the ratification of treaties. Incumbent presidents also called special sessions from time to time to allow senators to consider vacancies and other executive business. Special sessions are called by presidential proclamation. Except as noted below, all special sessions were convened to consider executive nominations.

Congress	Convened	Adjourned	Congress	Convened	Adjourned
2nd	March 4, 1791	March 4, 1791	40th	April 1, 1867	April 20, 1867
3rd	March 4, 1793[a]	March 4, 1793	41st	April 12, 1869	April 22, 1869
4th	June 8, 1795	June 26, 1795	42nd	May 10, 1871[c]	May 27, 1871
5th	March 4, 1797	March 4, 1797	43rd	March 4, 1873	March 26, 1873
5th	July 17, 1798	July 19, 1798	44th	March 5, 1875	March 24, 1875
7th	March 4, 1801	March 5, 1801	45th	March 5, 1877	March 17, 1877
11th	March 4, 1809	March 7, 1809	47th	March 4, 1881	May 20, 1881
15th	March 4, 1817	March 6, 1817	47th	October 10, 1881	October 29, 1881
19th	March 4, 1825	March 9, 1825	49th	March 4, 1885	April 2, 1885
21st	March 4, 1829	March 17, 1829	51st	March 4, 1889	April 2, 1889
25th	March 4, 1837	March 10, 1837	53rd	March 4, 1893	April 15, 1893
27th	March 4, 1841	March 15, 1841	55th	March 4, 1897	March 10, 1897
29th	March 4, 1845	March 20, 1845	57th	March 4, 1901	March 9, 1901
31st	March 5, 1849	March 23, 1849	58th	March 5, 1903	March 19, 1903
32nd	March 4, 1851	March 13, 1851	59th	March 4, 1905	March 18, 1905
33rd	March 4, 1853	April 11, 1853	61st	March 4, 1909	March 6, 1909
35th	March 4, 1857	March 14, 1857	63rd	March 4, 1913	March 17, 1913
35th	June 15, 1858	June 16, 1858	65th	March 5, 1917	March 16, 1917
36th	March 4, 1859	March 10, 1859	67th	March 4, 1921	March 15, 1921
36th	June 26, 1860[b]	June 28, 1860	69th	March 4, 1925	March 18, 1925
37th	March 4, 1861	March 28, 1861	71st	March 4, 1929	March 5, 1929
38th	March 4, 1863	March 14, 1863	71st	July 7, 1930[d]	July 21, 1930
39th	March 4, 1865	March 11, 1865	73rd	March 4, 1933	March 6, 1933

NOTES: a. To consider the Jay Treaty.
    b. To consider treaties.
    c. To consider the Washington Treaty.
    d. To consider the Naval Arms Treaty.
SOURCE: *1999–2000 Congressional Directory, 106th Congress* (Washington, D.C.: Government Printing Office, 1999).

Extraordinary Sessions of Congress since 1797

Article II, Section 3, of the Constitution provides that the president "may, on extraordinary Occasions, convene both Houses, or either of them."

This procedure occurs only if Congress is convened by presidential proclamation; it does not include the many special sessions of the Senate called primarily to confirm nominations prior to the Twentieth Amendment. *(See "Special sessions of Senate," p. 1144)*

Congress	Session	Date convened	Date of proclamation	Reason	President
5th	1st	May 15, 1797	March 25, 1797	Suspension of Relations with France	Adams
8th	1st	October 17, 1803	July 16, 1803	Louisiana Cession/Purchase	Jefferson
10th	1st	October 26, 1807	July 30, 1807	Relations with Great Britain	Jefferson
12th	1st	November 4, 1811	July 24, 1811	Relations with Great Britain	Jefferson
13th	3rd	September 19, 1814	August 8, 1814	War with Great Britain	Madison
25th	1st	September 4, 1837	May 15, 1837	Suspension of Species Payment	Van Buren
27th	1st	May 31, 1841	March 17, 1841	Condition of Finances and Revenue	Harrison
34th	2nd	August 21, 1856	August 18, 1856	Army Appropriations	Pierce
37th	1st	July 4, 1861	April 17, 1861	Insurrection of Southern States	Lincoln
45th	1st	October 15, 1877	May 5, 1877	Army Appropriations	Hayes
46th	1st	March 18, 1879	March 4, 1879	Appropriations	Hayes
53rd	1st	August 7, 1893	June 30, 1893	Repeal Silver Purchase Act	Cleveland
55th	1st	March 15, 1897	March 6, 1897	Dingley Tariff	McKinley
58th	1st	November 9, 1903	October 20, 1903	Cuban Reciprocity Treaty	Roosevelt
61st	1st	March 15, 1909	March 6, 1909	Payne-Aldrich Tariff	Taft
62nd	1st	April 4, 1911	March 4, 1911	Canadian Reciprocity	Taft
63rd	1st	April 7, 1913	March 17, 1913	Federal Reserve Act	Wilson
65th	1st	April 2, 1917	March 17, 1917	World War I	Wilson
66th	1st	May 19, 1919	May 7, 1919	High Cost of Living	Wilson
67th	1st	April 11, 1921	March 22, 1921	Emergency Agricultural Tariff	Harding
67th	3rd	November 20, 1922	November 9, 1922	Independent Merchant Marine	Harding
71st	1st	April 15, 1929	March 7, 1929	Smoot-Hawley Tariff	Hoover
73rd	1st	March 9, 1933	March 5, 1933	Recovery Legislation	Roosevelt
75th	2nd	November 15, 1937	October 12, 1937	Wages and Hours Act	Roosevelt
76th	2nd	September 21, 1939	September 13, 1939	Neutrality Legislation	Roosevelt
80th	1st	November 17, 1947	October 23, 1947	Domestic Legislation	Truman
80th	2nd	July 26, 1948	July 15, 1948	Domestic Legislation	Truman

NOTE: As of September 1999.

SOURCE: Senate Historical Office.

Congressional Information on the Internet

A huge array of congressional information is available for free at Internet sites operated by the federal government, colleges and universities, and commercial firms. The sites offer the full text of bills introduced in the House and Senate, voting records, campaign finance information, transcripts of selected congressional hearings, investigative reports, and much more.

THOMAS

The most important site for congressional information is THOMAS *(http://thomas.loc.gov)*, which is named for Thomas Jefferson and operated by the Library of Congress. THOMAS's highlight is its databases containing the full text of all bills introduced in Congress since 1989, the full text of the *Congressional Record* since 1989, and the status and summary information for all bills introduced since 1973.

THOMAS also offers special links to bills that have received or are expected to receive floor action during the current week and newsworthy bills that are pending or that have recently been approved. Finally, THOMAS has selected committee reports, answers to frequently asked questions about accessing congressional information, publications titled *How Our Laws Are Made* and *Enactment of a Law,* and links to lots of other congressional Web sites.

HOUSE OF REPRESENTATIVES

The U.S. House of Representatives site *(http://www.house.gov)* offers the schedule of bills, resolutions, and other legislative issues the House will consider in the current week. It also has updates about current proceedings on the House floor and a list of the next day's meeting of House committees. Other highlights include a database that helps users identify their representative, a directory of House members and committees, the House ethics manual, links to Web pages maintained by House members and committees, a calendar of congressional primary dates and candidate-filing deadlines for ballot access, the full text of all amendments to the Constitution that have been ratified and those that have been proposed but not ratified, and lots of information about Washington, D.C., for visitors.

Another key House site is The Office of the Clerk On-line Information Center *(http://clerkweb.house.gov)*, which has records of all roll-call votes taken since 1990. The votes are recorded by bill, so it is a lengthy process to compile a particular representative's voting record. The site also has lists of committee assignments, a telephone directory for members and committees, mailing label templates for members and committees, rules of the current Congress, election statistics from 1920 to the present, biographies of Speakers of the House, biographies of women who have served since 1917, and a virtual tour of the House Chamber.

One of the more interesting House sites is operated by the House Committee on Rules *(http://www.house.gov/rules)*. Its highlight is dozens of Congressional Research Service reports about the legislative process. Some of the available titles include *Legislative Research in Congressional Offices: A Primer, How to Follow Current Federal Legislation and Regulations, Hearings in the House of Representatives: A Guide for Preparation and Conduct, Investigative Oversight: An Introduction to the Law, Practice, and Procedure of Congressional Inquiry, How Measures Are Brought to the House Floor: A Brief Introduction, A Brief Introduction to the Federal Budget Process,* and *Presidential Vetoes 1789–1996: A Summary Overview.*

A final House site is operated by the office of the Law Revision Counsel *(http://uscode.house.gov)*. This site has a searchable version of the U.S. Code, which contains the text of public laws enacted by Congress, and a tutorial for searching the Code.

SENATE

At least in the Internet world, the Senate is not as active as the House. Its main Web site *(http://www.senate.gov)* has records of all roll-call votes taken since 1989 (arranged by bill), brief descriptions of all bills and joint resolutions introduced in the Senate during the past week, and a calendar of upcoming committee hearings. The site also provides the standing rules of the Senate, a directory of senators and their committee assignments, lists of nominations that the president has submitted to the Senate for approval, links to Web pages operated by senators and committees, and a virtual tour of the Senate.

GENERAL REFERENCE

Information about the membership, jurisdiction, and rules of each congressional committee is available at the U.S. Government Printing Office site *(http://www.access.gpo.gov/su_docs/legislative.html)*. It also has transcripts of selected congressional hearings, the full text of selected House and Senate reports, and the House and Senate rules manuals.

The U.S. General Accounting Office, the investigative arm of Congress, operates a site *(http://www.gao.gov)* that provides the full text of its reports from 1996 to the present. The reports cover a wide range of topics: aviation safety, combating terrorism, counternarcotics efforts in Mexico, defense contracting, electronic warfare, food assistance programs, Gulf War illness, health insurance, illegal aliens, information technology, long-term care, mass transit, Medicare, military readiness, money laundering, national parks, nuclear waste, organ donation, student loan defaults, and the Year 2000 computing crisis, among others.

The GAO Daybook is an excellent current awareness tool. This electronic mailing list distributes a daily list of reports and testimony released by the GAO. Subscriptions are available by sending an e-mail message to *majordomo@www.gao.gov,* and in the message area typing "subscribe daybook" (without the quotation marks).

Current budget and economic projections are provided at the Congressional Budget Office Web site *(http://www.cbo.gov)*. The site also has reports about the economic and budget outlook for the next decade, the president's budget proposals, federal civilian employment, Social Security privatization, tax reform, water use conflicts in the west, marriage and the federal income tax, and the role of foreign aid in development, among other topics. Other highlights include monthly budget updates, historical budget data, cost estimates for bills reported by congressional committees, and transcripts of congressional testimony by CBO officials.

The congressional Office of Technology Assessment was eliminated in 1995, but every report it ever issued is available at The OTA Legacy *(http://www.wws.princeton.edu:80/~ota)*, a site operated by the Woodrow Wilson School of Public and International Affairs at Princeton University. The site has more than 100,000 pages of detailed reports about aging, agricultural technology, arms control, biological research, cancer, computer security, defense technology, economic development, education, environmental protection, health and health technology, information technology, space, transportation, and many other subjects. The reports are organized in alphabetical, chronological, and topical lists.

CAMPAIGN FINANCE

Several Internet sites provide detailed campaign finance data for congressional elections. The official site is operated by the Federal Election Commission *(http://www.fec.gov)*, which regulates political spending. The site's highlight is its database of campaign reports filed from May 1996 to the present by House and presidential candidates, political action committees, and political party committees. Senate reports are not included because they are filed with the Secretary of the Senate. The reports in the FEC's database are scanned images of paper reports filed with the commission.

The FEC site also has summary financial data for House and Senate candidates in the current election cycle, abstracts of court decisions pertaining to federal election law from 1976 to 1997, a graph showing the number of political action committees (PACs) in existence each year from 1974 to the present, and a directory of national and state agencies that are responsible for releasing information about campaign financing, candidates on the ballot, election results, lobbying, and other issues. Another useful feature is a collection of brochures about federal election law, public funding of presidential elections, the ban on contributions by foreign nationals, independent expenditures supporting or opposing a candidate for federal office, contribution limits, filing a complaint, researching public records at the FEC, and other topics. Finally, the site provides the FEC's legislative recommendations, its annual report, a report about its first twenty years in existence, the FEC's monthly newsletter, several reports about voter registration, election results for the most recent presidential and congressional elections, and campaign guides for corporations and labor organizations, congressional candidates and committees, political party committees, and nonconnected committees.

The best online source for campaign finance data is FECInfo *(http://www.tray.com/fecinfo)*, which is operated by former Federal Election Commission employee Tony Raymond. FECInfo's searchable databases provide extensive itemized information about receipts and expenditures by federal candidates and political action committees from 1980 to the present. The data, which are obtained from the FEC, are quite detailed. For example, for candidates contributions can be searched by zip code. The site also has data on soft money contributions, lists of the top political action committees in various categories, lists of the top contributors from each state, and much more.

Another interesting site is Campaign Finance Data on the Internet *(http://www.soc.american.edu/campfin)*, which is operated by the American University School of Communication. It provides electronic files from the FEC that have been reformatted in .dbf format so they can be used in database programs such as Paradox, Access, and FoxPro. The files contain data on PAC, committee, and individual contributions to individual congressional candidates.

More campaign finance data is available from the Center for Responsive Politics *(http://www.opensecrets.org)*, a public interest organization. The center provides a list of all "soft money" donations to political parties of $100,000 or more in the current election cycle and data about "leadership" political action committees associated with individual politicians. Other databases at the site provide information about travel expenses that House members received from private sources for attending meetings and other events, activities of registered federal lobbyists, and activities of foreign agents who are registered in the United States.

Capitol Floor Plan

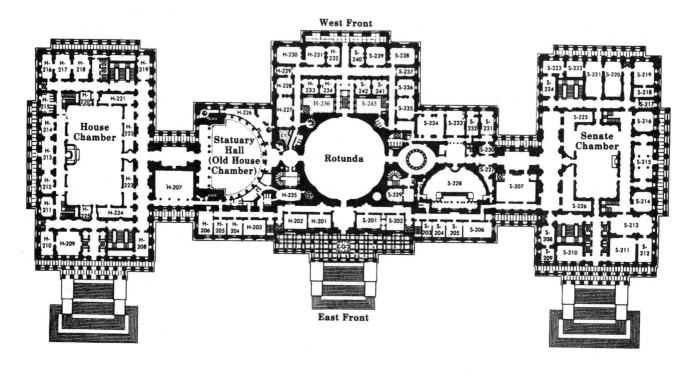

Scale:
0 16 32 48 64 Feet

H 207 House reception room

H 208 Ways and Means Committee

H 209–210 Speaker

H 216–218 Appropriations Committee

H 220 Speaker's floor office

H 221–224 Cloakrooms (lobbies)

H 227–233, 236 Speaker

S 207 Senators' conference room

S 213 Sentate reception room

S 214 Vice President's formal office

S 216 President's room

S 225–226 Cloakrooms (lobbies)

S 228 Old Senate chamber, 1810–1859

Map of Capitol Hill

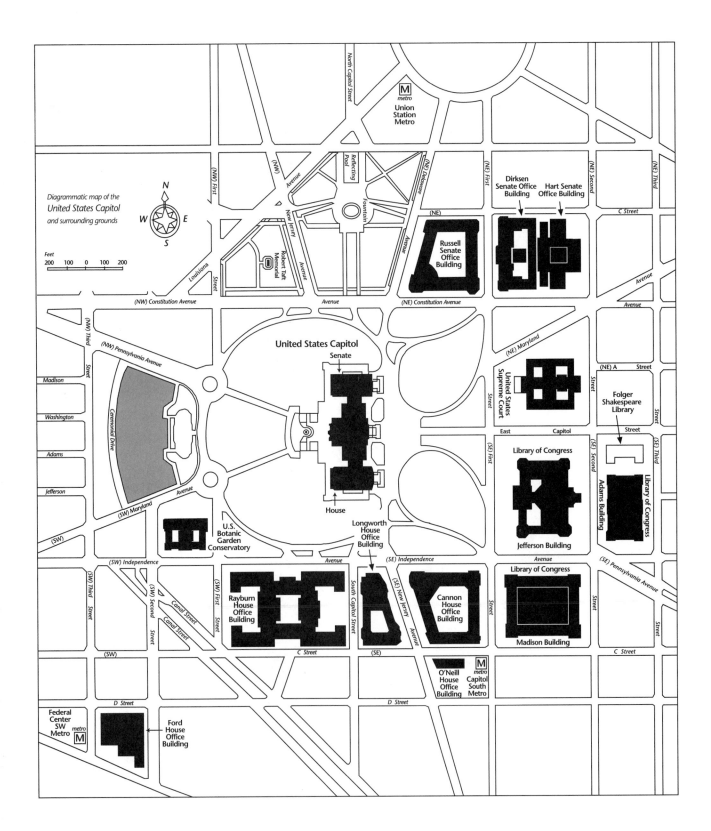

Diagrammatic map of the
United States Capitol
and surrounding grounds

N
W E
S

Feet
200 100 0 100 200

North Capitol Street

Union
Station
Metro

M
metro

Reflecting
Pool

Fountain

(NW) First Street

(NW) Avenue

(NE) Delaware Avenue

New Jersey Avenue

(NE) First Street

(NE) Second Street

(NE) Third Street

Dirksen
Senate Office
Building

Hart Senate
Office Building

C Street

(NE)

Russell
Senate
Office
Building

Robert Taft
Memorial

Louisiana Avenue

(NW) Constitution Avenue

Avenue

(NE) Constitution Avenue

Avenue

Avenue

Madison

Washington

Adams

Jefferson

(NW) Third Street

(NW) Pennsylvania Avenue

Ceremonial Drive

(SW) Maryland Avenue

United States Capitol

Senate

House

(NE) Maryland Avenue

United States
Supreme Court

First Street

(NE) A Street

Folger
Shakespeare
Library

(SE) Third Street

East   Capitol   Street

Library of Congress

(SE) First Street

(SE) Second Street

Adams Building

Library of Congress

Jefferson Building

(SW)

U.S.
Botanic
Garden
Conservatory

Longworth
House
Office
Building

(SE) Independence

(SW) Independence Avenue

Avenue

Library of Congress

(SE) Pennsylvania Avenue

Street

(SW) Third Street

(SW) Second Street

Canal Street

Canal Street

(SW) First Street

Rayburn
House
Office
Building

South Capitol Street

(SE) New Jersey Avenue

Cannon
House
Office
Building

First Street

Madison Building

C Street

(SW)

C Street

(SE)

O'Neill
House
Office
Building

M
metro

Capitol
South
Metro

D Street

D Street

Federal
Center
SW
Metro

M
metro

Ford
House
Office
Building

Members of Congress: 1789–1999

Members of Congress: 1789–1999

This biographical summary lists, alphabetically, all men and women who served in Congress as senators, representatives, resident commissioners, or territorial delegates from March 4, 1789, through October 1999—from the First Congress to the end of the First Session of the 106th Congress.

The material is organized as follows: name; relationship to other members, presidents, or vice presidents; party, state (of service); date of birth; date of death (if applicable); congressional service; service as House or Senate minority leader, House or Senate majority leader, Speaker of the House, or president pro tempore of the Senate (when elected); service as president, vice president, cabinet member, Supreme Court justice, governor, delegate to the Continental Congress, or chairman of the Democratic National Committee or the Republican National Committee.

If a member changed parties during his congressional service, party designation appearing after the member's name is that which applied at the end of such service and further breakdown is included after dates of congressional service. Party designation is multiple only if the member was elected by two or more parties at the same time. Where service date is left open, the member was serving in the 106th Congress.

Dates of service are inclusive and may cover more than one term—six years for senators and two years for representatives. Under the Constitution, terms of service from 1789 to 1933 were from March 4 to March 4; since 1934, service has been from January 3 to January 3. In actual practice, members often have been sworn in on other dates at the beginning of a Congress. The exact date is shown (where available) only if a member began or ended his service in midterm.

Only the dates of election of the Senate president pro tempore are included. Until March 12, 1890, the appointment or election of the president pro tempore was for the occasion only, resulting in more than one president pro tempore appearing per session or none at all. Since then, the president pro tempore serves until the Senate orders otherwise.

Presidential and vice-presidential terms from 1789 to 1933 were from March 4 to March 4; since 1934, the four-year term has been from January 20 to January 20.

The primary source of information for this list was U.S. Congress, Joint Committee on Printing, *Biographical Directory of the American Congress, 1774–1989* (Washington, D.C.: Government Printing Office, 1989), which made a number of changes from its previous edition. Most of these changes—reflected in the list below—pertain to party affiliation of members. Additional data were obtained from the *Biographical Directory of the American Congress, 1774–1996* (Alexandria, Va.: CQ Staff Directories, 1997); the files of the Joint Committee on Printing; the Congressional Directory; other Congressional Quarterly publications; and various newspapers.

PARTY ABBREVIATIONS

AD	Anti-Democrat	FSD	Free-Soil Democrat	P	Populist
Ad.D	Adams Democrat	FSil.	Free-Silver	PD	Popular Democrat
AF	Anti-Federalist	G	Greenbacker	PR	Progressive Republican
AJ	Anti-Jacksonian	I	Independent	Prog.	Progressive
AL	American Laborite	ID	Independent Democrat	Prohib.	Prohibitionist
ALD	Anti-Lecompton Democrat	IP	Independent Populist	R	Republican
ALot.	Anti-Lottery Democrat	IR	Independent Republican	Read	Readjuster
AM	Anti-Monopolist	IRad.	Independent Radical	Sil.R	Silver Republican
AMas.	Anti-Mason	IW	Independent Whig	Soc.	Socialist
AP	American Party	J	Jacksonian	SR	State Rights Party
C	Conservative	Jeff.R	Jeffersonian Republican	SRD	State Rights Democrat
Coal.	Coalitionist	L	Liberal	SRFT	State Rights Free-Trader
Confed. D	Confederate Democrat	Lab.	Laborite	U	Unionist
Const U	Constitutional Unionist	L&O	Law & Order	UD	Union Democrat
CR	Conservative Republican	LR	Liberal Republican	UL	Union Laborite
D	Democrat	N	Nullifier	UR	Union Republican
DFL	Democrat Farmer Labor	Nat.	Nationalist	UU	Unconditional Unionist
DR	Democratic Republican	New Prog.	New Progressive	UW	Union Whig
F	Federalist	Nonpart.	Nonpartisan	W	Whig
FL	Farmer Laborite	NR	National Republican	–	No party
FS	Free-Soiler	O	Opposition Party		

A

Aandahl, Fred George (R N.D.) April 9, 1897–April 7, 1966; House 1951–53; Gov. Jan. 4, 1945–Jan. 3, 1951.

Abbitt, Watkins Moorman (D Va.) May 21, 1908–July 13, 1998; House Feb. 17, 1948–73.

Abbot, Joel (R Ga.) March 17, 1776–Nov. 19, 1826; House 1817–25.

Abbott, Amos (W Mass.) Sept. 10, 1786–Nov. 2, 1868; House 1843–49.

Abbott, Joseph (D Texas) Jan. 15, 1840–Feb. 11, 1908; House 1887–97.

Abbott, Joseph Carter (R N.C.) July 15, 1825–Oct. 8, 1881; Senate July 14, 1868–71.

Abbott, Josiah Gardner (D Mass.) Nov. 1, 1814–June 2, 1891; House July 28, 1876–77.

Abbott, Nehemiah (R Maine) March 29, 1804–July 26, 1877; House 1857–59.

Abdnor, James (R S.D.) Feb. 13, 1923– ; House 1973–81; Senate 1981–87.

Abel, Hazel Hempell (R Neb.) July 10, 1888–July 30, 1966; Senate Nov. 8–Dec. 31, 1954.

Abele, Homer E. (R Ohio) Nov. 21, 1916– ; House 1963–65.

Abercrombie, James (UW Ala.) 1795–July 2, 1861; House 1851–55.

Abercrombie, John William (D Ala.) May 17, 1866–July 2, 1940; House 1913–17.

Abercrombie, Neil (D Hawaii) June 26, 1938– ; House Sept. 23, 1986–87, 1991– .

Abernethy, Charles Laban (D N.C.) March 18, 1872–Feb. 23, 1955; House Nov. 7, 1922–35.

Abernethy, Thomas Gerstle (D Miss.) May 16, 1903–June 11, 1998; House 1943–73.

Abourezk, James George (D S.D.) Feb. 24, 1931– ; House 1971–73; Senate 1973–79.

Abraham, Spencer (R Mich.) June 12, 1952– ; Senate 1995– .

Abzug, Bella Savitzky (D N.Y.) July 24, 1920–March 31, 1998; House 1971–77.

Acheson, Ernest Francis (R Pa.) Sept. 19, 1855–May 16, 1917; House 1895–1909.

Acker, Ephraim Leister (D Pa.) Jan. 11, 1827–May 12, 1903; House 1871–73.

Ackerman, Ernest Robinson (R N.J.) June 17, 1863–Oct. 18, 1931; House 1919–Oct. 18, 1931.

Ackerman, Gary Leonard (D N.Y.) Nov. 19, 1942– ; House March 1, 1983– .

Acklen, Joseph Hayes (D La.) May 20, 1850–Sept. 28, 1938; House Feb. 20, 1878–81.

Adair, Edwin Ross (R Ind.) Dec. 14, 1907–May 5, 1983; House 1951–71.

Adair, Jackson Leroy (D Ill.) Feb. 23, 1887–Jan. 19, 1956; House 1933–37.

Adair, John (J Ky.) Jan. 9, 1757–May 19, 1840; Senate Nov. 8, 1805–Nov. 18, 1806 (no party); House 1831–33; Gov. June 1, 1820–June 1, 1824 (Democratic Republican).

Adair, John Alfred McDowell (D Ind.) Dec. 22, 1864–Oct. 5, 1938; House 1907–17.

Adams, Alva Blanchard (D Colo.) Oct. 29, 1875–Dec. 1, 1941; Senate May 17, 1923–Nov. 30, 1924, 1933–Dec. 1, 1941.

Adams, Benjamin (F Mass.) Dec. 16, 1764–March 28, 1837; House Dec. 2, 1816–21.

Adams, Brockman "Brock" (D Wash.) Jan. 13, 1927– ; House 1965–Jan. 22, 1977; Chrmn. House Budget 1975–77; Senate 1987–93; Secy. of Transportation Jan. 23, 1977–July 22, 1979.

Adams, Charles Francis (son of John Quincy Adams, grandson of President John Adams) (R Mass.) Aug. 18, 1807–Nov. 21, 1886; House 1859–May 1, 1861.

Adams, Charles Henry (R N.Y.) April 10, 1824–Dec. 15, 1902; House 1875–77.

Adams, George Everett (R Ill.) June 18, 1840–Oct. 5, 1917; House 1883–91.

Adams, George Madison (nephew of Green Adams) (D Ky.) Dec. 20, 1837–April 6, 1920; House 1867–75.

Adams, Green (uncle of George Madison Adams) (O Ky.) Aug. 20, 1812–Jan. 18, 1884; House 1847–49 (Whig), 1859–61.

Adams, Henry Cullen (R Wis.) Nov. 28, 1850–July 9, 1906; House 1903–July 9, 1906.

Adams, John (J N.Y.) Aug. 26, 1778–Sept. 25, 1854; House March 4–Dec. 26, 1815 (Republican), 1833–35.

Adams, John Joseph (D N.Y.) Sept. 16, 1848–Feb. 16, 1919; House 1883–87.

Adams, John Quincy (son of President John Adams, father of Charles Francis Adams) (F Mass.) July 11, 1767–Feb. 23, 1848; Senate 1803–June 8, 1808; House 1831–Feb. 23, 1848; Secy. of State Sept. 22, 1817–March 3, 1825; President 1825–29 (Democratic Republican).

Adams, Parmenio (– N.Y.) Sept. 9, 1776–Feb. 19, 1832; House Jan. 7, 1824–27.

Adams, Robert Jr. (R Pa.) Feb. 26, 1849–June 1, 1906; House Dec. 19, 1893–June 1, 1906.

Adams, Robert Huntington (J Miss.) 1792–July 2, 1830; Senate Jan. 6, 1830–July 2, 1830.

Adams, Sherman (R N.H.) Jan. 8, 1899–Oct. 27, 1986; House 1945–47; Gov. Jan. 6, 1949–Jan. 1, 1953.

Adams, Silas (R Ky.) Feb. 9, 1839–May 5, 1896; House 1893–95.

Adams, Stephen (D Miss.) Oct. 17, 1807–May 11, 1857; House 1845–47; Senate March 17, 1852–57.

Adams, Wilbur Louis (D Del.) Oct. 23, 1884–Dec. 4, 1937; House 1933–35.

Adamson, William Charles (D Ga.) Aug. 13, 1854–Jan. 3, 1929; House 1897–Dec. 18, 1917.

Addabbo, Joseph Patrick (D N.Y.) March 17, 1925–April 10, 1986; House 1961–April 10, 1986.

Addams, William (D Pa.) April 11, 1777–May 30, 1858; House 1825–29.

Addonizio, Hugh Joseph (D N.J.) Jan. 31, 1914–Feb. 2, 1981; House 1949–June 30, 1962.

Aderholt, Robert (R Ala.) July 22, 1965– ; House 1997– .

Adgate, Asa (R N.Y.) Nov. 17, 1767–Feb. 15, 1832; House June 7, 1815–17.

Adkins, Charles (R Ill.) Feb. 7, 1863–March 31, 1941; House 1925–33.

Adrain, Garnett Bowditch (ALD N.J.) Dec. 15, 1815–Aug. 17, 1878; House 1857–61 (1857–59 Democrat).

Ahl, John Alexander (D Pa.) Aug. 16, 1813–April 25, 1882; House 1857–59.

Aiken, David Wyatt (father of Wyatt Aiken, cousin of William Aiken) (D S.C.) March 17, 1828–April 6, 1887; House 1877–87.

Aiken, George David (R Vt.) Aug. 20, 1892–Nov. 19, 1984; Senate Jan. 10, 1941–75; Chrmn. Senate Expenditures in the Executive Departments 1947–49; Chrmn. Senate Agriculture and Forestry 1953–55; Gov. Jan. 7, 1937–Jan. 9, 1941.

Aiken, William (cousin of David Wyatt Aiken) (D S.C.) Jan. 28, 1806–Sept. 7, 1887; House 1851–57; Gov. 1844–46.

Aiken, Wyatt (son of David Wyatt Aiken) (D S.C.) Dec. 14, 1863–Feb. 6, 1923; House 1903–17.

Ainey, William David Blakeslee (R Pa.) April 8, 1864–Sept. 4, 1932; House Nov. 7, 1911–15.

Ainslie, George (D Idaho) Oct. 30, 1838–May 19, 1913; House (Terr. Del.) 1879–83.

Ainsworth, Lucien Lester (D Iowa) June 21, 1831–April 19, 1902; House 1875–77.

Aitken, David Demerest (R Mich.) Sept. 5, 1853–May 26, 1930; House 1893–97.

Akaka, Daniel Kahikina (D Hawaii) Sept. 11, 1924– ; House 1977–May 16, 1990; Senate May 16, 1990– .

Akers, Thomas Peter (AP Mo.) Oct. 4, 1828–April 3, 1877; House Aug. 18, 1856–57.

Akin, Theron (PR N.Y.) May 23, 1855–March 26, 1933; House 1911–13.

Albaugh, Walter Hugh (R Ohio) Jan. 2, 1890–Jan. 21, 1942; House Nov. 8, 1938–39.

Albert, Carl Bert (cousin of Charles Wesley Vursell) (D Okla.) May 10, 1908– ; House 1947–77; House majority leader Jan. 10, 1962–71; Speaker Jan. 21, 1971–75, Jan. 14, 1975–77.

Albert, William Julian (R Md.) Aug. 4, 1816–March 29, 1879; House 1873–75.

Albertson, Nathaniel (D Ind.) June 10, 1800–Dec. 16, 1863; House 1849–51.

Albosta, Donald Joseph (D Mich.) Dec. 5, 1925– ; House 1979–85.

Albright, Charles (R Pa.) Dec. 13, 1830–Sept. 28, 1880; House 1873–75.

Albright, Charles Jefferson (R Ohio) May 9, 1816–Oct. 21, 1883; House 1855–57.

Alcorn, James Lusk (R Miss.) Nov. 4, 1816–Dec. 19, 1894; Senate Dec. 1, 1871–77; Gov. March 10, 1870–Nov. 30, 1871.

Alderson, John Duffy (D W.Va.) Nov. 29, 1854–Dec. 5, 1910; House 1889–95.

Aldrich, Cyrus (R Minn.) June 18, 1808–Oct. 5, 1871; House 1859–63.

Aldrich, James Franklin (son of William Aldrich) (R Ill.) April 6, 1853–March 8, 1933; House 1893–97.

Aldrich, Nelson Wilmarth (father of Richard Steere Aldrich, cousin of William Aldrich, great-grandfather of John Davidson "Jay" Rockefeller IV, grandfather of Vice Pres. Nelson Aldrich Rockefeller and Gov. Winthrop Rockefeller of Ark.) (R R.I.) Nov. 6, 1841–April 16, 1915; House 1879–Oct. 4, 1881; Senate Oct. 5, 1881–1911.

Aldrich, Richard Steere (son of Nelson Wilmarth Aldrich, great-uncle of John Davison "Jay" Rockefeller IV, uncle of Vice Pres. Nelson Aldrich Rockefeller of Ark.) (R R.I.) Feb. 29, 1884–Dec. 25, 1941; House 1923–33.

Aldrich, Truman Heminway (brother of William Farrington Aldrich) (R Ala.) Oct. 17, 1848–April 28, 1932; House June 9, 1896–97.

Aldrich, William (father of James Franklin Aldrich, cousin of Nelson Wilmarth Aldrich) (R Ill.) Jan. 19, 1820–Dec. 3, 1885; House 1877–83.

Aldrich, William Farrington (brother of Truman Heminway Aldrich) (R Ala.) March 11, 1853–Oct. 30, 1925; House March 13, 1896–97, Feb. 9, 1898–99, March 8, 1900–01.

Aleshire, Arthur William (D Ohio) Feb. 15, 1900–March 11, 1940; House 1937–39.

Alexander, Adam Rankin (F Tenn.) ?–?; House 1823–27.

Alexander, Armstead Milton (D Mo.) May 26, 1834–Nov. 7, 1892; House 1883–85.

Alexander, De Alva Stanwood (R N.Y.) July 17, 1846–Jan. 30, 1925; House 1897–1911.

Alexander, Evan Shelby (cousin of Nathaniel Alexander) (R N.C.) about 1767–Oct. 28, 1809; House Feb. 24, 1806–09.

Alexander, Henry Porteous (W N.Y.) Sept. 13, 1801–Feb. 22, 1867; House 1849–51.

Alexander, Hugh Quincy (D N.C.) Aug. 7, 1911–Sept. 17, 1989; House 1953–63.

Alexander, James Jr. (W Ohio) Oct. 17, 1789–Sept. 5, 1846; House 1837–39.

Alexander, John (R Ohio) April 16, 1777–June 28, 1848; House 1813–17.

Alexander, John Grant (R Minn.) July 16, 1893–Dec. 8, 1971; House 1939–41.

Alexander, Joshua Willis (D Mo.) Jan. 22, 1852–Feb. 27, 1936; House 1907–Dec. 15, 1919; Secy. of Commerce Dec. 16, 1919–March 4, 1921.

Alexander, Mark (J Va.) Feb. 7, 1792–Oct. 7, 1883; House 1819–33 (1819–29 no party).

Alexander, Nathaniel (cousin of Evan Shelby Alexander) (R N.C.) March 5, 1756–March 7, 1808; House 1803–Nov. 1805; Gov. Dec. 10, 1805–Dec. 1, 1807 (Democratic Republican).

Alexander, Syndenham Benoni (cousin of Adlai Ewing Stevenson and John Sharp Williams) (D N.C.) Dec. 8, 1840–June 14, 1921; House 1891–95.

Alexander, William Vollie Jr. (D Ark.) Jan. 16, 1934– ; House 1969–93.

Alford, Julius Caesar (W Ga.) May 10, 1799–Jan. 1, 1863; House Jan. 2–March 3, 1837 (State Rights Party), 1839–Oct. 1, 1841.

Alford, Thomas Dale (ID Ark.) Jan. 28, 1916– ; House 1959–63.

Alger, Bruce Reynolds (R Texas) June 12, 1918– ; House 1955–65.

Alger, Russell Alexander (R Mich.) Feb. 27, 1836–Jan. 24, 1907; Senate Sept. 27, 1902–Jan. 24, 1907; Gov. Jan. 1, 1885–Jan. 1, 1887; Secy. of War March 5, 1897–Aug. 1, 1899.

Allan, Chilton (W Ky.) April 6, 1786–Sept. 3, 1858; House 1831–37 (1831–35 Anti-Jacksonian).

Allard, Wayne (R Colo.) Dec. 2, 1943– ; House 1991–97; Senate 1997– .

Allee, James Frank (R Del.) Dec. 2, 1857–Oct. 12, 1938; Senate March 2, 1903–07.

Allen, Alfred Gaither (D Ohio) July 23, 1867–Dec. 9, 1932; House 1911–17.

Allen, Amos Lawrence (R Maine) March 17, 1837–Feb. 20, 1911; House Nov. 6, 1899–Feb. 20, 1911.

Allen, Asa Leonard (D La.) Jan. 5, 1891–Jan. 5, 1969; House 1937–53.

Allen, Charles (son of Joseph Allen, great-nephew of Samuel Adams) (FS Mass.) Aug. 9, 1797–Aug. 6, 1869; House 1849–53.

Allen, Charles Herbert (R Mass.) April 15, 1848–April 20, 1934; House 1885–89.

Allen, Clarence Emir (R Utah) Sept. 8, 1852–July 9, 1932; House Jan. 4, 1896–97.

Allen, Clifford Robertson (D Tenn.) Jan. 6, 1912–June 18, 1978; House Nov. 25, 1975–June 18, 1978.

Allen, Edward Payson (R Mich.) Oct. 28, 1839–Nov. 25, 1909; House 1887–91.

Allen, Elisha Hunt (son of Samuel Clesson Allen) (W Maine) Jan. 28, 1804–Jan. 1, 1883; House 1841–43.

Allen, George Felix (R Va.) March 8, 1952– ; House Nov. 12, 1991–93; Gov. Jan. 15, 1994–Jan. 17, 1998.

Allen, Heman (W Vt.) June 14, 1777–Dec. 11, 1844; House 1831–39 (1831–35 no party).

Allen, Heman (R Vt.) Feb. 23, 1779–April 7, 1852; House 1817–April 20, 1818.

Allen, Henry Crosby (R N.J.) May 13, 1872–March 7, 1942; House 1905–07.

Allen, Henry Dixon (D Ky.) June 24, 1854–March 9, 1924; House 1899–1903.

Allen, Henry Justin (R Kan.) Sept. 11, 1868–Jan. 17, 1950; Senate April 1, 1929–Nov. 30, 1930; Gov. Jan. 13, 1919–Jan. 8, 1923.

Allen, James Browning (husband of Maryon Pittman Allen) (D Ala.) Dec. 28, 1912–June 1, 1978; Senate 1969–June 1, 1978.

Allen, James Cameron (D Ill.) Jan. 29, 1822–Jan. 30, 1912; House 1853–July 18, 1856, Nov. 4, 1856–57, 1863–65.

Allen, John (father of John William Allen) (F Conn.) June 12, 1763–July 31, 1812; House 1797–99.

Allen, John Beard (R Wash.) May 18, 1845–Jan. 28, 1903; House (Terr. Del.) March 4–Nov. 11, 1889; Senate Nov. 20, 1889–93.

Allen, John Clayton (R Ill.) Feb. 14, 1860–Jan. 12, 1939; House 1925–33.

Allen, John James (brother of Robert Allen) (AJ Va.) Sept. 25, 1797–Sept. 18, 1871; House 1833–35.

Allen, John Joseph Jr. (R Calif.) Nov. 27, 1899–March 7, 1995; House 1947–59.

Allen, John Mills (D Miss.) July 8, 1846–Oct. 30, 1917; House 1885–1901.

Allen, John William (son of John Allen) (W Ohio) Aug. 1802–Oct. 5, 1887; House 1837–41.

Allen, Joseph (father of Charles Allen, nephew of Samuel Adams) (F Mass.) Sept. 2, 1749–Sept. 2, 1827; House Oct. 8, 1810–11.

Allen, Judson (D N.Y.) April 3, 1797–Aug. 6, 1880; House 1839–41.

Allen, Leo Elwood (R Ill.) Oct. 5, 1898–Jan. 19, 1973; House 1933–61; Chrmn. House Rules 1947–49, 1953–55.

Allen, Maryon Pittman (wife of James Browning Allen) (D Ala.) Nov. 30, 1925– ; Senate June 8–Nov. 7, 1978.

Allen, Nathaniel (father-in-law of Robert Lawson Rose) (– N.Y.) 1780–Dec. 22, 1832; House 1819–21.

Allen, Philip (D R.I.) Sept. 1, 1785–Dec. 16, 1865; Senate July 20, 1853–59; Gov. May 6, 1851–July 20, 1853.

Allen, Robert (– Tenn.) June 19, 1778–Aug. 19, 1844; House 1819–27.

Allen, Robert (brother of John James Allen) (J Va.) July 30, 1794–Dec. 30, 1859; House 1827–33.

Allen, Robert Edward Lee (D W.Va.) Nov. 28, 1865–Jan. 28, 1951; House 1923–25.

Allen, Robert Gray (D Pa.) Aug. 24, 1902–Aug. 9, 1963; House 1937–41.

Allen, Samuel Clesson (father of Elisha Hunt Allen) (F Mass.) Jan. 5, 1772–Feb. 8, 1842; House 1817–29.

Allen, Thomas (D Mo.) Aug. 29, 1813–April 8, 1882; House 1881–April 8, 1882.

Allen, Thomas (D Maine) April 16, 1945– ; House 1997– .

Allen, William (D Ohio) Dec. 18 or Dec. 27, 1803–July 11, 1879; House 1833–35 (Jacksonian); Senate 1837–49; Gov. Jan. 12, 1874–Jan. 10, 1876.

Allen, William (D Ohio) Aug. 13, 1827–July 6, 1881; House 1859–63.

Allen, William Franklin (D Del.) Jan. 19, 1883–June 14, 1946; House 1937–39.

Allen, William Joshua (son of Willis Allen) (D Ill.) June 9, 1829–Jan. 26, 1901; House June 2, 1862–65.

Allen, William Vincent (P Neb.) Jan. 28, 1847–Jan. 2, 1924; Senate 1893–99, Dec. 13, 1899–March 28, 1901.

Allen, Willis (father of William Joshua Allen) (D Ill.) Dec. 15, 1806–April 15, 1859; House 1851–55.

Alley, John Bassett (R Mass.) Jan. 7, 1817–Jan. 19, 1896; House 1859–67.

Allgood, Miles Clayton (D Ala.) Feb. 22, 1878–March 4, 1977; House 1923–35.

Allison, James Jr. (father of John Allison) (– Pa.) Oct. 4, 1772–June 17, 1854; House 1823–25.

Allison, John (son of James Allison Jr.) (W Pa.) Aug. 5, 1812–March 23, 1878; House 1851–53, 1855–57.

Allison, Robert (AMas. Pa.) March 10, 1777–Dec. 2, 1840; House 1831–33.

Allison, William Boyd (R Iowa) March 2, 1829–Aug. 4, 1908; House 1863–71; Senate 1873–Aug. 4, 1908.

Allott, Gordon Llewellyn (R Colo.) Jan. 2, 1907–Jan. 17, 1989; Senate 1955–73.

Almon, Edward Berton (D Ala.) April 18, 1860–June 22, 1933; House 1915–June 22, 1933.

Almond, James Lindsay Jr. (D Va.) June 15, 1898–April 14, 1986; House Jan. 22, 1946–April 17, 1948; Gov. Jan. 11, 1958–Jan. 13, 1962.

Alston, Lemuel James (R S.C.) 1760–1836; House 1807–11.

Alston, William Jeffreys (W Ala.) Dec. 31, 1800–June 10, 1876; House 1849–51.

Alston, Willis (nephew of Nathaniel Macon) (J N.C.) 1769–April 10, 1837; House 1799–1815 (Republican), 1825–31 (1825–29 Republican).

Alvord, James Church (W Mass.) April 14, 1808–Sept. 27, 1839; House 1839–Sept. 27, 1839.

Ambler, Jacob A. (R Ohio) Feb. 18, 1829–Sept. 22, 1906; House 1869–73.

Ambro, Jerome Anthony Jr. (D N.Y.) June 27, 1928–March 4, 1993; House 1975–81.

Amerman, Lemuel (D Pa.) Oct. 29, 1846–Oct. 7, 1897; House 1891–93.

Ames, Adelbert (father of Butler Ames, son-in-law of Benjamin Franklin Butler) (R Miss.) Oct. 31, 1835–April 12, 1933; Senate Feb. 23, 1870–Jan. 10, 1874; Gov. June 15, 1868–March 10, 1870 (Military), Jan. 4, 1874–March 20, 1876.

Ames, Butler (son of Adelbert Ames, grandson of Benjamin Franklin Butler) (R Mass.) Aug. 22, 1871–Nov. 6, 1954; House 1903–13.

Ames, Fisher (F Mass.) April 9, 1758–July 4, 1808; House 1789–97 (1789–95 no party).

Ames, Oakes (R Mass.) Jan. 10, 1804–May 8, 1873; House 1863–73.

Amlie, Thomas Ryum (Prog. Wis.) April 17, 1897–Aug. 22, 1973; House Oct. 13, 1931–33 (Republican), 1935–39.

Ammerman, Joseph Scofield (D Pa.) July 14, 1924–Oct. 14, 1993; House 1977–79.

Ancona, Sydenham Elnathan (D Pa.) Nov. 20, 1824–June 20, 1913; House 1861–67.

Andersen, Herman Carl (R Minn.) Jan. 27, 1897–July 26, 1978; House 1939–63.

Anderson, Albert Raney (IR Iowa) Nov. 8, 1837–Nov. 17, 1898; House 1887–89.

Anderson, Alexander Outlaw (son of Joseph Anderson) (D Tenn.) Nov. 10, 1794–May 23, 1869; Senate Feb. 26, 1840–41.

Anderson, Carl Carey (D Ohio) Dec. 2, 1877–Oct. 1, 1912; House 1909–Oct. 1, 1912.

Anderson, Chapman Levy (D Miss.) March 15, 1845–April 27, 1924; House 1887–91.

Anderson, Charles Arthur (D Mo.) Sept. 26, 1899–April 26, 1977; House 1937–41.

Anderson, Charles Marley (D Ohio) Jan. 5, 1845–Dec. 28, 1908; House 1885–87.

Anderson, Clinton Presba (D N.M.) Oct. 23, 1895–Nov. 11, 1975; House 1941–June 30, 1945; Senate 1949–73; Chrmn. Senate Interior and Insular Affairs 1961–63; Chrmn. Senate Aeronautical and Space Sciences 1963–73; Secy. of Agriculture June 30, 1945–May 10, 1948.

Anderson, George Alburtus (D Ill.) March 11, 1853–Jan. 31, 1896; House 1887–89.

Anderson, George Washington (R Mo.) May 22, 1832–Feb. 26, 1902; House 1865–69.

Anderson, Glenn Malcolm (D Calif.) Feb. 21, 1913–Dec. 13, 1994; House 1969–93; Chrmn. House Public Works and Transportation 1988–91.

Anderson, Hugh Johnston (D Maine) May 10, 1801–May 31, 1881; House 1837–41; Gov. Jan. 5, 1844–May 12, 1847.

Anderson, Isaac (R Pa.) Nov. 23, 1760–Oct. 27, 1838; House 1803–07.

Anderson, James Patton (D Wash.) Feb. 16, 1822–Sept. 20, 1872; House (Terr. Del.) 1855–57.

Anderson, John (J Maine) July 30, 1792–Aug. 21, 1853; House 1825–33 (1825–29 no party).

Anderson, John Alexander (R Kan.) June 26, 1834–May 18, 1892; House 1879–91 (1879–87 Republican, 1887–89 Independent Republican).

Anderson, John Bayard (R Ill.) Feb. 15, 1922– ; House 1961–81.

Anderson, John Zuinglius (R Calif.) March 22, 1904–Feb. 9, 1981; House 1939–53.

Anderson, Joseph (father of Alexander Outlaw Anderson) (– Tenn.) Nov. 5, 1757–April 17, 1837; Senate Sept. 26, 1797–1815; elected Pres. pro tempore Jan. 15, 1805, Feb. 28, 1805, March 2, 1805.

Anderson, Joseph Halstead (D N.Y.) Aug. 25, 1800–June 23, 1870; House 1843–47.

Anderson, Josiah McNair (W Tenn.) Nov. 29, 1807–Nov. 8, 1861; House 1849–51.

Anderson, LeRoy Hagen (D Mont.) Feb. 2, 1906–Sept. 25, 1991; House 1957–61.

Anderson, Lucian (UU Ky.) June 23, 1824–Oct. 18, 1898; House 1863–65.

Anderson, Richard Clough Jr. (R Ky.) Aug. 4, 1788–July 24, 1826; House 1817–21.

Anderson, Samuel (– Pa.) 1773–Jan. 17, 1850; House 1827–29.

Anderson, Simeon H. (father of William Clayton Anderson) (W Ky.) March 2, 1802–Aug. 11, 1840; House 1839–Aug. 11, 1840.

Anderson, Sydney (R Minn.) Sept. 18, 1881–Oct. 8, 1948; House 1911–25.

Anderson, Thomas Lilbourne (ID Mo.) Dec. 8, 1808–March 6, 1885; House 1857–61 (1857–59 American Party).

Anderson, Wendell Richard (D Minn.) Feb. 1, 1933– ; Senate Dec. 30, 1976–Dec. 29, 1978; Gov. Jan. 4, 1971–Dec. 29, 1976.

Anderson, William (R Pa.) 1762–Dec. 16, 1829; House 1809–15, 1817–19.

Anderson, William Black (I Ill.) April 2, 1830–Aug. 28, 1901; House 1875–77.

Anderson, William Clayton (son of Simeon H. Anderson, nephew of Albert Gallatin Talbott) (O Ky.) Dec. 26, 1826–Dec. 23, 1861; House 1859–61.

Anderson, William Coleman (R Tenn.) July 10, 1853–Sept. 8, 1902; House 1895–97.

Anderson, William Robert (D Tenn.) June 17, 1921– ; House 1965–73.

Andresen, August Herman (R Minn.) Oct. 11, 1890–Jan. 14, 1958; House 1925–33, 1935–Jan. 14, 1958.

Andrew, Abram Piatt Jr. (R Mass.) Feb. 12, 1873–June 3, 1936; House Sept. 27, 1921–June 3, 1936.

Andrew, John Forrester (D Mass.) Nov. 26, 1850–May 30, 1895; House 1889–93.

Andrews, Arthur Glenn (R Ala.) Jan. 15, 1909– ; House 1965–67.

Andrews, Charles (D Maine) Feb. 11, 1814–April 30, 1852; House 1851–April 30, 1852.

Andrews, Charles Oscar (D Fla.) March 7, 1877–Sept. 18, 1946; Senate Nov. 4, 1936–Sept. 18, 1946.

Andrews, Elizabeth Bullock (widow of George William Andrews) (D Ala.) Feb. 12, 1911– ; House April 4, 1972–73.

Andrews, George Rex (W N.Y.) Sept. 21, 1808–Dec. 5, 1873; House 1849–51.

Andrews, George William (husband of Elizabeth Bullock Andrews) (D Ala.) Dec. 12, 1906–Dec. 25, 1971; House March 14, 1944–Dec. 25, 1971.

Andrews, Ike Franklin (D N.C.) Sept. 2, 1925– ; House 1973–85.

Andrews, John Tuttle (D N.Y.) May 29, 1803–June 11, 1894; House 1837–39.

Andrews, Landaff Watson (W Ky.) Feb. 12, 1803–Dec. 23, 1887; House 1839–43.

Andrews, Mark (R N.D.) May 19, 1926– ; House Oct. 22, 1963–81; Senate 1981–87.

Andrews, Michael Allen (D Texas) Feb. 7, 1944– ; House 1983–95.

Andrews, Robert E. (D N.J.) Aug. 4, 1957– ; House Nov. 6, 1990– .

Andrews, Thomas H. (D Maine) March 22, 1953– ; House 1991–95.

Andrews, Samuel George (R N.Y.) Oct. 16, 1796–June 11, 1863; House 1857–59.

Andrews, Sherlock James (W Ohio) Nov. 17, 1801–Feb. 11, 1880; House 1841–43.

Andrews, Walter Gresham (R N.Y.) July 16, 1889–March 5, 1949; House 1931–49; Chrmn. House Armed Services 1947–49.

Andrews, William Ezekiel (R Neb.) Dec. 17, 1854–Jan. 19, 1942; House 1895–97, 1919–23.

Andrews, William Henry (R N.M.) Jan. 14, 1846–Jan. 16, 1919; House (Terr. Del.) 1905–Jan. 7, 1912.

Andrews, William Noble (R Md.) Nov. 13, 1876–Dec. 27, 1937; House 1919–21.

Andrus, John Emory (R N.Y.) Feb. 16, 1841–Dec. 26, 1934; House 1905–13.

Anfuso, Victor L'Episcopo (D N.Y.) March 10, 1905–Dec. 28, 1966; House 1951–53, 1955–63.

Angel, William G. (J N.Y.) July 17, 1790–Aug. 13, 1858; House 1825–27 (no party), 1829–33.

Angell, Homer Daniel (R Ore.) Jan. 12, 1875–March 31, 1968; House 1939–55.

Ankeny, Levi (R Wash.) Aug. 1, 1844–March 29, 1921; Senate 1903–09.

Annunzio, Frank (D Ill.) Jan. 12, 1915– ; House 1965–93; Chrmn. House Administration 1985–91.

Ansberry, Timothy Thomas (D Ohio) Dec. 24, 1871–July 5, 1943; House 1907–Jan. 9, 1915.

Ansorge, Martin Charles (R N.Y.) Jan. 1, 1882–Feb. 4, 1967; House 1921–23.

Anthony, Beryl Franklin Jr. (D Ark.) Feb. 21, 1938– ; House 1979–93.

Anthony, Daniel Read Jr. (R Kan.) Aug. 22, 1870–Aug. 4, 1931; House May 23, 1907–29.

Anthony, Henry Bowen (R R.I.) April 1, 1815–Sept. 2, 1884; Senate 1859–Sept. 2, 1884; elected Pres. pro tempore March 23, 1869, April 9, 1869, May 28, 1870, July 1, 1870, July 14, 1870, March 10, 1871, April 17, 1871, May 23, 1871, Dec. 21, 1871, Feb. 23, 1872, June 8, 1872, Dec. 4, 1872, Dec. 13, 1872, Dec. 20, 1872, Jan. 24, 1873, Jan. 23, 1875, Feb. 15, 1875; Gov. May 1, 1849–May 6, 1851 (Whig).

Anthony, Joseph Biles (J Pa.) June 19, 1795–Jan. 10, 1851; House 1833–37.

Antony, Edwin Le Roy (D Texas) Jan. 5, 1852–Jan. 16, 1913; House June 14, 1892–93.

Aplin, Henry Harrison (R Mich.) April 15, 1841–July 23, 1910; House Oct. 20, 1901–03.

Appleby, Stewart Hoffman (son of Theodore Frank Appleby) (R N.J.) May 17, 1890–Jan. 12, 1964; House Nov. 3, 1925–27.

Appleby, Theodore Frank (father of Stewart Hoffman Appleby) (R N.J.) Oct. 10, 1864–Dec. 15, 1924; House 1921–23.

Applegate, Douglas Earl (D Ohio) March 27, 1928– ; House 1977–95.

Appleton, John (D Maine) Feb. 11, 1815–Aug. 22, 1864; House 1851–53.

Appleton, Nathan (cousin of William Appleton) (W Mass.) Oct. 6, 1779–July 14, 1861; House 1831–33 (Anti-Jacksonian), June 9–Sept. 28, 1842.

Appleton, William (cousin of Nathan Appleton) (Const U Mass.) Nov. 16, 1786–Feb. 15, 1862; House 1851–55 (Whig), March 4–Sept. 27, 1861.

Apsley, Lewis Dewart (R Mass.) Sept. 29, 1852–April 11, 1925; House 1893–97.

Archer, John (father of Stevenson Archer, grandfather of Stevenson Archer born in 1827) (R Md.) May 5, 1741–Sept. 28, 1810; House 1801–07.

Archer, Stevenson (son of John Archer, father of Stevenson Archer, below) (R Md.) Oct. 11, 1786–June 26, 1848; House Oct. 26, 1811–17, 1819–21.

Archer, Stevenson (son of Stevenson Archer, above, grandson of John Archer) (D Md.) Feb. 28, 1827–Aug. 2, 1898; House 1867–75.

Archer, William Reynolds Jr. (R Texas) March 22, 1928– ; House 1971– ; Chrmn. House Ways and Means 1995– .

Archer, William Segar (nephew of Joseph Eggleston) (W Va.) March 5, 1789–March 28, 1855; House Jan. 3, 1820–35 (no party); Senate 1841–47.

Arends, Leslie Cornelius (R Ill.) Sept. 27, 1895–July 17, 1985; House 1935–Dec. 31, 1974.

Arens, Henry Martin (FL Minn.) Nov. 21, 1873–Oct. 6, 1963; House 1933–35.

Arentz, Samuel Shaw "Ulysses" (R Nev.) Jan. 8, 1879–June 17, 1934; House 1921–23, 1925–33.

Armey, Richard Keith (R Texas) July 7, 1940– ; House 1985– ; House majority leader 1995– .

Armfield, Robert Franklin (D N.C.) July 9, 1829–Nov. 9, 1898; House 1879–83.

Armstrong, David Hartley (D Mo.) Oct. 21, 1812–March 18, 1893; Senate Sept. 29, 1877–Jan. 26, 1879.

Armstrong, James (brother of John Armstrong Jr.) (– Pa.) Aug. 29, 1748–May 6, 1828; House 1793–95.

Armstrong, John Jr. (brother of James Armstrong) (– N.Y.) Nov. 25, 1758–April 1, 1843; Senate Nov. 6, 1800–Feb. 5, 1802, Nov. 10, 1803–June 30, 1804; Secy. of War Jan. 13, 1813–Sept. 27, 1814.

Armstrong, Moses Kimball (D Dakota) Sept. 19, 1832–Jan. 11, 1906; House (Terr. Del.) 1871–75.

Armstrong, Orland Kay (R Mo.) Oct. 2, 1893–April 15, 1987; House 1951–53.

Armstrong, William (D Va.) Dec. 23, 1782–May 10, 1865; House 1825–33.

Armstrong, William Hepburn (R Pa.) Sept. 7, 1824–May 14, 1919; House 1869–71.

Armstrong, William Lester (R Colo.) March 16, 1937– ; House 1973–79; Senate 1979–91.

Arnell, Samuel Mayes (R Tenn.) May 3, 1833–July 20, 1903; House July 24, 1866–71 (July 24, 1866–67 Unconditional Unionist).

Arnold, Benedict (brother-in-law of Matthias J. Bovee) (– N.Y.) Oct. 5, 1780–March 3, 1849; House 1829–31.

Arnold, Isaac Newton (R Ill.) Nov. 30, 1815–April 24, 1884; House 1861–65.

Arnold, Laurence Fletcher (D Ill.) June 8, 1891–Dec. 6, 1966; House 1937–43.

Arnold, Lemuel Hastings (great-great-uncle of Theodore Francis Green) (W R.I.) Jan. 29, 1792–June 27, 1852; House 1845–47; Gov. May 4, 1831–May 1, 1833 (Democratic Republican).

Arnold, Marshall (D Mo.) Oct. 21, 1845–June 12, 1913; House 1891–95.

Arnold, Samuel (D Conn.) June 1, 1806–May 5, 1869; House 1857–59.

Arnold, Samuel Greene (great-uncle of Theodore Francis Green) (R R.I.) April 12, 1821–Feb. 14, 1880; Senate Dec. 1, 1862–63.

Arnold, Samuel Washington (R Mo.) Sept. 21, 1879–Dec. 18, 1961; House 1943–49.

Arnold, Thomas Dickens (W Tenn.) May 3, 1798–May 26, 1870; House 1831–33 (Anti-Jacksonian), 1841–43.

Arnold, Warren Otis (R R.I.) June 3, 1839–April 1, 1910; House 1887–91, 1895–97.

Arnold, William Carlile (R Pa.) July 15, 1851–March 20, 1906; House 1895–99.

Arnold, William Wright (D Ill.) Oct. 14, 1877–Nov. 23, 1957; House 1923–Sept. 16, 1935.

Arnot, John Jr. (D N.Y.) March 11, 1831–Nov. 20, 1886; House 1883–Nov. 20, 1886.

Arrington, Archibald Hunter (uncle of Archibald Hunter Arrington Williams) (D N.C.) Nov. 13, 1809–July 20, 1872; House 1841–45.

Arthur, William Evans (D Ky.) March 3, 1825–May 18, 1897; House 1871–75.

Ash, Michael Woolston (J Pa.) March 5, 1789–Dec. 14, 1858; House 1835–37.

Ashbrook, Jean Spencer (widow of John Milan Ashbrook, daughter-in-law of William Albert Ashbrook) (R Ohio) Sept. 21, 1934– ; House July 12, 1982–83.

Ashbrook, John Milan (husband of Jean Spencer Ashbrook, son of William Albert Ashbrook) (R Ohio) Sept. 21, 1928–April 24, 1982; House 1961–April 24, 1982.

Ashbrook, William Albert (father of John Milan Ashbrook, father-in-law of Jean Spencer Ashbrook) (D Ohio) July 1, 1867–Jan. 1, 1940; House 1907–21, 1935–Jan. 1, 1940.

Ashcroft, John (R Mo.) May 9, 1942– ; Senate 1995– ; Gov. Jan. 14, 1985–Jan. 11, 1993.

Ashe, John Baptista (uncle of John Baptista Ashe of Tenn., Thomas Samuel Ashe and William Shepperd Ashe) (F N.C.) 1748–Nov. 27, 1802; House March 24, 1790–93; Cont. Cong. 1787.

Ashe, John Baptista (brother of William Shepperd Ashe, nephew of John Baptista Ashe of N.C. and cousin of Thomas Samuel Ashe) (W Tenn.) 1810–Dec. 29, 1857; House 1843–45.

Ashe, Thomas Samuel (nephew of John Baptista Ashe of N.C., cousin of John Baptista Ashe of Tenn. and William Shepperd Ashe) (D N.C.) July 19, 1812–Feb. 4, 1887; House 1873–77.

Ashe, William Shepperd (brother of John Baptista Ashe of Tenn., nephew of John Baptista Ashe of N.C., cousin of Thomas Samuel Ashe) (D N.C.) Sept. 14, 1814–Sept. 14, 1862; House 1849–55.

Ashley, Chester (D Ark.) June 1, 1790–April 29, 1848; Senate Nov. 8, 1844–April 29, 1848.

Ashley, Delos Rodeyn (R Nev.) Feb. 19, 1828–July 18, 1873; House 1865–69.

Ashley, Henry (– N.Y.) Feb. 19, 1778–Jan. 14, 1829; House 1825–27.

Ashley, James Mitchell (great-grandfather of Thomas William Ludlow Ashley) (R Ohio) Nov. 14, 1824–Sept. 16, 1896; House 1859–69; Gov. (Mont. Terr.) 1869–70.

Ashley, Thomas William Ludlow (great-grandson of James Mitchell Ashley) (D Ohio) Jan. 11, 1923– ; House 1955–81.

Ashley, William Henry (J Mo.) 1778–March 26, 1838; House Oct. 31, 1831–37.

Ashmore, John Durant (cousin of Robert Thomas Ashmore) (D S.C.) Aug. 18, 1819–Dec. 5, 1871; House 1859–Dec. 21, 1860.

Ashmore, Robert Thomas (cousin of John Durant Ashmore) (D S.C.) Feb. 22, 1904–Oct. 4, 1989; House June 2, 1953–69.

Ashmun, Eli Porter (father of George Ashmun) (– Mass.) June 24, 1770–May 10, 1819; Senate June 12, 1816–May 10, 1818.

Ashmun, George (son of Eli Porter Ashmun) (W Mass.) Dec. 25, 1804–July 16, 1870; House 1845–51.

Ashurst, Henry Fountai (D Ariz.) Sept. 13, 1874–May 31, 1962; Senate March 27, 1912–41.

Asper, Joel Funk (R Mo.) April 20, 1822–Oct. 1, 1872; House 1869–71.

Aspin, Les (D Wis.) July 21, 1938–May 21, 1995; House 1971–Jan. 20, 1993; Chrmn. House Armed Services 1985–93; Secy. of Defense Jan. 22, 1993–Feb. 2, 1994.

Aspinall, Wayne Norviel (D Colo.) April 3, 1896–Oct. 9, 1983; House 1949–73; Chrmn. House Interior and Insular Affairs 1959–73.

Aswell, James Benjamin (D La.) Dec. 23, 1869–March 16, 1931; House 1913–March 16, 1931.

Atchison, David Rice (W Mo.) Aug. 11, 1807–Jan. 26, 1886; Senate Oct. 14, 1843–55; elected Pres. pro tempore Aug. 8, 1846, Jan. 11, 1847, March 3, 1847, Feb. 2, 1848, June 1, 1848, June 26, 1848, July 29, 1848, Dec. 26, 1848, March 2, 1849, March 5, 1849, March 16, 1849, Dec. 20, 1852, March 4, 1853.

Atherton, Charles Gordon (son of Charles Humphrey Atherton) (D N.H.) July 4, 1804–Nov. 15, 1853; House 1837–43; Senate 1843–49 (also elected for the term beginning 1853 but never qualified).

Atherton, Charles Humphrey (father of Charles Gordon Atherton) (F N.H.) Aug. 14, 1773–Jan. 8, 1853; House 1815–17.

Atherton, Gibson (D Ohio) Jan. 19, 1831–Nov. 10, 1887; House 1879–83.

Atkeson, William Oscar (R Mo.) Aug. 24, 1854–Oct. 16, 1931; House 1921–23.

Atkins, Chester Greenough (D Mass.) April 14, 1948– ; House 1985–93.

Atkins, John DeWitt Clinton (D Tenn.) June 4, 1825–June 2, 1908; House 1857–59, 1873–83.

Atkinson, Archibald (D Va.) Sept. 15, 1792–Jan. 7, 1872; House 1843–49.

Atkinson, Eugene Vincent (D Pa.) April 5, 1927– ; House 1979–83 (Oct. 14, 1981–83 Republican.)

Atkinson, George Wesley (R W.Va.) June 29, 1845–April 4, 1925; House Feb. 26, 1890–91; Gov. March 4, 1897–March 4, 1901.

Atkinson, Louis Evans (R Pa.) April 16, 1841–Feb. 5, 1910; House 1883–93.

Atkinson, Richard Merrill (D Tenn.) Feb. 6, 1894–April 29, 1947; House 1937–39.

Atwater, John Wilbur (IP N.C.) Dec. 27, 1840–July 4, 1910; House 1899–1901.

Atwood, David (R Wis.) Dec. 15, 1815–Dec. 11, 1889; House Feb. 23, 1870–71.

Atwood, Harrison Henry (R Mass.) Aug. 26, 1863–Oct. 22, 1954; House 1895–97.

Auchincloss, James Coats (R N.J.) Jan. 19, 1885–Oct. 2, 1976; House 1943–65.

AuCoin, Les (D Ore.) Oct. 21, 1942– ; House 1975–93.

Auf der Heide, Oscar Louis (D N.J.) Dec. 8, 1874–March 29, 1945; House 1925–35.

Austin, Albert Elmer (stepfather of Clare Boothe Luce) (R Conn.) Nov. 15, 1877–Jan. 26, 1942; House 1939–41.

Austin, Archibald (R Va.) Aug. 11, 1772–Oct. 16, 1837; House 1817–19.

Austin, Richard Wilson (R Tenn.) Aug. 26, 1857–April 20, 1919; House 1909–19.

Austin, Warren Robinson (R Vt.) Nov. 12, 1877–Dec. 25, 1962; Senate April 1, 1931–Aug. 2, 1946.

Averett, Thomas Hamlet (D Va.) July 10, 1800–June 30, 1855; House 1849–53.

Averill, John Thomas (R Minn.) March 1, 1825–Oct. 3, 1889; House 1871–75.

Avery, Daniel (R N.Y.) Sept. 18, 1766–Jan. 30, 1842; House 1811–15, Sept. 30, 1816–17.

Avery, John (R Mich.) Feb. 29, 1824–Jan. 21, 1914; House 1893–97.

Avery, William Henry (R Kan.) Aug. 11, 1911– ; House 1955–65; Gov. Jan. 11, 1965–Jan. 9, 1967.

Avery, William Tecumsah (D Tenn.) Nov. 11, 1819–May 22, 1880; House 1857–61.

Avis, Samuel Brashear (R W.Va.) Feb. 19, 1872–June 8, 1924; House 1913–15.

Axtell, Samuel Beach (D Calif.) Oct. 14, 1819–Aug. 6, 1891; House 1867–71; Gov. (Utah Terr.) 1874–June 1875; Gov. (N.M. Terr.) 1875–78.

Aycrigg, John Bancker (W N.J.) July 9, 1798–Nov. 8, 1856; House 1837–39, 1841–43.

Ayer, Richard Small (R Va.) Oct. 9, 1829–Dec. 14, 1896; House Jan. 31, 1870–71.

Ayers, Roy Elmer (D Mont.) Nov. 9, 1882–May 23, 1955; House 1933–37; Gov. Jan. 4, 1937–Jan. 6, 1941.

Ayres, Steven Beckwith (ID N.Y.) Oct. 27, 1861–June 1, 1929; House 1911–13.

Ayres, William Augustus (D Kan.) April 19, 1867–Feb. 17, 1952; House 1915–21, 1923–Aug. 22, 1934.

Ayres, William Hanes (R Ohio) Feb. 5, 1916– ; House 1951–71.

B

Babbitt, Clinton (D Wis.) Nov. 16, 1831–March 11, 1907; House 1891–93.

Babbitt, Elijah (R Pa.) July 29, 1795–Jan. 9, 1887; House 1859–63.

Babcock, Alfred (W N.Y.) April 15, 1805–May 16, 1871; House 1841–43.

Babcock, Joseph Weeks (grandson of Joseph Weeks) (R Wis.) March 6, 1850–April 27, 1909; House 1893–1907.

Babcock, Leander (D N.Y.) March 1, 1811–Aug. 18, 1864; House 1851–53.

Babcock, William (AMas. N.Y.) 1785–Oct. 20, 1838; House 1831–33.

Babka, John Joseph (D Ohio) March 16, 1884–March 22, 1937; House 1919–21.

Bacchus, James (D Fla.) June 21, 1949– ; House 1991–95.

Bacharach, Isaac (R N.J.) Jan. 5, 1870–Sept. 5, 1956; House 1915–37.

Bachman, Nathan Lynn (D Tenn.) Aug. 2, 1878–April 23, 1937; Senate Feb. 28, 1933–April 23, 1937.

Bachman, Reuben Knecht (D Pa.) Aug. 6, 1834–Sept. 19, 1911; House 1879–81.

Bachmann, Carl George (R W.Va.) May 14, 1890–Jan. 22, 1980; House 1925–33.

Bachus, Spencer (R Ala.) Dec. 28, 1947– ; House 1993– .

Bacon, Augustus Octavius (cousin of William Schley Howard) (D Ga.) Oct. 20, 1839–Feb. 14, 1914; Senate 1895–Feb. 14, 1914; elected Pres. pro tempore Jan. 15, 1912 (to serve Jan. 15–Jan. 17, March 11–March 12, April 8, May 10, May 30–June 3, June 13–July 5, Aug. 1–Aug. 10, Aug. 27–Dec. 15, 1912; Jan. 5–Jan. 18, Feb. 2–Feb. 15, 1913).

Bacon, Ezekiel (son of John Bacon, father of William Johnson Bacon) (R Mass.) Sept. 1, 1776–Oct. 18, 1870; House Sept. 16, 1807–13.

Bacon, Henry (D N.Y.) March 14, 1846–March 25, 1915; House Dec. 6, 1886–89, 1891–93.

Bacon, John (father of Ezekiel Bacon, grandfather of William Johnson Bacon) (R Mass.) April 5, 1738–Oct. 25, 1820; House 1801–03.

Bacon, Mark Reeves (R Mich.) Feb. 29, 1852–Aug. 20, 1941; House March 4–Dec. 13, 1917.

Bacon, Robert Low (R N.Y.) July 23, 1884–Sept. 12, 1938; House 1923–Sept. 12, 1938.

Bacon, William Johnson (son of Ezekiel Bacon, grandson of John Bacon) (R N.Y.) Feb. 18, 1803–July 3, 1889; House 1877–79.

Badger, De Witt Clinton (D Ohio) Aug. 7, 1858–May 20, 1926; House 1903–05.

Badger, George Edmund (W N.C.) April 17, 1795–May 11, 1866; Senate Nov. 25, 1846–55; Secy. of the Navy March 6–Sept. 11, 1841.

Badger, Luther (– N.Y.) April 10, 1785–1869; House 1825–27.

Badham, Robert Edward (R Calif.) June 9, 1929– ; House 1977–89.

Badillo, Herman (D N.Y.) Aug. 21, 1929– ; House 1971–Dec. 31, 1977.

Baer, George Jr. (F Md.) 1763–April 3, 1834; House 1797–1801, 1815–17.

Baer, John Miller (R N.D.) March 29, 1886–Feb. 18, 1970; House July 10, 1917–21.

Baesler, Scotty (D Ky.) July 9, 1941– ; House 1993–99.

Bafalis, Louis Arthur (R Fla.) Sept. 28, 1929–   ; House 1973–83.

Bagby, Arthur Pendleton (D Ala.) 1794–Sept. 21, 1858; Senate Nov. 24, 1841–June 16, 1848; Gov. Nov. 21, 1837–Nov. 22, 1841.

Bagby, John Courts (D Ill.) Jan. 24, 1819–April 4, 1896; House 1875–77.

Bagley, George Augustus (R N.Y.) July 22, 1826–May 12, 1915; House 1875–79.

Bagley, John Holroyd Jr. (D N.Y.) Nov. 26, 1832–Oct. 23, 1902; House 1875–77, 1883–85.

Bailey, Alexander Hamilton (R N.Y.) Aug. 14, 1817–April 20, 1874; House Nov. 30, 1867–71.

Bailey, Cleveland Monroe (D W.Va.) July 15, 1886–July 13, 1965; House 1945–47, 1949–63.

Bailey, David Jackson (D Ga.) March 11, 1812–June 14, 1897; House 1851–55 (1851–53 State Rights Party).

Bailey, Donald Allen (D Pa.) July 21, 1945–   ; House 1979–83.

Bailey, Goldsmith Fox (R Mass.) July 17, 1823–May 8, 1862; House 1861–May 8, 1862.

Bailey, James Edmund (D Tenn.) Aug. 15, 1822–Dec. 29, 1885; Senate Jan. 19, 1877–81.

Bailey, Jeremiah (W Maine) May 1, 1773–July 6, 1853; House 1835–37.

Bailey, John (– Mass.) 1786–June 26, 1835; House Dec. 13, 1824–31.

Bailey, John Mosher (R N.Y.) Aug. 24, 1838–Feb. 21, 1916; House Nov. 5, 1878–81.

Bailey, Joseph (D Pa.) March 18, 1810–Aug. 26, 1885; House 1861–65.

Bailey, Joseph Weldon (father of Joseph Weldon Bailey Jr.) (D Texas) Oct. 6, 1862–April 13, 1929; House 1891–1901; Senate 1901–Jan. 3, 1913.

Bailey, Joseph Weldon Jr. (son of Joseph Weldon Bailey) (D Texas) Dec. 15, 1892–July 17, 1943; House 1933–35.

Bailey, Josiah William (D N.C.) Sept. 14, 1873–Dec. 15, 1946; Senate 1931–Dec. 15, 1946.

Bailey, Ralph Emerson (R Mo.) July 14, 1878–April 8, 1948; House 1925–27.

Bailey, Theodorus (– N.Y.) Oct. 12, 1758–Sept. 6, 1828; House 1793–97, 1799–1801, Oct. 6, 1801–03; Senate 1803–Jan. 16, 1804.

Bailey, Warren Worth (D Pa.) Jan. 8, 1855–Nov. 9, 1928; House 1913–17.

Bailey, Wendell (R Mo.) July 30, 1940–   ; House 1981–83.

Bailey, Willis Joshua (R Kan.) Oct. 12, 1854–May 19, 1932; House 1899–1901; Gov. Jan. 12, 1903–Jan. 9, 1905.

Baird, Brian (D Wash.) March 7, 1956–   ; House 1999–   .

Baird, David (father of David Baird Jr.) (R N.J.) April 7, 1839–Feb. 25, 1927; Senate Feb. 23, 1918–19.

Baird, David Jr. (son of David Baird) (R N.J.) Oct. 10, 1881–Feb. 28, 1955; Senate Nov. 30, 1929–Dec. 2, 1930.

Baird, Joseph Edward (R Ohio) Nov. 12, 1865–June 14, 1942; House 1929–31.

Baird, Samuel Thomas (D La.) May 5, 1861–April 22, 1899; House 1897–April 22, 1899.

Baker, Bill (R Calif.) June 14, 1940–   ; House 1993–97.

Baker, Caleb (– N.Y.) 1762–June 26, 1849; House 1819–21.

Baker, Charles Simeon (R N.Y.) Feb. 18, 1839–April 21, 1902; House 1885–91.

Baker, David Jewett (D Ill.) Sept. 7, 1792–Aug. 6, 1869; Senate Nov. 12–Dec. 11, 1830.

Baker, Edward Dickinson (R Ore.) Feb. 24, 1811–Oct. 21, 1861; House 1845–Jan. 15, 1847 (Whig Ill.), 1849–51 (Whig Ill.); Senate Oct. 2, 1860–Oct. 21, 1861.

Baker, Ezra (R N.J.) ?–?; House 1815–17.

Baker, Henry Moore (R N.H.) Jan. 11, 1841–May 30, 1912; House 1893–97.

Baker, Howard Henry (husband of Irene Bailey Baker, father of Howard Henry Baker Jr.) (R Tenn.) Jan. 12, 1902–Jan. 7, 1964; House 1951–Jan. 7, 1964.

Baker, Howard Henry Jr. (son of Howard Henry Baker, stepson of Irene Bailey Baker, son-in-law of Everett McKinley Dirksen) (R Tenn.) Nov. 15, 1925–   ; Senate 1967–85; Senate minority leader 1977–81; Senate majority leader 1981–85.

Baker, Irene Bailey (widow of Howard Henry Baker, stepmother of Howard Henry Baker Jr.) (R Tenn.) Nov. 17, 1901–April 2, 1994; House March 10, 1964–65.

Baker, Jacob Thompson (D N.J.) April 13, 1847–Dec. 7, 1919; House 1913–15.

Baker, Jehu (D Ill.) Nov. 4, 1822–March 1, 1903; House 1865–69 (Republican), 1887–89 (Republican), 1897–99.

Baker, John (F Va.) ?–Aug. 18, 1823; House 1811–13.

Baker, John Harris (brother of Lucien Baker) (R Ind.) Feb. 28, 1832–Oct. 21, 1915; House 1875–81.

Baker, LaMar (R Tenn.) Dec. 29, 1915–   ; House 1971–75.

Baker, Lucien (brother of John Harris Baker) (R Kan.) June 8, 1846–June 21, 1907; Senate 1895–1901.

Baker, Osmyn (W Mass.) May 18, 1800–Feb. 9, 1875; House Jan. 14, 1840–45.

Baker, Richard Hugh (R La.) May 22, 1948–   ; House 1987–   .

Baker, Robert (D N.Y.) April 1862–June 15, 1943; House 1903–05.

Baker, Stephen (R N.Y.) Aug. 12, 1819–June 9, 1875; House 1861–63.

Baker, William (P Kan.) April 29, 1831–Feb. 11, 1910; House 1891–97.

Baker, William Benjamin (R Md.) July 22, 1840–May 17, 1911; House 1895–1901.

Baker, William Henry (R N.Y.) Jan. 17, 1827–Nov. 25, 1911; House 1875–79.

Bakewell, Charles Montague (R Conn.) April 24, 1867–Sept. 19, 1957; House 1933–35.

Bakewell, Claude Ignatius (R Mo.) Aug. 9, 1912–March 18, 1987; House 1947–49, March 9, 1951–53.

Baldacci, John (D Maine) Jan. 30, 1955–   ; House 1995–   .

Baldrige, Howard Malcolm (R Neb.) June 23, 1894–Jan. 19, 1985; House 1931–33.

Baldus, Alvin James (D Wis.) April 27, 1926–   ; House 1975–81.

Baldwin, Abraham (F Ga.) Nov. 22, 1754–April 4, 1807; House 1789–99; Senate 1799–April 4, 1807; elected Pres. pro tempore Dec. 7, 1801, April 17, 1802; Cont. Cong. 1785, 1787–88.

Baldwin, Augustus Carpenter (UD Mich.) Dec. 24, 1817–Jan. 21, 1903; House 1863–65.

Baldwin, Harry Streett (D Md.) Aug. 21, 1894–Oct. 19, 1952; House 1943–47.

Baldwin, Henry (– Pa.) Jan. 14, 1780–April 21, 1844; House 1817–May 8, 1822; Assoc. Justice Supreme Court Jan. 18, 1830–April 21, 1844.

Baldwin, Henry Alexander (R Hawaii) Jan. 12, 1871–Oct. 8, 1946; House (Terr. Del.) March 25, 1922–23.

Baldwin, Henry Porter (R Mich.) Feb. 22, 1814–Dec. 31, 1892; Senate Nov. 17, 1879–81; Gov. Jan. 6, 1869–Jan. 1, 1873.

Baldwin, John (– Conn.) April 5, 1772–March 27, 1850; House 1825–29.

Baldwin, John Denison (R Mass.) Sept. 28, 1809–July 8, 1883; House 1863–69.

Baldwin, John Finley Jr. (R Calif.) June 28, 1915–March 9, 1966; House 1955–March 9, 1966.

Baldwin, Joseph Clark (R N.Y.) Jan. 11, 1897–Oct. 27, 1957; House March 11, 1941–47.

Baldwin, Melvin Riley (D Minn.) April 12, 1838–April 15, 1901; House 1893–95.

Baldwin, Raymond Earl (R Conn.) Aug. 31, 1893–Oct. 4, 1986; Senate Dec. 27, 1946–Dec. 16, 1949; Gov. Jan. 4, 1939–Jan. 8, 1941, Jan. 6, 1943–Dec. 27, 1946.

Baldwin, Roger Sherman (son of Simeon Baldwin) (W Conn.) Jan. 4, 1793–Feb. 19, 1863; Senate Nov. 11, 1847–51; Gov. May 1844–May 6, 1846.

Baldwin, Simeon (father of Roger Sherman Baldwin) (F Conn.) Dec. 14, 1761–May 26, 1851; House 1803–05.

Baldwin, Tammy (D Wis.) Feb. 11, 1962–   ; House 1999–   .

Ball, Edward (W Ohio) Nov. 6, 1811–Nov. 22, 1872; House 1853–57.

Ball, Joseph Hurst (R Minn.) Nov. 3, 1905–Dec. 18, 1993; Senate Oct. 14, 1940–Nov. 17, 1942, 1943–49.

Ball, Lewis Heisler (R Del.) Sept. 21, 1861–Oct. 18, 1932; House 1901–03; Senate March 3, 1903–05, 1919–25.

Ball, Thomas Henry (D Texas) Jan. 14, 1859–May 7, 1944; House 1897–Nov. 16, 1903.

Ball, Thomas Raymond (R Conn.) Feb. 12, 1896–June 16, 1943; House 1939–41.

Ball, William Lee (R Va.) Jan. 2, 1781–Feb. 28, 1824; House 1817–Feb. 28, 1824.

Ballenger, Cass (great-great-grandson of Lewis Cass) (R N.C.) Dec. 6, 1926–   ; House 1987–   .

Ballentine, John Goff (D Tenn.) May 20, 1825–Nov. 23, 1915; House 1883–87.

Ballou, Latimer Whipple (R R.I.) March 1, 1812–May 9, 1900; House 1875–81.

Baltz, William Nicolas (D Ill.) Feb. 5, 1860–Aug. 22, 1943; House 1913–15.

Bandstra, Bert Andrew (D Iowa) Jan. 25, 1922–Oct. 23, 1995; House 1965–67.

Bankhead, John Hollis (father of John Hollis Bankhead II and William Brockman Bankhead, grandfather of Walter Will Bankhead) (D Ala.) Sept. 13, 1842–March 1, 1920; House 1887–1907; Senate June 18, 1907–March 1, 1920.

Bankhead, John Hollis II (son of John Hollis Bankhead, brother of William Brockman Bankhead, father of Walter Will Bankhead) (D Ala.) July 8, 1872–June 12, 1946; Senate 1931–June 12, 1946.

Bankhead, Walter Will (son of John Hollis Bankhead II, grandson of John Hollis Bankhead, nephew of William Brockman Bankhead) (D Ala.) July 21, 1897–   ; House Jan. 3–Feb. 1, 1941.

Bankhead, William Brockman (son of John Hollis Bankhead, brother of John Hollis Bankhead II, uncle of Walter Will Bankhead) (D Ala.) April 12, 1874–Sept. 15, 1940; House 1917–Sept. 15, 1940; House majority leader 1935–June 4, 1936; Speaker June 4, 1936–37, Jan. 5, 1937–Sept. 15, 1940.

Banks, John (AMas. Pa.) Oct. 17, 1793–April 3, 1864; House 1831–36.

Banks, Linn (D Va.) Jan. 23, 1784–Jan. 13, 1842; House April 28, 1838–Dec. 6, 1841.

Banks, Nathaniel Prentice (R Mass.) Jan. 30, 1816–Sept. 1, 1894; House 1853–Dec. 24, 1857, Dec. 4, 1865–73, 1875–79, 1889–91 (1853–55 Democrat, 1855–57 American Party, March 4–Dec. 24, 1857 Republican, Dec. 4, 1865–67 Union Republican, 1867–73 Republican, 1875–77 Independent); Speaker Feb. 2, 1856–57; Gov. Jan. 6, 1858–Jan. 2, 1861.

Banning, Henry Blackstone (D Ohio) Nov. 10, 1836–Dec. 10, 1881; House 1873–79 (1873–75 Liberal Republican).

Bannon, Henry Towne (R Ohio) June 5, 1867–Sept. 6, 1950; House 1905–09.

Banta, Parke Monroe (R Mo.) Nov. 21, 1891–May 12, 1970; House 1947–49.

Barber, Hiram Jr. (R Ill.) March 24, 1835–Aug. 5, 1924; House 1879–81.

Barber, Isaac Ambrose (R Md.) Jan. 26, 1852–March 1, 1909; House 1897–99.

Barber, Joel Allen (R Wis.) Jan. 17, 1809–June 17, 1881; House 1871–75.

Barber, Laird Howard (D Pa.) Oct. 25, 1848–Feb. 16, 1928; House 1899–1901.

Barber, Levi (R Ohio) Oct. 16, 1777–April 23, 1833; House 1817–19, 1821–23.

Barber, Noyes (uncle of Edwin Barbour Morgan and Christopher Morgan) (– Conn.) April 28, 1781–Jan. 3, 1844; House 1821–35.

Barbour, Henry Ellsworth (R Calif.) March 8, 1877–March 21, 1945; House 1919–33.

Barbour, James (brother of Philip Pendleton Barbour, cousin of John Strode Barbour) (AD/SR Va.) June 10, 1775–June 7, 1842; Senate Jan. 2, 1815–March 7, 1825; elected Pres. pro tempore Feb. 15, 1819; Gov. Jan. 3, 1812–Dec. 1, 1814; Secy. of War March 7, 1825–May 23, 1828.

Barbour, John Strode (father of John Strode Barbour Jr., cousin of James Barbour and Philip Pendleton Barbour) (J Va.) Aug. 8, 1790–Jan. 12, 1855; House 1823–33 (1823–27 no party).

Barbour, John Strode Jr. (son of John Strode Barbour) (D Va.) Dec. 29, 1820–May 14, 1892; House 1881–87; Senate 1889–May 14, 1892.

Barbour, Lucien (R Ind.) March 4, 1811–July 19, 1880; House 1855–57.

Barbour, Philip Pendleton (brother of James Barbour, cousin of John Strode Barbour) (J Va.) May 25, 1783–Feb. 25, 1841; House Sept. 19, 1814–25 (Republican), 1827–Oct. 15, 1830 (1827–29 Republican); Speaker Dec. 4, 1821–23; Assoc. Justice Supreme Court May 12, 1836–Feb. 25, 1841.

Barbour, William Warren (R N.J.) July 31, 1888–Nov. 22, 1943; Senate Dec. 1, 1931–37, Nov. 9, 1938–Nov. 22, 1943.

Barca, Peter W. (D Wis.) Aug. 7, 1955–   ; House June 8, 1993–95.

Barchfeld, Andrew Jackson (R Pa.) May 18, 1863–Jan. 28, 1922; House 1905–17.

Barcia, James A. (D Mich.) Feb. 25, 1952–   ; House 1993–   .

Barclay, Charles Frederick (R Pa.) May 9, 1844–March 9, 1914; House 1907–11.

Barclay, David (D Pa.) 1823–Sept. 10, 1889; House 1855–57.

Bard, David (R Pa.) 1744–March 12, 1815; House 1795–99, 1803–March 12, 1815.

Bard, Thomas Robert (R Calif.) Dec. 8, 1841–March 5, 1915; Senate Feb. 7, 1900–05.

Barden, Graham Arthur (D N.C.) Sept. 25, 1896–Jan. 29, 1967; House 1935–61; Chrmn. House Education and Labor 1950–53, 1955–61.

Barham, John All (R Calif.) July 17, 1843–Jan. 22, 1926; House 1895–1901.

Baring, Walter Stephan Jr. (D Nev.) Sept. 9, 1911–July 13, 1975; House 1949–53, 1957–73.

Barker, Abraham Andrews (UR Pa.) March 30, 1816–March 18, 1898; House 1865–67.

Barker, David Jr. (– N.H.) Jan. 8, 1797–April 1, 1834; House 1827–29.

Barker, Joseph (R Mass.) Oct. 19, 1751–July 5, 1815; House 1805–09.

Barkley, Alben William (D Ky.) Nov. 24, 1877–April 30, 1956; House 1913–27; Senate 1927–Jan. 19, 1949, 1955–April 30, 1956; Senate majority leader July 22, 1937–47; Senate minority leader 1947–49; Vice President 1949–53.

Barksdale, Ethelbert (brother of William Barksdale) (D Miss.) Jan. 4, 1824–Feb. 17, 1893; House 1883–87.

Barksdale, William (brother of Ethelbert Barksdale) (D Miss.) Aug. 21, 1821–July 2, 1863; House 1853–Jan. 12, 1861.

Barlow, Bradley (G Vt.) May 12, 1814–Nov. 6, 1889; House 1879–81.

Barlow, Charles Averill (P Calif.) March 17, 1858–Oct. 3, 1927; House 1897–99.

Barlow, Stephen (– Pa.) June 13, 1779–Aug. 24, 1845; House 1827–29.

Barlow, Tom (D Ky.) Aug. 7, 1940–   ; House 1993–95.

Barnard, Daniel Dewey (W N.Y.) July 16, 1797–April 24, 1861; House 1827–29 (no party), 1839–45.

Barnard, Druie Douglas Jr. (D Ga.) March 20, 1922–   ; House 1977–93.

Barnard, Isaac Dutton (J Pa.) July 18, 1791–Feb. 28, 1834; Senate 1827–Dec. 6, 1831.

Barnard, William Oscar (R Ind.) Oct. 25, 1852–April 8, 1939; House 1909–11.

Barnes, Demas (D N.Y.) April 4, 1827–May 1, 1888; House 1867–69.

Barnes, George Thomas (D Ga.) Aug. 14, 1833–Oct. 24, 1901; House 1885–91.

Barnes, James Martin (D Ill.) Jan. 9, 1899–June 8, 1958; House 1939–43.

Barnes, Lyman Eddy (D Wis.) June 30, 1855–Jan. 16, 1904; House 1893–95.

Barnes, Michael Darr (D Md.) Sept. 3, 1943– ; House 1979–87.

Barnett, William (R Ga.) March 4, 1761–April 1832; House Oct. 5, 1812–15.

Barney, John (F Md.) Jan. 18, 1785–Jan. 26, 1857; House 1825–29.

Barney, Samuel Stebbins (R Wis.) Jan. 31, 1846–Dec. 31, 1919; House 1895–1903.

Barnhart, Henry A. (D Ind.) Sept. 11, 1858–March 26, 1934; House Nov. 3, 1908–19.

Barnitz, Charles Augustus (AMas. Pa.) Sept. 11, 1780–Jan. 8, 1850; House 1833–35.

Barnum, William Henry (D Conn.) Sept. 17, 1818–April 30, 1889; House 1867–May 18, 1876; Senate May 18, 1876–79; Chrmn. Dem. Nat. Comm. 1877–89.

Barnwell, Robert (father of Robert Woodward Barnwell) (F S.C.) Dec. 21, 1761–Oct. 24, 1814; House 1791–93; Cont. Cong. 1789.

Barnwell, Robert Woodward (son of Robert Barnwell) (– S.C.) Aug. 10, 1801–Nov. 5, 1882; House 1829–33; Senate June 4–Dec. 8, 1850.

Barr, Bob (R Ga.) Nov. 5, 1948– ; House 1995– .

Barr, Joseph Walker (D Ind.) Jan. 17, 1918–Feb. 23, 1996; House 1959–61; Secy. of the Treasury Dec. 21, 1968–Jan. 20, 1969.

Barr, Samuel Fleming (R Pa.) June 15, 1829–May 29, 1919; House 1881–85.

Barr, Thomas Jefferson (ID N.Y.) 1812–March 27, 1881; House Jan. 17, 1859–61.

Barrere, Granville (nephew of Nelson Barrere) (R Ill.) July 11, 1829–Jan. 13, 1889; House 1873–75.

Barrere, Nelson (uncle of Granville Barrere) (W Ohio) April 1, 1808–Aug. 20, 1883; House 1851–53.

Barret, John Richard (D Mo.) Aug. 21, 1825–Nov. 2, 1903; House 1859–June 8, 1860, Dec. 3, 1860–61.

Barrett, Frank Aloysius (R Wyo.) Nov. 10, 1892–May 30, 1962; House 1943–Dec. 31, 1950; Senate 1953–59; Gov. Jan. 1, 1951–Jan. 3, 1953.

Barrett, Thomas M. (D Wis.) Dec. 8, 1953– ; House 1993– .

Barrett, William (R Neb.) Feb. 9, 1929– ; House 1991– .

Barrett, William Aloysius (D Pa.) Aug. 14, 1896–April 12, 1976; House 1945–47, 1949–April 12, 1976.

Barrett, William Emerson (R Mass.) Dec. 29, 1858–Feb. 12, 1906; House 1895–99.

Barringer, Daniel Laurens (uncle of Daniel Moreau Barringer) (– N.C.) Oct. 1, 1788–Oct. 16, 1852; House Dec. 4, 1826–35.

Barringer, Daniel Moreau (nephew of Daniel Laurens Barringer) (W N.C.) July 30, 1806–Sept. 1, 1873; House 1843–49.

Barrow, Alexander (W La.) March 27, 1801–Dec. 29, 1846; Senate 1841–Dec. 29, 1846.

Barrow, Middleton Pope (grandson of Wilson Lumpkin) (D Ga.) Aug. 1, 1839–Dec. 23, 1903; Senate Nov. 15, 1882–83.

Barrow, Washington (W Tenn.) Oct. 5, 1807–Oct. 19, 1866; House 1847–49.

Barrows, Samuel June (R Mass.) May 26, 1845–April 21, 1909; House 1897–99.

Barry, Alexander Grant (R Ore.) Aug. 23, 1892–Dec. 28, 1952; Senate Nov. 9, 1938–39.

Barry, Frederick George (D Miss.) Jan. 12, 1845–May 7, 1909; House 1885–89.

Barry, Henry W. (R Miss.) April 1840–June 7, 1875; House Feb. 23, 1870–75.

Barry, Robert Raymond (R N.Y.) May 15, 1915–June 14, 1988; House 1959–65.

Barry, William Bernard (D N.Y.) July 21, 1902–Oct. 20, 1946; House Nov. 5, 1935–Oct. 20, 1946.

Barry, William Taylor (R Ky.) Feb. 5, 1784–Aug. 30, 1835; House Aug. 8, 1810–11; Senate Dec. 16, 1814–May 1, 1816; Postmaster Gen. April 6, 1829–April 30, 1835.

Barry, William Taylor Sullivan (D Miss.) Dec. 10, 1821–Jan. 29, 1868; House 1853–55.

Barstow, Gamaliel Henry (AMas. N.Y.) July 20, 1784–March 30, 1865; House 1831–33.

Barstow, Gideon (– Mass.) Sept. 7, 1783–March 26, 1852; House 1821–23.

Bartholdt, Richard (R Mo.) Nov. 2, 1855–March 19, 1932; House 1893–1915.

Bartine, Horace Franklin (R Nev.) March 21, 1848–Aug. 27, 1918; House 1889–93.

Bartlett, Bailey (F Mass.) Jan. 29, 1750–Sept. 9, 1830; House Nov. 27, 1797–1801.

Bartlett, Charles Lafayette (D Ga.) Jan. 31, 1853–April 21, 1938; House 1895–1915.

Bartlett, Dewey Follett (R Okla.) March 28, 1919–March 1, 1979; Senate 1973–79; Gov. Jan. 9, 1967–Jan. 11, 1971.

Bartlett, Edward Lewis "Bob" (D Alaska) April 20, 1904–Dec. 11, 1968; House (Terr. Del.) 1945–59; Senate 1959–Dec. 11, 1968.

Bartlett, Franklin (D N.Y.) Sept. 10, 1847–April 23, 1909; House 1893–97.

Bartlett, George Arthur (D Nev.) Nov. 30, 1869–June 1, 1951; House 1907–11.

Bartlett, Harry Stephen "Steve" (R Texas) Sept. 19, 1947– ; House 1983–March 11, 1991.

Bartlett, Ichabod (– N.H.) July 24, 1786–Oct. 19, 1853; House 1823–29.

Bartlett, Josiah Jr. (son of Gov. Josiah Bartlett of N.H.) (R N.H.) Aug. 29, 1768–April 16, 1838; House 1811–13.

Bartlett, Roscoe G. (R Md.) June 3, 1926– ; House 1993– .

Bartlett, Thomas Jr. (D Vt.) June 18, 1808–Sept. 12, 1876; House 1851–53.

Bartley, Mordecai (– Ohio) Dec. 16, 1783–Oct. 10, 1870; House 1823–31; Gov. Dec. 3, 1844–Dec. 12, 1846 (Whig).

Barton, Bruce (R N.Y.) Aug. 5, 1886–July 5, 1967; House Nov. 2, 1937–41.

Barton, David (– Mo.) Dec. 14, 1783–Sept. 28, 1837; Senate Aug. 10, 1821–31.

Barton, Joe Linus (R Texas) Sept. 15, 1949– ; House 1985– .

Barton, Richard Walker (W Va.) 1800–March 15, 1859; House 1841–43.

Barton, Samuel (J N.Y.) July 27, 1785–Jan. 29, 1858; House 1835–37.

Barton, Silas Reynolds (R Neb.) May 21, 1872–Nov. 7, 1916; House 1913–15.

Barton, William Edward (cousin of Courtney Walker Hamlin) (D Mo.) April 11, 1868–July 29, 1955; House 1931–33.

Barwig, Charles (D Wis.) March 19, 1837–Feb. 15, 1912; House 1889–95.

Bashford, Coles (I Ariz.) Jan. 24, 1816–April 25, 1878; House (Terr. Del.) 1867–69; Gov. March 25, 1856–Jan. 4, 1858 (Republican Wis.).

Bass, Lyman Kidder (R N.Y.) Nov. 13, 1836–May 11, 1889; House 1873–77.

Bass, Perkins (R N.H.) Oct. 6, 1912– ; House 1955–63.

Bass, Ross (D Tenn.) March 17, 1918–Jan. 1, 1993; House 1955–Nov. 3, 1964; Senate Nov. 4, 1964–Jan. 2, 1967.

Bassett, Burwell (R Va.) March 18, 1764–Feb. 26, 1841; House 1805–13, 1815–19, 1821–29.

Bassett, Edward Murray (D N.Y.) Feb. 7, 1863–Oct. 27, 1948; House 1903–05.

Bassett, Richard (grandfather of Richard Henry Bayard and James Asheton Bayard Jr., father-in-law of Joshua Clayton) (– Del.) April 2, 1745–Aug. 15, 1815; Senate 1789–93; Gov. Jan. 9, 1799–March 3, 1801 (Federalist).

Bate, William Brimage (D Tenn.) Oct. 7, 1826–March 9, 1905; Senate 1887–March 9, 1905; Gov. Jan. 15, 1883–Jan. 17, 1887.

Bateman, Ephraim (– N.J.) July 9, 1780–Jan. 28, 1829; House 1815–23; Senate Nov. 10, 1826–Jan. 12, 1829.

Bateman, Herbert Harvell (R Va.) Aug. 7, 1928– ; House 1983– .

Bates, Arthur Laban (nephew of John Milton Thayer) (R Pa.) June 6, 1859–Aug. 26, 1934; House 1901–13.

Bates, Edward (brother of James Woodson Bates) (– Mo.) Sept. 4, 1793–March 25, 1869; House 1827–29; Atty. Gen. March 5, 1861–Sept. 1864.

Bates, George Joseph (father of William Henry Bates) (R Mass.) Feb. 25, 1891–Nov. 1, 1949; House 1937–Nov. 1, 1949.

Bates, Isaac Chapman (W Mass.) Jan. 23, 1779–March 16, 1845; House 1827–35 (no party); Senate Jan. 13, 1841–March 16, 1845.

Bates, James (J Maine) Sept. 24, 1789–Feb. 25, 1882; House 1831–33.

Bates, James Woodson (brother of Edward Bates) (– Ark.) Aug. 25, 1788–Dec. 26, 1846; House (Terr. Del.) Dec. 21, 1819–23.

Bates, Jim (D Calif.) July 21, 1941– ; House 1983–91.

Bates, Joseph Bengal (D Ky.) Oct. 29, 1893–Sept. 10, 1965; House June 4, 1938–53.

Bates, Martin Waltham (D Del.) Feb. 24, 1786–Jan. 1, 1869; Senate Jan. 14, 1857–59.

Bates, William Henry (son of George Joseph Bates) (R Mass.) April 26, 1917–June 22, 1969; House Feb. 14, 1950–June 22, 1969.

Bathrick, Elsworth Raymond (D Ohio) Jan. 6, 1863–Dec. 23, 1917; House 1911–15, March 4–Dec. 23, 1917.

Battin, James Franklin (R Mont.) Feb. 13, 1925–Sept. 27, 1996; House 1961–Feb. 27, 1969.

Battle, Laurie Calvin (D Ala.) May 10, 1912– ; House 1947–55.

Baucus, Max Sieben (D Mont.) Dec. 11, 1941– ; House 1975–Dec. 14, 1978; Senate Dec. 15, 1978– ; Chrmn. Senate Environment and Public Works 1993–95.

Bauman, Robert Edmund (R Md.) April 4, 1937– ; House Aug. 21, 1973–81.

Baumhart, Albert David Jr. (R Ohio) June 15, 1908– ; House 1941–Sept. 2, 1942, 1955–61.

Baxter, Portus (R Vt.) Dec. 4, 1806–March 4, 1868; House 1861–67.

Bay, William Van Ness (D Mo.) Nov. 23, 1818–Feb. 10, 1894; House 1849–51.

Bayard, James Asheton Sr. (father of Richard Henry Bayard and James Asheton Bayard Jr., grandfather of Thomas Francis Bayard Sr., great-grandfather of Thomas Francis Bayard Jr.) (F Del.) July 28, 1767–Aug. 6, 1815; House 1797–1803; Senate Nov. 13, 1804–13.

Bayard, James Asheton Jr. (son of James Asheton Bayard Sr., brother of Richard Henry Bayard, grandson of Richard Bassett, father of Thomas Francis Bayard Sr., grandfather of Thomas Francis Bayard Jr.) (D Del.) Nov. 15, 1799–June 13, 1880; Senate 1851–Jan. 29, 1864, April 5, 1867–69.

Bayard, Richard Henry (son of James Asheton Bayard Sr., brother of Joseph Asheton Bayard Jr., grandson of Richard Bassett) (W Del.) Sept. 26, 1796–March 4, 1868; Senate June 17, 1836–Sept. 19, 1839, Jan. 12, 1841–45.

Bayard, Thomas Francis Sr. (son of James Asheton Bayard Jr., father of Thomas Francis Bayard Jr.) (D Del.) Oct. 29, 1828–Sept. 28, 1898; Senate 1869–March 6, 1885; elected Pres. pro tempore Oct. 10, 1881; Secy. of State March 7, 1885–March 6, 1889.

Bayard, Thomas Francis Jr. (son of Thomas Francis Bayard Sr., grandson of James Ashton Bayard Jr.) (D Del.) June 4, 1868–July 12, 1942; Senate Nov. 8, 1922–29.

Bayh, Birch Evan (father of Evan Bayh) (D Ind.) Jan. 22, 1928– ; Senate 1963–81; Chrmn. Senate Select Committee on Intelligence Activities 1978–81.

Bayh, Evan (son of Birch Evan Bayh) (D Ind.) Dec. 26, 1955– ; Senate 1999– ; Gov. Jan. 9, 1989–Jan. 13, 1997.

Baylies, Francis (brother of William Baylies) (– Mass.) Oct. 16, 1783–Oct. 28, 1852; House 1821–27.

Baylies, William (brother of Francis Baylies) (J Mass.) Sept. 15, 1776–Sept. 27, 1865; House March 4–June 28, 1809, 1813–17 (1809–17 Federalist), 1833–35 (Anti-Jacksonian).

Baylor, Robert Emmett Bledsoe (nephew of Jesse Bledsoe) (J Ala.) May 10, 1793–Jan. 6, 1874; House 1829–31.

Bayly, Thomas (F Md.) Sept. 13, 1775–1829; House 1817–23.

Bayly, Thomas Henry (son of Thomas Monteagle Bayly) (D Va.) Dec. 11, 1810–June 23, 1856; House May 6, 1844–June 23, 1856.

Bayly, Thomas Monteagle (father of Thomas Henry Bayly) (F Va.) March 26, 1775–Jan. 7, 1834; House 1813–15.

Bayne, Thomas McKee (R Pa.) June 14, 1836–June 16, 1894; House 1877–91.

Beach, Clifton Bailey (R Ohio) Sept. 16, 1845–Nov. 15, 1902; House 1895–99.

Beach, Lewis (D N.Y.) March 30, 1835–Aug. 10, 1886; House 1881–Aug. 10, 1886.

Beakes, Samuel Willard (D Mich.) Jan. 11, 1861–Feb. 9, 1927; House 1913–March 3, 1917, Dec. 13, 1917–19.

Beale, Charles Lewis (R N.Y.) March 5, 1824–Jan. 29, 1900; House 1859–61.

Beale, James Madison Hite (D Va.) Feb. 7, 1786–Aug. 2, 1866; House 1833–37 (Jacksonian), 1849–53.

Beale, Joseph Grant (R Pa.) March 26, 1839–May 21, 1915; House 1907–09.

Beale, Richard Lee Turberville (D Va.) May 22, 1819–April 21, 1893; House 1847–49, Jan. 23, 1879–81.

Beales, Cyrus William (R Pa.) Dec. 16, 1877–Nov. 14, 1927; House 1915–17.

Beall, James Andrew "Jack" (D Texas) Oct. 25, 1866–Feb. 12, 1929; House 1903–15.

Beall, James Glenn (father of John Glenn Beall Jr.) (R Md.) June 5, 1894–Jan. 14, 1971; House 1943–53; Senate 1953–65.

Beall, John Glenn Jr. (son of James Glenn Beall) (R Md.) June 19, 1927– ; House 1969–71; Senate 1971–77.

Beall, Reasin (R Ohio) Dec. 3, 1769–Feb. 20, 1843; House April 20, 1813–June 7, 1814.

Beam, Harry Peter (D Ill.) Nov. 23, 1892–Dec. 31, 1967; House 1931–Dec. 6, 1942.

Beaman, Fernando Cortez (R Mich.) June 28, 1814–Sept. 27, 1882; House 1861–71.

Beamer, John Valentine (R Ind.) Nov. 17, 1896–Sept. 8, 1964; House 1951–59.

Bean, Benning Moulton (J N.H.) Jan. 9, 1782–Feb. 6, 1866; House 1833–37.

Bean, Curtis Coe (R Ariz.) Jan. 4, 1828–Feb. 1, 1904; House (Terr. Del.) 1885–87.

Beard, Edward Peter (D R.I.) Jan. 20, 1940– ; House 1975–81.

Beard, Robin Leo Jr. (R Tenn.) Aug. 21, 1939– ; House 1973–83.

Beardsley, Samuel (D N.Y.) Feb. 6, 1790–May 6, 1860; House 1831–March 29, 1836 (Jacksonian), 1843–Feb. 29, 1844.

Beatty, John (– N.J.) Dec. 10, 1749–May 30, 1826; House 1793–95; Cont. Cong. 1784–85.

Beatty, John (R Ohio) Dec. 16, 1828–Dec. 21, 1914; House Feb. 5, 1868–73.

Beatty, William (D Pa.) 1787–April 12, 1851; House 1837–41.

Beaty, Martin (AJ Ky.) ?–?; House 1833–35.

Beaumont, Andrew (J Pa.) Jan. 24, 1790–Sept. 30, 1853; House 1833–37.

Becerra, Xavier (D Calif.) Jan. 26, 1958– ; House 1993– .

Beck, Erasmus Williams (D Ga.) Oct. 21, 1833–July 22, 1898; House Dec. 2, 1872–73.

Beck, James Burnie (D Ky.) Feb. 13, 1822–May 3, 1890; House 1867–75; Senate 1877–May 3, 1890.

Beck, James Montgomery (R Pa.) July 9, 1861–April 12, 1936; House Nov. 8, 1927–Sept. 30, 1934.

Beck, Joseph David (R Wis.) March 14, 1866–Nov. 8, 1936; House 1921–29.

Becker, Frank John (R N.Y.) Aug. 27, 1899–Sept. 4, 1981; House 1953–65.

Beckham, John Crepps Wickliffe (grandson of Charles Anderson Wickliffe, cousin of Robert Charles Wickliffe) (D Ky.) Aug. 5, 1869–Jan. 9, 1940; Senate 1915–21; Gov. Feb. 3, 1900–Dec. 10, 1907.

Beckner, William Morgan (D Ky.) June 19, 1841–March 14, 1910; House Dec. 3, 1894–95.

Beckwith, Charles Dyer (R N.J.) Oct. 22, 1838–March 27, 1921; House 1889–91.

Beckworth, Lindley Garrison "Gary" Sr. (D Texas) June 30, 1913–March 9, 1984; House 1939–53, 1957–67.

Bede, James Adam (R Minn.) Jan. 13, 1856–April 11, 1942; House 1903–09.

Bedell, Berkley Warren (D Iowa) March 5, 1921– ; House 1975–87.

Bedinger, George Michael (uncle of Henry Bedinger) (R Ky.) Dec. 10, 1756–Dec. 7, 1843; House 1803–07.

Bedinger, Henry (nephew of George Michael Bedinger) (D Va.) Feb. 3, 1812–Nov. 26, 1858; House 1845–49.

Bee, Carlos (D Texas) July 8, 1867–April 20, 1932; House 1919–21.

Beebe, George Monroe (D N.Y.) Oct. 28, 1836–March 1, 1927; House 1875–79.

Beecher, Philemon (– Ohio) 1775–Nov. 30, 1839; House 1817–21, 1823–29.

Beedy, Carroll Lynwood (R Maine) Aug. 3, 1880–Aug. 30, 1947; House 1921–35.

Beekman, Thomas (– N.Y.) ?–?; House 1829–31.

Beeman, Joseph Henry (D Miss.) Nov. 17, 1833–July 31, 1909; House 1891–93.

Beermann, Ralph Frederick (R Neb.) Aug. 13, 1912–Feb. 17, 1977; House 1961–65.

Beers, Cyrus (D N.Y.) June 21, 1786–June 5, 1850; House Dec. 3, 1838–39.

Beers, Edward McMath (R Pa.) May 27, 1877–April 21, 1932; House 1923–April 21, 1932.

Beeson, Henry White (D Pa.) Sept. 14, 1791–Oct. 28, 1863; House May 31, 1841–43.

Begg, James Thomas (R Ohio) Feb. 16, 1877–March 26, 1963; House 1919–29.

Begich, Nicholas Joseph (D Alaska) April 6, 1932–?; House 1971–72. (Disappeared on an airplane flight Oct. 16, 1972, and presumed dead; congressional seat declared vacant Dec. 29, 1972.)

Begole, Josiah Williams (R Mich.) Jan. 20, 1815–June 5, 1896; House 1873–75; Gov. Jan. 1, 1883–Jan. 1, 1885.

Beidler, Jacob Atlee (R Ohio) Nov. 2, 1852–Sept. 13, 1912; House 1901–07.

Beilenson, Anthony Charles (D Calif.) Oct. 26, 1932– ; House 1977–97; Chrmn. House Permanent Select Committee on Intelligence 1989–91.

Beirne, Andrew (D Va.) 1771–March 16, 1845; House 1837–41.

Beiter, Alfred Florian (D N.Y.) July 7, 1894–March 11, 1974; House 1933–39, 1941–43.

Belcher, Hiram (W Maine) Feb. 23, 1790–May 6, 1857; House 1847–49.

Belcher, Nathan (D Conn.) June 23, 1813–June 2, 1891; House 1853–55.

Belcher, Page Henry (R Okla.) April 21, 1899–Aug. 2, 1980; House 1951–73.

Belden, George Ogilvie (– N.Y.) March 28, 1797–Oct. 9, 1833; House 1827–29.

Belden, James Jerome (R N.Y.) Sept. 30, 1825–Jan. 1, 1904; House Nov. 8, 1887–95, 1897–99.

Belford, James Burns (cousin of Joseph McCrum Belford) (R Colo.) Sept. 28, 1837–Jan. 10, 1910; House Oct. 3, 1876–Dec. 13, 1877, 1879–85.

Belford, Joseph McCrum (cousin of James Burns Belford) (R N.Y.) Aug. 5, 1852–May 3, 1917; House 1897–99.

Belknap, Charles Eugene (R Mich.) Oct. 17, 1846–Jan. 16, 1929; House 1889–91, Nov. 3, 1891–93.

Belknap, Hugh Reid (R Ill.) Sept. 1, 1860–Nov. 12, 1901; House Dec. 27, 1895–99.

Bell, Alphonzo (R Calif.) Sept. 19, 1914– ; House 1961–77.

Bell, Charles Henry (nephew of Samuel Bell, cousin of James Bell) (R N.H.) Nov. 18, 1823–Nov. 11, 1893; Senate March 13–June 18, 1879; Gov. June 2, 1881–June 7, 1883.

Bell, Charles Jasper (D Mo.) Jan. 16, 1885–Jan. 21, 1978; House 1935–49.

Bell, Charles Keith (nephew of Reese Bowen Brabson) (D Texas) April 18, 1853–April 21, 1913; House 1893–97.

Bell, Charles Webster (PR Calif.) June 11, 1857–April 19, 1927; House 1913–15.

Bell, Hiram (W Ohio) April 22, 1808–Dec. 21, 1855; House 1851–53.

Bell, Hiram Parks (D Ga.) Jan. 19, 1827–Aug. 17, 1907; House 1873–75, March 13, 1877–79.

Bell, James (son of Samuel Bell, uncle of Samuel Newell Bell, cousin of Charles Henry Bell) (R N.H.) Nov. 13, 1804–May 26, 1857; Senate July 30, 1855–May 26, 1857.

Bell, James Martin (AJ Ohio) Oct. 16, 1796–April 4, 1849; House 1833–35.

Bell, John (W Ohio) June 19, 1796–May 4, 1869; House Jan. 7–March 3, 1851.

Bell, John (W Tenn.) Feb. 15, 1797–Sept. 10, 1869; House 1827–41 (no party); Speaker June 2, 1834–35; Senate Nov. 22, 1847–59; Secy. of War March 5–Sept. 13, 1841.

Bell, John Calhoun (P Colo.) Dec. 11, 1851–Aug. 12, 1933; House 1893–1903.

Bell, John Junior (D Texas) May 15, 1910–Jan. 24, 1963; House 1955–57.

Bell, Joshua Fry (W Ky.) Nov. 26, 1811–Aug. 17, 1870; House 1845–47.

Bell, Peter Hansbrough (D Texas) May 12, 1812–March 8, 1898; House 1853–57; Gov. Dec. 21, 1849–Nov. 23, 1853.

Bell, Samuel (father of James Bell, grandfather of Samuel Newell Bell, uncle of Charles Henry Bell) (W N.H.) Feb. 9, 1770–Dec. 23, 1850; Senate 1823–35 (1823–34 no party); Gov. June 3, 1819–June 5, 1823 (Democratic Republican).

Bell, Samuel Newell (grandson of Samuel Bell, nephew of James Bell) (D N.H.) March 25, 1829–Feb. 8, 1889; House 1871–73, 1875–77.

Bell, Theodore Arlington (D Calif.) July 25, 1872–Sept. 4, 1922; House 1903–05.

Bell, Thomas Montgomery (D Ga.) March 17, 1861–March 18, 1941; House 1905–31.

Bellamy, John Dillard (D N.C.) March 24, 1854–Sept. 25, 1942; House 1899–1903.

Bellinger, Joseph (R S.C.) 1773–Jan. 10, 1830; House 1817–19.

Bellmon, Henry Louis (R Okla.) Sept. 3, 1921– ; Senate 1969–81; Gov. Jan. 14, 1963–Jan. 9, 1967, Jan. 12, 1987– .

Belmont, Oliver Hazard Perry (brother of Perry Belmont) (D N.Y.) Nov. 12, 1858–June 10, 1908; House 1901–03.

Belmont, Perry (brother of Oliver Hazard Perry Belmont) (D N.Y.) Dec. 28, 1851–May 25, 1947; House 1881–Dec. 1, 1888.

Belser, James Edwin (D Ala.) Dec. 22, 1805–Jan. 16, 1859; House 1843–45.

Beltzhoover, Frank Eckels (D Pa.) Nov. 6, 1841–June 2, 1923; House 1879–83, 1891–95.

Bender, George Harrison (R Ohio) Sept. 29, 1896–June 18, 1961; House 1939–49, 1951–Dec. 15, 1954; Senate Dec. 16, 1954–57.

Benedict, Charles Brewster (D N.Y.) Feb. 7, 1828–Oct. 3, 1901; House 1877–79.

Benedict, Cleveland Keith (R W.Va.) March 21, 1935– ; House 1981–83.

Benedict, Henry Stanley (R Calif.) Feb. 20, 1878–July 10, 1930; House Nov. 7, 1916–17.

Benet, Christie (D S.C.) Dec. 26, 1879–March 30, 1951; Senate July 6–Nov. 5, 1918.

Benham, John Samuel (R Ind.) Oct. 24, 1863–Dec. 11, 1935; House 1919–23.

Benitez, Jaime (PD P.R.) Oct. 29, 1908– ; House (Res. Comm.) 1973–77.

Benjamin, Adam Jr. (D Ind.) Aug. 6, 1935–Sept. 7, 1982; House 1977–Sept. 7, 1982.

Benjamin, John Forbes (R Mo.) Jan. 23, 1817–March 8, 1877; House 1865–71.

Benjamin, Judah Philip (D La.) Aug. 6, 1811–May 6, 1884; Senate 1853–Feb. 4, 1861 (1853–59 Whig).

Benner, George Jacob (D Pa.) April 13, 1859–Dec. 30, 1930; House 1897–99.

Bennet, Augustus Witschief (son of William Stiles Bennet) (R N.Y.) Oct. 7, 1897–June 5, 1983; House 1945–47.

Bennet, Benjamin (R N.J.) Oct. 31, 1764–Oct. 8, 1840; House 1815–19.

Bennet, Hiram Pitt (CR Colo.) Sept. 2, 1826–Nov. 11, 1914; House (Terr. Del.) Aug. 19, 1861–65.

Bennet, William Stiles (father of Augustus Witschief Bennet) (R N.Y.) Nov. 9, 1870–Dec. 1, 1962; House 1905–11, Nov. 2, 1915–17.

Bennett, Charles Edward (D Fla.) Dec. 2, 1910– ; House 1949–93; Chrmn. House Standards of Official Conduct 1977–81.

Bennett, Charles Goodwin (R N.Y.) Dec. 11, 1863–May 25, 1914; House 1895–99.

Bennett, David Smith (R N.Y.) May 3, 1811–Nov. 6, 1894; House 1869–71.

Bennett, Granville Gaylord (R Dakota) Oct. 9, 1833–June 28, 1910; House (Terr. Del.) 1879–81.

Bennett, Hendley Stone (D Miss.) April 7, 1807–Dec. 15, 1891; House 1855–57.

Bennett, Henry (R N.Y.) Sept. 29, 1808–May 10, 1868; House 1849–59 (1849–57 Whig).

Bennett, John Bonifas (R Mich.) Jan. 10, 1904–Aug. 9, 1964; House 1943–45, 1947–Aug. 9, 1964.

Bennett, Joseph Bentley (R Ky.) April 21, 1859–Nov. 7, 1923; House 1905–11.

Bennett, Marion Tinsley (son of Philip Allen Bennett) (R Mo.) June 6, 1914– ; House Jan. 12, 1943–49.

Bennett, Philip Allen (father of Marion Tinsley Bennett) (R Mo.) March 5, 1881–Dec. 7, 1942; House 1941–Dec. 7, 1942.

Bennett, Risden Tyler (D N.C.) June 18, 1840–July 21, 1913; House 1883–87.

Bennett, Robert Foster (son of Wallace Foster Bennett) (R Utah) Sept. 18, 1933– ; Senate 1993– .

Bennett, Thomas Warren (I Idaho) Feb. 16, 1831–Feb. 2, 1893; House (Terr. Del.) 1875–June 23, 1876; Gov. (Idaho Terr.) Sept. 1871–Dec. 4, 1875.

Bennett, Wallace Foster (father of Robert Foster Bennett) (R Utah) Nov. 13, 1898–Dec. 19, 1993; Senate 1951–Dec. 20, 1974.

Benny, Allan (D N.J.) July 12, 1867–Nov. 6, 1942; House 1903–05.

Benson, Alfred Washburn (R Kan.) July 15, 1843–Jan. 1, 1916; Senate June 11, 1906–Jan. 23, 1907.

Benson, Carville Dickinson (D Md.) Aug. 24, 1872–Feb. 8, 1929; House Nov. 5, 1918–21.

Benson, Egbert (F N.Y.) June 21, 1746–Aug. 24, 1833; House 1789–93 (no party), March 4–Aug. 2, 1813; Cont. Cong. 1784, 1787–88.

Benson, Elmer Austin (FL Minn.) Sept. 22, 1895–March 13, 1985; Senate Dec. 27, 1935–Nov. 3, 1936; Gov. Jan. 4, 1937–Jan. 2, 1939.

Benson, Samuel Page (R Maine) Nov. 28, 1804–Aug. 12, 1876; House 1853–57 (1853–55 Whig).

Bentley, Alvin Morell (R Mich.) Aug. 30, 1918–April 10, 1969; House 1953–61.

Bentley, Helen Delich (R Md.) Nov. 28, 1923– ; House 1985–95.

Bentley, Henry Wilbur (D N.Y.) Sept. 30, 1838–Jan. 27, 1907; House 1891–93.

Benton, Charles Swan (D N.Y.) July 12, 1810–May 4, 1882; House 1843–47.

Benton, Jacob (R N.H.) Aug. 19, 1814–Sept. 29, 1892; House 1867–71.

Benton, Lemuel (great-grandfather of George William Dargan) (R S.C.) 1754–May 18, 1818; House 1793–99 (1793–95 no party).

Benton, Maecenas Eason (D Mo.) Jan. 29, 1848–April 27, 1924; House 1897–1905.

Benton, Thomas Hart (father-in-law of John Charles Fremont) (D Mo.) March 14, 1782–April 10, 1858; Senate Aug. 10, 1821–51; House 1853–55.

Benton, William (D Conn.) April 1, 1900–March 18, 1973; Senate Dec. 17, 1949–53.

Bentsen, Ken (nephew of Lloyd Bentsen) (D Texas) June 3, 1959– ; House 1995– .

Bentsen, Lloyd Millard Jr. (uncle of Ken Bentsen) (D Texas) Feb. 11, 1921– ; House Dec. 4, 1948–55; Senate 1971–Jan. 20, 1993; Chrmn. Senate Finance 1987–93; Secy. Of the Treasury Jan. 22, 1993–Dec. 22, 1994.

Bereuter, Douglas K. (R Neb.) Oct. 6, 1939– ; House 1979– .

Bergen, Christopher Augustus (R N.J.) Aug. 2, 1841–Feb. 18, 1905; House 1889–93.

Bergen, John Teunis (second cousin of Teunis Garret Bergen) (J N.Y.) 1786–March 9, 1855; House 1831–33.

Bergen, Teunis Garret (second cousin of John Teunis Bergen) (D N.Y.) Oct. 6, 1806–April 24, 1881; House 1865–67.

Berger, Victor Luitpold (Soc. Wis.) Feb. 28, 1860–Aug. 7, 1929; House 1911–13, 1923–29.

Bergland, Robert Selmer (D Minn.) July 22, 1928– ; House 1971–Jan. 22, 1977; Secy. of Agriculture Jan. 23, 1977–Jan. 20, 1981.

Berkley, Shelley (D Nev.) Jan. 20, 1951– ; House 1999– .

Berlin, William Markle (D Pa.) March 29, 1880–Oct. 14, 1962; House 1933–37.

Berman, Howard Lawrence (D Calif.) April 15, 1941– ; House 1983– .

Bernard, John Toussaint (FL Minn.) March 6, 1893–Aug. 6, 1983; House 1937–39.

Bernhisel, John Milton (W Utah) July 23, 1799–Sept. 28, 1881; House (Terr. Del.) 1851–59, 1861–63.

Berrien, John Macpherson (W Ga.) Aug. 23, 1781–Jan. 1, 1856; Senate 1825–March 9, 1829 (Jacksonian), 1841–May 1845, Nov. 13, 1845–May 28, 1852; Atty. Gen. March 9, 1829–July 20, 1831.

Berry, Albert Seaton (D Ky.) May 13, 1836–Jan. 6, 1908; House 1893–1901.

Berry, Campbell Polson (cousin of James Henderson Berry) (D Calif.) Nov. 7, 1834–Jan. 8, 1901; House 1879–83.

Berry, Ellis Yarnal (R S.D.) Oct. 6, 1902–April 1, 1999; House 1951–71.

Berry, George Leonard (D Tenn.) Sept. 12, 1882–Dec. 4, 1948; Senate May 6, 1937–Nov. 8, 1938.

Berry, James Henderson (cousin of Campbell Polson Berry) (D Ark.) May 15, 1841–Jan. 30, 1913; Senate March 20, 1885–1907; Gov. Jan. 13, 1883–Jan. 17, 1885.

Berry, John (D Ohio) April 26, 1833–May 18, 1879; House 1873–75.

Berry, Robert Marion (D Ark.) Aug. 27, 1942– ; House 1997– .

Beshlin, Earl Hanley (D/Prohib. Pa.) April 28, 1870–July 12, 1971; House Nov. 8, 1917–19.

Bethune, Edwin Ruthvin Jr. (R Ark.) Dec. 19, 1935– ; House 1979–85.

Bethune, Lauchlin (J N.C.) April 15, 1785–Oct. 10, 1874; House 1831–33.

Bethune, Marion (R Ga.) April 8, 1816–Feb. 20, 1895; House Dec. 22, 1870–71.

Betton, Silas (F N.H.) Aug. 26, 1768–Jan. 22, 1822; House 1803–07.

Betts, Jackson Edward (R Ohio) May 26, 1904–August 13, 1993; House 1951–73.

Betts, Samuel Rossiter (R N.Y.) June 8, 1787–Nov. 2, 1868; House 1815–17.

Betts, Thaddeus (W Conn.) Feb. 4, 1789–April 7, 1840; Senate 1839–April 7, 1840.

Beveridge, Albert Jeremiah (R Ind.) Oct. 6, 1862–April 27, 1927; Senate 1899–1911.

Beveridge, John Lourie (R Ill.) July 6, 1824–May 3, 1910; House Nov. 7, 1871–Jan. 4, 1873; Gov. Jan. 23, 1873–Jan. 8, 1877.

Bevill, Tom (D Ala.) March 27, 1921– ; House 1967–97.

Biaggi, Mario (D N.Y.) Oct. 26, 1917– ; House 1969–Aug. 8, 1988.

Bibb, George Mortimer (J Ky.) Oct. 30, 1776–April 14, 1859; Senate 1811–Aug. 23, 1814 (no party), 1829–35; Secy. of the Treasury July 4, 1844–March 7, 1845.

Bibb, William Wyatt (R Ga.) Oct. 2, 1781–July 9, 1820; House Jan. 26, 1807–Nov. 6, 1813; Senate Nov. 6, 1813–Nov. 9, 1816; Gov. Nov. 9, 1819–July 10, 1820 (Democratic Republican Ala.)

Bibighaus, Thomas Marshal (W Pa.) March 17, 1817–June 18, 1853; House 1851–53.

Bible, Alan Harvey (D Nev.) Nov. 20, 1909–Sept. 12, 1988; Senate Dec. 2, 1954–Dec. 17, 1974; Chrmn. Senate District of Columbia 1959–69; Chrmn. Senate Select Committee on Small Business 1969–75.

Bicknell, Bennet (D N.Y.) Nov. 14, 1781–Sept. 15, 1841; House 1837–39.

Bicknell, George Augustus (D Ind.) Feb. 6, 1815–April 11, 1891; House 1877–81.

Biddle, Charles John (nephew of Richard Biddle) (D Pa.) April 30, 1819–Sept. 28, 1873; House July 2, 1861–63.

Biddle, John (– Mich.) March 2, 1792–Aug. 25, 1859; House (Terr. Del.) 1829–Feb. 21, 1831.

Biddle, Joseph Franklin (R Pa.) Sept. 14, 1871–Dec. 3, 1936; House Nov. 8, 1932–33.

Biddle, Richard (uncle of Charles John Biddle) (AMas. Pa.) March 25, 1796–July 6, 1847; House 1837–40.

Biden, Joseph Robinette Jr. (D Del.) Nov. 20, 1942– ; Senate 1973– ; Chrmn. Senate Judiciary 1987–95.

Bidlack, Benjamin Alden (D Pa.) Sept. 8, 1804–Feb. 6, 1849; House 1841–45.

Bidwell, Barnabas (R Mass.) Aug. 23, 1763–July 27, 1833; House 1805–July 13, 1807.

Bidwell, John (R Calif.) Aug. 5, 1819–April 4, 1900; House 1865–67.

Biemiller, Andrew John (D Wis.) July 23, 1906–April 3, 1982; House 1945–47, 1949–51.

Biermann, Frederick Elliott (D Iowa) March 20, 1884–July 1, 1968; House 1933–39.

Biery, James Soloman (R Pa.) March 2, 1839–Dec. 3, 1904; House 1873–75.

Biester, Edward George Jr. (R Pa.) Jan. 5, 1931– ; House 1967–77.

Bigby, John Summerfield (R Ga.) Feb. 13, 1832–March 28, 1898; House 1871–73.

Bigelow, Abijah (F Mass.) Dec. 5, 1775–April 5, 1860; House Oct. 8, 1810–15.

Bigelow, Herbert Seely (D Ohio) Jan. 4, 1870–Nov. 11, 1951; House 1937–39.

Bigelow, Lewis (F Mass.) Aug. 18, 1785–Oct. 2, 1838; House 1821–23.

Biggert, Judy (R Ill.) Aug. 15, 1936– ; House 1999– .

Biggs, Asa (D N.C.) Feb. 4, 1811–March 6, 1878; House 1845–47; Senate 1855–May 5, 1858.

Biggs, Benjamin Thomas (D Del.) Oct. 1, 1821–Dec. 25, 1893; House 1869–73; Gov. Jan. 18, 1887–Jan. 20, 1891.

Biggs, Marion (D Calif.) May 2, 1823–Aug. 2, 1910; House 1887–91.

Bigler, William (brother of Gov. John Bigler of Calif.) (D Pa.) Jan. 1, 1814–Aug. 9, 1880; Senate Jan. 14, 1856–61; Gov. Jan. 20, 1852–Jan. 16, 1855.

Bilbo, Theodore Gilmore (D Miss.) Oct. 13, 1877–Aug. 21, 1947; Senate 1935–Aug. 21, 1947; Gov. Jan. 18, 1916–Jan. 20, 1920, Jan. 17, 1928–Jan. 19, 1932.

Bilbray, Brian P. (nephew of James Bilbray) (R Calif.) Jan. 28, 1951– ; House 1995– .

Bilbray, James Hubert (D Nev.) May 19, 1938– ; House 1987–95.

Bilirakis, Michael (R Fla.) July 16, 1930– ; House 1983– .

Billinghurst, Charles (R Wis.) July 27, 1818–Aug. 18, 1865; House 1855–59.

Billmeyer, Alexander (D Pa.) Jan. 7, 1841–May 24, 1924; House Nov. 4, 1902–03.

Binderup, Charles Gustav (D Neb.) March 5, 1873–Aug. 19, 1950; House 1935–39.

Bines, Thomas (R N.J.) ?–April 9, 1826; House Nov. 2, 1814–15.

Bingaman, Jesse Francis Jr. "Jeff" (D N.M.) Oct. 3, 1943– ; Senate 1983– .

Bingham, Henry Harrison (R Pa.) Dec. 4, 1841–March 22, 1912; House 1879–March 22, 1912.

Bingham, Hiram (father of Jonathan Brewster Bingham) (R Conn.) Nov. 19, 1875–June 6, 1956; Senate Dec. 17, 1924–33; Gov. Jan. 7–Jan. 8, 1925.

Bingham, John Armor (R Ohio) Jan. 21, 1815–March 19, 1900; House 1855–63, 1865–73.

Bingham, Jonathan Brewster (son of Hiram Bingham) (D N.Y.) April 24, 1914–July 3, 1986; House 1965–83.

Bingham, Kinsley Scott (R Mich.) Dec. 16, 1808–Oct. 5, 1861; House 1847–51 (Democrat); Senate 1859–Oct. 5, 1861; Gov. Jan. 3, 1855–Jan. 5, 1859.

Bingham, William (F Pa.) March 8, 1752–Feb. 7, 1804; Senate 1795–1801; elected Pres. pro tempore Feb. 16, 1797; Cont. Cong. 1786–88.

Binney, Horace (AJ Pa.) Jan. 4, 1780–Aug. 12, 1875; House 1833–35.

Birch, William Fred (R N.J.) Aug. 30, 1870–Jan. 25, 1946; House Nov. 5, 1918–19.

Bird, John (F N.Y.) Nov. 22, 1768–Feb. 2, 1806; House 1799–July 25, 1801.

Bird, John Taylor (D N.J.) Aug. 16, 1829–May 6, 1911; House 1869–73.

Bird, Richard Ely (R Kan.) Nov. 4, 1878–Jan. 10, 1955; House 1921–23.

Birdsall, Ausburn (D N.Y.) ?–July 10, 1903; House 1847–49.

Birdsall, Benjamin Pixley (R Iowa) Oct. 26, 1858–May 26, 1917; House 1903–09.

Birdsall, James (R N.Y.) 1783–July 20, 1856; House 1815–17.

Birdsall, Samuel (D N.Y.) May 14, 1791–Feb. 8, 1872; House 1837–39.

Birdseye, Victory (W N.Y.) Dec. 25, 1782–Sept. 16, 1853; House 1815–17 (Republican), 1841–43.

Bisbee, Horatio Jr. (R Fla.) May 1, 1839–March 27, 1916; House 1877–Feb. 20, 1879, Jan. 22–March 3, 1881, June 1, 1882–85.

Bishop, Cecil William "Runt" (R Ill.) June 29, 1890–Sept. 21, 1971; House 1941–55.

Bishop, James (W N.J.) May 11, 1816–May 10, 1895; House 1855–57.

Bishop, Phanuel (R Mass.) Sept. 3, 1739–Jan. 6, 1812; House 1799–1807.

Bishop, Roswell Peter (R Mich.) Jan. 6, 1843–March 4, 1920; House 1895–1907.

Bishop, Sanford D. Jr. (D Ga.) Feb. 4, 1947– ; House 1993– .

Bishop, William Darius (D Conn.) Sept. 14, 1827–Feb. 4, 1904; House 1857–59.

Bissell, William Harrison (ID Ill.) April 25, 1811–March 18, 1860; House 1849–55 (1849–53 Democrat); Gov. Jan. 12, 1857–March 18, 1860 (Republican).

Bixler, Harris Jacob (R Pa.) Sept. 16, 1870–March 29, 1941; House 1921–27.

Black, Edward Junius (father of George Robison Black) (D Ga.) Oct. 30, 1806–Sept. 1, 1846; House 1839–41 (Whig), Jan. 3, 1842–45.

Black, Eugene (D Texas) July 2, 1879–May 22, 1975; House 1915–29.

Black, Frank Swett (R N.Y.) March 8, 1853–March 22, 1913; House 1895–Jan. 7, 1897; Gov. Jan. 1, 1897–Jan. 1, 1899.

Black, George Robison (son of Edward Junius Black) (D Ga.) March 24, 1835–Nov. 3, 1886; House 1881–83.

Black, Henry (W Pa.) Feb. 25, 1783–Nov. 28, 1841; House June 28–Nov. 28, 1841.

Black, Hugo Lafayette (D Ala.) Feb. 27, 1886–Sept. 25, 1971; Senate 1927–Aug. 19, 1937; Assoc. Justice Supreme Court Aug. 19, 1937–Sept. 17, 1971.

Black, James (D Pa.) March 6, 1793–June 21, 1872; House Dec. 5, 1836–37 (Jacksonian), 1843–47.

Black, James Augustus (D S.C.) 1793–April 3, 1848; House 1843–April 3, 1848.

Black, James Conquest Cross (D Ga.) May 9, 1842–Oct. 1, 1928; House 1893–March 4, 1895, Oct. 2, 1895–97.

Black, John (W Miss.) ?–Aug. 29, 1854; Senate Nov. 12, 1832–March 3, 1833 (no party), Nov. 22, 1833–Jan. 22, 1838.

Black, John Charles (D Ill.) Jan. 27, 1839–Aug. 17, 1915; House 1893–Jan. 12, 1895.

Black, Loring Milton Jr. (D N.Y.) May 17, 1886–May 21, 1956; House 1923–35.

Blackburn, Benjamin Bentley (R Ga.) Feb. 14, 1927– ; House 1967–75.

Blackburn, Edmond Spencer (R N.C.) Sept. 22, 1868–March 10, 1912; House 1901–03, 1905–07.

Blackburn, Joseph Clay Stiles (D Ky.) Oct. 1, 1838–Sept. 12, 1918; House 1875–85; Senate 1885–97, 1901–07.

Blackburn, Robert E. Lee (R Ky.) April 9, 1870–Sept. 20, 1935; House 1929–31.

Blackburn, William Jasper (R La.) July 24, 1820–Nov. 10, 1899; House July 18, 1868–69.

Blackledge, William (father of William Salter Blackledge) (R N.C.) ?–Oct. 19, 1828; House 1803–09, 1811–13.

Blackledge, William Salter (son of William Blackledge) (– N.C.) 1793–March 21, 1857; House Feb. 7, 1821–23.

Blackmar, Esbon (W N.Y.) June 19, 1805–Nov. 19, 1857; House Dec. 4, 1848–49.

Blackmon, Fred Leonard (D Ala.) Sept. 15, 1873–Feb. 8, 1921; House 1911–Feb. 8, 1921.

Blackney, William Wallace (R Mich.) Aug. 28, 1876–March 14, 1963; House 1935–37, 1939–53.

Blackwell, Lucien E. (D Pa.) Aug. 1, 1931– ; House Nov. 13, 1991–95.

Blackwell, Julius W. (D Tenn.) ?–?; House 1839–41, 1843–45.

Blagojevich, Rod R. (D Ill.) Dec. 10, 1956– ; House 1997– .

Blaine, James Gillespie (R Maine) Jan. 31, 1830–Jan. 27, 1893; House 1863–July 10, 1876; Speaker 1869–73, Dec. 1, 1873–75; Senate July 10, 1876–March 5, 1881; Secy. of State March 7–Dec. 19, 1881, March 7, 1889–June 4, 1892.

Blaine, John James (R Wis.) May 4, 1875–April 16, 1934; Senate 1927–33; Gov. Jan. 3, 1921–Jan. 3, 1927.

Blair, Austin (R Mich.) Feb. 8, 1818–Aug. 6, 1894; House 1867–73; Gov. Jan. 2, 1861–Jan. 4, 1865.

Blair, Bernard (W N.Y.) May 24, 1801–May 7, 1880; House 1841–43.

Blair, Francis Preston Jr. (D Mo.) Feb. 19, 1821–July 8, 1875; House 1857–59 (Republican), June 8–25, 1860, 1861–July 1862, 1863–June 10, 1864; Senate Jan. 20, 1871–73.

Blair, Henry William (R N.H.) Dec. 6, 1834–March 14, 1920; House 1875–79, 1893–95; Senate June 20, 1879–85, March 10, 1885–91.

Blair, Jacob Beeson (UU W.Va.) April 11, 1821–Feb. 12, 1901; House Dec. 2, 1861–63 (U Va.), Dec. 7, 1863–65.

Blair, James (J S.C.) 1790–April 1, 1834; House 1821–May 8, 1822 (no party), 1829–April 1, 1834.

Blair, James Gorrall (LR Mo.) Jan. 1, 1825–March 1, 1904; House 1871–73.

Blair, John (J Tenn.) Sept. 13, 1790–July 9, 1863; House 1823–35 (1823–25 no party).

Blair, Samuel Steel (R Pa.) Dec. 5, 1821–Dec. 8, 1890; House 1859–63.

Blaisdell, Daniel (F N.H.) Jan. 22, 1762–Jan. 10, 1833; House 1809–11.

Blake, Harrison Gray Otis (R Ohio) March 17, 1818–April 16, 1876; House Oct. 11, 1859–63.

Blake, John Jr. (R N.Y.) Dec. 5, 1762–Jan. 13, 1826; House 1805–09.

Blake, John Lauris (R N.J.) March 25, 1831–Oct. 10, 1899; House 1879–81.

Blake, Thomas Holdsworth (– Ind.) June 14, 1792–Nov. 28, 1849; House 1827–29.

Blakeney, Albert Alexander (R Md.) Sept. 28, 1850–Oct. 15, 1924; House 1901–03, 1921–23.

Blakley, William Arvis (D Texas) Nov. 17, 1898–Jan. 5, 1976; Senate Jan. 15–April 28, 1957, Jan. 3–June 14, 1961.

Blanchard, George Washington (R Wis.) Jan. 26, 1884–Oct. 2, 1964; House 1933–35.

Blanchard, James Johnston (D Mich.) Aug. 8, 1942– ; House 1975–83; Gov. Jan. 1, 1983–91.

Blanchard, John (W Pa.) Sept. 30, 1787–March 9, 1849; House 1845–49.

Blanchard, Newton Crain (D La.) Jan. 29, 1849–June 22, 1922; House 1881–March 12, 1894; Senate March 12, 1894–97; Gov. May 10, 1904–May 18, 1908.

Bland, Oscar Edward (R Ind.) Nov. 21, 1877–Aug. 3, 1951; House 1917–23.

Bland, Richard Parks (D Mo.) Aug. 19, 1835–June 15, 1899; House 1873–95, 1897–June 15, 1899.

Bland, Schuyler Otis (D Va.) May 4, 1872–Feb. 16, 1950; House July 2, 1918–Feb. 16, 1950; Chrmn. House Merchant Marine and Fisheries 1949–50.

Bland, Theodorick (– Va.) March 21, 1742–June 1, 1790; House 1789–June 1, 1790; Cont. Cong. 1780–83.

Bland, William Thomas (grandson of John George Jackson, cousin of James Monroe Jackson) (D Mo.) Jan. 21, 1861–Jan. 15, 1928; House 1919–21.

Blanton, Leonard Ray (D Tenn.) April 10, 1930–Nov. 22, 1996; House 1967–73; Gov. Jan. 18, 1975–Jan. 17, 1979.

Blanton, Thomas Lindsay (D Texas) Oct. 25, 1872–Aug. 11, 1957; House 1917–29, May 20, 1930–37.

Blatnik, John Anton (D Minn.) Aug. 17, 1911–Dec. 17, 1991; House 1947–Dec. 31, 1974; Chrmn. House Public Works 1971–75.

Blaz, Ben Garrido (R Guam) Feb. 14, 1928– ; House 1985–93.

Bleakley, Orrin Dubbs (R Pa.) May 15, 1854–Dec. 3, 1927; House March 4–April 3, 1917.

Blease, Coleman Livingston (D S.C.) Oct. 8, 1868–Jan. 19, 1942; Senate 1925–31; Gov. Jan. 17, 1911–Jan. 14, 1915.

Bledsoe, Jesse (uncle of Robert Emmett Bledsoe Baylor) (R Ky.) April 6, 1776–June 25, 1836; Senate 1813–Dec. 24, 1814.

Bleecker, Harmanus (F N.Y.) Oct. 9, 1779–July 19, 1849; House 1811–13.

Bliley, Thomas Jerome Jr. (R Va.) Jan. 28, 1932– ; House 1981– ; Chrmn. House Commerce 1995– .

Bliss, Aaron Thomas (R Mich.) May 22, 1837–Sept. 16, 1906; House 1889–91; Gov. Jan. 1, 1901–Jan. 1, 1905.

Bliss, Archibald Meserole (D N.Y.) Jan. 25, 1838–March 19, 1923; House 1875–83, 1885–89.

Bliss, George (D Ohio) Jan. 1, 1813–Oct. 24, 1868; House 1853–55, 1863–65.

Bliss, Philemon (R Ohio) July 28, 1813–Aug. 25, 1889; House 1855–59.

Blitch, Iris Faircloth (D Ga.) April 25, 1912–August 19, 1993; House 1955–63.

Blodgett, Rufus (D N.J.) Oct. 9, 1834–Oct. 3, 1910; Senate 1887–93.

Bloodworth, Timothy (– N.C.) 1736–Aug. 24, 1814; House April 6, 1790–91; Senate 1795–1801; Cont. Cong. 1786.

Bloom, Isaac (– N.Y.) 1716–April 26, 1803; House March 4–April 26, 1803.

Bloom, Sol (D N.Y.) March 9, 1870–March 7, 1949; House 1923–March 7, 1949.

Bloomfield, Joseph (R N.J.) Oct. 18, 1753–Oct. 3, 1823; House 1817–21; Gov. Oct. 31, 1801–Oct. 28, 1802, Oct. 29, 1803–Oct. 29, 1812.

Blouin, Michael Thomas (D Iowa) Nov. 7, 1945– ; House 1975–79.

Blount, James Henderson (D Ga.) Sept. 12, 1837–March 8, 1903; House 1873–93.

Blount, Thomas (brother of William Blount, uncle of William Grainger Blount) (R N.C.) May 10, 1759–Feb. 7, 1812; House 1793–99 (1793–95 no party), 1805–09, 1811–Feb. 7, 1812.

Blount, William (father of William Grainger Blount, brother of Thomas Blount) (– Tenn.) March 26, 1749–March 21, 1800; Senate Aug. 2, 1796–July 8, 1797; Cont. Cong. 1782–83, 1786–87 (N.C.).

Blount, William Grainger (son of William Blount, nephew of Thomas Blount) (R Tenn.) 1784–May 21, 1827; House Dec. 8, 1815–19.

Blow, Henry Taylor (R Mo.) July 15, 1817–Sept. 11, 1875; House 1863–67 (1863–65 Unconditional Unionist).

Blue, Richard Whiting (R Kan.) Sept. 8, 1841–Jan. 28, 1907; House 1895–97.

Blumenauer, Earl (D Ore.) Aug. 16, 1949– ; House May 30, 1996– .

Blunt, Roy (R Mo.) Jan. 10, 1950– ; House 1997– .

Blute, Peter I. (R Mass.) Jan. 28, 1956– ; House 1993–97.

Boardman, Elijah (father of William Whiting Boardman) (D Conn.) March 7, 1760–Aug. 18, 1823; Senate 1821–Aug. 18, 1823.

Boardman, William Whiting (son of Elijah Boardman) (W Conn.) Oct. 10, 1794–Aug. 27, 1871; House Dec. 7, 1840–43.

Boarman, Alexander "Aleck" (LR La.) Dec. 10, 1839–Aug. 30, 1916; House Dec. 3, 1872–73.

Boatner, Charles Jahleal (D La.) Jan. 23, 1849–March 21, 1903; House 1889–95, June 10, 1896–97.

Bockee, Abraham (J N.Y.) Feb. 3, 1784–June 1, 1865; House 1829–31, 1833–37.

Bocock, Thomas Stanley (D Va.) May 18, 1815–Aug. 5, 1891; House 1847–61.

Boden, Andrew (R Pa.) ?–Dec. 20, 1835; House 1817–21.

Bodine, Robert Nall (D Mo.) Dec. 17, 1837–March 16, 1914; House 1897–99.

Bodle, Charles (J N.Y.) 1787–Oct. 31, 1835; House 1833–35.

Boehlert, Sherwood Louis (R N.Y.) June 28, 1936– ; House 1983– .

Boehne, John William (father of John William Boehne Jr.) (D Ind.) Oct. 28, 1856–Dec. 27, 1946; House 1909–13.

Boehne, John William Jr. (son of John William Boehne) (D Ind.) March 2, 1895–July 5, 1973; House 1931–43.

Boehner, John A. (R Ohio) Nov. 7, 1949– ; House 1991– .

Boen, Haldor Erickson (P Minn.) Jan. 2, 1851–July 23, 1912; House 1893–95.

Boggs, Corinne Claiborne "Lindy" (widow of Thomas Hale Boggs Sr.) (D La.) March 13, 1916– ; House March 20, 1973–91.

Boggs, James Caleb (R Del.) May 15, 1909–March 26, 1993; House 1947–53; Senate 1961–73; Gov. Jan. 20, 1953–Dec. 30, 1960.

Boggs, Thomas Hale Sr. (husband of Corinne Claiborne Boggs) (D La.) Feb. 15, 1914–?; House 1941–43, 1947–73; House majority leader 1971–73. (Disappeared on an airplane flight Oct. 16, 1972, and presumed dead; congressional seat declared vacant Jan. 3, 1973.)

Bogy, Lewis Vital (D Mo.) April 9, 1813–Sept. 20, 1877; Senate 1873–Sept. 20, 1877.

Bohn, Frank Probasco (R Mich.) July 14, 1866–June 1, 1944; House 1927–33.

Boies, William Dayton (R Iowa) Jan. 3, 1857–May 31, 1932; House 1919–29.

Boileau, Gerald John (Prog. Wis.) Jan. 15, 1900–Jan. 30, 1981; House 1931–39 (1931–35 Republican).

Bokee, David Alexander (W N.Y.) Oct. 6, 1805–March 15, 1860; House 1849–51.

Boland, Edward Patrick (D Mass.) Oct. 1, 1911– ; House 1953–89; Chrmn. House Permanent Select Committee on Intelligence 1977–85.

Boland, Patrick Joseph (husband of Veronica Grace Boland) (D Pa.) Jan. 6, 1880–May 18, 1942; House 1931–May 18, 1942.

Boland, Veronica Grace (widow of Patrick Joseph Boland) (D Pa.) March 18, 1899–June 19, 1982; House Nov. 19, 1942–43.

Boles, Thomas (R Ark.) July 16, 1837–March 13, 1905; House June 22, 1868–71, Feb. 9, 1872–73.

Bolles, Stephen (R Wis.) June 25, 1866–July 8, 1941; House 1939–July 8, 1941.

Bolling, Richard Walker (great-great-grandson of John Williams Walker, great-great-nephew of Percy Walker) (D Mo.) May 17, 1916–April 21, 1991; House 1949–83; Chrmn. House Rules 1979–83.

Bolton, Chester Castle (husband of Frances Payne Bolton, father of Oliver Payne Bolton) (R Ohio) Sept. 5, 1882–Oct. 29, 1939; House 1929–37, Jan. 3–Oct. 29, 1939.

Bolton, Frances Payne (widow of Chester Castle Bolton, granddaughter of Henry B. Payne, mother of Oliver Payne Bolton) (R Ohio) March 29, 1885–March 9, 1977; House Feb. 27, 1940–69.

Bolton, Oliver Payne (son of Chester Castle Bolton and Frances Payne Bolton, great-grandson of Henry B. Payne) (R Ohio) Feb. 22, 1917–Dec. 13, 1972; House 1953–57, 1963–65.

Bolton, William P. (D Md.) July 2, 1885–Nov. 22, 1964; House 1949–51.

Bond, Charles Grosvenor (nephew of Charles Henry Grosvenor) (R N.Y.) May 29, 1877–Jan. 10, 1974; House 1921–23.

Bond, Christopher Samuel "Kit" (R Mo.) March 6, 1939– ; Senate 1987– ; Chrmn. Senate Small Business 1995– ; Gov. Jan. 8, 1973–Jan. 10, 1977, Jan. 12, 1981–Jan. 14, 1985.

Bond, Shadrack (– Ill.) Nov. 24, 1773–April 12, 1832; House (Terr. Del.) Dec. 3, 1812–Aug. 2, 1813; Gov. Oct. 6, 1818–Dec. 5, 1822 (Democratic Republican).

Bond, William Key (W Ohio) Oct. 2, 1792–Feb. 17, 1864; House 1835–41.

Bone, Homer Truett (D Wash.) Jan. 25, 1883–March 11, 1970; Senate 1933–Nov. 13, 1944.

Boner, William Hill (D Tenn.) Feb. 14, 1945– ; House 1979–Oct. 5, 1987.

Bonham, Milledge Luke (D S.C.) Dec. 25, 1813–Aug. 27, 1890; House 1857–Dec. 21, 1860; Gov. Dec. 17, 1862–Dec. 20, 1864 (Confederate Democrat).

Bonilla, Henry (R Texas) Jan. 2, 1954– ; House 1993– .

Bonin, Edward John (R Pa.) Dec. 23, 1904–Dec. 20, 1990; House 1953–55.

Bonior, David Edward (D Mich.) June 6, 1945– ; House 1977– .

Bonker, Don Leroy (D Wash.) March 7, 1937– ; House 1975–89.

Bonner, Herbert Covington (D N.C.) May 16, 1891–Nov. 7, 1965; House Nov. 5, 1940–Nov. 7, 1965; Chrmn. House Merchant Marine and Fisheries 1955–66.

Bono, Mary (widow of Sonny Bono) (R Calif.) Oct. 24, 1961– ; House April 21, 1998– .

Bono, Sonny (husband of Mary Bono) (R Calif.) Feb. 16, 1935–Jan. 5, 1998; House 1995–Jan. 5, 1998.

Bonynge, Robert William (R Colo.) Sept. 8, 1863–Sept. 22, 1939; House Feb. 16, 1904–09.

Boody, Azariah (W N.Y.) April 21, 1815–Nov. 18, 1885; House March 4–Oct. 1853.

Boody, David Augustus (D N.Y.) Aug. 13, 1837–Jan. 20, 1930; House March 4–Oct. 13, 1891.

Booher, Charles Ferris (D Mo.) Jan. 31, 1848–Jan. 21, 1921; House Feb. 19–March 3, 1889, 1907–Jan. 21, 1921.

Booker, George William (C Va.) Dec. 5, 1821–June 4, 1883; House Jan. 26, 1870–71.

Boon, Ratliff (D Ind.) Jan. 18, 1781–Nov. 20, 1844; House 1825–27 (no party), 1829–39 (1829–37 Jacksonian); Gov. Sept. 12–Dec. 5, 1822 (Democrat).

Boone, Andrew Rechmond (D Ky.) April 4, 1831–Jan. 26, 1886; House 1875–79.

Booth, Newton (AM Calif.) Dec. 30, 1825–July 14, 1892; Senate 1875–81; Gov. Dec. 8, 1871–Feb. 27, 1875 (Republican).

Booth, Walter (FS Conn.) Dec. 8, 1791–April 30, 1870; House 1849–51.

Boothman, Melvin Morella (R Ohio) Oct. 16, 1846–March 5, 1904; House 1887–91.

Booze, William Samuel (R Md.) Jan. 9, 1862–Dec. 6, 1933; House 1897–99.

Borah, William Edgar (R Idaho) June 29, 1865–Jan. 19, 1940; Senate 1907–Jan. 19, 1940.

Borchers, Charles Martin (D Ill.) Nov. 18, 1869–Dec. 2, 1946; House 1913–15.

Borden, Nathaniel Briggs (W Mass.) April 15, 1801–April 10, 1865; House 1835–39 (1835–37 Jacksonian, 1837–39 Democrat), 1841–43.

Boreing, Vincent (R Ky.) Nov. 24, 1839–Sept. 16, 1903; House 1899–Sept. 16, 1903.

Boreman, Arthur Inghram (R W.Va.) July 24, 1823–April 19, 1896; Senate 1869–75; Gov. June 20, 1863–Feb. 26, 1869.

Boren, David Lyle (son of Lyle H. Boren) (D Okla.) April 21, 1941– ; Senate 1979–Nov. 15, 1994; Chrmn. Senate Select Committee on Intelligence Activities 1987– ; Gov. Jan. 13, 1975–Jan. 3, 1979.

Boren, Lyle H. (father of David Lyle Boren) (D Okla.) May 11, 1909–July 2, 1992; House 1937–47.

Borland, Charles Jr. (– N.Y.) June 29, 1786–Feb. 23, 1852; House Nov. 8, 1821–23.

Borland, Solon (D Ark.) Sept. 21, 1808–Jan. 1, 1864; Senate March 30, 1848–April 3, 1853.

Borland, William Patterson (D Mo.) Oct. 14, 1867–Feb. 20, 1919; House 1909–Feb. 20, 1919.

Borski, Robert Anthony Jr. (D Pa.) Oct. 20, 1948– ; House 1983– .

Borst, Peter I. (J N.Y.) April 24, 1797–Nov. 14, 1848; House 1829–31.

Bosch, Albert Henry (R N.Y.) Oct. 30, 1908– ; House 1953–Dec. 31, 1960.

Boschwitz, Rudolf Eli "Rudy" (R Minn.) Nov. 7, 1930– ; Senate Dec. 30, 1978–91.

Bosco, Douglas Harry (D Calif.) July 28, 1946– ; House 1983–91.

Bosone, Reva Zilpha Beck (D Utah) April 2, 1895–July 21, 1983; House 1949–53.

Boss, John Linscom Jr. (F R.I.) Sept. 7, 1780–Aug. 1, 1819; House 1815–19.

Bossier, Pierre Evariste John Baptiste (D La.) March 22, 1797–April 24, 1844; House 1843–April 24, 1844.

Boswell, Leonard (D Iowa) Jan. 10, 1934– ; House 1997– .

Boteler, Alexander Robinson (O Va.) May 16, 1815–May 8, 1892; House 1859–61.

Botkin, Jeremiah Dunham (P Kan.) April 24, 1849–Dec. 29, 1921; House 1897–99.

Botts, John Minor (W Va.) Sept. 16, 1802–Jan. 8, 1869; House 1839–43, 1847–49.

Bottum, Joseph H. (R S.D.) Aug. 7, 1903–July 4, 1984; Senate July 11, 1962–63.

Boucher, Frederick C. (D Va.) Aug. 1, 1946– ; House 1983– .

Bouck, Gabriel (nephew of Joseph Bouck) (D Wis.) Dec. 16, 1828–Feb. 21, 1904; House 1877–81.

Bouck, Joseph (uncle of Gabriel Bouck) (J N.Y.) July 22, 1788–March 30, 1858; House 1831–33.

Boude, Thomas (F Pa.) May 17, 1752–Oct. 24, 1822; House 1801–03.

Boudinot, Elias (– N.J.) May 2, 1740–Oct. 24, 1821; House 1789–95; Cont. Cong. 1778, 1781–83.

Bouldin, James Wood (brother of Thomas Tyler Bouldin) (D Va.) 1792–March 30, 1854; House March 15, 1834–39 (March 15, 1834–37 Jacksonian).

Bouldin, Thomas Tyler (brother of James Wood Bouldin) (J Va.) 1781–Feb. 11, 1834; House 1829–33, Aug. 26, 1833–Feb. 11, 1834.

Bouligny, Charles Dominique Joseph (uncle of John Edward Bouligny) (– La.) Aug. 22, 1773–March 4, 1833; Senate Nov. 19, 1824–29.

Bouligny, John Edward (nephew of Charles Dominique Joseph Bouligny) (AP La.) Feb. 5, 1824–Feb. 20, 1864; House 1859–61.

Boulter, Eldon Beau (R Texas) Feb. 23, 1942– ; House 1985–89.

Bound, Franklin (R Pa.) April 9, 1829–Aug. 8, 1910; House 1885–89.

Bouquard, Marilyn Laird Lloyd. (See Lloyd, Marilyn Laird.)

Bourne, Benjamin (F R.I.) Sept. 9, 1755–Sept. 17, 1808; House Aug. 31, 1790–96 (Aug. 31, 1790–95 no party).

Bourne, Jonathan Jr. (R Ore.) Feb. 23, 1855–Sept. 1, 1940; Senate 1907–13.

Bourne, Shearjasub (– Mass.) June 14, 1746–March 11, 1806; House 1791–95.

Boutell, Henry Sherman (R Ill.) March 14, 1856–March 11, 1926; House Nov. 23, 1897–1911.

Boutelle, Charles Addison (R Maine) Feb. 9, 1839–May 21, 1901; House 1883–1901.

Boutwell, George Sewel (R Mass.) Jan. 28, 1818–Feb. 27, 1905; House 1863–March 12, 1869; Senate March 17, 1873–77; Gov. Jan. 11, 1851–Jan. 14, 1853 (Democrat); Secy. of the Treasury March 12, 1869–March 16, 1873.

Bovee, Matthias Jacob (brother-in-law of Benedict Arnold) (J N.Y.) July 24, 1793–Sept. 12, 1872; House 1835–37.

Bow, Frank Townsend (R Ohio) Feb. 20, 1901–Nov. 13, 1972; House 1951–Nov. 13, 1972.

Bowden, George Edwin (nephew of Lemuel Jackson Bowden) (R Va.) July 6, 1852–Jan. 22, 1908; House 1887–91.

Bowden, Lemuel Jackson (uncle of George Edwin Bowden) (R Va.) Jan. 16, 1815–Jan. 2, 1864; Senate 1863–Jan. 2, 1864.

Bowdle, Stanley Eyre (D Ohio) Sept. 4, 1868–April 6, 1919; House 1913–15.

Bowdon, Franklin Welsh (uncle of Sydney Johnston Bowie) (D Ala.) Feb. 17, 1817–June 8, 1857; House Dec. 7, 1846–51.

Bowen, Christopher Columbus (R S.C.) Jan. 5, 1832–June 23, 1880; House July 20, 1868–71.

Bowen, David Reece (D Miss.) Oct. 21, 1932– ; House 1973–83.

Bowen, Henry (son of Rees Tate Bowen, nephew of John Warfield Johnston, cousin of William Bowen Campbell) (R Va.) Dec. 26, 1841–April 29, 1915; House 1883–85 (Readjuster), 1887–89.

Bowen, John Henry (R Tenn.) Sept. 1780–Sept. 25, 1822; House 1813–15.

Bowen, Rees Tate (father of Henry Bowen) (D Va.) Jan. 10, 1809–Aug. 29, 1879; House 1873–75.

Bowen, Thomas Mead (R Colo.) Oct. 26, 1835–Dec. 30, 1906; Senate 1883–89; Gov. (Idaho Terr.) 1871.

Bower, Gustavus Miller (D Va.) Dec. 12, 1790–Nov. 17, 1864; House 1843–45.

Bower, William Horton (D N.C.) June 6, 1850–May 11, 1910; House 1893–95.

Bowers, Eaton Jackson (D Miss.) June 17, 1865–Oct. 26, 1939; House 1903–11.

Bowers, George Meade (R W.Va.) Sept. 13, 1863–Dec. 7, 1925; House May 9, 1916–23.

Bowers, John Myer (F N.Y.) Sept. 25, 1772–Feb. 24, 1846; House May 26–Dec. 20, 1813.

Bowers, William Wallace (R Calif.) Oct. 20, 1834–May 2, 1917; House 1891–97.

Bowersock, Justin De Witt (R Kan.) Sept. 19, 1842–Oct. 27, 1922; House 1899–1907.

Bowie, Richard Johns (W Md.) June 23, 1807–March 12, 1888; House 1849–53.

Bowie, Sydney Johnston (nephew of Franklin Welsh Bowdon) (D Ala.) July 26, 1865–May 7, 1928; House 1901–07.

Bowie, Thomas Fielder (great-nephew of Walter Bowie, brother-in-law of Reverdy Johnson) (D Md.) April 7, 1808–Oct. 30, 1869; House 1855–59.

Bowie, Walter (great-uncle of Thomas Fielder Bowie) (R Md.) 1748–Nov. 9, 1810; House March 24, 1802–05.

Bowler, James Bernard (D Ill.) Feb. 5, 1875–July 18, 1957; House July 7, 1953–July 18, 1957.

Bowles, Chester Bliss (D Conn.) April 5, 1901–May 25, 1986; House 1959–61; Gov. Jan. 5, 1949–Jan. 3, 1951.

Bowles, Henry Leland (R Mass.) Jan. 6, 1866–May 17, 1932; House Sept. 29, 1925–29.

Bowlin, James Butler (D Mo.) Jan. 16, 1804–July 19, 1874; House 1843–51.

Bowling, William Bismarck (D Ala.) Sept. 24, 1870–Dec. 27, 1946; House Dec. 14, 1920–Aug. 16, 1928.

Bowman, Charles Calvin (R Pa.) Nov. 14, 1852–July 3, 1941; House 1911–Dec. 12, 1912.

Bowman, Frank Llewellyn (R W.Va.) Jan. 21, 1879–Sept. 15, 1936; House 1925–33.

Bowman, Selwyn Zadock (R Mass.) May 11, 1840–Sept. 30, 1928; House 1879–83.

Bowman, Thomas (D Iowa) May 25, 1848–Dec. 1, 1917; House 1891–93.

Bowne, Obadiah (W N.Y.) May 19, 1822–April 27, 1874; House 1851–53.

Bowne, Samuel Smith (D N.Y.) April 11, 1800–July 9, 1865; House 1841–43.

Bowring, Eva Kelly (R Neb.) Jan. 9, 1892–Jan. 8, 1985; Senate April 16–Nov. 7, 1954.

Box, John Calvin (D Texas) March 28, 1871–May 17, 1941; House 1919–31.

Boxer, Barbara (D Calif.) Nov. 11, 1940– ; House 1983–93; Senate 1993– .

Boyce, William Henry (D Del.) Nov. 28, 1855–Feb. 6, 1942; House 1923–25.

Boyce, William Waters (D S.C.) Oct. 24, 1818–Feb. 3, 1890; House 1853–Dec. 21, 1860.

Boyd, Adam (R N.J.) March 21, 1746–Aug. 15, 1835; House 1803–05, March 8, 1808–13.

Boyd, Alexander (F N.Y.) Sept. 14, 1764–April 8, 1857; House 1813–15.

Boyd, Allen (D Fla.) June 6, 1945– ; House 1997– .

Boyd, John Frank (R Neb.) Aug. 8, 1853–May 28, 1945; House 1907–09.

Boyd, John Huggins (W N.Y.) July 31, 1799–July 2, 1868; House 1851–53.

Boyd, Linn (D Ky.) Nov. 22, 1800–Dec. 17, 1859; House 1835–37 (Jacksonian), 1839–55; Speaker Dec. 1, 1851–53, Dec. 5, 1853–55.

Boyd, Sempronius Hamilton (R Mo.) May 28, 1828–June 22, 1894; House 1863–65 (Unconditional Unionist), 1869–71.

Boyd, Thomas Alexander (R Ill.) June 25, 1830–May 28, 1897; House 1877–81.

Boyden, Nathaniel (C N.C.) Aug. 16, 1796–Nov. 20, 1873; House 1847–49 (Whig), July 13, 1868–69.

Boyer, Benjamin Markley (D Pa.) Jan. 22, 1823–Aug. 16, 1887; House 1865–69.

Boyer, Lewis Leonard (D Ill.) May 19, 1886–March 12, 1944; House 1937–39.

Boykin, Frank William (D Ala.) Feb. 21, 1885–March 12, 1969; House July 30, 1935–63.

Boylan, John Joseph (D N.Y.) Sept. 20, 1878–Oct. 5, 1938; House 1923–Oct. 5, 1938.

Boyle, Charles Augustus (D Ill.) Aug. 13, 1907–Nov. 4, 1959; House 1955–Nov. 4, 1959.

Boyle, Charles Edmund (D Pa.) Feb. 4, 1836–Dec. 15, 1888; House 1883–87.

Boyle, John (R Ky.) Oct. 28, 1774–Feb. 28, 1835; House 1803–09.

Brabson, Reese Bowen (uncle of Charles Keith Bell) (O Tenn.) Sept. 16, 1817–Aug. 16, 1863; House 1859–61.

Brace, Jonathan (F Conn.) Nov. 12, 1754–Aug. 26, 1837; House Dec. 3, 1798–1800.

Brackenridge, Henry Marie (W Pa.) May 11, 1786–Jan. 18, 1871; House Oct. 13, 1840–41.

Bradbury, George (F Mass.) Oct. 10, 1770–Nov. 7, 1823; House 1813–17.

Bradbury, James Ware (D Maine) June 10, 1802–Jan. 6, 1901; Senate 1847–53.

Bradbury, Theophilus (F Mass.) Nov. 13, 1739–Sept. 6, 1803; House 1795–July 24, 1797.

Brademas, John (D Ind.) March 2, 1927– ; House 1959–81.

Bradford, Allen Alexander (R Colo.) July 23, 1815–March 12, 1888; House (Terr. Del.) 1865–67, 1869–71.

Bradford, Taul (grandson of Micah Taul) (D Ala.) Jan. 20, 1835–Oct. 28, 1883; House 1875–77.

Bradford, William (– R.I.) Nov. 4, 1729–July 6, 1808; Senate 1793–Oct. 1797; elected Pres. pro tempore July 6, 1797; Cont. Cong. (elected but did not attend) 1776.

Bradley, Edward (D Mich.) April 1808–Aug. 5, 1847; House March 4–Aug. 5, 1847.

Bradley, Frederick Van Ness (R Mich.) April 12, 1898–May 24, 1947; House 1939–May 24, 1947; Chrmn. House Merchant Marine and Fisheries 1947.

Bradley, Michael Joseph (D Pa.) May 24, 1897–Nov. 27, 1979; House 1937–47.

Bradley, Nathan Ball (R Mich.) May 28, 1831–Nov. 8, 1906; House 1873–77.

Bradley, Stephen Row (father of William Czar Bradley) (– Vt.) Feb. 20, 1754–Dec. 9, 1830; Senate Oct. 17, 1791–95, Oct. 15, 1801–13; elected Pres. pro tempore Dec. Dec. 14, 1802, Feb. 25, 1803, March 2, 1803, Dec. 28, 1808.

Bradley, Thomas Joseph (D N.Y.) Jan. 2, 1870–April 1, 1901; House 1897–1901.

Bradley, Thomas Wilson (R N.Y.) April 6, 1844–May 30, 1920; House 1903–13.

Bradley, William Czar (son of Stephen Row Bradley) (– Vt.) March 23, 1782–March 3, 1867; House 1813–15 (Republican), 1823–27.

Bradley, William O'Connell (R Ky.) March 18, 1847–May 23, 1914; Senate 1909–May 23, 1914; Gov. Dec. 10, 1895–Dec. 12, 1899.

Bradley, William Warren "Bill" (D N.J.) July 28, 1943– ; Senate 1979–97.

Bradley, Willis Winter (R Calif.) June 28, 1884–Aug. 27, 1954; House 1947–49.

Bradshaw, Samuel Carey (W Pa.) June 10, 1809–June 9, 1872; House 1855–57.

Brady, James Dennis (R Va.) April 3, 1843–Nov. 30, 1900; House 1885–87.

Brady, James Henry (R Idaho) June 12, 1862–Jan. 13, 1918; Senate Feb. 6, 1913–Jan. 13, 1918; Gov. Jan. 4, 1909–Jan. 2, 1911.

Brady, Jasper Ewing (W Pa.) March 4, 1797–Jan. 26, 1871; House 1847–49.

Brady, Kevin (R Texas) April 11, 1955– ; House 1997– .

Brady, Nicholas Frederick (R N.J.) April 11, 1930– ; Senate April 12–Dec. 20, 1982; Secy. of the Treasury Sept. 15, 1988–93.

Brady, Robert A. (D Pa.) April 7, 1945– ; House May 21, 1998– .

Bragg, Edward Stuyvesant (D Wis.) Feb. 20, 1827–June 20, 1912; House 1877–83, 1885–87.

Bragg, John (D Ala.) Jan. 14, 1806–Aug. 10, 1878; House 1851–53.

Bragg, Thomas (D N.C.) Nov. 9, 1810–Jan. 21, 1872; Senate 1859–March 6, 1861; Gov. Jan. 1, 1855–Jan. 1, 1859.

Brainerd, Lawrence (FS Vt.) March 16, 1794–May 9, 1870; Senate Oct. 14, 1854–55.

Brainerd, Samuel Myron (R Pa.) Nov. 13, 1842–Nov. 21, 1898; House 1883–85.

Bramblett, Ernest King (R Calif.) April 25, 1901–Dec. 27, 1966; House 1947–55.

Branch, John (uncle of Lawrence O'Bryan Branch, great-uncle of William Augustus Blount Branch) (D N.C.) Nov. 4, 1782–Jan. 3, 1863; Senate 1823–March 9, 1829; House May 12, 1831–33; Gov. Dec. 6, 1817–Dec. 7, 1820 (Democratic Republican); Secy. of the Navy March 9, 1829–March 12, 1831.

Branch, Lawrence O'Bryan (father of William Augustus Blount Branch, nephew of John Branch) (D N.C.) Nov. 28, 1820–Sept. 17, 1862; House 1855–61.

Branch, William Augustus Blount (son of Lawrence O'Bryan Branch, great-nephew of John Branch) (D N.C.) Feb. 26, 1847–Nov. 18, 1910; House 1891–95.

Brand, Charles (R Ohio) Nov. 1, 1871–May 23, 1966; House 1923–33.

Brand, Charles Hillyer (D Ga.) April 20, 1861–May 17, 1933; House 1917–May 17, 1933.

Brandegee, Augustus (father of Frank Bosworth Brandegee) (R Conn.) July 15, 1828–Nov. 10, 1904; House 1863–67.

Brandegee, Frank Bosworth (son of Augustus Brandegee) (R Conn.) July 8, 1864–Oct. 14, 1924; House Nov. 5, 1902–May 10, 1905; Senate May 10, 1905–Oct. 14, 1924; elected Pres. pro tempore May 25, 1912 (to serve May 25, 1912).

Brantley, William Gordon (D Ga.) Sept. 18, 1860–Sept. 11, 1934; House 1897–1913.

Brasco, Frank James (D N.Y.) Oct. 15, 1932– ; House 1967–75.

Bratton, John (– S.C.) March 7, 1831–Jan. 12, 1898; House Dec. 8, 1884–85.

Bratton, Robert Franklin (D Md.) May 3, 1845–May 10, 1894; House 1893–May 10, 1894.

Bratton, Sam Gilbert (D N.M.) Aug. 19, 1888–Sept. 22, 1963; Senate 1925–June 24, 1933.

Brawley, William Huggins (cousin of John James Hemphill, great-uncle of Robert Witherspoon Hemphill) (D S.C.) May 13, 1841–Nov. 15, 1916; House 1891–Feb. 12, 1894.

Braxton, Elliott Muse (D Va.) Oct. 8, 1823–Oct. 2, 1891; House 1871–73.

Bray, William Gilmer (R Ind.) June 17, 1903–June 4, 1979; House 1951–75.

Brayton, William Daniel (R R.I.) Nov. 6, 1815–June 30, 1887; House 1857–61.

Breaux, John Berlinger (D La.) March 1, 1944– ; House Sept. 30, 1972–87; Senate 1987– .

Breazeale, Phanor (D La.) Dec. 29, 1858–April 29, 1934; House 1899–1905.

Breck, Daniel (brother of Samuel Breck) (W Ky.) Feb. 12, 1788–Feb. 4, 1871; House 1849–51.

Breck, Samuel (brother of Daniel Breck) (– Pa.) July 17, 1771–Aug. 31, 1862; House 1823–25.

Breckinridge, Clifton Rodes (son of John Cabell Breckinridge, great-grandson of John Breckinridge) (D Ark.) Nov. 22, 1846–Dec. 3, 1932; House 1883–Sept. 5, 1890, Nov. 4, 1890–Aug. 14, 1894.

Breckinridge, James (brother of John Breckinridge, great-great-great-uncle of John Bayne Breckinridge, cousin of John Brown of Va. and Ky., James Brown, and Francis Preston) (F Va.) March 7, 1763–May 13, 1833; House 1809–17.

Breckinridge, James Douglas (– Ky.) ?–May 6, 1849; House Nov. 21, 1821–23.

Breckinridge, John (brother of James Breckinridge, grandfather of John Cabell Breckinridge and William Campbell Preston Breckinridge, great-grandfather of Clifton Rodes Breckinridge, great-great-grandfather of John Bayne Breckinridge, cousin of John Brown of Va. and Ky., James Brown, and Francis Preston) (R Ky.) Dec. 2, 1760–Dec. 14, 1806; Senate 1801–Aug. 7, 1805; Atty. Gen. Aug. 7, 1805–Dec. 14, 1806.

Breckinridge, John Bayne (great-great-grandson of John Breckinridge, great-great-great-nephew of James Breckinridge, great-nephew of William Campbell Preston Breckinridge) (D Ky.) Nov. 29, 1913–July 29, 1979; House 1973–79.

Breckinridge, John Cabell (grandson of John Breckinridge, father of Clifton Rodes Breckinridge, cousin of Henry Donnel Foster) (D Ky.) Jan. 21, 1821–May 17, 1875; House 1851–55; Senate March 4–Dec. 4, 1861; Vice President 1857–61.

Breckinridge, William Campbell Preston (grandson of John Breckinridge, uncle of Levin Irving Handy, great-uncle of John Bayne Breckinridge) (D Ky.) Aug. 28, 1837–Nov. 18, 1904; House 1885–95.

Breeding, James Floyd (D Kan.) Sept. 28, 1901–Oct. 17, 1977; House 1957–63.

Breen, Edward G. (D Ohio) June 10, 1908–May 8, 1991; House 1949–Oct. 1, 1951.

Breese, Sidney (D Ill.) July 15, 1800–June 27, 1878; Senate 1843–49.

Brehm, Walter Ellsworth (R Ohio) May 25, 1892–Aug. 24, 1971; House 1943–53.

Breitung, Edward (R Mich.) Nov. 10, 1831–March 3, 1887; House 1883–85.

Bremner, Robert Gunn (D N.J.) Dec. 17, 1874–Feb. 5, 1914; House 1913–Feb. 5, 1914.

Brengle, Francis (W Md.) Nov. 26, 1807–Dec. 10, 1846; House 1843–45.

Brennan, Joseph Edward (D Maine) Nov. 2, 1934–   ; House 1987–91; Gov. Jan. 3, 1979–Jan. 7, 1987.

Brennan, Martin Adlai (D Ill.) Sept. 21, 1879–July 4, 1941; House 1933–37.

Brennan, Vincent Morrison (R Mich.) April 22, 1890–Feb. 4, 1959; House 1921–23.

Brenner, John Lewis (D Ohio) Feb. 2, 1832–Nov. 1, 1906; House 1897–1901.

Brent, Richard (uncle of William Leigh Brent, nephew of Daniel Carroll) (– Va.) 1757–Dec. 30, 1814; House 1795–99, 1801–03; Senate 1809–Dec. 30, 1814.

Brent, William Leigh (nephew of Richard Brent) (– La.) Feb. 20, 1784–July 7, 1848; House 1823–29.

Brentano, Lorenzo (R Ill.) Nov. 4, 1813–Sept. 18, 1891; House 1877–79.

Brenton, Samuel (R Ind.) Nov. 22, 1810–March 29, 1857; House 1851–53 (Whig), 1855–March 29, 1857.

Brents, Thomas Hurley (R Wash.) Dec. 24, 1840–Oct. 23, 1916; House (Terr. Del.) 1879–85.

Bretz, John Lewis (D Ind.) Sept. 21, 1852–Dec. 25, 1920; House 1891–95.

Brevard, Joseph (– S.C.) July 19, 1766–Oct. 11, 1821; House 1819–21.

Brewer, Francis Beattie (R N.Y.) Oct. 8, 1820–July 29, 1892; House 1883–85.

Brewer, John Hart (R N.J.) March 29, 1844–Dec. 21, 1900; House 1881–85.

Brewer, Mark Spencer (R Mich.) Oct. 22, 1837–March 18, 1901; House 1877–81, 1887–91.

Brewer, Willis (D Ala.) March 15, 1844–Oct. 30, 1912; House 1897–1901.

Brewster, Daniel Baugh (D Md.) Nov. 23, 1923–   ; House 1959–63; Senate 1963–69.

Brewster, David P. (D N.Y.) June 15, 1801–Feb. 20, 1876; House 1839–43.

Brewster, Henry Colvin (R N.Y.) Sept. 7, 1845–Jan. 29, 1928; House 1895–99.

Brewster, Ralph Owen (R Maine) Feb. 22, 1888–Dec. 25, 1961; House 1935–41; Senate 1941–Dec. 31, 1952; Gov. Jan. 8, 1925–Jan. 2, 1929.

Brewster, William (D Okla.) Nov. 8, 1941–   ; House 1991–97.

Brice, Calvin Stewart (D Ohio) Sept. 17, 1845–Dec. 15, 1898; Senate 1891–97; Chrmn. Dem. Nat. Comm. 1889–92.

Brick, Abraham Lincoln (R Ind.) May 27, 1860–April 7, 1908; House 1899–April 7, 1908.

Bricker, John William (R Ohio) Sept. 6, 1893–March 22, 1986; Senate 1947–59; Chrmn. Senate Interstate and Foreign Commerce 1953–55; Gov. Jan. 9, 1939–Jan. 8, 1945.

Brickner, George H. (D Wis.) Jan. 21, 1834–Aug. 12, 1904; House 1889–95.

Bridges, George Washington (– Tenn.) Oct. 9, 1825–March 16, 1873; House Feb. 25–March 3, 1863.

Bridges, Henry Styles (R N.H.) Sept. 9, 1898–Nov. 26, 1961; Senate 1937–Nov. 26, 1961; Chrmn. Senate Appropriations 1947–49, 1953–55; Senate minority leader Jan. 8, 1952–53; elected Pres. pro tempore Jan. 3, 1953; Gov. Jan. 3, 1935–Jan. 7, 1937.

Bridges, Samuel Augustus (D Pa.) Jan. 27, 1802–Jan. 14, 1884; House March 6, 1848–49, 1853–55, 1877–79.

Briggs, Clay Stone (D Texas) Jan. 8, 1876–April 29, 1933; House 1919–April 29, 1933.

Briggs, Frank Obadiah (son of James Frankland Briggs) (R N.J.) Aug. 12, 1851–May 8, 1913; Senate 1907–13.

Briggs, Frank Parks (D Mo.) Feb. 25, 1894–Sept. 23, 1992; Senate Jan. 18, 1945–47.

Briggs, George (R N.Y.) May 6, 1805–June 1, 1869; House 1849–53 (Whig), 1859–61.

Briggs, George Nixon (W Mass.) April 12, 1796–Sept. 11, 1861; House 1831–43 (1831–35 Anti-Jacksonian); Gov. Jan. 3, 1844–Jan. 11, 1851.

Briggs, James Frankland (father of Frank Obadiah Briggs) (R N.H.) Oct. 23, 1827–Jan. 21, 1905; House 1877–83.

Brigham, Elbert Sidney (R Vt.) Oct. 19, 1877–July 5, 1962; House 1925–31.

Brigham, Elijah (F Mass.) July 7, 1751–Feb. 22, 1816; House 1811–Feb. 22, 1816.

Brigham, Lewis Alexander (R N.J.) Jan. 2, 1831–Feb. 19, 1885; House 1879–81.

Bright, Jesse David (D Ind.) Dec. 18, 1812–May 20, 1875; Senate 1845–Feb. 5, 1862; elected Pres. pro tempore Dec. 5, 1854, June 11, 1856, June 12, 1860.

Bright, John Morgan (D Tenn.) Jan. 20, 1817–Oct. 3, 1911; House 1871–81.

Brinkerhoff, Henry Roelif (cousin of Jacob Brinkerhoff) (D Ohio) Sept. 23, 1787–April 30, 1844; House 1843–April 30, 1844.

Brinkerhoff, Jacob (cousin of Henry Roelif Brinkerhoff) (D Ohio) Aug. 31, 1810–July 19, 1880; House 1843–47.

Brinkley, Jack Thomas (D Ga.) Dec. 22, 1930–   ; House 1967–83.

Brinson, Samuel Mitchell (D N.C.) March 20, 1870–April 13, 1922; House 1919–April 13, 1922.

Brisbin, John (D Pa.) July 13, 1818–Feb. 3, 1880; House Jan. 13–March 3, 1851.

Bristow, Francis Marion (O Ky.) Aug. 11, 1804–June 10, 1864; House Dec. 4, 1854–55 (Whig), 1859–61.

Bristow, Henry (R N.Y.) June 5, 1840–Oct. 11, 1906; House 1901–03.

Bristow, Joseph Little (R Kan.) July 22, 1861–July 14, 1944; Senate 1909–15.

Britt, Charles Robin (D N.C.) June 29, 1942–   ; House 1983–85.

Britt, James Jefferson (R N.C.) March 4, 1861–Dec. 26, 1939; House 1915–17, March 1–3, 1919.

Britten, Frederick Albert (R Ill.) Nov. 18, 1871–May 4, 1946; House 1913–35.

Broadhead, James Overton (D Mo.) May 29, 1819–Aug. 7, 1898; House 1883–85.

Brock, Lawrence (D Neb.) Aug. 16, 1906–Aug. 28, 1968; House 1959–61.

Brock, William Emerson (grandfather of William Emerson Brock III) (D Tenn.) March 14, 1872–Aug. 5, 1950; Senate Sept. 2, 1929–31.

Brock, William Emerson III (grandson of William Emerson Brock) (R Tenn.) Nov. 23, 1930–   ; House 1963–71; Senate 1971–77; Chrmn. Rep. Nat. Comm. 1977–81; Secy. of Labor April 29, 1985–Oct. 31, 1987.

Brockenbrough, William Henry (D Fla.) Feb. 23, 1812–Jan. 28, 1850; House Jan. 24, 1846–47.

Brockson, Franklin (D Del.) Aug. 6, 1865–March 16, 1942; House 1913–15.

Brockway, John Hall (W Conn.) Jan. 31, 1801–July 29, 1870; House 1839–43.

Brodbeck, Andrew R. (D Pa.) April 11, 1860–Feb. 27, 1937; House 1913–15, 1917–19.

Broderick, Case (cousin of David Colbreth Broderick and Andrew Kennedy) (R Kan.) Sept. 23, 1839–April 1, 1920; House 1891–99.

Broderick, David Colbreth (cousin of Andrew Kennedy and Case Broderick) (D Calif.) Feb. 4, 1820–Sept. 16, 1859; Senate 1857–Sept. 16, 1859.

Brodhead, John (J N.H.) Oct. 5, 1770–April 7, 1838; House 1829–33.

Brodhead, John Curtis (D N.Y.) Oct. 27, 1780–Jan. 2, 1859; House 1831–33 (Jacksonian), 1837–39.

Brodhead, Joseph Davis (son of Richard Brodhead) (– Pa.) Jan. 12, 1859–April 23, 1920; House 1907–09.

Brodhead, Richard (father of Joseph Brodhead) (D Pa.) Jan. 5, 1811–Sept. 16, 1863; House 1843–49; Senate 1851–57.

Brodhead, William McNulty (D Mich.) Sept. 12, 1941– ; House 1975–83.

Brogden, Curtis Hooks (R N.C.) Nov. 6, 1816–Jan. 5, 1901; House 1877–79; Gov. July 11, 1874–Jan. 1, 1877.

Bromberg, Frederick George (LR Ala.) June 19, 1837–Sept. 4, 1930; House 1873–75.

Bromwell, Henry Pelham Holmes (R Ill.) Aug. 26, 1823–Jan. 7, 1903; House 1865–69.

Bromwell, Jacob Henry (R Ohio) May 11, 1848–June 4, 1924; House Dec. 3, 1894–1903.

Bromwell, James Edward (R Iowa) March 26, 1920– ; House 1961–65.

Bronson, David (W Maine) Feb. 8, 1800–Nov. 20, 1863; House May 31, 1841–43.

Bronson, Isaac Hopkins (D N.Y.) Oct. 16, 1802–Aug. 13, 1855; House 1837–39.

Broocks, Moses Lycurgus (D Texas) Nov. 1, 1864–May 27, 1908; House 1905–07.

Brooke, Edward William III (R Mass.) Oct. 26, 1919– ; Senate 1967–79.

Brooke, Walker (W Miss.) Dec. 25, 1813–Feb. 18, 1869; Senate Feb. 18, 1852–53.

Brookhart, Smith Wildman (R Iowa) Feb. 2, 1869–Nov. 15, 1944; Senate Nov. 7, 1922–April 12, 1926, 1927–33 (Nov. 7, 1922–25 Progressive Republican).

Brooks, Charles Wayland (R Ill.) March 8, 1897–Jan. 14, 1957; Senate Nov. 22, 1940–49; Chrmn. Senate Rules and Administration 1947–49.

Brooks, David (F N.Y.) 1756–Aug. 30, 1838; House 1797–99.

Brooks, Edward Schroeder (R Pa.) June 14, 1867–July 12, 1957; House 1919–23.

Brooks, Edwin Bruce (cousin of Edmund Howard Hinshaw) (R Ill.) Sept. 20, 1868–Sept. 18, 1933; House 1919–23.

Brooks, Franklin Eli (R Colo.) Nov. 19, 1860–Feb. 7, 1916; House 1903–07.

Brooks, George Merrick (R Mass.) July 26, 1824–Sept. 22, 1893; House Nov. 2, 1869–May 13, 1872.

Brooks, Jack Bascom (D Texas) Dec. 18, 1922– ; House 1953–95; Chrmn. House Government Operations 1975–89; Chrmn. House Judiciary 1989–95.

Brooks, James (D N.Y.) Nov. 10, 1810–April 30, 1873; House 1849–53 (Whig), 1863–April 7, 1866, 1867–April 30, 1873.

Brooks, Joshua Twing (D Pa.) Feb. 27, 1884–Feb. 7, 1956; House 1933–37.

Brooks, Micah (R N.Y.) May 14, 1775–July 7, 1857; House 1815–17.

Brooks, Overton (nephew of John Holmes Overton) (D La.) Dec. 21, 1897–Sept. 16, 1961; House 1937–Sept. 16, 1961; Chrmn. House Science and Astronautics 1959–61.

Brooks, Preston Smith (D S.C.) Aug. 5, 1819–Jan. 27, 1857; House 1853–July 15, 1856, Aug. 1, 1856–Jan. 27, 1857.

Brookshire, Elijah Voorhees (D Ind.) Aug. 15, 1856–April 14, 1936; House 1889–95.

Broom, Jacob (son of James Madison Broom) (AP Pa.) July 25, 1808–Nov. 28, 1864; House 1855–57.

Broom, James Madison (father of Jacob Broom) (F Del.) 1776–Jan. 15, 1850; House 1805–07.

Broomall, John Martin (R Pa.) Jan. 19, 1816–June 3, 1894; House 1863–69.

Broomfield, William S. (R Mich.) April 28, 1922– ; House 1957–93.

Brophy, John Charles (R Wis.) Oct. 8, 1901–Dec. 26, 1976; House 1947–49.

Brosius, Marriott (R Pa.) March 7, 1843–March 16, 1901; House 1889–March 16, 1901.

Brotzman, Donald Glenn (R Colo.) June 28, 1922– ; House 1963–65, 1967–75.

Broughton, Joseph Melville (D N.C.) Nov. 17, 1888–March 6, 1949; Senate Dec. 31, 1948–March 6, 1949; Gov. Jan. 9, 1941–Jan. 4, 1945.

Broussard, Edwin Sidney (brother of Robert Foligny Broussard) (D La.) Dec. 4, 1874–Nov. 19, 1934; Senate 1921–33.

Broussard, Robert Foligny (brother of Edwin Sidney Broussard) (D La.) Aug. 17, 1864–April 12, 1918; House 1897–1915; Senate 1915–April 12, 1918.

Browder, Glen (D Ala.) Jan. 15, 1943– ; House April 18, 1989–97.

Brower, John Morehead (R N.C.) July 19, 1845–Aug. 5, 1913; House 1887–91.

Brown, Aaron Venable (D Tenn.) Aug. 15, 1795–March 8, 1859; House 1839–45; Gov. Oct. 14, 1845–Oct. 16, 1847; Postmaster Gen. March 7, 1857–March 8, 1859.

Brown, Albert Gallatin (D Miss.) May 31, 1813–June 12, 1880; House 1839–41, 1847–53; Senate Jan. 7, 1854–Jan. 12, 1861; Gov. Jan. 10, 1844–Jan. 10, 1848.

Brown, Anson (W N.Y.) 1800–June 14, 1840; House 1839–June 14, 1840.

Brown, Arthur (R Utah) March 8, 1843–Dec. 12, 1906; Senate Jan. 22, 1896–97.

Brown, Bedford (D N.C.) June 6, 1795–Dec. 6, 1870; Senate Dec. 9, 1829–Nov. 16, 1840.

Brown, Benjamin (nephew of John Brown) (F Mass.) Sept. 23, 1756–Sept. 17, 1831; House 1815–17.

Brown, Benjamin Gratz (grandson of John Brown of Va. and Ky.) (UU Mo.) May 28, 1826–Dec. 13, 1885; Senate Nov. 13, 1863–67; Gov. Jan. 9, 1871–Jan. 8, 1873 (Liberal Republican).

Brown, Charles (D Pa.) Sept. 23, 1797–Sept. 4, 1883; House 1841–43, 1847–49.

Brown, Charles Elwood (R Ohio) July 4, 1834–May 22, 1904; House 1885–89.

Brown, Charles Harrison (D Mo.) Oct. 22, 1920– ; House 1957–61.

Brown, Clarence J. (father of Clarence J. Brown Jr.) (R Ohio) July 14, 1893–Aug. 23, 1965; House 1939–Aug. 23, 1965.

Brown, Clarence J. Jr. (son of Clarence J. Brown) (R Ohio) June 18, 1927– ; House Nov. 2, 1965–83.

Brown, Corrine (D Fla.) Nov. 11, 1946– ; House 1993– .

Brown, Elias (J Md.) May 9, 1793–July 7, 1857; House 1829–31.

Brown, Ernest S. (R Nev.) Sept. 25, 1903–July 23, 1965; Senate Oct. 1–Dec. 1, 1954.

Brown, Ethan Allen (– Ohio) July 4, 1776–Feb. 24, 1852; Senate Jan. 3, 1822–25; Gov. Dec. 14, 1818–Jan. 4, 1822 (Democratic Republican).

Brown, Foster Vincent (father of Joseph Edgar Brown) (R Tenn.) Dec. 24, 1852–March 26, 1937; House 1895–97.

Brown, Fred Herbert (D N.H.) April 12, 1879–Feb. 3, 1955; Senate 1933–39; Gov. Jan. 4, 1923–Jan. 1, 1925.

Brown, Garry Eldridge (R Mich.) Aug. 12, 1923–Aug. 27, 1998; House 1967–79.

Brown, George Edward Jr. (D Calif.) March 6, 1920–July 15, 1999; House 1963–71, 1973–July 15, 1999; Chrmn. House Science, Space, and Technology 1991–95.

Brown, George Hanks (Hank) (R Colo.) Feb. 12, 1940– ; House 1981–91; Senate 1991–97.

Brown, George Houston (W N.J.) Feb. 12, 1810–Aug. 1, 1865; House 1851–53.

Brown, James (brother of John Brown of Va. and Ky., cousin of John Breckinridge, James Breckinridge, and Francis Preston) (– La.) Sept. 11, 1776–April 7, 1835; Senate Feb. 5, 1813–17, 1819–Dec. 10, 1823.

Brown, James Sproat (D Wis.) Feb. 1, 1824–April 15, 1878; House 1863–65.

Brown, James W. (son-in-law of Thomas Marshall Howe) (IR Pa.) July 14, 1844–Oct. 23, 1909; House 1903–05.

Brown, Jason Brevoort (D Ind.) Feb. 26, 1839–March 10, 1898; House 1889–95.

Brown, Jeremiah (W Pa.) April 14, 1785–March 2, 1858; House 1841–45.

Brown, John (uncle of Benjamin Brown, grandfather of John Brown Francis) (F R.I.) Jan. 27, 1736–Sept. 20, 1803; House 1799–1801; Cont. Cong. (elected but did not attend) 1784, 1785.

Brown, John (R Md.) ?–Dec. 13, 1815; House 1809–10.

Brown, John (brother of James Brown, grandfather of Benjamin Gratz Brown, cousin of John Breckinridge, James Breckinridge, and Francis Preston) (– Va./Ky.) Sept. 12, 1757–Aug. 29, 1837; House 1789–June 1, 1792 (Ky. district of Va.); Senate June 18, 1792–1805 (Ky.); elected Pres. pro tempore Oct. 17, 1803, Jan. 23, 1804; Cont. Cong. (Ky. district of Va.) 1787–88.

Brown, John (– Pa.) Aug. 12, 1772–Oct. 12, 1845; House 1821–25.

Brown, John Brewer (D Md.) May 13, 1836–May 16, 1898; House Nov. 8, 1892–93.

Brown, John Robert (R Va.) Jan. 14, 1842–Aug. 4, 1927; House 1887–89.

Brown, John W. (J N.Y.) Oct. 11, 1796–Sept. 6, 1875; House 1833–37.

Brown, John Young (nephew of Bryan Rust Young and William Singleton Young) (D Ky.) June 28, 1835–Jan. 11, 1904; House 1859–61, 1873–77; Gov. Sept. 1, 1891–Dec. 10, 1895.

Brown, John Young (D Ky.) Feb. 1, 1900–June 16, 1985; House 1933–35.

Brown, Joseph Edgar (son of Foster Vincent Brown) (R Tenn.) Feb. 11, 1880–June 13, 1939; House 1921–23.

Brown, Joseph Emerson (D Ga.) April 15, 1821–Nov. 30, 1894; Senate May 26, 1880–91; Gov. Nov. 6, 1857–June 17, 1865.

Brown, Lathrop (D N.Y.) Feb. 26, 1883–Nov. 28, 1959; House 1913–15.

Brown, Milton (W Tenn.) Feb. 28, 1804–May 15, 1883; House 1841–47.

Brown, Norris (R Neb.) May 2, 1863–Jan. 5, 1960; Senate 1907–13.

Brown, Paul (D Ga.) March 31, 1880–Sept. 24, 1961; House July 5, 1933–61.

Brown, Prentiss Marsh (D Mich.) June 18, 1889–Dec. 19, 1973; House 1933–Nov. 18, 1936; Senate Nov. 19, 1936–43.

Brown, Robert (R Pa.) Dec. 25, 1744–Feb. 26, 1823; House Dec. 4, 1798–1815.

Brown, Seth W. (R Ohio) Jan. 4, 1841–Feb. 24, 1923; House 1897–1901.

Brown, Sherrod (D Ohio) Nov. 9, 1952– ; House 1993–97.

Brown, Titus (– N.H.) Feb. 11, 1786–Jan. 29, 1849; House 1825–29.

Brown, Webster Everett (R Wis.) July 16, 1851–Dec. 14, 1929; House 1901–07.

Brown, William (– Ky.) April 19, 1779–Oct. 6, 1833; House 1819–21.

Brown, William Gay (father of William Gay Brown Jr.) (UU W.Va.) Sept. 25, 1800–April 19, 1884; House 1845–49 (Democrat Va.), 1861–63 (Unionist Va.), Dec. 7, 1863–65.

Brown, William Gay Jr. (son of William Gay Brown) (D W.Va.) April 7, 1856–March 9, 1916; House 1911–March 9, 1916.

Brown, William John (D Ind.) Aug. 15, 1805–March 18, 1857; House 1843–45, 1849–51.

Brown, William Ripley (R Kan.) July 16, 1840–March 3, 1916; House 1875–77.

Brown, William Wallace (R Pa.) April 22, 1836–Nov. 4, 1926; House 1883–87.

Brownback, Sam (R Kan.) Sept. 12, 1956– ; House 1995–Nov. 6, 1996; Senate Nov. 27, 1996– .

Browne, Charles (D N.J.) Sept. 28, 1875–Aug. 17, 1947; House 1923–25.

Browne, Edward Everts (R Wis.) Feb. 16, 1868–Nov. 23, 1945; House 1913–31.

Browne, George Huntington (D/Const U R.I.) Jan. 6, 1811–Sept. 26, 1885; House 1861–63.

Browne, Thomas Henry Bayly (R Va.) Feb. 8, 1844–Aug. 27, 1892; House 1887–91.

Browne, Thomas McLelland (R Ind.) April 19, 1829–July 17, 1891; House 1877–91.

Browning, Gordon Weaver (D Tenn.) Nov. 22, 1889–May 23, 1976; House 1923–35; Gov. Jan. 15, 1937–Jan. 16, 1939, Jan. 17, 1949–Jan. 15, 1953.

Browning, Orville Hickman (R Ill.) Feb. 10, 1806–Aug. 10, 1881; Senate June 26, 1861–Jan. 12, 1863; Secy. of the Interior Sept. 1, 1866–March 4, 1869.

Browning, William John (R N.J.) April 11, 1850–March 24, 1920; House Nov. 7, 1911–March 24, 1920.

Brownlow, Walter Preston (nephew of William Gannaway Brownlow) (R Tenn.) March 27, 1851–July 8, 1910; House 1897–July 8, 1910.

Brownlow, William Gannaway (uncle of Walter Preston Brownlow) (R Tenn.) Aug. 29, 1805–April 29, 1877; Senate 1869–75; Gov. April 5, 1865–Feb. 25, 1869.

Brownson, Charles Bruce (R Ind.) Feb. 5, 1914–Aug. 4, 1988; House 1951–59.

Broyhill, James Thomas (R N.C.) Aug. 19, 1927– ; House 1963–July 14, 1986; Senate July 14–Nov. 10, 1986.

Broyhill, Joel Thomas (R Va.) Nov. 4, 1919– ; House 1953–Dec. 31, 1974.

Bruce, Blanche Kelso (R Miss.) March 1, 1841–March 17, 1898; Senate 1875–81.

Bruce, Donald Cogley (R Ind.) April 27, 1921–Aug. 31, 1969; House 1961–65.

Bruce, Phineas (F Mass.) June 7, 1762–Oct. 4, 1809; elected to the House for the term beginning 1803 but did not serve.

Bruce, Terry L. (D Ill.) March 25, 1944– ; House 1985–93.

Bruce, William Cabell (D Md.) March 12, 1860–May 9, 1946; Senate 1923–29.

Brucker, Ferdinand (D Mich.) Jan. 8, 1858–March 3, 1904; House 1897–99.

Bruckner, Henry (D N.Y.) June 17, 1871–April 14, 1942; House 1913–Dec. 31, 1917.

Brumbaugh, Clement Laird (D Ohio) Feb. 28, 1863–Sept. 28, 1921; House 1913–21.

Brumbaugh, David Emmert (R Pa.) Oct. 8, 1894–April 22, 1977; House Nov. 2, 1943–47.

Brumm, Charles Napoleon (father of George Franklin Brumm) (R Pa.) June 9, 1838–Jan. 11, 1917; House 1881–89 (1881–85 Greenbacker), 1895–99, Nov. 6, 1906–Jan. 4, 1909.

Brumm, George Franklin (son of Charles Napoleon Brumm) (R Pa.) Jan. 24, 1880–May 29, 1934; House 1923–27, 1929–May 29, 1934.

Brundidge, Stephen Jr. (D Ark.) Jan. 1, 1857–Jan. 14, 1938; House 1897–1909.

Brunner, David B. (D Pa.) March 7, 1835–Nov. 29, 1903; House 1889–93.

Brunner, William Frank (D N.Y.) Sept. 15, 1887–April 23, 1965; House 1929–Sept. 27, 1935.

Brunsdale, Clarence Norman (R N.D.) July 9, 1891–Jan. 27, 1978; Senate Nov. 19, 1959–Aug. 7, 1960; Gov. Jan. 3, 1951–Jan. 9, 1957.

Brush, Henry (– Ohio) June 1778–Jan. 19, 1855; House 1819–21.

Bruyn, Andrew DeWitt (D N.Y.) Nov. 18, 1790–July 27, 1838; House 1837–July 27, 1838.

Bryan, Guy Morrison (D Texas) Jan. 12, 1821–June 4, 1901; House 1857–59.

Bryan, Henry H. (– Tenn.) ?–May 7, 1835; House 1819–21 (elected for the term beginning 1821 but did not serve).

Bryan, James Wesley (Prog. Wash.) March 11, 1874–Aug. 26, 1956; House 1913–15.

Bryan, John Heritage (– N.C.) Nov. 4, 1798–May 19, 1870; House 1825–29.

Bryan, Joseph (R Ga.) Aug. 18, 1773–Sept. 12, 1812; House 1803–06.

Bryan, Joseph Hunter (R N.C.) ?–?; House 1815–19.

Bryan, Nathan (R N.C.) 1748–June 4, 1798; House 1795–June 4, 1798.

Bryan, Nathan Philemon (brother of William James Bryan) (D Fla.) April 23, 1872–Aug. 8, 1935; Senate 1911–17.

Bryan, Richard H. (D Nev.) July 16, 1937– ; Senate 1989– ; Gov. Jan. 3, 1983–Jan. 3, 1989; Chrmn. Senate Select Committee on Ethics 1993–95.

Bryan, William James (brother of Nathan Philemon Bryan) (D Fla.) Oct. 10, 1876–March 22, 1908; Senate Dec. 26, 1907–March 22, 1908.

Bryan, William Jennings (father of Ruth Bryan Owen) (D Neb.) March 19, 1860–July 26, 1925; House 1891–95; Secy. of State March 5, 1913–June 9, 1915.

Bryant, Ed (R Tenn.) Sept. 7, 1948– ; House 1995– .

Bryant, John Wiley (D Texas) Feb. 22, 1947– ; House 1983–97.

Bryce, Lloyd Stephens (D N.Y.) Sept. 4, 1851–April 2, 1917; House 1887–89.

Bryson, Joseph Raleigh (D S.C.) Jan. 18, 1893–March 10, 1953; House 1939–March 10, 1953.

Buchanan, Andrew (D Pa.) April 8, 1780–Dec. 2, 1848; House 1835–39 (1835–37 Jacksonian).

Buchanan, Frank (D Ill.) June 14, 1862–April 18, 1930; House 1911–17.

Buchanan, Frank (husband of Vera Daerr Buchanan) (D Pa.) Dec. 1, 1902–April 27, 1951; House May 21, 1946–April 27, 1951.

Buchanan, Hugh (D Ga.) Sept. 15, 1823–June 11, 1890; House 1881–85.

Buchanan, James (D Pa.) April 23, 1791–June 1, 1868; House 1821–31 (no party); Senate Dec. 6, 1834–March 5, 1845; Secy. of State March 10, 1845–March 7, 1849; President 1857–61.

Buchanan, James (R N.J.) June 17, 1839–Oct. 30, 1900; House 1885–93.

Buchanan, James Paul (cousin of Edward William Pou) (D Texas) April 30, 1867–Feb. 22, 1937; House April 5, 1913–Feb. 22, 1937.

Buchanan, John Alexander (D Va.) Oct. 7, 1843–Sept. 2, 1921; House 1889–93.

Buchanan, John Hall Jr. (R Ala.) March 19, 1928– ; House 1965–81.

Buchanan, Vera Daerr (widow of Frank Buchanan) (D Pa.) July 20, 1902–Nov. 26, 1955; House July 24, 1951–Nov. 26, 1955.

Bucher, John Conrad (J Pa.) Dec. 28, 1792–Oct. 15, 1851; House 1831–33.

Buck, Alfred Eliab (R Ala.) Feb. 7, 1832–Dec. 4, 1902; House 1869–71.

Buck, Charles Francis (D La.) Nov. 5, 1841–Jan. 19, 1918; House 1895–97.

Buck, Clayton Douglass (great-great-nephew of John Middleton Clayton) (R Del.) March 21, 1890–Jan. 27, 1965; Senate 1943–49; Chrmn. Senate District of Columbia 1947–49; Gov. Jan. 15, 1929–Jan. 19, 1937.

Buck, Daniel (father of Daniel Azro Ashley Buck) (F Vt.) Nov. 9, 1753–Aug. 16, 1816; House 1795–97.

Buck, Daniel Azro Ashley (son of Daniel Buck) (– Vt.) April 19, 1789–Dec. 24, 1841; House 1823–25, 1827–29.

Buck, Ellsworth Brewer (R N.Y.) July 3, 1892–Aug. 14, 1970; House June 6, 1944–49.

Buck, Frank Henry (D Calif.) Sept. 23, 1887–Sept. 17, 1942; House 1933–Sept. 17, 1942.

Buck, John Ransom (R Conn.) Dec. 6, 1835–Feb. 6, 1917; House 1881–83, 1885–87.

Buckalew, Charles Rollin (D Pa.) Dec. 28, 1821–May 19, 1899; Senate 1863–69; House 1887–91.

Buckbee, John Theodore (R Ill.) Aug. 1, 1871–April 23, 1936; House 1927–April 23, 1936.

Buckingham, William Alfred (R Conn.) May 28, 1804–Feb. 5, 1875; Senate 1869–Feb. 5, 1875; Gov. May 5, 1858–May 2, 1866.

Buckland, Ralph Pomeroy (R Ohio) Jan. 20, 1812–May 27, 1892; House 1865–69.

Buckler, Richard Thompson (FL Minn.) Oct. 27, 1865–Jan. 23, 1950; House 1935–43.

Buckley, Charles Anthony (D N.Y.) June 23, 1890–Jan. 22, 1967; House 1935–65; Chrmn. House Public Works 1951–53, 1955–65.

Buckley, Charles Waldron (R Ala.) Feb. 18, 1835–Dec. 4, 1906; House July 21, 1868–73.

Buckley, James Lane (C N.Y.) March 9, 1923– ; Senate 1971–77.

Buckley, James Richard (D Ill.) Nov. 18, 1870–June 22, 1945; House 1923–25.

Buckley, James Vincent (D Ill.) May 15, 1894–July 30, 1954; House 1949–51.

Buckman, Clarence Bennett (R Minn.) April 1, 1851–March 1, 1917; House 1903–07.

Buckner, Alexander (– Mo.) 1785–June 6, 1833; Senate 1831–June 6, 1833.

Buckner, Aylett Hawes (nephew of Aylett Hawes, cousin of Richard Hawes and Albert Gallatin Hawes) (D Mo.) Dec. 14, 1816–Feb. 5, 1894; House 1873–85.

Buckner, Aylette (son of Richard Aylett Buckner) (W Ky.) July 21, 1806–July 3, 1869; House 1847–49.

Buckner, Richard Aylett (father of Aylette Buckner) (– Ky.) July 16, 1763–Dec. 8, 1847; House 1823–29.

Budd, James Herbert (D Calif.) May 18, 1851–July 30, 1908; House 1883–85; Gov. Jan. 11, 1895–Jan. 3, 1899.

Budge, Hamer Harold (R Idaho) Nov. 21, 1910– ; House 1951–61.

Buechner, John William "Jack" (R Mo.) June 6, 1940– ; House 1987–91.

Buel, Alexander Woodruff (D Mich.) Dec. 13, 1813–April 19, 1868; House 1849–51.

Buell, Alexander Hamilton (D N.Y.) July 14, 1801–Jan. 29, 1853; House 1851–Jan. 29, 1853.

Buffett, Howard Homan (R Neb.) Aug. 13, 1903–April 30, 1964; House 1943–49, 1951–53.

Buffinton, James (R Mass.) March 16, 1817–March 7, 1875; House 1855–63, 1869–March 7, 1875.

Buffington, Joseph (W Pa.) Nov. 27, 1803–Feb. 3, 1872; House 1843–47.

Buffum, Joseph Jr. (– N.H.) Sept. 23, 1784–Feb. 24, 1874; House 1819–21.

Bugg, Robert Malone (W Tenn.) Jan. 20, 1805–Feb. 18, 1887; House 1853–55.

Bulkeley, Morgan Gardner (cousin of Edwin Denison Morgan) (R Conn.) Dec. 26, 1837–Nov. 6, 1922; Senate 1905–11; Gov. Jan. 10, 1889–Jan. 4, 1893.

Bulkley, Robert Johns (D Ohio) Oct. 8, 1880–July 21, 1965; House 1911–15; Senate Dec. 1, 1930–39.

Bull, John (– Mo.) 1803–Feb. 1863; House 1833–35.

Bull, Melville (R R.I.) Sept. 29, 1854–July 5, 1909; House 1895–1903.

Bullard, Henry Adams (W La.) Sept. 9, 1788–April 17, 1851; House 1831–Jan. 4, 1834 (Anti-Jacksonian), Dec. 5, 1850–51.

Bulloch, William Bellinger (R Ga.) 1777–May 6, 1852; Senate April 8–Nov. 6, 1813.

Bullock, Robert (D Fla.) Dec. 8, 1828–July 27, 1905; House 1889–93.

Bullock, Stephen (F Mass.) Oct. 10, 1735–Feb. 2, 1816; House 1797–99.

Bullock, Wingfield (– Ky.) ?–Oct. 13, 1821; House 1821–Oct. 13, 1821.

Bulow, William John (D S.D.) Jan. 13, 1869–Feb. 26, 1960; Senate 1931–43; Gov. Jan. 4, 1927–Jan. 6, 1931.

Bulwinkle, Alfred Lee (D N.C.) April 21, 1883–Aug. 31, 1950; House 1921–29, 1931–Aug. 31, 1950.

Bumpers, Dale Leon (D Ark.) Aug. 12, 1925– ; Senate 1975–99; Chrmn. Senate Small Business 1987–95; Gov. Jan. 12, 1971–Jan. 2, 1975.

Bunch, Samuel (White supporter Tenn.) Dec. 4, 1786–Sept. 5, 1849; House 1833–37 (1833–35 Jacksonian).

Bundy, Hezekiah Sanford (R Ohio) Aug. 15, 1817–Dec. 12, 1895; House 1865–67, 1873–75, Dec. 4, 1893–95.

Bundy, Solomon (R N.Y.) May 22, 1823–Jan. 13, 1889; House 1877–79.

Bunker, Berkeley Lloyd (D Nev.) Aug. 12, 1906–Jan. 21, 1999; Senate Nov. 27, 1940–Dec. 6, 1942; House 1945–47.

Bunn, Benjamin Hickman (D N.C.) Oct. 19, 1844–Aug. 25, 1907; House 1889–95.

Bunn, Jim (R Ore.) Dec. 12, 1956– ; House 1995–97.

Bunnell, Frank Charles (R Pa.) March 19, 1842–Sept. 11, 1911; House Dec. 24, 1872–73 (no party), 1885–89.

Bunner, Rudolph (– N.Y.) Aug. 17, 1779–July 16, 1837; House 1827–29.

Bunning, James Paul David (R Ky.) Oct. 23, 1931– ; House 1987–99; Senate 1999– .

Bunting, Thomas Lathrop (D N.Y.) April 24, 1844–Dec. 27, 1898; House 1891–93.

Burch, John Chilton (D Calif.) Feb. 1, 1826–Aug. 31, 1885; House 1859–61.

Burch, Thomas Granville (D Va.) July 3, 1869–March 20, 1951; House 1931–May 31, 1946; Senate May 31–Nov. 5, 1946.

Burchard, Horatio Chapin (R Ill.) Sept. 22, 1825–May 14, 1908; House Dec. 6, 1869–79.

Burchard, Samuel Dickinson (D Wis.) July 17, 1836–Sept. 1, 1901; House 1875–77.

Burchill, Thomas Francis (D N.Y.) Aug. 3, 1882–March 28, 1960; House 1943–45.

Burd, George (– Pa.) 1793–Jan. 13, 1844; House 1831–35.

Burdett, Samuel Swinfin (R Mo.) Feb. 21, 1836–Sept. 24, 1914; House 1869–73.

Burdick, Clark (R R.I.) Jan. 13, 1868–Aug. 27, 1948; House 1919–33.

Burdick, Jocelyn Birch (widow of Quentin Northrop Burdick, daughter-in-law of Usher Lloyd Burdick, sister-in-law of Robert Woodrow Levering,) (D N.D.) Feb. 6, 1922– ; Senate Sept. 16–Dec. 14, 1992.

Burdick, Quentin Northrop (husband of Jocelyn Birch Burdick, son of Usher Lloyd Burdick, brother-in-law of Robert Woodrow Levering) (D N.D.) June 19, 1908–Sept. 8, 1992; House 1959–Aug. 8, 1960; Senate Aug. 8, 1960–Sept. 8, 1992; Chrmn. Senate Environment and Public Works 1987–92.

Burdick, Theodore Weld (R Iowa) Oct. 7, 1836–July 16, 1898; House 1877–79.

Burdick, Usher Lloyd (father of Quentin Northrop Burdick, father-in-law of Jocelyn Birch Burdick, father-in-law of Robert Woodrow Levering) (R N.D.) Feb. 21, 1879–Aug. 19, 1960; House 1935–45, 1949–59.

Burgener, Clair Walter (R Calif.) Dec. 5, 1921– ; House 1973–83.

Burges, Dempsey (R N.C.) 1751–Jan. 13, 1800; House 1795–99.

Burges, Tristam (great-great-uncle of Theodore Francis Green) (AJ R.I.) Feb. 26, 1770–Oct. 13, 1853; House 1825–35 (1825–31 no party).

Burgess, George Farmer (D Texas) Sept. 21, 1861–Dec. 31, 1919; House 1901–17.

Burgin, William Olin (D N.C.) July 28, 1877–April 11, 1946; House 1939–April 11, 1946.

Burk, Henry (R Pa.) Sept. 26, 1850–Dec. 5, 1903; House 1901–Dec. 5, 1903.

Burke, Aedanus (– S.C.) June 16, 1743–March 30, 1802; House 1789–91.

Burke, Charles Henry (R S.D.) April 1, 1861–April 7, 1944; House 1899–1907, 1909–15.

Burke, Edmund (D N.H.) Jan. 23, 1809–Jan. 25, 1882; House 1839–45.

Burke, Edward Raymond (D Neb.) Nov. 28, 1880–Nov. 4, 1968; House 1933–35; Senate 1935–41.

Burke, Frank Welsh (D Ky.) June 1, 1920– ; House 1959–63.

Burke, J. Herbert (R Fla.) Jan. 14, 1913–June 16, 1993; House 1967–79.

Burke, James Anthony (D Mass.) March 30, 1910–Oct. 13, 1983; House 1959–79.

Burke, James Francis (R Pa.) Oct. 21, 1867–Aug. 8, 1932; House 1905–15.

Burke, John Harley (D Calif.) June 2, 1894–May 14, 1951; House 1933–35.

Burke, Michael Edmund (D Wis.) Oct. 15, 1863–Dec. 12, 1918; House 1911–17.

Burke, Raymond Hugh (R Ohio) Nov. 4, 1881–Aug. 18, 1954; House 1947–49.

Burke, Robert Emmet (D Texas) Aug. 1, 1847–June 5, 1901; House 1897–June 5, 1901.

Burke, Thomas A. (D Ohio) Oct. 30, 1898–Dec. 5, 1971; Senate Nov. 10, 1953–Dec. 2, 1954.

Burke, Thomas Henry (D Ohio) May 6, 1904–Sept. 12, 1959; House 1949–51.

Burke, William Joseph (R Pa.) Sept. 25, 1862–Nov. 7, 1925; House 1919–23.

Burke, Yvonne Brathwaite (D Calif.) Oct. 5, 1932– ; House 1973–79.

Burkett, Elmer Jacob (R Neb.) Dec. 1, 1867–May 23, 1935; House 1899–March 4, 1905; Senate 1905–11.

Burkhalter, Everett Glen (D Calif.) Jan. 19, 1897–May 24, 1975; House 1963–65.

Burleigh, Edwin Chick (R Maine) Nov. 27, 1843–June 16, 1916; House June 21, 1897–1911; Senate 1913–June 16, 1916; Gov. Jan. 2, 1889–Jan. 4, 1893.

Burleigh, Henry Gordon (R N.Y.) June 2, 1832–Aug. 10, 1900; House 1883–87.

Burleigh, John Holmes (son of William Burleigh) (R Maine) Oct. 9, 1822–Dec. 5, 1877; House 1873–77.

Burleigh, Walter Atwood (R Dakota) Oct. 25, 1820–March 7, 1896; House (Terr. Del.) 1865–69.

Burleigh, William (father of John Holmes Burleigh) (– Maine) Oct. 24, 1785–July 2, 1827; House 1823–July 2, 1827.

Burleson, Albert Sidney (D Texas) June 7, 1863–Nov. 24, 1937; House 1899–March 6, 1913; Postmaster Gen. March 5, 1913–March 4, 1921.

Burleson, Omar Truman (D Texas) March 19, 1906–May 14, 1991; House 1947–Dec. 31, 1978; Chrmn. House Administration 1955–68.

Burlingame, Anson (R Mass.) Nov. 14, 1820–Feb. 23, 1870; House 1855–61 (1855–57 American Party).

Burlison, William Dean (D Mo.) March 15, 1933– ; House 1969–81.

Burnell, Barker (W Mass.) Jan. 30, 1798–June 15, 1843; House 1841–June 15, 1843.

Burnes, Daniel Dee (D Mo.) Jan. 4, 1851–Nov. 2, 1899; House 1893–95.

Burnes, James Nelson (D Mo.) Aug. 22, 1827–Jan. 23, 1889; House 1883–Jan. 23, 1889.

Burnet, Jacob (F N.J.) Feb. 22, 1770–May 10, 1853; Senate Dec. 10, 1828–31.

Burnett, Edward (D Mass.) March 16, 1849–Nov. 5, 1925; House 1887–89.

Burnett, Henry Cornelius (D Ky.) Oct. 5, 1825–Oct. 1, 1866; House 1855–Dec. 3, 1861.

Burnett, John Lawson (D Ala.) Jan. 20, 1854–May 13, 1919; House 1899–May 13, 1919.

Burney, William Evans (D Colo.) Sept. 11, 1893–Jan. 29, 1969; House Nov. 5, 1940–41.

Burnham, Alfred Avery (R Conn.) March 8, 1819–April 11, 1879; House 1859–63.

Burnham, George (R Calif.) Dec. 28, 1868–June 28, 1939; House 1933–37.

Burnham, Henry Eben (R N.H.) Nov. 8, 1844–Feb. 8, 1917; Senate 1901–13.

Burns, Conrad (R Mont.) Jan. 25, 1935– ; Senate 1989– .

Burns, John Anthony (D Hawaii) March 30, 1909–April 5, 1975; House (Terr. Del.) 1957–Aug. 21, 1959; Gov. Dec. 3, 1962–Dec. 2, 1974.

Burns, Joseph (J Ohio) March 11, 1800–May 12, 1875; House 1857–59.

Burns, Robert (D N.H.) Dec. 12, 1792–June 26, 1866; House 1833–37.

Burnside, Ambrose Everett (R R.I.) May 23, 1824–Sept. 13, 1881; Senate 1875–Sept. 13, 1881; Gov. May 29, 1866–May 25, 1869.

Burnside, Maurice Gwinn (D W.Va.) Aug. 23, 1902– ; House 1949–53, 1955–57.

Burnside, Thomas (R Pa.) July 28, 1782–March 25, 1851; House Oct. 10, 1815–April 1816.

Burr, Aaron (cousin of Theodore Dwight, father-in-law of Gov. Joseph Alston of S.C.) (D N.Y.) Feb. 6, 1756–Sept. 14, 1836; Senate 1791–97; Vice President 1801–05.

Burr, Albert George (D Ill.) Nov. 8, 1829–June 10, 1882; House 1867–71.

Burr, Richard M. (R N.C.) Nov. 30, 1955– ; House 1995– .

Burrell, Orlando (R Ill.) July 26, 1826–June 7, 1921; House 1895–97.

Burrill, James Jr. (great-grandfather of Theodore Francis Green) (– R.I.) April 25, 1772–Dec. 25, 1820; Senate 1817–Dec. 25, 1820.

Burroughs, Sherman Everett (R N.H.) Feb. 6, 1870–Jan. 27, 1923; House June 7, 1917–Jan. 27, 1923.

Burroughs, Silas Mainville (R N.Y.) July 16, 1810–June 3, 1860; House 1857–June 3, 1860.

Burrows, Daniel (uncle of Lorenzo Burrows) (– Conn.) Oct. 26, 1766–Jan. 23, 1858; House 1821–23.

Burrows, Joseph Henry (G Mo.) May 15, 1840–April 28, 1914; House 1881–83.

Burrows, Julius Caesar (R Mich.) Jan. 9, 1837–Nov. 16, 1915; House 1873–75, 1879–83, 1885–Jan. 23, 1895; Senate Jan. 24, 1895–1911.

Burrows, Lorenzo (nephew of Daniel Burrows) (W N.Y.) March 15, 1805–March 6, 1885; House 1849–53.

Bursum, Holm Olaf (R N.M.) Feb. 10, 1867–Aug. 7, 1953; Senate March 11, 1921–25.

Burt, Armistead (D S.C.) Nov. 13, 1802–Oct. 30, 1883; House 1843–53.

Burtness, Olger Burton (R N.D.) March 14, 1884–Jan. 20, 1960; House 1921–33.

Burton, Charles Germman (R Mo.) April 4, 1846–Feb. 25, 1926; House 1895–97.

Burton, Clarence Godber (D Va.) Dec. 14, 1886–Jan. 18, 1982; House Nov. 2, 1948–53.

Burton, Danny Lee (R Ind.) June 21, 1938– ; House 1983– ; Chrmn. House Government Reform 1997– .

Burton, Harold Hitz (R Ohio) June 22, 1888–Oct. 28, 1964; Senate 1941–Sept. 30, 1945; Assoc. Justice Supreme Court Oct. 1, 1945–Oct. 13, 1958.

Burton, Hiram Rodney (R Del.) Nov. 13, 1841–June 17, 1927; House 1905–09.

Burton, Hutchins Gordon (– N.C.) 1782–April 21, 1836; House Dec. 6, 1819–March 23, 1824; Gov. Dec. 7, 1824–Dec. 8, 1827 (Federalist).

Burton, John Lowell (brother of Phillip Burton, brother-in-law of Sala Burton) (D Calif.) Dec. 15, 1932– ; House June 25, 1974–83.

Burton, Joseph Ralph (R Kan.) Nov. 16, 1850–Feb. 27, 1923; Senate 1901–June 4, 1906.

Burton, Laurence Junior (R Utah) Oct. 30, 1926– ; House 1963–71.

Burton, Phillip (brother of John Lowell Burton, husband of Sala Burton) (D Calif.) June 1, 1926–April 10, 1983; House Feb. 18, 1964–April 10, 1983.

Burton, Sala (widow of Phillip Burton, sister-in-law of John Lowell Burton) (D Calif.) April 1, 1925–Feb. 1, 1987; House June 21, 1983–Feb. 1, 1987.

Burton, Theodore Elijah (R Ohio) Dec. 20, 1851–Oct. 28, 1929; House 1889–91, 1895–1909, 1921–Dec. 15, 1928; Senate 1909–15, Dec. 15, 1928–Oct. 28, 1929.

Burwell, William Armisted (R Va.) March 15, 1780–Feb. 16, 1821; House Dec. 1, 1806–Feb. 16, 1821.

Busbey, Fred Ernst (R Ill.) Feb. 8, 1895–Feb. 11, 1966; House 1943–45, 1947–49, 1951–55.

Busby, George Henry (D Ohio) June 10, 1794–Aug. 22, 1869; House 1851–53.

Busby, Thomas Jefferson (D Miss.) July 26, 1884–Oct. 18, 1964; House 1923–35.

Busey, Samuel Thompson (D Ill.) Nov. 16, 1835–Aug. 12, 1909; House 1891–93.

Bush, Alvin Ray (R Pa.) June 4, 1893–Nov. 5, 1959; House 1951–Nov. 5, 1959.

Bush, George Herbert Walker (son of Prescott Sheldon Bush) (R Texas) June 12, 1924– ; House 1967–71; Chrmn. Rep. Nat. Comm. Jan. 1973–Sept. 1974; Vice President 1981–89; President 1989–93.

Bush, Prescott Sheldon (father of George Herbert Walker Bush) (R Conn.) May 15, 1895–Oct. 8, 1972; Senate Nov. 4, 1952–Jan. 2, 1963.

Bushfield, Harlan John (husband of Vera Cahalan Bushfield) (R S.D.) Aug. 6, 1882–Sept. 27, 1948; Senate 1943–Sept. 27, 1948; Gov. Jan. 3, 1939–Jan. 5, 1943.

Bushfield, Vera Cahalan (widow of Harlan John Bushfield) (R S.D.) Aug. 9, 1889–April 16, 1976; Senate Oct. 6–Dec. 26, 1948.

Bushnell, Allen Ralph (D Wis.) July 18, 1833–March 29, 1909; House 1891–93.

Bushong, Robert Grey (grandson of Anthony Ellmaker Roberts) (R Pa.) June 10, 1883–April 6, 1951; House 1927–29.

Bustamante, Albert Garza (D Texas) April 8, 1935– ; House 1985–93.

Butler, Andrew Pickens (son of William Butler born in 1759, brother of William Butler born in 1790, uncle of Matthew Calbraith Butler) (SRD S.C.) Nov. 18, 1796–May 25, 1857; Senate Dec. 4, 1846–May 25, 1857.

Butler, Benjamin Franklin (grandfather of Butler Ames, father-in-law of Adelbert Ames) (R Mass.) Nov. 5, 1818–Jan. 11, 1893; House 1867–75, 1877–79; Gov. Jan. 4, 1883–Jan. 3, 1884 (Democrat/Greenback).

Butler, Chester Pierce (W Pa.) March 21, 1798–Oct. 5, 1850; House 1847–Oct. 5, 1850.

Butler, Ezra (R Vt.) Sept. 24, 1763–July 12, 1838; House 1813–15; Gov. Oct. 13, 1826–Oct. 10, 1828 (Democratic Republican).

Butler, Hugh Alfred (R Neb.) Feb. 28, 1878–July 1, 1954; Senate 1941–July 1, 1954; Chrmn. Senate Public Lands 1947–48; Chrmn. Senate Interior and Insular Affairs 1948–49, 1953–54.

Butler, James Joseph (D Mo.) Aug. 29, 1862–May 31, 1917; House 1901–June 28, 1902, Nov. 4, 1902–Feb. 26, 1903, 1903–05.

Butler, John Cornelius (R N.Y.) July 2, 1887–Aug. 13, 1953; House April 22, 1941–49, 1951–53.

Butler, John Marshall (R Md.) July 21, 1897–March 14, 1978; Senate 1951–63.

Butler, Josiah (R N.H.) Dec. 4, 1779–Oct. 27, 1854; House 1817–23.

Butler, Manley Caldwell (R Va.) June 2, 1925– ; House Nov. 7, 1972–83.

Butler, Marion (P N.C.) May 20, 1863–June 3, 1938; Senate 1895–1901.

Butler, Matthew Calbraith (son of William Butler born in 1790, grandson of William Butler born in 1759, nephew of Andrew Pickens Butler) (D S.C.) March 8, 1836–April 14, 1909; Senate 1877–95.

Butler, Mounce Gore (D Tenn.) May 11, 1849–Feb. 13, 1917; House 1905–07.

Butler, Pierce (D S.C.) July 11, 1744–Feb. 15, 1822; Senate 1789–Oct. 25, 1796, Nov. 4, 1802–Nov. 21, 1804; Cont. Cong. 1787.

Butler, Robert Reyburn (grandson of Roderick Randum Butler) (R Ore.) Sept. 24, 1881–Jan. 7, 1933; House Nov. 6, 1928–Jan. 7, 1933.

Butler, Roderick Randum (grandfather of Robert Reyburn Bulter) (R Tenn.) April 9, 1827–Aug. 18, 1902; House 1867–75, 1887–89.

Butler, Sampson Hale (D S.C.) Jan. 3, 1803–March 16, 1848; House 1839–Sept. 27, 1842.

Butler, Thomas (R La.) April 14, 1785–Aug. 7, 1847; House Nov. 16, 1818–21.

Butler, Thomas Belden (W Conn.) Aug. 22, 1806–June 8, 1873; House 1849–51.

Butler, Thomas Stalker (R Pa.) Nov. 4, 1855–May 26, 1928; House 1897–May 26, 1928 (1897–99 Independent Republican).

Butler, Walter Halben (D Iowa) Feb. 13, 1852–April 24, 1931; House 1891–93.

Butler, William (father of Andrew Pickens Butler and William Butler, below, grandfather of Matthew Calbraith Butler) (R S.C.) Dec. 17, 1759–Nov. 15, 1821; House 1801–13.

Butler, William (son of William Butler, above, brother of Andrew Pickens Butler, father of Matthew Calbraith Butler) (W S.C.) Feb. 1, 1790–Sept. 25, 1850; House 1841–43.

Butler, William Morgan (R Mass.) Jan. 29, 1861–March 29, 1937; Senate Nov. 13, 1924–Dec. 6, 1926; Chrmn. Rep. Nat. Comm. 1924–28.

Butler, William Orlando (D Ky.) April 19, 1791–Aug. 6, 1880; House 1839–43.

Butman, Samuel (– Maine) 1788–Oct. 9, 1864; House 1827–31.

Butterfield, Martin (R N.Y.) Dec. 8, 1790–Aug. 6, 1866; House 1859–61.

Butterworth, Benjamin (R Ohio) Oct. 22, 1837–Jan. 16, 1898; House 1879–83, 1885–91.

Button, Daniel Evan (R N.Y.) Nov. 1, 1917– ; House 1967–71.

Buttz, Charles Wilson (R S.C.) Nov. 16, 1837–July 20, 1913; House Nov. 7, 1876–77.

Buyer, Steve (R Ind.) Nov. 26, 1958– ; House 1993– ; Gov. 1971–75.

Bynum, Jesse Atherton (D N.C.) May 23, 1797–Sept. 23, 1868; House 1833–41 (1833–37 Jacksonian).

Bynum, William Dallas (D Ind.) June 26, 1846–Oct. 21, 1927; House 1885–95.

Byrd, Adam Monroe (D Miss.) July 6, 1859–June 21, 1912; House 1903–11.

Byrd, Harry Flood (father of Harry Flood Byrd Jr., nephew of Henry De La Warr Flood and Joel West Flood) (D Va.) June 10, 1887–Oct. 20, 1966; Senate 1933–Nov. 10, 1965; Gov. Feb. 1, 1926–Jan. 15, 1930.

Byrd, Harry Flood Jr. (son of Harry Flood Byrd) (I Va.) Dec. 20, 1914– ; Senate Nov. 12, 1965–83 (1965–71 Democrat); Chrmn. Senate Finance 1955–65.

Byrd, Robert Carlyle (D W.Va.) Nov. 20, 1917– ; House 1953–59; Senate 1959– ; Senate majority leader 1977–81, 1987–89; Senate minority leader 1981–87; elected Pres. pro tempore 1989–95; Chrmn. Senate Appropriations 1989–95.

Byrne, Emmet Francis (R Ill.) Dec. 6, 1896–Sept. 25, 1974; House 1957–59.

Byrne, James Aloysius (D Pa.) June 22, 1906–Sept. 3, 1980; House 1953–73.

Byrne, Leslie L. (D Va.) Oct. 27, 1946– ; House 1993–95.

Byrne, William Thomas (D N.Y.) March 6, 1876–Jan. 27, 1952; House 1937–Jan. 27, 1952.

Byrnes, James Francis (D S.C.) May 2, 1879–April 9, 1972; House 1911–25; Senate 1931–July 8, 1941; Assoc. Justice Supreme Court July 8, 1941–Oct. 3, 1942; Secy. of State July 3, 1945–Jan. 21, 1947; Gov. Jan. 16, 1951–Jan. 18, 1955.

Byrnes, John William (R Wis.) June 12, 1913–Jan. 12, 1985; House 1945–73.

Byrns, Joseph Wellington (father of Joseph Wellington Byrns Jr.) (D Tenn.) July 20, 1869–June 4, 1936; House 1909–June 4, 1936; House majority leader 1933–35; Speaker 1935–June 4, 1936.

Byrns, Joseph Wellington Jr. (son of Joseph Wellington Byrns) (D Tenn.) Aug. 15, 1903–March 8, 1973; House 1939–41.

Byrns, Samuel (D Mo.) March 4, 1848–July 9, 1914; House 1891–93.

Byron, Beverly Barton Butcher (widow of Goodloe Edgar Bryon, daughter-in-law of Katharine Edgar Byron and William Devereaux Byron) (D Md.) July 26, 1932– ; House 1979–93.

Byron, Goodloe Edgar (son of Katharine Edgar Byron and William Devereux Byron, great-grandson of Louis Emory McComas, husband of Beverly Barton Butcher Byron) (D Md.) June 22, 1929–Oct. 11, 1978; House 1971–Oct. 11, 1978.

Byron, Katharine Edgar (widow of William Devereux Byron, mother of Goodloe Edgar Byron, granddaughter of Louis Emory McComas, mother-in-law of Beverly Barton Butcher Byron) (D Md.) Oct. 25, 1903–Dec. 28, 1976; House May 27, 1941–43.

Byron, William Devereaux (husband of Katharine Edgar Byron, father of Goodloe Edgar Byron, father-in-law of Beverly Barton Butcher Byron) (D Md.) May 15, 1895–Feb. 27, 1941; House 1939–Feb. 27, 1941.

C

Cabaniss, Thomas Banks (cousin of Thomas Chipman McRae) (D Ga.) Aug. 31, 1835–Aug. 14, 1915; House 1893–95.

Cabell, Earle (D Texas) Oct. 27, 1906–Sept. 24, 1975; House 1965–73.

Cabell, Edward Carrington (W Fla.) Feb. 5, 1816–Feb. 28, 1896; House Oct. 6, 1845–Jan. 24, 1846 (no party), 1847–53.

Cabell, George Craighead (D Va.) Jan. 25, 1836–June 23, 1906; House 1875–87.

Cabell, Samuel Jordan (R Va.) Dec. 15, 1756–Aug. 4, 1818; House 1795–1803.

Cable, Benjamin Taylor (D Ill.) Aug. 11, 1853–Dec. 13, 1923; House 1891–93.

Cable, John Levi (great-grandson of Joseph Cable) (R Ohio) April 15, 1884–Sept. 15, 1971; House 1921–25, 1929–33.

Cable, Joseph (great-grandfather of John Levi Cable) (D Ohio) April 17, 1801–May 1, 1880; House 1849–53.

Cabot, George (great-grandfather of Henry Cabot Lodge, great-great-grandfather of Henry Cabot Lodge Jr.) (– Mass.) Dec. 3, 1752–April 18, 1823; Senate 1791–June 9, 1796.

Cadmus, Cornelius Andrew (D N.J.) Oct. 7, 1844–Jan. 20, 1902; House 1891–95.

Cadwalader, John (D Pa.) April 1, 1805–Jan. 26, 1879; House 1855–57.

Cadwalader, Lambert (– N.J.) 1742–Sept. 13, 1823; House 1789–91, 1793–95; Cont. Cong. 1785–87.

Cady, Claude Ernest (D Mich.) May 28, 1878–Nov. 30, 1953; House 1933–35.

Cady, Daniel (uncle of John Watts Cady) (F N.Y.) April 29, 1773–Oct. 31, 1859; House 1815–17.

Cady, John Watts (nephew of Daniel Cady) (– N.Y.) June 28, 1790–Jan. 5, 1854; House 1823–25.

Caffery, Donelson (grandfather of Patrick Thomson Caffery) (D La.) Sept. 10, 1835–Dec. 30, 1906; Senate Dec. 31, 1892–1901.

Caffery, Patrick Thomson (grandson of Donelson Caffery) (D La.) July 6, 1932– ; House 1969–73.

Cage, Harry (J Miss.) ?–1859; House 1833–35.

Cahill, William Thomas (R N.J.) June 25, 1912–July 1, 1996; House 1959–Jan. 19, 1970; Gov. Jan. 20, 1970–Jan. 15, 1974.

Cahoon, William (AMas. Vt.) Jan. 12, 1774–May 30, 1833; House 1829–33.

Cain, Harry Pulliam (R Wash.) Jan. 10, 1906–March 3, 1979; Senate Dec. 26, 1946–53.

Cain, Richard Harvey (R S.C.) April 12, 1825–Jan. 18, 1887; House 1873–75, 1877–79.

Caine, John Thomas (PP Utah) Jan. 8, 1829–Sept. 20, 1911; House (Terr. Del.) Nov. 7, 1882–93 (1882–89 Democrat).

Cake, Henry Lutz (R Pa.) Oct. 6, 1827–Aug. 26, 1899; House 1867–71.

Calder, William Musgrave (R N.Y.) March 3, 1869–March 3, 1945; House 1905–15; Senate 1917–23.

Calderhead, William Alexander (R Kan.) Sept. 26, 1844–Dec. 18, 1928; House 1895–97, 1899–1911.

Caldwell, Alexander (R Kan.) March 1, 1830–May 19, 1917; Senate 1871–March 24, 1873.

Caldwell, Andrew Jackson (D Tenn.) July 22, 1837–Nov. 22, 1906; House 1883–87.

Caldwell, Ben Franklin (D Ill.) Aug. 2, 1848–Dec. 29, 1924; House 1899–1905, 1907–09.

Caldwell, Charles Pope (D N.Y.) June 18, 1875–July 31, 1940; House 1915–21.

Caldwell, George Alfred (D Ky.) Oct. 18, 1814–Sept. 17, 1866; House 1843–45, 1849–51.

Caldwell, Greene Washington (D N.C.) April 13, 1806–July 10, 1864; House 1841–43.

Caldwell, James (R Ohio) Nov. 30, 1770–May 1838; House 1813–17.

Caldwell, John Alexander (R Ohio) April 21, 1852–May 24, 1927; House 1889–May 4, 1894.

Caldwell, John Henry (D Ala.) April 4, 1826–Sept. 4, 1902; House 1873–77.

Caldwell, John William (D Ky.) Jan. 15, 1837–July 4, 1903; House 1877–83.

Caldwell, Joseph Pearson (W N.C.) March 5, 1808–June 30, 1853; House 1849–53.

Caldwell, Millard Fillmore (D Fla.) Feb. 6, 1897–Oct. 23, 1984; House 1933–41; Gov. Jan. 2, 1945–Jan. 4, 1949.

Caldwell, Patrick Calhoun (D S.C.) March 10, 1801–Nov. 22, 1855; House 1841–43.

Caldwell, Robert Porter (D Tenn.) Dec. 16, 1821–March 12, 1885; House 1871–73.

Caldwell, William Parker (D Tenn.) Nov. 8, 1832–June 7, 1903; House 1875–79.

Cale, Thomas (I Alaska) Sept. 17, 1848–Feb. 3, 1941; House (Terr. Del.) 1907–09.

Calhoon, John (W Ky.) 1797–?; House 1835–39.

Calhoun, John Caldwell (cousin of John Ewing Colhoun and Joseph Calhoun) (R S.C.) March 18, 1782–March 31, 1850; House 1811–Nov. 3, 1817; Senate Dec. 29, 1832–43, Nov. 26, 1845–March 31, 1850; Vice President 1825–Dec. 28, 1832 (Democratic Republican); Secy. of War Oct. 8, 1817–March 7, 1825; Secy. of State April 1, 1844–March 10, 1845.

Calhoun, Joseph (cousin of John Caldwell Calhoun and John Ewing Colhoun) (R S.C.) Oct. 22, 1750–April 14, 1817; House June 2, 1807–11.

Calhoun, William Barron (W Mass.) Dec. 29, 1796–Nov. 8, 1865; House 1835–43.

Calkin, Hervey Chittenden (D N.Y.) March 23, 1828–April 20, 1913; House 1869–71.

Calkins, William Henry (R Ind.) Feb. 18, 1842–Jan. 29, 1894; House 1877–Oct. 20, 1884.

Call, Jacob (– Ind.) ?–April 20, 1826; House Dec. 23, 1824–25.

Call, Richard Keith (uncle of Wilkinson Call) (– Fla.) Oct. 24, 1792–Sept. 14, 1862; House (Terr. Del.) 1823–25; Gov. (Fla. Terr.) 1835–40, 1841–44.

Call, Wilkinson (nephew of Richard Keith Call, cousin of James David Walker) (D Fla.) Jan. 9, 1834–Aug. 24, 1910; Senate 1879–97.

Callahan, Herbert Leon "Sonny" (R Ala.) Sept. 11, 1932– ; House 1985– .

Callahan, James Yancy (FSil. Okla.) Dec. 19, 1852–May 3, 1935; House (Terr. Del.) 1897–99.

Callan, Clair Armstrong (D Neb.) March 20, 1920– ; House 1965–67.

Callaway, Howard Hollis "Bo" (R Ga.) April 2, 1927– ; House 1965–67.

Callaway, Oscar (D Texas) Oct. 2, 1872–Jan. 31, 1947; House 1911–17.

Callis, John Benton (R Ala.) Jan. 3, 1828–Sept. 24, 1898; House July 21, 1868–69.

Calvert, Charles Benedict (U Md.) Aug. 24, 1808–May 12, 1864; House 1861–63.

Calvert, Ken (R Calif.) June 8, 1953– ; House 1993– .

Calvin, Samuel (W Pa.) July 30, 1811–March 12, 1890; House 1849–51.

Cambreleng, Churchill Caldom (D N.Y.) Oct. 24, 1786–April 30, 1862; House 1821–39 (1821–29 no party, 1829–37 Jacksonian).

Camden, Johnson Newlon (father of Johnson Newlon Camden Jr.) (D W.Va.) March 6, 1828–April 25, 1908; Senate 1881–87, Jan. 25, 1893–95.

Camden, Johnson Newlon Jr. (son of Johnson Newlon Camden) (D Ky.) Jan. 5, 1865–Aug. 16, 1942; Senate June 16, 1914–15.

Cameron, Angus (R Wis.) July 4, 1826–March 30, 1897; Senate 1875–81, March 14, 1881–85.

Cameron, James Donald (son of Simon Cameron) (R Pa.) May 14, 1833–Aug. 30, 1918; Senate March 20, 1877–97; Secy. of War May 22, 1876–March 3, 1877; Chrmn. Rep. Nat. Comm. 1879–80.

Cameron, Ralph Henry (R Ariz.) Oct. 21, 1863–Feb. 12, 1953; House (Terr. Del.) 1909–Feb. 18, 1912; Senate 1921–27.

Cameron, Ronald Brooks (D Calif.) Aug. 16, 1927– ; House 1963–67.

Cameron, Simon (father of James Donald Cameron) (R Pa.) March 8, 1799–June 26, 1889; Senate March 13, 1845–49 (no party), 1857–March 4, 1861, 1867–March 12, 1877; Secy. of War March 5, 1861–Jan. 14, 1862.

Caminetti, Anthony (D Calif.) July 30, 1854–Nov. 17, 1923; House 1891–95.

Camp, Albert Sidney (D Ga.) July 26, 1892–July 24, 1954; House Aug. 1, 1939–July 24, 1954.

Camp, David (R Mich.) July 9, 1953– ; House 1991– .

Camp, John Henry (R N.Y.) April 4, 1840–Oct. 12, 1892; House 1877–83.

Camp, John Newbold Happy (R Okla.) May 11, 1908–Sept. 27, 1987; House 1969–75.

Campbell, Albert James (D Mont.) Dec. 12, 1857–Aug. 9, 1907; House 1899–1901.

Campbell, Alexander (R Ohio) 1779–Nov. 5, 1857; Senate Dec. 11, 1809–13.

Campbell, Alexander (I Ill.) Oct. 4, 1814–Aug. 8, 1898; House 1875–77.

Campbell, Ben Nighthorse (R Colo.) April 13, 1933– ; House 1987–93 (Democrat); Senate 1993– (1993–March 3, 1995 Democrat); Chrmn. Senate Indian Affairs 1995– .

Campbell, Brookins (D Tenn.) 1808–Dec. 25, 1853; House March 4–Dec. 25, 1853.

Campbell, Carroll Ashmore Jr. (R S.C.) July 24, 1940– ; House 1979–87; Gov. Jan. 14, 1987–Jan. 11, 1995.

Campbell, Courtney Warren (D Fla.) April 29, 1895–Dec. 22, 1971; House 1953–55.

Campbell, Ed Hoyt (R Iowa) March 6, 1882–April 26, 1969; House 1929–33.

Campbell, Felix (D N.Y.) Feb. 28, 1829–Nov. 8, 1902; House 1883–91.

Campbell, George Washington (R Tenn.) Feb. 9, 1769–Feb. 17, 1848; House 1803–09; Senate Oct. 8, 1811–Feb. 11, 1814, Oct. 10, 1815–April 20, 1818; Secy. of the Treasury Feb. 9–Oct. 5, 1814.

Campbell, Guy Edgar (R Pa.) Oct. 9, 1871–Feb. 17, 1940; House 1917–33 (1917–23 Democrat).

Campbell, Howard Edmond (R Pa.) Jan. 4, 1890–Jan. 6, 1971; House 1945–47.

Campbell, Jacob Miller (R Pa.) Nov. 20, 1821–Sept. 27, 1888; House 1877–79, 1881–87.

Campbell, James Edwin (nephew of Lewis Davis Campbell) (D Ohio) July 7, 1843–Dec. 18, 1924; House June 20, 1884–89; Gov. Jan. 13, 1890–Jan. 11, 1892.

Campbell, James Hepburn (W Pa.) Feb. 8, 1820–April 12, 1895; House 1855–57, 1859–63.

Campbell, James Romulus (D Ill.) May 4, 1853–Aug. 12, 1924; House 1897–99.

Campbell, John (F Md.) Sept. 11, 1765–June 23, 1828; House 1801–11.

Campbell, John (brother of Robert Blair Campbell) (D S.C.) ?–May 19, 1845; House 1829–31 (Jacksonian), 1837–45 (1837–39 Nullifier).

Campbell, John Goulder (D Ariz.) June 25, 1827–Dec. 22, 1903; House (Terr. Del.) 1879–81.

Campbell, John Hull (AP Pa.) Oct. 10, 1800–Jan. 19, 1868; House 1845–47.

Campbell, John Pierce Jr. (AP Ky.) Dec. 8, 1820–Oct. 29, 1888; House 1855–57.

Campbell, John Wilson (R Ohio) Feb. 23, 1782–Sept. 24, 1833; House 1817–27.

Campbell, Lewis Davis (uncle of James Edwin Campbell) (D Ohio) Aug. 9, 1811–Nov. 26, 1882; House 1849–May 25, 1858 (1849–55 Whig, 1855–57 American Party, 1857–May 25, 1858 Republican), 1871–73.

Campbell, Philip Pitt (R Kan.) April 25, 1862–May 26, 1941; House 1903–23.

Campbell, Robert Blair (brother of John Campbell of S.C.) (N S.C.) ?–July 12, 1862; House 1823–25 (no party), Feb. 27, 1834–37.

Campbell, Samuel (– N.Y.) July 11, 1773–June 2, 1853; House 1821–23.

Campbell, Thomas Jefferson (W Tenn.) 1786–April 13, 1850; House 1841–43.

Campbell, Thompson (D Ill.) 1811–Dec. 6, 1868; House 1851–53.

Campbell, Timothy John (D N.Y.) Jan. 8, 1840–April 7, 1904; House Nov. 3, 1885–89, 1891–95.

Campbell, Tom (R Calif.) Aug. 14, 1952– ; House 1989–93; House Dec. 15, 1995– .

Campbell, William Bowen (cousin of Henry Bowen) (U Tenn.) Feb. 1, 1807–Aug. 19, 1867; House 1837–43 (Whig), July 24, 1866–67; Gov. Oct. 16, 1851–Oct. 16, 1853 (Whig).

Campbell, William W. (AP N.Y.) June 10, 1806–Sept. 7, 1881; House 1845–47.

Campbell, William Wildman (R Ohio) April 2, 1853–Aug. 13, 1927; House 1905–07.

Canady, Charles T. (R Fla.) June 22, 1954– ; House 1993– .

Canby, Richard Sprigg (W Ohio) Sept. 30, 1808–July 27, 1895; House 1847–49.

Candler, Allen Daniel (cousin of Ezekiel Samuel Candler Jr. and Milton Anthony Candler) (D Ga.) Nov. 4, 1834–Oct. 26, 1910; House 1883–91; Gov. Oct. 29, 1898–Oct. 25, 1902.

Candler, Ezekiel Samuel Jr. (nephew of Milton Anthony Candler, cousin of Allen Daniel Candler) (D Miss.) Jan. 18, 1862–Dec. 18, 1944; House 1901–21.

Candler, John Wilson (R Mass.) Feb. 10, 1828–March 16, 1903; House 1881–83, 1889–91.

Candler, Milton Anthony (uncle of Ezekiel Samuel Candler Jr., cousin of Allen Daniel Candler) (D Ga.) Jan. 11, 1837–Aug. 8, 1909; House 1875–79.

Canfield, Gordon (R N.J.) April 15, 1898–June 20, 1972; House 1941–61.

Canfield, Harry Clifford (D Ind.) Nov. 22, 1875–Feb. 9, 1945; House 1923–33.

Cannon, Arthur Patrick (D Fla.) May 22, 1904–Jan. 23, 1966; House 1939–47.

Cannon, Christopher (R Utah) Oct. 20, 1950– ; House 1997– .

Cannon, Clarence Andrew (D Mo.) April 11, 1879–May 12, 1964; House 1923–May 12, 1964; Chrmn. House Appropriations 1949–53, 1955–64.

Cannon, Frank Jenne (son of George Quayle Cannon) (R Utah) Jan. 25, 1859–July 25, 1933; House (Terr. Del.) 1895–Jan. 4, 1896; Senate Jan. 22, 1896–99.

Cannon, George Quayle (father of Frank Jenne Cannon) (R Utah) Jan. 11, 1827–April 12, 1901; House (Terr. Del.) 1873–81.

Cannon, Howard Walter (D Nev.) Jan. 26, 1912– ; Senate 1959–83; Chrmn. Senate Rules and Administration 1973–77; Chrmn. Senate Select Committee on Standards and Conduct 1975–77; Chrmn. Senate Commerce, Science, and Transportation 1978–81.

Cannon, Joseph Gurney (R Ill.) May 7, 1836–Nov. 12, 1926; House 1873–91, 1893–1913, 1915–23; Speaker Nov. 9, 1903–05, Dec. 4, 1905–07, Dec. 2, 1907–09, March 15, 1909–11.

Cannon, Marion (P Calif.) Oct. 30, 1834–Aug. 27, 1920; House 1893–95.

Cannon, Newton (R Tenn.) May 22, 1781–Sept. 16, 1841; House Sept. 16, 1814–17, 1819–23; Gov. Oct. 12, 1835–Oct. 14, 1839 (Whig).

Cannon, Raymond Joseph (D Wis.) Aug. 26, 1894–Nov. 25, 1951; House 1933–39.

Cantor, Jacob Aaron (D N.Y.) Dec. 6, 1854–July 2, 1921; House Nov. 4, 1913–15.

Cantrill, James Campbell (D Ky.) July 9, 1870–Sept. 2, 1923; House 1909–Sept. 2, 1923.

Cantwell, Maria (D Wash.) Oct. 13, 1958– ; House 1993–95.

Capehart, Homer Earl (R Ind.) June 6, 1897–Sept. 3, 1979; Senate 1945–63; Chrmn. Senate Banking and Currency 1953–55.

Capehart, James (D W.Va.) March 7, 1847–April 28, 1921; House 1891–95.

Caperton, Allen Taylor (son of Hugh Caperton) (D W.Va.) Nov. 21, 1810–July 26, 1876; Senate 1875–July 26, 1876.

Caperton, Hugh (father of Allen Taylor Caperton) (F Va.) April 17, 1781–Feb. 9, 1847; House 1813–15.

Capozzoli, Louis Joseph (D N.Y.) March 6, 1901–Oct. 8, 1982; House 1941–45.

Capper, Arthur (R Kan.) July 14, 1865–Dec. 19, 1951; Senate 1919–49; Chrmn. Senate Agriculture and Forestry 1947–49; Gov. Jan. 11, 1915–Jan. 13, 1919.

Capps, Lois D. (widow of Walter Capps) (D Calif.) Jan. 10 1938– ; House March 17, 1998– .

Capps, Walter (husband of Lois D. Capps) (D Calif.) May 5, 1934–Oct. 28, 1997; House 1997–Oct. 28, 1997.

Capron, Adin Ballou (R R.I.) Jan. 9, 1841–March 17, 1911; House 1897–1911.

Capstick, John Henry (R N.J.) Sept. 2, 1856–March 17, 1918; House 1915–March 17, 1918.

Capuano, Michael Everett (R Mass.) Jan. 9, 1952– ; House 1999– .

Caputo, Bruce Faulkner (R N.Y.) Aug. 7, 1943– ; House 1977–79.

Caraway, Hattie Wyatt (widow of Thaddeus Horatius Caraway) (D Ark.) Feb. 1, 1878–Dec. 21, 1950; Senate Nov. 13, 1931–Jan. 2, 1945.

Caraway, Thaddeus Horatius (husband of Hattie Wyatt Caraway) (D Ark.) Oct. 17, 1871–Nov. 6, 1931; House 1913–21; Senate 1921–Nov. 6, 1931.

Carden, Cap Robert (D Ky.) Dec. 17, 1866–June 13, 1935; House 1931–June 13, 1935.

Cardin, Benjamin Louis (D Md.) Oct. 5, 1943– ; House 1987– .

Carew, John Francis (nephew of Thomas Francis Magner) (D N.Y.) April 16, 1873–April 10, 1951; House 1913–Dec. 28, 1929.

Carey, Hugh Leo (D N.Y.) April 11, 1919– ; House 1961–Dec. 31, 1974; Gov. Jan. 1, 1975–Jan. 1, 1983.

Carey, John (R Ohio) April 5, 1792–March 17, 1875; House 1859–61.

Carey, Joseph Maull (father of Robert Davis Carey) (R Wyo.) Jan. 19, 1845–Feb. 5, 1924; House (Terr. Del.) 1885–July 10, 1890; Senate Nov. 15, 1890–95; Gov. Jan. 2, 1911–Jan. 4, 1915.

Carey, Robert Davis (son of Joseph Maull Carey) (R Wyo.) Aug. 12, 1878–Jan. 17, 1937; Senate Dec. 1, 1930–37; Gov. Jan. 6, 1919–Jan. 1, 1923.

Carleton, Ezra Child (D Mich.) Sept. 6, 1838–July 24, 1911; House 1883–87.

Carleton, Peter (R N.H.) Sept. 19, 1755–April 29, 1828; House 1807–09.

Carley, Patrick J. (D N.Y.) Feb. 2, 1866–Feb. 25, 1936; House 1927–35.

Carlile, John Snyder (U Va.) Dec. 16, 1817–Oct. 24, 1878; House 1855–57 (American Party), March 4–July 9, 1861; Senate July 9, 1861–65.

Carlin, Charles Creighton (D Va.) April 8, 1866–Oct. 14, 1938; House Nov. 5, 1907–19.

Carlisle, John Griffin (D Ky.) Sept. 5, 1835–July 31, 1910; House 1877–May 26, 1890; Speaker Dec. 3, 1883–85, Dec. 7, 1885–87, Dec. 5, 1887–89; Senate May 26, 1890–Feb. 4, 1893; Secy. of the Treasury March 7, 1893–March 5, 1897.

Carlson, Clifford Dale (R Ill.) Dec. 30, 1915–Aug. 28, 1977; House April 4, 1972–73.

Carlson, Frank (R Kan.) Jan. 23, 1893–May 30, 1987; House 1935–47; Senate Nov. 29, 1950–69; Chrmn. Senate Post Office and Civil Service 1953–55; Gov. Jan. 13, 1947–Nov. 28, 1950.

Carlton, Henry Hull (D Ga.) May 14, 1835–Oct. 26, 1905; House 1887–91.

Carlyle, Frank Ertel (D N.C.) April 7, 1897–Oct. 2, 1960; House 1949–57.

Carmack, Edward Ward (D Tenn.) Nov. 5, 1858–Nov. 9, 1908; House 1897–1901; Senate 1901–07.

Carman, Gregory Wright (R N.Y.) Jan. 31, 1937– ; House 1981–83.

Carmichael, Archibald Hill (D Ala.) June 17, 1864–July 15, 1947; House Nov. 14, 1933–37.

Carmichael, Richard Bennett (J Md.) Dec. 25, 1807–Oct. 21, 1884; House 1833–35.

Carnahan, Albert Sidney Johnson (D Mo.) Jan. 9, 1897–March 24, 1968; House 1945–47, 1949–61.

Carnes, Thomas Petters (– Ga.) 1762–May 5, 1822; House 1793–95.

Carney, Charles Joseph (D Ohio) April 17, 1913–Oct. 7, 1987; House Nov. 3, 1970–79.

Carney, William (R N.Y.) July 1, 1942– ; House 1979–87.

Carpenter, Cyrus Clay (R Iowa) Nov. 24, 1829–May 29, 1898; House 1879–83; Gov. Jan. 11, 1872–Jan. 13, 1876.

Carpenter, Davis (W N.Y.) Dec. 25, 1799–Oct. 22, 1878; House Nov. 8, 1853–55.

Carpenter, Edmund Nelson (R Pa.) June 27, 1865–Nov. 4, 1952; House 1925–27.

Carpenter, Levi D. (D N.Y.) Aug. 21, 1802–Oct. 27, 1856; House Nov. 5, 1844–45.

Carpenter, Lewis Cass (R S.C.) Feb. 20, 1836–March 6, 1908; House Nov. 3, 1874–75.

Carpenter, Matthew Hale (R Wis.) Dec. 22, 1824–Feb. 24, 1881; Senate 1869–75, 1879–Feb. 24, 1881; elected Pres. pro tempore March 12, 1873, March 26, 1873, Dec. 11, 1873, Dec. 23, 1874.

Carpenter, Terry McGovern (D Neb.) March 28, 1900–April 27, 1978; House 1933–35.

Carpenter, William Randolph (D Kan.) April 24, 1894–July 26, 1956; House 1933–37.

Carper, Thomas Richard (D Del.) Jan. 23, 1947– ; House 1983–93; Gov. Jan. 19, 1993– .

Carr, Francis (father of James Carr) (R Mass.) Dec. 6, 1751–Oct. 6, 1821; House April 6, 1812–13.

Carr, James (son of Francis Carr) (F Mass.) Sept. 9, 1777–Aug. 24, 1818; House 1815–17.

Carr, John (D Ind.) April 9, 1793–Jan. 20, 1845; House 1831–37 (Jacksonian), 1839–41.

Carr, Milton Robert "Bob" (D Mich.) March 27, 1943– ; House 1975–81, 1983–95.

Carr, Nathan Tracy (D Ind.) Dec. 25, 1833–May 28, 1885; House Dec. 5, 1876–77.

Carr, Wooda Nicholas (D Pa.) Feb. 6, 1871–June 28, 1953; House 1913–15.

Carrier, Chester Otto (R Ky.) May 5, 1897–Sept. 24, 1980; House Nov. 30, 1943–45.

Carrigg, Joseph Leonard (R Pa.) Feb. 23, 1901–Feb. 6, 1989; House Nov. 6, 1951–59.

Carroll, Charles (cousin of Daniel Carroll) (– Md.) Sept. 19, 1737–Nov. 14, 1832; Senate 1789–Nov. 30, 1792; Cont. Cong. 1776–78.

Carroll, Charles Holker (W N.Y.) May 4, 1794–June 8, 1865; House 1843–47.

Carroll, Daniel (uncle of Richard Brent, cousin of Charles Carroll) (– Md.) July 22, 1730–May 7, 1796; House 1789–91; Cont. Cong. 1781–83.

Carroll, James (D Md.) Dec. 2, 1791–Jan. 16, 1873; House 1839–41.

Carroll, John Albert (D Colo.) July 30, 1901–Aug. 31, 1983; House 1947–51; Senate 1957–63.

Carroll, John Michael (D N.Y.) April 27, 1823–May 8, 1901; House 1871–73.

Carson, Henderson Haverfield (R Ohio) Oct. 25, 1893–Oct. 5, 1971; House 1943–45, 1947–49.

Carson, Julia (D Ind.) July 8, 1938– ; House 1997– .

Carson, Samuel Price (– N.C.) Jan. 22, 1798–Nov. 2, 1838; House 1825–33.

Carss, William Leighton (FL Minn.) Feb. 15, 1865–May 31, 1931; House 1919–21 (Union Laborite), 1925–29.

Carter, Albert Edward (R Calif.) July 5, 1881–Aug. 8, 1964; House 1925–45.

Carter, Charles David (D Okla.) Aug. 16, 1868–April 9, 1929; House Nov. 16, 1907–27.

Carter, John (J S.C.) Sept. 10, 1792–June 20, 1850; House Dec. 11, 1822–29 (Dec. 11, 1822–27 no party).

Carter, Luther Cullen (R N.Y.) Feb. 25, 1805–Jan. 3, 1875; House 1859–61.

Carter, Steven V. (D Iowa) Oct. 8, 1915–Nov. 4, 1959; House Jan. 3–Nov. 4, 1959.

Carter, Thomas Henry (R Mont.) Oct. 30, 1854–Sept. 17, 1911; House (Terr. Del.) March 4–Nov. 7, 1889, (Rep.) Nov. 8, 1889–91; Senate 1895–1901, 1905–11; Chrmn. Rep. Nat. Comm. 1892–96.

Carter, Tim Lee (R Ky.) Sept. 2, 1910–March 27, 1987; House 1965–81.

Carter, Timothy Jarvis (D Maine) Aug. 18, 1800–March 14, 1838; House Sept. 4, 1837–March 14, 1838.

Carter, Vincent Michael (R Wyo.) Nov. 6, 1891–Dec. 30, 1972; House 1929–35.

Carter, William Blount (W Tenn.) Oct. 22, 1792–April 17, 1848; House 1835–41.

Carter, William Henry (R Mass.) June 15, 1864–April 23, 1955; House 1915–19.

Cartter, David Kellogg (D Ohio) June 22, 1812–April 16, 1887; House 1849–53.

Cartwright, Wilburn (D Okla.) Jan. 12, 1892–March 14, 1979; House 1927–43.

Caruth, Asher Graham (D Ky.) Feb. 7, 1844–Nov. 25, 1907; House 1887–95.

Caruthers, Robert Looney (W Tenn.) July 31, 1800–Oct. 2, 1882; House 1841–43.

Caruthers, Samuel (D Mo.) Oct. 13, 1820–July 20, 1860; House 1853–59 (1853–57 Whig).

Carville, Edward Peter (D Nev.) May 14, 1885–June 27, 1956; Senate July 25, 1945–47; Gov. Jan. 2, 1939–July 24, 1945.

Cary, George (– Ga.) Aug. 7, 1789–Sept. 10, 1843; House 1823–27.

Cary, George Booth (D Va.) 1811–March 5, 1850; House 1841–43.

Cary, Glover H. (D Ky.) May 1, 1885–Dec. 5, 1936; House 1931–Dec. 5, 1936.

Cary, Jeremiah Eaton (D N.Y.) April 30, 1803–June 1888; House 1843–45.

Cary, Samuel Fenton (IR Ohio) Feb. 18, 1814–Sept. 29, 1900; House Nov. 21, 1867–69.

Cary, Shepard (D Maine) July 3, 1805–Aug. 9, 1866; House May 10, 1844–45.

Cary, William Joseph (R Wis.) March 22, 1865–Jan. 2, 1934; House 1907–19.

Case, Charles (R Ind.) Dec. 21, 1817–June 30, 1883; House Dec. 7, 1857–61.

Case, Clifford Philip (R N.J.) April 16, 1904–March 5, 1982; House 1945–Aug. 16, 1953; Senate 1955–79.

Case, Francis Higbee (R S.D.) Dec. 9, 1896–June 22, 1962; House 1937–51; Senate 1951–June 22, 1962; Chrmn. Senate District of Columbia 1953–55.

Case, Walter (– N.Y.) 1776–Oct. 7, 1859; House 1819–21.

Casey, John Joseph (D Pa.) May 26, 1875–May 5, 1929; House 1913–17, 1919–21, 1923–25, 1927–May 5, 1929.

Casey, Joseph (W Pa.) Dec. 17, 1814–Feb. 10, 1879; House 1849–51.

Casey, Joseph Edward (D Mass.) Dec. 27, 1898–Sept. 1, 1980; House 1935–43.

Casey, Levi (R S.C.) about 1752–Feb. 3, 1807; House 1803–Feb. 3, 1807.

Casey, Lyman Rufus (R N.D.) May 6, 1837–Jan. 26, 1914; Senate Nov. 25, 1889–93.

Casey, Robert Randolph (D Texas) July 27, 1915–April 17, 1986; House 1959–Jan. 22, 1976.

Casey, Samuel Lewis (U Ky.) Feb. 12, 1821–Aug. 25, 1902; House March 10, 1862–63.

Casey, Zadoc (ID Ill.) March 7, 1796–Sept. 4, 1862; House 1833–43 (1833–37 Jacksonian, 1837–41 Democrat).

Caskie, John Samuels (D Va.) Nov. 8, 1821–Dec. 16, 1869; House 1851–59.

Cason, Thomas Jefferson (R Ind.) Sept. 13, 1828–July 10, 1901; House 1873–77.

Cass, Lewis (great-great-grandfather of Cass Ballenger) (D Mich.) Oct. 9, 1782–June 17, 1866; Senate 1845–May 29, 1848, 1849–57; elected Pres. pro tempore Dec. 4, 1854; Gov. (Mich. Terr.) 1813–31; Secy. of War Aug. 1, 1831–Oct. 5, 1836; Secy. of State March 6, 1857–Dec. 14, 1860.

Cassedy, George (– N.J.) Sept. 16, 1783–Dec. 31, 1842; House 1821–27.

Cassel, Henry Burd (R Pa.) Oct. 19, 1855–April 28, 1926; House Nov. 5, 1901–09.

Casserly, Eugene (D Calif.) Nov. 13, 1820–June 14, 1883; Senate 1869–Nov. 19, 1873.

Cassidy, George Williams (D Nev.) April 25, 1836–June 24, 1892; House 1881–85.

Cassidy, James Henry (R Ohio) Oct. 28, 1869–Aug. 23, 1926; House April 20, 1909–11.

Cassingham, John Wilson (D Ohio) June 22, 1840–March 14, 1930; House 1901–05.

Castellow, Bryant Thomas (D Ga.) July 29, 1876–July 23, 1962; House Nov. 8, 1932–37.

Castle, Curtis Harvey (P Calif.) Oct. 4, 1848–July 12, 1928; House 1897–99.

Castle, James Nathan (D Minn.) May 23, 1836–Jan. 2, 1903; House 1891–93.

Castle, Michael N. (R Del.) July 2, 1939– ; House 1993– ; Gov. Jan. 15, 1985–Dec. 31, 1992.

Castor, George Albert (R Pa.) Aug. 6, 1855–Feb. 19, 1906; House Feb. 16, 1904–Feb. 19, 1906.

Caswell, Lucien Bonaparte (R Wis.) Nov. 27, 1827–April 26, 1919; House 1875–83, 1885–91.

Catchings, Thomas Clendinen (D Miss.) Jan. 11, 1847–Dec. 24, 1927; House 1885–1901.

Cate, George Washington (D Wis.) Sept. 17, 1825–March 7, 1905; House 1875–77.

Cate, William Henderson (D Ark.) Nov. 11, 1839–Aug. 23, 1899; House 1889–March 5, 1890, 1891–93.

Cathcart, Charles William (D Ind.) July 24, 1809–Aug. 22, 1888; House 1845–49; Senate Dec. 6, 1852–53.

Catlin, George Smith (D Conn.) Aug. 24, 1808–Dec. 26, 1851; House 1843–45.

Catlin, Theron Ephron (R Mo.) May 16, 1878–March 19, 1960; House 1911–Aug. 12, 1912.

Catron, Thomas Benton (R N.M.) Oct. 6, 1840–May 15, 1921; House (Terr. Del.) 1895–97; Senate March 27, 1912–17.

Cattell, Alexander Gilmore (R N.J.) Feb. 12, 1816–April 8, 1894; Senate Sept. 19, 1866–71.

Caulfield, Bernard Gregory (D Ill.) Oct. 18, 1828–Dec. 19, 1887; House Feb. 1, 1875–77.

Caulfield, Henry Stewart (R Mo.) Dec. 9, 1873–May 11, 1966; House 1907–09; Gov. Jan. 14, 1929–Jan. 9, 1933.

Causey, John Williams (D Del.) Sept. 19, 1841–Oct. 1, 1908; House 1891–95.

Causin, John M. S. (W Md.) 1811–Jan. 30, 1861; House 1843–45.

Cavalcante, Anthony (D Pa.) Feb. 6, 1897–Oct. 29, 1966; House 1949–51.

Cavanaugh, James Michael (D Mont.) July 4, 1823–Oct. 30, 1879; House May 11, 1858–59 (Minn.), 1867–71 (Terr. Del.).

Cavanaugh, John Joseph III (D Neb.) Aug. 1, 1945– ; House 1977–81.

Cavicchia, Peter Angelo (R N.J.) May 22, 1879–Sept. 11, 1967; House 1931–37.

Cederberg, Elford Alfred (R Mich.) March 6, 1918– ; House 1953–Dec. 31, 1978.

Celler, Emanuel (D N.Y.) May 6, 1888–Jan. 15, 1981; House 1923–73; Chrmn. House Judiciary 1949–53, 1955–73.

Cessna, John (R Pa.) June 29, 1821–Dec. 13, 1893; House 1869–71, 1873–75.

Chabot, Steve (R Ohio) Jan. 22, 1953– ; House 1995– .

Chace, Jonathan (R R.I.) July 22, 1829–June 30, 1917; House 1881–Jan. 26, 1885; Senate Jan. 20, 1885–April 9, 1889.

Chadwick, E. Wallace (R Pa.) Jan. 17, 1884–Aug. 18, 1969; House 1947–49.

Chafee, John Hubbard (R R.I.) Oct. 22, 1922–Oct. 24, 1999; Senate Dec. 29, 1976–Oct. 24, 1999; Gov. Jan. 1, 1963–Jan. 7, 1969; Chrmn. Senate Environment and Public Works 1995–99.

Chaffee, Calvin Clifford (AP Mass.) Aug. 28, 1811–Aug. 8, 1896; House 1855–59.

Chaffee, Jerome Bunty (R Colo.) April 17, 1825–March 9, 1886; House (Terr. Del.) 1871–75; Senate Nov. 15, 1876–79.

Chalmers, James Ronald (son of Joseph Williams Chalmers) (I Miss.) Jan. 12, 1831–April 9, 1898; House 1877–April 29, 1882 (Democrat), June 25, 1884–85.

Chalmers, Joseph Williams (father of James Ronald Chalmers) (D Miss.) 1807–June 16, 1853; Senate Nov. 3, 1845–47.

Chalmers, William Wallace (R Ohio) Nov. 1, 1861–Oct. 1, 1944; House 1921–23, 1925–31.

Chamberlain, Charles Ernest (R Mich.) July 22, 1917– ; House 1957–Dec. 31, 1974.

Chamberlain, Ebenezer Mattoon (D Ind.) Aug. 20, 1805–March 14, 1861; House 1853–55.

Chamberlain, George Earle (D Ore.) Jan. 1, 1854–July 9, 1928; Senate 1909–21; Gov. Jan. 14, 1903–Feb. 28, 1909.

Chamberlain, Jacob Payson (R N.Y.) Aug. 1, 1802–Oct. 5, 1878; House 1861–63.

Chamberlain, John Curtis (F N.H.) June 5, 1772–Dec. 8, 1834; House 1809–11.

Chamberlain, William (F Vt.) April 27, 1755–Sept. 27, 1828; House 1803–05, 1809–11.

Chambers, David (– Ohio) Nov. 25, 1780–Aug. 8, 1864; House Oct. 9, 1821–23.

Chambers, Ezekiel Forman (– Md.) Feb. 28, 1788–Jan. 30, 1867; Senate Jan. 24, 1826–Dec. 20, 1834.

Chambers, George (AMas. Pa.) Feb. 24, 1786–March 25, 1866; House 1833–37.

Chambers, Henry H. (– Ala.) Oct. 1, 1790–Jan. 24, 1826; Senate 1825–Jan. 24, 1826.

Chambers, John (W Ky.) Oct. 6, 1780–Sept. 21, 1852; House Dec. 1, 1828–29 (no party), 1835–39; Gov. (Iowa Terr.) 1841–45.

Chambliss, Saxby (R Ga.) Nov. 10, 1943– ; House 1995– .

Champion, Edwin Van Meter (D Ill.) Sept. 18, 1890–Feb. 11, 1976; House 1937–39.

Champion, Epaphroditius (F Conn.) April 6, 1756–Dec. 22, 1834; House 1807–17.

Champlin, Christopher Grant (F R.I.) April 12, 1768–March 18, 1840; House 1797–1801; Senate June 26, 1809–Oct. 2, 1811.

Chandler, Albert Benjamin "Happy" (D Ky.) July 14, 1898–June 15, 1991; Senate Oct. 10, 1939–Nov. 1, 1945; Gov. Dec. 10, 1935–Oct. 9, 1939, Dec. 13, 1955–Dec. 8, 1959.

Chandler, John (brother of Thomas Chandler, uncle of Zachariah Chandler) (R Maine) Feb. 1, 1762–Sept. 25, 1841; House 1805–09 (Mass.); Senate June 14, 1820–29.

Chandler, Joseph Ripley (W Pa.) Aug. 22, 1792–July 10, 1880; House 1849–55.

Chandler, Rod Dennis (great-great-great-nephew of Zachariah Chandler) (R Wash.) July 13, 1942– ; House 1983–93.

Chandler, Thomas (brother of John Chandler, uncle of Zachariah Chandler) (J N.H.) Aug. 10, 1772–Jan. 28, 1866; House 1829–33.

Chandler, Thomas Alberter (R Okla.) July 26, 1871–June 22, 1953; House 1917–19, 1921–23.

Chandler, Walter "Clift" (D Tenn.) Oct. 5, 1887–Oct. 1, 1967; House 1935–Jan. 2, 1940.

Chandler, Walter Marion (R N.Y.) Dec. 8, 1867–March 16, 1935; House 1913–19 (1913–17 Progressive), 1921–23.

Chandler, William Eaton (R N.H.) Dec. 28, 1835–Nov. 30, 1917; Senate June 14, 1887–89, June 18, 1889–1901; Secy. of the Navy April 16, 1882–March 6, 1885.

Chandler, Zachariah (nephew of John Chandler and Thomas Chandler, grandfather of Frederick Hale, great-great-great-uncle of Rod Dennis Chandler) (R Mich.) Dec. 10, 1813–Nov. 1, 1879; Senate 1857–75, Feb. 22, 1879–Nov. 1, 1879; Secy. of the Interior Oct. 19, 1875–March 11, 1877; Chrmn. Rep. Nat. Comm. 1876–79.

Chaney, John (D Ohio) Jan. 12, 1790–April 10, 1881; House 1833–39 (1833–37 Jacksonian).

Chaney, John Crawford (R Ind.) Feb. 1, 1853–April 26, 1940; House 1905–09.

Chanler, John Winthrop (father of William Astor Chanler) (D N.Y.) Sept. 14, 1826–Oct. 19, 1877; House 1863–69.

Chanler, William Astor (son of John Winthrop Chanler) (D N.Y.) June 11, 1867–March 4, 1934; House 1899–1901.

Chapin, Alfred Clark (grandfather of Hamilton Fish Jr. born in 1926) (D N.Y.) March 8, 1848–Oct. 2, 1936; House Nov. 3, 1891–Nov. 16, 1892.

Chapin, Chester Williams (D Mass.) Dec. 16, 1798–June 10, 1883; House 1875–77.

Chapin, Graham Hurd (J N.Y.) Feb. 10, 1799–Sept. 8, 1843; House 1835–37.

Chapman, Andrew Grant (son of John Grant Chapman) (D Md.) Jan. 17, 1839–Sept. 25, 1892; House 1881–83.

Chapman, Augustus Alexandria (D Va.) March 9, 1803–June 7, 1876; House 1843–47.

Chapman, Bird Beers (D Neb.) Aug. 24, 1821–Sept. 21, 1871; House (Terr. Del.) 1855–57.

Chapman, Charles (W Conn.) June 21, 1799–Aug. 7, 1869; House 1851–53.

Chapman, Henry (D Pa.) Feb. 4, 1804–April 11, 1891; House 1857–59.

Chapman, Jim (D Texas) March 8, 1945– ; House Aug. 3, 1985–97.

Chapman, John (F Pa.) Oct. 18, 1740–Jan. 27, 1800; House 1797–1799.

Chapman, John Grant (father of Andrew Grant Chapman) (W Md.) July 5, 1798–Dec. 10, 1856; House 1845–49.

Chapman, Pleasant Thomas (R Ill.) Oct. 8, 1854–Jan. 31, 1931; House 1905–11.

Chapman, Reuben (D Ala.) July 15, 1799–May 16, 1882; House 1835–47 (1835–37 Jacksonian); Gov. Dec. 16, 1847–Dec. 17, 1849.

Chapman, Virgil Munday (D Ky.) March 15, 1895–March 8, 1951; House 1925–29, 1931–49; Senate 1949–March 8, 1951.

Chapman, William Williams (D Iowa) Aug. 11, 1808–Oct. 18, 1892; House (Terr. Del.) Sept. 10, 1838–Oct. 27, 1840.

Chappell, Absalom Harris (cousin of Lucius Quintus Cincinnatus Lamar) (W Ga.) Dec. 18, 1801–Dec. 11, 1878; House Oct. 2, 1843–45.

Chappell, John Joel (R S.C.) Jan. 19, 1782–May 23, 1871; House 1813–17.

Chappell, William Venroe Jr. (D Fla.) Feb. 3, 1922–March 30, 1989; House 1969–89.

Chappie, Eugene A. (R Calif.) March 28, 1920–May 31, 1992; House 1981–87.

Charles, William Barclay (R N.Y.) April 3, 1861–Nov. 25, 1950; House 1915–17.

Charlton, Robert Milledge (D Ga.) Jan. 19, 1807–Jan. 18, 1854; Senate May 31, 1852–53.

Chase, Dudley (uncle of Salmon Portland Chase and Dudley Chase Denison) (R Vt.) Dec. 30, 1771–Feb. 23, 1846; Senate 1813–Nov. 3, 1817 (Jefferson Democrat), 1825–31.

Chase, George William (W N.Y.) ?–April 17, 1867; House 1853–55.

Chase, Jackson Burton (R Neb.) Aug. 19, 1890–May 4, 1974; House 1955–57.

Chase, James Mitchell (R Pa.) Dec. 19, 1891–Jan. 1, 1945; House 1927–33.

Chase, Lucien Bonaparte (D Tenn.) Dec. 5, 1817–Dec. 4, 1864; House 1845–49.

Chase, Ray P. (R Minn.) March 12, 1880–Sept. 18, 1948; House 1933–35.

Chase, Salmon Portland (nephew of Dudley Chase, cousin of Dudley Chase Denison) (R Ohio) Jan. 13, 1808–May 7, 1873; Senate

1849–55 (Free-Soiler), March 4–6, 1861; Gov. Jan. 14, 1856–Jan. 9, 1860; Secy. of the Treasury March 7, 1861–June 30, 1864; Chief Justice United States Dec. 15, 1864–May 7, 1873.

Chase, Samuel (– N.Y.) ?–Aug. 3, 1838; House 1827–29.

Chastain, Elijah Webb (D Ga.) Sept. 25, 1813–April 9, 1874; House 1851–55 (1851–53 Unionist).

Chatham, Richard Thurmond (D N.C.) Aug. 16, 1896–Feb. 5, 1957; House 1949–57.

Chaves, Jose Francisco (R N.M.) June 27, 1833–Nov. 26, 1904; House (Terr. Del.) 1865–67, Feb. 20, 1869–71.

Chavez, Dennis (D N.M.) April 8, 1888–Nov. 18, 1962; House 1931–35; Senate May 11, 1935–Nov. 18, 1962; Chrmn. Senate Public Works 1949–53, 1955–62.

Cheadle, Joseph Bonaparte (R Ind.) Aug. 14, 1842–May 28, 1904; House 1887–91.

Cheatham, Henry Plummer (R N.C.) Dec. 27, 1857–Nov. 29, 1935; House 1889–93.

Cheatham, Richard (W Tenn.) Feb. 20, 1799–Sept. 9, 1845; House 1837–39.

Chelf, Frank Leslie (D Ky.) Sept. 22, 1907–Sept. 1, 1982; House 1945–67.

Cheney, Person Colby (R N.H.) Feb. 25, 1828–June 19, 1901; Senate Nov. 24, 1886–June 14, 1887; Gov. June 10, 1875–June 6, 1877.

Cheney, Richard Bruce (R Wyo.) Jan. 30, 1941– ; House 1979–March 17, 1989; Secy. of Defense March 21, 1989–Jan. 20, 1993.

Chenoweth, Helen (R Idaho) Jan. 27, 1938– ; House 1995– .

Chenoweth, John Edgar (R Colo.) Aug. 17, 1897–Jan. 2, 1986; House 1941–49, 1951–65.

Chesney, Chester Anton (D Ill.) March 9, 1916–Sept. 20, 1986; House 1949–51.

Chesnut, James Jr. (D S.C.) Jan. 18, 1815–Feb. 1, 1885; Senate Dec. 3, 1858–Nov. 10, 1860.

Chetwood, William (W N.J.) June 17, 1771–Dec. 17, 1857; House Dec. 5, 1836–37.

Cheves, Langdon (R S.C.) Sept. 17, 1776–June 26, 1857; House Dec. 31, 1810–15; Speaker Jan. 19, 1814–15.

Chickering, Charles Addison (R N.Y.) Nov. 26, 1843–Feb. 13, 1900; House 1893–Feb. 13, 1900.

Chilcott, George Miles (R Colo.) Jan. 2, 1828–March 6, 1891; House (Terr. Del.) 1867–69; Senate April 17, 1882–Jan. 27, 1883.

Child, Thomas Jr. (W N.Y.) March 22, 1818–March 9, 1869; elected to the House for the term beginning 1855 but never qualified or attended a session owing to illness.

Childs, Robert Andrew (R Ill.) March 22, 1845–Dec. 19, 1915; House 1893–95.

Childs, Timothy (W N.Y.) 1785–Nov. 8, 1847; House 1829–31 (Anti-Mason), 1835–39, 1841–43.

Chiles, Lawton Mainor Jr. (D Fla.) April 3, 1930–Dec. 12, 1998; Senate 1971–89; Chrmn. Senate Budget 1987–89; Gov. Jan. 8, 1991–Dec. 12, 1998.

Chilton, Horace (grandson of Thomas Chilton) (D Texas) Dec. 29, 1853–June 12, 1932; Senate June 10, 1891–March 22, 1892, 1895–1901.

Chilton, Samuel (W Va.) Sept. 7, 1804–Jan. 14, 1867; House 1843–45.

Chilton, Thomas (grandfather of Horace Chilton) (AJ Ky.) July 30, 1798–Aug. 15, 1854; House Dec. 22, 1827–31 (no party), 1833–35.

Chilton, William Edwin (D W.Va.) March 17, 1858–Nov. 7, 1939; Senate 1911–17.

Chindblom, Carl Richard (R Ill.) Dec. 21, 1870–Sept. 12, 1956; House 1919–33.

Chinn, Joseph William (J Va.) Nov. 16, 1798–Dec. 5, 1840; House 1831–35.

Chinn, Thomas Withers (cousin of Robert Enoch Withers) (W La.) Nov. 22, 1791–May 22, 1852; House 1839–41.

Chiperfield, Burnett Mitchell (father of Robert Bruce Chiperfield) (R Ill.) June 14, 1870–June 24, 1940; House 1915–17, 1929–33.

Chiperfield, Robert Bruce (son of Burnett Mitchell Chiperfield) (R Ill.) Nov. 20, 1899–April 9, 1971; House 1939–63; Chrmn. House Foreign Affairs 1953–55.

Chipman, Daniel (brother of Nathaniel Chipman, great-uncle of John Logan Chipman) (F Vt.) Oct. 22, 1765–April 23, 1850; House 1815–May 5, 1816.

Chipman, John Logan (grandson of Nathaniel Chipman, great-nephew of Daniel Chipman) (D Mich.) June 5, 1830–Aug. 17, 1893; House 1887–Aug. 17, 1893.

Chipman, John Smith (D Mich.) Aug. 10, 1800–July 27, 1869; House 1845–47.

Chipman, Nathaniel (brother of Daniel Chipman, grandfather of John Logan Chipman) (F Vt.) Nov. 15, 1752–Feb. 13, 1843; Senate Oct. 17, 1797–1803.

Chipman, Norton Parker (R D.C.) March 7, 1836–Feb. 1, 1924; House (Del.) April 21, 1871–75.

Chisholm, Shirley Anita (D N.Y.) Nov. 30, 1924– ; House 1969–83.

Chittenden, Martin (F Vt.) March 12, 1763–Sept. 5, 1840; House 1803–13; Gov. Oct. 23, 1813–Oct. 14, 1815.

Chittenden, Simeon Baldwin (R N.Y.) March 29, 1814–April 14, 1889; House Nov. 3, 1874–81 (Nov. 3, 1874–77 Independent Republican).

Chittenden, Thomas Cotton (W N.Y.) Aug. 30, 1788–Aug. 22, 1866; House 1839–43.

Choate, Rufus (W Mass.) Oct. 1, 1799–July 13, 1859; House 1831–June 30, 1834; Senate Feb. 23, 1841–45.

Chrisman, James Stone (D Ky.) Sept. 14, 1818–July 29, 1881; House 1853–55.

Christensen, Donna M. C. (D V.I.) Sept. 19, 1945– ; House (Terr. Del.) 1997– .

Christensen, Jon (R Neb.) Feb. 20, 1963– ; House 1995–99.

Christgau, Victor Laurence August (R Minn.) Sept. 20, 1894–Oct. 10, 1991; House 1929–33.

Christiancy, Isaac Peckham (R Mich.) March 12, 1812–Sept. 8, 1890; Senate 1875–Feb. 10, 1879.

Christianson, Theodore (R Minn.) Sept. 12, 1883–Dec. 9, 1948; House 1933–37; Gov. Jan. 6, 1925–Jan. 6, 1931.

Christie, Gabriel (R Md.) 1755–April 1, 1808; House 1793–97 (no party), 1799–1801.

Christopher, George Henry (D Mo.) Dec. 9, 1888–Jan. 23, 1959; House 1949–51, 1955–Jan. 23, 1959.

Christopherson, Charles Andrew (R S.D.) July 23, 1871–Nov. 2, 1951; House 1919–33.

Chrysler, Dick (R Mich.) April 29, 1942– ; House 1995–97.

Chudoff, Earl (D Pa.) Nov. 15, 1907–May 17, 1993; House 1949–Jan. 5, 1958.

Church, Denver Samuel (D Calif.) Dec. 11, 1862–Feb. 21, 1952; House 1913–19, 1933–35.

Church, Frank Forrester (D Idaho) July 25, 1924–April 7, 1984; Senate 1957–81; Chrmn. Senate Foreign Relations 1979–81.

Church, Marguerite Stitt (widow of Ralph Edwin Church) (R Ill.) Sept. 13, 1892–May 26, 1990; House 1951–63.

Church, Ralph Edwin (husband of Marguerite Stitt Church) (R Ill.) May 5, 1883–March 21, 1950; House 1935–41, 1943–March 21, 1950.

Churchill, George Bosworth (R Mass.) Oct. 24, 1866–July 1, 1925; House March 4–July 1, 1925.

Churchill, John Charles (R N.Y.) Jan. 17, 1821–June 4, 1905; House 1867–71.

Churchwell, William Montgomery (D Tenn.) Feb. 20, 1826–Aug. 18, 1862; House 1851–55.

Cilley, Bradbury (uncle of Jonathan Cilley and Joseph Cilley) (F N.H.) Feb. 1, 1760–Dec. 17, 1831; House 1813–17.

Cilley, Jonathan (nephew of Bradbury Cilley, brother of Joseph Cilley) (D Maine) July 2, 1802–Feb. 24, 1838; House 1837–Feb. 24, 1838.

Cilley, Joseph (nephew of Bradbury Cilley, brother of Jonathan Cilley) (D N.H.) Jan. 4, 1791–Sept. 16, 1887; Senate June 13, 1846–47.

Citron, William Michael (D Conn.) Aug. 29, 1896–June 7, 1976; House 1935–39.

Claflin, William (R Mass.) March 6, 1818–Jan. 5, 1905; House 1877–81; Gov. Jan. 7, 1869–Jan. 4, 1872; Chrmn. Rep. Nat. Comm. 1868–72.

Clagett, Clifton (R N.H.) Dec. 3, 1762–Jan. 25, 1829; House 1803–05 (Federalist), 1817–21.

Clagett, William Horace (uncle of Samuel Barrett Pettengill) (R Mont.) Sept. 21, 1838–Aug. 3, 1901; House (Terr. Del.) 1871–73.

Clague, Frank (R Minn.) July 13, 1865–March 25, 1952; House 1921–33.

Claiborne, James Robert (D Mo.) June 22, 1882–Feb. 16, 1944; House 1933–37.

Claiborne, John (son of Thomas Claiborne born in 1749, brother of Thomas Claiborne born in 1780) (R Va.) 1777–Oct. 9, 1808; House 1805–Oct. 9, 1808.

Claiborne, John Francis Hamtramck (nephew of William Charles Cole Claiborne and Nathaniel Herbert Claiborne, great-great-grandfather of Claiborne de Borda Pell, great-nephew of Thomas Claiborne born in 1749, great-grandfather of Herbert Claiborne Pell Jr., great-great-great-uncle of Corinne Claiborne Boggs) (J Miss.) April 24, 1807–May 17, 1884; House 1835–37, July 18, 1837–Feb. 5, 1838.

Claiborne, Nathaniel Herbert (brother of William Charles Cole Claiborne, nephew of Thomas Claiborne born in 1749, uncle of John Francis Hamtramck Claiborne, great-great-great-uncle of Corinne Claiborne Boggs) (AJ Va.) Nov. 14, 1777–Aug. 15, 1859; House 1825–37 (1825–31 Jacksonian).

Claiborne, Thomas (father of John Claiborne and Thomas Claiborne born in 1780, uncle of Nathaniel Herbert Claiborne and William Charles Cole Claiborne, great-uncle of John Francis Hamtramck Claiborne, great-great-great-great-great-uncle of Corinne Claiborne Boggs) (R Va.) Feb. 1, 1749–1812; House 1793–99, 1801–05.

Claiborne, Thomas (son of Thomas Claiborne born in 1749, brother of John Claiborne) (R Tenn.) May 17, 1780–Jan. 7, 1856; House 1817–19.

Claiborne, William Charles Cole (brother of Nathaniel Herbert Claiborne, nephew of Thomas Claiborne born in 1749, uncle of John Francis Hamtramck Claiborne, great-great-great-uncle of Corinne Claiborne Boggs) (D La.) 1775–Nov. 23, 1817; House 1797–1801 (Republican); Senate March 4–Nov. 23, 1817; Gov. 1801–03 (Miss. Terr.), 1804–12 (Orleans Terr.), July 30, 1812–Dec. 16, 1816 (Democratic Republican).

Clancy, Donald Daniel (R Ohio) July 24, 1921– ; House 1961–77.

Clancy, John Michael (D N.Y.) May 7, 1837–July 25, 1903; House 1889–95.

Clancy, John Richard (D N.Y.) March 8, 1859–April 21, 1932; House 1913–15.

Clancy, Robert Henry (R Mich.) March 14, 1882–April 23, 1962; House 1923–25 (Democrat), 1927–33.

Clapp, Asa William Henry (D Maine) March 6, 1805–March 22, 1891; House 1847–49.

Clapp, Moses Edwin (R Minn.) May 21, 1851–March 6, 1929; Senate Jan. 23, 1901–17.

Clardy, John Daniel (D Ky.) Aug. 30, 1828–Aug. 20, 1918; House 1895–99.

Clardy, Kit Francis (R Mich.) June 17, 1892–Sept. 5, 1961; House 1953–55.

Clardy, Martin Linn (D Mo.) April 26, 1844–July 5, 1914; House 1879–89.

Clark, Abraham (– N.J.) Feb. 15, 1726–Sept. 15, 1794; House 1791–Sept. 15, 1794; Cont. Cong. 1776–78, 1780–83, 1786–88.

Clark, Alvah Augustus (cousin of James Nelson Pidcock) (D N.J.) Sept. 13, 1840–Dec. 27, 1912; House 1877–81.

Clark, Ambrose Williams (R N.Y.) Feb. 19, 1810–Oct. 13, 1887; House 1861–65.

Clark, Amos Jr. (R N.J.) Nov. 8, 1828–Oct. 31, 1912; House 1873–75.

Clark, Charles Benjamin (R Wis.) Aug. 24, 1844–Sept. 10, 1891; House 1887–91.

Clark, Charles Nelson (R Mo.) Aug. 21, 1827–Oct. 4, 1902; House 1895–97.

Clark, Christopher Henderson (brother of James Clark, uncle of John Bullock Clark, great-uncle of John Bullock Clark Jr.) (R Va.) 1767–Nov. 21, 1828; House Nov. 5, 1804–July 1, 1806.

Clark, Clarence Don (R Wyo.) April 16, 1851–Nov. 18, 1930; House Dec. 1, 1890–93; Senate Jan. 23, 1895–1917.

Clark, Daniel (– Orleans) about 1766–Aug. 16, 1813; House (Terr. Del.) Dec. 1, 1806–09.

Clark, Daniel (R N.H.) Oct. 24, 1809–Jan. 2, 1891; Senate June 27, 1857–July 27, 1866; elected Pres. pro tempore April 26, 1864, Feb. 9, 1865.

Clark, David Worth (D Idaho) April 2, 1902–June 19, 1955; House 1935–39; Senate 1939–45.

Clark, Ezra Jr. (R Conn.) Sept. 12, 1813–Sept. 26, 1896; House 1855–59 (1855–57 American Party).

Clark, Frank (D Fla.) March 28, 1860–April 14, 1936; House 1905–25.

Clark, Frank Monroe (D Pa.) Dec. 24, 1915– ; House 1955–Dec. 31, 1974.

Clark, Franklin (D Maine) Aug. 2, 1801–Aug. 24, 1874; House 1847–49.

Clark, Henry Alden (R Pa.) Jan. 7, 1850–Feb. 15, 1944; House 1917–19.

Clark, Henry Selby (D N.C.) Sept. 9, 1809–Jan. 8, 1869; House 1845–47.

Clark, Horace Francis (ALD N.Y.) Nov. 29, 1815–June 19, 1873; House 1857–61 (1857–59 Democrat).

Clark, James (brother of Christopher Henderson Clark, uncle of John Bullock Clark, great-uncle of John Bullock Clark Jr.) (R Ky.) Jan. 16, 1770–Sept. 27, 1839; House 1813–16, Aug. 1, 1825–31; Gov. June 1, 1836–Sept. 27, 1839 (Whig).

Clark, James Beauchamp "Champ" (father of Joel Bennett Clark) (D Mo.) March 7, 1850–March 2, 1921; House 1893–95, 1897–March 2, 1921; House minority leader 1908–11, 1919–21; Speaker April 4, 1911–13, April 7, 1913–15, Dec. 6, 1915–17, April 2, 1917–19.

Clark, James West (R N.C.) Oct. 15, 1779–Dec. 20, 1843; House 1815–17.

Clark, Jerome Bayard (D N.C.) April 5, 1882–Aug. 26, 1959; House 1929–49.

Clark, Joel Bennett (son of James Beauchamp Clark) (D Mo.) Jan. 8, 1890–July 13, 1954; Senate Feb. 3, 1933–45.

Clark, John Bullock (father of John Bullock Clark Jr., nephew of Christopher Henderson Clark and James Clark) (D Mo.) April 17, 1802–Oct. 29, 1885; House Dec. 7, 1857–July 13, 1861.

Clark, John Bullock Jr. (son of John Bullock Clark, great-nephew of Christopher Henderson Clark and James Clark) (D Mo.) Jan. 14, 1831–Sept. 7, 1903; House 1873–83.

Clark, John Chamberlain (W N.Y.) Jan. 14, 1793–Oct. 25, 1852; House 1827–29 (no party), 1837–43 (1837–39 Democrat).

Clark, Joseph Sill (D Pa.) Oct. 21, 1901–Jan. 12, 1990; Senate 1957–69.

Clark, Lincoln (D Iowa) Aug. 9, 1800–Sept. 16, 1886; House 1851–53.

Clark, Linwood Leon (R Md.) March 21, 1876–Nov. 18, 1965; House 1929–31.

Clark, Lot (– N.Y.) May 23, 1788–Dec. 18, 1862; House 1823–25.

Clark, Richard Clarence "Dick" (D Iowa) Sept. 14, 1929– ; Senate 1973–79.

Clark, Robert (– N.Y.) June 12, 1777–Oct. 1, 1837; House 1819–21.

Clark, Rush (R Iowa) Oct. 1, 1834–April 29, 1879; House 1877–April 29, 1879.

Clark, Samuel (D Mich.) Jan. 1800–Oct. 2, 1870; House 1833–35 (J N.Y.), 1853–55.

Clark, Samuel Mercer (R Iowa) Oct. 11, 1842–Aug. 11, 1900; House 1895–99.

Clark, William (AMas. Pa.) Feb. 18, 1774–March 28, 1851; House 1833–37.

Clark, William Andrews (D Mont.) Jan. 8, 1839–March 2, 1925; Senate Dec. 4, 1899–May 15, 1900, 1901–07.

Clark, William Thomas (R Texas) June 29, 1831–Oct. 12, 1905; House March 31, 1870–May 13, 1872.

Clarke, Archibald Smith (brother of Staley Nichols Clarke) (R N.Y.) 1788–Dec. 4, 1821; House Dec. 2, 1816–17.

Clarke, Bayard (W N.Y.) March 17, 1815–June 20, 1884; House 1855–57.

Clarke, Beverly Leonidas (D Ky.) Feb. 11, 1809–March 17, 1860; House 1847–49.

Clarke, Charles Ezra (W N.Y.) April 8, 1790–Dec. 29, 1863; House 1849–51.

Clarke, Frank Gay (R N.H.) Sept. 10, 1850–Jan. 9, 1901; House 1897–Jan. 9, 1901.

Clarke, Freeman (R N.Y.) March 22, 1809–June 24, 1887; House 1863–65, 1871–75.

Clarke, James McClure (D N.C.) June 12, 1917–April 13, 1999; House 1983–85, 1987–91.

Clarke, James Paul (D Ark.) Aug. 18, 1854–Oct. 1, 1916; Senate 1903–Oct. 1, 1916; elected Pres. pro tempore March 13, 1913, Dec. 6, 1915; Gov. Jan. 18, 1895–Jan. 12, 1897.

Clarke, John Blades (D Ky.) April 14, 1833–May 23, 1911; House 1875–79.

Clarke, John Davenport (husband of Marian Williams Clarke) (R N.Y.) Jan. 15, 1873–Nov. 5, 1933; House 1921–25, 1927–Nov. 5, 1933.

Clarke, John Hopkins (W R.I.) April 1, 1789–Nov. 23, 1870; Senate 1847–53.

Clarke, Marian Williams (widow of John Davenport Clarke) (R N.Y.) July 29, 1880–April 8, 1953; House Dec. 28, 1933–35.

Clarke, Reader Wright (R Ohio) May 18, 1812–May 23, 1872; House 1865–69.

Clarke, Richard Henry (D Ala.) Feb. 9, 1843–Sept. 26, 1906; House 1889–97.

Clarke, Sidney (R Kan.) Oct. 16, 1831–June 18, 1909; House 1865–71.

Clarke, Staley Nichols (brother of Archibald Smith Clarke) (W N.Y.) May 24, 1794–Oct. 14, 1860; House 1841–43.

Clason, Charles Russell (R Mass.) Sept. 3, 1890–July 7, 1985; House 1937–49.

Classon, David Guy (R Wis.) Sept. 27, 1870–Sept. 6, 1930; House 1917–23.

Clausen, Don Holst (R Calif.) April 27, 1923– ; House Jan. 22, 1963–83.

Clawson, Delwin Morgan (R Calif.) Jan. 11, 1914–May 5, 1992; House June 11, 1963–Dec. 31, 1978.

Clawson, Isaiah Dunn (R N.J.) March 30, 1822–Oct. 9, 1879; House 1855–59 (1855–57 Whig).

Clay, Alexander Stephens (D Ga.) Sept. 25, 1853–Nov. 13, 1910; Senate 1897–Nov. 13, 1910.

Clay, Brutus Junius (U Ky.) July 1, 1808–Oct. 11, 1878; House 1863–65.

Clay, Clement Claiborne Jr. (son of Clement Comer Clay) (D Ala.) Dec. 13, 1816–Jan. 3, 1882; Senate Nov. 29, 1853–Jan. 21, 1861.

Clay, Clement Comer (father of Clement Claiborne Clay Jr.) (D Ala.) Dec. 17, 1789–Sept. 7, 1866; House 1829–35 (no party); Senate June 19, 1837–Nov. 15, 1841; Gov. Nov. 21, 1835–July 17, 1837.

Clay, Henry (father of James Brown Clay) (W Ky.) April 12, 1777–June 29, 1852; Senate Nov. 19, 1806–07 (no party), Jan. 4, 1810–11 (no party), Nov. 10, 1831–March 31, 1842, 1849–June 29, 1852; House 1811–Jan. 19, 1814 (Republican), 1815–21 (Republican), 1823–March 6, 1825 (Republican); Speaker Nov. 4, 1811–13, May 24, 1813–Jan. 19, 1814, Dec. 4, 1815–17, Dec. 1, 1817–19, Dec. 6, 1819–Oct. 28, 1820, Dec. 1, 1823–25; Secy. of State March 7, 1825–March 3, 1829.

Clay, James Brown (son of Henry Clay) (D Ky.) Nov. 9, 1817–Jan. 26, 1864; House 1857–59.

Clay, James Franklin (D Ky.) Oct. 29, 1840–Aug. 17, 1921; House 1883–85.

Clay, Joseph (R Pa.) July 24, 1769–Aug. 27, 1811; House 1803–08.

Clay, Matthew (R Va.) March 25, 1754–May 27, 1815; House 1797–1813, March 4–May 27, 1815.

Clay, William Lacy Sr. (D Mo.) April 30, 1931– ; House 1969– ; Chrmn. House Post Office and Civil Service 1991–95.

Claypool, Harold Kile (son of Horatio Clifford Claypool, cousin of John Barney Peterson) (D Ohio) June 2, 1886–Aug. 2, 1958; House 1937–43.

Claypool, Horatio Clifford (father of Harold Kile Claypool, cousin of John Barney Peterson) (D Ohio) Feb. 9, 1859–Jan. 19, 1921; House 1911–15, 1917–19.

Clayton, Augustin Smith (J Ga.) Nov. 27, 1783–June 21, 1839; House Jan. 21, 1832–35.

Clayton, Bertram Tracy (brother of Henry De Lamar Clayton) (D N.Y.) Oct. 19, 1862–May 30, 1918; House 1899–1901.

Clayton, Charles (R Calif.) Oct. 5, 1825–Oct. 4, 1885; House 1873–75.

Clayton, Eva (D N.C.) Sept. 16, 1934– ; House Nov. 4, 1992– .

Clayton, Henry De Lamar (brother of Bertram Tracy Clayton) (D Ala.) Feb. 10, 1857–Dec. 21, 1929; House 1897–May 25, 1914.

Clayton, John Middleton (nephew of Joshua Clayton, cousin of Thomas Clayton, great-great-uncle of Clayton Douglass Buck) (W Del.) July 24, 1796–Nov. 9, 1856; Senate 1829–Dec. 29, 1836 (no party), 1845–Feb. 23, 1849, 1853–Nov. 9, 1856; Secy. of State March 8, 1849–July 22, 1850.

Clayton, Joshua (father of Thomas Clayton, uncle of John Middleton Clayton, son-in-law of Richard Bassett) (– Del.) July 20, 1744–Aug. 11, 1798; Senate Jan. 19–Aug. 11, 1798; Gov. June 2, 1789–Jan. 13, 1796 (Federalist).

Clayton, Powell (R Ark.) Aug. 7, 1833–Aug. 25, 1914; Senate 1871–77; Gov. July 2, 1868–March 17, 1871.

Clayton, Thomas (son of Joshua Clayton, cousin of John Middleton Clayton) (W Del.) July 1777–Aug. 21, 1854; House 1815–17 (Federalist); Senate Jan. 8, 1824–27 (no party), Jan. 9, 1837–47.

Cleary, William Edward (D N.Y.) July 20, 1849–Dec. 20, 1932; House March 5, 1918–21, 1923–27.

Cleland, Max (D Ga.) Aug. 24, 1942– ; Senate 1997– .

Clemens, Jeremiah (D Ala.) Dec. 28, 1814–May 21, 1865; Senate Nov. 30, 1849–53.

Clemens, Sherrard (D Va.) April 28, 1820–June 30, 1881; House Dec. 6, 1852–53, 1857–61.

Clement, Robert Nelson (D Tenn.) Sept. 23, 1943– ; House Jan. 25, 1988– .

Clemente, Louis Gary (D N.Y.) June 10, 1908–May 13, 1968; House 1949–53.

Clements, Andrew Jackson (U Tenn.) Dec. 23, 1832–Nov. 7, 1913; House 1861–63.

Clements, Earle Chester (D Ky.) Oct. 22, 1896–March 12, 1985; House 1945–Jan. 6, 1948; Senate Nov. 27, 1950–57; Gov. Dec. 9, 1947–Nov. 27, 1950.

Clements, Isaac (R Ill.) March 31, 1837–May 31, 1909; House 1873–75.

Clements, Judson Claudius (D Ga.) Feb. 12, 1846–June 18, 1917; House 1881–91.

Clements, Newton Nash (D Ala.) Dec. 23, 1837–Feb. 20, 1900; House Dec. 8, 1880–81.

Clendenin, David (R Ohio) ?–?; House Oct. 11, 1814–17.

Cleveland, Chauncey Fitch (D Conn.) Feb. 16, 1799–June 6, 1887; House 1849–53; Gov. May 4, 1842–May 1844.

Cleveland, James Colgate (R N.H.) June 13, 1920–Dec. 3, 1995; House 1963–81.

Cleveland, Jesse Franklin (D Ga.) Oct. 25, 1804–June 22, 1841; House Oct. 5, 1835–39 (Oct. 5, 1835–37 Jacksonian).

Cleveland, Orestes (D N.J.) March 2, 1829–March 30, 1896; House 1869–71.

Clevenger, Cliff (R Ohio) Aug. 20, 1885–Dec. 13, 1960; House 1939–59.

Clevenger, Raymond Francis (D Mich.) June 6, 1926– ; House 1965–67.

Clever, Charles P. (D N.M.) Feb. 23, 1830–July 8, 1874; House (Terr. Del.) Sept. 2, 1867–Feb. 20, 1869.

Clifford, Nathan (D Maine) Aug. 18, 1803–July 25, 1881; House 1839–43; Atty. Gen. Oct. 17, 1846–March 17, 1848; Assoc. Justice Supreme Court Jan. 21, 1858–July 25, 1881.

Clift, Joseph Wales (R Ga.) Sept. 30, 1837–May 2, 1908; House July 25, 1868–69.

Clinch, Duncan Lamont (W Ga.) April 6, 1787–Nov. 27, 1849; House Feb. 15, 1844–45.

Cline, Cyrus (D Ind.) July 12, 1856–Oct. 5, 1923; House 1909–17.

Clinger, William Floyd Jr. (R Pa.) April 4, 1929– ; House 1979–97; Chrmn. House Government Reform and Oversight 1995–97.

Clingman, Thomas Lanier (D N.C.) July 27, 1812–Nov. 3, 1897; House 1843–45 (Whig), 1847–May 7, 1858 (Whig); Senate May 7, 1858–March 28, 1861.

Clinton, De Witt (half-brother of James Graham Clinton, cousin of George Clinton, nephew of Vice Pres. George Clinton) (R N.Y.) March 2, 1769–Feb. 11, 1828; Senate Feb. 9, 1802–Nov. 4, 1803; Gov. July 1, 1817–Jan. 1, 1823, Jan. 1, 1825–Feb. 11, 1828.

Clinton, George (cousin of De Witt Clinton and James Graham Clinton, son of Vice Pres. George Clinton) (R N.Y.) June 6, 1771–Sept. 16, 1809; House Feb. 14, 1805–09.

Clinton, James Graham (half-brother of De Witt Clinton, cousin of George Clinton, nephew of Vice Pres. George Clinton) (D N.Y.) Jan. 2, 1804–May 28, 1849; House 1841–45.

Clippinger, Roy (R Ill.) Jan. 13, 1886–Dec. 24, 1962; House Nov. 6, 1945–49.

Clopton, David (D Ala.) Sept. 29, 1820–Feb. 5, 1892; House 1859–Jan. 21, 1861.

Clopton, John (R Va.) Feb. 7, 1756–Sept. 11, 1816; House 1795–99, 1801–Sept. 11, 1816.

Clouse, Wynne F. (R Tenn.) Aug. 29, 1883–Feb. 19, 1944; House 1921–23.

Clover, Benjamin Hutchinson (P Kan.) Dec. 22, 1837–Dec. 30, 1899; House 1891–93.

Clowney, William Kennedy (N S.C.) March 21, 1797–March 12, 1851; House 1833–35, 1837–39.

Cluett, Ernest Harold (R N.Y.) July 13, 1874–Feb. 4, 1954; House 1937–43.

Clunie, Thomas Jefferson (D Calif.) March 25, 1852–June 30, 1903; House 1889–91.

Clyburn, James E. (D S.C.) July 21, 1940– ; House 1993– .

Clymer, George (– Pa.) March 16, 1739–Jan. 23, 1813; House 1789–91; Cont. Cong. 1776–77, 1780–82.

Clymer, Hiester (nephew of William Hiester, cousin of Isaac Ellmaker Hiester) (D Pa.) Nov. 3, 1827–June 12, 1884; House 1873–81.

Coad, Merwin (D Iowa) Sept. 28, 1924– ; House 1957–63.

Coady, Charles Pearce (D Md.) Feb. 22, 1868–Feb. 16, 1934; House Nov. 4, 1913–21.

Coats, Daniel Ray (R Ind.) May 16, 1943– ; House 1981–Jan. 1, 1989; Senate 1989–99.

Cobb, Amasa (R Wis.) Sept. 27, 1823–July 5, 1905; House 1863–71.

Cobb, Clinton Levering (R N.C.) Aug. 25, 1842–April 30, 1879; House 1869–75.

Cobb, David (– Mass.) Sept. 14, 1748–April 17, 1830; House 1793–95.

Cobb, George Thomas (D N.J.) Oct. 13, 1813–Aug. 12, 1870; House 1861–63.

Cobb, Howell (uncle of Howell Cobb, below) (R Ga.) Aug. 3, 1772–May 26, 1818; House 1807–12.

Cobb, Howell (nephew of Howell Cobb, above) (D Ga.) Sept. 7, 1815–Oct. 9, 1868; House 1843–51, 1855–57; Speaker Dec. 22, 1849–51; Gov. Nov. 5, 1851–Nov. 9, 1853 (Union Democrat); Secy. of the Treasury March 7, 1857–Dec. 8, 1860.

Cobb, James Edward (– Ala.) Oct. 5, 1835–June 2, 1903; House 1887–April 21, 1896.

Cobb, Seth Wallace (D Mo.) Dec. 5, 1838–May 22, 1909; House 1891–97.

Cobb, Stephen Alonzo (R Kan.) June 17, 1833–Aug. 24, 1878; House 1873–75.

Cobb, Thomas Reed (D Ind.) July 2, 1828–June 23, 1892; House 1877–87.

Cobb, Thomas Willis (– Ga.) 1784–Feb. 1, 1830; House 1817–21, 1823–Dec. 6, 1824; Senate Dec. 6, 1824–28.

Cobb, Williamson Robert Winfield (D Ala.) June 8, 1807–Nov. 1, 1864; House 1847–Jan. 30, 1861.

Cobey, William Wilfred Jr. (R N.C.) May 13, 1939– ; House 1985–87.

Coble, Howard (R N.C.) March 18, 1931– ; House 1985– .

Coburn, Frank Potter (D Wis.) Dec. 6, 1858–Nov. 2, 1932; House 1891–93.

Coburn, John (R Ind.) Oct. 27, 1825–Jan. 28, 1908; House 1867–75.

Coburn, Stephen (R Maine) Nov. 11, 1817–July 4, 1882; House Jan. 2–March 3, 1861.

Coburn, Tom (R Okla.) March 14, 1948– ; House 1995– .

Cochran, Alexander Gilmore (D Pa.) March 20, 1846–May 1, 1928; House 1875–77.

Cochran, Charles Fremont (D Mo.) Sept. 27, 1846–Dec. 19, 1906; House 1897–1905.

Cochran, James (grandfather of James Cochrane Dobbin) (R N.C.) about 1767–April 7, 1813; House 1809–13.

Cochran, James (F N.Y.) Feb. 11, 1769–Nov. 7, 1848; House 1797–99.

Cochran, John Joseph (D Mo.) Aug. 11, 1880–March 6, 1947; House Nov. 2, 1926–47.

Cochran, Thomas Cunningham (R Pa.) Nov. 30, 1877–Dec. 10, 1957; House 1927–35.

Cochran, William Thad (R Miss.) Dec. 7, 1937– ; House 1973–Dec. 26, 1978; Senate Dec. 27, 1978– .

Cochrane, Aaron Van Schaick (nephew of Isaac Whitbeck Van Schaick) (R N.Y.) March 14, 1858–Sept. 7, 1943; House 1897–1901.

Cochrane, Clark Betton (uncle of George Cochrane Hazelton and Gerry Whiting Hazelton) (R N.Y.) May 31, 1815–March 5, 1867; House 1857–61.

Cochrane, John (D N.Y.) Aug. 27, 1813–Feb. 7, 1898; House 1857–61.

Cocke, John (son of William Cocke, uncle of William Michael Cocke) (– Tenn.) 1772–Feb. 16, 1854; House 1819–27.

Cocke, William (father of John Cocke, grandfather of William Michael Cocke) (R Tenn.) 1748–Aug. 22, 1828; Senate Aug. 2, 1796–March 3, 1797, April 22–Sept. 26, 1797, 1799–1805.

Cocke, William Michael (grandson of William Cocke, nephew of John Cocke) (W Tenn.) July 16, 1815–Feb. 6, 1896; House 1845–49.

Cockerill, Joseph Randolph (D Ohio) Jan. 2, 1818–Oct. 23, 1875; House 1857–59.

Cockran, William Bourke (D N.Y.) Feb. 28, 1854–March 1, 1923; House 1887–89, Nov. 3, 1891–95, Feb. 23, 1904–09, 1921–March 1, 1923.

Cockrell, Francis Marion (brother of Jeremiah Vardaman Cockrell) (D Mo.) Oct. 1, 1834–Dec. 13, 1915; Senate 1875–1905.

Cockrell, Jeremiah Vardaman (brother of Francis Marion Cockrell) (D Texas) May 7, 1832–March 18, 1915; House 1893–97.

Cocks, William Willets (brother of Frederick Cocks Hicks) (R N.Y.) July 24, 1861–May 24, 1932; House 1905–11.

Codd, George Pierre (R Mich.) Dec. 7, 1869–Feb. 16, 1927; House 1921–23.

Codding, James Hodge (R Pa.) July 8, 1849–Sept. 12, 1919; House Nov. 5, 1895–99.

Coelho, Anthony Lee "Tony" (D Calif.) June 15, 1942– ; House 1979–June 15, 1989.

Coffee, Harry Buffington (D Neb.) March 16, 1890–Oct. 3, 1972; House 1935–43.

Coffee, John (J Ga.) Dec. 3, 1782–Sept. 25, 1836; House 1833–Sept. 25, 1836.

Coffee, John Main (D Wash.) Jan. 23, 1897– ; House 1937–47.

Coffeen, Henry Asa (D Wyo.) Feb. 14, 1841–Dec. 9, 1912; House 1893–95.

Coffey, Robert Lewis Jr. (D Pa.) Oct. 21, 1918–April 20, 1949; House Jan. 3–April 20, 1949.

Coffin, Charles Dustin (W Ohio) Sept. 9, 1805–Feb. 28, 1880; House Dec. 20, 1837–39.

Coffin, Charles Edward (R Md.) July 18, 1841–May 24, 1912; House Nov. 6, 1894–97.

Coffin, Frank Morey (D Maine) July 11, 1919– ; House 1957–61.

Coffin, Howard Aldridge (R Mich.) June 11, 1877–Feb. 28, 1956; House 1947–49.

Coffin, Peleg Jr. (– Mass.) Nov. 3, 1756–March 6, 1805; House 1793–95.

Coffin, Thomas Chalkley (D Idaho) Oct. 25, 1887–June 8, 1934; House 1933–June 8, 1934.

Coffroth, Alexander Hamilton (D Pa.) May 18, 1828–Sept. 2, 1906; House 1863–65, Feb. 19–July 18, 1866, 1879–81.

Coghlan, John Maxwell (R Calif.) Dec. 8, 1835–March 26, 1879; House 1871–73.

Cogswell, William (R Mass.) Aug. 23, 1838–May 22, 1895; House 1887–May 22, 1895.

Cohelan, Jeffrey (D Calif.) June 24, 1914–Feb. 15, 1999; House 1959–71.

Cohen, John Sanford (D Ga.) Feb. 26, 1870–May 13, 1935; Senate April 25, 1932–Jan. 11, 1933.

Cohen, William Sebastian (R Maine) Aug. 28, 1940– ; House 1973–79; Senate 1979–97; Secy. of Defense Jan. 24, 1997– .

Cohen, William Wolfe (D N.Y.) Sept. 6, 1874–Oct. 12, 1940; House 1927–29.

Coit, Joshua (F Conn.) Oct. 7, 1758–Sept. 5, 1798; House 1793–Sept. 5, 1798 (1793–95 no party).

Coke, Richard (nephew of Richard Coke Jr.) (D Texas) March 13, 1829–May 14, 1897; Senate 1877–95; Gov. Jan. 15, 1874–Dec. 1, 1876.

Coke, Richard Jr. (uncle of Richard Coke) (J Va.) Nov. 16, 1790–March 31, 1851; House 1829–33.

Colcock, William Ferguson (D S.C.) Nov. 5, 1804–June 13, 1889; House 1849–53.

Colden, Cadwallader David (– N.Y.) April 4, 1769–Feb. 7, 1834; House Dec. 12, 1821–23.

Colden, Charles J. (D Calif.) Aug. 24, 1870–April 15, 1938; House 1933–April 15, 1938.

Cole, Albert McDonald (R Kan.) Oct. 13, 1901–June 5, 1994; House 1945–53.

Cole, Cornelius (R Calif.) Sept. 17, 1822–Nov. 3, 1924; House 1863–65 (Union Republican); Senate 1867–73.

Cole, Cyrenus (R Iowa) Jan. 13, 1863–Nov. 14, 1939; House July 19, 1921–33.

Cole, George Edward (D Wash.) Dec. 23, 1826–Dec. 3, 1906; House (Terr. Del.) 1863–65; Gov. (Wash. Terr.) Nov. 1866–March 4, 1867.

Cole, Nathan (R Mo.) July 26, 1825–March 4, 1904; House 1877–79.

Cole, Orsamus (W Wis.) Aug. 23, 1819–May 5, 1903; House 1849–51.

Cole, Ralph Dayton (brother of Raymond Clinton Cole) (R Ohio) Nov. 30, 1873–Oct. 15, 1932; House 1905–11.

Cole, Raymond Clinton (brother of Ralph Dayton Cole) (R Ohio) Aug. 21, 1870–Feb. 8, 1957; House 1919–25.

Cole, William Clay (R Mo.) Aug. 29, 1897–Sept. 23, 1965; House 1943–49, 1953–55.

Cole, William Hinson (D Md.) Jan. 11, 1837–July 8, 1886; House 1885–July 8, 1886.

Cole, William Purington Jr. (D Md.) May 11, 1889–Sept. 22, 1957; House 1927–29, 1931–Oct. 26, 1942.

Cole, William Sterling (R N.Y.) April 18, 1904–March 15, 1987; House 1935–Dec. 1, 1957.

Coleman, Earl Thomas (R Mo.) May 29, 1943– ; House Nov. 2, 1976–93.

Coleman, Hamilton Dudley (R La.) May 12, 1845–March 16, 1926; House 1889–91.

Coleman, Nicholas Daniel (J Ky.) April 22, 1800–May 11, 1874; House 1829–31.

Coleman, Ronald D'Emory (D Texas) Nov. 29, 1941– ; House 1983–97.

Coleman, William Henry (R Pa.) Dec. 28, 1871–June 3, 1943; House 1915–17.

Colerick, Walpole Gillespie (D Ind.) Aug. 1, 1845–Jan. 11, 1911; House 1879–83.

Coles, Isaac (father of Walter Coles) (R Va.) March 2, 1747–June 3, 1813; House 1789–91 (no party), 1793–97 (1793–95 no party).

Coles, Walter (son of Isaac Coles) (D Va.) Dec. 8, 1790–Nov. 9, 1857; House 1835–45 (1835–37 Jacksonian).

Colfax, Schuyler (R Ind.) March 23, 1823–Jan. 13, 1885; House 1855–69; Speaker Dec. 7, 1863–65, Dec. 4, 1865–67, March 4, 1867–March 2, 1869; Vice President 1869–73.

Colhoun, John Ewing (cousin of John Caldwell Calhoun and Joseph Calhoun) (R S.C.) about 1749–Oct. 26, 1802; Senate 1801–Oct. 26, 1802.

Collamer, Jacob (R Vt.) Jan. 8, 1791–Nov. 9, 1865; House 1843–49 (Whig); Senate 1855–Nov. 9, 1865; Postmaster Gen. March 8, 1849–July 22, 1850.

Collier, Harold Reginald (R Ill.) Dec. 12, 1915– ; House 1957–75.

Collier, James William (D Miss.) Sept. 28, 1872–Sept. 28, 1933; House 1909–33.

Collier, John Allen (great-great-grandfather of Edwin Arthur Hall) (AMas. N.Y.) Nov. 13, 1787–March 24, 1873; House 1831–33.

Collin, John Francis (D N.Y.) April 30, 1802–Sept. 16, 1889; House 1845–47.

Collins, Barbara-Rose (D Mich.) April 13, 1939– ; House 1991–97.

Collins, Cardiss (widow of George Washington Collins) (D Ill.) Sept. 24, 1931– ; House June 5, 1973–97.

Collins, Ela (father of William Collins) (– N.Y.) Feb. 14, 1786–Nov. 23, 1848; House 1823–25.

Collins, Francis Dolan (D Pa.) March 5, 1841–Nov. 21, 1891; House 1875–79.

Collins, George Washington (husband of Cardiss Collins) (D Ill.) March 5, 1925–Dec. 8, 1972; House Nov. 3, 1970–Dec. 8, 1972.

Collins, James Mitchell (R Texas) April 29, 1916–July 21, 1989; House Aug. 24, 1968–83.

Collins, Mac (R Ga.) Oct. 15, 1944– ; House 1993– .

Collins, Patrick Andrew (D Mass.) March 12, 1844–Sept. 13, 1905; House 1883–89.

Collins, Ross Alexander (D Miss.) April 25, 1880–July 14, 1968; House 1921–35, 1937–43.

Collins, Samuel LaFort (R Calif.) Aug. 6, 1895–June 26, 1965; House 1933–37.

Collins, Susan (R Maine) Dec. 7, 1952– ; Senate 1997– .

Collins, William (son of Ela Collins) (D N.Y.) Feb. 22, 1818–June 18, 1878; House 1847–49.

Colmer, William Meyers (D Miss.) Feb. 11, 1890–Sept. 9, 1980; House 1933–73; Chrmn. House Rules 1967–73.

Colorado, Antonio J. (D P.R.) Sept. 8, 1939– ; House (Res. Comm.) March 4, 1992–Jan. 3, 1993.

Colquitt, Alfred Holt (son of Walter Terry Colquitt) (D Ga.) April 20, 1824–March 26, 1894; House 1853–55 (no party); Senate 1883–March 26, 1894; Gov. Jan. 12, 1877–Nov. 4, 1882.

Colquitt, Walter Terry (father of Alfred Holt Colquitt) (D Ga.) Dec. 27, 1799–May 7, 1855; House 1839–July 21, 1840 (Whig), Jan. 3, 1842–43 (Van Buren Democrat); Senate 1843–Feb. 1848.

Colson, David Grant (R Ky.) April 1, 1861–Sept. 27, 1904; House 1895–99.

Colston, Edward (F Va.) Dec. 25, 1786–April 23, 1852; House 1817–19.

Colt, LeBaron Bradford (R R.I.) June 25, 1846–Aug. 18, 1924; Senate 1913–Aug. 18, 1924.

Colton, Don Byron (R Utah) Sept. 15, 1876–Aug. 1, 1952; House 1921–33.

Combest, Larry Ed (R Texas) March 20, 1945– ; House 1985– ; Chrmn. House Permanent Select Committee on Intelligence, 1995–97; Chrmn. House Agriculture 1999– .

Combs, George Hamilton Jr. (D Mo.) May 2, 1899–Nov. 29, 1977; House 1927–29.

Combs, Jesse Martin (D Texas) July 7, 1889–Aug. 21, 1953; House 1945–53.

Comegys, Joseph Parsons (W Del.) Dec. 29, 1813–Feb. 1, 1893; Senate Nov. 19, 1856–Jan. 14, 1857.

Comer, Braxton Bragg (D Ala.) Nov. 7, 1848–Aug. 15, 1927; Senate March 5–Nov. 2, 1920; Gov. Jan. 14, 1907–Jan. 17, 1911.

Comingo, Abram (D Mo.) Jan. 9, 1820–Nov. 10, 1889; House 1871–75.

Comins, Linus Bacon (R Mass.) Nov. 29, 1817–Oct. 14, 1892; House 1855–59 (1855–57 American Party).

Compton, Barnes (great-grandson of Philip Key) (D Md.) Nov. 16, 1830–Dec. 4, 1898; House 1885–March 20, 1890, 1891–May 15, 1894.

Compton, C. H. Ranulf (R Conn.) Sept. 16, 1878–Jan. 26, 1974; House 1943–45.

Comstock, Charles Carter (D Mich.) March 5, 1818–Feb. 20, 1900; House 1885–87.

Comstock, Daniel Webster (R Ind.) Dec. 16, 1840–May 19, 1917; House March 4–May 19, 1917.

Comstock, Oliver Cromwell (R N.Y.) March 1, 1780–Jan. 11, 1860; House 1813–19.

Comstock, Solomon Gilman (R Minn.) May 9, 1842–June 3, 1933; House 1889–91.

Conable, Barber Benjamin Jr. (R N.Y.) Nov. 2, 1922– ; House 1965–85.

Conard, John (R Pa.) Nov. 1773–May 9, 1857; House 1813–15.

Condict, Lewis (R N.J.) March 3, 1772–May 26, 1862; House 1811–17, 1821–33.

Condit, Gary (D Calif.) April 21, 1948– ; House Sept. 20, 1989– .

Condit, John (father of Silas Condit) (R N.J.) July 8, 1755–May 4, 1834; House 1799–1803, March 4–Nov. 4, 1819; Senate Sept. 1, 1803–March 3, 1809, March 21, 1809–17.

Condit, Silas (son of John Condit) (AJ N.J.) Aug. 18, 1778–Nov. 29, 1861; House 1831–33.

Condon, Francis Bernard (D R.I.) Nov. 11, 1891–Nov. 23, 1965; House Nov. 4, 1930–Jan. 10, 1935.

Condon, Robert Likens (D Calif.) Nov. 10, 1912–June 3, 1976; House 1953–55.

Conger, Edwin Hurd (R Iowa) March 7, 1843–May 18, 1907; House 1885–Oct. 3, 1890.

Conger, Harmon Sweatland (W N.Y.) April 9, 1816–Oct. 22, 1882; House 1847–51.

Conger, James Lockwood (W Mich.) Feb. 18, 1805–April 10, 1876; House 1851–53.

Conger, Omar Dwight (R Mich.) April 1, 1818–July 11, 1898; House 1869–81; Senate 1881–87.

Conkling, Alfred (father of Frederick Augustus Conkling and Roscoe Conkling) (– N.Y.) Oct. 12, 1789–Feb. 5, 1874; House 1821–23.

Conkling, Frederick Augustus (son of Alfred Conkling, brother of Roscoe Conkling) (R N.Y.) Aug. 22, 1816–Sept. 18, 1891; House 1861–63.

Conkling, Roscoe (son of Alfred Conkling, brother of Frederick Augustus Conkling) (R N.Y.) Oct. 30, 1829–April 18, 1888; House 1859–63, 1865–March 4, 1867; Senate March 4, 1867–May 16, 1881.

Conlan, John Bertrand (R Ariz.) Sept. 17, 1930– ; House 1973–77.

Conn, Charles Gerard (D Ind.) Jan. 29, 1844–Jan. 5, 1931; House 1893–95.

Connally, Thomas Terry "Tom" (D Texas) Aug. 19, 1877–Oct. 28, 1963; House 1917–29; Senate 1929–53; Chrmn. Senate Foreign Relations 1949–53.

Connell, Charles Robert (son of William Connell) (R Pa.) Sept. 22, 1864–Sept. 26, 1922; House 1921–Sept. 26, 1922.

Connell, Richard Edward (D N.Y.) Nov. 6, 1857–Oct. 30, 1912; House 1911–Oct. 30, 1912.

Connell, William (father of Charles Robert Connell) (R Pa.) Sept. 10, 1827–March 21, 1909; House 1897–1903, Feb. 10, 1904–05.

Connell, William James (R Neb.) July 6, 1846–Aug. 16, 1924; House 1889–91.

Connelly, John Robert (D Kan.) Feb. 27, 1870–Sept. 9, 1940; House 1913–19.

Conner, James Perry (R Iowa) Jan. 27, 1851–March 19, 1924; House Dec. 4, 1900–09.

Conner, John Coggswell (D Texas) Oct. 14, 1842–Dec. 10, 1873; House March 31, 1870–73.

Conner, Samuel Shepard (R Mass.) about 1783–Dec. 17, 1820; House 1815–17.

Connery, Lawrence Joseph (brother of William Patrick Connery Jr.) (D Mass.) Oct. 17, 1895–Oct. 19, 1941; House Sept. 28, 1937–Oct. 19, 1941.

Connery, William Patrick Jr. (brother of Lawrence Joseph Connery) (D Mass.) Aug. 24, 1888–June 15, 1937; House 1923–June 15, 1937.

Conness, John (UR Calif.) Sept. 22, 1821–Jan. 10, 1909; Senate 1863–69 (elected as a Douglas Democrat).

Connolly, Daniel Ward (D Pa.) April 24, 1847–Dec. 4, 1894; House 1883–85.

Connolly, James Austin (R Ill.) March 8, 1843–Dec. 15, 1914; House 1895–99.

Connolly, James Joseph (R Pa.) Sept. 24, 1881–Dec. 10, 1952; House 1921–35.

Connolly, Maurice (D Iowa) March 13, 1877–May 28, 1921; House 1913–15.

Connor, Henry William (D N.C.) Aug. 5, 1793–Jan. 6, 1866; House 1821–41 (1821–33 no party, 1833–37 Jacksonian).

Conover, Simon Barclay (R Fla.) Sept. 23, 1840–April 19, 1908; Senate 1873–79.

Conover, William Sheldrick II (R Pa.) Aug. 27, 1928– ; House April 25, 1972–73.

Conrad, Charles Magill (W La.) Dec. 24, 1804–Feb. 11, 1878; Senate April 14, 1842–43; House 1849–August 17, 1850; Secy. of War Aug. 15, 1850–March 7, 1853.

Conrad, Frederick (R Pa.) 1759–Aug. 3, 1827; House 1803–07.

Conrad, Kent (D N.D.) March 12, 1948– ; Senate 1987– .

Conry, Joseph Aloysius (D Mass.) Sept. 12, 1868–June 22, 1943; House 1901–03.

Conry, Michael Francis (D N.Y.) April 2, 1870–March 2, 1917; House 1909–March 2, 1917.

Constable, Albert (D Md.) June 3, 1805–Sept. 18, 1855; House 1845–47.

Conte, Silvio Otto (R Mass.) Nov. 9, 1921–Feb. 8, 1991; House 1959–Feb. 8, 1991.

Contee, Benjamin (uncle of Alexander Contee Hanson, great-uncle of Thomas Contee Worthington) (– Md.) 1755–Nov. 30, 1815; House 1789–91; Cont. Cong. 1788.

Converse, George Leroy (D Ohio) June 4, 1827–March 30, 1897; House 1879–85.

Conway, Henry Wharton (cousin of Ambrose Hundley Sevier) (– Ark.) March 18, 1793–Nov. 9, 1827; House (Terr. Del.) 1823–Nov. 9, 1827.

Conway, Martin Franklin (R Kan.) Nov. 19, 1827–Feb. 15, 1882; House Jan. 29, 1861–63.

Conyers, John Jr. (D Mich.) May 16, 1929– ; House 1965– ; Chrmn. House Government Operations 1989–95.

Cook, Burton Chauncey (R Ill.) May 11, 1819–Aug. 18, 1894; House 1865–Aug. 26, 1871.

Cook, Daniel Pope (– Ill.) 1794–Oct. 16, 1827; House 1819–27.

Cook, George Washington (R Colo.) Nov. 10, 1851–Dec. 18, 1916; House 1907–09.

Cook, Joel (R Pa.) March 20, 1842–Dec. 15, 1910; House Nov. 5, 1907–Dec. 15, 1910.

Cook, John Calhoun (D Iowa) Dec. 26, 1846–June 7, 1920; House March 3, 1883, Oct. 9, 1883–85.

Cook, John Parsons (W Iowa) Aug. 31, 1817–April 17, 1872; House 1853–55.

Cook, Marlow Webster (R Ky.) July 27, 1926– ; Senate Dec. 17, 1968–Dec. 27, 1974.

Cook, Merrill (R Utah) May 6, 1946– ; House 1997– .

Cook, Orchard (R Mass.) March 24, 1763–Aug. 12, 1819; House 1805–11.

Cook, Philip (D Ga.) July 30, 1817–May 24, 1894; House 1873–83.

Cook, Robert Eugene (D Ohio) May 19, 1920–Nov. 28, 1988; House 1959–63.

Cook, Samuel Andrew (R Wis.) Jan. 28, 1849–April 4, 1918; House 1895–97.

Cook, Samuel Ellis (D Ind.) Sept. 30, 1860–Feb. 22, 1946; House 1923–25.

Cook, Zadock (R Ga.) Feb. 18, 1769–Aug. 3, 1863; House Dec. 2, 1816–19.

Cooke, Bates (AMas. N.Y.) Dec. 23, 1787–May 31, 1841; House 1831–33.

Cooke, Edmund Francis (R N.Y.) April 13, 1885–May 13, 1967; House 1929–33.

Cooke, Edward Dean (R Ill.) Oct. 17, 1849–June 24, 1897; House 1895–June 24, 1897.

Cooke, Eleutheros (AJ Ohio) Dec. 25, 1787–Dec. 27, 1864; House 1831–33.

Cooke, Thomas Burrage (R N.Y.) Nov. 21, 1778–Nov. 20, 1853; House 1811–13.

Cooksey, John (R L.A.) August 20, 1941– ; House 1997– .

Cooley, Harold Dunbar (D N.C.) July 26, 1897–Jan. 15, 1974; House July 7, 1934–67; Chrmn. House Agriculture 1949–53, 1955–67.

Cooley, Wes (R Ore.) March 28, 1932– ; House 1995–97.

Coolidge, Frederick Spaulding (father of Marcus Allen Coolidge) (D Mass.) Dec. 7, 1841–June 8, 1906; House 1891–93.

Coolidge, Marcus Allen (son of Frederick Spaulding Coolidge) (D Mass.) Oct. 6, 1865–Jan. 23, 1947; Senate 1931–37.

Coombs, Frank Leslie (R Calif.) Dec. 27, 1853–Oct. 5, 1934; House 1901–03.

Coombs, William Jerome (D N.Y.) Dec. 24, 1833–Jan. 12, 1922; House 1891–95.

Coon, Samuel Harrison (R Ore.) April 15, 1903–May 8, 1980; House 1953–57.

Cooney, James (D Mo.) July 28, 1848–Nov. 16, 1904; House 1897–1903.

Cooper, Allen Foster (R Pa.) June 16, 1862–April 20, 1917; House 1903–11.

Cooper, Charles Merian (D Fla.) Jan. 16, 1856–Nov. 14, 1923; House 1893–97.

Cooper, Edmund (brother of Henry Cooper) (U Tenn.) Sept. 11, 1821–July 21, 1911; House July 24, 1866–67.

Cooper, Edward (R W.Va.) Feb. 26, 1873–March 1, 1928; House 1915–19.

Cooper, George Byran (D Mich.) June 6, 1808–Aug. 29, 1866; House 1859–May 15, 1860.

Cooper, George William (D Ind.) May 21, 1851–Nov. 27, 1899; House 1889–95.

Cooper, Henry (brother of Edmund Cooper) (D Tenn.) Aug. 22, 1827–Feb. 4, 1884; Senate 1871–77.

Cooper, Henry Allen (R Wis.) Sept. 8, 1850–March 1, 1931; House 1893–1919, 1921–March 1, 1931.

Cooper, James (W Pa.) May 8, 1810–March 28, 1863; House 1839–43; Senate 1849–55.

Cooper, James Haynes Shofner (D Tenn.) June 19, 1954– ; House 1983–95.

Cooper, Jere (D Tenn.) July 20, 1893–Dec. 18, 1957; House 1929–Dec. 18, 1957; Chrmn. House Ways and Means 1955–57.

Cooper, John Gordon (R Ohio) April 27, 1872–Jan. 7, 1955; House 1915–37.

Cooper, John Sherman (R Ky.) Aug. 23, 1901–Feb. 21, 1991; Senate Nov. 6, 1946–49, Nov. 5, 1952–55, Nov. 7, 1956–73.

Cooper, Mark Anthony (cousin of Eugenius Aristides Nisbet) (D Ga.) April 20, 1800–March 17, 1885; House 1839–41 (Whig), Jan. 3, 1842–June 26, 1843.

Cooper, Richard Matlack (– N.J.) Feb. 29, 1768–March 10, 1843; House 1829–33.

Cooper, Samuel Bronson (D Texas) May 30, 1850–Aug. 21, 1918; House 1893–1905, 1907–09.

Cooper, Thomas (F Del.) 1764–1829; House 1813–17.

Cooper, Thomas Buchecker (D Pa.) Dec. 29, 1823–April 4, 1862; House 1861–April 4, 1862.

Cooper, William (F N.Y.) Dec. 2, 1754–Dec. 22, 1809; House 1795–97, 1799–1801.

Cooper, William Craig (R Ohio) Dec. 18, 1832–Aug. 29, 1902; House 1885–91.

Cooper, William Raworth (D N.J.) Feb. 20, 1793–Sept. 22, 1856; House 1839–41.

Copeland, Oren Sturman (R Neb.) March 16, 1887–April 10, 1958; House 1941–43.

Copeland, Royal Samuel (D N.Y.) Nov. 7, 1868–June 17, 1938; Senate 1923–June 17, 1938.

Copley, Ira Clifton (nephew of Richard Henry Whiting) (R Ill.) Oct. 25, 1864–Nov. 1, 1947; House 1911–23 (1915–17 Progressive).

Coppersmith, Sam (D Ariz.) May 22, 1955– ; House 1993–95.

Corbett, Henry Winslow (UR Ore.) Feb. 18, 1827–March 31, 1903; Senate 1867–73.

Corbett, Robert James (R Pa.) Aug. 25, 1905–April 25, 1971; House 1939–41, 1945–April 25, 1971.

Corcoran, Thomas Joseph (R Ill.) May 23, 1939–   ; House 1977–85.

Cordon, Guy (R Ore.) April 24, 1890–June 8, 1969; Senate March 4, 1944–55; Chrmn. Senate Interior and Insular Affairs 1954–55.

Cordova, Jorge Luis (New Prog. P.R.) April 20, 1907–Sept. 18, 1994; House (Res. Comm.) 1969–73.

Corker, Stephen Alfestus (D Ga.) May 7, 1830–Oct. 18, 1879; House Dec. 22, 1870–71.

Corlett, William Wellington (R Wyo.) April 10, 1842–July 22, 1890; House (Terr. Del.) 1877–79.

Corley, Manuel Simeon (R S.C.) Feb. 10, 1823–Nov. 20, 1902; House July 25, 1868–69.

Corliss, John Blaisdell (R Mich.) June 7, 1851–Dec. 24, 1929; House 1895–1903.

Corman, James Charles (D Calif.) Oct. 20, 1920–   ; House 1961–81.

Cornell, Robert John (D Wis.) Dec. 16, 1919–   ; House 1975–79.

Cornell, Thomas (R N.Y.) Jan. 27, 1814–March 30, 1890; House 1867–69, 1881–83.

Corning, Erastus (grandfather of Parker Corning) (D N.Y.) Dec. 14, 1794–April 9, 1872; House 1857–59, 1861–Oct. 5, 1863.

Corning, Parker (grandson of Erastus Corning) (D N.Y.) Jan. 22, 1874–May 24, 1943; House 1923–37.

Cornish, Johnston (D N.J.) June 13, 1858–June 26, 1920; House 1893–95.

Cornwell, David Lance (D Ind.) June 14, 1945–   ; House 1977–79.

Corrada-del Rio, Baltasar (New Prog. P.R.) April 10, 1935–   ; House (Res. Comm.) 1977–85.

Corwin, Franklin (nephew of Moses Bledso Corwin and Thomas Corwin) (R Ill.) Jan. 12, 1818–June 15, 1879; House 1873–75.

Corwin, Moses Bledso (brother of Thomas Corwin, uncle of Franklin Corwin) (W Ohio) Jan. 5, 1790–April 7, 1872; House 1849–51, 1853–55.

Corwin, Thomas (brother of Moses Bledso Corwin, uncle of Franklin Corwin) (R Ohio) July 29, 1794–Dec. 18, 1865; House 1831–May 30, 1840 (Whig), 1859–March 12, 1861; Senate 1845–July 20, 1850 (Whig); Gov. Dec. 16, 1840–Dec. 14, 1841 (Whig); Secy. of the Treasury July 23, 1850–March 6, 1853.

Cosden, Jeremiah (– Md.) 1768–Dec. 5, 1824; House 1821–March 19, 1822.

Cosgrove, John (D Mo.) Sept. 12, 1839–Aug. 15, 1925; House 1883–85.

Costello, Jerry Francis (D Ill.) Sept. 25, 1949–   ; House Aug. 11, 1988–   .

Costello, John Martin (D Calif.) Jan. 15, 1903–Aug. 28, 1976; House 1935–45.

Costello, Peter Edward (R Pa.) June 27, 1854–Oct. 23, 1935; House 1915–21.

Costigan, Edward Prentiss (D Colo.) July 1, 1874–Jan. 17, 1939; Senate 1931–37.

Cothran, James Sproull (D S.C.) Aug. 8, 1830–Dec. 5, 1897; House 1887–91.

Cotter, William Ross (D Conn.) July 18, 1926–Sept. 8, 1981; House 1971–Sept. 8, 1981.

Cottman, Joseph Stewart (IW Md.) Aug. 16, 1803–Jan. 28, 1863; House 1851–53.

Cotton, Aylett Rains (R Iowa) Nov. 29, 1826–Oct. 30, 1912; House 1871–75.

Cotton, Norris H. (R N.H.) May 11, 1900–Feb. 24, 1989; House 1947–Nov. 7, 1954; Senate Nov. 8, 1954–Dec. 31, 1974, Aug. 8–Sept. 18, 1975.

Cottrell, James La Fayette (D Ala.) Aug. 25, 1808–Sept. 7, 1885; House Dec. 7, 1846–47.

Coudert, Frederick René Jr. (R N.Y.) May 7, 1898–May 21, 1972; House 1947–59.

Coudrey, Harry Marcy (R Mo.) Feb. 28, 1867–July 5, 1930; House June 23, 1906–11.

Coughlin, Clarence Dennis (uncle of Robert Lawrence Coughlin) (R Pa.) July 27, 1883–Dec. 15, 1946; House 1921–23.

Coughlin, Robert Lawrence (nephew of Clarence Dennis Coughlin) (R Pa.) April 11, 1929–   ; House 1969–93.

Coulter, Richard (J Pa.) March 1788–April 21, 1852; House 1827–35 (1827–29 no party).

Courter, James Andrew (R N.J.) Oct. 14, 1941–   ; House 1979–91.

Courtney, William Wirt (D Tenn.) Sept. 7, 1889–April 6, 1961; House May 11, 1939–49.

Cousins, Robert Gordon (R Iowa) Jan. 31, 1859–June 20, 1933; House 1893–1909.

Couzens, James (R Mich.) Aug. 26, 1872–Oct. 22, 1936; Senate Nov. 29, 1922–Oct. 22, 1936.

Coverdell, Paul (R Ga.) Jan. 20, 1939–   ; Senate 1993–   .

Covert, James Way (D N.Y.) Sept. 2, 1842–May 16, 1910; House 1877–81, 1889–95.

Covington, George Washington (D Md.) Sept. 12, 1838–April 6, 1911; House 1881–85.

Covington, James Harry (D Md.) May 3, 1870–Feb. 4, 1942; House 1909–Sept. 30, 1914.

Covington, Leonard (R Md.) Oct. 30, 1768–Nov. 14, 1813; House 1805–07.

Covode, John (R Pa.) March 17, 1808–Jan. 11, 1871; House 1855–63 (1855–57 Whig), 1867–69, Feb. 9, 1870–Jan. 11, 1871.

Cowan, Edgar (R Pa.) Sept. 19, 1815–Aug. 31, 1885; Senate 1861–67.

Cowan, Jacob Pitzer (D Ohio) March 20, 1823–July 9, 1895; House 1875–77.

Cowen, Benjamin Sprague (W Ohio) Sept. 27, 1793–Sept. 27, 1860; House 1841–43.

Cowen, John Kissig (D Md.) Oct. 28, 1844–April 26, 1904; House 1895–97.

Cowger, William Owen (R Ky.) Jan. 1, 1922–Oct. 2, 1971; House 1967–71.

Cowgill, Calvin (R Ind.) Jan. 7, 1819–Feb. 10, 1903; House 1879–81.

Cowherd, William Strother (D Mo.) Sept. 1, 1860–June 20, 1915; House 1897–1905.

Cowles, Charles Holden (nephew of William Henry Harrison Cowles) (R N.C.) July 16, 1875–Oct. 2, 1957; House 1909–11.

Cowles, George Washington (R N.Y.) Dec. 6, 1823–Jan. 20, 1901; House 1869–71.

Cowles, Henry Booth (– N.Y.) March 18, 1798–May 17, 1873; House 1829–31.

Cowles, William Henry Harrison (uncle of Charles Holden Cowles) (D N.C.) April 22, 1840–Dec. 30, 1901; House 1885–93.

Cox, C. Christopher (R Calif.) Oct. 16, 1952–   ; House 1989–   .

Cox, Edward Eugene (D Ga.) April 3, 1880–Dec. 24, 1952; House 1925–Dec. 24, 1952.

Cox, Isaac Newton (D N.Y.) Aug. 1, 1846–Sept. 28, 1916; House 1891–93.

Cox, Jacob Dolson (R Ohio) Oct. 27, 1828–Aug. 4, 1900; House 1877–79; Gov. Jan. 8, 1866–Jan. 13, 1868; Secy. of the Interior March 5, 1869–Oct. 31, 1870.

Cox, James (R N.J.) June 14, 1753–Sept. 12, 1810; House 1809–Sept. 12, 1810.

Cox, James Middleton (D Ohio) March 31, 1870–July 15, 1957; House 1909–Jan. 12, 1913; Gov. Jan. 13, 1913–Jan. 11, 1915, Jan. 8, 1917–Jan. 10, 1921.

Cox, John W. Jr. (D Ill.) July 10, 1947–   ; House 1991–93.

Cox, Leander Martin (AP Ky.) May 7, 1812–March 19, 1865; House 1853–57 (1853–55 Whig).

Cox, Nicholas Nichols (D Tenn.) Jan. 6, 1837–May 2, 1912; House 1891–1901.

Cox, Samuel Sullivan (D N.Y.) Sept. 30, 1824–Sept. 10, 1889; House 1857–65 (Ohio), 1869–73, Nov. 4, 1873–May 20, 1885, Nov. 2, 1886–Sept. 10, 1889.

Cox, William Elijah (D Ind.) Sept. 6, 1861–March 11, 1942; House 1907–19.

Cox, William Ruffin (D N.C.) March 11, 1831–Dec. 26, 1919; House 1881–87.

Coxe, William Jr. (F N.J.) May 3, 1762–Feb. 25, 1831; House 1813–15.

Coyle, William Radford (R Pa.) July 10, 1878–Jan. 30, 1962; House 1925–27, 1929–33.

Coyne, James Kitchenman III (R Pa.) Nov. 17, 1946– ; House 1981–83.

Coyne, William Joseph (D Pa.) Aug. 24, 1936– ; House 1981– .

Crabb, George Whitfield (W Ala.) Feb. 22, 1804–Aug. 15, 1846; House Sept. 4, 1838–41.

Crabb, Jeremiah (F Md.) 1760–1800; House 1795–96.

Craddock, John Durrett (R Ky.) Oct. 26, 1881–May 20, 1942; House 1929–31.

Cradlebaugh, John (– Nev.) Feb. 22, 1819–Feb. 22, 1872; House (Terr. Del.) Dec. 2, 1861–63.

Crafts, Samuel Chandler (– Vt.) Oct. 6, 1768–Nov. 19, 1853; House 1817–25; Senate April 23, 1842–43; Gov. Oct. 10, 1828–Oct. 18, 1831 (National Republican).

Cragin, Aaron Harrison (R N.H.) Feb. 3, 1821–May 10, 1898; House 1855–59 (1855–57 American Party); Senate 1865–77.

Crago, Thomas Spencer (R Pa.) Aug. 8, 1866–Sept. 12, 1925; House 1911–13, 1915–21, Sept. 20, 1921–23.

Craig, Alexander Kerr (D Pa.) Feb. 21, 1828–July 29, 1892; House Feb. 26–July 29, 1892.

Craig, George Henry (R Ala.) Dec. 25, 1845–Jan. 26, 1923; House Jan. 9–March 3, 1885.

Craig, Hector (J N.Y.) 1775–Jan. 31, 1842; House 1823–25 (no party), 1829–July 12, 1830.

Craig, James (D Mo.) Feb. 28, 1818–Oct. 22, 1888; House 1857–61.

Craig, Larry Edwin (R Idaho) July 20, 1945– ; House 1981–91; Senate 1991– .

Craig, Robert (D Va.) 1792–Nov. 25, 1852; House 1829–33 (Jacksonian), 1835–41.

Craig, Samuel Alfred (R Pa.) Nov. 19, 1839–March 17, 1920; House 1889–91.

Craig, William Benjamin (D Ala.) Nov. 2, 1877–Nov. 27, 1925; House 1907–11.

Craige, Francis Burton (D N.C.) March 13, 1811–Dec. 30, 1875; House 1853–61.

Craik, William (F Md.) Oct. 31, 1761–prior to 1814; House Dec. 5, 1796–1801.

Crail, Joe (R Calif.) Dec. 25, 1877–March 2, 1938; House 1927–33.

Crain, William Henry (D Texas) Nov. 25, 1848–Feb. 10, 1896; House 1885–Feb. 10, 1896.

Craley, Nathaniel Nieman Jr. (D Pa.) Nov. 17, 1927– ; House 1965–67.

Cramer, Bud (D Ala.) Aug. 22, 1947– ; House 1991– .

Cramer, John (J N.Y.) May 17, 1779–June 1, 1870; House 1833–37.

Cramer, William Cato (R Fla.) Aug. 4, 1922– ; House 1955–71.

Cramton, Louis Convers (R Mich.) Dec. 2, 1875–June 23, 1966; House 1913–31.

Crane, Daniel Bever (brother of Philip Miller Crane) (R Ill.) Jan. 10, 1936– ; House 1979–85.

Crane, Joseph Halsey (W Ohio) Aug. 31, 1782–Nov. 13, 1851; House 1829–37 (1829–33 no party, 1833–35 Anti-Jacksonian).

Crane, Philip Miller (brother of Daniel Bever Crane) (R Ill.) Nov. 3, 1930– ; House Nov. 25, 1969– .

Crane, Winthrop Murray (R Mass.) April 23, 1853–Oct. 2, 1920; Senate Oct. 12, 1904–13; Gov. Jan. 4, 1900–Jan. 8, 1903.

Cranford, John Walter (D Texas) 1862–March 3, 1899; House 1897–March 3, 1899.

Cranston, Alan (D Calif.) June 19, 1914– ; Senate 1969–93; Chrmn. Senate Veterans' Affairs 1977–81, 1987–93.

Cranston, Henry Young (brother of Robert Bennie Cranston) (W R.I.) Oct. 9, 1789–Feb. 12, 1864; House 1843–47 (1843–45 Law & Order).

Cranston, Robert Bennie (brother of Henry Young Cranston) (W R.I.) Jan. 14, 1791–Jan. 27, 1873; House 1837–43, 1847–49.

Crapo, Michael D. (R Idaho) May 20, 1951– ; House 1993–99; Senate 1999– .

Crapo, William Wallace (R Mass.) May 16, 1830–Feb. 28, 1926; House Nov. 2, 1875–83.

Crary, Isaac Edwin (D Mich.) Oct. 2, 1804–May 8, 1854; House Jan. 26, 1837–41 (Jan. 26–March 3, 1837 Jacksonian).

Cravens, James Addison (second cousin of James Harrison Cravens) (D Ind.) Nov. 4, 1818–June 20, 1893; House 1861–65.

Cravens, James Harrison (second cousin of James Addison Cravens) (W Ind.) Aug. 2, 1802–Dec. 4, 1876; House 1841–43.

Cravens, Jordan Edgar (cousin of William Ben Cravens) (D Ark.) Nov. 7, 1830–April 8, 1914; House 1877–83 (1877–79 Independent Democrat).

Cravens, William Ben (father of William Fadjo Cravens, cousin of Jordan Edgar Cravens) (D Ark.) Jan. 17, 1872–Jan. 13, 1939; House 1907–13, 1933–Jan. 13, 1939.

Cravens, William Fadjo (son of William Ben Cravens) (D Ark.) Feb. 15, 1889–April 16, 1974; House Sept. 12, 1939–49.

Crawford, Coe Isaac (R S.D.) Jan. 14, 1858–April 25, 1944; Senate 1909–15; Gov. Jan. 8, 1907–Jan. 5, 1909.

Crawford, Fred Lewis (R Mich.) May 5, 1888–April 13, 1957; House 1935–53.

Crawford, George W. (W Ga.) Dec. 22, 1798–July 27, 1872; House Jan. 7–March 3, 1843; Gov. Nov. 8, 1843–Nov. 3, 1847; Secy. of War March 8, 1849–July 23, 1850.

Crawford, Joel (R Ga.) June 15, 1783–April 5, 1858; House 1817–21.

Crawford, Martin Jenkins (D Ga.) March 17, 1820–July 23, 1883; House 1855–Jan. 23, 1861.

Crawford, Thomas Hartley (J Pa.) Nov. 14, 1786–Jan. 27, 1863; House 1829–33.

Crawford, William (R Pa.) 1760–Oct. 23, 1823; House 1809–17.

Crawford, William Harris (– Ga.) Feb. 24, 1772–Sept. 15, 1834; Senate Nov. 7, 1807–March 23, 1813; elected Pres. pro tempore March 24, 1812; Secy. of War Aug. 1, 1815–Oct. 22, 1816; Secy. of the Treasury Oct. 22, 1816–March 6, 1825.

Crawford, William Thomas (D N.C.) June 1, 1856–Nov. 16, 1913; House 1891–95, 1899–May 10, 1900, 1907–09.

Creager, Charles Edward (R Okla.) April 28, 1873–Jan. 11, 1964; House 1909–11.

Creal, Edward Wester (D Ky.) Nov. 20, 1883–Oct. 13, 1943; House Nov. 5, 1935–Oct. 13, 1943.

Creamer, Thomas James (D N.Y.) May 26, 1843–Aug. 4, 1914; House 1873–75, 1901–03.

Crebs, John Montgomery (D Ill.) April 9, 1830–June 26, 1890; House 1869–73.

Creely, John Vaudain (IR Pa.) Nov. 14, 1839–Sept. 28, 1900; House 1871–73.

Creighton, William Jr. (R Ohio) Oct. 29, 1778–Oct. 1, 1851; House May 4, 1813–17, 1827–28, 1829–33.

Cremeans, Frank A. (R Ohio) April 5, 1943– ; House 1995–97.

Creswell, John Angel James (R Md.) Nov. 18, 1828–Dec. 23, 1891; House 1863–65; Senate March 9, 1865–67; Postmaster Gen. March 6, 1869–July 6, 1874.

Cretella, Albert William (R Conn.) April 22, 1897–May 24, 1979; House 1953–59.

Crippa, Edward David (R Wyo.) April 8, 1899–Oct. 20, 1960; Senate June 24–Nov. 28, 1954.

Crisfeld, John Woodland (U Md.) Nov. 8, 1806–Jan. 12, 1897; House 1847–49 (Whig), 1861–63.

Crisp, Charles Frederick (father of Charles Robert Crisp) (D Ga.) Jan. 29, 1845–Oct. 23, 1896; House 1883–Oct. 23, 1896; Speaker Dec. 8, 1891–93, Aug. 7, 1893–95.

Crisp, Charles Robert (son of Charles Frederick Crisp) (D Ga.) Oct. 19, 1870–Feb. 7, 1937; House Dec. 19, 1896–97, 1913–Oct. 7, 1932.

Crist, Henry (R Ky.) Oct. 20, 1764–Aug. 11, 1844; House 1809–11.

Critcher, John (D Va.) March 11, 1820–Sept. 27, 1901; House 1871–73.

Crittenden, John Jordan (uncle of Thomas Theodore Crittenden) (U Ky.) Sept. 10, 1786–July 26, 1863; Senate 1817–19 (no party), 1835–41 (Whig), March 31, 1842–June 12, 1848 (Whig), 1855–61 (Whig); House 1861–63; Gov. June 1, 1848–July 1850 (Whig); Atty. Gen. March 5–Sept. 13, 1841, July 22, 1850–March 3, 1853.

Crittenden, Thomas Theodore (nephew of John Jordan Crittenden) (D Mo.) Jan. 1, 1832–May 29, 1909; House 1873–75, 1877–79; Gov. Jan. 10, 1881–Jan. 12, 1885.

Crocheron, Henry (brother of Jacob Crocheron) (R N.Y.) Dec. 26, 1772–Nov. 8, 1819; House 1815–17.

Crocheron, Jacob (brother of Henry Crocheron) (J N.Y.) Aug. 23, 1774–Dec. 27, 1849; House 1829–31.

Crocker, Alvah (R Mass.) Oct. 14, 1801–Dec. 26, 1874; House Jan. 2, 1872–Dec. 26, 1874.

Crocker, Samuel Leonard (W Mass.) March 31, 1804–Feb. 10, 1883; House 1853–55.

Crockett, David (father of John Wesley Crockett) (AJ Tenn.) Aug. 17, 1786–March 6, 1836; House 1827–31 (no party), 1833–35.

Crockett, George William Jr. (D Mich.) Aug. 10, 1909–Sept. 7, 1997; House Nov. 12, 1980–91.

Crockett, John Wesley (son of David Crockett) (W Tenn.) July 10, 1807–Nov. 24, 1852; House 1837–41.

Croft, George William (father of Theodore Gaillard Croft) (D S.C.) Dec. 20, 1846–March 10, 1904; House 1903–March 10, 1904.

Croft, Theodore Gaillard (son of George William Croft) (D S.C.) Nov. 26, 1874–March 23, 1920; House May 17, 1904–05.

Croll, William Martin (D Pa.) April 9, 1866–Oct. 21, 1929; House 1923–25.

Cromer, George Washington (R Ind.) May 13, 1856–Nov. 8, 1936; House 1899–1907.

Cronin, Paul William (R Mass.) March 14, 1938–April 5, 1997; House 1973–75.

Crook, Thurman Charles (D Ind.) July 18, 1891–Oct. 23, 1981; House 1949–51.

Crooke, Philip Schuyler (R N.Y.) March 2, 1810–March 17, 1881; House 1873–75.

Crosby, Charles Noel (D Pa.) Sept. 29, 1876–Jan. 26, 1951; House 1933–39.

Crosby, John Crawford (D Mass.) June 15, 1859–Oct. 14, 1943; House 1891–93.

Cross, Edward (D Ark.) Nov. 11, 1798–April 6, 1887; House 1839–45.

Cross, Oliver Harlan (D Texas) July 13, 1868–April 24, 1960; House 1929–37.

Crosser, Robert (D Ohio) June 7, 1874–June 3, 1957; House 1913–19, 1923–55; Chrmn. House Interstate and Foreign Commerce 1949–53.

Crossland, Edward (D Ky.) June 30, 1827–Sept. 11, 1881; House 1871–75.

Crouch, Edward (R Pa.) Nov. 9, 1764–Feb. 2, 1827; House Oct. 12, 1813–15.

Crounse, Lorenzo (R Neb.) Jan. 27, 1834–May 13, 1909; House 1873–77; Gov. Jan. 13, 1893–Jan. 3, 1895.

Crouse, George Washington (R Ohio) Nov. 23, 1832–Jan. 5, 1912; House 1887–89.

Crow, Charles Augustus (R Mo.) March 31, 1873–March 20, 1938; House 1909–11.

Crow, William Evans (father of William Josiah Crow) (R Pa.) March 10, 1870–Aug. 2, 1922; Senate Oct. 24, 1921–Aug. 2, 1922.

Crow, William Josiah (son of William Evans Crow) (R Pa.) Jan. 22, 1902–Oct. 13, 1974; House 1947–49.

Crowe, Eugene Burgess (D Ind.) Jan. 5, 1878–May 12, 1970; House 1931–41.

Crowell, John (– Ala.) Sept. 18, 1780–June 25, 1846; House (Terr. Del.) Jan. 29, 1818–19, (Rep.) Dec. 14, 1819–21.

Crowell, John (W Ohio) Sept. 15, 1801–March 8, 1883; House 1847–51.

Crowley, Joseph (D N.Y.) March 16, 1962– ; House 1999– .

Crowley, Joseph Burns (D Ohio) July 19, 1858–June 25, 1931; House 1899–1905.

Crowley, Miles (D Texas) Feb. 22, 1859–Sept. 22, 1921; House 1895–97.

Crowley, Richard (R N.Y.) Dec. 14, 1836–July 22, 1908; House 1879–83.

Crowninshield, Benjamin Williams (brother of Jacob Crowninshield) (– Mass.) Dec. 27, 1772–Feb. 3, 1851; House 1823–31; Secy. of the Navy Jan. 16, 1815–Sept. 30, 1818.

Crowninshield, Jacob (brother of Benjamin Williams Crowninshield) (R Mass.) March 31, 1770–April 15, 1808; House 1803–April 15, 1808.

Crowther, Frank (R N.Y.) July 10, 1870–July 20, 1955; House 1919–43.

Crowther, George Calhoun (R Mo.) Jan. 26, 1849–March 18, 1914; House 1895–97.

Croxton, Thomas (D Va.) March 8, 1822–July 3, 1903; House 1885–87.

Crozier, John Hervey (W Tenn.) Feb. 10, 1812–Oct. 25, 1889; House 1845–49.

Crozier, Robert (R Kan.) Oct. 13, 1827–Oct. 2, 1895; Senate Nov. 24, 1873–Feb. 12, 1874.

Crudup, Josiah (– N.C.) Jan. 13, 1791–May 20, 1872; House 1821–23.

Cruger, Daniel (R N.Y.) Dec. 22, 1780–July 12, 1843; House 1817–19.

Crump, Edward Hull (D Tenn.) Oct. 2, 1874–Oct. 16, 1954; House 1931–35.

Crump, George William (– Va.) Sept. 26, 1786–Oct. 1, 1848; House Jan. 21, 1826–27.

Crump, Rousseau Owen (R Mich.) May 20, 1843–May 1, 1901; House 1895–May 1, 1901.

Crumpacker, Edgar Dean (father of Maurice Edgar Crumpacker, cousin of Shepard J. Crumpacker Jr.) (R Ind.) May 27, 1851–May 19, 1920; House 1897–1913.

Crumpacker, Maurice Edgar (son of Edgar Dean Crumpacker, cousin of Shepard J. Crumpacker Jr.) (R Ore.) Dec. 19, 1886–July 24, 1927; House 1925–July 24, 1927.

Crumpacker, Shepard J. Jr. (cousin of Edgar Dean Crumpacker and Maurice Edgar Crumpacker) (R Ind.) Feb. 13, 1917–Oct. 14, 1986; House 1951–57.

Crutchfield, William (R Tenn.) Nov. 16, 1824–Jan. 24, 1890; House 1873–75.

Cubin, Barbara (R Wyo.) Nov. 30, 1946– ; House 1995– .

Culberson, Charles Allen (son of David Browning Culberson) (D Texas) June 10, 1855–March 19, 1925; Senate 1899–1923; Gov. Jan. 15, 1895–Jan. 17, 1899.

Culberson, David Browning (father of Charles Allen Culberson) (D Texas) Sept. 29, 1830–May 7, 1900; House 1875–97.

Culbertson, William Constantine (R Pa.) Nov. 25, 1825–May 24, 1906; House 1889–91.

Culbertson, William Wirt (R Ky.) Sept. 22, 1835–Oct. 31, 1911; House 1883–85.

Culbreth, Thomas (R Md.) April 13, 1786–April 16, 1843; House 1817–21.

Culkin, Francis Dugan (R N.Y.) Nov. 10, 1874–Aug. 4, 1943; House Nov. 6, 1928–Aug. 4, 1943.

Cullen, Elisha Dickerson (AP Del.) April 23, 1799–Feb. 8, 1862; House 1855–57.

Cullen, Thomas Henry (D N.Y.) March 29, 1868–March 1, 1944; House 1919–March 1, 1944.

Cullen, William (R Ill.) March 4, 1826–Jan. 17, 1914; House 1881–85.

Cullom, Alvan (brother of William Cullom, uncle of Shelby Moore Cullom) (D Tenn.) Sept. 4, 1797–July 20, 1877; House 1843–47.

Cullom, Shelby Moore (nephew of Alvan Cullom and William Cullom) (R Ill.) Nov. 22, 1829–Jan. 28, 1914; House 1865–71; Senate 1883–1913; Senate majority leader 1911–13; Gov. Jan. 8, 1877–Feb. 8, 1883.

Cullom, William (brother of Alvan Cullom, uncle of Shelby Moore Cullom) (W Tenn.) June 4, 1810–Dec. 6, 1896; House 1851–55.

Cullop, William Allen (D Ind.) March 28, 1853–Oct. 9, 1927; House 1909–17.

Culpepper, John (F N.C.) 1761–Jan. 1841; House 1807–Jan. 2, 1808, Feb. 23, 1808–09, 1813–17, 1819–21, 1823–25, 1827–29.

Culver, Charles Vernon (R Pa.) Sept. 6, 1830–Jan. 10, 1909; House 1865–67.

Culver, Erastus Dean (W N.Y.) March 15, 1803–Oct. 13, 1889; House 1845–47.

Culver, John Chester (D Iowa) Aug. 8, 1932– ; House 1965–75; Senate 1975–81.

Cumback, William (R Ind.) March 24, 1829–July 31, 1905; House 1855–57.

Cumming, Thomas William (D N.Y.) 1814 or 1815–Oct. 13, 1855; House 1853–55.

Cummings, Amos Jay (D N.Y.) May 15, 1841–May 2, 1902; House 1887–89, Nov. 5, 1889–Nov. 21, 1894, Nov. 5, 1895–May 2, 1902.

Cummings, Elijah E. (D Md.) Jan. 18, 1951– ; House April 25, 1996– .

Cummings, Fred Nelson (D Colo.) Sept. 18, 1864–Nov. 10, 1952; House 1933–41.

Cummings, Henry Johnson Brodhead (R Iowa) May 21, 1831–April 16, 1909; House 1877–79.

Cummings, Herbert Wesley (D Pa.) July 13, 1873–March 4, 1956; House 1923–25.

Cummins, Albert Baird (R Iowa) Feb. 15, 1850–July 30, 1926; Senate Nov. 24, 1908–July 30, 1926; elected Pres. pro tempore May 19, 1919, March 7, 1921; Gov. Jan. 16, 1902–Nov. 24, 1908.

Cummins, John D. (D Ohio) 1791–Sept. 11, 1849; House 1845–49.

Cunningham, Francis Alanson (D Ohio) Nov. 9, 1804–Aug. 16, 1864; House 1845–47.

Cunningham, Glenn Clarence (R Neb.) Sept. 10, 1912– ; House 1957–71.

Cunningham, John Edward III (R Wash.) March 27, 1931– ; House May 17, 1977–79.

Cunningham, Paul Harvey (R Iowa) June 15, 1890–July 16, 1961; House 1941–59.

Cunningham, Randy "Duke" (R Calif.) Dec. 8, 1941– ; House 1991– .

Curley, Edward Walter (D N.Y.) May 23, 1873–Jan. 6, 1940; House Nov. 5, 1935–Jan. 6, 1940.

Curley, James Michael (D Mass.) Nov. 20, 1874–Nov. 12, 1958; House 1911–Feb. 4, 1914, 1943–47; Gov. Jan. 3, 1935–Jan. 7, 1937.

Curlin, William Prather Jr. (D Ky.) Nov. 30, 1933– ; House Dec. 4, 1971–73.

Currie, Gilbert Archibald (R Mich.) Sept. 19, 1882–June 5, 1960; House 1917–21.

Currier, Frank Dunklee (R N.H.) Oct. 30, 1853–Nov. 25, 1921; House 1901–13.

Curry, Charles Forrest (father of Charles Forrest Curry Jr.) (R Calif.) March 14, 1858–Oct. 10, 1930; House 1913–Oct. 10, 1930.

Curry, Charles Forrest Jr. (son of Charles Forrest Curry) (R Calif.) Aug. 13, 1893–Oct. 7, 1972; House 1931–33.

Curry, George (R N.M.) April 3, 1861–Nov. 27, 1947; House Jan. 8, 1912–13; Gov. (N.M. Terr.) 1907–11.

Curry, Jabez Lamar Monroe (D Ala.) June 5, 1825–Feb. 12, 1903; House 1857–Jan. 21, 1861.

Curtin, Andrew Gregg (D Pa.) April 22, 1815–Oct. 7, 1894; House 1881–87; Gov. Jan. 15, 1861–Jan. 15, 1867 (Republican).

Curtin, Willard Sevier (R Pa.) Nov. 18, 1905–Feb. 4, 1996; House 1957–67.

Curtis, Carl Thomas (R Neb.) March 15, 1905– ; House 1939–Dec. 31, 1954; Senate Jan. 1, 1955–79.

Curtis, Carlton Brandaga (R Pa.) Dec. 17, 1811–March 17, 1883; House 1851–55 (Democrat), 1873–75.

Curtis, Charles (R Kan.) Jan. 25, 1860–Feb. 8, 1936; House 1893–Jan. 28, 1907; Senate Jan. 29, 1907–13, 1915–29; elected Pres. pro tempore Dec. 4, 1911 (to serve Dec. 4–Dec. 12, 1911); Senate majority leader Nov. 28, 1925–29; Vice President 1929–33.

Curtis, Edward (W N.Y.) Oct. 25, 1801–Aug. 2, 1856; House 1837–41.

Curtis, George Martin (R Iowa) April 1, 1844–Feb. 9, 1921; House 1895–99.

Curtis, Laurence (R Mass.) Sept. 3, 1893–July 11, 1989; House 1953–63.

Curtis, Newton Martin (R N.Y.) May 21, 1835–Jan. 8, 1910; House Nov. 3, 1891–97.

Curtis, Samuel Ryan (R Iowa) Feb. 3, 1805–Dec. 25, 1866; House 1857–Aug. 4, 1861.

Curtis, Thomas Bradford (R Mo.) May 14, 1911–Jan. 10, 1993; House 1951–69.

Cusack, Thomas (D Ill.) Oct. 5, 1858–Nov. 19, 1926; House 1899–1901.

Cushing, Caleb (W Mass.) Jan. 17, 1800–Jan. 2, 1879; House 1835–43; Atty. Gen. March 7, 1853–March 3, 1857.

Cushman, Francis Wellington (R Wash.) May 8, 1867–July 6, 1909; House 1899–July 6, 1909.

Cushman, John Paine (F N.Y.) March 8, 1784–Sept. 16, 1848; House 1817–19.

Cushman, Joshua (– Maine) April 11, 1761–Jan. 27, 1834; House 1819–21 (Mass.), 1821–25.

Cushman, Samuel (D N.H.) June 8, 1783–May 20, 1851; House 1835–39 (1835–37 Jacksonian).

Cutcheon, Byron M. (R Mich.) May 11, 1836–April 12, 1908; House 1883–91.

Cuthbert, Alfred (brother of John Alfred Cuthbert) (R Ga.) Dec. 23, 1785–July 9, 1856; House Dec. 13, 1813–Nov. 9, 1816, 1821–27; Senate Jan. 12, 1835–43.

Cuthbert, John Alfred (brother of Alfred Cuthbert) (– Ga.) June 3, 1788–Sept. 22, 1881; House 1819–21.

Cutler, Augustus William (D N.J.) Oct. 22, 1827–Jan. 1, 1897; House 1875–79.

Cutler, Manasseh (F Mass.) May 13, 1742–July 28, 1823; House 1801–05.

Cutler, William Parker (R Ohio) July 12, 1812–April 11, 1889; House 1861–63.

Cutting, Bronson Murray (R N.M.) June 23, 1888–May 6, 1935; Senate Dec. 29, 1927–Dec. 6, 1928, 1929–May 6, 1935.

Cutting, Francis Brockholst (D N.Y.) Aug. 6, 1804–June 26, 1870; House 1853–55.

Cutting, John Tyler (R Calif.) Sept. 7, 1844–Nov. 24, 1911; House 1891–93.

Cutts, Charles (F N.H.) Jan. 31, 1769–Jan. 25, 1846; Senate June 21, 1810–March 3, 1813, April 2–June 10, 1813.

Cutts, Marsena Edgar (R Iowa) May 22, 1833–Sept. 1, 1883; House 1881–Sept. 1, 1883.

Cutts, Richard (R Mass.) June 28, 1771–April 7, 1845; House 1801–13.

D

Daddario, Emilio Quincy (D Conn.) Sept. 24, 1918– ; House 1959–71.

Daggett, David (F Conn.) Dec. 31, 1764–April 12, 1851; Senate May 13, 1813–19.

Daggett, Rollin Mallory (R Nev.) Feb. 22, 1831–Nov. 12, 1901; House 1879–81.

Dague, Paul Bartram (R Pa.) May 19, 1898–Dec. 2, 1974; House 1947–67.

Dahle, Herman Bjorn (R Wis.) March 30, 1855–April 25, 1920; House 1899–1903.

Daily, Samuel Gordon (R Neb.) 1823–Aug. 15, 1866; House (Terr. Del.) May 18, 1860–65.

Dale, Harry Howard (D N.Y.) Dec. 3, 1868–Nov. 17, 1935; House 1913–Jan. 6, 1919.

Dale, Porter Hinman (R Vt.) March 1, 1867–Oct. 6, 1933; House 1915–Aug. 11, 1923; Senate Nov. 7, 1923–Oct. 6, 1933.

Dale, Thomas Henry (R Pa.) June 12, 1846–Aug. 21, 1912; House 1905–07.

D'Alesandro, Thomas Jr. (father of Nancy Pelosi) (D Md.) Aug. 1, 1903–Aug. 23, 1987; House 1939–May 16, 1947.

Dallas, George Mifflin (great-great-great-uncle of Claiborne de Borda Pell) (D Pa.) July 10, 1792–Dec. 31, 1864; Senate Dec. 13, 1831–33; Vice President 1845–49.

Dallinger, Frederick William (R Mass.) Oct. 2, 1871–Sept. 5, 1955; House 1915–25, Nov. 2, 1926–Oct. 1, 1932.

Dalton, Tristram (– Mass.) May 28, 1738–May 30, 1817; Senate 1789–91; Cont. Cong. (elected but did not attend) 1783, 1784.

Daly, John Burrwood (D Pa.) Feb. 13, 1872–March 12, 1939; House 1935–March 12, 1939.

Daly, William Davis (D N.J.) June 4, 1851–July 31, 1900; House 1899–July 31, 1900.

Dalzell, John (R Pa.) April 19, 1845–Oct. 2, 1927; House 1887–1913.

D'Amato, Alfonse Martello (R N.Y.) Aug. 1, 1937– ; Senate 1981–99; Chrmn. Senate Banking, Housing, and Urban Affairs 1995–99.

D'Amours, Norman Edward (D N.H.) Oct. 14, 1937– ; House 1975–85.

Damrell, William Shapleigh (R Mass.) Nov. 29, 1809–May 17, 1860; House 1855–59 (1855–57 American Party).

Dana, Amasa (D N.Y.) Oct. 19, 1792–Dec. 24, 1867; House 1839–41, 1843–45.

Dana, Judah (D Maine) April 25, 1772–Dec. 27, 1845; Senate Dec. 7, 1836–37.

Dana, Samuel (R Mass.) June 26, 1767–Nov. 20, 1835; House Sept. 22, 1814–15.

Dana, Samuel Whittlesey (F Conn.) Feb. 13, 1760–July 21, 1830; House Jan. 3, 1797–May 10, 1810 (no party); Senate May 10, 1810–21.

Danaher, John Anthony (R Conn.) Jan. 9, 1899–Sept. 22, 1990; Senate 1939–45.

Dane, Joseph (– Maine) Oct. 25, 1778–May 1, 1858; House Nov. 6, 1820–23.

Danford, Lorenzo (R Ohio) Oct. 18, 1829–June 19, 1899; House 1873–79, 1895–June 19, 1899.

Danforth, Henry Gold (R N.Y.) June 14, 1854–April 8, 1918; House 1911–17.

Danforth, John Claggett (R Mo.) Sept. 5, 1936– ; Senate Dec. 27, 1976–95; Chrmn. Senate Commerce, Science, and Transportation 1985–87.

Daniel, Charles Ezra (D S.C.) Nov. 11, 1895–Sept. 13, 1964; Senate Sept. 6–Dec. 23, 1954.

Daniel, Henry (J Ky.) March 15, 1786–Oct. 5, 1873; House 1827–33.

Daniel, John Reeves Jones (D N.C.) Jan. 13, 1802–June 22, 1868; House 1841–53.

Daniel, John Warwick (D Va.) Sept. 5, 1842–June 29, 1910; House 1885–87; Senate 1887–June 29, 1910.

Daniel, Price Marion (D Texas) Oct. 10, 1910–Aug. 25, 1988; Senate 1953–Jan. 14, 1957; Gov. Jan. 15, 1957–Jan. 15, 1963.

Daniel, Robert Williams Jr. (R Va.) March 17, 1936– ; House 1973–83.

Daniel, Wilbur Clarence "Dan" (D Va.) May 12, 1914–Jan. 23, 1988; House 1969–Jan. 23, 1988.

Daniell, Warren Fisher (D N.H.) June 26, 1826–July 30, 1913; House 1891–93.

Daniels, Charles (R N.Y.) March 24, 1825–Dec. 20, 1897; House 1893–97.

Daniels, Dominick Vincent (D N.J.) Oct. 18, 1908–July 17, 1987; House 1959–77.

Daniels, Milton John (R Calif.) April 18, 1838–Dec. 1, 1914; House 1903–05.

Danielson, George Elmore (D Calif.) Feb. 20, 1915–Sept. 12, 1998; House 1971–March 9, 1982.

Dannemeyer, William Edwin (R Calif.) Sept. 22, 1929– ; House 1979–93.

Danner, Joel Buchanan (D Pa.) 1804–July 29, 1885; House Dec. 2, 1850–51.

Danner, Pat (D Mo.) Jan. 13, 1934– ; House 1993– .

Darby, Ezra (R N.J.) June 7, 1768–Jan. 27, 1808; House 1805–Jan. 27, 1808.

Darby, Harry (R Kan.) Jan. 23, 1895–Jan. 17, 1987; Senate Dec. 2, 1949–Nov. 28, 1950.

Darby, John Fletcher (W Mo.) Dec. 10, 1803–May 11, 1882; House 1851–53.

Darden, Colgate Whitehead Jr. (D Va.) Feb. 11, 1897–June 9, 1981; House 1933–37, 1939–March 1, 1941; Gov. Jan. 21, 1942–Jan. 16, 1946.

Darden, George "Buddy" (D Ga.) Nov. 22, 1943– ; House Nov. 8, 1983–95.

Dargan, Edmund Strother (D Ala.) April 15, 1805–Nov. 22, 1879; House 1845–47.

Dargan, George William (great-grandson of Lemuel Benton) (D S.C.) May 11, 1841–June 29, 1898; House 1883–91.

Darling, Mason Cook (D Wis.) May 18, 1801–March 12, 1866; House June 9, 1848–49.

Darling, William Augustus (R N.Y.) Dec. 27, 1817–May 26, 1895; House 1865–67.

Darlington, Edward (cousin of Isaac Darlington and William Darlington, second cousin of Smedley Darlington) (AMas. Pa.) Sept. 17, 1795–Nov. 21, 1884; House 1833–39.

Darlington, Isaac (cousin of Edward Darlington and William Darlington, second cousin of Smedley Darlington) (F Pa.) Dec. 13, 1781–April 27, 1839; House 1817–19.

Darlington, Smedley (second cousin of Edward Darlington, Isaac Darlington, and William Darlington) (R Pa.) Dec. 24, 1827–June 24, 1899; House 1887–91.

Darlington, William (cousin of Edward Darlington and Isaac Darlington, second cousin of Smedley Darlington) (R Pa.) April 28, 1782–April 23, 1863; House 1815–17, 1819–23.

Darragh, Archibald Bard (R Mich.) Dec. 23, 1840–Feb. 21, 1927; House 1901–09.

Darragh, Cornelius (W Pa.) 1809–Dec. 22, 1854; House March 26, 1844–47.

Darrall, Chester Bidwell (R La.) June 24, 1842–Jan. 1, 1908; House 1869–Feb. 20, 1878, 1881–83.

Darrow, George Potter (R Pa.) Feb. 4, 1859–June 7, 1943; House 1915–37, 1939–41.

Daschle, Thomas Andrew (D S.D.) Dec. 9, 1947– ; House 1979–87; Senate 1987– ; Senate minority leader 1995– .

Daub, Harold John "Hal" Jr. (R Neb.) April 23, 1941– ; House 1981–89.

Daugherty, James Alexander (D Mo.) Aug. 30, 1847–Jan. 26, 1920; House 1911–13.

Daughton, Ralph Hunter (D Va.) Sept. 23, 1885–Dec. 22, 1958; House Nov. 7, 1944–47.

Davee, Thomas (D Maine) Dec. 9, 1797–Dec. 9, 1841; House 1837–41.

Davenport, Franklin (F N.J.) Sept. 1755–July 27, 1832; Senate Dec. 5, 1798–99; House 1799–1801.

Davenport, Frederick Morgan (R N.Y.) Aug. 27, 1866–Dec. 26, 1956; House 1925–33.

Davenport, Harry James (D Pa.) Aug. 28, 1902–Dec. 19, 1977; House 1949–51.

Davenport, Ira (R N.Y.) June 28, 1841–Oct. 6, 1904; House 1885–89.

Davenport, James (brother of John Davenport of Conn.) (F Conn.) Oct. 12, 1758–Aug. 3, 1797; House Dec. 5, 1796–Aug. 3, 1797.

Davenport, James Sanford (D Okla.) Sept. 21, 1864–Jan. 3, 1940; House Nov. 16, 1907–09, 1911–17.

Davenport, John (brother of James Davenport) (F Conn.) Jan. 16, 1752–Nov. 28, 1830; House 1799–1817.

Davenport, John (– Ohio) Jan. 9, 1788–July 18, 1855; House 1827–29.

Davenport, Samuel Arza (R Pa.) Jan. 15, 1834–Aug. 1, 1911; House 1897–1901.

Davenport, Stanley Woodward (D Pa.) July 21, 1861–Sept. 26, 1921; House 1899–1901.

Davenport, Thomas (AJ Va.) ?–Nov. 18, 1838; House 1825–35 (1825–29 no party, 1829–33 Jacksonian).

Davey, Martin Luther (D Ohio) July 25, 1884–March 31, 1946; House Nov. 5, 1918–21, 1923–29; Gov. Jan. 14, 1935–Jan. 9, 1939.

Davey, Robert Charles (D La.) Oct. 22, 1853–Dec. 26, 1908; House 1893–95, 1897–Dec. 26, 1908.

Davidson, Alexander Caldwell (D Ala.) Dec. 26, 1826–Nov. 6, 1897; House 1885–89.

Davidson, Irwin Delmore (D/L N.Y.) Jan. 2, 1906–Aug. 1, 1981; House 1955–Dec. 31, 1956.

Davidson, James Henry (R Wis.) June 18, 1858–Aug. 6, 1918; House 1897–1913, 1917–Aug. 6, 1918.

Davidson, Robert Hamilton McWhorta (D Fla.) Sept. 23, 1832–Jan. 18, 1908; House 1877–91.

Davidson, Thomas Green (D La.) Aug. 3, 1805–Sept. 11, 1883; House 1855–61.

Davidson, William (F N.C.) Sept. 12, 1778–Sept. 16, 1857; House Dec. 2, 1818–21.

Davies, Edward (AMas. Pa.) Nov. 1779–May 18, 1853; House 1837–41.

Davies, John Clay (D N.Y.) May 1, 1920– ; House 1949–51.

Davila, Felix Cordova (U P.R.) Nov. 20, 1878–Dec. 3, 1938; House (Res. Comm.) Aug. 7, 1917–April 11, 1932.

Davis, Alexander Mathews (D Va.) Jan. 17, 1833–Sept. 25, 1889; House 1873–March 5, 1874.

Davis, Amos (brother of Garrett Davis) (AJ Ky.) Aug. 15, 1794–June 11, 1835; House 1833–35.

Davis, Charles Russell (R Minn.) Sept. 17, 1849–July 29, 1930; House 1903–25.

Davis, Clifford (D Tenn.) Nov. 18, 1897–June 8, 1970; House Feb. 15, 1940–65.

Davis, Cushman Kellogg (R Minn.) June 16, 1838–Nov. 27, 1900; Senate 1887–Nov. 27, 1900; Gov. Jan. 7, 1874–Jan. 7, 1876.

Davis, Danny K. (D Ill.) Sept. 6, 1941– ; House 1997– .

Davis, David (cousin of Henry Winter Davis) (I Ill.) March 9, 1815–June 26, 1886; Senate 1877–83; elected Pres. pro tempore Oct. 13, 1881; Assoc. Justice Supreme Court Dec. 10, 1862–March 4, 1877.

Davis, Ewin Lamar (D Tenn.) Feb. 5, 1876–Oct. 23, 1949; House 1919–33.

Davis, Garrett (brother of Amos Davis) (D Ky.) Sept. 10, 1801–Sept. 22, 1872; House 1839–47 (Whig); Senate Dec. 10, 1861–Sept. 22, 1872 (1861–67 Unionist).

Davis, George Royal (R Ill.) Jan. 3, 1840–Nov. 25, 1899; House 1879–85.

Davis, George Thomas (W Mass.) Jan. 12, 1810–June 17, 1877; House 1851–53.

Davis, Glenn Robert (R Wis.) Oct. 28, 1914–Sept. 21, 1988; House April 22, 1947–57, 1965–Dec. 31, 1974.

Davis, Henry Gassaway (brother of Thomas Beall Davis, grandfather of Davis Elkins) (D W.Va.) Nov. 16, 1823–March 11, 1916; Senate 1871–83.

Davis, Henry Winter (cousin of David Davis) (UU Md.) Aug. 16, 1817–Dec. 30, 1865; House 1855–61 (American Party), 1863–65.

Davis, Horace (R Calif.) March 16, 1831–July 12, 1916; House 1877–81.

Davis, Jack (R Ill.) Sept. 6, 1935– ; House 1987–89.

Davis, Jacob Cunningham (D Ill.) Sept. 16, 1820–Dec. 25, 1883; House Nov. 4, 1856–57.

Davis, Jacob Erastus (D Ohio) Oct. 31, 1905– ; House 1941–43.

Davis, James Curran (D Ga.) May 17, 1895–Dec. 18, 1981; House 1947–63.

Davis, James Harvey "Cyclone" (D Texas) Dec. 24, 1853–Jan. 31, 1940; House 1915–17.

Davis, James John (R Pa.) Oct. 27, 1873–Nov. 22, 1947; Senate Dec. 2, 1930–45; Secy. of Labor March 5, 1921–Nov. 30, 1930.

Davis, Jeff (D Ark.) May 6, 1862–Jan. 3, 1913; Senate 1907–Jan. 3, 1913; Gov. Jan. 8, 1901–Jan. 8, 1907.

Davis, Jefferson Finis (D Miss.) June 3, 1808–Dec. 6, 1889; House 1845–June 1846; Senate Aug. 10, 1847–Sept. 23, 1851, 1857–Jan. 21, 1861; Secy. of War March 7, 1853–March 6, 1857.

Davis, Jim (D Fla.) Oct. 11, 1957– ; House 1997– .

Davis, John (W Mass.) Jan. 13, 1787–April 19, 1854; House 1825–Jan. 14, 1834 (no party); Senate 1835–Jan. 5, 1841, March 24, 1845–53; Gov. Jan. 9, 1834–March 1, 1835, Jan. 7, 1841–Jan. 17, 1843.

Davis, John (D Pa.) Aug. 7, 1788–April 1, 1878; House 1839–41.

Davis, John (P Kan.) Aug. 9, 1826–Aug. 1, 1901; House 1891–95.

Davis, John Givan (ALD Ind.) Oct. 10, 1810–Jan. 18, 1866; House 1851–55 (Democrat), 1857–61 (1857–59 Democrat).

Davis, John James (father of John William Davis of W.Va.) (ID W.Va.) May 5, 1835–March 19, 1916; House 1871–75 (1871–73 Democrat).

Davis, John Wesley (D Ind.) April 16, 1799–Aug. 22, 1859; House 1835–37 (Jacksonian), 1839–41, 1843–47; Speaker Dec. 1, 1845–47; Gov. (Ore. Terr.) 1853, 1854.

Davis, John William (son of John James Davis) (D W.Va.) April 13, 1873–March 24, 1955; House 1911–Aug. 29, 1913.

Davis, John William (D Ga.) Sept. 12, 1916–Oct. 3, 1992; House 1961–75.

Davis, Joseph Jonathan (D N.C.) April 13, 1828–Aug. 7, 1892; House 1875–81.

Davis, Lowndes Henry (D Mo.) Dec. 13, 1836–Feb. 4, 1920; House 1879–85.

Davis, Mendel Jackson (D S.C.) Oct. 23, 1942– ; House April 27, 1971–81.

Davis, Noah (R N.Y.) Sept. 10, 1818–March 20, 1902; House 1869–July 15, 1870.

Davis, Reuben (D Miss.) Jan. 18, 1813–Oct. 14, 1890; House 1857–Jan. 12, 1861.

Davis, Richard David (D N.Y.) 1799–June 17, 1871; House 1841–45.

Davis, Robert Lee (R Pa.) Oct. 29, 1893– ; House Nov. 8, 1932–33.

Davis, Robert Thompson (R Mass.) Aug. 28, 1823–Oct. 29, 1906; House 1883–89.

Davis, Robert William (R Mich.) July 31, 1932– ; House 1979–93.

Davis, Robert Wyche (D Fla.) March 15, 1849–Sept. 15, 1929; House 1897–1905.

Davis, Roger (R Pa.) Oct. 2, 1762–Nov. 20, 1815; House 1811–15.

Davis, Samuel (F Mass.) 1774–April 20, 1831; House 1813–15.

Davis, Thomas (D R.I.) Dec. 18, 1806–July 26, 1895; House 1853–55.

Davis, Thomas Beall (brother of Henry Gassaway Davis) (D W.Va.) April 25, 1828–Nov. 26, 1911; House June 6, 1905–07.

Davis, Thomas M. III (R Va.) Jan. 5, 1949– ; House 1995– .

Davis, Thomas Terry (R Ky.) ?–Nov. 15, 1807; House 1797–1803.

Davis, Thomas Treadwell (grandson of Thomas Tredwell) (R N.Y.) Aug. 22, 1810–May 2, 1872; House 1863–67 (1863–65 Unionist).

Davis, Timothy (R Iowa) March 29, 1794–April 27, 1872; House 1857–59.

Davis, Timothy (R Mass.) April 12, 1821–Oct. 23, 1888; House 1855–59 (1855–57 American Party).

Davis, Warren Ransom (N S.C.) May 8, 1793–Jan. 29, 1835; House 1827–Jan. 29, 1835 (1827–31 Jacksonian).

Davis, William Morris (R Pa.) Aug. 16, 1815–Aug. 5, 1891; House 1861–63.

Davison, George Mosby (R Ky.) March 23, 1855–Dec. 18, 1912; House 1897–99.

Davy, John Madison (R N.Y.) June 29, 1835–April 21, 1909; House 1875–77.

Dawes, Beman Gates (son of Rufus Dawes, brother of Vice President Charles Gates Dawes) (R Ohio) Jan. 14, 1870–May 15, 1953; House 1905–09.

Dawes, Henry Laurens (R Mass.) Oct. 30, 1816–Feb. 5, 1903; House 1857–75 (no party); Senate 1875–93.

Dawes, Rufus (father of Vice President Charles Gates Dawes and Beman Gates Dawes) (R Ohio) July 4, 1838–Aug. 2, 1899; House 1881–83.

Dawson, Albert Foster (R Iowa) Jan. 26, 1872–March 9, 1949; House 1905–11.

Dawson, John (R Va.) 1762–March 31, 1814; House 1797–March 31, 1814; Cont. Cong. 1788.

Dawson, John Bennett (D La.) March 17, 1798–June 26, 1845; House 1841–June 26, 1845.

Dawson, John Littleton (D Pa.) Feb. 7, 1813–Sept. 18, 1870; House 1851–55, 1863–67.

Dawson, William (D Mo.) March 17, 1848–Oct. 12, 1929; House 1885–87.

Dawson, William Adams (R Utah) Nov. 5, 1903–Nov. 7, 1981; House 1947–49, 1953–59.

Dawson, William Crosby (W Ga.) Jan. 4, 1798–May 5, 1856; House Nov. 7, 1836–Nov. 13, 1841 (Nov. 7, 1836–37 State Rights Party); Senate 1849–55.

Dawson, William Johnson (– N.C.) ?–1798; House 1793–95.

Dawson, William Levi (D Ill.) April 26, 1886–Nov. 9, 1970; House 1943–Nov. 9, 1970; Chrmn. House Expenditures in the Executive Departments 1949–52; Chrmn. House Government Operations 1952–53, 1955–71.

Day, Rowland (J N.Y.) March 6, 1779–Dec. 23, 1853; House 1823–25 (no party), 1833–35.

Day, Stephen Albion (R Ill.) July 13, 1882–Jan. 5, 1950; House 1941–45.

Day, Timothy Crane (R Ohio) Jan. 8, 1819–April 15, 1869; House 1855–57.

Dayan, Charles (J N.Y.) July 8, 1792–Dec. 25, 1877; House 1831–33.

Dayton, Alston Gordon (R W.Va.) Oct. 18, 1857–July 30, 1920; House 1895–March 16, 1905.

Dayton, Jonathan (F N.J.) Oct. 16, 1760–Oct. 9, 1824; House 1791–99 (no party); Speaker Dec. 7, 1795–97, May 15, 1797–99; Senate 1799–1805; Cont. Cong. 1787–88.

Dayton, William Lewis (W N.J.) Feb. 17, 1807–Dec. 1, 1864; Senate July 2, 1842–51.

Deal, Joseph Thomas (D Va.) Nov. 19, 1860–March 7, 1942; House 1921–29.

Deal, Nathan (R Ga.) Aug. 25, 1942– ; House 1993– (1993–April 10, 1995 Democrat).

Dean, Benjamin (D Mass.) Aug. 14, 1824–April 9, 1897; House March 28, 1878–79.

Dean, Ezra (D Ohio) April 9, 1795–Jan. 25, 1872; House 1841–45.

Dean, Gilbert (D N.Y.) Aug. 14, 1819–Oct. 12, 1870; House 1851–July 3, 1854.

Dean, Josiah (R Mass.) March 6, 1748–Oct. 14, 1818; House 1807–09.

Dean, Sidney (R Conn.) Nov. 16, 1818–Oct. 29, 1901; House 1855–59 (1855–57 American Party).

Deane, Charles Bennett (D N.C.) Nov. 1, 1898–Nov. 24, 1969; House 1947–57.

Dear, Cleveland (D La.) Aug. 22, 1888–Dec. 30, 1950; House 1933–37.

Dearborn, Henry (father of Henry Alexander Scammell Dearborn) (D Mass.) Feb. 23, 1751–June 6, 1829; House 1793–97 (1793–95 no party); Secy. of War March 5, 1801–March 7, 1809.

Dearborn, Henry Alexander Scammell (son of Henry Dearborn) (AJ Mass.) March 3, 1783–July 29, 1851; House 1831–33.

De Armond, David Albaugh (D Mo.) March 18, 1844–Nov. 23, 1909; House 1891–Nov. 23, 1909.

Deberry, Edmund (W N.C.) Aug. 14, 1787–Dec. 12, 1859; House 1829–31 (no party), 1833–45 (1833–35 Anti-Jacksonian), 1849–51.

Deboe, William Joseph (R Ky.) June 30, 1849–June 15, 1927; Senate 1897–1903.

De Bolt, Rezin A. (D Mo.) Jan. 20, 1828–Oct. 30, 1891; House 1875–77.

Deckard, Huey Joel (R Ind.) March 7, 1942– ; House 1979–83.

Decker, Perl D. (D Mo.) Sept. 10, 1875–Aug. 22, 1934; House 1913–19.

Deconcini, Dennis Webster (D Ariz.) May 8, 1937– ; Senate 1977–95; Chrmn. Senate Select Committee on Intelligence Activities 1993–95.

Deemer, Elias (R Pa.) Jan. 3, 1838–March 29, 1918; House 1901–07.

Deen, Braswell Drue (D Ga.) June 28, 1893–Nov. 28, 1981; House 1933–39.

Deering, Nathaniel Cobb (R Iowa) Sept. 2, 1827–Dec. 11, 1887; House 1877–83.

DeFazio, Peter Anthony (D Ore.) May 27, 1947– ; House 1987– .

De Forest, Henry Schermerhorn (R N.Y.) Feb. 16, 1847–Feb. 13, 1917; House 1911–13.

De Forest, Robert Elliott (D Conn.) Feb. 20, 1845–Oct. 1, 1924; House 1891–95.

Defrees, Joseph Hutton (R Ind.) May 13, 1812–Dec. 21, 1885; House 1865–67.

Degener, Edward (R Texas) Oct. 20, 1809–Sept. 11, 1890; House March 31, 1870–71.

Degetau, Frederico (R P.R.) Dec. 5, 1862–Jan. 20, 1914; House (Res. Comm.) 1901–05.

DeGette, Diana (D Colo.) July 29, 1957– ; House 1997– .

De Graff, John Isaac (D N.Y.) Oct. 2, 1783–July 26, 1848; House 1827–29 (no party), 1837–39.

De Graffenreid, Reese Calhoun (D Texas) May 7, 1859–Aug. 29, 1902; House 1897–Aug. 29, 1902.

Degraffenried, Edward (D Ala.) June 30, 1899–Nov. 5, 1974; House 1949–53.

De Haven, John Jefferson (R Calif.) March 12, 1849–Jan. 26, 1913; House 1889–Oct. 1, 1890.

Deitrick, Frederick Simpson (D Mass.) April 9, 1875–May 24, 1948; House 1913–15.

De Jarnette, Daniel Coleman (ID Va.) Oct. 18, 1822–Aug. 20, 1881; House 1859–61.

De Lacy, Emerson Hugh (D Wash.) May 9, 1910–Aug. 19, 1986; House 1945–47.

De la Garza, Eligio "Kika" II (D Texas) Sept. 22, 1927– ; House 1965–97; Chrmn. House Agriculture 1981–95.

Delahunt, William D. (D Mass) July 18, 1941– ; House 1997– .

De la Matyr, Gilbert (G Ind.) July 8, 1825–May 17, 1892; House 1879–81.

De la Montanya, James (D N.Y.) March 20, 1798–April 29, 1849; House 1839–41.

Delaney, James Joseph (D N.Y.) March 19, 1901–May 24, 1987; House 1945–47, 1949–Dec. 31, 1978; Chrmn. House Rules 1977–78.

Delaney, John Joseph (D N.Y.) Aug. 21, 1878–Nov. 18, 1948; House March 5, 1918–19, 1931–Nov. 18, 1948.

Delano, Charles (R Mass.) June 24, 1820–Jan. 23, 1883; House 1859–63.

Delano, Columbus (R Ohio) June 4, 1809–Oct. 23, 1896; House 1845–47 (Whig), 1865–67, June 3, 1868–69; Secy. of the Interior Nov. 1, 1870–Sept. 30, 1875.

De Lano, Milton (R N.Y.) Aug. 11, 1844–Jan. 2, 1922; House 1887–91.

Delaplaine, Isaac Clason (D N.Y.) Oct. 27, 1817–July 17, 1866; House 1861–63.

De Large, Robert Carlos (R S.C.) March 15, 1842–Feb. 14, 1874; House 1871–Jan. 24, 1873.

DeLauro, Rosa (D Conn.) March 2, 1943– ; House 1991– .

DeLay, Thomas Dale (R Texas) April 8, 1947– ; House 1985– .

DeMint, James (R S.C.) Sept. 2, 1951– ; House 1999– .

Delgado, Francisco Afan (Nat. P.I.) Jan. 25, 1886–Oct. 27, 1964; House (Res. Comm.) 1935–Feb. 14, 1936.

Dellay, Vincent John (D N.J.) June 23, 1907– ; House 1957–59 (1957 Republican).

Dellenback, John Richard (R Ore.) Nov. 6, 1918– ; House 1967–75.

Dellet, James (W Ala.) Feb. 18, 1788–Dec. 21, 1848; House 1839–41, 1843–45.

Dellums, Ronald Vernie (D Calif.) Nov. 24, 1935– ; House 1971–Feb. 6, 1998; Chrmn. House District of Columbia 1979–93; Chrmn. House Armed Services 1993–95.

De Lugo, Ron (D V.I.) Aug. 2, 1930– ; House (Terr. Del.) 1973–79, 1981–95.

Deming, Benjamin F. (AMas. Vt.) 1790–July 11, 1834; House 1833–July 11, 1834.

Deming, Henry Champion (R Conn.) May 23, 1815–Oct. 8, 1872; House 1863–67.

De Mott, John (D N.Y.) Oct. 7, 1790–July 31, 1870; House 1845–47.

De Motte, Mark Lindsey (R Ind.) Dec. 28, 1832–Sept. 23, 1908; House 1881–83.

Dempsey, John Joseph (D N.M.) June 22, 1879–March 11, 1958; House 1935–41, 1951–March 11, 1958; Gov. Jan. 1, 1943–Jan. 1, 1947.

Dempsey, Stephen Wallace (R N.Y.) May 8, 1862–March 1, 1949; House 1915–31.

De Muth, Peter Joseph (D Pa.) Jan. 1, 1892–April 3, 1993; House 1937–39.

DeNardis, Lawrence Joseph (R Conn.) March 18, 1938– ; House 1981–83.

Denby, Edwin (grandson of Graham Newell Fitch) (R Mich.) Feb. 18, 1870–Feb. 8, 1929; House 1905–11; Secy. of the Navy March 6, 1921–March 10, 1924.

Deneen, Charles Samuel (R Ill.) May 4, 1863–Feb. 5, 1940; Senate Feb. 26, 1925–31; Gov. Jan. 9, 1905–Feb. 3, 1913.

Denholm, Frank Edward (D S.D.) Nov. 29, 1923– ; House 1971–75.

Denison, Charles (nephew of George Denison) (D Pa.) Jan. 23, 1818–June 27, 1867; House 1863–June 27, 1867.

Denison, Dudley Chase (nephew of Dudley Chase, cousin of Salmon Portland Chase) (R Vt.) Sept. 13, 1819–Feb. 10, 1905; House 1875–79 (1875–77 Independent Republican).

Denison, Edward Everett (R Ill.) Aug. 28, 1873–June 17, 1953; House 1915–31.

Denison, George (uncle of Charles Denison) (– Pa.) Feb. 22, 1790–Aug. 20, 1831; House 1819–23.

De Nivernais, Edward James. (*See* Livernash, Edward James.)

Denney, Robert Vernon (R Neb.) April 11, 1916–June 26, 1981; House 1967–71.

Denning, William (– N.Y.) April 1740–Oct. 30, 1819; House 1809–10.

Dennis, David Worth (R Ind.) June 7, 1912–Jan. 6, 1999; House 1969–75.

Dennis, George Robertson (D Md.) April 8, 1822–Aug. 13, 1882; Senate 1873–79.

Dennis, John (father of John Dennis, below, uncle of Littleton Purnell Dennis) (F Md.) Dec. 17, 1771–Aug. 17, 1806; House 1797–1805.

Dennis, John (son of John Dennis, above) (W Md.) 1807–Nov. 1, 1859; House 1837–41.

Dennis, Littleton Purnell (nephew of John Dennis born in 1771, cousin of John Dennis born in 1807) (AJ Md.) July 21, 1786–April 14, 1834; House 1833–April 14, 1834.

Dennison, David Short (R Ohio) July 29, 1918– ; House 1957–59.

Denny, Arthur Armstrong (R Wash.) June 20, 1822–Jan. 9, 1899; House (Terr. Del.) 1865–67.

Denny, Harmar (great-grandfather of Harmar Denny Denny Jr.) (AMas. Pa.) May 13, 1794–Jan. 29, 1852; House Dec. 15, 1829–37.

Denny, Harmar Denny Jr. (great-grandson of Harmar Denny) (R Pa.) July 2, 1886–Jan. 6, 1966; House 1951–53.

Denny, James William (D Md.) Nov. 20, 1838–April 12, 1923; House 1899–1901, 1903–05.

Denny, Walter McKennon (D Miss.) Oct. 28, 1853–Nov. 5, 1926; House 1895–97.

Denoyelles, Peter (R N.Y.) 1766–May 6, 1829; House 1813–15.

Denson, William Henry (D Ala.) March 4, 1846–Sept. 26, 1906; House 1893–95.

Dent, George (F Md.) 1756–Dec. 2, 1813; House 1793–1801 (1793–95 no party).

Dent, John Herman (D Pa.) March 10, 1908–April 9, 1988; House Jan. 21, 1958–79.

Dent, Stanley Hubert Jr. (D Ala.) Aug. 16, 1869–Oct. 6, 1938; House 1909–21.

Dent, William Barton Wade (D Ga.) Sept. 8, 1806–Sept. 7, 1855; House 1853–55.

Denton, George Kirkpatrick (father of Winfield Kirkpatrick Denton) (D Ind.) Nov. 17, 1864–Jan. 4, 1926; House 1917–19.

Denton, Jeremiah Andrew Jr. (R Ala.) July 15, 1924– ; Senate Jan. 2, 1981–87.

Denton, Winfield Kirkpatrick (son of George Kirkpatrick Denton) (D Ind.) Oct. 28, 1896–Nov. 2, 1971; House 1949–53, 1955–67.

Denver, James William (father of Matthew Rombach Denver) (D Calif.) Oct. 23, 1817–Aug. 9, 1892; House 1855–57; Gov. (Kansas Terr.) June 7, 1857–58.

Denver, Matthew Rombach (son of James William Denver) (D Ohio) Dec. 21, 1870–May 13, 1954; House 1907–13.

Depew, Chauncey Mitchell (R N.Y.) April 23, 1834–April 5, 1928; Senate 1899–1911.

De Priest, Oscar (R Ill.) March 9, 1871–May 12, 1951; House 1929–35.

De Rouen, René Louis (D La.) Jan. 7, 1874–March 27, 1942; House Aug. 23, 1927–41.

Derounian, Steven Boghos (R N.Y.) April 6, 1918–   ; House 1953–65.

Derrick, Butler Carson Jr. (D S.C.) Sept. 30, 1936–   ; House 1975–95.

Dershem, Franklin Lewis (D Pa.) March 5, 1865–Feb. 14, 1950; House 1913–15.

Derwinski, Edward Joseph (R Ill.) Sept. 15, 1926–   ; House 1959–83; Secy. of Veterans Affairs March 15, 1989–Sept. 26, 1992.

De Saussure, William Ford (D S.C.) Feb. 22, 1792–March 13, 1870; Senate May 10, 1852–53.

Desha, Joseph (brother of Robert Desha) (R Ky.) Dec. 9, 1768–Oct. 11, 1842; House 1807–19; Gov. June 1, 1824–June 1, 1828 (Democratic Republican).

Desha, Robert (brother of Joseph Desha) (J Tenn.) Jan. 14, 1791–Feb. 6, 1849; House 1827–31.

Destrehan, Jean Noel (– La.) 1754–1823; Senate Sept. 3–Oct. 1, 1812.

Deuster, Peter Victor (D Wis.) Feb. 13, 1831–Dec. 31, 1904; House 1879–85.

Deutsch, Peter (D Fla.) April 1, 1957–   ; House 1993–   .

Devereux, James Patrick Sinnott (R Md.) Feb. 20, 1903–Aug. 5, 1988; House 1951–59.

De Veyra, Jaime Carlos (Nat. P.I.) Nov. 4, 1873–March 7, 1963; House (Res. Comm.) 1917–23.

Devine, Samuel Leeper (R Ohio) Dec. 21, 1915–June 27, 1997; House 1959–81.

Devitt, Edward James (R Minn.) May 5, 1911–March 2, 1992; House 1947–49.

De Vries, Marion (D Calif.) Aug. 15, 1865–Sept. 11, 1939; House 1897–Aug. 20, 1900.

Dewalt, Arthur Granville (D Pa.) Oct. 11, 1854–Oct. 26, 1931; House 1915–21.

Dewart, Lewis (father of William Lewis Dewart) (J Pa.) Nov. 14, 1780–April 26, 1852; House 1831–33.

D'Ewart, Wesley Abner (R Mont.) Oct. 1, 1889–Sept. 2, 1973; House June 5, 1945–55.

Dewart, William Lewis (son of Lewis Dewart) (D Pa.) June 21, 1821–April 19, 1888; House 1857–59.

Deweese, John Thomas (R N.C.) June 4, 1835–July 4, 1906; House July 6, 1868–Feb. 28, 1870.

Dewey, Charles Schuveldt (R Ill.) Nov. 10, 1880–Dec. 27, 1980; House 1941–45.

Dewey, Daniel (F Mass.) Jan. 29, 1766–May 26, 1815; House 1813–Feb. 24, 1814.

DeWine, Michael (R Ohio) Jan. 5, 1947–   ; House 1983–91; Senate 1995–   .

De Witt, Alexander (AP Mass.) April 2, 1798–Jan. 13, 1879; House 1853–57 (1853–55 Free-Soiler).

De Witt, Charles Gerrit (J N.Y.) Nov. 7, 1789–April 12, 1839; House 1829–31.

De Witt, David Miller (D N.Y.) Nov. 25, 1837–June 23, 1912; House 1873–75.

De Witt, Francis Byron (R Ohio) March 11, 1849–March 21, 1929; House 1895–97.

De Witt, Jacob Hasbrouck (– N.Y.) Oct. 2, 1784–Jan. 30, 1867; House 1819–21.

De Wolf, James (R R.I.) March 18, 1764–Dec. 21, 1837; Senate 1821–Oct. 31, 1825.

Dexter, Samuel (F Mass.) May 14, 1761–May 4, 1816; House 1793–95 (no party); Senate 1799–May 30, 1800; Secy. of War May 13–Dec. 31, 1800; Secy. of the Treasury Jan. 1–May 13, 1801.

Dezendorf, John Frederick (R Va.) Aug. 10, 1834–June 22, 1894; House 1881–83.

Dial, Nathaniel Barksdale (D S.C.) April 24, 1862–Dec. 11, 1940; Senate 1919–25.

Diaz-Balart, Lincoln (R Fla.) Aug. 13, 1954–   ; House 1993–   .

Dibble, Samuel (D S.C.) Sept. 16, 1837–Sept. 16, 1913; House June 9, 1881–May 31, 1882, 1883–91.

Dibrell, George Gibbs (D Tenn.) April 12, 1822–May 9, 1888; House 1875–85.

Dick, Charles William Frederick (R Ohio) Nov. 3, 1858–March 13, 1945; House Nov. 8, 1898–March 23, 1904; Senate March 23, 1904–11.

Dick, John (father of Samuel Bernard Dick) (R Pa.) June 17, 1794–May 29, 1872; House 1853–59 (1853–55 Whig).

Dick, Samuel Bernard (son of John Dick) (R Pa.) Oct. 26, 1836–May 10, 1907; House 1879–81.

Dickens, Samuel (R N.C.) ?–1840; House Dec. 2, 1816–17.

Dickerman, Charles Heber (D Pa.) Feb. 3, 1843–Dec. 17, 1915; House 1903–05.

Dickerson, Mahlon (brother of Philemon Dickerson) (R N.J.) April 17, 1770–Oct. 5, 1853; Senate 1817–Jan. 30, 1829; Gov. Oct. 26, 1815–Feb. 1, 1817; Secy. of the Navy July 1, 1834–June 30, 1838.

Dickerson, Philemon (brother of Mahlon Dickerson) (D N.J.) Jan. 11, 1788–Dec. 10, 1862; House 1833–Nov. 3, 1836 (Jacksonian), 1839–41; Gov. Nov. 3, 1836–Oct. 27, 1837 (Democrat).

Dickerson, William Worth (D Ky.) Nov. 29, 1851–Jan. 31, 1923; House June 21, 1890–93.

Dickey, Henry Luther (D Ohio) Oct. 29, 1832–May 23, 1910; House 1877–81.

Dickey, Jay (R Ark.) Dec. 14, 1939–   ; House 1993–   .

Dickey, Jesse Column (W Pa.) Feb. 27, 1808–Feb. 19, 1890; House 1849–51.

Dickey, John (father of Oliver James Dickey) (W Pa.) June 23, 1794–March 14, 1853; House 1843–45, 1847–49.

Dickey, Oliver James (son of John Dickey) (R Pa.) April 6, 1823–April 21, 1876; House Dec. 7, 1868–73.

Dickinson, Clement Cabell (D Mo.) Dec. 6, 1849–Jan. 14, 1938; House Feb. 1, 1910–21, 1923–29, 1931–35.

Dickinson, Daniel Stevens (D N.Y.) Sept. 11, 1800–April 12, 1866; Senate Nov. 30, 1844–51.

Dickinson, David W. (nephew of William Hardy Murfree) (W Tenn.) June 10, 1808–April 27, 1845; House 1833–35 (Jacksonia), 1843–45.

Dickinson, Edward (W Mass.) Jan. 1, 1803–June 16, 1874; House 1853–55.

Dickinson, Edward Fenwick (D Ohio) Jan. 21, 1829–Aug. 25, 1891; House 1869–71.

Dickinson, John Dean (– N.Y.) June 28, 1767–Jan. 28, 1841; House 1819–23, 1827–31.

Dickinson, Lester Jesse (cousin of Fred Dickinson Letts) (R Iowa) Oct. 29, 1873–June 4, 1968; House 1919–31; Senate 1931–37.

Dickinson, Philemon (– N.J.) April 5, 1739–Feb. 4, 1809; Senate Nov. 23, 1790–93; Cont. Cong. 1782–83 (Del.).

Dickinson, Rodolphus (D Ohio) Dec. 28, 1797–March 20, 1849; House 1847–March 20, 1849.

Dickinson, William Louis (R Ala.) June 5, 1925–   ; House 1965–93.

Dicks, Norman DeValois (D Wash.) Dec. 16, 1940–   ; House 1977–   .

Dickson, David (W Miss.) ?–July 31, 1836; House 1835–July 31, 1836.

Dickson, Frank Stoddard (R Ill.) Oct. 6, 1876–Feb. 24, 1953; House 1905–07.

Dickson, John (AMas. N.Y.) June 1, 1783–Feb. 22, 1852; House 1831–35.

Dickson, Joseph (F N.C.) April 1745–April 14, 1825; House 1799–1801.

Dickson, Samuel (W N.Y.) March 29, 1807–May 3, 1858; House 1855–57.

Dickson, William (R Tenn.) May 5, 1770–Feb. 1816; House 1801–07.

Dickson, William Alexander (D Miss.) July 20, 1861–Feb. 25, 1940; House 1909–13.

Dickstein, Samuel (D N.Y.) Feb. 5, 1885–April 22, 1954; House 1923–Dec. 30, 1945.

Diekema, Gerrit John (R Mich.) March 27, 1859–Dec. 20, 1930; House March 17, 1908–11.

Dies, Martin (father of Martin Dies Jr.) (D Texas) March 13, 1870–July 13, 1922; House 1909–19.

Dies, Martin Jr. (son of Martin Dies) (D Texas) Nov. 5, 1900–Nov. 14, 1972; House 1931–45, 1953–59.

Dieterich, William Henry (D Ill.) March 31, 1876–Oct. 12, 1940; House 1931–33; Senate 1933–39.

Dietrich, Charles Elmer (D Pa.) July 30, 1889–May 20, 1942; House 1935–37.

Dietrich, Charles Henry (R Neb.) Nov. 26, 1853–April 10, 1924; Senate March 28, 1901–05; Gov. Jan. 3–May 1, 1901.

Dietz, William (– N.Y.) June 28, 1778–Aug. 24, 1848; House 1825–27.

Difenderfer, Robert Edward (D Pa.) June 7, 1849–April 25, 1923; House 1911–15.

Diggs, Charles Coles Jr. (D Mich.) Dec. 2, 1922–Aug. 24, 1998; House 1955–June 3, 1980; Chrmn. House District of Columbia 1973–79.

Dill, Clarence Cleveland (D Wash.) Sept. 21, 1884–Jan. 14, 1978; House 1915–19; Senate 1923–35.

Dillingham, Paul Jr. (father of William Paul Dillingham) (D Vt.) Aug. 10, 1799–July 26, 1891; House 1843–47; Gov. Oct. 13, 1865–Oct. 13, 1867 (Republican).

Dillingham, William Paul (son of Paul Dillingham Jr.) (R Vt.) Dec. 12, 1843–July 12, 1923; Senate Oct. 18, 1900–July 12, 1923; Gov. Oct. 4, 1888–Oct. 2, 1890.

Dillon, Charles Hall (R S.D.) Dec. 18, 1853–Sept. 15, 1929; House 1913–19.

Dilweg, LaVern Ralph (D Wis.) Nov. 1, 1903–Jan. 2, 1968; House 1943–45.

Dimmick, Milo Melankthon (brother of William Harrison Dimmick) (D Pa.) Oct. 30, 1811–Nov. 22, 1872; House 1849–53.

Dimmick, William Harrison (brother of Milo Melankthon Dimmick) (D Pa.) Dec. 20, 1815–Aug. 2, 1861; House 1857–61.

Dimock, Davis Jr. (D Pa.) Sept. 17, 1801–Jan. 13, 1842; House 1841–Jan. 13, 1842.

Dimond, Anthony Joseph (D Alaska) Nov. 30, 1881–May 28, 1953; House (Terr. Del.) 1933–45.

Dingell, John David (father of John David Dingell Jr.) (D Mich.) Feb. 2, 1894–Sept. 19, 1955; House 1933–Sept. 19, 1955.

Dingell, John David Jr. (son of John David Dingell) (D Mich.) July 8, 1926– ; House Dec. 13, 1955– ; Chrmn. House Energy and Commerce 1981–95.

Dingley, Nelson Jr. (R Maine) Feb. 15, 1832–Jan. 13, 1899; House Sept. 12, 1881–Jan. 13, 1899; Gov. Jan. 7, 1874–Jan. 5, 1876.

Dinsmoor, Samuel (R N.H.) July 1, 1766–March 15, 1835; House 1811–13; Gov. June 2, 1831–June 5, 1834 (Jacksonian).

Dinsmore, Hugh Anderson (D Ark.) Dec. 24, 1850–May 2, 1930; House 1893–1905.

Dioguardi, Joseph J. (R N.Y.) Sept. 20, 1940– ; House 1985–89.

Dirksen, Everett McKinley (father-in-law of Howard H. Baker Jr.) (R Ill.) Jan. 4, 1896–Sept. 7, 1969; House 1933–49; Chrmn. House District of Columbia 1947–49; Senate 1951–Sept. 7, 1969; Senate minority leader 1959–Sept. 7, 1969.

Disney, David Tiernan (D Ohio) Aug. 25, 1803–March 14, 1857; House 1849–55.

Disney, Wesley Ernest (D Okla.) Oct. 31, 1883–March 26, 1961; House 1931–45.

Ditter, John William (R Pa.) Sept. 5, 1888–Nov. 21, 1943; House 1933–Nov. 21, 1943.

Diven, Alexander Samuel (R N.Y.) Feb. 10, 1809–June 11, 1896; House 1861–63.

Dix, John Adams (son-in-law of John Jordan Morgan) (D N.Y.) July 24, 1798–April 21, 1879; Senate Jan. 27, 1845–49; Secy. of the Trea-

sury Jan. 15–March 6, 1861; Gov. Jan. 1, 1873–Jan. 1, 1875 (Republican).

Dixon, Alan John (D Ill.) July 7, 1927– ; Senate 1981–93.

Dixon, Archibald (W Ky.) April 2, 1802–April 23, 1876; Senate Sept. 1, 1852–55.

Dixon, Henry Aldous (R Utah) June 29, 1890–Jan. 22, 1967; House 1955–61.

Dixon, James (R Conn.) Aug. 5, 1814–March 27, 1873; House 1845–49 (Whig); Senate 1857–69.

Dixon, Joseph (R N.C.) April 9, 1828–March 3, 1883; House Dec. 5, 1870–71.

Dixon, Joseph Andrew (D Ohio) June 3, 1879–July 4, 1942; House 1937–39.

Dixon, Joseph Moore (R Mont.) July 31, 1867–May 22, 1934; House 1903–07; Senate 1907–13; Gov. Jan. 3, 1921–Jan. 4, 1925.

Dixon, Julian Carey (D Calif.) Aug. 8, 1934– ; House 1979– ; Chrmn. House Standards of Official Conduct 1985–91.

Dixon, Lincoln (D Ind.) Feb. 9, 1860–Sept. 16, 1932; House 1905–19.

Dixon, Nathan Fellows (grandfather of Nathan Fellows Dixon born in 1847, father of Nathan Fellows Dixon, below) (W R.I.) Dec. 13, 1774–Jan. 29, 1842; Senate 1839–Jan. 29, 1842.

Dixon, Nathan Fellows (son of Nathan Fellows Dixon, above, father of Nathan Fellows Dixon, below) (R R.I.) May 1, 1812–April 11, 1881; House 1849–51 (Whig), 1863–71.

Dixon, Nathan Fellows (son of Nathan Fellows Dixon, above, grandson of Nathan Fellows Dixon born in 1774) (R R.I.) Aug. 28, 1847–Nov. 8, 1897; House Feb. 12–March 3, 1885; Senate April 10, 1889–95.

Dixon, William Wirt (D Mont.) June 3, 1838–Nov. 13, 1910; House 1891–93.

Doan, Robert Eachus (R Ohio) July 23, 1831–Feb. 24, 1919; House 1891–93.

Doan, William (D Ohio) April 4, 1792–June 22, 1847; House 1839–43.

Dobbin, James Cochrane (grandson of James Cochran of North Carolina) (D N.C.) Jan. 17, 1814–Aug. 4, 1857; House 1845–47; Secy. of the Navy March 8, 1853–March 6, 1857.

Dobbins, Donald Claude (D Ill.) March 20, 1878–Feb. 14, 1943; House 1933–37.

Dobbins, Samuel Atkinson (R N.J.) April 14, 1814–May 26, 1886; House 1873–77.

Dockery, Alexander Monroe (D Mo.) Feb. 11, 1845–Dec. 26, 1926; House 1883–99; Gov. Jan. 14, 1901–Jan. 9, 1905.

Dockery, Alfred (father of Oliver Hart Dockery) (W N.C.) Dec. 11, 1797–Dec. 7, 1875; House 1845–47, 1851–53.

Dockery, Oliver Hart (son of Alfred Dockery) (R N.C.) Aug. 12, 1830–March 21, 1906; House July 13, 1868–71.

Dockweiler, John Francis (D Calif.) Sept. 19, 1895–Jan. 31, 1943; House 1933–39.

Dodd, Christopher John (son of Thomas Joseph Dodd) (D Conn.) May 27, 1944– ; House 1975–81; Senate 1981– ; Gen. Chrmn. Dem. Nat. Comm. 1994–97.

Dodd, Edward (R N.Y.) Aug. 25, 1805–March 1, 1891; House 1855–59 (1855–57 Whig).

Dodd, Thomas Joseph (father of Christopher John Dodd) (D Conn.) May 15, 1907–May 24, 1971; House 1953–57; Senate 1959–Jan. 2, 1971.

Doddridge, Philip (– Va.) May 17, 1773–Nov. 19, 1832; House 1829–Nov. 19, 1832.

Dodds, Francis Henry (R Mich.) June 9, 1858–Dec. 23, 1940; House 1909–13.

Dodds, Ozro John (D Ohio) March 22, 1840–April 18, 1882; House Oct. 8, 1872–73.

Dodge, Augustus Caesar (son of Henry Dodge) (D Iowa) Jan. 2, 1812–Nov. 20, 1883; House (Terr. Del.) Oct. 28, 1840–Dec. 28, 1846; Senate Dec. 7, 1848–Feb. 22, 1855.

Dodge, Grenville Mellen (R Iowa) April 12, 1831–Jan. 3, 1916; House 1867–69.

Dodge, Henry (father of Augustus Caesar Dodge) (D Wis.) Oct. 12, 1782–June 19, 1867; House (Terr. Del.) 1841–45; Senate June 8, 1848–57; Gov. (Wis. Terr.) 1836–41, 1845–48.

Dodge, William Earle (R N.Y.) Sept. 4, 1805–Feb. 9, 1883; House April 7, 1866–67.

Doe, Nicholas Bartlett (W N.Y.) June 16, 1786–Dec. 6, 1856; House Dec. 7, 1840–41.

Doggett, Lloyd (D Texas) Oct. 6, 1946– ; House 1995– .

Doig, Andrew Wheeler (D N.Y.) July 24, 1799–July 11, 1875; House 1839–43.

Dole, Robert Joseph (R Kan.) July 22, 1923– ; House 1961–69; Senate 1969–June 11, 1996; Chrmn. Senate Finance 1981–85; Senate majority leader 1985–87, 1995–June 11, 1996; Senate minority leader 1987–95; Chrmn. Rep. Nat. Comm. Jan. 1971–Jan. 1973.

Dollinger, Isidore (D N.Y.) Nov. 13, 1903– ; House 1949–Dec. 31, 1959.

Dolliver, James Isaac (nephew of Jonathan Prentiss Dolliver) (R Iowa) Aug. 31, 1894–Dec. 10, 1978; House 1945–57.

Dolliver, Jonathan Prentiss (uncle of James Isaac Dolliver) (R Iowa) Feb. 6, 1858–Oct. 15, 1910; House 1889–Aug. 22, 1900; Senate Aug. 22, 1900–Oct. 15, 1910.

Dolph, Joseph Norton (uncle of Frederick William Mulkey) (R Ore.) Oct. 19, 1835–March 10, 1897; Senate 1883–95.

Domengeaux, James (D La.) Jan. 6, 1907–April 11, 1988; House 1941–April 15, 1944, Nov. 7, 1944–49.

Domenici, Peter Vichi (R N.M.) May 7, 1932– ; Senate 1973– ; Chrmn. Senate Budget 1981–87, 1995– .

Dominick, Frederick Haskell (D S.C.) Feb. 20, 1877–March 11, 1960; House 1917–33.

Dominick, Peter Hoyt (nephew of Howard Alexander Smith) (R Colo.) July 7, 1915–March 18, 1981; House 1961–63; Senate 1963–75.

Donahey, Alvin Victor (D Ohio) July 7, 1873–April 8, 1946; Senate 1935–41; Gov. Jan. 8, 1923–Jan. 14, 1929.

Dondero, George Anthony (R Mich.) Dec. 16, 1883–Jan. 29, 1968; House 1933–57; Chrmn. House Public Works 1947–49, 1953–55.

Donley, Joseph Benton (R Pa.) Oct. 10, 1838–Jan. 23, 1917; House 1869–71.

Donnan, William G. (R Iowa) June 30, 1834–Dec. 4, 1908; House 1871–75.

Donnell, Forrest C. (R Mo.) Aug. 20, 1884–March 3, 1980; Senate 1945–51; Gov. Jan. 13, 1941–Jan. 8, 1945.

Donnell, Richard Spaight (grandson of Richard Dobbs Spaight, nephew of Richard Dobbs Spaight Jr.) (W N.C.) Sept. 20, 1820–June 3, 1867; House 1847–49.

Donnelly, Brian Joseph (D Mass.) March 2, 1946– ; House 1979–93.

Donnelly, Ignatius (R Minn.) Nov. 3, 1831–Jan. 1, 1901; House 1863–69.

Donohoe, Michael (D Pa.) Feb. 22, 1864–Jan. 17, 1958; House 1911–15.

Donohue, Harold Daniel (D Mass.) June 18, 1901–Nov. 4, 1984; House 1947–Dec. 31, 1974.

Donovan, Dennis D. (D Ohio) Jan. 31, 1859–April 21, 1941; House 1891–95.

Donovan, James George (D N.Y.) Dec. 15, 1898–April 6, 1987; House 1951–57.

Donovan, Jeremiah (D Conn.) Oct. 18, 1857–April 22, 1935; House 1913–15.

Donovan, Jerome Francis (D N.Y.), Feb. 1, 1872–Nov. 2, 1949; House March 5, 1918–21.

Dooley, Calvin (D Calif.) Jan. 11, 1954– ; House 1991– .

Dooley, Edwin Benedict (R N.Y.) April 13, 1905–Jan. 25, 1982; House 1957–63.

Dooling, Peter Joseph (D N.Y.) Feb. 15, 1857–Oct. 18, 1931; House 1913–21.

Doolittle, Dudley (D Kan.) June 21, 1881–Nov. 14, 1957; House 1913–19.

Doolittle, James Rood (R Wis.) Jan. 3, 1815–July 23, 1897; Senate 1857–69.

Doolittle, John T. (R Calif.) Oct. 30, 1950– ; House 1991– .

Doolittle, William Hall (R Wash.) Nov. 6, 1848–Feb. 26, 1914; House 1893–97.

Doremus, Frank Ellsworth (D Mich.) Aug. 31, 1865–Sept. 4, 1947; House 1911–21.

Dorgan, Byron Leslie (D N.D.) May 14, 1942– ; House 1981– ; Senate Dec. 15, 1992– .

Dorn, Francis Edwin (R N.Y.) April 18, 1911–Sept. 17, 1987; House 1953–61.

Dorn, William Jennings Bryan (D S.C.) April 14, 1916– ; House 1947–49, 1951–Dec. 31, 1974; Chrmn. House Veterans' Affairs 1973–75.

Dornan, Robert Kenneth (R Calif.) April 3, 1933– ; House 1977–83, 1985–97.

Dorr, Charles Phillips (R W.Va.) Aug. 12, 1852–Oct. 8, 1914; House 1897–99.

Dorsey, Clement (– Md.) 1778–Aug. 6, 1848; House 1825–31.

Dorsey, Frank Joseph Gerard (D Pa.) April 26, 1891–July 13, 1949; House 1935–39.

Dorsey, George Washington Emery (R Neb.) Jan. 25, 1842–June 12, 1911; House 1885–91.

Dorsey, John Lloyd Jr. (D Ky.) Aug. 10, 1891–March 22, 1960; House Nov. 4, 1930–31.

Dorsey, Stephen Wallace (R Ark.) Feb. 28, 1842–March 20, 1916; Senate 1873–79.

Dorsheimer, William (D N.Y.) Feb. 5, 1832–March 26, 1888; House 1883–85.

Doty, James Duane (cousin of Morgan Lewis Martin) (ID Wis.) Nov. 5, 1799–June 13, 1865; House (Terr. Del.) Jan. 14, 1839–41 (Democrat), (Rep.) 1849–53 (1849–51 Democrat); Gov. (Wis. Terr.) 1841–44, (Utah Terr.) 1863–65.

Doubleday, Ulysses Freeman (J N.Y.) Dec. 15, 1792–March 11, 1866; House 1831–33, 1835–37.

Dougherty, Charles (D Fla.) Oct. 15, 1850–Oct. 11, 1915; House 1885–89.

Dougherty, Charles Francis (R Pa.) June 26, 1937– ; House 1979–83.

Dougherty, John (D Mo.) Feb. 25, 1857–Aug. 1, 1905; House 1899–1905.

Doughton, Robert Lee (D N.C.) Nov. 7, 1863–Oct. 1, 1954; House 1911–53; Chrmn. House Ways and Means 1949–53.

Douglas, Albert (R Ohio) April 25, 1852–March 14, 1935; House 1907–11.

Douglas, Beverly Browne (D Va.) Dec. 21, 1822–Dec. 22, 1878; House 1875–Dec. 22, 1878.

Douglas, Chuck (R N.H.) Dec. 2, 1942– ; House 1989–91.

Douglas, Emily Taft (wife of Paul Howard Douglas) (D Ill.) April 10, 1899–Jan. 28, 1994; House 1945–47.

Douglas, Fred James (R N.Y.) Sept. 14, 1869–Jan. 1, 1949; House 1937–45.

Douglas, Helen Gahagan (D Calif.) Nov. 25, 1900–June 28, 1980; House 1945–51.

Douglas, Lewis Williams (D Ariz.) July 2, 1894–March 7, 1974; House 1927–March 4, 1933.

Douglas, Paul Howard (husband of Emily Taft Douglas) (D Ill.) March 26, 1892–Sept. 24, 1976; Senate 1949–67.

Douglas, Stephen Arnold (D Ill.) April 23, 1813–June 3, 1861; House 1843–47; Senate 1847–June 3, 1861.

Douglas, William Harris (R N.Y.) Dec. 5, 1853–Jan. 27, 1944; House 1901–05.

Douglass, John Joseph (D Mass.) Feb. 9, 1873–April 5, 1939; House 1925–35.

Doutrich, Isaac Hoffer (R Pa.) Dec. 19, 1871–May 28, 1941; House 1927–37.

Dovener, Blackburn Barrett (R W.Va.) April 20, 1842–May 9, 1914; House 1895–1907.

Dow, John Goodchild (D N.Y.) May 6, 1905– ; House 1965–69, 1971–73.

Dowd, Clement (D N.C.) Aug. 27, 1832–April 15, 1898; House 1881–85.

Dowdell, James Ferguson (D Ala.) Nov. 26, 1818–Sept. 6, 1871; House 1853–59.

Dowdney, Abraham (D N.Y.) Oct. 31, 1841–Dec. 10, 1886; House 1885–Dec. 10, 1886.

Dowdy, Charles Wayne (D Miss.) July 27, 1943– ; House July 9, 1981–89.

Dowdy, John Vernard (D Texas) Feb. 11, 1912–April 12, 1995; House Sept. 23, 1952–73.

Dowell, Cassius Clay (R Iowa) Feb. 29, 1864–Feb. 4, 1940; House 1915–35, 1937–Feb. 4, 1940.

Downey, Sheridan (son of Stephen Wheeler Downey) (D Calif.) March 11, 1884–Oct. 25, 1961; Senate 1939–Nov. 30, 1950.

Downey, Stephen Wheeler (father of Sheridan Downey) (R Wyo.) July 25, 1839–Aug. 3, 1902; House (Terr. Del.) 1879–81.

Downey, Thomas Joseph (D N.Y.) Jan. 28, 1949– ; House 1975–93.

Downing, Charles (– Fla.) ?–1845; House (Terr. Del.) 1837–41.

Downing, Finis Ewing (D Ill.) Aug. 24, 1846–March 8, 1936; House 1895–June 5, 1896.

Downing, Thomas Nelms (D Va.) Feb. 1, 1919– ; House 1959–77.

Downs, Le Roy Donnelly (D Conn.) April 11, 1900–Jan. 18, 1970; House 1941–43.

Downs, Solomon Weathersbee (D La.) 1801–Aug. 14, 1854; Senate 1847–53.

Dowse, Edward (– Mass.) Oct. 22, 1756–Sept. 3, 1828; House 1819–May 26, 1820.

Dox, Peter Myndert (grandson of John Nicholas) (D Ala.) Sept. 11, 1813–April 2, 1891; House 1869–73.

Doxey, Charles Taylor (R Ind.) July 13, 1841–April 30, 1898; House Jan. 17–March 3, 1883.

Doxey, Wall (D Miss.) Aug. 8, 1892–March 2, 1962; House 1929–Sept. 28, 1941; Senate Sept. 29, 1941–43.

Doyle, Clyde Gilman (D Calif.) July 11, 1887–March 14, 1963; House 1945–47, 1949–March 14, 1963.

Doyle, Mike (D Pa.) Aug. 5, 1953– ; House 1995– .

Doyle, Thomas Aloysius (D Ill.) Jan. 9, 1886–Jan. 29, 1935; House Nov. 6, 1923–31.

Drake, Charles Daniel (R Mo.) April 11, 1811–April 1, 1892; Senate 1867–Dec. 19, 1870.

Drake, John Reuben (R N.Y.) Nov. 28, 1782–March 21, 1857; House 1817–19.

Drane, Herbert Jackson (D Fla.) June 20, 1863–Aug. 11, 1947; House 1917–33.

Draper, Joseph (J Va.) Dec. 25, 1794–June 10, 1834; House Dec. 6, 1830–31, Dec. 6, 1832–33.

Draper, William Franklin (R Mass.) April 9, 1842–Jan. 28, 1910; House 1893–97.

Draper, William Henry (R N.Y.) June 24, 1841–Dec. 7, 1921; House 1901–13.

Drayton, William (J S.C.) Dec. 30, 1776–May 24, 1846; House May 17, 1825–33 (May 17, 1825–27 no party).

Dreier, David Timothy (R Calif.) July 5, 1952– ; House 1981– ; Chrmn. House Rules 1999– .

Dresser, Solomon Robert (R Pa.) Feb. 1, 1842–Jan. 21, 1911; House 1903–07.

Drew, Ira Walton (D Pa.) Aug. 31, 1878–Feb. 12, 1972; House 1937–39.

Drew, Irving Webster (R N.H.) Jan. 8, 1845–April 10, 1922; Senate Sept. 2–Nov. 5, 1918.

Drewry, Patrick Henry (D Va.) May 24, 1875–Dec. 21, 1947; House April 27, 1920–Dec. 21, 1947.

Driggs, Edmund Hope (D N.Y.) May 2, 1865–Sept. 27, 1946; House Dec. 6, 1897–1901.

Driggs, John Fletcher (R Mich.) March 8, 1813–Dec. 17, 1877; House 1863–69.

Drinan, Robert Frederick (D Mass.) Nov. 15, 1920– ; House 1971–81.

Driscoll, Daniel Angelus (D N.Y.) March 6, 1875–June 5, 1955; House 1909–17.

Driscoll, Denis Joseph (D Pa.) March 27, 1871–Jan. 18, 1958; House 1935–37.

Driscoll, Michael Edward (R N.Y.) Feb. 9, 1851–Jan. 19, 1929; House 1899–1913.

Driver, William Joshua (D Ark.) March 2, 1873–Oct. 1, 1948; House 1921–39.

Dromgoole, George Coke (uncle of Alexander Dromgoole Sims) (D Va.) May 15, 1797–April 27, 1847; House 1835–41 (1835–37 Jacksonian), 1843–April 27, 1847.

Drukker, Dow Henry (R N.J.) Feb. 7, 1872–Jan. 11, 1963; House April 7, 1914–19.

Drum, Augustus (D Pa.) Nov. 26, 1815–Sept. 15, 1858; House 1853–55.

Dryden, John Fairfield (R N.J.) Aug. 7, 1839–Nov. 24, 1911; Senate Jan. 29, 1902–07.

Dubois, Fred Thomas (D Idaho) May 29, 1851–Feb. 14, 1930; House (Terr. Del.) 1887–July 3, 1890; Senate 1891–97, 1901–07 (1887–97 Republican, 1901 Silver Republican).

Du Bose, Dudley McIver (D Ga.) Oct. 28, 1834–March 2, 1883; House 1871–73.

Dudley, Charles Edward (– N.Y.) May 23, 1780–Jan. 23, 1841; Senate Jan. 15, 1829–33.

Dudley, Edward Bishop (– N.C.) Dec. 15, 1789–Oct. 30, 1855; House Nov. 10, 1829–31; Gov. Dec. 31, 1836–Jan. 1, 1841 (Whig).

Duell, Rodolphus Holland (R N.Y.) Dec. 20, 1824–Feb. 11, 1891; House 1859–63, 1871–75.

Duer, William (W N.Y.) May 25, 1805–Aug. 25, 1879; House 1847–51.

Duff, James Henderson (R Pa.) Jan. 21, 1883–Dec. 20, 1969; Senate Jan. 18, 1951–57; Gov. Jan. 21, 1947–Jan. 16, 1951.

Duffey, Warren Joseph (D Ohio) Jan. 24, 1886–July 7, 1936; House 1933–July 7, 1936.

Duffy, Francis Ryan (D Wis.) June 23, 1888–Aug. 16, 1979; Senate 1933–39.

Duffy, James Patrick Bernard (D N.Y.) Nov. 25, 1878–Jan. 8, 1969; House 1935–37.

Dugro, Philip Henry (D N.Y.) Oct. 3, 1855–March 1, 1920; House 1881–83.

Duke, Richard Thomas Walker (C Va.) June 6, 1822–July 2, 1898; House Nov. 8, 1870–73.

Dulles, John Foster (R N.Y.) Feb. 25, 1888–May 24, 1959; Senate July 7–Nov. 8, 1949; Secy. of State Jan. 21, 1953–April 22, 1959.

Dulski, Thaddeus Joseph (D N.Y.) Sept. 27, 1915–Oct. 11, 1988; House 1959–Dec. 31, 1974; Chrmn. House Post Office and Civil Service 1967–75.

Dumont, Ebenezer (U Ind.) Nov. 23, 1814–April 16, 1871; House 1863–67.

Dunbar, James Whitson (R Ind.) Oct. 17, 1860–May 19, 1943; House 1919–23, 1929–31.

Dunbar, William (D La.) 1805–March 18, 1861; House 1853–55.

Duncan, Alexander (D Ohio) 1788–March 23, 1853; House 1837–41, 1843–45.

Duncan, Daniel (W Ohio) July 22, 1806–May 18, 1849; House 1847–49.

Duncan, James (– Pa.) 1756–June 24, 1844; elected to the House for the term beginning 1821 but resigned before Congress assembled.

Duncan, James Henry (W Mass.) Dec. 5, 1793–Feb. 8, 1869; House 1849–53.

Duncan, John James (father of John J. "Jimmy" Duncan) (R Tenn.) March 24, 1919–June 21, 1988; House 1965–June 21, 1988.

Duncan, John J. "Jimmy" Jr. (son of John James Duncan) (R Tenn.) July 21, 1947– ; House Nov. 8, 1988– .

Duncan, Joseph (J Ill.) Feb. 22, 1794–Jan. 15, 1844; House 1827–Sept. 21, 1834; Gov. Dec. 3, 1834–Dec. 7, 1838 (Whig).

Duncan, Richard Meloan (D Mo.) Nov. 10, 1889–Aug. 1, 1974; House 1933–43.

Duncan, Robert Blackford (D Ore.) Dec. 4, 1920– ; House 1963–67, 1975–81.

Duncan, William Addison (D Pa.) Feb. 2, 1836–Nov. 14, 1884; House 1883–Nov. 14, 1884.

Duncan, William Garnett (W Ky.) March 2, 1800–May 25, 1875; House 1847–49.

Dungan, James Irvine (D Ohio) May 29, 1844–Dec. 28, 1931; House 1891–93.

Dunham, Cyrus Livingston (D Ind.) Jan. 16, 1817–Nov. 21, 1877; House 1849–55.

Dunham, Ransom Williams (R Ill.) March 21, 1838–Aug. 19, 1896; House 1883–89.

Dunlap, George Washington (U Ky.) Feb. 22, 1813–June 6, 1880; House 1861–63.

Dunlap, Robert Pickney (D Maine) Aug. 17, 1794–Oct. 20, 1859; House 1843–47; Gov. Jan. 1, 1834–Jan. 3, 1838.

Dunlap, William Claiborne (J Tenn.) Feb. 25, 1798–Nov. 16, 1872; House 1833–37.

Dunn, Aubert Culberson (D Miss.) Nov. 20, 1896–Jan. 4, 1987; House 1935–37.

Dunn, George Grundy (R Ind.) Dec. 20, 1812–Sept. 4, 1857; House 1847–49 (Whig), 1855–57.

Dunn, George Hedford (W Ind.) Nov. 15, 1794–Jan. 12, 1854; House 1837–39.

Dunn, James Whitney (R Mich.) July 21, 1943– ; House 1981–83.

Dunn, Jennifer (R Wash.) July 29, 1941– ; House 1993– .

Dunn, John Thomas (D N.J.) June 4, 1838–Feb. 22, 1907; House 1893–95.

Dunn, Matthew Anthony (D Pa.) Aug. 15, 1886–Feb. 13, 1942; House 1933–41.

Dunn, Poindexter (D Ark.) Nov. 3, 1834–Oct. 12, 1914; House 1879–89.

Dunn, Thomas Byrne (R N.Y.) March 16, 1853–July 2, 1924; House 1913–23.

Dunn, William McKee (R Ind.) Dec. 12, 1814–July 24, 1887; House 1859–63.

Dunnell, Mark Hill (R Minn.) July 2, 1823–Aug. 9, 1904; House 1871–83, 1889–91.

Dunphy, Edward John (D N.Y.) May 12, 1856–July 29, 1926; House 1889–95.

Dunwell, Charles Tappan (R N.Y.) Feb. 13, 1852–June 12, 1908; House 1903–June 12, 1908.

Du Pont, Henry Algernon (cousin of Thomas Coleman du Pont) (R Del.) July 30, 1838–Dec. 31, 1926; Senate June 13, 1906–17.

Du Pont, Pierre Samuel "Pete" IV (R Del.) Jan. 22, 1935– ; House 1971–77; Gov. Jan. 18, 1977–Jan. 15, 1985.

Du Pont, Thomas Coleman (cousin of Henry Algernon du Pont) (R Del.) Dec. 11, 1863–Nov. 11, 1930; Senate July 7, 1921–Nov. 7, 1922, 1925–Dec. 9, 1928.

Dupre, Henry Garland (D La.) July 28, 1873–Feb. 21, 1924; House Nov. 8, 1910–Feb. 21, 1924.

Durand, George Harman (D Mich.) Feb. 21, 1838–June 8, 1903; House 1875–77.

Durbin, Richard Joseph (D Ill.) Nov. 21, 1944– ; House 1983–97; Senate 1997– .

Durborow, Allan Cathcart Jr. (D Ill.) Nov. 10, 1857–March 10, 1908; House 1891–95.

Durell, Daniel Meserve (R N.H.) July 20, 1769–April 29, 1841; House 1807–09.

Durenberger, David Ferdinand (R Minn.) Aug. 19, 1934– ; Senate Nov. 8, 1978–95; Chrmn. Senate Select Committee on Intelligence Activities 1985–87.

Durey, Cyrus (R N.Y.) May 16, 1864–Jan. 4, 1933; House 1907–11.

Durfee, Job (– R.I.) Sept. 20, 1790–July 26, 1847; House 1821–25.

Durfee, Nathaniel Briggs (R R.I.) Sept. 29, 1812–Nov. 9, 1872; House 1855–59 (1855–57 American Party).

Durgan, George Richard (D Ind.) Jan. 20, 1872–Jan. 13, 1942; House 1933–35.

Durham, Carl Thomas (D N.C.) Aug. 28, 1892–April 29, 1974; House 1939–61.

Durham, Milton Jameson (D Ky.) May 16, 1824–Feb. 12, 1911; House 1873–79.

Durkee, Charles (R Wis.) Dec. 10, 1805–Jan. 14, 1870; House 1849–53 (Free-Soiler); Senate 1855–61; Gov. (Utah Terr.) 1865–69.

Durkin, John Anthony (D N.H.) March 29, 1936– ; Senate Sept. 18, 1975–Dec. 29, 1980.

Durno, Edwin Russell (R Ore.) Jan. 26, 1899–Nov. 20, 1976; House 1961–63.

Duval, Isaac Harding (R W.Va.) Sept. 1, 1824–July 10, 1902; House 1869–71.

Duval, William Pope (R Ky.) 1784–March 19, 1854; House 1813–15; Gov. (Fla. Terr.) 1822–34.

Duvall, Gabriel (R Md.) Dec. 6, 1752–March 6, 1844; House Nov. 11, 1794–March 28, 1796 (Nov. 11, 1794–95 no party); Assoc. Justice Supreme Court Nov. 23, 1811–Jan. 14, 1835.

Dwight, Henry Williams (– Mass.) Feb. 26, 1788–Feb. 21, 1845; House 1821–31.

Dwight, Jeremiah Wilbur (father of John Wilbur Dwight) (R N.Y.) April 17, 1819–Nov. 26, 1885; House 1877–83.

Dwight, John Wilbur (son of Jeremiah Wilbur Dwight) (R N.Y.) May 24, 1859–Jan. 19, 1928; House Nov. 2, 1902–13.

Dwight, Theodore (cousin of Aaron Burr) (F Conn.) Dec. 15, 1764–June 12, 1846; House Dec. 1, 1806–07.

Dwight, Thomas (F Mass.) Oct. 29, 1758–Jan. 2, 1819; House 1803–05.

Dwinell, Justin (– N.Y.) Oct. 28, 1785–Sept. 17, 1850; House 1823–25.

Dworshak, Henry Clarence (R Idaho) Aug. 29, 1894–July 23, 1962; House 1939–Nov. 5, 1946; Senate Nov. 6, 1946–49, Oct. 14, 1949–July 23, 1962.

Dwyer, Bernard James (D N.J.) Jan. 24, 1921–Oct. 31, 1998; House 1981–93.

Dwyer, Florence Price (R N.J.) July 4, 1902–Feb. 29, 1976; House 1957–73.

Dyal, Kenneth Warren (D Calif.) July 9, 1910–May 12, 1978; House 1965–67.

Dyer, David Patterson (uncle of Leonidas Carstarphen Dyer) (R Mo.) Feb. 12, 1838–April 29, 1924; House 1869–71.

Dyer, Leonidas Carstarphen (nephew of David Patterson Dyer) (R Mo.) June 11, 1871–Dec. 15, 1957; House 1911–June 19, 1914, 1915–33.

Dymally, Mervyn Malcolm (D Calif.) May 12, 1926– ; House 1981–93.

Dyson, Royden Patrick "Roy" (D Md.) Nov. 15, 1948– ; House 1981–91.

E

Eagan, John Joseph (D N.J.) Jan. 22, 1872–June 13, 1956; House 1913–21, 1923–25.

Eager, Samuel Watkins (R N.Y.) April 8, 1789–Dec. 23, 1860; House Nov. 2, 1830–31.

Eagle, Joe Henry (D Texas) Jan. 23, 1870–Jan. 10, 1963; House 1913–21, Jan. 28, 1933–37.

Eagleton, Thomas Francis (D Mo.) Sept. 4, 1929– ; Senate Dec. 28, 1968–87; Chrmn. Senate District of Columbia 1971–77.

Eames, Benjamin Tucker (R R.I.) June 4, 1818–Oct. 6, 1901; House 1871–79.

Earhart, Daniel Scofield (D Ohio) May 28, 1907–Jan. 2, 1976; House Nov. 3, 1936–37.

Earle, Elias (uncle of Samuel Earle and John Baylis Earle, great-grandfather of John Laurens Manning Irby and Joseph Haynsworth Earle) (R S.C.) June 19, 1762–May 19, 1823; House 1805–07, 1811–15, 1817–21.

Earle, John Baylis (nephew of Elias Earle, cousin of Samuel Earle) (R S.C.) Oct. 23, 1766–Feb. 3, 1863; House 1803–05.

Earle, Joseph Haynsworth (great-grandson of Elias Earle, cousin of John Laurens Manning Irby, nephew of William Lowndes Yancey) (D S.C.) April 30, 1847–May 20, 1897; Senate March 4–May 20, 1897.

Earle, Samuel (nephew of Elias Earle, cousin of John Baylis Earle) (R S.C.) Nov. 28, 1760–Nov. 24, 1833; House 1795–97.

Earll, Jonas Jr. (cousin of Nehemiah Hezekiah Earll) (J N.Y.) 1786–Oct. 28, 1846; House 1827–31.

Earll, Nehemiah Hezekiah (cousin of Jonas Earll Jr.) (D N.Y.) Oct. 5, 1787–Aug. 26, 1872; House 1839–41.

Early, Joseph Daniel (D Mass.) Jan. 31, 1933– ; House 1975–93.

Early, Peter (R Ga.) June 20, 1773–Aug. 15, 1817; House Jan. 10, 1803–07; Gov. Nov. 5, 1813–Nov. 10, 1815 (Democratic Republican).

Earnshaw, Manuel (I P.I.) Nov. 19, 1862–Feb. 13, 1936; House (Res. Comm.) 1913–17.

Earthman, Harold Henderson (D Tenn.) April 13, 1900–Feb. 26, 1987; House 1945–47.

East, John Porter (R N.C.) May 5, 1931–June 29, 1986; Senate 1981–June 29, 1986.

Eastland, James Oliver (D Miss.) Nov. 28, 1904–Feb. 19, 1986; Senate June 30–Sept. 28, 1941, 1943–Dec. 27, 1978; Chrmn. Senate Judiciary 1956–78; elected Pres. pro tempore July 28, 1972.

Eastman, Ben C. (D Wis.) Oct. 24, 1812–Feb. 2, 1856; House 1851–55.

Eastman, Ira Allen (nephew of Nehemiah Eastman) (D N.H.) Jan. 1, 1809–March 21, 1881; House 1839–43.

Eastman, Nehemiah (uncle of Ira Allen Eastman) (– N.H.) June 16, 1782–Jan. 11, 1856; House 1825–27.

Easton, Rufus (– Mo.) May 4, 1774–July 5, 1834; House (Terr. Del.) Sept. 17, 1814–Aug. 5, 1816.

Eaton, Charles Aubrey (uncle of William Robb Eaton) (R N.J.) March 29, 1868–Jan. 23, 1953; House 1925–53; Chrmn. House Foreign Affairs 1947–49.

Eaton, John Henry (R Tenn.) June 18, 1790–Nov. 17, 1856; Senate Sept. 5, 1818–21, Sept. 27, 1821–March 9, 1829; Secy. of War March 9, 1829–June 18, 1831; Gov. (Fla. Terr.) 1834–36.

Eaton, Lewis (– N.Y.) ?–?; House 1823–25.

Eaton, Thomas Marion (R Calif.) Aug. 3, 1896–Sept. 16, 1939; House Jan. 3–Sept. 16, 1939.

Eaton, William Robb (nephew of Charles Aubrey Eaton) (R Colo.) Dec. 17, 1877–Dec. 16, 1942; House 1929–33.

Eaton, William Wallace (D Conn.) Oct. 11, 1816–Sept. 21, 1898; Senate Feb. 5, 1875–81; House 1883–85.

Eberharter, Herman Peter (D Pa.) April 29, 1892–Sept. 9, 1958; House 1937–Sept. 9, 1958.

Echols, Leonard Sidney (R W.Va.) Oct. 30, 1871–May 9, 1946; House 1919–23.

Eckart, Dennis Edward (D Ohio) April 6, 1950– ; House 1981–93.

Eckert, Charles Richard (D Pa.) Jan. 20, 1868–Oct. 26, 1959; House 1935–39.

Eckert, Fred J. (R N.Y.) May 6, 1941– ; House 1985–87.

Eckert, George Nicholas (W Pa.) July 4, 1802–June 28, 1865; House 1847–49.

Eckhardt, Robert Christian (cousin of Richard Mifflin Kleberg Sr., great-nephew of Rudolph Kleberg, nephew of Harry McLeary Wurzbach) (D Texas) July 16, 1913– ; House 1967–81.

Eckley, Ephraim Ralph (R Ohio) Dec. 9, 1811–March 27, 1908; House 1863–69.

Ecton, Zales Nelson (R Mont.) April 1, 1898–March 3, 1961; Senate 1947–53.

Eddy, Frank Marion (R Minn.) April 1, 1856–Jan. 13, 1929; House 1895–1903.

Eddy, Norman (D Ind.) Dec. 10, 1810–Jan. 28, 1872; House 1853–55.

Eddy, Samuel (– R.I.) March 31, 1769–Feb. 3, 1839; House 1819–25.

Edelstein, Morris Michael (D N.Y.) Feb. 5, 1888–June 4, 1941; House Feb. 6, 1940–June 4, 1941.

Eden, John Rice (D Ill.) Feb. 1, 1826–June 9, 1909; House 1863–65, 1873–79, 1885–87.

Edgar, Robert William (D Pa.) May 29, 1943– ; House 1975–87.

Edge, Walter Evans (R N.J.) Nov. 20, 1873–Oct. 29, 1956; Senate 1919–Nov. 21, 1929; Gov. Jan. 15, 1917–May 16, 1919, Jan. 18, 1944–Jan. 21, 1947.

Edgerton, Alfred Peck (brother of Joseph Ketchum Edgerton) (D Ohio) Jan. 11, 1813–May 14, 1897; House 1851–55.

Edgerton, Alonzo Jay (R Minn.) June 7, 1827–Aug. 9, 1896; Senate March 12–Oct. 30, 1881.

Edgerton, Joseph Ketchum (brother of Alfred Peck Edgerton) (D Ind.) Feb. 16, 1818–Aug. 25, 1893; House 1863–65.

Edgerton, Sidney (R Ohio) Aug. 17, 1818–July 19, 1900; House 1859–63; Gov. (Mont. Terr.) 1865, 1866.

Edie, John Rufus (W Pa.) Jan. 14, 1814–Aug. 27, 1888; House 1855–59.

Edmands, John Wiley (W Mass.) March 1, 1809–Jan. 31, 1877; House 1853–55.

Edmiston, Andrew (D W.Va.) Nov. 13, 1892–Aug. 28, 1966; House Nov. 28, 1933–43.

Edmond, William (F Conn.) Sept. 28, 1755–Aug. 1, 1838; House Nov. 13, 1797–1801.

Edmonds, George Washington (R Pa.) Feb. 22, 1864–Sept. 28, 1939; House 1913–25, 1933–35.

Edmondson, Edmond Augustus (brother of James Howard Edmondson) (D Okla.) April 7, 1919–Dec. 8, 1990; House 1953–73.

Edmondson, James Howard (brother of Edmond Augustus Edmondson) (D Okla.) Sept. 27, 1925–Nov. 17, 1971; Senate Jan. 7, 1963–Nov. 3, 1964; Gov. Jan. 12, 1959–Jan. 6, 1963.

Edmunds, George Franklin (R Vt.) Feb. 1, 1828–Feb. 27, 1919; Senate April 3, 1866–Nov. 1, 1891; elected Pres. pro tempore March 3, 1883, Jan. 14, 1884.

Edmunds, Paul Carrington (D Va.) Nov. 1, 1836–March 12, 1899; House 1889–95.

Edmundson, Henry Alonzo (D Va.) June 14, 1814–Dec. 16, 1890; House 1849–61.

Edsall, Joseph E. (D N.J.) 1789–1865; House 1845–49.

Edwards, Benjamin (father of Ninian Edwards, grandfather of Benjamin Edwards Grey) (– Md.) Aug. 12, 1753–Nov. 13, 1829; House Jan. 2–March 3, 1795.

Edwards, Caldwell (P Mont.) Jan. 8, 1841–July 23, 1922; House 1901–03.

Edwards, Charles Gordon (D Ga.) July 2, 1878–July 13, 1931; House 1907–17, 1925–July 13, 1931.

Edwards, Chet (D Texas) Nov. 24, 1951– ; House 1991– .

Edwards, Don (D Calif.) Jan. 6, 1915– ; House 1963–95.

Edwards, Don Calvin (R Ky.) July 13, 1861–Sept. 19, 1938; House 1905–11.

Edwards, Edward Irving (D N.J.) Dec. 1, 1863–Jan. 26, 1931; Senate 1923–29; Gov. Jan. 20, 1920–Jan. 15, 1923.

Edwards, Edwin Washington (husband of Elaine Schwartzenburg Edwards) (D La.) Aug. 7, 1927– ; House Oct. 18, 1965–May 9, 1972; Gov. May 9, 1972–March 10, 1980, March 12, 1984–May 14, 1988, Jan. 8, 1992–Jan. 8, 1996.

Edwards, Elaine Schwartzenburg (wife of Edwin Washington Edwards) (D La.) March 8, 1929– ; Senate Aug. 1–Nov. 13, 1972.

Edwards, Francis Smith (AP N.Y.) May 28, 1817–May 20, 1899; House 1855–Feb. 28, 1857.

Edwards, Henry Waggaman (– Conn.) Oct. 1779–July 22, 1847; House 1819–23; Senate Oct. 8, 1823–27; Gov. May 4, 1833–May 7, 1834, May 6, 1835–May 2, 1838.

Edwards, John (– Ky.) 1748–1837; Senate June 18, 1792–95.

Edwards, John (D N.Y.) Aug. 6, 1781–Dec. 28, 1850; House 1837–39.

Edwards, John (great-uncle of John Edwards Leonard) (W Pa.) 1786–June 26, 1843; House 1839–43 (1839–41 AMas.).

Edwards, John (LR Ark.) Oct. 24, 1805–April 8, 1894; House 1871–Feb. 9, 1872.

Edwards, John (D N.C.) June 10, 1953– ; Senate 1999– .

Edwards, John Cummins (D Mo.) June 24, 1804–Sept. 14, 1888; House 1841–43; Gov. Nov. 20, 1844–Nov. 27, 1848.

Edwards, Marvin Henry "Mickey" (R Okla.) July 12, 1937– ; House 1977–93.

Edwards, Ninian (son of Benjamin Edwards) (R Ill.) March 17, 1775–July 20, 1833; Senate Dec. 3, 1818–24; Gov. 1809–18 (Ill. Terr.), Dec. 6, 1826–Dec. 6, 1830.

Edwards, Samuel (– Pa.) March 12, 1785–Nov. 21, 1850; House 1819–27.

Edwards, Thomas McKey (R N.H.) Dec. 16, 1795–May 1, 1875; House 1859–63.

Edwards, Thomas Owen (W Ohio) March 29, 1810–Feb. 5, 1876; House 1847–49.

Edwards, Weldon Nathaniel (R N.C.) Jan. 25, 1788–Dec. 18, 1873; House Feb. 7, 1816–27.

Edwards, William Jackson "Jack" (R Ala.) Sept. 20, 1928– ; House 1965–85.

Edwards, William Posey (R Ga.) Nov. 9, 1835–June 28, 1900; House July 25, 1868–69.

Efner, Valentine (J N.Y.) May 5, 1776–Nov. 20, 1865; House 1835–37.

Egbert, Albert Gallatin (D Pa.) April 13, 1828–March 28, 1896; House 1875–77.

Egbert, Joseph (D N.Y.) April 10, 1807–July 7, 1888; House 1841–43.

Ege, George (F Pa.) March 9, 1748–Dec. 14, 1829; House Dec. 8, 1796–Oct. 1797.

Eggleston, Benjamin (R Ohio) Jan. 3, 1816–Feb. 9, 1888; House 1865–69.

Eggleston, Joseph (uncle of William Segar Archer) (R Va.) Nov. 24, 1754–Feb. 13, 1811; House Dec. 3, 1798–1801.

Ehlers, Vernon J. (R Mich.) Feb. 6, 1934– ; House Jan. 25, 1994– .

Ehrlich, Robert Jr. (R Md.) Nov. 25, 1957– ; House 1995– .

Eicher, Edward Clayton (D Iowa) Dec. 16, 1878–Nov. 29, 1944; House 1933–Dec. 2, 1938.

Eickhoff, Anthony (D N.Y.) Sept. 11, 1827–Nov. 5, 1901; House 1877–79.

Eilberg, Joshua (D Pa.) Feb. 12, 1921– ; House 1967–79.

Einstein, Edwin (R N.Y.) Nov. 18, 1842–Jan. 24, 1905; House 1879–81.

Ekwall, William Alexander (R Ore.) June 14, 1887–Oct. 16, 1956; House 1935–37.

Ela, Jacob Hart (R N.H.) July 18, 1820–Aug. 21, 1884; House 1867–71.

Elam, Joseph Barton (D La.) June 12, 1821–July 4, 1885; House 1877–81.

Elder, James Walter (D La.) Oct. 5, 1882–Dec. 16, 1941; House 1913–15.

Eldredge, Charles Augustus (D Wis.) Feb. 27, 1820–Oct. 26, 1896; House 1863–75.

Eldredge, Nathaniel Buel (D Mich.) March 28, 1813–Nov. 27, 1893; House 1883–87.

Eliot, Samuel Atkins (great-grandfather of Thomas Hopkinson Eliot) (W Mass.) March 5, 1798–Jan. 29, 1862; House Aug. 22, 1850–51.

Eliot, Thomas Dawes (R Mass.) March 20, 1808–June 14, 1870; House April 17, 1854–1855 (Whig), 1859–69.

Eliot, Thomas Hopkinson (great-grandson of Samuel Atkins Eliot) (D Mass.) June 14, 1907–Oct. 14, 1991; House 1941–43.

Elizalde, Joaquin Miguel (– P.I.) Aug. 2, 1896–Feb. 9, 1965; House (Res. Comm.) Sept. 29, 1938–Aug. 9, 1944.

Elkins, Davis (son of Stephen Benton Elkins, grandson of Henry Gassaway Davis) (R W.Va.) Jan. 24, 1876–Jan. 5, 1959; Senate Jan. 9–Jan. 31, 1911, 1919–25.

Elkins, Stephen Benton (father of Davis Elkins) (R W.Va.) Sept. 26, 1841–Jan. 4, 1911; House (Terr. Del. N.M.) 1873–77; Senate 1895–Jan. 4, 1911; Secy. of War Dec. 17, 1891–March 5, 1893.

Ellenbogen, Henry (D Pa.) April 3, 1900–July 4, 1985; House 1933–Jan. 3, 1938.

Ellender, Allen Joseph (D La.) Sept. 24, 1890–July 27, 1972; Senate 1937–July 27, 1972; Chrmn. Senate Agriculture and Forestry 1951–53, 1955–71; elected Pres. pro tempore Jan. 22, 1971; Chrmn. Senate Appropriations 1971–72.

Ellerbe, James Edwin (D S.C.) Jan. 12, 1867–Oct. 24, 1917; House 1905–13.

Ellery, Christopher (R R.I.) Nov. 1, 1768–Dec. 2, 1840; Senate May 6, 1801–05.

Ellett, Henry Thomas (D Miss.) March 8, 1812–Oct. 15, 1887; House Jan. 26–March 3, 1847.

Ellett, Tazewell (D Va.) Jan. 1, 1856–May 19, 1914; House 1895–97.

Ellicott, Benjamin (R N.Y.) April 17, 1765–Dec. 10, 1827; House 1817–19.

Elliott, Alfred James (D Calif.) June 1, 1895–Jan. 17, 1973; House May 4, 1937–49.

Elliott, Carl Atwood (D Ala.) Dec. 20, 1913–Jan. 9, 1999; House 1949–65.

Elliott, Douglas Hemphill (R Pa.) June 3, 1921–June 19, 1960; House April 26–June 19, 1960.

Elliott, James (F Vt.) Aug. 18, 1775–Nov. 10, 1839; House 1803–09.

Elliott, James Thomas (R Ark.) April 22, 1823–July 28, 1875; House Jan. 13–March 3, 1869.

Elliott, John (– Ga.) Oct. 24, 1773–Aug. 9, 1827; Senate 1819–25.

Elliott, John Milton (D Ky.) May 20, 1820–March 26, 1879; House 1853–59.

Elliott, Mortimer Fitzland (D Pa.) Sept. 24, 1839–Aug. 5, 1920; House 1883–85.

Elliott, Richard Nash (R Ind.) April 25, 1873–March 21, 1948; House June 26, 1917–31.

Elliott, Robert Brown (R S.C.) Aug. 11, 1842–Aug. 9, 1884; House 1871–Nov. 1, 1874.

Elliott, William (D S.C.) Sept. 3, 1838–Dec. 7, 1907; House 1887–Sept. 23, 1890, 1891–93, 1895–June 4, 1896, 1897–1903.

Ellis, Caleb (F N.H.) April 16, 1767–May 6, 1816; House 1805–07.

Ellis, Chesselden (D N.Y.) 1808–May 10, 1854; House 1843–45.

Ellis, Clyde Taylor (D Ark.) Dec. 21, 1908–Feb. 9, 1980; House 1939–43.

Ellis, Edgar Clarence (R Mo.) Oct. 2, 1854–March 15, 1947; House 1905–09, 1921–23, 1925–27, 1929–31.

Ellis, Ezekiel John (D La.) Oct. 15, 1840–April 25, 1889; House 1875–85.

Ellis, Hubert Summers (R W.Va.) July 6, 1887–Dec. 3, 1959; House 1943–49.

Ellis, Powhatan (– Miss.) Jan. 17, 1790–March 18, 1863; Senate Sept. 28, 1825–Jan. 28, 1826, 1827–July 16, 1832.

Ellis, William Cox (– Pa.) May 5, 1787–Dec. 13, 1871; House (elected to the term beginning 1821 but resigned before Congress assembled), 1823–25.

Ellis, William Russell (R Ore.) April 23, 1850–Jan. 18, 1915; House 1893–99, 1907–11.

Ellis, William Thomas (D Ky.) July 24, 1845–Jan. 8, 1925; House 1889–95.

Ellison, Andrew (D Ohio) 1812–about 1860; House 1853–55.

Ellison, Daniel (R Md.) Feb. 14, 1886–Aug. 20, 1960; House 1943–45.

Ellmaker, Amos (– Pa.) Feb. 2, 1787–Nov. 28, 1851; elected to the House for the term beginning 1815 but did not qualify.

Ellsberry, William Wallace (D Ohio) Dec. 18, 1833–Sept. 7, 1894; House 1885–87.

Ellsworth, Charles Clinton (R Mich.) Jan. 29, 1824–June 25, 1899; House 1877–79.

Ellsworth, Franklin Fowler (R Minn.) July 10, 1879–Dec. 23, 1942; House 1915–21.

Ellsworth, Matthew Harris (R Ore.) Sept. 17, 1899–Feb. 7, 1986; House 1943–57.

Ellsworth, Oliver (father of William Wolcott Ellsworth) (– Conn.) April 29, 1745–Nov. 26, 1807; Senate 1789–March 8, 1796; Cont. Cong. 1778–83; Chief Justice United States March 8, 1796–Dec. 15, 1800.

Ellsworth, Robert Fred (R Kan.) June 11, 1926– ; House 1961–67.

Ellsworth, Samuel Stewart (D N.Y.) Oct. 13, 1790–June 4, 1863; House 1845–47.

Ellsworth, William Wolcott (son of Oliver Ellsworth) (– Conn.) Nov. 10, 1791–Jan. 15, 1868; House 1829–July 8, 1834; Gov. May 2, 1838–May 4, 1842 (Whig).

Ellwood, Reuben (R Ill.) Feb. 21, 1821–July 1, 1885; House 1883–July 1, 1885.

Ellzey, Lawrence Russell (D Miss.) March 20, 1891–Dec. 7, 1977; House March 15, 1932–35.

Elmendorf, Lucas Conrad (R N.Y.) 1758–Aug. 17, 1843; House 1797–1803.

Elmer, Ebenezer (brother of Jonathan Elmer, father of Lucius Quintius Cincinnatus Elmer) (R N.J.) Aug. 23, 1752–Oct. 18, 1843; House 1801–07.

Elmer, Jonathan (brother of Ebenezer Elmer, uncle of Lucius Quintius Cincinnatus Elmer) (– N.J.) Nov. 29, 1745–Sept. 3, 1817; Senate 1789–91; Cont. Cong. 1777–78, 1781–83, 1787–88.

Elmer, Lucius Quintius Cincinnatus (son of Ebenezer Elmer, nephew of Jonathan Elmer) (D N.J.) Feb. 3, 1793–March 11, 1883; House 1843–45.

Elmer, William Price (R Mo.) March 2, 1871–May 11, 1956; House 1943–45.

Elmore, Franklin Harper (D S.C.) Oct. 15, 1799–May 29, 1850; House Dec. 10, 1836–39 (State Rights Democrat); Senate April 11–May 28, 1850.

Elsaesser, Edward Julius (R N.Y.) March 10, 1904–Jan. 7, 1983; House 1945–49.

Elston, Charles Henry (R Ohio) Aug. 1, 1891–Sept. 25, 1980; House 1939–53.

Elston, John Arthur (R Calif.) Feb. 10, 1874–Dec. 15, 1921; House 1915–Dec. 15, 1921 (1915–17 Progressive).

Eltse, Ralph Roscoe (R Calif.) Sept. 13, 1885–March 18, 1971; House 1933–35.

Elvins, Politte (R Mo.) March 16, 1878–Jan. 14, 1943; House 1909–11.

Ely, Alfred (R N.Y.) Feb. 15, 1815–May 18, 1892; House 1859–63.

Ely, Frederick David (R Mass.) Sept. 24, 1838–Aug. 6, 1921; House 1885–87.

Ely, John (D N.Y.) Oct. 8, 1774–Aug. 20, 1849; House 1839–41.

Ely, Smith Jr. (D N.Y.) April 17, 1825–July 1, 1911; House 1871–73, 1875–Dec. 11, 1876.

Ely, William (F Mass.) Aug. 14, 1765–Oct. 9, 1817; House 1805–15.

Embree, Elisha (W Ind.) Sept. 28, 1801–Feb. 28, 1863; House 1847–49.

Emerich, Martin (D Ill.) April 27, 1846–Sept. 27, 1922; House 1903–05.

Emerson, Henry Ivory (R Ohio) March 15, 1871–Oct. 28, 1953; House 1915–21.

Emerson, Jo Ann (widow of Bill Emerson) (R Mo.) Sept. 16, 1950– ; House Nov. 5, 1996– .

Emerson, Louis Woodard (R N.Y.) July 25, 1857–June 10, 1924; House 1899–1903.

Emerson, Norvell William "Bill" (husband of Jo Ann Emerson) (R Mo.) Jan. 1, 1938–June 22, 1996; House 1981–June 22, 1996.

Emery, David Farnham (R Maine) Sept. 1, 1948– ; House 1975–83.

Emott, James (F N.Y.) March 9, 1771–April 7, 1850; House 1809–13.

Emrie, Jonas Reece (R Ohio) April 25, 1812–June 5, 1869; House 1855–57.

Engel, Albert Joseph (R Mich.) Jan. 1, 1888–Dec. 2, 1959; House 1935–51.

Engel, Eliot L. (D N.Y.) Feb. 18, 1947– ; House 1989– .

England, Edward Theodore (R W.Va.) Sept. 29, 1869–Sept. 9, 1934; House 1927–29.

Engle, Clair (D Calif.) Sept. 21, 1911–July 30, 1964; House Aug. 31, 1943–59; Chrmn. House Interior and Insular Affairs 1955–59; Senate 1959–July 30, 1964.

Englebright, Harry Lane (son of William Fellows Englebright) (R Calif.) Jan. 2, 1884–May 13, 1943; House Aug. 31, 1926–May 13, 1943.

Englebright, William Fellows (father of Harry Lane Englebright) (R Calif.) Nov. 23, 1855–Feb. 10, 1915; House Nov. 6, 1906–11.

English, Glenn Lee Jr. (D Okla.) Nov. 30, 1940– ; House 1975–Jan. 7, 1994.

English, James Edward (D Conn.) March 13, 1812–March 2, 1890; House 1861–65; Senate Nov. 27, 1875–May 17, 1876; Gov. May 1, 1867–May 5, 1869, May 4, 1870–May 16, 1871.

English, Karan (D Ariz.) March 23, 1949– ; House 1993–95.

English, Phil (R Pa.) June 20, 1956– ; House 1995– .

English, Thomas Dunn (D N.J.) June 29, 1819–April 1, 1902; House 1891–95.

English, Warren Barkley (D Calif.) May 1, 1840–Jan. 9, 1913; House April 4, 1894–95.

English, William Eastin (son of William Hayden English) (D Ind.) Nov. 3, 1850–April 29, 1926; House May 22, 1884–85.

English, William Hayden (father of William Eastin English) (D Ind.) Aug. 27, 1822–Feb. 7, 1896; House 1853–61.

Enloe, Benjamin Augustine (D Tenn.) Jan. 18, 1848–July 8, 1922; House 1887–95.

Enochs, William Henry (R Ohio) March 29, 1842–July 13, 1893; House 1891–July 13, 1893.

Ensign, John (R Nev.) March 25, 1958– ; House 1995–99.

Enzi, Michael B. (R Wyo.) Feb. 1, 1944– ; Senate 1997– .

Epes, James Fletcher (cousin of Sydney Parham Epes) (D Va.) May 23, 1842–Aug. 24, 1910; House 1891–95.

Epes, Sydney Parham (cousin of James Fletcher Epes and William Bacon Oliver) (D Va.) Aug. 20, 1865–March 3, 1900; House 1897–March 23, 1898 (no party), 1899–March 3, 1900.

Eppes, John Wayles (R Va.) April 7, 1773–Sept. 13, 1823; House 1803–11, 1813–15; Senate 1817–Dec. 4, 1819.

Erdahl, Arlen Ingolf (R Minn.) Feb. 27, 1931– ; House 1979–83.

Erdman, Constantine Jacob (grandson of Jacob Erdman) (D Pa.) Sept. 4, 1846–Jan. 15, 1911; House 1893–97.

Erdman, Jacob (grandfather of Constantine Jacob Erdman) (D Pa.) Feb. 22, 1801–July 20, 1867; House 1845–47.

Erdreich, Ben (D Ala.) Dec. 9, 1938– ; House 1983–93.

Erickson, John Edward (D Mont.) March 14, 1863–May 25, 1946; Senate March 13, 1933–Nov. 6, 1934; Gov. Jan. 5, 1925–March 13, 1933.

Erk, Edmund Frederick (R Pa.) April 17, 1872–Dec. 14, 1953; House Nov. 4, 1930–33.

Erlenborn, John Neal (R Ill.) Feb. 8, 1927– ; House 1965–85.

Ermentrout, Daniel (D Pa.) Jan. 24, 1837–Sept. 17, 1899; House 1881–89, 1897–Sept. 17, 1899.

Ernst, Richard Pretlow (R Ky.) Feb. 28, 1858–April 13, 1934; Senate 1921–27.

Errett, Russell (R Pa.) Nov. 10, 1817–April 7, 1891; House 1877–83.

Ertel, Allen Edward (D Pa.) Nov. 7, 1936– ; House 1977–83.

Ervin, James (R S.C.) Oct. 17, 1778–July 7, 1841; House 1817–21.

Ervin, Joseph Wilson (brother of Samuel James Ervin Jr.) (D N.C.) March 3, 1901–Dec. 25, 1945; House Jan. 3–Dec. 25, 1945.

Ervin, Samuel James Jr. (brother of Joseph Wilson Ervin) (D N.C.) Sept. 27, 1896–April 23, 1985; House Jan. 22, 1946–47; Senate June 5, 1954–Dec. 31, 1974; Chrmn. Senate Government Operations 1972–74.

Esch, John Jacob (R Wis.) March 20, 1861–April 27, 1941; House 1899–1921.

Esch, Marvin Lionel (R Mich.) Aug. 4, 1927– ; House 1967–77.

Eshleman, Edwin Duing (R Pa.) Dec. 4, 1920–Jan. 10, 1985; House 1967–77.

Eshoo, Anna G. (D Calif.) Dec. 13, 1942– ; House 1993– .

Eslick, Edward Everett (husband of Willa McCord Blake Eslick) (D Tenn.) April 19, 1872–June 14, 1932; House 1925–June 14, 1932.

Eslick, Willa McCord Blake (widow of Edward Everett Eslick) (D Tenn.) Sept. 8, 1878–Feb. 18, 1961; House Aug. 4, 1932–33.

Espy, Albert Michael "Mike" (D Miss.) Nov. 30, 1953– ; House 1987–Jan. 22, 1993; Secy. of Agriculture Jan. 22, 1993–Dec. 31, 1994.

Essen, Frederick (R Mo.) April 22, 1863–Aug. 18, 1946; House Nov. 5, 1918–19.

Estabrook, Experience (– Neb.) April 30, 1813–March 26, 1894; House (Terr. Del.) 1859–May 18, 1860.

Estep, Harry Allison (R Pa.) Feb. 1, 1884–Feb. 28, 1968; House 1927–33.

Esterly, Charles Joseph (R Pa.) Feb. 8, 1888–Sept. 3, 1940; House 1925–27, 1929–31.

Estil, Benjamin (– Va.) March 13, 1780–July 14, 1853; House 1825–27.

Estopinal, Albert (D La.) Jan. 30, 1845–April 28, 1919; House Nov. 3, 1908–April 28, 1919.

Esty, Constantine Canaris (R Mass.) Dec. 26, 1824–Dec. 27, 1912; House Dec. 2, 1872–73.

Etheridge, Bob R. (D N.C.) Aug. 7, 1941– ; House 1997– .

Etheridge, Emerson (O Tenn.) Sept. 28, 1819–Oct. 21, 1902; House 1853–57 (1853–55 Whig, 1855–57 American Party), 1859–61.

Eustis, George Jr. (brother of James Biddle Eustis) (AP La.) Sept. 28, 1828–March 15, 1872; House 1855–59.

Eustis, James Biddle (brother of George Eustis Jr.) (D La.) Aug. 27, 1834–Sept. 9, 1899; Senate Jan. 12, 1876–79, 1885–91.

Eustis, William (R Mass.) June 10, 1753–Feb. 6, 1825; House 1801–05, Aug. 21, 1820–23; Secy. of War March 7, 1809–Jan. 13, 1813; Gov. May 31, 1823–Feb. 6, 1825.

Evans, Alexander (W Md.) Sept. 13, 1818–Dec. 5, 1888; House 1847–53.

Evans, Alvin (R Pa.) Oct. 4, 1845–June 19, 1906; House 1901–05.

Evans, Billy Lee (D Ga.) Nov. 10, 1941– ; House 1977–83.

Evans, Charles Robley (D Nev.) Aug. 9, 1866–Nov. 30, 1954; House 1919–21.

Evans, Daniel Jackson (R Wash.) Oct. 16, 1925– ; Senate Sept. 12, 1983–89; Gov. Jan. 11, 1965–Jan. 12, 1977.

Evans, David Ellicott (– N.Y.) March 19, 1788–May 17, 1850; House March 4–May 2, 1827.

Evans, David Reid (R S.C.) Feb. 20, 1769–March 8, 1843; House 1813–15.

Evans, David Walter (D Ind.) Aug. 17, 1946– ; House 1975–83.

Evans, Frank Edward (D Colo.) Sept. 6, 1923– ; House 1965–79.

Evans, George (W Maine) Jan. 12, 1797–April 6, 1867; House July 20, 1829–41 (no party); Senate 1841–47.

Evans, Henry Clay (R Tenn.) June 18, 1843–Dec. 12, 1921; House 1889–91.

Evans, Hiram Kinsman (R Iowa) March 17, 1863–July 9, 1941; House June 4, 1923–25.

Evans, Isaac Newton (R Pa.) July 29, 1827–Dec. 3, 1901; House 1877–79, 1883–87.

Evans, James La Fayette (R Ind.) March 27, 1825–May 28, 1903; House 1875–79.

Evans, John Morgan (D Mont.) Jan. 7, 1863–March 12, 1946; House 1913–21, 1923–33.

Evans, Joshua Jr. (J Pa.) Jan. 20, 1777–Oct. 2, 1846; House 1829–33.

Evans, Josiah James (D S.C.) Nov. 27, 1786–May 6, 1858; Senate 1853–May 6, 1858.

Evans, Lane Allen (D Ill.) Aug. 4, 1951– ; House 1983– .

Evans, Lemuel Dale (AP Texas) Jan. 8, 1810–July 1, 1877; House 1855–57.

Evans, Lynden (D Ill.) June 28, 1858–May 6, 1926; House 1911–13.

Evans, Marcellus Hugh (D N.Y.) Sept. 22, 1884–Nov. 21, 1953; House 1935–41.

Evans, Melvin Herbert (R V.I.) Aug. 7, 1917–Nov. 27, 1984; House (Terr. Del.) 1979–81.

Evans, Nathan (W Ohio) June 24, 1804–Sept. 27, 1879; House 1847–51.

Evans, Robert Emory (R Neb.) July 15, 1856–July 8, 1925; House 1919–23.

Evans, Thomas (F Va.) ?–?; House 1797–1801.

Evans, Thomas Beverley Jr. (R Del.) Nov. 5, 1931– ; House 1977–83.

Evans, Thomas Cooper (R Iowa) May 26, 1924– ; House 1981–87.

Evans, Walter (nephew of Burwell Clark Ritter) (R Ky.) Sept. 18, 1842–Dec. 30, 1923; House 1895–99.

Evans, William Elmer (R Calif.) Dec. 14, 1877–Nov. 12, 1959; House 1927–35.

Evarts, William Maxwell (grandson of Roger Sherman) (R N.Y.) Feb. 6, 1818–Feb. 28, 1901; Senate 1885–91; Atty. Gen. July 15, 1868–March 3, 1869; Secy. of State March 12, 1877–March 7, 1881.

Everett, Edward (father of William Everett) (W Mass.) April 11, 1794–Jan. 15, 1865; House 1825–35 (no party); Senate 1853–June 1, 1854; Gov. Jan. 13, 1836–Jan. 18, 1840; Secy. of State Nov. 6, 1852–March 3, 1853.

Everett, Horace (W Vt.) July 17, 1779–Jan. 30, 1851; House 1829–43 (1829–35 no party).

Everett, Robert Ashton (D Tenn.) Feb. 24, 1915–Jan. 26, 1969; House Feb. 1, 1958–Jan. 26, 1969.

Everett, Robert William (D Ga.) March 3, 1839–Feb. 27, 1915; House 1891–93.

Everett, Terry (R Ala.) Feb. 15, 1937– ; House 1993– .

Everett, William (son of Edward Everett) (D Mass.) Oct. 10, 1839–Feb. 16, 1910; House April 25, 1893–95.

Everhart, James Bowen (son of William Everhart) (R Pa.) July 26, 1821–Aug. 23, 1888; House 1883–87.

Everhart, William (father of James Bowen Everhart) (W Pa.) May 17, 1785–Oct. 30, 1868; House 1853–55.

Evins, John Hamilton (D S.C.) July 18, 1830–Oct. 20, 1884; House 1877–Oct. 20, 1884.

Evins, Joseph Landon (D Tenn.) Oct. 24, 1910–March 31, 1984; House 1947–77; Chrmn. House Select Committee on Small Business 1963–75; Chrmn. House Small Business 1975–77.

Ewart, Hamilton Glover (R N.C.) Oct. 23, 1849–April 28, 1918; House 1889–91.

Ewing, Andrew (brother of Edwin Hickman Ewing) (D Tenn.) June 17, 1813–June 16, 1864; House 1849–51.

Ewing, Edwin Hickman (brother of Andrew Ewing) (W Tenn.) Dec. 2, 1809–April 24, 1902; House 1845–47.

Ewing, John (W Ind.) May 19, 1789–April 6, 1858; House 1833–35 (no party), 1837–39.

Ewing, John Hoge (W Pa.) Oct. 5, 1796–June 9, 1887; House 1845–47.

Ewing, Presley Underwood (W Ky.) Sept. 1, 1822–Sept. 27, 1854; House 1851–Sept. 27, 1854.

Ewing, Thomas (father of Thomas Ewing, below) (W Ohio) Dec. 28, 1789–Oct. 26, 1871; Senate 1831–37, July 20, 1850–51; Secy. of the Treasury March 4–Sept. 11, 1841; Secy. of the Interior March 8, 1849–July 22, 1850.

Ewing, Thomas (son of Thomas Ewing, above) (D Ohio) Aug. 7, 1829–Jan. 21, 1896; House 1877–81.

Ewing, Thomas W. (R Ill.) Sept. 19, 1935– ; House July 10, 1991– .

Ewing, William Lee Davidson (– Ill.) Aug. 31, 1795–March 25, 1846; Senate Dec. 30, 1835–37; Gov. Nov. 17–Dec. 3, 1834.

Exon, John James (D Neb.) Aug. 9, 1921– ; Senate 1979–97; Gov. Jan. 7, 1971–Jan. 3, 1979.

F

Faddis, Charles Isiah (D Pa.) June 13, 1890–April 1, 1972; House 1933–Dec. 4, 1942.

Fair, James Graham (D Nev.) Dec. 3, 1831–Dec. 28, 1894; Senate 1881–87.

Fairbanks, Charles Warren (R Ind.) May 11, 1852–June 4, 1918; Senate 1897–1905; Vice President 1905–09.

Fairchild, Benjamin Lewis (R N.Y.) Jan. 5, 1863–Oct. 25, 1946; House 1895–97, 1917–19, 1921–23, Nov. 6, 1923–27.

Fairchild, George Winthrop (R N.Y.) May 6, 1854–Dec. 31, 1924; House 1907–19.

Faircloth, Lauch (R N.C.) Jan. 14, 1928– ; Senate 1993–99.

Fairfield, John (D Maine) Jan. 30, 1797–Dec. 24, 1847; House 1835–Dec. 24, 1838; Senate 1843–Dec. 24, 1847; Gov. Jan. 2, 1839–Jan. 6, 1841, Jan. 5, 1842–March 7, 1843.

Fairfield, Louis William (R Ind.) Oct. 15, 1858–Feb. 20, 1930; House 1917–25.

Faison, John Miller (D N.C.) April 17, 1862–April 21, 1915; House 1911–15.

Falconer, Jacob Alexander (Prog. Wash.) Jan. 26, 1869–July 1, 1928; House 1913–15.

Faleomavaega, Eni F. H. (D Am Samoa) Aug. 15, 1943– ; House 1991– .

Fall, Albert Bacon (R N.M.) Nov. 26, 1861–Nov. 30, 1944; Senate March 27, 1912–March 4, 1921; Secy. of the Interior March 5, 1921–March 4, 1923.

Fallon, George Hyde (D Md.) July 24, 1902–March 21, 1980; House 1945–71; Chrmn. House Public Works 1965–71.

Fannin, Paul Jones (R Ariz.) Jan. 29, 1907– ; Senate 1965–77; Gov. Jan. 5, 1959–Jan. 4, 1965.

Faran, James John (D Ohio) Dec. 29, 1808–Dec. 12, 1892; House 1845–49.

Farbstein, Leonard (D N.Y.) Oct. 12, 1902– ; House 1957–71.

Faris, George Washington (R Ind.) June 9, 1854–April 17, 1914; House 1895–1901.

Farlee, Isaac Gray (– N.J.) May 18, 1787–Jan. 12, 1855; House 1843–45.

Farley, Ephraim Wilder (W Maine) Aug. 29, 1817–April 3, 1880; House 1853–55.

Farley, James Indus (D Ind.) Feb. 24, 1871–June 16, 1948; House 1933–39.

Farley, James Thompson (D Calif.) Aug. 6, 1829–Jan. 22, 1886; Senate 1879–85.

Farley, Michael Francis (D N.Y.) March 1, 1863–Oct. 8, 1921; House 1915–17.

Farlin, Dudley (J N.Y.) Sept. 2, 1777–Sept. 26, 1837; House 1835–37.

Farnsley, Charles Rowland Peaslee (D Ky.) March 28, 1907–June 19, 1990; House 1965–67.

Farnsworth, John Franklin (R Ill.) March 27, 1820–July 14, 1897; House 1857–61, 1863–73.

Farnum, Billie Sunday (D Mich.) April 11, 1916–Nov. 18, 1979; House 1965–67.

Farquhar, John Hanson (R Ind.) Dec. 20, 1818–Oct. 1, 1873; House 1865–67.

Farquhar, John McCreath (R N.Y.) April 17, 1832–April 24, 1918; House 1885–91.

Farr, Evarts Worcester (R N.H.) Oct. 10, 1840–Nov. 30, 1880; House 1879–Nov. 30, 1880.

Farr, John Richard (R Pa.) July 18, 1857–Dec. 11, 1933; House 1911–19, Feb. 25–March 3, 1921.

Farr, Sam (D Calif.) July 4, 1941– ; House June 16, 1993– .

Farrelly, John Wilson (son of Patrick Farrelly) (W Pa.) July 7, 1809–Dec. 20, 1860; House 1847–49.

Farrelly, Patrick (father of John Wilson Farrelly) (– Pa.) 1770–Jan. 12, 1826; House 1821–Jan. 12, 1826.

Farrington, James (D N.H.) Oct. 1, 1791–Oct. 29, 1859; House 1837–39.

Farrington, Joseph Rider (husband of Mary Elizabeth Pruett Farrington) (R Hawaii) Oct. 15, 1897–June 19, 1954; House (Terr. Del.) 1943–June 19, 1954.

Farrington, Mary Elizabeth Pruett (widow of Joseph Rider Farrington) (R Hawaii) May 30, 1898–July 21, 1984; House (Terr. Del.) July 31, 1954–57.

Farrow, Samuel (R S.C.) 1759–Nov. 18, 1824; House 1813–15.

Farwell, Charles Benjamin (R Ill.) July 1, 1823–Sept. 23, 1903; House 1871–May 6, 1876, 1881–83; Senate Jan. 19, 1887–91.

Farwell, Nathan Allen (cousin of Owen Lovejoy) (R Maine) Feb. 24, 1812–Dec. 9, 1893; Senate Oct. 27, 1864–65.

Farwell, Sewall Spaulding (R Iowa) April 26, 1834–Sept. 21, 1909; House 1881–83.

Fary, John George (D Ill.) April 11, 1911–June 7, 1984; House July 8, 1975–83.

Fascell, Dante Bruno (D Fla.) March 9, 1917–Nov. 28, 1998; House 1955–93; Chrmn. House Foreign Affairs 1984–93.

Fassett, Jacob Sloat (– N.Y.) Nov. 13, 1853–April 21, 1924; House 1905–11.

Fattah, Chaka (D Pa.) Nov. 21, 1956– ; House 1995– .

Faulkner, Charles James (father of Charles James Faulkner, below) (D W.Va.) July 6, 1806–Nov. 1, 1884; House 1851–59 (1851–55 Whig) (Va.), 1875–77.

Faulkner, Charles James (son of Charles James Faulkner, above) (D W.Va.) Sept. 21, 1847–Jan. 13, 1929; Senate 1887–99.

Fauntroy, Walter Edward (D D.C.) Feb. 6, 1933– ; House (Delegate) March 23, 1971–91.

Faust, Charles Lee (R Mo.) April 24, 1879–Dec. 17, 1928; House 1921–Dec. 17, 1928.

Favrot, George Kent (D La.) Nov. 26, 1868–Dec. 26, 1934; House 1907–09, 1921–25.

Fawell, Harris Walter (R Ill.) March 25, 1929– ; House 1985–99.

Fay, Francis Ball (W Mass.) June 12, 1793–Oct. 6, 1876; House Dec. 13, 1852–53.

Fay, James Herbert (D N.Y.) April 29, 1899–Sept. 10, 1948; House 1939–41, 1943–45.

Fay, John (– N.Y.) Feb. 10, 1773–June 21, 1855; House 1819–21.

Fazio, Victor Herbert Jr. (D Calif.) Oct. 11, 1942– ; House 1979–99.

Fearing, Paul (F N.W. Terr.) Feb. 28, 1762–Aug. 21, 1822; House (Terr. Del.) 1801–03.

Featherston, Winfield Scott (D Miss.) Aug. 8, 1820–May 28, 1891; House 1847–51.

Featherstone, Lewis Porter (Lab. Ark.) July 28, 1851–March 14, 1922; House March 5, 1890–91.

Feazel, William Crosson (D La.) June 10, 1895–March 16, 1965; Senate May 18–Dec. 30, 1948.

Feely, John Joseph (D Ill.) Aug. 1, 1875–Feb. 15, 1905; House 1901–03.

Feighan, Edward Farrell (nephew of Michael Aloysius Feighan) (D Ohio) Oct. 22, 1947– ; House 1983–93.

Feighan, Michael Aloysius (uncle of Edward Farrell Feighan) (D Ohio) Feb. 16, 1905–March 19, 1992; House 1943–71.

Feingold, Russell D. (D Wis.) March 2, 1953– ; Senate 1993– .

Feinstein, Dianne (D Calif.) June 22, 1933– ; Senate Nov. 10, 1992– .

Felch, Alpheus (D Mich.) Sept. 28, 1804–June 13, 1896; Senate 1847–53; Gov. Jan. 5, 1846–March 3, 1847.

Felder, John Myers (N S.C.) July 7, 1782–Sept. 1, 1851; House 1831–35 (1831–33 Jacksonian).

Fellows, Frank (R Maine) Nov. 7, 1889–Aug. 27, 1951; House 1941–Aug. 27, 1951.

Fellows, John R. (D N.Y.) July 29, 1832–Dec. 7, 1896; House 1891–Dec. 31, 1893.

Felton, Charles Norton (R Calif.) Jan. 1, 1828–Sept. 13, 1914; House 1885–89; Senate March 19, 1891–93.

Felton, Rebecca Latimer (wife of William Harrell Felton) (D Ga.) June 10, 1835–Jan. 24, 1930; Senate Nov. 21–Nov. 22, 1922.

Felton, William Harrell (husband of Rebecca Latimer Felton) (ID Ga.) June 1, 1823–Sept. 24, 1909; House 1875–81.

Fenerty, Clare Gerald (R Pa.) July 25, 1895–July 1, 1952; House 1935–37.

Fenn, Edward Hart (R Conn.) Sept. 12, 1856–Feb. 23, 1939; House 1921–31.

Fenn, Stephen Southmyd (D Idaho) March 28, 1820–April 13, 1892; House (Terr. Del.) June 23, 1876–79.

Fenner, James (R R.I.) Jan. 22, 1771–April 17, 1846; Senate 1805–Sept. 1807; Gov. May 6, 1807–May 1, 1811 (Democratic Republican), May 5, 1824–May 4, 1831 (Democratic Republican), May 2, 1843–May 6, 1845 (Law & Order Whig).

Fenton, Ivor David (R Pa.) Aug. 3, 1889–Oct. 23, 1986; House 1939–63.

Fenton, Lucien Jerome (R Ohio) May 7, 1844–June 28, 1922; House 1895–99.

Fenton, Reuben Eaton (R N.Y.) July 4, 1819–Aug. 25, 1885; House 1853–55 (Democrat), 1857–Dec. 20, 1864 (Democrat); Senate 1869–75; Gov. Jan. 1, 1865–Jan. 1, 1869 (Union Republican).

Fenwick, Millicent Hammond (R N.J.) Feb. 25, 1910–Sept. 16, 1992; House 1975–83.

Ferdon, John William (R N.Y.) Dec. 13, 1826–Aug. 5, 1884; House 1879–81.

Ferguson, Fenner (D Neb.) April 25, 1814–Oct. 11, 1859; House (Terr. Del.) 1857–59.

Ferguson, Homer (R Mich.) Feb. 25, 1889–Dec. 17, 1982; Senate 1943–55.

Ferguson, Phillip Colgan (D Okla.) Aug. 15, 1903–Aug. 8, 1978; House 1935–41.

Fergusson, Harvey Butler (D N.M.) Sept. 9, 1848–June 10, 1915; House (Terr. Del.) 1897–99, (Rep.) Jan. 8, 1912–15.

Fernald, Bert Manfred (R Maine) April 3, 1858–Aug. 23, 1926; Senate Sept. 12, 1916–Aug. 23, 1926; Gov. Jan. 6, 1909–Jan. 4, 1911.

Fernandez, Antonio Manuel (D N.M.) Jan. 17, 1902–Nov. 7, 1956; House 1943–Nov. 7, 1956.

Fernandez, Joachim Octave (D La.) Aug. 14, 1896–Aug. 8, 1978; House 1931–41.

Fernos-Isern, Antonio (PD P.R.) May 10, 1895–Jan. 19, 1974; House (Res. Comm.) Sept. 11, 1946–65.

Ferraro, Geraldine Anne (D N.Y.) Aug. 26, 1935– ; House 1979–85.

Ferrell, Thomas Merrill (D N.J.) June 20, 1844–Oct. 20, 1916; House 1883–85.

Ferris, Charles Goadsby (D N.Y.) about 1796–June 4, 1848; House Dec. 1, 1834–35 (Jacksonian), 1841–43.

Ferris, Scott (D Okla.) Nov. 3, 1877–June 8, 1945; House Nov. 16, 1907–21.

Ferris, Woodbridge Nathan (D Mich.) Jan. 6, 1853–March 23, 1928; Senate 1923–March 23, 1928; Gov. Jan. 1, 1913–Jan. 1, 1917.

Ferriss, Orange (R N.Y.) Nov. 26, 1814–April 11, 1894; House 1867–71.

Ferry, Orris Sanford (LR/D Conn.) Aug. 15, 1823–Nov. 21, 1875; House 1859–61 (Republican); Senate 1867–Nov. 21, 1875 (1867–73 Republican).

Ferry, Thomas White (R Mich.) June 10, 1827–Oct. 13, 1896; House 1865–71; Senate 1871–83; elected Pres. pro tempore March 9, 1875, March 19, 1875, Dec. 20, 1875, March 5, 1877, Feb. 26, 1878, April 17, 1878, March 3, 1879.

Fess, Simeon Davison (R Ohio) Dec. 11, 1861–Dec. 23, 1936; House 1913–23; Senate 1923–35; Chrmn. Rep. Nat. Comm. 1930–32.

Fessenden, Samuel Clement (brother of Thomas Amory Deblois Fessenden and William Pitt Fessenden) (R Maine) March 7, 1815–April 18, 1882; House 1861–63.

Fessenden, Thomas Amory Deblois (brother of Samuel Clement Fessenden and William Pitt Fessenden) (R Maine) Jan. 23, 1826–Sept. 28, 1868; House Dec. 1, 1862–63.

Fessenden, William Pitt (brother of Samuel Clement Fessenden and Thomas Amory Deblois Fessenden) (R Maine) Oct. 16, 1806–Sept. 8, 1869; House 1841–43 (Whig); Senate Feb. 10, 1854–July 1, 1864 (Feb. 10, 1854–59 Whig), 1865–Sept. 8, 1869; Secy. of the Treasury July 5, 1864–March 3, 1865.

Few, William (– Ga.) June 8, 1748–July 16, 1828; Senate 1789–93; Cont. Cong. 1780–82, 1786–88.

Ficklin, Orlando Bell (D Ill.) Dec. 16, 1808–May 5, 1886; House 1843–49, 1851–53.

Fiedler, Roberta Frances "Bobbi" (neé Horowitz) (R Calif.) April 22, 1937– ; House 1981–87.

Fiedler, William Henry Frederick (D N.J.) Aug. 25, 1847–Jan. 1, 1919; House 1883–85.

Field, David Dudley (D N.Y.) Feb. 13, 1805–April 13, 1894; House Jan. 11–March 3, 1877.

Field, Moses Whelock (R Mich.) Feb. 10, 1828–March 14, 1889; House 1873–75.

Field, Richard Stockton (son of Richard Stockton) (R N.J.) Dec. 31, 1803–May 25, 1870; Senate Nov. 21, 1862–Jan. 14, 1863.

Field, Scott (D Texas) Jan. 26, 1847–Dec. 20, 1931; House 1903–07.

Field, Walbridge Abner (R Mass.) April 26, 1833–July 15, 1899; House 1877–March 28, 1878 (no party), 1879–81.

Fielder, George Bragg (D N.J.) July 24, 1842–Aug. 14, 1906; House 1893–95.

Fields, Cleo (D La.) Nov. 22, 1962– ; House 1993–97.

Fields, Jack Milton Jr. (R Texas) Feb. 3, 1952– ; House 1981–97.

Fields, William Craig (R N.Y.) Feb. 13, 1804–Oct. 27, 1882; House 1867–69.

Fields, William Jason (D Ky.) Dec. 29, 1874–Oct. 21, 1954; House 1911–Dec. 11, 1923; Gov. Dec. 11, 1923–Dec. 13, 1927.

Fiesinger, William Louis (D Ohio) Oct. 25, 1877–Sept. 11, 1953; House 1931–37.

Fillmore, Millard (W N.Y.) Jan. 7, 1800–March 8, 1874; House 1833–35, 1837–43; Vice President 1849–July 10, 1850; President July 10, 1850–53.

Filner, Bob (D Calif.) Sept. 4, 1942– ; House 1993– .

Finch, Isaac (– N.Y.) Oct. 13, 1783–June 23, 1845; House 1829–31.

Finck, William Edward (D Ohio) Sept. 1, 1822–Jan. 25, 1901; House 1863–67, Dec. 7, 1874–75.

Findlay, James (brother of John Findlay and William Findlay) (J Ohio) Oct. 12, 1770–Dec. 28, 1835; House 1825–33 (1825–29 no party).

Findlay, John (brother of James Findlay and William Findlay) (– Pa.) March 31, 1766–Nov. 5, 1838; House Oct. 9, 1821–27.

Findlay, John Van Lear (D Md.) Dec. 21, 1839–April 19, 1907; House 1883–87.

Findlay, William (brother of James Findlay and John Findlay) (R Pa.) June 20, 1768–Nov. 12, 1846; Senate Dec. 10, 1821–27; Gov. Dec. 16, 1817–Dec. 19, 1820 (Democratic Republican).

Findley, Paul (R Ill.) June 23, 1921– ; House 1961–83.

Findley, William (R Pa.) 1741 or 1742–April 4, 1821; House 1791–99 (1791–95 no party), 1803–17.

Fine, John (D N.Y.) Aug. 26, 1794–Jan. 4, 1867; House 1839–41.

Fine, Sidney Asher (D N.Y.) Sept. 14, 1903–April 13, 1982; House 1951–Jan. 2, 1956.

Finerty, John Frederick (ID Ill.) Sept. 10, 1846–June 10, 1908; House 1883–85.

Fingerhut, Eric D. (D Ohio) May 6, 1959– ; House 1993–95.

Finkelnburg, Gustavus Adolphus (LR Mo.) April 6, 1837–May 18, 1908; House 1869–73 (1869–71 Republican).

Finley, Charles (son of Hugh Franklin Finley) (R Ky.) March 26, 1865–March 18, 1941; House Feb. 15, 1930–33.

Finley, David Edward (D S.C.) Feb. 28, 1861–Jan. 26, 1917; House 1899–Jan. 26, 1917.

Finley, Ebenezer Byron (nephew of Stephen Ross Harris) (D Ohio) July 31, 1833–Aug. 22, 1916; House 1877–81.

Finley, Hugh Franklin (father of Charles Finley) (R Ky.) Jan. 18, 1833–Oct. 16, 1909; House 1887–91.

Finley, Jesse Johnson (D Fla.) Nov. 18, 1812–Nov. 6, 1904; House April 19, 1876–77, Feb. 20–March 3, 1879, 1881–June 1, 1882.

Finnegan, Edward Rowan (D Ill.) June 5, 1905–Feb. 2, 1971; House 1961–Dec. 6, 1964.

Finney, Darwin Abel (R Pa.) Aug. 11, 1814–Aug. 25, 1868; House 1867–Aug. 25, 1868.

Fino, Paul Albert (R N.Y.) Dec. 15, 1913– ; House 1953–Dec. 31, 1968.

Fischer, Israel Frederick (R N.Y.) Aug. 17, 1858–March 16, 1940; House 1895–99.

Fish, Hamilton (father of Hamilton Fish, below, grandfather of Hamilton Fish born in 1888, great-grandfather of Hamilton Fish Jr. born in 1926) (W N.Y.) Aug. 3, 1808–Sept. 7, 1893; House 1843–45; Senate 1851–57; Gov. Jan. 1, 1849–Jan. 1, 1851; Secy. of State March 17, 1869–March 12, 1877.

Fish, Hamilton (son of Hamilton Fish, above, father of Hamilton Fish born in 1888, grandfather of Hamilton Fish Jr. born in 1926) (R N.Y.) April 17, 1849–Jan. 15, 1936; House 1909–11.

Fish, Hamilton (son of Hamilton Fish born in 1849, father of Hamilton Fish Jr., below, grandson of Hamilton Fish born in 1808) (R N.Y.) Dec. 7, 1888–Jan. 18, 1991; House Nov. 2, 1920–45.

Fish, Hamilton Jr. (son of Hamilton Fish born in 1888, above, grandson of Hamilton Fish born in 1849, great-grandson of Hamilton Fish born in 1808) (R N.Y.) June 3, 1926–July 23, 1996; House 1969–95.

Fishburne, John Wood (cousin of Fontaine Maury Maverick) (D Va.) March 8, 1868–June 24, 1937; House 1931–33.

Fisher, Charles (R N.C.) Oct. 20, 1789–May 7, 1849; House Feb. 11, 1819–21, 1839–41.

Fisher, David (W Ohio) Dec. 3, 1794–May 7, 1886; House 1847–49.

Fisher, George (– N.Y.) March 17, 1788–March 26, 1861; House 1829–Feb. 5, 1830.

Fisher, George Purnell (U Del.) Oct. 13, 1817–Feb. 10, 1899; House 1861–63.

Fisher, Horatio Gates (R Pa.) April 21, 1838–May 8, 1890; House 1879–83.

Fisher, Hubert Frederick (D Tenn.) Oct. 6, 1877–June 16, 1941; House 1917–31.

Fisher, John (R N.Y.) March 13, 1806–March 28, 1882; House 1869–71.

Fisher, Joseph Lyman (D Va.) Jan. 11, 1914–Feb. 19, 1992; House 1975–81.

Fisher, Ovie Clark (D Texas) Nov. 22, 1903–Dec. 9, 1994; House 1943–Dec. 31, 1974.

Fisher, Spencer Oliver (D Mich.) Feb. 3, 1843–June 1, 1919; House 1885–89.

Fisk, James (R Vt.) Oct. 4, 1763–Nov. 17, 1844; House 1805–09, 1811–15; Senate Nov. 4, 1817–Jan. 8, 1818.

Fisk, Jonathan (R N.Y.) Sept. 26, 1778–July 13, 1832; House 1809–11, 1813–March 1815.

Fitch, Asa (F N.Y.) Nov. 10, 1765–Aug. 24, 1843; House 1811–13.

Fitch, Ashbel Parmelee (D N.Y.) Oct. 8, 1838–May 4, 1904; House 1887–Dec. 26, 1893 (1887–89 Republican).

Fitch, Graham Newell (grandfather of Edwin Denby) (D Ind.) Dec. 5, 1809–Nov. 29, 1892; House 1849–53; Senate Feb. 4, 1857–61.

Fitch, Thomas (R Nev.) Jan. 27, 1838–Nov. 12, 1923; House 1869–71.

Fite, Samuel McClary (D Tenn.) June 12, 1816–Oct. 23, 1875; House March 4–Oct. 23, 1875.

Fithian, Floyd James (D Ind.) Nov. 3, 1928– ; House 1975–83.

Fithian, George Washington (D Ill.) July 4, 1854–Jan. 21, 1921; House 1889–95.

Fitzgerald, Frank Thomas (D N.Y.) May 4, 1857–Nov. 25, 1907; House March 4–Nov. 4, 1889.

Fitzgerald, John Francis (grandfather of John Fitzgerald Kennedy, Robert Francis Kennedy and Edward Moore Kennedy, great-grandfather of Joseph Patrick Kennedy II) (D Mass.) Feb. 11, 1863–Oct. 2, 1950; House 1895–1901, March 4–Oct. 23, 1919.

Fitzgerald, John Joseph (D N.Y.) March 10, 1872–May 13, 1952; House 1899–Dec. 31, 1917.

Fitzgerald, Peter G. (R Ill.) Oct. 20, 1960– ; Senate 1999– .

Fitzgerald, Roy Gerald (R Ohio) Aug. 25, 1875–Nov. 16, 1962; House 1921–31.

Fitzgerald, Thomas (D Mich.) April 10, 1796–March 25, 1855; Senate June 8, 1848–49.

Fitzgerald, William (J Tenn.) Aug. 6, 1799–March 1864; House 1831–33.

Fitzgerald, William Joseph (D Conn.) March 2, 1887–May 6, 1947; House 1937–39, 1941–43.

Fitzgerald, William Thomas (R Ohio) Oct. 13, 1858–Jan. 12, 1939; House 1925–29.

Fitzgibbons, John (D N.Y.) July 10, 1868–Aug. 4, 1941; House 1933–35.

Fitzhenry, Louis (D Ill.) June 13, 1870–Nov. 18, 1935; House 1913–15.

Fitzpatrick, Benjamin (D Ala.) June 30, 1802–Nov. 21, 1869; Senate Nov. 25, 1848–Nov. 30, 1849, Jan. 14, 1853–55, Nov. 26, 1855–Jan. 21, 1861; elected Pres. pro tempore Dec. 7, 1857, March 29, 1858, June 14, 1858, Jan. 25, 1859, March 9, 1859, Dec. 19, 1859, Feb. 20, 1860, June 26, 1860; Gov. Nov. 22, 1841–Dec. 10, 1845.

Fitzpatrick, James Martin (D N.Y.) June 27, 1869–April 10, 1949; House 1927–45.

Fitzpatrick, Morgan Cassius (D Tenn.) Oct. 29, 1868–June 25, 1908; House 1903–05.

Fitzpatrick, Thomas Young (D Ky.) Sept. 20, 1850–Jan. 21, 1906; House 1897–1901.

Fitzsimons, Thomas (– Pa.) 1741–Aug. 26, 1811; House 1789–95; Cont. Cong. 1782–83.

Fjare, Orvin Benonie (R Mont.) April 16, 1918–   ; House 1955–57.

Flack, William Henry (R N.Y.) March 22, 1861–Feb. 2, 1907; House 1903–Feb. 2, 1907.

Flagler, Thomas Thorn (W N.Y.) Oct. 12, 1811–Sept. 6, 1897; House 1853–57.

Flaherty, Lawrence James (R Calif.) July 4, 1878–June 13, 1926; House 1925–June 13, 1926.

Flaherty, Thomas Aloysius (D Mass.) Dec. 21, 1898–April 27, 1965; House Dec. 14, 1937–43.

Flake, Floyd Harold (D N.Y.) Jan. 30, 1945–   ; House 1987–Nov. 15, 1997.

Flanagan, De Witt Clinton (D N.J.) Dec. 28, 1870–Jan. 15, 1946; House June 18, 1902–03.

Flanagan, James Winright (R Texas) Sept. 5, 1805–Sept. 28, 1887; Senate March 30, 1870–75.

Flanagan, Michael Patrick (R Ill.) Nov. 9, 1962–   ; House 1995–97.

Flanders, Alvan (R Wash.) Aug. 2, 1825–March 14, 1884; House (Terr. Del.) 1867–69; Gov. (Wash. Terr.) 1869–70.

Flanders, Benjamin Franklin (U La.) Jan. 26, 1816–March 13, 1896; House Dec. 3, 1862–63; Military Gov. June 6, 1867–Jan. 8, 1868.

Flanders, Ralph Edward (R Vt.) Sept. 28, 1880–Feb. 19, 1970; Senate Nov. 1, 1946–59.

Flannagan, John William Jr. (D Va.) Feb. 20, 1885–April 27, 1955; House 1931–49.

Flannery, John Harold (D Pa.) April 19, 1898–June 3, 1961; House 1937–Jan. 3, 1942.

Fleeger, George Washington (R Pa.) March 13, 1839–June 25, 1894; House 1885–87.

Fleetwood, Frederick Gleed (R Vt.) Sept. 27, 1868–Jan. 28, 1938; House 1923–25.

Fleger, Anthony Alfred (D Ohio) Oct. 21, 1900–July 16, 1963; House 1937–39.

Fleming, William Bennett (D Ga.) Oct. 29, 1803–Aug. 19, 1886; House Feb. 10–March 3, 1879.

Fleming, William Henry (D Ga.) Oct. 18, 1856–June 9, 1944; House 1897–1903.

Fletcher, Charles Kimball (R Calif.) Dec. 15, 1902–Sept. 29, 1985; House 1947–49.

Fletcher, Duncan Upshaw (D Fla.) Jan. 6, 1859–June 17, 1936; Senate 1909–June 17, 1936.

Fletcher, Ernest L. (R Ky.) Nov. 12, 1952–   ; House 1999–   .

Fletcher, Isaac (D Vt.) Nov. 22, 1784–Oct. 19, 1842; House 1837–41.

Fletcher, Loren (R Minn.) April 10, 1833–April 15, 1919; House 1893–1903, 1905–07.

Fletcher, Richard (W Mass.) Jan. 8, 1788–June 21, 1869; House 1837–39.

Fletcher, Thomas (R Ky.) Oct. 21, 1779–?; House Dec. 2, 1816–17.

Fletcher, Thomas Brooks (D Ohio) Oct. 10, 1879–July 1, 1945; House 1925–29, 1933–39.

Flick, James Patton (R Iowa) Aug. 28, 1845–Feb. 25, 1929; House 1889–93.

Flint, Frank Putnam (R Calif.) July 15, 1862–Feb. 11, 1929; Senate 1905–11.

Flippo, Ronnie Gene (D Ala.) Aug. 15, 1937–   ; House 1977–91.

Flood, Daniel John (D Pa.) Nov. 26, 1903–May 28, 1994; House 1945–47, 1949–53, 1955–Jan. 31, 1980.

Flood, Henry De La Warr (brother of Joel West Flood, uncle of Harry Flood Byrd) (D Va.) Sept. 2, 1865–Dec. 8, 1921; House 1901–Dec. 8, 1921.

Flood, Joel West (brother of Henry De La Warr Flood, uncle of Harry Flood Byrd) (D Va.) Aug. 2, 1894–April 27, 1964; House Nov. 8, 1932–33.

Flood, Thomas Schmeck (R N.Y.) April 12, 1844–Oct. 28, 1908; House 1887–91.

Florence, Elias (W Ohio) Feb. 15, 1797–Nov. 21, 1880; House 1843–45.

Florence, Thomas Birch (D Pa.) Jan. 26, 1812–July 3, 1875; House 1851–61.

Florio, James Joseph (D N.J.) Aug. 29, 1937–   ; House 1975–Jan. 16, 1990; Gov. Jan. 16, 1990–Jan. 18, 1994.

Flournoy, Thomas Stanhope (W Va.) Dec. 15, 1811–March 12, 1883; House 1847–49.

Flower, Roswell Pettibone (D N.Y.) Aug. 7, 1835–May 12, 1899; House Nov. 8, 1881–83, 1889–Sept. 16, 1891; Gov. Jan. 1, 1892–Jan. 1, 1895.

Flowers, Walter (D Ala.) April 12, 1933–April 12, 1984; House 1969–79.

Floyd, Charles Albert (D N.Y.) 1791–Feb. 20, 1873; House 1841–43.

Floyd, John (– Ga.) Oct. 3, 1769–June 24, 1839; House 1827–29.

Floyd, John (R Va.) April 24, 1783–Aug. 17, 1837; House 1817–29; Gov. March 4, 1830–March 31, 1834 (Democrat).

Floyd, John Charles (D Ark.) April 14, 1858–Nov. 4, 1930; House 1905–15.

Floyd, John Gelston (grandson of William Floyd) (D N.Y.) Feb. 5, 1806–Oct. 5, 1881; House 1839–43, 1851–53.

Floyd, William (grandfather of John Gelston Floyd) (– N.Y.) Dec. 17, 1734–Aug. 4, 1821; House 1789–91; Cont. Cong. 1774–76, 1779–83.

Flye, Edwin (R Maine) March 4, 1817–July 12, 1886; House Dec. 4, 1876–77.

Flynn, Dennis Thomas (R Okla.) Feb. 13, 1861–June 19, 1939; House (Terr. Del.) 1893–97, 1899–1903.

Flynn, Gerald Thomas (D Wis.) Oct. 7, 1910–May 14, 1990; House 1959–61.

Flynn, Joseph Vincent (D N.Y.) Sept. 2, 1883–Feb. 6, 1940; House 1915–19.

Flynt, John James Jr. (D Ga.) Nov. 8, 1914–   ; House Nov. 2, 1954–79; Chrmn. House Standards of Official Conduct 1975–77.

Focht, Benjamin Kurtz (R Pa.) March 12, 1863–March 27, 1937; House 1907–13, 1915–23, 1933–March 27, 1937.

Foelker, Otto Godfrey (R N.Y.) Dec. 29, 1875–Jan. 18, 1943; House Nov. 3, 1908–11.

Foerderer, Robert Hermann (R Pa.) May 16, 1860–July 26, 1903; House 1901–July 26, 1903.

Fogarty, John Edward (D R.I.) March 23, 1913–Jan. 10, 1967; House 1941–Dec. 7, 1944; Feb. 7, 1945–Jan. 10, 1967.

Fogg, George Gilman (R N.H.) May 26, 1813–Oct. 5, 1881; Senate Aug. 31, 1866–67.

Foglietta, Thomas Michael (D Pa.) Dec. 3, 1928–   ; House 1981–Nov. 12, 1997 (1981–83 Independent).

Foley, James Bradford (D Ind.) Oct. 18, 1807–Dec. 5, 1886; House 1857–59.

Foley, John Robert (D Md.) Oct. 16, 1917–   ; House 1959–61.

Foley, Mark (R Fla.) Sept. 8, 1954–   ; House 1995–   .

Foley, Thomas Stephen (D Wash.) March 6, 1929– ; House 1965–95; Chrmn. House Agriculture 1975–81; House majority leader 1987–June 6, 1989; Speaker June 6, 1989–95.

Folger, Alonzo Dillard (brother of John Hamlin Folger) (D N.C.) July 9, 1888–April 30, 1941; House 1939–April 30, 1941.

Folger, John Hamlin (brother of Alonzo Dillard Folger) (D N.C.) Dec. 18, 1880–July 19, 1963; House June 14, 1941–49.

Folger, Walter Jr. (R Mass.) June 12, 1765–Sept. 8, 1849; House 1817–21.

Follett, John Fassett (D Ohio) Feb. 18, 1831–April 15, 1902; House 1883–85.

Fong, Hiram Leong (R Hawaii) Oct. 1, 1907– ; Senate Aug. 21, 1959–77.

Foot, Samuel Augustus (– Conn.) Nov. 8, 1780–Sept. 15, 1846; House 1819–21, 1823–25, 1833–May 9, 1834; Senate 1827–33; Gov. May 7, 1834–May 6, 1835 (Whig).

Foot, Solomon (R Vt.) Nov. 19, 1802–March 28, 1866; House 1843–47 (Whig); Senate 1851–March 28, 1866 (1851–57 Whig); elected Pres. pro tempore Feb. 16, 1861, March 23, 1861, July 18, 1861, Jan. 15, 1862, March 31, 1862, June 19, 1862, Feb. 18, 1863, March 4, 1863, Dec. 18, 1863, Feb. 23, 1864, April 11, 1864.

Foote, Charles Augustus (– N.Y.) April 15, 1785–Aug. 1, 1828; House 1823–25.

Foote, Ellsworth Bishop (R Conn.) Jan. 12, 1898–Jan. 18, 1977; House 1947–49.

Foote, Henry Stuart (D Miss.) Feb. 28, 1804–May 19, 1880; Senate 1847–Jan. 8, 1852; Gov. Jan. 10, 1852–Jan. 5, 1854.

Foote, Wallace Turner Jr. (R N.Y.) April 7, 1864–Dec. 17, 1910; House 1895–99.

Foraker, Joseph Benson (R Ohio) July 5, 1846–May 10, 1917; Senate 1897–1909; Gov. Jan. 11, 1886–Jan. 13, 1890.

Foran, Martin Ambrose (D Ohio) Nov. 11, 1844–June 28, 1921; House 1883–89.

Forand, Aime Joseph (D R.I.) May 23, 1895–Jan. 18, 1972; House 1937–39, 1941–61.

Forbes, Michael P. (D N.Y.) July 16, 1952– ; House 1995– (1995–99 Republican).

Ford, Aaron Lane (D Miss.) Dec. 21, 1903–July 8, 1983; House 1935–43.

Ford, George (D Ind.) Jan. 11, 1846–Aug. 30, 1917; House 1885–87.

Ford, Gerald Rudolph Jr. (R Mich.) July 14, 1913– ; House 1949–Dec. 6, 1973; House minority leader 1965–Dec. 6, 1973; Vice President Dec. 6, 1973–Aug. 9, 1974; President Aug. 9, 1974–77.

Ford, Harold Eugene (D Tenn.) (father of Harold Eugene Ford Jr.) May 20, 1945– ; House 1975–97.

Ford, Harold Eugene Jr. (D Tenn.) (son of Harold Eugene Ford) May 11, 1977– ; House 1997– .

Ford, James (J Pa.) May 4, 1783–Aug. 18, 1859; House 1829–33.

Ford, Leland Merritt (R Calif.) March 8, 1893–Nov. 27, 1965; House 1939–43.

Ford, Melbourne Haddock (D Mich.) June 30, 1849–April 20, 1891; House 1887–89, March 4–April 20, 1891.

Ford, Nicholas (G Mo.) June 21, 1833–June 18, 1897; House 1879–83.

Ford, Thomas Francis (D Calif.) Feb. 18, 1873–Dec. 26, 1958; House 1933–45.

Ford, Wendell Hampton (D Ky.) Sept. 8, 1924– ; Senate Dec. 28, 1974–99; Chrmn. Senate Rules and Administration 1987–95; Gov. Dec. 7, 1971–Dec. 28, 1974.

Ford, William David (D Mich.) Aug. 6, 1927– ; House 1965–95; Chrmn. House Post Office and Civil Service 1981–91; Chrmn. House Education and Labor 1991–95.

Ford, William Donnison (D N.Y.) 1779–Oct. 1, 1833; House 1819–21.

Fordney, Joseph Warren (R Mich.) Nov. 5, 1853–Jan. 8, 1932; House 1899–1923.

Foreman, Edgar Franklin (R N.M.) Dec. 22, 1933– ; House 1963–65 (Texas), 1969–71.

Forester, John B. (White supporter Tenn.) ?–Aug. 31, 1845; House 1833–37 (1833–35 Jacksonian).

Forker, Samuel Carr (D N.J.) March 16, 1821–Feb. 10, 1900; House 1871–73.

Forman, William St. John (D Ill.) Jan. 20, 1847–June 10, 1908; House 1889–95.

Fornance, Joseph (D Pa.) Oct. 18, 1804–Nov. 24, 1852; House 1839–43.

Fornes, Charles Vincent (D N.Y.) Jan. 22, 1844–May 22, 1929; House 1907–13.

Forney, Daniel Munroe (son of Peter Forney, uncle of William Henry Forney) (R N.C.) May 1784–Oct. 15, 1847; House 1815–18.

Forney, Peter (father of Daniel Munroe Forney, grandfather of William Henry Forney) (R N.C.) April 21, 1756–Feb. 1, 1834; House 1813–15.

Forney, William Henry (grandson of Peter Forney, nephew of Daniel Munroe Forney) (D Ala.) Nov. 9, 1823–Jan. 16, 1894; House 1875–93.

Forrest, Thomas (– Pa.) 1747–March 20, 1825; House 1819–21, Oct. 8, 1822–23.

Forrest, Uriah (– Md.) 1756–July 6, 1805; House 1793–Nov. 8, 1794; Cont. Cong. 1787.

Forrester, Elijah Lewis (D Ga.) Aug. 16, 1896–March 19, 1970; House 1951–65.

Forsyth, John (J Ga.) Oct. 22, 1780–Oct. 21, 1841; House 1813–Nov. 23, 1818 (Republican), 1823–Nov. 7, 1827 (Republican); Senate Nov. 23, 1818–Feb. 17, 1819 (Republican), Nov. 9, 1829–June 27, 1834; Gov. Nov. 7, 1827–Nov. 4, 1829 (Democratic Republican); Secy. of State July 1, 1834–March 3, 1841.

Forsythe, Albert Palaska (G Ill.) May 24, 1830–Sept. 2, 1906; House 1879–81.

Forsythe, Edwin Bell (R N.J.) Jan. 17, 1916–March 29, 1984; House Nov. 3, 1970–March 29, 1984.

Fort, Franklin William (R N.J.) March 30, 1880–June 20, 1937; House 1925–31.

Fort, Greenbury Lafayette (R Ill.) Oct. 17, 1825–Jan. 13, 1883; House 1873–81.

Fort, Tomlinson (– Ga.) July 14, 1787–May 11, 1859; House 1827–29.

Forward, Chauncey (brother of Walter Forward) (J Pa.) Feb. 4, 1793–Oct. 19, 1839; House Dec. 4, 1826–31 (Dec. 4, 1826–29 no party).

Forward, Walter (brother of Chauncey Forward) (– Pa.) Jan. 24, 1786–Nov. 24, 1852; House Oct. 8, 1822–25; Secy. of the Treasury Sept. 13, 1841–March 1, 1843.

Fosdick, Nicoll (– N.Y.) Nov. 9, 1785–May 7, 1868; House 1825–27.

Foss, Eugene Noble (brother of George Edmund Foss) (D Mass.) Sept. 24, 1858–Sept. 13, 1939; House March 22, 1910–Jan. 4, 1911; Gov. Jan. 5, 1911–Jan. 8, 1914.

Foss, Frank Herbert (R Mass.) Sept. 20, 1865–Feb. 15, 1947; House 1925–35.

Foss, George Edmund (brother of Eugene Noble Foss) (R Ill.) July 2, 1863–March 15, 1936; House 1895–1913, 1915–19.

Fossella, Vito J. (great-grandson of James O' Leary) (R NY) March 9, 1965– ; House Nov. 5, 1997– .

Foster, A. Lawrence (W N.Y.) ?–?; House 1841–43.

Foster, Abiel (F N.H.) Aug. 8, 1735–Feb. 6, 1806; House 1789–91 (no party), 1795–1803; Cont. Cong. 1783–85.

Foster, Addison Gardner (R Wash.) Jan. 28, 1837–Jan. 16, 1917; Senate 1899–1905.

Foster, Charles (R Ohio) April 12, 1828–Jan. 9, 1904; House 1871–79; Gov. Jan. 12, 1880–Jan. 14, 1884; Secy. of the Treasury Feb. 25, 1891–March 6, 1893.

Foster, David Johnson (R Vt.) June 27, 1857–March 21, 1912; House 1901–March 21, 1912.

Foster, Dwight (brother of Theodore Foster) (F Mass.) Dec. 7, 1757–April 29, 1823; House 1793–June 6, 1800 (no party); Senate June 6, 1800–March 2, 1803.

Foster, Ephraim Hubbard (W Tenn.) Sept. 17, 1794–Sept. 6, 1854; Senate Sept. 17, 1838–39; Oct. 17, 1843–45.

Foster, George Peter (D Ill.) April 3, 1858–Nov. 11, 1928; House 1899–1905.

Foster, Henry Allen (D N.Y.) May 7, 1800–May 11, 1889; House 1837–39; Senate Nov. 30, 1844–Jan. 27, 1845.

Foster, Henry Donnel (cousin of John Cabell Breckinridge) (D Pa.) Dec. 19, 1808–Oct. 16, 1880; House 1843–47, 1871–73.

Foster, Israel Moore (R Ohio) Jan. 12, 1873–June 10, 1950; House 1919–25.

Foster, John Hopkins (R Ind.) Jan. 31, 1862–Sept. 5, 1917; House May 16, 1905–09.

Foster, Lafayette Sabine (R Conn.) Nov. 22, 1806–Sept. 19, 1880; Senate 1855–67; elected Pres. pro tempore March 7, 1865.

Foster, Martin David (D Ill.) Sept. 3, 1861–Oct. 20, 1919; House 1907–19.

Foster, Murphy James (cousin of Jared Young Sanders) (D La.) Jan. 12, 1849–June 12, 1921; Senate 1901–13; Gov. May 16, 1892–May 21, 1900 (Anti-Lottery Democrat).

Foster, Nathaniel Greene (AP Ga.) Aug. 25, 1809–Oct. 19, 1869; House 1855–57 (affiliated with the Democratic Party).

Foster, Stephen Clark (R Maine) Dec. 24, 1799–Oct. 5, 1872; House 1857–61.

Foster, Theodore (brother of Dwight Foster) (F R.I.) April 29, 1752–Jan. 13, 1828; Senate June 7, 1790–1803.

Foster, Thomas Flournoy (W Ga.) Nov. 23, 1790–Sept. 14, 1848; House 1829–35 (no party), 1841–43.

Foster, Wilder De Ayr (R Mich.) Jan. 8, 1819–Sept. 20, 1873; House Dec. 4, 1871–Sept. 20, 1873.

Fouke, Philip Bond (D Ill.) Jan. 23, 1818–Oct. 3, 1876; House 1859–63.

Foulkes, George Ernest (D Mich.) Dec. 25, 1878–Dec. 13, 1960; House 1933–35.

Foulkrod, William Walker (R Pa.) Nov. 22, 1846–Nov. 13, 1910; House 1907–Nov. 13, 1910.

Fountain, Lawrence H. (D N.C.) April 23, 1913– ; House 1953–83.

Fowler, Charles Newell (R N.J.) Nov. 2, 1852–May 27, 1932; House 1895–1911.

Fowler, Hiram Robert (D Ill.) Feb. 7, 1851–Jan. 5, 1926; House 1911–15.

Fowler, John (R Ky.) 1755–Aug. 22, 1840; House 1797–1807.

Fowler, John Edgar (P N.C.) Sept. 8, 1866–July 4, 1930; House 1897–99.

Fowler, Joseph Smith (U Tenn.) Aug. 31, 1820–April 1, 1902; Senate July 24, 1866–71.

Fowler, Orin (W Mass.) July 19, 1791–Sept. 3, 1852; House 1849–Sept. 3, 1852.

Fowler, Samuel (grandfather of Samuel Fowler, below) (J N.J.) Oct. 30, 1779–Feb. 20, 1844; House 1833–37.

Fowler, Samuel (grandson of Samuel Fowler, above) (D N.J.) March 22, 1851–March 17, 1919; House 1889–93.

Fowler, Tillie (R Fla.) Dec. 23, 1942– ; House 1993– .

Fowler, Wyche Jr. (D Ga.) Oct. 6, 1940– ; House April 6, 1977–87; Senate 1987–93.

Fox, Andrew Fuller (D Miss.) April 26, 1849–Aug. 29, 1926; House 1897–1903.

Fox, John (D N.Y.) June 30, 1835–Jan. 17, 1914; House 1867–71.

Fox, Jon D. (R Pa.) April 22, 1947– ; House 1995–99.

Frahm, Sheila (R Kan.) March 22, 1945– ; Senate June 11, 1996–Nov. 27, 1996.

France, Joseph Irvin (R Md.) Oct. 11, 1873–Jan. 26, 1939; Senate 1917–23.

Franchot, Richard (R N.Y.) June 2, 1816–Nov. 23, 1875; House 1861–63.

Francis, George Blinn (R N.Y.) Aug. 12, 1883–May 20, 1967; House 1917–19.

Francis, John Brown (grandson of John Brown of R.I.) (W R.I.) May 31, 1791–Aug. 9, 1864; Senate Jan. 25, 1844–45; Gov. May 1, 1833–May 2, 1838 (Democrat).

Francis, William Bates (D Ohio) Oct. 25, 1860–Dec. 5, 1954; House 1911–15.

Frank, Augustus (nephew of William Patterson of N.Y. and George Washington Patterson) (R N.Y.) July 17, 1826–April 29, 1895; House 1859–65.

Frank, Barney (D Mass.) March 31, 1940– ; House 1981– .

Frank, Nathan (R Mo.) Feb. 23, 1852–April 5, 1931; House 1889–91.

Frankhauser, William Horace (R Mich.) March 5, 1863–May 9, 1921; House March 4–May 9, 1921.

Franklin, Benjamin Joseph (D Mo.) March 1839–May 18, 1898; House 1875–79; Gov. (Ariz. Terr.) April 18, 1896–July 29, 1897.

Franklin, Jesse (brother of Meshack Franklin) (R N.C.) March 24, 1760–Aug. 31, 1823; House 1795–97 (no party); Senate 1799–1805, 1807–13; elected Pres. pro tempore March 10, 1804; Gov. Dec. 7, 1820–Dec. 7, 1821 (Democratic Republican).

Franklin, John Rankin (W Md.) May 6, 1820–Jan. 11, 1878; House 1853–55.

Franklin, Meshack (brother of Jesse Franklin) (R N.C.) 1772–Dec. 18, 1839; House 1807–15.

Franklin, William Webster (R Miss.) Dec. 13, 1941– ; House 1983–87.

Franks, Bob (R N.J.) Sept. 21, 1951– ; House 1993– .

Franks, Gary (R Conn.) Feb. 9, 1953– ; House 1991–97.

Fraser, Donald MacKay (DFL Minn.) Feb. 20, 1924– ; House 1963–79.

Frazer, Victor O. (I V.I.) May 24, 1943– ; House (Delegate) 1995–97.

Frazier, James Beriah (father of James Beriah Frazier Jr.) (D Tenn.) Oct. 18, 1856–March 28, 1937; Senate March 21, 1905–11; Gov. Jan. 19, 1903–March 21, 1905.

Frazier, James Beriah Jr. (son of James Beriah Frazier) (D Tenn.) June 23, 1890–Oct. 30, 1978; House 1949–63.

Frazier, Lynn Joseph (R N.D.) Dec. 21, 1874–Jan. 11, 1947; Senate 1923–41; Gov. Jan. 3, 1917–Nov. 23, 1921.

Frear, James Archibald (R Wis.) Oct. 24, 1861–May 28, 1939; House 1913–35.

Frear, Joseph Allen Jr. (D Del.) March 7, 1903–Jan. 15, 1993; Senate 1949–61.

Frederick, Benjamin Todd (D Iowa) Oct. 5, 1834–Nov. 3, 1903; House 1885–87.

Fredericks, John Donnan (R Calif.) Sept. 10, 1869–Aug. 26, 1945; House May 1, 1923–27.

Free, Arthur Monroe (R Calif.) Jan. 15, 1879–April 1, 1953; House 1921–33.

Freedley, John (W Pa.) May 22, 1793–Dec. 8, 1851; House 1847–51.

Freeman, Chapman (R Pa.) Oct. 8, 1832–March 22, 1904; House 1875–79.

Freeman, James Crawford (R Ga.) April 1, 1820–Sept. 3, 1885; House 1873–75.

Freeman, John D. (U Miss.) ?–Jan. 17, 1886; House 1851–53.

Freeman, Jonathan (uncle of Nathaniel Freeman Jr.) (F N.H.) March 21, 1745–Aug. 20, 1808; House 1797–1801.

Freeman, Nathaniel Jr. (nephew of Jonathan Freeman) (R Mass.) May 1, 1766–Aug. 22, 1800; House 1795–99 (1795–97 Federalist).

Freeman, Richard Patrick (R Conn.) April 24, 1869–July 8, 1944; House 1915–33.

Freer, Romeo Hoyt (R W.Va.) Nov. 9, 1846–May 9, 1913; House 1899–1901.

Frelinghuysen, Frederick (father of Theodore Frelinghuysen, great-uncle of Frederick Theodore Frelinghuysen, great-great-great-grandfather of Peter Hood Ballantine Frelinghuysen Jr.) (– N.J.) April 13, 1753–April 13, 1804; Senate 1793–Nov. 12, 1796; Cont. Cong. 1779.

Frelinghuysen, Frederick Theodore (nephew and adopted son of Theodore Frelinghuysen, great-nephew of Frederick Frelinghuysen, uncle of Joseph Sherman Frelinghuysen, great-grandfather of Peter Hood Ballantine Frelinghuysen Jr.) (R N.J.) Aug. 4, 1817–May 20, 1885; Senate Nov. 12, 1866–69, 1871–77; Secy. of State Dec. 19, 1881–March 6, 1885.

Frelinghuysen, Joseph Sherman (nephew of Frederick Theodore Frelinghuysen, cousin of Peter Hood Ballantine Frelinghuysen Jr.) (R N.J.) March 12, 1869–Feb. 8, 1948; Senate 1917–23.

Frelinghuysen, Peter Hood Ballantine Jr. (cousin of Joseph Sherman Frelinghuysen, great-grandson of Frederick Theodore Frelinghuysen, great-great-nephew of Theodore Frelinghuysen, great-great-great-grandson of Frederick Frelinghuysen) (R N.J.) Jan. 17, 1916– ; House 1953–75.

Frelinghuysen, Rodney (son of Peter Hood Ballantine Frelinghuysen) (R N.J.) April 29, 1946– ; House 1995– .

Frelinghuysen, Theodore (son of Frederick Frelinghuysen, uncle and adoptive father of Frederick Theodore Frelinghuysen, great-great-uncle of Peter Hood Ballantine Frelinghuysen Jr.) (N.J.) March 28, 1787–April 12, 1862; Senate 1829–35.

Fremont, John Charles (son-in-law of Thomas Hart Benton) (D Calif.) Jan. 21, 1813–July 13, 1890; Senate Sept. 9, 1850–51; Gov. (Ariz. Terr.) 1878–81.

French, Burton Lee (R Idaho) Aug. 1, 1875–Sept. 12, 1954; House 1903–09, 1911–15, 1917–33.

French, Carlos (D Conn.) Aug. 6, 1835–April 14, 1903; House 1887–89.

French, Ezra Bartlett (R Maine) Sept. 23, 1810–April 24, 1880; House 1859–61.

French, John Robert (R N.C.) May 28, 1819–Oct. 2, 1890; House July 6, 1868–69.

French, Richard (D Ky.) June 20, 1792–May 1, 1854; House 1835–37 (Jacksonian), 1843–45, 1847–49.

Frenzel, William Eldridge (R Minn.) July 31, 1928– ; House 1971–91.

Frey, Louis Jr. (R Fla.) Jan. 11, 1934– ; House 1969–79.

Frey, Oliver Walter (D Pa.) Sept. 7, 1887–Aug. 26, 1939; House Nov. 7, 1933–39.

Frick, Henry (W Pa.) March 17, 1795–March 1, 1844; House 1843–March 1, 1844.

Friedel, Samuel Nathaniel (D Md.) April 18, 1898–March 21, 1979; House 1953–71; Chrmn. House Administration 1968–71.

Fries, Frank William (D Ill.) May 1, 1893–July 17, 1980; House 1937–41.

Fries, George (D Ohio) 1799–Nov. 13, 1866; House 1845–49.

Frisa, Daniel (R N.Y.) April 27, 1955– ; House 1995–97.

Frist, Bill (R Tenn.) Feb. 22, 1952– ; Senate 1995– .

Froehlich, Harold Vernon (R Wis.) May 12, 1932– ; House 1973–75.

Fromentin, Eligius (R La.) ?–Oct. 6, 1822; Senate 1813–19.

Frost, Joel (– N.Y.) ?–Sept. 11, 1827; House 1823–25.

Frost, Jonas Martin (D Texas) Jan. 1, 1942– ; House 1979– .

Frost, Richard Graham (D Mo.) Dec. 29, 1851–Feb. 1, 1900; House 1879–March 2, 1883.

Frost, Rufus Smith (R Mass.) July 18, 1826–March 6, 1894; House 1875–July 28, 1876.

Frothingham, Louis Adams (R Mass.) July 13, 1871–Aug. 23, 1928; House 1921–Aug. 23, 1928.

Fry, Jacob Jr. (D Pa.) June 10, 1802–Nov. 28, 1866; House 1835–39 (1835–37 Jacksonian).

Fry, Joseph Jr. (J Pa.) Aug. 4, 1781–Aug. 15, 1860; House 1827–31 (1827–29 no party).

Frye, William Pierce (grandfather of Wallace Humphrey White Jr.) (R Maine) Sept. 2, 1830–Aug. 8, 1911; House 1871–March 17, 1881; Senate March 18, 1881–Aug. 8, 1911; elected Pres. pro tempore Feb. 7, 1896, March 7, 1901, Dec. 5, 1907.

Fugate, Thomas Bacon (D Va.) April 10, 1899–Sept. 22, 1980; House 1949–53.

Fulbright, James Franklin (D Mo.) Jan. 24, 1877–April 5, 1948; House 1923–25, 1927–29, 1931–33.

Fulbright, James William (D Ark.) April 9, 1905–Feb. 9, 1995; House 1943–45; Senate 1945–Dec. 31, 1974; Chrmn. Senate Banking and Currency 1955–59; Chrmn. Senate Foreign Relations 1959–75.

Fulkerson, Abram (D Va.) May 13, 1834–Dec. 17, 1902; House 1881–83 (elected as a Readjuster Democrat).

Fulkerson, Frank Ballard (R Mo.) March 5, 1866–Aug. 30, 1936; House 1905–07.

Fuller, Alvan Tufts (R Mass.) Feb. 27, 1878–April 30, 1958; House 1917–Jan. 5, 1921 (1917–19 Independent Republican); Gov. Jan. 8, 1925–Jan. 3, 1929.

Fuller, Benoni Stinson (D Ind.) Nov. 13, 1825–April 14, 1903; House 1875–79.

Fuller, Charles Eugene (R Ill.) March 31, 1849–June 25, 1926; House 1903–13, 1915–June 25, 1926.

Fuller, Claude Albert (D Ark.) Jan. 20, 1876–Jan. 8, 1968; House 1929–39.

Fuller, George (D Pa.) Nov. 7, 1802–Nov. 24, 1888; House Dec. 2, 1844–45.

Fuller, Hawden Carlton (R N.Y.) Aug. 28, 1895–Jan. 29, 1990; House Nov. 2, 1943–49.

Fuller, Henry Mills (W Pa.) Jan. 3, 1820–Dec. 26, 1860; House 1851–53, 1855–57.

Fuller, Philo Case (W N.Y.) Aug. 14, 1787–Aug. 16, 1855; House 1833–Sept. 2, 1836 (1833–35 Anti-Mason).

Fuller, Thomas James Duncan (D Maine) March 17, 1808–Feb. 13, 1876; House 1849–57.

Fuller, Timothy (R Mass.) July 11, 1778–Oct. 1, 1835; House 1817–25.

Fuller, William Elijah (R Iowa) March 30, 1846–April 23, 1918; House 1885–89.

Fuller, William Kendall (J N.Y.) Nov. 24, 1792–Nov. 11, 1883; House 1833–37.

Fullerton, David (uncle of David Fullerton Robison) (– Pa.) Oct. 4, 1772–Feb. 1, 1843; House 1819–May 15, 1820.

Fulmer, Hampton Pitts (husband of Willa Lybrand Fulmer) (D S.C.) June 23, 1875–Oct. 19, 1944; House 1921–Oct. 19, 1944.

Fulmer, Willa Lybrand (widow of Hampton Pitts Fulmer) (D S.C.) Feb. 3, 1884–May 13, 1968; House Nov. 7, 1944–45.

Fulton, Andrew Steele (brother of John Hall Fulton) (W Va.) Sept. 29, 1800–Nov. 22, 1884; House 1847–49.

Fulton, Charles William (brother of Elmer Lincoln Fulton) (R Ore.) Aug. 24, 1853–Jan. 27, 1918; Senate 1903–09.

Fulton, Elmer Lincoln (brother of Charles William Fulton) (D Okla.) April 22, 1865–Oct. 4, 1939; House Nov. 16, 1907–09.

Fulton, James Grove (R Pa.) March 1, 1903–Oct. 6, 1971; House 1945–Oct. 6, 1971.

Fulton, John Hall (brother of Andrew Steele Fulton) (J Va.) ?–Jan. 28, 1836; House 1833–35.

Fulton, Richard Harmon (D Tenn.) Jan. 27, 1927– ; House 1963–Aug. 14, 1975.

Fulton, William Savin (D Ark.) June 2, 1795–Aug. 15, 1844; Senate Sept. 18, 1836–Aug. 15, 1844; Gov. (Ark. Terr.) 1835–36.

Funderburk, David (R N.C.) April 28, 1944– ; House 1995–97.

Funk, Benjamin Franklin (father of Frank Hamilton Funk) (R Ill.) Oct. 17, 1838–Feb. 14, 1909; House 1893–95.

Funk, Frank Hamilton (son of Benjamin Franklin Funk) (R Ill.) April 5, 1869–Nov. 24, 1940; House 1921–27.

Funston, Edward Hogue (R Kan.) Sept. 16, 1836–Sept. 10, 1911; House March 21, 1884–Aug. 2, 1894.

Fuqua, Don (D Fla.) Aug. 20, 1933– ; House 1963–87; Chrmn. House Science and Technology 1979–87.

Furcolo, Foster (D Mass.) July 29, 1911– ; House 1949–Sept. 30, 1952; Gov. Jan. 3, 1957–Jan. 5, 1961.

Furlong, Robert Grant (D Pa.) Jan. 4, 1886–March 19, 1973; House 1943–45.

Furlow, Allen John (R Minn.) Nov. 9, 1890–Jan. 29, 1954; House 1925–29.

Furse, Elizabeth (D Ore.) Oct. 13, 1936– ; House 1993–99.

Fuster, Jaime B. (D P.R.) Jan. 12, 1941– ; House (Res. Comm.) 1985–March 4, 1992.

Fyan, Robert Washington (D Mo.) March 11, 1835–July 28, 1896; House 1883–85, 1891–95.

G

Gabaldon, Isauro (Nat. P.I.) Dec. 8, 1875–Dec. 21, 1942; House (Res. Comm.) 1920–July 16, 1928.

Gage, Joshua (R Mass.) Aug. 7, 1763–Jan. 24, 1831; House 1817–19.

Gahn, Harry Conrad (R Ohio) April 26, 1880–Nov. 2, 1962; House 1921–23.

Gaillard, John (uncle of Theodore Gaillard Hunt) (R S.C.) Sept. 5, 1765–Feb. 26, 1826; Senate Dec. 6, 1804–Feb. 26, 1826; elected Pres. pro tempore Feb. 28, 1810, April 17, 1810, April 18, 1814, Nov. 25, 1814, March 6, 1817, March 31, 1818, Jan. 25, 1820, Feb. 1, 1822, Feb. 19, 1823, May 21, 1824, March 9, 1825.

Gaines, John Pollard (W Ky.) Sept. 22, 1795–Dec. 9, 1857; House 1847–49; Gov. (Ore. Terr.) 1850–53.

Gaines, John Wesley (D Tenn.) Aug. 24, 1860–July 4, 1926; House 1897–1909.

Gaines, Joseph Holt (R W.Va.) Sept. 3, 1864–April 12, 1951; House 1901–11.

Gaines, William Embre (R Va.) Aug. 30, 1844–May 4, 1912; House 1887–89.

Gaither, Nathan (J Ky.) Sept. 15, 1788–Aug. 12, 1862; House 1829–33.

Galbraith, John (D Pa.) Aug. 2, 1794–June 15, 1860; House 1833–37 (Jacksonian), 1839–41.

Gale, George (father of Levin Gale) (– Md.) June 3, 1756–Jan. 2, 1815; House 1789–91.

Gale, Levin (son of George Gale) (– Md.) April 24, 1784–Dec. 18, 1834; House 1827–29.

Gale, Richard Pillsbury (R Minn.) Oct. 30, 1900–Dec. 4, 1973; House 1941–45.

Galifianakis, Nick (D N.C.) July 22, 1928– ; House 1967–73.

Gallagher, Cornelius Edward (D N.J.) March 2, 1921– ; House 1959–73.

Gallagher, James A. (R Pa.) Jan. 16, 1869–Dec. 8, 1957; House 1943–45, 1947–49.

Gallagher, Thomas (D Ill.) July 6, 1850–Feb. 24, 1930; House 1909–21.

Gallagher, William James (D Minn.) May 13, 1875–Aug. 13, 1946; House 1945–Aug. 13, 1946.

Gallatin, Albert (– Pa.) Jan. 29, 1761–Aug. 12, 1849; Senate Dec. 2, 1793–Feb. 28, 1794; House 1795–1801; Secy. of the Treasury May 14, 1801–Feb. 8, 1814.

Gallegly, Elton William (R Calif.) March 7, 1944– ; House 1987– .

Gallegos, José Manuel (D N.M.) Oct. 30, 1815–April 21, 1875; House (Terr. Del.) 1853–July 23, 1856, 1871–73.

Gallinger, Jacob Harold (R N.H.) March 28, 1837–Aug. 17, 1918; House 1885–89; Senate 1891–Aug. 17, 1918; Senate minority leader 1913–Aug. 17, 1918; elected Pres. pro tempore Feb. 12, 1912 (to serve Feb. 12–Feb. 14, April 26–April 27, May 7, July 6–July 31, Aug. 12–Aug. 26, 1912; Dec. 16, 1912–Jan. 4, 1913; Jan. 19–Feb. 1, Feb. 16–March 3, 1913).

Gallivan, James Ambrose (D Mass.) Oct. 22, 1866–April 3, 1928; House April 7, 1914–April 3, 1928.

Gallo, Dean Anderson (R N.J.) Nov. 23, 1935–Nov. 6, 1994; House 1985–Nov. 6, 1994.

Galloway, Samuel (R Ohio) March 20, 1811–April 5, 1872; House 1855–57.

Gallup, Albert (D N.Y.) Jan. 30, 1796–Nov. 5, 1851; House 1837–39.

Gamble, James (D Pa.) Jan. 28, 1809–Feb. 22, 1883; House 1851–55.

Gamble, John Rankin (brother of Robert Jackson Gamble, uncle of Ralph Abernethy Gamble) (R S.D.) Jan. 15, 1848–Aug. 14, 1891; House March 4–Aug. 14, 1891.

Gamble, Ralph Abernethy (son of Robert Jackson Gamble, nephew of John Rankin Gamble) (R N.Y.) May 6, 1885–March 4, 1959; House Nov. 2, 1937–57.

Gamble, Robert Jackson (brother of John Rankin Gamble, father of Ralph Abernethy Gamble) (R S.D.) Feb. 7, 1851–Sept. 22, 1924; House 1895–97, 1899–1901; Senate 1901–13.

Gamble, Roger Lawson (W Ga.) 1787–Dec. 20, 1847; House 1833–35 (Jacksonian); 1841–43.

Gambrell, David Henry (D Ga.) Dec. 20, 1929– ; Senate Feb. 1, 1971–Nov. 7, 1972.

Gambrill, Stephen Warfield (D Md.) Oct. 2, 1873–Dec. 19, 1938; House Nov. 4, 1924–Dec. 19, 1938.

Gammage, Robert Alton (D Texas) March 13, 1938– ; House 1977–79.

Gandy, Harry Luther (D S.D.) Aug. 13, 1881–Aug. 15, 1957; House 1915–21.

Ganly, James Vincent (D N.Y.) Sept. 13. 1878–Sept. 7, 1923; House 1919–21, March 4–Sept. 7, 1923.

Gannett, Barzillai (R Mass.) June 17, 1764–1832; House 1809–12.

Ganske, Greg (R Iowa) March 31, 1949– ; House 1995– .

Ganson, John (D N.Y.) Jan. 1, 1818–Sept. 28, 1874; House 1863–65.

Gantz, Martin Kissinger (D Ohio) Jan. 28, 1862–Feb. 10, 1916; House 1891–93.

Garber, Harvey Cable (D Ohio) July 6, 1866–March 23, 1938; House 1903–07.

Garber, Jacob Aaron (R Va.) Jan. 25, 1879–Dec. 2, 1953; House 1929–31.

Garber, Milton Cline (R Okla.) Nov. 30, 1867–Sept. 12, 1948; House 1923–33.

Garcia, Robert (D N.Y.) Jan. 9, 1933– ; House Feb. 21, 1978–Jan. 7, 1990 (in Feb. 21, 1978, special election, registered as a Democrat but elected as a Republican-Liberal).

Gard, Warren (D Ohio) July 2, 1873–Nov. 1, 1929; House 1913–21.

Gardenier, Barent (F N.Y.) ?–Jan. 10, 1822; House 1807–11.

Gardner, Augustus Peabody (uncle of Henry Cabot Lodge Jr. and John Davis Lodge) (R Mass.) Nov. 5, 1865–Jan. 14, 1918; House Nov. 3, 1902–May 15, 1917.

Gardner, Edward Joseph (D Ohio) Aug. 7, 1898–Dec. 7, 1950; House 1945–47.

Gardner, Francis (R N.H.) Dec. 27, 1771–June 25, 1835; House 1807–09.

Gardner, Frank (D Ind.) May 8, 1872–Feb. 1, 1937; House 1923–29.

Gardner, Gideon (R Mass.) May 30, 1759–March 22, 1832; House 1809–11.

Gardner, James Carson (R N.C.) April 8, 1933– ; House 1967–69.

Gardner, John James (R N.J.) Oct. 17, 1845–Feb. 7, 1921; House 1893–1913.

Gardner, Mills (R Ohio) Jan. 30, 1830–Feb. 20, 1910; House 1877–79.

Gardner, Obadiah (D Maine) Sept. 13, 1852–July 24, 1938; Senate Sept. 23, 1911–13.

Gardner, Washington (R Mich.) Feb. 16, 1845–March 31, 1928; House 1899–1911.

Garfield, James Abram (R Ohio) Nov. 19, 1831–Sept. 19, 1881; House 1863–Nov. 8, 1880; President March 4–Sept. 19, 1881.

Garfielde, Selucius (R Wash.) Dec. 8, 1822–April 13, 1881; House (Terr. Del.) 1869–73.

Garland, Augustus Hill (D Ark.) June 11, 1832–Jan. 26, 1899; Senate 1877–March 6, 1885; Gov. Nov. 12, 1874–Jan. 11, 1877; Atty. General March 6, 1885–March 5, 1889.

Garland, David Shepherd (R Va.) Sept. 27, 1769–Oct. 7, 1841; House Jan. 17, 1810–11.

Garland, James (C Va.) June 6, 1791–Aug. 8, 1885; House 1835–41 (1835–37 Jacksonian, 1837–39 Democrat).

Garland, Mahlon Morris (R Pa.) May 4, 1856–Nov. 19, 1920; House 1915–Nov. 19, 1920.

Garland, Peter Adams (R Maine) June 16, 1923– ; House 1961–63.

Garland, Rice (W La.) about 1795–1861; House April 28, 1834–July 21, 1840 (April 28, 1834–35 no party, 1835–37 Anti-Jacksonian).

Garmatz, Edward Alexander (D Md.) Feb. 7, 1903–July 22, 1986; House July 15, 1947–73; Chrmn. House Merchant Marine and Fisheries 1966–73.

Garn, Edwin Jacob "Jake" (R Utah) Oct. 12, 1932– ; Senate Dec. 21, 1974–93; Chrmn. Senate Banking, Housing, and Urban Affairs 1981–87.

Garner, Alfred Buckwalter (R Pa.) March 4, 1873–July 30, 1930; House 1909–11.

Garner, John Nance (D Texas) Nov. 22, 1868–Nov. 7, 1967; House 1903–33; House minority leader 1929–31; Speaker Dec. 7, 1931–33; Vice President 1933–Jan. 20, 1941.

Garnett, James Mercer (brother of Robert Selden Garnett, grandfather of Muscoe Russell Hunter Garnett, cousin of Charles Fenton Mercer) (R Va.) June 8, 1770–April 23, 1843; House 1805–09.

Garnett, Muscoe Russell Hunter (grandson of James Mercer Garnett) (D Va.) July 25, 1821–Feb. 14, 1864; House Dec. 1, 1856–61.

Garnett, Robert Selden (brother of James Mercer Garnett, cousin of Charles Fenton Mercer) (R Va.) April 26, 1789–Aug. 15, 1840; House 1817–27.

Garnsey, Daniel Greene (– N.Y.) June 17, 1779–May 11, 1851; House 1825–29.

Garrett, Abraham Ellison (D Tenn.) March 6, 1830–Feb. 14, 1907; House 1871–73.

Garrett, Clyde Leonard (D Texas) Dec. 16, 1885–Dec. 18, 1959; House 1937–41.

Garrett, Daniel Edward (D Texas) April 28, 1869–Dec. 13, 1932; House 1913–15, 1917–19, 1921–Dec. 13, 1932.

Garrett, Finis James (D Tenn.) Aug. 26, 1875–May 25, 1956; House 1905–29; House minority leader 1923–29.

Garrison, Daniel (– N.J.) April 3, 1782–Feb. 13, 1851; House 1823–27.

Garrison, George Tankard (D Va.) Jan. 14, 1835–Nov. 14, 1889; House 1881–83, March 20, 1884–85.

Garrow, Nathaniel (– N.Y.) April 25, 1780–March 3, 1841; House 1827–29.

Garth, William Willis (D Ala.) Oct. 28, 1828–Feb. 25, 1912; House 1877–79.

Gartner, Fred Christian (R Pa.) March 14, 1896–Sept. 1, 1972; House 1939–41.

Gartrell, Lucius Jeremiah (uncle of Choice Boswell Randell) (D Ga.) Jan. 7, 1821–April 7, 1891; House 1857–Jan. 23, 1861.

Garvin, William Swan (D Pa.) July 25, 1806–Feb. 20, 1883; House 1845–47.

Gary, Frank Boyd (D S.C.) March 9, 1860–Dec. 7, 1922; Senate March 6, 1908–09.

Gary, Julian Vaughan (D Va.) Feb. 25, 1892–Sept. 6, 1973; House March 6, 1945–65.

Gasque, Allard Henry (husband of Elizabeth "Bessie" Hawley Gasque) (D S.C.) March 8, 1873–June 17, 1938; House 1923–June 17, 1938.

Gasque, Elizabeth "Bessie" Hawley (widow of Allard Henry Gasque) (Mrs. A. J. Van Exem) (D S.C.) Feb. 26, 1896–Nov. 2, 1989; House Sept. 13, 1938–39.

Gassaway, Percy Lee (D Okla.) Aug. 30, 1885–May 15, 1937; House 1935–37.

Gaston, Athelston (D Pa.) April 24, 1838–Sept. 23, 1907; House 1899–1901.

Gaston, William (F N.C.) Sept. 19, 1778–Jan. 23, 1844; House 1813–17.

Gates, Seth Merrill (W N.Y.) Oct. 10, 1800–Aug. 24, 1877; House 1839–43.

Gathings, Ezekiel Candler (D Ark.) Nov. 10, 1903–May 2, 1979; House 1939–69.

Gatlin, Alfred Moore (– N.C.) April 20, 1790–?; House 1823–25.

Gause, Lucien Coatsworth (D Ark.) Dec. 25, 1836–Nov. 5, 1880; House 1875–79.

Gavagan, Joseph Andrew (D N.Y.) Aug. 20, 1892–Oct. 18, 1968; House Nov. 5, 1929–Dec. 30, 1943.

Gavin, Leon Harry (R Pa.) Feb. 25, 1893–Sept. 15, 1963; House 1943–Sept. 15, 1963.

Gay, Edward James (grandfather of Edward James Gay, below) (D La.) Feb. 3, 1816–May 30, 1889; House 1885–May 30, 1889.

Gay, Edward James (grandson of Edward James Gay, above) (D La.) May 5, 1878–Dec. 1, 1952; Senate Nov. 6, 1918–21.

Gaydos, Joseph Matthew (D Pa.) July 3, 1926– ; House Nov. 5, 1968–93.

Gayle, John (W Ala.) Sept. 11, 1792–July 21, 1859; House 1847–49; Gov. Nov. 26, 1831–Nov. 21, 1835 (Democrat).

Gayle, June Ward (D Ky.) Feb. 22, 1865–Aug. 5, 1942; House Jan. 15, 1900–01.

Gaylord, James Madison (– Ohio) May 29, 1811–June 14, 1874; House 1851–53.

Gazlay, James William (– Ohio) July 23, 1784–June 8, 1874; House 1823–25.

Gear, John Henry (R Iowa) April 7, 1825–July 14, 1900; House 1887–91, 1893–95; Senate 1895–July 14, 1900; Gov. Jan. 17, 1878–Jan. 12, 1882.

Gearhart, Bertrand Wesley (R Calif.) May 31, 1890–Oct. 11, 1955; House 1935–49.

Gearin, John McDermeid (D Ore.) Aug. 15, 1851–Nov. 12, 1930; Senate Dec. 13, 1905–Jan. 23, 1907.

Geary, Thomas J. (D Calif.) Jan. 18, 1854–July 6, 1929; House Dec. 9, 1890–95.

Gebhard, John (– N.Y.) Feb. 22, 1782–Jan. 3, 1854; House 1821–23.

Geddes, George Washington (D Ohio) July 16, 1824–Nov. 9, 1892; House 1879–87.

Geddes, James (F N.Y.) July 22, 1763–Aug. 19, 1838; House 1813–15.

Geelan, James Patrick (D Conn.) Aug. 11, 1901–Aug. 10, 1982; House 1945–47.

Gehrmann, Bernard John (Prog. Wis.) Feb. 13, 1880–July 12, 1958; House 1935–43.

Geissenhainer, Jacob Augustus (D N.J.) Aug. 28, 1839–July 20, 1917; House 1889–95.

Gejdenson, Samuel (D Conn.) May 20, 1948– ; House 1981– .

Gekas, George William (R Pa.) April 14, 1930– ; House 1983– .

Gensman, Lorraine Michael (R Okla.) Aug. 26, 1878–May 27, 1954; House 1921–23.

Gentry, Brady Preston (D Texas) March 25, 1896–Nov. 9, 1966; House 1953–57.

Gentry, Meredith Poindexter (W Tenn.) Sept. 15, 1809–Nov. 2, 1866; House 1839–43, 1845–53.

George, Henry Jr. (D N.Y.) Nov. 3, 1862–Nov. 14, 1916; House 1911–15.

George, James Zachariah (D Miss.) Oct. 20, 1826–Aug. 14, 1897; Senate 1881–Aug. 14, 1897.

George, Melvin Clark (R Ore.) May 13, 1849–Feb. 22, 1933; House 1881–85.

George, Myron Virgil (R Kan.) Jan. 6, 1900–April 11, 1972; House Nov. 7, 1950–59.

George, Newell Adolphus (D Kan.) Sept. 24, 1904–Oct. 22, 1992; House 1959–61.

George, Walter Franklin (D Ga.) Jan. 29, 1878–Aug. 4, 1957; Senate Nov. 22, 1922–57; Chrmn. Senate Finance 1949–53; elected Pres. pro tempore Jan. 5, 1955; Chrmn. Senate Foreign Relations 1955–57.

Gephardt, Richard A. (D Mo.) Jan. 31, 1941– ; House 1977– ; House majority leader June 14, 1989–95; House minority leader 1995– .

Geran, Elmer Hendrickson (D N.J.) Oct. 24, 1875–Jan. 12, 1954; House 1923–25.

Geren, Peter (D Texas) Jan. 29, 1952– ; House Sept. 20, 1989–97.

Gerlach, Charles Lewis (R Pa.) Sept. 14, 1895–May 5, 1947; House 1939–May 5, 1947.

German, Obadiah (R N.Y.) April 22, 1766–Sept. 24, 1842; Senate 1809–15.

Gernerd, Fred Benjamin (R Pa.) Nov. 22, 1879–Aug. 7, 1948; House 1921–23.

Gerry, Elbridge (great-grandfather of Peter Goelet Gerry, grandfather of Elbridge Gerry, below) (– Mass.) July 17, 1744–Nov. 23, 1814; House 1789–93; Cont. Cong. 1776–80, 1783–85; Gov. June 2, 1810–June 5, 1812 (Democratic Republican); Vice President 1813–Nov. 23, 1814 (Democratic Republican).

Gerry, Elbridge (grandson of Elbridge Gerry, above) (D Maine) Dec. 6, 1813–April 10, 1886; House 1849–51.

Gerry, James (D Pa.) Aug. 14, 1796–July 19, 1873; House 1839–43.

Gerry, Peter Goelet (great-grandson of Elbridge Gerry) (D R.I.) Sept. 18, 1879–Oct. 31, 1957; House 1913–15; Senate 1917–29, 1935–47.

Gest, William Harrison (R Ill.) Jan. 7, 1838–Aug. 9, 1912; House 1887–91.

Gettys, Thomas Smithwick (D S.C.) June 19, 1912– ; House Nov. 3, 1964–Dec. 31, 1974.

Getz, James Lawrence (D Pa.) Sept. 14, 1821–Dec. 25, 1891; House 1867–73.

Geyer, Henry Sheffie (W Mo.) Dec. 9, 1790–March 5, 1859; Senate 1851–57.

Geyer, Lee Edward (D Calif.) Sept. 9, 1888–Oct. 11, 1941; House 1939–Oct. 11, 1941.

Gholson, James Herbert (AJ Va.) 1798–July 2, 1848; House 1833–35.

Gholson, Samuel Jameson (D Miss.) May 19, 1808–Oct. 16, 1883; House Dec. 1, 1836–37 (Jacksonian), July 18, 1837–Feb. 5, 1838.

Gholson, Thomas Jr. (R Va.) ?–July 4, 1816; House Nov. 7, 1808–July 4, 1816.

Giaimo, Robert Nicholas (D Conn.) Oct. 15, 1919– ; House 1959–81; Chrmn. House Budget 1977–81.

Gibbons, Jim (R Nev.) Dec. 16, 1944– ; House 1997– .

Gibbons, Sam Melville (D Fla.) Jan. 20, 1920– ; House 1963–97; Chrmn. House Ways and Means 1994–95.

Gibbs, Florence Reville (widow of Willis Benjamin Gibbs) (D Ga.) April 4, 1890–Aug. 19, 1964; House Oct. 1, 1940–41.

Gibbs, Willis Benjamin (husband of Florence Reville Gibbs) (D Ga.) April 15, 1889–Aug. 7, 1940; House 1939–Aug. 7, 1940.

Gibson, Charles Hopper (cousin of Henry Richard Gibson) (D Md.) Jan. 19, 1842–March 31, 1900; House 1885–91; Senate Nov. 19, 1891–97.

Gibson, Ernest Willard (father of Ernest William Gibson Jr.) (R Vt.) Dec. 29, 1872–June 20, 1940; House Nov. 6, 1923–Oct. 19, 1933; Senate Nov. 21, 1933–June 20, 1940.

Gibson, Ernest William Jr. (son of Ernest Willard Gibson) (R Vt.) March 6, 1901–Nov. 4, 1969; Senate June 24, 1940–41; Gov. Jan. 9, 1947–Jan. 16, 1950.

Gibson, Eustace (D W.Va.) Oct. 4, 1842–Dec. 10, 1900; House 1883–87.

Gibson, Henry Richard (cousin of Charles Hopper Gibson) (R Tenn.) Dec. 24, 1837–May 25, 1938; House 1895–1905.

Gibson, James King (C Va.) Feb. 18, 1812–March 30, 1879; House Jan. 28, 1870–71.

Gibson, John Strickland (D Ga.) Jan. 3, 1893–Oct. 19, 1960; House 1941–47.

Gibson, Paris (D Mont.) July 1, 1830–Dec. 16, 1920; Senate March 7, 1901–05.

Gibson, Randall Lee (D La.) Sept. 10, 1832–Dec. 15, 1892; House 1875–83; Senate 1883–Dec. 15, 1892.

Giddings, De Witt Clinton (D Texas) July 18, 1827–Aug. 19, 1903; House May 13, 1872–75, 1877–79.

Giddings, Joshua Reed (R Ohio) Oct. 6, 1795–May 27, 1864; House Dec. 3, 1838–March 22, 1842 (Whig); Dec. 5, 1842–59 (Dec. 5, 1842–49 Whig, 1849–55 Free-Soiler).

Giddings, Napoleon Bonaparte (D Neb.) Jan. 2, 1816–Aug. 3, 1897; House (Terr. Del.) Jan. 5–March 3, 1855.

Gifford, Charles Laceille (R Mass.) March 15, 1871–Aug. 23, 1947; House Nov. 7, 1922–Aug. 23, 1947.

Gifford, Oscar Sherman (R S.D.) Oct. 20, 1842–Jan. 16, 1913; House (Terr. Del. Dakota) 1885–89, (Rep.) Nov. 2, 1889–91.

Gilbert, Abijah (R Fla.) June 18, 1806–Nov. 23, 1881; Senate 1869–75.

Gilbert, Edward (D Calif.) about 1819–Aug. 2, 1852; House Sept. 11, 1850–51.

Gilbert, Ezekiel (F N.Y.) March 25, 1756–July 17, 1841; House 1793–97 (1793–95 no party).

Gilbert, George Gilmore (father of Ralph Waldo Emerson Gilbert) (D Ky.) Dec. 24, 1849–Nov. 9, 1909; House 1899–1907.

Gilbert, Jacob H. (D N.Y.) June 17, 1920–Feb. 27, 1981; House March 8, 1960–71.

Gilbert, Newton Whiting (R Ind.) May 24, 1862–July 5, 1939; House 1905–Nov. 6, 1906.

Gilbert, Ralph Waldo Emerson (son of George Gilmore Gilbert) (D Ky.) Jan. 17, 1882–July 30, 1939; House 1921–29, 1931–33.

Gilbert, Sylvester (R Conn.) Oct. 20, 1755–Jan. 2, 1846; House Nov. 16, 1818–19.

Gilbert, William Augustus (W N.Y.) Jan. 25, 1815–May 25, 1875; House 1855–Feb. 27, 1857.

Gilchrest, Wayne T. (R Md.) April 15, 1946– ; House 1991– .

Gilchrist, Fred Cramer (R Iowa) June 2, 1868–March 10, 1950; House 1931–45.

Gildea, James Hilary (D Pa.) Oct. 21, 1890–June 5, 1988; House 1935–39.

Giles, William Branch (R Va.) Aug. 12, 1762–Dec. 4, 1830; House Dec. 7, 1790–Oct. 2, 1798 (no party), 1801–03; Senate Aug. 11, 1804–15; Gov. March 4, 1827–March 4, 1830.

Giles, William Fell (D Md.) April 8, 1807–March 21, 1879; House 1845–47.

Gilfillan, Calvin Willard (R Pa.) Feb. 20, 1832–Dec. 2, 1901; House 1869–71.

Gilfillan, John Bachop (R Minn.) Feb. 11, 1835–Aug. 19, 1924; House 1885–87.

Gilhams, Clarence Chauncey (R Ind.) April 11, 1860–June 5, 1912; House Nov. 6, 1906–09.

Gill, John Jr. (D Md.) June 9, 1850–Jan. 27, 1918; House 1905–11.

Gill, Joseph John (R Ohio) Sept. 21, 1846–May 22, 1920; House Dec. 4, 1899–Oct. 31, 1903.

Gill, Michael Joseph (D Mo.) Dec. 5, 1864–Nov. 1, 1918; House June 19, 1914–15.

Gill, Patrick Francis (D Mo.) Aug. 16, 1868–May 21, 1923; House 1909–11, Aug. 12, 1912–13.

Gill, Thomas Ponce (D Hawaii) April 21, 1922– ; House 1963–65.

Gillen, Courtland Craig (D Ind.) July 3, 1880–Sept. 1, 1954; House 1931–33.

Gillespie, Dean Milton (R Colo.) May 3, 1884–Feb. 2, 1949; House March 7, 1944–47.

Gillespie, Eugene Pierce (D Pa.) Sept. 24, 1852–Dec. 16, 1899; House 1891–93.

Gillespie, James (R N.C.) ?–Jan. 11, 1805; House 1793–99 (1793–95 no party), 1803–Jan. 11, 1805.

Gillespie, James Frank (D Ill.) April 18, 1869–Nov. 26, 1954; House 1933–35.

Gillespie, Oscar William (D Texas) June 20, 1858–Aug. 23, 1927; House 1903–11.

Gillet, Charles William (R N.Y.) Nov. 26, 1840–Dec. 31, 1908; House 1893–1905.

Gillet, Ransom Hooker (D N.Y.) Jan. 27, 1800–Oct. 24, 1876; House 1833–37.

Gillett, Frederick Huntington (R Mass.) Oct. 16, 1851–July 31, 1935; House 1893–1925; Speaker May 19, 1919–21, April 11, 1921–23, Dec. 3, 1923–25; Senate 1925–31.

Gillett, James Norris (R Calif.) Sept. 20, 1860–April 20, 1937; House 1903–Nov. 4, 1906; Gov. Jan. 8, 1907–Jan. 3, 1911.

Gillette, Edward Hooker (son of Francis Gillette) (G Iowa) Oct. 1, 1840–Aug. 14, 1918; House 1879–81.

Gillette, Francis (father of Edward Hooker Gillette) (FS Conn.) Dec. 14, 1807–Sept. 30, 1879; Senate May 24, 1854–55.

Gillette, Guy Mark (D Iowa) Feb. 3, 1879–March 3, 1973; House 1933–Nov. 3, 1936; Senate Nov. 4, 1936–45, 1949–55.

Gillette, Wilson Darwin (R Pa.) July 1, 1880–Aug. 7, 1951; House Nov. 4, 1941–Aug. 7, 1951.

Gillie, George W. (R Ind.) Aug. 15, 1880–July 3, 1963; House 1939–49.

Gilligan, John Joyce (D Ohio) March 22, 1921– ; House 1965–67; Gov. Jan. 11, 1971–Jan. 13, 1975.

Gillis, James Lisle (D Pa.) Oct. 2, 1792–July 8, 1881; House 1857–59.

Gillmor, Paul E. (R Ohio) Feb. 1, 1939– ; House 1989– .

Gillon, Alexander (– S.C.) 1741–Oct. 6, 1794; House 1793–Oct. 6, 1794; Cont. Cong. (elected but did not attend) 1784.

Gilman, Benjamin Arthur (R N.Y.) Dec. 6, 1922– ; House 1973– ; Chrmn. House International Relations 1995– .

Gilman, Charles Jervis (great-nephew of John Taylor Gilman and Nicholas Gilman) (R Maine) Feb. 26, 1824–Feb. 5, 1901; House 1857–59.

Gilman, Nicholas (brother of John Taylor Gilman and great-uncle of Charles Jervis Gilman) (R N.H.) Aug. 3, 1755–May 2, 1814; House 1789–97 (no party); Senate 1805–May 2, 1814; Cont. Cong. 1787–89.

Gilmer, George Rockingham (J Ga.) April 11, 1790–Nov. 16, 1859; House 1821–23 (no party), Oct. 1, 1827–29 (no party), 1833–35; Gov. Nov. 4, 1829–Nov. 9, 1831 (Jacksonian), Nov. 8, 1837–Nov. 6, 1839 (Whig).

Gilmer, John Adams (O N.C.) Nov. 4, 1805–May 14, 1868; House 1857–61 (1857–59 American Party).

Gilmer, Thomas Walker (D Va.) April 6, 1802–Feb. 28, 1844; House 1841–Feb. 16, 1844 (1841–43 Whig); Gov. March 31, 1840–March 1, 1841 (Whig); Secy. of the Navy Feb. 19–Feb. 28, 1844.

Gilmer, William Franklin "Dixie" (D Okla.) June 7, 1901–June 9, 1954; House 1949–51.

Gilmore, Alfred (son of John Gilmore) (D Pa.) June 9, 1812–June 29, 1890; House 1849–53.

Gilmore, Edward (D Mass.) Jan. 4, 1867–April 10, 1924; House 1913–15.

Gilmore, John (father of Alfred Gilmore) (J Pa.) Feb. 18, 1780–May 11, 1845; House 1829–33.

Gilmore, Samuel Louis (D La.) July 30, 1859–July 18, 1910; House March 30, 1909–July 18, 1910.

Gingery, Don (D Pa.) Feb. 19, 1884–Oct. 15, 1961; House 1935–39.

Gingrich, Newt (R Ga.) June 17, 1943– ; House 1979–99; Speaker 1995–99.

Ginn, Ronald Bryan (D Ga.) May 31, 1934– ; House 1973–83.

Gist, Joseph (– S.C.) Jan. 12, 1775–March 8, 1836; House 1821–27.

Gittins, Robert Henry (D N.Y.) Dec. 14, 1869–Dec. 25, 1957; House 1913–15.

Glascock, John Raglan (D Calif.) Aug. 25, 1845–Nov. 10, 1913; House 1883–85.

Glascock, Thomas (D Ga.) Oct. 21, 1790–May 19, 1841; House Oct. 5, 1835–39 (Oct. 5, 1835–37 Jacksonian).

Glasgow, Hugh (R Pa.) Sept. 8, 1769–Jan. 31, 1818; House 1813–17.

Glass, Carter (D Va.) Jan. 4, 1858–May 28, 1946; House Nov. 4, 1902–Dec. 16, 1918; Senate Feb. 2, 1920–May 28, 1946; elected Pres. pro tempore July 10, 1941, Jan. 5, 1943; Secy. of the Treasury Dec. 16, 1918–Feb. 1, 1920.

Glass, Presley Thornton (D Tenn.) Oct. 18, 1824–Oct. 9, 1902; House 1885–89.

Glatfelter, Samuel Feiser (D Pa.) April 7, 1858–April 23, 1927; House 1923–25.

Glen, Henry (F N.Y.) July 13, 1739–Jan. 6, 1814; House 1793–1801 (1793–95 no party).

Glenn, John Herschel Jr. (D Ohio) July 18, 1921– ; Senate Dec. 24, 1974–99; Chrmn. Senate Governmental Affairs 1987–95.

Glenn, Milton Willits (R N.J.) June 18, 1903–Dec. 14, 1967; House Nov. 5, 1957–65.

Glenn, Otis Ferguson (R Ill.) Aug. 27, 1879–March 11, 1959; Senate Dec. 3, 1928–33.

Glenn, Thomas Louis (P Idaho) Feb. 2, 1847–Nov. 18, 1918; House 1901–03.

Glickman, Daniel Robert (D Kan.) Nov. 24, 1944– ; House 1977–95; Chrmn. House Permanent Select Committee on Intelligence, 1993–95; Secy. of Agriculture March 20, 1995– .

Gloninger, John (F Pa.) Sept. 19, 1758–Jan. 22, 1836; House March 4–Aug. 2, 1813.

Glossbrenner, Adam John (D Pa.) Aug. 31, 1810–March 1, 1889; House 1865–69.

Glover, David Delano (D Ark.) Jan. 18, 1868–April 5, 1952; House 1929–35.

Glover, John Milton (nephew of John Montgomery Glover) (D Mo.) June 23, 1852–Oct. 20, 1929; House 1885–89.

Glover, John Montgomery (uncle of John Milton Glover) (D Mo.) Sept. 4, 1822–Nov. 15, 1891; House 1873–79.

Glynn, James Peter (R Conn.) Nov. 12, 1867–March 6, 1930; House 1915–23, 1925–March 6, 1930.

Glynn, Martin Henry (D N.Y.) Sept. 27, 1871–Dec. 14, 1924; House 1899–1901; Gov. Oct. 17, 1913–Jan. 1, 1915.

Goddard, Calvin (F Conn.) July 17, 1768–May 2, 1842; House May 14, 1801–05.

Godshalk, William (R Pa.) Oct. 25, 1817–Feb. 6, 1891; House 1879–83.

Godwin, Hannibal Lafayette (D N.C.) Nov. 3, 1873–June 9, 1929; House 1907–21.

Goebel, Herman Philip (R Ohio) April 5, 1853–May 4, 1930; House 1903–11.

Goeke, John Henry (D Ohio) Oct. 28, 1869–March 25, 1930; House 1911–15.

Goff, Abe McGregor (R Idaho) Dec. 21, 1899–Nov. 23, 1984; House 1947–49.

Goff, Guy Despard (son of Nathan Goff, father of Louise Goff Reece, father-in-law of Brazilla Carroll Reece) (R W.Va.) Sept. 13, 1866–Jan. 7, 1933; Senate 1925–31.

Goff, Nathan (father of Guy Despard Goff, grandfather of Louise Goff Reece) (R W.Va.) Feb. 9, 1843–April 24, 1920; House 1883–89; Senate April 1, 1913–19; Secy. of the Navy Jan. 7–March 6, 1881.

Goggin, William Leftwich (W Va.) May 31, 1807–Jan. 3, 1870; House 1839–43, April 25, 1844–45, 1847–49.

Gold, Thomas Ruggles (F N.Y.) Nov. 4, 1764–Oct. 24, 1827; House 1809–13, 1815–17.

Golden, James Stephen (R Ky.) Sept. 10, 1891–Sept. 6, 1971; House 1949–55.

Golder, Benjamin Martin (R Pa.) Dec. 23, 1891–Dec. 30, 1946; House 1925–33.

Goldfogle, Henry Mayer (D N.Y.), May 23, 1856–June 1, 1929; House 1901–15, 1919–21.

Goldsborough, Charles (great-grandfather of Thomas Alan Goldsborough and Winder Laird Henry) (F Md.) July 15, 1765–Dec. 13, 1834; House 1805–17; Gov. Jan. 8–Dec. 20, 1819.

Goldsborough, Phillips Lee (R Md.) Aug. 6, 1865–Oct. 22, 1946; Senate 1929–35; Gov. Jan. 10, 1912–Jan. 12, 1916.

Goldsborough, Robert Henry (great-grandfather of Winder Laird Henry) (W Md.) Jan. 4, 1779–Oct. 5, 1836; Senate May 21, 1813–19 (Federalist), Jan. 13, 1835–Oct. 5, 1836.

Goldsborough, Thomas Alan (great-grandson of Charles Goldsborough) (D Md.) Sept. 16, 1877–June 16, 1951; House 1921–April 5, 1939.

Goldthwaite, George Thomas (D Ala.) Dec. 10, 1809–March 16, 1879; Senate 1871–77.

Goldwater, Barry Morris (father of Barry Morris Goldwater Jr.) (R Ariz.) Jan. 1, 1909–May 29, 1998; Senate 1953–65, 1969–87; Chrmn. Senate Select Committee on Intelligence Activities 1981–85; Chrmn. Senate Armed Services 1985–87.

Goldwater, Barry Morris Jr. (son of Barry Morris Goldwater) (R Calif.) July 15, 1938– ; House April 29, 1969–83.

Goldzier, Julius (D Ill.) Jan. 20, 1854–Jan. 20, 1925; House 1893–95.

Golladay, Edward Isaac (brother of Jacob Shall Golladay) (D Tenn.) Sept. 9, 1830–July 11, 1897; House 1871–73.

Golladay, Jacob Shall (brother of Edward Isaac Golladay) (D Ky.) Jan. 19, 1819–May 20, 1887; House Dec. 5, 1867–Feb. 28, 1870.

Gonzalez, Charlie (son of Henry Barbosa Gonzalez) (D Texas) May 5, 1945– ; House 1999– .

Gonzalez, Henry Barbosa (father of Charlie Gonzalez) (D Texas) May 3, 1916– ; House Nov. 4, 1961–99; Chrmn. House Banking, Housing, and Urban Affairs 1989–95.

Gooch, Daniel Linn (D Ky.) Oct. 28, 1853–April 12, 1913; House 1901–05.

Gooch, Daniel Wheelwright (R Mass.) Jan. 8, 1820–Nov. 11, 1891; House Jan. 31, 1858–Sept. 1, 1865, 1873–75.

Good, James William (R Iowa) Sept. 24, 1866–Nov. 18, 1929; House 1909–June 15, 1921; Secy. of War March 6–Nov. 18, 1929.

Goodall, Louis Bertrand (R Maine) Sept. 23, 1851–June 26, 1935; House 1917–21.

Goode, John Jr. (D Va.) May 27, 1829–July 14, 1909; House 1875–81.

Goode, Patrick Gaines (W Ohio) May 10, 1798–Oct. 17, 1862; House 1837–43.

Goode, Samuel (– Va.) March 21, 1756–Nov. 14, 1822; House 1799–1801.

Goode, Virgil (D Va.) Oct. 17, 1946– ; House 1997– .

Goode, William Osborne (D Va.) Sept. 16, 1798–July 3, 1859; House 1841–43, 1853–July 3, 1859.

Goodell, Charles Ellsworth (R N.Y.) March 16, 1926–Jan. 21, 1987; House May 26, 1959–Sept. 9, 1968; Senate Sept. 10, 1968–71.

Goodenow, John Milton (– Ohio) 1782–July 20, 1838; House 1829–April 9, 1830.

Goodenow, Robert (brother of Rufus King Goodenow) (W Maine) April 19, 1800–May 15, 1874; House 1851–53.

Goodenow, Rufus King (brother of Robert Goodenow) (W Maine) April 24, 1790–March 24, 1863; House 1849–51.

Goodhue, Benjamin (F Mass.) Sept. 20, 1748–July 28, 1814; House 1789–June 1796 (no party); Senate June 11, 1796–Nov. 8, 1800.

Goodin, John Randolph (D Kan.) Dec. 14, 1836–Dec. 18, 1885; House 1875–77.

Gooding, Frank Robert (R Idaho) Sept. 16, 1859–June 24, 1928; Senate Jan. 15, 1921–June 24, 1928; Gov. Jan. 2, 1905–Jan. 4, 1908.

Goodlatte, Robert W. (R Va.) Sept. 22, 1952– ; House 1993– .

Goodling, George Atlee (father of William Franklin Goodling) (R Pa.) Sept. 26, 1896–Oct. 17, 1982; House 1961–65, 1967–75.

Goodling, William Franklin (son of George Atlee Goodling) (R Pa.) Dec. 5, 1927– ; House 1975– ; Chrmn. House Education and the Workforce 1995– .

Goodnight, Isaac Herschel (D Ky.) Jan. 31, 1849–July 24, 1901; House 1889–95.

Goodrich, Chauncey (brother of Elizur Goodrich) (F Conn.) Oct. 20, 1759–Aug. 18, 1815; House 1795–1801; Senate Oct. 25, 1807–May 1813.

Goodrich, Elizur (brother of Chauncey Goodrich) (F Conn.) March 24, 1761–Nov. 1, 1849; House 1799–1801.

Goodrich, John Zacheus (W Mass.) Sept. 27, 1804–April 19, 1885; House 1851–55.

Goodrich, Milo (R N.Y.) Jan. 3, 1814–April 15, 1881; House 1871–73.

Goodwin, Angier Louis (R Mass.) Jan. 30, 1881–June 20, 1975; House 1943–55.

Goodwin, Forrest (R Maine) June 14, 1862–May 28, 1913; House March 4–May 28, 1913.

Goodwin, Godfrey Gummer (R Minn.) Jan. 11, 1873–Feb. 16, 1933; House 1925–Feb. 16, 1933.

Goodwin, Henry Charles (R N.Y.) June 25, 1824–Nov. 12, 1860; House Nov. 7, 1854–55 (Whig), 1857–59.

Goodwin, John Noble (R Ariz.) Oct. 18, 1824–April 29, 1887; House (Rep. Maine) 1861–63, (Terr. Del.) 1865–67; Gov. (Ariz. Terr.) 1863–65.

Goodwin, Philip Arnold (R N.Y.) Jan. 20, 1882–June 6, 1937; House 1933–June 6, 1937.

Goodwin, Robert Kingman (R Iowa) May 23, 1905–Feb. 21, 1983; House March 5, 1940–41.

Goodwin, William Shields (D Ark.) May 2, 1866–Aug. 9, 1937; House 1911–21.

Goodwyn, Albert Taylor (P Ala.) Dec. 17, 1842–July 2, 1931; House April 22, 1896–97.

Goodwyn, Peterson (R Va.) 1745–Feb. 21, 1818; House 1803–Feb. 21, 1818.

Goodyear, Charles (D N.Y.) April 26, 1804–April 9, 1876; House 1845–47, 1865–67.

Goodykoontz, Wells (R W.Va.) June 3, 1872–March 2, 1944; House 1919–21.

Gordon, Barton Jennings (D Tenn.) Jan. 24, 1949– ; House 1985– .

Gordon, George Washington (D Tenn.) Oct. 5, 1836–Aug. 9, 1911; House 1907–Aug. 9, 1911.

Gordon, James (– N.Y.) Oct. 31, 1739–Jan. 17, 1810; House 1791–95.

Gordon, James (– Miss.) Dec. 6, 1833–Nov. 28, 1912; Senate Dec. 27, 1909–Feb. 22, 1910.

Gordon, John Brown (D Ga.) Feb. 6, 1832–Jan. 9, 1904; Senate 1873–May 26, 1880, 1891–97; Gov. Nov. 9, 1886–Nov. 8, 1890.

Gordon, Robert Bryarly (D Ohio) Aug. 6, 1855–Jan. 3, 1923; House 1899–1903.

Gordon, Samuel (D N.Y.) April 28, 1802–Oct. 28, 1873; House 1841–43, 1845–47.

Gordon, Thomas Sylvy (D Ill.) Dec. 17, 1893–Jan. 22, 1959; House 1943–59; Chrmn. House Foreign Affairs 1957–59.

Gordon, William (F N.H.) April 12, 1763–May 8, 1802; House 1797–June 12, 1800.

Gordon, William (D Ohio) Dec. 15, 1862–Jan. 16, 1942; House 1913–19.

Gordon, William Fitzhugh (J Va.) Jan. 13, 1787–Aug. 28, 1858; House Jan. 25, 1830–35.

Gore, Albert Arnold (father of Albert Arnold Gore Jr.) (D Tenn.) Dec. 26, 1907–Dec. 5, 1998; House 1939–Dec. 4, 1944, 1945–53; Senate 1953–71.

Gore, Albert Arnold Jr. (son of Albert Arnold Gore) (D Tenn.) March 31, 1948– ; House 1977–85; Senate 1985–Jan. 2, 1993; Vice President 1993– .

Gore, Christopher (F Mass.) Sept. 21, 1758–March 1, 1827; Senate May 5, 1813–May 30, 1816; Gov. May 1, 1809–June 2, 1810.

Gore, Thomas Pryor (D Okla.) Dec. 10, 1870–March 16, 1949; Senate Dec. 11, 1907–21, 1931–37.

Gorham, Benjamin (AJ Mass.) Feb. 13, 1775–Sept. 27, 1855; House Nov. 6, 1820–23 (no party), July 23, 1827–31 (no party), 1833–35.

Gorman, Arthur Pue (D Md.) March 11, 1839–June 4, 1906; Senate 1881–99, 1903–June 4, 1906.

Gorman, George Edmund (D Ill.) April 13, 1873–Jan. 13, 1935; House 1913–15.

Gorman, James Sedgwick (D Mich.) Dec. 28, 1850–May 27, 1923; House 1891–95.

Gorman, John Jerome (R Ill.) June 2, 1883–Feb. 24, 1949; House 1921–23, 1925–27.

Gorman, Willis Arnold (D Ind.) Jan. 12, 1816–May 20, 1876; House 1849–53; Gov. (Minn. Terr.) 1853–57.

Gorski, Chester Charles (D N.Y.) June 22, 1906–April 25, 1975; House 1949–51.

Gorski, Martin (D Ill.) Oct. 30, 1886–Dec. 4, 1949; House 1943–Dec. 4, 1949.

Gorton, Thomas Slade III (R Wash.) Jan. 8, 1928– ; Senate 1981–87, 1989– .

Goss, Edward Wheeler (R Conn.) April 27, 1893–Dec. 27, 1972; House Nov. 4, 1930–35.

Goss, James Hamilton (R S.C.) Aug. 9, 1820–Oct. 31, 1886; House July 18, 1868–69.

Goss, Porter (R Fla.) Nov. 26, 1938– ; House 1989– ; Chrmn. House Permanent Select Committee on Intelligence, 1997– .

Gossett, Charles Clinton (D Idaho) Sept. 2, 1888–Sept. 20, 1974; Senate Nov. 17, 1945–47; Gov. Jan. 1–Nov. 17, 1945.

Gossett, Ed Lee (D Texas) Jan. 27, 1902– ; House 1939–July 31, 1951.

Gott, Daniel (W N.Y.) July 10, 1794–July 6, 1864; House 1847–51.

Gould, Arthur Robinson (R Maine) March 16, 1857–July 24, 1946; Senate Nov. 30, 1926–31.

Gould, Herman Day (W N.Y.) Jan. 16, 1799–Jan. 26, 1852; House 1849–51.

Gould, Norman Judd (grandson of Norman Buel Judd) (R N.Y.) March 15, 1877–Aug. 20, 1964; House Nov. 2, 1915–23.

Gould, Samuel Wadsworth (D Maine) Jan. 1, 1852–Dec. 19, 1935; House 1911–13.

Goulden, Joseph Aloysius (D N.Y.) Aug. 1, 1844–May 3, 1915; House 1903–11, 1913–May 3, 1915.

Gourdin, Theodore (R S.C.) March 20, 1764–Jan. 17, 1826; House 1813–15.

Govan, Andrew Robison (– S.C.) Jan. 13, 1794–June 27, 1841; House Dec. 4, 1822–27.

Gove, Samuel Francis (R Ga.) March 9, 1822–Dec. 3, 1900; House June 25, 1868–69.

Grabowski, Bernard Francis (D Conn.) June 11, 1923– ; House 1963–67.

Gradison, Willis David Jr. (R Ohio) Dec. 28, 1928– ; House 1975–Jan. 31, 1993.

Grady, Benjamin Franklin (D N.C.) Oct. 10, 1831–March 6, 1914; House 1891–95.

Graff, Joseph Verdi (R Ill.) July 1, 1854–Nov. 10, 1921; House 1895–1911.

Graham, Daniel Robert "Bob" (D Fla.) Nov. 9, 1936– ; Senate 1987– ; Gov. Jan. 2, 1979–Jan. 3, 1987.

Graham, Frank Porter (D N.C.) Oct. 14, 1886–Feb. 16, 1972; Senate March 29, 1949–Nov. 26, 1950.

Graham, George Scott (R Pa.) Sept. 13, 1850–July 4, 1931; House 1913–July 4, 1931.

Graham, James (brother of William Alexander Graham) (W N.C.) Jan. 7, 1793–Sept. 25, 1851; House 1833–March 29, 1836 (1833–35 no party), Dec. 5, 1836–43, 1845–47.

Graham, James Harper (R N.Y.) Sept. 18, 1812–June 23, 1881; House 1859–61.

Graham, James McMahon (D Ill.) April 14, 1852–Oct. 23, 1945; House 1909–15.

Graham, John Hugh (D N.Y.) April 1, 1835–July 11, 1895; House 1893–95.

Graham, Lindsey (R S.C.) July 9, 1955– ; House 1995– .

Graham, Louis Edward (R Pa.) Aug. 4, 1880–Nov. 9, 1965; House 1939–55.

Graham, William (W Ind.) March 16, 1782–Aug. 17, 1858; House 1837–39.

Graham, William Alexander (brother of James Graham) (W N.C.) Sept. 5, 1804–Aug. 11, 1875; Senate Nov. 25, 1840–43; Gov. Jan. 1, 1845–Jan. 1, 1849; Secy. of the Navy Aug. 2, 1850–July 25, 1852.

Graham, William Harrison (R Pa.) Aug. 3, 1844–March 2, 1923; House Nov. 29, 1898–1903, 1905–11.

Graham, William Johnson (R Ill.) Feb. 7, 1872–Nov. 10, 1937; House 1917–June 7, 1924.

Gramm, Phil (R Texas) July 8, 1942– ; House 1979–Jan. 5, 1983, Feb. 22, 1983–85 (1979–Jan. 5, 1983, Democrat); Senate 1985– ; Chrmn. Senate Banking, Housing, and Urban Affairs 1999– .

Grammer, Elijah Sherman (R Wash.) April 3, 1868–Nov. 19, 1936; Senate Nov. 22, 1932–33.

Grams, Rod (R Minn.) Feb. 4, 1948– ; House 1993–95; Senate 1995– .

Granahan, Kathryn Elizabeth (widow of William Thomas Granahan) (D Pa.) Dec. 7, 1906–July 10, 1979; House Nov. 6, 1956–63.

Granahan, William Thomas (husband of Kathryn Elizabeth Granahan) (D Pa.) July 26, 1895–May 25, 1956; House 1945–47, 1949–May 25, 1956.

Granata, Peter Charles (R Ill.) Oct. 28, 1898–Sept. 29, 1973; House 1931–April 5, 1932.

Grandy, Frederick Lawrence (R Iowa) June 29, 1948– ; House 1987–95.

Granfield, William Joseph (D Mass.) Dec. 18, 1889–May 28, 1959; House Feb. 11, 1930–37.

Granger, Amos Phelps (cousin of Francis Granger) (R N.Y.) June 3, 1789–Aug. 20, 1866; House 1855–59 (1855–57 Whig).

Granger, Bradley Francis (R Mich.) March 12, 1825–Nov. 4, 1882; House 1861–63.

Granger, Daniel Larned Davis (D R.I.) May 30, 1852–Feb. 14, 1909; House 1903–Feb. 14, 1909.

Granger, Francis (cousin of Amos Phelps Granger) (W N.Y.) Dec. 1, 1792–Aug. 31, 1868; House 1835–37, 1839–March 5, 1841, Nov. 27, 1841–43; Postmaster Gen. March 8–Sept. 13, 1841.

Granger, Kay (R Texas) Jan. 18, 1943– ; House 1997– .

Granger, Miles Tobey (D Conn.) Aug. 12, 1817–Oct. 21, 1895; House 1887–89.

Granger, Walter Keil (D Utah) Oct. 11, 1888–April 21, 1978; House 1941–53.

Grant, Abraham Phineas (D N.Y.) April 5, 1804–Dec. 11, 1871; House 1837–39.

Grant, George McInvale (D Ala.) July 11, 1897–Nov. 4, 1982; House June 14, 1938–65.

Grant, James William (R Fla.) Feb. 21, 1943– ; House 1987–91 (1987–Feb. 21, 1989 Democrat).

Grant, John Gaston (R N.C.) Jan. 1, 1858–June 21, 1923; House 1909–11.

Grant, Robert Allen (R Ind.) July 31, 1905–March 2, 1998; House 1939–49.

Grantland, Seaton (D Ga.) June 8, 1782–Oct. 18, 1864; House 1835–39 (1835–37 Jacksonian).

Grassley, Charles Ernest (R Iowa) Sept. 17, 1933– ; House 1975–81; Senate 1981– .

Grasso, Ella Tambussi (D Conn.) May 10, 1919–Feb. 5, 1981; House 1971–75; Gov. Jan. 8, 1975–Dec. 31, 1980.

Gravel, Maurice Robert "Mike" (D Alaska) May 13, 1930– ; Senate 1969–Jan. 2, 1981.

Gravely, Joseph Jackson (R Mo.) Sept. 25, 1828–April 28, 1872; House 1867–69.

Graves, Alexander (D Mo.) Aug. 25, 1844–Dec. 23, 1916; House 1883–85.

Graves, Dixie Bibb (wife of Gov. David Bibb Graves of Ala.) (D Ala.) July 26, 1882–Jan. 21, 1965; Senate Aug. 20, 1937–Jan. 10, 1938.

Graves, William Jordan (W Ky.) 1805–Sept. 27, 1848; House 1835–41.

Gray, Edward Winthrop (R N.J.) Aug. 18, 1870–June 10, 1942; House 1915–19.

Gray, Edwin (F Va.) July 18, 1743–?; House 1799–1813.

Gray, Finly Hutchinson (D Ind.) July 21, 1863–May 8, 1947; House 1911–17, 1933–39.

Gray, George (D Del.) May 4, 1840–Aug. 7, 1925; Senate March 18, 1885–99.

Gray, Hiram (D N.Y.) July 10, 1801–May 6, 1890; House 1837–39.

Gray, John Cowper (– Va.) 1783–May 18, 1823; House Aug. 28, 1820–21.

Gray, Joseph Anthony (D Pa.) Feb. 25, 1884–May 8, 1966; House 1935–39.

Gray, Kenneth James (D Ill.) Nov. 14, 1924– ; House 1955–Dec. 31, 1974, 1985–89.

Gray, Oscar Lee (D Ala.) July 2, 1865–Jan. 2, 1936; House 1915–19.

Gray, William Herbert III (D Pa.) Aug. 20, 1941– ; House 1979–Sept. 11, 1991; Chrmn. House Budget 1985–89.

Grayson, William (father of William John Grayson, uncle of Alexander Dalrymple Orr) (– Va.) about 1740–March 12, 1790; Senate 1789–March 12, 1790; Cont. Cong. 1785–87.

Grayson, William John (son of William Grayson, cousin of Alexander Dalrymple Orr) (N S.C.) Nov. 2, 1788–Oct. 4, 1863; House 1833–37.

Greeley, Horace (W N.Y.) Feb. 3, 1811–Nov. 29, 1872; House Dec. 4, 1848–49.

Green, Bryam (– N.Y.) April 15, 1786–Oct. 18, 1865; House 1843–45.

Green, Edith Starrett (D Ore.) Jan. 17, 1910–April 21, 1987; House 1955–Dec. 31, 1975.

Green, Frederick William (D Ohio) Feb. 18, 1816–June 18, 1879; House 1851–55.

Green, Gene (D Texas) Oct. 17, 1947– ; House 1993– .

Green, Henry Dickinson (D Pa.) May 3, 1857–Dec. 29, 1929; House Nov. 7, 1899–1903.

Green, Innis (J Pa.) Feb. 26, 1776–Aug. 4, 1839; House 1827–31 (1827–29 no party).

Green, Isaiah Lewis (R Mass.) Dec. 28, 1761–Dec. 5, 1841; House 1805–09, 1811–13.

Green, James Stephen (D Mo.) Feb. 28, 1817–Jan. 19, 1870; House 1847–51; Senate Jan. 12, 1857–61.

Green, Mark (R Wis.) June 1, 1960– ; House 1999– .

Green, Robert Alexis (D Fla.) Feb. 10, 1892–Feb. 9, 1973; House 1925–Nov. 25, 1944.

Green, Robert Stockton (D N.J.) March 25, 1831–May 7, 1895; House 1885–Jan. 17, 1887; Gov. Jan. 18, 1887–Jan. 21, 1890.

Green, Sedgwick William "Bill" (R N.Y.) Oct. 16, 1929– ; House Feb. 21, 1978–93.

Green, Theodore Francis (great-nephew of Samuel Greene Arnold, great-great-nephew of Tristam Burges, great-grandson of James Burrill Jr., great-great-grandson of Jonathan Arnold, great-great-nephew of Lemuel Hastings Arnold) (D R.I.) Oct. 2, 1867–May 19, 1966; Senate 1937–61; Chrmn. Senate Rules and Administration 1955–57; Chrmn. Senate Foreign Relations 1957–59; Gov. Jan. 3, 1933–Jan. 5, 1937.

Green, Wharton Jackson (grandson of Jesse Wharton, cousin of Matt Whitaker Ransom) (D N.C.) Feb. 28, 1831–Aug. 6, 1910; House 1883–87.

Green, William Joseph (son of William Joseph Green Jr.) (D Pa.) June 24, 1938– ; House April 28, 1964–77.

Green, William Joseph Jr. (father of William Joseph Green III) (D Pa.) March 5, 1910–Dec. 21, 1963; House 1945–47, 1949–Dec. 21, 1963.

Green, William Raymond (R Iowa) Nov. 7, 1856–June 11, 1947; House June 5, 1911–March 31, 1928.

Green, Willis (W Ky.) ?–?; House 1839–45.

Greene, Albert Collins (W R.I.) April 15, 1792–Jan. 8, 1863; Senate 1845–51.

Greene, Frank Lester (R Vt.) Feb. 10, 1870–Dec. 17, 1930; House July 30, 1912–23; Senate 1923–Dec. 17, 1930.

Greene George Woodward (D N.Y.) July 4, 1831–July 21, 1895; House 1869–Feb. 17, 1870.

Greene, Ray (F R.I.) Feb. 2, 1765–Jan. 11, 1849; Senate Nov. 13, 1797–March 5, 1801.

Greene, Thomas Marston (– Miss.) Feb. 26, 1758–Feb. 7, 1813; House (Terr. Del.) Dec. 6, 1802–03.

Greene, William Laury (P Neb.) Oct. 3, 1849–March 11, 1899; House 1897–March 11, 1899.

Greene, William Stedman (R Mass.) April 28, 1841–Sept. 22, 1924; House May 31, 1898–Sept. 22, 1924.

Greenhalge, Frederic Thomas (R Mass.) July 19, 1842–March 5, 1896; House 1889–91; Gov. Jan. 3, 1894–March 5, 1896.

Greenleaf, Halbert Stevens (D N.Y.) April 12, 1827–Aug. 25, 1906; House 1883–85, 1891–93.

Greenman, Edward Whitford (D N.Y.) Jan. 26, 1840–Aug. 3, 1908; House 1887–89.

Greenup, Christopher (R Ky.) 1750–April 27, 1818; House Nov. 9, 1792–97 (Nov. 9, 1792–95 no party); Gov. June 1, 1804–June 1, 1808.

Greenway, Isabella Selmes (later Mrs. Harry Orland King) (D Ariz.) March 22, 1886–Dec. 18, 1953; House Oct. 3, 1933–37.

Greenwood, Alfred Burton (D Ark.) July 11, 1811–Oct. 4, 1889; House 1853–59.

Greenwood, Arthur Herbert (D Ind.) Jan. 31, 1880–April 26, 1963; House 1923–39.

Greenwood, Ernest (D N.Y.) Nov. 25, 1884–June 15, 1955; House 1951–53.

Greenwood, James C. (R Pa.) May 4, 1951– ; House 1993– .

Greever, Paul Ranous (D Wyo.) Sept. 28, 1891–Feb. 16, 1943; House 1935–39.

Gregg, Alexander White (D Texas) Jan. 31, 1855–April 30, 1919; House 1903–19.

Gregg, Andrew (grandfather of James Xavier McLanahan) (R Pa.) June 10, 1755–May 20, 1835; House 1791–1807 (no party); Senate 1807–13; elected Pres. pro tempore June 26, 1809.

Gregg, Curtis Hussey (D Pa.) Aug. 9, 1865–Jan. 18, 1933; House 1911–13.

Gregg, James Madison (D Ind.) June 26, 1806–June 16, 1869; House 1857–59.

Gregg, Judd Alan (R N.H.) Feb. 14, 1947– ; House 1981–89; Senate 1993– ; Gov. Jan. 4, 1989–Jan. 7, 1993.

Gregory, Dudley Sanford (W N.J.) Feb. 5, 1800–Dec. 8, 1874; House 1847–49.

Gregory, Noble Jones (brother of William Voris Gregory) (D Ky.) Aug. 30, 1897–Sept. 26, 1971; House 1937–59.

Gregory, William Voris (brother of Noble Jones Gregory) (D Ky.) Oct. 21, 1877–Oct. 10, 1936; House 1927–Oct. 10, 1936.

Greig, John (W N.Y.) Aug. 6, 1779–April 9, 1858; House May 21–Sept. 25, 1841.

Greigg, Stanley Lloyd (D Iowa) May 7, 1931– ; House 1965–67.

Grennell, George Jr. (W Mass.) Dec. 25, 1786–Nov. 19, 1877; House 1829–39 (1829–31 no party, 1831–35 Anti-Jacksonian).

Gresham, Walter (D Texas) July 22, 1841–Nov. 6, 1920; House 1893–95.

Grey, Benjamin Edwards (grandson of Benjamin Edwards) (W Ky.) ?–?; House 1851–55.

Grider, George William (D Tenn.) Oct. 1, 1912–March 20, 1991; House 1965–67.

Grider, Henry (D Ky.) July 16, 1796–Sept. 7, 1866; House 1843–47 (Whig), 1861–Sept. 7, 1866 (1861–65 Unionist).

Griest, William Walton (R Pa.) Sept. 22, 1858–Dec. 5, 1929; House 1909–Dec. 5, 1929.

Griffin, Anthony Jerome (D N.Y.) April 1, 1866–Jan. 13, 1935; House March 5, 1918–Jan. 13, 1935.

Griffin, Charles Hudson (great-great-grandson of Isaac Griffin) (D Miss.) May 9, 1926–Sept. 10, 1989; House March 12, 1968–73.

Griffin, Daniel Joseph (D N.Y.) March 26, 1880–Dec. 11, 1926; House 1913–Dec. 31, 1917.

Griffin, Isaac (great-grandfather of Eugene McLanahan Wilson, great-great-grandfather of Charles Hudson Griffin) (R Pa.) Feb. 27, 1756–Oct. 12, 1827; House May 24, 1813–17.

Griffin, John King (D S.C.) Aug. 13, 1789–Aug. 1, 1841; House 1831–41 (1831–39 Nullifier).

Griffin, Levi Thomas (D Mich.) May 23, 1837–March 17, 1906; House Dec. 4, 1893–95.

Griffin, Michael (R Wis.) Sept. 9, 1842–Dec. 29, 1899; House Nov. 5, 1894–99.

Griffin, Robert Paul (R Mich.) Nov. 6, 1923– ; House 1957–May 10, 1966; Senate May 11, 1966–Jan. 2, 1979.

Griffin, Samuel (– Va.) ?–Nov. 3, 1810; House 1789–95.

Griffin, Thomas (F Va.) 1773–Oct. 7, 1837; House 1803–05.

Griffith, Francis Marion (D Ind.) Aug. 21, 1849–Feb. 8, 1927; House Dec. 6, 1897–1905.

Griffith, John Keller (D La.) Oct. 16, 1882–Sept. 25, 1942; House 1937–41.

Griffith, Samuel (D Pa.) Feb. 14, 1816–Oct. 1, 1893; House 1871–73.

Griffiths, Martha Wright (D Mich.) Jan. 29, 1912– ; House 1955–Dec. 31, 1974.

Griffiths, Percy Wilfred (R Ohio) March 30, 1893–June 12, 1983; House 1943–49.

Griggs, James Mathews (D Ga.) March 29, 1861–Jan. 5, 1910; House 1897–Jan. 5, 1910.

Grigsby, George Barnes (D Alaska) Dec. 2, 1874–May 9, 1962; House (Terr. Del.) June 3, 1920–March 1, 1921.

Grimes, James Wilson (R Iowa) Oct. 20, 1816–Feb. 7, 1872; Senate 1859–Dec. 6, 1869; Gov. Dec. 9, 1854–Jan. 13, 1858 (Whig).

Grimes, Thomas Wingfield (D Ga.) Dec. 18, 1844–Oct. 28, 1905; House 1887–91.

Grinnell, Joseph (brother of Moses Hicks Grinnell) (W Mass.) Nov. 17, 1788–Feb. 7, 1885; House Dec. 7, 1843–51.

Grinnell, Josiah Bushnell (R Iowa) Dec. 22, 1821–March 31, 1891; House 1863–67.

Grinnell, Moses Hicks (brother of Joseph Grinnell) (W N.Y.) March 3, 1803–Nov. 24, 1877; House 1839–41.

Grisham, Wayne Richard (R Calif.) Jan. 10, 1923– ; House 1979–83.

Griswold, Dwight Palmer (R Neb.) Nov. 27, 1893–April 12, 1954; Senate Nov. 5, 1952–April 12, 1954; Gov. Jan. 9, 1941–Jan. 9, 1947.

Griswold, Gaylord (F N.Y.) Dec. 18, 1767–March 1, 1809; House 1803–05.

Griswold, Glenn Hasenfratz (D Ind.) Jan. 20, 1890–Dec. 5, 1940; House 1931–39.

Griswold, Harry Wilbur (R Wis.) May 19, 1886–July 4, 1939; House Jan. 3–July 4, 1939.

Griswold, John Ashley (D N.Y.) Nov. 18, 1822–Feb. 22, 1902; House 1869–71.

Griswold, John Augustus (R N.Y.) Nov. 11, 1822–Oct. 31, 1872; House 1863–69 (1863–65 Democrat).

Griswold, Matthew (grandson of Roger Griswold) (R Pa.) June 6, 1833–May 19, 1919; House 1891–93, 1895–97.

Griswold, Roger (grandfather of Matthew Griswold) (F Conn.) May 21, 1762–Oct. 25, 1812; House 1795–1805; Gov. May 9, 1811–Oct. 25, 1812.

Griswold, Stanley (– Ohio) Nov. 14, 1763–Aug. 21, 1815; Senate May 18–Dec. 11, 1809.

Groesbeck, William Slocum (D Ohio) July 24, 1815–July 7, 1897; House 1857–59.

Gronna, Asle Jorgenson (R N.D.) Dec. 10, 1858–May 4, 1922; House 1905–Feb. 2, 1911; Senate Feb. 2, 1911–21.

Groome, James Black (D Md.) April 4, 1838–Oct. 5, 1893; Senate 1879–85; Gov. March 4, 1874–Jan. 12, 1876.

Gross, Chester Heilman (R Pa.) Oct. 13, 1888–Jan. 9, 1973; House 1939–41, 1943–49.

Gross, Ezra Carter (– N.Y.) July 11, 1787–April 9, 1829; House 1819–21.

Gross, Harold Royce (R Iowa) June 30, 1899–Sept. 22, 1987; House 1949–75.

Gross, Samuel (– Pa.) Nov. 10, 1776–March 19, 1839; House 1819–23.

Grosvenor, Charles Henry (uncle of Charles Grosvenor Bond) (R Ohio) Sept. 20, 1833–Oct. 30, 1917; House 1885–91, 1893–1907.

Grosvenor, Thomas Peabody (F N.Y.) Dec. 20, 1778–April 24, 1817; House Jan. 29, 1813–17.

Grotberg, John E. (R Ill.) March 23, 1925–Nov. 15, 1986; House 1985–Nov. 15, 1986.

Grout, Jonathan (– Mass.) July 23, 1737–Sept. 8, 1807; House 1789–91.

Grout, William Wallace (R Vt.) May 24, 1836–Oct. 7, 1902; House 1881–83, 1885–1901.

Grove, William Barry (F N.C.) Jan. 15, 1764–March 30, 1818; House 1791–1803 (1791–1801 no party).

Grover, Asa Porter (D Ky.) Feb. 18, 1819–July 20, 1887; House 1867–69.

Grover, James Russell Jr. (R N.Y.) March 5, 1919– ; House 1963–75.

Grover, La Fayette (D Ore.) Nov. 29, 1823–May 10, 1911; House Feb. 15–March 3, 1859; Senate 1877–83; Gov. Sept. 14, 1870–Feb. 1, 1877.

Grover, Martin (D N.Y.) Oct. 20, 1811–Aug. 23, 1875; House 1845–47.

Grow, Galusha Aaron (R Pa.) Aug. 31, 1823–March 31, 1907; House 1851–63 (1851–57 Democrat), Feb. 26, 1894–1903; Speaker July 4, 1861–63.

Gruening, Ernest (D Alaska) Feb. 6, 1887–June 26, 1974; Senate 1959–69; Gov. (Alaska Terr.) 1939–53.

Grundy, Felix (D Tenn.) Sept. 11, 1777–Dec. 19, 1840; House 1811–14 (Republican); Senate Oct. 19, 1829–July 4, 1838 (Jacksonian), Nov. 19, 1839–Dec. 19, 1840; Atty. Gen. Sept. 1–Dec. 1, 1838.

Grundy, Joseph Ridgway (R Pa.) Jan. 13, 1863–March 3, 1961; Senate Dec. 11, 1929–Dec. 1, 1930.

Guarini, Frank Joseph Jr. (D N.J.) Aug. 20, 1924– ; House 1979–93.

Gubser, Charles Samuel (R Calif.) Feb. 1, 1916– ; House 1953–Dec. 31, 1974.

Gude, Gilbert (R Md.) March 9, 1923– ; House 1967–77.

Gudger, James Madison Jr. (father of Katherine Gudger Langley, father-in-law of John Wesley Langley) (D N.C.) Oct. 22, 1855–Feb. 29, 1920; House 1903–07, 1911–15.

Gudger, Vonno Lamar Jr. (D N.C.) April 30, 1919– ; House 1977–81.

Guenther, Richard William (R Wis.) Nov. 30, 1845–April 5, 1913; House 1881–89.

Guernsey, Frank Edward (R Maine) Oct. 15, 1866–Jan. 1, 1927; House Nov. 3, 1908–17.

Guevara, Pedro (Nat. P.I.) Feb. 23, 1879–Jan. 19, 1937; House (Res. Comm.) 1923–Feb. 14, 1936.

Guffey, Joseph F. (D Pa.) Dec. 29, 1870–March 6, 1959; Senate 1935–47.

Guggenheim, Simon (R Colo.) Dec. 30, 1867–Nov. 2, 1941; Senate 1907–13.

Guill, Ben Hugh (R Texas) Sept. 8, 1909–Jan. 15, 1994; House May 6, 1950–51.

Guion, Walter (D La.) April 3, 1849–Feb. 7, 1927; Senate April 22–Nov. 5, 1918.

Gunckel, Lewis B. (R Ohio) Oct. 15, 1826–Oct. 3, 1903; House 1873–75.

Gunderson, Steven Craig (R Wis.) May 10, 1951– ; House 1981–97.

Gunn, James (– Ga.) March 13, 1753–July 30, 1801; Senate 1789–1801; Cont. Cong. (elected but did not attend) 1787.

Gunn, James (– Idaho) March 6, 1843–Nov. 5, 1911; House 1897–99.

Gunter, Thomas Montague (D Ark.) Sept. 18, 1826–Jan. 12, 1904; House June 16, 1874–83.

Gunter, William Dawson Jr. (D Fla.) July 16, 1934– ; House 1973–75.

Gurley, Henry Hosford (– La.) May 20, 1788–March 16, 1833; House 1823–31.

Gurley, John Addison (R Ohio) Dec. 9, 1813–Aug. 19, 1863; House 1859–63.

Gurney, Edward John (R Fla.) Jan. 12, 1914–May 14, 1996; House 1963–69; Senate 1969–Dec. 31, 1974.

Gurney, John Chandler "Chan" (R S.D.) May 21, 1896–March 9, 1985; Senate 1939–51; Chrmn. Senate Armed Services 1947–49.

Gustine, Amos (D Pa.) 1789–March 3, 1844; House May 4, 1841–43.

Guthrie, James (D Ky.) Dec. 5, 1792–March 13, 1869; Senate 1865–Feb. 7, 1868; Secy. of the Treasury March 7, 1853–March 6, 1857.

Gutierrez, Luis V. (D Ill.) Dec. 10, 1954– ; House 1993– .

Gutknecht, Gil (R Minn.) March 20, 1951– ; House 1995– .

Guyer, Tennyson (R Ohio) Nov. 29, 1913–April 12, 1981; House 1973–April 12, 1981.

Guyer, Ulysses Samuel (R Kan.) Dec. 13, 1868–June 5, 1943; House Nov. 4, 1924–25, 1927–June 5, 1943.

Guyon, James Jr. (– N.Y.) Dec. 24, 1778–March 9, 1846; House Jan. 14, 1820–21.

Gwin, William McKendree (D Calif.) Oct. 9, 1805–Sept. 3, 1885; House 1841–43 (Miss.); Senate Sept. 9, 1850–55, Jan. 13, 1857–61.

Gwinn, Ralph Waldo (R N.Y.) March 29, 1884–Feb. 27, 1962; House 1945–59.

Gwynne, John William (R Iowa) Oct. 20, 1889–July 5, 1972; House 1935–49.

H

Habersham, Richard Wylly (W Ga.) Dec. 1786–Dec. 2, 1842; House 1839–Dec. 2, 1842.

Hackett, Richard Nathaniel (D N.C.) Dec. 4, 1866–Nov. 22, 1923; House 1907–09.

Hackett, Thomas C. (D Ga.) ?–Oct. 8, 1851; House 1849–51.

Hackley, Aaron Jr. (–N.Y.) May 6, 1783–Dec. 28, 1868; House 1819–21.

Hackney, Thomas (D Mo.) Dec. 11, 1861–Dec. 24, 1946; House 1907–09.

Hadley, Lindley Hoag (R Wash.) June 19, 1861–Nov. 1, 1948; House 1915–33.

Hadley, William Flavius Lester (R Ill.) June 15, 1847–April 25, 1901; House Dec. 2, 1895–97.

Hagan, George Elliott (D Ga.) May 24, 1916–Dec. 26, 1990; House 1961–73.

Hagans, John Marshall (R W.Va.) Aug. 13, 1838–June 17, 1900; House 1873–75.

Hagedorn, Thomas Michael (R Minn.) Nov. 27, 1943– ; House 1975–83.

Hagel, Chuck (R Neb.) Oct. 4, 1946– ; Senate 1997– .

Hagen, Harlan Francis (D Calif.) Oct. 8, 1914– ; House 1953–67.

Hagen, Harold Christian (R Minn.) Nov. 10, 1901–March 19, 1957; House 1943–55 (1943–45 Farmer Laborite).

Hager, Alva Lysander (R Iowa) Oct. 29, 1850–Jan. 29, 1923; House 1893–99.

Hager, John Sharpenstein (D Calif.) March 12, 1818–March 19, 1890; Senate Dec. 23, 1873–75.

Haggott, Warren Armstrong (R Colo.) May 18, 1864–April 29, 1958; House 1907–09.

Hahn, John (R Pa.) Oct. 30, 1776–Feb. 26, 1823; House 1815–17.

Hahn, Michael (R La.) Nov. 24, 1830–March 15, 1886; House Dec. 3, 1862–63 (Unionist), 1885–March 15, 1886; Gov. March 4, 1864–March 3, 1865 (State Rights Free-Trader).

Haight, Charles (D N.J.) Jan. 4, 1838–Aug. 1, 1891; House 1867–71.

Haight, Edward (D N.Y.) March 26, 1817–Sept. 15, 1885; House 1861–63.

Haile, William (– Miss.) 1797–March 7, 1837; House July 10, 1826–Sept. 12, 1828.

Hailey, John (D Idaho) Aug. 29, 1835–April 10, 1921; House (Terr. Del.) 1873–75, 1885–87.

Hainer, Eugene Jerome (R Neb.) Aug. 16, 1851–March 17, 1929; House 1893–97.

Haines, Charles Delemere (D N.Y.) June 9, 1856–April 11, 1929; House 1893–95.

Haines, Harry Luther (D Pa.) Feb. 1, 1880–March 29, 1947; House 1931–39, 1941–43.

Haldeman, Richard Jacobs (D Pa.) May 19, 1831–Oct. 1, 1886; House 1869–73.

Hale, Artemas (W Mass.) Oct. 20, 1783–Aug. 3, 1882; House 1845–49.

Hale, Eugene (father of Frederick Hale) (R Maine) June 9, 1836–Oct. 27, 1918; House 1869–79; Senate 1881–1911.

Hale, Fletcher (R N.H.) Jan. 22, 1883–Oct. 22, 1931; House 1925–Oct. 22, 1931.

Hale, Frederick (son of Eugene Hale, grandson of Zachariah Chandler, cousin of Robert Hale) (R Maine) Oct. 7, 1874–Sept. 28, 1963; Senate 1917–41.

Hale, James Tracy (R Pa.) Oct. 14, 1810–April 6, 1865; House 1859–65.

Hale, John Blackwell (D Mo.) Feb. 27, 1831–Feb. 1, 1905; House 1885–87.

Hale, John Parker (FS N.H.) March 31, 1806–Nov. 19, 1873; House 1843–45 (Democrat); Senate 1847–53, July 30, 1855–65.

Hale, Nathan Wesley (R Tenn.) Feb. 11, 1860–Sept. 16, 1941; House 1905–09.

Hale, Robert (cousin of Frederick Hale) (R Maine) Nov. 29, 1889–Nov. 30, 1976; House 1943–59.

Hale, Robert Safford (R N.Y.) Sept. 24, 1822–Dec. 14, 1881; House Dec. 3, 1866–67, 1873–75.

Hale, Salma (R N.H.) March 7, 1787–Nov. 19, 1866; House 1817–19.

Hale, William (F N.H.) Aug. 6, 1765–Nov. 8, 1848; House 1809–11, 1813–17.

Haley, Elisha (D Conn.) Jan. 21, 1776–Jan. 22, 1860; House 1835–39 (1835–37 Jacksonian).

Haley, James Andrew (D Fla.) Jan. 4, 1899–Aug. 6, 1981; House 1953–77; Chrmn. House Interior and Insular Affairs 1973–77.

Hall, Albert Richardson (R Ind.) Aug. 27, 1884–Nov. 29, 1969; House 1925–31.

Hall, Augustus (D Iowa) April 29, 1814–Feb. 1, 1861; House 1855–57.

Hall, Benton Jay (D Iowa) Jan. 13, 1835–Jan. 5, 1894; House 1885–87.

Hall, Bolling (R Ga.) Dec. 25, 1767–Feb. 25, 1836; House 1811–17.

Hall, Chapin (R Pa.) July 12, 1816–Sept. 12, 1879; House 1859–61.

Hall, Darwin Scott (R Minn.) Jan. 23, 1844–Feb. 23, 1919; House 1889–91.

Hall, David McKee (D N.C.) May 16, 1918–Jan. 29, 1960; House 1959–Jan. 29, 1960.

Hall, Durward Gorham (R Mo.) Sept. 14, 1910– ; House 1961–73.

Hall, Edwin Arthur (great-grandson of John Allen Collier) (R N.Y.) Feb. 11, 1909– ; House Nov. 7, 1939–53.

Hall, George (– N.Y.) May 12, 1770–March 20, 1840; House 1819–21.

Hall, Hiland (W Vt.) July 20, 1795–Dec. 18, 1885; House Jan. 1, 1833–43 (Jan. 1–Jan. 3, 1833 no party, 1833–35 Anti-Jacksonian); Gov. Oct. 10, 1858–Oct. 12, 1860 (Republican).

Hall, Homer William (R Ill.) July 22, 1870–Sept. 22, 1954; House 1927–33.

Hall, James Knox Polk (D Pa.) Sept. 30, 1844–Jan. 5, 1915; House 1899–Nov. 29, 1902.

Hall, Joseph (J Maine) June 26, 1793–Dec. 31, 1859; House 1833–37.

Hall, Joshua Gilman (R N.H.) Nov. 5, 1828–Oct. 31, 1898; House 1879–83.

Hall, Katie Beatrice Green (D Ind.) April 3, 1938– ; House Nov. 2, 1982–85.

Hall, Lawrence Washington (D Ohio) 1819–Jan. 18, 1863; House 1857–59.

Hall, Leonard Wood (R N.Y.) Oct. 2, 1900–June 2, 1979; House 1939–Dec. 31, 1952; Chrmn. Rep. Nat. Comm. April 1953–Feb. 1957.

Hall, Nathan Kelsey (W N.Y.) March 28, 1810–March 2, 1874; House 1847–49; Postmaster Gen. July 23, 1850–Sept. 13, 1852.

Hall, Norman (D Pa.) Nov. 17, 1829–Sept. 29, 1917; House 1887–89.

Hall, Obed (R N.H.) Dec. 23, 1757–April 1, 1828; House 1811–13.

Hall, Osee Matson (D Minn.) Sept. 10, 1847–Nov. 26, 1914; House 1891–95.

Hall, Philo (R S.D.) Dec. 31, 1865–Oct. 7, 1938; House 1907–09.

Hall, Ralph Moody (D Texas) May 3, 1923– ; House 1981– .

Hall, Robert Bernard (R Mass.) Jan. 28, 1812–April 15, 1868; House 1855–59 (1855–57 American Party).

Hall, Robert Samuel (D Miss.) March 10, 1879–June 10, 1941; House 1929–33.

Hall, Sam Blakeley Jr. (D Texas) Jan. 11, 1924–April 10, 1994; House June 19, 1976–May 27, 1985.

Hall, Thomas (R N.D.) June 6, 1869–Dec. 4, 1958; House Nov. 4, 1924–33.

Hall, Thomas H. (J N.C.) June 1773–June 30, 1853; House 1817–25 (Republican), 1827–35 (1827–29 no party).

Hall, Tim Lee (D Ill.) June 11, 1925– ; House 1975–77.

Hall, Tony Patrick (D Ohio) Jan. 16, 1942– ; House 1979– .

Hall, Uriel Sebree (son of William Augustus Hall, nephew of Willard Preble Hall) (D Mo.) April 12, 1852–Dec. 30, 1932; House 1893–97.

Hall, Willard (R Del.) Dec. 24, 1780–May 10, 1875; House 1817–Jan. 22, 1821.

Hall, Willard Preble (brother of William Augustus Hall, uncle of Uriel Sebree Hall) (D Mo.) May 9, 1820–Nov. 3, 1882; House 1847–53; Gov. Jan. 31, 1864–Jan. 2, 1865 (Unionist).

Hall, William (J Tenn.) Feb. 11, 1775–Oct. 7, 1856; House 1831–33; Gov. April 16–Oct. 1, 1829 (Democratic Republican).

Hall, William Augustus (father of Uriel Sebree Hall, brother of Willard Preble Hall) (D Mo.) Oct. 15, 1815–Dec. 15, 1888; House Jan. 20, 1862–65.

Hall, Wilton Earle (D S.C.) March 11, 1901–Feb. 25, 1980; Senate Nov. 20, 1944–45.

Halleck, Charles Abraham (R Ind.) Aug. 22, 1900–March 3, 1986; House Jan. 29, 1935–69; House majority leader 1947–49, 1953–55; House minority leader 1959–65.

Hallock, John Jr. (D N.Y.) July 1783–Dec. 6, 1840; House 1825–29.

Halloway, Ransom (W N.Y.) about 1793–April 6, 1851; House 1849–51.

Hallowell, Edwin (D Pa.) April 2, 1844–Sept. 13, 1916; House 1891–93.

Halpern, Seymour (R N.Y.) Nov. 19, 1913–Jan. 10, 1997; House 1959–73.

Halsell, John Edward (D Ky.) Sept. 11, 1826–Dec. 26, 1899; House 1883–87.

Halsey, George Armstrong (R N.J.) Dec. 7, 1827–April 1, 1894; House 1867–69, 1871–73.

Halsey, Jehiel Howell (son of Silas Halsey, brother of Nicoll Halsey) (– N.Y.) Oct. 7, 1788–Dec. 5, 1867; House 1829–31.

Halsey, Nicoll (son of Silas Halsey, brother of Jehiel Howell Halsey) (J N.Y.) March 8, 1782–March 3, 1865; House 1833–35.

Halsey, Silas (father of Jehiel Howell Halsey and Nicoll Halsey) (R N.Y.) Oct. 6, 1743–Nov. 19, 1832; House 1805–07.

Halsey, Thomas Jefferson (R Mo.) May 4, 1863–March 17, 1951; House 1929–31.

Halstead, William (W N.J.) June 4, 1794–March 4, 1878; House 1837–39, 1841–43.

Halterman, Frederick (R Pa.) Oct. 22, 1831–March 22, 1907; House 1895–97.

Halvorson, Kittel (P Minn.) Dec. 15, 1846–July 12, 1936; House 1891–93.

Hambleton, Samuel (D Md.) Jan. 8, 1812–Dec. 9, 1886; House 1869–73.

Hamburg, Dan (D Calif.) Oct. 6, 1948– ; House 1993–95.

Hamer, Thomas Lyon (uncle of Thomas Ray Hamer) (D Ohio) July 1800–Dec. 2, 1846; House 1833–39 (1833–37 Jacksonian).

Hamer, Thomas Ray (nephew of Thomas Lyon Hamer) (R Idaho) May 4, 1864–Dec. 22, 1950; House 1909–11.

Hamill, James Alphonsus (D N.J.) March 30, 1877–Dec. 15, 1941; House 1907–21.

Hamill, Patrick (D Md.) April 28, 1817–Jan. 15, 1895; House 1869–71.

Hamilton, Andrew Holman (D Ind.) June 7, 1834–May 9, 1895; House 1875–79.

Hamilton, Andrew Jackson (brother of Morgan Calvin Hamilton) (ID Texas) Jan. 28, 1815–April 11, 1875; House 1859–61; Military Gov. 1862–65; Provisional Gov. June 17, 1865–Aug. 9, 1866.

Hamilton, Charles Mann (R N.Y.) Jan. 23, 1874–Jan. 3, 1942; House 1913–19.

Hamilton, Charles Memorial (R Fla.) Nov. 1, 1840–Oct. 22, 1875; House July 1, 1868–71.

Hamilton, Cornelius Springer (R Ohio) Jan. 2, 1821–Dec. 22, 1867; House March 4–Dec. 22, 1867.

Hamilton, Daniel Webster (D Iowa) Dec. 20, 1861–Aug. 21, 1936; House 1907–09.

Hamilton, Edward La Rue (R Mich.) Dec. 9, 1857–Nov. 2, 1923; House 1897–1921.

Hamilton, Finley (D Ky.) June 19, 1886–Jan. 10, 1940; House 1933–35.

Hamilton, James Jr. (– S.C.) May 8, 1786–Nov. 15, 1857; House Dec. 13, 1822–29; Gov. Dec. 9, 1830–Dec. 13, 1832 (State Rights Democrat).

Hamilton, John (R Pa.) Nov. 25, 1754–Aug. 22, 1837; House 1805–07.

Hamilton, John M. (D W.Va.) March 16, 1855–Dec. 27, 1916; House 1911–13.

Hamilton, John Taylor (D Iowa) Oct. 16, 1843–Jan. 25, 1925; House 1891–93.

Hamilton, Lee Herbert (D Ind.) April 20, 1931– ; House 1965–99; Chrmn. House Permanent Select Committee on Intelligence 1985–87; Chrmn. House Foreign Affairs 1993–95.

Hamilton, Morgan Calvin (brother of Andrew Jackson Hamilton) (R Texas) Feb. 25, 1809–Nov. 21, 1893; Senate March 31, 1870–77.

Hamilton, Norman Rond (D Va.) Nov. 13, 1877–March 26, 1964; House 1937–39.

Hamilton, Robert (D N.J.) Dec. 9, 1809–March 14, 1878; House 1873–77.

Hamilton, William Thomas (D Md.) Sept. 8, 1820–Oct. 26, 1888; House 1849–55; Senate 1869–75; Gov. Jan. 14, 1880–Jan. 9, 1884.

Hamlin, Courtney Walker (cousin of William Edward Barton) (D Mo.) Oct. 27, 1858–Feb. 16, 1950; House 1903–05, 1907–19.

Hamlin, Edward Stowe (W Ohio) July 6, 1808–Nov. 23, 1894; House Oct. 8, 1844–45.

Hamlin, Hannibal (R Maine) Aug. 27, 1809–July 4, 1891; House 1843–47 (Democrat); Senate June 8, 1848–Jan. 7, 1857 (Democrat), 1857–Jan. 17, 1861, 1869–81; Gov. Jan. 8–Feb. 25, 1857; Vice President 1861–65.

Hamlin, Simon Moulton (D Maine) Aug. 10, 1866–July 27, 1939; House 1935–37.

Hammer, William Cicero (D N.C.) March 24, 1865–Sept. 26, 1930; House 1921–Sept. 26, 1930.

Hammerschmidt, John Paul (R Ark.) May 4, 1922– ; House 1967–93.

Hammett, William Henry (D Miss.) March 25, 1799–July 9, 1861; House 1843–45.

Hammond, Edward (D Md.) March 17, 1812–Oct. 19, 1882; House 1849–53.

Hammond, Jabez Delno (R N.Y.) Aug. 2, 1778–Aug. 18, 1855; House 1815–17.

Hammond, James Henry (D S.C.) Nov. 15, 1807–Nov. 13, 1864; House 1835–Feb. 26, 1836 (Nullifier); Senate Dec. 7, 1857–Nov. 11, 1860; Gov. Dec. 8, 1842–Dec. 7, 1844 (Democrat).

Hammond, John (R N.Y.) Aug. 17, 1827–May 28, 1889; House 1879–83.

Hammond, Nathaniel Job (D Ga.) Dec. 26, 1833–April 20, 1899; House 1879–87.

Hammond, Peter Francis (D Ohio) June 30, 1887–April 2, 1971; House Nov. 3, 1936–37.

Hammond, Robert Hanna (D Pa.) April 28, 1791–June 2, 1847; House 1837–41.

Hammond, Samuel (R Ga.) Sept. 21, 1757–Sept. 11, 1842; House 1803–Feb. 2, 1805; Gov. (Upper Louisiana Terr.) 1805–24.

Hammond, Thomas (D Ind.) Feb. 27, 1843–Sept. 21, 1909; House 1893–95.

Hammond, Winfield Scott (D Minn.) Nov. 17, 1863–Dec. 30, 1915; House 1907–Jan. 6, 1915; Gov. Jan. 7–Dec. 30, 1915.

Hammons, David (D Maine) May 12, 1808–Nov. 7, 1888; House 1847–49.

Hammons, Joseph (J N.H.) March 3, 1787–March 29, 1836; House 1829–33.

Hampton, James Giles (W N.J.) June 13, 1814–Sept. 22, 1861; House 1845–49.

Hampton, Moses (W Pa.) Oct. 28, 1803–June 27, 1878; House 1847–51.

Hampton, Wade (grandfather of Wade Hampton, below) (R S.C.) 1752–Feb. 4, 1835; House 1795–97, 1803–05.

Hampton, Wade (grandson of Wade Hampton, above, son-in-law of George McDuffie) (D S.C.) March 28, 1818–April 11, 1902; Senate 1879–91; Gov. Dec. 14, 1876–Feb. 26, 1879.

Hanback, Lewis (R Kan.) March 27, 1839–Sept. 7, 1897; House 1883–87.

Hanbury, Harry Alfred (R N.Y.) Jan. 1, 1863–Aug. 22, 1940; House 1901–03.

Hance, Kent Ronald (D Texas) Nov. 14, 1942– ; House 1979–85.

Hanchett, Luther (R Wis.) Oct. 25, 1825–Nov. 24, 1862; House 1861–Nov. 24, 1862.

Hancock, Clarence Eugene (R N.Y.) Feb. 13, 1885–Jan. 3, 1948; House Nov. 8, 1927–47.

Hancock, Franklin Wills Jr. (D N.C.) Nov. 1, 1894–Jan. 23, 1969; House Nov. 4, 1930–39.

Hancock, George (– Va.) June 13, 1754–July 18, 1820; House 1793–97.

Hancock, John (D Texas) Oct. 24, 1824–July 19, 1893; House 1871–77, 1883–85.

Hancock, Milton D. "Mel" (R Mo.) Sept. 14, 1929– ; House 1989–97.

Hand, Augustus Cincinnatus (D N.Y.) Sept. 4, 1803–March 8, 1878; House 1839–41.

Hand, Thomas Millet (R N.J.) July 7, 1902–Dec. 26, 1956; House 1945–Dec. 26, 1956.

Handley, William Anderson (D Ala.) Dec. 15, 1834–June 23, 1909; House 1871–73.

Handy, Levin Irving (nephew of William Campbell Preston Breckenridge) (D Del.) Dec. 24, 1861–Feb. 3, 1922; House 1897–99.

Hanks, James Millander (D Ark.) Feb. 12, 1833–May 24, 1909; House 1871–73.

Hanley, James Michael (D N.Y.) July 19, 1920– ; House 1965–81; Chrmn. House Post Office and Civil Service 1979–81.

Hanly, James Franklin (R Ind.) April 4, 1863–Aug. 1, 1920; House 1895–97; Gov. Jan. 9, 1905–Jan. 11, 1909.

Hanna, John (R Ind.) Sept. 3, 1827–Oct. 24, 1882; House 1877–79.

Hanna, John Andre (grandfather of Archibald McAllister) (R Pa.) 1762–July 23, 1805; House 1797–July 23, 1805.

Hanna, Louis Benjamin (R N.D.) Aug. 9, 1861–April 23, 1948; House 1909–Jan. 7, 1913; Gov. Jan. 8, 1913–Jan. 3, 1917.

Hanna, Marcus Alonzo (father of Ruth Hanna McCormick) (R Ohio) Sept. 24, 1837–Feb. 15, 1904; Senate March 5, 1897–Feb. 15, 1904; Chrmn. Rep. Nat. Comm. 1896–1904.

Hanna, Richard Thomas (D Calif.) June 9, 1914– ; House 1963–Dec. 31, 1974.

Hanna, Robert (W Ind.) April 6, 1786–Nov. 16, 1858; Senate Aug. 19, 1831–Jan. 3, 1832.

Hannaford, Mark Warren (D Calif.) Feb. 7, 1925–June 2, 1985; House 1975–79.

Hannegan, Edward Allen (D Ind.) June 25, 1807–Feb. 25, 1859; House 1833–37; Senate 1843–49.

Hanrahan, Robert Paul (R Ill.) Feb. 25, 1934– ; House 1973–75.

Hansbrough, Henry Clay (R N.D.) Jan. 30, 1848–Nov. 16, 1933; House Nov. 2, 1889–91; Senate 1891–1909.

Hansen, Clifford Peter (R Wyo.) Oct. 16, 1912– ; Senate 1967–Dec. 31, 1978; Gov. Jan. 6, 1963–Jan. 2, 1967.

Hansen, George Vernon (R Idaho) Sept. 14, 1930– ; House 1965–69, 1975–85.

Hansen, James Vear (R Utah) Aug. 14, 1932– ; House 1981– ; Chrmn. House Standards of Official Conduct 1997–99.

Hansen, John Robert (D Iowa) Aug. 24, 1901–Sept. 23, 1974; House 1965–67.

Hansen, Julia Butler (D Wash.) June 14, 1907–May 3, 1988; House Nov. 8, 1960–Dec. 31, 1974.

Hansen, Orval Howard (R Idaho) Aug. 3, 1926– ; House 1969–75.

Hanson, Alexander Contee (F Md.) Feb. 27, 1786–April 23, 1819; House 1813–16; Senate Dec. 20, 1816–April 23, 1819.

Haralson, Hugh Anderson (D Ga.) Nov. 13, 1805–Sept. 25, 1854; House 1843–51.

Haralson, Jeremiah (R Ala.) April 1, 1846–about 1916; House 1875–77.

Hard, Gideon (W N.Y.) April 29, 1797–April 27, 1885; House 1833–37 (1833–35 Anti-Mason).

Hardeman, Thomas Jr. (D Ga.) Jan. 12, 1825–March 6, 1891; House 1859–Jan. 23, 1861 (Opposition), 1883–85.

Harden, Cecil Murray (R Ind.) Nov. 21, 1894–Dec. 5, 1984; House 1949–59.

Hardenbergh, Augustus Albert (D N.J.) May 18, 1830–Oct. 5, 1889; House 1875–79, 1881–83.

Hardin, Benjamin (cousin of Martin Davis Hardin) (W Ky.) Feb. 29, 1784–Sept. 24, 1852; House 1815–17 (Republican), 1819–23 (Republican), 1833–37 (1833–35 Anti-Jacksonian).

Hardin, John J. (son of Martin Davis Hardin) (W Ill.) Jan. 6, 1810–Feb. 23, 1847; House 1843–45.

Hardin, Martin Davis (cousin of Benjamin Hardin, father of John J. Hardin) (F Ky.) June 21, 1780–Oct. 8, 1823; Senate Nov. 13, 1816–17.

Harding, Aaron (D Ky.) Feb. 20, 1805–Dec. 24, 1875; House 1861–67 (1861–65 Unionist).

Harding, Abner Clark (R Ill.) Feb. 10, 1807–July 19, 1874; House 1865–69.

Harding, Benjamin Franklin (D Ore.) Jan. 4, 1823–June 16, 1899; Senate Sept. 12, 1862–65.

Harding, John Eugene (R Ohio) June 27, 1877–July 26, 1959; House 1907–09.

Harding, Ralph R. (D Idaho) Sept. 9, 1929– ; House 1961–65.

Harding, Warren Gamaliel (R Ohio) Nov. 2, 1865–Aug. 2, 1923; Senate 1915–Jan. 13, 1921; President 1921–Aug. 2, 1923.

Hardwick, Thomas William (D Ga.) Dec. 9, 1872–Jan. 31, 1944; House 1903–Nov. 2, 1914; Senate Nov. 4, 1914–19; Gov. June 25, 1921–June 30, 1923.

Hardy, Alexander Merrill (R Ind.) Dec. 16, 1847–Aug. 31, 1927; House 1895–97.

Hardy, Guy Urban (R Colo.) April 4, 1872–Jan. 26, 1947; House 1919–33.

Hardy, John (D N.Y.) Sept. 19, 1835–Dec. 9, 1913; House Dec. 5, 1881–85.

Hardy, Porter Jr. (D Va.) June 1, 1903–April 19, 1995; House 1947–69.

Hardy, Rufus (D Texas) Dec. 16, 1855–March 13, 1943; House 1907–23.

Hare, Butler Black (father of James Butler Hare) (D S.C.) Nov. 25, 1875–Dec. 30, 1967; House 1925–33, 1939–47.

Hare, Darius Dodge (D Ohio) Jan. 9, 1843–Feb. 10, 1897; House 1891–95.

Hare, James Butler (son of Butler Black Hare) (D S.C.) Sept. 4, 1918–July 16, 1966; House 1949–51.

Hare, Silas (D Texas) Nov. 13, 1827–Nov. 26, 1907; House 1887–91.

Hargis, Denver David (D Kan.) July 22, 1921– ; House 1959–61.

Harkin, Thomas Richard (D Iowa) Nov. 19, 1939– ; House 1975–85; Senate 1985– .

Harlan, Aaron (cousin of Andrew Jackson Harlan) (W Ohio) Sept. 8, 1802–Jan. 8, 1868; House 1853–59.

Harlan, Andrew Jackson (cousin of Aaron Harlan) (D Ind.) March 29, 1815–May 19, 1907; House 1849–51, 1853–55.

Harlan, Byron Berry (D Ohio) Oct. 22, 1886–Nov. 11, 1949; House 1931–39.

Harlan, James (W Ky.) June 22, 1800–Feb. 18, 1863; House 1835–39.

Harlan, James (R Iowa) Aug. 26, 1820–Oct. 5, 1899; Senate Dec. 31, 1855–Jan. 12, 1857 (Free-Soiler), Jan. 29, 1857–May 15, 1865, 1867–73; Secy. of the Interior May 15, 1865–Aug. 31, 1866.

Harless, Richard Fielding (D Ariz.) Aug. 6, 1905–Nov. 24, 1970; House 1943–49.

Harman, Jane (D Calif.) June 28, 1945– ; House 1993–99.

Harmanson, John Henry (D La.) Jan. 15, 1803–Oct. 24, 1850; House 1845–Oct. 24, 1850.

Harmer, Alfred Crout (R Pa.) Aug. 8, 1825–March 6, 1900; House 1871–75, 1877–March 6, 1900.

Harmon, Randall S. (D Ind.) July 19, 1903–Aug. 18, 1982; House 1959–61.

Harness, Forest Arthur (R Ind.) June 24, 1895–July 29, 1974; House 1939–49.

Harper, Alexander (W Ohio) Feb. 5, 1786–Dec. 1, 1860; House 1837–39, 1843–47, 1851–53.

Harper, Francis Jacob (D Pa.) March 5, 1800–March 18, 1837; House March 4–18, 1837.

Harper, James (W Pa.) March 28, 1780–March 31, 1873; House 1833–37 (1833–35 no party).

Harper, James Clarence (D N.C.) Dec. 6, 1819–Jan. 8, 1890; House 1871–73.

Harper, John Adams (R N.H.) Nov. 2, 1779–June 18, 1816; House 1811–13.

Harper, Joseph Morrill (J N.H.) June 21, 1787–Jan. 15, 1865; House 1831–35; Gov. Feb. 28–June 2, 1831.

Harper, Robert Goodloe (– Md.) Jan. 1765–Jan. 14, 1825; House Feb. 1795–March 1801 (S.C.); Senate Jan.–Dec. 1816.

Harper, William (J S.C.) Jan. 17, 1790–Oct. 10, 1847; Senate March 8–Nov. 29, 1826.

Harreld, John William (R Okla.) Jan. 24, 1872–Dec. 26, 1950; House Nov. 8, 1919–21; Senate 1921–27.

Harries, William Henry (D Minn.) Jan. 15, 1843–July 23, 1921; House 1891–93.

Harrington, Henry William (D Ind.) Sept. 12, 1825–March 20, 1882; House 1863–65.

Harrington, Michael Joseph (D Mass.) Sept. 2, 1936– ; House Sept. 30, 1969–79.

Harrington, Vincent Francis (D Iowa) May 16, 1903–Nov. 29, 1943; House 1937–Sept. 5, 1942.

Harris, Benjamin Gwinn (D Md.) Dec. 13, 1805–April 4, 1895; House 1863–67.

Harris, Benjamin Winslow (father of Robert Orr Harris) (R Mass.) Nov. 10, 1823–Feb. 7, 1907; House 1873–83.

Harris, Charles Murray (D Ill.) April 10, 1821–Sept. 20, 1896; House 1863–65.

Harris, Christopher Columbus (D Ala.) Jan. 28, 1842–Dec. 28, 1935; House May 11, 1914–15.

Harris, Claude Jr. (D Ala.) June 29, 1940–Oct. 2, 1994; House 1987–93.

Harris, Fred Roy (D Okla.) Nov. 13, 1930– ; Senate Nov. 4, 1964–Jan. 2, 1973; Chrmn. Dem. Nat. Comm. 1969–70.

Harris, George Emrick (R Miss.) Jan. 6, 1827–March 19, 1911; House Feb. 23, 1870–73.

Harris, Henry Richard (D Ga.) Feb. 2, 1828–Oct. 15, 1909; House 1873–79, 1885–87.

Harris, Henry Schenck (D N.J.) Dec. 27, 1850–May 2, 1902; House 1881–83.

Harris, Herbert Eugene II (D Va.) April 14, 1926– ; House 1975–81.

Harris, Ira (grandfather of Henry Riggs Rathbone) (R N.Y.) May 31, 1802–Dec. 2, 1875; Senate 1861–67.

Harris, Isham Green (D Tenn.) Feb. 10, 1818–July 8, 1897; House 1849–53; Senate 1877–July 8, 1897; elected Pres. pro tempore March 22, 1893, Jan. 10, 1895; Gov. Nov. 3, 1857–March 12, 1862.

Harris, James Morrison (AP Md.) Nov. 20, 1817–July 16, 1898; House 1855–61.

Harris, John (cousin of Robert Harris) (R N.Y.) Sept. 26, 1760–Nov. 1824; House 1807–09.

Harris, John Spafford (R La.) Dec. 18, 1825–Jan. 25, 1906; Senate July 8, 1868–71.

Harris, John Thomas (cousin of John Hill of Virginia) (D Va.) May 8, 1823–Oct. 14, 1899; House 1859–61 (Independent Democrat), 1871–81.

Harris, Mark (– Maine) Jan. 27, 1779–March 2, 1843; House Dec. 2, 1822–23.

Harris, Oren (D Ark.) Dec. 20, 1903–Feb. 5, 1997; House 1941–Feb. 2, 1966; Chrmn. House Interstate and Foreign Commerce 1957–66.

Harris, Robert (cousin of John Harris) (– Pa.) Sept. 5, 1768–Sept. 3, 1851; House 1823–27.

Harris, Robert Orr (son of Benjamin Winslow Harris) (R Mass.) Nov. 8, 1854–June 13, 1926; House 1911–13.

Harris, Sampson Willis (D Ala.) Feb. 23, 1809–April 1, 1857; House 1847–57.

Harris, Stephen Ross (uncle of Ebenezer Byron Finley) (R Ohio) May 22, 1824–Jan. 15, 1905; House 1895–97.

Harris, Thomas K. (R Tenn.) ?–March 18, 1816; House 1813–15.

Harris, Thomas Langrell (D Ill.) Oct. 29, 1816–Nov. 24, 1858; House 1849–51, 1855–Nov. 24, 1858.

Harris, Wiley Pope (D Miss.) Nov. 9, 1818–Dec. 3, 1891; House 1853–55.

Harris, William Alexander (father of William Alexander Harris, below) (D Va.) Aug. 24, 1805–March 28, 1864; House 1841–43.

Harris, William Alexander (son of William Alexander Harris, above) (P Kan.) Oct. 29, 1841–Dec. 20, 1909; House 1893–95; Senate 1897–1903.

Harris, William Julius (great-grandson of Charles Hooks) (D Ga.) Feb. 3, 1868–April 18, 1932; Senate 1919–April 18, 1932.

Harris, Winder Russell (D Va.) Dec. 3, 1888–Feb. 24, 1973; House April 8, 1941–Sept. 15, 1944.

Harrison, Albert Galliton (D Mo.) June 26, 1800–Sept. 7, 1839; House 1835–39 (1835–37 Jacksonian).

Harrison, Benjamin (grandson of William Henry Harrison, son of John Scott Harrison, grandfather of William Henry Harrison born in 1896) (R Ind.) Aug. 20, 1833–March 13, 1901; Senate 1881–87; President 1889–93.

Harrison, Burr Powell (son of Thomas Walter Harrison) (D Va.) July 2, 1904–Dec. 29, 1973; House Nov. 6, 1946–63.

Harrison, Byron Patton "Pat" (D Miss.) Aug. 29, 1881–June 22, 1941; House 1911–19; Senate 1919–June 22, 1941; elected Pres. pro tempore Jan. 6, 1941.

Harrison, Carter Bassett (brother of William Henry Harrison born in 1773) (R Va.) ?–April 18, 1808; House 1793–99 (1793–95 no party).

Harrison, Carter Henry (D Ill.) Feb. 15, 1825–Oct. 28, 1893; House 1875–79.

Harrison, Francis Burton (D N.Y.) Dec. 18, 1873–Nov. 21, 1957; House 1903–05, 1907–Sept. 1, 1913.

Harrison, Frank Girard (D Pa.) Feb. 2, 1940– ; House 1983–85.

Harrison, George Paul (D Ala.) March 19, 1841–July 17, 1922; House Nov. 6, 1894–97.

Harrison, Horace Harrison (R Tenn.) Aug. 7, 1829–Dec. 20, 1885; House 1873–75.

Harrison, John Scott (son of William Henry Harrison born in 1773, father of Benjamin Harrison) (R Ohio) Oct. 4, 1804–May 25, 1878; House 1853–57 (1853–55 Whig).

Harrison, Richard Almgill (U Ohio) April 8, 1824–July 30, 1904; House July 4, 1861–63.

Harrison, Robert Dinsmore (R Neb.) Jan. 26, 1897–June 11, 1977; House Dec. 4, 1951–59.

Harrison, Samuel Smith (J Pa.) 1780–April 1853; House 1833–37.

Harrison, Thomas Walter (father of Burr Powell Harrison) (D Va.) Aug. 5, 1856–May 9, 1935; House Nov. 7, 1916–Dec. 15, 1922, 1923–29.

Harrison, William Henry (father of John Scott Harrison, brother of Carter Basset Harrison, grandfather of Benjamin Harrison, great-great-grandfather of William Henry Harrison born in 1896) (– Ohio) Feb. 9, 1773–April 4, 1841; House (Terr. Del.) 1799–May 14, 1800, (Rep.) Oct. 8, 1816–19; Senate 1825–May 20, 1828; Gov. (Ind. Terr.) 1801–13; President March 4–April 4, 1841.

Harrison, William Henry (great-great-grandson of William Henry Harrison, grandson of Benjamin Harrison and Alvin Saunders) (R Wyo.) Aug. 10, 1896–Oct. 8, 1990; House 1951–55, 1961–65, 1967–69.

Harsha, William Howard (R Ohio) Jan. 1, 1921– ; House 1961–81.

Hart, Alphonso (R Ohio) July 4, 1830–Dec. 23, 1910; House 1883–85.

Hart, Archibald Chapman (D N.J.) Feb. 27, 1873–July 24, 1935; House Nov. 5, 1912–March 3, 1913, July 22, 1913–17.

Hart, Edward Joseph (D N.J.) March 25, 1893–April 20, 1961; House 1935–55; Chrmn. House Merchant Marine and Fisheries 1950–53.

Hart, Elizur Kirke (D N.Y.) April 8, 1841–Feb. 18, 1893; House 1877–79.

Hart, Emanuel Bernard (D N.Y.) Oct. 27, 1809–Aug. 29, 1897; House 1851–53.

Hart, Gary Warren (D Colo.) Nov. 28, 1936– ; Senate 1975–87.

Hart, Joseph Johnson (D Pa.) April 18, 1859–July 13, 1926; House 1895–97.

Hart, Michael James (D Mich.) July 16, 1877–Feb. 14, 1951; House Nov. 3, 1931–35.

Hart, Philip Aloysius (D Mich.) Dec. 10, 1912–Dec. 26, 1976; Senate 1959–Dec. 26, 1976.

Hart, Roswell (R N.Y.) Aug. 4, 1824–April 20, 1883; House 1865–67.

Hart, Thomas Charles (R Conn.) June 12, 1877–July 4, 1971; Senate Feb. 15, 1945–Nov. 5, 1946.

Harter, Dow Watters (D Ohio) Jan. 2, 1885–Sept. 4, 1971; House 1933–43.

Harter, John Francis (R N.Y.) Sept. 1, 1897–Dec. 20, 1947; House 1939–41.

Harter, Michael Daniel (grandson of Robert Moore) (D Ohio) April 6, 1846–Feb. 22, 1896; House 1891–95.

Hartke, Rupert Vance (D Ind.) May 31, 1919– ; Senate 1959–77; Chrmn. Senate Veterans' Affairs 1971–77.

Hartley, Fred Allan Jr. (R N.J.) Feb. 22, 1902–May 11, 1969; House 1929–49; Chrmn. House Eduction and Labor 1947–49.

Hartley, Thomas (F Pa.) Sept. 7, 1748–Dec. 21, 1800; House 1789–Dec. 21, 1800 (1789–93 no party).

Hartman, Charles Sampson (Sil.R Mont.) March 1, 1861–Aug. 3, 1929; House 1893–99 (1893–97 Republican).

Hartman, Jesse Lee (R Pa.) June 18, 1853–Feb. 17, 1930; House 1911–13.

Hartnett, Thomas Forbes (R S.C.) Aug. 7, 1941– ; House 1981–87.

Hartridge, Julian (D Ga.) Sept. 9, 1829–Jan. 8, 1879; House 1875–Jan. 8, 1879.

Hartzell, William (D Ill.) Feb. 20, 1837–Aug. 14, 1903; House 1875–79.

Harvey, David Archibald (R Okla.) March 20, 1845–May 24, 1916; House (Terr. Del.) Nov. 4, 1890–93.

Harvey, James (R Mich.) July 4, 1922– ; House 1961–Jan. 31, 1974.

Harvey, James Madison (R Kan.) Sept. 21, 1833–April 15, 1894; Senate Feb. 2, 1874–77; Gov. Jan. 11, 1869–Jan. 13, 1873.

Harvey, Jonathan (brother of Matthew Harvey) (– N.H.) Feb. 25, 1780–Aug. 23, 1859; House 1825–31.

Harvey, Matthew (brother of Jonathan Harvey) (– N.H.) June 21, 1781–April 7, 1866; House 1821–25; Gov. June 3, 1830–Feb. 28, 1831 (Jacksonian).

Harvey, Ralph (R Ind.) Aug. 9, 1901–Nov. 7, 1991; House Nov. 4, 1947–59, 1961–67.

Hasbrouck, Abraham Bruyn (cousin of Abraham Joseph Hasbrouck) (– N.Y.) Nov. 29, 1791–Feb. 24, 1879; House 1825–27.

Hasbrouck, Abraham Joseph (cousin of Abraham Bruyn Hasbrouck) (R N.Y.) Oct. 16, 1773–Jan. 12, 1845; House 1813–15.

Hasbrouck, Josiah (R N.Y.) March 5, 1755–March 19, 1821; House April 28, 1803–05, 1817–19.

Hascall, Augustus Porter (W N.Y.) June 24, 1800–June 27, 1872; House 1851–53.

Haskell, Dudley Chase (grandfather of Otis Halbert Holmes) (R Kan.) March 23, 1842–Dec. 16, 1883; House 1877–Dec. 16, 1883.

Haskell, Floyd Kirk (D Colo.) Feb. 7, 1916–Aug. 25, 1998; Senate 1973–79.

Haskell, Harry Garner Jr. (R Del.) May 27, 1921– ; House 1957–59.

Haskell, Reuben Locke (R N.Y.) Oct. 5, 1878–Oct. 2, 1971; House 1915–Dec. 31, 1919.

Haskell, William T. (nephew of Charles Ready) (W Tenn.) July 21, 1818–March 12, 1859; House 1847–49.

Haskin, John Bussing (ALD N.Y.) Aug. 27, 1821–Sept. 18, 1895; House 1857–61 (1857–59 Democrat).

Haskins, Kittredge (R Vt.) April 8, 1836–Aug. 7, 1916; House 1901–09.

Hastert, John Dennis (R Ill.) Jan. 2, 1942– ; House 1987– ; Speaker 1999– .

Hastings, Alcee L. (D Fla.) Sept. 5, 1936– ; House 1993– .

Hastings, Daniel Oren (R Del.) March 5, 1874–May 9, 1966; Senate Dec. 10, 1928–Jan. 2, 1937.

Hastings, George (D N.Y.) March 13, 1807–Aug. 29, 1866; House 1853–55.

Hastings, James Fred (R N.Y.) April 10, 1926– ; House 1969–Jan. 20, 1976.

Hastings, John (D Ohio) 1778–Dec. 8, 1854; House 1839–43.

Hastings, Richard "Doc" (R Wash.) Feb. 7, 1941– ; House 1995– .

Hastings, Serranus Clinton (D Iowa) Nov. 22, 1813–Feb. 18, 1893; House Dec. 28, 1846–47.

Hastings, Seth (father of William Soden Hastings) (F Mass.) April 8, 1762–Nov. 19, 1831; House Aug. 24, 1801–07.

Hastings, William Soden (son of Seth Hastings) (W Mass.) June 3, 1798–June 17, 1842; House 1837–June 17, 1842.

Hastings, William Wirt (D Okla.) Dec. 31, 1866–April 8, 1938; House 1915–21, 1923–35.

Hatch, Carl Atwood (D N.M.) Nov. 27, 1889–Sept. 15, 1963; Senate Oct. 10, 1933–Jan. 2, 1949.

Hatch, Herschel Harrison (R Mich.) Feb. 17, 1837–Nov. 30, 1920; House 1883–85.

Hatch, Israel Thompson (D N.Y.) June 30, 1808–Sept. 24, 1875; House 1857–59.

Hatch, Jethro Ayers (R Ind.) June 18, 1837–Aug. 3, 1912; House 1895–97.

Hatch, Orrin Grant (R Utah) March 22, 1934– ; Senate 1977– ; Chrmn. Senate Labor and Human Resources 1981–87; Chrmn. Senate Judiciary 1995– .

Hatch, William Henry (D Mo.) Sept. 11, 1833–Dec. 23, 1896; House 1879–95.

Hatcher, Charles Floyd (D Ga.) July 1, 1939– ; House 1981–93.

Hatcher, Robert Anthony (D Mo.) Feb. 24, 1819–Dec. 4, 1886; House 1873–79.

Hatfield, Henry Drury (R W.Va.) Sept. 15, 1875–Oct. 23, 1962; Senate 1929–35; Gov. March 4, 1913–March 4, 1917.

Hatfield, Mark Odom (R Ore.) July 12, 1922– ; Senate Jan. 10, 1967–97; Chrmn. Senate Appropriations 1981–87; Gov. Jan. 12, 1959–Jan. 9, 1967; Chrmn. Senate Appropriations 1995–97.

Hatfield, Paul Gerhart (D Mont.) April 29, 1928– ; Senate Jan. 22–Dec. 14, 1978.

Hathaway, Samuel Gilbert (J N.Y.) July 18, 1780–May 2, 1867; House 1833–35.

Hathaway, William Dodd (D Maine) Feb. 21, 1924– ; House 1965–73; Senate 1973–79.

Hathorn, Henry Harrison (R N.Y.) Nov. 28, 1813–Feb. 20, 1887; House 1873–77.

Hathorn, John (R N.Y.) Jan. 9, 1749–Feb. 19, 1825; House 1789–91 (no party), 1795–97; Cont. Cong. (elected but did not attend) 1788.

Hatton, Robert Hopkins (O Tenn.) Nov. 2, 1826–May 31, 1862; House 1859–61.

Haugen, Gilbert Nelson (R Iowa) April 21, 1859–July 18, 1933; House 1899–1933.

Haugen, Nils Pederson (R Wis.) March 9, 1849–April 23, 1931; House 1887–95.

Haughey, Thomas (R Ala.) 1826–Aug. 5, 1869; House July 21, 1868–69.

Haun, Henry Peter (D Calif.) Jan. 18, 1815–June 6, 1860; Senate Nov. 3, 1859–March 4, 1860.

Haven, Nathaniel Appleton (F N.H.) July 19, 1762–March 13, 1831; House 1809–11.

Haven, Solomon George (W N.Y.) Nov. 27, 1810–Dec. 24, 1861; House 1851–57.

Havenner, Franck Roberts (D Calif.) Sept. 20, 1882–July 24, 1967; House 1937–41 (1937–39 Progressive), 1945–53.

Havens, Harrison Eugene (R Mo.) Dec. 15, 1837–Aug. 16, 1916; House 1871–75.

Havens, James Smith (D N.Y.) May 28, 1859–Feb. 27, 1927; House April 19, 1910–11.

Havens, Jonathan Nicoll (R N.Y.) June 18, 1757–Oct. 25, 1799; House 1795–Oct. 25, 1799.

Hawes, Albert Gallatin (brother of Richard Hawes, nephew of Aylett Hawes, great-uncle of Harry Bartow Hawes, cousin of Aylett Hawes Buckner) (J Ky.) April 1, 1804–March 14, 1849; House 1831–37.

Hawes, Aylett (uncle of Richard Hawes, Albert Gallatin Hawes and Aylett Hawes Buckner) (R Va.) April 21, 1768–Aug. 31, 1833; House 1811–17.

Hawes, Harry Bartow (great-nephew of Albert Gallatin Hawes) (D Mo.) Nov. 15, 1869–July 31, 1947; House 1921–Oct. 15, 1926; Senate Dec. 6, 1926–Feb. 3, 1933.

Hawes, Richard (brother of Albert Gallatin Hawes, nephew of Aylett Hawes, cousin of Aylett Hawes Buckner) (W Ky.) Feb. 6, 1797–May 25, 1877; House 1837–41.

Hawk, Robert Moffett Allison (R Ill.) April 23, 1839–June 29, 1882; House 1879–June 29, 1882.

Hawkes, Albert Wahl (R N.J.) Nov. 20, 1878–May 9, 1971; Senate 1943–49.

Hawkes, James (– N.Y.) Dec. 13, 1776–Oct. 2, 1865; House 1821–23.

Hawkins, Augustus Freeman (D Calif.) Aug. 31, 1907– ; House 1963–91; Chrmn. House Administration 1981–84; Chrmn. House Education and Labor 1984–91.

Hawkins, Benjamin (uncle of Micajah Thomas Hawkins) (– N.C.) Aug. 15, 1754–June 6, 1816; Senate Nov. 27, 1789–95; Cont. Cong. 1781–83, 1787.

Hawkins, George Sydney (D Fla.) 1808–March 15, 1878; House 1857–Jan. 21, 1861.

Hawkins, Isaac Roberts (R Tenn.) May 16, 1818–Aug. 12, 1880; House July 24, 1866–71 (July 24, 1866–67 Unionist).

Hawkins, Joseph (Ad.D N.Y.) Nov. 14, 1781–April 20, 1832; House 1829–31.

Hawkins, Joseph H. (R Ky.) ?–1823; House March 29, 1814–15.

Hawkins, Micajah Thomas (nephew of Benjamin Hawkins and Nathaniel Macon) (D N.C.) May 20, 1790–Dec. 22, 1858; House Dec. 15, 1831–41 (Dec. 15, 1831–37 Jacksonian).

Hawkins, Paula (R Fla.) Jan. 24, 1927– ; Senate Jan. 1, 1981–87.

Hawks, Charles Jr. (R Wis.) July 7, 1899–Jan. 6, 1960; House 1939–41.

Hawley, John Baldwin (R Ill.) Feb. 9, 1831–May 24, 1895; House 1869–75.

Hawley, Joseph Roswell (R Conn.) Oct. 31, 1826–March 17, 1905; House Dec. 2, 1872–75, 1879–81; Senate 1881–1905; Gov. May 2, 1866–May 1, 1867.

Hawley, Robert Bradley (R Texas) Oct. 25, 1849–Nov. 28, 1921; House 1897–1901.

Hawley, Willis Chatman (R Ore.) May 5, 1864–July 24, 1941; House 1907–33.

Haws, John Henry Hobart (W N.Y.) 1809–Jan. 27, 1858; House 1851–53.

Hay, Andrew Kessler (W N.J.) Jan. 19, 1809–Feb. 7, 1881; House 1849–51.

Hay, James (D Va.) Jan. 9, 1856–June 12, 1931; House 1897–Oct. 1, 1916.

Hay, John Breese (R Ill.) Jan. 8, 1834–June 16, 1916; House 1869–73.

Hayakawa, Samuel Ichiye (R Calif.) July 18, 1906–Feb. 27, 1992; Senate 1977–83.

Hayden, Carl Trumbull (D Ariz.) Oct. 2, 1877–Jan. 25, 1972; House Feb. 19, 1912–27; Senate 1927–69; Chrmn. Senate Rules and Administration 1949–53; Chrmn. Senate Appropriations 1955–69; elected Pres. pro tempore Jan. 3, 1957.

Hayden, Edward Daniel (R Mass.) Dec. 27, 1833–Nov. 15, 1908; House 1885–89.

Hayden, Moses (– N.Y.) 1786–Feb. 13, 1830; House 1823–27.

Hayes, Charles Arthur (D Ill.) Feb. 17, 1918–April 8, 1997; House Aug. 23, 1983–93.

Hayes, Everis Anson (R Calif.) March 10, 1855–June 3, 1942; House 1905–19.

Hayes, James A. (R La.) Dec. 21, 1946– ; House 1987–97 (1987–Dec. 1, 1995 Democrat).

Hayes, Philip Cornelius (R Ill.) Feb. 3, 1833–July 13, 1916; House 1877–81.

Hayes, Philip Harold (D Ind.) Sept. 1, 1940– ; House 1975–77.

Hayes, Robin (R N.C.) Aug. 14, 1945– ; House 1999– .

Hayes, Rutherford Birchard (R Ohio) Oct. 4, 1822–Jan. 17, 1893; House 1865–July 20, 1867; Gov. Jan. 13, 1868–Jan. 8, 1872, Jan. 10, 1876–March 2, 1877; President 1877–81.

Hayes, Walter Ingalls (D Iowa) Dec. 9, 1841–March 14, 1901; House 1887–95.

Haymond, Thomas Sherwood (W Va.) Jan. 15, 1794–April 5, 1869; House Nov. 8, 1849–51.

Haymond, William Summerville (D Ind.) Feb. 20, 1823–Dec. 24, 1885; House 1875–77.

Hayne, Arthur Peronneau (brother of Robert Young Hayne) (D S.C.) March 12, 1788 or 1790–Jan. 7, 1867; Senate May 11–Dec. 2, 1858.

Hayne, Robert Young (brother of Arthur Peronneau Hayne, son-in-law of Charles Pinckney) (J S.C.) Nov. 10, 1791–Sept. 24, 1839; Senate 1823–Dec. 13, 1832 (1823–29 no party); Gov. Dec. 13, 1832–Dec. 11, 1834 (State Rights Democrat).

Haynes, Charles Eaton (– Ga.) April 15, 1784–Aug. 29, 1841; House 1825–31, 1835–39.

Haynes, Martin Alonzo (R N.H.) July 30, 1842–Nov. 28, 1919; House 1883–87.

Haynes, William Elisha (cousin of George William Palmer) (D Ohio) Oct. 19, 1829–Dec. 5, 1914; House 1889–93.

Hays, Charles (R Ala.) Feb. 2, 1834–June 24, 1879; House 1869–77.

Hays, Edward Dixon (R Mo.) April 28, 1872–July 25, 1941; House 1919–23.

Hays, Edward Retilla (R Iowa) May 26, 1847–Feb. 28, 1896; House Nov. 4, 1890–91.

Hays, Lawrence Brooks (D Ark.) Aug. 9, 1898–Oct. 11, 1981; House 1943–59.

Hays, Samuel (D Pa.) Sept. 10, 1783–July 1, 1868; House 1843–45.

Hays, Samuel Lewis (D Va.) Oct. 20, 1794–March 17, 1871; House 1841–43.

Hays, Wayne Levere (D Ohio) May 13, 1911–Feb. 10, 1989; House 1949–Sept. 1, 1976; Chrmn. House Administration 1971–76.

Hayward, Monroe Leland (R Neb.) Dec. 22, 1840–Dec. 5, 1899; elected to the Senate March 8, 1988, to fill a vacancy but died before qualifying.

Hayward, William Jr. (– Md.) 1787–Oct. 19, 1836; House 1823–25.

Haywood, William Henry Jr. (D N.C.) Oct. 23, 1801–Oct. 7, 1852; Senate 1843–July 25, 1846.

Hayworth, Donald (D Mich.) Jan. 13, 1898–Feb. 25, 1982; House 1955–57.

Hayworth, J. D. (R Ariz.) July 12, 1958– ; House 1995– .

Hazard, Nathaniel (– R.I.) 1776–Dec. 17, 1820; House 1819–Dec. 17, 1820.

Hazeltine, Abner (W N.Y.) June 10, 1793–Dec. 20, 1879; House 1833–37 (1833–35 Anti-Mason).

Hazeltine, Ira Sherwin (G Mo.) July 13, 1821–Jan. 13, 1899; House 1881–83.

Hazelton, George Cochrane (brother of Gerry Whiting Hazelton, nephew of Clark Betton Cochrane) (R Wis.) Jan. 3, 1832–Sept. 4, 1922; House 1877–83.

Hazelton, Gerry Whiting (brother of George Cochrane Hazelton, nephew of Clark Betton Cochrane) (R Wis.) Feb. 24, 1829–Sept. 29, 1920; House 1871–75.

Hazelton, John Wright (R N.J.) Dec. 10, 1814–Dec. 20, 1878; House 1871–75.

Hazlett, James Miller (R Pa.) Oct. 14, 1864–Nov. 8, 1941; House March 4–Oct. 20, 1927.

Heald, William Henry (R Del.) Aug. 27, 1864–June 3, 1939; House 1909–13.

Healey, Arthur Daniel (D Mass.) Dec. 29, 1889–Sept. 16, 1948; House 1933–Aug. 3, 1942.

Healey, James Christopher (D N.Y.) Dec. 24, 1909–Dec. 16, 1981; House Feb. 7, 1956–65.

Healy, Joseph (– N.H.) Aug. 21, 1776–Oct. 10, 1861; House 1825–29.

Healy, Ned Romeyn (D Calif.) Aug. 9, 1905–Sept. 10, 1977; House 1945–47.

Heard, John Thaddeus (D Mo.) Oct. 29, 1840–Jan. 27, 1927; House 1885–95.

Hearst, George (father of William Randolph Hearst) (D Calif.) Sept. 3, 1820–Feb. 28, 1891; Senate March 23–Aug. 4, 1886, 1887–Feb. 28, 1891.

Hearst, William Randolph (son of George Hearst) (D N.Y.) April 29, 1863–Aug. 14, 1951; House 1903–07.

Heath, James P. (J Md.) Dec. 21, 1777–June 12, 1854; House 1833–35.

Heath, John (R Va.) May 8, 1758–Oct. 13, 1810; House 1793–97.

Heaton, David (R N.C.) March 10, 1823–June 25, 1870; House July 15, 1868–June 25, 1870.

Heaton, Robert Douglas (R Pa.) July 1, 1873–June 11, 1933; House 1915–19.

Heatwole, Joel Prescott (R Minn.) Aug. 22, 1856–April 4, 1910; House 1895–1903.

Hebard, William (W Vt.) Nov. 29, 1800–Oct. 20, 1875; House 1849–53.

Hebert, Felix (R R.I.) Dec. 11, 1874–Dec. 14, 1969; Senate 1929–35.

Hebert, Felix Edward (D La.) Oct. 12, 1901–Dec. 29, 1979; House 1941–77; Chrmn. House Armed Services 1971–75.

Hechler, Ken (D W.Va.) Sept. 20, 1914– ; House 1959–77.

Hecht, Jacob Chic (R Nev.) Nov. 30, 1928– ; Senate 1983–89.

Heckler, Margaret M. (R Mass.) June 21, 1931– ; House 1967–83; Secy. Health and Human Services March 9, 1983–Dec. 13, 1985.

Hedge, Thomas (R Iowa) June 24, 1844–Nov. 28, 1920; House 1899–1907.

Hedrick, Erland Harold (D W.Va.) Aug. 9, 1894–Sept. 20, 1954; House 1945–53.

Heffernan, James Joseph (D N.Y.) Nov. 8, 1888–Jan. 27, 1967; House 1941–53.

Hefley, Joel M. (R Colo.) April 18, 1935– ; House 1987– .

Heflin, Howell Thomas (nephew of James Thomas Heflin) (D Ala.) June 19, 1921– ; Senate 1979–97; Chrmn. Senate Select Committee on Ethics 1987–91.

Heflin, James Thomas (uncle of Howell Thomas Heflin, nephew of Robert Stell Heflin) (D Ala.) April 9, 1869–April 22, 1951; House May 10, 1904–Nov. 1, 1920; Senate Nov. 3, 1920–31.

Heflin, Robert Stell (uncle of James Thomas Heflin) (R Ala.) April 15, 1815–Jan. 24, 1901; House 1869–71.

Hefner, Willie Gathrel "Bill" (D N.C.) April 11, 1930– ; House 1975–99.

Heftel, Cecil Landau (D Hawaii) Sept. 30, 1924– ; House 1977–July 11, 1986.

Heidinger, James Vandaveer (R Ill.) July 17, 1882–March 22, 1945; House 1941–March 22, 1945.

Heilman, William (great-grandfather of Charles Marion La Follette) (R Ind.) Oct. 11, 1824–Sept. 22, 1890; House 1879–83.

Heineman, Fred (R N.C.) Dec. 28, 1929– ; House 1995–97.

Heiner, Daniel Brodhead (R Pa.) Dec. 30, 1854–Feb. 14, 1944; House 1893–97.

Heinke, George Henry (R Neb.) July 22, 1882–Jan. 2, 1940; House 1939–Jan. 2, 1940.

Heintz, Victor (R Ohio) Nov. 20, 1876–Dec. 27, 1968; House 1917–19.

Heinz, Henry John III (R Pa.) Oct. 23, 1938–April 4, 1991; House Nov. 2, 1971–77; Senate 1977–April 4, 1991.

Heiskell, John Netherland (D Ark.) Nov. 2, 1872–Dec. 28, 1972; Senate Jan. 6–Jan. 29, 1913.

Heitfeld, Henry (P Idaho) Jan. 12, 1859–Oct. 21, 1938; Senate 1897–1903.

Helgesen, Henry Thomas (R N.D.) June 26, 1857–April 10, 1917; House 1911–April 10, 1917.

Heller, Louis Benjamin (D N.Y.) Feb. 10, 1905–Oct. 30, 1993; House Feb. 15, 1949–July 21, 1954.

Helm, Harvey (D Ky.) Dec. 2, 1865–March 3, 1919; House 1907–March 3, 1919.

Helmick, William (R Ohio) Sept. 6, 1817–March 31, 1888; House 1859–61.

Helms, Jesse Alexander (R N.C.) Oct. 18, 1921– ; Senate 1973– ; Chrmn. Senate Agriculture, Nutrition, and Forestry 1981–87; Chrmn. Senate Foreign Relations 1995– .

Helms, William (R N.J.) ?–1813; House 1801–11.

Helstoski, Henry (D N.J.) March 21, 1925– ; House 1965–77.

Helvering, Guy Tresillian (D Kan.) Jan. 10, 1878–July 4, 1946; House 1913–19.

Hemenway, James Alexander (R Ind.) March 8, 1860–Feb. 10, 1923; House 1895–1905; Senate March 4, 1905–09.

Hemphill, John (uncle of John James Hemphill, great-great-uncle of Robert Witherspoon Hemphill) (SRD Texas) Dec. 18, 1803–Jan. 4, 1862; Senate 1859–July 1861.

Hemphill, John James (cousin of William Huggins Brawley, nephew of John Hemphill, great-uncle of Robert Witherspoon Hemphill) (D S.C.) Aug. 25, 1849–May 11, 1912; House 1883–93.

Hemphill, Joseph (J Pa.) Jan. 7, 1770–May 29, 1842; House 1801–03 (Federalist), 1819–26 (Federalist), 1829–31.

Hemphill, Robert Witherspoon (great-great-nephew of John Hemphill, great-nephew of John James Hemphill and William Huggins Brawley, great-great-grandson of Robert Witherspoon) (D S.C.) May 10, 1915–Dec. 25, 1983; House 1957–May 1, 1964.

Hempstead, Edward (– Mo.) June 3, 1780–Aug. 10, 1817; House (Terr. Del.) Nov. 9, 1812–Sept. 17, 1814.

Hendee, George Whitman (R Vt.) Nov. 30, 1832–Dec. 6, 1906; House 1873–79; Gov. Feb. 7–Oct. 6, 1870.

Henderson, Archibald (F N.C.) Aug. 7, 1768–Oct. 21, 1822; House 1799–1803.

Henderson, Bennett H. (R Tenn.) Sept. 5, 1784–?; House 1815–17.

Henderson, Charles Belknap (D Nev.) June 8, 1873–Nov. 8, 1954; Senate Jan. 12, 1918–21.

Henderson, David Bremner (R Iowa) March 14, 1840–Feb. 25, 1906; House 1883–1903; Speaker Dec. 4, 1899–1901, Dec. 2, 1901–03.

Henderson, David Newton (D N.C.) April 16, 1921– ; House 1961–77; Chrmn. House Post Office and Civil Service 1975–77.

Henderson, James Henry Dickey (UR Ore.) July 23, 1810–Dec. 13, 1885; House 1865–67.

Henderson, James Pinckney (D Texas) March 31, 1808–June 4, 1858; Senate Nov. 9, 1857–June 4, 1858; Gov. Feb. 19, 1846–Dec. 21, 1847.

Henderson, John (W Miss.) Feb. 28, 1797–Sept. 15, 1857; Senate 1839–45.

Henderson, John Brooks (U Mo.) Nov. 16, 1826–April 12, 1913; Senate Jan. 17, 1862–69.

Henderson, John Earl (R Ohio) Jan. 4, 1917–Dec. 3, 1994; House 1955–61.

Henderson, John Steele (D N.C.) Jan. 6, 1846–Oct. 9, 1916; House 1885–95.

Henderson, Joseph (J Pa.) Aug. 2, 1791–Dec. 25, 1863; House 1833–37.

Henderson, Samuel (F Pa.) Nov. 27, 1764–Nov. 17, 1841; House Oct. 11, 1814–15.

Henderson, Thomas (F N.J.) Aug. 15, 1743–Dec. 15, 1824; House 1795–97; Cont. Cong. (elected but did not attend) 1779.

Henderson, Thomas Jefferson (R Ill.) Nov. 29, 1824–Feb. 6, 1911; House 1875–95.

Hendon, William Martin (R N.C.) Nov. 9, 1944– ; House 1981–83, 1985–87.

Hendrick, John Kerr (D Ky.) Oct. 10, 1849–June 20, 1921; House 1895–97.

Hendricks, Joseph Edward (D Fla.) Sept. 24, 1903–Oct. 20, 1974; House 1937–49.

Hendricks, Thomas Andrews (nephew of William Hendricks) (D Ind.) Sept. 7, 1819–Nov. 25, 1885; House 1851–55; Senate 1863–69; Gov. Jan. 15, 1873–Jan. 8, 1877; Vice President Nov. 4–Nov. 25, 1885.

Hendricks, William (uncle of Thomas Andrews Hendricks) (– Ind.) Nov. 12, 1782–May 16, 1850; House Dec. 11, 1816–July 25, 1822; Senate 1825–37; Gov. Dec. 5, 1822–Feb. 12, 1825 (Democratic Republican).

Hendrickson, Robert Clymer (R N.J.) Aug. 12, 1898–Dec. 7, 1964; Senate 1949–55.

Hendrix, Joseph Clifford (D N.Y.) May 25, 1853–Nov. 9, 1904; House 1893–95.

Henkle, Eli Jones (D Md.) Nov. 24, 1828–Nov. 1, 1893; House 1875–81.

Henley, Barclay (son of Thomas Jefferson Henley) (D Calif.) March 17, 1843–Feb. 15, 1914; House 1883–87.

Henley, Thomas Jefferson (father of Barclay Henley) (D Ind.) April 2, 1810–Jan. 2, 1865; House 1843–49.

Henn, Bernhart (D Iowa) 1817–Aug. 30, 1865; House 1851–55.

Henney, Charles William Francis (D Wis.) Feb. 2, 1884–Nov. 16, 1969; House 1933–35.

Hennings, Thomas Carey Jr. (D Mo.) June 25, 1903–Sept. 13, 1960; House 1935–Dec. 31, 1940; Senate 1951–Sept. 13, 1960; Chrmn. Senate Rules and Administration 1957–60.

Henry, Charles Lewis (R Ind.) July 1, 1849–May 2, 1927; House 1895–99.

Henry, Daniel Maynadier (D Md.) Feb. 19, 1823–Aug. 31, 1899; House 1877–81.

Henry, Edward Stevens (R Conn.) Feb. 10, 1836–Oct. 10, 1921; House 1895–1913.

Henry, John (– Md.) Nov. 1750–Dec. 16, 1798; Senate 1789–Dec. 10, 1797; Gov. Nov. 17, 1797–Nov. 14, 1798; Cont. Cong. 1778–80, 1785–86.

Henry, John (W Ill.) Nov. 1, 1800–April 28, 1882; House Feb. 5–March 3, 1847.

Henry, John Flournoy (– Ky.) Jan. 17, 1793–Nov. 12, 1873; House Dec. 11, 1826–27.

Henry, Lewis (R N.Y.) June 8, 1885–July 23, 1941; House April 11, 1922–23.

Henry, Patrick (uncle of Patrick Henry, below) (D Miss.) Feb. 12, 1843–May 18, 1930; House 1897–1901.

Henry, Patrick (nephew of Patrick Henry, above) (D Miss.) Feb. 15, 1861–Dec. 28, 1933; House 1901–03.

Henry, Paul Brentwood (R Mich.) July 9, 1942–July 31, 1993; House 1985–July 31, 1993.

Henry, Robert Kirkland (R Wis.) Feb. 9, 1890–Nov. 20, 1946; House 1945–Nov. 20, 1946.

Henry, Robert Lee (D Texas) May 12, 1864–July 9, 1931; House 1897–1917.

Henry, Robert Pryor (– Ky.) Nov. 24, 1788–Aug. 25, 1826; House 1823–Aug. 25, 1826.

Henry, Thomas (W Pa.) 1779–July 20, 1849; House 1837–43 (1837–41 AMas.).

Henry, William (W Vt.) March 22, 1788–April 16, 1861; House 1847–51.

Henry, Winder Laird (great-grandson of Charles Goldsborough and Robert Henry Goldsborough) (D Md.) Dec. 20, 1864–July 5, 1940; House Nov. 6, 1894–95.

Hensley, Walter Lewis (D Mo.) Sept. 3, 1871–July 18, 1946; House 1911–19.

Hepburn, William Peters (great-grandson of Matthew Lyon) (R Iowa) Nov. 4, 1833–Feb. 7, 1916; House 1881–87, 1893–1909.

Herbert, Hilary Abner (D Ala.) March 12, 1834–March 6, 1919; House 1877–93; Secy. of the Navy March 7, 1893–March 5, 1897.

Herbert, John Carlyle (F Md.) Aug. 16, 1775–Sept. 1, 1846; House 1815–19.

Herbert, Philemon Thomas (D Calif.) Nov. 1, 1825–July 23, 1864; House 1855–57.

Hereford, Frank (D W.Va.) July 4, 1825–Dec. 21, 1891; House 1871–Jan. 31, 1877; Senate Jan. 31, 1877–81.

Herger, Walter William "Wally" (R Calif.) May 20, 1945– ; House 1987– .

Herkimer, John (R N.Y.) 1773–June 8, 1848; House 1817–19, 1823–25.

Herlong, Albert Sydney Jr. (D Fla.) Feb. 14, 1909–Dec. 27, 1995; House 1949–69.

Hermann, Binger (R Ore.) Feb. 19, 1843–April 15, 1926; House 1885–97, June 1, 1903–07.

Hernandez, Benigno Cardenas (R N.M.) Feb. 13, 1862–Oct. 18, 1954; House 1915–17, 1919–21.

Hernandez, Joseph Marion (– Fla.) Aug. 4, 1793–June 8, 1857; House (Terr. Del.) Sept. 30, 1822–23.

Herndon, Thomas Hord (D Ala.) July 1, 1828–March 28, 1883; House 1879–March 28, 1883.

Herndon, William Smith (D Texas) Nov. 27, 1835–Oct. 11, 1903; House 1871–75.

Herod, William (W Ind.) March 31, 1801–Oct. 20, 1871; House Jan. 25, 1837–39.

Herrick, Anson (son of Ebenezer Herrick) (D N.Y.) Jan. 21, 1812–Feb. 6, 1868; House 1863–65.

Herrick, Ebenezer (father of Anson Herrick) (– Maine) Oct. 21, 1785–May 7, 1839; House 1821–27.

Herrick, Joshua (D Maine) March 18, 1793–Aug. 30, 1874; House 1843–45.

Herrick, Manuel (R Okla.) Sept. 20, 1876–Feb. 29, 1952; House 1921–23.

Herrick, Richard Platt (W N.Y.) March 23, 1791–June 20, 1846; House 1845–June 20, 1846.

Herrick, Samuel (R Ohio) April 14, 1779–June 4, 1852; House 1817–21.

Herring, Clyde LaVerne (D Iowa) May 3, 1879–Sept. 15, 1945; Senate Jan. 15, 1937–43; Gov. Jan. 12, 1933–Jan. 14, 1937.

Hersey, Ira Greenlief (R Maine) March 31, 1858–May 6, 1943; House 1917–29.

Hersey, Samuel Freeman (R Maine) April 12, 1812–Feb. 3, 1875; House 1873–Feb. 3, 1875.

Hersman, Hugh Steel (D Calif.) July 8, 1872–March 7, 1954; House 1919–21.

Hertel, Dennis Mark (D Mich.) Dec. 7, 1948– ; House 1981–93.

Herter, Christian Archibald (R Mass.) March 28, 1895–Dec. 30, 1966; House 1943–53; Gov. Jan. 8, 1953–Jan. 3, 1957; Secy. of State April 22, 1959–Jan. 20, 1961.

Heselton, John Walter (R Mass.) March 17, 1900–Aug. 19, 1962; House 1945–59.

Hess, William Emil (R Ohio) Feb. 13, 1898–July 14, 1986; House 1929–37, 1939–49, 1951–61.

Hewitt, Abram Stevens (D N.Y.) July 31, 1822–Jan. 18, 1903; House 1875–79, 1881–Dec. 30, 1886; Chrmn. Dem. Nat. Comm. 1876–77.

Hewitt, Goldsmith Whitehouse (D Ala.) Feb. 14, 1834–May 27, 1895; House 1875–79, 1881–85.

Heyburn, Weldon Brinton (R Idaho) May 23, 1852–Oct. 17, 1912; Senate 1903–Oct. 17, 1912.

Hibbard, Ellery Albee (cousin of Harry Hibbard) (D N.H.) July 31, 1826–July 24, 1903; House 1871–73.

Hibbard, Harry (cousin of Ellery Albee Hibbard) (D N.H.) June 1, 1816–July 28, 1872; House 1849–55.

Hibshman, Jacob (– Pa.) Jan. 31, 1772–May 19, 1852; House 1819–21.

Hickenlooper, Bourke Blakemore (R Iowa) July 21, 1896–Sept. 4, 1971; Senate 1945–69; Gov. Jan. 14, 1943–Jan. 11, 1945.

Hickey, Andrew James (R Ind.) Aug. 27, 1872–Aug. 20, 1942; House 1919–31.

Hickey, John Joseph (D Wyo.) Aug. 22, 1911–Sept. 22, 1970; Senate 1961–Nov. 6, 1962; Gov. Jan. 5, 1959–Jan. 2, 1961.

Hickman, John (R Pa.) Sept. 11, 1810–March 23, 1875; House 1855–63 (1855–59 Democrat, 1859–61 Anti-Lecompton Democrat).

Hicks, Floyd Verne (D Wash.) May 29, 1915– ; House 1965–77.

Hicks, Frederick Cocks (original name: Frederick Hicks Cocks, brother of William Willets Cocks) (R N.Y.) March 6, 1872–Dec. 14, 1925; House 1915–23.

Hicks, Josiah Duane (R Pa.) Aug. 1, 1844–May 9, 1923; House 1893–99.

Hicks, Louise Day (D Mass.) Oct. 16, 1923– ; House 1971–73.

Hicks, Thomas Holliday (U Md.) Sept. 2, 1798–Feb. 14, 1865; Senate Dec. 29, 1862–Feb. 14, 1865; Gov. Jan. 13, 1858–Jan. 8, 1862 (American Party).

Hiestand, Edgar Willard (R Calif.) Dec. 3, 1888–Aug. 19, 1970; House 1953–63.

Hiestand, John Andrew (R Pa.) Oct. 2, 1824–Dec. 13, 1890; House 1885–89.

Hiester, Daniel (brother of John Hiester, cousin of Joseph Hiester, uncle of William Hiester and Daniel Hiester, below) (R Md.) June

25, 1747–March 7, 1804; House 1789–July 1, 1796 (no party Pa.), 1801–March 7, 1804.

Hiester, Daniel (son of John Hiester, nephew of Daniel Hiester, above) (– Pa.) 1774–March 8, 1834; House 1809–11.

Hiester, Isaac Ellmaker (son of William Hiester, cousin of Hiester Clymer) (W Pa.) May 29, 1824–Feb. 6, 1871; House 1853–55.

Hiester, John (father of Daniel Hiester born in 1774, brother of Daniel Hiester born in 1747, cousin of Joseph Hiester, uncle of William Hiester) (R Pa.) April 9, 1745–Oct. 15, 1821; House 1807–09.

Hiester, Joseph (cousin of John Hiester and Daniel Hiester born in 1747, grandfather of Henry Augustus Muhlenberg) (R Pa.) Nov. 18, 1752–June 10, 1832; House Dec. 1, 1797–1805, 1815–Dec. 1820; Gov. Dec. 19, 1820–Dec. 16, 1823 (Democratic Republican).

Hiester, William (father of Isaac Ellmaker Hiester, uncle of Hiester Clymer, nephew of John Hiester and Daniel Hiester born in 1747) (AMas. Pa.) Oct. 10, 1790–Oct. 13, 1853; House 1831–37.

Higby, William (R Calif.) Aug. 18, 1813–Nov. 27, 1887; House 1863–69.

Higgins, Anthony (R Del.) Oct. 1, 1840–June 26, 1912; Senate 1889–95.

Higgins, Edwin Werter (R Conn.) July 2, 1874–Sept. 24, 1954; House Oct. 2, 1905–13.

Higgins, John Patrick (D Mass.) Feb. 19, 1893–Aug. 2, 1955; House 1935–Sept. 30, 1937.

Higgins, William Lincoln (R Conn.) March 8, 1867–Nov. 19, 1951; House 1933–37.

Hightower, Jack English (D Texas) Sept. 6, 1926– ; House 1975–85.

Hilborn, Samuel Greeley (R Calif.) Dec. 9, 1834–April 19, 1899; House Dec. 5, 1892–April 4, 1894, 1895–99.

Hildebrandt, Fred Herman (D S.D.) Aug. 2, 1874–Jan. 26, 1956; House 1933–39.

Hildebrant, Charles Quinn (R Ohio) Oct. 17, 1864–March 31, 1953; House 1901–05.

Hiler, John Patrick (R Ind.) April 24, 1953– ; House 1981–91.

Hill, Baron (D Ind.) June 23, 1953– ; House 1999– .

Hill, Benjamin Harvey (cousin of Hugh Lawson White Hill) (D Ga.) Sept. 14, 1823–Aug. 16, 1882; House May 5, 1875–77; Senate 1877–Aug. 16, 1882.

Hill, Charles Augustus (R Ill.) Aug. 23, 1833–May 29, 1902; House 1889–91.

Hill, Clement Sidney (W Ky.) Feb. 13, 1813–Jan. 5, 1892; House 1853–55.

Hill, David Bennett (D N.Y.) Aug. 29, 1843–Oct. 20, 1910; Senate Jan. 7, 1892–97; Gov. Jan. 6, 1885–Jan. 1, 1892.

Hill, Ebenezer J. (R Conn.) Aug. 4, 1845–Sept. 27, 1917; House 1895–1913, 1915–Sept. 27, 1917.

Hill, Hugh Lawson White (cousin of Benjamin Harvey Hill) (D Tenn.) March 1, 1810–Jan. 18, 1892; House 1847–49.

Hill, Isaac (J N.H.) April 6, 1788–March 22, 1851; Senate 1831–May 30, 1836; Gov. June 2, 1836–June 5, 1839.

Hill, John (D N.C.) April 9, 1797–April 24, 1861; House 1839–41.

Hill, John (cousin of John Thomas Harris) (W Va.) July 18, 1800–April 19, 1880; House 1839–41.

Hill, John (R N.J.) June 10, 1821–July 24, 1884; House 1867–73, 1881–83.

Hill, John Boynton Philip Clayton (R Md.) May 2, 1879–May 23, 1941; House 1921–27.

Hill, Joseph Lister (D Ala.) Dec. 29, 1894–Dec. 21, 1984; House Aug. 14, 1923–Jan. 11, 1938; Senate Jan. 11, 1938–Jan. 2, 1969; Chrmn. Senate Labor and Public Welfare 1955–69.

Hill, Joshua (R Ga.) Jan. 10, 1812–March 6, 1891; House 1857–Jan. 23, 1861 (American Party); Senate Feb. 1, 1871–73.

Hill, Knute (D Wash.) July 31, 1876–Dec. 3, 1963; House 1933–43.

Hill, Mark Langdon (– Maine) June 30, 1772–Nov. 26, 1842; House 1819–21 (Mass.), 1821–23.

Hill, Nathaniel Peter (R Colo.) Feb. 18, 1832–May 22, 1900; Senate 1879–85.

Hill, Ralph (R Ind.) Oct. 12, 1827–Aug. 20, 1899; House 1865–67.

Hill, Rick (R Mont.) Dec. 30, 1946– ; House 1997– .

Hill, Robert Potter (D Okla.) April 18, 1874–Oct. 29, 1937; House 1913–15 (Ill.), Jan. 3–Oct. 29, 1937.

Hill, Samuel Billingsley (D Wash.) April 2, 1875–March 16, 1958; House Sept. 25, 1923–June 25, 1936.

Hill, William David (D Ohio) Oct. 1, 1833–Dec. 26, 1906; House 1879–81, 1883–87.

Hill, William Henry (F N.C.) May 1, 1767–1809; House 1799–1803.

Hill, William Henry (R N.Y.) March 23, 1877–July 24, 1972; House 1919–21.

Hill, William Luther (D Fla.) Oct. 17, 1873–Jan. 5, 1951; Senate July 1–Nov. 3, 1936.

Hill, William Silas (R Colo.) Jan. 20, 1886–Aug. 28, 1972; House 1941–59; Chrmn. House Select Committee on Small Business 1953–55.

Hill, Wilson Shedric (D Miss.) Jan. 19, 1863–Feb. 14, 1921; House 1903–09.

Hilleary, Van (R Tenn.) June 20, 1959– ; House 1995– .

Hillelson, Jeffrey Paul (R Mo.) March 9, 1919– ; House 1953–55.

Hillen, Solomon Jr. (D Md.) July 10, 1810–June 26, 1873; House 1839–41.

Hillhouse, James (– Conn.) Oct. 20, 1754–Dec. 29, 1832; House 1791–96; Senate Dec. 1796–June 10, 1810; elected Pres. pro tempore Feb. 28, 1801; Cont. Cong. (elected but did not attend) 1786, 1788.

Hilliard, Benjamin Clark (D Colo.) Jan. 9, 1868–Aug. 7, 1951; House 1915–19.

Hilliard, Earl F. (D Ala.) April 9, 1942– ; House 1993– .

Hilliard, Henry Washington (W Ala.) Aug. 4, 1808–Dec. 17, 1892; House 1845–51.

Hillings, Patrick Jerome (R Calif.) Feb. 19, 1923–July 20, 1994; House 1951–59.

Hillis, Elwood Haynes (R Ind.) March 6, 1926– ; House 1971–87.

Hillyer, Junius (D Ga.) April 23, 1807–June 21, 1886; House 1851–55 (1851–53 Unionist).

Himes, Joseph Hendrix (R Ohio) Aug. 15, 1885–Sept. 9, 1960; House 1921–23.

Hinchey, Maurice D. (D N.Y.) Oct. 27, 1938– ; House 1993–99.

Hindman, Thomas Carmichael (D Ark.) Jan. 28, 1828–Sept. 27, 1868; House 1859–61.

Hindman, William (F Md.) April 1, 1743–Jan. 19, 1822; House Jan. 30, 1793–99 (no party); Senate Dec. 12, 1800–Nov. 19, 1801; Cont. Cong. 1785–88.

Hinds, Asher Crosby (R Maine) Feb. 6, 1863–May 1, 1919; House 1911–17.

Hinds, James (R Ark.) Dec. 5, 1833–Oct. 22, 1868; House June 22–Oct. 22, 1868.

Hinds, Thomas (D Miss.) Jan. 9, 1780–Aug. 23, 1840; House Oct. 21, 1828–31.

Hinebaugh, William Henry (Prog. Ill.) Dec. 16, 1867–Sept. 22, 1943; House 1913–15.

Hines, Richard (– N.C.) ?–Nov. 20, 1851; House 1825–27.

Hines, William Henry (D Pa.) March 15, 1856–Jan. 17, 1914; House 1893–95.

Hinojosa, Ruben (D Texas) Aug. 20, 1940– ; House 1997– .

Hinrichsen, William Henry (D Ill.) May 27, 1850–Dec. 18, 1907; House 1897–99.

Hinshaw, Andrew Jackson (R Calif.) Aug. 4, 1923– ; House 1973–77.

Hinshaw, Edmund Howard (cousin of Edwin Bruce Brooks) (R Neb.) Dec. 8, 1860–June 15, 1932; House 1903–11.

Hinshaw, John Carl Williams (R Calif.) July 28, 1894–Aug. 5, 1956; House 1939–Aug. 5, 1956.

Hinson, Jon Clifton (R Miss.) March 16, 1942–July 21, 1995; House 1979–April 13, 1981.

Hires, George (R N.J.) Jan. 26, 1835–Feb. 16, 1911; House 1885–89.

Hiscock, Frank (R N.Y.) Sept. 6, 1834–June 18, 1914; House 1877–87; Senate 1887–93.

Hise, Elijah (D Ky.) July 4, 1802–May 8, 1867; House Dec. 3, 1866–May 8, 1867.

Hitchcock, Gilbert Monell (son of Phineas Warrener Hitchcock) (D Neb.) Sept. 18, 1859–Feb. 3, 1934; House 1903–05, 1907–11; Senate 1911–23.

Hitchcock, Herbert Emery (D S.D.) Aug. 22, 1867–Feb. 17, 1958; Senate Dec. 29, 1936–Nov. 8, 1938.

Hitchcock, Peter (– Ohio) Oct. 19, 1781–March 4, 1854; House 1817–19.

Hitchcock, Phineas Warrener (father of Gilbert Monell Hitchcock) (R Neb.) Nov. 30, 1831–July 10, 1881; House (Terr. Del.) 1865–March 1, 1867; Senate 1871–77.

Hitt, Robert Roberts (R Ill.) Jan. 16, 1834–Sept. 20, 1906; House Nov. 7, 1882–Sept. 20, 1906.

Hoag, Truman Harrison (D Ohio) April 9, 1816–Feb. 5, 1870; House 1869–Feb. 5, 1870.

Hoagland, Moses (D Ohio) June 19, 1812–April 16, 1865; House 1849–51.

Hoagland, Peter (D Neb.) Nov. 17, 1941– ; House 1989–95.

Hoar, Ebenezer Rockwood (son of Samuel Hoar, brother of George Frisbie Hoar, father of Sherman Hoar, uncle of Rockwood Hoar) (R Mass.) Feb. 21, 1816–Jan. 31, 1895; House 1873–75; Atty. Gen. March 5, 1869–June 23, 1870.

Hoar, George Frisbie (son of Samuel Hoar, brother of Ebenezer Rockwood Hoar, father of Rockwood Hoar, uncle of Sherman Hoar) (R Mass.) Aug. 29, 1826–Sept. 30, 1904; House 1869–77; Senate 1877–Sept. 30, 1904.

Hoar, Rockwood (son of George Frisbie Hoar, nephew of Ebenezer Rockwood Hoar, cousin of Sherman Hoar, grandson of Samuel Hoar) (R Mass.) Aug. 24, 1855–Nov. 1, 1906; House March 1, 1905–Nov. 1, 1906.

Hoar, Samuel (father of Ebenezer Rockwood Hoar and George Frisbie Hoar, grandfather of Sherman Hoar and Rockwood Hoar) (W Mass.) May 18, 1778–Nov. 2, 1856; House 1835–37.

Hoar, Sherman (son of Ebenezer Rockwood Hoar, nephew of George Frisbee Hoar, cousin of Rockwood Hoar, grandson of Samuel Hoar) (D Mass.) July 30, 1860–Oct. 7, 1898; House 1891–93.

Hoard, Charles Brooks (R N.Y.) June 5, 1805–Nov. 20, 1886; House 1857–61.

Hobart, Aaron (– Mass.) June 26, 1787–Sept. 19, 1858; House Nov. 24, 1820–27.

Hobart, John Sloss (F N.Y.) May 6, 1738–Feb. 4, 1805; Senate Jan. 11–April 16, 1798.

Hobbie, Selah Reeve (J N.Y.) March 10, 1797–March 23, 1854; House 1827–29.

Hobbs, Samuel Francis (D Ala.) Oct. 5, 1887–May 31, 1952; House 1935–51.

Hoblitzell, Fetter Schrier (D Md.) Oct. 7, 1838–May 2, 1900; House 1881–85.

Hoblitzell, John Dempsey Jr. (R W.Va.) Dec. 30, 1912–Jan. 6, 1962; Senate Jan. 25–Nov. 4, 1958.

Hobson, David L. (R Ohio) Oct. 17, 1936– ; House 1991– .

Hobson, Richmond Pearson (D Ala.) Aug. 17, 1870–March 16, 1937; House 1907–15.

Hoch, Daniel Knabb (D Pa.) Jan. 31, 1866–Oct. 11, 1960; House 1943–47.

Hoch, Homer (R Kan.) July 4, 1879–Jan. 30, 1949; House 1919–33.

Hochbrueckner, George Joseph (D N.Y.) Sept. 20, 1938– ; House 1987–95.

Hodges, Asa (R Ark.) Jan. 22, 1822–June 6, 1900; House 1873–75.

Hodges, Charles Drury (D Ill.) Feb. 4, 1810–April 1, 1884; House Jan. 4–March 3, 1859.

Hodges, George Tisdale (R Vt.) July 4, 1789–Aug. 9, 1860; House Dec. 1, 1856–57.

Hodges, James Leonard (– Mass.) April 24, 1790–March 8, 1846; House 1827–33.

Hodges, Kaneaster Jr. (D Ark.) Aug. 20, 1928– ; Senate Dec. 10, 1977–79.

Hoeffel, Joseph M. III (D Pa.) Sept. 3, 1950– ; House 1999– .

Hoekstra, Peter (R Mich.) Oct. 30, 1953– ; House 1993– .

Hoeppel, John Henry (D Calif.) Feb. 10, 1881–Sept. 21, 1976; House 1933–37.

Hoeven, Charles Bernard (R Iowa) March 30, 1895–Nov. 9, 1980; House 1943–65.

Hoey, Clyde Roark (D N.C.) Dec. 11, 1877–May 12, 1954; House Dec. 16, 1919–21; Senate 1945–May 12, 1954; Gov. Jan. 7, 1937–Jan. 9, 1941.

Hoffecker, John Henry (father of Walter Oakley Hoffecker) (R Del.) Sept. 12, 1827–June 16, 1900; House 1899–June 16, 1900.

Hoffecker, Walter Oakley (son of John Henry Hoffecker) (R Del.) Sept. 20, 1854–Jan. 23, 1934; House Nov. 6, 1900–01.

Hoffman, Carl Henry (R Pa.) Aug. 12, 1896–Nov. 30, 1980; House May 21, 1946–47.

Hoffman, Clare Eugene (R Mich.) Sept. 10, 1875–Nov. 3, 1967; House 1935–63; Chrmn. House Expenditures in the Executive Departments 1947–49; Chrmn. House Government Operations 1953–55.

Hoffman, Elmer Joseph (R Ill.) July 7, 1899–June 25, 1976; House 1959–65.

Hoffman, Harold Giles (R N.J.) Feb. 7, 1896–June 4, 1954; House 1927–31; Gov. Jan. 15, 1935–Jan. 18, 1938.

Hoffman, Henry William (AP Md.) Nov. 10, 1825–July 28, 1895; House 1855–57.

Hoffman, Josiah Ogden (W N.Y.) May 3, 1793–May 1, 1856; House 1837–41.

Hoffman, Michael (J N.Y.) Oct. 11, 1787–Sept. 27, 1848; House 1825–33 (1825–29 no party).

Hoffman, Richard William (R Ill.) Dec. 23, 1893–July 6, 1975; House 1949–57.

Hogan, Earl Lee (D Ind.) March 13, 1920– ; House 1959–61.

Hogan, John (D Mo.) Jan. 2, 1805–Feb. 5, 1892; House 1865–67.

Hogan, Lawrence Joseph (R Md.) Sept. 30, 1928– ; House 1969–75.

Hogan, Michael Joseph (R N.Y.) April 22, 1871–May 7, 1940; House 1921–23.

Hogan, William (J N.Y.) July 17, 1792–Nov. 25, 1874; House 1831–33.

Hoge, John (brother of William Hoge) (R Pa.) Sept. 10, 1760–Aug. 4, 1824; House Nov. 2, 1804–05.

Hoge, John Blair (D W.Va.) Feb. 2, 1825–March 1, 1896; House 1881–83.

Hoge, Joseph Pendleton (D Ill.) Dec. 15, 1810–Aug. 14, 1891; House 1843–47.

Hoge, Solomon Lafayette (R S.C.) July 11, 1836–Feb. 23, 1909; House April 8, 1869–71, 1875–77.

Hoge, William (brother of John Hoge) (R Pa.) 1762–Sept. 25, 1814; House 1801–Oct. 15, 1804, 1807–09.

Hogeboom, James Lawrence (– N.Y.) Aug. 25, 1766–Dec. 23, 1839; House 1823–25.

Hogg, Charles Edgar (father of Robert Lynn Hogg) (D W.Va.) Dec. 21, 1852–June 14, 1935; House 1887–89.

Hogg, David (R Ind.) Aug. 21, 1886–Oct. 23, 1973; House 1925–33.

Hogg, Herschel Millard (R Colo.) Nov. 21, 1853–Aug. 27, 1934; House 1903–07.

Hogg, Robert Lynn (son of Charles Edgar Hogg) (R W.Va.) Dec. 30, 1893–July 21, 1973; House Nov. 4, 1930–33.

Hogg, Samuel (R Tenn.) April 18, 1783–May 28, 1842; House 1817–19.

Hoidale, Einar (D Minn.) Aug. 17, 1870–Dec. 5, 1952; House 1933–35.

Hoke, Martin R. (R Ohio) May 18, 1952– ; House 1993–97.

Holaday, William Perry (R Ill.) Dec. 14, 1882–Jan. 29, 1946; House 1923–33.

Holbrock, Greg John (D Ohio) June 21, 1906–Sept. 4, 1992; House 1941–43.

Holbrook, Edward Dexter (D Idaho) May 6, 1836–June 17, 1870; House (Terr. Del.) 1865–69.

Holcombe, George (– N.J.) March 1786–Jan. 14, 1828; House 1821–Jan. 14, 1828.

Holden, Tim (D Pa.) March 5, 1957– ; House 1993– .

Holifield, Chester Earl (D Calif.) Dec. 3, 1903–Feb. 6, 1995; House 1943–Dec. 31, 1974; Chrmn. House Government Operations 1971–75.

Holladay, Alexander Richmond (D Va.) Sept. 18, 1811–Jan. 29, 1877; House 1849–53.

Holland, Cornelius (J Maine) July 9, 1783–June 2, 1870; House Dec. 6, 1830–33.

Holland, Edward Everett (D Va.) Feb. 26, 1861–Oct. 23, 1941; House 1911–21.

Holland, Elmer Joseph (D Pa.) Jan. 8, 1894–Aug. 9, 1968; House May 19, 1942–43, Jan. 24, 1956–Aug. 9, 1968.

Holland, James (R N.C.) 1754–May 19, 1823; House 1795–97, 1801–11.

Holland, Kenneth Lamar (D S.C.) Nov. 24, 1934– ; House 1975–83.

Holland, Spessard Lindsey (D Fla.) July 10, 1892–Nov. 6, 1971; Senate Sept. 25, 1946–71; Gov. Jan. 7, 1941–Jan. 2, 1945.

Holleman, Joel (D Va.) Oct. 1, 1799–Aug. 5, 1844; House 1839–40.

Hollenbeck, Harold Capistran (R N.J.) Dec. 29, 1938– ; House 1977–83.

Holley, John Milton (W N.Y.) Nov. 10, 1802–March 8, 1848; House 1847–March 8, 1848.

Holliday, Elias Selah (R Ind.) March 5, 1842–March 13, 1936; House 1901–09.

Hollings, Ernest Frederick (D S.C.) Jan. 1, 1922– ; Senate Nov. 9, 1966– ; Chrmn. Senate Budget 1979–81; Chrmn. Senate Commerce, Science, and Transportation 1987–95; Gov. Jan. 20, 1959–Jan. 15, 1963.

Hollingsworth, David Adams (R Ohio) Nov. 21, 1844–Dec. 3, 1929; House 1909–11, 1915–19.

Hollis, Henry French (D N.H.) Aug. 30, 1869–July 7, 1949; Senate March 13, 1913–19.

Hollister, John Baker (R Ohio) Nov. 7, 1890–Jan. 4, 1979; House Nov. 3, 1931–37.

Holloway, Clyde Cecil (R La.) Nov. 28, 1943– ; House 1987–93.

Holloway, David Pierson (R Ind.) Dec. 7, 1809–Sept. 9, 1883; House 1855–57.

Holman, Rufus Cecil (R Ore.) Oct. 14, 1877–Nov. 27, 1959; Senate 1939–45.

Holman, William Steele (D Ind.) Sept. 6, 1822–April 22, 1897; House 1859–65, 1867–77, 1881–95, March 4–April 22, 1897.

Holmes, Adoniram Judson (R Iowa) March 2, 1842–Jan. 21, 1902; House 1883–89.

Holmes, Charles Horace (R N.Y.) Oct. 24, 1827–Oct. 2, 1874; House Dec. 6, 1870–71.

Holmes, David (R Miss.) March 10, 1770–Aug. 20, 1832; House 1797–1809 (no party Va.); Senate Aug. 30, 1820–Sept. 25, 1825; Gov. 1809–17 (Miss. Terr.), Dec. 10, 1817–Jan. 5, 1820, Jan. 7–July 25, 1826 (Democratic Republican).

Holmes, Elias Bellows (W N.Y.) May 22, 1807–July 31, 1866; House 1845–49.

Holmes, Gabriel (– N.C.) 1769–Sept. 26, 1829; House 1825–Sept. 26, 1829; Gov. Dec. 7, 1821–Dec. 7, 1824 (Democratic Republican).

Holmes, Isaac Edward (D S.C.) April 6, 1796–Feb. 24, 1867; House 1839–51.

Holmes, John (– Maine) March 14, 1773–July 7, 1843; House 1817–March 15, 1820 (Mass.); Senate June 13, 1820–27, Jan. 15, 1829–33.

Holmes, Otis Halbert (grandson of Dudley Chase Haskell) (R Wash.) Feb. 22, 1902–July 27, 1977; House 1943–59.

Holmes, Pehr Gustaf (R Mass.) April 9, 1881–Dec. 19, 1952; House 1931–47.

Holmes, Sidney Tracy (R N.Y.) Aug. 14, 1815–Jan. 16, 1890; House 1865–67.

Holmes, Uriel (F Conn.) Aug. 26, 1764–May 18, 1827; House 1817–18.

Holsey, Hopkins (D Ga.) Aug. 25, 1779–March 31, 1859; House Oct. 5, 1835–39 (Oct. 5, 1835–37 Jacksonian).

Holt, Hines (W Ga.) April 27, 1805–Nov. 4, 1865; House Feb. 1–March 3, 1841.

Holt, Joseph Franklin III (R Calif.) July 6, 1924–July 14, 1997; House 1953–61.

Holt, Marjorie Sewell (R Md.) Sept. 17, 1920– ; House 1973–87.

Holt, Orrin (D Conn.) March 13, 1792–June 20, 1855; House Dec. 5, 1836–39 (Dec. 5, 1836–37 Jacksonian).

Holt, Rush Dew (father of Rush D. Holt) (D W.Va.) June 19, 1905–Feb. 8, 1955; Senate June 21, 1935–41.

Holt, Rush D. (son of Rush Dew Holt) (D N.J.) Oct. 15, 1948– ; House 1999– .

Holten, Samuel (– Mass.) June 9, 1738–Jan. 2, 1816; House 1793–95; Cont. Cong. 1778–80, 1783–85, 1787.

Holton, Hart Benton (R Md.) Oct. 13, 1835–Jan. 4, 1907; House 1883–85.

Holtzman, Elizabeth (D N.Y.) Aug. 11, 1941– ; House 1973–81.

Holtzman, Lester (D N.Y.) June 1, 1913– ; House 1953–Dec. 31, 1961.

Honeyman, Nan Wood (D Ore.) July 15, 1881–Dec. 10, 1970; House 1937–39.

Hood, George Ezekial (D N.C.) Jan. 25, 1875–March 8, 1960; House 1915–19.

Hook, Enos (D Pa.) Dec. 3, 1804–July 15, 1841; House 1839–April 18, 1841.

Hook, Frank Eugene (D Mich.) May 26, 1893–June 21, 1982; House 1935–43, 1945–47.

Hooker, Charles Edward (D Miss.) 1825–Jan. 8, 1914; House 1875–83, 1887–95, 1901–03.

Hooker, James Murray (D Va.) Oct. 29, 1873–Aug. 6, 1940; House Nov. 8, 1921–25.

Hooker, Warren Brewster (R N.Y.) Nov. 24, 1856–March 5, 1920; House 1891–Nov. 10, 1898.

Hooks, Charles (great-grandfather of William Julius Harris) (R N.C.) Feb. 20, 1768–Oct. 18, 1843; House Dec. 2, 1816–17, 1819–25.

Hooley, Darlene (D Ore.) April 4, 1939– ; House 1997– .

Hooper, Benjamin Stephen (Read. Va.) March 6, 1835–Jan. 17, 1898; House 1883–85.

Hooper, Joseph Lawrence (R Mich.) Dec. 22, 1877–Feb. 22, 1934; House Aug. 18, 1925–Feb. 22, 1934.

Hooper, Samuel (R Mass.) Feb. 3, 1808–Feb. 14, 1875; House Dec. 2, 1861–Feb. 14, 1875.

Hooper, William Henry (D Utah) Dec. 25, 1813–Dec. 30, 1882; House (Terr. Del.) 1859–61, 1865–73.

Hope, Clifford Ragsdale (R Kan.) June 9, 1893–May 16, 1970; House 1927–57; Chrmn. House Agriculture 1947–49, 1953–55.

Hopkins, Albert Cole (R Pa.) Sept. 15, 1837–June 9, 1911; House 1891–95.

Hopkins, Albert Jarvis (R Ill.) Aug. 15, 1846–Aug. 23, 1922; House Dec. 7, 1885–1903; Senate 1903–09.

Hopkins, Benjamin Franklin (R Wis.) April 22, 1829–Jan. 1, 1870; House 1867–Jan. 1, 1870.

Hopkins, David William (R Mo.) Oct. 31, 1897–Oct. 14, 1968; House Feb. 5, 1929–33.

Hopkins, Francis Alexander (D Ky.) May 27, 1853–June 5, 1918; House 1903–07.

Hopkins, George Washington (D Va.) Feb. 22, 1804–March 1, 1861; House 1835–47 (1835–37 Jacksonian, 1837–39 Democrat, 1839–41 Conservative), 1857–59.

Hopkins, James Herron (D Pa.) Nov. 3, 1832–June 17, 1904; House 1875–77, 1883–85.

Hopkins, Larry Jones (R Ky.) Oct. 25, 1933– ; House 1979–93.

Hopkins, Nathan Thomas (R Ky.) Oct. 27, 1852–Feb. 11, 1927; House Feb. 18–March 3, 1897.

Hopkins, Samuel (R Ky.) April 9, 1753–Sept. 16, 1819; House 1813–15.

Hopkins, Samuel Isaac (Lab. Va.) Dec. 12, 1843–Jan. 15, 1914; House 1887–89.

Hopkins, Samuel Miles (F N.Y.) May 9, 1772–March 9, 1837; House 1813–15.

Hopkins, Stephen Tyng (R N.Y.) March 25, 1849–March 3, 1892; House 1887–89.

Hopkinson, Joseph (F Pa.) Nov. 12, 1770–Jan. 15, 1842; House 1815–19.

Hopwood, Robert Freeman (R Pa.) July 24, 1856–March 1, 1940; House 1915–17.

Horan, Walter Franklin (R Wash.) Oct. 15, 1898–Dec. 19, 1966; House 1943–65.

Horn, Henry (J Pa.) 1786–Jan. 12, 1862; House 1831–33.

Horn, Joan Kelly (D Mo.) Oct. 18, 1936– ; House 1991–93.

Horn, Steve (R Calif.) May 31, 1931– ; House 1993– .

Hornbeck, John Westbrook (W Pa.) Jan. 24, 1804–Jan. 16, 1848; House 1847–Jan. 16, 1848.

Hornor, Lynn Sedwick (D W.Va.) Nov. 3, 1874–Sept. 23, 1933; House 1931–Sept. 23, 1933.

Horr, Ralph Ashley (R Wash.) Aug. 12, 1884–Jan. 26, 1960; House 1931–33.

Horr, Roswell Gilbert (R Mich.) Nov. 26, 1830–Dec. 19, 1896; House 1879–85.

Horsey, Outerbridge (F Del.) March 5, 1777–June 9, 1842; Senate Jan. 12, 1810–21.

Horsford, Jerediah (W N.Y.) March 8, 1791–Jan. 14, 1875; House 1851–53.

Horton, Frank Jefferson (R N.Y.) Dec. 12, 1919– ; House 1963–93.

Horton, Frank Ogilvie (R Wyo.) Oct. 18, 1882–Aug. 17, 1948; House 1939–41.

Horton, Thomas Raymond (W N.Y.) April 1822–July 26, 1894; House 1855–57.

Horton, Valentine Baxter (R Ohio) Jan. 29, 1802–Jan. 14, 1888; House 1855–59, 1861–63.

Hoskins, George Gilbert (R N.Y.) Dec. 24, 1824–June 12, 1893; House 1873–77.

Hosmer, Craig (R Calif.) May 6, 1915–Oct. 11, 1982; House 1953–Dec. 31, 1974.

Hosmer, Hezekiah Lord (F N.Y.) June 7, 1765–June 9, 1814; House 1797–99.

Hostetler, Abraham Jonathan (D Ind.) Nov. 22, 1818–Nov. 24, 1899; House 1879–81.

Hostetter, Jacob (– Pa.) May 9, 1754–June 29, 1831; House Nov. 16, 1818–21.

Hostettler, John (R Ind.) July 19, 1961– ; House 1995– .

Hotchkiss, Giles Waldo (R N.Y.) Oct. 25, 1815–July 5, 1878; House 1863–67, 1869–71.

Hotchkiss, Julius (D Conn.) July 11, 1810–Dec. 23, 1878; House 1867–69.

Houck, Jacob Jr. (D N.Y.) Jan. 14, 1801–Oct. 2, 1857; House 1841–43.

Hough, David (F N.H.) March 13, 1753–April 18, 1831; House 1803–07.

Hough, William Jervis (D N.Y.) March 20, 1795–Oct. 4, 1869; House 1845–47.

Houghton, Alanson Bigelow (grandfather of Amory Houghton Jr.) (R N.Y.) Oct. 10, 1863–Sept. 15, 1941; House 1919–Feb. 28, 1922.

Houghton, Amory Jr. (grandson of Alanson Bigelow Houghton) (R N.Y.) Aug. 7, 1926– ; House 1987– .

Houghton, Sherman Otis (R Calif.) April 10, 1828–Aug. 31, 1914; House 1871–75.

Houk, George Washington (D Ohio) Sept. 25, 1825–Feb. 9, 1894; House 1891–Feb. 9, 1894.

Houk, John Chiles (son of Leonidas Campbell Houk) (R Tenn.) Feb. 26, 1860–June 3, 1923; House Dec. 7, 1891–95.

Houk, Leonidas Campbell (father of John Chiles Houk) (R Tenn.) June 8, 1836–May 25, 1891; House 1879–May 25, 1891.

House, John Ford (D Tenn.) Jan. 9, 1827–June 28, 1904; House 1875–83.

Houseman, Julius (D Mich.) Dec. 8, 1832–Feb. 8, 1891; House 1883–85.

Houston, Andrew Jackson (son of Samuel Houston) (D Texas) June 21, 1854–June 26, 1941; Senate April 21–June 26, 1941.

Houston, George Smith (D Ala.) Jan. 17, 1811–Dec. 31, 1879; House 1841–49, 1851–Jan. 21, 1861; Senate March 4–Dec. 31, 1879; Gov. Nov. 24, 1874–Nov. 28, 1878.

Houston, Henry Aydelotte (D Del.) July 10, 1847–April 5, 1925; House 1903–05.

Houston, John Mills (D Kan.) Sept. 15, 1890–April 29, 1975; House 1935–43.

Houston, John Wallace (uncle of Robert Griffith Houston) (W Del.) May 4, 1814–April 26, 1896; House 1845–51.

Houston, Robert Griffith (nephew of John Wallace Houston) (R Del.) Oct. 13, 1867–Jan. 29, 1946; House 1925–33.

Houston, Samuel (father of Andrew Jackson Houston, cousin of David Hubbard) (D Texas) March 2, 1793–July 26, 1863; House 1823–27 (no party Tenn.); Senate Feb. 21, 1846–59; Gov. Oct. 1, 1827–April 16, 1829 (Tenn.), Dec. 21, 1859–March 16, 1861.

Houston, Victor Stewart Kaleoaloha (R Hawaii) July 22, 1876–July 31, 1959; House (Terr. Del.) 1927–33.

Houston, William Cannon (D Tenn.) March 17, 1852–Aug. 30, 1931; House 1905–19.

Hovey, Alvin Peterson (R Ind.) Sept. 6, 1821–Nov. 23, 1891; House 1887–Jan. 17, 1889; Gov. Jan. 14, 1889–Nov. 21, 1891.

Howard, Benjamin (R Ky.) 1760–Sept. 18, 1814; House 1807–April 10, 1810; Gov. (La. Terr.) 1810–12.

Howard, Benjamin Chew (son of John Eager Howard) (D Md.) Nov. 5, 1791–March 6, 1872; House 1829–33 (Jacksonian), 1835–39 (1835–37 Jacksonian).

Howard, Edgar (D Neb.) Sept. 16, 1858–July 19, 1951; House 1923–35.

Howard, Everette Burgess (D Okla.) Sept. 19, 1873–April 3, 1950; House 1919–21, 1923–25, 1927–29.

Howard, Guy Victor (R Minn.) Nov. 28, 1879–Aug. 20, 1954; Senate Nov. 4, 1936–37.

Howard, Jacob Merritt (R Mich.) July 10, 1805–April 2, 1871; House 1841–43 (Whig); Senate Jan. 17, 1862–71.

Howard, James John (D N.J.) July 24, 1927–March 25, 1988; House 1965–March 25, 1988; Chrmn. House Public Works and Transportation 1981–88.

Howard, John Eager (father of Benjamin Chew Howard) (F Md.) June 4, 1752–Oct. 12, 1827; Senate Nov. 30, 1796–1803; elected Pres. pro tempore Nov. 21, 1800; Gov. Nov. 24, 1788–Nov. 14, 1791; Cont. Cong. 1788.

Howard, Jonas George (D Ind.) May 22, 1825–Oct. 5, 1911; House 1885–89.

Howard, Milford Wriarson (P Ala.) Dec. 18, 1862–Dec. 28, 1937; House 1895–99.

Howard, Tilghman Ashurst (D Ind.) Nov. 14, 1797–Aug. 16, 1844; House Aug. 5, 1839–July 1, 1840.

Howard, Volney Erskine (D Texas) Oct. 22, 1809–May 14, 1889; House 1849–53.

Howard, William (D Ohio) Dec. 31, 1817–June 1, 1891; House 1859–61.

Howard, William Alanson (R Mich.) April 8, 1813–April 10, 1880; House 1855–59, May 15, 1860–61; Gov. (Dakota Terr.) 1878–80.

Howard, William Marcellus (D Ga.) Dec. 6, 1857–July 5, 1932; House 1897–1911.

Howard, William Schley (cousin of Augustus Octavius Bacon) (D Ga.) June 29, 1875–Aug. 1, 1953; House 1911–19.

Howe, Albert Richards (R Miss.) Jan. 1, 1840–June 1, 1884; House 1873–75.

Howe, Allan Turner (D Utah) Sept. 6, 1927– ; House 1975–77.

Howe, James Robinson (R N.Y.) Jan. 27, 1839–Sept. 21, 1914; House 1895–99.

Howe, John W. (W Pa.) 1801–Dec. 1, 1873; House 1849–53.

Howe, Thomas Marshall (father-in-law of James W. Brown) (W Pa.) April 20, 1808–July 20, 1877; House 1851–55.

Howe, Thomas Y. Jr. (D N.Y.) 1801–July 15, 1860; House 1851–53.

Howe, Timothy Otis (R Wis.) Feb. 24, 1816–March 25, 1883; Senate 1861–79; Postmaster Gen. Jan. 5, 1882–March 25, 1883.

Howell, Benjamin Franklin (R N.J.) Jan. 27, 1844–Feb. 1, 1933; House 1895–1911.

Howell, Charles Robert (D N.J.) April 23, 1904–July 5, 1973; House 1949–55.

Howell, Edward (J N.Y.) Oct. 16, 1792–Jan. 30, 1871; House 1833–35.

Howell, Elias (father of James Bruen Howell) (W Ohio) 1792–May 1844; House 1835–37.

Howell, George (D Pa.) June 28, 1859–Nov. 19, 1913; House 1903–Feb. 10, 1904.

Howell, George Evan (R Ill.) Sept. 21, 1905–Jan. 18, 1980; House 1941–Oct. 5, 1947.

Howell, James Bruen (son of Elias Howell) (R Iowa) July 4, 1816–June 17, 1880; Senate Jan. 18, 1870–71.

Howell, Jeremiah Brown (R R.I.) Aug. 28, 1771–Feb. 5, 1822; Senate 1811–17.

Howell, Joseph (R Utah) Feb. 17, 1857–July 18, 1918; House 1903–17.

Howell, Nathaniel Woodhull (F N.Y.) Jan. 1, 1770–Oct. 15, 1851; House 1813–15.

Howell, Robert Beecher (R Neb.) Jan. 21, 1864–March 11, 1933; Senate 1923–March 11, 1933.

Howey, Benjamin Franklin (nephew of Charles Creighton Stratton) (R N.J.) March 17, 1828–Feb. 6, 1895; House 1883–85.

Howland, Benjamin (R R.I.) July 27, 1755–May 1, 1821; Senate Oct. 29, 1804–09.

Howland, Leonard Paul (R Ohio) Dec. 5, 1865–Dec. 23, 1942; House 1907–13.

Hoxworth, Stephen Arnold (D Ill.) May 1, 1860–Jan. 25, 1930; House 1913–15.

Hoyer, Steny Hamilton (D Md.) June 14, 1939– ; House June 3, 1981– .

Hruska, Roman Lee (R Neb.) Aug. 16, 1904–April 25, 1999; House 1953–Nov. 8, 1954; Senate Nov. 8, 1954–Dec. 27, 1976.

Hubard, Edmund Wilcox (D Va.) Feb. 20, 1806–Dec. 9, 1878; House 1841–47.

Hubbard, Asahel Wheeler (father of Elbert Hamilton Hubbard) (R Iowa) Jan. 19, 1819–Sept. 22, 1879; House 1863–69.

Hubbard, Carroll Jr. (D Ky.) July 7, 1937– ; House 1975–93.

Hubbard, Chester Dorman (father of William Pallister Hubbard) (R W.Va.) Nov. 25, 1814–Aug. 23, 1891; House 1865–69 (1865–67 Unconditional Unionist).

Hubbard, David (cousin of Samuel Houston) (D Ala.) 1792–Jan. 20, 1874; House 1839–41, 1849–51.

Hubbard, Demas Jr. (R N.Y.) Jan. 17, 1806–Sept. 2, 1873; House 1865–67.

Hubbard, Elbert Hamilton (son of Asahel Wheeler Hubbard) (R Iowa) Aug. 19, 1849–June 4, 1912; House 1905–June 4, 1912.

Hubbard, Henry (J N.H.) May 3, 1784–June 5, 1857; House 1829–35; Senate 1835–41; Gov. June 2, 1842–June 6, 1844 (Democrat).

Hubbard, Joel Douglas (R Mo.) Nov. 6, 1860–May 26, 1919; House 1895–97.

Hubbard, John Henry (R Conn.) March 24, 1804–July 30, 1872; House 1863–67.

Hubbard, Jonathan Hatch (F Vt.) May 7, 1768–Sept. 20, 1849; House 1809–11.

Hubbard, Levi (R Mass.) Dec. 19, 1762–Feb. 18, 1836; House 1813–15.

Hubbard, Richard Dudley (D Conn.) Sept. 7, 1818–Feb. 28, 1884; House 1867–69; Gov. Jan. 3, 1877–Jan. 9, 1879.

Hubbard, Samuel Dickinson (W Conn.) Aug. 10, 1799–Oct. 8, 1855; House 1845–49; Postmaster Gen. Sept. 14, 1852–March 7, 1853.

Hubbard, Thomas Hill (R N.Y.) Dec. 5, 1781–May 21, 1857; House 1817–19, 1821–23.

Hubbard, William Pallister (son of Chester Dorman Hubbard) (R W.Va.) Dec. 24, 1843–Dec. 5, 1921; House 1907–11.

Hubbell, Edwin Nelson (D N.Y.) Aug. 13, 1815–?; House 1865–67.

Hubbell, James Randolph (R Ohio) July 13, 1824–Nov. 26, 1890; House 1865–67.

Hubbell, Jay Abel (R Mich.) Sept. 15, 1829–Oct. 13, 1900; House 1873–83.

Hubbell, William Spring (D N.Y.) Jan. 17, 1801–Nov. 16, 1873; House 1843–45.

Hubbs, Orlando (R N.C.) Feb. 18, 1840–Dec. 5, 1930; House 1881–83.

Huber, Robert James (R Mich.) Aug. 29, 1922– ; House 1973–75.

Huber, Walter B. (D Ohio) June 29, 1903–Aug. 8, 1982; House 1945–51.

Hubley, Edward Burd (D Pa.) 1792–Feb. 23, 1856; House 1835–39 (1835–37 Jacksonian).

Huck, Winnifred Sprague Mason (daughter of William Ernest Mason) (R Ill.) Sept. 14, 1882–Aug. 24, 1936; House Nov. 7, 1922–23.

Huckaby, Thomas Jerald (D La.) July 19, 1941– ; House 1977–93.

Hudd, Thomas Richard (D Wis.) Oct. 2, 1835–June 22, 1896; House March 8, 1886–89.

Huddleston, George (father of George Huddleston Jr.) (D Ala.) Nov. 11, 1869–Feb. 29, 1960; House 1915–37.

Huddleston, George Jr. (son of George Huddleston) (D Ala.) March 19, 1920–Sept. 14, 1971; House 1955–65.

Huddleston, Walter Darlington (D Ky.) April 15, 1926– ; Senate 1973–85.

Hudnut, William Herbert III (R Ind.) Oct. 17, 1932– ; House 1973–75.

Hudson, Charles (W Mass.) Nov. 14, 1795–May 4, 1881; House May 3, 1841–49.

Hudson, Grant Martin (R Mich.) July 23, 1868–Oct. 26, 1955; House 1923–31.

Hudson, Thomas Jefferson (P Kan.) Oct. 30, 1839–Jan. 4, 1923; House 1893–95.

Hudspeth, Claude Benton (D Texas) May 12, 1877–March 19, 1941; House 1919–31.

Huff, George Franklin (R Pa.) July 16, 1842–April 18, 1912; House 1891–93, 1895–97, 1903–11.

Huffington, Michael (R Calif.) Sept. 3, 1947–   ; House 1993–95.

Huffman, James Wylie (D Ohio) Sept. 13, 1894–May 20, 1980; Senate Oct. 8, 1945–Nov. 5, 1946.

Hufty, Jacob (F N.J.) ?–May 20, 1814; House 1809–May 20, 1814 (1809–13 Republican).

Huger, Benjamin (F S.C.) 1768–July 7, 1823; House 1799–1805, 1815–17.

Huger, Daniel (father of Daniel Elliott Huger) (– S.C.) Feb. 20, 1742–July 6, 1799; House 1789–93; Cont. Cong. 1786–88.

Huger, Daniel Elliott (son of Daniel Huger) (SRD S.C.) June 28, 1779–Aug. 21, 1854; Senate 1843–45.

Hughes, Charles (D N.Y.) Feb. 27, 1822–Aug. 10, 1887; House 1853–55.

Hughes, Charles James Jr. (D Colo.) Feb. 16, 1853–Jan. 11, 1911; Senate 1909–Jan. 11, 1911.

Hughes, Dudley Mays (D Ga.) Oct. 10, 1848–Jan. 20, 1927; House 1909–17.

Hughes, George Wurtz (D Md.) Sept. 30, 1806–Sept. 3, 1870; House 1859–61.

Hughes, Harold Everett (D Iowa) Feb. 10, 1922–Oct. 23, 1996; Senate 1969–75; Gov. Jan. 17, 1963–Jan. 1, 1969.

Hughes, James (D Ind.) Nov. 24, 1823–Oct. 21, 1873; House 1857–59.

Hughes, James Anthony (R W.Va.) Feb. 27, 1861–March 2, 1930; House 1901–15, 1927–March 2, 1930.

Hughes, James Frederic (D Wis.) Aug. 7, 1883–Aug. 9, 1940; House 1933–35.

Hughes, James Hurd (D Del.) Jan. 14, 1867–Aug. 29, 1953; Senate 1937–43.

Hughes, James Madison (D Mo.) April 7, 1809–Feb. 26, 1861; House 1843–45.

Hughes, Thomas Hurst (– N.J.) Jan. 10, 1769–Nov. 10, 1839; House 1829–33.

Hughes, William (D N.J.) April 3, 1872–Jan. 30, 1918; House 1903–05, 1907–Sept. 27, 1912; Senate 1913–Jan. 30, 1918.

Hughes, William John (D N.J.) Oct. 17, 1932–   ; House 1975–95.

Hughston, Jonas Abbott (W N.Y.) 1808–Nov. 10, 1862; House 1855–57.

Hugunin, Daniel Jr. (– N.Y.) Feb. 6, 1790–June 21, 1850; House Dec. 15, 1825–27.

Hukriede, Theodore Waldemar (R Mo.) Nov. 9, 1878–April 14, 1945; House 1921–23.

Hulbert, George Murray (D N.Y.) May 14, 1881–April 26, 1950; House 1915–Jan. 1, 1918.

Hulbert, John Whitefield (F Mass.) June 1, 1770–Oct. 19, 1831; House Sept. 26, 1814–17.

Hulburd, Calvin Tilden (R N.Y.) June 5, 1809–Oct. 25, 1897; House 1863–69.

Hulick, George Washington (R Ohio) June 29, 1833–Aug. 13, 1907; House 1893–97.

Huling, James Hall (R W.Va.) March 24, 1844–April 23, 1918; House 1895–97.

Hulings, Willis James (R Pa.) July 1, 1850–Aug. 8, 1924; House 1913–15 (Progressive), 1919–21.

Hull, Cordell (D Tenn.) Oct. 2, 1871–July 23, 1955; House 1907–21, 1923–31; Senate 1931–March 3, 1933; Chrmn. Dem. Nat. Comm. 1921–24; Secy. of State March 4, 1933–Nov. 30, 1944.

Hull, Harry Edward (R Iowa) March 12, 1864–Jan. 16, 1938; House 1915–25.

Hull, John Albert Tiffin (R Iowa) May 1, 1841–Sept. 26, 1928; House 1891–1911.

Hull, Merlin (R Wis.) Dec. 18, 1870–May 17, 1953; House 1929–31 (Republican), 1935–May 17, 1953 (1935–47 Progressive).

Hull, Morton Denison (R Ill.) Jan. 13, 1867–Aug. 20, 1937; House April 3, 1923–33.

Hull, Noble Andrew (D Fla.) March 11, 1827–Jan. 28, 1907; House 1879–Jan. 22, 1881.

Hull, William Edgar (R Ill.) Jan. 13, 1866–May 30, 1942; House 1923–33.

Hull, William Raleigh Jr. (D Mo.) April 17, 1906–Aug. 15, 1977; House 1955–73.

Hulshof, Kenny (R Mo.) May 22, 1958–   ; House 1997–   .

Humphrey, Augustin Reed (R Neb.) Feb. 18, 1859–Dec. 10, 1937; House Nov. 7, 1922–23.

Humphrey, Charles (– N.Y.) Feb. 14, 1792–April 17, 1850; House 1825–27.

Humphrey, Gordon John (R N.H.) Oct. 9, 1940–   ; Senate 1979–91.

Humphrey, Herman Leon (R Wis.) March 14, 1830–June 10, 1902; House 1877–83.

Humphrey, Hubert Horatio Jr. (husband of Muriel Buck Humphrey) (D Minn.) May 27, 1911–Jan. 13, 1978; Senate 1949–Dec. 29, 1964, 1971–Jan. 13, 1978; Vice President 1965–69.

Humphrey, James (R N.Y.) Oct. 9, 1811–June 16, 1866; House 1859–61, 1865–June 16, 1866.

Humphrey, James Morgan (D N.Y.) Sept. 21, 1819–Feb. 9, 1899; House 1865–69.

Humphrey, Muriel Buck (widow of Hubert Horatio Humphrey Jr.) (D Minn.) Feb. 20, 1912–Sept. 20, 1998; Senate Jan. 25–Nov. 7, 1978.

Humphrey, Reuben (R N.Y.) Sept. 2, 1757–Aug. 12, 1831; House 1807–09.

Humphrey, William Ewart (R Wash.) March 31, 1862–Feb. 14, 1934; House 1903–17.

Humphreys, Andrew (D Ind.) March 30, 1821–June 14, 1904; House Dec. 5, 1876–77.

Humphreys, Benjamin Grubb (father of William Yerger Humphreys) (D Miss.) Aug. 17, 1865–Oct. 16, 1923; House 1903–Oct. 16, 1923.

Humphreys, Parry Wayne (R Tenn.) 1778–Feb. 12, 1839; House 1813–15.

Humphreys, Robert (D Ky.) Aug. 20, 1893–Dec. 31, 1977; Senate June 21–Nov. 6, 1956.

Humphreys, William Yerger (son of Benjamin Grubb Humphreys) (D Miss.) Sept. 9, 1890–Feb. 26, 1933; House Nov. 27, 1923–25.

Hungate, William Leonard (D Mo.) Dec. 24, 1922–   ; House Nov. 3, 1964–77.

Hungerford, John Newton (R N.Y.) Dec. 31, 1825–April 2, 1883; House 1877–79.

Hungerford, John Pratt (R Va.) Jan. 2, 1761–Dec. 21, 1833; House March 4–Nov. 29, 1811, 1813–17.

Hungerford, Orville (D N.Y.) Oct. 29, 1790–April 6, 1851; House 1843–47.

Hunt, Carleton (nephew of Theodore Gaillard Hunt) (D La.) Jan. 1, 1836–Aug. 14, 1921; House 1883–85.

Hunt, Hiram Paine (W N.Y.) May 23, 1796–Aug. 14, 1865; House 1835–37, 1839–43.

Hunt, James Bennett (D Mich.) Aug. 13, 1799–Aug. 15, 1857; House 1843–47.

Hunt, John Edmund (R N.J.) Nov. 25, 1908–Sept. 22, 1989; House 1967–75.

Hunt, John Thomas (D Mo.) Feb. 2, 1860–Nov. 30, 1916; House 1903–07.

Hunt, Jonathan (– Vt.) Aug. 12, 1787–May 15, 1832; House 1827–May 15, 1832.

Hunt, Lester Callaway (D Wyo.) July 8, 1892–June 19, 1954; Senate 1949–June 19, 1954; Gov. Jan. 4, 1943–Jan. 3, 1949.

Hunt, Samuel (F N.H.) July 8, 1765–July 7, 1807; House Dec. 6, 1802–05.

Hunt, Theodore Gaillard (nephew of John Gaillard, uncle of Carleton Hunt) (W La.) Oct. 23, 1805–Nov. 15, 1893; House 1853–55.

Hunt, Washington (W N.Y.) Aug. 5, 1811–Feb. 2, 1867; House 1843–49; Gov. Jan. 1, 1851–Jan. 1, 1853.

Hunter, Allan Oakley (R Calif.) June 15, 1916–May 2, 1995; House 1951–55.

Hunter, Andrew Jackson (D Ill.) Dec. 17, 1831–Jan. 12, 1913; House 1893–95, 1897–99.

Hunter, Duncan Lee (R Calif.) May 31, 1948– ; House 1981– .

Hunter, John (R S.C.) 1732–1802; House 1793–95 (no party); Senate Dec. 8, 1796–Nov. 26, 1798.

Hunter, John Feeney (D Ohio) Oct. 19, 1896–Dec. 19, 1957; House 1937–43.

Hunter, John Ward (– N.Y.) Oct. 15, 1807–April 16, 1900; House Dec. 4, 1866–67.

Hunter, Morton Craig (R Ind.) Feb. 5, 1825–Oct. 25, 1896; House 1867–69, 1873–79.

Hunter, Narsworthy (– Miss.) ?–March 11, 1802; House (Terr. Del.) 1801–March 11, 1802.

Hunter, Richard Charles (D Neb.) Dec. 3, 1884–Jan. 23, 1941; Senate Nov. 7, 1934–35.

Hunter, Robert Mercer Taliaferro (– Va.) April 21, 1809–July 18, 1887; House 1837–43 (State Rights Whig), 1845–47; Senate 1847–March 28, 1861; Speaker Dec. 16, 1839–41.

Hunter, Whiteside Godfrey (R Ky.) Dec. 25, 1841–Nov. 2, 1917; House 1887–89, 1895–97, Nov. 10, 1903–05.

Hunter, William (R Vt.) Jan. 3, 1754–Nov. 30, 1827; House 1817–19.

Hunter, William (F R.I.) Nov. 26, 1774–Dec. 3, 1849; Senate Oct. 28, 1811–21.

Hunter, William Forrest (W Ohio) Dec. 10, 1808–March 30, 1874; House 1849–53.

Hunter, William H. (D Ohio) ?–1842; House 1837–39.

Huntington, Abel (J N.Y.) Feb. 21, 1777–May 18, 1858; House 1833–37.

Huntington, Benjamin (– Conn.) April 19, 1736–Oct. 16, 1800; House 1789–91; Cont. Cong. 1780, 1782–83, 1788.

Huntington, Ebenezer (F Conn.) Dec. 26, 1754–June 17, 1834; House Oct. 11, 1810–11, 1817–19.

Huntington, Jabez Williams (W Conn.) Nov. 8, 1788–Nov. 1, 1847; House 1829–Aug. 16, 1834 (no party); Senate May 4, 1840–Nov. 1, 1847.

Hunton, Eppa (D Va.) Sept. 22, 1822–Oct. 11, 1908; House 1873–81; Senate May 28, 1892–95.

Huntsman, Adam (J Tenn.) Feb. 11, 1786–Aug. 23, 1849; House 1835–37.

Huot, Joseph Oliva (D N.H.) Aug. 11, 1917–Aug. 5, 1983; House 1965–67.

Hurd, Frank Hunt (D Ohio) Dec. 25, 1840–July 10, 1896; House 1875–77, 1879–81, 1883–85.

Hurlbut, Stephen Augustus (R Ill.) Nov. 29, 1815–March 27, 1882; House 1873–77.

Hurley, Denis Michael (R N.Y.) March 14, 1843–Feb. 26, 1899; House 1895–Feb. 26, 1899.

Husted, James William (R N.Y.) March 16, 1870–Jan. 2, 1925; House 1915–23.

Husting, Paul Oscar (D Wis.) April 25, 1866–Oct. 21, 1917; Senate 1915–Oct. 21, 1917.

Hutcheson, Joseph Chappell (D Texas) May 18, 1842–May 25, 1924; House 1893–97.

Hutchins, John (cousin of Wells Andrews Hutchins) (R Ohio) July 25, 1812–Nov. 20, 1891; House 1859–63.

Hutchins, Waldo (D N.Y.) Sept. 30, 1822–Feb. 8, 1891; House Nov. 4, 1879–85.

Hutchins, Wells Andrews (cousin of John Hutchins) (D Ohio) Oct. 8, 1818–Jan. 25, 1895; House 1863–65.

Hutchinson, Asa (R Ark.) Dec. 3, 1950– ; House 1997– .

Hutchinson, Elijah Cubberley (R N.J.) Aug. 7, 1855–June 25, 1932; House 1915–23.

Hutchinson, J. Edward (R Mich.) Oct. 13, 1914–July 22, 1985; House 1963–77.

Hutchinson, John Guiher (D W.Va.) Feb. 4, 1935– ; House June 3, 1980–81.

Hutchinson, Tim (R Ark.) Aug. 11, 1949– ; House 1993–97; Senate 1997– .

Hutchison, Kay Bailey (R Texas) July 22, 1943– ; Senate June 14, 1993– .

Hutto, Earl Dewitt (D Fla.) May 12, 1926– ; House 1979–95.

Hutton, John Edward (D Mo.) March 28, 1828–Dec. 28, 1893; House 1885–89.

Huyler, John (D N.J.) April 9, 1808–Jan. 9, 1870; House 1857–59.

Hyde, DeWitt Stephen (R Md.) March 21, 1909–April 25, 1986; House 1953–59.

Hyde, Henry John (R Ill.) April 18, 1924– ; House 1975– ; Chrmn. House Judiciary 1995– .

Hyde, Ira Barnes (R Mo.) Jan. 18, 1838–Dec. 6, 1926; House 1873–75.

Hyde, Samuel Clarence (R Wash.) April 22, 1842–March 7, 1922; House 1895–97.

Hyman, John Adams (R N.C.) July 23, 1840–Sept. 14, 1891; House 1875–77.

Hyneman, John M. (R Pa.) April 25, 1771–April 16, 1816; House 1811–Aug. 2, 1813.

Hynes, William Joseph (LR Ark.) March 31, 1843–April 2, 1915; House 1873–75.

I

Ichord, Richard Howard II (D Mo.) June 27, 1926–Dec. 25, 1992; House 1961–81; Chrmn. House Internal Security 1969–74.

Iglesias, Santiago (formerly Santiago Iglesias Pantin) (Coal. P.R.) Feb. 22, 1872–Dec. 5, 1939; House (Res. Comm.) 1933–Dec. 5, 1939.

Igoe, James Thomas (D Ill.) Oct. 23, 1883–Dec. 2, 1971; House 1927–33.

Igoe, Michael Lambert (D Ill.) April 16, 1885–Aug. 21, 1967; House Jan. 3–June 2, 1935.

Igoe, William Leo (D Mo.) Oct. 19, 1879–April 20, 1953; House 1913–21.

Ihrie, Peter Jr. (– Pa.) Feb. 3, 1796–March 29, 1871; House Oct. 13, 1829–33.

Ikard, Frank Neville (D Texas) Jan. 30, 1913–May 1, 1991; House Sept. 8, 1951–Dec. 15, 1961.

Ikirt, George Pierce (D Ohio) Nov. 3, 1852–Feb. 12, 1927; House 1893–95.

Ilsley, Daniel (R Mass.) May 30, 1740–May 10, 1813; House 1807–09.

Imhoff, Lawrence E. (D Ohio) Dec. 28, 1895–April 18, 1988; House 1933–39, 1941–43.

Imlay, James Henderson (F N.J.) Nov. 26, 1764–March 6, 1823; House 1797–1801.

Ingalls, John James (R Kan.) Dec. 29, 1833–Aug. 16, 1900; Senate 1873–91; elected Pres. pro tempore Feb. 25, 1887, March 7, 1889, April 2, 1889, Feb. 28, 1890, April 3, 1890.

Inge, Samuel Williams (nephew of William Marshall Inge) (D Ala.) Feb. 22, 1817–June 10, 1868; House 1847–51.

Inge, William Marshall (uncle of Samuel Williams Inge) (J Tenn.) 1802–1846; House 1833–35.

Ingersoll, Charles Jared (brother of Joseph Reed Ingersoll) (D Pa.) Oct. 3, 1782–May 14, 1862; House 1813–15 (Republican), 1841–49.

Ingersoll, Colin Macrae (son of Ralph Isaacs Ingersoll) (D Conn.) March 11, 1819–Sept. 13, 1903; House 1851–55.

Ingersoll, Ebon Clark (R Ill.) Dec. 12, 1831–May 31, 1879; House May 20, 1864–71.

Ingersoll, Joseph Reed (brother of Charles Jared Ingersoll) (W Pa.) June 14, 1786–Feb. 20, 1868; House 1835–37, Oct. 12, 1841–49.

Ingersoll, Ralph Isaacs (father of Colin Macrae Ingersoll) (– Conn.) Feb. 8, 1789–Aug. 26, 1872; House 1825–33.

Ingham, Samuel (D Conn.) Sept. 5, 1793–Nov. 10, 1881; House 1835–39 (1835–37 Jacksonian).

Ingham, Samuel Delucenna (R Pa.) Sept. 16, 1779–June 5, 1860; House 1813–July 6, 1818, Oct. 8, 1822–29; Secy. of the Treasury March 6, 1829–June 20, 1831.

Inglis, Bob (R S.C.) Oct. 11, 1959– ; House 1993–99.

Inhofe, James Mountain (R Okla.) Nov. 17, 1934– ; House 1987–Nov. 15, 1994; Senate Nov. 17, 1994– .

Inouye, Daniel Ken (D Hawaii) Sept. 7, 1924– ; House Aug. 21, 1959–63; Senate 1963– ; Chrmn. Senate Select Committee on Intelligence Activities 1976–78; Chrmn. Senate Indian Affairs 1993–1995.

Inslee, Jay (D Wash.) Feb. 9, 1951– ; House 1993–95, 1999– .

Irby, John Laurens Manning (great-grandson of Elias Earle) (D S.C.) Sept. 10, 1854–Dec. 9, 1900; Senate 1891–97.

Iredell, James (J N.C.) Nov. 2, 1788–April 13, 1853; Senate Dec. 15, 1828–31; Gov. Dec. 8, 1827–Dec. 12, 1828 (Democratic Republican).

Ireland, Andrew Poysell "Andy" (R Fla.) Aug. 23, 1930– ; House 1977–93 (1977–July 5, 1984, Democrat).

Ireland, Clifford Cady (R Ill.) Feb. 14, 1878–May 24, 1930; House 1917–23.

Irion, Alfred Briggs (D La.) Feb. 18, 1833–May 21, 1903; House 1885–87.

Irvin, Alexander (W Pa.) Jan. 18, 1800–March 20, 1874; House 1847–49.

Irvin, James (W Pa.) Feb. 18, 1800–Nov. 28, 1862; House 1841–45.

Irvin, William W. (J Ohio) 1778–March 28, 1842; House 1829–33.

Irvine, William (– Pa.) Nov. 3, 1741–July 29, 1804; House 1793–95; Cont. Cong. 1786–88.

Irvine, William (R N.Y.) Feb. 14, 1820–Nov. 12, 1882; House 1859–61.

Irving, Theodore Leonard (D Mo.) March 24, 1898–March 8, 1962; House 1949–53.

Irving, William (R N.Y.) Aug. 15, 1766–Nov. 9, 1821; House Jan. 22, 1814–19.

Irwin, Donald Jay (D Conn.) Sept. 7, 1926– ; House 1959–61, 1965–69.

Irwin, Edward Michael (R Ill.) April 14, 1869–Jan. 30, 1933; House 1925–31.

Irwin, Harvey Samuel (R Ky.) Dec. 10, 1844–Sept. 3, 1916; House 1901–03.

Irwin, Jared (R Pa.) Jan. 19, 1768–Sept. 20, 1818; House 1813–17.

Irwin, Thomas (J Pa.) Feb. 22, 1785–May 14, 1870; House 1829–31.

Irwin, William Wallace (W Pa.) 1803–Sept. 15, 1856; House 1841–43.

Isacks, Jacob C. (J Tenn.) ?–?; House 1823–33 (1823–29 no party).

Isacson, Leo (AL N.Y.) April 20, 1910–Sept. 21, 1996; House Feb. 17, 1948–49.

Isakson, Johnny (R Ga.) Dec. 27, 1944– ; House Feb. 25, 1999– .

Istook, Ernest (R Okla.) Feb. 11, 1950– ; House 1993– .

Ittner, Anthony Friday (R Mo.) Oct. 8, 1837–Feb. 22, 1931; House 1877–79.

Iverson, Alfred Sr. (D Ga.) Dec. 3, 1798–March 4, 1873; House 1847–49; Senate 1855–Jan. 28, 1861.

Ives, Irving McNeil (R N.Y.) Jan. 24, 1896–Feb. 24, 1962; Senate 1947–59.

Ives, Willard (D N.Y.) July 7, 1806–April 19, 1896; House 1851–53.

Izac, Edouard Victor Michel (D Calif.) Dec. 18, 1891–Jan. 18, 1990; House 1937–47.

Izard, Ralph (– S.C.) Jan. 23, 1741 or 1742–May 30, 1804; Senate 1789–95; elected Pres. pro tempore May 31, 1794; Cont. Cong. 1782–83.

Izlar, James Ferdinand (D S.C.) Nov. 25, 1832–May 26, 1912; House April 12, 1894–95.

J

Jack, Summers Melville (R Pa.) July 18, 1852–Sept. 16, 1945; House 1899–1903.

Jack, William (D Pa.) July 29, 1788–Feb. 28, 1852; House 1841–43.

Jackson, Alfred Metcalf (D Kan.) July 14, 1860–June 11, 1924; House 1901–03.

Jackson, Amos Henry (R Ohio) May 10, 1846–Aug. 30, 1924; House 1903–05.

Jackson, Andrew (R Tenn.) March 15, 1767–June 8, 1845; House Dec. 5, 1796–Sept. 1797 (no party); Senate Sept. 26, 1797–April 1798, 1823–Oct. 14, 1825; Gov. (Fla. Terr.) March 10–July 18, 1821; President 1829–37 (Democrat).

Jackson, David Sherwood (D N.Y.) 1813–Jan. 20, 1872; House 1847–April 19, 1848.

Jackson, Donald Lester (R Calif.) Jan. 23, 1910–May 27, 1981; House 1947–61.

Jackson, Ebenezer Jr. (– Conn.) Jan. 31, 1796–Aug. 17, 1874; House Dec. 1, 1834–35.

Jackson, Edward Brake (son of George Jackson, brother of John George Jackson) (– Va.) Jan. 25, 1793–Sept. 8, 1826; House Oct. 23, 1820–23.

Jackson, Fred Schuyler (R Kan.) April 19, 1868–Nov. 21, 1931; House 1911–13.

Jackson, George (father of John George Jackson and Edward Brake Jackson) (R Va.) Jan. 9, 1757–May 17, 1831; House 1795–97, 1799–1803.

Jackson, Henry Martin (D Wash.) May 31, 1912–Sept. 1, 1983; House 1941–53; Senate 1953–Sept. 1, 1983; Chrmn. Senate Interior and Insular Affairs 1963–77; Chrmn. Senate Energy and Natural Resources 1977–81; Chrmn. Dem. Nat. Comm. 1960–61.

Jackson, Howell Edmunds (D Tenn.) April 8, 1832–Aug. 8, 1895; Senate 1881–April 14, 1886; Assoc. Justice Supreme Court March 4, 1893–Aug. 8, 1895.

Jackson, Jabez Young (son of James Jackson born in 1757, uncle of James Jackson born in 1819) (D Ga.) July 1790–?; House Oct. 5, 1835–39 (1835–37 Jacksonian).

Jackson, James (father of Jabez Young Jackson, grandfather of James Jackson, below) (R Ga.) Sept. 21, 1757–March 19, 1806; House 1789–91 (no party); Senate 1793–95 (no party), 1801–March 19, 1806; Gov. Jan. 12, 1798–March 3, 1801 (Democratic Republican).

Jackson, James (grandson of James Jackson, above, nephew of Jabez Young Jackson) (D Ga.) Oct. 18, 1819–Jan. 13, 1887; House 1857–Jan. 23, 1861.

Jackson, James Monroe (cousin of William Thomas Bland) (D W.Va.) Dec. 3, 1825–Feb. 14, 1901; House 1889–Feb. 3, 1890.

Jackson, James Streshley (U Ky.) Sept. 27, 1823–Oct. 8, 1862; House March 4–Dec. 13, 1861.

Jackson, Jesse Jr. (D Ill.) March 11, 1965– ; House Dec. 14, 1995– .

Jackson, John George (son of George Jackson, brother of Edward Brake Jackson, grandfather of William Thomas Bland) (R Va.) Sept. 22, 1777–March 28, 1825; House 1803–Sept. 28, 1810, 1813–17.

Jackson, Joseph Webber (SR Ga.) Dec. 6, 1796–Sept. 29, 1854; House March 4, 1850–53 (March 4, 1850–51 Democrat).

Jackson, Oscar Lawrence (R Pa.) Sept. 2, 1840–Feb. 16, 1920; House 1885–89.

Jackson, Richard Jr. (F R.I.) July 3, 1764–April 18, 1838; House Nov. 11, 1808–15.

Jackson, Samuel Dillon (D Ind.) May 28, 1895–March 8, 1951; Senate Jan. 28–Nov. 13, 1944.

Jackson, Thomas Birdsall (D N.Y.) March 24, 1797–April 23, 1881; House 1837–41.

Jackson, William (W Mass.) Sept. 2, 1783–Feb. 27, 1855; House 1833–37 (1833–35 Anti-Mason).

Jackson, William Humphreys (father of William Purnell Jackson) (R Md.) Oct. 15, 1839–April 3, 1915; House 1901–05, 1907–09.

Jackson, William Purnell (son of William Humphreys Jackson) (R Md.) Jan. 11, 1868–March 7, 1939; Senate Nov. 29, 1912–Jan. 28, 1914.

Jackson, William Terry (W N.Y.) Dec. 29, 1794–Sept. 15, 1882; House 1849–51.

Jackson-Lee, Sheila (D Texas) Jan. 12, 1950– ; House 1995– .

Jacobs, Andrew (father of Andrew Jacobs Jr., father-in-law of Martha Elizabeth Keys) (D Ind.) Feb. 22, 1906–Nov. 12, 1992; House 1949–51.

Jacobs, Andrew Jr. (son of Andrew Jacobs, husband of Martha Elizabeth Keys) (D Ind.) Feb. 24, 1932– ; House 1965–73, 1975–97.

Jacobs, Ferris Jr. (R N.Y.) March 20, 1836–Aug. 30, 1886; House 1881–83.

Jacobs, Israel (– Pa.) June 9, 1726–about Dec. 10, 1796; House 1791–93.

Jacobs, Orange (R Wash.) May 2, 1827–May 21, 1914; House (Terr. Del.) 1875–79.

Jacobsen, Bernhard Martin (father of William Sebastian Jacobsen) (D Iowa) March 26, 1862–June 30, 1936; House 1931–June 30, 1936.

Jacobsen, William Sebastian (son of Bernhard Martin Jacobsen) (D Iowa) Jan. 15, 1887–April 10, 1955; House 1937–43.

Jacobstein, Meyer (D N.Y.) Jan. 25, 1880–April 18, 1963; House 1923–29.

Jacoway, Henderson Madison (D Ark.) Nov. 7, 1870–Aug. 4, 1947; House 1911–23.

Jadwin, Cornelius Comegys (R Pa.) March 27, 1835–Aug. 17, 1913; House 1881–83.

James, Addison Davis (grandfather of John Albert Whitaker) (R Ky.) Feb. 27, 1850–June 10, 1947; House 1907–09.

James, Amaziah Bailey (R N.Y.) July 1, 1812–July 6, 1883; House 1877–81.

James, Benjamin Franklin (R Pa.) Aug. 1, 1885–Jan. 26, 1961; House 1949–59.

James, Charles Tillinghast (D R.I.) Sept. 15, 1805–Oct. 17, 1862; Senate 1851–57.

James, Craig T. (R Fla.) May 5, 1941– ; House 1989–93.

James, Darwin Rush (R N.Y.) May 14, 1834–Nov. 19, 1908; House 1883–87.

James, Francis (W Pa.) April 4, 1799–Jan. 4, 1886; House 1839–43 (1839–41 Anti-Mason).

James, Hinton (D N.C.) April 24, 1884–Nov. 3, 1948; House Nov. 4, 1930–31.

James, Ollie Murray (D Ky.) July 27, 1871–Aug. 28, 1918; House 1903–13; Senate 1913–Aug. 28, 1918.

James, Rorer Abraham (D Va.) March 1, 1859–Aug. 6, 1921; House June 15, 1920–Aug. 6, 1921.

James, William Francis (R Mich.) May 23, 1873–Nov. 17, 1945; House 1915–35.

Jameson, John (D Mo.) March 6, 1802–Jan. 24, 1857; House Dec. 12, 1839–41, 1843–45, 1847–49.

Jamieson, William Darius (D Iowa) Nov. 9, 1873–Nov. 18, 1949; House 1909–11.

Janes, Henry Fisk (AMas. Vt.) Oct. 10, 1792–June 6, 1879; House Dec. 2, 1834–37.

Jarman, John (R Okla.) July 17, 1915–Jan. 15, 1982; House 1951–77 (1951–Jan. 24, 1975, Democrat).

Jarman, Pete (D Ala.) Oct. 31, 1892–Feb. 17, 1955; House 1937–49.

Jarnagin, Spencer (W Tenn.) 1792–June 25, 1853; Senate Oct. 17, 1843–47.

Jarrett, Benjamin (R Pa.) July 18, 1881–July 20, 1944; House 1937–43.

Jarrett, William Paul (D Hawaii) Aug. 22, 1877–Nov. 10, 1929; House (Terr. Del.) 1923–27.

Jarvis, Leonard (J Maine) Oct. 19, 1781–Oct. 18, 1854; House 1829–37.

Jarvis, Thomas Jordan (D N.C.) Jan. 18, 1836–June 17, 1915; Senate April 19, 1894–Jan. 23, 1895; Gov. Feb. 5, 1879–Jan. 21, 1885.

Javits, Jacob Koppel (R N.Y.) May 18, 1904–March 7, 1986; House 1947–Dec. 31, 1954; Senate Jan. 9, 1957–81.

Jayne, William (– Dakota) Oct. 8, 1826–March 20, 1916; House (Terr. Del.) 1863–June 17, 1864; Gov. (Terr.) 1861–63.

Jefferis, Albert Webb (R Neb.) Dec. 7, 1868–Sept. 14, 1942; House 1919–23.

Jeffers, Lamar (D Ala.) April 16, 1888–June 1, 1983; House June 7, 1921–35.

Jefferson, William J. (D La.) March 14, 1947– ; House 1991– .

Jeffords, Elza (R Miss.) May 23, 1826–March 19, 1885; House 1883–85.

Jeffords, James Merrill (R Vt.) May 11, 1934– ; House 1975–89; Senate 1989– ; Chrmn. Senate Labor and Human Resources 1997–99; Chrmn. Senate Health, Education, Labor and Pensions 1999– .

Jeffrey, Harry Palmer (R Ohio) Dec. 26, 1901–Jan. 4, 1997; House 1943–45.

Jeffries, James Edmund (R Kan.) June 1, 1925– ; House 1979–83.

Jeffries, Walter Sooy (R N.J.) Oct. 16, 1893–Oct. 11, 1954; House 1939–41.

Jenckes, Thomas Allen (R R.I.) Nov. 2, 1818–Nov. 4, 1875; House 1863–71.

Jenckes, Virginia Ellis (D Ind.) Nov. 6, 1877–Jan. 9, 1975; House 1933–39.

Jenifer, Daniel (W Md.) April 15, 1791–Dec. 18, 1855; House 1831–33 (Anti-Jacksonian), 1835–41 (1835–37 Anti-Jacksonian).

Jenison, Edward Halsey (R Ill.) July 27, 1907–June 24, 1996; House 1947–53.

Jenkins, Albert Gallatin (D Va.) Nov. 10, 1830–May 21, 1864; House 1857–61.

Jenkins, Edgar Lanier (D Ga.) Jan. 4, 1933– ; House 1977–93.

Jenkins, John James (R Wis.) Aug. 24, 1843–June 8, 1911; House 1895–1909.

Jenkins, Lemuel (– N.Y.) Oct. 20, 1789–Aug. 18, 1862; House 1823–25.

Jenkins, Mitchell (R Pa.) Jan. 24, 1896–Sept. 15, 1977; House 1947–49.

Jenkins, Robert (R Pa.) July 10, 1769–April 18, 1848; House 1807–11.

Jenkins, Thomas Albert (R Ohio) Oct. 28, 1880–Dec. 21, 1959; House 1925–59.

Jenkins, Timothy (D N.Y.) Jan. 29, 1799–Dec. 24, 1859; House 1845–49, 1851–53.

Jenkins, William L. (R Tenn.) Nov. 29, 1936– ; House 1997– .

Jenks, Arthur Byron (R N.H.) Oct. 15, 1866–Dec. 14, 1947; House 1937–June 9, 1938, 1939–43.

Jenks, George Augustus (D Pa.) March 26, 1836–Feb. 10, 1908; House 1875–77.

Jenks, Michael Hutchinson (W Pa.) May 21, 1795–Oct. 16, 1867; House 1843–45.

Jenner, William Ezra (R Ind.) July 21, 1908–March 9, 1985; Senate Nov. 14, 1944–45, 1947–59; Chrmn. Senate Rules and Administration 1953–55.

Jenness, Benning Wentworth (– N.H.) July 14, 1806–Nov. 16, 1879; Senate Dec. 1, 1845–June 13, 1846.

Jennings, David (– Ohio) 1787–1834; House 1825–May 25, 1826.

Jennings, John Jr. (R Tenn.) June 6, 1880–Feb. 27, 1956; House Dec. 30, 1939–51.

Jennings, Jonathan (– Ind.) 1784–July 26, 1834; House Dec. 2, 1822–31; Gov. Nov. 7, 1816–Sept. 12, 1822 (Democratic Republican).

Jennings, William Pat (D Va.) Aug. 20, 1919–Aug. 2, 1994; House 1955–67.

Jenrette, John Wilson Jr. (D S.C.) May 19, 1936– ; House Nov. 5, 1975–Dec. 10, 1980.

Jensen, Benton Franklin (R Iowa) Dec. 16, 1892–Feb. 5, 1970; House 1939–65.

Jepsen, Roger William (R Iowa) Dec. 23, 1928– ; Senate 1979–85.

Jett, Thomas Marion (D Ill.) May 1, 1862–Jan. 10, 1939; House 1897–1903.

Jewett, Daniel Tarbox (R Mo.) Sept. 14, 1807–Oct. 7, 1906; Senate Dec. 19, 1870–Jan. 20, 1871.

Jewett, Freeborn Garrettson (J N.Y.) Aug. 4, 1791–Jan. 27, 1858; House 1831–33.

Jewett, Hugh Judge (brother of Joshua Husband Jewett) (D Ohio) July 1, 1817–March 6, 1898; House 1873–June 23, 1874.

Jewett, Joshua Husband (brother of Hugh Judge Jewett) (D Ky.) Sept. 30, 1815–July 14, 1861; House 1855–59.

Jewett, Luther (F Vt.) Dec. 24, 1772–March 8, 1860; House 1815–17.

Joelson, Charles Samuel (D N.J.) Jan. 27, 1916–Aug. 17, 1999; House 1961–Sept. 4, 1969.

Johansen, August Edgar (R Mich.) July 21, 1905–April 16, 1995; House 1955–65.

John, Chris (D La.) Jan. 5, 1960– ; House 1997– .

Johns, Joshua Leroy (R Wis.) Feb. 27, 1881–March 16, 1947; House 1939–43.

Johns, Kensey Jr. (– Del.) Dec. 10, 1791–March 28, 1857; House Oct. 2, 1827–31.

Johnson, Adna Romulus (R Ohio) Dec. 14, 1860–June 11, 1938; House 1909–11.

Johnson, Albert (R Wash.) March 5, 1869–Jan. 17, 1957; House 1913–33.

Johnson, Albert Walter (R Pa.) April 17, 1906–Sept. 1, 1998; House Nov. 5, 1963–77.

Johnson, Andrew (father-in-law of David Trotter Patterson) (R Tenn.) Dec. 29, 1808–July 31, 1875; House 1843–53 (Democrat); Senate Oct. 8, 1857–March 4, 1862 (Democrat), March 4–July 31, 1875; Gov. Oct. 17, 1853–Nov. 3, 1857 (Democrat), March 12, 1862–March 4, 1865 (Military); Vice President March 4–April 15, 1865; President April 15, 1865–69.

Johnson, Anton Joseph (R Ill.) Oct. 20, 1878–April 16, 1958; House 1939–49.

Johnson, Ben (D Ky.) May 20, 1858–June 4, 1950; House 1907–27.

Johnson, Byron Lindberg (D Colo.) Oct. 12, 1917– ; House 1959–61.

Johnson, Calvin Dean (R Ill.) Nov. 22, 1898–Oct. 13, 1985; House 1943–45.

Johnson, Cave (D Tenn.) Jan. 11, 1793–Nov. 23, 1866; House 1829–37 (Jacksonian), 1839–45; Postmaster Gen. March 7, 1845–March 5, 1849.

Johnson, Charles (R N.Y.) ?–July 23, 1802; House 1801–July 23, 1802.

Johnson, Charles Fletcher (D Maine) Feb. 14, 1859–Feb. 15, 1930; Senate 1911–17.

Johnson, Dewey William (FL Minn.) March 14, 1899–Sept. 18, 1941; House 1937–39.

Johnson, Don (D Ga.) Jan. 30, 1948– ; House 1993–95.

Johnson, Eddie Bernice (D Texas) Dec. 3, 1935– ; House 1993– .

Johnson, Edwin Carl (D Colo.) Jan. 1, 1884–May 30, 1970; Senate 1937–55; Chrmn. Senate Interstate and Foreign Commerce 1949–53; Gov. Jan. 10, 1933–Jan. 2, 1937, Jan. 11, 1955–Jan. 8, 1957.

Johnson, Edwin Stockton (D S.D.) Feb. 26, 1857–July 19, 1933; Senate 1915–21.

Johnson, Francis (– Ky.) June 19, 1776–May 16, 1842; House Nov. 13, 1820–27.

Johnson, Fred Gustus (R Neb.) Oct. 16, 1876–April 30, 1951; House 1929–31.

Johnson, Frederick Avery (– N.Y.) Jan. 2, 1833–July 17, 1893; House 1883–87.

Johnson, George William (D W.Va.) Nov. 10, 1869–Feb. 24, 1944; House 1923–25, 1933–43.

Johnson, Glen Dale (D Okla.) Sept. 11, 1911–Feb. 10, 1983; House 1947–49.

Johnson, Grove Lawrence (father of Hiram Warren Johnson) (R Calif.) March 27, 1841–Feb. 1, 1926; House 1895–97.

Johnson, Harold Terry (D Calif.) Dec. 2, 1907–March 16, 1988; House 1959–81; Chrmn. House Public Works and Transportation 1977–81.

Johnson, Harvey Hull (D Ohio) Sept. 7, 1808–Feb. 4, 1896; House 1853–55.

Johnson, Henry (W La.) Sept. 14, 1783–Sept. 4, 1864; Senate Jan. 12, 1818–May 27, 1824 (Republican), Feb. 12, 1844–49; House Sept. 25, 1834–39; Gov. Dec. 13, 1824–Dec. 15, 1828 (Democratic Republican).

Johnson, Henry Underwood (R Ind.) Oct. 28, 1850–June 4, 1939; House 1891–99.

Johnson, Herschel Vespasian (D Ga.) Sept. 18, 1812–Aug. 16, 1880; Senate Feb. 4, 1848–49; Gov. Nov. 9, 1853–Nov. 6, 1857.

Johnson, Hiram Warren (son of Grove Lawrence Johnson) (R Calif.) Sept. 2, 1866–Aug. 6, 1945; Senate March 16, 1917–Aug. 6, 1945; Gov. Jan. 3, 1911–March 15, 1917.

Johnson, Jacob (R Utah) Nov. 1, 1847–Aug. 15, 1925; House 1913–15.

Johnson, James (R Va.) ?–Dec. 7, 1825; House 1813–Feb. 1, 1820.

Johnson, James (brother of Richard Mentor Johnson and John Telemachus Johnson, uncle of Robert Ward Johnson) (– Ky.) Jan. 1, 1774–Aug. 13, 1826; House 1825–Aug. 13, 1826.

Johnson, James (U Ga.) Feb. 12, 1811–Nov. 20, 1891; House 1851–53; Provisional Gov. June 17–Dec. 14, 1865 (Democrat).

Johnson, James Augustus (D Calif.) May 16, 1829–May 11, 1896; House 1867–71.

Johnson, James Hutchins (D N.H.) June 3, 1802–Sept. 2, 1887; House 1845–49.

Johnson, James Leeper (W Ky.) Oct. 30, 1818–Feb. 12, 1877; House 1849–51.

Johnson, James Paul (R Colo.) June 2, 1930– ; House 1973–81.

Johnson, Jay (D Wis.) Sept. 30, 1943– ; House 1997–99.

Johnson, Jed Joseph (father of Jed Joseph Johnson Jr.) (D Okla.) July 31, 1888–May 8, 1963; House 1927–47.

Johnson, Jed Joseph Jr. (son of Jed Joseph Johnson) (D Okla.) Dec. 17, 1939–Dec. 16, 1993; House 1965–67.

Johnson, Jeromus (– N.Y.) Nov. 2, 1775–Sept. 7, 1846; House 1825–29.

Johnson, John (ID Ohio) 1805–Feb. 5, 1867; House 1851–53.

Johnson, John Telemachus (brother of James Johnson born in 1774 and Richard Mentor Johnson, uncle of Robert Ward Johnson) (– Ky.) Oct. 5, 1788–Dec. 17, 1856; House 1821–25.

Johnson, Joseph (uncle of Waldo Porter Johnson) (D Va.) Dec. 19, 1785–Feb. 27, 1877; House 1823–27 (no party), Jan. 21–March 3, 1833 (no party), 1835–41 (1835–37 Jacksonian), 1845–47; Gov. Jan. 16, 1852–Dec. 31, 1856.

Johnson, Joseph Travis (D S.C.) Feb. 28, 1858–May 8, 1919; House 1901–April 19, 1915.

Johnson, Justin Leroy (R Calif.) April 8, 1888–March 26, 1961; House 1943–57.

Johnson, Lester Roland (D Wis.) June 16, 1901–July 24, 1975; House Oct. 13, 1953–65.

Johnson, Luther Alexander (D Texas) Oct. 29, 1875–June 6, 1965; House 1923–July 17, 1946.

Johnson, Lyndon Baines (D Texas) Aug. 27, 1908–Jan. 22, 1973; House April 10, 1937–49; Senate 1949–Jan. 3, 1961; Senate minority leader 1953–55; Senate majority leader 1955–61; Chrmn. Senate Aeronautical and Space Sciences 1958–61; Vice President 1961–Nov. 22, 1963; President Nov. 22, 1963–69.

Johnson, Magnus (FL Minn.) Sept. 19, 1871–Sept. 13, 1936; Senate July 16, 1923–25; House 1933–35.

Johnson, Martin Nelson (R N.D.) March 3, 1850–Oct. 21, 1909; House 1891–99; Senate March 4–Oct. 21, 1909.

Johnson, Nancy Lee (R Conn.) Jan. 5, 1935– ; House 1983– ; Chrwmn. House Standards of Official Conduct 1995–97.

Johnson, Noadiah (J N.Y.) 1795–April 4, 1839; House 1833–35.

Johnson, Noble Jacob (R Ind.) Aug. 23, 1887–March 17, 1968; House 1925–31, 1939–July 1, 1948.

Johnson, Paul Burney (D Miss.) March 23, 1880–Dec. 26, 1943; House 1919–23; Gov. Jan. 16, 1940–Dec. 26, 1943.

Johnson, Perley Brown (W Ohio) Sept. 8, 1798–Feb. 9, 1870; House 1843–45.

Johnson, Philip (D Pa.) Jan. 17, 1818–Jan. 29, 1867; House 1861–Jan. 29, 1867.

Johnson, Reverdy (brother-in-law of Thomas Fielder Bowie) (D Md.) May 21, 1796–Feb. 10, 1876; Senate 1845–March 7, 1849 (Whig), 1863–July 10, 1868; Atty Gen. March 8, 1849–July 20, 1850.

Johnson, Richard Mentor (brother of James Johnson born in 1774 and John Telemachus Johnson, uncle of Robert Ward Johnson) (R Ky.) Oct. 17, 1780–Nov. 19, 1850; House 1807–19, 1829–37; Senate Dec. 10, 1819–29; Vice President 1837–41.

Johnson, Robert Davis (D Mo.) Aug. 12, 1883–Oct. 23, 1961; House Sept. 29, 1931–33.

Johnson, Robert Ward (nephew of James Johnson born in 1774, John Telemachus Johnson and Richard Mentor Johnson) (D Ark.) July 22, 1814–July 26, 1879; House 1847–53; Senate July 6, 1853–61.

Johnson, Royal Cleaves (R S.D.) Oct. 3, 1882–Aug. 2, 1939; House 1915–33.

Johnson, Samuel Robert (R Texas) Oct. 11, 1930– ; House May 22, 1991– .

Johnson, Thomas Francis (D Md.) June 26, 1909–Feb. 1, 1988; House 1959–63.

Johnson, Timothy Peter (D S.D.) Dec. 28, 1946– ; House 1987–97; Senate 1997– .

Johnson, Tom Loftin (D Ohio) July 18, 1854–April 10, 1911; House 1891–95.

Johnson, Waldo Porter (nephew of Joseph Johnson) (D Mo.) Sept. 16, 1817–Aug. 14, 1885; Senate March 17, 1861–Jan. 10, 1862.

Johnson, William Cost (W Md.) Jan. 14, 1806–April 14, 1860; House 1833–35 (Anti-Jacksonian), 1837–43.

Johnson, William Richard (R Ill.) May 15, 1875–Jan. 2, 1938; House 1925–33.

Johnson, William Samuel (– Conn.) Oct. 7, 1727–Nov. 14, 1819; Senate 1789–March 4, 1791; Cont. Cong. 1785–87.

Johnson, William Ward (R Calif.) March 9, 1892–June 8, 1963; House 1941–45.

Johnston, Charles (W N.Y.) Feb. 14, 1793–Sept. 1, 1845; House 1839–41.

Johnston, Charles Clement (brother of Joseph Eggleston Johnston, uncle of John Warfield Johnston) (J Va.) April 30, 1795–June 17, 1832; House 1831–June 17, 1832.

Johnston, David Emmons (D W.Va.) April 10, 1845–July 7, 1917; House 1899–1901.

Johnston, Harry A. (D Fla.) Dec. 2, 1931– ; House 1989–97.

Johnston, James Thomas (R Ind.) Jan. 19, 1839–July 19, 1904; House 1885–89.

Johnston, John Bennett Jr. (father-in-law of Timothy J. Roemer) (D La.) June 10, 1932– ; Senate Nov. 14, 1972–97; Chrmn. Senate Energy and Natural Resources 1987–95.

Johnston, John Brown (D N.Y.) July 10, 1882–Jan. 11, 1960; House 1919–21.

Johnston, John Warfield (uncle of Henry Bowen, nephew of Charles Clement Johnston and Joseph Eggleston Johnston) (D Va.) Sept.

9, 1818–Feb. 27, 1889; Senate Jan. 26, 1870–March 3, 1871, March 15, 1871–83.

Johnston, Joseph Eggleston (brother of Charles Clement Johnston, uncle of John Warfield Johnston) (D Va.) Feb. 3, 1807–March 21, 1891; House 1879–81.

Johnston, Joseph Forney (D Ala.) March 23, 1843–Aug. 8, 1913; Senate Aug. 6, 1907–Aug. 8, 1913; Gov. Dec. 1, 1896–Dec. 1, 1900.

Johnston, Josiah Stoddard (– La.) Nov. 24, 1784–May 19, 1833; House 1821–23; Senate Jan. 15, 1824–May 19, 1833.

Johnston, Olin DeWitt Talmadge (father of Elizabeth Johnston Patterson) (D S.C.) Nov. 18, 1896–April 18, 1965; Senate 1945–April 18, 1965; Chrmn. Senate Post Office and Civil Service 1949–53, 1955–65; Gov. Jan. 15, 1935–Jan. 17, 1939, Jan. 19, 1943–Jan. 2, 1945.

Johnston, Rienzi Melville (cousin of Benjamin Edward Russell) (D Texas) Sept. 9, 1849–Feb. 28, 1926; Senate Jan. 4–29, 1913.

Johnston, Rowland Louis (R Mo.) April 23, 1872–Sept. 22, 1939; House 1929–31.

Johnston, Samuel (– N.C.) Dec. 15, 1733–Aug. 17, 1816; Senate Nov. 27, 1789–93; Cont. Cong. 1780–81; Gov. Dec. 20, 1787–Dec. 17, 1789 (Federalist).

Johnston, Thomas Dillard (D N.C.) April 1, 1840–June 22, 1902; House 1885–89.

Johnston, Walter Eugene III (R N.C.) March 3, 1936– ; House 1981–83.

Johnston, William (D Ohio) 1819–May 1, 1866; House 1863–65.

Johnstone, George (D S.C.) April 18, 1846–March 8, 1921; House 1891–93.

Jolley, John Lawlor (R S.D.) July 14, 1840–Dec. 14, 1926; House Dec. 7, 1891–93.

Jonas, Benjamin Franklin (D La.) July 19, 1834–Dec. 21, 1911; Senate 1879–85.

Jonas, Charles Andrew (father of Charles Raper Jonas) (R N.C.) Aug. 14, 1876–May 25, 1955; House 1929–31.

Jonas, Charles Raper (son of Charles Andrew Jonas) (R N.C.) Dec. 9, 1904–Sept. 28, 1988; House 1953–73.

Jonas, Edgar Allan (R Ill.) Oct. 14, 1885–Nov. 14, 1965; House 1949–55.

Jones, Alexander Hamilton (R N.C.) July 21, 1822–Jan. 29, 1901; House July 6, 1868–71.

Jones, Andrieus Aristieus (D N.M.) May 16, 1862–Dec. 20, 1927; Senate 1917–Dec. 20, 1927.

Jones, Ben (D Ga.) Aug. 30, 1941– ; House 1989–93.

Jones, Benjamin (J Ohio) April 13, 1787–April 24, 1861; House 1833–37.

Jones, Burr W. (D Wis.) March 9, 1846–Jan. 7, 1935; House 1883–85.

Jones, Charles William (D Fla.) Dec. 24, 1834–Oct. 11, 1897; Senate 1875–87.

Jones, Daniel Terryll (D N.Y.) Aug. 17, 1800–March 29, 1861; House 1851–55.

Jones, Ed (D Tenn.) April 20, 1912– ; House March 25, 1969–89.

Jones, Evan John (R Pa.) Oct. 23, 1872–Jan. 9, 1952; House 1919–23.

Jones, Francis (R Tenn.) ?–?; House 1817–23.

Jones, Frank (D N.H.) Sept. 15, 1832–Oct. 2, 1902; House 1875–79.

Jones, George (– Ga.) Feb. 25, 1766–Nov. 13, 1838; Senate Aug. 27–Nov. 7, 1807.

Jones, George Wallace (D Iowa) April 12, 1804–July 22, 1896; House (Terr. Del.) 1835–April 1836 (no party Mich.), 1837–Jan. 14, 1839 (no party Wis.); Senate Dec. 7, 1848–59.

Jones, George Washington (D Tenn.) March 15, 1806–Nov. 14, 1884; House 1843–59.

Jones, George Washington (G Texas) Sept. 5, 1828–July 11, 1903; House 1879–83.

Jones, Hamilton Chamberlain (D N.C.) Sept. 26, 1884–Aug. 10, 1957; House 1947–53.

Jones, Homer Raymond (R Wash.) Sept. 3, 1893–Nov. 26, 1970; House 1947–49.

Jones, Isaac Dashiell (W Md.) Nov. 1, 1806–July 5, 1893; House 1841–43.

Jones, James (F Ga.) ?–Jan. 11, 1801; House 1799–Jan. 11, 1801.

Jones, James (– Va.) Dec. 11, 1772–April 25, 1848; House 1819–23.

Jones, James Chamberlain (W Tenn.) April 20, 1809–Oct. 29, 1859; Senate 1851–57; Gov. Oct. 15, 1841–Oct. 14, 1845.

Jones, James Henry (D Texas) Sept. 13, 1830–March 22, 1904; House 1883–87.

Jones, James Kimbrough (D Ark.) Sept. 29, 1839–June 1, 1908; House 1881–Feb. 19, 1885; Senate March 4, 1885–1903; Chrmn. Dem. Nat. Comm. 1896–1904.

Jones, James Robert (D Okla.) May 5, 1939–   ; House 1973–87; Chrmn. House Budget 1981–85.

Jones, James Taylor (D Ala.) July 20, 1832–Feb. 15, 1895; House 1877–79, Dec. 3, 1883–89.

Jones, Jehu Glancy (D Pa.) Oct. 7, 1811–March 24, 1878; House 1851–53, Feb. 4, 1854–Oct. 30, 1858.

Jones, John James (D Ga.) Nov. 13, 1824–Oct. 19, 1898; House 1859–Jan. 23, 1861.

Jones, John Marvin (D Texas) Feb. 26, 1886–March 4, 1976; House 1917–Nov. 20, 1940.

Jones, John Percival (R Nev.) Jan. 27, 1829–Nov. 27, 1912; Senate 1873–1903.

Jones, John Sills (R Ohio) Feb. 12, 1836–April 11, 1903; House 1877–79.

Jones, John William (W Ga.) April 14, 1806–April 27, 1871; House 1847–49.

Jones, John Winston (D Va.) Nov. 22, 1791–Jan. 29, 1848; House 1835–45 (1835–37 Jacksonian); Speaker Dec. 4, 1843–45.

Jones, Morgan (D N.Y.) Feb. 26, 1830–July 13, 1894; House 1865–67.

Jones, Nathaniel (D N.Y.) Feb. 17, 1788–July 20, 1866; House 1837–41.

Jones, Owen (D Pa.) Dec. 29, 1819–Dec. 25, 1878; House 1857–59.

Jones, Paul Caruthers (D Mo.) March 12, 1901–Feb. 10, 1981; House Nov. 2, 1948–69.

Jones, Phineas (R N.J.) April 18, 1819–April 19, 1884; House 1881–83.

Jones, Robert Emmett Jr. (D Ala.) June 12, 1912–June 4, 1997; House Jan. 28, 1947–77; Chrmn. House Public Works and Transportation 1975–77.

Jones, Robert Franklin (R Ohio) June 25, 1907–June 22, 1968; House 1939–Sept. 2, 1947.

Jones, Roland (D La.) Nov. 18, 1813–Feb. 5, 1869; House 1853–55.

Jones, Seaborn (D Ga.) Feb. 1, 1788–March 18, 1864; House 1833–35 (Jacksonian), 1845–47.

Jones, Stephanie Tubbs (D Ohio) Sept. 10, 1949–   ; House 1999–   .

Jones, Thomas Laurens (D Ky.) Jan. 22, 1819–June 20, 1887; House 1867–71, 1875–77.

Jones, Walter (R Va.) Dec. 18, 1745–Dec. 31, 1815; House 1797–99, 1803–11.

Jones, Walter Beaman (D N.C.) Aug. 19, 1913–Sept. 15, 1992; House Feb. 5, 1966–Sept. 15, 1992; Chrmn. House Merchant Marine and Fisheries 1981–92.

Jones, Walter B. Jr. (son of Walter Beaman Jones) (R N.C.) Feb. 10, 1943–   ; House 1995–   .

Jones, Wesley Livsey (R Wash.) Oct. 9, 1863–Nov. 19, 1932; House 1899–1909; Senate 1909–Nov. 19, 1932.

Jones, William (R Pa.) 1760–Sept. 6, 1831; House 1801–03; Secy. of the Navy Jan. 19, 1813–Dec. 1, 1814.

Jones, William Atkinson (D Va.) March 21, 1849–April 17, 1918; House 1891–April 17, 1918.

Jones, William Carey (Sil.R Wash.) April 5, 1855–June 14, 1927; House 1897–99.

Jones, William Theopilus (R Wyo.) Feb. 20, 1842–Oct. 9, 1882; House (Terr. Del.) 1871–73.

Jones, Woodrow Wilson (D N.C.) Jan. 26, 1914–   ; House Nov. 7, 1950–57.

Jonkman, Bartel John (R Mich.) April 28, 1884–June 13, 1955; House Feb. 19, 1940–49.

Jontz, James Prather (D Ind.) Dec. 18, 1951–   ; House 1987–93.

Jordan, Barbara Charline (D Texas) Feb. 21, 1936–Jan. 17, 1996; House 1973–79.

Jordan, Benjamin Everett (D N.C.) Sept. 8, 1896–March 15, 1974; Senate April 19, 1958–73; Chrmn. Senate Rules and Administration 1963–72.

Jordan, Isaac M. (D Ohio) May 5, 1835–Dec. 3, 1890; House 1883–85.

Jordan, Leonard Beck (R Idaho) May 15, 1899–June 30, 1983; Senate Aug. 6, 1962–Jan. 2, 1973; Gov. Jan. 1, 1951–Jan. 3, 1955.

Jorden, Edwin James (R Pa.) Aug. 30, 1863–Sept. 7, 1903; House Feb. 23–March 4, 1895.

Jorgensen, Joseph (R Va.) Feb. 11, 1844–Jan. 21, 1888; House 1877–83.

Joseph, Antonio (D N.M.) Aug. 25, 1846–April 19, 1910; House (Terr. Del.) 1885–95.

Jost, Henry Lee (D Mo.) Dec. 6, 1873–July 13, 1950; House 1923–25.

Joy, Charles Frederick (R Mo.) Dec. 11, 1849–April 13, 1921; House 1893–April 3, 1894, 1895–1903.

Joyce, Charles Herbert (R Vt.) Jan. 30, 1830–Nov. 22, 1916; House 1875–83.

Joyce, James (R Ohio) July 2, 1870–March 25, 1931; House 1909–11.

Judd, Norman Buel (grandfather of Norman Judd Gould) (R Ill.) Jan. 10, 1815–Nov. 11, 1878; House 1867–71.

Judd, Walter Henry (R Minn.) Sept. 25, 1898–Feb. 13, 1994; House 1943–63.

Judson, Andrew Thompson (J Conn.) Nov. 29, 1784–March 17, 1853; House 1835–July 4, 1836.

Julian, George Washington (R Ind.) May 5, 1817–July 7, 1899; House 1849–51 (Free-Soiler), 1861–71.

Junkin, Benjamin Franklin (R Pa.) Nov. 12, 1822–Oct. 9, 1908; House 1859–61.

Juul, Niels (R Ill.) April 27, 1859–Dec. 4, 1929; House 1917–21.

K

Kading, Charles August (R Wis.) Jan. 14, 1874–June 19, 1956; House 1927–33.

Kahn, Florence Prag (widow of Julius Kahn) (R Calif.) Nov. 9, 1866–Nov. 16, 1948; House 1925–37.

Kahn, Julius (husband of Florence Prag Kahn) (R Calif.) Feb. 28, 1861–Dec. 18, 1924; House 1899–1903, 1905–Dec. 18, 1924.

Kalanianaole, Jonah Kuhio (R Hawaii) March 26, 1871–Jan. 7, 1922; House (Terr. Del.) 1903–Jan. 7, 1922.

Kalbfleisch, Martin (D N.Y.) Feb. 8, 1804–Feb. 12, 1873; House 1863–65.

Kane, Elias Kent (– Ill.) June 7, 1794–Dec. 12, 1835; Senate 1825–Dec. 12, 1835.

Kane, Nicholas Thomas (D N.Y.) Sept. 12, 1846–Sept. 14, 1887; House March 4–Sept. 14, 1887.

Kanjorski, Paul E. (D Pa.) April 2, 1937–   ; House 1985–   .

Kaptur, Marcia Carolyn "Marcy" (D Ohio) June 17, 1946–   ; House 1983–   .

Karch, Charles Adam (D Ill.) March 17, 1875–Nov. 6, 1932; House 1931–Nov. 6, 1932.

Karnes, David Kemp (R Neb.) Dec. 12, 1948–   ; Senate March 13, 1987–89.

Karst, Raymond Willard (D Mo.) Dec. 31, 1902–Oct. 4, 1987; House 1949–51.

Karsten, Frank Melvin (D Mo.) Jan. 7, 1913–May 14, 1992; House 1947–69.

Karth, Joseph Edward (D Minn.) Aug. 26, 1922– ; House 1959–77.

Kasem, George Albert (D Calif.) April 6, 1919– ; House 1959–61.

Kasich, John Richard (R Ohio) May 13, 1952– ; House 1983– ; Chrmn. House Budget 1995– .

Kassebaum, Nancy Landon (R Kan.) July 29, 1932– ; Senate Dec. 23, 1978–97; Chrwmn. Senate Labor and Human Resources 1995–97.

Kasson, John Adam (R Iowa) Jan. 11, 1822–May 19, 1910; House 1863–67, 1873–77, 1881–July 13, 1884.

Kasten, Robert Walter Jr. (R Wis.) June 19, 1942– ; House 1975–79; Senate 1981–93.

Kastenmeier, Robert William (D Wis.) Jan. 24, 1924– ; House 1959–91.

Kaufman, David Spangler (D Texas) Dec. 18, 1813–Jan. 31, 1851; House March 30, 1846–Jan. 31, 1851.

Kavanagh, Edward (J Maine) April 27, 1795–Jan. 22, 1844; House 1831–35; Gov. March 7, 1843–Jan. 1, 1844 (Democrat).

Kavanaugh, William Marmaduke (D Ark.) March 3, 1866–Feb. 21, 1915; Senate Jan. 29–March 3, 1913.

Kaynor, William Kirk (R Mass.) Nov. 29, 1884–Dec. 20, 1929; House March 4–Dec. 20, 1929.

Kazen, Abraham Jr. (D Texas) Jan. 17, 1919–Nov. 29, 1987; House 1967–85.

Kean, Hamilton Fish (father of Robert Winthrop Kean, brother of John Kean) (R N.J.) Feb. 27, 1862–Dec. 27, 1941; Senate 1929–35.

Kean, John (brother of Hamilton Fish Kean, uncle of Robert Winthrop Kean) (R N.J.) Dec. 4, 1852–Nov. 4, 1914; House 1883–85, 1887–89; Senate 1899–1911.

Kean, Robert Winthrop (son of Hamilton Fish Kean, nephew of John Kean) (R N.J.) Sept. 28, 1893–Sept. 21, 1980; House 1939–59.

Kearney, Bernard William (R N.Y.) May 23, 1889–June 3, 1976; House 1943–59.

Kearns, Carroll Dudley (R Pa.) May 7, 1900–June 11, 1976; House 1947–63.

Kearns, Charles Cyrus (R Ohio) Feb. 11, 1869–Dec. 17, 1931; House 1915–31.

Kearns, Thomas (R Utah) April 11, 1862–Oct. 18, 1918; Senate Jan. 23, 1901–05.

Keating, Edward (D Colo.) July 9, 1875–March 18, 1965; House 1913–19.

Keating, Kenneth Barnard (R N.Y.) May 18, 1900–May 5, 1975; House 1947–59; Senate 1959–65.

Keating, William John (R Ohio) March 30, 1927– ; House 1971–Jan. 3, 1974.

Kee, James (son of John Kee and Maude Elizabeth Kee) (D W.Va.) April 15, 1917–March 11, 1989; House 1965–73.

Kee, John (husband of Maude Elizabeth Kee, father of James Kee) (D W.Va.) Aug. 22, 1874–May 8, 1951; House 1933–May 8, 1951; Chrmn. House Foreign Affairs 1949–51.

Kee, Maude Elizabeth (widow of John Kee, mother of James Kee) (D W.Va.) ?–Feb. 16, 1975; House July 17, 1951–65.

Keefe, Frank Bateman (R Wis.) Sept. 23, 1887–Feb. 5, 1952; House 1939–51.

Keeney, Russell Watson (R Ill.) Dec. 29, 1897–Jan. 11, 1958; House 1957–Jan. 11, 1958.

Keese, Richard (– N.Y.) Nov. 23, 1794–Feb. 7, 1883; House 1827–29.

Kefauver, Carey Estes (D Tenn.) July 26, 1903–Aug. 10, 1963; House Sept. 13, 1939–49; Senate 1949–Aug. 10, 1963.

Kehoe, James Nicholas (D Ky.) July 15, 1862–June 16, 1945; House 1901–05.

Kehoe, James Walter (D Fla.) April 25, 1870–Aug. 20, 1938; House 1917–19.

Kehr, Edward Charles (D Mo.) Nov. 5, 1837–April 20, 1918; House 1875–77.

Keifer, Joseph Warren (R Ohio) Jan. 30, 1836–April 22, 1932; House 1877–85, 1905–11; Speaker Dec. 5, 1881–83.

Keightley, Edwin William (R Mich.) Aug. 7, 1843–May 4, 1926; House 1877–79.

Keim, George May (uncle of William High Keim) (D Pa.) March 23, 1805–June 10, 1861; House March 17, 1838–43.

Keim, William High (nephew of George May Keim) (R Pa.) June 13, 1813–May 18, 1862; House Dec. 7, 1858–59.

Keister, Abraham Lincoln (R Pa.) Sept. 10, 1852–May 26, 1917; House 1913–17.

Keith, Hastings (R Mass.) Nov. 22, 1915– ; House 1959–73.

Keitt, Laurence Massillon (D S.C.) Oct. 4, 1824–June 4, 1864; House 1853–July 16, 1856, Aug. 6, 1856–Dec. 1860.

Keliher, John Austin (D Mass.) Nov. 6, 1866–Sept. 20, 1938; House 1903–11.

Keller, Kent Ellsworth (D Ill.) June 4, 1867–Sept. 3, 1954; House 1931–41.

Keller, Oscar Edward (IR Minn.) July 30, 1878–Nov. 21, 1927; House July 1, 1919–27.

Kelley, Augustine Bernard (D Pa.) July 9, 1883–Nov. 20, 1957; House 1941–Nov. 20, 1957.

Kelley, Harrison (R Kan.) May 12, 1836–July 24, 1897; House Dec. 2, 1889–91.

Kelley, John Edward (P S.D.) March 27, 1853–Aug. 5, 1941; House 1897–99.

Kelley, Patrick Henry (R Mich.) Oct. 7, 1867–Sept. 11, 1925; House 1913–23.

Kelley, William Darrah (R Pa.) April 12, 1814–Jan. 9, 1890; House 1861–Jan. 9, 1890.

Kellogg, Charles (– N.Y.) Oct. 3, 1773–May 11, 1842; House 1825–27.

Kellogg, Francis William (R Ala.) May 30, 1810–Jan. 13, 1879; House 1859–65 (Mich.), July 22, 1868–69.

Kellogg, Frank Billings (R Minn.) Dec. 22, 1856–Dec. 21, 1937; Senate 1917–23; Secy. of State March 5, 1925–March 28, 1929.

Kellogg, Orlando (W N.Y.) June 18, 1809–Aug. 24, 1865; House 1847–49, 1863–Aug. 24, 1865.

Kellogg, Stephen Wright (R Conn.) April 5, 1822–Jan. 27, 1904; House 1869–73.

Kellogg, William (R Ill.) July 8, 1814–Dec. 20, 1872; House 1857–63.

Kellogg, William Pitt (R La.) Dec. 8, 1830–Aug. 10, 1918; Senate July 9, 1868–Nov. 1, 1872, 1877–83; House 1883–85; Gov. Jan. 13, 1873–Jan. 8, 1877.

Kelly, Edna Flannery (D N.Y.) Aug. 20, 1906–Dec. 14, 1997; House Nov. 8, 1949–69.

Kelly, Edward Austin (D Ill.) April 3, 1892–Aug. 30, 1969; House 1931–43, 1945–47.

Kelly, George Bradshaw (D N.Y.) Dec. 12, 1900–June 26, 1971; House 1937–39.

Kelly, James (F Pa.) July 17, 1760–Feb. 4, 1819; House 1805–09.

Kelly, James Kerr (D Ore.) Feb. 16, 1819–Sept. 15, 1903; Senate 1871–77.

Kelly, John (D N.Y.) April 20, 1822–June 1, 1886; House 1855–Dec. 25, 1858.

Kelly, Melville Clyde (R Pa.) Aug. 4, 1883–April 29, 1935; House 1913–15, 1917–35.

Kelly, Richard (R Fla.) July 31, 1924– ; House 1975–81.

Kelly, Sue W. (R N.Y.) Sept. 26, 1936– ; House 1995– .

Kelly, William (– Ala.) Sept. 22, 1786–Aug. 24, 1834; Senate Dec. 12, 1822–25.

Kelsey, William Henry (R N.Y.) Oct. 2, 1812–April 20, 1879; House 1855–59 (1855–57 Whig), 1867–71.

Kelso, John Russell (IRad. Mo.) March 23, 1831–Jan. 26, 1891; House 1865–67.

Kem, James Preston (R Mo.) April 2, 1890–Feb. 24, 1965; Senate 1947–53.

Kem, Omar Madison (P Neb.) Nov. 13, 1855–Feb. 13, 1942; House 1891–97.

Kemble, Gouverneur (D N.Y.) Jan. 25, 1786–Sept. 16, 1875; House 1837–41.

Kemp, Bolivar Edwards (D La.) Dec. 28, 1871–June 19, 1933; House 1925–June 19, 1933.

Kemp, Jack French (R N.Y.) July 13, 1935– ; House 1971–89; Secy. of Housing and Urban Development Feb. 13, 1989–Jan. 20, 1993.

Kempshall, Thomas (W N.Y.) about 1796–Jan. 14, 1865; House 1839–41.

Kempthorne, Dirk (R Idaho) Oct. 29, 1951– ; Senate 1993–99; Gov. Jan. 8, 1999– .

Kenan, Thomas (R N.C.) Feb. 26, 1771–Oct. 22, 1843; House 1805–11.

Kendall, Charles West (D Nev.) April 22, 1828–June 25, 1914; House 1871–75.

Kendall, Elva Roscoe (R Ky.) Feb. 14, 1893–Jan. 29, 1968; House 1929–31.

Kendall, John Wilkerson (father of Joseph Morgan Kendall) (D Ky.) June 26, 1834–March 7, 1892; House 1891–March 7, 1892.

Kendall, Jonas (father of Joseph Gowing Kendall) (– Mass.) Oct. 27, 1757–Oct. 22, 1844; House 1819–21.

Kendall, Joseph Gowing (son of Jonas Kendall) (– Mass.) Oct. 27, 1788–Oct. 2, 1847; House 1829–33.

Kendall, Joseph Morgan (son of John Wilkerson Kendall) (D Ky.) May 12, 1863–Nov. 5, 1933; House April 21, 1892–93, 1895–Feb. 18, 1897.

Kendall, Nathan Edward (R Iowa) March 17, 1868–Nov. 5, 1936; House 1909–13; Gov. Jan. 13, 1921–Jan. 15, 1925.

Kendall, Samuel Austin (R Pa.) Nov. 1, 1859–Jan. 8, 1933; House 1919–Jan. 8, 1933.

Kendrick, John Benjamin (D Wyo.) Sept. 6, 1857–Nov. 3, 1933; Senate 1917–Nov. 3, 1933; Gov. Jan. 4, 1915–Feb. 26, 1917.

Kenna, John Edward (D W.Va.) April 10, 1848–Jan. 11, 1893; House 1877–83; Senate 1883–Jan. 11, 1893.

Kennedy, Ambrose (R R.I.) Dec. 1, 1875–March 10, 1967; House 1913–23.

Kennedy, Ambrose Jerome (D Md.) Jan. 6, 1893–Aug. 29, 1950; House Nov. 8, 1932–41.

Kennedy, Andrew (cousin of Case Broderick) (D Ind.) July 24, 1810–Dec. 31, 1847; House 1841–47.

Kennedy, Anthony (brother of John Pendleton Kennedy) (AP Md.) Dec. 21, 1810–July 31, 1892; Senate 1857–63.

Kennedy, Charles Augustus (R Iowa) March 24, 1869–Jan. 10, 1951; House 1907–21.

Kennedy, Edward Moore (father of Patrick J. Kennedy, brother of John Fitzgerald Kennedy and Robert Francis Kennedy, grandson of John Francis Fitzgerald, uncle of Joseph Patrick Kennedy II) (D Mass.) Feb. 22, 1932– ; Senate Nov. 7, 1962– ; Chrmn. Senate Judiciary 1979–81; Chrmn. Senate Labor and Human Resources 1987–95.

Kennedy, James (R Ohio) Sept. 3, 1853–Nov. 9, 1928; House 1903–11.

Kennedy, John Fitzgerald (brother of Edward Moore Kennedy and Robert Francis Kennedy, grandson of John Francis Fitzgerald, uncle of Joseph Patrick Kennedy II and Patrick J. Kennedy) (D Mass.) May 29, 1917–Nov. 22, 1963; House 1947–53; Senate 1953–Dec. 22, 1960; President 1961–Nov. 22, 1963.

Kennedy, John Lauderdale (R Neb.) Oct. 27, 1854–Aug. 30, 1946; House 1905–07.

Kennedy, John Pendleton (brother of Anthony Kennedy) (W Md.) Oct. 25, 1795–Aug. 18, 1870; House April 25, 1838–39, 1841–45; Secy. of the Navy July 26, 1852–March 7, 1853.

Kennedy, Joseph Patrick II (son of Robert Francis Kennedy, cousin of Patrick J. Kennedy, nephew of Edward Moore Kennedy and John Fitzgerald Kennedy, great-grandson of John Francis Fitzgerald) (D Mass.) Sept. 24, 1952– ; House 1987–99.

Kennedy, Martin John (D N.Y.) Aug. 29, 1892–Oct. 27, 1955; House March 11, 1930–45.

Kennedy, Michael Joseph (D N.Y.) Oct. 25, 1897–Nov. 1, 1949; House 1939–43.

Kennedy, Patrick J. (son of Edward Moore Kennedy, cousin of Joseph Patrick Kennedy II, nephew of John Fitzgerald Kennedy and Robert F. Kennedy, great-grandson of John Francis Fitzgerald) (D R.I.) July 14, 1967– ; House 1995– .

Kennedy, Robert Francis (father of Joseph Patrick Kennedy II, brother of Edward Moore Kennedy and John Fitzgerald Kennedy, uncle of Patrick J. Kennedy, grandson of John Francis Fitzgerald (D N.Y.) Nov. 20, 1925–June 6, 1968; Senate 1965–June 6, 1968; Atty. Gen. Jan. 21, 1961–Sept. 3, 1964.

Kennedy, Robert Patterson (R Ohio) Jan. 23, 1840–May 6, 1918; House 1887–91.

Kennedy, William (R N.C.) July 31, 1768–Oct. 11, 1834; House 1803–05, 1809–11, Jan. 30, 1813–15.

Kennedy, William (D Conn.) Dec. 19, 1854–June 19, 1918; House 1913–15.

Kennelly, Barbara Bailey (D Conn.) July 10, 1936– ; House Jan. 25, 1982–99.

Kennett, Luther Martin (W Mo.) March 15, 1807–April 12, 1873; House 1855–57.

Kenney, Edward Aloysius (D N.J.) Aug. 11, 1884–Jan. 27, 1938; House 1933–Jan. 27, 1938.

Kenney, Richard Rolland (D Del.) Sept. 9, 1856–Aug. 14, 1931; Senate 1897–1901.

Kennon, William Sr. (cousin of William Kennon Jr.) (J Ohio) May 14, 1793–Nov. 2, 1881; House 1829–33, 1835–37.

Kennon, William Jr. (cousin of William Kennon Sr.) (D Ohio) June 12, 1802–Oct. 19, 1867; House 1847–49.

Kent, Everett (D Pa.) Nov. 15, 1888–Oct. 13, 1963; House 1923–25, 1927–29.

Kent, Joseph (R Md.) Jan. 14, 1779–Nov. 24, 1837; House 1811–15, 1819–Jan. 6, 1826; Senate 1833–Nov. 24, 1837; Gov. Jan. 9, 1826–Jan. 15, 1829 (Democratic Republican).

Kent, Moss (F N.Y.) April 3, 1766–May 30, 1838; House 1813–17.

Kent, William (I Calif.) March 29, 1864–March 13, 1928; House 1911–17 (1911–13 Progressive Republican).

Kenyon, William Scheuneman (R N.Y.) Dec. 13, 1820–Feb. 10, 1896; House 1859–61.

Kenyon, William Squire (R Iowa) June 10, 1869–Sept. 9, 1933; Senate April 12, 1911–Feb. 24, 1922.

Keogh, Eugene James (D N.Y.) Aug. 30, 1907–May 26, 1989; House 1937–67.

Kern, Frederick John (D Ill.) Sept. 6, 1864–Nov. 9, 1931; House 1901–03.

Kern, John Worth (D Ind.) Dec. 20, 1849–Aug. 17, 1917; Senate 1911–17; Senate majority leader 1913–17.

Kernan, Francis (D N.Y.) Jan. 14, 1816–Sept. 7, 1892; House 1863–65; Senate 1875–81.

Kerr, Daniel (R Iowa) June 18, 1836–Oct. 8, 1916; House 1887–91.

Kerr, James (D Pa.) Oct. 2, 1851–Oct. 31, 1908; House 1889–91.

Kerr, John (father of John Kerr Jr., cousin of Bartlett Yancey, great-uncle of John Hosea Kerr) (R Va.) Aug. 4, 1782–Sept. 29, 1842; House 1813–15, Oct. 30, 1815–17.

Kerr, John Jr. (son of John Kerr) (W N.C.) Feb. 10, 1811–Sept. 5, 1879; House 1853–55.

Kerr, John Bozman (son of John Leeds Kerr) (W Md.) March 5, 1809–Jan. 27, 1878; House 1849–51.

Kerr, John Hosea (great-nephew of John Kerr) (D N.C.) Dec. 31, 1873–June 21, 1958; House Nov. 6, 1923–53.

Kerr, John Leeds (father of John Bozman Kerr) (W Md.) Jan. 15, 1780–Feb. 21, 1844; House 1825–29 (no party), 1831–33 (no party); Senate Jan. 5, 1841–43.

Kerr, Joseph (– Ohio) 1765–Aug. 22, 1837; Senate Dec. 10, 1814–15.

Kerr, Josiah Leeds (R Md.) Jan. 10, 1861–Sept. 27, 1920; House Nov. 6, 1900–01.

Kerr, Michael Crawford (D Ind.) March 15, 1827–Aug. 19, 1876; House 1865–73, 1875–Aug. 19, 1876; Speaker Dec. 6, 1875–Aug. 19, 1876.

Kerr, Robert Samuel (D Okla.) Sept. 11, 1896–Jan. 1, 1963; Senate 1949–Jan. 1, 1963; Chrmn. Senate Aeronautical and Space Sciences 1961–63; Gov. Jan. 11, 1943–Jan. 13, 1947.

Kerr, Winfield Scott (R Ohio) June 23, 1852–Sept. 11, 1917; House 1895–1901.

Kerrey, Robert (D Neb.) Aug. 27, 1943– ; Senate 1989– ; Gov. Jan. 6, 1983–Jan. 9, 1987.

Kerrigan, James (ID N.Y.) Dec. 25, 1828–Nov. 1, 1899; House 1861–63.

Kerry, John Forbes (D Mass.) Dec. 22, 1943– ; Senate 1985– .

Kershaw, John (R S.C.) Sept. 12, 1765–Aug. 4, 1829; House 1813–15.

Kersten, Charles Joseph (R Wis.) May 26, 1902–Oct. 31, 1972; House 1947–49, 1951–55.

Ketcham, John Clark (R Mich.) Jan. 1, 1873–Dec. 4, 1941; House 1921–33.

Ketcham, John Henry (R N.Y.) Dec. 21, 1832–Nov. 4, 1906; House 1865–73, 1877–93, 1897–Nov. 4, 1906.

Ketchum, William Matthew (R Calif.) Sept. 2, 1921–June 24, 1978; House 1973–June 24, 1978.

Ketchum, Winthrop Welles (R Pa.) June 29, 1820–Dec. 6, 1879; House 1875–July 19, 1876.

Kettner, William (D Calif.) Nov. 20, 1864–Nov. 11, 1930; House 1913–21.

Key, David McKendree (D Tenn.) Jan. 27, 1824–Feb. 3, 1900; Senate Aug. 18, 1875–Jan. 19, 1877; Postmaster Gen. March 13, 1877–Aug. 24, 1880.

Key, John Alexander (D Ohio) Dec. 30, 1871–March 4, 1954; House 1913–19.

Key, Philip (cousin of Philip Barton Key, great-grandfather of Barnes Compton) (– Md.) 1750–Jan. 4, 1820; House 1791–93.

Key, Philip Barton (cousin of Philip Key) (F Md.) April 12, 1757–July 28, 1815; House 1807–13.

Keyes, Elias (– Vt.) April 14, 1758–July 9, 1844; House 1821–23.

Keyes, Henry Wilder (R N.H.) May 23, 1863–June 19, 1938; Senate 1919–37; Gov. Jan. 3, 1917–Jan. 2, 1919.

Keys, Martha Elizabeth (wife of Andrew Jacobs Jr., daughter-in-law of Andrew Jacobs Sr.) (D Kan.) Aug. 10, 1930– ; House 1975–79.

Kidder, David (W Maine) Dec. 8, 1787–Nov. 1, 1860; House 1823–27.

Kidder, Jefferson Parish (R Dakota) June 4, 1815–Oct. 2, 1883; House (Terr. Del.) 1875–79.

Kidwell, Zedekiah (D Va.) Jan. 4, 1814–April 27, 1872; House 1853–57.

Kiefer, Andrew Robert (R Minn.) May 25, 1832–May 1, 1904; House 1893–97.

Kiefner, Charles Edward (R Mo.) Nov. 25, 1869–Dec. 13, 1942; House 1925–27, 1929–31.

Kiess, Edgar Raymond (R Pa.) Aug. 26, 1875–July 20, 1930; House 1913–July 20, 1930.

Kilbourne, James (R Ohio) Oct. 19, 1770–April 9, 1850; House 1813–17.

Kilburn, Clarence Evans (R N.Y.) April 13, 1893–May 20, 1975; House Feb. 13, 1940–65.

Kilday, Paul Joseph (D Texas) March 29, 1900–Oct. 12, 1968; House 1939–Sept. 24, 1961.

Kildee, Dale Edward (D Mich.) Sept. 16, 1929– ; House 1977– .

Kilgore, Constantine Buckley (D Texas) Feb. 20, 1835–Sept. 23, 1897; House 1887–95.

Kilgore, Daniel (D Ohio) 1793–Dec. 12, 1851; House Dec. 1, 1834–July 4, 1838 (Dec. 1, 1834–37 Jacksonian).

Kilgore, David (R Ind.) April 3, 1804–Jan. 22, 1879; House 1857–61.

Kilgore, Harley Martin (D W.Va.) Jan. 11, 1893–Feb. 28, 1956; Senate 1941–Feb. 28, 1956; Chrmn. Senate Judiciary 1955–56.

Kilgore, Joe Madison (D Texas) Dec. 10, 1918–Feb. 10, 1999; House 1955–65.

Kille, Joseph (D N.J.) April 12, 1790–March 1, 1865; House 1839–41.

Killinger, John Weinland (R Pa.) Sept. 18, 1824–June 30, 1896; House 1859–63, 1871–75, 1877–81.

Kilpatrick, Carolyn Cheeks (D Mich.) June 25, 1945– ; House 1997– .

Kim, Jay C. (R Calif.) March 27, 1939– ; House 1993–99.

Kimball, Alanson Mellen (R Wis.) March 12, 1827–May 26, 1913; House 1875–77.

Kimball, Henry Mahlon (R Mich.) Aug. 27, 1878–Oct. 19, 1935; House Jan. 3–Oct. 19, 1935.

Kimball, William Preston (D Ky.) Nov. 4, 1857–Feb. 24, 1926; House 1907–09.

Kimmel, William (D Md.) Aug. 15, 1812–Dec. 28, 1886; House 1877–81.

Kincaid, John (J Ky.) Feb. 15, 1791–Feb. 7, 1873; House 1829–31.

Kincheloe, David Hayes (D Ky.) April 9, 1877–April 16, 1950; House 1915–Oct. 5, 1930.

Kind, Ron (D Wis.) March 16, 1963– ; House 1997– .

Kindel, George John (D Colo.) March 2, 1855–Feb. 28, 1930; House 1913–15.

Kindness, Thomas Norman (R Ohio) Aug. 26, 1929– ; House 1975–87.

Kindred, John Joseph (D N.Y.) July 15, 1864–Oct. 23, 1937; House 1911–13, 1921–29.

King, Adam (J Pa.) 1790–May 6, 1835; House 1827–33.

King, Andrew (D Mo.) March 20, 1812–Nov. 18, 1895; House 1871–73.

King, Austin Augustus (U Mo.) Sept. 21, 1802–April 22, 1870; House 1863–65; Gov. Nov. 27, 1848–Jan. 3, 1853 (Democrat).

King, Carleton James (R N.Y.) June 15, 1904–Nov. 19, 1977; House 1961–Dec. 31, 1974.

King, Cecil Rhodes (D Calif.) Jan. 13, 1898–March 17, 1974; House Aug. 25, 1942–69.

King, Cyrus (half-brother of Rufus King) (F Mass.) Sept. 6, 1772–April 25, 1817; House 1813–17.

King, Daniel Putnam (W Mass.) Jan. 8, 1801–July 25, 1850; House 1843–July 25, 1850.

King, David Sjodahl (son of William Henry King) (D Utah) June 20, 1917– ; House 1959–63, 1965–67.

King, Edward John (R Ill.) July 1, 1867–Feb. 17, 1929; House 1915–Feb. 17, 1929.

King, George Gordon (W R.I.) June 9, 1807–July 17, 1870; House 1849–53.

King, Henry (brother of Thomas Butler King, uncle of John Floyd King) (J Pa.) July 6, 1790–July 13, 1861; House 1831–35.

King, James Gore (son of Rufus King, brother of John Alsop King) (W N.J.) May 8, 1791–Oct. 3, 1853; House 1849–51.

King, John (J N.Y.) 1775–Sept. 1, 1836; House 1831–33.

King, John Alsop (son of Rufus King, brother of James Gore King) (W N.Y.) Jan. 3, 1788–July 7, 1867; House 1849–51; Gov. Jan. 1, 1857–Jan. 1, 1859 (Republican).

King, John Floyd (son of Thomas Butler King, nephew of Henry King) (D La.) April 20, 1842–May 8, 1915; House 1879–87.

King, John Pendleton (J Ga.) April 3, 1799–March 19, 1888; Senate Nov. 21, 1833–Nov. 1, 1837.

King, Karl Clarence (R Pa.) Jan. 26, 1897–April 16, 1974; House Nov. 6, 1951–57.

King, Perkins (J N.Y.) Jan. 12, 1784–Nov. 29, 1875; House 1829–31.

King, Peter T. (R N.Y.) April 5, 1944– ; House 1993– .

King, Preston (R N.Y.) Oct. 14, 1806–Nov. 12, 1865; House 1843–47 (Democrat), 1849–53 (Free-Soiler); Senate 1857–63.

King, Rufus (half-brother of Cyrus King, father of John Alsop King and James Gore King) (F N.Y.) March 24, 1755–April 29, 1827; Senate July 16, 1789–May 20, 1796 (no party), 1813–25; Cont. Cong. 1784–87 (Mass.).

King, Rufus H. (W N.Y.) Jan. 20, 1820–Sept. 13, 1890; House 1855–57.

King, Samuel Wilder (R Hawaii) Dec. 17, 1886–March 24, 1959; House (Terr. Del.) 1935–43; Gov. (Hawaii Terr.) Feb. 28, 1953–July 31, 1957.

King, Thomas Butler (brother of Henry King, father of John Floyd King) (W Ga.) Aug. 27, 1800–May 10, 1864; House 1839–43, 1845–50.

King, William Henry (father of David Sjodahl King) (D Utah) June 3, 1863–Nov. 27, 1949; House 1897–99, April 2, 1900–01; Senate 1917–41; elected Pres. pro tempore Nov. 19, 1940.

King, William Rufus deVane (D Ala.) April 7, 1786–April 18, 1853; House 1811–Nov. 4, 1816 (no party N.C.); Senate Dec. 14, 1819–April 15, 1844 (Dec. 14, 1819–21 Republican, 1821–April 15, 1844 Republican/Jacksonian), July 1, 1848–Dec. 20, 1852; elected Pres. pro tempore July 1, 1836, Jan. 28, 1837, March 7, 1837, Oct. 13, 1837, July 2, 1838, Feb. 25, 1839, July 3, 1840, March 3, 1841, March 4, 1841, May 6, 1850, July 11, 1850; Vice President March 4–April 18, 1853.

King, William Smith (R Minn.) Dec. 16, 1828–Feb. 24, 1900; House 1875–77.

Kingsbury, William Wallace (D Minn.) June 4, 1828–April 17, 1892; House (Terr. Del.) 1857–May 11, 1858.

Kingston, Jack (R Ga.) April 24, 1955– ; House 1993– .

Kinkaid, Moses Pierce (R Neb.) Jan. 24, 1856–July 6, 1922; House 1903–July 6, 1922.

Kinkead, Eugene Francis (D N.J.) March 27, 1876–Sept. 6, 1960; House 1909–Feb. 4, 1915.

Kinnard, George L. (J Ind.) 1803–Nov. 26, 1836; House 1833–Nov. 26, 1836.

Kinney, John Fitch (D Utah) April 2, 1816–Aug. 16, 1902; House (Terr. Del.) 1863–65.

Kinsella, Thomas (D N.Y.) Dec. 31, 1832–Feb. 11, 1884; House 1871–73.

Kinsey, Charles (R N.J.) 1773–June 25, 1849; House 1817–19, Feb. 2, 1820–21.

Kinsey, William Medcalf (R Mo.) Oct. 28, 1846–June 20, 1931; House 1889–91.

Kinsley, Martin (– Mass.) June 2, 1754–June 20, 1835; House 1819–21.

Kinzer, John Roland (R Pa.) March 28, 1874–July 25, 1955; House Jan. 28, 1930–47.

Kipp, George Washington (D Pa.) March 28, 1847–July 24, 1911; House 1907–09, March 4–July 24, 1911.

Kirby, William Fosgate (D Ark.) Nov. 16, 1867–July 26, 1934; Senate Nov. 8, 1916–21.

Kirk, Andrew Jackson (R Ky.) March 19, 1866–May 25, 1933; House Feb. 13, 1926–27.

Kirkland, Joseph (– N.Y.) Jan. 18, 1770–Jan. 26, 1844; House 1821–23.

Kirkpatrick, Littleton (D N.J.) Oct. 19, 1797–Aug. 15, 1859; House 1843–45.

Kirkpatrick, Sanford (D Iowa) Feb. 11, 1842–Feb. 13, 1932; House 1913–15.

Kirkpatrick, Snyder Solomon (R Kan.) Feb. 21, 1848–April 5, 1909; House 1895–97.

Kirkpatrick, William (R N.Y.) Nov. 7, 1769–Sept. 2, 1832; House 1807–09.

Kirkpatrick, William Huntington (son of William Sebring Kirkpatrick) (R Pa.) Oct. 2, 1885–Nov. 28, 1970; House 1921–23.

Kirkpatrick, William Sebring (father of William Huntington Kirkpatrick) (R Pa.) April 21, 1844–Nov. 3, 1932; House 1897–99.

Kirkwood, Samuel Jordan (R Iowa) Dec. 20, 1813–Sept. 1, 1894; Senate Jan. 13, 1866–67, 1877–March 7, 1881; Gov. Jan. 11, 1860–Jan. 14, 1864, Jan. 13, 1876–Feb. 1, 1877; Secy. of the Interior March 8, 1881–April 17, 1882.

Kirtland, Dorrance (R N.Y.) July 28, 1770–May 23, 1840; House 1817–19.

Kirwan, Michael Joseph (D Ohio) Dec. 2, 1886–July 27, 1970; House 1937–July 27, 1970.

Kissel, John (R N.Y.) July 31, 1864–Oct. 3, 1938; House 1921–23.

Kitchell, Aaron (R N.J.) July 10, 1744–June 25, 1820; House 1791–93, Jan. 29, 1795–97, 1799–1801; Senate 1805–March 12, 1809.

Kitchen, Bethuel Middleton (R W.Va.) March 21, 1812–Dec. 15, 1895; House 1867–69.

Kitchens, Wade Hampton (D Ark.) Dec. 26, 1878–Aug. 22, 1966; House 1937–41.

Kitchin, Alvin Paul (nephew of Claude Kitchin and William Walton Kitchin, grandson of William Hodges Kitchin) (D N.C.) Sept. 13, 1908–Oct. 22, 1983; House 1957–63.

Kitchin, Claude (son of William Hodges Kitchin, brother of William Walton Kitchin, uncle of Alvin Paul Kitchin) (D N.C.) March 24, 1869–May 31, 1923; House 1901–May 31, 1923; House majority leader 1915–19; House minority leader 1921–23.

Kitchin, William Hodges (father of Claude Kitchin and William Walton Kitchin, grandfather of Alvin Paul Kitchin) (D N.C.) Dec. 22, 1837–Feb. 2, 1901; House 1879–81.

Kitchin, William Walton (son of William Hodges Kitchin, brother of Claude Kitchin, uncle of Alvin Paul Kitchin) (D N.C.) Oct. 9, 1866–Nov. 9, 1924; House 1897–Jan. 11, 1909; Gov. Jan. 12, 1909–Jan. 15, 1913.

Kittera, John Wilkes (father of Thomas Kittera) (F Pa.) Nov. 1752–June 6, 1801; House 1791–1801 (1791–95 no party).

Kittera, Thomas (son of John Wilkes Kittera) (– Pa.) March 21, 1789–June 16, 1839; House Oct. 10, 1826–27.

Kittredge, Alfred Beard (R S.D.) March 28, 1861–May 4, 1911; Senate July 11, 1901–09.

Kittredge, George Washington (D N.H.) Jan. 31, 1805–March 6, 1881; House 1853–55.

Kleberg, Richard Mifflin Sr. (nephew of Rudolph Kleberg, cousin of Robert Christian Eckhardt) (D Texas) Nov. 18, 1887–May 8, 1955; House Nov. 24, 1931–45.

Kleberg, Rudolph (great-uncle of Robert Christian Eckhardt, uncle of Richard Mifflin Kleberg Sr.) (D Texas) June 26, 1847–Dec. 28, 1924; House April 7, 1896–1903.

Kleczka, Gerald Daniel (D Wis.) Nov. 26, 1943– ; House April 10, 1984– .

Kleczka, John Casimir (R Wis.) May 6, 1885–April 21, 1959; House 1919–23.

Klein, Arthur George (D N.Y.) Aug. 8, 1904–Feb. 20, 1968; House July 29, 1941–45, Feb. 19, 1946–Dec. 31, 1956.

Klein, Herb (D N.J.) June 24, 1930– ; House 1993–95.

Kleiner, John Jay (D Ind.) Feb. 8, 1845–April 8, 1911; House 1883–87.

Kleppe, Thomas Savig (R N.D.) July 1, 1919– ; House 1967–71; Secy. of the Interior Oct. 17, 1975–Jan. 20, 1977.

Klepper, Frank B. (R Mo.) June 22, 1864–Aug. 4, 1933; House 1905–07.

Kline, Ardolph Loges (R N.Y.) Feb. 21, 1858–Oct. 13, 1930; House 1921–23.

Kline, Isaac Clinton (R Pa.) Aug. 18, 1858–Dec. 2, 1947; House 1921–23.

Kline, Marcus Charles Lawrence (D Pa.) March 26, 1855–March 10, 1911; House 1903–07.

Klingensmith, John Jr. (D Pa.) 1785–?; House 1835–39 (1835–37 Jacksonian).

Klink, Ron (D Pa.) Sept. 23, 1951– ; House 1993– .

Kloeb, Frank Le Blond (grandson of Francis Celeste Le Blond) (D Ohio) June 16, 1890–March 11, 1976; House 1933–Aug. 19, 1937.

Klotz, Robert (D Pa.) Oct. 27, 1819–May 1, 1895; House 1879–83.

Kluczynski, John Carl (D Ill.) Feb. 15, 1896–Jan. 26, 1975; House 1951–Jan. 26, 1975.

Klug, Scott L. (R Wis.) Jan. 16, 1953– ; House 1991–99.

Kluttz, Theodore Franklin (D N.C.) Oct. 4, 1848–Nov. 18, 1918; House 1899–1905.

Knapp, Anthony Lausett (brother of Robert McCarty Knapp) (D Ill.) June 14, 1828–May 24, 1881; House Dec. 12, 1861–65.

Knapp, Charles (father of Charles Junius Knapp) (R N.Y.) Oct. 8, 1797–May 14, 1880; House 1869–71.

Knapp, Charles Junius (son of Charles Knapp) (R N.Y.) June 30, 1845–June 1, 1916; House 1889–91.

Knapp, Charles Luman (R N.Y.) July 4, 1847–Jan. 3, 1929; House Nov. 5, 1901–11.

Knapp, Chauncey Langdon (R Mass.) Feb. 26, 1809–May 31, 1898; House 1855–59 (1855–57 American Party).

Knapp, Robert McCarty (brother of Anthony Lausett Knapp) (D Ill.) April 21, 1831–June 24, 1889; House 1873–75, 1877–79.

Knickerbocker, Herman (F N.Y.) July 27, 1779–Jan. 30, 1855; House 1809–11.

Kniffin, Frank Charles (D Ohio) April 26, 1894–April 30, 1968; House 1931–39.

Knight, Charles Landon (R Ohio) June 18, 1867–Sept. 26, 1933; House 1921–23.

Knight, Jonathan (W Pa.) Nov. 22, 1787–Nov. 22, 1858; House 1855–57.

Knight, Nehemiah (father of Nehemiah Rice Knight) (R R.I.) March 23, 1746–June 13, 1808; House 1803–June 13, 1808.

Knight, Nehemiah Rice (son of Nehemiah Knight) (W R.I.) Dec. 31, 1780–April 18, 1854; Senate Jan. 9, 1821–41 (Jan. 9, 1821–35 Republican); Gov. May 7, 1817–Jan. 9, 1821 (Democratic Republican).

Knollenberg, Joe (R Mich.) Nov. 28, 1933– ; House 1993– .

Knopf, Philip (R Ill.) Nov. 18, 1847–Aug. 14, 1920; House 1903–09.

Knott, James Proctor (D Ky.) Aug. 29, 1830–June 18, 1911; House 1867–71, 1875–83; Gov. Sept. 4, 1883–Aug. 30, 1887.

Knowland, Joseph Russell (father of William Fife Knowland) (R Calif.) Aug. 5, 1873–Feb. 1, 1966; House Nov. 8, 1904–15.

Knowland, William Fife (son of Joseph Russell Knowland) (R Calif.) June 26, 1908–Feb. 23, 1974; Senate Aug. 26, 1945–59; Senate majority leader Aug. 4, 1953–55; Senate minority leader 1955–59.

Knowles, Freeman Tulley (P S.D.) Oct. 10, 1846–June 1, 1910; House 1897–99.

Knowlton, Ebenezer (R Maine) Dec. 6, 1815–Sept. 10, 1874; House 1855–57.

Knox, James (R Ill.) July 4, 1807–Oct. 8, 1876; House 1853–57 (1853–55 Whig).

Knox, Philander Chase (R Pa.) May 6, 1853–Oct. 12, 1921; Senate June 10, 1904–March 4, 1909, 1917–Oct. 12, 1921; Atty. Gen. April 5, 1901–June 30, 1904; Secy. of State March 6, 1909–March 5, 1913.

Knox, Samuel (UU Mo.) March 21, 1815–March 7, 1905; House June 10, 1864–65.

Knox, Victor Alfred (R Mich.) Jan. 13, 1899–Dec. 13, 1976; House 1953–65.

Knox, William Shadrach (R Mass.) Sept. 10, 1843–Sept. 21, 1914; House 1895–1903.

Knutson, Coya Gjesdal (DFL Minn.) Aug. 22, 1912–Oct. 10, 1996; House 1955–59.

Knutson, Harold (R Minn.) Oct. 20, 1880–Aug. 21, 1953; House 1917–49; Chrmn. House Ways and Means 1947–49.

Koch, Edward Irving (D/L N.Y.) Dec. 12, 1924– ; House 1969–Dec. 31, 1977.

Kocialkowski, Leo Paul (D Ill.) Aug. 16, 1882–Sept. 27, 1958; House 1933–43.

Kogovsek, Raymond Peter (D Colo.) Aug. 19, 1941– ; House 1979–85.

Kohl, Herbert (D Wis.) Feb. 7, 1935– ; Senate 1989– .

Kolbe, James Thomas (R Ariz.) June 28, 1942– ; House 1985– .

Kolter, Joseph Paul (D Pa.) Sept. 3, 1926– ; House 1983–93.

Konig, George (D Md.) Jan. 26, 1865–May 31, 1913; House 1911–May 31, 1913.

Konnyu, Ernest Leslie (R Calif.) May 17, 1937– ; House 1987–89.

Konop, Thomas Frank (D Wis.) Aug. 17, 1879–Oct. 17, 1964; House 1911–17.

Koontz, William Henry (R Pa.) July 15, 1830–July 4, 1911; House July 18, 1866–69.

Kopetski, Michael (D Ore.) Oct. 27, 1949– ; House 1991–95.

Kopp, Arthur William (R Wis.) Feb. 28, 1874–June 2, 1967; House 1909–13.

Kopp, William Frederick (R Iowa) June 20, 1869–Aug. 24, 1938; House 1921–33.

Kopplemann, Herman Paul (D Conn.) May 1, 1880–Aug. 11, 1957; House 1933–39, 1941–43, 1945–47.

Korbly, Charles Alexander (D Ind.) March 24, 1871–July 26, 1937; House 1909–15.

Korell, Franklin Frederick (R Ore.) July 23, 1889–June 7, 1965; House Oct. 18, 1927–31.

Kornegay, Horace Robinson (D N.C.) March 12, 1924– ; House 1961–69.

Kostmayer, Peter Houston (D Pa.) Sept. 27, 1946– ; House 1977–81, 1983–93.

Kowalski, Frank (D Conn.) Oct. 18, 1907–Oct. 11, 1974; House 1959–63.

Kramer, Charles (D Calif.) April 18, 1879–Jan. 20, 1943; House 1933–43.

Kramer, Kenneth Bentley (R Colo.) Feb. 19, 1942– ; House 1979–87.

Kraus, Milton (R Ind.) June 26, 1866–Nov. 18, 1942; House 1917–23.

Krebs, Jacob (– Pa.) March 13, 1782–Sept. 26, 1847; House Dec. 4, 1826–27.

Krebs, John Hans (D Calif.) Dec. 17, 1926– ; House 1975–79.

Krebs, Paul Joseph (D N.J.) May 26, 1912–Sept. 17, 1996; House 1965–67.

Kreider, Aaron Shenk (R Pa.) June 26, 1863–May 19, 1929; House 1913–23.

Kreidler, Mike (D Wash.) Sept. 28, 1943– ; House 1993–95.

Kremer, George (– Pa.) Nov. 21, 1775–Sept. 11, 1854; House 1823–29.

Kribbs, George Frederic (D Pa.) Nov. 8, 1846–Sept. 8, 1938; House 1891–95.

Kronmiller, John (R Md.) Dec. 6, 1858–June 19, 1928; House 1909–11.

Krueger, Otto (R N.D.) Sept. 7, 1890–June 6, 1963; House 1953–59.

Krueger, Robert Charles (D Texas) Sept. 19, 1935– ; House 1975–79; Senate Jan. 5, 1993–June 5, 1993.

Kruse, Edward H. (D Ind.) Oct. 22, 1918– ; House 1949–51.

Kuchel, Thomas Henry (R Calif.) Aug. 15, 1910–Nov. 21, 1994; Senate Jan. 2, 1953–69.

Kucinich, Dennis J. (D Ohio) Oct. 8, 1946– ; House 1997– .

Kuhns, Joseph Henry (W Pa.) Sept. 1800–Nov. 16, 1883; House 1851–53.

Kulp, Monroe Henry (R Pa.) Oct. 23, 1858–Oct. 19, 1911; House 1895–99.

Kunkel, Jacob Michael (D Md.) July 13, 1822–April 7, 1870; House 1857–61.

Kunkel, John Christian (grandfather of John Crain Kunkel) (R Pa.) Sept. 18, 1816–Oct. 14, 1870; House 1855–59 (1855–57 Whig).

Kunkel, John Crain (grandson of John Christian Kunkel, great-grandson of John Sergeant, great-great-grandson of Robert Whitehill) (R Pa.) July 21, 1898–July 27, 1970; House 1939–51, May 16, 1961–67.

Kunz, Stanley Henry (D Ill.) Sept. 26, 1864–April 23, 1946; House 1921–31, April 5, 1932–33.

Kupferman, Theodore Roosevelt (R N.Y.) May 12, 1920– ; House Feb. 8, 1966–69.

Kurtz, Jacob Banks (R Pa.) Oct. 31, 1867–Sept. 18, 1960; House 1923–35.

Kurtz, William Henry (D Pa.) Jan. 31, 1804–June 24, 1868; House 1851–55.

Kustermann, Gustav (R Wis.) May 24, 1850–Dec. 25, 1919; House 1907–11.

Kuykendall, Andrew Jackson (R Ill.) March 3, 1815–May 11, 1891; House 1865–67.

Kuykendall, Dan Heflin (R Tenn.) July 9, 1924– ; House 1967–75.

Kuykendall, Steven (R Calif.) Jan. 27, 1947– ; House 1999– .

Kvale, Ole Juulson (father of Paul John Kvale) (FL Minn.) Feb. 6, 1869–Sept. 11, 1929; House 1923–Sept. 11, 1929.

Kvale, Paul John (son of Ole Juulson Kvale) (FL Minn.) March 27, 1896–June 14, 1960; House Oct. 16, 1929–39.

Kyl, John Henry (father of Jon Llewellyn Kyl) (R Iowa) May 9, 1919– ; House Dec. 15, 1959–65, 1967–73.

Kyl, Jon Llewellyn (son of John Henry Kyl) (R Ariz.) April 25, 1942– ; House 1987–95; Senate 1995– .

Kyle, James Henderson (I S.D.) Feb. 24, 1854–July 1, 1901; Senate 1891–July 1, 1901.

Kyle, John Curtis (D Miss.) July 17, 1851–July 6, 1913; House 1891–97.

Kyle, Thomas Barton (R Ohio) March 10, 1856–Aug. 13, 1915; House 1901–05.

Kyros, Peter N. (D Maine) July 11, 1925– ; House 1967–75.

L

La Branche, Alcee Louis (D La.) 1806–Aug. 17, 1861; House 1843–45.

Lacey, Edward Samuel (R Mich.) Nov. 26, 1835–Oct. 2, 1916; House 1881–85.

Lacey, John Fletcher (R Iowa) May 30, 1841–Sept. 29, 1913; House 1889–91, 1893–1907.

Lacock, Abner (R Pa.) July 9, 1770–April 12, 1837; House 1811–13; Senate 1813–19.

Ladd, Edwin Freemont (R N.D.) Dec. 13, 1859–June 22, 1925; Senate 1921–June 22, 1925.

Ladd, George Washington (G Maine) Sept. 28, 1818–Jan. 30, 1892; House 1879–83.

La Dow, George Augustus (D Ore.) March 18, 1826–May 1, 1875; House March 4–May 1, 1875.

LaFalce, John Joseph (D N.Y.) Oct. 6, 1939– ; House 1975– ; Chrmn. House Small Business 1987–95.

Lafean, Daniel Franklin (R Pa.) Feb. 7, 1861–April 18, 1922; House 1903–13, 1915–17.

Lafferty, Abraham Walter (R Ore.) June 10, 1875–Jan. 15, 1964; House 1911–15.

Laffoon, Polk (D Ky.) Oct. 24, 1844–Oct. 22, 1906; House 1885–89.

Laflin, Addison Henry (R N.Y.) Oct. 24, 1823–Sept. 24, 1878; House 1865–71.

La Follette, Charles Marion (great-grandson of William Heilman) (R Ind.) Feb. 27, 1898–June 27, 1974; House 1943–47.

La Follette, Robert Marion (father of Robert Marion La Follette Jr.) (R Wis.) June 14, 1855–June 18, 1925; House 1885–91; Senate Jan. 2, 1906–June 18, 1925; Gov. Jan. 7, 1901–Jan. 1, 1906.

La Follette, Robert Marion Jr. (son of Robert Marion La Follette) (Prog. Wis.) Feb. 6, 1895–Feb. 24, 1953; Senate Sept. 30, 1925–47 (Sept. 30, 1925–35 Republican).

La Follette, William Leroy (R Wash.) Nov. 30, 1860–Dec. 20, 1934; House 1911–19.

Lafore, John Armand Jr. (R Pa.) May 25, 1905– ; House Nov. 5, 1957–61.

Lagan, Matthew Diamond (D La.) June 20, 1829–April 8, 1901; House 1887–89, 1891–93.

Lagomarsino, Robert John (R Calif.) Sept. 4, 1926– ; House March 5, 1974–93.

LaGuardia, Fiorello Henry (R N.Y.) Dec. 11, 1882–Sept. 20, 1947; House 1917–Dec. 31, 1919 (Republican), 1923–33 (1923–25 Republican, 1925–27 American Laborite).

Lahm, Samuel (D Ohio) April 22, 1812–June 16, 1876; House 1847–49.

LaHood, Ray (R Ill.) Dec. 6, 1945– ; House 1995– .

Laidlaw, William Grant (R N.Y.) Jan. 1, 1840–Aug. 19, 1908; House 1887–91.

Laird, James (R Neb.) June 20, 1849–Aug. 17, 1889; House 1883–Aug. 17, 1889.

Laird, Melvin Robert (R Wis.) Sept. 1, 1922– ; House 1953–Jan. 21, 1969; Secy. of Defense Jan. 22, 1969–Jan. 29, 1973.

Laird, William Ramsey III (D W.Va.) June 2, 1916–Jan. 7, 1974; Senate March 13–Nov. 6, 1956.

Lake, William Augustus (AP Miss.) Jan. 6, 1808–Oct. 15, 1861; House 1855–57.

Lamar, Henry Graybill (J Ga.) July 10, 1798–Sept. 10, 1861; House Dec. 7, 1829–33.

Lamar, James Robert (D Mo.) March 28, 1866–Aug. 11, 1923; House 1903–05, 1907–09.

Lamar, John Basil (D Ga.) Nov. 5, 1812–Sept. 15, 1862; House March 4–July 29, 1843.

Lamar, Lucius Quintus Cincinnatus (uncle of William Bailey Lamar, cousin of Absalom Harris Chappell) (D Miss.) Sept. 17, 1825–Jan. 23, 1893; House 1857–Dec. 1860, 1873–77; Senate 1877–March 6, 1885; Secy. of the Interior March 6, 1885–Jan. 10, 1888; Assoc. Justice Supreme Court Jan. 18, 1888–Jan. 23, 1893.

Lamar, William Bailey (nephew of Lucius Quintus Cincinnatus Lamar) (D Fla.) June 12, 1853–Sept. 26, 1928; House 1903–09.

Lamb, Alfred William (D Mo.) March 18, 1824–April 29, 1888; House 1853–55.

Lamb, John (D Va.) June 12, 1840–Nov. 21, 1924; House 1897–1913.

Lamb, John Edward (D Ind.) Dec. 26, 1852–Aug. 23, 1914; House 1883–85.

Lambert, John (R N.J.) Feb. 24, 1746–Feb. 4, 1823; House 1805–09; Senate 1809–15; Gov. Nov. 15, 1802–Oct. 29, 1803 (Democratic Republican).

Lambertson, William Purnell (R Kan.) March 23, 1880–Oct. 26, 1957; House 1929–45.

Lambeth, John Walter (D N.C.) Jan. 10, 1896–Jan. 12, 1961; House 1931–39.

Lamison, Charles Nelson (D Ohio) 1826–April 24, 1896; House 1871–75.

Lamneck, Arthur Philip (D Ohio) March 12, 1880–April 23, 1944; House 1931–39.

Lampert, Florian (R Wis.) July 8, 1863–July 18, 1930; House Nov. 5, 1918–July 18, 1930.

Lamport, William Henry (R N.Y.) May 27, 1811–July 21, 1891; House 1871–75.

Lampson, Nick (D Texas) Feb. 14, 1945– ; House 1997– .

Lancaster, Columbia (D Wash.) Aug. 26, 1803–Sept. 15, 1893; House (Terr. Del.) April 12, 1854–55.

Lancaster, Harold Martin (D N.C.) March 24, 1943– ; House 1987–95.

Landers, Franklin (D Ind.) March 22, 1825–Sept. 10, 1901; House 1875–77.

Landers, George Marcellus (D Conn.) Feb. 22, 1813–March 27, 1895; House 1875–79.

Landes, Silas Zephaniah (D Ill.) May 15, 1842–May 23, 1910; House 1885–89.

Landgrebe, Earl Frederick (R Ind.) Jan. 21, 1916–June 29, 1986; House 1969–75.

Landis, Charles Beary (brother of Frederick Landis) (R Ind.) July 9, 1858–April 24, 1922; House 1897–1909.

Landis, Frederick (brother of Charles Beary Landis) (R Ind.) Aug. 18, 1872–Nov. 15, 1934; House 1903–07.

Landis, Gerald Wayne (R Ind.) Feb. 23, 1895–Sept. 6, 1971; House 1939–49.

Landrieu, Mary L. (D La.) Nov. 23, 1955– ; Senate 1997– .

Landrum, John Morgan (D La.) July 3, 1815–Oct. 18, 1861; House 1859–61.

Landrum, Phillip Mitchell (D Ga.) Sept. 10, 1907–Nov. 19, 1990; House 1953–77.

Landry, Joseph Aristide (W La.) July 10, 1817–March 9, 1881; House 1851–53.

Landy, James (D Pa.) Oct. 13, 1813–July 25, 1875; House 1857–59.

Lane, Amos (father of James Henry Lane) (J Ind.) March 1, 1778–Sept. 2, 1849; House 1833–37.

Lane, Edward (D Ill.) March 27, 1842–Oct. 30, 1912; House 1887–95.

Lane, Harry (grandson of Joseph Lane, nephew of LaFayette Lane) (D Ore.) Aug. 28, 1855–May 23, 1917; Senate 1913–May 23, 1917.

Lane, Henry Smith (R Ind.) Feb. 24, 1811–June 18, 1881; House Aug. 3, 1840–43 (Whig); Senate 1861–67; Gov. Jan. 14–16, 1861.

Lane, James Henry (son of Amos Lane) (R Kan.) June 22, 1814–July 11, 1866; House 1853–55 (Democrat Ind.); Senate April 4, 1861–July 11, 1866.

Lane, Joseph (father of LaFayette Lane, grandfather of Harry Lane) (D Ore.) Dec. 14, 1801–April 19, 1881; House (Terr. Del.) June 2, 1851–Feb. 14, 1859 (no party); Senate Feb. 14, 1859–61; Gov. (Ore. Terr.) 1849–50, May 16–May 19, 1853.

Lane, Joseph Reed (R Iowa) May 6, 1858–May 1, 1931; House 1899–1901.

Lane, LaFayette (son of Joseph Lane, uncle of Harry Lane) (D Ore.) Nov. 12, 1842–Nov. 23, 1896; House Oct. 25, 1875–77.

Lane, Thomas Joseph (D Mass.) July 6, 1898–June 14, 1994; House Dec. 30, 1941–63.

Langdon, Chauncey (F Vt.) Nov. 8, 1763–July 23, 1830; House 1815–17.

Langdon, John (– N.H.) June 26, 1741–Sept. 18, 1819; Senate 1789–1801; elected Pres. pro tempore April 6, 1789, Nov. 5, 1792, March 1, 1793; Cont. Cong. 1775–76, 1787; Gov. June 6, 1805–June 8, 1809, June 7, 1810–June 5, 1812 (Democratic Republican).

Langen, Odin Elsford Stanley (R Minn.) Jan. 5, 1913–July 6, 1976; House 1959–71.

Langer, William (R N.D.) Sept. 30, 1886–Nov. 8, 1959; Senate 1941–Nov. 8, 1959; Chrmn. Senate Post Office and Civil Service 1947–49; Chrmn. Senate Judiciary 1953–55; Gov. Dec. 31, 1932–July 17, 1934 (Independent), Jan. 6, 1937–Jan. 5, 1939 (Independent).

Langham, Jonathan Nicholas (R Pa.) Aug. 4, 1861–May 21, 1945; House 1909–15.

Langley, John Wesley (husband of Katherine Gudger Langley, son-in-law of James Madison Gudger Jr.) (R Ky.) Jan. 14, 1868–Jan. 17, 1932; House 1907–Jan. 11, 1926.

Langley, Katherine Gudger (wife of John Wesley Langley, daughter of James Madison Gudger Jr.) (R Ky.) Feb. 14, 1888–Aug. 15, 1948; House 1927–31.

Langston, John Mercer (R Va.) Dec. 14, 1829–Nov. 15, 1897; House Sept. 23, 1890–91.

Lanham, Fritz Garland (son of Samuel Willis Tucker Lanham) (D Texas) Jan. 3, 1880–July 31, 1965; House April 19, 1919–47.

Lanham, Henderson Lovelace (D Ga.) Sept. 14, 1888–Nov. 10, 1957; House 1947–Nov. 10, 1957.

Lanham, Samuel Willis Tucker (father of Fritz Garland Lanham) (D Texas) July 4, 1846–July 29, 1908; House 1883–93, 1897–Jan. 15, 1903; Gov. Jan. 20, 1903–Jan. 15, 1907.

Laning, Jay Ford (R Ohio) May 15, 1853–Sept. 1, 1941; House 1907–09.

Lankford, Menalcus (R Va.) March 14, 1883–Dec. 27, 1937; House 1929–33.

Lankford, Richard Estep (D Md.) July 22, 1914– ; House 1955–65.

Lankford, William Chester (D Ga.) Dec. 7, 1877–Dec. 10, 1964; House 1919–33.

Lanman, James (R Conn.) June 14, 1767–Aug. 7, 1841; Senate 1819–25.

Lanning, William Mershon (R N.J.) Jan. 1, 1849–Feb. 16, 1912; House 1903–June 6, 1904.

Lansing, Frederick (R N.Y.) Feb. 16, 1838–Jan. 31, 1894; House 1889–91.

Lansing, Gerrit Yates (J N.Y.) Aug. 4, 1783–Jan. 3, 1862; House 1831–37.

Lansing, William Esselstyne (R N.Y.) Dec. 29, 1821–July 29, 1883; House 1861–63, 1871–75.

Lantaff, William Courtland (D Fla.) July 31, 1913–Jan. 28, 1970; House 1951–55.

Lantos, Thomas Peter (father-in-law of Richard Swett) (D Calif.) Feb. 1, 1928– ; House 1981– .

Lanzetta, James Joseph (D N.Y.) Dec. 21, 1894–Oct. 27, 1956; House 1933–35, 1937–39.

Lapham, Elbridge Gerry (R N.Y.) Oct. 18, 1814–Jan. 8, 1890; House 1875–July 29, 1881; Senate Aug. 2, 1881–85.

Lapham, Oscar (D R.I.) June 29, 1837–March 29, 1926; House 1891–95.

Laporte, John (J Pa.) Nov. 4, 1798–Aug. 22, 1862; House 1833–37.

Larcade, Henry Dominique Jr. (D La.) July 12, 1890–March 15, 1966; House 1943–53.

Largent, Steve (R Okla.) Sept. 28, 1955– ; House Nov. 29, 1994– .

Larned, Simon (R Mass.) Aug. 3, 1753–Nov. 16, 1817; House Nov. 5, 1804–05.

LaRocco, Larry (D Idaho) Aug. 25, 1946– ; House 1991–95.

Larrabee, Charles Hathaway (D Wis.) Nov. 9, 1820–Jan. 20, 1883; House 1859–61.

Larrabee, William Henry (D Ind.) Feb. 21, 1870–Nov. 16, 1960; House 1931–43.

Larrazolo, Octaviano Ambrosio (R N.M.) Dec. 7, 1859–April 7, 1930; Senate Dec. 7, 1928–29; Gov. Jan. 1, 1919–Jan. 1, 1921.

Larrinaga, Tulio (U P.R.) Jan. 15, 1847–April 28, 1917; House (Res. Comm.) 1905–11.

Larsen, William Washington (D Ga.) Aug. 12, 1871–Jan. 5, 1938; House 1917–33.

Larson, John B. (D Conn.) July 22, 1948– ; House 1999– .

Larson, Oscar John (R Minn.) May 20, 1871–Aug. 1, 1957; House 1921–25.

La Sere, Emile (D La.) 1802–Aug. 14, 1882; House Jan. 29, 1846–51.

Lash, Israel George (R N.C.) Aug. 18, 1810–April 1, 1878; House July 20, 1868–71.

Lassiter, Francis Rives (great-nephew of Francis Everod Rives) (D Va.) Feb. 18, 1866–Oct. 31, 1909; House April 19, 1900–03, 1907–Oct. 31, 1909.

Latham, George Robert (UU W.Va.) March 9, 1832–Dec. 16, 1917; House 1865–67.

Latham, Henry Jepson (R N.Y.) Dec. 10, 1908– ; House 1945–Dec. 31, 1958.

Latham, Louis Charles (D N.C.) Sept. 11, 1840–Oct. 16, 1895; House 1881–83, 1887–89.

Latham, Milton Slocum (D Calif.) May 23, 1827–March 4, 1882; House 1853–55; Senate March 5, 1860–63; Gov. Jan. 9–Jan. 14, 1860.

Latham, Tom (R Iowa) July 14, 1948– ; House 1995– .

Lathrop, Samuel (– Mass.) May 1, 1772–July 11, 1846; House 1819–27.

Lathrop, William (R Ill.) April 17, 1825–Nov. 19, 1907; House 1877–79.

Latimer, Asbury Churchwell (D S.C.) July 31, 1851–Feb. 20, 1908; House 1893–1903; Senate 1903–Feb. 20, 1908.

Latimer, Henry (F Del.) April 24, 1752–Dec. 19, 1819; House Feb. 14, 1794–Feb. 7, 1795 (no party); Senate Feb. 7, 1795–Feb. 28, 1801.

LaTourette, Steven C. (R Ohio) July 22, 1954– ; House 1995– .

Latta, Delbert Leroy (R Ohio) March 5, 1920– ; House 1959–89.

Latta, James Polk (D Neb.) Oct. 31, 1844–Sept. 11, 1911; House 1909–Sept. 11, 1911.

Lattimore, William (– Miss.) Feb. 9, 1774–April 3, 1843; House (Terr. Del.) 1803–07, 1813–17.

Laughlin, Greg H. (R Texas) Jan. 21, 1942– ; House 1989–97 (1989–June 26, 1995 Democrat).

Laurance, John (– N.Y.) 1750–Nov. 11, 1810; House 1789–93; Senate Nov. 9, 1796–Aug. 1800; elected Pres. pro tempore Dec. 6, 1798; Cont. Cong. 1785–87.

Lausche, Frank John (D Ohio) Nov. 14, 1895–April 21, 1990; Senate 1957–69; Gov. Jan. 8, 1945–Jan. 13, 1947, Jan. 10, 1949–Jan. 3, 1957.

Lautenberg, Frank Raleigh (D N.J.) Jan. 23, 1924– ; Senate Dec. 27, 1982– .

Law, Charles Blakeslee (R N.Y.) Feb. 5, 1872–Sept. 15, 1929; House 1905–11.

Law, John (son of Lyman Law, grandson of Amasa Learned) (D Ind.) Oct. 28, 1796–Oct. 7, 1873; House 1861–65.

Law, Lyman (father of John Law) (F Conn.) Aug. 19, 1770–Feb. 3, 1842; House 1811–17.

Lawler, Frank (D Ill.) June 25, 1842–Jan. 17, 1896; House 1885–91.

Lawler, Joab (J Ala.) June 12, 1796–May 8, 1838; House 1835–May 8, 1838.

Lawrence, Abbott (W Mass.) Dec. 16, 1792–Aug. 18, 1855; House 1835–37, 1839–Sept. 18, 1840.

Lawrence, Cornelius Van Wyck (cousin of Effingham Lawrence) (J N.Y.) Feb. 28, 1791–Feb. 20, 1861; House 1833–May 14, 1834.

Lawrence, Effingham (cousin of Cornelius Van Wyck Lawrence) (D La.) March 2, 1820–Dec. 9, 1878; House March 3, 1875.

Lawrence, George Pelton (R Mass.) May 19, 1859–Nov. 21, 1917; House Nov. 2, 1897–1913.

Lawrence, George Van Eman (son of Joseph Lawrence) (R Pa.) Nov. 13, 1818–Oct. 2, 1904; House 1865–69, 1883–85.

Lawrence, Henry Franklin (R Mo.) Jan. 31, 1868–Jan. 12, 1950; House 1921–23.

Lawrence, John Watson (D N.Y.) Aug. 1800–Dec. 20, 1888; House 1845–47.

Lawrence, Joseph (father of George Van Eman Lawrence) (W Pa.) 1786–April 17, 1842; House 1825–29 (no party), 1841–April 17, 1842.

Lawrence, Samuel (brother of William Thomas Lawrence) (– N.Y.) May 23, 1773–Oct. 20, 1837; House 1823–25.

Lawrence, Sidney (D N.Y.) Dec. 31, 1801–May 9, 1892; House 1847–49.

Lawrence, William (D Ohio) Sept. 2, 1814–Sept. 8, 1895; House 1857–59.

Lawrence, William (R Ohio) June 26, 1819–May 8, 1899; House 1865–71, 1873–77.

Lawrence, William Thomas (brother of Samuel Lawrence) (– N.Y.) May 7, 1788–Oct. 25, 1859; House 1847–49.

Laws, Gilbert Lafayette (R Neb.) March 11, 1838–April 25, 1907; House Dec. 2, 1889–91.

Lawson, John Daniel (R N.Y.) Feb. 18, 1816–Jan. 24, 1896; House 1873–75.

Lawson, John William (D Va.) Sept. 13, 1837–Feb. 21, 1905; House 1891–93.

Lawson, Thomas Graves (D Ga.) May 2, 1835–April 16, 1912; House 1891–97.

Lawyer, Thomas (R N.Y.) Oct. 14, 1785–May 21, 1868; House 1817–19.

Laxalt, Paul Dominique (R Nev.) Aug. 2, 1922– ; Senate Dec. 18, 1974–87; Gov. Jan. 2, 1967–Jan. 4, 1971; Gen. Chrmn. Rep. Nat. Comm. 1983–86.

Lay, Alfred Morrison (D Mo.) May 20, 1836–Dec. 8, 1879; House March 4–Dec. 8, 1879.

Lay, George Washington (W N.Y.) July 26, 1798–Oct. 21, 1860; House 1833–37 (1833–35 Anti-Mason).

Layton, Caleb Rodney (R Del.) Sept. 8, 1851–Nov. 11, 1930; House 1919–23.

Layton, Fernando Coello (D Ohio) April 11, 1847–June 22, 1926; House 1891–97.

Lazaro, Ladislas (D La.) June 5, 1872–March 30, 1927; House 1913–March 30, 1927.

Lazear, Jesse (D Pa.) Dec. 12, 1804–Sept. 2, 1877; House 1861–65.

Lazio, Rick A. (R N.Y.) March 13, 1958– ; House 1993– .

Lea, Clarence Frederick (D Calif.) July 11, 1874–June 20, 1964; House 1917–49.

Lea, Luke (brother of Pryor Lea, great-grandfather of Luke Lea, below) (White supporter Tenn.) Jan. 21, 1783–June 17, 1851; House 1833–37 (1833–35 Jacksonian).

Lea, Luke (great-grandson of Luke Lea, above) (D Tenn.) April 12, 1879–Nov. 18, 1945; Senate 1911–17.

Lea, Pryor (brother of Luke Lea) (J Tenn.) Aug. 31, 1794–Sept. 14, 1879; House 1827–31.

Leach, Anthony Claude "Buddy" Jr. (D La.) March 30, 1934– ; House 1979–81.

Leach, DeWitt Clinton (R Mich.) Nov. 23, 1822–Dec. 21, 1909; House 1857–61.

Leach, James Albert Smith (R Iowa) Oct. 15, 1942– ; House 1977– ; Chrmn. House Banking and Financial Services 1995– .

Leach, James Madison (D N.C.) Jan. 17, 1815–June 1, 1891; House 1859–61 (Opposition Party), 1871–75.

Leach, Robert Milton (R Mass.) April 2, 1879–Feb. 18, 1952; House Nov. 4, 1924–25.

Leadbetter, Daniel Parkhurst (D Ohio) Sept. 10, 1797–Feb. 26, 1870; House 1837–41.

Leahy, Edward Laurence (D R.I.) Feb. 9, 1886–July 22, 1953; Senate Aug. 24, 1949–Dec. 18, 1950.

Leahy, Patrick Joseph (D Vt.) March 31, 1940– ; Senate 1975– ; Chrmn. Senate Agriculture, Nutrition, and Forestry 1987–95.

Leake, Eugene Walter (D N.J.) July 13, 1877–Aug. 23, 1959; House 1907–09.

Leake, Shelton Farrar (ID Va.) Nov. 30, 1812–March 4, 1884; House 1845–47 (Democrat), 1859–61.

Leake, Walter (R Miss.) May 25, 1762–Nov. 17, 1825; Senate Dec. 10, 1817–May 15, 1820; Gov. Jan. 7, 1822–Nov. 17, 1825.

Learned, Amasa (grandfather of John Law) (– Conn.) Nov. 15, 1750–May 4, 1825; House 1791–95.

Leary, Cornelius Lawrence Ludlow (U Md.) Oct. 22, 1813–March 21, 1893; House 1861–63.

Leath, James Marvin (D Texas) May 6, 1931– ; House 1979–91.

Leatherwood, Elmer O. (R Utah) Sept. 4, 1872–Dec. 24, 1929; House 1921–Dec. 24, 1929.

Leavenworth, Elias Warner (R N.Y.) Dec. 20, 1803–Nov. 25, 1887; House 1875–77.

Leavitt, Humphrey Howe (J Ohio) June 18, 1796–March 15, 1873; House Dec. 6, 1830–July 10, 1834.

Leavitt, Scott (R Mont.) June 16, 1879–Oct. 19, 1966; House 1923–33.

Leavy, Charles Henry (D Wash.) Feb. 16, 1884–Sept. 25, 1952; House 1937–Aug. 1, 1942.

Le Blond, Francis Celeste (grandfather of Frank Le Blond Kloeb) (D Ohio) Feb. 14, 1821–Nov. 9, 1902; House 1863–67.

LeBoutillier, John (R N.Y.) May 26, 1953–   ; House 1981–83.

Lecompte, Joseph (J Ky.) Dec. 15, 1797–April 25, 1851; House 1825–33 (1825–31 no party).

Le Compte, Karl Miles (R Iowa) May 25, 1887–Sept. 30, 1972; House 1939–59; Chrmn. House Administration 1947–49, 1953–55.

Lederer, Raymond Francis (D Pa.) May 19, 1938–   ; House 1977–April 29, 1981.

Lee, Barbara (D Calif.) July 16, 1946–   ; House April 21, 1998–   .

Lee, Blair (great-grandson of Richard Henry Lee) (D Md.) Aug. 9, 1857–Dec. 25, 1944; Senate Jan. 28, 1914–17.

Lee, Frank Hood (D Mo.) March 29, 1873–Nov. 20, 1952; House 1933–35.

Lee, Gary Alcide (R N.Y.) Aug. 18, 1933–   ; House 1979–83.

Lee, Gideon (J N.Y.) April 27, 1778–Aug. 21, 1841; House Nov. 4, 1835–37.

Lee, Gordon (D Ga.) May 29, 1859–Nov. 7, 1927; House 1905–27.

Lee, Henry (brother of Richard Bland Lee, grandfather of William Henry Fitzhugh Lee) (F Va.) Jan. 29, 1756–March 25, 1818; House 1799–1801; Cont. Cong. 1786–88; Gov. Dec. 1, 1791–Dec. 1, 1794.

Lee, John (– Md.) Jan. 30, 1788–May 17, 1871; House 1823–25.

Lee, Joshua (J N.Y.) 1783–Dec. 19, 1842; House 1835–37.

Lee, Joshua Bryan (D Okla.) Jan. 23, 1892–Aug. 10, 1967; House 1935–37; Senate 1937–43.

Lee, Moses Lindley (R N.Y.) May 29, 1805–May 19, 1876; House 1859–61.

Lee, Richard Bland (brother of Henry Lee) (– Va.) Jan. 20, 1761–March 12, 1827; House 1789–95.

Lee, Richard Henry (great-grandfather of Blair Lee) (– Va.) Jan. 20, 1732–June 19, 1794; Senate 1789–Oct. 8, 1792; elected Pres. pro tempore April 18, 1792; Cont. Cong. 1774–79, 1784–85, 1787.

Lee, Robert Emmett (D Pa.) Oct. 12, 1868–Nov. 19, 1916; House 1911–15.

Lee, Robert Quincy (D Texas) Jan. 12, 1869–April 18, 1930; House 1929–April 18, 1930.

Lee, Silas (F Mass.) July 3, 1760–March 1, 1814; House 1799–Aug. 20, 1801.

Lee, Thomas (J N.J.) Nov. 28, 1780–Nov. 2, 1856; House 1833–37.

Lee, Warren Isbell (R N.Y.) Feb. 5, 1876–Dec. 25, 1955; House 1921–23.

Lee, William Henry Fitzhugh (grandson of Henry Lee) (D Va.) May 31, 1837–Oct. 15, 1891; House 1887–Oct. 15, 1891.

Leech, James Russell (R Pa.) Nov. 19, 1888–Feb. 5, 1952; House 1927–Jan. 29, 1932.

Leedom, John Peter (D Ohio) Dec. 20, 1847–March 18, 1895; House 1881–83.

Leet, Isaac (D Pa.) 1801–June 10, 1844; House 1839–41.

LeFante, Joseph Anthony (D N.J.) Sept. 8, 1928–   ; House 1977–Dec. 14, 1978.

Le Fever, Jacob (father of Frank Jacob Le Fevre) (R N.Y.) April 20, 1830–Feb. 4, 1905; House 1893–97.

Le Fever, Joseph (R Pa.) April 3, 1760–Oct. 17, 1826; House 1811–13.

Le Fevre, Benjamin (D Ohio) Oct. 8, 1838–March 7, 1922; House 1879–87.

Le Fevre, Frank Jacob (son of Jacob Le Fever) (R N.Y.) Nov. 30, 1874–April 29, 1941; House 1905–07.

Le Fevre, Jay (R N.Y.) Sept. 6, 1893–April 26, 1970; House 1943–51.

Lefferts, John (R N.Y.) Dec. 17, 1785–Sept. 18, 1829; House 1813–15.

Leffler, Isaac (brother of Shepherd Leffler) (– Va.) Nov. 7, 1788–March 8, 1866; House 1827–29.

Leffler, Shepherd (brother of Isaac Leffler) (D Iowa) April 24, 1811–Sept. 7, 1879; House Dec. 28, 1846–51.

Leftwich, Jabez (– Va.) Sept. 22, 1765–June 22, 1855; House 1821–25.

Leftwich, John William (D Tenn.) Sept. 7, 1826–March 6, 1870; House July 24, 1866–67.

Legarda Y Tuason, Benito (– P.I.) Sept. 27, 1853–Aug. 27, 1915; House (Res. Comm.) Nov. 22, 1907–13.

Legare, George Swinton (D S.C.) Nov. 11, 1869–Jan. 31, 1913; House 1903–Jan. 31, 1913.

Legare, Hugh Swinton (D S.C.) Jan. 2, 1797–June 20, 1843; House 1837–39; Atty. Gen. Sept. 13, 1841–June 20, 1843.

Leggett, Robert Louis (D Calif.) July 26, 1926–Aug. 13, 1997; House 1963–79.

Lehlbach, Frederick Reimold (nephew of Herman Lehlbach) (R N.J.) Jan. 31, 1876–Aug. 4, 1937; House 1915–37.

Lehlbach, Herman (uncle of Frederick Reimold Lehlbach) (R N.J.) July 3, 1845–Jan. 11, 1904; House 1885–91.

Lehman, Herbert Henry (D N.Y.) March 28, 1878–Dec. 5, 1963; Senate Nov. 9, 1949–57; Gov. Jan. 1, 1933–Dec. 3, 1942.

Lehman, Richard Henry (D Calif.) July 20, 1948–   ; House 1983–95.

Lehman, William (D Fla.) Oct. 4, 1913–   ; House 1973–93.

Lehman, William Eckart (D Pa.) Aug. 21, 1821–July 19, 1895; House 1861–63.

Lehr, John Camillus (D Mich.) Nov. 18, 1878–Feb. 17, 1958; House 1933–35.

Leib, Michael (R Pa.) Jan. 8, 1760–Dec. 8, 1822; House 1799–Feb. 14, 1806 (no party); Senate Jan. 9, 1809–Feb. 14, 1814.

Leib, Owen D. (D Pa.) ?–June 17, 1848; House 1845–47.

Leidy, Paul (D Pa.) Nov. 13, 1813–Sept. 11, 1877; House Dec. 7, 1857–59.

Leigh, Benjamin Watkins (W Va.) June 18, 1781–Feb. 2, 1849; Senate Feb. 26, 1834–July 4, 1836.

Leighty, Jacob D. (R Ind.) Nov. 15, 1839–Oct. 18, 1912; House 1895–97.

Leiper, George Gray (J Pa.) Feb. 3, 1786–Nov. 18, 1868; House 1829–31.

Leisenring, John (R Pa.) June 3, 1853–Jan. 19, 1901; House 1895–97.

Leiter, Benjamin Franklin (R Ohio) Oct. 13, 1813–June 17, 1866; House 1855–59.

Leland, George Thomas "Mickey" (D Texas) Nov. 27, 1944–Aug. 7, 1989; House 1979–Aug. 7, 1989.

Lemke, William (R N.D.) Aug. 13, 1878–May 30, 1950; House 1933–41 (Nonpartisan Republican), 1943–May 30, 1950.

Le Moyne, John Valcoulon (D Ill.) Nov. 17, 1828–July 27, 1918; House May 6, 1876–77.

Lenahan, John Thomas (D Pa.) Nov. 15, 1852–April 28, 1920; House 1907–09.

L'Engle, Claude (D Fla.) Oct. 19, 1868–Nov. 6, 1919; House 1913–15.

Lennon, Alton Asa (D N.C.) Aug. 17, 1906–Dec. 28, 1986; Senate July 10, 1953–Nov. 28, 1954; House 1957–73.

Lenroot, Irvine Luther (R Wis.) Jan. 31, 1869–Jan. 26, 1949; House 1909–April 17, 1918; Senate April 18, 1918–27.

Lent, James (J N.Y.) 1782–Feb. 22, 1833; House 1829–Feb. 22, 1833.

Lent, Norman Frederick (R/C N.Y.) March 23, 1931–   ; House 1971–93.

Lentz, John Jacob (D Ohio) Jan. 27, 1856–July 27, 1931; House 1897–1901.

Leonard, Fred Churchill (R Pa.) Feb. 16, 1856–Dec. 5, 1921; House 1895–97.

Leonard, George (F Mass.) July 4, 1729–July 26, 1819; House 1789–91 (no party), 1795–97.

Leonard, John Edwards (great-nephew of John Edwards of Pa.) (R La.) Sept. 22, 1845–March 15, 1878; House 1877–March 15, 1878.

Leonard, Moses Gage (D N.Y.) July 10, 1809–March 20, 1899; House 1843–45.

Leonard, Stephen Banks (D N.Y.) April 15, 1793–May 8, 1876; House 1835–37 (Jacksonian), 1839–41.

Lesher, John Vandling (D Pa.) July 27, 1866–May 3, 1932; House 1913–21.

Lesinski, John (father of John Lesinski Jr.) (D Mich.) Jan. 3, 1885–May 27, 1950; House 1933–May 27, 1950.

Lesinski, John Jr. (son of John Lesinski) (D Mich.) Dec. 28, 1914– ; House 1951–65; Chrmn. House Education and Labor 1949–50.

Lessler, Montague (R N.Y.) Jan. 1, 1869–Feb. 17, 1938; House Jan. 7, 1902–03.

Lester, Posey Green (D Va.) March 12, 1850–Feb. 9, 1929; House 1889–93.

Lester, Rufus Ezekiel (D Ga.) Dec. 12, 1837–June 16, 1906; House 1889–June 16, 1906.

Letcher, John (D Va.) March 29, 1813–Jan. 26, 1884; House 1851–59; Gov. Jan. 1, 1860–Dec. 31, 1863.

Letcher, Robert Perkins (– Ky.) Feb. 10, 1788–Jan. 24, 1861; House 1823–33, Aug. 6, 1834–35; Gov. June 1, 1840–June 1, 1844.

Letts, Fred Dickinson (cousin of Lester Jesse Dickinson) (R Iowa) April 26, 1875–Jan. 19, 1965; House 1925–31.

Lever, Asbury Francis (D S.C.) Jan. 5, 1875–April 28, 1940; House Nov. 5, 1901–Aug. 1, 1919.

Levering, Robert Woodrow (son-in-law of Usher L. Burdick, brother-in-law of Quentin N. Burdick, brother-in-law of Jocelyn Birch Burdick) (D Ohio) Oct. 3, 1914– ; House 1959–61.

Levin, Carl Milton (brother of Sander Martin Levin) (D Mich.) June 28, 1934– ; Senate 1979– .

Levin, Lewis Charles (AP Pa.) Nov. 10, 1808–March 14, 1860; House 1845–51.

Levin, Sander Martin (brother of Carl Milton Levin) (D Mich.) Sept. 6, 1931– ; House 1983– .

Levine, Meldon Edises "Mel" (D Calif.) June 7, 1943– ; House 1983–93.

Levitas, Elliott Harris (D Ga.) Dec. 26, 1930– ; House 1975–85.

Levy, David. (*See* Yulee, David Levy.)

Levy, David A. (R N.Y.) Dec. 18, 1953– ; House 1993–95.

Levy, Jefferson Monroe (D N.Y.) April 16, 1852–March 6, 1924; House 1899–1901, 1911–15.

Levy, William Mallory (D La.) Oct. 31, 1827–Aug. 14, 1882; House 1875–77.

Lewis, Abner (W N.Y.) ?–?; House 1845–47.

Lewis, Barbour (R Tenn.) Jan. 5, 1818–July 15, 1893; House 1873–75.

Lewis, Burwell Boykin (D Ala.) July 7, 1838–Oct. 11, 1885; House 1875–77, 1879–Oct. 1, 1880.

Lewis, Charles Jeremy "Jerry" (R Calif.) Oct. 21, 1934– ; House 1979–99.

Lewis, Charles Swearinger (D Va.) Feb. 26, 1821–Jan. 22, 1878; House Dec. 4, 1854–55.

Lewis, Clarke (D Miss.) Nov. 8, 1840–March 13, 1896; House 1889–93.

Lewis, David John (D Md.) May 1, 1869–Aug. 12, 1952; House 1911–17, 1931–39.

Lewis, Dixon Hall (D Ala.) Aug. 10, 1802–Oct. 25, 1848; House 1829–April 22, 1844 (State Rights Democrat); Senate April 22, 1844–Oct. 25, 1848.

Lewis, Earl Ramage (R Ohio) Feb. 22, 1887–Feb. 1, 1956; House 1939–41, 1943–49.

Lewis, Edward Taylor (D La.) Oct. 26, 1834–April 26, 1927; House 1883–85.

Lewis, Elijah Banks (D Ga.) March 27, 1854–Dec. 10, 1920; House 1897–1909.

Lewis, Fred Ewing (R Pa.) Feb. 8, 1865–June 27, 1949; House 1913–15.

Lewis, James Hamilton (D Ill.) May 18, 1863–April 9, 1939; House 1897–99 (Wash.); Senate March 26, 1913–19, 1931–April 9, 1939.

Lewis, John Francis (R Va.) March 1, 1818–Sept. 2, 1895; Senate Jan. 26, 1870–75.

Lewis, John Henry (R Ill.) July 21, 1830–Jan. 6, 1929; House 1881–83.

Lewis, John R. (D Ga.) Feb. 21, 1940– ; House 1987– .

Lewis, John William (R Ky.) Oct. 14, 1841–Dec. 20, 1913; House 1895–97.

Lewis, Joseph Jr. (F Va.) 1772–March 30, 1834; House 1803–17.

Lewis, Joseph Horace (D Ky.) Oct. 29, 1824–July 6, 1904; House May 10, 1870–73.

Lewis, Lawrence (D Colo.) June 22, 1879–Dec. 9, 1943; House 1933–Dec. 9, 1943.

Lewis, Robert Jacob (R Pa.) Dec. 30, 1864–July 24, 1933; House 1901–03.

Lewis, Ron (R Ky.) Sept. 14, 1946– ; House May 26, 1994– .

Lewis, Thomas (F Va.) ?–?; House 1803–March 5, 1804.

Lewis, Thomas F. (R Fla.) Oct. 26, 1924– ; House 1983–95.

Lewis, William (R Ky.) Sept. 22, 1868–Aug. 8, 1959; House April 24, 1948–49.

Lewis, William J. (D Va.) July 4, 1766–Nov. 1, 1828; House 1817–19.

Libbey, Harry (R Va.) Nov. 22, 1843–Sept. 30, 1913; House 1883–87 (1883–85 Readjuster).

Libonati, Roland Victor (D Ill.) Dec. 29, 1900– ; House Dec. 31, 1957–65.

Lichtenwalner, Norton Lewis (D Pa.) June 1, 1889–May 3, 1960; House 1931–33.

Lichtenwalter, Franklin Herbert (R Pa.) March 28, 1910–March 4, 1973; House Sept. 9, 1947–51.

Lieb, Charles (D Ind.) May 20, 1852–Sept. 1, 1928; House 1913–17.

Liebel, Michael Jr. (D Pa.) Dec. 12, 1870–Aug. 8, 1927; House 1915–17.

Lieberman, Joseph I. (D Conn.) Feb. 24, 1942– ; Senate 1989– .

Lightfoot, Jim Ross (R Iowa) Sept. 27, 1938– ; House 1985–97.

Ligon, Robert Fulwood (D Ala.) Dec. 16, 1823–Oct. 11, 1901; House 1877–79.

Ligon, Thomas Watkins (D Md.) May 10, 1810–Jan. 12, 1881; House 1845–49; Gov. Jan. 11, 1854–Jan. 13, 1858.

Lilley, George Leavens (R Conn.) Aug. 3, 1859–April 21, 1909; House 1903–Jan. 5, 1909; Gov. Jan. 6–April 21, 1909.

Lilley, Mial Eben (R Pa.) May 30, 1850–Feb. 28, 1915; House 1905–07.

Lilly, Samuel (D N.J.) Oct. 28, 1815–April 3, 1880; House 1853–55.

Lilly, Thomas Jefferson (D W.Va.) June 3, 1878–April 2, 1956; House 1923–25.

Lilly, William (R Pa.) June 3, 1821–Dec. 1, 1893; House March 4–Dec. 1, 1893.

Lincoln, Abraham (R Ill.) Feb. 12, 1809–April 15, 1865; House 1847–49 (Whig); President 1861–April 15, 1865.

Lincoln, Blanche Lambert (D Ark.) Sept. 30, 1960– ; House 1993–97; Senate 1999– .

Lincoln, Enoch (son of Levi Lincoln, brother of Levi Lincoln Jr.) (R Maine) Dec. 28, 1788–Oct. 8, 1829; House Nov. 4, 1818–21 (Mass.), 1821–26; Gov. Jan. 3, 1827–Oct. 8, 1829.

Lincoln, Levi (father of Enoch Lincoln and Levi Lincoln Jr.) (R Mass.) May 15, 1749–April 14, 1820; House Dec. 15, 1800–March 5, 1801; Cont. Cong. (elected but did not attend) 1781; Atty. Gen. March 5, 1801–March 3, 1805; Gov. Dec. 10, 1808–May 1, 1809 (Democratic Republican).

Lincoln, Levi Jr. (son of Levi Lincoln, brother of Enoch Lincoln) (W Mass.) Oct. 25, 1782–May 29, 1868; House Feb. 17, 1834–March 16, 1841 (Feb. 17, 1834–35 Anti-Jacksonian); Gov. May 26, 1825–Jan. 9,

1834 (May 26, 1825–29 Anti-Democrat, 1829–Jan. 9, 1834 National Republican).

Lincoln, William Slosson (R N.Y.) Aug. 13, 1813–April 21, 1893; House 1867–69.

Lind, James Francis (D Pa.) Oct. 17, 1900–   ; House 1949–53.

Lind, John (D Minn.) March 25, 1854–Sept. 18, 1930; House 1887–93 (Republican), 1903–05; Gov. Jan. 2, 1899–Jan. 7, 1901.

Lindbergh, Charles Augustus (R Minn.) Jan. 20, 1859–May 24, 1924; House 1907–17.

Linder, John (R Ga.) Sept. 9, 1942–   ; House 1993–   .

Lindley, James Johnson (W Mo.) Jan. 1, 1822–April 18, 1891; House 1853–57.

Lindquist, Francis Oscar (R Mich.) Sept. 27, 1869–Sept. 25, 1924; House 1913–15.

Lindsay, George Henry (father of George Washington Lindsay) (D N.Y.) Jan. 7, 1837–May 25, 1916; House 1901–13.

Lindsay, George Washington (son of George Henry Lindsay) (D N.Y.) March 28, 1865–March 15, 1938; House 1923–35.

Lindsay, John Vliet (R N.Y.) Nov. 24, 1921–   ; House 1959–Dec. 31, 1965.

Lindsay, William (D Ky.) Sept. 4, 1835–Oct. 15, 1909; Senate Feb. 15, 1893–1901.

Lindsey, Stephen Decatur (R Maine) March 3, 1828–April 26, 1884; House 1877–83.

Lindsley, James Girard (R N.Y.) March 19, 1819–Dec. 4, 1898; House 1885–87.

Lindsley, William Dell (D Ohio) Dec. 25, 1812–March 11, 1890; House 1853–55.

Lineberger, Walter Franklin (R Calif.) July 20, 1883–Oct. 9, 1943; House 1921–27.

Linehan, Neil Joseph (D Ill.) Sept. 23, 1895–Aug. 23, 1967; House 1949–51.

Link, Arthur Albert (D N.D.) May 24, 1914–   ; House 1971–73; Gov. Jan. 2, 1973–Jan. 7, 1981.

Link, William Walter (D Ill.) Feb. 12, 1884–Sept. 23, 1950; House 1945–47.

Linn, Archibald Ladley (W N.Y.) Oct. 15, 1802–Oct. 10, 1857; House 1841–43.

Linn, James (R N.J.) 1749–Jan. 5, 1821; House 1799–1801.

Linn, John (R N.J.) Dec. 3, 1763–Jan. 5, 1821; House 1817–Jan. 5, 1821.

Linn, Lewis Fields (J Mo.) Nov. 5, 1796–Oct. 3, 1843; Senate Oct. 25, 1833–Oct. 3, 1843.

Linney, Romulus Zachariah (R N.C.) Dec. 26, 1841–April 15, 1910; House 1895–1901.

Linthicum, John Charles (D Md.) Nov. 26, 1867–Oct. 5, 1932; House 1911–Oct. 5, 1932.

Linton, William Seelye (R Mich.) Feb. 4, 1856–Nov. 22, 1927; House 1893–97.

Lipinski, William Oliver (D Ill.) Dec. 22, 1937–   ; House 1983–   .

Lippitt, Henry Frederick (R R.I.) Oct. 12, 1856–Dec. 28, 1933; Senate 1911–17.

Lipscomb, Glenard Paul (R Calif.) Aug. 19, 1915–Feb. 1, 1970; House Nov. 10, 1953–Feb. 1, 1970.

Lisle, Marcus Claiborne (D Ky.) Sept. 23, 1862–July 7, 1894; House 1893–July 7, 1894.

Litchfield, Elisha (– N.Y.) July 12, 1785–Aug. 4, 1859; House 1821–25.

Littauer, Lucius Nathan (R N.Y.) Jan. 20, 1859–March 2, 1944; House 1897–1907.

Little, Chauncey Bundy (D Kan.) Feb. 10, 1877–Sept. 29, 1952; House 1925–27.

Little, Edward Campbell (R Kan.) Dec. 14, 1858–June 27, 1924; House 1917–June 27, 1924.

Little, Edward Preble (D Mass.) Nov. 7, 1791–Feb. 6, 1875; House Dec. 13, 1852–53.

Little, John (R Ohio) April 25, 1837–Oct. 18, 1900; House 1885–87.

Little, John Sebastian (D Ark.) March 15, 1853–Oct. 29, 1916; House Dec. 3, 1894–Jan. 1907; Gov. Jan. 8–Feb. 11, 1907.

Little, Joseph James (D N.Y.) June 5, 1841–Feb. 11, 1913; House Nov. 3, 1891–93.

Little, Peter (R Md.) Dec. 11, 1775–Feb. 5, 1830; House 1811–13, Sept. 2, 1816–29.

Littlefield, Charles Edgar (R Maine) June 21, 1851–May 2, 1915; House June 19, 1899–Sept. 30, 1908.

Littlefield, Nathaniel Swett (D Maine) Sept. 20, 1804–Aug. 15, 1882; House 1841–43, 1849–51.

Littlejohn, De Witt Clinton (R N.Y.) Feb. 7, 1818–Oct. 27, 1892; House 1863–65.

Littlepage, Adam Brown (D W.Va.) April 14, 1859–June 29, 1921; House 1911–13, 1915–19.

Littleton, Martin Wiley (D N.Y.) Jan. 12, 1872–Dec. 19, 1934; House 1911–13.

Litton, Jerry Lon (D Mo.) May 12, 1937–Aug. 3, 1976; House 1973–Aug. 3, 1976.

Lively, Robert Maclin (D Texas) Jan. 6, 1855–Jan. 15, 1929; House July 23, 1910–11.

Livermore, Arthur (son of Samuel Livermore, brother of Edward St. Loe Livermore) (R N.H.) July 29, 1766–July 1, 1853; House 1817–21, 1823–25.

Livermore, Edward St. Loe (son of Samuel Livermore, brother of Arthur Livermore) (F Mass.) April 5, 1762–Sept. 15, 1832; House 1807–11.

Livermore, Samuel (father of Arthur Livermore and Edward St. Loe Livermore) (F N.H.) May 14, 1732–May 18, 1803; House 1789–93 (no party); Senate 1793–June 12, 1801; elected Pres. pro tempore May 6, 1796, Dec. 2, 1799; Cont. Cong. 1780–82, 1785–86.

Livernash, Edward James (subsequently Edward James de Nivernais) (D/UL Calif.) Feb. 14, 1866–June 1, 1938; House 1903–05.

Livingston, Edward (cousin of Gov. William Livingston of N.J.) (– La.) May 28, 1764–May 23, 1836; House 1795–1801 (N.Y.), 1823–29; Senate 1829–May 24, 1831; Secy. of State May 24, 1831–May 29, 1833.

Livingston, Henry Walter (F N.Y.) 1768–Dec. 22, 1810; House 1803–07.

Livingston, Leonidas Felix (D Ga.) April 3, 1832–Feb. 11, 1912; House 1891–1911.

Livingston, Robert Le Roy (F N.Y.) 1778–1836; House 1809–May 6, 1812.

Livingston, Robert Linligthgow Jr. (R La.) April 30, 1943–   ; House Sept. 7, 1977–Feb. 28, 1999; Chrmn. House Appropriations 1995–99.

Lloyd, Edward (R Md.) July 22, 1779–June 2, 1834; House Dec. 3, 1806–09 (no party); Senate 1819–Jan. 14, 1826; Gov. June 9, 1809–Nov. 16, 1811 (Democratic Republican).

Lloyd, James (F Md.) 1745–1820; Senate Dec. 11, 1797–Dec. 1, 1800.

Lloyd, James (F Mass.) Dec. 1769–April 5, 1831; Senate June 9, 1808–May 1, 1813, June 5, 1822–May 23, 1826.

Lloyd, James Frederick (D Calif.) Sept. 27, 1922–   ; House 1975–81.

Lloyd, James Tilghman (D Mo.) Aug. 28, 1857–April 3, 1944; House June 1, 1897–1917.

Lloyd, Marilyn Laird (also known as Marilyn Laird Lloyd Bouquard) (D Tenn.) Jan. 3, 1929–   ; House 1975–95.

Lloyd, Sherman Parkinson (R Utah) Jan. 11, 1914–Dec. 15, 1979; House 1963–65, 1967–73.

Lloyd, Wesley (D Wash.) July 24, 1883–Jan. 10, 1936; House 1933–Jan. 10, 1936.

Loan, Benjamin Franklin (R Mo.) Oct. 4, 1819–March 30, 1881; House 1863–69 (1863–65 Unconditional Unionist).

Lobeck, Charles Otto (D Neb.) April 6, 1852–Jan. 30, 1920; House 1911–19.

LoBiondo, Frank A. (R N.J.) May 12, 1946– ; House 1995– .

Locher, Cyrus (D Ohio) March 8, 1878–Aug. 17, 1929; Senate April 5–Dec. 14, 1928.

Locke, Francis (nephew of Matthew Locke) (– N.C.) Oct. 31, 1776–Jan. 8, 1823; elected to the Senate but resigned Dec. 5, 1815, without having qualified.

Locke, John (– Mass.) Feb. 14, 1764–March 29, 1855; House 1823–29.

Locke, Matthew (uncle of Francis Locke, great-great-great-grandfather of Effiegene Locke Wingo) (R N.C.) 1730–Sept. 7, 1801; House 1793–99 (1793–95 no party).

Lockhart, James (D Ind.) Feb. 13, 1806–Sept. 7, 1857; House 1851–53, March 4–Sept. 7, 1857.

Lockhart, James Alexander (D N.C.) June 2, 1850–Dec. 24, 1905; House 1895–June 5, 1896.

Lockwood, Daniel Newton (D N.Y.) June 1, 1844–June 1, 1906; House 1877–79, 1891–95.

Lodge, Henry Cabot (grandfather of Henry Cabot Lodge Jr. and John Davis Lodge, great-grandson of George Cabot) (R Mass.) May 12, 1850–Nov. 9, 1924; House 1887–93; Senate 1893–Nov. 9, 1924; Senate minority leader Aug. 24, 1918–19; Senate majority leader 1919–Nov. 9, 1924; elected Pres. pro tempore March 25, 1912 (to serve March 25–March 26, 1912).

Lodge, Henry Cabot Jr. (grandson of Henry Cabot Lodge, brother of John Davis Lodge, nephew of Augustus Peabody Gardner, great-great-great-grandson of George Cabot) (R Mass.) July 5, 1902–Feb. 27, 1985; Senate 1937–Feb. 3, 1944, 1947–53.

Lodge, John Davis (grandson of Henry Cabot Lodge, brother of Henry Cabot Lodge Jr., nephew of Augustus Peabody Gardner, great-great-great-grandson of George Cabot) (R Conn.) Oct. 20, 1903–Oct. 29, 1985; House 1947–51; Gov. Jan. 3, 1951–Jan. 5, 1955.

Loeffler, Thomas Gilbert (R Texas) Aug. 1, 1946– ; House 1979–87.

Lofgren, Zoe (D Calif.) Dec. 21, 1947– ; House 1995– .

Lofland, James Rush (R Del.) Nov. 2, 1823–Feb. 10, 1894; House 1873–75.

Loft, George William (D N.Y.) Feb. 6, 1865–Nov. 6, 1943; House Nov. 4, 1913–17.

Loftin, Scott Marion (D Fla.) Sept. 14, 1878–Sept. 22, 1953; Senate May 26–Nov. 3, 1936.

Logan, George (R Pa.) Sept. 9, 1753–April 9, 1821; Senate July 13, 1801–07.

Logan, Henry (D Pa.) April 14, 1784–Dec. 26, 1866; House 1835–39 (1835–37 Jacksonian).

Logan, John Alexander (R Ill.) Feb. 9, 1826–Dec. 26, 1886; House 1859–April 2, 1862 (Democrat), 1867–71; Senate 1871–77, 1879–Dec. 26, 1886.

Logan, Marvel Mills (D Ky.) Jan. 7, 1874–Oct. 3, 1939; Senate 1931–Oct. 3, 1939.

Logan, William (R Ky.) Dec. 8, 1776–Aug. 8, 1822; Senate 1819–May 28, 1820.

Logan, William Turner (D S.C.) June 21, 1874–Sept. 15, 1941; House 1921–25.

Logue, James Washington (D Pa.) Feb. 22, 1863–Aug. 27, 1925; House 1913–15.

London, Meyer (Soc. N.Y.) Dec. 29, 1871–June 6, 1926; House 1915–19, 1921–23.

Lonergan, Augustine (D Conn.) May 20, 1874–Oct. 18, 1947; House 1913–15, 1917–21, 1931–33; Senate 1933–39.

Long, Alexander (D Ohio) Dec. 24, 1816–Nov. 28, 1886; House 1863–65.

Long, Cathy (widow of Gillis William Long) (D La.) Feb. 7, 1924– ; House April 4, 1985–87.

Long, Chester Isaiah (R Kan.) Oct. 12, 1860–July 1, 1934; House 1895–97, 1899–March 4, 1903; Senate 1903–09.

Long, Clarence Dickinson (D Md.) Dec. 11, 1908–Sept. 18, 1994; House 1963–85.

Long, Edward Henry Carroll (W Md.) Sept. 28, 1808–Oct. 16, 1865; House 1845–47.

Long, Edward Vaughn (D Mo.) July 18, 1908–Nov. 6, 1972; Senate Sept. 23, 1960–Dec. 27, 1968.

Long, George Shannon (brother of Huey Pierce "the Kingfish" Long, borther-in-law of Rose McConnell Long, uncle of Russell Billiu Long, cousin of Gillis William Long) (D La.) Sept. 11, 1883–March 22, 1958; House 1953–March 22, 1958.

Long, Gillis William (husband of Catherine Long, cousin of Huey Pierce "the Kingfish" Long, Rose McConnell Long, Russell Billiu Long and George Shannon Long) (D La.) May 4, 1923–Jan. 20, 1985; House 1963–65, 1973–Jan. 20, 1985.

Long, Huey Pierce "the Kingfish" (husband of Rose McConnell Long, father of Russell Billiu Long, brother of George Shannon Long, cousin of Gillis William Long) (D La.) Aug. 30, 1893–Sept. 10, 1935; Senate Jan. 25, 1932–Sept. 10, 1935; Gov. May 21, 1928–Jan. 25, 1932.

Long, Jefferson Franklin (R Ga.) March 3, 1836–Feb. 4, 1901; House Dec. 22, 1870–71.

Long, Jill (D Ind.) July 15, 1952– ; House April 5, 1989–95.

Long, John (– N.C.) Feb. 26, 1785–Aug. 11, 1857; House 1821–29.

Long, John Benjamin (D Texas) Sept. 8, 1843–April 27, 1924; House 1891–93.

Long, John Davis (R Mass.) Oct. 27, 1838–Aug. 28, 1915; House 1883–89; Gov. Jan. 8, 1880–Jan. 4, 1883; Secy. of the Navy March 6, 1897–April 30, 1902.

Long, Lewis Marshall (D Ill.) June 22, 1883–Sept. 9, 1957; House 1937–39.

Long, Oren Ethelbirt (D Hawaii) March 4, 1889–May 6, 1965; Senate (Terr. Sen.) 1956–59, (Sen.) Aug. 21, 1959–63; Gov. (Hawaii Terr.) 1951–53.

Long, Rose McConnell (widow of Huey Pierce "the Kingfish" Long, mother of Russell Billiu Long, daughter-in-law of George Shannon Long) (D La.) April 8, 1892–May 27, 1970; Senate Jan. 31, 1936–Jan. 2, 1937.

Long, Russell Billiu (son of Huey Pierce "the Kingfish" Long and Rose McConnell Long, nephew of George Shannon Long) (D La.) Nov. 3, 1918– ; Senate Dec. 31, 1948–87; Chrmn. Senate Finance 1965–81.

Long, Speedy Oteria (D La.) June 16, 1928– ; House 1965–73.

Longfellow, Stephen (– Maine) June 23, 1775–Aug. 2, 1849; House 1823–25.

Longley, James B. Jr. (R Maine) July 7, 1951– ; House 1995–97.

Longnecker, Henry Clay (R Pa.) April 17, 1820–Sept. 16, 1871; House 1859–61.

Longworth, Nicholas (nephew of Bellamy Storer) (R Ohio) Nov. 5, 1869–April 9, 1931; House 1903–13, 1915–April 9, 1931; House majority leader 1923–25; Speaker Dec. 7, 1925–27, Dec. 5, 1927–29, April 15, 1929–31.

Longyear, John Wesley (R Mich.) Oct. 22, 1820–March 11, 1875; House 1863–67.

Loofbourow, Frederick Charles (R Utah) Feb. 8, 1874–July 8, 1949; House Nov. 4, 1930–33.

Loomis, Andrew Williams (W Ohio) June 27, 1797–Aug. 24, 1873; House March 4–Oct. 20, 1837.

Loomis, Arphaxed (D N.Y.) April 9, 1798–Sept. 15, 1885; House 1837–39.

Loomis, Dwight (R Conn.) July 27, 1821–Sept. 17, 1903; House 1859–63.

Lord, Bert (R N.Y.) Dec. 4, 1869–May 24, 1939; House 1935–May 24, 1939.

Lord, Frederick William (D N.Y.) Dec. 11, 1800–May 24, 1860; House 1847–49.

Lord, Henry William (R Mich.) March 8, 1821–Jan. 25, 1891; House 1881–83.

Lord, Scott (D N.Y.) Dec. 11, 1820–Sept. 10, 1885; House 1875–77.

Lore, Charles Brown (D Del.) March 16, 1831–March 6, 1911; House 1883–87.

Lorimer, William (R Ill.) April 27, 1861–Sept. 13, 1934; House 1895–1901, 1903–June 17, 1909; Senate June 18, 1909–July 13, 1912.

Loring, George Bailey (R Mass.) Nov. 8, 1817–Sept. 14, 1891; House 1877–81.

Loser, Joseph Carlton (D Tenn.) Oct. 1, 1892–July 31, 1984; House 1957–63.

Lott, Chester Trent (R Miss.) Oct. 9, 1941– ; House 1973–89; Senate 1989– ; Senate majority leader June 12, 1996– .

Loud, Eugene Francis (R Calif.) March 12, 1847–Dec. 19, 1908; House 1891–1903.

Loud, George Alvin (R Mich.) June 18, 1852–Nov. 13, 1925; House 1903–13, 1915–17.

Loudenslager, Henry Clay (R N.J.) May 22, 1852–Aug. 12, 1911; House 1893–Aug. 12, 1911.

Loughridge, William (R Iowa) July 11, 1827–Sept. 26, 1889; House 1867–71, 1873–75.

Lounsbery, William (D N.Y.) Dec. 25, 1831–Nov. 8, 1905; House 1879–81.

Louttit, James Alexander (R Calif.) Oct. 16, 1848–July 26, 1906; House 1885–87.

Love, Francis Johnson (R W.Va.) Jan. 23, 1901– ; House 1947–49.

Love, James (AJ Ky.) May 12, 1795–June 12, 1874; House 1833–35.

Love, John (R Va.) ?–Aug. 17, 1822; House 1807–11.

Love, Peter Early (D Ga.) July 7, 1818–Nov. 8, 1866; House 1859–Jan. 23, 1861.

Love, Rodney Marvin (D Ohio) July 18, 1908–May 5, 1996; House 1965–67.

Love, Thomas Cutting (W N.Y.) Nov. 30, 1789–Sept. 17, 1853; House 1835–37.

Love, William Carter (R N.C.) 1784–1835; House 1815–17.

Love, William Franklin (D Miss.) March 29, 1850–Oct. 16, 1898; House 1897–Oct. 16, 1898.

Lovejoy, Owen (cousin of Nathan Allen Farwell) (R Ill.) Jan. 6, 1811–March 25, 1864; House 1857–March 25, 1864.

Lovering, Henry Bacon (D Mass.) April 8, 1841–April 5, 1911; House 1883–87.

Lovering, William Croad (R Mass.) Feb. 25, 1835–Feb. 4, 1910; House 1897–Feb. 4, 1910.

Lovett, John (F N.Y.) Feb. 20, 1761–Aug. 12, 1818; House 1813–17.

Lovette, Oscar Byrd (R Tenn.) Dec. 20, 1871–July 6, 1934; House 1931–33.

Lovre, Harold Orrin (R S.D.) Jan. 30, 1904–Jan. 17, 1972; House 1949–57.

Low, Frederick Ferdinand (R Calif.) June 30, 1828–July 21, 1894; House June 3, 1862–63; Gov. Dec. 10, 1863–Dec. 5, 1867 (Union Republican).

Low, Philip Burrill (R N.Y.) May 6, 1836–Aug. 23, 1912; House 1895–99.

Lowden, Frank Orren (R Ill.) Jan. 26, 1861–March 20, 1943; House Nov. 6, 1906–11; Gov. Jan. 8, 1917–Jan. 10, 1921.

Lowe, David Perley (R Kan.) Aug. 22, 1823–April 10, 1882; House 1871–75.

Lowe, William Manning (G Ala.) June 12, 1842–Oct. 12, 1882; House 1879–81, June 3–Oct. 12, 1882.

Lowell, Joshua Adams (D Maine) March 20, 1801–March 13, 1874; House 1839–43.

Lowenstein, Allard Kenneth (D N.Y.) Jan. 16, 1929–March 14, 1980; House 1969–71.

Lower, Christian (R Pa.) Jan. 7, 1740–Dec. 19, 1806; House 1805–Dec. 19, 1806.

Lowery, William David (R Calif.) May 2, 1947– ; House 1981–93.

Lowey, Nita M. (D N.Y.) July 5, 1937– ; House 1989– .

Lowndes, Lloyd Jr. (great-nephew of Edward Lloyd) (R Md.) Feb. 21, 1845–Jan. 8, 1905; House 1873–75; Gov. Jan. 8, 1896–Jan. 10, 1900.

Lowndes, Thomas (brother of William Lowndes) (F S.C.) Jan. 22, 1766–July 8, 1843; House 1801–05.

Lowndes, William (brother of Thomas Lowndes) (R S.C.) Feb. 11, 1782–Oct. 27, 1822; House 1811–May 8, 1822.

Lowrey, Bill Green (D Miss.) May 25, 1862–Sept. 2, 1947; House 1921–29.

Lowrie, Walter (D Pa.) Dec. 10, 1784–Dec. 14, 1868; Senate 1819–25.

Lowry, Michael Edward (D Wash.) March 8, 1939– ; House 1979–89; Gov. Jan. 13, 1993–Jan. 15, 1997.

Lowry, Robert (D Ind.) April 2, 1824–Jan. 27, 1904; House 1883–87.

Loyall, George (J Va.) May 29, 1789–Feb. 24, 1868; House March 9, 1830–31 (no party), 1833–37.

Lozier, Ralph Fulton (D Mo.) Jan. 28, 1866–May 28, 1945; House 1923–35.

Lucas, Edward (brother of William Lucas) (J Va.) Oct. 20, 1780–March 4, 1858; House 1833–37.

Lucas, Frank D. (R Okla.) Jan. 6, 1960– ; House May 17, 1994– .

Lucas, John Baptiste Charles (R Pa.) Aug. 14, 1758–Aug. 17, 1842; House 1803–05.

Lucas, Ken (D Ky.) Aug. 22, 1933– ; House 1999– .

Lucas, Scott Wike (D Ill.) Feb. 19, 1892–Feb. 22, 1968; House 1935–39; Senate 1939–51; Senate majority leader 1949–51.

Lucas, William (brother of Edward Lucas) (D Va.) Nov. 30, 1800–Aug. 29, 1877; House 1839–41, 1843–45.

Lucas, William Vincent (R S.D.) July 3, 1835–Nov. 10, 1921; House 1893–95.

Lucas, Wingate Hezekiah (D Texas) May 1, 1908–May 26, 1989; House 1947–55.

Luce, Clare Boothe (stepdaughter of Albert Elmer Austin) (R Conn.) April 10, 1903–Oct. 9, 1987; House 1943–47.

Luce, Robert (R Mass.) Dec. 2, 1862–April 17, 1946; House 1919–35, 1937–41.

Luckey, Henry Carl (D Neb.) Nov. 22, 1868–Dec. 31, 1956; House 1935–39.

Lucking, Alfred (D Mich.) Dec. 18, 1856–Dec. 1, 1929; House 1903–05.

Ludlow, Louis Leon (D Ind.) June 24, 1873–Nov. 28, 1950; House 1929–49.

Luecke, John Frederick (D Mich.) July 4, 1889–March 21, 1952; House 1937–39.

Lufkin, Willfred Weymouth (R Mass.) March 10, 1879–March 28, 1934; House Nov. 6, 1917–June 30, 1921.

Lugar, Richard G. (R Ind.) April 4, 1932– ; Senate 1977– ; Chrmn. Senate Foreign Relations 1985–87; Chrmn. Senate Agriculture, Nutrition, and Forestry 1995– .

Luhring, Oscar Raymond (R Ind.) Feb. 11, 1879–Aug. 20, 1944; House 1919–23.

Lujan, Manuel Jr. (R N.M.) May 12, 1928– ; House 1969–89; Secy. of Interior Feb. 8, 1989–Jan. 20, 1993.

Luken, Charles (son of Thomas Andrew Luken) (D Ohio) July 18, 1951– ; House 1991– .

Luken, Thomas Andrew (father of Charles Luken) (D Ohio) July 9, 1925– ; House March 5, 1974–75, 1977–91.

Lukens, Donald Edgar "Buz" (R Ohio) Feb. 11, 1931– ; House 1967–71, 1987–Oct. 24, 1990.

Lumpkin, Alva Moore (D S.C.) Nov. 13, 1886–Aug. 1, 1941; Senate July 22–Aug. 1, 1941.

Lumpkin, John Henry (nephew of Wilson Lumpkin) (D Ga.) June 13, 1812–July 10, 1860; House 1843–49, 1855–57.

Lumpkin, Wilson (uncle of John Henry Lumpkin, grandfather of Middleton Pope Barrow) (– Ga.) Jan. 14, 1783–Dec. 28, 1870; House 1815–17, 1827–31; Senate Nov. 22, 1837–41; Gov. Nov. 9, 1831–Nov. 4, 1835 (Union Democrat).

Luna, Tranquilino (R N.M.) Feb. 25, 1849–Nov. 20, 1892; House (Terr. Del.) 1881–March 5, 1884.

Lundeen, Ernest (FL Minn.) Aug. 4, 1878–Aug. 31, 1940; House 1917–19 (Republican), 1933–37; Senate 1937–Aug. 31, 1940.

Lundin, Frederick (R Ill.) May 18, 1868–Aug. 20, 1947; House 1909–11.

Lundine, Stanley Nelson (D N.Y.) Feb. 4, 1939– ; House March 2, 1976–87.

Lungren, Daniel Edward (R Calif.) Sept. 22, 1946– ; House 1979–89.

Lunn, George Richard (D N.Y.) June 23, 1873–Nov. 27, 1948; House 1917–19.

Lusk, Georgia Lee (D N.M.) May 12, 1893–Jan. 5, 1971; House 1947–49.

Lusk, Hall Stoner (D Ore.) Sept. 21, 1883–May 15, 1983; Senate March 16–Nov. 8, 1960.

Luther, William P. "Bill" (D Minn.) June 27, 1945– ; House 1995– .

Luttrell, John King (D Calif.) June 27, 1831–Oct. 4, 1893; House 1873–79.

Lybrand, Archibald (R Ohio) May 23, 1840–Feb. 7, 1910; House 1897–1901.

Lyle, Aaron (R Pa.) Nov. 17, 1759–Sept. 24, 1825; House 1809–17.

Lyle, John Emmett Jr. (D Texas) Sept. 4, 1910– ; House 1945–55.

Lyman, Joseph (R Iowa) Sept. 13, 1840–July 9, 1890; House 1885–89.

Lyman, Joseph Stebbins (– N.Y.) Feb. 14, 1785–March 21, 1821; House 1819–21.

Lyman, Samuel (F Mass.) Jan. 25, 1749–June 5, 1802; House 1795–Nov. 6, 1800.

Lyman, Theodore (IR Mass.) Aug. 23, 1833–Sept. 9, 1897; House 1883–85.

Lyman, William (R Mass.) Dec. 7, 1755–Sept. 2, 1811; House 1793–97 (1793–95 no party).

Lynch, John (R Maine) Feb. 18, 1825–July 21, 1892; House 1865–73.

Lynch, John (D Pa.) Nov. 1, 1843–Aug. 17, 1910; House 1887–89.

Lynch, John Roy (R Miss.) Sept. 10, 1847–Nov. 2, 1939; House 1873–77, April 29, 1882–83.

Lynch, Thomas (D Wis.) Nov. 21, 1844–May 4, 1898; House 1891–95.

Lynch, Walter Aloysius (D N.Y.) July 7, 1894–Sept. 10, 1957; House Feb. 20, 1940–51.

Lynde, William Pitt (D Wis.) Dec. 16, 1817–Dec. 18, 1885; House June 5, 1848–49, 1875–79.

Lyon, Asa (F Vt.) Dec. 31, 1763–April 4, 1841; House 1815–17.

Lyon, Caleb (I N.Y.) Dec. 7, 1822–Sept. 8, 1875; House 1853–55; Gov. (Idaho Terr.) 1864–66.

Lyon, Chittenden (son of Matthew Lyon) (J Ky.) Feb. 22, 1787–Nov. 23, 1842; House 1827–35 (1827–29 no party).

Lyon, Francis Strother (W Ala.) Feb. 25, 1800–Dec. 31, 1882; House 1835–39 (1835–37 Anti-Jacksonian).

Lyon, Homer Le Grand (D N.C.) March 1, 1879–May 31, 1956; House 1921–29.

Lyon, Lucius (D Mich.) Feb. 26, 1800–Sept. 24, 1851; House (Terr. Del.) 1833–35, (Rep.) 1843–45; Senate Jan. 26, 1837–39.

Lyon, Matthew (father of Chittenden Lyon, great-grandfather of William Peters Hepburn) (R Ky.) July 14, 1746–Aug. 1, 1822; House 1797–1801 (Vt.), 1803–11.

Lytle, Robert Todd (nephew of John Rowan) (J Ohio) May 19, 1804–Dec. 22, 1839; House 1833–March 10, 1834, Dec. 27, 1834–35.

M

Maas, Melvin Joseph (R Minn.) May 14, 1898–April 13, 1964; House 1927–33, 1935–45.

MacCrate, John (R N.Y.) March 29, 1885–June 9, 1976; House 1919–Dec. 30, 1920.

MacDonald, John Lewis (D Minn.) Feb. 22, 1838–July 13, 1903; House 1887–89.

Macdonald, Moses (D Maine) April 8, 1815–Oct. 18, 1869; House 1851–55.

Macdonald, Torbert Hart (D Mass.) June 6, 1917–May 21, 1976; House 1955–May 21, 1976.

MacDonald, William Josiah (Prog. Mich.) Nov. 17, 1873–March 29, 1946; House Aug. 26, 1913–15.

MacDougall, Clinton Dugald (R N.Y.) June 14, 1839–May 24, 1914; House 1873–77.

Mace, Daniel (R Ind.) Sept. 5, 1811–July 26, 1867; House 1851–57 (1851–55 Democrat).

MacGregor, Clarence (R N.Y.) Sept. 16, 1872–Feb. 18, 1952; House 1919–Dec. 31, 1928.

MacGregor, Clark (R Minn.) July 12, 1922– ; House 1961–71.

Machen, Hervey Gilbert (D Md.) Oct. 14, 1916–Nov. 29, 1994; House 1965–69.

Machen, Willis Benson (D Ky.) April 10, 1810–Sept. 29, 1893; Senate Sept. 27, 1872–73.

Machir, James (F Va.) ?–June 25, 1827; House 1797–99.

Machrowicz, Thaddeus Michael (D Mich.) Aug. 21, 1899–Feb. 17, 1970; House 1951–Sept. 18, 1961.

Machtley, Ronald K. (R R.I.) July 13, 1948– ; House 1989–95.

Maciejewski, Anton Frank (D Ill.) Jan. 3, 1893–Sept. 25, 1949; House 1939–Dec. 8, 1942.

Macintyre, Archibald Thompson (D Ga.) Oct. 27, 1822–Jan. 1, 1900; House 1871–73.

Maciora, Lucien John (D Conn.) Aug. 17, 1902–Oct. 19, 1993; House 1941–43.

Mack, Connie III (step-grandson of Tom Connally, grandson of Morris Sheppard, great-grandson of John Levi Sheppard) (R Fla.) Oct. 29, 1940– ; House 1983–89; Senate 1989– .

Mack, Peter Francis Jr. (D Ill.) Nov. 1, 1916–July 4, 1986; House 1949–63.

Mack, Russell Vernon (R Wash.) June 13, 1891–March 28, 1960; House June 7, 1947–March 28, 1960.

MacKay, James Armstrong (D Ga.) June 25, 1919– ; House 1965–67.

MacKay, Kenneth Hood "Buddy" Jr. (D Fla.) March 22, 1933– ; House 1983–89; Gov. Dec. 13, 1998–Jan. 5, 1999.

Mackey, Edmund William McGregor (R S.C.) March 8, 1846–Jan. 27, 1884; House 1875–July 19, 1876 (Independent Republican), May 31, 1882–Jan. 27, 1884.

Mackey, Levi Augustus (D Pa.) Nov. 25, 1819–Feb. 8, 1889; House 1875–79.

Mackie, John C. (D Mich.) June 1, 1920– ; House 1965–67.

MacKinnon, George Edward (R Minn.) April 22, 1906–May 1, 1995; House 1947–49.

MacLafferty, James Henry (R Calif.) Feb. 27, 1871–June 9, 1937; House Nov. 7, 1922–25.

Maclay, Samuel (brother of William Maclay, father of William Plunkett Maclay) (R Pa.) June 17, 1741–Oct. 5, 1811; House 1795–97 (no party); Senate 1803–Jan. 4, 1809.

Maclay, William (brother of Samuel Maclay, uncle of William Plunkett Maclay) (– Pa.) July 20, 1737–April 16, 1804; Senate 1789–91.

Maclay, William (R Pa.) March 22, 1765–Jan. 4, 1825; House 1815–19.

Maclay, William Brown (D N.Y.) March 20, 1812–Feb. 19, 1882; House 1843–49, 1857–61.

Maclay, William Plunkett (son of Samuel Maclay, nephew of William Maclay) (R Pa.) Aug. 23, 1774–Sept. 2, 1842; House Oct. 8, 1816–21.

Macon, Nathaniel (uncle of Willis Alston and Micajah Thomas Hawkins, great-grandfather of Charles Henry Martin of North Carolina) (R N.C.) Dec. 17, 1757–June 29, 1837; House 1791–Dec. 13, 1815 (no party); Senate Dec. 13, 1815–Nov. 14, 1828; Speaker Dec. 7, 1801–03, Oct. 17, 1803–05, Dec. 2, 1805–07; elected Pres. pro tempore May 20, 1826, Jan. 2, 1827, March 2, 1827; Cont. Cong. (elected but did not attend) 1785.

Macon, Robert Bruce (D Ark.) July 6, 1859–Oct. 9, 1925; House 1903–13.

Macy, John B. (D Wis.) March 26, 1799–Sept. 24, 1856; House 1853–55.

Macy, William Kingsland (R N.Y.) Nov. 21, 1889–July 15, 1961; House 1947–51.

Madden, Martin Barnaby (R Ill.) March 21, 1855–April 27, 1928; House 1905–April 27, 1928.

Madden, Ray John (D Ind.) Feb. 25, 1892–Sept. 28, 1987; House 1943–77; Chrmn. House Rules 1973–77.

Maddox, John W. (D Ga.) June 3, 1848–Sept. 27, 1922; House 1893–1905.

Madigan, Edward Rell (R Ill.) Jan. 13, 1936–Dec. 7, 1994; House 1973–March 8, 1991; Secy. of Agriculture March 12, 1991–Jan. 20, 1993.

Madison, Edmond Haggard (R Kan.) Dec. 18, 1865–Sept. 18, 1911; House 1907–Sept. 18, 1911.

Madison, James (R Va.) March 16, 1751–June 28, 1836; House 1789–97 (1789–95 no party); Cont. Cong. 1780–83, 1787–88; Secy. of State May 2, 1801–March 3, 1809; President 1809–17 (Democratic Republican).

Maffett, James Thompson (R Pa.) Feb. 2, 1837–Dec. 19, 1912; House 1887–89.

Magee, Clare (D Mo.) March 31, 1899–Aug. 7, 1969; House 1949–53.

Magee, James McDevitt (R Pa.) April 5, 1877–April 16, 1949; House 1923–27.

Magee, John (J N.Y.) Sept. 3, 1794–April 5, 1868; House 1827–31 (1827–29 no party).

Magee, John Alexander (D Pa.) Oct. 14, 1827–Nov. 18, 1903; House 1873–75.

Magee, Walter Warren (R N.Y.) May 23, 1861–May 25, 1927; House 1915–May 25, 1927.

Maginnis, Martin (D Mont.) Oct. 27, 1841–March 27, 1919; House (Terr. Del.) 1873–85.

Magner, Thomas Francis (uncle of John Francis Carew) (D N.Y.) March 8, 1860–Dec. 22, 1945; House 1889–95.

Magnuson, Donald Hammer (D Wash.) March 7, 1911–Oct. 5, 1979; House 1953–63.

Magnuson, Warren Grant (D Wash.) April 12, 1905–May 20, 1989; House 1937–Dec. 13, 1944; Senate Dec. 14, 1944–81; Chrmn. Senate Interstate and Foreign Commerce 1955–61; Chrmn. Senate Commerce 1961–77; Chrmn. Senate Commerce, Science, and Transportation 1977–78; Chrmn. Senate Appropriations 1978–81; elected Pres. pro tempore Jan. 15, 1979.

Magoon, Henry Sterling (R Wis.) Jan. 31, 1832–March 3, 1889; House 1875–77.

Magrady, Frederick William (R Pa.) Nov. 24, 1863–Aug. 27, 1954; House 1925–33.

Magruder, Allan Bowie (D La.) 1775–April 15, 1822; Senate Sept. 3, 1812–13.

Magruder, Patrick (R Md.) 1768–Dec. 24, 1819; House 1805–07.

Maguire, Gene Andrew (D N.J.) March 11, 1939– ; House 1975–81.

Maguire, James George (D Calif.) Feb. 22, 1853–June 20, 1920; House 1893–99.

Maguire, John Arthur (D Neb.) Nov. 29, 1870–July 1, 1939; House 1909–15.

Mahan, Bryan Francis (D Conn.) May 1, 1856–Nov. 16, 1923; House 1913–15.

Mahany, Rowland Blennerhassett (R N.Y.) Sept. 28, 1864–May 2, 1937; House 1895–99.

Maher, James Paul (D N.Y.) Nov. 3, 1865–July 31, 1946; House 1911–21.

Mahon, Gabriel Heyward Jr. (D S.C.) Nov. 11, 1889–June 11, 1962; House Nov. 3, 1936–39.

Mahon, George Herman (D Texas) Sept. 22, 1900–Nov. 19, 1985; House 1935–79; Chrmn. House Appropriations 1964–77.

Mahon, Thaddeus Maclay (R Pa.) May 21, 1840–May 31, 1916; House 1893–1907.

Mahone, William (Read. Va.) Dec. 1, 1826–Oct. 8, 1895; Senate 1881–87.

Mahoney, Peter Paul (D N.Y.) June 25, 1848–March 27, 1889; House 1885–89.

Mahoney, William Frank (D Ill.) Feb. 22, 1856–Dec. 27, 1904; House 1901–Dec. 27, 1904.

Mailliard, William Somers (R Calif.) June 10, 1917–June 10, 1992; House 1953–March 5, 1974.

Main, Verner Wright (R Mich.) Dec. 16, 1885–July 6, 1965; House Dec. 17, 1935–37.

Maish, Levi (D Pa.) Nov. 22, 1837–Feb. 26, 1899; House 1875–79, 1887–91.

Major, James Earl (D Ill.) Jan. 5, 1887–Jan. 4, 1972; House 1923–25, 1927–29, 1931–Oct. 6, 1933.

Major, Samuel Collier (D Mo.) July 2, 1869–July 28, 1931; House 1919–21, 1923–29, March 4–July 28, 1931.

Majors, Thomas Jefferson (R Neb.) June 25, 1841–July 11, 1932; House Nov. 5, 1878–79.

Malbone, Francis (F R.I.) March 20, 1759–June 4, 1809; House 1793–97 (no party); Senate March 4–June 4, 1809.

Malby, George Roland (R N.Y.) Sept. 16, 1857–July 5, 1912; House 1907–July 5, 1912.

Mallary, Richard Walker (R Vt.) Feb. 21, 1929– ; House Jan. 7, 1972–75.

Mallary, Rollin Carolas (– Vt.) May 27, 1784–April 15, 1831; House Jan. 13, 1820–April 15, 1831.

Mallory, Francis (W Va.) Dec. 12, 1807–March 26, 1860; House 1837–39, Dec. 28, 1840–43.

Mallory, Meredith (D N.Y.) ?–?; House 1839–41.

Mallory, Robert (U Ky.) Nov. 15, 1815–Aug. 11, 1885; House 1859–65 (1859–61 Opposition Party).

Mallory, Rufus (R Ore.) Jan. 10, 1831–April 30, 1914; House 1867–69.

Mallory, Stephen Russell (father of Stephen Russell Mallory, below) (D Fla.) 1813–Nov. 9, 1873; Senate 1851–Jan. 21, 1861.

Mallory, Stephen Russell (son of Stephen Russell Mallory, above) (D Fla.) Nov. 2, 1848–Dec. 23, 1907; House 1891–95; Senate May 15, 1897–Dec. 23, 1907.

Malone, George Wilson (R Nev.) Aug. 7, 1890–May 19, 1961; Senate 1947–59.

Maloney, Carolyn B. (D N.Y.) Feb. 19, 1948– ; House 1993– .

Maloney, Francis Thomas (D Conn.) March 31, 1894–Jan. 16, 1945; House 1933–35; Senate 1935–Jan. 16, 1945.

Maloney, Franklin John (R Pa.) March 29, 1899–Sept. 15, 1958; House 1947–49.

Maloney, James H. (D Conn.) Sept. 17, 1948– ; House 1997– .

Maloney, Paul Herbert (D La.) Feb. 14, 1876–March 26, 1967; House 1931–Dec. 15, 1940, 1943–47.

Maloney, Robert Sarsfield (R Mass.) Feb. 3, 1881–Nov. 8, 1934; House 1921–23.

Manahan, James (R Minn.) March 12, 1866–Jan. 8, 1932; House 1913–15.

Manasco, Carter (D Ala.) Jan. 3, 1902–Feb. 5, 1992; House June 24, 1941–49.

Manderson, Charles Frederick (R Neb.) Feb. 9, 1837–Sept. 28, 1911; Senate 1883–95; elected Pres. pro tempore March 2, 1891.

Mangum, Willie Person (W N.C.) May 10, 1792–Sept. 7, 1861; House 1823–March 18, 1826 (no party); Senate 1831–Nov. 26, 1836 (Jacksonian), Nov. 25, 1840–53; elected Pres. pro tempore May 31, 1842.

Mankin, Helen Douglas (D Ga.) Sept. 11, 1896–July 25, 1956; House Feb. 12, 1946–47.

Manlove, Joe Jonathan (R Mo.) Oct. 1, 1876–Jan. 31, 1956; House 1923–33.

Mann, Abijah Jr. (J N.Y.) Sept. 24, 1793–Sept. 6, 1868; House 1833–37.

Mann, David (D Ohio) Sept. 25, 1939– ; House 1993–95.

Mann, Edward Coke (D S.C.) Nov. 21, 1880–Nov. 11, 1931; House Oct. 7, 1919–21.

Mann, Horace (FS Mass.) May 4, 1796–Aug. 2, 1859; House April 3, 1848–53 (1848–51 Whig).

Mann, James (D La.) June 22, 1822–Aug. 26, 1868; House July 18–Aug. 26, 1868.

Mann, James Robert (R Ill.) Oct. 20, 1856–Nov. 30, 1922; House 1897–Nov. 30, 1922; House minority leader 1911–19.

Mann, James Robert (D S.C.) April 27, 1920– ; House 1969–79.

Mann, Job (D Pa.) March 31, 1795–Oct. 8, 1873; House 1835–37 (Jacksonian), 1847–51.

Mann, Joel Keith (J Pa.) Aug. 1, 1780–Aug. 28, 1857; House 1831–35.

Manning, John Jr. (D N.C.) July 30, 1830–Feb. 12, 1899; House Dec. 7, 1870–71.

Manning, Richard Irvine (cousin of John Peter Richardson II) (J S.C.) May 1, 1789–May 1, 1836; House Dec. 8, 1834–May 1, 1836; Gov. Dec. 3, 1824–Dec. 9, 1826 (Democratic Republican).

Manning, Vannoy Hartrog (D Miss.) July 26, 1839–Nov. 3, 1892; House 1877–83.

Mansfield, Joseph Jefferson (D Texas) Feb. 9, 1861–July 12, 1947; House 1917–July 12, 1947.

Mansfield, Michael Joseph "Mike" (D Mont.) March 16, 1903– ; House 1943–53; Senate 1953–77; Chrmn. Senate Rules and Administration 1961–63; Senate majority leader 1961–77.

Manson, Mahlon Dickerson (D Ind.) Feb. 20, 1820–Feb. 4, 1895; House 1871–73.

Mansur, Charles Harley (D Mo.) March 6, 1835–April 16, 1895; House 1887–93.

Mantle, Lee (R Mont.) Dec. 13, 1851–Nov. 18, 1934; Senate Jan. 16, 1895–99.

Manton, Thomas J. (D N.Y.) Nov. 3, 1932– ; House 1985–99.

Manzanares, Francisco Antonio (D N.M.) Jan. 25, 1843–Sept. 17, 1904; House (Terr. Del.) March 5, 1884–85.

Manzullo, Donald (R Ill.) March 24, 1944– ; House 1993– .

Mapes, Carl Edgar (R Mich.) Dec. 26, 1874–Dec. 12, 1939; House 1913–Dec. 12, 1939.

Marable, John Hartwell (– Tenn.) Nov. 18, 1786–April 11, 1844; House 1825–29.

Maraziti, Joseph James (R N.J.) June 15, 1912–May 20, 1991; House 1973–75.

Marcantonio, Vito Anthony (AL N.Y.) Dec. 10, 1902–Aug. 9, 1954; House 1935–37 (Republican), 1939–51.

Marchand, Albert Gallatin (son of David Marchand) (D Pa.) Feb. 27, 1811–Feb. 5, 1848; House 1839–43.

Marchand, David (father of Albert Gallatin Marchand) (R Pa.) Dec. 10, 1776–March 11, 1832; House 1817–21.

Marcy, Daniel (D N.H.) Nov. 7, 1809–Nov. 3, 1893; House 1863–65.

Marcy, William Learned (J N.Y.) Dec. 12, 1786–July 4, 1857; Senate 1831–Jan. 1, 1833; Gov. Jan. 1, 1833–Jan. 1, 1839; Secy. of War March 6, 1845–March 4, 1849; Secy. of State March 8, 1853–March 6, 1857.

Mardis, Samuel Wright (J Ala.) June 12, 1800–Nov. 14, 1836; House 1831–35.

Margolies-Mezvinsky, Marjorie (wife of Edward Maurice Mezvinsky) (D Pa.) June 21, 1942– ; House 1993–95.

Marion, Robert (R S.C.) 1766–March 22, 1811; House 1805–Dec. 4, 1810.

Markell, Henry (son of Jacob Markell) (– N.Y.) Feb. 7, 1792–Aug. 30, 1831; House 1825–29.

Markell, Jacob (father of Henry Markell) (F N.Y.) May 8, 1770–Nov. 26, 1852; House 1813–15.

Markey, Edward John (D Mass.) July 11, 1946– ; House Nov. 2, 1976– .

Markham, Henry Harrison (R Calif.) Nov. 16, 1840–Oct. 9, 1923; House 1885–87; Gov. Jan. 8, 1891–Jan. 11, 1895.

Markley, Philip Swenk (– Pa.) July 2, 1789–Sept. 12, 1834; House 1823–27.

Marks, Marc Lincoln (R Pa.) Feb. 12, 1927– ; House 1977–83.

Marks, William (– Pa.) Oct. 13, 1778–April 10, 1858; Senate 1825–31.

Marland, Ernest Whitworth (D Okla.) May 8, 1874–Oct. 3, 1941; House 1933–35; Gov. Jan. 14, 1935–Jan. 9, 1939.

Marlenee, Ronald Charles (R Mont.) Aug. 8, 1935– ; House 1977–93.

Marquette, Turner Mastin (R Neb.) July 19, 1831–Dec. 22, 1894; House March 2–3, 1867.

Marr, Alem (J Pa.) June 18, 1787–March 29, 1843; House 1829–31.

Marr, George Washington Lent (R Tenn.) May 25, 1779–Sept. 5, 1856; House 1817–19.

Marriott, David Daniel (R Utah) Nov. 2, 1939– ; House 1977–85.

Marsalis, John Henry (D Colo.) May 9, 1904–June 26, 1971; House 1949–51.

Marsh, Benjamin Franklin (R Ill.) 1839–June 2, 1905; House 1877–83, 1893–1901, 1903–June 2, 1905.

Marsh, Charles (father of George Perkins Marsh) (F Vt.) July 10, 1765–Jan. 11, 1849; House 1815–17.

Marsh, George Perkins (son of Charles Marsh) (W Vt.) March 15, 1801–July 23, 1882; House 1843–May 1849.

Marsh, John Otho Jr. (D Va.) Aug. 7, 1926– ; House 1963–71.

Marshall, Alexander Keith (AP Ky.) Feb. 11, 1808–April 28, 1884; House 1855–57.

Marshall, Alfred (D Maine) about 1797–Oct. 2, 1868; House 1841–43.

Marshall, Edward Colston (D Calif.) June 29, 1821–July 9, 1893; House 1851–53.

Marshall, Fred (D Minn.) March 13, 1906–June 5, 1985; House 1949–63.

Marshall, George Alexander (D Ohio) Sept. 14, 1851–April 21, 1899; House 1897–99.

Marshall, Humphrey (grandfather of Humphrey Marshall, below, father of Thomas Alexander Marshall, cousin of John Marshall) (F Ky.) 1760–July 1, 1841; Senate 1795–1801.

Marshall, Humphrey (grandson of Humphrey Marshall, above) (AP Ky.) Jan. 13, 1812–March 28, 1872; House 1849–Aug. 4, 1852 (Whig), 1855–59.

Marshall, James William (D Va.) March 31, 1844–Nov. 27, 1911; House 1893–95.

Marshall, John (uncle of Thomas Francis Marshall, cousin of Humphrey Marshall) (F Va.) Sept. 24, 1755–July 6, 1835; House 1799–June 7, 1800; Secy. of State June 6, 1800–Feb. 4, 1801; Chief Justice United States Feb. 4, 1801–July 6, 1835.

Marshall, Leroy Tate (R Ohio) Nov. 8, 1883–Nov. 22, 1950; House 1933–37.

Marshall, Lycurgus Luther (R Ohio) July 9, 1888–Jan. 12, 1958; House 1939–41.

Marshall, Samuel Scott (D Ill.) March 12, 1821–July 26, 1890; House 1855–59, 1865–75.

Marshall, Thomas Alexander (son of Humphrey Marshall) (AJ Ky.) Jan. 15, 1794–April 17, 1871; House 1831–35.

Marshall, Thomas Francis (nephew of John Marshall) (W Ky.) June 7, 1801–Sept. 22, 1864; House 1841–43.

Marshall, Thomas Frank (R N.D.) March 7, 1854–Aug. 20, 1921; House 1901–09.

Marston, Gilman (R N.H.) Aug. 20, 1811–July 3, 1890; House 1859–63, 1865–67; Senate March 4–June 18, 1889.

Martin, Alexander (– N.C.) 1740–Nov. 2, 1807; Senate 1793–99; Gov. Dec. 17, 1789–Dec. 14, 1792 (Federalist); Cont. Cong. (elected but did not attend) 1786.

Martin, Augustus Newton (D Ind.) March 23, 1847–July 11, 1901; House 1889–95.

Martin, Barclay (uncle of Lewis Tillman) (D Tenn.) Dec. 17, 1802–Nov. 8, 1890; House 1845–47.

Martin, Benjamin Franklin (D W.Va.) Oct. 2, 1828–Jan. 20, 1895; House 1877–81.

Martin, Charles (D Ill.) May 20, 1856–Oct. 28, 1917; House March 4–Oct. 28, 1917.

Martin, Charles Drake (D Ohio) Aug. 5, 1829–Aug. 27, 1911; House 1859–61.

Martin, Charles Henry (great-grandson of Nathaniel Macon) (P N.C.) Aug. 28, 1848–April 19, 1931; House June 5, 1896–99.

Martin, Charles Henry (D Ore.) Oct. 1, 1863–Sept. 22, 1946; House 1931–35; Gov. Jan. 14, 1935–Jan. 9, 1939.

Martin, David O'Brien (R N.Y.) April 26, 1944– ; House 1981–93.

Martin, David Thomas (R Neb.) July 9, 1907–May 15, 1997; House 1961–Dec. 31, 1974.

Martin, Eben Wever (R S.D.) April 12, 1855–May 22, 1932; House 1901–07, Nov. 3, 1908–15.

Martin, Edward (R Pa.) Sept. 18, 1879–March 19, 1967; Senate 1947–59; Chrmn. Senate Public Works 1953–55; Gov. Jan. 19, 1943–Jan. 2, 1947.

Martin, Edward Livingston (D Del.) March 29, 1837–Jan. 22, 1897; House 1879–83.

Martin, Elbert Sevier (brother of John Preston Martin) (ID Va.) about 1829–Sept. 3, 1876; House 1859–61.

Martin, Frederick Stanley (W N.Y.) April 25, 1794–June 28, 1865; House 1851–53.

Martin, George Brown (grandson of John Preston Martin) (D Ky.) Aug. 18, 1876–Nov. 12, 1945; Senate Sept. 7, 1918–19.

Martin, James Douglas (R Ala.) Sept. 1, 1918– ; House 1965–67.

Martin, James Grubbs (R N.C.) Dec. 11, 1935– ; House 1973–85; Gov. Jan. 5, 1985–Jan. 9, 1993.

Martin, James Stewart (R Ill.) Aug. 19, 1826–Nov. 20, 1907; House 1873–75.

Martin, John (D Kan.) Nov. 12, 1833–Sept. 3, 1913; Senate 1893–95.

Martin, John Andrew (D Colo.) April 10, 1868–Dec. 23, 1939; House 1909–13, 1933–Dec. 23, 1939.

Martin, John Cunningham (D Ill.) April 29, 1880–Jan. 27, 1952; House 1939–41.

Martin, John Mason (son of Joshua Lanier Martin) (D Ala.) Jan. 20, 1837–June 16, 1898; House 1885–87.

Martin, John Preston (brother of Elbert Sevier Martin, grandfather of George Brown Martin) (D Ky.) Oct. 11, 1811–Dec. 23, 1862; House 1845–47.

Martin, Joseph John (R N.C.) Nov. 21, 1833–Dec. 18, 1900; House 1879–Jan. 29, 1881.

Martin, Joseph William Jr. (R Mass.) Nov. 3, 1884–March 6, 1968; House 1925–67; House minority leader 1939–47, 1949–53, 1955–59; Speaker 1947–49, 1953–55; Chrmn. Rep. Nat. Comm. 1940–42.

Martin, Joshua Lanier (father of John Mason Martin) (D Ala.) Dec. 5, 1799–Nov. 2, 1856; House 1835–39 (1835–37 Jacksonian); Gov. Dec. 10, 1845–Dec. 16, 1847 (Independent).

Martin, Lewis J. (D N.J.) Feb. 22, 1844–May 5, 1913; House March 4–May 5, 1913.

Martin, Lynn Morley (R Ill.) Dec. 26, 1939– ; House 1981–91; Secy. of Labor Feb. 22, 1991–Jan. 20, 1993.

Martin, Morgan Lewis (cousin of James Duane Doty) (D Wis.) March 31, 1805–Dec. 10, 1887; House (Terr. Del.) 1845–47.

Martin, Patrick Minor (R Calif.) Nov. 25, 1924–July 18, 1968; House 1963–65.

Martin, Robert Nicols (– Md.) Jan. 14, 1798–July 20, 1870; House 1825–27.

Martin, Thomas Ellsworth (R Iowa) Jan. 18, 1893–June 27, 1971; House 1939–55; Senate 1955–61.

Martin, Thomas Staples (D Va.) July 29, 1847–Nov. 12, 1919; Senate 1895–Nov. 12, 1919; Senate minority leader 1911–13, March 4–Nov. 12, 1919; Senate majority leader 1917–19.

Martin, Whitmell Pugh (D La.) Aug. 12, 1867–April 6, 1929; House 1915–April 6, 1929 (1915–19 Progressive).

Martin, William Dickinson (J S.C.) Oct. 20, 1789–Nov. 17, 1833; House 1827–31.

Martin, William Harrison (D Texas) May 23, 1823–Feb. 3, 1898; House Nov. 4, 1887–91.

Martindale, Henry Clinton (AMas. N.Y.) May 6, 1780–April 22, 1860; House 1823–31 (no party), 1833–35.

Martine, James Edgar (D N.J.) Aug. 25, 1850–Feb. 26, 1925; Senate 1911–17.

Martinez, Matthew Gilbert (D. Calif.) Feb. 14, 1929– ; House July 15, 1982– .

Martini, Bill (R N.J.) Feb. 10, 1947– ; House 1995–97.

Marvin, Dudley (W N.Y.) May 9, 1786–June 25, 1856; House 1823–29, 1847–49.

Marvin, Francis (R N.Y.) March 8, 1828–Aug. 14, 1905; House 1893–95.

Marvin, James Madison (R N.Y.) Feb. 27, 1809–April 25, 1901; House 1863–69.

Marvin, Richard Pratt (W N.Y.) Dec. 23, 1803–Jan. 11, 1892; House 1837–41.

Mascara, Frank R. (D Pa.) Jan. 19, 1930– ; House 1995– .

Mason, Armistead Thomson (son of Stevens Thomson Mason) (R Va.) Aug. 4, 1787–Feb. 6, 1819; Senate Jan. 3, 1816–17.

Mason, Harry Howland (D Ill.) Dec. 16, 1873–March 10, 1946; House 1935–37.

Mason, James Brown (F R.I.) Jan. 1775–Aug. 31, 1819; House 1815–19.

Mason, James Murray (D Va.) Nov. 3, 1798–April 28, 1871; House 1837–39 (Jacksonian); Senate Jan. 21, 1847–March 28, 1861; elected Pres. pro tempore Jan. 6, 1857, March 4, 1857.

Mason, Jeremiah (F N.H.) April 27, 1768–Oct. 14, 1848; Senate June 10, 1813–June 16, 1817.

Mason, John Calvin (D Ky.) Aug. 4, 1802–Aug. 1865; House 1849–53, 1857–59.

Mason, John Thomson (D Md.) May 9, 1815–March 28, 1873; House 1841–43.

Mason, John Young (J Va.) April 18, 1799–Oct. 3, 1859; House 1831–Jan. 11, 1837; Secy. of the Navy March 26, 1844–March 10, 1845, Sept. 10, 1846–March 7, 1849; Atty. Gen. March 6, 1845–Sept. 9, 1846.

Mason, Jonathan (F Mass.) Sept. 12, 1756–Nov. 1, 1831; Senate Nov. 14, 1800–03; House 1817–May 15, 1820.

Mason, Joseph (R N.Y.) March 30, 1828–May 31, 1914; House 1879–83.

Mason, Moses Jr. (J Maine) June 2, 1789–June 25, 1866; House 1833–37.

Mason, Noah Morgan (R Ill.) July 19, 1882–March 29, 1965; House 1937–63.

Mason, Samson (W Ohio) July 24, 1793–Feb. 1, 1869; House 1835–43.

Mason, Stevens Thomson (father of Armistead Thomson Mason) (R Va.) Dec. 29, 1760–May 10, 1803; Senate Nov. 18, 1794–May 10, 1803 (Nov. 18, 1794–1803 no party).

Mason, William (J N.Y.) Sept. 10, 1786–Jan. 13, 1860; House 1835–37.

Mason, William Ernest (father of Winnifred Sprague Mason Huck) (R Ill.) July 7, 1850–June 16, 1921; House 1887–91, 1917–June 16, 1921; Senate 1897–1903.

Massey, William Alexander (R Nev.) Oct. 7, 1856–March 5, 1914; Senate July 1, 1912–Jan. 29, 1913.

Massey, Zachary David (R Tenn.) Nov. 14, 1864–July 13, 1923; House Nov. 8, 1910–11.

Massingale, Samuel Chapman (D Okla.) Aug. 2, 1870–Jan. 17, 1941; House 1935–Jan. 17, 1941.

Masters, Josiah (R N.Y.) Nov. 22, 1763–June 30, 1822; House 1805–09.

Mathews, Frank Asbury Jr. (R N.J.) Aug. 3, 1890–Feb. 5, 1964; House Nov. 6, 1945–49.

Mathews, George (– Ga.) Aug. 30, 1739–Aug. 30, 1812; House 1789–91; Gov. Nov. 7, 1793–Jan. 15, 1796 (Democratic Republican).

Mathews, George Arthur (R Dakota) June 4, 1852–April 19, 1941; House (Terr. Del.) March 4–Nov. 2, 1889.

Mathews, Harlan (D Tenn.) Jan. 17, 1927– ; Senate Jan. 5, 1993–Dec. 1, 1994.

Mathews, James (D Ohio) June 4, 1805–March 30, 1887; House 1841–45.

Mathews, Vincent (F N.Y.) June 29, 1766–Aug. 23, 1846; House 1809–11.

Mathewson, Elisha (R R.I.) April 18, 1767–Oct. 14, 1853; Senate Oct. 26, 1807–11.

Mathias, Charles McCurdy Jr. (R Md.) July 24, 1922– ; House 1961–69; Senate 1969–87; Chrmn. Senate Rules and Administration 1981–87.

Mathias, Robert Bruce (R Calif.) Nov. 17, 1930– ; House 1967–75.

Mathiot, Joshua (W Ohio) April 4, 1800–July 30, 1849; House 1841–43.

Mathis, Marvin Dawson (D Ga.) Nov. 30, 1940– ; House 1971–81.

Matlack, James (– N.J.) Jan. 11, 1775–Jan. 16, 1840; House 1821–25.

Matson, Aaron (– N.H.) 1770–July 18, 1855; House 1821–25.

Matson, Courtland Cushing (D Ind.) April 25, 1841–Sept. 4, 1915; House 1881–89.

Matsui, Robert Takeo (D Calif.) Sept. 17, 1941– ; House 1979– .

Matsunaga, Spark Masayuki (D Hawaii) Oct. 8, 1916–April 15, 1990; House 1963–77; Senate 1977–April 15, 1990.

Matteson, Orsamus Benajah (R N.Y.) Aug. 28, 1805–Dec. 22, 1889; House 1849–51 (Whig), 1853–Feb. 27, 1857 (Whig), March 4, 1857–59.

Matthews, Charles (R Pa.) Oct. 15, 1856–Dec. 12, 1932; House 1911–13.

Matthews, Donald Ray "Billy" (D Fla.) Oct. 3, 1907– ; House 1953–67.

Matthews, Nelson Edwin (R Ohio) April 14, 1852–Oct. 13, 1917; House 1915–17.

Matthews, Stanley (uncle of Henry Watterson) (R Ohio) July 21, 1824–March 22, 1889; Senate March 21, 1877–79; Assoc. Justice Supreme Court May 17, 1881–March 22, 1889.

Matthews, William (F Md.) April 26, 1755–?; House 1797–99.

Mattingly, Mack Francis (R Ga.) Jan. 7, 1931– ; Senate 1981–87.

Mattocks, John (W Vt.) March 4, 1777–Aug. 14, 1847; House 1821–23 (no party), 1825–27 (no party), 1841–43; Gov. Oct. 13, 1843–Oct. 11, 1844.

Mattoon, Ebenezer (F Mass.) Aug. 19, 1755–Sept. 11, 1843; House Feb. 2, 1801–03.

Mattox, James Albon (D Texas) Aug. 29, 1943– ; House 1977–83.

Maurice, James (D N.Y.) Nov. 7, 1814–Aug. 4, 1884; House 1853–55.

Maury, Abram Poindexter (cousin of Fontaine Maury Maverick) (W Tenn.) Dec. 26, 1801–July 22, 1848; House 1835–39 (1835–37 White supporter).

Maverick, Fontaine Maury (cousin of Abram Poindexter Maury, nephew of James Luther Slayden, cousin of John Wood Fishburne) (D Texas) Oct. 23, 1895–June 7, 1954; House 1935–39.

Mavroules, Nicholas (D Mass.) Nov. 1, 1929– ; House 1979–93.

Maxey, Samuel Bell (D Texas) March 30, 1825–Aug. 16, 1895; Senate 1875–87.

Maxwell, Augustus Emmett (grandfather of Emmett Wilson) (D Fla.) Sept. 21, 1820–May 5, 1903; House 1853–57.

Maxwell, George Clifford (father of John Patterson Bryan Maxwell, uncle of George Maxwell Robeson) (R N.J.) May 31, 1771–March 16, 1816; House 1811–13.

Maxwell, John Patterson Bryan (son of George Clifford Maxwell, uncle of George Maxwell Robeson) (W N.J.) Sept. 3, 1804–Nov. 14, 1845; House 1837–39, 1841–43.

Maxwell, Lewis (AJ Va.) April 17, 1790–Feb. 13, 1862; House 1827–33 (1827–31 no party).

Maxwell, Samuel (P Neb.) May 20, 1825–Feb. 11, 1901; House 1897–99.

Maxwell, Thomas (J N.Y.) Feb. 16, 1792–Nov. 4, 1864; House 1829–31.

May, Andrew Jackson (– Ky.) June 24, 1875–Sept. 6, 1959; House 1931–47.

May, Catherine Dean Barnes (R Wash.) May 18, 1914– ; House 1959–71.

May, Edwin Hyland Jr. (R Conn.) May 28, 1924– ; House 1957–59.

May, Henry (D Md.) Feb. 13, 1816–Sept. 25, 1866; House 1853–55, 1861–63.

May, Mitchell (D N.Y.) July 10, 1870–March 24, 1961; House 1899–1901.

May, William L. (D Ill.) about 1793–Sept. 29, 1849; House Dec. 1, 1834–39 (Dec. 1, 1834–37 Jacksonian).

Mayall, Samuel (D Maine) June 21, 1816–Sept. 17, 1892; House 1853–55.

Maybank, Burnet Rhett (D S.C.) March 7, 1899–Sept. 1, 1954; Senate Nov. 5, 1941–Sept. 1, 1954; Chrmn. Senate Banking and Currency 1949–53; Gov. Jan. 17, 1939–Nov. 4, 1941.

Maybury, William Cotter (D Mich.) Nov. 20, 1848–May 6, 1909; House 1883–87.

Mayfield, Earle Bradford (D Texas) April 12, 1881–June 23, 1964; Senate 1923–29.

Mayham, Stephen Lorenzo (D N.Y.) Oct. 8, 1826–March 3, 1908; House 1869–71, 1877–79.

Maynard, Harry Lee (D Va.) June 8, 1861–Oct. 23, 1922; House 1901–11.

Maynard, Horace (R Tenn.) Aug. 30, 1814–May 3, 1882; House 1857–63 (1857–59 American Party, 1859–61 Opposition Party, 1861–63 Unionist), July 24, 1866–75 (1866–67 Unconditional Unionist); Postmaster Gen. Aug. 25, 1880–March 7, 1881.

Maynard, John (W N.Y.) ?–March 24, 1850; House 1827–29 (no party), 1841–43.

Mayne, Wiley (R Iowa) Jan. 19, 1917– ; House 1967–75.

Mayo, Robert Murphy (Read. Va.) April 28, 1836–March 29, 1896; House 1883–March 20, 1884.

Mayrant, William (R S.C.) ?–?; House 1815–Oct. 21, 1816.

Mays, Dannite Hill (D Fla.) April 28, 1852–May 9, 1930; House 1909–13.

Mays, James Henry (D Utah) June 29, 1868–April 19, 1926; House 1915–21.

Mazzoli, Romano Louis (D Ky.) Nov. 2, 1932– ; House 1971–95.

McAdoo, William (D N.J.) Oct. 25, 1853–June 7, 1930; House 1883–91.

McAdoo, William Gibbs (D Calif.) Oct. 31, 1863–Feb. 1, 1941; Senate 1933–Nov. 8, 1938; Secy. of the Treasury March 6, 1913–Dec. 15, 1918.

McAleer, William (D Pa.) Jan. 6, 1838–April 19, 1912; House 1891–95 (1891–93 Democrat, 1893–95 Independent Democrat), 1897–1901.

McAllister, Archibald (grandson of John Andre Hanna) (D Pa.) Oct. 12, 1813–July 18, 1883; House 1863–65.

McAndrews, James (D Ill.) Oct. 22, 1862–Aug. 31, 1942; House 1901–05, 1913–21, 1935–41.

McArdle, Joseph A. (D Pa.) June 29, 1903–Dec. 27, 1967; House 1939–Jan. 5, 1942.

McArthur, Clifton Nesmith (grandson of James Willis Nesmith) (R Ore.) June 10, 1879–Dec. 9, 1923; House 1915–23.

McArthur, Duncan (– Ohio) Jan. 14, 1772–April 29, 1839; House (elected but never qualified and resigned April 5, 1813), 1823–25; Gov. Dec. 18, 1830–Dec. 7, 1832 (National Republican).

McBride, George Wycliffe (brother of John Rogers McBride) (R Ore.) March 13, 1854–June 18, 1911; Senate 1895–1901.

McBride, John Rogers (brother of George Wycliffe McBride) (R Ore.) Aug. 22, 1832–July 20, 1904; House 1863–65.

McBryde, Archibald (F N.C.) Sept. 28, 1766–Feb. 15, 1816; House 1809–13.

McCain, John Sidney III (R Ariz.) Aug. 29, 1936– ; House 1983–87; Senate 1987– ; Chrmn. Senate Indian Affairs 1995; Chrmn. Senate Commerce, Science, and Transportation 1997– .

McCall, John Ethridge (R Tenn.) Aug. 14, 1859–Aug. 8, 1920; House 1895–97.

McCall, Samuel Walker (R Mass.) Feb. 28, 1851–Nov. 4, 1923; House 1893–1913; Gov. Jan. 6, 1916–Jan. 2, 1919.

McCandless, Alfred A. (R Calif.) July 23, 1927– ; House 1983–95.

McCandless, Lincoln Loy (D Hawaii) Sept. 18, 1859–Oct. 5, 1940; House (Terr. Del.) 1933–35.

McCarran, Patrick Anthony "Pat" (D Nev.) Aug. 8, 1876–Sept. 28, 1954; Senate 1933–Sept. 28, 1954; Chrmn. Senate Judiciary 1949–53.

McCarthy, Carolyn (D N.Y.) Jan. 5, 1944– ; House 1997– .

McCarthy, Dennis (R N.Y.) March 19, 1814–Feb. 14, 1886; House 1867–71.

McCarthy, Eugene Joseph (D Minn.) March 29, 1916– ; House 1949–59; Senate 1959–71.

McCarthy, John Henry (D N.Y.) Nov. 16, 1850–Feb. 5, 1908; House 1889–Jan. 14, 1891.

McCarthy, John Jay (R Neb.) July 19, 1857–March 30, 1943; House 1903–07.

McCarthy, Joseph Raymond (R Wis.) Nov. 14, 1908–May 2, 1957; Senate 1947–May 2, 1957; Chrmn. Senate Government Operations 1953–55.

McCarthy, Karen (D Mo.) March 18, 1947– ; House 1995– .

McCarthy, Kathryn O'Loughlin. (See O'Loughlin, Kathryn Ellen.)

McCarthy, Richard Dean (D N.Y.) Sept. 24, 1927–May 5, 1995; House 1965–71.

McCarty, Andrew Zimmerman (W N.Y.) July 14, 1808–April 23, 1879; House 1855–57.

McCarty, Johnathan (AJ Ind.) Aug. 3, 1795–March 30, 1852; House 1831–37 (1831–35 Jacksonian).

McCarty, Richard (– N.Y.) Feb. 19, 1780–May 18, 1844; House 1821–23.

McCarty, William Mason (W Va.) about 1789–Dec. 20, 1863; House Jan. 25, 1840–41; Gov. (Fla. Terr.) 1827.

McCauslen, William Cochran (D Ohio) 1796–March 13, 1863; House 1843–45.

McClammy, Charles Washington (D N.C.) May 29, 1839–Feb. 26, 1896; House 1887–91.

McClean, Moses (D Pa.) June 17, 1804–Sept. 30, 1870; House 1845–47.

McCleary, James Thompson (R Minn.) Feb. 5, 1853–Dec. 17, 1924; House 1893–1907.

McCleery, James (R La.) Dec. 2, 1837–Nov. 5, 1871; House March 4–Nov. 5, 1871.

McClellan, Abraham (D Tenn.) Oct. 4, 1789–May 3, 1866; House 1837–43.

McClellan, Charles A. O. (D Ind.) May 25, 1835–Jan. 31, 1898; House 1889–93.

McClellan, George (D N.Y.) Oct. 10, 1856–Feb. 20, 1927; House 1913–15.

McClellan, George Brinton (D N.Y.) Nov. 23, 1865–Nov. 30, 1940; House 1895–Dec. 21, 1903.

McClellan, John Little (D Ark.) Feb. 25, 1896–Nov. 28, 1977; House 1935–39; Senate 1943–Nov. 28, 1977; Chrmn. Senate Expenditures in the Executive Departments 1949–52; Chrmn. Senate Government Operations 1952–53, 1955–72; Chrmn. Senate Appropriations 1972–77.

McClellan, Robert (D N.Y.) Oct. 2, 1806–June 28, 1860; House 1837–39, 1841–43.

McClelland, Robert (D Mich.) Aug. 1, 1807–Aug. 30, 1880; House 1843–49; Gov. Jan. 1, 1851–March 7, 1853; Secy. of the Interior March 8, 1853–March 9, 1857.

McClelland, William (D Pa.) March 2, 1842–Feb. 7, 1892; House 1871–73.

McClenachan, Blair (R Pa.) ?–May 8, 1812; House 1797–99.

McClernand, John Alexander (D Ill.) May 30, 1812–Sept. 20, 1900; House 1843–51, Nov. 8, 1859–Oct. 28, 1861.

McClintic, James Vernon (D Okla.) Sept. 8, 1878–April 22, 1948; House 1915–35.

McClintock, Charles Blaine (R Ohio) May 25, 1886–Feb. 1, 1965; House 1929–33.

McClory, Robert (R Ill.) Jan. 31, 1908–July 24, 1988; House 1963–83.

McCloskey, Augustus (D Texas) Sept. 23, 1878–July 21, 1950; House 1929–Feb. 10, 1930.

McCloskey, Francis Xavier (D Ind.) June 12, 1939– ; House 1983–85, May 1, 1985–95.

McCloskey, Paul Norton "Pete" Jr. (R Calif.) Sept. 29, 1927– ; House Dec. 12, 1967–83.

McClure, Addison S. (R Ohio) Oct. 10, 1839–April 17, 1903; House 1881–83, 1895–97.

McClure, Charles (D Pa.) 1804–Jan. 10, 1846; House 1837–39, Dec. 7, 1840–41.

McClure, James Albertus (R Idaho) Dec. 27, 1924– ; House 1967–73; Senate 1973– ; Chrmn. Senate Energy and Natural Resources 1981–87.

McClurg, Joseph Washington (R Mo.) Feb. 22, 1818–Dec. 2, 1900; House 1863–68 (1863–65 Unconditional Unionist); Gov. Jan. 12, 1869–Jan. 9, 1871.

McCoid, Moses Ayres (R Iowa) Nov. 5, 1840–May 19, 1904; House 1879–85.

McCollister, John Yetter (R Neb.) June 10, 1921– ; House 1971–77.

McCollum, Ira William "Bill" Jr. (R Fla.) July 12, 1944– ; House 1981– .

McComas, Louis Emory (grandfather of Katherine Edgar Byron, great-grandfather of Goodloe Edgar Byron) (R Md.) Oct. 28, 1846–Nov. 10, 1907; House 1883–91; Senate 1899–1905.

McComas, William (W Va.) 1795–June 3, 1865; House 1833–37 (1833–35 Jacksonian).

McConnell, Addison Mitchell "Mitch" Jr. (R Ky.) Feb. 20, 1942– ; Senate 1985– ; Chrmn. Senate Select Committee on Ethics 1995–97; Chrmn. Senate Rules and Administration 1999– .

McConnell, Felix Grundy (D Ala.) April 1, 1809–Sept. 10, 1846; House 1843–Sept. 10, 1846.

McConnell, Samuel Kerns Jr. (R Pa.) April 6, 1901–April 11, 1985; House Jan. 18, 1944–Sept. 1, 1957; Chrmn. House Education and Labor 1953–55.

McConnell, William John (R Idaho) Sept. 18, 1839–March 30, 1925; Senate Dec. 18, 1890–91; Gov. Jan. 2, 1893–Jan. 4, 1897.

McCook, Anson George (R N.Y.) Oct. 10, 1835–Dec. 30, 1917; House 1877–83.

McCord, Andrew (R N.Y.) about 1754–1808; House 1803–05.

McCord, James Nance (D Tenn.) March 17, 1879–Sept. 2, 1968; House 1943–45; Gov. Jan. 16, 1945–Jan. 17, 1949.

McCord, Myron Hawley (R Wis.) Nov. 26, 1840–April 27, 1908; House 1889–91; Gov. (Ariz. Terr.) 1897–98.

McCorkle, Joseph Walker (D Calif.) June 24, 1819–March 18, 1884; House 1851–53.

McCorkle, Paul Grier (D S.C.) Dec. 19, 1863–June 2, 1934; House Feb. 24–March 3, 1917.

McCormack, John William (D Mass.) Dec. 21, 1891–Nov. 22, 1980; House Nov. 6, 1928–71; House majority leader Sept. 26, 1940–47, 1949–53, 1955–Jan. 10, 1962; Speaker Jan. 9, 1963–65, Jan. 4, 1965–67, Jan. 10, 1967–71.

McCormack, Mike (D Wash.) Dec. 14, 1921– ; House 1971–81.

McCormick, Henry Clay (R Pa.) June 30, 1844–May 26, 1902; House 1887–91.

McCormick, James Robinson (D Mo.) Aug. 1, 1824–May 19, 1897; House Dec. 17, 1867–73.

McCormick, John Watts (R Ohio) Dec. 20, 1831–June 25, 1917; House 1883–85.

McCormick, Joseph Medill (husband of Ruth Hanna McCormick) (R Ill.) May 16, 1877–Feb. 25, 1925; House 1917–19; Senate 1919–Feb. 25, 1925.

McCormick, Nelson B. (P Kan.) Nov. 20, 1847–April 10, 1914; House 1897–99.

McCormick, Richard Cunningham (R N.Y.) May 23, 1832–June 2, 1901; House (Unionist Terr. Del. Ariz.) 1869–75, (Rep.) 1895–97; Gov. (Unionist Ariz. Terr.) 1866.

McCormick, Ruth Hanna (daughter of Marcus Alonzo Hanna, wife of Joseph Medill McCormick and of Albert Gallatin Simms) (R Ill.) March 27, 1880–Dec. 31, 1944; House 1929–31.

McCormick, Washington Jay (R Mont.) Jan. 4, 1884–March 7, 1949; House 1921–23.

McCowen, Edward Oscar (R Ohio) June 29, 1877–Nov. 4, 1953; House 1943–49.

McCoy, Robert (– Pa.) ?–June 7, 1849; House Nov. 22, 1831–33.

McCoy, Walter Irving (D N.J.) Dec. 8, 1859–July 17, 1933; House 1911–Oct. 3, 1914.

McCoy, William (J Va.) ?–1864; House 1811–33 (1811–29 Republican).

McCracken, Robert McDowell (R Idaho) March 15 1874–May 16, 1934; House 1915–17.

McCrary, George Washington (R Iowa) Aug. 29, 1835–June 23, 1890; House 1869–77; Secy. of War March 12, 1877–Dec. 10, 1879.

McCrate, John Dennis (D Maine) Oct. 1, 1802–Sept. 11, 1879; House 1845–47.

McCreary, George Deardorff (R Pa.) Sept. 28, 1846–July 26, 1915; House 1903–13.

McCreary, James Bennett (D Ky.) July 8, 1838–Oct. 8, 1918; House 1885–97; Senate 1903–09; Gov. Aug. 31, 1875–Aug. 31, 1879, Dec. 12, 1911–Dec. 7, 1915.

McCreary, John (– S.C.) 1761–Nov. 4, 1833; House 1819–21.

McCredie, William Wallace (R Wash.) April 27, 1862–May 10, 1935; House Nov. 2, 1909–11.

McCreery, Thomas Clay (D Ky.) Dec. 12, 1816–July 10, 1890; Senate Feb. 19, 1868–71, 1873–79.

McCreery, William (R Md.) 1750–March 8, 1814; House 1803–09.

McCreery, William (J Pa.) May 17, 1786–Sept. 27, 1841; House 1829–31.

McCrery, James O. III (R La.) Sept. 18, 1949– ; House April 26, 1988– .

McCulloch, George (D Pa.) Feb. 22, 1792–April 6, 1861; House Nov. 20, 1839–41.

McCulloch, John (W Pa.) Nov. 15, 1806–May 15, 1879; House 1853–55.

McCulloch, Philip Doddridge Jr. (D Ark.) June 23, 1851–Nov. 26, 1928; House 1893–1903.

McCulloch, Roscoe Conkling (R Ohio) Nov. 27, 1880–March 17, 1958; House 1915–21; Senate Nov. 5, 1929–Nov. 30, 1930.

McCulloch, William Moore (R Ohio) Nov. 24, 1901–Feb. 22, 1980; House Nov. 4, 1947–73.

McCullogh, Welty (R Pa.) Oct. 10, 1847–Aug. 31, 1889; House 1887–89.

McCullough, Hiram (D Md.) Sept. 26, 1813–March 4, 1885; House 1865–69.

McCullough, Thomas Grubb (– Pa.) April 20, 1785–Sept. 10, 1848; House Oct. 17, 1820–21.

McCumber, Porter James (R N.D.) Feb. 3, 1858–May 18, 1933; Senate 1899–1923.

McCurdy, David Keith (D Okla.) March 30, 1950– ; House 1981–95; Chrmn. House Permanent Select Committee on Intelligence 1991–93.

McDade, Joseph Michael (R Pa.) Sept. 29, 1931– ; House 1963–99.

McDaniel, William (D Mo.) ?–Dec. 14, 1866; House Dec. 7, 1846–47.

McDannold, John James (D Ill.) Aug. 29, 1851–Feb. 3, 1904; House 1893–95.

McDearmon, James Calvin (D Tenn.) June 13, 1844–July 19, 1902; House 1893–97.

McDermott, Allan Langdon (D N.J.) March 30, 1854–Oct. 26, 1908; House Dec. 3, 1900–07.

McDermott, James Thomas (D Ill.) Feb. 13, 1872–Feb. 7, 1938; House 1907–July 21, 1914, 1915–17.

McDermott, James (D Wash.) Dec. 28, 1936– ; House 1989– ; Chrmn. House Standards of Official Conduct 1993–95.

McDill, Alexander Stuart (R Wis.) March 18, 1822–Nov. 12, 1875; House 1873–75.

McDill, James Wilson (R Iowa) March 4, 1834–Feb. 28, 1894; House 1873–77; Senate March 8, 1881–83.

McDonald, Alexander (R Ark.) April 10, 1832–Dec. 13, 1903; Senate June 22, 1868–71.

McDonald, Edward Francis (D N.J.) Sept. 21, 1844–Nov. 5, 1892; House 1891–Nov. 5, 1892.

McDonald, Jack H. (R Mich.) June 28, 1932– ; House 1967–73.

McDonald, John (R Md.) May 24, 1837–Jan. 30, 1917; House 1897–99.

McDonald, Joseph Ewing (D Ind.) Aug. 29, 1819–June 21, 1891; House 1849–51; Senate 1875–81.

McDonald, Lawrence Patton (D Ga.) April 1, 1935–Sept. 1, 1983; House 1975–Sept. 1, 1983.

McDonough, Gordon Leo (R Calif.) Jan. 2, 1895–June 25, 1968; House 1945–63.

McDougall, James Alexander (D Calif.) Nov. 19, 1817–Sept. 3, 1867; House 1853–55; Senate 1861–67.

McDowell, Alexander (R Pa.) March 4, 1845–Sept. 30, 1913; House 1893–95.

McDowell, Harris Brown Jr. (D Del.) Feb. 10, 1906– ; House 1955–57, 1959–67.

McDowell, James (D Va.) Oct. 13, 1795–Aug. 24, 1851; House March 6, 1846–51; Gov. Jan. 1, 1843–Jan. 1, 1846.

McDowell, James Foster (D Ind.) Dec. 3, 1825–April 18, 1887; House 1863–65.

McDowell, John Anderson (D Ohio) Sept. 25, 1853–Oct. 2, 1927; House 1897–1901.

McDowell, John Ralph (R Pa.) Nov. 6, 1902–Dec. 11, 1957; House 1939–41, 1947–49.

McDowell, Joseph (father of Joseph Jefferson McDowell, cousin of Joseph McDowell, below) (R N.C.) Feb. 15, 1756–Feb. 5, 1801; House 1797–99; Cont. Cong. (elected but did not attend) 1787.

McDowell, Joseph (P G) (cousin of Joseph McDowell, above) (– N.C.) Feb. 25, 1758–March 7, 1799; House 1793–95.

McDowell, Joseph Jefferson (son of Joseph McDowell) (D Ohio) Nov. 13, 1800–Jan. 17, 1877; House 1843–47.

McDuffie, George (father-in-law of Wade Hampton) (D S.C.) Aug. 10, 1790–March 11, 1851; House 1821–34 (no party); Senate Dec. 23, 1842–Aug. 17, 1846; Gov. Dec. 11, 1834–Dec. 10, 1836 (State Rights Democrat).

McDuffie, John (D Ala.) Sept. 25, 1883–Nov. 1, 1950; House 1919–March 2, 1935.

McDuffie, John Van (R Ala.) May 16, 1841–Nov. 18, 1896; House June 4, 1890–91.

McEnery, Samuel Douglas (D La.) May 28, 1837–June 28, 1910; Senate 1897–June 28, 1910; Gov. Oct. 16, 1881–May 20, 1888.

McEttrick, Michael Joseph (ID Mass.) June 22, 1848–Dec. 31, 1921; House 1893–95.

McEwan, Thomas Jr. (R N.J.) Feb. 26, 1854–Sept. 11, 1926; House 1895–99.

McEwen, Robert Cameron (R N.Y.) Jan. 5, 1920–June 15, 1997; House 1965–81.

McEwen, Robert D. (R Ohio) Jan. 12, 1950– ; House 1981–93.

McFadden, Louis Thomas (R Pa.) July 25, 1876–Oct. 1, 1936; House 1915–35.

McFadden, Obadiah Benton (D Wash.) Nov. 18, 1815–June 25, 1875; House (Terr. Del.) 1873–75.

McFall, John Joseph (D Calif.) Feb. 20, 1918– ; House 1957–Dec. 31, 1978.

McFarlan, Duncan (R N.C.) ?–Sept. 7, 1816; House 1805–07.

McFarland, Ernest William (D Ariz.) Oct. 9, 1894–June 8, 1984; Senate 1941–53; Senate majority leader 1951–53; Gov. Jan. 3, 1955–Jan. 5, 1959.

McFarland, William (D Tenn.) Sept. 15, 1821–April 12, 1900; House 1875–77.

McFarlane, William Doddridge (D Texas) July 17, 1894–Feb. 18, 1980; House 1933–39.

McGann, Lawrence Edward (D Ill.) Feb. 2, 1852–July 22, 1928; House 1891–Dec. 27, 1895.

McGarvey, Robert Neill (R Pa.) Aug. 14, 1888–June 28, 1952; House 1947–49.

McGaughey, Edward Wilson (W Ind.) Jan. 16, 1817–Aug. 6, 1852; House 1845–47, 1849–51.

McGavin, Charles (R Ill.) Jan. 10, 1874–Dec. 17, 1940; House 1905–09.

McGee, Gale William (D Wyo.) March 17, 1915–April 9, 1992; Senate 1959–77; Chrmn. Senate Post Office and Civil Service 1969–77.

McGehee, Daniel Rayford (D Miss.) Sept. 10, 1883–Feb. 9, 1962; House 1935–47.

McGill, George (D Kan.) Feb. 12, 1879–May 14, 1963; Senate Dec. 1, 1930–39.

McGillicuddy, Daniel John (D Maine) Aug. 27, 1859–July 30, 1936; House 1911–17.

McGinley, Donald Francis (D Neb.) June 30, 1920– ; House 1959–61.

McGlennon, Cornelius Augustine (D N.J.) Dec. 10, 1878–June 13, 1931; House 1919–21.

McGlinchey, Herbert Joseph (D Pa.) Nov. 7, 1904– ; House 1945–47.

McGovern, George Stanley (D S.D.) July 19, 1922– ; House 1957–61; Senate 1963–81.

McGovern, James P. (D-Mass.) Nov. 20, 1959– ; House 1997– .

McGowan, Jonas Hartzell (R Mich.) April 2, 1837–July 5, 1909; House 1877–81.

McGranery, James Patrick (D Pa.) July 8, 1895–Dec. 23, 1962; House 1937–Nov. 17, 1943; Atty. Gen. May 27, 1952–Jan. 20, 1953.

McGrath, Christopher Columbus (D N.Y.) May 15, 1902–July 7, 1986; House 1949–53.

McGrath, James Howard (D R.I.) Nov. 28, 1903–Sept. 2, 1966; Senate 1947–Aug. 23, 1949; Chrmn. Senate District of Columbia 1949–51; Gov. Jan. 7, 1941–Oct. 6, 1945; Chrmn. Dem. Nat. Comm. 1947–49; Atty. Gen. Aug. 24, 1949–April 7, 1952.

McGrath, John Joseph (D Calif.) July 23, 1872–Aug. 25, 1951; House 1933–39.

McGrath, Raymond Joseph (R N.Y.) March 27, 1942– ; House 1981–93.

McGrath, Thomas Charles Jr. (D N.J.) April 22, 1927–Jan. 15, 1994; House 1965–67.

McGregor, J. Harry (R Ohio) Sept. 30, 1896–Oct. 7, 1958; House Feb. 27, 1940–Oct. 7, 1958.

McGrew, James Clark (R W.Va.) Sept. 14, 1813–Sept. 18, 1910; House 1869–73.

McGroarty, John Steven (D Calif.) Aug. 20, 1862–Aug. 7, 1944; House 1935–39.

McGugin, Harold Clement (R Kan.) Nov. 22, 1893–March 7, 1946; House 1931–35.

McGuire, Bird Segle (cousin of William Neville) (R Okla.) Oct. 13, 1865–Nov. 9, 1930; House (Terr. Del.) 1903–07, (Rep.) Nov. 16, 1907–15.

McGuire, John Andrew (D Conn.) Feb. 28, 1906–May 28, 1976; House 1949–53.

McHale, Paul (D Pa.) July 26, 1950– ; House 1993–99.

McHatton, Robert Lytle (– Ky.) Nov. 17, 1788–May 20, 1835; House Dec. 7, 1826–29.

McHenry, Henry Davis (son of John Hardin McHenry) (D Ky.) Feb. 27, 1826–Dec. 17, 1890; House 1871–73.

McHenry, John Geiser (D Pa.) April 26, 1868–Dec. 27, 1912; House 1907–Dec. 27, 1912.

McHenry, John Hardin (father of Henry Davis McHenry) (W Ky.) Oct. 13, 1797–Nov. 1, 1871; House 1845–47.

McHugh, John M. (R N.Y.) Sept. 29, 1948– ; House 1993– .

McHugh, Matthew Francis (D N.Y.) Dec. 6, 1938– ; House 1975–93.

McIlvaine, Abraham Robinson (W Pa.) Aug. 14, 1804–Aug. 22, 1863; House 1843–49.

McIlvaine, Joseph (– N.J.) Oct. 2, 1769–Aug. 19, 1826; Senate Nov. 12, 1823–Aug. 19, 1826.

McIndoe, Walter Duncan (R Wis.) March 30, 1819–Aug. 22, 1872; House Jan. 26, 1863–67.

McInnis, Scott (R Colo.) May 9, 1953– ; House 1993– .

McIntire, Clifford Guy (R Maine) May 4, 1908–Oct. 1, 1974; House Oct. 22, 1951–65.

McIntire, Rufus (J Maine) Dec. 19, 1784–April 28, 1866; House Sept. 10, 1827–35 (Sept. 10, 1827–29 no party).

McIntire, William Watson (R Md.) June 30, 1850–March 30, 1912; House 1897–99.

McIntosh, David M. (R Ind.) June 8, 1958– ; House 1995– .

McIntosh, Robert John (R Mich.) Sept. 16, 1922– ; House 1957–59.

McIntyre, John Joseph (D Wyo.) Dec. 17, 1904–Nov. 30, 1974; House 1941–43.

McIntyre, Mike (D N.C.) August 6, 1956– ; House 1997– .

McIntyre, Thomas James (D N.H.) Feb. 20, 1915–Aug. 8, 1992; Senate Nov. 7, 1962–79.

McJunkin, Ebenezer (R Pa.) March 28, 1819–Nov. 10, 1907; House 1871–Jan. 1, 1875.

McKaig, William McMahon (D Md.) July 29, 1845–June 6, 1907; House 1891–95.

McKay, James Iver (D N.C.) 1793–Sept. 4, 1853; House 1831–49 (1831–37 Jacksonian).

McKay, Koln Gunn (D Utah) Feb. 23, 1925– ; House 1971–81.

McKean, James Bedell (nephew of Samuel McKean) (R N.Y.) Aug. 5, 1821–Jan. 5, 1879; House 1859–63.

McKean, Samuel (uncle of James Bedell McKean) (J Pa.) April 7, 1787–Dec. 14, 1841; House 1823–29 (no party); Senate 1833–39.

McKee, George Colin (R Miss.) Oct. 2, 1837–Nov. 17, 1890; House 1869–75.

McKee, John (– Ala.) 1771–Aug. 12, 1832; House 1823–29.

McKee, Samuel (R Ky.) Oct. 13, 1774–Oct. 16, 1826; House 1809–17.

McKee, Samuel (R Ky.) Nov. 5, 1833–Dec. 11, 1898; House 1865–67 (Unconditional Unionist), June 22, 1868–69.

McKeighan, William Arthur (P Neb.) Jan. 19, 1842–Dec. 15, 1895; House 1891–95.

McKellar, Kenneth Douglas (D Tenn.) Jan. 29, 1869–Oct. 25, 1957; House Nov. 9, 1911–17; Senate 1917–53; elected Pres. pro tempore Jan. 6, 1945, Jan. 3, 1949; Chrmn. Senate Appropriations 1949–53.

McKenna, Joseph (R Calif.) Aug. 10, 1843–Nov. 21, 1926; House 1885–March 28, 1892; Atty. Gen. March 5, 1897–Jan. 25, 1898; Assoc. Justice Supreme Court Jan. 26, 1898–Jan. 5, 1925.

McKennan, Thomas McKean Thompson (W Pa.) March 31, 1794–July 9, 1852; House 1831–39 (Anti-Mason), May 30, 1842–43; Secy. of the Interior Aug. 15–Aug. 26, 1850.

McKenney, William Robertson (D Va.) Dec. 2, 1851–Jan. 3, 1916; House 1895–May 2, 1896.

McKenty, Jacob Kerlin (D Pa.) Jan. 19, 1827–Jan. 3, 1866; House Dec. 3, 1860–61.

McKenzie, Charles Edgar (D La.) Oct. 3, 1896–June 7, 1956; House 1943–47.

McKenzie, James Andrew (uncle of John McKenzie Moss) (D Ky.) Aug. 1, 1840–June 25, 1904; House 1877–83.

McKenzie, John Charles (R Ill.) Feb. 18, 1860–Sept. 17, 1941; House 1911–25.

McKenzie, Lewis (C Va.) Oct. 7, 1810–June 28, 1895; House Feb. 16–March 3, 1863 (Unionist), Jan. 31, 1870–71.

McKeon, Howard P. "Buck" (R Calif.) Sept. 9, 1939– ; House 1993– .

McKeon, John (D N.Y.) March 29, 1808–Nov. 22, 1883; House 1835–37 (Jacksonian), 1841–43.

McKeough, Raymond Stephen (D Ill.) April 29, 1888–Dec. 16, 1979; House 1935–43.

McKeown, Thomas Deitz (D Okla.) June 4, 1878–Oct. 22, 1951; House 1917–21, 1923–35.

McKernan, John Rettie Jr. (R Maine) May 20, 1948– ; House 1983–87; Gov. Jan. 7, 1987–Jan. 5, 1995.

McKevitt, James Douglas "Mike" (R Colo.) Oct. 26, 1928– ; House 1971–73.

McKibbin, Joseph Chambers (D Calif.) May 14, 1824–July 1, 1896; House 1857–59.

McKim, Alexander (uncle of Isaac McKim) (R Md.) Jan. 10, 1748–Jan. 18, 1832; House 1809–15.

McKim, Isaac (nephew of Alexander McKim) (D Md.) July 21, 1775–April 1, 1838; House Jan. 4, 1823–25 (no party), 1833–April 1, 1838 (1833–37 Jacksonian).

McKiniry, Richard Francis (D N.Y.) March 23, 1878–May 30, 1950; House 1919–21.

McKinlay, Duncan E. (R Calif.) Oct. 6, 1862–Dec. 30, 1914; House 1905–11.

McKinley, John (J Ala.) May 1, 1780–July 19, 1852; Senate Nov. 27, 1826–31 (no party), March 4–April 22, 1837; House 1833–35; Assoc. Justice Supreme Court Jan. 9, 1838–July 19, 1852.

McKinley, William (R Va.) ?–?; House Dec. 21, 1810–11.

McKinley, William Brown (R Ill.) Sept. 5, 1856–Dec. 7, 1926; House 1905–13, 1915–21; Senate 1921–Dec. 7, 1926.

McKinley, William Jr. (R Ohio) Jan. 29, 1843–Sept. 14, 1901; House 1877–May 27, 1884, 1885–91; Gov. Jan. 11, 1892–Jan. 13, 1896; President 1897–Sept. 14, 1901.

McKinney, Cynthia A. (D Ga.) March 17, 1955– ; House 1993– .

McKinney, James (R Ill.) April 14, 1852–Sept. 29, 1934; House Nov. 7, 1905–13.

McKinney, John Franklin (D Ohio) April 12, 1827–June 13, 1903; House 1863–65, 1871–73.

McKinney, Luther Franklin (D N.H.) April 25, 1841–July 30, 1922; House 1887–89, 1891–93.

McKinney, Stewart Brett (R Conn.) Jan. 30, 1931–May 7, 1987; House 1971–May 7, 1987.

McKinnon, Clinton Dotson (D Calif.) Feb. 5, 1906– ; House 1949–53.

McKissock, Thomas (W N.Y.) April 17, 1790–June 26, 1866; House 1849–51.

McKneally, Martin Boswell (R N.Y.) Dec. 31, 1914–June 14, 1992; House 1969–71.

McKnight, Robert (R Pa.) Jan. 20, 1820–Oct. 25, 1885; House 1859–63.

McLachlan, James (R Calif.) Aug. 1, 1852–Nov. 21, 1940; House 1895–97, 1901–11.

McLain, Frank Alexander (D Miss.) Jan. 29, 1852–Oct. 10, 1920; House Dec. 12, 1898–1909.

McLanahan, James Xavier (grandson of Andrew Gregg) (D Pa.) 1809–Dec. 16, 1861; House 1849–53.

McLane, Louis (father of Robert Milligan McLane) (– Del.) May 28, 1786–Oct. 7, 1857; House 1817–27; Senate 1827–April 16, 1829; Secy. of the Treasury Aug. 8, 1831–May 28, 1833; Secy. of State May 29, 1833–June 30, 1834.

McLane, Patrick (D Pa.) March 14, 1875–Nov. 13, 1946; House 1919–Feb. 25, 1921.

McLane, Robert Milligan (son of Louis McLane) (D Md.) June 23, 1815–April 16, 1898; House 1847–51, 1879–83; Gov. Jan. 9, 1884–March 27, 1885; Chrmn. Dem. Nat. Comm. 1852–54.

McLaughlin, Charles Francis (D Neb.) June 19, 1887–Feb. 5, 1976; House 1935–43.

McLaughlin, James Campbell (R Mich.) Jan. 26, 1858–Nov. 29, 1932; House 1907–Nov. 29, 1932.

McLaughlin, Joseph (R Pa.) June 9, 1867–Nov. 21, 1926; House 1917–19, 1921–23.

McLaughlin, Melvin Orlando (R Neb.) Aug. 8, 1876–June 18, 1928; House 1919–27.

McLaurin, Anselm Joseph (D Miss.) March 26, 1848–Dec. 22, 1909; Senate Feb. 7, 1894–95, 1901–Dec. 22, 1909; Gov. Jan. 20, 1896–Jan. 16, 1900.

McLaurin, John Lowndes (D S.C.) May 9, 1860–July 29, 1934; House Dec. 5, 1892–May 31, 1897; Senate June 1, 1897–1903.

McLean, Alney (R Ky.) June 10, 1779–Dec. 30, 1841; House 1815–17, 1819–21.

McLean, Donald Holman (R N.J.) March 18, 1884–Aug. 19, 1975; House 1933–45.

McLean, Finis Ewing (brother of John McLean of Ill., uncle of James David Walker) (W Ky.) Feb. 19, 1806–April 12, 1881; House 1849–51.

McLean, George Payne (R Conn.) Oct. 7, 1857–June 6, 1932; Senate 1911–29; Gov. Jan. 9, 1901–Jan. 7, 1903.

McLean, James Henry (R Mo.) Aug. 13, 1829–Aug. 12, 1886; House Dec. 15, 1882–83.

McLean, John (brother of William McLean) (R Ohio) March 11, 1785–April 4, 1861; House 1813–16; Postmaster Gen. July 1, 1823–March 9, 1829; Assoc. Justice Supreme Court Jan. 11, 1830–April 4, 1861.

McLean, John (brother of Finis Ewing McLean, uncle of James David Walker) (– Ill.) Feb. 4, 1791–Oct. 14, 1830; House Dec. 3, 1818–19; Senate Nov. 23, 1824–25, 1829–Oct. 14, 1830.

McLean, Samuel (D Mont.) Aug. 7, 1826–July 16, 1877; House (Terr. Del.) Jan. 6, 1865–67.

McLean, William (brother of John McLean of Ohio) (– Ohio) Aug. 10, 1794–Oct. 12, 1839; House 1823–29.

McLean, William Pinkney (D Texas) Aug. 9, 1836–March 13, 1925; House 1873–75.

McLemore, Atkins Jefferson "Jeff" (D Texas) March 13, 1857–March 4, 1929; House 1915–19.

McLene, Jeremiah (J Ohio) 1767–March 19, 1837; House 1833–37.

McLeod, Clarence John (R Mich.) July 3, 1895–May 15, 1959; House Nov. 2, 1920–21, 1923–37, 1939–41.

McLoskey, Robert Thaddeus (R Ill.) June 26, 1907– ; House 1963–65.

McMahon, Gregory (R N.Y.) March 19, 1915–June 27, 1989; House 1947–49.

McMahon, James O'Brien (born James O'Brien) (D Conn.) Oct. 6, 1903–July 28, 1952; Senate 1945–July 28, 1952.

McMahon, John A. (nephew of Clement Laird Vallandigham) (D Ohio) Feb. 19, 1833–March 8, 1923; House 1875–81.

McManus, William (– N.Y.) 1780–Jan. 18, 1835; House 1825–27.

McMaster, William Henry (R S.D.) May 10, 1877–Sept. 14, 1968; Senate 1925–31; Gov. Jan. 4, 1921–Jan. 6, 1925.

McMillan, Alexander (– N.C.) ?–1817; House 1817.

McMillan, J. Alex (R N.C.) May 9, 1932– ; House 1985–95.

McMillan, Clara Gooding (widow of Thomas Sanders McMillan) (D S.C.) Aug. 17, 1894–Nov. 8, 1976; House Nov. 7, 1939–41.

McMillan, James (R Mich.) May 12, 1838–Aug. 10, 1902; Senate 1889–Aug. 10, 1902.

McMillan, John Lanneau (D S.C.) April 12, 1898–Sept. 3, 1979; House 1939–73; Chrmn. House District of Columbia 1949–53, 1955–73.

McMillan, Samuel (R N.Y.) Aug. 6, 1850–May 6, 1924; House 1907–09.

McMillan, Samuel James Renwick (R Minn.) Feb. 22, 1826–Oct. 3, 1897; Senate 1875–87.

McMillan, Thomas Sanders (husband of Clara Gooding McMillan) (D S.C.) Nov. 27, 1888–Sept. 29, 1939; House 1925–Sept. 29, 1939.

McMillan, William (– N.W. Terr.) March 2, 1764–May 1804; House (Terr. Del.) Nov. 24, 1800–01.

McMillen, Charles Thomas (D Md.) May 26, 1952– ; House 1987–93.

McMillen, Rolla Coral (R Ill.) Oct. 5, 1880–May 6, 1961; House June 13, 1944–51.

McMillin, Benton (D Tenn.) Sept. 11, 1845–Jan. 8, 1933; House 1879–Jan. 6, 1899; Gov. Jan. 16, 1899–Jan. 19, 1903.

McMorran, Henry Gordon (R Mich.) June 11, 1844–July 19, 1929; House 1903–13.

McMullen, Chester Bartow (D Fla.) Dec. 6, 1902–Nov. 3, 1953; House 1951–53.

McMullen, Fayette (D Va.) May 18, 1805–Nov. 8, 1880; House 1849–57; Gov. (Wash. Terr.) 1857–61.

McMurray, Howard Johnstone (D Wis.) March 3, 1901–Aug. 14, 1961; House 1943–45.

McNagny, William Forgy (D Ind.) April 19, 1850–Aug. 24, 1923; House 1893–95.

McNair, John (D Pa.) June 8, 1800–Aug. 12, 1861; House 1851–55.

McNamara, Patrick Vincent (D Mich.) Oct. 4, 1894–April 30, 1966; Senate 1955–April 30, 1966; Chrmn. Senate Public Works 1963–66.

McNary, Charles Linza (R Ore.) June 12, 1874–Feb. 25, 1944; Senate May 29, 1917–Nov. 5, 1918, Dec. 18, 1918–Feb. 25, 1944; Senate minority leader 1933–44.

McNary, William Sarsfield (D Mass.) March 29, 1863–June 26, 1930; House 1903–07.

McNeely, Thompson Ware (D Ill.) Oct. 5, 1835–July 23, 1921; House 1869–73.

McNeill, Archibald (– N.C.) ?–1849; House 1821–23, 1825–27.

McNulta, John (R Ill.) Nov. 9, 1837–Feb. 22, 1900; House 1873–75.

McNulty, Frank Joseph (D N.J.) Aug. 10, 1872–May 26, 1926; House 1923–25.

McNulty, James Francis Jr. (D Ariz.) Oct. 18, 1925– ; House 1983–85.

McNulty, Michael R. (D N.Y.) Sept. 16, 1947– ; House 1989– .

McPherson, Edward (R Pa.) July 31, 1830–Dec. 14, 1895; House 1859–63.

McPherson, Isaac Vanbert (R Mo.) March 8, 1868–Oct. 31, 1931; House 1919–23.

McPherson, John Rhoderic (D N.J.) May 9, 1833–Oct. 8, 1897; Senate 1877–95.

McPherson, Smith (R Iowa) Feb. 14, 1848–Jan. 17, 1915; House 1899–June 6, 1900.

McQueen, John (D S.C.) Feb. 9, 1804–Aug. 30, 1867; House Feb. 12, 1849–Dec. 21, 1860.

McRae, John Jones (D Miss.) Jan. 10, 1815–May 31, 1868; Senate Dec. 1, 1851–March 17, 1852; House Dec. 7, 1858–Jan. 12, 1861; Gov. Jan. 10, 1854–Nov. 16, 1857.

McRae, Thomas Chipman (cousin of Thomas Banks Cabaniss) (D Ark.) Dec. 21, 1851–June 2, 1929; House Dec. 7, 1885–1903; Gov. Jan. 11, 1921–Jan. 13, 1925.

McReynolds, Samuel Davis (D Tenn.) April 16, 1872–July 11, 1939; House 1923–July 11, 1939.

McRoberts, Samuel (D Ill.) April 12, 1799–March 27, 1843; Senate 1841–March 27, 1843.

McRuer, Donald Campbell (R Calif.) March 10, 1826–Jan. 29, 1898; House 1865–67.

McShane, John Albert (D Neb.) Aug. 25, 1850–Nov. 10, 1923; House 1887–89.

McSherry, James (– Pa.) July 29, 1776–Feb. 3, 1849; House 1821–23.

McSpadden, Clem Rogers (D Okla.) Nov. 9, 1925– ; House 1973–75.

McSwain, John Jackson (D S.C.) May 1, 1875–Aug. 6, 1936; House 1921–Aug. 6, 1936.

McSween, Harold Barnett (D La.) July 19, 1926– ; House 1959–63.

McSweeney, John (D Ohio) Dec. 19, 1890–Dec. 13, 1969; House 1923–29, 1937–39, 1949–51.

McVean, Charles (J N.Y.) 1802–Dec. 22, 1848; House 1833–35.

McVey, Walter Lewis Jr. (R Kan.) Feb. 19, 1922– ; House 1961–63.

McVey, William Estus (R Ill.) Dec. 13, 1885–Aug. 10, 1958; House 1951–Aug. 10, 1958.

McVicker, Roy Harrison (D Colo.) Feb. 20, 1924–Sept. 15, 1973; House 1965–67.

McWilliams, John Dacher (R Conn.) July 23, 1891–March 30, 1975; House 1943–45.

McWillie, William (D Miss.) Nov. 17, 1795–March 3, 1869; House 1849–51; Gov. Nov. 16, 1857–Nov. 21, 1859.

Meacham, James (W Vt.) Aug. 16, 1810–Aug. 23, 1856; House Dec. 3, 1849–Aug. 23, 1856.

Mead, Cowles (– Ga.) Oct. 18, 1776–May 17, 1844; House March 4–Dec. 24, 1805.

Mead, James Michael (D N.Y.) Dec. 27, 1885–March 15, 1964; House 1919–Dec. 2, 1938; Senate Dec. 3, 1938–47.

Meade, Edwin Ruthven (D N.Y.) July 6, 1836–Nov. 28, 1889; House 1875–77.

Meade, Hugh Allen (D Md.) April 4, 1907–July 8, 1949; House 1947–49.

Meade, Richard Kidder (D Va.) July 29, 1803–April 20, 1862; House Aug. 5, 1847–53.

Meade, Wendell Howes (R Ky.) Jan. 18, 1912–June 2, 1986; House 1947–49.

Meader, George (R Mich.) Sept. 13, 1907–Oct. 15, 1994; House 1951–65.

Means, Rice William (R Colo.) Nov. 16, 1877–Jan. 30, 1949; Senate Dec. 1, 1924–27.

Mebane, Alexander (– N.C.) Nov. 26, 1744–July 5, 1795; House 1793–95.

Mechem, Edwin Leard (R N.M.) July 2, 1912– ; Senate Nov. 30, 1962–Nov. 3, 1964; Gov. Jan. 1, 1951–Jan. 1, 1955, Jan. 1, 1957–Jan. 1, 1959, Jan. 1, 1961–Nov. 30, 1962.

Medill, William (D Ohio) Feb. 1802–Sept. 2, 1865; House 1839–43; Gov. July 13, 1853–Jan. 14, 1856.

Meech, Ezra (D Vt.) July 26, 1773–Sept. 23, 1856; House 1810–21, 1825–27.

Meeds, Lloyd (D Wash.) Dec. 11, 1927– ; House 1965–79.

Meehan, Martin T. (D Mass.) Dec. 30, 1956– ; House 1993– .

Meek, Carrie P. (D Fla.) April 29, 1926– ; House 1993– .

Meeker, Jacob Edwin (R Mo.) Oct. 7, 1878–Oct. 16, 1918; House 1915–Oct. 16, 1918.

Meekison, David (D Ohio) Nov. 14, 1849–Feb. 12, 1915; House 1897–1901.

Meeks, Gregory W. (D N.Y.) Sept. 25, 1953– ; House Feb. 5, 1998– .

Meeks, James Andrew (D Ill.) March 7, 1864–Nov. 10, 1946; House 1933–39.

Meigs, Henry (– N.Y.) Oct. 28, 1782–May 20, 1861; House 1819–21.

Meigs, Return Jonathan Jr. (R Ohio) Nov. 17, 1764–March 29, 1825; Senate Dec. 12, 1808–May 1, 1810; Gov. Dec. 8, 1810–March 24, 1814 (Democratic Republican); Postmaster Gen. April 11, 1814–June 30, 1823.

Meiklejohn, George de Rue (R Neb.) Aug. 26, 1857–April 19, 1929; House 1893–97.

Melcher, John (D Mont.) Sept. 6, 1924– ; House June 24, 1969–77; Senate 1977–89.

Mellen, Prentiss (– Mass.) Oct. 11, 1764–Dec. 31, 1840; Senate June 5, 1818–May 15, 1820.

Mellish, David Batcheller (R N.Y.) Jan. 2, 1831–May 23, 1874; House 1873–May 23, 1874.

Menefee, Richard Hickman (W Ky.) Dec. 4, 1809–Feb. 21, 1841; House 1837–39.

Menendez, Robert (D N.J.) Jan. 1, 1954– ; House 1993– .

Menges, Franklin (R Pa.) Oct. 26, 1858–May 12, 1956; House 1925–31.

Menzies, John William (U Ky.) April 12, 1819–Oct. 3, 1897; House 1861–63.

Mercer, Charles Fenton (cousin of Robert Selden Garnett) (W Va.) June 16, 1778–May 4, 1858; House 1817–Dec. 26, 1839 (1817–31 Federalist, 1831–35 Anti-Jacksonian).

Mercer, David Henry (R Neb.) July 9, 1857–Jan. 10, 1919; House 1893–1903.

Mercer, John Francis (– Md.) May 17, 1759–Aug. 30, 1821; House Feb. 5, 1792–April 13, 1794; Cont. Cong. 1783–84 (Va.); Gov. Nov. 10, 1801–Nov. 15, 1803 (Democratic Republican).

Mercur, Ulysses (R Pa.) Aug. 12, 1818–June 6, 1887; House 1865–Dec. 2, 1872.

Meredith, Elisha Edward (D Va.) Dec. 26, 1848–July 29, 1900; House Dec. 9, 1891–97.

Meriwether, David (father of James Meriwether, grandfather of James A. Meriwether) (R Ga.) April 10, 1755–Nov. 16, 1822; House Dec. 6, 1802–07.

Meriwether, David (D Ky.) Oct. 30, 1800–April 4, 1893; Senate July 6–Aug. 31, 1852; Gov. (N.M. Terr.) 1853–55.

Meriwether, James (son of David Meriwether born in 1775, uncle of James A. Meriwether) (– Ga.) 1789–1854; House 1825–27.

Meriwether, James A. (nephew of James Meriwether, grandson of David Meriwether born in 1775) (W Ga.) Sept. 20, 1806–April 18, 1852; House 1841–43.

Merriam, Clinton Levi (R N.Y.) March 25, 1824–Feb. 18, 1900; House 1871–75.

Merrick, William Duhurst (father of William Matthew Merrick) (W Md.) Oct. 25, 1793–Feb. 5, 1857; Senate Jan. 4, 1838–45.

Merrick, William Matthew (son of William Duhurst Merrick) (D Md.) Sept. 1, 1818–Feb. 4, 1889; House 1871–73.

Merrill, D. Bailey (R Ind.) Nov. 22, 1912– ; House 1953–55.

Merrill, Orsamus Cook (R Vt.) June 18, 1775–April 12, 1865; House 1817–Jan. 12, 1820.

Merriman, Truman Adams (D N.Y.) Sept. 5, 1839–April 16, 1892; House 1885–89 (1885–87 Independent Democrat).

Merrimon, Augustus Summerfield (D N.C.) Sept. 15, 1830–Nov. 14, 1892; Senate 1873–79.

Merritt, Edwin Albert (R N.Y.) July 25, 1860–Dec. 4, 1914; House Nov. 5, 1912–Dec. 4, 1914.

Merritt, Matthew Joseph (D N.Y.) April 2, 1895–Sept. 29, 1946; House 1935–45.

Merritt, Samuel Augustus (D Idaho) Aug. 15, 1827–Sept. 8, 1910; House (Terr. Del.) 1871–73.

Merritt, Schuyler (R Conn.) Dec. 16, 1853–April 1, 1953; House Nov. 6, 1917–31, 1933–37.

Merrow, Chester Earl (R N.H.) Nov. 15, 1906–Feb. 10, 1974; House 1943–63.

Merwin, Orange (– Conn.) April 7, 1777–Sept. 4, 1853; House 1825–29.

Mesick, William Smith (R Mich.) Aug. 26, 1856–Dec. 1, 1942; House 1897–1901.

Meskill, Thomas Joseph (R Conn.) Jan. 30, 1928– ; House 1967–71; Gov. Jan. 6, 1971–Jan. 8, 1975.

Metcalf, Arunah (R N.Y.) Aug. 15, 1771–Aug. 15, 1848; House 1811–13.

Metcalf, Jack (R Wash.) Nov. 30, 1927– ; House 1995–97.

Metcalf, Jesse Houghton (R R.I.) Nov. 16, 1860–Oct. 9, 1942; Senate Nov. 5, 1924–37.

Metcalf, Lee Warren (D Mont.) Jan. 28, 1911–Jan. 12, 1978; House 1953–61; Senate 1961–Jan. 12, 1978.

Metcalf, Victor Howard (R Calif.) Oct. 10, 1853–Feb. 20, 1936; House 1899–July 1, 1904; Secy. of Commerce and Labor July 1, 1904–Dec. 16, 1906; Secy of the Navy Dec. 17, 1906–Nov. 30, 1908.

Metcalfe, Henry Bleecker (D N.Y.) Jan. 20, 1805–Feb. 7, 1881; House 1875–77.

Metcalfe, Lyne Shackelford (R Mo.) April 21, 1822–Jan. 31, 1906; House 1877–79.

Metcalfe, Ralph Harold (D Ill.) May 29, 1910–Oct. 10, 1978; House 1971–Oct. 10, 1978.

Metcalfe, Thomas (W Ky.) March 20, 1780–Aug. 18, 1855; House 1819–June 1, 1828 (no party); Senate June 23, 1848–49; Gov. June 1, 1828–June 1, 1832 (National Republican).

Metz, Herman August (D N.Y.) Oct. 19, 1867–May 17, 1934; House 1913–15.

Metzenbaum, Howard Morton (D Ohio) June 4, 1917– ; Senate Jan. 4–Dec. 23, 1974, Dec. 29, 1976–95.

Meyer, Adolph (D La.) Oct. 19, 1842–March 8, 1908; House 1891–March 8, 1908.

Meyer, Herbert Alton (R Kan.) Aug. 30, 1886–Oct. 2, 1950; House 1947–Oct. 2, 1950.

Meyer, John Ambrose (D Md.) May 15, 1899–Oct. 2, 1969; House 1941–43.

Meyer, William Henry (D Vt.) Dec. 29, 1914–Dec. 16, 1983; House 1959–61.

Meyers, Benjamin Franklin (D Pa.) July 6, 1833–Aug. 11, 1918; House 1871–73.

Meyers, Jan (R Kan.) July 20, 1928– ; House 1985–97; Chrwmn. House Small Business 1995–97.

Meyner, Helen Stevenson (D N.J.) March 5, 1929–Nov. 2, 1997; House 1975–79.

Mezvinsky, Edward Maurice (D Iowa) Jan. 17, 1937– ; House 1973–77.

Mfume, Kweisi (D Md.) Oct. 24, 1948– ; House 1987–Feb. 18, 1996.

Mica, Daniel Andrew (D Fla.) Feb. 4, 1944– ; House 1979–89.

Mica, John L. (R Fla.) Jan. 27, 1943– ; House 1993– .

Michaelson, Magne Alfred (R Ill.) Sept. 7, 1878–Oct. 26, 1949; House 1921–31.

Michalek, Anthony (R Ill.) Jan. 16, 1878–Dec. 21, 1916; House 1905–07.

Michel, Robert Henry (R Ill.) March 2, 1923– ; House 1957–95; House minority leader 1981–95.

Michener, Earl Cory (R Mich.) Nov. 30, 1876–July 4, 1957; House 1919–33, 1935–51; Chrmn. House Judiciary 1947–49.

Mickey, J. Ross (D Ill.) Jan. 5, 1856–March 20, 1928; House 1901–03.

Middlesworth, Ner (W Pa.) Dec. 12, 1783–June 2, 1865; House 1853–55.

Middleton, George (D N.J.) Oct. 14, 1800–Dec. 31, 1888; House 1863–65.

Middleton, Henry (R S.C.) Sept. 28, 1770–June 14, 1846; House 1815–19; Gov. Dec. 10, 1810–Dec. 10, 1812.

Miers, Robert Walter (D Ind.) Jan. 27, 1848–Feb. 20, 1930; House 1897–1905.

Mikulski, Barbara Ann (D Md.) July 20, 1936– ; House 1977–87; Senate 1987– .

Mikva, Abner Joseph (D Ill.) Jan. 21, 1926– ; House 1969–73, 1975–Sept. 26, 1979.

Miles, Frederick (R Conn.) Dec. 19, 1815–Nov. 20, 1896; House 1879–83, 1889–91.

Miles, John Esten (D N.M.) July 28, 1884–Oct. 7, 1971; House 1949–51; Gov. Jan. 1, 1939–Jan. 1, 1943.

Miles, Joshua Weldon (D Md.) Dec. 9, 1858–March 4, 1929; House 1895–97.

Miles, William Porcher (D S.C.) July 4, 1822–May 11, 1899; House 1857–Dec. 1860.

Milford, Dale (D Texas) Feb. 18, 1926–Dec. 26, 1997; House 1973–79.

Millard, Charles Dunsmore (R N.Y.) Dec. 1, 1873–Dec. 11, 1944; House 1931–Sept. 29, 1937.

Millard, Joseph Hopkins (R Neb.) April 20, 1836–Jan. 13, 1922; Senate March 28, 1901–07.

Millard, Stephen Columbus (R N.Y.) Jan. 14, 1841–June 21, 1914; House 1883–87.

Milledge, John (R Ga.) 1757–Feb. 9, 1818; House Nov. 22, 1792–93 (no party), 1795–99 (no party), 1801–May 1802; Senate June 19, 1806–Nov. 14, 1809; elected Pres. pro tempore Jan. 30, 1809; Gov. Nov. 4, 1802–Sept. 23, 1806 (Democratic Republican).

Millen, John (D Ga.) 1804–Oct. 15, 1843; House March 4–Oct. 15, 1843.

Millender-McDonald, Juanita (D Calif.) Sept. 7, 1938– ; House April 16, 1996– .

Miller, Arthur Lewis (R Neb.) May 24, 1892–March 16, 1967; House 1943–59; Chrmn. House Interior and Insular Affairs 1953–55.

Miller, Bert Henry (D Idaho) Dec. 15, 1879–Oct. 8, 1949; Senate Jan. 3–Oct. 8, 1949.

Miller, Clarence Benjamin (R Minn.) March 13, 1872–Jan. 10, 1922; House 1909–19.

Miller, Clarence E. (R Ohio) Nov. 1, 1917– ; House 1967–93.

Miller, Clement Woodnutt (nephew of Thomas Woodnutt Miller) (D Calif.) Oct. 28, 1916–Oct. 7, 1962; House 1959–Oct. 7, 1962.

Miller, Daniel (R Fla.) May 30, 1942– ; House 1993– .

Miller, Daniel Fry (W Iowa) Oct. 4, 1814–Dec. 9, 1895; House Dec. 20, 1850–51.

Miller, Daniel H. (J Pa.) ?–1846; House 1823–31 (1823–27 no party).

Miller, Edward Edwin (R Ill.) July 22, 1880–Aug. 1, 1946; House 1923–25.

Miller, Edward Tylor (R Md.) Feb. 1, 1895–Jan. 20, 1968; House 1947–59.

Miller, Gary G. (R Calif.) Oct. 16, 1948– ; House 1999– .

Miller, George (D Calif.) May 17, 1945– ; House 1975– ; Chrmn. House Interior and Insular Affairs 1991–95; Chrmn. House Merchant Marine and Fisheries 1993–95.

Miller, George Funston (R Pa.) Sept. 5, 1809–Oct. 21, 1885; House 1865–69.

Miller, George Paul (D Calif.) Jan. 15, 1891–Dec. 29, 1982; House 1945–73; Chrmn. House Science and Astronautics 1961–73.

Miller, Homer Virgil Milton (D Ga.) April 29, 1814–May 31, 1896; Senate Feb. 24–March 3, 1871.

Miller, Howard Shultz (D Kan.) Feb. 27, 1879–Jan. 2, 1970; House 1953–55.

Miller, Jack Richard (R Iowa) June 6, 1916–Aug. 29, 1994; Senate 1961–73.

Miller, Jacob Welsh (W N.J.) Aug. 29, 1800–Sept. 30, 1862; Senate 1841–53.

Miller, James Francis (D Texas) Aug. 1, 1830–July 3, 1902; House 1883–87.

Miller, James Monroe (R Kan.) May 6, 1852–Jan. 20, 1926; House 1899–1911.

Miller, Jesse (father of William Henry Miller) (J Pa.) 1800–Aug. 20, 1850; House 1833–Oct. 30, 1836.

Miller, John (– N.Y.) Nov. 10, 1774–March 31, 1862; House 1825–27.

Miller, John (D Mo.) Nov. 25, 1781–March 18, 1846; House 1837–43; Gov. Jan. 20, 1826–Nov. 14, 1832 (Jacksonian).

Miller, John Elvis (D Ark.) May 15, 1888–Jan. 30, 1981; House 1931–Nov. 14, 1937; Senate Nov. 15, 1937–March 31, 1941.

Miller, John Franklin (uncle of John Franklin Miller, below) (R Calif.) Nov. 21, 1831–March 8, 1886; Senate 1881–March 8, 1886.

Miller, John Franklin (nephew of John Franklin Miller, above) (R Wash.) June 9, 1862–May 28, 1936; House 1917–31.

Miller, John Gaines (W Mo.) Nov. 29, 1812–May 11, 1856; House 1851–May 11, 1856.

Miller, John Krepps (D Ohio) May 25, 1819–Aug. 11, 1863; House 1847–51.

Miller, John Ripin (R Wash.) May 23, 1938– ; House 1985–93.

Miller, Joseph (D Ohio) Sept. 9, 1819–May 27, 1862; House 1857–59.

Miller, Killian (W N.Y.) July 30, 1785–Jan. 9, 1859; House 1855–57.

Miller, Louis Ebenezer (R Mo.) April 30, 1899–Nov. 1, 1952; House 1943–45.

Miller, Lucas Miltiades (D Wis.) Sept. 15, 1824–Dec. 4, 1902; House 1891–93.

Miller, Morris Smith (father of Rutger Bleecker Miller) (F N.Y.) July 31, 1779–Nov. 16, 1824; House 1813–15.

Miller, Orrin Larrabee (R Kan.) Jan. 11, 1856–Sept. 11, 1926; House 1895–97.

Miller, Pleasant Moorman (R Tenn.) ?–1849; House 1809–11.

Miller, Rutger Bleecker (son of Morris Smith Miller) (J N.Y.) July 28, 1805–Nov. 12, 1877; House Nov. 9, 1836–37.

Miller, Samuel Franklin (R N.Y.) May 27, 1827–March 16, 1892; House 1863–65, 1875–77.

Miller, Samuel Henry (R Pa.) April 19, 1840–Sept. 4, 1918; House 1881–85, 1915–17.

Miller, Smith (D Ind.) May 30, 1804–March 21, 1872; House 1853–57.

Miller, Stephen Decatur (N S.C.) May 8, 1787–March 8, 1838; House Jan. 2, 1817–19 (no party); Senate 1831–March 2, 1833; Gov. Dec. 10, 1828–Dec. 9, 1830 (Democrat).

Miller, Thomas Byron (R Pa.) Aug. 11, 1896–March 20, 1976; House May 9, 1942–45.

Miller, Thomas Ezekiel (R S.C.) June 17, 1849–April 8, 1938; House Sept. 24, 1890–91.

Miller, Thomas Woodnutt (uncle of Clement Woodnutt Miller) (R Del.) June 26, 1886–May 5, 1973; House 1915–17.

Miller, Ward MacLaughlin (R Ohio) Nov. 29, 1902–March 11, 1984; House Nov. 8, 1960–61.

Miller, Warner (R N.Y.) Aug. 12, 1838–March 21, 1918; House 1879–July 26, 1881; Senate July 27, 1881–87.

Miller, Warren (R W.Va.) April 2, 1847–Dec. 29, 1920; House 1895–99.

Miller, William Edward (R N.Y.) March 22, 1914–June 24, 1983; House 1951–65; Chrmn. Rep. Nat. Comm. June 1960–July 1964.

Miller, William Henry (son of Jesse Miller) (D Pa.) Feb. 28, 1829–Sept. 12, 1870; House 1863–65.

Miller, William Jennings (R Conn.) March 12, 1899–Nov. 22, 1950; House 1939–41, 1943–45, 1947–49.

Miller, William Starr (AP N.Y.) Aug. 22, 1793–Nov. 9, 1854; House 1845–47.

Milligan, Jacob Le Roy (D Mo.) March 9, 1889–March 9, 1951; House Feb. 14, 1920–21, 1923–35.

Milligan, John Jones (W Del.) Dec. 10, 1795–April 20, 1875; House 1831–39 (1831–33 Anti-Jacksonian).

Milliken, Charles William (D Ky.) Aug. 15, 1827–Oct. 16, 1915; House 1873–77.

Milliken, Seth Llewellyn (R Maine) Dec. 12, 1831–April 18, 1897; House 1883–April 18, 1897.

Milliken, William H. Jr. (R Pa.) Aug. 19, 1897–July 4, 1969; House 1959–65.

Millikin, Eugene Donald (R Colo.) Feb. 12, 1891–July 26, 1958; Senate Dec. 20, 1941–57; Chrmn. Senate Finance 1947–49, 1953–55.

Millington, Charles Stephen (R N.Y.) March 13, 1855–Oct. 25, 1913; House 1909–11.

Mills, Daniel Webster (R Ill.) Feb. 25, 1838–Dec. 16, 1904; House 1897–99.

Mills, Elijah Hunt (F Mass.) Dec. 1, 1776–May 5, 1829; House 1815–19; Senate June 12, 1820–27.

Mills, Newt Virgus (D La.) Sept. 27, 1899–May 7, 1996; House 1937–43.

Mills, Ogden Livingston (R N.Y.) Aug. 23, 1884–Oct. 11, 1937; House 1921–27; Secy. of the Treasury Feb. 13, 1932–March 4, 1933.

Mills, Roger Quarles (D Texas) March 30, 1832–Sept. 2, 1911; House 1873–March 28, 1892; Senate March 29, 1892–99.

Mills, Wilbur Daigh (D Ark.) May 24, 1909–May 2, 1992; House 1939–77; Chrmn. House Ways and Means 1958–75.

Mills, William Oswald (R Md.) Aug. 12, 1924–May 24, 1973; House May 27, 1971–May 24, 1973.

Millson, John Singleton (D Va.) Oct. 1, 1808–March 1, 1874; House 1849–61.

Millspaugh, Frank Crenshaw (R Mo.) Jan. 14, 1872–July 8, 1947; House 1921–Dec. 5, 1922.

Millward, William (R Pa.) June 30, 1822–Nov. 28, 1871; House 1855–57 (Whig), 1859–61.

Milnes, Alfred (R Mich.) May 28, 1844–Jan. 15, 1916; House Dec. 2, 1895–97.

Milnes, William Jr. (C Va.) Dec. 8, 1827–Aug. 14, 1889; House Jan. 27, 1870–71.

Milnor, James (F Pa.) June 20, 1773–April 8, 1844; House 1811–13.

Milnor, William (F Pa.) June 26, 1769–Dec. 13, 1848; House 1807–11, 1815–17, 1821–May 8, 1822.

Milton, John Gerald (D N.J.) Jan. 21, 1881–April 14, 1977; Senate Jan. 18–Nov. 8, 1938.

Milton, William Hall (D Fla.) March 2, 1864–Jan. 4, 1942; Senate March 27, 1908–09.

Minahan, Daniel Francis (D N.J.) Aug. 8, 1877–April 29, 1947; House 1919–21, 1923–25.

Miner, Ahiman Louis (W Vt.) Sept. 23, 1804–July 19, 1886; House 1851–53.

Miner, Charles (F Pa.) Feb. 1, 1780–Oct. 26, 1865; House 1825–29.

Miner, Henry Clay (D N.Y.) March 23, 1842–Feb. 22, 1900; House 1895–97.

Miner, Phineas (– Conn.) Nov. 27, 1777–Sept. 15, 1839; House Dec. 1, 1834–35.

Mineta, Norman Yoshio (D Calif.) Nov. 12, 1931– ; House 1975–Oct. 10, 1995; Chrmn. House Public Works and Transportation 1993–95.

Minge, David (D Minn.) March 19, 1942– ; House 1993– .

Minish, Joseph George (D N.J.) Sept. 1, 1916– ; House 1963–85.

Mink, Patsy Takemoto (D Hawaii) Dec. 6, 1927– ; House 1965–77, Sept. 27, 1990– .

Minor, Edward Sloman (R Wis.) Dec. 13, 1840–July 26, 1924; House 1895–1907.

Minshall, William Edwin Jr. (R Ohio) Oct. 24, 1911–Oct. 15, 1990; House 1955–Dec. 31, 1974.

Minton, Sherman (D Ind.) Oct. 20, 1890–April 9, 1965; Senate 1935–41; Assoc. Justice Supreme Court Oct. 12, 1949–Oct. 15, 1956.

Mitchel, Charles Burton (D Ark.) Sept. 19, 1815–Sept. 20, 1864; Senate March 4–July 11, 1861.

Mitchell, Alexander (father of John Lendrum Mitchell) (D Wis.) Oct. 18, 1817–April 19, 1887; House 1871–75.

Mitchell, Alexander Clark (R Kan.) Oct. 11, 1860–July 7, 1911; House March 4–July 7, 1911.

Mitchell, Anderson (W N.C.) June 13, 1800–Dec. 24, 1876; House April 27, 1842–43.

Mitchell, Arthur Wergs (D Ill.) Dec. 22, 1883–May 9, 1968; House 1935–43.

Mitchell, Charles F. (W N.Y.) about 1808–?; House 1837–41.

Mitchell, Charles Le Moyne (D Conn.) Aug. 6, 1844–March 1, 1890; House 1883–87.

Mitchell, Donald Jerome (R N.Y.) May 8, 1923– ; House 1973–83.

Mitchell, Edward Archibald (R Ind.) Dec. 2, 1910–Dec. 11, 1979; House 1947–49.

Mitchell, George Edward (J Md.) March 3, 1781–June 28, 1832; House 1823–27 (no party), Dec. 7, 1829–June 28, 1832.

Mitchell, George John (D Maine) Aug. 20, 1933– ; Senate May 19, 1980–95; Senate majority leader 1989–95.

Mitchell, Harlan Erwin (D Ga.) Aug. 17, 1924– ; House Jan. 8, 1958–61.

Mitchell, Henry (J N.Y.) 1784–Jan. 12, 1856; House 1833–35.

Mitchell, Hugh Burnton (D Wash.) March 22, 1907–June 10, 1996; Senate Jan. 10, 1945–Dec. 25, 1946; House 1949–53.

Mitchell, James Coffield (– Tenn.) March 1786–Aug. 7, 1843; House 1825–29.

Mitchell, James S. (– Pa.) 1784–1844; House 1821–27.

Mitchell, John (– Pa.) March 8, 1781–Aug. 3, 1849; House 1825–29.

Mitchell, John Hipple (R Ore.) June 22, 1835–Dec. 8, 1905; Senate 1873–79, Nov. 18, 1885–97, 1901–Dec. 8, 1905.

Mitchell, John Inscho (R Pa.) July 28, 1838–Aug. 20, 1907; House 1877–81; Senate 1881–87.

Mitchell, John Joseph (D Mass.) May 9, 1873–Sept. 13, 1925; House Nov. 8, 1910–11, April 15, 1913–15.

Mitchell, John Lendrum (son of Alexander Mitchell) (D Wis.) Oct. 19, 1842–June 29, 1904; House 1891–93; Senate 1893–99.

Mitchell, John Murry (R N.Y.) March 18, 1858–May 31, 1905; House June 2, 1896–99.

Mitchell, John Ridley (D Tenn.) Sept. 26, 1877–Feb. 26, 1962; House 1931–39.

Mitchell, Nahum (F Mass.) Feb. 12, 1769–Aug. 1, 1853; House 1803–05.

Mitchell, Parren James (D Md.) April 29, 1922– ; House 1971–87; Chrmn. House Small Business 1981–87.

Mitchell, Robert (J Ohio) 1778–Nov. 13, 1848; House 1833–35.

Mitchell, Stephen Mix (– Conn.) Dec. 9, 1743–Sept. 30, 1835; Senate Dec. 2, 1793–95; Cont. Cong. 1785–88.

Mitchell, Thomas Rothmaler (J S.C.) May 1783–Nov. 2, 1837; House 1821–23 (no party), 1825–29 (no party), 1831–33.

Mitchell, William (R Ind.) Jan. 19, 1807–Sept. 11, 1865; House 1861–63.

Mitchill, Samuel Latham (R N.Y.) Aug. 20, 1764–Sept. 7, 1831; House 1801–Nov. 22, 1804, Dec. 4, 1810–13; Senate Nov. 23, 1804–09.

Mize, Chester Louis (R Kan.) Dec. 25, 1917–Jan. 11, 1994; House 1965–71.

Mizell, Wilmer David (R N.C.) Aug. 13, 1930–Feb. 21, 1999; House 1969–75.

Moakley, John Joseph (D Mass.) April 27, 1927– ; House 1973– (elected as an Independent Democrat, changed party affiliation to Democrat effective Jan. 2, 1973); Chrmn. House Rules 1989–95.

Mobley, William Carlton (D Ga.) Dec. 7, 1906–Oct. 14, 1981; House March 2, 1932–33.

Moeller, Walter Henry (D Ohio) March 15, 1910–April 13, 1999; House 1959–63, 1965–67.

Moffatt, Seth Crittenden (R Mich.) Aug. 10, 1841–Dec. 22, 1887; House 1885–Dec. 22, 1887.

Moffet, John (D Pa.) April 5, 1831–June 19, 1884; House March 4–April 9, 1869.

Moffett, Anthony John "Toby" Jr. (D Conn.) Aug. 18, 1944– ; House 1975–83.

Moffitt, Hosea (F N.Y.) Nov. 17, 1757–Aug. 31, 1825; House 1813–17.

Moffitt, John Henry (R N.Y.) Jan. 8, 1843–Aug. 14, 1926; House 1887–91.

Molinari, Guy Victor (father of Susan Molinari, father-in-law of L. William Paxon) (R N.Y.) Nov. 23, 1928– ; House 1981–Jan. 1, 1990.

Molinari, Susan (wife of L. William Paxon, daughter of Guy Victor Molinari) (R N.Y.) March 27, 1958– ; House March 27, 1990–Aug. 1, 1997.

Mollohan, Alan Bowlby (son of Robert Homer Mollohan) (D W.Va.) May 14, 1943– ; House 1983– .

Mollohan, Robert Homer (father of Alan Bowlby Mollohan) (D W.Va.) Sept. 18, 1909–Aug. 3, 1999; House 1953–57, 1969–83.

Molony, Richard Sheppard (D Ill.) June 28, 1811–Dec. 14, 1891; House 1851–53.

Monagan, John Stephen (D Conn.) Dec. 23, 1911– ; House 1959–73.

Monaghan, Joseph Patrick (D Mont.) March 26, 1906–July 4, 1985; House 1933–37.

Monahan, James Gideon (R Wis.) Jan. 12, 1855–Dec. 5, 1923; House 1919–21.

Monast, Louis (R R.I.) July 1, 1863–April 16, 1936; House 1927–29.

Mondale, Walter Frederick "Fritz" (D Minn.) Jan. 5, 1928– ; Senate Dec. 30, 1964–Dec. 30, 1976; Vice–President 1977–81.

Mondell, Franklin Wheeler (R Wyo.) Nov. 6, 1860–Aug. 6, 1939; House 1895–97, 1899–1923; House majority leader 1919–23.

Monell, Robert (J N.Y.) 1786–Nov. 29, 1860; House 1819–21 (no party), 1829–Feb. 21, 1831.

Money, Hernando De Soto (D Miss.) Aug. 26, 1839–Sept. 18, 1912; House 1875–85, 1893–97; Senate Oct. 8, 1897–1911.

Monkiewicz, Boleslaus Joseph (R Conn.) Aug. 8, 1898–July 2, 1971; House 1939–41, 1943–45.

Monroe, James (uncle of James Monroe, below) (– Va.) April 28, 1758–July 4, 1831; Senate Nov. 9, 1790–May 27, 1794; Cont. Cong. 1783–86; Gov. Dec. 1, 1799–Dec. 1, 1802 (Democratic Republican), Jan. 16–April 3, 1811 (Democratic Republican); Secy. of State April 6, 1811–Sept. 30, 1814, Feb. 28, 1815–March 3, 1817; Secy. of War Oct. 1, 1814–Feb. 28, 1815; President 1817–25 (Democratic Republican).

Monroe, James (nephew of James Monroe, above) (W N.Y.) Sept. 10, 1799–Sept. 7, 1870; House 1839–41.

Monroe, James (R Ohio) July 18, 1821–July 6, 1898; House 1871–81.

Monroney, Almer Stillwell Mike (D Okla.) March 2, 1902–Feb. 13, 1980; House 1939–51; Senate 1951–69; Chrmn. Senate Post Office and Civil Service 1965–69.

Monson, David Smith (R Utah) June 20, 1945– ; House 1985–87.

Montague, Andrew Jackson (D Va.) Oct. 3, 1862–Jan. 24, 1937; House 1913–Jan. 24, 1937; Gov. Jan. 1, 1902–Feb. 1, 1906.

Montet, Numa Francois (D La.) Sept. 17, 1892–Oct. 12, 1985; House Aug. 6, 1929–37.

Montgomery, Alexander Brooks (D Ky.) Dec. 11, 1837–Dec. 27, 1910; House 1887–95.

Montgomery, Daniel Jr. (R Pa.) Oct. 30, 1765–Dec. 30, 1831; House 1807–09.

Montgomery, Gillespie V. "Sonny" (D Miss.) Aug. 5, 1920– ; House 1967–97; Chrmn. House Veterans' Affairs 1981–95.

Montgomery, John (R Md.) 1764–July 17, 1828; House 1807–April 29, 1811.

Montgomery, John Gallagher (D Pa.) June 27, 1805–April 24, 1857; House March 4–April 24, 1857.

Montgomery, Samuel James (R Okla.) Dec. 1, 1896–June 4, 1957; House 1925–27.

Montgomery, Thomas (R Ky.) 1779–April 2, 1828; House 1813–15, Aug. 1, 1820–23.

Montgomery, William (– Pa.) Aug. 3, 1736–May 1, 1816; House 1793–95; Cont. Cong. (elected but did not attend) 1784.

Montgomery, William (D N.C.) Dec. 29, 1789–Nov. 27, 1844; House 1835–41 (1835–37 Jacksonian).

Montgomery, William (D Pa.) April 11, 1818–April 28, 1870; House 1857–61.

Montoya, Joseph Manuel (D N.M.) Sept. 24, 1915–June 5, 1978; House April 9, 1957–Nov. 3, 1964; Senate Nov. 4, 1964–77.

Montoya, Nestor (R N.M.) April 14, 1862–Jan. 13, 1923; House 1921–Jan. 13, 1923.

Moody, Arthur Edson Blair (D Mich.) Feb. 13, 1902–July 20, 1954; Senate April 23, 1951–Nov. 4, 1952.

Moody, Gideon Curtis (R S.D.) Oct. 16, 1832–March 17, 1904; Senate Nov. 2, 1889–91.

Moody, James Montraville (R N.C.) Feb. 12, 1858–Feb. 5, 1903; House 1901–Feb. 5, 1903.

Moody, Jim (D Wis.) Sept. 2, 1935– ; House 1983–93.

Moody, Malcolm Adelbert (R Ore.) Nov. 30, 1854–March 19, 1925; House 1899–1903.

Moody, William Henry (R Mass.) Dec. 23, 1853–July 2, 1917; House Nov. 5, 1895–May 1, 1902; Secy. of the Navy May 1, 1902–June 30, 1904; Atty. Gen. July 1, 1904–Dec. 17, 1906; Assoc. Justice Supreme Court Dec. 17, 1906–Nov. 20, 1910.

Moon, John Austin (D Tenn.) April 22, 1855–June 26, 1921; House 1897–1921.

Moon, John Wesley (R Mich.) Jan. 18, 1836–April 5, 1898; House 1893–95.

Moon, Reuben Osborne (R Pa.) July 22, 1847–Oct. 25, 1919; House Nov. 2, 1903–13.

Mooney, Charles Anthony (D Ohio) Jan. 5, 1879–May 29, 1931; House 1919–21, 1923–May 29, 1931.

Mooney, William Crittenden (R Ohio) June 15, 1855–July 24, 1918; House 1915–17.

Moor, Wyman Bradbury Seavy (D Maine) Nov. 11, 1811–March 10, 1869; Senate Jan. 5–June 7, 1848.

Moore, Allen Francis (R Ill.) Sept. 30, 1869–Aug. 18, 1945; House 1921–25.

Moore, Andrew (father of Samuel McDowell Moore) (– Va.) 1752–April 14, 1821; House 1789–97, March 5–Aug. 11, 1804; Senate Aug. 11, 1804–09.

Moore, Arch Alfred Jr. (R W.Va.) April 16, 1923– ; House 1957–69; Gov. Jan. 13, 1969–Jan. 17, 1977, Jan. 14, 1985–Jan. 16, 1989.

Moore, Arthur Harry (D N.J.) July 3, 1879–Nov. 18, 1952; Senate 1935–Jan. 17, 1938; Gov. Jan. 19, 1926–Jan. 15, 1929, Jan. 19, 1932–Jan. 3, 1935, Jan. 18, 1938–Jan. 21, 1941.

Moore, Charles Ellis (R Ohio) Jan. 3, 1884–April 2, 1941; House 1919–33.

Moore, Dennis (D Kan.) Nov. 8, 1945– ; House 1999– .

Moore, Edward Hall (R Okla.) Nov. 19, 1871–Sept. 2, 1950; Senate 1943–49.

Moore, Eliakim Hastings (R Ohio) June 19, 1812–April 4, 1900; House 1869–71.

Moore, Ely (D N.Y.) July 4, 1798–Jan. 27, 1860; House 1835–39 (1835–37 Jacksonian).

Moore, Gabriel (– Ala.) about 1785–1845; House 1821–29; Senate 1831–37; Gov. Nov. 25, 1829–March 3, 1831.

Moore, Heman Allen (D Ohio) Aug. 27, 1809–April 3, 1844; House 1843–April 3, 1844.

Moore, Henry Dunning (W Pa.) April 13, 1817–Aug. 11, 1887; House 1849–53.

Moore, Horace Ladd (D Kan.) Feb. 25, 1837–May 1, 1914; House Aug. 2, 1894–95.

Moore, Jesse Hale (R Ill.) April 22, 1817–July 11, 1883; House 1869–73.

Moore, John (W La.) 1788–June 17, 1867; House Dec. 17, 1840–43, 1851–53.

Moore, John Matthew (D Texas) Nov. 18, 1862–Feb. 3, 1940; House June 6, 1905–13.

Moore, John William (D Ky.) June 9, 1877–Dec. 11, 1941; House Nov. 3, 1925–29, June 1, 1929–33.

Moore, Joseph Hampton (R Pa.) March 8, 1864–May 2, 1950; House Nov. 6, 1906–Jan. 4, 1920.

Moore, Laban Theodore (O Ky.) Jan. 13, 1829–Nov. 9, 1892; House 1859–61.

Moore, Littleton Wilde (D Texas) March 25, 1835–Oct. 29, 1911; House 1887–93.

Moore, Nicholas Ruxton (R Md.) July 21, 1756–Oct. 7, 1816; House 1803–11, 1813–15.

Moore, Orren Cheney (R N.H.) Aug. 10, 1839–May 12, 1893; House 1889–91.

Moore, Oscar Fitzallen (R Ohio) Jan. 27, 1817–June 24, 1885; House 1855–57.

Moore, Paul John (D N.J.) Aug. 5, 1868–Jan. 10, 1938; House 1927–29.

Moore, Robert (grandfather of Michael Daniel Harter) (R Pa.) March 30, 1778–Jan. 14, 1831; House 1817–21.

Moore, Robert Lee (D Ga.) Nov. 27, 1867–Jan. 14, 1940; House 1923–25.

Moore, Robert Walton (D Va.) Feb. 6, 1859–Feb. 8, 1941; House May 27, 1919–31.

Moore, Samuel (R Pa.) Feb. 8, 1774–Feb. 18, 1861; House Oct. 13, 1818–May 20, 1822.

Moore, Samuel McDowell (son of Andrew Moore) (AJ Va.) Feb. 9, 1796–Sept. 17, 1875; House 1833–35.

Moore, Sydenham (D Ala.) May 25, 1817–May 31, 1862; House 1857–Jan. 21, 1861.

Moore, Thomas (R S.C.) 1759–July 11, 1822; House 1801–13, 1815–17.

Moore, Thomas Love (– Va.) ?–1862; House Nov. 13, 1820–23.

Moore, Thomas Patrick (– Ky.) 1797–July 21, 1853; House 1823–29.

Moore, William (R N.J.) Dec. 25, 1810–April 26, 1878; House 1867–71.

Moore, William Henson III (R La.) Oct. 4, 1939– ; House Jan. 7, 1975–87.

Moore, William Robert (R Tenn.) March 28, 1830–June 12, 1909; House 1881–83.

Moore, William Sutton (R Pa.) Nov. 18, 1822–Dec. 30, 1877; House 1873–75.

Moorehead, Tom Van Horn (R Ohio) April 12, 1898–Oct. 21, 1979; House 1961–63.

Moores, Merrill (R Ind.) April 21, 1856–Oct. 21, 1929; House 1915–25.

Moorhead, Carlos John (R Calif.) May 6, 1922– ; House 1973–97.

Moorhead, James Kennedy (R Pa.) Sept. 7, 1806–March 6, 1884; House 1859–69.

Moorhead, William Singer (D Pa.) April 8, 1923–Aug. 3, 1987; House 1959–81.

Moorman, Henry DeHaven (D Ky.) June 9, 1880–Feb. 3, 1939; House 1927–29.

Moran, Edward Carleton Jr. (D Maine) Dec. 29, 1894–July 12, 1967; House 1933–37.

Moran, James P. Jr. (D Va.) May 16, 1945– ; House 1991– .

Moran, Jerry (R Kan.) May 29, 1954– ; House 1997– .

Morano, Albert Paul (R Conn.) Jan. 18, 1908–Dec. 16, 1987; House 1951–59.

Morehead, Charles Slaughter (W Ky.) July 7, 1802–Dec. 21, 1868; House 1847–51; Gov. Sept. 1, 1855–Aug. 30, 1859 (American Party).

Morehead, James Turner (W Ky.) May 24, 1797–Dec. 28, 1854; Senate 1841–47; Gov. Feb. 22, 1834–June 1, 1836 (Democrat).

Morehead, James Turner (W N.C.) Jan. 11, 1799–May 5, 1875; House 1851–53.

Morehead, John Henry (D Neb.) Dec. 3, 1861–May 31, 1942; House 1923–35; Gov. Jan. 9, 1913–Jan. 4, 1917.

Morehead, John Motley (R N.C.) July 20, 1866–Dec. 13, 1923; House 1909–11.

Morella, Constance Albanese (R Md.) Feb. 12, 1931– ; House 1987– .

Morey, Frank (R La.) July 11, 1840–Sept. 22, 1889; House 1869–June 8, 1876.

Morey, Henry Lee (R Ohio) April 8, 1841–Dec. 29, 1902; House 1881–June 20, 1884, 1889–91.

Morgan, Charles Henry (R Mo.) July 5, 1842–Jan. 4, 1912; House 1875–79 (Democrat), 1883–85 (Democrat), 1893–95 (Democrat), 1909–11.

Morgan, Christopher (brother of Edwin Barbour Morgan, nephew of Noyes Barber) (W N.Y.) June 4, 1808–April 3, 1877; House 1839–43.

Morgan, Daniel (F Va.) 1736–July 6, 1802; House 1797–99.

Morgan, Dick Thompson (R Okla.) Dec. 6, 1853–July 4, 1920; House 1909–July 4, 1920.

Morgan, Edwin Barber (brother of Christopher Morgan, nephew of Noyes Barber) (R N.Y.) May 2, 1806–Oct. 13, 1881; House 1853–59 (1853–57 Whig).

Morgan, Edwin Dennison (cousin of Morgan Gardner Bulkeley) (R N.Y.) Feb. 8, 1811–Feb. 14, 1883; Senate 1863–69; Chrmn. Rep. Nat. Comm. 1856–64, 1872–76; Gov. Jan. 1, 1859–Jan. 1, 1863.

Morgan, George Washington (D Ohio) Sept. 20, 1820–July 26, 1893; House 1867–June 3, 1868, 1869–73.

Morgan, James (R N.J.) Dec. 29, 1756–Nov. 11, 1822; House 1811–13.

Morgan, James Bright (D Miss.) March 14, 1833–June 18, 1892; House 1885–91.

Morgan, John Jordan (father-in-law of John Adams Dix) (J N.Y.) 1770–July 29, 1849; House 1821–25 (no party), Dec. 1, 1834–35.

Morgan, John Tyler (D Ala.) June 20, 1824–June 11, 1907; Senate 1877–June 11, 1907.

Morgan, Lewis Lovering (D La.) March 2, 1876–June 10, 1950; House Nov. 5, 1912–17.

Morgan, Robert Burren (D N.C.) Oct. 5, 1925– ; Senate 1975–81.

Morgan, Stephen (R Ohio) Jan. 25, 1854–Feb. 9, 1928; House 1899–1905.

Morgan, Thomas Ellsworth (D Pa.) Oct. 13, 1906–July 31, 1995; House 1945–77; Chrmn. House Foreign Affairs 1959–75; Chrmn. House International Relations 1975–77.

Morgan, William Mitchell (R Ohio) Aug. 1, 1870–Sept. 17, 1935; House 1921–31.

Morgan, William Stephen (D Va.) Sept. 7, 1801–Sept. 3, 1878; House 1835–39 (1835–37 Jacksonian).

Morin, John Mary (R Pa.) April 18, 1868–March 3, 1942; House 1913–29.

Moritz, Theodore Leo (D Pa.) Feb. 10, 1892–March 13, 1982; House 1935–37.

Morphis, Joseph Lewis (R Miss.) April 17, 1831–July 29, 1913; House Feb. 23, 1870–73.

Morrell, Daniel Johnson (R Pa.) Aug. 8, 1821–Aug. 20, 1885; House 1867–71.

Morrell, Edward de Veaux (R Pa.) Aug. 7, 1863–Sept. 1, 1917; House Nov. 6, 1900–07.

Morril, David Lawrence (R N.H.) June 10, 1772–Jan. 28, 1849; Senate 1817–23; Gov. June 3, 1824–June 7, 1827.

Morrill, Anson Peaslee (brother of Lot Myrick Morrill) (R Maine) June 10, 1803–July 4, 1887; House 1861–63; Gov. Jan. 3, 1855–Jan. 2, 1856.

Morrill, Edmund Needham (R Kan.) Feb. 12, 1834–March 14, 1909; House 1883–91; Gov. Jan. 14, 1895–Jan. 11, 1897.

Morrill, Justin Smith (R Vt.) April 14, 1810–Dec. 28, 1898; House 1855–67 (1855–57 Whig, 1857–67 Republican); Senate 1867–Dec. 28, 1898 (1867–73 Union Republican).

Morrill, Lot Myrick (brother of Anson Peaslee Morrill) (R Maine) May 3, 1813–Jan. 10, 1883; Senate Jan. 17, 1861–69, Oct. 30, 1869–July 7, 1876; Gov. Jan. 8, 1858–Jan. 2, 1861; Secy. of the Treasury July 7, 1876–March 9, 1877.

Morrill, Samuel Plummer (R Maine) Feb. 11, 1816–Aug. 4, 1892; House 1869–71.

Morris, Calvary (W Ohio) Jan. 15, 1798–Oct. 13, 1871; House 1837–43.

Morris, Daniel (R N.Y.) Jan. 4, 1812–April 22, 1889; House 1863–67.

Morris, Edward Joy (R Pa.) July 16, 1815–Dec. 31, 1881; House 1843–45 (Whig), 1857–June 8, 1861.

Morris, Gouverneur (half–brother of Lewis Morris, uncle of Lewis Robert Morris) (F N.Y.) Jan. 31, 1752–Nov. 6, 1816; Senate April 3, 1800–03; Cont. Cong. 1778–79.

Morris, Isaac Newton (son of Thomas Morris of Ohio, brother of Jonathan David Morris) (D Ill.) Jan. 22, 1812–Oct. 29, 1879; House 1857–61.

Morris, James Remley (son of Joseph Morris) (D Ohio) Jan. 10, 1819–Dec. 24, 1899; House 1861–65.

Morris, Jonathan David (son of Thomas Morris of Ohio, brother of Isaac Newton Morris) (D Ohio) Oct. 8, 1804–May 16, 1875; House 1847–51.

Morris, Joseph (father of James Remley Morris) (D Ohio) Oct. 16, 1795–Oct. 23, 1854; House 1843–47.

Morris, Joseph Watkins (D Ky.) Feb. 26, 1879–Dec. 21, 1937; House Nov. 30, 1923–25.

Morris, Lewis Robert (nephew of Gouverneur Morris) (F Vt.) Nov. 2, 1760–Dec. 29, 1825; House 1797–1803.

Morris, Mathias (W Pa.) Sept. 12, 1787–Nov. 9, 1839; House 1835–39.

Morris, Robert (father of Thomas Morris of N.Y.) (– Pa.) Jan. 20, 1734–May 8, 1806; Senate 1789–95; Cont. Cong. 1775–78.

Morris, Robert Page Walter (R Minn.) June 30, 1853–Dec. 16, 1924; House 1897–1903.

Morris, Samuel Wells (D Pa.) Sept. 1, 1786–May 25, 1847; House 1837–41.

Morris, Thomas (son of Robert Morris) (F N.Y.) Feb. 26, 1771–March 12, 1849; House 1801–03.

Morris, Thomas (father of Isaac Newton Morris and Jonathan David Morris) (J Ohio) Jan. 3, 1776–Dec. 7, 1844; Senate 1833–39.

Morris, Thomas Gayle (D N.M.) Aug. 20, 1919– ; House 1959–69.

Morris, Toby (D Okla.) Feb. 28, 1899–Sept. 1, 1973; House 1947–53, 1957–61.

Morrison, Bruce Andrew (D Conn.) Oct. 8, 1944– ; House 1983–91.

Morrison, Cameron A. (D N.C.) Oct. 5, 1869–Aug. 20, 1953; Senate Dec. 13, 1930–Dec. 4, 1932; House 1943–45; Gov. Jan. 12, 1921–Jan. 14, 1925.

Morrison, George Washington (D N.H.) Oct. 16, 1809–Dec. 21, 1888; House Oct. 8, 1850–51, 1853–55.

Morrison, James Hobson (D La.) Dec. 8, 1908– ; House 1943–67.

Morrison, James Lowery Donaldson (D Ill.) April 12, 1816–Aug. 14, 1888; House Nov. 4, 1856–57.

Morrison, John Alexander (D Pa.) Jan. 31, 1814–July 25, 1904; House 1851–53.

Morrison, Martin Andrew (D Ind.) April 15, 1862–July 9, 1944; House 1909–17.

Morrison, Sidney Wallace (R Wash.) May 13, 1933– ; House 1981–93.

Morrison, William Ralls (D Ill.) Sept. 14, 1824–Sept. 29, 1909; House 1863–65, 1873–87.

Morrissey, John (D N.Y.) Feb. 12, 1831–May 1, 1878; House 1867–71.

Morrow, Dwight Whitney (R N.J.) Jan. 11, 1873–Oct. 5, 1931; Senate Dec. 3, 1930–Oct. 5, 1931.

Morrow, Jeremiah (W Ohio) Oct. 6, 1771–March 22, 1852; House Oct. 17, 1803–13 (Republican), Oct. 13, 1840–43; Senate 1813–19 (Republican); Gov. Dec. 28, 1822–Dec. 19, 1826 (Jacksonian).

Morrow, John (R Va.) ?–?; House 1805–09.

Morrow, John (D N.M.) April 19, 1865–Feb. 25, 1935; House 1923–29.

Morrow, William W. (R Calif.) July 15, 1843–July 24, 1929; House 1885–91.

Morse, Elijah Adams (R Mass.) May 25, 1841–June 5, 1898; House 1889–97.

Morse, Elmer Addison (R Wis.) May 11, 1870–Oct. 4, 1945; House 1907–13.

Morse, Frank Bradford (R Mass.) Aug. 7, 1921–Dec. 18, 1994; House 1961–May 1, 1972.

Morse, Freeman Harlow (R Maine) Feb. 19, 1807–Feb. 5, 1891; House 1843–45 (Whig), 1857–61.

Morse, Isaac Edward (D La.) May 22, 1809–Feb. 11, 1866; House Dec. 2, 1844–51.

Morse, Leopold (– Mass.) Aug. 15, 1831–Dec. 15, 1892; House 1877–85, 1887–89.

Morse, Oliver Andrew (R N.Y.) March 26, 1815–April 20, 1870; House 1857–59.

Morse, Wayne Lyman (D Ore.) Oct. 20, 1900–July 22, 1974; Senate 1945–69 (1945–57 Republican).

Morton, Jackson (brother of Jeremiah Morton) (W Fla.) Aug. 10, 1794–Nov. 20, 1874; Senate 1849–55.

Morton, Jeremiah (brother of Jackson Morton) (W Va.) Sept. 3, 1799–Nov. 28, 1878; House 1849–51.

Morton, Levi Parsons (R N.Y.) May 16, 1824–May 16, 1920; House 1879–March 21, 1881; Vice President 1889–93; Gov. Jan. 1, 1895–Jan. 1, 1897.

Morton, Marcus (R Mass.) Dec. 19, 1784–Feb. 6, 1864; House 1817–21; Gov. Feb. 6–May 26, 1825, Jan. 18, 1840–Jan. 7, 1841, Jan. 17, 1843–Jan. 3, 1844.

Morton, Oliver Hazard Perry Throck (R Ind.) Aug. 4, 1823–Nov. 1, 1877; Senate 1867–Nov. 1, 1877; Gov. Jan. 16, 1861–Jan. 23, 1867.

Morton, Rogers Clark Ballard (brother of Thruston Ballard Morton) (R Md.) Sept. 19, 1914–April 19, 1979; House 1963–Jan. 29, 1971; Chrmn. Rep. Nat. Comm. April 1969–Jan. 1971; Secy. of the Interior Jan. 29, 1971–April 30, 1975; Secy. of Commerce May 1, 1975–Feb. 2, 1976.

Morton, Thruston Ballard (brother of Rogers Clark Ballard Morton) (R Ky.) Aug. 19, 1907–August 14, 1982; House 1947–53; Senate 1957–69; Chrmn. Rep. Nat. Comm. April 1959–June 1961.

Moseley, Jonathan Ogden (F Conn.) April 9, 1762–Sept. 9, 1838; House 1805–21.

Moseley, William Abbott (W N.Y.) Oct. 20, 1798–Nov. 19, 1873; House 1843–47.

Moseley-Braun, Carol (D Ill.) Aug. 16, 1947– ; Senate 1993–99.

Moser, Guy Louis (D Pa.) Jan. 23, 1866–May 9, 1961; House 1937–43.

Moses, Charles Leavell (D Ga.) May 2, 1856–Oct. 10, 1910; House 1891–97.

Moses, George Higgins (R N.H.) Feb. 9, 1869–Dec. 20, 1944; Senate Nov. 6, 1918–33; elected Pres. pro tempore March 6, 1925, Dec. 15, 1927.

Moses, John (D N.D.) June 12, 1885–March 3, 1945; Senate Jan. 3–March 3, 1945; Gov. Jan. 5, 1939–Jan. 4, 1945.

Mosgrove, James (G Pa.) June 14, 1821–Nov. 27, 1900; House 1881–83.

Mosher, Charles Adams (R Ohio) May 7, 1906–Nov. 16, 1984; House 1961–77.

Mosier, Harold Gerard (D Ohio) July 24, 1889–Aug. 7, 1971; House 1937–39.

Moss, Frank Edward (D Utah) Sept. 23, 1911– ; Senate 1959–77; Chrmn. Senate Aeronautical and Space Sciences 1973–77.

Moss, Hunter Holmes Jr. (R W.Va.) May 26, 1874–July 15, 1916; House 1913–July 15, 1916.

Moss, John Emerson (D Calif.) April 13, 1915–Dec. 5, 1997; House 1953–Dec. 31, 1978.

Moss, John McKenzie (nephew of James Andrew McKenzie) (R Ky.) Jan. 3, 1868–June 11, 1929; House March 25, 1902–03.

Moss, Ralph Wilbur (D Ind.) April 21, 1862–April 26, 1919; House 1909–17.

Mott, Gordon Newell (R Nev.) Oct. 21, 1812–April 27, 1887; House (Terr. Del.) 1863–Oct. 31, 1864.

Mott, James (R N.J.) Jan. 18, 1739–Oct. 18, 1823; House 1801–05.

Mott, James Wheaton (R Ore.) Nov. 12, 1883–Nov. 12, 1945; House 1933–Nov. 12, 1945.

Mott, Luther Wright (R N.Y.) Nov. 30, 1874–July 10, 1923; House 1911–July 10, 1923.

Mott, Richard (R Ohio) July 21, 1804–Jan. 22, 1888; House 1855–59.

Mottl, Ronald Milton (D Ohio) Feb. 6, 1934– ; House 1975–83.

Moulder, Morgan Moore (D Mo.) Aug. 31, 1904–Nov. 12, 1976; House 1949–63.

Moulton, Mace (D N.H.) May 2, 1796–May 5, 1867; House 1845–47.

Moulton, Samuel Wheeler (D Ill.) Jan. 20, 1821–June 3, 1905; House 1865–67 (Republican), 1881–85.

Mouser, Grant Earl (father of Grant Earl Mouser Jr.) (R Ohio) Sept. 11, 1868–May 6, 1949; House 1905–09.

Mouser, Grant Earl Jr. (son of Grant Earl Mouser) (R Ohio) Feb. 20, 1895–Dec. 21, 1943; House 1929–33.

Mouton, Alexander (D La.) Nov. 19, 1804–Feb. 12, 1885; Senate Jan. 12, 1837–March 1, 1842; Gov. Jan. 30, 1843–Feb. 12, 1846.

Mouton, Robert Louis (D La.) Oct. 20, 1892–Nov. 26, 1956; House 1937–41.

Moxley, William James (R Ill.) May 22, 1851–Aug. 4, 1938; House Nov. 23, 1909–11.

Moynihan, Daniel Patrick (D N.Y.) March 16, 1927– ; Senate 1977– ; Chrmn. Senate Environment and Public Works 1992; Chrmn. Senate Finance 1993–95.

Moynihan, Patrick Henry (R Ill.) Sept. 25, 1869–May 20, 1946; House 1933–35.

Mozley, Norman Adolphus (R Mo.) Dec. 11, 1865–May 9, 1922; House 1895–97.

Mrazek, Robert Jan (D N.Y.) Nov. 6, 1945– ; House 1983–93.

Mruk, Joseph (R N.Y.) Nov. 6, 1903–Jan. 21, 1995; House 1943–45.

Mudd, Sydney Emanuel (father of Sydney Emanuel Mudd, below) (R Md.) Feb. 12, 1858–Oct. 21, 1911; House March 20, 1890–91, 1897–1911.

Mudd, Sydney Emanuel (son of Sydney Emanuel Mudd, above) (R Md.) June 20, 1885–Oct. 11, 1924; House 1915–Oct. 11, 1924.

Muhlenberg, Francis Swaine (son of John Peter Gabriel Muhlenberg, nephew of Frederick Augustus Conrad Muhlenberg) (NR Ohio) April 22, 1795–Dec. 17, 1831; House Dec. 19, 1828–29.

Muhlenberg, Frederick Augustus (great-great-grandson of Frederick Augustus Conrad Muhlenberg, great-great-great-nephew of John Peter Gabriel Muhlenberg) (R Pa.) Sept. 25, 1887–Jan. 19, 1980; House 1947–49.

Muhlenberg, Frederick Augustus Conrad (brother of John Peter Gabriel Muhlenberg, uncle of Francis Swaine Muhlenberg and Henry Augustus Philip Muhlenberg, great-great-grandfather of Frederick Augustus Muhlenberg) (– Pa.) Jan. 1, 1750–June 4, 1801; House 1789–97; Speaker April 1, 1789–91, Dec. 2, 1793–95; Cont. Cong. 1779–80.

Muhlenberg, Henry Augustus (son of Henry Augustus Philip Muhlenberg, grandson of Joseph Hiester) (D Pa.) July 21, 1823–Jan. 9, 1854; House 1853–Jan. 9, 1854.

Muhlenberg, Henry Augustus Philip (father of Henry Augustus Muhlenberg, nephew of John Peter Gabriel Muhlenberg and Frederick Augustus Conrad Muhlenberg) (D Pa.) May 13, 1782–Aug. 11, 1844; House 1829–Feb. 9, 1838 (1829–37 Jacksonian).

Muhlenberg, John Peter Gabriel (father of Francis Swaine Muhlenberg, brother of Frederick Augustus Conrad Muhlenberg, uncle of Henry Augustus Philip Muhlenberg, great-great-great-uncle of Frederick Augustus Muhlenberg) (– Pa.) Oct. 1, 1746–Oct. 1, 1807; House 1789–91, 1793–95, 1799–1801; Senate March 4–June 30, 1801.

Muldowney, Michael Joseph (R Pa.) Aug. 10, 1889–March 30, 1947; House 1933–35.

Muldrow, Henry Lowndes (D Miss.) Feb. 8, 1837–March 1, 1905; House 1877–85.

Mulkey, Frederick William (nephew of Joseph Norton Dolph) (R Ore.) Jan. 6, 1874–May 5, 1924; Senate Jan. 23–March 3, 1907, Nov. 6–Dec. 17, 1918.

Mulkey, William Oscar (D Ala.) July 27, 1871–June 30, 1943; House June 29, 1914–15.

Muller, Nicholas (D N.Y.) Nov. 15, 1836–Dec. 12, 1917; House 1877–81, 1883–87, 1899–Dec. 1, 1902.

Mullin, Joseph (W N.Y.) Aug. 6, 1811–May 17, 1882; House 1847–49.

Mullins, James (R Tenn.) Sept. 15, 1807–June 26, 1873; House 1867–69.

Multer, Abraham Jacob (D N.Y.) Dec. 24, 1900–Nov. 4, 1986; House Nov. 4, 1947–Dec. 31, 1967.

Mumford, George (R N.C.) ?–Dec. 31, 1818; House 1817–Dec. 31, 1818.

Mumford, Gurdon Saltonstall (R N.Y.) Jan. 29, 1764–April 30, 1831; House 1805–11.

Mumma, Walter Mann (R Pa.) Nov. 20, 1890–Feb. 25, 1961; House 1951–Feb. 25, 1961.

Mundt, Karl Earl (R S.D.) June 3, 1900–Aug. 16, 1974; House 1939–Dec. 30, 1948; Senate Dec. 31, 1948–73.

Mungen, William (D Ohio) May 12, 1821–Sept. 9, 1887; House 1867–71.

Murch, Thompson Henry (G Maine) March 29, 1838–Dec. 15, 1886; House 1879–83.

Murdock, John Robert (D Ariz.) April 20, 1885–Feb. 14, 1972; House 1937–53; Chrmn. House Interior and Insular Affairs 1951–53.

Murdock, Orrice Abram Jr. "Abe" (D Utah) July 18, 1893–Sept. 15, 1979; House 1933–41; Senate 1941–47.

Murdock, Victor (R Kan.) March 18, 1871–July 8, 1945; House May 26, 1903–15.

Murfree, William Hardy (uncle of David W. Dickinson) (R N.C.) Oct. 2, 1781–Jan. 19, 1827; House 1813–17.

Murkowski, Frank Hughes (R Alaska) March 28, 1933– ; Senate 1981– ; Chrmn. Senate Veterans' Affairs 1985–87; Chrmn. Senate Energy and Natural Resources 1995– .

Murphey, Charles (U Ga.) May 9, 1799–Jan. 16, 1861; House 1851–53.

Murphy, Arthur Phillips (R Mo.) Dec. 10, 1870–Feb. 1, 1914; House 1905–07, 1909–11.

Murphy, Austin John (D Pa.) June 17, 1927– ; House 1977–95.

Murphy, Benjamin Franklin (R Ohio) Dec. 24, 1867–March 6, 1938; House 1919–33.

Murphy, Edward Jr. (D N.Y.) Dec. 15, 1836–Aug. 3, 1911; Senate 1893–99.

Murphy, Everett Jerome (R Ill.) July 24, 1852–April 10, 1922; House 1895–97.

Murphy, George Lloyd (R Calif.) July 4, 1902–May 3, 1992; Senate Jan. 1, 1965–Jan. 2, 1971.

Murphy, Henry Cruse (D N.Y.) July 5, 1810–Dec. 1, 1882; House 1843–45, 1847–49.

Murphy, James Joseph (D N.Y.) Nov. 3, 1898–Oct. 19, 1962; House 1949–53.

Murphy, James William (D Wis.) April 17, 1858–July 11, 1927; House 1907–09.

Murphy, Jeremiah Henry (D Iowa) Feb. 19, 1835–Dec. 11, 1893; House 1883–87.

Murphy, John (J Ala.) 1785–Sept. 21, 1841; House 1833–35; Gov. Nov. 25, 1825–Nov. 25, 1829.

Murphy, John Michael (D N.Y.) Aug. 3, 1926– ; House 1963–81; Chrmn. House Merchant Marine and Fisheries 1977–81.

Murphy, John William (D Pa.) April 26, 1902–March 28, 1962; House 1943–July 17, 1946.

Murphy, Maurice J. Jr. (R N.H.) Oct. 3, 1927– ; Senate Dec. 7, 1961–Nov. 6, 1962.

Murphy, Morgan Francis (D Ill.) April 16, 1932– ; House 1971–81.

Murphy, Nathan Oakes (R Ariz.) Oct. 14, 1849–Aug. 22, 1908; House (Terr. Del.) 1895–97; Gov. (Ariz. Terr.) 1892–94, 1898–1902.

Murphy, Richard Louis (D Iowa) Nov. 6, 1875–July 16, 1936; Senate 1933–July 16, 1936.

Murphy, William Thomas (D Ill.) Aug. 7, 1899–Jan. 29, 1978; House 1959–71.

Murray, Ambrose Spencer (brother of William Murray) (R N.Y.) Nov. 27, 1807–Nov. 8, 1885; House 1855–59 (1855–57 Whig).

Murray, George Washington (R S.C.) Sept. 22, 1853–April 21, 1926; House 1893–95, June 4, 1896–97.

Murray, James Cunningham (D Ill.) May 16, 1917– ; House 1955–57.

Murray, James Edward (D Mont.) May 3, 1876–March 23, 1961; Senate Nov. 7, 1934–61; Chrmn. Senate Labor and Public Welfare 1951–53; Chrmn. Senate Interior and Insular Affairs 1955–61.

Murray, John (cousin of Thomas Murray Jr.) (R Pa.) 1768–March 7, 1834; House Oct. 14, 1817–21.

Murray, John L. (D Ky.) Jan. 25, 1806–Jan. 31, 1842; House 1837–39.

Murray, Patty (D Wash.) Oct. 11, 1950– ; Senate 1993– .

Murray, Reid Fred (R Wis.) Oct. 16, 1887–April 29, 1952; House 1939–April 29, 1952.

Murray, Robert Maynard (D Ohio) Nov. 28, 1841–Aug. 2, 1913; House 1883–85.

Murray, Thomas Jefferson (D Tenn.) Aug. 1, 1894–Nov. 28, 1971; House 1943–67; Chrmn. House Post Office and Civil Service 1949–53, 1955–67.

Murray, Thomas Jr. (cousin of John Murray) (– Pa.) 1770–Aug. 26, 1823; House Oct. 9, 1821–23.

Murray, William (brother of Ambrose Spencer Murray) (D N.Y.) Oct. 1, 1803–Aug. 25, 1875; House 1851–55.

Murray, William Francis (D Mass.) Sept. 7, 1881–Sept. 21, 1918; House 1911–Sept. 28, 1914.

Murray, William Henry David (D Okla.) Nov. 21, 1869–Oct. 15, 1956; House 1913–17; Gov. Jan. 12, 1931–Jan. 14, 1935.

Murray, William Vans (F Md.) Feb. 9, 1760–Dec. 11, 1803; House 1791–97 (1791–95 no party).

Murtha, John Patrick Jr. (D Pa.) Jan. 17, 1932– ; House Feb. 5, 1974– .

Muskie, Edmund Sixtus (D Maine) March 28, 1914–March 26, 1996; Senate 1959–May 7, 1980; Chrmn. Senate Budget 1975–79; Gov. Jan. 5, 1955–Jan. 3, 1959; Secy. of State May 8, 1980–Jan. 18, 1981.

Musselwhite, Harry Webster (D Mich.) May 23, 1868–Dec. 14, 1955; House 1933–35.

Musto, Raphael John (D Pa.) March 30, 1929– ; House April 15, 1980–81.

Mutchler, Howard (son of William Mutchler) (D Pa.) Feb. 12, 1859–Jan. 4, 1916; House Aug. 7, 1893–95, 1901–03.

Mutchler, William (father of Howard Mutchler) (D Pa.) Dec. 21, 1831–June 23, 1893; House 1875–77, 1881–85, 1889–June 23, 1893.

Myers, Amos (R Pa.) April 23, 1824–Oct. 18, 1893; House 1863–65.

Myers, Francis John (D Pa.) Dec. 18, 1901–July 5, 1956; House 1939–45; Senate 1945–51.

Myers, Gary Arthur (R Pa.) Aug. 16, 1937– ; House 1975–79.

Myers, Henry Lee (D Mont.) Oct. 9, 1862–Nov. 11, 1943; Senate 1911–23.

Myers, John Thomas (R Ind.) Feb. 8, 1927– ; House 1967–97.

Myers, Leonard (R Pa.) Nov. 13, 1827–Feb. 11, 1905; House 1863–69, April 9, 1869–75.

Myers, Michael Joseph "Ozzie" (D Pa.) May 4, 1943– ; House Nov. 2, 1976–Oct. 2, 1980.

Myers, William Ralph (D Ind.) June 12, 1836–April 18, 1907; House 1879–81.

Myrick, Sue (R N.C.) Aug. 1, 1941– ; House 1995– .

N

Nabers, Benjamin Duke (U Miss.) Nov. 7, 1812–Sept. 6, 1878; House 1851–53.

Nadler, Jerrold (D N.Y.) June 13, 1947– ; House Nov. 4, 1992– .

Nagle, David Ray (D Iowa) April 15, 1943– ; House 1987–93.

Naphen, Henry Francis (D Mass.) Aug. 14, 1852–June 8, 1905; House 1899–1903.

Napier, John Light (R S.C.) May 16, 1947– ; House 1981–83.

Napolitano, Grace (D Calif.) Dec. 4, 1936– ; House 1999– .

Narey, Harry Elsworth (R Iowa) May 15, 1885–Aug. 18, 1962; House Nov. 3, 1942–43.

Nash, Charles Edmund (R La.) May 23, 1844–June 21, 1913; House 1875–77.

Natcher, William Huston (D Ky.) Sept. 11, 1909–March 29, 1994; House Aug. 1, 1953–March 29, 1994; Chrmn. House Appropriations 1993–94.

Naudain, Arnold (– Del.) Jan. 6, 1790–Jan. 4, 1872; Senate Jan. 13, 1830–June 16, 1836.

Naylor, Charles (W Pa.) Oct. 6, 1806–Dec. 24, 1872; House June 29, 1837–41.

Neal, Henry Safford (R Ohio) Aug. 25, 1828–July 13, 1906; House 1877–83.

Neal, John Randolph (D Tenn.) Nov. 26, 1836–March 26, 1889; House 1885–89.

Neal, Lawrence Talbot (D Ohio) Sept. 22, 1844–Nov. 2, 1905; House 1873–77.

Neal, Richard E. (D Mass.) Feb. 14, 1949– ; House 1989– .

Neal, Stephen Lybrook (D N.C.) Nov. 7, 1934– ; House 1975–95.

Neal, William Elmer (R W.Va.) Oct. 14, 1875–Nov. 12, 1959; House 1953–55, 1957–59.

Neale, Raphael (– Md.) ?–Oct. 19, 1833; House 1819–25.

Nedzi, Lucien Norbert (D Mich.) May 28, 1925– ; House Nov. 7, 1961–81; Chrmn. House Select Committee on Intelligence 1975.

Neece, William Henry (D Ill.) Feb. 26, 1831–Jan. 3, 1909; House 1883–87.

Needham, James Carson (R Calif.) Sept. 17, 1864–July 11, 1942; House 1899–1913.

Neeley, George Arthur (D Kan.) Aug. 1, 1879–Jan. 1, 1919; House Nov. 11, 1912–15.

Neely, Matthew Mansfield (D W.Va.) Nov. 9, 1874–Jan. 18, 1958; House Oct. 14, 1913–21, 1945–47; Senate 1923–29, 1931–Jan. 12, 1941, 1949–Jan. 18, 1958; Chrmn. Senate District of Columbia 1951–53, 1955–59; Gov. Jan. 13, 1941–Jan. 15, 1945.

Negley, James Scott (R Pa.) Dec. 22, 1826–Aug. 7, 1901; House 1869–75, 1885–87.

Neill, Robert (D Ark.) Nov. 12, 1838–Feb. 16, 1907; House 1893–97.

Nelligan, James Leo (R Pa.) Feb. 14, 1929– ; House 1981–83.

Nelsen, Ancher (R Minn.) Oct. 11, 1904–Nov. 30, 1992; House 1959–Dec. 31, 1974.

Nelson, Adolphus Peter (R Wis.) March 28, 1872–Aug. 21, 1927; House Nov. 5, 1918–23.

Nelson, Arthur Emanuel (R Minn.) May 10, 1892–April 11, 1955; Senate Nov. 18, 1942–43.

Nelson, Charles Pembroke (son of John Edward Nelson) (R Maine) July 2, 1907–June 8, 1962; House 1949–57.

Nelson, Clarence William "Bill" (D Fla.) Sept. 29, 1942– ; House 1979–91.

Nelson, Gaylord Anton (D Wis.) June 4, 1916– ; Senate Jan. 8, 1963–81; Chrmn. Senate Select Committee on Small Business 1975–81; Gov. Jan. 5, 1959–Jan. 7, 1963.

Nelson, Homer Augustus (D N.Y.) Aug. 31, 1829–April 25, 1891; House 1863–65.

Nelson, Hugh (R Va.) Sept. 30, 1768–March 18, 1836; House 1811–Jan. 14, 1823.

Nelson, Jeremiah (AJ Mass.) Sept. 14, 1769–Oct. 2, 1838; House 1805–07 (Federalist), 1815–25 (Federalist), 1831–33.

Nelson, John (son of Roger Nelson) (– Md.) June 1, 1794–Jan. 18, 1860; House 1821–23; Atty. Gen. July 1, 1843–March 3, 1845.

Nelson, John Edward (father of Charles Pembroke Nelson) (R Maine) July 12, 1874–April 11, 1955; House March 27, 1922–33.

Nelson, John Mandt (R Wis.) Oct. 10, 1870–Jan. 29, 1955; House Sept. 4, 1906–19, 1921–33.

Nelson, Knute (R Minn.) Feb. 2, 1843–April 28, 1923; House 1883–89; Senate 1895–April 28, 1923; Gov. Jan. 4, 1893–Jan. 31, 1895.

Nelson, Roger (father of John Nelson) (R Md.) 1759–June 7, 1815; House Nov. 6, 1804–May 14, 1810.

Nelson, Thomas Amos Rogers (O Tenn.) March 19, 1812–Aug. 24, 1873; House 1859–61.

Nelson, Thomas Maduit (R Va.) Sept. 27, 1782–Nov. 10, 1853; House Dec. 4, 1816–19.

Nelson, William (W N.Y.) June 29, 1784–Oct. 3, 1869; House 1847–51.

Nelson, William Lester (D Mo.) Aug. 4, 1875–Dec. 31, 1946; House 1919–21, 1925–33, 1935–43.

Nes, Henry (W Pa.) May 20, 1799–Sept. 10, 1850; House 1843–45 (Independent Democrat), 1847–Sept. 10, 1850.

Nesbit, Walter (D Ill.) May 1, 1878–Dec. 6, 1938; House 1933–35.

Nesbitt, Wilson (R S.C.) ?–May 13, 1861; House 1817–19.

Nesmith, James Willis (cousin of Joseph Gardner Wilson, grandfather of Clifton Nesmith McArthur) (D Ore.) July 23, 1820–June 17, 1885; Senate 1861–67; House Dec. 1, 1873–75.

Nethercutt, George (R Wash.) Oct. 7, 1944– ; House 1995– .

Neuberger, Maurine Brown (widow of Richard Lewis Neuberger) (D Ore.) Jan. 9, 1907– ; Senate Nov. 9, 1960–67.

Neuberger, Richard Lewis (husband of Maurine Brown Neuberger) (D Ore.) Dec. 26, 1912–March 9, 1960; Senate 1955–March 9, 1960.

Neumann, Mark W. (R Wis.) Feb. 27, 1954– ; House 1995–99.

Neville, Joseph (– Va.) 1730–March 4, 1819; House 1793–95.

Neville, William (cousin of Bird Segle McGuire) (P Neb.) Dec. 29, 1843–April 5, 1909; House Dec. 4, 1899–1903.

Nevin, Robert Murphy (R Ohio) May 5, 1850–Dec. 17, 1912; House 1901–07.

New, Anthony (R Ky.) 1747–March 2, 1833; House 1793–1805 (1793–95 no party Va.), 1811–13, 1817–19, 1821–23.

New, Harry Stewart (R Ind.) Dec. 31, 1858–May 9, 1937; Senate 1917–23; Chrmn. Rep. Nat. Comm. 1907–08; Postmaster Gen. March 4, 1923–March 5, 1929.

New, Jeptha Dudley (D Ind.) Nov. 28, 1830–July 9, 1892; House 1875–77, 1879–81.

Newberry, John Stoughton (father of Truman Handy Newberry) (R Mich.) Nov. 18, 1826–Jan. 2, 1887; House 1879–81.

Newberry, Truman Handy (son of John Stoughton Newberry) (R Mich.) Nov. 5, 1864–Oct. 3, 1945; Senate 1919–Nov. 18, 1922; Secy. of the Navy Dec. 1, 1908–March 5, 1909.

Newberry, Walter Cass (D Ill.) Dec. 23, 1835–July 20, 1912; House 1891–93.

Newbold, Thomas (R N.J.) Aug. 2, 1760–Dec. 18, 1823; House 1807–13.

Newcomb, Carman Adam (R Mo.) July 1, 1830–April 6, 1902; House 1867–69.

Newell, William Augustus (R N.J.) Sept. 5, 1817–Aug. 8, 1901; House 1847–51 (Whig), 1865–67; Gov. Jan. 20, 1857–Jan. 17, 1860, (Wash. Terr.) 1880–84.

Newhall, Judson Lincoln (R Ky.) March 26, 1870–July 23, 1952; House 1929–31.

Newhard, Peter (D Pa.) July 26, 1783–Feb. 19, 1860; House 1839–43.

Newlands, Francis Griffith (D Nev.) Aug. 28, 1848–Dec. 24, 1917; House 1893–1903; Senate 1903–Dec. 24, 1917.

Newman, Alexander (D Va.) Oct. 5, 1804–Sept. 8, 1849; House March 4–Sept. 8, 1849.

Newnan, Daniel (– Ga.) about 1780–Jan. 16, 1851; House 1831–33.

Newsham, Joseph Parkinson (R La.) May 24, 1837–Oct. 22, 1919; House July 18, 1868–69, May 23, 1870–71.

Newsome, John Parks (D Ala.) Feb. 13, 1893–Nov. 10, 1961; House 1943–45.

Newton, Cherubusco (D La.) May 15, 1848–May 26, 1910; House 1887–89.

Newton, Cleveland Alexander (R Mo.) Sept. 3, 1873–Sept. 17, 1945; House 1919–27.

Newton, Eben (W Ohio) Oct. 16, 1795–Nov. 6, 1885; House 1851–53.

Newton, Thomas Jr. (R Va.) Nov. 21, 1768–Aug. 5, 1847; House 1801–29, March 4, 1829–March 9, 1830, 1831–33.

Newton, Thomas Willoughby (W Ark.) Jan. 18, 1804–Sept. 22, 1853; House Feb. 6–March 3, 1847.

Newton, Walter Hughes (R Minn.) Oct. 10, 1880–Aug. 10, 1941; House 1919–June 30, 1929.

Newton, Willoughby (W Va.) Dec. 2, 1802–May 23, 1874; House 1843–45.

Ney, Bob (R Ohio) July 5, 1954– ; House 1995– .

Niblack, Silas Leslie (cousin of William Ellis Niblack) (D Fla.) March 17, 1825–Feb. 13, 1883; House Jan. 29–March 3, 1873.

Niblack, William Ellis (cousin of Silas Leslie Niblack) (D Ind.) May 19, 1822–May 7, 1893; House Dec. 7, 1857–61, 1865–75.

Nicholas, John (brother of Wilson Cary Nicholas, uncle of Robert Carter Nicholas) (R Va.) about 1757–Dec. 31, 1819; House 1793–1801 (1793–95 no party).

Nicholas, Robert Carter (nephew of John Nicholas and Wilson Cary Nicholas) (D La.) 1793–Dec. 24, 1857; Senate Jan. 13, 1836–41.

Nicholas, Wilson Cary (brother of John Nicholas, uncle of Robert Carter Nicholas) (R Va.) Jan. 31, 1761–Oct. 10, 1820; Senate Dec. 5, 1799–May 22, 1804; House 1807–Nov. 27, 1809; Gov. Dec. 1, 1814–Dec. 1, 1816.

Nicholls, John Calhoun (D Ga.) April 25, 1834–Dec. 25, 1893; House 1879–81, 1883–85.

Nicholls, Samuel Jones (D S.C.) May 7, 1885–Nov. 23, 1937; House Sept. 14, 1915–21.

Nicholls, Thomas David (ID Pa.) Sept. 16, 1870–Jan. 19, 1931; House 1907–11.

Nichols, Charles Archibald (R Mich.) Aug. 25, 1876–April 25, 1920; House 1915–April 25, 1920.

Nichols, John (I N.C.) Nov. 14, 1834–Sept. 22, 1917; House 1887–89.

Nichols, John Conover (D Okla.) Aug. 31, 1896–Nov. 7, 1945; House 1935–July 3, 1943.

Nichols, Matthias H. (R Ohio) Oct. 3, 1824–Sept. 15, 1862; House 1853–59 (1853–55 Democrat).

Nichols, Richard (R Kan.) April 29, 1926– ; House 1991–93.

Nichols, William Flynt (D Ala.) Oct. 16, 1918–Dec. 13, 1988; House 1967–Dec. 13, 1988.

Nicholson, Alfred Osborn Pope (D Tenn.) Aug. 31, 1808–March 23, 1876; Senate Dec. 25, 1840–Feb. 7, 1842, 1859–61.

Nicholson, Donald William (R Mass.) Aug. 11, 1888–Feb. 16, 1968; House Nov. 18, 1947–59.

Nicholson, John (R N.Y.) 1765–Jan. 20, 1820; House 1809–11.

Nicholson, John Anthony (D Del.) Nov. 17, 1827–Nov. 4, 1906; House 1865–69.

Nicholson, Joseph Hopper (R Md.) May 15, 1770–March 4, 1817; House 1799–March 1, 1806.

Nicholson, Samuel Danford (R Colo.) Feb. 22, 1859–March 24, 1923; Senate 1921–March 24, 1923.

Nickles, Donald Lee (R Okla.) Dec. 6, 1948– ; Senate 1981– .

Nicoll, Henry (D N.Y.) Oct. 23, 1812–Nov. 28, 1879; House 1847–49.

Niedringhaus, Frederick Gottlieb (uncle of Henry Frederick Niedringhaus) (R Mo.) Oct. 21, 1837–Nov. 25, 1922; House 1889–91.

Niedringhaus, Henry Frederick (nephew of Frederick Gottlieb Niedringhaus) (R Mo.) Dec. 15, 1864–Aug. 3, 1941; House 1927–33.

Nielson, Howard Curtis (R Utah) Sept. 12, 1924– ; House 1983–91.

Niles, Jason (R Miss.) Dec. 19, 1814–July 7, 1894; House 1873–75.

Niles, John Milton (D Conn.) Aug. 20, 1787–May 31, 1856; Senate Dec. 21, 1835–39, 1843–49; Postmaster Gen. May 26, 1840–March 3, 1841.

Niles, Nathaniel (– Vt.) April 3, 1741–Oct. 31, 1828; House Oct. 17, 1791–95.

Nimtz, F. Jay (R Ind.) Dec. 1, 1915–Dec. 6, 1990; House 1957–59.

Nisbet, Eugenius Aristides (cousin of Mark Anthony Cooper) (W Ga.) Dec. 7, 1803–March 18, 1871; House 1839–Oct. 12, 1841.

Niven, Archibald Campbell (D N.Y.) Dec. 8, 1803–Feb. 21, 1882; House 1845–47.

Nix, Robert Nelson Cornelius Sr. (D Pa.) Aug. 9, 1905–June 22, 1987; House May 20, 1958–79; Chrmn. House Post Office and Civil Service 1977–79.

Nixon, George Stuart (R Nev.) April 2, 1860–June 5, 1912; Senate 1905–June 5, 1912.

Nixon, John Thompson (R N.J.) Aug. 31, 1820–Sept. 28, 1889; House 1859–63.

Nixon, Richard Milhous (R Calif.) Jan. 9, 1913–April 22, 1994; House 1947–Nov. 30, 1950; Senate Dec. 1, 1950–Jan. 1, 1953; Vice President 1953–61; President 1969–Aug. 9, 1974.

Noble, David Addison (D Mich.) Nov. 9, 1802–Oct. 13, 1876; House 1853–55.

Noble, James (R Ind.) Dec. 16, 1785–Feb. 26, 1831; Senate Dec. 11, 1816–Feb. 26, 1831.

Noble, Warren Perry (D Ohio) June 14, 1820–July 9, 1903; House 1861–65.

Noble, William Henry (D N.Y.) Sept. 22, 1788–Feb. 5, 1850; House 1837–39.

Nodar, Robert Joseph Jr. (R N.Y.) March 23, 1916–Sept. 11, 1974; House 1947–49.

Noell, John William (father of Thomas Estes Noell) (UU Mo.) Feb. 22, 1816–March 14, 1863; House 1859–March 14, 1863 (1859–63 Democrat).

Noell, Thomas Estes (son of John William Noell) (D Mo.) April 3, 1839–Oct. 3, 1867; House 1865–Oct. 3, 1867 (1865–67 Republican).

Nolan, John Ignatius (husband of Mae Ella Nolan) (R Calif.) Jan. 14, 1874–Nov. 18, 1922; House 1913–Nov. 18, 1922.

Nolan, Mae Ella (widow of John Ignatius Nolan) (R Calif.) Sept. 20, 1886–July 9, 1973; House Jan. 23, 1923–25.

Nolan, Michael Nicholas (D N.Y.) May 4, 1833–May 31, 1905; House 1881–83.

Nolan, Richard Michael (D Minn.) Dec. 17, 1943– ; House 1975–81.

Nolan, William Ignatius (R Minn.) May 14, 1874–Aug. 3, 1943; House June 17, 1929–33.

Noland, James Ellsworth (D Ind.) April 22, 1920–Aug. 12, 1992; House 1949–51.

Noonan, Edward Thomas (D Ill.) Oct. 23, 1861–Dec. 19, 1923; House 1899–1901.

Noonan, George Henry (R Texas) Aug. 20, 1828–Aug. 17, 1907; House 1895–97.

Norbeck, Peter (R S.D.) Aug. 27, 1870–Dec. 20, 1936; Senate 1921–Dec. 20, 1936; Gov. Jan. 2, 1917–Jan. 4, 1921.

Norblad, Albin Walter Jr. (R Ore.) Sept. 12, 1908–Sept. 20, 1964; House Jan. 11, 1946–Sept. 20, 1964.

Norcross, Amasa (R Mass.) Jan. 26, 1824–April 2, 1898; House 1877–83.

Norman, Fred Barthold (R Wash.) March 21, 1882–April 18, 1947; House 1943–45, Jan. 3–April 18, 1947.

Norrell, Catherine Dorris (widow of William Frank Norrell) (D Ark.) March 30, 1901–Aug. 26, 1981; House April 18, 1961–63.

Norrell, William Frank (husband of Catherine Dorris Norrell) (D Ark.) Aug. 29, 1896–Feb. 15, 1961; House 1939–Feb. 15, 1961.

Norris, Benjamin White (R Ala.) Jan. 22, 1819–Jan. 26, 1873; House July 21, 1868–69.

Norris, George William (IR Neb.) July 11, 1861–Sept. 2, 1944; House 1903–13 (Republican); Senate 1913–43 (1913–37 Republican).

Norris, Moses Jr. (D N.H.) Nov. 8, 1799–Jan. 11, 1855; House 1843–47; Senate 1849–Jan. 11, 1855.

North, Solomon Taylor (R Pa.) May 24, 1853–Oct. 19, 1917; House 1915–17.

North, William (F N.Y.) 1755–Jan. 3, 1836; Senate May 5–Aug. 17, 1798.

Northup, Anne M. (R Ky.) Jan. 22, 1948– ; House 1997– .

Northway, Stephen Asa (R Ohio) June 19, 1833–Sept. 8, 1898; House 1893–Sept. 8, 1898.

Norton, Daniel Sheldon (U Minn.) April 12, 1829–July 13, 1870; Senate 1865–July 13, 1870.

Norton, Ebenezer Foote (J N.Y.) Nov. 7, 1774–May 11, 1851; House 1829–31.

Norton, Eleanor Holmes (D D.C.) June 13, 1937–   ; House (Delegate) 1991–   .

Norton, Elijah Hise (D Mo.) Nov. 24, 1821–Aug. 6, 1914; House 1861–63.

Norton, James (D S.C.) Oct. 8, 1843–Oct. 14, 1920; House Dec. 6, 1897–1901.

Norton, James Albert (D Ohio) Nov. 11, 1843–July 24, 1912; House 1897–1903.

Norton, Jesse Olds (R Ill.) Dec. 25, 1812–Aug. 3, 1875; House 1853–57 (1853–55 Whig), 1863–65.

Norton, John Nathaniel (D Neb.) May 12, 1878–Oct. 5, 1960; House 1927–29, 1931–33.

Norton, Mary Teresa (D N.J.) March 7, 1875–Aug. 2, 1959; House 1925–51; Chrmn. House Administration 1949–51.

Norton, Miner Gibbs (R Ohio) May 11, 1857–Sept. 7, 1926; House 1921–23.

Norton, Nelson Ira (R N.Y.) March 30, 1820–Oct. 28, 1887; House Dec. 6, 1875–77.

Norton, Patrick Daniel (R N.D.) May 17, 1876–Oct. 14, 1953; House 1913–19.

Norton, Richard Henry (D Mo.) Nov. 6, 1849–March 15, 1918; House 1889–93.

Norvell, John (D Mich.) Dec. 21, 1789–April 24, 1850; Senate Jan. 26, 1837–41.

Norwood, Charlie (R Ga.) July 27, 1941–   ; House 1995–   .

Norwood, Thomas Manson (D Ga.) April 26, 1830–June 19, 1913; Senate Nov. 14, 1871–77; House 1885–89.

Nott, Abraham (F S.C.) Feb. 5, 1768–June 19, 1830; House 1799–1801.

Nourse, Amos (– Maine) Dec. 17, 1794–April 7, 1877; Senate Jan. 16–March 3, 1857.

Nowak, Henry James (D N.Y.) Feb. 21, 1935–   ; House 1975–93.

Noyes, John (F Vt.) April 2, 1764–Oct. 26, 1841; House 1815–17.

Noyes, Joseph Cobham (W Maine) Sept. 22, 1798–July 28, 1868; House 1837–39.

Nuckolls, Stephen Friel (D Wyo.) Aug. 16, 1825–Feb. 14, 1879; House (Terr. Del.) Dec. 6, 1869–71.

Nuckolls, William Thompson (J S.C.) Feb. 23, 1801–Sept. 27, 1855; House 1827–33.

Nugen, Robert Hunter (D Ohio) July 16, 1809–Feb. 28, 1872; House 1861–63.

Nugent, John Frost (D Idaho) June 28, 1868–Sept. 18, 1931; Senate Jan. 22, 1918–Jan. 14, 1921.

Nunn, David Alexander (R Tenn.) July 26, 1833–Sept. 11, 1918; House 1867–69, 1873–75.

Nunn, Samuel Augustus (great-nephew of Carl Vinson) (D Ga.) Sept. 8, 1938–   ; Senate Nov. 8, 1972–97; Chrmn. Senate Armed Services 1987–95.

Nussle, James (R Iowa) June 27, 1960–   ; House 1991–   .

Nute, Alonzo (R N.H.) Feb. 12, 1826–Dec. 24, 1892; House 1889–91.

Nutting, Newton Wright (R N.Y.) Oct. 22, 1840–Oct. 15, 1889; House 1883–85, 1887–Oct. 15, 1889.

Nye, Frank Mellen (R Minn.) March 7, 1852–Nov. 29, 1935; House 1907–13.

Nye, Gerald Prentice (R N.D.) Dec. 19, 1892–July 17, 1971; Senate Nov. 14, 1925–45.

Nye, James Warren (R Nev.) June 10, 1815–Dec. 25, 1876; Senate Dec. 16, 1864–73; Gov. (Nev. Terr.) 1861–64.

Nygaard, Hjalmar Carl (R N.D.) March 24, 1906–July 18, 1963; House 1961–July 18, 1963.

O

Oakar, Mary Rose (D Ohio) March 5, 1940–   ; House 1977–93.

Oakey, Peter Davis (R Conn.) Feb. 25, 1861–Nov. 18, 1920; House 1915–17.

Oakley, Thomas Jackson (F N.Y.) Nov. 10, 1783–May 11, 1857; House 1813–15, 1827–May 9, 1828.

Oakman, Charles Gibb (R Mich.) Sept. 4, 1903–Oct. 28, 1973; House 1953–55.

Oates, William Calvin (D Ala.) Nov. 30, 1835–Sept. 9, 1910; House 1881–Nov. 5, 1894; Gov. Dec. 1, 1894–Dec. 1, 1896.

Oberstar, James Louis (D Minn.) Sept. 10, 1934–   ; House 1975–   .

Obey, David Ross (D Wis.) Oct. 3, 1938–   ; House April 1, 1969–   ; Chrmn. House Appropriations 1994–95.

O'Brien, Charles Francis Xavier (D N.J.) March 7, 1879–Nov. 14, 1940; House 1921–25.

O'Brien, George Donoghue (D Mich.) Jan. 1, 1900–Oct. 25, 1957; House 1937–39, 1941–47, 1949–55.

O'Brien, George Miller (R Ill.) June 17, 1917–July 17, 1986; House 1973–July 17, 1986.

O'Brien, James (ID N.Y.) March 13, 1841–March 5, 1907; House 1879–81.

O'Brien, James Henry (D N.Y.) July 15, 1860–Sept. 2, 1924; House 1913–15.

O'Brien, Jeremiah (– Maine) Jan. 21, 1778–May 30, 1858; House 1823–29.

O'Brien, Joseph John (R N.Y.) Oct. 9, 1897–Jan. 23, 1953; House 1939–45.

O'Brien, Leo William (D N.Y.) Sept. 21, 1900–May 4, 1982; House April 1, 1952–67.

O'Brien, Thomas Joseph (D Ill.) April 30, 1878–April 14, 1964; House 1933–39, 1943–April 14, 1964.

O'Brien, William James (D Md.) May 28, 1836–Nov. 13, 1905; House 1873–77.

O'Brien, William Smith (D W.Va.) Jan. 8, 1862–Aug. 10, 1948; House 1927–29.

Ocampo, Pablo (– P.I.) Jan. 25, 1853–Feb. 5, 1925; House (Res. Comm.) Nov. 22, 1907–Nov. 22, 1909.

Ochiltree, Thomas Peck (I Texas) Oct. 26, 1837–Nov. 25, 1902; House 1883–85.

O'Connell, David Joseph (D N.Y.) Dec. 25, 1868–Dec. 29, 1930; House 1919–21, 1923–Dec. 29, 1930.

O'Connell, Jeremiah Edward (D R.I.) July 8, 1883–Sept. 18, 1964; House 1923–27, 1929–May 9, 1930.

O'Connell, Jerry Joseph (D Mont.) June 14, 1909–Jan. 16, 1956; House 1937–39.

O'Connell, John Matthew (D R.I.) Aug. 10, 1872–Dec. 6, 1941; House 1933–39.

O'Connell, Joseph Francis (D Mass.) Dec. 7, 1872–Dec. 10, 1942; House 1907–11.

O'Connor, Charles (R Okla.) Oct. 26, 1878–Nov. 15, 1940; House 1929–31.

O'Connor, James (D La.) April 4, 1870–Jan. 7, 1941; House June 5, 1919–31.

O'Connor, James Francis (D Mont.) May 7, 1878–Jan. 15, 1945; House 1937–Jan. 15, 1945.

O'Connor, John Joseph (D N.Y.) Nov. 23, 1885–Jan. 26, 1960; House Nov. 6, 1923–39.

O'Connor, Michael Patrick (D S.C.) Sept. 29, 1831–April 26, 1881; House 1879–81 (received credentials for the term beginning 1881 but died pending a contest).

O'Conor, Herbert Romulus (D Md.) Nov. 17, 1896–March 4, 1960; Senate 1947–53; Gov. Jan. 11, 1939–Jan. 3, 1947.

O'Daniel, Wilbert Lee "Pappy" (D Texas) March 11, 1890–May 11, 1969; Senate Aug. 4, 1941–49; Gov. Jan. 17, 1939–Aug. 4, 1941.

O'Day, Caroline Love Goodwin (D N.Y.) June 22, 1875–Jan. 4, 1943; House 1935–43.

Oddie, Tasker Lowndes (R Nev.) Oct. 20, 1870–Feb. 17, 1950; Senate 1921–33; Gov. Jan. 2, 1911–Jan. 4, 1915.

Odell, Benjamin Baker Jr. (R N.Y.) Jan. 14, 1854–May 9, 1926; House 1895–99; Gov. Jan. 1, 1901–Jan. 1, 1905.

Odell, Moses Fowler (D N.Y.) Feb. 24, 1818–June 13, 1866; House 1861–65.

Odell, Nathaniel Holmes (D N.Y.) Oct. 10, 1828–Oct. 30, 1904; House 1875–77.

O'Donnell, James (R Mich.) March 25, 1840–March 17, 1915; House 1885–93.

O'Ferrall, Charles Triplett (D Va.) Oct. 21, 1840–Sept. 22, 1905; House May 5, 1884–Dec. 28, 1893; Gov. Jan. 1, 1894–Jan. 1, 1898.

Ogden, Aaron (F N.J.) Dec. 3, 1756–April 19, 1839; Senate Feb. 28, 1801–03; Gov. Oct. 29, 1812–Oct. 29, 1813.

Ogden, Charles Franklin (R Ky.) ?–April 10, 1933; House 1919–23.

Ogden, David A. (F N.Y.) Jan. 10, 1770–June 9, 1829; House 1817–19.

Ogden, Henry Warren (D La.) Oct. 21, 1842–July 23, 1905; House May 12, 1894–99.

Ogle, Alexander (father of Charles Ogle, grandfather of Andrew Jackson Ogle) (R Pa.) Aug. 10, 1766–Oct. 14, 1832; House 1817–19.

Ogle, Andrew Jackson (grandson of Alexander Ogle, nephew of Charles Ogle) (W Pa.) March 25, 1822–Oct. 14, 1852; House 1849–51.

Ogle, Charles (son of Alexander Ogle, uncle of Andrew Jackson Ogle) (W Pa.) 1798–May 10, 1841; House 1837–May 10, 1841 (1837–41 Anti-Mason).

Oglesby, Richard James (cousin of Woodson Ratcliffe Oglesby) (R Ill.) July 25, 1824–April 24, 1899; Senate 1873–79; Gov. Jan. 16, 1865–Jan. 11, 1869, Jan. 13–Jan. 23, 1873, Jan. 30, 1885–Jan. 14, 1889.

Oglesby, Woodson Ratcliffe (cousin of Richard James Oglesby) (D N.Y.) Feb. 9, 1867–April 30, 1955; House 1913–17.

O'Gorman, James Aloysius (D N.Y.) May 5, 1860–May 17, 1943; Senate 1911–17.

O'Grady, James Mary Early (R N.Y.) March 31, 1863–Nov. 3, 1928; House 1899–1901.

O'Hair, Frank Trimble (D Ill.) March 12, 1870–Aug. 3, 1932; House 1913–15.

O'Hara, Barratt (D Ill.) April 28, 1882–Aug. 11, 1969; House 1949–51, 1953–69.

O'Hara, James Edward (R N.C.) Feb. 26, 1844–Sept. 15, 1905; House 1883–87.

O'Hara, James Grant (D Mich.) Nov. 8, 1925–March 13, 1989; House 1959–77.

O'Hara, Joseph Patrick (R Minn.) Jan. 23, 1895–March 4, 1975; House 1941–59.

Ohliger, Lewis Philip (D Ohio) Jan. 3, 1843–Jan. 9, 1923; House Dec. 5, 1892–93.

O'Konski, Alvin Edward (R Wis.) May 26, 1904–July 8, 1987; House 1943–73.

Olcott, Jacob Van Vechten (R N.Y.) May 17, 1856–June 1, 1940; House 1905–11.

Olcott, Simeon (F N.H.) Oct. 1, 1735–Feb. 22, 1815; Senate June 17, 1801–05.

Oldfield, Pearl Peden (widow of William Allan Oldfield) (D Ark.) Dec. 2, 1876–April 12, 1962; House Jan. 9, 1929–31.

Oldfield, William Allan (husband of Pearl Peden Oldfield) (D Ark.) Feb. 4, 1874–Nov. 19, 1928; House 1909–Nov. 19, 1928.

Olds, Edson Baldwin (D Ohio) June 3, 1802–Jan. 24, 1869; House 1849–55.

O'Leary, Denis (D N.Y.) Jan. 22, 1863–Sept. 27, 1943; House 1913–Dec. 31, 1914.

O'Leary, James Aloysius (D N.Y.) April 23, 1889–March 16, 1944; House 1935–March 16, 1944.

Olin, Abram Baldwin (son of Gideon Olin, cousin of Henry Olin) (R N.Y.) Sept. 21, 1808–July 7, 1879; House 1857–63.

Olin, Gideon (father of Abram Baldwin Olin, uncle of Henry Olin) (R Vt.) Nov. 2, 1743–Jan. 21, 1823; House 1803–07.

Olin, Henry (nephew of Gideon Olin, cousin of Abram Baldwin Olin) (– Vt.) May 7, 1768–Aug. 16, 1837; House Dec. 13, 1824–25.

Olin, James R. (D Va.) Feb. 28, 1920– ; House 1983–93.

Oliver, Andrew (D N.Y.) Jan. 16, 1815–March 6, 1889; House 1853–57.

Oliver, Daniel Charles (D N.Y.) Oct. 6, 1865–March 26, 1924; House 1917–19.

Oliver, Frank (D N.Y.) Oct. 2, 1883–Jan. 1, 1968; House 1923–June 18, 1934.

Oliver, George Tener (R Pa.) Jan. 26, 1848–Jan. 22, 1919; Senate March 17, 1909–17.

Oliver, James Churchill (D Maine) Aug. 6, 1895–Dec. 25, 1986; House 1937–43 (Republican), 1959–61.

Oliver, John (D Mass.) Aug. 6, 1895–Dec. 25, 1986; House 1937–43 (Republican), 1959–61.

Oliver, Mordecai (W Mo.) Oct. 22, 1819–April 25, 1898; House 1853–57.

Oliver, Samuel Addison (R Iowa) July 21, 1833–July 7, 1912; House 1875–79.

Oliver, William Bacon (cousin of Sydney Parham Epes) (D Ala.) May 23, 1867–May 27, 1948; House 1915–37.

Oliver, William Morrison (D N.Y.) Oct. 15, 1792–July 21, 1863; House 1841–43.

Olmsted, Marlin Edgar (R Pa.) May 21, 1847–July 19, 1913; House 1897–1913.

Olney, Richard (D Mass.) Jan. 5, 1871–Jan. 15, 1939; House 1915–21.

O'Loughlin, Kathryn Ellen (later married and served as Kathryn O'Loughlin McCarthy) (D Kan.) April 24, 1894–Jan. 16, 1952; House 1933–35.

Olpp, Archibald Ernest (R N.J.) May 12, 1882–July 26, 1949; House 1921–23.

Olsen, Arnold (D Mont.) Dec. 17, 1916–Oct. 9, 1990; House 1961–71.

Olson, Alec Gehard (DFL Minn.) Sept. 11, 1930– ; House 1963–67.

Olver, John W. (D Mass.) Sept. 3, 1936– ; House June 18, 1991– .

O'Mahoney, Joseph Christopher (D Wyo.) Nov. 5, 1884–Dec. 1, 1962; Senate Jan. 1, 1934–53, Nov. 29, 1954–61; Chrmn. Senate Interior and Insular Affairs 1949–53.

O'Malley, Matthew Vincent (D N.Y.) June 26, 1878–May 26, 1931; House March 4–May 26, 1931.

O'Malley, Thomas David Patrick (D Wis.) March 24, 1903–Dec. 19, 1979; House 1933–39.

O'Neal, Emmet (D Ky.) April 14, 1887–July 18, 1967; House 1935–47.

O'Neal, Maston Emmett Jr. (D Ga.) July 19, 1907–Jan. 9, 1990; House 1965–71.

O'Neall, John Henry (D Ind.) Oct. 30, 1838–July 15, 1907; House 1887–91.

O'Neil, Joseph Henry (D Mass.) March 23, 1853–Feb. 19, 1935; House 1889–95.

O'Neill, Charles (R Pa.) March 21, 1821–Nov. 25, 1893; House 1863–71, 1873–Nov. 25, 1893.

O'Neill, Edward Leo (D N.J.) July 10, 1903–Dec. 12, 1948; House 1937–39.

O'Neill, Harry Patrick (D Pa.) Feb. 10, 1889–June 24, 1953; House 1949–53.

O'Neill, John (D Ohio) Dec. 17, 1822–May 25, 1905; House 1863–65.

O'Neill, John Joseph (D Mo.) June 25, 1846–Feb. 19, 1898; House 1883–89, 1891–93, April 3, 1894–95.

O'Neill, Thomas Phillip "Tip" Jr. (D Mass.) Dec. 9, 1912–Jan. 5, 1994; House 1953–87; House majority leader 1973–77; Speaker Jan. 4, 1977–79, Jan. 15, 1979–81, Jan. 5, 1981–87.

O'Reilly, Daniel (ID N.Y.) June 3, 1838–Sept. 23, 1911; House 1879–81.

Ormsby, Stephen (R Ky.) 1759–1844; House 1811–13, April 20, 1813–17.

Orr, Alexander Dalrymple (nephew of William Grayson, cousin of William John Grayson (R Ky.) Nov. 6, 1761–June 21, 1835; House Nov. 8, 1792–97 (Nov. 8, 1792–95 no party).

Orr, Benjamin (F Mass.) Dec. 1, 1772–Sept. 3, 1828; House 1817–19.

Orr, Jackson (R Iowa) Sept. 21, 1832–March 15, 1926; House 1871–75.

Orr, James Lawrence (D S.C.) May 12, 1822–May 5, 1873; House 1849–59; Speaker Dec. 7, 1857–59; Gov. Nov. 29, 1865–July 6, 1868 (Republican).

Orr, Robert Jr. (– Pa.) March 5, 1786–May 22, 1876; House Oct. 11, 1825–29.

Orth, Godlove Stein (R Ind.) April 22, 1817–Dec. 16, 1882; House 1863–71, 1873–75, 1879–Dec. 16, 1882.

Ortiz, Solomon Porfirio (D Texas) June 3, 1938– ; House 1983– .

Orton, William (D Utah) Sept. 22, 1949– ; House 1991–97.

Osborn, Thomas Ward (R Fla.) March 9, 1836–Dec. 18, 1898; Senate June 25, 1868–73.

Osborne, Edwin Sylvanus (R Pa.) Aug. 7, 1839–Jan. 1, 1900; House 1885–91.

Osborne, Henry Zenas (R Calif.) Oct. 4, 1848–Feb. 8, 1923; House 1917–Feb. 8, 1923.

Osborne, John Eugene (D Wyo.) June 19, 1858–April 24, 1943; House 1897–99; Gov. Jan. 2, 1893–Jan. 7, 1895.

Osborne, Thomas Burr (W Conn.) July 8, 1798–Sept. 2, 1869; House 1839–43.

Osgood, Gayton Pickman (J Mass.) July 4, 1797–June 26, 1861; House 1833–35.

O'Shaunessy, George Francis (D R.I.) May 1, 1868–Nov. 28, 1934; House 1911–19.

Ose, Doug (R Calif.) June 27, 1955– ; House 1999– .

Osias, Camilo (Nat. P.I.) March 23, 1889–May 20, 1976; House (Res. Comm.) 1929–35.

Osmer, James H. (R Pa.) Jan. 23, 1832–Oct. 3, 1912; House 1879–81.

Osmers, Frank Charles Jr. (R N.J.) Dec. 30, 1907–May 21, 1977; House 1939–43, Nov. 6, 1951–65.

Ostertag, Harold Charles (R N.Y.) June 22, 1896–May 2, 1985; House 1951–65.

O'Sullivan, Eugene Daniel (D Neb.) May 31, 1883–Feb. 7, 1968; House 1949–51.

O'Sullivan, Patrick Brett (D Conn.) Aug. 11, 1887–Nov. 10, 1978; House 1923–25.

Otero, Mariano Sabino (nephew of Miguel Antonio Otero) (R N.M.) Aug. 29, 1844–Feb. 1, 1904; House (Terr. Del.) 1879–81.

Otero, Miguel Antonio (uncle of Mariano Sabino Otero) (D N.M.) June 21, 1829–May 30, 1882; House (Terr. Del.) July 23, 1856–61.

Otey, Peter Johnston (D Va.) Dec. 22, 1840–May 4, 1902; House 1895–May 4, 1902.

Otis, Harrison Gray (F Mass.) Oct. 8, 1765–Oct. 28, 1848; House 1797–1801; Senate 1817–May 30, 1822.

Otis, John (W Maine) Aug. 3, 1801–Oct. 17, 1856; House 1849–51.

Otis, John Grant (P Kan.) Feb. 10, 1838–Feb. 22, 1916; House 1891–93.

Otis, Norton Prentiss (R N.Y.) March 18, 1840–Feb. 20, 1905; House 1903–Feb. 20, 1905.

Otjen, Theobald (R Wis.) Oct. 27, 1851–April 11, 1924; House 1895–1907.

O'Toole, Donald Lawrence (D N.Y.) Aug. 1, 1902–Sept. 12, 1964; House 1937–53.

Ottinger, Richard Lawrence (D N.Y.) Jan. 27, 1929– ; House 1965–71, 1975–85.

Oury, Granville Henderson (D Ariz.) March 12, 1825–Jan. 11, 1891; House (Terr. Del.) 1881–85.

Outhwaite, Joseph Hodson (D Ohio) Dec. 5, 1841–Dec. 9, 1907; House 1885–95.

Outland, George Elmer (D Calif.) Oct. 8, 1906–March 2, 1981; House 1943–47.

Outlaw, David (cousin of George Outlaw) (W N.C.) Sept. 14, 1806–Oct. 22, 1868; House 1847–53.

Outlaw, George (cousin of David Outlaw) (– N.C.) ?–Aug. 15, 1825; House Jan. 19–March 3, 1825.

Overman, Lee Slater (D N.C.) Jan. 3, 1854–Dec. 12, 1930; Senate 1903–Dec. 12, 1930.

Overmyer, Arthur Warren (D Ohio) May 31, 1879–March 8, 1952; House 1915–19.

Overstreet, James (– S.C.) Feb. 11, 1773–May 24, 1822; House 1819–May 24, 1822.

Overstreet, James Whetstone (D Ga.) Aug. 28, 1866–Dec. 4, 1938; House Oct. 3, 1906–07, 1917–23.

Overstreet, Jesse (R Ind.) Dec. 14, 1859–May 27, 1910; House 1895–1909.

Overton, Edward Jr. (R Pa.) Feb. 4, 1836–Sept. 18, 1903; House 1877–81.

Overton, John Holmes (uncle of Overton Brooks) (D La.) Sept. 17, 1875–May 14, 1948; House May 12, 1931–33; Senate 1933–May 14, 1948.

Overton, Walter Hampden (J La.) 1788–Dec. 24, 1845; House 1829–31.

Owen, Allen Ferdinand (W Ga.) Oct. 9, 1816–April 7, 1865; House 1849–51.

Owen, Emmett Marshall (D Ga.) Oct. 19, 1877–June 21, 1939; House 1933–June 21, 1939.

Owen, George Washington (– Ala.) Oct. 20, 1796–Aug. 18, 1837; House 1823–29.

Owen, James (R N.C.) Dec. 7, 1784–Sept. 4, 1865; House 1817–19.

Owen, Robert Dale (D Ind.) Nov. 7, 1801–June 24, 1877; House 1843–47.

Owen, Robert Latham (D Okla.) Feb. 3, 1856–July 19, 1947; Senate Dec. 11, 1907–25.

Owen, Ruth Bryan (later Mrs. Borge Rohde, daughter of William Jennings Bryan) (D Fla.) Oct. 2, 1885–July 26, 1954; House 1929–33.

Owen, William Dale (R Ind.) Sept. 6, 1846–1906; House 1885–91.

Owens, Douglas Wayne (D Utah) May 2, 1937– ; House 1973–75, 1987–93.

Owens, George Welshman (D Ga.) Aug. 29, 1786–March 2, 1856; House 1835–39 (1835–37 Jacksonian).

Owens, James W. (D Ohio) Oct. 24, 1837–March 30, 1900; House 1889–93.

Owens, Major Robert Odell (D N.Y.) June 28, 1936– ; House 1983– .

Owens, Thomas Leonard (R Ill.) Dec. 21, 1897–June 7, 1948; House 1947–June 7, 1948.

Owens, William Claiborne (D Ky.) Oct. 17, 1849–Nov. 18, 1925; House 1895–97.

Owsley, Bryan Young (W Ky.) Aug. 19, 1798–Oct. 27, 1849; House 1841–43.

Oxley, Michael Garver (R Ohio) Feb. 11, 1944– ; House June 25, 1981– .

P

Pace, Stephen (D Ga.) March 9, 1891–April 5, 1970; House 1937–51.

Pacheco, Romualdo (R Calif.) Oct. 31, 1831–Jan. 23, 1899; House 1877–Feb. 7, 1878, 1879–83; Gov. Feb. 27–Dec. 9, 1875.

Packard, Jasper (R Ind.) Feb. 1, 1832–Dec. 13, 1899; House 1869–75.

Packard, Ronald C. (R Calif.) Jan. 19, 1931– ; House 1983– .

Packer, Asa (D Pa.) Dec. 29, 1805–May 17, 1879; House 1853–57.

Packer, Horace Billings (R Pa.) Oct. 11, 1851–April 13, 1940; House 1897–1901.

Packer, John Black (R Pa.) March 21, 1824–July 7, 1891; House 1869–77.

Packwood, Robert William (R Ore.) Sept. 11, 1932– ; Senate 1969–Oct. 1, 1995; Chrmn. Senate Commerce, Science, and Transportation 1981–85; Chrmn. Senate Finance 1985–87, 1995.

Paddock, Algernon Sidney (R Neb.) Nov. 9, 1830–Oct. 17, 1897; Senate 1875–81, 1887–93.

Paddock, George Arthur (R Ill.) March 24, 1885–Dec. 29, 1964; House 1941–43.

Padgett, Lemuel Phillips (D Tenn.) Nov. 28, 1855–Aug. 2, 1922; House 1901–Aug. 2, 1922.

Pagan, Bolivar (Coal. P.R.) May 16, 1897–Feb. 9, 1961; House (Res. Comm.) Dec. 26, 1939–45.

Page, Carroll Smalley (R Vt.) Jan. 10, 1843–Dec. 3, 1925; Senate Oct. 21, 1908–23; Gov. Oct. 2, 1890–Oct. 6, 1892.

Page, Charles Harrison (D R.I.) July 19, 1843–July 21, 1912; House Feb. 21–March 3, 1887, 1891–93, April 5, 1893–95.

Page, Henry (D Md.) June 28, 1841–Jan. 7, 1913; House 1891–Sept. 3, 1892.

Page, Horace Francis (R Calif.) Oct. 20, 1833–Aug. 23, 1890; House 1873–83.

Page, John (R Va.) April 17, 1743–Oct. 11, 1808; House 1789–97 (1789–95 no party); Gov. Dec. 1, 1802–Dec. 1, 1805 (Democratic Republican).

Page, John (W N.H.) May 21, 1787–Sept. 8, 1865; Senate June 8, 1836–37; Gov. June 5, 1839–June 2, 1842 (Democrat).

Page, Robert (F Va.) Feb. 4, 1765–Dec. 8, 1840; House 1799–1801.

Page, Robert Newton (D N.C.) Oct. 26, 1859–Oct. 3, 1933; House 1903–17.

Page, Sherman (J N.Y.) May 9, 1779–Sept. 27, 1853; House 1833–37.

Paige, Calvin DeWitt (R Mass.) May 20, 1848–April 24, 1930; House Nov. 26, 1913–25.

Paige, David Raymond (D Ohio) April 8, 1844–June 30, 1901; House 1883–85.

Paine, Elijah (F Vt.) Jan. 21, 1757–April 28, 1842; Senate 1795–Sept. 1, 1801 (1795–1801 no party).

Paine, Halbert Eleazer (R Wis.) Feb. 4, 1826–April 14, 1905; House 1865–71.

Paine, Robert Treat (AP N.C.) Feb. 18, 1812–Feb. 8, 1872; House 1855–57.

Paine, William Wiseham (D Ga.) Oct. 10, 1817–Aug. 5, 1882; House Dec. 22, 1870–71.

Palen, Rufus (W N.Y.) Feb. 25, 1807–April 26, 1844; House 1839–41.

Palfrey, John Gorham (W Mass.) May 2, 1796–April 26, 1881; House 1847–49.

Pallone, Frank Jr. (D N.J.) Oct. 30, 1951– ; House Nov. 8, 1988– .

Palmer, Alexander Mitchell (D Pa.) May 4, 1872–May 11, 1936; House 1909–15; Atty. Gen. March 5, 1919–March 5, 1921.

Palmer, Beriah (R N.Y.) 1740–May 20, 1812; House 1803–05.

Palmer, Cyrus Maffet (R Pa.) Feb. 12, 1887–Aug. 16, 1959; House 1927–29.

Palmer, Francis Wayland "Frank" (R Iowa) Oct. 11, 1827–Dec. 3, 1907; House 1869–73.

Palmer, George William (nephew of John Palmer, cousin of William Elisha Haynes) (R N.Y.) Jan. 13, 1818–March 2, 1916; House 1857–61.

Palmer, Henry Wilber (R Pa.) July 10, 1839–Feb. 15, 1913; House 1901–07, 1909–11.

Palmer, John (uncle of George William Palmer) (D N.Y.) Jan. 29, 1785–Dec. 8, 1840; House 1817–19 (Republican), 1837–39.

Palmer, John McAuley (D Ill.) Sept. 13, 1817–Sept. 25, 1900; Senate 1891–97; Gov. Jan. 11, 1869–Jan. 13, 1873 (Republican).

Palmer, John William (R Mo.) Aug. 20, 1866–Nov. 3, 1958; House 1929–31.

Palmer, Thomas Witherell (R Mich.) Jan. 25, 1830–June 1, 1913; Senate 1883–89.

Palmer, William Adams (R Vt.) Sept. 12, 1781–Dec. 3, 1860; Senate Oct. 20, 1818–25; Gov. Oct. 18, 1831–Nov. 2, 1835 (Anti-Mason Democrat).

Palmisano, Vincent Luke (D Md.) Aug. 5, 1882–Jan. 12, 1953; House 1927–39.

Panetta, Leon Edward (D Calif.) June 28, 1938– ; House 1977–Jan. 21, 1993; Chrmn. House Budget 1989–93.

Pantin, Santiago Iglesias. (*See* Iglesias, Santiago.)

Pappas, Michael (R N.J.) Dec. 29, 1960– ; House 1997–99.

Paredes, Quintin (Nat. P.I.) Sept. 9, 1884–Jan. 30, 1973; House (Res. Comm.) Feb. 14, 1936–Sept. 29, 1938.

Park, Frank (D Ga.) March 3, 1864–Nov. 20, 1925; House Nov. 5, 1913–25.

Parke, Benjamin (– Ind.) Sept. 22, 1777–July 12, 1835; House (Terr. Del.) Dec. 12, 1805–March 1, 1808.

Parker, Abraham X. (R N.Y.) Nov. 14, 1831–Aug. 9, 1909; House 1881–89.

Parker, Amasa Junius (D N.Y.) June 2, 1807–May 13, 1890; House 1837–39.

Parker, Andrew (D Pa.) May 21, 1805–Jan. 15, 1864; House 1851–53.

Parker, Homer Cling (D Ga.) Sept. 25, 1885–June 22, 1946; House Sept. 10, 1931–35.

Parker, Hosea Washington (D N.H.) May 30, 1833–Aug. 21, 1922; House 1871–75.

Parker, Isaac (F Mass.) June 17, 1768–July 25, 1830; House 1797–99.

Parker, Isaac Charles (R Mo.) Oct. 15, 1838–Nov. 17, 1896; House 1871–75.

Parker, James (R Mass.) 1768–Nov. 9, 1837; House 1813–15, 1819–21.

Parker, James (grandfather of Richard Wayne Parker) (J N.J.) March 3, 1776–April 1, 1868; House 1833–37.

Parker, James Southworth (R N.Y.) June 3, 1867–Dec. 19, 1933; House 1913–Dec. 19, 1933.

Parker, John Mason (R N.Y.) June 14, 1805–Dec. 16, 1873; House 1855–59 (1855–57 Whig).

Parker, Josiah (F Va.) May 11, 1751–March 11, 1810; House 1789–1801 (1789–95 no party).

Parker, Mike (R Miss.) Oct. 31, 1949– ; House 1989–99 (1993–Nov. 10, 1995, Democrat).

Parker, Nahum (R N.H.) March 4, 1760–Nov. 12, 1839; Senate 1807–June 1, 1810.

Parker, Richard (D Va.) Dec. 22, 1810–Nov. 10, 1893; House 1849–51.

Parker, Richard Elliott (J Va.) Dec. 27, 1783–Sept. 10, 1840; Senate Dec. 12, 1836–March 13, 1837.

Parker, Richard Wayne (grandson of James Parker) (R N.J.) Aug. 6, 1848–Nov. 28, 1923; House 1895–1911, Dec. 1, 1914–19, 1921–23.

Parker, Samuel Wilson (W Ind.) Sept. 9, 1805–Feb. 1, 1859; House 1851–55.

Parker, Severn Eyre (– Va.) July 19, 1787–Oct. 21, 1836; House 1819–21.

Parker, William Henry (– S.D.) May 5, 1847–June 26, 1908; House 1907–June 26, 1908.

Parks, Gorham (J Maine) May 27, 1794–Nov. 23, 1877; House 1833–37.

Parks, Tilman Bacon (D Ark.) May 14, 1872–Feb. 12, 1950; House 1921–37.

Parmenter, William (D Mass.) March 30, 1789–Feb. 25, 1866; House 1837–45.

Parran, Thomas (R Md.) Feb. 12, 1860–March 29, 1955; House 1911–13.

Parrett, William Fletcher (D Ind.) Aug. 10, 1825–June 30, 1895; House 1889–93.

Parris, Albion Keith (cousin of Virgil Delphini Parris) (R Maine) Jan. 19, 1788–Feb. 11, 1857; House 1815–Feb. 3, 1818 (Mass.); Senate 1827–Aug. 26, 1828; Gov. Jan. 5, 1822–Jan. 3, 1827 (Democratic Republican).

Parris, Stanford E. (R Va.) Sept. 9, 1929– ; House 1973–75, 1981–91.

Parris, Virgil Delphini (cousin of Albion Keith Parris) (SRD Maine) Feb. 18, 1807–June 13, 1874; House May 29, 1838–41.

Parrish, Isaac (D Ohio) March 1804–Aug. 9, 1860; House 1839–41, 1845–47.

Parrish, Lucian Walton (D Texas) Jan. 10, 1878–March 27, 1922; House 1919–March 27, 1922.

Parrott, John Fabyan (– N.H.) Aug. 8, 1767–July 9, 1836; House 1817–19; Senate 1819–25.

Parrott, Marcus Junius (R Kan.) Oct. 27, 1828–Oct. 4, 1879; House (Terr. Del.) 1857–Jan. 29, 1861.

Parsons, Claude VanCleve (D Ill.) Oct. 7, 1895–May 23, 1941; House Nov. 4, 1930–41.

Parsons, Edward Young (D Ky.) Dec. 12, 1841–July 8, 1876; House 1875–July 8, 1876.

Parsons, Herbert (R N.Y.) Oct. 28, 1869–Sept. 16, 1925; House 1905–11.

Parsons, Richard Chappel (R Ohio) Oct. 10, 1826–Jan. 9, 1899; House 1873–75.

Partridge, Donald Barrows (R Maine) June 7, 1891–June 5, 1946; House 1931–33.

Partridge, Frank Charles (R Vt.) May 7, 1861–March 2, 1943; Senate Dec. 23, 1930–March 31, 1931.

Partridge, George (– Mass.) Feb. 8, 1740–July 7, 1828; House 1789–Aug. 14, 1790; Cont. Cong. 1779–85.

Partridge, Samuel (D N.Y.) Nov. 29, 1790–March 30, 1883; House 1841–43.

Paschal, Thomas Moore (D Texas) Dec. 15, 1845–Jan. 28, 1919; House 1893–95.

Pasco, Samuel (D Fla.) June 28, 1834–March 13, 1917; Senate May 19, 1887–April 18, 1899.

Pascrell, Bill Jr. (D N.J.) Jan. 25, 1937– ; House 1997– .

Pashayan, Charles "Chip" Jr. (R Calif.) March 27, 1941– ; House 1979–91.

Passman, Otto Ernest (D La.) June 27, 1900–Aug. 13, 1988; House 1947–77.

Pastor, Ed (D Ariz.) June 28, 1943– ; House Oct. 3, 1991– .

Pastore, John Orlando (D R.I.) March 17, 1907– ; Senate Dec. 19, 1950–Dec. 28, 1976; Gov. Oct. 6, 1945–Dec. 19, 1950.

Paterson, John (R N.Y.) 1744–July 19, 1808; House 1803–05.

Paterson, William (– N.J.) Dec. 24, 1745–Sept. 9, 1806; Senate 1789–Nov. 13, 1790; Cont. Cong. (elected but did not attend) 1780, 1787; Gov. Oct. 30, 1790–March 4, 1793 (Federalist); Assoc. Justice Supreme Court March 11, 1793–Sept. 9, 1806.

Patman, John William Wright (father of William Neff Patman) (D Texas) Aug. 6, 1893–March 7, 1976; House 1929–March 7, 1976; Chrmn. House Select Committee on Small Business 1949–53, 1955–63; Chrmn. House Banking and Currency 1963–75.

Patman, William Neff (son of John William Wright Patman) (D Texas) March 26, 1927– ; House 1981–85.

Patrick, Luther (D Ala.) Jan. 23, 1894–May 26, 1957; House 1937–43, 1945–47.

Patten, Edward James (D N.J.) Aug. 22, 1905–Sept. 17, 1994; House 1963–81.

Patten, Harold Ambrose (D Ariz.) Oct. 6, 1907–Sept. 6, 1969; House 1949–55.

Patten, John (R Del.) April 26, 1746–Dec. 26, 1800; House 1793–Feb. 14, 1794 (no party), 1795–97; Cont. Cong. 1786.

Patten, Thomas Gedney (D N.Y.) Sept. 12, 1861–Feb. 23, 1939; House 1911–17.

Patterson, David Trotter (D Tenn.) Feb. 28, 1818–Nov. 3, 1891; Senate May 4, 1865–69.

Patterson, Edward White (D Kan.) Oct. 4, 1895–March 6, 1940; House 1935–39.

Patterson, Elizabeth Johnston (daughter of Olin DeWitt Talmadge Johnston) (D S.C.) Nov. 18, 1939– ; House 1987–93.

Patterson, Ellis Ellwood (D Calif.) Nov. 28, 1897–Aug. 25, 1985; House 1945–47.

Patterson, Francis Ford Jr. (R N.J.) July 30, 1867–Nov. 30, 1935; House Nov. 2, 1920–27.

Patterson, George Robert (R Pa.) Nov. 9, 1863–March 21, 1906; House 1901–March 21, 1906.

Patterson, George Washington (brother of William Patterson, uncle of Augustus Frank) (R N.Y.) Nov. 11, 1799–Oct. 15, 1879; House 1877–79.

Patterson, Gilbert Brown (D N.C.) May 29, 1863–Jan. 26, 1922; House 1903–07.

Patterson, James O'Hanlon (D S.C.) June 25, 1857–Oct. 25, 1911; House 1905–11.

Patterson, James Thomas (R Conn.) Oct. 20, 1908–Feb. 7, 1989; House 1947–59.

Patterson, James Willis (R N.H.) July 2, 1823–May 4, 1893; House 1863–67; Senate 1867–73.

Patterson, Jerry Mumford (D Calif.) Oct. 25, 1934– ; House 1975–85.

Patterson, John (half-brother of Thomas Patterson) (– Ohio) Feb. 10, 1771–Feb. 7, 1848; House 1823–25.

Patterson, John James (R S.C.) Aug. 8, 1830–Sept. 28, 1912; Senate 1873–79.

Patterson, Josiah (father of Malcolm Rice Patterson) (D Tenn.) April 14, 1837–Feb. 10, 1904; House 1891–97.

Patterson, Lafayette Lee (D Ala.) Aug. 23, 1888–March 3, 1987; House Nov. 6, 1928–33.

Patterson, Malcolm Rice (son of Josiah Patterson) (D Tenn.) June 7, 1861–March 8, 1935; House 1901–Nov. 5, 1906; Gov. Jan. 17, 1907–Jan. 26, 1911.

Patterson, Roscoe Conkling (R Mo.) Sept. 15, 1876–Oct. 22, 1954; House 1921–23; Senate 1929–35.

Patterson, Thomas (half-brother of John Patterson) (R Pa.) Oct. 1, 1764–Nov. 16, 1841; House 1817–25.

Patterson, Thomas J. (W N.Y.) about 1808–?; House 1843–45.

Patterson, Thomas MacDonald (D Colo.) Nov. 4, 1839–July 23, 1916; House (Terr. Del.) 1875–Aug. 1, 1876; (Rep.) Dec. 13, 1877–79; Senate 1901–07.

Patterson, Walter (– N.Y.) ?–?; House 1821–23.

Patterson, William (brother of George Washington Patterson, uncle of Augustus Frank) (W N.Y.) June 4, 1789–Aug. 14, 1838; House 1837–Aug. 14, 1838.

Patterson, William (J Ohio) 1790–Aug. 17, 1868; House 1833–37.

Pattison, Edward Worthington (D N.Y.) April 29, 1932–Aug. 22, 1990; House 1975–79.

Pattison, John M. (D Ohio) June 13, 1847–June 18, 1906; House 1891–93; Gov. Jan. 8–June 18, 1906.

Patton, Charles Emory (son of John Patton, brother of John Patton Jr., cousin of William Irvin Swoope) (– Pa.) July 5, 1859–Dec. 15, 1937; House 1911–15.

Patton, David Henry (D Ind.) Nov. 26, 1837–Jan. 17, 1914; House 1891–93.

Patton, John (father of Charles Emory Patton and John Patton Jr., uncle of William Irvin Swoope) (R Pa.) Jan. 6, 1823–Dec. 23, 1897; House 1861–63, 1887–89.

Patton, John Jr. (son of John Patton, brother of Charles Emory Patton, cousin of William Irvin Swoope) (R Mich.) Oct. 30, 1850–May 24, 1907; Senate May 5, 1894–Jan. 14, 1895.

Patton, John Denniston (D Pa.) Nov. 28, 1829–Feb. 22, 1904; House 1883–85.

Patton, John Mercer (D Va.) Aug. 10, 1797–Oct. 29, 1858; House Nov. 25, 1830–April 7, 1838 (Nov. 25, 1830–37 Jacksonian); Gov. March 18–March 31, 1841 (State Rights Whig).

Patton, Nat (D Texas) Feb. 26, 1884–July 27, 1957; House 1935–45.

Paul, John (father of John Paul, below) (Read. Va.) June 30, 1839–Nov. 1, 1901; House 1881–Sept. 5, 1883.

Paul, John (son of John Paul, above) (R Va.) Dec. 9, 1883–Feb. 13, 1964; House Dec. 15, 1922–23.

Paul, Ronald Ernest (R Texas) Aug. 20, 1935– ; House April 3, 1976–77, 1979–85, 1997– .

Paulding, William Jr. (R N.Y.) March 7, 1770–Feb. 11, 1854; House 1811–13.

Pawling, Levi (F Pa.) July 25, 1773–Sept. 7, 1845; House 1817–19.

Paxon, L. William (husband of Susan Molinari, son-in-law of Guy Molinari) (R N.Y.) April 29, 1954– ; House 1989–99.

Payne, Donald M. (D N.J.) July 16, 1934– ; House 1989– .

Payne, Frederick George (R Maine) July 24, 1904–June 15, 1978; Senate 1953–59; Gov. Jan. 5, 1949–Dec. 25, 1952.

Payne, Henry B. (grandfather of Frances Payne Bolton, great-grandfather of Oliver Payne Bolton) (D Ohio) Nov. 30, 1810–Sept. 9, 1896; House 1875–77; Senate 1885–91.

Payne, Lewis Franklin Jr. (D Va.) July 9, 1945– ; House June 21, 1988–97.

Payne, Sereno Elisha (R N.Y.) June 26, 1843–Dec. 10, 1914; House 1883–87, 1889–Dec. 10, 1914; House majority leader 1899–1911.

Payne, William Winter (D Ala.) Jan. 2, 1807–Sept. 2, 1874; House 1841–47.

Paynter, Lemuel (D Pa.) 1788–Aug. 1, 1863; House 1837–41.

Paynter, Thomas Hanson (D Ky.) Dec. 9, 1851–March 8, 1921; House 1889–Jan. 5, 1895; Senate 1907–13.

Payson, Lewis Edwin (R Ill.) Sept. 17, 1840–Oct. 4, 1909; House 1881–91.

Peace, Roger Craft (D S.C.) May 19, 1899–Aug. 20, 1968; Senate Aug. 5–Nov. 4, 1941.

Pearce, Charles Edward (R Mo.) May 29, 1842–Jan. 30, 1902; House 1897–1901.

Pearce, Dutee Jerauld (AMas. R.I.) April 3, 1789–May 9, 1849; House 1825–37 (1825–33 no party).

Pearce, James Alfred (D Md.) Dec. 8, 1805–Dec. 20, 1862; House 1835–39 (Whig), 1841–43 (Whig); Senate 1843–Dec. 20, 1862 (1843–61 Whig).

Pearce, John Jamison (R Pa.) Feb. 28, 1826–May 26, 1912; House 1855–57.

Pearre, George Alexander (R Md.) July 16, 1860–Sept. 19, 1923; House 1899–1911.

Pearson, Albert Jackson (D Ohio) May 20, 1846–May 15, 1905; House 1891–95.

Pearson, Herron Carney (D Tenn.) July 31, 1890–April 24, 1953; House 1935–43.

Pearson, James Blackwood (R Kan.) May 7, 1920– ; Senate Jan. 31, 1962–Dec. 23, 1978.

Pearson, John James (W Pa.) Oct. 25, 1800–May 30, 1888; House Dec. 5, 1836–37.

Pearson, Joseph (F N.C.) 1776–Oct. 27, 1834; House 1809–15.

Pearson, Richmond (R N.C.) Jan. 26, 1852–Sept. 12, 1923; House 1895–99, May 10, 1900–01.

Pease, Donald James (D Ohio) Sept. 26, 1931– ; House 1977–93.

Pease, Edward A. (R Ind.) May 22, 1951– ; House 1997– .

Pease, Henry Roberts (R Miss.) Feb. 19, 1835–Jan. 2, 1907; Senate Feb. 3, 1874–75.

Peaslee, Charles Hazen (D N.H.) Feb. 6, 1804–Sept. 18, 1866; House 1847–53.

Peavey, Hubert Haskell (R Wis.) Jan. 12, 1881–Nov. 21, 1937; House 1923–35.

Peck, Erasmus Darwin (R Ohio) Sept. 16, 1808–Dec. 25, 1876; House April 23, 1870–73.

Peck, George Washington (D Mich.) June 4, 1818–June 30, 1905; House 1855–57.

Peck, Jared Valentine (D N.Y.) Sept. 21, 1816–Dec. 25, 1891; House 1853–55.

Peck, Lucius Benedict (D Vt.) Nov. 17, 1802–Dec. 28, 1866; House 1847–51.

Peck, Luther Christopher (W N.Y.) Jan. 1800–Feb. 5, 1876; House 1837–41.

Peckham, Rufus Wheeler (D N.Y.) Dec. 20, 1809–Nov. 22, 1873; House 1853–55.

Peddie, Thomas Baldwin (R N.J.) Feb. 11, 1808–Feb. 16, 1889; House 1877–79.

Peden, Preston Elmer (D Okla.) June 28, 1914–June 27, 1985; House 1947–49.

Peek, Harmanus (– N.Y.) June 24, 1782–Sept. 27, 1838; House 1819–21.

Peel, Samuel West (D Ark.) Sept. 13, 1831–Dec. 18, 1924; House 1883–93.

Peelle, Stanton Judkins (R Ind.) Feb. 11, 1843–Sept. 4, 1928; House 1881–May 22, 1884.

Peery, George Campbell (D Va.) Oct. 28, 1873–Oct. 14, 1952; House 1923–29; Gov. Jan. 17, 1934–Jan. 19, 1938.

Peffer, William Alfred (P Kan.) Sept. 10, 1831–Oct. 7, 1912; Senate 1891–97.

Pegram, John (R Va.) Nov. 16, 1773–April 8, 1831; House April 21, 1818–19.

Peirce, Joseph (F N.H.) June 25, 1748–Sept. 12, 1812; House 1801–02.

Peirce, Robert Bruce Fraser (R Ind.) Feb. 17, 1843–Dec. 5, 1898; House 1881–83.

Pelham, Charles (R Ala.) March 12, 1835–Jan. 18, 1908; House 1873–75.

Pell, Claiborne de Borda (son of Herbert Claiborne Pell Jr., great-great grandson of John Francis Hamtramck Claiborne, great-great-great-nephew of George Mifflin Dallas, great-great-great-great-nephew of William Charles Cole Claiborne and Nathaniel Herbert Claiborne) (D R.I.) Nov. 22, 1918– ; Senate 1961–97; Chrmn. Senate Rules and Administration 1978–81; Chrmn. Senate Foreign Relations 1987–95.

Pell, Herbert Claiborne Jr. (great-grandson of John Francis Hamtramck Claiborne, great-great-great-nephew of William Charles Cole Claiborne and Nathaniel Herbert Claiborne, father of Claiborne de Borda Pell) (D N.Y.) Feb. 16, 1884–July 17, 1961; House 1919–21.

Pelly, Thomas Minor (R Wash.) Aug. 22, 1902–Nov. 21, 1973; House 1953–73.

Pelosi, Nancy (daughter of Thomas D'Alesandro Jr.) (D Calif.) March 26, 1940– ; House June 9, 1987– .

Pelton, Guy Ray (W N.Y.) Aug. 3, 1824–July 24, 1890; House 1855–57.

Pence, Lafayette (P Colo.) Dec. 23, 1857–Oct. 22, 1923; House 1893–95.

Pendleton, Edmund Henry (AJ N.Y.) 1788–Feb. 25, 1862; House 1831–33.

Pendleton, George Cassety (D Texas) April 23, 1845–Jan. 19, 1913; House 1893–97.

Pendleton, George Hunt (son of Nathanael Greene Pendleton) (D Ohio) July 19, 1825–Nov. 24, 1889; House 1857–65; Senate 1879–85.

Pendleton, James Monroe (R R.I.) Jan. 10, 1822–Feb. 16, 1889; House 1871–75.

Pendleton, John Overton (D W.Va.) July 4, 1851–Dec. 24, 1916; House 1889–Feb. 26, 1890, 1891–95.

Pendleton, John Strother (W Va.) March 1, 1802–Nov. 19, 1868; House 1845–49.

Pendleton, Nathanael Green (father of George Hunt Pendleton) (W Ohio) Aug. 25, 1793–June 16, 1861; House 1841–43.

Penington, John Brown (D Del.) Dec. 20, 1825–June 1, 1902; House 1887–91.

Penn, Alexander Gordon (D La.) May 10, 1799–May 7, 1866; House Dec. 30, 1850–53.

Penniman, Ebenezer Jenckes (W Mich.) Jan. 11, 1804–April 12, 1890; House 1851–53.

Pennington, Alexander Cumming McWhorter (cousin of William Pennington) (W N.J.) July 2, 1810–Jan. 25, 1867; House 1853–57.

Pennington, William (cousin of Alexander Cumming McWhorter Pennington) (R N.J.) May 4, 1796–Feb. 16, 1862; House 1859–61; Speaker Feb. 1, 1860–61; Gov. Oct. 27, 1837–Oct. 27, 1843 (Democratic Republican).

Penny, Timothy Joseph (DFL Minn.) Nov. 19, 1951– ; House 1983–95.

Pennybacker, Isaac Samuels (cousin of Green Berry Samuels) (D Va.) Sept. 3, 1805–Jan. 12, 1847; House 1837–39; Senate Dec. 3, 1845–Jan. 12, 1847.

Penrose, Boies (R Pa.) Nov. 1, 1860–Dec. 31, 1921; Senate 1897–Dec. 31, 1921.

Pepper, Claude Denson (D Fla.) Sept. 8, 1900–May 30, 1989; Senate Nov. 4, 1936–51; House 1963–May 30, 1989; Chrmn. House Rules 1983–89.

Pepper, George Wharton (R Pa.) March 16, 1867–May 24, 1961; Senate Jan. 9, 1922–27.

Pepper, Irvin St. Clair (D Iowa) June 10, 1876–Dec. 22, 1913; House 1911–Dec. 22, 1913.

Perce, Legrand Winfield (R Miss.) June 19, 1836–March 16, 1911; House Feb. 23, 1870–73.

Percy, Charles Harting (father-in-law of John Davison "Jay" Rockefeller IV) (R Ill.) Sept. 27, 1919– ; Senate 1967–85; Chrmn. Senate Foreign Relations 1981–85.

Percy, Le Roy (D Miss.) Nov. 9, 1860–Dec. 24, 1929; Senate Feb. 23, 1910–13.

Perea, Francisco (cousin of Pedro Perea) (R N.M.) Jan. 9, 1830–May 21, 1913; House (Terr. Del.) 1863–65.

Perea, Pedro (cousin of Francisco Perea) (R N.M.) April 22, 1852–Jan. 11, 1906; House (Terr. Del.) 1899–1901.

Perham, Sidney (R Maine) March 27, 1819–April 10, 1907; House 1863–69; Gov. Jan. 4, 1871–Jan. 7, 1874.

Perkins, Bishop (D N.Y.) Sept. 5, 1787–Nov. 20, 1866; House 1853–55.

Perkins, Bishop Walden (R Kan.) Oct. 18, 1841–June 20, 1894; House 1883–91; Senate Jan. 1, 1892–93.

Perkins, Carl Christopher "Chris" (son of Carl Dewey Perkins) (D Ky.) Aug. 6, 1954– ; House 1985–93 (elected Nov. 6, 1984, to fill a vacancy in the 98th Congress and to the 99th Congress but was not sworn in until Jan. 3, 1985).

Perkins, Carl Dewey (father of Carl Christopher "Chris" Perkins) (D Ky.) Oct. 15, 1912–Aug. 3, 1984; House 1949–Aug. 3, 1984; Chrmn. House Education and Labor 1967–84.

Perkins, Elias (F Conn.) April 5, 1767–Sept. 27, 1845; House 1801–03.

Perkins, George Clement (R Calif.) Aug. 23, 1839–Feb. 26, 1923; Senate July 26, 1893–1915; Gov. Jan. 8, 1880–Jan. 10, 1883.

Perkins, George Douglas (R Iowa) Feb. 29, 1840–Feb. 3, 1914; House 1891–99.

Perkins, James Breck (R N.Y.) Nov. 4, 1847–March 11, 1910; House 1901–March 11, 1910.

Perkins, Jared (W N.H.) Jan. 5, 1793–Oct. 15, 1854; House 1851–53.

Perkins, John Jr. (D La.) July 1, 1819–Nov. 28, 1885; House 1853–55.

Perkins, Randolph (R N.J.) Nov. 30, 1871–May 25, 1936; House 1921–May 25, 1936.

Perky, Kirtland Irving (D Idaho) Feb. 8, 1867–Jan. 9, 1939; Senate Nov. 18, 1912–Feb. 5, 1913.

Perlman, Nathan David (R N.Y.) Aug. 2, 1887–June 29, 1952; House Nov. 2, 1920–27.

Perrill, Augustus Leonard (D Ohio) Jan. 20, 1807–June 2, 1882; House 1845–47.

Perry, Aaron Fyfe (R Ohio) Jan. 1, 1815–March 11, 1893; House 1871–72.

Perry, Eli (D N.Y.) Dec. 25, 1799–May 17, 1881; House 1871–75.

Perry, John Jasiel (R Maine) Aug. 2, 1811–May 2, 1897; House 1855–57, 1859–61.

Perry, Nehemiah (D N.J.) March 30, 1816–Nov. 1, 1881; House 1861–65.

Perry, Thomas Johns (D Md.) Feb. 17, 1807–June 27, 1871; House 1845–47.

Perry, William Hayne (D S.C.) June 9, 1839–July 7, 1902; House 1885–91.

Person, Seymour Howe (R Mich.) Feb. 2, 1879–April 7, 1957; House 1931–33.

Persons, Henry (ID Ga.) Jan. 30, 1834–June 17, 1910; House 1879–81.

Pesquera, José Lorenzo (Nonpart. P.R.) Aug. 10, 1882–July 25, 1950; House (Res. Comm.) April 15, 1932–33.

Peter, George (F Md.) Sept. 28, 1779–June 22, 1861; House Oct. 7, 1816–19, 1825–27.

Peters, Andrew James (D Mass.) April 3, 1872–June 26, 1938; House 1907–Aug. 15, 1914.

Peters, John Andrew (uncle of John Andrew Peters, below) (R Maine) Oct. 9, 1822–April 2, 1904; House 1867–73.

Peters, John Andrew (nephew of John Andrew Peters, above) (R Maine) Aug. 13, 1864–Aug. 22, 1953; House Sept. 8, 1913–Jan. 2, 1922.

Peters, Mason Summers (P Kan.) Sept. 3, 1844–Feb. 14, 1914; House 1897–99.

Peters, Samuel Ritter (R Kan.) Aug. 16, 1842–April 21, 1910; House 1883–91.

Petersen, Andrew Nicholas (R N.Y.) March 10, 1870–Sept. 28, 1952; House 1921–23.

Peterson, Collin C. (D Minn.) June 29, 1944– ; House 1991– .

Peterson, Hugh (D Ga.) Aug. 21, 1898–Oct. 3, 1961; House 1935–47.

Peterson, James Hardin (D Fla.) Feb. 11, 1894–March 28, 1978; House 1933–51; Chrmn. House Public Lands 1949–51.

Peterson, John Barney (cousin of Horatio Clifford Claypool and Harold Kile Claypool) (D Ind.) July 4, 1850–July 16, 1944; House 1913–15.

Peterson, John E. (R Pa.) Dec. 25, 1938– ; House 1997– .

Peterson, Morris Blaine (D Utah) March 26, 1906–July 15, 1985; House 1961–63.

Peterson, Pete (D Fla.) June 26, 1935– ; House 1991–97.

Petri, Thomas Evert (R Wis.) May 28, 1940– ; House April 3, 1979– .

Petrie, George (ID N.Y.) Sept. 8, 1793–May 8, 1879; House 1847–49.

Petrikin, David (D Pa.) Dec. 1, 1788–March 1, 1847; House 1837–41.

Pettengill, Samuel Barrett (nephew of William Horace Clagett) (D Ind.) Jan. 19, 1886–March 20, 1974; House 1931–39.

Pettibone, Augustus Herman (R Tenn.) Jan. 21, 1835–Nov. 26, 1918; House 1881–87.

Pettigrew, Ebenezer (W N.C.) March 10, 1783–July 8, 1848; House 1835–37.

Pettigrew, Richard Franklin (R S.D.) July 23, 1848–Oct. 5, 1926; House (Terr. Del.) 1881–83; Senate Nov. 2, 1889–1901.

Pettis, Jerry Lyle (husband of Shirley Neal Pettis) (R Calif.) July 18, 1916–Feb. 14, 1975; House 1967–Feb. 14, 1975.

Pettis, Shirley Neal (widow of Jerry Lyle Pettis) (R Calif.) July 12, 1924– ; House April 29, 1975–79.

Pettis, Solomon Newton (R Pa.) Oct. 10, 1827–Sept. 18, 1900; House Dec. 7, 1868–69.

Pettis, Spencer Darwin (J Mo.) 1802–Aug. 28, 1831; House 1829–Aug. 28, 1831.

Pettit, John (D Ind.) June 24, 1807–Jan. 17, 1877; House 1843–49; Senate Jan. 11, 1853–55.

Pettit, John Upfold (R Ind.) Sept. 11, 1820–March 21, 1881; House 1855–61.

Pettus, Edmund Winston (D Ala.) July 6, 1821–July 27, 1907; Senate 1897–July 27, 1907.

Peyser, Peter A. (D N.Y.) Sept. 7, 1921– ; House 1971–77 (Republican), 1979–83.

Peyser, Theodore Albert (D N.Y.) Feb. 18, 1873–Aug. 8, 1937; House 1933–Aug. 8, 1937.

Peyton, Balie (brother of Joseph Hopkins Peyton) (White supporter Tenn.) Nov. 26, 1803–Aug. 18, 1878; House 1833–37 (1833–35 Jacksonian).

Peyton, Joseph Hopkins (brother of Balie Peyton) (W Tenn.) May 20, 1808–Nov. 11, 1845; House 1843–Nov. 11, 1845.

Peyton, Samuel Oldham (D Ky.) Jan. 8, 1804–Jan. 4, 1870; House 1847–49, 1857–61.

Pfeifer, Joseph Lawrence (D N.Y.) Feb. 6, 1892–April 19, 1974; House 1935–51.

Pfeiffer, William Louis (R N.Y.) May 29, 1907–July 22, 1985; House 1949–51.

Pfost, Gracie Bowers (D Idaho) March 12, 1906–Aug. 11, 1965; House 1953–63.

Pheiffer, William Townsend (R N.Y.) July 15, 1898–Aug. 16, 1986; House 1941–43.

Phelan, James (D Tenn.) Dec. 7, 1856–Jan. 30, 1891; House 1887–Jan. 30, 1891.

Phelan, James Duval (D Calif.) April 20, 1861–Aug. 7, 1930; Senate 1915–21.

Phelan, Michael Francis (D Mass.) Oct. 22, 1875–Oct. 12, 1941; House 1913–21.

Phelps, Charles Edward (C Md.) May 1, 1833–Dec. 27, 1908; House 1865–69 (1865–67 Unconditional Unionist).

Phelps, Darwin (R Pa.) April 17, 1807–Dec. 14, 1879; House 1869–71.

Phelps, David (D Ill.) Oct. 26, 1947– ; House 1999– .

Phelps, Elisha (father of John Smith Phelps) (– Conn.) Nov. 16, 1779–April 6, 1847; House 1819–21, 1825–29.

Phelps, James (son of Lancelot Phelps) (D Conn.) Jan. 12, 1822–Jan. 15, 1900; House 1875–83.

Phelps, John Smith (son of Elisha Phelps) (D Mo.) Dec. 22, 1814–Nov. 20, 1886; House 1845–63; Gov. Jan. 8, 1877–Jan. 10, 1881.

Phelps, Lancelot (father of James Phelps) (D Conn.) Nov. 9, 1784–Sept. 1, 1866; House 1835–39 (1835–37 Jacksonian).

Phelps, Oliver (R N.Y.) Oct. 21, 1749–Feb. 21, 1809; House 1803–05.

Phelps, Samuel Shethar (W Vt.) May 13, 1793–March 25, 1855; Senate 1839–51, Jan. 17, 1853–March 16, 1854.

Phelps, Timothy Guy (R Calif.) Dec. 20, 1824–June 11, 1899; House 1861–63.

Phelps, William Wallace (D Minn.) June 1, 1826–Aug. 3, 1873; House May 11, 1858–59.

Phelps, William Walter (R N.J.) Aug. 24, 1839–June 17, 1894; House 1873–75 (no party), 1883–89.

Philbin, Philip Joseph (D Mass.) May 29, 1898–June 14, 1972; House 1943–71.

Philips, John Finis (D Mo.) Dec. 31, 1834–March 13, 1919; House 1875–77, Jan. 10, 1880–81.

Phillips, Alfred Noroton (D Conn.) April 23, 1894–Jan. 18, 1970; House 1937–39.

Phillips, Dayton Edward (R Tenn.) March 29, 1910–Oct. 23, 1980; House 1947–51.

Phillips, Fremont Orestes (R Ohio) March 16, 1856–Feb. 21, 1936; House 1899–1901.

Phillips, Henry Myer (D Pa.) June 30, 1811–Aug. 28, 1884; House 1857–59.

Phillips, John (F Pa.) ?–?; House 1821–23.

Phillips, John (R Calif.) Sept. 11, 1887–Dec. 18, 1983; House 1943–57.

Phillips, Philip (D Ala.) Dec. 13, 1807–Jan. 14, 1884; House 1853–55.

Phillips, Stephen Clarendon (W Mass.) Nov. 4, 1801–June 26, 1857; House Dec. 1, 1834–Sept. 28, 1838.

Phillips, Thomas Wharton (father of Thomas Wharton Phillips Jr.) (R Pa.) Feb. 23, 1835–July 21, 1912; House 1893–97.

Phillips, Thomas Wharton Jr. (son of Thomas Wharton Phillips) (R Pa.) Nov. 21, 1874–Jan. 2, 1956; House 1923–27.

Phillips, William Addison (R Kan.) Jan. 14, 1824–Nov. 30, 1893; House 1873–79.

Philson, Robert (– Pa.) 1759–July 25, 1831; House 1819–21.

Phipps, Lawrence Cowle (R Colo.) Aug. 30, 1862–March 1, 1958; Senate 1919–31.

Phister, Elijah Conner (D Ky.) Oct. 8, 1822–May 16, 1887; House 1879–83.

Phoenix, Jonas Phillips (W N.Y.) Jan. 14, 1788–May 4, 1859; House 1843–45, 1849–51.

Pickens, Andrew (grandfather of Francis Wilkinson Pickens) (– S.C.) Sept. 13, 1739–Aug. 11, 1817; House 1793–95.

Pickens, Francis Wilkinson (grandson of Andrew Pickens) (D S.C.) April 7, 1805–Jan. 25, 1869; House Dec. 8, 1834–43 (Dec. 8, 1834–39 Nullifier); Gov. Dec. 14, 1860–Dec. 17, 1862 (State Rights Democrat).

Pickens, Israel (R Ala.) Jan. 30, 1780–April 24, 1827; House 1811–17 (N.C.); Senate Feb. 17–Nov. 27, 1826; Gov. Nov. 9, 1821–Nov. 25, 1825 (Democratic Republican).

Pickering, Charles W. "Chip" Jr. (R-Miss.) Aug. 10, 1963– ; House 1997– .

Pickering, Timothy (F Mass.) July 17, 1745–Jan. 29, 1829; Senate 1803–11; House 1813–17; Postmaster Gen. Aug. 19, 1791–Jan. 2, 1795; Secy. of War Jan. 2–Dec. 10, 1795; Secy. of State Dec. 10, 1795–May 12, 1800.

Pickett, Charles Edgar (R Iowa) Jan. 14, 1866–July 20, 1930; House 1909–13.

Pickett, Owen Bradford (D Va.) Aug. 31, 1930– ; House 1987– .

Pickett, Thomas Augustus (D Texas) Aug. 14, 1906–June 7, 1980; House 1945–June 30, 1952.

Pickle, James Jarrell "Jake" (D Texas) Oct. 11, 1913– ; House Dec. 21, 1963–95.

Pickler, John Alfred (R S.D.) Jan. 24, 1844–June 13, 1910; House Nov. 2, 1889–97.

Pickman, Benjamin Jr. (F Mass.) Sept. 30, 1763–Aug. 16, 1843; House 1809–11.

Pidcock, James Nelson (cousin of Alvah Augustus Clark) (D N.J.) Feb. 8, 1836–Dec. 17, 1899; House 1885–89.

Pierce, Charles Wilson (R Ala.) Oct. 7, 1823–Feb. 18, 1907; House July 21, 1868–69.

Pierce, Franklin (D N.H.) Nov. 23, 1804–Oct. 8, 1869; House 1833–37; Senate 1837–Feb. 28, 1842; President 1853–57.

Pierce, Gilbert Ashville (R N.D.) Jan. 11, 1839–Feb. 15, 1901; Senate Nov. 21, 1889–91; Gov. (Dakota Terr.) 1884–86.

Pierce, Henry Lillie (R Mass.) Aug. 23, 1825–Dec. 17, 1896; House Dec. 1, 1873–77.

Pierce, Ray Vaughn (R N.Y.) Aug. 6, 1840–Feb. 4, 1914; House 1879–Sept. 18, 1880.

Pierce, Rice Alexander (D Tenn.) July 3, 1848–July 12, 1936; House 1883–85, 1889–93, 1897–1905.

Pierce, Wallace Edgar (R N.Y.) Dec. 9, 1881–Jan. 3, 1940; House 1939–Jan. 3, 1940.

Pierce, Walter Marcus (D Ore.) May 30, 1861–March 27, 1954; House 1933–43; Gov. Jan. 8, 1923–Jan. 10, 1927.

Pierson, Isaac (– N.J.) Aug. 15, 1770–Sept. 22, 1833; House 1827–31.

Pierson, Jeremiah Halsey (– N.Y.) Sept. 13, 1766–Dec. 12, 1855; House 1821–23.

Pierson, Job (J N.Y.) Sept. 23, 1791–April 9, 1860; House 1831–35.

Pigott, James Protus (D Conn.) Sept. 11, 1852–July 1, 1919; House 1893–95.

Pike, Austin Franklin (R N.H.) Oct. 16, 1819–Oct. 8, 1886; House 1873–75; Senate 1883–Oct. 8, 1886.

Pike, Frederick Augustus (R Maine) Dec. 9, 1816–Dec. 2, 1886; House 1861–69.

Pike, James (R N.H.) Nov. 10, 1818–July 26, 1895; House 1855–59 (1855–57 American Party).

Pike, Otis Grey (D N.Y.) Aug. 31, 1921– ; House 1961–79; Chrmn. House Select Committee on Intelligence 1975–76.

Pilcher, John Leonard (D Ga.) Aug. 27, 1898–Aug. 20, 1981; House Feb. 4, 1953–65.

Pile, William Anderson (R Mo.) Feb. 11, 1829–July 7, 1889; House 1867–69; Gov. (N.M. Terr.) 1869, 1870.

Piles, Samuel Henry (R Wash.) Dec. 28, 1858–March 11, 1940; Senate 1905–11.

Pillion, John Raymond (R N.Y.) Aug. 10, 1904–Dec. 31, 1978; House 1953–65.

Pilsbury, Timothy (D Texas) April 12, 1789–Nov. 23, 1858; House March 30, 1846–49.

Pinckney, Charles (father of Henry Laurens Pinckney, father-in-law of Robert Young Hayne) (R S.C.) Oct. 26, 1757–Oct. 29, 1824; Senate Dec. 6, 1798–1801; House 1819–21; Cont. Cong. 1785–87; Gov. Jan. 26, 1789–Dec. 5, 1792, Dec. 8, 1796–Dec. 6, 1798, Dec. 9, 1806–Dec. 10, 1808.

Pinckney, Henry Laurens (son of Charles Pinckney) (N S.C.) Sept. 24, 1794–Feb. 3, 1863; House 1833–37.

Pinckney, John McPherson (D Texas) May 4, 1845–April 24, 1905; House Nov. 17, 1903–April 24, 1905.

Pinckney, Thomas (F S.C.) Oct. 23, 1750–Nov. 2, 1828; House Nov. 23, 1797–1801; Gov. Feb. 20, 1787–Jan. 26, 1789.

Pindall, James (F Va.) about 1783–Nov. 22, 1825; House 1817–July 26, 1820.

Pindar, John Sigsbee (D N.Y.) Nov. 18, 1835–June 30, 1907; House 1885–87, Nov. 4, 1890–91.

Pine, William Bliss (R Okla.) Dec. 30, 1877–Aug. 25, 1942; Senate 1925–31.

Pinero, Jesus T. (PD P.R.) April 16, 1897–Nov. 19, 1952; House (Res. Comm.) 1945–Sept. 2, 1946; Gov. 1946–48.

Pinkney, William (R Md.) March 17, 1764–Feb. 25, 1822; House March 4–Nov. 1791 (no party), 1815–April 18, 1816 (no party); Senate Dec. 21, 1819–Feb. 25, 1822; Atty. Gen. Dec. 11, 1811–Feb. 10, 1814.

Piper, William (R Pa.) Jan. 1, 1774–1852; House 1811–17.

Piper, William Adam (D Calif.) May 21, 1826–Aug. 5, 1899; House 1875–77.

Pirce, William Almy (R R.I.) Feb. 29, 1824–March 5, 1891; House 1885–Jan. 25, 1887.

Pirnie, Alexander (R N.Y.) April 16, 1903–June 12, 1982; House 1959–73.

Pitcher, Nathaniel (J N.Y.) 1777–May 25, 1836; House 1819–23 (no party), 1831–33.

Pitkin, Timothy (F Conn.) Jan. 21, 1766–Dec. 18, 1847; House Sept. 16, 1805–19.

Pitman, Charles Wesley (W Pa.) ?–June 8, 1871; House 1849–51.

Pitney, Mahlon (R N.J.) Feb. 5, 1858–Dec. 9, 1924; House 1895–Jan. 10, 1899; Assoc. Justice Supreme Court March 18, 1912–Dec. 31, 1922.

Pittenger, William Alvin (R Minn.) Dec. 29, 1885–Nov. 26, 1951; House 1929–33, 1935–37, 1939–47.

Pittman, Key (D Nev.) Sept. 19, 1872–Nov. 10, 1940; Senate Jan. 29, 1913–Nov. 10, 1940; elected Pres. pro tempore March 9, 1933, Jan. 7, 1935.

Pitts, Joseph R. (R Pa.) Oct. 10, 1939– ; House 1997– .

Plaisted, Harris Merrill (R Maine) Nov. 2, 1828–Jan. 31, 1898; House Sept. 13, 1875–77; Gov. Jan. 13, 1881–Jan. 3, 1883 (Democrat).

Plant, David (– Conn.) March 29, 1783–Oct. 18, 1851; House 1827–29.

Plants, Tobias Avery (R Ohio) March 17, 1811–June 19, 1887; House 1865–69.

Plater, Thomas (F Md.) May 9, 1769–May 1, 1830; House 1801–05.

Platt, Edmund (R N.Y.) Feb. 2, 1865–Aug. 7, 1939; House 1913–June 7, 1920.

Platt, James Henry Jr. (R Va.) July 13, 1837–Aug. 13, 1894; House Jan. 26, 1870–75.

Platt, Jonas (F N.Y.) June 30, 1769–Feb. 22, 1834; House 1799–1801.

Platt, Orville Hitchcock (R Conn.) July 19, 1827–April 21, 1905; Senate 1879–April 21, 1905.

Platt, Thomas Collier (R N.Y.) July 15, 1833–March 6, 1910; House 1873–77; Senate March 4–May 16, 1881, 1897–1909.

Plauche, Vance Gabriel (D La.) Aug. 25, 1897–April 2, 1976; House 1941–43.

Pleasants, James (R Va.) Oct. 24, 1769–Nov. 9, 1836; House 1811–Dec. 14, 1819; Senate Dec. 14, 1819–Dec. 15, 1822; Gov. Dec. 1, 1822–Dec. 10, 1825.

Ploeser, Walter Christian (R Mo.) Jan. 7, 1907– ; House 1941–49; Chrmn. House Select Committee on Small Business 1947–49.

Plowman, Thomas Scales (D Ala.) June 8, 1843–July 26, 1919; House 1897–Feb. 9, 1898.

Plumb, Preston B. (R Kan.) Oct. 12, 1837–Dec. 20, 1891; Senate 1877–Dec. 20, 1891.

Plumb, Ralph (R Ill.) March 29, 1816–April 8, 1903; House 1885–89.

Plumer, Arnold (D Pa.) June 6, 1801–April 28, 1869; House 1837–39, 1841–43.

Plumer, George (– Pa.) Dec. 5, 1762–June 8, 1843; House 1821–27.

Plumer, William (father of William Plumer Jr.) (F N.H.) June 25, 1759–Dec. 22, 1850; Senate June 17, 1802–07; Gov. June 5, 1812–June 3, 1813, June 6, 1816–June 3, 1819 (Democratic Republican).

Plumer, William Jr. (son of William Plumer) (– N.H.) Feb. 9, 1789–Sept. 18, 1854; House 1819–25.

Plumley, Charles Albert (son of Frank Plumley) (R Vt.) April 14, 1875–Oct. 31, 1964; House Jan. 16, 1934–51.

Plumley, Frank (father of Charles Albert Plumley) (R Vt.) Dec. 17, 1844–April 30, 1924; House 1909–15.

Plummer, Franklin E. (J Miss.) ?–Sept. 24, 1847; House 1831–35.

Poage, William Robert (D Texas) Dec. 28, 1899–Jan. 3, 1987; House 1937–Dec. 31, 1978; Chrmn. House Agriculture 1967–75.

Podell, Bertram L. (D N.Y.) Dec. 27, 1925– ; House Feb. 20, 1968–75.

Poehler, Henry (D Minn.) Aug. 22, 1833–July 18, 1912; House 1879–81.

Poff, Richard Harding (R Va.) Oct. 19, 1923– ; House 1953–Aug. 29, 1972.

Poindexter, George (– Miss.) 1779–Sept. 5, 1853; House (Terr. Del.) 1807–13; (Rep.) Dec. 10, 1817–19; Senate Oct. 15, 1830–35; elected

Pres. pro tempore June 28, 1834; Gov. Jan. 5, 1820–Jan. 7, 1822 (Democratic Republican).

Poindexter, Miles (R Wash.) April 22, 1868–Sept. 21, 1946; House 1909–11; Senate 1911–23.

Poinsett, Joel Roberts (D S.C.) March 2, 1779–Dec. 12, 1851; House 1821–March 7, 1825; Secy. of War March 7, 1837–March 5, 1841.

Polanco-Abreu, Santiago (PD P.R.) Oct. 30, 1920–Jan. 18, 1988; House 1965–69.

Poland, Luke Potter (R Vt.) Nov. 1, 1815–July 2, 1887; Senate Nov. 21, 1865–67; House 1867–75, 1883–85.

Polk, Albert Fawcett (D Del.) Oct. 11, 1869–Feb. 14, 1955; House 1917–19.

Polk, James Gould (D Ohio) Oct. 6, 1896–April 28, 1959; House 1931–41, 1949–April 28, 1959.

Polk, James Knox (brother of William Hawkins Polk) (D Tenn.) Nov. 2, 1795–June 15, 1849; House 1825–39 (1825–27 no party, 1827–37 Jacksonian); Speaker Dec. 7, 1835–37, Sept. 4, 1837–39; Gov. Oct. 14, 1839–Oct. 15, 1841; President 1845–49.

Polk, Rufus King (D Pa.) Aug. 23, 1866–March 5, 1902; House 1899–March 5, 1902.

Polk, Trusten (D Mo.) May 29, 1811–April 16, 1876; Senate 1857–Jan. 10, 1862; Gov. Jan. 5–Feb. 27, 1857.

Polk, William Hawkins (brother of James Knox Polk) (ID Tenn.) May 24, 1815–Dec. 16, 1862; House 1851–53.

Pollard, Ernest Mark (R Neb.) April 15, 1869–Sept. 24, 1939; House July 18, 1905–09.

Pollard, Henry Moses (R Mo.) June 14, 1836–Feb. 24, 1904; House 1877–79.

Pollock, Howard Wallace (R Alaska) April 11, 1920– ; House 1967–71.

Pollock, James (W Pa.) Sept. 11, 1810–April 19, 1890; House April 5, 1844–49; Gov. Jan. 16, 1855–Jan. 19, 1858.

Pollock, William Pegues (D S.C.) Dec. 9, 1870–June 2, 1922; Senate Nov. 6, 1918–19.

Polsley, Daniel Haymond (R W.Va.) Nov. 28, 1803–Oct. 14, 1877; House 1867–69.

Pombo, Richard W. (R Calif.) Jan. 8, 1961– ; House 1993– .

Pomerene, Atlee (D Ohio) Dec. 6, 1863–Nov. 12, 1937; Senate 1911–23.

Pomeroy, Charles (R Iowa) Sept. 3, 1825–Feb. 11, 1891; House 1869–71.

Pomeroy, Earl (D N.D.) Sept. 2, 1952– ; House 1993– .

Pomeroy, Samuel Clarke (R Kan.) Jan. 3, 1816–Aug. 27, 1891; Senate April 4, 1861–73.

Pomeroy, Theodore Medad (R N.Y.) Dec. 31, 1824–March 23, 1905; House 1861–69; Speaker March 3, 1869.

Pond, Benjamin (R N.Y.) 1768–Oct. 6, 1814; House 1811–13.

Pool, Joe Richard (D Texas) Feb. 18, 1911–July 14, 1968; House 1963–July 14, 1968.

Pool, John (uncle of Walter Freshwater Pool) (R N.C.) June 16, 1826–Aug. 16, 1884; Senate July 4, 1868–73.

Pool, Walter Freshwater (nephew of John Pool) (R N.C.) Oct. 10, 1850–Aug. 25, 1883; House March 4–Aug. 25, 1883.

Poole, Theodore Lewis (R N.Y.) April 10, 1840–Dec. 23, 1900; House 1895–97.

Pope, James Pinckney (D Idaho) March 31, 1884–Jan. 23, 1966; Senate 1933–39.

Pope, John (W Ky.) 1770–July 12, 1845; Senate 1807–13; House 1837–43; elected Pres. pro tempore Feb. 23, 1811; Gov. (Ark. Terr.) 1829–35.

Pope, Nathaniel (– Ill.) Jan. 5, 1784–Jan. 22, 1850; House (Terr. Del.) Sept. 5, 1816–Sept. 5, 1818.

Pope, Patrick Hamilton (J Ky.) March 17, 1806–May 4, 1841; House 1833–35.

Poppleton, Earley Franklin (D Ohio) Sept. 29, 1834–May 6, 1899; House 1875–77.

Porter, Albert Gallatin (R Ind.) April 20, 1824–May 3, 1897; House 1859–63; Gov. Jan. 10, 1881–Jan. 12, 1885.

Porter, Alexander (W La.) June 24, 1785–Jan. 13, 1844; Senate Dec. 19, 1833–Jan. 5, 1837.

Porter, Augustus Seymour (nephew of Peter Buell Porter) (W Mich.) Jan. 18, 1798–Sept. 18, 1872; Senate Jan. 20, 1840–45.

Porter, Charles Howell (R Va.) June 21, 1833–July 9, 1897; House Jan. 26, 1870–73.

Porter, Charles Orlando (D Ore.) April 4, 1919– ; House 1957–61.

Porter, Gilchrist (W Mo.) Nov. 1, 1817–Nov. 1, 1894; House 1851–53, 1855–57.

Porter, Henry Kirke (IR Pa.) Nov. 24, 1840–April 10, 1921; House 1903–05.

Porter, James (R N.Y.) April 18, 1787–Feb. 7, 1839; House 1817–19.

Porter, John (– Pa.) ?–?; House Dec. 8, 1806–11.

Porter, John Edward (R Ill.) June 1, 1935– ; House Jan. 22, 1980– .

Porter, Peter Augustus (grandson of Peter Buell Porter) (IR N.Y.) Oct. 10, 1853–Dec. 15, 1925; House 1907–09.

Porter, Peter Buell (grandfather of Peter Augustus Porter, uncle of Augustus Seymour Porter) (R N.Y.) Aug. 14, 1773–March 20, 1844; House 1809–13, 1815–Jan. 23, 1816; Secy. of War May 26, 1828–March 9, 1829.

Porter, Stephen Geyer (R Pa.) May 18, 1869–June 27, 1930; House 1911–June 27, 1930.

Porter, Timothy H. (– N.Y.) ?–about 1840; House 1825–27.

Portman, Rob (R Ohio) Dec. 19, 1955– ; House May 5, 1993– .

Posey, Francis Blackburn (R Ind.) April 28, 1848–Oct. 31, 1915; House Jan. 29–March 3, 1889.

Posey, Thomas (– La.) July 9, 1750–March 19, 1818; Senate Oct. 8, 1812–Feb. 4, 1813; Gov. (Ind. Terr.) 1813–16.

Poshard, Glenn (D Ill.) Oct. 30, 1945– ; House 1989–99.

Post, George Adams (D Pa.) Sept. 1, 1854–Oct. 31, 1925; House 1883–85.

Post, James Douglass (D Ohio) Nov. 25, 1863–April 1, 1921; House 1911–15.

Post, Jotham Jr. (F N.Y.) April 4, 1771–May 15, 1817; House 1813–15.

Post, Morton Everel (D Wyo.) Dec. 25, 1840–March 19, 1933; House (Terr. Del.) 1881–85.

Post, Philip Sidney (R Ill.) March 19, 1833–Jan. 6, 1895; House 1887–Jan. 6, 1895.

Poston, Charles Debrille (R Ariz.) April 20, 1825–June 24, 1902; House (Terr. Del.) Dec. 5, 1864–65.

Potter, Allen (D Mich.) Oct. 2, 1818–May 8, 1885; House 1875–77.

Potter, Charles Edward (R Mich.) Oct. 30, 1916–Nov. 23, 1979; House Aug. 26, 1947–Nov. 4, 1952; Senate Nov. 5, 1952–59.

Potter, Clarkson Nott (D N.Y.) April 25, 1825–Jan. 23, 1882; House 1869–75, 1877–79.

Potter, Elisha Reynolds (father of Elisha Reynolds Potter, below) (F R.I.) Nov. 5, 1764–Sept. 26, 1835; House Nov. 15, 1796–97, 1809–15.

Potter, Elisha Reynolds (son of Elisha Reynolds Potter, above) (L&O R.I.) June 20, 1811–April 10, 1882; House 1843–45.

Potter, Emery Davis (D Ohio) Oct. 7, 1804–Feb. 12, 1896; House 1843–45, 1849–51.

Potter, John Fox (R Wis.) May 11, 1817–May 18, 1899; House 1857–63.

Potter, Orlando Brunson (D N.Y.) March 10, 1823–Jan. 2, 1894; House 1883–85.

Potter, Robert (J N.C.) about 1800–March 2, 1842; House 1829–Nov. 1831.

Potter, Samuel John (R R.I.) June 29, 1753–Oct. 14, 1804; Senate 1803–Oct. 14, 1804.

Potter, William Wilson (D Pa.) Dec. 18, 1792–Oct. 28, 1839; House 1837–Oct. 28, 1839.

Pottle, Emory Bemsley (R N.Y.) July 4, 1815–April 18, 1891; House 1857–61.

Potts, David Jr. (AMas. Pa.) Nov. 27, 1794–June 1, 1863; House 1831–39.

Potts, David Matthew (R N.Y.) March 12, 1906–Sept. 11, 1976; House 1947–49.

Potts, Richard (– Md.) July 19, 1753–Nov. 26, 1808; Senate Jan. 10, 1793–Oct. 24, 1796; Cont. Cong. 1781.

Pou, Edward William (cousin of James Paul Buchanan) (D N.C.) Sept. 9, 1863–April 1, 1934; House 1901–April 1, 1934.

Poulson, C. Norris (R Calif.) July 23, 1895–Sept. 25, 1982; House 1943–45, 1947–June 11, 1953.

Pound, Thaddeus Coleman (R Wis.) Dec. 6, 1833–Nov. 21, 1914; House 1877–83.

Powell, Adam Clayton Jr. (D N.Y.) Nov. 29, 1908–April 4, 1972; House 1945–Feb. 28, 1967, 1969–71; Chrmn. House Education and Labor 1961–67.

Powell, Alfred H. (– Va.) March 6, 1781–1831; House 1825–27.

Powell, Cuthbert (son of Levin Powell) (W Va.) March 4, 1775–May 8, 1849; House 1841–43.

Powell, Joseph (D Pa.) June 23, 1828–April 24, 1904; House 1875–77.

Powell, Lazarus Whitehead (D Ky.) Oct. 6, 1812–July 3, 1867; Senate 1859–65; Gov. Sept. 2, 1851–Sept. 1, 1855.

Powell, Levin (father of Cuthbert Powell) (F Va.) 1737–Aug. 23, 1810; House 1799–1801.

Powell, Paulus (D Va.) 1809–June 10, 1874; House 1849–59.

Powell, Samuel (R Tenn.) July 10, 1776–Aug. 2, 1841; House 1815–17.

Powell, Walter Eugene (R Ohio) April 25, 1931– ; House 1971–75.

Power, Thomas Charles (R Mont.) May 22, 1839–Feb. 16, 1923; Senate Jan. 2, 1890–95.

Powers, Caleb (R Ky.) Feb. 1, 1869–July 25, 1932; House 1911–19.

Powers, David Lane (R N.J.) July 29, 1896–March 28, 1968; House 1933–Aug. 30, 1945.

Powers, Gershom (J N.Y.) July 11, 1789–June 25, 1831; House 1829–31.

Powers, Horace Henry (R Vt.) May 29, 1835–Dec. 8, 1913; House 1891–1901.

Powers, Llewellyn (R Maine) Oct. 14, 1836–July 28, 1908; House 1877–79, April 8, 1901–July 28, 1908; Gov. Jan. 6, 1897–Jan. 2, 1901.

Powers, Samuel Leland (R Mass.) Oct. 26, 1848–Nov. 30, 1929; House 1901–05.

Poydras, Julien de Lallande (– Orleans) April 3, 1740–June 14, 1824; House (Terr. Del.) 1809–11.

Pracht, Charles Frederick (R Pa.) Oct. 20, 1880–Dec. 22, 1950; House 1943–45.

Prall, Anning Smith (D N.Y.) Sept. 17, 1870–July 23, 1937; House Nov. 6, 1923–35.

Pratt, Charles Clarence (R Pa.) April 23, 1854–Jan. 27, 1916; House 1909–11.

Pratt, Daniel Darwin (R Ind.) Oct. 26, 1813–June 17, 1877; Senate 1869–75.

Pratt, Eliza Jane (D N.C.) March 5, 1902–May 13, 1981; House May 25, 1946–47.

Pratt, Harcourt Joseph (R N.Y.) Oct. 23, 1866–May 21, 1934; House 1925–33.

Pratt, Harry Hayt (R N.Y.) Nov. 11, 1864–Nov. 13, 1932; House 1915–19.

Pratt, Henry Otis (R Iowa) Feb. 11, 1838–May 22, 1931; House 1873–77.

Pratt, James Timothy (D Conn.) Dec. 14, 1802–April 11, 1887; House 1853–55.

Pratt, Joseph Marmaduke (R Pa.) Sept. 4, 1891–July 19, 1946; House Jan. 18, 1944–45.

Pratt, Le Gage (D N.J.) Dec. 14, 1852–March 9, 1911; House 1907–09.

Pratt, Ruth Sears Baker (R N.Y.) Aug. 24, 1877–Aug. 23, 1965; House 1929–33.

Pratt, Thomas George (W Md.) Feb. 18, 1804–Nov. 9, 1869; Senate Jan. 12, 1850–57; Gov. Jan. 6, 1845–Jan. 3, 1848.

Pratt, Zadock (D N.Y.) Oct. 30, 1790–April 6, 1871; House 1837–39, 1843–45.

Pray, Charles Nelson (R Mont.) April 6, 1868–Sept. 12, 1963; House 1907–13.

Prentiss, John Holmes (brother of Samuel Prentiss) (D N.Y.) April 17, 1784–June 26, 1861; House 1837–41.

Prentiss, Samuel (brother of John Holmes Prentiss) (W Vt.) March 31, 1782–Jan. 15, 1857; Senate 1831–April 11, 1842.

Prentiss, Seargeant Smith (– Miss.) Sept. 30, 1808–July 1, 1850; House May 30, 1838–39.

Prescott, Cyrus Dan (R N.Y.) Aug. 15, 1836–Oct. 23, 1902; House 1879–83.

Pressler, Larry Lee (R S.D.) March 29, 1942– ; House 1975–79; Senate 1979–97; Chrmn. Senate Commerce, Science, and Transportation 1995–97.

Preston, Francis (father of William Campbell Preston, uncle of William Ballard Preston and William Preston, cousin of James Breckinridge, John Breckinridge, James Brown, and John Brown of Virginia and Kentucky) (R Va.) Aug. 2, 1765–May 26, 1836; House 1793–97 (1793–95 no party).

Preston, Jacob Alexander (W Md.) March 12, 1796–Aug. 2, 1868; House 1843–45.

Preston, Prince Hulon Jr. (D Ga.) July 5, 1908–Feb. 8, 1961; House 1947–61.

Preston, William (nephew of Francis Preston, cousin of William Ballard Preston and William Campbell Preston) (W Ky.) Oct. 16, 1816–Sept. 21, 1887; House Dec. 6, 1852–55.

Preston, William Ballard (nephew of Francis Preston, cousin of William Preston and William Campbell Preston) (W Va.) Nov. 25, 1805–Nov. 16, 1862; House 1847–49; Secy. of the Navy March 8, 1849–July 22, 1850.

Preston, William Campbell (son of Francis Preston, cousin of William Preston and William Ballard Preston) (W S.C.) Dec. 27, 1794–May 22, 1860; Senate Nov. 26, 1833–Nov. 29, 1842 (Nov. 26, 1833–37 Nullifier).

Preyer, Lunsford Richardson (D N.C.) Jan. 11, 1919– ; House 1969–81.

Price, Andrew (D La.) April 2, 1854–Feb. 5, 1909; House Dec. 2, 1889–97.

Price, Charles Melvin (D Ill.) Jan. 1, 1905–April 22, 1988; House 1945–April 22, 1988; Chrmn. House Standards of Official Conduct 1969–75; Chrmn. House Armed Services 1975–85.

Price, David Eugene (D N.C.) Aug. 17, 1940– ; House 1987–95; 1997– .

Price, Emory Hilliard (D Fla.) Dec. 3, 1899–Feb. 11, 1976; House 1943–49.

Price, Hiram (R Iowa) Jan. 10, 1814–May 30, 1901; House 1863–69, 1877–81.

Price, Hugh Hiram (son of William Thompson Price) (R Wis.) Dec. 2, 1859–Dec. 25, 1904; House Jan. 18–March 3, 1887.

Price, Jesse Dashiell (D Md.) Aug. 15, 1863–May 14, 1939; House Nov. 3, 1914–19.

Price, Robert Dale (R Texas) Sept. 7, 1927– ; House 1967–75.

Price, Rodman McCamley (D N.J.) May 5, 1816–June 7, 1894; House 1851–53; Gov. Jan. 17, 1854–Jan. 20, 1857.

Price, Samuel (O W.Va.) July 28, 1805–Feb. 25, 1884; Senate Aug. 26, 1876–Jan. 26, 1877.

Price, Sterling (D Mo.) Sept. 20, 1809–Sept. 29, 1867; House 1845–Aug. 12, 1846; Gov. Jan. 3, 1853–Jan. 5, 1857.

Price, Thomas Lawson (D Mo.) Jan. 19, 1809–July 15, 1870; House Jan. 21, 1862–63.

Price, William Pierce (D Ga.) Jan. 29, 1835–Nov. 4, 1908; House Dec. 22, 1870–73.

Price, William Thompson (father of Hugh Hiram Price) (R Wis.) June 17, 1824–Dec. 6, 1886; House 1883–Dec. 6, 1886.

Pridemore, Auburn Lorenzo (D Va.) June 27, 1837–May 17, 1900; House 1877–79.

Priest, James Percy (D Tenn.) April 1, 1900–Oct. 12, 1956; House 1941–Oct. 12, 1956 (1941–43 Independent Democrat); Chrmn. House Interstate and Foreign Commerce 1955–57.

Prince, Charles Henry (R Ga.) May 9, 1837–April 3, 1912; House July 25, 1868–69.

Prince, George Washington (R Ill.) March 4, 1854–Sept. 26, 1939; House Dec. 2, 1895–1913.

Prince, Oliver Hillhouse (– Ga.) 1787–Oct. 9, 1837; Senate Nov. 7, 1828–29.

Prince, William (– Ind.) 1772–Sept. 8, 1824; House 1823–Sept. 8, 1824.

Prindle, Elizur H. (R N.Y.) May 6, 1829–Oct. 7, 1890; House 1871–73.

Pringey, Joseph Colburn (R Okla.) May 22, 1858–Feb. 11, 1935; House 1921–23.

Pringle, Benjamin (W N.Y.) Nov. 9, 1807–June 7, 1887; House 1853–57.

Pritchard, George Moore (son of Jeter Connelly Pritchard) (R N.C.) Jan. 4, 1886–April 24, 1955; House 1929–31.

Pritchard, Jeter Connelly (father of George Moore Pritchard) (R N.C.) July 12, 1857–April 10, 1921; Senate Jan. 23, 1895–1903.

Pritchard, Joel McFee (R Wash.) May 5, 1925–Oct. 9, 1997; House 1973–85.

Proctor, Redfield (R Vt.) June 1, 1831–March 4, 1908; Senate Nov. 2, 1891–March 4, 1908; Gov. Oct. 3, 1878–Oct. 7, 1880; Secy. of War March 5, 1889–Nov. 5, 1891.

Proffit, George H. (W Ind.) Sept. 7, 1807–Sept. 7, 1847; House 1839–43.

Prokop, Stanley A. (D Pa.) July 29, 1909–Nov. 11, 1977; House 1959–61.

Prosser, William Farrand (R Tenn.) March 16, 1834–Sept. 23, 1911; House 1869–71.

Prouty, Solomon Francis (R Iowa) Jan. 17, 1854–July 16, 1927; House 1911–15.

Prouty, Winston Lewis (R Vt.) Sept. 1, 1906–Sept. 10, 1971; House 1951–59; Senate 1959–Sept. 10, 1971.

Proxmire, William (D Wis.) Nov. 11, 1915– ; Senate Aug. 28, 1957–89; Chrmn. Senate Banking, Housing, and Urban Affairs 1975–81, 1987–89.

Pruyn, John Van Schaick Lansing (D N.Y.) June 22, 1811–Nov. 21, 1877; House Dec. 7, 1863–65, 1867–69.

Pryce, Deborah (R Ohio) July 29, 1951– ; House 1993– .

Pryor, David Hampton (D Ark.) Aug. 29, 1934– ; House Nov. 8, 1966–73; Senate 1979–97; Gov. Jan. 14, 1975–Jan. 3, 1979.

Pryor, Luke (D Ala.) July 5, 1820–Aug. 5, 1900; Senate Jan. 7–Nov. 23, 1880 (no party); House 1883–85.

Pryor, Roger Atkinson (D Va.) July 19, 1828–March 14, 1919; House Dec. 7, 1859–61.

Pucinski, Roman Conrad (D Ill.) May 13, 1919– ; House 1959–73.

Pugh, George Ellis (D Ohio) Nov. 28, 1822–July 19, 1876; Senate 1855–61.

Pugh, James Lawrence (D Ala.) Dec. 12, 1820–March 9, 1907; House 1859–Jan. 21, 1861 (no party); Senate Nov. 24, 1880–97.

Pugh, John (R Pa.) June 2, 1761–July 13, 1842; House 1805–09.

Pugh, John Howard (R N.J.) June 23, 1827–April 30, 1905; House 1877–79.

Pugh, Samuel Johnson (R Ky.) Jan. 28, 1850–April 17, 1922; House 1895–1901.

Pugsley, Cornelius Amory (D N.Y.) July 17, 1850–Sept. 10, 1936; House 1901–03.

Pugsley, Jacob Joseph (R Ohio) Jan. 25, 1838–Feb. 5, 1920; House 1887–91.

Pujo, Arsène Paulin (D La.) Dec. 16, 1861–Dec. 31, 1939; House 1903–13.

Pulitzer, Joseph (D N.Y.) April 10, 1847–Oct. 29, 1911; House 1885–April 10, 1886.

Purcell, Graham Boynton Jr. (D Texas) May 5, 1919– ; House Jan. 27, 1962–73.

Purcell, William Edward (D N.D.) Aug. 3, 1856–Nov. 23, 1928; Senate Feb. 1, 1910–Feb. 1, 1911.

Purdy, Smith Meade (D N.Y.) July 31, 1796–March 30, 1870; House 1843–45.

Purman, William James (R Fla.) April 11, 1840–Aug. 14, 1928; House 1873–Jan. 25, 1875, 1875–77.

Purnell, Fred Sampson (R Ind.) Oct. 25, 1882–Oct. 21, 1939; House 1917–33.

Pursell, Carl Duane (R Mich.) Dec. 19, 1932– ; House 1977–93.

Purtell, William Arthur (R Conn.) May 6, 1897–May 31, 1978; Senate Aug. 29–Nov. 4, 1952, 1953–59.

Purviance, Samuel Anderson (R Pa.) Jan. 10, 1809–Feb. 14, 1882; House 1855–59 (1855–57 Whig).

Purviance, Samuel Dinsmore (F N.C.) Jan. 7, 1774–about 1806; House 1803–05.

Puryear, Richard Clauselle (AP N.C.) Feb. 9, 1801–July 30, 1867; House 1853–57 (1853–55 Whig).

Pusey, William Henry Mills (D Iowa) July 29, 1826–Nov. 15, 1900; House 1883–85.

Putnam, Harvey (W N.Y.) Jan. 5, 1793–Sept. 20, 1855; House Nov. 7, 1838–39, 1847–51.

Pyle, Gladys (R S.D.) Oct. 4, 1890–March 14, 1989; Senate Nov. 9, 1938–39.

Q

Quackenbush, John Adam (R N.Y.) Oct. 15, 1828–May 11, 1908; House 1889–93.

Quarles, James Minor (O Tenn.) Feb. 8, 1823–March 3, 1901; House 1859–61.

Quarles, Joseph Very (R Wis.) Dec. 16, 1843–Oct. 7, 1911; Senate 1899–1905.

Quarles, Julian Minor (D Va.) Sept. 25, 1848–Nov. 18, 1929; House 1899–1901.

Quarles, Tunstall (R Ky.) about 1770–Jan. 7, 1855; House 1817–June 15, 1820.

Quay, Matthew Stanley (R Pa.) Sept. 30, 1833–May 28, 1904; Senate 1887–99, Jan. 16, 1901–May 28, 1904; Chrmn. Rep. Nat. Comm. 1888–91.

Quayle, James Danforth "Dan" (R Ind.) Feb. 4, 1947– ; House 1977–81; Senate 1981–Jan. 3, 1989; Vice President 1989–93.

Quayle, John Francis (D N.Y.) Dec. 1, 1868–Nov. 27, 1930; House 1923–Nov. 27, 1930.

Quezon, Manuel Luis (Nat. P.I.) Aug. 19, 1878–Aug. 1, 1944; House (Res. Comm.) Nov. 23, 1909–Oct. 15, 1916; Pres. (P.I.) 1935–44.

Quie, Albert Harold (R Minn.) Sept. 18, 1923– ; House Feb. 18, 1958–79; Gov. Jan. 1, 1979–Jan. 3, 1983.

Quigg, Lemuel Ely (R N.Y.) Feb. 12, 1863–July 1, 1919; House Jan. 30, 1894–99.

Quigley, James Michael (D Pa.) March 30, 1918– ; House 1955–57, 1959–61.

Quillen, James Henry (R Tenn.) Jan. 11, 1916– ; House 1963–97.

Quin, Percy Edwards (D Miss.) Oct. 30, 1872–Feb. 4, 1932; House 1913–Feb. 4, 1932.

Quincy, Josiah (F Mass.) Feb. 4, 1772–July 1, 1864; House 1805–13.

Quinn, Jack (R N.Y.) April 13, 1951– ; House 1993– .

Quinn, James Leland (D Pa.) Sept. 8, 1875–Nov. 12, 1960; House 1935–39.

Quinn, John (D N.Y.) Aug. 9, 1839–Feb. 23, 1903; House 1889–91.

Quinn, Peter Anthony (D N.Y.) May 10, 1904–Dec. 23, 1974; House 1945–47.

Quinn, Terence John (D N.Y.) Oct. 16, 1836–June 18, 1878; House 1877–June 18, 1878.

Quinn, Thomas Vincent (D N.Y.) March 16, 1903–March 1, 1982; House 1949–Dec. 30, 1951.

Quitman, John Anthony (D Miss.) Sept. 1, 1799–July 17, 1858; House 1855–July 17, 1858; Gov. Dec. 3, 1835–Jan. 7, 1836, Jan. 10, 1850–Feb. 3, 1851.

R

Rabaut, Louis Charles (D Mich.) Dec. 5, 1886–Nov. 12, 1961; House 1935–47, 1949–Nov. 12, 1961.

Rabin, Benjamin J. (D N.Y.) June 3, 1896–Feb. 22, 1969; House 1945–Dec. 31, 1947.

Race, John Abner (D Wis.) May 12, 1914–Nov. 10, 1983; House 1965–67.

Radanovich, George P. (R Calif.) June 20, 1955– ; House 1995– .

Radcliffe, Amos Henry (R N.J.) Jan. 16, 1870–Dec. 29, 1950; House 1919–23.

Radcliffe, George Lovic Pierce (D Md.) Aug. 22, 1877–July 29, 1974; Senate 1935–47.

Radford, William (D N.Y.) June 24, 1814–Jan. 18, 1870; House 1863–67.

Radwan, Edmund Patrick (R N.Y.) Sept. 22, 1911–Sept. 7, 1959; House 1951–59.

Ragon, Heartsill (D Ark.) March 20, 1885–Sept. 15, 1940; House 1923–June 16, 1933.

Ragsdale, James Willard (D S.C.) Dec. 14, 1872–July 23, 1919; House 1913–July 23, 1919.

Rahall, Nick Joe II (D W.Va.) May 20, 1949– ; House 1977– .

Railsback, Thomas Fisher (R Ill.) Jan. 22, 1932– ; House 1967–83.

Raines, John (R N.Y.) May 6, 1840–Dec. 16, 1909; House 1889–93.

Rainey, Henry Thomas (D Ill.) Aug. 20, 1860–Aug. 19, 1934; House 1903–21, 1923–Aug. 19, 1934; House majority leader 1931–33; Speaker March 9, 1933–Aug. 19, 1934.

Rainey, John William (D Ill.) Dec. 21, 1880–May 4, 1923; House April 2, 1918–May 4, 1923.

Rainey, Joseph Hayne (R S.C.) June 21, 1832–Aug. 2, 1887; House Dec. 12, 1870–79.

Rainey, Lilius Bratton (D Ala.) July 27, 1876–Sept. 27, 1959; House Sept. 30, 1919–23.

Rains, Albert M. (D Ala.) March 11, 1902–March 22, 1991; House 1945–65.

Raker, John Edward (D Calif.) Feb. 22, 1863–Jan. 22, 1926; House 1911–Jan. 22, 1926.

Ralston, Samuel Moffett (D Ind.) Dec. 1, 1857–Oct. 14, 1925; Senate 1923–Oct. 14, 1925; Gov. Jan. 13, 1913–Jan. 8, 1917.

Ramey, Frank Marion (R Ill.) Sept. 23, 1881–March 27, 1942; House 1929–31.

Ramey, Homer Alonzo (R Ohio) March 2, 1891–April 13, 1960; House 1943–49.

Ramsay, Robert Lincoln (D W.Va.) March 24, 1877–Nov. 14, 1956; House 1933–39, 1941–43, 1949–53.

Ramsey, Alexander (R Minn.) Sept. 8, 1815–April 22, 1903; House 1843–47 (Whig Pa.); Senate 1863–75; Gov. April 2, 1849–53 (Minn. Terr.), Jan. 2, 1860–July 10, 1863; Secy. of War Dec. 10, 1879–March 5, 1881.

Ramsey, John Rathbone (R N.J.) April 25, 1862–April 10, 1933; House 1917–21.

Ramsey, Robert (W Pa.) Feb. 15, 1780–Dec. 12, 1849; House 1833–35, 1841–43.

Ramsey, William (D Pa.) Sept. 7, 1779–Sept. 29, 1831; House 1827–Sept. 29, 1831 (1827–29 no party).

Ramsey, William Sterrett (D Pa.) June 12, 1810–Oct. 17, 1840; House 1839–Oct. 17, 1840.

Ramseyer, Christian William (R Iowa) March 13, 1875–Nov. 1, 1943; House 1915–33.

Ramspeck, Robert C. Word (D Ga.) Sept. 5, 1890–Sept. 10, 1972; House Oct. 2, 1929–Dec. 31, 1945.

Ramstad, James (R Minn.) May 6, 1946– ; House 1991– .

Randall, Alexander (W Md.) Jan. 3, 1803–Nov. 21, 1881; House 1841–43.

Randall, Benjamin (W Maine) Nov. 14, 1789–Oct. 11, 1859; House 1839–43.

Randall, Charles Hiram (Prohib. Calif.) July 23, 1865–Feb. 18, 1951; House 1915–21.

Randall, Charles Sturtevant (R Mass.) Feb. 20, 1824–Aug. 17, 1904; House 1889–95.

Randall, Clifford Ellsworth (R Wis.) Dec. 25, 1876–Oct. 16, 1934; House 1919–21.

Randall, Samuel Jackson (D Pa.) Oct. 10, 1828–April 13, 1890; House 1863–April 13, 1890; Speaker Dec. 4, 1876–77, Oct. 15, 1877–79, March 18, 1879–81.

Randall, William Harrison (UU Ky.) July 15, 1812–Aug. 1, 1881; House 1863–67.

Randall, William Joseph (D Mo.) July 16, 1909– ; House March 3, 1959–77.

Randell, Choice Boswell (nephew of Lucius Jeremiah Gartrell) (D Texas) Jan. 1, 1857–Oct. 19, 1945; House 1901–13.

Randolph, James Fitz (father of Theodore Fitz Randolph) (– N.J.) June 26, 1791–Jan. 25, 1872; House Dec. 1, 1827–33.

Randolph, James Henry (R Tenn.) Oct. 18, 1825–Aug. 22, 1900; House 1877–79.

Randolph, Jennings (D W.Va.) March 8, 1902–May 8, 1998; House 1933–47; Senate Nov. 5, 1958–85; Chrmn. Senate Public Works 1966–77; Chrmn. Senate Environment and Public Works 1977–81.

Randolph, John (– Va.) June 2, 1773–May 24, 1833; House 1799–1813, 1815–17, 1819–Dec. 26, 1825, 1827–29, March 4–May 24, 1833; Senate Dec. 26, 1825–27.

Randolph, Joseph Fitz (W N.J.) March 14, 1803–March 20, 1873; House 1837–43.

Randolph, Theodore Fitz (son of James Fitz Randolph) (D N.J.) June 24, 1826–Nov. 7, 1883; Senate 1875–81; Gov. Jan. 19, 1869–Jan. 16, 1872.

Randolph, Thomas Mann (son-in-law of Pres. Thomas Jefferson) (R Va.) Oct. 1, 1768–June 20, 1828; House 1803–07; Gov. Dec. 1, 1819–Dec. 1, 1822.

Raney, John Henry (R Mo.) Sept. 28, 1849–Jan. 23, 1928; House 1895–97.

Rangel, Charles Bernard (D N.Y.) June 1, 1930– ; House 1971– .

Rankin, Christopher (– Miss.) 1788–March 14, 1826; House 1819–March 14, 1826.

Rankin, Jeannette (R Mont.) June 11, 1880–May 18, 1973; House 1917–19, 1941–43.

Rankin, John Elliott (D Miss.) March 29, 1882–Nov. 26, 1960; House 1921–53; Chrmn. House Veterans' Affairs 1949–53.

Rankin, Joseph (D Wis.) Sept. 25, 1833–Jan. 24, 1886; House 1883–Jan. 24, 1886.

Ranney, Ambrose Arnold (R Mass.) April 17, 1821–March 5, 1899; House 1881–87.

Ransdell, Joseph Eugene (D La.) Oct. 7, 1858–July 27, 1954; House Aug. 29, 1899–1913; Senate 1913–31.

Ransier, Alonzo Jacob (R S.C.) Jan. 3, 1834–Aug. 17, 1882; House 1873–75.

Ransley, Harry Clay (R Pa.) Feb. 5, 1863–Nov. 7, 1941; House Nov. 2, 1920–37.

Ransom, Matt Whitaker (cousin of Wharton Jackson Green) (D N.C.) Oct. 8, 1826–Oct. 8, 1904; Senate Jan. 30, 1872–95; elected Pres. pro tempore Jan. 7, 1895.

Rantoul, Robert Jr. (D Mass.) Aug. 13, 1805–Aug. 7, 1852; Senate Feb. 1–March 3, 1851; House March 4, 1851–Aug. 7, 1852.

Rapier, James Thomas (R Ala.) Nov. 13, 1837–May 31, 1883; House 1873–75.

Rarick, John Richard (D La.) Jan. 29, 1924– ; House 1967–75.

Rariden, James (W Ind.) Feb. 14, 1795–Oct. 20, 1856; House 1837–41.

Ratchford, William Richard (D Conn.) May 24, 1934– ; House 1979–85.

Rathbone, Henry Riggs (grandson of Ira Harris) (R Ill.) Feb. 12, 1870–July 15, 1928; House 1923–July 15, 1928.

Rathbun, George Oscar (D N.Y.) 1803–Jan. 5, 1870; House 1843–47.

Rauch, George Washington (D Ind.) Feb. 22, 1876–Nov. 4, 1940; House 1907–17.

Raum, Green Berry (R Ill.) Dec. 3, 1829–Dec. 18, 1909; House 1867–69.

Ravenel, Arthur Jr. (R S.C.) March 29, 1927– ; House 1987–95.

Rawlins, Joseph Lafayette (D Utah) March 28, 1850–May 24, 1926; House (Terr. Del.) 1893–95; Senate 1897–1903.

Rawls, Morgan (D Ga.) June 29, 1829–Oct. 18, 1906; House 1873–March 24, 1874.

Rawson, Charles Augustus (R Iowa) May 29, 1867–Sept. 2, 1936; Senate Feb. 24–Dec. 1, 1922.

Ray, George Washington (R N.Y.) Feb. 3, 1844–Jan. 10, 1925; House 1883–85, 1891–Sept. 11, 1902.

Ray, John Henry (R N.Y.) Sept. 27, 1886–May 21, 1975; House 1953–63.

Ray, Joseph Warren (R Pa.) May 25, 1849–Sept. 15, 1928; House 1889–91.

Ray, Ossian (R N.H.) Dec. 13, 1835–Jan. 28, 1892; House Jan. 8, 1881–85.

Ray, Richard Belmont (D Ga.) Feb. 2, 1927–May 29, 1999; House 1983–1993.

Ray, William Henry (R Ill.) Dec. 14, 1812–Jan. 25, 1881; House 1873–75.

Rayburn, Samuel Taliaferro (D Texas) Jan. 6 1882–Nov. 16, 1961; House 1913–Nov. 16, 1961; House majority leader 1937–Sept. 16, 1940; House minority leader 1947–49, 1953–55; Speaker Sept. 16, 1940–43, Jan. 6, 1943–47, 1949–53, Jan. 5, 1955–59, Jan. 7, 1959–Nov. 16, 1961.

Rayfiel, Leo Frederick (D N.Y.) March 22, 1888–Nov. 18, 1978; House 1945–Sept. 13, 1947.

Raymond, Henry Jarvis (R N.Y.) Jan. 24, 1820–June 18, 1869; House 1865–67; Chrmn. Rep. Nat. Comm. 1864–66.

Raymond, John Baldwin (R Dakota) Dec. 5, 1844–Jan. 3, 1886; House (Terr. Del.) 1883–85.

Rayner, Isidor (D Md.) April 11, 1850–Nov. 25, 1912; House 1887–89, 1891–95; Senate 1905–Nov. 25, 1912.

Rayner, Kenneth (W N.C.) June 20, 1808–March 4, 1884; House 1839–45.

Rea, David (D Mo.) Jan. 19, 1831–June 13, 1901; House 1875–79.

Rea, John (R Pa.) Jan. 27, 1755–Feb. 26, 1829; House 1803–11, May 11, 1813–15.

Read, Almon Heath (D Pa.) June 12, 1790–June 3, 1844; House March 18, 1842–June 3, 1844.

Read, George (– Del.) Sept. 18, 1733–Sept. 21, 1798; Senate 1789–Sept. 18, 1793; Cont. Cong. 1774–77.

Read, Jacob (F S.C.) 1752–July 17, 1816; Senate 1795–1801; elected Pres. pro tempore Nov. 22, 1797; Cont. Cong. 1783–85.

Read, Nathan (F Mass.) July 2, 1759–Jan. 20, 1849; House Nov. 25, 1800–03.

Read, William Brown (D Ky.) Dec. 14, 1817–Aug. 5, 1880; House 1871–75.

Reade, Edwin Godwin (AP N.C.) Nov. 13, 1812–Oct. 18, 1894; House 1855–57.

Reading, John Roberts (D Pa.) Nov. 1, 1826–Feb. 14, 1886; House 1869–April 13, 1870.

Ready, Charles (uncle of William T. Haskell) (W Tenn.) Dec. 22, 1802–June 4, 1878; House 1853–59.

Reagan, John Henninger (D Texas) Oct. 8, 1818–March 6, 1905; House 1857–61, 1875–87; Senate 1887–June 10, 1891.

Reames, Alfred Evan (D Ore.) Feb. 5, 1870–March 4, 1943; Senate Feb. 1–Nov. 8, 1938.

Reams, Henry Frazier (I Ohio) Jan. 15, 1897–Sept. 15, 1971; House 1951–55.

Reavis, Charles Frank (R Neb.) Sept. 5, 1870–May 26, 1932; House 1915–June 3, 1922.

Reber, John (R Pa.) Feb. 1, 1858–Sept. 26, 1931; House 1919–23.

Redden, Monroe Minor (D N.C.) Sept. 24, 1901–Dec. 16, 1987; House 1947–53.

Redfield, William Cox (D N.Y.) June 18, 1858–June 13, 1932; House 1911–13; Secy. of Commerce March 5, 1913–Oct. 31, 1919.

Reding, John Randall (D N.H.) Oct. 18, 1805–Oct. 8, 1892; House 1841–45.

Redlin, Rolland W. (D N.D.) Feb. 29, 1920– ; House 1965–67.

Redmond, Bill (R N.M.) Jan. 28, 1955– ; House May 20, 1997–99.

Reece, Brazilla Carroll (husband of Louise Goff Reece, son-in-law of Guy Despard Goff) (R Tenn.) Dec. 22, 1889–March 19, 1961; House 1921–31, 1933–47, 1951–March 19, 1961; Chrmn. Rep. Nat. Comm. 1946–48.

Reece, Louise Goff (widow of Brazilla Carroll Reece, daughter of Guy Despard Goff, granddaughter of Nathan Goff) (R Tenn.) Nov. 6, 1898–May 14, 1970; House May 16, 1961–63.

Reed, Charles Manning (W Pa.) April 3, 1803–Dec. 16, 1871; House 1843–45.

Reed, Chauncey William (R Ill.) June 2, 1890–Feb. 9, 1956; House 1935–Feb. 9, 1956; Chrmn. House Judiciary 1953–55.

Reed, Clyde Martin (R Kan.) Oct. 19, 1871–Nov. 8, 1949; Senate 1939–Nov. 8, 1949; Gov. Jan. 14, 1929–Jan. 12, 1931.

Reed, Daniel Alden (R N.Y.) Sept. 15, 1875–Feb. 19, 1959; House 1919–Feb. 19, 1959; Chrmn. House Ways and Means 1953–55.

Reed, David Aiken (R Pa.) Dec. 21, 1880–Feb. 10, 1953; Senate Aug. 8, 1922–35.

Reed, Edward Cambridge (J N.Y.) March 8, 1793–May 1, 1883; House 1831–33.

Reed, Eugene Elliott (D N.H.) April 23, 1866–Dec. 15, 1940; House 1913–15.

Reed, Isaac (W Maine) Aug. 22, 1809–Sept. 19, 1887; House June 25, 1852–53.

Reed, James Alexander (D Mo.) Nov. 9, 1861–Sept. 8, 1944; Senate 1911–29.

Reed, James Byron (D Ark.) Jan. 2, 1881–April 27, 1935; House Oct. 20, 1923–29.

Reed, John (father of John Reed, below) (F Mass.) Nov. 11, 1751–Feb. 17, 1831; House 1795–1801.

Reed, John (son of John Reed, above) (W Mass.) Sept. 2, 1781–Nov. 25, 1860; House 1813–17 (Federalist), 1821–41 (1821–35 Federalist, 1835–37 Anti-Mason).

Reed, John F. "Jack" (D R.I.) Nov. 12, 1949– ; House 1991–97; Senate 1997– .

Reed, Joseph Rea (R Iowa) March 12, 1835–April 2, 1925; House 1889–91.

Reed, Philip (R Md.) 1760–Nov. 2, 1829; Senate Nov. 25, 1806–13; House 1817–19, March 19, 1822–23.

Reed, Robert Rentoul (W Pa.) March 12, 1807–Dec. 14, 1864; House 1849–51.

Reed, Stuart Felix (R W.Va.) Jan. 8, 1866–July 4, 1935; House 1917–25.

Reed, Thomas Brackett (R Maine) Oct. 18, 1839–Dec. 7, 1902; House 1877–Sept. 4, 1899; Speaker Dec. 2, 1889–91, Dec. 2, 1895–97, March 15, 1897–99.

Reed, Thomas Buck (– Miss.) May 7, 1787–Nov. 26, 1829; Senate Jan. 28, 1826–27, March 4–Nov. 26, 1829.

Reed, William (F Mass.) June 6, 1776–Feb. 18, 1837; House 1811–15.

Reeder, William Augustus (R Kan.) Aug. 28, 1849–Nov. 7, 1929; House 1899–1911.

Rees, Edward Herbert (R Kan.) June 3, 1886–Oct. 25, 1969; House 1937–61; Chrmn. House Post Office and Civil Service 1947–49, 1953–55.

Rees, Rollin Raymond (R Kan.) Jan. 10, 1865–May 30, 1935; House 1911–13.

Rees, Thomas Mankell (D Calif.) March 26, 1925– ; House Dec. 15, 1965–77.

Reese, David Addison (W Ga.) March 3, 1794–Dec. 16, 1871; House 1853–55.

Reese, Seaborn (D Ga.) Nov. 28, 1846–March 1, 1907; House Dec. 4, 1882–87.

Reeves, Albert Lee Jr. (R Mo.) May 31, 1906–April 15, 1987; House 1947–49.

Reeves, Henry Augustus (D N.Y.) Dec. 7, 1832–March 4, 1916; House 1869–71.

Reeves, Walter (R Ill.) Sept. 25, 1848–April 9, 1909; House 1895–1903.

Regan, Kenneth Mills (D Texas) March 6, 1893–Aug. 15, 1959; House Aug. 23, 1947–55.

Regula, Ralph Straus (R Ohio) Dec. 3, 1924– ; House 1973– .

Reid, Charles Chester (D Ark.) June 15, 1868–May 20, 1922; House 1901–11.

Reid, Charlotte Thompson (R Ill.) Sept. 27, 1913– ; House 1963–Oct. 7, 1971.

Reid, David Settle (nephew of Thomas Settle) (D N.C.) April 19, 1813–June 19, 1891; House 1843–47; Senate Dec. 6, 1854–59; Gov. Jan. 1, 1851–Dec. 6, 1854.

Reid, Frank R. (R Ill.) April 18, 1879–Jan. 25, 1945; House 1923–35.

Reid, Harry (D Nev.) Dec. 2, 1939– ; House 1983–87; Senate 1987– .

Reid, James Wesley (D N.C.) June 11, 1849–Jan. 1, 1902; House Jan. 28, 1885–Dec. 31, 1886.

Reid, John William (D Mo.) June 14, 1821–Nov. 22, 1881; House March 4–Dec. 2, 1861.

Reid, Ogden Rogers (D N.Y.) June 24, 1925– ; House 1963–75 (1963–March 22, 1972, Republican).

Reid, Robert Raymond (R Ga.) Sept. 8, 1789–July 1, 1841; House Feb. 18, 1819–23; Gov. (Fla. Terr.) 1839–41.

Reifel, Benjamin (R S.D.) Sept. 19, 1906–Jan. 2, 1990; House 1961–71.

Reilly, James Bernard (D Pa.) Aug. 12, 1845–May 14, 1924; House 1875–79, 1889–95.

Reilly, John (D Pa.) Feb. 22, 1836–April 19, 1904; House 1875–77.

Reilly, Michael Kieran (D Wis.) July 15, 1869–Oct. 14, 1944; House 1913–17, Nov. 4, 1930–39.

Reilly, Thomas Lawrence (D Conn.) Sept. 20, 1858–July 6, 1924; House 1911–15.

Reilly, Wilson (– Pa.) Aug. 8, 1811–Aug. 26, 1885; House 1857–59.

Reily, Luther (D Pa.) Oct. 17, 1794–Feb. 20, 1854; House 1837–39.

Reinecke, Edwin (R Calif.) Jan. 7, 1924– ; House 1965–Jan. 21, 1969.

Relfe, James Hugh (D Mo.) Oct. 17, 1791–Sept. 14, 1863; House 1843–47.

Remann, Frederick (R Ill.) May 10, 1847–July 14, 1895; House March 4–July 14, 1895.

Rencher, Abraham (W N.C.) Aug. 12, 1798–July 6, 1883; House 1829–39 (1829–33 Jacksonian, 1833–37 Anti-Jacksonian), 1841–43; Gov. (N.M. Terr.) 1857–61.

Resa, Alexander John (D Ill.) Aug. 4, 1887–July 4, 1964; House 1945–47.

Resnick, Joseph Yale (D N.Y.) July 13, 1924–Oct. 6, 1969; House 1965–69.

Reuss, Henry Schoellkopf (D Wis.) Feb. 22, 1912– ; House 1955–83; Chrmn. House Banking, Currency, and Housing 1975–77; Chrmn. House Banking, Finance, and Urban Affairs 1977–81.

Revels, Hiram Rhodes (R Miss.) Sept. 27, 1827–Jan. 16, 1901; Senate Feb. 23, 1870–71.

Revercomb, William Chapman (R W.Va.) July 20, 1895–Oct. 6, 1979; Senate 1943–49, Nov. 7, 1956–59; Chrmn. Senate Public Works 1947–49.

Reyburn, John Edgar (father of William Stuart Reyburn) (R Pa.) Feb. 7, 1845–Jan. 4, 1914; House Feb. 18, 1890–97, Nov. 6, 1906–March 31, 1907.

Reyburn, William Stuart (son of John Edgar Reyburn) (R Pa.) Dec. 17, 1882–July 25, 1946; House May 23, 1911–13.

Reyes, Silvestre (D Texas) Nov. 10, 1944– ; House 1997– .

Reynolds, Edwin Ruthvin (R N.Y.) Feb. 16, 1816–July 4, 1908; House Dec. 5, 1860–61.

Reynolds, Gideon (W N.Y.) Aug. 9, 1813–July 13, 1896; House 1847–51.

Reynolds, James B. (R Tenn.) 1779–June 10, 1851; House 1815–17, 1823–25.

Reynolds, John (D Ill.) Feb. 26, 1788–May 8, 1865; House Dec. 1, 1834–37 (Jacksonian), 1839–43 (Democrat); Gov. Dec. 6, 1830–Nov. 17, 1834.

Reynolds, John Hazard (ALD N.Y.) June 21, 1819–Sept. 24, 1875; House 1859–61.

Reynolds, John Merriman (R Pa.) March 5, 1848–Sept. 14, 1933; House 1905–Jan. 17, 1911.

Reynolds, Joseph (J N.Y.) Sept. 14, 1785–Sept. 24, 1864; House 1835–37.

Reynolds, Mel (D Ill.) Jan. 8, 1952– ; House 1993–Oct. 1, 1995.

Reynolds, Robert Rice (D N.C.) June 18, 1884–Feb. 13, 1963; Senate Dec. 5, 1932–45.

Reynolds, Samuel Williams (R Neb.) Aug. 11, 1890–March 20, 1988; Senate July 3–Nov. 7, 1954.

Reynolds, Thomas M. (R N.Y.) Sept. 3, 1950– ; House 1999– .

Rhea, John (R Tenn.) 1753–May 27, 1832; House 1803–15, 1817–23.

Rhea, John Stockdale (D Ky.) March 9, 1855–July 29, 1924; House 1897–March 25, 1902, 1903–05.

Rhea, William Francis (D Va.) April 20, 1858–March 23, 1931; House 1899–1903.

Rhett, Robert Barnwell (formerly Robert Barnwell Smith) (D S.C.) Dec. 24, 1800–Sept. 14, 1876; House 1837–49; Senate Dec. 18, 1850–May 7, 1852.

Rhinock, Joseph Lafayette (D Ky.) Jan. 4, 1863–Sept. 20, 1926; House 1905–11.

Rhodes, George Milton (D Pa.) Feb. 24, 1898–Oct. 23, 1978; House 1949–69.

Rhodes, John Jacob (father of John Jacob Rhodes III) (R Ariz.) Sept. 18, 1916– ; House 1953–83; House minority leader Dec. 7, 1974–81.

Rhodes, John Jacob III (son of John Jacob Rhodes) (R Ariz.) Sept. 8, 1943– ; House 1987–93.

Rhodes, Marion Edwards (R Mo.) Jan. 4, 1868–Dec. 25, 1928; House 1905–07, 1919–23.

Ribicoff, Abraham Alexander (D Conn.) April 9, 1910–Feb. 22, 1998; House 1949–53; Senate 1963–81; Chrmn. Senate Government Operations 1975–77; Chrmn. Senate Governmental Affairs 1977–81; Gov. Jan. 5, 1955–Jan. 21, 1961; Secy. of Health, Education and Welfare Jan. 21, 1961–July 13, 1962.

Ricaud, James Barroll (AP Md.) Feb. 11, 1808–Jan. 24, 1866; House 1855–59.

Rice, Alexander Hamilton (R Mass.) Aug. 30, 1818–July 22, 1895; House 1859–67; Gov. Jan. 5, 1876–Jan. 1, 1879.

Rice, Americus Vespucius (D Ohio) Nov. 18, 1835–April 4, 1904; House 1875–79.

Rice, Benjamin Franklin (R Ark.) May 26, 1828–Jan. 19, 1905; Senate June 23, 1868–73.

Rice, Edmund (brother of Henry Mower Rice) (D Minn.) Feb. 14, 1819–July 11, 1889; House 1887–89.

Rice, Edward Young (D Ill.) Feb. 8, 1820–April 16, 1883; House 1871–73.

Rice, Henry Mower (brother of Edmund Rice) (D Minn.) Nov. 29, 1817–Jan. 15, 1894; House (Terr. Del.) 1853–57; Senate May 11, 1858–63.

Rice, John Birchard (R Ohio) June 23, 1832–Jan. 14, 1893; House 1881–83.

Rice, John Blake (R Ill.) May 28, 1809–Dec. 17, 1874; House 1873–Dec. 17, 1874.

Rice, John Hovey (R Maine) Feb. 5, 1816–March 14, 1911; House 1861–67.

Rice, John McConnell (D Ky.) Feb. 19, 1831–Sept. 18, 1895; House 1869–73.

Rice, Theron Moses (G Mo.) Sept. 21, 1829–Nov. 7, 1895; House 1881–83.

Rice, Thomas (F Mass.) March 30, 1768–Aug. 25, 1854; House 1815–19.

Rice, William Whitney (R Mass.) March 7, 1826–March 1, 1896; House 1877–87.

Rich, Carl West (R Ohio) Sept. 12, 1898–June 26, 1972; House 1963–65.

Rich, Charles (R Vt.) Sept. 13, 1771–Oct. 15, 1824; House 1813–15.

Rich, John Tyler (R Mich.) April 23, 1841–March 28, 1926; House April 5, 1881–83; Gov. Jan. 1, 1893–Jan. 1, 1897.

Rich, Robert Fleming (R Pa.) June 23, 1883–April 28, 1968; House Nov. 4, 1930–43, 1945–51.

Richard, Gabriel (– Mich.) Oct. 15, 1767–Sept. 13, 1832; House (Terr. Del.) 1823–25.

Richards, Charles Lenmore (D Nev.) Oct. 3, 1877–Dec. 22, 1953; House 1923–25.

Richards, Jacob (R Pa.) 1773–July 20, 1816; House 1803–09.

Richards, James Alexander Dudley (D Ohio) March 22, 1845–Dec. 4, 1911; House 1893–95.

Richards, James Prioleau (D S.C.) Aug. 31, 1894–Feb. 21, 1979; House 1933–57; Chrmn. House Foreign Affairs 1951–53, 1955–57.

Richards, John (brother of Matthias Richards) (R Pa.) April 18, 1753–Nov. 13, 1822; House 1795–97.

Richards, John (– N.Y.) April 13, 1765–April 18, 1850; House 1823–25.

Richards, Mark (R Vt.) July 15, 1760–Aug. 10, 1844; House 1817–21.

Richards, Matthias (brother of John Richards) (R Pa.) Feb. 26, 1758–Aug. 4, 1830; House 1807–11.

Richardson, David Plunket (R N.Y.) May 28, 1833–June 21, 1904; House 1879–83.

Richardson, George Frederick (D Mich.) July 1, 1850–March 1, 1923; House 1893–95.

Richardson, Harry Alden (R Del.) Jan. 1, 1853–June 16, 1928; Senate 1907–13.

Richardson, James Daniel (D Tenn.) March 10, 1843–July 24, 1914; House 1885–1905; House minority leader 1899–1903.

Richardson, James Montgomery (D Ky.) July 1, 1858–Feb. 9, 1925; House 1905–07.

Richardson, John Peter (J S.C.) April 14, 1801–Jan. 24, 1864; House Dec. 19, 1836–39; Gov. Dec. 10, 1840–Dec. 8, 1842.

Richardson, John Smythe (D S.C.) Feb. 29, 1828–Feb. 24, 1894; House 1879–83.

Richardson, Joseph (– Mass.) Feb. 1, 1778–Sept. 25, 1871; House 1827–31.

Richardson, William (D Ala.) May 8, 1839–March 31, 1914; House Aug. 6, 1900–March 31, 1914.

Richardson, William Alexander (D Ill.) Jan. 16, 1811–Dec. 27, 1875; House Dec. 6, 1847–Aug. 25, 1856, 1861–Jan. 29, 1863; Senate Jan. 30, 1863–65.

Richardson, William Blaine (D N.M.) Nov. 15, 1947– ; House 1983–Feb. 13, 1997; Secy. of Energy Aug. 18, 1998– .

Richardson, William Emanuel (D Pa.) Sept. 3, 1886–Nov. 3, 1948; House 1933–37.

Richardson, William Merchant (R Mass.) Jan. 4, 1774–March 15, 1838; House Nov. 4, 1811–April 18, 1814.

Richmond, Frederick William (D N.Y.) Nov. 15, 1923– ; House 1975–August 25, 1982.

Richmond, Hiram Lawton (R Pa.) May 17, 1810–Feb. 19, 1885; House 1873–75.

Richmond, James Buchanan (D Va.) Feb. 27, 1842–April 30, 1910; House 1879–81.

Richmond, Jonathan (– N.Y.) July 31, 1774–July 28, 1853; House 1819–21.

Ricketts, Edwin Darlington (R Ohio) Aug. 3, 1867–July 3, 1937; House 1915–17, 1919–23.

Riddick, Carl Wood (R Mont.) Feb. 25, 1872–July 9, 1960; House 1919–23.

Riddle, Albert Gallatin (R Ohio) May 28, 1816–May 16, 1902; House 1861–63.

Riddle, George Read (D Del.) 1817–March 29, 1867; House 1851–55; Senate Feb. 2, 1864–March 29, 1867.

Riddle, Haywood Yancey (D Tenn.) June 20, 1834–March 28, 1879; House Dec. 14, 1875–79.

Riddleberger, Harrison Holt (Read. Va.) Oct. 4, 1844–Jan. 24, 1890; Senate 1883–89.

Rider, Ira Edgar (D N.Y.) Nov. 17, 1868–May 29, 1906; House 1903–05.

Ridge, Thomas Joseph (R Pa.) Aug. 26, 1945– ; House 1983–95; Gov. Jan. 17, 1995– .

Ridgely, Edwin Reed (P Kan.) May 9, 1844–April 23, 1927; House 1897–1901.

Ridgely, Henry Moore (F Del.) Aug. 6, 1779–Aug. 6, 1847; House 1811–15; Senate Jan. 12, 1827–29.

Ridgway, Joseph (W Ohio) May 6, 1783–Feb. 1, 1861; House 1837–43.

Ridgway, Robert (C Va.) April 21, 1823–Oct. 16, 1870; House Jan. 27–Oct. 16, 1870.

Riegle, Donald Wayne Jr. (D Mich.) Feb. 4, 1938– ; House 1967–Dec. 30, 1976 (1967–73 Republican); Senate Dec. 30, 1976–95; Chrmn. Senate Banking, Housing, and Urban Affairs 1989–95.

Riehlman, Roy Walter (R N.Y.) Aug. 26, 1899–July 16, 1978; House 1947–65.

Rife, John Winebrenner (R Pa.) Aug. 14, 1846–April 17, 1908; House 1889–93.

Riggs, Frank (R Calif.) Sept. 5, 1950– ; House 1991–93, 1995–99.

Riggs, James Milton (D Ill.) April 17, 1839–Nov. 18, 1933; House 1883–87.

Riggs, Jetur Rose (ALD N.J.) June 20, 1809–Nov. 5, 1869; House 1859–61.

Riggs, Lewis (D N.Y.) Jan. 16, 1789–Nov. 6, 1870; House 1841–43.

Rigney, Hugh McPheeters (D Ill.) July 31, 1873–Oct. 12, 1950; House 1937–39.

Riker, Samuel (R N.Y.) April 8, 1743–May 19, 1823; House Nov. 5, 1804–05, 1807–09.

Riley, Bob (R Ala.) Oct. 3, 1944– ; House 1997– .

Riley, Corinne Boyd (widow of John Jacob Riley) (D S.C.) July 4, 1893–April 12, 1979; House April 10, 1962–63.

Riley, John Jacob (husband of Corinne Boyd Riley) (D S.C.) Feb. 1, 1895–Jan. 1, 1962; House 1945–49, 1951–Jan. 1, 1962.

Rinaker, John Irving (R Ill.) Nov. 1, 1830–Jan. 15, 1915; House June 5, 1896–97.

Rinaldo, Matthew John (R N.J.) Sept. 1, 1931– ; House 1973–93.

Ringgold, Samuel (R Md.) Jan. 15, 1770–Oct. 18, 1829; House Oct. 15, 1810–15, 1817–21.

Riordan, Daniel Joseph (D N.Y.) July 7, 1870–April 28, 1923; House 1899–1901, Nov. 6, 1906–April 28, 1923.

Ripley, Eleazar Wheelock (brother of James Wheelock Ripley) (D La.) April 15, 1782–March 2, 1839; House 1835–March 2, 1839 (1835–37 Jacksonian).

Ripley, James Wheelock (brother of Eleazar Wheelock Ripley) (J Maine) March 12, 1786–June 17, 1835; House Sept. 11, 1826–March 12, 1830 (Sept. 11, 1826–29 no party).

Ripley, Thomas C. (W N.Y.) ?–?; House Dec. 7, 1846–47.

Risenhoover, Theodore Marshall (D Okla.) Nov. 3, 1934– ; House 1975–79.

Risk, Charles Francis (R R.I.) Aug. 19, 1897–Dec. 26, 1943; House Aug. 6, 1935–37, 1939–41.

Risley, Elijah (W N.Y.) May 7, 1787–Jan. 9, 1870; House 1849–51.

Ritchey, Thomas (D Ohio) Jan. 19, 1801–March 9, 1863; House 1847–49, 1853–55.

Ritchie, Byron Foster (son of James Monroe Ritchie) (D Ohio) Jan. 29, 1853–Aug. 22, 1928; House 1893–95.

Ritchie, David (R Pa.) Aug. 19, 1812–Jan. 24, 1867; House 1853–59 (1853–57 Whig).

Ritchie, James Monroe (father of Byron Foster Ritchie) (R Ohio) July 28, 1829–Aug. 17, 1918; House 1881–83.

Ritchie, John (D Md.) Aug. 12, 1831–Oct. 27, 1887; House 1871–73.

Ritter, Burwell Clark (uncle of Walter Evans) (D Ky.) Jan. 6, 1810–Oct. 1, 1880; House 1865–67.

Ritter, Donald Lawrence (R Pa.) Oct. 21, 1940– ; House 1979–93.

Ritter, John (D Pa.) Feb. 6, 1779–Nov. 24, 1851; House 1843–47.

Rivera, Luis Muñoz (U P.R.) July 17, 1859–Nov. 15, 1916; House (Res. Comm.) 1911–Nov. 15, 1916.

Rivers, Lucius Mendel (D S.C.) Sept. 28, 1905–Dec. 28, 1970; House 1941–Dec. 28, 1970; Chrmn. House Armed Services 1965–71.

Rivers, Lynn (D Mich.) Dec. 19, 1956– ; House 1995– .

Rivers, Ralph Julian (D Alaska) May 23, 1903–Aug. 14, 1976; House 1959–67.

Rivers, Thomas (AP Tenn.) Sept. 18, 1819–March 18, 1863; House 1855–57.

Rives, Francis Everod (great-uncle of Francis Rives Lassiter) (D Va.) Jan. 14, 1792–Dec. 26, 1861; House 1837–41.

Rives, William Cabell (W Va.) May 4, 1793–April 25, 1868; House 1823–29 (no party); Senate Dec. 10, 1832–Feb. 22, 1834 (Jacksonian), 1836–39 (Jacksonian), Jan. 18, 1841–45.

Rives, Zeno John (R Ill.) Feb. 22, 1874–Sept. 2, 1939; House 1905–07.

Rixey, John Franklin (D Va.) Aug. 1, 1854–Feb. 8, 1907; House 1897–Feb. 8, 1907.

Rizley, Ross (R Okla.) July 5, 1892–March 4, 1969; House 1941–49.

Roach, Sidney Crain (R Mo.) July 25, 1876–June 29, 1934; House 1921–25.

Roach, William Nathaniel (D N.D.) Sept. 25, 1840–Sept. 7, 1902; Senate 1893–99.

Roane, John (father of John Jones Roane) (J Va.) Feb. 9, 1766–Nov. 15, 1838; House 1809–15 (Republican), 1827–31, 1835–37.

Roane, John Jones (son of John Roane) (J Va.) Oct. 31, 1794–Dec. 18, 1869; House 1831–33.

Roane, William Henry (D Va.) Sept. 17, 1787–May 11, 1845; House 1815–17 (Republican); Senate March 14, 1837–41.

Roark, Charles Wickliffe (R Ky.) Jan. 22, 1887–April 5, 1929; House March 4–April 5, 1929.

Robb, Edward (D Mo.) March 19, 1857–March 13, 1934; House 1897–1905.

Robb, Charles Spittal (son-in-law of Lyndon Baines Johnson) (D Va.) June 26, 1939– ; Senate 1989– ; Gov. Jan. 16, 1982–Jan. 18, 1986.

Robbins, Asher (W R.I.) Oct. 26, 1757–Feb. 25, 1845; Senate Oct. 31, 1825–39.

Robbins, Edward Everett (R Pa.) Sept. 27, 1860–Jan. 25, 1919; House 1897–99, 1917–Jan. 25, 1919.

Robbins, Gaston Ahi (D Ala.) Sept. 26, 1858–Feb. 22, 1902; House 1893–March 13, 1896, 1899–March 8, 1900.

Robbins, George Robbins (R N.J.) Sept. 24, 1808–Feb. 22, 1875; House 1855–59 (1855–57 Whig).

Robbins, John (D Pa.) 1808–April 27, 1880; House 1849–55, 1875–77.

Robbins, William McKendree (D N.C.) Oct. 26, 1828–May 5, 1905; House 1873–79.

Roberts, Anthony Ellmaker (grandfather of Robert Grey Bushong) (R Pa.) Oct. 29, 1803–Jan. 25, 1885; House 1855–59 (1855–57 Independent Whig).

Roberts, Brigham Henry (D Utah) March 13, 1857–Sept. 27, 1933; House 1899–Jan. 25, 1900.

Roberts, Charles Boyle (D Md.) April 19, 1842–Sept. 10, 1899; House 1875–79.

Roberts, Charles Patrick "Pat" (R Kan.) April 20, 1936– ; House 1981–97; Senate 1997– ; Chrmn. House Agriculture 1995–97.

Roberts, Clint Ronald (R S.D.) Jan. 30, 1935– ; House 1981–83.

Roberts, Edwin Ewing (R Nev.) Dec. 12, 1870–Dec. 11, 1933; House 1911–19.

Roberts, Ellis Henry (R N.Y.) Sept. 30, 1827–Jan. 8, 1918; House 1871–75.

Roberts, Ernest William (R Mass.) Nov. 22, 1858–Feb. 27, 1924; House 1899–1917.

Roberts, Herbert Ray (D Texas) March 28, 1913–April 13, 1992; House Jan. 30, 1962–81; Chrmn. House Veterans' Affairs 1975–81.

Roberts, Jonathan (R Pa.) Aug. 16, 1771–July 24, 1854; House 1811–Feb. 24, 1814; Senate Feb. 24, 1814–21.

Roberts, Kenneth Allison (D Ala.) Nov. 1, 1912–May 9, 1989; House 1951–65.

Roberts, Robert Whyte (D Miss.) Nov. 28, 1784–Jan. 4, 1865; House 1843–47.

Roberts, William Randall (D N.Y.) Feb. 6, 1830–Aug. 9, 1897; House 1871–75.

Robertson, Absalom Willis (D Va.) May 27, 1887–Nov. 1, 1971; House 1933–Nov. 5, 1946; Senate Nov. 6, 1946–Dec. 30, 1966; Chrmn. Senate Banking and Currency 1959–67.

Robertson, Alice Mary (R Okla.) Jan. 2, 1854–July 1, 1931; House 1921–23.

Robertson, Charles Raymond (R N.D.) Sept. 5, 1889–Feb. 18, 1951; House 1941–43, 1945–49.

Robertson, Edward Vivian (R Wyo.) May 27, 1881–April 15, 1963; Senate 1943–49.

Robertson, Edward White (father of Samuel Matthews Robertson) (D La.) June 13, 1823–Aug. 2, 1887; House 1877–83, March 4–Aug. 2, 1887.

Robertson, George (R Ky.) Nov. 18, 1790–May 16, 1874; House 1817–21.

Robertson, John (brother of Thomas Bolling Robertson) (W Va.) April 13, 1787–July 5, 1873; House Dec. 8, 1834–39 (Dec. 8, 1834–35 no party).

Robertson, Samuel Matthews (son of Edward White Robertson) (D La.) Jan. 1, 1852–Dec. 24, 1911; House Dec. 5, 1887–1907.

Robertson, Thomas Austin (D Ky.) Sept. 9, 1848–July 18, 1892; House 1883–87.

Robertson, Thomas Bolling (brother of John Robertson) (R La.) Feb. 27, 1779–Oct. 5, 1828; House April 30, 1812–April 20, 1818; Gov. Dec. 18, 1820–Nov. 15, 1822 (Democratic Republican).

Robertson, Thomas James (R S.C.) Aug. 3, 1823–Oct. 13, 1897; Senate July 15, 1868–77.

Robertson, William Henry (R N.Y.) Oct. 10, 1823–Dec. 6, 1898; House 1867–69.

Robeson, Edward John Jr. (D Va.) Aug. 9, 1890–March 10, 1966; House May 2, 1950–59.

Robeson, George Maxwell (nephew of George Clifford Maxwell) (R N.J.) March 16, 1829–Sept. 27, 1897; House 1879–83; Secy. of the Navy June 26, 1869–March 12, 1877.

Robie, Reuben (D N.Y.) July 15, 1799–Jan. 21, 1872; House 1851–53.

Robinson, Arthur Raymond (R Ind.) March 12, 1881–March 17, 1961; Senate Oct. 20, 1925–35.

Robinson, Christopher (R R.I.) May 15, 1806–Oct. 3, 1889; House 1859–61.

Robinson, Edward (W Maine) Nov. 25, 1796–Feb. 19, 1857; House April 28, 1838–39.

Robinson, George Dexter (R Mass.) Jan. 20, 1834–Feb. 22, 1896; House 1877–Jan. 7, 1884; Gov. Jan. 3, 1884–Jan. 5, 1887.

Robinson, James Carroll (D Ill.) Aug. 19, 1823–Nov. 3, 1886; House 1859–65, 1871–75.

Robinson, James Kenneth (R Va.) May 14, 1916–April 8, 1990; House 1971–85.

Robinson, James McClellan (D Ind.) May 31, 1861–Jan. 16, 1942; House 1897–1905.

Robinson, James Sidney (R Ohio) Oct. 14, 1827–Jan. 14, 1892; House 1881–Jan. 12, 1885.

Robinson, James Wallace (R Ohio) Nov. 26, 1826–June 28, 1898; House 1873–75.

Robinson, James William (D Utah) Jan. 19, 1878–Dec. 2, 1964; House 1933–47.

Robinson, John Buchanan (R Pa.) May 23, 1846–Jan. 28, 1933; House 1891–97.

Robinson, John Larne (D Ind.) May 3, 1813–March 21, 1860; House 1847–53.

Robinson, John McCracken (J Ill.) April 10, 1794–April 25, 1843; Senate Dec. 11, 1830–41.

Robinson, John Seaton (D Neb.) May 4, 1856–May 25, 1903; House 1899–1903.

Robinson, Jonathan (brother of Moses Robinson) (R Vt.) Aug. 11, 1756–Nov. 3, 1819; Senate Oct. 10, 1807–15.

Robinson, Joseph Taylor (D Ark.) Aug. 26, 1872–July 14, 1937; House 1903–Jan. 14, 1913; Senate 1913–July 14, 1937; Senate minority leader 1923–33; Senate majority leader 1933–July 14, 1937; Gov. Jan. 15–March 10, 1913.

Robinson, Leonidas Dunlap (D N.C.) April 22, 1867–Nov. 7, 1941; House 1917–21.

Robinson, Milton Stapp (R Ind.) April 20, 1832–July 28, 1892; House 1875–79.

Robinson, Moses (brother of Jonathan Robinson) (– Vt.) March 20, 1741–May 26, 1813; Senate Oct. 17, 1791–Oct. 15, 1796; Gov. (Va. Terr.) 1789–90.

Robinson, Orville (D N.Y.) Oct. 28, 1801–Dec. 1, 1882; House 1843–45.

Robinson, Thomas Jr. (D Del.) 1800–Oct. 28, 1843; House 1839–41.

Robinson, Thomas John Bright (R Iowa) Aug. 12, 1868–Jan. 27, 1958; House 1923–33.

Robinson, Tommy Franklin (R Ark.) March 7, 1942– ; House 1985–91 (1985–July 28, 1989 Democrat).

Robinson, William Erigena (D N.Y.) May 6, 1814–Jan. 23, 1892; House 1867–69, 1881–85.

Robison, David Fullerton (nephew of David Fullerton) (W Pa.) May 28, 1816–June 24, 1859; House 1855–57.

Robison, Howard Winfield (R N.Y.) Oct. 30, 1915–Sept. 26, 1987; House Jan. 14, 1958–75.

Robsion, John Marshall (father of John Marshall Robsion Jr.) (R Ky.) Jan. 2, 1873–Feb. 17, 1948; House 1919–Jan. 10, 1930, 1935–Feb. 17, 1948; Senate Jan. 11–Nov. 30, 1930.

Robsion, John Marshall Jr. (son of John Marshall Robsion) (R Ky.) Aug. 28, 1904–Feb. 14, 1990; House 1953–59.

Rochester, William Beatty (D N.Y.) Jan. 29, 1789–June 14, 1838; House 1821–April 1823.

Rockefeller, John Davison "Jay" IV (great-grandson of Nelson Wilmarth Aldrich, great-nephew of Richard Steere Aldrich, nephew of Vice Pres. Nelson Aldrich Rockefeller and Gov. Winthrop Rockefeller of Ark., son-in-law of Charles Harting Percy) (D W.Va.) June 18, 1937– ; Senate Jan. 15, 1985– ; Chrmn. Senate Veterans' Affairs 1993–95; Gov. Jan. 17, 1977–Jan. 14, 1985.

Rockefeller, Lewis Kirby (R N.Y.) Nov. 25, 1875–Sept. 18, 1948; House Nov. 2, 1937–43.

Rockhill, William (D Ind.) Feb. 10, 1793–Jan. 15, 1865; House 1847–49.

Rockwell, Francis Williams (son of Julius Rockwell) (R Mass.) May 26, 1844–June 26, 1929; House Jan. 17, 1884–91.

Rockwell, Hosea Hunt (D N.Y.) May 31, 1840–Dec. 18, 1918; House 1891–93.

Rockwell, John Arnold (W Conn.) Aug. 27, 1803–Feb. 10, 1861; House 1845–49.

Rockwell, Julius (father of Francis Williams Rockwell) (W Mass.) April 26, 1805–May 19, 1888; House 1843–51; Senate June 3, 1854–Jan. 31, 1855.

Rockwell, Robert Fay (R Colo.) Feb. 11, 1886–Sept. 29, 1950; House Dec. 9, 1941–49.

Roddenbery, Seaborn Anderson (D Ga.) Jan. 12, 1870–Sept. 25, 1913; House Feb. 16, 1910–Sept. 25, 1913.

Rodenberg, William August (R Ill.) Oct. 30, 1865–Sept. 10, 1937; House 1899–1901, 1903–13, 1915–23.

Rodey, Bernard Shandon (R N.M.) March 1, 1856–March 10, 1927; House (Terr. Del.) 1901–05.

Rodgers, Robert Lewis (R Pa.) June 2, 1875–May 9, 1960; House 1939–47.

Rodino, Peter Wallace Jr. (D N.J.) June 7, 1909– ; House 1949–89; Chrmn. House Judiciary 1973–89.

Rodman, William (R Pa.) Oct. 7, 1757–July 27, 1824; House 1811–13.

Rodney, Caesar Augustus (cousin of George Brydges Rodney) (R Del.) Jan. 4, 1772–June 10, 1824; House 1803–05, 1821–Jan. 24, 1822; Senate Jan. 24, 1822–Jan. 29, 1823; Atty. Gen. Jan. 20, 1807–Dec. 11, 1811.

Rodney, Daniel (– Del.) Sept. 10, 1764–Sept. 2, 1846; House Oct. 1, 1822–23; Senate Nov. 8, 1826–Jan. 12, 1827; Gov. Jan. 18, 1814–Jan. 21, 1817 (Federalist).

Rodney, George Brydges (cousin of Caesar Augustus Rodney) (W Del.) April 2, 1803–June 18, 1883; House 1841–45.

Rodriguez, Ciro D. (D Texas) Dec. 9, 1946– ; House April 17, 1997– .

Roe, Dudley George (D Md.) March 23, 1881–Jan. 4, 1970; House 1945–47.

Roe, James A. (D N.Y.) July 9, 1896–April 22, 1967; House 1945–47.

Roe, Robert A. (D N.J.) Feb. 28, 1924– ; House Nov. 4, 1969–93; Chrmn. House Science, Space, and Technology 1987–91; Chrmn. House Public Works and Transportation 1991–93.

Roemer, Charles Elson III "Buddy" (D La.) Oct. 4, 1943– ; House 1981–March 14, 1988; Gov. March 14, 1988–Jan. 13, 1992 (March 11, 1991– Republican).

Roemer, Timothy J. (son-in-law of John Bennett Johnston Jr.) (D Ind.) Oct. 30, 1956– ; House 1991– .

Rogan, James E. (R Calif.) Aug. 21, 1957– ; House 1997– .

Rogers, Andrew Jackson (D N.J.) July 1, 1828–May 22, 1900; House 1863–67.

Rogers, Anthony Astley Cooper (D Ark.) Feb. 14, 1821–July 27, 1899; House 1869–71.

Rogers, Byron Giles (D Colo.) Aug. 1, 1900–Dec. 31, 1983; House 1951–71.

Rogers, Charles (W N.Y.) April 30, 1800–Jan. 13, 1874; House 1843–45.

Rogers, Dwight Laing (father of Paul Grant Rogers) (D Fla.) Aug. 17, 1886–Dec. 1, 1954; House 1945–Dec. 1, 1954.

Rogers, Edith Nourse (widow of John Jacob Rogers) (R Mass.) 1881–Sept. 10, 1960; House June 30, 1925–Sept. 10, 1960; Chrmn. House Veterans' Affairs 1947–49, 1953–55.

Rogers, Edward (D N.Y.) May 30, 1787–May 29, 1857; House 1839–41.

Rogers, George Frederick (D N.Y.) March 19, 1887–Nov. 20, 1948; House 1945–47.

Rogers, Harold Dallas (R Ky.) Dec. 31, 1937– ; House 1981– .

Rogers, James (D S.C.) Oct. 24, 1795–Dec. 21, 1873; House 1835–37 (Jacksonian), 1839–43.

Rogers, John (D N.Y.) May 9, 1813–May 11, 1879; House 1871–73.

Rogers, John Henry (D Ark.) Oct. 9, 1845–April 16, 1911; House 1883–91.

Rogers, John Jacob (husband of Edith Nourse Rogers) (R Mass.) Aug. 18, 1881–March 28, 1925; House 1913–March 28, 1925.

Rogers, Paul Grant (son of Dwight Laing Rogers) (D Fla.) June 4, 1921– ; House Jan. 11, 1955–79.

Rogers, Sion Hart (D N.C.) Sept. 30, 1825–Aug. 14, 1874; House 1853–55 (Whig), 1871–73.

Rogers, Thomas Jones (father of William Findlay Rogers) (R Pa.) 1781–Dec. 7, 1832; House March 3, 1818–April 20, 1824.

Rogers, Walter Edward (D Texas) July 19, 1908– ; House 1951–67.

Rogers, Will (D Okla.) Dec. 12, 1898–Aug. 3, 1983; House 1933–43.

Rogers, William Findlay (son of Thomas Jones Rogers) (D N.Y.) March 1, 1820–Dec. 16, 1899; House 1883–85.

Rogers, William Nathaniel (D N.H.) Jan. 10, 1892–Sept. 25, 1945; House 1923–25, Jan. 5, 1932–37.

Rogers, William Vann Jr. (D Calif.) Oct. 20, 1911–July 9, 1993; House 1943–May 23, 1944.

Rohrabacher, Dana (R Calif.) June 21, 1947– ; House 1989– .

Rohrbough, Edward Gay (R W.Va.) 1874–Dec. 12, 1956; House 1943–45, 1947–49.

Rollins, Edward Henry (R N.H.) Oct. 3, 1824–July 31, 1889; House 1861–67; Senate 1877–83.

Rollins, James Sidney (U Mo.) April 19, 1812–Jan. 9, 1888; House 1861–65 (1861–63 Constitutional Unionist).

Rolph, Thomas (R Calif.) Jan. 17, 1885–May 10, 1956; House 1941–45.

Roman, James Dixon (W Md.) Aug. 11, 1809–Jan. 19, 1867; House 1847–49.

Romeis, Jacob (R Ohio) Dec. 1, 1835–March 8, 1904; House 1885–89.

Romero, Trinidad (R N.M.) June 15, 1835–Aug. 28, 1918; House (Terr. Del.) 1877–79.

Romero-Barceló, Carlos A. (D P.R.) Sept. 4, 1932– ; House (Res. Comm.) 1993– .

Romjue, Milton Andrew (D Mo.) Dec. 5, 1874–Jan. 23, 1968; House 1917–21, 1923–43.

Romulo, Carlos Peña (– P.I.) Jan. 14, 1899–Dec. 15, 1985; House (Res. Comm.) Aug. 10, 1944–July 4, 1946.

Ronan, Daniel John (D Ill.) July 13, 1914–Aug. 13, 1969; House 1965–Aug. 13, 1969.

Roncalio, Teno (D Wyo.) March 23, 1916– ; House 1965–67, 1971–Dec. 30, 1978.

Roncallo, Angelo Dominick (R N.Y.) May 28, 1927– ; House 1973–75.

Rooney, Frederick Bernard (D Pa.) Nov. 6, 1925– ; House July 30, 1963–79.

Rooney, John James (D N.Y.) Nov. 29, 1903–Oct. 26, 1975; House June 6, 1944–Dec. 31, 1974.

Roosevelt, Franklin Delano Jr. (son of Pres. Franklin Delano Roosevelt, brother of James Roosevelt) (D N.Y.) Aug. 17, 1914–Aug. 17, 1988; House May 17, 1949–55 (1949–51 Liberal).

Roosevelt, James (son of Pres. Franklin Delano Roosevelt, brother of Franklin Delano Roosevelt Jr.) (D Calif.) Dec. 23, 1907–Aug. 13, 1991; House 1955–Sept. 30, 1965.

Roosevelt, James I. (uncle of Robert Barnwell Roosevelt) (D N.Y.) Dec. 14, 1795–April 5, 1875; House 1841–43.

Roosevelt, Robert Barnwell (nephew of James I. Roosevelt, uncle of Theodore Roosevelt) (D N.Y.) Aug. 7, 1829–June 14, 1906; House 1871–73.

Root, Elihu (R N.Y.) Feb. 15, 1845–Feb. 7, 1937; Senate 1909–15; Secy. of War Aug. 1, 1899–Jan. 31, 1904; Secy. of State July 19, 1905–Jan. 27, 1909.

Root, Erastus (J N.Y.) March 16, 1773–Dec. 24, 1846; House 1803–05 (Republican), 1809–11 (Republican), Dec. 26, 1815–17 (Republican), 1831–33.

Root, Joseph Mosley (FS Ohio) Oct. 7, 1807–April 7, 1879; House 1845–51 (1845–49 Whig).

Roots, Logan Holt (R Ark.) March 26, 1841–May 30, 1893; House June 22, 1868–71.

Rose, Charles Grandison III (D N.C.) Aug. 10, 1939– ; House 1973–97; Chrmn. House Administration 1991–95.

Rose, John Marshall (R Pa.) May 18, 1856–April 22, 1923; House 1917–23.

Rose, Robert Lawson (son of Robert Selden Rose, son-in-law of Nathaniel Allen) (W N.Y.) Oct. 12, 1804–March 14, 1877; House 1847–51.

Rose, Robert Selden (father of Robert Lawson Rose) (AMas. N.Y.) Feb. 24, 1774–Nov. 24, 1835; House 1823–27 (no party), 1829–31.

Rosecrans, William Starke (D Calif.) Sept. 6, 1819–March 11, 1898; House 1881–85.

Rosenbloom, Benjamin Louis (R W.Va.) June 3, 1880–March 22, 1965; House 1921–25.

Rosenthal, Benjamin Stanley (D N.Y.) June 8, 1923–Jan. 4, 1983; House Feb. 20, 1962–Jan. 4, 1983.

Rosier, Joseph (D W.Va.) Jan. 24, 1870–Oct. 7, 1951; Senate Jan. 3, 1941–Nov. 17, 1942.

Ros-Lehtinen, Ileana (R Fla.) July 15, 1952– ; House Sept. 6, 1989– .

Ross, Edmund Gibson (R Kan.) Dec. 7, 1826–May 8, 1907; Senate July 19, 1866–71; Gov. (N.M. Terr.) 1885–89 (Democrat).

Ross, Henry Howard (– N.Y.) May 9, 1790–Sept. 14, 1862; House 1825–27.

Ross, James (F Pa.) July 12, 1762–Nov. 27, 1847; Senate April 24, 1794–1803; elected Pres. pro tempore March 1, 1799.

Ross, John (father of Thomas Ross) (R Pa.) Feb. 24, 1770–Jan. 31, 1834; House 1809–11, 1815–Feb. 24, 1818.

Ross, Jonathan (R Vt.) April 30, 1826–Feb. 23, 1905; Senate Jan. 11, 1899–Oct. 18, 1900.

Ross, Lewis Winans (D Ill.) Dec. 8, 1812–Oct. 20, 1895; House 1863–69.

Ross, Miles (D N.J.) April 30, 1827–Feb. 22, 1903; House 1875–83.

Ross, Robert Tripp (R N.Y.) June 4, 1903–Oct. 1, 1981; House 1947–49, Feb. 19, 1952–53.

Ross, Sobieski (R Pa.) May 16, 1828–Oct. 24, 1877; House 1873–77.

Ross, Thomas (son of John Ross) (D Pa.) Dec. 1, 1806–July 7, 1865; House 1849–53.

Ross, Thomas Randolph (D Ohio) Oct. 26, 1788–June 28, 1869; House 1819–25.

Rossdale, Albert Berger (R N.Y.) Oct. 23, 1878–April 17, 1968; House 1921–23.

Rostenkowski, Daniel David "Dan" (D Ill.) Jan. 2, 1928– ; House 1959–95; Chrmn. House Ways and Means 1981–94.

Roth, Tobias Anton "Toby" (R Wis.) Oct. 10, 1938– ; House 1979–97.

Roth, William Victor Jr. (R Del.) July 22, 1921– ; House 1967–Dec. 31, 1970; Senate Jan. 1, 1971– ; Chrmn. Senate Governmental Affairs 1981–87, 1995–96; Chrmn. Senate Finance 1995– .

Rothermel, John Hoover (D Pa.) March 7, 1856–Aug. 1922; House 1907–15.

Rothman, Steven R. (D N.J.) Oct. 14, 1952– ; House 1997– .

Rothwell, Gideon Frank (D Mo.) April 24, 1836–Jan. 18, 1894; House 1879–81.

Roudebush, Richard Lowell (R Ind.) Jan. 18, 1918–Jan. 28, 1995; House 1961–71.

Roukema, Margaret Scafati "Marge" (R N.J.) Sept. 19, 1929– ; House 1981– .

Rouse, Arthur Blythe (D Ky.) June 20, 1874–Jan. 25, 1956; House 1911–27.

Roush, John Edward (D Ind.) Sept. 12, 1920– ; House 1959–69, 1971–77.

Rousseau, Lovell Harrison (UU Ky.) Aug. 4, 1818–Jan. 7, 1869; House 1865–July 21, 1866, Dec. 3, 1866–67.

Rousselot, John Harbin (R Calif.) Nov. 1, 1927– ; House 1961–63, June 30, 1970–83.

Routzohn, Harry Nelson (R Ohio) Nov. 4, 1881–April 14, 1953; House 1939–41.

Rowan, John (uncle of Robert Todd Lytle) (R Ky.) July 12, 1773–July 13, 1843; House 1807–09; Senate 1825–31.

Rowan, Joseph (D N.Y.) Sept. 8, 1870–Aug. 3, 1930; House 1919–21.

Rowan, William A. (D Ill.) Nov. 24, 1882–May 31, 1961; House 1943–47.

Rowbottom, Harry Emerson (R Ind.) Nov. 3, 1884–March 22, 1934; House 1925–31.

Rowe, Edmund (R Ohio) Dec. 21, 1892–Oct. 4, 1972; House 1943–45.

Rowe, Frederick William (R N.Y.) March 19, 1863–June 20, 1946; House 1915–21.

Rowe, Peter (D N.Y.) March 10, 1807–April 17, 1876; House 1853–55.

Rowell, Jonathan Harvey (R Ill.) Feb. 10, 1833–May 15, 1908; House 1883–91.

Rowland, Alfred (D N.C.) Feb. 9, 1844–Aug. 2, 1898; House 1887–91.

Rowland, Charles Hedding (R Pa.) Dec. 20, 1860–Nov. 24, 1921; House 1915–19.

Rowland, James Roy Jr. (D Ga.) Feb. 3, 1926– ; House 1983–95.

Rowland, John G. (R Conn.) May 24, 1957– ; House 1985–91; Gov. Jan. 4, 1995– .

Roy, Alphonse (D N.H.) Oct. 26, 1897–Oct. 5, 1967; House June 9, 1938–39.

Roy, William Robert (D Kan.) Feb. 23, 1926– ; House 1971–75.

Roybal, Edward Ross (D Calif.) Feb. 10, 1916– ; House 1963–93.

Roybal-Allard, Lucille (D Calif.) June 12, 1941– ; House 1993– .

Royce, Ed (R Calif.) Oct. 12, 1951– ; House 1993– .

Royce, Homer Elihu (R Vt.) June 14, 1819–April 24, 1891; House 1857–61.

Royer, William Howard (R Calif.) April 11, 1920– ; House April 3, 1979–81.

Royse, Lemuel Willard (R Ind.) Jan. 19, 1847–Dec. 18, 1946; House 1895–99.

Rubey, Thomas Lewis (D Mo.) Sept. 27, 1862–Nov. 2, 1928; House 1911–21, 1923–Nov. 2, 1928.

Rucker, Atterson Walden (D Colo.) April 3, 1847–July 19, 1924; House 1909–13.

Rucker, Tinsley White (D Ga.) March 24, 1848–Nov. 18, 1926; House Jan. 11–March 3, 1917.

Rucker, William Waller (D Mo.) Feb. 1, 1855–May 30, 1936; House 1899–1923.

Rudd, Eldon Dean (R Ariz.) July 15, 1920– ; House 1977–87.

Rudd, Stephen Andrew (D N.Y.) Dec. 11, 1874–March 31, 1936; House 1931–March 31, 1936.

Rudman, Warren Bruce (R N.H.) May 13, 1930– ; Senate Dec. 29, 1980–93; Chrmn. Senate Select Committee on Ethics 1985–87.

Ruffin, James Edward (D Mo.) July 24, 1893–April 9, 1977; House 1933–35.

Ruffin, Thomas (D N.C.) Sept. 9, 1820–Oct. 13, 1863; House 1853–61.

Ruggles, Benjamin (R Ohio) Feb. 21, 1783–Sept. 2, 1857; Senate 1815–33.

Ruggles, Charles Herman (– N.Y.) Feb. 10, 1789–June 16, 1865; House 1821–23.

Ruggles, John (J Maine) Oct. 8, 1789–June 20, 1874; Senate Jan. 20, 1835–41.

Ruggles, Nathaniel (F Mass.) Nov. 11, 1761–Dec. 19, 1819; House 1813–19.

Rumple, John Nicholas William (R Iowa) March 4, 1841–Jan. 31, 1903; House 1901–Jan. 31, 1903.

Rumsey, David (W N.Y.) Dec. 25, 1810–March 12, 1883; House 1847–51.

Rumsey, Edward (W Ky.) Nov. 5, 1796–April 6, 1868; House 1837–39.

Rumsfeld, Donald Henry (R Ill.) July 9, 1932– ; House 1963–May 25, 1969; Secy. of Defense Nov. 20, 1975–Jan. 20, 1977.

Runk, John (W N.J.) July 3, 1791–Sept. 22, 1872; House 1845–47.

Runnels, Harold Lowell (D N.M.) March 17, 1924–Aug. 5, 1980; House 1971–Aug. 5, 1980.

Rupley, Arthur Ringwalt (R Pa.) Nov. 13, 1868–Nov. 11, 1920; House 1913–15.

Ruppe, Philip Edward (R Mich.) Sept. 29, 1926– ; House 1967–79.

Ruppert, Jacob Jr. (D N.Y.) Aug. 5, 1867–Jan. 13, 1939; House 1899–1907.

Rush, Bobby L. (D Ill.) Nov. 23, 1946– ; House 1993– .

Rusk, Harry Welles (D Md.) Oct. 17, 1852–Jan. 28, 1926; House Nov. 2, 1886–97.

Rusk, Jeremiah McLain (R Wis.) June 17, 1830–Nov. 21, 1893; House 1871–77; Gov. Jan. 2, 1882–Jan. 7, 1889; Secy. of Agriculture March 6, 1889–March 6, 1893.

Rusk, Thomas Jefferson (D Texas) Dec. 5, 1803–July 29, 1857; Senate Feb. 21, 1846–July 29, 1857; elected Pres. pro tempore March 14, 1857.

Russ, John (– Conn.) Oct. 29, 1767–June 22, 1833; House 1819–23.

Russell, Benjamin Edward (cousin of Rienzi Melville Johnston) (D Ga.) Oct. 5, 1845–Dec. 4, 1909; House 1893–97.

Russell, Charles Addison (R Conn.) March 2, 1852–Oct. 23, 1902; House 1887–Oct. 23, 1902.

Russell, Charles Hinton (R Nev.) Dec. 27, 1903–Sept. 13, 1989; House 1947–49; Gov. Jan. 1, 1951–Jan. 5, 1959.

Russell, Daniel Lindsay (G N.C.) Aug. 7, 1845–May 14, 1908; House 1879–81; Gov. Jan. 12, 1897–Jan. 15, 1901.

Russell, David Abel (W N.Y.) 1780–Nov. 24, 1861; House 1835–41.

Russell, Donald Stuart (D S.C.) Feb. 22, 1906–Feb. 22, 1998; Senate April 22, 1965–Nov. 8, 1966; Gov. Jan. 15, 1963–April 22, 1965.

Russell, Gordon James (D Texas) Dec. 22, 1859–Sept. 14, 1919; House Nov. 4, 1902–June 14, 1910.

Russell, James McPherson (father of Samuel Lyon Russell) (W Pa.) Nov. 10, 1786–Nov. 14, 1870; House Dec. 21, 1841–43.

Russell, Jeremiah (D N.Y.) Jan. 26, 1786–Sept. 30, 1867; House 1843–45.

Russell, John (R N.Y.) Sept. 7, 1772–Aug. 2, 1842; House 1805–09.

Russell, John Edwards (D Mass.) Jan. 20, 1834–Oct. 28, 1903; House 1887–89.

Russell, Jonathan (– Mass.) Feb. 27, 1771–Feb. 17, 1832; House 1821–23.

Russell, Joseph (D N.Y.) ?–?; House 1845–47, 1851–53.

Russell, Joseph James (D Mo.) Aug. 23, 1854–Oct. 22, 1922; House 1907–09, 1911–19.

Russell, Joshua Edward (R Ohio) Aug. 9, 1867–June 21, 1953; House 1915–17.

Russell, Leslie W. (– N.Y.) April 15, 1840–Feb. 3, 1903; House March 4–Sept. 11, 1891.

Russell, Richard Brevard Jr. (D Ga.) Nov. 2, 1897–Jan. 21, 1971; Senate Jan. 12, 1933–Jan. 21, 1971; elected Pres. pro tempore Jan. 3, 1969; Chrmn. Senate Armed Services 1951–53, 1955–69; Chrmn. Senate Appropriations 1969–71; Gov. June 27, 1931–Jan. 10, 1933.

Russell, Richard Manning (D Mass.) March 3, 1891–Feb. 27, 1977; House 1935–37.

Russell, Sam Morris (D Texas) Aug. 9, 1889–Oct. 19, 1971; House 1941–47.

Russell, Samuel Lyon (son of James McPherson Russell) (W Pa.) July 30, 1816–Sept. 27, 1891; House 1853–55.

Russell, William (W Ohio) 1782–Sept. 28, 1845; House 1827–33 (Jacksonian), 1841–43.

Russell, William Augustus (R Mass.) April 22, 1831–Jan. 10, 1899; House 1879–85.

Russell, William Fiero (D N.Y.) Jan. 14, 1812–April 29, 1896; House 1857–59.

Russo, Martin Anthony (D Ill.) Jan. 23, 1944– ; House 1975–93.

Rust, Albert (D Ark.) ?–April 3, 1870; House 1855–57, 1859–61.

Ruth, Earl Baker (R N.C.) Feb. 7, 1916–Aug. 15, 1989; House 1969–75.

Rutherford, Albert Greig (R Pa.) Jan. 3, 1879–Aug. 10, 1941; House 1937–Aug. 10, 1941.

Rutherford, J. T. (D Texas) May 30, 1921– ; House 1955–63.

Rutherford, Robert (R Va.) Oct. 20, 1728–Oct. 1803; House 1793–97 (1793–95 no party).

Rutherford, Samuel (D Ga.) March 15, 1870–Feb. 4, 1932; House 1925–Feb. 4, 1932.

Rutherfurd, John (– N.J.) Sept. 20, 1760–Feb. 23, 1840; Senate 1791–Dec. 5, 1798.

Rutledge, John Jr. (F S.C.) 1766–Sept. 1, 1819; House 1797–1803.

Ryall, Daniel Bailey (D N.J.) Jan. 30, 1798–Dec. 17, 1864; House 1839–41.

Ryan, Elmer James (D Minn.) May 26, 1907–Feb. 1, 1958; House 1935–41.

Ryan, Harold Martin (D Mich.) Feb. 6, 1911– ; House Feb. 13, 1962–65.

Ryan, James Wilfrid (D Pa.) Oct. 16, 1858–Feb. 26, 1907; House 1899–1901.

Ryan, Leo Joseph (D Calif.) May 5, 1925–Nov. 18, 1978; House 1973–Nov. 18, 1978.

Ryan, Paul (R Wis.) Jan. 29, 1970– ; House 1999– .

Ryan, Thomas (R Kan.) Nov. 25, 1837–April 5, 1914; House 1877–April 4, 1889.

Ryan, Thomas Jefferson (R N.Y.) June 17, 1890–Nov. 10, 1968; House 1921–23.

Ryan, William (D N.Y.) March 8, 1840–Feb. 18, 1925; House 1893–95.

Ryan, William Fitts (D N.Y.) June 28, 1922–Sept. 17, 1972; House 1961–Sept. 17, 1972.

Ryan, William Henry (D N.Y.) May 10, 1860–Nov. 18, 1939; House 1899–1909.

Ryon, John Walker (D Pa.) March 4, 1825–March 12, 1901; House 1879–81.

Ryter, John Francis (D Conn.) Feb. 4, 1914–Feb. 5, 1978; House 1945–47.

Ryun, Jim (R Kan.) April 29, 1947– ; House Nov. 27, 1996– .

S

Sabath, Adolph Joachim (D Ill.) April 4, 1866–Nov. 6, 1952; House 1907–Nov. 6, 1952; Chrmn. House Rules 1949–53.

Sabin, Alvah (W Vt.) Oct. 23, 1793–Jan. 22, 1885; House 1853–57.

Sabin, Dwight May (R Minn.) April 25, 1843–Dec. 22, 1902; Senate 1883–89; Chrmn. Rep. Nat. Comm. 1883–84.

Sabine, Lorenzo (W Mass.) Feb. 28, 1803–April 14, 1877; House Dec. 13, 1852–53.

Sabo, Martin Olav (D Minn.) Feb. 28, 1938– ; House 1979– ; Chrmn. House Budget 1993–95.

Sackett, Frederick Mosley (R Ky.) Dec. 17, 1868–May 18, 1941; Senate 1925–Jan. 9, 1930.

Sackett, William Augustus (W N.Y.) Nov. 18, 1811–Sept. 6, 1895; House 1849–53.

Sacks, Leon (D Pa.) Oct. 7, 1902–March 11, 1972; House 1937–43.

Sadlak, Antoni Nicholas (R Conn.) June 13, 1908–Oct. 18, 1969; House 1947–59.

Sadler, Thomas William (D Ala.) April 17, 1831–Oct. 29, 1896; House 1885–87.

Sadowski, George Gregory (D Mich.) March 12, 1903–Oct. 9, 1961; House 1933–39, 1943–51.

Sage, Ebenezer (R N.Y.) Aug. 16, 1755–Jan. 20, 1834; House 1809–15.

Sage, Russell (W N.Y.) Aug. 4, 1816–July 22, 1906; House 1853–57.

Saiki, Patricia Fukuda (R Hawaii) May 28, 1930– ; House 1987–91.

Sailly, Peter (R N.Y.) April 20, 1754–March 16, 1826; House 1805–07.

St. George, Katharine Price Collier (R N.Y.) July 12, 1896–May 2, 1983; House 1947–65.

St Germain, Fernand Joseph (D R.I.) Jan. 9, 1928– ; House 1961–89; Chrmn. House Banking, Finance, and Urban Affairs 1981–89.

St. John, Charles (R N.Y.) Oct. 8, 1818–July 6, 1891; House 1871–75.

St. John, Daniel Bennett (W N.Y.) Oct. 8, 1808–Feb. 18, 1890; House 1847–49.

St. John, Henry (D Ohio) July 16, 1783–May 1869; House 1843–47.

St. Martin, Louis (D La.) May 17, 1820–Feb. 9, 1893; House 1851–53, 1885–87.

St. Onge, William Leon (D Conn.) Oct. 9, 1914–May 1, 1970; House 1963–May 1, 1970.

Salinger, Pierre Emil George (D Calif.) June 14, 1925– ; Senate Aug. 4–Dec. 31, 1964.

Salmon, Joshua S. (D N.J.) Feb. 2, 1846–May 6, 1902; House 1899–May 6, 1902.

Salmon, Matt (R Ariz.) Jan. 21, 1958– ; House 1995– .

Salmon, William Charles (D Tenn.) April 3, 1868–May 13, 1925; House 1923–25.

Saltonstall, Leverett (great-grandfather of Leverett Saltonstall, below) (W Mass.) June 13, 1783–May 8, 1845; House Dec. 5, 1838–43.

Saltonstall, Leverett (great-grandson of Leverett Saltonstall, above) (R Mass.) Sept. 1, 1892–June 17, 1979; Senate Jan. 4, 1945–67; Chrmn. Senate Armed Services 1953–55; Gov. Jan. 5, 1939–Jan. 3, 1945.

Samford, William James (D Ala.) Sept. 16, 1844–June 11, 1901; House 1879–81; Gov. Dec. 26, 1900–June 11, 1901.

Sammons, Thomas (grandfather of John Henry Starin) (R N.Y.) Oct. 1, 1762–Nov. 20, 1838; House 1803–07, 1809–13.

Sample, Samuel Caldwell (W Ind.) Aug. 15, 1796–Dec. 2, 1855; House 1843–45.

Sampson, Ezekiel Silas (R Iowa) Dec. 6, 1831–Oct. 7, 1892; House 1875–79.

Sampson, Zabdiel (R Mass.) Aug. 22, 1781–July 19, 1828; House 1817–July 26, 1820.

Samuel, Edmund William (R Pa.) Nov. 27, 1857–March 7, 1930; House 1905–07.

Samuels, Green Berry (cousin of Isaac Samuels Pennybacker) (D Va.) Feb. 1, 1806–Jan. 5, 1859; House 1839–41.

Sanborn, John Carfield (R Idaho) Sept. 28, 1885–May 16, 1968; House 1947–51.

Sanchez, Loretta (D Calif.) Jan. 7, 1960– ; House 1997– .

Sandager, Harry (R R.I.) April 12, 1887–Dec. 24, 1955; House 1939–41.

Sanders, Archie Dovell (R N.Y.) June 17, 1857–July 15, 1941; House 1917–33.

Sanders, Bernard (I Vt.) Sept. 8, 1941– ; House 1991– .

Sanders, Everett (R Ind.) March 8, 1882–May 12, 1950; House 1917–25; Chrmn. Rep. Nat. Comm. 1932–34.

Sanders, Jared Young (father of Jared Young Sanders Jr., cousin of Murphy James Foster) (D La.) Jan. 29, 1867–March 23, 1944; House 1917–21; Gov. May 18, 1908–May 14, 1912.

Sanders, Jared Young Jr. (son of Jared Young Sanders) (D La.) April 20, 1892–Nov. 29, 1960; House May 1, 1934–37, 1941–43.

Sanders, Morgan Gurley (D Texas) July 14, 1878–Jan. 7, 1956; House 1921–39.

Sanders, Newell (R Tenn.) July 12, 1850–Jan. 26, 1939; Senate April 11, 1912–Jan. 24, 1913.

Sanders, Wilbur Fiske (R Mont.) May 2, 1834–July 7, 1905; Senate Jan. 1, 1890–93.

Sandford, James T. (– Tenn.) ?–?; House 1823–25.

Sandford, Thomas (R Ky.) 1762–Dec. 10, 1808; House 1803–07.

Sandidge, John Milton (D La.) Jan. 7, 1817–March 30, 1890; House 1855–59.

Sandlin, John Nicholas (D La.) Feb. 24, 1872–Dec. 25, 1957; House 1921–37.

Sandlin, Max (D Texas) Sept. 29, 1952– ; House 1997– .

Sandman, Charles William Jr. (R N.J.) Oct. 23, 1921–Aug. 26, 1985; House 1967–75.

Sands, Joshua (F N.Y.) Oct. 12, 1757–Sept. 13, 1835; House 1803–05, 1825–27.

Sanford, John (father of Stephen Sanford, grandfather of John Sanford, below) (D N.Y.) June 3, 1803–Oct. 4, 1857; House 1841–43.

Sanford, John (son of Stephen Sanford, grandson of John Sanford, above) (R N.Y.) Jan. 18, 1851–Sept. 26, 1939; House 1889–93.

Sanford, John W. A. (D Ga.) Aug. 28, 1798–Sept. 12, 1870; House March 4–July 25, 1835.

Sanford, Jonah (great-grandfather of Rollin Brewster Sanford) (J N.Y.) Nov. 30, 1790–Dec. 25, 1867; House Nov. 3, 1830–31.

Sanford, Mark (R S.C.) May 28, 1960– ; House 1995– .

Sanford, Nathan (D N.Y.) Nov. 5, 1777–Oct. 17, 1838; Senate 1815–21, Jan. 14, 1826–31.

Sanford, Rollin Brewster (great-grandson of Jonah Sanford) (R N.Y.) May 18, 1874–May 16, 1957; House 1915–21.

Sanford, Stephen (son of John Sanford born in 1803, father of John Sanford born in 1851) (R N.Y.) May 26, 1826–Feb. 13, 1913; House 1869–71.

Sanford, Terry (D N.C.) Aug. 20, 1917–April 18, 1998; Senate Nov. 4, 1986–93; Gov. Jan. 5, 1961–Jan. 8, 1965; Chrmn. Senate Select Committee on Ethics 1991–93.

Sangmeister, George E. (D Ill.) Feb. 16, 1931– ; House 1989–95.

Santangelo, Alfred Edward (D N.Y.) June 4, 1912–March 30, 1978; House 1957–63.

Santini, James David (D Nev.) Aug. 13, 1937– ; House 1975–83.

Santorum, Rick (R Pa.) May 10, 1958– ; House 1991–95; Senate 1995– .

Sapp, William Fletcher (nephew of William Robinson Sapp) (R Iowa) Nov. 20, 1824–Nov. 22, 1890; House 1877–81.

Sapp, William Robinson (uncle of William Fletcher Sapp) (R Ohio) March 4, 1804–Jan. 3, 1875; House 1853–57 (1853–55 Whig).

Sarasin, Ronald Arthur (R Conn.) Dec. 31, 1934– ; House 1973–79.

Sarbacher, George William Jr. (R Pa.) Sept. 30, 1919–March 4, 1973; House 1947–49.

Sarbanes, Paul Spyros (D Md.) Feb. 3, 1933– ; House 1971–77; Senate 1977– .

Sargent, Aaron Augustus (R Calif.) Sept. 28, 1827–Aug. 14, 1887; House 1861–63, 1869–73; Senate 1873–79.

Sarpalius, William "Bill" (D Texas) Jan. 10, 1948– ; House 1989–95.

Sasscer, Lansdale Ghiselin (D Md.) Sept. 30, 1893–Nov. 5, 1964; House Feb. 3, 1939–53.

Sasser, James Ralph (D Tenn.) Sept. 30, 1936– ; Senate 1977–95; Chrmn. Senate Budget 1989–95.

Satterfield, Dave Edward Jr. (father of David Edward Satterfield III) (D Va.) Sept. 11, 1894–Dec. 27, 1946; House Nov. 2, 1937–Feb. 15, 1945.

Satterfield, David Edward III (son of Dave Edward Satterfield Jr.) (D Va.) Dec. 2, 1920–Sept. 30, 1988; House 1965–81.

Sauerhering, Edward (R Wis.) June 24, 1864–March 1, 1924; House 1895–99.

Saulsbury, Eli (brother of Willard Saulsbury, uncle of Willard Saulsbury Jr.) (D Del.) Dec. 29, 1817–March 22, 1893; Senate 1871–89.

Saulsbury, Willard Sr. (brother of Eli Saulsbury, father of Willard Saulsbury Jr., below) (D Del.) June 2, 1820–April 6, 1892; Senate 1859–71.

Saulsbury, Willard Jr. (son of Willard Saulsbury Sr., above, nephew of Eli Saulsbury) (D Del.) April 17, 1861–Feb. 20, 1927; Senate 1913–19; elected Pres. pro tempore Dec. 14, 1916.

Saund, Daliph Singh (D Calif.) Sept. 20, 1899–April 22, 1973; House 1957–63.

Saunders, Alvin (grandfather of William Henry Harrison of Wyoming) (R Neb.) July 12, 1817–Nov. 1, 1899; Senate March 5, 1877–83; Gov. (Neb. Terr.) 1861–67.

Saunders, Edward Watts (D Va.) Oct. 20, 1860–Dec. 16, 1921; House Nov. 6, 1906–Feb. 29, 1920.

Saunders, Romulus Mitchell (D N.C.) March 3, 1791–April 21, 1867; House 1821–27 (Republican), 1841–45.

Sauthoff, Harry (Prog. Wis.) June 3, 1879–June 16, 1966; House 1935–39, 1941–45.

Savage, Charles Raymon (D Wash.) April 12, 1906–Jan. 14, 1976; House 1945–47.

Savage, Gus (D Ill.) Oct. 30, 1925– ; House 1981–93.

Savage, John (R N.Y.) Feb. 22, 1779–Oct. 19, 1863; House 1815–19.

Savage, John Houston (D Tenn.) Oct. 9, 1815–April 5, 1904; House 1849–53, 1855–59.

Savage, John Simpson (D Ohio) Oct. 30, 1841–Nov. 24, 1884; House 1875–77.

Sawtelle, Cullen (D Maine) Sept. 25, 1805–Nov. 10, 1887; House 1845–47, 1849–51.

Sawyer, Frederick Adolphus (R S.C.) Dec. 12, 1822–July 31, 1891; Senate July 16, 1868–73.

Sawyer, Harold Samuel (R Mich.) March 21, 1920– ; House 1977–85.

Sawyer, John Gilbert (R N.Y.) June 5, 1825–Sept. 5, 1898; House 1885–91.

Sawyer, Lemuel (R N.C.) 1777–Jan. 9, 1852; House 1807–13, 1817–23, 1825–29.

Sawyer, Lewis Ernest (D Ark.) June 24, 1867–May 5, 1923; House March 4–May 5, 1923.

Sawyer, Philetus (R Wis.) Sept. 22, 1816–March 29, 1900; House 1865–75; Senate 1881–93.

Sawyer, Samuel Locke (ID Mo.) Nov. 27, 1813–March 29, 1890; House 1879–81.

Sawyer, Samuel Tredwell (W N.C.) 1800–Nov. 29, 1865; House 1837–39.

Sawyer, Thomas Charles (D Ohio) Aug. 15, 1945– ; House 1987– .

Sawyer, William (D Ohio) Aug. 5, 1803–Sept. 18, 1877; House 1845–49.

Saxbe, William Bart (R Ohio) June 24, 1916– ; Senate 1969–Jan. 3, 1974; Atty. Gen. Jan. 4, 1974–Feb. 3, 1975.

Saxton, Hugh James (R N.J.) Jan. 22, 1943– ; House 1985– (elected Nov. 6, 1984, to fill a vacancy in the 98th Congress and to the 99th Congress but was not sworn in until Jan. 3, 1985).

Say, Benjamin (R Pa.) Aug. 28, 1755–April 23, 1813; House Nov. 16, 1808–June 1809.

Sayers, Joseph Draper (D Texas) Sept. 23, 1841–May 15, 1929; House 1885–Jan. 16, 1899; Gov. Jan. 17, 1899–Jan. 20, 1903.

Sayler, Henry Benton (cousin of Milton Sayler) (R Ind.) March 31, 1836–June 18, 1900; House 1873–75.

Sayler, Milton (cousin of Henry Benton Sayler) (D Ohio) Nov. 4, 1831–Nov. 17, 1892; House 1873–79.

Saylor, John Phillips (R Pa.) July 23, 1908–Oct. 28, 1973; House Sept. 13, 1949–Oct. 28, 1973.

Scales, Alfred Moore (D N.C.) Nov. 26, 1827–Feb. 9, 1892; House 1857–59, 1875–Dec. 30, 1884; Gov. Jan. 21, 1885–Jan. 17, 1889.

Scamman, John Fairfield (D Maine) Oct. 24, 1786–May 22, 1858; House 1845–47.

Scanlon, Thomas Edward (D Pa.) Sept. 18, 1896–Aug. 9, 1955; House 1941–45.

Scarborough, Charles Joseph (R Fla.) April 9, 1963– ; House 1995– .

Scarborough, Robert Bethea (D S.C.) Oct. 29, 1861–Nov. 23, 1927; House 1901–05.

Schadeberg, Henry Carl (R Wis.) Oct. 12, 1913–Dec. 11, 1985; House 1961–65, 1967–71.

Schaefer, Daniel (R Colo.) Jan. 25, 1936– ; House March 29, 1983–99.

Schaefer, Edwin Martin (D Ill.) May 14, 1887–Nov. 8, 1950; House 1933–43.

Schafer, John Charles (R Wis.) May 7, 1893–June 9, 1962; House 1923–33, 1939–41.

Schaffer, Robert W. (R Colo.) July 24, 1962– ; House 1997– .

Schakowsky, Jan (D Ill.) May 26, 1944– ; House 1999– .

Schall, Thomas David (R Minn.) June 4, 1878–Dec. 22, 1935; House 1915–25; Senate 1925–Dec. 22, 1935.

Schell, Richard (D N.Y.) May 15, 1810–Nov. 10, 1879; House Dec. 7, 1874–75.

Schenck, Abraham Henry (uncle of Isaac Teller) (R N.Y.) Jan. 22, 1775–June 1, 1831; House 1815–17.

Schenck, Ferdinand Schureman (J N.J.) Feb. 11, 1790–May 16, 1860; House 1833–37.

Schenck, Paul Fornshell (R Ohio) April 19, 1899–Nov. 30, 1968; House Nov. 6, 1951–65.

Schenck, Robert Cumming (R Ohio) Oct. 4, 1809–March 23, 1890; House 1843–51 (Whig), 1863–Jan. 5, 1871.

Schenk, Lynn (D Calif.) Jan. 5, 1945– ; House 1993–95.

Scherer, Gordon Harry (R Ohio) Dec. 26, 1906–Aug. 13, 1988; House 1953–63.

Scherle, William Joseph (R Iowa) March 14, 1923– ; House 1967–75.

Schermerhorn, Abraham Maus (W N.Y.) Dec. 11, 1791–Aug. 22, 1855; House 1849–53.

Schermerhorn, Simon Jacob (D N.Y.) Sept. 25, 1827–July 21, 1901; House 1893–95.

Scheuer, James Haas (D/L N.Y.) Feb. 6, 1920– ; House 1965–73, 1975–93.

Schiff, Steven Harvey (R N.M.) March 18, 1947–March 25, 1998; House 1989–March 25, 1998.

Schiffler, Andrew Charles (R W.Va.) Aug. 10, 1889–March 27, 1970; House 1939–41, 1943–45.

Schirm, Charles Reginald (R Md.) Aug. 12, 1864–Nov. 2, 1918; House 1901–03.

Schisler, Darwin Gale (D Ill.) March 2, 1933– ; House 1965–67.

Schleicher, Gustave (D Texas) Nov. 19, 1823–Jan. 10, 1879; House 1875–Jan. 10, 1879.

Schley, William (J Ga.) Dec. 15, 1786–Nov. 20, 1858; House 1833–July 1, 1835; Gov. Nov. 4, 1835–Nov. 8, 1837 (Unionist).

Schmidhauser, John Richard (D Iowa) Jan. 3, 1922– ; House 1965–67.

Schmitt, Harrison Hagan (R N.M.) July 3, 1935– ; Senate 1977–83.

Schmitz, John George (R Calif.) Aug. 12, 1930– ; House June 30, 1970–73.

Schneebeli, Gustav Adolphus (R Pa.) May 23, 1853–Feb. 6, 1923; House 1905–07.

Schneebeli, Herman Theodore (R Pa.) July 7, 1907–May 6, 1982; House April 26, 1960–77.

Schneider, Claudine (R R.I.) March 25, 1947– ; House 1981–91.

Schneider, George John (Prog. Wis.) Oct. 30, 1877–March 12, 1939; House 1923–33 (Republican), 1935–39.

Schoeppel, Andrew Frank (R Kan.) Nov. 23, 1894–Jan. 21, 1962; Senate 1949–Jan. 21, 1962; Gov. Jan. 11, 1943–Jan. 13, 1947.

Schoolcraft, John Lawrence (W N.Y.) 1804–July 7, 1860; House 1849–53.

Schoonmaker, Cornelius Corneliusen (grandfather of Marius Schoonmaker) (– N.Y.) June 1745–96; House 1791–93.

Schoonmaker, Marius (grandson of Cornelius Corneliusen Schoonmaker) (W N.Y.) April 24, 1811–Jan. 5, 1894; House 1851–53.

Schroeder, Patricia Scott (D Colo.) July 30, 1940– ; House 1973–77.

Schuette, William Duncan (R Mich.) Oct. 13, 1953– ; House 1985–91.

Schuetz, Leonard William (D Ill.) Nov. 16, 1887–Feb. 13, 1944; House 1931–Feb. 13, 1944.

Schulte, William Theodore (D Ind.) Aug. 19, 1890–Dec. 7, 1966; House 1933–43.

Schulze, Richard Taylor (R Pa.) Aug. 7, 1929– ; House 1975–93.

Schumaker, John Godfrey (D N.Y.) June 27, 1826–Nov. 23, 1905; House 1869–71, 1873–77.

Schumer, Charles Ellis (D N.Y.) Nov. 23, 1950– ; House 1981–99; Senate 1999– .

Schuneman, Martin Gerretsen (R N.Y.) Feb. 10, 1764–Feb. 21, 1827; House 1805–07.

Schureman, James (F N.J.) Feb. 12, 1756–Jan. 22, 1824; House 1789–91 (no party), 1797–99 (no party), 1813–15; Senate 1799–Feb. 16, 1801; Cont. Cong. 1786–87.

Schurz, Carl (R Mo.) March 2, 1829–May 14, 1906; Senate 1869–75; Secy. of the Interior March 12, 1877–March 7, 1881.

Schuyler, Karl Cortlandt (R Colo.) April 3, 1877–July 31, 1933; Senate Dec. 7, 1932–33.

Schuyler, Philip Jeremiah (son of Philip John Schuyler) (F N.Y.) Jan. 21, 1768–Feb. 21, 1835; House 1817–19.

Schuyler, Philip John (father of Philip Jeremiah Schuyler) (– N.Y.) Nov. 20, 1733–Nov. 18, 1804; Senate 1789–91, 1797–Jan. 3, 1798; Cont. Cong. 1775, 1777, 1779–80.

Schwabe, George Blaine (brother of Max Schwabe) (R Okla.) July 26, 1886–April 2, 1952; House 1945–49, 1951–April 2, 1952.

Schwabe, Max (brother of George Blaine Schwabe) (R Mo.) Dec. 6, 1905– ; House 1943–49.

Schwartz, Henry Herman "Harry" (D Wyo.) May 18, 1869–April 24, 1955; Senate 1937–43.

Schwartz, John (ALD Pa.) Oct. 27, 1793–June 20, 1860; House 1859–June 20, 1860.

Schweiker, Richard Schultz (R Pa.) June 1, 1926– ; House 1961–69; Senate 1969–81; Secy. of Health and Human Services Jan. 22, 1981–Feb. 3, 1983.

Schwellenbach, Lewis Baxter (D Wash.) Sept. 20, 1894–June 10, 1948; Senate 1935–Dec. 16, 1940; Secy. of Labor July 1, 1945–June 10, 1948.

Schwengel, Frederick Delbert (R Iowa) May 28, 1906–April 1, 1993; House 1955–65, 1967–73.

Schwert, Pius Louis (D N.Y.) Nov. 22, 1892–March 11, 1941; House 1939–March 11, 1941.

Scoblick, James Paul (R Pa.) May 10, 1909–Dec. 4, 1981; House Nov. 5, 1946–49.

Scofield, Glenni William (R Pa.) March 11, 1817–Aug. 30, 1891; House 1863–75.

Scott, Byron Nicholson (D Calif.) March 21, 1903– ; House 1935–39.

Scott, Charles Frederick (R Kan.) Sept. 7, 1860–Sept. 18, 1938; House 1901–11.

Scott, Charles Lewis (D Calif.) Jan. 23, 1827–April 30, 1899; House 1857–61.

Scott, David (– Pa.) ?–?; elected to the House for term beginning 1817 but resigned before Congress assembled.

Scott, Frank Douglas (R Mich.) Aug. 25, 1878–Feb. 12, 1951; House 1915–27.

Scott, George Cromwell (R Iowa) Aug. 8, 1864–Oct. 6, 1948; House Nov. 5, 1912–15, 1917–19.

Scott, Hardie (son of John Roger Kirkpatrick Scott) (R Pa.) June 7, 1907– ; House 1947–53.

Scott, Harvey David (R Ind.) Oct. 18, 1818–July 11, 1891; House 1855–57.

Scott, Hugh Doggett Jr. (R Pa.) Nov. 11, 1900–July 21, 1994; House 1941–45, 1947–59; Senate 1959–77; Senate minority leader Sept. 24, 1969–77; Chrmn. Rep. Nat. Comm. 1948–49.

Scott, John (– Mo.) May 18, 1785–Oct. 1, 1861; House (Terr. Del.) Aug. 6, 1816–Jan. 13, 1817, Aug. 4, 1817–March 3, 1821, (Rep.) Aug. 10, 1821–27.

Scott, John (father of John Scott, below) (J Pa.) Dec. 25, 1784–Sept. 22, 1850; House 1829–31.

Scott, John (son of John Scott, above) (R Pa.) July 24, 1824–Nov. 29, 1896; Senate 1869–75.

Scott, John Guier (D Mo.) Dec. 26, 1819–May 16, 1892; House Dec. 7, 1863–65.

Scott, John Roger Kirkpatrick (father of Hardie Scott) (R Pa.) July 6, 1873–Dec. 9, 1945; House 1915–Jan. 5, 1919.

Scott, Lon Allen (R Tenn.) Sept. 25, 1888–Feb. 11, 1931; House 1921–23.

Scott, Nathan Bay (R W.Va.) Dec. 18, 1842–Jan. 2, 1924; Senate 1899–1911.

Scott, Owen (D Ill.) July 6, 1848–Dec. 21, 1928; House 1891–93.

Scott, Ralph James (D N.C.) Oct. 15, 1905–Aug. 5, 1983; House 1957–67.

Scott, Robert C. (D Va.) April 30, 1947– ; House 1993– .

Scott, Thomas (– Pa.) 1739–March 2, 1796; House 1789–91, 1793–95.

Scott, William Kerr (D N.C.) April 17, 1896–April 16, 1958; Senate Nov. 29, 1954–April 16, 1958; Gov. Jan. 6, 1949–Jan. 8, 1953.

Scott, William Lawrence (D Pa.) July 2, 1828–Sept. 19, 1891; House 1885–89.

Scott, William Lloyd (R Va.) July 1, 1915–Feb. 14, 1997; House 1967–73; Senate 1973–Jan. 1, 1979.

Scoville, Jonathan (D N.Y.) July 14, 1830–March 4, 1891; House Nov. 12, 1880–83.

Scranton, George Whitfield (second cousin of Joseph Augustine Scranton) (R Pa.) May 11, 1811–March 24, 1861; House 1859–March 24, 1861.

Scranton, Joseph Augustine (great-grandfather of William Warren Scranton, second cousin of George Whitfield Scranton) (R Pa.) July 26, 1838–Oct. 12, 1908; House 1881–83, 1885–87, 1889–91, 1893–97.

Scranton, William Warren (great-grandson of Joseph Augustine Scranton) (R Pa.) July 19, 1917– ; House 1961–63; Gov. Jan. 15, 1963–Jan. 17, 1967.

Scrivner, Errett Power (R Kan.) March 20, 1898–May 5, 1978; House Sept. 14, 1943–59.

Scroggy, Thomas Edmund (R Ohio) March 18, 1843–March 6, 1915; House 1905–07.

Scrugham, James Graves (D Nev.) Jan. 19, 1880–June 23, 1945; House 1933–Dec. 7, 1942; Senate Dec. 7, 1942–June 23, 1945; Gov. Jan. 1, 1923–Jan. 3, 1927.

Scudder, Henry Joel (uncle of Townsend Scudder) (R N.Y.) Sept. 18, 1825–Feb. 10, 1886; House 1873–75.

Scudder, Hubert Baxter (R Calif.) Nov. 5, 1888–July 4, 1968; House 1949–59.

Scudder, Isaac Williamson (R N.J.) 1816–Sept. 10, 1881; House 1873–75.

Scudder, John Anderson (R N.J.) March 22, 1759–Nov. 6, 1836; House Oct. 31, 1810–11.

Scudder, Townsend (nephew of Henry Joel Scudder) (D N.Y.) July 26, 1865–Feb. 22, 1960; House 1899–1901, 1903–05.

Scudder, Tredwell (– N.Y.) Jan. 1, 1778–Oct. 31, 1834; House 1817–19.

Scudder, Zeno (W Mass.) Aug. 18, 1807–June 26, 1857; House 1851–March 4, 1854.

Scull, Edward (R Pa.) Feb. 5, 1818–July 10, 1900; House 1887–93.

Scully, Thomas Joseph (D N.J.) Sept. 19, 1868–Dec. 14, 1921; House 1911–21.

Scurry, Richardson (D Texas) Nov. 11, 1811–April 9, 1862; House 1851–53.

Seaman, Henry John (AP N.Y.) April 16, 1805–May 3, 1861; House 1845–47.

Searing, John Alexander (D N.Y.) May 14, 1805–May 6, 1876; House 1857–59.

Sears, William Joseph (D Fla.) Dec. 4, 1874–March 30, 1944; House 1915–29, 1933–37.

Sears, Willis Gratz (R Neb.) Aug. 16, 1860–June 1, 1949; House 1923–31.

Seastrand, Andrea (R Calif.) Aug. 5, 1941– ; House 1995–97.

Seaton, Frederick Andrew (R Neb.) Dec. 11, 1909–Jan. 16, 1974; Senate Dec. 10, 1951–Nov. 4, 1952; Secy. of the Interior June 8, 1956–Jan. 20, 1961.

Seaver, Ebenezer (R Mass.) July 5, 1763–March 1, 1844; House 1803–13.

Sebastian, William King (D Ark.) 1812–May 20, 1865; Senate May 12, 1848–July 11, 1861.

Sebelius, Keith George (R Kan.) Sept. 10, 1916–Aug. 5, 1982; House 1969–81.

Seccombe, James (R Ohio) Feb. 12, 1893–Aug. 23, 1970; House 1939–41.

Secrest, Robert Thompson (D Ohio) Jan. 22, 1904–May 15, 1994; House 1933–Aug. 3, 1942, 1949–Sept. 26, 1954, 1963–67.

Seddon, James Alexander (D Va.) July 13, 1815–Aug. 19, 1880; House 1845–47, 1849–51.

Sedgwick, Charles Baldwin (R N.Y.) March 15, 1815–Feb. 3, 1883; House 1859–63.

Sedgwick, Theodore (F Mass.) May 9, 1746–Jan. 24, 1813; House 1789–June 1796 (no party), 1799–1801; Speaker Dec. 2, 1799–1801; Senate June 11, 1796–99; elected Pres. pro tempore June 27, 1798; Cont. Cong. 1785–86, 1788.

Seeley, John Edward (R N.Y.) Aug. 1, 1810–March 30, 1875; House 1871–73.

Seely-Brown, Horace Jr. (R Conn.) May 12, 1908–April 9, 1982; House 1947–49, 1951–59, 1961–63.

Seelye, Julius Hawley (I Mass.) Sept. 14, 1824–May 12, 1895; House 1875–77.

Seerley, John Joseph (D Iowa) March 13, 1852–Feb. 23, 1931; House 1891–93.

Segar, Joseph Eggleston (U Va.) June 1, 1804–April 30, 1880; House March 15, 1862–63.

Seger, George Nicholas (R N.J.) Jan. 4, 1866–Aug. 26, 1940; House 1923–Aug. 26, 1940.

Seiberling, Francis (cousin of John Frederick Seiberling) (R Ohio) Sept. 20, 1870–Feb. 1, 1945; House 1929–33.

Seiberling, John Frederick (cousin of Francis Seiberling) (D Ohio) Sept. 8, 1918–   ; House 1971–87.

Selby, Thomas Jefferson (D Ill.) Dec. 4, 1840–March 10, 1917; House 1901–03.

Selden, Armistead Inge Jr. (D Ala.) Feb. 20, 1921–Nov. 14, 1985; House 1953–69.

Selden, Dudley (J N.Y.) ?–Nov. 7, 1855; House 1833–July 1, 1834.

Seldomridge, Harry Hunter (D Colo.) Oct. 1, 1864–Nov. 2, 1927; House 1913–15.

Sells, Sam Riley (R Tenn.) Aug. 2, 1871–Nov. 2, 1935; House 1911–21.

Selvig, Conrad George (R Minn.) Oct. 11, 1877–Aug. 2, 1953; House 1927–33.

Selye, Lewis (IR N.Y.) July 11, 1803–Jan. 27, 1883; House 1867–69.

Semmes, Benedict Joseph (– Md.) Nov. 1, 1789–Feb. 10, 1863; House 1829–33.

Semple, James (D Ill.) Jan. 5, 1798–Dec. 20, 1866; Senate Dec. 4, 1843–47.

Sener, James Beverley (R Va.) May 18, 1837–Nov. 18, 1903; House 1873–75.

Seney, George Ebbert (D Ohio) May 29, 1832–June 11, 1905; House 1883–91.

Seney, Joshua (– Md.) March 4, 1756–Oct. 20, 1798; House 1789–May 1, 1792; Cont. Cong. 1788.

Senner, George Frederick Jr. (D Ariz.) Nov. 24, 1921–   ; House 1963–67.

Sensenbrenner, Frank James Jr. (R Wis.) June 14, 1943–   ; House 1979–   ; Chrmn. House Science 1997–   .

Senter, William Tandy (W Tenn.) May 12, 1801–Aug. 28, 1848; House 1843–45.

Sergeant, John (grandfather of John Sergeant Wise and Richard Alsop Wise, great-grandfather of John Crain Kunkel, father-in-law of Henry Alexander Wise) (W Pa.) Dec. 5, 1779–Nov. 23, 1852; House Oct. 10, 1815–23 (Federalist), 1827–29 (Federalist), 1837–Sept. 15, 1841.

Serrano, José E. (D N.Y.) Oct. 24, 1943–   ; House March 28, 1990–   .

Sessinghaus, Gustavus (R Mo.) Nov. 8, 1838–Nov. 16, 1887; House March 2–3, 1883.

Sessions, Jeff (R Ala.) Dec. 24, 1946–   ; Senate 1997–   .

Sessions, Pete (R-Texas) March 22, 1955–   ; House 1997–   .

Sessions, Walter Loomis (R N.Y.) Oct. 4, 1820–May 27, 1896; House 1871–75, 1885–87.

Settle, Evan Evans (D Ky.) Dec. 1, 1848–Nov. 16, 1899; House 1897–Nov. 16, 1899.

Settle, Thomas (uncle of David Settle Reid, grandfather of Thomas Settle, below) (R N.C.) March 9, 1789–Aug. 5, 1857; House 1817–21.

Settle, Thomas (grandson of Thomas Settle, above) (R N.C.) March 10, 1865–Jan. 20, 1919; House 1893–97.

Severance, Luther (W Maine) Oct. 26, 1797–Jan. 25, 1855; House 1843–47.

Sevier, Ambrose Hundley (cousin of Henry Wharton Conway) (D Ark.) Nov. 4, 1801–Dec. 31, 1848; House (Terr. Del.) Feb. 13, 1828–June 15, 1836; Senate Sept. 18, 1836–March 15, 1848; elected Pres. pro tempore Dec. 27, 1845.

Sevier, John (R Tenn.) Sept. 23, 1745–Sept. 24, 1815; House June 16, 1790–91 (no party N.C.), 1811–Sept. 24, 1815; Gov. March 30, 1796–Sept. 23, 1801 (Democratic Republican), Sept. 23, 1803–Sept. 19, 1809 (Democratic Republican).

Sewall, Charles S. (D Md.) 1779–Nov. 3, 1848; House Oct. 1, 1832–33 (Jacksonian), Jan. 2–March 3, 1843.

Sewall, Samuel (F Mass.) Dec. 11, 1757–June 8, 1814; House Dec. 7, 1796–Jan. 10, 1800.

Seward, James Lindsay (D Ga.) Oct. 30, 1813–Nov. 21, 1886; House 1853–59.

Seward, William Henry (R N.Y.) May 16, 1801–Oct. 10, 1872; Senate 1849–61 (1849–55 Whig); Secy. of State March 6, 1861–March 4, 1869; Gov. Jan. 1, 1839–Jan. 1, 1843 (Whig).

Sewell, William Joyce (R N.J.) Dec. 6, 1835–Dec. 27, 1901; Senate 1881–87, 1895–Dec. 27, 1901.

Sexton, Leonidas (R Ind.) May 19, 1827–July 4, 1880; House 1877–79.

Seybert, Adam (R Pa.) May 16, 1773–May 2, 1825; House Oct. 10, 1809–15, 1817–19.

Seymour, David Lowrey (D N.Y.) Dec. 2, 1803–Oct. 11, 1867; House 1843–45, 1851–53.

Seymour, Edward Woodruff (son of Origen Storrs Seymour) (D Conn.) Aug. 30, 1832–Oct. 16, 1892; House 1883–87.

Seymour, Henry William (R Mich.) July 21, 1834–April 7, 1906; House Feb. 14, 1888–89.

Seymour, Horatio (uncle of Origen Storrs Seymour) (– Vt.) May 31, 1778–Nov. 21, 1857; Senate 1821–33.

Seymour, John (R Calif.) Dec. 3, 1937–; Senate Jan. 10, 1991–Nov. 3, 1992.

Seymour, Origen Storrs (father of Edward Woodruff Seymour, nephew of Horatio Seymour) (D Conn.) Feb. 9, 1804–Aug. 12, 1881; House 1851–55.

Seymour, Thomas Hart (D Conn.) Sept. 29, 1807–Sept. 3, 1868; House 1843–45; Gov. May 4, 1850–Oct. 13, 1853.

Seymour, William (J N.Y.) about 1780–Dec. 28, 1848; House 1835–37.

Shackelford, John Williams (D N.C.) Nov. 16, 1844–Jan. 18, 1883; House 1881–Jan. 18, 1883.

Shackleford, Dorsey William (D Mo.) Aug. 27, 1853–July 15, 1936; House Aug. 29, 1899–1919.

Shadegg, John (R Ariz.) Oct. 22, 1949–   ; House 1995–   .

Shafer, Jacob K. (D Idaho) Dec. 26, 1823–Nov. 22, 1876; House (Terr. Del.) 1869–71.

Shafer, Paul Werntz (R Mich.) April 27, 1893–Aug. 17, 1954; House 1937–Aug. 17, 1954.

Shaffer, Joseph Crockett (R Va.) Jan. 19, 1880–Oct. 19, 1958; House 1929–31.

Shafroth, John Franklin (D Colo.) June 9, 1854–Feb. 20, 1922; House 1895–Feb. 15, 1904 (1895–97 Republican, 1897–1903 Silver Republican); Senate 1913–19; Gov. Jan. 12, 1909–Jan. 14, 1913.

Shallenberger, Ashton Cokayne (D Neb.) Dec. 23, 1862–Feb. 22, 1938; House 1901–03, 1915–19, 1923–29, 1931–35; Gov. Jan. 7, 1909–Jan. 5, 1911.

Shallenberger, William Shadrack (R Pa.) Nov. 24, 1839–April 15, 1914; House 1877–83.

Shamansky, Robert Norton (D Ohio) April 18, 1927–   ; House 1981–83.

Shanklin, George Sea (D Ky.) Dec. 23, 1807–April 1, 1883; House 1865–67.

Shanks, John Peter Cleaver (R Ind.) June 17, 1826–Jan. 23, 1901; House 1861–63, 1867–75.

Shanley, James Andrew (D Conn.) April 1, 1896–April 4, 1965; House 1935–43.

Shannon, James Michael (D Mass.) April 4, 1952– ; House 1979–85.

Shannon, Joseph Bernard (D Mo.) March 17, 1867–March 28, 1943; House 1931–43.

Shannon, Richard Cutts (R N.Y.) Feb. 12, 1839–Oct. 5, 1920; House 1895–99.

Shannon, Thomas (brother of Wilson Shannon) (– Ohio) Nov. 15, 1786–March 16, 1843; House Dec. 4, 1826–27.

Shannon, Thomas Bowles (R Calif.) Sept. 21, 1827–Feb. 21, 1897; House 1863–65.

Shannon, Wilson (brother of Thomas Shannon) (D Ohio) Feb. 24, 1802–Aug. 30, 1877; House 1853–55; Gov. Dec. 13, 1838–Dec. 16, 1840, Dec. 14, 1842–April 15, 1844, Aug. 10, 1855–Aug. 18, 1856 (Kansas Terr.).

Sharon, William (R Neb.) Jan. 9, 1821–Nov. 13, 1885; Senate 1875–81.

Sharp, Edgar Allan (R N.Y.) June 3, 1876–Nov. 27, 1948; House 1945–47.

Sharp, Philip Riley (D Ind.) July 15, 1942– ; House 1975–95.

Sharp, Solomon P. (R Ky.) 1780–Nov. 7, 1825; House 1813–17.

Sharp, William Graves (D Ohio) March 14, 1859–Nov. 17, 1922; House 1909–July 23, 1914.

Sharpe, Peter (– N.Y.) ?–?; House 1823–25.

Shartel, Cassius McLean (R Mo.) April 27, 1860–Sept. 27, 1943; House 1905–07.

Shattuc, William Bunn (R Ohio) June 11, 1841–July 13, 1911; House 1897–1903.

Shaw, Aaron (D Ill.) Dec. 19, 1811–Jan. 7, 1887; House 1857–59, 1883–85.

Shaw, Albert Duane (R N.Y.) Dec. 21, 1841–Feb. 10, 1901; House Nov. 6, 1900–Feb. 10, 1901.

Shaw, Eugene Clay Jr. (R Fla.) April 19, 1939– ; House 1981– .

Shaw, Frank Thomas (D Md.) Oct. 7, 1841–Feb. 24, 1923; House 1885–89.

Shaw, George Bullen (R Wis.) March 12, 1854–Aug. 27, 1894; House 1893–Aug. 27, 1894.

Shaw, Guy Loren (R Ill.) May 16, 1881–May 19, 1950; House 1921–23.

Shaw, Henry (son of Samuel Shaw) (R Mass.) 1788–Oct. 17, 1857; House 1817–21.

Shaw, Henry Marchmore (D N.C.) Nov. 20, 1819–Nov. 1, 1864; House 1853–55, 1857–59.

Shaw, John Gilbert (D N.C.) Jan. 16, 1859–July 21, 1932; House 1895–97.

Shaw, Samuel (father of Henry Shaw) (R Vt.) Dec. 1768–Oct. 23, 1827; House Sept. 6, 1808–13.

Shaw, Tristram (D N.H.) May 23, 1786–March 14, 1843; House 1839–43.

Shays, Christopher (R Conn.) Oct. 18, 1945– ; House Sept. 9, 1987– .

Sheafe, James (F N.H.) Nov. 16, 1755–Dec. 5, 1829; House 1799–1801; Senate 1801–June 14, 1802.

Sheakley, James (D Pa.) April 24, 1829–Dec. 10, 1917; House 1875–77; Gov. (Alaska Terr.) 1893–97.

Sheats, Charles Christopher (R Ala.) April 10, 1839–May 27, 1904; House 1873–75.

Sheehan, Timothy Patrick (R Ill.) Feb. 21, 1909– ; House 1951–59.

Sheffer, Daniel (D Pa.) May 24, 1783–Feb. 16, 1880; House 1837–39.

Sheffey, Daniel (F Va.) 1770–Dec. 3, 1830; House 1809–17.

Sheffield, William Paine (father of William Paine Sheffield, below) (R R.I.) Aug. 30, 1820–June 2, 1907; House 1861–63; Senate Nov. 19, 1884–Jan. 20, 1885.

Sheffield, William Paine (son of William Paine Sheffield, above) (R R.I.) June 1, 1857–Oct. 19, 1919; House 1909–11.

Shelby, Richard Craig (R Ala.) May 6, 1934– ; House 1979–87 (Democrat); Senate 1987– (1979–Nov. 9, 1994 Democrat); Chrmn. Senate Select Committee on Intelligence Activities 1997– .

Shelden, Carlos Douglas (R Mich.) June 10, 1840–June 24, 1904; House 1897–1903.

Sheldon, Lionel Allen (R La.) Aug. 30, 1828–Jan. 17, 1917; House 1869–75; Gov. (N.M. Terr.) 1881–85.

Sheldon, Porter (R N.Y.) Sept. 29, 1831–Aug. 15, 1908; House 1869–71.

Shell, George Washington (D S.C.) Nov. 13, 1831–Dec. 15, 1899; House 1891–95.

Shellabarger, Samuel (R Ohio) Dec. 10, 1817–Aug. 7, 1896; House 1861–63, 1865–69, 1871–73.

Shelley, Charles Miller (D Ala.) Dec. 28, 1833–Jan. 20, 1907; House 1877–81, Nov. 7, 1882–Jan. 9, 1885.

Shelley, John Francis (D Calif.) Sept. 3, 1905–Sept. 1, 1974; House Nov. 8, 1949–Jan. 7, 1964.

Shelton, Samuel Azariah (R Mo.) Sept. 3, 1858–Sept. 13, 1948; House 1921–23.

Shepard, Charles Biddle (D N.C.) Dec. 5, 1808–Oct. 25, 1843; House 1837–41 (1837–39 Whig).

Shepard, William (F Mass.) Dec. 1, 1737–Nov. 16, 1817; House 1797–1803.

Shepard, William Biddle (W N.C.) May 14, 1799–June 20, 1852; House 1829–37 (no party).

Shepherd, Karen (D Utah) July 5, 1940– ; House 1993–95.

Shepler, Matthias (D Ohio) Nov. 11, 1790–April 7, 1863; House 1837–39.

Shepley, Ether (J Maine) Nov. 2, 1789–Jan. 15, 1877; Senate 1833–March 3, 1836.

Sheppard, Harry Richard (D Calif.) Jan. 10, 1885–April 28, 1969; House 1937–65.

Sheppard, John Levi (father of Morris Sheppard, great-grandfather of Connie Mack III) (D Texas) April 13, 1852–Oct. 11, 1902; House 1899–Oct. 11, 1902.

Sheppard, Morris (son of John Levi Sheppard) (D Texas) May 28, 1875–April 9, 1941; House Nov. 15, 1902–Feb. 3, 1913; Senate Feb. 3, 1913–April 9, 1941.

Shepperd, Augustine Henry (W N.C.) Feb. 24, 1792–July 11, 1864; House 1827–39, 1841–43, 1847–51.

Sherburne, John Samuel (R N.H.) 1757–Aug. 2, 1830; House 1793–97.

Sheredine, Upton (– Md.) 1740–Jan. 14, 1800; House 1791–93.

Sheridan, George Augustus (LR La.) Feb. 22, 1840–Oct. 7, 1896; House 1873–75.

Sheridan, John Edward (D Pa.) Sept. 15, 1902–Nov. 12, 1987; House Nov. 7, 1939–47.

Sherley, Joseph Swagar (D Ky.) Nov. 28, 1871–Feb. 13, 1941; House 1903–19.

Sherman, Brad (D Calif.) Oct. 24, 1954– ; House 1997– .

Sherman, James Schoolcraft (R N.Y.) Oct. 24, 1855–Oct. 30, 1912; House 1887–91, 1893–1909; Vice President 1909–Oct. 30, 1912.

Sherman, John (R Ohio) May 10, 1823–Oct. 22, 1900; House 1855–March 21, 1861; Senate March 21, 1861–March 8, 1877, 1881–March 4, 1897; elected Pres. pro tempore Dec. 7, 1885; Secy. of the Treasury March 10, 1877–March 3, 1881; Secy. of State March 6, 1897–April 27, 1898.

Sherman, Judson W. (R N.Y.) 1808–Nov. 12, 1881; House 1857–59.

Sherman, Lawrence Yates (R Ill.) Nov. 8, 1858–Sept. 15, 1939; Senate March 26, 1913–21.

Sherman, Roger (grandfather of William Maxwell Evarts) (– Conn.) April 19, 1721–July 23, 1793; House 1789–91; Senate June 13, 1791–July 23, 1793; Cont. Cong. 1774–81, 1784.

Sherman, Socrates Norton (R N.Y.) July 22, 1801–Feb. 1, 1873; House 1861–63.

Sherrill, Eliakim (W N.Y.) Feb. 16, 1813–July 4, 1863; House 1847–49.

Sherrod, William Crawford (D Ala.) Aug. 17, 1835–March 24, 1919; House 1869–71.

Sherwin, John Crocker (R Ill.) Feb. 8, 1838–Jan. 1, 1904; House 1879–83.

Sherwood, Donald L. (R Pa.) March 5, 1941– ; House 1999– .

Sherwood, Henry (D Pa.) Oct. 9, 1813–Nov. 10, 1896; House 1871–73.

Sherwood, Isaac R. (D Ohio) Aug. 13, 1835–Oct. 15, 1925; House 1873–75 (Republican), 1907–21, 1923–25.

Sherwood, Samuel (F N.Y.) April 24, 1779–Oct. 31, 1862; House 1813–15.

Sherwood, Samuel Burr (F Conn.) Nov. 26, 1767–April 27, 1833; House 1817–19.

Shiel, George Knox (D Ore.) 1825–Dec. 12, 1893; House July 30, 1861–63.

Shields, Benjamin Glover (D Ala.) 1808–?; House 1841–43.

Shields, Ebenezer J. (W Tenn.) Dec. 22, 1778–April 21, 1846; House 1835–39 (1835–37 White supporter).

Shields, James (uncle of James Shields, below) (J Ohio) April 13, 1762–Aug. 13, 1831; House 1829–31.

Shields, James (nephew of James Shields, above) (D Mo.) May 10, 1810–June 1, 1879; Senate March 6–15, 1849 (Ill.), Oct. 27, 1849–55 (Ill.), May 11, 1858–59 (Minn.), Jan. 27–March 3, 1879.

Shields, John Knight (D Tenn.) Aug. 15, 1858–Sept. 30, 1934; Senate 1913–25.

Shimkus, John (R Ill.) Feb. 21, 1958– ; House 1997– .

Shinn, William Norton (J N.J.) Oct. 24, 1782–Aug. 18, 1871; House 1833–37.

Shipherd, Zebulon Rudd (F N.Y.) Nov. 15, 1768–Nov. 1, 1841; House 1813–15.

Shipley, George Edward (D Ill.) April 21, 1927– ; House 1959–79.

Shipstead, Henrik (R Minn.) Jan. 8, 1881–June 26, 1960; Senate 1923–47 (1923–41 Farmer Laborite).

Shiras, George III (IR Pa.) Jan. 1, 1859–March 24, 1942; House 1903–05.

Shively, Benjamin Franklin (D Ind.) March 20, 1857–March 14, 1916; House Dec. 1, 1884–85 (National Anti-Monopolist), 1887–93; Senate 1909–March 14, 1916.

Shober, Francis Edwin (father of Francis Emanuel Shober) (D N.C.) March 12, 1831–May 29, 1896; House 1869–73.

Shober, Francis Emanuel (son of Francis Edwin Shober) (D N.Y.) Oct. 24, 1860–Oct. 7, 1919; House 1903–05.

Shoemaker, Francis Henry (FL Minn.) April 25, 1889–July 24, 1958; House 1933–35.

Shoemaker, Lazarus Denison (R Pa.) Nov. 5, 1819–Sept. 9, 1893; House 1871–75.

Shonk, George Washington (R Pa.) April 26, 1850–Aug. 14, 1900; House 1891–93.

Short, Dewey Jackson (R Mo.) April 7, 1898–Nov. 19, 1979; House 1929–31, 1935–57; Chrmn. House Armed Services 1953–55.

Short, Don Levingston (R N.D.) June 22, 1903–May 10, 1982; House 1959–65.

Shorter, Eli Sims (D Ala.) March 15, 1823–April 29, 1879; House 1855–59.

Shortridge, Samuel Morgan (R Calif.) Aug. 3, 1861–Jan. 15, 1952; Senate 1921–33.

Shott, Hugh Ike (R W.Va.) Sept. 3, 1866–Oct. 12, 1953; House 1929–33; Senate Nov. 18, 1942–43.

Shoup, George Laird (great-grandfather of Richard Gardner Shoup) (R Idaho) June 15, 1836–Dec. 21, 1904; Senate Dec. 18, 1890–1901; Gov. April 1889–90 (Idaho Terr.), Oct. 1–Dec. 1890.

Shoup, Richard Gardner (great-grandson of George Laird Shoup) (R Mont.) Nov. 29, 1923–Nov. 25, 1995; House 1971–75.

Shouse, Jouett (D Kan.) Dec. 10, 1879–June 2, 1968; House 1915–19.

Showalter, Joseph Baltzell (R Pa.) Feb. 11, 1851–Dec. 3, 1932; House April 20, 1897–1903.

Shower, Jacob (D Md.) Feb. 22, 1803–May 25, 1879; House 1853–55.

Shows, C. Ronald "Ronnie" (D Miss) Jan. 26, 1947– ; House 1999– .

Shreve, Milton William (R Pa.) May 3, 1858–Dec. 23, 1939; House 1913–15, 1919–33.

Shriver, Garner E. (R Kan.) July 6, 1912–March 1, 1998; House 1961–77.

Shuford, Alonzo Craig (P N.C.) March 1, 1858–Feb. 8, 1933; House 1895–99.

Shuford, George Adams (D N.C.) Sept. 5, 1895–Dec. 8, 1962; House 1953–59.

Shull, Joseph Horace (D Pa.) Aug. 17, 1848–Aug. 9, 1944; House 1903–05.

Shultz, Emanuel (R Ohio) July 25, 1819–Nov. 5, 1912; House 1881–83.

Shumway, Norman David (R Calif.) July 28, 1934– ; House 1979–91.

Shuster, E. G. "Bud" (R Pa.) Jan. 23, 1932– ; House 1973– ; Chrmn. House Transportation and Infrastructure 1995– .

Sibal, Abner Woodruff (R Conn.) April 11, 1921– ; House 1961–65.

Sibley, Henry Hastings (son of Solomon Sibley) (– Minn.) Feb. 20, 1811–Feb. 18, 1891; House (Terr. Del.) Oct. 30, 1848–49 (Wis.), July 7, 1849–53; Gov. May 24, 1858–Jan. 2, 1860.

Sibley, Jonas (– Mass.) March 7, 1762–Feb. 5, 1834; House 1823–25.

Sibley, Joseph Crocker (R Pa.) Feb. 18, 1850–May 19, 1926; House 1893–95 (Democrat), 1899–1907 (1899–1901 Democrat).

Sibley, Mark Hopkins (W N.Y.) 1796–Sept. 8, 1852; House 1837–39.

Sibley, Solomon (father of Henry Hastings Sibley) (– Mich.) Oct. 7, 1769–April 4, 1846; House (Terr. Del.) Nov. 20, 1820–23.

Sickles, Carlton Ralph (D Md.) June 15, 1921– ; House 1963–67.

Sickles, Daniel Edgar (D N.Y.) Oct. 20, 1819–May 3, 1914; House 1857–61, 1893–95.

Sickles, Nicholas (J N.Y.) Sept. 11, 1801–May 13, 1845; House 1835–37.

Siegel, Isaac (R N.Y.) April 12, 1880–June 29, 1947; House 1915–23.

Sieminski, Alfred Dennis (D N.J.) Aug. 23, 1911–Dec. 13, 1990; House 1951–59.

Sikes, Robert Lee Fulton (D Fla.) June 3, 1906–Sept. 28, 1994; House 1941–Oct. 19, 1944, 1945–79.

Sikorski, Gerald Edward "Gerry" (DFL Minn.) April 26, 1948– ; House 1983–93.

Siler, Eugene (R Ky.) June 26, 1900–Dec. 5, 1987; House 1955–65.

Siljander, Mark Deli (R Mich.) June 11, 1951– ; House April 21, 1981–87.

Sill, Thomas Hale (– Pa.) Oct. 11, 1783–Feb. 7, 1856; House March 14, 1826–27, 1829–31.

Silsbee, Nathaniel (D Mass.) Jan. 14, 1773–July 14, 1850; House 1817–21; Senate May 31, 1826–35.

Silvester, Peter (grandfather of Peter Henry Silvester) (– N.Y.) 1734–Oct. 15, 1808; House 1789–93.

Silvester, Peter Henry (grandson of Peter Silvester) (W N.Y.) Feb. 17, 1807–Nov. 29, 1882; House 1847–51.

Simkins, Eldred (R S.C.) Aug. 30, 1779–Nov. 17, 1831; House Jan. 24, 1818–21.

Simmons, Furnifold McLendel (D N.C.) Jan. 20, 1854–April 30, 1940; House 1887–89; Senate 1901–31.

Simmons, George Abel (W N.Y.) Sept. 8, 1791–Oct. 27, 1857; House 1853–57.

Simmons, James Fowler (W R.I.) Sept. 10, 1795–July 10, 1864; Senate 1841–47, 1857–Aug. 15, 1862.

Simmons, James Samuel (nephew of Milton George Urner) (R N.Y.) Nov. 25, 1861–Nov. 28, 1935; House 1909–13.

Simmons, Robert Glenmore (R Neb.) Dec. 25, 1891–Dec. 27, 1969; House 1923–33.

Simms, Albert Gallatin (husband of Ruth Hanna McCormick) (R N.M.) Oct. 8, 1882–Dec. 29, 1964; House 1929–31.

Simms, William Emmett (D Ky.) Jan. 2, 1822–June 25, 1898; House 1859–61.

Simon, Joseph (R Ore.) Feb. 7, 1851–Feb. 14, 1935; Senate Oct. 8, 1898–1903.

Simon, Paul Martin (D Ill.) Nov. 29, 1928–   ; House 1975–85; Senate 1985–97.

Simonds, William Edgar (R Conn.) Nov. 24, 1842–March 14, 1903; House 1889–91.

Simons, Samuel (D Conn.) 1792–Jan. 13, 1847; House 1843–45.

Simonton, Charles Bryson (D Tenn.) Sept. 8, 1838–June 10, 1911; House 1879–83.

Simonton, William (W Pa.) Feb. 12, 1788–May 17, 1846; House 1839–43.

Simpkins, John (R Mass.) June 27, 1862–March 27, 1898; House 1895–March 27, 1898.

Simpson, Alan Kooi (son of Milward Lee Simpson) (R Wyo.) Sept. 2, 1931–   ; Senate Jan. 1, 1979–97; Chrmn. Senate Veterans' Affairs 1981–85, 1995–97.

Simpson, Edna Oakes (widow of Sidney Elmer "Sid" Simpson) (R Ill.) Oct. 28, 1891–May 15, 1984; House 1959–61.

Simpson, James Jr. (R Ill.) Jan. 7, 1905–Feb. 29, 1960; House 1933–35.

Simpson, Jeremiah "Jerry" (P Kan.) March 31, 1842–Oct. 23, 1905; House 1891–95, 1897–99.

Simpson, Kenneth Farrand (R N.Y.) May 4, 1895–Jan. 25, 1941; House Jan. 3–Jan. 25, 1941.

Simpson, Michael (R Idaho) Sept. 8, 1950–   ; House 1999–   .

Simpson, Milward Lee (father of Alan Kooi Simpson) (R Wyo.) Nov. 12, 1897–June 10, 1993; Senate Nov. 6, 1962–67; Gov. Jan. 3, 1955–Jan. 5, 1959.

Simpson, Richard Franklin (D S.C.) March 24, 1798–Oct. 28, 1882; House 1843–49.

Simpson, Richard Murray (R Pa.) Aug. 30, 1900–Jan. 7, 1960; House May 11, 1937–Jan. 7, 1960.

Simpson, Sidney Elmer "Sid" (husband of Edna Oakes Simpson) (R Ill.) Sept. 20, 1894–Oct. 26, 1958; House 1943–Oct. 26, 1958; Chrmn. House District of Columbia 1953–55.

Sims, Alexander Dromgoole (nephew of George Coke Dromgoole) (D S.C.) June 12, 1803–Nov. 22, 1848; House 1845–Nov. 22, 1848.

Sims, Hugo Sheridan Jr. (D S.C.) Oct. 14, 1921–   ; House 1949–51.

Sims, Leonard Henly (D Mo.) Feb. 6, 1807–Feb. 28, 1886; House 1845–47.

Sims, Thetus Willrette (D Tenn.) April 25, 1852–Dec. 17, 1939; House 1897–1921.

Sinclair, James Herbert (R N.D.) Oct. 9, 1871–Sept. 5, 1943; House 1919–35.

Singiser, Theodore Frelinghuysen (R Idaho) March 15, 1845–Jan. 23, 1907; House (Terr. Del.) 1883–85.

Singleton, James Washington (D Ill.) Nov. 23, 1811–April 4, 1892; House 1879–83.

Singleton, Otho Robards (D Miss.) Oct. 14, 1814–Jan. 11, 1889; House 1853–55, 1857–Jan. 12, 1861, 1875–87.

Singleton, Thomas Day (N S.C.) ?–Nov. 25, 1833; House March 3–Nov. 25, 1833 (served without having qualified).

Sinnickson, Clement Hall (great-nephew of Thomas Sinnickson) (R N.J.) Sept. 16, 1834–July 24, 1919; House 1875–79.

Sinnickson, Thomas (great-uncle of Clement Hall Sinnickson, uncle of Thomas Sinnickson, below) (F N.J.) Dec. 21, 1744–May 15, 1817; House 1789–91 (no party), 1797–99.

Sinnickson, Thomas (nephew of Thomas Sinnickson, above) (– N.J.) Dec. 13, 1786–Feb. 17, 1873; House Dec. 1, 1828–29.

Sinnott, Nicholas John (R Ore.) Dec. 6, 1870–July 20, 1929; House 1913–May 31, 1928.

Sipe, William Allen (D Pa.) July 1, 1844–Sept. 10, 1935; House Dec. 5, 1892–95.

Sirovich, William Irving (D N.Y.) March 18, 1882–Dec. 17, 1939; House 1927–Dec. 17, 1939.

Sisisky, Norman (D Va.) June 9, 1927–   ; House 1983–   .

Sisk, Bernice Frederic (D Calif.) Dec. 14, 1910–Oct. 25, 1995; House 1955–79.

Sisson, Frederick James (D N.Y.) March 31, 1879–Oct. 20, 1949; House 1933–37.

Sisson, Thomas Upton (D Miss.) Sept. 22, 1869–Sept. 26, 1923; House 1909–23.

Sites, Frank Crawford (D Pa.) Dec. 24, 1864–May 23, 1935; House 1923–25.

Sitgreaves, Charles (D N.J.) April 22, 1803–March 17, 1878; House 1865–69.

Sitgreaves, Samuel (F Pa.) March 16, 1764–April 4, 1827; House 1795–98.

Sittler, Edward Lewis Jr. (R Pa.) April 21, 1908–Dec. 26, 1978; House 1951–53.

Skaggs, David Evans (D Colo.) Feb. 22, 1943–   ; House 1987–99.

Skeen, Joseph Richard (R N.M.) June 30, 1927–   ; House 1981–   .

Skelton, Charles (D N.J.) April 19, 1806–May 20, 1879; House 1851–55.

Skelton, Isaac Newton "Ike" IV (D Mo.) Dec. 20, 1931–   ; House 1977–   .

Skiles, William Woodburn (R Ohio) Dec. 11, 1849–Jan. 9, 1904; House 1901–Jan. 9, 1904.

Skinner, Charles Rufus (R N.Y.) Aug. 4, 1844–June 30, 1928; House Nov. 8, 1881–85.

Skinner, Harry (brother of Thomas Gregory Skinner) (P N.C.) May 25, 1855–May 19, 1929; House 1895–99.

Skinner, Richard (R Vt.) May 30, 1778–May 23, 1833; House 1813–15; Gov. Oct. 13, 1820–Oct. 10, 1823 (Democratic Republican).

Skinner, Thomas Gregory (brother of Harry Skinner) (D N.C.) Jan. 22, 1842–Dec. 22, 1907; House Nov. 20, 1883–87, 1889–91.

Skinner, Thomson Joseph (R Mass.) May 24, 1752–Jan. 20, 1809; House Jan. 27, 1797–99, 1803–Aug. 10, 1804.

Skubitz, Joe (R Kan.) May 6, 1906–   ; House 1963–Dec. 31, 1978.

Slack, John Mark Jr. (D W.Va.) March 18, 1915–March 17, 1980; House 1959–March 17, 1980.

Slade, Charles (J Ill.) ?–July 26, 1834; House 1833–July 26, 1834.

Slade, William (W Vt.) May 9, 1786–Jan. 18, 1859; House Nov. 1, 1831–43 (Nov. 1, 1831–37 Anti-Mason); Gov. Oct. 11, 1844–Oct. 9, 1846.

Slater, James Harvey (D Ore.) Dec. 28, 1826–Jan. 28, 1899; House 1871–73; Senate 1879–85.

Slattery, James Charles (D Kan.) Aug. 4, 1948–   ; House 1983–95.

Slattery, James Michael (D Ill.) July 29, 1878–Aug. 28, 1948; Senate April 14, 1939–Nov. 21, 1940.

Slaughter, Daniel French Jr. (R Va.) May 20, 1925–Oct. 2, 1998; House 1985–Nov. 5, 1991.

Slaughter, Louise M. (D N.Y.) Aug. 14, 1929–   ; House 1987–   .

Slaughter, Roger Caldwell (D Mo.) July 17, 1905–June 2, 1974; House 1943–47.

Slayden, James Luther (uncle of Fontaine Maury Maverick) (D Texas) June 1, 1853–Feb. 24, 1924; House 1897–1919.

Slaymaker, Amos (F Pa.) March 11, 1755–June 12, 1837; House Oct. 11, 1814–15.

Slemons, William Ferguson (D Ark.) March 15, 1830–Dec. 10, 1918; House 1875–81.

Slemp, Campbell (father of Campbell Bascom Slemp) (R Va.) Dec. 2, 1839–Oct. 13, 1907; House 1903–Oct. 13, 1907.

Slemp, Campbell Bascom (son of Campbell Slemp) (R Va.) Sept. 4, 1870–Aug. 7, 1943; House Dec. 17, 1907–23.

Slidell, John (D La.) 1793–July 26, 1871; House 1843–Nov. 10, 1845; Senate Dec. 5, 1853–Feb. 4, 1861.

Slingerland, John I. (W N.Y.) March 1, 1804–Oct. 26, 1861; House 1847–49.

Sloan, Andrew (R Ga.) June 10, 1845–Sept. 22, 1883; House March 24, 1874–75.

Sloan, Andrew Scott (brother of Ithamar Conkey Sloan) (R Wis.) June 12, 1820–April 8, 1895; House 1861–63.

Sloan, Charles Henry (R Neb.) May 2, 1863–June 2, 1946; House 1911–19, 1929–31.

Sloan, Ithamar Conkey (brother of Andrew Scott Sloan) (R Wis.) May 9, 1822–Dec. 24, 1898; House 1863–67.

Sloan, James (R N.J.) ?–Nov. 1811; House 1803–09.

Sloane, John (– Ohio) 1779–May 15, 1856; House 1819–29.

Sloane, Jonathan (W Ohio) Nov. 1785–April 25, 1854; House 1833–37 (1833–35 Anti-Mason).

Slocum, Henry Warner (D N.Y.) Sept. 24, 1827–April 14, 1894; House 1869–73, 1883–85.

Slocumb, Jesse (F N.C.) 1780–Dec. 20, 1820; House 1817–Dec. 20, 1820.

Sloss, Joseph Humphrey (D Ala.) Oct. 12, 1826–Jan. 27, 1911; House 1871–75.

Small, Frank Jr. (R Md.) July 15, 1896–Oct. 24, 1973; House 1953–55.

Small, John Humphrey (D N.C.) Aug. 29, 1858–July 13, 1946; House 1899–1921.

Small, William Bradbury (R N.H.) May 17, 1817–April 7, 1878; House 1873–75.

Smalls, Robert (R S.C.) April 5, 1839–Feb. 22, 1915; House 1875–79, July 19, 1882–83, March 18, 1884–87.

Smart, Ephraim Knight (D Maine) Sept. 3, 1813–Sept. 29, 1872; House 1847–49, 1851–53.

Smart, James Stevenson (R N.Y.) June 14, 1842–Sept. 17, 1903; House 1873–75.

Smathers, George Armistead (nephew of William Howell Smathers) (D Fla.) Nov. 14, 1913– ; House 1947–51; Senate 1951–69; Chrmn. Senate Select Committee on Small Business 1967–69.

Smathers, William Howell (uncle of George Armistead Smathers) (D N.J.) Jan. 7, 1891–Sept. 24, 1955; Senate April 15, 1937–43.

Smelt, Dennis (R Ga.) about 1750–?; House Sept. 1, 1806–11.

Smilie, John (R Pa.) 1741–Dec. 30, 1812; House 1793–95 (no party), 1799–Dec. 30, 1812.

Smith, Abraham Herr (R Pa.) March 7, 1815–Feb. 16, 1894; House 1873–85.

Smith, Adam (D Wash.) June 15, 1965– ; House 1997– .

Smith, Addison Taylor (R Idaho) Sept. 5, 1862–July 5, 1956; House 1913–33.

Smith, Albert (D Maine) Jan. 3, 1793–May 29, 1867; House 1839–41.

Smith, Albert (W N.Y.) June 22, 1805–Aug. 27, 1870; House 1843–47.

Smith, Albert Lee Jr. (R Ala.) Aug. 31, 1931– ; House 1981–83.

Smith, Arthur (– Va.) Nov. 15, 1785–March 30, 1853; House 1821–25.

Smith, Ballard (R Va.) ?–?; House 1815–21.

Smith, Benjamin A. II (D Mass.) March 26, 1916–Sept. 26, 1991; Senate Dec. 27, 1960–Nov. 6, 1962.

Smith, Bernard (– N.J.) July 5, 1776–July 16, 1835; House 1819–21.

Smith, Caleb Blood (W Ind.) April 16, 1808–Jan. 7, 1864; House 1843–49; Secy. of the Interior March 5, 1861–Dec. 31, 1862.

Smith, Charles Bennett (D N.Y.) Sept. 14, 1870–May 21, 1939; House 1911–19.

Smith, Charles Brooks (R W.Va.) Feb. 24, 1844–Dec. 7, 1899; House Feb. 3, 1890–91.

Smith, Christopher Henry (R N.J.) March 4, 1953– ; House 1981– .

Smith, Clyde Harold (husband of Margaret Chase Smith) (R Maine) June 9, 1876–April 8, 1940; House 1937–April 8, 1940.

Smith, Daniel (R Tenn.) Oct. 28, 1748–June 6, 1818; Senate Oct. 6, 1798–99, 1805–March 31, 1809.

Smith, David Highbaugh (D Ky.) Dec. 19, 1854–Dec. 17, 1928; House 1897–1907.

Smith, Delazon (D Ore.) Oct. 5, 1816–Nov. 19, 1860; Senate Feb. 14–March 3, 1859.

Smith, Dennis Alan "Denny" (cousin of Steven Douglas Symms) (R Ore.) Jan. 19, 1938– ; House 1981–91.

Smith, Dietrich Conrad (R Ill.) April 4, 1840–April 18, 1914; House 1881–83.

Smith, Edward Henry (D N.Y.) May 5, 1809–Aug. 7, 1885; House 1861–63.

Smith, Ellison DuRant (D S.C.) Aug. 1, 1866–Nov. 17, 1944; Senate 1909–Nov. 17, 1944.

Smith, Frances Ormand Jonathan (D Maine) Nov. 23, 1806–Oct. 14, 1876; House 1833–39 (1833–37 Jacksonian).

Smith, Francis Raphael (D Pa.) Sept. 25, 1911–Dec. 9, 1982; House 1941–43.

Smith, Frank Ellis (D Miss.) Feb. 21, 1918–Aug. 2, 1997; House 1951–Nov. 14, 1962.

Smith, Frank Leslie (R Ill.) Nov. 24, 1867–Aug. 30, 1950; House 1919–21; elected to the Senate for the term beginning 1927 but was not permitted to qualify and resigned Feb. 9, 1928.

Smith, Frank Owens (D Md.) Aug. 27, 1859–Jan. 29, 1924; House 1913–15.

Smith, Frederick Cleveland (R Ohio) July 29, 1884–July 16, 1956; House 1939–51.

Smith, George (R Pa.) ?–?; House 1809–13.

Smith, George Joseph (R N.Y.) Nov. 7, 1859–Dec. 24, 1913; House 1903–05.

Smith, George Luke (R La.) Dec. 11, 1837–July 9, 1884; House Nov. 24, 1873–75.

Smith, George Ross (R Minn.) May 28, 1864–Nov. 7, 1952; House 1913–17.

Smith, George Washington (R Ill.) Aug. 18, 1846–Nov. 30, 1907; House 1889–Nov. 30, 1907.

Smith, Gerrit (FS N.Y.) March 6, 1797–Dec. 28, 1874; House 1853–Aug. 7, 1854.

Smith, Gomer Griffith (D Okla.) July 11, 1896–May 26, 1953; House Dec. 10, 1937–39.

Smith, Gordon (R Ore.) May 25, 1952– ; Senate 1997– .

Smith, Green Clay (son of John Speed Smith) (UU Ky.) July 4, 1826–June 29, 1895; House 1863–66; Gov. (Mont. Terr.) 1866–69.

Smith, H. Allen (R Calif.) Oct. 8, 1909– ; House 1957–73.

Smith, Henry (Lab. Wis.) July 22, 1838–Sept. 16, 1916; House 1887–89.

Smith, Henry Cassorte (R Mich.) June 2, 1856–Dec. 7, 1911; House 1899–1903.

Smith, Henry P. III (R N.Y.) Sept. 29, 1911–Oct. 1, 1995; House 1965–75.

Smith, Hezekiah Bradley (D N.J.) July 24, 1816–Nov. 3, 1887; House 1879–81.

Smith, Hiram Ypsilanti (R Iowa) March 22, 1843–Nov. 4, 1894; House Dec. 2, 1884–85.

Smith, Hoke (D Ga.) Sept. 2, 1855–Nov. 27, 1931; Senate Nov. 16, 1911–21; Secy. of the Interior March 6, 1893–Sept. 1, 1896; Gov. June 29, 1907–June 26, 1909, July 1–Nov. 16, 1911.

Smith, Horace Boardman (R N.Y.) Aug. 18, 1826–Dec. 26, 1888; House 1871–75.

Smith, Howard Alexander (uncle of Peter H. Dominick) (R N.J.) Jan. 30, 1880–Oct. 27, 1966; Senate Dec. 7, 1944–59; Chrmn. Senate Labor and Public Welfare 1953–55.

Smith, Howard Worth (D Va.) Feb. 2, 1883–Oct. 3, 1976; House 1931–67; Chrmn. House Rules 1955–67.

Smith, Isaac (F N.J.) 1740–Aug. 29, 1807; House 1795–97.

Smith, Isaac (R Pa.) Jan. 4, 1761–April 4, 1834; House 1813–15.

Smith, Israel (R Vt.) April 4, 1759–Dec. 2, 1810; House Oct. 17, 1791–97 (no party), 1801–03 (no party); Senate 1803–Oct. 1, 1807; Gov. Oct. 9, 1807–Oct. 14, 1808 (Democratic Republican).

Smith, James Jr. (D N.J.) June 12, 1851–April 1, 1927; Senate 1893–99.

Smith, James Strudwick (R N.C.) Oct. 15, 1790–Aug. 1859; House 1817–21.

Smith, James Vernon (R Okla.) July 23, 1926–June 23, 1973; House 1967–69.

Smith, Jedediah Kilburn (R N.H.) Nov. 7, 1770–Dec. 17, 1828; House 1807–09.

Smith, Jeremiah (brother of Samuel Smith of N.H., uncle of Robert Smith) (F N.H.) Nov. 29, 1759–Sept. 21, 1842; House 1791–July 26, 1797 (1791–95 no party); Gov. June 8, 1809–June 7, 1810.

Smith, John (R Ohio) about 1735–July 30, 1824; Senate April 1, 1803–April 25, 1808.

Smith, John (R Va.) May 7, 1750–March 5, 1836; House 1801–15.

Smith, John (R N.Y.) Feb. 12, 1752–Aug. 12, 1816; House Feb. 6, 1800–Feb. 23, 1804 (no party); Senate Feb. 23, 1804–13.

Smith, John (father of Worthington Curtis Smith) (D Vt.) Aug. 12, 1789–Nov. 26, 1858; House 1839–41.

Smith, John Ambler (R Va.) Sept. 23, 1847–Jan. 6, 1892; House 1873–75.

Smith, John Armstrong (R Ohio) Sept. 23, 1814–March 7, 1892; House 1869–73.

Smith, John Cotton (F Conn.) Feb. 12, 1765–Dec. 7, 1845; House Nov. 17, 1800–Aug. 1806; Gov. Oct. 25, 1812–May 8, 1817.

Smith, John Hyatt (I N.Y.) April 10, 1824–Dec. 7, 1886; House 1881–83.

Smith, John Joseph (D Conn.) Jan. 25, 1904–Feb. 16, 1980; House 1935–Nov. 4, 1941.

Smith, John M. C. (R Mich.) Feb. 6, 1853–March 30, 1923; House 1911–21, June 28, 1921–March 30, 1923.

Smith, John Quincy (R Ohio) Nov. 5, 1824–Dec. 30, 1901; House 1873–75.

Smith, John Speed (father of Green Clay Smith) (– Ky.) July 1, 1792–June 6, 1854; House Aug. 6, 1821–23.

Smith, John T. (D Pa.) ?–?; House 1843–45.

Smith, John Walter (D Md.) Feb. 5, 1845–April 19, 1925; House 1899–Jan. 12, 1900; Senate March 25, 1908–21; Gov. Jan. 10, 1900–Jan. 13, 1904.

Smith, Joseph Francis (D Pa.) Jan. 24, 1920–May 14, 1999; House July 28, 1981–83.

Smith, Joseph Luther (D W.Va.) May 22, 1880–Aug. 23, 1962; House 1929–45.

Smith, Joseph Showalter (D Ore.) June 20, 1824–July 13, 1884; House 1869–71.

Smith, Josiah (R Mass.) Feb. 26, 1738–April 4, 1803; House 1801–03.

Smith, Lamar Seeligson (R Texas) Nov. 19, 1947– ; House 1987– ; Chrmn. House Standards of Official Conduct 1999– .

Smith, Larkin (R Miss.) June 26, 1944– ; House Jan. 3–Aug. 13, 1989.

Smith, Lawrence Henry (R Wis.) Sept. 15, 1892–Jan. 22, 1958; House Aug. 29, 1941–Jan. 22, 1958.

Smith, Lawrence Jack (D Fla.) April 25, 1941– ; House 1983–93.

Smith, Linda (R Wash.) July 16, 1950– ; House 1995–97.

Smith, Madison Roswell (D Mo.) July 9, 1850–June 18, 1919; House 1907–09.

Smith, Marcus Aurelius (D Ariz.) Jan. 24, 1851–April 7, 1924; House (Terr. Del.) 1887–95, 1897–99, 1901–03, 1905–09; Senate March 27, 1912–21.

Smith, Margaret Chase (widow of Clyde Harold Smith) (R Maine) Dec. 14, 1897–May 29, 1995; House June 3, 1940–49; Senate 1949–73.

Smith, Martin Fernand (D Wash.) May 28, 1891–Oct. 25, 1954; House 1933–43.

Smith, Nathan (brother of Nathaniel Smith, uncle of Truman Smith) (W Conn.) Jan. 8, 1770–Dec. 6, 1835; Senate 1833–Dec. 6, 1835.

Smith, Nathaniel (brother of Nathan Smith, uncle of Truman Smith) (F Conn.) Jan. 6, 1762–March 9, 1822; House 1795–99.

Smith, Neal Edward (D Iowa) March 23, 1920– ; House 1959–95; Chrmn. House Small Business 1977–81.

Smith, Nick (R Mich.) Nov. 5, 1934– ; House 1993– .

Smith, O'Brien (R S.C.) about 1756–April 27, 1811; House 1805–07.

Smith, Oliver Hampton (W Ind.) Oct. 23, 1794–March 19, 1859; House 1827–29 (no party); Senate 1837–43.

Smith, Perry (D Conn.) May 12, 1783–June 8, 1852; Senate 1837–43.

Smith, Peter (R Vt.) Oct. 31, 1945– ; House 1989–91.

Smith, Ralph Tyler (R Ill.) Oct. 6, 1915–Aug. 13, 1972; Senate Sept. 17, 1969–Nov. 3, 1970.

Smith, Robert (nephew of Jeremiah Smith and Samuel Smith of N.H.) (D Ill.) June 12, 1802–Dec. 21, 1867; House 1843–49 (1843–47 Democrat, 1847–49 Independent Democrat), 1857–59.

Smith, Robert Barnwell. (*See* Rhett, Robert Barnwell.)

Smith, Robert Clinton (R N.H.) March 30, 1941– ; House 1985–91; Senate 1991– (July 13, 1999–Nov. 1, 1999 Independent); Chrmn. Senate Select Committee on Ethics 1997– .

Smith, Robert Freeman (R Ore.) June 16, 1931– ; House 1983–95, 1997–99; Chrmn. House Agriculture 1997–99.

Smith, Samuel (R Md.) July 27, 1752–April 22, 1839; House 1793–1803 (no party), Jan. 31, 1816–Dec. 17, 1822; Senate 1803–15, Dec. 17, 1822–33; elected Pres. pro tempore Dec. 2, 1805, March 18, 1806, March 2, 1807, April 16, 1808, May 15, 1828, March 13, 1829, May 29, 1830, March 1, 1831.

Smith, Samuel (R Pa.) ?–?; House Nov. 7, 1805–11.

Smith, Samuel (brother of Jeremiah Smith, uncle of Robert Smith) (F N.H.) Nov. 11, 1765–April 25, 1842; House 1813–15.

Smith, Samuel A. (J Pa.) 1795–May 15, 1861; House Oct. 13, 1829–33.

Smith, Samuel Axley (D Tenn.) June 26, 1822–Nov. 25, 1863; House 1853–59.

Smith, Samuel William (R Mich.) Aug. 23, 1852–June 19, 1931; House 1897–1915.

Smith, Sylvester Clark (R Calif.) Aug. 26, 1858–Jan. 26, 1913; House 1905–Jan. 26, 1913.

Smith, Thomas (F Pa.) ?–Jan. 29, 1846; House 1815–17.

Smith, Thomas (D Ind.) May 1, 1799–April 12, 1876; House 1839–41, 1843–47.

Smith, Thomas Alexander (D Md.) Sept. 3, 1850–May 1, 1932; House 1905–07.

Smith, Thomas Francis (D N.Y.) July 24, 1865–April 11, 1923; House April 12, 1917–21.

Smith, Thomas Vernor (D Ill.) April 26, 1890–May 24, 1964; House 1939–41.

Smith, Truman (nephew of Nathan Smith and Nathaniel Smith) (W Conn.) Nov. 27, 1791–May 3, 1884; House 1839–43, 1845–49; Senate 1849–May 24, 1854.

Smith, Virginia Dodd (R Neb.) June 30, 1911– ; House 1975–91.

Smith, Walter Inglewood (R Iowa) July 10, 1862–Jan. 27, 1922; House Dec. 3, 1900–March 15, 1911.

Smith, William (– Md.) April 12, 1728–March 27, 1814; House 1789–91; Cont. Cong. 1777.

Smith, William (R S.C.) about 1762–June 26, 1840; Senate Dec. 4, 1816–23, Nov. 29, 1826–31.

Smith, William (R S.C.) Sept. 20, 1751–June 22, 1837; House 1797–99.

Smith, William (– Va.) ?–?; House 1821–27.

Smith, William (D Va.) Sept. 6, 1797–May 18, 1887; House 1841–43, 1853–61; Gov. Jan. 1, 1846–Jan. 1, 1849 (Democrat), Jan. 1, 1864–April 1, 1865 (Confederate Democrat).

Smith, William Alden (R Mich.) May 12, 1859–Oct. 11, 1932; House 1895–Feb. 9, 1907; Senate Feb. 9, 1907–19.

Smith, William Alexander (R N.C.) Jan. 9, 1828–May 16, 1888; House 1873–75.

Smith, William Ephraim (D Ga.) March 14, 1829–March 11, 1890; House 1875–81.

Smith, William Jay (R Tenn.) Sept. 24, 1823–Nov. 29, 1913; House 1869–71.

Smith, William Loughton (F S.C.) 1758–Dec. 19, 1812; House 1789–July 10, 1797.

Smith, William Nathan Harrell (O N.C.) Sept. 24, 1812–Nov. 14, 1889; House 1859–61.

Smith, William Orlando (R Pa.) June 13, 1859–May 12, 1932; House 1903–07.

Smith, William Robert (D Texas) Aug. 18, 1863–Aug. 16, 1924; House 1903–17.

Smith, William Russell (AP Ala.) March 27, 1815–Feb. 26, 1896; House 1851–57 (1851–53 Unionist, 1853–55 Democrat).

Smith, William Stephens (F N.Y.) Nov. 8, 1755–June 10, 1816; House 1813–15.

Smith, Willis (D N.C.) Dec. 19, 1887–June 26, 1953; Senate Nov. 27, 1950–June 26, 1953.

Smith, Wint (R Kan.) Oct. 7, 1892–April 27, 1976; House 1947–61.

Smith, Worthington Curtis (son of John Smith of Vt.) (R Vt.) April 23, 1823–Jan. 2, 1894; House 1867–73.

Smithers, Nathaniel Barratt (UU Del.) Oct. 8, 1818–Jan. 16, 1896; House Dec. 7, 1863–65.

Smithwick, John Harris (D Fla.) July 17, 1872–Dec. 2, 1948; House 1919–27.

Smoot, Reed (R Utah) Jan. 10, 1862–Feb. 9, 1941; Senate 1903–33.

Smyser, Martin Luther (R Ohio) April 3, 1851–May 6, 1908; House 1889–91, 1905–07.

Smyth, Alexander (R Va.) 1765–April 17, 1830; House 1817–25, 1827–April 17, 1830.

Smyth, George Washington (D Texas) May 16, 1803–Feb. 21, 1866; House 1853–55.

Smyth, William (R Iowa) Jan. 3, 1824–Sept. 30, 1870; House 1869–Sept. 30, 1870.

Snapp, Henry (father of Howard Malcolm Snapp) (R Ill.) June 30, 1822–Nov. 26, 1895; House Dec. 4, 1871–73.

Snapp, Howard Malcolm (son of Henry Snapp) (R Ill.) Sept. 27, 1855–Aug. 14, 1938; House 1903–11.

Sneed, William Henry (AP Tenn.) Aug. 27, 1812–Sept. 18, 1869; House 1855–57.

Snell, Bertrand Hollis (R N.Y.) Dec. 9, 1870–Feb. 2, 1958; House Nov. 2, 1915–39; House minority leader 1931–39.

Snider, Samuel Prather (R Minn.) Oct. 9, 1845–Sept. 24, 1928; House 1889–91.

Snodgrass, Charles Edward (nephew of Henry Clay Snodgrass) (D Tenn.) Dec. 28, 1866–Aug. 3, 1936; House 1899–1903.

Snodgrass, Henry Clay (uncle of Charles Edward Snodgrass) (D Tenn.) March 29, 1848–April 22, 1931; House 1891–95.

Snodgrass, John Fryall (D Va.) March 2, 1804–June 5, 1854; House 1853–June 5, 1854.

Snook, John Stout (D Ohio) Dec. 18, 1862–Sept. 19, 1952; House 1901–05, 1917–19.

Snover, Horace Greeley (R Mich.) Sept. 21, 1847–July 21, 1924; House 1895–99.

Snow, Donald Francis (R Maine) Sept. 6, 1877–Feb. 12, 1958; House 1929–33.

Snow, Herman Wilber (D Ill.) July 3, 1836–Aug. 25, 1914; House 1891–93.

Snow, William W. (D N.Y.) April 27, 1812–Sept. 3, 1886; House 1851–53.

Snowbarger, Vincent (R Kan.) Sept. 16, 1949– ; House 1997–99.

Snowe, Olympia Jean Bouchles (R Maine) Feb. 21, 1947– ; House 1979–95; Senate 1995– .

Snyder, Adam Wilson (D Ill.) Oct. 6, 1799–May 14, 1842; House 1837–39.

Snyder, Charles Philip (D W.Va.) June 9, 1847–Aug. 21, 1915; House May 15, 1883–89.

Snyder, Homer Peter (R N.Y.) Dec. 6, 1863–Dec. 30, 1937; House 1915–25.

Snyder, John (– Pa.) Jan. 29, 1793–Aug. 15, 1850; House 1841–43.

Snyder, John Buell (D Pa.) July 30, 1877–Feb. 24, 1946; House 1933–Feb. 24, 1946.

Snyder, Marion Gene (R Ky.) Jan. 26, 1928– ; House 1963–65, 1967–87.

Snyder, Melvin Claude (R W.Va.) Oct. 29, 1898– ; House 1947–49.

Snyder, Oliver P. (R Ark.) Nov. 13, 1833–Nov. 22, 1882; House 1871–75.

Snyder, Victor F. (D Ark.) Sept. 27, 1947– ; House 1997– .

Solarz, Stephen Joshua (D N.Y.) Sept. 12, 1940– ; House 1975–93.

Sollers, Augustus Rhodes (W Md.) May 1, 1814–Nov. 26, 1862; House 1841–43, 1853–55.

Solomon, Gerald Brooks Hunt (R N.Y.) Aug. 14, 1930– ; House 1979–99; Chrmn. House Rules 1995–99.

Somers, Andrew Lawrence (D N.Y.) March 21, 1895–April 6, 1949; House 1925–April 6, 1949; Chrmn. House Public Lands 1949.

Somers, Peter J. (D Wis.) April 12, 1850–Feb. 15, 1924; House Aug. 27, 1893–95.

Somes, Daniel Eton (R Maine) May 20, 1815–Feb. 13, 1888; House 1859–61.

Sorg, Paul John (D Ohio) Sept. 23, 1840–May 28, 1902; House May 21, 1894–97.

Sosnowski, John Bartholomew (R Mich.) Dec. 8, 1883–July 16, 1968; House 1925–27.

Souder, Mark (R Ind.) July 18, 1950– ; House 1995– .

Soule, Nathan (J N.Y.) ?–?; House 1831–33.

Soule, Pierre (D La.) Aug. 31, 1801–March 26, 1870; Senate Jan. 21–March 3, 1847, 1849–April 11, 1853.

South, Charles Lacy (D Texas) July 22, 1892–Dec. 20, 1965; House 1935–43.

Southall, Robert Goode (D Va.) Dec. 26, 1852–May 25, 1924; House 1903–07.

Southard, Henry (father of Isaac Southard and Samuel Lewis Southard) (R N.J.) Oct. 7, 1747–May 22, 1842; House 1801–11, 1815–21.

Southard, Isaac (son of Henry Southard, brother of Samuel Lewis Southard) (AJ N.J.) Aug. 30, 1783–Sept. 18, 1850; House 1831–33.

Southard, James Harding (R Ohio) Jan. 20, 1851–Feb. 20, 1919; House 1895–1907.

Southard, Milton Isaiah (D Ohio) Oct. 20, 1836–May 4, 1905; House 1873–79.

Southard, Samuel Lewis (son of Henry Southard, brother of Isaac Southard) (W N.J.) June 9, 1787–June 26, 1842; Senate Jan. 26, 1821–23 (Republican), 1833–June 26, 1842; elected Pres. pro tempore March 11, 1841; Secy. of the Navy Sept. 16, 1823–March 3, 1829; Gov. Oct. 26, 1832–Feb. 27, 1833 (Republican).

Southgate, William Wright (W Ky.) Nov. 27, 1800–Dec. 26, 1849; House 1837–39.

Southwick, George Newell (R N.Y.) March 7, 1863–Oct. 17, 1912; House 1895–99, 1901–11.

Sowden, William Henry (D Pa.) June 6, 1840–March 3, 1907; House 1885–89.

Spaight, Richard Dobbs (grandfather of Richard Spaight Donnell, father of Richard Dobbs Spaight Jr.) (R N.C.) March 25, 1758–Sept. 6, 1802; House Dec. 10, 1798–1801; Cont. Cong. 1783–85; Gov. Dec. 14, 1792–Nov. 19, 1795 (Anti-Federalist).

Spaight, Richard Dobbs Jr. (son of Richard Dobbs Spaight, uncle of Richard Spaight Donnell) (– N.C.) 1796–May 2, 1850; House 1823–25; Gov. Dec. 10, 1835–Dec. 31, 1836 (Democrat).

Spalding, Burleigh Folsom (R N.D.) Dec. 3, 1853–March 17, 1934; House 1899–1901, 1903–05.

Spalding, George (R Mich.) Nov. 12, 1836–Sept. 13, 1915; House 1895–99.

Spalding, Rufus Paine (R Ohio) May 3, 1798–Aug. 29, 1886; House 1863–69.

Spalding, Thomas (R Ga.) March 26, 1774–Jan. 5, 1851; House Dec. 24, 1805–06.

Spangler, David (W Ohio) Dec. 2, 1796–Oct. 18, 1856; House 1833–37 (1833–35 Anti-Jacksonian).

Spangler, Jacob (R Pa.) Nov. 28, 1767–June 17, 1843; House 1817–April 20, 1818.

Sparkman, John Jackson (D Ala.) Dec. 20, 1899–Nov. 16, 1985; House 1937–Nov. 5, 1946; Senate Nov. 6, 1946–79; Chrmn. Senate Select Committee on Small Business 1950–53, 1955–67; Chrmn. Senate Banking and Currency 1967–71; Chrmn. Senate Banking, Housing, and Urban Affairs 1971–75; Chrmn. Senate Foreign Relations 1975–78.

Sparkman, Stephen Milancthon (D Fla.) July 29, 1849–Sept. 26, 1929; House 1895–1917.

Sparks, Charles Isaac (R Kan.) Dec. 20, 1872–April 30, 1937; House 1929–33.

Sparks, William Andrew Jackson (D Ill.) Nov. 19, 1828–May 7, 1904; House 1875–83.

Spaulding, Elbridge Gerry (R N.Y.) Feb. 24, 1809–May 5, 1897; House 1849–51 (Whig), 1859–63.

Spaulding, Oliver Lyman (R Mich.) Aug. 2, 1833–July 30, 1922; House 1881–83.

Speaks, John Charles (R Ohio) Feb. 11, 1859–Nov. 6, 1945; House 1921–31.

Spearing, James Zacharie (D La.) April 23, 1864–Nov. 2, 1942; House April 22, 1924–31.

Specter, Arlen (R Pa.) Feb. 12, 1930– ; Senate 1981– ; Chrmn. Senate Select Committee on Intelligence Activities 1995–97; Chrmn. Senate Veterans' Affairs 1997– .

Speed, Thomas (R Ky.) Oct. 25, 1768–Feb. 20, 1842; House 1817–19.

Speer, Emory (ID Ga.) Sept. 3, 1848–Dec. 13, 1918; House 1879–83.

Speer, Peter Moore (R Pa.) Dec. 29, 1862–Aug. 3, 1933; House 1911–13.

Speer, Robert Milton (D Pa.) Sept. 8, 1838–Jan. 17, 1890; House 1871–75.

Speer, Thomas Jefferson (R Ga.) Aug. 31, 1837–Aug. 18, 1872; House 1871–Aug. 18, 1872.

Speight, Jesse (D Miss.) Sept. 22, 1795–May 1, 1847; House 1829–37 (no party N.C.); Senate 1845–May 1, 1847.

Spellman, Gladys Noon (D Md.) March 1, 1918–June 19, 1988; House 1975–Feb. 24, 1981.

Spence, Brent (D Ky.) Dec. 24, 1874–Sept. 18, 1967; House 1931–63; Chrmn. House Banking and Currency 1949–53, 1955–63.

Spence, Floyd Davidson (R S.C.) April 9, 1928– ; House 1971– ; Chrmn. House Armed Services 1995– .

Spence, John Selby (uncle of Thomas Ara Spence) (W Md.) Feb. 29, 1788–Oct. 24, 1840; House 1823–25 (no party), 1831–33; Senate Dec. 31, 1836–Oct. 24, 1840.

Spence, Thomas Ara (nephew of John Selby Spence) (W Md.) Feb. 20, 1810–Nov. 10, 1877; House 1843–45.

Spencer, Ambrose (father of John Canfield Spencer) (– N.Y.) Dec. 13, 1765–March 13, 1848; House 1829–31.

Spencer, Elijah (– N.Y.) 1775–Dec. 15, 1852; House 1821–23.

Spencer, George Eliphaz (R Ala.) Nov. 1, 1836–Feb. 19, 1893; Senate July 13, 1868–79.

Spencer, George Lloyd (D Ark.) March 27, 1893–Jan. 14, 1981; Senate April 1, 1941–43.

Spencer, James Bradley (D N.Y.) April 26, 1781–March 26, 1848; House 1837–39.

Spencer, James Grafton (D Miss.) Sept. 13, 1844–Feb. 22, 1926; House 1895–97.

Spencer, John Canfield (son of Ambrose Spencer) (R N.Y.) Jan. 8, 1788–May 18, 1855; House 1817–19; Secy. of War Oct. 12, 1841–March 3, 1843; Secy. of the Treasury March 8, 1843–May 2, 1844.

Spencer, Richard (J Md.) Oct. 29, 1796–Sept. 3, 1868; House 1829–31.

Spencer, Selden Palmer (R Mo.) Sept. 16, 1862–May 16, 1925; Senate Nov. 6, 1918–May 16, 1925.

Spencer, William Brainerd (D La.) Feb. 5, 1835–Feb. 12, 1882; House June 8, 1876–Jan. 8, 1877.

Sperry, Lewis (D Conn.) Jan. 23, 1848–June 22, 1922; House 1891–95.

Sperry, Nehemiah Day (R Conn.) July 10, 1827–Nov. 13, 1911; House 1895–1911.

Spight, Thomas (D Miss.) Oct. 25, 1841–Jan. 5, 1924; House July 5, 1898–1911.

Spink, Cyrus (R Ohio) March 24, 1793–May 31, 1859; House March 4–May 31, 1859.

Spink, Solomon Lewis (R Dakota) March 20, 1831–Sept. 22, 1881; House (Terr. Del.) 1869–71.

Spinner, Francis Elias (R N.Y.) Jan. 21, 1802–Dec. 31, 1890; House 1855–61 (1855–57 Democrat).

Spinola, Francis Barretto (D N.Y.) March 19, 1821–April 14, 1891; House 1887–April 14, 1891.

Spong, William Belser Jr. (D Va.) Sept. 29, 1920–Oct. 8, 1997; Senate Dec. 31, 1966–73.

Spooner, Henry Joshua (R R.I.) Aug. 6, 1839–Feb. 9, 1918; House Dec. 5, 1881–91.

Spooner, John Coit (R Wis.) Jan. 6, 1843–June 11, 1919; Senate 1885–91, 1897–April 30, 1907.

Sprague, Charles Franklin (grandson of Peleg Sprague of Maine) (R Mass.) June 10, 1857–Jan. 30, 1902; House 1897–1901.

Sprague, Peleg (F N.H.) Dec. 10, 1756–April 20, 1800; House Dec. 15, 1797–99.

Sprague, Peleg (grandfather of Charles Franklin Sprague) (– Maine) April 27, 1793–Oct. 13, 1880; House 1825–29; Senate 1829–Jan. 1, 1835.

Sprague, William (W Mich.) Feb. 23, 1809–Sept. 19, 1868; House 1849–51.

Sprague, William (uncle of William Sprague, below) (W R.I.) Nov. 3, 1799–Oct. 19, 1856; House 1835–37; Senate Feb. 18, 1842–Jan. 17, 1844; Gov. May 2, 1838–May 1, 1839.

Sprague, William (nephew of William Sprague, above) (R R.I.) Sept. 12, 1830–Sept. 11, 1915; Senate 1863–75; Gov. May 29, 1860–March 3, 1863 (Unionist).

Sprague, William Peter (R Ohio) May 21, 1827–March 3, 1899; House 1871–75.

Spratt, John McKee Jr. (D S.C.) Nov. 1, 1942– ; House 1983– .

Sprigg, James Cresap (brother of Michael Cresap Sprigg) (W Ky.) 1802–Oct. 3, 1852; House 1841–43.

Sprigg, Michael Cresap (brother of James Cresap Sprigg) (J Md.) July 1, 1791–Dec. 18, 1845; House 1827–31.

Sprigg, Richard Jr. (nephew of Thomas Sprigg) (R Md.) ?–?; House May 5, 1796–99, 1801–Feb. 11, 1802.

Sprigg, Thomas (uncle of Richard Sprigg Jr.) (R Md.) 1747–Dec. 13, 1809; House 1793–97.

Spriggs, John Thomas (D N.Y.) April 5, 1825–Dec. 23, 1888; House 1883–87.

Springer, Raymond Smiley (R Ind.) April 26, 1882–Aug. 28, 1947; House 1939–Aug. 28, 1947.

Springer, William Lee (R Ill.) April 12, 1909–Sept. 20, 1992; House 1951–73.

Springer, William McKendree (D Ill.) May 30, 1836–Dec. 4, 1903; House 1875–95.

Sproul, Elliott Wilford (R Ill.) Dec. 28, 1856–June 22, 1935; House 1921–31.

Sproul, William Henry (R Kan.) Oct. 14, 1867–Dec. 27, 1932; House 1923–31.

Spruance, Presley (W Del.) Sept. 11, 1785–Feb. 13, 1863; Senate 1847–53.

Squire, Watson Carvosso (R Wash.) May 18, 1838–June 7, 1926; Senate Nov. 20, 1889–97; Gov. (Wash. Terr.) 1884–87.

Stabenow, Deborah (D Mich.) April 29, 1950– ; House 1997– .

Stack, Edmund John (D Ill.) Jan. 31, 1874–April 12, 1957; House 1911–13.

Stack, Edward John (D Fla.) April 29, 1910–Nov. 3, 1989; House 1979–81.

Stack, Michael Joseph (D Pa.) Sept. 29, 1888–Dec. 14, 1960; House 1935–39.

Stackhouse, Eli Thomas (D S.C.) March 27, 1824–June 14, 1892; House 1891–June 14, 1892.

Staebler, Neil Oliver (D Mich.) July 11, 1905– ; House 1963–65.

Stafford, Robert Theodore (R Vt.) Aug. 8, 1913– ; House 1961–Sept. 16, 1971; Senate Sept. 16, 1971–89; Chrmn. Senate Environment and Public Works 1981–87; Gov. Jan. 8, 1959–Jan. 5, 1961.

Stafford, William Henry (R Wis.) Oct. 12, 1869–April 22, 1957; House 1903–11, 1913–19, 1921–23, 1929–33.

Staggers, Harley Orrin (father of Harley Orrin Staggers Jr.) (D W.Va.) Aug. 3, 1907–Aug. 20, 1991; House 1949–81; Chrmn. House Interstate and Foreign Commerce 1966–81.

Staggers, Harley Orrin Jr. (son of Harley Orrin Staggers) (D W.Va.) Feb. 22, 1951– ; House 1983–93.

Stahle, James Alonzo (R Pa.) Jan. 11, 1829–Dec. 21, 1912; House 1895–97.

Stahlnecker, William Griggs (D N.Y.) June 20, 1849–March 26, 1902; House 1885–93.

Stalbaum, Lynn Ellsworth (D Wis.) May 15, 1920–June 17, 1999; House 1965–67.

Stalker, Gale Hamilton (R N.Y.) Nov. 7, 1889–Nov. 4, 1985; House 1923–35.

Stallings, Jesse Francis (D Ala.) April 4, 1856–March 18, 1928; House 1893–1901.

Stallings, Richard Howard (D Idaho) Oct. 10, 1940– ; House 1985–93.

Stallworth, James Adams (D Ala.) April 7, 1822–Aug. 31, 1861; House 1857–Jan. 21, 1861.

Stanard, Edwin Obed (R Mo.) Jan. 5, 1832–March 12, 1914; House 1873–75.

Stanbery, William (AJ Ohio) Aug. 10, 1788–Jan. 23, 1873; House Oct. 9, 1827–33 (Oct. 9, 1827–29 no party, 1829–31 Jacksonian).

Standifer, James (W Tenn.) ?–Aug. 20, 1837; House 1823–25 (no party), 1829–Aug. 20, 1837 (1829–35 Jacksonian, 1835–37 White supporter).

Standiford, Elisha David (D Ky.) Dec. 28, 1831–July 26, 1887; House 1873–75.

Stanfield, Robert Nelson (R Ore.) July 9, 1877–April 13 1945; Senate 1921–27.

Stanfill, William Abner (R Ky.) Jan. 16, 1892–June 12, 1971; Senate Nov. 19, 1945–Nov. 5, 1946.

Stanford, Leland (R Calif.) March 9, 1824–June 21, 1893; Senate 1885–June 21, 1893; Gov. Jan. 10, 1862–Dec. 10, 1863.

Stanford, Richard (grandfather of William Robert Webb) (R N.C.) March 2, 1767–April 9, 1816; House 1797–April 9, 1816.

Stangeland, Arlan Ingehart (R Minn.) Feb. 8, 1930– ; House March 1, 1977–91.

Stanley, Augustus Owsley (D Ky.) May 21, 1867–Aug. 12, 1958; House 1903–15; Senate May 19, 1919–25; Gov. Dec. 7, 1915–May 19, 1919.

Stanley, Thomas Bahnson (D Va.) July 16, 1890–July 10, 1970; House Nov. 5, 1946–Feb. 3, 1953; Chrmn. House Administration 1951–53; Gov. Jan. 20, 1954–Jan. 11, 1958.

Stanley, Winifred Claire (R N.Y.) Aug. 14, 1909–Feb. 29, 1996; House 1943–45.

Stanly, Edward (son of John Stanly) (W N.C.) Jan. 10, 1810–July 12, 1872; House 1837–43, 1849–53.

Stanly, John (father of Edward Stanly) (F N.C.) April 9, 1774–Aug. 2, 1834; House 1801–03, 1809–11.

Stanton, Benjamin (R Ohio) June 4, 1809–June 2, 1872; House 1851–53 (Whig), 1855–61.

Stanton, Frederick Perry (D Tenn.) Dec. 22, 1814–June 4, 1894; House 1845–55; Gov. (Kan. Terr.) 1858–61.

Stanton, James Vincent (D Ohio) Feb. 27, 1932– ; House 1971–77.

Stanton, John William (R Ohio) Feb. 20, 1924– ; House 1965–83.

Stanton, Joseph Jr. (R R.I.) July 19, 1739–1807; Senate June 7, 1790–93 (no party); House 1801–07.

Stanton, Richard Henry (D Ky.) Sept. 9, 1812–March 20, 1891; House 1849–55.

Stanton, William Henry (D Pa.) July 28, 1843–March 28, 1900; House Nov. 7, 1876–77.

Starin, John Henry (grandson of Thomas Sammons) (R N.Y.) Aug. 27, 1825–March 21, 1909; House 1877–81.

Stark, Benjamin (D Ore.) June 26, 1820–Oct. 10, 1898; Senate Oct. 29, 1861–Sept. 12, 1862.

Stark, Fortney Hillman "Pete" Jr. (D Calif.) Nov. 11, 1931– ; House 1973– ; Chrmn. House District of Columbia 1993–95.

Stark, William Ledyard (P Neb.) July 29, 1853–Nov. 11, 1922; House 1897–1903.

Starkey, Frank Thomas (D Minn.) Feb. 18, 1892–May 14, 1968; House 1945–47.

Starkweather, David Austin (D Ohio) Jan. 21, 1802–July 12, 1876; House 1839–41, 1845–47.

Starkweather, George Anson (D N.Y.) May 19, 1794–Oct. 15, 1879; House 1847–49.

Starkweather, Henry Howard (R Conn.) April 29, 1826–Jan. 28, 1876; House 1867–Jan. 28, 1876.

Starnes, Joe (D Ala.) March 31, 1895–Jan. 9, 1962; House 1935–45.

Starr, John Farson (R N.J.) March 25, 1818–Aug. 9, 1904; House 1863–67.

Staton, David Michael (R W.Va.) Feb. 11, 1940– ; House 1981–83.

Stauffer, Simon Walter (R Pa.) Aug. 13, 1888–Sept. 26, 1975; House 1953–55, 1957–59.

Steagall, Henry Bascom (D Ala.) May 19, 1873–Nov. 22, 1943; House 1915–Nov. 22, 1943.

Stearns, Asahel (F Mass.) June 17, 1774–Feb. 5, 1839; House 1815–17.

Stearns, Cliff (R Fla.) April 16, 1941– ; House 1989– .

Stearns, Foster Waterman (R N.H.) July 29, 1881–June 4, 1956; House 1939–45.

Stearns, Ozora Pierson (R Minn.) Jan. 15, 1831–June 2, 1896; Senate Jan. 23–March 3, 1871.

Stebbins, Henry George (D N.Y.) Sept. 15, 1811–Dec. 9, 1881; House 1863–Oct. 24, 1864.

Steck, Daniel Frederic (D Iowa) Dec. 16, 1881–Dec. 31, 1950; Senate April 12, 1926–31.

Stedman, Charles Manly (D N.C.) Jan. 29, 1841–Sept. 23, 1930; House 1911–Sept. 23, 1930.

Stedman, William (F Mass.) Jan. 21, 1765–Aug. 31, 1831; House 1803–July 16, 1810.

Steed, Thomas Jefferson (D Okla.) March 2, 1904–June 8, 1983; House 1949–81.

Steele, George Washington (R Ind.) Dec. 13, 1839–July 12, 1922; House 1881–89, 1895–1903; Gov. (Okla. Terr.) 1890–91.

Steele, Henry Joseph (D Pa.) May 10, 1860–March 19, 1933; House 1915–21.

Steele, John (– N.C.) Nov. 1, 1764–Aug. 14, 1815; House April 19, 1790–93.

Steele, John Benedict (D N.Y.) March 28, 1814–Sept. 24, 1866; House 1861–65.

Steele, John Nevett (AJ Md.) Feb. 22, 1796–Aug. 13, 1853; House May 29, 1834–37.

Steele, Leslie Jasper (D Ga.) Nov. 21, 1868–July 24, 1929; House 1927–July 24, 1929.

Steele, Robert Hampton (R Conn.) Nov. 3, 1938– ; House Nov. 3, 1970–75.

Steele, Thomas Jefferson (D Iowa) March 19, 1853–March 20, 1920; House 1915–17.

Steele, Walter Leak (D N.C.) April 18, 1823–Oct. 16, 1891; House 1877–81.

Steele, William Gaston (D N.J.) Dec. 17, 1820–April 22, 1892; House 1861–65.

Steele, William Randolph (D Wyo) July 24, 1842–Nov. 30, 1901; House (Terr. Del.) 1873–77.

Steelman, Alan Watson (R Texas) March 15, 1942– ; House 1973–77.

Steenerson, Halvor (R Minn.) June 30, 1852–Nov. 22, 1926; House 1903–23.

Steenrod, Lewis (D Va.) May 27, 1810–Oct. 3, 1862; House 1839–45.

Steers, Newton Ivan Jr. (R Md.) Jan. 13, 1917–Feb. 11, 1993; House 1977–79.

Stefan, Karl (R Neb.) March 1, 1884–Oct. 2, 1951; House 1935–Oct. 2, 1951.

Steiger, Sam (R Ariz.) March 10, 1929– ; House 1967–77.

Steiger, William Albert (R Wis.) May 15, 1938–Dec. 4, 1978; House 1967–Dec. 4, 1978.

Steiwer, Frederick (R Ore.) Oct. 13, 1883–Feb. 3, 1939; Senate 1927–Jan. 31, 1938.

Stenger, William Shearer (D Pa.) Feb. 13, 1840–March 29, 1918; House 1875–79.

Stengle, Charles Irwin (D N.Y.) Dec. 5, 1869–Nov. 23, 1953; House 1923–25.

Stenholm, Charles Walter (D Texas) Oct. 26, 1938– ; House 1979– .

Stennis, John Cornelius (D Miss.) Aug. 3, 1901–April 23, 1995; Senate Nov. 5, 1947–89; Chrmn. Senate Select Committee on Standards and Conduct 1966–75; Chrmn. Senate Armed Services 1969–81; elected Pres. pro tempore Jan. 6, 1987; Chrmn. Senate Appropriations 1987–89.

Stephens, Abraham P. (D N.Y.) Feb. 18, 1796–Nov. 25, 1859; House 1851–53.

Stephens, Alexander Hamilton (great-great-uncle of Robert Grier Stephens Jr.) (D Ga.) Feb. 11, 1812–March 4, 1883; House Oct. 2, 1843–59 (Oct. 2, 1843–51 Whig, 1853–55 Whig, 1851–53 Unionist), Dec. 1, 1873–Nov. 4, 1882; Gov. Nov. 4, 1882–March 4, 1883.

Stephens, Ambrose Everett Burnside (R Ohio) June 3, 1862–Feb. 12, 1927; House 1919–Feb. 12, 1927.

Stephens, Dan Voorhees (D Neb.) Nov. 4, 1868–Jan. 13, 1939; House Nov. 7, 1911–19.

Stephens, Hubert Durrett (D Miss.) July 2, 1875–March 14, 1946; House 1911–21; Senate 1923–35.

Stephens, John Hall (D Texas) Nov. 22, 1847–Nov. 18, 1924; House 1897–1917.

Stephens, Philander (J Pa.) 1788–July 8, 1842; House 1829–33.

Stephens, Robert Grier Jr. (great-great-nephew of Alexander Hamilton Stephens) (D Ga.) Aug. 14, 1913– ; House 1961–77.

Stephens, William Dennison (P Calif.) Dec. 26, 1859–April 25, 1944; House 1911–July 22, 1916 (1911–15 Republican); Gov. March 15, 1917–Jan. 9, 1923 (Republican).

Stephenson, Benjamin (D Ill.) ?–Oct. 10, 1822; House (Terr. Del.) Sept. 3, 1814–17.

Stephenson, Isaac (brother of Samuel Merritt Stephenson) (R Wis.) June 18, 1829–March 15, 1918; House 1883–89; Senate May 17, 1907–15.

Stephenson, James (F Va.) March 20, 1764–Aug. 7, 1833; House 1803–05, 1809–11, Oct. 28, 1822–25.

Stephenson, Samuel Merritt (brother of Isaac Stephenson) (R Mich.) Dec. 23, 1831–July 31, 1907; House 1889–97.

Sterett, Samuel (– Md.) 1758–July 12, 1833; House 1791–93.

Sterigere, John Benton (J Pa.) July 31, 1793–Oct. 13, 1852; House 1827–31 (1827–29 no party).

Sterling, Ansel (brother of Micah Sterling) (– Conn.) Feb. 3, 1782–Nov. 6, 1853; House 1821–25.

Sterling, Bruce Foster (D Pa.) Sept. 28, 1870–April 26, 1945; House 1917–19.

Sterling, John Allen (brother of Thomas Sterling) (R Ill.) Feb. 1, 1857–Oct. 17, 1918; House 1903–13, 1915–Oct. 17, 1918.

Sterling, Micah (brother of Ansel Sterling) (– N.Y.) Nov. 5, 1784–April 11, 1844; House 1821–23.

Sterling, Thomas (brother of John Allen Sterling) (R S.D.) Feb. 21, 1851–Aug. 26, 1930; Senate 1913–25.

Stetson, Charles (D Maine) Nov. 2, 1801–March 27, 1863; House 1849–51.

Stetson, Lemuel (D N.Y.) March 13, 1804–May 17, 1868; House 1843–45.

Stevens, Aaron Fletcher (R N.H.) Aug. 9, 1819–May 10, 1887; House 1867–71.

Stevens, Bradford Newcomb (D Ill.) Jan. 3, 1813–Nov. 10, 1885; House 1871–73.

Stevens, Charles Abbot (brother of Moses Tyler Stevens, cousin of Isaac Ingalls Stevens) (R Mass.) Aug. 9, 1816–April 7, 1892; House Jan. 27–March 3, 1875.

Stevens, Frederick Clement (R Minn.) Jan. 1, 1861–July 1, 1923; House 1897–1915.

Stevens, Hestor Lockhart (D Mich.) Oct. 1, 1803–May 7, 1864; House 1853–55.

Stevens, Hiram Sanford (D Ariz.) March 20, 1832–March 22, 1893; House (Terr. Del.) 1875–79.

Stevens, Isaac Ingalls (cousin of Charles Abbot Stevens and Moses Tyler Stevens) (D Wash.) March 25, 1818–Sept. 1, 1862; House (Terr. Del.) 1857–61; Gov. (Wash. Terr.) 1853–57.

Stevens, James (– Conn.) July 4, 1768–April 4, 1835; House 1819–21.

Stevens, Moses Tyler (brother of Charles Abbot Stevens, cousin of Isaac Ingalls Stevens) (D Mass.) Oct. 10, 1825–March 25, 1907; House 1891–95.

Stevens, Raymond Bartlett (D N.H.) June 18, 1874–May 18, 1942; House 1913–15.

Stevens, Robert Smith (D N.Y.) March 27, 1824–Feb. 23, 1893; House 1883–85.

Stevens, Thaddeus (R Pa.) April 4, 1792–Aug. 11, 1868; House 1849–53 (Whig), 1859–Aug. 11, 1868.

Stevens, Theodore F. "Ted" (R Alaska) Nov. 18, 1923– ; Senate Dec. 24, 1968– ; Chrmn. Senate Select Committee on Ethics 1983–85; Chrmn. Senate Rules and Administration 1995–96; Chrmn. Senate Governmental Affairs 1996–97; Chrmn. Senate Appropriations 1997– .

Stevenson, Adlai Ewing (great-grandfather of Adlai Ewing Stevenson III, grandfather of Gov. Adlai Ewing Stevenson II of Ill.) (D Ill.) Oct. 23, 1835–June 14, 1914; House 1875–77, 1879–81; Vice President 1893–97.

Stevenson, Adlai Ewing III (great-grandson of Adlai Ewing Stevenson, son of Adlai Ewing Stevenson II of Ill.) (D Ill.) Oct. 10, 1930– ; Senate Nov. 17, 1970–81; Chrmn. Senate Select Committee on Ethics 1977–81.

Stevenson, Andrew (father of John White Stevenson) (J Va.) Jan. 21, 1784–Jan. 25, 1857; House 1821–June 2, 1834 (1821–29 no party); Speaker Dec. 3, 1827–29, Dec. 7, 1829–31, Dec. 5, 1831–33, Dec. 2, 1833–June 2, 1834.

Stevenson, James S. (– Pa.) 1780–Oct. 16, 1831; House 1825–29.

Stevenson, Job Evans (R Ohio) Feb. 10, 1832–July 24, 1922; House 1869–73.

Stevenson, John White (son of Andrew Stevenson) (D Ky.) May 4, 1812–Aug. 10, 1886; House 1857–61; Senate 1871–77; Gov. Sept. 8, 1867–Feb. 13, 1871.

Stevenson, William Francis (D S.C.) Nov. 23, 1861–Feb. 12, 1942; House 1917–33.

Stevenson, William Henry (R Wis.) Sept. 23, 1891–March 19, 1978; House 1941–49.

Steward, Lewis (D Ill.) Nov. 21, 1824–Aug. 27, 1896; House 1891–93.

Stewart, Alexander (R Wis.) Sept. 12, 1829–May 24, 1912; House 1895–1901.

Stewart, Andrew (father of Andrew Stewart, below) (W Pa.) June 11, 1791–July 16, 1872; House 1821–29 (no party), 1831–35 (Anti-Mason), 1843–49.

Stewart, Andrew (son of Andrew Stewart, above) (R Pa.) April 6, 1836–Nov. 9, 1903; House 1891–Feb. 26, 1892.

Stewart, Arthur Thomas "Tom" (D Tenn.) Jan. 11, 1892–Oct. 10, 1972; Senate Jan. 16, 1939–49.

Stewart, Bennett McVey (D Ill.) Aug. 6, 1912–April 26, 1988; House 1979–81.

Stewart, Charles (D Texas) May 30, 1836–Sept. 21, 1895; House 1883–93.

Stewart, David (W Md.) Sept. 13, 1800–Jan. 5, 1858; Senate Dec. 6, 1849–Jan. 12, 1850.

Stewart, David Wallace (R Iowa) Jan. 22, 1887–Feb. 10, 1974; Senate Aug. 7, 1926–27.

Stewart, Donald Wilbur (D Ala.) Feb. 8, 1940– ; Senate Nov. 7, 1978–81.

Stewart, Jacob Henry (R Minn.) Jan. 15, 1829–Aug. 25, 1884; House 1877–79.

Stewart, James (F N.C.) Nov. 11, 1775–Dec. 29, 1821; House Jan. 5, 1818–19.

Stewart, James Augustus (D Md.) Nov. 24, 1808–April 3, 1879; House 1855–61.

Stewart, James Fleming (R N.J.) June 15, 1851–Jan. 21, 1904; House 1895–1903.

Stewart, John (R Pa.) ?–1820; House Jan. 15, 1801–05.

Stewart, John (D Conn.) Feb. 10, 1795–Sept. 16, 1860; House 1843–45.

Stewart, John David (D Ga.) Aug. 2, 1833–Jan. 28, 1894; House 1887–91.

Stewart, John George (R Del.) June 2, 1890–May 24, 1970; House 1935–37.

Stewart, John Knox (R N.Y.) Oct. 20, 1853–June 27, 1919; House 1899–1903.

Stewart, John Wolcott (R Vt.) Nov. 24, 1825–Oct. 29, 1915; House 1883–91; Senate March 24–Oct. 21, 1908; Gov. Oct. 6, 1870–Oct. 3, 1872.

Stewart, Paul (D Okla.) Feb. 27, 1892–Nov. 13, 1950; House 1943–47.

Stewart, Percy Hamilton (D N.J.) Jan. 10, 1867–June 30, 1951; House Dec. 1, 1931–33.

Stewart, Thomas Elliott (CR N.Y.) Sept. 22, 1824–Jan. 9, 1904; House 1867–69.

Stewart, William (R Pa.) Sept. 10, 1810–Oct. 17, 1876; House 1857–61.

Stewart, William Morris (Sil.R Nev.) Aug. 9, 1827–April 23, 1909; Senate Dec. 15, 1864–75 (Republican), 1887–1905 (1887–93 Republican).

Stigler, William Grady (D Okla.) July 7, 1891–Aug. 21, 1952; House March 28, 1944–Aug. 21, 1952.

Stiles, John Dodson (D Pa.) Jan. 15, 1822–Oct. 29, 1896; House June 3, 1862–65, 1869–71.

Stiles, William Henry (grandson of Joseph Clay) (D Ga.) Jan. 1, 1808–Dec. 20, 1865; House 1843–45.

Stillwell, Thomas Neel (R Ind.) Aug. 29, 1830–Jan. 14, 1874; House 1865–67.

Stiness, Walter Russell (R R.I.) March 13, 1854–March 17, 1924; House 1915–23.

Stinson, K. William (R Wash.) April 20, 1930– ; House 1963–65.

Stivers, Moses Dunning (R N.Y.) Dec. 30, 1828–Feb. 2, 1895; House 1889–91.

Stobbs, George Russell (R Mass.) Feb. 7, 1877–Dec. 23, 1966; House 1925–31.

Stockbridge, Francis Brown (R Mich.) April 9, 1826–April 30, 1894; Senate 1887–April 30, 1894.

Stockbridge, Henry Jr. (R Md.) Sept. 18, 1856–March 22, 1924; House 1889–91.

Stockdale, Thomas Ringland (D Miss.) March 28, 1828–Jan. 8, 1899; House 1887–95.

Stockman, David Alan (R Mich.) Nov. 10, 1946– ; House 1977–Jan. 27, 1981.

Stockman, Lowell (R Ore.) April 12, 1901–Aug. 9, 1962; House 1943–53.

Stockman, Steve (R Texas) Nov. 14, 1956– ; House 1995–97.

Stockslager, Strother Madison (D Ind.) May 7, 1842–June 1, 1930; House 1881–85.

Stockton, John Potter (son of Robert Field Stockton, grandson of Richard Stockton) (D N.J.) Aug. 2, 1826–Jan. 22, 1900; Senate March 15, 1865–March 27, 1866, 1869–75.

Stockton, Richard (father of Robert Field Stockton, grandfather of John Potter Stockton) (F N.J.) April 17, 1764–March 7, 1828; Senate Nov. 12, 1796–99; House 1813–15.

Stockton, Robert Field (son of Richard Stockton, father of John Potter Stockton) (D N.J.) Aug. 20, 1795–Oct. 7, 1866; Senate 1851–Jan. 10, 1853.

Stoddard, Ebenezer (– Conn.) May 6, 1785–Aug. 19, 1847; House 1821–25.

Stoddert, John Truman (J Md.) Oct. 1, 1790–July 19, 1870; House 1833–35.

Stokely, Samuel (W Ohio) Jan. 25, 1796–May 23, 1861; House 1841–43.

Stokes, Edward Lowber (R Pa.) Sept. 29, 1880–Nov. 8, 1964; House Nov. 3, 1931–35.

Stokes, James William (D S.C.) Dec. 12, 1853–July 6, 1901; House 1895–June 1, 1896, Nov. 3, 1896–July 6, 1901.

Stokes, Louis (D Ohio) Feb. 23, 1925– ; House 1969–99; Chrmn. House Standards of Official Conduct 1981–85, 1991–93; Chrmn. House Permanent Select Committee on Intelligence 1987–89.

Stokes, Montfort (– N.C.) March 12, 1762–Nov. 4, 1842; Senate Dec. 4, 1816–23; Gov. Dec. 18, 1830–Dec. 6, 1832.

Stokes, William Brickly (R Tenn.) Sept. 9, 1814–March 14, 1897; House 1859–61 (Opposition Party), July 24, 1866–71 (July 24, 1866–67 Unconditional Unionist).

Stoll, Philip Henry (D S.C.) Nov. 5, 1874–Oct. 29, 1958; House Oct. 7, 1919–23.

Stone, Alfred Parish (D Ohio) June 28, 1813–Aug. 2, 1865; House Oct. 8, 1844–45.

Stone, Charles Warren (R Pa.) June 29, 1843–Aug. 15, 1912; House Nov. 4, 1890–99.

Stone, Claudius Ulysses (D Ill.) May 11, 1879–Nov. 13, 1957; House 1911–17.

Stone, David (R N.C.) Feb. 17, 1770–Oct. 7, 1818; House 1799–1801 (no party); Senate 1801–Feb. 17, 1807, 1813–Dec. 24, 1814; Gov. Dec. 12, 1808–Dec. 5, 1810 (Democratic Republican).

Stone, Eben Francis (R Mass.) Aug. 3, 1822–Jan. 22, 1895; House 1881–87.

Stone, Frederick (grandson of Michael Jenifer Stone) (D Md.) Feb. 7, 1820–Oct. 17, 1899; House 1867–71.

Stone, James W. (D Ky.) 1813–Oct. 13, 1854; House 1843–45, 1851–53.

Stone, John Wesley (R Mich.) July 18, 1838–March 24, 1922; House 1877–81.

Stone, Joseph Champlin (R Iowa) July 30, 1829–Dec. 3, 1902; House 1877–79.

Stone, Michael Jenifer (grandfather of Frederick Stone) (– Md.) 1747–1812; House 1789–91.

Stone, Richard Bernard (D Fla.) Sept. 22, 1928– ; Senate Jan. 1, 1975–Dec. 31, 1980.

Stone, Ulysses Stevens (R Okla.) Dec. 17, 1878–Dec. 8, 1962; House 1929–31.

Stone, William (– Tenn.) Jan. 26, 1791–Feb. 18, 1853; House Sept. 14, 1837–39.

Stone, William Alexis (R Pa.) April 18, 1846–March 1, 1920; House 1891–Nov. 9, 1898; Gov. Jan. 17, 1899–Jan. 20, 1903.

Stone, William Henry (D Mo.) Nov. 7, 1828–July 9, 1901; House 1873–77.

Stone, William Joel (D Mo.) May 7, 1848–April 14, 1918; House 1885–91; Senate 1903–April 14, 1918; Gov. Jan. 9, 1893–Jan. 11, 1897.

Stone, William Johnson (D Ky.) June 26, 1841–March 12, 1923; House 1885–95.

Storer, Bellamy (father of Bellamy Storer, below) (W Ohio) March 26, 1796–June 1, 1875; House 1835–37.

Storer, Bellamy (son of Bellamy Storer, above, uncle of Nicholas Longworth) (R Ohio) Aug. 28, 1847–Nov. 12, 1922; House 1891–95.

Storer, Clement (R N.H.) Sept. 20, 1760–Nov. 21, 1830; House 1807–09; Senate June 27, 1817–19.

Storke, Thomas More (D Calif.) Nov. 23, 1876–Oct. 12, 1971; Senate Nov. 9, 1938–39.

Storm, Frederic (R N.Y.) July 2, 1844–June 9, 1935; House 1901–03.

Storm, John Brutzman (D Pa.) Sept. 19, 1838–Aug. 13, 1901; House 1871–75, 1883–87.

Storrs, Henry Randolph (brother of William Lucius Storrs) (F N.Y.) Sept. 3, 1787–July 29, 1837; House 1817–21, 1823–31.

Storrs, William Lucius (brother of Henry Randolph Storrs) (W Conn.) March 25, 1795–June 25, 1861; House 1829–33 (no party), 1839–June 1840.

Story, Joseph (R Mass.) Sept. 18, 1779–Sept. 10, 1845; House May 23, 1808–09; Assoc. Justice Supreme Court Feb. 3, 1812–Sept. 10, 1845.

Stoughton, William Lewis (R Mich.) March 20, 1827–June 6, 1888; House 1869–73.

Stout, Byron Gray (D Mich.) Jan. 12, 1829–June 19, 1896; House 1891–93.

Stout, Lansing (D Ore.) March 27, 1828–March 4, 1871; House 1859–61.

Stout, Tom (D Mont.) May 20, 1879–Dec. 26, 1965; House 1913–17.

Stover, John Hubler (R Mo.) April 24, 1833–Oct. 27, 1889; House Dec. 7, 1868–69.

Stow, Silas (R N.Y.) Dec. 21, 1773–Jan. 19, 1827; House 1811–13.

Stowell, William Henry Harrison (R Va.) July 26, 1840–April 27, 1922; House 1871–77.

Stower, John G. (J N.Y.) ?–?; House 1827–29.

Strader, Peter Wilson (D Ohio) Nov. 6, 1818–Feb. 25, 1881; House 1869–71.

Strait, Horace Burton (R Minn.) Jan. 26, 1835–Feb. 25, 1894; House 1873–79, 1881–87.

Strait, Thomas Jefferson (D S.C.) Dec. 25, 1846–April 18, 1924; House 1893–99.

Stranahan, James Samuel Thomas (W N.Y.) April 25, 1808–Sept. 3, 1898; House 1855–57.

Strang, Michael Lathrop (R Col.) June 17, 1929– ; House 1985–87.

Strange, Robert (D N.C.) Sept. 20, 1796–Feb. 19, 1854; Senate Dec. 5, 1836–Nov. 16, 1840.

Stratton, Charles Creighton (uncle of Benjamin Franklin Howey) (W N.J.) March 6, 1796–March 30, 1859; House 1837–39, 1841–43; Gov. Jan. 21, 1845–Jan. 18, 1848.

Stratton, John (F Va.) Aug. 19, 1769–May 10, 1804; House 1801–03.

Stratton, John Leake Newbold (R N.J.) Nov. 27, 1817–May 17, 1899; House 1859–63.

Stratton, Nathan Taylor (D N.J.) March 17, 1813–March 9, 1887; House 1851–55.

Stratton, Samuel Studdiford (D N.Y.) Sept. 27, 1916–Sept. 13, 1990; House 1959–89.

Stratton, William Grant (R Ill.) Feb. 26, 1914– ; House 1941–43, 1947–49; Gov. Jan. 12, 1953–Jan. 9, 1961.

Straub, Christian Markle (D Pa.) 1804–?; House 1853–55.

Straus, Isidor (D N.Y.) Feb. 6, 1845–April 15, 1912; House Jan. 30, 1894–95.

Strawbridge, James Dale (R Pa.) April 7, 1824–July 19, 1890; House 1873–75.

Street, Randall S. (– N.Y.) 1780–Nov. 21, 1841; House 1819–21.

Strickland, Randolph (R Mich.) Feb. 4, 1823–May 5, 1880; House 1869–71.

Strickland, Ted (D Ohio) Aug. 4, 1941– ; House 1993–95, 1997– .

Stringer, Lawrence Beaumont (D Ill.) Feb. 24, 1866–Dec. 5, 1942; House 1913–15.

Stringfellow, Douglas R. (R Utah) Sept. 24, 1922–Oct. 19, 1966; House 1953–55.

Strode, Jesse Burr (R Neb.) Feb. 18, 1845–Nov. 10, 1924; House 1895–99.

Strohm, John (W Pa.) Oct. 16, 1793–Sept. 12, 1884; House 1845–49.

Strong, Caleb (– Mass.) Jan. 9, 1745–Nov. 7, 1819; Senate 1789–June 1, 1796; Gov. May 30, 1800–May 29, 1807, June 5, 1812–May 30, 1816; Cont. Cong. (elected but did not attend) 1780.

Strong, James (– N.Y.) 1783–Aug. 8, 1847; House 1819–21, 1823–31.

Strong, James George (R Kan.) April 23, 1870–Jan. 11, 1938; House 1919–33.

Strong, Julius Levi (R Conn.) Nov. 8, 1828–Sept. 7, 1872; House 1869–Sept. 7, 1872.

Strong, Luther Martin (R Ohio) June 23, 1838–April 26, 1903; House 1893–97.

Strong, Nathan Leroy (R Pa.) Nov. 12, 1859–Dec. 14, 1939; House 1917–35.

Strong, Selah Brewster (D N.Y.) May 1, 1792–Nov. 29, 1872; House 1843–45.

Strong, Solomon (F Mass.) March 2, 1780–Sept. 16, 1850; House 1815–19.

Strong, Stephen (D N.Y.) Oct. 11, 1791–April 15, 1866; House 1845–47.

Strong, Sterling Price (D Texas) Aug. 17, 1862–March 28, 1936; House 1933–35.

Strong, Theron Rudd (cousin of William Strong of Pa.) (D N.Y.) Nov. 7, 1802–May 14, 1873; House 1839–41.

Strong, William (R Vt.) 1763–Jan. 28, 1840; House 1811–15, 1819–21.

Strong, William (cousin of Theron Rudd Strong) (D Pa.) May 6, 1808–Aug. 19, 1895; House 1847–51; Assoc. Justice Supreme Court March 14, 1870–Dec. 14, 1880.

Strother, George French (father of James French Strother of Va., great-grandfather of James French Strother of W.Va.) (R Va.) 1783–Nov. 28, 1840; House 1817–Feb. 10, 1820.

Strother, James French (son of George French Strother, grandfather of James French Strother, below) (W Va.) Sept. 4, 1811–Sept. 20, 1860; House 1851–53.

Strother, James French (grandson of James French Strother, above, great-grandson of George French Strother) (R W.Va.) June 29, 1868–April 10, 1930; House 1925–29.

Strouse, Myer (D Pa.) Dec. 16, 1825–Feb. 11, 1878; House 1863–67.

Strowd, William Franklin (P N.C.) Dec. 7, 1832–Dec. 12, 1911; House 1895–99.

Struble, Isaac S. (R Iowa) Nov. 3, 1843–Feb. 17, 1913; House 1883–91.

Strudwick, William Francis (F N.C.) ?–1812; House Nov. 28, 1796–97.

Stuart, Alexander Hugh Holmes (cousin of Archibald Stuart) (W Va.) April 2, 1807–Feb. 13, 1891; House 1841–43; Secy. of the Interior Sept. 12, 1850–March 7, 1853.

Stuart, Andrew (D Ohio) Aug. 3, 1823–April 30, 1872; House 1853–55.

Stuart, Archibald (cousin of Alexander Hugh Holmes Stuart) (D Va.) Dec. 2, 1795–Sept. 20, 1855; House 1837–39.

Stuart, Charles Edward (D Mich.) Nov. 25, 1810–May 19, 1887; House Dec. 6, 1847–49, 1851–53; Senate 1853–59; elected Pres. pro tempore June 9, 1856.

Stuart, David (D Mich.) March 12, 1816–Sept. 12, 1868; House 1853–55.

Stuart, John Todd (D Ill.) Nov. 10, 1807–Nov. 23, 1885; House 1839–43 (Whig), 1863–65.

Stuart, Philip (F Md.) 1760–Aug. 14, 1830; House 1811–19.

Stubblefield, Frank Albert (D Ky.) April 5, 1907–Oct. 14, 1977; House 1959–Dec. 31, 1974.

Stubbs, Henry Elbert (D Calif.) March 4, 1881–Feb. 28, 1937; House 1933–Feb. 28, 1937.

Stuckey, Williamson Sylvester Jr. (D Ga.) May 25, 1935– ; House 1967–77.

Studds, Gerry Eastman (D Mass.) May 12, 1937– ; House 1973–97; Chrmn. House Merchant Marine and Fisheries 1992–93.

Studley, Elmer Ebenezer (D N.Y.) Sept. 24, 1869–Sept. 6, 1942; House 1933–35.

Stull, Howard William (R Pa.) April 11, 1876–April 22, 1949; House April 26, 1932–33.

Stump, Herman (D Md.) Aug. 8, 1837–Jan. 9, 1917; House 1889–93.

Stump, Robert Lee "Bob" (R Ariz.) April 4, 1927– ; House 1977– (1977–83 Democrat); Chrmn. House Veterans' Affairs 1995– .

Stupak, Bart (D Mich.) Feb. 29, 1952– ; House 1993– .

Sturgeon, Daniel (D Pa.) Oct. 27, 1789–July 3, 1878; Senate Jan. 14, 1840–51.

Sturges, Jonathan (father of Lewis Burr Sturges) (– Conn.) Aug. 23, 1740–Oct. 4, 1819; House 1789–93; Cont. Cong. 1786.

Sturges, Lewis Burr (son of Jonathan Sturges) (F Conn.) March 15, 1763–March 30, 1844; House Sept. 16, 1805–17.

Sturgiss, George Cookman (R W.Va.) Aug. 16, 1842–Feb. 26, 1925; House 1907–11.

Sturtevant, John Cirby (R Pa.) Feb. 20, 1835–Dec. 20, 1912; House 1897–99.

Sullivan, Christopher Daniel (D N.Y.) July 14, 1870–Aug. 3, 1942; House 1917–41.

Sullivan, George (F N.H.) Aug. 29, 1771–April 14, 1838; House 1811–13.

Sullivan, John Andrew (D Mass.) May 10, 1868–May 31, 1927; House 1903–07.

Sullivan, John Berchmans (husband of Leonor Kretzer Sullivan) (D Mo.) Oct. 10, 1897–Jan. 29, 1951; House 1941–43, 1945–47, 1949–Jan. 29, 1951.

Sullivan, Leonor Kretzer (wife of John Berchmans Sullivan) (D Mo.) Aug. 21, 1902–Sept. 1, 1988; House 1953–77; Chrmn. House Merchant Marine and Fisheries 1973–77.

Sullivan, Maurice Joseph (D Nev.) Dec. 7, 1884–Aug. 9, 1953; House 1943–45.

Sullivan, Patrick Joseph (R Wyo.) March 17, 1865–April 8, 1935; Senate Dec. 5, 1929–Nov. 20, 1930.

Sullivan, Patrick Joseph (R Pa.) Oct. 12, 1877–Dec. 31, 1946; House 1929–33.

Sullivan, Timothy Daniel (D N.Y.) July 23, 1862–Aug. 31, 1913; House 1903–July 27, 1906 (also elected to the term beginning 1913 but never took his seat).

Sullivan, William Van Amberg (D Miss.) Dec. 18, 1857–March 21, 1918; House 1897–May 31, 1898; Senate May 31, 1898–1901.

Sulloway, Cyrus Adams (R N.H.) June 8, 1839–March 11, 1917; House 1895–1913, 1915–March 11, 1917.

Sulzer, Charles August (brother of William Sulzer) (D Alaska) Feb. 24, 1879–April 28, 1919; House (Terr Del.) 1917–Jan. 7, 1919, March 4–April 28, 1919.

Sulzer, William (brother of Charles August Sulzer) (D N.Y.) March 18, 1863–Nov. 6, 1941; House 1895–Dec. 31, 1912; Gov. Jan. 1–Oct. 17, 1913.

Summers, George William (W Va.) March 4, 1804–Sept. 19, 1868; House 1841–45.

Summers, John William (R Wash.) April 29, 1870–Sept. 25, 1937; House 1919–33.

Sumner, Charles (R Mass.) Jan. 6, 1811–March 11, 1874; Senate April 24, 1851–March 11, 1874 (1851–57 Free-Soiler).

Sumner, Charles Allen (D Calif.) Aug. 2, 1835–Jan. 31, 1903; House 1883–85.

Sumner, Daniel Hadley (D Wis.) Sept. 15, 1837–May 29, 1903; House 1883–85.

Sumner, Jessie (R Ill.) July 17, 1898–Aug. 10, 1994; House 1939–47.

Sumners, Hatton William (D Texas) May 30, 1875–April 19, 1962; House 1913–47.

Sumter, Thomas (grandfather of Thomas De Lage Sumter) (R S.C.) Aug. 14, 1734–June 1, 1832; House 1789–93 (no party), 1797–Dec. 15, 1801; Senate Dec. 15, 1801–Dec. 16, 1810; Cont. Cong. (elected but did not attend) 1783.

Sumter, Thomas De Lage (grandson of Thomas Sumter) (D S.C.) Nov. 14, 1809–July 2, 1874; House 1839–43.

Sundquist, Donald Kenneth (R Tenn.) March 15, 1936– ; House 1983–95; Gov. Jan. 21, 1995– .

Sundstrom, Frank Leander (R N.J.) Jan. 5, 1901–May 23, 1980; House 1943–49.

Sunia, Fofo Iosefa Fiti (D American Samoa) March 13, 1937– ; House 1981–89.

Sununu, John (R N.H.) Sept. 10, 1964– ; House 1997– .

Sutherland, Daniel Alexander (R Alaska) April 17, 1869–March 24, 1955; House (Terr. Del.) 1921–31.

Sutherland, George (R Utah) March 25, 1862–July 18, 1942; House 1901–03; Senate 1905–17; Assoc. Justice Supreme Court Oct. 2, 1922–Jan. 17, 1938.

Sutherland, Howard (R W.Va.) Sept. 8, 1865–March 12, 1950; House 1913–17; Senate 1917–23.

Sutherland, Jabez Gridley (D Mich.) Oct. 6, 1825–Nov. 20, 1902; House 1871–73.

Sutherland, Joel Barlow (J Pa.) Feb. 26, 1792–Nov. 15, 1861; House 1827–37.

Sutherland, Josiah (D N.Y.) June 12, 1804–May 25, 1887; House 1851–53.

Sutherland, Roderick Dhu (P Neb.) April 27, 1862–Oct. 18, 1915; House 1897–1901.

Sutphin, William Halstead (D N.J.) Aug. 30, 1887–Oct. 14, 1972; House 1931–43.

Sutton, James Patrick "Pat" (D Tenn.) Oct. 31, 1915– ; House 1949–55.

Swan, Samuel (– N.J.) 1771–Aug. 24, 1844; House 1821–31.

Swank, Fletcher B. (D Okla.) April 24, 1875–March 16, 1950; House 1921–29, 1931–35.

Swann, Edward (D N.Y.) March 10, 1862–Sept. 19, 1945; House Nov. 4, 1902–03.

Swann, Thomas (D Md.) Feb. 3, 1809–July 24, 1883; House 1869–79; Gov. Jan. 10, 1866–Jan. 13, 1869 (Union Democrat).

Swanson, Charles Edward (R Iowa) Jan. 3, 1879–Aug. 22, 1970; House 1929–33.

Swanson, Claude Augustus (D Va.) March 31, 1862–July 7, 1939; House 1893–Jan. 30, 1906; Senate Aug. 1, 1910–33; Gov. Feb. 1, 1906–Feb. 1, 1910; Secy. of the Navy March 4, 1933–July 7, 1939.

Swanwick, John (R Pa.) 1740–Aug. 1, 1798; House 1795–Aug. 1, 1798.

Swart, Peter (R N.Y.) July 5, 1752–Nov. 3, 1829; House 1807–09.

Swartz, Joshua William (R Pa.) June 9, 1867–May 27, 1959; House 1925–27.

Swasey, John Philip (R Maine) Sept. 4, 1839–May 27, 1928; House Nov. 3, 1908–11.

Swearingen, Henry (D Ohio) about 1792–?; House Dec. 3, 1838–41.

Sweat, Lorenzo De Medici (D Maine) May 26, 1818–July 26, 1898; House 1863–65.

Sweeney, David McCann "Mac" (R Texas) Sept. 15, 1955– ; House 1985–89.

Sweeney, John E. (R N.Y.) Aug. 9, 1955– ; House 1999– .

Sweeney, Martin Leonard (father of Robert E. Sweeney) (D Ohio) April 15, 1885–May 1, 1960; House Nov. 3, 1931–43.

Sweeney, Robert E. (son of Martin Leonard Sweeney) (D Ohio) Nov. 4, 1924– ; House 1965–67.

Sweeney, William Northcut (D Ky.) May 5, 1832–April 21, 1895; House 1869–71.

Sweeny, George (D Ohio) Feb. 22, 1796–Oct. 10, 1877; House 1839–43.

Sweet, Burton Erwin (R Iowa) Dec. 10, 1867–Jan. 3, 1957; House 1915–23.

Sweet, Edwin Forrest (D Mich.) Nov. 21, 1847–April 2, 1935; House 1911–13.

Sweet, John Hyde (R Neb.) Sept. 1, 1880–April 4, 1964; House April 9, 1940–41.

Sweet, Thaddeus C. (R N.Y.) Nov. 16, 1872–May 1, 1928; House Nov. 6, 1923–May 1, 1928.

Sweet, Willis (R Idaho) Jan. 1, 1856–July 9, 1925; House Oct. 1, 1890–95.

Sweetser, Charles (D Ohio) Jan. 22, 1808–April 14, 1864; House 1849–53.

Sweney, Joseph Henry (R Iowa) Oct. 2, 1845–Nov. 11, 1918; House 1889–91.

Swett, Richard (son-in-law of Thomas Peter Lantos) (D N.H.) May 1, 1957– ; House 1991–95.

Swick, Jesse Howard (R Pa.) Aug. 6, 1879–Nov. 17, 1952; House 1927–35.

Swift, Allen Byron (D Wash.) Sept. 12, 1935– ; House 1979–95.

Swift, Benjamin (W Vt.) April 3, 1781–Nov. 11, 1847; House 1827–31 (no party); Senate 1833–39.

Swift, George Robinson (D Ala.) Dec. 19, 1887–Sept. 10, 1972; Senate June 15–Nov. 5, 1946.

Swift, Oscar William (R N.Y.) April 11, 1869–June 30, 1940; House 1915–19.

Swift, Zephaniah (F Conn.) Feb. 27, 1759–Sept. 27, 1823; House 1793–97 (1793–95 no party).

Swigert, John Leonard (R Colo.) Aug. 30, 1931–Dec. 27, 1982; elected to the House for the term beginning 1983 but did not serve.

Swinburne, John (R N.Y.) May 30, 1820–March 28, 1889; House 1885–87.

Swindall, Charles (R Okla.) Feb. 13, 1876–June 19, 1939; House Nov. 2, 1920–21.

Swindall, Patrick Lynn (R Ga.) Oct. 18, 1950– ; House 1985–89.

Swing, Philip David (R Calif.) Nov. 30, 1884–Aug. 8, 1963; House 1921–33.

Switzer, Robert Mauck (R Ohio) March 6, 1863–Oct. 28, 1952; House 1911–19.

Swoope, Jacob (F Va.) ?–1832; House 1809–11.

Swoope, William Irvin (nephew of John Patton) (R Pa.) Oct. 3, 1862–Oct. 9, 1930; House 1923–27.

Swope, Guy Jacob (D Pa.) Dec. 26, 1892–July 25, 1969; House 1937–39; Gov. (P.R.) Feb. 3–Aug. 6, 1941.

Swope, John Augustus (D Pa.) Dec. 25, 1827–Dec. 6, 1910; House Dec. 23, 1884–85, Nov. 3, 1885–87.

Swope, King (R Ky.) Aug. 10, 1893–April 23, 1961; House Aug. 2, 1919–21.

Swope, Samuel Franklin (AP Ky.) March 1, 1809–April 19, 1865; House 1855–57 (affiliated with the Republican Party in 1856).

Sykes, George (D N.J.) Sept. 20, 1802–Feb. 25, 1880; House 1843–45, Nov. 4, 1845–47.

Symes, George Gifford (R Colo.) April 28, 1840–Nov. 3, 1893; House 1885–89.

Symington, James Wadsworth (son of Stuart Symington, grandson of James Wolcott Wadsworth Jr., great-grandson of James Wolcott Wadsworth) (D Mo.) Sept. 28, 1927– ; House 1969–77.

Symington, William Stuart (father of James Wadsworth Symington, son-in-law of James Wolcott Wadsworth Jr.) (D Mo.) June 26, 1901–Dec. 14, 1988; Senate 1953–Dec. 27, 1976.

Symms, Steven Douglas (R Idaho) April 23, 1938– ; House 1973–81; Senate 1981–93.

Synar, Michael Lynn (D Okla.) Oct. 17, 1950–Jan. 9, 1996; House 1979–95.

Sypher, Jacob Hale (R La.) June 22, 1837–May 9, 1905; House July 18, 1868–69, Nov. 7, 1870–75.

T

Taber, John (R N.Y.) May 5, 1880–Nov. 22, 1965; House 1923–63; Chrmn. House Appropriations 1947–49, 1953–55.

Taber, Stephen (son of Thomas Taber II) (D N.Y.) March 7, 1821–April 23, 1886; House 1865–69.

Taber, Thomas II (father of Stephen Taber) (J N.Y.) May 19, 1785–March 21, 1862; House Nov. 5, 1828–29.

Tabor, Horace Austin Warner (R Colo.) Nov. 26, 1830–April 10, 1899; Senate Jan. 27–March 3, 1883.

Tackett, Boyd Anderson (D Ark.) May 9, 1911–Feb. 23, 1985; House 1949–53.

Taffe, John (R Neb.) Jan. 30, 1827–March 14, 1884; House 1867–73.

Taft, Charles Phelps (brother of Pres. William Howard Taft, uncle of Robert Alphonso Taft, great-uncle of Robert Taft Jr.) (R Ohio) Dec. 21, 1843–Dec. 31, 1929; House 1895–97.

Taft, Kingsley Arter (R Ohio) July 19, 1903–March 28, 1970; Senate Nov. 5, 1946–47.

Taft, Robert Alphonso (son of Pres. William Howard Taft, father of Robert Taft Jr., nephew of Charles Phelps Taft) (R Ohio) Sept. 8, 1889–July 31, 1953; Senate 1939–July 31, 1953; Chrmn. Senate Labor and Public Welfare 1947–49; Senate majority leader Jan. 3–July 31, 1953.

Taft, Robert Jr. (son of Robert Alphonso Taft, grandson of Pres. William Howard Taft, great-nephew of Charles Phelps Taft) (R Ohio) Feb. 26, 1917–Dec. 7, 1993; House 1963–65, 1967–71; Senate 1971–Dec. 28, 1976.

Taggart, Joseph (D Kan.) June 15, 1867–Dec. 3, 1938; House Nov. 7, 1911–17.

Taggart, Samuel (F Mass.) March 24, 1754–April 25, 1825; House 1803–17.

Taggart, Thomas (D Ind.) Nov. 17, 1856–March 6, 1929; Senate March 20–Nov. 7, 1916; Chrmn. Dem. Nat. Comm. 1904–08.

Tague, Peter Francis (D Mass.) June 4, 1871–Sept. 17, 1941; House 1915–19, Oct. 23, 1919–25.

Tait, Charles (R Ga.) Feb. 1, 1768–Oct. 7, 1835; Senate Nov. 27, 1809–19.

Talbert, William Jasper (D S.C.) Oct. 6, 1846–Feb. 5, 1931; House 1893–1903.

Talbot, Isham (R Ky.) 1773–Sept. 25, 1837; Senate Jan. 3, 1815–19, Oct. 19, 1820–25.

Talbot, Joseph Edward (R Conn.) March 18, 1901–April 30, 1966; House Jan. 20, 1942–47.

Talbot, Silas (F N.Y.) Jan. 11, 1751–June 30, 1813; House 1793–95.

Talbott, Albert Gallatin (uncle of William Clayton Anderson) (D Ky.) April 4, 1808–Sept. 9, 1887; House 1855–59.

Talbott, Joshua Frederick Cockey (D Md.) July 29, 1843–Oct. 5, 1918; House 1879–85, 1893–95, 1903–Oct. 5, 1918.

Talcott, Burt Lacklen (R Calif.) Feb. 22, 1920– ; House 1963–77.

Talcott, Charles Andrew (D N.Y.) June 10, 1857–Feb. 27, 1920; House 1911–15.

Talent, James M. (R Mo.) Oct. 18, 1956– ; House 1993– ; Chrmn. House Small Business 1997– .

Taliaferro, Benjamin (F Ga.) 1750–Sept. 3, 1821; House 1799–1802.

Taliaferro, James Piper (D Fla.) Sept. 30, 1847–Oct. 6, 1934; Senate April 20, 1899–1911.

Taliaferro, John (W Va.) 1768–Aug. 12, 1852; House 1801–03 (Republican), Nov. 29, 1811–13 (Republican), March 24, 1824–31 (Republican), 1835–43.

Talle, Henry Oscar (R Iowa) Jan. 12, 1892–March 14, 1969; House 1939–59.

Tallmadge, Benjamin (father of Frederick Augustus Tallmadge) (F Conn.) Feb. 25, 1754–March 7, 1835; House 1801–17.

Tallmadge, Frederick Augustus (son of Benjamin Tallmadge) (W N.Y.) Aug. 29, 1792–Sept. 17, 1869; House 1847–49.

Tallmadge, James Jr. (R N.Y.) Jan. 20, 1778–Sept. 29, 1853; House June 6, 1817–19.

Tallmadge, Nathaniel Pitcher (D N.Y.) Feb. 8, 1795–Nov. 2, 1864; Senate 1833–June 17, 1844 (1833–39 Jacksonian); Gov. (Wis. Terr.) 1844–45.

Tallman, Peleg (R Mass.) July 24, 1764–March 12, 1840; House 1811–13.

Tallon, Robert Mooneyhan Jr. "Robin" (D S.C.) Aug. 8, 1946– ; House 1983–93.

Talmadge, Herman Eugene (D Ga.) Aug. 9, 1913– ; Senate 1957–81; Chrmn. Senate Agriculture and Forestry 1971–77; Chrmn. Senate Agriculture, Nutrition, and Forestry 1977–81; Gov. Jan. 14–March 18, 1947, Nov. 17, 1948–Jan. 11, 1955.

Tancredo, Tom (R Colo.) Dec. 20, 1945– ; House 1999– .

Tannehill, Adamson (R Pa.) May 23, 1750–Dec. 23, 1820; House 1813–15.

Tanner, Adolphus Hitchcock (R N.Y.) May 23, 1833–Jan. 14, 1882; House 1869–71.

Tanner, John (D Tenn.) Sept. 22, 1944– ; House 1989– .

Tappan, Benjamin (D Ohio) May 25, 1773–April 20, 1857; Senate 1839–45.

Tappan, Mason Weare (R N.H.) Oct. 20, 1817–Oct. 25, 1886; House 1855–61 (1855–57 American Party).

Tarbox, John Kemble (D Mass.) May 6, 1838–May 28, 1887; House 1875–77.

Tarr, Christian (R Pa.) May 25, 1765–Feb. 24, 1833; House 1817–21.

Tarsney, John Charles (D Mo.) Nov. 7, 1845–Sept. 4, 1920; House 1889–Feb. 17, 1896.

Tarsney, Timothy Edward (D Mich.) Feb. 4, 1849–June 8, 1909; House 1885–89.

Tarver, Malcolm Connor (D Ga.) Sept. 25, 1885–March 5, 1960; House 1927–47.

Tate, Farish Carter (D Ga.) Nov. 20, 1856–Feb. 7, 1922; House 1893–1905.

Tate, Magnus (F Va.) 1760–March 30, 1823; House 1815–17.

Tate, Randy (R Wash.) Nov. 23, 1965– ; House 1995–97.

Tatgenhorst, Charles Jr. (R Ohio) Aug. 19, 1883–Jan. 13, 1961; House Nov. 8, 1927–29.

Tatom, Absalom (R N.C.) 1742–Dec. 20, 1802; House 1795–June 1, 1796.

Tattnall, Edward Fenwick (– Ga.) 1788–Nov. 21, 1832; House 1821–27.

Tattnall, Josiah (R Ga.) 1762–June 6, 1803; Senate Feb. 20, 1796–99; Gov. Nov. 7, 1801–Nov. 4, 1802 (Democratic Republican).

Tauke, Thomas Joseph (R Iowa) Oct. 11, 1950– ; House 1979–91.

Taul, Micah (grandfather of Taul Bradford) (R Ky.) May 14, 1785–May 27, 1850; House 1815–17.

Taulbee, William Preston (D Ky.) Oct. 22, 1851–March 11, 1890; House 1885–89.

Tauriello, Anthony Francis (D N.Y.) Aug. 14, 1899–Dec. 21, 1983; House 1949–51.

Tauscher, Ellen O. (D Calif.) Nov. 15, 1951– ; House 1997– .

Tauzin, Wilbert Joseph "Billy" (R La.) June 14, 1943– ; House May 17, 1980– (1980–Aug. 6, 1995 Democrat).

Tavenner, Clyde Howard (D Ill.) Feb. 4, 1882–Feb. 6, 1942; House 1913–17.

Tawney, James Albertus (R Minn.) Jan. 3, 1855–June 12, 1919; House 1893–1911.

Tayler, Robert Walker (R Ohio) Nov. 26, 1852–Nov. 25, 1910; House 1895–1903.

Taylor, Abner (R Ill.) 1829–April 13, 1903; House 1889–93.

Taylor, Alexander Wilson (R Pa.) March 22, 1815–May 7, 1893; House 1873–75.

Taylor, Alfred Alexander (son of Nathaniel Green Taylor, brother of Robert Love Taylor) (R Tenn.) Aug. 6, 1848–Nov. 25, 1931; House 1889–95; Gov. Jan. 15, 1921–Jan. 16, 1923.

Taylor, Arthur Herbert (D Ind.) Feb. 29, 1852–Feb. 20, 1922; House 1893–95.

Taylor, Benjamin Irving (D N.Y.) Dec. 21, 1877–Sept. 5, 1946; House 1913–15.

Taylor, Caleb Newbold (R Pa.) July 27, 1813–Nov. 15, 1887; House 1867–69, April 13, 1870–71.

Taylor, Charles H. (R N.C.) Jan. 23, 1941– ; House 1991– .

Taylor, Chester William (son of Samuel Mitchell Taylor) (D Ark.) July 16, 1883–July 17, 1931; House Oct. 31, 1921–23.

Taylor, Dean Park (R N.Y.) Jan. 1, 1902–Oct. 16, 1977; House 1943–61.

Taylor, Edward Livingston Jr. (R Ohio) Aug. 10, 1869–March 10, 1938; House 1905–13.

Taylor, Edward Thomas (D Colo.) June 19, 1858–Sept. 3, 1941; House 1909–Sept. 3, 1941.

Taylor, Ezra Booth (R Ohio) July 9, 1823–Jan. 29, 1912; House Dec. 13, 1880–93.

Taylor, Gene (R Mo.) Feb. 10, 1928–Oct. 27, 1998; House 1973–89.

Taylor, Gene (D Miss.) Sept. 17, 1953– ; House Oct. 24, 1989– .

Taylor, George (D N.Y.) Oct. 19, 1820–Jan. 18, 1894; House 1857–59.

Taylor, George Washington (D Ala.) Jan. 16, 1849–Dec. 21, 1932; House 1897–1915.

Taylor, Glen Hearst (D Idaho) April 12, 1904–April 28, 1984; Senate 1945–51.

Taylor, Herbert Worthington (R N.J.) Feb. 19, 1869–Oct. 15, 1931; House 1921–23, 1925–27.

Taylor, Isaac Hamilton (R Ohio) April 18, 1840–Dec. 18, 1936; House 1885–87.

Taylor, James Alfred (D W.Va.) Sept. 25, 1878–June 9, 1956; House 1923–27.

Taylor, James Willis (R Tenn.) Aug. 28, 1880–Nov. 14, 1939; House 1919–Nov. 14, 1939.

Taylor, John (R Va.) Dec. 19, 1793–Aug. 20, 1824; Senate Oct. 18, 1792–May 11, 1794 (no party), June 4–Dec. 7, 1803, Dec. 18, 1822–Aug. 21, 1824.

Taylor, John (R S.C.) May 4, 1770–April 16, 1832; House 1807–Dec. 30, 1810; Senate Dec. 31, 1810–Nov. 1816; Gov. Dec. 9, 1826–Dec. 10, 1828 (Democratic Republican).

Taylor, John (R S.C.) ?–?; House 1815–17.

Taylor, John Clarence (D S.C.) March 2, 1890–March 25, 1983; House 1933–39.

Taylor, John James (D N.Y.) April 27, 1808–July 1, 1892; House 1853–55.

Taylor, John Lampkin (W Ohio) March 7, 1805–Sept. 6, 1870; House 1847–55.

Taylor, John May (D Tenn.) May 18, 1838–Feb. 17, 1911; House 1883–87.

Taylor, John W. (R N.Y.) March 26, 1784–Sept. 18, 1854; House 1813–33; Speaker Nov. 15, 1820–21, Dec. 5, 1825–27.

Taylor, Jonathan (D Ohio) 1796–April 1848; House 1839–41.

Taylor, Joseph Danner (R Ohio) Nov. 7, 1830–Sept. 19, 1899; House Jan. 2, 1883–85, 1887–93.

Taylor, Miles (D La.) July 16, 1805–Sept. 23, 1873; House 1855–Feb. 5, 1861.

Taylor, Nathaniel Green (father of Alfred Alexander Taylor and Robert Love Taylor) (U Tenn.) Dec. 29, 1819–April 1, 1887; House March 30, 1854–55 (Whig), July 24, 1866–67.

Taylor, Nelson (D N.Y.) June 8, 1821–Jan. 16, 1894; House 1865–67.

Taylor, Robert (– Va.) April 29, 1763–July 3, 1845; House 1825–27.

Taylor, Robert Love (son of Nathaniel Green Taylor, brother of Alfred Alexander Taylor) (D Tenn.) July 31, 1850–March 31, 1912; House 1879–81; Senate 1907–March 31, 1912; Gov. Jan. 17, 1887–Jan. 19, 1891, Jan. 21, 1897–Jan. 16, 1899.

Taylor, Roy Arthur (D N.C.) Jan. 31, 1910–Feb. 28, 1995; House June 25, 1960–77.

Taylor, Samuel Mitchell (father of Chester William Taylor) (D Ark.) May 25, 1852–Sept. 13, 1921; House Jan. 15, 1913–Sept. 13, 1921.

Taylor, Vincent Albert (R Ohio) Dec. 6, 1845–Dec. 2, 1922; House 1891–93.

Taylor, Waller (R Ind.) before 1786–Aug. 26, 1826; Senate Dec. 11, 1816–25.

Taylor, William (D N.Y.) Oct. 12, 1791–Sept. 16, 1865; House 1833–39.

Taylor, William (D Va.) April 5, 1788–Jan. 17, 1846; House 1843–Jan. 17, 1846.

Taylor, William Penn (AJ Va.) ?–?; House 1833–35.

Taylor, Zachary (R Tenn.) May 9, 1849–Feb. 19, 1921; House 1885–87.

Tazewell, Henry (father of Littleton Waller Tazewell) (– Va.) Nov. 27, 1753–Jan. 24, 1799; Senate Dec. 29, 1794–Jan. 24, 1799; elected Pres. pro tempore Feb. 20, 1795, Dec. 7, 1795.

Tazewell, Littleton Waller (son of Henry Tazewell) (– Va.) Dec. 17, 1774–May 6, 1860; House Nov. 26, 1800–01; Senate Dec. 7, 1824–July 16, 1832; elected Pres. pro tempore July 9, 1832; Gov. March 31, 1834–April 30, 1836 (Democrat).

Teague, Charles McKevett (R Calif.) Sept. 18, 1909–Jan. 1, 1974; House 1955–Jan. 1, 1974.

Teague, Olin Earl (D Texas) April 6, 1910–Jan. 23, 1981; House Aug. 24, 1946–Dec. 31, 1978; Chrmn. House Veterans' Affairs 1955–73; Chrmn. House Science and Astronautics 1973–75; Chrmn. House Science and Technology 1975–79.

Teese, Frederick Halstead (D N.J.) Oct. 21, 1823–Jan. 7, 1894; House 1875–77.

Teigan, Henry George (FL Minn.) Aug. 7, 1881–March 12, 1941; House 1937–39.

Tejeda, Frank Mariano (D Texas) Oct. 2, 1945–Jan. 30, 1997; House 1993–Jan. 30, 1997.

Telfair, Thomas (R Ga.) March 2, 1780–Feb. 18, 1818; House 1813–17.

Teller, Henry Moore (D Colo.) May 23, 1830–Feb. 23, 1914; Senate Nov. 15, 1876–April 17, 1882 (Republican), 1885–1909 (1885–97 Republican, 1897–1903 Silver Republican); Secy. of the Interior April 18, 1882–March 3, 1885.

Teller, Isaac (nephew of Abraham Henry Schenck) (W N.Y.) Feb. 7, 1799–April 30, 1868; House Nov. 7, 1854–55.

Teller, Ludwig (D N.Y.) June 22, 1911–Oct. 4, 1965; House 1957–61.

Temple, Henry Wilson (R Pa.) March 31, 1864–Jan. 11, 1955; House 1913–15 (Progressive), Nov. 2, 1915–33.

Temple, William (D Del.) Feb. 28, 1814–May 28, 1863; House March 4–May 28, 1863.

Templeton, Thomas Weir (R Pa.) Nov. 8, 1867–Sept. 5, 1935; House 1917–19.

Tener, John Kinley (R Pa.) July 25, 1863–May 19, 1946; House 1909–Jan. 16, 1911; Gov. Jan. 17, 1911–Jan. 19, 1915.

Tenerowicz, Rudolph Gabriel (D Mich.) June 14, 1890–Aug. 31, 1963; House 1939–43.

Ten Eyck, Egbert (– N.Y.) April 18, 1779–April 11, 1844; House 1823–Dec. 15, 1825.

Ten Eyck, John Conover (R N.J.) March 12, 1814–Aug. 24, 1879; Senate 1859–65.

Ten Eyck, Peter Gansevoort (D N.Y.) Nov. 7, 1873–Sept. 2, 1944; House 1913–15, 1921–23.

Tenney, Samuel (F N.H.) Nov. 27, 1748–Feb. 6, 1816; House Dec. 8, 1800–07.

Tenzer, Herbert (D N.Y.) Nov. 1, 1905–March 24, 1993; House 1965–69.

Terrell, George Butler (D Texas) Dec. 5, 1862–April 18, 1947; House 1933–35.

Terrell, James C. (U Ga.) Nov. 7, 1806–Dec. 1, 1835; House March 4–July 8, 1835.

Terrell, Joseph Meriwether (D Ga.) June 6, 1861–Nov. 17, 1912; Senate Nov. 17, 1910–July 14, 1911; Gov. Oct. 25, 1902–June 29, 1907.

Terrell, William (R Ga.) 1778–July 4, 1855; House 1817–21.

Terry, David Dickson (son of William Leake Terry) (D Ark.) Jan. 31, 1881–Oct. 7, 1963; House Dec. 19, 1933–Jan. 2, 1943.

Terry, John Hart (R N.Y.) Nov. 14, 1924– ; House 1971–73.

Terry, Lee (R Neb.) Jan. 29, 1962– ; House 1999– .

Terry, Nathaniel (F Conn.) Jan. 30, 1768–June 14, 1844; House 1817–19.

Terry, William (D Va.) Aug. 14, 1824–Sept. 5, 1888; House 1871–73, 1875–77.

Terry, William Leake (father of David Dickson Terry) (D Ark.) Sept. 27, 1850–Nov. 4, 1917; House 1891–1901.

Test, John (– Ind.) Nov. 12, 1771–Oct. 9, 1849; House 1823–27, 1829–31.

Tewes, Donald Edgar (R Wis.) Aug. 4, 1916– ; House 1957–59.

Thacher, Thomas Chandler (D Mass.) July 20, 1858–April 11, 1945; House 1913–15.

Thatcher, George (F Mass.) April 12, 1754–April 6, 1824; House 1789–1801 (1789–95 no party); Cont. Cong. 1787–89.

Thatcher, Maurice Hudson (R Ky.) Aug. 15, 1870–Jan. 6, 1973; House 1923–33.

Thatcher, Samuel (F Mass.) July 1, 1776–July 18, 1872; House Dec. 6, 1802–05.

Thayer, Andrew Jackson (D Ore.) Nov. 27, 1818–April 28, 1873; House March 4–July 30, 1861.

Thayer, Eli (father of John Alden Thayer) (R Mass.) June 11, 1819–April 15, 1899; House 1857–61.

Thayer, Harry Irving (R Mass.) Sept. 10, 1869–March 10, 1926; House 1925–March 10, 1926.

Thayer, John Alden (son of Eli Thayer) (D Mass.) Dec. 22, 1857–July 31, 1917; House 1911–13.

Thayer, John Milton (uncle of Arthur Laban Bates) (R Neb.) Jan. 24, 1820–March 19, 1906; Senate March 1, 1867–71; Gov. 1875–79 (Wyo. Terr.), Jan. 6, 1887–Jan. 15, 1891, May 5, 1891–Feb. 8, 1892.

Thayer, John Randolph (D Mass.) March 9, 1845–Dec. 19, 1916; House 1899–1905.

Thayer, Martin Russell (R Pa.) Jan. 27, 1819–Oct. 14, 1906; House 1863–67.

Theaker, Thomas Clarke (R Ohio) Feb. 1, 1812–July 16, 1883; House 1859–61.

Thibodeaux, Bannon Goforth (– La.) Dec. 22, 1812–March 5, 1866; House 1845–49.

Thill, Lewis Dominic (R Wis.) Oct. 18, 1903–May 6, 1975; House 1939–43.

Thistlewood, Napoleon Bonaparte (R Ill.) March 30, 1837–Sept. 15, 1915; House Feb. 15, 1908–13.

Thom, William Richard (D Ohio) July 7, 1885–Aug. 28, 1960; House 1933–39, 1941–43, 1945–47.

Thomas, Albert (husband of Lera Millard Thomas) (D Texas) April 12, 1898–Feb. 15, 1966; House 1937–Feb. 15, 1966.

Thomas, Benjamin Franklin (U Mass.) Feb. 12, 1813–Sept. 27, 1878; House June 11, 1861–63.

Thomas, Charles Randolph (father of Charles Randolph Thomas, below) (R N.C.) Feb. 7, 1827–Feb. 18, 1891; House 1871–75.

Thomas, Charles Randolph (son of Charles Randolph Thomas, above) (D N.C.) Aug. 21, 1861–March 8, 1931; House 1899–1911.

Thomas, Charles Spalding (D Colo.) Dec. 6, 1849–June 24, 1934; Senate Jan. 15, 1913–21; Gov. Jan. 10, 1899–Jan. 8, 1901.

Thomas, Christopher Yancy (R Va.) March 24, 1818–Feb. 11, 1879; House March 5, 1874–75.

Thomas, Craig (R Wyo.) Feb. 17, 1933– ; House May 2, 1989–95; Senate 1995– .

Thomas, David (R N.Y.) June 11, 1762–Nov. 27, 1831; House 1801–May 1, 1808.

Thomas, Elbert Duncan (D Utah) June 17, 1883–Feb. 11, 1953; Senate 1933–51; Chrmn. Senate Labor and Public Welfare 1949–51.

Thomas, Francis (R Md.) Feb. 3, 1799–Jan. 22, 1876; House 1831–41 (1831–37 Jacksonian), 1861–69 (1861–63 Unionist, 1863–67 Unconditional Unionist); Gov. Jan. 3, 1841–Jan. 6, 1845 (Democrat).

Thomas, George Morgan (R Ky.) Nov. 23, 1828–Jan. 7, 1914; House 1887–89.

Thomas, Henry Franklin (R Mich.) Dec. 17, 1843–April 16, 1912; House 1893–97.

Thomas, Isaac (R Tenn.) Nov. 4, 1784–Feb. 2, 1859; House 1815–17.

Thomas, James Houston (D Tenn.) Sept. 22, 1808–Aug. 4, 1876; House 1847–51, 1859–61.

Thomas, Jesse Burgess (R Ill.) 1777–May 3, 1853; House (Terr. Del.) Oct. 22, 1808–09 (no party Ind.); Senate Dec. 3, 1818–29.

Thomas, John (R Idaho) Jan. 4, 1874–Nov. 10, 1945; Senate June 30, 1928–33, Jan. 27, 1940–Nov. 10, 1945.

Thomas, John Chew (F Md.) Oct. 15, 1764–May 10, 1836; House 1799–1801.

Thomas, John Lewis Jr. (UU Md.) May 20, 1835–Oct. 15, 1893; House Dec. 4, 1865–67.

Thomas, John Parnell (R N.J.) Jan. 16, 1895–Nov. 19, 1970; House 1937–Jan. 2, 1950; Chrmn. House Un-American Activities 1947–49.

Thomas, John Robert (R Ill.) Oct. 11, 1846–Jan. 19, 1914; House 1879–89.

Thomas, John William Elmer (D Okla.) Sept. 8, 1876–Sept. 19, 1965; House 1923–27; Senate 1927–51; Chrmn. Senate Agriculture and Forestry 1949–51.

Thomas, Lera Millard (widow of Albert Thomas) (D Texas) Aug. 3, 1900–July 23, 1993; House March 26, 1966–67.

Thomas, Lot (R Iowa) Oct. 17, 1843–March 17, 1905; House 1899–1905.

Thomas, Ormsby Brunson (R Wis.) Aug. 21, 1832–Oct. 24, 1904; House 1885–91.

Thomas, Philemon (– La.) Feb. 9, 1763–Nov. 18, 1847; House 1831–35.

Thomas, Phillip Francis (D Md.) Sept. 12, 1810–Oct. 2, 1890; House 1839–41, 1875–77; Gov. Jan. 3, 1848–Jan. 6, 1851; Secy. of the Treasury Dec. 12, 1860–Jan. 14, 1861.

Thomas, Richard (F Pa.) Dec. 30, 1744–Jan. 19, 1832; House 1795–1801.

Thomas, Robert Lindsay (D Ga.) Nov. 20, 1943– ; House 1983–93.

Thomas, Robert Young Jr. (D Ky.) July 13, 1855–Sept. 3, 1925; House 1909–Sept. 3, 1925.

Thomas, William Aubrey (R Ohio) June 7, 1866–Sept. 8, 1951; House Nov. 8, 1904–11.

Thomas, William David (R N.Y.) March 22, 1880–May 17, 1936; House Jan. 30, 1934–May 17, 1936.

Thomas, William Marshall (R Calif.) Dec. 6, 1941– ; House 1979– ; Chrmn. House Oversight 1995–1999; Chrmn. House Administration 1999– .

Thomason, Robert Ewing (D Texas) May 30, 1879–Nov. 8, 1973; House 1931–July 31, 1947.

Thomasson, William Poindexter (W Ky.) Oct. 8, 1797–Dec. 29, 1882; House 1843–47.

Thompson, Albert Clifton (R Ohio) Jan. 23, 1842–Jan. 26, 1910; House 1885–91.

Thompson, Benjamin (W Mass.) Aug. 5, 1798–Sept. 24, 1852; House 1845–47, 1851–Sept. 24, 1852.

Thompson, Bennie (D Miss.) Jan. 28, 1948– ; House April 20, 1993– .

Thompson, Charles James (R Ohio) Jan. 24, 1862–March 27, 1932; House 1919–31.

Thompson, Charles Perkins (D Mass.) July 30, 1827–Jan. 19, 1894; House 1875–77.

Thompson, Charles Winston (D Ala.) Dec. 30, 1860–March 20, 1904; House 1901–March 20, 1904.

Thompson, Chester Charles (D Ill.) Sept. 19, 1893–Jan. 30, 1971; House 1933–39.

Thompson, Clark Wallace (D Texas) Aug. 6, 1896–Dec. 16, 1981; House June 24, 1933–35, Aug. 23, 1947–67.

Thompson, Fountain Land (D N.D.) Nov. 18, 1854–Feb. 4, 1942; Senate Nov. 10, 1909–Jan. 31, 1910.

Thompson, Frank Jr. (D N.J.) July 26, 1918–July 22, 1989; House 1955–Dec. 29, 1980; Chrmn. House Administration 1976–80.

Thompson, Fred (R Tenn.) Aug. 19, 1942– ; Senate Dec. 9, 1994– ; Chrmn. Senate Governmental Affairs 1997– .

Thompson, George Western (D Va.) May 14, 1806–Feb. 24, 1888; House 1851–July 30, 1852.

Thompson, Hedge (– N.J.) Jan. 28, 1780–July 23, 1828; House 1827–July 23, 1828.

Thompson, Jacob (D Miss.) May 15, 1810–March 24, 1885; House 1839–51; Secy. of the Interior March 10, 1857–Jan. 8, 1861.

Thompson, James (D Pa.) Oct. 1, 1806–Jan. 28, 1874; House 1845–51.

Thompson, Joel (F N.Y.) Oct. 3, 1760–Feb. 8, 1843; House 1813–15.

Thompson, John (R N.Y.) March 20, 1749–1823; House 1799–1801, 1807–11.

Thompson, John (R N.Y.) July 4, 1809–June 1, 1890; House 1857–59.

Thompson, John Burton (AP Ky.) Dec. 14, 1810–Jan. 7, 1874; House Dec. 7, 1840–43 (Whig), 1847–51 (Whig); Senate 1853–59.

Thompson, John McCandless (brother of William George Thompson) (R Pa.) Jan. 4, 1829–Sept. 3, 1903; House Dec. 22, 1874–75, 1877–79.

Thompson, Joseph Bryan (D Okla.) April 29, 1871–Sept. 18, 1919; House 1913–Sept. 18, 1919.

Thompson, Michael (D Calif.) Jan. 24, 1951– ; House 1999– .

Thompson, Philip (– Ky.) Aug. 20, 1789–Nov. 25, 1836; House 1823–25.

Thompson, Philip Burton Jr. (D Ky.) Oct. 15, 1845–Dec. 15, 1909; House 1879–85.

Thompson, Philip Rootes (R Va.) March 26, 1766–July 27, 1837; House 1801–07.

Thompson, Richard Wigginton (W Ind.) June 9, 1809–Feb. 9, 1900; House 1841–43, 1847–49; Secy. of the Navy March 13, 1877–Dec. 20, 1880.

Thompson, Robert Augustine (father of Thomas Larkin Thompson) (D Va.) Feb. 14, 1805–Aug. 31, 1876; House 1847–49.

Thompson, Ruth (R Mich.) Sept. 15, 1887–April 5, 1970; House 1951–57.

Thompson, Standish Fletcher (R Ga.) Feb. 5, 1925– ; House 1967–73.

Thompson, Theo Ashton (D La.) March 31, 1916–July 1, 1965; House 1953–July 1, 1965.

Thompson, Thomas Larkin (son of Robert Augustine Thompson) (D Calif.) May 31, 1838–Feb. 1, 1898; House 1887–89.

Thompson, Thomas Weston (F N.H.) March 15, 1766–Oct. 1, 1821; House 1805–07; Senate June 24, 1814–17.

Thompson, Waddy Jr. (W S.C.) Jan. 8, 1798–Nov. 23, 1868; House Sept. 10, 1835–41 (Sept. 10, 1835–37 Anti-Jacksonian).

Thompson, Wiley (J Ga.) Sept. 23, 1781–Dec. 28, 1835; House 1821–33.

Thompson, William (D Iowa) Nov. 10, 1813–Oct. 6, 1897; House 1847–June 29, 1850.

Thompson, William George (brother of John McCandless Thompson) (R Iowa) Jan. 17, 1830–April 2, 1911; House Oct. 14, 1879–83.

Thompson, William Henry (D Neb.) Dec. 14, 1853–June 6, 1937; Senate May 24, 1933–Nov. 6, 1934.

Thompson, William Howard (D Kan.) Oct. 14, 1871–Feb. 9, 1928; Senate 1913–19.

Thomson, Alexander (– Pa.) Jan. 12, 1788–Aug. 2, 1848; House Dec. 6, 1824–May 1, 1826.

Thomson, Charles Marsh (Prog. Ill.) Feb. 13, 1877–Dec. 30, 1943; House 1913–15.

Thomson, Edwin Keith (R Wyo) Feb. 8, 1919–Dec. 9, 1960; House 1955–Dec. 9, 1960; did not seek nomination but was elected to the Senate for the term beginning 1961, did not serve.

Thomson, John (J Ohio) Nov. 20, 1780–Dec. 2, 1852; House 1825–27 (no party), 1829–37.

Thomson, John Renshaw (D N.J.) Sept. 25, 1800–Sept. 12, 1862; Senate 1853–Sept. 12, 1862.

Thomson, Mark (F N.J.) 1739–Dec. 14, 1803; House 1795–99.

Thomson, Vernon Wallace (R Wis.) Nov. 5, 1905–April 12, 1988; House 1961–Dec. 31, 1974; Gov. Jan. 7, 1957–Jan. 5, 1959.

Thone, Charles (R Neb.) Jan. 4, 1924– ; House 1971–79; Gov. Jan. 4, 1979–Jan. 6, 1983.

Thorington, James (W Iowa) May 7, 1816–June 13, 1887; House 1855–57.

Thorkelson, Jacob (R Mont.) Sept. 24, 1876–Nov. 20, 1945; House 1939–41.

Thornberry, William Homer (D Texas) Jan. 9, 1909–Dec. 27, 1995; House 1949–Dec. 20, 1963.

Thornberry, William M. "Mac" (R Texas) July 15, 1958– ; House 1995– .

Thornburgh, Jacob Montgomery (R Tenn.) July 3, 1837–Sept. 19, 1890; House 1873–79.

Thornton, Anthony (D Ill.) Nov. 9, 1814–Sept. 10, 1904; House 1865–67.

Thornton, John Randolph (D La.) Aug. 25, 1846–Dec. 28, 1917; Senate Dec. 7, 1910–15.

Thornton, Raymond Hoyt Jr. (R Ark.) July 16, 1928– ; House 1973–79 (Democrat), 1991–97.

Thorp, Robert Taylor (R Va.) March 12, 1850–Nov. 26, 1938; House May 2, 1896–97, March 23, 1898–99.

Thorpe, Roy Henry (R Neb.) Dec. 13, 1874–Sept. 19, 1951; House Nov. 7, 1922–23.

Throckmorton, James Webb (D Texas) Feb. 1, 1825–April 21, 1894; House 1875–79, 1883–87; Gov. Aug. 9, 1866–Aug. 8, 1867.

Throop, Enos Thompson (R N.Y.) Aug. 21, 1784–Nov. 1, 1874; House 1815–June 4, 1816; Gov. March 12, 1829–Jan. 1, 1833 (Jacksonian).

Thropp, Joseph Earlston (R Pa.) Oct. 4, 1847–July 27, 1927; House 1899–1901.

Thruston, Buckner (R Ky.) Feb. 9, 1763–Aug. 30, 1845; Senate 1805–Dec. 18, 1809.

Thune, John (R S.D.) Jan. 7, 1961– ; House 1997– .

Thurman, Allen Granberry (D Ohio) Nov. 13, 1813–Dec. 12, 1895; House 1845–47; Senate 1869–81; elected Pres. pro tempore April 15, 1879, April 7, 1880, May 6, 1880.

Thurman, John Richardson (W N.Y.) Oct. 6, 1814–July 24, 1854; House 1849–51.

Thurman, Karen L. (D Fla.) Jan. 12, 1951– ; House 1993– .

Thurmond, James Strom (R S.C.) Dec. 5, 1902– ; Senate Dec. 24, 1954–April 4, 1956 (Democrat), Nov. 7, 1956– (Nov. 7, 1956–Sept. 16, 1964 Democrat); elected Pres. pro tempore Jan, 5, 1981–87, 1995– ; Gov. Jan. 21, 1947–Jan. 16, 1951 (Democrat); Chrmn. Senate Armed Services 1995–99.

Thurston, Benjamin Babcock (AP R.I.) June 29, 1804–May 17, 1886; House 1847–49 (Democrat), 1851–57 (1851–55 Democrat).

Thurston, John Mellen (R Neb.) Aug. 21, 1847–Aug. 9, 1916; Senate 1895–1901.

Thurston, Lloyd (R Iowa) March 27, 1880–May 7, 1970; House 1925–39.

Thurston, Samuel Royal (D Ore.) April 15, 1816–April 9, 1851; House (Terr. Del.) 1849–51.

Thye, Edward John (R Minn.) April 26, 1896–Aug. 28, 1969; Senate 1947–59; Chrmn. Senate Select Committee on Small Business 1953–55; Gov. April 27, 1943–Jan. 8, 1947.

Tiahrt, Todd (R Kan.) June 15, 1951– ; House 1995– .

Tibbatts, John Wooleston (D Ky.) June 12, 1802–July 5, 1852; House 1843–47.

Tibbits, George (F N.Y.) Jan. 14, 1763–July 19, 1849; House 1803–05.

Tibbott, Harve (R Pa.) May 27, 1885–Dec. 31, 1969; House 1939–49.

Tichenor, Isaac (F Vt.) Feb. 8, 1754–Dec. 11, 1838; Senate Oct. 18, 1796–Oct. 1797, 1815–21; Gov. Oct. 1797–Oct. 9, 1807, Oct. 17, 1808–Oct. 14, 1809.

Tiernan, Robert Owens (D R.I.) Feb. 24, 1929– ; House March 28, 1967–75.

Tierney, John (D Mass.) Sept. 18, 1951– ; House 1997– .

Tierney, William Laurence (D Conn.) Aug. 6, 1876–April 13, 1958; House 1931–33.

Tiffin, Edward (R Ohio) June 19, 1766–Aug. 9, 1829; Senate 1807–09; Gov. March 3, 1803–March 4, 1807 (Democratic Republican).

Tift, Nelson (D Ga.) July 23, 1810–Nov. 21, 1891; House July 25, 1868–69.

Tilden, Daniel Rose (W Ohio) Nov. 5, 1804–March 4, 1890; House 1843–47.

Tillinghast, Joseph Leonard (cousin of Thomas Tillinghast) (W R.I.) 1791–Dec. 30, 1844; House 1837–43.

Tillinghast, Thomas (cousin of Joseph Leonard Tillinghast) (R R.I.) Aug. 21, 1742–Aug. 26, 1821; House Nov. 13, 1797–99 (Federalist), 1801–03.

Tillman, Benjamin Ryan (brother of George Dionysius Tillman) (D S.C.) Aug. 11, 1847–July 3, 1918; Senate 1895–July 3, 1918; Gov. Dec. 4, 1890–Dec. 4, 1894.

Tillman, George Dionysius (brother of Benjamin Ryan Tillman) (D S.C.) Aug. 21, 1826–Feb. 2, 1902; House 1879–June 19, 1882, 1883–93.

Tillman, John Newton (D Ark.) Dec. 13, 1859–March 9, 1929; House 1915–29.

Tillman, Lewis (nephew of Barclay Martin) (R Tenn.) Aug. 18, 1816–May 3, 1886; House 1869–71.

Tillotson, Thomas (– N.Y.) 1750–May 5, 1832; elected to the House for the term beginning 1801 but did not qualify or take his seat, resigned Aug. 10, 1801.

Tilson, John Quillin (R Conn.) April 5, 1866–Aug. 14, 1958; House 1909–13, 1915–Dec. 3, 1932; House majority leader 1925–31.

Timberlake, Charles Bateman (R Colo.) Sept. 25, 1854–May 31, 1941; House 1915–33.

Tincher, Jasper Napoleon (R Kan.) Nov. 2, 1878–Nov. 6, 1951; House 1919–27.

Tinkham, George Holden (R Mass.) Oct. 29, 1870–Aug. 28, 1956; House 1915–43.

Tipton, John (D Ind.) Aug. 14, 1786–April 5, 1839; Senate Jan. 3, 1832–39.

Tipton, Thomas Foster (R Ill.) Aug. 29, 1833–Feb. 7, 1904; House 1877–79.

Tipton, Thomas Weston (R Neb.) Aug. 5, 1817–Nov. 26, 1899; Senate March 1, 1867–75.

Tirrell, Charles Quincy (R Mass.) Dec. 10, 1844–July 31, 1910; House 1901–July 31, 1910.

Titus, Obadiah (D N.Y.) Jan. 20, 1789–Sept. 2, 1854; House 1837–39.

Tobey, Charles William (R N.H.) July 22, 1880–July 24, 1953; House 1933–39; Senate 1939–July 24, 1953; Chrmn. Senate Banking and Currency 1947–49; Chrmn. Senate Interstate and Foreign Commerce 1953; Gov. Jan. 3, 1929–Jan. 1, 1931.

Tod, John (D Pa.) 1779–March 27, 1830; House 1821–24.

Todd, Albert May (D Mich.) June 3, 1850–Oct. 6, 1931; House 1897–99.

Todd, John Blair Smith (D Dakota) April 4, 1814–Jan. 5, 1872; House (Terr. Del.) Dec. 9, 1861–63, June 17, 1864–65.

Todd, Lemuel (R Pa.) July 29, 1817–May 12, 1891; House 1855–57, 1873–75.

Todd, Paul Harold Jr. (D Mich.) Sept. 22, 1921– ; House 1965–67.

Tolan, John Harvey (D Calif.) Jan. 15, 1877–June 30, 1947; House 1935–47.

Toland, George Washington (W Pa.) Feb. 8, 1796–Jan. 30, 1869; House 1837–43.

Toll, Herman (D Pa.) March 15, 1907–July 26, 1967; House 1959–67.

Tollefson, Thor Carl (R Wash.) May 2, 1901–Dec. 30, 1982; House 1947–65.

Tolley, Harold Sumner (R N.Y.) Jan. 16, 1894–May 20, 1956; House 1925–27.

Tomlinson, Gideon (– Conn.) Dec. 31, 1780–Oct. 8, 1854; House 1819–27; Senate 1831–37; Gov. May 2, 1827–March 2, 1831 (Democratic Republican).

Tomlinson, Thomas Ash (W N.Y.) March 1802–June 18, 1872; House 1841–43.

Tompkins, Arthur Sidney (R N.Y.) Aug. 26, 1865–Jan. 20, 1938; House 1899–1903.

Tompkins, Caleb (brother of Daniel D. Tompkins) (R N.Y.) Dec. 22, 1759–Jan. 1, 1846; House 1817–21.

Tompkins, Christopher (AJ Ky.) March 24, 1780–Aug. 9, 1858; House 1831–35.

Tompkins, Cydnor Bailey (father of Emmett Tompkins) (R Ohio) Nov. 8, 1810–July 23, 1862; House 1857–61.

Tompkins, Daniel D. (brother of Caleb Tompkins) (– N.Y.) June 21, 1774–June 11, 1825; elected to the House for the term beginning 1805 but resigned before taking seat; Gov. July 1, 1807–Feb. 24, 1817; Vice President 1817–25.

Tompkins, Emmett (son of Cydnor Bailey Tompkins) (R Ohio) Sept. 1, 1853–Dec. 18, 1917; House 1901–03.

Tompkins, Patrick Watson (W Miss.) 1804–May 8, 1953; House 1847–49.

Tongue, Thomas H. (R Ore.) June 23, 1844–Jan. 11, 1903; House 1897–Jan. 11, 1903.

Tonry, Richard Alvin (D La.) June 25, 1935– ; House Jan. 3–May 4, 1977.

Tonry, Richard Joseph (D N.Y.) Sept. 30, 1893–Jan. 17, 1971; House 1935–37.

Toole, Joseph Kemp (D Mont.) May 12, 1851–March 11, 1929; House (Terr. Del.) 1885–89; Gov. Nov. 8, 1889–Jan. 2, 1893, Jan. 7, 1901–April 1, 1908.

Toombs, Robert (D Ga.) July 2, 1810–Dec. 15, 1885; House 1845–53 (Whig); Senate 1853–Feb. 4, 1861.

Toomey, Patrick J. (R Pa.) Nov. 17, 1961– ; House 1999– .

Torkildsen, Peter G. (R Mass.) Jan. 28, 1958– ; House 1993–97.

Torrens, James H. (D N.Y.) Sept. 12, 1874–April 5, 1952; House Feb. 29, 1944–47.

Torres, Estaban Edward (D Calif.) Jan. 27, 1930– ; House 1983–99.

Torricelli, Robert Guy (D N.J.) Aug. 26, 1951– ; House 1983–97; Senate 1997– .

Toucey, Isaac (D Conn.) Nov. 15, 1792–July 30, 1869; House 1835–39; Senate May 12, 1852–57; Gov. May 6, 1846–May 5, 1847; Atty. Gen. June 21, 1848–March 3, 1849; Secy. of the Navy March 7, 1857–March 6, 1861.

Tou Velle, William Ellsworth (D Ohio) Nov. 23, 1862–Aug. 14, 1951; House 1907–11.

Towe, Harry Lancaster (R N.J.) Nov. 3, 1898–Feb. 8, 1991; House 1943–Sept. 7, 1951.

Towell, David Gilmer (R Nev.) June 9, 1937– ; House 1973–75.

Tower, John Goodwin (R Texas) Sept. 29, 1925–April 5, 1991; Senate June 15, 1961–85; Chrmn. Senate Armed Services 1981–85.

Towey, Frank William Jr. (D N.J.) Nov. 5, 1895–Sept. 4, 1979; House 1937–39.

Towne, Charles Arnette (D N.Y.) Nov. 21, 1858–Oct. 22, 1928; House 1895–97 (Republican Minn.), 1905–07; Senate Dec. 5, 1900–Jan. 28, 1901 (Minn.).

Towner, Horace Mann (R Iowa) Oct. 23, 1855–Nov. 23, 1937; House 1911–April 1, 1923; Gov. (P.R.) 1923–29.

Towns, Edolphus "Ed" (D N.Y.) July 21, 1934– ; House 1983– .

Towns, George Washington Bonaparte (D Ga.) May 4, 1801–July 15, 1854; House 1835–Sept. 1, 1836 (Jacksonian), 1837–39, Jan. 5, 1846–47; Gov. Nov. 3, 1847–Nov. 5, 1851.

Townsend, Amos (R Ohio) 1821–March 17, 1895; House 1877–83.

Townsend, Charles Champlain (R Pa.) Nov. 24, 1841–July 10, 1910; House 1889–91.

Townsend, Charles Elroy (R Mich.) Aug. 15, 1856–Aug. 3, 1924; House 1903–11; Senate 1911–23.

Townsend, Dwight (D N.Y.) Sept. 26, 1826–Oct. 29, 1899; House Dec. 5, 1864–65, 1871–73.

Townsend, Edward Waterman (D N.J.) Feb. 10, 1855–March 15, 1942; House 1911–15.

Townsend, George (R N.Y.) 1769–Aug. 17, 1844; House 1815–19.

Townsend, Hosea (R Colo.) June 16, 1840–March 4, 1909; House 1889–93.

Townsend, John Gillis Jr. (R Del.) May 31, 1871–April 10, 1964; Senate 1929–41; Gov. Jan. 17, 1917–Jan. 18, 1921.

Townsend, Martin Ingham (R N.Y.) Feb. 6, 1810–March 8, 1903; House 1875–79.

Townsend, Washington (R Pa.) Jan. 20, 1813–March 18, 1894; House 1869–77.

Townshend, Norton Strange (D Ohio) Dec. 25, 1815–July 13, 1895; House 1851–53.

Townshend, Richard Wellington (D Ill.) April 30, 1840–March 9, 1889; House 1877–March 9, 1889.

Tracewell, Robert John (R Ind.) May 7, 1852–July 28, 1922; House 1895–97.

Tracey, Charles (D N.Y.) May 27, 1847–March 24, 1905; House Nov. 8, 1887–95.

Tracey, John Plank (R Mo.) Sept. 18, 1836–July 24, 1910; House 1895–97.

Tracy, Albert Haller (brother of Phineas Lyman Tracy) (– N.Y.) June 17, 1793–Sept. 19, 1859; House 1819–25.

Tracy, Andrew (W Vt.) Dec. 15, 1797–Oct. 28, 1868; House 1853–55.

Tracy, Henry Wells (IR Pa.) Sept. 24, 1807–April 11, 1886; House 1863–65.

Tracy, Phineas Lyman (brother of Albert Haller Tracy) (AMas. N.Y.) Dec. 25, 1786–Dec. 22, 1876; House Nov. 5, 1827–33 (Nov. 5, 1827–29 no party).

Tracy, Uri (R N.Y.) Feb. 8, 1764–July 21, 1838; House 1805–07, 1809–13.

Tracy, Uriah (F Conn.) Feb. 2, 1755–July 19, 1807; House 1793–Oct. 13, 1796 (no party); Senate Oct. 13, 1796–July 19, 1807; elected Pres. pro tempore May 14, 1800.

Traeger, William Isham (R Calif.) Feb. 26, 1880–Jan. 20, 1935; House 1933–35.

Traficant, James A. Jr. (D Ohio) May 8, 1941– ; House 1985– .

Trafton, Mark (AP Mass.) Aug. 1, 1810–March 8, 1901; House 1855–57.

Train, Charles Russell (R Mass.) Oct. 18, 1817–July 28, 1885; House 1859–63.

Trammell, Park (D Fla.) April 9, 1876–May 8, 1936; Senate 1917–May 8, 1936; Gov. Jan. 7, 1913–Jan. 2, 1917.

Transue, Andrew Jackson (D Mich.) Jan. 12, 1903–June 24, 1995; House 1937–39.

Traxler, Jerome Bob (D Mich.) July 21, 1931– ; House April 16, 1974–93.

Traynor, Philip Andrew (D Del.) May 31, 1874–Dec. 5, 1962; House 1941–43, 1945–47.

Treadway, Allen Towner (R Mass.) Sept. 16, 1867–Feb. 16, 1947; House 1913–45.

Treadway, William Marshall (D Va.) Aug. 24, 1807–May 1, 1891; House 1845–47.

Tredwell, Thomas (grandfather of Thomas Treadwell Davis) (– N.Y.) Feb. 6, 1743–Dec. 30, 1831; House May 1791–95.

Treen, David Conner (R La.) July 16, 1928– ; House 1973–March 10, 1980; Gov. March 10, 1980–March 12, 1984.

Treloar, William Mitchellson (R Mo.) Sept. 21, 1850–July 3, 1935; House 1895–97.

Tremain, Lyman (R N.Y.) June 14, 1819–Nov. 30, 1878; House 1873–75.

Trezvant, James (J Va.) ?–Sept. 2, 1841; House 1825–31.

Tribble, Samuel Joelah (D Ga.) Nov. 15, 1869–Dec. 8, 1916; House 1911–Dec. 8, 1916.

Trible, Paul Seward Jr. (R Va.) Dec. 29, 1946– ; House 1977–83; Senate 1983–89.

Trigg, Abram (brother of John Johns Trigg) (R Va.) 1750–?; House 1797–1809.

Trigg, Connally Findlay (D Va.) Sept. 18, 1847–April 23, 1907; House 1885–87.

Trigg, John Johns (brother of Abram Trigg) (R Va.) 1748–May 17, 1804; House 1797–May 17, 1804.

Trimble, Carey Allen (R Ohio) Sept. 13, 1813–May 4, 1887; House 1859–63.

Trimble, David (R Ky.) June 1782–Oct. 20, 1842; House 1817–27.

Trimble, James William (D Ark.) Feb. 3, 1894–March 10, 1972; House 1945–67.

Trimble, John (R Tenn.) Feb. 7, 1812–Feb. 23, 1884; House 1867–69.

Trimble, Lawrence Strother (D Ky.) Aug. 26, 1825–Aug. 9, 1904; House 1865–71.

Trimble, South (D Ky.) April 13, 1864–Nov. 23, 1946; House 1901–07.

Trimble, William Allen (– Ohio) April 4, 1786–Dec. 13, 1821; Senate 1819–Dec. 13, 1821.

Triplett, Philip (W Ky.) Dec. 24, 1799–March 30, 1852; House 1839–43.

Trippe, Robert Pleasant (AP Ga.) Dec. 21, 1819–July 22, 1900; House 1855–59.

Trotter, James Fisher (D Miss.) Nov. 5, 1802–March 9, 1866; Senate Jan. 22–July 10, 1838.

Trotti, Samuel Wilds (D S.C.) July 18, 1810–June 24, 1856; House Dec. 17, 1842–43.

Troup, George Michael (R Ga.) Sept. 8, 1780–April 26, 1856; House 1807–15; Senate Nov. 13, 1816–Sept. 23, 1818, 1829–Nov. 8, 1833; Gov. Nov. 7, 1823–Nov. 7, 1827 (Democratic Republican).

Trout, Michael Carver (D Pa.) Sept. 30, 1810–June 25, 1873; House 1853–55.

Troutman, William Irvin (R Pa.) Jan. 13, 1905–Jan. 27, 1971; House 1943–Jan. 2, 1945.

Trowbridge, Rowland Ebenezer (R Mich.) June 18, 1821–April 20, 1881; House 1861–63, 1865–69.

Truax, Charles Vilas (D Ohio) Feb. 1, 1887–Aug. 9, 1935; House 1933–Aug. 9, 1935.

Truman, Harry S. (D Mo.) May 8, 1884–Dec. 26, 1972; Senate 1935–Jan. 17, 1945; Vice President Jan. 20–April 12, 1945; President April 12, 1945–53.

Trumbo, Andrew (W Ky.) Sept. 15, 1797–Aug. 21, 1871; House 1845–47.

Trumbull, Jonathan Jr. (– Conn.) March 26, 1740–Aug. 7, 1809; House 1789–95; Speaker Oct. 24, 1791–93; Senate 1795–June 10, 1796; Gov. Dec. 1, 1797–Aug. 7, 1809.

Trumbull, Joseph (W Conn.) Dec. 7, 1782–Aug. 4, 1861; House Dec. 1, 1834–35 (no party), 1839–43; Gov. May 2, 1849–May 4, 1850.

Trumbull, Lyman (– Ill.) Oct. 12, 1813–June 25, 1896; Senate 1855–73.

Tsongas, Paul Efthemios (D Mass.) Feb. 14, 1941–Jan. 18, 1997; House 1975–79; Senate 1979–85.

Tuck, Amos (W N.H.) Aug. 2, 1810–Dec. 11, 1879; House 1847–53 (1847–49 Independent, 1849–51 Free-Soiler).

Tuck, William Munford (D Va.) Sept. 28, 1896–June 9, 1983; House April 14, 1953–69; Gov. June 16, 1946–Jan. 18, 1950.

Tucker, Ebenezer (– N.J.) Nov. 15, 1758–Sept. 5, 1845; House 1825–29.

Tucker, George (cousin of Henry St. George Tucker) (– Va.) Aug. 20, 1775–April 10, 1861; House 1819–25.

Tucker, Henry St. George (father of John Randolph Tucker, grandfather of Henry St. George Tucker, below, cousin of George Tucker, nephew of Thomas Tudor Tucker) (R Va.) Dec. 29, 1780–Aug. 28, 1848; House 1815–19.

Tucker, Henry St. George (son of John Randolph Tucker, grandson of Henry St. George Tucker, above) (D Va.) April 5, 1853–July 23, 1932; House 1889–97, March 21, 1922–July 23, 1932.

Tucker, James Guy Jr. (D Ark.) June 13, 1943– ; House 1977–79; Gov. Dec. 12, 1992–July 15, 1996.

Tucker, John Randolph (son of Henry St. George Tucker born in 1780, father of Henry St. George Tucker born in 1853) (D Va.) Dec. 24, 1823–Feb. 13, 1897; House 1875–87.

Tucker, Starling (J S.C.) 1770–Jan. 3, 1834; House 1817–31 (1817–27 Republican).

Tucker, Thomas Tudor (uncle of Henry St. George Tucker born in 1780) (– S.C.) June 25, 1745–May 2, 1828; House 1789–93; Cont. Cong. 1787–88.

Tucker, Tilghman Mayfield (D Miss.) Feb. 5, 1802–April 3, 1859; House 1843–45; Gov. Jan. 10, 1842–Jan. 10, 1844.

Tucker, Walter R. III (D Calif.) May 28, 1957– ; House 1993–Dec. 15, 1995.

Tufts, John Quincy (R Iowa) July 12, 1840–Aug. 10, 1908; House 1875–77.

Tully, Pleasant Britton (D Calif.) March 21, 1829–March 24, 1897; House 1883–85.

Tumulty, Thomas James (D N.J.) March 2, 1913–Nov. 23, 1981; House 1955–57.

Tunnell, James Miller (D Del.) Aug. 2, 1879–Nov. 14, 1957; Senate 1941–47.

Tunney, John Varick (D Calif.) June 26, 1934– ; House 1965–Jan. 2, 1971; Senate Jan. 2, 1971–Jan. 1, 1977.

Tupper, Stanley Roger (R Maine) Jan. 25, 1921– ; House 1961–67.

Turley, Thomas Battle (D Tenn.) April 5, 1845–July 1, 1910; Senate July 20, 1897–1901.

Turnbull, Robert (D Va.) Jan. 11, 1850–Jan. 22, 1920; House March 8, 1910–13.

Turner, Benjamin Sterling (R Ala.) March 17, 1825–March 21, 1894; House 1871–73.

Turner, Charles Henry (D N.Y.) May 26, 1861–Aug. 31, 1913; House Dec. 9, 1889–91.

Turner, Charles Jr. (R Mass.) June 20, 1760–May 16, 1839; House June 28, 1809–13.

Turner, Clarence Wyly (D Tenn.) Oct. 22, 1866–March 23, 1939; House Nov. 7, 1922–23, 1933–March 23, 1939.

Turner, Daniel (son of James Turner of N.C.) (– N.C.) Sept. 21, 1796–July 21, 1860; House 1827–29.

Turner, Erastus Johnson (R Kan.) Dec. 26, 1846–Feb. 10, 1933; House 1887–91.

Turner, George (Fus./Sil.R/D/P Wash.) Feb. 25, 1850–Jan. 26, 1932; Senate 1897–1903.

Turner, Henry Gray (D Ga.) March 20, 1839–June 9, 1904; House 1881–97.

Turner, James (father of Daniel Turner) (R N.C.) Dec. 20, 1766–Jan. 15, 1824; Senate 1805–Nov. 21, 1816; Gov. Dec. 6, 1802–Dec. 10, 1805.

Turner, James (J Md.) Nov. 7, 1783–March 28, 1861; House 1833–37.

Turner, Jim (D Texas) Feb. 6, 1946– ; House 1997– .

Turner, Oscar (father of Oscar Turner, below) (ID Ky.) Feb. 3, 1825–Jan. 22, 1896; House 1879–85 (1879–81 Independent Democrat, 1881–83 Democrat).

Turner, Oscar (son of Oscar Turner, above) (D Ky.) Oct. 19, 1867–July 17, 1902; House 1899–1901.

Turner, Smith Spangler (D Va.) Nov. 21, 1842–April 8, 1898; House Jan. 30, 1894–97.

Turner, Thomas (D Ky.) Sept. 10, 1821–Sept. 11, 1900; House 1877–81.

Turner, Thomas Johnston (D Ill.) April 5, 1815–April 4, 1874; House 1847–49.

Turney, Hopkins Lacy (D Tenn.) Oct. 3, 1797–Aug. 1 1857; House 1837–43; Senate 1845–51.

Turney, Jacob (D Pa.) Feb. 18, 1825–Oct. 4, 1891; House 1875–79.

Turpie, David (D Ind.) July 8, 1828–April 21, 1909; Senate Jan. 14–March 3 1863, 1887–99.

Turpin, Charles Murray (R Pa.) March 4, 1878–June 4, 1946; House June 4, 1929–37.

Turpin, Louis Washington (D Ala.) Feb. 22, 1849–Feb. 3, 1903; House 1889–June 4, 1890, 1891–95.

Turrill, Joel (J N.Y.) Feb. 22, 1794–Dec. 28, 1859; House 1833–37.

Tuten, James Russell (D Ga.) July 23, 1911–Aug. 16, 1968; House 1963–67.

Tuthill, Joseph Hasbrouck (nephew of Selah Tuthill) (D N.Y.) Feb. 25, 1811–July 27, 1877; House 1871–73.

Tuthill, Selah (uncle of Joseph Hasbrouck Tuthill) (– N.Y.) Oct. 26, 1771–Sept. 7, 1821; House March 4–Sept. 7, 1821.

Tuttle, William Edgar Jr. (D N.J.) Dec. 10, 1870–Feb. 11, 1923; House 1911–15.

Tweed, William Marcy (D N.Y.) April 3, 1823–April 12, 1878; House 1853–55.

Tweedy, John Hubbard (W Wis.) Nov. 9, 1814–Nov. 12, 1891; House (Terr. Del.) 1847–May 29, 1848.

Tweedy, Samuel (AJ Conn.) March 8, 1776–July 1, 1868; House 1833–35.

Twichell, Ginery (R Mass.) Aug. 26, 1811–July 23, 1883; House 1867–73.

Twyman, Robert Joseph (R Ill.) June 18, 1897–June 28, 1976; House 1947–49.

Tydings, Joseph Davies (adoptive son of Millard Evelyn Tydings) (D Md.) May 4, 1928– ; Senate 1965–71; Chrmn. Senate District of Columbia 1969–71.

Tydings, Millard Evelyn (adoptive father of Joseph Davies Tydings) (D Md.) April 6, 1890–Feb. 9, 1961; House 1923–27; Senate 1927–51; Chrmn. Senate Armed Services 1949–51.

Tyler, Asher (W N.Y.) May 10, 1798–Aug. 1, 1875; House 1843–45.

Tyler, David Gardiner (son of John Tyler, grandson of Gov. John Tyler of Va.) (D Va.) July 12, 1846–Sept. 5, 1927; House 1893–97.

Tyler, James Manning (R Vt.) April 27, 1835–Oct. 13, 1926; House 1879–83.

Tyler, John (father of David Gardiner Tyler, son of Gov. John Tyler of Va.) (R Va.) March 29, 1790–Jan. 18, 1862; House Dec. 16, 1817–21; Senate 1827–Feb. 29, 1836; elected Pres. pro tempore March 3, 1835; Gov. Dec. 10, 1825–March 4, 1827 (Democratic Republican); Vice President March 4–April 6, 1841 (Whig); President April 6, 1841–45 (Whig).

Tyndall, William Thomas (R Mo.) Jan. 16, 1862–Nov. 26, 1928; House 1905–07.

Tyner, James Noble (R Ind.) Jan. 17, 1826–Dec. 5, 1904; House 1869–75; Postmaster Gen. July 13, 1876–March 12, 1877.

Tyson, Jacob (– N.Y.) Oct. 8, 1773–July 16, 1848; House 1823–25.

Tyson, Joe Roberts (W Pa.) Feb. 8, 1803–June 27, 1858; House 1855–57.

Tyson, John Russell (D Ala.) Nov. 28, 1856–March 27, 1923; House 1921–March 27, 1923.

Tyson, Lawrence Davis (D Tenn.) July 4, 1861–Aug. 24, 1929; Senate 1925–Aug. 24, 1929.

U

Udall, Mark (D Colo.) July 18, 1950– ; House 1999– .

Udall, Morris King (father of Mark Emery Udall, brother of Stewart

Lee Udall, uncle of Thomas S. Udall) (D Ariz.) June 15, 1922–Dec. 12, 1998; House May 2, 1961–May 4, 1991; Chrmn. House Interior and Insular Affairs 1977–91.

Udall, Stewart Lee (brother of Morris King Udall) (D Ariz.) Jan. 31, 1920– ; House 1955–Jan. 18, 1961; Secy. of the Interior Jan. 21, 1961–Jan. 20, 1969.

Udall, Thomas (D N.M.) May 18, 1948– ; House 1999– .

Udree, Daniel (R Pa.) Aug. 5, 1751–July 15, 1828; House Oct. 12, 1813–15, Dec. 26, 1820–21, Dec. 10, 1822–25.

Ullman, Albert Conrad (D Ore.) March 9, 1914–Oct. 11, 1986; House 1957–81; Chrmn. House Ways and Means 1975–81.

Umstead, William Bradley (D N.C.) May 13, 1895–Nov. 7, 1954; House 1933–39; Senate Dec. 18, 1946–Dec. 30, 1948; Gov. Jan. 8, 1953–Nov. 7, 1954.

Underhill, Charles Lee (R Mass.) July 20, 1867–Jan. 28, 1946; House 1921–33.

Underhill, Edwin Stewart (D N.Y.) Oct. 7, 1861–Feb. 7, 1929; House 1911–15.

Underhill, John Quincy (D N.Y.) Feb. 19, 1848–May 21, 1907; House 1899–1901.

Underhill, Walter (W N.Y.) Sept. 12, 1795–Aug. 17, 1866; House 1849–51.

Underwood, John William Henderson (D Ga.) Nov. 20, 1816–July 18, 1888; House 1859–Jan. 23, 1861.

Underwood, Joseph Rogers (brother of Warner Lewis Underwood, grandfather of Oscar Wilder Underwood) (W Ky.) Oct. 24, 1791–Aug. 23, 1876; House 1835–43; Senate 1847–53.

Underwood, Mell Gilbert (D Ohio) Jan. 30, 1892–March 8, 1972; House 1923–April 10, 1936.

Underwood, Oscar Wilder (grandson of Joseph Rogers Underwood, great-nephew of Warner Lewis Underwood) (D Ala.) May 6, 1862–Jan. 25, 1929; House 1895–June 9, 1896, 1897–1915; House majority leader 1911–15; Senate 1915–27; Senate minority leader April 27, 1920–23.

Underwood, Robert A. (D Guam) July 13, 1948– ; House (Delegate) 1993– .

Underwood, Thomas Rust (D Ky.) March 3, 1898–June 29, 1956; House 1949–March 17, 1951; Senate March 19, 1951–Nov. 4, 1952.

Underwood, Warner Lewis (brother of Joseph Rogers Underwood, great-uncle of Oscar Wilder Underwood) (AP Ky.) Aug. 7, 1808–March 12, 1872; House 1855–59.

Unsoeld, Jolene (D Wash.) Dec. 3, 1931– ; House 1989–95.

Updegraff, Jonathan Taylor (R Ohio) May 13, 1822–Nov. 30, 1882; House 1879–Nov. 30, 1882.

Updegraff, Thomas (R Iowa) April 3, 1834–Oct. 4, 1910; House 1879–83, 1893–99.

Updike, Ralph Eugene (R Ind.) May 27, 1894–Sept. 16, 1953; House 1925–29.

Upham, Charles Wentworth (cousin of George Baxter Upham and Jabez Upham) (W Mass.) May 4, 1802–June 15, 1875; House 1853–55.

Upham, George Baxter (brother of Jabez Upham, cousin of Charles Wentworth Upham) (F N.H.) Dec. 27 1768–Feb. 10, 1848; House 1801–03.

Upham, Jabez (brother of George Baxter Upham, cousin of Charles Wentworth Upham) (F Mass.) Aug. 23, 1764–Nov. 8, 1811; House 1807–10.

Upham, Nathaniel (R N.H.) June 9, 1774–July 10, 1829; House 1817–23.

Upham, William (W Vt.) Aug. 5, 1792–Jan. 14, 1853; Senate 1843–Jan. 14, 1853.

Upshaw, William David (D Ga.) Oct. 15, 1866–Nov. 21, 1952; House 1919–27.

Upson, Charles (R Mich.) March 19, 1821–Sept. 5, 1885; House 1863–69.

Upson, Christopher Columbus (D Texas) Oct. 17, 1829–Feb. 8, 1902; House April 15, 1879–83.

Upson, William Hanford (R Ohio) Jan. 11, 1823–April 13, 1910; House 1869–73.

Upton, Charles Horace (U Va.) Aug. 23, 1812–June 17, 1877; House May 23, 1861–Feb. 27, 1862.

Upton, Frederick Stephen (R Mich.) April 23, 1953– ; House 1987– .

Upton, Robert William (R N.H.) Feb. 3, 1884–April 28, 1972; Senate Aug. 14, 1953–Nov. 7, 1954.

Urner, Milton George (uncle of James Samuel Simmons) (R Md.) July 29, 1839–Feb. 9, 1926; House 1879–83.

Utt, James Boyd (R Calif.) March 11, 1899–March 1, 1970; House 1953–March 1, 1970.

Utter, George Herbert (R R.I.) July 24, 1854–Nov. 3, 1912; House 1911–Nov. 3, 1912; Gov. Jan. 3, 1905–Jan. 1, 1907.

Utterback, Hubert (cousin of John Gregg Utterback) (D Iowa) June 28, 1880–May 12, 1942; House 1935–37.

Utterback, John Gregg (cousin of Hubert Utterback) (D Maine) July 12, 1872–July 11, 1955; House 1933–35.

V

Vail, George (D N.J.) July 21, 1809–May 23, 1875; House 1853–57.

Vail, Henry (D N.Y.) 1782–June 25, 1853; House 1837–39.

Vail, Richard Bernard (R Ill.) Aug. 31, 1895–July 29, 1955; House 1947–49, 1951–53.

Vaile, William Newell (R Colo.) June 22, 1876–July 2, 1927; House 1919–July 2, 1927.

Valentine, Edward Kimble (R Neb.) June 1, 1843–April 11, 1916; House 1879–85.

Valentine, Itimous Thaddeus Jr. "Tim" (D N.C.) March 15, 1926– ; House 1983–95.

Valk, William Weightman (AP N.Y.) Oct. 12, 1806–Sept. 20, 1879; House 1855–57.

Vallandigham, Clement Laird (uncle of John A. McMahon) (D Ohio) July 29, 1820–June 17, 1871; House May 25, 1858–63.

Van Aernam, Henry (R N.Y.) March 11, 1819–June 1, 1894; House 1865–69, 1879–83.

Van Alen, James Isaac (half-brother of Martin Van Buren) (R N.Y.) 1776–Dec. 23, 1870; House 1807–09.

Van Alen, John Evert (F N.Y.) 1749–March 1807; House 1793–99 (1793–95 no party).

Van Alstyne, Thomas Jefferson (D N.Y.) July 25, 1827–Oct. 26, 1903; House 1883–85.

Van Auken, Daniel Myers (D Pa.) Jan. 15, 1826–Nov. 7, 1908; House 1867–71.

Van Buren, John (D N.Y.) May 13, 1799–Jan. 16, 1855; House 1841–43.

Van Buren, Martin (half-brother of James Isaac Van Alen) (– N.Y.) Dec. 5, 1782–July 24, 1862; Senate 1821–Dec. 20, 1828; Gov. Jan. 1–March 12, 1829 (Jeffersonian Republican); Secy. of State March 28, 1829–March 23, 1831; Vice President 1833–37 (Democrat); President 1837–41 (Democrat).

Vance, John Luther (D Ohio) July 19, 1839–June 10, 1921; House 1875–77.

Vance, Joseph (W Ohio) March 21, 1786–Aug. 24, 1852; House 1821–35 (1821–33 no party, 1833–35 Anti-Jacksonian), 1843–47; Gov. Dec. 12, 1836–Dec. 13, 1838.

Vance, Robert Brank (uncle of Zebulon Baird Vance and Robert Brank Vance, below) (– N.C.) 1793–1827; House 1823–25.

Vance, Robert Brank (nephew of Robert Brank Vance, above, brother of Zebulon Baird Vance) (D N.C.) April 24, 1828–Nov. 28, 1899; House 1873–85.

Vance, Robert Johnstone (D Conn.) March 15, 1854–June 15, 1902; House 1887–89.

Vance, Zebulon Baird (brother of Robert Brank Vance born in 1828, nephew of Robert Brank Vance born in 1793) (D N.C.) May 13, 1830–April 14, 1894; House Dec. 7, 1858–61; Senate 1879–April 14, 1894; Gov. Sept. 8, 1862–May 29, 1865, Jan. 1, 1877–Feb. 5, 1879.

Van Cortlandt, Philip (brother of Pierre Van Cortlandt Jr.) (R N.Y.) Aug. 21, 1749–Nov. 1, 1831; House 1793–1809 (1793–95 no party).

Van Cortlandt, Pierre Jr. (brother of Philip Van Cortlandt) (R N.Y.) Aug. 29, 1762–July 13, 1848; House 1811–13.

Van Deerlin, Lionel (D Calif.) July 25, 1914– ; House 1963–81.

Vandenberg, Arthur Hendrick (R Mich.) March 22, 1884–April 18, 1951; Senate March 31, 1928–April 18, 1951; elected Pres. pro tempore Jan. 4, 1947; Chrmn. Senate Foreign Relations 1947–49.

Vandergriff, Tommy Joe "Tom" (D Texas) Jan. 29, 1926– ; House 1983–85.

Vander Jagt, Guy Adrian (R Mich.) Aug. 26, 1931– ; House Nov. 8, 1966–93.

Vanderpoel, Aaron (D N.Y.) Feb. 5, 1799–July 18, 1870; House 1833–37 (Jacksonian), 1839–41.

Vander Veen, Richard Franklin (D Mich.) Nov. 26, 1922– ; House Feb. 18, 1974–77.

Vanderveer, Abraham (D N.Y.) 1781–July 21, 1839; House 1837–39.

Vandever, William (R Calif.) March 31, 1817–July 23, 1893; House 1859–Sept. 24, 1861 (Iowa), 1887–91.

Vandiver, Willard Duncan (D Mo.) March 30, 1854–May 30, 1932; House 1897–1905.

Van Duzer, Clarence Dunn (D Nev.) May 4, 1866–Sept. 28, 1947; House 1903–07.

Van Dyke, Carl Chester (D Minn.) Feb. 18, 1881–May 20, 1919; House 1915–May 20, 1919.

Van Dyke, John (W N.J.) April 3, 1807–Dec. 24, 1878; House 1847–51.

Van Dyke, Nicholas (F Del.) Dec. 20, 1770–May 21, 1826; House Oct. 6, 1807–11; Senate 1817–May 21, 1826.

Van Eaton, Henry Smith (D Miss.) Sept. 14, 1826–May 30, 1898; House 1883–87.

Van Gaasbeck, Peter (– N.Y.) Sept. 27, 1754–1797; House 1793–95.

Van Horn, Burt (R N.Y.) Oct. 28, 1823–April 1, 1896; House 1861–63, 1865–69.

Van Horn, George (D N.Y.) Feb. 5, 1850–May 3, 1904; House 1891–93.

Van Horn, Robert Thompson (R Mo.) May 19, 1824–Jan. 3, 1916; House 1865–71, 1881–83, Feb. 27, 1896–97.

Van Horne, Archibald (R Md.) ?–1817; House 1807–11.

Van Horne, Espy (– Pa.) 1795–Aug. 25, 1829; House 1825–29.

Van Horne, Isaac (R Pa.) Jan. 13, 1754–Feb. 2, 1834; House 1801–05.

Van Houten, Isaac B. (J N.Y.) June 4, 1776–Aug. 16, 1850; House 1833–35.

Vanik, Charles Albert (D Ohio) April 7, 1913– ; House 1955–81.

Vanmeter, John Inskeep (W Ohio) Feb. 1798–Aug. 3, 1875; House 1843–45.

Van Ness, John Peter (R N.Y.) 1770–March 7, 1846; House Oct. 6, 1801–Jan. 17, 1803.

Van Nuys, Frederick (D Ind.) April 16, 1874–Jan. 25, 1944; Senate 1933–Jan. 25, 1944.

Van Pelt, William Kaiser (R Wis.) March 10, 1905–June 2, 1996; House 1951–65.

Van Rensselaer, Henry Bell (son of Stephen Van Rensselaer) (W N.Y.) May 14, 1810–March 23, 1864; House 1841–43.

Van Rensselaer, Jeremiah (father of Solomon Van Vechten Van Rensselaer, cousin of Killian Killian Van Rensselaer) (– N.Y.) Aug. 27, 1738–Feb. 19, 1810; House 1789–91.

Van Rensselaer, Killian Killian (cousin of Jeremiah Van Rensselaer, uncle of Solomon Van Vechten Van Renssealer) (F N.Y.) June 9, 1763–June 18, 1845; House 1801–11.

Van Rensselaer, Solomon Van Vechten (son of Jeremiah Van Rensselaer, nephew of Killian Killian Van Rensselaer) (F N.Y.) Aug. 6, 1774–April 23, 1852; House 1819–Jan. 14, 1822.

Van Rensselaer, Stephen (father of Henry Bell Van Rensselaer) (– N.Y.) Nov. 1, 1764–Jan. 26, 1839; House Feb. 27, 1822–29.

Van Sant, Joshua (D Md.) Dec. 31, 1803–April 8, 1884; House 1853–55.

Van Schaick, Isaac Whitbeck (uncle of Aaron Van Schaick Cochrane) (R Wis.) Dec. 7, 1817–Aug. 22, 1901; House 1885–87, 1889–91.

Van Swearingen, Thomas (– Va.) May 5, 1784–Aug. 19, 1822; House 1819–Aug. 19, 1822.

Van Trump, Philadelph (D Ohio) Nov. 15, 1810–July 31, 1874; House 1867–73.

Van Valkenburgh, Robert Bruce (R N.Y.) Sept. 4, 1821–Aug. 1, 1888; House 1861–65.

Van Voorhis, Henry Clay (R Ohio) May 11, 1852–Dec. 12, 1927; House 1893–1905.

Van Voorhis, John (R N.Y.) Oct. 22, 1826–Oct. 20, 1905; House 1879–83, 1893–95.

Van Vorhes, Nelson Holmes (R Ohio) Jan. 23, 1822–Dec. 4, 1882; House 1875–79.

Van Winkle, Marshall (great-nephew of Peter Godwin Van Winkle) (R N.J.) Sept. 28, 1869–May 10, 1957; House 1905–07.

Van Winkle, Peter Godwin (great-uncle of Marshall Van Winkle) (U W.Va.) Sept. 7, 1808–April 15, 1872; Senate Aug. 4, 1863–69.

Van Wyck, Charles Henry (R Neb.) May 10, 1824–Oct. 24, 1895; House 1859–63, 1867–69, Feb. 17, 1870–71 (N.Y.); Senate 1881–87.

Van Wyck, William William (– N.Y.) Aug. 9, 1777–Aug. 27, 1840; House 1821–25.

Van Zandt, James Edward (R Pa.) Dec. 18, 1898–Jan. 6, 1986; House 1939–Sept. 24, 1943, 1947–63.

Vardaman, James Kimble (D Miss.) July 26, 1861–June 25, 1930; Senate 1913–19; Gov. Jan. 19, 1904–Jan. 21, 1908.

Vare, William Scott (R Pa.) Dec. 24, 1867–Aug. 7, 1934; House April 24, 1912–Jan. 2, 1923, 1923–27; elected to the Senate for the term beginning 1927 but was not permitted to qualify.

Varnum, John (F Mass.) June 25, 1778–July 23, 1836; House 1825–31.

Varnum, Joseph Bradley (R Mass.) Jan. 29, 1750 or 1751–Sept. 21, 1821; House 1795–June 29, 1811 (no party); Speaker Oct. 26, 1807–09, May 22, 1809–11; Senate June 29, 1811–17; elected Pres. pro tempore Dec. 6, 1813.

Vaughan, Horace Worth (D Texas) Dec. 2, 1867–Nov. 10, 1922; House 1913–15.

Vaughan, William Wirt (D Tenn.) July 2, 1831–Aug. 19, 1878; House 1871–73.

Vaughn, Albert Clinton Sr. (R Pa.) Oct. 9, 1894–Sept. 1, 1951; House Jan. 3–Sept. 1, 1951.

Vaux, Richard (D Pa.) Dec. 19, 1816–March 22, 1895; House May 20, 1890–91.

Veeder, William Davis (D N.Y.) May 19, 1835–Dec. 2, 1910; House 1877–79.

Vehslage, John Herman George (D N.Y.) Dec. 20, 1842–July 21, 1904; House 1897–99.

Velázquez, Nydia M. (D N.Y.) March 22, 1953– ; House 1993– .

Velde, Harold Himmel (R Ill.) April 1, 1910–Sept. 1, 1985; House 1949–57; Chrmn. House Un-American Activities 1953–55.

Venable, Abraham Bedford (uncle of Abraham Watkins Venable) (– Va.) Nov. 20, 1758–Dec. 26, 1811; House 1791–99; Senate Dec. 7, 1803–June 7, 1804.

Venable, Abraham Watkins (nephew of Abraham Bedford Venable) (D N.C.) Oct. 17, 1799–Feb. 24, 1876; House 1847–53.

Venable, Edward Carrington (D Va.) Jan. 31, 1853–Dec. 8, 1908; House 1889–Sept. 23, 1890.

Venable, William Webb (D Miss.) Sept. 25, 1880–Aug. 2, 1948; House Jan. 4, 1916–21.

Vento, Bruce Frank (DFL Minn.) Oct. 7, 1940– ; House 1977– .

Verplanck, Daniel Crommelin (father of Gulian Crommelin Verplanck) (R N.Y.) March 19, 1762–March 29, 1834; House Oct. 17, 1803–09.

Verplanck, Gulian Crommelin (son of Daniel Crommelin Verplanck) (J N.Y.) Aug. 6, 1786–March 18, 1870; House 1825–33 (1825–29 no party).

Verree, John Paul (R Pa.) March 9, 1817–June 27, 1889; House 1859–63.

Vest, George Graham (D Mo.) Dec. 6, 1830–Aug. 9, 1904; Senate 1879–1903.

Vestal, Albert Henry (R Ind.) Jan. 18, 1875–April 1, 1932; House 1917–April 1, 1932.

Veysey, Victor Vincent (R Calif.) April 14, 1915– ; House 1971–75.

Vibbard, Chauncey (D N.Y.) Nov. 11, 1811–June 5, 1891; House 1861–63.

Vickers, George (D Md.) Nov. 19, 1801–Oct. 8, 1879; Senate March 7, 1868–73.

Vidal, Michel (R La.) Oct. 1, 1824–?; House July 18, 1868–69.

Viele, Egbert Ludoricus (D N.Y.) June 17, 1825–April 22, 1902; House 1885–87.

Vigorito, Joseph Phillip (D Pa.) Nov. 10, 1918– ; House 1965–77.

Vilas, William Freeman (D Wis.) July 9, 1840–Aug. 27, 1908; Senate 1891–97; Postmaster Gen. March 7, 1885–Jan. 16, 1888; Secy. of the Interior Jan. 16, 1888–March 6, 1889.

Vincent, Beverly Mills (D Ky.) March 28, 1890–Aug. 15, 1980; House 1937–45.

Vincent, Bird J. (R Mich.) March 6, 1880–July 18, 1931; House 1923–July 18, 1931.

Vincent, Earl W. (R Iowa) March 27, 1886–May 22, 1953; House June 4, 1928–29.

Vincent, William Davis (P Kan.) Oct. 11, 1852–Feb. 28, 1922; House 1897–99.

Vining, John (– Del.) Dec. 23, 1758–Feb. 1802; House 1789–93; Senate 1793–Jan. 19, 1798; Cont. Cong. 1784–85.

Vinson, Carl (great-uncle of Samuel Augustus Nunn) (D Ga.) Nov. 18, 1883–June 1, 1981; House Nov. 3, 1914–65; Chrmn. House Armed Services 1949–53, 1955–65.

Vinson, Frederick Moore (D Ky.) Jan. 22, 1890–Sept. 8, 1953; House Jan. 12, 1924–29, 1931–May 12, 1938; Secy. of the Treasury July 23, 1945–June 23, 1946; Chief Justice United States June 24, 1946–Sept. 8, 1953.

Vinton, Samuel Finley (W Ohio) Sept. 25, 1792–May 11, 1862; House 1823–37 (1823–33 no party, 1833–35 Anti-Jacksonian), 1843–51.

Visclosky, Peter (D Ind.) Aug. 13, 1949– ; House 1985– .

Vitter, David (R La.) May 16, 1961– ; House June 8, 1999– .

Vivian, Weston Edward (D Mich.) Oct. 25, 1924– ; House 1965–67.

Voigt, Edward (R Wis.) Dec. 1, 1873–Aug. 26, 1934; House 1917–27.

Voinovich, George V. (R Ohio) July 15, 1936– ; Senate 1999– ; Gov. Jan. 14, 1991–Jan. 1, 1999.

Volk, Lester David (R N.Y.) Sept. 17, 1884–April 30, 1962; House Nov. 2, 1920–23.

Volkmer, Harold Lee (D Mo.) April 4, 1931– ; House 1977–97.

Vollmer, Henry (D Iowa) July 28, 1867–Aug. 25, 1930; House Feb. 10, 1914–15.

Volstead, Andrew John (R Minn.) Oct. 31, 1860–Jan. 20, 1947; House 1903–23.

Voorhees, Charles Stewart (son of Daniel Wolsey Voorhees) (D Wash.) June 4, 1853–Dec. 26, 1909; House (Terr. Del.) 1885–89.

Voorhees, Daniel Wolsey (father of Charles Stewart Voorhees) (D Ind.) Sept. 26, 1827–April 10, 1897; House 1861–Feb. 23, 1866, 1869–73; Senate Nov. 6, 1877–97.

Voorhis, Charles Henry (R N.J.) March 13, 1833–April 15, 1896; House 1879–81.

Voorhis, Horace Jeremiah "Jerry" (D Calif.) April 6, 1901–Sept. 11, 1984; House 1937–47.

Vorys, John Martin (R Ohio) June 16, 1896–Aug. 25, 1968; House 1939–59.

Vose, Roger (F N.H.) Feb. 24, 1763–Oct. 26, 1841; House 1813–17.

Vreeland, Albert Lincoln (R N.J.) July 2, 1901–May 3, 1975; House 1939–43.

Vreeland, Edward Butterfield (R N.Y.) Dec. 7, 1856–May 8, 1936; House Nov. 7, 1899–1913.

Vroom, Peter Dumont (D N.J.) Dec. 12, 1791–Nov. 18, 1873; House 1839–41; Gov. Nov. 6, 1829–Oct. 26, 1832, Oct. 25, 1833–Oct. 28, 1836.

Vucanovich, Barbara Farrell (R Nev.) June 22, 1921– ; House 1983–97.

Vursell, Charles Wesley (cousin of Carl Bert Albert) (R Ill.) Feb. 8, 1881–Sept. 21, 1974; House 1943–59.

W

Wachter, Frank Charles (R Md.) Sept. 16, 1861–July 1, 1910; House 1899–1907.

Waddell, Alfred Moore (D N.C.) Sept. 16, 1834–March 17, 1912; House 1871–79.

Waddill, Edmund Jr. (R Va.) May 22, 1855–April 9, 1931; House April 12, 1890–91.

Waddill, James Richard (D Mo.) Nov. 22, 1842–June 14, 1917; House 1879–81.

Wade, Benjamin Franklin (brother of Edward Wade) (R Ohio) Oct. 27, 1800–March 2, 1878; Senate March 15, 1851–69 (1851–57 Whig); elected Pres. pro tempore March 2, 1867.

Wade, Edward (brother of Benjamin Franklin Wade) (R Ohio) Nov. 22, 1802–Aug. 13, 1866; House 1853–61 (1853–55 Free-Soiler).

Wade, Martin Joseph (D Iowa) Oct. 20, 1861–April 16, 1931; House 1903–05.

Wade, William Henry (R Mo.) Nov. 3, 1835–Jan. 13, 1911; House 1885–91.

Wadleigh, Bainbridge (R N.H.) Jan. 4, 1831–Jan. 24, 1891; Senate 1873–79.

Wadsworth, James Wolcott (father of James Wolcott Wadsworth Jr., great-grandfather of James Wadsworth Symington) (R N.Y.) Oct. 12, 1846–Dec. 24, 1926; House Nov. 8, 1881–85, 1891–1907.

Wadsworth, James Wolcott Jr. (son of James Wolcott Wadsworth, grandfather of James Wadsworth Symington, father-in-law of Stuart Symington) (R N.Y.) Aug. 12, 1877–June 21, 1952; Senate 1915–27; House 1933–51.

Wadsworth, Jeremiah (– Conn.) July 12, 1743–April 30, 1804; House 1789–95; Cont. Cong. 1788.

Wadsworth, Peleg (F Mass.) May 6, 1748–Nov. 12, 1829; House 1793–1807.

Wadsworth, William Henry (R Ky.) July 4, 1821–April 2, 1893; House 1861–65 (Unionist), 1885–87.

Wagener, David Douglas (D Pa.) Oct. 11, 1792–Oct. 1, 1860; House 1833–41 (1833–37 Jacksonian).

Waggaman, George Augustus (– La.) 1782–March 31, 1843; Senate Nov. 15, 1831–35.

Waggonner, Joseph David Jr. (D La.) Sept. 7, 1918– ; House Dec. 19, 1961–79.

Wagner, Earl Thomas (D Ohio) April 27, 1908–March 6, 1990; House 1949–51.

Wagner, Peter Joseph (W N.Y.) Aug. 14, 1795–Sept. 13, 1884; House 1839–41.

Wagner, Robert Ferdinand (D N.Y.) June 8, 1877–May 4, 1953; Senate 1927–June 28, 1949.

Wagoner, George Chester Robinson (R Mo.) Sept. 3, 1863–April 27, 1946; House Feb. 26, 1901–03.

Wainwright, Jonathan Mayhew (R N.Y.) Dec. 10, 1864–June 3, 1945; House 1923–31.

Wainwright, Stuyvesant II (R N.Y.) March 16, 1921– ; House 1953–61.

Wait, John Turner (R Conn.) Aug. 27, 1811–April 21, 1899; House April 12, 1876–87.

Wakefield, James Beach (R Minn.) March 21, 1825–Aug. 25, 1910; House 1883–87.

Wakeman, Abram (W N.Y.) May 31, 1824–June 29, 1889; House 1855–57.

Wakeman, Seth (R N.Y.) Jan. 15, 1811–Jan. 4, 1880; House 1871–73.

Walbridge, David Safford (R Mich.) July 30, 1802–June 15, 1868; House 1855–59.

Walbridge, Henry Sanford (cousin of Hiram Walbridge) (W N.Y.) April 8, 1801–Jan. 27, 1869; House 1851–53.

Walbridge, Hiram (cousin of Henry Sanford Walbridge) (D N.Y.) Feb. 2, 1821–Dec. 6, 1870; House 1853–55.

Walcott, Frederic Collin (R Conn.) Feb. 19, 1869–April 27, 1949; Senate 1929–35.

Walden, Greg (R Ore.) Jan. 10, 1957– ; House 1999– .

Walden, Hiram (D N.Y.) Aug. 21, 1800–July 21, 1880; House 1849–51.

Walden, Madison Miner (R Iowa) Oct. 6, 1836–July 24, 1891; House 1871–73.

Waldholz, Enid Greene (R Utah) Oct. 5, 1958– ; House 1995–97.

Waldie, Jerome Russell (D Calif.) Feb. 15, 1925– ; House June 7, 1966–75.

Waldo, George Ernest (R N.Y.) Jan. 11, 1851–June 16, 1942; House 1905–09.

Waldo, Loren Pinckney (D Conn.) Feb. 2, 1802–Sept. 8, 1881; House 1849–51.

Waldon, Alton R. Jr. (D N.Y.) Dec. 21, 1936– ; House July 29, 1986–87.

Waldow, William Frederick (R N.Y.) Aug. 26, 1882–April 16, 1930; House 1917–19.

Waldron, Alfred Marpole (R Pa.) Sept. 21, 1865–June 28, 1952; House 1933–35.

Waldron, Henry (R Mich.) Oct. 11, 1819–Sept. 13, 1880; House 1855–61, 1871–77.

Wales, George Edward (– Vt.) May 13, 1792–Jan. 8, 1860; House 1825–29.

Wales, John (W Del.) July 31, 1783–Dec. 3, 1863; Senate Feb. 3, 1849–51.

Walgren, Douglas (D Pa.) Dec. 28, 1940– ; House 1977–91.

Walker, Amasa (R Mass.) May 4, 1799–Oct. 29, 1875; House Dec. 1, 1862–63.

Walker, Benjamin (F N.Y.) 1753–Jan. 13, 1818; House 1801–03.

Walker, Charles Christopher Brainerd (D N.Y.) June 27, 1824–Jan. 26, 1888; House 1875–77.

Walker, David (brother of George Walker, grandfather of James David Walker) (R Ky.) ?–March 1, 1820; House 1817–March 1, 1820.

Walker, E. S. Johnny (D N.M.) June 18, 1911– ; House 1965–69.

Walker, Felix (R N.C.) July 19, 1753–1828; House 1817–23.

Walker, Francis (brother of John Walker) (– Va.) June 22, 1764–March 1806; House 1793–95.

Walker, Freeman (– Ga.) Oct. 25, 1780–Sept. 23, 1827; Senate Nov. 6, 1819–Aug. 6, 1821.

Walker, George (brother of David Walker, great-uncle of James David Walker) (– Ky.) 1763–1819; Senate Aug. 30–Dec. 16, 1814.

Walker, Gilbert Carlton (D Va.) Aug. 1, 1833–May 11, 1885; House 1875–79; Gov. (Provisional) Sept. 21, 1869–Jan. 1, 1870, Jan. 1, 1870–Jan. 1, 1874 (Conservative).

Walker, Isaac Pigeon (D Wis.) Nov. 2, 1815–March 29, 1872; Senate June 8, 1848–55.

Walker, James Alexander (R Va.) Aug. 27, 1832–Oct. 21, 1901; House 1895–99.

Walker, James David (grandson of David Walker, nephew of Finis Ewing McLean and John McLean born in 1791, cousin of Wilkinson Call, great-nephew of George Walker) (D Ark.) Dec. 13, 1830–Oct. 17, 1906; Senate 1879–85.

Walker, James Peter (D Mo.) March 14, 1851–July 19, 1890; House 1887–July 19, 1890.

Walker, John (brother of Francis Walker) (– Va.) Feb. 13, 1744–Dec. 2, 1809; Senate March 31–Nov. 9, 1790; Cont. Cong. 1780.

Walker, John Randall (D Ga.) Feb. 23, 1874–?; House 1913–19.

Walker, John Williams (father of Percy Walker, great-great-grandfather of Richard Walker Bolling) (D Ala.) Aug. 12, 1783–April 23, 1823; Senate Dec. 14, 1819–Dec. 12, 1822.

Walker, Joseph Henry (R Mass.) Dec. 21, 1829–April 3, 1907; House 1889–99.

Walker, Lewis Leavell (R Ky.) Feb. 15, 1873–June 30, 1944; House 1929–31.

Walker, Percy (son of John Williams Walker, great-great-uncle of Richard Walker Bolling) (AP Ala.) Dec. 1812–Dec. 31, 1880; House 1855–57.

Walker, Prentiss Lafayette (R Miss.) Aug. 23, 1917–June 5, 1998; House 1965–67.

Walker, Robert Jarvis Cochran (R Pa.) Oct. 20, 1838–Dec. 19, 1903; House 1881–83.

Walker, Robert John (D Miss.) July 19, 1801–Nov. 11, 1869; Senate 1835–March 5, 1845; Secy. of the Treasury March 8, 1845–March 5, 1849; Gov. (Kan. Terr.) April–Dec. 1857.

Walker, Robert Smith (R Pa.) Dec. 23, 1942– ; House 1977–97; Chrmn. House Science 1995–97.

Walker, Walter (D Colo.) April 3, 1883–Oct. 8, 1956; Senate Sept. 26–Dec. 6, 1932.

Walker, William Adams (D N.Y.) June 5, 1805–Dec. 18, 1861; House 1853–55.

Wall, Garret Dorset (father of James Walter Wall) (J N.J.) March 10, 1783–Nov. 22, 1850; Senate 1835–41.

Wall, James Walter (son of Garret Dorset Wall) (D N.J.) May 26, 1820–June 9, 1872; Senate Jan. 14–March 3, 1863.

Wall, William (R N.Y.) March 20, 1800–April 20, 1872; House 1861–63.

Wallace, Alexander Stuart (R S.C.) Dec. 30, 1810–June 27, 1893; House May 27, 1870–77.

Wallace, Daniel (D S.C.) May 9, 1801–May 13, 1859; House June 12, 1848–53.

Wallace, David (W Ind.) April 24, 1799–Sept. 4, 1859; House 1841–43; Gov. Dec. 6, 1837–Dec. 9, 1840.

Wallace, James M. (R Pa.) 1750–Dec. 17, 1823; House Oct. 10, 1815–21.

Wallace, John Winfield (R Pa.) Dec. 20, 1818–June 24, 1889; House 1861–63, 1875–77.

Wallace, Jonathan Hasson (D Ohio) Oct. 31, 1824–Oct. 28, 1892; House May 27, 1884–85.

Wallace, Nathaniel Dick (D La.) Oct. 27, 1845–July 16, 1894; House Dec. 9, 1886–87.

Wallace, Robert Minor (D Ark.) Aug. 6, 1856–Nov. 9, 1942; House 1903–11.

Wallace, Rodney (R Mass.) Dec. 21, 1823–Feb. 27, 1903; House 1889–91.

Wallace, William Andrew (D Pa.) Nov. 28, 1827–May 22, 1896; Senate 1875–81.

Wallace, William Copeland (R N.Y.) May 21, 1856–Sept. 4, 1901; House 1889–91.

Wallace, William Henson (R Idaho) July 19, 1811–Feb. 7, 1879; House (Terr. Del. Wash.) 1861–63, (Terr. Del. Idaho) Feb. 1, 1864–65; Gov. (Idaho Terr.) 1863.

Walley, Samuel Hurd (W Mass.) Aug. 31, 1805–Aug. 27, 1877; House 1853–55.

Wallgren, Monrad Charles (D Wash.) April 17, 1891–Sept. 18, 1961; House 1933–Dec. 19, 1940; Senate Dec. 19, 1940–Jan. 9, 1945; Gov. Jan. 8, 1945–Jan. 10, 1949.

Wallhauser, George Marvin (R N.J.) Feb. 10, 1900–Aug. 4, 1993; House 1959–65.

Wallin, Samuel (R N.Y.) July 31, 1856–Dec. 1, 1917; House 1913–15.

Walling, Ansel Tracy (D Ohio) Jan. 10, 1824–June 22, 1896; House 1875–77.

Wallop, Malcolm (R Wyo.) Feb. 27, 1933– ; Senate 1977–95; Chrmn. Senate Select Committee on Ethics 1981–83.

Walls, Josiah Thomas (R Fla.) Dec. 30, 1842–May 5, 1905; House 1871–Jan. 29, 1873 (no party), 1873–April 19, 1876.

Waln, Robert (F Pa.) Feb. 22, 1765–Jan. 24, 1836; House Dec. 3, 1798–1801.

Walsh, Allan Bartholomew (D N.J.) Aug. 29, 1874–Aug. 5, 1953; House 1913–15.

Walsh, Arthur (D N.J.) Feb. 26, 1896–Dec. 13, 1947; Senate Nov. 26, 1943–Dec. 7, 1944.

Walsh, David Ignatius (D Mass.) Nov. 11, 1872–June 11, 1947; Senate 1919–25, Dec. 6, 1926–47; Gov. Jan. 8, 1914–Jan. 6, 1916.

Walsh, James Joseph (D N.Y.) May 22, 1858–May 8, 1909; House 1895–June 2, 1896.

Walsh, James T. (R N.Y.) June 19, 1947– ; House 1989– .

Walsh, John Richard (D Ind.) May 22, 1913–Jan. 23, 1975; House 1949–51.

Walsh, Joseph (R Mass.) Dec. 16, 1875–Jan. 13, 1946; House 1915–Aug. 2, 1922.

Walsh, Michael (D N.Y.) March 8, 1810–March 17, 1859; House 1853–55.

Walsh, Patrick (D Ga.) Jan. 1, 1840–March 19, 1899; Senate April 2, 1894–95.

Walsh, Thomas James (D Mont.) June 12, 1859–March 2, 1933; Senate 1913–March 2, 1933.

Walsh, Thomas Yates (W Md.) 1809–Jan. 20, 1865; House 1851–53.

Walsh, William (D Md.) May 11, 1828–May 17, 1892; House 1875–79.

Walsh, William Francis (R/C N.Y.) July 11, 1912– ; House 1973–79.

Walter, Francis Eugene (D Pa.) May 26, 1894–May 31, 1963; House 1933–May 31, 1963; Chrmn. House Un-American Activities 1955–63.

Walters, Anderson Howell (R Pa.) May 18, 1862–Dec. 7, 1927; House 1913–15, 1919–23, 1925–27.

Walters, Herbert Sanford (D Tenn.) Nov. 17, 1891–Aug. 17, 1973; Senate Aug. 20, 1963–Nov. 3, 1964.

Walthall, Edward Cary (D Miss.) April 4, 1831–April 21, 1898; Senate March 9, 1885–Jan. 24, 1894, 1895–April 21, 1898.

Walton, Charles Wesley (R Maine) Dec. 9, 1819–Jan. 24, 1900; House 1861–May 26, 1862.

Walton, Eliakim Persons (R Vt.) Feb. 17, 1812–Dec. 19, 1890; House 1857–63.

Walton, George (cousin of Matthew Walton) (– Ga.) 1749–Feb. 2, 1804; Senate Nov. 16, 1795–Feb. 20, 1796; Cont. Cong. 1776–77, 1780–81; Gov. Jan. 7–Nov. 9, 1789 (Democratic Republican).

Walton, Matthew (cousin of George Walton) (R Ky.) ?–Jan. 18, 1819; House 1803–07.

Walton, William Bell (D N.M.) Jan. 23, 1871–April 14, 1939; House 1917–19.

Walworth, Reuben Hyde (– N.Y.) Oct. 26, 1788–Nov. 27, 1867; House 1821–23.

Wamp, Zach (R Tenn.) Oct. 28, 1957– ; House 1995– .

Wampler, Fred (D Ind.) Oct. 15, 1909– ; House 1959–61.

Wampler, William Creed (R Va.) April 21, 1926– ; House 1953–55, 1967–83.

Wanger, Irving Price (R Pa.) March 5, 1852–Jan. 14, 1940; House 1893–1911.

Warburton, Herbert Birchby (R Del.) Sept. 21, 1916–July 30, 1983; House 1953–55.

Warburton, Stanton (R Wash.) April 13, 1865–Dec. 24, 1926; House 1911–13.

Ward, Aaron (uncle of Elijah Ward) (D N.Y.) July 5, 1790–March 2, 1867; House 1825–29 (no party), 1831–37 (Jacksonian), 1841–43.

Ward, Andrew Harrison (D Ky.) Jan. 3, 1815–April 16, 1904; House Dec. 3, 1866–67.

Ward, Artemas (father of Artemas Ward Jr.) (– Mass.) Nov. 26, 1727–Oct. 28, 1800; House 1791–95; Cont. Cong. 1780–81.

Ward, Artemas Jr. (son of Artemas Ward) (F Mass.) Jan. 9, 1762–Oct. 7, 1847; House 1813–17.

Ward, Charles Bonnell (R N.Y.) April 27, 1879–May 27, 1946; House 1915–25.

Ward, David Jenkins (D Md.) Sept. 17, 1871–Feb. 18, 1961; House June 6, 1939–45.

Ward, Elijah (nephew of Aaron Ward) (D N.Y.) Sept. 16, 1816–Feb. 7, 1882; House 1857–59, 1861–65, 1875–77.

Ward, Hallett Sydney (D N.C.) Aug. 31, 1870–March 31, 1956; House 1921–25.

Ward, Hamilton (R N.Y.) July 3, 1829–Dec. 28, 1898; House 1865–71.

Ward, James Hugh (D Ill.) Nov. 30, 1853–Aug. 15, 1916; House 1885–87.

Ward, Jasper Delos (R Ill.) Feb. 1, 1829–Aug. 6, 1902; House 1873–75.

Ward, Jonathan (R N.Y.) Sept. 21, 1768–Sept. 28, 1842; House 1815–17.

Ward, Marcus Lawrence (R N.J.) Nov. 9, 1812–April 25, 1884; House 1873–75; Gov. Jan. 16, 1866–Jan. 19, 1869; Chrmn. Rep. Nat. Comm. 1866–68.

Ward, Matthias (D Texas) Oct. 13, 1805–Oct. 5, 1861; Senate Sept. 27, 1858–Dec. 5, 1859.

Ward, Mike (D Ky.) Jan. 7, 1951– ; House 1995–97.

Ward, Thomas (R N.J.) about 1759–March 4, 1842; House 1813–17.

Ward, Thomas Bayless (D Ind.) April 27, 1835–Jan. 1, 1892; House 1883–87.

Ward, William (R Pa.) Jan. 1, 1837–Feb. 27, 1895; House 1877–83.

Ward, William Lukens (R N.Y.) Sept. 2, 1856–July 16, 1933; House 1897–99.

Ward, William Thomas (W Ky.) Aug. 9, 1808–Oct. 12, 1878; House 1851–53.

Wardwell, Daniel (J N.Y.) May 28, 1791–March 27, 1878; House 1831–37.

Ware, John Haines III (R Pa.) Aug. 29, 1908–July 31, 1997; House Nov. 3, 1970–75.

Ware, Nicholas (R Ga.) 1769–Sept. 7, 1824; Senate Nov. 10, 1821–Sept. 7, 1824.

Ware, Orie Solomon (D Ky.) May 11, 1882–Dec. 16, 1974; House 1927–29.

Warfield, Henry Ridgely (– Md.) Sept. 14, 1774–March 18, 1839; House 1819–25.

Warner, Adoniram Judson (D Ohio) Jan. 13, 1834–Aug. 12, 1910; House 1879–81, 1883–87.

Warner, Hiram (D Ga.) Oct. 29, 1802–June 30, 1881; House 1855–57.

Warner, John De Witt (D N.Y.) Oct. 30, 1851–May 27, 1925; House 1891–95.

Warner, John William (R Va.) Feb. 18, 1927– ; Senate Jan. 2, 1979– ; Chrmn. Senate Rules and Administration 1996–99; Chrmn. Senate Armed Services 1999– .

Warner, Levi (brother of Samuel Larkin Warner) (D Conn.) Oct. 10, 1831–April 12, 1911; House Dec. 4, 1876–79.

Warner, Richard (D Tenn.) Sept. 19, 1835–March 4, 1915; House 1881–85.

Warner, Samuel Larkin (brother of Levi Warner) (R Conn.) June 14, 1828–Feb. 6, 1893; House 1865–67.

Warner, Vespasian (R Ill.) April 23, 1842–March 31, 1925; House 1895–1905.

Warner, Willard (R Ala.) Sept. 4, 1826–Nov. 23, 1906; Senate July 13, 1868–71.

Warner, William (R Mo.) June 11, 1840–Oct. 4, 1916; House 1885–89; Senate March 18, 1905–11.

Warnock, William Robert (R Ohio) Aug. 29, 1838–July 30, 1918; House 1901–05.

Warren, Cornelius (W N.Y.) March 15, 1790–July 28, 1849; House 1847–49.

Warren, Edward Allen (D Ark.) May 2, 1818–July 2, 1875; House 1853–55, 1857–59.

Warren, Francis Emroy (R Wyo.) June 20, 1844–Nov. 24, 1929; Senate Nov. 18, 1890–93, 1895–Nov. 24, 1929; Gov. Feb. 1885–86 (Wyo. Terr.), March 1889–Sept. 1890 (Wyo. Terr.), Sept. 11–Nov. 24, 1890.

Warren, Joseph Mabbett (D N.Y.) Jan. 28, 1813–Sept. 9, 1896; House 1871–73.

Warren, Lindsay Carter (D N.C.) Dec. 16, 1889–Dec. 28, 1976; House 1925–Oct. 31, 1940.

Warren, Lott (W Ga.) Oct. 30, 1797–June 17, 1861; House 1839–43.

Warren, William Wirt (D Mass.) Feb. 27, 1834–May 2, 1880; House 1875–77.

Warwick, John George (D Ohio) Dec. 23, 1830–Aug. 14, 1892; House 1891–Aug. 14, 1892.

Washburn, Cadwallader Colden (brother of Israel Washburn Jr., Elihu Benjamin Washburne and William Drew Washburn) (R Wis.) April 22, 1818–May 15, 1882; House 1855–61, 1867–71; Gov. Jan. 1, 1872–Jan. 5, 1874.

Washburn, Charles Grenfill (R Mass.) Jan. 28, 1857–May 25, 1928; House Dec. 18, 1906–11.

Washburn, Henry Dana (R Ind.) March 28, 1832–Jan. 26, 1871; House Feb. 23, 1866–69.

Washburn, Israel Jr. (brother of Elihu Benjamin Washburne, Cadwallader Colden Washburn and William Drew Washburn) (R Maine) June 6, 1813–May 12, 1883; House 1851–Jan. 1, 1861 (1851–55 Whig); Gov. Jan. 2, 1861–Jan. 7, 1863.

Washburn, William Barrett (R Mass.) Jan. 31, 1820–Oct. 5, 1887; House 1863–Dec. 5, 1871; Senate April 29, 1874–75; Gov. Jan. 3, 1872–April 17, 1874.

Washburn, William Drew (brother of Israel Washburn Jr., Elihu Benjamin Washburne and Cadwallader Colden Washburn) (R Minn.) Jan. 14, 1831–July 29, 1912; House 1879–85; Senate 1889–95.

Washburne, Elihu Benjamin (brother of Israel Washburn Jr., Cadwallader Colden Washburn and William Drew Washburn) (R Ill.) Sept. 23, 1816–Oct. 23, 1887; House 1853–March 6, 1869 (1853–55 Whig); Secy. of State March 5–March 16, 1869.

Washington, Craig (D Texas) Oct. 12, 1941– ; House Jan. 23, 1990–95.

Washington, George Corbin (great-nephew of Pres. George Washington) (AJ Md.) Aug. 20, 1789–July 17, 1854; House 1827–33 (no party), 1835–37.

Washington, Harold (D Ill.) April 15, 1922–Nov. 25, 1987; House 1981–April 30, 1983.

Washington, Joseph Edwin (D Tenn.) Nov. 10, 1851–Aug. 28, 1915; House 1887–97.

Washington, William Henry (W N.C.) Feb. 7, 1813–Aug. 12, 1860; House 1841–43.

Wasielewski, Thaddeus Francis Boleslaw (D Wis.) Dec. 2, 1904–April 25, 1976; House 1941–47.

Waskey, Frank Hinman (D Alaska) April 20, 1875–Jan. 18, 1964; House (Terr. Del.) Aug. 14, 1906–07.

Wason, Edward Hills (R N.H.) Sept. 2, 1865–Feb. 6, 1941; House 1915–33.

Waterman, Charles Winfield (R Colo.) Nov. 2, 1861–Aug. 27, 1932; Senate 1927–Aug. 27, 1932.

Waters, Maxine (D Calif.) Aug. 31, 1938– ; House 1991– .

Waters, Russell Judson (R Calif.) June 6, 1843–Sept. 25, 1911; House 1899–1901.

Watkins, Albert Galiton (D Tenn.) May 5, 1818–Nov. 9, 1895; House 1849–53 (Whig), 1855–59.

Watkins, Arthur Vivian (R Utah) Dec. 18, 1886–Sept. 1, 1973; Senate 1947–59.

Watkins, Elton (D Ore.) July 6, 1881–June 24, 1956; House 1923–25.

Watkins, George Robert (R Pa.) May 21, 1902–Aug. 7, 1970; House 1965–Aug. 7, 1970.

Watkins, John Thomas (D La.) Jan. 15, 1854–April 25, 1925; House 1905–21.

Watkins, Wesley Wade (R Okla.) Dec. 15, 1938– ; House 1977–91 (Democrat), 1997– .

Watmough, John Goddard (AJ Pa.) Dec. 6, 1793–Nov. 27, 1861; House 1831–35.

Watres, Laurence Hawley (R Pa.) July 18, 1882–Feb. 6, 1964; House 1923–31.

Watson, Albert William (R S.C.) Aug. 30, 1922–Sept. 25, 1994; House 1963–Feb. 1, 1965 (Democrat), June 15, 1965–71.

Watson, Clarence Wayland (D W.Va.) May 8, 1864–May 24, 1940; Senate Feb. 1, 1911–13.

Watson, Cooper Kinderdine (R Ohio) June 18, 1810–May 20, 1880; House 1855–57.

Watson, David Kemper (R Ohio) June 8, 1849–Sept. 28, 1918; House 1895–97.

Watson, Henry Winfield (R Pa.) June 24, 1856–Aug. 27, 1933; House 1915–Aug. 27, 1933.

Watson, James (F N.Y.) April 6, 1750–May 15, 1806; Senate Aug. 17, 1798–March 19, 1800.

Watson, James Eli (R Ind.) Nov. 2, 1864–July 29, 1948; House 1895–97, 1899–1909; Senate Nov. 8, 1916–33; Senate majority leader 1929–33.

Watson, Lewis Findlay (R Pa.) April 14, 1819–Aug. 25, 1890; House 1877–79, 1881–83, 1889–Aug. 25, 1890.

Watson, Thomas Edward (D Ga.) Sept. 5, 1856–Sept. 26, 1922; House 1891–93 (Populist); Senate 1921–Sept. 26, 1922.

Watson, Walter Allen (D Va.) Nov. 25, 1867–Dec. 24, 1919; House 1913–Dec. 24, 1919.

Watt, Melvin (D N.C.) Aug. 26, 1945– ; House 1993– .

Watterson, Harvey Magee (father of Henry Watterson) (D Tenn.) Nov. 23, 1811–Oct. 1, 1891; House 1839–43.

Watterson, Henry (son of Harvey Magee Watterson, nephew of Stanley Matthews) (D Ky.) Feb. 16, 1840–Dec. 22, 1921; House Aug. 12, 1876–77.

Watts, J. C. (R Okla.) Nov. 18, 1957– ; House 1995– .

Watts, John (– N.Y.) Aug. 27, 1749–Sept. 3, 1836; House 1793–95.

Watts, John Clarence (D Ky.) July 9, 1902–Sept. 24, 1971; House April 14, 1951–Sept. 24, 1971.

Watts, John Sebrie (R N.M.) Jan. 19, 1816–June 11, 1876; House (Terr. Del.) 1861–63.

Waugh, Daniel Webster (R Ind.) March 7, 1842–March 14, 1921; House 1891–95.

Waxman, Henry Arnold (D Calif.) Sept. 12, 1939– ; House 1975– .

Wayne, Anthony (father of Isaac Wayne) (– Ga.) Jan. 1, 1745–Dec. 15, 1796; House 1791–March 21, 1792.

Wayne, Isaac (son of Anthony Wayne) (– Pa.) 1772–Oct. 25, 1852; House 1823–25.

Wayne, James Moore (J Ga.) 1790–July 5, 1867; House 1829–Jan. 13, 1835; Assoc. Justice Supreme Court Jan. 14, 1835–July 5, 1867.

Weadock, Thomas Addis Emmet (D Mich.) Jan. 1, 1850–Nov. 18, 1938; House 1891–95.

Weakley, Robert (R Tenn.) July 20, 1764–Feb. 4, 1845; House 1809–11.

Wearin, Otha Donner (D Iowa) Jan. 10, 1903–April 3, 1990; House 1933–39.

Weatherford, Zadoc Lorenzo (D Ala.) Feb. 4, 1888–May 21, 1983; House Nov. 5, 1940–41.

Weaver, Archibald Jerard (grandfather of Phillip Hart Weaver) (R Neb.) April 15, 1843–April 18, 1887; House 1883–87.

Weaver, Claude (D Okla.) March 19, 1867–May 19, 1954; House 1913–15.

Weaver, James Baird (G Iowa) June 12, 1833–Feb. 6, 1912; House 1879–81, 1885–89.

Weaver, James Dorman (R Pa.) Sept. 27, 1920– ; House 1963–65.

Weaver, James Howard (D Ore.) Aug. 8, 1927– ; House 1975–87.

Weaver, Phillip Hart (grandson of Archibald Jerard Weaver) (R Neb.) April 9, 1919–April 16, 1989; House 1955–63.

Weaver, Walter Lowrie (R Ohio) April 1, 1851–May 26, 1909; House 1897–1901.

Weaver, Zebulon (D N.C.) May 12, 1872–Oct. 29, 1948; House 1917–March 1, 1919, March 4, 1919–29, 1931–47.

Webb, Edwin Yates (D N.C.) May 23, 1872–Feb. 7, 1955; House 1903–Nov. 10, 1919.

Webb, William Robert (grandson of Richard Stanford) (D Tenn.) Nov. 11, 1842–Dec. 19, 1926; Senate Jan. 24–March 3, 1913.

Webber, Amos Richard (R Ohio) Jan. 21, 1852–Feb. 25, 1948; House Nov. 8, 1904–07.

Webber, George Washington (R Mich.) Nov. 25, 1825–Jan. 15, 1900; House 1881–83.

Weber, Edward Ford (R Ohio) July 26, 1931– ; House 1981–83.

Weber, John Baptiste (R N.Y.) Sept. 21, 1842–Dec. 18, 1926; House 1885–89.

Weber, John Vincent (R Minn.) July 24, 1952– ; House 1981–93.

Webster, Daniel (W Mass.) Jan. 18, 1782–Oct. 24, 1852; House 1813–17 (Federalist N.H.), 1823–May 30, 1827 (Federalist); Senate May 30, 1827–Feb. 22, 1841 (1827–33 Federalist), 1845–July 22, 1850; Secy. of State March 6, 1841–May 8, 1843, July 23, 1850–Oct. 24, 1852.

Webster, Edwin Hanson (UU Md.) March 31, 1829–April 24, 1893; House 1859–July 1865 (1859–61 American Party, 1861–63 Unionist).

Webster, John Stanley (R Wash.) Feb. 22, 1877–Dec. 24, 1962; House 1919–May 8, 1923.

Webster, Taylor (D Ohio) Oct. 1, 1800–April 27, 1876; House 1833–39 (1833–37 Jacksonian).

Wedemeyer, William Walter (R Mich.) March 22, 1873–Jan. 2, 1913; House 1911–Jan. 2, 1913.

Weeks, Charles Sinclair (son of John Wingate Weeks of Mass.) (R Mass.) June 15, 1893–Feb. 7, 1972; Senate Feb. 8–Dec. 19, 1944; Secy. of Commerce Jan. 21, 1953–Nov. 10, 1958.

Weeks, Edgar (cousin of John Wingate Weeks of Mass.) (R Mich.) Aug. 3, 1839–Dec. 17, 1904; House 1899–1903.

Weeks, John Eliakim (R Vt.) June 14, 1853–Sept. 10, 1949; House 1931–33; Gov. Jan. 6, 1927–Jan. 8, 1931.

Weeks, John Wingate (great-uncle of John Wingate Weeks, below) (J N.H.) March 31, 1781–April 3, 1853; House 1829–33.

Weeks, John Wingate (father of Sinclair Weeks, cousin of Edgar Weeks, great-nephew of John Wingate Weeks, above) (R Mass.) April 11, 1860–July 12, 1926; House 1905–March 4, 1913; Senate 1913–19; Secy. of War March 5, 1921–Oct. 13, 1925.

Weeks, Joseph (grandfather of Joseph Weeks Babcock) (D N.H.) Feb. 13, 1773–Aug. 4, 1845; House 1835–39 (1835–37 Jacksonian).

Weems, Capell Lane (R Ohio) July 7, 1860–Jan. 5, 1913; House Nov. 3, 1903–09.

Weems, John Crompton (– Md.) 1778–Jan. 20, 1862; House Feb. 1, 1826–29.

Wefald, Knud (FL Minn.) Nov. 3, 1869–Oct. 25, 1936; House 1923–27.

Weichel, Alvin F. (R Ohio) Sept. 11, 1891–Nov. 27, 1956; House 1943–55; Chrmn. House Merchant Marine and Fisheries 1947–49, 1953–55.

Weicker, Lowell Palmer Jr. (R Conn.) May 16, 1931– ; House 1969–71; Senate 1971–89; Chrmn. Senate Small Business 1981–87; Gov. Jan. 9, 1991–Jan. 4, 1995.

Weideman, Carl May (D Mich.) March 5, 1898–March 5, 1972; House 1933–35.

Weightman, Richard Hanson (D N.M.) Dec. 28, 1816–Aug. 10, 1861; House (Terr. Del.) 1851–53.

Weiner, Anthony D. (D N.Y.) Sept. 4, 1964– ; House 1999– .

Weis, Jessica McCullough (R N.Y.) July 8, 1901–May 1, 1963; House 1959–63.

Weiss, Samuel Arthur (D Pa.) April 15, 1902–Feb. 1, 1977; House 1941–Jan. 7, 1946.

Weiss, Theodore S. (D N.Y.) Sept. 17, 1927–Sept. 14, 1992; House 1977–Sept. 14, 1992.

Weisse, Charles Herman (D Wis.) Oct. 24, 1866–Oct. 8, 1919; House 1903–11.

Welborn, John (R Mo.) Nov. 20, 1857–Oct. 27, 1907; House 1905–07.

Welch, Adonijah Strong (R Fla.) April 12, 1821–March 14, 1889; Senate June 25, 1868–69.

Welch, Frank (R Neb.) Feb. 10, 1835–Sept. 4, 1878; House 1877–Sept. 4, 1878.

Welch, John (W Ohio) Oct. 28, 1805–Aug. 5, 1891; House 1851–53.

Welch, Philip James (D Mo.) April 4, 1895–April 26, 1963; House 1949–53.

Welch, Richard Joseph (R Calif.) Feb. 13, 1869–Sept. 10, 1949; House Aug. 31, 1926–Sept. 10, 1949; Chrmn. House Public Lands 1947–49.

Welch, William Wickham (AP Conn.) Dec. 10, 1818–July 30, 1892; House 1855–57.

Weldon, Dave (R Fla.) Aug. 31, 1953– ; House 1995– .

Weldon, Wayne Curtis (R Pa.) July 22, 1947– ; House 1987– .

Welker, Herman (R Idaho) Dec. 11, 1906–Oct. 30, 1957; Senate 1951–57.

Welker, Martin (R Ohio) April 25, 1819–March 15, 1902; House 1865–71.

Wellborn, Marshall Johnson (D Ga.) May 29, 1808–Oct. 16, 1874; House 1849–51.

Wellborn, Olin (D Texas) June 18, 1843–Dec. 6, 1921; House 1879–87.

Weller, Jerry (R Ill.) July 7, 1957– ; House 1995– .

Weller, John B. (D Calif.) Feb. 22, 1812–Aug. 17, 1875; House 1839–45 (Democrat Ohio); Senate Jan. 30, 1852–57; Gov. Jan. 8, 1858–Jan. 9, 1860.

Weller, Luman Hamlin (G Iowa) Aug. 24, 1833–March 2, 1914; House 1883–85.

Weller, Ovington Eugene (R Md.) Jan. 23, 1862–Jan. 5, 1947; Senate 1921–27.

Weller, Royal Hurlburt (D N.Y.) July 2, 1881–March 1, 1929; House 1923–March 1, 1929.

Welling, Milton Holmes (D Utah) Jan. 25, 1876–May 28, 1947; House 1917–21.

Wellington, George Louis (R Md.) Jan. 28, 1852–March 20, 1927; House 1895–97; Senate 1897–1903.

Wells, Alfred (R N.Y.) May 27, 1814–July 18, 1867; House 1859–61.

Wells, Daniel Jr. (D Wis.) July 16, 1808–March 18, 1902; House 1853–57.

Wells, Erastus (D Mo.) Dec. 2, 1823–Oct. 2, 1893; House 1869–77, 1879–81.

Wells, Guilford Wiley (IR Miss.) Feb. 14, 1840–March 21, 1909; House 1875–77.

Wells, John (W N.Y.) July 1, 1817–May 30, 1877; House 1851–53.

Wells, John Sullivan (– N.H.) Oct. 18, 1803–Aug. 1, 1860; Senate Jan. 16–March 3, 1855.

Wells, Owen Augustine (D Wis.) Feb. 4, 1844–Jan. 29, 1935; House 1893–95.

Wells, William Hill (F Del.) Jan. 7, 1769–March 11, 1829; Senate Jan. 17, 1799–Nov. 6, 1804, May 28, 1813–17.

Wellstone, Paul (D Minn.) July 21, 1944– ; Senate 1991– .

Welsh, George Austin (R Pa.) Aug. 9, 1878–Oct. 22, 1970; House 1923–May 31, 1932.

Weltner, Charles Longstreet (D Ga.) Dec. 17, 1927–Aug. 31, 1992; House 1963–67.

Welty, Benjamin Franklin (D Ohio) Aug. 9, 1870–Oct. 23, 1962; House 1917–21.

Wemple, Edward (D N.Y.) Oct. 23, 1843–Dec. 18, 1920; House 1883–85.

Wendover, Peter Hercules (R N.Y.) Aug. 1, 1768–Sept. 24, 1834; House 1815–21.

Wene, Elmer H. (D N.J.) May 1, 1892–Jan. 25, 1957; House 1937–39, 1941–45.

Wentworth, John (R Ill.) March 5, 1815–Oct. 16, 1888; House 1843–51 (Democrat), 1853–55 (Democrat), 1865–67.

Wentworth, Tappan (W Mass.) Feb. 24, 1802–June 12, 1875; House 1853–55.

Werdel, Thomas Harold (R Calif.) Sept. 13, 1905–Sept. 30, 1966; House 1949–53.

Werner, Theodore B. (D S.D.) June 2, 1892–Jan. 24, 1988; House 1933–37.

Wertz, George M. (R Pa.) July 19, 1856–Nov. 19, 1928; House 1923–25.

West, Charles Franklin (D Ohio) Jan. 12, 1895–Dec. 27, 1955; House 1931–35.

West, George (R N.Y.) Feb. 17, 1823–Sept. 20, 1901; House 1881–83, 1885–89.

West, Joseph Rodman (R La.) Sept. 19, 1822–Oct. 31, 1898; Senate 1871–77.

West, Milton Horace (D Texas) June 30, 1888–Oct. 28, 1948; House April 22, 1933–Oct. 28, 1948.

West, William Stanley (– Ga.) Aug. 23, 1849–Dec. 22, 1914; Senate March 2–Nov. 3, 1914.

Westbrook, John (D Pa.) Jan. 9, 1789–Oct. 8, 1852; House 1841–43.

Westbrook, Theodoric Romeyn (D N.Y.) Nov. 20, 1821–Oct. 6, 1885; House 1853–55.

Westcott, James Diament Jr. (D Fla.) May 10, 1802–Jan. 19, 1880; Senate July 1, 1845–49.

Westerlo, Rensselaer (F N.Y.) April 29, 1776–April 18, 1851; House 1817–19.

Westland, Aldred John (R Wash.) Dec. 14, 1904–Nov. 3, 1982; House 1953–65.

Wethered, John (W Md.) May 8, 1809–Feb. 15, 1888; House 1843–45.

Wetmore, George Peabody (R R.I.) Aug. 2, 1846–Sept. 11, 1921; Senate 1895–1907, Jan. 22, 1908–13; Gov. May 26, 1885–May 31, 1887.

Wever, John Madison (R N.Y.) Feb. 24, 1847–Sept. 27, 1914; House 1891–95.

Wexler, Robert (D Fla.) Jan. 2, 1961– ; House 1997– .

Weygand, Robert A. (D R.I.) May 10, 1948– ; House 1997– .

Weymouth, George Warren (R Mass.) Aug. 25, 1850–Sept. 7, 1910; House 1897–1901.

Whalen, Charles William Jr. (R Ohio) July 31, 1920– ; House 1967–79.

Whaley, Kellian Van Rensalear (UU W.Va.) May 6, 1821–May 20, 1876; House 1861–63 (Unionist Va.), Dec. 7, 1863–67.

Whaley, Richard Smith (D S.C.) July 15, 1874–Nov. 8, 1951; House April 29, 1913–21.

Whalley, John Irving (R Pa.) Sept. 14, 1902–March 8, 1980; House Nov. 8, 1960–73.

Whallon, Reuben (J N.Y.) Dec. 7, 1776–April 15, 1843; House 1833–35.

Wharton, Charles Stuart (R Ill.) April 22, 1875–Sept. 4, 1939; House 1905–07.

Wharton, James Ernest (R N.Y.) Oct. 4, 1899–Jan. 12, 1990; House 1951–65.

Wharton, Jesse (grandfather of Wharton Jackson Green) (R Tenn.) July 29, 1782–July 22, 1833; House 1807–09; Senate March 17, 1814–Oct. 10, 1815.

Wheat, Alan Dupree (D Mo.) Oct. 16, 1951– ; House 1983–95.

Wheat, William Howard (R Ill.) Feb. 19, 1879–Jan. 16, 1944; House 1939–Jan. 16, 1944.

Wheaton, Horace (D N.Y.) Feb. 24, 1803–June 23, 1882; House 1843–47.

Wheaton, Laban (F Mass.) March 13, 1754–March 23, 1846; House 1809–17.

Wheeler, Burton Kendall (D Mont.) Feb. 27, 1882–Jan. 6, 1975; Senate 1923–47.

Wheeler, Charles Kennedy (D Ky.) April 18, 1863–June 15, 1933; House 1897–1903.

Wheeler, Ezra (D Wis.) Dec. 23, 1820–Sept. 19, 1871; House 1863–65.

Wheeler, Frank Willis (R Mich.) March 2, 1853–Aug. 9, 1921; House 1889–91.

Wheeler, Grattan Henry (AMas. N.Y.) Aug. 25, 1783–March 11, 1852; House 1831–33.

Wheeler, Hamilton Kinkaid (R Ill.) Aug. 5, 1848–July 19, 1918; House 1893–95.

Wheeler, Harrison H. (D Mich.) March 22, 1839–July 28, 1896; House 1891–93.

Wheeler, John (D N.Y.) Feb. 11, 1823–April 1, 1906; House 1853–57.

Wheeler, Joseph (D Ala.) Sept. 10, 1836–Jan. 25, 1906; House 1881–June 3, 1882, Jan. 15–March 3, 1883, 1885–April 20, 1900.

Wheeler, Loren Edgar (R Ill.) Oct. 7, 1862–Jan. 8, 1932; House 1915–23, 1925–27.

Wheeler, Nelson Platt (R Pa.) Nov. 4, 1841–March 3, 1920; House 1907–11.

Wheeler, William Almon (R N.Y.) June 30, 1819–June 4, 1887; House 1861–63, 1869–77; Vice President 1877–81.

Wheeler, William McDonald (D Ga.) July 11, 1915– ; House 1947–55.

Whelchel, Benjamin Frank (D Ga.) Dec. 16, 1895–May 11, 1954; House 1935–45.

Wherry, Kenneth Spicer (R Neb.) Feb. 28, 1892–Nov. 29, 1951; Senate 1943–Nov. 29, 1951; Senate minority leader 1949–Nov. 29, 1951.

Whipple, Thomas Jr. (– N.H.) 1787–Jan. 23, 1835; House 1821–29.

Whitacre, John Jefferson (D Ohio) Dec. 28, 1860–Dec. 2, 1938; House 1911–15.

Whitaker, John Albert (grandson of Addison Davis James) (D Ky.) Oct. 31, 1901–Dec. 15, 1951; House April 17, 1948–Dec. 15, 1951.

Whitcomb, James (D Ind.) Dec. 1, 1795–Oct. 4, 1852; Senate 1849–Oct. 4, 1852; Gov. Dec. 6, 1843–Dec. 27, 1849.

White, Addison (cousin of John White) (W Ky.) May 1, 1824–Feb. 4, 1909; House 1851–53.

White, Albert Smith (R Ind.) Oct. 24, 1803–Sept. 24, 1864; House 1837–39 (Whig), 1861–63; Senate 1839–45 (Whig).

White, Alexander (– Va.) 1738–Sept. 19, 1804; House 1789–93.

White, Alexander (R Ala.) Oct. 16, 1816–Dec. 13, 1893; House 1851–53 (Whig), 1873–75.

White, Alexander Colwell (R Pa.) Dec. 12, 1833–June 11, 1906; House 1885–87.

White, Allison (D Pa.) Dec. 21, 1816–April 5, 1886; House 1857–59.

White, Bartow (– N.Y.) Nov. 7, 1776–Dec. 12, 1862; House 1825–27.

White, Benjamin (D Maine) May 13, 1790–June 7, 1860; House 1843–45.

White, Campbell Patrick (J N.Y.) Nov. 30, 1787–Feb. 12, 1859; House 1829–35.

White, Cecil Fielding (D Calif.) Dec. 12, 1900–March 29, 1992; House 1949–51.

White, Chilton Allen (D Ohio) Feb. 6, 1826–Dec. 7, 1900; House 1861–65.

White, Compton Ignatius (father of Compton Ignatius White Jr.) (D Idaho) July 31, 1877–March 31, 1956; House 1933–47, 1949–51.

White, Compton Ignatius Jr. (son of Compton Ignatius White) (D Idaho) Dec. 19, 1920–Oct. 19, 1998; House 1963–67.

White, David (– Ky.) 1785–Oct. 19, 1834; House 1823–25.

White, Dudley Allen (R Ohio) Jan. 3, 1901–Oct. 14, 1957; House 1937–41.

White, Edward Douglass Sr. (son of James White, father of Edward Douglass White) (W La.) March 1795–April 18, 1847; House 1829–Nov. 15, 1834 (no party), 1839–43; Gov. Feb. 2, 1835–Feb. 4, 1839.

White, Edward Douglass (grandson of James White, son of Edward Douglas White Sr.) (D La.) Nov. 3, 1845–May 19, 1921; Senate 1891–March 12, 1894; Assoc. Justice Supreme Court March 12, 1894–Dec. 18, 1910; Chief Justice United States Dec. 19, 1910–May 19, 1921.

White, Francis (F Va.) ?–Nov. 1826; House 1813–15.

White, Francis Shelley "Frank" (D Ala.) March 13, 1847–Aug. 1, 1922; Senate May 11, 1914–15.

White, Frederick Edward (D Iowa) Jan. 19, 1844–Jan. 14, 1920; House 1891–93.

White, George (D Ohio) Aug. 21, 1872–Dec. 15, 1953; House 1911–15, 1917–19; Chrmn. Dem. Nat. Comm. 1920–21; Gov. Jan. 12, 1931–Jan. 14, 1935.

White, George Elon (R Ill.) March 7, 1848–May 17, 1935; House 1895–99.

White, George Henry (R N.C.) Dec. 18, 1852–Dec. 28, 1918; House 1897–1901.

White, Harry (R Pa.) Jan. 12, 1834–June 23, 1920; House 1877–81.

White, Hays Baxter (R Kan.) Sept. 21, 1855–Sept. 29, 1930; House 1919–29.

White, Hugh (W N.Y.) Dec. 25, 1798–Oct. 6, 1870; House 1845–51.

White, Hugh Lawson (J Tenn.) Oct. 30, 1773–April 10, 1840; Senate Oct. 28, 1825–Jan. 13, 1840 (Oct. 28, 1825–29 no party); elected Pres. pro tempore Dec. 3, 1832.

White, James (father of Edward Douglass White Sr., grandfather of Edward Douglass White) (– Tenn.) June 16, 1749–Oct. 1809; House (Terr. Del.) Sept. 3, 1794–June 1, 1796; Cont. Cong. 1786–88 (N.C.).

White, James Bain (R Ind.) June 26, 1835–Oct. 9, 1897; House 1887–89.

White, James Bamford (D Ky.) June 6, 1842–March 25, 1931; House 1901–03.

White, John (cousin of Addison White, uncle of John Daugherty White) (W Ky.) Feb. 14, 1802–Sept. 22, 1845; House 1835–45; Speaker May 31, 1841–43.

White, John Daugherty (nephew of John White) (R Ky.) Jan. 16, 1849–Jan. 5, 1920; House 1875–77, 1881–85.

White, Joseph Livingston (W Ind.) ?–Jan. 12, 1861; House 1841–43.

White, Joseph M. (– Fla.) May 10, 1781–Oct. 19, 1839; House (Terr. Del.) 1825–37.

White, Joseph Worthington (D Ohio) Oct. 2, 1822–Aug. 6, 1892; House 1863–65.

White, Leonard (F Mass.) May 3, 1767–Oct. 10, 1849; House 1811–13.

White, Michael Doherty (R Ind.) Sept. 8, 1827–Feb. 6, 1917; House 1877–79.

White, Milo (R Minn.) Aug. 17, 1830–May 18, 1913; House 1883–87.

White, Phineas (– Vt.) Oct. 30, 1770–July 6, 1847; House 1821–23.

White, Richard Crawford (D Texas) April 29, 1923–Feb. 18, 1998; House 1965–83.

White, Rick (R Wash.) Nov. 6, 1953–   ; House 1995–99.

White, Samuel (F Del.) Dec. 1770–Nov. 4, 1809; Senate Feb. 28, 1801–Nov. 4, 1809.

White, Sebastian Harrison (D Colo.) Dec. 24, 1864–Dec. 21, 1945; House Nov. 15, 1927–29.

White, Stephen Mallory (D Calif.) Jan. 19, 1853–Feb. 21, 1901; Senate 1893–99.

White, Stephen Van Culen (R N.Y.) Aug. 1, 1831–Jan. 18, 1913; House 1887–89.

White, Wallace Humphrey Jr. (grandson of William Pierce Frye) (R Maine) Aug. 6, 1877–March 31, 1952; House 1917–31; Senate 1931–49; Senate minority leader 1945–47; Senate majority leader 1947–49; Chrmn. Senate Interstate and Foreign Commerce 1947–49.

White, Wilbur McKee (R Ohio) Feb. 22, 1890–Dec. 31, 1973; House 1931–33.

White, William John (R Ohio) Oct. 7, 1850–Feb. 16, 1923; House 1893–95.

Whiteaker, John (D Ore.) May 4, 1820–Oct. 2, 1902; House 1879–81; Gov. March 3, 1859–Sept. 10, 1862.

Whitehead, Joseph (D Va.) Oct. 31, 1867–July 8, 1938; House 1925–31.

Whitehead, Thomas (D Va.) Dec. 27, 1825–July 1, 1901; House 1873–75.

Whitehill, James (son of John Whitehill, nephew of Robert Whitehill) (R Pa.) Jan. 31, 1762–Feb. 26, 1822; House 1813–Sept. 1, 1814.

Whitehill, John (father of James Whitehill, brother of Robert Whitehill) (R Pa.) Dec. 11, 1729–Sept. 16, 1815; House 1803–07.

Whitehill, Robert (brother of John Whitehill, uncle of James Whitehill, great-great-grandfather of John Crain Kunkel) (R Pa.) July 21, 1738–April 8, 1813; House Nov. 7, 1805–April 8, 1813.

Whitehouse, John Osborne (D N.Y.) July 19, 1817–Aug. 24, 1881; House 1873–77.

Whitehurst, George William (R Va.) March 12, 1925–   ; House 1969–87.

Whitelaw, Robert Henry (D Mo.) Jan. 30, 1854–July 27, 1937; House Nov. 4, 1890–91.

Whiteley, Richard Henry (R Ga.) Dec. 22, 1830–Sept. 26, 1890; House Dec. 22, 1870–75.

Whiteley, William Gustavus (D Del.) Aug. 7, 1819–April 23, 1886; House 1857–61.

Whitener, Basil Lee (D N.C.) May 14, 1915–March 20, 1989; House 1957–69.

Whiteside, Jenkin (R Tenn.) 1772–Sept. 25, 1822; Senate April 11, 1809–Oct. 8, 1811.

Whiteside, John (R Pa.) 1773–July 28, 1830; House 1815–19.

Whitfield, Edward (R Ky.) May 25, 1943–   ; House 1995–   .

Whitfield, John Wilkins (D Kan.) March 11, 1818–Oct. 27, 1879; House (Terr. Del.) Dec. 20, 1854–Aug. 1, 1856, Dec. 9, 1856–57.

Whiting, Justin Rice (D Mich.) Feb. 18, 1847–Jan. 31, 1903; House 1887–95.

Whiting, Richard Henry (uncle of Ira Clifton Copley) (R Ill.) Jan. 17, 1826–May 24, 1888; House 1875–77.

Whiting, William (R Mass.) March 3, 1813–June 29, 1873; House March 4–June 29, 1873.

Whiting, William (R Mass.) May 24, 1841–Jan. 9, 1911; House 1883–89.

Whitley, Charles Orville (D N.C.) Jan. 3, 1927–   ; House 1977–Dec. 31, 1986.

Whitley, James Lucius (R N.Y.) May 24, 1872–May 17, 1959; House 1929–35.

Whitman, Ezekiel (F Maine) March 9, 1776–Aug. 1, 1866; House 1809–11 (Mass.), 1817–21 (Mass.), 1821–June 1, 1822.

Whitman, Lemuel (– Conn.) June 8, 1780–Nov. 13, 1841; House 1823–25.

Whitmore, Elias (– N.Y.) March 2, 1772–Dec. 26, 1853; House 1825–27.

Whitmore, George Washington (R Texas) Aug. 26, 1824–Oct. 14, 1876; House March 30, 1870–71.

Whitney, Thomas Richard (AP N.Y.) May 2, 1807–April 12, 1858; House 1855–57.

Whittaker, Robert Russell (R Kan.) Sept. 18, 1939– ; House 1979–91.

Whittemore, Benjamin Franklin (R S.C.) May 18, 1824–Jan. 25, 1894; House July 18, 1868–Feb. 24, 1870.

Whitten, Jamie Lloyd (D Miss.) April 18, 1910–Sept. 9, 1995; House Nov. 4, 1941–95; Chrmn. House Appropriations 1978–93.

Whitthorne, Washington Curran (D Tenn.) April 19, 1825–Sept. 21, 1891; House 1871–83, 1887–91; Senate April 16, 1886–87.

Whittington, William Madison (D Miss.) May 4, 1878–Aug. 20, 1962; House 1925–51; Chrmn. House Public Works 1949–51.

Whittlesey, Elisha (uncle of William Augustus Whittlesey, cousin of Frederick Whittlesey and Thomas Tucker Whittlesey) (W Ohio) Oct. 19, 1783–Jan. 7, 1863; House 1823–July 9, 1838 (1823–33 no party, 1833–35 Anti-Mason).

Whittlesey, Frederick (cousin of Elisha Whittlesey and Thomas Tucker Whittlesey) (AMas. N.Y.) June 12, 1799–Sept. 19, 1851; House 1831–35.

Whittlesey, Thomas Tucker (cousin of Elisha Whittlesey and Frederick Whittlesey) (D Conn.) Dec. 8, 1798–Aug. 20, 1868; House April 29, 1836–39 (April 29, 1836–37 Jacksonian).

Whittlesey, William Augustus (nephew of Elisha Whittlesey) (D Ohio) July 14, 1796–Nov. 6, 1866; House 1849–51.

Whyte, William Pinkney (D Md.) Aug. 9, 1824–March 17, 1908; Senate July 13, 1868–69, 1875–81, June 8, 1906–March 17, 1908; Gov. Jan. 10, 1872–March 4, 1874.

Wick, William Watson (D Ind.) Feb. 23, 1796–May 19, 1868; House 1839–41, 1845–49.

Wicker, Roger (R Miss.) July 5, 1951– ; House 1995– .

Wickersham, James (R Alaska) Aug. 24, 1857–Oct. 24, 1939; House (Terr. Del.) 1909–17, Jan. 7–March 3, 1919, March 1–3, 1921, 1931–33.

Wickersham, Victor Eugene (D Okla.) Feb. 9, 1906–March 15, 1988; House April 1, 1941–47, 1949–57, 1961–65.

Wickes, Eliphalet (R N.Y.) April 1, 1769–June 7, 1850; House 1805–07.

Wickham, Charles Preston (R Ohio) Sept. 15, 1836–March 18, 1925; House 1887–91.

Wickliffe, Charles Anderson (grandfather of Robert Charles Wickliffe and John Crepps Wickliffe Beckham) (U Ky.) June 8, 1788–Oct. 31, 1869; House 1823–33 (1823–27 no party, 1827–33 Jacksonian), 1861–63; Gov. Oct. 5, 1839–June 1, 1840 (Whig); Postmaster Gen. Oct. 13, 1841–March 6, 1845.

Wickliffe, Robert Charles (grandson of Charles Anderson Wickliffe, cousin of John Crepps Wickliffe Beckham) (D La.) May 1, 1874–June 11, 1912; House 1909–June 11, 1912.

Widgery, William (R Mass.) about 1753–July 31, 1822; House 1811–13.

Widnall, William Beck (R N.J.) March 17, 1906–Dec. 28, 1983; House Feb. 6, 1950–Dec. 31, 1974.

Wier, Roy William (D Minn.) Feb. 25, 1888–June 27, 1963; House 1949–61.

Wigfall, Louis Tresvant (D Texas) April 21, 1816–Feb. 18, 1874; Senate Dec. 5, 1859–March 23, 1861.

Wiggins, Charles Edward (R Calif.) Dec. 3, 1927– ; House 1967–79.

Wigginton, Peter Dinwiddie (D Calif.) Sept. 6, 1839–July 7, 1890; House 1875–77, Feb. 7, 1878–79.

Wigglesworth, Richard Bowditch (R Mass.) April 25, 1891–Oct. 22, 1960; House Nov. 6, 1928–Nov. 13, 1958.

Wike, Scott (D Ill.) April 6, 1834–Jan. 15, 1901; House 1875–77, 1889–93.

Wilber, David (father of David Forrest Wilber) (R N.Y.) Oct. 5, 1820–April 1, 1890; House 1873–75, 1879–81, 1887–April 1, 1890.

Wilber, David Forrest (son of David Wilber) (R N.Y.) Dec. 7, 1859–Aug. 14, 1928; House 1895–99.

Wilbour, Isaac (R R.I.) April 25, 1763–Oct. 4, 1837; House 1807–09; Gov. May 7, 1806–May 6, 1807 (Democratic Republican).

Wilcox, James Mark (D Fla.) May 21, 1890–Feb. 3, 1956; House 1933–39.

Wilcox, Jeduthun (father of Leonard Wilcox) (F N.H.) Nov. 18, 1768–July 18, 1838; House 1813–17.

Wilcox, John A. (U Miss.) April 18, 1819–Feb. 7, 1864; House 1851–53.

Wilcox, Leonard (son of Jeduthun Wilcox) (D N.H.) Jan. 29, 1799–June 18, 1850; Senate March 1, 1842–43.

Wilcox, Robert William (– Hawaii) Feb. 15, 1855–Oct. 23, 1903; House (Terr. Del.) Nov. 6, 1900–03.

Wilde, Richard Henry (R Ga.) Sept. 24, 1789–Sept. 10, 1847; House 1815–17, Feb. 7–March 3, 1825, Nov. 17, 1827–35.

Wilder, Abel Carter (R Kan.) March 18, 1828–Dec. 22, 1875; House 1863–65.

Wilder, William Henry (R Mass.) May 14, 1855–Sept. 11, 1913; House 1911–Sept. 11, 1913.

Wildman, Zalmon (J Conn.) Feb. 16, 1775–Dec. 10, 1835; House March 4–Dec. 10, 1835.

Wildrick, Isaac (D N.J.) March 3, 1803–March 22, 1892; House 1849–53.

Wiley, Alexander (R Wis.) May 26, 1884–May 26, 1967; Senate 1939–63; Chrmn. Senate Judiciary 1947–49; Chrmn. Senate Foreign Relations 1953–55.

Wiley, Ariosto Appling (brother of Oliver Cicero Wiley) (D Ala.) Nov. 6, 1848–June 17, 1908; House 1901–June 17, 1908.

Wiley, James Sullivan (D Maine) Jan. 22, 1808–Dec. 21, 1891; House 1847–49.

Wiley, John McClure (D N.Y.) Aug. 11, 1846–Aug. 13, 1912; House 1889–91.

Wiley, Oliver Cicero (brother of Ariosto Appling Wiley) (D Ala.) Jan. 30, 1851–Oct. 18, 1917; House Nov. 3, 1908–09.

Wiley, William Halsted (R N.J.) July 10, 1842–May 2, 1925; House 1903–07, 1909–11.

Wilfley, Xenophon Pierce (D Mo.) March 18, 1871–May 4, 1931; Senate April 30–Nov. 5, 1918.

Wilkin, James Whitney (father of Samuel Jones Wilkin) (R N.Y.) 1762–Feb. 23, 1845; House June 7, 1815–19.

Wilkin, Samuel Jones (son of James Whitney Wilkin) (AJ N.Y.) Dec. 17, 1793–March 11, 1866; House 1831–33.

Wilkins, Beriah (D Ohio) July 10, 1846–June 7, 1905; House 1883–89.

Wilkins, William (D Pa.) Dec. 20, 1779–June 23, 1865; Senate 1831–June 30, 1834 (Jacksonian); House 1843–Feb. 14, 1844; Secy. of War Feb. 15, 1844–March 4, 1845.

Wilkinson, Morton Smith (R Minn.) Jan. 22, 1819–Feb. 4, 1894; Senate 1859–65; House 1869–71.

Wilkinson, Theodore Stark (D La.) Dec. 18, 1847–Feb. 1, 1921; House 1887–91.

Willard, Charles Wesley (R Vt.) June 18, 1827–June 8, 1880; House 1869–75.

Willard, George (R Mich.) March 20, 1824–March 26, 1901; House 1873–77.

Willcox, Washington Frederick (D Conn.) Aug. 22, 1834–March 8, 1909; House 1889–93.

Willett, William Forte Jr. (D N.Y.) Nov. 27, 1869–Feb. 12, 1938; House 1907–11.

Willey, Calvin (– Conn.) Sept. 15, 1776–Aug. 23, 1858; Senate May 4, 1825–31.

Willey, Earle Dukes (R Del.) July 21, 1889–March 17, 1950; House 1943–45.

Willey, Waitman Thomas (R W.Va.) Oct. 18, 1811–May 2, 1900; Senate July 9, 1861–63 (Va.), Aug. 4, 1863–71 (Aug. 4, 1863–65 Unionist).

Willford, Albert Clinton (D Iowa) Sept. 21, 1877–March 10, 1937; House 1933–35.

Williams, Abram Pease (R Calif.) Feb. 3, 1832–Oct. 17, 1911; Senate Aug. 4, 1886–87.

Williams, Alpheus Starkey (D Mich.) Sept. 20, 1810–Dec. 21, 1878; House 1875–Dec. 21, 1878.

Williams, Andrew (R N.Y.) Aug. 27, 1828–Oct. 6, 1907; House 1875–79.

Williams, Archibald Hunter Arrington (nephew of Archibald Hunter Arrington) (D N.C.) Oct. 22, 1842–Sept. 5, 1895; House 1891–93.

Williams, Arthur Bruce (R Mich.) Jan. 27, 1872–May 1, 1925; House June 19, 1923–May 1, 1925.

Williams, Benjamin (– N.C.) Jan. 1, 1751–July 20, 1814; House 1793–95; Gov. Nov. 23, 1799–Dec. 6, 1802, Dec. 1, 1807–Dec. 12, 1808 (Democratic Republican).

Williams, Charles Grandison (R Wis.) Oct. 18, 1829–March 30, 1892; House 1873–83.

Williams, Christopher Harris (grandfather of John Sharp Williams) (W Tenn.) Dec. 18, 1798–Nov. 27, 1857; House 1837–43, 1849–53.

Williams, Clyde (D Mo.) Oct. 13, 1873–Nov. 12, 1954; House 1927–29, 1931–43.

Williams, David Rogerson (R S.C.) March 8, 1776–Nov. 17, 1830; House 1805–09, 1811–13; Gov. Dec. 10, 1814–Dec. 5, 1816 (Democrat Republican).

Williams, Elihu Stephen (R Ohio) Jan. 24, 1835–Dec. 1, 1903; House 1887–91.

Williams, George Fred (D Mass.) July 10, 1852–July 11, 1932; House 1891–93.

Williams, George Henry (R Ore.) March 26, 1823–April 4, 1910; Senate 1865–71; Atty. Gen. Jan. 10, 1872–May 15, 1875.

Williams, George Howard (R Mo.) Dec. 1, 1871–Nov. 25, 1963; Senate May 25, 1925–Dec. 5, 1926.

Williams, George Short (R Del.) Oct. 21, 1877–Nov. 22, 1961; House 1939–41.

Williams, Guinn (D Texas) April 22, 1871–Jan. 9, 1948; House May 13, 1922–33.

Williams, Harrison Arlington Jr. (D N.J.) Dec. 10, 1919– ; House Nov. 3, 1953–57; Senate 1959–March 11, 1982; Chrmn. Senate Labor and Public Welfare 1971–77; Chrmn. Senate Human Resources 1977–79; Chrmn. Senate Labor and Human Resources 1979–81.

Williams, Henry (D Mass.) Nov. 30, 1805–May 8, 1887; House 1839–41, 1843–45.

Williams, Hezekiah (D Maine) July 28, 1798–Oct. 23, 1856; House 1845–49.

Williams, Isaac Jr. (R N.Y.) April 5, 1777–Nov. 9, 1860; House Dec. 20, 1813–15, 1817–19, 1823–25.

Williams, James (D Del.) Aug. 4, 1825–April 12, 1899; House 1875–79.

Williams, James Douglas (D Ind.) Jan. 16, 1808–Nov. 20, 1880; House 1875–Dec. 1, 1876; Gov. Jan. 8, 1877–Nov. 20, 1880.

Williams, James Robert (D Ill.) Dec. 27, 1850–Nov. 8, 1923; House Dec. 2, 1889–95, 1899–1905.

Williams, James Wray (D Md.) Oct. 8, 1792–Dec. 2, 1842; House 1841–Dec. 2, 1842.

Williams, Jared (– Va.) March 4, 1766–Jan. 2, 1831; House 1819–25.

Williams, Jared Warner (D N.H.) Dec. 22, 1796–Sept. 29, 1864; House 1837–41; Senate Nov. 29, 1853–July 15, 1854; Gov. June 3, 1847–June 7, 1849.

Williams, Jeremiah Norman (D Ala.) May 29, 1829–May 8, 1915; House 1875–79.

Williams, John (F N.Y.) Sept. 1752–July 22, 1806; House 1795–99.

Williams, John (brother of Lewis Williams and Robert Williams, father of Joseph Lanier Williams, cousin of Marmaduke Williams) (R Tenn.) Jan. 29, 1778–Aug. 10, 1837; Senate Oct. 10, 1815–23.

Williams, John (D N.Y.) Jan. 7, 1807–March 26, 1875; House 1855–57.

Williams, John Bell (D Miss.) Dec. 4, 1918–March 25, 1983; House 1947–Jan. 16, 1968; Gov. Jan. 16, 1968–Jan. 18, 1972.

Williams, John James (R Del.) May 17, 1904–Jan. 11, 1988; Senate 1947–Dec. 31, 1970.

Williams, John McKeown Snow (R Mass.) Aug. 13, 1818–March 19, 1886; House 1873–75.

Williams, John Patrick (D Mont.) Oct. 30, 1937– ; House 1979–97.

Williams, John Sharp (grandson of Christopher Harris Williams) (D Miss.) July 30, 1854–Sept. 27, 1932; House 1893–1909; House minority leader 1903–08; Senate 1911–23.

Williams, John Stuart (D Ky.) July 10, 1818–July 17, 1898; Senate 1879–85.

Williams, Jonathan (– Pa.) May 20, 1750–May 16, 1815; House March 4–May 16, 1815.

Williams, Joseph Lanier (son of John Williams of Tenn., nephew of Lewis Williams and Robert Williams) (W Tenn.) Oct. 23, 1810–Dec. 14, 1865; House 1837–43.

Williams, Lawrence Gordon (R Pa.) Sept. 15, 1913–July 13, 1975; House 1967–75.

Williams, Lemuel (F Mass.) June 18, 1747–Nov. 8, 1828; House 1799–1805.

Williams, Lewis (brother of John Williams of Tenn. and Robert Williams, cousin of Marmaduke Williams, uncle of Joseph Lanier Williams) (W N.C.) Feb. 1, 1782–Feb. 23, 1842; House 1815–Feb. 23, 1842 (1815–35 Republican).

Williams, Lyle (R Ohio) Aug. 23, 1942– ; House 1979–85.

Williams, Marmaduke (cousin of John Williams of Tenn., Lewis Williams and Robert Williams) (R N.C.) April 6, 1774–Oct. 29, 1850; House 1803–09.

Williams, Morgan B. (R Pa.) Sept. 17, 1831–Oct. 13, 1903; House 1897–99.

Williams, Nathan (R N.Y.) Dec. 19, 1773–Sept. 25, 1835; House 1805–07.

Williams, Reuel (D Maine) June 2, 1783–July 25, 1862; Senate 1837–Feb. 15, 1843.

Williams, Richard (R Ore.) Nov. 15, 1836–June 19, 1914; House 1877–79.

Williams, Robert (brother of John Williams of Tenn. and Lewis Williams, cousin of Marmaduke Williams, uncle of Joseph Lanier Williams) (R N.C.) July 12, 1773–Jan. 25, 1836; House 1797–1803; Gov. (Miss. Terr.) 1805–09.

Williams, Seward Henry (R Ohio) Nov. 7, 1870–Sept. 2, 1922; House 1915–17.

Williams, Sherrod (W Ky.) 1804–?; House 1835–41.

Williams, Thomas (R Pa.) Aug. 28, 1806–June 16, 1872; House 1863–69.

Williams, Thomas (D Ala.) Aug. 11, 1825–April 13, 1903; House 1879–85.

Williams, Thomas Hickman (D Miss.) Jan. 20, 1801–May 3, 1851; Senate Nov. 12, 1838–39.

Williams, Thomas Hill (R Miss.) 1780–1840; Senate Dec. 10, 1817–29.

Williams, Thomas Scott (F Conn.) June 26, 1777–Dec. 15, 1861; House 1817–19.

Williams, Thomas Sutler (R Ill.) Feb. 14, 1872–April 5, 1940; House 1915–Nov. 11, 1929.

Williams, Thomas Wheeler (W Conn.) Sept. 28, 1789–Dec. 31, 1874; House 1839–43.

Williams, William (D N.Y.) Sept. 6, 1815–Sept. 10, 1876; House 1871–73.

Williams, William (R Ind.) May 11, 1821–April 22, 1896; House 1867–75.

Williams, William Brewster (R Mich.) July 28, 1826–March 4, 1905; House Dec. 1, 1873–77.

Williams, William Elza (D Ill.) May 5, 1857–Sept. 13, 1921; House 1899–1901, 1913–17.

Williams, William Robert (R N.Y.) Aug. 11, 1884–May 9, 1972; House 1951–59.

Williamson, Ben Mitchell (D Ky.) Oct. 16, 1864–June 23, 1941; Senate Dec. 1, 1930–31.

Williamson, Hugh (F N.C.) Dec. 5, 1735–May 22, 1819; House March 19, 1790–93; Cont. Cong. 1782–85, 1788.

Williamson, John Newton (R Ore.) Nov. 8, 1855–Aug. 29, 1943; House 1903–07.

Williamson, William (R S.D.) Oct. 7, 1875–July 15, 1972; House 1921–33.

Williamson, William Durkee (– Maine) July 31, 1779–May 27, 1846; House 1821–23; Gov. May 29–Dec. 25, 1821.

Willie, Asa Hoxie (D Texas) Oct. 11, 1829–March 16, 1899; House 1873–75.

Willis, Albert Shelby (D Ky.) Jan. 22, 1843–Jan. 6, 1897; House 1877–87.

Willis, Benjamin Albertson (D N.Y.) March 24, 1840–Oct. 14, 1886; House 1875–79.

Willis, Edwin Edward (D La.) Oct. 2, 1904–Oct. 24, 1972; House 1949–69; Chrmn. House Un-American Activities 1963–69.

Willis, Francis (– Ga.) Jan. 5, 1745–Jan. 25, 1829; House 1791–93.

Willis, Frank Bartlett (R Ohio) Dec. 28, 1871–March 30, 1928; House 1911–Jan. 9, 1915; Senate Jan. 14, 1921–March 30, 1928; Gov. Jan. 11, 1915–Jan. 8, 1917.

Willis, Jonathan Spencer (R Del.) April 5, 1830–Nov. 24, 1903; House 1895–97.

Willis, Raymond Eugene (R Ind.) Aug. 11, 1875–March 21, 1956; Senate 1941–47.

Willits, Edwin (R Mich.) April 24, 1830–Oct. 22, 1896; House 1877–83.

Willoughby, Westel Jr. (R N.Y.) Nov. 20, 1769–Oct. 3, 1844; House Dec. 13, 1815–17.

Wilmot, David (R Pa.) Jan. 20, 1814–March 16, 1868; House 1845–51 (Democrat); Senate March 14, 1861–63.

Wilshire, William Wallace (D Ark.) Sept. 8, 1830–Aug. 19, 1888; House 1873–June 16, 1874 (Republican), 1875–77.

Wilson, Alexander (R Va.) ?–?; House Dec. 4, 1804–09.

Wilson, Benjamin (D W.Va.) April 30, 1825–April 26, 1901; House 1875–83.

Wilson, Charles (D Texas) June 1, 1933– ; House 1973–Oct. 8, 1996.

Wilson, Charles Herbert (D Calif.) Feb. 15, 1917–July 21, 1984; House 1963–81.

Wilson, Earl (R Ind.) April 18, 1906–April 27, 1990; House 1941–59, 1961–65.

Wilson, Edgar (Sil.R Idaho) Feb. 25, 1861–Jan. 3, 1915; House 1895–97 (Republican), 1899–1901.

Wilson, Edgar Campbell (son of Thomas Wilson of Va., father of Eugene McLanahan Wilson) (AJ Va.) Oct. 18, 1800–April 24, 1860; House 1833–35.

Wilson, Emmett (grandson of Augustus Emmett Maxwell) (D Fla.) Sept. 17, 1882–May 29, 1918; House 1913–17.

Wilson, Ephraim King (father of Ephraim King Wilson, below) (J Md.) Sept. 15, 1771–Jan. 2, 1834; House 1827–31 (1827–29 no party).

Wilson, Ephraim King (son of Ephraim King Wilson, above) (D Md.) Dec. 22, 1821–Feb. 24, 1891; House 1873–75; Senate 1885–Feb. 24, 1891.

Wilson, Eugene McLanahan (son of Edgar Campbell Wilson, grandson of Thomas Wilson of Va., great-grandson of Isaac Griffin) (D Minn.) Dec. 25, 1833–April 10, 1890; House 1869–71.

Wilson, Francis Henry (R N.Y.) Feb. 11, 1844–Sept. 25, 1910; House 1895–Sept. 30, 1897.

Wilson, Frank Eugene (D N.Y.) Dec. 22, 1857–July 12, 1935; House 1899–1905, 1911–15.

Wilson, George Allison (R Iowa) April 1, 1884–Sept. 8, 1953; Senate Jan. 14, 1943–49; Gov. Jan. 12, 1939–Jan. 14, 1943.

Wilson, George Howard (D Okla.) Aug. 21, 1905–July 16, 1985; House 1949–51.

Wilson, George Washington (R Ohio) Feb. 22, 1840–Nov. 27, 1909; House 1893–97.

Wilson, Heather (R N.M.) Dec. 30, 1960– ; House June 25, 1998– .

Wilson, Henry (– Pa.) 1778–Aug. 14, 1826; House 1823–Aug. 14, 1826.

Wilson, Henry (R Mass.) Feb. 16, 1812–Nov. 22, 1875; Senate Jan. 31, 1855–73 (1855–59 Free-Soiler/American Party/Democrat); Vice President 1873–Nov. 22, 1875.

Wilson, Isaac (– N.Y.) June 25, 1780–Oct. 25, 1848; House 1823–Jan. 7, 1824.

Wilson, James (father of James Wilson, below) (F N.H.) Aug. 16, 1766–Jan. 4, 1839; House 1809–11.

Wilson, James (son of James Wilson, above) (W N.H.) March 18, 1797–May 29, 1881; House 1847–Sept. 9, 1850.

Wilson, James (– Pa.) April 28, 1779–July 19, 1868; House 1823–39.

Wilson, James (father of John Lockwood Wilson) (R Ind.) April 9, 1825–Aug. 8, 1867; House 1857–61.

Wilson, James (R Iowa) Aug. 16, 1835–Aug. 26, 1920; House 1873–77, 1883–85; Secy. of Agriculture March 6, 1897–March 5, 1913.

Wilson, James Clifton (D Texas) June 21, 1874–Aug. 3, 1951; House 1917–19.

Wilson, James Falconer (R Iowa) Oct. 19, 1828–April 22, 1895; House Oct. 8, 1861–69; Senate 1883–95.

Wilson, James Jefferson (R N.J.) 1775–July 28, 1834; Senate 1815–Jan. 8, 1821.

Wilson, Jeremiah Morrow (R Ind.) Nov. 25, 1828–Sept. 24, 1901; House 1871–75.

Wilson, John (– S.C.) Aug. 11, 1773–Aug. 13, 1828; House 1821–27.

Wilson, John (F Mass.) Jan. 10, 1777–Aug. 9, 1848; House 1813–15, 1817–19.

Wilson, John Frank (D Ariz.) May 7, 1846–April 7, 1911; House (Terr. Del.) 1899–1901, 1903–05.

Wilson, John Haden (D Pa.) Aug. 20, 1867–Jan. 28, 1946; House 1919–21.

Wilson, John Henry (R Ky.) Jan. 30, 1846–Jan. 14, 1923; House 1889–93.

Wilson, John Lockwood (son of James Wilson of Ind.) (R Wash.) Aug. 7, 1850–Nov. 6, 1912; House Nov. 20, 1889–Feb. 18, 1895; Senate Feb. 19, 1895–99.

Wilson, John Thomas (R Ohio) April 16, 1811–Oct. 6, 1891; House 1867–73.

Wilson, Joseph Franklin (D Texas) March 18, 1901–Oct. 13, 1968; House 1947–55.

Wilson, Joseph Gardner (cousin of James Willis Nesmith) (R Ore.) Dec. 13, 1826–July 2, 1873; House March 4–July 2, 1873.

Wilson, Nathan (R N.Y.) Dec. 23, 1758–July 25, 1834; House June 3, 1808–09.

Wilson, Pete (R Calif.) Aug. 23, 1933– ; Senate 1983–Jan. 7, 1991; Gov. Jan. 7, 1991–Jan. 4, 1999.

Wilson, Riley Joseph (D La.) Nov. 12, 1871–Feb. 23, 1946; House 1915–37.

Wilson, Robert (U Mo.) Nov. 1803–May 10, 1870; Senate Jan. 17, 1862–Nov. 13, 1863.

Wilson, Robert Carlton (R Calif.) April 5, 1916– ; House 1953–81.

Wilson, Robert Patterson Clark (D Mo.) Aug. 8, 1834–Dec. 21, 1916; House Dec. 2, 1889–93.

Wilson, Stanyarne (D S.C.) Jan. 10, 1860–Feb. 14, 1928; House 1895–1901.

Wilson, Stephen Fowler (R Pa.) Sept. 4, 1821–March 30, 1897; House 1865–69.

Wilson, Thomas (father of Edgar Campbell Wilson, grandfather of Eugene McLanahan Wilson) (F Va.) Sept. 11, 1765–Jan. 24, 1826; House 1811–13.

Wilson, Thomas (R Pa.) 1772–Oct. 4, 1824; House May 4, 1813–17.

Wilson, Thomas (D Minn.) May 16, 1827–April 3, 1910; House 1887–89.

Wilson, Thomas Webber (D Miss.) Jan. 24, 1893–Jan. 31, 1948; House 1923–29.

Wilson, William (R Pa.) ?–?; House 1815–19.

Wilson, William (– Ohio) March 19, 1773–June 6, 1827; House 1823–June 6, 1827.

Wilson, William Bauchop (D Pa.) April 2, 1862–May 25, 1934; House 1907–13; Secy. of Labor March 4, 1913–March 4, 1921.

Wilson, William Edward (D Ind.) March 9, 1870–Sept. 29, 1948; House 1923–25.

Wilson, William Henry (R Pa.) Dec. 6, 1877–Aug. 11, 1937; House 1935–37.

Wilson, William Lyne (D W.Va.) May 3, 1843–Oct. 17, 1900; House 1883–95; Postmaster Gen. April 4, 1895–March 5, 1897.

Wilson, William Warfield (R Ill.) March 2, 1868–July 22, 1942; House 1903–13, 1915–21.

Winans, Edwin Baruch (D Mich.) May 16, 1826–July 4, 1894; House 1883–87; Gov. Jan. 1, 1891–Jan. 1, 1893.

Winans, James January (R Ohio) June 7, 1818–April 28, 1879; House 1869–71.

Winans, John (D Wis.) Sept. 27, 1831–Jan. 17, 1907; House 1883–85.

Winchester, Boyd (D Ky.) Sept. 23, 1836–May 18, 1923; House 1869–73.

Windom, William (R Minn.) May 10, 1827–Jan. 29, 1891; House 1859–69; Senate July 15, 1870–Jan. 22, 1871, March 4, 1871–March 7, 1881, Nov. 15, 1881–83; Secy. of the Treasury March 8–Nov. 13, 1881, March 7, 1889–Jan. 29, 1891.

Winfield, Charles Henry (D N.Y.) April 22, 1822–June 10, 1888; House 1863–67.

Wing, Austin Eli (– Mich.) Feb. 3, 1792–Aug. 27, 1849; House (Terr. Del.) 1825–29, 1831–33.

Wingate, Joseph Ferdinand (D Maine) June 29, 1786–?; House 1827–31.

Wingate, Paine (– N.H.) May 14, 1739–March 7, 1838; Senate 1789–93; House 1793–95; Cont. Cong. 1788.

Wingo, Effiegene Locke (widow of Otis Theodore Wingo, great-great-great-granddaughter of Matthew Locke) (D Ark.) April 13, 1883–Sept. 19, 1962; House Nov. 4, 1930–33.

Wingo, Otis Theodore (husband of Effiegene Locke Wingo) (D Ark.) June 18, 1877–Oct. 21, 1930; House 1913–Oct. 21, 1930.

Winn, Edward Lawrence "Larry" Jr. (R Kan.) Aug. 22, 1919– ; House 1967–85.

Winn, Richard (R S.C.) 1750–Dec. 19, 1818; House 1793–97 (1793–95 no party), Jan. 24, 1803–13.

Winn, Thomas Elisha (D Ga.) May 21, 1839–June 5, 1925; House 1891–93.

Winslow, Samuel Ellsworth (R Mass.) April 11, 1862–July 11, 1940; House 1913–25.

Winslow, Warren (D N.C.) Jan. 1, 1810–Aug. 16, 1862; House 1855–61; Gov. Dec. 6, 1854–Jan. 1, 1855.

Winstead, William Arthur (D Miss.) Jan. 6, 1904–March 4, 1995; House 1943–65.

Winston, Joseph (R N.C.) June 17, 1746–April 21, 1815; House 1793–95 (no party), 1803–07.

Winter, Charles Edwin (R Wyo.) Sept. 13, 1870–April 22, 1948; House 1923–29.

Winter, Elisha I. (F N.Y.) July 15, 1781–June 30, 1849; House 1813–15.

Winter, Thomas Daniel (R Kan.) July 7, 1896–Nov. 7, 1951; House 1939–47.

Winthrop, Robert Charles (W Mass.) May 12, 1809–Nov. 16, 1894; House Nov. 9, 1840–May 25, 1842, Nov. 29, 1842–July 30, 1850; Senate July 30, 1850–Feb. 1, 1851; Speaker Dec. 6, 1847–49.

Wirth, Timothy Endicott (D Colo.) Sept. 22, 1939– ; House 1975–87; Senate 1987–93.

Wise, George Douglas (cousin of John Sergeant Wise and Richard Alsop Wise, nephew of Henry Alexander Wise) (D Va.) June 4, 1831–Feb. 4, 1898; House 1881–April 10, 1890, 1891–95.

Wise, Henry Alexander (father of John Sergeant Wise and Richard Alsop Wise, uncle of George Douglas Wise, son-in-law of John Sergeant) (D Va.) Dec. 3, 1806–Sept. 12, 1876; House 1833–Feb. 12, 1844 (1833–37 Jacksonian, 1837–43 Whig); Gov. Jan. 1, 1856–Dec. 31, 1859.

Wise, James Walter (D Ga.) March 3, 1868–Sept. 8, 1925; House 1915–25.

Wise, John Sergeant (son of Henry Alexander Wise, grandson of John Sergeant, brother of Richard Alsop Wise, cousin of George Douglas Wise) (Read. Va.) Dec. 27, 1846–May 12, 1913; House 1883–85.

Wise, Morgan Ringland (D Pa.) June 7, 1825–April 13, 1903; House 1879–83.

Wise, Richard Alsop (son of Henry Alexander Wise, grandson of John Sergeant, brother of John Sergeant Wise, cousin of George Douglas Wise) (R Va.) Sept. 2, 1843–Dec. 21, 1900; House April 26, 1898–99, March 12–Dec. 21, 1900.

Wise, Robert Ellsworth Jr. (D W.Va.) Jan. 6, 1948– ; House 1983– .

Witcher, John Seashoal (R W.Va.) July 15, 1839–July 8, 1906; House 1869–71.

Witherell, James (R Vt.) June 16, 1759–Jan. 9, 1838; House 1807–May 1, 1808.

Withers, Garrett Lee (D Ky.) June 21, 1884–April 30, 1953; Senate Jan. 20, 1949–Nov. 26, 1950; House Aug. 2, 1952–April 30, 1953.

Withers, Robert Enoch (cousin of Thomas Withers Chinn) (D Va.) Sept. 18, 1821–Sept. 21, 1907; Senate 1875–81.

Witherspoon, Robert (great-great-grandfather of Robert Witherspoon Hemphill) (R S.C.) Jan. 29, 1767–Oct. 11, 1837; House 1809–11.

Witherspoon, Samuel Andrew (D Miss.) May 4, 1855–Nov. 24, 1915; House 1911–Nov. 24, 1915.

Withrow, Gardner Robert (R Wis.) Oct. 5, 1892–Sept. 23, 1964; House 1931–39 (1931–35 Republican, 1935–39 Progressive), 1949–61.

Witte, William Henry (D Pa.) Oct. 4, 1817–Nov. 24, 1876; House 1853–55.

Wofford, Harris Llewellyn (D Pa.) April 9, 1926– ; Senate May 9, 1991–95.

Wofford, Thomas Albert (D S.C.) Sept. 27, 1908–Feb. 25, 1978; Senate April 5–Nov. 6, 1956.

Wolcott, Edward Oliver (R Colo.) March 26, 1848–March 1, 1905; Senate 1889–1901.

Wolcott, Jesse Paine (R Mich.) March 3, 1893–Jan. 28, 1969; House 1931–57; Chrmn. House Banking and Currency 1947–49, 1953–55.

Wolcott, Josiah Oliver (D Del.) Oct. 31, 1877–Nov. 11, 1938; Senate 1917–July 2, 1921.

Wold, John Schiller (R Wyo.) Aug. 31, 1916– ; House 1969–71.

Wolf, Frank Rudolph (R Va.) Jan. 30, 1939– ; House 1981– .

Wolf, George (– Pa.) Aug. 12, 1777–March 11, 1840; House Dec. 9, 1824–29; Gov. Dec. 15, 1829–Dec. 15, 1835 (Jacksonian).

Wolf, Harry Benjamin (D Md.) June 16, 1880–Feb. 17, 1944; House 1907–09.

Wolf, Leonard George (D Iowa) Oct. 29, 1925–March 28, 1970; House 1959–61.

Wolf, William Penn (R Iowa) Dec. 1, 1833–Sept. 19, 1896; House Dec. 6, 1870–71.

Wolfe, Simeon Kalfius (D Ind.) Feb. 14, 1824–Nov. 18, 1888; House 1873–75.

Wolfenden, James (R Pa.) July 25, 1889–April 8, 1949; House Nov. 6, 1928–47.

Wolff, Joseph Scott (D Mo.) June 14, 1878–Feb. 27, 1958; House 1923–25.

Wolff, Lester Lionel (D N.Y.) Jan. 4, 1919– ; House 1965–81.

Wolford, Frank Lane (D Ky.) Sept. 2, 1817–Aug. 2, 1895; House 1883–87.

Wolpe, Howard Eliot III (D Mich.) Nov. 2, 1939– ; House 1979–93.

Wolverton, Charles Anderson (R N.J.) Oct. 24, 1880–May 16, 1969; House 1927–59; Chrmn. House Interstate and Foreign Commerce 1947–49, 1953–55.

Wolverton, John Marshall (R W.Va.) Jan. 31, 1872–Aug. 19, 1944; House 1925–27, 1929–31.

Wolverton, Simon Peter (D Pa.) Jan. 28, 1837–Oct. 25, 1910; House 1891–95.

Won Pat, Antonio Borja (D Guam) Dec. 10, 1908–May 1, 1987; House 1973–85.

Wood, Abiel (R Mass.) July 22, 1772–Oct. 26, 1834; House 1813–15.

Wood, Alan Jr. (nephew of John Wood) (R Pa.) July 6, 1834–Oct. 31, 1902; House 1875–77.

Wood, Amos Eastman (D Ohio) Jan. 2, 1810–Nov. 19, 1850; House Dec. 3, 1849–Nov. 19, 1850.

Wood, Benjamin (brother of Fernando Wood) (D N.Y.) Oct. 13, 1820–Feb. 21, 1900; House 1861–65, 1881–83.

Wood, Benson (R Ill.) March 31, 1839–Aug. 27, 1915; House 1895–97.

Wood, Bradford Ripley (D N.Y.) Sept. 3, 1800–Sept. 26, 1889; House 1845–47.

Wood, Ernest Edward (D Mo.) Aug. 24, 1875–Jan. 10, 1952; House 1905–June 23, 1906.

Wood, Fernando (brother of Benjamin Wood) (D N.Y.) June 14, 1812–Feb. 14, 1881; House 1841–43, 1863–65, 1867–Feb. 14, 1881.

Wood, Ira Wells (R N.J.) June 19, 1856–Oct. 5, 1931; House Nov. 8, 1904–13.

Wood, John (uncle of Alan Wood Jr.) (R Pa.) Sept. 6, 1816–May 28, 1898; House 1859–61.

Wood, John Jacob (– N.Y.) Feb. 16, 1784–May 20, 1874; House 1827–29.

Wood, John M. (R Maine) Nov. 17, 1813–Dec. 24, 1864; House 1855–59.

Wood, John Stephens (D Ga.) Feb. 8, 1885–Sept. 12, 1968; House 1931–35, 1945–53; Chrmn. House Un-American Activities 1949–53.

Wood, John Travers (R Idaho) Nov. 25, 1878–Nov. 2, 1954; House 1951–53.

Wood, Reuben Terrell (D Mo.) Aug. 7, 1884–July 16, 1955; House 1933–41.

Wood, Silas (– N.Y.) Sept. 14, 1769–March 2, 1847; House 1819–29.

Wood, Thomas Jefferson (D Ind.) Sept. 30, 1844–Oct. 13, 1908; House 1883–85.

Wood, Walter Abbott (R N.Y.) Oct. 23, 1815–Jan. 15, 1892; House 1879–83.

Wood, William Robert (R Ind.) Jan. 5, 1861–March 7, 1933; House 1915–33.

Woodard, Frederick Augustus (D N.C.) Feb. 12, 1854–May 8, 1915; House 1893–97.

Woodbridge, Frederick Enoch (R Vt.) Aug. 29, 1818–April 25, 1888; House 1863–69.

Woodbridge, William (W Mich.) Aug. 20, 1780–Oct. 20, 1861; House (no party Terr. Del.) 1819–Aug. 9, 1820; Senate 1841–47; Gov. Jan. 7, 1840–Feb. 23, 1841.

Woodburn, William (R Nev.) April 14, 1838–Jan. 15, 1915; House 1875–77, 1885–89.

Woodbury, Levi (D N.H.) Dec. 22, 1789–Sept. 4, 1851; Senate March 16, 1825–31 (no party), 1841–Nov. 20, 1845; Gov. June 5, 1823–June 2, 1824 (Democratic Republican); Secy. of the Navy May 23, 1831–June 30, 1834; Secy. of the Treasury July 1, 1834–March 2, 1841; Assoc. Justice Supreme Court Sept. 23, 1845–Sept. 4, 1851.

Woodcock, David (– N.Y.) 1785–Sept. 18, 1835; House 1821–23, 1827–29.

Woodford, Stewart Lyndon (R N.Y.) Sept. 3, 1835–Feb. 14, 1913; House 1873–July 1, 1874.

Woodhouse, Chase Going (D Conn.) 1890–Dec. 12, 1984; House 1945–47, 1949–51.

Woodman, Charles Walhart (R Ill.) March 11, 1844–March 18, 1898; House 1895–97.

Woodruff, George Catlin (D Conn.) Dec. 1, 1805–Nov. 21, 1885; House 1861–63.

Woodruff, John (R Conn.) Feb. 12, 1826–May 20, 1868; House 1855–57 (American Party), 1859–61.

Woodruff, Roy Orchard (R Mich.) March 14, 1876–Feb. 12, 1953; House 1913–15 (Progressive), 1921–53.

Woodruff, Thomas M. (AP N.Y.) May 3, 1804–March 28, 1855; House 1845–47.

Woodrum, Clifton Alexander (D Va.) April 27, 1887–Oct. 6, 1950; House 1923–Dec. 31, 1945.

Woods, Frank Plowman (R Iowa) Dec. 11, 1868–April 25, 1944; House 1909–19.

Woods, Henry (brother of John Woods born in 1761) (F Pa.) 1764–1826; House 1799–1803.

Woods, James Pleasant (D Va.) Feb. 4, 1868–July 7, 1948; House Feb. 25, 1919–23.

Woods, John (brother of Henry Woods) (F Pa.) 1761–Dec. 16, 1816; elected to the House for the term beginning 1815 but never attended or qualified.

Woods, John (– Ohio) Oct. 18, 1794–July 30, 1855; House 1825–29.

Woods, Samuel Davis (R Calif.) Sept. 19, 1845–Dec. 24, 1915; House Dec. 3, 1900–03.

Woods, William (– N.Y.) 1790–Aug. 7, 1837; House Nov. 3, 1823–25.

Woodson, Samuel Hughes (father of Samuel Hughes Woodson, below) (– Ky.) Sept. 15, 1777–July 28, 1827; House 1821–23.

Woodson, Samuel Hughes (son of Samuel Hughes Woodson, above) (AP Mo.) Oct. 24, 1815–June 23, 1881; House 1857–61.

Woodward, George Washington (D Pa.) March 26, 1809–May 10, 1875; House Nov. 21, 1867–71.

Woodward, Gilbert Motier (D Wis.) Dec. 25, 1835–March 13, 1913; House 1883–85.

Woodward, Joseph Addison (son of William Woodward) (D S.C.) April 11, 1806–Aug. 3, 1885; House 1843–53.

Woodward, William (father of Joseph Addison Woodward) (R S.C.) ?–?; House 1815–17.

Woodworth, James Hutchinson (R Ill.) Dec. 4, 1804–March 26, 1869; House 1855–57.

Woodworth, Laurin Dewey (R Ohio) Sept. 10, 1837–March 13, 1897; House 1873–77.

Woodworth, William W. (D N.Y.) March 16, 1807–Feb. 13, 1873; House 1845–47.

Woodyard, Harry Chapman (R W.Va.) Nov. 13, 1867–June 21, 1929; House 1903–11, Nov. 7, 1916–23, 1925–27.

Woolsey, Lynn (D Calif.) Nov. 3, 1937– ; House 1993– .

Woomer, Ephraim Milton (R Pa.) Jan. 14, 1844–Nov. 29, 1897; House 1893–97.

Wooten, Dudley Goodall (D Texas) June 19, 1860–Feb. 7, 1929; House July 13, 1901–03.

Worcester, Samuel Thomas (R Ohio) Aug. 30, 1804–Dec. 6, 1882; House July 4, 1861–63.

Word, Thomas Jefferson (W Miss.) ?–?; House May 30, 1838–39.

Works, John Downey (R Calif.) March 29, 1847–June 6, 1928; Senate 1911–17.

Worley, Francis Eugene (D Texas) Oct. 10, 1908–Dec. 17, 1974; House 1941–April 3, 1950.

Worman, Ludwig (F Pa.) 1761–Oct. 17, 1822; House 1821–Oct. 17, 1822.

Wortendyke, Jacob Reynier (D N.J.) Nov. 27, 1818–Nov. 7, 1868; House 1857–59.

Worthington, Henry Gaither (R Nev.) Feb. 9, 1828–July 29, 1909; House Oct. 31, 1864–65.

Worthington, John Tolley Hood (D Md.) Nov. 1, 1788–April 27, 1849; House 1831–33 (Jacksonian), 1837–41.

Worthington, Nicholas Ellsworth (D Ill.) March 30, 1836–March 4, 1916; House 1883–87.

Worthington, Thomas (R Ohio) July 16, 1773–June 20, 1827; Senate April 1, 1803–07, Dec. 15, 1810–Dec. 1, 1814; Gov. Dec. 8, 1814–Dec. 14, 1818 (Democratic Republican).

Worthington, Thomas Contee (nephew of Benjamin Contee) (– Md.) Nov. 25, 1782–April 12, 1847; House 1825–27.

Wortley, George Cornelius (R N.Y.) Dec. 8, 1926– ; House 1981–89.

Wren, Thomas (R Nev.) Jan. 2, 1826–Feb. 5, 1904; House 1877–79.

Wright, Ashley Bascom (R Mass.) May 25, 1841–Aug. 14, 1897; House 1893–Aug. 14, 1897.

Wright, Augustus Romaldus (D Ga.) June 16, 1813–March 31, 1891; House 1857–59.

Wright, Charles Frederick (brother of Myron Benjamin Wright) (R Pa.) May 3, 1856–Nov. 10, 1925; House 1899–1905.

Wright, Daniel Boone (D Miss.) Feb. 17, 1812–Dec. 27, 1887; House 1853–57.

Wright, Edwin Ruthvin Vincent (D N.J.) Jan. 2, 1812–Jan. 21, 1871; House 1865–67.

Wright, George Grover (brother of Joseph Albert Wright) (R Iowa) March 24, 1820–Jan. 11, 1896; Senate 1871–77.

Wright, George Washington (I Calif.) June 4, 1816–April 7, 1885; House Sept. 11, 1850–51.

Wright, Hendrick Bradley (G Pa.) April 24, 1808–Sept. 2, 1881; House 1853–55 (Democrat), July 4, 1861–63 (Democrat), 1877–81 (1877–79 Democrat).

Wright, James Assion (D Pa.) Aug. 11, 1902–Nov. 7, 1963; House 1941–45.

Wright, James Claude Jr. (D Texas) Dec. 22, 1922– ; House 1955–June 30, 1989; House majority leader 1977–87; Speaker Jan. 6, 1987–June 6, 1989.

Wright, John Crafts (– Ohio) Aug. 17, 1783–Feb. 13, 1861; House 1823–29.

Wright, John Vines (D Tenn.) June 28, 1828–June 11, 1908; House 1855–61.

Wright, Joseph Albert (brother of George Grover Wright) (U Ind.) April 17, 1810–May 11, 1867; House 1843–45 (Democrat); Senate Feb. 24, 1862–Jan. 14, 1863; Gov. Dec. 5, 1849–Jan. 12, 1857.

Wright, Myron Benjamin (brother of Charles Frederick Wright) (R Pa.) June 12, 1847–Nov. 13, 1894; House 1889–Nov. 13, 1894.

Wright, Robert (R Md.) Nov. 20, 1752–Sept. 7, 1826; Senate Nov. 19, 1801–Nov. 12, 1806; House Nov. 29, 1810–17, 1821–23; Gov. Nov. 12, 1806–May 6, 1809 (Democratic Republican).

Wright, Samuel Gardiner (W N.J.) Nov. 18, 1781–July 30, 1845; House March 4–July 30, 1845.

Wright, Silas Jr. (J N.Y.) May 24, 1795–Aug. 27, 1847; House 1827–Feb. 16, 1829 (no party); Senate Jan. 4, 1833–Nov. 26, 1844; Gov. Jan. 1, 1845–Jan. 1, 1847.

Wright, William (D N.J.) Nov. 13, 1794–Nov. 1, 1866; House 1843–47 (Whig); Senate 1853–59, 1863–Nov. 1, 1866.

Wright, William Carter (D Ga.) Jan. 6, 1866–June 11, 1933; House Jan. 24, 1918–33.

Wu, David (D Ore.) April 8, 1955– ; House 1999– .

Wurts, John (– Pa.) Aug. 13, 1792–April 23, 1861; House 1825–27.

Wurzbach, Harry McLeary (uncle of Robert Christian Eckhardt) (R Texas) May 19, 1874–Nov. 6, 1931; House 1921–29, Feb. 10, 1930–Nov. 6, 1931.

Wyant, Adam Martin (R Pa.) Sept. 15, 1869–Jan. 5, 1935; House 1921–33.

Wyatt, Joseph Peyton Jr. (D Texas) Oct. 12, 1941– ; House 1979–81.

Wyatt, Wendell (R Ore.) June 15, 1917– ; House Nov. 3, 1964–75.

Wyden, Ronald Lee (D Ore.) May 3, 1949– ; House 1981–Feb. 5, 1996; Senate Feb. 6, 1996– .

Wydler, John Waldemar (R N.Y.) June 9, 1924–Aug. 4, 1987; House 1963–81.

Wylie, Chalmers Pangburn (R Ohio) Nov. 23, 1920–Aug. 14, 1998; House 1967–93.

Wyman, Louis Crosby (R N.H.) March 16, 1917– ; House 1963–65, 1967–Dec. 31, 1974; Senate Dec. 31, 1974–75.

Wynkoop, Henry (– Pa.) March 2, 1737–March 25, 1816; House 1789–91; Cont. Cong. 1779–82.

Wynn, Albert R. (D Md.) Sept. 10, 1951– ; House 1993– .

Wynn, William Joseph (D Calif.) June 12, 1860–Jan. 4, 1935; House 1903–05.

Wynns, Thomas (R N.C.) 1764–June 3, 1825; House Dec. 7, 1802–07.

Y

Yancey, Bartlett (cousin of John Kerr) (R N.C.) Feb. 19, 1785–Aug. 30, 1828; House 1813–17.

Yancey, Joel (J Ky.) Oct. 21, 1773–April 1838; House 1827–31.

Yancey, William Lowndes (uncle of Joseph Haynsworth Earle) (D Ala.) Aug. 10, 1814–July 28, 1863; House Dec. 2, 1844–Sept. 1, 1846.

Yangco, Teodoro Rafael (Nat. P.I.) Nov. 9, 1861–April 20, 1939; House (Res. Comm.) 1917–March 3, 1920.

Yaple, George Lewis (D Mich.) Feb. 20, 1851–Dec. 16, 1939; House 1883–85.

Yarborough, Ralph Webster (D Texas) June 8, 1903–Jan. 27, 1996; Senate April 29, 1957–71; Chrmn. Senate Labor and Public Welfare 1969–71.

Yardley, Robert Morris (R Pa.) Oct. 9, 1850–Dec. 8, 1902; House 1887–91.

Yates, John Barentse (R N.Y.) Feb. 1, 1784–July 10, 1836; House 1815–17.

Yates, Richard (father of Richard Yates) (R Ill.) Jan. 18, 1818–Nov. 27, 1873; House 1851–55 (Whig); Senate 1865–71; Gov. Jan. 14, 1861–Jan. 16, 1865.

Yates, Richard (son of Richard Yates) (R Ill.) Dec. 12, 1860–April 11, 1936; House 1919–33; Gov. Jan. 14, 1901–Jan. 9, 1905.

Yates, Sidney Richard (D Ill.) Aug. 27, 1909– ; House 1949–63, 1965–99.

Yatron, Gus (D Pa.) Oct. 16, 1927– ; House 1969–93.

Yeaman, George Helm (U Ky.) Nov. 1, 1829–Feb. 23, 1908; House Dec. 1, 1862–65.

Yeates, Jesse Johnson (D N.C.) May 29, 1829–Sept. 5, 1892; House 1875–79, Jan. 29–March 3, 1881.

Yell, Archibald (D Ark.) 1797–Feb. 22, 1847; House Aug. 1, 1836–39 (Aug. 1, 1836–37 Jacksonian), 1845–July 1, 1846; Gov. Nov. 4, 1840–April 29, 1844.

Yoakum, Charles Henderson (D Texas) July 10, 1849–Jan. 1, 1909; House 1895–97.

Yocum, Seth Hartman (G Pa.) Aug. 2, 1834–April 19, 1895; House 1879–81.

Yoder, Samuel S. (D Ohio) Aug. 16, 1841–May 11, 1921; House 1887–91.

Yon, Thomas Alva (D Fla.) March 14, 1882–Feb. 16, 1971; House 1927–33.

York, Tyre (ID N.C.) May 4, 1836–Jan. 28, 1916; House 1883–85.

Yorke, Thomas Jones (W N.J.) March 25, 1801–April 4, 1882; House 1837–39, 1841–43.

Yorty, Samuel William (D Calif.) Oct. 1, 1909–June 5, 1998; House 1951–55.

Yost, Jacob (R Va.) April 1, 1853–Jan. 25, 1933; House 1887–89, 1897–99.

Yost, Jacob Senewell (D Pa.) July 29, 1801–March 7, 1872; House 1843–47.

Youmans, Henry Melville (D Mich.) May 15, 1832–July 8, 1920; House 1891–93.

Young, Andrew Jackson Jr. (D Ga.) March 12, 1932– ; House 1973–Jan. 29, 1977.

Young, Augustus (W Vt.) March 20, 1784–June 17, 1857; House 1841–43.

Young, Bryan Rust (brother of William Singleton Young, uncle of John Young Brown born in 1835) (W Ky.) Jan. 14, 1800–May 14, 1882; House 1845–47.

Young, Charles William "Bill" (R Fla.) Dec. 16, 1930– ; House 1971– ; Chrmn. House Appropriations 1999– .

Young, Clarence Clifton (R Nev.) Nov. 7, 1922– ; House 1953–57.

Young, Donald Edwin (R Alaska) June 9, 1933– ; House March 6, 1973– ; Chrmn. House Resources 1995– .

Young, Ebenezer (– Conn.) Dec. 25, 1783–Aug. 18, 1851; House 1829–35.

Young, Edward Lunn (R S.C.) Sept. 7, 1920– ; House 1973–75.

Young, George Morley (R N.D.) Dec. 11, 1870–May 27, 1932; House 1913–Sept. 2, 1924.

Young, Hiram Casey (D Tenn.) Dec. 14, 1828–Aug. 17, 1899; House 1875–81, 1883–85.

Young, Horace Olin (R Mich.) Aug. 4, 1850–Aug. 5, 1917; House 1903–May 16, 1913.

Young, Isaac Daniel (R Kan.) March 29, 1849–Dec. 10, 1927; House 1911–13.

Young, James (D Texas) July 18, 1866–April 29, 1942; House 1911–21.

Young, James Rankin (R Pa.) March 10, 1847–Dec. 18, 1924; House 1897–1903.

Young, John (W N.Y.) June 12, 1802–April 23, 1852; House Nov. 9, 1836–37, 1841–43; Gov. Jan. 1, 1847–Jan. 1, 1849.

Young, John Andrew (D Texas) Nov. 10, 1916– ; House 1957–79.

Young, John Duncan (D Ky.) Sept. 22, 1823–Dec. 26, 1910; House 1873–75.

Young, John Smith (D La.) Nov. 4, 1834–Oct. 11, 1916; House Nov. 5, 1878–79.

Young, Lafayette (R Iowa) May 10, 1848–Nov. 15, 1926; Senate Nov. 12, 1910–April 11, 1911.

Young, Milton Ruben (R N.D.) Dec. 6, 1897–May 31, 1983; Senate March 12, 1945–81; elected Pres. pro tempore Dec. 4, 1980 (to serve Dec. 5, 1980).

Young, Pierce Manning Butler (D Ga.) Nov. 15, 1836–July 6, 1896; House July 25, 1868–69, Dec. 22, 1870–75.

Young, Richard (R N.Y.) Aug. 6, 1846–June 9, 1935; House 1909–11.

Young, Richard Montgomery (D Ill.) Feb. 20, 1798–Nov. 28, 1861; Senate 1837–43.

Young, Robert Anton III (D Mo.) Nov. 27, 1923– ; House 1977–87.

Young, Samuel Hollingsworth (R Ill.) Dec. 26, 1922– ; House 1973–75.

Young, Stephen Marvin (D Ohio) May 4, 1889–Dec. 1, 1984; House 1933–37, 1941–43, 1949–51; Senate 1959–71.

Young, Thomas Lowry (R Ohio) Dec. 14, 1832–July 20, 1888; House 1879–83; Gov. March 2, 1877–Jan. 14, 1878.

Young, Timothy Roberts (D Ill.) Nov. 19, 1811–May 12, 1898; House 1849–51.

Young, William Albin (– Va.) May 17, 1860–March 12, 1928; House 1897–April 26, 1898, 1899–March 12, 1900.

Young, William Singleton (brother of Bryan Rust Young, uncle of John Young Brown born in 1835) (– Ky.) April 10, 1790–Sept. 20, 1827; House 1825–Sept. 20, 1827.

Youngblood, Harold Francis (R Mich.) Aug. 7, 1907–May 10, 1983; House 1947–49.

Youngdahl, Oscar Ferdinand (R Minn.) Oct. 13, 1893–Feb. 3, 1946; House 1939–43.

Younger, Jesse Arthur (R Calif.) April 11, 1893–June 20, 1967; House 1953–June 20, 1967.

Yulee, David Levy (formerly David Levy) (D Fla.) June 12, 1810–Oct. 10, 1886; House (Terr. Del.) 1841–45 (Whig Democrat); Senate July 1, 1845–51, 1855–Jan. 21, 1861.

Z

Zablocki, Clement John (D Wis.) Nov. 18, 1912–Dec. 3, 1983; House 1949–Dec. 3, 1983; Chrmn. House International Relations 1977–79; Chrmn. House Foreign Affairs 1979–83.

Zeferetti, Leo C. (D N.Y.) July 15, 1927– ; House 1975–83.

Zelenko, Herbert (D N.Y.) March 16, 1906–Feb. 23, 1979; House 1955–63.

Zeliff, William (R N.H.) June 12, 1936– ; House 1991–97.

Zenor, William Tayor (D Ind.) April 30, 1846–June 2, 1916; House 1897–1907.

Ziegler, Edward Danner (D Pa.) March 3, 1844–Dec. 21, 1931; House 1899–1901.

Zihlman, Frederick Nicholas (R Md.) Oct. 2, 1879–April 22, 1935; House 1917–31.

Zimmer, Richard (R N.J.) Aug. 16, 1944– ; House 1991–97.

Zimmerman, Orville (D Mo.) Dec. 31, 1880–April 7, 1948; House 1935–April 7, 1948.

Zion, Roger Herschel (R Ind.) Sept. 17, 1921– ; House 1967–75.

Zioncheck, Marion Anthony (D Wash.) Dec. 5, 1901–Aug. 7, 1936; House 1933–Aug. 7, 1936.

Zollicoffer, Felix Kirk (AP Tenn.) May 19, 1812–Jan. 19, 1862; House 1853–59 (1853–55 Whig).

Zorinsky, Edward (D Neb.) Nov. 11, 1928–March 6, 1987; Senate Dec. 28, 1976–March 6, 1987.

Zschau, Edwin Van Wyck (R Calif.) Jan. 6, 1940– ; House 1983–87.

Zwach, John Matthew (R Minn.) Feb. 8, 1907–Nov. 11, 1990; House 1967–75.

Selected Bibliography

A

Aaron, Henry J., Barry P. Bosworth, and Gary Burtless. *Can America Afford to Grow Old? Paying for Social Security.* Washington, D.C.: Brookings Institution, 1989.

Aaron, Henry J., and John B. Shoven. *Should the United States Privatize Social Security?* Cambridge, Mass.: MIT Press, 1999.

Aberbach, Joel D. *Keeping a Watchful Eye: The Politics of Congressional Oversight.* Washington, D.C.: Brookings Institution, 1990.

Abraham, Henry J. *Justices, Presidents, and Senators: A History of the U.S. Supreme Court Appointments from Washington to Clinton.* New York: Rowman and Littlefield, 1999.

Abramowitz, Alan, and Jeffrey A. Segal. *Senate Elections.* Ann Arbor: University of Michigan Press, 1992.

Abramson, Paul R., John H. Aldrich, and David W. Rohde. *Change and Continuity in the 1996 and 1998 Elections.* Washington, D.C.: CQ Press, 1999.

Abshire, David M. *Foreign Policy Makers: President vs. Congress.* Beverly Hills, Calif.: Sage Publications, 1979.

Aikman, Lonnelle. *We, the People: The Story of the United States Capitol.* 13th ed. Washington, D.C.: United States Capitol Historical Society, 1985.

Aldrich, John H. *Why Parties? The Origin and Transformation of Political Parties in America.* Chicago: University of Chicago Press, 1995.

Alexander, De Alva S. *History and Procedure of the House of Representatives.* Boston: Houghton Mifflin, 1916.

Alexander, Herbert E. *Financing Politics: Money, Elections, and Political Reform.* 4th ed. Washington, D.C.: CQ Press, 1992.

Alexander, Herbert E., and Anthony Corrado. *Financing the 1992 Election.* Armonk, N.Y.: Sharpe, 1995.

Almanac of Federal PACs. Washington, D.C.: Amward Publications, 1990– .

The Almanac of the Unelected: Staff of the U.S. Congress. Washington, D.C.: Almanac of the Unelected, 1988– .

Amar, Akhil R. *The Bill of Rights: Creation and Reconstruction.* New Haven, Conn.: Yale University Press, 1998.

Amer, Mildred L. *House Committee on Standards of Official Conduct: A Brief History of Its Evolution and Jurisdiction.* Washington, D.C.: Congressional Research Service, 1997.

———. *Selected Courtesies and Privileges Extended to Former Members of the House of Representatives.* Washington, D.C.: Congressional Research Service, 1990.

American Lobbyists Directory. Detroit: Gale Research, 1990– .

American Political Science Association. Committee on Political Parties. *Toward a More Responsible Two-Party System: A Report.* New York: Rinehart, 1950.

American Political Science Association, and the American Historical Association. *This Constitution: From Ratification to the Bill of Rights.* Washington, D.C.: CQ Press, 1988.

———. *This Constitution: Our Enduring Legacy.* Washington, D.C.: CQ Press, 1986.

Andrews, Charles M. *The Colonial Period of American History.* 4 vols. New Haven, Conn.: Yale University Press, 1934.

Angle, Paul M. *The Library of Congress: An Account, Historical and Descriptive.* Kingsport, Tenn.: Kingsport Press, 1958.

Antieau, Chester J. *The Intended Significance of the Fourteenth Amendment.* Buffalo, N.Y.: W. S. Hein, 1997.

Arnold, R. Douglas. *Congress and the Bureaucracy: A Theory of Influence.* New Haven, Conn.: Yale University Press, 1979.

———. *The Logic of Congressional Action.* New Haven, Conn.: Yale University Press, 1990.

Asher, Herbert B. *Presidential Elections and American Politics: Voters, Candidates, and Campaigns since 1952.* 4th ed. Chicago: University of Chicago Press, 1988.

B

Bacchus, William I. *Inside the Legislative Process.* Boulder, Colo.: Westview Press, 1983.

Bach, Stanley, and Steven S. Smith. *Managing Uncertainty in the House of Representatives: Adaptation and Innovation of Special Rules.* Washington, D.C.: Brookings Institution, 1988.

Bacon, Donald C., Roger H. Davidson, and Morton Keller, eds. *The Encyclopedia of the United States Congress.* New York: Simon & Schuster, 1995.

Bailey, Christopher J. *The Republican Party in the U.S. Senate, 1974–84.* Manchester, England: Manchester University Press, 1988.

Bailyn, Bernard. *The Ideological Origin of the American Revolution.* Enl. ed., Cambridge, Mass., Harvard University Press, 1992.

Baker, Gordon E. *The Reapportionment Revolution: Representation, Political Power, and the Supreme Court.* New York: Random House, 1966.

Baker, Richard A., and Roger H. Davidson, eds. *First among Equals: Outstanding Senate Leaders of the Twentieth Century.* Washington, D.C.: Congressional Quarterly, 1991.

———. *The Senate of the United States: A Bicentennial History.* Malabar, Fla.: Krieger, 1988.

Baker, Ross K. *Friend and Foe in the U.S. Senate.* New York: Free Press, 1980.

———. *House and Senate.* 2nd ed. New York: Norton, 1995.

Barbash, Fred. *The Founding: A Dramatic Account of the Writing of the Constitution.* New York: Linden Press/Simon and Schuster, 1987.

Barber, James David, ed. *Choosing the President.* Englewood Cliffs, N.J.: Prentice Hall, 1974.

Barnhart, Michael, ed. *Congress and United States Foreign Policy: Controlling the Use of Force in the Nuclear Age.* Albany: State University of New York Press, 1987.

Barry, John M. *The Ambition and the Power.* New York: Viking Penguin, 1989.

Barth, Alan. *Government by Investigation.* New York: Viking, 1955.

Baum, Lawrence. *The Supreme Court.* 6th ed. Washington, D.C.: CQ Press, 1998.

Baumgartner, Frank R., and Beth L. Leech. *Basic Interests: The Importance of Groups in Politics and in Political Science.* Princeton, N.J.: Princeton University Press, 1998.

Bayh, Birch. *One Heartbeat Away: Presidential Disability and Succession.* Indianapolis: Bobbs-Merrill, 1968.

Beacham, Walton, ed. *Beacham's Guide to Key Lobbyists: An Analysis of Their Issues and Impact.* Washington, D.C.: Beacham Publishing, 1989.

Beard, Charles A. *An Economic Interpretation of the Constitution of the United States.* New York: Macmillan, 1935.

———, ed. *The Enduring Federalist.* Garden City, N.Y.: Doubleday, 1948.

Beard, Edmund, and Stephen Horn. *Congressional Ethics: The View from the House.* Washington, D.C.: Brookings Institution, 1975.

Beck, Carl. *Contempt of Congress: A Study of the Prosecutions Initiated by the Committee on Un-American Activities, 1945–1957.* New Orleans: Hauser Press, 1959.

Beck, Deborah, Paul Taylor, Jeffrey Stanger, and Douglas Rivlin. "Issue Advocacy Advertising during the 1996 Campaign: A Catalog." Philadelphia: University of Pennsylvania, Annenberg Public Policy Center, 1997.

Bell, Daniel, and Lester Thurow. *The Deficits: How Big? How Long? How Dangerous?* New York: New York University Press, 1985.

Bell, Roger. *Last among Equals: Hawaii Statehood and American Politics.* Honolulu: University of Hawaii Press, 1984.

Benedict, Michael L. *The Impeachment and Trial of Andrew Johnson.* New York: Norton, 1973.

Benenson, Robert, et al. *Jigsaw Politics: Shaping the House after the 1990 Census.* Washington, D.C.: Congressional Quarterly, 1990.

Benson, Paul R., Jr. *Supreme Court and the Commerce Clause, 1937–1970.* Port Washington, N.Y.: Dunellen Publishing, 1970.

Bentley, Eric, ed. *Thirty Years of Treason: Excerpts from Hearings before the House Un-American Activities Committee, 1938–1968.* New York: Viking, 1971.

Benton, Thomas H. *Thirty Years' View.* 2 vols. New York: Greenwood Press, 1968.

Berelson, Bernard, Paul F. Lazarsfeld, and William A. McPhee. *Voting: A Study of Opinion Formation in a Presidential Campaign.* Chicago: University of Chicago Press, 1954.

Berg, John C. *Unequal Struggle: Class, Gender, Race, and Power in the U.S. Congress.* Boulder, Colo.: Westview Press, 1995.

Berger, Raoul. *Congress v. the Supreme Court.* Cambridge, Mass.: Harvard University Press, 1969.

———. *Executive Privilege.* Cambridge, Mass.: Harvard University Press, 1974.

———. *Impeachment: The Constitutional Problems.* Cambridge, Mass.: Harvard University Press, 1973.

Berman, Daniel M. *How a Bill Becomes a Law: Congress Enacts Civil Rights Legislation.* New York: Macmillan, 1966.

Berman, Larry. *The Office of Management and Budget and the Presidency, 1921–1979.* Princeton, N.J.: Princeton University Press, 1979.

Bernstein, Robert A. *Elections, Representation, and Congressional Voting Behavior: The Myth of Constituency Control.* Englewood Cliffs, N.J.: Prentice Hall, 1989.

Berry, Jeffrey M. *The Interest Group Society.* 3rd ed. New York: Longman, 1997.

———. *Lobbying for the People: The Political Behavior of Public Interest Groups.* Princeton, N.J.: Princeton University Press, 1977.

———. *The New Liberalism: The Rising Power of Citizen Groups.* Washington, D.C.: Brookings Institution, 1999.

Bessette, Joseph M. *The Mild Voice of Reason: Deliberative Democracy and American National Government.* Chicago: University of Chicago Press, 1994.

Best, Judith. *The Case against Direct Election of the President: A Defense of the Electoral College.* Ithaca, N.Y.: Cornell University Press, 1975.

———. *The Choice of the People: Debating the Electoral College.* Lanham, Md.: Rowman and Littlefield, 1996.

Beth, Loren P. *The Development of the American Constitution, 1877–1917.* New York: Harper and Row, 1971.

Bianco, William T. *Trust: Representatives and Constituents.* Ann Arbor: University of Michigan Press, 1994

Bibby, John F. *Congress Off the Record: The Candid Analysis of Seven Members.* Washington, D.C.: American Enterprise Institute, 1983.

Bibby, John F., and Roger H. Davidson. *On Capitol Hill.* Hinsdale, Ill.: Dryden, 1972.

Bibby, John F., and L. Sandy Maisel. *Two Parties, or More? The American Party System.* Boulder, Co.: Westview Press, 1998.

Bickel, Alexander M. *The Least Dangerous Branch: The Supreme Court at the Bar of Politics.* 2nd ed. New Haven: Yale University Press, 1986.

———. *Reform and Continuity: The Electoral College, the Convention, and the Party System.* Rev ed. New York: Harper and Row, 1971.

Bickford, Charlene B., and Kenneth R. Bowling. *Birth of the Nation: The First Federal Congress, 1789–1791.* Washington, D.C.: First Federal Congress Project, George Washington University; New York: Second Circuit Committee on the Bicentennial of the United States Constitution, 1989.

Biersack, Robert, Paul S. Herrnson, and Clyde Wilcox. *After the Revolution: PACs, Lobbies, and the Republican Congress.* Boston: Allyn and Bacon, 1999.

Binder, Sarah A., and Steven S. Smith. *Politics or Principle? Filibustering in the United States Senate.* Washington, D.C.: Brookings Institution, 1997.

Birnbaum, Jeffrey H. *The Lobbyists: How Influence Peddlers Get Their Way in Washington.* New York: Times Books, 1992.

Birnbaum, Jeffrey H., and Alan S. Murray. *Showdown at Gucci Gulch: Lawmakers, Lobbyists, and the Unlikely Triumph of Tax Reform.* New York: Vintage Books, 1987.

Biskupic, Joan, and Elder Witt. *Congressional Quarterly's Guide to the U.S. Supreme Court.* 3rd ed. Washington, D.C.: Congressional Quarterly, 1997.

Bisnow, Mark. *In the Shadow of the Dome: Chronicles of a Capitol Hill Aide.* New York: William Morrow, 1990.

Blanchard, Robert O., ed. *Congress and the News Media.* New York: Hastings House, 1974.

Blechman, Barry M. *The Politics of National Security: Congress and U.S. Defense Policy.* New York: Oxford University Press, 1990.

Blechman, Barry M., and Stephen S. Kaplan. *Force without War: U.S. Armed Forces as a Political Instrument.* Washington, D.C.: Brookings Institution, 1978.

Bolling, Richard W. *House Out of Order.* New York: Dutton, 1965.

———. *Power in the House: A History of the Leadership of the House of Representatives.* New York: Dutton, 1968.

Bond, James E. *No Easy Walk to Freedom: Reconstruction and the Ratification of the Fourteenth Amendment.* Westport, Conn.: Praeger, 1997.

Bond, Jon R., and Richard Fleisher. *President in the Legislative Arena.* Chicago: University of Chicago Press, 1990.

Bone, Hugh A. *American Politics and the Party' System.* New York: McGraw-Hill, 1955.

Bork, Robert H. *The Antitrust Paradox.* New York: Basic Books, 1978.

———. *The Tempting of America: The Political Seduction of the Law.* New York: Free Press, 1990.

Bowen, Catherine D. *Miracle at Philadelphia: The Story of the Constitutional Convention, May to September 1787.* Boston: Little, Brown, 1966.

Bowles, Nigel. *The White House and Capitol Hill: The Politics of Presidential Persuasion.* New York: Oxford University Press, 1987.

Bowling, Kenneth R. *The Creation of Washington, D.C.: The Idea and Location of the American Capital.* Fairfax, Va.: George Mason University Press, 1991.

Brady, David W. *Critical Elections and Congressional Policy-Making.* Stanford, Calif.: Stanford University Press, 1988.

Brady, David W., and Craig Volden. *Revolving Gridlock: Politics and Policy from Carter to Clinton.* Boulder, Colo.: Westview Press, 1998.

Brant, Irving. *Impeachment: Trials and Errors.* New York: Knopf, 1972.

———. *James Madison: Father of the Constitution, 1787–1800.* Indianapolis: Bobbs-Merrill, 1950.

Breckenridge, Adam C. *Congress Against the Court.* Lincoln: University of Nebraska Press, 1970.

Broder, David S. *Behind the Front Page: A Candid Look at How the News Is Made.* New York: Simon and Schuster, 1987.

Bronner, Ethan. *Battle for Justice: How the Bork Nomination Shook America.* New York: Norton, 1989.

Brown, Glenn. *History of the United States Capitol.* 2 vols. Washington, D.C.: Government Printing Office, 1903. Reprint New York: Da Capo Press, 1970.

Brown, Richard E. *The GAO: Untapped Source of Congressional Power.* Knoxville: University of Tennessee Press, 1970.

Brown, William H. *House Practice: A Guide to the Rules, Precedents and Procedures of the House.* Washington, D.C.: Government Printing Office, 1996.

Browne, William P. *Cultivating Congress: Constituents, Issues, Interests, and Agricultural Policymaking*. Lawrence: University Press of Kansas, 1995

Bryan, Wilhelmus B. *A History of the National Capital*. 2 vols. New York: Macmillan, 1914–1916.

Burdette, Franklin L. *Filibustering in the Senate*. New York: Russell & Russell, 1965.

Burnham, Walter D. *Presidential Ballots, 1836–1892*. Baltimore: Johns Hopkins University Press, 1955.

Burns, James MacGregor. *Congress on Trial*. New York: Harper and Brothers, 1949.

———. *Leadership*. New York: Harper and Row, 1978.

Busbey, L. White. *Uncle Joe Cannon*. New York: Henry Holt, 1927.

Butler, Anne M., and Wendy Wolff. *United States Senate Election, Expulsion, and Censure Cases, 1793–1990*. Washington, D.C.: Government Printing Office, 1995.

Byrd, Robert C. *The Senate, 1789–1989: Addresses on the History of the United States Senate*. 2 vols. Washington, D.C.: Government Printing Office, 1988.

C

Caeser, James W. *Presidential Selection: Theory and Development*. Princeton, N.J.: Princeton University Press, 1979.

Cain, Bruce, John Ferejohn, and Morris Fiorina. *The Personal Vote: Constituency Service and Electoral Independence*. Cambridge, Mass.: Harvard University Press, 1987.

Campbell, Angus. *The Voter Decides*. New York: Harper and Row, 1954.

Campbell, Angus, Philip E. Converse, Warren E. Miller, and Donald E. Stokes. *The American Voter*. New York: Wiley, 1960.

Campbell, James E. *The Presidential Pulse of Congressional Elections*. 2nd ed. Lexington: University Press of Kentucky, 1997.

Cannon, Clarence, ed. *Cannon's Procedure in the House of Representatives*. Washington, D.C.: Government Printing Office, 1963.

Canon, David T. *Actors, Athletes, and Astronauts: Political Amateurs in the United State Congress*. Chicago: University of Chicago Press, 1990.

Cantor, Joseph E. *Campaign Financing*. Washington, D.C.: Congressional Research Service, 1998.

———. *Congressional Campaign Spending: 1976–1996*. Washington, D.C.: Congressional Research Service, 1997.

———. *Political Action Committees: Their Role in Financing Congressional Elections*. Washington, D.C.: Congressional Research Service, 1998.

Cantor, Joseph E., Denis S. Rutkus, and Kevin B. Greely. *Free and Reduced-Rate Television Time for Political Candidates*. Washington, D.C.: Congressional Research Service, 1997.

Caplan, Russell L. *Constitutional Brinksmanship: Amending the Constitution by National Convention*. New York: Oxford University Press, 1988.

Cappella, Joseph N., and Kathleen H. Jamieson. *Spiral of Cynicism: The Press and the Public Good*. New York: Oxford University Press, 1997.

Carr, Robert K. *The Supreme Court and Judicial Review*. New York: Farrar and Rinehart, 1942.

Carroll, Holbert N. *The House of Representatives and Foreign Affairs*. Pittsburgh: University of Pittsburgh Press, 1958.

Carter, Stephen L. *The Confirmation Mess: Cleaning up the Federal Appointment Process*. New York: Basic Books, 1994.

Center for Responsive Politics. "Who's Paying? Stats at-a-Glance on the Funding of U.S. Elections." Washington, D.C.: Center for Responsive Politics, 1997.

Cheever, Daniel S., and H. Field Haviland, Jr. *American Foreign Policy and the Separation of Powers*. Cambridge, Mass.: Harvard University Press, 1952.

Chiu, Chang-Wei. *The Speaker of the House of Representatives since 1896*. New York: Columbia University Press, 1928.

Choate, Pat. *Agents of Influence*. New York: Knopf, 1990.

Chubb, John E., and Paul E. Peterson, eds. *Can the Government Govern?* Washington, D.C.: Brookings Institution, 1989.

Cigler, Allan J., and Burdett A. Loomis. *Interest Group Politics*. 5th ed. Washington, D.C.: CQ Press, 1998.

Clancy, Paul, and Shirley Elder. *Tip: A Biography of Thomas P. O'Neill, Speaker of the House*. New York: Macmillan, 1980.

Clark, Champ. *My Quarter Century of American Politics*. 2 vols. New York: Harper and Brothers, 1920.

Clark, Peter, and Susan H. Evans. *Covering Campaigns: Journalism in Congressional Elections*. Stanford, Calif.: Stanford University Press, 1983.

Claude, Richard. *The Supreme Court and the Electoral Process*. Baltimore: Johns Hopkins University Press, 1970.

Clausen, Aage R. *How Congressmen Decide: A Policy Focus*. New York: St. Martin's, 1973.

Clawson, Dan, Alan Neustadtl, and Denise Scott. *Money Talks: Corporate PACs and Political Influence*. New York: Basic Books, 1992.

Clawson, Dan, Alan Neustadtl, and Mark Weller. *Dollars and Votes: How Business Campaign Contributions Subvert Democracy*. Philadelphia, Pa.: Temple, 1998

Cohen, Richard E. *Washington at Work: Back Rooms and Clean Air*. Needham Heights, Mass.: Allyn and Bacon, 1995.

Cole, John Y. *Jefferson's Legacy: A Brief History of the Library of Congress*. Washington, D.C.: Government Printing Office, 1993.

Collier, Christopher, and James L. Collier. *Decision in Philadelphia: The Constitutional Convention of 1787*. New York: Ballantine, 1986.

Collier, Kenneth. *Between the Branches: The White House Office of Legislative Affairs*. Pittsburgh: University of Pittsburgh Press, 1997.

Conant, Michael. *The Constitution and the Economy: Objective Theory and Critical Commentary*. Norman: University of Oklahoma Press, 1991.

Congressional Quarterly. *Congressional Elections, 1946–1996*. Washington, D.C.: Congressional Quarterly, 1998.

———. *Congressional Pay and Perquisites: History, Facts, and Controversy*. Washington, D.C.: Congressional Quarterly, 1992.

———. *Congressional Quarterly's Guide to U.S. Elections*. 3rd ed. Washington, D.C.: Congressional Quarterly, 1994.

———. *The Iran-Contra Puzzle*. Washington, D.C.: Congressional Quarterly, 1987.

———. *The Washington Lobby*. 5th ed. Washington, D.C.: Congressional Quarterly, 1987.

———. *Watergate: Chronology of a Crisis*. Washington, D.C.: Congressional Quarterly, 1974, Reprint 1999.

Congressional Quarterly Almanac. Washington, D.C.: Congressional Quarterly, 1948– .

Congressional Quarterly Weekly Report. Washington, D.C.: Congressional Quarterly, 1956–1998.

Connelly, William F., Jr., and John J. Pitney, Jr. *Congress' Permanent Minority? Republicans in the U.S. House*. Lanham, Md.: Rowman and Littlefield, 1994.

Conway, M. Margaret. *Political Participation in the United States*. 2nd ed. Washington, D.C.: CQ Press, 1991.

Cook, Timothy E. *Making Laws and Making News: Media Strategies in the U.S. House of Representatives*. Washington, D.C.: Brookings Institution, 1989.

Cooper, Joseph. *Congress and Its Committees: A Historical Approach to the Role of Committees in the Legislative Process*. New York: Garland Publishing, 1988.

Cooper, Joseph, and G. Calvin Mackenzie. *The House at Work*. Austin: University of Texas Press, 1981.

Corrado, Anthony, Thomas E. Mann, Daniel R. Ortiz, Trevor Potter, and Frank J. Sorauf, eds. *Campaign Finance Reform: A Sourcebook*. Washington, D.C.: Brookings Institution, 1997.

Corson, John J., and R. Shale Paul. *Men Near the Top: Filling Key Posts in the Federal Service*. Baltimore: Johns Hopkins University Press, 1966.

Cortner, Richard C. *The Apportionment Cases*. Knoxville: University of Tennessee Press, 1970.

———. *The Supreme Court and the Second Bill of Rights: The Fourteenth Amendment and the Nationalization of Civil Liberties*. Madison: University of Wisconsin Press, 1981.

Corwin, Edward S. *The Commerce Power vs. States Rights*. Princeton, N.J.: Princeton University Press, 1936.

———. *The Constitution and What It Means Today*. 14th ed. Revised by Harold W. Chase and Craig R. Ducat. Princeton, N.J.: Princeton University Press, 1978.

———. *The Doctrine of Judicial Review: Its Legal and Historical Basis and Other Essays*. Princeton, N.J.: Princeton University Press, 1914. Reprint. Gloucester, Mass.: Peter Smith, 1963.

———. *The President: Office and Powers, 1787–1984*. 5th ed. New York: New York University Press, 1984.

Corwin, Edward S., and Louis W. Koenig. *The Presidency Today*. New York: New York University Press, 1956.

Cotton, Norris. *In the Senate: Amidst the Conflict and the Turmoil*. New York: Dodd, Mead, 1978.

Cox, Gary W., and Mathew D. McCubbins. *Legislative Leviathan: Party Government in the House*. Berkeley: University of California Press, 1993.

Cox, Gary W., and Samuel Kernell, ed. *The Politics of Divided Government*. Boulder, Colo.: Westview Press, 1991.

CQ Weekly. Washington, D.C.: Washington, D.C.: Congressional Quarterly, 1998– .

Crabb, Cecil V., Jr., and Pat M. Holt. *Invitation to Struggle: Congress, the President, and Foreign Policy*. 4th ed. Washington, D.C.: CQ Press, 1992.

———. *The President's Removal Power under the Constitution*. New York: National Municipal League, 1927.

Cranford, John. *Budgeting for America*. 2nd ed. Washington, D.C.: Congressional Quarterly, 1989.

Cronin, Thomas E., and Rexford G. Tugwell, eds. *The Presidency Reappraised*. 2nd ed. New York: Praeger, 1977.

Crosskey, William W. *Politics and the Constitution in the History of the United States*. Chicago: University of Chicago Press, 1953.

Cummings, Milton C. *Congressmen and the Electorate: Elections for the U.S. House and the President, 1920–1964*. New York: Free Press, 1966.

Currie, James T. *The United States House of Representatives*. Malabar, Fla.: Krieger, 1988.

Curtis, Michael K. *No State Shall Abridge: The Fourteenth Amendment and the Bill of Rights*. Durham, N.C.: Duke University Press, 1986.

D

Dahl, Robert A. *Congress and Foreign Policy*. New York: Harcourt, Brace, 1950.

Davidson, Chandler, ed. *Minority Vote Dilution*. Washington, D.C.: Howard University Press, 1984.

Davidson, Roger H. *The Role of the Congressman*. New York: Pegasus, 1969.

———, ed. *Postreform Congress*. New York: St. Martin's, 1992.

Davidson, Roger H., and Walter J. Oleszek. *Congress against Itself*. Bloomington: Indiana University Press, 1977.

———. *Congress and Its Members*. 7th ed. Washington, D.C.: CQ Press, 2000.

Davis, Horace. *A Judicial Veto*. Boston: Houghton Mifflin, 1914. Reprint. New York: Da Capo Press, 1971.

Deering, Christopher J., and Steven S. Smith. *Committees in Congress*. 3rd ed. Washington, D.C.: CQ Press, 1997.

DeGrazia, Alfred. *Essay on Apportionment and Representative Government*. Washington, D.C.: American Enterprise Institute, 1963. Reprint. Westport, Conn.: Greenwood Press, 1983.

Derthick, Martha, and Paul J. Quirk. *The Politics of Deregulation*. Washington, D.C.: Brookings Institution, 1985.

Deschler, Lewis. *Deschler's Procedure in the U.S. House of Representatives*. 3rd ed. Washington, D.C.: Government Printing Office, 1979.

———. *Precedents of the House of Representatives*. Washington, D.C.: Government Printing Office, 1977– .

———. *Procedure in the House of Representatives*. Washington, D.C.: Government Printing Office, 1982; 1987 supplement.

Dewitt, David M. *Impeachment and Trial of Andrew Johnson*. New York: Russell & Russell, 1967.

Dexter, Lewis A. *The Sociology and Politics of Congress*. Chicago: Rand McNally, 1969.

Dodd, Lawrence C., and Bruce I. Oppenheimer, eds. *Congress Reconsidered*. 5th ed. Washington, D.C.: CQ Press, 1989.

———. *Congress Reconsidered*. 6th ed. Washington, D.C.: CQ Press, 1997.

Dole, Bob. *Historical Almanac of the United States Senate*. Washington, D.C.: Government Printing Office, 1989.

Drew, Elizabeth. *Politics and Money: The New Road to Corruption*. New York: Macmillan, 1983.

———. *Senator*. New York: Simon and Schuster, 1979.

Duncan, Philip, and Brian Nutting, eds. *Politics in America 2000: The 106th Congress*. Washington, D.C.: Congressional Quarterly, 1999.

Dwyer, Paul E. *Salaries of Members of Congress: Congressional Votes, 1967–1989*. Washington, D.C.: Congressional Research Service, 1989.

E

Eagleton, Thomas J. *War and Presidential Power*. New York: Liveright, 1974.

Early, Stephen T. *Constitutional Courts of the United States*. Totowa, N.J.: Littlefield Adams, 1977.

Eberling, Ernest J. *Congressional Investigations: A Study of the Origin and Development of the Power of Congress to Investigate and Punish for Contempt*. New York: Columbia University Press, 1928.

Edwards, George C., III. *At the Margins: Presidential Leadership of Congress*. New Haven, Conn.: Yale University Press, 1989.

———. *The Public Presidency: The Pursuit of Popular Support*. New York: St. Martin's, 1983.

Edwards, George C., III, John H. Kessel, and Bert A. Rockman, eds. *Researching the Presidency: Vital Questions, New Approaches*. Pittsburgh: University of Pittsburgh Press, 1993.

Ehrenhalt, Alan. *The United States of Ambition: Politicians, Power, and the Pursuit of Office*. New York: Times Books, 1991.

Eismeier, Theodore J., and Philip H. Pollock, III. *Business, Money and the Rise of Corporate PACs in American Elections*. New York: Quorum Books, 1988.

Eisner, Robert. *How Real Is the Federal Deficit?* New York: Free Press, 1986.

Elving, Ronald D. *Conflict and Compromise: How Congress Makes the Law*. New York: Simon & Schuster, 1995.

———, ed. *Congress and the Great Issues, 1945–1995*. Washington, D.C.: Congressional Quarterly, 1996.

Endersby, James W., and Karen M. McCurdy. "Committee Assignments in the U.S. Senate." *Legislative Studies Quarterly* 21 (1996): 219–234.

Epstein, Lee, and Jack Knight. *The Choices Justices Make*. Washington, D.C.: CQ Press, 1998.

Epstein, Lee, and Thomas G. Walker. *Constitutional Law for a Changing America: Institutional Powers and Constraints*. 3rd ed. Washington, D.C.: CQ Press, 1998.

———. *Constitutional Law for a Changing America: Rights, Liberties, and Justice*. 3rd ed. Washington, D.C.: CQ Press, 1998.

Ervin, Sam J., Jr. *Role of the Supreme Court: Policy Maker or Adjudicator?* Washington, D.C.: American Enterprise Institute, 1970.

Eskridge, William N. *Dynamic Statutory Interpretation*. Cambridge, Mass.: Harvard University Press, 1994.

Etzioni, Amitai. *Capital Corruption: The New Attack on American Democracy.* New York: Harcourt Brace Jovanovich, 1984.

Evans, C. Lawrence. *Leadership in Committee: A Comparative Analysis of Leadership Behavior in the U.S. Senate.* Ann Arbor: University of Michigan Press, 1991.

Evans, C. Lawrence, and Walter J. Oleszek. *Congress under Fire: Reform Politics and the Republican Majority.* Boston: Houghton Mifflin, 1997.

Evans, Rowland, and Robert Novak. *Lyndon B. Johnson: The Exercise of Power.* New York: New American Library, 1966.

Fallon, Richard, Daniel J. Meltzer, and David L. Shapiro. *Hart and Wechsler's The Federal Courts and the Federal System.* 4th ed. Westbury, N.Y.: Foundation Press, 1996.

Farrand, Max, ed. *The Records of the Federal Convention of 1787.* 4 vols. New Haven, Conn.: Yale University Press, 1973.

Federal Election Commission. "Annual Report." Washington, D.C., 1974– .

———. "Twenty Year Report." Washington, D.C., 1995.

F

Feerick, John D. *The Twenty-fifth Amendment: Its Complete History and Applications.* 2nd ed. New York: Fordham University Press, 1992.

Fenno, Richard F., Jr. *Congressmen in Committees.* Boston: Little, Brown, 1973.

———. *The Emergence of a Senate Leader: Pete Domenici and the Reagan Budget.* Washington, D.C.: CQ Press, 1991.

———. *Home Style: House Members in Their Districts.* Boston: Little, Brown, 1978.

———. *The Making of a Senator: Dan Quayle.* Washington, D.C.: CQ Press, 1989.

———. *The Power of the Purse: Appropriations Politics in Congress.* Boston: Little, Brown, 1966.

———. *The Presidential Odyssey of John Glenn.* Washington, D.C.: CQ Press, 1990.

———. *The President's Cabinet: An Analysis of the Period from Wilson to Eisenhower.* Cambridge, Mass.: Harvard University Press, 1959.

———. *Senators on the Campaign Trail: The Politics of Representative.* Norman: University of Oklahoma Press, 1996.

Fiellin, Alan. "The Functions of Informal Groups in Legislative Institutions." *Journal of Politics* (February 1962): 72–91.

Findley, William. *Review of the Revenue System Adopted by the First Congress.* Philadelphia: T. Dobson, 1794. Reprint. New York: Kelley, 1971.

Fiorina, Morris P. *Congress: Keystone of the Washington Establishment.* 2nd ed. New Haven, Conn.: Yale University Press, 1989.

———. *Divided Government.* New York: Maxwell Macmillan International, 1992.

———. *Representatives, Roll Calls, and Constituencies.* Lexington, Mass.: D. C. Heath, 1974.

———. *Retrospective Voting in American National Elections.* New Haven, Conn.: Yale University Press, 1981.

Fiorina, Morris P., and David W. Rohde, eds. *Home Style and Washington Work: Studies of Congressional Politics.* Ann Arbor: University of Michigan Press, 1989.

Fisher, Louis. *American Constitutional Law.* 3rd ed. Durham, N.C.: Carolina Academic Press, 1999.

———. *Constitutional Conflicts between Congress and the President.* 4th ed. Lawrence.: University Press of Kansas, 1997.

———. *The Politics of Shared Power: Congress and the Executive.* 4th ed. College Station: Texas A & M University Press, 1998.

———. *President and Congress: Power and Policy.* New York: Free Press, 1972.

———. *Presidential Spending Power.* Princeton, N.J.: Princeton University Press, 1975.

———. *Presidential War Power.* Lawrence: University Press of Kansas, 1995.

Flanigan, William H., and Nancy H. Zingale. *Political Behavior of the American Electorate.* 9th ed. Washington, D.C.: CQ Press, 1998.

Foley, Michael. *The New Senate: Liberal Influence on a Conservative Institution, 1959–1972.* New Haven: Conn.: Yale University Press, 1980.

Foley, Michael, and John E. Owens. *Congress and the Presidency: Institutional Politics in a Separated System.* New York: Manchester University Press, 1996.

Follett, Mary P. *The Speaker of the House of Representatives.* New York: Longmans, Green, 1896. Reprint. New York: Burt Franklin Reprints, 1974.

Foreman, Christopher H., Jr. *Signals from the Hill: Congressional Oversight and the Challenge of Social Regulation.* New Haven, Conn.: Yale University Press, 1988.

Forte, David F. *The Supreme Court in American Politics: Judicial Activism vs. Judicial Restraint.* Lexington, Mass.: D. C. Heath, 1972.

Fowler, Linda. *Candidates, Congress, and the American Democracy.* Ann Arbor: University of Michigan Press, 1993.

Fowler, Linda, and Robert D. McClure. *Political Ambition: Who Decides to Run for Congress.* New Haven, Conn.: Yale University Press, 1989.

Fox, Harrison W., Jr., and Susan W. Hammond. *Congressional Staffs: The Invisible Force in American Lawmaking.* New York: Free Press, 1977.

Franck, Thomas M., ed. *The Tethered Presidency: Congressional Restraints on Executive Power.* New York: New York University Press, 1981.

Franck, Thomas M., and Edward Weisband. *Foreign Policy by Congress.* New York: Oxford University Press, 1979.

Frankfurter, Felix. *The Commerce Clause under Marshall, Taney, and Waite.* Chapel Hill: University of North Carolina Press, 1937.

Frantzich, Stephen E. *Write Your Congressman: Constituent Communications and Representation.* New York: Praeger, 1986.

Frary, Ihna T. *They Built the Capitol.* Plainview, N.Y.: Books for Libraries, 1940.

Friedman, Leon, and Fred L. Israel, eds. *The Justices of the United States Supreme Court: Their Lives and Major Opinions.* 5 vols. New York: Chelsea House, 1997.

Fritz, Sara, and Dwight Morris. *Gold-Plated Politics: Running for Congress in the 1990s.* Washington, D.C.: CQ Press, 1992.

Froman, Lewis A., Jr. *The Congressional Process: Strategies, Rules, and Procedures.* Boston: Little, Brown, 1967.

———. *Congressmen and Their Constituencies.* Chicago: Rand-McNally, 1963.

Fuller, Hubert B. *The Speakers of the House.* Boston: Little, Brown, 1909.

Furlong, William L., and Margaret E. Scranton. *The Dynamics of Foreign Policymaking: The President, the Congress, and the Panama Canal Treaties.* Boulder, Colo.: Westview Press, 1984.

G

Galloway, George B. *Congress at the Crossroads.* New York: Crowell, 1946.

———. *History of the House of Representatives.* 2nd ed. Revised by Sidney Wise. New York: Crowell, 1976.

———. *The Legislative Process in Congress.* New York: Crowell, 1953.

Garay, Ronald. *Congressional Television: A Legislative History.* Westport, Conn.: Greenwood Press, 1984.

Garthoff, Raymond L. *Policy versus Law: The Reinterpretation of the ABM Treaty.* Washington, D.C.: Brookings Institution, 1987.

Gavit, Bernard C. *Commerce Clause of the United States Constitution.* New York: AMS Press, 1970.

Gellhorn, Walter. *When Americans Complain: Governmental Grievance Procedures.* Cambridge, Mass.: Harvard University Press, 1966.

Gerhardt, Michael J. *The Federal Impeachment Process: A Constitutional and Historical Analysis.* Princeton, N.J.: Princeton University Press, 1996.

Gertzog, Irwin N. *Congressional Women: Their Recruitment, Integration, and Behavior.* 2nd ed. Westport, Conn.: Praeger, 1995.

Getz, Robert S. *Congressional Ethics: The Conflict of Interest Issue.* New York: D. Van Nostrand, 1966.

Gillespie, Ed, and Bob Schellhas, eds. *Contract with America: The Bold Plan by Rep. Newt Gingrich, Rep. Dick Armey and the House Republicans to Change the Nation.* New York: Times Books, 1994.

Gilmour, John B. *Reconcilable Differences? Congress, the Budget Process, and the Deficit.* Berkeley: University of California Press, 1990.

Ginsberg, Benjamin, and Martin Shefter. *Politics by Other Means: Politicians, Prosecutors, and the Press from Watergate to Whitewater.* Rev. ed. New York: Norton, 1999.

Glaser, James M. *Race, Campaign Politics, and the Realignment in the South.* New Haven, Conn.: Yale University Press, 1996.

Goehlert, Robert U., and Fenton S. Martin. *The United States Congress: An Annotated Bibliography, 1980–1939.* Washington, D.C.: Congressional Quarterly, 1995.

Goehlert, Robert U., Fenton S. Martin, and John R. Sayre. *Members of Congress: A Bibliography.* Washington, D.C.: Congressional Quarterly, 1996.

Goidel, Robert K., Donald A. Gross, and Todd G. Shields. *Money Matters: Consequences of Campaign Finance Reform in U.S. House Elections.* Lanham, Md.: Rowan and Littlefield, 1999.

Goldfarb, Ronald L. *The Contempt Power.* New York: Columbia University Press, 1963.

Goldstein, Kenneth M. *Interest Groups, Lobbying, and Participation in America.* New York: Cambridge University Press, 1999.

Goldwin, Robert A., and Art Kaufman, eds. *Separation of Powers: Does It Still Work?* Washington, D.C.: American Enterprise Institute, 1986.

Goldwin, Robert A., and Robert A. Licht, eds. *Foreign Policy and the Constitution.* Washington, D.C.: AEI Press, 1990.

Goodman, Walter. *The Committee: The Extraordinary Career of the House Committee on Un-American Activities.* New York: Farrar, Straus and Giroux, 1968.

Goodrum, Charles A. *The Congressional Research Service of the United States Congress.* Washington, D.C.: Library of Congress, 1974.

Goodrum, Charles A., and Helen W. Dalrymple. *Guide to the Library of Congress.* Rev. ed. Washington, D.C.: Library of Congress, 1988.

———. *The Library of Congress.* Boulder, Colo.: Westview Press, 1982.

———. *Treasures of the Library of Congress.* Rev. ed. New York: Abrams, 1991.

Goodwin, George, Jr. *The Little Legislatures: Committees of Congress.* Amherst: University of Massachusetts Press, 1970.

Graber, Doris A. *Mass Media and American Politics.* 5th ed. Washington, D.C.: CQ Press, 1997.

———, ed. *Media Power in Politics.* 3rd ed. Washington, D.C.: CQ Press, 1994.

Gramlich, Edward M. *Is It Time to Reform Social Security?* Ann Arbor: University of Michigan Press, 1998.

Green, John C., Paul Herrnson, Lynda Powell, and Clyde Wilcox. "Individual Congressional Campaign Contributors: Wealthy, Conservative and Reform-Minded." Washington, D.C.: Center for Responsive Politics, 1998.

Green, John C., and Daniel M. Shea. *The State of the Parties: The Changing Role of Contemporary American Parties.* 3rd ed. Lanham, Md.: Rowan and Littlefield, 1999.

Grofman, Bernard, ed. *Race and Redistricting in the 1990s.* New York: Agathon Press, 1998.

Groseclose, Tim, and Charles Stewart. "The Value of Committee Seats in the House, 1947–1991." *American Journal of Political Science* 42 (April 1998): 453–474.

H

Haass, Richard N. *Intervention: The Use of American Military Force in the Post-Cold War World.* Washington, D.C.: Brookings Institution, 1998.

Hacker, Andrew. *Congressional Districting: The Issue of Equal Representation.* Rev. ed. Washington, D.C.: Brookings Institution, 1964.

Hall, Richard L. *Participation in Congress.* New Haven, Conn.: Yale University Press, 1996.

Hall, Richard L., and C. Lawrence Evans. "The Power of Subcommittees." *Journal of Politics* 52 (May 1990): 335–355.

Hamilton, Alexander, James Madison, and John Jay. *The Federalist Papers.* New York: New American Library, 1961.

Hamilton, Howard D. *Legislative Apportionment: Key to Power.* New York: Harper and Row, 1964.

Hamilton, James. *The Power to Probe: A Study of Congressional Investigations.* New York: Random House, 1976.

Hansen, John M. *Gaining Access: Congress and the Farm Lobby.* Chicago: University of Chicago Press, 1991.

Hanson, Royce. *The Political Thicket: Reapportionment and Constitutional Democracy.* Englewood Cliffs, N.J.: Prentice-Hall, 1966.

Hardaway, Robert M. *The Electoral College and the Constitution: The Case for Preserving Federalism.* Westport, Conn.: Praeger, 1994.

Hardeman, D. B., and Donald C. Bacon. *Rayburn: A Biography.* Austin: Texas Monthly Press, 1987.

Harris, Fred R. *Deadlock or Decision: The U.S. Senate and the Rise of National Politics.* New York: Oxford University Press, 1993.

Harris, Joseph P. *The Advice and Consent of the Senate: A Study of the Confirmation of Appointments by the United States Senate.* Westport, Conn.: Greenwood Press, 1968.

———. *Congressional Control of Administration.* Washington, D.C.: Brookings Institution, 1964.

Harris, Richard A., and Sidney M. Milkis. *The Politics of Regulatory Change: A Tale of Two Agencies.* 2nd ed. New York: Oxford University Press, 1996.

Hasbrouck, Paul D. *Party Government in the House of Representatives.* New York: Macmillan, 1927.

Hawkins, Betsy W. *Setting Course: A Congressional Management Guide.* 6th ed. Washington, D.C.: Congressional Management Foundation, 1996.

Haworth, Paul L. *The Hayes-Tilden Disputed Presidential Election of 1876.* Cleveland: Burrows, 1906.

Hayes, Michael T. *Lobbyists and Legislators: A Theory of Political Markets.* New Brunswick, N.J.: Rutgers University Press, 1984.

Haynes, George H. *The Senate of the United States: Its History and Practice.* 2 vols. Boston: Houghton Mifflin, 1938.

Hazelton, George C., Jr. *The National Capitol.* New York: F. Taylor, 1902.

Heard, Alexander. *The Costs of Democracy.* Chapel Hill: University of North Carolina Press, 1960.

Heard, Alexander, and Michael Nelson, eds. *Presidential Selection.* Durham, N.C.: Duke University Press, 1987.

Heard, Alexander, and Donald S. Strong. *Southern Primaries and Elections, 1920–1949.* University: University of Alabama Press, 1950. Reprint. Plainview, N.Y.: Books for Libraries Press, 1970.

Hecht, Marie B. *John Quincy Adams: A Personal History of an Independent Man.* New York: Macmillan, 1972.

Heclo, Hugh. *A Government of Strangers: Executive Politics in Washington.* Washington, D.C.: Brookings Institution, 1977.

Heinz, John P., et al. *The Hollow Core: Private Interests in National Policy Making.* Cambridge, Mass.: Harvard University Press, 1993.

Henkin, Louis. *Foreign Affairs and the Constitution.* New York: Norton, 1972.

Henry, H. Lon. *Congress: America's Privileged Class.* Rocklin, Calif.: Prima Publishing, 1994.

Herring, Edward P. *Presidential Leadership: The Political Relations of the Congress and Chief Executive.* Westport, Conn.: Greenwood Press, 1972.

Herrnson, Paul S. *Congressional Elections: Campaigning at Home and in Washington.* 2nd ed. Washington, D.C.: CQ Press, 1998.

Herrnson, Paul S., Shaiko, Ronald G., Wilcox, Clyde. eds., *The Interest*

Group Connection: Electioneering, Lobbying, and Policymaking In Washington. Chatham, N.J.: Chatham House, 1998.

Hertzke, Allen D., and Ronald M. Peters, Jr. *The Atomistic Congress: An Interpretation of Congressional Change.* New York: Sharpe, 1992.

Hess, Stephen, *Live from Capitol Hill! Studies of Congress and the Media.* Washington, D.C.: Brookings Institution, 1991.

———. *The Ultimate Insiders: U.S. Senators in the National Media.* Washington, D.C.: Brookings Institution, 1986.

———. *The Washington Reporters: Newswork.* Washington, D.C.: Brookings Institution, 1981.

Hibbing, John R. *Congressional Careers: Contours of Life in the U.S. House of Representatives.* Chapel Hill: University of North Carolina Press, 1991.

Hibbing, John R., and Elizabeth Theiss-Morse. *Congress as Public Enemy: Public Attitudes toward American Political Institutions.* New York: Cambridge University Press, 1995.

Highsmith, Carol M., and Ted Landphair. *The Library of Congress: America's Memory.* Golden, Colo.: Fulcrum, 1994.

Hinckley, Barbara. *Congressional Elections.* Washington, D.C.: CQ Press, 1981.

———. *Less Than Meets the Eye: Foreign Policymaking and the Myth of the Assertive Congress.* Chicago: University of Chicago Press, 1994.

———. *The Seniority System in Congress.* Bloomington: Indiana University Press, 1971.

———. *Stability and Change in Congress.* 4th ed. New York: Harper and Row, 1988.

Hinds, Asher C., ed. *Hinds' Precedents of the House of Representatives of the United States.* 11 vols. Washington, D.C.: Government Printing Office, 1907–1941.

Holt, Pat M. *Secret Intelligence and Public Policy: A Dilemma of Democracy.* Washington, D.C.: CQ Press, 1995.

———. *The War Powers Resolution: The Role of Congress in U.S. Armed Intervention.* Washington, D.C.: American Enterprise Institute, 1978.

Horn, Stephen. *Unused Power: The Work of the Senate Committee on Appropriations.* Washington, D.C.: Brookings Institution, 1970.

Hrebenar, Ronald J. *Interest Group Politics in America.* 3rd ed. Armonk, N.Y.: Sharpe, 1997.

Hughes, Charles E. *The Supreme Court of the United States.* New York: Columbia University Press, 1928.

Huitt, Ralph K., and Robert L. Peabody. *Congress: Two Decades of Analysis.* New York: Harper and Row, 1972.

Hupman, Richard D. *Senate Election, Expulsion, and Censure Cases from 1789 to 1972.* 92nd Cong., 1st sess., S Doc 92-7.

Hutson, James H., ed. *Supplement to Max Farrand's The Records of the Federal Convention of 1787.* New Haven, Conn.: Yale University Press, 1987.

I

Ippolito, Dennis S. *The Budget and National Politics.* San Francisco: Freeman, 1978.

J

Jackson, Brooks. *Broken Promise: Why the Federal Election Commission Failed. A Twentieth Century Fund Report.* New York: Priority Press, 1990.

———. *Honest Graft: Big Money and the American Political Process.* Rev. ed. Washington, D.C.: Farragut, 1990.

Jackson, Robert H. *The Struggle for Judicial Supremacy: A Study of a Crisis in American Power Politics.* New York: Random House, 1941.

Jacobs, Jerald A., ed. *Federal Lobbying.* Washington, D.C.: Bureau of National Affairs, 1989.

Jacobson, Gary C. *The Electoral Origins of Divided Government: Competi-*

tion in U.S. House Elections, 1946–1986. Boulder, Colo.: Westview Press, 1990.

———. *Money in Congressional Elections.* New Haven, Conn.: Yale University Press, 1980.

———. *The Politics of Congressional Elections.* 4th ed. New York: Longman, 1997.

Jacobson, Gary C., and Samuel Kernell. *Strategy and Choice in Congressional Elections.* 2nd ed. New Haven, Conn.: Yale University Press, 1983.

Jennings, Bruce, and Daniel Callahan, eds. *Representation and Responsibility: Exploring Legislative Ethics.* New York: Plenum Press, 1985.

Jentleson, Bruce W. *American Foreign Policy: The Dynamics of Choice in the 21st Century.* New York: Norton, 1999.

Johannes, John R. *To Serve the People: Congress and Constituency Service.* Lincoln: University of Nebraska Press, 1984.

Johnson, Cathy M. *The Dynamics of Conflict between Bureaucrats and Legislators.* Armonk, N.Y.: Sharpe, 1992.

Johnson, Loch K. *The Making of International Agreements: Congress Confronts the Executive.* New York: New York University Press, 1984.

———. *A Season of Inquiry: The Senate Intelligence Investigation.* Lexington: University Press of Kentucky, 1985.

Jones, Charles O. *The Minority Party in Congress.* Boston: Little, Brown, 1970.

———. *Party and Policy-Making: The House Republican Policy Committee.* New Brunswick, N.J.: Rutgers University Press, 1964.

———. *The Presidency in a Seperated System.* Washington, D.C.: Brookings Institution, 1994.

———. *Separate but Equal Branches: Congress and the Presidency.* 2nd ed. New York.: Chatham House, 1999.

———. *The United States Congress: People, Place, and Policy.* Homewood, Ill.: Dorsey, 1982.

Jones, Rochelle, and Peter Woll. *The Private World of Congress.* New York: Free Press, 1979.

Josephy, Alvin M., Jr. *On the Hill: A History of the American Congress.* New York: Simon and Schuster, 1980.

K

Kahn, Ronald. *The Supreme Court and Constitutional Theory: 1953–1993.* Lawrence: University Press of Kansas, 1994.

Kallenbach, Joseph E. *Federal Cooperation with the States under the Commerce Clause.* Ann Arbor: University of Michigan Press, 1942.

Kaptur, Marcy. *Women of Congress: A Twentieth-Century Odyssey.* Washington, D.C.: Congressional Quarterly, 1996.

Katz, Jonathan, and Brian Sala. "Careerism, Committee Assignments, and the Electoral Connection." *American Political Science Review* 90 (March 1996): 21–33.

Katz, William L. *Constitutional Amendments.* New York: Franklin Watts, 1974.

Katzmann, Robert A. *Courts and Congress.* Washington, D.C.: Brookings Institution, 1997.

Kazee, Thomas E., ed. *Who Runs for Congress? Ambition, Context, and Candidate Emergence.* Washington, D.C.: CQ Press, 1994.

Kelly, Alfred H., Winfred A. Harbison, and Herman Belz. *The American Constitution: Its Origins and Development.* 7th ed. New York: Norton, 1991.

Kennon, Donald R., and Richard Striner. *Washington Past and Present: A Guide to the Nation's Capital.* 2nd ed. Washington, D.C.: U.S. Capitol Historical Society, 1983.

Kernell, Samuel. *Going Public: New Strategies of Presidential Leadership.* 3rd ed. Washington, D.C.: CQ Press, 1997.

Key, V. O. *The Responsible Electorate.* New York: Vintage Books, 1966.

Kiewiet, D. Roderick, and Mathew D. McCubbins. *The Logic of Delegation: Congressional Parties and the Appropriations Process.* Chicago: University of Chicago Press, 1991.

Kimmel, Lewis H. *Federal Budget and Fiscal Policy, 1789–1958.* Washington, D.C.: Brookings Institution, 1959.

King, Anthony, ed. *Both Ends of the Avenue: The Presidency, the Executive Branch, and Congress in the 1980s.* Washington, D.C.: American Enterprise Institute, 1983.

King, David C. *Turf Wars: How Congressional Committees Claim Jurisdiction.* Chicago: University of Chicago Press, 1997.

Kingdon, John W. *Congressmen's Voting Decisions.* 3rd ed. Ann Arbor: University of Michigan Press, 1989.

Kofmehl, Kenneth. *Professional Staffs of Congress.* 3rd ed. West Lafayette, Ind.: Purdue University Press, 1977.

Koh, Harold H. *The National Security Constitution: Sharing Power after the Iran-Contra Affair.* New Haven, Conn.: Yale University Press, 1990.

Kolodny, Robin. *Pursuing Majorities: Congressional Campaign Committees in American Politics.* Norman: University of Oklahoma Press, 1998.

Koopman, Douglas L. *Hostile Takeover: The House Republican Party, 1980–1995.* Lanham, Md.: Rowman and Littlefield, 1996.

Korn, Jessica. *The Power of Separation: American Constitutionalism and the Myth of the Legislative Veto.* Princeton, N.J.: Princeton University Press, 1996.

Kornacki, John J., ed. *Leading Congress: New Styles, New Strategies.* Washington, D.C.: CQ Press, 1990.

Kozak, David C. *Contexts of Congressional Decision Behavior.* Lanham, Md.: University Press of America, 1984.

Krasno, Jonathan S. *Challengers, Competition, and Reelection: Comparing Senate and House Elections.* New Haven, Conn.: Yale University Press, 1994.

Krehbiel, Keith. *Information and Legislative Organization.* Ann Arbor: University of Michigan Press, 1991.

———. *Pivotal Politics: A Theory of U.S. Lawmaking.* Chicago: University of Chicago Press, 1998.

Krislov, Samuel. *Supreme Court in the Political Process.* New York: Macmillan, 1965.

Krousser, J. Morgan. *Colorblind Justice: Minority Voting Rights and the Undoing of the Second Reconstruction.* Chapel Hill: University of North Carolina Press, 1999.

Kubiak, Greg D. *The Gilded Dome: The U.S. Senate and Campaign Finance Reform.* Norman: University of Oklahoma Press, 1994.

Kurland, Philip B. *Watergate and the Constitution.* Chicago: University of Chicago Press, 1978.

Kuroda, Tadahisa. *The Origins of the Twelfth Amendment: The Electoral College in the Early Republic, 1787–1804.* Westport, Conn.: Greenwood Press, 1994.

L

Ladd, Everett C., and Charles D. Hadley. *Transformation of the American Party System.* 2nd ed. New York: Norton, 1978.

Leech, Margaret. *Reveille in Washington.* New York: Grosset & Dunlap, 1941.

LeLoup, Lance. *The Fiscal Congress: Legislative Control of the Budget.* Westport, Conn.: Greenwood Press, 1980.

Leonard, Thomas C. *The Power of the Press: The Birth of American Political Reporting.* New York: Oxford University Press, 1986.

Letwin, William. *Law and Economic Policy in America: The Evolution of the Sherman Antitrust Act.* Chicago: University of Chicago Press, 1959.

Leuchtenburg, William E. *The Supreme Court Reborn: The Constitutional Revolution in the Age of Roosevelt.* New York: Oxford University Press, 1995.

Levinson, Stanford, ed. *Responding to Imperfection: The Theory and Practice of Constitutional Amendment.* Princeton, N.J.: Princeton University Press, 1995.

Levitan, Sar A., and Martha R. Cooper. *Business Lobbies: The Public Good and the Bottom Line.* Baltimore: Johns Hopkins University Press, 1983.

Levy, Leonard W., ed. *Essays in the Making of the Constitution.* New York: Oxford University Press, 1969.

Levy, Leonard W., Kenneth L. Karst, and Dennis J. Mahoney, eds. *Encyclopedia of the American Constitution.* New York: Macmillan, 1986.

Lewinson, Paul. *Race, Class and Party: A History of Negro Suffrage and White Politics in the South.* New York: Oxford University Press, 1932.

Light, Paul C. *The President's Agenda: Domestic Policy Choice from Kennedy to Clinton.* 3rd ed. Baltimore: Johns Hopkins University Press, 1999.

Lindsay, James M. *Congress and the Politics of U.S. Foreign Policy.* Baltimore: Johns Hopkins University Press, 1994.

Linsky, Martin. *Impact: How the Press Affects Federal Policymaking.* New York: Norton, 1986.

Loewenberg, Gerhard, Samuel C. Patterson, and Malcolm E. Jewell. *Handbook of Legislative Research.* Cambridge, Mass.: Harvard University Press, 1985.

Longley, Lawrence D., and Alan G. Braun. *The Politics of Electoral College Reform.* 2nd ed. New Haven, Conn.: Yale University Press, 1975.

Longley, Lawrence D., and Walter J. Oleszek. *Bicameral Politics: Conference Committees in Congress.* New Haven, Conn.: Yale University Press, 1989.

Loomis, Burdett A. *The Contemporary Congress.* New York: St. Martin's, 1996.

———. *The New American Politician.* New York: Basic Books, 1988.

Loss, Richard, ed. *Corwin on the Constitution.* Ithaca, N.Y.: Cornell University Press, 1981.

Lowi, Theodore J. *The Personal President: Power Invested, Promise Unfilled.* Ithaca: Cornell University Press, 1985.

Luce, Robert. *Legislative Principles.* Boston: Houghton Mifflin, 1930. Reprint. New York: Da Capo Press, 1971.

———. *Legislative Procedure: Parliamentary practices and the Course of Business in the Framing of Statutes.* Boston: Houghton Mifflin, 1922. Reprint. New York: Da Capo Press, 1972.

Lutz, Donald. *Origins of American Constitutionalism.* Baton Rouge: Louisiana State University Press, 1988.

M

Maass, Arthur. *Congress and the Common Good.* New York: Basic Books, 1983.

MacBride, Roger L. *The American Electoral College.* 2nd ed. Caldwell, Idaho: Caxton Printers, 1963.

Mackaman, Frank H., ed. *Understanding Congressional Leadership.* Washington, D.C.: CQ Press, 1981.

Mackenzie, G. Calvin. *The Politics of Presidential Appointments.* New York: Free Press, 1981.

———, ed. *The In-and-Outers: Presidential Appointees and Transient Government in Washington.* Baltimore: Johns Hopkins University Press, 1987.

MacNeil, Neil. *Dirksen: Portrait of a Public Man.* New York: World Publishing, 1970.

Madison, James. *Notes of Debates in the Federal Convention of 1787.* Athens: Ohio University Press, 1966.

Madison, James, Alexander Hamilton, and John Jay. *The Federalist.* New York: New American Library, 1961.

Magleby, David B., and Candice J. Nelson. *The Money Chase: Congressional Campaign Finance Reform.* Washington, D.C.: Brookings Institution, 1990.

Maisel, L. Sandy, ed. *The Parties Respond: Changes in American Parties and Campaigns.* 2nd ed. Boulder: Westview Press, 1994.

Makinson, Larry. "The Big Picture: Money Follows Power Shift on Capitol Hill." Washington, D.C.: Center for Responsive Politics, 1997.

Makinson, Larry, and Joshua F. Goldstein. *The Cash Constituents of Congress.* 2nd ed. Washington, D.C.: Congressional Quarterly, 1994.

————. *Open Secrets: The Encyclopedia of Congressional Money and Politics.* 4th ed. Washington, D.C.: Congressional Quarterly, 1996.

Malbin, Michael J. *Parties, Interest Groups, and Campaign Finance Laws.* Washington, D.C.: American Enterprise Institute, 1980.

————. *Unelected Representatives: Congressional Staff and the Future of Representative Government.* New York: Basic Books, 1980.

————, ed. *Money and Politics in the United States: Financing Elections in the 1980s.* Chatham, N.J.: Chatham House/American Enterprise Institute, 1984.

Maltese, John A. *The Selling of Supreme Court Nominees.* Baltimore: Johns Hopkins University Press, 1995.

Maltzman, Forrest. *Competing Principals: Committees, Parties, and the Organization of Congress.* Ann Arbor: University of Michigan Press, 1997.

Manley, John F. *The Politics of Finance: The House Committee on Ways and Means.* Boston: Little, Brown, 1970.

Mann, Thomas E. *Unsafe at Any Margin: Interpreting Congressional Elections.* Washington, D.C.: American Enterprise Institute, 1978.

————, ed. *A Question of Balance: The President, the Congress, and Foreign Policy.* Washington, D.C.: Brookings Institution, 1990.

Mann, Thomas E., and Norman J. Ornstein, eds. *Congress, the Press, and the Public.* Washington, D.C.: Brookings Institution, 1994.

————. *The New Congress.* Washington, D.C.: American Enterprise Institute, 1981.

————. *Renewing Congress: A First Report.* Washington, D.C.: Brookings Institution and American Enterprise Institute, 1992.

————. *Renewing Congress: A Second Report.* Washington, D.C.: Brookings Institution and American Enterprise Institute, 1993.

Mansbridge, Jane J. *Why We Lost the ERA.* Chicago: University of Chicago Press, 1986.

Mansfield, Harvey C. *The Comptroller General: A Study in the Law and Practice of Financial Administration.* New Haven, Conn.: Yale University Press, 1939.

Margolis, Lawrence. *Executive Agreements and Presidential Power in Foreign Policy.* New York: Praeger, 1985.

Martin, Fenton S., and Robert U. Goehlert. *How to Research Congress.* Washington, D.C.: Congressional Quarterly, 1996.

Maskell, Jack. *Expulsion and Censure Actions Taken by the Full Senate against Members.* Washington, D.C.: Congressional Research Service, Library of Congress, 1990, 1993.

————. *Removal of Members of Congress from Office and the Issue of Recall of Legislators.* Washington, D.C.: Congressional Research Service, 1999.

————. *Reports Concerning Investigations and/or Disciplinary Recommendations from the House Committee on Standards of Official Conduct since Its Inception in 1968.* Washington, D.C.: Congressional Research Service, 1989.

Matthews, Donald R. *U.S. Senators and Their World.* Chapel Hill: University of North Carolina Press, 1960.

Maxey, Margaret N., and Robert L. Kuhn, *Regulatory Reform: New Vision and Old Curse.* New York: Praeger, 1985.

Mayhew, David R. *Congress: The Electoral Connection.* New Haven, Conn.: Yale University Press, 1974.

————. *Divided We Govern: Party Control, Lawmaking, and Investigations, 1946–1990.* New Haven, Conn.: Yale University Press, 1991.

————. *Party Loyalty among Congressmen: The Difference between Democrats and Republicans 1947–1962.* Cambridge, Mass.: Harvard University Press, 1966.

Mayo, Bernard. *Henry Clay: Spokesman of the New West.* Boston: Houghton Mifflin, 1937.

McConachie, Lauros G. *Congressional Committees: A Study of the Origins and Development of Our National and Local Legislative Methods.* New York: Crowell, 1898.

McDougal, Jim, and Curtis Wilkie. *Arkansas Mischief: The Birth of a National Scandal.* New York: Henry Holt, 1998.

McGeary, M. Nelson. *The Developments of Congressional Investigative Power.* New York: Octagon Books, 1973.

McGovney, Dudley O. *The American Suffrage Medley.* Chicago: University of Chicago Press, 1949.

McGown, Ada C. *The Congressional Conference Committee.* New York: Columbia University Press, 1927.

McLaughlin, Andrew C. *The Confederation and the Constitution, 1783–1789.* New York: Collier Books, 1962.

McLoughlin, Merrill, ed. *The Impeachment and Trial of President Clinton: The Official Transcripts, from the House Judiciary Committee Hearings to the Senate Trial.* New York: Time Books, 1999.

Mee, Charles L., Jr. *The Genius of the People.* New York: Harper and Row, 1987.

Merriner, James L., and Thomas P. Senter. *Against Long Odds: Citizens Who Challenge Congressional Incumbents.* Westport, Conn.: Praeger, 1999.

Mezey, Michael L. *Congress, the President, and Public Policy.* Boulder, Colo.: Westview Press, 1989.

Milbrath, Lester W. *The Washington Lobbyists.* Chicago: Rand McNally, 1963.

Milkis, Sidney M., and Michael Nelson. *The American Presidency: Origins and Development, 1776–1998.* 3rd ed. Washington, D.C.: Congressional Quarterly, 1999.

Miller, Clem. *Member of the House: Letters of a Congressman.* New York: Scribner's, 1962.

Miller, James A. *Running in Place: Inside the Senate.* New York: Simon and Schuster, 1986.

Mills, Gregory B., and John L. Palmer. *The Deficit Dilemma: Budget Policy in the Reagan Era.* Washington, D.C.: Urban Institute Press, 1984.

Milton, George F. *The Use of Presidential Power.* Boston: Little, Brown, 1944.

Moe, Ronald C. *Presidential Succession.* Washington, D.C.: Congressional Research Service, 1979.

Moore, Blaine F. *Supreme Court and Unconstitutional Legislation.* New York: Columbia University Press, 1913. Reprint. New York: AMS Press, 1968.

Morgan, Donald G. *Congress and the Constitution: A Study of Responsibility.* Cambridge, Mass.: Harvard University Press, 1966.

Morris, Dwight, and Murielle E. Gamache. *Handbook of Campaign Spending: Money in the 1992 Congressional Races.* Washington, D.C.: Congressional Quarterly, 1994.

Munson, Richard. *The Cardinals of Capitol Hill: The Men and Women Who Control Federal Spending.* New York: Grove Press, 1993.

Murphy, Walter F. *Congress and the Court: A Case Study in the American Political Process.* Chicago: University of Chicago Press, 1962.

Muskie, Edmund S., Kenneth Rush, and Kenneth W. Thompson, eds. *The President, the Congress and Foreign Policy.* Lanham, Md.: University Press of America, 1986.

Mutch, Robert E. *Campaigns, Congress, and Courts: The Making of Federal Campaign Finance Law.* New York: Praeger, 1988.

Myrdal, Gunnar. *An American Dilemma: The Negro Problem and Modern Democracy.* New York: Harper & Row, 1944.

N

Nelson, Garrison, ed. *Committees in the U.S. Congress 1947–1992.* 2 vols. Washington, D.C.: Congressional Quarterly, 1993–1994.

Nelson, Josephus, and Judith Farley. *Full Circle: Ninety Years of Service in the Main Reading Room.* Washington, D.C.: Library of Congress, 1991.

Nelson, Michael, ed. *Congressional Quarterly's Guide to the Presidency.* 2nd ed. Washington, D.C.: Congressional Quarterly, 1996.

————. *The Presidency and the Political System.* 5th ed. Washington, D.C.: CQ Press, 1998.

Neustadt, Richard E. *Presidential Power and the Modern Presidents: The*

Politics of Leadership from Roosevelt to Reagan. New York: Free Press, 1990.

Nevins, Allan. *The American States during and after the Revolution, 1775–1789.* New York: Macmillan, 1924.

Newman, Roger K., ed. *The Constitution and Its Amendments.* New York: Macmillan Reference USA, 1999.

Nichols, Roy F. *The Invention of the American Political Parties.* New York: Macmillan, 1967.

Nickels, Ilona B. *Parliamentary Reference Sources: An Introductory Guide.* Washington, D.C.: Congressional Research Service, 1986.

Nie, Norman H., Sidney Verba, and John R. Petrocik. *The Changing American Voter.* Cambridge, Mass.: Harvard University Press, 1976.

Noonan, John T., Jr. *Bribes: The Intellectual History of a Moral Idea.* Berkeley: University of California Press, 1984.

Nugent, Margaret L., and John R. Johannes. *Money, Elections, and Democracy: Reforming Congressional Campaign Finance.* Boulder, Colo.: Westview, 1990.

O

O'Brien, David. *Storm Center: The Supreme Court in American Politics.* 4th ed. New York: Norton, 1996.

Ogden, August R. *The Dies Committee: A Study of the Special House Committees for Investigation of Un-American Activities, 1938–1944.* Washington, D.C.: Catholic University of America Press, 1945.

Ogden, Frederic D. *The Poll Tax in the South.* University: University of Alabama Press, 1958.

Ogul, Morris. *Congress Oversees the Bureaucracy: Studies in Legislative Supervision.* Pittsburgh: University of Pittsburgh, 1976.

Oleszek, Walter J. *Congressional Procedures and the Policy Process.* 4th ed. Washington, D.C.: CQ Press, 1996.

———. *Majority and Minority Whips of the Senate: History and Development of the Party Whip System in the United States Senate.* Washington, D.C.: Government Printing Office, 1979.

Olson, Mancur. *The Logic of Collective Action.* Cambridge, Mass.: Harvard University Press, 1965.

O'Neill, Thomas P., Jr., with William Novak. *Man of the House: The Life and Political Memoirs of Speaker Tip O'Neill.* New York: Random House, 1987.

Onuf, Peter S., ed. *Ratifying, Amending, and Interpreting the Constitution.* New York: Garland Publications, 1991.

Orfield, Lester B. *Amending the Federal Constitution.* New York: Da Capo Press, 1971.

Ornstein, Norman J. *Campaign Finance: An Illustrated Guide.* Washington, D.C.: American Enterprise Institute, 1997.

———, ed. *Congress in Change: Evolution and Reform.* New York: Praeger, 1975.

Ornstein, Norman J., and Shirley Elder. *Interest Groups, Lobbying, and Policymaking.* Washington, D.C.: CQ Press, 1978.

Ornstein, Norman J., Thomas E. Mann, and Michael J. Malbin. *Vital Statistics on Congress, 1997–1998.* Washington, D.C.: Congressional Quarterly, 1998.

P

Palazzolo, Daniel J. *Done Deal? The Politics of the 1997 Budget Agreement.* New York: Chatham House, 1999.

———. *The Speaker and the Budget: Leadership in the Post-Reform House of Representatives.* Pittsburgh: University of Pittsburgh Press, 1992.

Parker, Frank R. *Black Votes Count: Political Empowerment in Mississippi after 1965.* Chapel Hill: University of North Carolina Press, 1990.

Parker, Glenn R. *Characteristics of Congress: Politics and Congressional Behavior.* Englewood Cliffs, N.J.: Prentice-Hall, 1989.

———. *Congress and the Rent-Seeking Society.* Ann Arbor: University of Michigan, 1996.

———. *Homeward Bound: Exploring Changes in Congressional Behavior.* Pittsburgh: University of Pittsburgh Press, 1986.

———. *Institutional Change, Discretion, and the Making of Modern Congress: An Economic Interpretation.* Ann Arbor: University of Michigan, 1992.

———, ed. *Studies of Congress.* Washington, D.C.: CQ Press, 1985.

Parker, Glenn R., and Suzanne L. Parker. *Factions in House Committees.* Knoxville: University of Tennessee Press, 1985.

Patterson, Bradley H., Jr. *The Ring of Power: The White House Staff and Its Expanding Role in Government.* New York: Basic Books, 1988.

Paul, Roland A. *American Military Commitments Abroad.* New Brunswick, N.J.: Rutgers University Press, 1973.

Peabody, Robert L. *Leadership in Congress: Stability, Succession and Change.* Boston: Little, Brown, 1976.

Peabody, Robert L., and Nelson W. Polsby. *New Perspectives on the House of Representatives.* 4th ed. Baltimore: Johns Hopkins University Press, 1992.

Peabody, Robert L., et al. *To Enact a Law: Congress and Campaign Financing.* New York: Praeger, 1972.

Pechman, Joseph A. *Federal Tax Policy.* 5th ed. Washington, D.C.: Brookings Institution, 1987.

Peirce, Neal R., and Lawrence D. Longley. *The People's President: The Electoral College in American History and the Direct Vote Alternative.* Rev. ed. New Haven, Conn.: Yale University Press, 1981.

Peters, Ronald M., Jr. *The American Speakership: The Office in Historical Perspective.* 2nd ed. Baltimore: Johns Hopkins University Press, 1997.

———, ed. *The Speaker: Leadership in the U.S. House of Representatives.* Washington, D.C.: Congressional Quarterly, 1995.

Peters, William. *A More Perfect Union: The Making of the United States Constitution.* New York: Crown, 1987.

Peterson, Mark A. *Legislating Together: The White House and Capitol Hill from Eisenhower to Reagan.* Cambridge, Mass.: Harvard University Press, 1990.

———, ed. *The President, the Congress, and the Making of Foreign Policy.* Norman: University of Oklahoma Press, 1994.

Phillips, Kevin. *The Politics of Rich and Poor: Wealth in the American Electorate in the Reagan Aftermath.* New York: Random House, 1990.

Polsby, Nelson W. "The Institutionalization of the U.S. House of Representatives." *American Political Science Review* 62, no. 1 (March 1968): 144–168.

———, ed. *Congressional Behavior.* New York: Random House, 1971.

Pomper, Gerald M., et al. *The Election of 1996: Reports and Interpretations.* Chatham, N.J.: Chatham House, 1997.

Poole, Keith T., and Howard Rosenthal. *Congress: A Political-Economic History of Roll Call Voting.* New York: Oxford University Press, 1997.

Porter, J. A. *City of Washington: Its Origin and Administration.* New York: Johnson Reprint, 1973.

Pressman, Jeffrey L. *House vs. Senate: Conflict in the Appropriation Process.* New Haven, Conn.: Yale University Press, 1966.

Price, David E. *Who Makes the Laws?* Cambridge, Mass.: Schenkman, 1972.

Pritchett, C. Herman. *Congress versus the Supreme Court, 1957–1960.* Minneapolis: University of Minnesota Press, 1961.

———. *The Roosevelt Court: A Study in Judicial Politics and Values, 1937–1947.* New York: Macmillan, 1948.

R

Ragsdale, Bruce A., and Joel D. Treese. *Black Americans in Congress, 1870–1989.* Office of the Historian, U.S. House of Representatives. Washington, D.C.: Government Printing Office, 1990.

Rakove, Jack N. *The Beginnings of National Politics: An Interpretive History of the Constitutional Congress.* New York: Knopf, 1979.

Ranney, Austin. *Channels of Power: The Impact of Television on American Politics.* New York: Basic Books, 1983.

Redman, Eric. *The Dance of Legislation.* New York: Simon and Schuster, 1973.

Reedy, George E. *The U.S. Senate: Paralysis or a Search for Consensus?* New York: Crown, 1986.

Reeves, Andree E. *Congressional Committee Chairmen: Three Who Made an Evolution.* Lexington: University of Kentucky Press, 1993.

Rehnquist, William H. *Grand Inquests: The Historic Impeachments of Justice Samuel Chase and President Andrew Johnson.* New York: Morrow, 1992.

Reichley, James. *The Life of the Parties: A History of American Political Parties.* New York: Free Press, 1992.

Reid, T. R. *Congressional Odyssey: The Saga of a Senate Bill.* New York: Freeman, 1980.

Reveley, W. Taylor, III. *War Powers of the President and Congress: Who Holds the Arrows and Olive Branch?* Charlottesville: University Press of Virginia, 1981.

Reynolds, George G. *Distribution of Power to Regulate Interstate Carriers between the Nation and the States.* New York: AMS Press, 1928.

Richardson, Jeremy J., ed. *Pressure Groups.* New York: Oxford University Press, 1993.

Riddick, Floyd M. *The United States Congress: Organization and Procedure.* Manassas, Va.: National Capitol Publishers, 1949.

Riddick, Floyd M., and Alan S. Frumin. *Riddick's Senate Procedure: Precedents and Practices.* Rev. ed. 101st Cong., 2nd sess., 1992. Senate Doc. 101-28. Washington, D.C.: Government Printing Office, 1992.

Riddle, Donald H. *The Truman Committee: A Study in Congressional Responsibility.* New Brunswick, N.J.: Rutgers University Press, 1964.

Rieselbach, Leroy N. *Congressional Politics: The Evolving Legislative System.* 2nd ed. Boulder, Colo.: Westview, 1995.

———. *Congressional Reform: The Changing Modern Congress.* Washington, D.C.: CQ Press, 1994.

———. *Legislative Reform: The Policy Impact.* Lexington, Mass.: Lexington Books, 1978.

Ripley, Randall B., and Grace A. Franklin. *Congress, the Bureaucracy, and Public Policy.* 5th ed. Pacific Grove, Calif.: Brooks/Cole, 1991.

Ripley, Randall B., and James M. Lindsay. *Congress Resurgent: Foreign and Defense Policy on Capitol Hill.* Ann Arbor: University of Michigan Press, 1993.

Ritchie, Donald A. *Press Gallery: Congress and the Washington Correspondents.* Cambridge, Mass.: Harvard University Press, 1991.

Robinson, James A. *Congress and Foreign Policy Making.* Homewood, Ill.: Dorsey, 1967.

———. *The House Rules Committee.* Indianapolis: Bobbs-Merrill, 1963.

Rogers, Lindsay. *The American Senate.* New York: Knopf, 1926.

Rohde, David W. *Parties and Leaders in the Postreform House.* Chicago: University of Chicago Press, 1991.

Rosati, Jerel A. *Readings in the Politics of U.S. Foreign Policy.* New York: Harcourt Brace, 1998.

Rosenstone, Steven J., and John Mark Hansen. *Mobilization, Participation, and Democracy in America.* New York: Macmillan, 1993.

Rosner, Jeremy D. *The New Tug-of-War: Congress, the Executive Branch, and National Security.* Washington, D.C.: Carnegie Endowment for International Peace, 1995.

Rossiter, Clinton. *1787: The Grand Convention.* New York: Macmillan, 1966.

Rothenberg, Lawrence S. *Linking Citizens to Government: Interest Group Politics at Common Cause.* New York: Cambridge University Press, 1992

Rothman, David J. *Politics and Power: The United States Senate, 1869–1901.* Cambridge, Mass.: Harvard University Press, 1966.

Rothstein, Samuel. "The Origins of Legislative Reference Services in the United States." *Legislative Studies Quarterly* 25, no. 3 (August 1990): 401–411.

Rourke, John. *Congress and the Presidency in U.S. Foreign Policymaking: A Study of Interaction and Influence, 1945–1982.* Boulder, Colo.: Westview Press, 1983.

Rovere, Richard H. *Senator Joe McCarthy.* Cleveland: World Publishing, 1968.

Rubin, Irene. *The Politics of Public Budgeting: Getting and Spending, Borrowing and Balancing.* 3rd ed. Chatham, N.J.: Chatham House Publishers, 1997.

Rudman, Warren B. *COMBAT: Twelve Years in the U.S. Senate.* New York: Random House, 1996.

Rush, Mark. *Does Redistricting Make a Difference? Partisan Representation and Electoral Behavior.* Baltimore: Johns Hopkins University Press, 1993.

S

Sabato, Larry J. *Feeding Frenzy: How American Journalism Has Transformed American Politics.* New York: Free Press, 1991.

———. *PAC Power: Inside the World of Political Action Committees.* New York: Norton, 1984.

———. *Paying for Elections: The Campaign Finance Thicket.* New York: Priority Press/Twentieth Century Fund, 1989.

Savage, James D. *Balanced Budgets and American Politics.* Ithaca, N.Y.: Cornell University Press, 1988.

Schattschneider, Elmer E. *Party Government.* New York: Holt, Rinehart & Winston, 1942.

———. *The Semisovereign People: A Realist's View of Democracy in America.* New York: Holt, Rinehart and Winston, 1960.

Scher, Richard K., Jon L. Mills, and John J. Hotaling. *Voting Rights and Democracy: The Law and Politics of Districting.* Chicago: Nelson-Hall, 1997.

Schick, Allen. *Crisis in the Budget Process: Exercising Political Choice.* Washington, D.C.: American Enterprise Institute, 1986.

———. *The Federal Budget: Politics, Policy, Process.* Washington, D.C.: Brookings Institution, 1995.

Schlesinger, Arthur M., Jr. *The Imperial Presidency.* Boston: Houghton Mifflin, 1989.

———, ed. *History of U.S. Political Parties.* 4 vols. New York: Bowker, 1981.

Schlesinger, Arthur M., Jr., and Roger Burns, eds. *Congress Investigates: A Documented History, 1792–1974.* 5 vols. New York: Bowker, 1975.

Schlesinger, Joseph A. *Political Parties and the Winning of Office.* Ann Arbor: University of Michigan Press, 1991.

Schlozman, Kay L., and John Tierney. *Organized Interests and American Democracy.* New York: Harper and Row, 1986.

Schmeckebier, Laurence F. *Congressional Apportionment.* Washington, D.C.: Brookings Institution, 1941. Reprint. Westport, Conn.: Greenwood Press, 1976.

———. *The District of Columbia: Its Government and Administration.* Baltimore: Johns Hopkins University Press, 1928.

Schmidhauser, John R. *The Supreme Court and Congress: Conflict and Interaction, 1945–1968.* New York: Free Press, 1972.

Schubert, Glendon, ed. *Reapportionment.* New York: Scribner's, 1965.

Schwab, Larry M. *The Impact of Congressional Reapportionment and Redistricting.* Lanham, Md.: University Press of America, 1988.

Shea, Daniel M., and John C. Green. *The State of the Parties: The Changing Role of Contemporary American Parties.* Lanham, Md.: Rowan and Littlefield, 1994.

Shelley, Mack C. *The Permanent Majority: The Conservative Coalition in the United States Congress.* University: University of Alabama Press, 1983.

Sheppard, Burton D. *Rethinking Congressional Reform: The Reform Roots of the Special Interest Congress.* Cambridge, Mass.: Schenkman, 1985.

Shepsle, Kenneth A. *The Giant Jigsaw Puzzle: Democratic Committee Assignments in the Modern House.* Chicago: University of Chicago Press, 1978.

Shepsle, Kenneth A., and Barry R. Weingast. "The Institutional Foundations of Committee Power." *American Political Science Review* 81 (June 1987): 85–104.

Shuman, Howard E. *Politics and the Budget: The Struggle between the President and the Congress*. 3rd ed. Englewood Cliffs, N.J.: Prentice Hall, 1992.

Sibley, Joel, ed. *Encyclopedia of the American Legislative System: Studies of the Principle Structures, Processes, and Policies of Congress and State Legislatures since the Colonial Era*. New York: Scribner's, 1994.

Siff, Ted, and Alan Weil. *Ruling Congress: How House and Senate Rules Govern the Legislative Process*. New York: Grossman, 1975.

Silva, Ruth C. *Presidential Succession*. Ann Arbor: University of Michigan Press, 1951.

Silverstein, Gordon. *Imbalance of Power: Constitutional Interpretation and the Making of Foreign Policy*. New York: Oxford University Press, 1997.

Simon, Paul. *Advice and Consent: Clarence Thomas, Robert Bork, and the Intriguing History of the Supreme Court's Nomination Battles*. Washington, D.C.: National Press Books, 1992.

———. *The Glass House: Politics and Morality in the Nation's Capital*. New York: Continuum, 1984.

Simpson, Andrew L. *The Library of Congress*. New York: Chelsea House, 1989.

Sinclair, Barbara. *Congressional Realignment, 1925–1978*. Austin: University of Texas, 1983.

———. *Legislators, Leaders, and Lawmaking: The U.S. House of Representatives in the Post Reform Era*. Baltimore: Johns Hopkins University Press, 1995.

———. *Majority Leadership in the U.S. House*. Baltimore: Johns Hopkins University Press, 1983.

———. *The Transformation of the U.S. Senate*. Baltimore: Johns Hopkins University Press, 1989.

———. *Unorthodox Lawmaking: New Legislative Processes in the U.S. Congress*. Washington, D.C.: CQ Press, 1997.

Sindler, Allan P. *Unchosen Presidents: The Vice-President and Other Frustrations of Presidential Succession*. Berkeley: University of California Press, 1976.

Smith, David G. *The Convention and the Constitution*. New York: St. Martin's, 1965.

Smith, Hedrick. *The Power Game: How Washington Works*. New York: Random House, 1988.

Smith, Page. *A New Age Now Begins: A People's History of the American Revolution*. 2 vols. New York: McGraw-Hill, 1976.

Smith, Steven S. *The American Congress*. Boston: Houghton Mifflin, 1995.

———. *Call to Order: Floor Politics in the House and Senate*. Washington, D.C.: Brookings Institution, 1989.

Smyrl, Marc E. *Conflict or Codetermination? Congress, the President, and the Power to Make War*. Cambridge, Mass.: Ballinger, 1988.

Sofaer, Abraham D. *War, Foreign Affairs, and Constitutional Power: The Origins*. Cambridge, Mass.: Ballinger, 1976.

———. *Decline and Resurgence of Congress*. Washington, D.C.: Brookings Institution, 1981.

Sorauf, Frank J. *Inside Campaign Finance: Myths and Realities*. New Haven, Conn.: Yale University Press, 1992.

———. *Money in American Elections*. Glenview, Ill.: Scott, Foresman/Little, Brown, 1988.

Spanier, John, and Joseph Nogee, eds. *Congress, the Presidency, and American Foreign Policy*. Elmsford, N.Y.: Pergamon, 1981.

Spitzer, Robert J. *President and Congress: Executive Hegemony at the Crossroads of American Government*. Philadelphia: Temple University Press, 1993.

Stein, Robert M., and Kenneth N. Bickers. *Perpetuating the Pork Barrel: Policy Subsystems and American Democracy*. New York: Cambridge University Press, 1995.

Steinberg, Alfred. *Sam Rayburn*. New York: Hawthorne Books, 1975.

Stern, Philip M. *The Best Congress Money Can Buy*. New York: Pantheon Books, 1988.

Stewart, James B. *Blood Sport: The President and His Adversaries*. New York: Simon and Schuster, 1996.

Stockman, David A. *The Triumph of Politics: Why the Reagan Revolution Failed*. New York: Harper and Row, 1986.

Strahan, Randall W. *New Ways and Means: Reform and Change in a Congressional Committee*. Chapel Hill: University of North Carolina Press, 1990.

Strom, Gerald S. *The Logic of Lawmaking: A Spatial Theory Approach*. Baltimore: Johns Hopkins University Press, 1990.

Sullivan, Terry O. *Procedural Structure: A Success and Influence in Congress*. New York: Praeger, 1984.

Sundquist, James L. *Constitutional Reform and Effective Government*. Rev. ed. Washington, D.C.: Brookings Institution, 1992.

———. *The Decline and Resurgence of Congress*. Washington, D.C.: Brookings Institution, 1981.

———. *Dynamics of the Party System: Alignment and Realignment of Political Parties in the United States*. Rev. ed. Washington, D.C.: Brookings Institution, 1983.

———, ed. *Back to Gridlock: Governance in the Clinton Years*. Washington, D.C.: Brookings Institution, 1995.

Swanstrom, Roy. *The United States Senate, 1787–1801*. 100th Cong., 1st sess., 1988. S Doc 100-31. Washington, D.C.: Government Printing Office, 1988.

Swift, Elaine K. *The Making of an American Senate: A Reconstitutive Change in Congress, 1787–1841*. Ann Arbor: University of Michigan Press, 1996.

Swindler, William F. *Court and Constitution in the Twentieth Century: The New Legality, 1932–1968*. Indianapolis: Bobbs-Merrill, 1970.

———. *Court and Constitution in the Twentieth Century: The Old Legality, 1889–1932*. Indianapolis: Bobbs-Merrill, 1969.

Swisher, Carl B. *American Constitutional Development*. 2nd ed. Cambridge, Mass.: Houghton Mifflin, 1954.

T

Tacheron, Donald G., and Morris K. Udall. *The Job of the Congressman: An Introduction to Service in the U.S. House of Representatives*. 2nd ed. New York: Macmillan, 1970.

Tarrance, V. Lance, Jr., Walter De Vries, and Donna L. Mosher. *Checked and Balanced: How Ticket-Splitters Are Shaping the New Balance of Power in American Politics*. Grand Rapids, Mich.: Eerdmans, 1998.

Taylor, Telford. *Grand Inquest: The Story of Congressional Investigations*. New York: Ballantine Books, 1961.

Teixeira, Ruy A. *The Disappearing American Voter*. Washington, D.C.: Brookings Institution, 1992.

Thayer, George. *Who Shakes the Money Tree? American Campaign Financing from 1789 to the Present*. New York: Simon and Schuster, 1973.

Thernstrom, Abigail M. *Whose Votes Count? Affirmative Action and Minority Voting Rights*. Cambridge, Mass.: Harvard University Press, 1987.

Thomas, Norman C., and Joseph A. Pika. *The Politics of the Presidency*. 4th ed. Washington, D.C.: CQ Press, 1997.

Thompson, Dennis F. *Ethics in Congress: From Individual to Institutional Corruption*. Washington, D.C.: Brookings Institution, 1995.

Thurber, James A., ed. *Divided Democracy: Cooperation and Conflict between the President and Congress*. Washington, D.C.: CQ Press, 1991.

———. *Rivals for Power: Presidential-Congressional Relations*. Washington, D.C.: CQ Press, 1996.

Tiefer, Charles. *Congressional Practice and Procedure: A Reference, Research, and Legislative Guide*. Westport, Conn.: Greenwood Press, 1989.

Tienken, Robert L. *House of Representatives Exclusion, Censure, and Expulsion Cases from 1789 to 1973*. Washington, D.C.: Government Printing Office, 1973.

Tindall, William. *Standard History of the City of Washington from a Study of the Original Sources*. Knoxville, Tenn.: H. W. Crew, 1914.

Tocqueville, Alexis de. *Democracy in America*. 2 vols. New York: Schocken Books, 1967.

Tolchin, Susan, and Martin Tolchin. *Dismantling America: The Rush to Deregulate*. Boston: Houghton Mifflin, 1983.

———. *To the Victor: Political Patronage from the Clubhouse to the White House*. New York: Random House, 1971.

Trask, Roger R. *Defender of the Public Interest: The General Accounting Office, 1921–1966*. Washington, D.C.: Government Printing Office, 1996.

Treverton, Gregory F. *Covert Action: The Limits of Intervention in the Postwar World*. New York: Basic Books, 1987.

Tribe, Laurence H. *God Save This Honorable Court: How the Choice of Justices Can Change Our Lives*. New York: Random House, 1985.

Truman, David B. *The Governmental Process*. 2nd ed. New York: Knopf, 1971.

———, ed. *The Congress and America's Future*. 2nd ed. Englewood Cliffs, N.J.: Prentice-Hall, 1973.

Tugwell, Rexford G. *The Enlargement of the Presidency*. Garden City, N.Y.: Doubleday, 1960.

Twentieth Century Fund. *Obstacle Course: The Report of the Twentieth Century Fund Task Force on the Presidential Appointment Process*. New York: Twentieth Century Fund Press, 1996.

U

Unekis, Joseph K., and Leroy N. Rieselbach. *Congressional Committee Politics: Continuity and Change*. New York: Praeger, 1984.

U.S. Congress. House. *Constitution, Jefferson's Manual, and Rules of the House of Representatives*. Washington, D.C.: Government Printing Office, 1797– .

———. *The History and Operation of the House Majority Whip Organization*. 94th Cong., 1st sess., 1975. H Doc 94-162. Washington, D.C.: Government Printing Office, 1975.

———. *History of the House of Representatives, 1789–1994*. Washington, D.C.: Government Printing Office, 1994.

———. *Manual on Legislative Procedure in the U.S. House of Representatives*. 6th ed. Washington: Government Printing Office, 1986.

———. Commission on the Bicentenary. *Women in Congress, 1917–1990*. Washington, D.C.: Government Printing Office, 1991.

———. Committee on Governmental Reform and Oversight. *Minority Rights, Prerogatives and Protections in the Committee on Government Reform and Oversight*. Washington, D.C.: Government Printing Office, 1997.

———. Committee on Rules. *A History of the Committee on Rules: 1st to 97th Congress, 1789–1981*. 97th Cong., 2nd sess., 1982. Washington, D.C.: Government Printing Office, 1982.

———. Committee on Standards of Official Conduct. *Ethics Manual for Members, Officers, and Employees of the U.S. House of Representatives*. 102nd Cong., 2nd sess., 1992. Washington, D.C.: Government Printing Office, 1992.

———. *Historical Summary of Conduct Cases in the House of Representatives*. Washington, D.C.: Government Printing Office, 1992.

———. Office of Inspector General. *Fire Protection Systems Do Not Adequately Protect the House*. Audit Report 98–HOC–20, Dec. 18, 1998.

U.S. Congress. Senate. *Majority and Minority Leaders of the Senate: History and Development of the Offices of the Floor Leaders*. Prepared by Floyd M. Riddick. 100th Cong., 2nd sess., 1988. S Doc Y1.1/3:100-29. Washington, D.C.: Government Printing Office, 1988.

———. *The United States Congress and Capitol: A Walking Tour Handbook*. 2 vols. Washington, D.C.: Government Printing Office, 1999.

———. Committee on Rules and Administration. *Senate Manual Containing the Standing Rules, Orders, Laws, and Resolutions Affecting the Business of the United States Senate*. Washington, D.C.: Government Printing Office, 1967– .

———. Select Committee on Ethics. *In re: The Matter of Senator Alan Cranston, Senator Dennis DeConcini, Senator John Glenn, Senator John McCain, Senator Donald Riegle. Prepared Text of the Opening Statement of Special Counsel Robert S. Bennett*. 101st Cong., 2nd sess., 1990, committee print. Washington, D.C.: Government Printing Office, 1990.

———. *Interpretive Rulings of the Select Committee on Ethics*. Washington, D.C.: Government Printing Office, 1993.

———. *Senate Ethics Manual*. Washington, D.C.: Government Printing Office, 1996.

———. Temporary Select Committee to Study the Senate Committee System. *First Report, with Recommendations; Structure of the Senate Committee System: Jurisdictions, Numbers and Sizes, and Limitations on Memberships and Chairmanships, Referral Procedures, and Scheduling*. 94th Cong., 2nd sess., 1976. S Rept 94-1395. Washington, D.C.: Government Printing Office, 1976.

U.S. General Accounting Office. *The U.S. General Accounting Office: Responsibilities and Services to Congress*. Washington, D.C.: Government Printing Office, 1985.

V

Van Beek, Stephen D. *Post-Passage Politics: Bicameral Resolution in Congress*. Pittsburgh: University of Pittsburgh, 1995.

Van Doren, Carl. *The Great Rehearsal: The Story of the Making and Ratifying of the Constitution of the United States*. New York: Viking, 1948.

Van Tassel, Emily Field, and Paul Finkelman. *Impeachable Offenses: A Documentary History from 1787 to Present*. Washington, D.C.: Congressional Quarterly, 1999.

Vermeer, Jan P., ed. *Campaigns in the News: Mass Media and Congressional Elections*. Westport, Conn.: Greenwood Press, 1987.

Vogler, David J. *The Third House: Conference Committees in the United States Congress*. Evanston, Ill.: Northwestern University Press, 1971.

Vose, Clement E. *Constitutional Change: Amendment Politics and Supreme Court Litigation since 1900*. Lexington, Mass.: Lexington Books, 1972.

W

Walker, Jack L. *Mobilizing Interest Groups in America: Patrons, Professions, and Social Movements*. Ann Arbor: University of Michigan, 1991.

Warren, Charles. *The Making of the Constitution*. Boston: Little, Brown, 1928.

———. *The Supreme Court in United States History*. Rev. ed. 2 vols. Boston: Little, Brown, 1926.

Washington Representatives. Washington, D.C.: Columbia Books, 1990– .

Watson, Richard A. *Presidential Vetoes and Public Policy*. Lawrence: University Press of Kansas, 1993.

Wattenberg, Martin P. *The Decline of American Political Parties: 1952–1994*. Cambridge, Mass.: Harvard University Press, 1996.

Weeks, Kent M. *Adam Clayton Powell and the Supreme Court*. New York: Dunellen, 1971.

Weidenbaum, Murray L. *Federal Budgeting, The Choice of Government Programs*. Washington, D.C.: American Enterprise Institute, 1964.

West, Darrell M. *Congress and Economic Policymaking*. Pittsburgh: University of Pittsburgh Press, 1987.

West, Robin. *Progressive Constitutionalism: Reconstructing the Fourteenth Amendment*. Durham, N.C.: Duke University Press, 1994.

Westlye, Mark C. *Senate Elections and Campaign Intensity*. Baltimore: Johns Hopkins University Press, 1991.

Whalen, Charles, and Barbara Whalen. *The Longest Debate: A Legislative History of the 1964 Civil Rights Act*. Washington, D.C.: Seven Locks Press, 1985.

White, Joseph, and Aaron Wildavsky. *The Deficit and the Public Interest: The Search for Responsible Budgeting in the 1980s*. Berkeley: University of California Press, 1989.

White, Theodore H. *Breach of Faith: The Fall of Richard Nixon*. New York: Dell, 1975.

White, William S. *Citadel: The Story of the U.S. Senate.* New York: Harpers & Brothers, 1956.

Wilcox, Francis O. *Congress, the Executive, and Foreign Policy.* New York: Harper and Row, 1971.

Wildavsky, Aaron, and Naomi Caiden. *The New Politics of the Budgetary Process.* 3rd ed. New York: Longman, 1997.

Williams, T. Harry. *Hayes: The Diary of a President, 1875–1881.* New York: McKay, 1964.

Williams, Walter. *The Congressional Budget Office: A Critical Link in Budget Reform.* Seattle: Institute of Government Research, University of Washington, 1974.

Wilmerding, Lucius, Jr. *The Electoral College.* New Brunswick, N.J.: Rutgers University Press, 1958.

———. *The Spending Power: A History of the Efforts of Congress to Control Expenditures.* New Haven, Conn.: Yale University Press, 1943.

Wilson, Woodrow. *Congressional Government: A Study in American Politics.* Boston: Houghton Mifflin, 1885. Reprint. Cleveland: Meridian, 1956.

Wiltz, John E. *In Search of Peace: The Senate Munitions Inquiry, 1934–1936.* Baton Rouge: Louisiana State University Press, 1963.

Witte, John. *The Politics and Development of the Federal Income Tax.* Madison: University of Wisconsin Press, 1985.

Wolanin, Barbara A. *Constantino Brumidi: Artist of the Capitol.* Washington, D.C.: Government Printing Office, 1998.

Wolfinger, Raymond E., and Steven J. Rosenstone. *Who Votes?* New Haven, Conn.: Yale University Press, 1980.

Wolpe, Bruce C., and Bertram J. Levine. *Lobbying Congress: How the System Works.* 2nd ed. Washington, D.C.: Congressional Quarterly, 1996.

Wood, Gordon S. *The Creation of the American Republic, 1776–1787.* New York: Norton, 1972.

Woodward, Bob. *The Final Days.* New York: Touchstone Books, 1989.

Woodward, Bob, and Carl Bernstein. *All the President's Men.* New York: Touchstone Books, 1987.

Wormuth, Francis D., and Edwin B. Firmage. *To Chain the Dog of War: The War Power of Congress in History and Law.* 2nd ed. Urbana: University of Illinois Press, 1989.

Wright, Gerald C., Leroy N. Rieselbach, and Lawrence C. Dodd, eds. *Congress and Policy Change.* New York: Agathon Press, 1986.

Wright, James. *You and Your Congressman.* Rev. ed. New York: Capricorn Books, 1976.

Wright, John R. *Interest Groups & Congress: Lobbying, Contributions, and Influence.* Boston, Ma.: Allyn and Bacon, 1996.

Y

Young, James S. *The Washington Community, 1800–1828.* New York: Columbia University Press, 1966.

Z

Zeidenstein, Harvey. *Direct Election of the President.* Lexington, Mass.: D. C. Heath, 1973.

Zorack, John L. *The Lobbying Handbook.* Washington. D.C.: Professional Lobbying and Consulting Center, 1990.

Illustration Credits and Acknowledgments

1. Constitutional Beginnings

1 Library of Congress 8 Library of Congress
11 Library of Congress 14 Library of Congress
18 Library of Congress 24 Library of
Congress 29 Library of Congress 32 Library
of Congress 34 Senate Historical Office
36 Library of Congress

2. History of the House

40 National Portrait Gallery, Smithsonian
Institution 42 Architect of the Capitol
46 Library of Congress 48 Library of
Congress 50 Library of Congress 52 Library
of Congress 54 AP/Wide World Photos
62 no credit 65 U.S. Information Agency.
Courtesy of the Sam Rayburn Library
69 no credit 73 Sue Klemens 79 R. Michael
Jenkins, Congressional Quarterly 81 © 1994
by Herblock in *The Washington Post*
84 Congressional Quarterly 86 Douglas
Graham, Congressional Quarterly

3. History of the House

90 Senate Historical Office 93 Library of
Congress 97 Library of Congress
98 National Archives 100 Library of Congress
103 Senate Historical Office 107 no credit
110 Library of Congress 112 Library of
Congress 117 Library of Congress
121 Senate Historical Office 123 The Strom
Thurmond Institute 128 Senate Historical
Office 131 no credit 137 Nathaniel Harari,
Congressional Quarterly 142 Scott J. Ferrell,
Congressional Quarterly

4. Power of the Purse

151 Mary Fackelman, White House 155 Scott J.
Ferrell, Congressional Quarterly 156 Scott J.
Ferrell, Congressional Quarterly 159 AP/
Wide World Photos 170 White House
175 UPI/Bettman 179 Congressional
Quarterly 181 Rick Wilking, Reuters

5. Foreign Policy Powers

187 Senate Historical Office 190 Scott J.
Ferrell, Congressional Quarterly
195 R. Michael Jenkins, Congressional
Quarterly 196 AP/Wide World Photos
205 Senate Historical Office 210 The White
House 214 Jimmy Carter Library 220 AP/
Wide World Photos 226 Library of Congress
227 Library of Congress 230 Diana Walker
232 Department of Defense
235 Congressional Quarterly 243 Ken Heinen

6. Congressional Investigations

250 Library of Congress 255 U.S. Information
Agency 263 "Now where?" Cartoon by Le
Pelley/Library of Congress 268 Library of
Congress 270 Library of Congress
274 Senate Historical Office 276 AP/Wide
World Photos 278 Scott J. Ferrell,
Congressional Quarterly

7. The Senate's Confirmation Power

283 R. Michael Jenkins, Congressional
Quarterly 285 Library of Congress
288 Library of Congress 290 Library of
Congress 293 Collection of the Supreme
Court of the United States 297 Paul Conklin
299 R. Michael Jenkins, Congressional
Quarterly 303 National Archives 304 Ken
Heinen

8. Regulation of Commerce

309 Library of Congress 312 Senate Historical
Office 317 Library of Congress
322 *Evansville Courier;* Franklin D. Roosevelt
Library 328 Library of Congress

9. Impeachment Power

332 Senate Historical Office 335 Library of
Congress 337 Reuters/Senate Historical
Office 341 National Portrait Gallery
342 Library of Congress 344 Scott J. Ferrell,
Congressional Quarterly 346 Douglas
Graham, Congressional Quarterly
350 R. Michael Jenkins, Congressional
Quarterly 352 WETA

10. Constitutional Amendments

356 Library of Congress 365 Library of
Congress 370 Library of Congress

11. Power to Select the President

380 National Archives 386 Library of
Congress 393 White House

12. Seat of Government

399 Historical Society of Washington,
D.C. 403 Air Photographics

13. Miscellaneous Powers

407 Doug Mills, Reuters 410 Library of
Congress

14. Party Leadership in Congress

415 Library of Congress 419 Douglas
Graham, Congressional Quarterly
425 Library of Congress 427 National Portrait
Gallery, Smithsonian Institution 431 Library
of Congress 433 no credit 436 Associated
Press 440 Reuters 443 AP/Wide World
Photos 447 Douglas Graham, Congressional
Quarterly 449 AP/Wide World Photos
452 Scott J. Ferrell, Congressional Quarterly
458 Library of Congress 461 Kathleen Beall,
Congressional Quarterly 463 Scott J. Ferrell,
Congressional Quarterly

15. The Legislative Process

472 Douglas Graham, Congressional
Quarterly 482 C-SPAN 484 Scott J. Ferrell,
Congressional Quarterly 495 Douglas
Graham, Congressional Quarterly
500 Warren K. Leffler, *U.S. News and World
Report* 505 Scott J. Ferrell, Congressional
Quarterly 514 Douglas Graham,

Congressional Quarterly 521 Douglas
Graham, Congressional Quarterly
532 R. Michael Jenkins, Congressional
Quarterly

16. The Committee System

538 Douglas Graham, Congressional Quarterly
545 no credit 558 Douglas Graham,
Congressional Quarterly 562 Douglas
Graham, Congressional Quarterly 566 Scott J.
Ferrell, Congressional Quarterly 572 Scott J.
Ferrell, Congressional Quarterly
577 R. Michael Jenkins, Congressional
Quarterly

17. Congressional Staff

582 U.S. Senate Historical Office 591 Scott J.
Ferrell, Congressional Quarterly 595 Douglas
Graham, Congressional Quarterly
598 Douglas Graham, Congressional Quarterly
599 Scott J. Ferrell, Congressional Quarterly
603 R. Michael Jenkins, Congressional
Quarterly 605 R. Michael Jenkins,
Congressional Quarterly

18. Constituency Pressures

609 LBJ Library 614 AP/Wide World Photos
615 Mike Segar, Reuters 618 Congressional
Quarterly

19. The Media

626 Douglas Graham, Congressional Quarterly
629 Scott J. Ferrell, Congressional Quarterly
633 Douglas Graham, Congressional
Quarterly 634 Senate Historical Office
635 Scott J. Ferrell, Congressional Quarterly

20. Internal Pressures

640 (both) no credit 645 Scott J. Ferrell,
Congressional Quarterly 647 U.S. Information Agency

21. The President

656 Dwight D. Eisenhower Library 658 John
F. Kennedy Library 663 Franklin D. Roosevelt
Library 665 National Republican
Congressional Committee 671 Reuters

22. The Supreme Court

674 Ken Heinen 677 U.S. Supreme Court
679 U.S. Supreme Court 681 AP/Ron
Edmonds 685 Library of Congress 687 Ken
Heinen

23. Lobbying

692 Library of Congress 698 Library of
Congress 701 Douglas Graham,
Congressional Quarterly 707 Teresa Zabala
710 Scott J. Ferrell, Congressional Quarterly
712 R. Michael Jenkins, Congressional
Quarterly 716 R. Michael Jenkins,
Congressional Quarterly 723 Scott J. Ferrell,
Congressional Quarterly

24. Capitol and Office Buildings

725 no credit   731 Library of Congress
735 Library of Congress   738 Architect of the
Capitol   740 Architect of the Capitol
741 Douglas Graham, Congressional Quarterly
742 Scott J. Ferrell, Congressional Quarterly
743 John L. Moore

25. Library of Congress

750 Library of Congress   751 Library of
Congress   753 R. Michael Jenkins,
Congressional Quarterly

26. Supporting Organizations

756 no credit   761 Scott J. Ferrell,
Congressional Quarterly

27. Pay and Honoraria

763 Architect of the Capitol   771 Karen
Ruckman   773 Pete Souza, White House
775 R. Michael Jenkins, Congressional
Quarterly   781 Richard Ellis, Congressional
Quarterly

28. Allowances and Other Benefits

784 Library of Congress   790 Toshiyuki
Aizawa, Reuters   794 Douglas Graham,
Congressional Quarterly   798 Architect of the
Capitol   799 Scott J. Ferrell, Congressional
Quarterly   802 Library of Congress

29. Who Elects Congress

805 Courtesy of the League of Women Voters
810 Library of Congress   813 National
Archives   818 Library of Congress

30. Political Parties and Elections

826 Wood engraving in *Harper's Weekly,* May
19, 1860, Library of Congress   832 Dorthea
Lange, Library of Congress   834 Bill Finney
835 Scott J. Ferrell, Congressional Quarterly

31. Who Gets Elected

843 James Watts, Congressional Quarterly
846 Scott J. Ferrell, Congressional Quarterly

32. Campaign Financing

857 Douglas Graham, Congressional Quarterly
866 © 1996 by Herblock, in *The Washington
Post*   869 Douglas Graham, Congressional
Quarterly   871 Library of Congress   877 no
credit   880 Gerald R. Ford Library   881 no
credit   886 R. Michael Jenkins, Congressional
Quarterly

33. Reapportionment and Redistricting

894 National Portrait Gallery   901 Library of
Congress   907 R. Michael Jenkins,
Congressional Quarterly

34. Seating and Disciplining

913 R. Michael Jenkins, Congressional
Quarterly   922 Library of Congress   927 Scott
J. Ferrell, Congressional Quarterly/C-SPAN
928 Library of Congress   932 Steven
Karafyllakis   933 R. Michael Jenkins,
Congressional Quarterly   940 Robert Giroux,
Reuters

35. Ethics and Criminal Prosecutions

947 no credit   952 no credit   955 no credit
956 AP/Wide World Photos   960 Sue Klemens
967 AP/Wide World Photos
970 Congressional Quarterly   976 no credit
977 no credit   981 R. Michael Jenkins
986 Steve Karafyllakis

Index

F

F-22 fighter planes, 193
Fair Employment Practices Commission, 63
Fair Employment Practices Office, 602
Fair Labor Standards Act of 1938, 62, 323, 325, 600, 602 (box)
Fairbanks, Charles W., 134 (table)
Fairchild Industries, 946
Faircloth, Lauch, 973
Faleomavaega, Eni F. H., 851
Fall, Albert B., 267, 289, 352, 634
Fallon, George H., 736 (box)
Family and Medical Leave Act of 1993, 602, 602 (box)
Family policy, 441 (box)
Farley, James A., 658, 666
Farm Credit Administration, 326
Farrand, Max, 675
Fascell, Dante B., 211–212, 238
"Fast-track" procedures, 423, 475 (box)
Faulkner, C. J., 105
Fauntroy, Walter E., 401, 402, 851, 966, 974 (box)
Fazio, Vic
    appropriations, 622
    congressional pay, 771, 774, 775
    Joint Taxation staff, 594
    Murphy reprimand, 938
    party leadership, 446, 451
FBI. *See* Federal Bureau of Investigation
FEC. *See* Federal Election Commission
FECA. *See* Federal Election Campaign Act
Federal aid to education, 105, 710
Federal Aviation Administration, 326
Federal budget. *See* Budget, U.S.
Federal Bureau of Investigation (FBI)
    Abscam scandal, 76, 139, 527, 722, 953, 955–957
    campaign finance investigation, 578–579
    executive privilege issues, 260, 262
    intelligence oversight, 242, 245
    Senate investigations, 132–133, 275
    Watergate scandal, 274
    White House files controversy, 262, 279, 344
Federal Contested Elections Act of 1969, 833
Federal contractors
    patronage, 665–667
    political contributions, 873
Federal Corrupt Practices Act of 1910, 872, 917
Federal Corrupt Practices Act of 1925, 70, 856, 872–875
    Watergate scandal, 877
Federal courts. *See also* Supreme Court
    constitutional basis, 31–33, 405
    establishment, 405, 675
    judges
        impeachments, 332–333, 347–350
        new judgeships, 405–406, 684
        pay, 405, 769
        tenure, 335, 684
    jurisdiction
        congressional staff grievances, 602
        injunctions in labor disputes, 321
        suits against states, 363
    political question doctrine, 261 (box)
    redistricting, 902, 904–905
Federal debt. *See* Budget, U.S.
Federal Deposit Insurance Corporation, 326
Federal Election Campaign Act (FECA) of 1971
    FEC enforcement, 882 (box)
    limits, disclosure, 854, 856, 858, 875–876
Federal Election Campaign Act Amendments of 1974
    Court test, 858, 869, 880–882
    FEC enforcement, 44 (box)

provisions, 879–880
    soft money, 867–868
    Watergate effect, 856
Federal Election Campaign Act Amendments of 1976, 779, 882–884
Federal Election Campaign Act Amendments of 1979, 699, 856, 868, 884–885
Federal Election Commission (FEC)
    agency history (box), 882–883
    appointments, 295
    business PACs, 699
    campaign finance reports, 854, 858, 859
    Durenberger ethics case, 933
    motor-voter report, 821
    soft money, 868
    structure, 879, 881–884
Federal employees
    D.C. voting rights, 401
    eligibility of members of Congress, 21
    ethics rules, 945 (box), 949, 951
    impeachment exemptions, 333
    lobbying restrictions, 718, 981
    patronage, 281–282, 288–289, 292, 665–667, 800–801
    political fund-raising, 871, 873
    state taxes, 148 (box)
Federal Financing Bank, 165 (box)
Federal government (general)
    claims, 526–527
    congressional oversight, 577–579
    shutdowns, 83, 162–163, 179, 182, 442, 463, 476
Federal Home Loan Bank Board, 326
Federal Housing Finance Board, 326
Federal lands disposal, 215
Federal Maritime Commission, 326
Federal Power Commission, 291, 301, 313, 314, 326
Federal Regulation of Lobbying Act of 1946, 64, 716, 717–718, 720
Federal Reserve Act of 1913, 267
Federal Reserve System, 326
Federal-state relations
    Articles of Confederation, 12–14
    CBO estimates of federal mandates, 758, 759
    commerce regulation
        employees, 329
        gun control, 329–330
        health, morals police power, 316–320
        insurance, 328–329
        navigation, 307, 309, 311
        railroad rates, 313–314
        wages and hours, 321
        wartime powers, 294
    constitutional basis, 15
        amendment process, 33
        congressional pay, 20
        militia regulation, 25
        powers of Congress, 22
        state powers, 32–33
        suits against states, 363, 686
        supremacy clause, 22, 31–32
    grants, 157 (box), 160
    Prohibition enforcement, 368
    Supreme Court decisions, 680, 681–682
        judicial review of state laws, 675, 687
        jurisdiction changes, 686
    tax immunities (box), 148
Federal Tort Claims Act of 1946, 526–527
Federal Trade Commission
    antitrust law history, 324
    appointments, 289, 301–302
    as regulatory agency, 326
    utilities investigations, 719, 720
Federal Trade Commission Act of 1914, 267

The Federalist papers, 34 (box), 35
    Constitution amendment, 357–358
    foreign policy powers, 185
    general welfare clause, 157
    House apportionment, 892–893
    impeachment, 332, 333
    judicial review, 675
    political parties, factions, 692, 825
    press freedom, 627
    qualifications of members, 918
    seat of government, 395
    Senate confirmation power, 283–284
    Senate elections, 90
    Senate removal power, 298
    treaty power, 198
    war powers, 221
Federalist Party
    Constitution ratification, 34–36
    history, 40–41, 94–95, 825
    judicial appointments, 676 (box)
    presidential election of 1800, 364, 380–381
    Senate history, 94–95
Federation of American Scientists, 245
Feingold, Russell, 512 (box), 857
Feinstein, Dianne, 141, 843, 863, 864
Felton, Rebecca L., 841
Fenn, E. Hart, 60, 898
Fenno, Richard F., Jr., 613
Ferraro, Geraldine, 844, 959
Fiedler, Bobbi, 960
Fiellin, Alan, 651
Fifteenth Amendment
    historical context, provisions, 359, 366–367
    minority voting rights, 366–367, 677, 807, 811, 812, 816
    ratification, 358 (box), 362, 810
    redistricting, 903
    women's voting rights, 368
Fifth Amendment
    citizenship revocation, 409
    committee witness rights, 254–255
    equal protection implication, 679
    freedom of contract, 320
    and immunity, 256–257
    provisions, 363
    state actions, 366 (box)
    wartime commerce regulation, 315
Filburn, Roscoe C., 325
Filibusters. *See also* Cloture
    history
        civil rights bills, 119–120
        lame-duck sessions, 115–116
        post–Civil War era, 104–108
        Progressive era, 111–112
        reforms, 129, 130–131
        slavery, 99
    House-Senate differences, 470
    individual record, 106, 518
    Senate floor procedures, 512 (box), 513, 516–520
        conference reports, 521, 528
        dilatory tactics, 516–517 (box)
        limited on budget bills, 528
        in morning hour, 511–512
        postcloture, 131–132, 519–520
        scheduling, 510 (box)
        summary, 106–107
        track system, 508–509, 519
        veto override attempts, 532
Fillmore, Millard
    appointments, 286 (table), 287
    Capitol expansion, 733
    inaugural sites, 732 (box)
    vetoes, 669
    votes as vice president, 134 (table)